PRESIDENTIAL PROFILES
THE EISENHOWER YEARS

Michael S. Mayer

Facts On File
An imprint of Infobase Publishing

The Eisenhower Years

Facts On File, Inc.
An imprint of Infobase Publishing
132 West 31st Street
New York NY 10001

Library of Congress Cataloging-in-Publication Data

Mayer, Michael S.
    The Eisenhower years / Michael S. Mayer.
        p. cm.—(Presidential profiles)
    Includes bibliographical references and index.
    ISBN 978-0-8160-5387-2 (hc : alk. paper) 1. United States—Politics and government—1953–1961. 2. United States—Politics and government—1953–1961—Sources. 3. Eisenhower, Dwight D. (Dwight David), 1890–1969. 4. Eisenhower, Dwight D. (Dwight David), 1890–1969—Political and social views. 5. United States—History—1953–1961—Biography. [1. United States—Politics and government—1953–1961. 2. United States—Politics and government—1953–1961—Sources. 3. Eisenhower, Dwight D. (Dwight David), 1890–1969. 4. Eisenhower, Dwight D. (Dwight David), 1890–1969—Political and social views.] I. Title.
    E835.M35 2009
    973.921—dc22   2008038110

CONTENTS

CONTRIBUTING EDITORS

Robert J. Babbitz
University of Pennsylvania

Catherine A. Barnes
Columbia University

James Lewis Baughman
Columbia University

Jason Berger
University of Virginia

Miriam D. Bluestone
Rutgers University

Rachel Burd
City University of New York

Frank D'Angelo
City University of New York

Glenn B. Davis
Columbia University

Thomas G. Denton
Ohio University

Alexander C. Dill
Harvard University

Elliot Figman
University of Massachusetts

Joshua B. Freeman
Rutgers University

Rebecca S. Greene
Columbia University

Steven L. Goulden
University of Chicago

Thomas L. Harrison
Columbia University

Joseph C. Holub
University of California, Berkeley

Joseph P. Lawrence
Columbia University

Michael L. Levine
Rutgers University

Frank H. Milburn
Franconia College

Thomas O'Brien
New York University

Arthur E. Scherr
Columbia University

Eleanora W. Schoenebaum
Columbia University

Martin J. Swanson
University of Virginia

Selma Yampolsky
University of Wisconsin

PREFACE

❧

This project proved more daunting and considerably more time-consuming than I ever imagined. In the process, I came to the realization that many standard reference works are astonishingly unreliable. Simple things, such as dates, where someone attended college, or what jobs he or she held and when, could be difficult to verify, even in our modern age. I have made every effort to be accurate and have not provided dates, job titles, etc., without corroborating them with two reliable sources. Given the limitations on time and resources, as well as the nature of human endeavor, I do not promise that this volume is without error, but I have made every reasonable effort to avoid it.

Most people find biography interesting. That is because people are endlessly fascinating and complex. Unsympathetic figures have admirable traits; appealing figures have flaws, sometimes ghastly ones. The biographies included in this volume certainly bear this out. Even some of the least promising figures turn out to have done interesting things. Surprisingly enough, one seemingly colorless Republican senator from the Midwest invented the jukebox. Moreover, for all the emphasis historians have recently placed on large historical forces, it is, in the end, people who make history.

As I progressed with this project, I found that I was writing a pointillist history of the 1950s. Each biography constitutes a dab; taken altogether, they tell the story of an era as limitlessly complicated and absorbing as those who populated it. A glance at the chronology included in this volume belies the image of the 1950s as an era of quiescence. It is impossible to consider an era dull when it encompasses great achievements in medicine, the social sciences, and literature; a series of crises in the cold war; the birth of the modern Civil Rights movement; the beginning of rock and roll; bitter political divisions; and the dawn of the space race.

It is a cliché to note that every work of scholarship is a cooperative effort, but in this undertaking, I accumulated an unusually large number of debts that require acknowledgment. First I should mention Owen Lancer, editor in chief at Facts On File, who recruited me to this project and who bore with me as I slogged through the alphabet. I owe a debt of gratitude to countless librarians and archivists all over the country who located seemingly irretrievable parcels of information. In some cases, I contacted family members to verify some aspect of a person's life or career. Simply to list all of them would take considerably more space than allotted to this preface. Inadequate though it seems, it will have to do to say that I appreciate the help given by everyone. Some of these people, however, provided assistance that cannot go unmentioned. I should begin by thanking the staff of the Mansfield Library at my home institution, the University of Montana. In particular, Donna McCrea, the university archivist, proved impressively knowledgeable and astonishingly resourceful in helping me track down obscure facts about largely forgotten people. The Russell Kirk Center proved unusually receptive and helpful; Annette Kirk was helpful and gracious beyond any normal expectation. Margaret Calhoon, the senior archivist and curator of Georgia Power (a Southern Company) and Elaine McConnell, the rare-book curator at the United

States Military Academy at West Point, provided me with information I had just about despaired of ever finding. In addition to assistance from archivists and librarians, I received much-appreciated support from President George Dennison of the University of Montana and then-Provost Lois Muir of the same institution. Several research assistants helped track down obscure information; David Zierler, Melissa Cuzzart, and Shannon Michael did outstanding work.

Two people bore the greatest burden of this project. My wife, Susan Mayer, suffered my absence at times and places I should have been present while I struggled to complete the manuscript. Her company, Litigation Abstract, Inc., also provided technical assistance. Stewart Justman, a professor of liberal studies at the University of Montana and a literary critic of extraordinary ability, endured endless recountings of things I had discovered. He listened, read drafts of more than a few entries, discussed, argued, policed my propensity for wisecracks, and provided support in countless ways. To them go my boundless thanks.

For all of the valuable assistance I received, I must claim sole responsibility for any errors of fact or eccentricities of interpretation.

Michael S. Mayer
Missoula, Montana

INTRODUCTION

❧

Dwight D. Eisenhower assumed the presidency in January 1953 at a time of bitter partisan divisions and disillusionment. Problems at home and abroad had undermined the presidency of Harry S. Truman, who, by the time he left office, had lost the confidence of the American people. In the aftermath of victory over the Axis powers, the United States found itself engaged in a cold war with its wartime ally, the Soviet Union. The United States could do little more than watch as the Soviets consolidated their hold on Eastern Europe. Faced with these unexpected developments, some, particularly on the Republican right, blamed the diplomacy of President Franklin D. Roosevelt at the Yalta Conference. American interests suffered reverses in Asia, as well. Mao Zedong's (Mao Tse-tung's) Communists drove the Nationalist Chinese government from the mainland. The cold war turned hot when North Korea invaded South Korea and the United States intervened to prevent the fall of South Korea. The stakes ratcheted up when the Communist Chinese entered the conflict and the war settled into a bloody stalemate.

At home, revelations of real and imagined Soviet espionage whipped the American public into a state of fear. Alger Hiss was convicted of perjury, and Julius and Ethel Rosenberg were convicted of espionage. An FBI raid turned up classified documents from the State Department in the office of a small magazine devoted to American policy in Asia. Demagogues in both parties attempted to use the resulting anxieties for political purpose. None did so more spectacularly or more recklessly than Sen. Joseph R. McCarthy (R-Wis.). Corruption plagued the Truman administration; several of Truman's top aides were implicated in scandals involving conflict of interest, and a number of high-ranking officials in the Bureau of Internal Revenue were dismissed or had to resign after it was revealed that they declined to prosecute tax evasion cases in exchange for money or political favors.

After 20 years of Democratic rule, dissatisfaction with the Truman administration seemed to open the door for the Republicans. Sen. Karl Mundt (R-S.C.) summed up the Republican strategy going into the presidential election of 1952 with the formula K_1C_2 (Korea, communism, and corruption). On the stump, Republican speakers hammered home their indictment of the Truman administration. The Republicans, however, needed to decide on a candidate. Conservatives in the party ardently supported Sen. Robert A. Taft of Ohio; the Eastern, or liberal, wing of the party backed Gen. Eisenhower. After a bitter struggle for the nomination, the Republicans nominated Eisenhower. The Democratic nominee, Adlai Stevenson, was not only saddled with the unpopularity of the Truman administration but had to run against a widely popular hero of World War II. In addition to being sick of Truman, the country did "like Ike," and Eisenhower won in a landslide. Republicans also gained control of both houses of Congress.

Eisenhower's presidency has undergone a radical reassessment by professional historians over the last 25 years. Once considered a detached, incompetent, genial former general utterly out of his

President-elect Dwight D. Eisenhower inspects the living quarters of troops of the ROK's Capital Division, December 4, 1952. *(Dwight D. Eisenhower Library and Museum)*

depth as president, Eisenhower is now commonly regarded as an engaged, informed, and effective president. Moreover, the popular impression of the era over which he presided, that of a quiet, uneventful age of "Happy Days," obscures the reality of a country undergoing profound social and economic change at home and engaged in a colossal global struggle with the Soviet Union abroad. To be sure, the United States had emerged from World War II as the most powerful and prosperous country in the world. During the Eisenhower era, the country experienced an economic boom and a baby boom; Americans were moving to prefabricated houses in the suburbs; veterans attending college on the G.I. Bill opened the door to the middle and professional classes for millions; college graduates flocked to take comfortable and secure jobs with large corporations. Yet, for all their wealth and power, Americans worried about the expansion of Soviet communism, about communist spies and sympathizers at home, and about the possibility of nuclear annihilation. Indeed, the 1950s was, as historian Carl Degler put it, an age of "affluence and anxiety."

The image of Eisenhower as a disengaged, bumbling, grandfather-in-chief had a certain currency during Eisenhower's tenure in office, but grew more and more entrenched until the late 1960s and early 1970s, when the war in Vietnam and domestic unrest at home caused some historians to question the liberal consensus that had held sway since the end of World War II. In their search for alternatives, dissenting historians found one in Eisenhower, a president who ended one war and did not begin another, who presided over years of domestic tranquility, who cut defense budgets, and who warned of the influence of the military-industrial complex. At the same time, the opening of vast collections of papers at the Eisenhower Library in Abilene, Kan., in the late 1960s and early 1970s also influenced the direction of historical research. Changing political perspectives and access to new information combined to create an active interest in the Eisenhower presidency.

As the first products of this new scholarly interest appeared in the early 1970s, a fresh picture of Eisenhower began to emerge. Two themes dominated this revisionist scholarship. The first presented Eisenhower as far more engaged, intelligent, and articulate than had been commonly acknowledged; the second portrayed him as more politically conservative than generally believed. Not long after the publication of this first wave of revisionist scholarship, still more collections at the Eisenhower Library were opened to researchers. These included Eisenhower's personal papers as president and the papers of several of his top advisors. The availability of this new material generated another wave of historical writing that supported one of the early revisionist theses and called into question the other. Eisenhower's own papers strongly reinforced the idea that Eisenhower was a crafty politician, an informed and engaged leader, as well as a capable wordsmith. The opening of higher-level documentation called into question, however, the assertion that Eisenhower was a die-hard conservative. Indeed, explorations in the archives indicated that, although a fiscal conservative, Eisenhower fell well within the consensus on domestic politics established by Franklin Roosevelt and the New Deal.

Since then, historians have crafted yet another image of the 34th president. Eisenhower appears to have been something of an American Disraeli. Just as the conservative British reformer stole the Liberals' thunder, Eisenhower preserved, strengthened, and expanded the basic structure of the New Deal. During Eisenhower's presidency, social security benefits were increased and coverage was expanded. The minimum wage and unemployment benefits were increased. The administration undertook huge new public works projects, including the Saint Lawrence Seaway and the National Highway System. Eisenhower also proposed new initiatives in public health and education, including plans for health reinsurance and federal aid for the construction of new schools, which Congress refused to pass. Finally, the administration made some real, if limited, progress in the area of civil rights for African Americans.

In evaluating Eisenhower's tenure in the White House, the first question to consider relates to Eisenhower's approach to the presidency. The once conventional view held that Eisenhower differed fundamentally from Franklin Roosevelt and Harry Truman, who expanded the powers of the office. There was some truth to this. Eisenhower had a healthy respect for the constitutionally ordained separation of powers, and he did not seek to expand the powers of the presidency at the expense of other branches of government. However, even had he aspired to the kind of expansive role Roosevelt had played, it was not necessarily available to him. The Democrats controlled Congress for the last six of Eisenhower's eight years as president. Moreover, Eisenhower presided over a deeply divided party.

A second issue to consider is Eisenhower's management of the White House. As chief executive, Eisenhower was very much in command of his administration. Contrary to the once prevailing image, his chief of staff, Sherman Adams, neither kept information from Eisenhower nor made major policy decisions. Rather, he controlled the flow of paper and expedited the president's wishes. Eisenhower did indeed delegate authority, but he reserved the final say on policy to himself. He then left the articulation and implementation of policy to his subordinates. Fred Greenstein, a political scientist, has argued that Eisenhower practiced a "hidden hand" style of leadership. Eisenhower assembled a capable cabinet and let them do their jobs, within the broad

lines of policies he established. His hand remained invisible to the public, and he was perfectly willing to let subordinates take credit for successful policies. This served Eisenhower's purposes, because the subordinates were also available to take the blame when things went wrong. When farmers were upset with the administration's agricultural policy, Secretary of Agriculture Ezra Taft Benson absorbed the abuse. When conservative Republicans resented the administration's patronage practices, they went after Sherman Adams. After Eisenhower dispatched federal troops to Little Rock, Ark., to enforce a court order requiring the admission of black students to Central High School, Attorney General Herbert Brownell took most of the heat. Eisenhower remained largely untouched. A striking example of his approach came when Eisenhower suggested to his press secretary, Jim Hagerty, a possible answer to a question that would almost certainly come up in Hagerty's next

During the 1956 campaign for reelection, Washington, D.C., November 1, 1956 *(Dwight D. Eisenhower Library and Museum)*

press briefing. Hagerty objected, "But if I answer that way, I'll catch hell." Eisenhower walked around the desk, put his arm around Hagerty, and said, "Better you, my boy, than me."

Eisenhower's relations with Senator Joseph McCarthy, the red-baiting junior senator from Wisconsin, demonstrated Eisenhower's hidden-hand style of leadership. McCarthy had burst on the scene in 1950 with spectacular charges that Communists had infiltrated and subverted the federal government. The election of a Republican to the White House did not pacify McCarthy, and the senator from Wisconsin almost immediately made trouble for the new administration. McCarthy opposed the nomination of James B. Conant, the president of Harvard, whom Eisenhower selected to be high commissioner to Germany, largely because Conant had opposed a congressional investigation into subversive activities on his campus. McCarthy also opposed the nomination of Walter Bedell Smith, who had served as Eisenhower's chief of staff during World War II, to become undersecretary of state, because Smith had defended John Paton Davies, Jr., a diplomat whom McCarthy alleged was a communist. McCarthy took even greater exception to the nomination of Charles E. Bohlen as ambassador to the Soviet Union. In McCarthy's view, and that of others on the Republican right, Bohlen had been

Senator Joseph McCarthy offers to give reporters a list of State Department employees he says are undergoing a security-loyalty check. *(Library of Congress)*

involved in what they regarded as President Franklin Roosevelt's "sell-out" of Eastern Europe at Yalta. A career foreign service officer, Bohlen had been at Yalta and during his confirmation hearings refused to repudiate the accords. Eisenhower despised McCarthy and his methods. He believed, however, that if a president attacked McCarthy directly, it would serve only to give McCarthy more publicity and would likely lead the Senate to rally around one of its own. Therefore, Eisenhower resisted pressure from some of his aides and his brother, Milton, to speak out publicly against McCarthy. Rather, he maneuvered behind the scenes first to oppose and then to help bring down the demagogue from Wisconsin. In an effort to gain confirmation for Conant, Eisenhower called McCarthy and sent Vice President Richard M. Nixon to talk to the senator. As a result of these overtures, McCarthy agreed not to make a floor fight, even though he remained "much opposed" to the nomination and voted against it. With respect to the nomination of Eisenhower's old friend Walter "Beetle" Smith, Eisenhower called Taft, the majority leader in the Senate, and told him to put an end to McCarthy's attack on the nominee. Taft did so, and Smith won confirmation. By working behind the scenes through Taft, Eisenhower denied McCarthy the headlines he so craved. In the case of Bohlen, Eisenhower persuaded Taft to put aside his natural inclination to oppose the nominee. Nevertheless, McCarthy obtained FBI raw files that contained vague and unsubstantiated rumors about Bohlen's personal life. McCarthy demanded that the Senate be given access not just to the FBI report but to the "entire file"; Eisenhower refused. The president once again delegated Nixon to talk to McCarthy. Nixon could not convince McCarthy to stop his active opposition to the nomination, but he did persuade the senator to moderate the attack somewhat. During the bitter debate in the Senate over Bohlen's nomination, Eisenhower publicly defended the nominee and worked behind the scenes to shore up support for Bohlen's confirmation. At Eisenhower's behest, Taft rallied a number conservative Republicans who would otherwise almost certainly have opposed the nomination. As a result, Bohlen won confirmation easily. Yet another example of Eisenhower's approach came in April 1954 when he met with Joe Meek, a conservative

Republican and the party's nominee in the upcoming election for the Senate seat held by Paul Douglas (D-Ill.). The president agreed to support Meek on two conditions: that Meek support the administration's program if he won and that Meek not invite McCarthy to campaign for him.

In particular, Eisenhower cooperated with McCarthy's opponents in the Senate during the Army–McCarthy hearings. The hearings grew out of McCarthy's failed attempt to substantiate his charges that a "radar spy ring" existed at Fort Monmouth. The senator then turned his attention to the case of Dr. Irving Peress, a draftee dentist who had refused to sign a loyalty oath. After Peress refused to answer McCarthy's questions, he was promoted, according to the requirements of the doctors' draft law, and given an honorable discharge. Early in 1954, McCarthy called Gen. Ralph Zwicker, Peress's commanding officer, to testify before his committee. "Who," demanded McCarthy, "promoted Peress?" When Zwicker, a decorated war hero, professed not to know the answer, the senator browbeat and insulted him. Following this performance, Secretary of the Army Robert T. Stevens met with McCarthy and Karl Mundt (R-S. Dak.) at Sen. Everett Dirksen's (R-Ill.) office and agreed to release the names of those associated with Peress's promotion and to permit Zwicker to testify further in exchange for a promise that McCarthy would not abuse the general. McCarthy announced that Stevens had capitulated, and the press reported that the administration had surrendered to the senator. Stevens offered to resign, but Eisenhower would not hear of it. Instead, he told Stevens to admit that the army had made an administrative error. In the meantime, Eisenhower met with Dirksen and Mundt and got them to agree to keep McCarthy in line. The administration also responded by releasing a chronology that traced the efforts of McCarthy and his aide, Roy Cohn, to gain preferential treatment for Cohn's friend and associate, G. David Schine, who had recently been inducted into the army. McCarthy retaliated by charging that the army held Schine hostage in an effort to coerce the senator into dropping his investigation. During several weeks of nationally televised hearings, McCarthy's boorish behavior and his disregard for decency or procedure helped turn the American

public against him. Before and during the hearings, Eisenhower repeatedly urged Republican leaders in the Senate to maintain order and proper procedures. When McCarthy attempted to expand the inquiry to include the actions of members of the White House staff, Eisenhower asserted "executive privilege" and refused to allow them to testify. During the hearings, Eisenhower and his administration worked closely with anti-McCarthy senators to help bring down the demagogue from Wisconsin. In December 1954, with the congressional elections behind them, the Senate voted 67-22 to censure McCarthy for behavior that brought the Senate into "dishonor and disrepute."

Some historians have questioned whether Eisenhower's tactics were the best or most expeditious way to put a halt to McCarthy's antics. Others, in particular Fred Greenstein, contend that "it is difficult to see how . . . another technique would have worked faster and more decisively in the context of the time." Robert Griffith, one of the most incisive historians to write about McCarthy, argues that Eisenhower's approach "arose in part from his realistic, if cynical, respect for McCarthy's support among Senate Republicans, in part from his personal dislike for the philippic mode. It also derived, however, from his sophisticated analysis of the relationships between McCarthy, the media, and the presidency." It seems clear that Eisenhower certainly was not the only, perhaps not even the most significant, factor in bringing about the ultimate downfall of the junior senator from Wisconsin, but it seems equally clear that he played a consequential role.

Earlier evaluations of Eisenhower criticized his lack of interest in party politics. More recent scholarship has made a persuasive case that Eisenhower actively led his party and attempted to strengthen its moderate wing. He found wielding patronage distasteful and left that largely to subordinates. He did, however, use his own immense popularity as an effective political tool by threatening to withhold his political support in an effort to keep congressional Republicans in line on key legislative items. When the House of Representatives rejected the administration's Health Reinsurance Plan, Eisenhower demanded the names of the Republicans who voted against it. "If any of those fellows who voted against that bill expect me to do anything for them in this campaign," the president fumed, "they are going to be very much surprised."

Yet one element of the indictment remains—Eisenhower failed to remake the Republican Party in his own, moderate, image. Part of that failure lay in the fact that Eisenhower always cared more about governing than building his own party. Perhaps the larger part of that failure, however, was that the party was deeply split along geographical and ideological lines, and the conservative wing of the party was particularly strong in Congress. Given those circumstances, one must ask whether anyone could have prevented the ultimate triumph of the right wing of the party.

The characterization of Eisenhower as an active, capable, and informed chief executive and a skilled politician has become an accepted paradigm. Toward what ends did he use that energy and political skill? Eisenhower frequently described his politics and policies as middle-of-the-road, and that was a reasonably accurate assessment. As mentioned above, the Democrats controlled Congress for three-quarters of his presidency. Had Eisenhower wanted to dismantle the New Deal, he never had the votes. Even when the Republicans controlled Congress from 1953 to 1955, there were more than enough Democratic and liberal Republican votes in Congress to block any attempt to repeal the New Deal. Beyond that, the American public did not want to see the New Deal undone. Roosevelt had established a broad consensus in favor of the notion that the federal government had responsibility both for the basic welfare of the American people and for the maintenance of prosperity. In a letter responding to criticism from his older brother, Edgar, a fervently right-wing Republican, Eisenhower lectured:

> Should any party attempt to abolish social security and eliminate labor laws and farm programs, you would not hear of that party again in our political history. There is a tiny splinter group, of course, that believes you can do these things. Among them are H. L. Hunt . . . , and a few other Texas oil millionaires, and an occasional politician and businessman from other areas. Their number is negligible and they are stupid.

Simply noting, however, that neither Congress nor the American people wanted to eliminate the New Deal obscured an important point. Eisenhower never intended to dismantle the New Deal. He was part of that broad consensus.

The 34th president never came up with a catchy name for his domestic program. He tried "moderate progressivism," "progressive moderation," and "dynamic conservatism." None of those had the ring of the New Deal, the Fair Deal, or the Great Society, but they did describe Eisenhower's approach. As the first Republican president after the New Deal, Eisenhower consolidated, preserved, and expanded its basic structure. He established the New Deal consensus as truly bipartisan. Republican national candidates had stopped running against the New Deal after 1936, but they never held power until after the elections of 1952, in which they won the White House and slender majorities in both houses of Congress. People wondered what the Republicans would actually do with power. Eisenhower provided the answer.

While Eisenhower had no intention of turning back the clock to 1932, he believed that big government threatened free enterprise and individual initiative. Unlike some more recent conservatives, he did not limit these concerns to domestic programs. He worried that ever-expanding defense budgets would distort the economy, require high taxes, and stifle private enterprise. Accordingly, he strove mightily to balance the budget, but he was no doctrinaire economic conservative. Eisenhower managed to produce budget surpluses in 1956 and 1957 and to balance the budget in 1960 (there would be only one balanced budget between that time and the late 1990s—in 1969). Four of his five deficits came during recessions, including the highest peacetime deficit to that time, in 1959. In short, Eisenhower used Keynesian counter-cyclical spending to combat economic downturns. One student of fiscal policy, Iwan Morgan, has described Eisenhower with considerable accuracy as a "passive and half-hearted Keynesian." Even passive and half-hearted Keynesianism has never been a characteristic of doctrinaire economic conservatives.

Aside from the question of the budget, Eisenhower forged an impressive overall economic record. Opponents at the time, and some historians since, have pointed out that, during the 1950s, economic growth in the United States lagged behind that of many other industrial countries. That, of course, missed the point that, unlike Great Britain, Europe, and Japan, the United States did not have to rebuild after World War II. Indeed, the American economy had expanded markedly during the war. The fact that the rate of growth in America was slower than in countries undergoing reconstruction during the 1950s was both inevitable and virtually meaningless. Family income rose sharply during Eisenhower's two terms, and median family income increased more than twice as much as the increase in the cost of living. Inflation averaged under 2 percent from 1953 to 1961. Especially in light of subsequent economic performance, Eisenhower's record has led a number of historians to give him high marks as a "manager of prosperity."

Eisenhower understood, as he made clear in the letter to his brother Edgar, that any attempt to abolish the New Deal would amount to political suicide. Beyond that, he personally believed that government had a role in people's lives. He believed in the maintenance of a basic welfare state; he believed that the government had a responsibility to maintain prosperity; and he believed in federal activity, as the Republican leader in the Senate, Robert Taft, put it, "where the objective is clearly beyond the power of that state or community to achieve." Eisenhower himself probably best summed up his approach when he stated that government should be liberal where people are concerned and conservative in dealing with their money.

In agriculture, Eisenhower attempted to cut back on the policies of the Roosevelt and Truman administrations. When Eisenhower took office, the government had accumulated huge stores of surplus grain, cotton, tobacco, and other commodities. The surplus resulted from policies intended to maintain the purchasing power of farmers relative to other groups in the economy. If, at harvest time, prices for a supported crop had fallen below the designated price, a farmer who had planted no more than the number of acres fixed by the government could get a loan from the government for the supported price of the crop. The crop served as collateral. If the market price rose, the farmer paid back the government and took the crop. If the price fell, the farmer

held on to the money and let the government keep the crop. As a result, the federal government found itself with huge stores of basic commodities.

Eisenhower's secretary of agriculture, Ezra Taft Benson, proposed a sliding scale of price supports (from 75 to 90 percent of parity) that was intended to move agriculture toward an open market and reduce the surplus. Farmers screamed bloody murder. In actuality, Eisenhower's predecessor had not supported full parity prices; during the Truman administration, agricultural price supports were pegged at 90 percent of parity. Reducing the subsidies left the already existing surplus stores of commodities in place. Attempts to sell off the surplus had not been especially successful, and storage costs had become expensive. Moreover, the very existence of mountains of stored commodities further depressed agricultural prices. To deal with the situation, the Eisenhower administration recommended that the surplus be given away through school lunch programs, disaster relief, stockpiles against a national emergency, and foreign aid. Eisenhower also favored reforestation of fallow acres, even if it required federal repurchase or regulation of private property.

Congress passed modest reductions in price supports in 1954. In 1956, the administration sent to Congress an agricultural bill that provided farmers with either cash or like compensation if they would leave land fallow. In that respect, it did not differ from New Deal policies, but Eisenhower also provided farmers with payment for putting land back into ungrazed grass, forest, or water storage. The Democrat-dominated Congress passed a bill including the administration program as well as a provision restoring subsidies to 90 percent of parity. Eisenhower vetoed the bill, and Congress could not muster the votes to override his veto. Eventually, Congress passed legislation establishing Eisenhower's Soil Bank. In spite of Eisenhower's reduction of agricultural subsidies, he left the basic structure of the farm program intact.

In other areas, Eisenhower oversaw the preservation and expansion of basic elements of the New Deal. In his first State of the Union message, he called for expanding "safeguards against the privations that too often come with unemployment, old age, illness, and accident." During his first year in the White House, the president proposed broadening social security to cover self-employed farmers, doctors, dentists, lawyers, and others. The proposal also included an increase in monthly benefits and a liberalized retirement earnings provision. Congress took no action, and Eisenhower renewed the recommendation in a special message to Congress the following year. Legislation in 1954 brought 10 million self-employed workers into the system, the largest expansion of Social Security since its inception. The new law also raised benefits.

In 1956, Congress amended the Social Security Act to include disability insurance, funded through the payroll tax and administered by the states. Disability insurance was expanded to include dependants of the disabled in 1958. As pressure built up to add medical care for the aged (Medicare), Sen. John F. Kennedy, running for the presidency, gave a speech at Hyde Park, by then a shrine to Franklin D. Roosevelt, on the 25th anniversary of the Social Security Act. Standing within sight of Roosevelt's grave, Kennedy ended a long-standing feud with Eleanor Roosevelt and endorsed Medicare. In response, the administration produced a plan, drawn up by Arthur Flemming, the secretary of health, education, and welfare. It provided for 180 days of hospitalization and covered most other medical expenses. The plan differed from Democratic proposals in that it would be paid for through the social security system, administered by private companies, and would include a means test. The plan encountered opposition from the left and the right. The American Medical Association branded it socialist; the AFL-CIO claimed that it was a boondoggle for insurance companies. Two conservative Democrats, Sen. Robert S. Kerr of Oklahoma and Wilbur Mills of Arkansas, chair of the House Ways and Means Committee, drew up a third alternative. Funded from general revenues, it provided federal grants to enable states to pay for medical care of elderly welfare recipients or elderly persons unable to pay their own medical bills. Ultimately, Eisenhower signed the Kerr-Mills bill, and it became law.

Under Eisenhower, the minimum wage was increased from 75 cents to $1 an hour, one of the largest percentage increases in history. After listening to various proposals from the cabinet, Eisenhower decided to propose an increase of 90 cents and compromise on $1. Congress passed the increase in 1955.

In some areas, Eisenhower expanded the legacy of the New Deal. His administration undertook several huge public works projects. Although these represented an expansion of New Deal style programs, they did not constitute a radical departure from past practice. Since the 1920s, Republican and Democratic presidents alike had advocated a project to convert the Saint Lawrence River into an inland waterway connecting the Great Lakes with the Atlantic Ocean. The Eisenhower administration proposed, and Congress passed, legislation establishing the Saint Lawrence Seaway Development Corporation to cooperate with Canada in building the Saint Lawrence Seaway. The project was completed in 1959.

If Eisenhower tended towards fiscal conservatism, he also proved to be a wise investor. The largest public works project of his administration was the interstate highway system. By the 1950s, overland transportation in America was little short of a disaster. Since World War II, the railroads had been in chronic financial trouble and had steadily cut passenger service. Highways, traditionally the preserve of state and local governments, had become increasingly inadequate. The continuing development of the automobile and inexpensive fuel made driving ever more attractive, and the resulting increase in traffic placed greater demands on roads. In addition, trucks offered the least expensive, quickest, and most convenient means of moving goods. Yet American highways had not kept pace with advances in, or America's reliance on, automobiles and trucks. Of American cities, only New York, Los Angeles, and Chicago had high-speed expressways. The country lacked four-lane highways to link its cities. The need was clear, and only the federal government could build a unified system of highways. In addition, the resources required for such an undertaking exceeded the capabilities of state and local governments. All of this fit Eisenhower's idea of an appropriate role for the federal government. Moreover, such a massive public works program would enable Eisenhower to respond to swings in the economy and in unemployment. Finally, the system could make evacuation of cities possible in the event of nuclear war and would facilitate the movement of military traffic.

President Eisenhower signs H.R. 8127, the 1954 Highway Legislation, May 6, 1954. *(Dwight D. Eisenhower Library and Museum)*

Eisenhower appointed a commission headed by Gen. Lucius Clay to study the situation. The commission recommended the construction of an extensive national highway system with federal and state money. Conservatives opposed the undertaking. Roads had always been a function of the states, they argued, and the cost of the project was staggering. Eisenhower overcame conservative opposition by stressing the value of the highway system to civil defense. In Congress, his legislative leaders won votes by making concessions to representatives from major urban areas. In the end, Congress passed the Federal Highway Act of 1956, which provided for the construction of 42,000 miles of limited access,

four- to eight-lane roads linking America's major cities. Federal taxes on fuels, tires, and commercial vehicles paid for the National System of Interstate and Defense Highways. By the end of Eisenhower's presidency, 7,500 miles of the system had been opened.

With reference to these public works projects, a prominent historian, William L. O'Neill, has called Eisenhower "a master builder." In subsequent decades, the United States, in effect, lived off of the investments made during the Eisenhower years. As O'Neill has pointed out, spending for infrastructure "has long been only a fraction of what it was in the 1950s." In the years since Eisenhower left office, the United States not only has failed substantially to expand the infrastructure Eisenhower bequeathed, but has maintained it poorly.

In another area, federally funded public housing, Eisenhower continued along a path similar to the one Truman had followed. In 1949, Congress passed a law providing for construction of 810,000 units of public housing over the next six years. When Truman left office, fewer than one-quarter of those units had been built; Truman had never requested construction of more than 75,000 units in a single year. The new Eisenhower administration submitted a request for 35,000 new housing starts in fiscal year 1954, which prompted the immediate and strenuous opposition of conservative Republicans in the Congress. The House stripped all public housing from the bill, but the Senate restored the administration's original request. The conference committee settled on the construction of 20,000 new units.

In 1954, the administration requested legislation to guarantee the construction of 1 million units of housing that year, largely through federal mortgage insurance, urban renewal, and lower requirements for down payments on federally insured loans for low-income housing. The measure also proposed continuing the federal public housing program for four years, with the construction of 35,000 units in each of the four years. When congressional Republican leaders objected, Eisenhower defended it as a basic need of the people. Once again, the House eliminated all public housing from the measure, and the Senate restored the president's original request. The conference committee produced a compromise that authorized 35,000 new housing starts in fiscal year 1955 but limited new public housing starts to the number of units of slum clearance. Eisenhower signed the bill; in doing so, however, he indicated that the job was "not all finished. . . . We shall need to continue our public housing program until the needs can be met by private industry."

Eisenhower's proposals for housing were more modest than Truman's, but the urgent housing shortage Truman faced had abated. If Eisenhower did not get everything he wanted from Congress, he got much of what he requested. If he asked for a bit less than Truman, the need was less acute. In many respects, Eisenhower's housing policy rep-

resented a continuation of the policy he inherited. His approach to housing issues was similar to his trimming of agricultural subsidies. In both cases, despite alterations and reductions, the basic structure of policy he inherited remained intact.

The Eisenhower administration proposed several new programs to improve public health. In 1953, Eisenhower sent a message to Congress that emphasized the need for expanded health insurance for the American people. While 92 million people had private health insurance, three-quarters of families with annual incomes below $2,000 had no insurance coverage. The following year, Eisenhower proposed a health reinsurance program. The plan set up a fund that would be used to assume 75 percent of any "abnormal losses" incurred by any approved private health insurance carriers that resulted from offering coverage to high-risk customers. The purpose of the plan was to reduce the cost of insurance and thereby make it available to more people. Ever concerned about what it regarded as socialized medicine, the American Medical Association lobbied hard against the program. So, too, did the major insurance companies, and the Chicago-based companies were especially effective in persuading midwestern Republicans. Liberal Democrats, who advocated a more extensive, centralized program, also joined in the opposition. Thus, opponents in Congress from the left and right combined to kill the plan.

The defeat of the reinsurance plan infuriated Eisenhower. "How in the hell," he demanded, "is the American Medical Association going to stop socialized medicine if they oppose bills such as this?" The president continued: "I don't believe the people of the United States are going to stand for being deprived of the opportunity to get medical insurance. If they don't get a bill like this, they will go for socialized medicine sooner or later and the Medical Association will have no one to blame but itself." This reaction revealed much about Eisenhower's approach to social issues. He supported basic social programs because he believed in them and because he believed that the American people demanded them. He also supported such programs because he feared that, in their absence, demands for change would take a direction he did not support or would go further than he deemed wise.

Along those lines, Eisenhower supported a limited federal role in the distribution of the Salk polio vaccine. Eisenhower was determined that "no child in the United States would be denied . . . [the vaccine] for want of ability to pay." Congress acted favorably on Eisenhower's request to appropriate $30 million in grants for distribution of the vaccine to children from the poorest families. Eisenhower also approved a plan for the orderly distribution of the vaccine. Under the management of Oveta Culp Hobby, the secretary of health, education, and welfare, distribution of the vaccine became something of a public relations nightmare. That did not, however, change the fundamental fact of Eisenhower's support for an active, if limited, federal role.

Eisenhower also supported federal activity in other areas relating to public health. He obtained an increase in federal spending on hospitals and other medical facilities. Spending for public health, medical research, and hospital construction increased from $290 million in 1954 to almost $1 billion in 1960.

Education became a pressing issue during the 1950s. As the children of the baby boom reached school age, their sheer numbers created a crisis in education. School districts struggled vainly to find funding for enough teachers, classrooms, and textbooks to meet the demand. Recognizing that schools were a jealously guarded responsibility of local government, the Eisenhower administration sought the least controversial means for providing federal aid. A primary objection to federal aid to schools was that the federal government might dictate who would teach and what might be taught in schools. Therefore, in 1955, the Eisenhower administration proposed an ambitious federal initiative to provide aid in the least sensitive area, the construction of new classrooms. The proposal became hopelessly entangled with issues of school desegregation and whether federal funds should go to parochial schools. Conservatives regarded any federal involvement with schools as a threat to local control. Southerners worried that federal aid would act as the thin edge of the wedge of desegregation (the government might withhold federal funds to segregated schools). Adding weight to that concern, Adam Clayton Powell, Jr., an African-American member of Congress from Harlem,

offered an amendment that would have prohibited federal aid to segregated schools. Catholics opposed federal assistance that excluded parochial schools. Confronted with determined opposition from these constituencies and their representatives, Congress rejected Eisenhower's school construction bill.

In 1958, after the Soviet Union launched Sputnik and many Americans frantically worried that the United States had fallen behind the Soviets in technology, Eisenhower proposed and Congress passed the National Defense Education Act. The act provided low-interest loans for deserving college students and for grants to improve the teaching of math and science in the public schools. At least one historian has argued that the National Defense Education Act constituted the most significant federal contribution to education since the Morrill Land Grant Act. If so, its significance derived not from the nature or amount of the aid, but from the fact that it expanded the New Deal's conception of federal responsibility for the national welfare to include education.

Historians have generally given Eisenhower low marks in the area of civil rights. Yet much of the criticism misses the mark. Eisenhower certainly was no drum major for civil rights, but he and his administration made important, if limited, contributions to the cause of civil rights. Eisenhower talked less about the issue than his predecessor or his successor, but his concrete accomplishments exceeded those of either Harry Truman or John Kennedy.

The Eisenhower administration appointed African Americans in unprecedented numbers and to unprecedented positions in the executive branch. Before Eisenhower became president, those few blacks in government service generally held either one of a few specific posts in domestic affairs that dealt with "Negro matters" or foreign-service assignments in black African countries. Eisenhower continued that type of appointment, but he also named African Americans to positions in no way connected to racial issues and appointed blacks to positions previously held only by whites. The appointment of E. Frederic Morrow as administrative officer for the Special Projects Group made Morrow the first African American to hold an executive position in the White House. Lois Lippman became the first black secretary to work in the White House.

African Americans took new positions throughout the executive branch. J. Ernest Wilkins received an appointment as assistant secretary of labor and, in that capacity, would become the first African American to represent a department of the executive branch in a cabinet meeting. African Americans held positions as chief of the Parole Board, chairman of the President's Employment Policy Committee, registrar of the Treasury, and associate general counsel in the Post Office Department. Eisenhower also appointed African Americans to less visible posts in the middle levels of government.

Not long after Eisenhower took office, the *Pittsburgh Courier*, one of the nation's leading black newspapers, rejoiced that "there are far more Negro faces around here now than at any time in the past twenty years." The *Courier* observed a marked contrast to the way things had been under Franklin Roosevelt and particularly Harry Truman.

Although Eisenhower opposed a compulsory federal Fair Employment Practices Commission, he set out to eliminate discrimination in employment by the federal government. Toward that end, he replaced an ineffective committee created by Truman with a new President's Committee on Government Employment Policy. In practice, Eisenhower's committee was only somewhat more effective than Truman's had been.

Eisenhower also attempted to deal with discrimination practiced by firms holding contracts with the federal government. As a first step, Eisenhower created a President's Committee on Government Contracts. Following the recommendation of that committee, Eisenhower issued an executive order requiring that all contracts with the federal government contain a clause prohibiting contractors from discriminating in hiring or promotion. The order further required that any subcontract contain a similar clause.

Eisenhower also made good on Truman's promise to desegregate the armed forces. There had been some limited progress in this area before Eisenhower became president, but most of that progress came about in response to the exigencies of combat in Korea, not executive action. Immediately upon taking office, Eisenhower moved to end segregation in the military. Even before the Supreme Court ruled segregated schools unconstitutional, the Eisenhower administration ordered the elimination of segregation in schools on military bases. The Eisenhower administration also undertook to desegregate Veterans Administration hospitals and civilian employees on military bases. Eisenhower's policies encountered opposition and did not always proceed quickly or without hitches. By the late 1950s, however, the official policy of nondiscrimination in the armed forces had gone a long way toward becoming a reality. The military had become one of the most integrated institutions in American life.

One of the most significant efforts the administration made to advance the cause of civil rights was its effort to desegregate Washington, D.C. When Eisenhower took office, Washington was a rigidly segregated city. During the campaign of 1952, Eisenhower had pledged to end segregation in the nation's capital. Upon taking office, the new president set about redeeming that pledge. Toward that end, he decided to make the District's Board of Commissioners a force for change. The commissioners began by taking steps to eliminate discriminatory hiring practices by the D.C. government itself. Next, in late 1953, the Board of Commissioners added a clause to all contracts with the District government forbidding discrimination in hiring or promotion by contractors and subcontractors.

The President's Committee on Government Contracts played an important role in the attempt to stamp out discrimination by quasi-public entities in the District. The committee entered long and arduous negotiations with the Capital Transit Company, which provided Washington's bus service, and the Chesapeake and Potomac Telephone Company. Eventually, the committee gained concessions from both companies that opened jobs previously held only by whites to African Americans.

On another front, the Justice Department, under the leadership of Attorney General Herbert Brownell, entered a case against the Thompson restaurant chain. At issue were laws passed by Congress during Reconstruction that forbade discrimination in places of public accommodation in the District of Columbia. Although ignored for decades, these laws remained on the books. Attorneys for the Thompson restaurants argued that the laws had fallen into disuse and were therefore not enforceable. The attorney general himself appeared before the Supreme Court to argue for enforcement of the so-called lost laws. The Supreme Court ruled unanimously in favor of the government's position.

While the Thompson case was pending before the Supreme Court, Eisenhower invited owners of Washington's hotels and theaters to the White House and tried to persuade them to end segregation voluntarily in their establishments. The hotel owners were particularly recalcitrant. Even after the Thompson ruling, service for African Americans remained uncertain in Washington's hotels, and the fight for equal treatment in hotels passed to private organizations.

Eisenhower proved more persuasive in dealing with owners of movie theaters. In the 1950s, downtown movie theaters charged more than suburban theaters, basing their higher prices on the fact that first-run movies often took a year to make it to suburban theaters. Moreover, major studios owned some downtown movie palaces. Accordingly, Eisenhower asked leaders of the motion picture industry to desegregate the theaters they owned or controlled in Washington and to deny first-run films to other theaters in the District that continued to exclude African Americans or to segregate. Coupled with the efforts of local activists, the result was the rapid opening of major downtown theaters to black customers.

Eisenhower fell well short of his stated goal of ending "every vestige" of segregation in Washington. Yet his administration began the process and made significant progress towards that end. After the first year and a half of Eisenhower's presidency, African Americans faced a far less inhospitable environment in the nation's capital.

The initiatives to desegregate the armed forces, to eliminate discrimination among employees of the federal government, and to desegregate the nation's capital all came during the first 16 months of the Eisenhower administration. Its policy was one of active intervention in areas where the federal government had unquestioned authority and the executive branch had unilateral power. Eisenhower wanted neither to raise the issue of federalism nor to engage in a noisy battle with Congress. Where the executive did not exert unilateral authority, the administration relied primarily on attempts at conciliation and persuasion. This strategy produced substantial, if limited, gains.

Eisenhower seemed pleased with the results, but his approach became almost irrelevant on May 17, 1954. On that date, in *Brown v. Board of Education of Topeka*, the Supreme Court ruled that segregation in public schools violated the equal protection clause of the Fourteenth Amendment. When Eisenhower entered the White House, the federal government had already entered the school segregation cases on the side of the black school children and filed a brief arguing against segregation. In response to a set of questions set forth by the Court, the Eisenhower administration filed a brief asserting that the Fourteenth Amendment "forbade all distinctions based on race or color." During oral arguments before the Supreme Court, Assistant Attorney General J. Lee Rankin argued that "segregation in public schools cannot be maintained under the Fourteenth Amendment." When the Supreme Court asked for further arguments on how to implement its decision outlawing segregation, Eisenhower took an active role in shaping the government's brief. In that instance, he toned down the brief prepared by two activist subordinates (Solicitor General Simon E. Soboleff and Philip Elman, a lawyer in the Justice Department). Even with Eisenhower's modifications, however, the government brief argued for a somewhat more specific decree than the one the Court finally issued.

Without doubt, however, Eisenhower's most important contribution to the outcome of *Brown* was the appointment of Earl Warren to replace Chief Justice Fred Vinson. Warren proved instrumental in obtaining the unanimous decision in *Brown*. Some historians have contended that Warren's actions surprised and dismayed the president. In fact, Eisenhower was very involved in the nomination of Warren and, indeed, in all appellate judicial appointments. The often repeated story that Eisenhower came to regard the appointment of Warren as his greatest mistake simply has no basis in truth. Herbert Brownell, who worked more closely with Eisenhower on such matters than anyone, denied that Eisenhower ever said anything to that effect. The source for Eisenhower's supposed comment was an oral history interview with Ralph

Supreme Court Justices (left to right) William O. Douglas, Stanley Reed, Chief Justice Earl Warren, Hugo Black, Felix Frankfurter, and others stand with President Eisenhower on the White House steps, 1953 *(Library of Congress)*

Cake, a right-wing Republican from the West Coast who detested Warren. Eisenhower did occasionally grumble about some of the Warren Court's decisions, particularly in the area of internal security, but he never lost confidence in Warren. To the contrary, Eisenhower told his press secretary, Jim Hagerty, in 1956 that Warren was becoming one of the great chief justices in history.

Historians have criticized Eisenhower for failing to endorse the *Brown* decision. Eisenhower always maintained that it was not his job to pass judgment on decisions of the Supreme Court; it was his job to enforce them. If he commented on the Court's decisions, he reasoned, inevitably he would be led to express his disagreement with a decision of the Court. This, in turn, would lead to questions about

his willingness to enforce that decision. Eisenhower's position seems to have been based on principle; nonetheless, many southerners took it as an expression of displeasure with the Court's ruling.

Whatever the wisdom of refusing to comment on the Court's decision, Eisenhower did have reservations about *Brown*. He considered it an unwise exercise of federal power and an example of questionable judicial activism. He also thought that federal coercion would prove an ineffective means to end segregation and would therefore set back the cause of desegregation. Eisenhower favored a gradual end to segregation and hoped to avoid the use of coercive federal power. Whatever his disagreements with the Court's approach, however, he did not disagree with the basic principle established in *Brown*.

Moreover, when federal authority was challenged in Little Rock, Ark., Eisenhower acted forcefully. A federal district court ordered the admission of nine black students to Little Rock's Central High School in 1957. When first the governor of Arkansas and then a mob prevented the black students from entering Central High, Eisenhower nationalized the Arkansas National Guard and sent paratroopers from the elite 101st Airborne Division to enforce the federal court's order.

The Eisenhower administration did more to advance civil rights than enforce federal court orders. Brownell submitted civil rights legislation to Congress in 1956. The Democratic party controlled Congress, and the Democratic leadership wanted no part of an internecine battle over civil rights during an election year. The majority leader in the Senate, Lyndon Johnson, buried the bill in committee. The administration resubmitted its proposals in 1957. Without the immediate pressure of an election, Johnson concluded that some bill would have to pass for the good of both the Democratic party and his own presidential ambitions. Johnson guided the bill through Congress, but in the process, he removed the bill's most far-reaching provisions and effectively gutted it. As it passed, the bill created a Civil Rights Division in the Justice Department, established a Civil Rights Commission, and contained provisions to protect voting rights. The bill Johnson engineered was a shadow

President Eisenhower meets with civil rights leaders at the White House, June 23, 1958. Left to right: Lester Granger, Martin Luther King, Jr., E. Frederic Morrow, President Eisenhower, A. Philip Randolph, Attorney General William Rogers, Rocco Siciliano, and Roy Wilkins *(Dwight D. Eisenhower Library and Museum)*

of the administration's proposal, but it was, nevertheless, the first civil rights legislation to pass Congress since Reconstruction. In 1960, Eisenhower went back to Congress and got stronger protection for black voting rights. Like the Civil Rights Act of 1957, the Civil Rights Act of 1960 proved insufficient to protect black voters in the South. However, Eisenhower's two civil rights laws paved the way for the Civil Rights Act of 1964 and the Voting Rights Act of 1965.

Eisenhower's appointments to the federal judiciary in the South constituted his greatest contribution to civil rights. The liberals and moderates he appointed to the areas most affected by the *Brown* decision insured an ongoing process of desegregation. When compared to appointments made by his predecessor and successor, Eisenhower's achievement stands out in dramatic relief. One of these nominees in particular, Simon E. Sobeloff, won confirmation over bitter and determined opposition by segregationists. The judges Eisenhower appointed to the Fourth and Fifth Circuit Courts of Appeal oversaw the dismantling of the system of segregation in the South. In appointing these judges, Eisenhower accomplished his purpose. They would enforce the Supreme Court's mandate, but, by the very nature of the American legal system, the process would be a gradual one.

In spite of the myriad domestic problems he faced, Eisenhower devoted the majority of his time as president to foreign policy. He took office at a time when the cold war burned hot in Korea, when relations with the Soviet Union seemed to threaten to explode into a mushroom cloud, and when new nations began to emerge from the wreckage of European colonialism. In a dangerous and unstable world, the Eisenhower administration charted a course for the United States that would influence much of the rest of the century.

Much as was the case in domestic policy, Eisenhower inherited a consensus in foreign policy from his predecessor. With the Truman Doctrine and the Marshall Plan, Truman had established a consensus in favor of the policy of containment. Eisenhower functioned within that consensus in foreign policy; indeed, he had helped to create it. He passed on the consensus intact to his successor, John F. Kennedy. Nevertheless, as was the case with domestic policy,

and perhaps to an even greater extent, Eisenhower differed in his methods and style from both his predecessor and successor. While Truman and Kennedy tended to provoke confrontation, Eisenhower sought to downplay international tensions. Despite that significant difference in style, Eisenhower pursued the same objectives and fought the cold war with the same commitment as presidents before and after him.

Eisenhower came to the White House with broad experience in foreign policy. He had commanded a multinational military coalition during World War II, and the concerns of international politics had been the very essence of his job as supreme allied commander. Dealing with Joseph Stalin, Winston Churchill, and Franklin D. Roosevelt provided him an advanced education in diplomacy at the summit. In addition, he handled with great skill the problems of an international military alliance, which included managing strains on that alliance created by nationalist egomaniacs like Field Marshal Bernard Law Montgomery of Great Britain and General George S. Patton of the United States. After the war, Eisenhower served as the army chief of staff and supreme commander of the North Atlantic Treaty Organization (NATO). In short, he had been a major figure in American defense and foreign policy since World War II. He knew world leaders on a personal, often fairly intimate, basis, and his knowledge of and relationships with these leaders informed his foreign policy.

For secretary of state, Eisenhower chose John Foster Dulles, who was typical of Eisenhower's appointments to his cabinet. Capable and forceful, Dulles was ready to take the credit when things went well and, more important from Eisenhower's perspective, available to take the blame when things went wrong. While Eisenhower made the final decisions with respect to foreign policy, he allowed Dulles to articulate and implement those policies. In general, it should be said, the two men agreed on the basics of foreign policy. Dulles was inclined to take a somewhat harder line on some issues, but the president and his secretary of state were very much in accord with respect to their general approach.

Some of the earliest revisionist works on Eisenhower were written by New Left historians in the late 1960s and early 1970s. Disillusioned by the pol-

White House conference with (left to right) John Foster Dulles, Winston Churchill, President Eisenhower, and Anthony Eden, June 25, 1954 *(Dwight D. Eisenhower Library and Museum)*

icies of the Kennedy and Johnson administrations that led to the war in Vietnam, New Left historians searched the past for an alternative and found one in Eisenhower, a president who ended one war and did not begin another. The idea of a military man as a man of peace held a strong attraction for these dissenting historians. While that image contained an element of truth, it was overdrawn. Eisenhower was a dedicated cold warrior. Although reluctant to commit American forces, he was willing to use covert operations to achieve his goals. Setting aside the overstatement, at least some part of the New Left analysis of Eisenhower remains persuasive. In his conduct of the cold war, Eisenhower differed from Truman before him and Kennedy after in that he sought to avoid confrontation and to defuse tensions. A good example came in July 1954, when Chinese Communists shot down a British commercial airliner. Two U.S. aircraft carriers from the Asian fleet (which were off the coast of Indochina in response to the crisis faced by the French army

at Dien Bien Phu) were sent to aid any survivors. The ships came under attack by Communist Chinese fighter planes, and they shot down two of the Chinese planes. Rather than play up the incident, Eisenhower maneuvered to ease tensions. By any standard, it was a far more serious incident than when the Soviet Union shot down Korean Air Lines flight 007 in the 1980s. Unlike the situation facing President Ronald W. Reagan in the 1980s, the United States was directly involved; American carriers had been attacked while on a rescue mission, and they had shot down two Chinese planes. Yet, while most people have probably heard of the incident involving KAL 007, very few are aware of the earlier episode. Rather than ratcheting up the tension, Eisenhower sought to calm things down.

Despite differences in style, Eisenhower's approach to foreign policy had much more in common with Truman than it did with that of the right wing of his own party. The Republican party was deeply divided between the eastern (also known as the liberal or internationalist) wing of the party and the conservative, or midwestern, wing. Like the Democrats, liberal Republicans placed their faith in multilateral defense pacts and regarded the developed nations of Europe as the primary area of American interest. Eastern Republicans also supported Truman's basic approach to the cold war, including the Truman Doctrine and Marshall Plan, large defense budgets, universal military training, and conscription. In contrast, conservative Republicans rejected both the Europe-first orientation of the Roosevelt and Truman administrations and collective security arrangements. They preferred to see the United States chart its own course and look after its own interests; moreover, they believed that the future lay not in Europe but across the Pacific. Conservative Republicans opposed universal military training and conscription in peacetime as threats to individual liberty and to the republic. On all of these issues, both during the Truman years and his own administration, Eisenhower sided with the eastern Republicans and the Democrats.

At the same time, Eisenhower believed that the Truman administration had failed to balance its conduct of the cold war and America's international commitments with the country's limited resources. Especially in the earliest days of the cold war, Eisenhower thought that Truman and his advisors had overestimated the military aspect of the Soviet threat, which he regarded, at least in the short term, as primarily political and economic. Further, Eisenhower repeatedly expressed concern about the high level of defense spending by the Truman administration.

His critique of the Truman administration's conduct of the cold war formed the basis for Eisenhower's foreign policy. He came into office determined to reduce defense budgets and did so. Not only did Eisenhower think that Truman spent more on the military than was necessary to provide adequate defense, he worried about what such huge defense budgets would do to the economy and ultimately to democratic institutions. Eisenhower's "New Look" defense policy, which relied on air power, technology, and the nuclear deterrent, grew largely out of his desire to keep defense spending in check. The New Look provided for an expanded strategic air force and reductions in conventional forces. Sec-

retary of Defense Charles E. Wilson summed up the policy with the unfortunate phrase "more bang for the buck." Expensive though weapons systems were, they offered a less expensive means of projecting force than the use of conventional forces. In addition to Eisenhower's determination to cut military costs, the New Look was a reaction to the Korean War, which cost American lives and treasure, was divisive at home, and strained relations with America's allies. Eisenhower regarded "our young men" as "our most valued, our most costly asset," and he proclaimed his intention not to "use them any more than we have to." Finally, preparing to fight a conventional war in Europe, where the Soviets had natural strategic and logistical advantages and where the Soviets enjoyed an enormous advantage in men and conventional weapons, struck Eisenhower as senseless. In contrast, the New Look focused on situations in which the United States had the natural advantage.

In typical fashion, Eisenhower delegated the articulation of the New Look to Dulles. In an address to the Council on Foreign Relations in January 1954, the secretary of state explained that the United States would deter further communist aggression by aiding local defenses and developing "massive retaliatory power." This, he explained, would enable the United States to "retaliate, instantly, by means and at places of our choosing." The New Look would provide "maximum deterrent at a bearable cost." This did not mean that the United States would resort to all-out nuclear war to meet every exigency. Local defenses, perhaps supplemented by tactical nuclear weapons if necessary, would often serve as an adequate deterrent in most circumstances. Behind all other defenses, however, lay the threat of an all-out nuclear response to deter communist aggression.

Truman's proposed defense budget for fiscal year 1954 was $45 billion, a level Eisenhower regarded as unsustainable. While Eisenhower regarded the Soviet Union as a threat, he doubted that Soviet leaders would risk a general war. Rather, he believed that the United States faced a prolonged period of international tension. In that long struggle, he thought, excessive defense spending threatened to weaken the American economy by contributing to budget deficits and inflation. Further, the taxes needed to support such high levels of defense spending would hamper the free enterprise system and foster the growth of statism. Eisenhower and his administration reduced Truman's defense budget for 1954 to $43.2 billion and projected spending $40 billion for defense in 1955 and $35 billion in 1956. By ending the war in Korea and implementing the New Look, the Eisenhower administration was able to reduce defense budgets substantially. Spending for defense fell to $37.5 billion in 1955 and roughly $33.5 billion in 1957. Eisenhower's last defense budget was $40 billion. In his farewell address, Eisenhower observed that the cold war had resulted in a larger military and enormous military spending. "The conjunction of an immense military establishment and a large arms industry," the president pointed out, "is new in the American experience," and its "total influence—economic, political, even spiritual—is felt in every city, every statehouse, every office of the federal government." While recognizing the necessity of a large and powerful military establishment, he warned that "we must not fail to comprehend its grave implications." "In the councils of government," he admonished, "we must guard against the acquisition of unwarranted influence, whether sought or unsought, by the military-industrial complex."

The most pressing matter facing Eisenhower when he became president was the ongoing war in Korea. Eisenhower worried that the war drained American resources and raised doubts about the credibility of the United States. Thus, he wanted to end the war. Toward that end, Dulles hinted to the Indian prime minister, Jawaharlal Nehru, that, if the negotiations in Korea collapsed, the United States might widen the war and resort to nuclear weapons. Two weeks later, the North Koreans and Chinese acceded to the western demand for the voluntary repatriation of prisoners, which removed the last substantial obstacle to an armistice. Eisenhower and Dulles were convinced that their nuclear diplomacy brought the Communists to an agreement. That analysis underestimated other factors, but, in all probability, the Eisenhower administration's threats to use nuclear weapons constituted one of several factors that pushed the Chinese and North Koreans to agree to a settlement. Some historians have suggested that the warnings the administration intended to pass on to the Chinese through India may not even have reached the Chinese, but, in any case, the Chinese certainly knew of Eisenhower's campaign rhetoric, which called for a more aggressive policy in Korea. On the other hand, any impact those threats might have had was most likely offset, at least partly, by the Chinese belief that the Soviet nuclear arsenal would deter the United States from using nuclear weapons. The continuing heavy toll of casualties suffered by the Chinese and North Koreans certainly provided an incentive for them to seek a truce. Moreover, Stalin died in March 1953, and the Soviet Union's new leaders pressed their allies to end the war at an early date. Finally, having prevented the forcible reunification of Korea under the auspices of the Western powers, China's leader, Mao Zedong, could claim a victory of sorts. Even if the administration's nuclear diplomacy did not account alone, or even primarily, for the end of hostilities, the armistice ended a bloody stalemate that was unpopular at home, caused problems with allies, and cost an enormous amount of money as well as tens of thousands of American lives.

Eisenhower inherited a cold war and a divided Europe from his predecessor. Stalin's death and hints about the possibility of "peaceful coexistence" from the collective leadership that succeeded him prompted Eisenhower to explore the possibility of reaching an accord with the Soviet Union. Some of his advisors, Dulles in particular, remained skeptical of Soviet intentions. Nonetheless, Eisenhower did not want to miss the opportunity if, indeed, it existed. In April 1953, Eisenhower delivered a major speech, titled "A Chance for Peace," to the American Society of Newspaper Editors, in which he eloquently discussed the cost of the arms race and outlined the conditions for a general reduction in tensions. Ultimately, however, Eisenhower and his administration became convinced that the Soviet "peace offensive" amounted to nothing more than a cynical attempt to divide the Western alliance, and little came of the "chance for peace." The use of Soviet tanks to put down rioting in East Germany in June 1953 served to confirm the Eisenhower administration's skepticism about Soviet intentions.

The British prime minister, Winston Churchill, pushed for an early summit meeting with the new leaders of the Soviet Union. Eisenhower turned aside Churchill's calls for an early summit and focused on building the Western alliance. Toward that end, he adopted a plan to rearm West Germany and integrate its forces into the European Defense Community. The plan encountered opposition from the French, who remained worried about the prospect of German rearmament. Never enthusiastic about a European Defense Community, the British took the opportunity to suggest that West Germany be admitted to NATO. The British suggestion prevailed, and the Paris Accords of October 1954 provided for West German sovereignty and the creation of a West German army integrated into the defense structure of NATO. The Federal Republic of Germany formally entered NATO in May 1955. The Soviet Union responded by forming its own military organization comprising Eastern European nations, known as the Warsaw Pact.

For all his doubts about the intentions of the Soviets, Eisenhower repeatedly expressed his concern about the escalating nuclear arms race. In December 1953, three months after the Soviet Union detonated a thermonuclear device, Eisenhower gave a speech at the United Nations General Assembly in which he called on all nuclear powers to donate a set amount of fissionable material to be used for peaceful purposes under the auspices of the United Nations. The Soviets rejected "Atoms for Peace," as the initiative became known, which put the United States in a favorable light, but, even had the Soviets accepted it, the proposal would have done nothing to halt the arms race.

The Soviet Union surprised the West in 1955, however, by agreeing to conclude a peace treaty with Austria. The treaty provided for the end of military occupation and established Austria as an independent, neutral nation. Seeing the possibility of an opening, European nations urged Eisenhower to hold a summit conference with the Soviet Union. Eisenhower remained skeptical, and Dulles warned about the possibility of a trap set by the communists. Nevertheless, Eisenhower somewhat reluctantly agreed to a summit meeting at Geneva in July 1955. At the summit, Eisenhower proposed that the Unites States and Soviet Union exchange blueprints of military installations and permit mutual aerial surveillance. Britain and France joined the so-called

Open Skies initiative, but the Soviets rejected it. Geneva produced no agreements of substance, but it did establish a warmer diplomatic climate. The "Spirit of Geneva" represented the first thaw in the cold war.

By the middle of the decade, various successes gave the administration cause to be confident in their conduct of the cold war. The Soviets had failed to prevent the rearmament of West Germany and its incorporation into NATO; they had settled for the neutralization of Austria; and their "peace offensive" had been upstaged by Eisenhower's proposal for "Open Skies" at Geneva. Further, Khrushchev's secret speech at the Twentieth Party Congress in February 1956 acknowledged the failures of socialism, denounced Stalin's crimes, and repudiated the doctrine of inevitable conflict between socialism and capitalism, opting instead for "peaceful coexistence." The Eisenhower administration obtained a copy of the speech and released it to the *New York Times*. In an effort to keep up the pressure on the Soviet Union, the United States sent radio broadcasts encouraging the "captive peoples" of Eastern Europe to liberate themselves from the Soviet Union.

In late October 1956, strikes, demonstrations, and rioting broke out in Poland, which led to the return to power of Władysław Gomułka, whom the Soviets had ousted from the Polish government and imprisoned in 1949 because of his "Titoist" leanings. Back in government, Gomułka had the temerity to insist that the Soviet model was not the only road to socialism. A furious Khrushchev threatened to send Soviet troops into Poland but then backed off when the Poles reassured him that their nation would remain within the Soviet bloc.

Inspired by events in Poland, young Hungarians took to the streets on October 23 demanding the return to power of Imre Nagy, a reformer whom the Soviets had deposed a year earlier. Seizing an opportunity presented by the Western alliance's preoccupation with the Suez crisis, Khrushchev decided to send Soviet troops and tanks to crush the rebellion. Hungarian street fighters met the tanks with stones and firebombs in a heroic but futile effort to turn back the Soviet invaders. As the fighting escalated, the Central Committee named Nagy premier on October 24, but even that failed to satisfy the protesters. On October 30, Nagy's government promised to establish a multiparty system and hold free elections. The Soviet government responded with an announcement that "socialist nations can build their relations only on the principle of full equality, respect of territorial integrity, state independence and sovereignty, and noninterference." Attempting to allay Soviet anxieties and prevent an escalation of violence, Eisenhower issued a statement denying that the United States regarded new governments in Eastern Europe as "potential military allies." Events, however, moved the situation beyond the point where Eisenhower's assurances could satisfy the Soviets. On November 1, Nagy announced the withdrawal of Hungary from the Warsaw Pact, declared his nation's neutrality, and appealed to the United Nations to defend that neutrality. In the United Nations Security Council, the Soviet Union vetoed an American backed resolution calling on the Soviet Union to withdraw its forces from Hungary. At this point, Khrushchev sent a massive Soviet force into Hungary and installed a puppet government. Approximately 20,000 Hungarians died in the ruthless repression of the Hungarian independence movement. Nagy was arrested and later executed. Hungarian appeals for help from the West went unanswered. Eisenhower concluded that any overt American intervention in the Hungarian crisis would lead to war with the Soviet Union. Further, in such an intervention, all tactical and logistical advantages would have rested with the Soviet Union. For all the compassion he felt for the Hungarian people, he was not willing to risk a general war.

Eisenhower's perpetual attempts to contain the U.S. defense budget encountered a particularly difficult test after the Soviet Union launched the first man-made satellite, *Sputnik*, in October 1957. The next month, the Soviets launched *Sputnik II*, which weighed over 1,000 pounds and carried a live dog. In addition, Khrushchev bragged about the development of an intercontinental ballistic missile (ICBM). Many in the United States, including many leading politicians, panicked. Democrats, in particular, criticized Eisenhower for allowing America's defense to deteriorate. Eisenhower responded calmly both to the Soviet launch of *Sputnik* and to the storm of criticism at home.

Well before the launch of *Sputnik*, in the spring of 1957, the National Security Council commissioned a panel, headed by H. Rowan Gaither of the Ford Foundation, to study Soviet offensive capabilities. Presented to the president in November, after the launch of *Sputnik*, the report presented a grim evaluation of the relative strength of the United States and the Soviet Union. It predicted that, by 1959, the USSR would be able to launch 100 ICBMs carrying nuclear warheads against the United States. In addition, it warned that the manned bombers of the Strategic Air Command would be vulnerable to such an attack. Extrapolating from existing trends, the report warned that the Soviets would achieve nuclear and technological superiority by 1960. It recommended that the United States embark on a program to develop

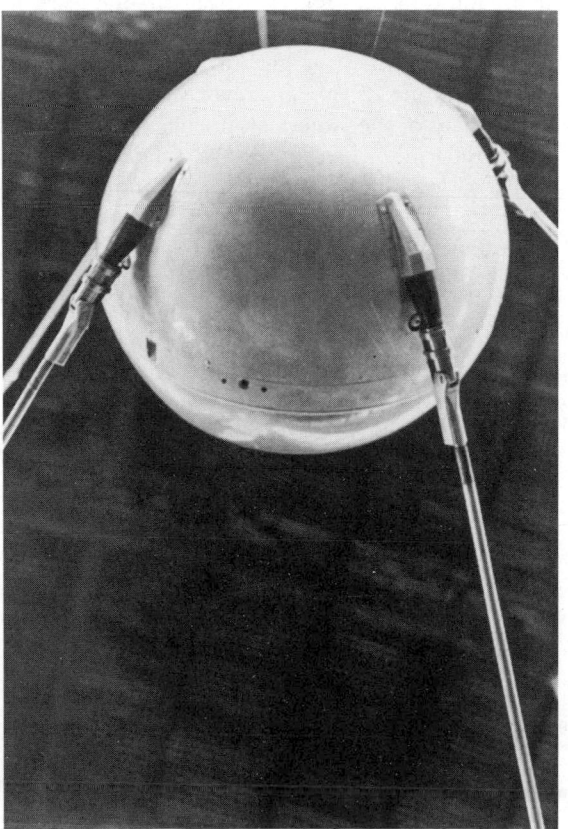

Sputnik I, the first artificial satellite, launched by the Soviet Union on October 4, 1957 *(NASA)*

missiles, develop an early warning system, and build a national system of fallout shelters to protect the civilian population. In addition, the report urged an expansion of America's conventional forces. Eisenhower thought the report unduly pessimistic and rejected many of the panel's findings. The president particularly objected to the $40 billion price tag for the committee's recommendations. Eisenhower's suspicions turned out to be correct; the report was erroneous. Nevertheless, the report was leaked to the press, which fueled the panic over *Sputnik*.

In the aftermath of *Sputnik*, Eisenhower appointed James R. Killian, Jr., president of the Massachusetts Institute of Technology, as special assistant for science and technology. At the same time, the president established the President's Science Advisory Committee (PSAC) to advise him on scientific matters and named Killian to head it. In addition, and mostly to calm public fears, he asked for a supplemental appropriation of $1.2 billion to make the Strategic Air Command less vulnerable. None of this, however, did much to ease the anxiety of the American public. To the public's further alarm, in December 1957, the Navy's Vanguard rocket lifted a few feet off the launch pad and exploded. That was followed by a series of rockets exploding on the launching pad and rockets fired with faulty trajectories. On January 31, 1958, the United States launched *Explorer*, the first successful American satellite. It went higher than *Sputnik* but weighed only 18 pounds (the first *Sputnik* weighed 184 pounds).

In his response to *Sputnik*, Eisenhower refused to succumb to panic, assessed the military and technological situations accurately, rejected hysterical responses, and held the line on reckless increases in defense spending. The historian Stephen Ambrose called Eisenhower's response to *Sputnik* "one of his finest hours." Further, Ambrose doubted that "any other man could have done what Eisenhower did." Ambrose's assessment both of Eisenhower's evaluation of the situation and his policies in response to it, while perhaps a bit breathless, sensibly gave Eisenhower credit for saving "his country untold billions of dollars and no one knows how many war scares." Yet the fact remains that, however sure his judgment and grasp of policy, Eisenhower was less successful in reassuring the American public. This

was, in part, because, as Robert Divine pointed out in his account of *Sputnik*, Eisenhower's assessment relied on classified information he could not make available to the public without compromising American intelligence capabilities. Thus, Eisenhower could not explain the reasons for his seeming lack of concern, and contemporaries, as Divine put it, "saw [Eisenhower's] calm reaction as proof of his complacency, if not senility, and condemned him for a lack of leadership." Divine concluded that, even while "the passage of time has confirmed the wisdom of the president's response," Eisenhower was unable to convince the public. As a result, he was forced to approve some increases in defense spending that he regarded as unnecessary.

Europe once again became a flash point in the cold war in November 1958, when Khrushchev announced that the Soviet Union intended, at an early date, to sign a separate peace treaty with the German Democratic Republic (East Germany) and extend formal recognition to that country. This would have terminated the occupation rights of the United States, Great Britain, and France in West Berlin and, as Khrushchev pointed out, would have left them to deal with East Germany for access to the city. Eisenhower refrained from making a public statement in response. Later that month, Khrushchev proposed that West Berlin be established as a "free city" under the United Nations and that the occupying powers withdraw all military forces from the city. He set a six-month deadline for the Western powers to negotiate a settlement along those lines. If no agreement were reached by May 27, 1959, declared the Soviet premier, the Soviet Union would unilaterally proceed to sign a treaty with East Germany.

Khrushchev was not acting on some whim. West Berlin was an irritant to him; it served as a constant reminder of the disparity in standards of living between East and West Germany. In addition, a steady flow of East Germans, including many intellectuals and skilled workers, fled to the West by entering the western sector of Berlin. During the decade before Khrushchev's ultimatum, nearly 3 million East Germans found refuge in West Berlin. On the other hand, the vulnerability of the small Western enclave, surrounded by hostile territory and hostile forces, provided Khrushchev with some leverage against the Western powers.

The Western allies disagreed on how to respond to Khrushchev's ultimatum. Eisenhower thought it important to "leave no doubt in the Soviets' minds of our intentions" not to yield on Berlin, yet he wanted to avoid any provocation. He fully intended to resolve the matter through diplomacy. Among America's allies, the British took the most conciliatory position. While drawing the line at formal diplomatic recognition of the German Democratic Republic, they leaned toward working out some sort of an arrangement with the East Germans short of formal recognition. The French, once again under the leadership of Charles de Gaulle, adopted a somewhat ambiguous position. De Gaulle did not much like the idea of a reunified Germany but thought it best for the West to take a firm stand on West Berlin. He was content to await developments before embarking on a specific course. The West German chancellor, Konrad Adenauer, took the hardest line. He strongly objected to any move toward recognizing the German Democratic Republic and therefore accepting a permanent division of Germany. The willingness of the British to engage the East Germans short of formal recognition caused him considerable alarm.

Eisenhower and Dulles managed to compose allied differences and obtained a statement from NATO supporting Western access to West Berlin. They also got France, Great Britain, and West Germany to join the United States in coordinated replies to the Soviet Union, which asserted that the agreements reached by the allies regarding Germany at the end of World War II could be terminated only by mutual consent. In January 1959, Eisenhower and Dulles proposed negotiations with the Soviets on the German question at the foreign-minister level to be held in mid-April. The carefully calculated offer of negotiations in advance of Khrushchev's deadline gave the Soviet leader room to back down without losing face, and, over the succeeding weeks, Khrushchev cautiously retreated from his confrontational position. A significant step came when the Soviet premier agreed to a conference of foreign ministers from the United States, Soviet Union, Great Britain, France, Poland, and Czechoslovakia.

In the meantime, pressures began to build for a summit meeting between Eisenhower and Khrushchev. The British prime minister, Harold Macmil-

Nikita Khrushchev and President Eisenhower about to board a helicopter to Camp David, September 15, 1959 *(Dwight D. Eisenhower Library and Museum)*

lan, went to the Soviet Union in March 1959 and reported that Khrushchev was willing to push back the deadline of May 27 in exchange for a summit conference. Eisenhower, who had always maintained his willingness to meet Soviet leaders but insisted that there be a reasonable chance of progress toward agreements, resisted calls for a summit.

Before the foreign ministers' conference convened on May 11, Dulles's failing health forced him to resign. Increasingly incapacitated by the stomach cancer that would soon kill him, the secretary of state informed Eisenhower in April that he was no longer able to meet the physical demands of his job. Eisenhower quickly made arrangements for Christian A. Herter, a former governor of Massachusetts then serving as undersecretary of state, to succeed Dulles, who submitted his formal letter of resignation on April 15. The administration announced Herter's appointment three days later.

Herter had served as acting secretary of state during Dulles's illness, but he had neither Dulles's stature nor his rapport with Eisenhower. At the foreign ministers' meeting in Geneva, negotiations quickly bogged down. The ministers quietly took a recess from their stalled talks to attend Dulles's funeral in Washington, D.C., on May 27, ironically the original deadline for Khrushchev's ultimatum.

Although Eisenhower continued to resist what he later described as "a summit without more than a blind hope to justify it," Macmillan continued to press for a summit meeting. All the while, Khrushchev alternated between belligerent bluster and occasional hints of accommodation. With the foreign ministers' talks deadlocked in late June, Eisenhower issued an invitation to Khrushchev to visit the United States. Khrushchev quickly accepted, and the trip was arranged for September. Eisenhower maintained that his meeting with Khrushchev would be an informal conversation between himself and the Soviet leader, a "prelude to a summit." The agreement for a meeting between the two leaders did nothing to further the foreign ministers' talks, which ground to an unsatisfactory and inconclusive end on August 5. Eisenhower had one more bit of business to take care of before Khrushchev came to the United States. The president visited western Europe to reassure leaders there that he would not make any deals with Khrushchev without consulting the Europeans.

After a whirlwind tour of the United States in mid-September, Khrushchev went to Camp David to meet with Eisenhower. The Soviet leader pushed hard for a summit, but Eisenhower refused to negotiate under the threat of Soviet recognition of East Germany. Finally, Eisenhower agreed to pull back from his demand for progress in lower level talks and to attend a summit in the spring of 1960. Khrushchev withdrew his demand for a fixed deadline and his plan for a separate peace treaty with East Germany. The face-to-face meeting settled little; essentially, the two leaders agreed to continue negotiations. That, however, proved enough to defuse the crisis. Thanks to Eisenhower's resolute but cautious diplomacy, the Berlin crisis ended not with a bang but a whimper.

Perhaps Eisenhower's handling of the Berlin crisis can best be appreciated by comparing his response to a virtually identical ultimatum Khrushchev issued to Kennedy three years later. Kennedy took a belligerent stand, sent a 1,500-man battle group over the autobahn to West Berlin to demonstrate American resolve to defend West Berlin, appointed Gen. Curtis LeMay (an outspoken advocate of big bombers) to head the air force, and made a terrifying speech to the nation. The United States and Soviet Union faced off like gunfighters in the old West, and rattled their nuclear weapons. Ultimately, Kennedy settled for negotiations, which, like those in 1958 and 1959, failed to resolve the German question.

Throughout the Berlin crisis, Eisenhower faced considerable pressure to increase conventional forces and military spending, yet he steadfastly refused to yield to such calls. Democrats in Congress used the incident to attack the reductions in conventional forces and defense spending Eisenhower proposed in 1958. In particular, Democrats opposed the administration's plans to cut 55,000 men from the military during what they described as a time of crisis. Some Democrats, most notably those with presidential ambitions in 1960, called for a $3 billion increase in the defense budget. In a meeting with Republican congressional leaders on March 10, 1959, Eisenhower rejected the idea that the dispute over Berlin was "a great crisis." With respect to Democratic demands to know why he was reducing American forces, Eisenhower cited other uses for the $250 million those men would cost. He mentioned schools, hospitals, and other needs. Then he asked the Republican leaders to look at the matter another way: "What would these 55,000 men do if we had them? Certainly they are not going to fight a land war in Europe. How could a land war be fought successfully against the great number of divisions that are available on the other side of the Curtain?" "It is perfectly clear," the president went on, "that you can't provide security with a checkbook. . . . If these people decide to put another $3 billion into the budget every time Russia tries to push, they might as well go all the way to a garrison state." If the Democrats wanted to add such huge sums to the budget, the president thought that "they at least ought to raise taxes to pay for it," but, he mused, "they don't have the courage." Eisenhower dismissed the Democratic posturing as "a hysteria that is largely political."

The president did not restrict such comments to meetings with aides or congressional leaders. On March 11, the day after his meeting with Republican legislative leaders, Eisenhower held a press conference in which he faced hostile questioning about his intent to reduce the size of the army. A clearly irritated Eisenhower responded: "What would you do with more ground forces in Europe? Does anyone here have an idea? Would you start a ground war? We are certainly not going to fight a ground war in Europe. What good would it do to send a few more thousands or even a few divisions of troops to Europe?" In the end, Eisenhower skillfully navigated the Berlin crisis, both at home and abroad. He avoided a war without yielding anything to the Soviets, while at the same time managing to avoid unnecessary increases in military spending.

Part of the resolution of the Berlin crisis was a summit scheduled for spring 1960, the agenda for which included disarmament. Eisenhower had repeatedly expressed concern about the escalating nuclear arms race but had failed to reach an agreement, even within his administration, on a workable proposal for disarmament. In October 1957, Isidor Rabi, a physicist from Columbia University, told Eisenhower that, given the advantage the United States enjoyed over the Soviets in nuclear technology, a suspension of nuclear testing would serve the interest of the United States. Although other top scientists, including Edward Teller and Ernest Lawrence, strongly disagreed, the idea of a test ban appealed strongly to Eisenhower. It would save money and maintain America's lead in technology. Further, the public, both in the United States and abroad, had become increasingly concerned about the radioactive fallout generated by atmospheric testing of nuclear weapons, a concern that Eisenhower shared. Until 1958, the Eisenhower administration made any suspension of nuclear weapons testing contingent on the willingness of the Soviets to agree to a verifiable limit on the production of nuclear weapons and a reduction of conventional forces. The Soviet Union consistently rejected those conditions.

Several factors, however, led Eisenhower to reexamine that position. Public worries about the dangers of fallout continued to exert pressure on the administration. Congressional hearings on the dangers radioactive fallout posed to public health heightened the public's concern. Changes within the administration, too, opened the door to a reconsideration of the policy on testing. James Killian and the PSAC provided an alternative source of technical advice to the Atomic Energy Commission's strong opposition to a test ban. Ironically, the resignation of Harold Stassen, Eisenhower's special assistant for disarmament and one of the strongest voices in the administration in favor of a test ban, also helped pave the way for rethinking the policy on testing. Dulles, who jealously guarded his turf, resented what he regarded as Stassen's encroachments into the State Department's territory. The secretary of state, therefore, often opposed Stassen's proposals. With Stassen's departure, however, Dulles seemed more willing to consider a test ban; indeed, Dulles emerged as one of its strongest supporters in the administration. In February 1958, Eisenhower considered releasing a statement announcing a unilateral cessation of testing. Only the strenuous opposition of Lewis Strauss, the head of the Atomic Energy Commission, persuaded him not to do so.

After completing a series of nuclear tests in which they exploded 11 bombs in two weeks during March 1958, the Soviets announced a unilateral suspension of testing and called on the United States to do the same. Even before the Soviets made the announcement, the CIA had learned of their intention to do so. Knowledge of the upcoming Soviet announcement sparked an intense debate within the administration. While the Atomic Energy Commission and the Defense Department insisted on the necessity of continued testing to maintain the United States' advantage in nuclear weaponry, Dulles warned that the Soviet proposal put the United States in an unfavorable light with respect to world opinion. While sympathetic to Dulles's position, Eisenhower ultimately yielded to the AEC and Defense Department. For one thing, the president regarded the timing of the Soviet offer with suspicion. It came after the Soviet Union had completed an extensive series of tests and just as the United States was about to embark on one. Such considerations led Eisenhower to reject the Soviet offer as a "gimmick."

Even as he decided to reject the Soviet proposal, Eisenhower fully understood the propaganda advantage the Soviets stood to gain. He was particularly frustrated that, as he put it, the "United States . . . seeking peace, is unable to achieve an advantageous impact on world opinion." Acting on the report of a panel headed by nuclear physicist Hans Bethe, which concluded that the technology existed to detect most nuclear testing without extensive on-site inspections, Eisenhower proposed technical talks with the Soviets on the means to verify a permanent ban on the testing of nuclear weapons. Eisenhower then invited the nuclear powers (Great Britain and the Soviet Union) to enter into negotiations for a test ban treaty and announced that the United States would suspend testing for a year if the Soviets would do the same. Khrushchev accepted Eisenhower's offer to negotiate. The timing allowed the United States to complete its scheduled round of testing. Eisenhower ordered a moratorium on testing to begin on October 31, 1958.

The Conference on the Discontinuance of Nuclear Weapons Tests got under way in Geneva on October 31, 1958, and stalled immediately. Going into the talks, Eisenhower's scientific advisers informed him that off-site technological monitoring systems had proved less effective than predicted, particularly for smaller underground tests. Consequently, at the talks, the United States insisted on an extensive regime of inspections. Khrushchev accused the United States of manipulating the data to justify more intrusive inspections. Despite these frustrations, Eisenhower was determined to achieve a ban on nuclear testing, and he hoped for some actual disarmament as well. On February 11, 1959, he announced his willingness to accept a treaty that would end all testing in the atmosphere, the oceans, and outer space and provide for monitoring of underground tests. In March, the Soviets indicated a willingness to accept Eisenhower's proposal if the United States also agreed to a moratorium on low-kiloton tests underground. The unverifiable cessation of small underground tests for an indeterminate period ran counter to a long-accepted American position, but Eisenhower decided to counter with an offer of an unsupervised moratorium of underground testing for one year, which he was willing to extend to two years. In April 1959, Eisenhower proposed a ban on atmospheric testing as a first step, pending an agreement on a verifiable comprehensive test ban.

Eisenhower resisted pressure from the Atomic Energy Commission and the Defense Department to resume testing after the moratorium expired on October 31, 1959. In discussions within the administration regarding a resumption of American testing, Eisenhower became particularly heated in his insistence that he would approve no atmospheric testing. When George Kistiakowsky, a chemist from Harvard University who replaced Killian on the PSAC in mid-1959, reported that there was no pressing need for testing in the immediate future, Eisenhower extended the moratorium on American testing to the end of 1959. The British and Soviets followed suit. When the technical talks broke up amid a flurry of mutual acrimony and accusations in late 1959, Eisenhower announced that the United States would not resume testing without advance notification. Khrushchev responded that the Soviets would not resume testing unless the West did. For the remainder of his presidency, Eisenhower refused to approve any nuclear testing. Early in 1960, Kistiakowsky suggested a ban on atmospheric and underwater testing accompanied by a suspension of underground tests registering above 4.75 on the Richter scale. The threshold was sufficiently high that it required at least some on-site inspections in the Soviet Union for verification. Eisenhower announced the new position in February 1960, accompanied by a proposal for a joint effort by American, British, and Soviet scientists to improve seismic detection techniques so that the threshold might be progressively lowered. In March, the Soviets agreed to the concept, with the condition that the Western powers agree to a four- or five-year moratorium on all tests below the 4.75 threshold pending completion of the joint research project. In a contentious meeting with his top security advisers, Eisenhower insisted that the international political advantages of an agreement banning atmospheric testing and large underground tests, even with problems monitoring the cessation of smaller underground tests, far outweighed any impediments it might pose to the American program of developing nuclear weapons. He preferred a moratorium of one year but was willing to extend it to two years, contingent on other powers' reciprocation. The president thought it best to do it through executive action, rather than a formal treaty, because he was nearing the end of his presidency and thought it best not to tie the hands of his successor. In addition, he wanted to avoid potential opposition in the Senate. Macmillan signed on to Eisenhower's position, and the two leaders thought that any remaining details could be ironed out at the upcoming summit in Paris. Eisenhower issued a statement on March 29 setting forth his position. At a press conference the following month, Eisenhower announced that he, Macmillan, and de Gaulle had agreed that disarmament should be the main topic at the summit meeting.

Indeed, many had high hopes for the Paris Summit, but those hopes were dashed. Beginning in 1956, Eisenhower had authorized overflights of the Soviet Union by high-altitude U-2 aircraft to gather intelligence. These flights were scheduled to be replaced by reconnaissance satellites, due to become operational in 1960. The U-2 had the ability to fly at an altitude of 70,000 feet, which placed it out of the range of Soviet interceptors or surface-to-air missiles. Although Soviet radar could detect the flights, Eisenhower and Dulles figured that the Soviets would not publicly complain, because to do so would be to admit the limitations of their air

defenses. Still, Eisenhower recognized the provocative nature of such flights and therefore insisted that each operation be cleared with him. As he moved toward détente with the Soviets at the end of the 1950s, Eisenhower carefully weighed the diplomatic risks of each flight against the potential yield of intelligence, and he countermanded most of the missions proposed to him. In a meeting with aides in early 1960, he said that his "one tremendous asset" going into the upcoming summit was his "reputation for honesty." If the Soviets shot down one of those aircraft while he was engaged in "apparently sincere deliberations," it would destroy the president's effectiveness. However, the U-2 flights provided valuable hard intelligence. Moreover, they confirmed his suspicions about the limitations of the Soviets' long-range missile program, which, in turn, solidified his resolve to hold the line on defense spending, despite demands for increased spending from the military and congressional Democrats. In addition, the overflights provided evidence that refuted Democratic charges that Eisenhower had allowed the Soviets to gain a dangerous advantage in missiles. Thus, in April, he approved one final U-2 flight.

On May 1, 1960, the Soviets shot down a U-2 aircraft piloted by Francis Gary Powers. Eisenhower's military and intelligence advisers informed him that, in the event of a mishap, the pilot would most likely

U-2 "Dragon Lady" *(National Archives)*

not survive and had a suicide pin in case he did. Any evidence of espionage would be eradicated by self-destruct systems in the aircraft. The CIA neglected to inform the president that the self-destruct mechanism required the pilot to activate it. Upon learning of the missing aircraft, Eisenhower decided to leave the next move to Khrushchev. The president figured that if the Soviet premier were sincere about the summit, he would downplay the incident, much as Eisenhower himself had done when the Chinese shot down the British airliner in 1954. When Khrushchev announced on May 5 that Soviet forces had shot down a spy plane, Eisenhower authorized release of a prearranged cover story that a high-altitude NASA weather plane had been missing since May 1. Khrushchev then went before the Supreme Soviet on May 7 and announced that he had both the pilot, who had survived, and the intact wreckage of the spy plane. Further, he announced that the pilot would be tried for espionage. Khrushchev said that he was prepared to grant that Eisenhower had no knowledge of the mission and blamed the flight on "militarists" in the American government. To accept the out that Khrushchev offered would have served to confirm charges by his political opponents that Eisenhower was out of touch. Eisenhower initially acquiesced in the efforts of his advisers to insulate him from responsibility, but these efforts only made the situation worse. The inept and confusing efforts to keep the president clear of the incident played into Khrushchev's claims that militarists in the Pentagon were out of control and into Democratic campaign charges that Eisenhower was out of touch. In the end, Eisenhower decided to accept responsibility. On May 9, Eisenhower met with congressional leaders, explained the U-2 and its history, and told them that "we will now just have to endure the storm." Herter announced on May 9 that Eisenhower had authorized U-2 overflights for several years. He justified them as an effort to prevent another Pearl Harbor. At a press conference two days later, Eisenhower defended the flights as an effort to protect the United States against a surprise attack and stressed that he saw no reason why this dispute over "an unarmed nonmilitary" plane should jeopardize progress on important issues at the upcoming summit.

Khrushchev's motives remain a mystery. His actions seemed to indicate that he intended to tor-pedo the summit, but he had consistently pushed for it. The flight clearly infuriated Khrushchev, who was already facing opposition to his policy of "peaceful coexistence" from hard-liners at home and the Chinese abroad. Further, a recent trip to France had convinced him that he would not be able to divide the allies on the question of Berlin. In an effort to shore up his own position, he issued a series of angry public statements denouncing American aggression and warning that the Soviet Union would do whatever was necessary to defend its sovereignty. He also threatened to retaliate against any nation that provided bases for the U-2. There was, however, something disingenuous about his fury; after all, Soviet satellites flew over the United States daily, and some of the photographs taken from those satellites had appeared in Soviet newspapers. In his column for the *New York Times*, James Reston speculated that, having realized that Eisenhower had no intention of pulling out of Berlin, Khrushchev used the U-2 incident to blame the United States for the failure of the summit. De Gaulle thought that the Soviet leader had second thoughts about having Eisenhower address the Soviet people on television. Another possible explanation is that Soviet scientists arrived at the same conclusion Kistiakowsky had—that a test ban would benefit the Americans. Eisenhower himself suspected that Khrushchev intended to use the incident to drive a wedge between the NATO allies.

On the day before the opening session of the summit, Khrushchev circulated a set of demands that he must have known Eisenhower could not possibly accept, including a formal apology for the U-2 incident, punishment for those responsible, and a promise that there would be no more such flights over Soviet territory. In fact, Eisenhower had ordered an end to the U-2 overflights before he left for Paris. He intended to announce the cessation at the opening of the summit in a speech that stressed America's desire to negotiate a settlement of the Berlin issue and a test ban treaty. Khrushchev's demands, however, placed Eisenhower's attempt at conciliation in a very different light. The president had no intention of appearing to give in to Khrushchev's demands. Moreover, if Eisenhower's assessment of Khrushchev's motives was right, the

Soviet leader had miscalculated. The crisis, if any-thing, drew the Allies closer together.

At the opening session of the summit on May 16, de Gaulle had hardly called the meeting to order when Khrushchev demanded to speak. The Soviet premier launched into a highly emotional tirade against the United States and insisted on receiving satisfaction concerning the U-2 incident before proceeding to other matters. At the end of his harangue, Khrushchev withdrew the invitation for Eisenhower's visit to the Soviet Union that summer. A furious Eisenhower refused to apologize for attempting to protect the security of his country. Yet he did assure the Soviet leader that he had unilaterally suspended further overflights for the rest of his administration. Khrushchev refused to be placated. Macmillan and de Gaulle tried unsuccessfully to move to other matters, but the Soviets walked out. The summit collapsed even before it began.

The U-2 incident and the failed summit thwarted Eisenhower's ambition to achieve a significant thaw in the cold war during the last months of his administration. Negotiations in Geneva over a test ban dragged on until August but failed to reach any agreement on the question of on-site inspections or the duration of the moratorium on small-yield underground tests. It was Eisenhower's greatest disappointment as president.

While many historians have praised Eisenhower's restraint in dealing with the Soviet Union and the cold war in Europe, some have argued that he exercised less restraint in his use of force in the Third World. While such an analysis contains an element of truth, it presents too stark a dichotomy and too simple a picture of the Eisenhower administration's foreign policy. In some respects, the restraint and caution with which Eisenhower managed relations with the Soviets, particularly in Europe, was less evident in his dealings with the Third World. On the other hand, Eisenhower's policies with respect to the Middle East, Asia, and Latin America demonstrated similar objectives—to limit risks for the United States and not to allow local problems to lead to a major confrontation between superpowers.

From early in his administration, Eisenhower faced a series of crises in Asia. On September 3, 1954, the Communist Chinese initiated a sustained bombardment of the Quemoy and Matsu islands, located just off the coast of mainland China but held by the Nationalist Chinese. These islands were considerably closer to the coast of China than to Taiwan (Formosa), to which the Nationalist Chinese fled in 1949. Quemoy and Matsu had little strategic value for the defense of Taiwan, but the Nationalist leader, Chiang Kai-shek (Jiang Jieshi), placed large garrisons on the islands and used them to launch raids against the mainland and against Chinese Communist shipping.

The Eisenhower administration remained uncertain about what, exactly, the Communist Chinese intended with respect to the offshore islands. The Joint Chiefs of Staff informed Eisenhower that the islands were not necessary to the defense of Taiwan and that Chiang could not hold them without help from the United States. The Joint Chiefs recommended putting American forces on the islands and conducting bombing raids on the mainland. Eisenhower flatly rejected their recommendation. Nevertheless, Dulles had earlier warned that any attack on the offshore islands might provoke an American military response. Moreover, the China Lobby, which had support within the right wing of the Republican party, wanted an aggressive response. In late October, the mainland Chinese appeared to be preparing for an invasion. During the next month, the Chinese bombed other small islands held by the Nationalists and continued their buildup across from Quemoy and Matsu.

A this point, the Chinese upped the ante by announcing that 13 American pilots who had been shot down over China during the Korean war had been convicted of espionage. The action outraged many in the United States. Sen. William Knowland (R-Calif.), a leading voice for the China Lobby (critics derisively referred to him as the Senator from Taiwan), demanded a blockade of China. Eisenhower thought the idea foolish and, in a press conference, lectured that "the hard way is to have the courage to be patient." The administration explicitly stated its commitment to defend Taiwan and the Pescadore (Penghu [P'eng-hu]) Islands, which lay near Taiwan, but said nothing about other islands. The shelling of Quemoy and Matsu continued, and in December Dulles negotiated the Mutual Defense Treaty with Chiang, in which the two parties agreed that an armed attack on one would be regarded as an act of war against the other. At Eisenhower's insistence, however, the treaty limited the American commitment to defending Taiwan, the Pescadores, and "such other territories as may be determined by mutual agreement." In addition, Dulles extracted from Chiang a pledge not to launch an attack on the mainland without American approval.

The crisis intensified in January 1955. Chiang warned of the possibility of "war at any time," and, on the other side of the Straits of Formosa, the mainland Chinese announced that an invasion of Taiwan was "imminent." On January 10, the Communist Chinese bombed the Tachen Islands. The following week, they seized Ichiang, an island just north of the Tachens. Faced with the prospect of a Chinese invasion of the Tachens, Eisenhower decided that the United States would not defend that island group. At the same time, he made a decision to ask Congress for a resolution authorizing him to use American forces to defend Taiwan and the Pescadores. Dulles wanted to include Quemoy and Matsu in the resolution, but Eisenhower refused. On January 24, Eisenhower sent a message to Congress asking for a resolution granting him authority to use armed force, "if in his judgment it became necessary," to defend Taiwan, the Pescadores, and "closely related localities." The resolution did not mention Quemoy or Matsu, and Eisenhower refused to commit himself publicly beyond a statement that he would not commit American troops to defend Quemoy and Matsu unless he became convinced that an attack on the islands was a precursor to an attack on Taiwan. Congress overwhelmingly passed the resolution.

Chiang wanted assurances of an American commitment to defend Quemoy and Matsu if he withdrew from the Tachens. Eisenhower, however, would give no such guarantee. On January 19, Eisenhower agreed to Dulles's proposal that the United States provide assistance if the Nationalists evacuated the Tachens. Chiang reluctantly agreed to abandon the islands, and the evacuation, which began on February 4, was completed in less than a week. Much to everyone's relief, the Chinese Communists did not attack.

The question of Quemoy and Matsu remained. Eisenhower's deliberately ambiguous diplomacy

may have, as intended, left the Chinese uncertain about American intentions, but it had the same effect on America's allies. Western European countries thought it reckless to risk a war over those islands and were alarmed at the prospect that the United States might do so. The British prime minister, Winston Churchill, understood why the United States could not permit Chiang "and his adherents . . . to be liquidated and massacred by Communist China," but he thought that a very different matter from Chiang's ability to hold the offshore islands and use them as bridgeheads for Nationalist actions against the mainland.

Eisenhower explained his thinking on the offshore islands in a letter to General Alfred M. Gruenther, supreme commander of NATO forces, on February 1, 1955. "Now, if the solution we adopt should state flatly that we would defend the principal islands of the offshore group (Quemoy and the Matsus)," he wrote, "we would not please the Chinese Nationalists, but we would frighten Europe and of course even further infuriate the Chinese Communists. . . . By announcing this as a policy we would be compelled to maintain in the area, at great cost, forces that could assure the defense of islands that are almost within wading distance of the mainland." From a military perspective, the matter was simple, but there were other considerations. Eisenhower understood that the Europeans considered Americans "reckless," but he noted that a large majority of Americans did not want to allow Taiwan to fall to the Communists. Indeed, some wanted more aggressive action. Eisenhower saw himself as caught between "the truculent and the timid, the jingoists and the pacifists." A further consideration was the morale of the Nationalists on Taiwan. All of this accounted for the nature of the congressional resolution "passed by Congress at my request." "The wording as to areas outside Taiwan and the Pescadores" Eisenhower explained, "is vague. In view of what I have just said, you can understand why this is so."

Dulles raised the stakes on March 15, when he stated that the United States was prepared to use tactical atomic weapons in the event of an attack on Taiwan. At a news conference on March 16, Eisenhower said that he saw no reason why nuclear weapons "shouldn't be used exactly as you would use a bullet or anything else." In his memoirs, Eisenhower wrote that "I hoped this answer would have some effect in persuading the Chinese Communists of the strength of our determination." Whatever their effect on the Chinese, such statements certainly alarmed European leaders; but, in fact, Eisenhower did not want to go to war over barren rocks in the Straits of Formosa. In a meeting with some top advisers on April 1, Eisenhower stated that war with China over Quemoy and Matsu was "undesirable." He explained that America's allies would not support a war over the islands and that public opinion in the United States was divided. The president also worried about the effect such a war would have on the American economy. From Eisenhower's perspective, a "desirable solution" would be for Chiang to pull voluntarily back from the islands, in exchange for which Eisenhower was willing to station American forces on Taiwan. At the very least, Eisenhower hoped to persuade Chiang to reduce the number of forces on Quemoy and Matsu.

Through mid-April, Eisenhower and Dulles tried to move Chiang towards this position. Chiang, however, intended to keep his forces on the islands and wanted an American commitment to defend Quemoy and Matsu. Finally, on April 23, Zhou Enlai (Chou En-lai), the Chinese foreign minister, offered to negotiate, and Eisenhower took up the offer. The Chinese reduced their shelling of the islands and by mid-May stopped it entirely. In addition, the Chinese released the American prisoners, and talks between Chinese and American representatives began on August 1. The talks failed to resolve the issue of the offshore islands, but served to end the crisis.

Eisenhower and Dulles regarded the incident as an example of the effectiveness of atomic diplomacy. Subsequent decades have failed to produce agreement among historians. Many have criticized Eisenhower and Dulles for taking the country to the brink of war over the offshore islands. Richard V. Damms concedes that the threat to use atomic weapons may have contributed to the Chinese decision to seek a relaxation of tensions but concludes that "the threat of massive retaliation did not deter the PRC [People's Republic of China] from seizing the offshore islands." Further, the incident led Mao "to initiate China's own atomic bomb programme"

and "seriously strained relations between the United States and its European allies." In contrast, Robert A. Divine lauds Eisenhower for introducing "a note of deliberate ambiguity into American policy." Eisenhower, he maintains, "used a measured nuclear threat to warn the Chinese without insulting them or provoking them into an attack." "The beauty of Eisenhower's policy," concludes Divine, "is that to this day no one can be sure whether or not he would have responded militarily to an invasion of the offshore islands." Stephen E. Ambrose considers Eisenhower's handling of the crisis a "tour de force." "He never had to use the bomb; he did not plunge the world into war; he kept the peace without losing any territory or prestige." According to Ambrose, in addition to keeping the world in the dark about his intentions, Eisenhower himself did not know whether he would have used nuclear weapons. The commander in chief kept his options open, and he never knew "just how he would respond to an invasion of Quemoy and Matsu, because he insisted on waiting to see the precise nature of the attack before deciding how to react." From Eisenhower's perspective, he achieved his objectives. At the end of the day, Chiang held Quemoy and Matsu; the United States had clearly committed to defend Taiwan; and a war had been avoided.

The diplomacy of Eisenhower and Dulles ended the crisis of the moment, but did not resolve the underlying issue of the offshore islands, which heated up again in 1958. Chiang had built up his forces on the islands, despite protests from the mainland Chinese, and on August 23, the Communist Chinese once again began shelling the islands. By that time, however, the Soviet Union had a formidable nuclear capacity, which changed the context of the crisis. Eisenhower strengthened American naval forces in the region but refused to give Chiang a commitment to defend the islands. The Communist Chinese escalated the crisis by using aircraft to bomb the islands and by initiating a blockade. Dulles wanted a clear statement of the administration's intention to defend the islands, but Eisenhower worried that, given such an assurance, Chiang might deliberately provoke a confrontation and thus drag the United States into war with Communist China. Dulles also supported the use of tactical atomic weapons, but Eisenhower thought otherwise. If the United States used atomic weapons, he argued, the Soviets might retaliate with atomic weapons against Taiwan, and the use of atomic weapons would result in "a worldwide feeling of revulsion against the United States."

As was the case with the first confrontation over the islands, Eisenhower had to balance a myriad of considerations. The Asia-Firsters in his own party demanded strong action. Many Americans, however, could not fathom going to war over small islands half a world away. Further complicating matters, the British held to the position they had taken during the first crisis in the Formosa Straights: the islands were not worth a world war.

Much as he did in the earlier confrontation over Quemoy and Matsu, Eisenhower pursued a diplomacy of ambiguity. The key to an American response was whether Eisenhower judged an attack on the islands to be a forerunner of an attack on Taiwan. In any event, if his hand were forced, Eisenhower was willing to consider military measures only to thwart the mainland Chinese invasion; he rejected the idea of attacks on the mainland to punish China, at least in the initial phase. In the meantime, he authorized the use of the United States Navy to escort Nationalist Chinese ships to resupply the garrisons on Quemoy and Matsu.

Eisenhower approved a statement, issued by Dulles on September 4, that warned of a possible American retaliation in the event of an outright invasion of the islands. The statement also invited Communist China to resume talks on the status of Taiwan. On September 6, Zhou Enlai indicated the willingness of the People's Republic of China to resume negotiations. On September 11, however, Eisenhower gave a nationally televised speech apparently intended to reassure the Asia-First wing of the Republican party as well as Chiang. The president said that the United States was bound by its treaties and that there would be no retreat. With respect to the upcoming talks, he promised that "there is not going to be any appeasement." At the same time, he assured the country that "I believe there is not going to be any war." The speech provoked some harsh criticism at home and abroad.

Amid continued shelling of the islands, talks resumed in mid-September. In early October, the Communist Chinese suspended their shelling of the islands. Eisenhower took the opportunity to send Dulles to Taiwan to persuade Chiang to reduce his garrisons on the islands. While the Chinese Nationalist leader refused to withdraw, he did agree to issue a statement renouncing the use of force to regain the mainland. The Chinese Communists responded favorably. They announced that they would fire on Nationalist resupply convoys only on odd days of the month, effectively permitting resupply on the even days. Ultimately, Chiang reduced his garrison, although not to the degree Eisenhower recommended, and the Communists ceased their bombardment.

As was the case with the first crisis, historians have drawn differing conclusions about the way Eisenhower handled the incident. Damms argued that the episode "raised questions about the credibility of Eisenhower's nuclear strategy." In contrast, Ambrose concluded that "the crisis passed, without war, without retreat, without putting an intolerable strain on NATO, and without a loss of face by the ChiNats [Nationalist Chinese] or the United States. Eisenhower had used a combination of threats, firmness, and resolve, combined with a willingness to negotiate and be reasonable, to achieve an outcome satisfactory to him."

One of the most complex and vexing set of issues confronting the Eisenhower administration related to the disintegration of the European colonial empires and the emergence of new, independent nations, 37 of which came into existence between 1946 and 1960. Eisenhower personally found colonialism repugnant, and neither he nor Dulles had any intention of supporting colonialism in Africa, Asia, or the Middle East. On the other hand, the administration needed to maintain the cooperation of the British and the French, particularly in Europe but elsewhere as well. Further complicating matters, American policy under Eisenhower sought to prevent the emerging nations from turning to communism, and, while he recognized the burden European colonialism placed on that effort, his administration often opposed communist-led nationalist movements. Eisenhower gave considerable thought to the appropriate tactics for meeting what he regarded as communist aggression in the developing nations. Nuclear war was unacceptable, and Korea had demonstrated the pitfalls of conventional war. Moreover, Eisenhower had been greatly impressed by the effectiveness of covert operations during World War II and turned to covert operations as a low-risk, low-cost means of meeting communist challenges in what came to be known at the Third World.

The administration's first encounter with Third World nationalism came in Iran, where in May 1951 the nationalist government of Prime Minister Mohammed Mossadeq nationalized the country's oil industry, including the Anglo-Iranian Oil Company, of which the British government owned 52 percent. The British government shut down the refinery at Abadan (then the world's largest), withdrew its technicians, and organized an international boycott of Iranian oil. The boycott had a ruinous effect on Iran's economy. Oil accounted for roughly 30 percent of Iran's national income and as much as 60 percent of its foreign exchange. Iranian oil production fell to something over an eighth of what it had been. However devastating the consequences of the boycott and the withdrawal of technicians, they served to harden Mossadeq's resolve not to submit. "It is better," he said, "to be independent and produce only one ton of oil in a year than to produce 32 million tons and be a slave to Britain." Western diplomats found Mossadeq a strange, rather ridiculous, figure; he conducted business in his pajamas, broke into tears at the drop of a hat, and was given to fainting spells. That perception, however, clouded their view of a man who was the product of a wealthy landowning family and was, as the historian Robert Divine described him, "a shrewd politician who exploited the nationalist grievances that all Iranians felt towards the British." Fearing that any concessions would make him appear to be a British pawn, Mossadeq refused to compromise, and, in October 1952, broke off diplomatic relations with Great Britain. In the meantime, Mossadeq used the situation to gain more extensive powers from the Iranian parliament.

The British prime minister, Winston Churchill, hoped that the incoming Eisenhower administration might resolve the crisis. Mossadeq, on the other hand, urged Eisenhower to give economic aid to Iran and to break the British embargo by buying Iranian oil. Pointing out that Mossadeq had accepted the support of Tudeh, the Iranian communist party, and had come to rely more heavily on the communists, the British urged a covert operation to overthrow Mossadeq. The Iranian prime minister's rejection of American proposals designed to resolve the dispute moved Eisenhower in that direction. Ultimately, Mossadeq's intransigence in negotiations with the British, his strained relations with the pro-Western shah, his overtures to Iranian communists, and his gestures towards the Soviet Union convinced Eisenhower of the need to remove him. The president authorized a covert operation, planned by the CIA.

In March 1953, Mossadeq asked the parliament to make him commander in chief of the Iranian army. When the parliament refused, Mossadeq, on July 19, 1953, dissolved parliament, called for a plebiscite, and began to rule by decree. The Tudeh Party staged riots in the streets of Teheran. Adding to Eisenhower's concern, Mossadeq accepted $20 million in aid from the Soviet Union, and at the end of July, the Tudeh Party announced its support for Mossadeq, which Mossadeq accepted. In the plebiscite, held on August 5, Mossadeq won 99.4 percent of the vote. The shah removed Mossadeq and appointed a general to be the new prime minister. Mossadeq began arresting political opponents, and rioting in support of Mossadeq spread through the streets of Teheran. With events turning against him, the shah fled to Italy.

American agents cultivated the support of military officers loyal to the shah and organized street demonstrations against Mossadeq. Facing a crisis, Mossadeq, whose policies had alienated many intellectuals and a substantial portion of the middle class, found few willing to support him. The army arrested Mossadeq, and the shah returned in triumph on August 22. The Eisenhower administration quickly extended $45 million in economic aid to Iran. The new Iranian government quickly restored relations with Great Britain and in 1954 agreed to pay $25 million to the Anglo-Iranian Oil Company for its assets that had been seized. The United States brokered an agreement that provided for a new international consortium to develop Iran's oil industry. The Anglo-Iranian Oil Company and American oil companies each enjoyed a 40 percent stake of the consortium, which divided profits equally with the Iranian government.

In the short term, at least from the perspective of Washington, the covert operation to overthrow Mossadeq was a remarkable success. The American-backed coup removed a leader who had strained relations with the West and seemed to be moving towards the Soviet Union. It also brought American companies a significant role in the development of Iranian oil, from which they had previously been excluded. Finally, it achieved all this with minimal risk or cost. On the other hand, the United States backed a coup against a democratically elected leader, and, over the long term, the operation served to tie the United States to a repressive regime.

Another example of Eisenhower's use of covert action in the Third World came the following year in Guatemala, where the United States supported the overthrow of the leftist government of President Jacobo Arbenz Guzmán. A wealthy landowner and former colonel in the Army, Arbenz embarked on a program to promote economic diversification, unionization, and land reform. In 1952, the Guatemalan National Assembly approved a plan of agrarian reform that provided for the expropriation and redistribution of uncultivated land on large estates. The measure provided for owners to be compensated with government bonds equivalent to the value of the land declared for tax purposes. The United Fruit Company, an American concern, objected to the $3 per acre price offered in compensation, and officials of the company lobbied the United States government to intervene. Some historians have made much of the ties between some members of the Eisenhower administration and United Fruit. Far more significant, however,

Some of the anti-Arbenz Guatemalan troops *(National Archives)*

was the concern among policy makers that Guatemala might slip into the communist orbit. Arbenz included communists in his coalition and accused the United States of using germ warfare in Korea. In an operation similar to the one that led to the ouster of Mossadeq in Iran, the CIA armed and trained a group of Guatemalan exiles led by Colonel Carlos Castillo Armas, who had been exiled after an unsuccessful coup in 1950. The Eisenhower administration worked to isolate Arbenz diplomatically and pressed European nations to withhold economic and military assistance to Guatemala. At a meeting of the Organization of American States in Caracas, Venezuela, in March 1954, Dulles obtained approval of a resolution declaring that communist control of any American state presented a threat to the hemisphere.

Worried about an invasion, Arbenz bought weapons from the Soviet bloc. The Eisenhower administration pointed to that arms purchase as proof that Arbenz planned to export communist revolution in the region. The administration also gave military assistance to Honduras and Nicaragua and blockaded Guatemalan ports. On June 18, 1954, Castillo Armas and his force of roughly 150 men invaded Guatemala while planes supplied by the CIA bombed the capital. Arbenz appealed to the United Nations Security Council, and France and Great Britain seemed willing to hear Guatemala's case. Dulles, however, warned them that such a position would lead the United States to pursue "an independent line concerning such matters as Egypt and North Africa." The Security Council ultimately voted 5-4, with Britain and France abstaining, not to place Guatemala on its agenda. After the Guatemalan army called on Arbenz to resign, he fled, and Castillo Armas became president. Castillo Armas outlawed the communist party and restored confiscated property to the owners from whom it had been taken.

Once more, a covert operation seemed to produce a great success. A nuisance had been removed and with little cost or risk. As was the case with Iran, however, there was a downside to the operation. Student and labor groups organized protests in various locations throughout Latin America. Some governments voiced their displeasure at the ouster of Arbenz. Perhaps most important, the military government in Guatemala committed extensive abuses of human rights throughout the following decades. In the short term, indeed even to the end of the Eisenhower administration, the action seemed a great success from the perspective of the White House.

The French struggle to hold on to its colonial possession in Indochina provided yet another test for the diplomacy of the Eisenhower administration. During World War II, the Japanese had occupied French Indochina, and after the war, Ho Chi Minh, a communist who had led a nationalist movement in Vietnam against the French before the war and the resistance to the Japanese during the war, demanded independence for his country. As the French attempted to reimpose their colonial rule after the war, they encountered fierce opposition from an insurgent movement led by Ho and his Viet Minh. Primarily in an effort to get the French to cooperate in building a Western alliance in Europe, the Truman administration began aiding the French. Mao's victory in the Chinese civil war and the outbreak of the Korean war convinced the Truman administration to increase substantially American aid to the French. By the time Eisenhower became president, the United States was paying for a significant majority of the cost of the French effort in Indochina.

Eisenhower had no sympathy for the French effort to maintain its colonial rule in Indochina. As distasteful as Eisenhower found British colonialism, he detested French colonialism even more. He regarded the French as both inept and particularly brutal colonizers. Dulles and Eisenhower repeatedly urged the French to grant freedom to Indochina. Both the president and the secretary of state, however, believed that the region could not be allowed to fall under communist control. Further, American policy remained limited by the need for French cooperation in Europe. Domestic politics also played a role in shaping the administration's policy. The Eisenhower administration had to deal with the Republican right, which considered Asia to be the primary area of American interest and had fiercely attacked Truman and his administration for the "loss" of China. Setting aside strategic questions, the further expansion of communism in Asia would have generated serious political problems for the administration at home.

The situation in Indochina came to a head in early 1954, when the French concentrated their forces in northwestern Vietnam and the Viet Minh surrounded a large French garrison at Dien Bien Phu. While the Viet Minh occupied the high ground around the garrison and pounded the French position, the beleaguered French government sought military assistance from the United States. Given the various pressures on him and his administration, Eisenhower did not reject the request but established several conditions for American aid. He insisted that any intervention be part of a multinational force (that included Asian countries) and that the French grant independence to the associated states of Laos, Cambodia, and Vietnam upon the defeat of the Communists. Further, he would not commit the United States unless he received prior approval from Congress and the British agreed to participate. As Eisenhower figured, such conditions never materialized. The British opposed any intervention, and the French refused to continue fighting only to give up their colonies in the end.

As the Geneva Conference, called to discuss Asian issues, got under way on April 26, 1954, and the French garrison at Dien Bien Phu desperately attempted to stave off impending defeat, Eisenhower remained disinclined to send American ground troops to Indochina. He realized that even a French military defeat did not mean that Indochina had to fall to the Communists. Although resigned to part of Vietnam coming under the control of the Communists, he wanted to aid that part of Vietnam that remained noncommunist after the Geneva Conference had finished its work. At the same time, Eisenhower resisted the increasing pressure from the Republican right to intervene militarily.

The French garrison surrendered on May 7. The Geneva Accords provided for the independence of Laos and Cambodia, and the Viet Minh agreed to withdraw their forces from those countries. Vietnam was also granted independence and divided at the 17th parallel. The Viet Minh withdrew to north of the dividing line, and the French withdrew to the south. National reunification elections were scheduled to take place in 1956, under the auspices of an international commission. The United States began to aid the South Vietnamese government and sent military advisers to Laos and Cambodia. When Ngo Dinh Diem became prime minister of South Vietnam in 1954 and expanded his power, the Eisenhower administration supported him. Ultimately, Diem ousted the emperor and was elected president of the Republic of Vietnam.

Eisenhower and Dulles remained concerned about the possibility of expanding communist influence in Southeast Asia. In September 1954, Dulles negotiated the Manila Pact, which created the Southeast Asia Treaty Organization. The members, which included the United States, France, Great Britain, Australia, New Zealand, Pakistan, and the Philippines, agreed to consult in the event of common danger or threat to peace and security in the region.

Throughout the crisis in French Indochina, Eisenhower faced pressure, particularly from the Republican right, to intervene. Both the president's politics and his military training argued against such a course. In a draft of his presidential memoirs, Eisenhower wrote that "the jungles of Indochina . . . would have swallowed up division after division of United States troops. . . . Furthermore, the presence of ever more numbers of white men in uniform probably would have aggravated rather than assuaged Asiatic resentments." Interestingly enough, he cut that passage when he published the volume in 1965, because the United States was by then escalating its military commitment to Vietnam and he did not want publicly to criticize the conduct of a successor, President Johnson. In another unpublished portion of his memoirs, Eisenhower wrote that it was important that the United States not support French colonialism, because "among all the powerful nations of the world the United States [was] the only one with a tradition of anti-colonialism." That standing, he maintained, was "an asset of incalculable value to the Free World." By his reckoning, "the moral position of the United States was more to be guarded than the Tonkin Delta, indeed than all of Indochina."

This opinion was not something Eisenhower conceived in retrospect. In a letter he wrote to Alfred Gruenther on April 26, 1954, as the situation became increasingly desperate for the French garrison at Dien Bien Phu, Eisenhower stated

As you know, you and I started more than three years ago trying to convince the French that they could not win the Indo-China war and particularly could not get real American support in that region unless they would unequivocally pledge independence to the Associated States upon the achievement of military victory. Along with this—indeed as a corollary to it—this administration has been arguing that no Western power can go into Asia militarily, except as one of a concert of powers, which concert must include local Asiatic peoples.

To contemplate anything else is to lay ourselves open to the charge of imperialism and colonialism or—at the very least—of objectionable paternalism. Even, therefore, if we could by some sudden stroke assure the saving of the Dien Bien Phu garrison, I think that under the conditions proposed by the French, the free world would lose more than it would gain.

On the same day he wrote to Gruenther, Eisenhower told Republican congressional leaders that if one United States combat soldier were put into Indochina "the entire prestige of the United States would be at stake, not only in that area but throughout the world." The United States would be forced into a position of having to win, and the president was not sure if that would be possible without "hitting full force." He then commented on what a "terrible" decision that would be. After examining the military options and finding them unsatisfactory, he made the decision not to go to war in Indochina.

The legacy of colonialism also provided the backdrop for the Suez Crisis in 1956, one of the most difficult tests the Eisenhower administration confronted in foreign policy. After a coup overthrew Egypt's pro-Western monarchy in 1952, Gamal Abdel Nasser emerged as the leader of that country. Nasser espoused radical Arab nationalism and asserted his leadership of the Arab world. Eisenhower and Dulles recognized Arab nationalism as a force to be reckoned with, especially in light of their conclusion that the French and British would not be able to maintain their influence in the region, which supplied two-thirds of Western Europe's oil. Therefore, the American administration urged its allies to accommodate change in the area and to make efforts to mitigate the legacy of colonialism. Underlying all other concerns, however, Eisenhower and

Dulles worried about the potential for the expansion of Soviet influence in the region.

Accordingly, in 1954, the administration encouraged the British to accede to Nasser's demand that they abandon British military bases around the Suez Canal. The following year, the United States sponsored the Baghdad Pact, signed by Great Britain, Turkey, Iran, Iraq, and Pakistan, which was designed to deter the Soviet Union from expanding its influence in the region as the British departed. Eisenhower and Dulles held out some hope that Nasser might eventually join the pact, but instead he denounced it as Western imperialism. Moreover, American and British attempts to broker a comprehensive peace between Israel and its Arab neighbors ran aground on Nasser's Pan-Arabism and his militant hostility to Israel. Following an Israeli reprisal raid in Gaza in February 1955, Nasser sought Western aid in building up his military. When he did not get what he wanted form the West, Nasser arranged to buy Soviet weapons through Czechoslovakia.

Eisenhower and Dulles came to regard the Egyptian leader as a threat to stability in the region. Nevertheless, they maintained the hope that the United States could influence Nasser through economic aid. Late in 1955, the United States and Great Britain proposed a package of over $400 million in grants and loans to build a high dam on the Nile River at Aswan that would provide hydroelectric power and irrigation. Fearing Western influence over Egypt's economy, Nasser hesitated to accept the loan. The proposal also encountered resistance in the United States. Southern members of Congress opposed what amounted to a subsidy for Egyptian cotton, which competed with the cotton produced in their home states. Further opposition came from anticommunists, who questioned the wisdom of aiding a neutralist who bought arms from the Soviet Union. Finally, the pro-Israel lobby objected to aiding a leader who had declared his commitment to the destruction of Israel.

By March 1956, the administration decided to take a harder line with respect to Nasser. After the Egyptian leader further antagonized the American administration by recognizing Communist China in May, the United States withdrew the offer to finance the dam and increased aid to pro-Western Arab governments in the region. Nasser responded by nationalizing the Suez Canal Company, owned largely by the British and French, and declared that he would use the revenue from the operation of the Suez Canal to finance the Aswan Dam. Intent on recovering their property and convinced of the necessity of removing Nasser from power, Britain and France immediately contemplated military action. The French had an additional reason to favor Nasser's removal—they bitterly resented his support of the Algerian rebellion against French rule.

As much as Eisenhower and Dulles disapproved of Nasser's seizure of the Suez Canal, they hoped to resolve the situation by using economic and diplomatic pressure to force the Egyptian leader to compensate the British and French, and also by establishing an international authority to oversee operation of the canal. Military intervention, the American administration warned, would simply inflame Arab nationalism, threaten Western interests in the region, and provide an opportunity for the expansion of Soviet influence. Further, a military adventure might result in the closure of the canal and thereby disrupt the supply of oil from the Middle East, which would have devastating consequences for the economies of Western Europe. Thus, Eisenhower urged the British and French to exercise restraint. In an exchange of letters with the British prime minister, Anthony Eden, Eisenhower argued against the use of military force unless public opinion in Great Britain and the United States solidly supported it and until "every possible means of protecting our vital interests has been exhausted without result." More important was Eisenhower's contention that "I really do not see how a successful result could be achieved by forcible means." European economies, he pointed out, would suffer if a war disrupted the supply of oil from the Middle East, and opinion in the Middle East, North Africa, Asia, and Africa would "be consolidated against the West to a degree which, I fear, could not be overcome in a generation." Eisenhower suggested exerting economic pressure and exploiting "Arab rivalries" to lessen Nasser's influence outside Egypt, the latter of which was possible only "if we do not make Nasser an Arab hero."

In late October, however, the British and French, without informing the United States,

entered an agreement with Israel (which had been plagued by cross-border raids by Egyptian commandos and alarmed by an alliance between Egypt, Syria, and Jordan) to take military action to restore the canal to British and French control and to remove Nasser from power. On October 29, Israeli forces launched an operation in the Sinai peninsula that expelled the Egyptian army from Gaza, from which the commando raids had been launched, and took Sharm el-Sheikh, which broke the Egyptian blockade in the Gulf of Aqaba. The next day, the British and French issued an ultimatum demanding that belligerents withdraw their forces to positions 10 miles from the Canal and allow the British and French to move into positions along the waterway. Otherwise, the British and French would take such positions by force. The Israelis immediately agreed. As expected, Nasser refused, and the British and French launched air strikes against Egyptian bases on October 31. They also sent an invasion fleet toward Port Said with the stated intent of keeping the canal open. Before the force could land, however, Nasser blocked the canal by scuttling ships in it, and, a few days later, Syrian forces cut the oil pipeline from Iraq to the Mediterranean.

Furious at the Anglo-French military adventure and at not being informed of it in advance, Eisenhower sought to impose a cease-fire through the United Nations. In the first place, Eisenhower thought the action of the British and French smacked of colonialism. Beyond that, he had concerns about the implications the invasion had for the cold war. He believed it necessary for the United States to disassociate itself from European colonialism in order not to push newly independent nations and the Arab world into the Soviet orbit. In addition, Eisenhower found it frustrating that the Suez Crisis diverted the world's attention from the Soviet Union's savage repression of the movement for reform in Hungary. The opportunity to trumpet the evils of the Soviet system was diminished by the competing din, with its echoes of European colonialism, generated by Suez.

The United States offered a resolution in the United Nations [UN] Security Council calling on Israel and Egypt to cease fire, on Israel to withdraw to its preexisting borders, and on all members of the UN to refrain from using force in the Middle East. The British and French vetoed it. A resolution by the Soviet Union calling on Israel to withdraw also encountered a British and French veto. Eisenhower thought it of paramount importance to prevent the Soviets from seizing the leadership of the opposition to the use of force in the Middle East. At the same time, he did not want the British and French to be, as he later put it, "branded as naked aggressors without provocation." In an effort to balance these concerns, the United States offered a resolution in the General Assembly that called for an immediate cease-fire, the withdrawal of all troops to the positions they held before the military action began, a ban on arms shipments to the area in which the hostilities were taking place, and action to open the Suez Canal. The UN adopted the American resolution.

In deference to the UN resolution, the Israelis halted their operations in the Sinai on November 4. They had achieved their objectives by taking control of the Gaza Strip and breaking the Egyptian blockade. Great Britain and France, however, were less successful. British and French paratroopers landed near the canal on November 5 but encountered resistance from Egyptian forces. Compounding matters, the Soviet premier, Nikolai Bulganin, threatened the use of force against invaders. Bulganin also wrote Eisenhower proposing that the United States and Soviet Union join forces to intervene to stop the fighting. The White House issued a statement calling the idea "unthinkable." With the British and French claiming control of the Canal area, the British government declared a cease-fire on November 6. Eisenhower phoned Eden and urged him to yield to a UN peacekeeping force.

After the cease-fire, Eisenhower kept pressure on Great Britain, France, and Israel to withdraw. He blocked financial aid to stabilize the pound and held up a plan to ease the impact of oil shortages in Western Europe by increasing production in the Western Hemisphere. The British and French forces withdrew from Egypt in December; the Israelis withdrew in March 1957. In the first few days after the cease-fire, the Soviet Union raised the possibility of its sending "volunteers" to Egypt. Eisenhower sternly warned Bulganin that "any such action would be directly contrary to the resolutions of the General Assembly of the United Nations" and that the United States would "oppose any such effort."

Eisenhower's management of the Suez Crisis produced mixed results. His primary objectives were to prevent both a larger war and the expansion of Soviet influence in the Middle East. While his policy did avert a general war and temporarily raised American standing in the Arab world, it ultimately failed in its two overarching objectives: to contain Nasserism and to prevent the expansion of Soviet influence in the region. Despite suffering a humiliating military defeat, Nasser not only remained in power but increased his reputation in the Arab world for having stood up to European imperialism. The Soviet Union gained a substantial foothold in the Arab world by issuing military threats against Britain and France and by financing the Aswan Dam. With respect to relations with America's allies, too, Eisenhower's actions yielded uneven outcomes. The experience made clear to Great Britain the extent to which it depended on American military and economic support, and Harold Macmillan, who replaced Anthony Eden as prime minister in January 1957, worked assiduously to restore the special relationship. On the other hand, France, already angered by American policy in Indochina, concluded that it could not depend on the United States to support vital French interests and that it must chart an independent course.

In the aftermath of Suez, Eisenhower and Dulles worried that the decline of French and British influence in the Mideast created a power vacuum that the Soviets might exploit. Further, the Arab-Israeli conflict threatened to explode into war at any time, and that would have provided another opportunity for the Soviets to expand their influence in the region. Should the Soviets gain control of the Middle East, Eisenhower reasoned, it "would be disastrous to Europe because of its oil requirements." In addition, Nasser's radical Arab nationalism posed a threat to Western interests and pro-Western Arab regimes in the area.

The administration's response was the Eisenhower Doctrine, announced in January 1957. Eisenhower requested $200 million from Congress in military and economic aid to be spent at the administration's discretion over the following two years. He also sought congressional approval to send American troops to any nation facing "overt armed aggression by any country controlled by

International Communism" that requested assistance. Some congressional leaders questioned the wisdom of granting the president a blank check; others simply opposed additional foreign aid; supporters of Israel objected to providing aid to Arab nations. Ultimately, however, the Middle East Resolution passed both houses of Congress, and Eisenhower signed it into law on March 9.

While the Eisenhower Doctrine focused on the threat of external communist aggression, Eisenhower recognized that Nasserism posed the most significant and immediate threat to Western interests in the Middle East, although he linked Nasser's "growing ambition" to "the sense of power he has gained out of his associations with the Soviets." Those concerns quickly came to fruition, and Eisenhower had to consider the conditions under which he would apply the doctrine that bore his name. In 1957, elections in Jordan resulted in a victory for Arab nationalists. The new government recommended abrogating the Anglo-Jordanian mutual defense treaty of 1948 and establishing diplomatic relations with the Soviet Union and Communist China. King Hussein foiled an attempted coup by Nasserite and leftist elements on April 13, after which he dismissed the prime minister and imposed martial law. The ousted prime minister established a government-in-exile in Syria, and his supporters rioted in Amman. King Hussein appealed to the Eisenhower administration for assistance. Under the authority granted him by the Middle East Resolution, the president immediately gave $10 million in economic aid to Jordan and moved the Sixth Fleet into the Eastern Mediterranean.

Developments in Jordan and Syria, which struck an arms deal with the Soviet Union and moved closer to Nasser, worried the pro-Western government of Camille Chamoun in Lebanon. A member of his country's Maronite Christian population, Chamoun's six-year term was scheduled to end in September 1958. It would have required a constitutional amendment for him to succeed himself, and Muslims in Lebanon (as well as Syria and Egypt) strongly opposed such an amendment as well as a second term. Chamoun had aligned Lebanon with the United States in the cold war and supported the Eisenhower Doctrine; Lebanese Muslims sympathized with Nasser. A victory for Chamoun's supporters in the parliamentary elections in 1957 amidst charges of fraud from Muslims at least opened the door to the possibility of amending the constitution. Complicating matters for the fragile peace in Lebanon, Syria and Egypt formed the United Arab Republic in January 1958, raising the specter of the expansion of Nasserism. When Chamoun floated the idea of amending the constitution in late April, Muslims rioted in the streets. By early May, bands of Christian and Muslim militia clashed in the streets. Lebanon complained to the United States that arms smuggled in from Syria, Egypt, and the Soviet Union threatened to spark a civil war. Moreover, Nasser tried to take advantage of the situation by broadcasting anti-Chamoun propaganda into Lebanon. Chamoun requested help under the Eisenhower Doctrine.

Dulles and Eisenhower understood the internal divisions in Lebanon and doubted either that it was actually under attack by the United Arab Republic or that the UAR was dominated by international communism. At least initially, Dulles was particularly skeptical that grounds existed to support an intervention. Further, the president and secretary of state were sensitive to the impact a military intervention might have in the Arab world. They understood that an American intervention risked dissipating the goodwill built up by the administration's actions during the Suez Crisis. On the other hand, they were concerned that a failure to respond to Chamoun's request would raise doubts about the reliability of the United States as an ally among pro-Western governments in the Middle East and elsewhere. Eisenhower informed the Lebanese leader that he would send American troops, but only if Chamoun first sought help from the United Nations in resolving the crisis and renounced his ambition for a second term. While Chamoun tried to meet these conditions, Eisenhower sent the Sixth Fleet to the Eastern Mediterranean. Eisenhower had, as he put it at the time, "little, if any, enthusiasm for our intervening." While he placed little faith in the Lebanese leader, Eisenhower held out some hope that Chamoun would be able to stabilize the situation by himself. At the same time, Eisenhower decided that, should Chamoun formally request American military assistance, he would need to respond in order to maintain American credibility.

For a time, it seemed that American intervention was unlikely. On May 22, Lebanese officials requested an emergency session of the UN Security Council, which passed a resolution on June 10 providing for an observation team to prevent the infiltration of arms and men into Lebanon. While the UN worked to find a solution and even Nasser seemed to seek a reduction of tensions, events in Iraq further destabilized the region. On July 14, 1957, pro-Nasser forces overthrew Iraq's pro-Western monarchy and executed the king and crown prince. Hussein in Jordan and Saud in Saudi Arabia urged the United States to send troops to the region. In Lebanon, political violence between Chamoun's supporters and opponents escalated, and Chamoun, claiming that his nation faced a threat from communism and Nasserism, again appealed to the United States for help under the Eisenhower Doctrine. Turkey, Iran, Pakistan, and Saudi Arabia also urged the Americans and British to intervene. On July 15, Eisenhower ordered 14,000 marines and army personnel to that country and announced that the United States was acting to prevent communist aggression in that country. That same day, the United States introduced a draft resolution in the United Nations asking that the international body assume responsibility for the defense of Lebanon. The Soviet Union vetoed the resolution.

As events in Lebanon unfolded, King Hussein of Jordan discovered and thwarted a plot to overthrow him on June 14. He requested aid from the British, who sent paratroopers to Jordan on July 17 to shore up Hussein's regime. The British prime minister, Harold Macmillan, wanted American participation, but Eisenhower refused beyond providing airlift capabilities to the British.

In the short term, at least, the bloodless operation achieved its objectives. The United States pressed Chamoun to hold elections, and the pro-Western Gen. Faud Chehab won election as president in August, at which point American forces began to withdraw. The last American forces left Lebanon on October 25. As Eisenhower wrote to Macmillan, "Without firing a shot in anger, and in close and friendly collaboration with the local authorities, our forces have achieved what they were sent to Lebanon and Jordan to do, at the request of the respective Governments. They have preserved the independence of these two small countries against aggressive subversive forces directed from outside. Our action has proved to the world, and especially to the smaller nations, that we stand by our pledges and that we have the courage to carry out our solemn undertakings, regardless of the threats made against us."

On the surface, Eisenhower's willingness to send American forces to Lebanon appeared to contrast starkly with his more cautious, restrained response to crises in the Far East and elsewhere. In fact, however, Eisenhower calculated that there was little possibility of a clash with the Soviets over Lebanon (Syria, he thought, might be a different matter). Moreover, in Lebanon, there was not as much indigenous resistance as in, say, Indochina. The intervention in Lebanon also served to demonstrate the sufficiency of American conventional capabilities, not so much to the Soviets but to domestic critics of the New Look, to pro-Western states in the region (most significantly King Saud), and, most importantly, to Nasser. Further, Eisenhower reckoned that the Middle East fell within the vital interests of the United States. Setting aside the strategic reasons for the intervention, Eisenhower handled the tactical aspects with the skill of a professional. The show of military force was calculated to gain maximum effect with minimum risk. Eisenhower made sure that the American military commitment was limited in scope; the orders under which the American forces operated restricted their activities to securing the airfield and the capital. The operation was also limited in duration. In an address to the American people that evening, Eisenhower expressed the hope that the United Nations would move quickly and "permit the early withdrawal of United States forces." The former general calculated the level of military force with the intent to discourage opposition, and, indeed, the marines landed without incident. Eisenhower's calculations with respect to the Soviets also proved accurate. They limited their response to diplomatic bluster. The crisis ended, and Eisenhower achieved his basic objectives without risking a general war. Nevertheless, even before withdrawing the American troops, Eisenhower ordered a reconsideration of the administration's policy in the Middle East. Opposition to Arab nationalism, the most powerful force in the region, Eisenhower conceded, was futile, and setting the United States against it only inflamed popular sentiment in the region. Therefore, he argued, the United States "must either work with it or change it, or do some of both." "The question," as the president put it, "is how to take a sympathetic position regarding the Arabs without agreeing to the destruction of Israel."

During the final two years of Eisenhower's presidency, preventing the expansion of communism in Latin America again emerged as a major focus of foreign policy. After the overthrow of the Arbenz government in Guatemala, Eisenhower and Dulles were occupied primarily with various crises in Europe, the Middle East, and Asia. Although Latin America did not claim the focused attention of the administration, it did not drop entirely off the administration's radar. Serving as his brother's special envoy, Milton Eisenhower went on a fact-finding trip of Latin America in 1954. The trip convinced him that traditional foreign aid served to strengthen the existing order but did not facilitate necessary social change. He recommended expanded trade and investment, increased technical aid, and cultural exchanges. Above all, Milton believed that the United States should encourage democratic governments. Congress, however, balked at providing the funds for the kind of aid and exchanges Milton recommended. In response to Milton's report, the Eisenhower administration increased by twofold the flow of private and public capital into the region, strengthened the role of the Organization of American States, promoted common markets, and established the Inter-American Development Bank (founded to make loans with conditions requiring social reform). Subsequent trips to Latin America in 1958 and 1960 confirmed Milton's views. All of this formed the basis for what John F. Kennedy would later call the Alliance for Progress. Nevertheless, discontent with the existing order seethed in the region, and politicians in the United States tended to ignore unrest in Latin America unless it threatened to topple a pro-American government.

In Cuba, Fidel Castro led a revolt against Fulgencio Batista, the country's brutal and corrupt dictator. Eisenhower's attempts to press Batista to institute reforms availed nothing. The young and charismatic Castro and his cause struck a sympathetic chord throughout Latin America. Even in the United States, many found Castro's promises of free elections, schools, housing, and economic reform far more appealing than the reactionary despotism of Batista. While Eisenhower had reservations about Castro, he withheld support from Batista. American policy denied arms to both sides in Cuba.

Despite concerns from the CIA about the involvement of communists in Castro's movement, Eisenhower rejected recommendations that the United States side with Batista as the lesser of two evils. Eisenhower figured that "our only hope, if any, lay with some kind of nondictatorial 'third force,'" but no such third force emerged. Throughout the closing months of 1958, Batista's armed forces lost ground to the rebels. Castro entered Havana on New Year's Day 1959, and Batista fled the country. The United States quickly recognized the new regime, but Castro immediately proceeded to alienate the United States by purging liberals from his government, by staging mass executions, and by signing a trade and aid agreement with the Soviet Union. Within two weeks after taking power, Castro legalized the Communist Party. On January 21, Castro's first prime minister resigned in protest over mass executions and the anti-Americanism of Castro's speeches. Castro made himself premier on February 13, and, at the end of the month announced that he was postponing the promised elections for two years. Allen Dulles, director of the CIA, reported to Eisenhower that Castro's government was not dominated by communists but that the communists had "worked their way into the labor unions, the armed forces, and other organizations."

In the past, the United States had sent marines to dispatch troublesome governments in Latin America, a step Eisenhower refused even to consider. As he wrote to his brother, Edgar Eisenhower, a successful lawyer and conservative Republican who had complained about the president's policy in Panama:

You are contemplating a trip to Costa Rica. Should we use the old method of sending Marines into any Latin American country as a means of asserting and enforcing our interpretation of any difficulty that might arise, any North American would have a most unpleasant time if he should undertake such a journey.

In addition, Castro was popular throughout Latin America and had many supporters in the United States. The costs of an American military intervention were too high.

The Eisenhower administration remained somewhat puzzled by Castro. Herter met Castro during the latter's trip to the United States in April 1959 and found him "very much like a child in many ways" and "quite immature regarding problems of government." At the same time, Herter noted that the Cuban leader spoke in English "with restraint and considerable personal appeal." The CIA found Castro's assurances that he would remain in the Western camp unconvincing and reported the "probability" that land reform in Cuba would likely "adversely affect certain American owned properties." On the other hand, the agency warned that it "would be a serious mistake to underestimate this man" and thought that there was some possibility of "developing a constructive relationship with him." Eisenhower scrawled on the report, "File. We will check in a year!!"

By January 1960, the confiscation of American property, the Cuban invasion of Haiti, and Castro's continuing verbal attacks on the United States led Eisenhower and his administration to conclude that they had to do something about the Cuban leader. Castro, however, was not Arbenz. The masses of Latin America regarded him as an enormously appealing figure, and Castro dismissed attempts to link him with the communists as an example of the American propensity to regard any Latin American reformer as a communist. Further, the opposition to Castro, in Cuba and among exiles in Florida, was deeply divided; therefore, the prospect of uniting the opposition in exile behind an alternative to Castro seemed remote. Finally, the American administration could expect no help from other Latin American countries. In private, rulers of Latin American countries told Eisenhower that they hoped the United States would get rid of Castro, but they would not speak out in public against the widely popular Cuban leader.

Another matter complicated American policy towards Cuba. Several Latin American governments pressed for action against Rafael Trujillo, the dictator of the Dominican Republic, as a condition for supporting any move against Castro. Eisenhower, who found Trujillo's regime repulsive, explored ways of persuading the Dominican tyrant to step down. He even considered setting up a trust fund for Trujillo but drew the line at offering him asylum in the United States. In any case, Trujillo had no intention of resigning, and the American administration worried that forcing him out might lead to chaos and ultimately a communist takeover. Whatever their concerns about him, the administration did not worry about Trujillo entering a mutual security agreement with the Soviet Union.

In the Caracas Declaration of 1954, the Organization of American States had committed itself to oppose the intrusion of communism into the Western hemisphere. However, proving that Castro was a communist remained something of a problem, not the least because the Eisenhower administration itself was not entirely convinced. Events in Cuba, however, moved them in that direction.

Once again, Eisenhower turned to the CIA and covert operations to handle a troublesome situation. Eisenhower told Allen Dulles to develop a "program" to get rid of Castro. Eisenhower made it clear to the CIA that he did not want Castro removed until a government in exile had been formed. Simply killing Castro, Eisenhower thought, would do nothing more than elevate either Raúl Castro or Che Guevara to leadership, and he regarded either as a worse alternative. The CIA nevertheless undertook a series of attempts to assassinate Castro, apparently without Eisenhower's knowledge. In March 1960, Eisenhower approved a program that included the creation of a "responsible and unified" Cuban government in exile, a "propaganda offensive" against Castro's government, the development of a "covert intelligence and action organization in Cuba," and the training of a "paramilitary force outside of Cuba for future guerilla action."

In the meantime, Latin American governments used Castro as an argument for increased economic and military aid to their countries. In February 1960, Eisenhower made a personal goodwill trip of Latin America in an effort to persuade governments there that they did not need more weapons but that they did need to undertake social and economic reforms. He also hoped to counter Castro's appeal to the masses. Eisenhower's appeals for reform fell on deaf ears, and his attempt to rally support against Castro failed.

Eisenhower's greatest concern was that Castro would allow Khrushchev to use Cuba as a base for Soviet strategic weapons, but he thought that unlikely. After all, he figured that the Soviet leader had to know that the United States "could not tolerate" such a development. Nevertheless, the Soviet Union expanded its influence in Cuba. The two nations concluded a trade and credit agreement in February 1960. In July, Khrushchev threatened to use his rockets to protect Cuba from a military attack. At the same time, the Soviet premier denied any interest in placing Soviet missiles in Cuba; his ICBMs, he bragged, made that unnecessary.

Eisenhower began to move against Castro. By law, the United States bought approximately half of Cuba's sugar crop at premium prices. In July 1960, Eisenhower signed legislation that gave the president temporary authority to reduce the amount of sugar Cuba could export to the United States. Eisenhower cut the remaining sugar quota for that year by 95 percent. At a meeting of the American Foreign Ministers in August, the Eisenhower administration took advantage of Khrushchev's bluster and got the conference to condemn any "intervention or the threat of intervention . . . from an extra-continental power in the affairs of the American Republics." It specifically warned against any attempt by "the Sino-Soviet powers" to intervene in the Western hemisphere. The conference also issued a condemnation of the Dominican Republic and called on members of the OAS to break diplomatic relations. The United States quickly did so.

Eisenhower also recognized the need for reform in Latin America to prevent the spread of communism. In early September 1960, Congress approved the administration's request for $600 million in non-military aid to Latin America. On September 13, the Special Committee of the Organization of American States adopted the Act of Bogotá, which called for cooperative measures to improve land, to reform tax structures, and to build education systems, public health facilities, and community facilities.

While the administration attempted to use diplomatic measures and to improve conditions to prevent the spread of communism, it also prepared to take additional economic measures against Cuba and began the evacuation of American citizens. Yet, despite pressure from some Republican leaders in Congress and from Nixon, Eisenhower rejected the use of American military force to remove Castro. At a meeting of Republican congressional leaders, and in words reminiscent of his letter to Edgar about Panama, he said, "If we were to try to accomplish our aims by force, we would see all of [Latin America] tending to fall away and some would be Communist within two years. . . . If the United States does not conduct itself in precisely the right way vis-à-vis Cuba, we could lose all of South America."

Nonetheless, in August, after learning that Cuba was importing arms form Czechoslovakia, Eisenhower authorized an expansion of the program to train Cuban exiles. The president was disappointed that there had been no progress on developing a government-in-exile and remained firm that he would approve no action without a credible, popular alternative to Castro's government. By December, there were roughly 600 exiles training in Guatemala; once again, Eisenhower told the CIA that he would approve no plan to use the force unless he had evidence of a government-in-exile.

On January 2, 1961, Castro accused the United States embassy in Havana of harboring spies and ordered almost all of the personnel at the embassy to leave Cuba within 24 hours. An outraged Eisenhower broke off diplomatic relations. The exiles training in Guatemala would not be ready to go until March, and a legitimate government-in-exile was nowhere to be found. The CIA, however, worried that the brigade could not be held together much past that date if no action were taken. Andrew Goodpaster, Eisenhower's staff secretary, warned that the CIA was creating a relatively large military force that was not officially responsible to any government and that the operation would build a momentum of its own. Eisenhower replied that the CIA was creating an asset, not committing the United States to a course of policy. In his memoirs, Eisenhower recalled that, in the absence of a credible leader and alternative government, "it was impossible to make specific plans for a military invasion." Eisenhower bequeathed to his successor a band of Cuban exiles training to overthrow Castro's government.

In many respects, Eisenhower compiled an impressive record as president. He was the only president since the advent of polls whose popularity did not decline. He presided over a time of peace and prosperity for most Americans. At the same time, Eisenhower was by no means universally successful; nor were his policies always prescient. By the 1950s, the white middle class had begun to flee the cities for the suburbs. In the process, they left behind an increasingly black and poor population. The migration stripped the cities of their tax base at a time when the need for public services was growing. This process began under Truman, continued under Eisenhower, and did not receive serious federal attention until the Johnson administration. If Eisenhower was less than farsighted in the minimal attention he paid to the problems of cities, he failed utterly in his attempt to unite and to redefine the Republican party in his own moderate image. His cautious contributions to the advancement of civil rights for African Americans, however important, certainly did not make equality a reality and failed to satisfy the demands of the burgeoning Civil Rights movement. Historians continue to debate whether Eisenhower could have reined in McCarthy and McCarthyism earlier and thereby saved the nation a good deal of anguish. In foreign policy, Eisenhower ended one war and did not begin another. He resisted the temptation of sending American combat forces into Indochina. The Geneva summit represented the first thaw in the cold war. Historians such as Robert Divine have lauded his restraint in dealing with major crises and with the Soviet Union. Eisenhower was particularly cautious when it came to putting American troops in harm's way. In his memoirs, Eisenhower proudly pointed out that, under his stewardship, not a single member of the American armed forces had died in combat after the end of the Korean War and communism did not expand into new territories. This did not, he wrote, happen by accident. For all that, some historians have argued that Eisenhower demonstrated less restraint when dealing with the Third World. There, he sometimes resorted to more aggressive measures, although usually with covert operations rather than the use of American military force. Moreover, interventions in Iran and Guatemala

President Dwight D. Eisenhower *(Dwight D. Eisenhower Library and Museum)*

that looked like successes in the short term had long-term negative consequences.

Whatever its limitations and failures, however, Eisenhower's presidency was not, as William V. Shannon described it, "the time of the great Postponement." It was not even only, in the words of Charles Alexander, "a good job of holding the line." Eisenhower presided over eight years of peace, prosperity, and progress. As the first Republican president after Franklin Roosevelt, he preserved, strengthened, and expanded the basic structure of the New Deal. He eliminated no major federal programs and embarked on several new initiatives. After Eisenhower, the broad consensus in favor of the basic structures of the New Deal became truly bipartisan.

In some areas, Eisenhower essentially maintained programs he inherited. The regulatory structures of the New Deal remained in place, and Eisenhower retained the Tennessee Valley Authority. In others areas, such as farm subsidies and public housing, Eisenhower cut back on New Deal and

Fair Deal programs; but he did not eliminate the programs themselves. In still other areas, Eisenhower oversaw an expansion of New Deal policies. His administration expanded the coverage of Social Security and raised benefits. He oversaw passage of a substantial increase in the minimum wage and an increase in unemployment benefits. He undertook large public works projects, such as the Saint Lawrence Seaway and the national highway system. In the area of health, he supported a federal role in the distribution of the Salk vaccine and an expansion of federal spending for hospitals and research. In addition, Eisenhower could claim credit for some real progress in civil rights.

In some instances, Eisenhower proposed extensions of the policies of Roosevelt and Truman but failed to win legislative approval. The administration's proposals for federal aid for the construction of schools and for a federal health reinsurance program died in Congress.

William Bragg Ewald has asserted that Eisenhower's greatest achievement was that "many terrible things that could have happened didn't." As a result, according to Ewald, "Dwight Eisenhower's presidency gave America eight good years." Eight years of peace, prosperity, and relative domestic tranquility looks pretty good, particularly compared to the performance of subsequent presidents. Perhaps that is why Stephen Ambrose lent his assent to the judgment of "millions of Americans," who "felt that the country was damned lucky to have him."

Abernathy, Ralph D(avid)

(1926–1990) *minister, civil rights leader*
Born on his parents' 500-acre farm in Marengo Co.,
Ala., on March 11, 1926, Ralph Abernathy was the
10th of 12 children. He received a B.S. from Alabama State College in 1950 and an M.A. in sociology from Atlanta University in 1951. Ordained a
Baptist minister in 1948, Abernathy became pastor
of the First Baptist Church in Montgomery, Ala.
in 1951.

Active in civic affairs and a member of the
NAACP, Abernathy readily agreed to help organize
a boycott of Montgomery's racially segregated bus
system following the arrest of ROSA PARKS, a black
seamstress, on December 1, 1955, for violation of
the city's bus segregation ordinance. Abernathy
helped contact other black ministers, set up planning meetings, and prepared for the boycott, which
began on December 5. He urged the formation of
a permanent organization to manage the protest
and suggested the name Montgomery Improvement Association (MIA) for the body, which was
established on the first day of the boycott. MARTIN
LUTHER KING, JR., a young Baptist minister relatively new to Montgomery, was chosen to lead the
MIA. Abernathy was named to the executive board
and the program committee.

Abernathy and King had already become
close friends by the time the Montgomery boycott
started. "From the beginning of the protest," King
later declared, "[Abernathy] was my closest associate and most trusted friend." Abernathy took charge

of much MIA business when King was out of town,
was a close adviser to King throughout the 381-day
boycott, and organized regular mass meetings of
Montgomery's blacks.

On November 13, 1956, the Supreme Court
ruled that bus segregation in Montgomery was
unconstitutional. Abernathy then helped organize a
program of mass training in nonviolent techniques
to prepare the black community for integration.
On December 21, 1956, the day after the Supreme
Court's desegregation order arrived in Montgomery, Abernathy and King rode on an integrated bus.
A month of retaliatory violence by whites followed.
In the early hours of January 10, 1957, while King
and Abernathy were in Atlanta for a meeting, Abernathy's home and church, along with three other
black churches and the home of another minister,
were bombed.

The historic Montgomery boycott marked
the beginning of an era of nonviolent direct action
by southern blacks against racial segregation and
discrimination. It also inaugurated a partnership
between King and Abernathy. Early in 1957, the
two helped found the Southern Christian Leadership Conference (SCLC). Abernathy was appointed
financial secretary-treasurer, while King was named
president. Under the auspices of the SCLC, the
two ministers preached a philosophy of nonviolent
resistance to Jim Crow practices and began organizing nonviolent training institutes and voter registration drives among southern blacks. The burly
Abernathy was regarded as less intellectual than

King and as having more of a common touch in his preaching and speaking, but the two became alter egos. Beginning with Montgomery, King consulted Abernathy before making any important decision. In 1961, at King's urging, Abernathy moved to Atlanta in order to be closer to King, who had moved there the year before, and to the SCLC's Atlanta headquarters.

During the next seven years, Abernathy remained King's chief aide and confidant, helping him direct desegregation and voter registration campaigns in Albany, Ga., in 1962, Birmingham, Ala., in 1963 and Selma, Ala., in 1965. Abernathy became vice-president of SCLC in 1965 and was with King when the latter was assassinated in Memphis, Tenn., on April 4, 1968. Abernathy succeeded King as president of the SCLC and led a Poor People's Campaign in Washington, D.C., in the spring and summer of 1968. Abernathy resigned the presidency of SCLC in 1977. He ran unsuccessfully for a congressional seat from Georgia in 1978, and in 1980 surprised many by endorsing Ronald Reagan for president. Abernathy went on to found the Foundation for Economic Enterprises Development, an organization dedicated to improving economic opportunities for African Americans, and served as pastor to the West Hunter Street Baptist Church in Atlanta until 1983, when he suffered the first of several strokes. The publication of his autobiography, *And the Walls Came Tumbling Down*, in 1989 generated controversy for its discussion of King's sexual infidelities. Abernathy died on April 17, 1990, in Atlanta.

—CAB

Acheson, Dean G(ooderham)

(1893–1971) *secretary of state, lawyer*

Born on April 11, 1893, in Middletown, Conn., Acheson attended Groton and Yale (class of 1916). Following his graduation from Harvard Law School in 1918, Acheson became private secretary to Supreme Court Justice Louis Brandeis. He then entered law practice in Washington with the prestigious firm of Covington and Burling. In 1933, he was appointed undersecretary of the treasury but resigned after a few months in a disagreement with the administration over economic policy. Acheson

returned to public service in 1941 as assistant secretary of state. From 1944 to 1947, he served as undersecretary of state, the department's second-ranking post, and from 1949 to 1952 he was secretary of state.

While at the State Department, Acheson helped formulate the early American response to the cold war. Believing that the Soviet Union was bent on world conquest, he thought that attempts to negotiate with the Russians from a position of equality were useless. Instead, Acheson recommended that the United States give immense amounts of economic, political, and military aid to countries on the rim of the communist bloc to prevent or "contain" future Soviet expansion. In his view, Germany played a key role in the redevelopment of Europe. Acheson's ideas were reflected in the Marshall Plan of 1947.

Acheson firmly believed that America should negotiate from a position of overwhelming military strength maintained by a strong nuclear strike force, a large conventional army, and a series of regional alliances designed to rim the communist bloc. Faced with such awesome power, the Soviet Union, he believed, would be willing to negotiate differences. As secretary of state, Acheson was instrumental in the creation of the North Atlantic Treaty Organization (NATO), the rebuilding and rearming of Germany, and the development of atomic policy. Although he believed that the North Atlantic community represented the peak of cultural and political growth and therefore made it the focus of his diplomacy, Acheson spent a large portion of his time on Asian affairs. Following the fall of Chiang Kai-shek (Jiang Jieshi), Acheson pursued a nonrecognition policy toward Communist China. During his last years in the State Department, he also worked to prevent the widening of the Korean War.

Despite his vigorous anticommunism, Acheson was attacked as being "soft on communism" for his defense of Alger Hiss, for what rightists termed his "appeasement" of the Soviet Union, and for his "loss" of China. Acheson left office at the end of the Truman administration to return to his private law practice.

During the Eisenhower administration, Acheson attempted to defend his record against criticism by Secretary of State JOHN FOSTER DULLES and the right wing of the Republican Party while trying to articulate an alternative foreign policy for the Democratic Party. Acheson charged that the administration's New Look, a reliance on strategic nuclear weapons as America's prime deterrent, "was a fraud upon words and upon facts." It produced "doubts, fears and loss of confidence in our leadership." To him, "massive retaliation" implied unilateralism and a reversion to isolationism, for Dulles's threat that the United States would retaliate "by means and places of our own choosing" precluded any consultation with American allies. This policy, Acheson argued, showed that the United States would recklessly gamble its allies' future to win diplomatic victories.

Acheson maintained that massive retaliation was irrelevant to the past and future skirmishes of the cold war. Only unified ground action had checked Communist advances in Korea. During the 1956 presidential campaign, he charged that the Republican foreign policy of "bluff and bluster" did not save Dien Bien Phu or prevent Nasser from seizing the Suez Canal. He said that Eisenhower and Dulles could have continued Truman's foreign policy but instead had become "the prisoners of the primitive propaganda and slogans of the McCarthy-Taft-Knowland forces." Acheson recommended the return to a proper balance between conventional and nuclear weapons, the end of empty rhetorical threats, and a willingness to work with NATO to repair the alleged damage done to American prestige during Eisenhower's first term.

When the Communist Chinese resumed shelling the offshore islands of Quemoy and Matsu in 1958, Acheson denounced Eisenhower's foreign policy once again. He observed that the United States seemed to be "drifting, either dazed or indifferent, to war with China." Rejecting Dulles's position that Quemoy was crucial to the defense of Taiwan (Formosa), he maintained that the island traditionally belonged to the mainland. Its population was minimal and it had no strategic value. Acheson warned that Chiang Kai-shek was interested in the island only as a staging area to attack the Communist Chinese and would use the crisis to embroil the United States in a conflict with the Communist Chinese.

Maintaining his strong mistrust of the communists into the 1950s, the former secretary was skeptical of Eisenhower's attempts to relax tensions between the United States and the Soviet Union. He counseled the nation to be ever vigilant to meet any Soviet challenge and be cautious of being lured into making premature agreements that could be harmful in the future. He discounted the efficacy of summit conferences with the Soviets, writing in 1958 that the United States had nothing to negotiate with the Soviet Union. He opposed GEORGE KENNAN's call for negotiations on American and Soviet withdrawal from Eastern and Western Europe and the reunification and neutralization of Germany. Acheson thought neutralization would eventually push Germany into the Soviet camp, while withdrawal of American troops would leave NATO countries vulnerable to communist infiltration. As late as 1959 he opposed summit meetings, where he thought the Soviet Union would possess all the advantages. Soviet premier Nikita Khrushchev, he believed, would endeavor to obtain concessions from the West on Berlin and try to obtain American endorsement of the status quo in Eastern Europe. To make such an agreement, Acheson wrote, would be tantamount to another "Munich."

During the late 1950s, Acheson served as chairman of the Democratic Advisory Council's foreign policy committee. He spoke for the hard-line faction, which saw little possibility for accommodation with the Soviets. In contrast, such notable Democrats as ELEANOR ROOSEVELT and CHESTER BOWLES advocated closer relations with the USSR.

In the 1960s, Dean Acheson advised President JOHN F. KENNEDY during the Cuban missile crisis and President LYNDON B. JOHNSON on policy in Vietnam. Following the Tet offensive of early 1968, Johnson asked Acheson to make an independent study of U.S. involvement in Vietnam. Acheson concluded that the United States could not win the war without another major troop buildup, which the American people would not support. He advised the president to get out of Vietnam as soon as possible. His recommendation was a leading factor in Johnson's decision to de-escalate the war in March 1968. Acheson died on October 12, 1971.

—JB

Adams, John G(ibbons)

(1912–2003) *general counsel, Department of the Army*

Born in Ashland, Ky., on March 23, 1912, Adams earned a law degree from the University of South Dakota in 1935. He then worked for the South Dakota Department of Justice and served as vice president of the Young Republican National Federation. At the same time he owned and operated an oil company in Sioux Falls, S.Dak. In 1947 Adams moved to Washington as a clerk for the Senate Committee on Armed Services, and two years later, he became assistant general counsel for the Department of Defense. In 1953 he was named general counsel of the Department of the Army. That year the Senate Government Operations Committee's Permanent Investigations Subcommittee, chaired by Sen. JOSEPH MCCARTHY (R-Wis.), intensified its investigations of alleged subversive activity in the army. Adams soon came into conflict with the panel over what he regarded as its interference in army affairs.

In March 1954, the Army released a report, which Adams had helped draft, accusing the Investigations Subcommittee's counsel, ROY COHN of trying to exert pressure on the army to give special privileges to Pvt. G. DAVID SCHINE, a former special investigator for the subcommittee and a close friend of Cohn. Schine had been drafted in November 1953 and assigned to Fort Dix, N.J. McCarthy then called a press conference at which he accused Adams of trying to use Schine as a hostage to force McCarthy to call off his probe of communists in the army. The senator added that Adams had encouraged him to investigate the navy and air force instead. On March 16 the subcommittee voted to hold hearings on the dispute. In April Adams was named, along with Army Secretary ROBERT T. STEVENS and Assistant Defense Secretary H. STRUVE HENSEL, in formal charges filed by McCarthy.

During the Army-McCarthy hearings in April, May, and June, the army appointed JOSEPH N. WELCH as special counsel in the case. In testimony offered in May on the "abuse and pressure" he had received from Cohn on Schine's behalf, Adams alleged that Cohn had persistently sought to have his friend assigned to New York and had threatened to "wreck the army" if Schine were given overseas duty. Cohn and McCarthy testified that Adams had tried to blackmail them into dropping their investigations at Fort Monmouth, N.J., by threatening to circulate an embarrassing report about Cohn. Other testimony indicated that Adams had gone to great lengths to satisfy Cohn's demands. In the subcommittee's report, released in August, the Republican majority concluded that the charge of "improper influence" by McCarthy on behalf of Schine "was not established" and that Adams and Stevens had tried "to terminate or influence" the Fort Monmouth probe. Subcommittee Democrats, however, sharply condemned the actions of Cohn and McCarthy. In addition, they accused Stevens and Adams of following a "policy of appeasement" and of "weakness and lack of propriety."

Once a suitable period had passed after the Army-McCarthy hearings, Adams, under pressure from his superiors, resigned his position as the army's general counsel as of March 31, 1955. Adams began an unsuccessful career in the private practice of law. In 1958, the Eisenhower administration proposed Adams as a commissioner of the Interstate Commerce Commission, but Sen. STYLES BRIDGES announced his intention to block the appointment. Nevertheless, that same year, Adams became a senior attorney for the Civil Aeronautics Board. In 1965, Adams became a board member of the CAB and served until 1970. He joined a Washington, D.C., law firm for five years and then established a two-partner firm, from which he retired to write his account of the Army-McCarthy hearings. He died in Dallas, Tex., on June 26, 2003.

—TLH

Adams, Sherman

(1899–1986) *assistant to the president*

The son of a grocery store owner, Adams was born on January 8, 1899. He served in the U.S. Marine Corps during World War I and received a B.A. from Dartmouth College in 1920. He then began a career in the lumber industry, starting as a clerk and scaler in southern Vermont and ultimately becoming general manager of a lumber company in Lincoln, N.H. Following a 1938 hurricane that leveled many trees in New Hampshire, Adams was selected to tour the state urging an emergency salvage effort.

His success encouraged him to wage a campaign for the New Hampshire House of Representatives in 1940. He won the race and was reelected two years later. During his second term he became Speaker of the House.

In 1944, Adams was elected to the U.S. House of Representatives. There he compiled a moderately conservative domestic record. He did not establish a clear pattern of voting in foreign affairs. In 1946 Adams lost the New Hampshire Republican gubernatorial primary by 157 votes and returned to private life.

Two years later, Adams waged a successful gubernatorial campaign; he won reelection in 1950. As governor he consolidated government departments to promote efficiency and attempted to reduce the budget. To set an example of austerity, Adams arrived at his office at dawn and in the winter walked to and from work on snowshoes.

On September 30, 1951, Adams joined five other Republicans at the annual Governors Conference in endorsing DWIGHT D. EISENHOWER for their party's presidential nomination. The first primary was held in New Hampshire, and under Adams's leadership the Eisenhower forces won all the state's delegates to the Republican National Convention. With his home state's primary over, Adams campaigned for Eisenhower throughout the country. At the July convention he was the candidate's floor leader. He impressed Eisenhower with his penchant for hard work, mastery of detail, and skill in behind-the-scenes political combat.

Eisenhower asked Adams to be his campaign chief of staff. The governor accepted, and accompanied Eisenhower during the entire race. Adams decided when and where the candidate would speak and helped make major strategy decisions. Adams's endorsement of the proposal that Eisenhower pledge to go to Korea was an important factor in the presidential nominee's acceptance of the idea.

Shortly after the election, Eisenhower asked Adams to come to Washington as the president's chief of staff. As a former military officer, Eisenhower was accustomed to operating through channels of delegated authority and had been aided by highly competent chiefs of staff. As a result, Adams became one of the most powerful appointed officials in modern American history.

Adams was often given the tasks Eisenhower preferred not to do. Although the president directed patronage policy, it was Adams who dispensed jobs, making many enemies both within and without the Republican Party among disappointed office seekers and their sponsors. In 1953, for example, he offended WALTER REUTHER by rejecting his candidate for assistant secretary of labor. He was also influential in the firing of government officials and was believed to have had a significant role in the departures of Secretary of Health, Education and Welfare OVETA CULP HOBBY in 1955 and of Secretary of the Interior DOUGLAS McKAY in 1956. Even when he did not have a hand in a dismissal, he was often assigned to convey the news to the individual.

Eisenhower avoided partisan public attacks on Democrats and frequently turned the job over to Adams. In reply, Democrats often denounced him rather than the president. Adams also put pressure on members of Congress to advance administration bills. Since Adams performed the unpleasant tasks that Eisenhower did not want to do, the presidential assistant's public image was the opposite of Eisenhower's. The president was known as a fatherly, genial man above partisan politics. Adams, on the other hand, was regarded as a cold-blooded, ruthless partisan. He was often referred to as "Great Stone Face" or as the administration's "Abominable No-Man."

Stories of Adams's influence and his control over access to the president appeared regularly in newspaper columns during the 1950s and made their way into histories of the period. In fact, those stories greatly exaggerated the truth. Adams served as Eisenhower's gatekeeper; people whom Eisenhower decided not to see blamed Adams. Similarly, individuals whose requests were denied did the same. Adams did control the flow of paper, which made it possible for Eisenhower to focus on larger issues of policy, and this gave Adams an indirect but not insubstantial influence on policy.

Adams generally stood with the liberal wing of the Republican Party. Soon after Sen. JOSEPH McCARTHY (R-Wis.) began his attacks on the administration in 1953, Adams urged Eisenhower to prepare a counteroffensive. He reportedly was the first to suggest that the army compile a record of its disputes with McCarthy. The resulting dossier was used in the Army-McCarthy hearings. During Eisenhower's first term, Adams opposed the conservative bloc within the administration, led by Secretary of the Treasury GEORGE HUMPHREY, that stressed budget-balancing. He defended the Department of Health, Education and Welfare in its battles with Humphrey for additional funds and supported expanded social security and housing programs, federal aid for school construction, and high levels of foreign aid. After the president's reelection in 1956, Adams played a key role in replacing Humphrey with the more liberal ROBERT B. ANDERSON. At the same time he also had a hand in replacing conservatives such as Secretary of Defense CHARLES E. WILSON and Undersecretary of State HERBERT HOOVER, JR., with moderates NEIL H. MCELROY and CHRISTIAN HERTER, respectively. In 1957, Adams backed the president's civil rights legislation and played a significant role in the administration's reaction to the desegregation crisis in Little Rock, Ark.

Eisenhower had used corruption in the Truman administration as a major Republican issue during the 1952 campaign. He asserted that public officials must be untainted by unethical as well as illegal activities. Adams appeared to be a strict enforcer of the president's standards. An investigation by the House Judiciary Committee's Antitrust and Monopoly Subcommittee in 1955 revealed that PETER STROBEL, commissioner of the Public Buildings Service, had approved contracts awarded to companies that were clients of his private firm. Although subcommittee chairman Rep. EMANUEL CELLER (D-N.Y.) decided that Strobel had not acted illegally, Adams forced the commissioner to resign. In February 1958 the House Interstate and Foreign Commerce Committee's Legislative Oversight Subcommittee discovered that Federal Communications Commission member RICHARD A. MACK had received financial assistance from a friend seeking a license to operate a Miami television station. Adams immediately demanded Mack's resignation, which was tendered on March 3.

During 1958, serious questions arose concerning Adams's own public ethics. A congressional probe of his activities created the biggest scandal of the administration and culminated in Adams's resignation. In February 1958, the Legislative Oversight Subcommittee discovered that five years earlier Adams had apparently intervened with the Civil Aeronautics Board (CAB) on behalf of MURRAY CHOTINER, former campaign manager for Vice President Nixon and, in 1953, counsel for North American Airlines. Adams asked CAB chairman Herman B. Denny how the airline could delay the implementation of a board ruling revoking North American's operating license.

This matter was overshadowed in June and July 1958 when the panel probed the relationship between Adams and his old friend BERNARD GOLDFINE, a Boston textile magnate. Subcommittee staff members and witnesses charged that Adams received gifts from Goldfine during the early and mid 1950s while at the same time intervening on his friend's behalf with the Federal Trade Commission (FTC) and the Securities and Exchange Commission (SEC).

Goldfine, it was alleged, had paid over $3,000 in hotel bills for Adams between 1953 and 1958 and had given him a vicuña coat, two suits, and a $2,400 oriental rug. Meanwhile, Goldfine was facing FTC mislabeling charges against his textile firms. FTC officials testified that in 1954 Adams had asked the commission chairman about the charges and the following year arranged a meeting between Goldfine and agency officials. In February 1957, the FTC merely issued a cease-and-desist order against Goldfine, although agency lawyers had recommended a civil suit. In 1956, the SEC had considered action against Goldfine for not filing required financial reports on his real estate operations. After Adams had directed an inquiry on the matter to the SEC, proceedings against Goldfine were dropped.

The presidential assistant appeared before the legislative oversight panel on June 17. He acknowledged the payment of his hotel bills by Goldfine and the receipt of the coat, suits, and rug. (He stated that the rug was a loan, not a gift.) However, he contended that the gifts were merely tokens of a long-standing friendship. Adams said that his efforts on behalf of Goldfine had been routine responses to requests and that he had not used his influence on his friend's behalf. He conceded, however, that unfavorable implications could be drawn from his actions and that "if I had the decisions before me to make, I believe I would have acted a little more prudently."

President Eisenhower steadfastly defended Adams, but the presidential assistant received little additional support. He got backing from some Republican senators who were not up for reelection. However, the great majority of Republican congressmen running for office in 1958 believed that their candidacies would be damaged by Adams's presence in the White House, particularly since the administration had prided itself on its ethical standards. Moreover, conservative Republican, who had resented Adams, led the attack. Adams's position was further damaged when, on July 2, Goldfine's attorney revealed that the textile magnate had charged off the hotel bills and the rug as business expenses.

In late August, GOP national chairman MEADE ALCORN told the president that almost all party leaders and major financial backers believed Adams had to go. With great reluctance, Eisenhower finally agreed. The president understood that Adams had been "less than alert" in his dealings with Goldfine, but Eisenhower maintained that Adams was "not only honest, effective, and dedicated, but in most cases, *his attackers know this to be true.*"

On September 22, Adams submitted his resignation. Later that day he made a national television and radio address. He charged that he had been the victim of a "campaign of vilification" and asserted that he had "never influenced nor attempted to influence" any agency on any matter. Adams remained on the White House payroll into October to help the president's staff through its transition period. In late October, he flew home to Lincoln, N.H.

Adams became a part owner of a New Hampshire ski resort. In 1961, he published *First-Hand Report: The Story of the Eisenhower Administration*, detailing his years at the White House. He died in Hanover, N.H., on October 27, 1956.

—MSM

Aiken, George D(avid)

(1892–1984) *U.S. senator*

Born in Dummerston, Vt., on August 30, 1892, and raised on his father's farm near Brattleboro, Vt., Aiken had a strong interest in agriculture and joined the local branch of the National Grange while in high school. Subsequently he became a leading expert in the commercial cultivation of wildflowers. In 1930, Aiken was elected to the state House of Representatives and was chosen speaker of that body in 1933. He ran successfully for lieutenant governor in 1935 and for governor in 1937 and 1939. A moderate Republican, Aiken gained national attention in 1937, when he wrote an open letter to his party's national committee urging abandonment of a "hate-Roosevelt" policy for a more positive program.

Aiken won election to the U.S. Senate in 1940. He gained a reputation for integrity and independence and won each of his subsequent reelection bids with over 65 percent of the vote. During the 1940s Aiken opposed the use of subsidies to lower farm prices and sought to revive the food stamp program of the 1930s. He was an active proponent of the Saint Lawrence Seaway project and backed federal aid to education and minimum wage legislation. In June 1950, Aiken joined Sen. MARGARET CHASE SMITH (R-Maine) and five other senators in signing a "Declaration of Conscience," denouncing Sen. JOSEPH R. MCCARTHY's (R-Wis.) use of "fear, bigotry, ignorance and intolerance" in his investigations of domestic communists.

One of the leaders of the congressional farm bloc, Aiken served as chairman of the Agriculture and Forestry Committee from 1953 to 1955. In 1953, he backed President DWIGHT D. EISENHOWER's plan to reorganize the Agriculture Department, which strengthened the authority of Secretary of Agriculture EZRA TAFT BENSON. When Sen. WAYNE MORSE (I-Oreg.) said that the measure might create a one-man "super legislature," Aiken replied that the farmers had "no better friend on earth" than Benson. The following year Aiken endorsed the administration's omnibus farm program, which proposed to replace fixed price supports with lower, flexible supports to discourage overproduction.

Aiken introduced the Water Facilities Act of 1954. The measure provided federal aid to rural communities seeking to develop an adequate power supply. Aiken believed that this measure was essential for the prosperity of rural America, and he regarded its adoption as one of his most important achievements. During the same year, he sponsored the Small Watershed Act, which authorized the secretary of agriculture to cooperate with state and local authorities in implementing projects for improving methods of soil conservation.

In 1958, Aiken opposed an amendment to a farm surplus disposal bill, offered by senators WILLIAM E. JENNER (R-Ind.) and STYLES BRIDGES (R-N.H.), that would have barred the sale of farm surpluses to communist countries. He commented that the Jenner-Bridges amendment would give the USSR "an iron-clad guarantee that we'll never attempt to win any satellite away from her." Aiken supported the farm surplus law of 1959, which provided for the distribution of excess farm products through a food stamp program and other means.

Aiken broke with his more conservative Republican colleagues on a number of issues. In January 1954 he and Sen. Smith were the only Republicans who opposed Robert E. Lee's confirmation as a member of the Federal Communications Commission. Lee was a conservative allegedly indebted to Sen. McCarthy for his appointment. During the same year, he joined senators JOHN J. WILLIAMS (R-Del.) and HERBERT H. LEHMAN (D-N.Y.) in an unsuccessful effort to cut oil and gas depletion allowances from 27.5 percent to 15 percent.

In 1960, Aiken and seven other Republican senators offered a voluntary federal-state health insurance program for all Americans over 65. Under the plan, the state would have contracted with private firms for the coverage, and subscribers would have made payments based on income, with the federal and state governments sharing the remaining costs. Aiken's proposal was more liberal than the administration plan, which limited aid to single elderly persons with adjusted gross incomes of up to $2,500 a year and married couples with annual incomes up to $3,800. The plan finally adopted in August contained most of the basic features of Aiken's proposal but required a means test and permitted each state to determine the type and extent of medical assistance provided.

Aiken backed the Kennedy administration's minimum wage and school aid programs in 1961 but voted against Medicare in 1962. During the late 1960s, he received national attention for his opposition to the Johnson administration's Vietnam War policies. In 1970 he supported the Cooper-Church

amendment barring the use of American troops in Cambodia. Aiken retired from the Senate in 1975. He died of a stroke in Montpelier, Vt., in 1984.

—MLL

Albert, Carl (Bert)

(1908–2000) *U.S. congressman, House majority whip*

The son of a poor farmer and coal miner, Albert was born in McAlester, Okla., on May 10, 1908. Soon after his birth, his family moved to Bug Tussle, Okla., just north of McAlester. An extremely able student, he graduated Phi Beta Kappa from the University of Oklahoma in 1931 and won a Rhodes scholarship to study at Oxford, where he earned two law degrees. Upon his return to the United States in 1934, Albert worked as a law clerk, accountant, and lawyer until 1941, when he enlisted in the army. He served in the Pacific and rose to the rank of lieutenant colonel. In 1946, Albert, bucking a Republican tide, won a seat as a Democrat in the U.S. House of Representatives by a narrow 329-vote margin. He backed President HARRY S. TRUMAN's foreign policy and generally supported the administration's domestic programs. However, he opposed the anti–poll tax bill in 1947 and voted to override Truman's vetoes of the Taft-Hartley bill in 1947 and the communist-control bill in 1950.

Albert consistently backed the House's Democratic leadership. From the beginning of his congressional tenure, he carefully scrutinized the operations of the lower chamber to acquaint himself with its procedures and with the voting patterns of its members. Because of his loyalty and diligence, his Democratic colleagues tapped him for leadership positions. In August 1954, he became cochairman of the party's speakers committee for the forthcoming congressional campaign. The Democrats captured control of the House in the November elections, and in January 1955 Reps. SAM RAYBURN (D-Tex.) and JOHN W. McCORMACK (D-Mass.), the new speaker and majority leader, respectively, chose him to serve as majority whip.

As whip, Albert's functions were to familiarize himself with the sentiments of the Democratic members of the House, persuade wavering representatives to vote as the leadership wished, and make certain that Democratic members were on the floor for major votes. An undemonstrative, modest man, Albert worked behind the scenes using persuasion and compromise rather than threats to win support for the Democratic leadership's proposals.

Although some journalists described Albert as an effective bridge between northern liberals and southern conservatives, some congressional liberals viewed his desire to compromise as an indication of ineffective leadership. Moreover, Albert opposed civil rights bills in 1956 and 1957. Reacting to liberal complaints, not only about Albert but also about McCormack and Rayburn, the Democratic National Committee announced in 1956 its intention to appoint an advisory committee of noncongressional liberals to help shape the party's legislative program. However, when the Democratic congressional leadership refused to cooperate with the plan, it was abandoned.

As a representative of a predominantly rural state, one of Albert's major concerns was farm policy. Using his power as majority whip, member of the Agriculture Committee, and, beginning in 1955, chairman of its Wheat Subcommittee, he opposed the Eisenhower administration's program of reduced and flexible price supports. Soon after becoming majority whip, Albert predicted that the new Democratic House majority would vote to reestablish high, rigid supports. In May 1955 the lower chamber passed a bill supporting major crops at 90 percent of parity, but the measure did not reach the Senate floor that year. Eisenhower vetoed a similar bill, passed by both houses in 1956. In 1959 Albert backed a bill offering wheat growers the alternative of reducing their acreage by 25 percent and receiving 90 percent of parity price support or receiving 50 percent of parity with no production controls. Eisenhower also vetoed this measure.

Following Rayburn's death in 1961, McCormack became Speaker, and Albert replaced McCormack as majority leader. As leader, Albert played a significant role in advancing the Democratic legislative agenda in the 1960s. In particular, he was a central figure in obtaining passage of the Civil Rights Act of 1964 and Medicare. Albert gained national notoriety when he presided over the unruly Democratic National Convention in 1968. When McCormack retired in 1971, Albert succeeded him as Speaker. Although he hoped to serve as a uni-

fier of his party, Albert was less than successful in that regard. He sided against autocratic committee chairmen and, during his tenure, Congress did make some small adjustments in the seniority system. Although this won him plaudits among reformers, he often appeared weak, and he vacillated on important issues. Albert did not seek reelection in 1976 and returned to McAlester. For a short time, he was "of counsel" to the Washington law firm of Cohn and Marks. He died in McAlester on February 4, 2000.

—MSM

Alcorn, (Hugh) Meade (Jr.)

(1907–1992) *chairman, Republican National Committee*

The son of a distinguished Republican jurist from Connecticut, Meade Alcorn was born in Suffield, Conn., on October 20, 1907. He attended Dartmouth College and Yale University School of Law, where he received his LL.B. degree in 1933. That year Alcorn was admitted to the Connecticut bar and joined his father's law firm. He immediately became active in Republican politics, joining the Suffield Republican Committee. Alcorn served as a Republican representative in the Connecticut General Assembly from 1936 to 1942. He served as majority leader in 1939 and speaker in 1941. In 1942, he was appointed state attorney for Hartford Co., a post he held for six years. Alcorn ran unsuccessfully for lieutenant governor on the Republican ticket in 1948. He served as state chairman of the Connecticut "Eisenhower for President" committee in 1952 and was a delegate to the Republican National Convention, where he assisted Eisenhower's floor leader, SHERMAN ADAMS, in rounding up votes.

In 1953, Alcorn and other liberal Eisenhower supporters won election to the Republican National Committee. Two years later, the national chairman, LEONARD HALL, chose him to assist in making arrangements for the Republican National Convention in 1956. Together with Hall, Alcorn backed retention of RICHARD NIXON as vice president, despite criticism of his right-wing stands. Alcorn denounced Democratic attacks on the vice president and quieted Republican fears about his popularity by pointing to a Gallup poll showing that an

Eisenhower-Nixon ticket would win in November. That fall Alcorn worked hard for the Republican national ticket in Connecticut.

At a news conference in January 1957, President Eisenhower spoke of Alcorn as one of the party leaders responsible for "modern Republicanism." Alcorn described this as "enlightened conservatism" that favored government services without government restriction of individual liberty. When Leonard Hall resigned in January 1957, Eisenhower enthusiastically supported Alcorn for national chairman. Alcorn took office immediately.

The new chairman announced that his first priority was to elect a Republican Congress in 1958. Signs were unfavorable for the Republicans, however. Inflation, Little Rock, *Sputnik*, and contention over the budget eroded Eisenhower's popularity in 1957. Within the Republican party, conservatives became increasingly reactive. Sensing a rightward drift, Alcorn attempted to focus attention on charges that the Democrats had been the party of corruption and treason during the late 1940s and early 1950s. His charges backfired. In March 1958, Federal Communications Commission head RICHARD MACK, accused of taking bribes, was forced to resign under pressure from the White House. Alcorn's assertion that Mack was a Democrat did not change the fact that he had been a Republican appointee. Three months later, Sherman Adams, the president's chief of staff, was accused of accepting gifts while in office. The scandal grew throughout the summer, and financial contributions to the National Committee dropped off sharply. In August Alcorn conducted a secret survey of the Republican National Committee that indicated all members favored Adams's dismissal. Alcorn carried this information to the president, who asked Alcorn to convey the news to Adams. Adams resigned in September.

That month an election in normally Republican Maine saw Democratic Gov. Edmund Muskie swamp his Republican opponent. Alcorn's worst fears were realized in the congressional elections eight weeks later. Republicans lost 47 seats in the House and 13 in the Senate, a rout unmatched since the 1930s. In April 1959, Meade Alcorn resigned. He returned to private law practice and contin-

ued representing Connecticut on the Republican National Committee until 1961. Alcorn remained active with the law firm of Tyner, Cooper and Alcorn until his 80th birthday. He died in Suffield, Conn., on January 13, 1992.

—MSM

Aldrich, Winthrop W(illiams)
(1885–1974) *ambassador to Great Britain*

The son of a powerful conservative senator, Nelson W. Aldrich (R-R.I.), Aldrich was born on November 2, 1885, in Providence, R.I. He was descended from the Pilgrims and the noted theologian Roger Williams. After receiving a B.A. degree from Harvard in 1907 and an LL.B. from that institution three years later, he joined a prominent New York law firm. Aldrich served in the Naval Reserve during World War I. In 1919 he joined the law firm of Murray, Prentice, and Howland and became a specialist in finance and banking. In perhaps his most significant case, he successfully represented the Rockefeller family interests in their fight for control of Standard Oil of Indiana. In 1930, he became president of the Chase National Bank; four years later he rose to chairman of the board.

During World War II, Aldrich directed Allied relief efforts. As president of the International Chamber of Commerce during the Truman administration, he helped win conservative support for the Marshall Plan and the president's foreign aid proposals. Aldrich was an early supporter of Gen. DWIGHT D. EISENHOWER for president. In 1951 he helped survey potential Eisenhower support in Texas and reportedly raised large sums of money for the general during the 1952 election campaign.

Shortly after the election, Eisenhower named Aldrich ambassador to Great Britain. The Senate confirmed the appointment in February 1953. As ambassador, Aldrich took little part in the formulation of policy and served primarily as a spokesman for the administration. During the mid-1950s, he was particularly involved in discussions on the Middle East. After Egypt seized the Suez Canal and closed it to international shipping in July 1956, Aldrich attempted to forestall war between Great

Britain and France (the major investors in the canal) and Egypt. He warned that the United States would not back military efforts to reopen the waterway. His efforts failed; during late October the British, French, and Israelis attacked Egypt.

British public opinion deplored the American failure to join in the invasion. Aldrich vigorously sought to reestablish good will between the United States and Great Britain, but strained relations between the two nations compelled him to announce his retirement in December 1956. At a farewell dinner for Aldrich in February 1957, Prime Minister Harold Macmillan praised him for playing "a remarkable and indeed historic role during those weeks of anxious strain." Because of Aldrich's efforts, the prime minister asserted, the British government looked forward to reestablishing relations with the United States "on the old level."

Upon returning to the United States, Aldrich resumed his business activities. He died in New York City on February 25, 1974, at the age of 88.

—RJB

Allen, George V(enable)

(1903–1970) *ambassador to India and Nepal; assistant secretary of state for Near Eastern, South Asian, and African Affairs; U.S. Information Agency director*

Born in Durham, N.C., on November 3, 1903, Allen graduated from Duke University in 1924. He taught high school in Buncombe Co., N.C., for four years and simultaneously worked as a reporter for the *Asheville (N.C.) Times.* In 1930, he joined the Foreign Service. Prior to World War II, he held posts in Kingston, Shanghai, Athens, and Cairo. Recalled to Washington in 1938, Allen became assistant chief of the State Department's new Eastern division in 1942; two years later, he advanced to chief of the Middle Eastern division. Allen was a member of the first U.S. delegation to the United Nations in 1945. The following year, he was appointed ambassador to Iran. He served as assistant secretary of state for public affairs from 1948 to 1950 and was ambassador to Yugoslavia from 1950 to 1953. President DWIGHT D. EISENHOWER nominated him to succeed CHESTER BOWLES as ambassador to India and Nepal in February 1953.

During his two years in India, Allen attempted to allay fears that the Eisenhower administration was pursuing a pro-Pakistan policy at the expense of India. He was also called upon to explain the 1954 India-Communist Chinese mutual nonaggression agreement to the House Foreign Affairs Committee. Allen observed that India regarded Communist China with an uneasy mixture of fear and admiration. The United States, Allen urged the committee, should respond by increasing its aid to India to help make it "a source of strength to the free world."

In January 1955, President Eisenhower nominated Allen to be assistant secretary of state for Near Eastern, South Asian, and African Affairs. He was confirmed that month. In September Allen undertook his most important mission for the Eisenhower administration. During the spring of 1955, after several Egyptian raids across the armistice line along the Gaza Strip had provoked a large-scale Israeli reprisal, Egyptian premier Gamal Abdel Nasser had sent the United States several requests for military aid. Negotiations led to an impasse. The United States never officially turned down the request, but it continued to stall. Finally, in June 1955, Nasser threatened to ask the USSR for weapons. The State Department did not consider the threat seriously. By late September, the deal appeared all but consummated, and Secretary of State JOHN FOSTER DULLES hurriedly sent the Central Intelligence Agency's Middle Eastern expert, KERMIT ROOSEVELT, to urge Nasser to reconsider the Soviet arms deal. However, Roosevelt was unable to head off the arms accord, which the Soviets and the Egyptians formally signed on September 27, 1955.

The next day, Dulles sent Allen to Cairo in a final effort to turn Nasser around and discuss the ramifications of the pact. Allen believed his mission ill-conceived. As far as he was concerned, it could only appear to the Arab world as an American ultimatum to Nasser.

Allen's visit to Cairo was, according to historian Townsend Hoopes, "a reasonably cordial exercise in futility." At first Allen was something less than candid, explaining to Nasser that, while the United States could understand Egypt's policy of neutrality, it surely was not neutral to accept weapons from a single source. At this point, Nasser recounted his frustrations in getting a clear reply to his frequent pleas for U.S. arms. The Egyptian ruler further emphasized his country's need to maintain a military balance vis-à-vis Israel. Allen warned Nasser that Soviet arms would mean the introduction of Soviet technicians and advisers and argued that their presence might endanger Egyptian sovereignty. Nasser dismissed the threat. Leaving Cairo, Allen told reporters that, while the United States regretted the Egyptian-Soviet arms deal, it firmly believed that Nasser's sole purpose was to defend his country. Nevertheless, relations between the two nations remained severely strained.

Allen remained assistant secretary until October 1957, when the White House announced his appointment as director of the U.S. Information Agency (USIA). Taking over the agency at a time when its prestige and budget were at an all-time low, Allen attempted to change its often-criticized image. To counter charges that the USIA was naïve and propaganda-oriented, he attempted to adapt the agency's information to the needs and viewpoints of the recipient nations. This policy brought him into frequent conflict with his superiors in the State Department.

In 1961, Allen left the State Department and became president of the Tobacco Institute. During the next few years, he defended the tobacco industry against the early reports linking cigarette smoking to lung cancer. In 1966 President LYNDON JOHNSON named Allen a career ambassador and appointed him head of the Foreign Service Institute. He retired in 1969 and died in Durham, N.C., on July 11, 1970.

—RJB

Allen, Leo E(lwood)
(1898–1973) *U.S. congressman*

Allen was born on October 5, 1898, in Elizabeth, Ill. He received a B.A. degree from the University of Michigan in 1923 and the following year became a clerk in the Jo Daviess Co., Ill., Circuit Court. Admitted to the Illinois bar in 1929, he began practicing law in Galena the next year. Allen won election as a Republican to the U.S. House of Rep-

resentatives in 1932, where he established a record as an isolationist and opponent of New Deal domestic programs. After the Republicans gained control of the House in the 1946 elections, he served as chairman of the Rules Committee. In that post, he attempted to block universal military training legislation but failed to defeat the Selective Service Act of 1948. During the Truman administration, Allen compiled a consistently conservative record, backing the Taft-Hartley Act of 1947, the Internal Security Act of 1950, and the McCarran Act of 1952.

Allen again became chairman of the Rules Committee in 1953, following the Republican electoral sweep of the preceding year. As head of the committee, he defended Eisenhower's tax proposals against the attacks of Ways and Means Committee chairman Rep. DANIEL REED (R-N.Y.). Early in 1953, Reed's panel blocked an administration bill to extend an excess profits tax on corporations. In June the Rules Committee, under Allen's leadership, took the unusual step of reporting the bill to the floor without a favorable vote from the Ways and Means Committee. At about the same time, Allen blocked Reed's bill to cut income taxes, which the administration opposed.

Allen opposed a $1 minimum wage in 1955. He claimed that it would harm "2.5 million subnormals and elderly people" whom employers would not be willing to pay eight dollars a day. During the same year, he favored the deregulation of natural gas prices.

As a member of the Rules Committee, Allen formed part of the southern Democratic-Republican coalition that prevented many social welfare measures from reaching the House floor. In 1959, his vote helped produce a tie in the committee that blocked the progress of a $1 billion housing bill. The following year, he and the panel's other conservatives succeeded in stalling another housing bill. During the same year, they were also able to stop an aid-to-education measure. However, Allen and most of the other Republicans on the committee broke with the southern Democrats in 1957 and 1960 to enable the administration's civil rights bills to go to the House floor.

Allen declined to run for reelection in 1960. He died in Galena, Ill., on January 19, 1973.

—MLL

Allison, John M(oore)

(1905–1978) *assistant secretary of state for Far Eastern Affairs, ambassador to Japan, ambassador to Indonesia, ambassador to Czechoslovakia*

Allison was born on April 7, 1905, in Molton, Kans. After graduating from the University of Nebraska in 1927, Allison went to Japan to teach English. In 1930, he began his diplomatic career as a clerk in the American consulate in Shanghai. Between 1932 and 1941, Allison was alternately stationed in China and Japan. He was interned by the Japanese for six months following the attack on Pearl Harbor. Allison spent the remainder of World War II in London, where he participated in negotiations for shipping and transportation agreements. He returned to Washington in 1947 to become assistant secretary of state for Far Eastern affairs. In 1950 he served as special assistant to JOHN FOSTER DULLES in preliminary negotiations for the Japanese peace treaty. The treaty was signed in 1951.

Eisenhower nominated Allison ambassador to Japan in March 1954, and the Senate confirmed the nomination the following month. Allison's chief problem in the post was the issue of Japanese rearmament. Dulles exerted strong pressure on Allison to convince Japan to rearm itself as a primary bulwark against communist expansion in the Pacific. However, the Japanese were solidly opposed to the plan. They had not only accepted Gen. Douglas MacArthur's postwar idea that Japan should become the "Switzerland of Asia," but had also written it into a strongly antiwar constitution. Japanese constitutional experts argued that any military establishment would violate the postwar constitution. In addition, the Japanese faced severe economic problems well into the 1950s and thus maintained that the nation could not afford a strong defense force. Allison took a stand against the secretary of state on the rearmament issue. He strongly believed that Japan, as an autonomous nation, should not be reduced to a forward bastion of American strategic strength.

Allison's sympathy for the Japanese position considerably aided negotiations. On March 8, 1954, the two nations signed a mutual defense agreement. The United States agreed to give at least $100 million in finished weapons, industrial subsidies to munitions makers, and other types of economic aid. In return, Japan promised to rebuild its armed forces under U.S. guidance and make a "full contribution to the strength of the anti-Communist world." Allison disliked the provision permitting the United States to intervene in the Japanese budgetary process to guarantee $155 million annually for the support of American troops there. In April 1955, he reached an agreement with Prime Minister Shigeru Yoshida that the United States would assume one-third of the Japanese burden for American troops, in return for which Japan would spend more on its airfields and armed forces. However, Dulles disavowed the agreement in August.

Allison faced a more emotional problem in March 1954, when a Japanese fishing boat was contaminated with radioactive ash from an American nuclear bomb test in the South Pacific. One crew member died as a result. Allison was widely praised for the way he handled the delicate situation, which resulted in an American settlement of $2 million in January 1955.

Allison was appointed ambassador to Indonesia in April 1957. During the early years of the decade, he had been a strong anticommunist. However, by the time of this appointment, he had come to believe that foreign relations should not be defined simply in terms of anticommunist ideology. He maintained that nations generally acted on self-interest rather than political doctrine, and so he was not overly concerned with President Achmed Sukarno's left-wing tendencies. Because Washington feared Sukarno's overtures to the Soviet Union, Allison was unable to acquire the U.S. support he believed necessary to prevent a further drift to the left. When he recommended that the United States back Sukarno's bid for a UN resolution calling for Indonesian control over Western New Guinea, Washington recommended that the ambassador encourage regional uprisings against Sukarno.

Finding his advice disregarded by the State Department, Allison offered his resignation in September 1957. In a final attempt to influence policy, he sent a telegram in November recommending that the United States support the transfer of Western New Guinea to Indonesia after five years in exchange for economic concessions to the Dutch, who still owned the territory. The concessions included Indonesian adherence to the ANZUS Pact; a pledge from Sukarno to "control strictly" communist activity and "accept American assistance and guidance in anti-subversive activities"; and increased U.S. aid to Indonesia. The State Department rejected the proposal when Australia and the Netherlands opposed it.

Allison was appointed ambassador to Czechoslovakia in March 1958. He served there until 1960, when he resigned from the Foreign Service because of his wife's ill health. Allison retired to Honolulu, where he taught at the University of Hawaii. He died on October 28, 1978.

—JPL

Allott, Gordon (Llewellyn)
(1907–1989)   *U.S. senator*

The son of a federal meat inspector, Allott was born on January 2, 1907, in Pueblo, Colo. After graduating from the University of Colorado, he earned a law degree from the same institution in 1929 and was admitted to the bar later that year. He then set up a legal practice in Lamar, Colo., a wheat-belt trading center. During the 1930s and 1940s, Allott was active on state and national Republican committees. After serving as county attorney of Prowers County, city attorney of Lamar, and district attorney of the 15th judicial district, Allott won election as lieutenant governor in 1950.

A close friend of former Minnesota Gov. HAROLD STASSEN, Allott backed Stassen's unsuccessful bid for the presidential nomination in 1952. In 1954, Allott ran for the U.S. Senate on a platform supporting the Eisenhower administration's farm policy. With strong support from the state's farm sections, he won an upset victory against the popular Democrat, John Carroll.

Allott voted as a conservative Republican on most issues during the Eisenhower administration. However, he supported the Civil Rights Acts of 1957 and 1960. As a member of the Interior and Insular Affairs Committee, Allott helped win Senate approval of the Upper Colorado River Project in 1955. The project was one of the largest and most important federal reclamation efforts up to that time. Conservationists, however, objected to the Allott-backed proposal to flood much of the Dino-

saur National Monument in Colorado and Utah. This provision was deleted from the final version of the bill as passed by the House in 1956.

During the 1960s, Allott opposed most of the Democratic administrations' domestic legislative programs. In 1969 he won the chairmanship of the powerful Senate Republican Conference Committee. Allott lost his bid for reelection in 1972. He died in Englewood, Colo., on January 17, 1989.

—TLH

Almond, J(ames) Lindsay, Jr.
(1898–1986)   *governor of Virginia*

Born in Charlottesville, Va., on June 15, 1898, Almond earned his LL.B. at the University of Virginia in 1923. He practiced law in Roanoke for the next nine years. In 1932, he was elected judge of Roanoke's Hustings Court and served until 1945. He then successfully ran as a Democrat to fill a House seat vacated by the resignation of Clifton A. Woodrum (D-Va.). Reelected to a full term in 1946, Almond compiled a generally conservative record, voting to extend the draft and override President HARRY S. TRUMAN's veto of the Taft-Hartley bill. He resigned from Congress in April 1948 to complete a term as state attorney general after the occupant died in office.

Almond campaigned for a four-year term as attorney general in 1949 on a platform supporting an amendment that would have repealed the poll tax and placed increased restrictions on the right to vote. Although the amendment was defeated, Almond won handily. As attorney general, he expected to be the Byrd organization candidate for governor, but in January 1953 he withdrew his name at Sen. HARRY F. BYRD's (D-Va.) request. He won election to a second term as attorney general in November.

During 1952, Almond pleaded the state's case in *Davis v. County School Board of Prince Edward County.* The suit had been brought by African Americans demanding that the state law requiring segregated schools be struck down. Although privately conceding that African Americans had received an inferior education in the state, Almond opposed demands for school integration and rejected the NAACP's contention that separate but equal facilities were inherently discriminatory. Instead, he recommended the use of funds to equalize black facilities. A three-member federal court upheld the constitutionality of the Virginia statute but ordered the unequal facilities remedied. The case was later taken to the Supreme Court, where it became one of several argued as *Brown v. Board of Education*. Almond helped present Virginia's case before the high tribunal. In May 1954, the Supreme Court unanimously declared segregated schools unconstitutional.

In the wake of the decision, Virginia Gov. THOMAS B. STANLEY appointed a commission, headed by Garland Gray, to seek means to preserve the status quo in Virginia's schools. Issued in November 1955, the Gray Commission's report recommended that local authorities be permitted to close public schools threatened with integration. The state would then pay tuition for private schooling. These recommendations won approval in a referendum held in March 1956. Interpreting approval of the local option as total support for segregation, Sen. Byrd called for "massive resistance" to the Supreme Court's decision. The state would close schools threatened with integration regardless of local feeling. Segregationists relied on the theory of interposition to justify Virginia's resistance. According to this theory, a state had the right to interpose its authority between its people and the improper exercise of power by the federal government.

During the dispute over the *Brown* decision, Almond maintained a moderate position and in April 1956 stated that interposition had no legal validity. While such prominent Southerners as Texas Gov. ALLAN SHIVERS advocated a regional candidate for president in 1956 and the Byrd machine remained neutral, Almond worked for the 1956 Democratic national ticket.

When Almond announced his candidacy for governor in late 1956, Byrd concluded he could not stop the attorney general and so endorsed him. Running as the organization candidate, and recognizing a rightward drift in public sentiment, Almond campaigned on a platform of massive resistance. Yet, he remained skeptical of that position and surprised segregationists in October 1957 by saying there would be a degree of forced integration under federal mandate. Despite the statement, Almond

went on to win the governorship two-to-one over Republican Ted Dalton the following month.

In his inaugural address, Almond gave unqualified support for opposition to the *Brown* decision. "Against massive attacks," he stated, "we must marshall massive resistance." He warned that "integration anywhere means destruction everywhere." Almond sensed rising segregationist sentiment and in April sponsored legislation consolidating state control of pupil assignments and strengthening the governor's school closing authority. In September Almond closed nine schools that were under court order to integrate.

During the fall of 1958, moderate forces began demanding a change of position on school integration. In October the Virginia Parent-Teacher Association urged abandonment of interposition and adoption of the local option. Shortly thereafter, city newspapers began to withdraw support for massive resistance. By December 29 leading industrialists had become sufficiently alarmed by declining out-of-state investment to call on Almond and urge him to drop interposition. Attempting to stall until the direction of public opinion was clear, Almond refused to invoke laws that permitted him to reopen closed schools as segregated institutions. He also directed his attorney general to prepare a test case for the Virginia courts. According to historian Numan Bartley, Almond presumed that federal courts would strike down massive resistance and thought that it would be better received if the decision came from a state court. On January 19, 1959, both a federal district court and the Virginia Supreme Court of Appeals ruled that closing schools and withholding state funds from integrated institutions was unconstitutional.

While denouncing the decision, the governor maneuvered Virginia toward compliance with the order. He called a special session of the legislature in January and cautiously sounded a retreat from massive resistance. Closed schools were reopened, and three city systems began at least token desegregation. In the legislature, Almond prevented a resurgence of extremist forces led by the Byrd organization. A report by the Perrow Commission, packed with Almond-appointed moderates, recommended a 15-bill program to develop a policy of local option that held integration to token levels.

The legislature enacted the measures in April despite bitter opposition.

During the remaining years of his term, the breech between Almond and Byrd hardened, and the governor purged Byrd supporters at every opportunity. Forbidden by law to succeed himself, Almond ran his own antiorganization candidate for governor in the July 1961 Democratic primary. His effort failed, and Byrd maintained control of the statehouse. In 1962 Almond was appointed a judge of the Federal Patents Court, where he served until his retirement in 1973. He died in Richmond, Va., on April 15, 1986.

—MJS

Alsop, Joseph W(right), Jr.
(1910–1989) *journalist, author*

Born on October 11, 1910, in Avelon, Conn., Joseph Alsop was the eldest son of one of the most socially prominent families in Connecticut. His father was an insurance executive, and both his parents served several terms in the state legislature. Alsop attended the prestigious Groton School and graduated from Harvard magna cum laude in 1932. Family influence gained him a job as a reporter for the *New York Herald Tribune*. Alsop quickly proved to be one of the paper's top feature writers and in 1936 was sent to Washington, D.C., to cover the capital news. Alsop soon established a secure position for himself in the Washington political and social scene. From 1937 to 1940, he coauthored with Robert E. Kintner a syndicated column entitled "The Capitol Parade," which was distributed to almost 100 newspapers throughout the country. During the same period, he collaborated on several books dealing with various aspects of both domestic and foreign affairs.

Although an isolationist during the 1930s, Alsop adopted a strong interventionist stance well before America's entry into World War II. In 1940 he initiated lobbying efforts that proved decisive in convincing Roosevelt to honor Great Britain's urgent request for American warships. Alsop served briefly in the navy during World War II but soon resigned his commission in order to become an adviser and supporter of Gen. Claire Chennault and Generalissimo Chiang Kai-shek (Jiang Jieshi) in wartime China. Alsop's experience left him a strong supporter of Nationalist China and a vigorous anticommunist.

In 1946 Alsop resumed his work as a columnist, this time collaborating with his brother STEWART. Through their column, "Matter of Fact," they built a joint reputation as leading commentators of the day on foreign affairs. In both 1950 and 1952, they received recognition from the Overseas Press Club for "the best interpretation of foreign news." The Alsops took a strong stand against McCarthyism, maintaining that the real threat to the United States was not internal communist subversion, but external communist attack.

During the Eisenhower administration, the Alsops took a pessimistic view of world events. The column's doom-crying refrain was primarily the responsibility of Joseph Alsop. His New Year's message in 1954 was simply, "All is lost." In general, his favorite descriptions of the 1950s depicted an era poised dangerously on "the edge of the abyss."

In the autumn of 1953, Alsop journeyed to Asia, where he wrote ominously of the great power of Communist China and the harmful effects of the armistice in Korea. In November he called upon the American government to take a more active role in Vietnam. He warned that if the French pulled out, all of Indochina would soon fall under communist control. Alsop returned to Southeast Asia a number of times, always writing of its imminent collapse.

In 1956, Alsop turned his attention to the Middle East. He described the problems of Arab nationalism, growing Soviet involvement, and the plight of Palestinian refugees. He perceptively described the emerging crisis. The following year, he found himself in the Soviet Union. There he described the enormous strength of Soviet industry and what he thought was the illusory nature of de-Stalinization. "While somewhat more supple than their late master," he said, "Stalin's heirs have actually proven somewhat more adventurous."

In 1954, the brothers collaborated on a book entitled *We Accuse!*, which denounced the Atomic Energy Commission, and the commission's head LEWIS STRAUSS, in particular, for refusing to reinstate J. ROBERT OPPENHEIMER's security clearance. They defended Oppenheimer's prewar connections with left-wing organizations as a "brand of political folly that was a common highbrow reaction to the menace of Nazism." The Alsops pointed out that the scientist had quickly renounced the ties and had become what they saw as a prominent cold warrior, a position they both lauded. The two writers maintained that Oppenheimer had been brought to trial not because of his left-wing connections but because of his opposition to the development of the hydrogen bomb. The Alsops termed the administration's security system "inherently repugnant in its present standards and procedures to every high tradition of the American past." The two brothers predicted that if the system were not reformed quickly "lasting harm will begin to be done."

In March 1958, the Alsop brothers ended their 12-year partnership when Stewart took a job as a contributing editor for the *Saturday Evening Post.* Their reputation was then at its height. The column was distributed to almost 200 newspapers throughout the world. Several months earlier, *Newsweek* had called the brothers "possibly the most influential and provocative columnists in the business." After they ended their partnership, they collected a number of their articles into a book, *The Reporter's Trade,* which they introduced with a plea for the government to be more open with the press. They also praised Eisenhower for bringing the McCarthy era to a close but criticized him for not pouring enough money into the national defense effort. Joseph Alsop continued to write "Matter of Fact" alone, focusing on the cold war struggle between the United States and the USSR. During the last years of the decade, he was one of several prominent Americans to warn of a growing "missile gap" between the United States and the USSR (a claim that was inaccurate).

Alsop was a firm supporter of the Vietnam War. In 1964, he wrote what some critics thought was his best book, *From the Silent Earth,* a study of the Greek bronze age. Alsop retired in 1974, soon after his brother's death. Joseph Alsop died of cancer and emphysema on August 28, 1989 in Washington, D.C. —*JPL*

Alsop, Stewart (Johonnot) (Oliver)

(1914–1974) *journalist, author*

Alsop was born in Avon, Conn., on May 17, 1914, into a Connecticut family with a history of gov-

ernment service. His mother was a niece of Theodore Roosevelt and a cousin of both Franklin and ELEANOR ROOSEVELT. Stewart Alsop attended Groton and then Yale University, where he graduated in 1936. He became an editor for the Doubleday Doran publishing company in New York. Following the U.S. entry into World War II, he attempted to enlist in the army but was rejected on medical grounds. He then went to England and joined the rifle corps. In 1944, he was transferred to the U.S. Army. Alsop served in the Office of Strategic Services and parachuted into occupied France shortly after D-day. On his return to the United States, Stewart collaborated with his brother JOSEPH ALSOP on a syndicated column, "Matter of Fact." The partnership lasted until 1958.

In 1950 and 1952, both Alsops were cited by the Overseas Press Club for the "best interpretation of foreign news." In 1954 they joined forces to write *We Accuse!,* a defense of J. ROBERT OPPENHEIMER against security-risk charges investigated by the Atomic Energy Commission. The book won an award by the Author's Guild in 1955 for its contribution to civil liberties. When Stewart Alsop accepted a job as a contributing editor for the *Saturday Evening Post* in 1958, the brothers ended what had often been described as a "stormy partnership." Later that year, they published *The Reporter's Trade,* a collection of their columns introduced by a plea for government candor with the press.

In contrast to his brother, Stewart Alsop was a family man, a cautious writer, and a cheerful personality. Although he generally agreed with his brother's positions, he freely conceded that "Joe can play the organ of gloom better than I." During their partnership, his main contribution was a series of articles on ballistic missiles. He was the first to point out that the air force planned to fire an intercontinental ballistic missile (ICBM) in 1957 and the first to report the Soviet ICBM tests.

Alsop had announced his support for Eisenhower as a presidential candidate as early as April 1950. However, soon after Eisenhower took office, Alsop joined his brother in criticizing the president for placing budgetary considerations above defense requirements. They expressed this view in an early series of attacks on GEORGE HUMPHREY, Eisenhower's first secretary of the treasury. In his *Nixon and Eisenhower,* published in 1960, Alsop repeated the charge that the Eisenhower administration had failed "to maintain a genuine balance of power with the Communist bloc." However, he offset the charge with his judgement that "the Eisenhower years have been a settling-down period, a time of adjustment and stabilization after an era of enormous change."

Alsop continued working for the *Saturday Evening Post* until its close in 1968, when he began writing a weekly column for *Newsweek.* Although he was slow in advocating American withdrawal from Vietnam, he did not give the war the kind of support his brother did. In 1973 he wrote *Stay of Execution* about his impending death from leukemia. He continued his work for *Newsweek* until the eve of his death. His last articles expressed his concern over Watergate and his loss of faith in Richard Nixon, whom he had long admired. He died on May 26, 1974, in Bethesda, Md.

—JPL

Anastasia, Albert

(1902–1957) *organized crime figure*

Born Umberto Anastasia on September 26, 1902, in Tropea, Culabria, Italy, Umberto Anastasia joined the Mafia while in Italy. He jumped ship in New York in 1919 but later reentered the United States legally. Encouraged by official laxity, Anastasia and his three brothers subverted the Brooklyn longshoremen's union. He changed his name to Albert Anastasia in 1921, following his arrest for the murder of a fellow longshoreman. Anastasia spent 18 months on death row until, in what was to become a familiar gangland pattern, a new trial was granted on a technicality and a four important prosecution witnesses disappeared. Arrested again in 1923, he served two years for carrying a gun. Between 1921 and 1954, he was arrested 10 times, five for murder.

In the 1920s, Anastasia served under Giuseppe ("Joe the Boss") Masseria. Anastasia, however, was loyal to CHARLES ("LUCKY") LUCIANO and FRANK COSTELLO. Anastasia sided with Luciano when the latter attempted to depose the old-line families headed by Masseria and Salvatore Maranzano. When Luciano emerged victorious in what became known as the Castellammarese War, Luciano placed

Anastasia and Louis ("Lepke") Buchalter in charge of the enforcement arm of the National Crime Syndicate, known as Murder, Incorporated. Anastasia and Buchalter terrorized unions in New York's garment district, often extorting "sweetheart contracts" at gunpoint. Between 1931 and 1940, Murder Inc., allegedly committed 63 murders. Abe ("Kid Twist") Reles, a hit man for Murder, Inc., was arrested and agreed to testify against others in exchange for immunity from prosecution. His testimony led to the conviction of Buchalter and a number of hit men. Buchalter was sent to the electric chair in 1941. However, Anastasia went free when Brooklyn District Attorney William O'Dwyer, who had connections to organized crime, declined to prosecute him when Reles died after going out of a window in a room at the Half Moon Hotel while in police custody. O'Dwyer was censured by a grand jury for his conduct. From 1942 to 1944, Anastasia served in the army. After his discharge he bought a dress factory in order to establish a legitimate front.

In the early 1950s, Anastasia came into conflict with the head of his family, Vincent Mangano. When the latter vanished in 1951, Anastasia became head of the Mangano family.

During the 1950s, Anastasia's activities were the subject of two highly publicized congressional hearings. In 1950 and 1951, Sen. ESTES KEFAUVER (D-Tenn.) and his Senate Crime Investigating Committee probed what they thought was a massive crime conspiracy aided by official corruption. Anastasia was called to testify and was cited for contempt of Congress when he refused to tell the committee how he earned his living. The Kefauver Committee report accused O'Dwyer, who was then ambassador to Mexico, of aiding crime by not prosecuting Anastasia. Despite the publicity generated by Kefauver's campaign and the widespread belief that a criminal network had extended its power throughout the nation, the federal government took little action against organized crime. The FBI did not officially recognize the existence of a national crime syndicate. Director J. EDGAR HOOVER shunned Mafia cases. They were difficult to prosecute and did not result in a high rate of conviction.

In May 1956, ROBERT KENNEDY, chief counsel of the Senate Permanent Investigations Subcommittee, questioned Anastasia about racketeer domination of companies producing military uniforms under government contract. No action was taken on the matter. Kennedy later outlined another instance of Anastasia's penetration of labor. In 1955 private garbage collectors in New York formed an employer's association. According to Kennedy, Anastasia took control of this through Teamster Local 813 and maneuvered to monopolize the garbage industry through the employers' "adviser," Jimmy Squillante.

In the mid-1950s, Anastasia engaged in a struggle for power with VITO GENOVESE, who managed to secure the allegiance of Joseph Profaci, the boss of another family, and Carlo Gambino, Anastasia's underboss. The rivalry played out when Anastasia was shot to death in the barbershop of New York's Park Sheraton Hotel on October 25, 1957.

The following month, 58 known hoodlums were arrested in Appalachin, N.Y., at the largest Mafia conference ever held. Of these, 22 said their businesses dealt with labor-management relations. All were released for lack of evidence. It was later learned that Vito Genovese had called the conclave to ratify his control of America's largest Mafia "family" following the death of Anastasia and the retirement of Frank Costello.

Appalachin marked the beginning of an effort by the federal government against organized crime. Eisenhower's attorney general, WILLIAM T. ROGERS, established a special group within the Justice Department to investigate organized crime without asking Hoover. The section lasted only two years but provided a focus for anticrime activity. In the 1960s, Attorney General Robert Kennedy pressed for new wiretap legislation and encouraged a new policy of prosecuting mobsters under any and all available laws.

—MSM

Anderson, Clinton P(resba)

(1895–1975) *U.S. senator; chairman, Joint Congressional Committee on Atomic Energy*

A native of Centerville, S.Dak., Anderson was born on October 23, 1895. He studied at Dakota Wesleyan University from 1913 to 1915. After completing a year of pre-law studies at the University of Michigan, he attempted to enter military service but was rejected because of a tubercular condition. He then moved to New Mexico, where the climate helped him improve his health. From 1918 to 1922, he worked for the *Albuquerque Journal*, where he helped uncover evidence relating to the Teapot Dome scandal. He began a career in insurance in 1922 and eventually became president of his own firm. Anderson was appointed treasurer of New Mexico in 1933, and throughout the 1930s he helped administer various New Deal relief programs in the state.

In 1940, Anderson won election to the U.S. House as a representative at large. He led a congressional probe of national food shortages and black-marketing in the meat industry. President HARRY S. TRUMAN was so impressed by Anderson's investigations that he appointed the congressman secretary of agriculture in 1945. In 1948 Anderson won election to the Senate.

From the beginning of his Senate tenure, Anderson consistently voted with the Democratic liberals. An advocate of federal control of natural resources, he fought Eisenhower's concept of federal-state "partnership." In early 1953, the administration overturned Truman's designation of offshore oil lands as a navy reserve, thereby giving control of these fields back to the states. Anderson and other liberals staged an unsuccessful filibuster to protest the move and press for federal control. Administration backers succeeded in passing a bill supporting state ownership, but the Supreme Court eventually ruled in favor of limited control by those states whose colonial charters stipulated it.

Best known as an effective defender of New Mexico's interests, Anderson sponsored legislation that brought his state large sums of federal money for defense installations, land reclamation, and water resources. As chairman of the Joint Congressional Committee on Atomic Energy, he was particularly influential in bringing the nuclear power industry to New Mexico. He consistently supported programs for nuclear power projects and later contended that the government had not adequately funded them. In 1956, Anderson served as floor manager of the Upper Colorado River Storage Project, a plan to divert Colorado River water to New Mexico, particularly to Indian lands. Because of his efforts, the Senate raised the administration's suggested initial appropriation from $8 million to $13 million.

In 1959, Anderson led the fight against confirmation of LEWIS STRAUSS as secretary of commerce. An advocate of public power development, the senator opposed Strauss because he had backed the 1954 Dixon-Yates contract giving a private combine, rather than the Tennessee Valley Authority, the right to supply power to Atomic Energy Commission installations in the Tennessee Valley area. Anderson also objected to Strauss's refusal to support J. ROBERT OPPENHEIMER during the latter's security hearings in 1954. Partly as a result of Anderson's opposition, Strauss became the first cabinet appointee to be rejected by the Senate since 1925.

Anderson played a prominent role in the 1960s in both atomic affairs and the U.S. space program. In his final term in the Senate, he won the Goddard Memorial Trophy for "outstanding contributions to space flight programs that promoted American leadership in astronautics." He retired from the Senate in 1973 and died in Albuquerque, New Mexico, on November 11, 1975.

—TGD

Robert B. Anderson, secretary of the navy
(Dwight D. Eisenhower Library and Museum)

Anderson, Robert B(ernard)

(1910–1989) *secretary of the navy, deputy secretary of defense, secretary of the treasury*

Born in Burleson, Tex., on June 4, 1910, and raised on a farm in the cotton and cattle region of Texas, Anderson graduated from Weatherford College in 1927. To finance his law studies he taught Spanish, history, and mathematics in 1929 at a local high school. He won election to the state legislature the same day he graduated from the University of Texas Law School in 1932. Named state tax commissioner in 1934, Anderson successfully introduced a bill to organize the first social security agency in Texas. Three years later, he became general attorney for the vast W. I. Waggoner ranch, at that time the second richest in the nation. Appointed general manager four years later, he increased its holdings and introduced modern ranching methods.

During World War II, Anderson served as a civilian aide to the secretary of the army. In the 1940s, he was associated with several large business organizations, among them the American Petroleum Institute. Anderson was one of the oil industry's most effective witnesses before Congress. In 1949 he became chairman of the Texas State Board of Education.

President-elect Eisenhower designated Anderson secretary of the navy in December 1952. Early in the new administration, Eisenhower ordered an end to segregation on military bases and in schools in military bases. In June 1953, Rep. ADAM CLAYTON POWELL, JR. (D-N.Y.) charged that several figures in the administration had ignored or obstructed the president's order. Powell singled out shipyards in Charleston, S.C., and Norfolk, Va. Eisenhower's chief of staff, SHERMAN ADAMS, found Powell's charges to be essentially accurate and assigned MAXWELL RABB to handle the problem. Rabb met with Anderson, who ordered an end to segregation on 43 naval stations in the South. Over a weekend, the "white" and "colored" signs were removed from drinking fountains and lavatories. Mess halls were desegregated more gradually but expeditiously. The process went forward without a major incident. Anderson's handling of the situation greatly impressed Eisenhower. In November 1953 Eisenhower announced that the policy had been "completely effective."

Anderson was appointed deputy secretary of defense in March 1954. During his tenure, he helped Eisenhower formulate the Open Skies proposal delivered at the 1955 Geneva summit conference. The plan was designed to give the administration the psychological offensive following the Soviet Union's disarmament overture of May. It suggested that the United States and USSR exchange military blueprints and allow mutual air reconnaissance over their military installations. The Kremlin eventually rejected the proposal.

Anderson left his post in August 1955 to return to business, but Eisenhower called him into government service again in 1956 as his personal emissary to the Middle East. The former secretary attempted to initiate direct discussions between Israeli Prime Minister David Ben Gurion and Egyptian President Gamal Abdel Nasser in an effort to resolve outstanding differences. However, his efforts failed, and in October Israel, France, and Great Britain attacked Egypt.

Eisenhower had great political plans for Anderson. The president found the deeply religious, conservative, mild-mannered Anderson the ideal man to implement his own ideas for America and urged him to be his running mate in the 1956 campaign. Eisenhower also thought that Anderson, a Southerner and a Democrat, would improve Republican chances in the South. However, Anderson refused, pleading inexperience in partisan politics. Eisenhower confided to EMMET J. HUGHES before the 1960 election that he considered Anderson his number-one choice for the presidency.

Anderson replaced GEORGE HUMPHREY as secretary of the treasury in July 1957. In fiscal and monetary policy he was as conservative as his predecessor. He stood firmly behind the administration's desire to reduce the size of government and balance the budget in order to cut inflation and invigorate private enterprise. Anderson differed with Humphrey, however, in his more relaxed attitude toward increased defense spending and his more liberal approach to foreign economic policy.

Anderson's concern with preventing inflation was reflected in his response to the recession of 1957–58. Convinced that the recession would be short-lived, he opposed tax cuts to stimulate the economy because he believed they would be inflationary. His popularity with Democratic congressional leaders Rep. SAM RAYBURN (D-Tex.) and Sen. LYNDON B. JOHNSON (D-Tex.) helped him maintain this policy. In March 1958, he made a "gentleman's agreement" with Rayburn, pledging that each would consult the other before moving to reduce taxes.

The budget for fiscal 1959 reflected Anderson's continued fear of inflation. In the wake of the Soviet launch of *Sputnik* in October 1957, demands grew for increased military spending. Anderson supported the increase but insisted that the budget be tightened elsewhere. As a result, the 1959 budget put a ban on flood control and reclamation projects, reduced agricultural subsidies, and implemented a cutback on federal grants for urban renewal and welfare programs. However, increases in military spending, together with a small decline in revenue caused by the recession, produced a deficit of $12.5 billion, the largest during Eisenhower's presidency.

Conflict between the secretary of the treasury and the Democratic Congress over economic policy came to a head in August 1959. The House Ways and Means Committee shelved the president's request to raise interest rates on government bonds. Anderson argued that the only alternative to the repeal of interest rate ceilings was to force more of the national debt into inflationary short-term securities, to which the ceilings did not apply. Intent on exploiting the issue, the Democrats in the Senate lashed out against the move, stating that it would raise interest rates for all borrowers. Anderson refused to yield to the criticism. Congress refused to raise the rate on long-term obligations.

With the retirement and death of Secretary of State JOHN F. DULLES, Anderson became increasingly influential in the cabinet. He used his position to fight for a balanced budget and persuaded Eisenhower to oppose Secretary of State CHRISTIAN HERTER's attempts to arrange long-term financing of the Development Loan Fund. Anderson also convinced the president to insist that recipients of development loans spend their dollars in the United States. To reduce the balance of payment deficit, he insisted that the Allies remove their quotas against the importation of American goods and take on a greater share of the cost of defending their territories.

During the Kennedy administration, Anderson was a partner in the investment house of Loeb, Rhodes & Co. and a member of the presidential panel formed to study the U.S. foreign aid program. Anderson served as an informal consultant to President Johnson and advised him to pursue a conservative fiscal policy. Toward the end of his life, Anderson engaged in controversial activities, some of which led to legal difficulties. In 1987, he was disbarred and sentenced to jail after pleading guilty to charges of tax evasion related to an unregistered offshore bank he operated and allegations of money laundering. He also was reported to have been a lobbyist for Rev. Sun Myung Moon and his Church of Unification. Anderson died in New York on August 14, 1989.

—MSM

Arends, Les(lie) C(ornelius)

(1895–1985) *U.S. congressman*

Arends was born on September 27, 1895, in Melvin, Ill. After studying at Oberlin College for two years, he entered the army during World War I and received his discharge in 1919. Following in his father's footsteps, Arends became a farmer and banker in 1920. Seeking public office for the first time in 1934, he won election as a Republican to the U.S. House of Representatives from a prosperous agricultural region south of Chicago. Arends was a critic of what he believed was the dangerous centralization of power under the New Deal. He became Republican minority whip in 1943 and served as majority whip for two years after the Republican electoral victory of 1946.

Arends again became majority whip after the election in 1952. After the Republican defeat in the election of 1954, he again became minority whip.

Arends defended the administration's program to eliminate security risks from the government. In January 1954, Eisenhower maintained that under his program more than 2,200 communists had left the federal payroll. Congressional critics charged that Eisenhower was attempting to mislead the public into believing that all of these employees were commu-

nists, whereas many were social rather than political deviates. In February 1954, Sen. WAYNE MORSE (I-Oreg.) charged the president with responsibility for a "fascist big lie technique" and asked for a breakdown on how many of the security risks were communists. Two days later, Arends said there was no reason for a classification of the causes of the employees' dismissals and charged that Morse had "impeached the honesty and integrity" of the president.

In 1955, Arends denounced an unsuccessful Democratic effort to introduce a bill ending the administration's program of flexible farm price supports and restoring rigid supports at 90 percent of parity.

A strong supporter of private enterprise, Arends sought to minimize government intervention in the workings of the market economy. In 1955 he defended the sale of government-owned synthetic rubber plants to the highest-bidding private companies against Democratic charges that the sale might promote monopoly. Two years later, he unsuccessfully attempted to delete from a military public works bill a provision giving Congress a veto over the transfer of Defense Department work to private industry.

The second-ranking Republican on the Armed Services Committee through 1956 and subsequently the senior Republican on the panel, Arends was a staunch defender of large military appropriations.

Arends generally opposed the domestic programs of the Kennedy and Johnson administrations, although he voted for the Civil Rights Act of 1964. He also backed the Johnson administration's Vietnam War policy. Arends announced in 1974 that he would not seek reelection. He retained his post as minority leader until his retirement. Arends died in Naples, Fla., on July 17, 1985.

—MLL

Arendt, Hannah

(1906–1975) *philosopher, political scientist*

Born into a German-Jewish family in Hanover on October 14, 1906, Arendt earned a doctorate at the age of 22 from the University of Heidelberg. She studied under philosophers Karl Jaspers and Martin Heidegger. In 1933, she fled Hitler's Germany and went to Paris, where she worked for Youth Aliyah, a Zionist group that facilitated the rescue of Jewish children. After a brief detention in a French internment camp, she migrated to New York in 1941, accompanied by her mother and her husband. She found work as the research director for the Conference on Jewish Relations. In 1946 she became chief editor of Schocken Books, while also writing articles on diverse topics. From 1949 to 1952, she served as executive secretary of Jewish Cultural Reconstruction, Inc. She professed no personal religious affiliation, but always participated in Jewish cultural activities.

Arendt published *The Origins of Totalitarianism*, her first book in English, in 1951. Remarkable for its sweep and erudition, the book attempted to explain the rise of totalitarian governments, which she considered to be "the central event of our world." She regarded the totalitarian state as essentially different "from other forms of political oppression . . . such as despotism, tyranny, and dictatorship." It created "entirely new political institutions and destroyed all social, legal, and political traditions of the country." She traced the roots of totalitarianism to imperialism and anti-Semitism. The book established her reputation and won her several university teaching positions. In 1953, she delivered the Christian Gauss lectures at Princeton University, and in 1959 she became the first woman to be appointed a full professor at Princeton. She also held positions at Columbia University, the University of Chicago, and for a number of years before her death, at the New School for Social Research.

In articles written in the 1950s and published primarily in *Partisan Review*, Arendt struggled with the broad concepts of history and freedom, tradition and authority. Her work culminated in a lecture series given at the University of Chicago in 1956 and published in 1958 as *The Human Condition*. In it, Arendt made a distinction between labor, the products of which are consumed and forgotten, and work, the products of which are used and admired. The book noted with dismay the forces present in modern life that diminished workmanship into labor. For Arendt, however, neither labor nor work rose to the level of public activity. Neither the jobholder nor the businessman engaged in the political realm. Indeed, economic self-absorption led to the ruin of the political realm.

Reviews of her work were mixed. Many acknowledged its importance as a philosophical structure for understanding the contemporary political situation but complained of its obscurity. Arendt made her position much clearer in the epilogue to the 1958 edition of the *The Origins of Totalitarianism*, which she wrote in response to the Hungarian revolt in 1956. She hailed the revolt as "the first and yet unique instance of a people's uprising against total domination." It was important as a display of man's insuppressible freedom and his ability to act in the public realm, even under the most intolerable circumstances. However, she did not see the revolt as a portent of future uprisings. She attributed it to the temporary thawing of Soviet oppression, indicating that where oppression was total, rebellion might be impossible. The thaw left no room for optimism, since, according to Arendt, the period of de-Stalinization represented only a tactical maneuver on the part of the Soviet hierarchy and would be followed by a renewal of totalitarian policies. As evidence she cited the heavy-handed reaction to the Hungarian uprising and Khruschev's declarations that the Soviet Union had no need to fear the consequences of nuclear warfare.

In 1963, Arendt went to Jerusalem to report on the trial of Adolf Eichmann for the *New Yorker*. Her reports on the trial and a book published later that year, *Eichmann in Jerusalem: A Report on the Banality of Evil*, became the focal point of intense controversy. Arendt began her analysis of the roots of Eichmann's banality with his use of language; he "was generally incapable of uttering a single sentence that was not a cliché. The longer one listened to him, the more obvious it became that his inability to speak was closely connected to an inability to *think*. . . ." This and his inability to see the Final Solution in terms beyond his own advancement within the SS, argued Arendt, made it difficult to regard Eichmann as an example of pure evil; indeed, it was difficult to take him seriously. "Everybody," including the prosecutors, "could see that this man was not a 'monster,' but it was difficult indeed not to suspect that he was a clown." In the end, the "unspeakable horror" of Eichmann's deeds dwarfed the comic aspect. For Arendt, however, the real horror was the ease with which the modern bureaucratic state subverted an individual conscience. Eichmann was a "terrifyingly normal" example of modern man and the power of the totalitarian state. Some critics misread the work as an attempt to cast Eichmann in a more favorable light. Others misinterpreted the book as an indictment of Jews for going like sheep to the slaughter. Arendt developed this appraisal of bureaucracy into a deeply pessimistic evaluation of the modern world. America's involvement in Vietnam and the circumstances surrounding the Watergate affair only served to make her evaluation more severe. She died in New York City on December 4, 1975.

—MSM

Armour, Norman
(1887–1982) *ambassador to Guatemala*
Born on October 14, 1887, in Brighton, England, to American parents, Armour received his B.A. from Princeton in 1909 and graduated from Harvard Law School in 1913. He returned to Princeton for an M.A. in 1915 and entered the Foreign Service that same year. Assigned to Russia both prior to and during the Russian Revolution, he arranged for the escape of a princess whom he later married. Assigned as minister to Haiti in 1932, Armour oversaw the withdrawal of U.S. Marines and the return of the government to Haitians. Armour was appointed ambassador to Chile in 1938 and served as ambassador to Argentina and Spain during World War II. His experience in revolutionary Russia, fascist Spain, and post-revolutionary Chile instilled in him a loathing for rebellion and upheaval. He retired in 1945 only to be recalled by President HARRY S. TRUMAN in 1948 to become ambassador to Venezuela, where the U.S. was carrying on delicate oil negotiations. He retired again in 1951.

During the opening days of the Eisenhower administration, Armour joined other Foreign Service officers in protesting Sen. JOSEPH R. MCCARTHY'S (R-Wis.) attacks on the State Department. In March 1953, when Senate conservatives challenged CHARLES BOHLEN's nomination as ambassador to the USSR because of his ties to Truman's foreign policy, Armour and other career Foreign Service officers sent a letter to the Senate Foreign Relations Committee in support of Bohlen. In January 1954, Armour joined four other career diplomats in publicly deploring the "sinister" effects of McCarthy's "flimsy" attacks on the

Foreign Service. The diplomats further complained that the administration's loyalty-security and personnel policies might produce "a Foreign Service competent to serve a totalitarian government."

Armour was once again called out of retirement in 1954 to become ambassador to Guatemala. He arrived in that country just after the Central Intelligence Agency had helped overthrow the leftist regime of Jacobo Arbenz. Armour's task was to aid the rightist government in restoring the Guatemalan economy and to oversee the vast amounts of American economic aid given that country. Approaching 70 at the time of his recall to duty, Armour again retired in early May 1955, declaring that the post-revolutionary economic recovery of Guatemala was well under way.

In October 1956, Sen. J. WILLIAM FULBRIGHT (D-Ark.), chairman of a special Senate subcommittee investigating foreign aid, appointed Armour to a panel making on-the-spot studies of the program. Assigned to observe activities in Greece, Turkey, and Iran, Armour reported back to the committee in March 1957 that new foreign aid efforts were needed. Estimates by the North Atlantic Treaty Organization of Turkey's military capabilities were probably "overly optimistic," he said, while U.S. security interests in Greece were jeopardized because of unsettled relations between Greece and Cyprus. The United States, he warned, needed to provide "substantial assistance" for Iran to resist any Soviet aggression in the years ahead.

Armour retired from public life after his Mediterranean fact-finding mission, although he continued to advise the State Department and give lectures at Princeton and elsewhere. When he died in New York City on September 27, 1982, Armour was widely praised as a highly professional and polished diplomat.

—RJB

Ashmore, Harry S(cott)
(1916–1998) *journalist*
Born in Greenville, S.C., on July 27, 1917, Harry Ashmore was the son of a merchant whose ancestors served in the Confederate army. He became acquainted with the plight of southern blacks when, as a teenager, he worked on a cotton farm during

the summer. In 1937, he graduated from Clemson Agricultural College and began a career in journalism, covering the local courthouse for the Greenville *Piedmont*. Following service in the army during World War II, Ashmore was named associate editor of the Charlotte, N.C., *News*. He wrote editorials advocating two-party politics in the South, racial and religious tolerance, and the enfranchisement of African Americans. The *Arkansas Gazette* hired Ashmore as editor in 1947. He became executive editor the following year.

In 1953, the Ford Foundation commissioned Ashmore to head a team of scholars studying biracial education in the United States. The report, entitled *The Negro and the Schools* (1954), was published the day before the Supreme Court handed down its decision in *Brown v. Board of Education*, which struck down segregation in public schools. The study revealed that African Americans in segregated schools received an inferior education; it noted that a gap also existed in the North between the quality of education blacks were getting compared to whites. The report cautioned that desegregation was an explosive issue because of Americans' intense interest in education. It pointed to community attitudes as the most important factor in integration but noted that gradual desegregation had often proved more volatile than immediate integration. Both integrationists and segregationists used the study to support their positions.

In September 1957, when the Democratic governor of Arkansas, ORVAL FAUBUS, ordered national guardsmen to Little Rock to prevent the integration of Central High School, Ashmore endorsed President Eisenhower's use of federal troops to ensure desegregation. In an editorial, he wrote, "We are going to have to decide what kind of people we are— whether we obey the law only when we approve of it, or whether we obey it no matter how distasteful we find it." By mid-October, Ashmore had written more than 40 editorials and appeared on television and radio pleading for compliance. Faubus denounced him as an "ardent integrationist;" the White Citizens' Councils branded him "Public Enemy No. 1." In December 1957, segregationists attempted a boycott of *Gazette* advertisers to induce a change in the paper's editorial policies. Its circulation did drop for a short time, but throughout the incident, Hugh B. Patterson, Jr., the paper's publisher, backed Ash-

more. In May 1958, Ashmore received the Pulitzer Prize for editorial writing. The *Gazette* also received a Pulitzer Prize for carrying his work.

Ashmore's book, *An Epitaph for Dixie* (1958), appeared following the Little Rock crisis. As the title indicated, he argued that the Old South was dying. He predicted that its reliance on agriculture, its one-party political system, and its racial policies would crumble in the face of the demands of a growing, northern-oriented, industrialized society. Ashmore observed that a developing industrial elite would replace the old agrarian-based southern high society. These new leaders, anxious for immediate economic growth, would realize that a prosperous black citizenry was essential for southern prosperity and therefore would accept integration. Segregation, with all its political, social, and economic consequences, had to end so that African Americans could be integrated into the new system. Ashmore also predicted that, in the future, blacks would be more aggressive in demanding their rights.

From 1955 to 1956, Ashmore took a leave of absence to work in ADLAI STEVENSON's presidential campaign. In September 1959, he left the *Gazette* to become a director of the Center for the Study of Democratic Institutions. At the center, he concentrated his attention on race relations and the press, defending the growing militancy of the Civil Rights movement in the mid-1960s. He was also a prominent critic of the Johnson administration's policy in Vietnam. Ashmore left the center in 1974 amidst a financial crisis, which curbed its activities.

Ashmore served as editor in chief of the *Encyclopædia Britannica* and wrote a number of books, most of which dealt with race relations. He published *Hearts and Minds: The Anatomy of Racism from Roosevelt to Reagan* in 1982 and a memoir, *Civil Rights and Wrongs*, in 1994. He died in Santa Barbara, Calif., on January 20, 1998.

—JB

Avery, Sewell (Lee)

(1874–1960) *chairman of Montgomery Ward & Company*

The son of a wealthy lumberman, Avery was born on November 4, 1874, in Saginaw, Mich. Following his graduation from the University of Michigan in 1894, he managed one of his father's businesses, a plaster works, which was soon combined with other companies to form U.S. Gypsum Co. The enterprising Avery became its president at the age of 30. Twenty-eight years later, at the initiative of J. P. Morgan & Co., Avery assumed the board chairmanship of Montgomery Ward & Co. Avery turned the debt-ridden mail and retail department store chain into a once-again viable competitor. Operating in a highly autocratic fashion, he recruited the best marketers and upgraded Ward's merchandise line. By 1939 Ward's sales approached 75 percent of those of Sears Roebuck & Co., the leader in the field and the only department store chain surpassing Ward's in annual sales.

Politically, Avery was an extreme conservative. A frequent critic of Franklin D. Roosevelt and the New Deal, he engaged in a long struggle during World War II over the recognition of a retail employee's union. In a dramatic climax, President Roosevelt utilized special war powers in December 1943 and ordered the army to seize Ward's Chicago building. Army police bodily removed the intransigent Avery from his offices.

Following the war, Avery dictated company policy in anticipation of another Great Depression. This fear led him to suspend all expansion; between 1941 and 1957, Ward opened no new stores. He even kept the modernization of stores to a minimum in the interest of maintaining high liquidity.

Ward's earnings per share plummeted from $5.59 in 1950 to $2.62 in 1955. Its optimistic rival, Sears, expanded and increased its market share.

Ward suffered in other ways as a result of Avery's continued one-man rule. While Sears decentralized, Ward consolidated its management structure. Avery dominated its management past his 80th birthday. Subordinates quit or were fired at an unusually rapid rate; in August 1953, Avery caused the resignation of his 32nd vice president.

Avery's domination began to end in mid-1954. Between then and Ward's annual shareholders' meeting in May 1955, an investor from Florida, LOUIS E. WOLFSON, tried to buy controlling interest in Ward to exercise effective management. Wolfson planned to replace Avery. The battle ended with Wolfson's failure to secure more than 1 percent of Ward stock. Yet Wolfson's campaign itself placed enormous pressures on Avery, who at one point asked JAMES HOFFA, president of the Teamsters Union, to purchase shares on his behalf. Shareholders forced Avery's resignation at the annual meeting in 1955. His successor, John A. Barr, soon inaugurated an ambitious capital expansion program and decentralized operations on the Sears model. Despite Barr's initiatives, however, Ward's sales and earnings lagged through the decade.

Avery died in Chicago, Ill., on October 31, 1960.

—JLB

B

Barden, Graham A(rthur)

(1896–1967) *chairman, Education and Labor Committee*

Born on September 26, 1896, in Sampson Co., N.C., Barden served in the navy during World War I and then studied at the University of North Carolina at Chapel Hill, where he received an LL.B. in 1920. He practiced law in New Bern, N.C., while serving as judge of the Craven Co. Court from 1920 to 1924. Barden represented the county in the North Carolina General Assembly in 1933.

The following year, Barden won election as a Democrat to the U.S. House of Representatives, where he became known as a conservative and an opponent of organized labor. However, he did sponsor vocational rehabilitation and education bills. In 1949, as chairman of a subcommittee of the Education and Labor Committee, he introduced a school-aid bill that provided no assistance for either parochial schools or schools for racial minorities. Rep. John Lesinski (D-Mich.), chairman of the Education and Labor Committee, charged that the bill "dripped with bigotry and racial prejudice." In 1950, following Lesinski's death, Barden became chairman of the Education and Labor Committee.

Barden asserted that he "never knew the Republic to be endangered by a bill that was not passed." Because of this belief and his desire to control the education and labor panel, he called few meetings of the committee. To further enhance his dominance, he decided personally which subcommittee would receive each bill. By 1955, however, the number of liberals on the panel had increased sufficiently to enable a revolt against the chairman. Barden agreed to establish a regular schedule of committee meetings and to create subcommittees with specified areas of jurisdiction. He rejected the liberals' request that subcommittee chairmen be appointed on the basis of seniority. In practice, however, Barden did appoint chairmen on that basis—with the exception of Rep. ADAM CLAYTON POWELL, JR., (D-N.Y.), an African American whom he refused to appoint. Barden contended that his objections to Powell were of a personal rather than a racial nature.

In 1955, Barden backed a bill sponsored by the administration to raise the minimum wage from 75 to 90 cents an hour. During committee hearings, he opposed a greater increase, asserting that with a $1 minimum rate many firms might have to fire employees. However, the committee passed a $1 minimum wage bill, which became law in August. In 1960 another minimum wage bill failed to pass in part because Barden, the chairman of the House delegation in a Senate-House conference, insisted upon the $1.15 minimum voted by the House instead of the $1.25 minimum in the Senate version.

In 1960, the Education and Labor Committee considered a bill to legalize common-site picketing, which would have permitted unions to picket a firm at a construction site even if the effect was to stop the work of other firms at the same location. Barden opposed the measure, stating that employers on a construction site generally did not act as partners. He also said that it would have a "devastating effect . . . on the health and welfare of a community, or upon our national defense effort." The bill passed the Education and Labor Committee but was blocked by the Rules Committee.

In 1955, the Education and Labor Committee passed a bill sponsored by the Eisenhower administration providing federal aid for school construction. Barden backed the measure and sponsored it on the House floor the following year. However, he withdrew his sponsorship after the chamber adopted an amendment, offered by Rep. Powell, barring federal funds for segregated schools. The bill failed to pass Congress. Two years later Barden opposed a scholarship provision, designed to meet the Soviet technological threat, in a school-aid bill. The scholarship plan cleared the committee but was stricken on the House floor. The following year, Barden opposed a bill providing aid for school construction, which was passed by the Education and Labor Committee but blocked by the Rules Committee. In 1960, he attacked a Senate-passed measure eliminating the noncommunist affidavit requirement from the National Defense Education Act of 1958. The bill was pigeonholed in the Education and Labor Committee.

In January 1960, Barden announced that he would not seek reelection. He died of cancer in New Bern, N.C., on January 20, 1967.

—MLL

Bates, Daisy (Gatson)

(1922–1999) *president, Arkansas NAACP*

Daisy Gatson was born in 1922 and grew up on farms in eastern Arkansas. She attended Philander Smith College and Shorter College in Little Rock, Ark., and in 1941 founded the Arkansas *State Press* with her husband, L. C. Bates, to advance the cause of black rights. Daisy Bates first became known in the Civil Rights movement in 1946, when she was found guilty on contempt charges in circuit court for criticizing the trial of a black defendant. This conviction was overturned by the Arkansas Supreme Court.

When the U.S. Supreme Court ruled public school segregation to be unconstitutional in May 1954, a number of Arkansas school districts desegregated voluntarily. This process was supported by

Gov. FRANCIS A. CHERRY, who promised compliance with the law. In November 1954, ORVAL FAUBUS was elected governor, pledging not to "force" integration on those communities that opposed it. Faubus won reelection two years later, defeating a die-hard segregationist.

In response to the *Brown* decision, the Little Rock school board proposed a plan to gradually desegregate Little Rock's schools. After the NAACP unsuccessfully challenged the plan in court, the school board began implementing the plan by desegregating Central High School in September 1957.

Nine black students were selected by the NAACP and coached in Daisy Bates's home on nonviolent reaction to expected abuse by segregationists. Beginning in August 1957 and for the next two years, Daisy Bates served as the driving force behind Little Rock's integration effort. Her life was repeatedly threatened. In September, Gov. Faubus uttered his famous warning that "blood will run in the streets" if integration were attempted, and he called out the National Guard to keep black students from entering Central. Later in the month, President DWIGHT D. EISENHOWER federalized the Arkansas Guard and dispatched federal troops to maintain order and escort the African-American students through hostile mobs to Central High. Central was forcibly integrated, but in October Little Rock's City Council ordered the arrest of Daisy Bates and other civil rights activists on charges of failing to register as NAACP members under a new law. The defendants were convicted and fined in municipal court in December 1957. The Supreme Court overturned the conviction in 1960.

Little Rock remained under court order to desegregate all of its schools. Faubus closed all the city's high schools in September 1958. As they prepared to reopen on an integrated basis, Daisy Bates's home was bombed in July 1959. She escaped injury and wired Attorney General WILLIAM P. ROGERS, requesting federal protection. When this was denied, she telegraphed President Eisenhower, who referred her back to the Justice Department. All of Little Rock's high schools reopened on an integrated basis in September 1959, and the tide of violence began to ebb.

Daisy Bates told her story in a book, *The Long Shadow of Little Rock* (1962). She continued to be an activist and 10 years later denounced President RICHARD NIXON's cutoff of Office of Economic Opportunity funds for an Arkansas community as "economic genocide." In 1974 Bates was honored for her role in Little Rock by the National Black Political Convention. She died in Little Rock on November 4, 1999.

—MJS

Battle, John S(tewart)

(1890–1972) member, U.S. Civil Rights Commission
John S. Battle, the son of a Baptist minister, was born on July 11, 1890, in New Bern, N.C. He received his LL.B. at the University of Virginia in 1913. A member of the conservative Democratic Byrd machine in Virginia politics, he served for 19 years in the House of Delegates and state Senate, where he became chairman of the Finance Committee. In 1949, Sen. HARRY BYRD (D-Va.) picked the state senator as the organization's candidate for governor. Battle won the primary in August 1950 against the strongest liberal Democratic challenge to Byrd's dominance in decades and went on to win the general election in November. Fiscally liberal by the standards of the Byrd machine, Battle pioneered a $75 million public school building program.

Battle gained prominence at the Democratic National Convention in 1952, when he led rebellious southern delegations from Virginia, Louisiana, and South Carolina in refusing to sign a loyalty oath that required delegates to support the convention's presidential ticket, a pledge politically anathema in some southern states because of the fear that the convention would choose a supporter of civil rights. Battle insisted that the defiant delegates be seated. They were, and he went home a hero. He supported the nominee, ADLAI STEVENSON, while Virginia's Democratic Party remained neutral.

Although a firm segregationist, Battle refused Sen. Byrd's call for "massive resistance" to school desegregation. Fully formulated by 1957, Byrd's resistance program called for states to block federal integration orders they deemed illegal. Some states declared the Supreme Court's desegregation decision itself null and void. President Eisenhower

apparently noticed Battle's position. In August 1957, Congress created a six-member Civil Rights Commission to investigate voting rights violations as part of that year's Civil Rights Act. Trying to include a broad range of opinion, Eisenhower appointed Battle to the commission in November. During Senate confirmation hearings in February 1958, the former North Carolina governor described his job as exclusively fact-finding. The committee approved his appointment to the post at the beginning of March.

During the commission's first public hearings, Battle clashed with officials from Alabama attempting to obstruct its work. Six registrars from Montgomery refused to produce subpoenaed voting records, and Judge George Wallace threatened to jail registrars who complied. Battle assailed the officials, warning of new federal rights legislation if the defiance continued. He then joined the commission in asking Attorney General WILLIAM P. ROGERS to take appropriate legal action.

Battle dissented from the Civil Rights Commission's first report to Congress, presented in the summer of 1959. It recommended specific legislation to assure equal voting, educational, and housing rights. Battle thought this exceeded the commission's mandate. Insisting that existing civil rights guarantees were sufficient and should be enforced, Battle urged only the investigation of voting rights and did not favor sending federal registrars into the South. Battle contended that the commission's report was not factual and impartial as Congress had intended. The former North Carolina governor maintained that the document was only "an argument in advocacy of preconceived ideas in race relations."

Noting that the commission had completed its two-year term, Battle resisted Eisenhower's plea to stay on and resigned his position in October 1959. He returned to his law practice in Charlottesville, Va. Battle died there on April 9, 1972.

—MJS

Bazelon, David L(ionel)

(1909–1993) federal appellate judge
David L. Bazelon was born on September 3, 1909, in Superior, Wis. His father, the proprietor of the local general store, died two years later, leaving the family

virtually destitute. The family moved to Chicago, where Bazelon attended public schools, after which he spent a year at the University of Illinois. Bazelon received his B.S.L. from Northwestern University in 1931. He read law the following year and engaged in the private practice of law from 1932 to 1935, during which time he was also active in Democratic Party politics. In 1935 he became assistant U.S. attorney for the Northern District of Illinois, a position he held until 1940, when he returned to private practice as the senior member of the firm of Gottlieb and Schwartz. In 1946, he was appointed assistant U.S. attorney general in the U.S. Lands Division. He remained in the Justice Department for three years, during which time he also headed the Office of Alien Property (1947–49). President HARRY S. TRUMAN named him to a recess appointment on the U.S. Court of Appeals for the District of Columbia Circuit in 1949, making Bazelon the youngest person ever appointed to a federal judgeship. The Senate confirmed the nomination in 1950.

Over the years, Bazelon established a reputation as one of the most liberal federal judges in the nation. A judicial activist, he consistently advocated the protection of the rights of those accused of crimes and opening the judicial system to the findings of other disciplines, most notably psychology. His best known opinion, *Durham v. U.S.*, came in 1954 and involved the case of a mentally disturbed man convicted of burglary. In his written opinion, Bazelon attempted to revise the prevailing legal test for insanity. Under the existing rule, a criminal could claim insanity as a defense only if it could be proved that the defendant was unable to distinguish between right and wrong or if the criminal act was the product of an "irresistible impulse." The so-called "Durham rule" held that "an accused is not criminally responsible if his unlawful act was the product of a mental disease or defect." Bazelon always maintained that he did not create a new formula; rather, he attempted to "open the door to information." He hoped that his ruling would enable psychiatrists to present to juries insight into what motivated a criminal. In fact, the Durham rule proved unworkable, and even Bazelon became thoroughly disenchanted with the results of his own decision. The Court of Appeals abandoned the rule in 1972, with Bazelon

writing a separate concurring opinion. Based on the experience of almost two decades, the court, and Bazelon too, concluded that the Durham rule had given psychiatrists too great a role and too much leeway.

During the 1960s, Bazelon and future chief justice, WARREN E. BURGER, who was then a judge on the Court of Appeals for the District of Columbia Circuit, carried on a bitter and public debate over the rights of defendants in criminal cases. The elevation of Burger to the Supreme Court coincided with a waning of Bazelon's influence.

Bazelon stepped down as chief judge in 1978, several months before the law required him to retire, so that his friend and colleague, J. SKELLY WRIGHT, would have a longer tenure as chief judge. Bazelon took senior judge status in 1979 and remained on the court until his death in Washington, D.C., on February 19, 1993. He published *Questioning Authority: Justice and Criminal Law* in 1988.

—MSM

Beam, Jacob D(yneley)
(1908–1993) *deputy director, State Department Policy Planning Staff; ambassador to Poland*

Born in Princeton, N.J., on March 24, 1908, Beam, the son of a university professor, attended the Kent School in Connecticut and Princeton University, from which he graduated in 1929. Following a year of graduate study at Cambridge University, he joined the U.S. Foreign Service in 1931 as a clerk at the U.S. consulate in Geneva. From 1934 to 1940, he was assigned to the American embassy in Berlin. Beam served as secretary to the ambassador to Great Britain, John J. Winant, during World War II. From 1945 to 1947, he worked on the staff of the U.S. political adviser in Germany. Beam became consul general in Java in 1949, and during the early 1950s he was a U.S. Information Service officer in Belgrade. Beam temporarily headed the embassy in Moscow after Ambassador GEORGE F. KENNAN had been declared persona non grata in October 1952. He remained there through the tense period of Stalin's death, leaving in April 1953, when CHARLES BOHLEN became ambassador. Beam became deputy director of the State Department's policy planning staff that June.

President Eisenhower appointed Beam ambassador to Poland in June 1957. Along with his embassy responsibilities, the new American ambassador was given the task of negotiating with Communist China in the only official contact the United States had then had with that country. The primary issue under discussion was the shelling by the mainland Chinese of the offshore islands of Quemoy and Matsu, held by Nationalist China.

At talks held during the fall of 1958, Beam and his Chinese counterpart, Wang Ping-nan, found themselves deadlocked. Beam demanded an immediate cease-fire, after which the United States would negotiate to have the islands neutralized through a gradual Nationalist withdrawal. Wang, on the other hand, maintained that the cease-fire did not concern the United States because its troops were not under attack. He demanded that the Nationalists withdraw from the islands and that the U.S. remove its troops from Taiwan. Although the Communists did gradually stop the shelling, Beam and Wang failed to come to an agreement on the subject. Beam continued his contacts with the Chinese until he left his post in December 1961, when he was appointed deputy director of the U.S. Disarmament Agency.

President LYNDON B. JOHNSON appointed Beam ambassador to Czechoslovakia in 1968. The following year, President RICHARD M. NIXON appointed him ambassador to the Soviet Union. Beam held this post until his retirement in 1973. His service over five decades won him a reputation as a cool, professional diplomat with a keen sense of irony. After his retirement, Beam gave talks and wrote articles about the Soviet Union and arms control. He served as director of Radio Free Europe (1974–77) and published his memoirs, *Multiple Exposure*, in 1978. Beam died in Rockville, Md., on August 16, 1993.

—JB

Beck, Dave

(1894–1993) *union leader*

The son of a carpet cleaner, Beck was born in Stockton, Calif., on June 16, 1894. Forced to leave high school before graduation because of his family's financial difficulties, he went to work in a laundry and then became a laundry wagon driver. In 1917 he became a charter member of Seattle, Wash., Local 566 of the International Brotherhood of Teamsters (IBT). During World War I, Beck was a machinist's mate with the Naval Aviation Service. He resumed work as a laundry driver after the War; in 1923 he won election to the executive board of his local and two years later became its secretary-treasurer. Beck was chosen president of the local in 1927.

During the 1930s and 1940s, Beck moved up through the ranks of the IBT to become one of the most powerful Teamster leaders in the nation. Acknowledging his work in organizing the West Coast, the IBT elected him to the newly created position of executive vice president in 1947. When the IBT's president, Dan Tobin, retired in 1952, Beck was elected president. He also sat on the Executive Council of the American Federation of Labor (AFL) and became one of its vice presidents in 1953.

Described as a practical man with a "business rather than a social philosophy," Beck began a program to expand and consolidate the Teamsters' power. Under Tobin, the union had been composed of a series of locals with leaders interested only in their own affairs. When Beck took over, he employed the techniques he had used on the West Coast to forge a centralized structure. He formed regional conferences and merged small locals to centralize power. Along with the conferences, Beck established 15 trade divisions that sought contracts on an area-wide basis. Beck promised to double union membership by 1960 and alienated such labor leaders as WALTER REUTHER by his willingness to raid other unions. By 1955 the Teamsters controlled the nation's truck drivers in a tightly centralized organization guided by Beck and his right-hand man, JAMES HOFFA. In addition to trucking, the IBT represented workers in municipal government, canneries, breweries, and the taxi industry. Reflecting the union's national importance, in 1956 Beck moved its headquarters to Washington into a plush $5 million building facing the Capitol.

Beck had grave reservations about the merger of the AFL and the Congress of Industrial Organizations (CIO) in 1955. Although he headed the largest AFL union, he refused to take part in negotiations on the merger and was away "on Teamster business" when the pact was ratified. In a press conference, Beck maintained that the merger had proceeded too quickly and that many large problems remained. One of the major issues unresolved between Reuther, GEORGE MEANY, and Beck was the Teamster leader's refusal to sign the organization's no-raiding pact. Pushing to increase his membership, Beck hoped to achieve his goal through a series of alliances in a trade-union center apart from the AFL-CIO.

During 1956, Beck became the focus of a congressional investigation of union corruption. ROBERT KENNEDY, chief counsel of the Senate Permanent Investigations Subcommittee, learned that the union president had used $150,000 from the union treasury to improve his vast estate and had then sold his home to the IBT to repay the loan while arranging to live in it rent-free for the rest of his life. Beck had also used Teamster funds for personal purchases. In January and February 1957, Beck avoided testifying before the Select Committee on Improper Activities in the Labor or Management Field, first claiming to be sick and then leaving the country on winter cruises. On March 26, he finally appeared before the panel, headed by Sen. JOHN MCCLELLAN (D-Ark.), to answer the charges. Beck took the Fifth Amendment 65 times. The AFL-CIO expelled Beck from its Executive Council for refusing to answer the committee's questions. As a result of pressure from the IBT, Beck did not seek reelection that year.

Following his retirement, Beck became involved in a series of legal cases dealing with the charges aired before the committee. In 1957, he was convicted of embezzling $1,900 for the sale of a union-owned Cadillac. Two years later, he was indicted on charges of having violated the Taft-Hartley Act by borrowing $200,000 from trucking industry representatives, but he was acquitted in 1962. Between 1962 and 1965, he served a 30-month prison term after being convicted for filing a false federal income tax return. After his release, Beck became a successful real estate promoter in Seattle, where he died on December 26, 1993.

—JB

Bell, Daniel
(1919–   ) *sociologist*
Born Daniel Bolotsky on May 10, 1919, in New York City, Bell was the son of Polish-Jewish gar-

ment workers and grew up on New York's Lower East Side. A precocious student, Bell joined the Young People's Socialist League at the age of 13. Following his graduation from City College in 1938, he edited the Social Democratic *New Leader* from 1941 to 1945. In 1945, he briefly held the job of managing editor at *Common Sense*. Bell left journalism in the fall of 1945 to become an instructor in social sciences at the University of Chicago. Three years later, he became labor editor of *Fortune*. He continued in that post until 1958 while maintaining ties to the academic community as a part-time instructor at Columbia University. He assumed full-time teaching at Columbia in 1959, earned his Ph.D. from Columbia, and rose to the rank of professor by 1962.

During the 1950s, Bell was an articulate spokesmen for the growing centrist movement among postwar intellectuals. Along with other pluralist intellectuals, Bell argued that, in America, political parties and voluntary associations jockeyed for power and, in doing so, created a delicate balance. His most influential work of the decade was his introduction to *The New American Right* (1955), a collection of articles by scholars which publicized the view that McCarthyism was heir to the radical populist and agrarian agitation of an earlier time. Bell thought McCarthyism was a manifestation of the social tensions of the postwar period. Sen. McCarthy's attack on communists afforded an outlet for the "status anxieties" of various social groups. These included: the "new middle class" of German and Irish-Americans, which felt it had to prove its patriotism in light of World War II; the "soured patricians," members of old upper classes who saw their power diminishing; and the "new rich," uneasy with the way they acquired their wealth. Combined with an inbred American populism, "with its insistence on disclosure and leveling," these status anxieties produced support for McCarthy.

Bell argued that McCarthyism was unique in American life because it injected ideology into the mainstream of American politics. Previously, he maintained it had been confined to such tangential issues as Prohibition and Sunday blue laws. Bell feared that "the tendency to convert issues into ideologies, to invest them with moral color and high emotional charge, invites conflicts which can only derange a society." Bell's remedy was to return to the pragmatic, issue-oriented politics of the pre–New Deal age and a political system divorced from the intervention of moral issues.

In 1960, Bell published *The End of Ideology: On the Exhaustion of Political Ideas in the Fifties.* The work was soon acclaimed as a classic. In it, Bell adopted a position he described as "anti-ideological, but not conservative." For all his protestations, however, Bell's work reflected his disenchantment with traditional radicalism and radical ideologies. He emphasized the folly and danger of utopian ideologies and expressed his preference for the American party system, with its imperative not to turn "concrete issues" into "ideologically tinged conflicts" that had the potential to create disastrous divisions in the polity. Moreover, he believed that the problems facing modern America resisted ideological formulations; rather, they were more likely to be solved by "pragmatic compromise" and technological solutions.

During the 1960s, Bell continued to stress the effect of status anxiety on the development of American conservatism. He published a revised version of *The New American Right,* titled *The Radical Right,* in 1963. Toward the end of the decade, he grew increasingly pessimistic about government's ability to produce beneficial social change. In 1969, Bell left Columbia's sociology department for Harvard. He continued to publish prolifically. *The Coming of Post-Industrial Society* came out in 1973, *Social Sciences since the Second World War* in 1982, and *Communitarianism and Its Critics* in 1993.

—MSM

Bennett, Wallace F(oster)
(1898–1993) *U.S. senator*

Born into a Mormon family in Salt Lake City on November 13, 1898, Bennett attended a church high school and received a B.A. from the University of Utah in 1919. His college career was interrupted by service as a second lieutenant of infantry during World War I. After graduating, he worked as a high school principal and later entered his father's paint and glass firm. When his father died in 1938, Bennett became president and general manager of the business. In December 1948, he was elected president of the National Association of Manufacturers. The Mormon emphasis upon hard work and individual responsibility shaped his conservative political views. He opposed extensive social welfare programs and what he regarded as excessive government regulation of the economy. In 1950 he won a U.S. Senate seat by defeating the liberal incumbent, Sen. Elbert Thomas (D-Utah).

Serving on the Banking and Currency and Finance Committees, Bennett became a leading spokesman for the Eisenhower administration on matters of taxation and finance. In 1954 he supported the administration's tax revision bill that many Democrats criticized for allegedly providing more tax relief to big business than to individual taxpayers. When Democrats unsuccessfully attempted to reduce personal income taxes the following year, Bennett defended the measure passed in 1954 as "carefully balanced to bring some measure of relief to every part of our economy" and denounced the Democratic proposal as "the height of fiscal irresponsibility."

An opponent of strong federal controls over the economy, Bennett dissented from a majority report of the Banking and Currency Committee in May 1955 that recommended tightening existing regulations of the stock market and investigating the possibility of fraud and manipulation in the sharp rise of stock prices during the preceding 15 months. Bennett, along with Sens. HOMER E. CAPEHART (R-Ind.), JOHN W. BRICKER (R-Ohio), and J. Glenn Beall (R-Md.), denounced the majority for attempting "to disturb the economy" and "to weaken the confidence of the people in the Administration."

A persistent critic of social welfare programs, Bennett successfully offered in 1957 a floor amendment to a housing bill to retain the federal contribution to slum clearance and urban renewal at two-thirds of the cost rather than raising it to three-quarters, as proposed by the Banking and Currency panel. In both 1958 and 1959, he was among the minority on the Committee that voted against reporting out area redevelopment bills to aid regions suffering from chronic unemployment.

Bennett supported legislation to promote the economic growth of his state. In 1955, he backed a billion-dollar program to construct water storage facilities in the Upper Colorado River Basin, an important project for promoting agriculture and the production of minerals in Utah. The measure became law the following year. In 1956, he contributed an amendment to the Defense Production Act that directed the government to promote the geographical dispersal of defense-related industries. Tax incentives resulting from the amendment played a major role in attracting the missile industry to Utah.

During the early 1960s, Bennett helped defeat a truth-in-lending proposal in the Banking and Currency Committee. He voted against most of the Kennedy administration's social welfare programs, including the aid-to-education bill in 1961, Medicare in 1962, and mass transit aid in 1962 and 1963. During the Johnson presidency, Bennett opposed the bulk of the administration's Great Society programs but supported its civil rights measures. He strongly supported the Vietnam War. In 1974, Bennett announced that he would not seek reelection and resumed his career in business. He lived in Salt Lake City, where he died on December 19, 1993.

—MLL

Benson, Ezra Taft

(1899–1994) *secretary of agriculture*

Descended from Mormon pioneers who accompanied Brigham Young on the westward trek in 1847. Benson was born in Whitney, Idaho, on August 4, 1899. He grew up on a farm in Idaho and attended Utah State Agricultural College. He performed the required Mormon missionary service in Europe during 1922–23 and then returned to work on his father's farm while continuing his agricultural studies. He received a B.S. degree in 1926 from Brigham Young University. Benson took an M.S. degree in agricultural economics at Iowa State College the following year. In the early 1930s, he worked as a county agricultural agent for the University of Idaho Extension Service and later helped organize the Idaho Cooperative Council, of which he was secretary from 1933 to 1939. In the latter year, he went to Washington to assume the post of executive secretary of the National Council of Farm Cooperatives. Although Benson served with many government agencies during his tenure in Washington, including the National Farm Credit Committee and the National Agricultural Advisory

Commission, he was a sharp critic of President Franklin Roosevelt's farm policies. In 1943, Benson gave up his influential job when he was selected to become the youngest member of the Council of Twelve Apostles, the ruling group of the Mormon Church. Despite his church work, Benson served as director of the Farm Foundation from 1946 to 1950 and remained in the spotlight with zealous attacks on "paternalistic government" and calls to the cooperative movement to propagate the "free enterprise" system.

After DWIGHT D. EISENHOWER's victory in November 1952, observers thought that he would name his brother, MILTON S. EISENHOWER, to head the Department of Agriculture (USDA). But Milton was not interested in the job. Many prominent names were discussed until the president-elect settled on Benson, a relatively unknown figure nationally but highly recommended by farm leaders. At the time, the appointment was interpreted as a concession to the conservative wing of the Republican Party led by Sen. ROBERT A. TAFT (R-Ohio), whom Benson had supported for the Republican nomination. Nonetheless, Eisenhower assured Benson that he was in agreement with the new secretary's plans to decrease government interference in agriculture and to make research, education, and market development the USDA's prime responsibilities.

Farm policy constituted one of the most complex and intractable problems in postwar American politics. Despite a steady decline in farm population, advanced technology concentrated in ever larger farm units produced crops at a rate greater than the rise in demand, resulting in enormous surpluses. Democratic administrations bought and stored the farmers' surplus at a high cost to the taxpayers. In combination with production controls, this policy sought to ensure farmers, incomes at or near parity with the nonfarm population by subsidizing high prices in the market. Because of the relatively high demand created by postwar reconstruction and the Korean war, the surplus problem did not assume extraordinary proportions until the advent of the Eisenhower administration. By 1954, the government had enough cotton, wheat, and other commodities in storage to meet the needs of the market for an entire year. Not only was it expensive to store the crops, but their very presence depressed agricultural prices. At the same time, the price of manufactured goods purchased by farmers rose.

Secretary Benson believed that a return to the free market of supply and demand offered the best solution to the problems of overproduction and declining farm income. He argued that without artificial controls market prices would at first decline, thus encouraging farmers to cut production. According to Benson, government price supports had encouraged overproduction. Without supports, agriculture could be more efficient, and lower prices would stimulate consumption and ensure a higher standard of living for the general population. In addition, he believed that continued dependence on the federal government would prove morally corrupting to the farmer. In response to critics who noted that laissez-faire would drive smaller, less efficient farmers out of business—and thus destroy the cherished family farm ideal—Benson argued that, through education and marketing research, some small farmers could find new markets while others could find nonfarm work in their region. Besides, he pointed out, giant commercial farms, not small family unit, benefited most from existing price support policies.

President Eisenhower asked Benson to move slowly in his goal to reinstate the free market in American agriculture because of the considerable opposition radical changes in USDA policy would evoke in Congress and the farm states. In his election campaign, Eisenhower had been intentionally ambiguous about whether he would continue to support 90 percent of parity price supports after the law establishing that level expired in 1954. In January 1953, Benson aroused the ire of a number of farm-belt Republican senators at his confirmation hearings, when he refused to commit the administration to an extension of 90 percent of parity price supports for the six basic crops (wheat, corn, cotton, rice, peanuts, and tobacco) for three additional years. Criticism of Benson increased when, in February, at his first public speech as secretary, he told a meeting of cattle raisers concerned about falling beef prices that they should produce for a free market and consider price supports only as "disaster insurance" rather than as an encouragement to "uneconomic production."

Ezra Taft Benson, secretary of agriculture *(Dwight D. Eisenhower Library and Museum)*

Benson's reorganization of the USDA with the aid of the interim National Agricultural Advisory Commission established by President Eisenhower in July 1953 irritated Republican farm-bloc leaders whom Benson neglected to consult about new appointments. Granted greater powers than his predecessors, Benson angered Democrats in November by abolishing the Production and Marketing Administration (PMA), a New Deal stronghold, and the Bureau of Agricultural Economics (BAE). He also substantially reduced the authority of the Soil Conservation Service. In place of the PMA and the BAE, he set up the Commodity Stabilization Service to handle production control and price support functions and the Agricultural Marketing Service to handle marketing functions. Because of his desire to enlarge agricultural exports, Benson fostered the creation of the Foreign Agricultural Service to develop markets abroad. Finally, the secretary reorganized the USDA into four branches, each headed by an assistant secretary: federal-state relations, marketing and foreign agriculture, agricultural stabilization, and agricultural credit.

Benson's public statements and reorganization program as well as a steady decline in farm prices accelerated by the close of the Korean War elicited widespread calls for his resignation. President Eisenhower publicly declared his confidence in the secretary but privately cautioned Benson to moderate his attacks on high price supports.

In 1954, Benson presented Congress with a new farm package intended for implementation in 1955. He favored a new system of flexible price supports for basic commodities that could be gradually related to supply. As expected, members of the congressional farm bloc assailed Benson's recommendations, but they won the approval of a group of urban liberal Democrats.

In order to ensure the farm bill's passage, President Eisenhower took Benson's plan to the public, pointing out that a change from rigid to flexible price supports would affect less than one-fourth of the income received by farmers. In June 1954, Benson and Vice President RICHARD NIXON appeared on national television to inform the American people that a flexible price support program would merely implement legislation passed in 1949. Benson explained that, after World War II, the nation "stopped all-out production of munitions and ships [but] we didn't put a stop to all-out production of surplus food."

In August the Agricultural Act of 1954 finally passed after prolonged debate. Flexible price supports ranged from 82.5 percent to 90 percent of parity for basic crops—Benson had desired a minimum level of 75 percent—in 1955 and thereafter from 75 percent to 90 percent depending upon market prices. Of the six basic crops, only tobacco, which had no surplus problem, had a mandatory 90 percent support level. Surplus holdings of the Commodity Credit Corporation (CCC) were set aside, as Benson had requested, to be used for foreign and domestic disaster relief, school lunch programs, research, and other purposes. Benson's victory was marred, however, when in September the White House, concerned about the November elections, overruled his stringent controls on wheat acreage allotments. Nonetheless, the perception of Benson

as a political liability seemed to be refuted by the elections, in which pro-Benson congressmen ran better than his critics in the farm belt.

The success of a flexible price-support policy depended in large part upon unloading surpluses abroad. The Agricultural Trade Development and Assistance Act, passed in July 1954, met some of Benson's goals. The bill authorized the sale of surpluses abroad in exchange for foreign currencies with a provision allowing the CCC to take a $700-million annual loss in such transactions. The president could also send needy nations up to $300 million worth of surpluses over a three-year period. Another provision allowed the government to barter food for goods essential to national security.

The disposal of surpluses abroad, however, was politically complicated. If sold at price-supported domestic prices, most U.S. commodities could not compete with foreign producers in the world market. On the other hand, any dumping might violate the General Agreement on Tariffs and Trade (GATT) and disturb the equilibrium of international trade. Despite these difficulties, Benson undertook a series of foreign tours to Latin America, Canada, and Europe in 1955 in order to promote U.S. farm products.

Benson's aggressive program to expand trade ran into opposition from Secretary of State JOHN FOSTER DULLES, who did not wish to weaken the economies of American allies. Dulles's policy yielded some markets to allies and nonaligned nations in the interest of national security. In addition, the State Department steadfastly opposed trade with communist-bloc nations, which eliminated a potentially important market for American farmers. Benson, a fierce anticommunist was not inclined to confront Dulles on this particular issue, but expansion of exports remained one of the most consistent and possibly one of the most successful themes of his tenure.

By the late fall of 1955, Republicans were already worried about the 1956 elections. The decline in farm income by 20 percent since the peak of the Korean War, with no upturn in sight, was a major cause for concern. In 1955, a new protest movement, the National Farm Organization (NFO), was established. The NFO demanded 100 percent of parity and advocated collective bargaining for farmers. Leading Republicans concluded that the administration needed a new agricultural program to win the confidence of farmers. Benson refused to repudiate his price support policy.

Eisenhower hoped to promote conservation and at the same time aid farmers with a plan he called a Soil Bank. He wanted to pay farmers to retire land from production or to devote the land to conservation practices. The New Deal had paid farmers to take marginal land out of production, and some Republicans had advocated similar programs. Eisenhower thought that such a plan would both conserve soil and reduce surpluses, thereby raising agricultural prices. He also wanted the federal government to buy back marginal land on the Great Plains that had been homesteaded in the 19th century. Benson opposed adding to the public lands, and GEORGE HUMPHREY, the secretary of the treasury, disapproved of buying back land the government had given away. Benson, however, was willing to support the Soil Bank.

In December 1955, Benson announced the plan for the Soil Bank. Some of Benson's conservative supporters, opposed to federal subsidies, criticized the Soil Bank, while his opponents attacked it as insufficient to bring farm income up to nonfarm levels. Nonetheless, Benson both believed the Soil Bank could help stem overproduction and recognized its political value.

The administration offered its agricultural program to Congress in January 1956. It did not include Eisenhower's plan to buy back marginal lands, but it did offer farmers either cash or kind equivalent to the probable yield for land they left fallow (essentially the policy of the New Deal). It also included the Soil Bank, a longer-term program, which provided for farmers to receive payments over a period of years for land they put back into water storage or ungrazed grass or forest. Benson remained skeptical about the Conservation Reserve, as the program was officially named, but the president wanted it. Benson was more comfortable with the proposal to tie the Soil Bank to flexible price supports. Finally, the administration wanted to expand programs to dispose of the surplus.

The bill became entangled in election-year politics. Seeking the farm vote, Democrats in Congress introduced amendments calling for 90 percent of parity. Effectively, they offered the Soil Bank

in exchange for fixed and high parity payments. Congress passed an omnibus farm bill in April that included the Soil Bank, 90 percent parity supports for basic commodities, and higher supports for dairy products. Eisenhower vetoed the bill. After efforts to override the veto failed, Congress passed and Eisenhower signed a compromise that included the Soil Bank and provisions to dispose of the surplus, but also established floors on cotton and rice acreage, a cotton export program, and a two-price plan for rice. It also included mandatory supports for small grains and a temporary freeze on parity pricing.

Benson's reputation now rested largely on the performance of the Soil Bank. He knew there was little chance that it would be an immediate success. The program was expensive, and farmers might cultivate their reduced acreage more intensively. Through 1957, production continued to outstrip demand, farm income fell, and USDA spending exceeded its budget. Despite the surplus disposal program, high production kept CCC holdings constant.

The only major bill Benson presented to Congress in 1957 proposed to allow corn farmers to expand their acreage allotments and still remain eligible for price supports, provided they agreed to participate in the Soil Bank. Since the bill was considered too favorable to the corn area, a coalition of southern and urban congressmen combined to defeat the plan in March. In May, Benson suggested that the parity floors for price supports be lowered or the secretary be given the authority to set levels at anywhere from zero percent to 90 percent of parity.

Meanwhile, the secretary directed criticism at another area of congressional inaction. He charged that congressional unwillingness to fund the Rural Development Program (RDP), established in 1955, prejudiced the future of the family farm that figured so prominently in congressional rhetoric. Benson maintained that the program could alleviate rural poverty by teaching either modern farming techniques or nonfarm skills and by providing easier credit and health services. An ambitious RDP, Benson suggested, could cope with the dislocations that might be caused by the end of price supports. Rural development, however, did not receive substantial funding until the 1960s.

Benson persisted in his efforts to move toward a free market. In 1958, he and President Eisenhower proposed lowering the support scale for basics and dairy products to between 70 percent and 90 percent of parity. The secretary predicted that lower prices and increased sales would result and that production controls could be eased or perhaps eliminated for corn. The Democratic Congress, however, passed a freeze on price supports and acreage restrictions, prompting a presidential veto in March. The Agricultural Act of 1958, enacted in August, was another compromise. Benson and the administration got an eventual reduction of price support floors for corn, upland cotton, and rice from 75 percent to 65 percent of parity, while various congressional groups won removal of limits on corn production and a bar to further large cutbacks in rice and cotton allotments.

Despite a slight increase in farm income in 1958, overproduction continued, and discontent was widespread in the farm belt. On February 30, farm-bloc Republican congressmen requested Benson's resignation, stating that his farm policies would cost the Republicans 20 to 25 House seats in the elections. As in the past, Eisenhower stood by Benson. The secretary campaigned vigorously in the farm states, defending his program and asking voters whether they wanted "a truly American or a left-wing dominated Congress for the next two critical years," but Democrats won impressive gains in both the House and Senate. Large Democratic majorities ensured that Benson could not hope to maintain the limited successes he had achieved.

Nevertheless, Benson persuaded the president to propose his most far-reaching agricultural program yet: abandonment of both the parity concept and the idea of a statutory price-support floor based on parity. In his message to Congress in January 1959, Eisenhower suggested that price supports be used to prevent precipitate price drops rather than to sustain farm prices against long-range market trends. The president recommended that either supports for a commodity in a given year be fixed at some percentage of its average market prices during the three years preceding or that supports be made discretionary, to be fixed by the secretary at zero percent to 90 percent of parity. Not surprisingly, Congress ignored these proposals.

In October 1959, Benson made a trip to the Soviet Union. On his return, the secretary said that he was more convinced than ever of the "superiority of our system of privately owned family-sized farms, the profit system, freedom for the farmer to decide what to grow and market, and competitive markets."

Some conservative Republicans tried to persuade Benson to run for the presidential nomination in 1960. The secretary, however, did not want to remain in public life. Furthermore, it was clear that Vice President Nixon was the favorite to capture the nomination and that Benson was too unpopular in the party to be nominated. The Democrats were preparing the most comprehensive farm platform in history, which sought to capitalize on anti-Benson feeling, promising farmers full parity of income with the nonfarm population. Fearing the effect of Benson's legacy on the elections of 1960, several farm-belt members of the Republican National Committee got GOP National Chairman Sen. THRUSTON B. MORTON (R-Ky.) to ask for Benson's resignation in December 1959. Nixon tried to dissociate himself from Benson and successfully persuaded Eisenhower to moderate his final farm message to Congress. Yet the vice president had generally supported Benson, and his campaign platform advocated a continuation of the secretary's policies. Benson had hoped to campaign for the Nixon ticket, but the Republican nominee kept him on the sideline. Nonetheless, the secretary was able to get his views across by circulating a personal statement, "Where We Stand," at the GOP National Convention and with publication of his book, *Freedom to Farm*.

Benson returned to Salt Lake City in January 1961 to resume his work with the Council of Twelve Apostles. He continued his interest in agriculture, and in the mid-1960s he was a vigorous defender of the John Birch Society. After leaving Washington, however, Benson devoted most of his time to the church. In 1985, he became the 13th president, prophet, seer, and revelator of the Church of Jesus Christ of Latter-day Saints. He continued in that role even after becoming incapacitated in 1989; he was unable to speak and, at times, to recognize even friends and relatives. Death came at Benson's home in Salt Lake City on May 30, 1994.

—MSM

Benton, William (Burnett)

(1900–1973) *U.S. senator*

The descendant of a family that first settled in Connecticut during the 17th century, Benton was born in Minneapolis, Minn., on April 1, 1900. After service in the army during World War I, he entered Yale and received his degree in 1921. Benton turned down a Rhodes scholarship for a job as advertising copywriter with the George Batten agency in New York. During the 1920s, he rose in the advertising world, and in 1929, he helped found the firm of Benton and Bowles with his Yale schoolmate CHESTER BOWLES. The agency prospered in spite of, or some say because of, the Depression, pioneering in such fields as consumer surveys and sponsorship of soap operas.

In 1936, Benton left the advertising business to become vice president of the University of Chicago, then under the leadership of ROBERT HUTCHINS. Benton remained there for eight years, helping the university pioneer in the use of educational radio and movies. Benton also urged the University of Chicago to publish the *Encyclopædia Britannica* and provided the necessary working capital for the venture. In 1943, he became chairman of the *Encyclopædia Britannica*.

Benton served as assistant secretary of state from 1945 to 1947, supervising the State Department's overseas information program. At that post, he helped establish the United Nations Education, Scientific and Cultural Organization (UNESCO) and organized the Voice of America broadcasts. In 1949 Chester Bowles, then governor of Connecticut, appointed his former advertising partner to fill a Senate seat vacated by the retiring Raymond Baldwin. Benton won reelection to the remainder of the term in 1950 by a bare 1,100 margin. During his short career, Benton gained a reputation as one of the upper chamber's most liberal members. Moreover, he remained an amateur in a body that respected professionalism. He did not always follow the traditions and precedents of the Senate.

The freshman senator quickly emerged as a major opponent of Sen. JOSEPH R. MCCARTHY (R-Wis.). Angered at McCarthy's role in the Maryland senatorial campaign of 1950, during which McCarthy campaigned against Millard Tydings (D-Md.)—one of his most vocal critics—Benton began a personal crusade against the senator from Wisconsin. Benton regarded McCarthy's claims to knowledge of communist subversion as outright lies. Further, he was disgusted by McCarthy's denunciation of George Marshall as a communist sympathizer.

In August 1951, Benton presented a resolution asking for an investigation of McCarthy's actions in order to decide if he should be expelled. The following month, Benton presented a lengthy, biting indictment of the senator on the Senate floor. In words that even his lawyers thought libelous, he excoriated McCarthy for his charges against Marshall, saying that if the senator actually believed his "towering lies," Congress "might investigate the precedent of an expulsion proceeding against a senator thought to be of unsound mind." The Privileges and Elections Subcommittee reluctantly voted to investigate Benton's charges as well as McCarthy's countercharges. The senator from Wisconsin maintained that Benton had shielded security risks and had failed to report a $600 donation as part of his campaign funds. McCarthy refused to answer Benton's charges and testified before the panel only on his allegations against Benton.

In January 1953, the panel issued its report. It contained no recommendations but said that the probe raised questions about McCarthy's activities and charged that McCarthy had deliberately "set out to thwart the committee." The panel criticized Benton for accepting the $600 contribution but took no action. The Justice Department also cleared him of campaign irregularities.

While the congressional probe was in progress, Benton, hoping to bring his crusade to court, had in 1952 waived congressional immunity on his Senate speech against McCarthy. McCarthy then instituted a $2 million libel suit. The case, carried on during 1952 and 1953, proved inconclusive. In March 1954, McCarthy announced he had dropped the suit because his lawyers could find no one to testify that they believed Benton's charges. Benton's allies launched a campaign to gather signatures of "Believers"; 14,000 responded.

Benton lost his Senate seat in the election of 1952. Out of office, he criticized the Eisenhower administration. In 1956, he charged that the GOP had failed to keep a campaign pledge from 1952 to revise immigration restrictions and said the United States had been fortunate to "avoid disaster" under the Eisenhower administration's foreign policy.

Benton attempted a political comeback in 1958. During the spring, he ran for the Democratic senatorial nomination against his liberal friend Chester Bowles and conservative THOMAS DODD. The state party chairman, John Bailey, and Gov. ABRAHAM RIBICOFF supported Benton; they feared that Bowles's controversial views on foreign policy would weaken the ticket. At the convention in June, Benton and Bowles split the liberal vote, giving the nomination to Dodd. After his defeat, Benton returned to his business. From 1963 to 1968, he was the U.S. member of the executive board of UNESCO. He died in New York City on March 18, 1973.

—EWS

Bestor, Arthur E(ugene), Jr.

(1908–1994) *historian and educational critic*
Born in Chautauqua, N.Y., on September 20, 1908, Bestor received his B.A. and Ph.D. from Yale University in 1930 and 1938, respectively. He taught at Teachers College of Columbia University before moving to Stanford University and then the University of Illinois.

As a professional historian, he was perhaps best known for his early work on utopian communities of the 19th century. The American Historical Association awarded Bestor's book, *Backwoods Utopia*, the Albert J. Beveridge Prize in 1946. In the 1960s, he turned his scholarly attention to the field of constitutional history, specifically to the constitutional provisions for making war and peace and the role of the presidency in defining foreign relations. Bestor testified before several congressional committees regarding the intent of the framers of the Constitution with respect to the role of the Senate in the making of treaties.

He became best known by the general public, however, for his critiques of the American educational system. By the post–World War II era, progressive educational theories dominated public education in the United States. Progressive educational theories held that education should be "child-centered." Each child should learn at his or her own pace and by active engagement rather than by rote memorization. Further, each child should receive a basic liberal education and, beyond that, an education that would develop the child's particular abilities (including vocational training) and would allow the child to function effectively in society. By proposing to offer a basic liberal education for all and to meet the specific demands of each child, however, progressive education had promised more than it could deliver. By the mid-1950s, progressive education came under a withering attack. The year 1953 saw the publication of Albert Lynd's *Quackery in the Public Schools*, Robert Hutchins's *The Conflict in Education*, Paul Woodring's *Let's Talk Sense about Our Schools*, and Bestor's *Educational Wastelands*. Of these books, Bestor's was easily the most influential. He had first publicly criticized American education in the article "Liberal Education and a Liberal Nation," which appeared in *The American Scholar* in 1952. After that, he wrote several more harshly critical essays in *The New Republic*, *The Scientific Monthly*, and the *American Association of University Professors Bulletin*. His attack climaxed with the publication of *Educational Wastelands*. Two years later, Bestor came out with a revised and expanded version titled *The Restoration of Learning*.

In *Educational Wastelands*, Bestor denounced what he called a "retreat from learning." He maintained that the purpose of education was intellectual training, or "the deliberate cultivation of the ability to think." This, he argued, was best done through the academic disciplines, which evolved as systematic methods for solving problems. Modern schools, he contended, had subverted this purpose by separating the schools from scholarship and teacher training from the arts and sciences. He attacked progressive education's emphasis on life-adjustment as "a parody of education." To reform education, he called for the education of teachers to place a greater emphasis on training in subject matter and less on pedagogy. Bestor further advocated rigorous standards, greater attention to content, and a stronger commitment to liberal education.

When the Soviet Union launched *Sputnik* in 1957, many looked for something to blame for what they perceived as America's second-place standing in the space race. Progressive education became a favorite target, and Bestor's book gained a wide audience.

Bestor moved to the University of Washington in 1962 and taught there until his retirement in 1976, when he became professor emeritus. He was among the first constitutional scholars to call for the resignation of President RICHARD M. NIXON. Bestor died of lung cancer on December 13, 1994, in Seattle, Wash.

—MSM

Bethe, Hans A(lbrecht)
(1906–2005) *physicist*

The son of a distinguished physiologist, Bethe was born on July 2, 1906, in Strasbourg, Alsace-Lorraine. He was educated in Germany, where he received his doctorate in physics in 1928. He taught at various German universities, but because of his part-Jewish ancestry, fled the country in 1933. After a year in England, he settled in the United States and in 1937 joined the faculty of Cornell University, where his research into celestial energy aided scientists in developing the hydrogen bomb. From 1943 to 1946, Bethe worked on the Manhattan Project under the direction of J. ROBERT OPPENHEIMER. Although the project's primary goal was to build an atomic or fission bomb, work also proceeded on the development of the hydrogen bomb. The latter project was put aside in 1944 because of technical problems.

Bethe and Oppenheimer became leading spokesmen for "finite containment" in the postwar debate over continuation of research on the hydrogen bomb. These scientists believed that a large stockpile of American nuclear arms was necessary to contain Soviet aggression. However, they maintained that further technological advances would bring the supply of weapons to dangerous levels unwarranted by strategic considerations. Declaring that the Soviet Union was "largely imitative" in its atomic energy programs, they maintained that the United States could forego the hydrogen weapon without incurring a serious security risk. Instead, they suggested that work on the bomb be conducted only at a theoretical level. President HARRY S. TRUMAN rejected their advice, and, following recommendations of EDWARD TELLER, authorized production of the weapon in 1950. The outbreak of the Korean War changed Bethe's mind. Previously an outspoken opponent of the H-bomb, he agreed to devote himself to thermonuclear research at Cornell and Los Alamos. It was first exploded in November 1952.

During the early years of the Eisenhower administration, Bethe became a leading defender of Oppenheimer, who had been suspended from his post as an Atomic Energy Commission (AEC) consultant in 1953 as an alleged security risk. In part, this suspension was based on his failure to endorse a "crash" program for the development of the hydrogen bomb. When the suspension and subsequent hearings were publicized in April 1954, Bethe joined many outstanding scientists who declared their confidence in Oppenheimer and testified on his behalf. Following the AEC's decision not to reinstate Oppenheimer despite its finding that he was "loyal," Bethe released a statement by the American Physical Society denouncing the ruling as based on differences over nuclear weapons policy rather than on actual security risk.

In 1956, Bethe was appointed to the President's Science Advisory Committee (PSAC). Two years later, he became chairman of a special panel formed to study the possible effects of a nuclear test ban agreement between the United States and the Soviet Union and to research the efficiency of various methods of detecting atomic blasts. Bethe testified before the Senate Disarmament Subcommittee in April 1958 that the United States would gain "considerably" from a test ban if it included "a good inspection system with all the trimmings." He rejected Teller's testimony that the Soviet Union would benefit more than the United States and that adequate detection was impossible. Bethe maintained that if tests continued the USSR "will surely attain the same level of capability as we. . . . It is more advantageous to stop when . . . you are still ahead." He did, however, suggest that any ban include provisions for continued high-altitude tests to gain information on such explosions.

Bethe attended the 1958 U.S.-Soviet disarmament talks in Geneva, where the two delegations agreed that any test ban accord would include acoustical, radiological, seismic, and electromagnetic detection systems. A year later, in secret testimony before the Senate Disarmament Subcommittee, he recommended that a treaty also provide for satellite monitoring of explosions in outer space. The advocates of finite containment won a major victory in March 1960, when the United States and the USSR agreed to negotiate a ban on nuclear tests except for small underground ones considered unverifiable.

Bethe continued to serve as a presidential adviser during the Kennedy administration. Throughout his career, Bethe won many scientific honors, including the Max Planck Medal, West Germany's highest scientific honor, for his research on celestial energy. He received the AEC's Enrico Fermi Award in 1961 and the Nobel Prize in physics in 1967. Bethe continued to teach at Cornell until 1975.

Bethe died at his home in Ithaca, N.Y., on March 6, 2005.

—MDB

Bible, Alan D.

(1909–1988) *U.S. senator*

Bible was born on November 20, 1909, in Lovelock, Nev. He graduated from the University of Nevada at Reno in 1930 and from Georgetown University Law School in 1934. Bible gained admission to the Nevada bar in 1935 and, for the next two decades, engaged in the private practice of law when not holding public office. A protege and law partner of Sen. PATRICK MCCARRAN (D-Nev.), Bible served as district attorney of Storey County from 1935 to 1938 and, in the last year, received an appointment as deputy attorney general of Nevada. After serving as state attorney from 1942 to 1950, he resumed the private practice of law. When McCarran died in 1954, Bible was elected to serve out the remainder of his term. Bible won reelection to a full term in 1956.

During the Eisenhower administration, Bible voted as a moderately conservative Democrat, backing the party leadership in the Senate. He supported the Civil Rights Act of 1957 but only after voting for the elimination of a provision authorizing the attorney general to institute civil action for preventive relief in civil rights cases. He also voted to remove a similar enforcement provision from the Civil Rights Act of 1960. By the late 1950s, Bible was identified by *Congressional Quarterly* as one of a small number of Northern and Western Democrats who voted more than half the time with the conservative coalition of southern Democrats and Republicans.

As a representative of a state heavily dependent on mining, Bible continued McCarran's efforts to raise tariffs on lead and zinc. Calling attention to the depressed condition of the domestic minerals industry, Bible advocated the establishment of a national minerals policy to protect the industry from foreign competition. However, the administration feared that heavy tariff increases would hurt foreign countries whose economies the United States wished to aid. When Eisenhower presented a minerals plan in 1957 providing for low sliding-scale import taxes on lead and zinc and limiting government assistance for mining exploration, Bible called it a "joke." Eisenhower imposed import quotas on lead and zinc in 1958. Many regarded the move as a trade-off in exchange for the support of Western congressmen for the administration's reciprocal trade program. Bible never succeeded in getting the comprehensive subsidy program he had long desired.

During the Kennedy and Johnson administrations, Bible's numerous committee assignments attested to his great influence. He sat on the Appropriations, Interior and Insular Affairs, and Select Small Business Committees, as well as the Special Committee on Aging and the Democratic Steering Committee. He chaired the District of Columbia Committee from 1957 to 1968. Bible's record of support for the liberal legislation of the 1960s was mixed. He served in the Senate until his resignation in 1974, after which he returned to his law practice. He died in Auburn, Calif., on September 12, 1988.

—TLH

Biemiller, Andrew J(ohn)

(1906–1982) *union leader*

Born of Quaker parents on July 23, 1906, in Sandusky, Ohio, Andrew Biemiller graduated from Cornell University in 1926. After doing graduate work at the University of Pennsylvania, he taught history, specializing in the British trade union movement, at Syracuse University and the University of Pennsylvania. In 1932, he became a reporter for the *Milwaukee Leader.* From 1932 to 1942, he was labor-relations counselor and organizer for the Milwaukee Federation of Trade Councils and the Wisconsin State Federation of Labor. Biemiller won election as a Socialist-Progressive to the Wisconsin legislature in 1936, and served there until 1942, when he became assistant to the vice chairman for labor production of the War Production Board. Elected to Congress as a Democrat from Wisconsin's fifth district in 1944, he served from 1945 to 1946 and from 1949 to 1950. He was defeated for reelection in that traditionally Republican state in 1946 and 1952. Between terms, he worked as director of political education for the upholsterers' union.

During 1951 and 1952, Biemiller was a special assistant to the secretary of the interior and a public-relations counselor in Washington, D.C. In 1953, he joined the American Federation of Labor (AFL) as a legislative lobbyist. There he helped AFL president GEORGE MEANY negotiate the merger with the Congress of Industrial Organizations (CIO) that led to the creation of the AFL-CIO in 1955. Biemiller became director of the organization's department of legislation the following year.

As the AFL-CIO's chief lobbyist, Biemiller often opposed measures supported by the Eisenhower administration on Capitol Hill. In 1957, he challenged Eisenhower's minimum-wage bill, which extended coverage to 2.5 million additional workers, as "too little too late." Instead, he backed Rep. A. B. Kelley's (D-Pa.) unsuccessful measure that would have extended coverage to 9.7 million workers and raised the hourly wage to $1.25. Biemiller and the AFL-CIO favored Medicare financed through Social Security rather than Eisenhower's health reinsurance proposals, and he worked with House Speaker SAM RAYBURN (D-Tex.) to defeat the administration's program in 1957. The following year, he supported increased school construction as a means of combating the recession and attacked Eisenhower's failure to mention the proposal in his anti-recession message to Congress. In 1959 he called Eisenhower's four-year, $1-billion housing program inadequate and condemned the president's lack of action on unemployment. That year Biemiller focused his attention on defeating the Landrum-Griffin bill, which contained provisions limiting secondary boycotts. Despite Biemiller's

efforts, Eisenhower signed the measure into law in September.

During the 1950s, Biemiller became involved in the question of atomic energy control. He was chairman of the AFL-CIO's committee on atomic energy and a member of the labor-management advisory committee of the Atomic Energy Commission. Testifying before a congressional committee in May 1954, he supported Eisenhower's "Atoms-for-Peace" plan and recommended that Asian nations be included within its provisions for atomic energy development under control of the United Nations. Biemiller was concerned with the possibility of private monopolies of nuclear power and told Congress in 1955 that the government should prohibit them. The following year, he warned against the hazards of nuclear reactors and charged that the Atomic Energy Commission had underestimated their dangers and muzzled press reports of accidents.

Disappointed at Sen. LYNDON B. JOHNSON's (D-Tex.) failure to oppose the Landrum-Griffin Act, Biemiller supported Sen. JOHN F. KENNEDY (D-Mass.) for the Democratic presidential nomination in 1960. Biemiller maintained close contact with the White House during the Kennedy and Johnson administrations. He testified on Capitol Hill in support of Kennedy's manpower retraining, education, and foreign aid bills and lobbied for Johnson's Great Society legislation. Biemiller also supported the administration's policy in Vietnam. During the Nixon administration, he played an important role in blocking the appointment of southern judges Clement F. Haynsworth and G. Harrold Carswell to the U.S. Supreme Court. Biemiller left the AFL-CIO in 1979 and resided in Bethesda, Md., until his death there on April 3, 1982.

—AES

Bissell, Richard M(ervin), Jr.

(1909–1994) *special assistant to the director of Central Intelligence; deputy director of plans, Central Intelligence Agency*

Born in Hartford, Conn., on September 18, 1909, Bissell attended the elite Groton School and then went to Yale, where he graduated in 1932. From 1932 to 1933, he studied at the London School of

Economics. He then returned to Yale as an instructor and eventually assistant professor in economics. Bissell received his Ph.D. from that university in 1939. He was appointed assistant administrator of the Marshall Plan in 1948 and served there until 1951.

In 1954, Bissell joined the Central Intelligence Agency (CIA) as special assistant to Director ALLEN W. DULLES. Bissell was one of the few high-ranking members of the agency who had no background in wartime intelligence work. His major responsibility was to develop techniques for obtaining information on the strategic capabilities of the Soviet Union. He sided with Dulles in advocating the use of modern technology rather than operatives to gather data. He conceived and supervised the program of U-2 flights over the Soviet Union and helped develop the SR-71 high-altitude surveillance plane. He was also an early advocate of spy satellites. Bissell's U-2 program became public in May 1960, when pilot FRANCIS GARY POWERS was shot down over Soviet territory. The United States defended the mission and announced that it would continue overflights to prevent communist expansion.

In 1959, Bissell became deputy director for plans, responsible for coordinating covert operations. According to the report of the Senate Select Committee on Intelligence Activities, issued in 1975, at this post Bissell supervised plans to assassinate Congolese leader Patrice Lumumba as well as Cuban Premier Fidel Castro and his brother Raul. In September 1960, a CIA scientist, Joseph Scheider (whose real name was Sidney Gottlieb), acting on orders from Bissell, obtained poison and hypodermic needles from army stockpiles and flew to Leopoldville with instructions for CIA station officer Victor Hedgman to kill Lumumba. When this failed, Bissell asked a senior CIA officer, Michael Mulroney, to undertake the assignment. Mulroney refused to assassinate Lumumba, but he flew to the Congo and got two other CIA agents to attempt the assassination. Before the CIA could make further attempts, however, Lumumba was killed by Congolese opponents.

According to the Senate Select Committee's report, during the summer of 1960 Bissell sanctioned attempts on the lives of Raul and Fidel Castro. The decision to kill Raul was reversed before action could be taken, but an attempt was authorized on the life of the premier. The plan involved CIA cooperation with organized-crime leaders Sam Giancana and John Roselli, who were given money, poison, and electronic gear to give to hired assassins. Although the plan was never put into operation, the CIA did make several attempts on Castro's life during the early 1960s.

The origin of the orders to assassinate Lumumba and Castro was never clearly determined, because the system of executive command in the agency was purposefully ambiguous to permit "plausible denial." Bissell testified in 1975 that he had assumed he had the authority of Eisenhower and Dulles to assassinate Lumumba. He also said he had interpreted Dulles's original order to eliminate Castro as including possible assassination. However, Bissell also testified that he had not informed Eisenhower of the plot to kill Castro and that, to his knowledge, neither did Dulles. Bissell did say that he believed Dulles would have informed the president in an "oblique" way but admitted that this was "pure personal opinion." The committee was never able to discover Dulles's role in the action. It did conclude that Bissell had exceeded his delegated authority by engaging in the projects.

On March 17, 1960, Eisenhower ordered the CIA to help unify opposition to the Castro regime. Dulles turned the task over to Bissell, who proposed to train guerrillas in Guatemala to infiltrate Cuba and organize a popular revolt. When infiltration proved unworkable, Bissell proposed a full-scale invasion of the island by refugees trained and armed by the United States. Bissell organized the project in Guatemala. The plan called for not only the development of camps for training guerrillas but also the construction of airstrips. These would provide a base for CIA planes, which would drop arms to guerrillas already in Cuba and provide cover for the invasion. Eisenhower authorized only the formation and training of the exile force. He reserved the decision on whether or how to use it. Above all, Eisenhower emphasized the importance of finding a Cuban leader who could unify the opposition forces and form a credible government in exile. Without a proper political foundation, he believed, the enterprise was worthless. When Eisenhower left office, he remained skeptical about the force and the political preconditions necessary for its use. Nevertheless, he passed the exile force on to his successor.

The new president, JOHN F. KENNEDY, gave approval for the invasion, which took place on April 17, 1961. The operation was an abysmal failure; the exile force was defeated by April 19.

Bissell resigned in February 1962. Shortly thereafter he became head of the Institute for Defense Analysis. He remained there until 1964, when he became an executive of the United Aircraft Corp. Beginning in 1974, he worked as a self-employed management consultant. He died in Farmington, Conn., on February 7, 1994.

—MSM

Black, Eugene R(obert)

(1898–1992) *president, International Bank for Reconstruction and Development*

Born on May 1, 1898, in Atlanta, Ga., and raised there, Black received his B.A. from the University of Georgia in 1918 and served as an ensign in the navy during World War I. Black joined an Atlanta-based New York investment house in 1931 and two years later associated himself with the Chase National Bank of New York, where he became an expert on the bond market. From 1933 to 1947, Black was involved in Chase's international activities. He briefly served as undersecretary of the treasury in 1936. In 1947 President HARRY S. TRUMAN appointed Black an executive director of the International Bank for Reconstruction and Development (World Bank). The appointment of the conservative Black was welcomed by Wall Street, which disapproved of the bank's earlier liberal loan policies. Black become president of the World Bank in 1949.

During Black's presidency, the bank turned from an emphasis on European redevelopment loans to an emphasis on projects in underdeveloped nations. He emphasized education and the development of technological knowledge in directing the bank's investments. Under Black, the bank tried to avoid high-risk projects and instead opted for the development of "economies of scale," such as transportation facilities, power installations, irrigation, and land reclamation projects—prerequisites

for increased productivity in many sectors of the borrowing nations's economies. To prevent political pressures, the bank usually made loans only where they could be entrusted to a quasi-autonomous authority, not to the government of a recipient nation.

Black became deeply involved in the negotiations for financing the Aswan High Dam in 1955–56. The bank did a study in 1953–54 showing that the project was both technically sound and economically feasible. Black reported directly to President DWIGHT D. EISENHOWER that the construction of the dam was Egypt's highest economic and social priority and recommended joint financing by Great Britain, the United States, and the World Bank. He then attempted to counter President Gamal Abdel Nasser's fear that the agreement would infringe upon Egypt's sovereignty and to convince him to accept the plan. Black also had to persuade Secretary of State JOHN FOSTER DULLES to agree to the measure, despite Egypt's increasing closeness to the USSR.

Black's task became more difficult in May 1956, when Nasser's recognition of Communist China and rumors of Egypt's increased arms and financial dealings with the Russians further cooled the administration's enthusiasm for the project. He continued to promote the proposal, cautioning that the United States would lose a public relations battle and push Nasser into the arms of the Soviets if it refused aid. Nevertheless, Dulles decided to withdraw American support for the project in July.

Black also served as a mediator in disputes arising from the Suez conflict of 1956. In December 1958, he left for Cairo to negotiate a settlement of the British-French claims arising from Nasser's 1956 nationalization of the canal. Black's efforts ended triumphantly in February 1959 with the signing of an Anglo-Egyptian accord outlining terms of compensation to British property owners.

The Kennedy administration also used Black as mediator in the conflict between India and Pakistan in 1962. In 1963, Black retired from the World Bank but maintained close contacts with the business community. That year he served on the Clay Committee, formed to study the nation's foreign aid program. During the Johnson administration, Black served as presidential adviser on Southeast Asian economic affairs. He died on February 20, 1992, in Southampton, N.Y.

—ACD

Black, Hugo L(afayette)

(1886–1971) *associate justice, U.S. Supreme Court*

Born on February 27, 1886, in Harlan, Ala., and raised in rural Clay Co., Ala., Hugo Black received a two-year undergraduate law degree from the University of Alabama in 1906. He built a successful law practice in Birmingham and held several local offices there before winning election to the U.S. Senate in 1926. Reelected in 1932, Black quickly became an outspoken supporter of the New Deal. President Franklin D. Roosevelt selected the Alabaman as his first nominee to the Supreme Court in August 1937. Shortly after the Senate confirmed Black's appointment on August 17, a Pittsburgh newspaper published evidence of his membership in the Ku Klux Klan. The furor died down only after Black made a brief radio speech on October 1 stating that he had joined the Klan in 1923 but had resigned from it in 1925.

On the bench, Black favored expanded government power over the economy, and he voted to sustain the New Deal's economic and social welfare legislation. However, he opposed government intrusion on individual liberties guaranteed by the Bill of Rights and gradually emerged as one of the foremost defenders of civil liberties on the Court. Black insisted that the provisions of the Bill of Rights were absolutes that government could not abridge. He also contended that the Fourteenth Amendment had made the first eight Amendments fully applicable to the states as well as the federal government. The justice gave a special position to the First Amendment, for he believed the rights of free speech, press, and assembly formed the foundation of a free government. He argued that the amendment unequivocally barred all government interference with individual thought and expression. This led Black to oppose restrictions on obscenity, "subversive" speech, and even libel. Black was especially ardent in his defense of the First Amendment during the McCarthy era, when a majority of the Court often restricted the rights of free speech and association in loyalty-secu-

rity cases. In a famous dissent in the *Dennis* case (1951), for example, Black asserted that the Smith Act, which made it illegal to teach or advocate violent overthrow of the U.S. government, violated the First Amendment.

During the Eisenhower years, Black continued to express his absolutist views of the First Amendment. When the Court reconsidered the Smith Act in June 1957 and interpreted it in a manner that gave greater scope to freedom of speech but did not declare the act unconstitutional, Black wrote a separate opinion. He again argued that the statute was unconstitutional under the First Amendment.

The justice also opposed legislative investigations into subversion that probed individual beliefs. He repeatedly voted to overturn the contempt convictions of witnesses who refused to answer committee questions about their political ideas and associations. In June 1957, he joined the majority in two decisions setting limits on congressional and state investigative powers (*Watkins v. U.S.* and *Sweezy v. New Hampshire*) and dissented when the Court retreated from this position in two cases decided in June 1959 (*Uphaus v. Wyman* and *Barenblatt v. U.S.*). In his dissenting opinion in *Barenblatt*, Black contended that the chief aim of the House Un-American Activities Committee was to expose and try witnesses who were suspected communists and to punish them by humiliation and public scorn. As a result, the committee was not only violating individual rights of free association and expression, but was also illegally exercising a judicial function that the Constitution had assigned to the courts.

Justice Black spoke for the majority in two cases, decided in May 1957, that placed limits on the legal profession's power to regulate admission to its ranks. He overturned the refusal of state bar associations to admit candidates with actual or alleged communist backgrounds as a denial of due process of law.

Black's absolutist views generally led him to give wide scope to the constitutional rights guaranteed to those accused of crimes. He continually insisted that the states as well as the federal government must supply counsel to all indigent criminal defendants. In April 1956, he ruled that the states must also supply an indigent defendant with a free trial transcript if it was essential to appeal a criminal conviction. Black believed the Fifth Amendment's privilege against self-incrimination was beyond the reach of government. He dissented in February 1954, when the Court upheld a state gambling conviction, because he thought the defendant's Fifth Amendment rights had been denied. Black also wrote the majority opinion in a well-known case, *Thompson v. City of Louisville* (1960), which held it a denial of due process to convict an individual of loitering or vagrancy when there was no evidence to support the charge.

In the 1950s and 1960s, Black gave his full support to the Court's rulings overturning racial segregation and discrimination. He voted with the majority in May 1954 to hold segregated public schools unconstitutional *(Brown v. Board of Education)* and wrote the majority opinion in *Boynton v. Virginia* (1960), which extended the Court's earlier prohibition against segregation in interstate travel to cover accommodations in terminals used in interstate travel.

For much of his career, Black's literalist interpretation of the Bill of Rights led him in the direction of liberal activism. The same approach, however, could lead to different conclusions. For example, the Fourth Amendment prohibited only "unreasonable" searches and seizures, and Black was reluctant to restrict the power of the government on a term so open to interpretation, as can be seen in his vacillation on the exclusionary rule. He also balked at the creation of new rights. When a majority of the Court found a right of marital privacy in the "penumbras" of the first ten Amendments (*Griswold v. Connecticut,* 1965), Black dissented vigorously. Moreover, despite his absolutist reading of the First Amendment's protection of free speech, Black opposed extending that protection to symbolic speech, such as picketing.

One of the most controversial members of the Court, Black's commitment to judicial activism led him into sometimes bitter and even personal conflict with justices committed to judicial restraint, most notably FELIX FRANKFURTER and ROBERT JACKSON. Black's consistent adherence to his belief that the Court should turn to notions of reasonableness or social utility only when the text and historical context of the Constitution failed to resolve an issue made him an intellectual leader on the Court. He thus became an important figure in the effort to balance claims for an active judicial review with those of majoritarian democracy.

When he died in Bethesda, Md., on September 25, 1971, he was widely praised as a defender of civil liberties when such a position was rejected by a majority of his brethren on the Court and unpopular with the public. Whether they agreed or disagreed with Black, no one could question his influence on constitutional law.

—MSM

Blake, Eugene Carson
(1906–1985) *president, National Council of Churches of Christ in the U.S.A.*

The son of a Presbyterian elder, Eugene Carson Blake was born in St. Louis, Mo., on November 7, 1906. He received his A.B. degree with honors in philosophy at Princeton in 1928. After studying at Edinburgh University, he was awarded a Th.B. from Princeton Theological Seminary in 1932. During the next two decades, Blake held pulpits in Albany, N.Y., Pasadena, Calif., and New York, N.Y. In 1948 he was a delegate to the conference establishing the World Council of Churches, an organization founded to foster cooperation between 163 different Protestant and Orthodox denominations. Two years later, Blake helped form the National Council of Churches of Christ in the U.S.A. (NCCC), an organization of Protestant and Orthodox churches formed to promote ecumenism and coordinate church welfare programs, social research, and charity. He was elected stated elder of the United Presbyterian Church in the U.S. in 1951 and president of the NCCC in 1954.

During the 1950s, Blake was in the forefront of what church historian Harvey Cox called the "New Breed" of clergymen, social activists who led the struggle for civil liberties and civil rights. In December 1953, the General Council of the United Presbyterian Church in the U.S. sent a letter to its congregations decrying "assaults on basic human rights" in the United States. Defending the message, Blake pointed to two serious threats to religion in America: "anti-intellectualism . . . which tends to blur all distinctions except those of white and black" and the forces of "totalitarianism, communism, and fascism."

The following year, Black chaired a subcommittee of the NCCC that called for the adoption of procedural reforms in congressional investigating committees to protect individual freedom.

In February 1960, it was revealed that an air force training manual contained charges that the NCCC was communist infiltrated. Six Protestant leaders, including Blake, demanded apologies from Air Force Secretary Dudley C. Sharp and Rep. FRANCIS E. WALTER (D-Pa.), chairman of the House Un-American Activities Committee (HUAC). They also demanded assurances that the manual containing the allegations would not be reissued. Walter offered to let the six testify before the committee on the accuracy of the charges, but they refused on the grounds that HUAC was not the proper forum for discussing their protest. They maintained that there were other committees charged with the oversight of government operations. The manual was withdrawn without any determination as to the charges.

Blake was also active in the growing Civil Rights movement. In 1956, he sent a telegram to the Rev. Solomon S. Seay in Montgomery, Ala., assuring African Americans that he supported the Montgomery bus boycott. Two years later, he issued a statement declaring that desegregation in the South should be enforced "with troops and tanks if necessary." The view was rejected by Philip Howerton, moderator of the Presbyterian Church in the U.S. (Southern Presbyterian Church), who warned that force would result in "nothing but chaos."

In 1960, Blake was one of 13 prominent Protestant clergymen who, in an open letter to fellow pastors, condemned the use of anti-Catholicism in the presidential primary campaign.

Blake maintained his involvement in civil rights throughout the 1960s and continued to champion the union of Protestant denominations. He also emerged as a prominent opponent of the Vietnam War. Blake became secretary-general of the World Council of Churches in 1966 and served at that post until 1972. He died in Stanford, Conn., on July 31, 1985.

—SY

Blatnik, John A(nton)
(1911–1991) *U.S. congressman*

Blatnik was born in Chisholm, Minn., on August 17, 1911. After graduating from Chisholm High School, he taught in a one-room rural school before attending State Teachers College, where he earned a bachelor of education. He taught high school chemistry in Chisholm for two years and became assistant superintendent of schools of Saint Louis Co. from 1939 to 1941. He won election to the state senate in 1940 and served from 1941 to 1947. Overlapping with his two terms in the state senate, he served in the U.S. Army Air Corps and the Office of Strategic Services from August 1942 to 1946.

Blatnik won election as a Democrat to Congress in 1946 from the ore-mining region of northeastern Minnesota. In the House, he supported the labor and civil rights legislation of the Truman and Eisenhower administrations. A descendant of Slovene immigrants, Blatnik was particularly concerned with the loss of American influence in Yugoslavia following World War II. He denounced Eisenhower's foreign policy, describing it as based "almost entirely on armament" rather than economic aid and cultural exchange.

By the early 1950s, the high-grade iron ores that had made Blatnik's district the iron capital of the world were becoming seriously depleted, and steel manufacturers were turning to cheaper foreign sources. In an effort to counteract this trend, Blatnik fought for the long-postponed Saint Lawrence Seaway Project, which he viewed as a means of opening the isolated region to industrial development. In 1954, Congress finally authorized the construction of a deep-water navigation channel in the Saint Lawrence River, making it possible for large ships to sail from the Atlantic Ocean to Duluth, Minn., at the western end of the Great Lakes.

During the Eisenhower years, Blatnik also became known as a crusader for clean water legislation. As chairman of the Public Works Committee's Rivers and Harbors Subcommittee, he sponsored the Federal Water Pollution Control Act of 1956, steering it skillfully through the pro-industry committee and a hostile Congress. The act authorized federal grants for the construction of local sewage treatment plants and established a Water Pollution

Control Advisory Board within the Public Health Service. It gave federal investigators power to force polluting industries or cities to clean up rivers and streams, but only in cases of interstate pollution. Moreover, they were not given the legal right to inspect industrial plants or municipal waste treatment facilities. Although these jurisdictional limitations weakened the law, the act was a landmark in the fight for clean water. Through 1961, Blatnik was the principal sponsor of congressional efforts to strengthen the federal program.

During the 1960s, Blatnik maintained his liberal record on most issues, but he ceased to be a vigorous proponent of pollution-control legislation. The reasons for this about-face were not clear, but critics suggested that it resulted from the Federal Water Quality Control Administration's attempt to stop the Reserve Mining Co., the largest employer in Blatnik's district, from dumping industrial wastes into Lake Superior. Blatnik retired from Congress in 1974. After leaving Congress, Blatnik worked as a consultant both to the shipping industry and on environmental and economic development. He died in Forest Heights, Md., on December 17, 1991.

—TLH

Blossom, Virgil T(racey)

(1906–1965) *superintendent of schools, Little Rock, Ark.*

Born in Brookfield, Mo., in 1907, Blossom graduated from Missouri Valley College, which he attended on an athletic scholarship. Subsequently, he earned an M.S. from the University of Arkansas and attended classes at Northwestern University. In 1935 he took a job as a teacher and athletic director at Okmolgee, Oklahoma. Three years later, he became principal of Fayetteville High School in Arkansas. Blossom became Fayetteville's superintendent of schools in 1942. In the spring of 1953, he became superintendent of schools in Little Rock, Arkansas, while continuing to hold his position in Fayetteville. Following the Supreme Court's ruling in May 1954 that declared segregated schools unconstitutional, Blossom desegregated Fayetteville without incident. The following September, he took up his post in Little Rock on a full-time basis. He pursued his duties so energeti-

cally that in 1955 Little Rock citizens named him "Man of the Year."

While Blossom did not welcome desegregation, he thought it best to comply with the Supreme Court's ruling. During the summer of 1954, he developed a plan to desegregate public schools in Little Rock. At that time, Little Rock had only one high school for whites and one for blacks, but two new schools were under construction. Horace Mann, in the east, was being built in a predominantly black area. The other new school, Hall, was located in the affluent, predominantly white, western suburbs. At the time construction of the new schools began, the school board intended that Horace Mann would become the city's black high school. The old black high school would become a black junior high. Central, up to that time the only white school, would continue to serve whites, as would Hall.

Blossom's plan called for desegregation to begin at the high school level. After monitoring progress at the high schools, the school board would integrate the junior high schools. The final step would be the integration of elementary schools. In May 1955, the school board adopted a revised version of Blossom's plan. Integration would begin at the high school level in 1957 and then only at Central High, which drew from a predominantly working-class population. Integration would come to the junior high schools in 1959 or 1960, then, finally, to the elementary schools. The plan set no specific date for desegregation of the elementary schools but suggested 1963. The plan also allowed students to transfer out of schools in which their race would be a minority. This ensured that Horace Mann would have no white students.

The NAACP challenged the plan in court, but Judge John E. Miller ruled that the Blossom plan met the Supreme Court's requirement of a "prompt and reasonable start." At this point, it seemed reasonable to expect that desegregation would begin with little or no trouble. The school board had voluntarily developed a plan for desegregation, and a federal court had endorsed it. Moreover, the governor, ORVAL FAUBUS, had avoided direct involvement with the issue of desegregation. He had condoned the desegregation of public colleges and universities in Arkansas and had not intervened in Hoxie or Fayetteville. Facing reelection and a challenge from a segregationist opponent, however, Faubus moved to a tougher position on desegregation in 1956. Faubus won reelection, and voters passed three ballot measures designed to resist desegregation. Nevertheless, in March 1957, moderates defeated their segregationist opponents in elections to Little Rock's school board.

Throughout the summer of 1957, however, segregationist opposition grew. After some maneuvering in court, Faubus went on statewide television on September 2. His speech blamed Blossom for "forcing" desegregation on "the people." Further, until the legal issues were resolved, no black students would be admitted to white schools, and units of the Arkansas National Guard would enforce the order. The school board then lost its nerve and asked a federal judge to delay desegregation; the judge denied the request. On September 4, the National Guard blocked the entry of the black students. The school board again petitioned the court for delay and was again rejected. Moreover, the court issued a restraining order against Faubus, ordering him not to interfere with the desegregation of Central High. A meeting between President DWIGHT D. EISENHOWER and Faubus failed to resolve the situation. On September 20, the federal district court ruled that Faubus had acted unlawfully in obstructing the order to proceed with integration and enjoined the governor and officers of the National Guard from preventing the black students from attending classes. Faubus withdrew the guard.

The black students attended Central High on September 23, but rioting outside the school led school authorities to withdraw the students for their own safety. That night, the president went on national television and issued a proclamation commanding all persons obstructing the court orders to cease and desist. The next morning, a mob again gathered at Central High. Eisenhower nationalized the guard and sent 500 paratroopers of the 101st Airborne to ensure compliance with the court's orders. The black students attended Central High for the remainder of that year under the protection of the 101st and then the Arkansas National Guard.

Blossom remained the target of local extremists. He was nearly assassinated by a sniper and had his telephone disconnected to stem the tide of threatening calls. In September 1958, after failing to get a court order to halt further integration, Gov. Faubus closed Little Rock's secondary schools completely. Five of the six school board members friendly to Blossom resigned. Newly elected segregationists then fired the superintendent. Blossom moved to San Antonio, Tex., where he guided a rural school district through a period of expansion. He died of a heart attack in San Antonio, Tex., on January 15, 1965.

—MSM

Blough, Roger M(iles)
(1904–1985) *chairman, United States Steel Corporation*

The son of a truck farmer, Roger Blough was born on January 19, 1904, in Riverside, Pa. After graduating from Susquehanna University in 1925, he taught history at the high school in Hawley, Pa., for three years before deciding to go to law school. He graduated from Yale Law School in 1931 and joined the Wall Street firm of White and Case. Blough's association with U.S. Steel began in the late 1930s, when he served as an associate counsel for the corporation during a congressional investigation of the steel industry. Blough left White and Case in 1942 to become general solicitor for U.S. Steel. In 1951, he became executive vice president and a member of the board of directors. A close confidante of U.S. Steel's president, BENJAMIN FAIRLESS, Blough continued his ascent in the firm's hierarchy. When President HARRY S. TRUMAN seized the steel mills in 1952, Blough helped to plead the corporation's case before the U.S. Supreme Court. The Court ruled Truman's action unconstitutional, and the mills were returned to their owners. After the death of the company's general counsel in July 1953, Blough assumed the position, and, upon the retirement of Fairless in 1955, Blough became chairman of the board of directors and chief executive officer.

The world's largest steel-making enterprise and the producer of one-third of the nation's total steel capacity, U.S. Steel had total sales of $3.5 billion at the time of Blough's ascendancy. After mid-decade, however, U.S. Steel, along with the rest of the industry, was afflicted by a slowdown in orders for military hardware, autos, business construction and, after 1957, exports.

As chairman of the corporation, Blough supervised negotiations with the United Steel Workers of America (USW). In 1955, talks were held under the wage-reopening clause of a two-year pact signed in 1954. At midnight on June 30, steelworkers went on strike, but the next morning, Blough hastened to sign an agreement granting an average hourly wage increase of 15 cents. The contract also provided the union with protection against the unilateral introduction of labor-saving machinery by the company.

With the basic steel agreements due to expire in 1959, U.S. Steel conducted a massive public relations and advertising campaign that blamed the demands of the USW for inflation. The union, on the other hand, contended that the company enjoyed high profits as a result of several price increases since 1955, which outstripped by far increases in labor costs. The USW also insisted on a voice in determining the pace of technological change, since the company's closure of older plants in 1957 and 1958 resulted in layoffs for thousands of steel workers. Blough countered that the corporation had to hold the line on union demands in order to remain competitive.

The workers went out on a strike that lasted 116 days and required Eisenhower's intervention to settle. The contract, finally signed in January 1960, granted workers raises and other benefits costing 41 cents an hour over a 2½ year period. The benefits included increased and broadened pensions, continued supplemental unemployment benefits, and creation of a human relations research committee to study wage adjustment, job classification, incentive pay, and other problems. Blough maintained that the cost of the new wage package would be "well over one billion dollars."

In 1962, Blough engaged in a major confrontation with the Kennedy administration when he sought to increase steel prices. That year, the steel industry and the USW reached an agreement for a modest increase in wages, which pleased the Kennedy administration. Blough maintained that the cost of domestic labor was rising more rapidly than that of foreign producers. Moreover, the corpora-

tion's profits declined from $304.2 million in 1960 to $190.2 million in 1961. This, argued Blough, threatened the ability of the company to reinvest and to modernize. Blough therefore announced an increase of 3.5 percent in the price of steel. After a campaign of presidential pressure to roll back the price of steel, Inland Steel announced that it would not increase prices. Kaiser Steel also announced that it would not increase prices. Bethlehem Steel, the second largest producer in the country, then rescinded its price increase. U.S. Steel had no choice but to rescind its increase.

Blough retired from U.S. Steel in 1969. During his tenure as chairman of the board, his company's share of the sale of domestic steel declined from 30 percent to 25 percent. Moreover, imported steel increased to 16 percent of the market by 1968.

Immediately after leaving U.S. Steel, Blough returned to White and Case. He remained a partner in the firm until 1976. He died in Hawley, Pa., on October 8, 1985.

—MSM

Boggs, J(ames) Caleb

(1909–1993) *governor of Delaware*

The product of an old, established Delaware family, Boggs was born in Cheswold, Del., on May 15, 1909. He received an A.B. degree from the University of Delaware in 1931 and an LL.B. from Georgetown University six years later. He set up law practice in Dover, Del., and later helped found the Wilmington firm of Logan, Duffy and Boggs. Following service in the Army during World War II. Boggs was elected to Congress as a Republican in 1946. On Capitol Hill, he took a stand against what he termed the "waste and duplication" of the Truman administration, which he thought was "drifting towards socialism." He won reelection twice.

In November 1952, Boggs defeated the Democratic incumbent, Elbert N. Carvel, to win election as Delaware's governor. He continued to maintain his position against the growth of federal power and increased spending. During his first year in office, Boggs signed a bill requiring all communists and members of organizations appearing on the attorney general's subversive list who lived in or passed through Delaware to register with the state police.

The law proved unenforceable. In 1953, Boggs attempted civil service reform but was blocked by the state legislature. Three years later, he had considerably more success in getting through a program of extensive executive and judicial reform, school consolidation, and increased salaries for teachers.

Boggs received national attention in 1954, when he requested that Delaware's Board of Education comply with the Supreme Court's *Brown* decision outlawing segregation in public schools. His action made Delaware the scene of the first of many confrontations over desegregation. Although integration proceeded smoothly in the northern, industrialized sector of the state, it met with stiff resistance in the southern section. In September Boggs was forced to intervene when a plan bringing 11 black children into an all-white school in Milford, Del., resulted in a much publicized boycott. He temporarily halted implementation of the plan and ordered the arrest of Bryant W. Bowles, self-styled founder and president of the National Association for the Advancement of White People, whom Boggs alleged had come to the state specifically to organize the boycott. The governor justified the arrest as being directed against "organized mob rule and mass hysteria," though the state supreme court subsequently declared Bowles innocent.

Boggs was reelected governor in 1956, and in 1959 he served as chairman of the U.S. Governors Conference. He won election to the U.S. Senate in 1960, where he compiled a generally conservative record, although he was a strong supporter of the Civil Rights Act of 1964. In 1965, Boggs was appointed to the White House Conference on International Cooperation and in the same year joined Sen. MIKE MANSFIELD (D-Mont.) on a fact-finding tour of Asia, which resulted in a plea for a negotiated settlement in Vietnam. Boggs was defeated for reelection in 1972 and returned to his old law firm. He died in Wilmington, Del., on March 26, 1993.

—JPL

Boggs, T(homas) Hale
(1914–1972) *U.S. congressman*

The descendant of a colonial family, Boggs was born on February 15, 1914, in Long Beach, Miss. He received a law degree from Tulane University in 1937 and then entered private practice in New Orleans. In 1939, he helped form the People's League of Independent Voters, an organization of business and professional men established to combat the state's Democratic machine. In the 1940 Democratic House primary, Boggs ran successfully against the machine-backed incumbent and went on to win the general election. However, the former incumbent defeated him in the Democratic primary in 1942. Boggs joined the U.S. Naval Reserve in November 1943.

In 1946, Boggs was again elected to the House from New Orleans. A political protégé of the Democratic leader, Rep. SAM RAYBURN (D-Tex.), Boggs was appointed to the influential Ways and Means Committee. He became head of the panel's Subcommittee on Narcotics in 1951, and during that year, he successfully sponsored a bill to stiffen the penalties for violations of federal narcotics and marijuana laws. In January 1952, he lost the Louisiana Democratic gubernatorial primary.

A moderate southern Democrat, Boggs often broke with his more liberal party colleagues. In July 1953, he joined with conservatives on the Ways and Means Committee in an unsuccessful attempt to block an administration-sponsored effort to extend an excess-profits tax on corporations. Boggs also voted against the Civil Rights Acts of 1957 and 1960. In March 1959, as a member of the Joint Economic Committee, he dissented from a report of the panel's Democratic majority urging emphasis on the expansion of production and employment rather than the containment of inflation. In March 1960, Boggs voted with a majority on the Ways and Means Committee opposing the Forand bill, which would have provided medical care for the aged under Social Security.

The sugar industry was an important element of Louisiana's economy, and in March and April 1955, Boggs and Sen. ALLEN J. ELLENDER (D-La.) introduced a sugar quota bill intended to enlarge the domestic producers' share of excess market demand above estimated annual American consumption. A modified version of this measure became law in May 1956.

In 1957, Boggs became chairman of the Ways and Means Committee's Foreign Trade Policy Subcommittee, where he advocated liberal foreign trade programs. That December, he backed Eisenhower's request for a five-year extension of the Reciprocal Trade Agreements granting the president authority to cut tariffs by as much as 25 percent. In August 1958, Eisenhower signed a four-year extension bill permitting cuts up to 20 percent. Boggs's subcommittee began hearings on American investment in underdeveloped areas in December 1958. A month later, he introduced a bill to encourage investment in those regions by permitting investors to defer payment of U.S. corporate taxes on foreign earnings until the funds were returned to America. A modified version of this proposal passed the House in May 1960 but was rejected by the Senate Finance Committee. Another provision of the bill Boggs introduced in 1959 liberalized the terms by which U.S. firms with investments abroad could take credit for their foreign tax payments in computing their U.S. tax liability. That measure was introduced as a separate bill early in 1960. Sen. ALBERT GORE (D-Tenn.), a leading advocate of tax reform and an opponent of the foreign tax credit, denounced the proposal in May 1960 as an attempt to expand an already unjustified loophole. Nevertheless, the bill passed both chambers and was signed into law in September.

In 1962, Boggs succeeded Rep. CARL ALBERT (D-Okla.) as majority whip. During the mid-1960s his voting record became more liberal. He opposed the Civil Rights Act of 1964 but supported the Voting Rights Act of 1965 and the Civil Rights Act of 1968. Boggs also voted for antipoverty legislation. In 1971, he became majority leader following the retirement of House Speaker JOHN McCORMACK (D-Mass.). Boggs was a passenger in a plane that disappeared over Alaska on October 16, 1972. The craft was not located, and Boggs was presumed to have died in a crash.

—MLL

Bohlen, Charles E(ustis)

(1904–1974) *ambassador to the Soviet Union, ambassador to the Philippines*

The son of a well-to-do sportsman and a descendant of the first U.S. ambassador to France, Bohlen was born in Clayton, N.Y., on August 30, 1904. He was educated at Saint Paul's School and Harvard University. Two years after graduating from Harvard in 1927, he joined the Foreign Service and was posted as vice-consul in Prague. He remained there until 1931, when he was assigned to Paris as vice-consul and language officer. While in France, he took extensive courses in Russian history, language, and culture in preparation for a specialization in Soviet affairs. Upon the recommendation of William Bullitt, ambassador to the Soviet Union, Bohlen became part of the first America mission to the USSR in 1934. He served there intermittently until 1939, when he received a post to Tokyo. Bohlen was at the embassy during the Japanese attack on Pearl Harbor and, like the other members of the mission, was interned by the Japanese for six months after the attack. Upon his return to Washington, he became acting chief of the State Department's division of Eastern European affairs.

During World War II, Bohlen served as an adviser and chief interpreter at the Teheran Conference of 1943 and the Yalta and Potsdam Conferences of 1945. He also worked as liaison officer between the State Department and the White House. In 1947, Bohlen became personal adviser to Secretary of State George C. Marshall. Bohlen played an important role in developing the Marshall Plan and molding the Truman policy of containment of the Soviet Union. He became counselor of the Paris embassy in 1949. Two years later, he returned to Washington and served as an aide to JOHN FOSTER DULLES at the Japanese peace conference in San Francisco.

President Eisenhower nominated Bohlen as ambassador to the Soviet Union in 1953. Conservatives, led by Sens. JOSEPH McCARTHY (R-Wis.) and PATRICK McCARRAN (D-Nev.), bitterly opposed the nomination. They claimed that Bohlen was too closely associated with Truman's foreign policy to represent the Republican administration. They also charged that FBI reports contained damaging information about Bohlen's family life. McCarthy demanded that the FBI files be made available to the Senate. After initially refusing, Eisenhower agreed to allow two senators to examine the files and report to the Senate. Although the senators were never able to reveal specific instances of disloyalty, their charges seriously jeopardized confirmation. For many individuals in the State Department, the

Bohlen case became a test of the new Administration's willingness to defend the beleaguered department against McCarthy's continuing attacks.

At the confirmation hearings, Bohlen defended the Yalta agreements as the best that could have been achieved and refused to repudiate them. Dulles supported the appointment fully and denied that Bohlen had security problems. He conceded that the two men did not often agree on policy and specifically that they viewed the Yalta agreements in different lights. Nevertheless, he reminded the Foreign Relations Committee that as ambassador Bohlen would have little influence in policymaking. Eisenhower, too, defended the nomination, although he apparently had been asked by a high-ranking official, never identified, to withdraw it. McCarthy's attempt to prevent the appointment failed when several important conservatives, led by Sen. ROBERT TAFT (R-Ohio), rejected the Wisconsin senator's contention that Dulles had lied in defending Bohlen's security record. The Senate confirmed Bohlen in March 1953.

As ambassador, Bohlen's task was to inform the Kremlin of official U.S. positions and to gather as much information as possible about Soviet leadership and policy changes. During his tenure, he reported on the changes of leadership following Stalin's death in 1953 and on the Soviet reaction to the Suez Crisis and the Hungarian revolt of 1956. These reports often contained policy recommendations, but, according to Bohlen, Secretary of State Dulles rarely heeded them. In summing up his four years in the Soviet Union, the ambassador wrote, "I cannot say I accomplished much during my four years . . . nor can I think of any serious mistakes we made at the embassy."

In 1957, Dulles, apparently as a result of a commitment to appoint LLEWELLYN THOMPSON ambassador to the Soviet Union, announced that Bohlen had decided to give up his position. Bohlen, who had not considered this, thought of resigning from the Foreign Service. Instead, he accepted a post as ambassador to the Philippines. Despite Bohlen's protestations, rumors persisted that he was being "exiled" to the Philippines because of policy disagreements with Dulles. During his tour, Bohlen settled Philippine war claims against the United States and unsuccessfully attempted to convince Congress to give the Philippines jurisdiction over the prosecution of crimes committed by U.S. military personnel off U.S. bases.

In 1959, Secretary of State CHRISTIAN HERTER appointed Bohlen his special assistant for Soviet affairs. Herter dropped plans to make him a counselor or assistant secretary because he feared that conservative senators would oppose confirmation. As Herter's assistant, Bohlen was an adviser and interpreter at the abortive summit conference in May 1960.

During the 1960s, Bohlen served as a presidential adviser to both JOHN KENNEDY and LYNDON JOHNSON. He was named ambassador to France in 1962 and remained at that post until the end of 1967, when he was appointed deputy undersecretary of state for political affairs. Bohlen retired in January 1969 and died in Washington, D.C., on January 1, 1974.

—EWS

Bolton, Frances P(ayne Bingham)
(1885–1977) *U.S. congressman*

Born to one of Cleveland, Ohio's, oldest and wealthiest families, Frances Bingham was born on March 29, 1885. After marrying Chester C. Bolton, a steel executive, in 1907, she devoted both time and money to a variety of philanthropic enterprises, notably the Tuskegee Institute. With particular interest in nursing, Bolton persuaded the War Department, then headed by fellow Clevelander Newton D. Baker, to create the Army School of Nursing during World War I. Beginning in 1928, she participated in her husband's usually successful campaigns for the House. Upon her husband's death, Bolton ran as a Republican and won election to his seat in a special election in 1940.

One of the few women members of the House in the 1940s, Bolton fought for an end to discriminatory practices by the Armed Services. During World War II, she called for the desegregation, both by race and sex, of military nursing units. After the war, she argued for the inclusion of women in the Selective Service System in 1949.

Throughout her House career, Bolton served on the Foreign Affairs Committee. She led efforts that resulted in the restructuring of the committee's procedure. A frequent defender of the United Nations, she also advocated independence for colonial Africa in the late 1940s. Although a mild isolationist prior to Pearl Harbor, Bolton assumed more internationalist positions than those of most of her fellow Midwestern Republicans.

In February 1954, Bolton declined to join some GOP members of Congress in criticizing a plan—presented by Secretary of State JOHN FOSTER DULLES—for a conference that April at Geneva, which would have included a delegation from Communist China. Senate Majority Leader WILLIAM F. KNOWLAND, JR. (R-Calif.) led an assault upon Dulles's qualified support for Communist China's representation at talks on Indochina and Korea. Bolton, Sen. WALTER F. GEORGE (D-Ga.), Reps. James P. Richards (D-S.C.), and Franklin D. Roosevelt, Jr. (D-N.Y.) supported Dulles; they argued that China's presence at the discussions would not indicate American recognition of the Communist regime.

Bolton consistently supported foreign policy legislation favored by the White House. During the 84th Congress (1955–56), she voted for 93 percent of the foreign policy measures endorsed by the president, as measured by *Congressional Quarterly*. The average among Republicans in the House was 70 percent. She similarly led her fellow Republicans 79 percent to 56 percent in the 85th Congress (1957–58).

By the 1960s, Bolton was both the ranking woman representative and the ranking GOP member on the Foreign Affairs Committee. Her oldest son, Oliver P. Bolton, served three terms in the House from the nearby 11th District; they represented the only mother-son team in the lower chamber. Bolton encountered little opposition in winning reelection until 1968, when at age 83, she lost her seat due to redistricting. Bolton died in Lyndhurst, Ohio, on March 9, 1977.

—JLB

Bonner, Herbert C(ovington)
(1891–1965) *U.S. congressman*

Born in Washington, N.C., on May 16, 1891, Bonner worked as a salesman and a farmer before enlisting in the army during World War I. In 1924, he became secretary to Assemblyman Lindsay War-

ren. When Warren was elected to the U.S. House of Representatives, Bonner accompanied him to Washington. In 1940, Bonner was elected as a Democrat to fill Warren's unexpired term, vacated when the Congressman became controller general. In Congress, Bonner represented a district in eastern North Carolina consisting of small towns and textile mills until his death in 1965. During the 1940s, he led a number of congressional investigations, including one into postwar profiteering and another on waste in military installations.

While on Capitol Hill, Bonner compiled a record as an opponent of labor and civil rights legislation. He voted against the Civil Rights Acts of 1957 and 1960. Bonner also opposed federally financed public housing and measures to aid education. A conservative on foreign policy, he voted against lower tariffs requested by President DWIGHT D. EISENHOWER and most foreign aid bills except those specifically designed to curb communist aggression. Bonner was a strong anticommunist and supported measures, such as the Eisenhower Doctrine, that were designed to give the president the power to act swiftly against communist aggression throughout the world.

Bonner's major concern in Congress was the U.S. maritime industry. As chairman of the Merchant Marine and Fisheries Committee, he criticized what he thought were excessive union demands and the failure of management to modernize shipping. He also pleaded for increased federal aid to the industry. During 1956, Bonner was responsible for defeating amendments to the "50-50 law." This law, supported by the industry, required that at least half of all agricultural surpluses shipped as foreign aid be moved in American ships. In February, Bonner's committee issued a report concluding that the law did not impair the success of the aid program and was "vitally necessary" to American shipping.

Although a vocal supporter of the construction of a nuclear-powered merchant vessel, he objected to Eisenhower's proposal that the vessel be used as a "peace ship," carrying "practical knowledge of the usefulness of [atomic] science." Bonner called the president's plan "an international side-show, a Mississippi River Showboat" and proposed development of a second "practical" vessel. The final bill, signed into law in July 1956, combined Eisenhower's and Bonner's proposals. The first nuclear ship, the *Savannah*, was launched in 1962.

During the 1960s, Bonner pushed for compulsory arbitration in the shipping industry and increased federal subsidies for shipbuilding. Bonner died in Washington, D.C., on November 7, 1965.

—EWS

Boulware, Lemuel (Ricketts)

(1895–1990) *vice-president in charge of employee, community, and union relations, General Electric Company*

Born on June 3, 1895, in Springfield, Ky., Boulware graduated from the University of Wisconsin in 1916. He taught business administration briefly before embarking on a career as an industrial executive. He served as an infantry captain in World War I. During World War II, he joined the War Production Board as an operations vice chairman and met CHARLES E. WILSON of the General Electric Co. (GE). When Wilson became president of GE after the war, he brought Boulware into the company.

GE's relations with the United Electrical Workers had been relatively amicable from the mid-1930s through the war years. After the union won a major victory through a strike in 1946, however, the company sought to restrict future union gains by adopting a firmer approach toward bargaining. Boulware was charged with devising an aggressive employee-relations policy, which came to be known as "Boulwarism" after its inauguration in 1947. GE proceeded to carry out what its opponents called one of the best-financed, most highly organized, and longest antiunion campaigns in corporate history.

The principal element in the Boulware formula was what the company called "truthful offers." In an effort to end what Boulware described as "eastern bazaar haggling" and to deny unions the opportunity to claim that they had forced the company to raise its contract offers, GE put on the bargaining table everything it was willing to give. Under Boulware, GE listened closely to union demands, examined the wages and working conditions at competitor companies, conducted extensive research on all issues, and put forward a "fair, firm offer,"

with nothing withheld for future negotiations. As a result, the company's first offer was usually its last. Unions charged that GE with bargaining by ultimatum. However, Boulware denied that the company attempted to drive a bargain less favorable to its employees than could be achieved by the more conventional negotiating approach used by most large businesses.

Boulwarism also featured the extensive use of advertising and mass-marketing techniques. Fearing that unless the company communicated its proposals by every means available, employees and the public would learn only the unions' version of events, GE produced regular plant bulletins, sent management representatives to public gatherings, and placed full-page advertisements in the press of all communities in which its plans were located. With the aid of a large research staff, Boulware applied the techniques of market research to merchandise GE's "product"—its contract offers—on all fronts in order to make the most effective "sale" to employees and local communities.

Although several unions competed for jurisdiction over GE workers after 1949, the International Union of Electrical Workers (IUE) was the largest by far, and its president, JAMES CAREY, was GE's principal adversary during the 1950s. At the yearly contract rounds between 1950 and 1955, Carey usually failed to move the company from its initial bargaining position. He also failed to gain his membership's support for a strike in the face of effective publicity by the company. As a result, the IUE repeatedly ended up accepting GE's offer long after the expiration of the previous year's contract.

In 1955, with market forecasters predicting a long-term boom, GE planned new investments in plant, equipment, manpower, and research and prepared to expand into the fields of atomic power and computers. In a temporary departure from Boulwarism, the company also offered a five-year contract in 1955, including quarterly cost-of-living adjustments, a comprehensive medical insurance program, and an informal pledge not to launch any antiunion campaigns during the contract's annual escape periods. In 1956, Boulware became vice president for employee and public relations. In 1958, the agreement reached in 1955 was renegotiated after the recession of 1957 severely affected

GE's utility apparatus, industrial equipment, and appliance departments. Talks ended in a stalemate when the company refused the IUE's demands for supplemental unemployment benefits and joint union-management automation committees.

Boulwarism was revived after 1958, as GE prepared for a confrontation with the electrical workers union. The IUE went out on strike in 1960. The company responded with company-organized back-to-work movements, widely-publicized plant openings, and occasional use of police force. After three weeks, the IUE called off the strike. The labor editor of the *New York Times*, A. H. Raskin, called it "the worst setback any union has received in a nationwide strike since World War II."

Boulware retired in 1961. He published two books, one of which defended his approach to labor relations (*The Truth about Boulwarism*, 1969). Boulware died in Delray Beach, Fla., on November 7, 1990.

—TLH

Bowie, Robert R(ichardson)

(1909–) *director of policy planning, Department of State; assistant secretary of state for policy planning*
Born on August 24, 1909, in Baltimore, Md., Bowie graduated from Princeton in 1931, and, after receiving a law degree from Harvard three years later, returned to Baltimore to begin legal practice. He served as assistant director of the Maryland Legislative Council from 1940 to 1941 and as assistant attorney general of Maryland from 1941 to 1942. After service in the Army during World War II, Bowie became a professor of law at Harvard, where he remained intermittently until 1955. During the Truman administration, he was special assistant to the deputy military governor of Germany from 1945 to 1946 and served as director of the task force of the Hoover Commission on the Reorganization of the Federal Government in 1948. Bowie returned to Germany as general counsel and special adviser to the U.S. high commissioner in 1950 and 1951.

In 1953, Secretary of State JOHN FOSTER DULLES appointed Bowie director of policy planning in the State Department. Dulles frequently consulted Bowie, who often opposed the secretary's uncompromising anticommunism. Yet, despite Dulles's respect

for him, Bowie never exerted much influence over the secretary, and the planning staff wielded far less power than it had during the Truman administration.

At a series of conferences held in the spring and fall of 1953, Bowie helped formulate the administration's policy of "massive retaliation." Under this plan, the United States relied on strategic nuclear weapons rather than conventional warfare to prevent Soviet expansion and guard against a nuclear attack by the Soviets. The department reiterated its support for "containment" of communism in eastern Europe and upheld the use of nuclear weapons to prevent communist subversion in nonaligned nations. However, the administration rejected suggestions of "liberating" eastern Europe by force.

Bowie criticized Dulles's belligerent policy regarding Quemoy and Matsu in the spring of 1954 and disliked the secretary's willingness to discuss possible use of nuclear weapons against Communist China. Relying heavily on information supplied him by Chairman of the Joint Chiefs of Staff Adm. ARTHUR RADFORD, Dulles claimed that tactical nuclear weapons could "destroy military targets without endangering unrelated civilian centers." Astonished by Dulles's statements, Bowie gave him Central Intelligence Agency estimates that civilian casualties on the Chinese mainland would reach 12 to 14 million, even if the United States dropped tactical atomic bombs on only military targets.

In August 1955, President Eisenhower appointed Bowie assistant secretary of state for policy planning. The appointment was opposed by Republican Senate Policy Committee Chairman STYLES BRIDGES (R-N.H.), who accused Bowie of favoring Communist China's admission to the UN. However, the Senate Foreign Relations Committee approved Bowie after he swore that he had never advocated Communist China's replacement of Taiwan in the organization. The Senate confirmed Bowie's appointment in February 1956. He was involved in the decision not to build the Aswan Dam.

Following his retirement from the State Department in May 1957, Bowie returned to Harvard, where he taught international relations. He was director of the Harvard Center for International Affairs from 1957 to 1972 and Clarence Dillon Professor of International Affairs from 1972 until his retirement in 1980. In 1960, Bowie wrote a report for the Senate Foreign Relations Committee in which he argued that the United States should remain vigilant with respect to the Soviet Union, despite an apparent thaw in relations between the two countries and rising living standards in the Soviet Union that he thought might lead the Soviets to an accommodation with the United States. The report also advocated looking beyond the immediate points of conflict with the USSR and recommended a less direct competition between the two countries for the allegiance of uncommitted nations. In 1998, Bowie coauthored, with Richard H. Immerman, *Waging Peace: How Eisenhower Shaped an Enduring Cold War Strategy.*

While at Harvard, Bowie continued to serve the government. He was counselor to the State Department from 1966 to 1968 and served as deputy director at national intelligence for the CIA from 1977 to 1979. He is currently Dillon Professor Emeritus at Harvard.

—AES

Bowles, Chester
(1901–1986) *U.S. congressman*

The scion of a well-to-do Yankee family, Bowles was born on April 5, 1901, in Springfield, Mass. He graduated from Yale University in 1924 and then worked for a short time as a journalist for his hometown newspaper, the *Springfield Republican.* In 1925, he moved to New York to accept a position as a copywriter in an advertising agency. Four years later, he and WILLIAM BENTON founded their own agency, which prospered despite, or even perhaps because of, the depression.

With the outbreak of World War II, Bowles administered Connecticut's rationing program. His success impressed President Franklin D. Roosevelt, who invited him to Washington to serve as director of the Office of Price Administration in 1943. President HARRY S. TRUMAN appointed him Director of economic stabilization in 1945. Bowles also represented the United States at the first conference of the United Nations Education, Scientific and Cultural Organization in 1946 and served as special assistant to UN Secretary General Trygve Lie.

In 1948, Bowles was elected governor of Connecticut. Bowles lost his bid for reelection in 1950,

but President Truman named him ambassador to India the following year. There he defended the neutralist policies of Prime Minister Jawaharlal Nehru against criticism by American conservatives who equated neutralism with procommunism. Bowles joined other liberals in urging a shift from military to economic aid. He retired from government service at the end of the Truman administration.

During the early years of the Eisenhower administration, Bowles wrote numerous articles and books, including *The New Dimensions of Peace* (1953), *Africa's Challenge to America* (1956), and *Ideas, People and Peace* (1958), which established his reputation as a leading critic of American policy toward developing nations, particularly in the area of foreign aid. Bowles deplored the refusal of colonial powers to grant their territories independence. This, he maintained, led to discontent, which proved a fertile ground for communist subversion. He argued that foreign aid provided America's best deterrent against the spread of communism. Bowles charged that the Eisenhower administration's foreign aid program was stingy and its emphasis on military aid misguided. The small amount of foreign aid offered, he stated, was designed not to improve living standards but to gain support for the United States in the United Nations and win a popularity contest with the Soviet Union. Quite often the programs failed to meet such expectations. This, in turn, disillusioned Congress, which then slashed foreign aid. Bowles also criticized State Department officials for their ignorance of the cultures and languages of developing countries.

At a time when many liberals, defensive about their past connections with the Left, were becoming cold warriors, Bowles stood apart from them. He downplayed the Soviet threat and stressed the dangers of poverty and hunger. However, his plans for a successful foreign aid program did have some anti-Soviet overtones.

In 1958, Bowles began a political comeback by seeking the Democratic nomination for a Senate seat from Connecticut. Ironically, his old advertising partner, WILLIAM BENTON, who previously served in the Senate, entered the race along with Rep. THOMAS DODD (D-Conn.). Benton had the backing of the state party chairman, John Bailey, and Gov. ABRAHAM RIBICOFF, who feared that

Bowles's controversial stands on foreign policy would weaken the ticket that he headed. At the party's convention in June, Benton and Bowles split the liberal vote, permitting Dodd to win the nomination. Bowles then ran for a House seat in his traditionally Republican home distrct and won by a large margin. During his one term in Congress, he lobbied for improvements in foreign-aid programs.

In 1959, many liberals mentioned Bowles as a dark-horse candidate for the Democratic presidential nomination. However, his controversial stands limited his appeal. In late 1959, presidential aspirant Sen. JOHN F. KENNEDY (D-Mass.) elicited Bowles's support in the belief that his endorsement would aid him in a struggle with ADLAI STEVENSON. Bowles did endorse Kennedy, but his refusal to campaign for the senator against his old friend, Sen. HUBERT HUMPHREY (D-Minn.), alienated many Kennedy supporters. Bowles served as Kennedy's foreign policy adviser during the general election campaign in 1960.

When Kennedy became president, Bowles was appointed undersecretary of state. As a result of clashes with Attorney General ROBERT F. KENNEDY and many powerful members of the State Department and Congress, Bowles was forced to resign in November 1961. Kennedy then appointed him special adviser on Asian, African, and Latin American affairs. In December 1962, Bowles once again became ambassador to India. During the 1960s, Bowles lobbied for increased foreign aid for that nation but had little success in convincing presidents Kennedy and Johnson to follow his recommendations. Bowles retired in 1969 and returned to Connecticut. He lived there until his death in Essex, Conn., on May 25, 1986.

—JB

Braden, Spruille

(1894–1978) *chairman, Crime Committee of Greater New York*

Born on March 13, 1894, in Elkhorn, Mont., into a mining family—his father founded the Braden Copper Co.—Braden studied mining engineering at Yale University. After receiving a Ph.D. in 1914, Braden worked in a number of South Ameri-

can mining ventures and married the daughter of a prominent Chilean physician. During the 1920s, he advised South American governments in loan negotiations, participated in inter-American financial conferences, and served as an official of several large corporations.

In 1933, he was appointed U.S. delegate to the Seventh International Conference of American States. From 1935 to 1939, he headed the U.S. team at the Chaco Peace Conference, where he negotiated the settlement of the war between Bolivia and Paraguay. After serving as ambassador to Colombia from 1939 to 1942, he then became ambassador to Cuba. In 1945, he was made ambassador to Argentina and that same year was promoted to assistant secretary of state for American republic affairs. During the postwar period, Braden recommended a "hard-line" policy against all forms of dictatorship. His widely publicized efforts to press Argentine dictator Juan Domingo Perón to restore constitutional liberties, deliver over to the United States Nazi agents hiding in Argentina, and abide by the provisions of inter-American defense commitments disturbed State Department officials eager to restore friendly relations with Perón's government. Braden also made enemies in the Pentagon with his opposition to large military aid programs to Latin American nations, arguing that such programs wasted U.S. taxpayers' money and encouraged military adventurism among the Latins. "Bradenism" became a term that described a heavy-handed approach to negotiating with Latin American officials.

Braden left government service in July 1947, believing that his anticommunist, antifascist policies had been sabotaged by pro-communist, incompetent employees of the State Department. He then settled in New York City and worked as a lecturer and as a consultant to a number of large corporations, including Anaconda Copper, American Foreign Power, Lone Star Cement, and United Fruit. In February 1949, Braden became president of the American Arbitration Association.

Reacting to the growing concern over the activities of organized crime and corruption in government, a group of prominent citizens formed the New York City Anti-Crime Committee in January 1951. They asked Braden to act as the committee's unpaid chairman. Supported by the municipal government, the Anti-Crime Committee concentrated its investigations on organized crime's infiltration into labor, business, and politics. In February 1953, the panel issued its first report, citing evidence of organized crime's influence in the city's food, garment-trucking, and building industries. The committee's investigation of crime on the waterfront was instrumental in influencing the American Federation of Labor to expel the International Longshoremen's Association and to set up a new union in September 1953. Organized crime's role on the docks became a national issue, and the situation in the port of New York was dramatized in the successful film, *On the Waterfront* (1954). In July 1955, Braden warned that racketeers planned to take over the trucking industry and strongly criticized Teamsters president DAVID BECK for failure to take action against his vice president, JAMES HOFFA. The Anti-Crime Committee suspended its operations in December 1956 for lack of funds. Braden, however, was satisfied with the committee's work and believed that it had encouraged the public to demand more vigorous prosecution of official corruption.

During the 1950s, Braden was closely identified with some of the most right-wing elements in public life. In November 1954, he helped organize "10 Million Americans Mobilizing for Justice," an organization opposed to the Senate's proposed censure of Sen. JOSEPH MCCARTHY (R-Wis.). Braden also cooperated with the Senate Internal Security Subcommittee's investigations into communist subversion in the U.S. government. In December 1953, he told the subcommittee that communism could not be eliminated from Latin America until "insidious groups" and "bad characters" were removed from the State Department. He asserted that the official actions of Alger Hiss were "down the communist line" and noted that his own reports warning of communism were missing from the State Department's files. Testifying before the subcommittee again in November 1954, Braden stated that pro-communists were apparently still influencing State Department policy.

Braden spoke out strongly against the government of Guatemala's president, Jacobo Arbenz Guzmán, and urged the new Eisenhower administration to take action against it. In a widely reported talk to a symposium at Dartmouth College in March 1953, he criticized President DWIGHT D. EISENHOWER for failing to intervene in Guatemala to prevent what Braden described as a communist takeover. In subsequent years, Braden continued to speak out publicly on foreign affairs. He defended U.S. private investments in Latin America, arguing that, overall they helped rather than exploited the Latin American people. In addition, he believed that the United States had the responsibility to intervene in nations of the Western Hemisphere to protect U.S. businesses and to suppress communism. Finally, Braden was a leading opponent of American foreign aid programs. In June 1957, he testified against the Eisenhower administration's foreign aid package before the House Foreign Affairs Committee. Braden published his memoirs, *Diplomats and Demagogues*, in 1998. He died in Los Angeles on January 10, 1978.

—JCH

Braun, Wernher von

(1912–1977) *director, Guided Missile Development Division, Redstone Arsenal; director, Development Division, Army Ballistic Missile Agency*

Born to an aristocratic East Prussian family on March 23, 1912, in Wirsitz, Germany (now Wyrzysk, Poland), von Braun attended the French Gymnasium in Berlin (where his family moved after Wirsitz became part of Poland in 1920 as a result of the Treaty of Versailles). As a boy, he developed an interest in astronomy and rocketry. After attending secondary school near Weimar, he did his undergraduate work at Berlin's Charlottenburg Institute of Technology. Von Braun served as a volunteer assistant to Professor Hermann Oberth, a pioneer in rocketry, and joined the *Verein für Raumschiffart* (Spaceflight Society). From 1931 to 1932, von Braun took part in experiments with liquid-fueled rockets. Early on, he came to the recognition that the development of rocketry and space flight would cost huge amounts of money that only a government could provide. He also concluded that it was unlikely that any government would invest such an amount for purely scientific purposes. Von Braun signed a contract with army ordinance in 1932 and became technical director of the German army's rocket experiment station. While working for the army, he earned a doctorate from the University of Berlin in 1934. Von Braun and his team initially developed three series of rockets, the A-1, A-2, and A-3. Needing a larger facility, von Braun selected Peenemünde as the location for a new facility dedicated to the development of rocket-propelled weapons and aircraft for the German army and air force. By 1943, the facility employed 1,950 scientists, engineers, and technicians. The team at Peenemünde developed the V-1, a pilotless flying bomb, and the A-4 (later renamed the V-2), a large ballistic missile.

The V-2 made its first successful flight in October 1942. After the Royal Air Force bombed the facility at Peenemünde in August 1943, manufacture of the missiles moved to an underground facility in the Harz Mountains. The first V-2 was launched against England in September 1944. From 1943 to the end of the war, approximately 60,000 slave laborers worked at the underground facility; roughly 20,000 of them died. More people died building the V-2 than died from its use as a weapon.

The nature and extent of von Braun's commitment to the Nazi regime remain uncertain. He joined the Nazi Party in 1937 and accepted a commission in the SS in 1940. Heinrich Himmler promoted him three times, and von Braun became a major in the SS in June 1943. The Gestapo arrested him in 1944 and charged him with placing his commitment to space travel above the development of an effective weapon. He was released after two weeks because he was essential to the V-2 program. Although he had no direct administrative responsibility for the supervision of slave labor, he accepted the use of slave labor at Peenemünde and certainly was aware of the horrific treatment of the laborers at Nordhausen.

In 1945, von Braun and other members of his team fled the advancing Soviet army and headed for central Germany, where they surrendered to American forces. He later said he did this because the United States seemed more likely to support his research and because "the next time, I wanted to be on the winning side." The Americans, on the other hand, wanted to gain access to German advances in rocketry. Von Braun signed a contract with the U.S. Army and, together with 119 scientists and engineers who had worked with him in Germany, flew to the United States in September 1945.

Von Braun and his group of German scientists initially were sent to Fort Bliss, Tex., where they taught the army to handle captured V-2s. They also continued to work on the development of new missiles for research and military uses. In 1950, the army transferred von Braun's team and the Army Ordnance Guided Missile Center to the Redstone Arsenal in Huntsville, Ala. Von Braun became technical director and then chief of the Guided Missile Development Division.

During the Korean War, his group was directed to develop a surface-to-surface ballistic missile with a 500-mile range. The rocket, named the Redstone, had a shorter range than expected, but it laid the technical base for future developments in rocketry. The Redstone, which was capable of carrying a nuclear warhead, was successfully tested in August 1953. The missile became part of the U.S. Army's arsenal in 1958.

During the years when he worked on the Redstone, von Braun also became the leading advocate of space flight in the United States. He helped develop a series of articles on the subject for *Colliers* titled "Man Will Conquer Space Soon!" and appeared on camera for three episodes of the *Disneyland* television show devoted to travel in space. In numerous television appearances and in popular books he wrote or cowrote, von Braun pressed the case for space exploration. He became a naturalized American citizen in 1955.

In 1955, von Braun's team began elaborating on the Redstone to devise rockets capable of the higher speeds needed for intermediate range ballistic missiles (IRBMs). The result of this work was the Jupiter, which consisted of a Redstone with two additional stages. To attain the carrier capabilities needed to place a satellite in orbit, von Braun added a fourth stage, creating the Juno 1.

In February 1956, the Army Ballistic Missile Agency (ABMA) was established, incorporating the Redstone Arsenal's Guided Missile Division. Von Braun became director of the ABMA under the military command of General John B. Medaris. With the navy working on its own Polaris missile and the Vanguard rocket and the air force authorized to develop the Intercontinental Ballistic Missile, the ABMA was restricted to work on IRBMs and limited feasibility studies of missiles with greater ranges.

As had been the case in Germany, von Braun's primary efforts focused on the development of rockets as weaponry. However, he advocated the use of rockets for space exploration well before Soviet advances in the field convinced American officials of the importance of a space program. In 1951, von Braun proposed that the United States develop a doughnut-shaped space station, and, in *Mars Project*, published in 1952, he envisioned the eventual construction of an interplanetary space fleet. In 1955, he pointed out that, with a few relatively minor alterations, a Redstone missile could carry a small craft into orbit around the earth. President DWIGHT D. EISENHOWER, however, wanted to demonstrate America's peaceful intentions in space, and he announced that the navy's Vanguard rocket, which was based on the Viking (a scientific research rocket) would carry the first U.S. satellite. He preferred not to have the Redstone or Jupiter missiles, which had been designed to carry nuclear payloads, launch the satellite.

In April 1957, von Braun and Medaris proposed to the Defense Department's Research and Development Council a schedule for ABMA to use Jupiter missiles to launch satellites beginning that September. The Council initially rejected the proposal, but, things changed after the Soviet Union placed its *Sputnik* satellite into orbit in October 1957. The day after the Soviets launched *Sputnik*, Secretary of Defense NEIL MCELROY went to Huntsville, where von Braun told him that the United States could launch a satellite within 90 days. Von Braun received instructions to prepare to launch a satellite with a Jupiter rocket as a backup to the navy's effort. After the Vanguard exploded on the launchpad on December 6, a modified Jupiter rocket launched Explorer I, the first U.S. satellite, into orbit on January 31, 1958.

During testimony before the Senate Preparedness Subcommittee in December 1957, von Braun proposed that the United States establish a national space agency with a $1.5 billion annual budget. Such an agency, he told the subcommittee, could have "a man orbiting the earth on a returnable basis" within five years and could produce a manned

space station in 10 years. President Eisenhower endorsed the plan in the following spring. Congress passed a law creating the National Aeronautics and Space Administration (NASA), independent of the Defense Department, in July 1958. The army turned the Redstone Arsenal's rocket program over to the newly created NASA. Von Braun became director of NASA's facility in Huntsville, renamed the George C. Marshall Flight Center, in 1960.

In the early 1960s, von Braun played a large role in the U.S. space program. The first two Americans in space, Alan B. Shepard and Virgil I. Grissom, rode in capsules powered by Redstone launchers. Von Braun oversaw the development of the large *Saturn* rocket used by the Apollo missions. He was a leading advocate of the position that manned flight to the moon should be the focus for the American space program, and he participated in much of the decision making surrounding the Apollo missions. A frequent spokesman for NASA, his books and articles helped stimulate national interest in the space program. Von Braun served as the director of the Marshall Center until 1970 and moved to Washington, D.C., as associate director of NASA for two more years. He left the agency in 1972 to become vice president of engineering and development at Fairchild Industries. Von Braun died in Alexandria, Virginia, on June 16, 1977.

—MSM

Brennan, William J(oseph), Jr.
(1906–1997) *associate justice, U.S. Supreme Court*
The son of Irish immigrants, Brennan was born on April 25, 1906, in Newark, N.J. He received a B.S. from the Wharton School of Finance of the University of Pennsylvania in 1928. He earned a degree from Harvard law school in 1931, and then joined the Newark law firm of Pitney, Harbin, and Skinner, where he became a partner in 1937 and a specialist in labor law. A leader of a group of young attorneys who successfully promoted reform and streamlining of the New Jersey judicial system, Brennan was named a judge on the state Superior Court in 1949. The next year, Governor Alfred E. Driscoll appointed Brennan to the Appellate Division of the Superior Court. In 1952, Driscoll appointed Brennan to the New Jersey Supreme Court.

President Eisenhower announced Brennan's appointment to the U.S. Supreme Court to replace retiring Justice SHERMAN MINTON on September 29, 1956. Although a Democrat, Brennan had not been politically active, and he had the judicial experience and high standing within the legal profession that Eisenhower wanted in a Supreme Court candidate. Brennan began serving on the Court under a recess appointment on October 16. The Senate confirmed his nomination on March 19, 1957. Only Sen. JOSEPH R. MCCARTHY (R-Wis.), whose methods Brennan had criticized in two speeches in the mid-1950s, voted against him.

By the end of his first term on the Court, Brennan had clearly aligned himself with the liberals on the bench. In June 1957, his majority opinion in the highly controversial *Jencks* case held, that in federal criminal trials, the government must let the defense examine relevant reports previously made to the government by prosecution witnesses. On the same day, Brennan's opinion for the Court in the *E.I. du Pont de Nemours & Co.* case held that DuPont's ownership of 23 percent of General Motors stock had given it an illegal advantage when competing for sales of automotive finishes and fabrics to GM. Brennan voted with the majority in several cases handed down on June 17, 1957, a date critics referred to as "Red Monday." In *Yates v. U.S.*, the Court held that, while advocating and teaching a course of action designed to overthrow the government could be punished, advocating or teaching such a course of action as an "abstract doctrine" could not. This reversed the convictions of the top leaders of the communist party in California and effectively halted prosecutions under the Smith Act. The second decision, *Service v. Dulles*, ruled that, since the State Department had been unable to find formal grounds for dismissing JOHN STEWART SERVICE, it could not dismiss him because top officials wished to do so. In *Watkins v. U.S.*, the Court held that congressional investigations had to be related to an explicit legislative purpose; speaking for the majority, Chief Justice EARL WARREN wrote, "There is no Congressional power to expose for the sake of exposure."

Though he had joined the Court's libertarian wing in his votes, Brennan remained largely independent of it in his judicial philosophy. Unlike Justice HUGO BLACK, for example, Brennan did not consider First Amendment guarantees absolute but believed that these rights must be balanced against government interests. He insisted, however, that only a real and very substantial government need justified any curtailment of individual rights and thus usually favored the individual in loyalty-security cases. In June 1958, for example, Brennan dissented when the majority upheld the dismissal of municipal employees in Philadelphia and New York because they had refused to answer questions from superiors about their political activities. The justice declared that there had been no demonstration in either suit of a government security interest sufficient to justify the denial of the appellants' free speech rights. Brennan again dissented in two cases, decided a year later, in which the majority sustained the contempt convictions of witnesses who had failed to provide information during congressional and state investigations into possible subversion. The record in both cases, he asserted, showed the investigations had no valid legislative purpose but only the impermissible goal of exposure for exposure's sake.

Brennan's rejection of Black's absolutist reading of the First Amendment came to the fore in cases dealing with the law of obscenity, and in this area, Brennan emerged as the primary spokesman for the Court. In *Roth v. U.S.* (1957), Brennan, writing for the majority, declared that "obscenity is not within the area of constitutionally protected speech or press." This led him to define obscenity, which he characterized as material "which deals with sex in a manner appealing to prurient interests." Brennan's test for obscenity was "whether to the average person, applying contemporary community standards, the dominant theme of the material taken as a whole appeals to prurient interests." Moreover, any idea having "the slightest redeeming social importance" could claim protection of the First Amendment. Hugo Black and WILLIAM DOUGLAS dissented. Writing for the dissenters, Douglas argued that speech or writing might be suppressed only when they amounted to conduct or were "so closely brigaded with illegal actions as to be an inescapable part of it." For two decades after *Roth*, the Court struggled unsuccessfully to arrive at a working definition of obscenity.

In *Jacobellis v. Ohio* (1964), Brennan emphasized an element he had established as part of the *Roth* test. For material to be obscene, prosecutors had to establish that it was utterly without redeeming social importance. Brennan again spoke for the majority in a case upholding the conviction of a publisher for violating federal postal censorship laws (*Ginzburg v. U.S.*, 1966). In *Memoirs v. Massachusetts* (1966), Brennan's lead opinion held that for material to be found obscene, all elements of the *Roth* test had to "coalesce." Brennan consistently attempted to protect art while permitting the banning of obscenity. In 1973, with four Nixon appointments on the Court, Chief Justice WARREN BURGER revised the *Roth* test. Burger ruled that, in order to be found obscene, material did not need to be "utterly without redeeming social value"; it needed only to lack "serious artistic, political, or scientific value" (*Miller v. California*). Brennan entered a long dissent in which he asserted that the Court had failed to reach a workable definition of obscenity and that failure "has certainly taught that the outright suppression of obscenity cannot be reconciled with the fundamental principles of the First and Fourteenth Amendments."

In criminal rights cases, Brennan generally adopted a liberal position. He favored extending the right to counsel in state court criminal cases, and he voted in March 1960 to overturn the espionage conviction of Soviet Col. Rudolf I. Abel because he believed the evidence used against Abel had been illegally obtained. In March 1959, however, Brennan was part of a majority in two cases that decided that an individual could be tried in both federal and state courts for the same offense without violating the prohibition against double jeopardy.

During the heyday of the Warren Court in the 1960s, Brennan became an even more staunch liberal who believed the judiciary was constitutionally vested with the job of protecting the integrity and privacy of the individual from unnecessary interference by the government. He wrote significant opinions for the Court in cases involving reapportionment, freedom of the press, and the Fourteenth Amendment. Such decisions won him a reputation as a justice who was firmly committed to individual civil liberties and to the guarantees of procedural due process.

Brennan served long enough to see the Court take a more conservative direction in the 1980s. While he had often functioned behind the scenes as the architect who constructed majorities during the Warren era, Brennan later became more outspoken in his liberal views and his criticism of the direction of the Court. He retired from the Court in 1990 and died in Arlington, Va., on July 24, 1997. In his 34 years on the Court, Brennan wrote 533 majority opinions, 694 dissents, and 346 concurring opinions. Many of his dissents came during the later part of his career, as did most of the public attention he attracted. His greatest influence, however, came as the point man for the Warren Court.

—MSM

Brewster, Frank W.
(1898–1996) *vice president, International Brotherhood of Teamsters*

Born in Seattle, Wash., in 1898, Brewster was the son of a postman. He got his first job in 1913 driving a dray team. After serving two years in the army during and after World War I, he became recording secretary of his Teamsters Union local. When the Western Conference of Teamsters was formed in 1937, Brewster became its secretary. He succeeded DAVE BECK as president of the organization in 1953. During 1956, Brewster was involved in a dispute with Beck, then president of the International Brotherhood of Teamsters (IBT), and JAMES R. HOFFA, a vice president, over a mutual aid pact between the Teamsters and the International Longshoremen's Association. Beck and Hoffa favored the pact. Brewster, however, wanted no part of the "racketeering and communism of the longshore unions."

During the opening months of 1957, the Senate Government Operations Committee's Permanent Investigations Subcommittee probed charges of racketeering and illegal use of union funds in the IBT. Over a three-month period, subcommittee counsel ROBERT F. KENNEDY revealed evidence that Brewster had engaged in a variety of illegal activities. Brewster was charged with having used union funds to pay his personal bills (including several for maintenance of his racing stable and traveling expenses for his jockey). Testimony also revealed Brewster's links to organized crime.

Brewster initially refused to testify before the subcommittee and was cited for contempt of Congress in February. The following month, he appeared before the panel. He swore that he had "never conspired" to engage in any racket and knew of no "official or employee of the Teamsters who [had]." Brewster also denied any involvement with organized crime. Finally, he refused to admit that he had used union funds to pay personal bills. He acknowledged, however, that he had ordered his secretary to spend union money for plane tickets for his jockey. Brewster said he had intended to pay it back—although he had not yet done so.

In March, officials of the Western Conference gave Brewster a vote of confidence. They charged that the Senate investigation was being used by employers to prevent unions from obtaining the best possible hours, wages, and working conditions. Brewster was convicted of contempt of Congress in June 1957. The conviction was reversed in April 1958, when an appeals court ruled that the Senate committee had exceeded its jurisdiction in investigating rackets. In June, Brewster was deposed as head of the Western Conference in a power struggle with Jimmy Hoffa. After that, he served as president of Joint Council 28, which represented 46 Teamsters locals in Washington state until 1964. Upon his retirement, Brewster moved to Cathedral City, Calif., where he lived until his death in Rancho Mirage, Calif., on November 15, 1996.

—SY

Bricker, John W(illiam)

(1893–1986) *U.S. senator; chairman, Senate Commerce Committee*

John W. Bricker was born on September 6, 1893, in rural Madison Co., Ohio. He grew up there and received a B.A. from Ohio State University in 1916. During World War I, he served as an army chaplain. Bricker returned to Ohio State and earned a law degree in 1920. He then held several local elective offices as a Republican. He won election as state attorney general in 1932 but lost his bid for reelection. Bricker was elected governor in 1938. A whitemaned, handsome man, an effective speaker, and an efficient administrator, "Honest John" won reelection in 1940 and 1942 by wide margins. After a brief try

for the Republican presidential nomination in 1944, Bricker agreed to run for vice president. The GOP ticket lost in November. Two years later, Bricker won election to the U.S. Senate. There, he stood with the party's conservative "Old Guard." In 1952, as in 1940 and 1948, Bricker backed his fellow Ohioan, Sen. ROBERT A. TAFT (R-Ohio), for the Republican presidential nomination. Running for reelection in 1952, Bricker defeated the Democratic nominee, MICHAEL V. DiSALLE, by a comfortable margin.

Few members of the Old Guard created more problems for the Eisenhower administration than Bricker did between 1953 and 1954. In March 1953, he joined conservative Republicans voting against confirmation of CHARLES E. BOHLEN as ambassador to the Soviet Union. Bricker also initiated efforts to cut the administration's foreign-aid requests. In January 1954, he opposed funding for the Saint Lawrence Seaway, despite its expected benefits to Ohio's ports on Lake Erie. That December, he voted against the censure, quietly sought by the White House, of Sen. JOSEPH R. MCCARTHY (R-Wis.).

Yet no position more aggravated Eisenhower than did Bricker's sponsorship of an amendment to restrict the federal government's treaty-making powers. Bricker had advocated such a proposal since the Truman administration. As reported by the Judiciary Committee in June 1953, the Bricker amendment first voided any provision of treaties that conflicted with the Constitution. Second, it stipulated that "a treaty shall become effective as internal law in the United States only through legislation which would be valid in the absence of a treaty." Known as the "which clause," this section raised the possibility that a single state could nullify an international compact. More important, the amendment delimited Congress's powers. Because of a Supreme Court ruling in 1920, Congress appeared empowered to extend its authority over states in enacting social legislation whenever it was carrying out the obligations of a treaty. Bricker's article would have prevented Congress from passing laws on the basis of that precedent. Finally, the amendment made all executive understandings with foreign powers subject to Senate ratification.

Bricker and other Republican nationalists had condemned Franklin D. Roosevelt's secret agreements with the Soviet Union during World War

II. Bricker and others cited undisclosed, undebated understandings that accepted Soviet expansion into Eastern Europe immediately after the war. The Ohioan had long been a foe of those he called "One Worlders," generally liberal easterners like ELEANOR ROOSEVELT, who promoted international agreements in social and economic policy. Repeatedly, Bricker worked against American funding of the UN's International Labor Organization or its International Atomic Energy Commission. The UN's Covenant on Human Rights particularly incensed Bricker. This covenant, under negotiation between 1948 and 1954, included provisions that suspended such rights as freedom of speech during times of national emergency.

The fight for the Bricker amendment quickly evolved into a mass crusade. Many associations had long advocated a clarification of the statutory effect of treaties and world organizations upon domestic law. Others wanted to restrict the ability of presidents to make international agreements. The Republican platform in 1952 had endorsed Bricker's amendment, as had Taft, the American Bar Association (ABA), and especially its past president, Frank E. Holman. Besides the ABA, pro-amendment associations included the American Farm Bureau, American Legion, and the Daughters of the American Revolution. Special committees like the Vigilant Women for the Bricker Amendment organized spontaneously. Viewing it as a defense of states rights, Southerners opposed to federal civil rights legislation overwhelmingly backed the proposal.

The most pronounced critics of the measure tended to be liberal, long-standing internationalists. Advocates of a strong chief executive, they deemed the Bricker amendment a hazardous weakening of presidential powers. Opponents of the amendment also viewed the mass movement in support of it as "new isolationism."

Eisenhower regarded the Bricker amendment as foolishness and would have preferred simply to let the issue die. Given the widespread support for the amendment, particularly the nearly unanimous support within the Republican party, however, it would not go away. Without Eisenhower's opposition, the amendment would almost certainly have been adopted. Eisenhower met with Bricker several times in an attempt to persuade the senator to settle for innocuous language that Eisenhower could support, but to no avail. The president's supporters in the Senate blocked any action in 1953. Eisenhower, who believed that the amendment restricted presidential authority beyond what the Constitution intended, took a more public stand in opposition to the Bricker amendment in 1954. Administration officials worked out a compromise with Bricker in January, but after conferring with Holman, Bricker repudiated the compromise. Eisenhower then launched an all-out public campaign against the Bricker amendment. Bricker complained that Eisenhower's role in the debate was "highly improper," because, under the Constitution, the president had no formal role in the process of amending the Constitution. Eisenhower became so frustrated with the matter that he told JAMES HAGERTY that "if it's true that when you die the things that bothered you most are engraved on your skull, I am sure I'll have there the mud and dirt of France during [the] invasion and the name of Senator Bricker." Eisenhower's opposition led a number of his supporters in the Senate to withdraw their support for the amendment.

Ultimately, the administration beat the Bricker amendment. On February 25, 1954, Bricker's amendment was defeated 50–42. The next day, a milder version, sponsored by Sen. WALTER F. GEORGE (D-Ga.), fell one vote short of the necessary two-thirds majority. After that, Bricker inexplicably abandoned his crusade. He did reintroduce the amendment in 1955 but did not labor strenuously for it.

On domestic policy, Bricker figured prominently first as chairman (1953–55) and then as the ranking Republican (1955–59) of the Commerce Committee. Early in the fall of 1953, he acknowledged that he had accepted money from his Columbus law firm, which represented the Pennsylvania Railroad; he had done so even though his panel oversaw transportation policy.

Bricker attacked the two then-dominant television networks in February 1955 as a monopoly. In June 1956, however, he defended the major automobile manufacturers on the same charges during Judiciary Committee hearings. That July, Bricker blocked floor consideration of a new bill that policed the pricing policies of major producers.

Bricker unexpectedly lost his Senate seat in 1958. He had originally planned to retire from politics, but Eisenhower, despite the amendment quarrel, urged him to seek a third term. Bricker agreed. However, his victory was jeopardized when a group of Ohio business leaders met in June and determined to place a "right-to-work" (RTW) referendum on the November ballot. The RTW proposal would have prevented "union shop" labor contracts (those compelling employees to join unions after being hired). At the businessmen's gathering in June, Bricker objected vehemently to the initiative. The Ohio GOP would lose badly, he predicted, because it would invariably be identified with the pro-business RTW forces and against organized labor. Although he evaded the RTW issue, he lost to his Democratic opponent, Stephen M. Young, by just over 100,000 votes. But for the RTW issue, Bricker believed, he might have won by between 250,000 and 500,000 votes. Bricker quit active politics to practice law in Columbus. He died there on March 22, 1986.

—MSM

Bridges, Harry (Alfred) (Renton)

(1901–1990) *president, International Longshoremen's and Warehousemen's Union*

The son of a prosperous real estate agent, Bridges was born in Melbourne, Australia, on July 28, 1901. He spent five years as a seaman before beginning work on the San Francisco docks in 1922. In the early 1930s, Bridges emerged as a leader of the newly chartered local of the International Longshoreman's Association (ILA). He led a dock strike in 1934 that touched off a general strike in San Francisco. The strike propelled Bridges into the presidency first of the ILA local and then of the Pacific Coast District. In 1937, he led the Pacific Coast District out of the American Federation of Labor (AFL) and into the Congress of Industrial Organizations (CIO) as the International Longshoremen's and Warehousemen's Union (ILWU). Bridges became the ILWU's first president. Throughout this period, he was a member of the Industrial Workers of the World and remained close to the Communist Party. Bridges always denied that he belonged to the Communist Party, which would have been grounds for depor-

tation, but files of the Communist International opened in 1992 showed that Bridges was elected to the national Central Committee of the Communist Party in 1936. During the 1940s, Bridges became one of the most powerful labor figures on the West Coast, and his ILWU became an important base of communist strength in the CIO.

Beginning in 1939, Bridges was the target of a 16-year effort by the federal government to denaturalize and deport him. Although the CIO expelled the ILWU in 1949 because of communist domination, the Justice Department never proved that Bridges was a communist. However, in 1950, he was convicted of perjury. A jury ruled that he had obtained his U.S. citizenship in 1945 by fraud when he had denied he had ever been a communist. The Federal Appeals Court upheld the conviction in 1952, but in 1953 the Supreme Court ruled that Bridges had been indicted after the statute of limitations had run out.

Long an opponent of congressional investigations of alleged subversion, Bridges threatened in 1955 to shut down all of Hawaii's industries in a protest strike against a four-day hearing Sen. JAMES O. EASTLAND (D-Miss.) had planned to investigate subversion on the islands. However, only 3,000 of Hawaii's 24,000 ILWU members walked off their jobs when the probe began in November. At the hearings, Gov. Samuel W. King testified that ILWU leaders, including Bridges, were the core of the territory's communist problem. He expressed hope that the probe might lead to the ILWU being "listed as Communist-infiltrated" under the Communist Control Act of 1954 and that Hawaiian industry consequently would be freed "from the necessity of recognizing such organizations as legitimate labor unions. . . ." The power of Bridges's union was regarded as one of the obstacles to Hawaiian statehood.

In 1959, Bridges was called to testify on possible Communist Party affiliation before the House Un-American Activities Committee. He invoked the Fifth Amendment, saying he had been cleared of such charges in the past. In answering questions on the union's attitude toward China, Bridges said he personally would "object in every way I could" to shipment of U.S. arms to Nationalist China for the invasion of the Chinese mainland. However, he asserted it would be up to union members to decide whether the ILWU would boycott such shipments. He denied having joined Teamster president JAMES R. HOFFA in plans for a worldwide transport workers' union or having conferred with foreign communists during a trip abroad on how to institute a worldwide shipping boycott.

In October 1959, Bridges became the first labor leader to defy the Landrum-Griffin Act, when he refused to comply with Secretary of Labor JAMES P. MITCHELL's request that he report on communists and ex-convicts in the ILWU. Bridges maintained that the law "violates . . . at least the First and Fifth Amendments."

Bridges continued as president of the ILWU during the 1960s and 1970s. In 1960, he signed a five-and-one-half-year collective bargaining contract with the Pacific Maritime Association. Known as the M & M Agreement, it had a far-reaching impact on the nature of longshore work and the character of the industry. Bridges retired as head of the union in 1977. He died of emphysema in San Francisco, Calif., on March 30, 1990.

—SY

Bridges, (Henry) Styles
(1898–1961) *U.S. senator*

Born in West Pembroke, Maine, on September 9, 1898, Bridges was raised in Maine, where he attended public schools. He received a degree in agriculture from the University of Maine in 1918. After serving as an instructor at Sanderson Academy, in Ashfield, Mass., from 1918 to 1919, he worked as an agricultural agent until 1922, when he became executive secretary of the New Hampshire Farm Bureau Federation. Bridges served as editor of the *Granite Monthly Magazine* from 1924 to 1926 and director and secretary of the New Hampshire Investment Company from 1924 to 1929. He received an appointment to the New Hampshire Public Service Commission in 1930 and served until 1934, when he won the Republican gubernatorial nomination. Later that year, he easily won the general election and became the youngest governor in the nation. As governor, he balanced the budget while sponsoring state unemployment compensation and old-age benefits. In 1936, he bucked the Democratic tide and won election to the U.S. Senate.

Known from the beginning of his tenure as a vigorous conservative and anticommunist, Bridges assailed many of Franklin D. Roosevelt's domestic policies but supported Roosevelt's efforts early in World War II to supply the Allied powers. He was a foe of Secretary of State DEAN ACHESON and led the "Asia firsters" in denouncing the administration's refusal to give large-scale aid to Chiang Kai-shek (Jiang Jieshi) as a "sellout" to the Communists.

Bridges, called the Gray Eminence of the Republican Party, became the senior member of the GOP and its floor leader in the Senate in 1952. With the Republican victory in the election of 1952, he was named president pro tempore of the Senate and chairman of the Appropriations Committee, from which post he frequently pressed for cuts in the federal budget.

Bridges remained a strident anticommunist. When President DWIGHT D. EISENHOWER nominated CHARLES BOHLEN to be ambassador to the Soviet Union in February 1953, Bridges joined other conservatives in attempting to block the appointment. He seized the moment to attack the Yalta agreements of 1945, which Bohlen had helped negotiate, as a traitorous mishandling of American foreign policy and to denounce Bohlen as an "appeaser" of communists. Despite the efforts of conservatives, the Senate confirmed Bohlen in March.

Bridges was a strong supporter of Sen. JOSEPH R. MCCARTHY's (R-Wis.) attacks on alleged subversives in government and disdained Republican moderates' misgivings about McCarthy's tactics. When, in September 1954, the Senate Select Committee to Study Censure Charges filed a report recommending censure of McCarthy for his contempt of the Senate and his abuse of Gen. RALPH ZWICKER, Bridges began attempts to either dilute the resolution or defeat it entirely. First he pressed to delay the full Senate hearings on the resolution until after the elections that November. With that objective accomplished, he used the period of Senate inactivity to attempt to win moderate Republican support for McCarthy. He hoped to win enough Republican support to approach Democratic leaders and offer a compromise resolution so that the censure did not appear to be a partisan Democratic move. The support did not materialize; the Senate condemned McCarthy in December. One of 22 Republicans to vote against the measure, Bridges denounced the action as a blow against patriotic anticommunism.

Undaunted, Bridges carried his anticommunist battle to the White House. When President Eisenhower agreed to U.S. participation in a Geneva summit conference in 1955, Bridges avowed that all international conferences held the dangers of "appeasement, compromise and weakness"—particularly those conferences that included the USSR. Eisenhower, who had been threatened with the Bricker amendment that sought to curb his treaty-making power, promised Bridges and other Republican leaders that he would take no actions without congressional approval.

In 1956 Bridges introduced amendments that would have cut off all aid to Yugoslavia. He also ridiculed the neutralist positions of Prime Minister Jawaharlal Nehru and wanted to decrease U.S. assistance to India.

Bridges was a prominent political strategist in the Republican hierarchy, particularly as the chairman of the GOP Policy Committee from 1955 to 1961. Eisenhower's heart attack in 1955 occasioned major concerns within the party: the possibility of his death in office, the delegation of his responsibilities during the illness, and the status of the Republican ticket in 1956. Fully aware of the importance of the vice presidency, some conservatives, displeased with RICHARD NIXON because of his association with Eisenhower's moderate policies, hoped to advance Bridges as a candidate for the office. Bridges, however, strongly supported Nixon's remaining on the ticket. During Eisenhower's illnesses, Bridges advocated Nixon's assumption of some presidential duties, but he found his suggestions blocked by the White House chief of staff, SHERMAN ADAMS. The New Hampshire senator believed Nixon to be a strong candidate for president in 1960.

Bridges won a fifth term in the Senate in 1960. He supported those actions of the Kennedy administration that he believed challenged communism and advised a resumption of U.S. nuclear testing in 1961. He died in Concord, N.H., on November 26, 1961.

—TGD

Brown, Clarence
(1893–1965) *U.S. congressman*

Brown was born in Blanchester, Ohio, on July 14, 1893. As a boy, he sold popcorn and newspapers and served as a janitor in a bank. He studied at Washington and Lee University law school from 1913 to 1915. Rather than practice law, he became a newspaper publisher. In 1918, Brown was elected lieutenant governor of Ohio and served two two-year terms. He won the election for secretary of state in 1926. In 1932, he lost in the Republican gubernatorial primary. Two years later, he won the nomination for governor but was defeated in the general election. Brown headed Frank Knox's campaign for the vice presidency in 1936.

Brown won election to a seat in the U.S. House of Representatives in 1938. Before World War II, he generally opposed legislation aimed at reversing American neutrality. After the war, he opposed aid to Greece and Turkey on grounds of economy but was paired in favor of the Marshall Plan.

Brown compiled a consistently conservative record on domestic issues. He supported the establishment of the Un-American Activities Committee on a permanent basis in 1945, the Taft-Hartley Act in 1947, and the Internal Security Act in 1950. However, he backed a bill outlawing the poll tax in 1944 and the Fair Employment Practices Act of 1950.

In 1952, as in 1940 and 1948, Brown actively supported Sen. ROBERT A. TAFT (R-Ohio) for the Republican presidential nomination. He served as one of Taft's campaign managers and was one of the Ohio senator's major strategists in the struggle over contested delegate seats at the Republican National Convention. At the first session of the convention, he moved to exclude, on a technicality, Taft's Louisiana delegates from the provisions of the "Fair Play" amendment. This rule stipulated that contested delegates could not vote on any challenges to delegates' credentials. The defeat of Brown's proposal was an early signal that Taft's nomination bid would fail. Taft and many others regarded Brown's proposal as a major tactical error, because it appeared to be a crude, unprincipled attempt to strengthen the Ohioan's forces.

Brown was appointed to the Commission on Organization of the Executive Branch of the Government, unofficially known as the Second Hoover

Commission. An opponent of what he regarded as government encroachment on business, he concurred with the committee's report, issued in 1955, which urged substantial cutbacks in government activity. Its major proposals, echoing the general theme "get government out of business," included the transfer of federal lending agencies and power installations to private hands and the elimination of federal medical services. Testifying before the Government Operations Committee's Intergovernmental Relations Subcommittee in 1954, Brown criticized military commissaries as presenting "a real threat to free enterprise" because of their competition with private business.

A member of the Rules Committee, which had the power to block legislation on the way from its committee of original jurisdiction to the House floor, he generally joined the coalition of southern Democrats and conservative Republicans on the panel in their often successful efforts to kill liberal social welfare measures. He helped block housing bills in 1955, 1959, and 1960 and school aid and minimum wage bills in the latter year. However, in 1957 and 1960, he backed successful efforts to clear civil rights bills for consideration on the floor of the House.

As a member of the rules panel, Brown was a leading opponent of President JOHN F. KENNEDY's domestic legislation. Brown died of uremic poisoning in Washington, D.C., on August 23, 1965.

—MLL

Brown, Edmund G(erald)

(1905–1996) *governor of California*

The son of Gold Rush settlers, "Pat" Brown was born in San Francisco, Calif., on April 21, 1905. He attended public and parochial schools in San Francisco. Lacking the money to attend college, he worked in his father's cigar store–poker room establishment while studying law at night. He received his LL.B. from the San Francisco Law School in 1927 and opened a private practice in San Francisco. In 1928, Brown entered politics as an unsuccessful Republican candidate for the California Assembly. He switched parties during the New Deal and, after an unsuccessful bid for the office in 1939, won the first of two terms as San Francisco district attorney

in 1943. Brown was elected state attorney general in 1950 and again in 1954. As the only Democrat holding statewide office, he was the titular head of the state Democratic Party. During his eight years in office, he earned a reputation as a progressive but a tough criminal investigator.

In 1958, Brown entered the state's gubernatorial race against Republican Sen. WILLIAM F. KNOWLAND. Knowland's extreme conservatism enabled Brown to seize the center of the political spectrum. Brown described himself as a "responsible" liberal and advocated more ambitious state programs to keep pace with California's demographic and physical growth. Backed strongly by organized labor, which mobilized its ranks to help Brown and defeat a right-to-work initiative backed by his opponent, the Democrat won the November election by more than 1 million votes. He became the state's second Democratic governor in the century. Democrats also swept into all the top state offices except one and carried the first Democratic majorities in both houses of the legislature since 1889.

As governor, Brown undertook an ambitious bipartisan legislative program that easily passed the legislature. He took action on air pollution, problems confronting the elderly, prisons, highway safety, and atomic energy. Brown also established a state economic development commission, a consumers' council, and the state's first fair employment practices commission. The governor developed $200 million in new tax revenues and abolished the state's troublesome cross-filing primary election system, which allowed a voter to participate in any primary he chose, regardless of his registration. Brown also brought northern and southern California interests together to approve the $1.7 billion California Water Project in 1960. The project, the most costly in U.S. history, was designed to provide water from the northern part of the state for the burgeoning population of the south and the irrigated farmlands of the Central Valley.

At the time, Brown's plan was lauded as a spectacular achievement. By the 1970s, however, observers concluded that the plan had become unnecessary because of the slowdown in California's population increase and had caused ecological damage to northern rivers. One of Ralph Nader's research groups charged that the water project was a "special interest boondoggle" that ultimately cost close to $10 billion and placed greater burdens on the individual taxpayer than on the largest industrial and corporate farm users of the water.

During his early years as governor, Brown made a number of important enemies, who continued to plague him throughout his career. His unsuccessful effort to pass a tax on oil alienated California's powerful oil lobby. His attempts to subject unions to state regulations failed and weakened organized labor's support for his future political ambitions.

Brown's inconsistent position on the fate of CARYL CHESSMAN, a convicted rapist, hurt his standing both among conservatives and a large segment of liberal Democrats. Chessman, who had spent over a decade on San Quentin's Death Row, had become an international cause célèbre through repeated protestations of his innocence and publication of four popular books. In October 1959, Brown rejected a plea for clemency, but Chessman's life was spared for the seventh time by a stay of execution from the U.S. Supreme Court. In February 1960, Brown reprieved Chessman 10 days before his eighth scheduled date of execution because, Brown said, the State Department had informed him that President Eisenhower's visit to Uruguay might be disturbed by hostile demonstrations if Chessman were executed. In addition, Brown argued that he wanted the California legislature to consider abolition of the death penalty. Chessman was finally executed in May 1960 after Brown refused to grant another reprieve. Demonstrators at the execution attacked the governor as "the hangman of California."

Brown's power within California's Democratic Party declined after 1961, as President Kennedy looked to the Democratic Speaker of the assembly, Jesse Unruh, as his chief political operative in the state. Nonetheless, Brown won a spectacular reelection victory in November 1962 over former vice president RICHARD NIXON. Brown's second term coincided with the student revolt at the University of California at Berkeley, the Watts riot in 1965, and the growing farmworker movement. Conservative Republicans resented these developments and held Brown's "soft" liberalism partly responsible. In 1966, Brown lost his bid for a third

gubernatorial term to Ronald Reagan, a former movie star and conservative spokesman. Following his defeat, Brown served as head of the National Commission for the Reform of Federal Criminal Laws. He died in Beverly Hills, Calif., on February 16, 1996.

—JCH

Brown, Winthrop G(ilman)
(1907–1987) *ambassador to Laos*

Born on July 12, 1907, in Seal Harbor, Maine, Brown attended Yale law school, and after receiving his degree in 1929, practiced in New York. He joined the staff of the Lend-Lease Administration in 1941. Over the next five years, he represented the agency in missions in London and New Delhi. Brown was director of the Office of International Trade Policy from 1947 to 1950 and of the Office of International Materials Policy from 1950 to 1952. During the 1950s, he served as minister for Economic Affairs in London and New Delhi. In July 1960, he became an ambassador to Laos.

Brown arrived at his assignment shortly before a coup on August 9, led by Laotian Air Force Capt. Kong Le, toppled the pro-American government of Gen. Phoumi Nosavan. Brown sympathized with Le, whom he considered a sincere nationalist disturbed by Phoumi's corruption. The ambassador did not think Le a potential ally of the communist Pathet Lao, which controlled a large portion of the countryside, and he saw no danger to American interests from the new regime. Despite requests from the State Department that he take steps to have Le removed, Brown did not act, preferring to see how the situation developed.

Kong Le turned administrative power over to neutralist Prince Souvanna Phouma, who formed a government composed of opponents of Phoumi's pro-Western stance. Phoumi refused to accept Souvanna's offer of a position in the new regime. Instead, he decided to use his control of the Royal Laotian Army to retake the government by force.

Brown respected Souvanna and soon threw his support behind the neutralist leader. He questioned the possibility of developing a pro-Western government in light of the corruption of the previous regime and growing nationalist feelings in the country. However, many high State Department officials feared that Souvanna would make an alliance with the Left, and they demanded his replacement.

Because of the growing opposition to Souvanna in Washington, Brown was anxious to promote a rightist-neutralist coalition that would exclude pro-communists. At the same time, he attempted to prevent Phoumi from reestablishing his control through military action. Brown was unsuccessful in his efforts, because the Central Intelligence Agency continued to supply Phoumi with troops and material.

Unable to get U.S. military aid or assurances of diplomatic backing, Souvanna formed an alliance with the Pathet Lao in September. Hoping to reverse Souvanna's stand, Brown asked the State Department to grant him assistance. Washington did give both Souvanna and Phoumi loans but granted military aid only to Phoumi. Nevertheless, Brown still pushed for a reorientation of American policy. He risked his own diplomatic position by returning instructions to Washington and asking for clarification. In this way, he hoped to maintain a discussion of policy options.

By November, Brown and Washington were pursuing opposite policies. The State Department openly backed Phoumi, who had begun his military campaign against Souvanna. Brown opposed this action and asked for U.S. air support to reinforce Souvanna's troops, led by Kong Le. By the end of the month, he was able to persuade Washington to cut off aid to Phoumi. However, by that time the general had driven Souvanna to exile and Kong Le into an alliance with the communists.

Brown remained at his post into the Kennedy administration. Unlike his predecessor, JOHN F. KENNEDY, although reluctantly, supported a neutralist government in Laos. It was formed in June 1962. Brown, however, had little part in the negotiations leading to its creation. During the Johnson administration, he served as ambassador to Korea and special assistant to the Secretary of State. He was appointed deputy assistant secretary of state for East Asian and Pacific affairs in 1968. Brown retired from the Foreign Service two years later. He died in Washington, D.C., on May 25, 1987.

—EWS

Brownell, Herbert, Jr.
(1904–1996) *attorney general*

The son of a university teacher, Herbert Brownell, Jr., was born on February 20, 1904, in Peru, Neb. He grew up in Nebraska and attended the University of Nebraska, where he edited the college newspaper. He earned his law degree from Yale law school, where he was editor of the law review in 1927 and began his career with Root, Clark, Backner & Ballantine in Manhattan. In 1929, he joined the firm of Lord, Day and Lord, with which he was associated for 60 years. Brownell's specialty was hotel and restaurant law. He also served as counsel for New York's 1939 World's Fair.

Brownell became active in New York Republican politics early in his career. From 1933 to 1937, he represented a Manhattan district in the New York State Assembly. Brownell became politically prominent with the help of Manhattan district attorney THOMAS E. DEWEY. He managed Dewey's unsuccessful bid for the governorship in 1938 as well as his successful campaign in 1942. Accompanying Dewey to Albany, Brownell handled patronage but refused a cabinet post. He was manager of Dewey's unsuccessful presidential campaigns in 1944 and 1948, and he also served as chairman of the Republican National Committee from 1944–46.

During the campaign of 1952, Brownell was one of Gen. DWIGHT D. EISENHOWER's key advisers. He played a major role in the formulation of strategy at the convention, most notably in his recommendation that Eisenhower forces support a "Fair Play Amendment," under which many delegates backing Sen. ROBERT TAFT (R-Ohio) were unseated. Brownell also urged Eisenhower to select Sen. RICHARD NIXON (R-Calif.) as his running mate. After Eisenhower's election in November, Brownell continued in his crucial advisory role, proposing cabinet nominees and overseeing patronage. According to presidential assistant SHERMAN ADAMS, "Eisenhower at that time had more confidence in Brownell's political advice than he had in anyone else's." On November 21, the president-elect designated Brownell as his attorney general.

During Brownell's first year in office, the debate over communists in government continued to rage. A vigorous anticommunist, Brownell generated controversy with a speech he gave to the

Executives Club of Chicago on November 6, 1953, in which he alleged that Harry Dexter White, an assistant secretary of the Treasury whom President HARRY S. TRUMAN appointed to be executive director of the International Monetary Fund (IMF) in 1946, had not only been a spy but that evidence of his activities had been forwarded to the Truman White House before Truman named him to the IMF. Based on the testimony of Elizabeth Bentley and WHITTAKER CHAMBERS, White had been accused in 1948 of spying for the Soviet Union (a charge that would, in the 1990s, be supported by the release of the Venona transcripts). Brownell based his accusation on files in the Justice Department that both supported the allegations of spying and established that Gen. Harry Vaughn, Truman's military aide, had received a report from the FBI on White's activities in December 1945. Moreover, when Truman's nomination of White became public, the FBI sent Truman a second, more detailed report of White's activities.

Truman vehemently denied that White had been a communist and that he had seen the FBI reports. The former president accused Brownell of making the accusation for political purposes and accused him of "McCarthyism." Other prominent Democrats quickly echoed Truman's charges. However, Truman later admitted that he had, indeed, seen the reports, but only after it came out that a duplicate of the second report had gone to JAMES F. BYRNES, then the secretary of state. Truman then changed his story; he had fired White as soon as he discovered the latter's disloyalty. In fact, White had remained at the IMF for 11 months and then resigned without explanation. Moreover, Frank Coe, whom White had appointed as his assistant and whom the FBI had identified as a member of a Soviet espionage ring (a charge that would also be supported by the Venona transcripts), remained at the IMF until December 1952.

On November 10, Truman gave a speech in which he called Brownell a liar and denounced "fake crusaders who dig up and distort records of the past." In a press conference on November 11, Eisenhower said that he did not believe that Truman had knowingly appointed a communist to high office. The president went on to say that it was reckless and un-American to make accusations without being prepared to make the evidence available. However, he maintained that FBI files should not be released. At the same time, Eisenhower backed his attorney general and rejected suggestions that Brownell had impugned Truman's loyalty. In the meantime, the House Committee on Un-American Activities had subpoenaed Truman, and Eisenhower said that he would not have subpoenaed the former president. On the same day, Brownell explained that he criticized the "laxity" of the previous administration and had not intended to question Truman's loyalty.

On November 16, Truman gave an address on national television and radio, in which he acknowledged that he had received the FBI report on White in February 1946, after White's confirmation for the IMF. He further said that the FBI's charges were "impossible to prove." Truman then stated that he had appointed White to the IMF with the approval of the FBI in order not to disrupt ongoing FBI investigations or to alert White that he was under suspicion. The next day, in sworn testimony before the Senate Internal Security Subcommittee, J. EDGAR HOOVER, director of the FBI, contradicted Truman's version of events. Hoover testified that he told TOM CLARK, Truman's attorney general, that appointing White was "unwise"; he also stated that White's appointment actually hampered the FBI's investigation, because the IMF's premises were "extraterritorial" and therefore FBI agents could not enter them. Brownell also testified before the same subcommittee, and the administration partly declassified the FBI reports on White sent to the White House between November 1945 and February 1946. Brownell told the subcommittee that the FBI report received by the White House in December 1945 "constituted adequate warning to anyone who read it" that appointing White to the IMF constituted an "extreme danger to the security of the country." The attorney general also testified that, although a grand jury had not indicted White in 1948, "much of this evidence" against White had been obtained by wiretap and was therefore not admissible before a federal grand jury. The subcommittee took no action, and the White matter quickly faded from public attention.

In a letter to AL GRUENTHER, commander of NATO, Eisenhower wrote that "the White case was unquestionably distorted in the papers, and I am quite ready to admit that the manner of its presentation was probably not the best. However, so far as the plain, unvarnished fact is concerned, I can see no flaw in the entire line of argument and exposition that was presented publicly by Attorney General Brownell and J. Edgar Hoover."

On other issues involving communists and suspected subversives, Brownell consistently followed a hard line. In June 1953, he filed an immediate protest when Supreme Court Justice WILLIAM O. DOUGLAS granted a stay of execution to convicted spies JULIUS and ETHEL ROSENBERG. The full Court soon reversed the order. Brownell advised Eisenhower to reject calls for clemency. Brownell asked Congress in April 1954 to permit the death penalty for peacetime spying as well as wartime espionage.

In August 1953, Brownell declared that U.S. communists were "a greater menace now than at any time [because they] have gone underground since the Smith Act trials started. They are better organized and detection is more difficult." In line with his pledge to "utterly destroy all" Communist Party activities in the United States, Brownell from 1953 to 1955 proposed a body of anticommunist legislation for congressional enactment. He sought legislation to compel witnesses to testify if granted immunity from criminal prosecution. He requested a "greatly needed" amendment to the perjury law to make "willful giving of contradictory statements under oath" a crime. Existing law required the government to prove one of the statements false. He recommended increasing penalties for seditious conspiracy and advocating the forcible overthrow of the government to a maximum of 20 years imprisonment; he also sought authority for the government to revoke the citizenship of persons convicted of such offenses. Under his existing authority, Brownell added scores of left-wing organizations to the attorney general's list of subversive groups, a number that exceeded 300 by 1955.

The attorney general personally intervened in a split within the Justice Department in 1955 over a case involving the right of a fired government employee to confront his accuser. The department's brief, urging the Supreme Court to uphold

the 1951 U.S. Public Health Service's dismissal of Dr. John Peters on loyalty grounds, was signed by Brownell instead of Solicitor General SIMON SOBELOFF, who normally represented the government before the Supreme Court. Sobeloff argued that Peters's dismissal violated the Fifth Amendment's ban on depriving a person of liberty or property without due process of law, while Brownell maintained that the due process clause did not cover government jobs, since government security programs depended on undercover agents and secret informers. Sobeloff declined to argue the case. In June 1955, the Court overturned Peters's dismissal. The Court decided the case on procedural grounds; it held that the Loyalty Review Board had exceeded its authority by deciding to review a case that had not been appealed to it. The Court did not rule on the constitutional question of whether Peters had been denied due process of law.

Brownell singled out labor unions for special attention in his anticommunist offensive. In an interview in August 1953, he rejected the idea that communists were "concentrated in the clergy"; he said, "I suppose there are more in labor unions than anywhere else." In July 1955, he asked that the striking Union of Mine, Mill and Smelter Workers be stripped of its privileges before the National Labor Relations Board on the grounds that it was communist-dominated. In December, he urged the Subversive Activities Control Board to declare the striking United Electrical, Radio and Machine Workers (UE) "communist-infiltrated." The president of the EU, Albert Fitzgerald, denied Brownell's accusation and denounced him as "the nation's No. 1 strikebreaker."

In the area of antitrust policy, the Justice Department under Brownell differed in a number of ways from its Democratic predecessors. In June 1953, Brownell pledged that the Eisenhower administration would tolerate "no winking" at antitrust violations but would emphasize civil rather than criminal actions. He attempted to hire only top law school graduates for the department and the antitrust division under the so-called Honors Program. He promulgated a firm rule whereby lawyers who had worked for the division could not represent firms being sued by the division for a two-year period after leaving the Justice Department.

He also sought legislation raising from $5,000 to $50,000 the maximum fine for antitrust violations and enabling the government to sue for actual damages resulting from violations, since the government was the nation's "largest single purchaser of goods" and its losses could be substantial.

Among the firms prosecuted for antitrust violations by Brownell's department were the Westinghouse Electric Co. and the Aluminum Company of America (Alcoa). Perhaps the most ambitious suit filed during his tenure was against the General Motors Corp. (GM). The suit charged that GM, which sold 84 percent of all new buses in 1955, had conspired with four bus operating companies to maintain its monopoly. In June 1953, he pledged grand jury proceedings against several large international oil companies that allegedly formed a cartel to control distribution and prices. "The highest considerations of national security" was the explanation given for the dismissal.

In January 1956, the Justice Department signed a famous consent decree with the American Telephone and Telegraph Co. (AT&T). The original suit, filed by the Justice Department in 1949, had charged AT&T with monopolizing the telephone market via its control of the Western Electric Co., the leading manufacturer of telephone equipment, and called for the separation of the two companies. On taking office, Brownell met privately with AT&T's general counsel to discuss ways of ending the litigation without damaging AT&T. The settlement, reached in 1956, allowed AT&T to keep Western Electric and continue their previous arrangements. AT&T consented to license patents to all applicants at reasonable royalties. Brownell called the decree "a major victory" for the government, but *Business Week* commented that the "'major victory' turned out on second look to be hardly more than a slap on the wrist for the biggest corporation in the world."

Within the Eisenhower cabinet, Brownell was the most active proponent of expanding the role of the federal government in protecting civil rights. In December 1953, he filed an amicus curiae brief in *Brown v. Board of Education*, then before the Supreme Court. The brief supported the Court's authority to declare school segregation unconstitutional, as the Court eventually ruled in 1954. (The

new chief justice, EARL WARREN, had been chosen by President Eisenhower upon Brownell's recommendation.)

Brownell was the key administration figure behind the conception and passage of the Civil Rights Act of 1957. The proposed bill, put together by Justice Department lawyers early in 1956, would have created a Civil Rights Commission and a new civil rights division within the Justice Department. Its third section would have armed the government with injunctive power against civil rights violations and enabled the attorney general to join civil suits against individuals infringing on others' civil rights. A fourth section protected voting rights. Despite a lack of enthusiasm on the part of Eisenhower and much of the rest of the cabinet, Brownell won official backing for the proposals and defended them before the Judiciary Committees in Congress in the spring of 1956. The bill passed the House, but LYNDON JOHNSON, the majority leader in the Senate, killed the bill by consigning it to JAMES O. EASTLAND's Judiciary Committee. Johnson wanted no part of an issue that would divide the Democratic party in an election year.

Brownell played an active part in the Senate battle over the bill in the spring of 1957. He argued strongly against an amendment initiated by southern senators to require jury trials for persons charged with contempt of court for violating injunctions against interfering with individuals' voting rights. The administration's version left contempt decisions up to the discretion of a federal judge. It was widely assumed that southern juries would refuse to convict accused violators of civil rights laws. Brownell warned that the jury trial amendment guaranteed the "practical nullification" of the bill's effectiveness by "seriously weakening" the power of federal courts to enforce their orders. He pointed out that under "traditional rules of procedure" a "defendant is not entitled to jury trial in contempt proceedings" when the government sued for "preventive relief."

The Senate passed the jury trial amendment nevertheless, and also deleted the bill's controversial Part III. In the debates, southern senators attacked Brownell as the author of these allegedly punitive sections. The final bill retained the Civil Rights Commission, the new civil rights division for the

Justice Department, and the voting rights section with the jury trial amendment.

Brownell also played a vital advisory role in the school integration crisis in Little Rock, Ark., in September 1957. Gov. ORVAL FAUBUS precipitated the crisis when he ordered the Arkansas National Guard to prevent black students from entering the city's Central High School as part of a court-ordered integration plan. Acting on Brownell's advice, President Eisenhower dispatched regular army paratroopers to Little Rock to enforce the federal court's integration order.

Perhaps Brownell's most significant contribution to civil rights as attorney general was his role in the appointment of liberal and moderate judges to the federal judiciary in the South. With Brownell's advice, Eisenhower appointed Sobeloff, CLEMENT F. HAYNSWORTH, and Herbert S. Boreman to the Fourth Circuit Court of Appeals. He appointed ELBERT P. TUTTLE, JOHN MINOR WISDOM, and John R. Brown to the Fifth Circuit. Southerners blocked the Sobeloff nomination for more than a year and held up Haynsworth's confirmation for nine months.

Brownell resigned as attorney general in 1957 and returned to Lord, Day & Lord, serving as senior partner until he stepped down in 1977. He was of counsel to the firm from 1977–89. Brownell was president of the Association of the Bar of the City of New York in 1963 and later served as an adviser to Mayor JOHN V. LINDSAY, who had been his executive assistant in the Justice Department. He died in New York City on May 1, 1996.

—MSM

Bruce, David K(irkpatrick) E(ste)
(1898–1977) *observer to the European Defense Community Interim Commission and special representative to the European Coal and Steel Community, ambassador to Germany*

Born to a socially and politically prominent family in Baltimore, Md., on February 12, 1898, David Bruce was the son of William Cabell Bruce, a writer and author of a Pulitzer Prize–winning biography of Benjamin Franklin. William Bruce also served as U.S. senator from Maryland from 1923 to 1929. David Bruce attended Princeton University but left

during his second year to join the National Guard. He was sent to France, but World War I ended before he saw combat. After attending law school at the Universities of Virginia and Maryland, Bruce began practicing law in Baltimore in 1921. He won election to Maryland's House of Delegates in 1924 and served a single term. In 1926, he became vice counsel in Rome but returned to the United States the following year to join the Bankers Trust Co. He continued a close association with the Mellon family and also worked for W. AVERELL HARRIMAN. Bruce helped the Mellons establish the National Gallery of Art in the late 1930s and served as president of the museum. He won election to the Virginia House of Delegates in 1939. The following year, with World War II under way in Europe, he became chief representative of the American Red Cross in London.

Bruce did not serve long with the Red Cross. William J. Donovan recruited him to help set up the Office of Strategic Services (OSS), an intelligence agency that became the forerunner of the Central Intelligence Agency. Given the rank of colonel in the U.S. Army Air Corps, Bruce commanded OSS operations in Europe from 1943 until the end of the war. In June 1947, he became assistant secretary of commerce under his friend and business associate, W. Averell Harriman. Bruce went to Paris to administer the Marshall Plan in 1948, and became ambassador to France one year later. In April 1952, Bruce was named undersecretary of state and also assumed the posts of alternate governor of the International Monetary Fund and governor of the International Bank for Reconstruction and Development (World Bank).

In February 1953, President Eisenhower appointed Bruce observer at the Interim Commission of the European Defense Community (EDC) and special representative to the European Coal and Steel Community (ECSC). Bruce had long been a proponent of European integration and was an originator of the concept of a European army. In addition, he was well acquainted with European political leaders, particularly the French, whose consent was vital for the establishment of the EDC. Because he was a liberal and a leading financial contributor to the Democratic Party, conservative Republicans disapproved of the nomination, but the Senate easily confirmed him.

Based in Paris, Bruce's operation was established to convince Europeans of the merits of political, economic, and military integration. By the end of 1953, the six member-nations had created a single market for coal and steel. Despite early production difficulties and conflicts among the members, the economic union progressed, and in 1958 it gave way to the European Economic Community.

Bruce found the EDC negotiations more difficult. He traveled throughout Western Europe seeking support for a supranational army capable of resisting Soviet aggression without a heavy U.S. commitment. He concentrated most of his attention, however, on France. Although he had considerable popularity in that country, members of the French National Assembly criticized him for conducting a high-pressure lobbying campaign for the EDC. Opponents of EDC, including communists, Gaullist nationalists, and those fearful of German rearmament, combined to reject the EDC in the assembly in August 1954. The defeat of EDC was a personal setback for Bruce and effectively concluded his special role in Europe.

Bruce left the State Department in February 1955, but agreed to serve as a consultant. In August 1956, President Eisenhower named him to an eight-member board of consultants that periodically reviewed foreign intelligence activities. Six months later, he returned to full-time diplomatic work as ambassador to West Germany. Less popular in Germany than in France, Bruce nonetheless succeeded in cultivating an extremely close relationship with Chancellor Konrad Adenauer, although he neglected other West German politicians and trade union leaders.

Bruce resigned his diplomatic post in November 1959 to serve as a foreign policy adviser to the Democratic Party during the presidential election of 1960. In February 1961, President JOHN F. KENNEDY named him ambassador to Great Britain. Bruce thus became the first U.S. diplomat to hold the three most important European ambassadorships. He remained in London until February 1969. After a brief retirement, Bruce was appointed U.S. representative to the Vietnam peace talks in Paris in 1970, and in 1973 he went to Beijing as liaison officer to the People's Republic of China. President GERALD R. FORD appointed him ambassador to the North Atlantic Treaty Organization in 1974. He retired again in January 1976 and died in Washington, D.C., on December 5, 1977.

—MSM

Brucker, Wilber M(arion)
(1894–1968) *secretary of the army*

The son of a judge and Democratic congressman, Brucker was born in Saginaw, Mich., on June 23, 1894. He worked his way through the University of Michigan, from which he received a degree in law in 1916. He enlisted in the Michigan National Guard and served on the Mexican border from 1916 to 1917. After attending First Officers' Training Camp at Fort Sheridan, in Illinois, he was commissioned a second lieutenant in the Infantry. He served in France from 1917 to 1918. Upon leaving the service, he returned to Michigan and became assistant prosecuting attorney of Saginaw Co. in 1919, serving in that position until he became prosecuting attorney in 1923. He was assistant attorney general of Michigan from 1927 to 1928 and attorney general from 1928 to 1930. Brucker was elected governor and served a single term from 1930 to 1932. After losing his bid for reelection, he joined the Detroit law firm of Clark, Klein, Brucker, and Waples.

Brucker left private law practice upon his nomination as general counsel of the Defense Department in 1954. He gained publicity during the Army-McCarthy hearings of that year by laughing at Sen. JOSEPH R. MCCARTHY's (R-Wis.) accusation that President DWIGHT D. EISENHOWER was conducting "a conspiracy of silence" about military security. However, Brucker called for legislation to keep subversives out of defense plants and supervised the development of a Pentagon program to screen and review all personnel in the Defense Department. In 1955, NORMAN THOMAS and other civil libertarians attacked the army's security program for issuing less than honorable discharges to military personnel based on preinduction activities.

Appointed secretary of the army in June 1955, Brucker initially supported the administration's "New Look" policy, which stressed nuclear deterrence as the nation's primary defense. However, by 1957, he joined Army Chief of Staff MAXWELL D. TAYLOR in opposing the budget reductions the policy entailed. During testimony before the Senate Appropriations Committee, Brucker argued that the cutbacks would reduce troop strength, lower service standards, and limit research in biological and chemical warfare. Taking a vigorous stand in opposition to the emphasis on nuclear weapons, he stated that modern warfare would require the development of tactics to meet limited types of conflict. At the meeting of the Association of the U.S. Army in 1958, Brucker argued that, as nuclear stalemate was reached between the United States and the USSR, the possibilities of limited wars would be "most likely." A year later, he told members of Congress that the communists had been involved in 18 limited wars since 1945 and described the Soviet army as "modern, mobile and menacing." Before leaving office, Brucker initiated a reorganization plan for the army to enable it to adapt to either atomic or conventional war on any scale.

In 1957, after President Eisenhower issued an executive order placing the Arkansas National Guard under federal control and Secretary of Defense CHARLES E. WILSON ordered 1,000 troops into Little Rock, Ark., Brucker supervised the government's enforcement of the integration of Central High School. After the inauguration of JOHN F. KENNEDY in 1961, Brucker returned to Detroit and engaged in the private practice of law with Brucker and Brucker until his death at Grosse Pointe Farms, Mich., on October 28, 1968.

—MSM

Brundage, Percival F(lack)

(1892–1979) *director, Bureau of the Budget*
The son of a Protestant minister, Brundage was born on April 2, 1892. He graduated from Harvard in 1914 with a B.A. in the classics. He then took a job as an office boy with an accounting firm in New York. Following a night course in accounting, he joined another firm, Price, Waterhouse & Co., in 1916. Brundage remained with Price, Waterhouse for the next 38 years, advancing from staff accountant to partner in 1930 and senior partner by 1944. He joined the Eisenhower administration in May 1954 as deputy director of the budget; in April 1956 he was sworn in as successor to director ROWLAND HUGHES.

As budget director, Brundage spearheaded the administration's drive to get the government out of competition with private industry. In May 1956, the Budget Bureau reported that the federal government was operating 19,321 commercial and industrial facilities. At the end of October, Brundage disclosed that 492 of those facilities had been dropped or curtailed on the principle that "the government has ordinarily no right to compete in a private enterprise economy," even if "the apparent cost" to the government would be increased by shifting to private production. Brundage also announced that the government had sold over $1 billion of the assets of the liquidated Reconstruction Finance Corp.

Throughout 1957, Brundage was at the center of a controversy over the budget for fiscal 1958, the first he prepared. Presented in January 1957, the 1958 budget placed estimated expenditures at $71.8 billion, the highest ever in peacetime. Over the next few months, Brundage was in the paradoxical position of defending the administration's budget while President Eisenhower and Secretary of the Treasury GEORGE HUMPHREY were inviting Congress to make cuts.

In January, Brundage appeared before the Joint Economic Committee and characterized his budget as a "good budget and a fair compromise." In May, after months of congressional criticism, he said the budget had been "examined, analyzed and evaluated" and could be cut no further. However, some fiscal conservatives remained unsatisfied. Sen. HARRY BYRD (D-Va.), chairman of the Senate Finance Committee, called on President Eisenhower to replace Brundage with someone "dedicated to economy instead of . . . finding new ways to spend more money."

Brundage was also an adversary of congressional proposals for tax cuts, which he steadfastly opposed through 1957. In October, he argued that the projected surplus of $1.5 billion for fiscal 1958 was too small to allow for tax reductions. Ultimately, the recession of 1958 wiped out the expected surplus, and the 1958 budget instead ended up with a $2.8 billion deficit.

Brundage left the Budget Bureau in March 1958 and returned to Price, Waterhouse as a consultant. He died in Ridgewood, N.J., on July 16, 1979.

—TO

Buckley, William F(rank), Jr.
(1925–2008) *author*

The sixth of 10 children, Buckley was born in New York City on November 24, 1925. His father, William Frank Buckley, Sr., was a wealthy lawyer and oil executive. William F. Buckley, Jr., moved with his family from Mexico to Sharon, Conn., and then began his formal education in Paris. He attended private schools in England and began high school at the Catholic Beaumont College in England. During World War II, Buckley returned to the United States, where he attended Millbrook School in Millbrook, N.Y., from which he graduated in 1943. Buckley adopted his father's strong Catholic faith and his conservative politics. He enrolled at the National Autonomous University of Mexico in 1943, and left the following year to enter the army. Upon completing Officer Candidate School in 1944, he was commissioned as a second lieutenant in the U.S. Army. At the end of the war, Buckley enrolled at Yale University, where he won distinction as a debater and served as editor in chief of the *Yale Daily News*. He graduated from Yale in 1950.

One year later, Buckley gained early prominence with the publication of his first book, *God and Man at Yale*, a full-throated attack against his alma mater and the ideas he considered dominant at the school. Buckley argued that the overwhelming majority of Yale professors denigrated religion, advocated atheism or agnosticism, and championed secularism. He also maintained that the university taught collectivism and attacked or dismissed individualism. For example, Buckley pointed out that the overwhelming majority of professors in the economics department taught from a Keynesian perspective and used Keynesian textbooks. In one of his more controversial positions, Buckley dismissed "the superstitions of academic freedom." "I believe it to be an indisputable fact," Buckley wrote, "that most colleges and universities, and certainly Yale, the protests and pretensions of their educators . . . notwithstanding, do not practice . . . academic freedom." He pointed out that Yale would not tolerate a sociologist who "revealed himself as a racist." Similarly, he found it "inconceivable" that Yale would long tolerate a political scientist who "openly scorned democracy" and advocated totalitarianism. Buckley then called upon Yale's conservative alumni to assert control over the institution and make sure that their values were inculcated in the university's students.

Buckley was a member of the Central Intelligence Agency from July 1951 to April 1952. In 1954, he stirred up another controversy with his second book, *McCarthy and His Enemies*, the most important defense of McCarthyism to appear in print during the period. Buckley and his coauthor, L. Brent Bozell, combined a spirited justification of the charges of the Wisconsin senator with sharp thrusts at the alleged inconsistencies and unfair tactics of his opponents. Although acknowledging that McCarthy had been guilty of blunders and misconduct, they endorsed his contention that there was widespread communist subversion of the U.S. government. The authors concluded that "on McCarthyism hangs the hopes of America for effective resistance to communist infiltration."

In 1955, Buckley founded the *National Review*, which before long became the leading intellectual organ of American conservatism. In the "Publisher's Statement" of its inaugural issue, Buckley declared, "*National Review* is out of place in the sense that the United Nations and the League of Women Voters and the *New York Times* and Henry Steele Commager are in place." It "stands athwart history, yelling Stop!" Among the magazine's editors and contributors, many of them ex-communists, were the luminaries of the intellectual Right: RUSSELL KIRK, JAMES BURNHAM, WILLMOORE KENDALL, MAX EASTMAN, and WHITTAKER CHAMBERS.

As editor in chief, Buckley orchestrated their weekly denunciations of the manifestations of modern liberalism: big government, social welfare programs, civil rights laws, unbalanced budgets, containment, foreign aid, and contemporary mores. Its contributors included libertarians, economic conservatives, and traditionalists, but all shared a fierce anticommunism and an abhorrence of the welfare state. Buckley himself emerged as the premier polemicist of American conservative politics. Moving across a broad field of issues, he used wit, mockery, and verbal refinement to prick the hides of liberal targets, both institutional, such as Social Security and the United Nations, and personal, such as ELEANOR ROOSEVELT and ARTHUR SCHLESINGER, JR.

In 1959, Buckley published the only substantial exposition of his credo, *Up from Liberalism*. He criticized the materialistic limits of liberal thought and registered alarm at the centralization of power in the state to accomplish liberalism's social ends. He deplored "liberalism's total appetite for power" and "the root assumptions of liberal economic theory . . . that, economically speaking, the people are merely gatherers of money which is the right and duty of a central intelligence to distribute." Buckley's prescription for social progress derived from classical economics: "It is to maintain and wherever possible enhance the freedom of the individual to acquire property and dispose of that property in ways he decides on."

Buckley reached a wider audience with his syndicated newspaper column, "On the Right." Beginning in 1962 and continuing until his death, he wrote some 5,600 columns. He also hosted *Firing Line*, a television program on which he interviewed and debated guests in his provocative and entertaining style, from 1966 to 1999. It was one of the longest running programs in the history of television. Buckley ran for mayor of New York City on the Conservative Party ticket in 1965 but garnered only 13.4 percent of the vote. Over the course of his career, he wrote over 50 books. Buckley stepped down as editor of the *National Review* in 1990 but stayed on as editor at large. In addition, he continued to write his column and to publish essays and books, including novels and an autobiography. A founder of modern conservatism, his greatest contribution was to make conservative ideas respectable at a time when liberalism dominated American political discourse. Buckley died at his home in Stamford, Conn., on February 27, 2008.

—MSM

Bunche, Ralph J(ohnson)

(1904–1971) *director, United Nations Department of Trusteeship; United Nations undersecretary*

The son of a barber, Bunche was born in Detroit, Mich., on August 7, 1904. After his mother died and his father effectively abandoned the family, Bunche was raised by his maternal grandmother. Bunche moved with his family to New Mexico and then to Los Angeles, Calif. The intensely competitive

Bunche excelled in high school, where he played basketball and graduated valedictorian of his class at Jefferson High School. He attended the University of California, Southern Branch (later the University of California at Los Angeles), where he wrote for the campus newspaper, was president of the debating society, played football, starred at basketball, and graduated summa cum laude with a Phi Beta Kappa key in 1927. After receiving an M.A. from Harvard University in 1928, he began teaching political science at Howard University. Bunche continued to teach at Howard intermittently until 1950. He took a leave of absence from Howard in the fall of 1929 to begin work on his doctorate at Harvard. In 1934, he received his Ph.D. in government and international relations after completing a dissertation comparing French rule in Togoland and Dahomey. Bunche did postdoctoral work at Northwestern University, the London School of Economics, and Capetown University in South Africa. In 1936 he published a short book, *A World View of Race*. Two years later, he began working with Gunnar Myrdal, a Swedish sociologist commissioned by the Carnegie Corporation to undertake a massive study of African Americans. The study was published as *An American Dilemma: The Negro Problem and Modern Democracy* in 1944.

During World War II, Bunche was rejected for military service for physical reasons. He served in the Office of Strategic Services as senior social-science analyst and expert on Africa. Joining the State Department in 1944 as a colonial specialist, Bunche drew up the trusteeship section of the United Nations Charter at the Dumbarton Oaks Conference of 1944. He attended the first UN conference at San Francisco in 1945. From 1945 to 1947, Bunche was associate chief of the State Department's Division of Dependent Area Affairs.

At the request of UN Secretary General Trygve Lie, Bunche became director of the UN's trusteeship division in 1947. That year, he sat on the Special Committee on Palestine, which recommended creation of a Jewish national state. After fighting broke out between Israel and its Arab neighbors in 1948, the UN appointed Count Folke Bernadotte of Sweden to mediate the conflict. Bunche accompanied Bernadotte as his chief aide. After the assassination of Bernadotte in September 1948,

Bunche became the UN's chief mediator. Through 11 months of tireless negotiating, Bunche achieved an armistice between Israel and the Arab states. For his efforts, Bunche received the Nobel Peace Prize in 1950.

A forceful advocate for black civil rights in the United States, Bunche helped organize a conference in 1935 on "The Status of the Negro under the New Deal." At the conference, he criticized the administration of Franklin D. Roosevelt and its policies toward African Americans. In 1949, he turned down the offer of a position as an assistant secretary of state, stating that he did not want to expose himself or his family to the discrimination they would face in segregated Washington, D.C. That same year, Bunche received the Spingarn Medal from the NAACP.

In response to growing rightist criticism of the American delegation at the UN, ambassador HENRY CABOT LODGE began a loyalty investigation of the personnel, including Bunche, in 1953. The plan had the full support of Secretary General Lie, who authorized non-American employees to provide information to the FBI. When Dag Hammarskjöld replaced Lie in April, he ordered the FBI off UN territory. In response, the Eisenhower administration created the International Organizations Employees Loyalty Board to continue the probe. The board attempted to keep its efforts secret. Nevertheless, news leaked out in May 1954 that the board was investigating Bunche. Eisenhower opposed the probe and sent a presidential assistant, Maxwell Rabb, to warn Bunche about FBI reports and the board's queries and to offer his support. Bunche, however, decided to stand alone. At the hearing, he was confronted by two ex-communist witnesses on the payroll of the Justice Department, who charged him with communist connections. After two days of testimony, the board's chairman, Pierce J. Geraty, announced on May 28, 1954, that Bunche had been unanimously cleared of all charges.

Bunche was appointed undersecretary of the UN in August 1954, the highest post ever held by an American in the organization. Following the Israeli-Egyptian war in 1956, he organized the UN Emergency Force responsible for keeping the peace and served as a member of the three-man committee supervising the cease-fire. Bunche was criticized

for siding with the Egyptians and denounced by Israeli Prime Minister David Ben Gurion.

In April 1958, Bunche headed a special commission that successfully settled an Israeli-Jordanian dispute over Israel's Mt. Scopus enclave in Jordanian Jerusalem. After meeting in May with officials from both countries, Bunche persuaded the Jordanian government to lift a blockade of Israeli convoys to the Jewish community. The following month, Bunche was promoted to undersecretary for special political affairs, serving as Hammarskjöld's principal troubleshooter.

Bunche played a major role in the Congo crisis of 1960. Four days after the declaration of Congolese independence in June 1960, President Joseph Kasavubu and Premier Patrice Lumumba, facing civil war with breakaway Katanga province, petitioned for UN troops to preserve order and prevent unilateral intervention by Belgium. On July 14, the UN voted to send a force, and Bunche was assigned to organize the effort. He then remained in the Congo as Hammarskjöld's personal representative.

In that capacity, Bunche helped negotiate the agreement, disclosed on July 18, for Belgian officials in the Congo to accept orders from UN Forces and to limit their troops' actions to "the security needs of Belgian nationals." At the beginning of August, Bunche met with Premier Moise Tshombe, head of breakaway Katanga, to try to convince him to permit UN troops to enter the province to oust Belgian troops in the area. Bunche could not persuade Tshombe that the force would not be used as an advance guard for his rival, Lumumba. Bunche, therefore, advised Hammarskjöld against pressing the issue for fear of bloodshed.

During the summer, Bunche became embroiled in a dispute between the commanders of the UN Force, Gen. Henry Alexander (commander of Ghanaian UN troops) and Gen. Carl von Horn (UN force commander). In August, Alexander protested that von Horn was "unprepared to exercise any military authority at all, thus putting Ghanaian and other UN troops in an impossible position." Alexander's protest implied that Hammarskjöld and Bunche bore responsibility for the UN command's weakness. Bunche maintained that Alexander's criticisms were invalid because the general could not "comprehend the nature of an international peace force." Nevertheless, Bunche was replaced as Hammarskjöld's representative that month. UN officials denied that the move was connected with the dispute.

Bunche continued to advise Hammarskjöld on the Congo until the secretary general's death in September 1961. That month, he became temporary head of the organization, serving until the installation of U Thant as secretary general in November. Bunche served as a UN troubleshooter in Yemen during 1963 and in Cyprus during 1964. He also lent his prestige to the American Civil Rights movement. During the mid-1960s, he opposed attempts to link the Civil Rights movement with opposition to the Vietnam War. Bunche died in New York City on December 9, 1971.

—MSM

Burger, Warren Earl
(1907–1995) *lawyer and federal judge*

Born in Saint Paul, Minn., on September 17, 1907, Burger grew up in modest circumstances on a farm near Saint Paul and attended public schools. While working at a life insurance company, he attended night classes at the University of Minnesota for two years and at Saint Paul College of Law (now William Mitchell College of Law), from which he graduated in 1931. Burger practiced law with the firm of Boyesen, Otis & Faricy in Saint Paul from 1931 to 1953. During that time, he became active in Republican politics and worked on HAR-OLD STASSEN's successful campaigns for governor. He also supported Stassen's unsuccessful attempts to capture the Republican presidential nomination. Burger served as Stassen's floor manager at the Republican conventions in 1948 and in 1952, when he attracted the attention of HERBERT BROWNELL, one of Eisenhower's managers, who would later become attorney general in the Eisenhower administration.

After Eisenhower took office, Brownell appointed Burger as an assistant attorney general in charge of the Justice Department's Claims (later the Civil) Division in 1953. In 1955, Burger became involved in the case of Dr. John Plunnet Peters, a senior professor of medicine at Yale University and a part-time consultant to the Public Health Service.

After the departmental loyalty board twice cleared Peters, the Loyalty Review Board, on its own initiative, reviewed the case and found that a reasonable doubt existed as to Peters's loyalty. Peters went to court and, after he lost in federal district court, the firm of Arnold, Fortas & Porter agreed to represent him and took the case to the Supreme Court. When the case came before the solicitor general, SIMON E. SOBELOFF, he was uncomfortable with the fact that the names of informants against Peters had been withheld not only from Peters but from the Loyalty Review Board as well. Sobeloff proposed a confession of error. Ultimately Brownell decided to prosecute the case actively, and Sobeloff declined to argue the government's case. At this point, Brownell asked Burger to argue the case before the Supreme Court. The government lost the case, but the Supreme Court ducked the larger constitutional issue and held improper the Loyalty Review Board's procedure in reviewing a case that had not been appealed to it.

When Judge Harold Stephens of the United States Court of Appeals for the District of Columbia died, Eisenhower nominated Burger to fill the vacancy. The Senate approved him, and Burger joined the court in 1956. He quickly established a reputation as a moderate conservative for taking a hard line on matters relating to law and order and advocating a judicially conservative approach to reading statutes and the Constitution. On a deeply divided court, he led the wing that opposed the extension of rights to those accused of criminal acts. Rather, he preferred to give leeway to police, prosecutors, and trial judges. Burger frequently sparred with the court's more liberal members, particularly DAVID L. BAZELON, and vigorously opposed Bazelon's attempts to revise the legal standard of insanity in criminal cases.

In 1969, President RICHARD M. NIXON nominated Burger to be chief justice of the United States. The Senate overwhelmingly approved the nomination. Much to the disappointment of many conservatives, the Supreme Court during Burger's tenure as chief justice consolidated many of the major rulings of the Warren Court. Moreover, under Burger the Court struck down state antiabortion laws in *Roe v. Wade* (1973), upheld the Court-ordered use of busing to desegregate schools in *Swann v. Char-*

lotte-Mecklenburg (1971), and upheld affirmative action in *Bakke v. Board of Regents* (1978). In some regards, the Burger Court was at least as activist as its predecessor. It recognized new rights and created new constitutional doctrine regarding the right to privacy and gender as well as racial discrimination. Although uncomfortable with some of these trends, Burger wrote the opinions for the Court on decisions that validated busing to achieve desegregation and forced Nixon to turn over the White House tape recordings to Watergate investigators. Burger also wrote several significant opinions upholding First Amendment claims. In *Nebraska Press Association v. Stuart* (1976), he held that, given the constitutional bias against prior restraint, trial judges should use gag orders only as a matter of last resort. Judges, he reasoned, could take other steps to ensure a fair trial, such as sequestering the jury or changing the venue. In addition, he wrote for the majority in *Miami Herald Publishing Co. v. Tornillo* (1974), which struck down a Florida law requiring newspapers that had attacked the character of a political candidate to give free space for a reply. Burger did not, however, believe that the First Amendment protected obscenity. He attempted to end the court's 15-year struggle to construct a legal definition of obscenity in *Miller v. California* (1973). Writing for the majority, Burger restricted the scope of material protected by the First Amendment under WILLIAM J. BRENNAN's opinion for the majority in *Roth v. United States* (1957). Burger defined obscenity as "works which, taken as a whole, appeal to the prurient interest in sex, which portray sexual conduct in a patently offensive way and which, taken as a whole, do not have serious literary, artistic, political, or scientific value." Further, *Roth* held that juries should apply "contemporary community standards" in determining whether a particular work met the definition of obscenity; while Brennan had looked to the standards of the nation as a whole, Burger held that the standards should be those of the local community. On another First Amendment matter, Burger wrote the majority opinion in *Lemon v. Kurtzman* (1971), a major decision involving separation of church and state. In order to pass constitutional muster, he wrote, a law conferring some benefit on religion first "must have a secular legislative pur-

pose; second, its principal or primary effect must be one that neither advances nor inhibits religion; finally, the statute must not foster an excessive government entanglement with religion." Burger also continued to oppose the extension of protections to those accused of a crime, and the Burger Court did narrow some Warren Court decisions in that area.

Although his opinions were, in general, somewhat better than contemporary critics allowed, Burger was not the intellectual leader of the Court that bore his name. Another Nixon appointee, William H. Rehnquist, exerted more influence on the Court's conservatives; Brennan played a comparable role for the liberals. Burger voted with the minority more frequently than influential chief justices such as Warren. His difficult personality strained relations with colleagues and hampered him in constructing majorities on specific cases.

Burger loved the ceremonial aspects of his office and was an able administrator. He modernized procedures at the Supreme Court and made it a more efficient body. He took his title (chief justice of the United States) seriously and regarded himself as steward of the nation's judicial system. He was influential in the creation of the National Center for State Courts, the Institute for Court Management, and the National Institute of Corrections. These organizations educated and trained participants in the judicial process.

Burger retired as chief justice in 1986, and became chair of the Bicentennial Commission on the U.S. Constitution. He died in Washington, D.C., of congestive heart failure on June 25, 1995.

—MSM

Burke, Arleigh A(lbert)
(1901–1996) *chief of naval operations*
Of Swedish and Pennsylvania Dutch ancestry, Burke was born in Boulder, Colo., on October 19, 1901, and raised on a farm near Boulder. Intent on a naval career, Burke entered the U.S. Naval Academy at Annapolis and graduated in 1923. He served five years sea duty and then returned to the United States to study ordnance engineering at Annapolis. He received his M.S. in engineering from the University of Michigan in 1931. During the 1930s, Burke continued his career as an ordnance officer.

He served in the Pacific during World War II, where he gained a reputation for the speed at which he carried squadrons into combat. For his service in the war, he received numerous decorations, including the Navy Distinguished Service Medal, the Legion of Merit, and the Silver Star.

Burke was head of the research and development division of the Bureau of Ordnance in 1945. Three years later, he was promoted to an assistant to the chief of naval operations in the organizational research and policy division. Burke participated in the so-called Revolt of the Admirals in 1949, opposing the emphasis on the B-36 air force bomber in the armed forces unification plan. Reportedly because of his part in the action, Capt. Burke's promotion to rear admiral was postponed until July 1950. He served in combat during the Korean war, and in the summer of 1951, Burke served as a member of the UN Military Armistice Commission in Korea. In July 1951, he was named director of strategic plans of naval operations, the second highest post in the navy hierarchy. After a brief stint as commander of the Atlantic Fleet from November 1954 to June 1955, he was appointed chief of naval operations. In choosing Burke, Eisenhower passed over 38 admirals with more seniority.

Burke initially supported Eisenhower's "New Look" defense policy. The New Look grew out of a desire to limit the defense budget and prevent debilitating ground wars such as those in Korea. The policy placed primary emphasis on "massive retaliation," the use of nuclear weapons delivered by air force strategic bombers or missiles as America's major deterrent against aggression. In testimony before a Senate appropriations subcommittee in 1957, Burke vigorously endorsed the president's budget for fiscal 1958, maintaining that it would "give us the maximum in naval power for every dollar requested."

The launching of the Soviet satellite *Sputnik* in the fall of 1957 opened a debate on defense strategy among different branches of the military and between the military and the administration. Burke joined Generals MAXWELL TAYLOR and JAMES GAVIN of the army in urging the administration to reorient its defense policies. They pointed out that with the two superpowers gradually reaching nuclear parity, general warfare would be replaced by limited wars. Burke cautioned that the Soviet Union was still bent

on "engulfing the whole world," but because it had been thwarted by American nuclear power, it would not stage a large-scale attack. Instead it would adopt a "piecemeal approach to world domination." Burke opposed demands by the air force for an emphasis on missiles, and he pointed to the need to develop conventional forces such as the navy to meet the challenge of limited war. Anxious to preserve the twin roles of his service, he maintained that the navy could fight both limited and full-scale wars with the use of such weapons as aircraft carriers and submarines equipped with missiles.

Burke opposed the administration's defense budget and urged major increases to prepare the armed forces to fight both nuclear and limited wars. He alleged that the administration's continuous desire for budget reviews had forced the navy to submit smaller budget requests than needed.

Burke's call for a more varied defense strategy failed to carry much weight until the Kennedy administration, which emphasized "flexible response." Burke continued at his post until August 1961, when he retired from the navy. After his retirement, Burke served on the boards of several major corporations. He died in Bethesda, Md., on January 1, 1996.

—EWS

Burnham, James
(1905–1987) *journalist, writer*

The son of a railroad executive, Burnham was born on November 22, 1905, in Chicago. He received his B.A. from Princeton University in 1927, and attended Oxford University, where he earned an M.A. in 1929. From 1930 to 1954, he was professor of philosophy at New York University. He coedited the left-wing literary and philosophical review, *The Symposium*, from 1930 to 1933. In the latter year, Burnham became a Trotskyist. The Depression seems to have convinced him that capitalism was doomed and that communism was the solution to the problems that caused the collapse of capitalism, but he hated Stalin. In 1934, he became coeditor of the *New International*, a journal of American Trotskyists. At the end of the 1930s, forced collectivization, Stalin's purges, and the Nazi-Soviet pact convinced Burnham to reject Trotsky's belief that the USSR was a "progressive workers" state, which must be defended despite Stalin's actions. Quitting the *New International* in 1940, he forcefully broke away from Trotsky and renounced his former pro-Soviet sympathies.

Burnham was still viewed by many as a leftist, albeit anticommunist, when he wrote *The Managerial Revolution* in 1941. In that book, he argued that capitalism was entering a new phase, in which hired managers would wrest control of the means of production from the owners (shareholders). Capitalism was unable to marshal resources efficiently or fairly; therefore, resources had to be managed by a centralized authority. Thus, he predicted that Germany would defeat England and, after that, three superstates—one in Europe (Germany), one in Asia (Japan), and one in North and South America (the United States)—would emerge and engage in an endless struggle for world domination. For Burnham, the inevitable trend towards managerialism was manifested in the transfer of sovereignty from representative institutions to centralized administrative bodies. Burnham regarded the New Deal as an American, if incipient, version of managerialism.

With the emergence of the cold war, Burnham became intensely anticommunist. Initially, he joined with liberal anticommunists. In 1947, he published *The Struggle for the World*, which made a powerful case that communism's implacable goal of world conquest made it the greatest threat to stability in the world. That threat was magnified by the USSR's nuclear capability. He warned that the United States had to prepare for a struggle to the death with the Soviet Union. At the time he wrote *The Struggle for the World*, Burnham still considered himself on the left, but he was clearly moving rightward. He supported, with only minor reservations, aggressive attempts to root out communism at home. In foreign policy, he rejected containment and advocated liberation of communist nations by propaganda and subversion, which he called "polwar."

In *Containment or Liberation?* (1953), Burnham brilliantly exposed flaws in the argument for containment, but he was somewhat vague with respect to how liberation might be achieved. He proposed recognition of governments in exile, recruiting and military training of refugees, propaganda, and the threat of force from noncommunist allies.

The following year, Burnham published *The Web of Subversion*, in which he maintained that communist infiltration of the American government, particularly the State Department, since the 1930s accounted for events such as the Soviet domination of Eastern Europe and the fall of mainland China to the Communists.

Burnham claimed to be without bias for or against Sen. JOSEPH R. MCCARTHY (R-Wis.), although he believed that McCarthy's opponents were dupes of the communists. In November 1954, he did oppose efforts in the Senate to censure McCarthy. He believed, in retrospect, that McCarthyism had a larger significance than the question of communism in government. Burnham used the issue to introduce one of the major elements in postwar conservative thought. He wrote, "The issue was philosophical, metaphysical: what kind of community are we. And the Liberals were correct in labeling McCarthy The Enemy, and in destroying him. From the Liberal standpoint—secularist, egalitarian, relativist—the line is now drawn, Relativism must be Absolute."

Burnham revised his advocacy of the liberation of Eastern Europe after the Hungarian uprising of 1956. He remained conspicuously silent while the United States watched the USSR crush the Hungarian rebels and only later claimed that a properly timed U.S. ultimatum would have dissuaded the Russians from intervening. To the disappointment of his conservative colleagues, he now suggested a mutual withdrawal of North Atlantic Treaty Organization and Warsaw Pact divisions from Europe and the neutralization of central Europe.

When WILLIAM F. BUCKLEY, JR., began publishing the conservative *National Review* in 1955, Burnham became one of the original members of the editorial board. He soon emerged as Buckley's second in command. Although liberals tended to dismiss Burnham as a right-wing crank, some of his fellow editors at the *National Review* regarded him as too pragmatic. Buckley, however, continued to support Burnham, who contributed a regular column to the magazine for two decades. In it, Burnham focused on matters of defense and foreign policy and maintained an uncompromising anticommunist stand. He became disillusioned with the foreign policy of JOHN FOSTER DULLES and DWIGHT EISENHOWER. Burnham was initially impressed with JOHN F. KENNEDY's policy of flexible response and his aggressive anticommunism. That enthusiasm quickly waned. Burnham supported the war in Vietnam but was highly critical of what he regarded as a no-win policy. He believed that the war could be won and called for more aggressive military action to achieve that end.

Burnham was also concerned about the expansion of federal power. This led him to oppose the Supreme Court's ruling, in *Brown v. Board of Education* (1954), that segregated schools violated the Constitution. Although he was not himself a bigot, his opposition to federal power led him to support southern opposition to the decision and to civil rights measures in general.

Despite his profound conservatism, he occasionally adopted quirky positions. For example, he applauded the Woodstock festival and supported the treaty negotiated by President Jimmy Carter to transfer the Panama Canal to Panama. Such stands, along with his support for NELSON ROCKEFELLER, made him suspect to his colleagues at the *National Review*. Buckley, nevertheless, continued to support Burnham, who remained with the magazine until a massive stroke disabled him in 1978. He died in Kent, Conn., on July 28, 1987.

—MSM

Burns, Arthur F(rank)
(1904–1987) *chairman, Council of Economic Advisers*

Born in Stanislau, Austria, on April 27, 1904, Arthur Burns emigrated to the United States with his parents and grew up in Bayonne, N.J. He worked his way through Columbia University, earning a B.A., an M.A. in economics in 1925, and a Ph.D. in 1934. Burns began teaching at Rutgers University in 1927; by 1943, he had become a full professor. The following year, he joined the Columbia faculty as a full professor.

In addition to teaching, Burns produced studies for the National Bureau of Economic Research, a private organization engaged in statistical research on economic issues. Through his work with the National Bureau, of which he became director of research in 1948, he emerged as an acknowledged expert on business cycles.

During the mid- and late 1930s, American economists debated the theories of the British economist John Maynard Keynes, who advocated direct government intervention in the economy. Burns accepted some of Keynes's ideas but thought American Keynesians simplistic in their application of Keynes's theories. Burns maintained that each industry had its own cycle; when several turned downward at the same time, a depression resulted. Therefore, any intervention by the government, argued Burns, had to be highly selective. Among his studies were *Production Trends in the United States Since 1870* (1934), his doctoral dissertation, and *Measuring Business Cycles* (1946), written in collaboration with Wesley Mitchell, who had been his doctor, adviser, and whom Burns regarded as the principal influence on his thought.

In 1946, Burns published a critique of Keynesian economics. In general, Burns's economics were moderately conservative; he favored a free market and increased competition but also recognized that government had a role to play in fostering economic stability and leveling business cycles. In 1951, he praised the existing distribution of income in America and said that any future redistribution should not come by transferring income from the rich to the poor but by increasing the productivity of those at the bottom through encouragement of increased competition and small business. Burns criticized the "free money" policies of the Truman administration.

In March 1953, President Eisenhower appointed Burns a member of the Council of Economic Advisers. That August, Burns became chairman of the council. At the outset of his tenure, he had to defend the very existence of the council against congressional Republicans who had grown hostile to the agency during the Truman years. Burns managed to maintain the council and its staff intact, and he exercised a key role in the making of economic policy during Eisenhower's first term.

According to presidential assistant SHERMAN ADAMS, "Arthur Burns turned out to be a pleasant surprise. He and Eisenhower got along fine. They shared the same outlook and philosophy. Far from being the abstract and impractical professor, Burns had his feet planted solidly on the ground and had no difficulty in more than holding his own in arguments at the cabinet table with such hard-headed protagonists as [GEORGE] HUMPHREY and [JOSEPH] DODGE."

In 1953, Burns correctly predicted that the restrictive credit policies being pursued by the Treasury and the Federal Reserve would contribute to an economic slowdown. During the recession of 1953–54, Burns resisted a major recovery program. He thought that economic indicators pointed to a milder recession than most economists predicted. The administration subsequently applied the policies he recommended: liberalization of credit combined with tax cuts. The administration allowed the expiration of the excess profits tax and the Korean War increases in the personal income and excise rates. These reductions added $7.4 billion to disposable income and helped fuel the prosperity of 1954–55.

In general, Burns favored monetary over fiscal stimulation of the economy. "The more you can get out of monetary policy," he said, "the less you need to get out of fiscal policy, with its headaches about deficits, the public debt, and the like." Burns sought, with mixed success, to get the Federal Reserve to ease up on credit restrictions, particularly in the area of housing. He also backed a liberalization of the Federal Housing Authority's lending rules in order to stimulate housing starts and home modernization. To guard against inflation, however, Burns sometimes favored credit restrictions, as in January 1956, when he unsuccessfully argued at a cabinet meeting in favor of controls on consumer credit.

Since the late 1940s, Burns held that maintaining employment was the primary objective of government. He also believed that inflation represented a serious problem that government had to address. On the whole, Burns was more willing than President Eisenhower's more conservative advisers to resort to public works to promote economic expansion. He supported the idea of an ambitious highway-building program. In 1955, he helped prepare a plan to aid chronically depressed areas such as New England textile towns and the Appalachian coal country. The plan called for the formation of an area redevelopment agency within the Commerce Department to extend capital improvement loans to depressed communities. President Eisenhower originally favored the idea but withdrew his

support when Democrats in Congress expanded the proposal. Area redevelopment legislation remained stymied throughout the 1950s.

Burns left the Eisenhower administration in November 1956, and returned to his work at Columbia University and the National Bureau of Economic Research. He continued to advise the administration, as in March 1960 when he warned Vice President RICHARD NIXON that the Republicans would lose the November election unless the administration cut taxes to combat the current recession. Nixon took Burns's counsel to a cabinet meeting, but the president was reluctant to add to the already sizeable deficit and ruled out a tax reduction. The recession continued to the end of the year, and Nixon lost the presidential contest by a narrow margin to Sen. JOHN F. KENNEDY (D-Mass.).

Burns served on Kennedy's Advisory Committee on Labor-Management Policy. During the Kennedy-Johnson years, he frequently spoke out on economic policy, often in opposition to the fiscal activism of Democratic economic policymakers. Burns's version of economic stimulus called for a revision of progressive tax laws to lower rates on corporations and people with high incomes. He argued that this approach would provide more investment capital and generate more jobs. He steadily advocated less government spending to curb inflation and annual tax cuts to spur economic growth.

In January 1969, President Nixon named Burns counselor to the president and in October nominated him to succeed WILLIAM McCHESNEY MARTIN as chairman of the Board of Governors of the Federal Reserve System. Confirmed by the Senate in December, Burns took office on February 1, 1970. He served until the end of his term in 1978. President James Earl Carter, a Democrat, chose not to reappoint Burns, who took a position at the American Enterprise Institute. Burns served as ambassador to West Germany from 1981 to 1985. He died in Baltimore, Md., on June 6, 1987.

—MSM

Burton, Harold H(itz)

(1888–1964) *associate justice, U.S. Supreme Court*
Born on June 22, 1888, in Jamaica Plain, Mass., Harold H. Burton graduated from Bowdoin

College in 1909 and from Harvard Law School in 1912. After service in the army during World War I, he practiced law in Cleveland and became a member of the Ohio House of Representatives in 1929. Elected mayor of Cleveland in 1935 as a reform candidate, Burton won reelection twice by wide margins. A Republican, he ran successfully for the U.S. Senate in 1940, despite opposition from the state party leadership. In the Senate, Burton was an internationalist in foreign policy and a moderate on domestic issues. He served as a member of the Senate committee, headed by HARRY S. TRUMAN (D-Mo.), that investigated the defense effort in World War II. President Truman chose Burton as his first nominee to the Supreme Court in September 1945.

On the bench, Burton displayed a conservative orientation. He generally favored judicial restraint and usually voted to uphold government power, especially in loyalty-security cases. Burton did occasionally join the Court's more liberal justices to overturn some aspect of a government anticommunist program, but he based these decisions on narrow statutory or procedural grounds.

Burton adhered to this pattern during his years on the Warren Court. He dissented from a decision in 1956 upsetting state sedition laws and from a ruling in 1957 placing limits on state investigations of subversion. The justice also objected to a decision in 1958 that held the denial of passports to members of the Communist Party illegal. In the same month, Burton spoke for a five-man majority that upheld the dismissal of a public school teacher for incompetency after he had refused to tell school authorities whether he had once been an officer in a communist organization.

In 1953 Burton wrote the majority opinion in a case setting aside the perjury conviction of labor leader HARRY BRIDGES for allegedly having sworn falsely at his naturalization hearing in 1945 that he was not a communist. The justice based his decision on the ground that the statute of limitations had run out before Bridges was indicted. He concurred in a 1957 decision overturning the convictions of California Communist Party leaders under the Smith Act. However, he dissented from the majority opinion that the act did not outlaw the advocacy of the forcible overthrow of the government "as an abstract doctrine." That same year, Burton also took the narrow ground in a case in which the majority ruled that a federal criminal defendant was entitled to see statements government witnesses made to the FBI before trial. In a separate opinion, he said the trial judge should examine the statements before they were turned over to defense counsel and withhold those containing information pertaining to national security.

Burton also tended to uphold government power in criminal rights cases. He frequently voted to sustain convictions in which a defendant alleged that he had been denied the right to counsel or that his confession was coerced. Although Burton usually favored the government position in antitrust cases, he wrote the dissenting opinion when the majority held, in 1957, that the DuPont Co.'s acquisition of General Motors stock in 1917–19 violated the Clayton Antitrust Act. After his first term on the Court, Burton repeatedly voted to outlaw racial segregation and discrimination. In May 1954, he joined in the Court's *Brown* decision, which ruled public school segregation unconstitutional.

Burton retired from the Supreme Court in October 1958 because of ill health. Observers of the Court considered him to have been a largely conservative jurist but one with a certain flexibility and independence. A very conscientious and hardworking man, Burton had a reputation both on and off the Court for having a judicial temperament because of his capacity to keep an open mind on issues and to maintain an emotional distance from cases. Nonetheless, most legal scholars have ranked him a mediocre justice at best. Burton did not play a leading role on the Court; he was neither a great scholar nor an original thinker. Although his opinions improved during his years on the Court, they remained rather lackluster and tedious. Burton died in Washington, D.C., on October 28, 1964.

—CAB

Bush, Prescott S(heldon)
(1895–1972) *U.S. senator*

Bush was born on May 15, 1895, in Columbus, Ohio, where his father was a steel manufacturer. He attended St. George's School and received a B.A. from Yale University in 1917. After service in

World War I, Bush worked for a hardware firm in Saint Louis and the United States Rubber Co. He then became a vice president of W. A. Harriman and Co., a New York City investment firm, in 1926. When Brown Brothers merged with Harriman in 1930, Bush became a partner in the new firm.

From 1935 to 1952, Bush was the moderator of the Representative Town Meeting in Greenwich, Conn. During World War II, he served as campaign chairman for the United Service Organizations (USO) and the National War Fund, Inc. Because of his success as a fund-raiser, he was chosen chairman of the Connecticut Republican State Finance Committee in 1947. Three years later, Bush ran unsuccessfully for the U.S. Senate.

In 1952, Bush opposed Rep. ABRAHAM RIBI-COFF (D-Conn.) in a contest to fill the remainder of the term of the late Sen. Brien McMahon (D-Conn.). During the contest, Bush criticized Sen. JOSEPH R. MCCARTHY (R-Wis.), stating that there were "many, like myself, who approve heartily of his goals but hold reservations at times concerning his methods." He defeated Ribicoff in November by 30,000 votes. In 1956, Bush won a full term by defeating Rep. THOMAS J. DODD (D-Conn.) by 128,000 votes.

As a senator, Bush was a flexible conservative. In 1954, he defended the Dixon-Yates contract, stating that it was time for Congress to "contain" the Tennessee Valley Authority and prevent "this sprawling giant" from "groping its way across the country." In 1955, Bush attacked a public highway bill for, among other things, imposing new controls upon the states in the areas of highway construction and operation. In 1956, Bush opposed public power development at Niagara Falls. In 1958, Bush voted against an area redevelopment bill to aid economically distressed regions on the ground that "it would create a new channel into which to pour vast amounts of federal dollars in futile attempts" to cure unemployment.

On a number of issues, however, Bush broke with many of his conservative colleagues. In 1954, he offered a uniform code of committee behavior to prevent McCarthy's continued abuse of investigating committees; later that year he voted to condemn the senator from Wisconsin. In 1955, he expressed regret that a housing bill did not provide for a larger number of public housing units. Bush was a strong backer of President Eisenhower's civil rights bills. In 1957, he opposed an effort by southern senators to weaken a civil rights bill, proposed by the administration, by guaranteeing a jury trial to those accused of contempt for trying to prevent blacks from voting. Three years later, Bush and seven other Republicans joined northern Democrats in an unsuccessful effort to end a southern filibuster of a civil rights bill by invoking cloture. Bush also supported the nomination of Solicitor General SIMON E. SOBELOFF to the Fourth Circuit Court of Appeals, a nomination vigorously opposed by southern segregationists.

During his years in Congress, Bush gained a reputation as an expert on government finance and the national economy. Because of his banking background, he was named to Eisenhower's Commission on Foreign Economic Policy in 1953. Bush concurred with most of the panel's recommendations, including those urging an early termination of economic aid in the form of grants, continuation of a vigorous technical assistance program without huge expenditures, encouragement of U.S. private investment abroad by reducing taxes on income from such investment, and extension of reciprocal trade legislation.

In 1954, as chairman of the Banking and Currency Committee's Subcommittee on Securities, Bush backed the panel's bill amending the Securities Exchange Act. Enacted in August, it permitted a wider dissemination of information about securities before their sale and simplified the procedures involved in the registration of securities issues with the Securities and Exchange Commission. In 1957, he succeeded in amending a Banking and Currency Committee bill to require disclosure of the names of only those persons owning at least 5 percent of the outstanding stock of banks. Three years later, Bush supported an administration bill to remove the statutory ceiling of 4¼ percent on government bond interest rates. When Democrats blocked the measure, Bush denounced them for playing politics with the nation's credit. He asserted that, while interest rates had declined somewhat because of a slight recession in business, rates would rise again as the economy picked up steam.

Bush served as chairman of the Republican National Platform Committee in 1956. Four years later, he chaired the subcommittee that wrote the planks on business, labor, and the economy in the national platform.

Bush generally opposed President JOHN F. KENNEDY's domestic policies. In 1962, he criticized the administration's Trade Expansion Act, which gave the president increased power to cut tariffs through reciprocal agreements. In May 1962, Bush announced that he would not seek reelection for health reasons. He returned to Brown Brothers, Harriman and Co. Bush died in New York City on October 8, 1972.

—MLL

Bush, Vannevar

(1890–1974) *president, Carnegie Institution of Washington; chairman, Massachusetts Institute of Technology Corporation*

The son of a Universalist minister, Bush was born on March 11, 1890, in Everett, Mass. He earned both his B.S. and M.S. degrees from Tufts College in 1913, and received his Ph.D. in engineering jointly from Harvard and the Massachusetts Institute of Technology (MIT) in 1916. The following year, he worked in a special navy antisubmarine laboratory. Bush joined MIT's faculty in 1919 and became the institute's vice president and dean of its school of engineering in 1932. A prolific inventor, he designed a number of advanced mathematical analyzing instruments, including the differential analyzer, the forerunner of the computer. In 1939, he became the president of the Carnegie Institution of Washington.

In 1940, Bush served as chairman of the National Defense Research Committee (NDRC), formed at his suggestion to direct war-related scientific research. The following year, he became chairman of the Office of Scientific Research and Development (OSRD), which included the NDRC. Bush made no technical contribution to the war effort, but, as an administrator, he was responsible for the development of an array of new weapons, including radar, amphibious vehicles, and the atomic bomb. In June 1945, he advised President HARRY S. TRUMAN to use the atomic bomb against Japan without prior warning.

After the war, Bush continued to serve on government policy committees. He prepared recommendations on ways in which wartime research could be applied to peace. The report, "Science, the Endless Frontier," urged massive government support for basic research. His recommendations resulted in the establishment of the National Science Foundation in 1950. Bush opposed the development of the hydrogen bomb and urged negotiations to end the arms race.

In the 1950s, Bush was a vocal critic of abuses in security investigations, which he thought had retarded weapons research by undermining scientists' morale. He was particularly alarmed by the Oppenheimer security hearings in 1954. J. ROBERT OPPENHEIMER had directed the development of the atomic bomb and had served as chairman of the Atomic Energy Commission's (AEC) General Advisory Committee (GAC) in the early postwar period. Because of Oppenheimer's prewar involvement with leftist groups and his postwar reservations about the development of the hydrogen bomb, President DWIGHT D. EISENHOWER ordered his security clearance suspended in late 1953 pending a hearing. Bush objected to the charges and urged that they be "redrafted in such a way as to remove all implication that Oppenheimer was being tried for his opinions."

Following the AEC's decision to continue the suspension of Oppenheimer's clearance, Bush wrote in the *New York Times*, ". . . there should be no insistence that any individual cease his thinking at any time, or that he suppress his honest opinion in order slavishly to follow a policy abstractly laid down." In an address to the American Association for the Advancement of Science in December 1954, he declared that "useful men" were "denied the opportunity to contribute to our scientific efforts because of their youthful indiscretions." In an apparent reference to Sen. JOSEPH R. MCCARTHY (R-Wis.), he accused "ruthless, ambitious men" of using "our loyalty procedures for political purposes."

In 1957, Bush became chairman of the MIT Corporation and in 1959 its honorary chairman. He continued to write and lecture on national defense through the 1960s. In 1970, he and JAMES CONANT received the Atomic Pioneers Award from the AEC. After suffering a stroke, Bush died of pneumonia in Belmont, Mass., on June 28, 1974.

—MDB

Butler, John Marshall
(1897–1978) *U.S. senator*

Born in Baltimore, Md., on July 21, 1897, Butler attended public schools and served in the army during World War I. After attending Johns Hopkins University in 1919 and 1921, he went to work in his father's real estate business. He graduated from the University of Maryland Law School in 1926. That same year, he commenced the practice of law with the firm of Venable, Baetyer & Howard in Baltimore, where he would remain for 20 years. After serving as a member of the City Service Commission (1947–49), he won election to the U.S. Senate in 1950. That election, in which Butler defeated Millard E. Tydings (a four-term Democratic incumbent), received national attention for the unethical tactics employed by Sen. JOSEPH MCCARTHY against Tydings, who had chaired the Senate committee that dismissed McCarthy's initial charges that communists worked in the State Department. The defeat of Tydings contributed to the myth of McCarthy's invincibility. After all, Franklin D. Roosevelt had attempted to purge Tydings in the Democratic primary of 1938 and failed. In fact, however, Tydings was more vulnerable than he appeared. A southern Democrat who was hostile to labor and civil rights, Tydings had the support of neither labor nor black voters. Moreover, although Maryland's voter registration was overwhelmingly Democratic, Democratic vote totals had been declining in recent elections. Further, the growth of the Washington suburbs changed the complexion of the Democratic vote; the government workers and professionals who lived in those suburbs tended to be New Deal Democrats and unsympathetic to Tydings. Perhaps most important, in an off-year election, the Democratic governor, W. Preston Lane, headed the party's ticket. Lane had signed into law the state's first sales tax, which had proved extremely unpopular, and had

won renomination only after a bitter primary contest. Indeed, George P. Mahoney had gotten more votes in the primary election but lost because of the effect of the state's unit rule. In the general election, THEODORE ROOSEVELT MCKELDIN, the popular former mayor of Baltimore and a liberal Republican, handily defeated Lane. Even while going down to defeat, Tydings ran well ahead of Lane and every other Democrat on the state ticket.

Furious over McCarthy's campaign tactics, Tydings petitioned the Senate to disqualify Butler. The Senate convened a special election subcommittee to investigate the charges. The unanimous report found that Butler had used "despicable methods in unseating Tydings" and condemned McCarthy's activities in the campaign. It did not, however, recommend expulsion.

In the Senate, Butler compiled a generally conservative record. He supported attempts to return offshore oil lands to the states and voted for the Bricker amendment. He also introduced a bill that became the Communist Control Act of 1954. The McCarran Internal Security Act of 1950 required organizations designated as "communist action" and "communist front" by the Subversive Activities Control Board to register with the attorney general. Butler's bill proposed to mandate registration of a third group, "communist infiltrated" organizations. Liberals, led by HUBERT HUMPHREY, introduced an amendment that declared the communist party an "agency of a hostile foreign power" and therefore not entitled to the rights, privileges, and immunities legal bodies enjoyed. The amendment passed, as did the entire bill. After the Senate voted to censure McCarthy, the senator from Wisconsin unleashed an attack on the president, in which he apologized to the American people for having urged them to vote for Eisenhower. Butler, who had voted against censure, quickly distanced himself from McCarthy's diatribe, as did most of those who had opposed the censure motion.

Butler was reelected in 1956, and served until January 2, 1963, after he chose not to be a candidate for reelection in 1962. He resided in Baltimore until his death from a heart attack in Rocky Mount, N.C., on March 14, 1978.

—MSM

Butler, Paul M(ulholland)

(1905–1961) *chairman, Democratic National Committee*

Butler was born on June 15, 1905, in South Bend, Ind. He received an LL.B. degree from Notre Dame law school in 1927 and established a legal practice in South Bend. During the 1930s and 1940s, he gradually rose in the ranks of the state Democratic Party. In 1952 he ousted Frank McHale, a friend of President HARRY S. TRUMAN, as Democratic National Committeeman from Indiana. At the Democratic National Convention that year, Butler was one of the principal supporters of Gov. ADLAI E. STEVENSON of Illinois.

In 1954, Butler was elected chairman of the Democratic National Committee over Truman's strenuous opposition. The committee's functions were normally limited to raising money, organizing presidential nominating conventions, and providing assistance in the management of campaigns. However, in the absence of a Democratic president, Butler sought to transform the panel into an instrument of national party leadership. To accomplish this, he advocated more aggressive political attacks on the Eisenhower administration and pushed for the adoption of a clear-cut, liberal national platform.

The day after his election as chairman, Butler directly attacked President Eisenhower for failing to unite the nation. Until then, most Democrats had criticized only the men around the president. In 1956, Butler urged the party to adopt a strong civil rights platform and to endorse the Supreme Court's school desegregation decision of 1954. His strong stand earned him the enmity of southern leaders, who accused him of having dared the South to bolt the party.

Immediately after the presidential election of 1956, Butler asserted that Senate Majority Leader LYNDON B. JOHNSON (D-Tex.) and Speaker SAM RAYBURN (D-Tex.) were too moderate and too conciliatory towards the administration. Butler charged that congressional Democrats had not played "the true role of an opposition party from 1952 up to the [1956] presidential campaign." On November 27, 1956, the National Committee voted to create the Democratic Advisory Council to enable Northern liberals to circumvent those leaders in the formulation of Democratic legislative programs. Johnson and Rayburn refused to join the council, although Stevenson and Truman participated in its efforts.

Under Butler's chairmanship, the National Committee took several other measures to centralize and unify the party under its direction. It appointed six regional representatives to coordinate state and national programs, created a program for training precinct workers, and inaugurated executive leadership conferences for state and county party officials.

In 1960, the uneasy truce between Truman and Butler was broken when the former president charged Butler with rigging the national convention in favor of Sen. JOHN F. KENNEDY (D-Mass.). Truman resigned as a Missouri delegate before the gathering convened. Following Kennedy's nomination, Butler announced that he would not seek another term as committee chairman. At Kennedy's behest, the committee chose Sen. HENRY M. JACKSON (D-Wash.) to succeed Butler.

Butler retired from politics to practice law in Washington, D.C., where he died of a heart attack on December 30, 1961.

—MLL

Byrd, Harry F(lood)

(1887–1966) *U.S. senator*

Born on June 10, 1887, in Martinsburg, W. Va., Harry Byrd was the scion of a Virginia line dating back to 1674. His father was a lawyer, newspaper publisher, and one-time speaker of the Virginia House of Delegates. Byrd left school at the age of 15 to restore his father's paper, the *Winchester Star*, to solvency. At the age of 20, he established his own newspaper in Martinsburg, W. Va., and in 1923 acquired the Harrisonburg (Va.) *News-Record*. Byrd also became involved in apple growing. His chain of orchards in the Shenandoah Valley grew to one of the largest in the world.

Byrd entered the Virginia State Senate in 1915 and within a decade became the dominant figure in Virginia politics. He remained so for the next 40 years. A master political technician, Byrd built a durable personal fiefdom out of the existing Democratic machine based on farmers, rural businessmen, county courthouse cliques, and the virtual disenfranchisement of most black citizens. He won prominence by his key role in the defeat of a bond issue for roads in 1923. The "pay-as-you-go" principle of government finance became the trademark of Byrd's political career. He served as Virginia's governor from 1926 to 1930, and his frugal regime was considered innovative and successful. Appointed to the Senate in 1933 at the urging of President Franklin D. Roosevelt, Byrd ironically became one of the most bitter opponents of the New Deal. With his installment as chairman of the newly created Joint Committee on Reduction of Nonessential Federal Expenditures in 1941, he attained a forum for his sallies against unbalanced budgets and social welfare programs.

In the 1950s, Byrd was one of the Senate's most influential members, possessing two decades of experience and senior positions on the powerful Armed Services Committee and the Finance Committee. (He became chairman of the latter in 1955.) In the presidential election of 1952, he refused to endorse the Democratic ticket headed by ADLAI STEVENSON. Virginia's 12 electoral votes went to the Republican candidate, DWIGHT D. EISENHOWER.

Byrd's unflagging pursuit of economy in government frequently placed him in opposition to the Eisenhower administration as well as his fellow Democrats. He often voted against public works bills, including the great public works projects of the decade, the Saint Lawrence Seaway and the national highway program. He consistently fought to eliminate all economic assistance from foreign-aid packages. In 1955, Byrd opposed a salary increase for members of Congress and a $20 tax cut for lower income families. In 1957, he called upon President Eisenhower to make $5 billion in budget cuts and to replace Budget Director PERCIVAL F. BRUNDAGE for not pruning aggressively enough. Byrd also worked to block enactment of his Democratic colleagues' social measures. In 1960, he opposed federal aid to education, federal aid for areas beset by chronic unemployment, an increase in the minimum wage from $1 to $1.25 an hour, and Medicare.

In the wake of the Supreme Court's ruling in 1954 that struck down school segregation, Byrd moved to the forefront of the southern crusade to maintain segregation and states rights. His call for "massive resistance" in February 1956 became a rallying cry for those determined to oppose even token desegregation. In March, he helped mobilize the signing of the "Southern Manifesto," which denounced the Court's decision in the school segregation cases and pledged to "use all lawful means" to bring about its reversal. One hundred and one southern members of Congress signed the document.

Within Virginia, the Byrd organization was the backbone of the legislative effort to frustrate school desegregation. In 1956, the Virginia legislature enacted laws requiring the governor to close a public school rather than allow it to be integrated and providing tuition grants to students attending segregated private schools in their place. In September 1958, Gov. J. LINDSAY ALMOND ordered the closing of several public schools. In January 1959, the courts invalidated Virginia's massive resistance laws. Almond permitted the schools to reopen, but Byrd remained in adamant opposition.

A national symbol of unbudging resistance to integration, deficit-spending, and the welfare state, Byrd received demonstrations of support in the presidential elections of 1956 and 1960. Although not a declared candidate, he won 134,157 votes for president in 1956. In the election of 1960, he received the electoral votes of Mississippi, Alabama, and one Oklahoma Republican elector, for a total of 15.

The crumbling of massive resistance speeded the atrophy of the Byrd machine. The growth of the state's urban areas and the decline in the state's agricultural population gradually undermined its rural foundation, while legislative reapportionment and the repeal of the poll tax in the 1960s ended the systematic exclusion of potential contending groups that had aided the Byrd organization for half a century. Declining in influence and in failing health, Byrd resigned from the Senate in November 1965; his son, Harry F. Byrd, Jr., was appointed his successor. The elder Byrd died of a brain tumor on October 20, 1966, in Berryville, Va.

—TO

Byrd, Robert C(arlyle)

(1918–   ) *U.S. congressman and senator*

Born on January 15, 1918, in North Wilkesboro, N.C., and orphaned at the age of 10 months, Byrd was raised in West Virginia by his uncle, a poor coal miner. After graduating from high school, Byrd worked as a butcher. During World War II, he worked in shipyards in Maryland and Florida. In 1942, he was an active organizer for the Ku Klux Klan (KKK) but left the group after about a year. Byrd won a seat in the West Virginia House of Delegates in 1946 and was reelected in 1948. Two years later, he ran a successful campaign for the state Senate.

In 1952, Byrd sought a seat in the U.S. House of Representatives from his state's sixth congressional district, a coal mining region that included the city of Charleston. Byrd won the primary, but during the general election campaign, his opponent revealed that in 1946 Byrd had expressed a renewed interest in the Klan in a letter to its Imperial Wizard. Gov. Okey Patteson demanded that Byrd abandon the race, and the Democratic Party withdrew its backing. Byrd, however, renounced the KKK, continued his campaign, and defeated his Republican opponent with 55.6 percent of the vote.

As a representative, Byrd was most vocal in matters affecting coal miners and the coal industry, the major interest groups of his district. Having won election with labor's backing, he supported a proposal in the House to repeal the Taft-Hartley Act in 1953. Byrd also devoted considerable attention to protecting the coal industry against competition from alternative forms of energy. In 1953 and 1955, he unsuccessfully attempted to add oil import quotas to bills extending reciprocal trade laws. In June 1957, Byrd warned against importing natural gas from Canada, asserting that it "would create a serious impact upon the economy of the coal regions of West Virginia and neighboring states."

Byrd ran for the Senate in 1958. Making the recession the major issue in his campaign, he defeated the Republican incumbent, Sen. Chapman Rivercomb, with 59.2 percent of the vote. A moderate Democrat, Byrd voted with the upper chamber's southern Democratic–conservative Republican coalition on 42 percent of key roll calls in 1959 and 1960. In January 1959, he opposed a liberal effort to modify Senate Rule 22 to facilitate the invoking of cloture against southern filibusters. He voted for the Civil Rights Act of 1960 after opposing attempts to expand the scope of its coverage.

Byrd backed Sen. LYNDON B. JOHNSON's (D-Tex.) presidential bid in 1960, but when Johnson declined to enter the May West Virginia primary, he supported Sen. HUMBERT H. HUMPHREY (D-Minn.). Byrd denied the contention of some critics that his endorsement was influenced by Sen. JOHN F. KENNEDY's (D-Mass.) Catholicism.

An energetic and tireless worker, Byrd moved up in the Senate Democratic hierarchy during the 1960s and early-1970s. In 1971, he became majority whip. Byrd succeed JOHN MCCORMACK (D-Mass.) as majority leader in 1977. He is perhaps best known for his flowery oratorical style and his ability to bring pork barrel spending to his home state.

—MLL

Byrnes, James F(rancis)

(1879–1972) *governor of South Carolina*

The son of Irish immigrants, Byrnes was born on May 2, 1879, in Charleston, S.C. He was apprenticed as a law clerk at the age of 14. Byrnes became a court stenographer at 21, studied law in his spare time, and was admitted to the South Carolina bar in 1903. That year, he bought the *Aiken (S.C.) Journal and Review*, which he edited until 1907. A Democrat, Byrnes was elected solicitor of the second judicial circuit in 1908, and two years later won election to the U.S. House of Representatives, where he served until 1925. He ran unsuccessfully for the Senate in 1924, but won a seat six years later.

Following Roosevelt's election in 1932, Byrnes served as one of the president's chief legislative tacticians and the de facto leader of congressional Democrats. After 1936, however, Byrnes joined the southern Democratic opposition to the New Deal. With the advent of World War II in 1939, he muted his differences with the president and helped to repeal the Neutrality Act and pass the lend-lease bill. In 1941, Roosevelt appointed Byrnes associate justice of the Supreme Court. He stepped down 16 months later to head the Office of Economic Stabilization. In 1943, Byrnes became director of the Office of War Mobilization, where he supervised the production of war and civilian goods. Roosevelt described him as "assistant president on the home front."

Byrnes accompanied Roosevelt to the Yalta Conference in 1945, and, after Roosevelt's death, became secretary of state. He was one of Truman's closest advisers, helping make the decision to drop the atomic bomb on Japan and formulating policy toward the Soviet Union. As secretary of state, Byrnes sought a postwar settlement that would prevent Soviet control over Eastern Europe and retain the American atomic monopoly. Byrnes resigned in 1947 in a disagreement over Truman's domestic program, particularly regarding civil rights. After a period of silence, he denounced Truman's domestic policies and the movement toward a strong, centralized government.

In January 1950, Byrnes was elected governor of South Carolina on a states' rights platform. While in office, he pushed through the legislature a school administration reorganization plan, an anti-masking bill aimed at the Ku Klux Klan, a right-to-work law forbidding compulsory union membership, and a statute increasing support for state colleges. He also obtained immediate approval for a new mental health bond issue.

Byrnes's primary focus was on the restoration of states' rights, particularly what he believed was their right to maintain segregation. The governor thought three things were necessary to restore those rights: increased state responsibility toward African Americans to give them equal facilities and services without integration; a determined stand by states to prevent further federal inroads, particularly in civil rights and school segregation; and cooperative action by southern states to prevent the continued growth of federal power.

After the NAACP filed suit against the segregated schools of Clarendon Co., Byrnes proposed and the legislature passed a 3 percent sales tax and a $75 million school bond issue to upgrade black facilities. As a former justice of the Supreme Court, he understood the direction of recent rulings and hoped that equalization of facilities would enable him to preserve segregation. While developing his school equalization program, Byrnes had the legislature enact measures to counter possible federal intervention to desegregate local schools. School boards were authorized to transfer their property to private hands. A pupil-assignment law required students switching schools to receive written permission from both institutions. Byrnes created the first group in the South to map out

strategy to maintain segregation. Headed by state Sen. L. Marion Gressette, the so-called Gressette Committee suggested that South Carolina drop the state constitutional provision requiring free public schools. Byrnes approved the recommendation and called for action on the proposal in January 1952. The legislature responded, and voters ratified the amendment in the elections of November 1952.

Byrnes denounced the Supreme Court's ruling in *Brown v. Board of Education* (1954), which declared segregated school facilities unconstitutional. The ruling directly affected South Carolina, because a challenge to the school system of Clarendon Co. had been one of the cases that the Court decided in *Brown*. The governor maintained that the validity of the Constitution was ageless and that previous decisions supporting segregation should not be overturned. That year, he supported segregationist Lt. Gov. George Bell Timmerman for the Democratic gubernatorial nomination. In 1957, when Eisenhower sent troops into Little Rock, Ark., to desegregate its Central High School, Byrnes denounced the action. Byrnes maintained that "sensible Negroes" "know that when integration occurs, there will cease to be education for either the white or colored child."

In response to his desire to revive regional unity, Byrnes urged the South to become independent of the Democratic Party. In major addresses before the Virginia and Georgia legislatures in 1952, he denounced the growth of federal power under Truman, particularly its intrusion into the area of civil rights, and called on the South to put principle before party. When Eisenhower won the Republican nomination, Byrnes openly supported him and was responsible for the general's stronger showing in the South than any Republican candidate since Reconstruction. In September 1953, National Democratic Chairman Stephen A. Mitchell read Byrnes out of the party. In March 1956, Byrnes, Timmerman, and Sen. Strom Thurmond (D-S.C.) tried to force South Carolina to break with the national Democrats. When this movement collapsed in October, Byrnes endorsed Sen. Harry F. Byrd (D-Va.) for president. Following Eisenhower's reelection, Byrnes accused Attorney General Herbert Brownell of persuading the president to support black demands in return for votes.

Unable to serve a second term under South Carolina law, Byrnes retired in 1955. Throughout the remainder of the 1950s, he lent prestige and dignity to the segregationist cause. He supported conservative Sen. BARRY M. GOLDWATER (R-Ariz.) for president in 1964 and RICHARD NIXON in 1968. Byrnes died in Columbia, S.C., on April 9, 1972.

—MJS

Byrnes, John W(illiam)
(1913–1985) *U.S. congressman*

John Byrnes was born on June 12, 1913, in Green Bay, Wis. He received his B.A. from the University of Wisconsin in 1936 and his law degree from the same institution two years later. After practicing law briefly, he was appointed special deputy commissioner of banking for Wisconsin in 1938. He stayed in that post until his election to the state senate as a Republican in 1940. In 1943, he became majority leader and the next year won election to the U.S. House of Representatives.

A fiscal conservative, Byrnes vocally opposed Democratic social welfare programs and deficit-spending. He also advocated economy in government. Named to the Ways and Means Committee in 1947, Byrnes gradually rose to prominence in the House as a Republican spokesman on tax and fiscal policy.

During the 1950s, Byrnes was a Republican Party loyalist and usually a faithful supporter of the Eisenhower administration. In February 1953, he was one of only four members of the Ways and Means Committee to vote against an income tax cut being pushed by the committee's chairman, Rep. DANIEL REED (R-N.Y.), but opposed by the Eisenhower administration.

Byrnes generally favored tax measures designed to benefit specific sectors of business, such as the oil depletion allowance and the credit for stock dividend income. In 1954, the House passed his motion to give working parents a tax deduction of up to $600 for child care expenses. Four years later, however, Byrnes opposed the Keogh plan, a proposal to allow self-employed individuals to set up tax-sheltered retirement plans. He said that it provided no relief for millions of other persons who contributed to the Social Security system and were not permitted to deduct their contributions from their taxable income.

Byrnes was often in the forefront of efforts to curb federal spending. When the Eisenhower administration requested a $5 billion increase in the national debt ceiling in January 1958, Byrnes put forth a proposal to limit the rise to $3 billion. The House rejected Byrnes's measure, 275-114. In April, he again led the economy bloc in a battle over a Democratic bill expanding unemployment benefits. His proposal to limit benefits to workers currently insured lost in the Ways and Means Committee, 14-7. In 1960, he opposed the Democrats' proposal for Medicare and opposed a 7½ percent pay increase for federal workers.

In 1959, Byrnes became chairman of the House Republican Policy Committee after helping Rep. CHARLES A. HALLECK (R-Ind.) depose Rep. JOSEPH W. MARTIN (R-Mass.) as House minority leader. Over the next decade, Byrnes led Republican opposition to social legislation supported by the Kennedy and Johnson administrations, while working closely with Ways and Means Committee chairman Rep. WILBUR MILLS (D-Ark.) to round up a bipartisan consensus on tax measures. Byrnes retired in 1973 and resided in Arlington, Va., until his death in Marshfield, Wisc., on January 12, 1985.

—TO

Cabot, John M(oors)

(1901–1981) *assistant secretary of state for inter-American affairs, ambassador to Sweden, ambassador to Colombia, ambassador to Brazil*

A member of the prominent Cabot family of Boston, John Moors Cabot was born in Cambridge, Mass., on December 11, 1901. He graduated magna cum laude from Harvard University in 1923 and took a degree in modern history at Oxford University two years later. Cabot began his diplomatic career in 1927 as vice-counsel in Callao, Peru. Thereafter, he was posted to the Dominican Republic and Mexico. As chargé d'affaires in Belgrade from 1946 to 1947, he observed and reported the split between Yugoslavia and the Soviet Union. He served as United States consul general in Shanghai until the victory of the Chinese Communists in 1949.

In February 1953, President Eisenhower named Cabot assistant secretary of state for inter-American affairs. In his first month in office, Cabot led the U.S. delegation at the Inter-American Economic and Social Conference in Caracas, Venezuela. There Cabot outlined what all assumed was the official Eisenhower policy for the hemisphere. He recommended continued U.S. technical assistance, considerable movement of federal and particularly private funds to Latin America, and equitable trade relations. Speaking later in the United States, Cabot warned that import curbs on Latin American products damaged the ideals of Pan-Americanism and could serve only to abet communist subversion in the hemisphere. He argued that to deal effectively with the communists, the United States had to cut its ties with reactionary regimes and seize the leadership of social reform in Latin America.

Cabot failed to realize his designs. His efforts to make more use of the Export-Import Bank for long-term development loans were vetoed by Secretary of the Treasury GEORGE HUMPHREY, who wanted to restrict the bank's role and favored loans for short-term purposes only. The administration also imposed import restrictions on many Latin American products. His conflicts with Humphrey led to Cabot's resignation in February 1954.

Cabot was immediately named ambassador to Sweden. He became ambassador to Colombia in April 1957 and remained there until May 1959, when he was transferred to Brazil.

Cabot arrived there at a period when Brazilian-American relations were strained by growing nationalist feelings and the belief that the United States was insensitive to Latin American needs. Although he frequently spoke before Brazilian student groups in an effort to reduce hostility toward the United States, he could not restrain the government's development of an independent foreign policy.

President JOHN F. KENNEDY asked Cabot to stay on in Brazil because of the ambassador's sympathy for his administration's Latin American policy. However, Cabot's difficulties with the new Brazilian president forced him to leave his post in August 1961. He served as ambassador to Poland from December 1961 to August 1965 and retired from the State Department in 1966. Subsequently, he taught at the Fletcher School of Law and Diplomacy at Tufts University and the School of Foreign Service at Georgetown University. He died in New York City on February 23, 1981.

—JCH

Campbell, Joseph
(1900–1984) *member, Atomic Energy Commission; U.S. controller general*

Campbell was born on March 25, 1900, in New York City. He received an A.B. degree from Columbia University in 1924, and then began a career in accounting with the firm of Lingley, Baird and Dixon. He established his own firm nine years later. During the 1940s, he served as assistant treasurer of Columbia University and in 1949 was appointed treasurer and vice president.

President DWIGHT D. EISENHOWER appointed Campbell to the five-man Atomic Energy Commission (AEC) in 1953. During his year on the panel, he was involved in two major controversies of the early Eisenhower administration: the decision to deny scientist J. ROBERT OPPENHEIMER security clearance and the decision to approve the Dixon-Yates contract. In June 1954, Campbell voted with the four-man majority to deny Oppenheimer security clearance. The majority did not find him a security risk but nevertheless voted to deny clearance because of "fundamental defects" in character. It also found that "his association with . . . communists had extended far beyond the tolerable limits of prudence . . . expected of one holding high government position."

Campbell joined the AEC's chairman, LEWIS STRAUSS, in backing the Dixon-Yates contract in 1954. This agreement provided for a private utility to construct a hydroelectric plant near West Memphis, Ark. The company would then have sold power to AEC installations in the area, replacing the Tennessee Valley Authority (TVA) as the supplier. The contract aroused a storm of protest from advocates of public power, who opposed the replacement of power produced by the government-operated TVA. The contract was canceled in June 1955, after the Democrats had regained control of Congress and after revelations of possible improprieties in the negotiation of the contract.

In January 1955, Campbell was appointed to a 15-year term as controller general. A nonpolitical position involving no policymaking functions, the controller advised Congress on legislative matters, audited government programs, and offered recommendations designed to make government operations more efficient and effective. During the Eisenhower administration, Campbell testified against the president's highway program of 1955, warning that the moral-obligation bonds Eisenhower intended to use to finance the project were illegal under existing laws. Several years later, he criticized the air force's management of the $2-billion intercontinental ballistic missile program because the service had shifted responsibility for the project to private industry.

In December 1960, Campbell attempted to cut off funds to the State Department inspector general's office for withholding from Congress information on U.S. aid to Latin America. The administration, terming the data confidential, supported the State Department. Eisenhower ordered Secretary of State CHRISTIAN HERTER to ignore Campbell's order.

Campbell resigned his post in 1965, before his term expired. He died in Sarasota, Fla., on June 21, 1984.

—TLH

Cannon, Howard W(alter)
(1912–2002) *U.S. senator*

The son of a banker and rancher, Cannon was born on January 26, 1912, in Saint George, Utah. He received a law degree from the University of Arizona in 1937, and opened a practice in Utah the following year. After service in the army air corps during World War II, he became a partner in a Las Vegas legal firm. He was elected Las Vegas city attorney in 1949 and occupied that post for eight years. In 1956, he lost the Democratic primary for a U.S. House seat.

Two years later, Cannon entered the Nevada senatorial race against the Republican incumbent, George W. Malone. The campaign pitted Cannon, whose ties were with the new, growing industrial concerns of southern Nevada, against the conservative Malone, allied with the mining interests of the

North and West. Attacking the Republican as an isolationist and conservative, Cannon won the race with 56 percent of the vote. Cannon benefitted from the nationwide Democratic trend, but equally important was the backing of organized labor and the strong support he received from Las Vegas. These provided Cannon's political base throughout his career.

During his first two years in the Senate, Cannon compiled a moderately liberal record. In 1959, he supported two housing bills vetoed by President Eisenhower, who contended that they were too expensive. The following year, Cannon voted to override a presidential veto of an area redevelopment bill providing federal aid to depressed regions. In June 1959, he joined a majority of senators in rejecting the nomination of former Atomic Energy Commission Chairman Lewis L. Strauss as secretary of commerce on the ground that he had been excessively influenced by private business.

In 1959, Cannon opposed an effort by liberals to ease the Senate's filibuster rules. These required a two-thirds vote of the entire Senate to stop debate and provided that debate could not be shut off on proposals to consider changes in Senate rules. Liberals wanted to permit imposition of cloture by majority vote of the entire chamber and by 60 percent of those voting. Instead, Cannon backed a revision introduced by Senate Majority Leader Lyndon B. Johnson (D-Tex.) that would have permitted two-thirds of those voting to shut off debate on all measures, including rules changes.

A member of the Armed Services and Aeronautical and Space Committees, Cannon was a strong backer of military spending and the space program in the 1960s. He also supported President Johnson's Vietnam policies. Cannon served on the commerce committee for 24 years and played a role in deregulating the trucking and airline industries. He first received significant national attention in 1973 when, as chairman of the Rules and Administration Committee, he led its hearings on President Richard Nixon's nomination of Rep. Gerald Ford (R-Mich.) for vice president. During the fall of the following year, he chaired the panel's consideration of Nelson Rockefeller for the vice presidency.

Cannon lost his bid for reelection in 1982. He died in Las Vegas on March 7, 2002.

—MLL

Capehart, Homer E(arl)
(1897–1979) U.S. senator

The son of a tenant farmer, Capehart was born on June 6, 1897, in Algiers, Ind. He attended public schools and served in the army during World War I. After the war, he worked in farming and in the radio and phonograph business. In 1932, he began his own company, which developed the automatic record changer that made the jukebox possible. Ousted by the board of directors during the Great Depression, he took a job as vice president of the Rudolph Wurlitzer Corporation and head of its jukebox division. Capehart won election as a Republican to the U.S. Senate from Indiana in 1944 and quickly emerged as one of the chamber's more conservative and anticommunist members. He won reelection two times.

When Republicans took control of Congress in 1953, Capehart became chairman of the Senate Banking and Currency Committee. During the early weeks of the administration, Capehart opposed Eisenhower's plan for ending wage and price controls quickly and without provision for standby measures. Fearing a recurrence of the inflation that gripped the nation following the end of controls after World War II, Capehart immediately introduced a bill to set up emergency control machinery. The measure narrowly passed the Senate but died in the House.

Capehart was assigned to the Foreign Relations Committee in 1954. That February, he voted for the Bricker amendment, which limited the president's treaty-making powers. It was defeated by one vote. In 1955, Capehart attacked a resolution by Sen. Joseph R. McCarthy (R-Wis.) requiring Eisenhower to condition his participation in the Geneva summit conference on a Soviet agreement to put a discussion of Eastern Europe on the agenda. He also criticized Sen. Lyndon B. Johnson (D-Tex.) and Sen. Walter George (D-Ga.) for permitting the resolution to emerge from the Foreign Relations Committee. The measure was defeated on the floor of the Senate.

Following his reelection in 1956, Capehart became an increasingly strong supporter of administration policy. He backed the Civil Rights Act of 1957, which protected the voting rights of African Americans. The following year, he supported presidential assistant Sherman Adams in the face of conflict-of-interest charges. Capehart also supported the permanent establishment of the Small Business Administration and backed statehood for Alaska.

In 1959, a vice president of Wurlitzer Inc., testifying before the senate Committee on Improper Relations in the Labor or Management Field, charged that Capehart had been forced to deal with racketeers when he sold jukeboxes to that company in the 1930s. The Senator strongly refuted this. He joined other conservatives in voting down a national commission to deal with organized crime in 1960.

Capehart opposed most legislation proposed by the Kennedy administration. He gained national prominence in 1962, when he lambasted the administration's Cuban policy and warned of a Soviet buildup in the island. Capehart lost his bid for reelection that year to Democrat Birch Bayh. He returned to farming, manufacturing, and investment pursuits. He died in Indianapolis, Ind., on September 3, 1979.

—MJS

Carey, James B(arron)

(1911–1973) *president, International Union of Electrical, Radio and Machine Workers*

The son of a civil servant, James Carey was born on August 12, 1911, in Philadelphia. He began working in a local factory at the age of 14. Following graduation from high school, he got a job at the Philco Radio Co. in Philadelphia. In 1933, Carey and a group of supporters took over a company union at Philco and led a successful strike of the plant's 3,800 employees. Shortly afterward, he left his job to become an organizer in the radio industry for the American Federation of Labor (AFL). Carey favored industrial unionism, however, and he soon came into conflict with the federation's policy of assigning workers to separate craft brotherhoods. In March 1936, he helped organize a meeting of 28 AFL locals representing 30,000 electrical workers, which formed an independent union, the United Electrical, Radio and Machine Workers of America (UE). Six months later, Carey led the UE into the new Committee for Industrial Organization (CIO). In 1938, he was elected national secretary of the CIO, and in 1942 he became its secretary-treasurer.

A liberal anticommunist, Carey nevertheless ran the UE after 1936 in cooperation with communists. Following the Stalin-Hitler Pact in 1939, he broke with these elements, and in 1941 he was ousted from the union presidency by a coalition of communists and more conservative members. Thereafter, Carey led the anticommunist opposition within the UE, and with WALTER REUTHER of the United Auto Workers, he spearheaded a drive to purge the CIO of communist influence.

After World War II, Carey worked with the State Department and various European labor leaders to create the anticommunist International Confederation of Free Trade Unions. In 1949, the UE was expelled from the CIO, and the CIO presented Carey with a charter for a new union, the International Union of Electrical, Radio and Machine Workers (IUE). A long period of jurisdictional warfare followed between the UE, the IUE, and several AFL craft unions. During that time, the IUE won collective bargaining rights in a majority of plants in the electrical equipment industry.

Carey was a member of the committee that negotiated the merger of the AFL and CIO in 1955. He was elected a vice president of the new organization and general secretary of its industrial union department. He often represented the AFL-CIO at international labor functions during the 1950s.

At the same time, however, continuing jurisdictional conflict and employer resistance steadily weakened Carey's own union. In 1955, the IUE struck the Westinghouse Corp. after the company attempted to extend a three-year contract, negotiated in the previous year, to five years. The strike, which lasted six months and eventually involved more than 70,000 workers throughout the country, was the longest and most bitterly contested dispute in a major industry since 1941. Clashes between striking and nonstriking employees and police intervention also marked the strike as a notable exception to the relatively peaceful pattern of labor-management relations established in mass-production industries after the war.

Throughout the 1950s, Carey complained that his union was the victim of unfair labor practices on the part of the General Electric Co. IUE members termed the company's bargaining policy "Boulwarism," after the name of a GE vice president (LEMUEL BOULWARE), or "bargaining by ultimatum," since the company's first offer was its last. In 1960, Carey called a strike against GE that proved disastrous for the union. IUE called off the strike after three weeks. Following that defeat, the IUE lost 10 important plant elections affecting several thousand workers.

In 1965, rank-and-file insurgents defeated Carey for the presidency of the IUE. Shortly afterward, he left the union to become a labor representative of the United Nations Association, a position that he held until his retirement in 1972. Carey died in Silver Spring, Md., on September 11, 1973.

—TLH

Carlson, Frank
(1893–1987) *U.S. senator*

The son of Swedish immigrants, Carlson was born on January 23, 1893, in Concordia, Kans. He attended Kansas State College. After serving in the army during World War I, he returned to Concordia and bought a large wheat and livestock farm. He was elected to the state legislature as a Republican in 1929 and 1931. In 1935, Carlson won a seat in the U.S. House of Representatives from Kansas's sixth district. During the 1930s, he backed high parity for farmers but generally opposed New Deal measures. He also opposed amending the neutrality laws. Carlson was elected governor of Kansas in 1946 and was reelected in 1948. Two years later, he won election to the U.S. Senate.

A moderate Republican, Carlson was an early supporter of Gen. DWIGHT D. EISENHOWER for the Republican presidential nomination in 1952. After the Republican Convention, he acted as an intermediary between the Eisenhower forces and Sen. ROBERT A. TAFT (R-Ohio) in an effort to unite the party. Eisenhower appointed Carlson a special adviser during the campaign.

In August 1954, Carlson served on the committee of six "neutral" senators, known as the Select Committee to Study Censure, created to study charges of misconduct against Sen. JOSEPH R. MCCARTHY (R-Wis.). That November, he joined in its unanimous recommendation for censure. On November 12, during floor debate on the panel's report, Carlson charged that McCarthy had violated Senate rules by his attacks on the committee's conduct and motives.

In the Senate, Carlson was generally conservative on fiscal and welfare matters; however, typically for a farm-state Republican, he supported aid to farmers. First as chairman, and after 1955 as senior Republican, of the Post Office and Civil Service Committee, Carlson attempted to limit the salaries, benefits, and promotions of federal civil service workers. During the summer of 1954, he succeeded in placing restrictions on the number of permanent employees, promotions, and transfers in the federal service. The following year, he unsuccessfully offered a floor amendment to reduce pay increases for classified employees from 10 percent, as provided by a committee bill, to 6 percent. In 1957, he opposed another pay raise, again without success, charging that it would require a supplemental appropriation of half a billion dollars.

A supporter of 100 percent of parity price supports for wheat farmers, Carlson in 1954 opposed the administration's omnibus farm bill, which established flexible price supports. Two years later, he successfully introduced a proposal to give the secretary of agriculture discretionary authority to support wheat for domestic human consumption at 100 percent of parity. However, the president vetoed the bill to which the proviso was attached.

Carlson generally supported the administration's positions. In 1955, as a member of the three-member Post Office and Civil Service Committee's Government Employees Security Program Subcommittee, he defended President Eisenhower's security program against charges that its procedures failed to adequately protect the rights of federal employees and job applicants. The following year, Carlson criticized the committee's report, which recommended that the scope of the program's coverage be reduced from 6 million to 1.5 million employees. He supported the extension of the Reciprocal Trade Agreements Act in 1955 and voted against a medical insurance system financed through Social Security in 1960. Although he won reelection in 1956 and 1962, he never became a significant force in the Senate.

Carlson opposed most New Frontier programs in the early 1960s but backed the Kennedy administration's foreign policies. Subsequently, he voted against most of President Johnson's Great Society programs, but he supported the Civil Rights Act of 1964, the Voting Rights Act of 1965, and the Demonstration Cities plan in 1966. Carlson was not a critic of the Vietnam War. From time to time, however, he called for negotiations. In 1968, he decided not to seek reelection. Carlson was a favorite-son candidate at the Republican National Convention in August 1968. He returned to his farm in Concordia and died there on May 30, 1987.

—MLL

Carr, Francis P.

(1917–1971) *executive director, Permanent Investigations Subcommittee of the Senate Government Operations Committee*

Born in Newport, R.I., in 1917, Carr graduated from Brown University and received a law degree from the University of Pennsylvania in 1942. He then entered the FBI. As head of the New York field division's security matters section in the late-1940s, he directed the investigation of prominent leaders of the Communist Party. Carr resigned from the FBI in 1953 and was appointed executive director of the staff of the Senate Permanent Investigations Subcommittee, headed by Sen. JOSEPH R. McCARTHY (R-Wis.).

During 1954, Carr became embroiled in the dispute between the army and McCarthy. On March 15, 1954, Secretary of the Army ROBERT T. STEVENS charged that Carr, McCarthy, and subcommittee counsel ROY COHN had exerted pressure on the army to obtain special treatment for Pvt. G. DAVID SCHINE, a former aide to McCarthy.

On March 16, the Permanent Investigations Subcommittee voted to investigate the accusation. Carr was cleared of the charges in May on a straight party vote and was exempted from appearing before the panel. Democrats on the subcommittee opposed the action, maintaining it had been taken to help Carr avoid testifying.

On June 14, Carr voluntarily testified. He maintained that, in an effort to stop McCarthy's probe, Stevens had offered preferential treatment to Schine. Carr also testified that the secretary had been willing to reveal "some homosexuals" in the air force in return for information about McCarthy's next investigation.

The subcommittee issued its report in August. The Democrats denounced McCarthy's conduct, while the Republicans mildly criticized him. Democrats likewise rebuked Stevens more severely than Republicans for submitting to McCarthy's pressure. Members of both parties found no evidence of wrongdoing on Carr's part. In a dissenting opinion, Sen. CHARLES E. POTTER (D-Mich.) said he was not entirely blameless. After the hearings, Carr faded from public view. He died on June 16, 1971.

—SY

Carroll, John A(lbert)

(1901–1983) *U.S. senator*

Born in Denver, Colo., on July 30, 1901, Carroll attended public schools through eighth grade. He served in the army during World War I and later joined the Denver Police Department. He passed his high school equivalency exam and in 1929 received a law degree from Westminster Law College. As a young lawyer, he became involved in local Democratic politics and served as assistant U.S. district attorney for Denver from 1933 to 1934. He was district attorney of Denver from 1936 to 1940, when he lost a primary race for governor of Colorado. He practiced law until receiving an appointment as attorney for the Denver region of the Office of Price Administration. Carroll served in the army during World War II. He won election to the U.S. House of Representatives in 1946 and was reelected two years later. In 1950, he ran against Republican incumbent EUGENE D. MILLIKIN for the Senate and lost. After this, he served briefly in the Truman White House and returned to the practice of law.

After losing a second race for a Senate seat in 1954, Carroll finally won election to the Senate in 1956. During his one term, Carroll supported education, medical, social, and civil rights legislation. Carroll voted for the Civil Rights Act of 1957 and joined liberals in an unsuccessful attempt to strengthen the civil rights bill of 1960.

As a congressman from a Western state, Carroll was deeply concerned with resource development and conservation. He supported the controversial Hells Canyon Dam Project, which provided for federal construction and operation of a massive dam on the Snake River. In 1957, he sponsored a bill authorizing funds for the Fryingpan-Arkansas Project, a multiple-purpose reclamation effort designed to divert surplus water from the Colorado River Basin to the Arkansas River Basin. The project was vital to the development of southeastern Colorado. Carroll also supported unsuccessful efforts to limit billboards on highways.

In 1958, Carroll became a major defender of the Supreme Court, then under attack for its controversial decisions on civil liberties. During the mid-1950s, the Court had limited the power of both state and local government in subversion cases and strengthened the rights of individuals under arrest. In August 1958, Carroll opposed attempts to strip the Court of the power to review subversion cases. His motion to recommit killed an amendment declaring that "no act of Congress . . . should be construed by the Courts as nullifying state laws on the same subject unless Congress so specified or there was an unreconcilable difference between state and federal law." On a point of order, Carroll defeated a bill reversing the *Mallory* decision, which had invalidated the confession of a confessed rapist because of delays in his arraignment.

Carroll lost his bid for reelection in 1962 to Peter Dominik. He practiced law in Denver until 1968 and died in that city on August 30, 1983.

—MSM

Case, Clifford P(hilip)

(1904–1982) *U.S. congressman and senator*

The son of a Dutch Reformed minister, Case was born in Franklin Park, N.J., on April 16, 1904. He graduated from Rutgers University in 1925 and received an LL.B. from Columbia University in 1928. He joined the Wall Street law firm of Simpson, Thacher and Bartlett the same year and was a member of the firm from 1939 to 1953. From 1938 to 1942, Case served on the Common Council of Rahway, N.J.

In 1944, Case was elected to the U.S. House of Representatives. There he gained a reputation as a liberal Republican who frequently crossed party lines to support civil rights, education, and welfare legislation. He favored an anti–poll tax measure in 1945, opposed the establishment of a permanent Un-American Activities Committee in 1945, supported the creation of a Fair Employment Practices Commission in 1950, and voted against overriding President HARRY S. TRUMAN's veto of the McCarran immigration bill in 1952. On the other hand, he voted to override the president's veto of the Taft-Hartley bill in 1947 and helped draft the communist-control bill in 1948. Dissatisfied with the lack of significant influence of all but the most senior members of the House, Case resigned his seat in August 1953. He became president of the Ford Foundation's Fund for the Republic, established to defend civil liberties against cold war pressures for conformity.

In March 1954, Case resigned that post to run for the U.S. Senate. During the campaign, he faced opposition from labor, Old Guard Republicans, and supporters of Sen. JOSEPH R. MCCARTHY (R-Wis.), who labeled him a "left-wing socialist" and "darling of the Americans for Democratic Action." Stressing his opposition to McCarthy, Case narrowly defeated his liberal Democratic opponent in November.

As a senator, Case remained a member of the bloc of Northeastern liberal Republicans in Congress. In November 1956, he urged revision of the McCarran Immigration Act to eliminate "the senseless and serious discriminations against nationalities of Southern and Southeastern Europe." A strong supporter of civil rights, in 1957 Case opposed southern attempts to weaken the administration's civil rights bill by requiring a jury trial for contempt cases involving persons who had attempted to prevent blacks from voting. In March 1960, Case was one of eight Republicans who joined liberal Democrats in an unsuccessful effort to end a southern filibuster against another civil rights bill sponsored by the administration.

Case did not uniformly vote with the Senate's liberal Democrats. In 1959, he backed a $2.1-billion housing bill but declined to support an effort to override President Eisenhower's veto. The same year, he voted to confirm LEWIS STRAUSS as secretary of commerce, a choice opposed by many liberals on the ground that Strauss had been too close to private business interests as chairman of the Atomic Energy Commission.

Case continued his liberal record during the 1960s, backing most civil rights and social welfare legislation. He was also a leading spokesman for financial disclosure legislation for all three branches of the federal government. Case opposed the growth of right-wing influence in the Republican Party, and in 1964, he fought the nomination of conservative Sen. BARRY GOLDWATER (R-Ariz.) for president. During the later part of the decade, Case emerged as a critic of President LYNDON B. JOHNSON's Vietnam policies. After failing to win the Republican nomination for his seat in 1978, he returned to the practice of law and was a lecturer at Rutgers University. He died in Washington, D.C., on March 5, 1982.

—MLL

Celler, Emanuel

(1888–1981) *U.S. congressman; chairman, Judiciary Committee*

The son of a liquor distiller, Celler was born in Brooklyn, N.Y., on May 6, 1888. He graduated from Columbia University in 1910, and received his LL.B. there two years later. In 1922, he won election to Congress as a Democrat from New York's 10th congressional district, a predominately middle-class Jewish section of Brooklyn. In the House, Celler established a strong liberal record, introducing measures to curb the abuses of big business and advocating the liberalization of immigration laws. Celler was a fervent supporter of the New Deal and a strong defender of civil liberties. In 1945, he backed an unsuccessful anti–poll tax bill and opposed a measure making the Un-American Activities Committee a standing committee.

Celler maintained his liberal record during the Truman administration. He opposed the Taft-Hartley bill of 1947. Two years later, he became chairman of the Judiciary Committee, a position he held for the duration of his congressional tenure (except for 1953–55, when Republicans had a majority in the House). In 1949, Celler used his post as chairman of the Judiciary Committee to establish the Subcommittee on Antitrust and Monopoly. From 1949 to 1951, the panel conducted a series of well-

publicized investigations into insurance companies, the steel industry, and monopoly practices in baseball. In 1950, Celler helped steer the Celler-Kefauver antimerger bill through Congress. Celler was also a vocal opponent of Sen. JOSEPH R. McCARTHY's (R-Wis.) anticommunist crusade.

During the 1950s, Celler continued to be a leading congressional defender of civil liberties. He cast one of two votes against appropriations for the House Un-American Activities Committee in 1953 and 1954. In 1954, he opposed a bill, formulated as a tool in the anticommunist crusade, that allowed Congress to grant immunity to congressional witnesses under certain conditions. Critics maintained it had the effect of forcing witnesses to testify or face jail sentences. In a minority statement directed at McCarthy and his supporters, Celler and three other Democrats on the Judiciary Committee denounced the action. Despite his strong stand on the rights of witnesses in loyalty-security hearings, Celler did not oppose a 1954 bill banning the Communist Party. Although he described the measure as "palpably unconstitutional," he voted for it.

In May and June 1955, Celler's antitrust subcommittee held hearings on government policy toward mergers. The subcommittee's report maintained that the "third great merger movement" in U.S. history was already in progress and warned that previous periods of intensive merger activity had been followed by "devastating business collapse." Celler also opposed a proposal to grant antitrust immunity to companies involved in defense production. However, the bill was passed by both houses in August 1955.

Celler introduced a civil rights bill in 1956 that consisted of an antilynching provision and an omnibus civil rights bill. The Eisenhower administration sent a bill to Congress proposing the creation of a civil rights commission; the elevation of the Civil Rights Section of the Justice Department to the status of a division, headed by an assistant attorney general; authorization for the Justice Department to file civil suits to protect civil rights; and authorizing the Justice Department to file suits to protect voting rights. In a procedural maneuver, the administration's bill was substituted for Celler's. The bill passed the House, but LYNDON JOHNSON, the majority leader in the Senate, used procedural trickery to consign the bill to the deep freeze of JAMES O. EASTLAND's Judiciary Committee.

The following year, the Eisenhower administration sent the bill back to Congress. As it worked its way through the House, Celler criticized what he regarded as Eisenhower's lukewarm support for the measure. The House once again passed the bill, but the Senate removed Title III (the general civil rights provision) and added a jury trial provision to Title IV (voting rights). This amendment, offered by southerners, guaranteed a jury trial to those who violated court orders not to interfere with African Americans exercising their right to vote. Celler opposed the jury trial amendment, but it became part of the Civil Rights Act of 1957.

In 1959, Celler introduced the House version of a measure calling for financial aid for school desegregation and for authorization for the Department of Health, Education, and Welfare to develop desegregation plans. However, the proposals died in committee. He also failed to get those proposals included in the Civil Rights Act of 1960. Celler participated in the successful drive for a strong civil rights plank in the Democratic platform of 1960. The plank called for federal aid to desegregated school districts, federal authority to file civil suits to prevent any denial of civil rights, and a federal Fair Employment Practices Commission.

Celler continued to play an important role in civil rights legislation during the 1960s. He sponsored the Twenty-Fourth Amendment, ratified in 1964, which abolished the poll tax in federal elections, and was a principal author of the Civil Rights Act of 1964. He also helped secure passage of the Voting Rights Act of 1965, the Immigration and Naturalization Act of 1965, and the Civil Rights Act of 1968. After 50 years in the House, Celler was defeated in the 1972 Democratic congressional primary by Elizabeth Holtzman, a young Brooklyn lawyer. He died in Brooklyn on January 15, 1981.

—MSM

Chambers, (Jay) (Vivian) Whittaker
(1901–1961) *journalist*

The product of a vaguely bohemian and downwardly mobile family, Chambers was born in Philadelphia, on April 1, 1901, and grew up in Lynbrook, on the south shore of Long Island, N.Y. After attending Columbia University, Chambers joined the Communist Party in 1925. He wrote for the *Daily Worker*, the *New Masses*, and other communist publications from 1925 to 1929, when he resigned from the *Daily Worker* in the wake of factional wars within the Communist Party. After a brief period as a self-described "independent communist oppositionist," Chambers rejoined the party in 1931. He contributed short stories to the *New Masses* that won him acclaim as the "hottest literary Bolshevik" in New York. He became the editor of the *New Masses* in 1932. Beginning in 1928, Chambers also worked as a freelance translator. He translated *Bambi*, a children's novel by the Austrian writer Felix Salten, and a dozen other works, including novels by Heinrich Mann and Franz Werfel. In 1932, Chambers went underground as a Soviet spy.

The Soviet purges and show trials of 1937–38 caused Chambers to reconsider the cause he was serving. He left the Communist Party in 1938, joined *Time* magazine as an editor in 1939, and rose to senior editor in 1942.

Chambers appeared before the House Un-American Activities Committee in August 1948 and gave testimony that implicated Alger Hiss, a former official in the State Department, as a communist conspirator. When Hiss sued Chambers for libel, Chambers produced government documents—including the so-called Pumpkin Papers—given him by Hiss when they both worked for the Communist Party. Chambers's evidence was later used to convict Hiss of perjury (the statute of limitations prohibited an indictment for espionage).

When the Hiss-Chambers controversy broke, Chambers resigned his staff position at *Time*. After the Hiss case, Chambers retired from the public arena to give occasional congressional testimony and work on his farm in Maryland. In 1952, he wrote *Witness*, an autobiography in which he ruminated on the communist threat to the West, the concurrent battle between atheism and religion, and the more insidious danger of secular liberalism. The book was immediately praised as a contemporary spiritual and political testament by the American Right.

Chambers served as a prominent conservative spokesman during the 1950s. He sympathized with Sen. JOSEPH R. MCCARTHY's (R-Wis.) fight against communism but deplored the senator's style, and he refused to be aligned with McCarthy's faction. In a letter to WILLIAM F. BUCKLEY, Chambers warned that "Senator McCarthy will one day make some irreparable blunder which will play directly into the hands of our common enemy and discredit the whole anticommunist effort for a long while to come." Later, Chambers's *Witness* was among those books removed from the State Department's overseas libraries under pressure from Sen. McCarthy.

In August 1957, Chambers joined the staff of *National Review.* He continued to write about the communist threat and attacked American liberals as spiritually bankrupt, "man-mind oriented, rather than God-soul trusting" theorists who destroyed Western civilization from within. At the same time, however, he argued that the right, and particularly the Republican Party, had not formed a cohesive philosophy that could either attract the populace or offer solutions for an "anti-conservative," technology-dominated Amer-capitalism. Many on the right respected Chambers as a brilliant martyr redeemed from communism.

Chambers made his final public pronouncement on the Hiss case in 1959. He supported Hiss's attempt to secure a passport but demanded that Hiss finally confess the truth. In Chambers's words, "Hiss's defiance perpetuates and keeps a fracture in the community as a whole."

In the fall of 1959, Chambers enrolled as an undergraduate at Western Maryland College, where he studied Romance languages, ancient Greek, Russian, economics, and biology. At the same time, he stopped contributing to the *National Review.* Chambers cited a lack of time, given his new role as a student. The real, if unstated, reason was his differences with the magazine. In the late 1950s, Chambers adopted positions and played with ideas antithetical to the *National Review.* For example, Chambers supported the Supreme Court's ruling that the State Department could not constitutionally deny a passport to a citizen on the basis of his or her political beliefs. He also exhibited an interest in the arguments of John Kenneth Galbraith's *The Affluent Society.* Nevertheless, Chambers and Buckley remained close friends.

Chambers died of a heart attack in Westminster, Md., on July 9, 1961. A collection of his writings, *Cold Friday,* was published posthumously in 1964.

—MSM

Chandler, A(lbert) B(enjamin)
(1898–1991) *governor of Kentucky*

Born on July 14, 1898, in Corydon, Ky., and raised in rural poverty, Chandler worked in laundries and restaurants to earn his tuition for Transylvania College in Lexington. After taking his B.S. degree in 1921, he studied one year at Harvard Law School but left Cambridge and earned his LL.B. in 1924 from the University of Kentucky in Lexington. He then moved to Versailles, Ky., to practice law and play professional baseball. After terms as a state senator from 1929 to 1931 and lieutenant governor for the next four years, he was elected governor in 1935. Nicknamed "Happy" because of his ever-present smile, the gregarious, backslapping Chandler mixed a down-home campaign style with a brand of politics that vacillated between populist and archconservative. He brought about a much-needed reorganization of state government and eliminated a $20-million budget deficit. He also abolished the state sales tax, which he considered regressive. Some argued that his restrained fiscal policies prevented the rapid development of community welfare programs. Labor leaders criticized him for directing National Guardsmen to bring order to the Harlan Co. United Mine Workers' strikes of 1939.

After an unsuccessful attempt to win the Democratic nomination for a Senate seat in 1938, Chandler resigned the governorship in 1939 to have his successor appoint him to fill the Senate term of a deceased incumbent. He won election to a full term in 1942, but he resigned his seat to become the commissioner of baseball in 1945. He was commissioner when (with his consent) Jackie Robinson broke the color barrier in 1947. After receiving an insufficient vote of confidence from baseball owners, he resigned his post in 1951, and returned to Versailles to practice law; edit his newspaper, the

Woodford Sun; and prepare for reentry into political life.

In 1955, Chandler geared up for a run for the governorship against a candidate supported by his longtime foe, Sen. Earle Clements, and by the state Democratic Party. A mixture of grassroots campaigning and Chandler's extensive alliances proved stronger than the party organization, and the ex-governor won the primary by a slim margin. In the general election, Chandler amassed the largest plurality ever for a Kentucky governor. His inauguration was marked by banners carrying such slogans as "Happy for President in 1956 if Mama Says Yes."

Chandler mounted a presidential campaign in early 1956, but it developed little momentum. His support for the Dixiecrat ticket in the election of 1948 and his clearly visible support for presidential aspirant Sen. RICHARD B. RUSSELL (D-Ga.) in 1952 found scant support in national Democratic Party ranks. The governor solicited the endorsement of ex-president HARRY S. TRUMAN but was refused. He entered the national convention with only his own state's 30 delegates and left it with 36½ votes.

Chandler, whose opponent in the Democratic gubernatorial primary of 1955 accused him of equivocating on school integration, clarified his stance to the nation during the presidential campaign. He stated that Kentucky would abide by the Supreme Court's desegregation decision. In the fall of 1956, when disorders interrupted the integration of schools in several Kentucky cities, Gov. Chandler sent out National Guardsmen to keep the peace. He committed the state to obedience to the law and threatened to declare martial law if further disturbances warranted it.

In his second term as governor, Chandler continued the Kentucky state government's tradition of blatant political patronage, contrary to his campaign promise to replace "buddy" employment practices with a merit system. In 1958, he refused to support proposed legislation establishing a merit system, arguing that state government was "not ready" for the change. He infuriated not only his enemies, but also many allies when, in 1956, he allegedly ordered 20,000 state employees to vote and work for him in state and county presidential conventions or be dismissed if they refused. Chandler faced accusations of corruption throughout his

various political administrations. Political scientist Neal Peirce wrote that "major questions remain to this day [1975] as to how much Chandler benefited personally from his governorship."

Forbidden by Kentucky state law from running for a second consecutive term, Chandler retired from the statehouse and waited for the next election in four years. In the interim, however, he lost his charm with the voters, and he was defeated in the Democratic gubernatorial primaries of 1963, 1967, and 1971. After the last defeat, he declared his permanent retirement from politics. He died in Versailles on June 15, 1991.

—TGD

Chavez, Dennis
(1888–1962) *U.S. senator*

One of eighth children, Chavez was born in Los Chavez, N.Mex., on April 8, 1888. He dropped out of school in the eighth grade and worked at menial jobs. He served as an interpreter for Sen. A. A. James (D-N.Mex.) during the election of 1916 and, as a result, was given a job as a clerk in the U.S. Senate. While working in the upper house, Chavez passed a special entrance examination to attend Georgetown University. He received his LL.B. in 1920 and returned to Albuquerque, N.Mex., to practice law. After serving in the New Mexico House of Representatives, he won a seat in the U.S. House. Appointed to fill a vacant seat in the Senate in May 1935, Chavez won election in his own right in 1936, He became the Senate's first Spanish-surnamed member.

In the Senate, Chavez supported New and Fair Deal programs. He actively promoted Franklin D. Roosevelt's Good Neighbor Policy and sought to improve conditions in Puerto Rico. Chavez frequently voiced support for civil rights and fair employment measures, and, in 1943, he cosponsored an amendment granting equal rights for women. He was one of 10 senators who voted against overriding President HARRY S. TRUMAN's veto of the internal security bill of 1950.

Chavez's reelection in 1952 was contested by Patrick J. Hurley, who charged voting fraud. The following year, a Senate elections subcommittee recommended, by a two-to-one vote, that 20,000 votes cast for Chavez and 10,000 for Hurley be invalidated "for lack of secrecy" in voting places. The recommendation would have resulted in Chavez's defeat, but the Senate rejected the recommendation in March 1954.

During the Eisenhower administration, Chavez, as chairman of the Senate Defense Appropriations Subcommittee, opposed attempts by the administration to reduce the military budget. In 1956, he recommended increasing Eisenhower's proposed budget for the air force by $1.6 billion to speed up production of B-52 long-range bombers. In 1960, Chavez emphasized that his subcommittee's first responsibility was to provide the money needed to "keep America strong" in the light of recent events, particularly the Soviet Union's satellite launchings. Remarking that economy was of secondary importance, the Senator implicitly criticized the administration's desire to put budgetary considerations over security needs. He asked Chairman of the Joint Chiefs Gen. NATHAN TWINING to "tell us what you want" and his panel would not deprive him of "one dime if it is necessary for our national security."

Chavez had a mixed record of support for the administration on domestic issues. As chairman of the Public Works Committee, he initially opposed Eisenhower's plan for the construction of a highway system creating some 42,000 miles of controlled-access roads. The system was to be funded jointly by the state and federal government, with Washington paying 90 percent of the costs. The senator preferred Sen. ALBERT GORE's (D-Tenn.) more modest proposal, which would have been paid for from the general treasury funds, thus putting a lesser burden on the states. Nevertheless, Chavez agreed to cosponsor the Eisenhower measure, which became law in 1956.

The senator supported the Civil Rights Act of 1957. However, he voted against the administration's initial proposal, which would have given the attorney general broad powers to seek injunctions in any type of civil rights case with or without the consent of an alleged victim. As enacted, the law dealt only with voting rights.

Chavez favored statehood for Alaska and Hawaii. He enthusiastically supported the massive public housing bill of 1959 and the aid-to-

depressed-areas bill of 1960. He voted to override Eisenhower's veto in each case.

Chavez supported most of the Kennedy administration's social welfare legislation, including Medicare. He died of cancer in Washington, D.C., on November 18, 1962.

—AES

Cherry, Francis

(1908–1965) *governor of Arkansas; member, Subversive Activities Control Board*

The youngest of five children of a poor railroad conductor, Francis Cherry was born on September 5, 1908, in Fort Worth, Tex. He graduated from Oklahoma Agricultural and Mechanical College in 1930. He then worked at odd jobs for three years to earn tuition money for the University of Arkansas law school, where he obtained his LL.B. in 1936. In 1937, Cherry entered private practice and a short time later became a commissioner for the Workman's Compensation Commission. Five years later, he was elected chancellor and probate judge of the 12th chancery district in northeast Arkansas. He was the youngest person ever to hold that post.

Waiving his judicial deferment, Cherry was commissioned in the navy in 1944 and served for two years. He returned to the bench in 1946, and won reelection to another six-year term in 1948. He ran for the Arkansas Democratic gubernatorial nomination in 1952. Cherry was given little chance of success against the incumbent, but through the use of radio he won the primary and the general election.

Upon taking office, Cherry promoted a legislative program designed to encourage the economic development of the state. He also supported a constitutional amendment for revision of the property tax system. In addition, he encouraged industrial development.

Following the Supreme Court's ruling in May 1954 that struck down school desegregation, Cherry announced that he would comply with the decision. He stated, "Obviously it will take a good deal of time to work it out. I only hope that what has happened does not set back the advances Negroes have made in Arkansas in the past several years." He planned to appoint a governor's committee on segregation as a first step toward compliance. Cherry, however, had little role in Arkansas's desegregation battles. In August 1954 he lost the Democratic primary to ORVAL FAUBUS.

The following year, Eisenhower appointed Cherry to the Subversive Activities Control Board (SACB). The SACB was established in 1950 to determine if organizations were communist-affiliated. Under the Internal Security Act of 1950, which established the board, communist groups were required to register with the SACB. The registration issue became hotly debated during the 1950s, as the Supreme Court limited the scope of anticommunist legislation. In 1958, Cherry supported continued registration.

In 1961, Cherry recommended that the International Mine, Mill and Smelter Workers be declared a communist-affiliated organization. The full board upheld the findings in 1962. Cherry was appointed chairman of the SACB in 1963, and died of a heart ailment in Washington, D.C., on July 15, 1965.

—RB

Chessman, Caryl W(hittier)

(1921–1960) *convicted felon*

Caryl Chessman was born in Michigan on May 17, 1921, but grew up in Los Angeles. After a childhood scarred by the crippling of his mother and two suicide attempts by his father, Chessman began stealing food at age 15. He later served two terms in prison for armed robbery. In January 1948, Chessman was arrested, charged with robbery, kidnapping, sexual abuses, and attempted rape. Serving as his own counsel and claiming mistaken identity, Chessman was convicted on 17 counts and sentenced to die for kidnapping.

Chessman appealed the verdict on the grounds that he had been deprived of counsel and that his trial record was faulty. Over the next 12 years, his case went to the Supreme Court 16 times. Eleven rehearings were held in state and federal courts. By 1960, Supreme Court Justice WILLIAM O. DOUGLAS said, "The conclusion is irresistible that Chessman is playing a game with the courts." While on death row, Chessman wrote four books

in the 1950s. The first, *Cell 2455, Death Row*, became a best seller.

Chessman's case generated worldwide attention from many who opposed the death penalty and saw the series of stays followed by proposed dates of execution as cruel. Pleas that his life be spared came from such diverse individuals as Albert Schweitzer, Pablo Casals, and Brigitte Bardot and from newspapers such as the Vatican's *L'Osservatore Romano*. The case also prompted anti-American demonstrations.

On February 1960, just 10 hours before he was to die, California Gov. EDMUND G. BROWN granted Chessman his eighth stay of execution. The governor announced he had taken the action because Assistant Secretary of State Roy R. Rubottom, Jr., in a telegram to Brown, had relayed a statement by the Uruguayan government warning of possible hostile demonstrations there during President Eisenhower's visit, should Chessman be executed. Brown, a foe of capital punishment, also wanted the state legislature to consider abolishing California's death penalty. Sen. CLAIR ENGLE (D-Calif.) protested Brown's decision on the ground that justice to an individual should be based on the facts of the case and not "rest on international reaction." The chairman of the Senate Foreign Relations Committee, J. WILLIAM FULBRIGHT (D-Ark.), denounced the State Department for interfering in the affairs of a sovereign state.

While crowds kept vigil outside San Quentin, Chessman was executed on May 2, 1960. In many high schools and colleges, students observed a minute of silence in his memory. Chessman denied his guilt to the end.

—MJS

Chotiner, Murray M.

(1909–1974) *Republican political adviser*

Murray Chotiner was born in Pittsburgh, Pa., on October 4, 1909. After a year as an undergraduate, he enrolled in Southwestern College of Law in Los Angeles. He completed his LL.B. at the age of 20, making him the youngest graduate in the school's history. Following his admission to the California bar in 1931, he became a prominent criminal lawyer and political public relations man. He worked for HERBERT HOOVER's presidential campaign in

1932 and EARL WARREN's campaign for governor in 1942. Warren found Chotiner's ruthless partisanship distasteful, and the two men eventually parted ways.

In 1946, RICHARD NIXON, making his first run for the House against Rep. Jerry Voorhis (D-Calif.), retained Chotiner as an adviser. Although Chotiner was primarily occupied with the management of WILLIAM KNOWLAND's senatorial campaign that year, he advised Nixon to attack Voorhis for taking money from the CIO's political action committee (PAC). In fact, Voorhis had taken money from CIO-PAC in 1944, but the organization had declined either to endorse or support him financially in 1946 because of Voorhis's increasingly firm stands on labor unrest and the Soviet Union. However, the National Citizens Political Action Committee (NCPAC), a nonunion counterpart to CIO-PAC, did endorse Voorhis. Nixon blurred the distinction and played on concerns (shared by Voorhis) that the CIO was controlled by communists. As the campaign progressed, Nixon linked votes Voorhis had cast in Congress and positions he had taken to left-wing and communist groups. The tactic helped Nixon win the election.

In 1950, Chotiner managed Nixon's campaign for the U.S. Senate against Rep. Helen Gahagan Douglas (D-Calif.), who had waged a bitter campaign against the Democratic incumbent, Sheridan Downey, before the latter withdrew claiming poor health. Both Downey and Elias M. Boddy, who stepped in to challenge Douglas for the nomination, attacked her "left-wing" voting record and associations. In the general election, the Nixon campaign referred to Douglas as the "pink lady" and issued a flyer on pink paper comparing her votes to those of Vito Marcantonio of New York. Many regarded the abrasive and ruthless Chotiner as the inspiration for the attacks on Douglas. Nixon went on to an overwhelming victory in November.

Chotiner played an important role in the maneuvering that won Nixon the vice presidential nomination two years later, and Nixon asked Chotiner to manage his campaign for the vice presidency. When, in September 1952, Nixon was accused of improperly maintaining a "secret" political fund for his personal use, Chotiner aggressively defended him, both in public and behind the scenes.

Although independent investigation soon established that the fund was neither secret nor illegal, Republican presidential nominee Gen. DWIGHT D. EISENHOWER did not spring to Nixon's defense. Many senior Republicans wanted to drop Nixon from the ticket. Chotiner rejected such demands out of hand, and urged Nixon not to accept chastisement from Eisenhower. Chotiner advised his client to get his message across to the widest possible public and boosted Nixon's spirits by asserting that, if Nixon were forced off the ticket, he would call a press conference and identify those who had pressed Nixon to resign. The Republican National Committee (RNC) bought a half hour of time on television, and Nixon used it to give what became known as his "Checkers speech." In it, the candidate explained that the fund was not secret, that the money had been used for legitimate campaign expenses, and that an audit and a legal opinion by a leading firm in California supported these claims. He made a full financial disclosure and challenged his opponents to do the same. ADLAI STEVENSON, the Democratic nominee, had a similar fund, and Stevenson's running mate, JOHN SPARKMAN, had placed his wife on his Senate payroll. Nixon asked his audience to write or wire the Republican National Committee indicating whether they wanted him to remain on the ticket.

Nixon believed that he had "loused it up"; he had timed the speech poorly and neglected to give the RNC's address. Nevertheless, Chotiner and others assured him that the speech had been a success. Following the speech, Nixon's popularity rose, and Eisenhower publicly reaffirmed his support.

At the same time he was managing Nixon's campaign, Chotiner advised Knowland in his successful bid for reelection. Between 1952 and 1955, Chotiner worked with the RNC while continuing his law practice. During this time, he lectured to Republican "political schools" on campaign techniques. Chotiner advised candidates to attack their opponents from the outset. He also advised Nixon during the latter's barnstorming in the congressional elections of 1954.

Chotiner's aggressive campaigns and his penchant for playing at the boundaries of unethical practices made him many enemies. In 1956, the anti-Semitic press attacked Nixon for his association with "that Jew Chotiner," an attack that Chotiner turned to his and Nixon's advantage. That same year, as part of an inquiry into influence peddling in military procurement, the Senate Government Operations Committee's Permanent Investigations Subcommittee began looking into some of Chotiner's legal clients. On April 25, the subcommittee subpoenaed Chotiner, and Democrats on the subcommittee charged that he had used his ties to Nixon on behalf of his clients. Specifically, they alleged that Chotiner had asked officials to set aside the fraud conviction of two garment manufacturers accused of stealing government clothing material. Chotiner denied this but admitted that he had, "on one or two occasions," asked White House aides Maxwell Rabb and Charles Willis to obtain information for him in an airlines case. Further, Chotiner denied ever using "the name of the Vice President in connection with . . . any client." Eisenhower's press secretary, JAMES HAGERTY, declared that Chotiner had done nothing wrong, although Nixon refused to comment. The subcommittee's chair, Sen. JOHN MCCLELLAN (D-Ark.), demanded that Chotiner produce a list of his clients since 1953, which Chotiner refused to do on the ground of attorney/client privilege. Ultimately, the subcommittee did not recommend that an indictment be brought in the matter. Nevertheless, RNC Chairman LEONARD HALL dispensed with Chotiner's services in June.

Further light was cast on Chotiner's role in the airlines intervention in February 1958. Testifying before the House Subcommittee on Legislative Oversight, BERNARD SCHWARTZ charged that presidential assistant SHERMAN ADAMS had improperly intervened at the Civil Aeronautics Board in 1953 on behalf of Chotiner's client, North American Airlines. In June, President Eisenhower said that, since the case had finally been decided against North American Airlines, no government influence was evident. Chotiner's visible influence in the Eisenhower administration ended in 1958.

Chotiner continued to advise Nixon in subsequent campaigns, although he played a less central role than in 1946, 1950, or 1952. He worked for John Mitchell, Nixon's campaign manager, in 1968 and was President-elect Nixon's first choice as Republican National Chairman in 1969. When

opposition to the appointment developed, Chotiner took an obscure job as government counsel for trade negotiations. He died as result of an automobile accident in Washington, D.C., on January 30, 1974.

Chotiner established a reputation as one of the early political merchandisers who emerged in the years after World War II. He was a talented, intensely partisan, and ruthless operative who constantly skirted the bounds of ethical behavior.

—MSM

Church, Frank (Forrester)
(1924–1984) *U.S. senator*

The son of the owner of a sporting goods store, Frank Church was born in Boise, Idaho, on July 25, 1924. He attended public schools and was a champion debater in high school. He enrolled at Stanford University in 1942 but enlisted in the army the following year and served as a military intelligence officer in the China-Burma-India theater. Following his discharge in 1946, he returned to Stanford and graduated in 1947. The same year he graduated, Church married Bethine Clark, the daughter of Chase A. Clark, a former Democratic governor of Idaho. He also enrolled at Harvard Law School but, after a year, transferred to Stanford Law School. Upon graduating from law school in 1950, he returned to Boise to practice law. He also became active in the Democratic Party.

In 1956, Church became a candidate for the Democratic nomination for the Senate seat occupied by HERMAN WELKER (R-Ida.). During the campaign, Church was bitterly opposed by the Idaho Power Co. and other private utility concerns for his vigorous advocacy of public power, a crucial issue throughout the Far West during the 1950s. Church promised to fight for federal construction of a single high dam at Hells Canyon near the Idaho-Oregon border to generate low-rate hydroelectric power for the entire area. Backed by the Eisenhower administration, Welker proposed instead that the Idaho Power Co. go through with its plans to build three smaller privately financed dams. Aided by substantial contributions from out-of-state liberal groups and from the Senate Democratic Campaign Committee, Church upset Welker by a margin of 14 percent, although the Republican ticket carried the state in the presidential election that year. Church was only 32 when he took his seat and the fourth-youngest senator in the history of the Senate.

In June 1957, Church cosponsored a bill authorizing the Hells Canyon dam that passed the Senate but was subsequently sidetracked in a House committee. The same bill had been defeated the year before in the upper house by a coalition of southern Democrats and pro–private power Republicans. Majority Leader LYNDON B. JOHNSON (D-Tex.) convinced Church to cosponsor a jury-trial amendment weakening the Civil Rights Act of 1957 in exchange for southern support for the Hells Canyon project. The provision, requiring jury trials under certain conditions, was expected to cripple the ability of the courts and the Justice Department to protect voting rights, since it was assumed that southern juries would not convict in contempt cases relating to the civil rights of African Americans. The upper chamber passed the amendment on August 2 by a vote of 51-42. Its passage represented a victory for southern senators who, aware that they did not have the votes to prevent passage of the bill itself, adopted a strategy aimed at modifying it as much as possible. In the meantime, the Hells Canyon bill passed, with the support of five southern senators, on June 21.

In 1959, Church again lined up with Johnson in opposing an attempt by northern liberals to overhaul the Senate filibuster rule substantially by permitting the imposition of cloture by majority vote. Instead, he supported a slight revision of the rule, sponsored by Johnson and a bipartisan leadership group, enabling two-thirds of the senators present and voting (rather than two-thirds of the entire Senate membership) to shut off debate. The following year, however, Church joined the liberal bloc in an unsuccessful effort to strengthen the Civil Rights Act of 1960 by empowering the attorney general to enter private suits for school desegregation. On most issues, Church voted as a liberal during his freshman term in the Senate.

A talented orator, Church was selected to give the keynote speech at the Democratic National Convention in 1960. He condemned the slow rate of economic growth under President DWIGHT D.

EISENHOWER and called for increased military outlays so that the United States could negotiate with the USSR from a position of strength.

Church won reelection in 1962 and again in 1968 and 1974. During the 1960s, Church compiled a strong liberal record, voting for civil rights, school aid, minimum wage, and Medicare bills. As a member of the Interior and Insular Affairs Committee, he frequently supported conservation measures. Church emerged as one of the earliest and strongest Senate critics of President Lyndon B. Johnson's policies in Southeast Asia. In 1970, he coauthored a measure prohibiting President RICHARD M. NIXON from sending U.S. combat troops into Cambodia without the consent of Congress.

In 1975, Church headed a much publicized investigation of alleged abuse of power by the Central Intelligence Agency and the FBI. Partly on the strength of the publicity he gained as a result of these proceedings, he entered the presidential primaries in 1976.

Church won primaries in Nebraska, Idaho, Oregon, and Montana but fell far behind the eventual nominee, Jimmy Carter. Church ended his bid before the Democratic convention. Although generally liberal, he opposed gun control legislation and in 1979 disclosed the presence of Soviet combat troops in Cuba and demanded their withdrawal before the Senate ratified the SALT II treaty. Church also led the floor debate in support of the ratification of the Panama Canal Treaty in 1978. His support for the treaty returning the canal to Panama cost him dearly in his bid for reelection in 1980. Church narrowly lost his seat to Congressman Steve Symms (R-Idaho). After leaving the Senate, he practiced law with the firm of Whitman and Ransom in Bethesda, Md., until his death there on April 7, 1984.

—TLH

Clark, Joseph S(ill), Jr.

(1901–1990) *mayor of Philadelphia, U.S. senator*

A member of a prominent and well-to-do Philadelphia family, Clark was born in Philadelphia on October 21, 1901. He attended the Middlesex School and Harvard, where he received a B.S. degree in 1923. Three years later, he obtained an

LL.B. from the University of Pennsylvania in 1926 and began practicing law in Philadelphia.

In 1928, Clark broke with his family's long-standing Republican allegiance to endorse Al Smith for the presidency. Six years later, he made an unsuccessful race for the Philadelphia City Council. In 1934 and 1935, he was deputy attorney general of Pennsylvania. Clark served in the army air corps during World War II, rising to the rank of colonel.

During the postwar years, Clark and RICH-ARDSON DILWORTH led a Democratic reform movement, which sought to end the Republican machine's longtime dominance of Philadelphia government. Clark managed Dilworth's unsuccessful candidacy for mayor in 1947. After serving as chairman of the Philadelphia chapter of Americans for Democratic Action (ADA), Clark was elected city controller in 1949. In that post, he investigated official scandals and set the stage for a mayoral race in 1951. He won the election and became Philadelphia's first Democratic mayor in 67 years.

As mayor, Clark tried to bring professional, dedicated people into government without regard for party. His strict enforcement of civil service laws enabled many African Americans to get city jobs for the first time.

Clark focused much of his attention upon the revival of Philadelphia's economy, which had suffered as a result of corrupt government and the migration of textile manufacturers to the South. Under his administration, Philadelphia became a pioneer in planning designed to revive the decaying core city. Clark often used quasi-public corporations to achieve this goal. In February 1955, the nonprofit Food Distribution Center Corp., with both businessmen and city officials on its board, was chartered to erect a new food market. In 1958, another quasi-public corporation was formed to begin construction on an industrial park. The mayor also supported purely private attempts to revive the area. He backed the Pennsylvania Railroad's plan for an office building/shopping center complex on the site of its old station, and he worked, with limited success, to improve its design.

To facilitate economic growth, Clark established the Urban Traffic and Transportation Board (UTTB) to devise a plan for a balanced system of mass and highway transit. The UTTB's report,

submitted in December 1955, stressed the need for mass transit and urged the establishment of a regional organization to develop an integrated transportation network. Clark's successor, Richardson Dilworth, implemented the plan.

Clark also initiated some low-income housing projects and established the post of housing coordinator. He unsuccessfully attempted to procure a state law permitting the city to use its own crews to correct housing violations. Clark added an economist to his staff to deal with unemployment and tried but failed to get federal funds for job training.

In 1956, Clark decided to run for the Senate. Campaigning on a liberal platform, he defeated the incumbent, Sen. James Duff (R-Pa.), by a slim margin. In the Senate, Clark was a leading advocate of civil rights legislation. He criticized the administration's housing programs, asserting in 1957 that the legislation of that year did not provide housing for those who really needed it.

A strong supporter of federal aid to education, he unsuccessfully sought to create a loan fund for the construction of college teaching facilities in 1960. During the same year, Clark and Sen. MIKE MONRONEY (D-Okla.) succeeded in amending a Senate bill to double the amount of aid provided to public schools. In January 1960, Clark joined 11 colleagues in the Senate Democratic Conference in an unsuccessful bid to take power away from Majority Leader LYNDON B. JOHNSON (D-Tex.) and give the liberal Senate Democratic Policy Committee a greater role in formulating policy on legislation.

Clark was a floor manager for many of President JOHN F. KENNEDY's legislative proposals. He won reelection in 1962. During the mid-1960s, he sought to improve the efficiency of the Senate and promote ethics legislation for Congress. In the later part of the decade, he became an outspoken critic of the Johnson administration's policies in Vietnam. Clark was defeated in his bid for reelection in 1968. Between 1969 and 1971, he was president of the United World Federalists, U.S.A., and after 1969, he served as chairman of the Coalition on National Priorities and Military Policy. He continued to reside in Philadelphia until his death in that city on January 12, 1990.

—MLL

Clark, Mark W(ayne)

(1896–1984) *commander in chief, U.S. Army Forces in the Far East and UN Command in Korea*

The son of an Army colonel, Mark Clark was born on May 1, 1896, at Madison Barracks, N.Y. He received a B.S. from the U.S. Military Academy at West Point in 1917. After more than a decade of further military education and minor army posts, he was promoted to lieutenant colonel in 1940. Clark rose to chief of staff of the army ground forces in May 1942 and commanded all U.S. infantry in Europe for the remainder of World War II. Following the war, Clark headed occupation forces in Austria. He was named deputy secretary of state in 1947.

This dual military and diplomatic experience prepared Clark for his appointment as commander of U.S. and UN forces in Korea in April 1952. When President-elect DWIGHT D. EISENHOWER flew to Korea in December 1952, he received a briefing from Clark, who favored a decisive victory over North Korea. The UN commander advanced three proposals: bombarding the enemy with air and artillery without advancing; destroying Chinese supply bases in Manchuria; or simultaneously using air power against Manchuria while advancing ground forces to the Chinese border.

Anxious to end the war, Eisenhower followed none of these plans. He relied instead on diplomatic effort coupled with threats of massive American intervention and nuclear warfare. Clark served as the conduit for the diplomatic advances and threats. When North Korea stalled the peace talks at Panmunjom in May 1953, Clark, acting on instructions, proposed that, in the future, the peace commission decide disputes by majority vote. This plan proposed giving the neutral Indian delegate the decisive voice. If North Korea rejected this, he was prepared to terminate negotiations and resume the war "in new ways never yet tried in Korea." North Korea accepted, and the following month, Clark informed Washington that an armistice was near.

The intense anticommunist nationalism of South Korea's President Syngman Rhee was an obstruction to a final agreement. In June, Rhee threatened to reject the truce and attack North Korea without UN support. Clark convinced him of the futility of such an action. At the same time, he guaranteed Rhee's adherence to truce terms in a letter to North Korea. Sen. RALPH FLANDERS (R-Vt.) denounced Clark for this action, but Rhee capitulated. The Korean armistice was signed in July 1953.

Clark retired from the military the following month and advocated the use of nuclear weapons if North Korea broke the truce. Testifying before the Senate Internal Security Subcommittee one year later, Clark recommended that diplomatic relations with Russia be severed and that the USSR and its satellites be ousted from the UN. Eisenhower disavowed this position.

The inability of the United States to anticipate the Korean conflict in 1950 was widely regarded as an intelligence failure. After the war, amidst allegations of communist infiltration and gross inefficiency within the Central Intelligence Agency (CIA), Congress called for a full investigation. In July 1954, former President HERBERT HOOVER announced that Clark would head a Hoover Commission task force studying the "structure and administration" of the CIA. This headed off an independent investigation threatened by Sen. JOSEPH McCARTHY (R-Wis.). Clark said he would search out subversives but that he was primarily concerned with improving the agency's operating procedures.

In June 1955, his task force's findings were presented to the president and Congress in the Hoover Commission's Report. Clark expressed concern about the lack of adequate intelligence data from behind the Iron Curtain but dismissed charges of communist infiltration. Instead he accused the State Department of "timidity" in gathering intelligence. To correct "administrative flaws" within the CIA and insure that the agency operated within democratic limits, Clark proposed creating a permanent watchdog commission made up of U.S. senators, representatives, and presidential appointees. By implication, he criticized excessive reliance on spying and other covert action and called on the agency to strengthen its intelligence-gathering functions. The Clark report was the most critical evaluation made of the CIA until the 1970s. The Hoover Commission weakened Clark's proposal for a watchdog committee in its final report. President Eisenhower joined the CIA in opposing it in any form, and the proposal died.

Clark served as president of the Citadel Military College from 1954 to 1965. He died in Charleston, S.C., on April 17, 1984.

—MJS

Clark, Tom C(ampbell)

(1889–1977) *associate justice, U.S. Supreme Court*
Tom Clark was born in Dallas, Tex., on September 23, 1889. He grew up in a family of lawyers, served in the military during World War I, and graduated from the University of Texas in 1921 and its law school in 1922. After graduation, he worked in his father's law firm in Dallas and served as civil district attorney of Dallas from 1927 to 1933. Clark went to work for the Justice Department in 1937. During World War II, he coordinated the relocation of Japanese Americans and became an assistant attorney general in 1943, heading first the antitrust and later the criminal divisions. He worked with Sen. HARRY S. TRUMAN's (D-Mo.) investigation of the defense effort in an official capacity, and he supported Truman for the vice presidency in 1944. Shortly after the death of Franklin D. Roosevelt, President Truman appointed Clark attorney general.

In his four years as attorney general, Clark instituted over 160 antitrust suits and had a major part in the development of the administration's anticommunist campaign. He urged the establishment of loyalty programs both in and out of government, drafted the first attorney general's list of subversive political organizations, and initiated the prosecution of the leaders of the American Communist Party in 1948. When Truman nominated Clark to the Supreme Court in July 1949, there was considerable liberal opposition to the appointment, but the Senate soon confirmed him. Clark's accession to the bench helped create a five-member conservative bloc, which dominated the Court for the next four years.

Clark generally placed the needs of government ahead of individual liberties, especially in loyalty-security cases. In the mid-1950s, Clark entered strong objections when the Court began placing limits on government anticommunist efforts. Clark dissented vigorously when the Court handed down several decisions in June 1957 restricting the government's anticommunist activities. In *Watkins v. U.S.*, the justices overturned the conviction of a

man charged with contempt for refusing to answer questions before the House Un-American Activities Committee. The majority held that the First Amendment limited the investigative powers of Congress and that questions asked by congressional investigators had to be related to a legitimate legislative purpose. Clark alone dissented. He found himself alone in dissent again when, in *Yates v. U.S.*, the Court overturned the convictions of second-tier leaders of the Communist Party and narrowed the scope of the Smith Act. Clark also took the government's side in the case of Clinton E. Jencks, a labor union official who had filed a noncommunist affidavit with the National Labor Relations Board. Seeking to prove the affidavit false, the government used the testimony of paid FBI informers, which it refused to make available to the trial judge. The majority reversed the conviction, and, in yet another solo dissent, Clark openly called for Congress to pass a law overturning the Court's ruling. In addition, Clark dissented from the Court's decision that a federal employee could be summarily dismissed as a security risk only if he had a sensitive job.

In June 1959, Clark finally spoke for the majority in sustaining the contempt conviction of a minister who had refused to turn over to New Hampshire's attorney general the guest list of a summer camp suspected of being a communist meeting place. The justice ruled that the state's interest in discovering the presence of possible subversives outweighed any individual rights of privacy or association involved. Later that month, Clark once again dissented when the Court overturned a government industrial security program on the ground that neither the president nor Congress had authorized certain of the procedures used in the program.

In criminal rights cases, Clark also tended to uphold government power against claims of individual rights. In February 1954, for example, he voted to sustain a state gambling conviction based on illegally seized evidence. He joined the majority in two cases in March 1959, ruling that persons tried for the same offense in both federal and state courts had not been subjected to double jeopardy. Clark, however, was more flexible in this area than in loyalty-security matters and sometimes voted in support of defendants' rights. In April 1956, he was part of a five-justice majority that held that states must, under certain circumstances, supply indigent defendants with free trial transcripts on appeal.

Clark joined in the major Supreme Court decisions outlawing racial segregation, including the landmark *Brown* ruling of May 1954. He was one of six justices who voted to strike down Truman's decision to seize the nation's steel mills during the Korean War (*Youngstown Sheet and Tube Co. v. Sawyer*, 1952). In addition, he wrote a large number of opinions in the field of antitrust law.

During the 1960s, Clark took a liberal position in several important cases involving criminal rights. For example, he wrote the majority opinion in *Mapp v. Ohio* (1961), which excluded the use of evidence obtained through unreasonable searches and seizures in state criminal trials. In other matters, Clark wrote for the majority in *Abington School District v. Schempp* (1963), which banned recitation of the Lord's Prayer and Bible reading in public schools, and in a case sustaining the public accommodations section of the Civil Rights Act of 1964.

When he resigned from the Court in 1967, Clark was generally rated as, at best, an average jurist who had nonetheless grown during his 18 years on the bench and had become a productive member of the Court. He died on June 13, 1977, in New York City.

—MSM

Clay, Lucius D(ubignon)
(1897–1978) *presidential adviser*

The son of a politically prominent family, Clay was born in Marietta, Ga., on April 23, 1897. He attended West Point and, following his graduation in 1918, served as an army engineer. During World War II, he was promoted to brigadier general and coordinated the production and procurement of supplies for the army as director of material. In 1944, Clay was appointed deputy director for war programs and general administrator in the Office of War Mobilization and Reconversion.

Upon Gen. DWIGHT D. EISENHOWER's recommendation, Clay became deputy military governor of occupied Germany in April 1945. At that post, he helped establish the four occupation zones and undertook the reconstruction of the American sector. In January 1947, Clay became military governor of the American zone and commanding general of U.S. forces in Europe. During the Soviet blockade of Berlin in 1948, Clay oversaw the airlift that supplied the city for over a year. He also supervised German currency reform and the drafting of the West German constitution. Clay retired from the army in 1949, and a year later became chairman of the board and chief officer of the Continental Can Co. Under his leadership, the company prospered, becoming the largest manufacturer of containers in the United States.

An old friend of Eisenhower, Clay played an important role in the general's campaign for the presidency in 1952. In 1951, when Eisenhower was still commander of the North Atlantic Treaty Organization, Clay sought to convince him to run for the Republican presidential nomination. Clay then acted as liaison between the general and professional politicians campaigning for him in the United States. Following Eisenhower's nomination, Clay backed the choice of RICHARD NIXON as the vice presidential candidate. He urged the general to steer a middle course during the race to attract independent voters.

In the postelection period, Clay was one of the advisers, along with HERBERT BROWNELL and SHERMAN ADAMS, who aided Eisenhower in searching out and screening people for high executive positions. Among his recommendations were the appointments of JOHN FOSTER DULLES as secretary of state, GEORGE HUMPHREY as secretary of the treasury, and JOSEPH DODGE as director of the budget. During this period, he also helped organize the meetings between Commerce Secretary-designate SINCLAIR WEEKS and financial leaders that led to the decision to remove wage and price controls.

Clay continued to serve as a presidential adviser during the Eisenhower administration. In late 1954 and early 1955, he headed a presidential commission formed to plan a national highway program. The panel's report, issued in January 1955, called for a 42,000-mile interstate highway network to be built at a cost of $101 billion. The system was to be constructed in cooperation with the states but would rely heavily on federal funding. The report formed the basis for Eisenhower's legislative proposals, adopted in modified form as the Federal Highways Aid Act of 1956.

During the Kennedy administration, Clay served as a presidential adviser on Berlin. In 1962, he headed a committee formed to study U.S. foreign aid policy. In the late 1960s, Clay was a supporter of LYNDON JOHNSON's Vietnam policy. He retired as chairman of the board of Continental Can in 1970 and died in Chatham, Mass., on April 16, 1978.

—EWS

Clement, Frank G(oad)

(1920–1969) *governor of Tennessee*

The son of a lawyer, Clement was born in Dickson, Tenn., on June 2, 1920. He attended Cumberland University in Lebanon, Tenn., and received his LL.B. degree from Vanderbilt University in 1942. After spending a year in Chicago as a special agent for the FBI, he joined the army in 1943 and served within the United States throughout the war. In 1946, Clement was appointed general counsel for the Tennessee Railroad and Public Utilities Commission, where he earned a reputation as an outstanding attorney and a "champion of the people." He became involved in Democratic politics and, in 1952, was elected governor of Tennessee.

During the campaign, Clement's Bible-thumping, evangelical style of political oratory won him a degree of national attention. As governor, he strove primarily to enact educational reform. By March 1953, Clement had gained legislative approval of a $5 million bond issue to provide public-school children with free textbooks. He won reelection in 1954 under a new law granting the governor a four-year term (with the condition that he not seek immediate reelection). During his second term, Clement pushed through the legislature an annual appropriation of $20 million for increased aid to education. He also won legislative approval of a comprehensive public power policy, a new retirement system for state employees, and major reforms in mental health services. To pay for these programs, Clement had the state sales tax increased from 2 to 3 percent.

Much of Clement's tenure was devoted to the issue of school desegregation. After the Supreme Court's decision outlawing segregated schools in 1954, Clement made no secret of his own segregationist attitudes but swore to uphold the law. Thus, in 1955, he vetoed two segregation bills passed by the state legislature. When riots broke out in Clinton, Tenn., in the fall of 1956 over the admission of blacks to previously all-white schools, he responded by calling out the National Guard. Clement declared, "I am not doing this to promote integration or segregation. I am doing this to . . . preserve the peace." His willingness to uphold the law established his reputation as one of the southern governors least hostile to the *Brown* decision. In 1957, however, he recommended a five-point anti-integration program. The legislature passed the five bills and three additional measures; Clement signed all eight. Nevertheless, he helped to defeat an interposition resolution and vetoed a bill repealing the state's compulsory attendance law. His attempt to split the difference on the issue of desegregation may have been motivated, at least in part, by his own national political ambitions.

Clement delivered the keynote address at the Democratic National Convention in 1956. In it, he attacked the Republicans for fostering economic recession and favoring big business over the rights of the common man. The speech was most memorable, however, for its portrayal of Secretary of State JOHN FOSTER DULLES as "the greatest unguided missile in the history of American diplomacy" and its characterization of the Eisenhower-Nixon administration as "the vice-hatchet man slinging slander and spreading half-truths while the top man peers down the green fairways of indifference."

After his term as governor expired in 1959, Clement turned over the office to Buford Ellington, his handpicked successor. In 1962, Clement was elected to another term as governor. His national ambitions were finally destroyed when he ran unsuccessfully for the Senate in 1964 and again in 1966. He died in a car accident in Nashville on November 4, 1969.

—JPL

Cohn, Roy M(arcus)

(1927–1986) *chief counsel, Permanent Investigations Subcommittee of the Senate Government Operations Committee*

The son of a New York State Supreme Court judge and protégé of the boss of the Bronx Co. Democratic machine, Cohn was born on February 20,

1927, in New York City. He attended the Fieldston School, managed by the Ethical Culture Society. By the age of 20, he had graduated from Columbia College and Columbia Law School (in 1947). He had to wait until the next year, when he turned 21, to be admitted to the bar. With the help of his father's political connections, he was immediately hired as an assistant U.S. attorney for the southern district of New York. Over the next four years, Cohn specialized in the prosecution of subversive activities, working as a staff lawyer in the perjury trial of William Remington in 1950–51 and the espionage trial of JULIUS and ETHEL ROSENBERG in 1951.

In 1952, Cohn was transferred to Washington, D.C., where he served for four months as a special assistant to Attorney General James McGranery. Cohn drew up the perjury indictment of Owen Lattimore, whom Sen. JOSEPH R. MCCARTHY (R-Wis.) had charged in 1950 with heading a subversive ring in the State Department. Cohn also conducted a grand jury probe of subversion among employees of the United Nations Secretariat. This probe brought him to the attention of Sen. McCarthy, chairman of the Permanent Investigations Subcommittee, who hired him as chief counsel of the panel in January 1953.

Cohn's role in the subcommittee's sensational investigations of communist influence in government agencies was second only to that of McCarthy himself. A brash young man, he was known to pay little attention to the wishes of anyone on the subcommittee except McCarthy. The two worked closely together in coordinating publicity, scheduling hearings, and interrogating witnesses. The Wisconsin senator once remarked that Cohn was "as indispensable as I am."

Energetic and forceful, Cohn was a shrewd strategist with a sharp, retentive mind and a photographic memory. His interrogation of witnesses was relentless and often scornful. Many critics of McCarthy found the chief counsel at least as distasteful as the senator himself and regarded him as an arrogant thug with little or no regard for the ethics of his profession.

In April 1953, Cohn and the subcommittee's chief consultant, G. DAVID SCHINE, went on a 17-day, seven-country tour of Europe in search of pro-communist literature in the State Depart-

ment's overseas libraries. The trip received extensive publicity in both the American and European press. At the library in Vienna they asked that *The American Legion Magazine* be placed on the shelves. Then, after finding the works of Mark Twain at the Soviet Culture Center, they went back to the State Department library to see if it had the same books. In Munich, reporters overheard one of them telling a hotel clerk that they wanted separate rooms, since they did not work for the State Department, an allusion to alleged homosexuality among State Department employees. Critics of McCarthy's subcommittee charged the two men with distasteful, childish, and farcical behavior deleterious to America's reputation abroad. The tour prompted President Eisenhower to issue a warning against "book burners" in a commencement address at Dartmouth College in June 1953.

In the fall of 1953, McCarthy and Cohn began hearings on communist infiltration in the army. Meanwhile, the senator and his chief counsel, learning that Schine was to be drafted, tried unsuccessfully to procure a commission for him. After Schine was inducted into the army in November 1953 as a private, Cohn frequently contacted high-level army figures to obtain passes and easy assignments for Schine. McCarthy seemed to have little personal interest in Schine's fortunes, and his participation in or tolerance of these activities indicated the extent of Cohn's influence upon the senator.

On March 11, 1954, after McCarthy had escalated his attack on the army for allegedly tolerating the presence of subversive elements within its ranks, the army released a chronology of the efforts of McCarthy, Cohn, and other members of the subcommittee's staff on Schine's behalf. According to this account, Cohn had threatened to discredit the army through the subcommittee's investigation unless Schine received special treatment. McCarthy quickly counterattacked by alleging that the army was holding Schine as a "hostage" to block the congressional probe.

In April 1954, the Investigations Subcommittee began the so-called Army-McCarthy hearings to examine the charges and countercharges. Since Cohn was a principal in the investigation, he temporarily withdrew as the panel's counsel. During the hearings, Cohn was heard to threaten to "get" a minority member of the subcommittee, Sen. HENRY M. JACKSON (D-Wash.), for attacking McCarthy. On June 14, near the end of the investigation, Cohn unsuccessfully tried to prevent McCarthy from mentioning the fact that a member of Army Counsel JOSEPH WELCH's law firm had once belonged to a pro-communist group. (Cohn and McCarthy's lawyer, Edward Bennett Williams, had agreed not to raise the matter.) Welch turned the incident into a confrontation between himself and McCarthy, which severely damaged the senator's cause.

In August, the subcommittee's Republican majority issued a report stating that Cohn had been "unduly aggressive and insistent" in the Schine matter. The Democratic minority went further, insisting that he had "misused and abused the powers of his office and brought disrepute to the committee." In the meantime, Cohn, under strong pressure from Senate Republicans, resigned his position with the subcommittee on July 19.

Cohn joined the New York City law firm that became Saxe, Bacon & Bolan. His family's influence and his own considerable legal skills brought to the firm an impressive list of clients. Even Cohn's greatest detractors could not help but admire his technique in the courtroom. At the same time, he played close to the edge of ethical behavior and received several judicial reprimands for unethical conduct. In 1957, he became a professor of law at the New York Law School.

In order to avoid taxes, Cohn took a relatively small salary of $100,000 a year from his law firm. However, he received lavish perquisites such as a rent-free apartment in Manhattan, the use of a chauffeured Rolls-Royce, and a seemingly limitless expense account.

Cohn was tried in federal court on charges including fraud, conspiracy, and corporate manipulation in 1964, 1969, and 1971. All three trials ended in acquittal. He was also in constant trouble with the Internal Revenue Service. On June 23, 1986, not long before his death, he was disbarred. A five-judge panel of the Appellate Division of the New York Supreme Court found his conduct in four matters "unprofessional" and "unethical." The panel found his behavior in one of the cases "particularly reprehensible."

Cohn died on August 2, 1986, in Bethesda, Md. The reported cause of death was HTLV-3 virus, which would later be called HIV and recognized as the cause of AIDS.

Cohn was the author of *McCarthy* (1968), a defense of the senator from Wisconsin.

—MSM

Coleman, James P(lemon)
(1914–1991) *governor of Mississippi*

Born on a red-dirt farm in Ackerman, Miss., on January 9, 1914, James P. Coleman worked his way through the University of Mississippi and George Washington University law school. He received his LL.B. in 1939. While in Washington, D.C., Coleman worked as secretary to Rep. Aaron L. Ford (D-Miss.) and became friends with Rep. LYNDON B. JOHNSON (D-Tex.). Coleman returned to Mississippi and served first as a district attorney and then a circuit judge between 1939 and 1950. In October 1950, he was elected state attorney general. Coleman served as Democratic national committeeman in 1952 and kept the Mississippi delegation from bolting the Democratic National Convention over a proposed requirement that delegates promise to support the convention's ticket regardless of its stand on civil rights.

When the Supreme Court struck down segregated public schools in May 1954, Coleman, a staunch defender of segregation, asked for restraint. He cautioned against adoption of a strategy of "massive resistance," which called for the interposition of state power to prevent enforcement of the decision. Coleman avoided race-baiting and worked to restore stability after the murder of EMMETT TILL in August 1955. On September 1, U.S. Attorney General HERBERT BROWNELL announced an inquiry into alleged intimidation of black voters in Mississippi. Coleman denied any violations. In the tense atmosphere following Till's murder and Brownell's inquiry, Coleman's approach was cool and legalistic. He told a meeting of the White Citizens' Council that eliminating segregation through court action would take the government 2,000 years.

In 1955, Coleman ran for governor on a platform pledging continued segregation by legal means. He ran unopposed in the November election. Soon after he took office in 1956, Coleman announced that he regarded the school desegregation decisions "unconstitutional" and promised that Mississippi would "resist enforcement by every legal and constitutional means available." Nevertheless, he described the movement to nullify the Court's decision as "legal poppycock." In the face of an increasing rightward trend, however, the governor adopted a more segregationist position.

He endorsed interposition in January 1956 at a conference convened by Virginia's Gov. THOMAS STANLEY but refused to join a call for nullification. The following month, Coleman obtained legislative approval for a $78 million school budget—the largest in state history—to upgrade black schools and silence Northern critics. He also urged a bill giving businesses the right to choose their customers and providing segregated waiting rooms in intrastate travel.

The segregation laws failed to allay fears of integration, and, in 1956, the governor faced a restive state party divided over political strategy in the upcoming presidential election. In May, the Association of Citizens' Councils, a group of white supremacist organizations, formulated a resolution demanding that the state delegation to the Democratic National Convention accept only a presidential candidate who supported interposition. Coleman offered an alternative strategy he called "friendly persuasion." He maintained that southern leaders should focus on an acceptable compromise on issues relating to segregation and that they should do so within the privacy of committees. Inflammatory public rhetoric, Coleman argued, would only provoke Northern delegates into rigid positions. He further contended that political realities would force Northern party leaders to accommodate southern views. Supported by Sen. JOHN STENNIS (D-Miss.), Coleman's plea for an unpledged delegation prevailed. At the Democratic National Convention, southern delegates employed Coleman's strategy and won the adoption of a moderate civil rights plank in the platform.

Coleman attempted to conduct his and Mississippi's opposition to *Brown* in as orderly and dignified a manner as possible. Toward that end, he proposed a State Sovereignty Commission in June 1956. Coleman intended that the commission would impede desegregation but at the same time calm racial tensions, erode support for the citizens' councils, and avoid negative publicity in the national media. The legislature, however, saw the commission as a means of stamping out any opposition to segregation and granted the commission extraordinary authority "to do and perform any and all acts . . . necessary and proper to protect the sovereignty of the State of Mississippi." Under Coleman's successor, Ross Barnett, the commission became a means of imposing racial orthodoxy.

The kind of moderation Coleman advocated garnered little political support. He prevented the White Citizens' Councils from obtaining tax money and in April 1959 called in the FBI after the lynching of Mack Parker. When he supported a new constitution that did not mention race, the legislature defeated it. Although Coleman could not succeed himself, voters effectively repudiated him in 1960 by electing Barnett, a die-hard segregationist whom Coleman opposed. That same year, Coleman supported the candidacy of Sen. JOHN F. KENNEDY (D-Mass.) for the presidency.

Coleman won election to the state legislature in 1960 and served through 1964. He ran for governor in 1963 as a racial moderate but lost in the Democratic primary to Paul B. Johnson, Jr., Barnett's lieutenant governor. In 1965, President Lyndon B. Johnson, at the behest of Sen. JAMES O. EASTLAND (D-Miss.), appointed Coleman to the Fifth Circuit Court of Appeals. Coleman later became chief judge and served in that capacity until his retirement in 1981. He died in Ackerman, Miss., on September 28, 1991.

—MSM

Coleman, John S(trader)
(1897–1958) *president, U.S. Chamber of Commerce; chairman, board of directors*
The son of a hardware merchant, John S. Coleman was born in Charleston, W.Va., on October 12, 1897. He attended Washington, D.C.'s, Emerson Institute and worked at the Guaranty Trust Corp. of New York before World War I. He served in the army during the war. Coleman joined the sales staff of the Burroughs Adding Machine Corp.

in 1920, while studying law at night at Georgetown University. He received his LL.B. from that institution in 1924. After obtaining a million-dollar contract with the government for Burroughs, he rose rapidly through the company hierarchy, eventually becoming president in 1946. He greatly improved efficiency at Burroughs, doubling the number of workers and increasing production. Under Coleman's leadership, Burroughs Adding Corp. smoothly made the transition from adding machine production to more diversified operations and did pioneering work in the construction of computers.

A political conservative, who advocated less government regulation and interference in business affairs, he nevertheless urged greater cooperation between labor, management and government. Burroughs attempted to apply "human engineering" to his organization, maintaining that "the function of management is to operate a successful organization both economically and humanly . . . [and] to give every man a sense of function."

Coleman was an ardent advocate of free trade. During the 1940s, he directed a 10-year study for the Detroit Board of Commerce, which concluded in November 1952 that all U.S. tariffs should be abolished. However, he modified his position at the Chicago World Trade Conference in February 1953, calling instead for a gradual reduction of duties. Coleman saw the election of Dwight D. Eisenhower in 1952 as an opportunity for business to exercise its responsibility to the world by cooperating with the president to prevent another depression.

In March 1956, Coleman was elected president of the U.S. Chamber of Commerce; the following year, he became chairman of the board. During his two years in office, Coleman served as spokesman for the organization's pro-business philosophy. In a statement in February 1957, he proposed cuts in the federal budget, maintaining that $5 billion could be eliminated by reducing federal aid to education, college housing loans, funds to fight juvenile delinquency, and welfare grants. He charged that Secretary of Health, Education, and Welfare Marion Folsom had overestimated the national classroom shortage. Coleman contended that, given the present rate of school construction, the problem would be solved by 1960 and claimed that the federal government sought to provide aid as a way of controlling public schools. His position was backed by the National Association of Manufacturers, which represented smaller businessmen. Coleman also demanded that foreign aid and farm programs be scaled down.

Coleman died of a heart attack on April 13, 1958, in Detroit, Mich.

—AES

Collins, J(oseph) Lawton
(1896–1987) *U.S. special representative in Vietnam*

The son of Irish-Catholic parents, J. Lawton Collins was born in New Orleans on May 1, 1896. After graduating from the United States Military Academy in 1917, Collins commanded a battalion of the occupation forces in Germany during 1919. Collins served in various military capacities in the 1920s and 1930s, and, by the outbreak of World War II, he had achieved the rank of brigadier general. During World War II, he saw active duty in the Pacific, where he helped reorganize American defenses on Hawaii. He also commanded the 25th Division on Guadalcanal, where his aggressive tactics earned him the nickname "Lightning Joe." In June 1944, as commander of VII Corps, he led the breakout from the Normandy beachhead. Collins went on to command a number of successful operations in France and Germany and was promoted to lieutenant general in April 1945. After the war, he was assigned to the Pentagon and from 1948 to 1953 served as army chief of staff. In 1953, President Eisenhower appointed him U.S. representative to the North Atlantic Treaty Organization (NATO).

Following the partition of Vietnam in 1954, Collins became prominently involved in the policy debate over U.S. support of South Vietnam's Premier, Ngo Dinh Diem. On November 3, 1954, Eisenhower appointed Collins special United States representative to Vietnam with the "personal rank of Ambassador." From his arrival in Vietnam, Collins expressed doubts about Diem. Other American officials, including the principal American intelligence officer in Vietnam, Col. Edward Lansdale, supported Diem. Whatever his misgivings, Collins initiated a program aiding Diem in establishing security, in training the South Vietnamese Army, and in laying the groundwork for agrarian reform. He also helped Diem to engineer the effective exile of a major rival, Gen. Nguyen Van Hinh. Despite these efforts, Collins never established a working relationship with Diem. The Vietnamese leader refused to heed Collins's military and political advice.

By March 1955, Collins and other U.S. officials in both Saigon and Washington, distressed by Diem's refusal to institute suggested reforms, began to reconsider U.S. support for the premier. The immediate issue was the premier's refusal to reorganize the government to include representatives from South Vietnam's powerful political-religious sects. When Diem turned down the sects' demands for a coalition government in late March 1955, fighting broke out in the streets of Saigon between government forces and the sects, principally the Binh Xuyen.

Collins recommended that the United States consider alternatives to Diem, and in an exchange of messages with Secretary of State JOHN FOSTER DULLES argued forcefully for replacing Diem. Dulles and his advisers in the State Department were inclined to continue support for Diem, or at least not to discard him abruptly or completely. Eisenhower, who had confidence in both Dulles and Collins, allowed each to make his case and reserved judgment.

In mid-April, Collins was recalled to Washington for consultation. The general held to his position that continued support for Diem would be a "major error." He persuaded Eisenhower, and the State Department could do "nothing more than arrange a face-saving compromise" that would retain Diem as president in a largely titular role while real power passed to Dr. Phan Huy Quat of the Dai Viet party. At this point, however, fighting broke out in Saigon between the Binh Xuyen forces and the Vietnamese National Army, during which the VNA quickly gained the advantage. Diem's supporters, including senators MIKE MANSFIELD (D-Mont.) and WILLIAM KNOWLAND (D-Calif.) as well as Dulles, lobbied hard for Diem, and American policy reverted to support for the Vietnamese premier. Diem proceeded to crush the sects. Collins remained skeptical; he believed that Diem would become more unlikely to heed American advice to broaden the base of his government.

With the shift in American policy, Collins was replaced. He returned to Washington in May 1955, and shortly thereafter resumed his duties as U.S. representative to NATO.

Retiring from government service in 1957, he served until 1969 as a director of Charles Pfizer and Co., and as vice president of Pfizer International Subsidiaries until 1972. Throughout these years, Collins remained skeptical about U.S. policy in Vietnam and, as one of a small group of "dovish generals," opposed the continual escalation of American involvement in Southeast Asia.

He died of a heart attack on September 12, 1987, in Washington, D.C.

—MSM

Collins, (Thomas) LeRoy
(1909–1991) *governor of Florida*

A grocer's son, LeRoy Collins was born on March 10, 1909, in Tallahassee, Fla. He remained in Tallahassee until he graduated from high school in 1927. After high school, he studied at the Eastman School of Business in Poughkeepsie, N.Y., and spent a year at the Cumberland Law School in Lebanon, Tenn. After gaining admission to the Florida bar, Collins started his own practice in Tallahassee and clerked part-time for the Works Progress Administration. He won election as a Democrat to the Florida House of Representatives in 1934 and to the state senate in 1940. Except for two years in the navy during World War II, Collins served continuously in the legislature until 1954. In the state senate, he earned a reputation for moderate progressivism. A poll of Florida journalists twice named him the state's "most valuable senator."

Beginning in 1952, Collins's own political future became linked with that of Democratic Gov. Dan McCarty, who led a reform coalition of urban voters and minority groups supporting improvements in state services and the continuation of diversified economic development. Following McCarty's death in September 1953, Collins assumed the leadership of the faction.

In 1954, Collins ran for election to fill out the remaining two years of McCarty's term. In the Democratic primary, he defeated Gov. Charley E. Johns, who had been appointed to fill the remainder of McCarty's term and was commonly identified with the party's powerful, archconservative wing. Although Collins condemned Johns's failure to support an anti–Ku Klux Klan bill while he had been a state legislator in 1951, race relations were only a minor issue in the campaign. Collins won election in November without Republican opposition.

As governor, Collins fit the image-conscious, growth-oriented mold of what historians of the modern South term "business progressivism." He improved state services, upgraded Florida's educational systems, and reduced patronage through the extension of the civil service system. He also attempted to reapportion the state to give the growing urban centers more equitable representation, but his efforts failed.

Much of Collins's time was devoted to the issue of civil rights. When the Supreme Court struck down segregated public schools in the *Brown* decision (1954), Collins reacted cautiously. Although he said he favored segregated schools, he warned against "hysteria and political demagoguery." In April 1955, he told the legislature that no new laws were needed to protect segregation. Instead, he suggested that the legislators throw the state's weight behind orderly efforts to reverse the decision. Ignoring the governor, the legislature passed three segregationist measures, which Collins criticized but signed. They provided for the assignment of students to schools on the basis of health, safety, and education and not race.

During the gubernatorial campaign of 1956, in which the governor was opposed by a militant segregationist, Sumter Lowry, Collins became a more vocal advocate of the status quo, but he urged that it be maintained by lawful and peaceful means. He announced that he refused to "have the state torn asunder by rioting and disorder and violence and the sort of thing that [Lowry] is seeking to invite." Collins won the election handily. However, Florida's Democratic Party became even more fragmented. Collins's strength declined in his native northern Florida while it grew in urban and black districts.

Following the Supreme Court's ruling in May 1955 that local school authorities had the duty to implement desegregation, Collins called the legislature into session to enact a program to counter the decision. It passed a pupil placement law permitting appeals from decisions of local school boards and gave the governor emergency power to call out the militia to prevent or suppress violence. The legislature also adopted a resolution condemning the Supreme Court and asserting the state's right to regulate education. However, Collins opposed more radical antisegregation legislation. He criticized a joint legislative resolution passed in 1957 that nullified recent antisegregation Supreme Court edicts, announcing "it is anarchy and rebellion against the nation which must remain 'indivisible under God' if it is to survive. I decry it as an evil thing, whipped up by the demagogues and carried in the hot and erratic words of passion, prejudice and hysteria." Collins also lobbied against other extreme measures and in June 1957 vetoed a law providing for a local option on whether or not to close schools facing desegregation. During the crisis involving desegregation in Little Rock, Ark., in 1957, Collins pleaded for moderation in settling the issue. Before the Southern Governors Conference in late September, he asked that southerners consider Supreme Court rulings "the law of the land and insist that ours must be a land of the law." The southerner, he said, "must not sanction violence, defiance and disorder and, above all, he must abhor hate." The speech earned him widespread praise and contributed to his image as a leading southern moderate.

In his last years as governor, Collins acted increasingly like a national, rather than sectional, leader. He headed the National Governors Conference in May 1958, visited with Soviet Premier Nikita S. Khrushchev in July 1959, and became the first southern governor since the Civil War to serve as permanent chairman at the Democratic National Convention in July 1960. A few observers considered him a possibility for national office in 1960. Yet Collins's professed aspirations for national office were hurt by Florida's still slow adjustment to desegregation. Indeed, critics pointed out that, while Collins had talked about leading his people into compliance with the Court's decision, Florida had made less progress toward desegregation than Virginia, which pursued a policy of massive resistance.

Collins's career as an elected public official ended with his second term. Between 1961 and 1964, Collins was president of the National Association of

Broadcasters. In 1964, President LYNDON B. JOHN-SON appointed Collins to be the first head of the Community Relations Service, created by the Civil Rights Act of 1964 to promote peaceful compliance with the law. In that capacity, Collins played a central role in defusing the civil rights crisis at Selma in 1965. Later that year, Collins was appointed undersecretary of commerce.

Collins returned to Florida in 1966 to practice law, and when Sen. GEORGE SMATHERS (D-Fla.) decided not to seek reelection in 1968, Collins ran for the vacant senate seat. After narrowly defeating a conservative in the primary, he lost in the general election. Collins returned to Tallahassee, joined a prestigious law firm, wrote a book (*Forerunners Courageous: Stories of Frontier Florida*, 1971), and served on several government commissions. He died in Tallahassee on March 12, 1991.

—MSM

Conant, James B(ryant)

(1893–1978) *high commissioner for West Germany, ambassador to the Federal Republic of Germany*
Born in Dorchester, Mass., on March 26, 1893, Conant graduated from Harvard in 1913 and received his Ph.D. in chemistry there in 1916. During World War I, he supervised the production of poisonous gas for the Chemical Warfare Service. Conant joined the faculty at Harvard in 1919 and won recognition for his research in organic chemistry as well as for his influence as an educator. He became president of Harvard in 1933, a post he retained until 1953. During his tenure, Conant emphasized the need for general education for undergraduates and reformed the system of faculty promotion.

As chairman of the National Defense Research Committee in 1940 and, from 1941 to 1946, as deputy director of the Office of Scientific Research and Development, Conant coordinated war-related scientific research, particularly that involving the development of the atomic bomb. In 1945, he served on the presidential advisory committee that recommended deploying the atomic bomb against Japan without prior warning.

Between 1947 and 1950, Conant served on the General Advisory Committee (GAC) of the Atomic Energy Commission (AEC). During the period, he emerged as the panel's strongest, most outspoken opponent of the development of the hydrogen bomb. With the majority of committee members, he signed a statement denouncing the weapon for strategic as well as political reasons, saying that it could only be a "weapon of genocide."

Conant served as U.S. high commissioner for Germany from 1953 to 1955. His major tasks were to prepare West Germany for full independence, begin steps for its inclusion in the North Atlantic Treaty Organization, and protect U.S. claims of free access to the Russian sector, particularly in Berlin. Following the formal establishment of the Federal Republic of Germany in 1955, Conant was named U.S. ambassador there. He resigned the post in January 1957 and declined an offer to become ambassador to India.

During the early 1950s, Conant had frequently criticized anticommunist investigations in schools and government. In his final report as president of Harvard, he warned that the damage done by such investigations was "far greater than any conceivable harm" a communist teacher might do. He was particularly alarmed about the possible ramifications of the security hearing involving J. ROBERT OPPENHEIMER in 1954. The director of the wartime atomic bomb project, Oppenheimer had had his security clearance suspended in late 1953 because of his prewar left-wing politics and his postwar ambivalence about the development of the hydrogen bomb. During the security hearing, Conant testified that Oppenheimer had been "thoroughly loyal," and he pointed out that he, too, had opposed the bomb's development. However, the AEC voted to maintain the suspension.

During the late-1950s, Conant devoted himself to educational projects. In March 1957, he received a Carnegie Corp. grant to make a thorough study of U.S. secondary education. His report, released in 1960 as *The American High School Today*, affirmed the basic soundness of U.S. schools while stressing the need to study "solid" academic subjects, including languages. It further recommended consolidating small schools into larger, presumably more efficient, ones and creating a curriculum consisting of several levels that would serve the various intellectual abilities and future plans of students. In February 1960, Eisenhower appointed Conant to the Commission on National Goals. The Commission report, issued that November, concluded that to respond to the "Sino-Soviet threat" and the dangers of the nuclear age, the United States should strengthen itself domestically by ensuring individual freedoms. The report called on the federal government to "stimulate changes in attitude" concerning race and act against discriminatory voting practices.

Conant continued to write and lecture on education and foreign policy through the 1960s. In 1964, he wrote *Slums and Suburbs*, which described inner city schools as "social dynamite." Conant returned to Berlin as an advisor on education for 18 months beginning in 1964.

He eventually retired to New York City but continued to comment on national affairs. Conant was a vocal supporter of the Johnson administration's conduct of the war in Vietnam. He died on February 11, 1978, in Hanover, N.H.

—MDB

Cooper, (Leon) Jere

(1893–1957) *U.S. congressman; chairman, Ways and Means Committee*

Cooper was born on a farm in Dyer County, Tenn., on July 20, 1893. After receiving an LL.B. degree from Cumberland University in Lebanon, Tenn., in 1914, he was admitted to the state bar the same year and began practicing law in Dyersburg. After service in the army in World War I, Cooper won election to the Dyersburg City Council and in 1920 was appointed the town's attorney.

Cooper won a seat as a Democrat in the U.S. House of Representatives in 1928 and subsequently backed most New Deal and Fair Deal measures. He was also one of the leading congressional supporters of Secretary of State Cordell Hull's reciprocal trade program. He became a member of the Ways and Means Committee in 1932 and seven years later became chairman of the panel's subcommittee on taxation. Cooper developed a reputation as an expert on tax matters and played a key role in establishing the system of withholding taxes.

As the ranking minority member of the Ways and Means Committee during the first two years of the Eisenhower administration, Cooper was a leading critic of the president's tax bill in 1954. With many other Democrats, he denounced it for giving more relief to the wealthy than to the poor. On the floor of the House, he attacked the bill's dividend tax relief provision, stating that he "objected to the principle of providing more favorable treatment for unearned income than for earned income." Democratic efforts, backed by Cooper, to replace the dividend relief provision with a personal exemption increase were defeated in both houses.

In 1955, Cooper became chairman of the Ways and Means Committee as well as chairman of the Joint Internal Revenue Taxation Committee. Under his leadership, the Ways and Means panel appended to a corporate and excise tax extension measure a $20 income tax reduction for all persons entitled to a personal exemption. The Senate rejected the proposal. Cooper led the House delegation in a joint House-Senate conference on the bill and demanded reinstatement of the reduction. However, because of what he termed the government's need for revenue from corporate and excise taxes, he reluctantly struck the tax credit.

Cooper strongly backed the administration's request in 1953 for extension of reciprocal trade legislation. Representing a largely rural constituency, he asserted that "if there should be a decline in the exports of farm products so as to increase the supply available to our domestic market by only 7 or 8 percent, farm prices would fall as much as one-third."

Congress voted to renew the Reciprocal Trade Agreements Act for one year in 1953 and again in 1954. In 1955, Cooper, then the chairman of the Ways and Means Committee, introduced and helped to oversee passage of legislation to extend the reciprocal trade law for three years and to grant the president authority to cut tariffs by 5 percent during each of the three years.

Cooper died of a heart attack in Bethesda, Md., on December 18, 1957.

—MLL

Cooper, John S(herman)

(1901–1991) *U.S. senator, ambassador to India and Nepal*

Born in Somerset, Ky., on August 23, 1901, Cooper graduated from Yale in 1923 and attended Harvard

Law School from 1923 to 1925. He then returned to Kentucky, where he was admitted to the bar in 1928. That same year, he won election as a Republican to the state legislature. He sat as a county judge from 1930 until 1938. Cooper served in the army during World War II, and, in the immediate postwar period, he helped reorganize the German judicial system in Bavaria.

In 1945, Cooper won election as a circuit judge in Kentucky; he resigned in November 1946, having won a special election to fill the Senate seat vacated by the resignation of ALBERT B. CHANDLER. After failing to win reelection in 1948, Cooper briefly resumed the practice of law. He was a member of the U.S. delegation to the UN General Assembly from 1949 to 1951 and during that time also served as a consultant to Secretary of State DEAN ACHESON. Upon the death of Senator Virgil M. Chapman, Cooper won a special election to fill the remainder of his term. Cooper entered the Senate for the second time in November 1952, but in 1954 he once again failed to win reelection. President Eisenhower appointed him ambassador to India and Nepal in 1955. The following year, Cooper won a Senate seat in yet another special election, this one occasioned by the death of Alben W. Barkley. Cooper won reelection to a full term in 1960 and again in 1966.

Cooper early on established himself as one of the Senate's most liberal and independent Republicans. A critic of Sen. JOSEPH R. MCCARTHY's anticommunist campaign, Cooper was among the first Republicans to endorse McCarthy's censure.

During the 1950s, Cooper spoke frequently on international affairs and opposed the vehement anticommunist position of many of his colleagues as dangerously extreme. In January 1953, he was the only Republican who voted against the unsuccessful Bricker amendment, which would have limited the president's treaty-making powers. Two months later, Cooper opposed Sen. WILLIAM F. KNOWLAND's (R-Calif.) proposal that the U.S. blockade the coast of China and have the Soviet Union condemned in the United Nations as a "supporter of aggression in the Far East." In July 1958, he protested Eisenhower's decision to land U.S. troops in Lebanon.

Cooper was one of the few Republican defenders of the Tennessee Valley Authority (TVA), and

he advocated its expansion. In July 1954, he cast the sole Republican vote against Eisenhower's omnibus atomic energy bill, which included the Dixon-Yates contract providing for a private utility to replace the TVA as the Atomic Energy Commission's chief energy supplier in the Memphis, Tenn., region. Cooper also voted for a Democratic area redevelopment bill introduced in March 1959. The measure, which called for federal funds to stimulate business in economically depressed areas, was vetoed by Eisenhower, who sent Cooper a letter suggesting other methods of developing the region. However, Cooper maintained his original position and supported an unsuccessful attempt to override the veto in May 1960.

The senator was among the strongest Republican supporters of civil rights legislation. In January 1957, he voted for a proposal to ease cloture proceedings, an unsuccessful effort by advocates of civil rights to skirt the filibuster used by southern opponents of civil rights. Cooper opposed a southern attempt to weaken the Civil Rights Act of 1957 by guaranteeing a jury trial to persons accused of obstructing the voting rights of others. An amendment he proposed in July 1957 to let the attorney general decide whether or not to grant a jury trial in such cases was rejected by the Senate, 81-8. He also favored expansion of the Civil Rights Act of 1957 and 1960 to include school desegregation provisions, although the provision failed to make the final version of either act.

Republican liberals nominated Cooper for Senate Republican leader in December 1958, but he was defeated by Sen. EVERETT DIRKSEN (R-Ill.). In 1960, Cooper joined seven other Republican senators in offering a voluntary federal-state health insurance program for all Americans over 65. Under the plan, the state would have contracted with private firms for the coverage, and subscribers would have made payments based on income, with the federal and state governments sharing the remaining costs. Cooper's proposal was more liberal than the administration's plan, which limited aid to single elderly persons with adjusted gross incomes of up to $2,500 a year and married couples with annual incomes up to $3,800. The plan finally adopted in August contained most of the basic features of Cooper's proposal. However, it required a means test and permitted each state to determine the type and extent of medical assistance provided.

During the 1960s, Cooper continued to support civil rights legislation. He became a leading Republican critic of the Johnson administration's conduct of the Vietnam War and in 1970 cosponsored an amendment prohibiting the use of U.S. troops in Cambodia. Cooper did not stand for reelection in 1972.

After leaving the Senate, he served as ambassador to the German Democratic Republic from 1974 to 1976, after which he resumed the practice of law in Washington, D.C. He died in Washington on February 21, 1991.

—MDB

Corsi, Edward

(1896–1964) *special assistant to the State Department for Refugee and Immigration Problems*
Born in Abruzzi, Italy, on December 29, 1896, Corsi immigrated to the U.S. at the age of seven. His family settled on New York's Lower East Side, and Corsi attended both public and parochial schools. He also became active in Haarlem House, a settlement house in New York's Little Italy. Corsi worked his way through Fordham University School of Law, from which he graduated in 1922. He then began a career as a journalist for *Outlook* magazine and the *New York World.* President HERBERT HOOVER appointed him immigration commissioner at Ellis Island in 1931, where he improved and humanized procedures for handling immigrants. He served in that post until 1934, when New York's mayor, Fiorello La Guardia, appointed him director of emergency relief. The next year, Corsi became deputy city welfare director. Gov. THOMAS E. DEWEY appointed him state industrial commissioner in 1943. A lifelong Republican, Corsi ran unsuccessfully for a U.S. Senate seat in 1938 and for mayor of New York City in 1950.

In December 1954, Secretary of State JOHN FOSTER DULLES appointed Corsi a State Department consultant to help increase immigration under the Refugee Relief Act of 1953. Corsi was to work with SCOTT MCLEOD, the State Department's security director, to process the entry of 214,000 over-quota refugees into the United States in three

years. McLeod and Corsi repeatedly clashed over the administration of the program. The security director insisted on a thorough security check of all entrants, thus slowing down arrivals. Corsi, on the other hand, had elaborate plans to recruit refugees, facilitate the entry process, and shortcut the act's delaying provisions. In addition, the two men fought over authority; Corsi refused to be McLeod's assistant.

On February 28, Rep. FRANCIS E. WALTER (D-Pa.), chairman of the House Immigration Subcommittee, charged that Corsi had been associated with two allegedly left-wing organizations: the National Lawyers Guild and the American Committee for the Protection of the Foreign Born. Corsi denied the charges. On March 1, Walter admitted his error with respect to the Lawyers Guild but maintained his position on the other charge. Walter supported McLeod on his clash with Corsi and in a letter to Dulles demanded Corsi's ouster "forthwith." On March 16, McLeod offered Corsi the choice of being his deputy or heading an insignificant project surveying immigration in Latin America, Corsi did not respond.

At the beginning of April, Dulles notified Corsi that his appointment had been a 90-day assignment and would not be renewed. The secretary stressed that he did not question Corsi's loyalty and, in token of this, again offered him the job in Latin America. Corsi refused it, charging that his dismissal had been the result of pressure from Walter and McLeod.

Congressional liberals denounced Corsi's ouster and demanded an investigation of the incident. In press conferences and in testimony before a Senate Judiciary subcommittee, Dulles and McLeod defended their action. They maintained that Corsi had tried to bypass some provisions of the Refugee Relief Act and was incapable of administering the program. McLeod denied that he had known of Walter's demand when he made Corsi the Latin America job offer. Corsi, in turn, charged that the administration of the act was a national scandal. The law's administration was "wholly dominated by the psychology of security," Corsi declared. He said "refugees are investigated to death" because "the police job is the thing, not the admission of the refugees—that is just incidental."

New York's governor, AVERELL HARRIMAN, appointed Corsi to the New York State Unemployment Insurance Board in 1958. Corsi also served as director of the New York World's Fair. He practiced law in New York until his death in an automobile accident in Kensington, N.Y., on December 13, 1964.

—JB

Costello, Frank
(1891–1973) *organized crime figure*

Born Francesco Castiglia in Cosenza, Italy, on January 26, 1891, Frank Costello came to the United States in 1896 and settled in predominantly Italian East Harlem. He became aware early of ethnic power politics in Tammany Hall and changed his name to the Irish Costello in 1914. He was arrested twice by the age of 21, and in 1915 he received a one-year prison sentence for carrying a gun.

Costello became prominent as a bootlegger and controller of New York City slot machines during the early 1920s. Although a close friend of such rising organized crime figures as ALBERT ANASTASIA and Lucky Luciano, unlike these two, he preferred manipulation to violence. During the 1930s and 1940s, he cultivated Democratic leaders in Tammany Hall. Costello's rackets encountered little official opposition except during the administration of Mayor Fiorello La Guardia, who drove slot machines out of New York in 1935. Costello then moved his machines to New Orleans at the invitation of Sen. Huey P. Long (D-La.), who promised to legalize them. In 1936, after Luciano went to prison and Mafia leader VITO GENOVESE fled to Italy, Costello found himself head of the New York syndicate. He controlled Manhattan's organized crime for the next 10 years. In 1939, federal authorities tried Costello in New Orleans for tax evasion but lost the case because of lack of evidence.

The Senate Crime Investigating Committee's probe of organized crime in 1951 exposed the extent of Costello's racketeering and political influence. For eight days in February and March, Costello testified before the panel, led by Sen. ESTES KEFAUVER (D-Tenn.), on his role in New York City politics. Kefauver made public wiretaps documenting Costello's role in the Democratic nomination of

Thomas Aurelio for the State Supreme Court in 1943. Costello's influence over Tammany leaders also enabled William O'Dwyer to win the nomination and election for mayor in 1945.

No formal charges were brought against Costello because much of the evidence had been gained by wiretaps, legally inadmissible in court. However, when Costello walked out of the hearing room on March 15, on the ground that he had a sore throat, the committee cited him for contempt of Congress. Kefauver concluded that Costello was part of a national axis of crime including racketeers Meyer Lansky and Joe Adonis. In 1952, Costello was convicted on the contempt charge and sentenced to 18 months in prison and a $5,000 fine. He went free pending appeal. Later that year, the federal government began proceedings to revoke his citizenship on the ground that he had lied about his occupation on naturalization papers.

In 1953, Costello was indicted, and in May 1954 was convicted of evading $73,714 in income taxes. He received a five-year sentence and a $2,000 fine but was freed on bail in 1957. Publicity, time spent in prison, and legal appeals weakened Costello within the Mafia. Vying for leadership, Vito Genovese attempted to have him assassinated in May 1957, but Costello survived. After the killing of Anastasia in October, Costello retired. In February 1961, the Supreme Court upheld the revocation of his citizenship.

Costello was released from prison in June 1961. During the remaining years of his life, he stayed out of the public eye. According to the *New York Times*, however, Costello came out of retirement after the death of Vito Genovese in 1969 to lead the New York underworld. He was involved in long-range planning and mediation of disputes rather than day-to-day operations. Costello died of natural causes in New York City on February 1, 1973.

—MJS

Cotton, Norris
(1900–1989) *U.S. congressman and senator*

Born in Warren, N.H., on May 11, 1900, Cotton graduated from Wesleyan University in 1923 and was elected as a Republican to the New Hampshire House of Representatives the following year. From

1924 to 1928, he served as secretary to U.S. Sen. George H. Moses (R-N.H.) while attending George Washington University Law School. Cotton was admitted to the New Hampshire bar in 1928 and commenced the practice of law in Lebanon. From 1933 to 1939, he was district attorney for Grafton Co., and from 1939 to 1944 he sat as a justice in the municipal court of Lebanon. He again served in the state house of representatives in 1943 and 1945. Cotton was elected to the U.S. House of Representatives in 1946. There he compiled a conservative record, voting to override President HARRY S. TRUMAN's veto of the Taft-Hartley bill in 1947, to support the subversive activities control bill in 1948, and to oppose the administration's long-term housing bill in 1949.

Cotton won a special election to fill a vacant Senate seat in 1952. He continued his conservative voting pattern in the upper house, fighting measures extending the power of the federal government. In April 1955, he opposed a federal highway program financed through general treasury funds on the grounds that it would increase taxes and the public debt and would impose federal controls in areas previously left to the states. The proposal, passed by the Senate but rejected by the House, was a substitute for the Eisenhower administration's plan to finance highway construction through a federal bond issue.

In 1956, Cotton opposed a public power project at Niagara Falls, stating that "it is simply a question of private versus government enterprise, and I believe in private enterprise." He also voted against the area redevelopment bill of 1958.

Cotton supported the Eisenhower administration's federal employee security program. In June 1956, the Supreme Court ruled that, under a law passed in 1950, the president's executive order of April 1953, which permitted the dismissal of any federal employee for doubtful loyalty, could apply only to persons in sensitive positions. Following the decision, Cotton and Senators KARL E. MUNDT (R-S. Dak.), EDWARD MARTIN (R-Pa.), and WILLIAM F. KNOWLAND (R-Calif.) introduced a bill amending the act to extend the program to all government employees regardless of position. The measure was not reported to the Senate floor.

In June 1958, the House Interstate and Foreign Commerce Committee's Legislative Oversight Subcommittee began an investigation into the relationship between Boston industrialist BERNARD GOLDFINE and presidential assistant SHERMAN ADAMS, a probe that culminated in Adams's resignation. The following month, Goldfine acknowledged that he had paid hotel bills for Cotton and Sens. Frederick Payne (R-Me.) and STYLES BRIDGES (R-N.H.).

Cotton consistently opposed the domestic legislation of the Kennedy and Johnson administrations. A militant anticommunist, he backed American involvement in Vietnam throughout the 1960s. During the early 1970s, however, he became disenchanted with the war. He opposed U.S. military intervention in Cambodia and American support for the regime in Vietnam. Cotton served as chairman of the Republican Conference from 1973 to 1975. He declined to run for reelection in 1974, but returned to the Senate briefly when, on August 8, 1975, he was appointed to fill a vacancy caused by the contested election of November 5, 1974. He served until September 18, 1975. Cotton died in Lebanon, N.H., on February 24, 1989.

—MLL

Cousins, Norman
(1915–1990) *editor,* Saturday Review

Cousins was born in Union City, N.J., on June 24, 1915. He graduated from Teachers College at Columbia University in 1933, and the following year he was hired as an editor on the *New York Post.* After subsequently working as a book critic for *Current History*, he became the editor of the *Saturday Review of Literature* (later the *Saturday Review*), a liberal literary weekly, in 1942. Cousins expanded the magazine's format to include feature articles on current events and his own editorials on political and cultural problems, in addition to book reviews.

Although a supporter of American involvement in World War II, Cousins became a peace activist as a result of the atomic bombing of Hiroshima. On the night of August 6, 1945, the day the bomb was dropped, he composed a famous editorial for the *Review* titled "Modern Man Is Obsolete," in which he declared that human survival had become absolutely dependent on man's ability to avoid a new war. Believing that nuclear destruction could be averted only by the establishment of a new international order, Cousins helped found the United World Federalists in 1947, an organization that advocated transforming the United Nations into a world government with the authority to enforce disarmament.

During the late-1950s, Cousins played an important role in the protest against the atmospheric testing of nuclear bombs. In 1957, he helped organize the National Committee for a Sane Nuclear Policy (SANE), a coalition of pacifists and nonpacifists that called for the immediate cessation of nuclear testing. With Cousins as cochairman, SANE began by publicizing the threat of genetic damage and contamination of the food supply from atomic fallout. After the United States and the Soviet Union both suspended testing in 1958, the organization, which had grown to about 25,000 members, broadened its aims to include general disarmament. At the same time, SANE continued to work for a permanent test ban treaty, organizing mass demonstrations in support of his proposal throughout the country in 1959 and 1960.

In May 1960, one week after it held a rally that packed New York's Madison Square Garden, Sen. THOMAS DODD (D-Conn.) charged that SANE was infiltrated by communists. Cousins responded by suspending the organizer of the rally, whom Dodd had named as one of the "infiltrators," and proposing a resolution, adopted by SANE's national board, restricting membership in the organization to those "whose support is not qualified by adherence to communist or other totalitarian doctrine." Dodd later claimed that Cousins had agreed to supply his Senate Internal Security Subcommittee with the names of alleged communists in SANE, but Cousins denied having offered to cooperate with the investigation. Several leading peace activists condemned Cousins's actions as a capitulation to McCarthyism, and many resigned from SANE in protest.

In the following years, Cousins continued to work for a nuclear test ban treaty and to advocate disarmament through a world rule of law. During the late 1960s, he was active in the campaign for a negotiated settlement of the Vietnam War. In November 1971, Cousins resigned his post at the *Saturday Review* because of an editorial dispute with its new owners. The following year, he

founded *World* magazine. In 1973, Cousins bought the then-bankrupt *Saturday Review* and combined it with his new publication to form *Saturday Review/World*.

After recovering from a life-threatening form of arthritis, he became convinced of the importance of a positive attitude in the process of healing. He advanced this view in *Anatomy of an Illness* (1979), *The Healing Heart* (1983), and *Head First: The Biology of Hope* (1989). He died of a heart attack on November 30, 1990, in Los Angeles.

—TLH

Cross, Hugh
(1896–1972) *member and chairman, Interstate Commerce Commission*

The son of early Illinois pioneers, Cross was born on August 24, 1896, in Jerseyville, Ill. He received his law degree from the University of Illinois in 1921, and began legal practice in Jerseyville. In 1932, he won election as a Republican to the Illinois General Assembly, where he served four successive two-year terms. He was elected Speaker of the House in 1939. Cross was lieutenant governor from 1940 to 1948. In April 1949, President HARRY S. TRUMAN appointed him to serve out an unexpired term on the Interstate Commerce Commission (ICC). He was reappointed to a full seven-year term in December 1950. The commission rotated its chairmanship, and on the basis of his seniority, Cross became chairman in July 1955.

In November 1955, the Senate Permanent Investigations Subcommittee began closed hearings on possible conflict of interest involving Cross. Testimony revealed that Cross had contacted the heads of three railroads in an effort to secure for Railroad Transfer Service, Inc. a contract to haul passengers and baggage between Chicago's eight rail terminals. John Keeshin, a longtime friend of Cross, owned Railroad Transfer.

Paul E. Feucht, president of one of the lines, told the panel that Cross had telephoned him saying he was "very much interested in seeing that J. L. Keeshin got the new contract with the railroad." Even more damaging was the testimony of two other presidents who reported having heard rumors that Cross was unhappy in Washington and would resign his post to head Railroad Transfer if the company were awarded the contract. Keeshin told the subcommittee that he had discussed business with Cross but denied that he had offered the commissioner a job. Cross, too, denied charges that Keeshin had promised him a job in return for his favors. The subcommittee concluded that, although there was no evidence that Cross had acted corruptly or illegally, he had "behaved in an unwise manner involving impropriety." Both Democratic and Republican members of the panel agreed not to pursue the investigation if Cross resigned. On November 23, 1955, he sent a letter of resignation to President Eisenhower. Cross stated that he would have liked to defend himself "against the baseless charges" but was resigning effective immediately to protect the reputation of the ICC and because of his own and his wife's poor health. Eisenhower accepted the resignation. Although JAMES HAGERTY, Eisenhower's press secretary, and others denied it, rumors persisted that Cross had resigned under pressure from the administration.

Neither Congress nor the Justice Department showed any inclination to pursue the matter after Cross's resignation. After leaving Washington, Cross returned to Jerseyville, where he owned a farm. He was president of the Jersey County Abstract and Title Company from 1957 to 1962. Cross died in Jerseyville on October 15, 1972.

—MSM

Curran, Joseph E(dwin)

(1906–1981) *president, National Maritime Union*

The son of a cook, Joseph Curran was born in New York City on March 1, 1906. He went to sea at the age of 16. In 1935, he joined the International Seamen's Union (ISU) and sailed on the S.S. *California*. Discovering that West Coast seamen's wages and conditions were better than those on the East Coast, Curran led the crew of the *California* in a wildcat strike to obtain pay parity. Secretary of Labor Frances Perkins assured Curran that if the strike were ended, the crew's grievances would be heard. Instead, 64 seamen were fired. Curran then led a major strike. He refused to accept a settlement negotiated by the ISU. Instead, he broke away from the union to form the National Maritime Union

(NMU), taking 35,000 ISU members with him. The new organization became part of the Congress of Industrial Organizations (CIO). The 31-year old Curran was elected the first president of the NMU in 1937.

During World War II, Curran worked closely with Communist Party members in leading the union, although he himself was not a member of the party. In 1946, he joined a group of radicals, recently expelled from the Communist Party, in a successful drive to oust communists from the NMU. He then turned against his former supporters. In a bitter struggle, which culminated in violence, the followers of his rival, David Drummond, were expelled from the union.

Although the NMU joined the combined AFL-CIO in 1955, Curran was often at odds with the organization's president, GEORGE MEANY. In 1956, Curran voted to endorse the Democratic presidential ticket despite Meany's desire to have the organization remain neutral in the election. That year, he also gave his support to the International Longshoremen's Association's (ILA) organizing drive, despite the ILA's expulsion from the AFL because of corruption and the AFL's creation of a rival group, the International Brotherhood of Longshoremen. Curran also refused to support the expulsion of the Teamsters Union from the merged AFL-CIO and repeatedly attempted to have it reinstated. In 1958, despite Meany's objections, Curran joined the Teamsters and the ILA in sponsoring a Conference on Transportation Unity under the chairmanship of JAMES HOFFA. Curran did, however, agree to abide by an order of the AFL-CIO Executive Council not to enter into any formal or informal agreements with the Teamsters.

Curran was one of the American labor leaders who met Premier Nikita Khrushchev during the Soviet leader's visit to the United States in 1959. While most labor leaders denounced both Khrushchev personally and the communist system, Curran refused to condemn the premier. In 1960, he visited the Soviet Union and had an apparently cordial interview with the Soviet leader.

In 1960, the Department of Labor challenged Curran's reelection as president of the NMU on the grounds of election irregularities. These included illegal disqualification of candidates, electioneering at the polls, promotion of candidacies with union funds, and failure to provide secret ballots. The suit was a major test of the provisions of the Landrum-Griffin Act of 1959. The case was later dropped in return for Curran's admission of guilt on some charges and an agreement to conduct future elections according to the provisions of the law.

During the 1950s and 1960s, the NMU was threatened by a decline in jobs caused by ships registering under foreign flags. Curran responded by attempting to gain increased government subsidies for the shipping industry. Although he managed to gain higher wages and better working conditions for union members, he failed to win increased government subsidies.

In the late-1960s, a growing opposition movement within the union challenged his authority, and charges of irregularities in the union election of 1966 forced a rerun of that election three years later. Nevertheless, Curran remained in office until his retirement in 1973. He died of cancer in Boca Raton, Fla., on August 14, 1981.

—SY

Curtice, Harlow H(erbert)

(1893–1962) *president, General Motors Corporation*
Curtice was born in Eaton Rapids, Mich., on August 15, 1893. He began working at General Motors in 1914 as a bookkeeper for the AC Spark Plug Division. Within a year, he was named comptroller. By 1930, he had risen to president of the division. Transferring to the Buick Motor Division in 1933 as its president and general manager, he led the ailing section to produce GM's fourth largest-selling car in the prewar years. He became a vice president of the General Motors Corp. in 1940 and left Buick to become executive vice president in 1948.

When GM's president, CHARLES WILSON, went to Washington in 1953 as Secretary of Defense, Curtice succeeded him. During his tenure, Curtice maintained GM's position as the leading manufacturer in the automotive industry. By announcing a $1-billion expansion program early in 1954, he increased the company's postwar capital investment to $3 billion. In the middle of 1955, GM announced another $500-million expansion, bringing postwar investment to $4 billion. Predicting "another record

year for business generally," in January 1956 Curtice announced a further $1-billion growth expenditure.

GM's dominant position in the automobile industry attracted attention from Congress. Curtice testified before the Senate Banking and Currency Committee in March 1955, during its probe of rising stock market prices. Chairman J. WILLIAM FULBRIGHT (D-Ark.) wanted to know whether GM could force competitors out of business by lowering prices. Curtice responded that the automotive industry "is even more competitive today than at any time." The hearings were recessed indefinitely on March 23.

In December 1955, the Antitrust and Monopoly Subcommittee of the Senate Judiciary Committee investigated charges that GM engaged in monopolistic practices and coerced dealers. GM dealers specifically charged that the company used "almost diabolical pressure" to increase sales, including threats of eviction upon expiration of their short-term leases. Curtice responded by offering dealers a five-year franchise instead of the existing one-year contracts.

Two bills resulted from these hearings. One measure allowed car dealers to sue in federal court to recover damages from companies not acting in good faith in carrying out the terms of contracts with dealers. President Eisenhower signed it into law in August 1956. The other bill, which would have authorized Federal Trade Commission regulation of unfair trade practices in the automobile distributing industry, died in the Senate.

In July 1956, Attorney General HERBERT BROWNELL accused GM and four bus companies of conspiracy to monopolize bus sales. Curtice denied the charge.

In 1957, Curtice opposed the request of Michigan's governor, G. MENNEN WILLIAMS, for increased taxes on corporation profits in the state. Curtice warned that GM already had located several new plants outside of Michigan because of tax considerations. After being criticized for his statement, Curtice denied that it had been intended as a threat to remove GM from Michigan.

Disputes between the auto industry and the president of the United Auto Workers, WALTER P. REUTHER, raged during contract negotiations in

1957 and 1958. The Big Three auto companies—General Motors, Ford, and Chrysler—rejected outright a proposal made in August 1957 by Reuther to reduce prices in 1958 as an anti-inflationary measure. Of the three company heads, Curtice particularly was opposed to Reuther's later suggestion of profit sharing to counter a recession. Curtice called it "a radical scheme . . . foreign to the concepts of the American free enterprise system." The contract disputes continued after Curtice's retirement.

Curtice resigned as GM's president and chief executive on September 1, 1958, at the age of 65, under the company's automatic retirement plan. He died of heart failure in Flint, Mich., on November 3, 1962.

—RB

Curtis, Carl T(homas)

(1905–2000) *U.S. congressman and senator*

A descendant of early settlers and farmers in Nebraska, Curtis was born in Kearney Co., Neb., on March 15, 1905. He attended the University of Nebraska and Nebraska Wesleyan University. After briefly teaching public school in Minden, Neb., Curtis studied law and was admitted to the bar in 1930. He began the practice of law in Minden and served as county attorney for Kearney from 1931 to 1934. He ran successfully for the House of Representatives in 1938. A Republican from the most Republican state in the nation, Curtis compiled one of the most conservative records in Congress. Except on civil rights, he voted with southern Democrats on most economic and social issues.

During his years in the House, Curtis became increasingly interested in the problems of the Social Security system, and in 1947 he called for the "blanketing in" of all aged persons not receiving benefits, especially self-employed professionals, business owners, and employees of state and local governments. In 1953, as chairman of a special subcommittee on Social Security of the Ways and Means Committee, he helped draw up legislation embodying the new administration's proposals to extend old-age insurance coverage to 10 million additional persons. The Curtis plan, modeled on one put forward by the U.S. Chamber of Commerce, proposed replacing the insurance principle

of the system, by which each worker built up a retirement fund for his old age, with a pay-as-you-go policy, by which currently employed persons would support the aged with their payroll taxes. Opponents such as Secretary of Health, Education, and Welfare OVETA C. HOBBY described the plan as a "criminal raid on the Social Security Trust Fund" built up by contributions from individual earnings. The bill, passed in August 1954, was modified at the suggestion of the president to provide for greater coverage without drastically reforming the system.

After his election to the Senate in 1954, Curtis focused on what he viewed as the coercive role of labor unions in American society. As a member of the Rules and Administration Committee's Subcommittee on Elections, he participated in the drive to close loopholes in the campaign spending laws that permitted unions to use dues and manpower for partisan purposes under the guise of "education and information" programs. In May 1957, he replaced the deceased Sen. JOSEPH MCCARTHY (R-Wis.) on the Select Committee on Improper Activities in the Labor or Management Field. Eight months later, the AFL-CIO singled out Curtis and Senators BARRY GOLDWATER (R-Ariz.) and KARL MUNDT (R-S. Dak.) as having "demonstrated their anti-labor bias and . . . forfeiting any claim . . . of conducting themselves in a spirit of fairness or objectivity." Curtis and Mundt constantly pressed the committee to investigate the crime and violence associated with United Auto Workers (UAW) strikes. In August 1959, they finally succeeded in holding hearings on the UAW over the protest of the committee's counsel, ROBERT F. KENNEDY. When the committee issued its final report in 1960, Curtis joined other Republicans in denouncing the probe. They criticized its failure to investigate cases deeply, to fix responsibility for criminal action, or to recommend reform. The senators attributed this inaction to what they termed a close alliance between UAW President WALTER REUTHER and the Democratic Party.

Curtis won reelection in 1960, 1966, and 1972. In 1963, Curtis sat on five legislative committees—more than any other senator. He opposed most of the social welfare programs of the Kennedy and Johnson administrations and was one of

President RICHARD NIXON's staunchest supporters during the Watergate scandal. Curtis did not run for reelection in 1978. He returned to Lincoln, Neb., where he practiced law until his death there on January 21, 2000.

—TLH

Curtis, Thomas B(radford)
(1911–1993) *U.S. congressman*

The son and grandson of lawyers, Curtis was born in Saint Louis, Mo., on May 10, 1911. He earned his B.A. from Dartmouth College in 1932 and his LL.B. from Washington University in 1935. Upon graduation from law school, he joined his father's firm. After briefly serving on the Board of Election of Saint Louis County in 1942, Curtis served in the navy from 1942 to 1945. He ran unsuccessfully for several offices before winning election to Congress as a Republican from Saint Louis County. In the House, Curtis emerged as a fiscal conservative who favored ending price controls and cutting military spending and foreign aid.

With the opening of the Republican-controlled 83rd Congress in 1953, Curtis was assigned to the powerful House Ways and Means Committee. During the Eisenhower administration, he gradually established himself as a leading Republican spokesman on economic policy and revenue matters. A resolute foe of social welfare and defense measures that he believed contributed to an unbalanced budget, Curtis was often a lone dissenter on appropriations votes. Occasionally, his opposition to federal spending led him to take positions that other fiscal conservatives considered extreme. For example, in 1953, he suggested that Social Security be turned over to private industry. Curtis strongly supported civil rights legislation. He voted for the Civil Rights Acts of 1957 and 1960.

Curtis attracted attention in 1958 when he came to the defense of presidential assistant SHERMAN ADAMS, who was charged with securing favored treatment from federal regulatory agencies for Boston industrialist BERNARD GOLDFINE. Curtis declared that the Interstate and Foreign Commerce Committee's Legislative Oversight Subcommittee, which was investigating the matter, had taken defamatory testimony. He moved that the subcommittee be censured. This motion was ruled out of order by Speaker SAM RAYBURN. Later Curtis was one of only eight representatives who voted against citing Goldfine for contempt of Congress for his refusal to answer questions before the subcommittee.

As the senior Republican on the Joint Economic Committee and the second-ranking Republican on the Ways and Means Committee, Curtis maintained his record of fiscal conservatism during the Kennedy and Johnson administrations. He was particularly active in fighting tax increases and Medicare.

Curtis left the House in 1969 after an unsuccessful bid for a Senate seat. He was vice president and general counsel for the *Encyclopædia Britannica* from 1969 to 1973. In 1972, President RICHARD M. NIXON appointed him chairman of the Corporation for Public Broadcasting, a board set up to control the allocation of federal funds to public radio and television stations. He served as chairman of the Federal Election Commission from April 1975 to May 1976. He died in Allegan, Mich., on January 19, 1993.

—TLH

D

Daley, Richard J(oseph)
(1902–1976) *mayor of Chicago*

The grandson of Irish immigrants and son of a sheet-metal worker, Daley was born in Chicago on May 15, 1902, and grew up in the predominantly Irish Bridgeport section of Chicago's South Side. He graduated from the Christian Brothers' De La Salle Institute, a commercial high school, in 1919. Later, he studied in the evening at DePaul University and received a law degree in 1934.

At the age of 21, Daley became a precinct captain in the city's Democratic organization. After the Democrats won the municipal elections in 1923, he got a job as a clerk for the city council. During the same period, Daley became president of the Hamburg Social and Athletic Club, a sometimes violent neighborhood gang that was politically influential in his ward. When the ward boss was elected treasurer of Cook Co. (which included Chicago and its suburbs) in 1931, Daley became a clerk in the treasurer's office. He was elected to the Illinois House of Representatives in 1936 and ran successful races for the state senate in 1938 and 1942. Daley lost a race for county sheriff in 1946.

Following ADLAI E. STEVENSON's election as governor in 1948, Daley was appointed state director of revenue and served as the governor's representative to the legislature. During these years, he received significant press coverage, gaining a reputation as a young, reformist Democrat of the Stevenson type. In 1950, he left his post and ran a successful campaign for Cook Co. clerk.

Daley assumed the leadership of the Chicago party organization in July 1953, when he became chairman of the Cook Co. Democratic Central Committee. The party's electoral strength was based upon the work of precinct captains and their assistants in the wards. In exchange for their services, these party workers received patronage positions from their ward leaders. As county chairman, Daley controlled these leaders by personally determining the patronage each would receive. To preserve his patronage power, Daley minimized the number of civil service officeholders chosen by merit. He did this by making many temporary appointments. Daley also selected the party's candidates for local offices.

As chairman of the Democratic Committee, Daley had little difficulty in securing the organization's endorsement for mayor in December 1954. In the local Democratic primary held in February 1955, he defeated the incumbent Democratic mayor, Martin Kennelly, who had offended many party leaders by his efforts to combat municipal corruption. Two months later, Daley easily won the general election.

Daley's major goal during his first term was to revitalize Chicago's downtown business area through the construction of expressways, parking garages, and docking facilities as well as by enlarging O'Hare Airport to accommodate commercial traffic. He also attempted to stem the middle- and upper-class exodus to the suburbs by encouraging the construction of high-rise luxury apartments along the lakefront. Daley was able to fund his projects through the use of bonds and by procuring greater taxing authority for the city from the state legislature in the summer of 1955.

The mayor's critics contended that corruption was rampant under his administration and that he was doing little to alleviate the plight of slum dwellers or to halt the declining quality of the schools and the public transportation system. They also noted that his construction plans failed to stop the exodus to the suburbs. However, backed by his machine and with the support of the downtown business community and organized labor, he won reelection in the spring of 1959 with 71.4 percent of the vote.

Later that year, the city government was tarnished by scandals involving corruption in the traffic and municipal courts. In January 1960, these were overshadowed by revelations that policemen were participating in burglaries. Daley moved dramatically to repair the image of the city government. He fired the police commissioner and replaced him in February with Orlando W. Wilson, a professional criminologist from California. Daley granted Wilson far greater independence from City Hall than police commissioners traditionally had possessed, and the new chief began a major reorganization of his department.

Daley emerged as a major figure in national Democratic politics during his first six years as mayor. At the party's convention in 1956, he received his first national publicity by rounding up support in the Illinois delegation for Stevenson, who had backed Daley's bid for the mayoralty the previous year. In the general election, however, the combined efforts of Stevenson and Daley could not prevent the state from going to Eisenhower. In 1960, Daley rejected Stevenson's appeal for support in his third bid for the party's nomination. At the convention, Daley, who controlled about three-quarters of the state delegation, delivered the bulk of the votes from Illinois for Sen. JOHN F. KENNEDY (D-Mass.) to help him win a first-ballot victory.

In November 1960, a heavily Democratic Cook Co. vote overcame the traditional downstate Republican majority and enabled Kennedy to carry Illinois's crucial electoral votes by a narrow margin of 10,000 ballots. Many observers believed that Daley's machine, through widespread electoral fraud, had stolen the White House from the Republican candidate, Vice President RICHARD M. NIXON. Over 600 polling-place workers and Democratic precinct captains were charged with allowing ineligible voters to cast ballots in the name of deceased persons, permitting individuals to vote more than once, and other offenses. Most of the charges were eventually dropped. Mike Royko, in *Boss: Richard J. Daley of Chicago*, attributed the dismissal of charges to the fact that the judge in the case was a loyal organization Democrat. A recount in the 900 Cook Co. precincts using paper ballots significantly reduced the margins of defeat for some state and local Republican candidates, particularly in the case of Benjamin Adamowski, the Republican state's attorney who was seeking reelection. Adamowski had initiated investigations of corruption in the Chicago city government, and Royko contended that capturing his post and other state and local offices were Daley's primary goals. The recount did not substantially affect the presidential tally, and the Republicans did not press for further retabulations. None of the election results, including Adamowski's defeat, were overturned.

Expanded federal aid to cities during the 1960s enabled Daley to strengthen his political base, and he continued to win reelection easily. He dispensed urban renewal contracts to friendly builders and used antipoverty programs as an additional source of patronage. Daley had supporters among business leaders and Democratic liberals. Even as other major cities struggled to provide essential services, Daley made Chicago work. However, Daley largely ignored the growing problems of the black community in Chicago, which had become one of the most segregated cities in the country. Those issues commanded national attention when, during the summer of 1966, demonstrations for open housing in ethnic areas met with violence. Two years later, during the Democratic National Convention in Chicago, the city's police savagely attacked protesters in the streets. Although many, particularly liberal Democrats, criticized Daley, he continued to receive strong support from most Chicagoans. The mayor suffered a major political setback in 1976, when his handpicked gubernatorial candidate was soundly defeated by a Republican who, as a U.S. attorney, had successfully prosecuted a number of the mayor's political allies. Daley died of a heart attack in Chicago on December 20, 1976.

—MLL

Daniel, (Marion) Price
(1910–1988) *U.S. senator, governor of Texas*

Born in Dayton, Tex., on October 10, 1910, Price Daniel attended public schools and, after graduation, went to work as a reporter. He graduated from Baylor University in 1931 and from Baylor's law school in 1932. Upon receiving his degree, he began a law practice in Liberty, Tex., and became a member of the speakers' bureau of the Democratic national campaign. In 1938, Daniel won election to the Texas House of Representatives as a moderate New Deal Democrat. He served as Speaker in 1943. Daniel joined the army in 1943, serving in the Pacific theater and in Japan. Upon his discharge in 1946, he returned to Texas and won election as attorney general that year without opposition. While in office, Daniel established a reputation as a rackets-buster and champion of state claims to offshore oil. In 1952, he ran for the U.S. Senate on a platform supporting Texas's oil claims and opposing President HARRY S. TRUMAN's position on civil rights. He won 72 percent of the votes in the Democratic primary in July and won election without opposition in November. In the national election, Daniel joined Gov. ALLAN SHIVERS in supporting DWIGHT D. EISENHOWER for the presidency.

In the Senate, Daniel emerged as a moderate conservative who opposed government expansion and control of the economy except in agriculture. He voted against the Saint Lawrence Seaway Project in 1954 and the administration's highway bill in 1956. Daniel supported the Bricker amendment in 1954, which would have limited the president's treaty-making powers. The senator backed Eisenhower's proposal to deregulate the price of natural gas and voted against congressional salary increases in 1955.

A states' rights advocate and supporter of segregation, Daniel opposed the Supreme Court's decision in *Brown v. Board of Education* (1954), which struck down segregation in public schools, but he refused to take an extreme stand on the issue. He was instrumental in rewriting and moderating the "Southern Manifesto" of 1956. Early drafts of the document, as originally conceived by Sen. STROM THURMOND (D-S.C.), contained passages branding the ruling unconstitutional and approving interposition—the use of state power to nullify the decision. Several legislators refused to accept these drafts, and a committee was formed to modify it. The five-member panel, which included Thurmond, Senators RICHARD RUSSELL (D-Ga.), JOHN STENNIS (D-Miss.), WILLIAM FULBRIGHT (D-Ark.), and Daniel, drew up a far less dramatic document than the original. It denounced "the unwarranted decision of the Supreme Court" as a substitution of "naked power for established law" and backed the states "which have declared their intention to resist forced integration by any lawful means."

Daniel emerged as one of the leaders of the centrist wing of the Texas Democratic Party. Although conservative, this group refused to follow Gov. Allan Shivers's call to split the state Democrats from the national party. Daniel supported ADLAI STEVENSON for president in 1956 and, in September, joined centrists at the state convention in blocking both "Shivercrats" and liberals from positions of power. That year, he ran for governor. After narrowly winning a runoff in the Democratic primary against a liberal opponent, Ralph Yarborough, Daniel won election in November.

During his tenure, Daniel attempted to maintain his moderate stand on segregation. Texas refused to comply with the desegregation decision but also opposed joining the interposition crusade. In late 1956, a committee Shivers appointed to study segregation submitted a hard-line report, including proposals for the state to return to a completely segregated school system. The panel also recommended a pupil placement bill, an interposition resolution, and a referendum prohibiting desegregation unless 20 percent of the voters petitioned for it and a majority approved it. Daniel was not enthusiastic about the report, but legislative pressure and majority support for a return to white supremacy eventually forced him to support portions of it. When the legislature passed the pupil assignment and referendum bills in 1957, Daniel signed both. Four interposition resolutions remained stalled in the legislature. The two laws stemmed the progress of desegregation, which until that time had proceeded more rapidly in Texas than in any other southern state.

Daniel won reelection in 1958 and 1960. In 1962, John Connally defeated Daniel in the Democratic primary. Price Daniel retired from government in 1962 and resumed his private law practice. In 1967, LYNDON B. JOHNSON appointed Daniel to be director of the Office of Emergency Preparedness and assistant to the president for Federal-State Relations. Daniel also served on the National Security Council under Johnson and later served eight years on the Texas Supreme Court, after which he returned to the practice of law. He died in Liberty on August 25, 1988.

—MJS

Davies, John Paton, Jr.
(1908–1999) *Foreign Service officer*

The son of Baptist missionaries, Davies was born in Leshan (Kiating), China, on April 6, 1908. He spent his early years in China and studied at the University of Wisconsin and Yenching University before receiving his degree from Columbia in 1931. He then entered the Foreign Service. Davies served as a consul in a number of Chinese cities and, during the late-1930s and early-1940s, was adviser to Col. Joseph Stilwell.

As one of the highest ranking Foreign Service officials in China, Davies issued frequent reports and policy recommendations on the Chinese civil war. He described Chiang kai-shek's (Jiang Jieshi's) corruption and decadence and predicted that, because of his refusal to reform, the Communists would defeat him. Davies rejected the recommendations of Roosevelt's representative, Gen. Patrick Hurley, that the United States give unqualified support to the Nationalists. Davies believed that Hurley's statements weakened the American position. He recommended that the United States ignore ideology and deal with the Communists, not only because it would prevent the formation of a Sino-Soviet bloc but also because the United States would eventually have no other choice.

In 1945, Davies was appointed first secretary of the embassy in Moscow; from 1947 to 1951, he was a member of the State Department's policy planning staff. He then served with the U.S. High Com-

mission in Germany and was director of political affairs at the U.S. mission from 1951 to 1953. In 1953–54, he was a counselor and chargé d'affaires in Lima, Peru.

During the late-1940s and early-1950s, Sen. JOSEPH R. MCCARTHY (R-Wis.) frequently attacked Davies because of his views on foreign policy. The senator from Wisconsin denounced him as a pro-communist and charged him with the responsibility for "losing China." As a result of these and subsequent charges, Davies underwent eight security investigations from 1948 to 1953. He was cleared in each case.

In 1953, McCarthy resumed his attacks on Davies. In response, Secretary of State JOHN FOSTER DULLES suspended the diplomat and ordered a special security board to review his case. At the hearing, Gen. Hurley testified that Davies was one of the men who had sabotaged a Nationalist Chinese victory. The board recommended Davies's removal in August.

Four months later, Dulles dismissed Davies on the grounds that he lacked "judgment, discretion and reliability." Dulles stated that neither he nor the board had found Davies disloyal but that, under Eisenhower's security orders, "complete and unswerving loyalty was not enough. He must be reliable, trustworthy, of good character and conduct."

The secretary said that the board had recommended Davies's ouster because "his observation and evaluation of the facts [in reporting to superiors], his policy recommendations, his attitude with respect to existing policy and his disregard of proper forbearance and caution in making known his dissents . . . were not in accordance with the standard required of Foreign Service officers." Dulles later let it be known that he would furnish Davies a character reference if needed.

Following the dismissal, Davies and his family remained in Lima, where he opened a furniture business. In 1964, Davies returned to Washington and requested a review of his case. His name was cleared by the Johnson administration in November 1968.

Davies's dismissal was one of a series that purged many China experts from the State Department, including Oliver Edmund Clubb, JOHN CARTER VINCENT, and JOHN STEWART SERVICE.

Critics such as GEORGE KENNAN charged that the firings had a long-range detrimental effect on the department. In his opinion, they dissuaded talented individuals from entering the State Department because of the threat of dismissal at any time for disloyalty. Those men and women who remained became more cautious. Some observers would later attribute American problems in Southeast Asia, at least in part, to the dismissal of the "old China hands."

Upon Davies's return to Washington, he published *Foreign and Other Affairs* (1964), a book on the United States involvement in Vietnam. He also published *Dragon by the Tail: American, British, Japanese, and Russian Encounters with China and One Another* (1972). Davies lived in Spain in the 1970s and wrote newspaper articles and lectured. He died at his home in Asheville, N.C., on December 23, 1999.

—JD

Davis, Jimmie H(ouston)

(1904–2000) *governor of Louisiana*

The son of a poor sharecropper, Jimmie Davis was born in Jackson Parish, La., on September 11, 1904. He worked his way through college and graduate school singing and composing country-western music. After earning a B.A. from Louisiana College and an M.A. from Louisiana State University, he taught history at Dodd College. Davis entered politics in his home city of Shreveport, La., and made his way up the political ladder by winning friends and generating good will. He almost never took a determined stand on issues, preferring, as he put it, to "live and let live." In 1938, he won the race for safety commissioner, after a campaign in which he said nothing against his opponent but sang songs that he had composed. He was elected the Democratic governor of Louisiana in 1944. Again he did not run on issues, but rather he sang his compositions during the campaign. By the time of his campaign, they included such national hits as "You Are My Sunshine," "Bed Bug Blues," "Bear Cat Poppa," "High Powered Mama" and "Get Yourself a Car."

Davis accomplished little as governor. He preferred to put decisions off as long as possible. When forced to make a decision, he would often leave the state for long periods of time, occasionally going to Hollywood to work in movies. Louisiana law prohibited the governor from succeeding himself, and after his term expired, he resumed his singing career.

Davis tried to make a political comeback in the Democratic gubernatorial primary of December 1959. His leading opponent, deLESSEPS MORRISON, ran on his record as an efficient mayor of New Orleans. In contrast, Davis once again sang songs and campaigned on platitudes. Another candidate, State Sen. Willie Rainach, ran on a pro-segregationist platform. Morrison won the primary but was forced to face Davis in a runoff in January 1960. With Rainach out of the race, Davis attempted to appeal to the pro-segregationist vote. He charged Morrison with being soft on integration and labeled him an "NAACP candidate." Davis also took advantage of Morrison's sophisticated appearance to win the state's rural vote. He once said that Morrison "looks right taking Zsa Zsa Gabor to tea [but] looks all wrong to those Rednecks up in hill country." Davis won the runoff and went on to win the election.

In May 1960, a federal judge, J. SKELLY WRIGHT, ended years of delay by ordering New Orleans to desegregate its schools at the beginning of the fall term. The following month, the New Orleans School Board asked the governor to "interpose state sovereignty" between the judiciary and the school system to prevent integration. At first Davis refused, but as a result of pressure from staunch segregationists, he took action. Terming the order an unwarranted intrusion of the federal government in intrastate affairs, Davis pledged to resist the order, even at the risk of going to jail. He then worked with the legislature to pass a series of anti-integration laws. These included bills barring the use of state funds for integrated schools, permitting the governor to close integrated schools, and allowing the governor to close schools to prevent violence.

On August 17, Davis assumed administration of New Orleans schools and appointed his own superintendent. Ten days later, the federal court issued a temporary restraining order blocking Davis's action. It also struck down the segregation laws. This act strengthened the moderate faction on the New Orleans School Board, which acknowledged the inevitability of integration and was willing to accept gradual and limited desegregation. Judge Wright then granted this group their request to postpone desegregation until November. On November 4, four black students entered previously all-white schools amid jeering mobs. Four days later, the state legislature once again gave Gov. Davis the right to close the schools. However, Judge Wright struck down the law. By the spring of 1961, the resistance had broken down, as the schools resumed normal operations. Davis continued to back segregation, calling it "the most noble cause that had ever arisen during the lifetime of any man living in the world to date.

After Davis left office, he resumed his singing and business career. He tried a political comeback in November 1971, running for governor in the crowded Louisiana primary, but he did poorly in the race. He died on November 5, 2000, in Baton Rouge, La.

—JB

Davis, John (William)
(1873–1955) *attorney*

Born in Clarksburg, W.Va., on April 13, 1873, Davis attended private schools. He received a B.A. from Washington and Lee University in 1892. After graduating, he taught school and apprenticed in his father's law office before returning to Washington and Lee to earn a law degree in 1895. Following admission to the bar, he entered practice with his father in Clarksburg. Davis served a term in the West Virginia House of Delegates in 1899 and ran successfully as a Democrat for the U.S. House of Representatives in 1910. President Woodrow Wilson appointed him solicitor general in 1913. During the next five years, Davis frequently defended progressive legislation before the Supreme Court, earning a reputation as one of America's greatest solicitors general. In 1918, he was named ambassador to Great Britain and served as an adviser to Wilson at Versailles.

Davis became head of the Wall Street firm of Stetson, Jennings and Russell in 1921. The firm became known as Stetson, Jennings, Russell & Davis, then Davis, Polk, Wardwell, Gardiner & Reed, still later Davis, Polk, Wardwell, Sunderland & Kiendl, and finally Davis, Polk & Wardwell.

Over the next few decades, he achieved prominence as a corporation counsel who argued against the expansion of government power into the commercial sector. From 1922 to 1924, he served as president of the American Bar Association. In 1924, the deadlocked Democratic National Convention made Davis its presidential nominee on the 103rd ballot. He was badly defeated by Calvin Coolidge in November, winning only 136 electoral votes, all from the South.

Although he supported Franklin D. Roosevelt in 1932, Davis soon became disenchanted with the expansion of federal power under the New Deal and helped organize the anti–New Deal Liberty League in 1934. As a member of the Lawyers Vigilance Committee, he argued against the constitutionality of much New Deal legislation in the higher courts.

Davis believed deeply in states' rights and the strict construction of the Constitution. He was also a strong civil libertarian. During the 1940s and 1950s, he argued many important cases in the interest of his conservative principles. He battled for the rights of conscientious objectors during World War II and supported Alger Hiss in the postwar period. In 1952, he successfully argued before the Supreme Court against the constitutionality of President Truman's seizure of the steel mills (*Youngstown Sheet & Tube Co. v. Sawyer,* 1952).

During 1952–53, Davis defended South Carolina's school segregation in one of the cases known collectively as *Brown v. Board of Education.* He rejected THURGOOD MARSHALL's premise that the Fourteenth Amendment had outlawed segregation and that separate schools were not equal because they produced a sense of inferiority in black children. Davis maintained that the framers of the amendment had never intended it to be used to support integrated public schools. The same Congress that passed the Fourteenth Amendment, he pointed out, appropriated funds for segregated public schools in Washington, D.C. Davis maintained that if segregation were to be outlawed, it had to be done either by an act of Congress or by amending the Constitution. To undo state laws by judicial fiat, Davis insisted, would destroy the separation of powers established by the Constitution and would be an unconstitutional intrusion by the federal government into the affairs of the states.

Davis then challenged Marshall's contention that segregation produced feelings of inferiority in black children. He raised the question of whether having "three white children with 27 blacks would prevent the psychological distress segregation was charged with doing." Concluding, the elderly lawyer said that South Carolina "is convinced that the happiness, the progress, and the welfare of these children is best promoted in segregated schools." In May 1954, the Supreme Court unanimously ruled that segregated schools were unconstitutional. Davis remarked that the decision was "unworthy of the Supreme Court" and predicted that turmoil would result in the South following the decision.

In 1954, Davis defended J. ROBERT OPPENHEIMER against charges that he was a security risk. When the Atomic Energy Commission review board refused to clear Oppenheimer, Davis called the ruling not simply "unjust" but "silly."

During the course of his long legal career, Davis appeared before the Supreme Court more than any other 20th-century lawyer. Legal experts commonly ranked him as one of the finest advocates of the era. Davis died in Charleston, S.C., on March 24, 1955.

—MSM

Dawson, William L(evi)

(1886–1970) *U.S. congressman; chairman, Government Operations Committee; chairman, Committee on Executive Expenditures*

Dawson was born in Albany, Ga., on April 26, 1886. After graduating magna cum laude from Fisk University in 1909, he attended Kent College and Northwestern University law school. Following service in the army during World War I, he began practicing law in Chicago. In 1928, Dawson ran unsuccessfully as a Republican candidate for the U.S. House of Representatives. From 1933 to 1939, he served as alderman from Chicago's South Side. He became a Democrat in 1939, in part because his largely black constituency had switched its allegiance to the party of Franklin D. Roosevelt.

Dawson used his position to build a political machine that controlled politics in the black ghetto. In 1942, he defied the wishes of Chicago's Democratic mayor, Edward Kelly, who had aided

his political career, and ran for a seat in Congress. Using his ward position, Dawson won the race and continued to win election from the first congressional district until the time of his death. In Chicago's black ghetto, Dawson was the man to see for patronage jobs; he chose or appointed the aldermen of six wards.

Dawson could often determine the fate of white as well as black office holders. Angered by alleged police brutality and attempts to arrest petty gamblers, he determined to oppose Mayor Martin Kennelly's reelection in 1953. However, because he could find no alternative candidate, he did not openly break with the mayor. In 1955, he threw his support to RICHARD J. DALEY. With Dawson's support, Daley defeated Kennelly in the primary and went on to win the general election. In three of Dawson's pocket wards, Daley won by an almost 4 to 1 margin, and in the black 24th ward, he won by 18 to 1. Dawson's support proved to be a crucial element in Daley's victory.

In Congress, Dawson was a strong supporter of New and Fair Deal legislation and during the 1940s worked to outlaw the poll tax and segregation in the armed forces. During the 1950s, however, he became increasingly alienated from the emerging Civil Rights movement. He provided only lukewarm backing for civil rights legislation and refused to actively support an antilynching bill. In 1956, Dawson opposed an amendment by Rep. ADAM CLAYTON POWELL, JR. (D-N.Y.), to an aid-to-education bill denying federal funds to segregated schools. The congressman believed that the amendment would kill the proposal, a prediction confirmed when the measure went down to defeat in July.

Dawson's apathy toward civil rights measures earned him the anger of the president of the local branch of the NAACP, Willoughby Abner, who called him "soft" on civil rights. In reaction, Dawson used his patronage power to gain control of the NAACP chapter. In 1957, his handpicked candidate, Theodore Jones, took the presidency from Abner in an election dominated by the new "Dawson members."

During the Kennedy and Johnson years, Dawson joined other Northern urban Democrats in support of the administrations' social welfare legislation. Throughout the decade, young blacks, dissatisfied with Dawson's civil rights stand, attempted to unseat him, but he defeated all primary challengers by margins of at least two to one. He remained unbeaten until his death in Chicago, on November 9, 1970.

—AES

Dean, Arthur H(obson)

(1898–1987) *State Department negotiator*

Born in Ithaca, N.Y., on October 16, 1898, Dean worked his way through Cornell University and, following service in the Army during World War I, received his law degree there in 1923. That same year, he joined the law firm of Sullivan and Cromwell, in which JOHN FOSTER DULLES was a senior partner. Dean worked on cases involving American and British banking interests and became a partner in 1930. During World War II, Dean served as a coast guard instructor in navigation and piloting. After the war, Dean returned to Sullivan and Cromwell and became head of the firm in 1949, when Dulles resigned to become a U.S. senator. Dean was a member of the Institute of Pacific Relations in the early 1950s but resigned in 1952 after a Senate subcommittee report said that the effect of the institute's activities on public opinion had "served communist interests."

At the behest of Secretary of State Dulles, Dean went to Korea in October 1953 as chief allied negotiator in the peace talks with the North Koreans and the Chinese Communists. Dean opposed North Korean and Chinese suggestions that nations not involved in the war, including the USSR, be represented. Reiterating the UN's resolution of August 1953, he stressed that the peace conference should be attended only by the countries participating in the fighting. In December 1953, the Communist Chinese delegate accused the United States of perfidy in allowing South Korea to "release" 21,000 noncommunist North Korean and Communist Chinese prisoners of war into UN custody instead of sending them home. In responses to the charge, Dean temporarily suspended negotiations.

In January 1954, after Dean was reported to have told the *Providence Journal* that the United States should recognize the People's Republic of China, Sen. HERMAN WELKER (R-Ida.) accused Dean of supporting "appeasement" and of collaboration with Communist China. He also assailed Dean as the former "official spokesman" of the Institute of Pacific Relations. In March, Dulles asked Dean to resign from the Korean negotiations. However, the secretary still asked him to go to South Korea and review the political situation with President Syngman Rhee a week before the negotiations opened in Geneva in April 1954.

Dean returned to the full-time practice of law in 1954. He continued to recommend recognition of Communist China during the Quemoy-Matsu crisis of 1955. In an article in *Foreign Affairs*, he maintained that recognition would improve the United States' international position. Dean recommended consideration of Great Britain's two-China idea, which would recognize Communist rule on the mainland and Nationalist rule on Taiwan.

During the spring of 1958, Dean represented the United States in Geneva at the 87-nation Conference on the Law of the Sea. Upholding the traditional U.S. position, he initially called for a three-mile limit on national claims to the coastal sea. This stand was opposed by the USSR, Iceland, and several South American nations, which favored at least a 12-mile limit. In an attempt to break the deadlock, on April 15 Dean proposed that territorial limits be extended to six miles. He also asked for the establishment of an additional six-mile zone from which all foreign fishermen could be excluded except those who had fished the area regularly for 10 years preceding the signing of a new sea law convention. The proposal was voted down on April 28, and Dean gave formal notice that the United States would continue to observe the three-mile limit.

During the Kennedy administration, Dean represented the United States at the Geneva talks on ending nuclear weapons tests and advised the president on disarmament. He also served as a delegate to the UN General Assembly in the 1960s. In 1968, he became a member of the Senior Advisory Group on Vietnam, convened to consider the military's request for over 200,000 more troops for Vietnam. The panel recommended rejection of the request and the de-escalation of the war. Dean died in Glen Cove, N.Y., on November 30, 1987.

—RSG

DeLoach, Deke (Cartha) (Dekle)

(1920–   ) *FBI official*

Born into a poor family in Claxton, Ga., on July 20, 1920, DeLoach worked his way through Stetson University, from which he graduated in 1942. He joined the FBI and worked as an agent carrying out investigations of Communist Party members in Norfolk, Toledo, and Akron, Ohio. Dissatisfied with the work, he left the agency in 1944 to join the navy. Following the war, he returned to the bureau.

Assigned to FBI headquarters, DeLoach carried out security checks of potential employees in atomic energy projects. Later, he served as liaison between the FBI and various U.S. intelligence agencies. In 1951, DeLoach attended an international conference on intelligence matters and wrote a report on the meeting for Director J. EDGAR HOOVER. Hoover was impressed by the young man, and the two quickly became close friends. Hoover quickly promoted DeLoach to inspector and gave the young man sensitive special assignments, mainly disciplining agents who failed to comply with the bureau's strict code of personal behavior. He disciplined agents for major offenses such as trying to persuade communists to become FBI informers and allowing these overtures to be leaked. On other occasions, DeLoach punished agents for sexual infidelity.

In 1953, DeLoach became a special assistant in the office of Clyde Tolson, Hoover's right-hand man. That year, Hoover asked DeLoach to join the American Legion and guide the group's anticommunist crusade. Hoover did not object to the spirit of the legion's campaign. However, he opposed the legion's demands to investigate specific groups and individuals, preferring to choose the bureau's targets himself. He resented amateur attempts to compete with his organization. DeLoach took his task seriously and, using his FBI credentials, became a post commander, department commander, vice commander, and eventually national vice commander. At one point, he thought of running for national commander, but Hoover vetoed the proposal as "too political." DeLoach became chairman of the organization's public relations committee in 1958. There he exercised great influence over the organization's internal policy as well as public relations. The American Legion was a strong source of support for Hoover, and over the next 20 years, it often mobilized its forces to defend the director's controversial actions.

In 1959, DeLoach became assistant director of the crime records division which, despite its title, was responsible for public and congressional relations. He became one of the bureau's leading speakers, articulating a hard-hitting conservative view of the communist threat and the FBI's role in combating it. The personable DeLoach maintained a close relationship with key members of Congress and worked with them to further the interests of the bureau. DeLoach also improved relations with the press. Toward that end, he used his access to the FBI's massive files containing personal information on members of Congress. He often leaked information on individual congressmen to favorite reporters.

Upon the assassination of JOHN F. KENNEDY, DeLoach was appointed liaison to the White House. In December 1965, DeLoach became assistant to the director and assumed charge of all the bureau's investigative activities. He developed a close relationship with President LYNDON B. JOHNSON, who often preferred to communicate with DeLoach rather than Hoover. DeLoach had hoped to succeed Hoover as director. When it became apparent that Hoover was unwilling to retire, DeLoach accepted a lucrative offer to become an executive with Pepsico, Inc. He left the bureau in June 1970. In 1995, he published *Hoover's FBI: The Inside Story by Hoover's Trusted Lieutenant*.

—JB

DeSapio, Carmine G(erald)

(1908–2004) *chairman, New York County Democratic Committee*

The son of an Italian immigrant, DeSapio was born on New York City's Lower West Side on December 10, 1908. He attended local parochial schools and studied law at Fordham University. However, he was forced to give up his studies because of an attack of rheumatic fever. The illness resulted in an eye inflammation that required him to wear the tinted glasses that became his trademark. While still attending high school, DeSapio became interested in politics and joined the local Democratic club. A loyal member of New York's Tammany Hall, he worked his way up in the Democratic machine until he won a seat on its executive committee in 1943. He was elected to the citywide Board of Elections in 1946 and the following year was part of the four-man group that took over effective leadership of Tammany Hall. In 1949, he became the first Italian-American leader of Tammany Hall.

During the next five years, DeSapio expanded his control throughout New York City's five boroughs and amassed great power in the state. In 1953, he broke with Mayor Vincent Impellitteri over questions of patronage and charges that the mayor had been connected with organized crime. He instead backed ROBERT F. WAGNER, JR., for the Democratic mayoral nomination. The son of a popular liberal senator, Wagner was a favorite of New York liberals. With DeSapio's help, Wagner defeated Impellitteri in the primary and went on to win the general election.

During the 1950s, DeSapio sought to make Tammany Hall a force for liberalism while at the same time continuing to function as a political machine. He championed housing reform and health care legislation. Indebted to DeSapio for his election, Wagner turned patronage over to him. Under DeSapio's guidance, city appointments and elected offices were opened to minorities, and many qualified individuals were appointed to city positions. He democratized the organization's process of electing local political leaders and sought to sever Tammany's ties with organized crime. Unlike many traditional bosses, DeSapio relished public exposure and acclaim. He lectured in colleges, published articles, consented to be interviewed by the media, and enjoyed mingling openly with the powerful.

In 1954, DeSapio supported W. AVERELL HARRIMAN for governor of New York. The former ambassador was opposed by such Democrats as THOMAS FINLETTER and ELEANOR ROOSEVELT, who favored the nomination of Franklin D. Roosevelt, Jr. Using his control of the New York State Democratic Party, DeSapio pushed the nomination through the Democratic convention. With Harriman's victory at the polls, DeSapio emerged as the most powerful Democratic Party leader in the state. To add to DeSapio's prestige and power, Harriman appointed him secretary of

state and consulted him on patronage and other political matters. In addition, DeSapio served as an unofficial lobbyist for New York City in Albany and Washington.

Ironically, Harriman's victory over Roosevelt contributed to the decline of DeSapio's power. Eleanor Roosevelt held him responsible for her son's defeat and became increasingly hostile to DeSapio throughout the 1950s. She joined HERBERT LEHMAN and Thomas Finletter to found the New York Committee for Democratic Voters, a group formed to wrest power from DeSapio and Tammany Hall. DeSapio also contributed to his own political downfall. In July 1957, he unwittingly left an envelope containing $11,200 in large bills in a taxi. Although he denied the money was his, the cab driver publicly identified him as the source. Wagner's personal triumph in the election of 1957 released the mayor from obligations to his former sponsor, and the two men became rivals. At the same time, reform stirrings in his own district eroded DeSapio's power at its source. Most importantly, the gubernatorial and senatorial elections proved disastrous for DeSapio. Over the objections of reformers, DeSapio pushed the nomination of FRANK HOGAN for the Senate through the state convention. When Hogan and Harriman were defeated in the November election., DeSapio lost his upstate power base. His dictatorial conduct at the convention served as a catalyst for New York City reformers to organize to unseat DeSapio's supporters from elected positions.

In 1961, Wagner broke openly with DeSapio and accepted the support of the reform movement for his bid for reelection. Running on the issue of bossism, Wagner defeated DeSapio's candidate, Arthur Levitt, in the Democratic primary. DeSapio himself was defeated for his district leadership. Because only district leaders were eligible to serve as county leaders, DeSapio lost all his state and local posts. He attempted political comebacks in 1964 and 1965 but failed in both cases. In 1969, a federal jury convicted DeSapio of having conspired to induce a public official to misuse his office in return for a bribe. After serving a 17-month sentence, he was released in December 1972. DeSapio died in Manhattan on July 27, 2004.

—JB

Dewey, Thomas E(dmund)

(1902–1971) *governor of New York, presidential candidate*

Thomas E. Dewey was born on March 24, 1902, in Owosso, Mich., where his father was editor of the local Republican newspaper. Dewey earned a B.A. at the University of Michigan in 1923 and an LL.B. from Columbia Law School in 1925. His decision to embark on a legal career came only after seriously contemplating a career in opera. After graduating from law school, he entered private practice with Larkin, Rathbone & Perry, a Wall Street firm. In 1927 he went to work for McNamara & Seymour. In the late 1920s, he became active in Republican politics, associating himself with the "reform" element that battled the Tammany Hall Democratic machine. During this period, he met HERBERT BROWNELL, another lawyer with similar political leanings. Brownell would become Dewey's closest adviser and manager of Dewey's successful campaigns for governor and his unsuccessful campaigns for the presidency. In 1931, Dewey took a position as chief assistant U.S. attorney for the southern district of New York and served as acting U.S. attorney for the southern district of New York for five weeks in 1933, after which he returned to private practice. While in the U.S. attorney's office, Dewey played an important role in prosecuting organized-crime figures and corrupt politicians. In 1935, Gov. HERBERT H. LEHMAN named him special prosecutor to investigate racketeering and vice in New York. His activities as a "racket-busting" prosecutor made him a national hero and helped him launch a career in politics.

In 1937, running on Fiorello La Guardia's Fusion ticket, Dewey won election as district attorney for New York County. The next year, he challenged Lehman for the governorship and narrowly lost. His strong showing made him a serious contender, despite his youth, for the Republican presidential nomination in 1940. The outbreak of World War II in Europe, however, changed the dynamic of the presidential election. The Republicans chose Wendell L. Wilkie, an internationalist, over Dewey, who lacked experience in foreign policy, and Sen. ROBERT A. TAFT of Ohio, an isolationist. In 1942, Dewey won the Republican gubernatorial nomination, swept to victory in the general election, and became the first Republican governor of New York in 20 years. He easily won reelection in 1946 and 1950.

As governor, Dewey proved to be an efficient administrator, and, while no New Deal liberal, he believed that government could play a constructive role in promoting the public interest. Dewey oversaw a needed reapportionment of congressional and legislative districts, liberalized the state unemployment insurance law, undertook an ambitious expansion of public housing and highway programs, established a state university system, and introduced public health programs. A forceful and consistent proponent of civil rights for African Americans, Dewey sponsored the first state commission to end religious and racial discrimination in employment practices and was a major force behind passage of landmark civil rights legislation enacted by the state legislature in 1945. A fiscal conservative, Dewey maintained a balanced budget, even as he expanded social programs and the state's infrastructure.

Ably assisted by Brownell and others, Dewey built a national political organization. He became the leader of the Eastern, or internationalist, wing of the Republican party, which drew its support primarily from the Northeast and the West Coast. Dewey maintained that his progressive but fiscally conservative approach offered a viable alternative to the New Deal. Eastern Republicans vied for control of the party with the Midwestern, conservative, isolationist wing led by Taft. In the contest for the Republican nomination in 1944, Dewey brushed aside Wilkie in the Wisconsin primary and overcame JOHN BRICKER, a conservative senator from Ohio, at the convention. In an effort to placate conservatives, Dewey chose Bricker as his running mate. Initially, Dewey took the high road during the campaign. He proposed to remove not only the war but foreign policy from the partisanship of a campaign. Attacks by Roosevelt and his supporters, however, led Dewey to respond in kind. On November 8, Roosevelt won 36 of 48 states and garnered 342 electoral votes to Dewey's 99. In the popular vote, however, Dewey's 44.8 percent (against Roosevelt's 52.8 percent) represented the best showing by a Republican since the 1920s.

Dewey's respectable showing against Roosevelt made him a leading contender for the nomination in

1948. He consistently led Gallup polls of Republican voters, and Democratic strategists expected him to be the Republican nominee. Dewey strengthened his identification with the Eastern, internationalist wing of the party by supporting the Truman Doctrine and the Marshall Plan in 1947. The conservative wing of the party had always regarded Dewey warily. His support of the Truman administration's approach to the cold war reinforced their suspicions. On other matters of foreign policy, though, Dewey took positions closer to those of the Midwestern conservatives. In 1947 and 1948, he repeatedly called for more U.S. aid to Nationalist China and for greater attention to Asia generally.

In spite of Dewey's prominence, the road to the nomination in 1948 was not easy. HAROLD E. STASSEN upset Dewey in the Wisconsin and Nebraska primaries. Trapped by a pledge not to campaign while the New York legislature remained in session, Dewey made only brief appearances right before the primaries in those states. In contrast, Stassen campaigned tirelessly. In the Oregon primary that May, Dewey matched Stassen's efforts and performed well in a radio debate on the issue of outlawing the American Communist Party. He criticized the ban, which Stassen supported, as antithetical to a democratic society. Dewey won the primary and ended Stassen's hopes for the nomination, but he still faced a serious challenge from Taft. At the Republican National Convention in June, Stassen refused to throw his delegates to Taft, and Taft declined to withdraw in favor of a compromise candidate, Sen. ARTHUR H. VANDENBERG (R-Mich.). Division among his opponents and a strong showing on the first two ballots enabled Dewey to capture the nomination on the third ballot. He chose EARL WARREN, the popular governor of California, as his running mate.

Experts nearly unanimously predicted Dewey's election. Republicans had won both houses of Congress in 1946, and Truman's approval ratings remained low. Further, the Democrats were divided. Henry A. Wallace, whom Truman had fired from the cabinet after he split with the president over the cold war, was running on a third-party ticket. Truman's problems compounded when, despite the efforts of his managers, liberals succeeded in inserting a strong civil rights plank into the Democratic

platform at the convention. In response, southern delegates walked out and later formed a third party, the States' Rights Party, which nominated STROM THURMOND (D-S.C.).

In spite of the apparent strength of his position, Dewey had problems, too. Like their opponents, the Republicans were divided. In private, Dewey disapproved of the 80th Congress, led by Midwestern Republicans and relentlessly attacked by Truman, but he could ill afford to alienate such a substantial element of his party. Further, Truman called the Republican-controlled Congress into special session and effectively dared it to pass the progressive Republican party platform. Despite pleas from Dewey and Brownell, Congress refused to do so. Truman traveled all over the country denouncing the "do-nothing" 80th Congress. Foreign policy presented Dewey with another predicament. After the beginning of the Berlin airlift, Dewey consulted with Vandenberg and JOHN FOSTER DULLES and decided to avoid discussing foreign policy. Instead, the Republican nominee promoted national unity in a time of rising tensions with the Soviet Union.

Having taken foreign policy off the table and needing to tread carefully on domestic issues, Dewey found it hard to establish a base from which to attack Truman effectively. True to his meticulous personality, his campaign appearances ran like clockwork; cartoonists likened him to an adding machine. Although a skilled orator, he rarely appealed to emotions. He never attacked Truman by name and resisted suggestions that he emphasize the issue of domestic subversion. Most important, Dewey, as critics observed, campaigned like the incumbent. He did not begin campaigning until Labor Day. Even then, Truman gave twice as many speeches as his Republican opponent. Finally, Dewey held to an older notion of dignified statesmanship. Although he could display warmth and humor in private, he came across in public as formal, prim, and stiff. Alice Roosevelt Longworth quipped that Dewey looked like the groom on a wedding cake.

By mid-October Truman began to edge up in the Gallup polls. On October 25, Truman blasted Thurmond's Dixiecrats as "crackpots" and Wallace's supporters as part of a "contemptible communist minority." The president also compared Dewey and the Republicans to the fascists of the 1930s in Germany and Italy. Dewey's instinct was to respond, but his aides persuaded him not to change tactics and aggressively attack Truman. On November 2, voters reelected Truman with 49 percent to Dewey's 45 percent.

Between 1949 and 1952, Dewey continued to exert a powerful influence within the Republican party. He persisted in supporting the basic approach of the Truman administration to the cold war. Specifically, he backed the North Atlantic Treaty Organization and the U.S. intervention in Korea. When Taft emerged as the front-runner for the nomination in 1952, Dewey, who believed that Taft's unilateralist foreign policy would be disastrous for the party and the country, was instrumental in persuading Gen. DWIGHT D. EISENHOWER to run. Dewey lent key advisers, including Herbert Brownell, to the Draft Eisenhower Committee. Ultimately, Dewey and his advisers played a key role in denying the nomination to Taft and gaining it for Eisenhower. In the process, Dewey earned the undying hatred of Taft's supporters. Partly as a concession to the Taft wing, Dewey also played a significant role in securing the vice presidential nomination for Sen. RICHARD M. NIXON (R-Calif.). Once the story of Nixon's "slush fund" broke, Dewey urged Nixon to make a televised speech responding to the charges. Nixon delivered his famous "Checkers" speech, and effectively rebutted charges of corruption. Eisenhower decided to keep Nixon and easily defeated ADLAI STEVENSON in November.

Dewey chose not run for a fourth term as governor in 1952, and declined to serve in the Eisenhower administration. Instead, he returned to the private practice of law with the firm of Dewey, Ballantine, Bushby, Palmer & Wood. He remained active in the Republican party and served as an occasional adviser to President Eisenhower. Moreover, many of his former aides and advisers, including Dulles, Brownell, LEONARD HALL, WILLIAM ROGERS, GABRIEL HAUGE, Lawrence Walsh, and JAMES HAGERTY, held prominent positions in the Eisenhower administration. Dewey addressed the Republican National Conventions in 1956, 1960, 1964, and 1968. He also served on the Republican Coordinating Committee between 1965 and 1968. After Nixon won election to the presidency, he

offered Dewey an appointment as secretary of state or chief justice. Dewey declined. He died of a heart attack in Bal Harbour, Fla., on March 15, 1971.

—MSM

Dillon, C(larence) Douglas
(1909–2003) *ambassador to France, State Department officer*

Born in Geneva, Switzerland, on August 21, 1909, C. Douglas Dillon grew up amid affluence in New York City suburbs. He graduated from Groton School in 1927 and Harvard University (magna cum laude) in 1931. With help from his father, Dillon purchased a seat on the New York Stock Exchange in 1931. Seven years later, he became vice president of Dillon, Read and Co., the investment banking firm founded by his father. Dillon followed the firm's president, James V. Forrestal, into the Navy Department in 1940. During World War II, he saw action in the Pacific as a navy air operations officer. After the war, Dillon became board chairman of Dillon, Read. Under his guidance, the firm doubled its investment portfolio in six years.

A prominent Republican, Dillon worked with JOHN FOSTER DULLES in Gov. THOMAS DEWEY's 1948 presidential campaign. In December 1951, he initiated the "draft Eisenhower" movement in New Jersey and became a large financial contributor to the Republican presidential campaign in 1952.

President Eisenhower named Dillon ambassador to France in January 1953. Dillon frequently represented Secretary of State Dulles at the Geneva Conference on Indochina in 1954. He also assisted Special Ambassador DAVID BRUCE in attempting to persuade the French to accept European economic and military unity. Fearful of German rearmament and of sacrificing their sovereignty to a supranational army, the French rejected the European Defense Community in August 1954. At the end of the year, however, they agreed to a compromise solution: the admission of West Germany into the North Atlantic Treaty Organization under the aegis of the Western European Union.

In January 1957, Dillon became deputy undersecretary of state for economic affairs. During the course of that year, he was given supervisory authority over the entire U.S. foreign-aid program. In

Douglas Dillon, undersecretary of state *(Dwight D. Eisenhower Library and Museum)*

April, he was named alternate governor of the International Monetary Fund (IMF), and in December, he was appointed to the Development Loan Fund (DLF). Dillon was promoted to undersecretary of state for economic affairs in July 1958. His increased power reflected the Eisenhower administration's desire to devise a more ambitious and coherent foreign aid program. Vice President RICHARD M. NIXON, who was instrumental in choosing Dillon for the job of coordinating foreign aid, believed that Dillon could ably argue the case for increased expenditures before a skeptical Congress.

With his new authority, Dillon sought to revamp foreign-aid policy. The United States, he asserted, could no longer grant foreign aid on an emergency basis. In November 1957, he advocated a five-year extension of the Reciprocal Trade Agreements Act and more money for the DLF, especially for African and Asian nations. He also urged Congress to approve U.S. membership in the Organization for Trade Cooperation, an agency designed to administer the 38-nation General Agreement on Tariffs and Trade. Finally, he recommended more private investment and greater use of the Export-Import Bank to help underdeveloped nations.

Dillon's ambitious designs met with considerable success. In September 1957, the Inter-American Economic Conference called for a reduction of trade restrictions among member nations, increased efforts to stimulate investment capital, and intergovernmental cooperation on the problems of raw-material producers. Dillon encouraged the creation of regional common markets in Latin America, although he pointed out that the United States could not join because of conflicting agreements with other parts of the world. In August 1958, Dillon announced U.S. support of the Inter-American Development Institution, formed to provide development loans to Latin American countries.

In April 1959, Dillon became undersecretary of state, the second-ranking post in the State Department. He retained his authority over economic affairs and achieved two of his most notable successes in the last year of the Eisenhower administration. In September 1960, Dillon submitted a $500-million program to the Inter-American Economic Conference meeting in Bogotá, Colombia. Despite Cuban denunciations of the Act of Bogotá, all the other nations agreed to the proposal. The social development plan, a forerunner of President Kennedy's Alliance for Progress, was financed by the United States but administered by the Inter-American Development Bank. With its aims of modernizing Latin American economies, improving standards of living, and fostering land and tax reform, Dillon hoped that the plan could help democratize Latin America and thus make the rest of the hemisphere immune to communist revolution.

In December 1960, Dillon's persistent efforts to convince the Western Europeans to develop more ambitious foreign-aid programs led to the establishment of the Organization for Economic Cooperation and Development (OECD). Consisting of the United States, Canada, and 18 European nations, the OECD succeeded the Organization for European Economic Cooperation and marked the beginning of a coordinated foreign aid policy by the developed nations.

Although Dillon was a large contributor to Nixon's presidential campaign in 1960, President-elect Kennedy asked him to join his cabinet as secretary of the treasury. Dillon accepted Kennedy's offer and became the most important economic policy maker during the Kennedy administration. He continued at his post under the Johnson administration. Unable to achieve a rapport with Johnson, Dillon left the Treasury in March 1965 and returned to Dillon, Reed. In February 1967, he became president of the U.S. and Foreign Securities Corp.

After leaving Washington, Dillon's activities with the Metropolitan Museum of Art occupied most of his time. He served as president of the museum from 1970 to 1977 and chairman from 1977 to 1983. Even after stepping down as chairman, he continued his involvement with the museum. A passionate collector of 18th- and 19th-century French paintings, he donated his collection to the Metropolitan Museum. Dillon died in New York City on January 12, 2003.

—JCH

Dilworth, Richardson

(1898–1974) *mayor of Philadelphia*

Dilworth was born into a patrician family in Pittsburgh on August 29, 1898. After serving in the Marine Corps during World War I, he attended Yale, where he received his A.B. in 1921. Five years later, he earned his law degree from the same institution. Dilworth then began to practice law in Philadelphia. The colorful, outgoing trial lawyer also became involved in reform politics as a Democrat. Over the next 40 years, Dilworth opposed the entrenched Republican machine, which had dominated Philadelphia politics since the end of the 19th century.

In 1947, Dilworth ran for mayor on a platform denouncing municipal corruption. He lost to the Republican machine candidate, Mayor Bernard Samuels, by approximately 90,000 votes. Over the next two years, however, revelations of wholesale municipal corruption were uncovered, and in 1949 Dilworth was elected city treasurer. In 1951, he became district attorney at the same time that his political ally and friend, JOSEPH CLARK, became mayor. Dilworth and Clark received their support from a broad-based coalition of ethnic minority leaders, ideological liberals, and patrician Philadelphia families. Dilworth became mayor in 1956, when Clark went to the U.S. Senate.

During the 1950s, the two men ushered in what journalist Neal Peirce called "Philadelphia's modern Golden Age." Under the Clark and Dilworth administrations, Philadelphia reorganized its government and reformed its civil service. It began a reform of its transit system, encouraged industrial development, and undertook a large-scale public housing program.

The two men developed one of the largest urban-renewal projects in the nation. It was designed to rejuvenate the city's waterfront and rehabilitate the aging downtown area. Parks were created and the city's historic sites renovated. Dilworth often used public-interest corporations to coordinate and guide renewal efforts. These groups, independent of but close to municipal government, were composed not only of corporate and banking officials, but also of members of various interest groups. The businessmen on the board provided investors with confidence in the stability of projects, while the civic groups gave the efforts a broad political base.

Dilworth opposed segregation in private schools and defended the rights of organized labor. He endorsed federal aid for housing and in 1959 protested Eisenhower's veto of a $1.5-billion housing bill. The mayor also urged the development of a progressive national transportation policy. He recommended that commuter railroads be subsidized by low-interest loans; that rail taxation policies be coordinated among state, local, and federal governments; and that mass transit facilities be improved.

Dilworth resigned as mayor to run for governor in 1962. He lost to William Scranton but continued in public service as president of the Philadelphia Board of Education. Dilworth resigned from the school board in 1971. He died in Philadelphia of a brain tumor on January 23, 1974.

—SY

Dirksen, Everett McKinley

(1895–1969) *U.S. senator, Senate minority leader*

Born in Pekin, Ill., on January 4, 1895, Everett McKinley Dirksen grew up on his family's farm in central Illinois. After attending the University of Minnesota, he served in the army during World War I and received a battlefield commission. He returned to Pekin after the war and engaged in several business ventures. He won a seat on the city council in 1926. After running unsuccessfully in the Republican primary for a seat in the House of Representatives in 1930, he won a seat in the House in 1932, where he would serve until 1948. In Congress, Dirksen generally supported his party's Eastern internationalist wing. Dirksen found little fault in Roosevelt's conduct of foreign policy from 1933 to 1936. Beginning in 1937, however, he became increasingly critical of what he regarded as the president's interventionism. Then, in September 1941, he repudiated his isolationist position and threw his support behind Roosevelt. After World War II, Dirksen, an avid anticommunist, advocated American economic assistance to curtail Soviet influence. He played an important role in the passage of the first Marshall Plan appropriations in 1947. Because of problems with his health that threatened his eyesight, Dirksen did not run for reelection in 1948. In 1950, his health and eyesight restored, Dirksen defeated the heavily favored Democratic incumbent, Scott Lucas, in a race for the U.S. Senate.

A growing conviction that the Fair Deal was moving towards welfare statism and that government regulation was strangling economic freedom combined with increasing concerns over Truman's foreign policies and Dirksen's own anticommunism, to move the new senator's politics to the right.

Dirksen figured prominently in the battle for the Republican presidential nomination in 1952. A leading supporter of Sen. ROBERT A. TAFT (R-Ohio), he twice spoke for the Taft forces before the national convention, and he nominated Taft. Dirksen wanted the vice presidential spot and hoped that Taft would choose him as his running mate. From the rostrum, he rhetorically attacked the GOP's presidential nominee in 1944 and 1948, Gov. THOMAS E. DEWEY, who opposed Taft. Pointing to Dewey, seated before him, he cried, "We followed you before, and you took us down the path to defeat!" The convention fell into pandemonium. Despite Dirksen's histrionics, Dewey's candidate, DWIGHT D. EISENHOWER, won the nomination. The general did not seriously consider Dirksen for the

vice presidency, despite Taft's strong recommendation.

In the next three years, Eisenhower commanded only marginal loyalty from Dirksen, whose flannel-voiced orations and slippery positions on issues earned him the nickname "the Wizard of Ooze." During the campaign for the general election in 1952, Dirksen gave Eisenhower only lukewarm support. In the 83rd (1953–54) Congress, Taft, then majority leader, rewarded Dirksen with three important committee assignments: Appropriations, Judiciary, and Government Operations. Yet, neither Taft nor Eisenhower could count on Dirksen for crucial votes. In March 1953, he voted against the nomination of CHARLES E. BOHLEN to be ambassador to the Soviet Union, despite Taft's support for the appointment. The following month, Dirksen joined Taft in criticizing Eisenhower's first budget, because defense appropriations proved larger than hoped. Dirksen favored the Bricker amendment, which would have curbed the president's treaty-making powers. Long after Sen. JOHN W. BRICKER (R-Ohio) had all but abandoned the cause, Dirksen reintroduced the measure in early 1956. His initiative failed. In 1954, Dirksen reversed himself and supported Eisenhower's proposal for foreign aid and the Saint Lawrence Seaway.

Dirksen also opposed the Eisenhower administration during the Army-McCarthy hearings of 1954. From the time of his campaign for the Senate in 1950, Dirksen had been a vociferous proponent of Sen. JOSEPH R. McCARTHY's (R-Wis.) anticommunist investigations. Assigned to McCarthy's Permanent Investigations Subcommittee, he generally backed the Wisconsin senator's ambitious investigation of subversion in the army, and in 1954 attempted to forestall an open clash between McCarthy and the White House over the issue. In one last attempt to heal the growing breach between the army and McCarthy, Dirksen hosted a luncheon for Army Secretary ROBERT T. STEVENS and Republican members of the subcommittee. The stormy meeting failed to reconcile the differences between the administration on the one hand and McCarthy and his supporters on the other. As the meeting ended, KARL MUNDT (R-S.Dak.) read a "memorandum of understanding" that sounded like a surrender by Stevens. The episode infuriated some top members of the White House staff. The hearings began on April 22, 1954. In early May, Dirksen twice sought unsuccessfully to cut short the proceedings, the second time by proposing that once Stevens had completed his testimony, the subcommittee would then go immediately to McCarthy's testimony; the remaining hearings would be held in executive session. Stevens, however, wanted vindication, and Mundt joined the Democrats on the committee (who were happy to see an intramural brawl within the Republican party continue) to defeat Dirksen's motion. Thus, the public had an extended opportunity to observe McCarthy in action. In June, Dirksen motioned, again unsuccessfully, to end the hearings after one additional week of testimony. By then, however, McCarthy had all but destroyed his credibility.

Dirksen stood by McCarthy through the Senate vote that condemned him. In July 1954, he implored the Senate not to discipline McCarthy. He worked to alter the wording of the resolution from "censure" to "deplore." Visiting McCarthy during the fall, he asked his colleague to sign one of three letters of apology he had drafted, but McCarthy refused. In December, the Senate condemned McCarthy by a 67-22 vote; Dirksen joined 19 other GOP senators in voting against the motion. Dirksen received severe criticism from his colleagues and the national press for his advocacy of McCarthy's case.

Dirksen's political fortunes rose spectacularly within two years after McCarthy's fall. Soon after the vote to condemn McCarthy, Dirksen began to move away from the extreme right wing of the Republican party. Although erratic in his support for Eisenhower up to 1955, thereafter the senator identified his interests closely with those of the president. Up for reelection the same year as Eisenhower, Dirksen needed the popular president's endorsement. In addition, Dirksen's former sponsor, the very conservative owner of the *Chicago Tribune*, Robert McCormick, died in April 1955. Therefore, when Eisenhower appealed to Dirksen for help because WILLIAM KNOWLAND (R-Calif.) proved ineffective as minority leader, Dirksen answered the call. By early 1956, Dirksen stood apart from the party's "Old Guard," managing the administration's plan to sell old air force planes to Yugoslavia. Nevertheless,

Knowland and the conservative stalwarts prevented the Yugoslav arms sale. Dirksen also led administration forces backing a civil rights bill in 1956, a modified version of which passed the House in August. However, majority leader LYNDON JOHNSON buried the bill when it got to the Senate. Eisenhower warmly endorsed Dirksen for his labors, and in the fall, both men carried Illinois easily.

In January 1957, Dirksen became minority whip and Knowland's chief assistant. He assumed more and more of his chief's responsibilities as Knowland began his California gubernatorial campaign in 1958. Unlike Knowland, Dirksen established cordial relations with Eisenhower and supported the administration's programs. During the 85th Congress, the once-rebellious Dirksen ranked first in *Congressional Quarterly's* listing of senators voting in support of the administration. Dirksen even defended Eisenhower's aide, SHERMAN ADAMS, on the eve of his ouster for conflict of interest.

Dirksen succeeded Knowland as minority leader in January 1959. Most Republican moderates in the Senate opposed his succession as one engineered by the Old Guard and its powerful leader, STYLES BRIDGES (R-N.H.). The moderates' candidate, JOHN SHERMAN COOPER (R-Ky.), lost to Dirksen by a 20-14 vote in the party caucus. After his victory, Dirksen made the liberal THOMAS KUCHEL (R-Calif.) minority whip. As demanded by the younger caucus members, he redistributed at least one important committee assignment to each senator, no matter how low his seniority. Through these moves, as well as his mastery of legislative detail, compromise, and cajolery, Dirksen molded the once-fragmented Republican minority into a cohesive unit.

Dirksen worked for the administration with some success against overwhelming odds. The Democrats made spectacular gains in the 1958 elections; the Democratic majority in the Senate climbed from 48-47 to 64-34. Despite Republican losses, Dirksen and the president, working in concert, frustrated an ambitious legislative program promoted by majority leader LYNDON B. JOHNSON. For example, strong Republican support for presidential vetoes on two occasions in 1959 killed the Democrats' housing bill. Congress ultimately passed a measure acceptable to Eisenhower. Dirksen also played an important role in securing passage of the Civil Rights Act of 1960.

Dirksen served as minority leader through the 1960s. His national stature increased markedly when the GOP lost control of the executive branch after 1960. By the mid-1960s, Dirksen had earned much praise for his bipartisan support for initiatives of the Kennedy and Johnson administrations in civil rights and foreign policy. A colorful, dramatic speaker and storyteller, Dirksen enjoyed a national constituency that long remembered his oratorical flights. By 1967, however, his control over the Senate minority began to wane. Dirksen died in Washington, D.C., on September 7, 1969.

—MSM

DiSalle, Michael V(incent)
(1908–1981) *governor of Ohio*

The son of Italian immigrants, Michael DiSalle was born on January 6, 1908, in New York City. He grew up in Toledo, Ohio. After earning a law degree at Georgetown University in 1931, DiSalle entered Toledo Democratic politics and in 1947 was appointed mayor. Three years later, he lost the Democratic primary for the Senate nomination. In December 1950, President HARRY S. TRUMAN appointed him director of price stabilization. DiSalle left Washington in 1952 to return to Ohio and campaign for the U.S. Senate. Running ahead of the national ticket, he lost nonetheless to the popular Republican incumbent, JOHN W. BRICKER. DiSalle returned to Washington in early December to serve as administrator of the Economic Stabilization Agency for the remaining six weeks of the Truman presidency.

Out of office after 1953, DiSalle nevertheless commanded the loyalty of many state and national Democrats who were dissatisfied with Ohio Democratic Gov. FRANK J. LAUSCHE's leadership.

DiSalle played a major role in the Democratic vice presidential nomination in 1956. After ADLAI E. STEVENSON opened the vice presidential nomination to the convention, DiSalle agreed to nominate Sen. ESTES KEFAUVER (D-Tenn.). In so doing, he effectively committed 58 of Ohio's 64 votes to Kefauver, who narrowly defeated Sen. JOHN F. KENNEDY (D-Mass.) on the second ballot.

In the fall of 1956, DiSalle ran for the governorship of Ohio. During the campaign, he devoted several weeks to an effort to reinvigorate the state party's organization and allotted still more time to touring rural counties, expecting to gain from farmers' unhappiness with Eisenhower's agriculture policies. The strategy failed. Eisenhower swept all parts of the state, and Republican gubernatorial nominee, Attorney General C. William O'Neill, won 56 percent of the vote.

DiSalle's opportunity came two years later. Poorly staffed, indecisive, and ill, O'Neill proved an ineffective governor. In a monumental political error, he warmly endorsed a business coalition that placed on the November 1958 ballot a "right-to-work" proposal banning union shops. The referendum evoked vehement, well-organized union opposition and failed to engender expected support from Catholics and nonunion laborers. It lost by 1 million votes. In the face of a nationwide Democratic trend, both O'Neill and Sen. Bricker lost their campaigns for reelection. DiSalle was the first Democratic governor clearly identifiable with the politics of the national party since 1920.

DiSalle's sense of triumph proved short-lived. His predecessor's policy of borrowing to meet expenses (the state ran a $100 million budget deficit in 1958) forced DiSalle to raise corporate and sales taxes in 1959, an immensely unpopular decision. Yet, despite the increased revenues, DiSalle alienated union officials and liberal Democrats by delaying action on the expansion of social services. He gained nothing in popularity by opposing capital punishment and employing convicted murderers to work at the governor's mansion.

Kennedy maneuvered a reluctant DiSalle into endorsing his presidential candidacy in January 1960. Kennedy won the nomination and, with DiSalle's encouragement, selected the Senate majority leader, LYNDON B. JOHNSON (D-Tex.), as his running mate.

The Democratic ticket lost Ohio. Surveys later suggested that Kennedy's Catholicism hurt him, but most experts and DiSalle himself blamed the result on the governor's tax increase in 1959. The Republicans recaptured control of the legislature and made the governor's last two years in office difficult.

DiSalle lost his campaign for reelection in 1962 by a then-record margin of 555,669 votes. He returned to law practice in Columbus and remained active in Democratic politics. However, he never again sought elective office. In 1976, he moved his law practice to Washington, D.C. He died of a heart attack while visiting Pescara, Italy, on September 15, 1981.

—JLB

Dixon, Edgar H.

(1904–1962) *president, Middle Southern Utilities Inc.*
Dixon was born on December 16, 1904, in Hackensack, N.J. His formal schooling ended with graduation from Hackensack High School in 1922. Starting at Electric Bond and Share Co. as a $70-a-month clerk, he took night courses in English and accounting at New York University. By 1934, Dixon was serving as financial clerk and assistant treasurer of a number of Electric Bond's subsidiaries. He was secretary-treasurer and director of Electric Power and Light Corp. from 1935 to 1944 and served as president of the company from 1944 to 1949. Dixon became the first president of Middle Southern Utilities, Inc., in 1949. The company doubled its profits over the next 10 years.

In 1954, Middle Southern Utilities joined the Southern Co., headed by Eugene Yates, to form the Mississippi Valley Generating Co. Their purpose was to construct a plant at West Memphis, Ark., to sell 600,000 kilowatts of power annually to the Atomic Energy Commission (AEC). Dixon's firm owned 80 percent of Mississippi Valley and Yates's company owned 20 percent.

Under the terms of the proposed Dixon-Yates contract, power would be fed into the Tennessee Valley Authority (TVA) system for distribution to consumers, including the AEC. It marked the first time in its history that the TVA would act as a distributor rather a generator of power.

Dixon and Yates started negotiating with the AEC and the Bureau of the Budget in June 1954. Haste was required, because President Eisenhower had promised a 600,000-kilowatt reduction in the AEC's demand on TVA power by 1957. The two government agencies, therefore, solicited no other bids. They ignored a proposal by Walter von

Tresckow, head of an alternate power syndicate in New York, as well as the TVA's suggestion that it could supply the power for $5 million less than private sources. The TVA was not told the terms of the Dixon-Yates contract until after it had been negotiated.

Democratic senators denounced the agreement as an attempt to undermine the TVA. In late 1954, they uncovered possible violations of the Holding Company Act by Dixon's and Yates's southern subsidiaries. In February 1955, Sen. LISTER HILL (D-Ala.) discovered that Adolphe H. Wenzell, a vice president of the First Boston Corp., which was arranging financing for Dixon-Yates, was a consultant to the Bureau of the Budget at the time negotiations were in progress. His name did not appear on a list that the AEC had released revealing the names of those who had worked on the contract. Questioned by Sen. ESTES KEFAUVER (D-Tenn.) in hearings held by the Judiciary Committee's Subcommittee on Antitrust and Monopoly in July 1955, Director of the Budget ROWLAND HUGHES stated that he thought Wenzell's role too insignificant to mention.

After Wenzell openly acknowledged his dual role and stated that he had worked with Hughes, the president canceled the contract in July 1955. His action followed an announcement by Memphis that it intended to build a $100-million municipally owned power plant. The following year, Dixon and Yates brought suit against the United States for $3 million in reported expenditures. In June 1959, the U.S. Claims Court awarded the Mississippi Valley Generating Co. $1.8 million. The Supreme Court reversed that decision in January 1961. Throughout the controversy and thereafter, Dixon defended the contract. He remained one of the most sought-after utilities executives in the United States. He died in New York City on August 3, 1962.

—MJS

Dodd, Thomas J(oseph)

(1907–1971) *U.S. congressman and senator*
Dodd was born in Norwich, Conn., on May 15, 1907. He received a Bachelor of Philosophy from Providence College in 1930 and an LL.B. from the Yale Law School in 1933. From 1933 to 1935, he

was a special agent with the FBI. In 1935, Dodd organized the National Youth Administration in Connecticut, and from 1938 to 1945, he served as an assistant to the attorney general. During the postwar period, Dodd was executive trial counsel at the Nuremberg war crimes trials. He unsuccessfully sought the Connecticut Democratic gubernatorial nomination in 1946 and 1948.

In 1952, Dodd won election to the U.S. House of Representatives, where he proved to be one of Congress's staunchest anticommunists. In 1953, Dodd was named to the seven-man Select Committee to Investigate Soviet Seizure of the Baltic Countries, which held hearings in 1953 and early 1954. The following year, he was assigned to that panel's successor, the nine-member Select Committee on Communist Aggression. The committee's report, in August 1954, recommended that the United States call a conference of "free world" nations for the purpose of breaking off trade and diplomatic relations with communist countries. During the same year, he chaired a special subcommittee probing alleged incarceration and abuse of American citizens in Communist China. In November, Dodd suggested that the United States retaliate by urging the West to apply a trade embargo against mainland China. Two years later, he successfully amended a farm-surplus disposal bill to restrict surplus transactions to "friendly countries."

Although a strong anticommunist, in 1954 Dodd criticized a bill, recommended by Attorney General HERBERT BROWNELL, that would have permitted the attorney general to order wiretapping in suspected cases of espionage, sabotage, and other threats to national security. He voted for the bill only after the addition of an amendment requiring federal court approval for a tap. In a related issue, Dodd voted against a bill giving Congress and U.S. district courts authority to grant immunity to congressional and court witnesses. The measure was aimed at witnesses taking the Fifth Amendment against self-incrimination in hearings involving national security. Under the bill's provisions, such persons would have the alternatives of either testifying or going to jail. On the other hand, he backed the Communist Control Act of 1954, sponsored by Democratic liberals, which outlawed the Communist Party.

Dodd compiled a generally liberal record on domestic issues. A strong supporter of civil rights, in 1956 he backed a controversial amendment offered by Rep. ADAM CLAYTON POWELL, JR. (D-N.Y.) to a bill providing federal aid for school construction. The Powell amendment would have barred aid to states operating racially segregated schools. Dodd voted both for the amendment, which was adopted, and the final bill, which was defeated. In 1956, he also supported a civil rights bill sponsored by the administration aimed against racial discrimination, particularly in voting.

In 1956, Dodd unsuccessfully ran for the U.S. Senate. The following year, he represented three members of the Teamsters Union in an unsuccessful suit to block JAMES R. HOFFA's accession to the presidency of the organization. In 1958, he again ran for the Senate on a platform stressing the need for a strengthened military and a program to combat unemployment and inflation. He won by 146,000 votes.

Dodd maintained his strong anticommunist position as a senator. In a letter to President Eisenhower in January 1959, he warned against a bilateral conference with the Soviet Union on the ground that it would divide the United States from its allies. In 1960, he was a leader of opposition to the ratification of the Antarctic Treaty with the Soviet Union and 10 other nations. The purpose of the pact was to ensure that Antarctica would be used for peaceful purposes, but opponents maintained that the treaty did not have guarantees against Soviet military operations on that continent.

In 1960, Dodd and Sen. KENNETH B. KEATING (R-N.Y.), as members of the Judiciary Committee's Internal Security Subcommittee, introduced a four-part internal security bill. The measure widened the definition of illegal espionage and of foreign agents under the Foreign Agents Registration Act of 1958. It defined the Smith Act's (1940) prohibition against forming a group advocating the violent overthrow of the government as applying to the organization's ongoing activities as well as its initial formation. This represented an effort to overturn the Supreme Court's interpretation of the Smith Act in *Yates v. U.S.* (1957), which held that the statute did not outlaw advocacy of forcible overthrow of the government as an abstract doctrine. In addition, the bill permitted the secretary of state to declare certain areas off limits for travel and, after a hearing, to deny passports to communists and communist sympathizers whom he believed might endanger U.S. security. The House passed a similar bill, but the Senate did not act. Most of the Dodd-Keating proposals, however, became law in 1961 and 1962.

As chairman of the Internal Security Subcommittee, Dodd conducted an investigation in 1960 into alleged communist influence in the nuclear test-ban movement. He ordered Nobel Prize–winning chemist Dr. LINUS C. PAULING to produce the names of persons who helped him circulate a petition in 1957 calling for a test-ban agreement, but Pauling declined to do so.

Dodd backed most social welfare and civil rights legislation during his first two years in the Senate. He voted to override Eisenhower's vetoes of housing legislation in 1959 and of an area redevelopment bill in 1960. Dodd supported a boost in the minimum wage from $1 to $1.25, a bill to provide federal aid to schools, a health care program for the aged funded by Social Security, and the administration's Civil Rights bill in 1960.

During the early 1960s, Dodd, as chairman of the Judiciary Committee's Juvenile Delinquency Subcommittee, conducted a probe of the influence of television upon juvenile delinquency. Subsequently, he was a strong supporter of the Vietnam War and of gun-control legislation. In 1967, the Senate censured him for misuse of campaign funds. Dodd unsuccessfully ran for reelection as an independent in 1970. He died in Old Lyme, Conn., on May 24, 1971.

Dodge, Joseph M(orrell)

(1890–1964) *director of the budget*

Born in Detroit, Mich., on November 18, 1890, Joseph Dodge attended public high school. Upon graduating in 1908, he worked as a bank messenger and in various clerical positions before becoming a bank examiner for the Michigan State Banking Commission in 1911. In 1917, he joined a Dodge (no relation) auto dealership as general manager. He remained until 1932, when he returned to bank-

ing as vice president of the First National Bank of Detroit. The next year, he became president of the Bank of Detroit.

During World War II, Dodge held a number of posts with government agencies, the most important of which was chairman of the War Contracts Board. At the war's end, he went to Germany as financial adviser to Gen. LUCIUS CLAY, commander of the Allied military government. He returned to the Bank of Detroit in 1946. In 1949, President HARRY S. TRUMAN summoned Dodge to serve as financial adviser to Gen. Douglas MacArthur in Japan. Dodge's program of fiscal austerity helped stabilize the Japanese currency and rebuild the country's shattered economy.

In November 1952, Dodge was named budget director by President-elect DWIGHT D. EISENHOWER. Dodge's first public statement, on January 6, 1953, warned against expecting any "60-day miracle" in the way of budget cuts, but he devoted himself to reducing government spending. He directed all federal agencies to submit revised estimates of expenditures in order to cut the budget deficit of $9.9 billion projected by the outgoing Truman administration for fiscal 1954. Under Dodge, the deficit for that year was trimmed to $3.1 billion, although the total budget did not fall under $70 billion, as President-elect Eisenhower had pledged it would. Among Dodge's methods for raising revenues and cutting costs were increased rents in public housing and admissions to national parks as well as curtailed use of government automobiles. He also promoted economy in defense spending and opposed plans by Republican members of Congress to cut taxes on 1953 income.

Dodge resigned as budget director in April 1954 to return to his bank in Detroit. Later that year, he became involved in the congressional investigation of the controversial Dixon-Yates affair. EDGAR DIXON and EUGENE YATES were utility executives seeking a government contract to supply power to the Atomic Energy Commission. Dodge had originally suggested having a private company supply the power instead of the Tennessee Valley Authority and had named Adolphe Wenzell, a vice president of the First Boston Corp., to study the matter. The choice of Wenzell became a subject of controversy when it was revealed that First Boston was to finance the Dixon-Yates combine. Testifying before the Senate Subcommittee on Antitrust and Monopoly, Dodge maintained that Wenzell had not influenced his decision on the contract.

In the fall of 1954, Dodge returned to government as a special assistant to President Eisenhower on foreign economic policy. In January, he became chairman of the administration's Council on Foreign Economic Policy, which had been set up at his recommendation. He served in this post until July 1956. His major task was coordinating the disparate activities of the dozens of U.S. agencies involved in international economic affairs. Dodge died in Detroit on December 2,1964.

—TO

Doerfer, John C(harles)

(1904–1990) *commissioner, Federal Communications Commission*

The son of a German immigrant, John C. Doerfer was born in Milwaukee, Wis., on November 30, 1904. He worked his way through the University of Wisconsin, where he graduated in 1928. After receiving a law degree from Marquette in 1934, he then opened a private law practice in a suburb of Milwaukee. From 1940 to 1949, he served as city attorney of Milwaukee; in 1949 he became chairman of the state's Public Service Commission.

President Eisenhower named Doerfer to a one-year vacancy on the Federal Communications Commission (FCC) in 1953 and to a full seven-year term in 1954. At the time, some liberals denounced the appointment as an attempt by the administration to placate Sen. JOSEPH R. MCCARTHY (R-Wis.). The Senate, however, confirmed Doerfer in April.

In 1953, Doerfer promoted an FCC investigation of an Erie, Pa., TV station license owned by EDWARD LAMB, a wealthy attorney from Toledo with a leftist past. FCC hearings in 1954–55 proved embarrassing to Lamb's opponents. Government witnesses who had testified to Lamb's communist connections confessed to committing perjury at the request of an FCC attorney. Even McCarthy, initially enthused over the affair, admitted by early 1955 that the FCC had no case. In December 1955, an FCC examiner, Herbert Sharfman, exonerated Lamb and recommended renewal of the license.

Doerfer repeatedly expressed doubts about legislation that would have granted the FCC authority to regulate the national television networks. Rather, he believed competition between networks would eventually improve the content of programs. Under his chairmanship, the FCC issued and renewed station licenses without regard to earlier FCC precedents requiring "public interest," locally oriented news and cultural programming.

In February 1957, the FCC announced plans for testing a subscription television service (PAY-TV) in selected markets. This action aroused the opposition of the major networks and Congress. House Judiciary Committee Chairman EMANUEL CELLER (D-N.Y.) argued that the FCC did not have the power to conduct PAY-TV tests. At first, Doerfer stood firm with the 6-1 majority favoring the tests. In January 1958, however, he told a House committee that he did not favor PAY-TV if it threatened to replace free TV. By July 1958, Doerfer relented to pressure from Congress and the networks, and the FCC delayed indefinitely authorization of the tests.

In 1958, DREW PEARSON, a newspaper columnist, charged Doerfer with conflicts of interest. At the urging of Speaker SAM RAYBURN, in 1957 the House Committee on Interstate and Foreign Commerce had appointed a subcommittee, known as the Special Committee on Legislative Oversight, to investigate interference with the regulatory agencies. In January 1958, the subcommittee's chief counsel, BERNARD SCHWARTZ, submitted a memorandum urging a sweeping investigation of the FCC. The subcommittee declined to undertake the sort of investigation recommended by Schwartz, and someone leaked the memo to Pearson. At congressional hearings, it came out that station KWTV in Oklahoma City had reimbursed Doerfer for the first leg of a trip in 1954, and the National Association of Radio and Television Broadcasters reimbursed him for the second leg, to Spokane, Wash. Doerfer then submitted travel vouchers to the government for the trip. Doerfer attributed the double reimbursement to a mistake. It also came out that he had received travel expenses and an honorarium for speeches to broadcasting groups at several resorts. In addition, he received partial reimbursement for one of the trips from the government. Doerfer defended the trips and payments as "amenities." The hearings established neither illegality nor impropriety on Doerfer's part.

Doerfer survived criticism stemming from the exposés. Imprecise language in a 1952 amendment to the FCC Act could be interpreted to permit commissioners to accept honoraria, and the comptroller general supported Doerfer's interpretation. Thus, Eisenhower refused to remove Doerfer. In addition, Schwartz's tactics, both as an investigator and interrogator, also offended many and created sympathy for Doerfer. Attention soon turned away from Doerfer's hearings to another, more serious conflict-of-interest scandal involving another FCC Commissioner, Richard A. Mack. Nevertheless, the subcommittee warned Doerfer not to continue his close fraternization with the industry.

Subsequently, the FCC chairman had to deal with a series of scandals in the television industry. In fall 1959, several contestants on TV quiz shows (once the highest-rated programs) confessed to having been given questions and answers in advance. The quiz-show scandals shocked the nation and created demands for the criminal prosecution of the producer and overall reform. In October, Doerfer denied that the FCC had any responsibility for "policing" the shows. Rumors concerning irregularities involving quiz shows had reached the FCC in July 1958. The commission had asked the three networks about them, but the networks disclaimed knowledge of the alleged practices. Doerfer told a subcommittee of the House Commerce Committee that the best response to all "objectionable programming" would be "greater incentive for the exercise of self-regulatory restraints."

Early in March 1960, the *New York Herald Tribune* reported that Doerfer had spent a portion of his previous month's vacation aboard the yacht of George Storer, who owned five television stations and seven radio stations. Storer had also paid for a trip Doerfer took to Miami and Bimini in 1955.

Before the House Commerce Committee a day later, Doerfer admitted to accepting Storer's hospitality and defended his own actions. He had not clearly violated the law, but he had acted against the subcommittee's 1958 recommendation that he discontinue his close and remunerative contacts with broadcasting executives. This time, Eisenhower immediately requested and secured his resignation.

After resigning from the FCC, Doerfer took up legal practice in Washington, D.C. He moved to Florida in 1963, where he did legal work for Storer Broadcasting Company until 1974. He practiced law on a part-time basis until he retired in 1980. Doerfer died in Boston on June 5, 1992.

—MSM

Dorfman, Paul
(ca. 1902–1971) *labor figure*

A former prizefighter, member of Al Capone's mob, and associate of such underworld figures as John Dioguardi (Johnny Dio), Paul "Red" Dorfman was born around 1902. He took over the Waste Materials Handlers Federated Labor Union in 1939, following the murder of its president. That same year, he established the Union Casualty Agency with his stepson, Allan, and his wife as the principal agents. Already a leading crime figure in Chicago, Dorfman sought to expand his power through his close personal relationship with Jimmy Hoffa.

In late January 1959, the Senate Committee on Improper Relations in the Labor or Management Field, chaired by Sen. John McClellan (D-Ark.), investigated an insurance scheme ostensibly fashioned by Dorfman and Hoffa to swindle members of the Teamster's Union. According to the Committee, shortly after Dorfman established the Union Casualty Agency, the company bid to handle the welfare pension fund of the huge Central States Drivers Council and Local 1031 of the International Brotherhood of Electrical Workers. Hoffa arranged for Dorfman's company to obtain the contract. Testimony showed that the Dorfman family made $4 million in commissions and fees as a result of the deal. At the same time, the Teamster's benefits were reduced and their premiums raised in 1952. The committee's counsel, Robert F. Kennedy, revealed that a Chicago Internal Revenue agent had been discharged for having given his personal approval to Allan Dorfman's income tax returns.

Paul Dorfman repeatedly took the Fifth Amendment when he appeared in front of the Committee on January 30, 1959. Robert Kennedy asked him whether the contract that Hoffa gave him was a reward for Dorfman's aid in enabling the Teamster leader to amass power in the Chicago area. Although Dorfman refused to answer this question, the McClellan committee claimed that such a deal did occur.

The committee also charged that Dorfman had helped Hoffa increase his power in New York City. Dorfman persuaded his friend Anthony Doria, an official in the United Automobile Workers–American Federation of Labor (there was another group associated with the Congress of Industrial Organizations), to issue a charter for a new local in New York organized by Sam Zachman, a friend of Dorfman who had ties to organized crime. Involved in actually setting up the local was Johnny Dio, one of Hoffa's operatives and another close friend of Dorfman. Dio eventually pushed Zachman out and took over the union himself. He organized additional locals, staffed them with ex-convicts, and then became the union's regional director. The employees of the businesses organized were forced to join the union. The mostly black and Puerto Rican members paid a $25 initiation fee and a $3.50 a month dues; the companies paid them the minimum wage with no benefits. By setting up this extortion operation, Dorfman and Dio provided Hoffa with a power base in the New York area.

In December 1958, GEORGE MEANY placed Dorfman's union under AFL-CIO trusteeship. The federation president then removed Dorfman in August 1959 from his office as secretary-treasurer and from the union itself. Meany based his decision on the fact that the Dorfman family had derived personal advantage from union funds deposited in their insurance company.

Revelations of the activities of union officials such as Paul Dorfman led to a public demand for legislation to prevent such abuses. In September 1959, Congress passed the Landrum-Griffin Act. The law's anticorruption provision subjected union officials found guilty of misusing funds to stiff fines and prison terms. It also prohibited certain types of criminal offenders from holding union offices. However, it proved difficult to enforce.

Following the McClellan committee's revelations, the Dorfman insurance company was reorganized, allegedly to hide its activities. Paul Dorfman devoted most of his time to that business. In 1964, a grand jury in San Francisco indicted him and his son on a charge of extorting $100,000 from an insurance executive in San Francisco. The jury acquitted them on the charge. Allan Dorfman was tried with Jimmy Hoffa in 1964 on a charge of jury tampering and was acquitted. Paul Dorfman died in Chicago on March 12, 1971.

—JB

Douglas, Paul H(oward)
(1892–1976) *U.S. senator*

Born in Salem, Mass., on March 26, 1892, and reared on a farm in northern Maine, Paul Douglas worked his way through Bowdoin College, graduating in 1913. He obtained an M.A. (1915) and a Ph.D. (1921) in economics from Columbia University and taught economics at a number of colleges before joining the University of Chicago's faculty in 1920. Douglas won professional renown for his scholarly works, the most notable of which were *Wages of the Family* (1925), *Real Wages in the United States, 1890–1926* (1930), and *Theory of Wages* (1934). He entered the political arena in 1929, when he undertook an investigation of the Chicago utilities magnate, Samuel Insull, then at the peak of his power. Persistent in the face of harsh opposition from the financial and political establishment, Douglas displayed the doggedly independent liberalism that became his trademark as a political figure.

During the Depression, Douglas influenced public policy through his service on a variety of commissions and committees. In 1930, he was a secretary to the Pennsylvania Commission on Unemployment and the New York Committee to Stabilize Employment. From 1931 to 1933, he was a member of the Illinois Housing Commission, and he helped to formulate the state's Utilities Act of 1933, Old Age Pension Act of 1935, and Unemployment Insurance Act of 1937. He also participated in the drafting of the national Social Security Act of 1935.

In 1938, Douglas won election as a Chicago alderman with the support of intellectuals and upper–middle-class reformers from the Hyde Park area as well as the Democratic machine. In office, he alienated the regular organization with his exposures of graft and corruption and lost the Democratic nomination for the U.S. Senate in 1942 to a machine-backed candidate. Immediately following his defeats, Douglas enlisted in the Marine Corps as a private, despite his age (50) and his Quaker faith. (He had been a pacifist and opposed military preparation until Italy's invasion of Ethiopia in 1935.) Douglas served in the Pacific theater and left the service in 1946 as a decorated lieutenant colonel, recipient of the Purple Heart and Bronze Star. Despite five operations, he never recovered functional use of his left arm.

Douglas again ran for the Senate in 1948, on a platform advocating a federal housing program, federal aid to education, repeal of the Taft-Hartley Act, and support of President Truman's foreign policy. With the support of the Cook Co. Democratic machine, he defeated the Republican incumbent by 400,000 votes.

Douglas soon became a leader of the Senate's liberal bloc. His voting record consistently won the approval of the AFL-CIO and the Americans for Democratic Action. During the Eisenhower administration, Douglas called for a number of legislative initiatives, including civil rights, tax reform, stimulative economics, and social welfare. He frequently pointed out waste and extravagance in the military and in public works programs. He was frustrated as much by his Democratic colleagues in Congress as by the Republican administration. Douglas frequently stood alone in a crusade or in the company of a handful of fellow liberals.

One of the Senate's most outspoken proponents of civil rights legislation. Douglas persistently and unsuccessfully sought to pave the way for such laws by amending the Senate's Rule 22, which governed debate and enabled Southerners to filibuster civil rights proposals to death. Rule 22 required a two-thirds vote to limit debate. Douglas's efforts to substitute cloture by a simple majority consistently failed, as did moderate revisions, such as cloture by a three-fifths vote or after 15 days of debate.

During the first term of the Eisenhower administration, civil rights proposals got nowhere in the Senate. In August 1956, Douglas led a group of northern liberals who tried and failed to put a strong civil rights plank into the Democratic platform. Douglas was disinclined to moderate civil rights goals in order to mollify southern Demo-

crats. Commenting in the fall of 1957 on reports that forced school desegregation might lead southern segregationists to form a third party, he said he "would welcome it" because "it would mean getting the Dixiecrats out of our party."

Douglas supported the Civil Rights Act of 1957, although it was not so far-reaching as his own proposals. He joined the administration in fighting unsuccessfully against an amendment mandating a jury trial in cases in which a court injunction protecting black voting rights had been violated. He voted for the final bill in spite of its dilution, because it contained some protections for voting rights and established a civil rights division within the Justice Department.

In January 1959, Douglas headed a 15-member Senate group that introduced a measure empowering the attorney general to initiate lawsuits to halt illegal bias and providing $40 million a year to help finance school districts trying to desegregate in the face of state opposition. The bill failed to pass at the time, but its major provisions were included in the omnibus Civil Rights Act of 1964.

In economic affairs, Douglas was a vocal and knowledgeable spokesman for liberal Senate Democrats. He made several unsuccessful attempts to legislate sizable tax cuts to stimulate the economy and reduce unemployment. Douglas was also the Senate's foremost critic of tax loopholes. Named to the Finance Committee in 1956 after being kept off several years, Douglas and Sen. ALBERT GORE (D-Tenn.) were frequently a minority of two protesting the committee's enactment of tax preferences for corporations and wealthy individuals. Douglas's chief target was the 27½ percent oil depletion allowance. His efforts to reduce or eliminate this provision were easily defeated in the committee and on the Senate floor.

Douglas enjoyed more success in his promotion of area redevelopment legislation. Parallel to his continuous criticism of "pork barrel" public works projects that he considered expensive and unnecessary, he conceived and gathered support for an ambitious federal program to reinvigorate the economies of chronically depressed regions. The principal features of Douglas's area redevelopment plan were public works, technical assistance and long-term credit for local industry, and the retraining of jobless workers. Douglas first introduced his measure in 1955 with the textile and coal-producing areas of the Northeast in mind; in 1956, he broadened its scope to reach the depressed agricultural regions of the South as well.

Area redevelopment passed the Senate, 60-30, in 1956 but remained bottled up in the House Rules Committee when the 84th Congress adjourned. Congress passed it in 1958 and 1960. Both times it was vetoed by President Eisenhower, who objected to the breadth of the measure and said that it would "greatly diminish local responsibility." The Area Redevelopment Act was signed into law by President JOHN F. KENNEDY in 1961. Douglas listed it as his greatest achievement during his over 20 years in Congress.

A vigorous anticommunist, Douglas was a member of the Committee of One Million against the Admission of Communist China to the UN. In 1954, he called for U.S. intervention on the side of France in the Indochina war. He supported Secretary of State JOHN, FOSTER DULLES's efforts to build the Southeast Asia Treaty Organization. During Soviet Premier Nikita S. Khrushchev's visit to America in 1959, Douglas joined several other members of Congress on the Committee for Freedom of All Peoples, which called for Americans to observe Premier Khrushchev's visit with a period of mourning for victims of communist oppression.

Douglas won reelection in 1960 by a margin of 420,000 votes. In the next six years, he actively supported the Kennedy and Johnson administrations' social welfare programs. The senator continued his personal battles for tax reform and truth-in-lending legislation. In 1966, he lost his Senate seat to Republican Charles Percy. Douglas died in Washington, D.C., on September 24, 1976.

—TO

Douglas, William O(rville)

(1898–1980) *associate justice, U.S. Supreme Court*
The longest tenured justice in the history of the Supreme Court, William O. Douglas was born in Maine Township, Minn., on October 16, 1898. He grew up in Yakima, Wash., and worked his way through Whitman College. After his graduation in 1920, he taught school for two years. He then

worked his way through Columbia Law School, graduating second in his class in 1925. He worked briefly for a major Wall Street law firm and then taught at Columbia and Yale law schools, where he developed a reputation for his studies of bankruptcy. Named to the Securities and Exchange Commission (SEC) in January 1936, he became its chairman in 1937. On the SEC, Douglas pushed the reorganization of stock exchanges and instituted various reforms to protect investors. President Franklin Roosevelt appointed Douglas to the Supreme Court in March 1939. The Senate confirmed his nomination the following month.

In his earliest years on the Court, Douglas joined a majority of his colleagues in sanctioning the expansion of the power of the federal government over the economy and in sustaining various regulatory measures of the New Deal. A recognized expert in financial and corporate law, Douglas wrote many influential Court opinions in these areas. Yet, Douglas became best known as an ardent defender of individual liberties, whose commitment to personal freedoms grew over the years.

During World War II, Douglas's most significant decisions involved the regulation of business and bankruptcy law. At the same time, the war presented difficult issues for the Court, particularly for Douglas and his close ally, HUGO BLACK. For example, Black and Douglas struggled to balance the competing values of protection of civil liberties on the one hand and support for the wartime activities of the government and the president who appointed them on the other. Both justices supported compulsory flag-salute laws in *Minersville School District v. Gobitis* (1940). Two years later, however, in a case involving the validity of municipal license fees on transient merchants, including Jehovah's Witnesses, Black and Douglas, joined by Frank Murphy, took the extraordinary step of publicly repenting their vote in *Gobitis*. They then enthusiastically joined the majority in reversing the Gobitis decision in *West Virginia v. Barnette* (1943).

After the war, Black and Douglas consistently upheld civil liberties, particularly free speech. Douglas, who had earlier held that government could restrict free speech in certain circumstances, concluded that, under the First Amendment, government could regulate actions but could not prohibit any form of expression. In *Terminiello v. Chicago* (1949), Douglas wrote for the Court, reversing the conviction of a fascist, defrocked ex-priest whose words provoked a hostile crowd. Black and Douglas entered vigorous dissents in *Dennis v. U.S.* (1951), in which the majority upheld the convictions under the Smith Act of leaders of the American Communist Party for conspiring to teach and advocate the overthrow of the government. In *Yates v. U.S.* (1957), the Court reversed the convictions of a second group of Communist leaders. The majority found that the lower court's instructions to the jury failed to distinguish between advocacy of forcible overthrow of the government as an abstract doctrine and advocating action toward that end. Douglas and Black dissented in part; they would have struck down the Smith Act as a violation of the First Amendment.

With respect to obscenity, Douglas dissented when the majority upheld the conviction of Samuel Roth for mailing obscene materials (*Roth v. U.S.*, 1957). Writing for the majority, WILLIAM BRENNAN held that obscenity was not protected by the First Amendment and that banning obscene material was a "proper exercise of the postal power." Douglas filed a vigorous dissent, in which Black joined. He wrote that the standard established by the majority inflicted punishment "for thoughts provoked, not for overt acts or antisocial conduct" and therefore violated the First Amendment. Speech and writing, he argued might be suppressed only when they amounted to conduct or were "so closely brigaded with illegal action as to be an inescapable part of it."

Though he gave a special place to First Amendment rights, Justice Douglas was solicitous of other guarantees of individual rights. He generally interpreted the criminal procedure guarantees in the Bill of Rights broadly to the benefit of the individual. Throughout the 1950s, he favored extending the right to counsel to all. In *Ullman v. U.S.* (1956), the Justice dissented when the Court upheld a federal law under which the government could force a witness to testify in security cases by granting him immunity from prosecution. Douglas asserted that the Fifth Amendment made it unconstitutional for Congress to compel anyone to confess to a crime, even with a grant of immunity. Douglas also strongly

supported the right of equal protection under the law, and he unhesitatingly voted with his colleagues in May 1954 to hold that racial segregation violated the Fourteenth Amendment.

Often a controversial figure, Douglas became a center of conflict in June 1953, when he granted a stay of execution to convicted atomic spies JULIUS and ETHEL ROSENBERG. The month before, the Court had refused for the third time to review the Rosenbergs' conviction. Nevertheless, Douglas granted the stay when new legal arguments were presented on their behalf. Chief Justice FRED VINSON then called the Court into special session. After hearing arguments, the Court vacated Douglas's stay. Rep. William M. Wheeler (D-Ga.) introduced a resolution to impeach Douglas for his action, but the House Judiciary Committee killed the resolution.

In the 1960s, the majority of the Court came to adopt many of Douglas's positions on the rights of the criminally accused. Perhaps his greatest impact on the law came in *Griswold v. Connecticut* (1965), when he wrote for the majority in a decision striking down Connecticut's anti-contraceptive law on the ground that it violated a right of privacy he found in the "emanations" and "penumbras" of the First, Third, Fourth, Fifth, and Ninth Amendments. From the mid-1960s, however, Douglas's opinions came under increasing attack from legal scholars for their tendentiousness and for their lack of legal craftsmanship. In addition, his personal life generated controversy. In the early 1950s, he divorced his wife of 29 years; subsequently, he remarried three times. Douglas also began to travel widely and to explore the outdoors. He also wrote books intended for popular consumption about his various expeditions. These books won him a reputation as an outdoorsman and conservationist.

His controversial private life, his absolutist positions on legal matters, and the lack of care that marked his opinions, even on matters about which he cared deeply, resulted in a move, led by the House Minority Leader, GERALD FORD (R-Mich.), to impeach the justice in 1970. A subcommittee of the House Judiciary Committee rejected the charges. The experience, however, did little to moderate Douglas's positions or subdue his combative personality.

Douglas suffered a debilitating stroke in December 1974. He missed much of the Supreme Court's term, and though he returned the following term, his capacities were substantially and clearly diminished. He resigned in November 1975, after serving longer than any justice in history. Douglas remained in Washington, D.C., where he died on January 19, 1980.

While legal analysts unanimously conceded Douglas's brilliance, critics attacked his absolutist approach, his results-oriented jurisprudence, and the absence of formal legal analysis in his opinions. As a result of these traits and his abrasive personality, Douglas left an insubstantial intellectual legacy. Black, Douglas's close ally for many of his years on the Court, was the greater theoretician and legal craftsman. Indeed, Black developed most of the legal theories with which Douglas was associated. Supporters pointed to Douglas's mercurial intellect and his eloquent advocacy for the less powerful. He could be particularly eloquent in his defense of free speech. The fact remains, however, that his impact on jurisprudence was considerably less than that of his contemporaries such as FELIX FRANKFURTER, Black, and Brennan.

—MSM

Dowling, Walter C(ecil)

(1905–1977) *ambassador to South Korea, ambassador to West Germany*

Walter Dowling was born in Atkinson, Ga., on August 4, 1905. Following his graduation from Mercer University in 1925, Dowling worked as a bank clerk. He joined the Foreign Service in 1932, and, over the next 12 years, served as vice consul in Oslo, Lisbon, Rome, and Rio de Janeiro. In 1945, he was transferred to the office of the U.S. representative to the Advisory Council for Italy. The following year, Dowling was assigned to the State Department's division of South European affairs and by 1947 was its associate director. In 1949, he was appointed counselor of legation in Vienna. Three years later, Dowling became deputy U.S. high commissioner for Austria; in 1953, he represented the secretary of state in negotiations for an Austrian peace treaty. Dowling was appointed deputy U.S. high commissioner for Germany in July 1953, and in 1955 became minister-counselor of the American embassy at Bonn.

Eisenhower appointed Dowling ambassador to South Korea in May 1955. Six months later, the United States and South Korea signed a treaty of friendship, commerce, and navigation designed to further development of economic relations between the two countries. Relations between the United States and Korea became strained at the end of the decade because of repressive measures pushed through the South Korean parliament. In January 1959, Dowling was recalled to Washington to protest the tactics used in the passage of the Korean National Security Act, one of two measures abolishing local elections and suppressing opposition newspapers passed in December 1958 after specially hired guards had forcibly removed members of the opposition party from Parliament.

In February 1959, the State Department ordered Dowling to return to Seoul to mediate a dispute between South Korea and Japan. Japan's plan to return thousands of Koreans living in that country to Communist North Korea incensed South Korean President Syngman Rhee, who threatened to use military force to prevent the move. Dowling helped bring the two nations to the conference table. As a result, although thousands of Koreans were repatriated to North Korea, the condition of those remaining in Japan improved considerably, as did the relations between South Korea and Japan.

After a stint as assistant secretary of state for European affairs during the fall of 1959, Dowling became ambassador to West Germany. In November 1958, Soviet Premier Nikita Khrushchev had announced that the Soviet Union had decided "to renounce the remnants of the occupation regime in Berlin." He demanded that the three Western powers, the United States, France, and Great Britain, withdraw 10,000 men from their occupation zones, declare Berlin a demilitarized free city, and negotiate directly with East Germany on access to the city. He threatened that if the Western allies did not comply within six months, the USSR would give the East German government control of Western military supply routes to the city. The United States refused Khrushchev's demand that Berlin be made a "free city," opposed recognition of East Germany, and announced that, as one of the Allied occupation powers, it would maintain its access rights to all sectors of Berlin.

Immediately after assuming office, Dowling traveled to West Berlin to reassure the people there of continued American support. He reiterated the U.S. stand more dramatically in September 1960, when he forced East German border police to back down in their attempt to bar him from the Soviet sector of Berlin because he was not accredited to the East German government.

Dowling retired from the Foreign Service in 1963 because of poor health. In 1969, he became a visiting professor of political science at Mercer University and served there until his death in Savannah, Ga., on July 1, 1977.

Drucker, Peter F(erdinand)
(1909–2005) *author*

The son of a lawyer and university professor, Peter Drucker was born in Vienna, Austria, on November 19, 1909. After receiving a doctorate in law from the University of Frankfurt in 1931, he taught international law and constitutional history at that university while writing on finance and foreign affairs for the city's daily newspaper. Soon after Adolf Hitler came to power in 1933, Drucker left Germany for England and took a job with a bank in London. In 1937, he moved to the United States, where he made his living over the next 40 years as an author, teacher, and consultant to business enterprises. He taught first at Sarah Lawrence College from 1942 to 1948 and then at Bennington College. In 1950, he became professor of management at New York University.

In 1939, Drucker published *The End of Economic Man*, a critique of totalitarianism and a forecast of what it portended for the future of mankind. He offered a dismal vision in which no hope lay in either capitalism or socialism because they failed to satisfy man's need for noneconomic fulfillment. Fascism was a fraud, Drucker asserted, but it had succeeded because it gave individuals status and the illusion that their actions had heroic significance.

In *The Future of Industrial Man* (1942), Drucker continued to argue that individuals must be given status and purpose if a free industrial society were to survive. In his analysis, this could only be accomplished within an institution. To Drucker, the essential institution for America's future would be the corporation, which he considered the representative social phenomenon of the era. He applauded corporate managers for their commitment to objective analysis in the pursuit of profits. Indeed, Drucker likened a capitalist to a "good artist or scientist." This led him to conclude, "There has never been a more efficient, a more honest, a more capable and conscientious group of rulers than the professional managers of the great American corporations today."

Drucker gave a more detailed picture of modern business enterprise in *The Concept of the Corporation* (1946), which he undertook as a study of the General Motors Corp. (GM). Drucker held that workers should have no role in the management of the corporation; their sense of status and function might be enhanced by greater participation in activities peripheral to their jobs, such as community services, but not in the making of company policy. At the same time, he advocated fostering a sense of community among workers. Drucker regarded workers as a resource rather than a cost, and advocated creating a safety net for them. Drucker praised bigness as conducive to efficiency and social stability. He generally approved of GM's famous decentralized organization but placed emphasis on the exercise of leadership by top management and the generation of esprit de corps.

By the 1950s, Drucker's books, his prolific magazine writing, and his successful consulting ventures had established him as an important theorist of corporate capitalism and a seminal contributor to the study of management. His celebration of the corporation fused with the decade's dominant strain of thought. Drucker, however, warned against placing a premium on conformity, which could turn the corporate structure into an ossified bureaucracy. He maintained that a good manager understood the need for risk-taking.

Drucker frequently decried the growth of government into a "swollen monstrosity," and called the proliferation of new agencies a cancer on the political system. During the 1960s and 1970s, he maintained his steady output of articles and books, including *The Effective Executive* (1967), *The Age of Discontinuity: Guidelines to Our Changing Society*

(1969), and *The Unseen Revolution: How Pension Fund Socialism Came to America* (1976). In his characteristic fashion, Drucker mixed philosophic speculation on business, government, and society with practical analysis of managerial problems.

In 1971, Drucker became Clarke Professor of Social Sciences at Claremont Graduate School. He continued to publish a stream of books and popular articles. Of his more than 30 books, 13 concerned economics, politics, and society; 15 were about management. He published a volume of memoirs, *Adventures of a Bystander,* in 1979. Recent works included *Management Challenges for the 21st Century* (1999) and *Managing the Next Society* (2002). Many regarded him as the seminal thinker and writer on organizations and management.

Drucker was awarded the Presidential Medal of Freedom in 2002. He died in Claremont, Calif., on November 11, 2005, a few days short of his 96th birthday.

—TO

Dryden, Hugh L(atimer)

(1898–1965) *director, National Advisory Committee for Aeronautics; deputy administrator, National Aeronautics and Space Administration*

The son of a streetcar conductor, Dryden was born in Pocomoke City, Md., on July 2, 1898. He grew up in Baltimore and attended the city's public schools. He received his B.A. from Johns Hopkins in 1916 and his Ph.D. there three years later. He then took a job as the director of the aeronautics section of the National Bureau of Standards, where he had conducted research as a student. During the 1920s, Dryden made a significant scientific breakthrough by using wind tunnels to determine what the flow around airplane wings would be at speeds approaching and beyond the speed of sound. This work, together with studies of wind turbulence carried out in the 1930s, made him one of the key figures behind the revolutionary strides in aircraft design during the 1930s and 1940s. During World War II, Dryden headed a project that developed the first self-guided missile used in combat. He was appointed associate director of the Bureau of Standards in 1946 but resigned the following year to join the National Advisory Committee for Aeronautics

(NACA), an agency geared toward civilian research in aviation design. Dryden became director of the agency in 1949.

As director, Dryden was often called upon to justify research projects before congressional committees. In April 1953, he appeared before a House Appropriations subcommittee to explain projects intended to link a nuclear reactor to a comparatively conventional jet engine. Two years later, after it became known that the Soviet Union was working on an atomic-powered airplane, Dryden went before a Senate Armed Services subcommittee to request funds to expand NACA's facilities for the same research.

In response to the Soviet Union's successful launching of *Sputnik,* the first artificial satellite, in October 1957 and to the Gaither Report, warning of increasing Soviet advances in military-technology and scientific knowledge, Eisenhower called for the creation of a national space and aeronautics agency in April 1958. This Agency, which would absorb the functions of NACA, was designed to direct U.S. activities relating to all nonmilitary aspects of outer space. Dryden played a major role in drafting the legislation and presenting the proposal to Congress. The measure was signed into law in July.

Dryden, himself, had a conservative vision of the goals of the new National Aeronautics and Space Administration (NASA). He reported that its initial project would be the orbiting of a stargazing satellite and urged the development of satellites that could be used either for communications purposes or for the scientific investigation of the Moon. When questioned about the feasibility of sending men into space, Dryden dismissed the idea as a circus stunt. Because of his limited view of the agency's goals, he did not oppose NASA's modest budget.

Upon the creation of NASA, Dryden was appointed deputy administrator of the agency. He was initially shaken by his failure to receive the top post, but this disappointment waned when he learned that his position would permit him to concentrate on the technical aspects of space research. Despite his initial caution, Dryden came to express his full confidence that the United States could quickly develop a program of manned space exploration. Pointing to the complexity of the factors involved, he suggested that the best way to meet the goal lay in international cooperation.

Dryden continued at his post during the Kennedy administration and the early years of the Johnson presidency. He died in Washington, D.C., on December 2, 1965.

—EF

Dubinsky, David

(1892–1982) *president, International Ladies' Garment Workers' Union*

David Dubinsky was born on February 22, 1892, in Brest Litovsk, Poland (later the Soviet Union). His family moved to Łódź, Poland, when he was very young. In order to work in his father's bakery, Dubinsky had to join the city's semi-legal bakers' union. At the age of 15, he led a strike against the bakers, including his father. Arrested as a labor agitator, he was exiled to Siberia, but he managed to escape en route and emigrated to the United States in 1911. In New York, Dubinsky learned the cloak-cutting trade, joined the International Ladies' Garment Workers' Union (ILGWU), and was active in the Socialist Party. In 1922, he became a member of the union's executive board. Dubinsky tightly controlled his cutters' local and waged a successful 10-year battle against communists in the union. He became acting president in 1927 and was elected president in 1932. He became a vice president of the American Federation of Labor (AFL) in 1935.

In 1935, Dubinsky joined JOHN L. LEWIS and other advocates of industrial unions to form the Committee (later Congress) for Industrial Organization (CIO). Dubinsky vigorously backed the CIO's organizing drives among workers in mass-production industries but opposed its permanent formation as an alternative to the more conservative, craft-union-oriented AFL. For a short time, Dubinsky pulled his union out of the AFL in protest against its treatment of the CIO, but he rejoined it in 1940.

An enthusiastic supporter of Franklin D. Roosevelt's New Deal, Dubinsky joined Sidney Hillman and ALEX ROSE in forming the American Labor Party (ALP) to support the New Deal nationally while remaining outside the Democratic Party, which they thought dominated by urban bosses and southern conservatives. Because of growing communist strength in the ALP, Dubinsky, Hillman, and Rose left in 1944 to found New York State's Liberal Party. Dubinsky helped form Americans for Democratic Action three years later. By the onset of the cold war, he had repudiated his socialist past. Starting with HARRY S. TRUMAN in 1948, Dubinsky and the Liberal Party supported every Democratic candidate for president.

Dubinsky also played a major role in the AFL's international activities, helping to organize the International Federation of Trade Unions. Following World War II, the ILGWU spent $3 million abroad, much of it in Israel and Italy, where Dubinsky helped facilitate the merger of Catholic and socialist trade unions into one federation.

By the 1950s, the ILGWU's welfare programs were among the most extensive of any union in the country. The union had established its own health centers, radio stations, a major cooperative housing project on New York City's Lower East Side, and extensive recreational facilities. Dubinsky continued to expand the benefits throughout the decade. Following a strike in 1958, the union obtained severance pay for those workers whose companies closed down or moved out of New York. This was of crucial importance, because many small clothing manufacturers were fleeing the Northeast to the South, which was hostile to unions. Dubinsky also persuaded the employers to sew the famous "union label" into their garments. Both union and management hoped that labeling would persuade Americans to buy union-made garments. Their objective was to fight cheap imports and, just as importantly, hurt many of the nonunionized shops protected from ILGWU organizers through alliances with organized crime. The strike settlement in 1958 included provisions to equalize wages for workers outside the Northeast.

Dubinsky's leadership often earned the praise of his opponents at the bargaining table. ILGWU special teams cooperated with industry to encourage efficiency, and many employers acknowledged that the benefits Dubinsky won for his workers made them into a stable, contented workforce. Stability of employment became common in the 1950s for many ILGWU members for the first time. When negotiating, Dubinsky often took into consideration the financial status of an industry plagued with price-cutting competition from imports and nonunion shops in the South. Finally, many employers admired Dubinsky's campaign against labor racketeers.

In the 1920s and 1930s, Dubinsky waged a battle to purge his union of corrupt officials, who were often tied to organized crime. Although he was never completely successful in his campaign, by the late 1930s, the ILGWU had purged most criminal elements from its ranks. Dubinsky also sought to press the AFL, and after 1955 the AFL-CIO, to deal more forcefully with the criminal elements in member unions. In 1952, he successfully initiated the AFL's expulsion of the racketeer-infested International Longshoremen's Association. Dubinsky sat on the AFL-CIO's Committee on Ethical Practices that expelled the Teamsters Union in December 1957. That year, the Senate Select Committee on Improper Activities in the Labor or Management Field heard testimony that Dubinsky had cooperated with criminals to aid his union's past organization drives. Dubinsky denied the accusations.

In the 1960s, Dubinsky remained active in Liberal Party politics and aided John V. Lindsay's mayoral campaigns in 1965 and 1969. Dubinsky retired as president of the ILGWU in 1966. He died in New York City on September 17, 1982.

—JB

Dulles, Allen W(elsh)
(1893–1969) *director of Central Intelligence*

Allen Dulles was born in Watertown, N.Y., on April 7, 1893. The Dulles family had a background in diplomatic service. Allen's grandfather John W. Foster served as Benjamin Harrison's secretary of state. His uncle Robert Lansing held the same post in the Wilson administration; another uncle, John Walsh, had been minister to England. Dulles's father, however, was a Presbyterian minister who imbued his sons with a strong belief in the conflict of good and evil. Dulles attended private schools in upstate New York and Paris and then earned B.A. and M.A. degrees at Princeton University.

Beginning in 1916, Dulles served in a number of posts in the diplomatic service, including an assignment with the U.S. delegation to the Versailles Peace Conference of 1918–19. From 1922 to 1926, he served as the chief of the State Department's division of Near Eastern affairs. After receiving his LL.B. from George Washington University in 1926, he resigned from government work and joined his brother, JOHN FOSTER DULLES, at the law firm of Sullivan & Cromwell. He became a partner in the firm four years later. Allen Dulles observed with horror the rise of Hitler. In 1938, he ran an unsuccessful campaign for Congress in which he urged the need for America to face up to the Nazis.

With the outbreak of World War II, Dulles returned to government service as director of the Office of Strategic Services. He supervised espionage activities against Germany and played an important role in the surrender of German troops in Italy in 1945. After the war, he helped draft the National Security Act of 1947, which established the Central Intelligence Agency (CIA), and in 1948 he headed a three-man committee that studied the intelligence functions of the organization. In 1951, Dulles left his law practice to become the deputy director of the CIA, in charge of covert operations.

In 1953, President DWIGHT D. EISENHOWER appointed Dulles director of Central Intelligence, a position that gave him power not only to run the CIA but also to oversee all U.S. intelligence activities. Dulles's personal style quickly became the public's image of the CIA and its formal standard of behavior. Pipe-smoking, urbane, and educated in the Ivy League, like many early CIA officials, Dulles was able to impress upon his listeners in public and government circles the need for absolute secrecy in CIA operations. During his tenure, there was little outside oversight of his agency, largely because of his close relationship with Eisenhower and powerful congressional leaders who shared his views on secrecy.

During the Eisenhower administration, the CIA and State Department worked harmoniously because of the closeness of Allen Dulles and his brother, Secretary of State John Foster Dulles. The two men shared the view that the cold war was a moral crusade against communism. Both used their belief in the necessity for democracy to triumph over totalitarianism to justify their policies.

Under Dulles, the CIA helped overthrow several left-wing governments and establish regimes that supported the United States. The CIA's first major success occurred in Iran in 1953, when operatives, directed by Kermit Roosevelt, helped topple the leftist government of Prime Minister Mohammed Mossadeq.

Two years later, Dulles helped plot the overthrow of Guatemalan President Jacobo Arbenz, whose leftist government had roused the ire of the American administration. In June, a small army of exiled Guatemalans, trained and financed by the CIA, crossed the Honduras-Guatemala border to overthrow Arbenz. Three old airplanes, supplied by the CIA, provided the army with necessary air cover. When the invasion faltered, Dulles convinced Eisenhower to send two additional American planes to the small, crippled air force. As a result of the attack, Guatemalan army officials deserted Arbenz, and he was forced to capitulate. With CIA guidance, negotiations brought the rightist Col. Carlos Castillo-Armas into power. Castillo-Armas was assassinated in 1957.

In Iran and Guatemala, the CIA supported disaffected local groups. The agency also backed anticommunist regimes with little popular support. In South Vietnam, for example, the agency helped President Ngo Dinh Diem solidify his hold on the central government despite opposition from military and sect leaders.

During Dulles's tenure, intelligence-gathering operations were expanded and new technological means of surveillance, such as the U-2 and SR-71 spy planes, were developed. Emphasis was put on the use of technology rather than traditional operatives to collect data.

In 1975, the Senate Select Committee to Study Intelligence Activities (the Church committee) reported that, during Dulles's tenure, the CIA formulated a complicated system of responsibility for departmental actions. By issuing vague but suggestive instructions to subordinates, highly placed officials under examination could legitimately claim "plausible denial" of culpability in covert operations. The committee, therefore, had difficulty in determining Dulles's role in some of the CIA's more controversial projects. It found evidence that he authorized the assassination of Congolese leader

Patrice Lumumba and said he may have received suggestive, if not direct, encouragement for such action from President Eisenhower. Dulles sent the following message to the CIA station in Léopoldville in 1960: "We wish every possible support in eliminating Lumumba from any possibility of resuming a governmental position." CIA operatives, headed by RICHARD BISSELL, interpreted the cable as authorization to arrange Lumumba's death. Local Congolese, however, killed Lumumba before the CIA operation could materialize. In addition, the Select Committee revealed that Dulles and Eisenhower had urged the overthrow of Rafael Trujillo, the rightist dictator of the Dominican Republic.

Investigations by the Church committee and by the Rockefeller committee on CIA activities within the United States revealed that, during the Dulles years, some U.S. businesses, small foundations, and organizations were used as fronts for CIA activities. From 1952 to 1973, beginning with Dulles's approval of a "New York mail program," CIA officials intercepted, screened, opened, and sometimes photocopied millions of mailed items from selected countries, primarily those under communist control. Presumably with the tacit approval of three postmasters general, the agency monitored the correspondence of those on their "watch list," which included such individuals as Victor Reuther and LINUS PAULING.

A former CIA agent, Victor Marchetti, and an ex-State Department official, John D. Marks, claimed in their book *The CIA and the Cult of Intelligence* that in 1959 Dulles had revised the content of a CIA intelligence report describing Cuban premier Fidel Castro's rise to power as a natural development in the face of the excesses of the Batista regime and had sent Eisenhower a much darker analysis predicting that Castro would use extreme measures to solidify his power. In March 1960, the president authorized Dulles to initiate a series of measures designed to liberate the island from communist rule. Dulles, in turn, gave Bissell responsibility for handling the operation.

Bissell embellished upon the relatively cautious program Eisenhower endorsed on March 17. Bissell devised a plan to use exiles, trained at CIA bases in Guatemala, to infiltrate the island and overthrow the regime. When that proved unfeasible, he developed a plan to invade the island. Bissell also enlisted the aid of organized crime figures in an unsuccessful effort to assassinate Castro. The Senate Select Committee reported that "it is not entirely certain that Dulles was ever made aware of the true nature of the underworld plot."

After the election of 1960, Dulles and Bissell briefed President-elect JOHN F. KENNEDY on Cuba. Bissell informed the president-elect that the CIA was considering a "significant strike force to act as a catalyst" in provoking an uprising against Castro. In fact, the original program did not include a "significant strike force" and reckoned that it would be necessary to develop anti-Castro resistance within Cuba before contemplating any paramilitary infiltrations from the outside. Nevertheless, as planning got under way, Bissell increasingly turned his attention to the development of a strike force. As the CIA plans became more ambitious, neither Bissell nor Dulles had apprised Eisenhower of these developments. Kennedy approved the landing, and the disastrous Bay of Pigs invasion took place in April 1961. After the fiasco, Kennedy moved quickly to replace Dulles, who resigned in September 1961 and returned to his law practice. Dulles served on the Warren Commission, which investigated the Kennedy assassination. He died in Washington on January 29, 1969.

—MSM, JB, TCD

Dulles, John Foster
(1888–1959) *secretary of state*

Born on February 25, 1888, in Washington, D.C., Dulles was descended from a family of diplomats and clergymen. His maternal grandfather, John W. Foster, served as ambassador to Russia, Spain, and Mexico and was secretary of state under Benjamin Harrison. His uncle, Robert Lansing, was secretary of state in the Wilson administration. Dulles's paternal grandfather, John Welch Dulles, was a Presbyterian missionary in China. His father, Allen Dulles, taught philosophy at Auburn Theological Seminary and was a Presbyterian minister in Watertown, N.Y., where Foster grew up.

Dulles graduated from Princeton University in 1908 and spent a year studying at the Sorbonne. Although he had expressed an interest in entering the ministry, he decided to become a lawyer. He completed the three-year curriculum at George Washington University's law school in two years while earning the highest grades ever achieved at that school. Upon finishing law school in 1911, he joined the prestigious New York law firm of Sullivan & Cromwell. Dulles served as a special agent for the State Department in Central America in 1917. During World War I, he worked with the army intelligence service and was an assistant to the chairman of the War Trade Board.

Dulles went to the Versailles Peace Conference in 1919 as legal counsel to Bernard Baruch, the U.S. representative on the Reparations Commission. In that capacity, Dulles earned high praise for his role in convincing the British and French to lower their demands for reparations.

Upon Dulles's return from Paris, he became a partner in Sullivan & Cromwell. An austere man and a compulsive worker, Dulles established a distinguished record as a specialist in international law. After Germany defaulted on its reparations payments and France occupied the Ruhr Valley, Dulles served as special counsel to the Dawes Commission (after its chairman, Charles Dawes). Dulles became managing partner of Sullivan & Cromwell in 1927. Under his leadership, the firm opened offices in Berlin and Buenos Aires and expanded its office in Paris. For the next two decades, it would be the largest law firm in the world.

Throughout the 1930s, Dulles lectured and wrote on foreign affairs. Moreover, his firm had extensive dealings in Europe and particularly in Germany. Dulles attended a meeting of the World Council of Churches at Oxford in 1937. He came away from the conference impressed with the sincerity of the participants and the effectiveness of the World Council as a platform. Personally, Dulles deplored the excesses of the Nazis but maintained that it was up to Germans to deal with the matter. Further, he believed that the injustices of the Versailles treaty had led to Hitler's rise and the international friction of the late 1930s. He presented his views in *War, Peace and Change*, published in early 1939. Devoid of the moral tone that would later typify his work, the book was a systematic, legalistic inquiry into the reasons nations go to war. Dulles ascribed the troubled situation in Europe to the failure of the Treaty of Versailles. By insisting on the maintenance of the status quo, the victorious Allies had forced Germany to take violent action to achieve needed change. Dulles saw the threat to peace coming from the system of nation-states advancing their self-interest and suggested that war could be avoided through the creation of "international mechanisms" (which he did not clearly define) to manage change.

Throughout the late 1930s, Dulles remained a noninterventionist. He was deeply disturbed by the outbreak of war in Europe and believed the United States could avoid entering the struggle by developing a moral solution to the crisis. In 1940, he assumed the chairmanship of the Federal Council of Churchs' Commission on a Just and Durable Peace. Dulles's major goal was to create a more effective successor to the League of Nations. In May 1943, he set down an abstract plan for preventing war in a report titled "The Six Pillars of Peace." In contrast to his early works, it contained a strong moral theme. Dulles believed that peace could be achieved only when nations acted in conjunction with moral law. The United States had a particular moral obligation in guiding the postwar world and in forming the international organization that would maintain peace.

During the war, Dulles emerged as a leading spokesman on foreign policy for the eastern wing of the Republican party. In 1944, he served as a foreign policy adviser to the Republican presidential candidate, Governor THOMAS DEWEY of New York. A supporter of a bipartisan foreign policy, Dulles also undertook several diplomatic assignments for the Roosevelt and Truman administrations. In 1945, he was a member of the U.S. delegation to the UN Conference in San Francisco. From 1946 to 1950, he was a delegate to the UN General Assembly and an adviser to the State Department. Dulles served as Dewey's adviser during the presidential campaign in 1948 and backed the candidate's decision not to mount an aggressive attack on Truman's foreign policy. During the immediate postwar period, Dulles endorsed the Truman Doctrine, the Marshall Plan, and the North Atlantic Treaty, as well as the president's conduct of the Korean war.

In the last half of the decade, Dulles's assessment of the world situation changed. No longer did

he see peace threatened by the system of nation-states and the selfishness of all countries. Instead, it was jeopardized by the evil intentions and ideologies of specific states, particularly the Soviet Union. In an article in *Life* magazine in 1946, he warned that the Soviet Union would continue its expansionist policy. Dulles called for military measures to meet the threat, but more importantly, he preached a need for a spiritual rebirth and a recommitment to American institutions to counter the threat. Despite his hatred of communism, he urged a more conciliatory attitude toward the USSR, believing it might lift the Iron Curtain and permit the entrance of beneficent Western influence.

In 1949, Dewey appointed Dulles to fill a vacancy in the Senate created by the resignation of Robert Wagner. Dulles lost to HERBERT H. LEHMAN in a special election that fall to serve the remainder of the term. Dulles became a consultant for the State Department and in 1950–51 negotiated the U.S.-Japanese peace treaty. This agreement restored Japan's sovereignty and allowed U.S. bases to remain in that nation. Dulles was always proud of the treaty. He regarded it as "creative and curative," not harsh and vindictive, like the Treaty of Versailles.

During the early 1950s, Dulles, by then the Republican Party's most prominent foreign-policy figure, became increasingly critical of the Truman administration's foreign policy.

Dulles outlined his new position in a *Life* article in 1952. He contended that Truman's policy of containment had been only partly successful in preventing communist expansion and had failed to roll back the communist sphere of influence in Eastern Europe and China. Containment offered the American people only the status quo. Instead, Dulles suggested a policy of liberation for nations of the Eastern bloc. Dulles opposed Truman's reliance on conventional weapons, maintaining it would bankrupt the nation. He recommended that the United States rely on nuclear weapons when necessary. In his words, the primary way of countering communist aggression was "for the free world to develop the will and organize the means to retaliate instantly against open aggression by Red Armies, so that, if it occurred anywhere, we could and would strike back, where it hurt, by means of our own choosing."

Dulles's ideas impressed both moderate and conservative Republicans. In 1952, he was asked to draft the foreign policy plank in the Republican platform. There he condemned containment as "negative, futile and immoral" because it abandoned "countless human beings to despotic and godless terror." The party pledged the liberation of Eastern Europe. Dulles campaigned vigorously for the Eisenhower ticket but was rarely seen with the general or asked for his advice. Eisenhower had reservations about and was reluctant to associate himself too closely with Dulles's policy of liberation.

The press widely assumed that Dulles would be chosen as Eisenhower's secretary of state and, in fact, Eisenhower never seriously considered anyone else. He named Dulles secretary of state in late November.

Relations between the men were initially formal. The aloof Dulles had difficulty dealing with the president. Eisenhower, in turn, found his secretary of state dull, verbose, and legalistic in his discussions. Yet the two men developed a close relationship. Eisenhower spoke to Dulles daily.

Over the decade, the two men molded foreign policy. Contrary to some earlier accounts, Dulles did not dominate Eisenhower. The president was clearly in charge and made policy decisions. Nonetheless, Eisenhower had a high regard for Dulles and his opinions. Eisenhower once told EMMET HUGHES, "There's only one man I know who has seen *more* of the world and talked with more people and *knows* more than he does—and that's *me*." In general, Eisenhower and Dulles agreed on the basic outlines of foreign policy. Dulles sometimes took a harder line with respect to the Soviet Union or specific foreign policy conflicts. Moreover, Dulles had a penchant for encapsulating his ideas into catchy phrases ("massive retaliation," "agonizing reappraisals") that created controversy. At times, this caused Eisenhower some irritation. At other times, Eisenhower used Dulles as the bad cop while he came on as the reasonable good cop in international relations.

Dulles considered himself primarily the president's personal foreign policy adviser, and he jealously guarded his position within the White House. He objected to independent foreign policy initiatives by such advisers as HAROLD STASSEN in the field of disarmament and NELSON ROCKEFELLER in the field of Latin American relations. Each of these men resigned, in part, because the secretary frustrated their plans.

Because he thought of himself as an adviser, Dulles spent less time on the administration of the State Department. However, he did not, as some critics charged, attempt to run the state department out of his briefcase.

Dulles entered office well aware of the need for good relations with Congress. During his early life he had seen Woodrow Wilson's dream of American participation in the League of Nations destroyed by his inability to deal with Congress. After World War II, he saw DEAN ACHESON hampered by the same failure. Dulles was particularly concerned with maintaining good relations with the powerful Republican Right, led by such senators as WILLIAM JENNER, (R-Ind.), STYLES BRIDGES (R-N.H.), and JOSEPH McCARTHY (R-Wis.).

Soon after becoming secretary of state, he attempted to placate McCarthy, who had charged that the State Department harbored subversives. Dulles instituted strict security reviews under the direction of SCOTT McLEOD, a McCarthy supporter. Over the next few years, investigations resulted in the dismissal or forced resignation of several hundred State Department employees as security risks or because of drunkenness, homosexuality, incompetence, or "incompatibility." The last reason was used for those whose policy judgments displeased the Republican Right.

Those removed included JOHN P. DAVIES and JOHN CARTER VINCENT, China experts under attack as pro-Communist because they opposed all-out aid to Chiang Kai-shek (Jiang Jieshi) during the 1940s. Reviewing their files, Dulles found no security violations. Nevertheless, he refused to support these men and asked for their resignations on the grounds of lack of judgment, discretion, and reliability.

Dulles did, however, support the nomination of CHARLES E. BOHLEN to be ambassador to the USSR. Right-wing Republicans accused the diplomat of being a security risk and attacked him because of his role in the formation of the Yalta agreements. The Senate confirmed Bohlen's appointment, but while the Senate considered the nomination, Dulles insisted that he not be seen too frequently in Bohlen's company.

Dulles entered his office with the desire to implement a policy of boldness and action. No longer would the United States simply react to communist challenge; it would take the offensive against the adversary. Although he had no long-range plans to implement this idea, his policy initially dealt with four considerations: ending the Korean war without changing the status quo in the rest of Asia; developing anticommunist alliances in the Middle East; unifying western Europe; and maintaining the cold war against the Soviets.

Shortly after the inauguration, Dulles and Eisenhower took steps to end the Korean War. They intensified the pressure on China to accept a compromise agreement. In his State of the Union message, Eisenhower announced he would remove the Seventh Fleet from the Formosa Straits, thus "unleashing" Chiang Kai-shek for a possible attack on the mainland. The administration also revealed plans to increase U.S. air power in Korea, enlarge the South Korean Army, and place nuclear weapons on Okinawa. At the same time, Dulles firmly pushed South Korea into accepting an armistice by refusing to give in to President Syngman Rhee's demands for resumption of the war if Korean unification was not achieved within three months of an armistice. The agreement was signed on July 27, 1953.

In the Mideast, Dulles attempted to forestall communist expansion through the establishment of pro-Western governments and the formation of a military alliance similar to the North Atlantic Treaty Organization (NATO). The leftist government of Iranian Premier Mohammed Mossadeq was overthrown in August 1953 with the help of the Central Intelligence Agency (CIA). A pro-Western regime loyal to the Shah took its place. In attempting to form alliances, the secretary was frustrated by growing nationalism in Arab nations, particularly Egypt. Reacting to years of British colonial rule, Egyptian leader Gamal Abdel Nasser refused to accept membership in any mutual defense organization giving Great Britain or any other colonial power the right to return to Egypt if strategic interests were threatened. Nasser did not perceive the communist threat as serious and attempted to maintain a policy of neutrality to prevent domination by either the Western or Soviet bloc. In 1954, the British succeeded in forming the Baghdad Pact,

a military alliance with Turkey, Iran, Iraq, and Pakistan. Dulles, however, was reluctant to recognize the alliance, because he did not want to be associated with colonial powers. Fearing that American membership would antagonize Arab leaders, he sent an "observer" rather than an ambassador to the new organization.

As secretary of state, Dulles was particularly concerned with American policy in western Europe, which he thought would be the major battlefield of the cold war. Throughout his tenure, he attempted to promote European unification, maintaining that Europe, "the world's worst fire hazard," could not be rebuilt on the old system of nation-states. The secretary supported moves toward economic unification, including the formation of the European Iron and Steel Community, and he wanted them complemented by steps toward military unification. By the time Dulles came into office, an agreement on the formation of the European Defense Community (EDC), establishing an inter-European army, had already been initialed by the entities concerned: France, Germany, and the Benelux countries. However, popular opposition to the plan, particularly in France, which feared German rearmament, endangered ratification. During the early months of 1953, Dulles flew to various European capitals in an attempt to increase support for the EDC. Intent upon gaining acceptance, he suggested that a defeat of the proposal would result in "an agonizing reappraisal" of American commitments in Europe. However, his efforts failed. The proposal died in August 1954, when the French Assembly refused to consider the plan.

Dulles was particularly upset by the defeat because he believed it necessary to integrate West Germany into the mainstream of European politics as quickly as possible lest the nation make an accommodation with the Soviet bloc. Dulles's strident stand during the debate over the EDC, however, angered America's allies, and the secretary was forced to leave the negotiation of the German issue to the British. Over the next few months, Foreign Minister Anthony Eden laid the groundwork for the introduction of Germany into NATO while placing constraints on German rearmament to please the French. Dulles supported the plan, approved at a foreign minister's conference convened in London in September.

Although critics derided him as an unwavering and reflexive cold warrior, documents declassified over the last two decades have revealed that Dulles was more complex and flexible than his image as a Presbyterian crusader in the cold war. He was open to the possibility of genuine negotiations with the Soviets and recognized the process of change in the post-Stalin era. Dulles believed that, after Stalin's death, communist rulers in Eastern Europe would "experience far greater difficulty . . . in subordinating the impulse of nationalism" and urged American embassies "to sow doubt, confusion, uncertainty about [the] new regime." At the same time, he counseled caution. An overly exuberant response on the part of the West, he warned, could channel Russian nationalism into sympathy for the new leadership. When a series of anticommunist riots broke out in East Germany, Dulles made a point of explicitly and publicly stating that fomenting internal difficulties in the Soviet sphere did "not mean" encouraging "an armed revolt which would precipitate a massacre." Nevertheless, Dulles seems to have been more suspicious of a series of peace overtures by the post-Stalinist leadership than was Eisenhower. When Eisenhower determined to respond publicly to the gesture, Dulles recommended that the speech contain a list of "deeds," including political self-determination for Eastern Europe, to test the sincerity of the Russian proposals. These were included in the president's statement, which suggested the possibility of accommodation.

Along the same lines, Dulles had serious reservations about the summit conference with the Soviet leaders in 1955. He believed that the meeting would accomplish nothing and worried that it would antagonize the Republican right. The secretary urged that the United States require the USSR to begin withdrawal from Eastern Europe before serious talks began. Eisenhower, however, rejected his secretary's advice and accepted an invitation to meet with the Soviet leaders in July. Although Dulles had advised him to wear an "austere countenance" when photographed with Premier Nikolai Bulganin, the president conducted himself in a warm, friendly manner. The conference resolved none of the issues dividing the nations—Germany and disarmament—but the fact that the leaders of the two superpowers had discussed differences gave

hope of improved chances for peace and led to the "Spirit of Geneva," the first thaw in the cold war.

Dulles, however, had a pessimistic assessment of the meeting. He remained convinced that the Soviet Union had called the summit to gain strategic respite. The secretary believed that the Soviets had overextended themselves in the arms race and were hence forced toward conciliation with the West. He conceded that the new Soviet policy "might assume the force of an irreversible trend" and that it should be encouraged. However, he refused to accept the situation in Europe and warned that Russian actions did not justify "the free world relaxing its vigilance or substantially altering its programs for collective security."

Although Dulles and his defenders hailed his policies as a departure from those of the Truman administration, they were in essence continuations of containment. The major innovation was the introduction of the "New Look" defense policy, with its reliance on strategic deterrence or "massive retaliation" as it became known. Fashioned chiefly by Adm. ARTHUR RADFORD, chairman of the Joint Chiefs of Staff, the New Look was based on a desire to hold down defense costs and prevent debilitating ground wars such as those in Korea. It called for a greater reliance on the strategic air force and a reduction in conventional forces. Although its origins could be traced to Dulles's article, "The Policy of Boldness," which appeared in *Life* in 1952, the secretary had very little to do with the actual formulation. In military matters, he was content to rely on the Pentagon. Yet the secretary was given the task of explaining the New Look to the American people. In a speech before the Council on Foreign Relations in January 1954, Dulles told the audience that the use of conventional forces had traditionally given the enemy the initiative. The secretary promised that the United States could "depend upon a great capacity to retaliate instantly by means and at places of our own choosing."

Foreign policy observers had difficulty trying to understand what Dulles meant by this ambiguous statement. Many thought the secretary promised nuclear war for any Soviet infraction of the status quo. Dulles attempted to clarify the use of the term, but his several attempts at explanation confused the issue further. WALTER LIPPMANN, wrote that "official explanations of the New Look have become so voluminous that it is almost a career to keep up with them." That concept, with its ambiguity, played an important role in the development of Dulles's foreign policy. The secretary saw the threat of deterrence as a potent diplomatic weapon to brandish before the communists.

The New Look was tested twice during 1954: in Vietnam and in the Formosa Straits. During the spring of 1954, the French asked for direct American intervention in Vietnam to relieve their garrison at Dien Bien Phu, then under attack by the communist Vietminh. The French confided to Dulles their desire to reach a settlement in the Indochina war and told him they would restrict military operations to achieve that goal. The secretary opposed the French decision, believing it would further the expansion of communism in Southeast Asia. He also rejected Radford's call for bombing raids to relieve the fort, because the proposal was too narrow in scope.

Nevertheless, Eisenhower and Dulles believed that something should be done, and they began to formulate a response between March 24 and April 1. They considered a coalition of the United States, Great Britain, France, Australia, New Zealand, Thailand, the Philippines, and the Associated States of Indochina that would commit itself to defend Indochina and the rest of Southeast Asia against communism. Eisenhower and Dulles agreed that, if the United States were to intervene, it should do so only as part of a multinational coalition. Further, if the United States did intervene, they wanted, in keeping with the New Look, local and regional forces to do most of the ground fighting. The United States would provide air and naval support, train local forces, and furnish money and supplies. In a speech on March 29, Dulles publicly presented the concept, but did so in deliberately vague terms. "The United States," he said, "feels that the possibility of communist control should not be passively accepted, but should be met with united action."

Over the next month, Dulles attempted to generate congressional and allied support for his plan. Eisenhower and Dulles understood that if they did nothing and Indochina fell to the communists, they would be vulnerable to attack both from right-wing Republicans and Democrats. Further, in the aftermath of Korea, intervention without congressional authorization was not politically feasible. Contrary to what Chalmers Roberts and others have argued, Eisenhower and Dulles did not seek congressional authority for an immediate air strike to relieve the French garrison at Dien Bien Phu. Rather, they sought a congressional resolution that would give the president broad discretionary authority to use American power to prevent the "extension and expansion" of communism in Southeast Asia. Congressional leaders, however, wanted assurances that America's allies would participate and the United States would not have to bear most of the burden. They also wanted France to agree to grant the Indochinese independence. These conditions did not differ in any significant way from what Eisenhower and Dulles had in mind, but they did take unilateral action off the table. Since the French showed no inclination to meet Eisenhower's conditions that any force be multinational and that the French promise independence to the Indochinese, it was highly improbable that Eisenhower would have intervened on behalf of the French. The position of the congressional leaders, however, provided a convenient excuse. Moreover, the British did not agree that the fall of Indochina threatened the rest of Southeast Asia.

Dulles opposed sending a delegation to the Geneva Conference on Indochina in April 1954. Eisenhower, however, wanted an American presence and sent WALTER BEDELL SMITH as an observer but not a participant. Dulles spent a week at the conference, during which he refused to acknowledge the Communist Chinese delegation.

On July 20, the Geneva Conference reached an agreement on Vietnam. Under the Geneva Accords, as the agreement was known, Vietnam was temporarily divided along the 17th parallel, with the communists, led by Ho Chi Minh, controlling the north and a pro-Western government in the south. Neither North nor South Vietnam would enter into military alliances. The nation was to be reunified through free elections scheduled for 1956. The United States took note of the agreements and announced that it would "refrain from the . . . use of force" to upset them, but it did not sign the Geneva Accords. In a statement after the agreement had been reached, Smith announced that the United States "would view any renewal of the aggression in violation of the aforesaid agreements with grave concern and as seriously threatening international peace and security."

Over the next few months, Dulles worked to prevent communist expansion in Vietnam. In September, eight nations (the United States, Great Britain, France, Australia, New Zealand, Pakistan, Thailand, and the Philippines) formed the Southeast Asia Treaty Organization and pledged to resist communist aggression in the area. That fall, Dulles announced that the United States would give both economic and military aid to the government of South Vietnam. The United States backed the government of Prime Minister Ngo Dinh Diem and sent economic aid and military advisers, such as EDWARD LANSDALE, to help Diem solidify his position. The American government also supported Diem when he ousted the emperor, Bao Dai. In a shift from the New Look, the secretary began backing reliance on "local defense" to counter communist aggression. When, in 1955, the North Vietnamese proposed preliminary talks to plan the national elections called for the by Geneva Accords, Diem refused, and the Eisenhower administration, convinced that Ho would win such an election, backed Diem's position.

During the fall of 1954, Communist Chinese artillery began shelling the islands of Quemoy and Matsu located off the mainland coast and held by the Nationalist Chinese. Members of the administration differed on how to interpret the action. Dulles believed it was a possible prelude for an invasion of Taiwan; but several military leaders questioned the Communists' military capacity to stage such an action. The secretary joined Radford and most of the Joint Chiefs of Staff (except Gen. MATTHEW RIDGWAY) in proposing that Eisenhower permit Chiang to bomb the mainland. If Beijing retaliated, they suggested the United States send bombers to help the Nationalists. Eisenhower, however, rejected the proposal, preferring to work out a diplomatic solution to the crisis. Eisenhower did order airlifts to Taiwan and the Seventh Fleet to escort Nationalist supply ships. He also sent Dulles to negotiate a mutual security treaty between Nationalist China and the United States. The treaty declared that an armed attack against either nation would be regarded as an act of war against the other.

At Eisenhower's insistence, the treaty applied only to Taiwan and the Pescadores, thus omitting Quemoy and Matsu. The treaty also provided that the Nationalists would not unilaterally use force against the mainland.

In early 1955, the Chinese Communist air force raided the Tachen islands, held by the Nationalist Chinese. The Chinese Communists also captured an island near the Tachens and gave indications of preparing to invade Quemoy and Matsu. In late January, Eisenhower and Dulles met to discuss a congressional resolution granting the president authority to use American forces to defend Taiwan and the Pescadores. Dulles wanted to include Quemoy and Matsu, but Eisenhower overruled him. Congress passed the resolution by the end of the month. On April 23, at the conference of nonaligned nations in Bandung, Zhou Enlai (Chou En-lai) gave a conciliatory speech, and Eisenhower responded. Subsequently, the mainland Chinese reduced their shelling of the islands and by mid-May stopped it entirely. The crisis passed.

With the presidential campaign approaching in 1956, Dulles defended his conduct of foreign policy in an interview with *Life* magazine. He maintained that only unwavering opposition to the Soviet Union could avoid both war and surrender to communism. Dulles pointed to three occasions on which such a posture prevented both further Soviet aggression and war: the implied threat of the use of nuclear weapons to end the Korean War, a show of force that deterred the Chinese from entering the war in Indochina, and the firm stand the administration had taken on Quemoy and Matsu. "You have to take chances for peace," Dulles told *Life*, "just as you must take chances in war. Some say we were brought to the verge of war. The ability to get to the verge without getting into war is the necessary art. If you cannot master it, you inevitably get into war. If you try to run away from it, if you are scared to go to the brink, you are lost. . . . We walked to the brink and we looked it in the face. We took strong action." Critics pointed out that threats to use nuclear weapons over limited objectives had little force, because other nations knew that the United States would not be the first to resort to nuclear weapons in such instances.

The consequences of decolonization after World War II ranked among the most persistent and serious issues Dulles and Eisenhower faced. Between 1946 and 1960, 37 new nations emerged from colonial status in the Middle East, Asia, and Africa. Many of these nations chose to remain at least ostensibly neutral in the cold war. In April 1955, 29 "nonaligned" states met at the Bandung Conference and declared their support for "neutrality" and for the Soviet call for "peaceful coexistence." Dulles regarded neutralism as "immoral and shortsighted."

Above all, the United States wanted to make sure that the transition from colonialism to independence did not result in either an increase in communist influence or, worse still, communist control. The Middle East provided the most difficult test for this policy. In Egypt, Gamal Abdel Nasser and a group of young army officers overthrew King Farouk in 1952. Nasser pledged to regain control of the Suez Canal from Great Britain. Under pressure from the United States, the British agreed in 1954 to a phased withdrawal of their troops from the Suez Canal Zone. To maintain Western influence, the United States supported a military alliance of Great Britain, Turkey, Iran, Iraq, and Pakistan, known as the Baghdad Pact. Egypt, however, refused to join, and the bitter conflict between Arabs and Israelis made any hopes for peace in the region unlikely.

Egypt had requested American arms, which the United States refused to supply while British soldiers remained in the Suez Canal Zone. The Egyptian requests for arms were complicated by repeated incidents along the Israeli-Egyptian frontier, particularly at the armistice line along the Gaza Strip. A series of Arab raids and Israeli retaliations increased tensions in the fall of 1954. Several more substantial attacks by Egyptians in early 1955 led to a brigade-strength reprisal raid by Israelis against the Egyptian headquarters in Gaza at the end of February. Nasser used the occasion to renew his request for arms from the United States. When the United States offered arms but with conditions attached, Nasser turned to the Soviets, who arranged for Czechoslovakia to supply a massive shipment of arms to Egypt. In the meantime, the United States attempted to broker a peace agreement. The adversaries, however, did not cooperate. In response to repeated Egyptian raids, Israel launched a significant attack in September,

and Nasser responded by tightening his blockade of the Straits of Tiran. Israel decided on the need for a preventive war before the full effect of the Soviet arms could be brought to bear.

Dulles and Eisenhower attempted to win Nasser's loyalty by offering to provide funding for Nasser's dream of a dam on the Nile at Aswan. British intelligence, however, informed the Eisenhower administration that Nasser was urging the overthrow of pro-Western monarchies in Saudi Arabia, Iraq, and Jordan. Moreover, in May 1956, Nasser recognized Communist China. Domestically, the dam drew opposition from Zionists and Jewish Americans as well as southern members of Congress, who resisted a project that would increase competition for American cotton. Further, Eisenhower and Dulles worried that the arms deal with Czechoslovakia meant that Egypt had aligned with the Soviets. Thus, on July 19, 1956, Dulles informed the Egyptian ambassador that the United States would not fund the Aswan Dam. Nasser responded by seizing the Suez Canal and announced that he would use future proceeds to pay for the dam.

The seizure of the canal threatened British and French interests in the Middle East. The British and French depended on the Canal for shipment of most of their oil, and they began making plans to regain control of the waterway militarily. Eisenhower and Dulles urged a negotiated settlement. Dulles proposed an association of canal users to collect tolls and give to Egypt what it determined was a fair share of the revenues. The proposal angered both Egypt and the European nations. The British and French particularly resented the fact that they had not been consulted in advance.

Impatient with U.S. leadership, the British and French made common cause with the Israelis and decided to settle the matter militarily. In late October 1956, the Israeli army invaded the Sinai, while British and French forces seized the canal. Furious that the United States had not been consulted, worried that the military action would draw attention away from the Soviet invasion of Hungary, and concerned that the action might bring the Soviets into the Middle East, Eisenhower exerted pressure on the British, French, and Israelis to withdraw their forces. The United States joined with the Soviet Union at the UN to pass a resolution calling for the withdrawal of invading forces. Faced with the opposition of world opinion and the two superpowers, Britain, France, and Israel withdrew their forces. The Suez Crisis strained U.S. relations with the British; although the differences were soon composed. The crisis also created frictions with the French, which less easily and less quickly abated. Disagreements over Suez, however, did not seriously disrupt NATO.

Concerned about the expansion of Soviet influence in the Middle East, in January 1957 Eisenhower asked Congress for a joint resolution granting the president authority to send troops to the area if a pro-Western government required assistance against communist aggression. Congress quickly passed the resolution, which became known as the "Eisenhower Doctrine." When, in the aftermath of a military coup that overthrew the Hashemite monarchy in Iraq, the pro-Western Lebanese government feared a revolt in 1958, it requested American assistance, and Eisenhower sent American troops in a show of support for the government of President Camille Chamoun. American diplomats negotiated the withdrawal of American and British forces and a compromise between factions in Lebanon.

The night the UN voted to call for a cease-fire in the Suez Crisis, Dulles experienced severe abdominal pains and went to the hospital. He was diagnosed with cancer. In spite of Dulles's failing health during the second Eisenhower administration, he continued to exert a powerful influence on American policy. Responding to some sentiment in Congress and elsewhere in favor of reaching an accord with mainland China, Dulles gave a speech in June 1957 restating the U.S. policy of nonrecognition. In the meantime, after the Quemoy and Matsu crisis of 1955, Chiang Kai-shek (Jiang Jieshi) had reinforced his garrisons on the two islands. In 1958, Communist China once again began heavy shelling of the islands. Dulles favored an unequivocal statement of America's willingness to defend the islands, but Eisenhower rejected the idea of such a statement. With Eisenhower's approval, however, Dulles held a press conference in which his remarks would be attributable only to a "high official." In it, he declared an unequivocal determination to defend the islands. America's allies counseled caution, and

a growing segment of the American public also expressed concern over the possibility of war over the islands. Eisenhower resisted military advice to employ "low yield" nuclear weapons. Rather, he ordered the Seventh Fleet to escort Nationalist supply ships and an airlift of supplies to Taiwan. Soviet Premier Nikita Khrushchev sent a letter warning against any contemplated use of nuclear weapons and reminding Eisenhower that "the other side too has atomic and hydrogen weapons." Offended by the intemperate tone of the letter, Eisenhower had it returned to the Soviet embassy. Nevertheless, in a press conference at the end of September, Dulles, while maintaining that he had no intention to modify American policy, stated that the United States had no legal commitment to defend Quemoy and Matsu. He further remarked that the heavy concentration of forces on the islands was "rather foolish." In late October, after some frank discussions, Dulles and Chiang agreed that the Nationalist leader would refrain from the use of force against the mainland and withdraw some troops from the islands. Eisenhower suspended escorts of Nationalist ships, and the Chinese Communists relaxed the bombardment. Once again, war over the islands was avoided.

The last major foreign policy crisis in which Dulles was involved came when Khrushchev issued an ultimatum in November 1958. Unless talks on the final disposition of Germany began within six weeks, the Soviets would sign a peace treaty with East Germany, thus ending the agreements reached at the end of World War II. The Western allies would then have to negotiate access to West Berlin with East Germany. In early December, Dulles had to be hospitalized for his cancer. Although quite ill, he attended the NATO meeting of the council in mid-December. Dulles regarded Khrushchev's action as reckless and urged the Western nations not to negotiate under duress. However, he believed that a show of resolve could avoid war. At the end of March, the Soviet premier agreed to a conference of foreign ministers in May and withdrew his ultimatum.

His failing health forced Dulles to resign on April 15. He died in his sleep on May 24, 1959, in Washington, D.C.

—MSM

Durkin, Martin P(atrick)

(1894–1955) secretary of labor

Born on March 18, 1894, in Chicago, Durkin worked for four years as an apprentice steam fitter before becoming a journeyman plumber in Chicago Local 597 of the United Association of Journeymen and Apprentices of the Plumbing and Pipe Fitting Industry of the U.S. and Canada (UA). He served in the army during World War I. In 1922, Durkin became business manager of the largest local of the plumbers' union, Local 597, and in 1927 was made vice president of the Chicago Building Trades Council.

Appointed Illinois state director of labor in 1933 by Democratic Gov. Henry Horner, Durkin served in that post until 1941. As director, he streamlined his department and gained recognition as an administrator. He successfully pushed through legislation that established unemployment compensation and a state employment service, developed new safety rules for employees, and regulated minimum wages and maximum hours for women and children. Durkin went to Washington in 1941 as secretary-treasurer of the national office of the UA. In 1943, he succeeded George Meany as its president.

Eisenhower announced Durkin's appointment as secretary of labor in December 1952. The new Republican administration was acutely aware that, during the campaign, organized labor had called for the repeal of the Taft-Hartley Act and that demands for repeal, or at least revision, of the law would not end with the election. When he considered filling the post of secretary of labor, Eisenhower told Lucius Clay and Herbert Brownell that he wanted someone "from the ranks of labor itself." After considering a number of possibilities, Brownell and Clay accepted Harold Stassen's recommendation of Durkin.

The nomination prompted an angry response from some Republicans. Durkin was a Democrat and had actively worked for the campaign of Adlai E. Stevenson. Sen. Robert Taft called the nomination "incomprehensible," "incredible," and "an affront to millions of union members who had the courage to deny the edict of officers like Mr. Durkin that they vote for Stevenson." Republicans were not alone in their dismay over the nomina-

tion. African Americans protested the elevation of the leader of one of the most racist unions to the cabinet. Eisenhower described the nomination as an "experiment"; his chief of staff, Sherman Adams, described it as "an experiment doomed from the start to failure." The *New Republic* described the cabinet as "eight millionaires and one plumber."

Durkin and his views found little sympathy in the administration. The secretary's primary goal was to revise the Taft-Hartley Act, opposed by labor because of its restrictions on unions. Eisenhower himself, while rejecting total repeal of the measure, had supported amending the legislation to eliminate those provisions that could be used to "smash unions." However, in the White House, Eisenhower did not back Durkin when he clashed with other departments.

Durkin initially set up a committee of representatives of the public, business, and labor to study ways of revising the Taft-Hartley Act. However, quarrels led him to recess the panel. He blamed the representatives of employers for the committee's inability to function.

The secretary's problems with revising the statute soon narrowed to a clash between the Labor Department and the Commerce Department, headed by Sinclair Weeks. Durkin wanted to drop the act's requirement that union leaders sign noncommunist affidavits and to abolish "right-to-work" laws. He also wanted to give labor more control over membership and liberalize the ability to engage in secondary boycotts. Most important, he wanted to minimize the jurisdiction of state courts in labor disputes. Weeks, on the other hand, refused to concede anything above what Eisenhower had vaguely promised and wished to emphasize the power of states in disputes.

Because the two executive departments could not come to an agreement, presidential assistants Bernard Shanley and Gerald Morgan drew up a memorandum suggesting a position for the administration; most of its 19 points were concessions to Durkin. Their memorandum eventually became the basis for a draft message the president was to make to Congress. It was to have been forwarded to the legislature on July 31. However, Taft died that day, and because Taft had coauthored the original legislation, the White House thought that it would be tactless to submit the amendments. Shanley and Morgan, however, assured Durkin that the amendments would be publicly released shortly.

In the meantime, Weeks and others maneuvered behind the scenes to kill the message. Vice President RICHARD NIXON told Eisenhower that repealing the right-to-work provisions would alienate business leaders and southerners. On Aug. 3, the *Wall Street Journal* ran an exposé on the message under the headline "They Favor the Union." In response to the leak, the White House staff released a statement emphasizing that the text was only an early draft.

Durkin and Eisenhower had lunch on August 19. Durkin recalled that Eisenhower had promised to support the 19 amendments. According to Eisenhower's account, he urged Durkin not to think of himself as "a special pleader for labor" and to take a broader view of his responsibilities. On September 10, the president made it clear to Durkin that he would not support the amendments. Durkin resigned and publicly charged that Eisenhower had reneged on his promise to support the amendments. Durkin's eight months in office was the shortest tenure of any secretary of labor. At a press conference later that week, Eisenhower angrily denied having ever agreed to support the amendments.

Durkin returned to the presidency of the UA. He died in Washington, D.C., on Nov. 13, 1955, after operations for a brain tumor.

—MSM

Dworshak, Henry C(larence)
(1894–1962) *U.S. congressman and senator*

Henry Dworshak was born on August 29, 1894, in Duluth, Minn. He served in the army during World War I, after which he became manager of a printer supply business. In 1929, he began publishing a newspaper in Idaho. Dworshak won election as a Republican to the U.S. House of Representatives in 1938 and in 1946 was elected to complete a Senate term expiring in January 1949. He lost his bid for a full term in 1948, but after the Democrat who defeated him died in October 1949, Dworshak was appointed to fill the seat. The following year, he was elected to complete the final four years of the term.

Dworshak was one of the most conservative Republicans in Congress. In 1953, he joined 11 other Republicans voting against the confirmation of CHARLES, BOHLEN as ambassador to the Soviet Union. They maintained that Bohlen was associated with President HARRY S. TRUMAN's foreign policy, which they alleged was "soft on communism."

Dworshak was a strong supporter of Sen. JOSEPH R. MCCARTHY (R-Wis.). In April 1954, McCarthy, with the consent of the Government Operations Committee's Permanent Investigations Subcommittee, chose Dworshak to replace him as chairman during the Army-McCarthy hearings. Dworshak generally favored McCarthy during the probe. In late May, he introduced a motion that had the effect of removing FRANCIS CARR, the subcommittee's staff director, as a witness. Carr was one of McCarthy's staff members accused by the army of attempting to secure special favors for Pvt. G. DAVID SCHINE, a former consultant to the subcommittee. Despite the pleas of the army's counsel, JOSEPH L. WELCH, who wanted to question Carr, Dworshak's motion passed on a straight party vote. The following December, Dworshak voted against the Senate's condemnation of McCarthy.

An advocate of a balanced budget, Dworshak pressed for cuts in Post Office and Public Housing Administration appropriations in 1953. He favored defense budget reductions in 1954 and 1957. Dworshak also criticized the foreign-aid program. In 1957, the senator declared that "goodwill and friendship cannot be bought by American dollars alone."

In 1956, Dworshak opposed a bill, sponsored by Sen. WAYNE MORSE (D-Oreg.), authorizing federal construction of the Hells Canyon Dam. Nevertheless, the Interior and Insular Affairs Committee reported out the measure. Dworshak signed the panel's minority report, which stated that private erection of the dam was in the national interest and that there was no need to insist on a federal project when private construction could achieve similar benefits. The bill reported out of committee was defeated on the Senate floor, and the project was privately built.

Dworshak was a staunch opponent of President Kennedy's domestic policies. The Idaho senator died of a heart attack in Washington, D.C., on July 23, 1962.

—MLL

Eastland, James O(liver)

(1904–1986) *U.S. senator; chairman, Judiciary Committee*

The son of a well-to-do and influential district attorney, James Eastland was born in Doddsville, Miss., on November 28, 1904. He attended the University of Mississippi, Vanderbilt University, and the University of Alabama. After gaining admission to the Mississippi bar in 1927, he began a career as a lawyer. Eastland served as a Democrat in the Mississippi House of Representatives from 1928 to 1932. He then retired from politics and, beginning in 1934, practiced law and managed his family's cotton plantation in Ruleville.

Upon the death of Sen. Byron Patton Harrison in 1941, Gov. Paul B. Johnson appointed Eastland the vacant seat. He declined to run in the special election, but Eastland won a full term in 1942 and subsequently won reelection five times. An unswerving opponent of measures aimed at eliminating racial discrimination, Eastland denounced an anti–poll tax measure in 1944 and charged that "the driving force behind this bill is a bunch of communists." Four years later, he backed the states' rights presidential candidacy of Gov. STROM THURMOND.

Eastland devoted a major share of his activity in the Senate to defending Mississippi's cotton interests. During the 1940s, he introduced bills to ban the import of foreign cotton and to withhold government cotton from the domestic market. During the 1950s, as a member of the Agriculture and Forestry Committee, Eastland attempted to protect the cotton planters of the Deep South against competition from new growers in the Southwest. In 1953, Congress was considering reductions in acreage allotments to reduce cotton surpluses. Planters in California and Arizona requested special protection for new cotton growers in the form of an acreage reduction ceiling of 25 percent for their states. Eastland played a key role in working out a compromise, passed in January 1954, that gave California and Arizona bonus acreage but apportioned basic allotments among the states according to past production figures.

Even while supporting subsidies for cotton farmers in Mississippi, Eastland consistently opposed social welfare legislation. He also supported a strongly anticommunist foreign policy and the crusade against communist subversion at home. Although he did not publicly support Sen. JOSEPH MCCARTHY (R-Wis.) and voted for the censure of the junior senator from Wisconsin in December 1954, he, too, was convinced of the need to ferret out communist subversion. After becoming chairman of the Judiciary' Committee's Internal Security Subcommittee in 1955, Eastland began an investigation of communist infiltration of the news media. Eastland maintained that the press had to be free from control of the Communist Party or "any other conspiracy against the government of the United States." He also believed that communists influenced labor unions, civil rights groups, liberal political organizations, and the Supreme Court.

Eastland criticized the Supreme Court's ruling in *Cole v. Young* (1956), which restricted the application of the Internal Security Act of 1950 to employees in sensitive agencies. In response to that decision, he introduced a bill to apply the act to all federal jobs. The measure failed to win approval.

Eastland denounced the Supreme Court's school desegregation decision of 1954 as "an illegal, immoral, and sinful doctrine" and warned that the decision would lead to the "mongrelization of the white race." Further, he questioned whether people were "obligated morally or legally to obey a decision whose authorities rest not on law but upon the writings and teachings of pro-communist agitators." In 1955, he played a major role in the formation of the Federation for Constitutional Government, a short-lived attempt to unite the white Citizens' Councils and other local white-supremacist groups. He was a frequent and popular speaker before those organizations.

After becoming chairman of the Judiciary Committee in March 1956, Eastland posed a formidable obstacle to the passage of civil rights bills, which fell within the jurisdiction of that panel. In 1957, the administration's civil rights measure passed only after the Senate, in June, voted to bypass the committee and place the measure on the chamber's calendar. Throughout 1959, Eastland delayed another civil rights bill in committee. Liberals pressed Majority Leader LYNDON B. JOHNSON (D-Tex.) and Minority Leader EVERETT M. DIRKSEN (R-Ill.) to bring the measure to the floor, and the leaders announced in September that they would act early the following year to bring the legislation up for debate. In 1960, Johnson and Dirksen bypassed Eastland's Judiciary Committee to get the bill to the floor of the Senate. Southern senators filibustered, and an attempt to invoke cloture failed. Eventually, the Southerners abandoned their filibuster. Passed by Congress in April and signed by the president on May 6, the Civil Rights Act of 1960 provided for court-appointed referees to supervise voting procedures and imposed more stringent penalties for obstructing voting rights. That same year, Eastland bottled up an anti–poll tax amendment to the Constitution.

Disturbed by Supreme Court rulings in civil rights, internal security, and other areas, Eastland joined southerners and anticommunists who sought to restrict the Court's power. In 1956, he introduced a constitutional amendment providing that "there shall be no limitation upon the power of any state to regulate health, morals, education, marriage, and good order in the state." The Senate took no action on the proposal. Eastland claimed the communist influence on the Court was extensive, and in 1958, he asserted that Justices HUGO BLACK, WILLIAM DOUGLAS, and FELIX FRANKFURTER had taken a "pro-communist" position in the great majority of cases involving subversive activities. In 1959, after the Court overturned New York State's ban on exhibiting the movie *L'Amant de Lady Chatterley* (*Lady Chatterley's Lover*), Eastland offered a constitutional amendment barring infringement upon the right of a state "to decide on the basis of its own public policy questions of decency [and] morality." The Senate took no action on this proposed amendment, either.

Although not well known outside of Washington and Mississippi, Eastland wielded considerable power. He opposed most of the social welfare programs of the Kennedy and Johnson administrations, including an increase in the minimum wage, federal aid to education, Medicare, and Head Start. Most notably, Eastland used his chairmanship of the Senate Judiciary Committee to block civil rights legislation. It took deft parliamentary maneuvering to extricate the Civil Rights Act of 1964 and the Voting Rights Act of 1965 from his grip. He delayed for almost a year the confirmation of THURGOOD MARSHALL, a black lawyer who led the NAACP's legal fight against segregation, to a seat on the U.S. Circuit Court of Appeals. "The Chairman," as Eastland was known, also used his power to gain appointments to federal judgeships for conservative Southerners, particularly during the Kennedy administration.

Eastland declined to support Lyndon Johnson in the election of 1964, although he supported Johnson's policy on the war in Vietnam. After choosing not to stand for reelection in 1978, he returned to Doddsville, and lived in Mississippi until the end of his life. He died in Greenwood, Miss., on February 19, 1986.

—MSM

Eastman, Max F(orrester)

(1883–1969) *journalist, writer*

The son of two Congregational ministers, Max Eastman was born in Canandaigua, N.Y., on January 4, 1883. After graduating from Williams College in 1905, he did graduate work in philosophy under John Dewey at Columbia University. After completing all the requirements for a Ph.D., he did not file his dissertation. Through his sister, Crystal, he became associated with the pre–World War I bohemian Left in Greenwich Village. In 1912, he accepted an offer to become editor of the *Masses*, a failing monthly magazine. Eastman turned it into a brilliant and influential journal of Leftist politics and radical approaches to art. Eastman, along with other contributors to the *Masses*, opposed American entry into World War I and expressed those views in the magazine. Consequently, Eastman and six others were indicted for conspiring to obstruct military recruiting and other offenses under the Sedition Act. They escaped conviction thanks to two hung juries. Nevertheless, the revocation of its second-class mailing privilege effectively killed the *Masses* in 1917.

Eastman enthusiastically supported the Bolshevik seizure of power in October 1917, and in 1918, he and Crystal founded the pro-Bolshevik magazine, the *Liberator*. An admirer of Lenin, Eastman went to the Soviet Union in 1922, where he married the sister of a prominent official. In the power struggle that followed Lenin's death in 1924, Eastman supported Trotsky. Joseph Stalin became increasingly powerful, and Eastman left the Soviet Union later that year for western Europe, where he published extracts from what came to be known as Lenin's last "Testament," which warned against Stalin. In 1925, he published *Since Lenin Died*, an account of the methods the Stalinist faction had used to grab power. Eastman was devastated when Trotsky joined communist newspapers in Europe and the United States in denouncing the book.

After returning to the United States in 1927, Eastman supported himself by giving public lectures. He translated Trotsky's works into English and was influential in founding the first Trotskyist party in the United States; however, his position puzzled and angered some of his compatriots. *Marx and Lenin: The Science of Revolution* (1926) combined his attack on the corruption of Bolshevism under Stalin with probing questions about Marxism as an intellectual system. At the same time, however, it supported the communist revolution. His opposition to Stalin alienated Eastman from the majority of American leftists. The publication in 1934 of *Artists in Uniform*, an expose of Stalin's literary purges (conducted in the United States through John Reed Clubs), provoked the wrath of leftist publications in the United States. Eastman's disillusion with what he regarded as the unscientific Marxism practiced in the Soviet Union led him ultimately to reject Marxism itself. Two books published in 1940 elucidated his new position. *Marxism: Is It Science?* explained how he had been misled on that question and why he no longer believed in socialism. *Stalin's Russia* offered the most accurate and cogent indictment in English of Stalin's rule and the purges of the 1930s. Eastman moved to the Right and in 1941 began a long career as roving editor for *Reader's Digest*.

Although his political views gained more notoriety, he believed—and other critics concurred—that his major contribution came in literary studies. His *Enjoyment of Poetry* (1913) was long used as a standard college text. Edmund Wilson praised *The Literary Mind: Its Place in an Age of Science* (1931) for its incisive analysis of "the larger relations of art and science to one another, and of both to the society behind them." Eastman also published five volumes of his own verse.

By the 1950s, Eastman had emerged as a vociferous voice on the Right. Although concerned about internal subversion, he did not succumb to the idea that every reversal in foreign policy resulted from communist influence in Washington. He regarded Sen. JOSEPH R. MCCARTHY (R-Wis.) as clumsy, intemperate, and embarrassing to the Right, calling him "a misbehaved and sloppy-minded person functioning in a place where the prime demand was for a well-behaved and extremely accurate and exact mind." Eastman considered McCarthy incapable of doing "a necessary job in a mature and thoughtful way." Eastman, however, concluded that McCarthy's enemies were still more dangerous, because they refused to recognize the desperate nature of the West's struggle with communism. Further, they were compromised by their own past flirtations with the Left. Eastman said that he would gladly suffer McCarthyism's assaults on civil liberties in exchange for removing communists from the government.

Eastman reserved his greatest contempt for liberalism. He believed that liberalism, with its support of a growing welfare state and a declining free marketplace, might well destroy Western democracy before communism could. He advocated laissez-faire capitalism and decentralization of government.

In 1955, Eastman published *Reflections on the Failure of Socialism*, in which he analyzed what he believed were fallacies of Marxist and socialist thinking. First, he rejected socialism as naively utopian. Further, he regarded liberalism as equally dangerous. In an argument based on the writings of conservative European economists like F. A. HAYEK and Ludwig von Mises, Eastman contended that any planned economy led to the destruction of the free market, from which other liberties were derived. Nevertheless, Eastman tolerated a "mixed economy" so long as consumers and workers retained substantial control over the market.

Reflections on the Failure of Socialism won a wide audience among conservatives. In 1955, Eastman accepted the invitation of WILLIAM F. BUCKLEY, JR., to join the *National Review* as a member of the board of directors and a contributor. He continued to attack communism, but his avowedly nonreligious perspective isolated him from many other conservatives on the staff. Throughout his life, Eastman, an atheist, deeply distrusted organized religion and its potential for "ecclesiastical authoritarianism." He earlier had split with communism because he regarded it as a religion, and now he disagreed with conservatives such as WHITTAKER CHAMBERS who viewed the cold war as a battle of religion versus atheism. Eastman resigned from *National Review* in 1958, although he contributed articles until 1964.

Eastman continued to publish books and essays throughout the 1960s. Commenting on the "young rebels" of that period in an interview with Alden Whitman of the *New York Times*, he said that, though they shared some of the intensity of feeling of his own Greenwich Village rebels of the 1910s and 1920s, they "had no ultimate purpose."

He described them as detached from the working class, "the bohemian wing of the bourgeoisie." Eastman was working on another book when he died in Bridgetown, Barbados, on March 25, 1969.

—MSM

Eaton, Cyrus S(tephen)
(1883–1979) *industrialist*

Born in Pugwash Junction, Nova Scotia, Canada, on December 27, 1883, Cyrus Eaton was the son of a rural Baptist minister. He earned a divinity degree at McMaster University in 1905. Through his uncle, a Baptist minister in Cleveland, Eaton met John D. Rockefeller, Sr. Eaton became a protégé of Rockefeller and went on to found his own company, the Continental Gas and Electric Company, which emerged as a major supplier to western Canada and the upper Midwest in the United States. In 1913, Eaton became a U.S. citizen. He took up a partnership at Otis and Company, an investment house, and later consolidated his vast utilities holdings into the United Light and Power Company. He also moved into the rubber and steel industries. Eaton lost most of his personal fortune, about $100 million, in the stock market crash in 1929. He subsequently rebuilt his fortune. Eaton acquired substantial holdings in railroads, shipping, iron ore, coal, and steel; and he served on the board of directors of approximately 40 companies, including Goodyear Tire and Rubber, Youngstown Sheet and Tube, Fisher Body, and the Baltimore and Ohio Railroad.

For all his own aggressive (and sometimes litigious) business practices, he was suspicious of Wall Street's financial community and wrote articles criticizing American business practices and the failure of the capitalist system to take into account social concerns. With respect to politics, Eaton supported Franklin D. Roosevelt and HARRY S. TRUMAN.

During the 1950s, Eaton became increasingly critical of the cold war and the nuclear arms race, and his public comments on these matters often generated controversy. He opined, for example, that "the only people in the U.S. who believe that communism is a menace to the U.S. are the boys on the payroll of the FBI." Further, he denounced Secretary of State JOHN FOSTER DULLES for "blithely court[ing] the ultimate world catastrophe of the bomb without even consulting the Senate Foreign Relations Committee and the House Foreign Affairs Committee."

Eaton believed that "we must either learn to live with the communists or resign ourselves to perish with them." In an effort to foster intellectual exchange and growing understanding, he gathered a group of Soviet and American nuclear scientists at his cattle ranch near Pugwash in 1957. At the second "Pugwash Conference," in 1958, the conferees urged that nations either ban nuclear tests completely or at least establish tests for radioactivity and quotas for the production of weapons. Ultimately, he held more than 40 "Pugwash Conferences" at Pugwash and other locations around the world. Eaton made a number of trips to the Soviet Union and met with top Soviet leaders. In September 1958, he met for an hour and a half with Premier Nikita Khrushchev at the Kremlin. That same year, Eaton caused a furor when he entertained Jáanos Kádár, the Hungarian leader installed by Khrushchev after the Soviets brutally suppressed the Hungarian uprising. The Soviet bloc bestowed numerous awards on Eaton, including the Lenin Peace Prize in 1960. In the United States, many condemned the Cleveland industrialist's efforts at private diplomacy as naïve; some considered them subversive.

After Eaton had met briefly with Khrushchev in May 1960 at Paris's Orly Airport following the collapse of the Paris summit meeting, Sen. THOMAS DODD (D-Conn.) called for prosecution of Eaton under the Logan Act. The measure, passed in 1799, barred private citizens from dealing with foreign governments on U.S. policy matters. However, no action was taken on Dodd's demand.

Eaton continued to manage his investments and to serve on many boards through the 1960s and 1970s. He also attempted to establish economic ties with the Soviet bloc and was an early opponent of the war in Vietnam. When he died at Acadia Farms, his 850-acre holding at Northfield, Ohio, on May 10, 1979, his fortune was estimated at over $1 billion.

—MSM

Eaton, Frederick M(cCurdy)

(1905–1984) chairman, U.S. delegation, 10-nation Committee on Disarmament

Born in Akron, Ohio, on May 21, 1905, Frederick Eaton received a B.A. from Harvard University in 1927, and obtained a degree from its law school three years later. He was admitted to the New York bar in 1930 and went to work for the New York law firm of Cotton & Franklin. During World War II, Eaton was general counsel to the War Production Board and a member of the Combined Raw Materials Board and Combined Production and Resources Board. After the war, he joined the prestigious Wall Street law firm of Shearman and Sterling. He became a director of the New York Life Insurance Company and in 1954 was appointed a director of the New York City Bank Farmers Trust Company. He also served as special counsel to the secretary of the army during the Army-McCarthy hearings.

Eaton served as chairman of the U.S. delegation to the 10-nation Committee on Disarmament in 1960. When the panel first met on March 15, he served as spokesperson for the Western nations—the United States, Great Britain, France, Italy, and Canada. He presented a joint proposal for conventional and nuclear disarmament enforced by an international disarmament organization with the right of on-site inspection. Reflecting the Western nations' most immediate concern, it called for a total prohibition of orbiting satellites carrying nuclear weapons.

Soviet delegate Valerian A. Zorin rejected the plan on the grounds that it would require a prolonged study of the technical problems of inspection and put off practical disarmament indefinitely. The Soviets opposed early inspection measures as "espionage" and preferred enforcing disarmament controls after each phase of the plan was completed. Further, Zorin refused to give priority to the satellite agreement and insisted that the United States agree to remove its military bases from Europe before discussing the issue. The Soviets, in turn, offered a plan for total disarmament within four years. Eaton denounced the plan as a "grand but hollow design" and an "unenforceable scheme."

On April 14, in an attempt to break the deadlock, Eaton offered to terminate Western production of nuclear weapons and allow international inspection of Western atomic plants, In a dramatic move, he made public a list of U.S. atomic plants, challenging the Soviets to do the same. Eaton then proposed a joint U.S.-USSR inspection team be formed to check manpower reductions in the armed forces of the two nations. The USSR rejected the proposal.

On July 7, the Soviet Union presented still another proposal, calling for the evacuation of foreign military bases in Europe simultaneously with the demolition of nuclear delivery systems as the first stage in disarmament. Eaton rejected the plan. He claimed that, because of Russia's large conventional forces in Eastern Europe, the proposal would leave the small Western nations at the mercy of the USSR. Charging that the United States sought only "unilateral military advantages," the communist delegations withdrew from the committee on June 27, effectively ending negotiations. Eaton accused the Soviets of "torpedoing" the conference and said that their "refusal to continue the discussions is convincing proof that the present Soviet motivation is propaganda, pure propaganda."

After the disarmament conference, Eaton returned to the private practice of law. He became the senior partner of Shearman and Sterling and held that position until he retired in 1975. During the Johnson administration, Eaton headed an investigation of the intelligence community. Upon his retirement, Eaton moved to New Hampshire. He died in Dublin, N.H., on October 3, 1984.

—MSM

Egan, William Allen
(1914–1984) *governor of Alaska*

The son of a gold miner, William Egan was born on October 8, 1914, in Valdez, Alaska. He graduated from Valdez High School in 1932 and worked at odd jobs. He was elected as a Democrat to Alaska's territorial house of representatives in 1941 and served in the army from 1943 to 1946. Upon returning from the army, he bought a grocery store in Valdez. He served in the state house of representatives from 1947 until 1952, when he won election to the territorial senate. Eaton became territorial speaker in 1955.

Egan championed Alaskan statehood throughout his career. Pointing to Alaska's lack of adequate civil government and to its exploitation by the salmon industry, he believed that these problems could be solved only by statehood. In 1941, he cosponsored the first bill to submit the issue of statehood to Alaskan voters, but it was defeated. Five years later, Egan again introduced a bill providing for a referendum on statehood. This time the bill passed, and in the referendum held that year a majority of Alaskans voted for statehood.

When a coalition of Republicans and southern Democrats defeated statehood bills in the U.S. Congress during 1950, 1954, and 1955, the territorial legislature decided to force the issue. It called a constitutional convention, which met in 1955 and 1956. As president of that body, Egan was the principal architect of the constitution, signed in February 1956 and ratified by the voters in April, The document provided for only two elected statewide officials—the governor and secretary of state. The governor appointed all department heads and judges subject to legislative or judicial council approval. The size of the legislature was increased, and it met annually.

The convention also called for the election of a state delegation of two senators and one representative to go to Washington and lobby for statehood. Egan was elected as part of the all-Democratic delegation in October. Despite Republican fears that Alaska would remain a Democratic state, Congress voted for statehood in July 1958. The following month, Alaskans approved statehood five to one.

In November 1958, Egan was elected governor, defeating his Republican opponent by a large margin. Sworn into office in January 1959, a few months after statehood was proclaimed, Egan fell ill and was unable to assume his duties until April. During the early months of his administration, he presented a budget that increased aid for education, health, and welfare. He also ended the issuance of licenses for salmon traps, which he believed reduced the salmon crop and aided corporate fishing interests.

After winning reelection in 1962, Egan lost to Walter J. Hickel in 1966. Egan won a third term in 1970 but failed in his bid for reelection in 1974. He died in Anchorage, Alaska, on May 6, 1984.

—MJS

Einstein, Albert
(1879–1953) *theoretical physicist*

The son of nonreligious German-Jewish parents, Einstein was born in Ulm, Germany, on March 14, 1879. He moved to Switzerland as a young man and renounced his German citizenship. After graduating from the Swiss Federal Polytechnic in Zurich in 1900, he failed to obtain a teaching position and held a succession of temporary teaching jobs before finding work in 1902 as a patent office clerk in Berne. While working in the patent office, Einstein worked on problems in theoretical physics. Beginning in 1905, he published a series of papers that revolutionized modern physics. Perhaps the most famous of these dealt with his theory of special relativity, which Einstein used to conclude that matter and energy were physically equivalent, in effect interconvertible. This result, stated mathematically as $E = mc^2$, furnished an explanation for the liberation of energy in atomic explosions. The other papers dealt with Brownian motion as a final proof of the molecular nature of matter and the photoelectric effect, an important advance in quantum mechanics, which founded the photon theory of light.

Einstein received his doctorate from the University of Zurich in 1909, and taught at Zurich, Prague, and Leyden before accepting an offer to direct the Kaiser Wilhlem Institute of Sciences in Berlin in 1913. A Swiss citizen living in Berlin, he publicly opposed Germany's participation in World War I and supported socialism. In spite of this, he managed to avoid imprisonment.

During a solar eclipse in 1919, a British astronomer, Arthur Stanley Eddington, observed the light-bending effect predicted by Einstein. This made Einstein, already one of the world's most respected physicists, a celebrity. He received the Nobel Prize in 1921 for his work on the quantum theory. During the 1920s, Einstein became an active Zionist, traveling extensively to raise funds for Jewish settlement in Palestine. In 1933, he fled Nazi-dominated Germany and accepted a lifetime professorship at Princeton's Institute for Advanced Study.

Although World War I made him a pacifist, Einstein abandoned this position following the rise of fascism in Germany and Japan. In 1939, he signed a letter to Franklin D. Roosevelt urging the United States to develop an atomic bomb before the Germans did. His action led to the establishment of the Manhattan Project in 1942. However, Einstein did not take part in constructing the bomb. The bombings of Hiroshima and Nagasaki in 1945 horrified the physicist, and, during the postwar period, he became a leading voice for nuclear disarmament. As chairman of the Emergency Committee of Atomic Scientists, founded in 1946, Einstein sought to inform Americans of the realities of atomic warfare and the dangers of a nuclear arms race. He called on scientists to refrain from cooperation with the military and opposed the development of the hydrogen bomb.

Einstein was outspoken in his opposition to the anticommunist crusade of the late-1940s and early-1950s. In 1953, he urged clemency for JULIUS and ETHEL ROSENBERG, who were convicted of espionage and later executed. Einstein also spoke out against the abuses of congressional investigating committees. In a letter made public in June 1953, he told a New York City high school teacher who had refused to testify before the Senate Internal Security Subcommittee that "every intellectual who is called before one of the committees ought to refuse to testify." Einstein asserted that "it is shameful for a blameless citizen to submit to such an inquisition." His letter was cited by several witnesses who refused to testify before congressional committees later that year. In April 1954, when physicist J. ROBERT OPPENHEIMER's government security clearance was suspended, Einstein publicly affirmed his confidence in his colleague.

Einstein continued to advocate disarmament until the end of his life. Early in 1955, he and Nobel Prize winner Lord Bertrand Russell, the British mathematician and philosopher, drafted an international appeal against the further development or use of atomic weapons.

Einstein died in Princeton of a ruptured aorta on April 18, 1955. The Einstein-Russell statement, signed by six other Nobel Prize winners, was sent to various heads of state in July.

—MDB

Eisenhower, Dwight D(avid)

(1890–1969) *president of the United States*

Born into a Mennonite family in Dennison, Texas, on October 14, 1890, David Dwight Eisenhower grew up in Abilene, Kans., where his father worked at a local creamery. To avoid confusion with his father, David Jacob Eisenhower, the boy's mother, Ida, called him Dwight; from boyhood on, however, most people called him Ike. Although intelligent and ambitious, he was an above-average student, not an outstanding one, in school. He was also a talented athlete and an intense competitor. Eisenhower won an appointment to the U.S. Military Academy through the competitive examination process and in 1911 enrolled at West Point as Dwight David Eisenhower, in deference to his mother. He graduated in the middle of his class in 1915. His class rank would have been higher but for his considerable accumulation of demerits.

Much to his disappointment, Eisenhower did not go overseas during World War I. Rather, he served as a tank instructor. During the interwar years, he served on the staffs of generals Fox Conner, Douglas MacArthur, and George C. Marshall. Under the tutelage of Conner, a respected military intellectual, Eisenhower became a serious student of military science. Recognition of his status as a rising young officer came when Eisenhower received orders first to attend Command and General Staff School, where he finished first in his class, and then the Army War College. Although his superior officers held him in high regard, promotions in the peacetime army were hard to come by. He expected to face forced retirement as a lieutenant colonel—but World War II changed that.

Soon after America's entry into the war, Marshall, then serving as chief of staff, made Eisenhower head of the War Plans Division. In May 1942, Marshall placed the recently promoted Maj. Gen. Eisenhower in command of U.S. forces in Great Britain. Eisenhower commanded the Allied invasion of North Africa in 1942. He also led the Allied invasions of Sicily and Italy in 1943. Eisenhower's rank rose with his responsibilities. He was promoted to lieutenant general before assuming command of the North African invasion and to four-star general before the invasion of Sicily. In December 1943, President Franklin D. Roosevelt named Eisenhower

supreme commander of the Allied Expeditionary Force that would invade France in 1944. At the end of 1944, Eisenhower was promoted to five-star general, the rank he held when the German army surrendered on May 7, 1945. Eisenhower emerged from the war as the best known and most popular of American generals. He was a fine strategist, but his greatest strength as commander lay in his ability to handle complex multinational operations. That ability came to the fore in his skillful management of two contentious, egomaniacal, and nationalistic subordinates, Bernard L. Montgomery and George S. Patton.

Eisenhower served as head of the American zone of occupation in Germany from May to November 1945, when President HARRY S. TRUMAN appointed him Army Chief of Staff. Eisenhower held that position until he resigned from the army in 1948. That same year, he published his memoir of the war, *Crusade in Europe*. It became one of the best-selling and most widely translated books of the 20th century, and the proceeds from it provided Eisenhower with financial security. Also in 1948, Eisenhower became president of Columbia University, a position he held through 1950. In December 1950, Truman named him the first supreme commander of the allied forces in Europe being organized under the North Atlantic Treaty Organization (NATO), a post he assumed in January 1951.

During the early 1950s, a group of liberal, or Eastern, Republicans urged Eisenhower to run for president. They argued that Eisenhower alone could prevent the Midwestern, or conservative, wing from gaining control of the party, and ultimately the White House. Eisenhower initially resisted. By late 1951, however, he became convinced that the leading Republican candidate, Sen. ROBERT TAFT (R-Ohio), a unilateralist, would, as president, threaten collective security and American interests in Europe. Still, Eisenhower remained publicly uncommitted and continued his work in Europe. In the meantime, various liberal Republicans, including politicians like Gov. THOMAS E. DEWEY of New York and Sen. HENRY CABOT LODGE (R-Mass.) as well as business leaders like PAUL HOFFMAN and William Robinson, began to organize a campaign to secure the nomination for Eisenhower in 1952. They entered Eisenhower in the New Hampshire

Christmas at the White House, 1957 *(Dwight D. Eisenhower Library and Museum)*

primary, where, without campaigning, he won 50 percent of the Republican vote to Taft's 37 percent. In Minnesota, Eisenhower's name was not even on the ballot, and he finished a strong second to favorite son HAROLD STASSEN.

Nevertheless, Eisenhower would not get the nomination without a bitter struggle against Taft. Thus, after the treaty establishing the European Defense Community was signed on May 27, Eisenhower resigned as NATO commander and returned to the United States to campaign actively for the nomination. His campaign emphasized his status as a leader above politics. It also portrayed him as a straightforward, regular fellow, who stood for tra-

ditional American values. After some initial difficulties in adjusting to having speeches written for him, Eisenhower emerged as an effective campaigner. His greatest gift was the ability to project his winning personality to the public. Taft, for all his intellectual gifts, was a cold, unappealing personality and a poor speaker. Nevertheless, Taft could claim the allegiance of party loyalists. By the time of the Republican National Convention in July, the struggle for the nomination revolved around the seating of rival delegations from Georgia, Florida, Louisiana, and Texas. The regulars on the Republican National Committee seated most of the Taft delegations, but the Eisenhower campaign took the matter to the floor of the convention, where their so-called fair play amendment carried. After that, the general won the nomination on the first ballot and, on the advice of his campaign advisers, chose Sen. RICHARD M. NIXON of California as his running mate. Nixon balanced the ticket in several respects; he was young, from the West, and from the conservative wing of the party.

During the campaign, the Republicans ran on a formula described by Sen. KARL MUNDT (R-S. Dak.) as K_1C_2 (Korea, Communism, Corruption). The unpopular war in Korea, concerns about communists in government, and the scandals of the Truman administration had combined to drive Truman's approval ratings to record lows. Eisenhower pledged to "clean up the mess in Washington," but, for the most part, he took the high road and left the partisan attacks to Nixon. In foreign policy, Eisenhower believed that isolationism had contributed to the rise of Hitler and thus to the coming of World War II. By extension, he held that a refusal to remain engaged with the rest of the world, and Europe in particular, would encourage continued communist aggression and might ultimately lead to nuclear war. At home, he opposed further extensions of the New Deal on the ground that such extensions would undermine individual initiative and threaten the American way of life.

The crusade to "clean up the mess in Washington" hit a snag when, on September 18, the *New York Post*, one of the few newspapers supporting the Democratic nominee, ADLAI STEVENSON, ran a story that Nixon had a "secret" fund raised by California business leaders and had used it for personal expenses. In fact, the fund was not secret; Nixon had previously answered questions from reporters about it. Eisenhower had SHERMAN ADAMS arrange an audit by Price, Waterhouse. The candidate also let Nixon know that he favored a speech addressing the subject. Then, it came out that Stevenson had a similar fund, which muted Democratic criticism. Moreover, the audit showed that Nixon had not diverted any of the fund for personal use. The Republican National Committee bought 30 minutes of prime time on television for Nixon, who gave his famous "Checkers" speech.

Polls showed Eisenhower ahead, but after polls seemed to have predicted a Dewey victory in 1948,

no one put too much trust in them. In October, Eisenhower announced, "I shall go to Korea." For all practical purposes, that settled the election. Voters found the idea of the hero of World War II going to observe the Korean War firsthand enormously reassuring. Eisenhower won in a landslide. In the highest turnout to that time, he garnered slightly over 55 percent of the vote. He carried 41 states and won 442 electoral votes to Stevenson's 89. Eisenhower even cracked the solidly Democratic South. He took Texas, Virginia, Tennessee, and Oklahoma. The Republicans also won a narrow majority in the House and a tie in the Senate, which they controlled through the tiebreaking vote of the vice president.

The election of 1952 was more a rejection of the Truman administration and a personal victory for Eisenhower than it was an endorsement of the Republican party. The Democrats remained the majority party; they would win back both houses of Congress in 1954 and maintain that control for the rest of Eisenhower's two terms (and, indeed, through the 1960s and 1970s). Further complicating matters, Eisenhower represented the liberal wing of his party, but conservatives controlled the congressional delegation. Eisenhower and his administration had no intention of undoing the New Deal; rather, they wanted to limit its expansion. In contrast, a number of Republican conservatives in Congress demanded a wholesale assault on the New Deal. Further, while the president and the Eastern (or liberal, or internationalist) wing of the party favored a foreign policy that concentrated on Europe and relied on multilateral defense, the conservative wing placed its priority on Asia and preferred a unilateral approach.

Eisenhower assembled a cabinet of capable and successful people. Unlike many presidents, he did not appoint old cronies; indeed, he did not choose a single old friend. The secretary of state, JOHN FOSTER DULLES, was senior partner in Sullivan & Cromwell, one of the leading Wall Street law firms, and came to the post with a wealth of experience in foreign affairs. The position of attorney general went to HERBERT BROWNELL, another highly successful lawyer who had been involved in reform and Republican politics in New York and had managed Dewey's campaigns for governor and president. Brownell had also played major roles in persuading Eisenhower to run in the campaign of 1952. Eisenhower picked CHARLES E. WILSON, president of General Motors, to be secretary of defense and GEORGE M. HUMPHREY, president of the Mark A. Hannah Company, to be secretary of the treasury. The secretary of labor, MARTIN DURKIN, was president of the plumbers' union and a Stevenson Democrat. The quip that the cabinet consisted of "nine millionaires and a plumber," although clever, did not give a real sense of the nature of Eisenhower's cabinet.

Eisenhower also reorganized the White House. He named SHERMAN ADAMS, the crusty former governor of New Hampshire, to be chief of staff. He created a White House staff secretary's office and chose his former staff assistant at the Pentagon and NATO, Brig. Gen. Paul T. Carroll, to head it. When Carroll died in October 1954, Eisenhower selected another former NATO aide, Col. ANDREW J. GOODPASTER, to replace him.

As president, Eisenhower's first objective was to end the stalemated, unpopular war in Korea. Stalin's death in March 1953 created an opportunity. Eisenhower pressed both Communist China and South Korea to accept an armistice. He removed the Seventh Fleet from the Formosa Straits, thus "unleashing" Chiang Kai-shek (Jiang Jieshi). He also hinted darkly at the possible use of nuclear weapons. Finally, after considerable difficulty, an armistice was signed on July 27.

With respect to foreign policy in general, Eisenhower continued Truman's policy of containment of the Soviet Union. Like Truman, Eisenhower gave priority to Europe, which he believed was the primary area of American interest. In order to prevent communist expansion in that region, he encouraged the redevelopment and unification of Western Europe economically and militarily. Further, Eisenhower believed in a multilateral approach to defense. All of this brought Eisenhower into conflict with the right wing of his party, which opposed collective security and believed Asia to be the primary area of American interest. Throughout his presidency, Eisenhower faced a challenge from the China bloc, a group of conservative Republicans in Congress led by WILLIAM KNOWLAND (R-Calif.) in the Senate and WALTER JUDD (R-Minn.) in the House.

Conflict between Eisenhower and the conservative wing of his party surfaced immediately. Although conservative Republicans urged him to repudiate the Yalta accords, Eisenhower worried that to do so might cost Western access rights to Berlin. Moreover, he had no taste for the prospect of renouncing agreements he had carried out while army chief of staff. Further difficulties came when Eisenhower nominated CHARLES BOHLEN to be ambassador to the Soviet Union. The Republican right regarded him as too closely linked to the foreign policy of the Truman administration, and some suggested that he was a security risk. Eisenhower held his ground, and, with the cooperation of Taft, Bohlen won confirmation in March 1953.

Another sore point with the Right was that, in spite of the rhetoric of the campaign in 1952, during which Dulles in particular called for the "rollback" of communist influence and the "liberation of captive peoples," the United States often found itself powerless to control events in Europe. For example, the United States could realistically do nothing when East Germans rose to demand a greater degree of freedom after the death of Stalin in 1953.

The most serious challenge from the Republican right came when, in 1953, Sen. JOHN BRICKER (R-Ohio) proposed a constitutional amendment that would have limited the power of the president to make treaties. Sixty-two other senators cosponsored the measure, including 44 of the 47 Republicans in the body. Eisenhower vigorously opposed the measure, which would most likely have passed without his opposition. Procedural maneuvering kept the Bricker amendment off the floor throughout 1953, and Eisenhower managed to mobilize enough support to defeat the measure in a very close vote in February 1954.

Eisenhower intended to continue to wage the cold war, but he also wanted to balance the budget. Further, he worried that excessive defense spending would distort the American economy, and finally, he believed that the money could be better spent. Seizing on the death of Stalin as an opportunity, Eisenhower delivered a speech to the American Association of Newspaper Editors on April 16, 1953. In it, he proposed a reduction in the arms race and the use of the resulting savings to establish "a fund for world aid and reconstruction. . . . The monument to this new kind of war would be these: roads and schools, hospitals and homes, food and health." In contrast, "Every gun that is made, every warship launched, every rocket fired, signifies, in a final sense, a theft from those who hunger and are not fed, those who are cold and are not clothed." Indeed, the best the arms race could offer was a "life of perpetual fear and tension." This, he concluded, was "not a way of life at all, in any true sense," but rather, "humanity hanging from a cross of iron."

Eisenhower's concerns to balance the budget while providing an adequate defense, combined with the lessons of the unpopular limited war in Korea, led to reorientation of defense policy. The "New Look," as the policy was known, featured a greater reliance on technology, air power, and the nuclear deterrent. For one thing, these were areas where the United States enjoyed a substantial advantage. With respect to Europe in particular, the advantage in conventional forces belonged to the Soviet Union. In a different vein, Eisenhower believed that a strong economy constituted an essential element of defense, and, toward that end, he hoped to cut defense spending. The New Look provided a means to achieve deterrence at a lower cost. While Eisenhower rejected the idea of withdrawing U.S. forces from Europe immediately, he hoped that America's allies might be weaned from dependence on American conventional forces. The New Look did enable Eisenhower to reduce defense budgets throughout his two terms in office. In a policy paper approved in October 1954 (NSC 162/2) and in its budget for 1955, the administration began implementing the New Look. NSC 162/2 called for a 25 percent reduction in the size of the military by 1956, with most of the cuts coming from the army and navy. The air force, on the other hand, was enlarged and its budget increased. The end of the Korean War as well as the emphasis on air power, technology, and the nuclear deterrent enabled the administration to reduce the defense budget by roughly $4 billion.

Deterring the Soviets constituted only one aspect of managing the cold war. In the spring of 1954, the French, attempting to maintain their influence in Indochina, requested American military aid to relieve their garrison at Dien Bien Phu. In 1950, after the victory of Mao Zedong (Mao Tse-Tung) over the Nationalists in China and the outbreak of the Korean War, the Truman administration increased aid to the French to help their effort to defeat the insurgency of the Viet Minh. By the time Truman left office, the United States was paying for a good part of the cost of the French effort. While Eisenhower disliked colonialism and regarded French colonialism with particular contempt, he worried about the consequences of Vietnam falling to the Communists. Thus, he made substantial aid from the United States conditional on internationalizing the war and the promise of "unconditional independence" for the Associated States (Laos, Cambodia, and Vietnam). The British were not keen on involvement, and the French were unwilling to meet Eisenhower's conditions. Without intervention by the United States, the French garrison surrendered on May 7, 1954. The Geneva Accords, signed a few months later, granted full independence to Laos, Cambodia, and Vietnam. Vietnam was divided along the 17th parallel, with the Viet Minh in control in the North and the French-backed emperor, Bao Dai, at the head of the government in the South. Subsequently, the United States created the Southeast Asia Treaty Organization (SEATO). The members—the United States, France, Great Britain, Australia, New Zealand, Pakistan, and the Philippines—agreed to consult in the event of common danger.

During the fall of 1954, Eisenhower again resisted pressure to become engaged in a war in Asia. The Communist Chinese began shelling Quemoy and Matsu, two islands held by the Nationalists. In January 1955, Eisenhower and Dulles obtained a congressional resolution granting the president authority to use American forces to defend Taiwan and the Pescadores. Dulled wanted to include Quemoy and Matsu, but Eisenhower overruled him. On April 23, at the conference of nonaligned nations in Bandung, Zhou Enlai (Chou En-lai) gave a conciliatory speech, and Eisenhower responded. Subsequently, the mainland Chinese reduced their shelling of the islands and by mid-May stopped it entirely. The crisis passed.

Although a resolute cold warrior, Eisenhower hoped to reduce tensions between the United States and USSR. In 1955, the two countries agreed to end their occupation of Austria and create an independent, neutral country. That same year, the two countries, under the auspices of the United Nations, negotiated to prohibit the use and manufacture of nuclear weapons and reduce conventional forces. Those negotiations ultimately failed. In July 1955, the United States, USSR, Great Britain, and France met at a summit conference in Geneva. Eisenhower presented his "Open Skies" proposal, which called for an exchange of maps of military installations and for each side to submit to aerial inspections. The Soviets rejected the plan. In the end, the conference reached no agreements of substance, but it did produce, as Eisenhower reported to the American people, a "new spirit of conciliation and cooperation."

At the same time he sought to reduce tensions with the Soviets, Eisenhower had to confront the problems associated with the breakup of the old colonial empires and the emergence of new nations. If the president demonstrated restraint in dealing with the Soviets and Chinese, he was not always so restrained in dealing with radical nationalist revolutions in the Third World. In 1953, the CIA supported a successful coup against the elected leftist government of Mohammed Mossadeq in Iran. The following year, in Guatemala, the CIA once again supported a coup against an elected leftist government, this time that of Jacobo Arbenz Guzmán in Guatemala.

In domestic policy, Eisenhower fit within the broad consensus established by Franklin D. Roosevelt and the New Deal that the federal government was responsible for the functioning of the economy and for the basic welfare of the American people. Like his opposition to the Bricker amendment, this recognition brought Eisenhower into frequent conflict with the Republican right, which included his older brother, Edgar. A highly successful lawyer, Edgar was free with his criticism of Dwight's administration, and the two engaged in an ongoing debate. On November 8, 1954, Eisenhower wrote to Edgar: "Should any party attempt to abolish social security and eliminate labor laws and farm programs, you would not hear of that party again in our political history. There is a tiny splinter group, of course, that believes you can do these things. Among them are H. L. Hunt ... and a few other Texas oil millionaires, and an occasional politician

and businessman from other areas. Their number is negligible and they are stupid." Beyond an awareness that to position oneself beyond the boundaries of the New Deal consensus amounted to political suicide, Eisenhower himself was comfortable with that broad consensus. He believed in the maintenance of a basic welfare state; he believed that the government had a responsibility to maintain prosperity; and he believed in federal activity, as Republican senator Robert Taft put it, "where the objective is clearly beyond the power of the state or community to achieve." Indeed, Eisenhower had nothing but contempt for the right wing of his party and once scoffed that Frank Holman (the conservative president of the American Bar Association and an architect of the Bricker amendment) was "obsessed with saving the nation from Eleanor Roosevelt."

At the same time, Eisenhower had reservations about further expansions of the federal government. Near the end of his presidency, he summed up his views in a letter to Edgar's wife, Lucy Eisenhower. "Just about eight years ago," he wrote, "I finally decided I should come back to the United States to stand for the Presidency. I did so in the hope that I could stem what I thought was a clear drift towards paternalism, if not socialism, in our government's relation to its people. It has been a long, uphill struggle, and during the years I have learned some things. The first of these is that this country is not going to the right—that the economic and political affairs of our people are not going to be soon conducted as to take our nation back to the days of the 1890s. Indeed, this would be undesirable if we could do it."

Eisenhower searched for a catchy phrase to encapsulate his views. He tried "moderate progressivism," "progressive moderation," and "dynamic conservatism." All captured his intent, but none had the ring of Theodore Roosevelt's Square Deal, Franklin Roosevelt's New Deal, or Harry Truman's Fair Deal.

During his first term, Eisenhower focused his attention on holding down government expenditures, balancing the budget, and reducing taxes. Shortly after taking office, he removed wage and price controls established by the Truman administration. He also made modest reductions in Truman's budget and the projected deficit. He resisted, however, conservative calls for a tax cut, because he believed the revenues were necessary, given the cost of the war in Korea. With the end of the Korean War, the economy entered a recession at the end of 1953. Eisenhower responded with a moderate Keynesian approach. Eventually, the combination of the administration's efforts to hold down expenditures and an expanding economy produced a small budget surplus in 1956.

In agriculture, Eisenhower attempted to cut back on the policies of the Roosevelt and Truman administrations. By the time Eisenhower took office, the government had accumulated huge stores of surplus grain, cotton, tobacco, and other commodities, which itself had the effect of depressing agricultural prices. The Eisenhower administration adopted a policy of sliding price supports (ranging from 75 to 90 percent of parity) that was intended to move American farmers toward an open market and to reduce the surplus. Congress passed modest reductions in price supports in 1954, and in 1956 it passed an administration proposal to create a soil bank (the policy paid farmers for putting land into ungrazed grass, forest, or water storage). Agricultural interests aggressively opposed the reductions in subsidies, but, in fact, the Truman administration had never paid full parity prices. Under Truman, agricultural price supports had been pegged at 90 percent of parity. While reducing subsidies, Eisenhower left the basic program intact.

Eisenhower preferred to see the development of natural resources and the generation of power left to the states or private companies. He signed the Submerged Lands Act of 1953, which returned oil-bearing tidelands to the states. The administration reversed a decision, made during the Truman years, for the federal government to build a high dam at Hells Canyon on the Snake River. At the same time, the administration withdrew objections to a plan for the Idaho Power Company to build three low dams on the river. The Eisenhower administration also rescinded authorization of federally constructed dams on the Columbia River and the Coosa River. The latter project went to the Alabama Power Company, a rival of the Tennessee Valley Authority (TVA). Nevertheless, Eisenhower found it difficult to limit the growth of the TVA. The Atomic Energy Commission (AEC) proposed to sign a

contract to purchase power from the Mississippi Valley Generation Company (formed by EDGAR H. DIXON, president of the Middle South Utilities, and EUGENE A. YATES, chairman of the board of the Southern Company), rather than the TVA. The decision infuriated advocates of public power and created a minor scandal when it came out that a consultant to the Bureau of the Budget had been simultaneously advising the Dixon-Yates company. When the city of Memphis decided to build its own municipal power plant, which freed up power from the TVA for use by the AEC, Eisenhower took the opportunity to cancel the Dixon-Yates contract and thus avoided a major controversy.

If Eisenhower wanted to stop the spread of statism in some areas, he advocated modest expansions of government activities in others. In his first State of the Union message, he called for expanding "safeguards against the privations that too often come with unemployment, old age, illness and accident." The president proposed broadening Social Security to cover self-employed farmers, doctors, dentists, lawyers, and others. The proposal also included an increase in monthly benefits and a provision to liberalize limits on retirement earnings. Congress took no action that year, but in 1954 Congress passed legislation extending Social Security coverage to self-employed workers, thus bringing 10.5 million additional workers into the system. It was the greatest expansion of Social Security since its creation. The law also increased benefits. In 1955 Eisenhower sought an increase in the minimum wage and signed into law an increase from 75 cents to $1 an hour, one of the largest percentage increases in history.

Eisenhower also supported expansions in federal programs for public health. He proposed a plan to expand health insurance coverage by creating a federal fund to underwrite the risks of private health insurance carriers that extended coverage to high-risk customers. Ever vigilant against what it regarded as socialized medicine, the American Medical Association lobbied aggressively against the proposal. Liberal Democrats, who advocated some form of a national health system, also opposed it, as did major insurance companies. The plan for health reinsurance died in committee. Eisenhower was more successful in gaining congressional approval for a federal role in the distribution of the Salk polio vaccine.

With respect to federally funded public housing, Eisenhower largely continued the policies he inherited from the Truman administration. Truman had never requested more than 75,000 units in a year, and the housing shortage had abated. Eisenhower initially proposed the construction of 35,000 units for fiscal 1954, but conservative opposition in Congress forced him to settle for 20,000. In 1954, Eisenhower requested legislation to guarantee the construction of 1 million units of housing during that year, largely through federal mortgage insurance, urban renewal, and lower requirements for down payments on federally insured loans for low-income housing. The proposal also called for the construction of 35,000 units of public housing in each of the next four years. Eisenhower resisted conservative demands for the elimination of all provisions for public housing and settled for a compromise that linked the number of new units of public housing to the number of units of slum clearance.

In some areas, Eisenhower expanded the legacy of the New Deal. His administration undertook several large public works projects. Eisenhower proposed, and Congress passed, legislation providing for the construction of the Saint Lawrence Seaway. The project was completed in 1959. The largest public works project of his administration was the interstate highway system. By the time Eisenhower became president, overland transportation in the United States was woefully inadequate. Railroads had faced financial difficulties since the end of World War II, and highways constructed by state and local governments had not kept pace with the increasing demands created by the growing reliance on automobiles and trucks. Eisenhower appointed a commission headed by Gen. LUCIUS CLAY to study the situation. The commission recommended the construction of a national highway system using both federal and state money but acknowledged that the federal government would have to bear most of the cost. Eisenhower overcame the opposition of conservatives in Congress by emphasizing the importance of such a system to civil defense. The project called for construction of 42,000 miles of controlled-access highways linking major cities.

By the time Eisenhower left office, 7,500 miles of the system were in use.

Another area in which Eisenhower proposed expanding the New Deal was federal aid to education. The baby boom placed an unmanageable burden on locally funded schools. Publicly funded schools were a jealously guarded responsibility of local government. Conservatives and many local officials objected that federal aid might become a means for the federal government to dictate what was taught in schools and who taught it. In an effort to circumvent such objections, the Eisenhower administration recommended federal aid for the construction of new classrooms. Conservatives nonetheless believed that any federal involvement with public schools threatened local control, and Southerners worried that the federal government might use federal funds, more specifically the threat to withhold them, as a means to dismantle segregation. ADAM CLAYTON POWELL, JR., lent substance to those fears when he proposed an amendment that would have prohibited federal aid to segregated schools. Even after the defeat of the Powell Amendment, Congress rejected Eisenhower's school construction bill.

Eisenhower also made substantial contributions to civil rights in his first term. He appointed unprecedented numbers of African Americans to positions in the executive branch and appointed some to positions that had previously been held only by whites. For instance, Fred Morrow became the first African American to hold an executive position in the White House; Lois Lippman became the first black secretary to work there. Eisenhower named African Americans as assistant secretary of labor and chief of the parole board. Although he had opposed a compulsory Fair Employment Practices Commission, Eisenhower appointed a committee to eliminate discrimination in employment by the federal government and by contractors with the federal government. Eisenhower also put into effect Truman's unfulfilled promise to desegregate the armed forces and took steps to desegregate Washington, D.C.

Those early initiatives in civil rights marked a considerable advance over the policies of the Truman administration. In 1954, however, the Supreme Court changed the context of civil rights when, in *Brown v. Board of Education*, it declared segregated public schools unconstitutional. By the time Eisenhower entered the White House, the Truman administration's Justice Department had filed an amicus curiae brief in the school segregation cases. Eisenhower's Justice Department took the same position in the reargument of the cases in the fall of 1953. Eisenhower's most significant contribution to the *Brown* decision, and a somewhat inadvertent one, was the appointment of EARL WARREN as chief justice. While many have criticized Eisenhower for failing to endorse the decision, he always took the position that it was not his job to pass judgment on decisions of the Supreme Court; his job was to enforce them. In truth, Eisenhower had reservations about the expansion of federal authority and judicial activism inherent in the decision. He did not, as has frequently been asserted, disagree with the basic principle articulated in *Brown*.

In the initial aftermath of the *Brown* decision, Eisenhower moved cautiously. Southern intransigence finally convinced him to permit Attorney General Herbert Brownell to submit to Congress a four-part civil rights bill in 1956, but the Democratic leadership of Congress wanted no part of an internecine battle over civil rights in an election year. LYNDON JOHNSON, the majority leader in the Senate, employed clever procedural maneuvering to bury the bill in committee.

The issue of internal communist subversion brought Eisenhower into direct confrontation with the right wing of the Republican party and, in particular, the red-baiting junior senator from Wisconsin, JOSEPH R. MCCARTHY. The president personally detested McCarthy and his methods. Nevertheless, he refused to confront the senator publicly or directly, although some of his aides and his brother, Milton, urged him to do so. As Eisenhower himself put it, he did not take this position because he failed to love a good fight. Rather, he believed that if he publicly attacked McCarthy it would serve only to generate more publicity for the senator and would prompt the Senate to rally around one of its own. In addition, such an attack would also enrage the right wing of his own party and threaten his entire legislative agenda. Then, too, as a personal matter, he preferred not to "get down in the gutter with that guy."

Instead, Eisenhower worked behind the scenes and cooperated with McCarthy's opponents in an effort to bring the demagogue down. Eisenhower did publicly, if somewhat obliquely, attack McCarthy (or McCarthyism, as the cartoonist Herbert L. Block dubbed hysterical anticommunism) in a speech at the commencement of Dartmouth College, in which he urged the graduates not to join the "book burners." The remarks clearly referred to two of McCarthy's aides, ROY COHN and G. DAVID SCHINE, who conducted searches for subversive literature in overseas libraries run by the State Department. The president also responded to an article by J. B. MATTHEWS, the newly named head of the staff of the Committee on Government Operations, which McCarthy chaired. In that article, Matthews charged that "the largest single group supporting the communist apparatus in the United States today is composed of Protestant clergymen." In a letter to the National Conference of Christians and Jews, Eisenhower denounced the attack on the ministry as "unjustifiable and deplorable."

Eisenhower did not disagree with McCarthy over the need for national security or the reality of the threat of communist subversion, but Eisenhower believed that such matters were best handled through orderly administrative and judicial proceedings, not through sensation-seeking hearings or reckless partisan attacks. Eisenhower replaced Truman's loyalty program with a loyalty and security program. Truman's Executive Order 9835 provided for the dismissal of a government employee if, "on all the evidence, reasonable grounds exist for the belief that the person involved is disloyal to the Government of the United States." Truman later revised the standard for dismissal to whether there was "a reasonable doubt as to the loyalty of the person involved." Eisenhower's Executive Order 10450, issued in 1953, denied employment to anyone whose employment was not "clearly consistent with the national security." In December 1953, Eisenhower suspended J. ROBERT OPPENHEIMER's security clearance pending a full administrative review by the Atomic Energy Commission. The AEC found that Oppenheimer was loyal but a security risk and withdrew his clearance permanently.

The final break with McCarthy came after the senator launched an investigation of Eisenhower's beloved army. When McCarthy failed to find a spy ring he alleged existed at Fort Monmouth, he turned his attention to a dentist who had refused to answer routine screening questions but had, through an administrative error, been promoted before receiving an honorable discharge. McCarthy called Gen. RALPH ZWICKER before his committee and verbally abused the decorated war hero. ROBERT T. STEVENS, the secretary of the army, met with McCarthy and other Republican leaders in an effort to assure that future witnesses would be treated with respect, but McCarthy and the press portrayed the meeting as a capitulation on Stevens's part. At this point, Eisenhower moved more directly to bring down the senator from Wisconsin. He publicly lauded Zwicker's service, and the army released a chronology detailing attempts by Cohn and McCarthy to secure preferential treatment for Schine, who had been drafted. McCarthy countered by charging that the army was holding Schine hostage to hamstring his investigation. During the Army-McCarthy hearings in 1953, the president cooperated behind the scenes with McCarthy's opponents. When McCarthy threatened to subpoena members of the White House staff, Eisenhower, claiming executive privilege, refused to allow members of his staff to testify about advice they had given him. In addition, without mentioning McCarthy by name, Eisenhower made several statements in March to the effect that "we can't defeat communists by destroying the things in which we believe." The president also supported Sen. RALPH FLANDERS (R-Vt.), who had publicly attacked McCarthy. Working closely with the army and McCarthy's opponents in the Senate, Eisenhower helped bring down the junior senator from Wisconsin. The president played no direct role, however, in the Senate's decision to condemn McCarthy in December.

On the night of September 23, 1955, Eisenhower suffered a "moderately severe" heart attack, from which he made a full recovery. Nevertheless, he had not decided to run for a second term, and the issue of his health further complicated the issue. Milton was concerned that a second term might kill his brother. Ultimately, however, Eisenhower concluded that he was the "only man" who could keep the nomination out of the hands of the right wing of the party. Knowland had already announced his intention to run if Eisenhower did not. By December, Eisenhower felt strong enough to run, but he held off on his decision until he got a clean bill of health from his doctors in February 1956. Although he toyed with the idea of replacing Nixon on the ticket, he ultimately decided that Nixon would again be his running mate.

Eisenhower ran on a platform that emphasized the peace and prosperity his first term had brought the country. His Democratic opponent, Adlai Stevenson, had difficulty finding an issue that resonated with the public. As Stevenson's prospects for a victory receded, he grasped onto the issue of the president's health. He attacked Nixon in increasingly personal terms and warned that a Republican victory would make Nixon president "within the next four years." Eisenhower's obvious physical well-being negated the issue.

Toward the end of the campaign, two foreign policy crises further strengthened the president's position. Egypt's autocratic ruler, Gamal Abdel Nasser, nationalized the Suez Canal after failing to obtain American support for a dam at Aswan on the Nile. In late October, Great Britain, France, and Israel responded with a joint assault on Egypt. The attack caught Eisenhower by surprise. The United States, working with the Soviet Union, obtained a UN resolution condemning the attack. Faced with overwhelming international pressure, the British, French, and Israelis agreed to a cease-fire. The second crisis stemmed from unrest in the Soviet-dominated countries of eastern Europe. Labor unrest in Poland developed into national resistance to Soviet domination in mid-1956, which Khrushchev put down with force. In late October, Hungary, led by Imre Nagy, sought to withdraw from the Warsaw Pact. The Soviet premier, Nikita Khrushchev, sent in troops and tanks to restore Soviet rule. Hungarians took to the streets, throwing rocks and firebombs at the invading tanks; in the course of putting down the uprising, Soviets killed approximately 20,000 Hungarians. In spite of Republican talk of the need for "rollback" of communist influence during the campaign of 1952, Eisenhower could do little as the Soviets brutally repressed the Hungarian uprising. Nevertheless, these incidents reminded the American public of the dangerous state of the world and reinforced the public image of Eisenhower's sure hand at the helm of American foreign policy.

On November 6, Eisenhower won reelection by a landslide. He carried all but seven southern states, won nearly 58 percent of the popular vote, and swamped Stevenson in the electoral college by a vote of 457–74. In spite of the magnitude of Eisenhower's victory, the Democrats retained control of both houses of Congress. In fact, they picked up one seat in the Senate and two in the House.

Second terms tend to be less successful, and the first two years of Eisenhower's second term were beset with difficulties. The president's popularity reached a low point in 1958. However, his approval ratings rebounded in the last two years of his presidency. Some of Eisenhower's difficulties stemmed from a Democratic Congress that, freed from the prospect of another Eisenhower candidacy, became increasingly confrontational.

The president suffered a major defeat in the battle of the budget in 1957. Eisenhower submitted a budget for fiscal 1958 that called for grants for school construction, development of water resources, and a modest expansion of social welfare programs. The budget also provided for increases in defense and foreign aid. Conservative Republicans in Congress regarded Eisenhower's budget as a betrayal of traditional party values and demanded reductions in spending. They received support from Democrats who hoped to capitalize on public fears of inflationary spending. Thus, the Republican president found himself in the unusual position of asking the Democratic Congress to restore funds. Ultimately, Congress cut $4 billion in spending from the president's budget. Compounding his problems, a recession that began during 1957 and lasted into 1958 reduced tax revenues. This left the administration facing a projected $500-million deficit instead of a projected $1.8 billion surplus.

One of the most substantial blows to public confidence in Eisenhower's leadership came on October 4, 1957, when the Soviet Union launched *Sputnik*, Earth's first artificial satellite. Coming on the heels of the Soviet Union's successful test of an intercontinental ballistic missile, *Sputnik* dealt a devastating blow to the American sense of security, which, in turn, opened a debate over defense policy. Eisenhower faced open criticism from the military, which objected to his tight defense budgets. Military critics of the New Look, such as Gen. MAXWELL TAYLOR and Adm. ARLEIGH BURKE, joined by civilian critics such as HENRY KISSINGER, maintained that future conflicts would likely be limited wars and that greater numbers of conventional forces would be needed to fight them. Even the air force, the main beneficiary of the New Look, wanted to spend more money on an accelerated program to develop missiles and maintain U.S. superiority. Politicians, including STUART SYMINGTON (D-Mo.) and JOHN F. KENNEDY (D-Mass.), sensed an issue that could restore a Democrat to the White House and warned that Eisenhower had allowed a "missile gap" to develop. In fact, America's capacity to deliver nuclear weapons remained far superior to that of the Soviets.

In the wake of *Sputnik*, some wanted a crash program in education to produce more scientists. Others demanded a massive commitment to achieve superiority over the USSR in astronautics. Eisenhower remained unalarmed. Since 1956, U-2 spy planes had provided information on Soviet military capabilities, and the president was well aware of America's superior nuclear capability. He cautioned that despite a "high sense of urgency," the United States should not "mount our charger and . . . ride off in all directions at once." The president appointed JAMES KILLIAN as special assistant to the president for science and technology. Further, the budget Eisenhower submitted in 1958 called for increased spending on the missile program and on scientific and technical education. Nevertheless, the president warned that "to amass military power without regard to our economic capacity would be to defend ourselves against one kind of disaster by inviting another." Eisenhower attempted to reassure the nation without revealing sensitive intelligence data. These efforts suffered another blow on November 3, when the Soviets launched *Sputnik II*. The following day, a group of civilian consultants to the National Security Council, headed by H. ROWAN GAITHER of the Ford Foundation, presented a classified report critical of American defense policies. Eisenhower regarded the report as alarmist and rejected many of its finding. However, portions of the report leaked to the press, giving the president's critics more ammunition.

Eisenhower wanted to reserve space exploration for peaceful purposes and therefore resisted recommendations to combine the missile and space programs. Despite protests from the air force, the president placed the space program under the auspices of the National Aeronautics and Space Administration (NASA), a civilian agency he created in July 1958.

A recession that began in 1957 contributed to the president's political difficulties. As was the case with *Sputnik*, Eisenhower responded cautiously. He reversed cutbacks in defense spending and public works, accelerated federally funded projects already authorized, and liberalized restrictions on federally guaranteed mortgages. In addition, he asked for legislation to extend unemployment insurance from 26 weeks to 39 weeks, which Congress promptly enacted. However, Eisenhower resisted pressure from Democrats for massive spending on public works and from conservative Republicans for tax cuts. Although the recession had ended by April, Republicans suffered a devastating defeat in the congressional elections of 1958.

After the Democratic victory in 1958, it seemed that "the spenders" had gained the upper hand, but Eisenhower proved remarkably adept at holding down spending in 1959. After a record peacetime deficit of $12.4 billion in fiscal 1959, Eisenhower forged a coalition of Republicans and conservative Democrats to hold the line on the budget. Making effective use of the veto, Eisenhower produced a budget surplus of $1.3 billion for 1960.

Exacerbating Eisenhower's political difficulties, in June 1958, a subcommittee of the House Interstate and Foreign Commerce Committee alleged that SHERMAN ADAMS, the president's chief of staff, had used his influence on behalf of BERNARD GOLDFINE, an industrialist from New England who had tax and regulatory problems, in exchange for Goldfine paying some hotel bills for Adams. The brusque chief of staff assured Eisenhower that "I made a mistake, but I'm no crook." It turned out, however, that Adams had also accepted an expensive coat and other gifts from Goldfine. The day after Adams testified before the committee, Eisenhower issued a ringing endorsement of his aide. However, conservative Republicans in Congress, who had never liked Adams, began to demand his resigna-tion. With the election on the horizon and Republican prospects looking grim, many in the party blamed Adams. It became clear that Adams had to go. He announced his resignation on September 22, and Eisenhower accepted it with "deepest regret."

Civil rights emerged as a prominent issue during Eisenhower's second term. In 1957, Eisenhower resubmitted the civil rights bill Brownell had recommended the year before, and this time the president unequivocally endorsed all four proposals. The legislation called for the elevation of the Civil Rights Section in the Criminal Division of the Justice Department to the status of a division, headed by an assistant attorney general. It also provided for the creation of a Civil Rights Commission. The most controversial provision, Title III, would have granted authority to the attorney general to enter civil suits on behalf of people whose civil rights had been violated. The fourth proposal protected voting rights. Lyndon Johnson played a central role in getting the legislation passed, but he also gutted the measure by eliminating Title III and adding a provision for jury trials for those convicted of interfering with the voting rights of others. Eisenhower somewhat reluctantly signed the watered-down bill. The president was particularly chagrined over the jury-trial amendment, but he had nonetheless obtained passage of the first civil rights bill since Reconstruction. Eisenhower went back to Congress and eventually obtained passage in 1960 of a second civil rights measure designed to protect black voting rights.

The most dramatic confrontation over civil rights came in 1957, when Governor ORVAL FAUBUS of Arkansas defied a federal court order and used the Arkansas National Guard to block the admission of nine black students to Little Rock's Central High School. Eisenhower nationalized the Arkansas National Guard and sent a thousand paratroopers from the elite 101st Airborne to enforce the court's order.

Eisenhower's most significant contribution to civil rights was his appointment of liberal and moderate judges to the federal judiciary in the South. These judges insured an ongoing process of desegregation. Moreover, these appointments stand in marked contrast to those of Truman and Kennedy. Two of Eisenhower's appointments to the Fourth

Circuit Court of Appeals, Simon E. Sobeloff and Clement F. Haynsworth, were confirmed in spite of determined opposition by segregationists.

In foreign policy, Eisenhower began his second term dealing with the aftermath of the Suez Crisis. Eisenhower and Dulles worried that the Soviet Union might attempt to fill the power vacuum left by the decline of French and British influence in the Middle East. In addition, Nasser's appeal to Arab nationalism threatened pro-Western regimes, and the Arab-Israeli conflict threatened to explode into war at any time. In January 1957, Eisenhower asked Congress to approve a resolution granting the president authority to use American forces to support nations facing "overt armed aggression by any country controlled by international communism." He also asked for $200 million in military and economic aid to the area. This policy came to be known as the Eisenhower Doctrine.

Although the Eisenhower Doctrine was directed at communism, Eisenhower recognized that the most immediate threat to American interests in the region was Nasserism. After pro-Nasser elements won the Jordanian elections in 1957, King Hussein dismissed the prime minister and declared martial law. The ousted prime minister fled to Syria, where he plotted a return to power. King Hussein appealed to Eisenhower for help against what he claimed was "communist" subversion. Eisenhower responded with $20 million in aid. The following year, anti-Western elements gained power in Iraq and threatened the governments of Lebanon and Jordan. Pro-Nasser forces overthrew Iraq's pro-Western monarchy on July 14, 1958. This alarmed the already shaky government of Lebanese President Camille Chamoun. The day after the Iraqi coup, in response to a request from Chamoun, Eisenhower sent troops to Lebanon to prevent a possible coup by supporters of Nasser. Two days later, the United States assisted the airlift of British paratroopers to Jordan to support a nervous King Hussein. Eisenhower managed to arrange a political settlement in Lebanon, which enabled him to withdraw American forces within a few weeks. The interventions managed to maintain pro-Western governments in Lebanon and Jordan but did not stem Arab nationalism. Therefore, the administration reconsidered its policy and decided to "work

more closely with Arab nationalism and associate itself more closely with such aims and aspirations of the Arab people as are not contrary to the basic interests of the United States."

Just as the Lebanese crisis settled down, the Communist Chinese resumed shelling Quemoy and Matsu on August 23, 1958. Eisenhower resisted the advice of some advisers to use tactical nuclear weapons; instead, he ordered the Seventh Fleet to escort Nationalist supply ships. The shelling continued, and on September 11, Eisenhower gave a nationally televised speech in which he rejected "appeasement" but assured the country of his belief that "there is not going to be any war." Reaction to the speech was highly unfavorable. Neither public opinion in the United States nor any of America's allies supported a war over the islands. Some of those anxieties were misplaced; just as he had in the first crisis over Quemoy and Matsu, Eisenhower understood that the offshore islands had more psychological than strategic importance. In October, Dulles and Chiang reached an agreement that Chiang would not use force to regain the mainland. The Nationalist leader further agreed to withdraw some troops from the islands, and Eisenhower suspended escorts for Nationalist ships. The Communist Chinese responded to these signals by easing the bombardment of the islands.

The Suez Crisis left long-term strains on the Atlantic alliance. Although Eisenhower was able to restore relations with Great Britain, France (under Charles de Gaulle) embarked upon an independent foreign policy. This complicated matters when the Soviet premier, Nikita Khrushchev, issued an ultimatum regarding German reunification.

Khrushchev announced in November 1958 that, unless the West agreed to enter negotiations on a final settlement on Germany within six months, the USSR would recognize East Germany, and Western nations would have to deal with the East German regime for access to West Berlin. He also proposed withdrawing all foreign forces from Berlin and making it a free city under UN auspices. Eisenhower rejected advice to test Soviet intentions by sending American military forces through East Germany and into West Berlin. In public, the president initially took a firm stand. At the same time, he indicated to Khrushchev his willingness to negotiate. Khrushchev ultimately backed off his position and agreed to a foreign ministers conference in May 1959 and a trip to the United States in September. The foreign ministers conference recessed without resolving the outstanding issues.

Khrushchev's trip to the United States in September 1959 produced a thaw in relations between the superpowers. The visit attracted a good deal of publicity, but it produced little of substance. At a meeting between Eisenhower and the Soviet premier at Camp David, the two swapped war stories and discussed Berlin. Eisenhower consented to a summit conference the following spring and conceded that the allied position in Berlin was an "anomaly." In exchange, the Soviet leader agreed to put aside the separate treaty with East Germany and to begin negotiations over Berlin without a deadline. In many regards, it was a bravura performance by Eisenhower. He held the Western alliance together, conceded nothing of substance, and defused the crisis.

Pressure for a nuclear test ban had been building throughout the second half of the decade. In 1958, Eisenhower invited Great Britain and the USSR to enter into negotiations for a test ban treaty and also proposed suspending American testing for a year, provided that the Soviets did so as well. Khrushchev accepted. After a series of intense negotiations, in April 1959 Eisenhower proposed a ban on atmospheric testing as an interim step. Khrushchev rejected the offer. Both sides, however, seemed to be moving towards a test ban. The United States and USSR took the first step toward the limitation of nuclear weapons in December 1959, when they joined 10 other countries in signing the Antarctic Treaty, which established a nuclear-free zone in the Antarctic. This increased expectations for the Paris summit scheduled for May 1960.

After John Foster Dulles died of stomach cancer in May 1959, Eisenhower concentrated foreign policy in his own hands. He increasingly came to believe that his historic mission was to encourage a "just and lasting peace." As part of that mission, Eisenhower made a series of goodwill trips to Latin America, Asia, and Africa. He also made greater efforts to find an accommodation with the Soviets. By the middle of 1959, the press began to refer to the "new" Eisenhower. Indeed, both at home and abroad, Eisenhower rebounded from the difficulties of the first two years of his second term.

During the final two years of Eisenhower's presidency, preventing the expansion of communism in Latin America emerged as a major focus of administration policy. Toward that end, he initiated steps to bring down the government of Fidel Castro, the Cuban leader who had come to power in 1959. As Castro's revolution gathered strength, Eisenhower had attempted first to press Cuba's dictator, Fulgencio Batista, to institute reforms, and had then imposed an arms embargo and withdrawn political support. Although there were some concerns about communists within Castro's movement, the administration extended recognition to Castro's government in January 1959. Castro immediately proceeded to alienate the United States by purging liberals, his onetime allies, from his government, by staging mass executions, and by signing a trade and aid agreement with the Soviet Union. In response to the confiscation of American property in July 1959, Eisenhower cut Cuba's sugar quota by 700,000 tons. Later that year, he took steps to prohibit Cuban sugar from the U.S. market. In March 1960, he approved a plan by the Central Intelligence Agency to subvert Castro's regime and ultimately to replace it. The plan included support for the opposition in exile, propaganda, sabotage, and training a group of Cuban exiles to overthrow Castro's government.

In other parts of Latin America, however, the president focused his attention on preventing the expansion of communism through the use of massive and long-term economic aid. Sobered by the hostile reception to Vice President Richard Nixon's trip to the region in mid-1958, Eisenhower warned that the choice was "social evolution or revolution." The administration also began to place greater emphasis on promoting democracy in the region. MILTON EISENHOWER's fact-finding trip to the region reinforced the administration's new direction. In 1959 the Eisenhower administration supported a regional development bank, for which the United States provided most of the initial capital. In September 1960, the administration put forward a plan to assist health services, expand housing and educational facilities, and aid agriculture. It won the support of all Latin American nations except Cuba. These policies formed the basis for Kennedy's Alliance for Progress.

Two events marred Eisenhower's last months in office. In May, his summit meeting with Khrushchev was canceled after the Soviets shot down a U.S. intelligence plane over Soviet territory. Initial cover stories blew up when Khrushchev produced the pilot and spy equipment. Eisenhower took personal responsibility for the incident. Unappeased, Khrushchev issued a series of angry denunciations of American aggression. Perhaps the Soviet leader preferred to wait until a new president took office; perhaps he needed to appease hard-liners in his own country. At the opening session of the summit, Khrushchev angrily denounced the United States and demanded an apology for the U-2 overflights before he would move on to other issues. Even Eisenhower's assurance that he had suspended further U-2 overflights for the rest of his administration failed to satisfy the Soviet premier. The Soviets effectively walked out. The collapse of the Paris summit was one of the great disappointments of Eisenhower's presidency.

In June 1960, Eisenhower had to cancel a goodwill trip to Japan because anti-American riots erupted after the Japanese Diet ratified a defense treaty with the United States in January. The retention of U.S. military bases was especially contentious, and although the Japanese government managed to push the measure through the parliament, the prime minister was forced to resign.

Although Eisenhower had his reverses as well as his successes, he presided over eight years of peace and prosperity. In domestic affairs, his policies fell well within the New Deal consensus. He did not dismantle any basic structure he inherited from Roosevelt and Truman. In some areas, such as public housing, he essentially maintained existing policies. In other areas, for example farm subsidies, he cut but retained the basic program. In still other areas, he presided over expansions of the New Deal legacy. Examples included Social Security (an increase in benefits and expansion of the program), the minimum wage (one of the largest percentage increases in history), public works (the Saint Lawrence Seaway and the national highway system), public health (a federal role in the distribution of

the Salk vaccine), and civil rights (the desegregation of the armed forces and Washington, D.C., attempts to eliminate discrimination in hiring by the federal government, and the passage of the first civil rights legislation since Reconstruction). On occasion, he proposed an expansion of the New Deal but failed to get the program through Congress. Health reinsurance and school construction were his most significant unsuccessful efforts in that regard.

In all, Eisenhower as president was a classic Tory reformer. He was willing to reform in order to preserve the basics of the system. Perhaps this was best illustrated by his reaction to the defeat of his health reinsurance program. "How in the hell," he asked, "is the AMA going to stop socialized medicine if they oppose bills such as this?" Most of all, as the first Republican president since the New Deal, he preserved and expanded the structures of government he inherited from Roosevelt and Truman. In doing so, he made the New Deal consensus genuinely bipartisan. The fact was that the Republican party had stopped running against the New Deal after 1936, but they had not held power until Eisenhower's victory in 1952.

In foreign policy as well, Eisenhower inherited a consensus from his predecessor. In the shadow of the Greek and Turkish crises of 1947, Truman had established a consensus in favor of containment of the Soviet Union. Here, too, Eisenhower functioned within the broad consensus he inherited. Nevertheless, if the basic objective remained the same, there were differences in style and approach. Eisenhower pursued the cold war as vigorously as Truman before him and Kennedy after him. However, he was less likely to seek confrontation than either Truman or Kennedy and sought to play down tensions with the Soviet Union. To grasp the difference, one need only compare Eisenhower's handling of Khrushchev's ultimatum on Berlin to Kennedy's response to the same ultimatum from the same Soviet leader. In addition, Eisenhower held the line on defense budgets.

Eisenhower played only a small role in the presidential campaign of 1960. Although he remained unenthusiastic about Richard Nixon, he accepted the vice president's nomination as inevitable. Still, he waited until March to give his vice president a somewhat less than enthusiastic endorsement. In his address to the Republican convention, Eisenhower spoke of the achievements of his administration rather than about Nixon's qualifications for the presidency. Yielding to Nixon's wishes, Eisenhower did not actively enter the campaign until the very last days. Facing the dilemma of all vice presidents who wish to succeed the president they served, Nixon wanted to establish his own identity. At the same time, he had to do so without criticizing the policies of the administration he served. This dynamic strained an already tense relationship between Eisenhower and Nixon. Whatever reservations he had about Nixon, however, Eisenhower regarded Kennedy as unqualified and was anxious to help his party retain the White House. Not until late October did Eisenhower campaign extensively for Nixon, but even then he talked about his administration's achievements and not about Nixon's experience or personal qualities. On election day, Kennedy defeated Nixon in one of the closest elections in American history.

In the waning days of his presidency, Eisenhower chose not to read his last State of the Union message and sent it to be entered in the *Congressional Record.* Instead, he went on national television to deliver a farewell address. In it, he warned against the danger of communism, "a hostile ideology—global in scope, atheistic in character, ruthless in purpose, and insidious in method." "Unhappily," he told the nation, "the danger it poses promises to be of indefinite duration." He also admonished the American people to guard against the "unwarranted influence, whether sought or unsought, by the military-industrial complex." The "conjunction of an immense military establishment and a large arms industry," the old warrior observed, was "new in the American experience," and "the potential for the disastrous rise of misplaced power exists and will persist."

Eisenhower retired to his farm near Gettysburg, Pa., but he could not escape an endless stream of requests for his time, his name, and his advice. Republicans prevailed on him to appear at fundraisers; candidates sought his advice and support; organizations appealed for his endorsement; historians wanted interviews and archivists permission to organize his papers. The General, as he preferred to be called, published a highly readable memoir of his presidency in two large volumes, *Mandate for Change* (1963) and *Waging Peace* (1965). He also published a more personal account of his early years, *At Ease: Stories I Tell to Friends* (1967). Both Kennedy and Johnson called on Eisenhower for his advice. The disastrous invasion at the Bay of Pigs reinforced his misgivings about his successor. Eisenhower often cited the advice of his old mentor, Fox Conner: "Always take your job seriously, never yourself." After one visit to the Kennedy White House, he commented that the people there functioned on a different principle: "Take yourself seriously, and to hell with the job." Immediately after Kennedy was assassinated, Eisenhower met with Lyndon Johnson, who later recalled that he "was deeply moved that the former president should go into such specific detail and give me his recommendations and his support." Eisenhower consistently opposed Kennedy's increases in defense spending and watched with dismay the policy of his successors in Southeast Asia. The former president opposed Kennedy's decision to increase the number of American "advisers" in South Vietnam; yet Eisenhower thought it important not to lose Indochina to communism. He regarded Johnson's policy of gradual escalation as military folly and the product of a lack of political will. By June 1966 he saw a stalemate developing, something that, as a military professional, he considered unacceptable, and began to discuss disengagement.

A heart attack in the fall of 1965 forced Eisenhower to cut back on the active schedule he had maintained. After that, his health began to fail. He had gallbladder surgery in December 1966, followed by congestive heart failure in February 1967 and a stroke two months after that. After another heart attack, he entered Walter Reed Army Hospital on May 14, 1968. From the hospital, Eisenhower issued a statement warmly endorsing Nixon for president. On August 5, the former president rallied to put on a suit to make a brief televised address to the Republican National Committee from his suite at Walter Reed. He died on March 28, 1969.

During the decades after Eisenhower left office, historians' assessments of his presidency changed. Throughout the 1960s, most professional historians, a group dominated by Democrats, criticized his formalist view of the presidency and his lack of an activist domestic agenda. Eisenhower tended to rank near the bottom of presidents in polls of historians, who portrayed him as an incompetent, genial former general who was utterly out of his depth as president. The American involvement in Indochina and the domestic unrest of the 1960s, however, prompted some to question the postwar liberal consensus and to reexamine the 1940s and 1950s from a different perspective. In that context, some historians found Eisenhower an appealing figure. He ended one war and did not begin another; he cut defense spending and warned of the military-industrial complex. The image of a military man as a man of peace held a strong attraction, particularly for historians who came of age during the war in Vietnam. That image was somewhat overdrawn, but it contributed to a fundamental reconsideration of Eisenhower's presidency. At the same time that political considerations were leading historians to reassess Eisenhower and his presidency, large collections of documents at the Eisenhower Library were opened to researchers. Initial explorations led most of these scholars to conclude that Eisenhower was more active, intelligent, informed, and competent than he had been generally regarded. A good number of these scholars also concluded that Eisenhower was more conservative than he had typically been portrayed. The opening of enormous collections at the Eisenhower Library in the mid-1970s, including Eisenhower's own papers as president, reinforced the view that Eisenhower was more literate and able than the early accounts gave him credit for being. However, these documents called into question the notion that Eisenhower was really an Old Guard Republican. Indeed, Eisenhower's private papers revealed him to be a fiscal conservative, but one whose politics fell well within the broad political consensus established by Roosevelt and the New Deal. By the early 1980s, a growing body of scholarship depicting Eisenhower as a competent and engaged leader had become known as "Eisenhower revisionism" and came to dominate scholarship on the 1950s. Even as it established itself as something of a new orthodoxy, however, Eisenhower revisionism came to encompass so broad a range of views that it became meaningless. Once they had demolished the image of the bumbling, befuddled ex-general,

historians began to debate the nature and wisdom of Eisenhower's policies.

Whatever its limitations and failures, Eisenhower's presidency was not, as William V. Shannon described it, "the time of the great postponement." It was not even only, in the words of Charles Alexander, "a good job of holding the line." Eisenhower presided over a period of peace and prosperity, and, particularly compared to what came after him, that achievement should not be gainsaid. Perhaps that perspective led Stephen Ambrose to join in the judgment of "millions of Americans" who "felt that the country was damned lucky to have him."

—MSM

Eisenhower, Milton S(tover)

(1889–1985) *presidential adviser; president, Pennsylvania State University; president, Johns Hopkins University*

Born in Abilene, Kans., on September 15, 1899, Milton Eisenhower, the youngest brother of Dwight D. Eisenhower, enrolled at Kansas State University in 1919. Because he had to work to pay for his education, it took him six years to graduate. He earned money as a correspondent for the *Kansas City Star* and the *Topeka Daily Capital*, a contributor to the *Kansas Farmer* and the *Iowa Farmer*, and a proofreader for the alumni journal. Eisenhower was a member of Phi Kappa Phi (a scholastic honorary society for scientific schools), won several awards for public speaking, and was editor of the campus newspaper. Upon graduation, he became an instructor in the journalism school; he also took some graduate courses. After finishing first on an examination for the foreign service, Eisenhower received an appointment to a consular post in Edinburgh, Scotland. While there, he took courses at the University of Edinburgh.

When William M. Jardine, the president of Kansas State, became secretary of agriculture under Calvin Coolidge, he cabled Eisenhower and asked him to come to Washington as his assistant. Eisenhower hesitated to give up the security of the foreign service, so Jardine arranged for him to take a civil service examination. Eisenhower once again finished first and received an appointment in the Department of Agriculture in 1926. He became information director for the department two years later, and served under Jardine's successor, Arthur Hyde.

The advent of the Roosevelt administration brought a new secretary of agriculture, Henry A. Wallace. Eisenhower and Wallace quickly developed a strong mutual respect and a close personal relationship. Wallace, who was awkward and ill at ease in the social world of Washington, did not get on at all well with Roosevelt. Eisenhower, on the other hand, was by this time a polished veteran of official Washington and quickly established an easy rapport with the president. Wallace came to rely on Eisenhower to act as an intermediary with the president. Under the New Deal, the many agencies of the Agriculture Department promulgated often-conflicting policies. Wallace made Eisenhower coordinator of the Office of Land-Use Planning, a position "second in responsibility to the Secretary's" whose responsibility was to reconcile the various conflicts.

When Wallace became Roosevelt's vice president, Eisenhower clashed with the new secretary of agriculture, Claude R. Wickard. Eisenhower considered leaving the government, but Roosevelt kept him on board by giving him special assignments. Shortly after the attack on Pearl Harbor, the president asked Eisenhower to study all of the government's dissemination of information related to the war. Eisenhower recommended the creation of an Office of War Information. In March 1942, Roosevelt called Eisenhower in and told him that his new job would be to head the War Relocation Authority (WRA), which was responsible for relocating Japanese Americans from the West Coast to government relocation centers. Eisenhower would later recall this assignment as "the meanest, toughest, most unpleasant of my career." Less than a month after assuming his new post, Eisenhower wrote, "I feel most deeply that when the war is over . . . we as Americans are going to regret the avoidable injustices that may have been done." All attempts to humanize this inhumane program failed. Eisenhower reminded a meeting of governors from 10 western states that none of the Japanese Americans had been found guilty of anything. He proposed 50 to 75 small camps, modeled on the Civilian Conservation Corps (CCC). Some of the internees

would work in the camps, on reclamation projects, or in manufacturing; but he hoped that the majority would find work in the private sector. He pointed to the labor shortage in the intermountain states, especially in agriculture. The governors shouted down his proposals. Similarly, Eisenhower's hope that the Japanese Americans might be relocated to "small CCC sort of camps" gave way to objections by the army and War Department that larger camps took less manpower to keep under armed guard. Eisenhower was never comfortable with the assignment, and, after three months, Roosevelt relieved him of the burden and named him associate director of the Office of War Information (OWI). Before leaving the WRA, Eisenhower prepared a final report, in which he suggested that the president "issue a strong public statement in behalf of loyal American citizens" and urged "a more liberal wage policy" in the camps. Roosevelt ignored his recommendations. At the OWI, Milton played an important role in defending Dwight's reputation when many in the press criticized the general for a deal struck with Adm. Jean Darlan, deputy head of the Vichy government and commander in chief of its armed forces. Milton went to North Africa to oversee public relations, and the press coverage of Gen. Eisenhower became much more favorable.

When the president of Kansas State College stepped down in the spring of 1943, campus officials offered Eisenhower the position. After much deliberation, he accepted and took office on July 1, 1943. During his tenure, Eisenhower broadened the curriculum at Kansas State College of Agriculture and Applied Science (which later became Kansas State University). He added elements of a liberal education to buttress the technical education at the school. In early 1950, the trustees of another land-grant college, Penn State College (later University), offered the presidency of that institution to Eisenhower. He accepted and assumed his new post after the end of the academic year. His experience at Penn State was similar in many ways to that at Kansas State. Eisenhower set about transforming Penn State "from a leading agricultural and scientific college into a distinguished international university."

During the postwar years, Eisenhower continued to serve the government in various capacities. In 1945, President HARRY S. TRUMAN asked Eisenhower to help the new secretary of agriculture, Clinton P. Anderson, merge the War Food Administration and the Department of Agriculture. The president offered Eisenhower an appointment as either a special assistant to the president or undersecretary of agriculture. Milton declined either title but agreed to commute for three months to tackle the assignment. Later that year, Truman named Eisenhower to a three-member fact-finding board in the wage dispute between General Motors and the United Auto Workers. In March 1946, Truman appointed him to the Famine Emergency Committee. That same year, Eisenhower declined an offer from Truman to become an assistant secretary-general at the United Nations. Also in 1946, Eisenhower became chair of the U.S. National Commission for the United Nations Educational, Scientific, and Cultural Organization (UNESCO), a position he would hold for four years. In that capacity, he attended the first international conference of UNESCO as the vice-chair of the American delegation and also became a member of UNESCO's executive board.

Milton initially counseled his brother against running for president in 1952. However, after Dwight met with Sen. ROBERT TAFT (R-Ohio) and the senator rejected the concept of mutual security in Europe, both brothers concluded that Ike ought to leave open the prospect of the Republican presidential nomination. No one else seemed able to stop Taft from getting the nomination. Further, Milton became convinced that his brother was the only Republican who could win the general election, and he thought a change in administrations necessary after 20 years of Democratic rule. From the earliest stages of Dwight's political career, Milton served as his brother's closest adviser. The two men had enjoyed an extremely close relationship throughout their adult lives. Dwight thought highly of Milton's intelligence, knowledge, and ideas. Further, the younger Eisenhower had years of experience in Washington. Milton became a key figure in the movement to draft Ike and in the campaign. In an official capacity, he was a member of the Eisenhower for President steering committee and played a role at the Republican National Convention in July 1952.

In spite of their intimate relationship, Milton held no high official position in his brother's admin-istration. Both wanted to avoid any charges of nepotism. Ike often mused that he would have appointed Milton to the cabinet, either at Agriculture or State, had he not been the president's brother. At the same time, Milton's lack of an official position allowed him to serve as an adviser without portfolio. He had virtually unlimited access to the president, and he advised on virtually all matters; he helped write speeches, took on special assignments, and served as his brother's personal representative in Latin America. Most important of all, Milton functioned as his brother's sounding board. Ike trusted his brother's judgment and his ability to keep a confidence. For eight years, Milton spent most weekends at the White House. A direct line connected Milton's office at Penn State to the White House. During the week, he frequently wrote long letters to his brother on a wide variety of subjects. Throughout it all, Milton attempted to remain discretely in the background.

Sometimes Milton's role was more public. For instance, Ike named his brother, along with NELSON ROCKEFELLER and ARTHUR FLEMMING, to the President's Advisory Committee on Government Organization (PACGO). The committee studied the federal government and made recommendations to eliminate unnecessary duplication and improve efficiency in the structure of government. The work of PACGO led to the creation of the Department of Health, Education and Welfare; the United States Information Agency; the Agency for International Development; the Small Business Administration; and the National Aeronautics and Space Administration.

Milton served as his brother's special envoy to Latin America in 1954. A five-week trip convinced him that traditional foreign aid might strengthen the existing order but would not facilitate necessary social change. He recommended expanded trade and investment, increased technical aid, and cultural exchanges. Beyond that, he believed that the United States should not only help develop Latin America's economic infrastructure but also encourage democratic governments. Toward that end, he believed that U.S. aid should emphasize long-term development projects. He also stressed the need for better educational opportunities, better sanitation, and better health care. Milton made subsequent trips to Latin America in 1958 and 1960. He presented his views on inter-American relations in *The Wine Is Bitter* (1963). Influenced by Milton's initial report, the Eisenhower administration "doubled the flow of private and public capital," strengthened the role of the Organization of American States, promoted common markets, and established the Inter-American Bank (founded to make loans with conditions requiring social reform). The legislation and international agreements that JOHN F. KENNEDY would later call the Alliance for Progress were already enacted or well under way by the end of the Eisenhower administration.

When the president suffered a heart attack in 1955, a minor boomlet developed in support of Milton as the Republican candidate in 1956 if his brother could not run. The *New York Herald Tribune*, the *Chicago Sun-Times*, and three Republican governors came out in favor of Milton if Dwight were not available. A poll of Republican state chairmen indicated substantial support for Ike's younger brother. The president himself had long regarded Milton as "the most highly qualified man in the United States to be president," but Ike doubted that his younger brother was physically strong enough and thought that the American people would resent anything that appeared to create a dynasty. The boom proved embarrassing to Milton, and Ike's remarkable recovery put an end to speculation about the need for a successor.

As close as they were, the two brothers did not always agree. For example, Milton at times urged his brother to denounce Sen. JOSEPH MCCARTHY (R-Wis.). The president thought that such a course would elevate McCarthy, give him the publicity on which he thrived, and possibly rally the Senate to defend one of its own against the executive.

Despite his efforts to remain quietly in the background, Milton's role at times attracted public attention. He became a favorite target of conservative critics of the administration, who blamed him for what they regarded as the liberal bent of the administration. They pointed to his years of service to the New Deal as proof of his left-leaning views. McCarthy on several occasions attacked Milton's role in the administration. In January 1957, McCarthy denounced Milton as an "extreme radical" who "tops the list" of the "motley crowd" that influenced the president. Ironi-

cally, in his desperate search for an issue on which to attack the president in 1956, ADLAI STEVENSON, the Democratic nominee, charged that Milton used his influence to gain support for right-wing dictators in Latin America. Attacks on his brother, toward whom he had always felt protective, ignited Ike's legendary temper. In response to Stevenson's allegations, Ike broke from his usual practice of avoiding direct references to personalities and leveled a blast at Stevenson, who had failed to get his facts straight.

The death of his wife in 1955 left Milton devastated. He left Penn State in May 1956, and in July of that year accepted the presidency of Johns Hopkins University. During his years at Johns Hopkins, the school thrived, and Eisenhower enjoyed great popularity with the students, faculty, and trustees. On his watch, the endowment had doubled, the income tripled, and the university built and paid for buildings worth $75 million. When he retired in 1967 with the position of president emeritus, faculty salaries were fourth-highest in the nation, and the institution's place as one of the country's great universities was secure. These achievements brought him great satisfaction. Under Milton Eisenhower's unfortunate successor, the university's fortunes turned down. By 1971, the institution faced student unrest, a large budget deficit, salary freezes, and cutbacks in positions. The faculty revolted. The trustees asked Eisenhower to return to active leadership on an interim basis. Students and the faculty joined in urging Eisenhower to return. He did and turned the situation at Hopkins around within a year, at which point he stepped down again.

Milton's public service continued after his brother left the White House. During Kennedy's presidency, he negotiated with Fidel Castro for the release of prisoners taken at the Bay of Pigs. LYNDON JOHNSON chose him to chair the National Commission on the Causes and Prevention of Violence. Milton remained active in Republican politics and strongly opposed the more conservative direction it took beginning in 1964. He supported Sen. Charles McC. Mathias, Jr., a liberal Republican from Maryland, and endorsed John Anderson's bid for the presidency in 1980.

Eisenhower published something of a political memoir, *The President Is Calling*, in 1974, which he intended to advance his ideas about the need for structural reform in government. He died on May 2, 1985.

—MSM

Ellender, Allen J(oseph)
(1890–1972) *U.S. senator; chairman, Agriculture and Forestry Committee*

Born in Montegut, La., on Sept. 24, 1890, Allen Ellender graduated from Saint Aloysius College in New Orleans and earned a law degree from Tulane University in 1913. While in his twenties, he served as district attorney of Terrebonne Parish and established himself as the area's leading potato farmer. In 1924, Ellender won election to the state House of Representatives as a Democratic opponent of Huey P. Long, but he soon allied himself with the governor's populist administration. Emerging as a key figure in the Long machine, Ellender was Speaker of the House when Long, then a U.S. senator, was assassinated in 1935. Long's widow filled his unexpired term, and Ellender won election to the vacant seat in 1936. In office, he was appointed to the Agriculture Committee and coauthored the Agricultural Adjustment Act of 1937.

Abandoning Long-style populism early in his Senate career, Ellender became known chiefly as a spokesman for his state's wealthy sugar, rice, and cotton growers, whose interests he protected on the Agriculture Committee. As committee chairman during all but two years of the Eisenhower administration, he was particularly energetic in attempting to revise U.S. sugar marketing quotas to make them more favorable to domestic producers. In 1955, Ellender introduced legislation restricting the importation of lower-cost sugar from the Caribbean and thus guaranteed American growers a larger share of the domestic market. Five years later, in response to the confiscation of American-owned property by the Castro regime in Cuba, he helped secure the suspension of Cuban sugar quotas. Ellender also used his control of the Agriculture Committee to block the Eisenhower administration's attempt to lower price supports on basic farm commodities to bring them closer to world prices. Congress enacted most of the administration's program of flexible price supports in 1954. Two years

later, Ellender pushed through a bill restoring high, rigid supports on basic crops, but Eisenhower vetoed the measure.

Although a staunch southern conservative on most domestic issues, Ellender was an advocate of closer relations with the USSR and a critic of defense spending. In 1957, after a 28-nation trip abroad, he issued a controversial report praising Soviet society and attacking the whole concept of foreign aid as an "abysmal failure."

During the 1960s, Ellender continued to play a major role in the shaping of agriculture policy, while leading southern opposition to civil rights legislation. His long tenure increased his power in the Senate, and in 1971 he resigned the chairmanship of the Agriculture Committee to become chairman of the key Appropriations Committee. At the time of his death in Bethesda, Md., on July 27, 1972, Ellender was president pro tempore of the Senate and third in the line of presidential succession.

—TLH

Engle, Clair
(1911–1964) *U.S. congressman and senator; chairman, Interior and Insular Affairs Committee*

Engle was born in Bakersfield, Calif., on September 21, 1911. He received an LL.B. degree from the University of California in 1933. The following year, he won election as a county district attorney, the youngest in California's history. Reelected in 1938 and cited by state's attorney general, EARL WARREN, for his aggressiveness, Engle spent one term in the state Senate before successfully running as a Democrat for the U.S. House of Representatives in a special election in 1943. His district was the nation's largest, covering one-third of California from the Mojave Desert to Oregon. Engle specialized in water resources legislation and sponsored every expansion of the California Central Valley Reclamation Project between 1943 and 1957. In 1952, he wrote a pioneer authorization for research into conversion of salt water to fresh water. Engle was assigned to the Interior and Insular Affairs Committee in 1951. The following year, he chaired an Interior Affairs Subcommittee examining proposals to build a federal hydroelectric dam in Hells Canyon, Idaho. His astute questioning of witnesses on water rights resulted in the committee's unanimous vote against the power project. In 1953, he became ranking Democrat on the Interior and Insular Affairs panel.

Engle supported statehood for Hawaii in March 1953 and testified in its favor at Senate hearings. A strong opponent of racial discrimination, he supported the administration's civil rights bill in 1957. When President Eisenhower threatened to veto the measure in August after it had been weakened in the Senate, Engle charged that the chief executive was trying to maximize political mileage by appealing to both supporters and opponents of civil rights.

In 1955, Engle became chairman of the Interior and Insular Affairs Committee and assistant Democratic whip. As chairman, he backed the development of public power. In June 1956, Engle said that, according to legal views cited by the Library of Congress, the federal government could build power projects in Hells Canyon even though the Federal Power Commission had given the right to a private company. His committee then passed a Hells Canyon bill, but opponents of public power killed it in the Senate. During the same year, Engle backed a bill authorizing $760 million for Upper Colorado River reclamation and a power project backed by the administration. The bill was signed into law in April 1956.

Engle entered the race in 1958 for the Senate seat vacated by WILLIAM F. KNOWLAND. In an election complicated by California's cross-filing system, which permitted candidates to run as both Democrats and Republicans, Engle defeated Republican Gov. GOODWIN KNIGHT for the Democratic senatorial nomination and in the November election. Sen. Engle was assigned to committees on armed services, small business, and interstate commerce. In January 1959, the liberal freshman participated in a move to limit anti–civil rights filibustering. This effort failed when the Senate leadership succeeded in substituting a much weaker measure that did not offend Southerners.

In 1960, Engle led opposition to the Senate's ratification of the U.S.-Soviet Antarctica Treaty, which pledged "peaceful use" of the frozen continent. Testifying in June before the Senate Foreign Relations Committee, Engle charged the pact did not insure against secret Soviet military operations

and gave the USSR equal rights in an area where the United States had been predominant. Two months later, the Senate ratified the treaty.

Engle generally supported President JOHN F. KENNEDY's legislative program. He received a 100 percent rating from the liberal Americans for Democratic Action in 1961. Engle fell ill in 1963 and required repeated brain surgery. He voted from a wheelchair for the Johnson administration's landmark civil rights bill in June 1964. He died in Washington, D.C., on July 30, 1964.

—MJS

Ervin, Sam(uel) J(ames), Jr.
(1896–1985) *U.S. senator*

Born in Morgantown, N.C., on September 27, 1896, Ervin received an A.B. degree from the University of North Carolina at Chapel Hill in 1917. Following service in the army during World War I, he was admitted to the North Carolina bar in 1918. Ervin then enrolled at Harvard and obtained his LL.B. degree there in 1922.

Ervin returned to Morgantown, where he intermittently practiced law for 30 years. A Democrat, he was elected to the North Carolina General Assembly three times during the mid-1920s and early-1930s. After sitting on the Burke Co. Criminal Court from 1935 to 1937, he was appointed to the North Carolina Superior Court in 1937, where he served for six years. He returned to private practice in 1943. In January 1946, Ervin won a special election to fill a vacancy in the U.S. House of Representatives created by the death of his brother, but he did not run for reelection the following fall. In February 1948, he was appointed an associate justice of the North Carolina Supreme Court.

The governor of North Carolina appointed Ervin to fill a vacant Senate seat in June 1954. Because of Ervin's judicial experience, Minority Leader LYNDON B. JOHNSON (D-Tex.) tapped him to serve on a special six-member select committee created to investigate censure charges against Sen. JOSEPH R. MCCARTHY (R-Wis.). Ervin did not participate extensively in the questioning of witnesses during the panel's hearings. In September he concurred with the committee's recommendation to censure McCarthy. On November 10, as the Senate began its deliberations on the committee's recommendation, McCarthy inserted in the *Congressional Record* a statement asserting that the panel "had done the work of the Communist Party" and had "imitated Communist methods." Eight days later, Ervin made an unusually sharp attack on his colleague from Wisconsin, declaring that, if McCarthy believed these charges, he had "mental delusions," and, if he did not, he was suffering from "moral incapacity."

A strict constructionist, Ervin regarded himself as a defender of the rights of individuals and of the states under the Constitution against encroachment by federal government. He opposed government attacks upon southern racial discrimination as threats to these rights. In 1956, Ervin asserted that segregation was "not the offspring of racial bigotry or racial prejudice" but the result of the exercise of "a fundamental American freedom—the freedom of selecting one's associates." In 1957, he opposed the Eisenhower administration's civil rights bill, designed to protect black voting rights, claiming that it infringed upon the constitutional right of the states to determine voter qualifications. Ervin succeeded in weakening the measure by amending it to guarantee a jury trial in the cases of those accused of violating a court order and intimidating or coercing voters. Three years later, he participated in a southern filibuster against another administration civil rights bill, designed to protect black voting rights, which he denounced as giving special privileges to racially defined groups. At the Democratic National Convention in July 1960, Ervin unsuccessfully fought against the inclusion of a civil rights plank in the party platform.

If Ervin's constitutional arguments seemed a mere rationalization for racial discrimination, he did, on occasion, vote with liberals on issues relating to civil liberties. In the *Jencks* decision of June 1957, the Supreme Court ruled that defendants were entitled to see statements of prosecution witnesses. Many members of Congress criticized the Court, but Ervin defended the ruling, and in August he voted against Sen. EVERETT M. DIRKSEN's (R-Ill.) proposals aimed at limiting the effects of the decision. In April 1958, Ervin joined a nine-to-five majority of the Judiciary Committee that rejected an amendment applying the federal security program to nonsensitive as well as sensitive jobs.

Ervin's commitment to civil libertarianism had narrowly defined limits, and he opposed the reversal of criminal convictions based on procedural technicalities. For example, in June 1957, the Supreme Court established the so-called Mallory rule when it overturned a rape conviction on the ground that there had been unnecessary delay before arraignment. Fourteen months later, Ervin unsuccessfully proposed that trial judges be empowered to determine whether delays were reasonable and to make their decisions binding on appellate courts if founded upon substantial evidence.

Ervin was generally unsympathetic to organized labor. He opposed the repeal of state right-to-work laws. In 1957, Ervin was appointed to the Senate Select Committee on Improper Activities in the Labor or Management Field, which investigated corruption in the Teamsters and other unions for the next three years. In 1959, he and Sen. JOHN F. KENNEDY (D-Mass.) introduced a bill aimed at cleaning up the kind of labor racketeering and labor-management collusion exposed by the investigation. The measure contained provisions to eliminate corruption and ensure fair elections. Fearing that it would weaken support for the bill, the two men deliberately did not deal with major provisions in the Taft-Hartley Act affecting rights in collective bargaining. The Senate passed the measure with little modification in April. However, the House changed it dramatically. Finally enacted in September as the Labor Management Reporting and Disclosure Act, the bill also extended the Taft-Hartley Act's prohibitions against secondary boycotts.

During the early 1960s, Ervin opposed federal aid to parochial schools on the ground that it violated the constitutional separation of church and state. Although he continued to oppose most social welfare and civil rights legislation, Ervin earned the admiration of liberals in the late-1960s and early-1970s for his opposition to Richard Nixon's Omnibus D.C. Crime Bill, his probe of army surveillance of civilians, and his role in 1973 as chairman of the Watergate Committee. He declined to run for reelection in 1974. Ervin returned to North Carolina, where he practiced law and wrote. He died in Winston-Salem, N.C., on April 23, 1985.

—MLL

Fairless, Benjamin F(ranklin)

(1890–1962) *chairman of the board, United States Steel Corporation; president, American Iron and Steel Institute*

The son of poor Welsh immigrants, Benjamin Williams was born in Pigeon Run, Ohio, on May 3, 1890. His parents sent him to live with his aunt and uncle, Sarah and Jacob Fairless, at the age of five to provide access to better schooling. The Fairless family later adopted him and legally changed his name to Fairless. Benjamin worked his way through Ohio Northern University and, following his graduation in 1913, went to work as a surveyor for the Wheeling and Lake Erie Railroad. Soon after, however, he joined the Central Steel Co. as a civil engineer. Fairless rose rapidly, becoming president and general manager in 1928. When his company and several others merged to form the Republic Steel Corp. in 1930, he became its executive vice president. Fairless became president of the Carnegie-Illinois Steel Corp. in 1935. In January 1938, he was elected president and chairman of the executive committee of its parent company, U.S. Steel.

During World War II, Fairless served on various advisory boards, including the Iron and Steel Industry Advisory Committee and the War Production Board. In the postwar years, he defended U.S. Steel against government investigations of monopolistic trends. He criticized those who thought there was "something inherently vicious in bigness and growth and success" and described detractors of big business as people who "think small." During 1952,

Fairless helped negotiate the settlement of a 55-day strike that crippled the industry.

In May 1952, Fairless was elected chairman of the board and chief executive officer of U.S. Steel. He held these positions until May 1955, when he retired at the age of 65. He was subsequently named chairman of the executive advisory committee and continued as a member of the board. That same year, he became president of the American Iron and Steel Institute (AISI).

Fairless often represented the industry before government committees and served on various presidential committees. Early in 1955, he appeared before the Senate Banking and Currency Committee, during a "friendly" study of the stock market, to detail financial problems faced by U.S. Steel. He stressed restoration of "investor confidence" as a major concern. In late 1955, he served on a task force, established by presidential disarmament adviser HAROLD E. STASSEN, to study the role of the steel industry in determining disarmament policies. The steel industry executive also became a member of the presidential board of consultants to monitor and evaluate U.S. intelligence operations.

In 1954, Eisenhower named Fairless to head the Citizens Advisers on the Mutual Security Program. The panel was to study issues relating to the U.S. foreign-aid programs, especially those posed by a Soviet shift from direct intervention to the use of economic aid to extend its influence. During 1956–57, the committee made a 52-day tour of 21 countries. Its report, issued in March 1957, urged the continuation of the program. While acknowledging that military assistance was vital to prevent Communist expansion, the panel maintained that economic development was as important for future security. It recommended that economic aid be focused on long-term development and urged the formation of regional markets such as the European Economic Community. The advisers concluded that "foreign investment of private capital is far more desirable than investment by government" and urged increasing incentives for such investment "by providing more equitable taxation of foreign business income." The report also urged that foreign-aid programs be presented to each Congress, rather than to each session, to permit more efficient planning and utilization of funds.

Fairless continued to represent big steel through the remainder of the decade and conferred with Vice President RICHARD M. NIXON in 1959 in an unsuccessful effort to avert a steel strike. He remained AISI president until his death in Ligonier, Pa., on January 1, 1962.

—RB

Farland, Joseph S(impson)

(1914–2007) *ambassador to the Dominican Republic, ambassador to Panama*

The son of a banker, Farland was born in Clarksburg, W.Va., on August 11, 1914. He graduated from West Virginia University in 1936 and earned his law degree from the same institution two years later. Admitted to the bar, he practiced law in West Virginia until he became an FBI agent in 1942. Commissioned an officer in the navy in 1944, he did research on strategic issues relating to Asia. In 1946, Farland returned to West Virginia and became president of his father-in-law's coal company, Christopher Fuel Corporation. He also founded Farland Fuel Company and Farland Coal Corporation.

In 1956, Farland, who had been active in Republican politics in West Virginia, became deputy director of the Mutual Security Agency. The next year, President DWIGHT D. EISENHOWER nominated Farland to be ambassador to the Dominican Republic. The Senate confirmed him in May 1957. Farland failed to establish good relations with the Dominican Republic's dictator, Rafael Trujillo.

The ambassador made little secret of his distaste for Trujillo's authoritarian regime and met with dissidents.

Because of Farland's inability to deal with Trujillo, Eisenhower removed him from the Dominican Republic in 1960 and named him ambassador to Panama. The Senate confirmed the appointment in June 1960. Farland sympathized with Panamanian peasants and found fault with American foreign-aid programs. The ambassador objected to the policy of granting foreign aid to governments rather than private groups, which he believed prevented money from reaching the local level. He also was impatient with the State Department's bureaucracy, which insisted on surveys and other procedures that Farland thought delayed aid. During his tenure, Farland built roads so that small farmers could get their produce to market. He also helped Panamanians build vocational schools, low-income housing, and medical facilities.

Farland continued as ambassador to Panama under the administration of JOHN F. KENNEDY. The Kennedy administration rejected Farland's suggestion that Panamanians be given increased control of the Canal Zone, and the ambassador resigned in July 1963. Shortly after his departure, the *New Republic* praised him as "a figure from the romance of what we would like the American abroad to be."

Upon leaving the State Department, Farland joined the Washington law firm of Surrey and Morse. In 1964, he headed an advisory panel on Latin American affairs for BARRY GOLDWATER, the Republican nominee for the presidency. After the campaign, Farland returned to his law firm. President RICHARD M. NIXON appointed him ambassador to Pakistan in 1969. In that capacity, he participated in a ruse that kept secret the meeting in July 1971 between HENRY A. KISSINGER, Nixon's National Security Advisor, and Zhou Enlai (Chou En-lai), the Chinese premier. That meeting laid the groundwork for Nixon's trip to China in February 1972. Farland became ambassador to Iran in 1972 and left the foreign service in 1973, after which he returned to the private practice of law. He died at his home in Winchester, Va., on January 28, 2007.

—MSM

Fast, Howard M(elvin)
(1914–2003) *writer*

Born to Jewish parents in New York City on November 11, 1914, Fast spent his youth in self-described "utter poverty." He applied for service in the navy while still in his mid-teens but was rejected because of his age. Subsequently, he spent years drifting from job to job, mixing with multitudes of people, "fighting," and, most of all, reading. In his autobiography, *The Naked God,* Fast marked 1932, a year when he worked in a Harlem branch of the New York Public Library, as the point when his career as a writer truly opened up. Between the years 1932 and 1944, he wrote 13 books, including novels, biographies, stories, and juvenile publications. He showed particular interest in writing historical novels that probed the American past for new perspectives. They included *Two Valleys* (1933), about the frontier during the American Revolution; *Conceived in Liberty* (1939), which dealt with a private at Valley Forge; *The Unvanquished* (1942), concerning the development of George Washington as a leader; *Citizen Tom Paine* (1943); and *Freedom Road* (1944), the story of an African American who becomes a member of Congress during Reconstruction. He also wrote *Spartacus* (1951), a best-seller, which in 1960 was made into a film starring Kirk Douglas and directed by Stanley Kubrick. By the early 1940s, Fast's books were accumulating both critical praise and a substantial readership. During World War II, he worked for the Office of War Information.

In 1943, Fast became a member of the U.S. Communist Party, a commitment that drastically altered his career. Long before 1943, he had attended meetings of communist and radical groups, and in that year he firmly "came to accept the proposition that the truest and most consistent fighters in the anti-fascist struggle were the Communists." His full commitment to the party came at a time when the majority of American writers on the Left had long since abandoned the organization.

In 1949, the Civil Right Congress, a communist front group, scheduled a fund-raising concert in Peekskill, N.Y., at which the black singer PAUL ROBESON was the leading attraction. In a speech he gave not long before the scheduled concert, Robeson urged African Americans not to fight in a war against the Soviet Union. The remarks touched off a firestorm. Led by the local American Legion, hundreds of World War II veterans blocked roads, rocked cars, and threatened would-be concert goers, leading to cancellation of the event. When the concert was rescheduled, the governor of New York, THOMAS E. DEWEY, sent hundreds of state police to protect the concert, which went on in spite of a furious protest by a mob of veterans. After the concert, the veterans stoned the cars of those leaving the event. Although the police arrested the local officers of the American Legion, a grand jury refused to indict. Fast claimed, somewhat nonsensically given the facts, that "the Peekskill affair was an important step in the preparation for the fascization of America and for the creation of receptive soil for promulgation of World War III." After that time, Fast's name was regularly invoked as "the public face" of American Communists. In 1950, he was called before the House Committee of Un-American Activities (HUAC) as a member of the Anti-Fascist Refugee Committee. He was charged with contempt for refusing to answer the committee's questions and served a short time in prison in 1950. He ran a symbolic and futile campaign for Congress in 1952 on the American Labor Party ticket.

In 1953, Fast was called before Sen. JOSEPH MCCARTHY's (R-Wis.) Permanent Investigations Subcommittee of the Committee on Government Operations to testify on such subjects as alleged subversive books in the U.S. State Department libraries and alleged sabotage of Voice of America (VOA) broadcasts in Europe. As a result of the hearings, his books were removed from the libraries. McCarthy admonished VOA officials for suggesting that a few of his works might be suitable for overseas readers.

Although often vilified in America during the early 1950s, Fast was a literary hero in the USSR. The Soviets credited him with creating true "proletarian heroes" in his books and with portraying American history in a light favorable to a communist perspective. By his own account, millions of his books were printed in the USSR, two of his plays were performed there, and one of his books was transformed into an opera. In addition, two book-length critical studies of his work were published in the Soviet Union. In 1953, the Soviet government awarded Fast the Stalin Peace Prize. Meanwhile,

Fast found himself blacklisted in the United States. His books generally went out of print, and he could not find publishers for his new works. Only certain of his earlier works were still deemed suitable reading according to reviewers and publishers.

A dedicated communist, Fast wrote for party publications, attended meetings and conventions, and contributed considerable sums to party coffers until 1956. At that time, he broke from the organization after the publicity over what he termed the "revelations" in Nikita Khrushchev's report to the Russian Twentieth Congress, which detailed the atrocities of Stalin's dictatorship. Fast made no public pronouncement of his renunciation of communism until 1957. Later that year, he published *The Naked God*, a loosely constructed autobiography that attempted to explain his journey from "fellow traveler" to "deserter," He was called again to testify before HUAC in 1957 to serve as a public example of a "reformed" American communist.

During the late-1950s and the 1960s, Fast again found a market for his writing. He continued to publish novels, stories, and plays, worked in Hollywood, and contributed to mainstream American publications such as the *Saturday Evening Post* and *Ladies' Home Journal*.

Fast published a memoir, *Being Red*, in 1990. He died in Greenwich, Conn., on March 12, 2003.

—MSM

Faubus, Orval E(ugene)
(1910–1994) *governor of Arkansas*

The son of a socialist and liberal Democrat, Faubus was born on January 7, 1910, in Combs, a town in the Ozark mountains of northwestern Arkansas. He worked as a schoolteacher and itinerant fruit picker while attending State Vocational High School at Huntsville. Following graduation Faubus found employment in the lumber industry in Washington State. In 1936, he returned to Arkansas and ran unsuccessfully for the Democratic nomination for representative to the state assembly. He was elected Madison Co. circuit clerk in 1938 and reelected in 1940. Faubus served with distinction during World War II. He entered the army as a private in 1942 and left it in 1946 as a major. In May 1946, he became acting postmaster in Huntsville, Ark. He

bought the *Madison County Record* in 1947. Serving as both editor and publisher, he built the paper into the third-largest weekly in the state. During the gubernatorial campaign of 1948, Faubus and his paper supported the liberal Sidney McMath. After winning the election, McMath appointed Faubus to the state highway commission and to a salaried position as an administrative adviser to the governor. In March 1951, McMath named Faubus director of the Arkansas Highway Department. When McMath lost the Democratic primary in 1952, Faubus returned to his newspaper.

Denouncing incumbent Gov. FRANCIS CHERRY as the tool of special interests, Faubus defeated him in the Democratic gubernatorial primary in August 1954 and went on to win a two-year term in November. As governor, he instituted a populist program of social reform and economic development. Under his direction, the legislature reformed welfare laws, established a conservation commission, increased mental health facilities, and formed the Arkansas Industrial Development Commission, chaired by Winthrop Rockefeller, to encourage the industrialization of the state. Under Faubus, Arkansas also began complying with the Supreme Court's decision of 1954 that struck down segregation in public schools. Six out of seven state colleges were desegregated, as were schools in Fayetteville, Hoxi, and Charleston. Faubus cautiously avoided taking any position on desegregation.

Seeking a second term in 1956, Faubus faced a segregationist, Jim Johnson. Faubus began to modify his stand on racial integration. Following a statewide survey indicating that 85 percent of the people opposed desegregation, he announced that he "could not be a party to any attempt to force acceptance of change to which the people were so overwhelmingly opposed." During the fall, the governor campaigned for a law giving the state power to assign pupils to school by race and a resolution interposing state law against federal acts deemed illegal. Both measures passed, and Faubus won reelection. Faubus openly opposed forced integration and favored local option. Yet none of his proposals would have penalized communities that integrated their schools, and he consistently rejected calls to nullify the Supreme Court's decision.

Following the Little Rock School Board's decision to integrate Central High School in the fall of 1957, the Capital Citizens' Council launched an intensive propaganda campaign demanding that the governor intervene to prevent bloodshed and preserve segregation. On the other hand, Little Rock's school superintendent, VIRGIL BLOSSOM, asked the governor for a public commitment to law, order, and peaceful desegregation. Faubus steadfastly refused to take a public stand on the issue. Behind the scenes, he unsuccessfully attempted to persuade the Justice Department to intervene to delay desegregation.

Fearing that the matter would injure his chance for election to a third term, Faubus adopted a more extreme position. After attempts to delay desegregation through court action had failed, he ordered the National Guard to prevent the admission of black students to Central High School on September 2. Two days later, the Arkansas National Guard blocked the entry of nine black students. At this point, Judge Ronald N. Davies invited the Justice Department to join the case as a friend of the court. Lawyers from the Justice Department filed a petition requesting a preliminary injunction against Faubus and the commanding officers of the National Guard. Davies granted a temporary restraining order and set a full hearing for September 20.

In the meantime, Rep. BROOKS HAYS (D-Ark.), a moderate who represented the district that included Little Rock, offered to act as an intermediary between Faubus and the president. His efforts led to a meeting between Eisenhower and Faubus on September 14. Eisenhower believed that he had reached an accord with Faubus that the governor would instruct the guard to preserve order but to permit the black students to enter the school. Faubus first proved himself untrustworthy in the public statement he released after the meeting. Moreover, Faubus neither withdrew the guard nor changed their orders. After the hearing on September 20, Davies enjoined Faubus and officers of the guard from interfering with the court's order to desegregate Central High. Faubus withdrew the guard.

On the following Monday, September 23, a large mob converged on Central High. Authorities slipped eight black students past the mob and into Central High. News that the black students had entered the school intensified the rioting, and after three hours, the mob threatened to overwhelm the police guarding the school. Authorities decided to withdraw the black students. That evening, Eisenhower went on national television and condemned "the disgraceful occurrences of today." The orders of a federal court, he warned, could not "be flouted with impunity." He then issued a proclamation commanding "all persons engaged in such obstruction to cease and desist." The next morning, a mob once again gathered at Central High. After conferring with the White House, Mayor Woodrow Wilson Mann sent a wire requesting federal intervention. Eisenhower federalized the Arkansas National Guard and sent a thousand paratroopers from the 101st Airborne Division to Little Rock. On September 25, federal troops escorted the black students through a white mob and into the school. The highly trained, battle-hardened veterans of the 101st controlled the mob, and no one was seriously injured. Federal troops remained in Little Rock through November, but the guard remained throughout the school year.

Faubus took an increasingly demagogic position on school desegregation and easily won the Democratic primary in July 1958, assuring that he would be the first governor of Arkansas in 50 years to serve a third term. In August, the state legislature passed several bills granting the governor broad authority to prevent integration. On September 12, the Supreme Court, sitting in special session, ruled against a request by Little Rock's school board to delay desegregation. Faubus responded by signing the segregation bills passed by the state legislature and invoking the authority they granted him to close Little Rock's public schools. In late September, the citizens of Little Rock voted to close their schools rather than integrate them. The city's schools remained closed for a year. By early 1959, civic and business elites in Little Rock mobilized against the school closings. In a recall election, three moderates won reelection to the school board and three segregationists lost. The new school board voted to reopen the city's schools.

His defiance of federal authority made Faubus a hero to segregationists and a celebrity; he won reelection in 1960, 1962, and 1964. After retiring in 1967, Faubus attempted comebacks in 1970 and 1974 but lost both times in the Democratic primary. He died on December 14, 1994, in Conway, Ark.

—MSM

Ferguson, Homer
(1889–1982) *U.S. senator*

Ferguson was born on February 25, 1889, in Harrison City, Pa. He attended the University of Pittsburgh from 1910 to 1911 and received a law degree from the University of Michigan in 1913. Upon graduation, he was admitted to the bar and began to practice law in Detroit. He ran unsuccessfully for the state senate in 1926, but was appointed to a vacant judicial position on the Wayne County Circuit Court in 1929. He won election to that position the following year and reelection in 1935 and 1941. During this time, he also taught at the Detroit College of Law (1929–39). In 1939, he was appointed to sit as the sole member of a special grand jury to investigate corruption in the municipal government. His investigation resulted in over 300 indictments and the convictions of, among others, an ex-mayor, many high police officials, and a number of underworld figures. Ferguson emerged from the investigation with a reputation as an honest, dogged, and effective prosecutor. In 1942, he narrowly defeated the Democratic incumbent, Prentiss M. Brown, for a seat in the U.S. Senate.

In the Senate, Ferguson established himself as an aggressive investigator but an undistinguished legislator. In 1943, he was appointed to the Special Senate Committee to Investigate the National Defense Program, chaired by HARRY S. TRUMAN. Ferguson also served on the Joint Committee on the Investigation of the Pearl Harbor Attack in 1945–46. He joined with Sen. Ralph Owen Brewster (R-Maine) in a minority report challenging the majority's conclusion that blame rested with the military field commanders. Ferguson and Brewster contended that "high authorities in Washington" shared responsibility. During his early years in the Senate, Ferguson opposed most New Deal and Fair Deal measures proposed by Franklin D. Roosevelt and Truman. On foreign policy, he tended toward isolationism and protectionism. All in all, he was

a typical Midwestern conservative Republican. He won reelection in 1948.

As the cold war took shape, Ferguson became one of the first senators to raise the issue of communist subversion in government. He also supported legislation to require the registration of members of the American Communist Party. His efforts, however, were soon overshadowed by more spectacular anticommunists, most notably Senator JOSEPH MCCARTHY (R-Wis.). Although Ferguson initially supported McCarthy, he refrained from the sensational tactics favored by the junior senator from Wisconsin.

When ROBERT TAFT (R-Ohio) died and WILLIAM KNOWLAND (R-Calif.) replaced him as majority leader, Ferguson assumed the chairmanship of the Republican Policy Committee in June 1953. By this time, Ferguson had begun to distance himself from McCarthy, and he voted for the resolution to condemn McCarthy in December 1954. As part of the Republican congressional leadership, Ferguson moved closer to the administration's positions on many issues. For example, he initially led the opposition to the confirmation of CHARLES BOHLEN as ambassador to the USSR. A career diplomat, Bohlen had served as an adviser at the Yalta Conference in 1945. Like other conservative Republicans, Ferguson regarded him as a symbol of what they believed to be a "sellout" at Yalta and a representative of the "Truman-Acheson crowd" in the State Department. When it became clear, however, that the administration would not withdraw the nomination, he voted in favor of confirmation. Similarly, Ferguson reversed his position on the Bricker amendment, which would have limited the power of the executive to enter into treaties and other international agreements. Ferguson had supported the measure since it was first introduced by JOHN W. BRICKER (R-Ohio) in 1951. Faced with determined opposition from President Eisenhower, Ferguson worked with Knowland to find a compromise. The Senate narrowly rejected the Bricker amendment and then rejected the proposals put forward by Knowland and Ferguson. Ferguson also came to support the administration on foreign aid, immigration of refugees, and trade policy.

Ferguson narrowly lost his bid for reelection in 1954 to PATRICK V. MCNAMARA, a union official who had the support of Michigan's labor organizations. He served briefly as a legal consultant to the Department of Defense until Eisenhower named him ambassador to the Philippines in March 1955. In February 1956, Eisenhower appointed him an associate judge on the U.S. Court of Military Appeals. He took senior judge status in 1971. As a judge on the Court of Military Appeals, he consistently supported the constitutional rights of members of the armed services. Ferguson retired in 1976 and moved to Grosse Pointe, Mich., where he lived until his death on December 17, 1982.

—MSM

Fiedler, Leslie A(ron)
(1917–2003) *writer, educator*

The son of a Jewish pharmacist, Fiedler was born in Newark, N.J., on March 8, 1917. He began his interest in politics as a child. At 12, he read Thoreau and the following year Marx. As a student, Fiedler took part in pacifist and labor demonstrations, but he described his involvement as "tourism" that entailed no risks. Fiedler attended New York University, graduating magna cum laude with a B.A. in English in 1938. He did his graduate work at the University of Wisconsin, receiving his Ph.D. in English in 1941. That year he joined the faculty of Montana State University (later the University of Montana). During World War II, he served as a Japanese translator in the Pacific theater.

After the war, Fiedler returned to Montana State, where he immediately established a reputation for iconoclasm, offering a unique perspective on the American literary past that was both scorned and admired. In three collections of essays—*An End to Innocence* (1955), *Love and Death in the American Novel* (1960), and *No! In Thunder: Essays on Myth and Literature* (1960)—he traced patterns in American literature and contended that the bulk of American novelists clearly had been unable to write convincingly of mature, heterosexual love because they, like most Americans, were crippled by adolescent views of sexuality. American readers were often presented with an "innocent, homoerotic relationship between a white and a non-white male." American writers—mostly white males—clung to this "last believed-in stronghold of life without passion" in

order to justify their hatred of the "Fallen Woman" (one who feels and demonstrates passion). Concurrently, the portrayal of such relationships assuaged the guilt these writers felt for America's destruction of its non-whites. In the absence of such a relationship, readers were likely to find themes of pathological obsessions—rape, murder, betrayal—but rarely fully realized, honest, loving relationships.

Fiedler's view of the hypocrisy in American literary claims to innocence extended to his perspectives on American political events. Always politically minded as an author and educator, he wrote numerous articles in the 1950s that helped shape the general intellectual climate. Fiedler argued that members of the communist party were agents of a foreign power, rather than members of a legitimate dissenting group. Thus, he regarded Truman's Loyalty Program as an unfortunate necessity. He also charged that liberals as well as radicals were deluded by a "dream of innocence" that held "the man of good will is identical with the righteous man." Fiedler called on them to cast off their political innocence.

Perhaps Fiedler's most influential articles were three collected in *An End to Innocence*: "Hiss, Chambers and the Age of Innocence" (1950), "Afterthoughts on the Rosenbergs" (1953), and "McCarthy and the Intellectuals" (1954). The evidence against the Rosenbergs, wrote Fiedler, was "overwhelming." Only those who felt a need to elevate them into martyred "victims of the class struggle and the Cold War" could ignore their "palpable guilt." Fiedler was repelled by what he perceived to be the inauthenticity of the Rosenbergs. They had turned their lives and, indeed, their deaths, into "official clichés." At the same time, he deplored the execution of the Rosenbergs as a violation of the principle of human mercy.

Fiedler disdained the refusal of the Rosenbergs or Hiss to confess. One might, he thought, have expected them "to cry out their faith proudly before the tribunal." Instead, contrary to "their own early writings," they pleaded that "they had never advocated revolution." The betrayal of Hiss went beyond that. Fiedler regarded him as an ambitious member of the American elite who donated time to the Soviet Union to demonstrate that he had not "'sold out' to the bourgeois world in which he was making a splendid career." The fact that he profited immensely from the society he wanted to destroy made him Machiavellian rather than revolutionary. Further, for Fiedler, there was something juvenile about Hiss's refusal to confess. "The qualifying act of moral adulthood," wrote Fiedler, "is precisely this admission of responsibility for the past and its consequences." Hiss, Fiedler pointed out, was on trial for perjury and not treason. He "need not even have gone to prison," but, typical of the "Popular Front mind," he preferred to "pose as the Victim." Fiedler extended his indictment of Hiss to the whole generation of romantic liberals and radicals who were guilty not of struggling for a better world, "but for having substituted sentimentality for intelligence in that struggle."

Although disgusted by Sen. JOSEPH R. McCARTHY (R-Wis.), Fiedler declared that "to assess McCarthyism justly means to admit that good and evil are divided." Fiedler rebuked liberals for intellectual arrogance, for the supposition that they were immune to "political error," when, in fact, they had been wrong about communism. Liberals, wrote Fiedler, could not accept the "unpalatable truth" that "buffoons and bullies, those who *know* really nothing about the Soviet Union at all, were right—stupidly right. . . accidentally right, right for the wrong reasons, but damnably right."

Increasingly unhappy at Montana State University, Fiedler left in 1963 to become a professor at the State University of New York at Buffalo. There he continued his prodigious output of literary and cultural criticism, novels, and short stories. In 1967, he was arrested and convicted of "maintaining a premise" where marijuana was used. The New York Court of Appeals overturned the conviction in 1972. In spite of his long hair and beard, Fiedler maintained a detached and wary view of the counterculture. Further, he had little patience with what he regarded as the political cant of the New Left. Revolutionary communism, which attracted some academics in the late 1960s, held even less appeal for Fiedler; he had his fling as a Trotskyist and Schachtmanite in his youth. In 1972, SUNY Buffalo created a special chair for Fiedler, making him the Samuel Langhorne Clemens professor of English. He died in Buffalo on January 28, 2003.

—MSM

Finletter, Thomas K(night)
(1893–1980) *attorney*

A member of a prominent Philadelphia family and the son of a judge, Finletter was born in Philadelphia on November 11, 1893. He graduated from the University of Pennsylvania in 1915. After serving in the army during World War I, he received a law degree from the University of Pennsylvania in 1920. Upon gaining admission to the New York Bar in 1921, he joined the elite Wall Street firm of Cravath, Henderson & DeGersdorff. Finletter moved to Coudert Brothers in 1927 as a partner. He joined the State Department as a special assistant to the secretary of state in 1941. Two years later, he was appointed executive director of the Office of Foreign Economic Coordination, which supervised economic planning in Allied-controlled areas. During World War II, Finletter was also a consultant to the committee laying the foundation for the UN. In 1945, he attended the San Francisco conference, at which the UN was founded, as an aide to ADLAI STEVENSON.

In July 1947, President Truman appointed Finletter chairman of the Air Policy Commission (later known as the Finletter commission), formed to study all phases of national aviation policy in relation to security needs. The committee report, issued in 1948 as "Survival in the Air Age," predicted that by 1952, the Soviet Union would achieve nuclear and air parity with the United States. To meet the challenge, the report recommended that the United States expand the air force.

In May 1948, Finletter became chief of the Economic Administration Mission in London. He returned to Coudert Brothers in June 1949 but returned to government in April 1950 as secretary of the air force, a position he held until the end of the Truman administration. Although a supporter of a coordinated defense, Finletter emerged as the administration's leading advocate of air power as a first deterrent.

Finletter supported Stevenson for president in 1952. In the years following Stevenson's defeat, he headed an informal advisory panel, known as the "Finletter Group," which met regularly to discuss issues and suggest positions Stevenson should take as "leader of the loyal opposition." The group, which included ARTHUR SCHLESINGER JR., JOHN KENNETH GALBRAITH, and CHESTER BOWLES, provided Stevenson with material on such issues as civil rights, foreign affairs, and civil liberties. Although Stevenson did not want this group considered his personal brain trust, as the election of 1956 drew closer, the panel started preparing positions for the upcoming campaign and policies for a potential Stevenson administration. During the campaign of 1956, Finletter headed the New York State Stevenson for President Committee.

In January 1957, Democratic National Chairman PAUL BUTLER organized the Democratic Advisory Council with Finletter as one of its members. The group was created to limit the power of congressional leaders Rep. SAM RAYBURN (D-Tex.) and Sen. LYNDON B. JOHNSON (D-Tex.) and give liberals a greater voice in shaping legislative policy. However, the congressional leaders refused to join the panel, and so the council had little influence on legislation.

Finletter again actively supported Stevenson for president in 1960. He helped organize a draft-Stevenson movement and prepared speeches for the former governor, hoping they would get him the publicity needed to capture the nomination. Despite massive demonstrations for him at the convention, Stevenson never formally declared his candidacy, and his backers failed to win sufficient delegates to prevent Sen. JOHN F. KENNEDY's (D-Mass.) nomination on the first ballot.

Throughout the 1950s, Finletter spoke and wrote on foreign policy and defense issues. His book, *Power and Policy* (1954), criticized what he regarded as a failure of leadership that forfeited America's nuclear superiority. Predicting that by 1956 the Soviet Union would have enough nuclear weapons to totally destroy the United States, he urged the Eisenhower administration to build up a massive nuclear deterrent to discourage attack. He argued against cuts in the defense budget and recommended increased spending, particularly for the air force, which would bear the main burden of defense. Finletter's conclusions about the relative strength of the United States and USSR were mistaken.

In 1955, Finletter came out in opposition to the administration's disarmament proposals, which called for a reduction, first in conventional forces and then in nuclear weapons, supervised by an elaborate inspection system. The former air force secretary questioned whether such a system could ever be effective in dealing with a large country such as the Soviet Union, which was also controlled by a secretive government. Instead, he advocated enforced disarmament backed by a UN military force strong enough to compel compliance. The United States would give up its major deterrent—nuclear weapons—only after the enforcement system was completely developed.

At the end of the decade, Finletter continued to attack the administration, claiming that the Russians were ahead of the United States in defense and space research. He was one of the Democrats who claimed that a "missile gap" existed between the United States and the Soviet Union, and he urged Americans to reorient their priorities to regain their superiority. According to Finletter, money had to be channeled from consumer goods to education, science, natural resource development, and armaments. In his opinion, this could best be accomplished if the United States were led by a liberal Democrat. Once again, Finletter's claims of Soviet superiority were unfounded. His position derived either from erroneous information, excessive partisanship, or both.

During the 1950s, Finletter was extremely active in New York politics. He sought the Democratic nomination for senator in 1958 but was turned down by Tammany boss CARMINE DeSAPIO. To fight what they considered a blatant exercise of machine power, Finletter, HERBERT LEHMAN, and ELEANOR ROOSEVELT organized the New York Committee for Democratic Voters the following year. In 1961, the reform candidate for mayor, ROBERT WAGNER JR., defeated Arthur Levitt, DeSapio's handpicked nominee, effectively ending the boss's power in New York.

President Kennedy appointed Finletter ambassador to the North Atlantic Treaty Organization in 1961. He held that post until 1965, when he returned to law practice with Coudert Brothers. He retired in 1970, and died in New York City on April 24, 1980.

—MSM

Flanders, Ralph E(dward)
(1880–1970) *U.S. senator*

Born into a family of modest means on September 28, 1880, in Barnet, Vt., Flanders moved with his parents to Rhode Island and attended public schools in several communities. After graduating from a country school, he became an apprentice machinist in Providence. He learned mechanical engineering and drafting in the shop and studied mechanical drawing at night school. He also studied engineering through a correspondence school. A working engineer, Flanders also published articles on machine designing. His articles led to an appointment in 1905 as associate editor of *Machinery*, a position that took him to New York. Flanders published a book, *Gear-Cutting Machinery*, in 1909. He returned to Vermont in 1910 to work for the Jones and Lamson Machine Company. In 1933, he succeeded his father-in-law as president of the company. Throughout the 1920s and 1930s, he established a reputation as an industrialist who was concerned about economics and social problems. He advocated a responsible capitalism that would avoid drastic swings in production and employment and would provide higher standards of living for workers.

Flanders ran in the Republican primary for a seat in the U.S. Senate in 1940 but lost to GEORGE AIKEN. During World War II, he served in a number of federal agencies, including the Office of Price Administration, the Economic Stabilization Board, and the War Production Board. He was president of the Federal Reserve Board of Boston from 1944 to 1946. When Warren Austin (R-Vt.) resigned from the Senate in 1946, Vermont's governor appointed Flanders to fill the remaining months of Austin's term; later that year, he won election for a full term. He was reelected in 1952. While identified with the liberal wing of the Republican party, Flanders took a variety of positions that made him difficult to type. Although elected with the backing of organized labor, he supported the Taft-Hartley law, which labor opposed. In general, however, his record on domestic issues was liberal. A strong proponent of public housing, he voted for the Taft-Ellender-Wagner housing act. He also supported the Civil Rights Act of 1957. In 1954, he cosponsored, with Sen. IRVING IVES (R-N.Y.), a bill advocated by the administration to provide federal subsidies to reduce the cost of private health insurance. He also supported the Eisenhower administration's plan to provide aid to depressed areas. In foreign policy,

he joined internationalist Republicans in supporting the Truman Doctrine, the Marshall Plan, the Selective Service Act of 1948, the nomination of CHARLES BOHLEN as ambassador to the Soviet Union, the Eisenhower Doctrine, and the Atoms for Peace Treaty. However, he opposed the North Atlantic Treaty Organization Treaty and supported the Bricker amendment, which would have restricted the treaty-making power of the president and which Eisenhower strongly opposed.

A strong anticommunist, Flanders was nevertheless appalled by the reckless charges of Sen. JOSEPH MCCARTHY (R-Wis.). He criticized McCarthy in private but for the most part remained publicly silent. However, in early March 1954, after McCarthy turned his attack on the army, Flanders gave a speech in which he ridiculed the junior senator from Wisconsin: "He dons his war paint. He goes into his war dance. He emits his war-whoops. He goes forth to battle and proudly returns with the scalp of a pink army dentist." On June 1, with the Army-McCarthy hearings underway, Flanders compared McCarthy to Hitler and denounced him for spreading division and confusion. Flanders recognized that any move by the Senate to discipline McCarthy would have to be initiated by a Republican to avoid the appearance of partisanship. After giving notice to McCarthy, Flanders introduced a resolution on June 11 to strip McCarthy of his committee chairmanships. Many senators, including the Republican leadership and southern Democrats, opposed the measure on the ground that it would impinge on the seniority system. When the Senate Republican Policy Committee declared its unanimous opposition to the resolution, Flanders announced on July 16 that he intended to change his resolution to one calling for censure.

On the night of July 30, Flanders submitted a resolution charging McCarthy with refusing to answer questions about his finances before the Rules and Administration's Subcommittee on Privileges and Elections in 1952, with responsibility for the "irresponsible conduct" of two of McCarthy's aides (ROY COHN and G. DAVID SCHINE), and with abusing Gen. RALPH W. ZWICKER when the general appeared before McCarthy's subcommittee. Flanders and other senators subsequently added additional charges. The Senate voted on August

2 to refer the resolution to a special bipartisan committee. In November, the panel introduced a resolution to censure McCarthy for his refusal to appear before the Subcommittee on Privileges and Elections and for his abuse of Gen. Zwicker. The following month, the Senate voted to condemn McCarthy by a vote of 67-22. Flanders did not take a leading role in the debate.

Flanders chose not to seek reelection in 1958 and retired to Vermont to become a pig farmer. He published an autobiography, *Senator from Vermont* (1961), and lived quietly until his death in Springfield, Vt., on February 10, 1970.

—MSM

Flemming, Arthur S(herwood)

(1905–1996) *director, Office of Defense Mobilization; secretary, Department of Health, Education, and Welfare*

Born in Kingston, N.Y., on June 12, 1905, Flemming attended public schools and, after graduating from high school, worked for a year as a reporter before enrolling at Ohio Wesleyan University, from which he graduated in 1927. He then received a master's degree in political science from American University, where he taught government and served as debate coach. Flemming earned a law degree from George Washington University in 1933. The following year, he became director of American University's School of Public Affairs. He remained at this position until 1938, when he became executive officer of the university.

In 1939, Franklin D. Roosevelt appointed Flemming to the Civil Service Commission. He held this position until 1948. During World War II, Flemming also served as chief of labor supply for the Office of Production Management and member of the War Manpower Commission. In 1947, President HARRY S. TRUMAN appointed Flemming to the Hoover Commission, charged with evaluating the structure of the executive branch. Flemming left government service in 1948 to accept the presidency of Ohio Wesleyan University. Three years later, however, he took a leave of absence to become assistant to the director of Defense Mobilization, CHARLES WILSON, and chairman of the Manpower Policy Committee of the Office of Defense Mobilization (ODM). Both agencies supervised the organization of the nation's resources to fight the Korean War.

When President Eisenhower took office, he made ODM a permanent government agency and appointed Flemming its acting head. In June 1953, Flemming reluctantly accepted the directorship on a permanent basis. At that post, he prepared a comprehensive plan for national mobilization in the event of nuclear war. This included proposals for industrial mobilization, rationing, wage and price controls, and personnel training. He also prepared contingency plans in case of an oil shortage during the Suez Crisis of 1956. In February 1958, Flemming resigned his position with ODM and returned to Ohio Wesleyan as president. Throughout the Eisenhower administration, Flemming served on the President's Advisory Committee on Government Organization. He chaired that body from 1958 to 1961.

Upon the resignation of MARION FOLSOM in mid-1958, Eisenhower appointed Flemming secretary of health, education, and welfare (HEW).

Arthur S. Flemming, secretary of health, education, and welfare, 1958–1961 *(Dwight D. Eisenhower Library and Museum)*

Eisenhower's selection drew the praise of many liberals and moderates who were impressed with Flemming's commitment to the social welfare programs of the past administrations. Conservatives were nevertheless satisfied because of his administrative skills and his support for a balanced budget.

Flemming's background and attitudes differed from those of many of the men in the president's cabinet, which was drawn largely from the ranks of business. A quiet, withdrawn man, he had risen through the government bureaucracy. Although described as an "endurable do-gooder" and "spender," Flemming was adept at political maneuvering and in dealing with Congress.

As secretary of HEW, Flemming advocated increased federal aid to education to meet what he viewed as America's weakness in science and mathematics after the Soviet launching of *Sputnik* during the fall of 1957. The National Defense Education Act, passed one month after Flemming took office, offered loans to college students, particularly those interested in teaching, as well as matching grants to schools of all levels for laboratories, textbooks, and other facilities. It also provided fellowships for graduate students. Flemming backed the measure but urged the repeal of the loyalty oath requirement for the loan program. Not satisfied with the scope of the bill, Flemming, in 1959, proposed a program to spur school construction through $5 billion in loans and matching grants over a five-year period. Flemming's bill and several more ambitious Democratic-sponsored measures were debated in Congress in 1959 and 1960, but none ever passed.

Soon after becoming secretary, Flemming became embroiled in the school desegregation crisis. In September 1958, he warned areas practicing segregation that federal installations in the areas might be shut down if the schools were not integrated. In December, he denounced the closings of schools in Virginia and Arkansas as "indefensible."

Flemming opposed recommendations for medical care for the aged financed through Social Security. In May 1959, he offered the administration's own proposal calling for state programs subsidized by the federal government to provide health care for persons over 65. The states would have collected fees from those who could afford payments while the aged on relief would have free coverage.

Eligible persons would have been given the option of purchasing private insurance plans, which the federal and state governments would have subsidized up to 50 percent. Congress never passed the administration's proposal.

During his tenure as secretary of HEW, Flemming called for increased efforts to combat air and water pollution and the use of color additives in foods, drugs, and chemicals. In November 1959, he precipitated a national scare when he warned that certain cranberries from the Pacific Northwest had been contaminated by weed-killers linked to cancer. Occurring right before Thanksgiving, Flemming's action produced bans in numerous states. He defended his announcement by saying, "My position all along has been that when we in the government develop information of this nature, we have an obligation to make it available to the public."

Flemming became president of the University of Oregon in 1961 and remained there until 1968, when he assumed the presidency of Macalester College in St. Paul, Minn., which he held until 1971. Flemming remained active in public life, as well. He served as a consultant to Kennedy on Medicare and as a member of the Peace Corps National Advisory Commission under Kennedy and Johnson. In the late 1960s, he called for an increased commitment to the War on Poverty. During the Nixon administration, Flemming chaired the White House Conference on Aging in 1971 and served as a commissioner on aging. He chaired the U.S. Civil Rights Commission from 1972 to 1981.

A deeply religious man, Flemming was an active Methodist layman and headed the National Council of Churches of Christ in America. His career combined compassion for those in need with bureaucratic competence. His last years were devoted to advocacy on behalf of Social Security. He died in Alexandria, Va., on September 7, 1996.

—MSM

Flesch, Rudolf F(ranz)

(1911–1986) *educational researcher and critic*

Born in Vienna, Austria, on May 8, 1911, Flesch received a doctorate in law from the University of Vienna in 1933. After emigrating to the United States in 1938, he earned a Ph.D. in library science from Columbia University in 1943. The following year, he became an American citizen. Flesch began his career in educational research with the Readability Laboratory of the American Association of Adult Education at Columbia Teachers College. First in the scholarly *Marks of Readable Style: A Study in Adult Education* (1943) and then in the popular *The Art of Plain Talk* (1946), Flesch proposed a scientific method for writing easily understandable prose. He recommended a plain style, short paragraphs and sentences, and the use of colloquial English. Further, he drew a connection between such direct expression and liberal politics. His work won an audience not only among educators but among journalists, advertising copywriters, and business people. Shortly after World War II, Flesch moved to Dobbs Ferry, N.Y., and worked as a freelance writer, lecturer, and consultant. In 1951, he produced the influential *AP Writing Handbook* for the Associated Press, *How to Write Better,* and *The Art of Clear Thinking.*

Perhaps Flesch's most influential work was *Why Johnny Can't Read: And What You Can Do about It,* a polemic published in 1955. In it, Flesch contended that illiteracy and near-illiteracy were widespread and increasing in the United States, and he blamed the schools. Johnny could not read, according to Flesch, "for the simple reason that nobody ever showed him how." Flesch focused his criticism on what he maintained was the prevailing method of teaching children to begin to read. He contended that the universal acceptance of the sight or "look-and say" method (teaching children the meaning of whole words) accounted for the problem. He recommended instead the phonics approach, or teaching the correspondence of letters and sounds. Concern over the American education system grew exponentially after the Soviet launch of *Sputnik* in the fall of 1957. This brought the work of Flesch and other critics of public education to the attention of a broad public. Indeed, *Why Johnny Can't Read* had more influence on the public than it did on the educational establishment. However, it joined works by Arthur Bestor and James B. Conant as focal points in the debate over education in the late 1950s.

After achieving considerable fame with *Why Johnny Can't Read,* Flesch continued to lecture, pub-

lish articles, and write books. His works included *How to Be Brief* (1962), *The ABC of Style* (1965), *Say What You Mean* (1972), and *How to Write Plain English: A Book for Lawyers and Consumers* (1979). In 1981 he joined yet another round of debate over education with the publication of *Why Johnny Still Can't Read: A New Look at the Scandal of Our Schools.* As he had a quarter of a century earlier, he focused his attack on reading instruction and once again advocated phonics. Flesch died on October 5, 1986, in Dobbs Ferry, N.Y.

—MSM

Folsom, James E(lisha)
(1908–1987) *governor of Alabama*

Born on a farm in Coffee Co., Ala., on October 9, 1908, Folsom grew up in rural southeastern Alabama. After his father, a county official, died in 1919, the family suffered economic hardship. Folsom attended the University of Alabama and Howard College (now Samford University) and then joined the merchant marine. He returned to Alabama, where family connections helped him obtain a post in the Civil Works Administration in 1933. He then went to work in Washington, D.C., where he attended night classes at George Washington University.

Folsom returned to Alabama, settled in Cullman Co. in the northern part of the state, established himself as an insurance salesman, and entered electoral politics. His size (he stood six feet eight inches tall and weighed 245 pounds) earned him the nickname "Big Jim." His habit of kissing every woman on the campaign trail won him another nickname: "Kissing Jim." Folsom lost the first four elections in which he ran. In 1933, he failed to win a seat at the state Prohibition convention. He ran unsuccessfully for Congress in 1936 and 1938 and for governor in 1942. As a delegate to the Democratic National Convention in 1944, he split with the Alabama delegation and supported Henry Wallace for the vice presidential nomination.

Folsom developed a political style that made effective use of populist and rural symbols. When he campaigned for governor in 1946, a string band accompanied him on the campaign trail. He brandished an old mop and a galvanized pail to symbolize his promise to clean out the Capitol. He attacked the Big Mules, the large planters and industrialists who, according to Folsom, controlled the state. He promised legislative reapportionment, old-age pensions, aid to schools, repeal of the poll tax, the construction of highways to connect farms to markets, better pay for teachers, workers' compensation, and unemployment insurance. Folsom believed that race-baiting diverted attention from more important social issues, and adopted a moderate position on racial matters. He surprised the state's political establishment by winning a plurality in the Democratic primary and handily defeating his opponent in the runoff. In Alabama, the winning Democratic nomination was tantamount to winning the office, which he did in the general election.

In office, Folsom could not deliver on most of the promises he made during the campaign. He managed to achieve passage of a highway program and an increase in teachers' salaries, but the legislature blocked most of his program. Aside from opposition in the legislature, Folsom suffered from alcoholism, which undermined his effectiveness. As governor, he refused to engage in race-baiting and treated African Americans with respect. He opposed the Dixiecrat movement in 1948 and in 1949 pushed through the legislature a law, directed at the Ku Klux Klan, banning the wearing of masks in public. In his Christmas message of 1949, Folsom said, "Negroes constitute 35 percent of our population in Alabama. Are they getting 35 percent of the fair share of living? Are they getting adequate medical care to rid themselves of hookworm, rickets and social diseases?" Further, he denounced the "stirring of old hatred and prejudices and false alarms." Under state law, he was unable to succeed himself, and he returned to private life in 1951.

Folsom easily won a second term as governor in 1954, the year the Supreme Court handed down its decision in *Brown v. Board of Education*. Issues of civil rights and desegregation dominated that term. Folsom was not an integrationist. He preferred separate-but-equal facilities and once promised that Alabama would be the last state to integrate. Nevertheless, he maintained that the Supreme Court's decision striking down segregated public schools was the law and that integration was inevitable. At the Southern Governors' Conference in 1954, he

declined to sign a pledge to use every constitutional means to maintain segregation. In 1955, Folsom prevented the enactment of most bills introduced in the legislature designed to continue segregation. He ignored a resolution calling for Congress to curtail the federal judiciary and threatened to veto any measure censuring the Supreme Court. Folsom also vetoed three anti-NAACP (National Association for the Advancement of Colored People) measures. Nevertheless, a pupil placement act, which enabled local authorities to assign pupils on the basis of nonracial criteria that had the effect of impeding desegregation, became law without his signature.

Folsom failed to respond adequately when, in 1956, a federal court ordered the admission of AUTHERINE LUCY, a black student, to the University of Alabama. Her presence on campus led to three days of rioting. During this time, Folsom was on a weeklong drunken binge in Florida. That same year, Folsom infuriated his opponents by inviting a black member of Congress, ADAM CLAYTON POWELL, JR. (D-N.Y.), for a drink at the governor's mansion. When Folsom convened a special session of the legislature to deal with reapportionment, the lawmakers passed a series of segregationist measures, including a resolution interposing the state's authority between the people and the supposedly illegitimate exercise of federal authority and nullifying the Supreme Court's decision. The governor called the measure "hogwash" and likened it to "a hound dog baying at the moon and claiming it's got the moon treed." The legislature also enacted two constitutional amendments permitting the state to abandon its public school system.

By this time, the growing influence of the White Citizens' Council had changed political realities. In 1956, Folsom spoke in favor of segregation and signed a bill providing for private schools where districts had abandoned their public schools. At the same time, Folsom continued to call for moderation. In April 1956, he ran for Democratic national committeeman against Charles McKay, who chaired the White Citizens' Council, and suffered a crushing defeat. By 1957, Folsom offered only limited opposition to segregationist measures and signed a resolution nullifying the *Brown* decision. Although unable to succeed himself, Folsom suffered another political defeat in 1958 when his protégé, George Wallace, lost the Democratic nomination for governor to attorney general JOHN PATTERSON, a staunch segregationist.

Folsom attempted a comeback in 1962, but he lost to Wallace, who ran as a segregationist. In a televised appearance on election eve, Folsom was incoherent, perhaps because he was drunk. He never recovered. He ran for governor unsuccessfully in 1966, 1970, 1974, 1978, and 1982, receiving fewer votes in each election. In his last years, he suffered from heart disease and a series of strokes. He died in Cullman, Ala., on November 21, 1987.

—MSM

Folsom, Marion B(ayard)

(1893–1976) *undersecretary of the treasury; secretary, Department of Health, Education, and Welfare*

Born in McRae, Ga., on November 23, 1893, Marion Folsom graduated from the University of Georgia in 1912 and received an M.B.A. from Harvard University two years later. He served in the army during World War I. In 1921, he became assistant to George Eastman, president of Eastman Kodak, Co., and in 1935 was made treasurer. During the 1930s, Folsom developed the old-age pension plan for Kodak, which was later expanded to include 13 other firms under the title "the Rochester Plan."

Because of the wide interest in this program, President Franklin D. Roosevelt appointed Folsom to the President's Advisory Council on Economic Security in 1934 and to the Federal Council on Social Security in 1937. During World War II, Folsom served as a member of the War Manpower Commission and of the Committee for Economic Development (CED), headed by PAUL HOFFMAN. As a member of the CED, Folsom developed plans for the reconversion of the wartime to a peacetime economy with the objective of ensuring maximum production and full employment.

Eisenhower appointed Folsom undersecretary of the treasury in January 1953. During his tenure, he represented the Treasury on a cabinet committee to determine how federal employee benefits compared with private industry. As a result of the investigation, Folsom sponsored a life insurance program for civil service employees underwritten

Marion Folsom, secretary of health, education, and welfare, 1955–1958 *(Dwight D. Eisenhower Library and Museum)*

by private industry. The plan provided that federal employees would pay the rate generally contributed by workers in the private sector, and the Treasury would pay the remaining one-third of the cost. In August the president signed the bill making civil service life insurance mandatory unless an employee signed a statement saying he did not want to be covered. Between 1954 and 1961, the program covered almost 2.5 million employees.

In 1954, he worked with the Department of Health, Education, and Welfare on a study of old-age and survivors' insurance, which became the basis for a series of proposed changes in Social Security that Eisenhower recommended to Congress. Later that year, Congress acted on the recommendations and amended the Social Security Act to include self-employed workers and to increase benefits.

Folsom also helped revise the federal corporate income tax. The Income Tax Revision Act of 1954 enabled industry to make larger provisions for depreciation during the early years of an asset. According to Folsom, it contributed to the generally high level of private investment after 1954.

In 1955, Folsom succeeded OVETA CULP HOBBY as secretary of health, education, and welfare. The new secretary continued to support the Salk polio vaccine program instituted in 1955. He coordinated the effort to ensure that the country's demand for the vaccine was met, and in December 1956, he announced that there was no longer a shortage but a surplus of 17 million doses. During Folsom's tenure, federal support for medical research and for the training of nurses and public health personnel increased.

In 1956, Folsom served—along with Secretary of State JOHN FOSTER DULLES, Secretary of the Treasury GEORGE HUMPHREY, and Attorney General HERBERT BROWNELL—on the cabinet committee investigating narcotics traffic. In February, the committee disclosed that there were 60,000 addicts in the United States, 13 percent of them under the age of 21. The panel recommended that the states develop treatment programs and increase penalties for drug pushers and that the United States work with international agencies to control drug traffic.

From 1955 to 1958, Folsom lobbied for passage of the national defense education bill. The secretary believed that the United States lagged behind other major nations in the teaching of sciences and languages, and he calculated that there would be an inadequate supply of Ph.D.s over the next 10 years. He therefore called on Congress to pass a bill providing fellowships and loans to graduate students, grants to gifted high school students, and aid to states for teaching languages, mathematics, and the sciences. The bill also gave assistance to colleges and universities to establish training programs for teachers of modern, especially rare, languages. The National Defense Education Act became law in September 1954. It authorized the expenditure of $1 billion over a four-year period.

After resigning as secretary in 1958, Folsom, along with Henry T. Herald, president of the Ford Foundation, and John W. Gardner, president of the Carnegie Foundation, served on the New York State Committee on Higher Education. In December 1959, the panel recommended to Gov. NELSON A. ROCKEFELLER that the state increase its funds for public undergraduate and graduate education, limit expenditures for private institutions, and discontinue tuition-free higher education except for rebates to needy students. It also proposed making 11 state teachers colleges into liberal arts colleges and establishing a new state university system that included two graduate schools.

From 1958 to 1968, Folsom was director of Kodak. He also served as chairman of the Advisory Committee for Personnel for the U.S. Public Health Service in 1961 and 1962, and was chairman of the National Commission on Community Health Services from 1962 to 1967 and vice chairman of the White House Conference on Health in 1967. Folsom died in Rochester, N.Y., on September 28, 1976.

—RSG

Ford, Gerald R(udolph)

(1913–2006) *U.S. congressman*

Born in Omaha, Neb., on July 14, 1913, and raised by his stepfather in Grand Rapids, Mich., Ford was a football star at the University of Michigan, where he received a B.A. degree in 1935. Subsequently Ford studied law at Yale University and received an LL.B. degree in 1941. He briefly practiced law with a firm in Grand Rapids before joining the navy in 1942. After his discharge four years later, Ford returned home to resume his legal career.

In 1948, Ford's stepfather, a Republican county chairman, and Sen. Arthur H. Vandenberg (R-Mich.) urged Ford to challenge incumbent isolationist Rep. Bartel J. Jonkman (R-Mich.) in the Republican congressional primary. Ford won easily and went on to defeat his Democratic opponent with 61 percent of the vote. In subsequent elections, he never won less than 60 percent of the vote. Ford generally supported President HARRY S. TRUMAN'S foreign policy while opposing most of his domestic social welfare programs.

Although Ford's views and voting record were conservative, he was a political pragmatist and a party loyalist. In 1952, he was an early backer of DWIGHT D. EISENHOWER for the Republican presidential nomination, partly because he believed that Eisenhower would run better in Michigan than his conservative opponent, Sen. ROBERT H. TAFT (R-Ohio). Although Ford was a strong anticommunist, he did not join Sen. JOSEPH R. MCCARTHY (R-Wis.)

in criticizing the Eisenhower administration for allegedly tolerating subversives in its midst. According to *Congressional Quarterly*, in the 83rd and 84th Congresses (1953–54, 1955–56), Ford was among the five House Republicans who most frequently supported President Eisenhower.

Ford served on the Appropriations Committee and, as a member of that panel's Department of Defense Subcommittee, became an expert on military spending. A supporter of high defense appropriations, he unsuccessfully sought to add $80 million to the army's budget in 1957. Ford also strongly backed military assistance to friendly countries. In 1956, he deplored Congress's 33 percent cut of the president's request for foreign military aid. The following year, Ford criticized similar reductions, asserting that "we have made [them] in the wrong areas. . . . We ought to increase the [foreign aid] funds related to our own security and reduce the funds in those other non-military areas." In 1960, Ford headed a task force of the House Republican Policy Committee that produced recommendations—based on papers written by academic, professional, and legislative experts—for a comprehensive national security strategy.

During the 1950s, Ford's reputation for candor and honesty earned him the respect of his fellow Republicans. A congenial man, he also maintained cordial relations with the Democratic House leadership. In 1959, he was chosen to serve on a select committee that examined the budget of the Central Intelligence Agency. Hoping someday to become House Speaker, Ford turned down opportunities to run for the Senate in 1952 and 1954 and for governor of Michigan in 1956. However, the Republican Party's failure to win the congressional elections of 1954, 1956, and 1958 made him more receptive to other possibilities. In 1960, he allowed a group of Michigan Republicans to conduct a campaign on his behalf for the vice presidential nomination, but the Republican presidential nominee, RICHARD M. NIXON, chose HENRY CABOT LODGE as his running mate. Believing that many Midwestern Republicans would find Lodge too liberal, Ford did not think the choice a good one. As a party loyalist, however, he acceded to Nixon's request that he second Lodge's nomination at the national convention.

In January 1963, a group of young Republican representatives led a revolt against Minority Leader CHARLES A. HALLECK (R-Ind.) and chose Ford to replace Rep. Charles B. Hoeven (R-Iowa) as chairman of the Republican Conference Committee. Two years later, Ford defeated Halleck in a contest for minority leader, a position he held until 1973. In 1963, President LYNDON JOHNSON named Ford to the Warren Commission, which was formed to investigate the assassination of JOHN F. KENNEDY. After the resignation of Vice President Spiro Agnew in October 1973, President Richard M. Nixon nominated Ford to fill the vacancy. Ford won congressional approval and was sworn in as vice president on December 6. When Nixon resigned in the wake of the Watergate scandal, Ford became president on August 9, 1974. A month later, Ford granted a "full, free and absolute pardon" to Nixon. In retrospect, many have concluded that it was an act of statesmanship that helped the country move past the scandal and ensuing constitutional crisis; but at the time, Ford's action was widely criticized. After turning back a stiff challenge for the Republican nomination from Ronald W. Reagan, a former governor of California, Ford lost the general election in 1976 to Jimmy Carter.

In the years after he left the White House, Ford occasionally spoke out on major issues, published a memoir in 1979, and served on the boards of several major American corporations. He died at his home in Rancho Mirage, Calif., on December 26, 2006.

—MSM

Ford, Henry II
(1917–1987) *president, Ford Motor Company*

The grandson of pioneer auto manufacturer and industrialist Henry Ford and the son of the president of Ford Motor Company, Edsel Ford, Henry Ford II was born in Detroit on September 4, 1917. He was groomed from an early age for leadership in the family's enterprises. Henry Ford II attended Yale University but left before earning a degree. In August 1940, he took a job with Ford Motor Company as a mechanic. He became an ensign in the U.S. Naval Reserve in April 1941 and was on active duty during World War II. Although he volunteered for it, he never served overseas. When

Edsel Ford died in 1943 and the elder Henry Ford resumed control of the company, Secretary of the Navy Frank Knox worried that the 80-year-old Ford might no longer be capable of running a company essential to the war effort. Knox therefore discharged Henry Ford II so that he could help run the company. In September 1945, the elder Ford reluctantly stepped aside to let his grandson assume the presidency at the age of 28.

When Ford took over from his grandfather, the company was losing $9 million a month. The elder Henry Ford had been an autocratic manager. Unlike its rival, General Motors, which had developed formal administrative structures for running a large and diversified manufacturing operation, the Ford Company lacked such a structure. Indeed, the company did not even use modern accounting techniques to control costs. In addition, Ford Motor suffered from terrible labor relations. Finally, the company had failed to adapt to changing customer preferences. The younger Ford responded by reorganizing the company, delegating authority, and bringing in a management team known as the "Whiz Kids" for their successful administration of the mobilization of resources for the air force during World War II. The new management team, which included Robert S. McNamara (later secretary of defense in the Kennedy and Johnson administrations), modernized the firm's production facilities and marketing techniques. Ford also adopted a more flexible policy toward the demands of the United Auto Workers (UAW).

After government restrictions on auto production were lifted following the Korean War, Ford embarked on a campaign to overtake GM in production and sales. Ford and his "team" sought to move the company—hitherto essentially a producer of one popular car, the Ford, plus the less successful Lincoln and Mercury—into more diversified production. With the unprecedented demand for passenger cars in the early 1950s and with profits reaching an all-time high as a result, Ford thought the time ripe to break GM's domination of the middle-priced car market. In 1957, Ford introduced the Edsel, which proved to be one of the biggest marketing failures in corporate history. It lost the company about $350 million. Ford was more successful in offering other new models during the 1950s, but

the company failed to achieve first place among the Big Three auto makers.

Prior to the auto industry contract talks in 1955, UAW president WALTER REUTHER launched a campaign for a "guaranteed annual wage" to protect auto workers against interruptions in employment and selected Ford as the target company. The company refused to pay the guaranteed annual wage but, after first offering to sell workers stock on liberal terms and then advance them interest-free loans on the stock during layoffs, it devised a system of unemployment compensation to supplement government insurance. Ford's Supplemental Unemployment Benefit plan (SUB) was accepted by the union and later adopted by other automakers.

During the early 1950s, Henry Ford II was a leading advocate of "free trade" in the auto industry, calling for the abandonment of high tariffs on foreign car imports. With increasing competition from foreign-made small cars in the latter part of the decade, however, he began to reverse his position. A strong supporter of the Eisenhower administration, Ford was named by the president in 1953 to serve as an alternate delegate to the United Nations. In the fall of 1960, however, he came into conflict with the White House over the issue of trade policy. Despite pleas by the administration to cut down overseas spending, Ford proceeded with its plans to pay out $360 million to European stockholders for the public shares in its British affiliate. Secretary of the Treasury ROBERT ANDERSON personally urged Ford to hold up the stock purchase, but the company leadership refused to cooperate. The week the purchase went through, U.S. gold reserves dropped by $204 million.

Ford was president of Ford Motor Company from 1945 to 1963, except for a brief period in 1960 when McNamara held the position. In addition, Ford served as chairman of the board of directors from 1960 until he stepped down in 1980. Even after that, he continued to exercise considerable influence as chairman of the board's finance committee. In 1961, JOHN F. KENNEDY appointed him to the Advisory Committee on Labor-Management Policy. Ford, however, was an outspoken critic of Kennedy's intervention in the 1962 steel crisis. The auto magnate broke with a lifelong loyalty to the Republican party to support LYNDON B. JOHNSON's presidential candidacy in 1964. During the 1960s, Ford supported civil rights organizations and endorsed Johnson's antipoverty programs. In 1968, Johnson appointed him to be the first chairman of the National Alliance of Businessmen. The following year, Johnson awarded Ford the Medal of Freedom. RICHARD M. NIXON named him chairman of the National Center for Voluntary Action in 1970. Ford died of pneumonia in Detroit on September 29, 1987.

—MSM

Foster, William C(hapman)

(1897–1984) *chief delegate, Geneva Conference on the Prevention of Surprise Attacks*

Foster was born in Westfield, N.J., on April 27, 1897. He left the Massachusetts Institute of Technology at the end of his junior year to serve as a lieutenant and military aviator in World War I. After returning from military service, he graduated from MIT in 1918. In 1922, he joined Pressed and Welded Steel Products Company, where he was secretary-treasurer and later president. He remained with the company until 1946. Impressed by Foster's knowledge of the problems of small business, Secretary of Commerce W. AVERELL HARRIMAN convinced President HARRY S. TRUMAN to appoint Foster, a Republican, to be undersecretary of commerce in 1946. Two years later, when Harriman was named ambassador at large to western Europe to oversee the first operations of the Marshall Plan, Foster went along as general deputy in charge of the Paris headquarters. In June 1949, Foster became deputy administrator of the Economic Cooperation Administration (ECA). The following year, he became administrator. As undersecretary of defense from 1951 to 1953, Foster headed a panel that prepared a secret report on the comparative military strengths of the United States and USSR. Foster resigned in 1953 to become president of the Manufacturing Chemists Association. He joined Olin Mathieson Chemical Corp. in 1955 as executive vice president. Concurrently, he was chairman of the board of Reaction Motors and a director of Detroit Edison.

Foster returned to government service in 1958 to head the U.S. delegation to the Geneva Conference on the Prevention of Surprise Attacks. With only two months' notice, Foster familiarized himself with the U.S. position, which focused on technical matters: the definition of the "instruments of surprise attack" and the application of inspection and observation techniques to the problem.

Throughout the conference, convened in November, the Western and Eastern blocs differed significantly on what should be discussed. Foster, working on the premise that the major threat to security arose from long-range missiles and manned aircraft carrying thermonuclear weapons, stressed the need for technical weapons control. He therefore outlined a proposal for the development of a comprehensive inspection system to deal with existing weapons. In addition, he noted the danger of inadequate partial inspection, believing it could give one nation a temporary advantage, and cautioned that any step-by-step implementation of inspection systems would require careful negotiations to circumvent that problem.

The Soviets, on the other hand, emphasized disarmament rather than control, maintaining that the two could not be separated. Assuming that the chief danger of surprise attack came from concentrations of conventional forces, they demanded the liquidation of military bases on foreign soil, the reduction of conventional arms and troops, and the abolition of nuclear weapons. The Soviets were particularly anxious to create a nuclear-free zone in central Europe to prevent the rearming of West Germany. The USSR rejected the call for a comprehensive inspection system because it might compromise its security, and offered a system of self-inspection instead.

The conference ended in December with no agreement. Yet it did have long-range benefits. The technical papers the United States prepared for the meeting provided valuable data on weapons and inspection technology for future negotiations. More important, it marked the first time the United States had developed concrete proposals rather than vague principles for weapons control. It also was a major turning point in U.S. thought on the issue of disarmament and arms control. Instead of focusing on control of fissionable materials, the United States stressed the elimination of nuclear warfare through the control of the means of delivery of nuclear arms. Testifying before the Senate Subcommittee on Disarmament in January 1959, Foster said the conference had shown him the need to define the issues involved in control and disarmament more clearly. It had also given him valuable experience in dealing with the Soviets and in understanding the importance they placed on defending their security.

In September 1961, Foster was appointed director of the Arms Control and Disarmament Agency. At that post, he was involved in the negotiation of a partial nuclear test ban treaty, which the Senate ratified in September 1963. During the Johnson administration, Foster helped negotiate the nuclear nonproliferation treaty in 1968. He left office in January 1968 and became president of Porter International Co. in 1970. He died in Washington, D.C., on October 14, 1984.

—ACD

Frankfurter, Felix

(1882–1965) *associate justice, U.S. Supreme Court*
Born in Vienna, Austria, on November 15, 1882, Felix Frankfurter emigrated to the United States with his family at the age of 12. He graduated from the City College of New York in 1902 and, after serving a year on the city's tenement house commission, he entered Harvard Law School, from which he graduated first in the class of 1906. Upon graduation, he briefly worked for the prestigious law firm of Hornblower, Byrne, Miller & Potter before joining the staff of Henry L. Stimson, the U.S. attorney for the Southern District of New York. Frankfurter managed the campaign and wrote speeches for Stimson's unsuccessful campaign for governor on a Progressive-Republican ticket in 1910. A year later, President William Howard Taft named Stimson secretary of war, and Frankfurter became his special assistant. When Frankfurter accepted a position at Harvard Law School in 1914, he became the first Jewish member of its faculty. During World War I, Frankfurter took leave to serve as a special assistant to the secretary of war, Newton D. Baker. During his 25 years at Harvard, Frankfurter established a reputation as a noted scholar on the Supreme Court, the Constitution, and administrative law. He also maintained a wide range of activities that

won him a reputation as a leading liberal. He served as an adviser to the NAACP and the American Civil Liberties Union, supported labor unions, and fought to have the convictions of Italian anarchists Nicola Sacco and Bartolomeo Vanzetti overturned. Frankfurter sent many of his law students to clerk for Louis D. Brandeis, Oliver Wendell Holmes, Benjamin Cardozo, and Learned Hand. During World War I, Frankfurter established a relationship with Franklin D. Roosevelt, then assistant secretary of the navy. When Roosevelt became governor of New York in 1929, he sought Frankfurter's advice about legislation and people who might serve in his administration. When Roosevelt became president, Frankfurter advised him on legislation, appointments, and speeches. Frankfurter and his protégés exerted a powerful influence on New Deal legislation, particularly the Securities Exchange Act, the Social Security Act, and the Fair Labor Standards Act. Roosevelt named Frankfurter to the Supreme Court in January 1939.

On the Court, Justice Frankfurter became the leading advocate of judicial restraint. Legislatures, he had long contended, were the policymaking bodies in a democratic society, and the Court must defer to their judgments and sustain laws that did not clearly violate the Constitution, however unwise the justices might think them to be. On the Court, Frankfurter consistently upheld legislation regulating the economy. Deferring to the legislative branch, he also voted on a number of occasions to uphold laws curtailing civil liberties. Although it sometimes meant voting against causes he had earlier championed, Frankfurter insisted that judges must be disinterested and detached and must not read into the Constitution their own notions of good policy. Unlike fellow Roosevelt appointee Justice HUGO BLACK, Frankfurter did not give First Amendment rights any preferred position over other constitutional guarantees; nor did he consider any provisions in the Bill of Rights absolute. He insisted that the Court must balance the conflicting interests in each case, making its judgments without any doctrinaire presuppositions.

Frankfurter wrote the opinion for the majority in *Minersville School District v. Gobitis* (1940) upholding the suspension for public school of Jehovah's Witnesses because they refused to salute the flag, an action they maintained violated their right to free exercise of religion. Three years later, when the Court reversed that decision in *West Virginia v. Barnette* (1943), Frankfurter dissented. Frankfurter held that, in time of war, the courts should uphold the claims of government, if based on a reasonable construction of the Constitution.

Despite his commitment to judicial restraint, Frankfurter did not necessarily vote to uphold legislative encroachments on individual liberties. He spoke for a unanimous court in *Butler v. Michigan* (1957), which struck down a Michigan law banning obscene books unfit for young people. Frankfurter observed that the law attempted to "quarantine the general reading public against books not too rugged for grown men and women in order to shield juvenile innocence." "Surely," he concluded, "this is to burn the house to roast the pig." He therefore held that the law in question was "not reasonably restricted to the evil with which it is said to deal." Given his background as a professor, Frankfurter was particularly sensitive to matters of academic freedom. He voted with the majority in *Slochower v. Board of Higher Education of New York City* (1956), a decision that reversed the dismissal of a professor at Brooklyn college because he had invoked the Fifth Amendment before a congressional committee. In *Sweezy v. New Hampshire*, the Court overturned the contempt conviction of a professor in New Hampshire who, when called before the state's attorney general sitting as a one-man investigative committee, had refused to answer questions relating to the Progressive Party and about a lecture he gave at the University of New Hampshire. In a separate concurring opinion, Frankfurter delivered a powerful defense of academic freedom.

Frankfurter had a mixed record dealing with the loyalty and security cases of the 1950s. When he did vote against the government, he usually did so for narrow procedural or statutory reasons, rather than on broad constitutional grounds. In *Pennsylvania v. Nelson* (1956), he joined five other justices in overturning a Pennsylvania law outlawing sedition against the United States on the ground that Congress had preempted the field with the Smith Act. Frankfurter also joined the majority in *Watkins v. U.S.* (1957) in ruling that congressional investigations had to be clearly related to a legitimate legisla-

tive purpose. On a number of occasions, Frankfurter voted to uphold governmental action taken in the name of security, even though that action conflicted with claims of individual freedom. In *Beilan v. Board of Education* (1958), Frankfurter voted with the majority to uphold the dismissal of a Philadelphia schoolteacher discharged for "incompetence" after the teacher had refused to answer questions from the superintendent about possible affiliations with the communist party. The teacher had also invoked the Fifth Amendment before HUAC. The Court found that the dismissal was not for specific charges of disloyalty. That same year, the Court upheld the dismissal of an employee of New York's subway system who refused to answer questions under the protection of the Fifth Amendment (*Lerner v. Casey*). Once again Frankfurter joined the majority in a decision that turned on the fact that the plea of the Fifth had not been the key point in the dismissal.

The justice was far more willing to have the Court take an active role in overseeing federal criminal procedure and was especially exacting regarding search and seizure and confessions. Building on an opinion he had written in 1943, Frankfurter ruled in *Mallory v. U.S.* (1957) that when there was any unnecessary delay between the arrest and arraignment of a defendant, a confession obtained during that period was inadmissible in federal courts. However, Frankfurter contended that the Constitution placed fewer limits on state criminal procedures, and so he applied less rigid standards to the states.

Throughout his judicial career, Frankfurter voted in support of black Americans' claims for equality under the law. As a Jew and a naturalized citizen, Frankfurter had an unbounded faith in assimilation and cherished the ideal of a meritocratic social order. Racial discrimination appalled him. He actively promoted the careers of Charles Hamilton Houston and William Hastie, who had been his students and played major roles in guiding the NAACP's legal battle against segregation. In addition, Frankfurter hired the Court's first black law clerk, William Coleman, Jr., in 1948. He made a significant contribution to bringing about the Court's unanimous May 1954 decision in *Brown v. Board of Education*, which held segregated public schools unconstitutional. Frankfurter believed a unanimous opinion would be best for the Court and the country, and so he sought to delay a final decision until the Court had reached a consensus. He also was influential in separating the decision invalidating school segregation from the remedy. Frankfurter circulated several memos among the justices on the question of how to implement the decision. The Court's final decree, issued in May 1955, followed the gradualist approach Frankfurter favored and called for school boards to make a "prompt and reasonable start" toward desegregation and proceed "with all deliberate speed," a phrase the justice had suggested in one of his memos. When state officials later attempted to forestall school integration in Little Rock, Ark., Frankfurter joined in the Court's order in September 1958 mandating the resumption of school desegregation in that city. He also wrote a special concurring opinion affirming the supremacy of the law and condemning defiance and obstruction of its enforcement.

Frankfurter's views on racial issues never moved beyond the NAACP's original position that called for nondiscrimination and a color-blind legal system. He expressed grave doubts about the growing militancy of southern black college students and the sit-in protests. Regarding a case involving black protestors who had been jailed for trespassing on private property, Frankfurter remarked that "it will not advance the cause of constitutional equality for Negroes for the court to be taking short cuts to discriminate as partisans in favor of Negroes or even to appear to do so."

Throughout the postwar era, Frankfurter became increasingly estranged from fellow Roosevelt appointees Hugo Black and WILLIAM O. DOUGLAS. Moreover, by the 1960s, the Warren Court increasingly came to reject Frankfurter's approach to jurisprudence. He lost perhaps his greatest battle with Black over the incorporation of the Fourteenth Amendment (the application of the Bill of Rights to state governments through the Fourteenth Amendment's due process clause). Frankfurter's dissents in *Mapp v. Ohio* (1961) and *Baker v. Carr* (1962) expressed his commitment both to judicial restraint and to coordinate federalism. His retirement in 1962 and replacement by ARTHUR GOLDBERG marked a major turning point. Goldberg provided a dependable fifth vote for the liberal wing of the Court. Virtually none

of Frankfurter's major constitutional decisions survived the ensuing two decades.

As a professor of law and Supreme Court justice, Frankfurter made substantial contributions to debates over policy and jurisprudence. The scholarly consensus on his tenure as a justice, however, has not been kind. In the minds of many, Frankfurter's commitment to judicial restraint, particularly in the field of civil liberties, "uncoupled" him "from the locomotive of history," as Joseph Lash put it. Nevertheless, his commitment to judicial restraint and federalism constituted a significant legacy to the Court and to justices who would follow him on it. He died in Washington, D.C., on February 22, 1965.

—MSM

Freeman, Orville L(orthrop)
(1918–2003) *governor of Minnesota*

The son of a storekeeper, Freeman was born in Minneapolis on March 9, 1918. He graduated magna cum laude from the University of Minnesota in 1940. Following service with the marines during World War II, he returned to the university to obtain his law degree in 1946. While practicing law, he joined HUBERT HUMPHREY and other liberals in effecting a merger of the Democratic and Farmer-Labor parties in 1944. Freeman became the state chairman in 1948 and managed Humphrey's successful campaign for the Senate that year.

Freeman ran unsuccessfully for state attorney general in 1950 and for governor in 1952. He won election as governor in 1954 and reelection in 1956 and 1958. A fine administrator, he was responsible for major improvements in education and welfare: building schools, increasing space in state mental hospitals, and expanding state aid to local school districts. To finance this program, he had to raise property taxes to an all-time high and attempt to install pay-as-you-go income taxes. Freeman's tax policies and his decision to send state militia to close a strikebound meatpacking company contributed to his failure to win a fourth term in 1960.

As governor, Freeman opposed Secretary of Agriculture EZRA TAFT BENSON's policy of reducing price supports on agricultural commodities, which, the secretary maintained, aided only the larger farmers who could control production. In 1959, Freeman created the Minnesota Farm Policy Committee, composed of agricultural economists, to evaluate the Benson program. Its report called for the establishment of a national food policy with production goals set for domestic and foreign use. Once the production goal was determined, marketing allotments would be distributed to farmers on a graduated basis, with the largest farms receiving the proportionately largest reductions. The report also advocated the reduction of agricultural surpluses through overseas sales, the establishment of school lunch programs, and the granting of aid to depressed areas.

Freeman and Humphrey were early supporters of ADLAI STEVENSON for the Democratic presidential nomination in 1956 and assured their candidate of Farmer-Labor support in the Minnesota primary. Therefore, Stevenson campaigned very little in the state. Sen. ESTES KEFAUVER (D-Tenn.), running on the proposition that Freeman and Humphrey were political bosses, won an upset victory that slowed down Stevenson's drive for the nomination and damaged the governor's prestige. Following Stevenson's defeat in the November election, Freeman joined the Democratic Advisory Council, a panel of leading Democrats who prepared position papers for the party on important issues. He was considered one of the most liberal members of the panel, especially on agriculture, civil rights, and foreign-policy issues.

Freeman supported Humphrey for president in 1960, and after the senator's withdrawal from the primary race, he endorsed Sen. JOHN F. KENNEDY (D-Mass.). At the Democratic National Convention, the Minnesota delegation split between supporters of Kennedy and Stevenson. Freeman and Humphrey led the pro-Kennedy forces against the Stevenson supporters, headed by Sen. EUGENE McCARTHY (D-Minn.). Gov. Freeman placed Kennedy's name in nomination, calling him a "proven liberal" and a demonstrated leader. In the early part of the primary race, Kennedy considered Freeman a leading contender for vice president. However, he was reluctant to choose a northern liberal and instead selected Sen. LYNDON, JOHNSON (D-Tex.) as his running mate.

Freeman served as secretary of agriculture during the Kennedy and Johnson administrations and put into practice many of the recommendations his Farm Policy Committee made in 1959. He helped to establish the food stamps and school breakfast programs. He also worked to expand global markets for American farmers, promoted loans and grants for water and sewer systems in rural areas, and lobbied Congress to strengthen food safety regulations. Freeman served until the end of the Johnson administration, when he became chief executive of EDP Technology, a consulting company. He headed Business International Corporation from 1971 to 1985 and worked for a law firm in Washington, D.C., from 1985 to 1995. He returned to Minneapolis in 1995, where he was a visiting scholar at the Humphrey Institute of Public Affairs at the University of Minnesota. He died in Minneapolis of complications from Alzheimer's disease on February 20, 2003.

—JB

Fritchey, Clayton

(1904–2001) *deputy chairman, Democratic National Committee*

Born in Bellefontaine, Ohio, in 1904, Fritchey moved with his family to Baltimore in 1906. He began his career in journalism as a reporter for the *Baltimore American* in 1924. Three years later, he became city editor of the *Baltimore Post*. After working briefly for the *Pittsburgh Press*, he returned to the *Baltimore Post* as managing editor in 1931. He subsequently worked for the *Cleveland Press* and became editor of the *New Orleans Item* in 1944. Fritchey served as director of the Department of Defense's public relations bureau from 1950 to 1952. In that post, newsmen rated him as "competent, but not outstanding." An outspoken liberal Democrat, he was appointed an assistant to President HARRY S. TRUMAN in 1952. After the National Democratic Convention in July, Fritchey served as liaison between Truman and the presidential nominee, ADLAI E. STEVENSON. The Democratic National Chairman, STEPHEN MITCHELL, appointed Fritchey deputy chairman in December 1952. Fritchey served in that post until 1957, concerning himself principally with editing the national committee's official magazine, *Democratic Digest*.

Fritchey took a "no-holds-barred" approach to politics. In 1953, in an effort to draw attention to flimsy charges of corruption against HERBERT BROWNELL, Fritchey recklessly accused the attorney general of attempting to "divert attention" from those charges by alleging that communists had infiltrated the Truman administration. Further, in 1954, Fritchey paid a private investigator named Paul Hughes $2,300 for a 94-page report, filled with fabricated memos and documents, pertaining to purported "illegal activities" of Sen. JOSEPH McCARTHY (R-Wis.) and the Senate Government Operations Committee's Permanent Investigations Subcommittee. Fritchey's role came out at Hughes's trial for perjury in 1956.

Fritchey's aggressiveness was rewarded in August 1956, when Stevenson, making his second run for the presidency, named him press secretary for the campaign. As the campaign progressed, some accused Fritchey of spending too much time with Democratic officials and not enough with reporters. When Stevenson lost in November, Fritchey resigned his party post.

In 1957, Fritchey and three associates bought the *Arlington Sun* and renamed it the *Northern Virginia Sun*. Fritchey served as the publisher until 1961, when Stevenson became chief United States delegate to the United Nations and Fritchey accepted a position as director of public affairs for the United States mission. Upon Stevenson's death in 1965, Fritchey left the UN and began writing a syndicated column for *Newsday*. He retired in 1984 and died in Washington, D.C., on January 23, 2001.

—MSM

Fulbright, J(ames) William
(1905–1995) *U.S. senator*

The son of a wealthy banker and prominent businessman, Fulbright was born in Sumner, Mo., on April 9, 1905. He grew up in Fayetteville, Ark., in the northwestern part of the state. He graduated from the University of Arkansas in 1925 and spent the next three years at Oxford on a Rhodes scholarship. Upon his return to the United States in 1928,

Fulbright entered George Washington University law school. Following his graduation in 1934, he worked as an intern in the Justice Department's antitrust division, where he helped prosecute *Schechter Poultry Corp. v. U.S.* (1935). Fulbright left government service after a year to accept a position as law instructor at George Washington University.

In 1936, Fulbright returned to Fayetteville, where he combined teaching at the University of Arkansas with managing the family's businesses. Three years later, Fulbright, then 34, was appointed president of the university. He was the youngest university president in the United States. As president, he first gained national attention by raising university standards. He also spoke out in opposition to isolationists. When Homer Adkins was elected governor in 1940, he dismissed Fulbright from his post.

In 1942, Fulbright won a seat in the House of Representatives, where he was assigned to the Foreign Affairs Committee. Several months after taking his seat in Congress, he defended Franklin D. Roosevelt's war policies against an attack by Rep. CLARE BOOTHE LUCE (R-Conn.). In June 1943, Fulbright introduced a resolution supporting American participation in a postwar international organization dedicated to preserving peace. The resolution passed both houses of Congress by large margins.

Fulbright won a seat in the Senate in 1944. His campaign emphasized Fulbright's conservative positions on domestic issues. In the Senate, he continued to support internationalism and multilateralism in foreign policy and conservative, politically safe, positions on domestic affairs. He proposed that the UN be empowered to limit armaments and nuclear weapons and recommended abolition of the veto in the Security Council. He also advocated a stronger World Court, with power to make binding decisions. In addition, he became increasingly critical of the Truman administration for its hard line toward the USSR. Fulbright shifted his position, however, after the Soviets rejected an American plan to internationalize atomic weapons. He supported the Truman Doctrine, the Marshall Plan, and the North Atlantic Treaty. Domestically, he opposed civil rights legislation and supported several measures opposed by organized labor, including the Taft-Hartley Act.

In September 1945, Fulbright offered a bill for the educational exchange program that would bear his name. The bill passed in 1946.

Fulbright's relations with the Truman administration deteriorated further after Republicans won control of both houses of Congress in 1946, and Fulbright suggested that the president appoint Sen. ARTHUR VANDENBERG (R-Mich.) secretary of state (making him next in line to the presidency) and resign. Truman responded by calling the senator an "overeducated Oxford S.O.B." After winning reelection in 1950, Fulbright chaired a subcommittee of the Banking and Currency Committee, which conducted an investigation that uncovered substantial influence peddling in the Reconstruction Finance Corporation (RFC).

During the Eisenhower administration, Fulbright continued to support the economic interests of the South. He supported the Dixon-Yates power combine and opposed an increase in the minimum wage. Yet Fulbright was not a conservative who feared and wished to restrict government action. He instead wanted to reorient government from a concentration on defense and highway spending to an emphasis on housing, education, and antitrust programs.

Fulbright was an early critic of Sen. JOSEPH MCCARTHY (R-Wis.). In the early 1950s, McCarthy and Fulbright clashed over McCarthy's acceptance of $10,000 for writing a pamphlet for a company financed by the RFC (and therefore under the supervision of the Banking and Currency Committee, on which McCarthy served) and Truman's nomination of Philip C. Jessup to be a delegate to the United Nations. In 1953, Fulbright defended the Fulbright Fellowship program, which McCarthy charged with supporting pro-communists. Early in 1954, when McCarthy was at the height of his power, the Senate voted on further appropriations for McCarthy's Permanent Investigations Subcommittee. Only Fulbright opposed the bill.

Fulbright played a leading role in the Senate's condemnation of McCarthy in 1954. Because McCarthy's conduct in the Army-McCarthy hearings of the spring had alienated many important senators, Fulbright thought it would be an appropriate time to act against him. Believing that it

would be best if a Republican took the lead, Fulbright approached Sen. RALPH FLANDERS (R-Vt.), who agreed to sponsor a censure resolution. Fulbright helped Flanders prepare the measure, which stated simply that McCarthy had brought discredit to the Senate. Fulbright also did the bulk of the research on the legal and historical precedents for the censure action and handled negotiations with the Democratic leadership. When the original measure proved too vague to attract support, Fulbright amended it with a bill of particulars. In early November, a select committee, headed by Sen. ARTHUR WATKINS (R-Utah), recommended McCarthy's censure. When the final debate began at the end of the month, Fulbright took the Senate floor to denounce the hatred and fears engendered by McCarthy. On December 2, the Senate voted to condemn the senator from Wisconsin.

Fulbright remained an opponent of integration throughout the 1950s. In March 1956, he joined 18 other senators and 82 representatives in signing the "Southern Manifesto," which denounced the Supreme Court's 1954 decision outlawing segregated public schools. The congressmen maintained that the Court had "substituted naked power for established law" and laid the basis for interracial strife. They, therefore, pledged to resist integration by "any lawful means." Although considered inflammatory by many liberals, the statement was more moderate than the one originally proposed by Sen. STROM THURMOND (D-S.C.). That proposal had endorsed the theory of interposition (the use of state power to nullify the Court's decision) and had branded the Court's action illegal and unconstitutional. Fulbright had opposed that extreme language, and the manifesto was modified to gain his support. He voted against the Civil Rights Acts of 1957 and 1960.

During the 1950s, Fulbright frequently clashed with President Eisenhower and Secretary of State JOHN FOSTER DULLES over U.S. foreign affairs. He urged a reorientation of U.S. policy from one based on an ideological confrontation with the Soviet Union to one resting on big-power interests. He stressed the need to supply economic and technical rather than military aid to U.S. allies and questioned the administration's dependence on nuclear weapons for defense.

Fulbright also opposed the president's emphasis on the formation of defense pacts with underdeveloped nations. He disapproved of the Southeast Asian Treaty of 1954, which established the Southeast Asia Treaty Organization (SEATO), and the Formosa Resolution of 1955, giving the president the right to use force to defend Formosa (Taiwan) and the Pescadores. In 1957, the senator opposed the Eisenhower Doctrine, which authorized the president to use the armed forces to aid a Middle Eastern nation resisting "armed attack from any country controlled by international communism." Fulbright used the hearings on the resolution to denounce Eisenhower's approach, which he claimed would weaken Western influence in the Middle East. He regarded the Eisenhower Doctrine as disastrous to the North Atlantic Treaty Organization (NATO) and damaging to U.S. friendship with Great Britain and France. A resolution supporting the Eisenhower Doctrine passed the Senate in March 1957. Fulbright was one of 19 senators who voted against it.

Fulbright assumed the chair of the Senate Foreign Relations Committee in 1959. He held the chair until 1975, making him the longest serving chair of that committee in history.

Fulbright supported LYNDON B. JOHNSON for the presidency in 1960. When JOHN F. KENNEDY won the election, he considered Fulbright for secretary of state, but the senator's record as a segregationist effectively disqualified him. Throughout the 1960s, Fulbright urged an end to foreign policy based on the notion that the United States and USSR were locked in an inevitable ideological conflict. He argued that relations with the Soviets should be seen in terms of a traditional great-power rivalry. In spite of that perspective, he urged a belligerent response during the Cuban missile crisis of 1962. Fulbright became increasingly critical of the war in Vietnam. His friendship with Johnson gave way to hostility as he split with the president first over the intervention in the Dominican Republic and then over Vietnam. By the end of the decade, Fulbright had emerged as the leading symbol of congressional discontent with the war.

In his bid for a sixth term in 1974, Fulbright lost the Democratic primary to Dale Bumpers. After leaving the Senate, Fulbright went to work for the Washington law firm of Hogan & Hartson, where he lobbied for the interests of the governments of Japan and the United Arab Emirates. He retired from the firm in 1994 and died in Washington, D.C., on February 9, 1995.

—MSM

Funston, G(eorge) Keith
(1910–1992) *president, New York Stock Exchange*

Born in Waterloo, Iowa, on October 12, 1910, G. Keith Funston grew up in Sioux Falls, S.Dak., where his father owned the International Savings Bank. Funston won a scholarship to Trinity College in Connecticut and graduated as class valedictorian in 1932. After earning an M.B.A. from the Harvard Graduate School of Business Administration in 1934, he worked from 1935 to 1940 for the American Radiator Co., where he set up a sales incentive plan. In 1940, he joined the Sylvania Electric Products Co. as sales planning director. He then became director of purchasing. Funston left Sylvania to become a dollar-a-year man during World War II, serving at the War Production Board as special assistant, first to former investment banker Sidney Weinberg and then to chairman Donald Nelson. In 1944, he entered the U.S. Naval Reserve as a lieutenant commander. He was assigned to the Industrial Readjustment Branch of the Office of Procurement and Material. That same year, he was chosen president of Trinity College, a position he could not take up until the end of the war. A successful fund-raiser, Funston raised $5 million in six years for the small institution. Funston also served on the boards of directors of seven corporations until 1951, when, upon Weinberg's recommendation, he was selected as president of the New York Stock Exchange (NYSE).

The NYSE provided the physical environment for the buying and selling of stocks, but it also was responsible for "self-regulation," policing its members' ethical behavior in areas outside the purview of the Securities and Exchange Commission (SEC). The 40-year-old Funston had no background in the securities business when he took the $100,000-a-year post of NYSE president, but his wholesome image and success in selling and public relations equipped him for the task of representing the stock exchange to Washington and the public.

Funston undertook a crusade to improve the public image of the stock market that still suffered from the crash of 1929. Funston proclaimed himself "salesman of shares in America" and used the atmosphere of the cold war to link stock ownership with patriotism. During Funston's tenure at the NYSE, the number of investors in corporate stocks grew from more than 6 million in 1951 to more than 22 million in 1967. He touted the benefits of owning stocks through a massive advertising campaign. Not all of his innovations, however, were successful. In 1954, he introduced the Monthly Investment Plan (MIP) to encourage small investors by enabling them essentially to buy stocks on an installment basis for as little as $40 a month. The plan proved cumbersome, and high commission costs as well as competition from mutual funds limited the appeal of and participation in the MIP.

As the official spokesman of the NYSE's 1,300 members, Funston was quick to defend a free market in securities whenever the government attempted to tighten regulation. On January 4, 1954, the Federal Reserve Board raised the margin requirement from 50 percent of a stock's price to 60 percent. The next day, Funston criticized the board's action as "hard to understand" because "it comes at a time when industry is seeking new funds to build new plants and equipment."

During a speculative boom in 1955, the Senate Banking and Currency Committee conducted a study of the stock market. In March Funston testified that, despite the recent sharp rise in speculation, the market was healthy, for the high price level was "not the product of undue extension of credit or of unsound market activity but reflects the confident appraisal of the general public." Funston dismissed alarms that the current market conditions were similar to those that had caused the crash in 1929, and he opposed proposals to raise margin requirements.

Funston's tenure coincided with the largest bull market to that point. During the 1960s, he found it increasingly necessary to defend the exchange against criticisms of its "private club" exclusiveness, abuses in stock trading, and the laxity of its performance as self-regulator. He left the NYSE in April 1967 to become chairman of the Olin Mathieson Chemical Corp., a position he held until 1972. He died in Greenwich, Conn., on May 15, 1992.

—MSM

Gaither, H(orace) Rowan, Jr.

(1909–1961) *president, Ford Foundation; presidential adviser*

Born in Natchez, Miss., on November 23, 1909, H. Rowan Gaither obtained his B.A. from the University of California at Berkeley in 1929 and a law degree there four years later. He then moved to Washington, D.C., to serve as a special assistant to the Farm Credit Administration. In 1936, Gaither returned to California to practice law and teach at Berkeley's law school. During World War II, Gaither served as assistant director of the Radiation Laboratory of the Massachusetts Institute of Technology. Following the war, he returned to private law practice. He helped to establish the RAND Corporation, an independent, nonprofit organization to carry out research on national defense, initially for the air force. When RAND got under way in 1948, Gaither became chair of the board of trustees, a position he held until his death. At RAND, Gaither worked closely with the Ford Foundation, which funded many of the corporation's projects. In 1951, the Ford Foundation appointed Gaither associate director in charge of the investigation of human behavior and conduct. Two years later, he was elected president.

In 1954, the House Special Committee to Investigate Tax-Exempt Foundations heard testimony on charges that the Ford, Rockefeller, Carnegie, and other foundations supported subversive activities. On July 24, Gaither charged that the committee "maligned" the foundation with irresponsible testimony and called its accusations "erroneous and baseless . . . sheerest nonsense."

Gaither asked for an opportunity to appear before the committee to avert a damaging effect on the "morale, initiative and freedom of scientific, educational and charitable organizations." However, public hearings ended before representatives of the foundations were heard.

In December, the majority on the committee issued a report maintaining that, while the foundations did not support communist organizations, they "have directly supported 'subversion' in the true meaning of that term, namely, the process of undermining some of our vital protective concepts and principles." Gaither joined DEAN RUSK, president of the Rockefeller Foundation, in calling the report biased and unfounded.

Gaither took over the Ford Foundation at a time of turmoil and conflict. His skill at conciliation and his ability to forge consensuses proved incapable of resolving fundamental disagreements at the foundation. In 1956, Donald David replaced him as president, and Gaither was elevated to chairman of the board.

In the spring of 1957, Gaither headed a study, commissioned by the National Security Council (NSC), of Soviet offensive capabilities and American defense requirements. Gaither fell ill with cancer as the committee's work got under way and was unable to participate in the preparation of the committee's report. Nevertheless, the committee became known as the Gaither Committee and its findings as the Gaither Report. The report was presented to the National Security Council in early November, three days after Gaither had briefed the president. The Gaither panel presented a grim evaluation of the relative strengths of the United States and Soviet Union. The Soviet gross national product, although roughly one-third that of the United States, was growing at a faster rate. Moreover, Soviet military spending roughly equaled that of the United States. The Gaither group predicted that, because of increased Soviet military spending, the USSR would be able to launch 100 intercontinental ballistic missiles (ICBMs) carrying nuclear warheads against the United States by 1959. The report further warned that American manned bombers of the Strategic Air Command, except for those on alert status, would be vulnerable. The report recommended a comprehensive revision of defense policies and a substantial increase in military spending. Specifically, the report called for expanded missile programs, rapid development of an ICBM early warning system, and development of a national system of fallout shelters to protect the civilian population. The panel also predicted that future conflicts were more likely to be limited wars rather than all-out nuclear ones. Therefore, the panel recommended an expansion of conventional forces. Eisenhower regarded the report as unduly pessimistic and rejected many of the panel's findings. For example, he contended that American overseas bases provided a great capacity for dispersion of forces. Moreover, Eisenhower particularly objected to the $40-billion price tag for the committee's recommendations.

Amid the near hysteria over the Soviet launch of *Sputnik* on October 4, 1957, parts of the highly secret report were leaked to the press in November 1957. Despite growing demands for the release of the full report, led by Senate Majority Leader LYNDON B. JOHNSON, Eisenhower refused to do so, a position which Gaither supported. Moreover, Gaither refused to make public any information from the report. Subsequently, president JOHN F. KENNEDY also refused to release the report. Gaither died of cancer in Boston, Mass., on April 7, 1961.

—MSM

Galbraith, John Kenneth
(1908–2006) *economist*

Born on a farm near Iona Station, Ontario, Canada, on October 15, 1908, John Kenneth Galbraith

received a B.S. from Ontario Agricultural College in 1931 and his Ph.D. in economics from the University of California at Berkeley in 1934. After working over the summer for the Agricultural Adjustment Administration, he took a job as an instructor in the economics department at Harvard in the fall of 1934. He remained at Harvard until 1939. In the fall of 1937, he became a United States citizen, just before he went to Cambridge University for the 1937–38 academic year on a Social Science Research Council Fellowship in agricultural economics. In 1939 he became an assistant professor of economics at Princeton. After a year at Princeton, he went to Washington, D.C., to serve as economic adviser to Chester Davis, the agricultural member of the National Defense Advisory Committee. In 1941, Galbraith moved to the Office of Price Administration as director of price controls. He resigned in 1943 under fire from a variety of business and congressional critics. Later that year, HENRY LUCE hired Galbraith as an editor of *Fortune* magazine. Galbraith continued to work for *Fortune*, with interruptions, until 1948. In 1945, Galbraith directed the United States Strategic Bombing Survey, the purpose of which was to assess the effects of the air war against Germany and Japan. After the war, he served as director of the State Department's Office of Economic Security Policy, which controlled the economic affairs of the former Axis powers.

Galbraith returned to Harvard as a lecturer in economics in 1948. He became a full professor a year later and Paul M. Warburg professor of economics in 1959. During the 1950s, he published a number of highly influential analyses of the American economy. Through his trenchant expression and witty debunking of what he referred to as "conventional wisdom," Galbraith attracted a wide audience for his advocacy of Keynesian economics and liberal politics.

In *American Capitalism: The Concept of Countervailing Power* (1952), Galbraith argued that the classical model of small competing units did not apply to the modern American economy. Large corporations, he maintained, had come to dominate the American economy because only they could afford to make the large-scale investments in new processes, expensive equipment, and basic research necessary to sustain economic growth.

Nevertheless, he argued, big business would not go unchecked, because trade unions, farm organizations, consumer groups, and big government acted as "countervailing powers." For Galbraith, big government acted as the protector of social units too weak or unorganized to maintain a fair equilibrium. Galbraith's essentially sanguine picture of the structure of the American economy had enormous influence on perceptions of American society during the 1950s.

In 1955, Galbraith published *The Great Crash: 1929*, a lively account of the stock market crash that marked the beginning of the Great Depression. According to Galbraith, the cause of the market's collapse was the "speculative orgy" that preceded it. Galbraith argued that the crash did not cause the depression but that it helped to trigger the larger economic crisis. He maintained that had the economy not had grave underlying weaknesses, such as a severe maldistribution of income and a bad banking structure, the crash probably would not have precipitated such a deep depression. Galbraith's emphasis on "maldistribution," by which he meant the unequal distribution of wealth, ignored the fact that the distribution of wealth was more unequal in the first decade and a half of the 20th century than it had been in the 1920s, and no depression ensued. Moreover, Galbraith's analysis overlooked the significance of the fact that the economy of the 1920s was driven by sales of consumer durables.

In March 1955, Galbraith appeared before the Senate Banking and Currency Committee investigating that year's stock market boom. He told the committee that the speculative hysteria was unhealthy and was one of several factors that disturbingly resembled conditions preceding the crash in 1929. He urged raising margin requirements on stock purchases to 100 percent, a proposal sharply at variance from the recommendations of the stock exchange officials who testified. The stock market dropped the day after Galbraith's testimony, but the crash he predicted never came.

Galbraith's testimony infuriated the committee's senior Republican, Sen. Homer Capehart (R-Ind.), who later accused the economist of disparaging the American economy and "praising communism." In a public telegram, Galbraith accused the senator of taking some sentences from a pamphlet Galbraith had written out of context. In addition, the economist charged Capehart with omitting passages in the pamphlet critical of communism. The dispute flared briefly on the front pages and then died. Galbraith's most important work of the decade was *The Affluent Society* (1958), a critique of national priorities. In it, Galbraith questioned the national consensus that greater production and an abundance of goods provided adequately for America's needs. Liberals and conservatives, he maintained, agreed that unlimited economic growth, spurred by Keynesian demand management, could maintain high levels of employment, eliminate poverty, and provide an alternative to Marxist demands for redistribution of wealth. Galbraith concurred with other economists that the "uncertainties of economic life" that had dominated earlier eras had either been eliminated or were less "serious" in the United States after World War II. However, he saw different dangers: inflation and consumer debt. Further, Galbraith derided the American preoccupation with the variety and quantity of consumer goods, a craving he believed owed more to advertising than real need. In contrast to the affluent private sector, Galbraith painted a picture of squalor in the public sector. He pointed to the deterioration of the infrastructure of America's cities, as well as inadequate spending on schools, hospitals, libraries, parks, playgrounds, museums, and police, as examples of public undertakings neglected in pursuit of private abundance. Galbraith called for a rearrangement of national priorities and specifically urged an increase in progressive taxation and in spending on the public sector.

Galbraith returned to the topic of inflation in an essay in *The Liberal Hour* (1960). In his analysis, inflation resulted largely from price increases in a few highly concentrated industries, such as steel, automobiles, rubber, and machinery. Because of the power of the "largest and strongest firms" and the "largest and strongest unions," prices rose in an inflationary spiral, irrespective of market fluctuations. "Modern inflation," he wrote, "is not neutral." "Because of its inevitable identification with economic strength," Galbraith concluded, "it is inequitable, regressive, and reactionary." Galbraith rejected monetary adjustments as an ineffective response. Another possible solution, fiscal policy, he contended, severely cut demand, output, and employment and was therefore "worse than the disease." Instead, he proposed wage and price restraints applied to what he regarded as unwarranted increases in highly concentrated industries.

Throughout the 1950s, Galbraith lent his support to various liberal causes and the Democratic party. As a member of ADLAI STEVENSON's presidential campaign staff in 1952 and 1956, his primary function was to tutor the candidate in Keynesian economics. From 1956 to 1960, Galbraith chaired the Democratic Advisory Council's economic panel. An early supporter of Sen. JOHN F. KENNEDY's (D-Mass.) presidential nomination, Galbraith was rewarded after Kennedy won the presidency in 1960. The economist served as an unofficial economic adviser to the Kennedy administration and as ambassador to India from 1961 to 1963.

Returning to Harvard in 1963, he spent four years producing *The New Industrial State* (1967), another analysis of the political economy of the United States. In it, he argued that large corporations made up a "technostructure" necessary for continuing technological advances. However, they did not focus on maximizing profit in the way neoclassical economists believed. Rather, they controlled consumer demand through advertising and marketing. In addition, big business and government worked together to maintain economic stability. Thus, he concluded that the American economy did not differ all that much from Soviet economic planning and that the two systems might converge. For his own part, Galbraith argued for the nationalization of some industries, including defense contractors, and for a system of wage and price controls.

During the administrations of LYNDON B. JOHNSON and RICHARD M. NIXON, Galbraith continued to reach a broad readership with his books and polemical essays. Although he served as an advisor to Johnson, Galbraith split with him over the Vietnam War and emerged as an outspoken critic of the war and a prominent figure in the left wing of the Democratic party. He supported the candidacies of EUGENE MCCARTHY in 1968 and George McGovern in 1972.

Galbraith published *Economics and the Public Purpose* (1973), in which he argued for a new socialism. The free enterprise system, he maintained, no longer could support certain industries. His new socialism, however, would not nationalize banks and high-technology industries, as socialists had previously intended. Rather, it would nationalize housing, health, and other public service industries. Further, Galbraith called for public support of the arts and the conversion of some corporations and military contractors into public corporations. Ever the partisan Democrat, Galbraith criticized the economic policies of the Nixon administration and blamed the president for the economic downturn of the 1970s.

After retiring from Harvard in 1975, Galbraith continued to write and participate in Democratic party politics. His books from this period included *Annals of an Abiding Liberal* (1979), *A Life in Our Times* (1981), *A Journey through Economic Time* (1994), and *The Good Society: The Humane Agenda* (1996). Even as the political climate moved away from the sort of liberalism he espoused, Galbraith never changed his approach or attempted to distance himself from the label of liberalism. In a 1992 article in *Modern Maturity*, the magazine of the American Association of Retired Persons (AARP), he asserted that "there is no hope for liberals if they seek only to imitate conservatives, and no function, either." Galbraith died in Cambridge, Mass., on April 29, 2006.

—MSM

Gardner, Trevor
(1915–1963)   *assistant secretary of the air force for research and development*

Born in Cardiff, Wales, on August 24, 1915, Gardner became an American citizen in 1937 and received a B.S. degree in engineering from the University of Southern California during the same year. After earning his M.B.A. in 1939, Gardner became general manager and executive vice president of the General Tire and Rubber Co. of California in 1945. Three years later, he was named president of the Hycon Co., a manufacturer of electrical parts.

In the spring of 1953, Air Force Secretary HAROLD TALBOTT appointed Gardner special assistant to look into air force research and development. Gardner quickly found an area of particular interest in the long-range missile program. Through both official and unofficial efforts, he enormously speeded development of the nation's first intercontinental ballistic missiles (ICBMs) over the next few years.

While the budget-minded Republican administration was interested in reducing defense spending, Gardner questioned whether enough money was being allocated to develop a workable ICBM ahead of the Soviet Union. In June 1953, Secretary of Defense CHARLES WILSON joined Talbott in asking Gardner to widen his probe of the long-range missile program. However, while the defense secretary had economy in mind, Gardner was contemplating a crash development program for the Atlas missile estimated at $2.75 billion. By the fall of 1953, Gardner had created the Strategic Missiles Evaluation Committee (SMEC), a review committee chaired by Dr. John von Neumann of Princeton University. In February 1954, SMEC reported that an operational ICBM could be produced within six to eight years, but only if the project were accorded "the highest national priority." Gardner agreed with the panel's conclusions. He also urged Secretary Talbott to create a new, separate agency to oversee development of the ICBM. Gardner failed to get a separate agency, but he did get a new western development division within the air force's Air Research and Development Command to oversee the ICBM project. Gardner also successfully backed the appointment of Gen. Bernard Schriever to head the division. Nevertheless, Gardner and Schriever encountered resistance from the air force bureaucracy, which placed greater emphasis on the new B-52 bomber.

President Eisenhower nominated Trevor Gardner to be assistant air force secretary in August 1954. Sen. BOURKE HICKENLOOPER (R-Iowa) blocked confirmation because of allegations that Gardner had supported nuclear scientist Dr. J. ROBERT OPPENHEIMER in a dispute with the loyalty review board the same year. Talbott announced he would retain Gardner as his special assistant. In February 1955, President Eisenhower resubmitted the nomination; Hickenlooper withdrew his objection, and Gardner was quickly confirmed.

In the spring of 1955, Gardner and Schriever took their case to Congress. In testimony before a congressional committee, they told of the bureaucratic obstacles they faced and warned that

the Soviets might be winning the race to build an ICBM. After two members of the Joint Committee on Atomic Energy sent a letter to Eisenhower in June urging a crash program to develop the ICBM, the president had Gardner and Schriever present a special briefing on the ICBM to the National Security Council. After their presentation, Eisenhower authorized the NSC to give the ICBM "the highest national priority," which enabled Gardner and Schriever to overcome any bureaucratic impediments. Still, Eisenhower refused to authorize a cash program or to create either a separate agency or overall czar of the missile program.

The ICBM program also faced competition from intermediate range ballistic missiles (IRBMs). In March 1954, Eisenhower asked a panel of his scientific advisory committee to study defense in a thermonuclear age. The panel, headed by JAMES KILLIAN, the president of the Massachusetts Institute of Technology, reported its findings in February 1955. Although it supported the ICBM program and deemed progress on it "satisfactory," the report warned that ICBMs would not be militarily significant for perhaps 10 years. Therefore, it recommended the development of IRBMs. Eisenhower granted the IRBM program the same priority status as the ICBM program. Gardner, who believed that the government's efforts should be concentrated on developing an ICBM, disagreed with the president's decision.

In November 1955, Secretary Wilson created a Ballistic Missiles Committee within the Defense Department to preclude interservice rivalries from interfering with the development of ballistic missiles. The air force also established its own ballistic missile committee to work around the air staff, which still gave preference to the B-52.

Gardner believed the ICBM program should be more generously funded. In January 1956, he requested an additional $120 million in research funds for fiscal year 1956 and an additional $250 million for 1957. Air Force Secretary DONALD A. QUARLES rejected Gardner's proposal twice, and Gardner resigned in February. President Eisenhower accepted his resignation within a few days. Gardner then publicly stated he did not believe the United States could maintain military superiority over the Soviet Union at current spending levels. In a post-resignation appearance on television's *Meet the Press*, Gardner asserted that the Soviet Union led the United States in ICBM development and warned that the military budget for 1957 "guaranteed this nation the second-best air force in the world." He repeated these charges in June, testifying before the Senate Armed Services Committee's Air Force Subcommittee, chaired by Sen. STUART SYMINGTON (D-Mo.).

Following his resignation, Gardner returned to the presidency and chairmanship of the Hycon Co. From 1960 to 1961, he chaired the Air Force Space Task Force. Gardner died in Washington, D.C., on September 28, 1963.

—MSM

Gates, Thomas S(overeign), Jr.
(1906–1983) *secretary of the navy, deputy secretary of defense*

The son of an investment banker who later became president of the University of Pennsylvania, Thomas S. Gates, Jr., was born in Germantown, Pa., on April 10, 1906. He received his B.A. from the University of Pennsylvania in 1928 and joined his father's firm, Drexel and Co. The younger Gates became a partner in 1940. During World War II, Gates served in the Navy. He graduated from the Quonset Point Air Intelligence School in Rhode Island and helped organize naval air intelligence in Europe. Gates rose to the rank of lieutenant commander before being released from active duty in October 1945. After the war, he returned to Drexel.

Nominated by President DWIGHT EISENHOWER to be undersecretary of the navy in October 1953, Gates removed himself from an active role in banking and was confirmed without difficulty. Naval division heads reported directly to the undersecretary, and in 1955 Gates settled a dispute over the relationship between the navy and Marine Corps commands. Gates actively promoted a naval nuclear strike force as part of Eisenhower's "New Look" defense policy. In November 1956, he defended aircraft carriers under construction as more mobile and thus safer for launching aircraft than land-based runways.

Eisenhower named him secretary of the navy in March 1957. Days after his confirmation, Gates stated that aircraft carriers would be the navy's principal strike force. He accurately forecast the future importance of atomic submarines armed with missiles. Gates sacrificed funds for conventional vessels to begin building the nation's first atomic carrier.

After the Soviet Union launched *Sputnik* on October 4, 1957, the missile programs of the U.S. armed services faced mounting criticism. In response, Gates revealed plans for the submarine-based Polaris missile system. Following his own previous example, the secretary sacrificed projects on which the navy had spent over $680 million for the success of Polaris over the next two years.

Unhappy with the reorganization of the Defense Department in 1958 that increased the power of the secretary of defense at the expense of the service secretaries, Gates resigned from the navy in February 1959. In a resignation-eve speech, he pointed to the increased communist capacity to wage limited war and called for building the capacity of the navy and Marine Corps to counter limited aggression.

Gates became deputy defense secretary the following June. The next month, he testified before the House Armed Services Committee investigating charges that a "munitions lobby" heavily staffed by retired Pentagon officials sought to influence the awarding of defense contracts. Gates upheld the right of former officers to work in defense industries, denied feeling lobbying pressure, and said he closely watched for conflict of interest among ex-officers.

When NEIL MCELROY resigned as defense secretary in December, President Eisenhower appointed Gates to succeed him. Although expected to exercise a caretaker's role during the final year of the Eisenhower administration, Gates plunged into promoting greater cooperation between the Joint Chiefs of Staff and their civilian superiors. Much of Gates's year as defense secretary was devoted to defending the administration's $41-billion defense budget against Democratic charges of inadequacy and a "missile gap." In January 1960, Sen. STUART SYMINGTON (D-Mo.) led the attack, claiming the Soviets would soon boast a three-to-one missile lead over the United States. He called for a step-up in all missile programs and for an around-the-clock airborne bomber alert. Symington was supported by Strategic Air Command commander in chief Gen. Thomas Power. In hearings before the House Defense Appropriations Subcommittee and the Senate Armed Services Committee, the defense secretary countered by revealing new intelligence estimates of a much smaller gap and asserting that an adequate defense did not hinge on a missile-to-missile ratio. Although the Democratic Congress approved a defense budget roughly in line with the administration's requests in April, charges of a missile gap continued throughout the election year.

The Department of Defense was embarrassed in May when a U-2 spy plane was shot down over Soviet airspace. The incident came on the eve of summit talks between the United States and the USSR and led Soviet Premier Nikita S. Khrushchev to break off the meeting. Called before the Senate Foreign Relations Committee the following month, Gates defended the flights, which, he asserted, produced a wide range of vital information. He termed a military alert he had ordered during the summit as "absolutely essential" and denied that it was provocative.

After the elections of November 1960, the press reported that President-elect JOHN. F. KENNEDY seriously contemplated retaining Gates as defense secretary but eventually nominated Robert S. McNamara, the president of Ford Motor Co. Not wishing to commit McNamara to last-minute decisions made by the Eisenhower administration, the outgoing secretary suspended navy and air force projects for new supersonic aircraft and eliminated the proposed Skybolt missile system from the defense budget in January 1961.

Upon retiring, Gates joined Morgan and Company in New York, which later became Morgan Guaranty Trust Company. He became president in 1962 and chairman and chief executive officer in 1965. President RICHARD M. NIXON appointed him to chair the Advisory Commission on an All-Volunteer Force. In 1976 President GERALD R. FORD chose Gates to serve as chief of the United States Liaison Office in the People's Republic of China. Gates died in Philadelphia on March 25, 1983.

—MJS

Gavin, James M(aurice)

(1907–1990) *chief of research and development, Army General Staff*

Born of uncertain parentage in New York City on March 22, 1907, Gavin was adopted in 1909 by a coal miner and his wife, taken to live in Mount Carmel, Pa., and given their name. In 1924, he enlisted in the army as a private; the following year, he was admitted to U.S. Military Academy at West Point, from which he graduated in 1929. Gavin began his military career in the infantry but became an expert in air operations while teaching tactics at West Point in 1940. He became convinced of the importance of airborne warfare and became a paratrooper in 1941. After the United States entered World War II, Gavin entered an accelerated course at the Command and General Staff School. Upon completing the course in 1942, he was promoted to colonel and appointed chief of military operations of the Airborne Command at Fort Bragg, N.C. The following year, Gavin led the 505th Parachute Infantry Regiment in the invasion of Sicily. Promoted to brigadier general at age 36, he led the 82nd Airborne in the Normandy landing. Gavin was given command of the 82nd Airborne in August 1944 and led the division through the Battle of the Bulge and the Allied drive across Germany. In December 1945, he returned to Fort Bragg with his division, which he continued to command until he became chief of staff of the Fifth Army in 1948. In 1949, he was assigned to the Defense Department's Weapons Systems Evaluation Group. Two years later, he became chief of staff of allied forces in southern Europe. He returned to Germany in 1952 to command the VII Corps. In 1954, Gavin was appointed assistant chief of staff for plans and operations and was given the temporary rank of lieutenant general. He became chief of research and development for the army general staff, with the rank of deputy chief of staff, in 1955.

Gavin soon emerged as a prominent opponent of the Eisenhower administration's "New Look," which emphasized the nuclear deterrent and air power at the expense of conventional forces. Like Gen. MAXWELL TAYLOR, another famous paratrooper, Gavin argued for expanded conventional forces to fight limited wars. Gavin advocated the development of an antimissile missile and joined

Taylor in urging that the army's Nike-Zeus missile be armed with nuclear warheads and developed to destroy incoming ICBMs. In defending this plan against opposition from the air force, Gavin contended that the Strategic Air Command did not provide a sufficient deterrent and that, in the future, missiles would prove more effective. However, Gavin also intensely disliked Taylor, the army chief of staff, with whom he had a long-standing rivalry.

Gavin stirred a political controversy in January 1958 by announcing that he would retire on the grounds that he "could do more on the outside for national defense than on the inside." Gavin also suggested that his chances for promotion had been jeopardized by the position he had taken. However, Gavin denied that his decision was a result of difficulties over promotion and said that his real reason was his inability "to get something done about the deteriorating position of the army." In final testimony before the Senate Preparedness Subcommittee, chaired by Majority Leader LYNDON B. JOHNSON (D-Tex.), Gavin denounced the administration's policy, maintaining that army leaders "were asked to lead men into battle but denied necessary weapons." Gavin again warned that U.S. retaliatory power was declining in the face of Soviet missile production. Despite requests from Johnson and other powerful members of Congress that he remain, Gavin resigned effective March 1958.

Following his resignation, Gavin joined the industrial research and management consulting firm of Arthur Little, Inc., but continued as a prominent critic of Eisenhower's defense policy. In 1958, he published *War and Peace in the Space Age*, which warned that the United States would need to develop more flexible military policies to fight future wars, Gavin cautioned that America's reliance on strategic nuclear weapons had left it incapable of fighting limited wars. This, in turn, would lead to a series of political and military defeats and "invite general war." "Such a war," he predicted, "is one that no one will win."

In 1958, Gavin joined a group advising Sen. JOHN F. KENNEDY (D-Mass.), who was planning a bid for the presidency. The following year, Gavin supported the contention that a "missile gap" existed between the United States and the USSR.

Kennedy later used the allegation in his presidential campaign.

In 1961, Kennedy appointed Gavin ambassador to France. He resigned the post in 1962 because of the high personal expenses of running the embassy. Gavin returned to Arthur Little. As the United States escalated its military commitment, Gavin became a prominent critic of the Vietnam War. He had opposed intervention when he was in the army and, as the 1960s progressed, grew increasingly critical of American strategy and tactics. Gavin maintained that the United States had committed too large a portion of its resources to the war at the expense of other commitments. Further, he advocated an "enclave strategy," which would have limited American ground forces to defensive operations, as a prelude to withdrawal. In 1968 he coauthored *Crisis Now* with Arthur Hadley; the book called for an end to the war and a reallocation of resources to rebuild America's cities and to aid the poor. He retired in 1977 and published an account of his experiences during World War II, *On to Berlin*, in 1978. Gavin died in Baltimore on February 23, 1990.

—MSM

Genovese, Vito
(1897–1969) *organized crime figure*
Born in Rossiglione, Italy, on November 27, 1897, Vito Genovese immigrated to New York in 1913. He was arrested for the first time when he was 19, and he served a short prison term for carrying a pistol. During Prohibition, Genovese moved up in the underworld as an ally of Charles "Lucky" Luciano. The ambitious gangster preferred to maintain a low profile, hiding his illicit income behind a legitimate front. In 1925 he set up the Genovese Trading Co. Throughout his life, he portrayed himself as an honest junk dealer.

During the 1930s, Genovese rose in the hierarchy of the underworld. His primary activities involved gambling and extortion. He and Luciano were involved in a series of murders related to a struggle for power within the Italian underworld. After THOMAS E. DEWEY obtained a conviction against Luciano in 1936 for compulsory prostitution, the special prosecutor turned his attention to Genovese, particularly to the murder of Ferdinand Boccia in 1934. Genovese, who had become a naturalized citizen in 1936, fled the country the following year. He donated $250,000 to Italy's fascist government and received that country's highest civilian award from Benito Mussolini. After the Allied invasion of Italy, Genovese offered his services as a translator. He was jailed in 1944, when an investigation of black marketing turned up his role in the black market. While he was being held, word came of his indictment in the United States for the murder of Boccia. Military authorities returned Genovese to Brooklyn to stand trial, but the state's chief witness was found poisoned in jail, and prosecutors had to drop the charges.

In 1950–51 Sen. ESTES KEFAUVER (D-Tenn.) chaired sensational televised hearings into organized crime. The hearings identified Genovese as a major figure in the Mafia. Genovese tried to establish a stronger position within the Mafia in 1957, at least allegedly, through the attempted assassination of FRANK COSTELLO, reputed to be Luciano's successor, and the murder of ALBERT ANASTASIA, said to be Costello's "muscle." Costello retired after the attempt on his life.

In November 1957, Genovese convened an underworld conference in Apalachin, N.Y., to declare himself head of New York's organized crime. On the agenda was a directive from the Mafia's 12-man national commission, of which Genovese was a member, ordering the mob out of narcotics because of the high arrest risk. Police broke up the Apalachin meeting and arrested Genovese along with roughly 60 other underworld figures.

Genovese was summoned before the Senate Committee on Improper Activities in the Labor or Management Field in July 1958 to answer questions on his narcotics activities. He invoked the Fifth Amendment 150 times. Genovese was arrested five days later for conspiracy to transport and deal in narcotics. At his trial in 1959, he received a 15-year sentence. Genovese continued directing his criminal operations from Atlanta's federal prison.

During the 1960s, Joseph Valachi, a convicted mobster and member of Genovese's gang, went to the authorities claiming Genovese was trying to have him killed. In retaliation, Valachi testified before the Senate Permanent Investigations

Subcommittee for 10 weeks starting in September 1963. He sketched a nationwide crime syndicate in what Attorney General ROBERT F. KENNEDY called the biggest intelligence breakthrough of the century. Valachi also testified that Genovese continued to run a large criminal empire from behind bars. Federal authorities transferred Genovese to Leavenworth, in Kansas. With his health failing, Genovese was transferred to the medical facility at Springfield, where he died on February 14, 1969.

—MSM

George, Walter F(ranklin)
(1878–1957) *U.S. senator; chairman, Foreign Relations Committee; ambassador to the North Atlantic Treaty Organization*

The son of a tenant farmer, Walter George was born near Preston, Ga., on January 29, 1878. He distinguished himself in intercollegiate oratorical contests while attending Mercer University, a Baptist institution, from which he graduated in 1900. He received his law degree from the same institution a year later. In 1901, he moved to Vienna, Ga., and set up a law practice there. He became solicitor general for the Cordele Judiciary Circuit in 1907 and a judge of that circuit's Superior Court in 1912. George took a seat on the Georgia Court of Appeals (the state's highest court) in 1917. He resigned from the court in 1922 to run for the Senate seat left vacant by the death of the fiery populist Tom Watson. Supported by Atlanta business interests as well as South Georgia Watsonites, George was elected by a landslide and reelected in each of five subsequent contests.

In the Senate, George gradually rose to power through diligence, seniority, and quiet promotion of conservative policies. He became a member of the Finance Committee in 1927 and over the years established himself as the Senate's expert on taxes. Although a supporter of some early New Deal measures, including the Tennessee Valley Authority, the Social Security Act, and the Wagner Labor Relations Act, by Roosevelt's second term he had emerged as a leading foe of reform legislation. He mobilized opposition to housing and wage-hour bills and managed the defeat of Roosevelt's "court-packing" plan. In the election of 1938, Roosevelt campaigned against George in the Democratic primary as part of the so-called purge of key congressional conservatives obstructing his program, but the strategy backfired. George won reelection over a supporter of the New Deal, Lawrence Camp, and a rural demagogue, Eugene Talmadge.

George initially favored neutrality legislation and helped kill Roosevelt's request for cash-and-carry sales to European democracies in the event of a war. Hitler's invasion of Poland changed his mind, and, upon assuming the chairmanship of the Foreign Relations Committee in November 1940, George helped win passage of the president's lend-lease program. In August 1941, he resigned the Foreign Relations chairmanship to take over that of the Finance Committee. Except for the 1947–48 session, he held that position until 1953. During the Truman years, he was a powerful foe of the Fair Deal. George provided crucial support for Truman's foreign-policy initiatives, however, backing Greek-Turkish aid, the Marshall Plan, and the North Atlantic Treaty.

When the 83rd Congress convened in January 1953 with Republican majorities, the chairmanship of the Finance Committee passed to Sen. EUGENE MILLIKIN (R-Colo.) George remained the ranking Democrat on the Finance and Foreign Relations Committees, and his 30 years of service made him the Senate's most senior member. By the first term of the Eisenhower administration, George had become a pillar of the Senate "establishment." He carried himself with the manner of a southern aristocrat, in spite of his decidedly nonaristocratic background. George did not speak frequently on the floor of the Senate, but when he did, his thorough preparation and resonant voice compelled the respectful attention of his colleagues.

George played an important role in the controversy over the Bricker amendment, designed to limit the power of the president in making foreign policy and vigorously opposed by the Eisenhower administration. In response to criticism that a clause in the amendment would necessitate approval by every state for all foreign agreements, George proposed a substitute removing that requirement while mandating that all executive agreements win Senate ratification. The Eisenhower administration opposed George's version as well. In February 1954, George's bill fell one vote short of the two-thirds majority needed to pass the Senate.

For the most part, however, George served as an influential ally of the Eisenhower administration on matters of foreign policy. When Sen. WILLIAM KNOWLAND (R-Calif.) called for a blockade of mainland China in November 1954 in order to secure the release of 13 captured Americans, George endorsed the administration's refusal to take such action. After the Democrats won control of both houses in the election of 1954, George assumed the chairmanship of the Foreign Relations Committee. In January 1955, he sponsored a resolution giving the president unlimited authority to use U.S. armed forces to protect Taiwan and the Pescadores islands off China. The Senate passed the measure overwhelmingly.

Increasingly concerned about the peaceful settlement of international disputes, George spurred preparations for a four-power summit conference with his call for such a conclave during an appearance on *Meet the Press* on March 20, 1955. The White House and the State Department responded favorably to his suggestion that the summit meeting need not be put off until the Soviets made peaceful gestures in "deeds, not words," as the administration had previously demanded. The conference, involving the United States, the Soviet Union, Great Britain, and France, took place in July 1955.

In April 1955, George declared that "we ought to be willing to talk" with the Communist Chinese "because we certainly owe a high obligation to all mankind everywhere." Two months later, he proposed resumption of trade between Japan and China. Referring to complaints he had received from southern textile manufacturers about trading concessions made by the United States to Japan, he maintained that resumption of Japan-China trade would relax "cutthroat competition" against American companies.

George provided valuable service to the Eisenhower administration in the congressional battle over foreign aid in 1956. In June he led the effort in the Foreign Relations Committee to restore $1 billion cut by the House from the administration's $4.8-billion request. The committee refused to restore the total sum but did agree to put back $600 million. George then successfully steered the measure past efforts to reduce it on the Senate floor. The absence of any U.S. financial support for Egypt's Aswan Dam project was due partly to George's opposition. He based his stand on his objection to long-term aid commitments and to the possibility that the Aswan Dam would make 2 million acres available for cotton-growing, thereby cutting into U.S. cotton exports.

Republican control of the Senate in 1953–54 and George's growing preoccupation with foreign affairs meant that he had less influence on economic policy than he had enjoyed as chair of the Finance Committee. However, he continued to exert considerable influence on behalf of fiscal conservatism. In January 1953, he responded to the $78.5-billion budget submitted by the outgoing Truman administration by stating that "the principal duty of this Congress and the new administration is to see to it that the budget is cut." In March 1955, he voted against a temporary tax cut of $20 per taxpayer offered by his fellow Democrats. He was among the half-dozen southern Democrats providing the Republicans with the 50-44 margin by which the cut was rejected.

A lifelong segregationist, George opposed every civil rights measure, including antilynching bills. He was one of the leaders of the movement behind the "Southern Manifesto" of 1956. The strategists met in George's office to draft the statement, and George acted as the group's spokesman, presenting the declaration in the Senate on March 12. Signed by 19 senators and 77 representatives, the manifesto denounced the Supreme Court's decision on public school desegregation and pledged resistance to it by "all lawful means."

Facing a stiff primary challenge by white-supremacist HERMAN TALMADGE, George announced in May 1956 that he would not seek reelection. In July, in an unexpected move, he sponsored an amendment to a Social Security bill to qualify totally disabled workers for full Social Security benefits at age 50. The measure, which never would have passed without the southern conservative's surprise blessing, carried by a 47-45 vote.

In January 1957, President Eisenhower appointed George ambassador to the North Atlantic Treaty Organization. George served only briefly; he died of heart disease in Vienna, Ga. on August 4, 1957.

—MSM

Ginsberg, Allen
(1926–1997) *poet*

Born in Newark, N.J., on June 3, 1926, Ginsberg's childhood was scarred by the harrowing experience of watching his mother's psychological deterioration, first at home, then in a mental hospital. He expressed his anguish and love for her in the elegy, "Kaddish for Naomi Ginsberg" (1961). His father, Louis, was a teacher and poet of a more traditional style who was critical of Ginsberg's first attempts at poetry. The younger Ginsberg entered Columbia College in 1943 after briefly attending Montclair State College. While at Columbia, Ginsberg became good friends with the writers William S. Burroughs and JACK KEROUAC. He graduated in 1948. Ginsberg worked as a market research consultant between 1951 and 1953 while writing in his spare time.

In 1953, Ginsberg decided to move to San Francisco and devote himself completely to his poetry. Ginsberg became acquainted with such writers as Kenneth Rexroth, Michael McClure, and Gary Snyder, who shared his need to divorce himself from traditional styles and develop a new type of poetry.

The result of Ginsberg's search for a poetic voice was the long epic poem *Howl!*, one of the major literary and social documents of the 1950s. It both attacked American spiritual stagnation and affirmed personal joy. The famous opening of *Howl!*, which became Ginsberg's best-known poem, powerfully expressed the Beat perspective: "I saw the best minds of my generation destroyed by madness, starving hysterical naked,/dragging themselves through the negro streets at dawn looking for an angry fix."

The poem, with Kerouac's *On the Road*, signified the beginning of the San Francisco Renaissance and the Beat Generation, cultural and literary movements that, a decade later, powerfully influenced the counter culture of the 1960s. *On the Road* and *Howl!* seemed to galvanize the feelings of those who deplored American materialism and sought to restore a deep sense of community to their lives. Most literary reviewers scorned *Howl!*, rejecting its exuberant use of sexual and scatological language. A few applauded what they termed the important, "messianic" voice of the poem. Meanwhile, Ginsberg won a wide American audience. Lawrence Ferlinghetti published *Howl! And Other Poems* in 1956. The open celebration of homosexuality and drug use in *Howl!* led to its impoundment by U.S. Customs agents, and Ginsberg was tried on obscenity charges in 1957. After a long trial, at which a series of witnesses testified to the poem's literary merit, Judge Clayton Horn ruled that the poem met the test of "redeeming social importance."

Ginsberg wrote prolifically, and his poems appeared in both smaller and established publications during the late-1950s. He emerged as a cultural spokesman for a segment of American youth and left-oriented individuals in the 1960s. During those years, he advocated the liberalization of laws against nonaddictive drugs and proselytized for unrestricted sexual freedom. He also organized antiwar demonstrations and initiated efforts to halt ecological destruction and the spread of nuclear weapons. In 1974, Ginsberg's achievements as a poet were recognized with a National Book Award for his collection of poetry, *The Fall of America*.

From the 1960s through the 1980s, Ginsberg seemed to be in the forefront of whatever movement was fashionable. He championed the sexual revolution, the counterculture, and the antiwar movement in the 1960s. He demonstrated against the CIA and the Shah of Iran in the 1970s and protested against nuclear weapons and President Ronald Reagan in the 1980s. The publication of an anthology of his work, *Collected Poems*, in 1985 firmly established Ginsberg's reputation as a major American poet. He went on a book tour and appeared frequently on television, but instead of his familiar Beat or countercultural clothing, he wore a suit and tie. He acknowledged that his political judgments had not always been sound. "I thought," he admitted, "the North Vietnamese would be a lot better than they turned out to be." He further mused that "I shouldn't have been marching against the Shah of Iran because the mullahs have turned out to be a lot worse."

Even as he involved himself in a myriad of activities, he continued to write. Over the years, he published *Wichita Vortex Sutra* (1966), *Wales Visitation* (1967), *Don't Grow Old* (1976), *Composed on the Tongue* (1980), *Illuminated Poems* (1996), and *Luminous Dreams* (1997). Ginsberg died at his home in the East Village of Manhattan, on April 5, 1997.

—MSM

Gold, Ben

(1898–1985) *president, International Fur and Leather Workers Union of the United States and Canada*

Born in Bessarabia, Russia, on September 8, 1898, Gold immigrated to the United States in 1910 and joined the International Fur Workers Union of the United States and Canada (IFWU) two years later. He became a member of the Socialist Party in 1916. Gold joined the Communist Party at the time of its founding in 1919. He was elected manager of the IFWU's New York Joint Board in 1925. Two years later, in an effort to remove the communist influence, the American Federation of Labor (AFL) dissolved the Joint Board and expelled its leaders. However, the communists retained the loyalty of the rank-and-file fur workers. Led by Gold, the New York furriers affiliated with the communist-led Needle Trades Workers Industrial Union in 1929. When this group was disbanded in 1935, Gold and the fur workers returned to the IFWU. In 1937, Gold was elected president of the IFWU, which then left the AFL and joined the new Congress of Industrial Organizations (CIO). The IFWU merged with the National Leather Workers Association in 1939, and Gold became president of the International Fur and Leather Workers Union (IFLWU). Gold was an active and open member of the Communist Party and ran for the New York state assembly in 1931 and 1936 on the Communist ticket.

The IFLWU's opposition to the Marshall Plan and the Truman Doctrine, as well as its endorsement of Henry A. Wallace, alienated the union from Philip Murray, the president of the CIO. Murray condemned the leaders of the furriers' union at the CIO convention in October 1949. The CIO expelled the furriers and other communist-dominated unions in 1950.

Although the IFLWU easily repelled challenges to its hold on the fur trades in New York, the IFLWU decided to submit to the provisions of the Taft-Hartley Act in order to protect locals outside of New York against raids by other unions. Therefore, in 1950, the IFLWU instructed its officers to sign the noncommunist affidavits required by the Taft-Hartley Act. Gold publicly quit the party and signed the affidavit; in his statement, however, he proclaimed his continuing loyalty to the party's objectives. Two years later, he refused to tell the National Labor Relations Board (NLRB) whether his affidavit was truthful. He also refused to deny that he had supported the Communist Party after signing the affidavit. Federal authorities brought charges against Gold for lying on his noncommunist affidavit. A federal grand jury indicted him for perjury, and in April 1954, he was convicted and sentenced to one to three years in jail. The month after his conviction, he was reelected as president of the IFLWU. As a result, the NLRB prohibited the union from making use of its services in collective bargaining. Worried about the effect this ruling would have on the union, Gold resigned the presidency in October.

An equally divided U.S. Circuit Court of Appeals for the District of Columbia upheld Gold's conviction on March 9, 1956. A Supreme Court ruling, however, held that a union could not be deprived of NLRB services because a leader had falsified a noncommunist affidavit. In January 1957, the Supreme Court ordered that Gold be given a new trial because FBI agents had contacted three members of Gold's jury in relation to another investigation. In May, the Justice Department moved that the indictment against Gold be dismissed because "certain material evidence . . . [was] not available." Gold died in North Miami Beach, Fla., on July 23, 1985.

—MSM

Goldberg, Arthur J(oseph)

(1908–1990) *general counsel, Congress of Industrial Organizations; general counsel, United Steelworkers of America; secretary of labor; associate Supreme Court justice*

Born in Chicago on August 8, 1908, Goldberg was the youngest of 11 children of Russian-Jewish parents on Chicago's West Side. He graduated from a public high school at the age of 16 and attended Crane Junior College and took classes at DePaul University before enrolling in Northwestern University's law school, where he compiled the best academic record in the school's history to that point. He was editor of the law review and earned his B.S.L. (bachelor of science in law) in 1928 and J.S.D. the following year. In spite of Goldberg's stellar academic performance, Chicago's elite firms did not hire Jews. He joined Pritzger & Pritzger, a successful Chicago firm founded by highly assimilated German Jews. Although successful, he found his work there unsatisfying and in 1933 left to start his own practice. He was active in the local Civil Liberties Committee, which later became the Illinois Division of the American Civil Liberties Union. Although drawn to liberal causes, he rejected political radicalism and became an ardent supporter of Franklin D. Roosevelt and the New Deal. This led the Chicago branch of the Congress of Industrial Organizations (CIO) to ask him to represent them during a newspaper strike in 1938. The CIO sent other labor cases to Goldberg, who became well established as a labor lawyer. During World War II, he served with the Office of Strategic Services. He resumed the private practice of law in 1944.

With the cold war under way, liberals and radicals competed for control of the CIO. As the liberals gained the upper hand in 1948, the CIO ousted its general counsel, the radical Lee Pressman, and Philip Murray, president of the CIO, named Goldberg to replace him. Murray also named Goldberg general counsel for the United Steelworkers of America. Goldberg helped establish procedures by which the CIO expelled communist-dominated affiliates. In 1949, he negotiated a pension plan for the Steelworkers that served as a model for other unions. Over the next decade, he also became a leading lobbyist for organized labor. In 1955, Goldberg and J. Albert Woll, counsel for the American Federation of Labor (AFL), negotiated a merger of the AFL and CIO. The organizations agreed to retain previous organizing jurisdictions for each member union and to recognize the equal legitimacy of craft and industrial unions. A joint convention in December formally proclaimed the merger. Although Goldberg wanted the job of AFL-CIO general counsel, some leaders of the combined unions did not have full confidence in him, and he was made special counsel instead. He also served as general counsel for the AFL-CIO's Industrial Union Department.

During 1957 and 1958, the Senate Select Committee on Improper Activities in the Labor or Management Field, chaired by Sen. JOHN MCCLELLAN (D-Ark.), investigated corruption in organized labor. Goldberg helped formulate the AFL-CIO's ethical practices code, which led to the expulsion of the Teamsters and other scandal-ridden unions. In the course of the McClellan committee's work, Goldberg worked closely with Sen. JOHN F. KENNEDY (D-Mass.) in crafting moderate labor reform legislation that provided for full public disclosure of union finances. He also attempted to forestall the more extensive measures that were ultimately included in the Landrum-Griffin Act, including a ban on "hot cargo" contracts (under which union members were allowed to refuse to work with non-union materials), prohibition of secondary boycotts, restrictions on picketing, and expanded federal regulation of internal union affairs.

Throughout the 1950s, Goldberg continued to represent the United Steelworkers. Murray's successor as the union's president, DAVID MCDONALD, had neither the ability nor the skill to lead a large industrial union. He handled public relations and left important decisions to Goldberg. It was Goldberg who conducted the negotiations during a 116-day steel strike in 1959 and won important concessions from the industry on wages and working conditions. The new contract, signed in January 1960, also included Goldberg's proposal for a Human Relations Committee, composed of representatives of the union, the industry, and the public, that was intended to prevent future strikes.

Goldberg played a leading role in mobilizing labor behind Kennedy's campaign for the Democratic nomination. In December 1960, the president-elect chose Goldberg as his secretary of labor. The president of the AFL-CIO, GEORGE MEANY, had nominated five elected union officials for the post. Kennedy picked Goldberg because he was "from the unions but not of them" and could therefore be relied on to enforce the reform provisions of the Landrum-Griffin Act.

As secretary of labor, Goldberg intervened frequently in labor-management disputes to secure noninflationary wage settlements. He also worked to provide federal support for public-employee unionism and to aid the growth of unions in Latin America. As a result of his support for wage restraints, Goldberg's relations with organized labor began to deteriorate. Partly for this reason, Kennedy nominated him to a seat on the Supreme Court in 1962 upon the retirement of FELIX FRANKFURTER. On the Court, Goldberg consistently supported civil rights and the expansion of legal protections for criminal defendants and suspects. Perhaps his best-known opinion was *Escobedo v. Illinois* (1964), in which the Court overturned a conviction for murder on the ground that police had continued questioning a suspect and prevented him from speaking to his lawyer after he had repeatedly requested to do so. Goldberg also voted for legislative reapportionment. He spent only 34 months on the bench, during which time he continued to advise presidents Kennedy and LYNDON B. JOHNSON on national labor problems. In July 1965, Johnson persuaded a reluctant Goldberg to leave the Court to become ambassador to the United Nations. Goldberg hoped to negotiate a settlement to the Vietnam War, but Johnson ignored Goldberg's advice to end escalation of the war and seek a negotiated peace. Frustrated with his limited influence, Goldberg resigned in 1968 and resumed the practice of law with the New York firm of Paul, Weiss, Goldberg, Rifkind, Wharton & Garrison. He worked for HUBERT HUMPHREY's campaign for the presidency in 1968 and spoke out in opposition to American policy in Vietnam. Goldberg ran as the Democratic candidate for governor of New York in 1970. After losing the race by a lopsided margin to the incumbent, NELSON A. ROCKEFELLER, Goldberg returned to Washington, D.C., and practiced law until his death there on January 19, 1990.

—MSM

Goldfine, Bernard

(ca. 1889–1967) *businessman*

Born in the Russian town of Avanta in about 1889, Goldfine immigrated to the United States with his parents at the age of eight. He dropped out of high school after one year to work in his father's junk business. At the age of 19, he and a friend started the Strathmore Woolen Company in Boston. They bought and sold woolen remnants and prospered by supplying material for military uniforms during World War I. By the time of the Great Depression, Goldfine owned textile mills in four New England states and had substantial real estate holdings. The headquarters of his empire was in Lebanon, N.H. During the 1930s, he expanded his holdings by buying businesses and land at depressed prices. He also cultivated close relationships with the governors of New England states and with Boston's mayor, James M. Curley. Goldfine loved to demonstrate his connections and his political clout.

His love for politics and publicity led to the downfall of SHERMAN ADAMS, Eisenhower's chief of staff. In 1958, the Legislative Oversight Subcommittee of the House Interstate and Foreign Commerce Committee held hearings that produced evidence that Adams had accepted favors from Goldfine and had intervened with federal agencies on Goldfine's behalf. In 1953, the Federal Trade Commission (FTC) accused Goldfine's textile companies of mislabeling their products. Goldfine told Adams about the problem, and Adams called Edward F. Howrey, the chairman of the FTC. Howrey requested a full report on the matter, which he forwarded to Adams, who passed it on to Goldfine. Adams's secretary inquired about the matter a month later and learned that the case had been closed. The FTC brought similar charges the following year, and Adams arranged for Goldfine to meet with Howrey. Although some lawyers in the FTC had recommended a civil suit against Goldfine, the agency settled for a cease-and-desist order in 1957. Adams also inquired about Goldfine's problems with the Securities and Exchange Commission, which was investigating the East Boston Company, one of Goldfine's holdings, for failing to file annual financial reports. No further actions against Goldfine were taken. The Legislative Oversight Subcommittee also found that Goldfine had given Adams a vicuña coat and an oriental rug valued at $2,400. Goldfine had also paid $1,642.28 for hotel rooms used by Adams and members of his family.

Adams denied that Goldfine had received special treatment. He and Goldfine acknowledged the

gifts but described them as gifts given by one friend to another. At his own request, Adams appeared before the committee on June 17 and acknowledged having made mistakes in judgment, but he denied ever having used his position to influence government agencies. Goldfine testified before the subcommittee in July. The gregarious Goldfine said that he had declared the gifts to Adams and the hotel bills as business expenses on his tax returns but that he expected no favors in return. It turned out that Goldfine had also paid hotel bills for Sens. NORRIS COTTON (R-N.H.), STYLES BRIDGES (R-N.H.), and Frederick Payne (R-Maine). In addition, the textile manufacturer had also sent checks at Christmas "to some of the poor workers" in government. Goldfine refused to answer 22 questions from the subcommittee about his financial affairs and was cited for contempt of Congress. After Payne lost his bid for reelection in September, political pressure mounted, and Eisenhower asked Adams to resign.

In December 1958, Goldfine refused to submit records for an investigation of his taxes and was cited for contempt of court. He received a three-month sentence, which he served in 1960. For his contempt of Congress, Goldfine paid a fine and was given a suspended one-year sentence in 1959. While in prison in 1960, he was charged with evading over $790,000 in federal income taxes between 1953 and 1957. Lawyers questioned his mental competency to stand trial, and he was placed under psychiatric observation until he was determined fit. Goldfine pleaded guilty in 1961 to tax evasion and received a sentence of a year and a day in prison and a fine of $110,000. He suffered a slight stroke and was released in 1962, after serving seven and one-half months of his sentence. Goldfine settled federal tax claims of $3.5 million against himself and $6.8 million against his wife. He retired to his home in Chestnut Hill, Mass., and died in Boston on September 21, 1967.

—MSM

Goldwater, Barry M(orris)
(1909–1998) *U.S. senator*
Goldwater was born in Phoenix, Ariz., on January 1, 1909. His grandfather, a Jewish immigrant from an area of Poland then ruled by Russia, established a

mercantile store in Prescott, Ariz. Goldwater's father opened a branch of the family business in Phoenix. Although his father's side of the family was Jewish, Goldwater was raised in the Episcopalian faith of his mother. After a disastrous freshman year in high school, his parents sent him to Staunton Military Academy in Virginia, where he thrived on the rigorous discipline and graduated in the top half of his class. The faculty voted him best all-around cadet, which assured him an appointment to West Point. His mother, however, wanted him closer to home because his father was in poor health. Goldwater enrolled at the University of Arizona in the fall of 1928, but he left college the following spring, soon after his father died, and went to work in the family department store. He joined several service organizations and, in 1930, the officers reserve corps. In 1936, he and his brother assumed control of the family business. During World War II, Goldwater, who had learned to fly in 1930, served in the army air corps. Age and poor eyesight disqualified him as a combat pilot, but he trained pilots, supervised construction, and requisitioned supplies. When the shortage of pilots led to the creation of the Air Transport Command to ferry aircraft and supplies to war zones, Goldwater qualified and transferred to it. At the end of the war, he left the army as a lieutenant colonel. After the war, he founded the Arizona Air National Guard and eventually rose to the rank of major general in the air force reserve. He also became involved in the municipal reform movement in Phoenix and ran for city council in 1949. Goldwater won a seat and, in office, worked tirelessly to cut municipal spending. In 1952, he challenged Ernest W. McFarland, the Democratic incumbent, for a seat in the U.S. Senate. Although considered a long shot, Goldwater won by roughly 7,000 votes.

In the Senate, Goldwater aggressively supported limiting the power and spending of the federal government and sought to maintain the maximum freedom for the individual. He opposed high taxes, unbalanced budgets, agricultural price supports, federal aid to education, federal minimum wage laws, and the concentration of power in organized labor. In short, he resisted anything he thought threatened individualism or free enterprise. He supported increasing rights for women and giv-

ing offshore oil reserves to the states. In foreign policy, he advocated an aggressively anticommunist stance and urged retaliation against nations that traded with Communist China. He also argued for a reduction of foreign aid.

When he arrived in the Senate, ROBERT TAFT (R-Ohio) assigned him to the Banking and Currency and the Labor and Public Welfare Committees. The assignments chagrined the new senator from Arizona, who wanted the Armed Services and Interior Committees. In some regards, Goldwater was not particularly suited to the Senate. The legislative process seemed to bore him. He was not a skilled debater, and he refused to compromise his positions. However, he was personable, good-looking, vigorous, and eminently quotable. His image provided a refreshing contrast with that of the stuffy Taft. Since Goldwater's talents best equipped him to serve as a salesman for conservatism, his colleagues put him on the Republican Senate Campaign Committee.

Early in his first term, Goldwater clearly aligned himself with the conservative wing of the Republican party; nonetheless, he frequently found himself in accord with the administration. He supported Sen. JOSEPH R. MCCARTHY's (R-Wis.) crusade against communists in government and was one of 22 senators who voted against condemning McCarthy in December 1954. At the same time, he rejected McCarthy's accusations that Eisenhower was a communist appeaser. Moreover, there were a number of issues on which he clearly sided with the administration. His attack in 1953 on wage, rent, and price controls brought praise from Eisenhower. Goldwater also voted for an administration proposal extending Social Security coverage and benefits as well as one increasing the minimum wage. Goldwater took the lead in supporting the administration's "termination" policy, intended to eliminate the dependence of Native American tribes on the federal government and ultimately to abolish reservations. When it came to defense policy, Goldwater backed the New Look and its greater reliance on air power and the nuclear deterrent.

An indication of Goldwater's rising status in the party came in 1955, when Republican senators elected him chair of the Senate Republican Campaign Committee. The position greatly increased his national visibility, and he emerged as a leading voice for conservatism. During the 84th Congress in 1955–56, Goldwater supported the administration 66 percent of the time, slightly less frequently than the average Republican senator. Although he did not join some conservatives in publicly attacking the administration, he became increasingly impatient with its continuation of New Deal programs. Despite the growing differences between himself and Eisenhower, Goldwater campaigned for the president's reelection in 1956.

However, Goldwater began to challenge the administration in 1957. He opposed Eisenhower's request for a congressional resolution authorizing the president to send American forces to the Middle East to resist communist aggression. Goldwater openly rebelled against Eisenhower's budget for 1958, the largest peacetime budget request to that time. Speaking on the Senate floor, he attacked the budget as a "betrayal of the people's trust," not to mention campaign pledges and Republican Party principles. He accused the administration of following the course of Truman's administration and "demonstrating tendencies to bow to the siren song of socialism."

During the 1950s, Goldwater devoted a good deal of attention to his work on the Labor and Public Welfare Committee. An ardent foe of labor unions, he supported tightened federal and state control of their activities and the right of workers to elect not to join a union. He opposed organized labor's intervention in the political process. These positions led to clashes with WALTER REUTHER, president of the United Automobile Workers (UAW), and other union leaders. All of this came to national attention when Goldwater was named to the Senate Select Committee on Improper Activities in the Labor Management Field, chaired by JOHN McCLELLAN (D-Ark.). Created in 1957, the committee was charged to investigate corruption in labor unions. Over the objections of Goldwater and the Republican minority, the probe focused primarily on the Teamsters Union. Goldwater condemned the committee counsel, ROBERT F. KENNEDY, for refusing to investigate the UAW and Reuther, a staunch Democratic supporter, with equal vigor. At a Republican fund-raising dinner in 1957, Goldwater attacked Reuther and the UAW's political war chest as "more dangerous than Soviet Russia."

Reuther called the senator from Arizona "mentally unbalanced" and "this country's number-one political fanatic, peddler of class hatred, and union hater." The feud continued through Goldwater's campaign for reelection in 1958. McFarland, then governor of Arizona, looked forward confidently to a rematch with Goldwater. Organized labor poured resources into the campaign to defeat Goldwater, whose campaign stressed illicit union support for his opponent and won 56.1 percent of the vote.

In 1959, two members of the McClellan committee, JOHN KENNEDY (D-Mass.) and SAM ERVIN (D-N.C.), offered a bill that mandated secret ballots in union elections and full disclosure of financial transactions. Goldwater dismissed the measure as a "pantywaist bill." He called for tougher penalties for corrupt practices and a ban on unions coercing an employer to refuse to do business with another employer. Goldwater was the lone senator to vote against the Kennedy-Ervin bill. The House, however, rejected it in favor of a stronger substitute introduced by ROBERT GRIFFIN (R-Mich.) and PHILIP LANDRUM (D-Ga.). Goldwater supported the Landrum-Griffin bill, which became law in 1959.

Goldwater was reelected chair of the Republican Senate Campaign Committee in 1959 and stumped the country speaking for conservatism. He urged Republicans to return to the principles of Taft, a clear swipe at the Eisenhower administration. Some conservatives began to think about Goldwater as a candidate for president. Clarence Manion, the dean of Notre Dame's law school and a right-wing activist, urged Goldwater to write a book. When Goldwater demurred because he was not a writer, Manion arranged for L. Brent Bozell, an editor for WILLIAM F. BUCKLEY's *National Review* and Buckley's brother-in-law, to act as ghostwriter. Bozell pieced together the book from Goldwater's speeches, some of which Bozell had written. *The Conscience of a Conservative* came out in March 1960 and unexpectedly became a best seller. The book advocated "achieving the maximum amount of freedom for individuals that is consistent with the maintenance of social order." "Freedom for farmers" meant ending subsidies and price supports. "Freedom for labor" would be achieved by outlawing the closed shop and passing right-to-work laws. The book attacked the federal government as "a Leviathan, a vast national authority out of touch with the people, and out of their control" and championed states' rights as a "bulwark against the encroachments of individual freedom by Big Government." It demanded reductions in the federal bureaucracy and in federal spending, denounced the income tax as "confiscatory," and called for eliminating federal welfare programs, federal aid to education, and federal housing programs. Some of Goldwater's favorite and most frequently used lines appeared in the book: "I have little interest in streamlining government or in making it more efficient, for I mean to reduce its size. . . . My aim is not to pass laws, but to repeal them."

Civil rights posed an interesting problem. Goldwater distinguished civil rights from "human" or "natural" rights. *The Conscience of a Conservative* held that the Constitution protected only black voting rights, the right to contract, and the right to property. Further, the federal government had no constitutional authority to require states to "maintain racially mixed schools," because it had no constitutional power to interfere in education. Goldwater acknowledged that he agreed with the objectives of the *Brown* decision: "I believe that it *is* both wise and just for negro [sic] children to attend the same schools as whites, and that to deny them this opportunity carries with it strong implications of inferiority." However, he continued, "I am not prepared to impose that judgment . . . on the people of Mississippi or South Carolina." This position was no sophistry. Goldwater had been one of the first white merchants in Phoenix to employ African Americans, and he integrated the Arizona Air National Guard. A member of the Tucson chapter of the NAACP, he supported and contributed money to a lawsuit that successfully challenged de jure segregation in Phoenix's public schools. He also played an instrumental role in ending segregation in the city's restaurants. In spite of those beliefs, he voted for restrictive amendments to the Civil Rights Act of 1957.

By the time of the Republican National Convention in 1960, Goldwater had emerged as the recognized leader of the party's conservative wing. At the convention, he led an attack by conservatives on the compromise platform agreed to before the convention by Vice President RICHARD M. NIXON and New York's liberal governor, NELSON A. ROCKEFELLER. As a protest against Nixon's accommodation with Rockefeller, some enraged conservative delegates nominated Goldwater for president. However, Goldwater gave a speech asking that his name be withdrawn and calling for party unity. Nevertheless, he received 10 votes from the Louisiana delegation on the first ballot.

During the 1960s, Goldwater dominated the conservative wing of the Republican Party. His blunt statement of his positions thrilled conservatives and alarmed opponents. In an interview in 1963, he said, "You know, I think we ought to sell the TVA [Tennessee Valley Authority]." During the same interview, he casually proposed giving NATO commanders authority to use nuclear weapons. Goldwater later admitted that "there are words of mine floating around in the air that I would like to reach up and eat." Perhaps he had in mind a news conference in 1961 in which he said, "Sometimes I think this country would be better off if we could just saw off the Eastern Seaboard and let it float out to sea." Although he believed that segregation was morally wrong and favored withholding federal funds from public works projects in states that practiced discrimination, he opposed the Civil Rights Act of 1964 as a violation of states' rights and the individual's right to discriminate.

After a bitter struggle in which his opponents, particularly Rockefeller, portrayed him as a dangerous extremist, Goldwater captured the Republican nomination in 1964. Goldwater promised "a choice, not an echo." At the convention, his partisans booed and hooted Rockefeller's speech. Goldwater further alienated moderates in the party with his own acceptance speech, in which he famously declared that "extremism in defense of liberty is no vice and . . . moderation in the pursuit of justice is no virtue." In the general election, LYNDON JOHNSON overwhelmed Goldwater, who carried only six states and 36 percent of the popular vote.

Goldwater won election to the Senate again in 1968. He would win reelection in 1974 and 1980. During the Watergate crisis, he played a crucial role in persuading President Nixon to resign. Long before his retirement, Goldwater had come to be regarded as a respected elder statesman of his party.

He retired as chair of the Senate Armed Services Committee and could claim the lion's share of responsibility for the passage of the Defense Department Reorganization Act of 1986, which streamlined command channels at the Pentagon. Always true to his libertarian principles, Goldwater angered the New Right in the 1980s with his defense of a woman's right to choose an abortion and gay rights. In addition, he opposed efforts of disgruntled conservatives to limit the power of the courts.

Goldwater chose not to seek reelection in 1986 and retired to his home in Paradise Valley, a suburb of Phoenix. He suffered a major stroke in 1996 and died at home on May 29, 1998.

—MSM

Goodpaster, Andrew J(ackson)
(1915–2005) *White House staff secretary*

Goodpaster was born in Granite City, Ill., on February 12, 1915. After attending McKendree College in Lebanon, Ill., for two years, Goodpaster transferred to the U.S. Military Academy at West Point, from which he graduated second in his class in 1939. He served in various engineering assignments before World War II and then saw combat in North Africa and Italy as commander of the 48th Engineer Batallion.

Goodpaster was attached to the general staff of the War Department from 1944 to 1947 and then went to Princeton University, where he earned an M.A. in engineering in 1948 and a Ph.D. in international relations in 1950. He was the army's representative on the Joint Advanced Study Committee of the Joint Chiefs of Staff in 1950. Six months later, Goodpaster went to Europe as an aide to Gen. DWIGHT D. EISENHOWER in organizing the military forces of the North Atlantic Treaty Organization (NATO). He also worked with W. AVERELL HARRIMAN in developing a statement of political aims for NATO. In 1954, he took over the post of U.S. district engineer in San Francisco.

In September 1954, President Eisenhower appointed Col. Goodpaster White House staff secretary. His duties consisted of clearing all communications to the president and coordinating cabinet operations. He also served as liaison between the White House and the various departments and agencies concerned with defense and national security matters. Goodpaster's most important duty was handling all correspondence dealing with national security and supervising day-to-day operations of the National Security Council.

Eisenhower had enormous admiration for Goodpaster and absolute confidence in him. The president depended on his aides to provide accurate information, and Goodpaster's calm efficiency, remarkable intelligence, and ability to keep a confidence ideally suited him to Eisenhower's purposes. Goodpaster became the aide on whom Eisenhower relied most, and he was at the president's side constantly during working hours.

During the Quemoy and Matsu crisis of 1954–55, Goodpaster participated in meetings to evaluate the ability of the Nationalist Chinese to defend the offshore islands. When Eisenhower was not satisfied with the intelligence he was receiving, he sent Goodpaster to confer with the commander in chief of the Pacific Fleet. In July 1955, Goodpaster was Eisenhower's personal assistant at the Geneva summit.

The following year, Goodpaster served as liaison between the Pentagon, the Central Intelligence Agency, and the White House during the Suez Crisis. He also kept a close record of intelligence reports during the U.S. military action in Lebanon in 1958.

After the president was stricken with a heart attack in September 1955, his secretary reduced the amount of Eisenhower's work by delaying action on some measures and taking action on some "by direction of the President." When the president suffered a mild stroke in 1957, Goodpaster kept the White House running smoothly while the chief executive recovered.

Following the resignation of SHERMAN ADAMS in September 1958, Goodpaster's authority increased. All matters relating to the Defense and State Departments were funneled through either Goodpaster or Gordon Gray, the special assistant for national security affairs. Thus, in May 1960, it was Goodpaster who first brought Eisenhower the news of the downing of the U-2 spy plane over the Soviet Union.

Goodpaster remained in the White House during the early part of 1961 to aid JOHN F. KENNEDY in his transition to office. He then served with the army in Europe and in 1962 returned to Washington as special assistant to Gen. Maxwell Taylor. In 1967, he became senior U.S. Army member of the UN Military Staff Committee and directed special studies in the office of the Army Chief of Staff. From July 1967 to June 1968, he served as commandant of the National War College. Goodpaster was promoted to general in 1968. He served as deputy commander of U.S. forces in Vietnam from 1968 to 1969. At the request of president-elect Richard M. Nixon, President Lyndon B. Johnson called Goodpaster to Washington in December 1968 to help with the presidential transition. In March 1969, Goodpaster became Supreme Allied Commander of NATO forces in Europe and commander in chief of U.S. military forces in Europe. Goodpaster retired from the army in 1974 and became a senior fellow in security and strategic studies at the Woodrow Wilson International Center for Scholars. He was a founder of the Committee on the Present Danger, organized to put forward the idea that the military threat posed by the Soviet Union had been underestimated and that the United States needed to strengthen its defensive capabilities. In 1977, President Jimmy Carter called Goodpaster out of retirement to serve as commandant of West Point in the aftermath of a cheating scandal. Goodpaster served as commandant until 1981. Carter also asked Goodpaster to serve as a special representative to foreign governments following the Soviet invasion of Afghanistan. After that, Goodpaster became a senior fellow at the Eisenhower World Affairs Institute. He remained active until the end of his life and was working on his memoirs at the time of his death from prostate cancer on May 16, 2005, in Washington, D.C.

—MSM

Gordon, Thomas S(ylvy)
(1893–1959) *U.S. congressman; chairman, Foreign Affairs Committee*

Gordon was born in Chicago on December 17, 1893. He attended parochial schools and graduated from Saint Stanislaus College in 1912. After working in banking from 1916 to 1920, Gordon began working for *Dziennik Chicagoski*, a Polish language newspaper, in 1921. He started out as a clerk and advanced to office manager. His job with the newspaper helped him enter Democratic politics. While maintaining his association with the paper, he served as commissioner of Chicago West Parks from 1933 to 1936 and of public vehicle licenses from 1936 to 1939. Gordon was elected city treasurer in 1939 and won election to Congress in 1942 from Chicago's predominantly Polish eighth district. As a freshman, he was assigned to the Foreign Affairs Committee. He supported President Harry S. Truman's foreign policies and domestic welfare programs.

Gordon generally voted with the liberal Democrats in the House during the Eisenhower administration. In 1955, he supported a bill to restore rigid farm price supports and opposed a measure exempting producers of natural gas from federal public utility regulation under the Natural Gas Act. Two years later, Gordon was among 80 Democratic liberals backing a comprehensive legislative program that called, among other things, for civil rights measures, repeal of the Taft-Hartley Act, aid to depressed areas, and revision of immigration and naturalization standards to eliminate the national origins system.

In 1957, Gordon became chair of the Foreign Affairs Committee. During his first month in that post, he backed the administration's draft of the Eisenhower Doctrine for the Middle East. On January 5, 1957, President Eisenhower addressed a joint session of Congress to ask for authority to use U.S. armed forces to protect the Middle East from communist aggression. Minutes after the address, Gordon introduced a joint resolution authorizing the president to use U.S. forces "as he deems necessary to secure and protect the territorial integrity and political independence" of Middle East nations against countries "controlled by international communism." The House passed this administration-initiated version of the doctrine, but the Senate eliminated the clause permitting the president to use troops "as he deems necessary" and stated only that the United States was "prepared to use Armed Forces" if the president "determines the necessity." Gordon opposed the Senate alteration but preferred accepting its version to further debate. The House adopted the upper chamber's resolution.

Gordon backed the Mutual Security Act of 1957, which authorized over $3.3 billion in military and economic foreign aid for fiscal 1958. It introduced a new approach to foreign economic assistance, eliminating the grants-in-aid program and authorizing a new $500-million Development Loan Fund. Gordon defended the change against charges that the loans would really be grants because they could be repaid in foreign currencies. He criticized those who opposed foreign aid in all forms, stating that a "fortress America" could not survive economically.

Gordon stepped down as chairman of the Foreign Affairs Committee in February 1958 because of ill health. He died in Chicago of heart disease on January 22, 1959.

—MLL

Gore, Albert A(rnold)

(1907–1998) *U.S. senator*

Born in Granville, Tenn., on December 27, 1907, Albert Gore attended a one-room school and worked his way through Middle Tennessee State Teachers College. He ran unsuccessfully for superintendent of schools in Smith County, Tenn., in 1930 and went to work on his father's farm. When the man who defeated him died, Gore was chosen to fill the term. He took night classes in law at the YMCA in Nashville and received a law degree in 1936. Gore won election to Congress in 1938 as a Democrat and a strong supporter of the New Deal. In his first speech, however, he opposed the Roosevelt administration and the Democratic leadership by speaking against expanding the borrowing authority of the United States Housing Authority. In general, though, he supported the domestic and foreign policies of the Roosevelt and Truman administrations. In 1952, he challenged the aged Sen. Kenneth McKellar, chair of the Senate Appropriations Committee, who represented Tennessee's once-powerful Crump machine, in the Democratic primary. In a campaign that focused on his support for liberal economic policies and the Tennessee Valley Authority (TVA) as well his opponent's advanced age, Gore defeated McKellar and went on to win the general election in November.

Gore's florid style of speaking and his distinguished bearing suited him well for the Senate. In the upper house, he worked energetically on behalf of public power, highway construction, and tax reform. During the Eisenhower administration, his Senate votes paralleled the position of the liberal Americans for Democratic Action 70 percent of the time.

Gore played an important role in the controversial Dixon-Yates affair of 1954–55. The TVA proposed building a new steam plant at Fulton, Tenn., to supply power to the city of Memphis. The consumption of TVA power by the Atomic Energy Commission's (AEC) installations at Paduca meant that the city of Memphis would face a shortage of electricity within four years. Eisenhower, who preferred private development of power, could not see the justification for the federal government to pay for a plant to supply power to a particular city. He ordered JOSEPH DODGE, the director of the Bureau of the Budget, and LEWIS L. STRAUSS, chairman of the AEC, to explore the possibilities of having private industry build the plant. EDGAR H. DIXON, president of Middle South Utilities, and EUGENE YATES, chairman of the board of the Southern Company, organized the Mississippi Valley Generating Company to build a plant that would supply power to the TVA to replace the power the TVA sold to the AEC. The Dixon-Yates proposal was considered acceptable by the AEC, TVA, and Bureau of the Budget, and, upon the recommendation of the Bureau of the Budget, Eisenhower approved it.

Gore spearheaded the vocal Democratic efforts to cancel the contract. In November 1954, he charged that it "reeks of government subsidy," that there "is no private enterprise in it," and that Dixon-Yates's profits were "practically guaranteed" at an unreasonably high level. He also played up a conflict of interest on the part of a consultant to the Budget Bureau who recommended the contract. In January 1955, Gore and the other nine Democrats on the Joint Atomic Energy Committee urged that the contract be rejected as "not in the public interest." The AEC went ahead with the Dixon-Yates contract. Ultimately, the city of Memphis decided to build its own plant, which enabled Eisenhower to cancel the Dixon-Yates contract and thus avoid a continuing controversy.

Gore played a significant role in guiding the Federal-Aid Highway Act of 1956 and the Highway

Revenue Act of 1956 through the Senate. In 1955, the Eisenhower administration recommended construction of an interstate highway system and proposed financing the system through the sale of bonds. Sen. HARRY BYRD (D-Va.) opposed the plan, which, he declared, would "wreck our fiscal budget system." Byrd wanted to allow receipts from the federal gasoline tax to accumulate until there was enough money to pay for the roads. In an effort to find common ground, Gore crafted a bill calling for the Bureau of Public Roads to spend $10 billion over five years on an interstate highway system. The federal government would bear 75 percent of the cost of construction. The bill funded only a third of the program and required the Bureau of Public Roads to return to Congress for annual appropriations. Eisenhower seemed likely to oppose Gore's version, and Rep. George Hyde Fallon (D-Md.) drafted a plan that kept the general provisions of Gore's bill but extended the period through 1968 and paid for construction of the system by raising taxes on gasoline, diesel fuel, trucks, trailers, buses, and tires. Fallon's bill failed, but it passed the following year, and Gore introduced a similar bill in the Senate. After the conference committee reconciled the two bills, both houses passed the conference bill on June 25. The Federal-Aid Highway Act of 1956 authorized $25 billion over 12 years for the construction of a national system of interstate and defense highways; created a Highway Trust Fund, supported by increasing the federal tax on gas, diesel fuel, trucks, buses, and tires; and set the federal responsibility at 90 percent of the cost.

Gore did not always side with liberals. He called for the use of nuclear weapons in Korea; and, although moderate compared to those of most of his southern colleagues, his record on civil rights issues was mixed. In 1956, Gore, LYNDON JOHNSON (D-Tex.), and ESTES KEFAUVER (D-Tenn.) were the only senators from the old Confederate states who refused to sign the Southern Manifesto, which advocated resistance by all legal means to desegregation. Gore called it "a dangerous, deceptive propaganda move which encouraged southerners to defy the Government and to disobey its laws." Although he voted for the Civil Rights Act of 1957, Gore also voted for amendments that effectively emasculated the bill. He voted to eliminate a provision that would have

authorized the Justice Department to file civil suits to desegregate and voted to give jury trials to those who violated court orders protecting black voting rights. He also voted against attempts to amend the Senate's Rule 22, which required a two-thirds vote to end debate and allowed southerners to block civil rights legislation by filibustering.

Along with Sen. PAUL DOUGLAS (D-Ill.), Gore was the most persistent Senate advocate of tax reform. In 1957, he moved from the Public Works Committee to the tax-writing Finance Committee, where he and Douglas waged a usually futile struggle to close loopholes favoring the rich and corporations. Among the tax preferences they fought unsuccessfully to reduce or eliminate were the 27½ percent oil depletion allowance, the dividend credit, the foreign tax credit, and stock option abuses. In addition, they sought to institute withholding taxes at the source of interest and dividend income. Gore also frequently denounced the "tight money" policies of the Federal Reserve Board and strenuously opposed the Eisenhower administration's effort in 1959–60 to remove the 4½ percent interest rate ceiling on government bonds. He contended that higher interest rates only hurt consumers and enriched bankers.

A member of the Foreign Relations Committee, Gore expounded the liberal internationalism of his hero, Cordell Hull. Like Hull, he was a strong advocate of reciprocal trade agreements. He supported foreign aid and generally backed the foreign policy of the Eisenhower administration. In November 1958, Gore proposed that the United States suspend all nuclear tests for three years. As a delegate to the disarmament conferences of the late Eisenhower and early Kennedy years, he helped negotiate the limited nuclear test ban treaty, finally signed and ratified in 1963.

Gore's maverick bent and crusading fervor, particularly his attacks on the tax system, often brought him into conflict with Majority Leader Lyndon Johnson. At the Democratic caucus in January 1960, he led an abortive revolt against Johnson's autocratic powers. Charging that party identity had been blurred by the leadership's willingness to compromise with the Eisenhower administration, he proposed that the Democratic caucus instead of the majority leader choose Democratic Policy

Committee members and that the committee actually make policy instead of merely scheduling legislation. The caucus rejected Gore's motion by a 51-12 vote. Johnson did agree, however, to Sen. WILLIAM PROXMIRE's (D-Wis.) demand to hold periodic caucuses to discuss policy positions before bills came up on the floor.

Gore was a candidate for the vice presidential nomination in 1956 and 1960. In 1956, he finished third in the balloting behind Kefauver and Sen. JOHN F. KENNEDY (D-Mass.) before throwing his support to Kefauver. He was a hopeful again in 1960, but Kennedy chose Johnson instead as his running mate. Gore won reelection in 1958 against a white, supremacist challenge. While running for reelection in 1964, Gore voted against the Civil Rights Act of 1964, something he later said he regretted. Gore won reelection and became an outspoken critic of the war in Vietnam. He opposed RICHARD M. NIXON's nominations of CLEMENT F. HAYNSWORTH and G. Harold Carswell to the Supreme Court. His positions on school busing and the war became issues during his unsuccessful campaign for a fourth term in 1970. After losing to Rep. William E. Brock III (R-Tenn.), Gore returned to Tennessee, where he ran a profitable cattle-breeding farm and served on a number of corporate boards. He died in Carthage, Tenn., on December 5, 1998.

—MSM

Graham, Billy (William) (Franklin)
(1918–   ) *evangelist*

A descendant of pre-Revolutionary Scotch-Irish pioneers, Graham, was born near Charlotte, N.C., on November 7, 1918. He grew up on his father's farm near Charlotte, and, at the age of 16, experienced a religious conversion. In 1936, he enrolled at Bob Jones College, a fundamentalist school in Cleveland, Tenn. Uncomfortable with campus life at Bob Jones, Graham transferred to the Florida Bible Institute (later Trinity College), from which he graduated in 1940 with a Bachelor of Theology. While there, he was baptized at a Baptist church and began a lifelong membership in the Southern Baptist Convention. Ordained a Baptist minister in 1939, he began preaching on street corners and at rescue missions. Graham attended Wheaton College in Wheaton, Ill., from 1940 to 1943 and graduated with a B.A. in anthropology. Upon graduating, he took a pastorate at the Baptist church in Western Springs, a suburb of Chicago. While at Western Springs, he took over a weekly religious radio program, *Songs in the Night*, from another local pastor.

During World War II, fundamentalists staged a series of religious revivals. Graham traveled the country conducting Christian rallies. Youth for Christ, an organization that grew out of the rallies, was founded in 1945, and Graham became its vice president and first full-time evangelist. For the next several years, he spoke at rallies and organized Youth for Christ chapters throughout the United States, Canada, and Europe. He began to hold evangelistic rallies on his own and in 1948 resigned from the staff of Youth for Christ. Graham also became president of Northwestern Schools in Minneapolis in 1947, a position he held until 1951.

Already well known within the evangelical and fundamentalist communities, Graham came to national prominence in 1949 when he led a spectacular series of revival meetings in Los Angeles. Graham's success at winning converts drew the attention of William Randolph Hearst, who ordered his publications to "puff Graham." Successful campaigns in Boston and South Carolina led to coverage in *Time* and *Life* magazines. Graham's preaching connected popular anxieties about nuclear destruction with Biblical warnings of judgment for sin. His sermons often emphasized the determination of the Soviet Union to conquer the world for communism and atheism. He preached that the millennium was near and sometimes that it would come only after a devastating war with the Soviet Union. Americans, he taught, would emerge relatively unscathed from World War III if they adopted Christianity and were "born again." Although he stayed away from party politics, Graham preached often about the threat of domestic communist subversion and the need for traditional American values. Moreover, he urged evangelicals to compete with other organized groups for political influence.

Throughout the 1950s, Graham held evangelical campaigns he called "crusades" in all major U.S. cities as well as in Africa, Asia, South America, and Europe. Perhaps the most impressive were crusades in London in 1954 and New York in 1957. The

New York crusade marked a turning point for Graham. Up to that point, his revivals had been sponsored by fundamentalists; in New York, he accepted sponsorship of the local council of churches, which included Protestant liberals. It seemed a sign that Graham was moving toward the ecclesiastical center, and this led to a break with some more militant fundamentalists. In addition to the rallies, Graham had a weekly radio program, *The Hour of Decision*, and, for three years, a television show by the same name. As his varied activities became more complex, he incorporated the Billy Graham Evangelistic Association (BGEA) to run his ministry. BGEA published periodicals and books, released phonograph records, and acquired a movie production company. Edited tapes of his crusades became widely watched television specials.

Graham professed political neutrality during the campaign of 1952, but became a strong supporter of Eisenhower after the election. Secretary of State JOHN FOSTER DULLES endorsed Graham's world tours in 1954 and 1956. After his trip to India in 1956, Graham visited Eisenhower to inform him about the trip. Graham supported desegregation but favored a gradual process. In the early 1950s, he ordered that his rallies be desegregated and that his staff hire African Americans. In 1956 Eisenhower suggested that Graham use his influence with Protestant ministers to enlist them in the cause of peaceful desegregation, or at least to persuade them not to inflame public opinion against it. When, in his meetings with ministers, Graham used Eisenhower's name to support his plea for moderation, he received a letter from the president requesting that their exchange be kept confidential.

Graham's style of preaching became more subdued after the early 1950s. He called himself a Christian rather than a fundamentalist. Liberal theologians, such as REINHOLD NIEBUHR, criticized Graham's failure to promote social reform and characterized his ministry as a form of "Christian pietism quite irrelevant to the political life of man." On the other side of the spectrum, some fundamentalists condemned what they regarded as his move to the theological center. Still others found fault with Graham's use of gigantic rallies and the mass media. As the *Christian Century* complained, "At this strange new junction of Madison Avenue and the Bible Belt, the Holy Spirit is not overworked, he is overlooked." Despite his critics, by the late 1950s, polls consistently indicated that Graham was one of the "most admired" people in the United States.

Graham supported RICHARD M. NIXON in the election of 1960, but he maintained cordial relations with the administration of JOHN F. KENNEDY and supported Kennedy's actions during the Cuban missile crisis. Graham continued to advocate desegregation and denounced violence against the Freedom Riders; at the same time, he urged black leaders to proceed slowly. Although invited to the White House by every president since Truman, Graham enjoyed a particularly close relationship with Nixon. He held a series of religious services at the White House during Nixon's first term and delivered a short prayer at Nixon's second inauguration. The two men often appeared in public together. Graham remained loyal to Nixon as the revelations concerning the Watergate scandal continued to mount. After the release of the White House tapes in May 1974, however, Graham called reading them "a profoundly disturbing and disappointing experience." Still, upon Nixon's resignation, Graham urged Americans to pray for the disgraced president.

By the 1980s, Graham began to mix a message of social meliorism with his traditional premillennial fatalism. In 1982, he called the nuclear arms race "a moral and spiritual issue that must concern us all," and in *Approaching Hoofbeats*, published the following year, he reflected that he should have done more to further world peace and social justice. In 1992, Graham announced that he had Parkinson's disease and would cut back on his schedule. A decade later, the release of some of the Nixon tapes revealed that Graham had joined in making anti-Semitic comments during a meeting with Nixon in 1972. Graham lives in Montreat, N.C., where he and his late wife had made their home since 1945.

—MSM

Graham, Philip Leslie
(1915–1963) *publisher*

The son of a mining engineer and farmer, Graham was born on July 18, 1915, in Terry, S.Dak. He moved with his family to Florida, where his father managed a failed experimental sugarcane plantation. The senior Graham took over the land, began a successful dairy farm, eventually made a fortune in real estate, and became influential in state Democratic politics. The younger Graham earned his B.A. at the University of Florida in 1936 and his law degree from Harvard in 1939. At Harvard, he was editor of the law review and a protégé of FELIX FRANKFURTER. After graduating, he clerked for Justice STANLEY REED and then for (by this time, Justice) Frankfurter. Graham became one of the many Frankfurter students who went to work for the New Deal. He was an attorney for the Office of Lend-Lease Administration and the Office of Emergency Management. In 1940, he married Katharine Meyer, the daughter of Eugene Meyer, a wealthy banker and owner of the *Washington Post*. Graham served in intelligence with the army air corps during World War II and rose to the rank of major. After the war, at the behest of his father-in-law, Graham became the publisher of the *Post*, and under his leadership, the newspaper emerged as one of the country's most influential. Graham himself became a powerful figure in the liberal establishment and the consummate Washington insider. He used his position at the paper and the *Post* itself to further his own liberal, elitist vision and causes.

With Graham at the helm, the *Post* supported President HARRY S. TRUMAN's foreign policy and yet defended civil liberties during the emerging cold war (although Graham was more cautious in this regard than his editorial writer, Alan Barth). The paper was among the leaders in criticizing the antics of Sen. JOSEPH MCCARTHY (R-Wis.). Graham and the *Post* endorsed DWIGHT D. EISENHOWER in the presidential election of 1952, at least in part because the publisher thought that Eisenhower's election would bring McCarthy to heel. During the 1950s, the *Post* consistently supported civil rights, although the paper published little about African Americans or the black community in Washington and was slow to integrate its own offices.

Graham made the *Post* a financial as well as a journalistic success. The paper purchased its morning rival, the *Washington Times-Herald*, in 1954 and *Newsweek* magazine in 1961. In addition, the *Post* purchased its first television station in 1950 and developed an empire in radio and television broadcasting.

A charming and charismatic character, Graham established himself as a favorite guest at Georgetown cocktail parties. He could engage the paper's pressmen and drivers with equal ease. In addition to his personal magnetism, his success at the *Post* derived from his sound editorial judgment and his appreciation for good writing. Above all, though, he cultivated close contacts with people in power, most notably senators LYNDON B. JOHNSON (D-Tex.) and JOHN F. KENNEDY (D-Mass.). Graham urged Johnson to support a civil rights bill in 1957 and helped maneuver the legislation through Congress. He supported Johnson for the presidency in 1960 and played a role in Kennedy's selection of Johnson as his running mate. Graham became extremely close to Kennedy during the latter's tenure in the White House. The coverage of events in the *Post* and in *Newsweek* reflected Graham's intimate connection with the president.

Graham suffered from manic depression and could not work for several months in 1957. He was able to attend to his duties at the *Post* only sporadically in 1958 and 1959. As he reached the pinnacle of power and financial success in the early 1960s, he proved unable to handle it. He was verbally abusive to his family and friends and became increasingly resentful of his father-in-law, who before his death in 1959 had treated Graham like a favored son. Graham's public tirades against Meyer shocked those who knew how much the old man loved him. Moreover, his attacks on Meyer reflected an intense and growing anti-Semitism. Graham drank heavily and engaged in extramarital affairs with little effort at discretion. In 1963, he had a highly public affair with a young Australian woman who worked at *Newsweek* and announced his intention to marry her. That same year, at a conference of newspaper publishers in Phoenix, Ariz., he delivered a savage and obscene attack on his peers and disclosed one of Kennedy's affairs. After he began to disrobe, he was escorted from the stage and returned to Washington in a straitjacket. After a period of psychiatric care, he shot himself to death at Glen Welby, his estate near Middleburg, Va., on August 3, 1963.

—MSM

Green, Edith S(tarrett)

(1910–1987) *U.S. congresswoman*

Born on January 17, 1910, in Trent, S.Dak., Edith Louise Starrett moved with her parents to Oregon in 1916. She attended Willamette University from 1927 to 1929 and graduated from the University of Oregon in 1939. After working as an English teacher from 1930 to 1941 and a radio announcer from 1943 to 1947, she was director of public relations for the Oregon Education Association and ran unsuccessfully for secretary of state of Oregon in 1952. A Democrat, Green narrowly won a congressional seat in 1954 from a district including Portland and part of its suburbs.

In the House, she served on the Education and Labor Committee. Green supported a variety of liberal programs, including civil rights, tax reform, repeal of the Taft-Hartley Act, a higher minimum wage, equal pay for equal work performed by women, campaign finance disclosure, and public rather than private development of resources. However, her main efforts focused on education. In her first month in office, she introduced a bill to provide emergency federal assistance to states and territories for construction of urgently needed school facilities, but no action was taken on the proposal. Green also introduced the Library Services Act, which became law in June 1956 and helped to extend public library services to rural areas.

Green's interest in education was sometimes linked to her commitment to civil rights. In 1956, Green and seven other Democratic representatives asked President Eisenhower to declare that he would refuse to allocate federal funds to school systems that defied the Supreme Court's 1954 decision outlawing school segregation. The president, however, declined.

The successful launching of the Soviet satellite, *Sputnik*, in 1957 aroused American fears that the United States lagged behind the Soviet Union in educational programs, and in 1958 Congress approved an unprecedented educational appropriation, the National Defense Education Act (NDEA). Green helped shape and win passage of the measure, which provided more than $1 billion over a seven-year period for loans and grants to schools and students. In April 1959, she joined two college presidents in urging Congress to remove the loyalty oath required of NDEA fund recipients. No action was taken on the request.

Green supported the large defense expenditures she believed were necessary because of the cold war. She and seven other Democratic representatives drafted a resolution in 1959 against atomic exchange agreements between the United States and seven NATO countries. The group feared that such pacts would heighten the risk of war. In May 1960, she joined 27 other House Democrats who wrote the president urging him to oppose "any unwise cuts" in the mutual security appropriations bill.

Although Green had only narrowly won her first House race, her subsequent majorities never fell below 63 percent. Her strong base enabled her to play a role in national Democratic politics. At the convention in 1956, she seconded the nomination of ADLAI STEVENSON for president, and in 1960 she managed JOHN F. KENNEDY's (D-Mass.) successful campaign in the Oregon primary. She seconded the Massachusetts senator's nomination at the Los Angeles convention in 1960. Green maintained a record of solid support for the domestic policies of the Kennedy and Johnson administrations and continued to play an active role in education legislation. She spoke out forcefully against the war in Vietnam beginning in 1965. Green grew increasingly conservative in the late 1960s and early 1970s. She opposed busing as a means to achieve desegregation and voted against increasing payments to welfare recipients. She did not seek reelection in 1974 and supported GERALD FORD in the presidential election of 1976. After retiring from Congress, she was a professor of government at Warner Pacific College and served on the Oregon Board of Higher Education in 1979. She died in Tualatin, Oreg., on April 21, 1987.

—MSM

Green, Theodore Francis

(1867–1966) *U.S. senator; chairman, Foreign Relations Committee*

Born into a wealthy and aristocratic family in Providence, R.I., on October 2, 1867, Green graduated from Providence High School in 1883. He earned a B.A. from Brown University in 1887 and an M.A. from the same institution a year later.

After attending Harvard Law School from 1888 to 1890, he studied at the Universities of Bonn and Berlin from 1890 to 1892. Green was admitted to the Rhode Island bar in 1892 and joined his father's law firm two years later. His legal career was interrupted briefly by service in the Spanish-American War. Green was elected as a Democrat to the state house of representatives for the 1907–08 term. He ran unsuccessfully for the U.S. House of Representatives in 1920 and for governor in 1912, 1928, and 1930. The Great Depression helped him finally win the governorship in 1932. In office, he immediately obtained passage of legislation providing welfare and unemployment relief. Green won reelection in 1934, and helped establish the Democratic party as the dominant party in what had been a Republican state.

In 1936, Gov. Green won a seat in the U.S. Senate. He supported New Deal and Fair Deal legislation and was an internationalist in foreign affairs both before and after World War II. In addition to backing relief, recovery, and regulatory measures of the New Deal, Green supported Franklin D. Roosevelt's court-packing plan. In 1944 and 1945, as chairman of the Committee on Campaign Expenditures, Green led an investigation of violations of limitations on campaign spending prescribed by the Hatch Act. In 1945 the panel recommended repeal of the law as "unrealistic."

A member of the Foreign Relations Committee, Green compiled a record as an internationalist in foreign policy during the 1950s. He voted against the Bricker amendment, which would have limited the president's power to make treaties, and joined the panel's other Democrats in 1953 in opposing a resolution, inspired by Secretary of State JOHN FOSTER DULLES, annulling secret foreign agreements used to justify the "enslavement" of other peoples. The resolution represented an implicit attack on Democratic presidents Franklin D. Roosevelt and HARRY S. TRUMAN for allegedly making such agreements with the Soviet Union at Yalta and Potsdam. The resolution died in committee that March. Two years later, Green strongly supported a resolution, adopted by both houses, opposing all forms of colonialism.

In 1957, Green gave up the chair of the Rules and Administration Committee to become head of the Foreign Relations panel. He supported the Eisenhower Doctrine and Eisenhower's decision to send American forces to Lebanon in 1958. In 1957, he defended his committee's $250-million cut in the administration's foreign-aid request on the grounds that the reduction would not impair the national interest and would compel tighter administration of the program. However, when Congress, following action by the Senate and House appropriations committees, reduced the request by another $750 million, Green resisted the additional cuts. The following year, he and seven other Foreign Relations Committee members signed a letter to President Eisenhower asking for greater emphasis on economic aid and less on military assistance. Green split with Eisenhower over the latter's response to threats by Communist China against the Nationalist-held islands of Quemoy and Matsu. After that, the senator became increasingly critical of Eisenhower's foreign policy.

A loyal ally of the majority leader, LYNDON B. JOHNSON, Green was one of a handful of Democratic liberals who voted to eliminate the provision authorizing the Justice Department to enter civil suits on behalf of desegregation from the bill that became the Civil Rights Act of 1957. By the mid-1950s, Green's failing hearing, eyesight, and mental faculties made him overly dependent on his aides. In 1959, Green was over 90 years old and incapable of handling the responsibility of chairing the Foreign Relations Committee. He required the assistance of an aide to find his way around Capitol Hill; he had difficulty identifying colleagues on the Foreign Relations Committee without the aid of a seating chart; he would brief the press on closed meetings of the committee and compound the problem by presenting a garbled version of what had transpired. On the floor of the Senate, it was all he could do to mumble and stumble his way through speeches his aides had written for him. After the *Providence Journal* ran an editorial urging him to step down, Johnson persuaded him to relinquish the chair voluntarily to the second-ranking Democrat, Senator J. WILLIAM FULBRIGHT (D-Ark.). Green did not seek reelection in 1960 and died in Providence on May 19, 1966.

—MSM

Greenewalt, Crawford H(allock)

(1902–1993) *president and chairman of the executive committee, E.I. du Pont [DuPont] de Nemours & Co.*

The son of a physician and symphony pianist, Greenewalt was born on August 16, 1902. He graduated from the Massachusetts Institute of Technology in 1922 with a degree in chemical engineering and began his career with DuPont at the company's plant in Philadelphia. Two years later, he was transferred to the Experimental Station to work in high-pressure technology. In June 1926, he married Margaretta DuPont, the daughter of the company's president, Irénée DuPont. In the 1920s and 1930s, he helped supervise the development of nylon.

Greenewalt was elected to the board of directors in 1941 and named chemical director the same year. He became director of the Grasselli Chemical Department of DuPont in 1942. Greenewalt witnessed the first self-sustaining atomic chain reaction engineered by Enrico Fermi at the University of Chicago in 1942. Thereafter, he helped maintain a close contact between DuPont and the atomic project. DuPont was involved in the design, construction and operation of the plutonium plant near Hanford, Wash. During World War II, he served as adviser to the Chemical Warfare Service and the Manhattan Project.

After the war, Greenewalt was promoted, first to vice president in 1946, then to president, chairman of the executive committee, and member of the finance committee in 1948. He made large-scale research projects designed to produce "new nylons," the company's major objective in the postwar years. Toward that end, he persuaded DuPont's executive committee to commit $30 million to new research facilities and to fund research programs at universities. During his presidency, Greenewalt oversaw the development of the synthetic fibers Orlon, Dacron, and Lycra. The company also began to expand overseas.

During Greenewalt's tenure, the antitrust division of the Justice Department conducted several investigations of DuPont. A suit, begun in 1947, charging monopolistic practices in the manufacture and sale of cellophane, was thrown out in December 1953. A separate suit, filed in 1949, charged that DuPont's $560-million investment in General Motors, giving it a controlling share of the stock, violated the Clayton Antitrust Act. In 1951, the Supreme Court reversed the ruling of a federal district court that the government had failed to prove conspiracy. The court said that DuPont's control made it possible for the company to monopolize a substantial part of the market for auto fabrics and finishes. The case was then sent back to the lower court to determine an equitable remedy. In 1959, that court ruled that the company could keep its 23 percent interest but would have to give up voting rights in the stock. The Supreme Court rejected this decree in 1961 and ordered DuPont to divest itself of its 63 million shares (valued by that date at almost $3 billion) within 10 years.

During the 1950s, Greenewalt served on several government commissions. His most important assignment was as a member of the Commission on National Goals, formed in 1959. The panel report, released in November 1960, called for "extraordinary personal responsibility, sustained effort and sacrifice" from every American in the 1960s to help the United States achieve "high and difficult goals" in a period of "grave danger" ahead.

While approving the report, Greenewalt added his own statement cautioning that the goals would call for unprecedented expenditures that would create an unsupportable tax burden given the present economy. He therefore recommended improving the atmosphere for vigorous growth through, among other things, cutting income tax rates in the higher brackets, Although supporting the report's recommendation for free trade, he cautioned that it could lead to higher unemployment and the move to reduce tariffs should be taken cautiously.

By the late 1950s, DuPont had become overly reliant on textile fibers and faced slowing growth as well as diminishing returns from research on textiles. In 1961, Greenewalt urged the company to focus on developing new markets and announced a program to diversify the company's interests "beyond existing fields of interest and beyond chemistry." He stepped down as president in 1962 but continued to serve as chair of the board of directors until 1967. Even after resigning the chair, he remained on the board and continued to advocate the development of new product lines until his retirement in 1988. He died in Wilmington, Del., on September 27, 1993.

—MSM

Griffin, (Samuel) Marvin
(1907–1982) *governor of Georgia*

The son of a state legislator and founder of the Bainbridge *Post-Searchlight*, Griffin was born in Bainbridge, Ga., on September 4, 1907. He grew up in an atmosphere of small-town politics and journalism and worked as a page in the Georgia legislature at the age of 10. After receiving a B.A. from the Citadel in 1929, he taught at Randolph-Macon Academy in Front Royal, Va. When his father became ill in 1933, Griffin returned to Bainbridge to take over the family newspaper. He won election to the general assembly as a Democrat in 1934 and, after serving one term, ran unsuccessfully for the U.S. House of Representatives in 1936. He worked for the administration of Gov. E. D. ("Ed") Rivers and eventually became Rivers's executive secretary. Griffin enlisted in the army during World War II, served in the South Pacific, and rose to the rank of lieutenant colonel. In 1944, Georgia's governor, Ellis Arnall, appointed him adjutant general of the Georgia National Guard, a post he held until 1947. Griffin won a special election for lieutenant governor in 1948 and won reelection to a full term in 1950, during which he served under Georgia's segregationist governor, HERMAN TALMADGE.

In January 1954, anticipating that the Supreme Court would rule against segregation in public schools, Talmadge created the Georgia Commission on Education to develop a plan to maintain segregation. He also promoted a state constitutional amendment giving the state power to convert its public schools into a private system. State funds would then be used for tuition grants for private school students. Griffin strongly supported this plan and in 1954 gained Talmadge's informal support against eight other contenders in the Democratic primary for the gubernatorial nomination. Running as an extreme segregationist, he won the September primary and was elected in November.

Assuming office without a social, economic, or political program, Griffin focused his attention on preserving segregation. In April 1955, he opposed integration in a debate with New York State Attorney General JACOB K. JAVITS at the Harvard Law School. In December of that year, Griffin gained wide attention by requesting the state board of regents to prohibit schools under its jurisdiction from engaging in athletic events "where the races are mixed on such teams or where segregation is not required among spectators." The request was prompted by Georgia Tech's scheduled participation in the Sugar Bowl against a team from the University of Pittsburgh that had one black player. The board of regents turned down the governor's request but reaffirmed that games played in Georgia would remain segregated.

In September 1955, Griffin participated in a meeting of leading political figures in Georgia at which they decided to take over the foundering States' Rights Council and make it an effective organization in the service of white supremacy. During January 1956, Griffin and other state officials traveled through Georgia promoting the council and enlisting members. State employees were virtually compelled to contribute.

That month, Virginia's governor, THOMAS STANLEY, called a southern governors' conference to support the doctrine of interposition, which asserted that a state had a right to interpose its sovereignty between its people and illegal acts of the federal government. Griffin alone held an even more extreme position, urging outright nullification of the Supreme Court decision. In February 1956, he had the Georgia legislature invoke interposition and approve nullification.

Griffin refused to join the Dixiecrat call for a new political party. However, when he accepted nomination as Georgia's favorite-son candidate for president at the Democratic National Convention in August 1956, Griffin took advantage of the national coverage to denounce the Supreme Court in his acceptance speech.

In August 1957, Griffin went to Little Rock, Ark., where Central High School was scheduled to desegregate at the beginning of the school year, and gave a speech at a meeting of the Capital Citizens' Council. Griffin's address contended, in vague but inflammatory terms, that Georgia was using interposition to nullify the Supreme Court's decision in *Brown v. Board of Education*. Governor ORVAL FAUBUS of Arkansas steered clear of the meeting but invited Griffin to stay overnight at the governor's mansion. Faubus maintained that Griffin's speech shifted public opinion in Little Rock and that it limited his own options. When President Eisenhower ordered federal troops to enforce integration in Little Rock the following month, Gov. Griffin joined other southern leaders in urging the South to take unified political action to prevent desegregation. There were, however, limits to Griffin's commitment to segregation. When extreme segregationists urged him to defy federal court orders, Griffin declined, saying that "being in jail kind of crimps a governor's style."

Griffin's term was not devoted solely to preserving segregation. Upon taking office, he faced an expected deficit, so he reneged on a campaign promise and pushed through an increase in the state income tax. Under his administration, the Rural Roads Authority paved nearly 12,000 miles of rural roads. His administration also oversaw a 50 percent increase in funding for education, which included a 25 percent raise in teachers' salaries. Some of the increased spending on education went to larger appropriations for black schools and to reducing the disparity between the salaries of black and white teachers in an effort to resist desegregation by demonstrating the equality of black and white schools. By 1958, however, the governor found himself increasingly occupied defending his administration against charges of corruption. Some members of his administration were convicted on various charges. Prevented by law from succeeding himself, he retired in 1959. A grand jury in Fulton Co. investigated Griffin in 1960 but did not return an indictment. He attempted a comeback in the gubernatorial race of 1962, but he lost overwhelmingly in the Democratic primary. Griffin reemerged briefly in 1968 as the temporary vice presidential nominee of George Wallace's American Independent Party. Like many conservative southern Democrats, Griffin began supporting Republican presidential candidates in the 1970s. He endorsed GERALD FORD in 1976 and Ronald Reagan in 1980. Griffin died of lung cancer in Tallahassee, Fla., on June 13, 1982.

—MSM

Griffin, Robert P.

(1923–   ) *U.S. congressman*

The son of a factory worker, Griffin was born in Detroit, Mich., on November 6, 1923. He attended Central Michigan College of Education at Mount Pleasant, but left to enlist in the army in 1943. After serving in Europe for 14 months, he returned to Central Michigan College and graduated in 1947. By that time, he had decided to become a lawyer rather than a teacher. He enrolled at the University of Michigan Law School, where he was an associate editor of the *Michigan Law Review* and received his law degree in 1950. Griffin was admitted to the Michigan bar that same year and cofounded a law firm in Traverse City. He specialized in labor law.

In 1956, Griffin entered the Republican congressional primary in the ninth district against a conservative incumbent, Rep. Ruth Thompson. He won that contest and went on to defeat his Democratic opponent by 14,000 votes. Because of his expertise in labor matters, he asked for and was given an assignment on the Education and Labor Committee. In 1957, he broke with six conservative Republican members of the Education and Labor Committee and supported a bill, backed by the administration, that would have provided federal aid for school construction. The following year, he supported a measure establishing a seven-year program of federal loans and grants to schools and individual students. On the House floor, he succeeded in adding an amendment to include junior colleges among the institutions eligible for aid to improve instructional facilities in science, mathematics, and modern languages.

In 1959, Griffin earned the enmity of organized labor by cosponsoring a labor reform measure. The origins of the bill lay in the investigations of organized labor by Sen. JOHN McCLELLAN's (D-Ark.) Select Committee on Improper Activities in the Labor or Management Field. That probe, which revealed extensive corruption as well as collusion between management and labor leaders, generated public pressure for reform. Early in 1959, Eisenhower called for legislation to safeguard union contributions of workers, ensure secret ballots in union elections, and protect the public interest during labor disputes. The AFL-CIO supported a weaker measure, and Sen. JOHN F. KENNEDY (D-Mass.) proposed a bill along those lines. Kennedy's bill required labor unions to file annual financial reports, required that union elections be held by secret ballot and at regular intervals, and provided criminal penalties for bribery, extortion, misappropriation of union funds, and other practices.

President Eisenhower, Republican congressional leaders, and southern Democrats favored a more comprehensive bill including amendments strengthening some provisions of the Taft-Hartley Act. When the House Education and Labor Committee in July 1959 reported a measure that did not go much beyond Kennedy's proposal, Griffin and Rep. PHIL M. LANDRUM (D-Ga.) introduced their own bill, adding the desired amendments to the bill in the Senate. The most significant provisions of the original Landrum-Griffin bill were adopted by both houses in September. The amendments to the Taft-Hartley Act defined as an unfair labor practice a labor-management contract under which the employer agreed not to do business with another firm, restricted organizational and recognition picketing and secondary boycotts, brought several additional categories of workers within the scope of the Taft-Hartley Act's restrictions on picketing and secondary boycotts, and barred unions from picketing a retail store to protest that the store was handling the goods of a firm that the union was striking.

In 1960, Griffin opposed a bill to legalize common-site picketing in the construction industry. He also opposed efforts to increase the minimum wage by more than 15 cents above the existing $1 minimum, asserting that a larger increment would be harmful to marginal and physically handicapped workers and would cause serious economic dislocation.

In 1963, Griffin and several other younger Republican representatives led a revolt against the party's leadership in the House that resulted in the ouster of the chair of the House Republican Conference Committee and the election of Rep. GERALD R. FORD (R-Mich.) in his place. Two years later, the so-called Young Turks unseated the minority leader, CHARLES A. HALLECK (R-Ind.), and replaced him with Ford. Although Griffin voted much like other Republican members of the House, he split with his party and voted for Medicare after the Republican substitute failed. In 1966, Gov. GEORGE W. ROMNEY appointed Griffin to the seat left vacant by the death of Sen. PAT V. McNAMARA (D-Mich.). Griffin won a full term

in the elections that fall and reelection in 1972. In 1968, he led the successful opposition to President LYNDON B. JOHNSON's nomination of Associate Justice Abe Fortas to be chief justice. Griffin became minority whip in 1969, a position he held until he ran unsuccessfully for minority leader in 1976. After failing in his bid for a third full term in 1978, Griffin returned to Traverse City, Mich., where he continues to live.

—MSM

Gross, H(arold) R(oyce)
(1899–1987) *U.S. congressman*

Born on June 30, 1899, in Arispe, Iowa, Gross was raised on a farm in southern Iowa. After serving overseas in World War I, he attended Iowa State College and the University of Missouri School of Journalism. From 1921 to 1935, he worked on several newspapers as a reporter and editor. He was a radio news commentator from 1935 to 1948.

In the Republican primary of June 1948, Gross defeated the incumbent U.S. representative in Iowa's predominantly agricultural third congressional district and went on to win the general election. Gross quickly established himself as a persistent advocate of reductions in federal spending and in May 1950 voted for a $600-million cut in the national budget. In 1949 and 1950, however, Gross backed bills sponsored by the Truman administration providing for high farm price supports.

Gross opposed the internationalist and multilateral foreign policy of the Truman and Eisenhower administrations. In 1953, he unsuccessfully offered an amendment to an appropriations bill that would have cut America's contribution to the UN by 90 percent. Two years later, he opposed an extension of reciprocal trade legislation. In 1957, Gross voted against U.S. appropriations for the UN Emergency Force in the Middle East. During the same year, he opposed the Eisenhower Doctrine, which authorized the president to use force to help Middle Eastern nations repel communist aggression. In 1959, he offered an amendment to a mutual security bill that declared that the United States should have as little political connection with other nations as possible. It was rejected by voice vote.

Continuing to advocate fiscal frugality during the 1950s, Gross opposed an increase in the national debt limit in 1955, asserting that "the answer to financial stability on the part of the federal government is reduced spending, not steadily increasing debt." During the same year, he denounced congressional junkets and opposed increased salaries for judges and cabinet officers in the District of Columbia. His fiscal conservatism led him to oppose many social welfare expenditures. In 1956, he criticized a 37 percent increase in funds for the National Institutes of Health. Two years later, Gross asserted that the funds allotted by the Appropriations Committee for the Labor and Health, Education, and Welfare departments were excessive.

Gross nevertheless persisted in backing high farm price supports during the Eisenhower presidency and in 1954 voted against the administration's omnibus farm bill, which lowered support levels. He opposed the Civil Rights Act of 1957 but voted for the Civil Rights Act of 1960. According to *Congressional Quarterly*, Gross voted contrary to Eisenhower positions on key bills more often than he backed the administration.

Gross consistently opposed New Frontier and Great Society programs in the 1960s and continued his efforts to reduce U.S. financial support of the UN. During the 1960s and early 1970s, Gross retained his reputation as a leading opponent of what he regarded as excessive government spending. He did not run for reelection in 1974. Gross resided in Arlington, Va., until his death in Washington, D.C., on September 22, 1987.

—MLL

Gruening, Ernest H(enry)
(1887–1974) *U.S. senator*

Born on February 6, 1887, in New York City, Gruening graduated from the Hotchkiss School in 1903, Harvard College in 1907, and Harvard Medical School in 1912. He chose a career in journalism, beginning as a reporter for the *Boston American* in 1912. He then held a succession of jobs with several newspapers and became managing editor of the *New York Tribune* in 1917. After service in the Field Artillery Corps in 1918, he served as editor of several liberal journals during the 1920s and 1930s.

In that capacity, he espoused a number of controversial causes, including racial integration and birth control. He was editor of the *Nation* from 1920 to 1923. Gruening took time off from journalism to direct publicity for Robert La Follette's campaign for the presidency in 1924. After the election, he went to Mexico to report on conditions after the revolution for *Collier's Weekly*. In 1927, he helped found the *Portland (Maine) Evening News*, for which he served as editor until 1932. An opponent of American military intervention in Latin America, he published *Mexico and Its Heritage* (1927), a highly regarded account of the Mexican Revolution. He supported HERBERT HOOVER for the presidency in 1928. Gruening edited the *New York Post* from 1932 to 1933.

As the New Deal got under way, Gruening became a loyal Democrat. He served briefly as editor of the *New York Evening Post* in early 1934. Later that year, President Franklin D. Roosevelt appointed him director of the division of territories and island possessions in the Department of the Interior. Gruening simultaneously administered relief and reconstruction programs in Puerto Rico. In 1939, Roosevelt appointed him territorial governor of Alaska, a position he held until 1953.

Gruening later wrote that when he assumed the governorship, "Alaska was in the grip of absentee interests and had been for a quarter of a century." As governor, he proposed a tax system that weakened the influence of nonresident business interests, and he worked for improved transportation, particularly the construction of the Alcan Highway. Gruening also won legislation designed to protect Alaska's Eskimos from discrimination.

Gruening was also a leading advocate of statehood. He appeared on numerous occasions before congressional committees charged with weighing Alaska's possible admission to the union. Anticipating statehood, the Alaska territorial legislature called a constitutional convention, which assembled in September 1955 with Gruening as its keynote speaker. His address, titled "Let Us End American Colonialism," was widely circulated in pamphlet form by pro-statehood groups.

Gruening's campaign for statehood had to answer objections stemming from Alaska's remoteness, small population, and strategic military value.

President Eisenhower, who, endorsed statehood for Hawaii, had reservations about Alaska's lack of population and its strategic importance. In *The Battle for Alaska Statehood* (1967), Gruening attributed Eisenhower's opposition to "the assumption that Hawaii would elect Republicans and Alaska Democrats." In fact, although Eisenhower opposed Alaskan statehood in 1953 based largely on its lack of population, he recommended statehood for Alaska and Hawaii to Congress in January 1957.

To promote its cause, the Alaska legislature adopted the "Tennessee Plan," a device first used by Tennessee in 1796 to achieve statehood. Under the plan, the territory in November 1956 elected two senators, including Gruening, and one representative to the U.S. Congress to lobby for statehood. Their efforts met with success. In June 1958, Congress approved statehood for Alaska and Hawaii. Democrats won all statewide offices that November, and Gruening won a four-year Senate term. He won reelection in 1962.

In the Senate, Gruening vigorously represented Alaska's interests. He also called for a more vigorous congressional role in foreign policy, particularly in the area of foreign aid. In May 1960, the Senate accepted his amendment to a foreign-aid bill that required detailed explanations and cost projections for military assistance projects. However, his amendment requiring officials to give Congress detailed country-by-country budgets for all foreign-aid programs was defeated. In national affairs, Gruening supported a variety of progressive measures. He cosponsored Sen. PATRICK McNAMARA's program to provide medical care to the aged through Social Security. In addition, he supported most civil rights measures and government funding for the distribution of birth control information.

Initially enthusiastic about the election of JOHN F. KENNEDY, Gruening became disappointed with what he perceived to be Kennedy's lack of commitment to domestic issues. He staunchly supported the domestic programs of the Johnson administration, but he won prominence as one of the earliest congressional opponents of the Vietnam War. He spoke against Kennedy's policy in Indochina in 1963 and was one of two senators to vote against the Gulf of Tonkin Resolution in 1964. Making a bid for a third term, Gruening lost the Democratic primary

to Mike Gravel in 1968. Upon leaving the Senate, Gruening became president of an investment firm and a legislative consultant. He continued to oppose the war and campaigned for Sen. George McGovern (D-S.Dak.) in the presidential election of 1972. Gruening died in Washington, D.C., on June 26, 1974.

—MSM

Gruenther, Alfred M(aximilian)
(1899–1983) *supreme allied commander, Europe; president, American Red Cross*

The son of a small-town newspaper editor, Gruenther was born in Platte Center, Neb., on March 3, 1899. He attended the United States Military Academy at West Point and graduated fourth in the class of 1918. He completed field artillery school in 1919 and the following year was assigned to Fort Knox, Ky. While there, he took up bridge, which became a consuming passion for him. Later, he would serve as a referee for some of the great bridge matches of the 1930s and write a book, *Duplicate Contract Bridge*. After an inconspicuous early career (it took him 17 years of peacetime service to advance to captain), during which he mostly taught mathematics at West Point, Gruenther attended Command and General Staff School in 1937 and the Army War College in 1939. He attracted attention for his performance in the large-scale war games conducted in 1941, known as the Louisiana Maneuvers. As a result of his performance, he was promoted and made deputy chief of staff of the Third Army, whose chief of staff was DWIGHT D. EISENHOWER, then a brigadier general. When the United States entered World War II, Gruenther went to London as chief American planner for Operation Torch, the Allied invasion of North Africa. He won the Distinguished Service Medal for his role in planning the invasion. Subsequently, he served as deputy chief of staff under Gen. Eisenhower, who was then the supreme allied commander, and in 1943 became chief of staff of the Fifth Army under Gen. MARK W. CLARK. In that capacity, he contributed to the planning of the invasion of Italy and the campaign in the Apennines. When Clark became commander of the Fifteenth Army Group, Gruenther continued as his chief of staff. After the war, Gruenther served as deputy commanding general of the U.S. forces in Austria from 1945 to 1947. In all of his duties, he demonstrated a capacity to assimilate and analyze masses of information and to convert the product into precise operational plans.

In 1947, Gruenther returned to the United States, where he served as deputy commandant of the National War College and director of the staff of the Joint Chiefs of Staff. He then became the army's deputy chief of staff for plans and operations. In 1951, he assumed new duties as the first chief of staff at NATO headquarters and received his fourth star, making him the youngest four-star general in the history of the U.S. Army. Gruenther served as chief of staff under Eisenhower and then General MATTHEW B. RIDGWAY. In May 1953, he took over as commander of Supreme Headquarters Allied Powers, Europe (SHAPE).

As commander of SHAPE, Gruenther won respect as a diplomat as well as a military leader. Eisenhower recognized Gruenther's good relations with European leaders and used him as a personal envoy. Gruenther helped present the administration's support for European unity. In addition, he had to deal with European discomfort over Eisenhower's reduction of American conventional forces as part of the "New Look" defense policy. Eisenhower used Gruenther to help calm European leaders when many of them became concerned about the confrontation between the United States and the People's Republic of China over Quemoy and Matsu in the first half of 1955. Gruenther strongly supported the admission of Germany into NATO and the integration of German forces into NATO's force structure. The latter position, in particular, encountered stiff opposition on the part of some allies. Moreover, by the time Gruenther became Supreme Allied commander Europe (SACEUR), some analysts had begun to argue that NATO was a victim of its own success. Its military preparedness contributed to reducing the Soviet threat, but, consequently, some members of the alliance regarded it as less important. France withdrew the bulk of its ground forces from NATO to fight in North Africa.

After retiring from the army at the end of 1956, Gruenther became president of the American Red Cross from 1957 to 1964. He served on numerous boards of directors, as chairman of the English-Speaking Union of the United States from 1966 to 1968, and as a trustee of Eisenhower College in Seneca Falls, N.Y. Gruenther died of pneumonia in Washington, D.C., on May 30, 1983.

—MSM

Hagerty, James Campbell

(1909–1981) *White House press secretary*

The son of James A. Hagerty, chief political correspondent for the *New York Times*, James C. Hagerty was born on May 9, 1909, in Plattsburgh, N.Y. After graduating from Blair Academy in 1928, he went to work on the New York Stock Exchange. The stock market crash made him rethink his career plans, and he enrolled at Columbia University, where he received his B.A. in 1934. While at Columbia, he was campus correspondent for the *New York Times*. Upon graduation, he joined the city staff of that paper. He became a legislative correspondent and deputy bureau chief in Albany for the *Times* in 1938. When THOMAS E. DEWEY was elected governor, he named Hagerty as an executive assistant and press secretary. Hagerty also handled press relations for Dewey's two presidential campaigns.

When Eisenhower undertook his campaign for the presidency in 1952, he chose Hagerty as his principal spokesman and press adviser. After the election, Eisenhower selected Hagerty as his press secretary. From the outset, Eisenhower included Hagerty in key meetings and made sure that the press secretary was fully informed about developments and policies. Hagerty emerged as one of Eisenhower's most trusted advisers. He also generally enjoyed good relations with the working press. Hagerty and his assistants briefed reporters every morning and afternoon; they held many press briefings on weekends, too. In spite of occasional flashes of Hagerty's explosive temper, many in the White House press corps liked him; virtually all respected his competence. Hagerty initiated regularly scheduled presidential news conferences and instituted a new policy that allowed everything the president said at a press conference to be printed verbatim. He presided over the admission of newsreel and television cameras to presidential news conferences in 1955. Eisenhower and Hagerty saw this as an opportunity to get the administration's message directly to the people, unmediated by the press. Widely regarded as the very model of a modern press secretary, Hagerty's success derived from his own experience and ability as well as his close personal relationship with Eisenhower.

The press secretary's assured handling of difficult situations eased public anxiety and put the administration in the best possible light. Hagerty kept the press informed of the president's condition following Eisenhower's heart attack in September 1955 and his stroke in November 1957. In the days and weeks after the president's heart attack, Hagerty became a familiar figure to the public through frequent news briefings. He also relayed to the public information about the downing of a U-2 spy plane over the Soviet Union and the subsequent cancellation of the summit conference in 1960.

In addition to handling press relations, Hagerty offered advice on a range of domestic and political matters. For instance, he urged Eisenhower to denounce the attack on the Protestant clergy by J. B. MATTHEWS, a member of Sen. JOSEPH McCARTHY's staff. Hagerty arranged for the National Conference of Christians and Jews to send an outraged telegram to the president and drafted the president's reply. When Eisenhower considered running for a second term, Hagerty was one of the few people he consulted about the decision. In one instance where Eisenhower did not follow his press secretary's advice, Hagerty unsuccessfully urged Eisenhower to trumpet the successes of the U.S. space program.

Hagerty was sympathetic to black civil rights and willing to weigh in on the issue. In June 1955, Louis Lautier, a reporter for the *Baltimore Afro-American*, applied for membership in the National Press Club. Some members opposed the admission of an African American, and Merriman Smith, a reporter friendly to the administration, advised Hagerty, as a member of the administration, to stay out of the controversy. Hagerty replied that he was a voting member and would vote for Lautier's admission, a position that received the president's backing. During the debate over the administration's bill to provide federal aid for school construction in 1956, Hagerty urged the president to support the Powell amendment, which would have banned federal aid to school districts that continued to practice segregation. However, Eisenhower remained publicly neutral on the amendment.

With the end of the Eisenhower administration, Hagerty joined the American Broadcasting Company as vice president of the news division. In 1964, he became vice president of corporate relations, a title he held, despite suffering a stroke in 1975, until his death in Bronxville, N.Y., on April 11, 1981.

—MSM

Hall, Leonard W(ood)

(1900–1979) *chairman, Republican National Committee*

The son of a White House librarian, Hall was born on October 2, 1900, in Oyster Bay, N.Y. He earned his LL.B. at Georgetown University law school in 1920, was admitted to the New York bar in 1922, and began a lucrative law career in New York City. Hall entered politics as a GOP campaign worker in 1926. He served as state assemblyman in 1927–28 and again from 1934 to 1938. He was sheriff of Nassau Co. from 1929 to 1931. In 1939,

he won election to the U.S. House of Representatives, where he voted primarily with the internationalist Eastern wing of the Republican Party. Hall managed THOMAS DEWEY's unsuccessful presidential campaign in 1948. He did not seek reelection in 1952, but supported Gen. Eisenhower for the Republican presidential nomination and established a personal relationship with the general during the fall campaign.

Hall became Eisenhower's choice for Republican national chairman following C. WESLEY ROBERTS's resignation in March 1953. The decision was based not only on Hall's relationship with the president but on his high standing with party leaders on Capitol Hill. In addition, he had organized the Republican Campaign Congressional Committee to unify the party and increase its influence in Washington, and so was known by Republican leaders throughout the country. Just as important, Hall had experience in organizing campaigns, a significant factor for a party facing difficult midterm elections in 1954.

Both Sen. ROBERT TAFT (R-Ohio) and Thomas Dewey opposed Hall's selection. Taft objected to Hall's alliance with the Eastern wing of the party, while Dewey harbored ill feelings going back to the disappointing loss in 1948. However, as a result of pressure from the administration and House Speaker JOE MARTIN (R-Mass.), both men eventually agreed to subordinate their own feelings and support Hall, who was officially installed as chairman in April 1953.

Hall's first challenge was to maintain Republican control of Congress in the elections of 1954. Sen. JOSEPH R. MCCARTHY's (R-Wis.) anticommunist crusade presented a problem, particularly after his attack on the army. Hall initially endorsed McCarthy's attacks on communists and praised him as a "great asset" to the party. The Republican National Committee paid for a nine-city speaking tour by the senator. After McCarthy's abuse of Gen. RALPH ZWICKER, however, Hall emerged from a meeting with Eisenhower on March 2 and told reporters, "I don't think anyone would say generals in our army are not fighting communism." He also acknowledged that McCarthy could damage Republican chances in the upcoming elections. Attempting to make political capital out of the incident, ADLAI STEVENSON declared in a nationally broadcast speech that "a group of political plungers had persuaded the president that McCarthyism is the best Republican formula for political success." He also called the party "half McCarthy and half Eisenhower." McCarthy demanded equal time from the networks to respond. Hall, apparently acting with Eisenhower's support, moved to preempt McCarthy by asking for 30 minutes of equal time on behalf of the Republican National Committee. He then announced that Vice President RICHARD M. NIXON would deliver the Republican reply. The fall elections proved disastrous for the Republican Party. Democrats won control of both houses of Congress, and Republicans lost heavily in gubernatorial races as well.

In late 1955 and early 1956, Hall first urged Eisenhower to seek a second term and then, when the president demonstrated reluctance to commit himself to keeping Nixon on the ticket, Hall became a forceful advocate of retaining Nixon. He argued that keeping Nixon was necessary to placate conservatives in the party. Once Eisenhower had publicly indicated that Nixon should "chart his own course," Hall persuaded Nixon to express his desire for renomination directly to the president. After talking with Nixon, Eisenhower announced that the ticket would remain intact. Eisenhower won a lopsided victory over Stevenson in November, but, for the first time in over 100 years, the party of a victorious presidential candidate failed to win control of either house of Congress.

Adding to his difficulties, Hall became enmeshed in a scandal involving the General Services Administration (GSA). In 1955, EDMUND MANSURE, the administrator of the GSA, was charged with allowing political considerations to influence the awarding of contracts to upgrade a nickel plant in Nicaro, Cuba, owned by the U.S. government. In an appearance before the House Special Government Activities Subcommittee, Mansure testified that, early in the negotiations, he had submitted a list of contractors to Hall for approval. Although Mansure denied that the approval sought was on "a political basis," a confidential memo obtained by the subcommittee indicated that the Frederick Snare Company received the contract only after meeting with Hall and assuring him that no Democrats held

top positions in the company. Hall denied that he had ever "cleared any contractor, big or small, for work with the government." While it was never proved that Hall or any other Republican solicited financial contributions from any of the companies seeking the Nicaro contract, the top executives at Snare substantially increased their contributions to Republicans in the elections of 1954. The chair of the subcommittee offered Hall the opportunity to appear before the subcommittee, but Hall declined. If the charges against Hall were true, he most likely violated federal law; yet he never faced questioning by the subcommittee. Rumors circulated to the effect that Democrats had done much the same thing when they held the White House and were therefore unenthusiastic about pursuing the matter. Whatever their motives, the Democratic members of the subcommittee were curiously restrained.

Hall resigned as GOP chairman in January 1957 and returned to the private practice of law in Garden City, N.Y., and New York City. He supported New York's Gov. NELSON ROCKEFELLER's unsuccessful candidacies for the Republican presidential nomination in 1964 and 1968. Hall died in Glen Cove, N.Y., on June 2, 1979.

—MSM

Halleck, Charles A(braham)
(1900–1986) *U.S. congressman, House majority leader, House minority leader*

The son of two lawyers, Halleck was born in Demotte, Ind., on August 22, 1900. After graduating from high school and serving in the army during World War I, he enrolled in Indiana University, where he received his A.B. from the law department in 1922 and his LL.B. in 1924, finishing first in his law school class. The year he graduated from law school, he entered his parents' law firm and won election as prosecuting attorney for Indiana's 13th judicial district. He served for 10 years before winning a special election for a congressional seat in 1935. His campaign criticized the New Deal for expanding the role of the federal government. Although he favored "humanitarian legislation," he argued against federal welfare and for local control. In Congress, Halleck consistently supported the Republican leadership and voted with the midwestern, conservative wing of the party. His reliability led JOE MARTIN (R-Mass.), the powerful minority leader, to appoint Halleck to the House Rules Committee. In 1940 Halleck became Martin's informal assistant. With respect to foreign policy, Halleck remained an isolationist until the Japanese attack on Pearl Harbor.

As chairman of the Republican Congressional Campaign Committee (a post he assumed in 1943), Halleck contributed substantially to the Republican victory in the congressional elections of 1946. He raised money and stumped the country speaking for Republican candidates. Republican control of the House made Martin the Speaker in 1947, and Halleck was elected majority leader. Halleck was floor leader for the Taft-Hartley Act, a law restricting the political power of labor unions. A convert to internationalism after Pearl Harbor, Halleck supported aid for Greece and Turkey and voted for the Marshall Plan. In spite of his identification with the conservative wing of the party, Halleck endorsed THOMAS E. DEWEY, leader of the Eastern or liberal wing of the party, for the Republican presidential nomination in 1948. Apparently, he hoped to be Dewey's running mate, but that hope did not materialize. Moreover, Democrats won both houses of Congress that year, and Martin resumed the role of minority leader. Although no longer leader, Halleck remained an important member of the Republican leadership in the House.

When the Republicans won both houses behind Eisenhower's victory in 1952, Halleck again became majority leader. Although more conservative than Eisenhower, Halleck was first and foremost a party loyalist. While sympathetic to the efforts of conservative Republicans to enact a tax cut in 1953, he supported the administration's opposition to a reduction. Moreover, in spite of his criticism of foreign aid and reciprocal trade programs under Truman, he backed similar measures under Eisenhower.

When the Republicans lost control of both houses of Congress in the elections of 1954, Halleck considered challenging Martin for the position of minority leader. He sought Eisenhower's support, but the president, preferring to preserve party unity, urged Halleck not to run. Halleck entertained the possibility of running against the aging Martin for the leadership in 1957 but once again deferred

to the president. After the Democratic sweep in the 1958 elections, however, Eisenhower indicated that he would not stand in Halleck's way. Eisenhower believed that weak congressional leadership had contributed to the defeat in 1958, and his hands-off policy was, in effect, an endorsement of Halleck. Further, many conservatives in the party believed that Martin cooperated too easily with the Democratic Speaker, SAM RAYBURN (D-Tex.). On January 6, 1959, the House Republican caucus voted 74 to 70 to end Martin's 20-year reign and elected Halleck minority leader.

Halleck was a more aggressive and partisan minority leader than his predecessor. Shortly after assuming the leadership, he chose conservatives for two vacancies on the Rules Committee created when moderate Republicans, who had held the seats, lost their bids for reelection. The Rules Committee controlled the flow of legislation to the House floor, and Halleck's action made it more difficult for Rayburn to bring measures to a vote.

As leader, Halleck worked closely with Eisenhower and the minority leader in the Senate, EVERETT DIRKSEN (R-Ill.), to hold down federal spending. Eisenhower wielded the veto, and Halleck successfully held House Republicans together to sustain it. Halleck played a significant role in gaining passage of the Landrum-Griffin bill in the House. The Senate passed a measure that required labor unions to file annual financial reports, required that union elections be held by secret ballot and at regular intervals, and provided criminal penalties for bribery, extortion, misappropriation of union funds, and other practices. The House added restrictions on secondary boycotts and certain types of picketing. The bill ultimately passed by both houses closely resembled the measure that came out of the House. Halleck also led a successful effort to limit the area served by the Tennessee Valley Authority.

When the Democrats won the White House and retained control of both houses of Congress in 1960, Halleck assumed the role of opposition leader. He and Dirksen held frequent press conferences that became known as the "Ev and Charlie Show." Joining with southern Democrats, the Republican leadership managed to defeat a number of President JOHN F. KENNEDY's legislative proposals, including school aid and omnibus housing measures in 1961 and a farm bill in 1962. On the other hand, Halleck supported Kennedy's proposed civil rights measure and endorsed the more extensive civil rights bill backed by President LYNDON B. JOHNSON in 1964.

Halleck's hold on the leadership position began to slip in the early 1960s. In January 1963, GERALD FORD (R-Mich.), backed by a number of younger Republicans in the House, defeated Halleck's candidate for chair of the Republican Policy Committee. The Democratic landslide of 1964 further undermined Halleck's position. Ford defeated Halleck for the leadership in 1965. In 1968, Halleck announced that he would not run for reelection that year. Upon leaving the House, he returned to Indiana and resided in Rensselaer until his death in Lafayette, Ind., on March 3, 1986.

—MSM

Hannah, John A(lfred)
(1902–1991) *president, Michigan State University; assistant secretary of defense for manpower; chairman, Civil Rights Commission*

The son of a poultry breeder, Hannah was born in Grand Rapids, Mich., on October 9, 1902. He attended Grand Rapids Junior College and the University of Michigan before graduating from Michigan Agricultural College, later known as Michigan State University (MSU), in 1923. Upon graduation, he became a poultry specialist with the university's extension service. He took a leave from that position in 1933 to become managing director of the National Poultry Breeders and Hatchery Committee, formed under the auspices of the National Recovery Administration. In 1934, Hannah returned to his alma mater, first as secretary of the school's governing body and, beginning in 1941, as president. During his presidency, MSU grew from a small land-grant college with 6,000 students into a "megaversity" with an enrollment of over 42,000 and a budget of over $100 million. Although not a scholar, the president became well known for his ability to sell his institution to the Michigan legislature by emphasizing popular and practical courses. He also garnered large amounts of state and federal aid for increased enrollment and construction. By 1951, MSU's building bud-

get had reached $31 million, two-thirds from the state and federal governments. Funds also came from federally financed foreign-aid projects that the university directed in Asia, Africa, and Latin America. His critics claimed that he was sacrificing academic quality for expansion, but Hannah replied that his purpose was "not to de-emphasize scholarship but to emphasize its application." In another initiative, Hannah led MSU away from traditional racial discrimination. He directed that dormitories be racially integrated and that racial designations be removed from student records. He also refused to allow the school's athletic teams to play in places where minority athletes would not be accorded equal rights.

In 1953, President Eisenhower appointed Hannah assistant secretary of defense for manpower and personnel. During his short term in office, he was instrumental in ending segregation in civilian schools attended by children of members of the armed forces. He also attempted to raise the caliber of the armed forces by increasing intelligence requirements and extending training periods. Hannah returned to MSU in September 1954.

Three years later, Eisenhower appointed Hannah chairman of the newly formed Civil Rights Commission. He took office in February 1958. That year he announced that the panel would investigate violations of black voting rights in Alabama, Florida, and Mississippi. The commission's first report, released in September 1959, emphasized that many blacks were denied voting rights and recommended a series of legislative proposals to solve the problem. The panel suggested measures authorizing the temporary use of federal officials to register qualified voters in federal, general, special, or primary elections. It also recommended a census survey of voting statistics by race and that state and local authorities be required to preserve voting records. The commission urged that it be empowered to apply directly to federal courts for orders enforcing directives that witnesses appear and produce records.

Hannah and two other members of the group, Rev. Theodore M. Hesburgh and George M. Johnson, also proposed a constitutional amendment to abolish literacy tests in voting. They further recommended that federal aid be withheld from segregated colleges and universities. However, the commission's three southern members opposed the recommendations.

Hannah continued as chairman of the Civil Rights Commission during the Kennedy and Johnson years. In 1966, an article in *Ramparts* charged that a federally financed MSU project in South Vietnam had provided a cover for Central Intelligence Agency (CIA) operations between 1955 and 1959. Hannah admitted the possibility of CIA infiltration but denied that Michigan State University had knowingly tolerated or encouraged this.

In 1969, President RICHARD M. NIXON appointed Hannah director of the Agency for International Development (AID), the primary agency responsible for the U.S. foreign-aid program. He originally wanted to retain the presidency of MSU while at AID, but he ultimately resigned his presidency. Hannah served as head of AID until his retirement in 1973. After retiring, he continued his association with the agency as a consultant. Hannah served as director of the United Nations' World Food Council from 1975 to 1978. He died in Kalamazoo, Mich., on February 23, 1991.

—SY

Harlan, John Marshall
(1899–1971) *judge, U.S. Court of Appeals for the Second Circuit; associate justice, U.S. Supreme Court*
Born in Chicago on May 20, 1899, Harlan had a distinguished legal lineage. His father and great-grandfather were lawyers; his grandfather, for whom he was named, served on the U.S. Supreme Court. After receiving his B.A. from Princeton University in 1920, Harlan spent three years as a Rhodes scholar at Balliol College, Oxford, where he began his study of law. Upon returning to the United States, he earned his LL.B. from New York Law School in 1924. That same year, he won admission to the New York bar. Harlan began his career with Root, Clark, Buckner & Howland, one of the most prestigious law firms in New York City. When Emory Buckner, a senior member of the firm, became U.S. attorney for the Southern District of New York in 1925, Harlan served as his assistant for a year. Harlan was made a partner in Root, Clark, Buckner & Howland in 1931.

After Buckner died in 1941, Harlan became the firm's leading litigator, specializing in corporate and antitrust cases. During World War II, Harlan commanded the Operational Analysis Section of the army air corps in England. He also served on a committee planning the postwar occupation of Germany. Upon returning to private practice in 1945, he emerged as a recognized leader of the New York bar. He served as chief counsel to the New York State Crime Commission from 1951 to 1953 and held several top positions in the Association of the Bar of the City of New York. By the early 1950s, he had established a reputation as one of the nation's top antitrust litigators. Although never an especially active Republican, he had close ties to Gov. THOMAS E. DEWEY and the governor's trusted adviser, HERBERT BROWNELL, who became attorney general in the Eisenhower administration. President Eisenhower nominated Harlan to the U.S. Court of Appeals for the Second Circuit in January 1954, and Harlan took his seat on the bench in March. Less than a year later, Eisenhower nominated Harlan to the Supreme Court. In the Senate Judiciary Committee, Southerners held up the nomination, apparently out of fear that Harlan shared his grandfather's belief that the "Constitution is colorblind" and to express their dissatisfaction with the decision in *Brown v. Board of Education*. Nevertheless, the Senate voted overwhelmingly to confirm the nomination in March 1955. Harlan brought to the bench the same incisive intelligence and attention to detail that won him a reputation as a "lawyer's lawyer." As a justice, his careful, precisely reasoned opinions earned him virtually unanimous respect from lawyers and judges.

Harlan was a moderate-to-conservative voice on the liberal and activist Warren Court, although he joined in many of that Court's rulings. His votes in cases involving segregation confirmed the fears of southerners. He joined the Court's unanimous ruling in May 1955 that desegregation should begin at once and proceed "with all deliberate speed." He later voted to strike down segregation in public facilities. Indeed, he joined every opinion that invalidated state-supported segregation. In June 1958, Harlan spoke for a unanimous court in a decision reversing a fine of $100,000 imposed by the state of Alabama on the NAACP for refusing to turn over its membership lists (*NAACP v. Alabama*). Harlan's decision held that the right of free association was protected by the Constitution.

In his early years on the Court, Harlan often sided with the Court's more liberal members in opposing the government's position in loyalty and security cases, but he usually based his opinion on narrow, technical grounds, rather than the broad constitutional grounds espoused by HUGO BLACK and WILLIAM O. DOUGLAS. As a result, he often spoke for the Court in these matters. In *Cole v. Young* (1956), for example, Harlan wrote the majority opinion that reversed the dismissal of a federal food and drug inspector. Harlan's carefully crafted opinion maintained that the Internal Security Act of 1950 authorized the dismissal of a government employee as a security risk only if he held a sensitive job.

Harlan also wrote for the majority in *Yates v. U.S.* (1957), which reversed the conviction of 14 leaders of the California Communist Party under the Smith Act. The decision ruled that the Smith Act did not outlaw advocacy of the forcible overthrow of the government as an abstract doctrine. It banned such advocacy only when it amounted to incitement to action. This ruling made convictions of communists under the law's conspiracy clause extremely difficult. That same month (June 1957), Harlan joined the majority in *Watkins v. U.S.* to reverse the contempt conviction of a witness who had refused to answer questions about former communist associates before the House Un-American Activities Committee (HUAC). *Watkins* held that the questions had to be in furtherance of a legitimate function of Congress, such as legislation. Congress had no authority to expose the private affairs of individuals for the sake of exposure.

After *Watkins*, however, Harlan generally took a more pro-government position in most loyalty and security cases. In June 1959, he wrote for a five-member majority to sustain the contempt conviction of a professor who had refused to answer the questions of a HUAC subcommittee about his Communist Party membership and activities. Harlan held that the committee had not violated the professor's right to academic freedom and had met the requirements established by *Watkins* in its questioning of the witness.

In general, Harlan agreed with FELIX FRANKFURTER, with whom he developed a close personal as well as intellectual affinity, that the Court should play a limited role in the federal system. He argued that justices should exercise restraint. Social ills, he maintained, should be remedied through the political process and not through the courts. In *Reynolds v. Simms* (1964), he explicitly rejected the belief that "every major social ill in the country can find its cure in some constitutional 'principle.'" Further, he was concerned to maintain "the delicate balance of federal state relations," which he regarded as a "bulwark of freedom." In addition to his commitment to federalism, he believed in proceduralism. Harlan accepted that courts should follow precedent unless a compelling argument could be made that a past case had been decided in error.

In federal criminal cases, Harlan was willing to reverse convictions if the defendant had not been afforded proper procedural rights. He gave greater leeway to the states, however, and was inclined to accept state criminal procedures as constitutional, so long as they were "fundamentally fair." Harlan opposed the doctrine of "incorporation," which maintained that, under the Fourteenth Amendment, the states had to give defendants all the guarantees included in the Bill of Rights. In *Griffin v. Illinois* (1956), he dissented when the majority held that states must supply an indigent convicted person with a free trial transcript, even though the right of appeal in Illinois depended on having such a transcript.

Harlan also insisted that the Constitution placed differing limits on state and federal power to regulate obscenity. In a separate opinion in June 1957, he maintained that states had greater authority to regulate pornography than the federal government (see *Roth v. U.S.* [1957] and *Alberts v. California* [1957]).

After Frankfurter's retirement in 1962, Harlan became the Court's leading advocate of judicial restraint. Facing the emergence of a solid, liberal activist majority in the 1960s, Harlan frequently dissented. He dissented in the Court's decisions on reapportionment (*Baker v. Carr* [1962] and *Reynolds v. Simms* [1964]). Harlan also dissented in decisions invalidating Virginia's poll tax and upholding the power of Congress to grant suffrage to 18-year-olds. In addition, he departed from the majority in many of the cases regarding the rights of those accused of crimes. Harlan entered a vigorous dissent in *Miranda v. Arizona* (1966), which established rules for informing individuals of their rights when taken into police custody. Nevertheless, Harlan joined in many of the Warren Court's most famous decisions. He concurred in *Gideon v. Wainwright* (1962), which granted accused felons the right to counsel. Harlan also joined decisions that prohibited organized prayer in public schools (*Engel v. Vitale* [1962] and *Abington School District v. Schempp* [1963]) and voted with the majority to strike down Connecticut's law criminalizing the sale of contraceptives in *Griswold v. Connecticut* (1965).

Harlan retired in September 1971 because of ill health and died in Washington on December 29, 1971. Even Harlan's critics admired his legal learning and craft as well as his intellectual integrity. His carefully drawn opinions clearly set forth the issues in the case and the reasons for his judgment. Much as he had been a "lawyer's lawyer" in private practice, he was a "lawyer's judge" on the Court.

—MSM

Harlow, Bryce N(athaniel)

(1916–1987) *special assistant to the president, deputy assistant to the president*

Bryce Harlow was born on August 11, 1916, in Oklahoma City. After graduating from the University of Oklahoma in 1936 with a Phi Beta Kappa key, he entered graduate school in government at the University of Texas. After a year, he returned to Oklahoma City, enrolled in the M.A. program in government at the University of Oklahoma, and worked at Harlow Publishing Company, the family business. Harlow went to Washington, D.C., in 1938 as assistant librarian of the House of Representatives. In 1940, he took a position on the staff of Congressman Wesley E. Disney (D-Okla.) and joined the army reserve. In July 1941, Harlow was placed on active duty as an officer in the public information office of Army Chief of Staff Gen. George C. Marshall. When Marshall formed a congressional relations division in early 1942, he chose Brig. Gen. WILTON B. PERSONS to head it,

and Harlow joined Persons's staff. That same year, Harlow received his masters degree. After rising to the rank of lieutenant colonel, he left the military and in 1947 took a job on the staff of the House Armed Services Committee. He became chief clerk to the Armed Services Committee, but left Washington in 1951 to take a position as vice president of Harlow Publishing Company.

Harlow played a minor role in Eisenhower's campaign in Oklahoma and in 1953 accepted a position with the White House congressional liaison office, which was headed by Persons. Harlow's knowledge of the legislative process, his political instincts, and his personal popularity made him an effective lobbyist for the administration's legislative agenda. Harlow enjoyed good and productive working relationships with the powerful Democratic congressional leaders, SAM RAYBURN (D-Tex.), who became Speaker of the House after the Democrats took control in the elections of 1954, and LYNDON JOHNSON (D-Tex.), who became the majority leader in the Senate.

Harlow occupied a series of positions during Eisenhower's two terms. Early in the first administration, in addition to his work with Congress, Harlow became the president's chief speech writer. He also assumed the responsibility as liaison between the president and the various agencies and departments of the executive branch. In his various capacities, Harlow participated in discussions of policy regarding defense, science, and foreign affairs, as well as most domestic matters. When Persons succeeded SHERMAN ADAMS as chief of staff in September 1958, Harlow replaced Persons as head of the congressional liaison office.

One of the more liberal members of the White House staff, he was one of a group of presidential aides who urged the president to confront Sen. JOSEPH R. MCCARTHY (R-Wis.) more publicly. Harlow was also one of the more forceful advocates of black civil rights within the administration. He wrote the draft of Eisenhower's speech condemning the rioting that broke out in Little Rock, Ark., when black students, pursuant to a court order, attended Central High School. After a tour of the South and Southwest in the summer of 1958, he urged Eisenhower to take a strong public stand in favor of school desegregation.

After leaving the White House in January 1961, Harlow became a director of governmental relations for Procter & Gamble Company. Harlow supported RICHARD M. NIXON for the presidency in 1968, and, when Nixon won, he named Harlow assistant to the president for legislative and congressional affairs. By the end of Nixon's first year in office, Harlow was elevated to counselor to the president with cabinet rank. In his new position, Harlow no longer had responsibility for operational duties with Congress, but he retained overall responsibility for congressional relations. Harlow proved less effective than he had been in the 1950s, in part because of the strained relations between Nixon and the Democratic Congress. Harlow resigned in December 1970 and left the White House in 1971 to become a vice president of Procter & Gamble. Nixon called Harlow back to the White House in the spring of 1973 to deal with the burgeoning Watergate scandal. Given the circumstances, Harlow maintained congressional relations about as well as could be expected. He left the White House in 1974 and returned to Procter & Gamble. Harlow served as a consultant for President GERALD FORD and as strategist for Ford's unsuccessful campaign for reelection in 1976. In 1978, Harlow retired from Procter & Gamble and moved to Harpers Ferry, W.Va., where he lived until his death in Arlington, Va., on February 17, 1987.

—MSM

Harriman, W(illiam) Averell

(1891–1986) *governor of New York*

A son of Edward Henry Harriman, a financier and railroad magnate, Averell Harriman was born in New York City on November 15, 1891. Upon E. H. Harriman's death in 1909, Averell inherited an enormous fortune. At Groton and then Yale, where he received his B.A. in 1913, Harriman was an undistinguished student but an outstanding athlete. While a senior at Yale, Harriman was elected to the board of directors of the Union Pacific. Afer graduating, he went to work for the Union Pacific and became a vice president a year later. Anxious to make a name for himself independent of his father, he bought a rundown shipyard in 1917 and left the railroad to direct it. After World War I, Harriman

expanded his interests and presided over the creation of one of the largest merchant fleets in the world. He also formed the investment house of W. A. Harriman and Company in 1919 and joined with his brother to found a private bank, Harriman Brothers & Company, in 1920. The two financial concerns merged with Brown Brothers in 1931 to form Brown Brothers Harriman & Company. In 1932, Harriman returned to railroading as chairman of the board of the Union Pacific.

Although initially a Republican, Harriman switched parties in 1928. Harriman supported Franklin D. Roosevelt in 1932, and in 1934 Roosevelt appointed Harriman state chairman of the National Recovery Administration (NRA). Harriman later became the agency's special assistant administrator, and when Roosevelt dismissed the NRA's head, Hugh Johnson, Harriman ran the organization until the Supreme Court declared it unconstitutional in 1935. Harriman also served as a member of the Business Advisory Council of the Department of Commerce and its chair from 1937 to 1940. When World War II broke out in Europe, Harriman sought a post in Washington. In early 1941, Harriman became chief of the materials branch of the production division of the Office of Production Management. With the passage of lend-lease legislation in March 1941, Harriman was sent to London to facilitate the disbursement of lend-lease aid to Britain. When the Soviet Union entered the war, Harriman oversaw lend-lease aid to the USSR. Harriman served as ambassador to the Soviet Union from 1943 to 1946. After the death of presidential adviser Harry Hopkins, however, Harriman's influence declined. He served as ambassador to Great Britain from March to September 1946, when Truman named him to replace Henry A. Wallace as secretary of commerce. Harriman held that position until 1948. He then served as director of economic aid to Europe under the Marshall Plan from 1948 to 1953. In 1951, Truman named Harriman as director of the Mutual Security Administration, a post he also held until 1953.

As the Truman administration wound down, Harriman turned his attention to winning elective office. He sought the Democratic presidential nomination in 1952. A supporter of the New Deal and Fair Deal, he drew strong support from liberals, but he finished fourth on the first two ballots at the Democratic convention, upon which Harriman withdrew from the race. Two years later, Harriman ran for the Democratic gubernatorial nomination in New York. With the aid of CARMINE DESAPIO, the boss of New York City's Tammany Hall, Harriman defeated Rep. Franklin D. Roosevelt, Jr., for the Democratic nomination. With respect to substantive differences on policy, very little separated Harriman from his opponent in the general election, Sen. IRVING M. IVES, a liberal Republican. Ultimately, Harriman narrowly defeated Ives.

In response to the state's financial difficulties, Harriman instituted an austerity program, which was predictably unpopular. Harriman was nonetheless proud of his record as governor, pointing to programs to aid the elderly, an increase of 77 percent in state aid to education, a substantial increase in regents' scholarships, and increased benefits to workers. Even many of his supporters, however, considered the governor's accomplishments as modest, at best. Republican control of the legislature certainly limited what Harriman could accomplish. Harriman compounded his problems, however, with his own political ineptitude and his preoccupation with capturing the Democratic presidential nomination in 1956. In pursuit of the nomination, he continually attacked the foreign and domestic policies of the Eisenhower administration. Hoping to win the support of northern liberals, labor, and big cities, he staked out a position on the party's left wing, particularly with respect to civil rights for African Americans. Harriman thus encountered strong opposition from conservatives in the party as well as the powerful southern bloc. Neither Harriman nor Sen. ESTES KEFAUVER (D-Tenn.) could prevent ADLAI STEVENSON from winning the nomination for a second time.

Even after his defeat and despite his own rather advanced age, Harriman continued to nurture hopes of capturing the nomination in 1960. The first important step was his reelection as governor in 1958. A series of political defeats, however, diminished his chances. Liberals and reformers in the Democratic Party hoped to nominate either former Air Force Secretary THOMAS FINLETTER or Atomic Energy Commissioner Thomas Murray

(Harriman's choice) for the U.S. Senate in 1958. DeSapio supported FRANK HOGAN, the district attorney of Manhattan, and DeSapio dominated the Democratic state convention, which dutifully nominated Hogan. This not only weakened Harriman, but it left both Hogan and Harriman, who was running for reelection that year, vulnerable to charges that the Democratic Party was boss-dominated. Further, Harriman faced a formidable opponent in NELSON A. ROCKEFELLER, the grandson of John D. Rockefeller, a liberal Republican, and a dynamic campaigner. Rockefeller defeated Harriman decisively. Harriman announced that he no longer entertained any political ambitions.

Harriman supported JOHN F. KENNEDY for the Democratic nomination in 1960 and served as a foreign policy adviser to the candidate. After the election, Kennedy, concerned about Harriman's age and slight deafness, hesitated to appoint the former ambassador to a position in government. Ultimately, Harriman accepted a position as ambassador-at-large. Kennedy then named Harriman assistant secretary of state for Far Eastern affairs (1961–63). Harriman negotiated the neutralization of Laos in 1962. Harriman became undersecretary of state for political affairs in 1963 and that same year headed the American team that negotiated the nuclear test ban treaty. After the assassination of Kennedy, Harriman stayed on with the Johnson administration. In 1965, at his own request, his title reverted to ambassador-at-large. Johnson placed him in charge of the American effort to initiate talks to end the war in Vietnam. In 1968 he headed the United States delegation at the Paris peace talks. Although initially a hawk, Harriman pressed for an accommodation. When RICHARD M. NIXON became president, he replaced Harriman, who subsequently publicly advocated a complete American withdrawal. Harriman vigorously criticized the invasion of Cambodia in 1970 and in 1971 urged Congress to use its power to end the conflict.

His public career ended, Harriman continued to demonstrate an interest in foreign affairs. In 1982, he donated $10 million to the Russian Institute at Columbia University to promote American studies of the Soviet Union. He said that he did so because Soviet studies had declined in recent years, and that ignorance of the Soviet Union was "very dangerous." In June 1983, Harriman went to Moscow to meet with the Soviet leader, Uri V. Andropov. Harriman died at his home in Yorktown Heights, N.Y., on July 26, 1986.

—MSM

Harris, Oren

(1903–1997) *U.S. congressman; chairman, Interstate and Foreign Commerce Committee*

Born in Belton, Ark., on December 20, 1903, Oren Harris grew up in southern Arkansas. He graduated from Henderson-Brown College in 1929, and, after receiving his LL.B. from Cumberland University in 1930, he set up practice in El Dorado, Ark., a town whose economy was closely tied to the region's oil and natural gas industries. He was deputy prosecuting attorney of Union Co. from 1933 to 1936 and prosecuting attorney of the 13th judicial circuit from 1937 to 1940. In 1940, Harris won election as a Democrat to the U.S. House of Representatives. In 1952, he chaired a special House Commerce Committee investigation of television programs. Four years later, Harris acquired a 25 percent interest in an El Dorado TV station.

Like most of his southern colleagues, Harris usually voted as a Democrat but always supported his sectional interests. He opposed the Saint Lawrence Seaway project in May 1954 and an increase in the minimum wage in July 1955. He favored the Eisenhower administration's requests for foreign aid appropriations. Harris, who enjoyed close links to House Speaker SAM RAYBURN (D-Tex.), tended to vote with the majority of his fellow Democrats through the 1950s. However, he generally opposed consumer legislation and civil rights measures. In 1956, Harris joined 100 other southern members of Congress in signing the "Southern Manifesto," which called for defiance of the Supreme Court's decision in *Brown v. Board of Education*.

Through much of his House career, Harris closely identified himself with efforts to deregulate the oil and natural gas industry. Early in 1955, he and Sen. J. WILLIAM FULBRIGHT (D-Ark.) proposed a measure that would have exempted independent producers and gatherers of natural gas from the regulatory authority of the Federal Power Commission. Its waiver of price controls aroused determined

opposition from Northern urban and consumer groups. Yet the legislation enjoyed support from the White House and southern Democrats, and it passed both houses. In February 1956, however, Eisenhower reluctantly vetoed the bill following the attempted bribery of Sen. Frances Case (R-S.Dak.) by a gas producer. Harris unsuccessfully resubmitted his natural gas bill in the 85th Congress.

Assuming the chairmanship of the House Commerce Committee in January 1957, Harris became embroiled in an investigation of the federal regulatory agencies. At the urging of Speaker Rayburn, the House agreed in 1957 to establish a Special Subcommittee on Legislative Oversight to examine the actions of the independent commissions. Harris initially showed little interest in a detailed, critical inquiry because of his connections with the gas and TV industries. Instead, he selected the chairman, Rep. Morgan Moulder (D-Mo.), and chief counsel, BERNARD SCHWARTZ, because he considered them "safe," cautious inquisitors. Just in case they proved otherwise, Harris attended the subcommittee sessions as an ex officio member.

Schwartz, however, quickly upset Harris's well-laid plans. In leaks and official statements to the press in early 1958, Schwartz made detailed charges implicating high administration figures in conflicts of interest. Harris first tried to discredit Schwartz. He suggested to reporters that the counsel had, like some of those he accused, overbilled the government on expenses. When that tactic failed, Harris persuaded the subcommittee to dismiss Schwartz and had his papers seized. Moulder thereupon resigned in protest, and Harris made himself chairman.

Schwartz's charges, however, appeared too serious to be dismissed outright. Subpoenaed as a witness, he elaborated on cases he had made against two members of the Federal Communications Commission (FCC), RICHARD MACK and JOHN DOERFER, and the president's chief aide, SHERMAN ADAMS. Aware of the extensive news coverage Schwartz's testimony had received, Rayburn demanded that Harris pursue the allegations. Harris dutifully pledged "the most thorough investigation Capitol Hill has ever seen." Following hearings in March 1958, Harris demanded and secured Mack's dismissal. (As a result of the probe, Doerfer resigned in 1960.)

In the summer of 1958, Harris's panel pursued rumors that Sherman Adams had interceded with the Federal Trade Commission and the Securities and Exchange Commission on behalf of BERNARD GOLDFINE, who had given him gifts. Adams initially invoked "executive privilege" and refused to honor subpoenas issued by the House. But he soon relented and testified in June. To his detractors' surprise, Harris asked the key, incriminating questions. Adams acknowledged that he might have acted "more prudently" in inquiring of federal agencies about matters involving Goldfine. However, he said that it was "unwarranted and unfair" to charge that he had secured favored treatment for Goldfine from the agencies. Adams was forced to resign in September.

Another sensational offshoot of the Legislative Oversight Panel's labors was its probe of the TV industry. Under its authority to investigate the FCC, the Harris subcommittee took testimony in the fall of 1959 from quiz show participants which revealed that the programs had been rigged. The extension of the inquiry into 1960 added to the mounting pressure on broadcasters for greater self-regulation.

During the 1960s, Harris favored less government regulation by independent commissions and occasionally clashed with the Kennedy and Johnson administrations over the issue. In July 1965, President LYNDON B. JOHNSON named Harris U.S. judge of the Eastern and Western Arkansas District, a post he had long coveted. He assumed office in February 1966. Harris died in Little Rock, Ark., on February 5, 1997.

—JLB

Harris, Reed
(1909–1982) *deputy administrator, International Information Administration*

Reed Harris was born on November 5, 1909, in New York City. After attending a military academy in Virginia, Harris entered Columbia University in 1928. He became editor of the school newspaper, the *Spectator*, which, under his direction, made a radical departure from its former conservative tradition. The paper attacked the "semi-professionalism" of the university's football team and supported a group

of Columbia sociology students on a fact-finding mission in the Kentucky coal-mining region. His criticism of the university's food services prompted the college dean to expel him for a "long series of discourtesies, innuendos, and misrepresentations." Harris's case became a cause célèbre for liberals and journalists across America. The uproar over his expulsion compelled the university authorities to reinstate him, but he afterward dropped out of Columbia. Harris later summarized his views on college sports in his book, *King Football* (1932). In 1931, Harris turned to freelance journalism, working for the *New York Times* and the *New York Evening Journal*. In 1934, he became assistant director of the Federal Writers's Projects and executive editor for the Federal Emergency Relief Administration. Harris briefly left government service in 1938 and went to work at Robbins Travel House as a travel-book editor. He returned to the government as an administrative officer for the National Emergency Council in 1939. During World War II, Harris worked for the Office of War Information (OWI) from 1942 until he volunteered for the air force in 1944. Upon his separation from the service, he returned to the OWI, which was then being transferred to the State Department.

From 1950 to 1953, Harris served as deputy administrator of the International Information Administration. While at that post, he became embroiled in a dispute over the decision of the Voice of America (VOA) to discontinue Hebrew broadcasts to Israel. The move had been made for budgetary reasons. Nevertheless, before the order was issued, staff members asked Harris if the decision had been considered in the light of growing communist anti-Semitism, a theme they hoped to exploit in the broadcasts. The decision was confirmed and the order issued in December 1952. However, as a result of opposition from Sidney Glazer, chief of the Hebrew Service of the VOA, Gerald Dooher, acting chief of the South Asian and African Near East Service, and various members of Congress, the State Department reversed the decision.

In February 1953, the Senate Internal Security Subcommittee, chaired by Sen. JOSEPH R. MCCARTHY (R-Wis.), held hearings on Harris's decision. Using Dooher's testimony, McCarthy implied that Harris had aided the communists through his action. The chairman asked Dooher if he thought that "if Harris's order had been followed, [he] would have been performing a great service to the communist cause?" McCarthy later asked Dooher if he felt this action would have been the same "if [Harris] had been representing Joe Stalin." In both cases Dooher answered yes. Harris testified that the decision was made by a board, which concluded that there were more effective ways of communicating with the Israeli people.

McCarthy also questioned Harris on his college record and his book, *King Football*, which, in addition to its attack on the professionalization and commercialization of college football, contained a defense of academic freedom that included support for the right of communists to teach. Further, Harris had been listed as a sponsor of a dinner for the communist-dominated American Student Union in 1937. Harris frankly acknowledged his youthful affiliations (including membership in the socialist Student League for Industrial Democracy), swore that he had never been a communist, and declared that he had long since disavowed such radical beliefs. Harris countercharged that McCarthy was using "unfair tactics" by raising his activities in college and affiliations from many years before. McCarthy refused to accept Harris's political maturation and pressed on. Harris angrily responded that he resented "the tone of this inquiry very much, Mr. Chairman," because "it is my neck, my public neck, that you are, I think, very skillfully trying to wring." The comment got considerable play in the media.

Harris resigned his post in April 1953. McCarthy called his departure "the best thing that has happened there in a very long time." Harris then founded Publications Services Inc., a firm used by agencies for processing information. EDWARD R. MURROW made Harris his executive assistant at the United States Information Agency in 1961. Harris died of a heart attack in Washington, D.C., on October 15, 1982.

—MSM

Harris, Seymour E(dwin)
(1897–1974) *economist*

Harris was born on September 8, 1897 in New York City. Following his graduation from Harvard Uni-

versity in 1920, Harris taught economics at Princeton. He returned to Harvard in 1922 as a graduate student and instructor. He obtained a doctorate there in 1926. Harris then joined the faculty at Harvard and rose through the academic ranks, becoming a professor in 1945. His early work met with mixed reviews; critics pointed to a lack of clarity and poor organization that characterized Harris's books. During World War II, he served as a member of the Board of Economic Warfare in 1942 and worked for the Office of Price Administration from 1942 to 1943. Harris also advised several Latin American governments on fiscal matters.

During the postwar period, Harris served on the advisory boards of several government commissions and wrote two books, both published in 1947: *National Debt and the New Economic Policy* and *The New Economics*. Both expounded Keynesian economic theory. Harris also became interested in the problems of financing higher education. He recommended that college costs be borne primarily by tuition payments rather than tax dollars. In the 1950s, Harris showed great concern about New England's declining textile industry. He denounced reduced tariffs on Japanese textile imports in 1954 and urged greater government-labor cooperation to solve the problems of the region. In 1955, Harris became chair of the economics department at Harvard.

In 1952, Harris served as an adviser to Democratic candidate ADLAI STEVENSON, who had been his student at Princeton. Following his defeat, Stevenson made Harris his fiscal policy adviser in preparation for a political comeback. From 1953 to 1956, Harris was a member of an informal advisory panel, known as the "Finletter Group," which met regularly to discuss issues and suggest positions the Democrats should take.

During the Eisenhower administration, Harris was often called to testify before congressional committees on fiscal policy. He opposed the Republicans' emphasis on a balanced budget at the expense of full employment and government services. Harris also maintained that the president's policies put "excessive burdens on state and local governments." He did, however, support reductions in the defense budget.

After Stevenson was defeated for the Democratic presidential nomination in 1960, Harris became an adviser to JOHN F. KENNEDY. When Kennedy became president, Harris was named chair of a panel of economic advisers that met weekly with the secretary of the treasury. After Kennedy was assassinated, Harris published *Economics of the Kennedy Years and a Look Ahead* (1964), in which he credited Kennedy for the economic recovery of the early 1960s.

Harris left Harvard in 1963 to become chair of the economics department at the University of California, San Diego. He also served as an economic consultant to President LYNDON B. JOHNSON. Harris died in San Diego on October 27, 1974.

—MSM

Harrison, William K(elly), Jr.

(1895–1987) *senior United Nations delegate*

A direct descendant of President William Henry Harrison, William K. Harrison Jr. was born in Washington, D.C., on September 7, 1895. He graduated from West Point and served in France during World War I. After the war, Harrison remained in Europe, where he learned French and Spanish. He returned to the United States in 1920 to teach at West Point. Over the next 20 years, he served in various assignments in the United States and the Philippines, rising steadily in rank; by 1942, he held the temporary rank of brigadier general. During World War II, he commanded infantry in Europe and later served under Gen. Douglas MacArthur with the occupation troops in Japan. Harrison worked in the office of the chief of staff during 1949 and 1950. In January 1952, Gen. MATTHEW B. RIDGWAY placed Harrison, then deputy commander of the Eighth Army in Korea, on the Korean armistice delegation under the UN command. Harrison became chief UN delegate to the Korean truce negotiations in May 1952.

By the time Harrison took command of the delegation, only the issue of the repatriation of prisoners of war (POWs) blocked the signing of an agreement. The UN forces refused to repatriate prisoners who did not want to return to North Korea or Communist China. The communists, in turn, demanded the return of all prisoners and claimed they would use force if necessary to secure them.

In early 1952, the United Nations Command (UNC) altered its position from "voluntary repatriation" to "no forced repatriation." In March, the communists offered to drop their demand for the return of 38,000 civilian internees if the UNC would cease its demand for an accounting of the 52,000 UN prisoners the communists had classified as "sent home" or "released at the front." The Chinese then proposed that, in order to determine how many prisoners would accept repatriation willingly, new lists be prepared. Most of the prisoners held by the United Nations were interned at Koje Island (Geojedo), where a series of clashes between prisoners (whom the North Koreans continued to regard as combatants) and guards had taken place. During an attempt at screening, riots broke out followed by an attempted mass escape. In order to restore order, the UN forces had to open fire, resulting in the wounding and killing of some prisoners. The Chinese accused the UN of a "bloody yet cowardly massacre." On July 8, the communists offered an armistice if the UNC would forcibly repatriate all Chinese POWs. Five days later, the UNC announced the result of the screening. Of 132,000 North Korean prisoners and pro-communist South Korean internees, 76,600 demanded repatriation. Only 6,400 out of 20,800 Chinese prisoners of war chose to return to Communist China. Presentation of these results led to new heights of vituperation from the communist delegates. Meanwhile, the UN forces released 38,000 South Korean civilian internees. In an effort to offer a face-saving solution to the Communists, Harrison proposed that the 38,000 civilian internees be counted, so that the Communists could claim that 121,000 communist POWs had been released. The Communists rejected that proposal.

In September, Harrison presented three alternative proposals, "any one of which [would] lead to an armistice." The first would have allowed all non-repatriated prisoners, after identification in the demilitarized zone, to have the right to return to their captors. The second would have provided for all prisoners who opted against repatriation to be interviewed by neutral representatives in the demilitarized zone and to be allowed to choose the side to which they would go. The third would have placed all non-repatriated prisoners in the DMZ without any screening and allow them to go the side of their choice. The Chinese rejected the offer, and Harrison unilaterally recessed the plenary meeting.

In early 1953, the Communists proposed sending all non-repatriated prisoners to a neutral state within three months of the signing of a truce. For six months after that, agents of various combatant governments would be able to attempt to persuade prisoners to return to their native lands. After the end of six months, all remaining prisoners who refused repatriation would remain in custody of the neutral state until a postwar conference decided their fates. Harrison rejected the plan.

The talks produced some results in early April, when the two sides managed to negotiate an exchange of sick and wounded prisoners that took place at the end of April and early May. On May 7, the Communists proposed that a repatriation commission be formed of neutral nations (Czechoslovakia, Poland, Sweden, Switzerland, and India), each of which would provide equal numbers of armed personnel. That commission would take custody of non-repatriates in Korea, after which agents of the countries to which the prisoners declined to be repatriated would have four months to persuade the prisoners to come home, and the ultimate fate of the prisoners would be determined by a postwar conference. Speaking for the United Nations command, Harrison rejected the proposals, but he made a counterproposal on May 13. It provided that all Korean prisoners be released to civilian status on the signing of an armistice. Chinese and North Korean prisoners who declined repatriation would be turned over to a supervisory commission of neutral nations, the custodial forces and chair of which would be Indian. After 60 days, during which the Chinese and North Korean governments could try to convince them to return home, all non-repatriates would be granted civilian status (and therefore freedom). The Communists rejected the offer the day after it was made.

In late May, the United States, after consultation with its allies, devised a set of final proposals. They provided for the transfer of all prisoners to the supervisory commission of neutral nations, which would have an Indian chair and Indian custodial forces. An initial period of 60 days would allow for the repatriation of those who wished; those who

did not wish to return home would have 90 or 120 days to "explain," after which they would either be released as civilians or have their cases referred to the General Assembly. At the same time, in a message conveyed to China through the Indian government, the new administration in Washington hinted darkly at the possible use of nuclear weapons if the final offer were rejected.

On June 4, the Communists accepted the final plan with some minor changes. The Communists refused to accept the General Assembly as custodian on the ground that the UN was a belligerent. The agreement allowed two months for repatriation. After which, governments would have 90 days to persuade their nationals among remaining prisoners to return home. Then, a postwar conference would attempt to agree on the final disposition of the non-repatriates. If the conference could not agree after 30 days, prisoners who so desired would be sent to a neutral country, supervised by the Indian Red Cross or the supervisory commission of neutral nations.

Syngman Rhee, the South Korean president, opposed the repatriation agreement, and on June 18 ordered the release of 25,000 anticommunist Korean POWs. Following some stern admonitions from the United States, Rhee agreed to release no more prisoners. The armistice was signed on July 27, 1953. Harrison and Gen. MARK CLARK signed for the United States.

After signing the agreement, Harrison returned to military duty. In April 1954, he was named commander of the new Army Caribbean Forces. He retired in February 1957. Harrison was a Baptist lay evangelist and often preached at army religious services. A month after he retired, he became director of the Evangelical (Child) Welfare Agency. He held that position for three years and then moved to Largo, Fla., and later to Springfield, Pa. Harrison again emerged in the public eye during the presidential campaign of 1960. He attended a meeting in September that questioned whether a Catholic, such as Democratic presidential candidate JOHN F. KENNEDY, should be president because he might be the target of pressure from the Pope. Harrison died in a nursing home in Bryn Mawr, Pa., on May 25, 1987.

—MSM

Hart, Philip A(loysius)

(1912–1976) U.S. senator

Born into an Irish-Catholic family on December 10, 1912, in Bryn Mawr, Pa., Philip Hart was the son of a former landscape gardener who had worked his way up to the presidency of a small bank in suburban Philadelphia. Hart attended private schools and Georgetown University, where he roomed with the son of Walter O. Briggs, the Detroit auto-parts millionaire and owner of the Detroit Tigers baseball team. Hart graduated in 1934 and subsequently married his roommate's sister, who inherited a portion of the family's $100 million fortune. He received his law degree from the University of Michigan in 1937, was admitted to the Michigan bar in 1938, and commenced the practice of law in Detroit. He served in the army from 1941 to 1946, during which time he was wounded in the D-day assault on Utah Beach. Upon his discharge with the rank of lieutenant colonel, he resumed his law practice.

While in law school, Hart had befriended G. MENNEN ("Soapy") WILLIAMS, the heir to the Mennen toiletry fortune and an enthusiastic supporter of the New Deal. In 1948, Williams fashioned an alliance of Democratic liberals and organized labor, which carried him to the governorship. During this period, Williams steadily promoted Hart's political career, appointing him state corporation and securities commissioner in 1949. Hart served as state director of the Office of Price Stabilization from 1951 to 1952. In the latter year, he was named U.S. district attorney for the Eastern District of Michigan. In that post, he secured the conviction of six Michigan communist leaders for conspiracy to teach or advocate the violent overthrow of the government. In 1953, Hart became Williams's legal counsel and the following year made a successful bid for lieutenant governor. His reelection in 1956 made him the first Democrat to serve two terms in this office. In 1958, Hart was Williams's choice for the Senate nomination. Campaigning in favor of civil rights and tax reform, and with the strong backing of the state's labor unions, he beat the Republican incumbent, CHARLES E. POTTER, with 53 percent of the vote.

As a freshman senator, Hart quickly earned a reputation as one of the most liberal members of the upper house. During the opening days of the session in 1959, he joined a group of liberal insur-

gents in an unsuccessful attempt to ease Senate Rule 22—the so-called filibuster rule requiring the vote of two-thirds of the entire Senate membership to shut off debate—as a prelude to the enactment of civil rights legislation. Hart also took a firm stand against political censorship of the arts. When the American National Exhibition in Moscow was criticized because it included the works of artists who had been associated with alleged communist-front organizations, Hart declared that "it is the Soviet Union which has lost face by attempting political censorship of its artists. We do not want to get ourselves into that situation."

In January 1960, Hart was one of about a dozen liberal insurgents who organized a challenge to Majority Leader LYNDON B. JOHNSON in the Senate Democratic Conference. Hart supported a motion aimed at stripping Johnson of his power to appoint members of the Democratic Policy Committee, which scheduled legislation for floor action, by making it an elective body. He also voted against a motion confirming Johnson's power to fill vacancies on the Democratic Steering Committee, which made Democratic committee assignments. The reformers were defeated on both issues.

In the 1960s, Hart became a highly effective leader of the Democratic liberal bloc in the Senate, particularly on civil rights, antitrust, and consumer issues. During the Nixon administration, Hart's firm stands in favor of busing and handgun control aroused some of his constituents to mount unsuccessful recall campaigns in 1971 and 1972. Hart also opposed Nixon's nominations of CLEMENT F. HAYNSWORTH and G. Harold Carswell to the Supreme Court. After being diagnosed with cancer, Hart did not seek reelection in 1976. He succumbed to the disease on December 26, 1976, in Washington, D.C., as he neared the end of his third term in the Senate.

—TLH

Hauge, Gabriel

(1914–1981) administrative assistant to the president for domestic and economic affairs, special assistant to the president for economic affairs

The son of a Lutheran minister, Gabriel Hauge was born in Hawley, Minn., on March 7, 1914. He attended public schools and Concordia College, from which he graduated in 1935. He earned an M.A. from Harvard University three years later and taught economics as a lecturer at Harvard for two years before taking a similar position at Princeton University. Hauge entered the navy during World War II, serving as an officer on battleships in the Pacific. After the war, he returned to Harvard and earned his doctorate in economics in 1947. That same year, Hauge became chief of the Division of Research and Statistics at the New York State Banking Commission. He took time off from that job to serve as economic adviser to the Republican presidential nominee, Thomas E. Dewey, in 1948. Hauge left the banking commission in 1950 to accept a position as the assistant chairman of the executive committee at McGraw-Hill Publishing Company and an editor of *Business Week*.

In late 1951, Hauge joined "Citizens for Eisenhower," an exploratory committee hoping to persuade the general to run for the Republican nomination, and served as its research director. In June 1952, he became research director for the Eisenhower campaign. Hauge soon emerged as one of Eisenhower's principal speech writers. One of the more liberal members of the campaign staff, Hauge urged the candidate to distance himself from Sen. Joseph R. McCarthy (R-Wis.).

When Eisenhower won the election, Hauge joined the White House staff as Eisenhower's personal economic adviser. Officially, his title was administrative assistant to the president for economic affairs from 1953 to 1956, and special assistant to the president for economic affairs from 1956 to 1958. Soon after the inauguration, Hauge, along with Arthur Flemming and James Brownlee, developed a plan for dismantling all government price controls. The plan would have ended controls gradually and on a commodity-by-commodity basis. Eisenhower, however, moved more swiftly to end deregulation, and by the end of February 1953, all controls had been lifted.

Hauge explained and defended the administration's policies to groups of business leaders and economists. He sometimes drafted speeches for the president. In all, he emerged as a highly influential figure within the administration. Hauge advocated a role for the government in restraining inflation and

in stimulating the economy to prevent depressions. At the same time, he generally opposed government planning, price fixing, wage control, and rationing (except in time of war). Hauge frequently sided with Arthur Burns, the chief of the Council of Economic Advisers, against Secretary of the Treasury George Humphrey's insistence on balanced budgets. In general, the position of Hauge and Burns prevailed. For example, Hauge encouraged Eisenhower's view that construction of the interstate highway system could be used as a counter-recessionary measure. On the other hand, Hauge opposed the federal operation of the Hells Canyon Dam as an unwarranted interference with the private sector.

In spite of Eisenhower's high regard for Hauge, the latter's positions did not always persuade the president. In 1955, Eisenhower rejected a plan by Hauge and Burns for aid to depressed areas. Three years later, Eisenhower decided against a tax cut proposed by Hauge as an emergency antirecession measure. The new secretary of the treasury, Robert Anderson, opposed the measure, and, in this instance, his counsel prevailed.

Hauge left the government in 1958 to join Manufacturers Trust Company as chairman of its finance committee. In an unsuccessful effort to keep Hauge in the administration, Eisenhower offered him a post in the cabinet. Hauge nevertheless continued to consult with Eisenhower on economic policies. After Manufacturers Trust merged with Hanover Bank in 1961, Hague became vice chairman of the board. In that capacity, and then as president after 1963, he led an ultimately successful legal battle against the Justice Department, which had challenged the merger. Hauge became chairman in 1971, a position he held until his retirement in 1979. During his stewardship, the bank's assets grew from $7.7 billion in 1966 to $55 billion in 1980. The same period saw the bank expand from 200 offices in New York City to more than 700 offices in the United States and over 100 offices in foreign countries.

Even after leaving Washington, Hauge continued publicly to advocate monetary restraint by the Federal Reserve and free movement of goods and investment among nations. Although he was considered for several positions in the administration of Richard M. Nixon, Hauge chose to remain at

Manufacturers Hanover. Both GERALD R. FORD and Jimmy Carter consulted Hauge on economic matters. Hauge died in New York City on July 24, 1981.

—MSM

Hayden, Carl T(rumbull)

(1877–1972) *U.S. senator; chairman, Appropriations Committee*

Hayden was born on October 2, 1877, in Hayden's Ferry (now Tempe), Ariz., a town founded by his father. He attended Stanford University from 1896 to 1900 but left before completing his degree to return to Tempe in order to help his ailing father run the family mercantile and flour-milling businesses. Hayden served on the town council from 1902 to 1904, as treasurer of Maricopa Co. from 1904 to 1906, and as sheriff of Maricopa Co. from 1907 to 1912. He won election to the U.S. House of Representatives in 1912 as Arizona's first, and only, member. He held that seat until he went into the Senate. In the House, he established himself as a significant figure regarding water reclamation and land-use issues. One of his most significant achievements was his sponsorship of legislation to establish the Grand Canyon National Park. The son of a suffragette, he introduced a joint resolution in favor of a woman-suffrage amendment, which failed. Hayden also supported organized labor. During World War I, he served as a major in the army. He won election to the Senate in 1926 and served until January 3, 1969.

As a senator, he made few speeches but wielded considerable influence because of his seniority and his effectiveness in legislative maneuvering. A champion of water and land reclamation projects, he exerted powerful influence on federal policy in those areas. His signature achievement was his sponsorship of the Central Arizona Project (CAP), a plan to divert water from the Colorado River to Arizona. In the early 1950s, a CAP bill passed the Senate but failed in the House. Hayden continued to press for the project until Congress finally passed the Colorado River Basin Project Act in 1968, which included the Colorado River project and other land reclamation projects. During 1951 and 1952, as chairman of the Rules Committee

and then as a member of the Subcommittee on Privileges and Elections, Hayden was involved in an investigation of the activities of Sen. JOSEPH R. MCCARTHY (R-Wis.). The final report was critical of McCarthy's financial practices and denounced the Wisconsin senator's "disdain and contempt for the rules and wishes" of the Senate. Hayden also planned to demand that McCarthy either "stand aside" or be administered the oath of office "without prejudice" to further action by the Senate when the senator from Wisconsin presented himself to be sworn in at the beginning of the session in 1953. The plan collapsed when Republicans warned that if Hayden did so, they would ask DENNIS CHAVEZ (D-N.Mex.) to "stand aside" pending an investigation of his closely contested reelection, which was marked by charges of fraud and irregularities.

A party loyalist, Hayden supported the administrations of Franklin D. Roosevelt, HARRY S. TRUMAN, JOHN F. KENNEDY, and LYNDON B. JOHNSON. He consistently advocated federally supported highway construction and sponsored the Hayden-Cartwright Act of 1934. He was a coauthor of the Federal-Aid Highway Act of 1956, which called for the creation of over 42,000 miles of four-to-eight-lane, controlled-access roads linking major urban areas. On civil rights, however, he voted with the southern, conservative wing of the Democratic party. Hayden voted against legislation to eliminate the poll tax in 1948 and consistently refused to support ending southern filibusters against civil rights legislation.

Hayden was appointed to the Appropriations Committee his first term in the Senate and became its chairman in 1955, a post he held until 1969. In recognition of his long service, he was named dean of the Senate in 1957 and was president pro tempore of the Senate from the 1957 to 1969. In the 1960s, he moderated his opposition to civil rights legislation and supported the Civil Rights Act of 1964 and the Voting Rights Act of 1965, perhaps because of changing circumstances and perhaps because he was a party loyalist. He also supported Johnson on Medicare and issues relating to Social Security. In 1969, Hayden retired to Tempe. He died in Mesa, Ariz., on January 25, 1972.

—MSM

Hayek, Friedrich August
(1899–1992) *economist*

Born Friedrich August von Hayek in Vienna, Austria, on May 8, 1899, Hayek took his doctorate in jurisprudence at the University of Vienna in 1921 and a second doctorate in 1923. Although he enrolled as a law student, his interests focused on economics and psychology. He did postgraduate work at New York University from 1923 to 1924. Initially a socialist, Hayek was profoundly influenced by the publication in 1922 of Ludwig von Mises's *Die Gemeinwirtschaft*, later translated into English as *Socialism*. Mises argued that, without a market, there was no way to establish the value of the means of production and, therefore, no way to determine their proper uses. Along with a group that included Oskar Morgenstern and Eric Voegelin, Hayek attended Mises's informal seminar, which was the focal point of economic study and thought in Vienna. From 1927 to 1931, Hayek was director of the Austrian Institute for Trade Cycle Research; during those same years, he was privatdozent at the University of Vienna. He became the Tooke professor of economic science and statistics at the London School of Economics and Political Science in 1931. In the 1930s, he emerged a one of the most lucid and trenchant critics of the economic theories of John Maynard Keynes. As Hayek observed the crisis in Central Europe evolve during the 1930s, he chose to become a British subject in 1938.

A fervent anti-Nazi as well as a critic of the trend towards social democracy he observed in Great Britain, Hayek published *The Road to Serfdom* in 1944. In it, he argued that government planning inherently led to the "suppression of freedom" and ultimately to "dictatorship." "Economic control," he maintained, "is not merely control of a sector of human life which can be separated from the rest; it is the control of the means of all our ends. And whoever has sole control of the means must also determine which ends are to be served." Thus, all collectivism inevitably led to totalitarianism, and democratic socialism was "unachievable." In place of government planning and control, Hayek advocated individualism and classical liberalism. At the same time, he denied that this meant laissez-faire. Rather, he proposed that "government in all its actions [should be] bound by rules fixed and announced beforehand." More restrained in his antistatism than Mises, Hayek accepted government activities designed to facilitate competition and thus allowed for sanitary regulations, minimum wage laws, limits on working hours, and even social insurance. In all cases, however, the purpose of government intervention had to be the preservation of competition, private initiative, and private property. The book's publication in Great Britain aroused some controversy; its appearance in America created a sensation. After three publishing houses in the United States rejected the book, the University of Chicago Press published an American edition, printing 2,000 copies. Within a week, the press ordered a second printing of 5,000 copies. The book received lavish praise and was also the subject of almost hysterical attacks. It became a Book-of-the-Month Club selection; Reader's Digest condensed it.

In 1950, Hayek left the London School for the Committee on Social Thought at the University of Chicago. Four years later, he edited *Capitalism and the Historians*, which attacked contemporary trends in the writing of British economic history. He rejected "the legend of the deterioration of the position of the working classes in consequence of the rise of 'capitalism.'" ARTHUR SCHLESINGER, JR., somewhat incongruously fulminated: "Americans, one would think, have enough trouble with home-grown McCarthys without importing Viennese professors to add academic luster to the process." Keith Hutchinson, in the *Nation*, charged the book with "whitewashing the Industrial Revolution."

If liberals could wax apoplectic about Hayek, the Austrian economist had serious reservations about the emerging conservative movement. In his book, *The Constitution of Liberty* (1960), Hayek included an essay titled "Postscript: Why I Am Not a Conservative," in which he distinguished his position from that of the European Right. He criticized conservatism for lacking a coherent set of principles and for its hostility to innovation. In addition, he cited what he saw as conservatism's willingness to use the state for its own purposes, even to the point of acquiescing in socialism. He reiterated his case for limited government, free markets, and the fixed, impartial rule of law.

Hayek left the University of Chicago in 1961 and returned to Germany. He lived in Freiburg and taught at the university there until 1975, when he became an emeritus professor. He won the Nobel Prize in economics in 1974. Even after his retirement, Hayek continued to write; he published *The Fatal Conceit* in 1988. He died in Freiburg in 1992.

Haynsworth, Clement Furman, Jr.

(1912–1989) *judge, United States Court of Appeals for the Fourth Circuit*

The son of a lawyer, Clement F. Haynsworth was born in Greenville, S.C., on October 30, 1912. He graduated summa cum laude from Furman University, an institution founded by his great-grandfather, in 1933 and from Harvard Law School in 1936. Upon earning his law degree, he practiced law in the firm founded by his father and grandfather until he left to serve as a naval intelligence officer from 1942 to 1945. After the war, he returned to the family firm and became senior partner in 1946. The firm prospered under Haynsworth's leadership; it had a number of major corporate clients and became the largest law firm in South Carolina. Haynsworth served on numerous corporate boards. Increasingly disaffected from the national Democratic Party, Haynsworth supported Eisenhower in 1952 and again in 1956, although he was only mildly politically active. One of Haynsworth's friends and clients, Charles E. Daniel, owned a large construction company and had ties to the Eisenhower administration. In 1957 Eisenhower nominated Haynsworth to the U.S. Court of Appeals for the Fourth Circuit. Sen. STROM THURMOND (D-S.C.) had opposed nominating Haynsworth. Thurmond wanted the seat for Robert McC. Figg, the dean of the University of South Carolina Law School, who had represented the Clarendon County school board in *Brown v. Board of Education* (1954). When it became apparent that the administration would not nominate Figg, Thurmond, apparently concerned that Haynsworth might not be sufficiently segregationist, aggressively advanced the candidacy of Alfred Burgess. Nevertheless, Haynsworth, who had no public record as a segregationist or an anti-segregationist, was nominated and confirmed. He was sworn in on April 5, 1957. When SIMON E. SOBELOFF reached the mandatory retirement age and took

senior judge status in 1964, Haynsworth succeeded him as chief judge of the Fourth Circuit.

Throughout the late 1950s and early 1960s, Haynsworth consistently voted to end legal segregation. As the issue changed from desegregation to active efforts to promote integration, Haynsworth's votes took on a more conservative cast. He dissented from a ruling in 1962 that overturned a freedom of choice plan in Charlottesville, Va. In 1968, the Supreme Court reversed his decision upholding a freedom of choice plan for desegregation that allowed parents to choose their children's schools. On several other occasions, the Supreme Court overturned positions Haynsworth took on issues relating to desegregation. On the other hand, Haynsworth maintained his opposition to state supported segregation. He joined a unanimous decision in 1964 striking down the use of tax-financed state tuition grants to private, segregated schools and wrote a decision desegregating the North Carolina Dental Society.

RICHARD M. NIXON nominated Haynsworth to the Supreme Court in 1969. Civil rights groups attacked him as a segregationist, an irony given that much of the resistance to his nomination to the Fourth Circuit came from those who regarded him as insufficiently segregationist. Fred Graham, the Supreme Court reporter for the *New York Times*, wrote that those who attacked Haynsworth as a segregationist "seem to have overstated their case. He has never attempted to delay or thwart desegregation, but he has also never mustered . . . impatience and righteous indignation over the slow pace of desegregation." Supporters of organized labor attacked him as antilabor, identifying seven cases in which he had taken an antilabor position and had been reversed by the Supreme Court. Opponents also accused him of conflict of interest in a case involving Darlington Manufacturing Company because Haynsworth was part owner of a vending machine company that did business with Deering Milliken, the parent company of Darlington Manufacturing. Although Jerome Frank, perhaps the leading authority on when judges should recuse themselves, testified not only that Haynsworth had done nothing improper but that he had a duty to sit on the case, the charge of unethical behavior stuck. Despite the support of many prominent members of the legal community, including 16 past presidents of the American Bar Association, the Senate rejected Haynsworth by a vote of 55 to 45. Although he considered resigning from the Fourth Circuit after the Senate vote, Haynsworth ultimately remained on the bench. His subsequent performance on the court won widespread praise, even from some who voted against his nomination to the Supreme Court. He took senior judge status in 1981 and continued to serve on the Fourth Circuit until his death in Greenville on November 22, 1989.

—MSM

Hays, (Lawrence) Brooks
(1898–1981) *U.S. congressman*

Brooks Hays was born in London, Ark., on August 9, 1898. After graduating from the University of Arkansas in 1919 and George Washington University law school three years later, Brooks Hays opened a law practice in Russellville, Ark. He served in the army in 1918. Hays served as assistant state attorney general from 1925 to 1927 and ran unsuccessfully for governor in 1928 and 1930. After an unsuccessful run in a special election for congress in 1933, he was the National Recovery Administration's labor compliance officer for Arkansas in 1934 and assistant to the administrator for resettlement in 1935. From 1936 to 1942, he held various posts in the Farm Security Administration. Hays won election to the House of Representatives as a Democrat from Arkansas's fifth district, which included Little Rock, in 1942.

On Capitol Hill, Hays was one of a small group of southern moderates who often joined Northern Democrats in supporting social welfare legislation. In 1949 and 1950, he unsuccessfully urged the adoption of a compromise civil rights plan in place of Truman's proposal. In 1948, Truman called for a bill to outlaw lynching, measures against the poll tax, a compulsory Fair Employment Practices Commission (FEPC), an executive commission on civil rights, and the elevation of the civil rights section in the Justice Department to the status of a division. The following year, Hays proposed a compromise that won the support of several southern moderates. He called for a constitutional amendment to outlaw the poll tax, a modified antilynching law that would

permit federal intervention only when local authorities failed to act, the abandonment of attempts to legislate against segregation in interstate transportation, and establishment of a counseling service in the Department of Labor as an alternative to a compulsory FEPC. Truman rejected the compromise. Hays also played a role in crafting the civil rights plank in the Democratic platform of 1952.

Assigned to the Foreign Affairs Committee in 1951, Hays was an internationalist on most policy issues. He voted for Eisenhower's foreign-aid bills in 1953 and 1954, and in 1957 he convinced the committee to support an extension of the administration's foreign-aid authorization from one to three years. He also approved the Eisenhower Doctrine in 1957, which gave the president the power to use force to assist Middle Eastern nations threatened by communist aggression. Hays was an outspoken champion of the UN, describing it as the world's best hope for peace. In 1955 he served as a member of the U.S. delegation to the UN General Assembly.

After the Supreme Court struck down segregated public schools in 1954, Hays, like every southern moderate, was caught in a difficult, if not untenable, position. In 1956, he reluctantly signed the "Southern Manifesto," which denounced the Supreme Court's decision as a "clear abuse of judicial power" and pledged to use all legal means to resist it. When, in September 1957, Gov. ORVAL FAUBUS used the Arkansas National Guard to prevent the court-ordered desegregation of Little Rock's Central High School, the judge whose orders had been defied asked the Justice Department to intervene. At this point, Hays, whose district included Little Rock, offered to act as an intermediary. He arranged a meeting between the governor and the president on September 14. At the meeting, Eisenhower suggested that, rather than withdrawing the guard, Faubus simply change their orders to preserve order and allow the black students to enter the school. Eisenhower believed that he had gotten such a commitment from Faubus. In his public statements afer the conference, however, Faubus refused to commit either to removing the guardsmen or to changing their orders. Convinced that Faubus had deceived him, Eisenhower was furious. Under direct court order not to interfere with the desegregation of Central High, Faubus withdrew the guard. The black students entered Central High on September 23, but, faced with a threatening mob outside the school, authorities decided to withdraw the students for their own safety. That evening, Eisenhower went on national television and warned that he would use "whatever force may be necessary to prevent the obstruction of the orders of the court." When the mob again gathered outside the school the next day, the president nationalized the Arkansas National Guard and sent in 1,000 armed paratroopers to enforce the court's order.

In the months following the crisis at Little Rock, Hays called for compliance with all laws. As segregationist sentiment hardened, this position became politically untenable. In 1958, Dale Alford (an ophthalmologist, a member of the school board in Little Rock, and a segregationist) mounted a last-minute write-in campaign against Hays. While Faubus took no public role in the election, his organization weighed in on behalf of Alford, who defeated Hays. Both Sen. JOHN F. KENNEDY (D-Mass.) and Vice President RICHARD M. NIXON sent Hays letters of condolence.

After losing his seat, Hays was appointed a director of the Tennessee Valley Authority. He served there until February 1961, when he was appointed assistant secretary of state for congressional affairs. From December 1961 to February 1964, Hays was a special assistant to the president. During the last part of the decade, he taught at various universities. In 1972, he unsuccessfully ran for a seat in Congress from North Carolina. Hays lived in Chevy Chase, Md., until his death there on October 11, 1981.

—MSM

Hays, Wayne L(evere)

(1911–1989) *U.S. congressman*

The son of a farmer, Hays was born in Bannock, Ohio, on May 13, 1911. He graduated from Ohio State University in 1933 and studied at Duke University in 1935. He worked as a high school teacher in Ohio from 1934 to 1938. In 1939, he won election to the first of three consecutive two-year terms as mayor of Flushing, Ohio. While holding that office, he served as a Democrat in the state senate in 1941 and 1942. A member of the Officers Reserve

Corps of the U.S. Army since 1933, Hays was called to active duty in 1941 and received a medical discharge a year later. In 1945, he left the mayor's office to operate a farm in Belmont, Ohio. He also was Belmont Co. commissioner from 1945 to 1949. Hays won election to the U.S. House of Representatives in 1948. Representing a poor agricultural and industrial district in southeastern Ohio, Hays generally voted as a liberal on matters of domestic policy. He also supported President HARRY S. TRUMAN's foreign policy.

Although Hays voted for the Internal Security Act of 1950, he played something of a moderating role when he was appointed to the newly created Select Committee to Investigate Tax-Exempt Foundations in 1953. Established to determine whether tax-exempt educational and philanthropic foundations had financed subversive activities and propaganda, the panel held hearings during May and June 1954, which were marked by frequent clashes between the chairman, B. Carroll Reece (R-Tenn.), and Hays, who believed that witnesses and committee staff members were unfairly charging individuals and institutions with communist views and affiliations. Attempting to demonstrate that out-of-context quotations could be used to suggest communist sympathies, Hays read excerpts from encyclicals by Popes Leo XIII and Pius XI without attribution and induced a staff member to assert that they were "closely comparable to communist literature." Hays also demanded that the investigation be extended to include Facts Forum, a tax-exempt, right-wing radio and television production company funded by H. L. Hunt, an oil millionaire from Texas.

The committee's majority report found little evidence that the foundations directly supported communism. However, it asserted that they encouraged attacks on the American social and governmental system and promoted collectivist ideas. Hays and Rep. Gracie Pfost (D-Idaho), the other Democrat on the panel, filed a minority report charging that the "theme of prejudgment . . . characterized the entire course of this committee's activities" and that with few exceptions only antifoundation witnesses had been called.

Hays unsuccessfully tried to double the authorization for urban and public-works planning in the omnibus housing bill of 1954. Two years later, he attacked as too modest an administration program to create a $50-million revolving loan fund for depressed rural areas. In 1957, Hays was among 80 House Democrats who offered a list of liberal domestic and foreign policy programs for congressional action. He generally favored economic rather than military assistance to underdeveloped areas.

In the 1960s, Hays broke with many of his liberal colleagues over the Vietnam War, which he supported, and school busing to achieve integration, which he opposed. As Hays accumulated seniority on the House Administration Committee, which oversaw committee budgets, office expenses, and travel vouchers, he used his position to retaliate against other members he disliked or with whom he disagreed. Many members came to regard him as arrogant and abrasive, particularly after he assumed the chair of the Administration Committee in 1971. By 1976, Hays had become one of the most powerful and resented members of Congress. That year, the *Washington Post* reported that Elizabeth Ray, a 33-year-old clerk on the staff of the House Administration Committee, had been given her $14,000-a-year job to be Hays's mistress. In an effort to avoid an investigation by the House Ethics Committee, Hays first resigned his chairmanships and then resigned from the House. He returned to his farm in Belmont, where he bred Angus cattle and Tennessee walking horses. In 1978 he won election to the Ohio House of Representatives but lost his bid for reelection two years later. Hays became chairman of the Democratic Party in Belmont Co. in 1980 and remained active in local politics. He died in Wheeling, W.Va., on February 10, 1989.

—MSM

Hébert, F(elix) Edward
(1901–1979) *U.S. congressman*

Born in New Orleans, La., on October 12, 1901, Hébert attended public and parochial schools. He attended Tulane University from 1920 to 1924, which he left before completing his law degree. From 1918 to 1940, he worked as a journalist and editor in New Orleans. He became political editor of the *New Orleans States* in 1929 and used his front-page column to attack Gov. Huey P. Long. After becoming city editor in 1939, Hébert wrote a series

of articles exposing corruption in Louisiana state politics. In 1940, he defeated a longtime Democratic incumbent in the primary and easily won election to Congress from the state's first congressional district, which included eight wards in New Orleans plus Plaquemines and St. Bernard's Parishes.

In 1943, Hébert was assigned to the Naval Affairs Committee, which in 1947 was merged with the other service panels to form the Armed Services Committee. A staunch defender of segregation and an opponent of what he regarded as federal encroachment upon the rights of the states, he supported South Carolina Gov. STROM THURMOND's third-party presidential candidacy in 1948. That year Hébert was assigned to the House Committee on Un-American Activities (or House Un-American Activities Committee [HUAC]), but he lost that assignment the following year as a result of his support of Thurmond. As chairman of the Armed Services Committee's Subcommittee for Special Investigations, he led probes of wasteful procurement procedures in the military in 1949, 1951, and 1952.

Hébert continued to oppose what he regarded as unnecessary defense expenditures during the Eisenhower administration. In 1956, he opposed an administration-sponsored reorganization of the Defense Department that would have created an office of assistant secretary for research and development for each of the three services.

Despite his crusades against waste, Hébert was a leading advocate of a strong military establishment. A critic of the Eisenhower administration's efforts to reduce the manpower of the Armed Services, in 1959 he attacked Secretary of Defense NEIL McELROY for imposing a "gag" on military officers who opposed the cutbacks. That year, he went against the administration's wishes in voting to provide an additional $99 million to maintain the army's strength at 900,000 men.

In 1959, Hébert's subcommittee on special investigations probed the hiring of retired military officers by the defense industry. Critics of the practice charged that such officers exerted influence upon their former colleagues still in the military. In January 1960, the subcommittee released a report supporting legislation to check this syndrome. Hébert offered a bill barring military and civilian Defense Department personnel from accepting compensation for helping a private company secure a government defense contract within two years after their departure from the department. The measure imposed a $10,000 fine, two years imprisonment and denial of retirement pay during the period of violation for those found guilty. In the full Armed Services Committee, however, chairman CARL VINSON (D-Ga.) succeeded in eliminating the provisions for fine and imprisonment. Hébert unsuccessfully attempted to restore them on the House floor. The measure died in the Senate.

In spite of his opposition to wasteful defense spending, he repeatedly used his influence to procure federal projects in his district, including several military bases, a naval hospital, and a research center.

Throughout the 1950s, Hébert opposed all civil rights legislation and most social welfare legislation. He remained consistent in his opposition to such legislation during the Kennedy and Johnson administrations. Hébert's steadfast opposition to civil rights and social welfare legislation alienated him from members of the Democratic caucus and ultimately led to his fall from effective political power. He also persisted in his support of a powerful military and supported the war in Vietnam. Nonetheless, in 1970 he led a subcommittee investigation into a massacre in that had taken place at My Lai in 1968. His criticism of the Pentagon and State Department for concealing details of the incident won praise even from some of his critics. Upon the death of L. MENDEL RIVERS (D-S.C.) in 1971, Hébert became chair of the Armed Services Committee. His support of the war in Vietnam led to conflicts with junior Democrats in the House. In 1975, the Democratic caucus voted to strip Hébert and two other senior Democrats of their chairmanships. This greatly diminished his power. His demotion and failing health led him to decide not to seek reelection in 1976. He died in New Orleans on December 29, 1979.

—MSM

Hennings, Thomas C(arey), Jr.

(1903–1960) *U.S. senator; chairman, Rules and Administration Committee*

Born in St. Louis, Mo., on June 25, 1903. Hennings received a B.A. from Cornell University in 1924 and an LL.B. from Washington University in 1926.

He joined a law firm in a St. Louis the same year and, from 1929 to 1934, served as assistant circuit attorney in that city. Elected to the U.S. House of Representatives in 1934, he supported Franklin D. Roosevelt's domestic and foreign policies. In 1940, Hennings successfully ran for circuit attorney in St. Louis, but the following year he was called from the U.S. Naval Reserve to active duty. After his discharge in 1944, he resumed his post as circuit attorney.

In 1950, Hennings ran for the Senate against the incumbent Republican senator, Forrest C. Donnell. During the campaign, he warned that Sen. JOSEPH R. McCARTHY's (R-Wis.) activities posed a threat to freedom. Hennings defeated the incumbent by 90,000 votes. He won reelection in 1956.

During his early years in the Senate, Hennings continued his campaign against the Wisconsin Republican. He served on the Rules and Administration Committee's Subcommittee on Privileges and Elections, which in 1951 investigated the Maryland senatorial campaign of 1950, during which JOHN MARSHALL BUTLER defeated Sen. Millard E. Tydings (D-Md.) and McCarthy campaigned against Tydings. The subcommittee's report, later accepted by the full committee, was sharply critical of McCarthy's role in the election. In August 1951, Sen. WILLIAM BENTON (D-Conn.) introduced a resolution calling on the Rules Committee to consider the expulsion of McCarthy from the Senate, which was referred to the Subcommittee on Privileges and Elections. McCarthy released a letter questioning Hennings's qualifications to serve on the subcommittee, to which Hennings replied in a speech on the Senate floor. When Sen. Guy Gillette (D-Iowa) resigned from the subcommittee, Hennings assumed the chair. The report of the subcommittee, issued on January 2, 1953, sidestepped the issues of "McCarthyism" and communism in government. Instead, it focused on McCarthy's spotty finances. It also criticized McCarthy's "disdain and contempt for the rules and wishes of the entire Senate body, as well as the membership of the Subcommittee on Privileges and Elections." The report declined to offer any recommendations. Hennings did, however, forward the report to the Justice Department and the Internal Revenue Service. An investigation by the Justice Department found no basis on which to prosecute McCarthy.

Hennings continued to oppose McCarthy. In July 1953, he denounced the removal of books from United States Information Agency libraries under pressure from McCarthy. In July 1954, Hennings backed Sen. RALPH E. FLANDERS's (R-Vt.) resolution calling for McCarthy's censure. Wanting an immediate showdown and fearing that the resolution might be buried, Hennings was one of 12 senators who in August voted against referring it to a special panel.

After McCarthy's censure in December 1954, Hennings continued his opposition to what he regarded as threats to civil liberties. In the fall of 1955, the Judiciary Committee's Constitutional Rights Subcommittee, chaired by Hennings, began an investigation of the possible erosion of freedom in the United States, which included a critical examination of the federal government's loyalty program. The following year, as a member of the Internal Security Subcommittee of the Judiciary Committee, he was critical of the security panel's investigation of communist influence in the press. Hennings expressed doubts about the propriety of calling individuals whose communist activities had ended many years before. In 1958, he moved to table a bill passed by the House that would have barred federal courts from applying the federal preemption doctrine unless a federal and state statute were irreconcilably in conflict or unless Congress had specifically stated its intention to preempt a particular field of legislation. The immediate purpose of the bill was to enable states to pass anti-sedition laws. Hennings's motion failed, but a recommittal motion succeeded shortly thereafter.

Hennings was a persistent but unsuccessful proponent of election reform. As a member of the Rules and Administration Committee, in 1953 and 1955 he led efforts to pass legislation raising spending limits for national campaigns and tightening disclosure requirements. Neither attempt got beyond the committee. Hennings became chairman of the Rules and Administration Committee in 1957, and two years later the panel reported another reform measure. In an individual view filed with the committee's report, he criticized the bill for failing to bring primary elections within the scope of the reporting requirement. On the Senate floor the following year, Hennings successfully amended the bill to include primaries.

Consistently liberal in his voting, Hennings opposed a bill in 1956 designed to exempt independent natural gas producers from federal utility regulation. On the Judiciary Committee, he sought to expedite the Senate's consideration of the Eisenhower administration's civil rights bill in 1957 and opposed Southern efforts to weaken the measure. In 1960, Hennings cosponsored Sen. PAT McNAMARA's (D-Mich.) bill to provide medical care for the aged within the Social Security system. Hennings died in Washington, D.C., on September 13, 1960.

—MSM

Hensel, H(erman) Struve

(1901–1991)   *assistant secretary of defense for international security affairs*

The son of a stockbroker, Hensel was born in Hoboken, N.J., on August 22, 1901. He graduated from Princeton University in 1922 and received an LL.B. from Columbia University three years later. Over the next 15 years, he established a reputation as a leading corporate lawyer with the firms of Cravath Swaine and Milbank Tweed. In 1940, he organized and served as the first chief of the navy's legal division for procurement. He later became general counsel for the navy and in 1945 was appointed assistant secretary of the navy for materiel procurement. After a brief return to private law practice, he joined the Economic Cooperation Administration in 1948 and was sent to South America to enlist the cooperation of Argentina in the Marshall Plan.

In 1952, Hensel went to work for the Defense Department as general counsel. In 1954, he was made assistant secretary of defense for international security affairs. Shortly after the appointment, he was drawn into the dispute between the army and Sen. JOSEPH R. McCARTHY (R-Wis.). Early in the year, high officials in the Department of the Army began drawing up a "chronology" of McCarthy's efforts to gain preferential treatment for a recently inducted member of his staff, G. DAVID SCHINE. Hensel's only role in the preparation of the army's case was to sign a letter of transmittal forwarding the chronology to a member of McCarthy's permanent investigations subcommittee. McCarthy, however, charged that Hensel had helped write it in an attempt to "blackmail" McCarthy into calling off his investigations of alleged subversion in the military. In formal charges to this effect, filed with the subcommittee in April, McCarthy named Hensel as a co-principal along with Secretary of the Army ROBERT T. STEVENS and the army's counsel, JOHN G. ADAMS. At the same time, McCarthy added the charge that Hensel had a personal motive for discrediting him: to block an investigation of alleged conflict of interest involving Hensel's partnership in a ship supply firm while he was in charge of procurement for the navy during the war. Hensel labeled these charges "barefaced lies" and challenged McCarthy to drop his congressional immunity and repeat them in court.

On May 17, McCarthy admitted that he had no evidence to show that Hensel had been involved in the Schine affair. Shortly afterwards the subcommittee voted to dismiss the charges against him.

Hensel left the Defense Department in 1955 and returned to the private practice of law. He was a partner in the Coudert Brothers law firm from 1966 to 1977. He then retained an active interest in legal and corporate affairs until shortly before his death in Boca Raton, Fla., on May 27, 1991.

—MSM

Herberg, Will
(1901–1977) *philosopher, theologian*

The son of Russian-Jewish parents, Herberg was born in Liakhovichi, Russia, on June 30, 1901. His parents immigrated to the United States in 1904 and settled in a Jewish neighborhood in Brooklyn, New York. Herberg's father deserted the family in 1910, leaving the family in dire economic straits. After graduating from Boys' High School in 1918, Herberg enrolled in the College of the City of New York in September of that year. A brilliant but undisciplined student, he excelled in foreign languages, literature, mathematics, and physics. He failed, however, to meet a requirement in physical education and earned poor grades in hygiene and military science. All of that, combined with frequent absences from military science, led to

his suspension from CCNY in 1920. During the 1920s, Herberg emerged as a prominent figure in American communism; he was active in the Communist Young Workers League and, by the middle of the decade, was a member of its national executive committee. When the Communist Party split in 1929 over the issue of autonomy from the Soviet Union and Joseph Stalin's purge of Nikolay Bukharin, Herberg sided with those who favored an independent course. JAY LOVESTONE, Benjamin Gitlow, Herberg, and others of that faction were expelled from the American Communist Party (CPUSA) for being "right deviationists." After their expulsion, the Lovestonites, as they became known, formed an organization eventually known as the Independent Labor League of America (ILLA), which maintained that the singular circumstances of America required a uniquely American approach to the workers' struggle. Herberg became managing editor of the Lovestoneite publication first known as *Revolutionary Age* and later called *Workers' Age*. In 1933, Herberg took a position as education director of the International Ladies' Garment Workers' Union, a job he held until 1948. Herberg emerged during the 1930s as perhaps the leading spokesperson for the Lovestonites. He condemned with equal vigor Stalinism, the approach of Leon Trotsky, and democratic socialism.

By the end of the 1930s, Herberg became disillusioned with Stalin's purges, the Nazi-Soviet Pact, and American communism's subservience to Moscow. Profoundly influenced by REINHOLD NIEBUHR's *Moral Man and Immoral Society* (1932), Herberg concluded that the source of Stalinism's corruption lay in its failure to recognize the inherently sinful nature of human beings and the consequent inevitable imperfection of human institutions. In the early 1940s, after considering a conversion to Christianity, Herberg, at Niebuhr's urging, instead explored his own religious tradition. He undertook extensive study at the Jewish Theological Seminary, as a result of which Herberg came to regard himself as a democratic socialist and embraced Conservative Judaism.

Swayed by the arguments of the Jewish existentialist theologian Martin Buber as well as Christian neoorthodox theologians such as Niebuhr and Karl Barth, Herberg published his first book, *Judaism and Modern Man: An Interpretation of Jewish Religion,* in 1951. In it, he maintained that neither science, nor Marxism, nor psychoanalysis offered an answer to human despair. Humans could "transcend" their spiritual crisis only by making a great "leap of faith" toward a God unknowable through science or cognitive experience. This position, shaped by the teaching of Niebuhr and influenced by Herberg's deeply felt kinship with Jesuits like John Courtney Murray, led the journalist John Cogley perceptively, if somewhat irreverently, to introduce Herberg to an audience as "Reinhold Niebuhr, S.J."

By the late 1940s and into the 1950s, Herberg considered himself a liberal. Throughout the 1950s, however, he moved gradually towards Burkean conservatism. Like his fellow ex-communist, WHITTAKER CHAMBERS, Herberg saw the conflict between the free world and communist as a "struggle for the soul of modern man." Despite his own anticommunism, Herberg detested Sen. JOSEPH R. McCARTHY (R-Wis.), whom he regarded as an outgrowth of left-wing populism. According to Herberg, the advent of mass communications enabled political leaders to circumvent deliberative institutions and appeal directly to the masses. Early in the New Deal, Franklin D. Roosevelt had made use of the potential of mass communications and engaged in "government by rabble-rousing." Herberg wrote that "McCarthy, like Roosevelt, is impatient with the restraints and limitations of . . . proper constitutional channels." McCarthy's rise, concluded Herberg, demonstrated the danger of "irresponsible mass-democracy," something the founders of the American republic had intended to prevent by creating a carefully balanced government.

In 1955, Herberg published *Protestant-Catholic-Jew: An Essay in American Religious Sociology.* In it, he took as his starting point an apparent contradiction. Church attendance had never been higher, and America seemed to be undergoing a religious revival led by popularizers such as FULTON SHEEN, NORMAN VINCENT PEALE, and BILLY GRAHAM. At the same time, however, American life was becoming more secular. Thus the paradox: Americans were becoming at once more secular and more religious. Herberg found an explanation in the process of immigration and assimilation. He argued that, as the grandchildren of immigrants assimilated into a mainstream American culture, religion had become a means of identification, "a way of sociability or 'belonging,' rather than a way of reorienting one's life to God." Religion itself had become part of a larger American civic creed, which he called "the American Way of Life." Americans participated in that creed through identification with one of the three communities of faith. In the process, religion practiced by Americans had "lost much of its authentic Christian (or Jewish) content." "Faith in faith itself," rather than devotion to a specific creed, became the a means of participating in the American civic creed. Herberg decried what he regarded as a vacuous "faith in faith" rather than faith in God.

Throughout the first half of the 1950s, Herberg had published widely and spoken frequently at colleges. In 1955, he joined the faculty of Drew University, a Methodist school in New Jersey, as a professor of Judaic studies and social philosophy. In the following years, he edited three anthologies: *The Writings of Martin Buber* (1956), *Four Existentialist Theologians* (1958), and *Community, State and Church* (1960). Herberg received honorary doctorate degrees from Park College in 1956, Franklin and Marshall College in 1960, and Ohio Wesleyan University in 1963.

Although his centrist political views and identification with the Catholic church led him to support JOHN F. KENNEDY's campaign for the presidency in 1960, Herberg was becoming more conservative, and in 1961 he became a contributing editor to WILLIAM F. BUCKLEY's *National Review.* For the next 15 years, it served as the main outlet for Herberg's ideas and his substantial contributions to the emerging conservative movement in America. His strong commitment to social order led him to criticize the civil rights movement led by MARTIN LUTHER KING, JR. Despite his own opposition to racial discrimination, Herberg rejected the idea that one had a religious right to violate the law (although Herberg modified that position by the 1970s). Herberg also criticized the liberalizing tendencies of Pope John XXIII and the Second Vatican Council. Unlike some who found in the counterculture of the 1960s a new spirituality, Herberg dismissed it as self-indulgent and utterly devoid of lasting values.

When Herberg first appeared in *Who's Who in America*, he falsely claimed to have been born on August 7, 1907, in New York City and to have earned bachelor's, master's, and doctoral degrees from Columbia University. His motivation for the misrepresentation regarding his birth appears to have been in part to distance himself from his Russian roots and in part to claim a later birth date and thus to prolong his academic career. Thanks to his intellectual brilliance along with his comprehensive command of religious, political, and philosophical ideas and texts, neither his colleagues nor his students had any reason to doubt his academic credentials. Until very late in his life, no one suspected that he might not hold the degrees he claimed.

Herberg continued to speak out for conservative causes until his final illness. He died in Chatham, N.J., on March 26, 1977.

—MSM

Herter, Christian A(rchibald)

(1895–1966) *governor of Massachusetts, undersecretary of state, secretary of state*

The son of expatriate American artists, Adele and Albert Herter, Christian Herter was born in Paris France, on March 28, 1895. After receiving his primary education there, he went to the Browning School in New York and graduated from Harvard in 1915. Herter entered Columbia University's School of Architecture but left in 1916 to join the Foreign Service. He served as an attaché to the American embassy in Berlin and as head of the American legation in Brussels. After working for the State Department in Washington from 1917 to 1918, Herter negotiated a prisoner of war agreement with Germany in 1918 and in 1919 served as secretary to the Paris Peace Commission. He served as special assistant to HERBERT C. HOOVER, the head of the European Relief Council, in 1920 and 1921. When Hoover became secretary of commerce in 1921, he asked Herter to be his assistant. Herter held this post until 1924, when he left government service to become editor of the *Independent*. The *Independent* was sold in 1928, and Herter worked as an associate editor of the *Sportsman* until 1936. During the 1929–30 academic year, he was a lecturer on foreign affairs at Harvard University.

Herter served as a Republican in the Massachusetts House of Representatives from 1931 to 1943; for the last four of those years, he was speaker of the house. In 1942, he won election to the U.S. House of Representatives. He served in that body for 10 years. A member of the internationalist wing of the Republican Party, he supported the creation of the United Nations and the development of the Marshall Plan.

In 1952, Herter successfully ran for governor of Massachusetts. In the state house, he presented a liberal program establishing a state department of commerce, introducing a public housing program, and increasing aid to the elderly. Herter was reelected in 1954. However, the Republicans lost control of the lower house of the General Court, which prevented the enactment of the governor's proposed judicial reorganization.

In 1956, liberal Republicans, led by HAROLD STASSEN, proposed that Gov. Herter replace RICHARD NIXON as the party's vice presidential candidate. Although Eisenhower had pondered replacing Nixon, Herter was not one of his choices. Herter's identification with Harvard and the East Coast elite, his age (he was 61), and his health (he suffered from arthritis) all worked against him. Moreover, Republican party regulars rallied behind Nixon, so Eisenhower had SHERMAN ADAMS call Herter and offer him a position in the State Department if he withdrew from consideration for the vice presidency. Herter agreed and offered to nominate Nixon at the Republican convention. In 1957, Eisenhower appointed Herter undersecretary of state. Herter quickly developed a close relationship with Secretary of State JOHN FOSTER DULLES, who was already ill with the cancer that would ultimately kill him. When Dulles became too ill to continue as secretary of state, he recommended Herter as his successor. Eisenhower had some reservations about Herter's health and considered several other candidates, but ultimately Dulles's counsel prevailed. Eisenhower nominated Herter on April 18, 1959; the Senate unanimously approved the nomination in record time, and Herter took office four days later.

As secretary of state, Herter followed the same general approach to policy as Dulles, which had, in fact, always been guided ultimately by Eisenhower.

In some regards, however, Herter was more flexible than his predecessor. An early test of Herter's diplomacy came when Soviet premier Nikita S. Khrushchev challenged the Allied position in West Berlin. In November 1958, Khrushchev threatened to sign a peace treaty with East Germany, thereby terminating Allied rights in West Berlin, unless the Western Allies withdrew their troops from Berlin within six months and make it a "free city." The reaction of the various Western Allies to Khrushchev's ultimatum revealed significant disagreements. Eisenhower, first with Dulles and then with Herter, attempted to compose the differences. Khrushchev agreed to a conference of foreign ministers to discuss the German question to be followed by a summit meeting. In April 1959, Herter attended a meeting in Paris at which the Western foreign ministers announced that they were in complete agreement on strategy for the upcoming conference with the Soviet Union. Their plan called for a four-stage "permanent settlement in Europe." The first stage called for the unification of East and West Berlin through free elections. The second stage would see the establishment of a "mixed" German committee to expand technical contacts between the two Germanys. The third stage called for the election of an all-German assembly to establish a "liberal democratic and federative system," and the fourth stage called for the recognition of a unified Germany. The negotiations with the Soviets in May resulted in a deadlock, as did a second meeting in August.

Herter also failed to make much progress on the issue of disarmament. In early 1959, Eisenhower, who wanted a comprehensive nuclear test ban treaty with the Soviets, decided to try for the more limited objective of ending atmospheric testing. Khrushchev rejected the proposal, but the talks in Geneva continued. In March 1960, speaking before the National Press Club in Washington, Herter outlined a program that included proposals for disarmament under the supervision of an international controls panel and for talks leading to the eventual reduction of military forces. The Soviet Union rejected the proposal because of its provision for on-site inspection of missile stations and atomic installations.

On May 5, 1960, Khrushchev announced that the Soviet Union had downed an American U-2 plane on a reconnaissance mission over the USSR. The administration initially denied the charge. Herter argued that Washington should accept responsibility for the flights and explain why they were needed. On May 7, the State Department admitted that a flight over Soviet territory had been made by an "unarmed civilian U-2." Two day later, Herter defended the missions and indicated that they were necessary to prevent possible Soviet aggression and would continue. With the U-2 incident still dominating the headlines, Herter left for Geneva on May 12 to prepare for the meeting between Eisenhower, Khrushchev, and the British prime minister, Harold Macmillan. The summit collapsed five days later, when Khrushchev opened the meeting with a diatribe against Eisenhower and the United States and then walked out.

Cuba proved to be another intractable problem during Herter's tenure. He became secretary of state only months after Fidel Castro had come to power. As undersecretary of state, Herter had advised that the United States remain neutral in the Cuban conflict and that the Cuban dictator Fulgencio Batista would ultimately have to relinquish power. Batista's behavior led Eisenhower to impose an arms embargo and withdraw diplomatic support. After Castro came to power, his legalization of the Communist Party, his purge of liberals, and his mass executions alienated the Eisenhower administration. When the American Society of Newspaper Editors invited the new Cuban leader to the United States in April, Eisenhower demonstrated his revulsion at the executions by refusing to meet with Castro and having Nixon and Herter meet with him instead. When Castro later seized American properties, the State Department, on September 30, 1959, advised Americans to avoid all unnecessary travel to Cuba. Herter approved an embargo on most exports to Cuba in October. At the same time, he stepped up efforts to maintain relations with other Latin American nations. In August 1960, Castro began to accept Soviet weapons, and Herter obtained a resolution censuring the Cuban dictator from the Organization of American States. Castro then demanded that the United States reduce the number of personnel at its embassy in Havana, and the United States broke off diplomatic relations between the two countries on January 3, 1961.

Herter did not serve as secretary of state long enough to put his own stamp on U.S. foreign policy. Moreover, after the death of Dulles, Eisenhower moved to take more personal control over foreign policy. In addition, Herter never enjoyed the close relationship with Eisenhower that Dulles had. Nevertheless, he faithfully and competently carried out the foreign policy of his president. A model patrician, Herter was impeccably courteous and mild-mannered. Underneath that veneer, though, lay toughness and strength. An exceptionally tall man (he stood six feet six inches), he suffered from severe arthritis for the last 20 years of his life and frequently had to use crutches.

At the end of the Eisenhower presidency, Herter retired from public life. In February 1962, JOHN F. KENNEDY named Herter special U.S. representative for trade negotiations with Europe, a position he held until his death in Washington, D.C., on December 30, 1966.

—MSM

Hickenlooper, Bourke B(lakemore)
(1896–1971) *U.S. senator*

Born on July 21, 1896, in Blockton, Iowa, Hickenlooper attended public schools and Iowa State College at Ames. He left college in 1917 to enlist in the U.S. Army's Officer Training Camp at Fort Snelling, Minn. Commissioned a second lieutenant, he served in France from August 1918 to February 1919. After being honorably discharged, Hickenlooper returned to Iowa State, where he received a B.S. in industrial science in 1920, and then enrolled in the College of Law at the State University of Iowa at Iowa City. After earning his law degree in 1922 and gaining admission to the bar that same year, he practiced law in Cedar Rapids.

After failing in his initial try for public office, Hickenlooper won a seat as a Republican in the Iowa General Assembly, in which he served from 1934 to 1937. He was lieutenant governor from 1939 to 1942 and governor from 1943 to 1944, when he won election to the U.S. Senate. He was reelected in 1950, 1956, and 1962. His political success came in spite of a lack of charisma and a rather dour personality. In the Senate, Hickenlooper generally voted as a Midwestern conservative Republican. He favored

a strongly anticommunist foreign policy, aggressive measures to deal with domestic communist subversion, fiscal restraint, and minimal taxation. In one significant respect, Hickenlooper departed from Midwestern conservatism on foreign policy: he early on embraced internationalism and supported the Truman Doctrine, Marshall Plan, and NATO.

Like many conservative Republicans, Hickenlooper interpreted Eisenhower's victory in 1952 as a mandate to repudiate the Yalta agreements reached near the end of World War II. As a candidate, Eisenhower had criticized the agreements. As president, however, he had no intention of repudiating them. After all, Yalta provided the United States with its occupation rights in Vienna and West Berlin. Then, too, if the Americans could repudiate the agreements, so could the Soviets. Further, the British had made it clear that they would not join in repudiating the agreements, and doing so would alienate Democrats at home. On February 20, 1952, Eisenhower presented to Congress a proposed resolution that stopped short of disavowing Yalta. Instead, it criticized the Soviet Union for violating the agreements and rejected any "interpretations" of Yalta that "have been perverted to bring about the subjugation of free peoples." Hickenlooper and other Republicans on the Foreign Relations Committee believed that Eisenhower's resolution betrayed a fundamental Republican position. Hickenlooper wanted outright repudiation. Sen. ROBERT TAFT (R-Ohio) attempted to reach a compromise by proposing an amendment stipulating that the resolution did not "constitute any determination by Congress as to the validity or invalidity of any provisions of the said agreements." Democrats supported Eisenhower's version and opposed any amendment. The death of the Soviet dictator, Joseph Stalin, provided an opportunity to postpone any resolution on Yalta.

Hickenlooper found himself at odds with the Eisenhower administration on several other issues. He broke with the administration in 1953 over the nomination of CHARLES E. BOHLEN to be ambassador to the USSR. Hickenlooper linked the nominee to the hated Yalta accords and derided him as a representative of the State Department under Roosevelt and Truman. Hickenlooper joined 10 other Republican senators in voting against the nomination. In addition, he supported the anticommunist crusade of Sen. JOSEPH R. MCCARTHY (R-Wis.) and in December 1954 voted against the Senate's censure of the junior senator from Wisconsin.

Although he served many years in the Senate and exercised considerable influence, few measures bore Hickenlooper's name. One notable exception was the Atomic Energy Act of 1954. Hickenlooper had become chair of the Joint Congressional Committee on Atomic Energy in 1949, and he resumed the chair with the Republican victory in 1952. In 1954, he cosponsored legislation to amend the Atomic Energy Act of 1946 to require the Atomic Energy Commission to grant licenses to private corporations to produce and market power from nuclear sources.

Despite his earlier reservations about Eisenhower's foreign policy. Hickenlooper emerged as a consistent supporter of the administration. As a senator from a largely agricultural state that depended heavily on the price of corn and hay, he favored high price supports on those commodities. He nonetheless backed the administration's policy of flexible rather than rigid price supports. In addition, he supported civil rights legislation.

At the same time, Hickenlooper opposed most domestic welfare legislation and generally opposed expanding the power of the federal government.

In the 1960s, Hickenlooper's approach to policy changed little. He opposed federal aid to education, Medicare, and the War on Poverty, although he continued his general support for civil rights. He successfully added a controversial amendment to the Foreign Aid Act of 1962 that provided for the automatic denial of American aid to any foreign country that expropriated the property of U.S. citizens without adequate compensation. During the mid and late 1960s, Hickenlooper and Sen. J. WILLIAM FULBRIGHT (D-Ark.), cooperated to gain passage of a controversial consular treaty with the Soviet Union. As he had in the 1950s, he continued to oppose allowing U.S. trade with communist countries. In addition, he advocated strengthening the armed forces and supported American policy in Vietnam. Hickenlooper did not run for reelection in 1968 and died while visiting Shelter Island, N.Y., on September 4, 1971.

—MSM

Hill, (Joseph) Lister
(1894–1984) *U.S. senator; chairman, Labor and Welfare Committee*

The son of a prominent surgeon, Joseph Lister Hill was born in Montgomery, Ala., on December 27, 1894. Lister Hill, as he preferred to be known, was raised in his mother's Catholic faith and attended Catholic grade school. He graduated from the Starke University School in Montgomery and then earned an A.B. from the University of Alabama in 1914 and a law degree from the same institution in 1915. After receiving a second law degree from Columbia University in 1916, he returned to Montgomery to practice law. He served as president of the Montgomery Board of Education from 1917 to 1922. During World War I, Hill entered the army, rising from private to first lieutenant. After being discharged, he returned to Montgomery, resumed his law practice, and, as he became active in civic affairs and Democratic politics in heavily Protestant Alabama, announced his conversion to Methodism, the faith of his father's side of the family. He won a special election for a seat in the U.S. House of Representatives in 1923. In spite of his initial reservations about expanding the role of the federal government, Hill became an active supporter of Franklin D. Roosevelt and the New Deal. He was sponsor in the House of the bill that created the Tennessee Valley Authority (TVA), which contributed to greatly to the economic development of northern Alabama. In 1937, he ran successfully for the U.S. Senate seat vacated when Roosevelt appointed HUGO BLACK to the Supreme Court. Three years later, he became Democratic whip, and in 1940 he nominated Roosevelt at the Democratic National Convention. As a senator, he supported Roosevelt's foreign policy. In 1943, he helped write the resolution that put the Senate on record in favor of a future United Nations.

During the postwar era, Hill became a proponent of national health care. Perhaps his most significant achievement in that area came with the passage in 1946 of a bill he cosponsored with HAROLD BURTON (R-Ohio) that provided federal grants to state and local nonprofit organizations for the construction of hospitals. That same year, Hill resigned as whip rather than muster support for HARRY S. TRUMAN's civil rights proposals. Hill opposed attempts to abolish the poll tax, outlaw lynching, and limit debate in the Senate. He called for Truman to step aside in April 1948 but did not join the Dixiecrat defection from the Democratic party that year.

Hill won reelection in 1950 and 1956. During the 1950s, Hill continued his concern for legislation relating to health and medicine. His ability to influence policy in that area increased when he became chairman of the Senate Labor and Welfare Committee in 1955. In addition, he served as chairman of the Appropriations Committee's Subcommittee for Health and Welfare Agencies. In May 1955, he introduced a bill to provide free distribution of the new Salk polio vaccine to all children in the United States. The American Medical Association opposed the measure, as did Secretary of Health Education, and Welfare OVETA CULP HOBBY. The Eisenhower administration proposed instead a measure to provide free vaccines to needy children. The Senate Labor and Welfare Committee reported out Hill's bill, the Senate passed it, and Eisenhower signed it in August 1955. In 1956, Hill sponsored successful amendments to provide additional funding for the National Institutes of Health and for training nurses. He also introduced a bill, passed in 1960, that provided funds for international cooperation in medical research.

In addition to supporting federal funding for health, Hill advocated federal aid for education. In 1956, he cosponsored the Library Services Act, which appropriated federal funds to upgrade the nation's libraries. Hill also supported the National Defense Education Act, passed after the Soviet launch of *Sputnik*, that provided federal loans for college students and federal matching funds to promote the teaching of science, mathematics, and foreign languages in the schools.

Throughout the 1950s, Hill continued to advocate public, rather than private, development of power and other resources. In 1953, he opposed the administration's proposal to grant oil-rich submerged costal lands to the states because he believed that private oil companies would be the main beneficiaries. In January of that year, he participated in a 28-day filibuster against the administration's bill. In addition to supporting a measure, introduced by Sen. CLINTON ANDERSON (D-N.Mex.), that called

for federal control of submerged lands beyond the three-mile limit, Hill introduced an amendment to Anderson's proposal that would have set aside all federal revenue from offshore oil for national defense and education. Congress rejected Anderson's bill in April 1953.

Hill opposed the Dixon-Yates contract in 1954. EDGAR DIXON of Middle Southern Utilities and EUGENE YATES of the Southern Company had been given a contract by the Atomic Energy Commission (AEC) to build a steam plant near Memphis, Tenn. The plant would have supplied power for consumers in the Memphis area, including the TVA. Hill charged that the government was using Dixon and Yates "as hatchet men to destroy the TVA." In February 1955, Hill was appointed head of a subcommittee of the Appropriations Committee charged with handling AEC-TVA funds. During hearings that month, Hill disclosed that Adolphe H. Wenzell, a consultant to the Bureau of the Budget at the time of the negotiations, was also a vice president and director of the First Boston Corporation, which was arranging financing for the Dixon-Yates project. Hill accused Wenzell of a conflict of interest and denounced the budget director, ROWLAND HUGHES, for concealing the connection. Hughes acknowledged that Wenzell had participated in contract talks but denied having concealed anything. That same month, city officials in Memphis announced their intention to build a power plant, which made construction of the private plant unnecessary. Eisenhower canceled the Dixon-Yates contract in July.

While Hill supported much liberal domestic legislation, he opposed all civil rights measures. He publicly supported a futile resolution, passed by the Alabama legislature, declaring the Supreme Court's decision in *Brown v. Board of Education* (1954), which held segregated public schools unconstitutional, null, and void in the state. He joined 100 other southern members of Congress in signing the "Southern Manifesto," presented to Congress in March 1956. The document attacked the *Brown* decision as "a clear abuse of judicial power" and charged that the justices substituted "personal political and social ideas for the established laws of the land." Hill voted against the Civil Rights Acts of 1957 and 1960.

Afer nearly losing his seat to a conservative Republican challenger in 1962, Hill's voting record became increasingly conservative. While he continued to support health legislation, including Medicare, and social welfare programs designed to aid rural areas, he voted against most social programs aimed at urban problems. In addition, he continued to oppose all civil rights legislation. He declined to run for reelection in 1968. Hill returned to Montgomery, where he lived until his death there on December 20, 1984.

—MSM

Hill, Robert C(harles)

(1917–1978) *ambassador to Costa Rica, ambassador to El Salvador, special assistant to the undersecretary of state for mutual security affairs, assistant secretary of state for congressional relations, ambassador to Mexico*

The son of a physician, Hill was born in Littleton, N.H., on September 17, 1917. After graduating from the Taft School and then Dartmouth College in 1942, he worked as a junior executive for the Todd Shipbuilding Corp. and went to Washington, D.C., as the company's representative. In 1943, Hill joined the State Department as an officer of the Foreign Service Auxiliary and served as a vice-consul in Calcutta, India, from 1944 to 1945. After World War II, Hill briefly studied law at Boston University but left in 1947 to become a clerk to the Senate Banking and Currency Committee. Returning to the private sector in 1949, he joined W. R. Grace and Co., which operated sea and air transportation in Latin America.

In October 1953, Eisenhower appointed Hill ambassador to Costa Rica. While in that country, he was an official "observer" in the negotiation of a contract between Costa Rica and the powerful, American-based United Fruit Co. The youngest ambassador in American history, Hill served there for only about a year before being transferred to El Salvador, where he was ambassador from 1954 to 1955. During his stay in Latin America, he traveled extensively to familiarize himself with the problems of the population. In September 1955, Hill was named special assistant to HERBERT HOOVER

Jr., the undersecretary of state for mutual security affairs. After his confirmation in October, he spent the next five months coordinating foreign-aid programs and developing and presenting to Congress legislative proposals for the mutual security program. The young diplomat specialized in aid to Third World nations. As a result of his successful dealings with Congress, Hill was promoted to assistant secretary of state for congressional relations in February 1956.

As a legislative liaison officer, Hill's diplomatic skills helped smooth the passage of the administration's foreign-aid requests. During 1956 and 1957, observers credited Hill with playing an important part in getting Congress to approve aid to Yugoslavia over the objections of some conservatives, who argued that it would help communism. In May 1957, Hill confronted the issue of a Saudi Arabian ban on the assignment of Jewish servicemen to that country. Though some members of Congress from New York had charged the U.S. government with tacit compliance with the ban, Hill assured the representatives that the United States did "not condone" any foreign government's discrimination against U.S. citizens. However, he expressed doubt that the ban would soon be lifted.

In May 1957, Hill was confirmed as ambassador to Mexico. As in Costa Rica and El Salvador, Hill proved adept at winning the good will of the populace despite tensions between the two nations over aid, tariffs, and oil development. Aware of the value of the press, he visited Mexico's most important newspapers and its major television network to promote American-Mexican friendship. In October 1958, he scored a diplomatic triumph for the United States when he presented an interracial and international group of baseball stars at a Mexican movie festival. The ballplayers' appearance followed the showing of the movie *The Defiant Ones*, a film that stressed interracial harmony and that helped dampen the anti-American feeling.

Upon winning election to the New Hampshire State Legislature in November 1960, Hill resigned as ambassador to Mexico effective January 1961. After serving one term, Hill returned to private business, becoming director of a number of corporations, including United Fruit Co. He chaired the Republican National Committee's Foreign

Policy Task Force from 1965 to 1968 and served on the Republican Coordinating Committee's Task Force on National Security from 1967 to 1968. Hill returned to diplomatic service in 1969, when President RICHARD M. NIXON appointed him ambassador to Spain, a post he held until 1972, when he resigned to run for governor of New Hampshire. His campaign never caught on, and he dropped out of the race before the primary election. From 1973 to 1974, he was assistant secretary of defense for international security affairs. Hill became ambassador to Argentina in 1974 and held that post until his retirement in 1977. He died of a heart attack in Littleton, N.H., on November 28, 1978.

—MSM

Hobby, Oveta Culp
(1905–1995) *administrator, Federal Security Agency; secretary of health, education, and welfare*

The daughter of a prominent lawyer and state legislator, Oveta Culp was born in Killeen, Tex., on January 19, 1905. After studying at Mary Hardin Baylor College in Belton, Tex., she served as parliamentarian for the Texas House of Representatives from 1925 to 1931. During that time, she also took classes at the University of Texas, worked as a clerk of the State Banking Commission and later as a clerk in the judiciary committee, and served as assistant to the city attorney of Houston. She ran unsuccessfully for the state legislature in 1931 and later that year married William Pettus Hobby, a former governor of Texas (1917 to 1921) and the publisher of the *Houston Post*. After her marriage, Oveta Hobby immersed herself in the paper. She reviewed books, edited copy, and wrote editorials. She held the title of book editor from 1933 to 1936, assistant editor from 1936 to 1938, and executive vice president beginning in 1938. In addition, she published a text on parliamentary procedure, *Mr. Chairman* (1937), that was widely adopted by public schools in Texas and Louisiana.

In June 1941, Gen. David Searles asked Hobby to organize a section on women's activities for the army. Beginning in July 1941, she worked in Washington, D.C., as a dollar-a-year head of the Women's Interest Section of the War Department's Bureau of Public Relations. In September of that year, Gen.

George C. Marshall asked Hobby to plan a women's army. The following May, Congress created the Women's Auxiliary Army Corps (WAACS), and Secretary of War Henry Stimson appointed Hobby its director with the rank of major. In July 1943, she was promoted to colonel. The unit received full status in the army in late 1943, and the term "Auxiliary" was dropped from its title. By the end of the war, at least 100,000 women had served in the WAC. Hobby resigned from the corps one month after V-E Day.

Hobby returned to private life as executive vice president of the *Houston Post* as well as director of KPRC radio and KPRC-TV. She helped organize Democrats for Eisenhower in Texas, and, following Eisenhower's victory in the election of 1952, he appointed her to head the Federal Security Agency (FSA). At the time of the appointment, Eisenhower already intended to consolidate all functions

Oveta Culp Hobby, the first secretary of health, education, and welfare, 1953–1955 *(Dwight D. Eisenhower Library and Museum)*

relating to health, education, and welfare into one department with cabinet rank and to make Hobby its head. In April 1953, the new Department of Health, Education, and Welfare (HEW) was created, and Hobby became only the second woman to serve in the cabinet.

Hobby opposed socialized medicine as "undemocratic and economically unsound," but she nevertheless supported the administration's "health reinsurance" plan. Introduced in 1954, the plan set up a fund that would be used to assume 75 percent of any "abnormal losses" incurred by any approved private health insurance carriers that resulted from offering coverage to high-risk customers. The purpose of the plan was to reduce the cost of insurance and thereby make it available to more people. Ever concerned about what it regarded as socialized medicine, the American Medical Association lobbied hard against the program. So, too, did the major insurance companies. Liberal Democrats, who advocated a more extensive, centralized program, also joined in the opposition. Thus, opponents in Congress from the left and right combined to kill the plan.

As head of the FSA and later HEW, Hobby became embroiled in a controversy over segregation in federally funded schools run on military installations for dependents of military personnel. Soon after the new administration took office, CLARENCE MITCHELL, the NAACP's lobbyist on Capitol Hill, met with Hobby to protest the FSA's cooperation with local authorities in maintaining segregation in such schools. Hobby opposed swift action to desegregate locally run schools on military bases, but Eisenhower overruled her. In June 1953, Rep. ADAM CLAYTON POWELL, JR. (D-N.Y.), charged that Hobby had "virtually countermanded" Eisenhower's program for desegregating schools on military bases. An investigation by the White House staff indicated that there was some truth to the charge, and, once again, Eisenhower had to remedy the situation.

A strong anticommunist, Hobby supported the president's loyalty and security program. In 1954, she reported that the department had dismissed 238 employees as "security risks," of whom 114 were "suspected subversives." According to HEW, security risks included persons who "drank or gossiped too much or were found to be unstable mentally."

On April 12, 1955, Dr. Thomas Francis, Jr., director of the Poliomyelitis Vaccine Evaluation Center of the University of Michigan, announced the results of an extensive test demonstrating that a polio vaccine developed by Dr. JONAS SALK was "safe, effective, and potent." That same day, the federal government licensed six manufacturers to produce the vaccine under the supervision of the Public Health Service (PHS). Two weeks later, the government announced that the manufacturers would produce enough of the vaccine to immunize every child under nine by August 1. Even before the results of the test were known, however, the National Foundation for Infantile Paralysis had purchased 9 million doses and announced that it would turn this over to state health officials to inoculate all children in first and second grades at no charge. On April 14, Eisenhower directed Hobby to establish a voluntary system to allocate the vaccine fairly. Hobby secured an agreement from the drug manufacturers to distribute the vaccine in accordance with the government's plan once they had produced enough of the vaccine to fulfill the contract with the National Foundation.

The process was beset with problems. On April 27, the surgeon general temporarily banned the distribution of vaccine produced by one of laboratories after some people inoculated with that vaccine contracted polio. On May 6, the PHS halted the release of all new vaccine but recommended continuing injections with vaccine that had already been approved and distributed. The next day, the PHS ordered a suspension of vaccinations while it reexamined procedures for manufacturing and testing the vaccine. Further delays gave the impression of a program in chaos, and all the while the public was clamoring for the vaccine.

On May 16, Hobby sent a plan to the White House for distribution of the vaccine once the needs of the National Foundation's program for free inoculations of first and second graders had been met. The plan called for manufacturers to allocate vaccine for each state and for the states to establish systems to distribute the vaccine. The federal government would appropriate $28 million to purchase vaccine for the poor. Democrats criticized

Hobby for not producing a plan sooner. Sen. LISTER HILL (D-Ala.), who in May had introduced a bill to provide free inoculations for all children, led the charge. Sen. WAYNE MORSE (D-Oreg.) demanded that Hobby be dismissed for "gross incompetence." Ultimately, the Senate passed Hill's bill, and Eisenhower signed it in August.

In July 1955, at the height of the controversy over distribution of the Salk vaccine, Hobby resigned her cabinet post, citing her husband's illness as the reason. The timing gave the appearance that she resigned under pressure. Eisenhower made a point of demonstrating his support, and Secretary of the Treasury GEORGE HUMPHREY called her "the best man in the Cabinet."

Hobby returned to the *Houston Post* as president and editor. She became chairman of the board of the *Post* in 1965 and held that position until she sold the paper in 1983. Throughout the 1960s and 1970s, she served on the boards of numerous corporations and public bodies, including Mutual of New York, General Foods Corporation, Rice University, and the Corporation for Public Broadcasting. LYNDON B. JOHNSON appointed her to the National Advisory Commission of Selective Service. Hobby died in Houston, Tex., on August 16, 1995.

—MSM

Hodges, Luther H(artwell)

(1898–1974) *governor of North Carolina*

Born in Pittsylvania Co., Va., on March 9, 1898, Luther Hodges worked as an office boy while attending public school. He financed his studies at the University of North Carolina by selling books, firing furnaces, and waiting on tables. After serving in the army during World War I, Hodges returned to the university and graduated in 1919. That year, he became secretary to the general manager of Marshall Field & Co.'s eight textile mills in the Leaksville, Ky., area and rose through the company to become general manager of all Field textile mills in 1939. Three years later, he was elected a vice president.

In 1944, Hodges took charge of the textile division of the Office of Price Administration and in 1945 became a consultant to the secretary of agriculture. Retiring from the textile business in 1950,

Hodges headed the industry division of the Economic Cooperation Administration and served as State Department consultant at the International Management Conference in 1951. With little previous political experience, Hodges was elected lieutenant governor of North Carolina in 1952. When Gov. William B. Umstead died in November 1954, Hodges succeeded him. Hodges won election in his own right in 1956.

Dissatisfied with North Carolina's ranking of 44th out of the 48 states in per capita income, Hodges aggressively sought industrial development. In order to stimulate the state's economy, he initiated programs to court out-of-state industries by offering tax incentives and by creating the North Carolina Business Development Corporation in 1955 to make long-term credit more accessible. During his term in office, over $1 billion was invested in the state, and 140,000 new jobs were created. In another attempt to attract business and foster economic development, North Carolina, under Hodges's leadership, established a network of 18 industrial education centers. Later, these merged with a technical institute and two junior colleges to form the state's community college system.

Hodges became governor only months after the Supreme Court ruled segregated public schools unconstitutional. Although a segregationist, Hodges opposed the most extreme demands for nullification of the ruling. Nevertheless, he protected himself from a segregationist challenge by preempting the issue. With Hodges's backing, the legislature passed several measures in 1955 designed to retain segregation in the state's schools. A pupil placement law granted county and city boards the power to assign pupils to schools. This gave localities the option to comply with the Supreme Court's ruling but, at the same time, made it more difficult to achieve desegregation through litigation. Another measure transferred ownership and operation of state school buses to local school districts and undermined tenure by replacing continuing contracts for teachers with yearly contracts. In 1956, Hodges called a special session of the legislature to enact measures designed to prevent integration. The special session resulted in a new law allowing for local elections to close public schools in "intolerable situations" and another providing tuition grants for students attending private segregated schools.

Hodges also played a significant role in the crisis involving the desegregation of Central High School in Little Rock, Ark. The Southern Governors Conference was meeting in September 1957, when President Eisenhower sent federal troops to enforce a federal court order to admit black students to Central High. The conference authorized a committee of five, chaired by Hodges, to ask the president to withdraw the troops. When the delegation met with Eisenhower on October 1, Hodges challenged the desirability, rather than the legality, of sending the troops. Eisenhower replied that he would withdraw the federal troops if the governor of Arkansas, ORVAL FAUBUS, would agree to maintain order and carry out the court's mandate. The governors contacted Faubus, who agreed to announce that "the orders of the federal court will not be obstructed." Instead, Faubus, sent a wire declaring that he would resume responsibility for maintaining order and that "the orders of the federal court will not be obstructed by me." Eisenhower pronounced the wire "worthless." That evening, Eisenhower issued a statement thanking the southern governors for their efforts and explaining that Faubus had failed to commit himself to "use his full powers as Governor to prevent the obstruction of the orders of the . . . District Court." The next day, Faubus held a news conference and refused to give an inch, in spite of the urging of the committee of southern governors. Several members of the committee openly expressed their disapproval of Faubus. Hodges simply reported the failure of the negotiations in a nationwide broadcast and terminated his personal involvement. Federal troops remained in Little Rock until late November; federalized elements of the Arkansas National Guard remained on duty until the end of the school year.

During the latter part of the decade, Hodges continued to build up North Carolina's industry, developed the state's "research triangle" (consisting of the University of North Carolina, North Carolina State College, and Duke University), supported the minimum wage, and furthered highway safety.

During the presidential campaign of 1960, Hodges actively supported Sen. JOHN F. KENNEDY's (D-Mass.) candidacy. Hodges served as secretary of commerce from 1961 to 1965. He was not an especially influential member of the cabinet. After leaving government service, he returned to business, assuming the directorships of several major corporations. He died of a heart attack in Chapel Hill, N.C., on October 6, 1974.

—MSM

Hoffa, James R(iddle)
(1913–ca. 1975) *union leader*

The son of an itinerant coal driller, Hoffa was born in Brazil, Ind., on February 13, 1913. After the death of his father in 1920, Hoffa moved with his family to Detroit. He left school after the ninth grade to help support the family and worked as a stock boy in a department store and a freight handler in a grocery store. While working at the latter job, he organized his fellow workers into a labor union affiliated with the American Federation of Labor (AFL). In 1934, he took his local into the International Brotherhood of Teamsters and became a full-time organizer for the Teamsters. He became president of the local in 1937. That same year, Hoffa helped Farrell Dobbs, a radical Teamster from Minneapolis, set up the Central States Drivers Council. Hoffa became its chairman in 1940. That same year, Hoffa became president of the Michigan Conference of Teamsters. The next year, at the behest of the national leader of the Teamsters, Dan Tobin, Hoffa led goon squads to prevent Dobbs and his supporters from taking the Central Conference of Teamsters out of the AFL and into the more militant Congress of Industrial Organizations (CIO). When the CIO led a counterattack against Hoffa's base in Detroit, Hoffa allegedly sought help from Santo Perrone and "Scarface Joe" Bommarito, two gangsters based in Detroit.

Links to organized crime would color the rest of Hoffa's career. He stood trial in 1946 for extortion. The indictment alleged that he took part in a conspiracy to compel small grocers to purchase "permits" from the Teamsters to make deliveries with their own trucks. As part of a plea bargain, the charges were reduced and Hoffa received two years probation, in exchange for which he made restitution to the grocers. In 1951, the Kefauver crime commission exposed evidence that a Detroit local of the Teamsters acted as a front for organized crime to extort money from jukebox distributors.

Hoffa represented the contradictory traditions of militant trade unionism and corrupt business unionism. Although he obtained good settlements for his workers, Hoffa had no reservations about using strong-arm tactics to win contracts or to defeat rivals within the labor movement. His alliance with organized crime figures enabled Hoffa to intimidate workers, unionists, and employers. In addition, his connections with organized crime figures in other Midwestern cities enabled Hoffa to expand his geographic base. For example, in 1949 Hoffa worked out an agreement with Paul "Red" Dorfman, a former member of Al Capone's organization, that allowed Hoffa to expand his operations in Chicago. In exchange, Dorfman's son, Allan, was appointed insurance broker for the Central States Drivers Council's health and welfare fund.

Although his strength in the central states gave him a base from which he might have challenged Seattle's Dave Beck to succeed Tobin as president of the Teamsters in 1952, Hoffa supported Beck. In return, Beck gave Hoffa a free hand in the Midwest. Hoffa became one of nine vice presidents of the Teamsters in 1952 and president of the Central Conference of Teamsters the following year. By the middle of the decade, Hoffa had become the undisputed boss of the Teamsters in the Midwest. He personally approved all strikes, and an order from him could tie up all trucking in the region. He also controlled the finances of the Central States Drivers Council.

Hoffa used a web of political contacts as well as violence and intimidation to prevent authorities from interfering with his operations. Internal opponents encountered the same obstacles. Dissidents within the Teamsters found no support from Beck, and local officials, who were either on the take from Hoffa or intimidated by him, refused to prosecute those charged with intimidating dissidents.

In the second half of the 1950s, Hoffa extended his power to the East Coast and throughout the nation. He moved first to gain control of the Teamsters in the New York metropolitan area. With the help of two reputed organized crime figures, Tony "Ducks" Corallo and Johnny Dio, Hoffa set up a number of paper locals that gave him a majority on the local representative body, the Teamsters

Jimmy Hoffa, 1959 *(Library of Congress)*

Joint Council. He also secured control of the Philadelphia locals. Through an alliance with Tony Provenzano, an official of the Teamsters in New Jersey and a reputed mobster, Hoffa established his power in that state. In addition, Hoffa established ties with the International Longshoremen's Association, a union expelled from the AFL because of its corruption. This enabled Hoffa to tie up not only trucking but also the docks on the East Coast. When charges of corruption forced Beck to resign in 1957, Hoffa became president of the Teamsters. Some even believed that Hoffa leaked the evidence that discredited Beck.

Beginning in 1957, the Senate Committee on Improper Activities in the Labor or Management Field, chaired by Sen. John L. McClellan (D-Ark.), conducted an extended investigation into

Hoffa's activities as leader of the Teamsters. ROB-ERT F. KENNEDY, the committee's majority counsel, supervised the investigation and led the questioning of witnesses. The hearings documented Hoffa's ties with organized crime. On numerous occasions, Kennedy listed names of racketeers on Hoffa's payroll and asked if Hoffa was aware of their past and if he intended to remove them from their positions. Hoffa promised to dismiss those tied to organized crime, but he never did. The panel also uncovered evidence of how Teamsters officials enriched themselves by extorting money from companies with which the Teamsters had contracts in exchange for labor peace. Employers paid off the Teamsters officials by putting them on the payroll for nonexistent jobs. The committee further found that Hoffa personally profited from his connections with the Teamsters. Under his wife's name, he was part owner of a trucking business. The Taft-Hartley Act prohibited union officials from owning businesses with which their unions bargained. Hoffa also borrowed union money for personal investments by having a union member take out a loan and transfer it to him. Hoffa then invested the money, often in his wife's maiden name. On his income tax form, Hoffa annually listed $10,000 as "collections." At hearings, he told Kennedy that he won the money at the racetrack, but many believed that it came from kickbacks from employers who received favorable treatment from Hoffa and the union.

During the lengthy probe into his activities, Hoffa developed techniques to evade questioning. He conveniently could not remember transactions, events, and people. He dodged questions by expounding on his philosophy of labor relations. He scheduled plane flights for just after a hearing to limit questioning. Although his conduct frustrated members of the committee, enough evidence of Hoffa's wrongdoing emerged to convince Congress of the need for legislation to prevent corruption in organized labor. In 1959, Congress passed the Landrum-Griffin Act, which prevented individuals with criminal records from holding positions of leadership in unions. It also increased fines and prison sentences for union officials convicted of misusing union funds.

In 1957, the AFL-CIO expelled Hoffa and his union for unethical practices. The action did not bother Hoffa, who believed that, because the Teamsters was the largest union in the federation, it would hurt the AFL-CIO more than it would the Teamsters. The AFL-CIO would have to do without dues from the Teamsters, and the Teamsters would benefit from keeping the money. Moreover, Hoffa had cultivated contacts with leading officials of the AFL-CIO, and, in spite of GEORGE MEANY's order to isolate the Teamsters, leaders of the AFL-CIO did not cooperate.

During the late 1950s, the federal government tried to bring criminal charges against Hoffa. He was indicted for attempting to bribe a lawyer on the staff of the Senate committee investigating him. Although the case seemed open-and-shut, a Washington jury acquitted Hoffa. Halfway through the trial, a black newspaper featuring a pro-Hoffa article on the cover was delivered to the homes of black jurors. The great black fighter, Joe Louis, came to court and had his picture taken with his friend, Jimmy Hoffa. In addition, it later came out that four members of the jury had criminal records. In 1958, Hoffa was indicted twice for wiretapping fellow Teamsters. The first case ended in a hung jury; the second ended with an acquittal.

As president of the Teamsters, Hoffa centralized leadership of the union, expanded organizing activities, and moved into organization of white-collar employees. When ROBERT F. KENNEDY became attorney general in 1961, the Justice Department embarked on a relentless campaign against Hoffa. Hoffa was convicted of jury tampering and fraud in 1963 and 1964. Nevertheless, he managed to negotiate the first national contract in the trucking industry in 1964. Having exhausted his appeals, Hoffa began serving an eight-year prison sentence for jury tampering followed by an additional five years for fraud. He left the Teamsters in the hands of Frank Fitzsimmons, a loyal assistant, who had been vice president of the Teamsters since 1966. Nevertheless, Hoffa did not resign the presidency, and some speculated that he continued to exercise influence from prison. He retired in June 1971, upon which he received the title president emeritus and an award of $1.7 million in lieu of a pension. In December of that year, President RICHARD NIXON pardoned him on the condition that Hoffa not engage in union affairs until 1980. Before long, however, Hoffa initiated legal action in an effort to invalidate the provision keeping him out of union affairs. He also engaged in a feud with Fitzsimmons.

On July 30, 1975, Hoffa left a restaurant in the Detroit area. He called his wife and told her that Anthony Giacolone, an alleged member of organized crime in Detroit, had failed to meet him. Hoffa was never seen or heard from again.

—MSM

Hoffer, Eric

(1902–1983) *philosopher and longshoreman*

The only child of Alsatian immigrants, Hoffer was born in the Bronx, N.Y., on July 25, 1902. German was his first language, and he spoke English with a heavy accent. At the age of nine, he lost his eyesight; it inexplicably returned when he was 15. Hoffer never attended school. He lost both parents while he was still young. His mother died when Hoffer was a young boy, and, when his father died in 1920, Hoffer left New York for southern California. He lived for 10 years on skid row in Los Angeles, working at odd jobs and borrowing books from the public library to educate himself. He spent another 10 years picking crops in the valleys of California, during which time he borrowed books from libraries located along the rail lines. When the United States entered World War II, Hoffer attempted to join the military but was rejected because of a hernia. Instead, in an attempt to aid the war effort, he went to work as a longshoreman in San Francisco. He worked there until his retirement in 1967.

Steady employment enabled him to organize the ideas he had developed during 20 years of reading and travel into a book, published by Harpers in 1951, *The True Believer.* In it, he contemplated the origins of mass movements, from religions to Soviet communism and German fascism. The book reflected Hoffer's focus on the threat of totalitarianism, especially as manifested in Hitler's Germany and Stalin's Soviet Union. Hoffer found the origins of these "madhouses" in human psychology. He argued that fanaticism derived from frustration born of insecurity and self-hatred. Fanaticism found fertile soil in those who would commit themselves to any cause that offered significance to their meaningless lives. Mass movements, maintained Hoffer,

offered "a flight from the self." Hoffer wrote: "A man is likely to mind his own business when it is worth minding. When it is not, he takes his mind off his own meaningless affairs by minding other people's business." The book won wide critical acclaim and a large audience; its admirers included President DWIGHT EISENHOWER. Hoffer went on to write 10 more books. His second book, *The Passionate State of Mind* (1955), which featured a collection of philosophical aphorisms, also focused on the threat posed by totalitarianism and the true believer.

In the 1960s, Hoffer conducted seminars as an adjunct instructor at the University of California at Berkeley. He also published prolifically. *The Ordeal of Change* (1963), regarded by some as his best work, dealt with the fear of the new. *The Temper of Our Time* (1967) collected previously published pieces of social commentary. *Working and Thinking on the Waterfront* (1969) was a daily journal. Hoffer became something of a celebrity when he appeared on a television special with Eric Sevareid on CBS in 1967. On the program, Hoffer praised the embattled president, LYNDON B. JOHNSON, who invited Hoffer to the White House. This increased Hoffer's fame, but it also diminished his reputation with liberal intellectuals. That reputation took another blow when, serving as a member of Johnson's Commission on the Causes and Prevention of Violence from 1968 to 1969, Hoffer scolded black witnesses.

He continued to publish until the end of his life. His later works included: *First Things, Last Things* (1976), *Before the Sabbath* (1979), *Between the Devil and the Dragon* (1982), and *Truth Imagined* (1983). Hoffer was awarded the Presidential Medal of Freedom on February 23, 1983, and died in San Francisco on May 29 of that same year.

—MSM

Hoffman, Clare E(ugene)

(1875–1967) *U.S. congressman; chairman, Committee on Expenditures in the Executive Departments; chairman, Government Operations Committee*

Born in Vicksburg, Pa., on September 10, 1875, Hoffman attended public schools and received an LL.B. from Northwestern University in 1895. He intended to gain admission to the Michigan bar, but he was too young, so he took some business courses at Valparaiso University. In 1896 he was admitted to the bar in Michigan and commenced the practice of law in Allegan, Mich. He served as prosecuting attorney of Allegan Co. from 1904 to 1910. After that, he served as an attorney for the city. Hoffman chaired the Republican Party in Allegan Co. for several decades before he won election to the U.S. House of Representatives in 1934. His campaign emphasized individual initiative, and he maintained that business, unencumbered by the federal government, offered the best means to end the depression. He won election to 13 succeeding Congresses.

A conservative and an isolationist, Hoffman voted against most New Deal measures, including both Agricultural Adjustment Acts, Social Security, and the Wagner Act. He also earned the enmity of organized labor for a number of positions he took. Hoffman was the most vehement congressional critic of the sit-down strike in Flint, Mich., in 1937, and advocated the use of troops to end it. He also attacked the Congress of Industrial Organizations and its leader, JOHN L. LEWIS. Before the Japanese attack on Pearl Harbor, Hoffman repeatedly voted against measures that he feared would lead to American involvement in World War II, such as the Lend-Lease Act and the Selective Service Act. After Pearl Harbor, he supported defense measures.

After the war, Hoffman bitterly opposed many of President HARRY S. TRUMAN's policies. He criticized Truman for failing to root out communists in the government and became an outspoken supporter of Sen. JOSEPH R. McCARTHY (R-Wis.). Hoffman also opposed a Fair Employment Practices Commission, legislation to abolish the poll tax, and antilynching legislation as infringements on states' rights. In 1947, Hoffman became chair of the Committee on Expenditures in the Executive Departments. In that capacity, he led investigations of the disposal of surplus war property, federal enforcement of antiracketeering legislation, and a meatpacking strike in the Midwest. He also could claim a large share of the credit for the National Security Act, which reorganized the military. Republican leaders waived the rule limiting members to service on one standing committee in order to allow Hoffman to hold on to his seat on the Education and Labor Committee. In January 1947,

Hoffman introduced a bill that would have outlawed the closed shop, work slowdowns, picketing, dues, checkoffs, and certain types of strikes. Many of his ideas did not make it into the Taft-Hartley Act, passed later that year. Hoffman voted for the measure but considered it barely adequate.

The elections of 1952 put a Republican in the White House and gave the party control of both houses of Congress. Once again chair of the Committee on Expenditures, the name of which had been changed to the Committee on Government Operations, Hoffman focused his attention on gangsterism in labor unions, which he described as "twice as dangerous to the country" as communism. Hoffman appointed a special subcommittee of the Government Operations Committee, which included himself, to cooperate with a panel of the Education and Labor Committee in an investigation of labor corruption in Kansas City. In September, he signed the joint subcommittee's report recommending that a federal grand jury investigate. Hoffman also investigated JIMMY HOFFA of the International Brotherhood of Teamsters. Some of the evidence Hoffman developed was later used to help convict Hoffa of misusing union pension funds in 1964.

Hoffman came into conflict with other members of the Government Operations Committee when he asked chairs of subcommittees to reduce their staffs and expenditures after July 31, 1953. In retaliation, the committee voted 23-1 to limit Hoffman's power to appoint ad hoc panels for special investigations. On July 29, the full House voted 171-6 to allow the subcommittees of the Government Operations Committee to spend all the funds allotted to them.

Even with a Republican in the White House, Hoffman found much to criticize. He was one of the few Republican representatives to vote against the Eisenhower administration's civil rights bills in 1957 and 1960. In 1957, he also opposed a bill, sponsored by the administration, to provide federal aid for school construction. Along with five other Republicans on the Education and Labor Committee, Hoffman asserted that the classroom shortage was "nowhere near as serious" as supporters of the measure contended and that states and localities could cope with whatever needs existed. In 1960 Hoffman denounced a minimum-wage bill.

After 1955, with the Democrats again in control of Congress, Hoffman lost much of his ability to influence legislation. The Landrum-Griffin Act of 1959 limited secondary boycotts and picketing, ideas Hoffman had long advocated.

Hoffman was one of the few isolationist members of Congress of the 1930s who continued to take an isolationist position during the 1950s. In 1955, he abstained in the vote on the administration's Formosa resolution, stating, "I think it is a declaration of war, and I don't think the cost in lives will justify it." Two years later, Hoffman voted against the Eisenhower Doctrine for the Middle East, declaring that "the minding of our own business" was more essential than ever.

As a member of the Republican right, Hoffman criticized the appointment in 1957 of MEADE ALCORN, an exponent of what President Eisenhower called "modern Republicanism," as Republican national chairman. Hoffman said that Alcorn's appointment meant the "conservative wing of the Republican Party . . . was being liquidated." Early in 1958, after the administration submitted a record $71.8-billion budget, he contended that President Eisenhower and "his left-wing, free-spending, international one-world advisers propose to disinfect, fumigate, purify, renovate, unify and remake the Republican Party."

His health failing, Hoffman chose not to run for reelection in 1962. He retired to his home in Allegan, Mich., where he died on November 3, 1967.

—MSM

Hoffman, Paul G(ray)

(1891–1974) *U.S. delegate to the United Nations*
Paul Hoffman was born in Chicago on April 26, 1891, and grew up in Western Springs, Ill., a nearby suburb. He attended public schools in Western Springs and the University of Chicago, which he left after his freshman year. Hoffman then took a job with Halladay Cars in the Chicago suburbs and became a successful salesman. After moving to Los Angeles in 1911, he began selling Studebaker automobiles, and by 1915 Hoffman became district sales manager. He served in the army during World War I, rising from private to first lieutenant. After leaving the service, he returned to California and to Studebaker. In 1919, he purchased Studebaker's distributorship for southern California. By 1925, when Hoffman became vice president in charge of sales, he was reportedly doing $7 million worth of business annually. Its business curtailed by the Great Depression, Studebaker went into receivership in 1933. Hoffman helped draft the reorganization plan, and the company emerged from receivership two years later with Hoffman as its president. Hoffman held that post for 13 years. He maintained good relations with labor unions, emphasized fuel efficiency, and became a leading advocate for automobile safety. He persuaded other automakers to create and finance the Automotive Safety Foundation and became its first president. During World War II, Studebaker made airplane engines and heavy military trucks. After the war, Studebaker emerged as the most successful of the smaller automakers.

Hoffman had always believed that corporate executives should involve themselves in civic affairs. He became chairman of United China Relief in 1942. He also helped found the American Policy Commission (APC), a group of scholars, business leaders, and leaders of organized labor formed to seek solutions to current economic problems. During the war, the APC changed its name to the Committee for Economic Development (CED), and Hoffman became chairman. After the war, the CED concentrated on ensuring economic freedom but, at the same time, supported many reforms of the New Deal as well as governmental measures to expand international trade. A strong internationalist, Hoffman lobbied for the Marshall Plan, and in 1948 HARRY S. TRUMAN appointed Hoffman to be the first administrator of the European Recovery Program. In that capacity, Hoffman oversaw the distribution of approximately $10 billion for the economic development of Europe. A highly efficient administrator, Hoffman also demonstrated skill in dealing with members of Congress and European officials.

In November 1950, with the European Recovery Program well under way, Hoffman accepted an offer to become the first president of the Ford Foundation. During his time at the foundation, he initiated programs designed to deal with social problems such as poverty and racial injustice. He particularly expanded its operations in the area of education. The foundation's Fund for the Advancement of Education spent about $6 million a year on travel and study fellowships for high school and college teachers and on expanded liberal arts programs for students. In addition, the Ford Foundation for Adult Education spent over $25 million, a third of which went for educational radio and television, between 1951 and 1955. Under Hoffman's leadership, the foundation also created programs to aid Eastern European individuals and groups fleeing from or resisting communism.

In the early 1950s, Hoffman became an outspoken defender of civil liberties. His public denunciation of Sen. JOSEPH R. MCCARTHY (R-Wis.) brought criticism and congressional scrutiny to the Ford Foundation.

Hoffman was an early, enthusiastic supporter of DWIGHT D. EISENHOWER for president. As far back as 1949, he tried to persuade the general to run, believing that Eisenhower was the one man who could unite postwar America and lead a "moral crusade" to return the country to traditional values. In addition, Hoffman saw Eisenhower as a man able to reorient the Republican Party. "I think," he said, "[Eisenhower] is going to put 'new heart' in the Republican Party and recast it in the image of Abraham Lincoln. We can use a party which takes its orders neither from the NAM [National Association of Manufacturers] nor the CIO [Congress of Industrial Organizations]."

As chairman of the Advisory Committee of Citizens for Eisenhower in 1952, Hoffman, along with HENRY CABOT LODGE, led the efforts to persuade Eisenhower to run for the Republican presidential nomination. During March 1952, Hoffman campaigned for the general in New Hampshire, where Eisenhower's name had been entered on the primary ballot without his public consent. Hoffman told a large audience at the University of New Hampshire that a vote for Eisenhower was the only way to ensure the continuance of a vital two-party system. After Eisenhower's dramatic victory in the New Hampshire primary, Hoffman spent several days with the general in Europe, persuading him to return to the United States and campaign openly. During the primary and the general election race,

Hoffman gave a considerable number of speeches and press conferences. He repeatedly made the case that only Eisenhower could unify the Republican Party; ensure peace by negotiating with the Soviets; win the votes of the South, independents, and youths; and restore the domestic economy.

In early 1953, trustees of the Ford Foundation pressed Hoffman to resign, in large part because of his political activities. Hoffman returned to Studebaker as chairman of the board, only to discover that the company had problems with production, sales, and labor relations. After negotiating a merger with Packard, he yielded control to a new management team. During this time, Hoffman maintained a close personal relationship with the new president and served as an adviser. He also served as chairman of the Fund for the Republic, an organization dedicated to protecting civil liberties. In 1954, Hoffman urged Eisenhower to attack McCarthy directly. At the same time, he also criticized the administration for what he considered its reluctance to rid itself of subversive elements.

Hoffman urged Eisenhower to run for reelection in 1956, despite the president's earlier heart attack, and campaigned vigorously for Eisenhower's reelection. Sometimes his zeal for Eisenhower and modern Republicanism proved embarrassing. In an article that appeared in the October issue of *Collier's*, Hoffman described what he saw as Eisenhower's concern for transforming the Republican Party from a series of factions into a unified party. Hoffman maintained that Eisenhower could "achieve something unique in American politics, a party that is fundamentally pressure-proof; something profoundly superior to its rival, the Democratic Party, whose irreconcilable differences leave it permanently open to the pressures of contending narrow interest groups." Hoffman maintained that, although the president had unified the party to a great degree, "senators claiming the label Republican who embrace none or very little of the Eisenhower program and philosophy" remained within the party. He divided these individuals into "unappeasables," including McCarthy, Sen. WILLIAM E. JENNER (R-Ind.), and HERMAN WELKER (R-Ida.) and "faint hopes," including Sen. BARRY GOLDWATER (R-Ariz.). Upset by the article, Goldwater asked presidential aide SHERMAN ADAMS to clarify his standing with Eisenhower. Adams assured him that Eisenhower did not intend to avoid him. The president also assured Republicans that there was room for dissent within the party.

In 1956, Eisenhower appointed Hoffman a member of the U.S. delegation to the United Nations General Assembly. Conservatives, led by McCarthy, predictably opposed the nomination. Nevertheless, he won confirmation in July. During his tenure, he urged the UN to form a permanent military force. In March 1959, Hoffman called on the developed nations to increase their private and public foreign aid by 100 to 400 percent over the next 10 years to promote peace. He asked the United States in particular to raise aid from $1.4 billion per year to an aggregate of $30 to $40 billion over the next 10 years.

In 1958, Secretary General Dag Hammarskjöld named Hoffman director of the new UN Special Fund to assist the economic development of poor and underdeveloped nations. The post required him to raise $250 million in contributions from member nations annually. Hoffman advocated a capitalist approach to economic development and insisted that the program's fund must be used as seed money. After 1966, the Special Fund became known as the UN Development Program. Hoffman retired from the UN in 1972.

In addition to his career in business and government, he wrote several books, including *Marketing Used Cars* (1929), *Peace Can Be Won* (1951), and *World Without Want* (1962). Hoffman died in New York City on October 8, 1974.

—MSM

Hoffman, Walter E(dward)
(1907–1996) *U.S. district judge*
Born in Jersey City, N.J., on July 18, 1907, Walter Hoffman graduated from the University of Pennsylvania in 1928 and received his law degree from Washington and Lee University in 1931. He then entered private practice in Norfolk, Va. A Republican who made unsuccessful races for Congress and for state attorney general, he was among the first party leaders in Virginia to support DWIGHT D. EISENHOWER for the Republican presidential nomination in 1952. At the Republican National Con-

vention in Chicago, Hoffman's firmness in backing the general within the divided Virginia delegation reportedly contributed to Eisenhower's nomination. Eisenhower appointed Hoffman the U.S. district judge for the eastern district of Virginia in 1954. Hoffman took his seat that September.

On the bench, Judge Hoffman insisted on compliance with the U.S. Supreme Court's decision in the school desegregation case of May 1954. In September 1956, the Virginia legislature passed a series of laws designed to thwart school desegregation, including a pupil-placement act and a measure requiring the governor to close any public school faced with a final desegregation order. In January 1957, Hoffman held the pupil-placement law unconstitutional because it took race into consideration in the process of assigning pupils to schools. The next month, he enjoined school officials in Norfolk, Va., from assigning students to schools based on race. The order was stayed pending appeal. The U.S. Court of Appeals for the Fourth Circuit upheld Hoffman's decision, and the Supreme Court denied certiorari on October 21, 1957.

Hoffman ruled in June 1958 that his order should take effect no later than the beginning of the school year that fall. In July, the school board established criteria for evaluating the applications of black students applying to previously all-white schools. The criteria included academic, physical, and moral fitness as well as social adaptability. One hundred fifty-one black pupils applied for admission to previously all-white schools. On August 18, however, the State Supreme Court of Appeals issued an order restraining the schools from enrolling or placing students in Norfolk's public schools. That same day, the school board rejected all of the applicants. Although many were rejected on academic or technical grounds, 24 students applied to attend schools in areas where racial tensions were high, and the school board decided that assigning them to these schools would create "racial conflicts and grave administrative problems." The school board found that four more students would be so racially isolated in the schools to which they applied that they would suffer psychological harm. Of the students who applied for a transfer, 30 petitioned Hoffman to set aside the school board's decision. On August 25, Hoffman instructed the board that achievement tests and interviews could be used in determining suitability for transfer if they were fairly administered. Racial tension or the isolation of black students, however, did not constitute valid grounds for refusing a transfer. Hoffman ordered the board to reconsider the requests for transfer and to report back to him on August 29. The school board reluctantly agreed to assign 17 black students to six formerly all-white schools. At the same time, the board delayed the opening of schools until September 22, appealed to the Court of Appeals for the Fourth Circuit, and filed a motion requesting postponement of Hoffman's desegregation order until September 1959. Hoffman denied the motion on September 2 but reserved the right to reconsider his action pending the Supreme Court's decision in the case arising out of the desegregation crisis in Little Rock, Ark. (*Aaron v. Cooper*). The Supreme Court handed down its decision in *Aaron v. Cooper* on September 12, and on September 18, Hoffman filed a memorandum declaring that "there is no longer any legal or justifiable reason further to consider defendant's request for a one year deferment." The school board postponed the opening of the city's secondary schools until September 29 and asked the chief judge of the Fourth Circuit, SIMON E. SOBELOFF, for a stay of Hoffman's order; Sobeloff denied the stay but offered to convene a special session to hear an appeal on the merits of the case. The Fourth Circuit heard the appeal on September 27 and on the same day issued a decision affirming Hoffman's order.

Gov. J. LINDSAY ALMOND, JR., responded to the Fourth Circuit's decision by closing the six junior and senior high schools involved. Faced with court orders to desegregate elsewhere in the state, Almond closed schools in other districts. By the end of September, roughly 13,000 students had been locked out of public schools throughout Virginia. As a result, moderates began to exert pressure to end Virginia's policy of "massive resistance."

On January 19, 1959, both a three-judge federal court in Richmond (consisting of Sobeloff and CLEMENT F. HAYNSWORTH, JR., from the Fourth Circuit Court of Appeals and Hoffman) and the Virginia Supreme Court of Appeals handed down decisions declaring Virginia's school-closing law unconstitutional.

The governor then called a special session of the state legislature, which repealed the massive-resistance laws but passed other, less transparently defiant laws to try to discourage school desegregation. In Norfolk, after final orders from Hoffman, 17 black students finally began attending the reopened white public schools on February 2, 1959.

Hoffman also ruled against segregation in cases not involving the school system. In July 1955, for example, he ordered the desegregation of Virginia's Seashore State Park. Hoffman granted a preliminary injunction in August 1956 that prohibited the city of Portsmouth from operating a golf course that did not admit blacks. In January 1958, Hoffman joined a majority on a three-judge panel that found three of Virginia's anti-NAACP laws unconstitutional.

Hoffman's commitment to follow the rulings of the Supreme Court made him a favorite target for verbal abuse from Virginia's segregationists. He received a flood of phone calls and letters denouncing him, and he was socially ostracized. In response, Hoffman declared, "I will do my duty if it costs me my last friend on earth."

Norfolk began token desegregation of its schools in 1959, but the NAACP continued to challenge in court the city's plan for limited and gradual desegregation. The litigation finally ended in March 1966, when Hoffman approved a desegregation plan that resulted from negotiations between the school board, the NAACP, and the Justice Department.

Hoffman served as chief judge for the Eastern District of Virginia from 1961 to 1973. The chief judge of the Fourth Circuit Court of Appeals selected Hoffman to preside over the criminal trial of Vice President Spiro T. Agnew in 1973. Hoffman also served as the director of the Federal Judicial Center. He took senior judge status in 1974 and continued to sit until his death in Norfolk, Va., on November 21, 1996.

—MSM

Hofstadter, Richard
(1916–1970) *historian*

The son of a Jewish immigrant father and a Protestant mother, Richard Hofstadter was born in Buffalo, N.Y., on August 6, 1916. He grew up in that city, attended public schools, and graduated with honors from the University of Buffalo in 1937. Under pressure from his family, he prepared for a career in law. He worked as a clerk for Judge Irving R. Kauffmann and enrolled at the New York School of Law, but he found the study of law uninteresting and performed poorly. After one term, he withdrew and entered the graduate program in history at Columbia University, where he earned his Ph.D. in 1942. Both as an undergraduate and as a graduate student, he was involved in leftist politics and may have become a member of the communist party for a brief while. By 1939, however, he had become disillusioned with the communist party and with Marxism. At the same time, he maintained his intense dislike for capitalism. Hofstadter came to identify himself as a critic of liberalism from within the liberal tradition. As a graduate student, Hofstadter taught at Brooklyn College and the City University of New York. He defended his doctoral dissertation, "Social Darwinism in American Thought, 1860–1915," in 1942 and that same year took his first full-time academic appointment at the University of Maryland. Hofstadter returned to Columbia University as an assistant professor in 1946. He became a full professor in 1952.

Hofstadter published *The American Political Tradition and the Men Who Made It* in 1948. A collection of incisive, iconoclastic profiles of those who shaped American political history from the founders of the republic to Franklin D. Roosevelt, the book maintained that American leaders, despite disagreements on specific issues, "shared a belief in the rights of property, the philosophy of economic individualism, the value of competition." The book won a Pulitzer Prize and became assigned reading for a generation of students of American history.

Hofstadter's emphasis on the common assumptions and values held by Americans over time, rather than the conflicts that divided them, was a common theme of a group of postwar American historians known as the "consensus" school. Unlike those members of the consensus school who celebrated the fundamental accord they found in the American experience, however, Hofstadter never denied the reality of conflict in American history, and he criticized the inflexibility and intellectual stagna-

tion he believed consensus imposed on American political life.

In the 1950s, Hofstadter emerged as a leading academic critic and analyst of the American right and Sen. JOSEPH MCCARTHY (R-Wis.). In the spring of 1954, the directors of the American Civilization Program at Barnard College invited Hofstadter gave a talk on political dissent. He chose as his topic right-wing or, as he called it, pseudo-conservative dissent. The lecture was published in *The American Scholar* and later included in Daniel Bell's *The New American Right* (1955). In that highly influential essay, "The Pseudo-Conservative Revolt," Hofstadter wrote that "although they believe themselves to be conservatives and usually employ the rhetoric of conservatism," the people he identified as "pseudo-conservatives" demonstrated "signs of a serious and restless dissatisfaction with American life, traditions, and institutions." This manifested itself in pseudo-conservatives' "hyper-patriotism and hyper-conformism," their belief in an internal conspiracy permeating American life, their accusations that national leaders were guilty of betrayal, and their desire for authoritarian solutions. Indeed, "in the name of upholding traditional American values and institutions and in the process of defining them against more or less fictitious dangers," pseudo-conservatives "consciously or unconsciously aim[ed] at their abolition." Thus, they had "little in common with the temperate and compromising spirit of true conservatism."

While not denying the economic and political causes of this discontent, Hofstadter stressed its social and psychological elements. For Hofstadter, "the rootlessness and heterogeneity of American life" led to "a peculiar scramble for status" and a secure identity. This, in turn, gave rise to pseudo-conservatism's focus on "status politics," rather than traditional "interest politics." Since, however, it was difficult to give pragmatic expression to status politics, Hofstadter concluded that such discontent found expression not in legislative proposals, but in "grousing." He located intense concerns over status in certain groups, among them old-stock Anglo-Saxons, who felt displaced in modern America, and certain ethnic groups, whose members experienced anxiety about their Americanism and felt a need to prove it. Both groups found satisfaction in advertising their patriotism and challenging the loyalty of others. A decade later, Hofstadter acknowledged that he had "overstated the role of certain ethnic minorities in the right wing" and ignored the role of religious fundamentalism.

By the mid-1950s, Hofstadter's position had changed from that of *The American Political Tradition*. No longer did he criticize reform movements for the inadequacy and conservatism of their leadership. Instead, he drew connections between McCarthyism and what he regarded as earlier mass movements. In his widely read and enormously influential book, *The Age of Reform: From Bryan to F.D.R.* (1955), Hofstadter applied the critical concepts he had used to analyze the right wing in postwar America to Populism and Progressivism. He regarded the two movements suspiciously for responding emotionally rather than rationally to social change and for being motivated by status rather than economic concerns. Indeed, he found that elements of Populism and Progressivism, particularly Populism, seemed "very strongly to foreshadow some aspects of the cranky pseudo-conservatism" of the 1950s. According to Hofstadter, the Populists sought solace in a romanticized vision of America's agrarian past, spun conspiracy theories, and succumbed to panaceas such as free silver. He argued that the origins of the Progressive impulse lay in the status anxieties of a middle class afraid of vulgar plutocrats above and urban immigrants below. Moreover, Hofstadter found cause for alarm in the provincialism, chauvinism, and anti-Semitism of the Populists and the moralistic nostalgia of the Progressives. Hofstadter won his second Pulitzer Prize for *The Age of Reform*.

By the end of the 1950s, Hofstadter had become one of the most highly regarded and widely read historians of his era. His work ranged over a wide variety of subjects, something made possible by the fact that his research consisted of extensive reading in the historical literature and examination of published primary sources rather than archival research. Hofstadter offered interpretations based in large part on historical imagination rather than carefully researched theses. His engaging prose style carried readers along, even when Hofstadter failed to offer substantial supporting evidence. Columbia

University made him DeWitt Clinton Professor of American History in 1959.

In the 1960s, Hofstadter's scholarship continued to reflect his perception of the relationship between current events and history. He unequivocally stated that *Anti-Intellectualism in American Life* (1963) "was conceived in response to the political and intellectual conditions of the 1950s." In *The Paranoid Style in American Politics* (1965), he updated his analysis of "pseudo-conservatism" and offered a critique of the Goldwater phenomenon. He published two more traditional works of history, *The Progressive Historians* (1968) and *The Idea of a Party System* (1969), and was at work on a social history of America in the 18th century when he died of leukemia in New York City on October 24, 1970. A completed fragment of that work, *America in 1750: A Social Portrait*, was published posthumously in 1971.

—MSM

Hogan, Frank S(mithwick)
(1902–1974)   *district attorney*

The son of Irish immigrants, Frank Hogan was born in Waterbury, Conn., on January 17, 1902. He attended parochial school in Waterbury and worked his way through Columbia University, from which he graduated in 1924. After working for a year, he entered Columbia Law School, where he was an average student. Upon receiving his degree in 1928, Hogan joined a law firm in Manhattan's financial district. After a short time, he left to begin his own practice, specializing in insurance and real estate law, with Anthony J. Liebler. The practice struggled to get by, and in 1935, Hogan joined the staff of THOMAS E. DEWEY, who had been appointed special prosecutor to investigate organized crime. Dewey gained fame for his successful prosecutions of the mobster Charles ("Lucky") Luciano for racketeering and of James Hines, the Democratic party leader, for corruption. Dewey won election as district attorney for New York Co. (Manhattan), and when he took office in 1937, Hogan followed him as an assistant district attorney. When Dewey resigned to run for governor in 1941, Hogan gained the endorsement of the Republican, Democratic, and Labor parties and was elected to succeed him. Hogan won reelection every four years until 1973.

During his 32 years as Manhattan's district attorney, Hogan won acclaim as a model of an aggressive, nonpartisan prosecutor. He gained national attention for the successful prosecutions his office conducted against organized crime and corrupt politicians. In 1945, in the only case he personally tried as district attorney, Hogan won convictions against Joseph S. Fay and James Bove for corrupt union practices. After a years-long investigation of FRANK COSTELLO, the head of an organized crime family who had great influence with Tammany Hall, Hogan's office provided crucial information on Costello to Sen. ESTES KEFAUVER's Select Committee on Organized Crime. Hogan also secured convictions in 1951 against Joe Adonis, a gangster operating primarily in Brooklyn and New Jersey, and Frank Erickson ("King of the Bookmakers") in 1953. In addition, Hogan focused his attention on corrupt politicians. He oversaw the successful prosecution of James J. Moran, a deputy fire commissioner who had organized an extortion racket that victimized contractors with the city.

Hogan's office investigated and prosecuted some of the most highly publicized scandals of the 1950s, including college basketball's point-shaving scandal, the bribery ("payola") of radio disc jockeys, the television quiz-show scandals, and corruption in city government. During the 1960s, Hogan's office investigated payoffs in New York's State Liquor Authority and uncovered most of the evidence used by federal prosecutors to convict the city's water commissioner, James Marcus. In another famous incident, Hogan exposed Clifford Irving's scheme to profit from a fraudulent biography of HOWARD HUGHES.

Hogan twice ran for higher office. In 1949, Mayor William O'Dwyer, the Democratic incumbent, indicated that he would not seek reelection. Hogan gathered sufficient support, including that of Tammany Hall, to gain the nomination. O'Dwyer then changed his mind, and Hogan withdrew from the race. Hogan ran for reelection as district attorney instead and won easily.

In 1958, CARMINE DESAPIO, the boss of Tammany Hall, helped Hogan win the Democratic nomination for the U.S. Senate. DeSapio insisted

on Hogan, perhaps because he wanted to choose a new district attorney, who would have the power to appoint over a hundred assistants. Two other Democrats, however, sought the nomination, former Secretary of the Air Force THOMAS K. FINLETTER and Thomas Murray, former head of the Atomic Energy Commission, who had the support of Gov. AVERELL HARRIMAN. Hogan took little part in the bitter struggle for the nomination, but DeSapio's raw exercise of power to secure the nomination for Hogan at the Democratic state convention created a backlash. While Hogan's personal integrity was not an issue, his links to DeSapio and Tammany Hall engendered hostility from reformers in the Democratic party and hurt him in the general election, which he lost to KENNETH B. KEATING.

For most of his years in office, Hogan was America's most famous prosecutor. He built a well-deserved reputation for personal honesty, and the office he headed was respected for both its integrity and competence. Hogan's office maintained a high conviction rate, and the talented young lawyers Hogan hired went on to occupy high positions in the legal profession and on the bench of New York. By the late 1960s, however, the luster began to fade. Some came to regard Hogan as overzealous and out of touch. More seriously, some accused Hogan of pursuing personal agendas. Two of his prosecutions proved particularly controversial. In the first of these, Hogan brought obscenity charges against the comedian Lenny Bruce in 1964. Although Hogan obtained a conviction, an appeals court overturned the decision, ruling that "it was error to hold that the performances were without social merit." In the second matter, Hogan, a proud and active alumnus of Columbia, insisted on prosecuting hundreds of students involved in protests at the university in 1968, even though the university had withdrawn the charges. Toward the end of Hogan's tenure, the Knapp commission exposed systemic corruption in New York City's police department. The commission criticized prosecutors for failing to move against that corruption aggressively.

Seeking vindication, Hogan ran for a ninth term in 1973, even though he suffered a disabling stroke that summer. For the first time in many years, he faced a serious opponent in the primary. Unable to return to work after the stroke, Hogan was forced to rely on aides to run his office. Voters nevertheless reelected him by a two-to-one margin. Hogan resigned as district attorney the day after Christmas, less than two months after his reelection. He died in New York City on April 2, 1974.

—MSM

Holifield, Chet (Chester) (Earl)
(1903–1995) *U.S. congressman*

Born on December 3, 1903, in Mayfield, Ky., Holifield moved with his family to Springdale, Ark. He left high school before graduation, and after working in a tailor shop, established his own men's clothing business. He entered Democratic politics during the 1930s as a party leader in the Los Angeles area. In 1942, he won election as a Democrat to the U.S. House of Representatives from California's 19th district, a predominantly blue-collar area with a substantial Mexican-American population. On Capitol Hill, Holifield focused his attention on the problems of atomic energy development. A proponent of civilian control of the atom, he was placed on the newly created Joint Committee on Atomic Energy, which supervised the Atomic Energy Commission (AEC) in 1947. During the mid and late 1940s, Holifield was an outspoken opponent of the House Un-American Activities Committee and defended AEC chairman David Lilienthal and Edward U. Condon, nuclear physicist and director of the National Bureau of Standards, against charges of being "soft on communism."

During the Eisenhower administration, Holifield emerged as a leading champion of public development of atomic energy. In 1954, he opposed an administration-backed bill permitting the AEC to license private construction of atomic power plants. Holifield charged that the bill, which proposed a five-year period of compulsory patent sharing, "would set a pattern of monopoly" in the industrial use of atomic energy and contended that the period should be extended to at least 10 years. He also objected to its limitations on the AEC's authority to produce power, to its allegedly insufficient safeguards for protecting the public interest, and to a "built-in subsidy" for industry in the provision for government purchase of privately produced nuclear materials. However, the legislation passed Congress in essentially the form requested by the administration.

In 1956, Holifield supported a bill authorizing $400 million for expanding the construction of reactors by the AEC. He asserted that the building of reactors during the experimental stage should be undertaken by government rather than by private enterprise. The administration opposed the bill, and in July the House, by a vote of 203 to 191, recommitted the bill to the Joint Committee on Atomic Energy.

Holifield was a leading critic of the controversial Dixon-Yates contract. The dispute began in 1954, when the Tennessee Valley Authority (TVA) proposed building a new steam plant at Fulton, Tenn., to supply power to the city of Memphis. The consumption of TVA power by the Atomic Energy Commission's (AEC) installations at Paduca meant that the city of Memphis would face a shortage of electricity within four years. Eisenhower, who preferred private development of power, could not see the justification for the federal government to pay for a plant to supply power to a particular city. He ordered JOSEPH DODGE, the director of the Bureau of the Budget, and LEWIS L. STRAUSS, chairman of the AEC, to explore the possibilities of having private industry build the plant. EDGAR H. DIXON, president of Middle South Utilities, and EUGENE YATES, chairman of the board of the Southern Company, organized the Mississippi Valley Generating Company to build a plant that would supply power to the TVA to replace the power the TVA sold to the AEC. The Dixon-Yates proposal was considered acceptable by the AEC, TVA, and the Bureau of the Budget, and, upon the recommendation of the Bureau of the Budget, Eisenhower approved it.

Holifield was prominent among a group of liberals who argued that the private power would cost more than that provided by TVA, and he charged that Eisenhower was using the AEC to subsidize a private utility and undermine the government-owned agency. After the Democrats gained control of Congress in 1955, the Joint Committee on Atomic Energy recommended cancellation of the contract. When the city of Memphis decided to build its own municipal power plant, which freed up power from existing TVA facilities for use by the

AEC, the administration cancelled the Dixon-Yates contract.

In 1953, Holifield served as a member of the Commission on Organization of the Executive Branch of Government, chaired by former president HERBERT HOOVER. The commission's report of 1955 urged drastic cutbacks in many government activities. The leading dissident on the panel, Holifield charged the commission with exceeding its jurisdiction and distorting facts. He denounced its opposition to public power and its call for reductions in federal legal and lending services.

During 1957, as chairman of the Joint Committee on Atomic Energy's Special Subcommittee on Radiation, Holifield held hearings on the consequences of radioactive fallout from nuclear weapons. At the conclusion of the probe, he denounced the AEC for "playing down" the hazard of fallout. Meanwhile, in 1957 and 1958, the Government Operations Committee's Subcommittee on Military Operations, also chaired by Holifield, investigated civil defense policy. During the course of the hearings, Holifield emerged as a strong proponent of fallout shelters, and his subcommittee was instrumental in persuading the Office of Civil Defense to request $32 billion for the construction of shelters.

Holifield was one of the founders of a liberal House Democratic caucus in 1957. Among the measures the group endorsed were federal aid for housing, school construction, and medical education; assistance to depressed areas; repeal of the Taft-Hartley Act; and the elimination of the national origins system from immigration and naturalization laws. The caucus was formally organized as the Democratic Study Group in 1959, and, the following year, Holifield was chosen its chairman.

During the 1960s, Holifield rotated with Sen. JOHN O. PASTORE (D-R.I.) as chairman of the Joint Committee on Atomic Energy. In the early 1960s, he supported the Kennedy administration's program to spend billions of dollars on fallout shelters. A consistent supporter of nuclear power development, he also supported the administration's plan, passed by Congress in 1962, to permit the AEC to add electric generating facilities to its plutonium production reactor in Hanford, Wash. In 1970, Holifield supported appropriating $2 billion to develop a breeder reactor. After 1965, Holifield faced increasing criticism from former liberal allies for his support of the war in Vietnam and appropriation requests from the Pentagon. He became chair of the Government Operations Committee in 1971. In 1974, Holifield announced that he would not seek reelection. He returned to California, resumed the manufacture and sale of men's clothing, and died in Redlands, Calif., on February 6, 1995.

—MSM

Hollister, John B(aker)

(1890–1979) *executive director, Commission on the Organization of the Executive Branch; director, International Cooperation Administration, State Department*

Born in Cincinnati, Ohio, on November 7, 1890, Hollister graduated from Saint Paul's School in Concord, N.H., and from Yale University in 1911. After studying at the University of Munich, he attended Harvard Law School, where he received his degree in 1915. He was admitted to the Ohio bar and began practice in Cincinnati that same year. Following service in the artillery during World War I, he helped administer U.S. relief in Poland and Lithuania. He returned to Ohio to practice law. In 1924 joined with his lifelong friend, ROBERT A. TAFT, Taft's brother Charles, and John Stettinius to form the partnership of Taft, Stettinius, and Hollister. Hollister won a special election in 1931 to fill a vacancy in the House of Representatives created by the death of Nicholas Longworth (R-Ohio). A conservative Republican, Hollister's position on the House Banking and Currency Committee gave him a platform to oppose many New Deal measures. He was reelected twice but lost his bid for reelection in 1936. He returned to his law practice in 1937 but remained active in Republican politics throughout the 1930s and 1940s.

In 1953, HERBERT HOOVER appointed Hollister executive director of the Commission on the Organization of the Executive Branch. During the next two years, Hollister investigated the allocation of foreign aid by the State Department's Foreign Operations Administration (FOA). His report recommended cutting $360 million annually from foreign aid appropriations and increasing efficiency in the allotment of technical aid.

In April 1955, President Eisenhower, seeking to appease conservative Republicans, appointed Hollister head of the newly created International Cooperation Administration (ICA), a semiautonomous agency within the State Department that replaced the FOA. As director of the ICA, Hollister coordinated economic and military aid "except for matters which . . . requir[ed] final decision by the President."

As director, Hollister supported increased exports by Western nations to Soviet satellite nations in an effort to lessen their dependence on the USSR, a policy that drew the wrath of Sen. JOSEPH McCARTHY (R-Wis.). Hollister refused to appear in open hearings before the Senate Permanent Investigations Subcommittee on the issue but agreed to testify behind closed doors.

The administration requested that Congress appropriate $4.67 billion for mutual security for fiscal 1957, nearly $1.4 billion more than the amount authorized by Congress for the previous year and almost $2 billion more than Congress actually appropriated for foreign aid in fiscal 1956. The proposal encountered widespread opposition in Congress. In hearings before the House Foreign Affairs Committee in March and the Senate Foreign Relations Committee in April, Hollister defended the administration's proposal. After much maneuvering, Congress appropriated $3.8 billion for the mutual security program in fiscal 1957. Conservative Republicans generally opposed foreign aid, and other members of Congress objected to giving aid to "neutralist" nations such as India and Yugoslavia. In addition, Congress made its greatest cuts in military assistance. Congress cut $73 million from Eisenhower's requests for nonmilitary assistance and $982 million from his request for $3 billion in military aid.

In 1957, the administration included the creation of a Development Loan Fund (DLF) in its proposals for the mutual assistance program for 1958. The DLF would make public loans for the purpose of economic development to Third World countries, and those loans would be repayable in local currencies. Once again, Congress substantially cut the president's requests, but it did approve a modified version of the DLF. Although he publicly defended the administration's foreign-aid program, Hollister, a conservative Republican, disagreed

with the president on fundamental matters relating to foreign aid. After the passage of the foreign-aid bill, Hollister submitted his resignation in July 1957. Hollister's dissent became public as he was about to leave his post. In a directive issued on September 12, 1957, the day before his departure, Hollister criticized American assistance to government-owned enterprises. He argued that the ICA's policy was to administer American aid "in such a way as will encourage the development of the private sectors" of foreign countries.

After leaving the ICA, Hollister returned to his old law firm. He died in Cincinnati on January 4, 1979.

—MSM

Hook, Sidney
(1902–1989) *philosopher*

The son of an immigrant Jewish garment worker, Sidney Hook was born in Brooklyn, N.Y., on December 20, 1902, and grew up in Williamsburg, a neighborhood populated by Jewish immigrants. He graduated from City College of New York in 1923 and earned his Ph.D. in 1927 from Columbia University, where he studied philosophy under John Dewey. The same year he earned his degree, Hook joined the philosophy department at New York University and published his dissertation, *The Metaphysics of Pragmatism*. He became chair of that department in 1934.

During the 1930s, Hook gained prominence both as a radical intellectual and an activist. He published a translation of Lenin's works in 1927. In 1932, Hook organized a group of intellectuals to endorse William Z. Foster, the communist candidate, for president. Soon after, however, Hook grew increasingly disgusted by the practices of the Communist Party (CP) and broke with it in 1933. He moved toward the independent socialism of A. J. MUSTE and helped organize the American Workers Party in 1933, which merged with the Trotskyists in 1934. Hook also produced a prodigious body of intellectual work. He published *Towards the Understanding of Karl Marx* (1933), in which he drew a distinction between Marx and Marxism (by which he meant the practice and official orthodoxy of the Soviet Union). The CP's harsh attacks on the book contributed to Hook's ultimate break with the party. In *The Meaning of Marx* (1934), Hook reinterpreted Marx's understanding of Hegel's dialectic in terms of pragmatism. Like much of Hook's writing at this point in his career, the book attempted to find common ground in Marx and Dewey. *From Hegel to Marx* (1936) explored the intellectual genesis of Marxism.

By the late 1930s, Hook had become an outspoken critic not only of Joseph Stalin but of communism. As the decade drew to a close, he began to draw parallels between Nazism and Stalinism as forms of totalitarianism. In particular, Hook vigorously attacked Soviet science and Stalin's purges, both of which violated his commitment to free and open discourse. In 1939, along with Dewey, NORMAN THOMAS, and other leftist intellectuals, Hook organized the Committee for Cultural Freedom and issued a manifesto critical of Stalin's Soviet Union. During these years, Hook also began to extend his critique to Marx and Marxist thought.

As the cold war got under way, Hook identified himself as a social democrat and a "Cold War liberal." He believed that the West, despite its flaws, represented the best hope of freedom and expounded his views in books as well as articles in the *New York Times*, *Commentary*, and the *New Leader*. Hook maintained a kind of friendship with WHITTAKER CHAMBERS and supported his charges against Alger Hiss. In 1949, Hook published an article in *Commentary*, in which he called for the ouster of all communist teachers from American classrooms. He argued that communists were not unfit to teach because of their ideas but because they had committed "*professional misconduct* in joining a conspiratorial organization, one of whose declared purposes is corruption of the teaching process for political purposes." Hook worried that a still greater menace to American education lay in the "little army of 'progressive' intellectuals" who supported Soviet foreign policy, lent their names to various front groups, and opposed "even the mildest and most justified of administrative measures" to restrict communist academics. In *Heresy, Yes—Conspiracy, No* (published as articles in 1950 and 1951, later as a pamphlet, and then as a book in 1952), Hook maintained that communists had no right to teach because they did not subscribe to the principles of free and open debate and were engaged in a conspiracy, directed by an enemy power, to subvert academic freedom. Rather than teach, communists "indoctrinated" students. Extending the argument beyond the classroom, Hook maintained that communism was a "secret or underground movement which seeks to attain its ends not by normal political or educational processes, but by playing outside the rules of the game." Therefore, party members, who functioned as virtual "agents of a foreign power," were not entitled to the protection of civil liberties. At the same time, he argued for the necessity of distinguishing communist conspiracy from dissent or "heresy." For Hook, the First Amendment protected heresy; it did not protect conspiracy. Hook defended the Smith Act, which made it illegal to advocate the overthrow of the government by force or violence, because he thought it necessary to deal with American communists, whom he believed represented a "clear, present, flourishing, and extremely powerful" threat to "national survival." That threat derived not from their numbers or their ideas but because of their "organizational ties" to the Kremlin.

In 1950, Hook joined with a group of American and European intellectuals to found the Congress for Cultural Freedom. The organization encouraged Western intellectuals to unite against communist aggression and against myths that minimized the threat it posed. Many years later, it would come out that the CIA supported the Congress for Cultural Freedom; but the CIA's role was not known at the time, and the intellectuals involved did not need the CIA to instruct them in anticommunism. In 1951, Hook joined JAMES BURNHAM, ARTHUR SCHLESINGER, JR., the novelist James T. Farrell, and others in organizing the American Committee for Cultural Freedom (ACCF), an affiliate of the European Congress, which Hook regarded as a necessary counterbalance to those intellectuals who supported the Soviet Union or turned a blind eye to the threat of totalitarianism. Hook readily acknowledged that America was no "paradise of liberty," especially for African Americans, yet he found incomprehensible the inability of many European intellectuals to see the difference between an imperfect democracy and a "totalitarian inferno."

As a member of ACCF's committee on academic freedom, Hook supported the removal of communist teachers but maintained that academic tenure should be left in the hands of colleges and boards of education and not turned over to congressional bodies, such as the House Un-American Activities Committee. While condemning what he called the "cultural vigilantism" of Sen. JOSEPH McCARTHY (R-Wis.), he disagreed with liberals who derided the anticommunist activities of that era as a "witch hunt." Hook and the ACCF protested the government's refusal to permit Charlie Chaplin to reenter the United States and its probe of ARTHUR MILLER. They also criticized McCarthy's investigation of the Voice of America. Nevertheless, Hook and the ACCF attacked those writers they believed exploited civil liberties to the advantage of communism.

Hook defined himself as a secular humanist, which he explained meant that he adhered to "the view that morals are autonomous of religious belief, that they are relevant to truths about nature and human nature, truths that rest on scientific evidence." Rooted in pragmatism, Hook's philosophy held that action was fundamental to thought. Thought contemplated action and its consequences. That process resulted in the construction of norms, which could, in turn, be modified and applied in new contexts. Further, the point of any theoretical construct was to serve as a basis for action, and the consequences of that action would confirm or discredit the theory.

During the 1960s, Hook continued to write extensively on civil liberties, Marxism, American politics, progressive education, and philosophical theory. He supported the withdrawal of American forces from Vietnam, but only if North Vietnamese forces also withdrew. While he debated publicly with Bertrand Russell, Hook criticized American universities for refusing to allow Russell to teach in the United States because of his political views. The New Left frequently criticized him for his positions on the Vietnam War and academic freedom. Hook responded by publishing *Academic Freedom and Academic Anarchy* (1968), an attack on the New Left. In addition to his scholarly and public engagement, Hook held the chair of the philosophy department at NYU for 35 years, surrendering it only on his

retirement in 1969. As attempts to remedy past discrimination led to affirmative action, he criticized quotas in university admissions as perversions of the concept of equality of opportunity and as inconsistent with academic freedom. In 1973, he became a senior research fellow at the Hoover Institution on War, Revolution and Peace at Stanford University. Hook was awarded the Presidential Medal of Freedom in 1985 and published an autobiography, *Out of Step: An Unquiet Life in the 20th Century* in 1987. He died of congestive heart failure in Stanford, Calif., on July 12, 1989.

—MSM

Hoover, Herbert (Clark)

(1874–1964) *president of the United States; chairman, Commission on Organization of the Executive Branch*

Born in West Branch, Iowa, on August 10, 1874, and orphaned at the age of nine, Herbert Hoover migrated to California to live with relatives. He graduated from Stanford University in 1894. Over the next 20 years, Hoover made a fortune as a mining engineer and executive. He directed various Allied relief efforts during World War I and headed the U.S. Food Administration from 1917 to 1918; his personal assistants included ROBERT A. TAFT and LEWIS L. STRAUSS. Between 1921 and 1928, Hoover served with distinction as secretary of commerce. With a large national following originating from his World War I humanitarianism, and representing the Republican Party during an economic boom, Hoover easily won election to the presidency in 1928.

Hoover had the bad fortune to be president at the onset of the Great Depression. Although he took unprecedented actions to reverse an economic downturn (his was the first administration actively to intervene in the economy in peacetime), his approach was limited by his commitment to voluntary cooperation and his distrust of the coercive power of government. His efforts proved unsuccessful in reversing the downturn. Hoover also lacked the skilled, charismatic leadership necessary at a time of great national crisis. He could manipulate neither the Congress nor public opinion. The voters rejected him for reelection in 1932 by a wide margin. For the rest of Hoover's long life, Democratic orators and large numbers of people identified him and his party with the depression. Nevertheless, as Rexford Tugwell, one of Franklin D. Roosevelt's "Brain Trust," later confessed, "We didn't admit it at the time, but practically the whole New Deal was extrapolated from programs that Hoover started."

Hoover remained out of government through the Roosevelt administration. He became an increasingly strident critic of the New Deal and grew more conservative with age. He regarded the emerging American welfare state with its expanding bureaucracy as a threat not only to free enterprise but individual initiative and dignity. From his presidency onward, Hoover rejected coercive approaches to foreign policy. Above all, he hoped to avoid military conflict. He opposed American entry into World War II, and, for all his hatred of communism, did not become an avid cold warrior. Indeed, he opposed what he considered to be the excessive anticommunist rhetoric of HARRY S. TRUMAN and his administration. Hoover opposed the creation of the North Atlantic Treaty Organization, was critical of the conduct of the Korean War, and advocated withdrawing American forces from Europe.

Hoover returned to government after Roosevelt's death. In early 1946, Truman asked Hoover to draw up a program to deal with food shortages, and Hoover directed efforts to provide relief to wartorn Europe. The following year, Truman appointed Hoover to head a Commission on Organization of the Executive Branch of Government, which became known as the "Hoover Commission." The commission presented a series of recommendations in 1949 that focused on creating a more efficient, vertical organization of the executive branch.

The election of DWIGHT D. EISENHOWER, the first Republican president since Hoover, further improved the ex-president's national stature. Although Hoover had not supported Eisenhower for the presidential nomination and disagreed with him on many matters of policy, he and Eisenhower became good friends. Hoover attended White House functions as well as Western fishing outings and barbecues. The president named Hoover's eldest son, HERBERT HOOVER, JR., undersecretary of state in August 1954.

During the Eisenhower administration, Hoover chaired the Second Hoover Commission on the Organization of the Executive Branch. After receiving the appointment from Eisenhower in 1953, Hoover once again strove to make the executive branch less wasteful. But he also determined that a reformed administration would be one more accountable to the people through a better, more systematic presentation of official "facts and records" for public discussion. In addition, the second commission, unlike its predecessor, enjoyed the broader mandate of surveying policy as well as functional coordination.

The commission covered much ground in issuing its reports through the first half of 1955. Its 11 members, from both parties and several special study groups, studied such diverse problems as intelligence gathering, foreign aid, budget and accounting, military supply, administrative procedure, and water power. In all, the commission investigated 95 percent of all executive departments and agencies. Many of its findings related gross examples of mismanagement and poor planning. In April 1955, for example, the commission reported that the navy's supply of hamburger would last 60 years. Hoover promised that, if adopted, his panel's recommendations would save the government billions of dollars.

The Hoover commission's reports proved to be conservative in domestic policy. The panel uncovered about 3,000 examples of governmental competition with the private sector and requested that one-third of the programs be dismantled. Others, it declared, should be denied certain exclusive privileges. The Rural Electrification Administration, it proposed, should be forced to operate on a self-supporting basis. (Hoover himself privately wished to sell the popular Tennessee Valley Authority [TVA], a product of the New Deal era.) The commission also called for the dissolution of such federal lending programs as the Agricultural Marketing Act Revolving Fund and the Federal Farm Mortgage Act.

Eisenhower had mixed reactions to the commission's findings. He approved of certain structural reforms, in budgeting for example, but he refused to endorse the commission's more conservative recommendations. He politely ignored Hoover's idea (and own draft) of a message to Congress promoting them. Of the Second Hoover Commission's 314 suggestions, the administration adopted 64 percent (compared to the 72 percent adopted by the Truman administration).

Hoover, for his part, played the role of elder statesman practically to the very end of his life. He addressed and was well received by the Republican National Conventions in 1956 and 1960, while remaining an object of derision at Democratic ones. His public image did improve; in December 1959, a Gallup survey listed him ninth on a list of Most Admired Americans. Eisenhower's Democratic successor, JOHN F. KENNEDY, whose father, Joseph P. Kennedy, served on the Second Hoover Commission, consulted with Hoover. Throughout his life, Hoover published numerous works, including *Principles of Mining* (1909), *American Individualism* (1922), *The Challenge to Liberty* (1934), *The Memoirs of Herbert Hoover*, 3 vols. (1951–52), and *The Ordeal of Woodrow Wilson* (1958). He died in New York City on October 20, 1964.

—MSM

Hoover, Herbert, Jr.
(1903–1969) *special consultant to the secretary of state, undersecretary of state*

The son of the 31st president of the United States, Herbert Hoover, Jr., was born in London, England, on August 4, 1903. He graduated from Stanford University in 1925, received his M.B.A. from Harvard Business School in 1928, and remained at Harvard as an instructor for the next two years. Hoover worked as a communications engineer from 1929 to 1934 for Transcontinental and Western Air, Inc. In 1935, he was a teaching fellow at the California Institute of Technology. Like his father, Herbert Hoover Jr. was a mining engineer. After inventing a number of radio and electronic devices to detect oil, Hoover founded the United Geophysical Co. at Pasadena, Calif., in 1935, which employed over 1,000 persons prospecting all over the world. During World War II, Hoover's company became a major defense contractor. He invented several instruments to measure the vibration and strain in aircraft.

Hoover enjoyed such standing in the oil industry that he became a consultant to the governments of Venezuela, Brazil, Chile, and Peru. He played a central role in negotiating an agreement between Venezuela and several oil companies. As a result of his dealings with the oil producing nations, Hoover was asked to negotiate the settlement of the Iranian-British dispute over the Abadan oil fields in 1953–54.

The dispute began in May 1951, when the Iranian prime minister, Mohammad Mossadeq, nationalized the Anglo-Iranian Oil Company, of which the British government owned 52 percent. In October the British shut down the Abadan refinery and ordered British technicians to leave Iran. Great Britain refused to buy oil from Iran and placed legal obstacles in the way of any other country willing to do so. Without revenue from the sale of oil, Iran faced an economic crisis. Iran retaliated by ordering the British to close all their consulates in January 1952 and severed diplomatic relations with Great Britain in October. By the beginning of 1953, two

Herbert Hoover, Jr., undersecretary of state
(Dwight D. Eisenhower Library and Museum)

years of negotiations had failed to resolve the dispute. Late that year, a coup, supported by major segments of the Iranian population and the Central Intelligence Agency, overthrew Mossadeq and restored the Shah to power.

The State Department selected Hoover to arrange a settlement. Iran desperately wanted a resolution, because not only had the country lost revenue over the previous two years, but Britain and the United States had shifted much of their oil trade to other Middle Eastern countries. Nevertheless, the competing interests of various oil companies, the British and American governments, and Iran made the negotiations difficult. Hoover's skill and knowledge of the oil industry guided the negotiations to a successful settlement in the summer of 1954. Under the agreement, the Iranian government gained ownership of its nation's oil reserves. Iran paid the British $70 million. An international consortium of oil companies signed a 25-year agreement with Iran to manage production and sell the oil. The consortium agreed to pay the Anglo-Iranian Oil Company $600 million. Within the consortium, the old Anglo-Iranian Company got a 40 percent share, Royal Dutch Shell got 14 percent, the Compagnie Française des Petroles got 6 percent, and American companies (Gulf, Standard Oil of New Jersey, Texaco, and Socony-Mobil), which had previously been shut out of Iran, got 40 percent.

For his efforts, Hoover received the Presidential Medal of Freedom, and Eisenhower appointed him undersecretary of state in August 1954. Hoover proved to be less than adept as a diplomat. His interest in foreign affairs seemed not to extend past questions relating to the oil industry, and he lacked tact.

At the height of the Suez Crisis in 1956, Secretary of State JOHN FOSTER DULLES was recovering from an operation for the cancer that would eventually kill him, and Hoover was acting secretary of state. When Egypt's leader, Gamal Abdel Nasser, nationalized the Suez Canal in July 1956 and the British, French, and Israelis, contrary to the wishes of the American government, resorted to military action, the United States declined to support the weakening British pound and refused to provide oil to the British and French until they withdrew their forces from Egypt. Hoover's obvious lack of sympathy for the British position and his curt manner did little to repair relations with America's closest ally.

Hoover retired from the State Department in 1957, returned to Pasadena, Calif., and resumed his career as an engineer. He died in Pasadena on July 9, 1969.

—MSM

Hoover, J(ohn) Edgar
(1895–1972) *director, Federal Bureau of Investigation*

Born in Washington, D.C., on January 1, 1895, J. Edgar Hoover grew up in Washington, where his father worked for the Coast and Geodetic Survey. After graduating from high school in 1913, Hoover worked as an indexer for the Library of Congress and attended National University Law School (later George Washington University Law School) at night. He received his degree in 1916 and in 1917 went to work as a clerk for the Department of Justice. Hoover's ability and capacity for work impressed his superiors, who before long placed him in charge of the alien registration section of the Bureau of Investigation. His work there brought him to the attention of Attorney General A. Mitchell Palmer. After a series of bombings, including that of Palmer's house, in June 1919, the attorney general put Hoover in charge of the newly created General Intelligence Division of the Justice Department, created to study subversive activities. Hoover planned and directed the raids on radicals in November 1919 and January 1920 that became known as the Palmer raids. In 1921 Hoover became assistant director of the Bureau of Investigation. After the Teapot Dome scandals, which had tainted the Justice Department and its Bureau of Investigation, the new attorney general, Harlan Fiske Stone, recognized the need to clean house at the Bureau of Investigation and promoted Hoover to director. Hoover depoliticized the agency and introduced a merit system for recruiting agents. He brought in honest and capable people, shaped them into a disciplined unit, and built the bureau into a model of scientific law enforcement. He established a national fingerprint file in 1925 (which evolved into a world-renowned unit for the identification of fingerprints), a pioneering crime laboratory in 1932, and a training school for local police officers in 1935. Hoover also began a system for the collection and analysis of national crime statistics. The New Deal extended the authority of the federal government, and Hoover took advantage of the new political climate to expand the powers of his agency. In 1934, Congress granted the bureau, originally an investigative organization, authority over a long list of newly defined federal crimes and authorized its agents to make arrests and carry firearms. The capture of celebrity criminals like George "Machine Gun" Kelly and the killing of others (including "Pretty Boy" Floyd, "Ma" Barker and her son Fred, "Baby Face" Nelson, and John Dillinger) in shootouts made Hoover and his "G-men" national heroes. In 1935, the agency was renamed the Federal Bureau of Investigation (FBI).

As he became increasingly concerned over the rise of Adolf Hitler and the activities of American Nazis, President Franklin D. Roosevelt issued a secret presidential directive in 1934 authorizing the bureau to investigate activities of American Nazis and their sympathizers. Over the next two years, Roosevelt asked Hoover and the FBI to investigate various right-wing groups. In 1936 Roosevelt authorized the director to monitor communist activities. After Hitler's invasion of Poland in 1939, Roosevelt placed Hoover in charge of all domestic counterintelligence. During World War II, the FBI and Hoover enhanced their reputations with a carefully crafted public relations campaign and a number of spectacular arrests. Immediately after Pearl Harbor, the FBI rounded up German and Japanese agents, which accounted, at least in part, for the success in suppressing enemy espionage and sabotage during the war. When a German U-boat put ashore eight saboteurs on Long Island in 1942, Hoover's agents apprehended them all within 48 hours.

With the developing cold war, Hoover's agency became more involved in investigating communist subversion. The FBI had collected reports on communist infiltration during the late 1930s, but America's entry into World War II and the alliance with the Soviet Union rendered these insignificant to an administration preoccupied with maintaining the wartime alliance. As U.S. relations with the Soviets deteriorated after the war, however, fear of espionage and that American communists held sensitive positions in government led President HARRY S. TRUMAN to continue the FBI's surveillance of extremist organizations. Truman also established a Federal Loyalty Program for government employees that involved FBI background checks for all federal employees and applicants for federal jobs. Dissatisfied with Truman's response, however, Hoover lent his support to the House Un-American Activities Committee (HUAC), which conducted hearings on communists in government and in Hollywood. Investigations by the FBI provided important information for the prosecution of Alger Hiss for having lied about passing documents to the Soviets and for the prosecution under the Smith Act of leaders of the American Communist Party. In 1950, Hoover and his agents exposed the atomic scientist Klaus Fuchs as a spy, which resulted in the arrest and conviction of JULIUS and ETHEL ROSENBERG in 1951. Truman expanded the FBI's authority to engage in wiretaps in 1952, and Hoover stretched that authority to include opening mail and conducting illegal break-ins.

Throughout the cold war, Hoover conducted a large-scale, public campaign to warn the American citizenry against the dangers of communism. He published books and articles (largely written by FBI personnel), made speeches, and cooperated with anticommunist groups inside and outside of government. Typically for the master bureaucratic infighter, Hoover quickly distanced himself and his agency from allies who became liabilities, most notably in the case of Sen. JOSEPH R. MCCARTHY (R-Wis.). Hoover's best-selling book, *Masters of Deceit: The Story of Communism in America and How to Fight It* (1958), explained the history and objectives of communism and asked Americans to guard against communist subversion and report any evidence of it to the FBI. He had the bureau's public relations unit cooperate with authors and producers of movies and television programs that featured the FBI in an effort to ensure that the agency would be presented in a favorable light.

Shortly after the new Eisenhower administration took office, Hoover became embroiled in a heated controversy. In November 1953, he testified before the Senate Internal Security Subcommittee in support of Attorney General HERBERT BROWNELL's charge that Truman had appointed Harry Dexter White to be director of the International Monetary Fund after being informed that White was a communist. Brownell managed to produce evidence that the White House had received a damning FBI report on White before the latter assumed his position. Years later, the opening of Soviet archives after the fall of the Soviet Union and the release of the Venona decrypts would support the charge that White had passed information to the Soviets. At the time, the charges were extremely controversial and became the focus of intense partisan conflict. However, the controversy over the White affair burned hot briefly, quickly cooled, and passed from the public's attention.

After a series of Supreme Court decisions in 1956 effectively limited prosecutions under the Smith Act, Hoover created COINTELPRO (Counter Intelligence Program) to disrupt and neutralize the communist party in the United States. COINTELPRO used "dirty tricks," including illegal wiretaps and break-ins, leaking information about the party's activities, and sending letters to employers demanding the dismissal of communist employees. Hoover's campaign against MARTIN LUTHER KING, JR., began out of suspicion arising from the communist background of some of King's associates. It developed into a personal vendetta inspired by Hoover's racism, his outrage over King's personal conduct, and his resentment over King's criticism of the FBI regarding civil rights cases.

In the late 1950s, the FBI made a series of spectacular arrests. The agency uncovered Colonel Rudolph Abel, the head of a large Soviet espionage ring in 1957, which led to his arrest by the Immigration and Naturalization Service that June. The following year, the bureau broke another major spy operation. Hoover's fears of espionage led him to oppose increasing economic and cultural contacts with the Soviet Union and its allies.

From the Roosevelt through the Nixon administrations, Hoover provided presidents personal information about political opponents. In the 1950s, he informed Eisenhower about the activities of ELEANOR ROOSEVELT, NORMAN THOMAS, and Justice WILLIAM O. DOUGLAS, among others. Hoover used such services further to entrench his own position and that of his agency.

Despite congressional investigations of organized crime during the second half of the 1950s, Hoover refused to acknowledge the existence of the Mafia. According to some critics, he devoted little attention to the problem because convictions against organized crime required enormous resources and because convictions were difficult to obtain. Instead, Hoover focused the bureau's attention on crimes such as kidnapping, which attracted public attention, and auto theft, which was relatively easily solved.

In the 1960s, Hoover continued his crusade against domestic communism long after the issue had ceased to occupy the primary attention of the public or politicians. His reluctance to involve the bureau in civil rights matters became a point of criticism, and his campaign against King reached its climax when the FBI sent King tape recordings of his extramarital affairs and threatened to make them public. For many in the New Left and civil rights movements, Hoover became a symbol of unquestioning patriotism and repressive governmental authority. Ironically, Hoover's loyalty to his bureau made him an obstacle to the attempts of President RICHARD M. NIXON to use the FBI to cover up the Watergate affair.

Hoover died in Washington, D.C., on May 2, 1972. After Hoover's death, Sen. FRANK CHURCH's Select Committee to Study Governmental Operations with Respect to Intelligence Activities investigated Hoover's career and revealed the long history of harassment of dissidents. After examining his activities, the Church committee concluded that Hoover represented a classic case of the abuse of governmental authority. Perhaps a more balanced assessment would take into account Hoover's role in the professionalization of law enforcement and in maintaining national security in times of crisis, including World War II and the cold war, while weighing it against his undoubted abuses of power and his disregard for civil liberties.

—MSM

Hope, Clifford R(agsdale)

(1893–1970) *U.S. congressman; chairman,*
Agriculture Committee

Born in Birmingham, Iowa, on June 9, 1893, Hope moved with his family to Garden City, Kans., when he was 13. He attended Nebraska Wesleyan University and received an LL.B. degree in 1917 from Washburn Law School in Topeka, Kans. After gaining admission to the bar, he volunteered for military service. He served as a second lieutenant in World War I, and, upon his discharge in 1919, opened a law office in Garden City. He served in the Kansas state legislature from 1921 to 1927. In 1925 he became the youngest person ever to be chosen speaker of the house of representatives in Kansas.

Hope won election to the U.S. House of Representatives in 1926. For the next 30 years he served in the House and played an important role in shaping farm legislation, particularly in the post–World War II era. From his freshman term, he was a member of the Agriculture Committee. An early backer of Gov. Alf Landon's candidacy for the presidency, Hope was named to chair the Republican National Committee's farm division. After Landon captured the nomination in 1936, many observers anticipated that Hope would become secretary of agriculture if Landon won the election. When Republicans gained control of the House in the 1946 elections, Hope became chair of the House Agriculture Committee. He generally supported the Democratic program of high price supports and in 1948 backed a measure establishing 90 percent of parity for basic commodities. The following year, however, he opposed a plan, supported by the Truman administration, to give Secretary of Agriculture Charles Brannan increased authority to limit farm production.

A moderate Republican, Hope was one of 19 representatives who sent a letter to DWIGHT D. EISENHOWER in February 1952 urging him to seek the Republican presidential nomination. Following the Republican landslide of that year, Hope again became chairman of the Agriculture Committee. In 1953 he supported a bill sponsored by Eisenhower administration that increased the authority of the secretary of agriculture within his department. Hope also backed the administration's proposal authorizing the president to use farm products stored under the price support program to relieve famine conditions abroad. He warned that the program would fall into disrepute if the stored crops rotted while people starved.

In 1953, Hope introduced a measure reorganizing the Farm Credit Administration, divorcing it from the Agriculture Department and increasing "farmer participation and control of the farm credit system." The next year, Hope and Sen. GEORGE D. AIKEN (R-Vt.) introduced a bill authorizing the secretary of agriculture to cooperate with state and local agencies to improve soil conservation in the upriver watershed or "subwatershed" areas of streams and rivers.

In 1954, Hope opposed the major feature of the administration's omnibus farm program, which was the establishment of flexible price supports between 75 percent and 90 percent of parity for the six basic farm commodities. The bill that emerged from his committee retained 90 percent parity payment through 1955. The final measure provided flexibility but limited it to between 82.5 percent and 90 percent of parity. In 1955, as ranking minority member of the agriculture panel, Hope favored a Democratic-inspired proposal to reestablish 90 percent parity. However, he declined to join other Midwestern Republicans in publicly criticizing Secretary of Agriculture EZRA TAFT BENSON.

Hope did not run for reelection in 1956. He returned to Garden City, where he wrote a weekly newspaper column and was president of Great Plains Wheat, Inc., from 1959 to 1963. Hope died of a stroke in Garden City on May 16, 1970.

—MSM

Hughes, Emmet J(ohn)

(1920–1982) *administrative assistant to the*
president

The son of Irish Catholic parents, Hughes was born in Newark, N.J., on December 26, 1920. After graduating summa cum laude from Princeton University in 1941, he received a graduate fellowship in history from Columbia University. His graduate career was cut short when his adviser was appointed ambassador to Spain and Hughes accompanied him as his press attaché. During World War II, Hughes, while continuing to serve at the American embassy, enlisted in the army and served with the Office of

Strategic Services. He also published a revised version of his senior thesis at Princeton, *The Church and the Liberal Society*, in 1944. After the war, Hughes remained with the embassy until 1946. That year, he accepted a job with Time-Life; he was bureau chief in Rome from 1947 to 1948 and head of the bureau in Berlin from 1948 to 1949. He became articles editor for *Life* magazine in 1949.

Hughes took a leave of absence from *Life* in 1952 in order to volunteer as a speechwriter for the Republican presidential candidate, DWIGHT D. EISENHOWER. An independent liberal, Hughes nevertheless believed a Republican victory in 1952 was vital. He wrote some of the most significant speeches Eisenhower gave during the campaign. In a speech scheduled to be given in Wisconsin, Hughes included a passage that denounced the tactics of Sen. JOSEPH MCCARTHY (R-Wis.) and praised Secretary of Defense George C. Marshall, whom McCarthy had denounced as a "front man for traitors." At the urging of Wisconsin Republicans, particularly Gov. WALTER KOHLER, who was running for reelection, Eisenhower reluctantly agreed to remove the passage criticizing McCarthy and praising Marshall, and he gave the speech without it. The campaign, however, had already given the press copies of the uncut speech, and the omission generated considerable controversy. Hughes also wrote the speech in which Eisenhower promised "I shall go to Korea." Delivered in October, the speech contributed to Eisenhower's convincing victory in November.

During the transition period after the election, Hughes drafted speeches and statements. His principal duty, however, was to work with the president-elect on the inaugural address. When Eisenhower took office, Hughes assumed a position as assistant to the president. His primary responsibility consisted of writing speeches. Hughes helped to write "The Chance for Peace," a speech delivered in 1953 at a meeting of the American Society of Newspaper Editors that warned of the dangers of the arms race.

During his eight months in the White House, Hughes became increasingly disillusioned with the president and his administration. In particular, Hughes wanted Eisenhower publicly to denounce McCarthy. After McCarthy attacked the State Department, and his aides traveled through Europe to investigate subversive literature in U.S. libraries, Hughes once again urged the president to take the offensive against the junior senator from Wisconsin. Eisenhower, however, refused, as he put it, "to get in the gutter with that guy." Hughes took advantage of a request from the American Library Association for a presidential message by drafting a warning against McCarthy's excesses, and Eisenhower signed the letter. In general, however, Hughes was unable to persuade Eisenhower to mount a frontal assault against McCarthy.

In September 1953, Hughes, who maintained that he had never intended to stay on past the election, resigned and returned to Time-Life as a special European correspondent for *Life*. He continued his criticism of the administration. In November 1953, he sent a long letter to the president explaining that bickering within the cabinet made the administration appear indecisive. Hughes, nevertheless, readily accepted an invitation to speak at the Republican National Convention in 1956. He also joined the president's staff as a special assistant on speeches and campaign strategy. In that capacity, he drafted the speech, given on November 1, in which the president responded to the Suez Crisis by condemning the British, French, and Israeli action and urging the United Nations to intervene.

After Eisenhower's reelection, Hughes considered remaining with the administration. He would have liked a position as an adviser on foreign policy, but Secretary of State JOHN FOSTER DULLES blocked him from a major post in the State Department. The day after Eisenhower's second inaugural address, Hughes ended his career in the White House. While he occasionally worked on speeches and played a major role in drafting a presidential speech on foreign aid in May 1957, Hughes otherwise resumed his work with Time-Life. He was editor of *Fortune* magazine from 1956 to 1957 and chief foreign correspondent for Time-Life from 1957 to 1960. Hughes also vented his frustration against Eisenhower and Dulles in *America the Vincible* (1959), a book that criticized the direction of American foreign policy during Eisenhower's second term but saved its harshest criticism for Dulles.

From 1960 to 1963, he served as an adviser to the Rockefeller family. Hughes also published a memoir, *Ordeal by Power* (1962), that described the inner working of the administration and presented a highly unfavorable portrait of Eisenhower. In the days before presidential aides regularly published insider accounts of the administration they served, Hughes's book created something of a sensation. Based on the documentary evidence available at the Eisenhower Library, most historians today reject many of Hughes's conclusions and his portrayal of the president. At the time, however, the book enjoyed a favorable critical response. From 1963 to 1968, Hughes was a columnist and an editorial consultant for *Newsweek*. He served as a special assistant to Gov. NELSON ROCKEFELLER during the latter's unsuccessful bid for the Republican nomination in 1968 and worked as an aide to the governor until 1970, when Hughes joined the Eagleton Institute of Politics at Rutgers University. He held that position until he died of a heart attack in Princeton, N.J., on September 19, 1982.

—MSM

Hughes, Howard R(obard), Jr.
(1905–1976) *industrialist*

The son of a Texas oil wildcatter, Hughes was born in Houston, Tex., on December 24, 1905. His father, Howard Hughes, Sr., patented a rotary drill bit that revolutionized oil drilling; he then formed what would become the Hughes Tool Company. The bit made him a wealthy man. Hughes, Jr., attended Fessenden School and Thatcher School. Although he never graduated from high school, Hughes sat in on classes at California Institute of Technology and enrolled at Rice Institute. His mother died in 1922, and his father died in 1924. Upon his father's death, Hughes inherited 75 percent of the Hughes Tool company. He dropped out of Rice and, within a year, bought out the other 25 percent from various relatives. The income from his ownership of the company allowed Hughes to pursue other interests. In 1925, he moved to Los Angeles and began to produce films. He made several films of varying quality (*Two Arabian Nights*, made in 1927, won an Academy Award for director Lewis Milestone) before making an epic about fighter pilots in the

Royal Air Force during World War I, *Hell's Angels* (1930), which he wrote and directed. A series of unsuccessful films followed before he produced two classics, *The Front Page* (1931) and *Scarface* (1932).

From early on, Hughes demonstrated mechanical talent and a love for flying. He founded the Hughes Aircraft Company in 1933 and forged a distinguished career as an aviator. He set several speed records, including the fastest transcontinental flight (1936) and the fastest flight around the world (1938). His exploits made him a national hero and won him a ticker tape parade down Broadway as well as an invitation to the White House. In 1939, Hughes acquired stock in Trans World Airlines.

During World War II, Hughes joined with Henry J. Kaiser, a shipbuilder, to win a contract to build a huge troop and cargo carrier made of wood known as the H-4 Hercules and, more popularly, as the "Spruce Goose." The contract was canceled when it became obvious that the planes would not be available before the war ended. Hughes also received a contract for the XF-11 reconnaissance plane, which, like the H-4 Hercules, was not produced before the end of the war. Hughes also set up a film production company and made *The Outlaw* (1943), initially banned by censors and universally panned by critics after its release. Thanks largely to the controversy surrounding its release and to Jane Russell, whose anatomical gifts far exceeded her acting ability, the film made an enormous profit.

After the war, Hughes produced a couple of unsuccessful films. He also was determined to prove that the two planes he developed during the war, the XF-11 and the H-4 Hercules, were airworthy. With Hughes at the controls, the XF-11 prototype made its first flight on July 7, 1946. An engine malfunctioned, the plane crashed, and Hughes was nearly killed. He recovered quickly and immediately began flying again; he successfully flew the second prototype on April 6, 1947. The Senate War Investigating Committee questioned him in August 1947 on his failure to deliver on wartime contracts. On November 2, 1947, in an attempt to prove the H-4 airworthy, he piloted the plane on its only flight.

Hughes bought RKO Studios in 1948. His eccentric management style brought harsh criticism from within the company, and he sold his shares in 1955 for a profit. Movies constituted only one of his areas of interest. During the postwar era, he expanded TWA into a major international carrier.

A fervent anticommunist, Hughes used his positions as a producer and the head of a studio to blacklist suspected communist sympathizers. He fired Paul Jarrico, one of RKO's leading writers, in 1951 for refusing to cooperate with the House Un-American Activities Committee. Hughes even ordered Jarrico's name removed from the credits of a film he had recently written. Jarrico sued Hughes over the matter, but a court ruled in Hughes's favor in 1957. His anticommunism even led the reclusive Hughes to make a rare public appearance, when he addressed the American Legion's Hollywood post in January 1953. In his speech, he expressed the opinion that communists had infiltrated the motion picture industry and maintained that an individual's refusal to disclose whether or not he was a communist was sufficient to incriminate him. He further argued that those who defended the civil liberties of communists did not have the best interests of the nation at heart. In addition to the speech, Hughes lent his support to the Legion's ultimately successful efforts to bar Charlie Chaplin's film, *Limelight*, from American theaters because of Chaplin's left-wing sympathies.

Although his behavior had always been somewhat erratic, he became more so in the years after World War II. He suffered a nervous breakdown in 1958. In the late 1950s, because of increasing competition and poor management, TWA began to lose money. He sold TWA in 1966 for $566 million. In 1967, he bought the Desert Inn in Las Vegas and made it his home. He then proceeded to build an empire in Las Vegas that included several other casinos, a radio station, and real estate. Hughes took over Air West in 1970. To avoid taxes, he moved to the Bahamas that same year. He never returned to the United States. Hughes became a recluse, moving from one luxury hotel to another and finally settling in Acapulco, Mexico. He sold Hughes Tool Company to the public in 1972 for $150 million. In 1974, the government indicted him for alleged irregularities in his purchase of Air West. At the time, Hughes was living in the Bahamas and could not be extradited. Long a hypochondriac with an acute fear of germs, he became increasingly obsessed with such matters. His behavior crossed into the

bizarre; he refused medical attention, ate peculiar diets, and took drugs (apparently his addiction to painkillers dated from his recovery after the crash of the XF-11 in 1946). At the time of his death, he weighed only 94 pounds. As his health failed catastrophically, his aides put him on a plane to take him from Acapulco to Houston, but Hughes died in flight on April 5, 1976.

—MSM

Hughes, Rowland R(oberts)
(1896–1957) *director, Bureau of the Budget*
Born in Oakhurst, N.J., on March 28, 1896, Hughes graduated from Brown University in 1917. He worked for the National City Bank of New York from his senior year in college until he joined the Eisenhower administration in 1953. In the 10 years following his graduation, he worked at the bank's branches in Shanghai, Bombay, Osaka, and Tokyo. Recalled to New York in 1927, Hughes was made assistant controller in 1929 and controller in 1934. Beginning in the 1940s, he became an active member of the tax committees of the Controllers Institute of America, the American Bankers Association, and the Council of State Chambers of Commerce.

Hughes entered the Eisenhower administration in April 1953 as assistant director of the budget. He became deputy director in August and in April 1954 succeeded JOSEPH M. DODGE as director. Hughes's background and beliefs placed him in full accord with the administration's objective of reducing the size of the federal budget. Seeking to promote economy and efficiency by example, he reduced his own agency's appropriation request by $33,500 in May 1955. In July, the government announced that the federal deficit for fiscal year 1955 had been $300 million less than expected.

Hughes also vigorously sought to end government competition with private business wherever possible. On January 25, 1955, he directed all government agencies to complete by April 15 an inventory of their commercial activities and report by July 15 which of their manufacturing facilities could be shifted to the private sector.

Hughes was a key figure in the Dixon-Yates affair, the Eisenhower administration's most controversial attempt to replace government activity with private enterprise. The plan was to have a southern utilities combine construct a steam power plant near West Memphis, Ark., to supply power to Atomic Energy Commission installations in the area and to surrounding municipalities previously served by the Tennessee Valley Authority. The project had originated in the Budget Bureau when Hughes was second in command. Hughes took part in drawing up the contract with utility executives EDGAR DIXON and Eugene Yates, promoted it within the government, and defended it before congressional committees. His testimony, however, was ambiguous and contradictory. His appearance before the Joint Committee on Atomic Energy in November 1954 prompted the *New Republic* to remark that Hughes "proved to be as inept a witness as reporters could remember. He appeared to know so little about the major provisions of the Dixon-Yates contract, which he had approved, that with some justification Sen. CLINTON ANDERSON (D-N.Mex.) asked him if he had ever read it."

Early in 1955, critics of the contract charged that one of the officials responsible for drawing it up was guilty of conflict of interest. A consultant with the Bureau of the Budget, Adolphe Wenzell, was an employee of the First Boston Corp., which acted as a financial agent for the Dixon-Yates combine. Testifying before the Senate Antitrust and Monopoly Subcommittee in June, Hughes stated that Wenzell's role had been insignificant and that Wenzell had "never had anything to do with the policy of Dixon-Yates." Hughes also professed ignorance of the fact that First Boston was acting as a financial agent of Dixon-Yates. A few days later, however, Wenzell himself contradicted Hughes's statements, asserting that he had been called to Washington in January 1954 by Hughes to serve as an expert in the financing of the project, had attended some 20 meetings on the subject, and had made First Boston's interest in the contract "abundantly clear" to Hughes. The subcommittee report, issued in August 1955, concluded "the testimony that Hughes gave . . . defies understanding." By that date, President Eisenhower had ordered the contract canceled.

Within the Eisenhower administration, Hughes was the focal point of conflicting pressures to spend more in individual cases while balancing the total budget. On March 30, 1956, the day

before his retirement, Hughes submitted a memo to the president criticizing special interests and department heads, "special pleaders for particular expenditures," for lobbying for increased allocations "regardless of the impact on the budget as a whole." The chief offender, in Hughes's view, was Secretary of Defense CHARLES WILSON, who persistently sought larger appropriations for new projects. Such pressures undermined the administration's zeal for reducing expenditures, Hughes maintained. As it happened, the government enjoyed a $1.75-billion budget surplus for fiscal year 1956, the first surplus since 1951.

Hughes died of arteriosclerosis in San Francisco on April 2, 1957.

—TO

Humphrey, George M(agoffin)
(1890–1970) *secretary of the treasury*

Born in Cheboygan, Mich., on March 8, 1890, George Humphrey grew up in Saginaw, Mich., and attended the University of Michigan, from which he received a law degree in 1912. After gaining admission to the Michigan bar that same year, he commenced the practice of law with his father's firm. In 1918, he became general counsel for the M. A. Hanna Company of Cleveland, Ohio. Humphrey rose rapidly in the firm, becoming partner in 1920, vice president in 1922, and president in 1929. When Humphrey joined M. A. Hanna, it was a money-losing shipper of iron ore and coal in the Great Lakes region. Under his leadership, it became a prosperous, expanding industrial enterprise that branched out into mining and became involved in steel, rayon, plastics, oil, and copper production, and banking. Through mergers Humphrey placed the National Steel Co. and the Pittsburgh Consolidated Coal Co. under M. A. Hanna's corporate umbrella. By 1952, when Humphrey was elected chairman of the board, M. A. Hanna had assets totaling more than $120 million.

After World War II, Humphrey became active in public affairs. He was named chairman of the Department of Commerce's Business Advisory Council in 1946. The following year, President HARRY S. TRUMAN appointed him to a 12-member advisory board established by the Taft-Hartley Act.

In 1948, PAUL HOFFMAN, head of the Economic Cooperation Administration, chose Humphrey to head a five-member Reparations Survey Committee to advise the Allied powers regarding the dismantling of German industrial plants. Humphrey enthusiastically supported Sen. ROBERT A. TAFT's unsuccessful attempt to gain the Republican nomination in 1948. He supported Taft again in 1952, but DWIGHT D. EISENHOWER defeated Taft for the nomination, and Humphrey served as chair of the Republican finance committee. After Eisenhower won the election, he chose Humphrey as his secretary of the treasury on the recommendation of Gen. LUCIUS CLAY and Hoffman. The Senate confirmed his nomination, and Humphrey took the oath of office on January 21, 1953.

Although Eisenhower hardly knew Humphrey before designating him secretary of the treasury, the two men quickly established a warm personal rapport. The president frequently visited Humphrey's plantation in Thomasville, Ga., where they hunted quail and played golf. Eisenhower and Humphrey shared a common outlook on fundamental economic issues. Armed with the president's trust and his own forceful personality, Humphrey played a significant role in formulating policy during Eisenhower's first term. Nevertheless, Eisenhower' chief of staff, SHERMAN ADAMS, recalled that "while Eisenhower had great respect for Humphrey's judgment, it seemed to him that Humphrey was sometimes too quick to think of government economic problems in the terms of private industry and occasionally too impatient for fast action." Despite Humphrey's personal relationship with the president and his undoubted influence, historians have sometimes overestimated that influence. Indeed, his economic advice was, at times, less influential than that of ARTHUR BURNS, Eisenhower's first chair of the Council of Economic Advisers.

Humphrey's views were staunchly conservative. He believed that the federal government had become too large and intervened in too many areas of life. In addition, he worried that the expansion of government hindered economic growth and eroded individual initiative. He favored cutting taxes, because he believed that high taxes impeded investment, and held that chronic budget deficits posed a serious threat of inflation.

George Humphrey, secretary of the treasury
(Dwight D. Eisenhower Library and Museum)

During the winter of 1952–53, the incoming administration debated continuing the wage and price controls Truman had imposed after the beginning of the Korean war. The most vocal advocate of eliminating all controls, Humphrey maintained that they brought only economic stagnation. While some of Eisenhower's advisers worried about inflation, Humphrey argued that the elimination of controls would result in increased production that would absorb any wage increases. He further contended that a policy of tight money would forestall price inflation. Humphrey prevailed, and Eisenhower announced in his State of the Union message that all controls on prices and wages would be removed shortly. The ensuing decontrol did not result in a harmful increase in prices.

Eisenhower and Humphrey worried about the effects of constant deficits and intended to cut federal spending. Truman's proposed budget for fiscal year 1954 projected a deficit of $9.9 billion. It quickly became apparent, however, that the new administration would not be able to meet its election promises of a tax cut in 1953 and a balanced budget by 1954. Humphrey's commitment to balance the budget superseded his desire to cut taxes, and the administration essentially adhered to that priority. Seeking to reduce spending, Humphrey persistently argued for cuts in foreign aid and military spending as well as in social programs. The administration submitted a revised budget to Congress in April that cut the deficit to $3.1 billion. Most of the cuts in the budget came from defense spending. Taxes imposed to pay for the Korean War scheduled to expire in mid-1953 were extended to the end of the year. The budget did not please conservative Republicans in Congress. Taft, the majority leader in the Senate, and Daniel A. Reed (R-N.Y.), chair of the House Ways and Means Committee, led the call for greater reductions in spending and for tax relief. They wanted to allow both the excess profits tax and the increase in income tax to expire on July 1, 1953. Humphrey argued that allowing the excess profits tax and the income tax increase to expire on July 1 instead of December 1 of that year would cost the government revenue, exacerbate the deficit, and fuel inflation. Ultimately, the administration prevailed. When Taft first learned that the budget would not be balanced as soon as expected, he had a heated meeting with Eisenhower. Humphrey, an old Taft supporter, supported the president and did so in such as way as to prevent a rift between Taft and Eisenhower.

Humphrey believed in the efficacy of monetary policy in controlling inflation, and, in the interest of stability, he preferred long-term over short-term borrowing. When Humphrey took office, most of the national debt was in the form of short-term borrowing. This made it difficult to stabilize federal finances. In addition, short-term borrowing by the treasury tended to increase the supply of money and therefore increase inflationary pressure. In June 1953, Humphrey brought out an issue of 30-year bonds bearing an attractive interest rate of 3.25 percent. Democrats denounced that issue as deflationary. It did have the effect of drawing funds out of the mortgage market and therefore increasing the cost of financing a house. Thus, the increase in rates contributed, to a degree, to the economic slump in the summer and fall of 1953 that accompanied the end of the Korean War. The Federal Reserve eased the crisis by lowering the reserve requirements of member banks, thereby increasing the money available for loans. Humphrey urged relying on markets to end the recession. Burns, however, advocated increasing spending and cutting taxes. Eisenhower sided with Burns. Humphrey later admitted that he had tightened credit too much. As the administration moved to stimulate the economy, Humphrey proposed removing excise taxes on various luxury products, a measure Congress passed and Eisenhower signed in April 1954. Humphrey recommended exempting from taxation a portion of income derived from stock dividends. Liberal Democrats objected that this favored the wealthy. Humphrey countered that such a policy would stimulate equity financing as well as capital spending and thus ultimately benefit low-income families by creating jobs and stimulating prosperity. Congress passed that measure, too. The economy began a recovery by September 1954.

Humphrey was not entirely successful in his effort to reduce the concentration of short-term debt or in balancing the budget. Nevertheless, the administration held down deficits during the recession of 1953 and early 1954. The budget for fiscal 1955 showed a modest deficit of $1.2 billion, and the budget for fiscal 1956 produced a surplus of $1.75 billion. Going into the election of 1956, Humphrey and Eisenhower could legitimately claim that they had soundly managed the nation's financial affairs.

Despite his oft-repeated sermons about the desirability of tax reduction, Humphrey frequently used his influence to block tax cuts, particularly broad-based tax reductions initiated by Democrats in Congress. In March 1955, he attacked a Democratic plan to stimulate the economy by giving each taxpayer a $20 tax cut as "silly," "irresponsible," and a "political quickie gimmick." The House approved the tax cut, but the Senate rejected it. At the same time, Congress approved the administration's request to defer scheduled excise and corporate tax cuts for a year, which added $2.8 billion to government income. In 1956 and 1957, Humphrey's concern over the budget continued to override his discomfort over high taxes. He declared in a speech on February 1, 1956, that taxes should be cut as soon as possible because they were so high that they were curtailing the "very basis of our freedom—

incentive." However, he testified two days later before the Joint Economic Committee that the anticipated budget surplus for fiscal 1956 was too small to permit a tax cut.

Humphrey exercised influence in policy areas outside the normal authority of treasury secretaries. He sat on the National Security Council at the president's invitation. His fiscal conservatism often led him to oppose ambitious new weapons systems. He was unpersuaded by the arguments of some generals in favor of an increased, highly mobile force of ground troops equipped with sophisticated arms and materials. His cautionary counsel about the fiscal impact of such an expensive undertaking reinforced Eisenhower's view that high troop levels were not worth the expense. Humphrey was also a vigorous proponent of the Saint Lawrence Seaway, which he had supported for years as president of M. A. Hanna. The project, which converted the Saint Lawrence River into an inland waterway connecting the Great Lakes with the Atlantic Ocean by building a deepwater navigation channel, was completed in 1959.

In the first half of 1957, his last months as treasury secretary, Humphrey played a controversial and unconventional role in the battle over the budget for fiscal 1958. In January he declared to reporters that the $71.8 billion spending figure submitted by the administration was too high and invited Congress to make cuts in the administration's own requests, although he did not specify where. He said that the government must reduce "the terrific tax take we are taking out of this country," because "if we don't over a long period of time, I predict that you will have a depression that will curl your hair." In response to the stir caused by Humphrey's dire prophecy, Eisenhower, a week later, said that Humphrey was not talking about the near future but about the consequences of "long-term continuation of spending of the order of which we are now doing." He affirmed his "complete agreement" with his treasury secretary's view that Congress should make cuts in the budget. As it turned out, congressional conservatives enthusiastically slashed appropriations for several departments and programs more deeply than the administration found acceptable. The Eisenhower administration ended up pleading, with mixed success, for the restoration of money, particularly for foreign aid and defense. The appropriations bill passed in August totaled $4 billion less than the president's January request, a serious setback for Eisenhower.

In June 1957, Humphrey defended the Eisenhower administration's fiscal performance, asserting that it had cut government spending, balanced the budget, arrested inflation, achieved a "record-breaking tax reduction" of $7.4 billion in 1954, and "encouraged an expansion of enterprise to new high levels." He conceded that the administration had failed to cut non-defense spending below the levels of the Truman administration and to achieve "some of our debt management objectives."

Humphrey left the Treasury in July 1957 and became chairman of the board of National Steel. He also returned to M. A. Hanna as honorary chairman until the liquidation of the company in 1965. He died in Cleveland on January 20, 1970.

—MSM

Humphrey, Hubert H(oratio)
(1911–1978) *U.S. senator*

The son of a druggist, Hubert Humphrey was born in Wallace, S.Dak., on May 27, 1911. His father's reverence for William Jennings Bryan and Woodrow Wilson profoundly influenced him. He was a star debater and class valedictorian in high school, but he had to leave the University of Minnesota in 1931 to work in his father's drugstore. He became a registered pharmacist in 1933 and managed the store, while his father participated actively in South Dakota Democratic Party politics. Humphrey returned to the University of Minnesota in 1937, earning his B.A. in 1939 and an M.A. in political science from Louisiana State University a year later. His master's thesis, entitled "The Political Philosophy of the New Deal," was a tribute to Franklin D. Roosevelt's response to the depression.

After a brief teaching career, Humphrey plunged into Minnesota politics. He played a key role in the merger of the Farmer-Labor and Democratic Parties in 1944 and won election as mayor of Minneapolis the next year. As mayor, he waged a war against vices, created the first municipal fair-employment practices commission in the United

States, expanded the city's housing program, and took an active part in settling strikes. After winning reelection in 1947, Humphrey helped organize the liberal, anticommunist Americans for Democratic Action (ADA) and fought a successful battle to purge the communist faction from the Democratic-Farmer-Labor Party. He gained national attention at the Democratic National Convention in 1948 with a stirring oration in favor of a strong civil rights plank. Humphrey's speech, in which he called on the Democratic party to "get out of the shadow of states' rights and walk forthrightly into the bright sunshine of human rights," moved the convention to reject the Truman administration's modest civil rights plank in favor of the stronger one he favored. In November, Humphrey unseated Sen. Joseph Ball, the Republican incumbent.

Humphrey quickly moved into the vanguard of the Senate's liberal minority. He advocated legislation promoting civil rights, tax reform, aid to education, and organized labor. The first bill he introduced was a proposal to establish medical care for the aged, financed through the Social Security system. It did not pass, but years later, as vice president, he would help President LYNDON B. JOHNSON pass Medicare. In 1949, he joined an unsuccessful attempt to change Senate rules regarding the filibuster. That same year, he failed in an attempt to move civil rights legislation. He also made an unsuccessful effort to repeal the Taft-Hartley Act. At this point, early in his career, Humphrey alienated powerful conservatives in the Senate with his sharp verbal attacks and his effusive liberalism. Their hostility and his own ignorance of Senate procedures rendered Humphrey largely ineffective.

Taken aback by his succession of defeats and his ostracization by the established leaders of the Senate and of his party, Humphrey changed his approach. Working closely with then-senator Lyndon Johnson (D-Tex.), Humphrey toned down his rhetoric and moderated his intensely ideological approach. He set himself to his committee work and learned the rules of the Senate. Although he continued to sponsor dozens of bills each session, he accepted compromises when he saw a chance to make some modest gain, rather than holding out unsuccessfully for everything he wanted. For

example, he opposed an antidiscrimination amendment to the bill that became the Housing Act of 1954 because the amendment would have cost support from southerners necessary for passage of the bill. Humphrey became the liaison between the liberal wing of the Democratic Party and the Senate's fabled "inner club," dominated by southern conservatives. In this way, he eased his way into the Senate's "establishment."

Humphrey consistently supported the interests of farmers, who made up a large part of his constituency. He relentlessly opposed the Eisenhower administration's reduction of agricultural price supports. Partly in an effort to aid his rural constituents, Humphrey became a leading advocate of the distribution of American agricultural surplus to needy nations abroad, which, he argued, would "avert famine and combat communism." He was instrumental in passing Public Law 480, passed in 1954, which authorized the distribution of U.S. agricultural surpluses abroad. In 1961 he helped expand the law into the Food for Peace program. In another attempt to aid farmers, he proposed reducing surpluses with a domestic food stamp program.

On foreign policy, Humphrey generally supported the Eisenhower administration. He joined other Democrats, however, in criticizing the "New Look" defense policy's reliance on air power, technology, and the nuclear deterrent and argued against reductions in conventional forces. With Johnson's sponsorship, Humphrey became a member of the Foreign Relations Committee in 1953 and chair of that committee's Disarmament Subcommittee in 1955. As chair of the Disarmament Subcommittee, he held hearings in 1956 and 1958 on a ban on atmospheric nuclear testing.

Although strongly anticommunist, Humphrey heatedly denounced Republican red-baiters and, in particular, Sen. JOSEPH MCCARTHY (R-Wis.). At times, however, his own anticommunist zeal and jockeying for political advantage led him to outdo the right-wing Republicans. In 1950, he and other liberals sponsored an amendment to an omnibus internal security bill that granted the president authority to detain subversives in time of emergency. It was a vote he claimed immediately to regret. Nevertheless, facing a campaign for reelection in 1954, Humphrey introduced an amendment to the bill that became the Communist Control Act of 1954, a repressive measure opposed by the Eisenhower administration. Humphrey's amendment declared that the communist party was an "agency of a hostile foreign power" and therefore not entitled to the rights and immunities of legal bodies. To civil libertarians, who protested that the amendment represented a gross violation of civil liberties, Humphrey replied, "I do not intend to be half patriot." Supported by Lyndon Johnson, the amendment narrowly passed; the entire bill passed with only ESTES KEFAUVER (D-Tenn.) voting no. Although he continued to defend his actions at least as late as 1959, Humphrey later admitted that the Communist Control Act was "not one of the things I'm proudest of."

Whatever his disregard for the civil liberties of communists, Humphrey continued to be a leading supporter of civil rights for African Americans. His role as Johnson's bridge to the liberals in the Senate and his willingness to compromise in order to achieve some gains played out in the contribution he made to passage of the Civil Rights Act of 1957. The Senate substantially weakened the administration's civil rights bill, eliminating authority for the attorney general to enter civil suits and adding an amendment making it civil, rather than criminal, contempt to violate federal court orders enforcing voting rights. As Johnson's lieutenant, Humphrey was an important figure in forging the compromise that weakened the bill and avoided a filibuster by southern Democrats.

Humphrey had long considered a run for higher office, and in 1956 he mounted an abortive bid for his party's vice presidential nomination. Fully expecting that ADLAI STEVENSON would chose him for the second spot on the ticket, he was shocked when Stevenson announced that he would let the convention pick the vice presidential nominee. Unprepared for a floor fight, Humphrey ran a poor fifth on the first ballot and withdrew. He then threw his support to Kefauver, who became Stevenson's running mate.

When he opened his campaign on December 30, 1959, Humphrey became the first candidate to declare for the presidency in 1960. The most liberal of the Democratic hopefuls, he had recently burnished his foreign-policy credential by serving on the U.S. delegation to the United Nations General Assembly in 1956 and to UNESCO in 1958. In the latter capacity, he visited the Soviet Union and had a private meeting with the Soviet premier, Nikita Khrushchev, that lasted over eight hours. Humphrey's only active rival in the months before the convention was Sen. JOHN F. KENNEDY (D-Mass.), who ran a well-financed, tightly organized campaign. Humphrey's poorly organized and poorly financed campaign was no match. Kennedy defeated Humphrey in Wisconsin, and the West Virginia primary emerged as a crucial test. Kennedy needed a win in an overwhelmingly Protestant state to lay to rest questions about whether his Catholicism made him unelectable. Humphrey just needed a win. The candidates debated the state's depressed economic condition, but, given the stakes, the campaign devolved into bitter personal attacks. Humphrey emphasized Kennedy's wealth and privilege. Kennedy's supporters accused Humphrey of dodging the draft during World War II (he received a deferment because of a double hernia and color blindness). Kennedy won a decisive victory in West Virginia, and Humphrey withdrew from the race. After Kennedy captured the nomination, Humphrey supported him and won election to his third term in the Senate.

Humphrey became majority whip in 1961 and was a key figure in guiding through the Senate a variety of measures, some of which he had advocated for years, including the Peace Corps (enacted in 1961). He also played an important role in passing the Arms Control and Disarmament Agency that same year.

After Kennedy's assassination, Humphrey urged President Johnson to move ahead with the Civil Rights Act of 1964 and, as floor leader, cooperated with Johnson in breaking the southern filibuster that made passage of the measure possible. Johnson chose Humphrey as his running mate in 1964, and the Democratic ticket overwhelmed the Republican candidate, BARRY GOLDWATER, in November. Humphrey loyally served Johnson as vice president and cooperated with the congressional leadership to gain passage of Medicare and the Voting Rights Act of 1965. Although he initially had reservations about the growing American involvement in Vietnam, he became a fervent supporter of the war. When Johnson withdrew from the presidential race in 1968, Humphrey announced his candidacy and inherited much of Johnson's support. He ultimately won the nomination, despite challenges from antiwar candidates ROBERT F. KENNEDY, who was assassinated before the convention, and EUGENE MCCARTHY. In the general election, Humphrey was damaged by his association with the unpopular Johnson administration and the war as well as by the third-party candidacy of Gov. George Wallace of Alabama. Although trailing desperately in late September, Humphrey gained steadily in the polls. Ultimately, he lost the election by a narrow margin to RICHARD M. NIXON. Humphrey returned to Minnesota to teach at Macalester College. When Eugene McCarthy decided not to seek reelection to the Senate in 1970, Humphrey successfully ran for the vacant seat. Upon his return to the Senate, he once again espoused a number of liberal positions. He supported limiting the development of the antiballistic missile system and opposed Nixon's decision to impound funds appropriated by Congress for social programs. Humphrey announced his candidacy for the presidency in 1972 but gained little support. In 1975, he became chair of the Joint Economic Committee. He sponsored the Humphrey-Hawkins Full Employment and National Growth Act of 1978, passed after his death, which set general guidelines by which the nation could coordinate economic growth and established a goal of 3.5 percent unemployment within five years. Although a minor boom developed in support of a presidential bid in 1976, Humphrey decided to run for reelection to the Senate and won. He died of cancer in Waverly, Minn., on January 13, 1978.

—MSM

Hutcheson, Maurice A(lbert)

(1897–1983) *president, United Brotherhood of Carpenters and Joiners of America*

Born in Saginaw Co., Mich., on May 7, 1897, Maurice Hutcheson was the son of William Hutcheson, president of the United Brotherhood of Carpenters and Joiners (UBC) and one of the most powerful union leaders in the 20th century. The family moved to Indianapolis in 1913, when his father became president of the carpenters' union. In 1914, Maurice

became a carpenter's apprentice. After serving as a carpenter's mate in the navy during World War I, he worked as a journeyman from 1918 to 1928, when he became an auditor for the UBC. In 1938, he was elected first vice president of the UBC; he became president upon his father's retirement in 1952.

Shortly after assuming that office, Hutcheson took the union out of the American Federation of Labor (AFL) in a dispute over a no-raiding agreement the AFL had negotiated with the Congress of Industrial Organizations (CIO). He reaffiliated with the AFL a few weeks later and became a vice president of the federation and member of the Executive Council in 1953. When the AFL merged with the CIO in 1955, Hutcheson retained these positions. In 1954, Hutcheson negotiated an end to a long-standing jurisdictional feud with the International Association of Machinists.

In 1957, Hutcheson was charged with bribing an Indiana state highway official to obtain advanced information on the location of a planned highway. Hutcheson, it was maintained, then bought up the land and sold it to the state at a huge profit. A grand jury in Lake Co., Ind., failed to indict the union leader on the charges. However a grand jury in Marion Co. did indict on similar charges the following year.

While his case was pending, the Senate Committee on Improper Relations in the Labor or Management Field, chaired by Sen. JOHN MCCLELLAN (D-Ark.), ordered Hutcheson to testify on that case and on other questionable activities. These included charges that William Hutcheson had embezzled money from the UBC and that Maurice Hutcheson had conspired with JIMMY HOFFA to fix a jury. The committee also contended that Hutcheson had paid Max Raddock, whom it termed a "shrewd confidence man," $519,000 in union funds "with noticeably little return." According to an investigator for the committee, Hutcheson had used Raddock as a "fixer in a successful move to block the Lake Co., Ind., indictment." Hutcheson refused to testify on the grounds that it could prejudice the case pending in Indiana. The Senate cited him for contempt of Congress, and a federal district court convicted him in May 1960. He was sentenced to six months in prison and fined $500. The Supreme Court upheld that conviction.

In November 1959, two members of Baltimore Local 107 of the UBC asked the Marion Co. Circuit Court to appoint monitors to halt alleged corruption in their union. They accused Hutcheson and 13 other union officers of bribery, threatening opponents with injury or death, destroying possibly incriminating union records, withholding pensions of retired members who opposed them, and of not letting rivals speak at union conventions. The members also reported that the officials had accepted more than $100,000 in "gratuities" from employees and maintained that they had paid back income taxes for individuals who knew what they had done.

Hutcheson's legal difficulties jeopardized his position in the AFL-CIO. In 1958, the Executive Council asked him to explain his indictment in Indiana and his refusal to answer questions before the McClellan committee. Hutcheson absented himself from council meetings, but he sent AFL-CIO president GEORGE MEANY a letter denying any violation of the AFL-CIO's ethical code. JAMES B. CAREY, president of the International Union of Electrical Workers, proposed suspending Hutcheson until he appeared before the council, but the panel deferred action until Hutcheson appeared. The union never took disciplinary action against the UBC's leader.

Hutcheson was convicted in the Indiana highway case in 1960 and sentenced to 2-to-14 years imprisonment. This verdict was overturned in October 1963 by the Indiana Supreme Court, which held that the trial record contained insufficient evidence to establish a conspiracy.

During the 1960s, Hutcheson and other union leaders resisted efforts to eliminate racial discrimination in the construction trades. However, they eventually approved a compromise plan on the issue that made entry into trade unions based on merit. Hutcheson was appointed to a panel established by the labor and management Construction Industry Joint Conference to administer the compromise plan.

Hutcheson still faced a prison sentence for the contempt of Congress conviction. Meany, a long-time ally, and other labor leaders petitioned the federal district court to convert the sentence from prison to probation. In 1964, a federal district judge in Washington reduced the sentence to two years probation. Later that year, President LYNDON B. JOHNSON pardoned Hutcheson, who continued to serve as president of the UBC until his retirement in 1972. Upon retiring, Hutcheson moved to Florida, where he lived until his death in Lakeland, Fla., on January 9, 1983.

—JB

Hutchins, Robert M(aynard)

(1899–1977) *associate director, Ford Foundation; chief executive officer, Fund for the Republic; president, Center for the Study of Democratic Institutions*

The son of a Presbyterian minister who taught at Oberlin College and became president of Berea College, Hutchins was born in New York City on January 17, 1899. He moved with his family to Oberlin, Ohio, in 1907, when his father took up a teaching position there. After attending Oberlin College for two years, Hutchins left in 1917 to serve in the ambulance corps of the United States and Italy during World War I. Italy awarded him the *Croce di Guerra* for bravery under fire. Upon his discharge in 1919, he returned to the United States and enrolled at Yale University, where he earned an A.B. in 1921. After graduating, he taught at the Lake Placid School until 1923, when he became secretary to the Yale Corporation. Hutchins earned an LL.B. from Yale Law School in 1925 and immediately began teaching there. He was appointed acting dean in 1927 and dean in 1928. Influenced by legal realism, he revised the law school's curriculum to include a greater emphasis on legal philosophy and to rely less on the case method. He also introduced seminars that linked law and the social sciences. His tenure as dean was marked by Hutchins's dazzling style and energy. It also revealed some of Hutchins's shortcomings as an administrator. When alumni and some faculty members expressed reservations about the direction he was taking the law school, Hutchins brusquely dismissed their concerns.

Hutchins became president of the University of Chicago in 1929 and quickly emerged as perhaps the most outspoken, innovative, and controversial university president in the country. He argued that universities overemphasized research at the expense of teaching, advocated a strong core curriculum built around the "great books" of the Western tradition, and criticized the emphasis on vocational training as well as narrow specialization in undergraduate education. The faculty blocked implementation of many of Hutchins's ideas, but he did manage to make significant changes in the approach to the undergraduate curriculum. Hutchins also abolished intercollegiate football. Under Hutchins, Chicago was a place of considerable intellectual excitement, but his high-handed style brought him into constant conflict with the faculty. After an investigation in 1937–38, the American Association of University Professors criticized tenure and promotion practices at Chicago and recommended a number of changes. The university accepted those recommendations and incorporated them into university policy.

As Hutchins established a national reputation, his public advocacy of liberal positions brought him to the attention of President Franklin D. Roosevelt and his administration. Although considered for several positions in the New Deal, Hutchins refused to engage in the necessary political maneuvering. He did receive an offer to chair the Securities and Exchange Commission, which he turned down. Hutchins really wanted an appointment to the Supreme Court, but his chances for that evaporated when he opposed Roosevelt's rearmament policies in 1940 and 1941.

The conflicts and controversies at the University of Chicago began to wear on Hutchins, and he sought other outlets for his energy and creativity. He was chair of the board of editors of the *Encyclopædia Britannica* from 1943 until his retirement in 1974 and took a leave of absence from the University of Chicago in 1946 to serve as its editor. In spite of his own disregard for faculty governance, Hutchins emerged as a leading voice for freedom of speech and academic freedom in the late 1940s. Hutchins led the Commission for Freedom of the Press, funded by HENRY LUCE, which published seven volumes in 1946 and 1947 as well as a summary statement, *A Free and Responsible Press*. His opposition to loyalty oaths for faculty members led to an investigation by a subcommittee of the Illinois state legislature in 1949.

Hutchins left the University of Chicago in 1951 to take up a position as associate director of the Ford Foundation. In that capacity, he set up three semi-independent funds: the Fund for the Advancement of Education, the Fund for Adult Education, and the Fund for the Republic. Hutchins's outspoken positions on free speech and other issues brought him into conflict with the foundation's board. In 1954, the board, as a means of easing him out of the foundation, appointed him director of the Fund for the Republic and provided the fund with a $15-million terminal grant. Hutchins described the Fund for the Republic as a "wholly disowned subsidiary of the Ford Foundation." Cut loose from the foundation, the fund undertook "activities directed toward the elimination of restrictions on freedom of thought, inquiry, and expression . . . and the development of policies and procedures best adapted to protect those rights." It supported research on the federal loyalty and security program, blacklisting in the entertainment industry, civil rights, and civil liberties.

The fund's activities brought scrutiny from right-wing critics. FRANCIS E. WALTER (D-Pa.) of the House Un-American Activities Committee wrote Hutchins asking if the fund was "friend or foe in the fight against communism." Hutchins replied that the letter had cast "unjust and unwarranted" doubt on the integrity of the fund's officers. The national commander of the American Legion, Seaborn P. Collins, Jr., launched a verbal assault on the fund and on Hutchins. Hutchins aggressively defended himself and the fund against such attacks, but some members of his board worried about the danger to the fund and to their own reputations. With his job security uncertain and two-thirds of the Ford money gone, Hutchins reorganized the fund in 1959, moved it from New York City to Santa Barbara, Calif., and renamed it the Center for the Study of Democratic Institutions. According to Hutchins, the center was "directed at discovering whether and how a free and just society may be maintained under the strikingly new . . . considerations of the 20th century." Rather than giving grants for research, the center focused on creating ongoing discussions of basic issues, such as freedom and responsibility, education in a democracy, world peace, and the legal system. The center included practicing politicians as well as academics in its discussions and distributed pamphlets reporting on those discussions. It also published a journal titled *The Center*. In 1962, Hutchins became chair of the center's board as well as its president. He stepped down to become a senior life fellow in 1974 but returned as president in 1975. In the last number of years he headed the center, he struggled with diminishing funds. He died in Santa Barbara on May 14, 1977. The center closed two years after his death.

—MSM

I

Ives, Irving M(cNeil)

(1896–1962) *U.S. senator*

Ives was born of old New York stock in Bainbridge, N.Y., on January 24, 1896. He attended public schools and enrolled at Hamilton College. His college career was interrupted in 1917, when he enlisted in the army. After serving overseas during World War I, he was discharged as a first lieutenant and returned to Hamilton. Upon his graduation in 1920, he went into banking. He spent three years as a clerk for Guaranty Trust Company in New York City and then took a position as a manager with Manufacturers Trust Company in Norwich, N.Y. In 1930, he established his own insurance firm. That same year, with the support of a reform faction of the Republican party in Chenango County, he won election to the first of eight terms in the New York State Assembly. He became minority leader in 1935 and speaker in 1936. A revolt within the party cost him his speakership the next year, and he was demoted to majority leader, a position he held until he left the assembly in 1946.

In the legislature, he earned a reputation as a moderate liberal and a careful legislative craftsman. He supported social welfare legislation and laws to protect labor unions. In 1945, he cosponsored legislation to establish the nations's first Fair Employment Practices Commission (FEPC), empowered to prevent discrimination in employment on the basis of race, religion, or ethnicity. Ives hoped to gain the Republican nomination for the U.S. Senate in 1944 but failed when Gov. THOMAS E. DEWEY backed another candidate. Ives took a position as dean of

the new Industrial and Labor Relations School at Cornell in 1945. In 1946, he gained Dewey's support, captured the Republican nomination for New York's other Senate seat, and easily defeated former Gov. HERBERT LEHMAN in the general election. Ives was sufficiently popular with organized labor that the state American Federation of Labor withheld its customary endorsement of the Democratic candidate. His support of the FEPC drew the votes of many black and Jewish voters.

In the Senate, Ives quickly emerged as a leader of the liberal Republicans. An internationalist since World War I, he supported the Truman administration's policy of containment and voted for the Marshall Plan and the North Atlantic Treaty Organization. Nevertheless, he supported a resolution in 1950 criticizing the administration's Asian policy and demanding the resignation of Secretary of State DEAN ACHESON, whom Ives believed had lost the confidence of the America people. On domestic issues, Ives established himself as an expert on labor-management issues. While more liberal than many congressional Republicans on such matters, he did support the Taft-Hartley Act in 1947. At the same time, he led an effort to moderate the bill. While he supported bans on secondary boycotts, jurisdictional walkouts, and the closed shop, as well as a provision authorizing the president to seek injunctions to delay strikes for 80 days, he persuaded Sen. ROBERT A. TAFT (R-Ohio) to eliminate a provision that would have restricted industry-wide collective bargaining. His vote for the bill soured his relations with organized labor, and WIL-

LIAM GREEN, president of the American Federation of Labor, vowed to defeat Ives in 1952. In spite of Green's efforts, Ives won reelection with over 55 percent of the vote.

On another significant domestic issue, Ives deplored the reckless red-baiting of Sen. JOSEPH MCCARTHY (R-Wis.). In June 1950, he was one of seven Republican senators to sign a "Declaration of Conscience" charging that the Senate had been "debased to the level of a forum of hate and character assassination sheltered by the shield of Congressional immunity." When the Senate censured McCarthy in December 1954, Ives voted for the censure resolution.

Ives was among the first to enlist in the effort to persuade Gen. DWIGHT D. EISENHOWER to run for the Republican nomination in 1952. After Eisenhower's election, Ives consistently supported the president's foreign and domestic policies. He backed the administration's civil rights bills in 1956 and 1957 and was a key contributor to several important pieces of labor and social legislation. As chair of the Labor and Public Welfare Committee's Subcommittee on Welfare and Pension Plans, he conducted investigations that led to the passage in 1958 of legislation compelling pension plans to register with the Labor Department and submit annual reports on funding and operations.

In 1957 and 1958, Ives served as vice chair of Sen. JOHN L. MCCLELLAN's (D-Ark.) Select Committee on Improper Activities in the Labor or Management Field. The committee's investigations drew attention to widespread racketeering in certain labor unions and forced the resignation of DAVE BECK, the head of the International Brotherhood of Teamsters. In the wake of these disclosures, Ives cosponsored with Sen. JOHN F. KENNEDY (D-Mass.) a bill containing both strong provisions to eliminate corruption in labor unions and several amendments to the Taft-Hartley Act favored by the AFL-CIO. The bill passed the Senate by 88 to 1, but vigorous opposition from some business leaders and Secretary of Labor James P. Mitchell led to its defeat in the House. The Landrum-Griffin Act of 1959 contained many of the anticorruption measures but did not contain the changes in the Taft-Hartley Act favored by organized labor.

In 1954, Gov. Dewey persuaded a reluctant Ives to seek the governorship of New York. Ives lost to the Democratic candidate, W. AVERELL HARRIMAN, in the closest statewide election in a century. It was the only time Ives lost an election.

In 1958, Ives announced that he would not seek reelection due to ill health. He retired to Norwich, N.Y., where he died on February 24, 1962.

—MSM

J

Jackson, C(harles) D(ouglas)

(1902–1964) *special assistant to the president for cold war planning*

The son of a marble importer, C. D. Jackson was born in New York City on March 16, 1902. He attended the Sillig School in Switzerland for his early education and the Hill School in Pottstown, Pa., from which he graduated, from 1915 to 1920. From there he went to Princeton University, where he majored in French and earned his B.A. in 1924. He had intended to teach French, but his father died the year he graduated from college, and Jackson took over the family business. The business failed during the Great Depression, and Jackson sold it in 1931. That same year, he approached HENRY R. LUCE, the head of *Time* magazine, for a job. Luce hired him as an assistant to the president. Jackson remained with the Luce publishing empire for the rest of his life. Soon after the launch of *Life* magazine in 1936, Jackson became its general manager and served in that capacity from 1937 until 1940, when he became a vice president of Time, Inc. After serving in World War II, Jackson was managing director of Time-Life International, which placed him in charge of the company's news-gathering and publishing activities outside the United States. He became publisher of *Fortune* magazine in 1949, vice president in charge of general management in 1954, and administrative vice president in 1959. He was publisher of *Life* from 1960 until his death in 1964.

His long career with the Luce empire was interrupted frequently with government service. He took a year's leave of absence beginning in late 1940 to organize the Council for Democracy, an organization dedicated to countering isolationist sentiment. In 1942, he went to Turkey on a mission for the State Department and the Bureau of Economic Warfare. His task was to renew a contract for the purchase of Turkish chrome. On his arrival, Jackson found that the Turkish government had reached an agreement to sell its chrome to the Germans. Jackson successfully negotiated an acceleration of mining operations during the remaining months of the American contract with Turkey, and he managed to impede the subsequent shipments of chrome to Germany. In the spring of 1943, he became deputy chief of the Psychological Warfare Branch of Allied Headquarters for North Africa, Sicily, and Italy. In early 1944, he was assigned to London to help organize the Psychological Warfare Division (PWD) at the headquarters of Gen. DWIGHT D. EISENHOWER, who had recently been chosen supreme commander of the Allied Expeditionary Forces. The PWD planned and executed propaganda activities; a large part of that mission was to rally the people of France to support the Allied invasion in June 1944. The PWD also participated in denazification after the war.

Jackson returned to Time, Inc., in 1945. Six years later, he took another leave of absence to serve as president of the National Committee for a Free Europe. He returned to Europe and, under the auspices of Radio Free Europe, established radio broadcasts to Soviet-occupied Czechoslovakia and other countries in Eastern Europe under Soviet domination.

Eisenhower and Jackson had become friendly during the war, and they maintained the friendship after the war ended. Jackson became an early and active supporter of Eisenhower's candidacy for the presidency in 1952. With HERBERT BROWNELL and HAROLD STASSEN, Jackson served as a member of Eisenhower's unofficial strategy team. In addition to developing themes for speeches, he also researched and helped write them. Eisenhower credited Jackson with proposing that the candidate pledge to "go to Korea." Shortly after the election, Eisenhower appointed Jackson a special assistant for cold war planning. Jackson had a role in the preparation of the inaugural address and Eisenhower's first State of the Union message. When Eisenhower took office, Jackson became special assistant to the president to deal with psychological warfare.

Jackson's position involved him with many major issues early in the administration. When, in 1953, Eisenhower rejected appeals for clemency in the case of the convicted spies JULIUS and ETHEL ROSENBERG, Jackson objected to what he regarded as Eisenhower's failure to consider the opinion of America's allies. In March 1953, Jackson helped write the first major foreign-policy address Eisenhower gave as president. Delivered on April 16 and titled "The Chance for Peace," the speech responded to the Soviet "peace offensive" after the death of Joseph Stalin and intended to seize the psychological initiative on the issue of peace. It welcomed the recent Soviet statements regarding the need for peace and appealed to the new leaders of the Soviet Union for "clear and specific acts" to signify that they shared this goal. Jackson participated in the debate over the U.S. response to the growing demands for an end to the arms race. He joined J. ROBERT OPPENHEIMER in urging full disclosure of the realities of atomic warfare. Eisenhower, however, believed that such an approach would only alarm the American people and set off panicky demands for large, ineffectual defense appropriations. Instead, the president proposed establishing an international agency to increase the supply of fissionable materials and make it available to other nations for peaceful purposes. Jackson played a major part in the preparation of Eisenhower's

"Atoms for Peace" address to the United Nations in 1953, which presented that proposal to the world. He also accompanied Eisenhower to the Bermuda Conference in 1953 and the Berlin Conference in 1954, convened to discuss terms for peace treaties with Austria and Germany.

Jackson urged Eisenhower to publicly confront Sen. JOSEPH R. MCCARTHY (R-Wis.) and his reckless charges, but the president rejected Jackson's advice. Eisenhower did not want to "get down in the gutter" with the senator, and he believed that a public attack by the president would only give McCarthy more publicity, on which he fed, and possibly cause the Senate to rally around one of its own. Aware of Jackson's position, McCarthy called him a man who was "unsympathetic toward 'strong patriotism' and Americanism who would coddle communists and left-wingers in government and listen to their advice."

Jackson resigned his position in the White House in March 1954 to return to Time, Inc. He nevertheless served as a member of the U.S. delegation to the United Nations beginning in September 1954. In early 1964, he was one of the organizers of the International Executive Service Corps, a private initiative that sought to aid the development of business overseas by providing advice regarding management. Jackson served as chairman of the board of the International Executive Service Corps from June 1964 until his death. He was also involved in numerous civic, cultural, and social organizations and served on the boards of the Metropolitan Opera Association, the Lincoln Center for the Performing Arts, the Boston Symphony, the Carnegie Corporation, the United Negro College Fund, and Project Hope. Jackson died of cancer in New York City on September 18, 1964.

—MSM

Jackson, Henry M(artin)
(1912–1983) *U.S. senator*
The son of Norwegian immigrants, Jackson was born on May 31, 1912, in Everett, Wash., a mill town and minor seaport north of Seattle. His father was a small-time building contractor and an official in the local plasterers and cement masons union. The younger Jackson was nicknamed "Scoop," after

a comic-strip character of the time (a newspaper reporter who got others to do his work for him). After earning a law degree from the University of Washington in 1935 and gaining admission to the bar the same year, he began the practice of law in Everett, Wash. He won election as prosecuting attorney of Shohomish Co. in 1938. In that office, he quickly made a name for himself with raids on illegal gambling houses and bootleg liquor establishments. Based on his reputation as a crusading prosecutor and his avid support of the New Deal, he won election as a Democrat to the U.S. House of Representatives in 1940. An isolationist before the Japanese attack on Pearl Harbor, he became a committed internationalist afterward. Given that he was of draft age and single, Jackson felt political pressure to join the military and enlisted in the army as a private. He served only a few months before President Franklin D. Roosevelt ordered members of Congress to surrender their seats or leave active duty; Jackson returned to Congress. Like most politicians from the west coast, Jackson supported the internment of Japanese Americans. He was reelected five times and, during his time in the House, compiled one of the most liberal voting records in Congress. An effective advocate for his district's maritime interests, he developed expertise in areas of particular interest to the west, including public lands, reclamation, and the development of hydroelectric power. Jackson supported national health insurance and public power.

Jackson opposed the anticommunist investigations of the Truman administration. He voted against funding for the House Un-American Activities Committee and against overriding the president's veto of the Internal Security Act of 1950. However, he strongly supported Truman's anticommunist policies abroad. As a member of the Interior Subcommittee of the Appropriations Committee and the Joint Congressional Committee on Atomic Energy, he was instrumental in gaining public works projects for his state and in promoting the Pacific Northwest as a center for the defense industry.

In 1952, Jackson ran for the Senate against the Republican incumbent, Harry P. Cain. A charismatic war hero and one of the most vocal conservatives in the upper house, Cain had lost popularity among the state's voters for his opposition to federal funds for Washington's Grand Coulee Dam, the world's largest irrigation and hydroelectric project. Campaigning as a champion of public power and public development of atomic energy, Jackson stressed the state's strategic role in nuclear fission, created by its vast hydroelectric reserves. With the backing of the Grange, farm co-ops, and organized labor, he won the election, one of only two Senate contests in which a Democrat unseated a Republican in the Eisenhower landslide.

Arriving in the upper house in 1953, Jackson was assigned to the Government Operations Committee and its Permanent Investigations Subcommittee, both chaired by Sen. JOSEPH McCARTHY (R-Wis.). Although he initially raised no objections to the subcommittee's wide-ranging and sensational investigations of alleged communist subversion in the State Department and Armed Services, Jackson began to express cautious criticism of McCarthy's methods in June 1953. In July, Jackson and Senators JOHN McCLELLAN (D-Ark.) and STUART SYMINGTON (D-Mo.) made headlines by demanding the firing of committee staff director, J. B. MATTHEWS, who had written a magazine article accusing the Protestant clergy of being riddled with communist sympathizers. When McCarthy refused to permit a vote on the issue, the three Democrats resigned from the subcommittee. They returned in January 1954 after McCarthy permitted them to hire their own staff assistant, ROBERT F. KENNEDY, as minority counsel.

Jackson again came before the public eye during the nationally televised Army-McCarthy hearings of 1954. In March, the army charged McCarthy and his aide, ROY COHN, with threatening to use the investigations subcommittee to "wreck the Army" unless special privileges were given their recently drafted associate, G. DAVID SCHINE. McCarthy retaliated by accusing the army of trying to blackmail him into discontinuing his investigation of security leaks at Fort Monmouth, N.J. During the subcommittee's hearings in April, May, and June, Jackson pursued a methodically legalistic line of questioning aimed at uncovering clear-cut perjury on either side. No decisive conclusion emerged from the tumultuous proceedings, but Jackson did succeed in putting McCarthy on the defensive at several points.

For his role in the hearings, the Democratic leadership rewarded him with a seat on the Interior and Insular Affairs and the Armed Forces Committees. In January 1955, when the Democrats had regained control of the Senate, he was given a place on the Joint Committee on Atomic Energy, making him the only freshman senator with four committee assignments. On the Interior Committee, Jackson helped lead the fight for a federally financed Hells Canyon Dam. He was also involved throughout the 1950s in problems of power development, reclamation, national parks, and mining—issues of deep concern to his constituents.

During the Eisenhower administration, Jackson compiled a strong liberal and pro-labor record in the Senate. He received the highest ratings among his colleagues by the liberal Americans for Democratic Action (ADA), and he never voted against legislation favored by the AFL-CIO's Committee on Political Education (COPE). Although a consistent advocate of increased welfare spending, federal aid to education, national health insurance, and civil rights, Jackson did not take the lead on these issues. Instead, he focused on military affairs and defense policy, interests that arose from his conviction that "the cold war was going to be the greatest challenge of [our] time. Just as the challenge of the 1930s was the depression, now the predominant issue was the survival of the Western world." He consistently attacked the Eisenhower administration for spending too little on defense.

As a member of the Armed Forces and Atomic Energy Committees, Jackson became a strong critic of the administration's defense policies and a leading exponent of the thesis that a "missile gap" existed between the United States and the USSR. In January 1956, Jackson made a major Senate speech warning that the Russians were ahead of the United States in the development of an intermediate-range ballistic missile that would enable them to engage in what he called "nuclear blackmail." Coming at the beginning of an election year, the speech stirred up a raging controversy. From then on, Jackson relentlessly attacked the president and Defense Secretary CHARLES E. WILSON, insisting that the administration's defense policy was causing the United States to "lose our lead" in weapons technology. Stressing the urgent need to develop an intercontinental ballistic missile (ICBM), he advocated a crash program similar to the Manhattan Project that had produced the atomic bomb during World War II. Jackson also worked closely with Adm. HYMAN G. RICKOVER in promoting the nuclear submarine program, and he repeatedly came to Rickover's assistance when the navy attempted to force the admiral into retirement.

In 1959, Jackson chaired the newly created Government Operations Committee's National Policy Subcommittee, which conducted a two-year investigation of the government's methods in the making and conducting of foreign policy. As a result of these investigations, he became intimately acquainted with the inner workings of the Defense and State Departments and acquired an expertise that made him the foremost Democratic spokesman on defense matters. Jackson's ominous warnings of a missile gap were taken up by Sen. JOHN F. KENNEDY (D-Mass.) in the presidential campaign of 1960. They were later proved to have been erroneous.

During his first term in the Senate, Jackson began to develop a strongly personal, almost nonpartisan, appeal among Washington voters and the state's private interests. His popularity derived, in large part, from his ability to bring federal money and jobs to his constituents in the form of reclamation, defense, and aerospace projects. But it was also the result of his assiduous courting of businessmen and Republican voters. (Washington's blanket-primary system allowed Republicans to cross over and vote for Democrats.) During his reelection campaign in 1958, in which he won 68 percent of the vote, Jackson received contributions from important corporations that generally supported Republican candidates. He began a particularly close association with the Boeing Co., one of the country's largest defense contractors and the state's biggest private employer.

As chair of the Interior Committee's Subcommittee on Territories, Jackson led the successful fight for Alaskan statehood. The following year, he managed the bill granting statehood to Hawaii. Although sometimes criticized as the "senator from Boeing," Jackson had emerged as one of the Senate's acknowledged authorities on national security policy and a major figure in the Democratic Party.

Although Jackson had been mentioned as a vice presidential possibility in 1956, he emerged as a serious contender for the second spot on the Democratic ticket in 1960. Endorsed in the opening days of the Democratic National Convention by Mayor ROBERT WAGNER of New York, Gov. PAT BROWN of California, and Sen. MIKE MANSFIELD (D-Mont.), he was also Robert F. Kennedy's personal choice. John Kennedy, however, chose Sen. LYNDON B. JOHNSON (D-Tex.) in the belief that the ticket could not win without carrying Texas. Jackson was asked to serve as a chairman of the Democratic National Committee. He reluctantly accepted the post but found that Robert Kennedy was the real director of the Kennedy campaign. On election day, Jackson was unable to prevent RICHARD M. NIXON from carrying Washington, and he resigned from the committee as soon as the election was over.

Jackson's relations with the Kennedy administration were distant. In the early 1960s, he criticized proposals to control nuclear weapons that he thought might sacrifice American advantages over the Soviet Union. He reluctantly supported the Nuclear Test Ban Treaty in 1963. That same year, he succeeded to the chair of the Interior and Insular Affairs Committee. From that position, he oversaw passage of much of the environmental legislation of the 1960s.

Jackson enthusiastically supported the policy of the Kennedy and Johnson administrations in Southeast Asia. Like Kennedy, he considered Vietnam an important battlefield in the cold war, and, as the 1960s went on, his support for Lyndon Johnson's escalation of the war drove a wedge between Jackson and liberal Democrats. In the late 1960s, Jackson supported the development of an antiballistic missile (ABM) system. When Richard Nixon won the presidential election in 1968, he offered Jackson the position of secretary of defense, which Jackson declined. Jackson continued to support development of the ABM and a robust military. These positions led to opposition from the left wing of his party and a challenge in the Democratic primary of 1970, but Jackson easily captured the nomination and won reelection in the fall.

Jackson opposed Nixon's policy of détente with the Soviet Union. He criticized the Strategic Arms Limitation Talks (SALT I) treaty of 1972 for giving an advantage to the Soviet Union, and won approval for an amendment declaring that any future agreement must provide for numerical equality between American and Soviet weapons. At the same time, he supported Nixon's opening to China.

In the early 1970s, Jackson became widely known as a strong supporter of the state of Israel. A long-term critic of Soviet abuses of human rights, he called attention to Soviet restrictions on the right of Jews to emigrate. He cosponsored the Jackson-Vanik amendment in 1974, which made increased American trade with the Soviet Union conditional on the moderation of Soviet restrictions on emigration.

Jackson launched his first bid for the Democratic presidential nomination in 1972 but won only the Washington state caucuses. He mounted a better effort in 1976 but ultimately lost the nomination to Jimmy Carter. Jackson continued his opposition to the strategic arms limitation process and led the attack on SALT II in 1979. Even had Carter not withdrawn the treaty to protest the Soviet Union's invasion of Afghanistan, the treaty most likely would have failed in the Senate. In the late 1970s and 1980s, Jackson found new admirers among Republicans and neoconservative intellectuals. He agreed with President Ronald Reagan that communism and Soviet influence in Central America constituted a major strategic threat, and he supported the armed opposition to the Sandinista regime in Nicaragua. Despite the discomfort of many in his party with his positions on Central America and nuclear weapons, Jackson easily won reelection in 1982. He died unexpectedly, of a ruptured aorta, on September 1, 1983, in Everett, Wash.

—MSM

Jackson, Robert H(oughwout)

(1892–1954) *associate justice, U.S. Supreme Court*
Robert Jackson was born in Spring Creek, Pa., on February 13, 1892. At the age of five he moved with his family to Frewsburg, N.Y. Immediately upon graduating from high school, Jackson became a clerk in the law offices of his cousin, a prominent lawyer in Jamestown, N.Y., and an active Demo-

crat. Jackson did attend Albany Law School for a year, but essentially he learned the law through the apprentice system. After gaining admission to the bar in 1913, Jackson built a thriving practice in Jamestown and a reputation as one of the best trial lawyers in western New York. He was active in the bar association and in Democratic politics. After Franklin D. Roosevelt was elected as governor of New York, Jackson served as an adviser, and, after Roosevelt became president, Jackson accepted a position as general counsel of the Bureau of Internal Revenue in February 1934. Jackson moved to the Justice Department as assistant attorney general in charge of the tax division in March 1936. After only two months, he shifted to assistant attorney general in charge of the antitrust division. When Roosevelt appointed STANLEY REED to the Supreme Court in 1938, he named Jackson to replace Reed as solicitor general. As the "government's lawyer," Jackson won acclaim for his skill as an appellate advocate. In 1940, Roosevelt made Jackson attorney general. The next year, Chief Justice Charles Evans Hughes resigned, and Roosevelt elevated Justice Harlan Fiske Stone to the chief justiceship. In June 1941, Roosevelt appointed Jackson to fill the vacancy as an associate justice. The Senate confirmed Jackson a month later.

On the bench, Jackson did not gravitate toward other active New Dealers Roosevelt had elevated to the Court, such as HUGO BLACK, WILLIAM O. DOUGLAS, and Frank Murphy. He quickly established himself as a powerful advocate of both nationalism and judicial restraint. As such, he voted regularly with another Roosevelt appointee, FELIX FRANKFURTER. The issue of federalism was crucial to the New Deal, and Jackson consistently championed national over state power. He filed a concurring opinion in *Edwards v. California* (1941), which struck down California's so-called Okie law that limited the right of entry into the state by those who had no visible means of support. Jackson argued that the right to enter any state was a "privilege" of U.S. citizenship. "If national citizenship means less than this," wrote the new justice, "it means nothing." Based on his reading of the commerce clause of the Constitution, Jackson was willing to grant the federal government broad authority to regulate the economy. He wrote the majority opinion in *Wickard*

v. Filburn (1942), which upheld the second Agricultural Adjustment Act.

Jackson's record was more mixed when it came to civil liberties. He often eloquently defended the individual's freedom of thought, but he also contended that the government could limit the right of free speech if the speech involved was intrusive, aggressive, or a threat to public order. He wrote for the majority in *West Virginia Board of Education v. Barnette* (1943), which struck down a state statute requiring school children to salute the flag. When, in *Korematsu v. U.S.* (1944), the court upheld the conviction of an American-born citizen of Japanese descent for failing to report to a relocation center, Jackson dissented.

From May 1945 to October 1946, Jackson took a leave from the Court to act as chief U.S. prosecutor at the Nuremberg trials of senior Nazi officials. Jackson regarded it as the most important work of his life.

Jackson's commitment to judicial restraint brought him into ideological and personal conflict with other Roosevelt appointees, particularly Black. The feud with Black exploded into an embarrassingly public war in 1946. When Stone died in April 1946, HARRY S. TRUMAN appointed a loyal friend, FRED M. VINSON, to be chief justice. Jackson, who was in Nuremberg when Stone died and Truman pondered a replacement, believed that Black's active opposition had cost him the chief justiceship. He responded by issuing a blistering public attack on Black that harmed Jackson more than it did his adversary.

Influenced by his work at Nuremberg and by the emergence of the cold war, Jackson increasingly perceived a need to balance freedom and public order. In *Terminiello v. Chicago* (1949), he dissented from a majority ruling that overturned the conviction for a breach of the peace by a defrocked Catholic priest whose fascist and anti-Semitic speech "provoked a hostile mob and incited a friendly one, and threatened violence between the two." Jackson warned that the majority's "doctrinaire" view of the First Amendment would "convert the . . . Bill of Rights into a suicide pact." Similar concerns led Jackson to uphold federal measures to restrict communist activities. In *American Communications Association v. Douds* (1950), the Court upheld a section of the Taft-Hartley Act requiring officers of labor unions to sign affidavits affirming that they were not members of the communist party and did not believe in the unlawful overthrow of the government. Jackson concurred in part and dissented in part. He was willing to allow the government to inquire into membership in the communist party but drew the line at efforts by the government to inquire into private beliefs. The following year, in *Dennis v. U.S.*, he voted with the majority to affirm the conviction of officers of the communist party for conspiring to teach or advocate the overthrow of the government in violation of the Smith Act. Jackson unwaveringly supported the separation of church and state. He dissented when, in *Everson v. Board of Education of Ewing Township* (1947), the Court upheld a New Jersey statute that authorized school boards to reimburse parents of children who attended Catholic schools for the cost of transportation. Similarly, Jackson dissented from the majority's position in *Zorach v. Clauson* (1952), which upheld a New York law allowing release time for religious instruction during school hours providing that the instruction took place off school property.

While he had generally supported the expansion of civil rights for African Americans, Jackson had reservations about the school desegregation cases. After participating in the oral arguments, he did not think that the legislative history of the Fourteenth Amendment supported a decision striking down segregated public schools, and he considered filing a separate concurring opinion. Ultimately, Chief Justice EARL WARREN persuaded him of the need for unanimity. Although Jackson suffered a heart attack on April 1, 1954, he returned to the bench on May 17 to be present when Warren read the Court's decision. It was a dramatic demonstration of the Court's unity and of Jackson's support for the decision. Shortly after commencement of the fall term, Jackson suffered a second heart attack and died on October 8, 1954, in McLean, Va.

A superb prose stylist and legal craftsman, Jackson remains one of the most frequently quoted American jurists. His commitment to judicial restraint continues to influence American jurisprudence.

—MSM

Javits, Jacob K(oppel)
(1904–1986) *U.S. senator*

Javits's father, a rabbinical student in Austria, emigrated to New York City and worked as a janitor in a tenement and a Tammany Hall ward heeler on the Lower East Side. Jacob Javits was born on May 18, 1904, in New York City. After graduating from high school, he attended night classes at Columbia University and in 1923 enrolled in New York University Law School. He supported himself with part-time jobs and earned his J.D. in 1926. After gaining admission to the bar in 1927, he joined with his older brother to form the law firm of Javits and Javits, specializing in bankruptcy and corporate reorganization. The firm enjoyed considerable success. Repulsed by the corruption of Tammany Hall, he joined the Republican-Fusion party in the 1930s and was an avid supporter of Fiorello H. La Guardia. He served in the Chemical Warfare Department in Washington, D.C., during World War II and achieved the rank of lieutenant colonel. In 1945, he was the chief of research for the Republican-Liberal-Fusion ticket's unsuccessful mayoral candidate. The following year, the Republican party nominated him to run for a seat in the U.S. House of Representatives from the city's Upper West Side. Javits became the first Republican to carry the district since 1920.

Javits immediately established himself as among the most liberal Republicans in Congress. He regarded himself as a political descendant of Theodore Roosevelt and argued that a healthy political party had to have room for more than one point of view. His views led him to support the Truman administration on a number of controversial issues. He voted to uphold President HARRY S. TRUMAN's veto of the Taft-Hartley bill in 1947 and supported the Marshall Plan as well as the Truman Doctrine. An outspoken opponent of discrimination, he supported legislation to outlaw the poll tax in 1947 and 1949. Alarmed by its excesses, he also voted against funding for the House Un-American Activities Committee in 1948. In addition, Javits emerged as an early and enthusiastic supporter of the state of Israel.

After the Republican victory in 1952, Javits frequently had to defend his Republican credentials against colleagues who regarded him as too liberal.

He described himself as a mainstream Eisenhower Republican, but, in fact, he frequently took positions more liberal than those of the administration. In April 1954, Javits proposed an amendment to the administration's omnibus open housing bill that would have banned segregation in housing financed through federal mortgage insurance. The amendment failed.

In August, he criticized a bill, requested by Attorney General HERBERT BROWNELL, to give the Justice Department authority to grant immunity to congressional and court witnesses. Critics of the bill claimed that it would have the effect of compelling witnesses to testify or go to jail. Javits voted against the bill, but Congress passed it, and President Eisenhower signed it later in the month.

In 1954, Javits did not run for reelection and instead ran for attorney general of New York State. His opponent, Franklin D. Roosevelt Jr., was well-known, well-funded, and expected to win. Javits, however, combined support from the Jewish community, a strong showing with New York City's liberal vote, and traditionally Republican voters upstate to pull off the upset. As New York's attorney general, he supported legislation banning employment discrimination and a health insurance program for state employees. He also continued to speak out on national issues, backing aid to Israel, expanded federal public housing, and a higher federal minimum wage.

Javits sought the seat in the U.S. Senate vacated by the retirement of HERBERT LEHMAN (D-N.Y.). His bid ran into difficulty when, shortly before the Republican state committee met in September to choose a nominee, Julian G. Sourwine, former counsel to the Senate Internal Security Subcommittee, accused Javits of having been "mixed up" with a staff member of the communist *Daily Worker*. Javits aggressively countered the charge, and the convention unanimously selected him as the nominee on September 10. In November, he defeated his Democratic opponent, New York City's mayor, ROBERT F. WAGNER, by approximately 450,000 votes.

In the Senate, Javits resumed his role as a leading Republican congressional liberal. He endorsed the administration's civil rights bill in 1957 as "the minimum which should be enacted at this time." Three years later, Javits unsuccessfully sought to strengthen the administration's civil rights bill by expanding its voting rights provisions and establishing a permanent Commission on Equal Job Opportunity. In August 1959, Javits and Sen. HUGH SCOTT (R-Pa.) were the only two Republicans in the upper chamber who voted to override a veto of a public housing bill, which President Eisenhower had criticized as "extravagant." In May 1960, Javits was among five Republican senators to support an effort to override a presidential veto of an area redevelopment bill. The Senate sustained both vetoes.

Javits believed that government had a constructive role to play in improving the lives of citizens. He also believed in a mixed economy and attempted to support private enterprise. In 1960, liberal Democrats supported the Forand bill, which provided for the establishment of a medical care plan for the aged within the Social Security system. Javits and seven other Republicans offered a voluntary plan involving federal and state grants to subsidize the purchase of private health insurance.

In the area of foreign policy, Javits staunchly supported the administration. He backed the Eisenhower Doctrine for the Middle East in 1957. Two years later, Javits endorsed the administration's program of foreign military and economic assistance, and criticized Sen. MIKE MANSFIELD's (D-Mont.) proposal for reducing economic aid.

During the 1960s, despite his position as part of the liberal minority within the minority party, Javits became one of the most prominent figures in Congress by serving on as many committees and subcommittees as possible and by speaking out on a wide range of issues. Javits also continued his support of civil rights. As part of that effort, he backed an attempt to change the Senate rules to make it easier to end a filibuster in 1961. He supported a bill banning the discriminatory use of literacy tests in federal elections in 1962 and the civil rights bill offered by President JOHN F. KENNEDY in 1963. In addition, he repeatedly offered riders aimed at denying federal funds to institutions that practiced segregation. Javits backed President LYNDON B. JOHNSON's civil rights measures and much of the Great Society as well.

In 1962, Javits won reelection by almost 1 million votes. He backed NELSON ROCKEFELLER for the Republican nomination in 1964, and, when the conservative BARRY M. GOLDWATER won the nomination, Javits declined to endorse him. That decision did not hinder his own electoral chances. Javits won reelection in 1968, this time by more than a million votes.

Although Javits supported the Johnson administration's policy in Vietnam during the early and mid-1960s, by 1967 he began to have doubts and joined 22 other senators in calling for a peaceful resolution of the conflict. In 1970, Javits supported the Cooper-Church amendment to bar funds for combat operations in Cambodia and voted to repeal the Gulf of Tonkin Resolution. He also supported the McGovern-Hatfield amendment designed to end the war in 1971. The following year, he voted for a proposal to cut off funds for all combat operations in Southeast Asia by the end of 1972. Javits sponsored legislation in 1970 to limit the war-making powers of the president. It did not pass that year, but Javits persisted, and Congress passed the War Powers Act over Nixon's veto in 1973.

In the late 1960s and early 1970s, Javits became a leading advocate of consumer protection legislation. He cosponsored a bill in 1970 to create a consumer protection agency. The bill died on the Senate floor in 1972, again in 1974, and yet again in conference committee in 1975. While Javits opposed Nixon's policy in Southeast Asia, he responded cautiously as the Watergate scandal unfolded in 1973 and 1974. Javits maintained that Nixon was innocent until proven guilty. That position and the disastrous impact of Watergate on all Republicans in 1974 substantially reduced Javits's margin of victory when he ran for a fourth term in 1974. At this point, Javits increasingly turned his attention to world affairs and, in particular, to the Middle East.

By 1980, Javits's health had begun to fail. Moreover, as his party shifted to the right, his brand of liberal Republicanism grew more and more out of fashion. A conservative challenger, Alfonse D'Amato, defeated him in the Republican primary that year. Javits defiantly ran on the Liberal party ticket, but his presence split the liberal vote, handing D'Amato a victory in the general election. After the election, Javits retired from public life. He died in Palm Beach, Fla., on March 7, 1986.

—MSM

Jenner, William E(zra)
(1908–1985) *U.S. senator*

Born in Marengo, Ind., on July 21, 1908, Jenner graduated from Indiana University in 1930. While working as an elevator operator in the Old House Office Building, he took night classes at George Washington University and subsequently earned a law degree from Indiana University Law School. After gaining admission to the bar, he entered private practice in Indiana. He won election to the Indiana State Senate in 1934 and served in that body until 1942. Jenner became minority leader in 1937 and was president pro tempore and majority leader from 1938 to 1941. In 1942, he resigned his seat to serve in the army air corps during World War II. He left the service as a captain in 1944 and returned to Indiana. In November 1944, he won an election to fill the remaining weeks in the Senate term of Frederick Van Nuys (D-Ind.), who had died in office. Jenner did not stand for election for the full term. Instead, he resumed his law practice and became chair of the Republican State Committee. Jenner won a full term in the U.S. Senate in 1946.

Jenner was a member of the "Class of 1946," a group of Republican legislators elected in the Republican landslide of that year who supported a conservative domestic agenda and rejected the Europe-first orientation of the Truman administration's foreign policy. Like others of this group, Jenner believed that America's primary area of interest in foreign policy was in Asia. As such, he opposed the Marshall Plan and the establishment of the North Atlantic Treaty Organization. He also expressed outrage that the United States sent aid to socialist Great Britain. In contrast, Jenner vigorously supported increased aid to Nationalist China. One of the most vocal members of the so-called China bloc, he charged that the Truman administration's refusal to aid Chiang Kai-shek (Jiang Jieshi) led to the fall of China to the Communists. Jenner also supported Sen. JOSEPH R. MCCARTHY'S (R-Wis.) charges that a communist conspiracy in the State Department was responsible for the loss of China. Indeed, Jenner became McCarthy's closest ally. When the Tydings committee, created to investigate McCarthy's initial charges, issued its report, Jenner attacked it as "the most scandalous and brazen whitewash of treasonable conspiracy in our history." An outspoken critic of Gen. George C. Marshall, whom he blamed for the fall of China and for failing to stop the spread of communism elsewhere, Jenner described Marshall as "either an unsuspecting stooge or an actual coconspirator with the most treasonable array of political cutthroats ever turned loose in the executive branch of government." In 1950, Jenner voted against amending the National Security Act of 1947 to permit Marshall to become secretary of defense. In the debate over that measure, Jenner called Marshall a "living lie" and a "front man for traitors." The senator from Indiana also opposed President HARRY S. TRUMAN's dismissal of Gen. Douglas MacArthur in 1951 and called for the president's impeachment.

Jenner supported Sen. ROBERT A. TAFT of Ohio for the Republican nomination in 1952 and reluctantly backed DWIGHT D. EISENHOWER after the latter won the nomination. Nevertheless, Jenner, running for reelection, campaigned aggressively against the Democratic ticket. He warned that "if ADLAI [STEVENSON] gets into the White House, Alger [Hiss] gets out of jail." He charged that if Stevenson won, the "Red Network" would be able to operate safely. In typically harsh terms, he predicted that, in the event of a Democratic victory, the "bodies of thousands of American boys would be tossed onto Truman's funeral pyre in Asia."

Despite Jenner's efforts on behalf of the ticket, Eisenhower had little taste for the senator from Indiana. At a rally in Indianapolis on September 9, the candidate sat on the same podium with Jenner. In his speech, Eisenhower endorsed the entire Republican ticket but failed to mention Jenner by name. When Eisenhower finished, Jenner quickly jumped to his feet and embraced the nominee while photographers captured the moment. An embarrassed and furious Eisenhower demanded that Rep. CHARLES HALLECK (R-Ind.) "get me out of here." Eisenhower later told EMMET HUGHES that he "felt dirty from the touch of the man." Nevertheless, Democrats and even some Republicans criticized Eisenhower's unwillingness to publicly repudiate Jenner.

After the Republicans swept the elections in 1952, Taft, the new majority leader, appointed Jenner chair of the Internal Security Subcommittee in an effort to contain McCarthy's excesses. Although

Taft disliked Jenner, he believed that the senator from Indiana would submit to party discipline, something that McCarthy could not be counted on to do. Taft hoped that Jenner would continue to attack past Democratic administrations and not embarrass his own party. Initially, the strategy seemed to work. Jenner repeatedly denounced the Truman administration.

In July 1953, the Internal Security Subcommittee issued a report entitled "Interlocking Subversion in Government." Reprinted and circulated by the Republican National Committee, it attempted to document what Attorney General HERBERT BROWNELL called "the very successful communist espionage penetration in our government during World War II and thereafter." A noted civil libertarian, Norman Redlich, examined the charges in the February 6, 1954, edition of the *Nation*. He wrote that the report was a rehash of old charges and questioned the accuracy of the findings.

The Senate Internal Security Subcommittee also resumed the inquiry into the Harry Dexter White affair. Through documents and testimony provided by former Secretary of State JAMES BYRNES, Attorney General Herbert Brownell, and FBI Director J. EDGAR HOOVER, the panel concluded that President Truman had known that White was a communist when he had appointed him to head the International Monetary Fund. Truman defended his actions on national television, and little action was taken on the report. Many years later, the Verona decrypts firmly established that White engaged in espionage for the Soviets.

In early 1954, Jenner claimed that the Republican administration had found "heaps of evidence of the stupidity, the corruption, even the treason of its predecessors." Jenner said the Democrats had "permitted traitors to bring us close to military defeat." In a speech in Indiana he said, "The Fair Dealers and their communist brain trusts . . . put every possible handicap on our Armed Forces" and sent them to Korea where they "were supposed to be defeated."

From 1953 to 1955, Jenner's subcommittee investigated a wide range of alleged communist activities: subversion in the clergy, army, United Nations and, most particularly, the schools. Jenner proudly claimed that as a result of his probes many teachers had been dismissed. He complimented school systems, such as those in California and New York, for cooperating with his subcommittee in the task of rooting out communists.

Reacting to several decisions by the Supreme Court restricting investigations of subversion, Jenner cosponsored a bill in 1957 to limit the Court's power. One provision would have restored to congressional committees the investigative authority that the Court had limited in *Watkins v. U.S.* (1957). In *Watkins*, the Court held that congressional investigations had to be related to a legitimate function of Congress; congressional investigators had no power to expose for the sake of exposure. A second section would have effectively reversed the Court's decision in *Pennsylvania v. Nelson* (1956), which overturned a state sedition law on the ground that Congress had preempted the field with the Smith Act. A third provision would have reversed the Court's ruling in *Yates v. United States* (1957), which had narrowly interpreted the Smith Act by distinguishing between advocacy of the forcible overthrow of the government as an abstract doctrine and advocacy of action toward that end. Moreover, the bill would have barred the Court from accepting or deciding cases dealing with these and related matters in the future. Attorney General WILLIAM P. ROGERS and the American Bar Association condemned the Jenner bill; the Senate rejected it on August 20, 1958.

Even as the Senate moved to censure McCarthy, Jenner remained a loyal ally. In November 1954, he charged the Watkins committee, which had recommended censure of the Wisconsin Republican, with having failed to consider "the most important evidence"—that McCarthy "was fighting a conspiracy." Jenner maintained that the censure movement "was initiated by a communist conspiracy" and that the Watkins committee was aiding it. He interrupted the final debate on condemnation and personally attacked Sen. RALPH FLANDERS (R–Vt.), whose actions during the spring of 1954 had helped spur the censure movement. Jenner asked the Vermont Republican why he had referred to "Soviet tyrants and murderers as 'my friends, my brothers.'" The words Jenner cited came from a Voice of America broadcast that Flanders had made to the Soviet-bloc countries. Flanders retorted that Jenner had "taken leave of his

intelligence." He explained that the broadcast was directed to the Soviet people and not the government. Despite Jenner's efforts, the Senate voted to condemn McCarthy in December.

Jenner continued to be one of the leading members of the China bloc in the Senate. In May 1954 he called on the United States to arm 20 million Nationalist Chinese, Korean, Japanese, and other anticommunists in Asia to support Taiwan's attacks on the mainland and divert communist forces from Indochina. Jenner expressed outrage that the United States prevented Chiang Kai-shek from raiding the mainland and opposed any further attempts by the U.S. government to resume normal relations with communist China. He also asked the president to issue a "final statement" that the United States would not recognize Communist China or sanction its admission to the UN. During the dispute over Quemoy and Matsu in late 1954, Jenner supported a blockade of the mainland. On April 28, 1955, Jenner introduced a resolution that would have repudiated in advance any concessions that the United States might make to Beijing.

Jenner became increasingly dissatisfied with the Eisenhower administration. By 1956, he was making public his view that Eisenhower's leadership had "ruined" the Republican party. He thought the party should reconstitute itself as a conservative party. Near the end of 1957, Jenner surprised political observers and the leaders of his own party when he announced that he would not seek reelection in 1958. He returned to Indiana and resumed his law practice. His other interests included the Seaway Corporation, a land-development company, and four farms he owned. Jenner died in Bedford, Ind., on March 9, 1985.

—MSM

Johnson, Frank M(inis), Jr.
(1918–1999) *U.S. district judge*
Born at Haleyville, in the Republican hill country of northern Alabama, on October 30, 1918, Frank Johnson attended Birmingham-Southern College on a football scholarship and Massey Business College in Birmingham before enrolling in the pre-law program at the University of Alabama. He graduated at the top of his law school class at the Univer-

sity of Alabama in 1943. Later that year, he joined the army as a private, was commissioned as a lieutenant, won the Bronze Star for his actions during the Normandy invasion, and was mustered out a captain. He returned to Alabama, began a law practice in Jasper, and became active in Republican politics. In 1952, he headed the Alabama Veterans for Eisenhower and was a state campaign manager for DWIGHT D. EISENHOWER's presidential campaign. President Eisenhower appointed him U.S. attorney for the northern district of Alabama in 1953. Two years later, Eisenhower appointed him U.S. district judge for the middle district of Alabama. Johnson began his judicial service on November 7, 1955.

Judge Johnson decided several important civil rights cases and in the process won a reputation among most observers as a fair and principled jurist. On June 6, 1956, during the Montgomery bus boycott led by MARTIN LUTHER KING JR., Johnson joined the majority on a three-judge federal court that held Montgomery's law requiring segregated buses unconstitutional. Three years later, he struck down racial segregation in Montgomery's public parks. Johnson also handed down rulings ordering the desegregation of public schools and colleges, libraries, museums, depots, airports, restaurants, and other places of public accommodation.

In December 1958, Judge Johnson had the first of many run-ins with George C. Wallace, a former law school classmate who was then a state circuit court judge. On December 8, Wallace defied a subpoena from the U.S. Civil Rights Commission and refused to turn over voter registration records in two counties under his jurisdiction. In three separate decrees issued between December 11 and January 9, Johnson ordered Wallace to let agents of the commission examine the records. Wallace kept up his resistance but finally, on January 12 and 13, gave the records to county grand juries, which then let commission employees see the data. On January 26, Johnson dismissed contempt charges against Wallace, explaining that Wallace had complied with court orders, though indirectly, and that punishing him would only promote his political fortunes. In August 1960, Johnson also overturned a state court injunction blocking federal investigators from examining voter registration records in Montgomery. At the same time, he upheld the con-

stitutionality of the Civil Rights Act of 1960 against a challenge from the state.

With his evenhanded, considered approach, Johnson did not always decide civil rights cases in favor of African Americans or the federal government if he thought law or precedent was against them. In one of the first major tests of the Civil Rights Act of 1957, Johnson ruled in March 1959 against the Justice Department. He held that the law did not allow the federal government to bring a voting discrimination suit directly against the state of Alabama. The Fifth Circuit Court of Appeals upheld his interpretation, and, as a result of the adverse ruling, Congress included a provision to authorize voting rights suits against the states in the Civil Rights Act of 1960. In 1960, Johnson upheld the expulsion without a hearing of six black students from Alabama State College for having led sit-ins in Montgomery and Tuskegee. A higher court later reversed Johnson.

Throughout the 1960s, Judge Johnson's rulings pushed reluctant white Alabamans toward desegregation. In March 1961, he entered a sweeping decree, which served as a model for other federal courts, outlawing voting discrimination in Macon Co. Johnson enjoined a planned civil rights march from Selma to Montgomery in March 1965, but later in the month, he authorized the march and ordered the state to supply police protection to the demonstrators. The day after that march, one participant, Viola Liuzzo, was murdered. A jury in Lownes Co. failed to convict three Ku Klux Klansmen accused of the crime, despite a witness who testified that he saw one of the defendants commit the murder. The three were later tried on federal civil rights charges, but the jury declared itself deadlocked. Measuring his words carefully to avoid a mistrial, Johnson urged them to try again; the evidence, he instructed, could not be more clear. The jury brought in a conviction, and Johnson sentenced the defendants to the maximum term of three years in prison. Johnson ordered officials in various counties under his jurisdiction to prepare school desegregation plans and in March 1967 was a member of a three-judge court that placed all of Alabama under an order to desegregate its schools. His decisions made him a frequent target of criticism from George Wallace, who had become governor of Alabama. Wallace called him an "integratin', carpetbaggin', baldfaced liar." Johnson was socially ostracized and received countless threats. He was under 24-hour protection by federal marshals from 1961 to 1975. Johnson incurred Wallace's wrath again in the 1970s with decisions requiring the state to improve the state's institutions for the mentally ill and retarded as well as its prison system. Johnson also, in 1972, ordered the Alabama State Police, which had never had a black trooper, to end its "blatant and continuous discrimination." In 1977, President Jimmy Carter nominated Johnson to head the FBI, but Johnson withdrew after undergoing heart surgery. After recovering from that surgery, Johnson returned to the bench. He ruled in 1978 that the hiring practices of Alabama State University discriminated against whites, making him the first federal judge to find a black institution guilty of discrimination against whites. In 1979, Carter appointed Johnson to the Fifth Circuit Court of Appeals. Two years later, when the Fifth Circuit was divided in two, Johnson became a judge on the new Eleventh Circuit. He took senior judge status in 1992. Three years later, President Bill Clinton awarded him the Presidential Medal of Freedom. Johnson died of pneumonia at his home in Montgomery, Ala., on July 23, 1999.

—MSM

Johnson, Lyndon B(aines)

(1908–1973) *U.S. senator, Senate minority leader, Senate majority leader*

Born in Stonewall, Tex., on August 27, 1908, Lyndon Johnson was the eldest son of Sam Johnson, a small farmer and cattle speculator, and Rebecca Baines, the daughter of a prosperous lawyer. At the age of five, he moved from Stonewall, Tex., to nearby Johnson City, founded by his grandfather, a populist politician. Johnson worked his way through Southwest Texas State Teachers College and graduated with a B.S. in 1930. For the next two years, he taught in the Houston public school system.

In 1932, Johnson went to Washington, D.C., as secretary to Rep. Richard Kleberg (D-Tex.) of the 14th district. There he assiduously gathered information about the operation of Congress and took advantage of every opportunity to meet influential

people, including Reps. SAM RAYBURN (D-Tex.) and WRIGHT PATMAN (D-Tex.), who had both served in the Texas state legislature with his father. Three years later, President Franklin D. Roosevelt appointed him Texas Director of the National Youth Administration (NYA). The youngest state NYA director. Johnson proved a capable administrator and built up a political constituency through the gratitude he received from those who obtained NYA jobs.

In 1937, Johnson entered a special election for the congressional seat from Texas's 10th District, a relatively liberal area in a conservative state. He distinguished himself from his seven opponents by proclaiming total support for President Franklin D. Roosevelt's programs, including the president's plan to enlarge the Supreme Court. Johnson received twice the votes of his closest opponent. By making a favorable impression on Roosevelt, Johnson obtained a seat on the powerful Naval Affairs Committee and used it to procure public works projects for his district.

Power in the House was based on seniority, and the impatient Johnson did not want to travel the long road to preeminence. In 1941, he ran for a Senate seat in a special election but lost by 1,300 votes to Texas Gov. Wilbert L. "Pappy" O'Daniel. Immediately after Pearl Harbor, Johnson asked to be called up for active duty. He served as the president's special emissary in Australia and New Zealand for seven months and returned to Congress in July 1942, when Roosevelt recalled all legislators to their duties in Washington. Six years later, Johnson ran for the Senate again and defeated the conservative former governor, Coke Stevenson, in the Democratic primary by 87 votes, out of 1 million cast, despite the loser's charge of fraud.

In the Senate, Johnson shifted significantly to the right. His new, statewide constituency was much more conservative than the 10th district. Furthermore, Johnson wanted to associate himself with conservative Sen. RICHARD RUSSELL (D-Ga.), the most powerful figure in the Senate. To get closer to Russell, he requested an appointment to the Georgia senator's Armed Services Committee, which he received. With Russell's assistance, he became party whip in 1951.

After the majority leader, Ernest McFarland (D-Ariz.), was defeated in the elections of 1952,

Johnson devoted all of his energies to behind-the-scenes efforts to win the post while publicly feigning disinterest. He succeeded with the help of key public endorsements from Russell and Sen. Earle Clements (D-Ky.), who had ties to the liberal wing of the party. Because the Republicans had gained control of both houses of Congress in 1952, Johnson became the Senate minority leader.

The post of party leader was not highly coveted. It had historically been a largely titular office, a front for an informal inner club of powerful senators. McFarland, for example, had merely served as the spokesman for Russell, the real leader of the upper chamber's Democrats. Shortly after assuming the post, however, Johnson subtly expanded his powers to become the center of his party's power structure in the Senate. He reformed the seniority system so that every Democratic senator, including freshmen, was guaranteed a good committee assignment. In the name of a fairer distribution of committee seats, he gained discretionary power in making assignments that previous leaders had not possessed. By party rule, the leader was also chairman of the Democratic Policy Committee. Johnson severed its ties with and accountability to the party as a whole, making it a purely senatorial institution, fully under his control. He eliminated its function of determining legislative programs and limited its responsibility largely to that of determining the flow of legislation to the floor. This gave him considerable influence over senators seeking the passage of particular bills. Johnson virtually eliminated the Democratic Caucus, thereby ending group discussions of issues and depriving Democratic senators of a collective decision-making apparatus beyond the leader's control. Johnson channeled the funds of the Senate Democratic Campaign Committee into the smaller states, where they were more likely to have greater impact. This gave him a clear claim to the gratitude of senators elected with the help of the committee. He used his responsibility for assigning office space to reward cooperative senators with better offices and punish rebellious colleagues with cramped quarters.

Johnson supplemented these powers with an elaborate intelligence network that enabled him to learn the desires and needs of his fellow senators. He used this information to dangle before his party

Lyndon B. Johnson and Samuel Rayburn arrive at the White House to attend a Bipartisan Legislative Leadership meeting, December 13, 1955. *(Dwight D. Eisenhower Library and Museum)*

colleagues those rewards or (usually by implication) punishments most likely to influence their votes. Johnson also was extremely skilled in the art of persuasion on a one-to-one basis. Few Democratic senators were completely immune to what became known as the "Johnson Treatment."

Although Johnson succeeded in making himself a powerful party leader, his legislative goals were modest. In February 1953, he declared that Senate Democrats would engage in the "politics of responsibility" rather than the "politics of partisanship," which meant that despite the wishes of liberals in the party, he would not offer a comprehensive alternative to the administration's program. Johnson believed that only the president could initiate major legislation. In addition, his political base in Texas was conservative. Moreover, his style of behind-the-scenes manipulation was conducive to the politics of concession and compromise, not the formulation of ideological programs. Finally, Johnson thought that, given President Eisenhower's great popularity, it would be politically suicidal to attack him frontally.

Therefore, Johnson proceeded cautiously, challenging the administration on a selective basis and only when he believed that his party's conservatives and liberals could unite on the issue involved. He took strong stands in favor of strengthening the Social Security system and extending rural electrification while refusing to move to Eisenhower's left on such controversial issues as public power and civil rights. Often he presented the Democrats as the best ally of the president, supporting him against right-wing Republicans. In 1953, Sen. ROBERT A. TAFT (R-Ohio) demanded that a resolution, backed by the Eisenhower administration, denouncing Soviet "enslavement" of eastern Europe be amended to include condemnation of the Yalta and Potsdam agreements, an implied attack on the Democrats. Johnson denounced Taft for trying to "divide us in the face of the enemy" and praised Eisenhower for having issued "a clear call for America to speak with a united voice against the Soviet enslavement of free peoples."

Johnson's approach to Sen. JOSEPH R. McCAR-THY (R-Wis.) typified his cautiousness. He feared that a Democratic attack on the Wisconsin senator would unite Republicans and make it appear that the Democrats were trying to cover up the alleged subversive influences in the Truman administration. Johnson did not move against McCarthy until he believed that immediate success was possible. That time came after the Senate, in August 1954, voted to establish a select committee to investigate censure charges. The unanimous Democratic opposition to McCarthy in the censure vote of December 1954 resulted, in large measure, from Johnson's efforts. To avoid charges by McCarthy's supporters that Democrats were soft on communism, Johnson in 1954 suggested that the United States might withdraw from the United Nations if Communist China were admitted and that the nation should act against the left-wing government in Guatemala.

When Johnson became majority leader in 1955, he continued his policy of cautious compromise. During that year, he added protectionist provisions to a reciprocal trade bill to secure its passage. In 1955, he also opposed liberal Sen. PAUL DOUGLAS's (D-Ill.) effort to raise the minimum wage level in an administration bill from 90 cents to $1.25. Johnson agreed to increase the figure to $1. At the same time, however, he eliminated a provision extending minimum-wage coverage to additional workers because he feared that it would split the party along North-South lines. In July of that year, Johnson suffered a heart attack but recovered by the end of September.

In 1956, Johnson, with Rayburn's backing, headed an attempt to wrest control of the Texas Democratic Party from conservative Gov. ALLAN SHIVERS, who had led most of the organization to bolt from the national party in 1952 and support Eisenhower. To bolster this effort, he offered himself as Texas's favorite-son candidate for president. With the aid of Texas liberals, he won control of the state convention in May 1956 and was elected chairman of the delegation to the National Democratic Convention. Some of his advisers urged him to turn his favorite-son candidacy into an active, full-scale bid for the presidential nomination. Because he was a Southerner with a conservative political base, Johnson decided to forgo the primary popularity contests and rest his hopes on the possibility of a deadlocked convention. However, ADLAI E. STE-VENSON won the nomination on the first ballot.

In September 1956, the majority leader split with his Texas liberal allies of the previous spring, leaving the Johnson-Rayburn moderates with exclusive control of the state party. Under their leadership, the organization rejected both state interposition against the Supreme Court's school desegregation decision of 1954, the strategy favored by Shivers, and active implementation of the Court's ruling, the policy backed by the liberals.

In 1956, the Eisenhower administration submitted to Congress a four-part civil rights bill providing for the creation of a civil rights commission, the elevation of the Civil Rights Section of the Criminal Division in the Justice Department to the status of a division, authority for the attorney general to enter civil suits to enforce civil rights, and protection for voting rights. Johnson wanted nothing to do with a battle over civil rights that would divide his party in an election year. When the House passed the civil rights bill, he cleverly outmaneuvered liberals in the Senate and consigned the bill to oblivion by committing it to Sen. JAMES O. EASTLAND's (D-Miss.) Judiciary Committee. After the election, Johnson concluded that, for the sake of his party and for his own presidential ambitions, some form of civil rights bill would have to pass. He warned the southern Democrats that if they continued to block all civil rights legislation, the liberals might muster enough votes to change Rule 22 and eliminate the filibuster. Without the threat of a filibuster, he admonished, the South would face another Reconstruction. When the administration resubmitted the bill the following year, Johnson held his party together, weakened the bill sufficiently to avoid a southern filibuster, and oversaw passage of the first civil rights legislation since Reconstruction. In order to avoid the filibuster, Johnson eliminated Title III, which authorized the attorney general to initiate civil action for preventive relief in a wide range of civil rights matters. To achieve this, Johnson brokered a deal between Democrats from the mountain states and southern Democrats. Johnson promised the western Democrats that if they voted to remove Title III, he would persuade southern Democrats to vote for the Hells Canyon Dam project in Idaho. In addition, he had friendly senators add to Title IV, the section protecting voting rights, an amendment that required a jury trial for those held in contempt of court under the provisions of the act. Johnson's deft maneuvering guided the bill through the Senate, but he also effectively gutted the measure. To add to the frustration of Republicans, Johnson also managed to walk off with most of the credit.

In the furor after the Soviet Union launched *Sputnik* in October 1957, Johnson arranged for the Armed Services Committee's Defense Preparedness Subcommittee, which he chaired, to hold hearings. He did so, at least partly, in effort to neutralize STUART SYMINGTON (D-Mo.), a rival for the Democratic nomination in 1960 who intended to use hearings of the full Armed Services Committee to attack Eisenhower for allowing his concern with the budget to imperil the nation. Held from October 1957 to January 1958, Johnson's hearings eschewed direct partisan attacks on the president or the administration. Rather than rehash Democratic criticisms of Eisenhower's cuts in defense spending, the hearings focused on the new issues of space and the development of missiles and how the United States could close the gap. Johnson cautiously avoided partisan recriminations. He understood that taking the high road in this instance also made good politics. In a political masterstroke, Johnson used the hearings to put the Republican

administration on the defensive without launching a personal attack on the president or seeming to engage in partisan politics.

The Democratic sweep of the congressional elections in 1958 weakened Johnson's hold over his Democratic Senate colleagues. A number of liberal freshmen Democrats entered the upper house, strengthening the ranks of senators favoring a clear-cut alternative program. Meanwhile, President Eisenhower became more aggressive in his determination to minimize spending. Sen. EVERETT DIRKSEN (R-Ill.), the new Republican leader, was much more inclined than his predecessor, Sen. WILLIAM KNOWLAND (R-Calif.), to exert pressure in order to secure Republican unity. The approaching presidential election of 1960 intensified political polarization. Under these circumstances, Johnson, whose system of operation was founded on compromise, could not function at his best. Early in 1959, in an effort to please liberals, he introduced bills to fund the construction of airports and housing. On the floor, however, he angered liberals by cutting funds from both measures in an effort to secure veto-proof bills. Nevertheless, he still failed to get enough votes to override subsequent vetoes of these measures.

In 1960, Johnson made a bid for the Democratic presidential nomination. Johnson was indecisive about running because, as in 1956, he knew the disadvantages faced by Southerners in Democratic presidential politics and feared that a bid for the presidency might destroy his conservative Texas political base. Johnson decided to wait for front-runners Sen. JOHN F. KENNEDY (D-Mass.) and Sen. HUBERT H. HUMPHREY (D-Minn.) to eliminate each other in the primaries before announcing his candidacy. The strategy fell apart in May 1960, when Kennedy eliminated Humphrey in the West Virginia primary. Johnson's second-line strategy was to encourage all candidates to remain in the race in the hope of blocking a first-ballot victory for Kennedy at the Democratic National Convention in July. In a last-minute act of desperation, he and House Speaker Rayburn announced in late June that Congress would recess July 2 and reconvene between the Democratic Convention and the election. This was an act of political blackmail intended to convey the impression that if anyone but Johnson were nominated, the majority leader would stall liberal legislation to the detriment of the candidate. He did not announce his candidacy until July 5.

Johnson's bid failed in part because of his delay in announcing, but his lack of ties to the urban machines, labor unions, and minority groups that formed an essential part of the Democratic party also hurt him. Moreover, Johnson relied on gaining the support of members of his party in the Senate, whom he hoped would influence the selection of delegates. In essence, Johnson ran a traditional insider campaign for the nomination. Kennedy outflanked him by running outside the party organization. He used pollsters and carefully selected state primaries in which to run. The senators on whom Johnson relied had less influence on the selection of delegates than Johnson had expected.

Kennedy won the nomination on the first ballot with 806 votes to 409 for Johnson. Kennedy surprised many observers (and disappointed many liberals) by selecting Johnson as his vice presidential running mate. Having received only 9½ delegate votes from the South, the senator from Massachusetts selected the majority leader to strengthen the ticket in that region. In addition, Kennedy had been a lightweight in the Senate; Johnson was the heaviest of heavyweights. The Texan was a perfect ticket-balancer. Why Johnson decided to accept the candidacy for an almost powerless office remains something of a question, but several considerations seem to have moved him in that direction. For one thing, Johnson had been the most important figure in his party for eight years. If Kennedy won and Johnson remained as majority leader, Johnson's job would be to carry water for the administration. The vice presidency, on the other hand, would free him from his Texas constituency, thus enabling him to establish himself as a national figure, and thereby position him for a subsequent run for the White House. Moreover, if Kennedy lost, Johnson remained in the Senate and a leader of his party. Whatever his reasons for accepting the nomination, Johnson's presence on the ticked played an important role in Kennedy's narrow victory over Vice President RICHARD M. NIXON.

While vice president, Johnson served as chairman of the National Aeronautics and Space Council

and of the President's Committee on Equal Opportunity. Nevertheless, Johnson was excluded from the inner circle of the Kennedy administration and exercised little real influence. Most of his responsibilities involved goodwill foreign travel and ceremonial occasions. Accustomed to wielding power, he hated being vice president.

Immediately after Kennedy was assassinated on November 22, 1963, Johnson assumed the presidency with a keen sense of the requirements of the moment and a sure grasp of the legislative process. However, he inherited an administration of strangers, Ivy Leaguers who had adored Kennedy and condescended to Johnson, and now they resented him for sitting in Kennedy's chair. For his part, Johnson both admired and resented the Ivy League "intellectuals" he inherited from Kennedy, and he took great pleasure in humiliating them.

For all the suspicion with which liberals regarded Johnson, he was, on most domestic issues, more liberal than Kennedy. In his first State of the Union message, delivered just two months after the assassination, he declared an unconditional war on poverty. The theme of the speech was "let us continue," but he expanded Kennedy's modest programs and then proceeded to ram them through Congress. In the spring of 1964, Johnson gave a speech at the University of Michigan in which he called for a legislative program that would lead to a "Great Society." His first great achievement was passage of the Civil Rights Act of 1964. That was followed by the Economic Opportunity Act of 1964.

In November 1964, with Humphrey as his running mate, Johnson overwhelmed his conservative Republican adversary, Sen. BARRY M. GOLDWATER (R-Ariz.), with 61 percent of the popular vote. Taking the election as a mandate, Johnson demonstrated his mastery of the process by pushing through Congress a legislative agenda unequaled except by Franklin Roosevelt. In 1965 alone, Congress passed the Appalachian Regional Development Act, the Housing and Urban Development Act, Medicare, federal aid to elementary and secondary schools, the Higher Education Act, and the Voting Rights Act. After that, he added legislation to increase benefits and enlarge coverage of Social Security, to expand federal activity in the field of public health, and to create a department of transportation. The Great Society also included the Land and Water Conservation Act (1964), the National Wilderness Preservation Act (1964), the Truth in Packaging Act (1966), and the Truth in Lending Act (1968).

In spite of his achievements enacting his domestic policy, Great Society legislation did not always accomplish its purpose. Some on both the left and right questioned the approach of relying on centralized federal programs to address social problems. The Vietnam War, however, proved to be Johnson's political downfall. After the Rolling Thunder bombing in 1965, the American presence steadily escalated until well over half a million American troops were in Vietnam. As progress proved difficult and casualties mounted, the war became increasingly unpopular. Sen. EUGENE MCCARTHY (D-Minn.), running against the war, came close to defeating Johnson in the New Hampshire primary in 1968. In a national television broadcast on March 31, 1968, Johnson announced that he would not seek reelection.

Johnson retired from public life in January 1969 and set about writing his memoirs and supervising the establishment of the Johnson Library at the University of Texas in Austin. He died of a heart attack in Stonewall, Tex., on January 22, 1973.

—MSM

Jones, Howard P(alfrey)
(1899–1973) *ambassador to Indonesia*

Born in Chicago on January 2, 1899, Jones attended the University of Wisconsin for three years, after which he transferred to Columbia University, where he received an Litt.B. in 1921. He then began a career in journalism with the New York branch of the United Press. At the age of 24, Jones became the managing editor of the *Evansville (Ind.) Press*. A few years later, he was editor-in-chief of a chain of nine newspapers in Michigan. He did graduate work in public affairs at the University of Michigan from 1925 to 1927 and at Columbia from 1929 to 1930.

From 1933 to 1939, Jones served as executive director of the National Municipal League and editor of its publication. In 1938, after an unsuccessful

bid for a seat in the New York State Assembly, he was appointed to the state's civil service commission. Jones served in the U.S. Army from 1943 to 1947. He served on the staff of the Supreme Headquarters, Allied Expeditionary Forces, and rose to the rank of colonel. After the war, he played an important role in the reconstruction of Germany's financial institutions. He joined the Foreign Service in 1948. From 1949 to 1951, he was deputy director and then director of the Berlin office of the U.S. High Commissioner for Germany. In 1952, he was assigned to the Far East as counselor of embassy in Taipei, Taiwan (Formosa). Two years later, Jones became director of the U.S. operations mission to the Republic of Indonesia. As deputy assistant secretary of state for Far Eastern economic affairs from 1955 to 1958, he urged more technical assistance and private investment in Southeast Asia to prevent communist expansion.

Jones was named ambassador to Indonesia in January 1958, replacing JOHN M. ALLISON, who had been removed because he disagreed with the administration's policy toward President Achmed Sukarno. Under Sukarno, the Indonesian government seized a number of Dutch companies, embraced "nonalignment," and accepted increasing amounts of aid from the Soviet Union. Although U.S. policy towards Indonesia remained officially neutral, officials in the State Department had criticized Sukarno's policy of "guided democracy" and his increasing ties to the Soviet Union. In addition, the United States funneled covert aid to a rebel group attempting to overthrow Sukarno.

Shortly after arriving in Indonesia, Jones issued a statement that the United States had no intention of interfering in Indonesia's internal affairs. When an American pilot was shot down and captured after flying a mission for the rebels, Jones issued an official expression of regret "that a private American citizen has been involved as a paid soldier of fortune serving with the rebel forces." Soon after this, the administration cut off support for the rebels.

Jones recommended reaching an accommodation with Sukarno. After the Indonesian government defeated the rebels, Sukarno ended anti-American demonstrations. The United States reciprocated by initiating military and economic aid to Indonesia to counter the aid given by the Soviet Union.

Jones continued as ambassador to Indonesia after the Kennedy administration took office in 1961. At that time, tension was mounting between Indonesia and the Netherlands over the disputed territory of West Irian (the western half of the island of New Guinea). By late 1961, Sukarno threatened to use force to exert his country's control over the area. Jones played a central role in avoiding a war and persuading the Dutch and Indonesians to negotiate. In 1962, the two nations agreed to a resolution of the conflict; after a period of administration by the United Nations, Indonesia would assume control of the territory. Jones also took part in negotiations resulting in an agreement in 1963 between the Indonesian government and foreign oil companies that led to the nationalization of the oil industry with compensation to the foreign companies.

During the mid-1960s, relations between the United States and Indonesia became increasingly strained. Sukarno turned to his country's communist party for support. Jones believed that Sukarno was more a nationalist, but President LYNDON JOHNSON regarded Sukarno, who had established closer ties with Communist China and sent agents to destabilize Malaysia, as a communist threat. After Sukarno withdrew his country from the United Nations in 1965, Jones resigned in despair.

He accepted the chancellorship of the East-West Center, a cooperative organization with the University of Hawaii for the furtherance of understanding between the United States and the Far East. In 1971, Jones published *Indonesia: The Possible Dream*, in which he recounted his diplomatic career. He died in Stanford, Calif., on September 18, 1973.

—MSM

Judd, Walter H(enry)

(1898–1994) *U.S. congressman*

Born in Rising City, Neb., on September 25, 1898, Judd attended public schools and enrolled at the University of Nebraska. His college career was interrupted when he enlisted in the U.S. Army in 1918 as a private. Discharged in 1919 as a second lieutenant, he returned to school and earned his B.A. (1920) and M.D. (1923) degrees from the University of Nebraska. He was an instructor of zoology at the University of Omaha from 1920 to

1924. In 1925, he went to China as a medical missionary and worked there from 1925 to 1931. He did a fellowship in surgery at the Mayo Foundation from 1932 to 1934, after which he returned to his missionary work in China from 1934 to 1938. Judd returned to the U.S. after the Japanese takeover of his hospital in 1938. For the next two years, he toured the Midwest warning of Japanese aggression and calling for U.S. support of China. Discouraged by the widespread isolationist mood in this period, however, he settled down to a medical practice in Minneapolis in 1941. After Pearl Harbor, Judd's views became popular, and in 1942 he won a seat in the U.S. House of Representatives, defeating Oscar Youngdahl, the isolationist incumbent, in the Republican primary and two opponents in the general election.

During the postwar period, Judd emerged as an influential member of the House on foreign policy. Unlike many midwestern Republicans, he supported economic relief and development programs to help stabilize European countries after the war. He also emerged as a leader of the China bloc in Congress. An outspoken critic of the Truman administration's hands-off policy in the Chinese civil war, he continually pressed for support for Chiang Kai-shek (Jiang Jieshi). Judd blamed the State Department for Chiang's defeat in 1949; after 1950 he began to suggest that the loss was due to communist influence in the government.

Judd became a leading voice for the "China Lobby," a powerful pressure group composed of officials from the Nationalist embassy in Washington, paid propaganda agents, and a large number of American anticommunist business people, journalists, union leaders, and policy groups, who zealously promoted Chiang's cause in the United States. He also served as an adviser to the lobby's two main policy groups, the American China Policy Association and the China Emergency Committee, both of which worked closely with the congressional China bloc in the closing years of the Truman administration.

During the Eisenhower administration, the congressman continued to press for a hard-line policy on Communist China. In the summer of 1953, Judd, who chaired the Foreign Relations Committee's Subcommittee on Far Eastern Affairs, introduced a resolution opposing the admission of

Communist China to the United Nations (UN). The congressman believed that it would be "plain hypocrisy" to admit a regime "which brazenly went to war with the UN itself." More important, he argued, admission would have increased the prestige of the enemies of the United States and the UN. The House unanimously adopted the resolution in July.

In the fall of 1953, Judd and other leaders of the China Lobby formed the Committee for One Million against the Admission of Communist China to the UN. With the blessings of Eisenhower and the backing of the American Legion, the American Federation of Labor, and the General Federation of Women's Clubs, the committee collected the million signatures in just nine months.

Judd reacted vigorously to the Communist Chinese capture of two American flyers in 1954 and the resumption of hostilities between Nationalists and Communists in 1955. He objected to Eisenhower's call for a cease-fire between the two belligerents. In his opinion, such a move would have neutralized the Nationalist Chinese instead of permitting them to remain a threat to the mainland's flank and prevent communist expansion into Southeast Asia. He also urged Eisenhower not to permit relatives to visit the downed flyers and thus draw attention away from the conflict.

Shortly thereafter Judd helped reconstitute the Committee for One Million as the Committee of One Million against the Admission of Communist China to the UN. The organization then launched a broad campaign to rally public opinion against not only admission of China to the UN but also diplomatic recognition or trade relations with the Communist Chinese. In 1957, the committee organized a nationwide postcard mailing that helped kill proposed Senate hearings on trade with mainland China. In 1959, it issued a rebuttal to the Colon Report, a widely publicized private study urging closer U.S.-China relations.

Judd delivered the keynote address at the Republican National Convention in 1960. During the campaign, the committee of One Million supported the congressman as a possible secretary of state, but the effort died with JOHN F. KENNEDY's election.

During the Kennedy administration, Judd supported the president on several important foreign policy measures, including the Trade Expansion Act of 1962, but he opposed such programs as Medicare. Although he described himself as a "progressive conservative," Judd became associated with the Far Right during the early-1960s. He participated in the Christian Anti-Communist Crusade but was critical of the John Birch Society. In 1962, Judd narrowly lost his bid for an 11th term. Upon leaving Congress, he became a contributing editor to *Reader's Digest* in 1963, a position he held until his retirement in 1976. He continued to speak frequently on issues he engaged as a member of Congress and was a daily radio commentator on international relations for "Washington Report," sponsored by the American Security Council, from 1964 to 1969. Perhaps above all, Judd continued to oppose recognition of Communist China, even after President RICHARD M. NIXON initiated closer ties with the mainland in the early 1970s. In 1971, he bitterly assailed the decision by the United Nations General Assembly to admit mainland China as a member and to expel Taiwan. He held his peace, however, when Nixon visited China in February 1972. Judd resided in Mitchellville, Md., until his death there on February 13, 1994.

—MSM

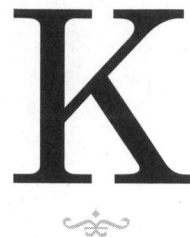

K

Keating, Kenneth B(arnard)
(1900–1975) *U.S. congressman and senator*

Born in Lima, N.Y., on May 18, 1900, Keating graduated from Genesee Wesleyan Seminary in 1915 and from the University of Rochester in 1919. Keating taught Latin in a high school for a year and then entered Harvard Law School. After earning his LL.B. from that institution in 1923 and gaining admission to the bar the same year, he established a successful law practice in Rochester. He had served as a sergeant in the U.S. Army during World War I and was commissioned a major in the army in 1942. From 1943 to 1946, he served in the China-Burma-India theater of operations and was promoted to full colonel in 1944. Keating returned to Rochester and won election to the U.S. House of Representatives in 1946 as a moderate Republican. He won reelection to the House five times before winning a seat in the Senate.

In the House, Keating established a record as a strong anticommunist and a supporter of many social welfare proposals and civil rights measures. He sponsored a bill in 1956 to limit judicial appeals by aliens sentenced to deportation. Two years later, he introduced a bill that would have given the president authority to deny passports to communists and others deemed dangerous to national security. In 1955, he introduced bills that would have granted 18-year-olds the right to vote and given the president the line-item veto (the power to veto specific items in appropriations bills). Keating also led efforts in the House to reform the immigration quota system. In 1956, he cosponsored a successful bill that limited bank mergers.

A consistent and strong supporter of civil rights, Keating defended the Supreme Court's ruling in the school desegregation cases at a time when many of his colleagues declined to take a stand. As a member of the Judiciary Committee, Keating played an important role in gaining passage of the Civil Rights Act of 1957, which established the Civil Rights Commission, created a Civil Rights Division in the Justice Department, and granted the government authority to seek injunctions against deprivation of voting rights.

An ardent supporter of the state of Israel, Keating opposed the Eisenhower administration's decision not to sell arms to Israel in 1956. He headed a committee of five that represented 50 Republican members of Congress who united in an unsuccessful attempt to exert pressure on the administration to reverse its decision.

Keating ran for a seat in the U.S. Senate in 1958 and defeated FRANK HOGAN, the district attorney of Manhattan. Before actually taking his seat, he joined an unsuccessful attempt by liberal Republicans in the Senate to unseat the party's conservative leaders, STYLES BRIDGES (R-N.H.) and EVERETT DIRKSEN (R-Ill.). In the Senate, Keating continued his strong support of civil rights. He played an important role in mustering support from moderate and conservative Republicans for the Voting Rights Act of 1960. During the course of that legislation, he unsuccessfully attempted to strengthen the bill by adding an amendment that would have provided technical assistance to areas desegregating their schools. In addition, he sponsored legislation attempting to deal with segregationist violence in the South.

In other matters, he introduced and fought for the bill that became the Twenty-third Amendment to the Constitution, which granted voters in the District of Columbia the right to vote in presidential elections and gave the capital as many votes in the electoral college as a state with the same population. Keating also supported legislation that attempted to control organized crime. He joined four other Republican senators voting with the Democratic majority in an unsuccessful attempt to override Eisenhower's veto of a bill to provide aid to depressed areas.

Keating and seven other Republican senators proposed a voluntary federal-state health insurance program for all Americans over the age of 65. Under the plan, the states would have contracted with private firms for the coverage and subscribers would have made payments based on income; federal and state governments would have shared the remaining costs. This proposal went further than the administration's plan, which limited aid to single elderly persons with adjusted gross incomes of up to $2,500 a year and married couples with incomes of up to $3,800. The plan finally adopted in August contained most of the features of Keating's proposal but required a means test and permitted each state to determine the type and extent of medical coverage provided.

Keating gained national attention in 1962, when he warned that the Soviet Union was building intercontinental ballistic missiles in Cuba. From the end of August through early October, he gave, by his own count, over 25 speeches on the subject, in which he criticized the Kennedy administration for failing to take action. President JOHN F. KENNEDY rejected the charge and demanded that Keating reveal his sources. After the U-2 overflights confirmed the presence of Soviet missiles and Kennedy announced the "quarantine" of Cuba, Keating supported the president's action.

Keating lost his bid for reelection in 1964 to ROBERT F. KENNEDY. His campaign suffered from the poor showing by the party's presidential nominee, BARRY GOLDWATER, in New York and, on the other hand, from Keating's refusal to support his own party's nominee. After his defeat, Keating

joined a leading New York law firm, Royall, Keogel & Rogers. He won election as associate judge of the New York State Court of Appeals in 1965 and served there until President RICHARD M. NIXON appointed him ambassador to India in 1969. Keating held that post until 1972, when he resigned to return to the United States and campaign for Nixon's reelection. Nixon appointed him ambassador to Israel in August 1973, and he served in that position until his death in New York City on May 5, 1975.

—MSM

Kefauver, C(arey) Estes
(1903–1963) *U.S. senator; chairman, Judiciary Committee, Subcommittee on Antitrust and Monopoly*

The scion of a socially prominent Tennessee family, Estes Kefauver was born in Madisonville, Tenn., on July 26, 1903. He attended the University of Tennessee, where he excelled in athletics, edited the campus newspaper, served as president of the student body, and graduated in 1924. After earning a law degree from Yale University in 1927, he returned to Tennessee and, for the next 12 years, practiced law in Chattanooga. He served as president of the Chattanooga Jaycees and helped organize the Volunteers, a political reform group. Kefauver ran unsuccessfully for the state senate in 1938. The following year, Gov. Prentice Cooper appointed him commissioner of finance and taxation. In a special election for a vacant House seat in the summer of 1939, he won the Democratic primary with organizational backing and defeated his isolationist Republican opponent in the general election.

In his nine-year career in the House, Kefauver established a generally liberal, pro-labor voting record unusual for a southern member of Congress. He stood out as a strong proponent of public power and a defender of the Tennessee Valley Authority (TVA), an advocate of internal congressional reform, and a critic of monopoly power. Most strikingly, however, Kefauver defected from the southern consensus on civil rights for African Americans. In 1942, he spoke on the floor in support of a bill that would have abolished the poll tax as a prerequisite to voting. This prompted the outspoken white supremacist,

John Rankin (D-Miss.), to rise on the floor of the House, point a finger at his colleague from Tennessee, and say, "Shame on you, Estes Kefauver."

Kefauver ran for the U.S. Senate in 1948. A poor speaker, he stumbled over words and spoke in sentences punctuated with awkward pauses. He also had a penchant for verbal gaffes. In addition, he had to face two candidates in the Democratic primary, one of whom, Tom Stewart, was the incumbent and the other had the support of the powerful statewide political machine headed by Edward Hull Crump, the mayor of Memphis. Kefauver's campaign emphasized personal contact with voters, and, with the two more conservative candidates vying for the same votes, he managed to win the primary. Kefauver went on to defeat his Republican opponent, B. Carroll Reece, in the general election.

In the Senate, Kefauver's generally liberal voting record and his moderation on civil rights marked him as a maverick among southern senators. As he had in the House, Kefauver consistently backed the Truman administration's foreign policy. The most significant legislative accomplishment of his early career was the Kefauver-Celler Act of 1950, which attempted to close a loophole in the Clayton Anti-Trust Act of 1914 by prohibiting one firm from acquiring the assets of another "if the effect would be substantially to lessen competition or to create monopoly."

Kefauver catapulted to national attention in 1950–51 with his sensational investigation of organized crime. The Kefauver committee conducted hearings in cities around the country and received extensive press coverage. The hearings established the pervasive influence of organized crime and its links to Democratic political machines. The climax of the investigation came with the hearings in New York, where a parade of gangsters, who very much looked and talked the part, testified before the committee. The dramatic hearings were carried live on national television and made Kefauver a national figure.

The hearings on organized crime thrust Kefauver to the forefront of Democratic politics but at the same time earned him the enmity of the leadership of his own party, because the hearings had sullied the reputations of many Democratic mayors. Capitalizing on his new national prominence

and the widespread dissatisfaction with the Truman administration, Kefauver sought the Democratic nomination in 1952. Few gave him any chance of defeating President Truman, but Kefauver won a stunning upset in the New Hampshire primary, defeating the sitting president by 3,873 votes. Two weeks later, Truman announced that he would not run for reelection. Kefauver's campaign focused on bringing the candidate into personal contact with as many voters as possible. He traveled from town to town, shaking hands with countless people. Although he refrained from directly attacking the Truman administration, his strongest talking point was his ability to clean up corruption in government. Kefauver won most of the subsequent primaries, losing only in Florida to Sen. RICHARD RUSSELL of Georgia and in the District of Columbia to AVERELL HARRIMAN, and went into the convention in July with a majority of the popular votes cast in the primaries and a plurality of delegates.

At the convention in Chicago, Kefauver encountered strong opposition from the party's leadership. His investigation of organized crime, which had caused problems for some Democratic machines, alienated party professionals and urban bosses. Largely because of Kefauver's position on civil rights, all southern delegations except Tennessee's opposed his candidacy. Moreover, Truman remained hostile to him. Truman and other party leaders threw their support to the governor of Illinois, ADLAI STEVENSON. Kefauver led on the first two ballots, but Stevenson won on the third. The circumstances of his defeat convinced Kefauver and many of his followers that the will of the people had been thwarted and that the party bosses had stolen the nomination from him.

Kefauver frequently opposed the new Eisenhower administration. In April 1953, for example, he participated in an unsuccessful filibuster by liberals to block a bill, backed by the administration, to return offshore oil deposits to the states. Nevertheless, he supported the administration's efforts to defeat the Bricker amendment, which would have limited the president's power to enter into treaties.

An outspoken critic of Sen. JOSEPH MCCARTHY (R-Wis.), Kefauver also resisted Democratic efforts to outdo the anticommunism of the Republican right. A group of liberal Democrats sponsored a bill that became the Communist Control Act of 1954, which included provisions outlawing the Communist Party and providing for detention of subversives in time of emergency. It passed the Senate by a vote of 81-1, with Kefauver casting the lone dissenting vote. Speaking against the bill, he argued that "a grievous wrong inflicted on us by the Republicans does not justify our inflicting an even greater wrong upon the protections given our people by the Bill of Rights."

Many believed that Kefauver's independent positions, particularly on civil rights, jeopardized his chances for reelection in 1954. His conservative challenger in the Democratic primary, Rep. Pat Sutton (D-Tenn.), called him a "coddler" of communists, a "left winger," and an integrationist. Sutton also attacked Kefauver's support for foreign aid and his opposition to the House Un-American Activities Committee. Although political observers predicted a close race, Kefauver overwhelmed Sutton in the primary and went on to defeat his Republican opponent easily in the general election.

After winning reelection, Kefauver became one of the leaders of the Democratic attack on the controversial Dixon-Yates contract. When the TVA proposed building a new steam plant at Fulton, Tenn., to supply power to the city of Memphis because the consumption of TVA power by the Atomic Energy Commission's (AEC) installations at Paduca would leave Memphis facing a shortage of electricity within four years, Eisenhower, who preferred private development of power, could not see the justification for the federal government to pay for a plant to supply power to a particular city. He ordered JOSEPH DODGE, director of the Bureau of the Budget, and LEWIS L. STRAUSS, chairman of the AEC, to explore the possibility of having private industry build the plant. EDGAR H. DIXON, president of Middle South Utilities, and EUGENE YATES, chairman of the board of the Southern Company, organized the Mississippi Valley Generating Company to build a plant that would supply power to the TVA to replace the power the TVA sold the AEC. The Dixon Yates proposal was considered acceptable by the AEC, TVA, and the Bureau of the Budget, and, upon the recommendation of the Bureau of the Budget, Eisenhower approved it.

Democratic senators lost no time denouncing the agreement as an attempt to undermine the TVA. Kefauver repeatedly spoke against what he characterized as the secrecy and conflict of interest surrounding the plan's inception, the alleged windfall for its private beneficiaries, and the harm he believed the plan would do to public power. He headed a special panel of the Judiciary Committee's Antitrust and Monopoly Subcommittee chosen to investigate the affair. During those hearings, Kefauver played a key role in the questioning of the director of the Bureau of the Budget that brought to light an apparent conflict of interest. A consultant to the Bureau of the Budget had simultaneously advised the Dixon-Yates company. Later that month, after the city of Memphis decided to build its own plant, Eisenhower cancelled the Dixon-Yates contract.

Kefauver made a second run for the presidency in 1956. As in 1952, political pundits gave him little chance. Most assumed that Stevenson would again be the Democratic nominee. Nevertheless, Kefauver won again in New Hampshire and then pulled a major upset over Stevenson in Minnesota. With the support of the Democratic establishment, Stevenson edged past Kefauver in the Florida primary. When Stevenson defeated him in California, effectively ending Kefauver's hopes, the Tennessean withdrew from the race and endorsed Stevenson.

At the Democratic convention in August, Stevenson unexpectedly threw the choice of a vice presidential running mate to the convention at large. Kefauver's supporters organized hastily on his behalf, and he won a dramatic victory over Sen. JOHN KENNEDY (D-Mass.). During the race that fall, Kefauver campaigned vigorously in the regions of his greatest popularity: the Middle West and the West. In his characteristic populist rhetoric, he attacked the Eisenhower administration for being dominated by special interests and "readers of the *Wall Street Journal*." He repeatedly denounced the farm policies of Secretary of Agriculture EZRA TAFT BENSON, whose department, he believed, injured the family farmer to favor "the food processors and meat packers and grain traders and big bankers and miscellaneous other millionaires." However, the Stevenson-Kefauver ticket could not overcome the great popularity of President Eisenhower and the widespread satisfaction with the conditions of peace and prosperity. The president won reelection in a landslide victory.

His defeat in 1956 effectively ended Kefauver's presidential ambitions. Thereafter, he devoted himself to his Senate duties and made his mark as Congress's most dedicated foe of monopoly in a generation. In the six years following his ascendancy to the chairmanship of the Antitrust and Monopoly Subcommittee in 1957, he conducted a series of well-publicized investigations into economic concentration. Kefauver focused on the problem of "administered prices," that is, prices of major products set artificially high, insensitive to market fluctuations. The subcommittee's hearings concerning administered prices in the steel, automobile, bread, drug, and electrical equipment industries, among others, filled 26 volumes and kept the issue before the public for six years. Kefauver frequently criticized the role of administered prices in inflation. He warned that growing corporate concentration hurt consumers and small businessmen and that the loss of economic freedom on their part ultimately could lead to the loss of political freedom.

Kefauver's voting record on civil rights questions was generally moderate. He supported attempts by liberals to modify the Senate's filibuster rule. In 1956, he was one of only three southern senators who refused to sign the "Southern Manifesto" denouncing the Supreme Court's decision striking down segregated public schools. He voted for the Civil Rights Act of 1957. Yet in the legislative struggle over the measure, Kefauver helped win Senate passage of the controversial jury trial amendment, mandating that individuals accused of violating a federal court injunction not to interfere with the voting rights of African Americans would be given a trial by jury. Opponents of the amendment charged that it intended to weaken federal protection of black voting rights, but Kefauver maintained that "any miscarriage of justice will not be remedied by eliminating the right to trial by jury." The final version of the bill permitted judges to try minor violations of the law but assured defendants another trial, by jury, if severe penalties were imposed. In spite of his positions on civil rights, which put him at odds with his southern colleagues in the Senate and with many of his constituents, Kefauver later admitted that he found it difficult to adjust to the

idea of integration. Moreover, his record on civil rights grew more conservative as he approached his bid for reelection in 1960. In 1959 he criticized the Civil Rights Commission's recommendations for specific legislation to ensure equal rights in voting, education, and housing. The following year, he voted with the southern bloc on a variety of amendments to weaken the Civil Rights Act of 1960, but he backed the final bill.

As in 1954, Kefauver entered his battle for reelection amid pessimistic speculation and again surprised observers with an overwhelming victory in the Democratic primary. His most significant achievement during the Kennedy administration was the passage of the Kefauver-Harris Drug Control Act (1962), which greatly strengthened federal regulations to ensure that drugs be proven safe and effective before being marketed. Due in large part to opposition from the Kennedy administration, however, the final version of the measure did not include provisions against excessive pricing of prescription drugs, which Kefauver had placed in the original bill. Another milestone was the passage of the Twenty-fourth Amendment outlawing the poll tax. A career-long opponent of the poll tax, Kefauver initiated the measure and guided it through the Senate. The requisite number of states ratified the amendment after his death. Kefauver collapsed on the floor of the Senate and died in Bethesda, Md., of an aortic aneurysm on August 10, 1963.

—MSM

Kennan, George F(rost)
(1904–2005) *foreign policy critic*

The descendant of a pre-Revolutionary Scotch-Irish family, Kennan was born in Milwaukee on February 16, 1904. He attended Saint John's Military Academy, graduated from Princeton University in 1925, and entered the Foreign Service the following year. From 1927 to 1931, he served in Central and Eastern Europe. Kennan was a member of the first American embassy to the USSR in 1933 and served there as third secretary until 1936. The young diplomat was then stationed in Prague and Berlin, where he remained until World War II began. From December 1941 to May 1942, he was interned by the Nazis. During the early years of the war, Kennan served at the American embassy in Portugal and in 1943 joined the European Advisory Commission in London, where he worked on plans for postwar Germany.

In 1944, Kennan was again posted to the USSR. While serving in Moscow, he sent Washington dispatches predicting that the Russians would seek military, economic, and ideological expansion in Western Europe and urged the United States to develop a firm policy to counteract it. As relations with the Soviets deteriorated, Kennan sent his famous "Long Telegram" to Washington. It explained to American policy makers, baffled by the course of Soviet policy, the origins of that policy, and it proposed a course of action. According to Kennan, Soviet foreign policy derived from internal factors, such as the "traditional and instinctive Russian sense of insecurity" and Marxist dogma, which provided the "justification for their instinctive fear of [the] outside world, for the dictatorship without which they did not know how to rule, . . . for sacrifices they felt bound to demand." Thus, he concluded, Soviet power was "impervious to the logic of reason" but "highly sensitive to the logic of force." As a result of Kennan's work, Secretary of State George C. Marshall appointed him head of the State Department's policy planning staff in 1947. That year he wrote an article for *Foreign Affairs* magazine, under the name of Mr. X, that expanded the case made in his Long Telegram and served as an outline for the Truman administration's Soviet policy. "Soviet pressure against the free institutions of the Western world," he wrote, could "be contained by the adroit and vigorous application of counterforce." That force, he elaborated, should primarily take the form of diplomatic and economic pressure as well as covert action. In his memoirs, Kennan wrote that he did not mean containment by military means but acknowledged that the language he used in the article "was at best ambiguous and lent itself to misinterpretation." When DEAN ACHESON became secretary of state in 1949, he appointed Kennan counselor of the department. However, the two quickly broke over the implementation of containment, and in 1955, Kennan took a leave of absence to carry on research at the Institute of Advanced Study in Princeton.

Kennan was appointed ambassador to the Soviet Union in the fall of 1951. His stay in Moscow was short; the Soviets declared him persona non grata for his statements criticizing the Russian treatment of Western diplomats. Kennan returned to the United States in October 1952 during the presidential campaign in which the Republican Party condemned containment as "negative, futile, and immoral." Instead, the Republicans, most prominently JOHN FOSTER DULLES, promised to extend the hope of liberation to Eastern Europe. In January 1953, while awaiting reassignment, Kennan delivered a speech in which he warned against any "government action that was designed to interfere with the internal affairs of another country" and spoke out in favor of containment rather than liberation. Kennan's public dissent from the policy of the incoming administration added to Dulles's discomfort at having the author of containment in a Republican administration. The new secretary of state took advantage of a rule requiring the reassignment of chiefs of missions within 90 days to force Kennan's retirement. Kennan then returned to the Institute at Princeton to write Russian history.

During the 1950s, Kennan was one of the foremost critics of the Eisenhower administration. Pointing out that communist expansion was ideological and economic, not military, he opposed reliance on military alliances such as the North Atlantic Treaty Organization. He also objected to Dulles's defining the struggle against the USSR in terms of a moral crusade.

At the end of 1957, Kennan delivered a series of lectures over the British Broadcasting Corp. that called for a reassessment of American policy toward the USSR. He suggested that, since Stalin's death in 1953, a liberalizing trend had appeared in Russia that made the Kremlin leaders more inclined to diplomatic negotiation than military conquest. Kennan dismissed the administration's idea of giving Germany nuclear arms to prevent Russian expansion. Instead, he called for a unified, disarmed, and neutral Germany and recommended that the United States use the threat of that possibility to negotiate with the Russians on the neutralization of Central and Eastern Europe. The Soviet Union and the United States could then withdraw or "disengage" their forces from the area.

Kennan's call for disengagement generated a debate among foreign policy officials. Dean Acheson and Henry Kissinger were among his most forceful critics. Acheson wrote that Kennan "has never, in my judgment, grasped the realities of power relationships, but takes a rather mystical attitude toward them." Disengagement, the former secretary of state claimed, would be the "new isolationism." Professor Kissinger argued that the Russians should still be considered a military threat to Western Europe and American troops should remain there as a major deterrent. Walter Lippmann, who had advocated disengagement in the late-1940s, praised Kennan's change of position.

In 1959, Kennan questioned the Eisenhower administration's reliance on nuclear weapons of indiscriminate mass destruction for America's defense. He proposed, instead, that the United States and Russia abolish them and that this country rely on conventional forces to defend itself.

During the Kennedy administration, Kennan served as ambassador to Yugoslavia. Long an advocate of policies designed to undermine the unity of the Soviet bloc, Kennan sought to strengthen Yugoslavia's ties to the West. When Congress rejected his appeals and passed legislation restricting trade with Yugoslavia, Kennan resigned his ambassadorship in May 1963. Two months later, he returned to the Institute for Advanced Study, where he continued to analyze and write about foreign policy until the end of his life. Kennan once again entered the public debate over foreign policy in the mid-1960s as a critic of American policy in Vietnam. He maintained that Vietnam was not vital to American strategic or diplomatic interests and that escalation of the war would inhibit the possibility of a negotiated settlement. In addition, he argued that the war would lead to a rapprochement between the Soviet Union and China. When, in 1966, Sen. J. William Fulbright (D-Ark.) held nationally televised hearings of the Senate Foreign Relations Committee on the war, he asked Kennan to testify. For all his opposition to the war in Vietnam, Kennan was scathingly critical of the student left of the 1960s, both for its methods of protest and its failure to present a coherent program.

Kennan was a leading expert on Russian history as well as an analyst of foreign policy. An elegant and prolific writer, Kennan produced 17 books. He won a Pulitzer Prize in 1956 for *Russia Leaves the War*. Its sequel, *The Decision to Intervene* (1957), also received a warm reception from critics. *American Diplomacy: 1900–1951* (1952), based on a series of lectures he gave at the University of Chicago in 1951, briefly and gracefully presented a realist critique of American foreign policy. The book found a large popular audience, and generations of college students cut their teeth on it. Kennan won a second Pulitzer Prize for *Memoirs: 1925–1950*, published in 1967; the second volume of his memoirs came out in 1972. Over the next three decades, he continued to produce essays, articles, and books. He published a volume of personal reflections, *Around the Cragged Hill*, in 1993. He wrote an opinion piece for the *New York Times* in 1997 criticizing the Clinton administration's support for the expansion of NATO and warning that such a step "would be the most fateful error of American policy in the entire post–cold war era." As the administration of George W. Bush prepared for a war with Iraq in September 2002, Kennan gave an interview in which he criticized that policy. Kennan died at home in Princeton, N.J., on March 17, 2005.

—MSM

Kennedy, John F(itzgerald)
(1917–1963) *U.S. senator*

The son of Joseph P. Kennedy, a millionaire stock market speculator and investment banker, John Kennedy was born in Brookline, Mass., on May 29, 1917. His maternal grandfather had been mayor of Boston, and his paternal grandfather had served in the Massachusetts State Senate. Kennedy graduated from Choate School and in 1935 began attending Princeton. He switched to Harvard one year later and graduated in 1940 with a degree in political science. While a student, Kennedy spent several summers in England, where his father was ambassador. Out of this experience, he conceived the topic for his senior thesis, "Appeasement in Europe," which warned against Great Britain's policy of appeasement. In 1940, with the assistance of Arthur Krock, he published the work as *Why England Slept*, and it became a best seller.

President Eisenhower and President-elect John F. Kennedy, December 6, 1960 *(Dwight D. Eisenhower Library and Museum)*

After a brief stint at Stanford business school, Kennedy joined the navy in 1941. In 1943, a Japanese destroyer sunk the PT boat under Kennedy's command. Following the war, he briefly worked as a reporter for International News Services but decided to pursue a political career. In 1946, he won the Democratic primary in Boston's 11th district against the machine candidate. Labeling himself as "fighting conservative," an anticommunist who supported the New Deal, he easily won the general election. He was reelected in 1948 and in 1950.

As a member of the House, Kennedy compiled an undistinguished record. Colleagues regarded him as a playboy and the lightweight son of a wealthy man. Assorted physical ailments, the most serious of which was Addison's disease (an adrenal insufficiency), contributed to his lack of attention to his official duties.

Kennedy usually voted with other Northern liberals in support of Fair Deal legislation. He supported federally funded housing and voted against the Taft-Hartley Act. However, he maintained a more conservative position on foreign policy and the issue of domestic communism. Kennedy created a minor incident in 1949, when he attacked President HARRY S. TRUMAN for what he considered the unnecessary loss of mainland China to the Communists. A year before Sen. JOSEPH R. McCARTHY (R-

Wis.) gave his famous speech in Wheeling, W.Va., Kennedy denounced the advice given by "the Lattimores and the Fairbanks." Owen Lattimore of Johns Hopkins, an expert on the Far East, and John King Fairbanks of Harvard, a leading authority on China, would become two of McCarthy's favorite targets. "What our young men have saved," Kennedy charged, "our diplomats and president have frittered away." In the same speech, he attacked the Yalta Accords and George Marshall. In 1950, he contributed to Rep. RICHARD M. NIXON's (R-Calif.) reelection campaign against Helen Gahagan Douglas. That November, he made a speech in which he praised McCarthy and supported the McCarran Internal Security Act.

In 1952, Kennedy ran for the U.S. Senate seat held by HENRY CABOT LODGE. Very little distinguished the two men on the issues, and the race became a conflict of personalities and campaign styles. Kennedy's campaign exhibited many of the characteristics of his later races. A staff of loyal workers headed by the candidate's family ran a well-financed and carefully planned effort. The Kennedy women gave teas attended by hundreds of women eager to meet the candidate. The candidate's father was able to enlist the support of several Taft Republicans who bitterly resented Lodge's role in persuading DWIGHT EISENHOWER to oppose Sen. ROBERT TAFT (R-Ohio) for the Republican nomination. T. Walter Taylor, a banker from Boston, and Basil Brewer, the publisher of the New Bedford *Standard-Times*, threw their support to Kennedy in an effort to defeat Lodge. Joe Fox, publisher of the isolationist *Boston Post*, also endorsed Kennedy, in his case after receiving a loan of $500,000 from Joseph Kennedy.

John Kennedy nonetheless had problems. Jewish voters distrusted him because of his own views on Israel and his father's opinions about Nazi Germany and reputed anti-Semitism. JOHN McCORMACK (D-Mass.), the majority leader in the House and a popular figure with Jewish voters in the state, helped with that. Kennedy's relationship with Joe McCarthy proved more tricky. McCarthy had both supporters and detractors among voters likely to support Kennedy. The candidate, aided by family money, managed to walk a tightrope on the issue. Joseph Kennedy had contributed money to McCar-

thy, who offered to campaign for Lodge on the condition that he would not attack Kennedy. Lodge, who detested McCarthy, declined the offer. When some of Kennedy's aides urged him to sign an anti-McCarthy manifesto during the campaign, his father objected and furiously charged that the aides were "trying to ruin Jack." Kennedy did not sign the document. In November, Kennedy defeated Lodge by 70,000 votes.

By the time he entered the Senate, Kennedy's health had improved. Cortisone controlled the Addison's disease, and two surgeries improved the condition of his back. In his early years as a senator, he focused primarily on the needs of his section, then in the midst of economic depression. Kennedy introduced several bills to aid Massachusetts's fishing, textile, building, and watch industries through tariff protection and increased federal aid. He also supported higher minimum-wage laws to force southern textile industries to maintain comparable labor costs with their competitors in New England. Despite his support for his section, he backed construction of the Saint Lawrence Seaway, which many in New England opposed because they feared it would reduce the role of the port of Boston. The only senator from New England to vote for the measure, he justified his stand by insisting that Canada was prepared to go on with the project alone. He also maintained that national economic and security interests should take precedence over sectionalism.

By 1954, Kennedy had become disillusioned with McCarthy's investigations, although he muted his criticism. In fact, Kennedy tried to find the middle of the road on issues relating to McCarthy and anticommunism. A member of the Senate Government Operations Committee, chaired by McCarthy, he voted against the witness immunity bill in August 1954 that would have given the Justice Department authority to grant immunity to witnesses testifying before Congress and in court. Critics of the measure claimed that it would have the effect of compelling witnesses to testify or go to jail. On the other hand, Kennedy was a cosponsor of the Communist Control Act of 1954. He was in the hospital for back surgery when the vote to condemn McCarthy came to the floor. Kennedy's aide, Theodore Sorensen, had prepared a speech for Kennedy in which the senator supported censure but only because McCarthy had supported ROY COHN in his confrontation with the army. The speech carefully asserted Kennedy's past support for McCarthy and declined to support censure based on past misconduct. When the Senate voted to condemn McCarthy, Kennedy did not go on record through the parliamentary device of "pairing," when two members on opposite sides of an issue agree not to vote on the matter. He was the only Democrat not to vote for condemnation or to pair with the majority.

In April 1954, while the besieged French garrison at Dien Bien Phu desperately tried to hold off the Viet Minh, Kennedy gave a speech in the Senate criticizing French colonialism and calling on the French to grant independence to the Associated States. He argued strongly against giving American military aid to the French. At the same time, he attacked the "New Look" defense policy for failing to provide the means to act in such situations.

Kennedy was absent from the Senate from November 1954 until May 1955 while recuperating from several spinal operations. During that period, he worked on a book, *Profiles In Courage*. Written largely by his staff, in particular Sorensen, the book presented seven studies of politicians who demonstrated fidelity to political principle in difficult circumstances. Published in early 1956, the book won a Pulitzer Prize and was a best seller.

In 1956, Kennedy waged a vigorous battle against John McCormack for the leadership of the Democratic Party in Massachusetts. Hoping to control the state delegation to the Democratic National Convention and thus influence the convention's choice for president, McCormack won the state's nonbinding presidential primary in 1956. Kennedy, on the other hand, supported the nomination of ADLAI STEVENSON. The Massachusetts state chairman, William H. Burke, Jr., a McCormack supporter, made a speech hinting that Stevenson backers were communists, to which Kennedy responded by campaigning against Burke's reelection. Kennedy's candidate, John M. Lynch, won the office by a large margin, solidifying Kennedy's leadership of the state party.

Kennedy nominated Stevenson for president at the Democratic National Convention in 1956. When Stevenson threw the vice presidential nomination open to the convention, Kennedy and a few aides organized a spirited campaign for the second place on the ticket. He lost to Sen. ESTES KEFAUVER (D-Tenn.) on the third ballot.

Over the next three years, Kennedy laid the groundwork for a presidential campaign in 1960. He made some 1,000 speeches in all parts of the nation, demonstrated his popularity by winning reelection to the Senate by almost a million votes in 1958, and carefully built a legislative record that would appeal to liberals and moderates in the Democratic Party.

Kennedy adopted a carefully crafted moderate position on civil rights. He voted for the final version of the Eisenhower administration's civil rights bill in 1957 and against eliminating the bill's most far-reaching provision, Title III, which authorized the attorney general to seek injunctions for a variety of violations of civil rights. Ultimately, southerners managed to remove Title III from the final bill. On the other hand, Kennedy voted for a successful amendment, backed by southern senators, that gave violators of injunctions enforcing voting rights the right to a jury trial.

Similarly, Kennedy sought to establish a balanced record on labor issues. While not wanting to appear too close to organized labor, he had no intention of alienating that base of support so important to any Democrat's presidential aspirations. The AFL-CIO's Committee on Political Education announced that he had voted "right" on 15 out of 16 important labor issues during the period. From 1957 to 1959, however, he played an active role in the McClellan committee's investigations of improper activities in labor unions, which earned him the opposition of a number of labor leaders. In 1959, Kennedy cosponsored a bill designed to correct some of the most blatant abuses uncovered by the McClellan committee. It also intended to head off calls for more stringent regulation of unions. Kennedy's measure called for unions to make full disclosure of their financial records and to file annual financial reports with the secretary of labor. The bill provided criminal penalties for bribery, extortion, and misappropriation of union funds. To pacify organized labor, it also modified certain provisions in the Taft-Hartley Act. Over Kennedy's opposition, the Senate added a requirement that union officers file an affidavit declaring that they were not communists. The Kennedy-Ives bill passed the Senate, but the House passed the Landrum-Griffin bill, which defined as an unfair labor practice a labor-management contract under which the employer agreed not to do business with another firm, prohibited secondary boycotts, restricted picketing, and expanded federal regulation of internal union affairs. The conference committee essentially adopted the Landrum-Griffin version, which won approval in both houses.

Kennedy took an increasing interest in foreign affairs. In 1957, he edged out Kefauver to win a coveted seat on the Foreign Relations Committee. He was particularly prominent in urging a reorientation of U.S. policies toward underdeveloped nations. Keenly aware of the force of anticolonialism in emerging nations, he published in 1957 an article in *Foreign Affairs* arguing that American leaders underrated the strength of nationalism in Asia and Africa and that the administration lacked a definable Middle Eastern policy.

Kennedy caused a controversy in July 1957, when he brought the Algerian question to the Senate floor and urged that the civil war there be ended with Algerian independence. He offered a resolution proposing that the United States negotiate the conflict. Members of both parties as well as representatives of the Eisenhower administration, which at the time was attempting to bring France within a Western European Union, criticized the speech for antagonizing France.

Kennedy was a cold warrior who saw communist expansion as a major threat to the United States. In 1957, he supported the Eisenhower Doctrine, which gave the president authority to use U.S. troops to protect Middle Eastern nations threatened by communist takeover. In August 1957, he introduced legislation providing funds for "educational materials" to inform the public of the nature of the communist threat. He urged Americans to support increased military expenditures for defense against the Soviet Union. Beginning in 1958, he alleged that a "missile gap" existed between the United States and the USSR and predicted it would grow more serious in the 1960s. He claimed that *Sputnik* and other technological advances gave the USSR the advantage in the world balance of power and warned of a Russian attack that would destroy the world. Kennedy questioned the value of trying to appease the Soviet Union and urged a strong military to prevent a "second Munich."

Kennedy began running for the Democratic nomination in 1960 almost as soon as the election of 1956 was over. He formally announced his candidacy in January 1960. The beneficiary of yet another well organized and lavishly funded campaign, Kennedy defeated Sen. Hubert Humphrey (D-Minn.), the leader of the party's liberal wing, in the West Virginia and Wisconsin primaries, proving that a Roman Catholic could win in heavily Protestant states. He then brushed aside a challenge from Sen. Lyndon Johnson (D-Tex.) at the convention. Kennedy captured the nomination on the first ballot and selected Johnson as his running mate. In the general election, he faced Vice President Richard M. Nixon. Kennedy made his attack on the Eisenhower administration's defense policies a focal point of his campaign. He called for larger defense budgets, an increase in conventional forces, and spending to close the "missile gap." During the campaign, Kennedy and Nixon engaged in the first televised debates between presidential candidates. In the end, Kennedy defeated Nixon in one of the closest popular votes in American history; he had a more comfortable margin of victory in the electoral college.

As president, Kennedy left a meager record in domestic affairs. The slimness of his margin in the popular vote and his own lack of legislative skill limited Kennedy's success in gaining passage of legislation relating to domestic matters. He made proposals for increased federal aid to education, medical care for the elderly, and urban renewal, most of which never got through Congress while he was president. The few measures Congress enacted during his term were not terribly significant. He did achieve legislation to increase the minimum wage, tax cuts, and the Trade Act of 1962.

On one of the most momentous domestic issues confronting his administration, civil rights, Kennedy took a cautious approach, not least because of the narrow margin of his electoral victory and the importance of the South in his coalition. He held off issuing an executive order banning discrimination in housing built with federal funds, which he had promised during the campaign, until after the congressional elections in 1962. Even then, the order was something less than he had promised. Kennedy resisted pressure from Freedom Riders and other activists to use the power of the federal government to end racial segregation and protect black voting rights. He acted reluctantly when Gov. Ross Barnett defied a court order to admit James Meredith to the University of Mississippi. Only after massive demonstrations in Birmingham, Ala., led by MARTIN LUTHER KING, JR., did Kennedy call for civil rights legislation. That legislation remained stalled in Congress at the time of his assassination. Perhaps most significantly, he appointed a number of segregationists to federal judgeships in the South.

In foreign affairs, Kennedy pursued an aggressively anticommunist foreign policy. Not long after assuming the presidency, he approved a disastrous invasion at the Bay of Pigs in an attempt to overthrow Cuba's communist dictator, Fidel Castro. After a harrowing meeting with the Soviet premier, Nikita Khrushchev, in Vienna, Kennedy faced off with Khrushchev over Berlin. The United States and Soviet Union engaged in another showdown when the Soviets placed missiles in Cuba. Kennedy declared a quarantine, and ultimately Khrushchev backed down. Kennedy honored his campaign promise to increase military spending and America's conventional forces. He used that capability to increase the American commitment to South Vietnam.

Kennedy was assassinated on November 22, 1963, in Dallas, Tex. The romantic image of Kennedy that emerged after his death has not withstood the scrutiny of historians.

—MSM

Kennedy, Robert F(rancis)

(1925–1968) *assistant counsel, Senate Permanent Subcommittee on Investigations of the Government Operations Committee; minority counsel; chief counsel, Senate Select Committee on Improper Activities in the Labor or Management Field*

The seventh of nine children of Joseph P. and Rose Fitzgerald Kennedy, Robert F. Kennedy was born in Brookline, Mass., on November 20, 1925, into one of the wealthiest families in the United States. He attended Portsmouth Priory and Milton Academy, from which he graduated in 1943. In his senior year at Milton, he joined the V-12 program, which

trained naval officers. Kennedy reported for duty at Harvard University in March 1944. He was transferred to the campus of Bates College for further training in November of that year. In June 1945, with the war in Europe over, he was transferred back to Harvard for more training. World War II had ended when, through the intercession of his father, Robert received permission to leave his officer training unit in February 1946 and enlisted in the Navy as a seaman aboard a destroyer named for his brother, Joseph Kennedy, Jr., who had been killed in the crash of a navy plane in August 1944. After the navy discharged him in May 1946, Kennedy returned to Harvard, graduated in 1948, and then went on to law school at the University of Virginia. Upon earning his law degree in 1951, he worked for the Department of Justice prosecuting graft and income-tax evasion cases. He resigned in mid-1952 to manage his brother JOHN F. KENNEDY's successful campaign for the U.S. Senate.

In 1953, Kennedy secured, through his father's friendship with Sen. JOSEPH R. McCARTHY (R-Wis.), an appointment as assistant counsel to the Senate Permanent Investigations Subcommittee, of which McCarthy was chairman. Kennedy's badgering tone with witnesses, while perhaps not so abusive as that of McCarthy or the committee's chief counsel, ROY COHN, nevertheless earned him the enmity of many liberals, intellectuals, and civil libertarians. Kennedy agreed with McCarthy about the nature of the communist threat and, at least to a degree, agreed with him with respect to tactics. Cohn and Kennedy, however, soon clashed. The two ambitious and ruthless young men took an immediate dislike to each other. Kennedy had wanted the job that went to Cohn; moreover, several biographers of Kennedy have suggested that he was offended by Cohn's homosexuality. Assigned to investigate Western trade with Communist China, Kennedy's work led to an announcement by McCarthy that he had personally negotiated an agreement with a group of Greek shipowners, who had promised that their vessels would no longer stop at ports in China or the Soviet bloc. Kennedy increasingly took issue with the way Cohn ran the operations of the subcommittee. When Cohn and G. DAVID SCHINE went on a highly publicized and much-ridiculed inspection tour of American embassies in Europe searching for subversives and subversive literature in U.S. Information Agency libraries, Kennedy warned McCarthy that Cohn's behavior would lead to disaster. Kennedy quit the committee's staff.

Kennedy went to work for the Hoover Commission, of which his father was a member. About the time Kennedy resigned in July 1953, the three Democrats on the subcommittee, JOHN MCCLELLAN (D-Ark.), HENRY JACKSON (D-Wash.), and STUART SYMINGTON (D-Mo.), began a boycott of the subcommittee. In January 1954, they agreed to return, and in February hired Kennedy as minority counsel. Kennedy returned to the subcommittee in time to become involved in the dispute between the army and McCarthy that began when Cohn allegedly attempted to obtain preferential treatment for Schine, who had been drafted. The army revealed what it maintained were Cohn's efforts to exert pressure on behalf of Schine, and McCarthy charged that the army was heavily infiltrated by communists.

The subcommittee held televised hearings on the dispute in April, May, and June. Kennedy used his position as minority counsel to go after Cohn, rather than McCarthy. At one point in the hearings, Kennedy fed questions to Sen. Jackson that indirectly attacked Cohn by mocking a grandiose plan, drawn up by Schine, to counter communism around the world through "psychological warfare." A furious Cohn confronted Kennedy, the two engaged in a shouting match, and only the intervention of other aides prevented a fistfight. When the hearings ended on June 17, Kennedy, working with James M. Landis, dean of Harvard Law School, wrote the minority report, which accused McCarthy of "gross misconduct." Later that year, Kennedy compiled evidence for Democrats to use in the debate over a resolution to censure McCarthy. Nevertheless, through it all, Kennedy's personal affection for McCarthy never wavered. When McCarthy died in May 1957, funeral services were held at Saint Matthew's Cathedral in Washington, D.C., in the Senate Chamber, and at Saint Mary's Roman Catholic Church in Appleton, Wis. Robert Kennedy attended all three.

Kennedy became chief counsel when the Democrats regained control of Congress in 1955 and continued to work for the subcommittee until late 1956. His work focused on conflict-of-interest cases involving figures in the Eisenhower administration. One investigation led to the resignation of HAROLD TALBOTT as secretary of the air force. During this period, a reporter, Clark Mollenhoff, brought Kennedy evidence of corruption in the Teamsters Union. Kennedy then began his own investigation, accumulating evidence of Teamsters president DAVE BECK's blatant misuse of funds. His findings led the Senate to create the Select Committee on Improper Activities in the Labor or Management Field in January 1957. Kennedy immediately became the committee's chief counsel.

The investigations of the Senate "rackets committee," as the select committee soon came to be called, uncovered glaring evidence of dishonesty and extortion in the Teamsters Union. Though Kennedy's initial target was Dave Beck, the hearings soon focused upon JAMES HOFFA, vice president of the Teamsters who succeeded Beck as president in 1957, when the latter refused to run for reelection because of charges of misuse of union funds. Kennedy's investigation revealed a complicated story of conflict of interest and collusion with underworld figures to further Hoffa's interests in the union. Repeated clashes between the union leader and the committee counsel provided the highlights of Hoffa's many appearances before the committee. The hearings ground on inconclusively, and Kennedy encountered criticism from Republicans on the committee who believed that, by focusing on Hoffa, he was deliberately deflecting attention from WALTER REUTHER of the United Auto Workers, who regularly supported Democratic candidates. Kennedy reluctantly began an investigation of the UAW that uncovered no wrongdoing. The hearings on the Teamsters brought the committee's chief counsel and his brother, who sat on the committee, national attention, not all of it favorable. Some constitutional scholars criticized Robert Kennedy's methods of questioning and maintained that he attempted to transform a claim of privilege under the Fifth Amendment into an admission of guilt.

Kennedy resigned as counsel to the rackets committee in September 1959 to manage his brother's race for the presidency. In early 1960, he published a book about his investigations, *The Enemy Within*. John Kennedy defeated HUBERT HUMPHREY in the primaries and turned aside a challenge from the majority leader in the Senate, LYNDON JOHNSON (D-Tex.) at the convention. In the general election, he won a narrow victory over Vice President RICHARD M. NIXON.

After winning the presidency, John Kennedy named his brother attorney general. In that office, Robert Kennedy continued his campaign against organized crime. He also resumed his war on Jimmy Hoffa. During his brother's presidency, the Justice Department dealt with matters relating to civil rights, organized crime, labor, economic monopoly, and juvenile delinquency. The attorney general and his brother responded cautiously as civil rights activists tried to involve the federal government in their struggle. Robert Kennedy served as his brother's closest adviser and participated in virtually all major decisions of the administration, including the response to the Cuban missile crisis.

The assassination of John Kennedy on November 22, 1963, devastated Robert. He briefly continued as attorney general under Johnson, but resigned in 1964 to run for a senate seat from New York. Kennedy defeated the Republican incumbent, KENNETH KEATING, by slightly over 700,000 votes. In that election, Kennedy benefited from the Johnson landslide; the president carried New York by 2.7 million votes. Although an early supporter of the American involvement in Vietnam, Kennedy came to question the efficacy of the American military effort. At the same time, he hesitated to break with the administration and make his doubts public. Kennedy declined entreaties from antiwar activists to challenge Johnson for the nomination. Not until Sen. EUGENE MCCARTHY (D-Minn.) made a strong showing in the New Hampshire primary did Kennedy enter the race. On June 5, 1968, the night he won the California primary, he was fatally shot by Sirhan Sirhan in Los Angeles.

—MSM

Kennon, Robert F(loyd)

(1902–1988) *governor of Louisiana*

Born in Minden, La., on August 21, 1902, Robert F. Kennon graduated from Minden High School in 1919. He earned a B.A. from Louisiana State University in 1923 and a law degree from the same institution in 1925. He was admitted to the Louisi-

ana bar that same year and set up a law practice in Minden. Kennon defeated the incumbent mayor of Minden in 1925, but did not stand for reelection when his term expired. He returned to the private practice of law until 1930, when he won election as district attorney for the 26th Judicial District in Louisiana. In addition to holding elective office, he organized a local company of the National Guard in 1925 and served as its captain. In 1940, he ran first in the primary for a position as a judge on the Second Circuit Court of Appeals, finishing ahead of the incumbent and another candidate. He defeated the incumbent in the runoff. The seat he won would not become vacant until January 1, 1942, however, and Kennon continued to serve as district attorney until he was called to active duty on January 5, 1941. He served in Europe during World War II and rose to the rank of lieutenant colonel. Upon his discharge from the service in May 1945, he returned to Louisiana, and, upon the death of Associate Justice Archibald T. Higgins, Kennon was appointed to Louisiana's Supreme Court to fill the unexpired term. Kennon served from October 1945 to January 1947. In 1948, he ran as an anti-Long candidate in the Democratic gubernatorial primary and lost to EARL K. LONG, brother of the late Huey Long. The anti-Long faction was composed primarily of oil and gas businessmen opposed to the pension plans and other share-the-wealth measures of the Long brothers. A few months after losing to Earl, in a special election to fill a vacant seat in the U.S. Senate, Kennon lost the Democratic nomination to Huey's 27-year-old son, RUSSELL LONG.

Kennon succeeded on his third try for governor. He defeated Carlos G. Spaht, who had the backing of the Long machine, in the Democratic primary of January 1952 and in the subsequent runoff. Campaigning on a platform that called for lowering the gasoline tax, economizing in government, and reducing the governor's power, Kennon won election over the Republican candidate, Harrison Bagwell, in April. He supported Sen. RICHARD B. RUSSELL (D-Ga.) for the Democratic presidential nomination in 1952. At the National Democratic Convention in July, Gov. Kennon led his delegation in refusing to sign an oath pledging to support the party's presidential and vice presidential nominees. Following the convention, he remarked there was "considerable uncertainty" in the South regarding the Democratic presidential nominee, ADLAI E. STEVENSON.

Louisiana was second only to Texas in oil lands claimed on the continental shelf. The Democratic platform supported federal ownership of these lands. When, in September, the Republican presidential candidate, DWIGHT D. EISENHOWER, promised to back state claims to the offshore oil, Kennon endorsed him. Later that month, the governor organized Louisiana "Democrats for Eisenhower" but refused to work with the state GOP. Eisenhower narrowly lost Louisiana in November.

Following the Republican president's inauguration in January 1953, Kennon testified for state claims to submerged oil lands before the Senate Interior and Insular Affairs Committee. When, in February, the panel pondered whether maritime or state law should apply to the tidelands oil areas, Kennon spoke up for the latter. Eisenhower signed the long-disputed bill turning offshore oil over to the states into law in May 1953. Kennon continued to dissociate himself from the national Democratic Party. He joined fellow southern Democratic Govs. ALLAN SHIVERS of Texas and JAMES F. BYRNES of South Carolina, who had also supported Eisenhower, in refusing to attend a national Democratic conference in September 1953.

When the U.S. Supreme Court declared public school segregation unconstitutional in May 1954, Kennon avoided rabble-rousing demagoguery and did not ask for new segregation laws. Hoping for an appointment to a federal judgeship, Kennon thought it unwise publicly to oppose the highest federal court. He did, however, sign those bills that came out of the legislature, including a measure to cut off state funds to schools that desegregated and a pupil placement law. Moreover, Kennon promised that segregation would be maintained within existing statutes and that the legislature would provide a school system "which will include segregation in fact." After the Supreme Court handed down its decision on the implementation of school desegregation (*Brown II*) in 1955, Kennon declared, "I am convinced the majority of the people of this state want their schools segregated. So long as I am governor, I will try to follow the wishes of the people." In 1956, Kennon defied an order by the Interstate Commerce Commission requiring integration of railroad and bus waiting rooms. The governor instructed all state and municipal officials to enforce state segregation laws.

In July 1954, Kennon was elected chairman of the U.S. Governors Conference. He conferred with his fellow executives on the president's proposed $50-billion interstate highway program. In December, Kennon presented Eisenhower with the governors' report calling for highway expenditures of $101 billion over the next 10 years. As the national elections approached in 1956, it became evident that Kennon and Shivers would again support Eisenhower. Prohibited by law from succeeding himself, Kennon endorsed anti-Long candidate Fred Preaus, who lost to Earl K. Long in the Democratic gubernatorial primary of 1956. Kennon joined Shivers in endorsing and campaigning for Eisenhower during his last year in office. Upon completing his term, Kennon returned to the private practice of law in Baton Rouge. When a judgeship on the United States Court of Appeals for the Fifth Circuit became vacant, Kennon made clear his desire for the appointment, but it went instead to JOHN MINOR WISDOM. Eisenhower's attorney general, HERBERT BROWNELL, later recalled that Kennon did not get the nomination because he was a segregationist. Kennon attempted to return to public life with an unsuccessful run for governor in 1963. He died in Baton Rouge on January 11, 1988.

—MSM

Kerouac, Jack
(1922–1969) *writer*

The son of French-Canadian parents, Kerouac was born Jean-Louis Lebris de Kerouac in the small town of Lowell, Mass., on March 12, 1922. English was his second language; as a boy, he first spoke joual, a dialect of French Canadians. At Lowell High School, he achieved success both as an athlete and as a student. After graduating, he spent a year at the Horace Mann School in Riverdale, N.Y., before taking up a scholarship at Columbia University in the fall of 1940. A star running back on the freshman football team until he suffered a broken leg, he was less successful as a student at Columbia. He left Columbia in the fall of 1941 and joined the merchant marine and later the navy, which discharged him after a brief stint for unspecified psychiatric reasons. After his discharge from the navy, he served in the merchant marine again before going back to Columbia in 1944. Although his return to college and to football proved fleeting, at Columbia he met a group of aspiring writers, including ALLEN GINS-BERG and William Burroughs. Kerouac had already written an unpublished book of short stories and an unpublished novel.

Sometime after his father's death from stomach cancer in 1946, Kerouac began work on what became his first published book, *The Town and the City* (1950). Powerfully influenced by the novels of Thomas Wolfe, this thinly veiled autobiographical recounting of his boyhood in Lowell revealed both the excesses of Kerouac's style and its powerful lyricism. The reviews were modest and the sales virtually nonexistent. In that novel, he used the word "beat" for the first time in his writing. Kerouac sometimes claimed that the word "beat" came from "beatific or beatitude." On other occasions, he maintained that it referred to being beaten down or in a state of despair. Kerouac coined the term "Beat Generation" to refer to the spiritual exhaustion of his companions. The term came to be used to describe a movement that gained a degree of popularity in the mid-1950s and opposed contemporary values, which its adherents believed were materialistic and patriotic. Kerouac objected to that use of the term, maintaining that it destroyed his meaning.

His next work, *On the Road* (1957), broke dramatically from traditional literary style. Originally composed at a typewriter on a long roll of Teletype paper, the novel attempted to capture in prose the spontaneous, improvisational style of bebop, a form of jazz pioneered by Charlie Parker and Dizzy Gillespie. Kerouac based the book on several trips across the country he made in the late 1940s with Neal Cassady, a young drifter from Denver. From its Beat opening ("I first met Dean not long after my wife and I split up. I had just gotten over a serious illness that I won't bother to talk about, except that it had something to do with the miserably weary split-up and my feeling that everything was dead"), the book offered an alternative vision of American life and an alternative lifestyle. Some found in it an expression of their own alienation

and yearning for the freedom symbolized by the open road. *On the Road* became, at least for some, a blueprint for a joyriding, drug-taking rebellion against the values of American society in the 1950s. Between 1951 and 1956, Kerouac composed many unpublished poems and novels, including a version of "On the Road" that would later be published as *Visions of Cody* in 1973. Some critics consider this to be the finest example of Kerouac's attempts at "spontaneous prose."

The publication of *On the Road* made Kerouac a literary celebrity, a status to which he reacted uncomfortably. In various public appearances, including on the *Tonight Show*, he was cast as a Beat icon. Many literary critics regarded the Beat phenomenon as a passing fad and refused to take Kerouac's work seriously. One night on the *David Susskind Show*, Truman Capote, after listening to Norman Mailer describe Kerouac's method of composition, famously remarked, "That's not writing, it's just . . . typing." The rejection by many critics and the association of his work with what he regarded as a fad deeply hurt him. Moreover, trying to live up to the image he presented in *On the Road* contributed to an already severe drinking problem. He continued to travel around the country and spent some time in San Francisco, where he established a close friendship with Gary Snyder, who interested Kerouac in Buddhism. His next book, *The Dharma Bums* (1958), described his experiences with Snyder and his steps, along with those of his friends, toward spiritual enlightenment. For all his enthusiasm for Buddhism, however, Kerouac remained a serious Catholic.

Through their lifestyle and their art, the Beats spawned a hoard of imitators. First in the San Francisco Bay area and Greenwich Village and then elsewhere, coffee shops sprang up where young women attired in black turtlenecks and black leotards joined young men in beards, khaki slacks, and sweaters to listen to cool jazz and hear readings of usually dreadful poetry. Similarly, would-be writers spewed out streams of undisciplined, often incoherent, prose in an effort to mimic Kerouac's style. Despite his belief that he produced more valid work when he wrote "without consciousness," Kerouac's best prose differed markedly from that of his imitators. Although his output was uneven in quality, an attention to detail, a grounding in European and

American literature, and an intense lyrical quality distinguished his best work.

Kerouac may be best remembered for his influence on the generation of the 1960s. In fact, however, his political ideas often differed considerably from those of the young people he influenced. In many respects a political conservative, his politics were libertarian rather than radical. Deeply influenced by his Catholic upbringing, Kerouac was anti-Semitic and anticommunist. He denounced the New Left, became friendly with WILLIAM F. BUCKLEY, and, throughout the Vietnam War, which he supported, insisted that he was "still a Marine" and ready to serve. In addition, he did not advocate the licentious sexuality often associated with the Beat lifestyle or the hippies of the 1960s. Indeed, this icon of the counterculture lived at his mother's house throughout much of his adult life.

Kerouac continued to write autobiographical novels in the 1960s. *Big Sur* (1962) depicted his attempt to break his drinking habit and reconnect with his talent as a writer by embarking on a solitary retreat to commune with nature in Bixby Canyon in the Big Sur region. The experiment failed, and he returned to San Francisco and to the bottle. The several novels that followed in the mid-1960s did not measure up to his earlier work. Beset by alcoholism and stung by both criticism of his political views and by what he regarded as the deliberate distortion of those views to the purposes of others, he withdrew from public life. He died of an abdominal hemorrhage in Saint Petersburg, Fla., on October 21, 1969.

—MSM

Kerr, Clark

(1911–2003) *president, University of California*

The son of an apple farmer, Clark Kerr was born in Reading, Pa., on May 17, 1911. He received a B.A. from Swarthmore College in 1932 and earned an M.A. from Stanford University the following year. He studied at the London School of Economics, taught economics at Antioch, and earned a Ph.D. from the University of California at Berkeley in 1939.

From 1939 to 1940, Kerr taught labor economics at Stanford University. In 1942, he undertook his first assignment arbitrating between unions and management in a wage dispute. Over the next 20 years, he became the most highly paid labor-management negotiator on the West Coast. After teaching for five years at the University of Washington, Kerr returned to the University of California in 1945. He established the Institute of Industrial Relations at Berkeley while teaching a full schedule. In 1950, the university's regents required that faculty members sign a loyalty oath. Although he signed it, Kerr was one of the most outspoken of faculty leaders in opposition to the oath. In 1952, with strong backing from the faculty, Kerr was named the first chancellor of the Berkeley campus. In the six years he held that position, he spurred the physical expansion of the campus and, partially in response to the circumstances of the cold war, encouraged scientific research. Kerr also continued to serve as a labor mediator. In April 1958, United Auto Workers president WALTER REUTHER chose Kerr to sit on an independent ethics panel to which union members could appeal disputes with their leaders.

Kerr became president of the University of California in September 1958. His tenure as chancellor and president coincided with the enormous expansion of higher education in the United States spurred by the G.I. Bill, widespread affluence, and, later in the decade, the response to *Sputnik*. Kerr developed California's Master Plan, which created a three-tier system of higher education. At the top were the University of California campuses, which drew students from the top 12.5 percent of the state's high school students and had responsibility for most graduate programs, professional schools, and research. The state college system focused on undergraduate education. Community colleges offered two-year programs for entering students (some of whom would transfer to four-year institutions) as well as vocational programs, and were open to every graduate of California's high schools. Kerr also oversaw the building of new campuses at Irvine, San Diego, and Santa Cruz.

The model of a modern educator, Kerr was appointed to President Eisenhower's Commission on National Goals in February 1960. Issued the following November, the commission's report stressed the need for Americans to make great sacrifices in the 1960s to defend freedom against anticipated communist expansion. In an individual report, Kerr said the nation should seek to eliminate racial discrimination by 1970.

Kerr coined the term "multiversity" for a series of lectures he gave at Harvard. He expanded upon the concept in a book, *The Uses of the University* (1963), which posited that "the knowledge industry" might do for the second half of the 20th century what railroads did for the second half of the 19th century. In response to new conditions and new demands, the multiversity, a vast complex of research, technology, and education, had emerged to replace the teaching colleges of the 19th century and the pure research university. Kerr held that the development of giant multiversities was inevitable. He nevertheless pointed out dangers he saw as attendant to the creation of "knowledge factories." Among those, he focused on the neglect of students in the form of large classes, the extension of the use of teaching assistants, and the selection and promotion of faculty on the basis of research alone.

Whatever reservations he may have held about the emerging multiversity, Kerr made the University of California into the largest research and doctorate-awarding institution in the country. It was ironic that, given his own warnings about such trends, Kerr's university became the object of increasing criticism for becoming impersonal, oblivious to students needs, and obsessed with funding and growth.

Those developments, coupled with increasing student activism, had catastrophic consequences for Kerr, his presidency, and the university. When Kerr became president, Berkeley was experiencing a growth of student activism. In addition to agitating about campus issues, students protested the execution of CARYL CHESSMAN and hearings held by the House Un-American Activities Committee in San Francisco. In the early 1960s, students were drawn increasingly to the civil rights movement. Several dozen students from Berkeley worked for the Mississippi Freedom Summer project in the summer of 1964. That fall, a concerned administration enforced a prohibition against soliciting on campus for noncampus political activity. In response, students organized the Free Speech Movement, which Kerr initially dismissed as "a ritual of hackneyed complaints." Large-scale demonstrations and the occupation of Sproul Hall led Gov. EDMUND G.

BROWN to call in the police, who arrested almost 800 demonstrators. Faced with mounting protests and an overwhelming vote by the faculty in opposition to the prohibition of political activity on campus, Kerr rescinded the ban. Although he often disagreed with the students' causes and disapproved of their actions, he refused to comply with an order from the regents in 1965 to take punitive measures against them and tendered his resignation. The regents backed down. Nevertheless, the continuing student activism at Berkeley generated resentment in some quarters and undermined Kerr's relationship with the regents and the state government.

Campaigning for governor in 1966, Ronald Reagan pledged to "clean up the mess in Berkeley." In January 1967, at the regents' first meeting after Reagan was sworn in as governor, the regents voted, 14 to 8, to fire Kerr. Kerr joked that he left the presidency of the University of California the same way he entered it, "fired with enthusiasm." In spite of the quip, he later called his dismissal the "most painful event" of his life. Kerr retained his position in Berkeley's School of Business Administration and later served on the Carnegie Commission on Higher Education and the Carnegie Council on Policy Studies. He championed the cause of economically disadvantaged students and advocated that federal aid to higher education be given to students rather than only to institutions. Kerr published a two-volume memoir of his years at the University of California, *The Gold and the Blue*, in 2001 and 2003. He died, following complications from a fall, in El Cerrito, Calif., on December 1, 2003.

—MSM

Kerr, Robert S(amuel)
(1896–1963) *U.S. senator*

The son of an ardent Progressive Democrat, Robert Kerr was born in a log cabin in Indian Territory, later the state of Oklahoma, on September 11, 1896. After graduating from high school, he taught school while he earned a two-year degree from East Central State Normal School in Ada, Okla. He studied law briefly at the University of Oklahoma, but financial exigencies forced him to drop out in 1916. He clerked in a law office until the United States entered World War I and he was commissioned a second lieutenant in the army. Although he never saw combat, Kerr served overseas in the field artillery. At end of the war, he returned to Oklahoma, where he struggled to make a living. After a business venture failed, Kerr passed the state bar examination in 1922 and began to practice law in Ada. After a few years, he entered the oil business with his brother-in-law, James L. Anderson. The firm had become so successful by 1929 that Kerr abandoned his law practice to devote his efforts to the Anderson-Kerr Drilling Company. Anderson-Kerr struck it rich in 1932 by drilling within Oklahoma City, where other oil firms feared possible property damage. Anderson retired in 1936, and Dean A. McGee, a former chief geologist with Phillips Petroleum, joined the firm. That same year, Kerr conducted a successful campaign to persuade the voters of Oklahoma City to extend the drilling area. Lucrative contracts with the Continental Oil Company and the Phillips Petroleum Company made Kerr a millionaire by the end of the Great Depression. In 1946, the company changed its name to Kerr-McGee Oil Industries, Inc., and expanded into all areas of the oil business except distribution. The company also established substantial interests in other natural resources, including gas, helium, potash, and beryllium. By the 1950s, Kerr-McGee controlled 25 percent of the known uranium reserves in the United States.

During the 1930s, Kerr became a leading spokesperson for the oil and gas industry in Oklahoma. He was also active in the Oklahoma National Guard and in the American Legion. Those activities provided a springboard into public life. In 1942, Kerr ran for the Democratic nomination for governor as a supporter of the New Deal and the war effort. He won both the primary and the general election by narrow margins. Kerr made his debut in national politics as the keynote speaker at the Democratic National Convention in 1944. At that convention, he also played a role in the selection of HARRY S. TRUMAN as the vice-presidential nominee.

Kerr won election to the Senate in 1948. As a member of that body, he generally endorsed the policies of the Truman administration and emerged as a leading advocate for the oil and gas industry. In 1950, he tried unsuccessfully to exempt natural gas from federal regulation. Although he aspired to national office, he focused primarily on the parochial interests of his state. He won assignment to the Public Works and Finance Committees, which placed him in a good position to further Oklahoma's interests. A keen mind, a forceful personality, and a mastery of detail enabled Kerr to rise rapidly in the Senate. An effective debater, his command of policy, combined with sarcasm, vituperation, and personal attacks, made opponents reluctant to take him on. Behind closed, doors, where the real business of the Senate took place, Kerr was equally effective as a bargainer. While effective, his style did not endear him to his colleagues. Sen. PAUL DOUGLAS (D-Ill.) observed that Kerr was "more feared than liked."

Kerr made an unsuccessful bid for the Democratic presidential nomination in 1952. After that, he committed himself entirely to his work in the Senate. He won reelection in 1954 and 1960. His close relationship with LYNDON JOHNSON, his party's leader in the Senate, and alliances with the powerful southern and western senators who dominated that body placed him at the center of power.

For all his national influence, he remained, above all, a voice for state and regional interests. He devoted himself to promoting federal projects to develop Oklahoma's natural resources. As chair of the Rivers and Harbors Subcommittee of the Public Works Committee, he pushed through a vast program of regional development projects, including hydroelectric plants, irrigation projects, an improved inland waterway system, pollution control, and recreational facilities. Indeed, the Arkansas River Navigation System, a $1.3-billion federal project in northeastern Oklahoma, defined his three terms in the Senate. His position on the Rivers and Harbors Subcommittee not only enabled him to serve Oklahoma's interests, but it gave him control over the fate of other senators' water projects. With the political IOUs thus accumulated, he wielded substantial power in other matters that concerned him, such as taxes and trade. For example, as the Senate's leading champion of the oil and gas industry, Kerr managed to rebuff any attempts to eliminate or reduce the 27.5 percent oil depletion allowance.

Kerr also used his considerable power to achieve enactment of special tax benefits for individuals. In 1955, the U.S. tax court ruled that Leo Sanders, a contractor from Oklahoma City, owed the government $955,000 in back taxes. The Supreme Court rejected Sanders's appeal in February 1956. Two months later, Kerr inserted in a tax measure a section that applied only to Sanders. The provision specified that, in Sanders's unique situation, the maximum tax rate was 33 percent, instead of 91 percent, and it further excused him from the large penalties he would have had to pay for failing to file proper returns. The measure passed, effectively relieving Sanders of most of the $955,000 he owed. Such power led Douglas to comment that Kerr was the "uncrowned king of the Senate."

Kerr opposed the Eisenhower administration on a number of issues involving the interests of his state. A strong protectionist, he fought to restrict foreign imports that injured Oklahoma's lead, zinc, and oil industries. This position led him to oppose the administration's proposals for freer trade. He voted against a three-year extension of the reciprocal trade bill sponsored by the administration in 1955 and in 1958 unsuccessfully sought to limit the president's authority to override decisions by the tariff commission. A supporter of high farm price supports, Kerr constantly criticized Secretary of Agriculture EZRA TAFT BENSON's policy of flexible price supports. In October 1953, he charged that Benson's failure to support cattle prices at 90 percent of parity had reduced farmers' share of the national income to the lowest level in 15 years. With typical vituperation, he said that Eisenhower "knew far too little about farm problems" and called for Benson's removal.

Kerr's desire for higher federal spending in such areas as public works and agriculture clashed with the administration's desire to cut budgets. In 1957, he launched a broad attack on the economic performance of the Eisenhower administration. In June, armed with a battery of statistics, he subjected Secretary of the Treasury GEORGE HUMPHREY and chairman of the Federal Reserve Board WILLIAM McCHESNEY MARTIN to intensive critical interrogation during Senate hearings. Kerr assailed the Eisenhower administration for allowing "big business to reinforce its position and its share of the economy; while the farm industry has been almost bankrupted, small business had been penalized and jeopardized and those in the lending business have

increased their share by 40 percent." Kerr's invective reached its peak during a debate in the Senate on July 15, when he said that if the country's fiscal experts were "marched . . . by Eisenhower for months" he would remain "uninformed" on fiscal matters because it took "brains" to understand them and "he doesn't have them."

Kerr played a central role in the enactment of legislation to provide medical care for the aged in 1960. He won passage in the Senate Finance Committee of a conservative substitute for a more sweeping proposal for medical care (Medicare) for the elderly sponsored by presidential candidate Sen. JOHN F. KENNEDY (D-Mass.) and favored by most Democratic senators. Kennedy's bill proposed to provide medical care to all people over the age of 65 and to pay for the program with an increase in Social Security taxes. The administration offered a plan that included 180 days of hospitalization and covered most other medical expenses, paid for through the Social Security system but administered by the states and private companies and limited to elderly people who could not afford to pay for their medical expenses. Kerr's plan provided for matching federal funds to the states to pay for medical care only for the elderly indigent, and it paid for the program out of general revenues. In August, the Senate voted down the administration plan on a party-line vote; it then defeated Medicare by a vote of 51-44, after which it passed Kerr's version by 91-2. After a conference committee reconciled the Kerr bill with a similar measure, sponsored by WILBUR MILLS (D-Ark.) and passed by the House, both houses passed the legislation. Upon receiving Eisenhower's signature, the Kerr-Mills Act became law.

Kerr supported Johnson's bid for the Democratic nomination in 1960. After losing the nomination to Kennedy, Johnson accepted Kennedy's offer of the vice presidential nomination. When the Democratic ticket won, Kerr replaced Johnson as chair of the Aeronautical and Space Sciences Committee. With that assignment and his position as ranking Democrat on the Finance and Public Works Committees, Kerr reached the peak of his power in the Senate. For the most part, he worked to support the administration's domestic program. Following Kennedy's request for an increase in spending for the space program, Kerr's committee doubled the appropriations for the National Aeronautics and Space Administration (NASA). As always, Kerr pursued his personal agenda as well; he engineered the appointment of James Webb, an employee of Kerr-McGee, as head of NASA. In return for his support of selected elements of Kennedy's legislative program, Kerr exacted from the administration a free hand with respect to water resources. In spite of this arrangement, the administration could not always count on Kerr's support; he managed the defeat of Medicare in 1962.

Kerr suffered a heart attack and died at Bethesda Naval Hospital on January 1, 1963.

—MSM

Keyserling, Leon H(yman)
(1908–1987) *economist*

Born in Charleston, S.C., on January 22, 1908, Keyserling attended Columbia University, where he was influenced by Rexford Tugwell, an institutional economist and later a prominent adviser to Franklin D. Roosevelt. Upon graduating in 1928 with a B.A. in economics, Keyserling enrolled in Harvard Law School, from which he graduated in 1931. He then enrolled as a doctoral student in economics at Columbia but did not complete his dissertation. As the New Deal got under way, he went to Washington and joined the Department of Agriculture in 1933. Later that year, he became administrative assistant to Sen. ROBERT F. WAGNER (D-N.Y.) and in that capacity helped draft several important New Deal measures. Keyserling was the primary drafter of Section 7A of the National Industrial Recovery Act (NIRA), which provided government support for collective bargaining. After the Supreme Court declared the NIRA unconstitutional, Congress reenacted Section 7A as part of the National Labor Relations Act of 1935 (the Wagner Act). Keyserling also played a significant role in crafting the Social Security Act of 1935 and the Housing Act of 1937. Wagner chaired the Democratic Platform Committee, and he had Keyserling draft the party platforms in 1936, 1940, and 1944. In addition, Keyserling occasionally wrote speeches for Roosevelt.

Keyserling worked in federal housing agencies from 1937 to 1946. He was general counsel to the U.S. Housing Authority from 1937 to 1938 and then deputy administrator and general counsel from 1938 to 1942. From 1941 to 1942, he was acting administrator. After the American entry into World War II, he became acting commissioner of the Federal Public Housing Authority. He served as general counsel to the National Housing Agency from 1942 to 1946. After the war, he played a role in the creation of the Department of Housing and Urban Development and drafted the National Housing Act of 1949.

At the end of the war, Keyserling played a role in drafting the Full Employment Act of 1946. The act established that full employment should be a focus of economic policy. It also created the Council of Economic Advisers. President HARRY S. TRUMAN appointed him vice chairman of the new Council of Economic Advisers (CEA) in 1946. When the Democrats lost the congressional elections of 1946, Keyserling became part of Clark Clifford's Monday night supper group, which attempted to influence the Truman administration to take a more liberal course. The group also developed strategy for the presidential campaign in 1948. In 1949, Keyserling became chair of the CEA. He held the position until the end of the Truman administration, but he exercised his greatest influence from the time he assumed the chair until the outbreak of the Korean War.

Keyserling's approach to the economy focused on growth. He repeated many of Tugwell's ideas about the need for balance in the economy, the danger of monopolies, and the benefits of planning, but Keyserling believed that growth could solve major economic problems, including depression and inflation. Above all, however, he believed that growth could solve social problems and do so without raising the question of redistribution of wealth. In other words, Keyserling maintained that if the economic pie could be expanded, even those with the smallest slices would still have enough to live decently, and the pie need not be re-sliced. Although he advocated increased government spending to stimulate demand, Keyserling always denied that he was a Keynesian economist.

With the advent of a Republican administration in 1953, Keyserling returned to his law practice and became a consulting economist. His clients included nearly all the public employee unions in New York City. He founded the Conference on Economic Progress, a tax-exempt nonprofit foundation dedicated to the study of public policy, and served as its director until 1972. After leaving Washington, Keyserling wrote profusely and lobbied for a variety of liberal causes, but he exercised little influence on policy. He was a low-tech economist, and high-tech economics began to dominate the field even while Keyserling was in office. Professional economists found Keyserling's economic analysis unsophisticated, and he was poorly equipped to engage the macroeconomists of the postwar era.

During the 1960s, he criticized the Kennedy administration for being too timid and for failing to pursue full employment. He continued to advocate liberal positions during the Johnson and Nixon administrations and helped to draft the Full Employment and Balanced Growth Act of 1978 (the Humphrey-Hawkins Act). He died in Washington, D.C., on August 9, 1987.

—MSM

Killian, James R(hyne)

(1904–1988) *president, Massachusetts Institute of Technology; member, Office for Defense Mobilization Science Advisory Committee; president's special assistant for science and technology; chairman, President's Science Advisory Committee; member, President's Science Advisory Committee*

Born in Blacksburg, S.C., on July 24, 1904, Killian attended Trinity College (now Duke University) before graduating from the Massachusetts Institute of Technology (MIT) in 1926 with a degree in engineering and business administration. He went to work for MIT's scientific journal, *Technology Review*, and became its editor in 1930. While serving in that post, he also helped found what became MIT Press. Killian left his position as editor in 1939 to become executive assistant to MIT's president, a position he held until 1943. He served as executive vice president from 1943 to 1948 and president-designate in 1948 before becoming president in 1949. Although he spent part of the next decade on leave to work for the government, he remained president until 1959.

As president, Killian promoted the school's ties with private business and its research in weapons technology. At the same time, he stressed broader training for scientists. During his presidency, MIT established a School of Humanities, a School of Industrial Management, and a Center for International Studies.

Killian also became an adviser to the federal government on matters pertaining to science. From 1951 to 1959, he served as chair of the Army Scientific Panel. He joined the Office of Defense Mobilization's Science Advisory Committee in 1951. Killian continued to work for the government under Eisenhower. In 1954 and 1955, he headed a panel of the Science Advisory Committee to study the problem of defending the United States against a surprise thermonuclear attack. After studying the matter for almost a year, the panel issued its report in February 1955. The report stressed the need for better delivery of nuclear warheads. It deemed progress on an intercontinental ballistic missile (ICBM) "satisfactory" but warned that there would not be enough ICBMs to have military significance until 1965. To prevent the Soviet Union from deploying ballistic missiles first, the report urged the development of intermediate range ballistic missiles (IRBM). Eisenhower ordered the National Security Council to give programs for both intermediate and intercontinental missiles "highest national priority" status. On December 15, 1955, however, Eisenhower instructed the secretary of defense to continue both programs but to give priority to the ballistic missile that could be developed first, and that was the intermediate range missile. Eisenhower came to trust and rely on Killian and gave him a number of assignments. He appointed Killian to chair the eight-member Board of Consultants, a committee with responsibility to oversee the Central Intelligence Agency. He also named Killian to a committee, headed by H. ROWAN GAITHER, JR., created to study civil defense.

The launching of the Soviet satellite, *Sputnik*, in October 1957 created a public outcry for an increased emphasis on science in education and an increase in defense spending. To coordinate an accelerated science program, Eisenhower appointed Killian to the newly created post of special assistant for science and technology. In that capacity,

Killian's task was to improve scientific education at all levels, to expand basic research programs, to coordinate scientific activities with allied nations, and to expedite the development of missiles.

At the same time, Eisenhower ordered the removal of the Science Advisory Committee from the Office of Defense Mobilization to the White House and appointed Killian to chair the expanded and reorganized President's Science Advisory Committee (PSAC). Killian took leave from MIT to assume his new responsibilities. He shared the president's view that the launch of *Sputnik* probably indicated that the Soviets were ahead in the development of an ICBM, but that this did not mean that the Soviets had surpassed the United States in science. Moreover, like Eisenhower, he worried that the reaction to *Sputnik* would lead to panic-driven spending that would damage the economy and result in little scientific achievement. Killian was involved in a wide range of studies and decisions involving issues relating to science and defense. He played a major role in shaping the American ballistic missile program. At the president's request in February 1958, Killian oversaw a study of the organization of the American space program. In commissioning the study, Killian acknowledged the necessity for military space programs to continue within the Defense Department, but he warned against limiting American efforts in space "to narrowly concerned military objectives." Completed in March 1958, the study recommended the creation of the National Aeronautics and Space Administration (NASA), which Congress enacted in July 1958. The committee also reported the possibility of a manned flight to the Moon before the end of the next decade.

Killian played a significant role in the Eisenhower administration's decision to pursue a nuclear test ban agreement with the Soviet Union. In March 1958, he appointed a committee of scientists, headed by HANS BETHE, to study the possible effects of such a ban and the adequacy of methods for detecting nuclear tests. The committee reported that the United States could benefit from a test ban monitored by a good detection system, a finding that helped allay the fears and refute the objections of many who had opposed the ban.

In July 1959, Killian resigned as Eisenhower's special assistant and as chair of the PSAC. He remained, however, a member of the PSAC until 1961. At the same time he resigned his major positions in government, he stepped down as president of MIT to become chair of the MIT Corporation. Even then, Eisenhower continued to call on him for national service. In February 1960, the president appointed Killian to the Commission on National Goals.

Killian continued to serve as a presidential adviser during subsequent presidential administrations. He chaired the Carnegie Commission on Educational Television from 1965 to 1967, which issued a report advocating the creation of a nationwide network of TV stations supported by the government. When Congress passed the Public Television Act of 1967, President LYNDON B. JOHNSON appointed Killian to the board of trustees of the Corporation for Public Broadcasting, a position he held from 1968 to 1975. Killian served as chair of the Corporation for Public Broadcasting in 1973 and 1974. Upon retiring as chair of the MIT Corporation in 1971, he was given the title of honorary chairman. His books included *Sputnik, Scientists and Eisenhower* (1977) and *The Education of a College President* (1985). He died in Cambridge, Mass., on January 29, 1988.

—MSM

King, Martin Luther, Jr.
(1929–1968) *minister; president, Montgomery Improvement Association; president, Southern Christian Leadership Conference*

The son of a Baptist minister, King was born Michael King, Jr., on January 15, 1929, in Atlanta. In 1934, Michael King, Sr., upon the dying request of his own father, changed both his name and that of his son to Martin Luther King. Martin Luther King, Jr., attended Morehouse College from 1944 to 1948. Although he found the emotionalism of his father's religion embarrassing and questioned some tenets of Baptist doctrine, the minister teachers at Morehouse and the example of his father led King to decide to enter the ministry. He was ordained during his senior year. Upon graduating from Morehouse, he enrolled at Crozer Theological Seminary in Pennsylvania. There, he began to move away from liberal Christian theology and toward the neoorthodoxy of REINHOLD NIEBUHR, which stressed original sin, the inherently sinful nature of humans, and the imperfectability of human society. King received his divinity degree from Crozer in 1951 and enrolled in the doctoral program in systematic theology at Boston University's School of Theology. He received his Ph.D. in 1955. Many years later, while conducting research for the publication of King's papers (the first volume of which appeared in 1992), scholars discovered that King had plagiarized substantial portions of his doctoral dissertation and some of his papers in graduate school.

While working on his dissertation, King contemplated an academic career but ultimately accepted an offer to become pastor of the Dexter Avenue Baptist Church in Montgomery, Ala. Upon moving to Montgomery in 1954, he spent much of his first year there completing his dissertation and tending to his new duties as pastor. Then came an event that would change his life. On December 1, 1955, ROSA PARKS, a black seamstress, an activist, and an officer in the local chapter of the National Association for the Advancement of Colored People (NAACP), was arrested for refusing to surrender her seat to a white man as required by Montgomery's segregation ordinance. Black leaders of Montgomery organized to protest Parks's arrest and formed the Montgomery Improvement Association (MIA). They planned a boycott of the city's buses and demanded that white passengers be seated from front to back and black passengers be seated from back to front on a first come, first serve basis. In addition, they demanded courteous treatment of black passengers and the hiring of some black drivers. Although new to Montgomery and not a primary force behind the protest, King emerged as its leader. The organizers of the protest turned to him because of his education, his ability as a speaker, and, perhaps most important, because he was not identified with any faction of Montgomery's divided black leadership and therefore could serve as a unifying force.

The boycott had an immediate impact. On December 5, the scheduled beginning of the boycott, only a handful of black riders, who normally accounted for 70 percent of the Montgomery City Line's passengers, took the buses. The MIA established a car pool consisting of some 300 vehicles to transport African Americans who depended on bus service and held twice-weekly meetings to communicate the latest developments, raise funds, and sustain morale. Encouraged by BAYARD RUSTIN and other veteran pacifists, King became an advocate of Mohandas Gandhi's precepts of nonviolence, which he expressed in Christian terms. He taught that the nonviolent resister refused to hate and quoted Booker T. Washington: "Let no man pull you so low as to make you hate him."

As the protest continued, white resistance increased. Negotiations between the MIA, city officials, and the bus company, which was losing large sums of money, broke down at the end of December. King was arrested for speeding on January 26, 1956. Four days later, a bomb tore apart the front of King's home. An angry mob gathered, and only an impassioned speech by King prevented violence. On February 1, a bomb exploded at the home of E. D. Nixon, one of the founders and leaders of the MIA. In late February, King and 88 other leaders of the boycott were indicted on a charge of conspiring to organize an illegal boycott. He was convicted on March 22, but his $500 fine was suspended pending appeal.

In the face of stiffening white resistance, the MIA expanded its demands to include an end of segregation on the city's buses. The MIA, with support from the NAACP, filed suit in federal court on February 1, 1956, challenging the constitutionality of the city ordinances and state laws that required segregation on local buses. On June 4, a three-judge federal court decided, by a two-to-one vote, that the segregation laws violated the equal protection clause of the Fourteenth Amendment. The city appealed to the U.S. Supreme Court. With its appeal pending, city officials moved to enjoin operation of the MIA's car pool. During a hearing on that issue on November 13, word arrived that the Supreme Court had held the laws requiring segregated buses unconstitutional. Nevertheless, a local judge issued an injunction against the car pool, and the MIA disbanded it. The black community of Montgomery continued the boycott until the Supreme Court's order arrived on December 20. The next day, at 5:55 A.M., King and several associates boarded a bus and began the integration of Montgomery's public transportation.

For the next month, elements of the white community engaged in a campaign of violence. A shotgun blast tore through the front of King's house in the early morning hours of December 23; a group of white men beat a 15-year-old black girl at a bus stop; snipers fired on an integrated bus. Four black churches and the homes of two ministers (including RALPH ABERNATHY's) were bombed on January 10, 1957. More bombings followed at the end of the month, including an unsuccessful attempt to dynamite King's home. The wave of violence finally aroused city officials, and police arrested seven white men for the bombing. The arrests, however, exhausted the resolve of the city's white leadership. An all-white jury failed to convict in the first two cases brought, despite signed confessions.

The bus boycott lasted 382 days. It almost bankrupted the Montgomery City Line, and it unified Montgomery's black community, but it did not end segregation on Montgomery's buses; it took a legal challenge, backed by the NAACP, to do that. The boycott also attracted national attention and thrust King into national prominence. Further, the experience helped establish nonviolence as King's basic philosophy. The young minister had shown interest in Gandhian techniques of nonviolent resistance since his student days, and from its start, the boycott was nonviolent. Moreover, from the beginning of the protest, King preached the doctrine of Christian love and forgiveness to his followers. Only gradually, however, did King develop a sophisticated comprehension of the connections between Christian love, Gandhian nonviolence, and the struggle to end segregation and discrimination in America. As the boycott unfolded and as his ideas coalesced, King made nonviolent direct action the explicit ideological framework of the protest. Moreover, the boycott provided evidence of the effectiveness of nonviolent direct action and established the technique as a major tactic of the Civil Rights movement.

Seeking to expand the use of nonviolent direct action, King and approximately 60 other black leaders from 10 southern states met in Atlanta on January 10–11, 1957, and formed the Southern Christian Leadership Conference (SCLC). At a meeting in New Orleans the following month, King became the founding president of SCLC.

In March 1957, King traveled to Ghana at the invitation of Prime Minister Kwame Nkrumah to attend the ceremonies celebrating that country's independence. There, he met Vice President RICHARD M. NIXON, with whom he established a cordial relationship. Nixon invited King to visit him in Washington.

Upon his return from Ghana, King and other civil rights leaders organized a Prayer Pilgrimage to Washington, D.C., to demand federal action on school desegregation and voting rights for African Americans. Held on May 17, 1957, the third anniversary of the *Brown* decision, the Prayer Pilgrimage turned out a much smaller crowd than organizers had expected. Nevertheless, it was the largest civil rights gathering to that time and provided a forum for King's first truly national address. Even though King was still very young and new to national leadership, and despite the presence of established civil rights leaders, such as ROY WILKINS of the NAACP, A. PHILIP RANDOLPH of the Brotherhood of Sleeping Car Porters, and James Farmer of the Congress of Racial Equality (CORE), as well as black celebrities, including Jackie Robinson, Sammy Davis, Jr., and Harry Belafonte, King's address dominated the event. Speaking to the crowd of between 15,000 and 25,000 demonstrators, King urged the federal government, northern white liberals, and southern moderates to take stronger action on behalf of civil rights. He stressed, first and foremost, the importance of the right to vote. His repeated call to "Give us the ballot" elicited enthusiastic responses from the audience. *Ebony* magazine proclaimed that King "emerged from the Pilgrimage as the No. 1 Negro leader of men."

Following up on the invitation Nixon had extended in Ghana, King, accompanied by Ralph Abernathy, met with the vice president and Secretary of Labor JAMES P. MITCHELL on June 13, 1957. King asked that Eisenhower make a speech in the South calling for compliance with the Supreme Court's ruling on school segregation and enforcement of black voting rights. If Eisenhower did not give such a speech, King urged Nixon to do so. Nixon replied that he might convene a meeting of the President's Committee on Government Contracts in the South. Nixon became so involved in a discussion of the administration's pending civil rights bill that he lost track of the time. The meeting lasted over two hours.

A year later, King was one of a group of black leaders who met with Eisenhower. The meeting, held on June 23, 1958, also included Randolph, Wilkins, and Lester Granger of the National Urban League. Randolph began by reading a prepared statement that included nine recommendations. King spoke next; he emphasized the power of moral leadership and specifically argued for a presidential pronouncement and a White House conference on race, both of which were included in Randolph's nine points. While the meeting produced little in the way of concrete gains, it further established King's place among civil rights leaders.

In September 1958, the publication of King's book, *Stride toward Freedom: The Montgomery Story*, contributed still further to King's prominence as a national civil rights leader. On September 20, while autographing copies of the book at a department store in Harlem, an apparently insane woman stabbed him in the chest. He recovered from the injury and was released from the hospital on October 3.

Following the Prayer Pilgrimage, King and SCLC undertook a voter registration campaign, but, unlike the NAACP, SCLC did not have the resources to mount effective campaigns at the local level. In addition, King was not an especially gifted organizer or administrator. Before 1960, SCLC lacked a clearly defined strategy. Perhaps King's most significant activity in the last years of the 1950s was his deepening study of nonviolence. In February 1959, he traveled to India at the invitation of the Gandhian National Memorial Fund. King met with Prime Minister Jawaharlal Nehru as well as students and followers of Gandhian nonviolent resistance. The trip solidified King's commitment to nonviolence, which for him became the one valid method of social change.

In January 1960, King and his family moved to Atlanta, where the SCLC had established its headquarters, and became co-pastor, with his father, of the Ebenezer Baptist Church. Soon after his arrival in Atlanta, the student-led lunch counter sit-ins spread throughout the South and gave new impetus to the southern Civil Rights movement. The SCLC sponsored a meeting of leaders of the sit-ins at Shaw University in Raleigh, N.C., in April 1960.

That meeting led to the formation of a new group, the Student Nonviolent Coordinating Committee (SNCC).

In October 1960, King was arrested in DeKalb County, Ga., for allegedly violating his probation by driving without a valid license, and he received a sentence of four months in a rural penal camp. On October 26, the Democratic candidate for the presidency, Sen. JOHN F. KENNEDY (D-Mass.), called King's wife to express his concern. A call from the candidate's brother, ROBERT F. KENNEDY, helped persuade the judge to grant bail. Although many historians have credited the incident with increasing the black vote for Kennedy in November, some recent research has questioned the incident's actual impact on black voting.

By 1960, King had emerged as a national symbol of the southern struggle for civil rights and the leading exponent of nonviolent direct action, which became the primary tactic of black protest in the early 1960s. Beginning with the sit-ins and the formation of SNCC, King often functioned as a mediator between increasingly militant student activists and more cautious national civil rights leaders. He also served as perhaps the primary channel of communication between black and white Americans.

King's tactical differences with SNCC surfaced in the course of a protest campaign, originally organized by SNCC, in Albany, Ga., during 1961 and 1962. Police Chief Laurie Pritchett reined in his police force, and they arrested demonstrators without the public exhibitions of violence that had spurred national outrage in other instances. At the request of the local movement, King came to Albany. After being arrested at demonstrations organized by the Albany Movement, King left jail and ultimately left Albany without achieving a victory. Some activists within the Civil Rights movement began to question his militancy and to challenge the dominant position he held in the movement.

In response to the defeat at Albany, King undertook a campaign in Birmingham, Ala. The demonstrations, organized by SCLC, began in January 1963 and constituted the largest civil rights protest to that time. King's arrest for leading a demonstration on April 12 helped push the Kennedy administration toward intervention in the conflict. While in jail, King wrote a public letter in response to a group of clergymen who had questioned the timing and wisdom of the protests. The "Letter from a Birmingham Jail" became one of King's most widely known statements.

King's leadership of the Civil Rights movement reached its peak in 1963. After the successful campaign in Birmingham, he gave his famous "I Have a Dream" speech in August at the March on Washington. At the end of 1963, *Time* magazine named him its man of the year. Such recognition helped establish King as the preeminent civil rights leader of his day, but it also provoked a hostile response from J. EDGAR HOOVER, the director of the FBI. With the approval of Attorney General Robert F. Kennedy and President John F. Kennedy, Hoover established extensive electronic surveillance of King's activities. That surveillance recorded a number of King's numerous extramarital affairs. Although Hoover regarded him as a dangerous radical, King was, in fact, a moderating force in a movement splintering under pressure from more militant black separatists and black nationalists. By this time, King had become an international figure, and he was awarded the Nobel Peace Prize in December 1964.

In early 1965, King and SCLC chose Selma, Ala., as the stage for protests designed to dramatize the need for federal enforcement of black voting rights. Several demonstrations encountered violent reactions from Sheriff Jim Clark's police force. On Sunday, March 7, John Lewis and Hosea Williams led a march from Selma to Montgomery, the state capital. After the marchers crossed the Edmund Pettus Bridge at the edge of the city, state troopers and mounted sheriff's deputies attacked them. Television cameras recorded the savage attack on the peaceful protestors. King, who was in Atlanta at the time of the march, returned to Selma and called for another demonstration on March 9, but a federal district judge issued an order prohibiting it. Officials from the Community Relations Service, after negotiating with King and local authorities, brokered a compromise whereby the marchers would cross the bridge, stop when met by police, and return to Selma. King led the march to the appointed point, stopped and prayed, and ordered the marchers to return to Selma. That decision, made without consulting SNCC's staff members, served further to alienate SNCC from King and SCLC. The Civil

Rights movement had begun to splinter, and King no longer served as a unifying figure.

After the events at Selma helped to spur enactment of the Voting Rights Act of 1965, King turned his attention to the problems of the ghettos in the North. In 1966, he led a campaign in Chicago to protest job discrimination, poor schools, and poor housing. The protests encountered opposition from Mayor RICHARD J. DALEY's powerful political machine and violence from white ethnic communities. In addition, the campaign was marred by violence from black youth gangs.

King came out publicly against the war in Vietnam in 1967, which caused the FBI to intensify its attempts to undermine him. The following year, King called for a Poor People's Campaign in Washington, but before it got under way, he was assassinated on April 4, 1968, in Memphis, Tenn., where he had come to support a strike by black sanitation workers.

—MSM

Kinsey, Alfred C(harles)
(1894–1956) *scientist*

Alfred Kinsey was born in Hoboken, N.J., on June 23, 1894. After taking a B.S. (magna cum laude) from Bowdoin College in 1916, Kinsey entered the graduate program in applied biology at Harvard, where he served as an instructor in zoology in 1917 and 1918 and an instructor in botany in 1918 and 1919. He was a Sheldon traveling fellow in 1919 and 1920, during which time he worked on a study of gall wasps for his doctoral dissertation. Upon completing his Sc.D. in entomology in 1920, he accepted an appointment as an assistant professor at Indiana University. Over the next 18 years, the zoology professor earned a reputation as a leading authority on the gall wasp and a successful author of high school biology textbooks (his *Introduction to Biology* and its subsequent editions sold half a million copies). He became an associate professor in 1922 and a full professor in 1929.

After students objected to the "health and hygiene" course taught at Indiana University, Kinsey volunteered in 1938 to develop a sex-education course based on a scientific approach. When teaching the course, he maintained a clinical attitude but nonetheless issued thundering denunciations of sexually repressive laws and attitudes. He also became increasingly concerned with the lack of scientific knowledge regarding human sexual behavior. Kinsey later recalled that he "was struck by the fact that a large area of living had not been studied on a broad objective basis," and he "started out to do so." He developed a fluidly structured questionnaire covering a variety of topics. (The final version consisted of between 300 and 521 separate items, depending on the number and variety of the respondent's sexual experiences.) In July 1938, Kinsey administered the first survey to students. In an effort to expand his statistical base, he went to big cities, especially Chicago, where he interviewed large numbers of prostitutes, homosexuals, and other people. Kinsey's work generated powerful opposition, and, under growing pressure from various sources, Kinsey stopped teaching the course, but he continued his interviews.

Up to this point, he financed his investigations with his own resources. In 1940, he received a grant from the National Research Council. Later, through the NRC, Kinsey received a grant of $40,000 a year for at least three years by the Rockefeller Foundation for his new Institute for Sex Research, which was affiliated with Indiana University. The grant enabled the Institute for Sex Research to expand its interviewing of volunteer subjects and to compile the data from those interviews into a variety of statistical categories. The information was recorded in a code devised by Kinsey and known only to him and his top assistants.

In 1948, Kinsey published *Sexual Behavior in the Human Male*, an 804-page report published by W. B. Saunders Company, a publisher of medical books. Based on interviews with 5,300 white males of different cultural, occupational, and economic groups, the study recorded physical, social, and economic data relating to the subjects; in addition, it documented their marital histories, sex education, nocturnal dreams, masturbation, animal contacts, heterosexual experiences, and homosexual experiences. Many of the report's conclusions contradicted popularly believed, or at least tacitly accepted, ideas about human sexuality. The study observed a correspondence between the sex habits of individuals and the social, educational, and religious groups to

which the individual belonged. For instance, Kinsey found that lower classes preferred more direct, genital sexuality.

The fundamental conclusion of the study was that American males found numerous and varied "outlets" for their sexuality and that the sexual practices of American males conflicted with existing laws, conventions, and moral codes. The report estimated that 90 percent of the male population practiced masturbation, even though many religious leaders, educators, and parents denounced it as immoral. The study further indicated that 85 percent of males had engaged in premarital intercourse, between 30 percent and 45 percent had engaged in extramarital intercourse, and that 70 percent had patronized prostitutes. According to Kinsey's statistics, 37 percent of males had engaged in homosexual contact to the point of orgasm at least once and that 17 percent of farm boys had sexual relations with animals. These figures varied according to age group and social class. Kinsey passed no judgment on these practices; he regarded sexual expression as biologically normal in whatever form it took.

The Kinsey Report, as it became known, became a best seller. The heavy tome sold 200,000 hardback copies in two months. Kinsey used the royalties to help fund the Institute, which also received increased funding from the Rockefeller Foundation. The new resources enabled Kinsey to hire and train a team of researchers to conduct more interviews.

Sexual Behavior in the Human Male created something of a furor. Some readers attacked Kinsey's efforts to avoid the social and moral implications of sexual behavior. Margaret Mead wrote, in the *New York Times*, that Kinsey's impersonal handling of the subject was "extraordinarily destructive of interpsychic and interpersonal relationships." Others criticized the soundness of his sampling methods. For instance, critics argued that Kinsey's use of prisoners distorted his sample.

The controversy surrounding the publication of the first study, however, paled beside the firestorm that erupted following the publication of the second study, *Sexual Behavior in the Human Female*, in 1953. Based on interviews with 5,940 white female volunteers dating back to 1938, the 842-page study found that the range of variation among females exceeded the range of variation among males. It further found that the sexual behavior of women was not so conditioned by the attitudes of the social groups to which they belonged as that of males. Kinsey's team found no basic differences in the physiological nature of male and female orgasms, but they did perceive differences in responsiveness to psychosexual stimuli. The report also found that "frigidity" occurred less frequently in females than previously supposed, and it concluded that an absence of orgasm in females generally resulted from insensitivity on the part of the woman's partner and not from physical malfunction. Kinsey found a somewhat lower incidence of masturbation, homosexuality, and extramarital intercourse in females than in males; still, he found that 62 percent had masturbated, 90 percent had petted before marriage, nearly half had engaged in sexual intercourse before marriage (apparently most with their future husbands), 26 percent had engaged in extramarital intercourse, and 13 percent had at least one homosexual experience that resulted in orgasm. He argued that such activities should be viewed as common and normal in a biological sense.

America's most famed theologian, REINHOLD NIEBUHR, denounced Kinsey's "naturalism" and his "moral anarchism." Representative Louis B. Heller (D-N.Y.) accused Kinsey of "hurling the insult of the century against our mothers, wives, daughters, and sisters." The House Select Committee to Investigate Tax-Exempt Foundations, created in 1953, opened hearings in May 1954 on alleged improper awarding of funds by American foundations. One focus of the investigation was the Rockefeller Foundation.

Dating back to the publication of *Sexual Behavior in the Human Male*, Kinsey also faced criticism from within the scientific community. Many challenged Kinsey's assumption that his sample constituted a representative one. The Rockefeller Foundation named a team of prominent statisticians in 1951 to review Kinsey's data and sampling technique. While the final report generally supported Kinsey's work, it did insist that he improve his sampling methodology. An infuriated Kinsey rejected their recommendations, and, soon after *Sexual Behavior in the Human Female* was published,

the Rockefeller Foundation ended its funding for the institute.

James H. Jones, a historian who has also written about the notorious Tuskegee experiment, published an exhaustive biography of Kinsey in 1997. Drawing on the Kinsey Institute archives and interviews with Kinsey's friends, former students, and colleagues, Jones found that Kinsey had engaged in extreme acts of sadomasochism and other unusual sexual practices from his teens until nearly the time he died. Kinsey also organized, participated in, and in some instances filmed various sexual activities involving interview subjects, colleagues (and their spouses), and prostitutes. The Kinsey who emerged from Jones's study was less an objective scientist than an impassioned advocate of more liberated sexuality, who set out to slay his own sexual dragons as well as what he regarded as the repressive norms of society.

Although plagued by heart trouble, Kinsey continued to work at a frantic pace after the publication of *Sexual Behavior in the Human Female*. His plans included a volume on homosexuality and one comparing the sex laws of the various states. He conducted his 7,985th interview on May 24, 1956; it turned out to be his last. Kinsey suffered a heart attack on June 1, 1956, which impaired even his legendary capacity for work. Ill with pneumonia that made his heart condition worse, he died of an embolism on August 25, 1956, in Bloomington, Ind.

—MSM

Kirk, Russell (Amos)
(1918–1994) *political writer*

The son of a railroad engineer, Kirk was born in Plymouth, Mich., on October 19, 1918. He grew up in a small town in Michigan's "stump country," a depressed agricultural area that timber companies had stripped of trees at the turn of the 20th century. As a youth, he embraced his parents' fear that the "assembly-line civilization" represented by Henry Ford would destroy his region's traditional family-oriented way of life. He entered Michigan State College (later University) on a scholarship in 1936. His experience in college confirmed his conservative tendencies. Brought up to revere traditional literary disciplines, he found the emphasis on technical skills at Michigan State completely unsatisfying, and he described the school as "an institution where humane learning was barely tolerated." Years later, he recalled that he refused to get a job while in college, a decision that forced him to subsist on peanut butter and crackers, so that he had time to read the classics that could not be found in the curriculum. He received his B.A. in 1940 and earned an M.A. from Duke University in 1941.

Kirk was drafted into the army in 1942 and stationed in Utah as a sergeant in the Chemical Warfare Service. His assignment left him with considerable free time to pursue his reading. Moreover, his observation of military inefficiency and governmental bureaucracy reinforced his conservative leanings. He also developed the Catholic sacramental vision that so profoundly influenced his political ideas.

In 1946, while still serving in the army, Kirk wrote an article attacking peacetime conscription. He feared that the New Dealers would seek to perpetuate a wartime economy by provoking a conflict with the Soviet Union. He also wrote articles on education, the humanities, and the conservative tradition. After leaving the army in 1946, Kirk taught at Michigan State. He took his doctorate at Saint Andrews University in Scotland in 1952. During his travels in Europe, he observed the disruption of deep traditions by the policies of liberal governments and the destruction of beautiful ancient buildings to make way for uniform, concrete housing projects, all of which influenced his dissertation on the Anglo-American conservative intellectual tradition.

In 1953, his dissertation was published as *The Conservative Mind: From Burke to Santayana.* Arguing against the then-common contention that the liberal tradition defined the American experience, Kirk identified within American political thought a conservative intellectual tradition, which traced its roots to Edmund Burke and in America was personified by John Adams, James Fenimore Cooper, Nathaniel Hawthorne, Herman Melville, John C. Calhoun, Henry Adams, and George Santayana. The book defended the values of tradition, authority, and community against the liberal faith in reason, equality, and individualism. Kirk defined conservatism as a body of belief that accepted social hierar-

chy as essential to the proper ordering of society and embraced traditional morality. Conservatives, he wrote, believed "that a divine intent rules society as well as conscience, forging an eternal chain of right and duty which links great and obscure, living and dead." In addition, he elaborated, "Civilized society requires orders and classes. The only true equality is moral equality." Also essential to conservative thought was the "persuasion that property and freedom are inseparably connected, and that economic levelling is not economic progress." The book was widely and favorably reviewed; it drew praise even from liberals. By identifying a conservative intellectual tradition in America, Kirk provided a basis around which conservatives could build a movement. Along with FRIEDRICH HAYEK's *The Road to Serfdom,* WHITTAKER CHAMBERS's *Witness,* and WILLIAM F. BUCKLEY's *God and Man at Yale, The Conservative Mind* became one of the founding documents of modern conservatism.

As a consequence of the book's reception, Kirk found himself in the unexpected position of founder of a movement. The so-called new conservatives, many of whom were academics, distinguished themselves from other conservatives by their emphasis on tradition and community rather than on untrammeled economic freedom. Kirk's political philosophy rejected the elevation of humans to a status "only a little lower than the angels" with the "power to become godlike," which he traced back to the Renaissance and the Enlightenment. Kirk disdained "the strutting Rationalism of the Enlightenment," with its emphasis on "the doctrines of progress, rationality, secularism, and political reform." In contrast to pride and preoccupation with the self, Kirk posited "culture," which he defined as "the elevation of character which distinguishes the civilized man from the brute." Specifically, he found an alternative to the pride of the Renaissance and Enlightenment in awe, humility, and reverence for classical and biblical ideas, which led to a quest for "the well-ordered commonwealth" of Plato through the "moral imagination" of Edmund Burke. According to Kirk, Plato taught "men how to bring their souls into harmony with divine order."

In 1954, Kirk published *A Program for Conservatives,* which focused on the role of conservatives in the contemporary world. By arguing that conservatism embraced family, church, and community rather than free enterprise and unfettered individualism, the book sparked a debate among conservatives between traditionalists and libertarians and led to a series of confrontations between Kirk and AYN RAND. Kirk rejected Rand's philosophy of "objectivism," which held that altruism was an illusion and that people should be concerned with their self-interest. In contrast, he maintained that "we human beings were made for brotherhood, and if we live only for our own petty little selves, our souls shrivel." His disagreement with libertarians led him to request the removal of his name from the masthead of William F. Buckley's magazine, the *National Review*, for which he had written since its founding in 1955. Kirk nevertheless continued to contribute his monthly column, "From the Academy," to the magazine until 1980.

In a number of books and articles he wrote throughout the 1950s, Kirk expressed his opposition to the tumult and spiritual vacuity of a mechanized age. He idealized small family businesses over corporate enterprises, dismissed the proposal to develop a project for landing on the Moon as both useless and impossible to carry out, and insisted that poverty was not a bad thing unless combined with the ugliness of modern urban slums and the degradation of modern social welfare programs. At the same time, Kirk rejected the radical right of the 1950s. He once called Robert Welch, the founder of the John Birch Society, a "likable, honest, courageous, energetic man," who was the "kiss of death" for conservatism because of his "silliness and injustice of utterance."

Kirk accepted a part-time position as research professor of politics at Long Island University in 1956. Limited to two months a year, the job effectively released him from those duties in the university he had always found distasteful. Thereafter, he spent most of his time carrying out his functions as justice of the peace in Mecosta, Mich. (population 200), delivering lectures throughout the country, and writing. He served as founding editor of a critical journal, *Modern Age: A Conservative Review*, from 1957 to 1959. In 1960, he founded *The University Bookman*, an educational quarterly, and edited the journal from its inception until his death in 1994. Above all, Kirk wrote prodigiously. For 13 years,

he wrote a newspaper column for the *Los Angeles Times* syndicate. His books include *Randolph of Roanoke* (1951), *Confessions of a Bohemian Tory* (1963), *Enemies of Permanent Things* (1969), *Eliot and His Age* (1971), *The Roots of American Order* (1974), and *Reclaiming a Patrimony* (1982).

Kirk died of congestive heart failure in Mecosta on April 29, 1994.

—MSM

Kissinger, Henry A(lfred)

(1923–   ) *foreign and military policy adviser*

The son of middle-class Jews, Heinz Kissinger was born in Fürth, Germany, on May 27, 1923. His family left Germany in 1938 to escape Nazi persecution and settled in New York City. Upon his arrival in New York, Kissinger adopted the name Henry; he took evening courses in accounting at the City College of New York and became a citizen of the United States in 1943. Kissinger served in the U.S. Army from 1943 to 1946 as an infantryman, intelligence specialist, and military administrator in occupied Germany. After leaving the military, he attended Harvard University, where he earned a B.A. summa cum laude in 1950, his M.A. in 1952, and his Ph.D. in 1954. Upon completing his doctorate, he became a member of the faculty at Harvard. Kissinger's first major article on national security appeared in the April 1955 issue of *Foreign Affairs*, a publication of the Council on Foreign Relations. In it, he criticized the Eisenhower administration's "New Look," which emphasized air power, technology, and the nuclear deterrent over conventional forces. The policy intended in part to avoid another Korean War and in part to reduce defense expenditures. Kissinger, however, contended that the threat of nuclear retaliation no longer provided a credible deterrent to Soviet aggression, particularly in areas peripheral to U.S. interests. "As Soviet nuclear strength increases," he wrote, "the number of areas that will seem worth the destruction of New York, Detroit, or Chicago will steadily diminish." The article led to an offer to be staff director of a study, sponsored by the Council on Foreign Relations, on the consequences of nuclear weapons for American foreign policy. The job included writing a book after the study was completed. Kissinger took leave from Harvard and began his work for the Council on Foreign Relations in 1955.

In 1957, Kissinger published his dissertation, a study of European diplomacy after the Napoleonic wars, as *A World Restored: Metternich, Castlereagh, and the Problems of Peace, 1812–1822*. The work focused on the structure of peace created by Castlereagh and Metternich in an era when the forces of revolution and nationalism threatened to disrupt the status quo. Kissinger respected Metternich's ability to establish "stability." "Whenever peace—conceived as the avoidance of war—has been the primary objective of a power or a group of powers," wrote Kissinger, "the international system has been at the mercy of the most ruthless member of the international community." Kissinger maintained that stability, rather than peace, should be the primary goal of diplomacy. "Stability," he argued, "reflects, not the absence of unsatisfied claims, but the absence of a grievance of such magnitude that redress will be sought in overturning the settlement rather than through an adjustment within its framework." However, maintaining stability, Kissinger contended, required not only balancing the claims of various states but "arrang[ing] the balance of forces as to deter aggression produced by causes other than the conditions of the settlement." The diplomacy of Metternich and Castlereagh "may not have fulfilled all the hopes of an idealistic generation," concluded Kissinger, "but it gave this generation something perhaps more precious: a period of stability which permitted their hopes to be realized without a major war or a permanent revolution."

The same year as *A World Restored* came out, Kissinger published *Nuclear Weapons and Foreign Policy*, the product of his work for the Council on Foreign Relations. The book began with the premise that the Soviet Union was an expansionist power dedicated to worldwide revolution and subverting American interests. From there, it considered the various approaches to containing Soviet aggression. Kissinger again criticized the Eisenhower administration's New Look defense policy that relied on air power, technology, and the nuclear deterrent to prevent a Soviet attack and to contain Soviet expansionism. As Kissinger saw it, the United States, since World War II, responded to the cold war with a "flight into technology," devising "ever more fearful weapons." But technology did not solve the problem, according to Kissinger; rather, it presented a dilemma: "The more powerful the weapons, . . . the greater becomes the reluctance to use them." Kissinger argued that a heavy reliance on nuclear weapons would not deter the Soviet Union, since no one believed that the United States would launch a nuclear strike, thereby risking retaliation on its own cities, to achieve a minor objective. Not only did such a defense posture fail to deter the Soviets, but it alarmed America's allies, who worried that the United States had become an undependable ally. Setting aside threats to minor interests, they questioned whether the United States would launch a nuclear strike and risk retaliation on its own cities to save even Bonn or Paris. The New Look derived, in part, according to Kissinger, out of an outmoded notion of unconditional surrender. Given the horrible destructive power of nuclear weapons and the Soviet possession of such weapons, nuclear war became unthinkable. Therefore, the only plausible wars would be those fought for limited, essentially political, objectives. To fight such wars, the United States needed a "spectrum of capabilities," ranging from conventional forces to the capacity to wage total nuclear war to provide the maximum credible threat to aggression. The ultimate purpose was to prevent all-out nuclear war, and therefore, in addition to strategic nuclear weapons, the United States needed adequate conventional forces, the capability to fight a limited nuclear war, and a doctrine to govern American responses to various forms of aggression. The book had enormous impact.

In 1956, midway through his book for the Council on Foreign Relations, Kissinger accepted an offer from NELSON A. ROCKEFELLER to direct a Special Studies Project of the Rockefeller Brothers Fund. The Special Studies Project gathered prominent Americans to examine America's future foreign and domestic problems. Kissinger participated in all the panels and personally wrote the project's final report on international security, issued in 1958 as "International Security: The Military Aspect." The report warned that the Soviets had dramatically improved their technological capacity and were approaching military parity with the United States. The panel members urged a national effort to develop a civil defense system and a $3-billion increase in defense spending. They also advocated developing a capability for covert operations. In 1960 Rockefeller based his presidential campaign's approach to security issues on the report.

Kissinger returned to Harvard in 1957; he received tenure in 1959 and became a full professor in the government department in 1962. As associate director of Harvard's Center for International Affairs from 1958 to 1960 and as director of the Defense Studies Program from 1958 to 1959, he established a wide range of contacts with influential policy makers, academics, military officials, and business leaders. He also strengthened his connections with the government. He served as a consultant to the Weapons Systems Evaluation Group of the Joint Chiefs of Staff from 1955 to 1960.

Kissinger published *The Necessity for Choice: Prospects of American Foreign Policy* in 1961. He restated his belief that the United States needed to respond to limited challenges with appropriate force levels. At the same time, he backed away from his advocacy of tactical nuclear weapons and emphasized conventional forces. He questioned the prospects for détente with the Soviet Union and recommended increased aid to important noncommunist nations "on the comparative scale of the Marshall Plan."

Kissinger served as an adviser to the Kennedy administration's National Security Council in 1961 and 1962. He was consultant to the Arms Control and Disarmament Agency from 1961 to 1968 and to the State Department from 1965 to 1969. In the latter capacity, he toured South Vietnam.

Kissinger served as assistant for national security affairs for Presidents RICHARD M. NIXON and GERALD FORD from 1969 to 1976 and secretary of state from 1973 to 1977. During the Nixon administration, he helped shape American policy in Vietnam, open contacts with Communist China, establish détente with the Soviet Union, and initiate peace talks in the Middle East. Kissinger developed a policy of warmer relations with the Soviet Union and began negotiations for the limitation of strategic arms (Strategic Arms Limitation Talks, or SALT). Those talks resulted in the Strategic Arms Limitation Treaty in 1972. He engineered a rapprochement between the United States and the Peoples Republic of China that led to the first

official contacts between the two countries since the Communists took power in 1949. Kissinger negotiated a cease-fire agreement providing for the withdrawal of U.S. forces from Vietnam in January 1973, for which he was awarded the Nobel Peace Prize in 1973 jointly with the chief North Vietnamese negotiator, Le Duc Tho. After the Arab-Israeli War of 1973, Kissinger engaged in shuttle diplomacy to bring about a disengagement of forces. Ultimately, his efforts led to a historic agreement between Israel and Egypt in 1975.

After leaving government service, he founded Kissinger Associates, an international consulting firm, of which he is chairman. He has continued to write and speak, particularly on matters relating to foreign policy. President Ronald W. Reagan appointed him to head a national commission on Central America. Kissinger's books include *The Troubled Partnership: A Reappraisal of the Atlantic Alliance* (1965), *American Foreign Policy* (1969), *The White House Years* (1979), *For the Record* (1981), *Years of Upheaval* (1982), and *Years of Renewal* (1999).

—MSM

Kistiakowsky, George B(ogdan)
(1900–1982) *president's special assistant for science and technology*

Born in Kiev, Ukraine (then part of Russia), on November 18, 1900, Kistiakowsky grew up in the Ukraine, where his father was a professor of law at the University of Kiev. Kistiakowsky attended private schools in Kiev and Moscow until the Russian Revolution of 1917, after which he joined the White Army and fought against the Bolsheviks. In 1919, Kistiakowsky fled to Yugoslavia and spent a year in the Balkans and Turkey. Ultimately, he made his way to Germany, where he entered the University of Berlin in 1920. After quickly completing his undergraduate work, he earned a doctorate in chemistry in 1925. The following year, he came to the United States to take up a two-year fellowship at Princeton University. He published a monograph, "Photochemical Processes," in 1927, and became an assistant professor at Princeton in 1928. At the invitation of JAMES B. CONANT, then chair of the chemistry department at Harvard University, Kistiakowsky took up a position as an assistant professor in 1930. Concentrating in the field of physical chemistry, in particular chemical kinetics, he published prolifically. He became a U.S. citizen in 1933 and advanced to associate professor that same year. In 1937, he became Abbott and James Lawrence professor of chemistry. He remained at Harvard for the rest of his career, during which he produced over 150 articles.

After World War II broke out in Europe, President Franklin D. Roosevelt established the National Defense Research Committee to provide scientific information to military leaders. Conant, by then president of Harvard, headed the chemistry division, and he appointed Kistiakowsky to lead its explosives unit. In 1944, Kistiakowsky became leader of the explosives division of the Manhattan Project. In that capacity, he oversaw the development of the conventional explosive device that triggered the first atomic bomb. When the war ended, Kistiakowsky returned to Harvard and served as chair of the chemistry department from 1947 to 1950.

In 1953, Kistiakowsky became a member of the Defense Department's ballistic missiles advisory committee, a position he held until 1958. In 1954, he urged that priority be given to the development of an intercontinental ballistic missile (ICBM). Eisenhower appointed him to the President's Science Advisory Committee (PSAC) in 1957. The following year, he participated in a conference with representatives of the USSR, held in Geneva, Switzerland, the purpose of which was to reduce the danger of a surprise attack. When JAMES R. KILLIAN, JR. resigned as the special assistant to the president for science and technology in 1959, Eisenhower appointed Kistiakowsky to replace him. Kistiakowsky took leave from Harvard to accept the appointment. As the president's science adviser, he chaired meetings of the PSAC, participated in the National Aeronautics and Space Council (NASC) and the National Security Council, and coordinated scientific matters of interest to the government. He advised the president on new weapons programs, on nuclear arms control, and on proposals to stop the testing of nuclear weapons.

A fiscal and political conservative, Kistiakowsky opposed the high defense budgets submitted by the Defense Department and NASC but urged spending for basic research. He was in accord with the Eisenhower administration's position that space exploration was less a matter of national prestige than of scientific progress. Consequently, he played down the importance of spectacular manned space missions and emphasized instead the development of unmanned probes.

Kistiakowsky supported Eisenhower's emphasis on the nuclear deterrent as America's first line of defense but also backed the administration's efforts to achieve a limited test ban treaty with the USSR. While he maintained that the United States needed to continue a limited degree of testing in order to develop a "clean bomb" (one that would produce lower levels of radioactive fallout), he did not believe it necessary to create a more destructive nuclear arsenal. To critics who argued that the Soviets would violate a test ban, Kistiakowsky replied that scientific research was close to producing seismic indicators sensitive enough to detect any possible violations by the Soviet Union. When the ongoing talks with the Soviets in Geneva broke down, Eisenhower announced that the United States would not resume testing and would provide notification of any intention to resume testing.

Although the government focused primarily on the physical sciences throughout the 1950s, under Kistiakowsky's leadership, the PSAC organized a life sciences panel in January 1960. Kistiakowsky added a panel on carcinogenic chemical additives in food after the disclosure that the cranberry crop in 1959 had been contaminated by an herbicide that likely had carcinogenic effects. As a result of the crisis, the powers of the Food and Drug Administration were expanded.

After JOHN F. KENNEDY's inauguration in 1961, Kistiakowsky handed over his duties as science adviser to Jerome Wiesner. After 1960, he devoted himself principally to his work at Harvard. Nevertheless, Kistiakowsky continued to serve on the PSAC through 1963. He also served on the advisory board of the U.S. Arms Control and Disarmament Agency from 1962 to 1969. In 1968, he severed his connections with the Pentagon to protest the U.S. involvement in Vietnam. Kistiakowsky served as vice president of the National Academy of Sciences from 1965 to 1972. He became professor emeritus in 1971. Even after his retirement, Kistiakowsky continued to play an active role in debates over nuclear policy. In 1977, he became chair of the Council for a Livable World, an organization dedicated to reducing nuclear armaments and preventing nuclear war. He publicly criticized the allocation of federal resources to defense and to the space program instead of to civilian technology programs. When he worked at the White House, he kept a diary, which he published in 1976 as *A Scientist at the White House*. He died in Cambridge, Mass., on December 7, 1982.

—MSM

Knight, Goodwin (Jess)

(1896–1970) *governor of California*

The descendent of early Western settlers, Knight was born in Provo, Utah, on December 9, 1896. He moved with his family to Los Angeles at the age of eight. He attended public schools. During his youth, he wrote a collection of boys' stories published in 1910. Knight worked as a grocery clerk, miner, and newspaper reporter before entering Stanford University. He withdrew from Stanford to serve in the navy during World War I, after which he returned to Stanford and graduated in 1919. He studied political science at Cornell University from 1919 to 1920. After gaining admission to the California bar in 1921, Knight commenced the practice of law in Los Angeles. He became active in Republican politics and took part in Hiram Johnson's campaign for the presidential nomination in 1920 and 1924. Knight was appointed to fill an unexpired term as judge of the superior court of Los Angeles Co. in 1935; he won election to the bench in 1936, where he served until 1946. He gained publicity for his handling of weddings and divorces for Hollywood actors. Knight garnered more publicity by hosting radio talk shows in Los Angeles and San Francisco. Possessed of an affable personality, Knight made effective use of radio, and later television, to further his political career.

In 1944, he sought the Republican nomination to the U.S. Senate but withdrew early and backed Fred Houser. Running with Gov. EARL WARREN at the top of the ticket, Knight won election as lieutenant governor in 1946. Despite his earlier support for Hiram Johnson, Knight had strong ties to the state Republican party's right wing and often

disagreed with Warren's more progressive policies. He opposed the governor's advocacy of prepaid health insurance and a fair-employment practices bill. Unlike Warren, he supported a loyalty oath for professors in the University of California system. Nevertheless, he ran with Warren again in 1950 and won reelection.

In September 1953, Warren announced that he would not seek a fourth term, and Knight immediately declared his candidacy. The next month, Knight succeeded to the governorship when Warren resigned upon being appointed chief justice of the United States. Conservatives in California welcomed Knight's accession, and the new governor promised to "conduct a business-like administration with emphasis on reducing spending." However, he proved a more liberal governor than most observers had predicted and conservatives had hoped. Indeed, his policies proved very similar to those of Warren. To cope with California's rapidly growing population, Knight supported highway programs, rapid transit systems for metropolitan areas, and development of water resources. He increased state aid for the disabled, higher education, mental health, and unemployment compensation. In October 1954, he announced the allocation of $100,000 to study health problems caused by smog. Knight also announced that he would veto any "right-to-work" legislation. At the same time, he maintained his position as a fervent anticommunist. The governor's attempts to placate both sides of the political spectrum proved effective; in particular, his gestures toward organized labor reaped rewards. With the strong backing of the American Federation of Labor, he won election to a full term in 1954 by more than 550,000 votes over the Democratic candidate, Richard Graves.

Although the titular head of the California Republican Party, Knight struggled for control with Vice President RICHARD NIXON and the archconservative Sen. WILLIAM KNOWLAND. In 1954 Knight and Knowland joined forces to gain control of the California Republican Party. The battle heated up in 1955, as the factions struggled for leadership positions going into the elections of 1956. Nixon suffered a resounding defeat when the faction led by Knight and Knowland not only won the chairmanship of the state party but the vice-chairmanship (the vice-chairman automatically became chairman the following year, which, in this case, was an election year). In October 1955, Knight announced that he would enter the 1956 Republican National Convention as a "favorite son" candidate should President Eisenhower decide not to run. In effect, this challenged Nixon's claim as Eisenhower's successor. Throughout early 1956, Knight withheld his endorsement of Nixon for a second term as vice president, and at the convention in August, he was one of the principal opponents of Nixon's renomination. With Knowland's help, Nixon fought off the challenge.

In January 1957, Knowland announced that he planned to give up his seat in the Senate; before long, it became clear that he planned to run against Knight for the gubernatorial nomination in 1958. Knight and Knowland engaged in a bitter campaign, marked by their disagreement over right-to-work laws, which Knowland supported. By November 1957, Knight, who was trailing badly in the polls and short of money, met with Eisenhower and Nixon. After the meeting, Knight announced that he was withdrawing from the race for governor and would instead seek the seat in the Senate vacated by Knowland. The aura of a backroom deal plagued both Knowland and Knight until election day.

Knight then encountered stiff opposition in the Republican primary from George Christopher, the mayor of San Francisco. Knight and Knowland won their primaries, but Knight once again stirred up internecine warfare when he refused to endorse Knowland. The bitter divisions in the party led to a disaster at the polls in 1958. Although some labor leaders supported him, Knight lost to Rep. CLAIR ENGLE (D-Calif.) by almost three-quarters of a million votes. Knowland lost to the Democratic attorney general, EDMUND (PAT) BROWN.

After his tenure as governor, Knight became a television news commentator in Los Angeles. He planned to run for governor again in 1962, but a case of hepatitis forced him to withdraw from the race for the Republican nomination in January. Subsequently, Knight became chairman of the board of the Imperial Bank of Los Angeles. He endorsed NELSON ROCKEFELLER for the presidential nomination in 1964 and briefly considered seeking the

governorship in 1966. He died of pneumonia on May 22, 1970, in Inglewood, Calif.

—MSM

Knowland, William F(ife)

(1908–1974) *U.S. senator, Senate majority leader, Senate minority leader*

The son of a newspaper publisher and a six-term member of the House of Representatives, Knowland was born in Alameda, Calif., on June 26, 1908. At the age of 12, he made speeches for presidential candidate Warren G. Harding. Knowland graduated from the University of California in 1929, after which he joined the staff of his father's paper, the *Oakland Tribune*. He won election as a Republican to the state assembly in 1932. Two years later, he won a seat in the state senate. Already a rising star in California politics, he became a member of the Republican National Committee in 1938 and was elected to chair its executive committee in 1941.

Drafted into the army in 1942, Knowland went to Officer Candidate School and rose to the rank of major. He was serving in Europe when, in 1945, Gov. EARL WARREN appointed him to fill the unexpired term of the recently deceased Sen. Hiram Johnson (R-Calif.). The army discharged him so that he could take up the appointment, upon which Knowland returned to the United States and assumed his duties as a senator. He won election in his own right the following year and rapidly emerged as a leader of the conservative wing of the Republican party. From his arrival in the Senate, Knowland established a reputation for fervent anticommunism and for equally passionate support of Nationalist China.

Knowland frequently clashed with the Truman administration. In 1947, he supported the Taft-Hartley bill, which outlawed the closed shop and secondary boycotts, gave the president authority to impose an 80-day "cooling off" period to prevent strikes that threatened the national interest, forbade union contributions to political parties, and required unions to submit annual financial reports to the secretary of labor. Knowland helped mobilize the votes to override Truman's veto. He also supported the Tidelands Oil Bill of 1946, which would have vested in the states control of submerged lands

Senator William Knowland talks to reporters outside the White House, October 12, 1957. *(Dwight D. Eisenhower Library and Museum)*

off their coasts, including offshore oil deposits. Truman vetoed the measure.

On other issues, however, Knowland took less conservative positions. He voted for the Full Employment Act of 1945 and supported civil rights legislation. Moreover, in an era when southern senators frequently used the filibuster or the threat of a filibuster to thwart liberal legislation, Knowland in 1947 offered a bill to invoke cloture by a majority vote rather than the traditional two-thirds.

In foreign policy, Knowland became a leader of the so-called China Lobby, an informal group

of people inside and outside of government who decried the "loss" of China to the Communists in 1949 and supported the return of Chiang Kai-shek (Jiang Jieshi) and the Nationalists from Taiwan (Formosa). Knowland criticized the State Department's white paper on China, which placed blame for the fall of China to the Communists on the corruption and incompetence of the Nationalists, as a "whitewash" of a "do-nothing policy." His preoccupation with China prompted some critics to dub him "the senator from Formosa." He did, however, break with most of his colleagues on the Republican right to support Truman's plan to provide aid to

Greece and Turkey in 1947 in an effort to thwart communist insurgencies in those countries.

Knowland initially supported Truman's decision to intervene in Korea, but he soon joined Gen. Douglas MacArthur and other critics of the administration's policies, which, Knowland argued, prevented a military victory. Indeed, the senator became perhaps the most bellicose critic of the administration's handling of the war.

Anticommunism shaped Knowland's domestic policies as well. Even though he disliked Sen. JOSEPH R. McCARTHY's (R–Wis.) carelessness with facts, Knowland nonetheless supported McCarthy's charges that communists had infiltrated the American government. In particular, he backed McCarthy's contention that communist sympathizers in the State Department, such as JOHN PATTON DAVIES, JR., were responsible for the fall of China to the Communists. Even before McCarthy burst on the scene with his spectacular denunciations in February 1950, Knowland charged that Owen Lattimore, an academic expert on China and an adviser to the State Department, advocated "a policy of appeasement" in Asia and espoused the communist party line.

Knowland made the speech nominating Nixon for the vice presidency at the Republican convention in 1952 and won reelection to the Senate later that year. The elections also brought Eisenhower to the White House and gave Republicans control of both houses of Congress. Knowland became chairman of the Republican Policy Committee in 1953 and frequently stood in for the ailing majority leader, ROBERT A. TAFT of Ohio. When Taft died in July 1953, Knowland took over as majority leader. Although Knowland adopted liberal positions on some issues, in particular civil rights, his conservative politics often brought him into conflict with the president. Not long after the Californian replaced Taft, Eisenhower remarked that "Knowland is the biggest disappointment I have found since I have been in politics."

In particular, Knowland's strident and inflexible position on China resulted in friction with the administration. Knowland vigorously opposed the admission of mainland China to the United Nations and exerted pressure on the Eisenhower administration to take a firm stand against membership for China. He repeatedly offered a resolution supporting American withdrawal from the United Nations if Communist China were admitted. In April 1954, the Chinese premier, Zhou Enlai (Chou En-lai), announced that his country desired peaceful relations with the United States and asked for negotiations on outstanding issues. Knowland warned against "another Munich." Pressure from Knowland and other members of the China Lobby led Secretary of State JOHN FOSTER DULLES to announce that the administration opposed the admission of Communist China to the UN. Unappeased, Knowland threatened to resign as majority leader if mainland China gained admission. China was also the focus of Knowland's concern over the Geneva Conference on Indochina and Korea in April 1954. As the administration prepared for the conference, Knowland argued that any negotiation with the Communist Chinese government would be tantamount to recognition. All of this led a frustrated Eisenhower to write to ALFRED M. GRUENTHER, then supreme Allied commander in Europe, that "Knowland has no foreign policy except to develop high blood pressure whenever he mentions the word 'Red China.'" Knowland's persistent pressure, along with that of other members of the China Lobby, nevertheless influenced the administration's policy. Dulles attended the conference only briefly and at one session refused to shake hands with Zhou Enlai. He downgraded the U.S. delegation to the status of observer, and instructed Undersecretary of State WALTER BEDELL SMITH not to take part in the negotiations.

When the Communist Chinese began shelling the offshore islands of Quemoy and Matsu during the fall of 1954, Knowland advocated a blockade of the Chinese coast. Eisenhower resisted the pressure from the China Lobby and took no military action.

Knowland's support of McCarthy further alienated him from the Eisenhower administration. He opposed a resolution, introduced by Sen. RALPH FLANDERS (R–Vt.), to strip McCarthy of his committee chairmanships. When Flanders later introduced a motion to censure McCarthy, Knowland successfully moved to have a special committee examine the charges. Contrary to Knowland's intentions, however, the committee unanimously recommended censure. When the majority of the Senate voted in favor of the resolution in December 1954, Knowland voted against it.

Knowland's leadership proved a frequent source of irritation to Eisenhower, and not only because of differences over policy. In fact, despite his frequent disagreements with Eisenhower, as his party's leader Knowland generally supported the administration's domestic policy. However, Knowland demonstrated no particular skill as majority leader. Moreover, after the Democrats won control of both houses of Congress in the elections of 1954, Knowland became minority leader. Never an effective party leader, he proved even less so when leading the minority.

In addition to disagreements over policy, Knowland's ambition led to clashes with Eisenhower, who remarked of Knowland: "It is a pity that his wisdom, his judgment, his tact, and his sense of humor lag so far behind his ambition." In 1956, Knowland announced that he would seek the Republican nomination if Eisenhower decided to retire. Immediately, the senator from California began jockeying for position with his long-time rival, Nixon. When Eisenhower decided to run for a second term, Knowland withdrew from the race.

In January 1957, Knowland announced that he planned to give up his seat in the Senate; before long, it became clear that he planned to run against California's incumbent Republican governor, GOODWIN KNIGHT, for the gubernatorial nomination in 1958. Knight and Knowland engaged in a bitter campaign, marked by their disagreement over right-to-work laws, which Knowland supported. By November 1957, Knight, who was trailing badly in the polls and short of money, met with Eisenhower and Nixon. After the meeting, Knight announced that he was withdrawing from the race for governor and would instead seek the seat in the Senate vacated by Knowland. The aura of a backroom deal plagued both Knowland and Knight until election day.

Knowland and Knight won their primaries, but Knight once again stirred up internecine warfare when he refused to endorse Knowland. The internal divisions led to a disaster for the Republican party at the polls in 1958. Knight lost to Rep. CLAIR ENGLE (D-Calif.), and Knowland lost to

the state's Democratic attorney general, EDMUND (PAT) BROWN.

After his defeat at the polls, Knowland returned to the *Oakland Tribune* in 1958. He became president and publisher of the paper when his father died in 1966. Although he never ran for elective office again, Knowland remained active in politics. He served on BARRY GOLDWATER's campaign staff in 1964 and supported fellow Californian Ronald Reagan for the Republican presidential nomination in 1968. Knowland died, an apparent suicide, at his summer home in Monte Rio, Calif., on February 23, 1974. The cause of death was a single gunshot to his head.

—MSM

Kohlberg, Alfred
(1887–1960) *China policy lobbyist*

The son of a dry-goods shopkeeper, Kohlberg was born in San Francisco, Calif., on January 27, 1887. He enrolled at the University of California in 1904 but never graduated. At first, he tried his hand at the printing business but soon joined his family's business. After being impressed by textiles from China at the Panama Pacific Expo in 1915, Kohlberg traveled frequently to the Far East and established a series of business contacts. He purchased linen kerchiefs from Ireland, exported them to China (where pieceworkers embroidered them), and then sold them in the United States. Critics would later charge that Kohlberg paid the Chinese workers extremely low wages. By the 1930s, Kohlberg ran a thriving business based in Manhattan that would make him a wealthy man.

Given his international connections, Kohlberg was acutely aware of the political crises brewing in Europe and Asia during the 1930s and became active in various causes. The descendant of German Jewish immigrants, he worked as a fund-raiser for the United Jewish Appeal beginning in 1939. His most passionate commitment, however, was to China. He served as chairman of the Executive Committee of the American Bureau for Medical Aid to China (ABMAC) and traveled repeatedly to China to report on operations for the United China Relief (UCR) during World War II. Under the auspices of ABMAC, he went to China to determine the merit of reports that Chiang Kai-shek's (Jiang Jieshi's) Nationalist government was beset with graft and corruption. At least to his own satisfaction, Kohlberg determined that such reports were grossly exaggerated. Kohlberg also came to resent the attitude he perceived among American diplomats with respect to the Nationalist cause. As he saw it, these diplomats calmly accepted that Chiang would inevitably lose to the Communists. Even more, he concluded that the predictions of Chiang's downfall were inspired by sympathy for Mao Zedong (Mao Tse-Tung) and his Communists. After expressing his concerns within the UCR and failing to convince the leadership of the organization, he resigned in 1943. He then joined the Institute of Pacific Relations (IPR), a private think tank with ties to the State Department, but he found what he considered sympathy for the Chinese Communists there too. In the meantime, Kohlberg became a highly engaged student of communism. He read resolutions of the Comintern and the *Daily Worker*; he met with ex-Communists, many of whom became friends. Kohlberg compared IPR reports of Nationalist abuses to those in the *Daily Worker*, and wrote a report to the IPR charging that "your employees have been putting over on you a not-too-well camouflaged Communist line." When the leaders of the IPR rejected his charges, Kohlberg resigned and took his case to the Senate Subcommittee on Internal Security.

During the years after World War II, Kohlberg emerged as the leader of the "China Lobby," an informal group of individuals who criticized American policy in the years leading up to the Communist victory in China. The China Lobby sought American support for the Chinese government in exile in Taiwan and demanded that those it held responsible for the fall of China to the Communists be held accountable. In 1946, Kohlberg helped to found and became the first vice president of the America China Policy Association (ACPA), which lobbied for increased aid to Nationalist China and for the removal of communist sympathizers from the U.S. government. Later, Kohlberg served as chairman of the board of ACPA. Finding his true calling as a lobbyist and propagandist, he generated press releases, wrote letters to Congress, and compiled reports exposing the pro-communist sympa-

thies of officers in the Far East Bureau of the State Department. He also contributed articles to *China Monthly*, perhaps the most pro-Nationalist journal of that time. In those articles, he maintained that Chiang was being "sold out by pro-communist U.S. Foreign Service officers." The officers he attacked included JOHN PATTON DAVIES, JR., JOHN CARTER VINCENT, and JOHN STEWART SERVICE. Another of Kohlberg's favorite targets was Owen Lattimore, an academic expert on the Far East and a sometime adviser to the State Department. Kohlberg also published *Plain Talk*, a journal devoted to criticizing U.S. policy toward China.

The release of the State Department's White Paper on China in 1949 and Kohlberg's response brought him to national prominence. He denounced the White Paper, "the real purpose" of which, he declared, seemed "to be to reveal to the chancelleries of the world the story of the American betrayal of the Republic of China. What could be of greater aid to the Soviet Union than this?" He further alleged a "great conspiracy" that was responsible for the fall of China to the Communists. A group of conservative Republican members of Congress, "known as the China Bloc," shared similar sentiments and demanded an investigation of alleged communist sympathizers in the government.

Kohlberg found an ally in Sen. JOSEPH R. McCARTHY (R-Wis.), who in 1950 charged that he knew of communists and communist sympathizers in the State Department. The ACPA and Kohlberg supplied files to support McCarthy's charges. Investigations by the Internal Security Subcommittee of the Senate Judiciary Committee, led by Sen. PAT McCARRAN (D-Nev.), resulted in a purge of the Far East Branch of the State Department. Those whose careers were cut short included Vincent, Service, Davies, and O. Edmund Clubb.

Kohlberg's fervent anticommunism extended to domestic issues, as well. He supported not only McCarthy's charges but his methods. Kohlberg served as a member of the Special Committee on Radio and Television of the Joint Committee against Communism in New York. In 1950, the organization published a pamphlet titled *Red Channels*, which resulted in the blacklisting of many actors, directors, and writers in radio and television. Kohlberg was a founding member of the American Jewish League against Communism, which he chaired, and became its honorary president in 1955.

Kohlberg supported ROBERT TAFT, the conservative senator from Ohio, for the Republican nomination in 1952. Once Eisenhower gained the nomination, however, Kohlberg endorsed him. After Eisenhower entered the White House, Kohlberg became increasingly dissatisfied with the president's foreign policy. By 1954, Kohlberg concluded that Eisenhower was insufficiently aggressive in combating communism and charged that the president had largely followed the policies of the Truman administration.

Although he suffered a heart attack in 1954 that forced him to restrict his activities, Kohlberg remained active in his political causes. In 1955, Kohlberg set up a Committee of Endorsers, which took out newspaper advertisements demanding a more aggressive policy to combat communism. At congressional hearings, Kohlberg presented the Committee of Endorsers' program, which called on the United States to use economic, political, psychological, and military means to defeat communism. He continued actively to espouse anticommunism and the cause of Nationalist China until he died of a heart attack in Manhattan on April 7, 1960.

—MSM

Kohler, Herbert (Vollrath)
(1891–1968) *businessman*

Kohler was born in Sheboygan, Wis., on October 21, 1891. His father, John M. Kohler, founded the Kohler Company, a manufacturer of plumbing ware, in 1873. Herbert Kohler received a Ph.B. from Yale University's Sheffield Scientific School in 1914 and went to work for the family business. He became president of the company in 1937 and succeeded his half-brother, Walter J. Kohler, Sr., a former governor of Wisconsin (1929–30), as the company's chairman of the board in 1940. Under Herbert Kohler's leadership, the company became the nation's largest manufacturer of plumbing fixtures.

In 1953, Local 833 of the United Auto Workers (UAW) won an election to represent Kohler employees at the enterprise's plant in Sheboygan,

Wis., replacing a company union. On April 5, 1954, the employees went on strike, demanding a closed shop, dues check-offs, a grievance arbitration procedure, and a 10-cent-an-hour wage increase. The company rejected the first three demands and offered a three-cent increase. For two months, the factory was closed by sometimes-violent mass picketing by the approximately 3,600 striking workers (out of 4,000 company employees). However, the company obtained an injunction from a state circuit court halting the mass picketing. In June the company reopened the plant and hired replacements for the employees who did not return to work. In 1955 a near-riot developed when a group of strikers prevented a shipment of clay from reaching the factory.

Although Kohler delegated responsibility for strike negotiations to others, the company's position reflected his views. As the strike wore on year after year, he gained a reputation among businessmen and conservatives as an heroic, beleaguered, old-fashioned individualist. He denounced WALTER REUTHER, president of the UAW, as "a Moscow-trained socialist" and charged that the union was trying to tell him how to run his company. He also accused the union of resorting to violence against non-strikers. After mass picketing ended and the strikers were fired and replaced, Kohler said the union no longer represented his company's employees. The Wisconsin judge who issued the anti–mass picketing injunction subsequently stated that, after the company won the injunction, Kohler lost interest in negotiating because he thought that he had won the strike. The union offered to submit the disputed issues to arbitration, and WALTER J. KOHLER, JR., governor of Wisconsin and nephew of the company's president, appealed unsuccessfully to Herbert Kohler to agree to arbitration. In 1958, the Old Timers Council of the National Association of Manufacturers (composed of former directors of the NAM) named Herbert Kohler "Man of the Year."

To liberals and labor union spokesmen, Kohler's position on the strike represented a throwback to the aggressive antiunion attitudes of 19th-century businessmen. Reuther denounced him as "the most reactionary, anti-labor, immoral employer in America." The UAW charged the Kohler Co. with, among other things, stockpiling weapons in anticipation of the strike, instigating violence, and attempting to intimidate the strikers by hiring detectives to spy on them and on union officials. The union ultimately spent $12 million on strike benefits alone during the walkout.

In February and March 1958, the strike received national attention when the Senate Select Committee on Improper Activities in the Labor or Management Field, chaired by Sen. JOHN MCCLELLAN (D-Ark.), investigated the strife in Sheboygan. Appearing as a witness, Kohler accused the union of "mob rule" and "night-riding vandalism" and asserted that his company was performing a public service by resisting such tactics. Reuther testified that the Kohler Co. was not negotiating in good faith, but he conceded that some of the union's tactics were "reprehensible." Sen. BARRY M. GOLDWATER (R-Ariz.), a member of the panel, denounced the UAW's methods, particularly its efforts to organize a boycott of Kohler products. Sen. PAT MCNAMARA (D-Mich.) resigned from the committee, charging that some of its Republican members were using the probe to attack the UAW.

In August 1960, the five-man National Labor Relations Board (NLRB) ruled that the Kohler Co. had engaged in unfair labor practices during the strike. The board stressed particularly the granting of a wage increase to non-striking employees in 1954, describing it as an attempt to undermine the union's bargaining effectiveness. The NLRB ordered the reinstatement of most of the strikers who had been fired. The strike officially ended when the board filed its ruling on September 2, 1960.

In January 1962, the U.S. Court of Appeals in Washington, D.C., upheld the NLRB ruling. Six months later, the Supreme Court refused to hear the company's appeal. The following month, Kohler resigned his post as president but continued as chairman and executive director. In December 1962, the Kohler Co. and the UAW agreed on a contract. The pact provided for expanded fringe benefits, a major medical plan, an improved pension plan, and an additional paid holiday, but not for a closed shop or a wage increase. Three years later, all issues relating to the strike were settled when the company and the union agreed on the amount of

back pay and pensions to be granted to employees who had been fired during the walkout.

Kohler died of cerebral thrombosis and pneumonia in Sheboygan, Wis., on July 28, 1968.

—MSM

Kohler, Walter J(odok), Jr.
(1904–1976) *governor of Wisconsin*

The son of Walter Jodok Kohler, Sr., a businessman and one-term Republican governor of Wisconsin (1929–30), Walter J. Kohler, Jr., was born in Sheboygan, Wis., on April 4, 1904. His grandfather, John M. Kohler, founded a company that made enamel bathroom and kitchen fixtures. Walter J. Kohler, Sr., became president of the family business in 1905. Under his leadership, the company expanded its range of produces and became known as a manufacturer of premium bathroom and kitchen fixtures and plumbing supplies. Walter J. Kohler, Jr., graduated from Yale University in 1925 and went to work for the Kohler Co. During World War II, he volunteered for the navy and served in the Pacific for four years. Kohler was discharged as lieutenant commander in 1945. He went to work at another of the family's companies, the Vollrath Co., but soon became involved in politics. He considered challenging JOSEPH R. MCCARTHY for the Republican nomination for a seat in the U.S. Senate in 1946 but ultimately decided against it. In 1948, he chaired the Wisconsin delegation to the Republican National Convention. Kohler ran for governor in 1950 and won.

Kohler disliked McCarthy and seriously considered challenging him in the Republican primary in 1952. Instead, under pressure from party regulars, he sought reelection as governor, put aside his reservations about McCarthy, and campaigned for the senator's reelection in 1952. Kohler said: "You can't write McCarthy off. You can like him or dislike him but the fact remains that all of the things he has said about the communists in government stack up to the point where there is too much smoke to repudiate McCarthy."

Kohler also supported the candidacy of DWIGHT D. EISENHOWER for the Republican nomination and campaigned for Eisenhower in the Wisconsin primary. He also helped to organize support for Eisenhower among the nation's governors. During the general election in 1952, Eisenhower had several scheduled stops in Wisconsin. The candidate asked speechwriter EMMET JOHN HUGHES to insert a tribute to George C. Marshall, whom McCarthy had accused of disloyalty, into one of the speeches. News of the planned statement reached Republican leaders in Wisconsin. On October 2, McCarthy, Kohler, and Henry Ringling, a Republican national committeeman from Wisconsin, flew to Peoria, Ill., to meet with Eisenhower before the campaign train traveled North. McCarthy made it clear that he did not want the reference to Marshall made in Wisconsin. The meeting became heated, and Eisenhower told McCarthy in no uncertain terms what he thought of the senator's anticommunist crusade. The presidential candidate also defended Marshall and stated his intent to retain the passage. The next day, as the train headed for Green Bay, Eisenhower again met with the Republicans from Wisconsin. He lectured them about "un-American methods in combating communism." On the way to Appleton, McCarthy's hometown, McCarthy and Kohler had another tense meeting with Eisenhower and SHERMAN ADAMS. As the train headed toward Milwaukee, Kohler pleaded with Adams to delete the statement about Marshall. The governor argued that it threatened to divide the party in Wisconsin and might jeopardize Republican chances in local and national elections. Adams agreed and brought Kohler to see Eisenhower. They were joined by Maj. Gen. WILTON B. ("Jerry") PERSONS, who sympathized with Kohler's position. Ike finally relented, although an adviser later described him as "purple with rage."

Kohler won reelection in 1952 and again in 1954, running both times against WILLIAM PROXMIRE. He supported a substantial expansion of Wisconsin's highway system and signed into law the largest tax cut, in terms of percentage, at any level of government between the presidencies of Calvin Coolidge and JOHN F. KENNEDY.

During his third term, Kohler was asked to help seek a resolution to the strike against his family's company, and he offered his services as a peacemaker. WALTER REUTHER, president of the United Automobile Workers, said that he would accept the governor's decision as "final and binding." However, Kohler's uncle, HERBERT V. KOHLER, flatly rejected the offer and denounced his nephew.

In 1957, Kohler ran for the seat in the U.S. Senate vacated by the death of McCarthy. Once again, Proxmire was his opponent. This time, however, Proxmire prevailed. Kohler returned to his position as president of the Vollrath Co. He remained interested in public affairs and was a member of the Council of Foreign Relations and chairman of the American Cancer Society. He died in Sheboygan on March 21, 1976.

—MSM

Krock, Arthur
(1886–1974) *journalist*

The son of a bookkeeper, Krock was born in Glasgow, Ky., a small market town, on November 16, 1886. After attending schools in Glasgow and Chicago, he enrolled at Princeton University but was forced to leave after one semester because of financial difficulties. He earned an A.A. degree at Lewis Institute in Chicago in 1906. Soon after completing his work at Lewis Institute, he began a career in journalism as a cub reporter for the *Louisville Herald.* When the paper had to retrench in 1908, Krock lost his job but quickly found another as night editor in Louisville for the Associated Press. He became the Washington correspondent for the *Louisville Times* in 1910. Within a year, he also represented the *Louisville Courier-Journal.* In 1915 he returned to Louisville as editorial manager for the two papers. Krock served as editor in chief of the *Louisville Times* from 1919 to 1923, during which time he covered the Versailles Conference. His reporting on the peace conference earned him the French Legion of Honor. Following an editorial dispute with the paper's owner in 1923, Krock left the *Louisville Times* and moved to New York, where he took up a position as assistant to Will Hays, head of the Motion Picture Producers and Distributors of America. Before long, he joined the editorial staff of the *New York World* and in 1923 became assistant to its publisher, Ralph Pulitzer. Krock joined the *New York Times* as an editorial writer in 1927 and became head of the paper's Washington bureau in January 1932. In addition to his administrative duties, he remained a correspondent and in 1933 began a signed, editorial-page column titled "In the Nation." He stepped down as head of the Washington bureau in 1953 but continued to write his column until his retirement in 1966.

A political conservative, Krock often criticized the New Deal, which he regarded as a threat to states' rights and free enterprise. Krock quickly recognized the growing importance of fiscal and monetary policy; he set about mastering the economic theories and policies of the New Deal and quickly became an acknowledged expert. He won two Pulitzer Prizes during the Roosevelt administration. The first came in 1935 for general excellence in reporting; the second came in 1937 for an interview with Franklin D. Roosevelt, in which the president discussed his accomplishments and plans, including his determination to add new members to the Supreme Court.

Krock had a close personal relationship with President HARRY S. TRUMAN, which began when Truman was a senator. Their friendship did not, however, prevent Krock from frequently attacking the administration. He opposed much of Truman's Fair Deal legislation, which Krock characterized as "more federal paternalism and . . . centralization." The columnist also criticized Truman for giving federal positions to friends and allies rather than to people qualified for the jobs. On the other hand, Krock praised Truman's forceful opposition to the nationwide strikes of coal miners, railway workers, and steelworkers; he also supported the president's efforts to contain communism (although he sometimes criticized Truman for not being aggressive enough in doing so). In 1951, Krock revealed that Truman had approached Gen. DWIGHT D. EISENHOWER with an offer to support the general for the Democratic presidential nomination in 1952 (Truman had made a similar offer to Eisenhower in 1948). Although Truman denied that the incident took place and Eisenhower refused to confirm it, Krock stood behind his story and maintained that his source was a "Democrat in an eminent public position." Years later he revealed that it had been Justice WILLIAM O. DOUGLAS.

Krock supported Eisenhower for the presidency in 1952 and looked forward to a conservative administration. After Eisenhower's election, however, Krock proved somewhat ambivalent about

the Eisenhower administration. During the early years of Eisenhower's presidency, Krock vacillated between charges that the president was acting tentatively and anticipation of the exertion of strong presidential leadership. By 1956, he criticized Eisenhower for his inability to lead the nation. Two years later, Krock was again defending the president against charges that he was "merely serving out his term." In his memoirs, Krock expressed a generally favorable, although not uncritical, view of the Eisenhower administration. His greatest criticism of Eisenhower was his failure to rein in the federal budget, the "steady increase" of which, Krock argued, established Eisenhower as "another of the great spenders."

The southern-born Krock responded cautiously to the Supreme Court's decision striking down segregated public schools. He called it a "milestone in more ways than one" because political and ideological differences on the Court had been submerged by agreement on the basic proposition that segregation in public schools harmed those segregated and therefore violated the equal protection clause of the Fourteenth Amendment. Krock found wisdom in the Court's decision to withhold relief and to order reargument on implementation in the fall. Gradualism was necessary, he maintained, because the ruling struck at the established social and political systems of the South. Localities would require time "to survey the acute problem which the Supreme Court has imposed on them and to decide how to resolve it." Krock predicted that the "problem will not instantly disappear" and asked that those who had pressed for the decision "be foremost in cooperating with those who are confronted with its incalculable consequences at first-hand." After defiance of a federal court order relating to the desegregation of Central High School in Little Rock, Ark., led Eisenhower to send federal troops to enforce the order, Krock wrote that the incident marked the end of a period in which the South tried to oppose the Court's ruling by legal, or "positive," means. He predicted that "the negative period of state and local resistance will now begin" and that some states would shut down their school systems.

Throughout the 1960s, Krock was a conservative voice on an increasingly liberal paper. He remained skeptical of presidential power and liberal economics. In addition to his two Pulitzer prizes, Krock won a special Pulitzer commendation in 1950 and a special Pulitzer citation in 1955. Soon after his retirement in 1966, he published a selection of his columns. Krock published his *Memoirs* in 1968, followed by two other books, *The Consent of the Governed and Other Deceits* (1971) and *Myself When Young: Growing Up in the 1890s* (1974). He received the Medal of Freedom in 1970. Although he personally liked President RICHARD M. NIXON, Krock was shocked and offended by the Watergate scandal. In the last year of his life, Krock complained that Nixon had betrayed the conservative cause. Krock died in Washington, D.C., on April 12, 1974.

Kuchel, Thomas H(enry)
(1910–1994) *U.S. senator*

The product of a pioneer family that helped found the southern California town of Anaheim and owned and edited the *Anaheim Gazette*, Kuchel was born in Anaheim on August 15, 1910. He graduated from the University of Southern California in 1932 and from the university's law school in 1935. That same year, he was admitted to the bar and began to practice law in Anaheim. He represented Orange Co. as a Republican in the state assembly from 1936 to 1939 and served in the state senate from 1940 to 1945. While still serving as a state senator, Kuchel volunteered for the U.S. Naval Reserve and was called to active duty as a lieutenant (junior grade) in 1942. He remained in the service until 1945. Gov. EARL WARREN appointed Kuchel to an unfilled term as state controller in February 1946. In November of that year, he won election to a full term. In 1950, Kuchel not only won the nomination of his own party for controller, but he won the Democratic nomination as well (then a common practice under California's cross-filing primary system). He ran unopposed in the general election. When RICHARD NIXON assumed the vice presidency in 1953, Warren named Kuchel to fill Nixon's seat in the U.S. Senate until the elections of 1954. Kuchel defeated Rep. Sam Yorty (D-Calif.) in the election to fill the remainder of Nixon's term. Kuchel won election to a full term in 1956 and was reelected in 1962.

Although he described himself as a "middle-of-the-road Eisenhower Republican," Kuchel took conservative, antiadministration positions on a number of issues during his first years in the Senate. He was one of the cosponsors of the Bricker amendment, which sought to curb the president's power to make treaties and to impose greater congressional regulation over the conduct of foreign affairs. Strenuous opposition by the administration led to the defeat of the Bricker amendment on February 25, 1954. One day later, a milder version sponsored by Sen. WALTER F. GEORGE (D-Ga.) fell one vote short of the two-thirds majority needed to pass a constitutional amendment. Kuchel also opposed the censure of Sen. JOSEPH R. McCARTHY (R-Wis.) in late 1954.

Kuchel soon moved away from his conservative positions and by the late 1950s became identified with the liberal Republican minority in the Senate. He supported the Air Pollution Control Act of 1955, which appropriated $5 million annually for five years for research by the Public Health Service. His political evolution reflected, in part, a recognition that California had a majority of registered Democrats and a large proportion of independent voters. Therefore, to be successful, a Republican candidate had to appeal to Democratic and independent voters. Kuchel's moderate course earned him the support not only of the business community, but also of some labor unions. In his bid for reelection in 1956, Kuchel followed the Warren tradition of personal, almost nonpartisan campaigning. He emphasized his independence from other Republican office seekers, formed his own campaign committee, and tapped independent sources of funds.

Although Kuchel's independence won him broad electoral support, it cost him influence within the state Republican party. When Warren's appointment as chief justice in 1953 removed him from California politics, it left the state's Republican party without a generally accepted leader. For several years, Sen. WILLIAM F. KNOWLAND, Gov. GOODWIN J. KNIGHT, and Vice President Nixon struggled for control of the party. Kuchel remained aloof from the contending factions. Even after the elections of 1958, in which Knowland lost his bid for the governorship and Knight was defeated for Knowland's seat in the Senate, leaving Kuchel as the only Republican holding a major statewide office, Kuchel did not become involved in the struggle for control of the party. Moreover, after that electoral debacle, conservatives gradually took over the party's organizational apparatus, and Kuchel's position in the party deteriorated. Furthermore, the repeal of California's cross-filing system in 1958 meant that he could no longer count on Democratic votes to secure the Republican nomination.

Following heavy Republican losses in the congressional elections of 1958, Kuchel joined a group of Republican liberals in challenging the conservative leadership of the party in the Senate. In an effort to avoid an intraparty conflict, Sen. EVERETT DIRKSEN (R-Ill.), the conservative candidate for minority leader, offered the post of whip to Kuchel, but the insurgents, led by Sen. GEORGE AIKEN (R-Vt.), refused the compromise. By the time the party caucus met in January 1959, the conservatives had enough votes to win all the leadership posts. Dirksen, however, in an effort to maintain unity, backed Kuchel instead of the conservative candidate for whip, KARL MUNDT (R-S.Dak.). With Dirksen's support, Kuchel won election as whip, a position he held until he left the Senate in 1969. Dirksen also arranged Kuchel's assignment to the important Senate Appropriations Committee.

As the Republican whip, Kuchel helped promote legislation on which the party's position had been determined by the Republican Policy Committee. Occasionally, this meant supporting legislation favored by the Republicans' southern Democratic partners in the Senate's conservative coalition. In 1959, for example, Kuchel introduced an amendment to a labor anticorruption bill that weakened a provision permitting the secretary of labor to seek federal court injunctions blocking unions from depriving their members of voting and other rights. Southern Democrats feared that this provision would serve as a precedent for civil rights action on behalf of black members of southern unions. However, Kuchel often voted against the majority of his party.

Kuchel joined liberals in an unsuccessful attempt to strengthen the Civil Rights Act of 1960 by empowering the attorney general to enter private suits for school desegregation. In the same year, he voted to override the president's veto of salary increases for federal employees, a measure opposed by most Republicans as fiscally irresponsible. As a result of these stands, Kuchel exerted little influence with most of his Republican colleagues in the Senate.

During the Kennedy and Johnson administrations, Kuchel continued to side with liberals on many domestic issues. In 1964, for example, he was one of only five Republicans to vote for Medicare, and he was influential in the passage of conservation measures. Kuchel also played a major role in obtaining passage of civil rights legislation in the mid-1960s. He was comanager on the floor for bills that became the Civil Rights Act of 1964 and the Voting Rights Act of 1965. His refusal to support Sen. BARRY GOLDWATER (R-Ariz.), the Republican nominee in 1964, led to an unsuccessful attempt to oust Kuchel as whip the following year. Kuchel further alienated members of his party by refusing to support Nixon for governor of California in 1962, George Murphy for the Senate in 1964, and Ronald Reagan for governor in 1966. When Kuchel came up for reelection in 1968, conservatives in California backed Max Rafferty, who defeated him for the Republican nomination. Kuchel returned to legal practice with a firm in Beverly Hills and subsequently became a lobbyist for Colombian sugar interests. He resided in Beverly Hills until his death on November 21, 1994.

—MSM

Ladejinsky, Wolf I(saac)

(1899–1975) *agricultural expert*

The son of a well-to-do Jewish miller and trader, Ladejinsky was born in Ekaterinopol, Ukraine, on March 15, 1899. He completed secondary studies at a local gymnasium, but the prospect of study at a university was disrupted by the outbreak of the Russian Revolution, during which his father's mill and property were confiscated and his brother killed. At the age of 21, Ladejinsky fled to Romania, where he found a clerical job with the Bucharest office of the Hebrew Immigrant Aid Society (HIAS). With the assistance of HIAS, he came to the United States in 1922 and settled in New York City. He had no money and spoke no English; over the next four years, he supported himself by making mattresses, washing windows, and selling newspapers. During this time, he saved his money and learned English. He enrolled in Columbia University in 1926, and graduated with a B.S. in 1928. That same year, he became a naturalized citizen. In 1930, he took a position as an interpreter with the Soviet Union's Amtorg Trading Corporation. He was fired without explanation after one year. Ladejinsky then earned a master's degree in agricultural economics from Columbia University in 1934. The following year, Ladejinsky joined the Office of Foreign Agricultural Relations in the U.S. Department of Agriculture. He published several articles on Soviet collective farms, denouncing Soviet agricultural policies under Stalin; he also published numerous articles on Asian agriculture. By the end of World War II, Ladejinsky had become one of the department's leading experts on Asian agriculture.

During the postwar period, Ladejinsky emerged as a major force behind land reform in Asia. In 1945, Gen. Douglas MacArthur called him to Japan as an adviser to the occupation government. Under Ladejinsky's direction, the old Japanese feudal system was abolished, and Japanese farmers were allowed to acquire land. Millions of acres were redistributed to peasants. He also went to China to help implement land reform there, but he was eventually forced out when the Communists took power. As an adviser to Chiang Kai-shek (Jiang Jieshi), Ladejinsky also aided land redistribution in Taiwan (Formosa). In 1950, he became an agricultural attaché with the U.S. embassy in Tokyo, and, by 1954, he was in charge of the American agricultural program in the Far East.

As a result of bureaucratic reorganization, agricultural attachés were transferred to the Department of Agriculture in 1954. Ladejinsky, therefore, had to undergo a security clearance, despite the fact that he had been given clearance by the State Department only seven months earlier. Under the Eisenhower administration's security program, department heads held responsibility for clearance. In December 1954, the Department of Agriculture informed Ladejinsky that he would not be reappointed to his post because he did not meet "technical standards and security requirements." Secretary of Agriculture Ezra Taft Benson based his decision in part on the different role agricultural attachés would play under the Department of Agriculture (as Benson put it, "It was agriculture we were interested in, not land reform"). With respect to "security requirements," Benson cited Ladejinsky's former employment with Amtorg, his connection with communist front organizations, an extended visit to the Soviet Union in 1939, and the fact that the attaché had family in the Ukraine. In particular, Benson maintained that Ladejinsky's family in the Ukraine gave the Soviet government sway over him. Many officials, including Sen. HUBERT HUMPHREY (D-Minn.) and Rep. WALTER JUDD (R-Minn.), came to Ladejinsky's defense. They pointed out that Ladejinsky's trip to the Soviet Union came at the request of the Agriculture Department and that his connection with communist front organizations amounted to nothing more than his name on their mailing lists. Prominent Japanese officials objected that the denial of Ladejinsky's clearance damaged American prestige in the Far East. Even behind-the-scenes maneuvering by the White House failed to persuade Benson to reconsider.

On January 5, 1955, in what amounted to a slap in the face to Benson, Ladejinsky received full security clearance by the Foreign Operations Administration (FOA) and was hired to supervise land reform projects in South Vietnam. Finally, Benson reversed his decision and apologized to Ladejinsky. When the functions of FOA were transferred to the International Cooperation Administration in May 1955, Ladejinsky was assigned to that agency.

Ladejinsky was forced to resign his post in February 1956, when he violated a rule forbidding employees of the FOA from investing in companies that received aid from the United States. He remained in South Vietnam as an adviser to President Ngo Dinh Diem until 1961. For the next three years, he worked as a consultant and regional specialist for the Ford Foundation. In 1964, he participated in a study by the World Bank of economic development in India, and he remained with the World Bank for the next decade, most of which he spent as a member of the World Bank's permanent resident mission in India. Ladejinsky died in Washington, D.C., on July 3, 1975.

—MSM

Landrum, Phil(lip) M(itchell)
(1907–1990) *U.S. congressman*

Landrum was born in Martin, Ga., a small village in the northeastern part of the state, on September 10, 1907. He attended public schools and Mercer University in Macon, Ga. In the early and mid-1930s, he worked as a coach in local high schools. From 1937 to 1941, he was superintendent of Nelson (Ga.) High School. While teaching, Landrum attended Piedmont College in Demorest, Ga., from which he graduated in 1939, and earned his LL.B. from the Atlanta Law School in 1941. Upon his admission to the bar in 1941, he commenced the practice of law in Canton, Ga. In 1942, he ran unsuccessfully for the Democratic nomination for a congressional seat. After enlisting in the army air corps as a private in 1942, he served in Europe and was discharged in June 1945 as a first lieutenant. Upon returning to civilian life, Landrum worked briefly for the Veterans Administration before being appointed assistant attorney general of Georgia in 1946, a position he held until 1947. Between 1947 and 1949, he served as executive secretary to Gov. M. E. Thompson. He then practiced law in Jasper, Ga. In 1952, Landrum defeated five other Democrats to win the party's nomination for a seat in the U.S. House of Representatives. He ran unopposed in November. As a member of the House, he represented a poor agricultural area of the state with an economy based on poultry raising and low-wage textile manufacturing.

Landrum established a conservative record in Congress. He opposed the development of public power and large-scale public works projects, such as the Saint Lawrence Seaway. He was the only Democrat on the Education and Labor Committee in 1955 to vote against raising the minimum wage from 75 cents to $1. He did, however, vote for the bill on the floor of the House.

Landrum vigorously opposed civil rights legislation. In March 1956, he joined 100 other southern members of Congress in signing the "Southern Manifesto," which denounced the Supreme Court's ruling that segregated public schools were unconstitutional and pledged "all lawful means" to bring about its reversal. In July 1956, he voted against a bill to provide federal aid for school construction that contained the Powell amendment, which barred schools practicing segregation from receiving such funds. Landrum also voted against the Civil Rights Acts of 1957 and 1960 and opposed extending the life of the Civil Rights Commission. He voted against granting statehood to Alaska in 1958 and Hawaii in 1959 because the admission of the new states would reduce the South's influence in Congress.

As a member of the House Education and Labor Committee, Landrum became involved in developing measures to deal with corruption in labor unions. Investigations in 1957 by the Senate Select Committee on Improper Activities in the Labor or Management Field, led by Sen. JOHN MCCLELLAN (D-Ark.), revealed extensive corruption and embezzlement in labor unions as well as collusion between management and labor leaders. In 1958, two members of the McClellan committee, JOHN KENNEDY (D-Mass.) and SAM ERVIN (D-N.C.), offered a bill that mandated secret ballots in union elections and full disclosure of financial transactions. The Senate passed the measure, but the House rejected it. Early in 1959, Eisenhower called for legislation to safeguard union contributions of workers, insure secret ballots in union elections, and protect the public interest during labor disputes. In July 1959, the House Education and Labor Committee reported out a bill, sponsored by Karl Elliot (D-Ala.), that focused on the prevention of financial and electoral misconduct by union leaders. Landrum, however, believed the bill "too weak" and demanded more extensive measures. Together with Rep. ROBERT P. GRIFFIN (R-Mich.), Landrum developed an alternative bill designed to strengthen the Taft-Hartley Act, which passed the House. In early August, President DWIGHT D. EISENHOWER made a special speech on radio and television supporting the Landrum-Griffin bill as "a good start toward a real labor reform law." Despite opposition from liberals and organized labor, the bill passed both houses of Congress, and Eisenhower signed it into law in September 1959. The new law contained a "bill of rights" for labor, set criminal penalties for the abuse of union offices, and guaranteed union members free elections. Its most controversial provisions amended the Taft-Hartley Act to: (1) expand the ban on secondary boycotts by prohibiting unions from using boycotts to coerce employers

to stop doing business with other firms; (2) extend secondary boycott provisions to additional workers; and (3) permit state agencies and courts to take jurisdiction under state law of cases the National Labor Relations Board refused to accept.

In December, Landrum urged further amendment of the Taft-Hartley Act to deal with "national emergencies," such as the steel strike of that year. He declared the Landrum-Griffin Act "only the beginning of real reform."

Landrum was a forceful advocate for the southern textile industry during the 1960s. He supported restrictions on textile imports and opposed increases in the minimum wage. Although he continued his opposition to civil rights legislation, Landrum played a leading role in obtaining passage of President LYNDON JOHNSON's domestic legislation. He played a decisive role in gaining passage in the House of the Equal Opportunity Act of 1964. In addition, he sponsored legislation in the House to enact Johnson's War on Poverty and played an instrumental role in gaining the support of southern members to insure its passage. Landrum also voted for Medicare in 1965. He did not stand for reelection in 1976. He returned to Jasper, Ga., where he resided until his death on November 19, 1990.

—MSM

Langer, William
(1886–1959) *U.S. senator; chairman, Judiciary Committee*

William Langer was born on his family's farm in Everest Township, near Casselton in the Dakota Territory on September 30, 1886. After graduating from Casselton High School as valedictorian in 1904, he received an LL.B. from the University of North Dakota in 1906, but, by statute, was too young to practice law. He then attended Columbia University, where he was valedictorian, and received a B.A. in 1910. After a failed venture in Mexico, he returned to North Dakota, where he was admitted to the bar in 1911, settled in Mandan, and served as assistant state's attorney for Morton Co. until 1914. He became state's attorney in 1914, and held that office until 1916, when he moved to Bismark, N.Dak., and set up a law practice there. Running as a Republican with backing from the

Non-Partisan League (NPL), he won election as state attorney general in 1916 and reelection two years later. The NPL, a farmers' alliance that advocated state cooperatives, steadily gained influence in the state's Republican Party. As attorney general, Langer aggressively enforced Prohibition and Sunday closing laws; he also energetically enforced compulsory school attendance and prosecuted vice. He broke with the NPL in 1919, accusing its leadership of advocating "socialism and free love," and the next year ran unsuccessfully for the Republican gubernatorial nomination. Langer returned to the practice of law in Bismark and, over the next decade, held a number of appointive offices. He served on the state parole board, the board of equalization, and the board of health (which he headed). After being defeated for the Republican nomination as attorney general in 1928, Langer made peace with the NPL.

In 1932, Langer captured the Republican nomination for governor. He endorsed Franklin D. Roosevelt for president, attacked the grain trade monopoly, unjust grain grading, and corruption in financial institutions and state government. In a difficult year for Republicans, Langer won in a landslide. Shortly after assuming office, he became embroiled in scandal and controversy. In 1934, he was found guilty in federal court of coercing state employees to buy subscriptions equal to 5 percent of their salaries to the NPL's newspaper, the *Leader*. Since a convicted felon was barred from holding state office, the lieutenant governor claimed the right to succeed Langer, who responded by declaring martial law and calling out the National Guard. Ultimately, on July 17th, 1934, the state's supreme court removed him from office. Langer appealed his conviction and won a new trial, which resulted in a hung jury. In 1935, yet another trial resulted in his acquittal.

Running as an independent with backing from the NPL, Langer won election as governor in 1936. Two years later, again endorsed by the NPL, Langer failed to unseat the incumbent, Sen. Gerald P. Nye (R-N.Dak.), in the Republican primary. Langer then filed as an independent in the general election and again lost to Nye. In 1940, this time running as a Republican with support from the NPL, Langer won a three-way race for a seat in the Senate. His opponents brought a series of charges to the Senate Committee on Elections and Privileges. Langer was allowed to take his seat "without prejudice" while the committee investigated the allegations. After reviewing the evidence in a voluminous report, the committee, in December 1941, recommended by a vote of 13 to 3 that Langer be denied his seat because he had demonstrated "continuous, contemptuous, and shameful disregard for public duty." In March 1942, however, the Senate as a whole voted to allow Langer to retain his seat.

In the Senate, Langer established a reputation as a maverick. A rigid isolationist both before and after World War II, he broke with other Republican isolationists on most social and economic issues. In foreign policy, Langer repeatedly opposed legislation, backed by Roosevelt, that moved the United States away from neutrality and prepared for war. In 1943, he accused the president of having led the country into war. He opposed the collective security proposals of Dumbarton Oaks in 1945 and was one of only two senators to vote against ratification of the United Nations charter. As relations with the Soviet Union deteriorated after the war, Langer opposed aid to Greece and Turkey, the Marshall Plan, the North Atlantic Treaty, and universal military training. His approach to the Korean conflict was somewhat schizophrenic. He asked for withdrawal of American ground forces in March 1951 but two years later attacked American allies for opposing action beyond the Yalu River.

In domestic politics, however, he voted against the Taft-Hartley Act in 1947 and supported high agricultural price supports, rural electrification, rural telephone service, as well as retirement benefits for postal workers. Langer consistently defended the interests of American Indians and civil service employees. He backed HARRY S. TRUMAN for the presidency in 1948.

Despite his eclectic positions, he remained popular with voters in North Dakota. He won reelection in 1946, 1952, and 1958. In the last of those elections, he carried every county in the state. Langer endorsed neither candidate in 1952 but appeared in North Dakota with Truman, who was campaigning for the Democratic nominee, ADLAI STEVENSON. Ironically, Eisenhower's victory helped Republicans capture both houses of

Congress, which made Langer chair of the Senate Judiciary Committee when Congress convened in 1953.

In general, Langer opposed the Eisenhower administration's legislative program. He supported the president less frequently than any Republican in the Senate. During the 83rd Congress, for example, *Congressional Quarterly* reported that he backed legislation endorsed by the White House only 29 percent of the time. In 1955, 1956, and 1958, Langer was the Republican senator who most frequently voted against the administration.

As chair of the Judiciary Committee, he headed the panel's special investigation of juvenile delinquency in 1953 and 1954. The hearings focused on the effect of mass media on children and, in particular, the relationship of the media to deviancy and delinquency. In January 1954, Langer used his position as chair of the Judiciary Committee to delay the confirmation of EARL WARREN as chief justice of the United States. Langer was angered by what he perceived to be a lack of patronage for his state. Claiming that he had no bias against Warren, Langer held hearings in which he allowed the most scurrilous charges to be aired. Senator ARTHUR V. WATKINS (R-Utah) declared the accusations to be "the biggest lot of tommyrot ever brought before a Senate committee." Although he eventually supported Warren, Langer voted against the nomination of JOHN M. HARLAN of New York as associate justice of the Supreme Court a year later.

Langer's support of public power brought him once again into conflict with the administration. When the Atomic Energy Commission's (AEC) consumption of power generated by the Tennessee Valley Authority (TVA) threatened the city of Memphis with an eventual shortage of electricity, the TVA proposed building a new steam plant to meet the growing demand. Eisenhower, who favored private development of power, ordered the director of the Bureau of the Budget, JOSEPH DODGE and the chairman of the AEC, LEWIS L. STRAUSS, to explore the possibility of having private industry build the plant. EDGAR H. DIXON, president of Middle South Utilities, and EUGENE A. YATES, chairman of the board of the Southern Company, formed the Mississippi Valley Generation Company

to build the plant to supply power to the TVA. The TVA, AEC, and Bureau of the Budget found the Dixon-Yates proposal acceptable, and Eisenhower approved it. The decision infuriated advocates of public power.

In August 1954, Langer insisted on investigating charges that Dixon had been involved in questionable business practices. When the Republican leadership in the Senate blocked Langer, he paid for hearings himself. Senators defending the administration, including EVERETT M. DIRKSEN (R-Ill.) and JOHN MARSHALL BUTLER (R-Md.), argued that Langer's funding of the hearings was improper. Langer simply ignored them. As chair of the Judiciary Committee's Antitrust Subcommittee, Langer took testimony in August and issued a report on Dixon's Mississippi Power and Light Company. The subcommittee's analysis cited "monopolistic trends and abuses" in Dixon's operations and attacked the administration's support of private power development. Dirksen, a member of the subcommittee, refused to sign the report. In July 1955, Langer accused Dixon of committing perjury when testifying on his role in the negotiation of the contract.

Langer's opposition to the Dixon-Yates contract resulted in his refusal to back Strauss's nomination as secretary of commerce in 1959. The nomination ultimately went down to defeat in the full Senate. Only two Republicans, Langer and MARGARET CHASE SMITH (R-Maine), voted against Strauss.

In December 1954, Langer voted against the condemnation of Sen. JOSEPH R. MCCARTHY (R-Wis.). The North Dakotan frequently disagreed with McCarthy on the rights of those accused of communist sympathies, but he felt a personal obligation to McCarthy for his help during Langer's campaign for the Republican nomination in 1952. McCarthy recorded a message defending the North Dakotan against charges from the right wing of the state's party that Langer was insufficiently anticommunist.

Langer joined Sen. HUBERT HUMPHREY (D-Minn.) in sponsoring a constitutional amendment that would have abolished the electoral college and provided for the direct popular election of the president. Langer also supported a national presidential primary. The Senate refused to act on Langer's proposal in 1955 and again in 1956.

Not only did Langer often disagree with Eisenhower on domestic matters, he also split with the administration over foreign policy. In February 1954, he voted for the Bricker amendment, designed to limit the treaty-making power of the president. When the Communist Chinese began shelling the offshore islands of Quemoy and Matsu in 1954 and Eisenhower sought a congressional resolution committing the United States to the defense of Taiwan (Formosa), Langer unsuccessfully offered an amendment that would have prohibited the use of American forces on the Chinese mainland, Quemoy, or Matsu. Langer, who had long opposed mutual security treaties, was the only senator to vote against ratification of the Southeast Asia Treaty Organization in February 1955. That same month, he was one of only six senators to vote against the China Mutual Defense Treaty. Langer later supported initiatives that would have restricted America's commitments to defend Taiwan.

In spite of his disagreements with the president and the administration, when the NPL filed in the Democratic column in 1956, Langer, who was not up for reelection that year, endorsed Eisenhower. By the late 1950s, Langer's health was failing, but he refused to relinquish his seat in the Senate. Angry over his independence, the state Republican party officially opposed his renomination in 1958 and backed another candidate. Langer nonetheless won the primary by a two-to-one majority and carried every county. Even though he did not make a single campaign appearance, he easily won the general election that fall. During the contest for the Republican nomination, Dirksen, contrary to his normal practice, had endorsed Langer, who returned the favor in January 1959 by supporting Dirksen for minority leader in the Senate. By 1959, Langer, who had suffered from diabetes for years, was blind. He died of a heart attack in Washington, D.C., on November 8, 1959.

—MSM

Lansdale, Edward G(eary)
(1908–1987) *air force officer*

The son of an automotive executive, Lansdale was born in Detroit on February 6, 1908. He attended the University of California at Los Angeles (UCLA) and obtained a commission in the army through the Reserve Officers' Training Corps. After leaving UCLA without graduating in 1931, he went to New York to find work as a journalist. He moved back to California in 1935 and began a career in advertising. When World War II broke out, he was working in San Francisco. He had resigned his commission and applied to have it reinstated. While he was waiting, a business acquaintance helped him get him a position in the Office of Strategic Services (OSS), the forerunner of the Central Intelligence Agency (CIA). Called to active duty in 1943, he was assigned to military intelligence but continued to work for the OSS. After the war, Lansdale received a commission in the regular army and went to the Philippines with the rank of major. There he was in charge of intelligence analysis for the Western Pacific. While still in the Philippines, he transferred to the newly created air force in 1947. In 1949, the air force effectively lent him to an interagency espionage group, the Office of Policy Coordination, which became part of the CIA in 1952. Lansdale became intrigued with the techniques of psychological warfare. Moreover, he became convinced that the cold war would be fought not through conventional warfare, but in a struggle for the loyalty of people in the emerging nations. For Lansdale, the answer to the revolutionary doctrine of the communists was not only military strength and foreign aid; local governments had to establish their legitimacy with their people.

In 1950, Lansdale, now a lieutenant colonel, returned to the Philippines, ostensibly as a military adviser. In fact, his mission was to help Ramon Magsaysay, the Philippine defense minister, establish a popular base. Lansdale helped Magsaysay defeat the communist-led insurgents known as the Huks. Convinced that the guerrilla war could not be won through the use of conventional military force alone, Lansdale counseled Magsaysay on counterinsurgency techniques. In addition to psychological warfare, Lansdale advocated the development of social, economic, and political programs to win the allegiance of the rural population. By the time Lansdale left the Philippines, the Philippine government had defeated the Huks, and Magsaysay had won the presidency by an overwhelming majority in 1953. His work in the Philippines earned Lansdale a reputation as an expert in counterinsurgency.

Lansdale's success in the Philippines prompted Eisenhower to send him to Vietnam in 1954 to prevent a communist takeover of that country. Lansdale's mission was to help the Vietnamese resist the communists, but not to help the French restore their colonial rule. An idealistic advocate of democracy, he undertook the mission with zeal. Lansdale arrived in South Vietnam in June, just as the Geneva accords divided the country into the communist-controlled North and non-communist South. A month after he arrived, Ngo Dinh Diem became prime minister of South Vietnam. Lansdale befriended the new prime minister and became Diem's close personal adviser. Lansdale organized the Saigon Military Mission, which operated independently of the CIA station in Saigon and of the U.S. embassy, and engaged in undercover operations against the North. He helped to organize the mass movement of refugees, the majority of whom were Catholics, from the North to the South. In addition, Lansdale developed a number of programs designed to prevent the expansion of the communist Viet Minh and broaden Diem's political base. He helped the new government set up plans for the quick integration of refugees from the North and aided in the development of programs to train governmental administrators for provinces vacated by the Viet Minh. Lansdale also trained the South Vietnamese Army in intelligence operations and psychological warfare. Perhaps most difficult of all, he attempted to temper Diem's autocratic impulses and educate him in the techniques of electoral politics.

Lansdale went to great lengths to assure the survival and success of Diem's government. He disbursed considerable sums of money to help neutralize Diem's political opponents and helped to prevent a coup against Diem by disgruntled army officers in 1954. Lansdale also sought to undermine the power of local warlords and gangsters, known as sect leaders. His advice helped Diem prevail in an armed confrontation with the sects in the spring of 1955. In the spring of 1955, Lansdale also defended Diem against the assessment by Eisenhower's personal representative, Gen. J. LAWTON COLLINS, that Diem could not win the necessary backing of the army or make the governmental reforms necessary to establish a broad political base. In addition, Lansdale defended Diem against the French, who

hated the premier because of his anti-French attitude. With the backing of the French, the head of state, Bao Dai, ordered Diem to leave office in April 1955. Diem, however, refused, and contemplated a coup against Bao Dai. Lansdale dissuaded him, and convinced the premier to hold a plebiscite in which voters could effectively choose between Bao Dai and Diem. In a referendum held on October 23, 1955, voters cast 98 percent of ballots to oust Bao Dai and replace him with Diem as chief of state. Three days later, Diem proclaimed the Republic of South Vietnam, with himself as its first president.

For all his efforts, Lansdale never enjoyed the success with Diem that he had with Magsaysay. Lansdale insisted that Diem permit a loyal opposition and warned Diem against forming his own political party, urging him instead to function as a nonpartisan national leader. Instead, the South Vietnamese leader placed family members in key positions, failed to broaden his base of support, and alienated much of South Vietnam with oppressive policies.

Lansdale left Vietnam in 1956 and went to the Pentagon as an assistant to the secretary of defense for covert operations. Whatever Diem's shortcomings, he remained in power, and that added to Lansdale's reputation. In 1960, Lansdale, then a brigadier general, returned to Vietnam for an inspection mission. His report criticized the Diem regime for not instituting needed political, economic, and social reforms. He reserved some of his harshest criticism for the United States for failing to support Diem with a full range of programs to solidify his support. The report impressed the new president, JOHN F. KENNEDY, who authorized an expanded counterinsurgency program and increased aid to the government in Saigon. Kennedy considered appointing Lansdale ambassador to South Vietnam, but officials in the departments of State and Defense insisted that the general was too controversial and independent. Kennedy used Lansdale as an adviser throughout his administration. After the failure of the invasion at the Bay of Pigs, Kennedy assigned Lansdale to undertake a reexamination of policy toward Cuba. Lansdale became part of Operation Mongoose, an effort to destabilize the Cuban government and to assassinate Fidel Castro. Military and diplomatic officials, always uncomfortable with Lansdale's unorthodox and freewheeling approach, arranged for his promotion to major general in 1963 and his retirement from active duty on October 31. At the urging of Vice President HUBERT H. HUMPHREY, President LYNDON JOHNSON sent Lansdale back to Vietnam in 1965 as a special assistant to the American ambassador. His assignment was to work on broadening the political base of the government, but he had little influence on policy-making decisions. Lansdale left Vietnam in 1968 and published his memoirs, *In the Midst of Wars: An American's Mission to Southeast Asia*, in 1972. He died at his home in McLean, Va., on February 23, 1987.

Throughout his career, Lansdale remained a controversial figure. To some, he exemplified the best kind of American military adviser, interested not only in warfare but in helping the nation on whose behalf he fought. William J. Lederer and Eugene Burdick represented him as such in their novel *The Ugly American* (1958). They based one of their characters, Col. Edwin B. Hillandale, on Lansdale. To others, however, Lansdale represented something else, the naive foreigner who did not understand the complexities of a foreign culture and whose well-intended efforts could have catastrophic consequences. With that idea in mind, Graham Greene apparently used Lansdale as a model for Alden Pyle, a character in *The Quiet American* (1955).

—MSM

Larson, Arthur L(ewis)

(1910–1993) *undersecretary of labor; director, United States Information Agency; special assistant to the president*

The son of a judge, Arthur Larson was born in Sioux Falls, S.Dak., on July 4, 1910. He graduated magna cum laude from Augustana College in 1931. The following year, he received a Rhodes scholarship and in 1935 earned a B.A. at Oxford in jurisprudence. Larson then returned to the United States and began practicing law in Milwaukee in 1935. Two years later, he accepted an appointment as assistant professor at the University of Tennessee Law School, where he specialized in labor law. During World War II, he worked as a counsel for the Office of Price Administration and for the Foreign Economic Administration. Larson joined the faculty of Cornell University Law School in 1948. Over the next four years, he served as a consultant on the law of corporations to the New York Law Revision Commission and published an 11-volume treatise, *The Law of Workmen's Compensation* (1952), which became the standard work in its field. In 1953, Larson became dean of the University of Pittsburgh Law School.

Eisenhower appointed Larson undersecretary of labor in March 1954. In that capacity, Larson emerged as one of the administration's leading liberals. Over the next two years, he lobbied for an extension of unemployment insurance benefits, an increase in disability payments under workers' compensation, and meaningful attempts to employ the elderly.

In 1956, Larson published *A Republican Looks at His Party*, which maintained that Eisenhower Republicanism represented the true center of American politics and urged the party to adopt its principles. Republicans, he argued, should accept a modified role for government in modern industrial society and should aim to appeal to urban voters, young people, and minorities. According to Larson, "New Republicanism" combined a commitment to free enterprise and an endorsement of social welfare legislation. The book so impressed Eisenhower that he asked Larson to help write his acceptance speech for the Republican National Convention in 1956. In addition, the book established Larson as the leading theorist of modern Republicanism. Larson later expanded on those ideas in *What We Are For* (1959).

In February 1957, Larson became head of the U.S. Information Agency (USIA). Eisenhower asked Congress for a substantial increase in funding for the agency, but the Democratic Congress proposed cuts in spending for the agency. Larson appeared before Congress in an unsuccessful effort to request a restoration of funding at least to the previous year's level. He continued at the USIA until October 1957, when Eisenhower appointed him a special assistant. Larson's primary responsibility was as a speechwriter, in particular on issues relating to science and national security. He resigned from the government in 1958 to become

Swearing-in of Arthur Larson as special assistant to the president, October 28, 1957 *(Dwight D. Eisenhower Library and Museum)*

James B. Duke professor of law and director of the Rule of Law Center at Duke University. Even after he left the government, he remained in contact with Eisenhower, served as a special consultant to the president until the end of the administration, and assisted with some of Eisenhower's speeches.

During the 1960s and 1970s, Larson served on a number of advisory commissions involving both economic and foreign policy. He was a consultant to President LYNDON B. JOHNSON, the State Department, and the United Nations. In addition, he published several books on economic and foreign policy. When the Republican party turned away from his New Republicanism and nominated BARRY GOLDWATER for the presidency in 1964, Larson refused to support the party's nominee. In 1968, he wrote *Eisenhower: The President Nobody Knew*, in which he generally praised Eisenhower's leadership as well as his approach to both foreign and domestic policy. He described Eisenhower as an active, engaged president, who was firmly in control of his administration. The book made headlines for Larson's assertion that Eisenhower had told him that he disagreed with the Supreme Court's decision in *Brown v. Board of Education*. In the first volume of his memoirs, published in 1963, Eisenhower had asserted that "there can be no question that the judgment of the Court was right." In the sec-

ond volume of Eisenhower's memoirs, published in 1965, the former president more explicitly stated that "I definitely agreed with the unanimous decision." Larson retired in 1980, but continued to be active until his death in Durham, N.C., on May 28, 1993. At the time he died, he was working on a volume of memoirs, which his son, Lex Larson, completed and published in 1997.

—MSM

Lausche, Frank J(ohn)
(1895–1990) *governor of Ohio, U.S. senator*

The son of Slovenian immigrants, Frank Lausche was born on November 14, 1895, in Cleveland, Ohio, and grew up in that city. His father died while Lausche was in his early teens, and the boy helped support his family by lighting streetlamps and selling newspapers. After attending Central Institute Prep School in 1915 and 1916, he played baseball in the minor leagues. He joined the army as a private in 1918 and earned a commission, serving as a second lieutenant during World War I. After his discharge from the army, Lausche attended Cleveland's John Marshall School of Law at night and earned his degree in 1920. The same year, he was admitted to the bar and began to practice law in Cleveland. He became active in Democratic party politics and twice failed to win election to the state legislature. In 1932 he was appointed to fill a vacancy on Cleveland's Municipal Court. He subsequently won election in his own right and served until 1937. He was elected to a seat on the city's Common Pleas Court in 1936 and served from 1937 to 1941. Lausche won election as mayor of Cleveland in 1941 with 71 percent of the vote. His reputation for honesty, independence, and fiscal restraint made him a popular figure, and he won reelection in 1943 by an even greater margin. He ran for governor of Ohio in 1944 and won easily. After his first term, he narrowly lost his bid for reelection in the Republican landslide of 1946 but then won four more terms, serving from 1949 to 1956.

Lausche's political independence allowed him to remain popular in a traditionally Republican state. Moreover, although the Republicans dominated the state legislature for most of Lausche's administration, he proved successful in gaining passage of much of his program, including legislation providing for conservation and restoration of the state's natural resources, expansion of the state's welfare program, increased funding for higher education, and construction of hospitals and penal institutions. He neutralized potential criticism from fiscally conservative Republicans by limiting state expenditures, even as he supported popular projects like the state turnpike. During his campaigns for governor, he ignored regular Democratic city organizations and organized labor while campaigning heavily in normally Republican areas. Since he owed the party machines and the unions nothing for his political success, he largely ignored them. His conservative positions on many issues did nothing to endear him to liberals and unions. For example, he favored "right-to-work" legislation, which unions bitterly opposed. At the same time, he supported civil rights and fair employment legislation.

Lausche's position as an independent contributed to his defeat of the incumbent, Sen. George H. Bender (R-Ohio), in 1956. Bender had the advantage of strong Republican candidates at the top of the state and national tickets, but Lausche outmaneuvered him by telling audiences that, if elected, he might vote with Republicans to organize the Senate in 1957. Bender indignantly accused him of "trying to grab Ike's coattails." Apparently Lausche succeeded; he won 52.9 percent of the vote, even as Eisenhower swept the state. When Congress convened in January 1957, Lausche voted with Senate Democrats, which denied Republicans control of the upper house.

Nonetheless, in the Senate, Lausche proved a strong supporter of Eisenhower. According to *Congressional Quarterly*, Lausche supported the administration more frequently than any other Democrat in the 85th Congress. His independence infuriated some in his own party. During the second session of the 85th Congress, Lausche voted 69 percent of the time against the majority of his fellow Democrats. He refused to endorse Sen. JOHN BRICKER's (R-Ohio) Democratic opponent in 1958. At the same time, Lausche enjoyed a close personal relationship with the majority leader, Sen. LYNDON B. JOHNSON (D-Tex.) and sometimes switched positions to save a piece of Democratic legislation. True to his

record of support for civil rights, Lausche voted for the Civil Rights Acts of 1957 and 1960.

Lausche easily won reelection in 1962. His conservative positions frequently put him at odds with his party. He voted against federal aid to education, the creation of the Department of Housing and Urban Development, and federal aid to urban mass transportation. His skepticism of Democratic spending programs offended powerful elements within Ohio's Democratic party. Organized labor, in particular, sought to defeat him. Lausche's refusal to endorse Carl Stokes in the latter's run for mayor of Cleveland alienated black voters. As a result, the State Democratic Central Committee endorsed John J. Gilligan for Lausche's seat in 1968. That May, Lausche lost the primary to Gilligan, who then lost in the general election to the Republican candidate, William B. Saxbe. Estranged from his party, Lausche endorsed RICHARD M. NIXON for the presidency in 1968 and again in 1972. In the latter race, he dismissed Nixon's opponent, Sen. George McGovern (D-S.Dak.), as "indecisive and inconsistent." Lausche never again held public office. He died in Cleveland on April 20, 1990.

—MSM

Leader, George M(ichael)

(1918–)   *governor of Pennsylvania*

Leader was born in York, Pa., on January 17, 1918. His family had farmed in York Co. for several generations, and his father was active in Democratic politics. He grew up on his parents' poultry farm and went to York High School before attending Gettysburg College and the University of Pennsylvania, where he earned a B.S. degree in education in 1939. When his father fell ill, Leader went to work for Guy A. Leader & Sons, the family farming business. He also followed his father into politics; he became a member of the York County Democratic Committee in 1940 and secretary of that body two years later. During World War II, Leader served in the navy as an ensign aboard the aircraft carrier USS *Randolph* in the Pacific theater. After the war, he returned to York Co. and purchased Willow Brook Farm, where he operated a successful chicken hatchery. He also embarked on a political career. In 1946 he became a justice of the peace and succeeded his father as chair of the county Democratic committee. At the time, his father was a state senator. When his father chose not to run for reelection in 1950, Leader ran for and won his father's seat in the state senate. He ran for state treasurer in 1952 but lost to his Republican opponent, Weldon Heyburn. Leader nonetheless proved himself a good campaigner and gained statewide recognition.

Leader ran for governor in 1954. He had the backing of the Democratic organizations in Pittsburgh and Philadelphia and was among the earliest candidates to make extensive use of media advertising and professional pollsters. He promised state aid for the creation of new jobs and attacked the 1 percent sales tax enacted under the administration of the incumbent Republican, Gov. John S. Fine. Running against Fine's lieutenant governor, Lloyd H. Wood, Leader focused his attack on the unpopular sales tax and won in a major upset.

Upon taking office on January 18, 1955, Leader inherited a budget deficit of $75 million from Fine. The public disliked Fine's sales tax, and Leader had campaigned against it. In April 1955, Leader called for a 1 percent state income tax and a tax on investments. Both parties opposed the levies, and after an impasse that lasted 17 months, Leader had to abandon his proposal. He then reluctantly asked for and got an increase in the sales tax to 3 percent. Given that he had campaigned against the sales tax, many voters felt betrayed, and Leader's popularity plummeted.

In spite of the setback on the issue of the budget and taxation, Leader pursued an ambitious agenda. Making good on his campaign pledge to involve the state in the creation of jobs, he oversaw the enactment in 1956 of the Pennsylvania Industrial Development Authority, which offered state financing to private enterprises as an incentive to locate in distressed areas. Leader also removed over 10,000 jobs from the civil service system, provided state support for the education of children with disabilities, expanded the state park system, increased payments for workers' compensation and unemployment compensation, and opened a vocational rehabilitation center in Johnstown. The cold war and, in particular, the launch of *Sputnik*, generated concern over education. Leader responded by expanding state aid to school districts and increas-

ing teachers' salaries by 20 percent. In addition, he increased support for the state's 14 colleges.

In addition, Leader established a record in support of civil rights. He signed legislation creating a Fair Employment Practices Council, established to police discrimination in employment. When a black family moved into the Levittown in Bucks Co. and encountered hostility, threats, and violence, Leader sent the state police to keep peace and ordered the state's attorney general to prosecute those who violated the rights of the black family.

In September 1955, Leader began speaking out on national issues. He became one of the first Democrats publicly to urge his party to criticize President DWIGHT D. EISENHOWER. The following month, he announced that he would support ADLAI E. STEVENSON for the Democratic presidential nomination in 1956. It seemed that Leader was positioning himself for a dark-horse candidacy for the vice presidential nomination, but he withdrew himself from consideration. He nevertheless campaigned energetically for Stevenson and attacked Vice President RICHARD M. NIXON. For all of Leader's efforts, Stevenson failed to carry Pennsylvania in the election, and Republicans won control of both houses of the state's legislature.

Pennsylvania's constitution limited governors to a single term, and Leader decided to run for the U.S. Senate in 1958. He had not, however, handled patronage to the satisfaction of the Democratic machine, and alienated himself from its leadership. In his bid for a Senate seat, he abandoned the city machines that had elected him and sought to identify himself with reformers in the party. He fired ward leaders in Philadelphia and announced his support for the candidacy of a reformer, RICHARDSON DILWORTH, the mayor of Philadelphia, for governor. Dilworth, however, declined to run. Leader won the Democratic primary but, in spite of a sweeping Democratic victory that year, lost in the general election to Rep. HUGH SCOTT (R-Pa.). Organization workers deserted Leader in large numbers. In Philadelphia, the successful Democratic candidate for governor, David L. Lawrence, ran 40,000 votes ahead of Leader. Scott defeated Leader by 113,000 votes, while Lawrence won the governorship by 80,000 votes. Leader failed to carry even York Co.

Following his defeat, Leader returned to Willow Brook Farm. He became a mortgage banker and founded Leader Nursing Homes, Inc. In the 1980s and 1990s, he and his family established retirement communities. He resides in Hummelstown, Pa.

—MSM

Lee, J(oseph) Bracken
(1899–1996) *governor of Utah*

Lee was born in Price, Utah, on January 7, 1899. Although ancestors on both sides of his family were active in the Mormon Church, his father was not, and Lee never belonged to the church. At the age of five, Lee moved with his family to Colorado but returned to Price, where he attended Carbon County High School. In April 1917, two months before his scheduled graduation, the United States entered World War I, and Lee enlisted in the army. Assigned to train troops in the United States, he rose to the rank of sergeant and served until March 1919. Immediately after leaving the service, he worked briefly as a postal clerk and then joined his father in the insurance and real estate business. Eventually, he became manager and owner of the agency. Lee also became active in Republican politics. After running unsuccessfully for mayor of Price in 1931, he ran again in 1935 and won by two votes. He was reelected five times and served from 1935 to 1947. In 1940, he unsuccessfully ran for the Republican gubernatorial nomination. Two years after that, he tried and failed to gain the Republican nomination for a seat in the U.S. House of Representatives. He won the gubernatorial nomination in 1944 but lost in the general election to Herbert B. Maw. Four years later, in a rematch against Maw, Lee promised to run the state on a conservative, businesslike basis and distanced himself from the Republican presidential nominee, New York's governor, Thomas E. Dewey. Lee defeated Maw and was the only Republican to win statewide office that year. A strict fiscal conservative, he cut a variety of state agencies and programs. His primary target for spending cuts, however, was education, and that earned him the opposition of virtually every educator in the state. Lee also made headlines with his opposition to the income tax, foreign aid, and the United Nations. A charismatic figure and a talented speaker, he had a penchant for personal and political invective that made him many enemies. His constituents admired Lee's willingness to speak his mind. He summed up his approach to politics with the slogan, "Do it honestly, do the best you know how, and let 'em holler."

Lee backed the conservative Robert A. Taft (R-Ohio) for the Republican presidential nomination in 1952. Lee, however, became enmeshed in the maneuvering over the seating of the rival Taft and Eisenhower delegations at the Republican National Convention. In May, Eisenhower's forces put together a two-page statement proposing that contested delegates be kept from voting on the right of others to be seated, a position that would serve to Eisenhower's advantage. They hoped to have the statement signed jointly by supporters of both Eisenhower and Taft. At the annual conference of governors, which took place just before the Republican convention, Gov. Dan Thornton of Colorado and Dewey of New York urged the 23 Republicans attending the annual conference of governors to sign a manifesto declaring that contested delegates should not vote on the seating of other delegates. Every Republican governor at the conference, including those who supported Taft, felt obliged to sign. The governors issued the manifesto on July 2, five days before the convention; Thornton, representing Eisenhower's supporters, read one page of the statement, and Lee, representing Taft's backers, read the other. In the general election, Lee backed Eisenhower, and, in November, Lee won reelection and Eisenhower carried Utah.

Throughout Eisenhower's presidency, Lee was one of his sharpest critics on the Republican right. During the first half of the decade, Lee was an outspoken supporter of Sen. Joseph R. McCarthy (R-Wis.) and opposed the Senate resolution to censure McCarthy in December 1954. Lee accused Eisenhower of steering America leftward and recommended the formation of a third, conservative party in 1956. As the presidential election year got under way, the governor continued to attack Eisenhower. He challenged the constitutionality of foreign aid and refused to pay federal income tax until Secretary of the Treasury George Humphrey successfully brought an action to compel the governor to pay. Lee's antics cost him dearly. He lost the Republican gubernatorial primary in 1956 to George Clyde, who ran as an Eisenhower Republican. Lee then entered the race as an independent and finished third in the general election.

Lee challenged Sen. ARTHUR V. WATKINS (R-Utah) for the Republican senatorial nomination in 1958. Watkins had chaired the committee investigating the charges that resulted in McCarthy's censure. After losing the primary, Lee entered the general election as an independent. His candidacy split the Republican vote and resulted in a victory for the Democratic candidate, Frank Moss. From 1960 to 1972, Lee served as mayor of Salt Lake City. In that capacity, he may have made his most significant contribution. While not deviating from his hard-line conservative positions, he matured as a politician and adopted a somewhat more temperate approach. As a result, he was more effective, and his tenure was marked by fiscal stability and capital improvements. Lee made unsuccessful bids for the U.S. Senate in 1962 and for governor in 1964. He died in Salt Lake City on October 20, 1996.

—MSM

Lee, Richard C(harles)

(1916–2003) *mayor of New Haven, Conn.*

Lee was born in New Haven, Conn., on March 12, 1916 and raised in a working-class section of the city. Following his graduation from high school in 1935, he worked as a city hall reporter for the *New Haven Journal-Courier.* Running as a Democrat, Lee won election to the board of aldermen in 1939. He served for a short time in the army during World War II before receiving a medical discharge. He then returned to New Haven to resume his position as alderman. Lee went to work for the *Yale News Digest* in 1943 and the following year was appointed director of Yale's public relations service. During the 1940s, he became prominent in local Democratic politics. In 1949 and 1951, he campaigned for mayor, losing by narrow margins both times.

Lee ran for mayor again in 1953. Realizing he would need a dramatic issue to galvanize support for his race, he focused his attention on urban renewal. He assembled a campaign staff of highly motivated young urban planners who drew up his proposal for "the rebirth of New Haven." Campaigning on that issue, Lee managed to win the general election in November by a narrow margin.

Lee began his program by enlisting the aid of noted French urban designer Maurice Rovital to help him draw up a master redevelopment plan. Rovital based his plans on the belief that the city would have to attract well-to-do suburbanites to its stores and recreational facilities to develop a viable economic base. Revitalization, therefore, depended on the growing interstate highway system that spanned southern Connecticut. Lee won authorization for the construction of a superhighway linking the Connecticut Turnpike to the heart of downtown New Haven. Working closely with Edward J. Logue, a young attorney he named as supervisor of the program, he then initiated massive slum clearance projects to permit the widening of local streets and the construction of new offices, department stores, middle-income apartments, and parking garages. He also began a program for developing low-income housing. To finance these projects, the mayor applied for federal assistance under the Federal Housing Act of 1954, which provided grants and loans for cities to purchase rundown property. After upgrading it, the city could sell the property to private developers.

In pursuit of his goals, Lee sought to gain control of the city bureaucracy. He had inherited a government made up of numerous independent departments. These agencies were often more responsive to the desires of powerful advisory committees, led by business leaders indifferent to Lee's goals, than to the mayor's office. Lee gradually appointed individuals loyal to him to head and staff the city's departments. The mayor then arranged for his supporters to sit on the advisory committees. Realizing that a large portion of his political strength lay in the Democratic organization, Lee maintained good relations with the local machine. He often appointed political regulars to city jobs, mingling them with the urban specialists he had brought in to reconstruct the city. By 1956, Lee controlled the city bureaucracy.

During the last half of the decade, Lee won massive electoral victories over his Republican rivals. His dependence on the Democratic machine thus ended, though he always had cordial relations with the party regulars. Lee, however, endeavored to keep politics out of urban renewal. He also tried to enlist the help of Yale and attempted to gain the support of the business community. When the city's chamber of commerce proved skeptical of his dream, Lee created an alternate business group to advise him.

By the end of the decade, New Haven was receiving more federal aid per capita than any other city in the country, and Lee had gained a reputation as one of the most imaginative mayors in the nation. Many pointed to his city as perhaps the most promising example of urban renewal. During the presidential campaign of 1960, Lee was an adviser to the Democratic candidate, JOHN F. KENNEDY. Lee continued to serve as mayor until 1970. Throughout the 1960s, New Haven continued to draw national attention for its urban renewal projects and its job-training programs for the poor. The city was the first to receive a grant from the newly created Office of Economic Opportunity. In addition, New Haven received grants from private foundations and corporations for various projects. Nevertheless, the city continued to lose industrial jobs and therefore its economic base. At the same time, an influx of African Americans from the South expanded its inner city. For all of Lee's programs, the city continued to suffer from disproportionate poverty and unemployment. A major race riot in 1967 tarnished the mayor's image as a visionary of urban renewal. After leaving public office in 1970, Lee taught political science at Yale and the University of Connecticut. He died in New Haven on February 2, 2003.

—MSM

Lehman, Herbert H(enry)
(1878–1963) *U.S. senator*

The son of wealthy German-Jewish immigrants, Lehman was born in New York City on March 28, 1878. His father was a founding partner of Lehman Brothers, a company that began as a cotton-trading concern and developed into a leading investment banking firm. After earning a B.A. from Williams College in 1899, Lehman went to work for J. Spencer Turner, a textile firm in New York, rising to became vice president and treasurer of the company in 1906. Two years later, he joined Lehman

Brothers as a partner. Having established himself in business, Lehman increasingly devoted himself to various philanthropic activities. Although he donated substantial sums to a variety of religious groups (Protestant, Catholic, and Jewish) as well as civic organizations (including the Boy Scouts and the National Association for the Advancement of Colored People), his primary philanthropic interest was the Joint Distribution Committee (JDC), organized by American Jews during World War I primarily to aid Jews in Eastern Europe. Lehman joined the army as a captain during World War I and served with the General Staff Corps in Washington, D.C. Upon leaving the service as a colonel, he returned to Lehman Brothers. In the 1920s, Lehman became vice chairman of the JDC and oversaw aid to reconstruct Jewish communities in Eastern Europe. He also acted as a mediator in the garment industry and forged close ties to labor groups, particularly the International Ladies' Garment Workers' Union (ILGWU) and the Amalgamated Clothing Workers. These unions subsequently provided enthusiastic support when Lehman entered politics.

Lehman became active in state Democratic politics in the 1920s. He served as treasurer to Gov. Alfred E. Smith's reelection campaign in 1924, headed Smith's campaign committee in 1926, and was director of the finance committee for Smith's presidential campaign in 1928. In 1928, Franklin D. Roosevelt was elected governor, and Lehman won election as lieutenant governor. Lehman and Roosevelt won reelection in 1930. In 1932, Roosevelt ran for the presidency, and Lehman, after gaining the Democratic nomination over the opposition of party bosses, was elected governor in a landslide. He won reelection in 1934 and 1936. A change in New York's constitution extended the governor's term to four years, and Lehman won a four-year term in 1938.

As governor, Lehman maintained close political ties to Roosevelt and oversaw New York's "Little New Deal," a set of state programs designed to promote relief and reform that resembled Roosevelt's New Deal. These state measures offered benefits to groups excluded from federal programs. In December 1942, Lehman resigned as governor a month before his term ended in order to accept an appointment as head of the newly established Office of Foreign Relief and Rehabilitation Operations; the following year, he became director general of the United Nations Relief and Rehabilitation Administration (UNRRA). Lehman resigned his post in March 1946 and ran for the Senate from New York. In addition to capturing the Democratic nomination, he also gained the endorsements of New York's Liberal Party and the American Labor Party. Nevertheless, dissatisfaction with the Truman administration led to a Republican tide that year, which swept the party into control of both houses of Congress. Lehman suffered what was to be the only electoral defeat of his career.

In 1949, Lehman defeated the Republican nominee, JOHN FOSTER DULLES, in a special election to fill the vacancy created by the resignation of Sen. ROBERT F. WAGNER (D-N.Y.). Lehman won election to a full term in 1950. In the Senate, Lehman quickly established himself as one of the leading liberals of the upper house. In general, he supported President HARRY S. TRUMAN's foreign policy and domestic policies. Lehman supported civil liberties, the rights of aliens, liberal immigration regulations, civil rights for African Americans, and the development of public power. Along those lines, he unsuccessfully opposed the Internal Security Act in 1950 and the McCarran-Walter Immigration Act in 1952.

Lehman consistently opposed the Eisenhower administration's policy of encouraging private, rather than public, development of power and resources. In April 1953, he participated in a 28-day filibuster against an administration-backed proposal to grant oil-rich submerged coastal lands to the states. The following year, he joined a filibuster against the Dixon-Yates contract, under which private companies were to provide power to the Tennessee Valley Authority (TVA) to make up for the power the TVA supplied to the Atomic Energy Commission. Eisenhower ultimately cancelled the Dixon-Yates contract. Lehman won another victory for public power when, in 1956, he sponsored a successful measure authorizing the New York State Power Authority to build and operate a $405 million project at Niagra Falls.

From the time Sen. JOSEPH R. MCCARTHY (R-Wis.) drew national attention with his sensational accusations of Communists in government, Lehman was among his most outspoken critics. On the Senate floor, he repeatedly confronted McCarthy and demanded proof for the senator's reckless charges. Lehman and McCarthy traded accusations in 1953, after McCarthy alleged that criticism of two of his aides, ROY M. COHN and G. DAVID SCHINE, were motivated by anti-Semitism. Soon after that, McCarthy read to the Senate a letter in which Lehman had expressed "complete confidence" in the loyalty of Alger Hiss. Lehman replied that the letter had been written months before any "real evidence" of Hiss's guilt had emerged and before Hiss's indictment and conviction for perjury. McCarthy also accused Lehman of hiring Communists and Communist sympathizers when he was director of the UNRRA. In June 1954, Lehman endorsed Sen. RALPH FLANDERS's (R-Vt.) resolution to censure McCarthy. Two months later, Lehman cosponsored a bill with Sen. WAYNE MORSE (I-Oreg.), clearly aimed at McCarthy, that would have required a code of procedure for all congressional committees. Morse and Lehman joined other senators as cosponsors of Sen. ESTES KEFAUVER's (D-Tenn.) proposed "Code of Conduct for Congressional Committees." The Senate did not adopt either proposal. In September 1954, Lehman supported the recommendation of the Watkins Committee that McCarthy be censured. On the final vote, Lehman voted for censure.

Even as he opposed McCarthy's anticommunist activities, Lehman supported the Communist Control Bill of 1954, one of the most repressive measures proposed during the cold war. Sponsored by a group of Democratic liberals in the Senate led by HUBERT H. HUMPHREY (D-Minn.), the bill declared the American Communist Party an "agency of a hostile foreign power" and therefore not entitled to the rights claimed by legal bodies. Lehman voted for the bill, which passed in August 1954.

In 1955 and 1956, Lehman increasingly turned his attention to civil rights for African Americans. In March 1956, he protested when the Democrats in the Senate gave the chair of the Judiciary Committee to a segregationist senator, JAMES O. EASTLAND (D-Miss.), on the traditional basis of seniority. In June, Lehman announced that he would sponsor an antisegregation amendment to a proposed appropriation of $1.6 billion for the construction of schools. The bill went down to defeat in the House the next month.

In July 1956, the House passed the administration's civil rights bill, which established a Civil Rights Commission and elevated the Civil Right Section of the Justice Department to the status of a division. When the bill came to the Senate, Lehman and others attempted to rescue it from Eastland's Judiciary Committee, but their effort failed by a vote of 76 to 6. The Judiciary Committee failed to report the bill, and Lehman blamed the administration for submitting its recommendations late in the session. He neglected to mention the role of Majority Leader LYNDON B. JOHNSON (D–Tex.) in burying the bill in Eastland's committee.

Lehman did not, however, exempt members of his own party from criticism for failing to support civil rights. In early 1956, he wrote to ADLAI STEVENSON "expressing [his] sense of disquietude" about Stevenson's cautious position on civil rights. Lehman continued his advocacy of civil rights at the Democratic National Convention in August 1956. He called for a floor fight on civil rights, but the convention instead accepted a draft from the platform committee that attempted to reconcile southern segregationists and northern liberals within the party. The Democratic platform stated simply that the *Brown* decision "brought consequences of vast importance to our nation as a whole and especially to communities directly affected."

Lehman declined to run for reelection in 1956. After leaving office, he returned to some of the issues with which he had been involved earlier in his career. In March 1958, he mediated a general strike by the ILGWU. Later that year, ELEANOR ROOSEVELT and Lehman formed the National Council for Industrial Peace to promote harmonious relations between labor and management and to oppose right-to-work laws. In January 1959, with the support of New York's mayor, ROBERT F. WAGNER, JR., Roosevelt and Lehman formed the New York Committee for Democratic Voters. The group aimed to wrest control of the state party from the "hands of the old-style party professional," specifically CARMINE DESAPIO, the leader of Tammany Hall. The reformers achieved their goal in 1961, when they won several municipal offices and

defeated DeSapio for his position as district leader. Because only district leaders could serve as county leaders, DeSapio also lost his post as leader of Manhattan Co. Lehman remained active in reform politics until his death at his home in New York City on December 5, 1963.

—MSM

LeMay, Curtis E(merson)
(1906–1990) *air force vice chief of staff*

The son of an ironworker, LeMay was born in Columbus, Ohio, on November 15, 1906. He wanted a military career but failed to secure an appointment to West Point, so he enrolled at the school of engineering at Ohio State University, where he joined the Reserve Officers Training Corps. LeMay left without graduating to take up a commission as second lieutenant in the reserve field artillery in 1928. He volunteered for the army air corps and received his wings in October 1929. While serving in the army air corps, he completed his degree in civil engineering at Ohio State in 1934. After receiving a promotion to first lieutenant in 1935, he transferred to Second Bomb Group in 1937 and became one of the first pilots to qualify on the new B-17 heavy bomber. Promoted to captain in 1940 and to major in 1941, he received the Distinguished Flying Cross for flying experimental missions.

Like many other officers, LeMay's career took off with the advent of World War II. He became a lieutenant colonel in January 1942 and a colonel in March of that year. An innovator in the use of strategic bombers, he led a raid that took off from England and bombed Regensburg, Germany. He received promotion to brigadier general in September 1943 and to major general in March 1944. In August 1944, he was ordered to the China-Burma-India theater and later to the Pacific, where he planned the B-29 raids on Tokyo and other Japanese cities. LeMay was transferred to the staff of Gen. Carl A. Spaatz, head of the U.S. Strategic Air Forces, in August 1945, where he helped plan the atomic bombings of Hiroshima and Nagasaki. In December 1945, LeMay became deputy chief of air staff for research and development. In that capacity, he supported research on supersonic aircraft and missiles. He also helped oversee the introduction of jet bombers. When the air force became a separate branch of the service in 1947, LeMay was named to command of air forces in Europe and received a temporary promotion to lieutenant general. He directed the Berlin airlift of 1948 to 1949. While the airlift continued, LeMay returned to the United States in October 1948 to assume command of the Strategic Air Command (SAC). He modernized SAC and imposed a regimen of strict discipline and intense training. Under his command, SAC became a highly motivated, extremely efficient, and powerful fighting force.

LeMay strenuously advocated the position that strategic bombers should serve as the primary deterrent to Soviet aggression. He repeatedly warned that the Soviet Union was cutting into the American lead in strategic air power and opposed efforts by the Eisenhower administration to limit SAC's budget. Eisenhower's chief of staff, SHERMAN ADAMS, credited LeMay's testimony before STEWART SYMINGTON'S (D-Mo.) subcommittee of the Senate Armed Services Committee with persuading Congress to appropriate an additional $900 million for additional B-52 bombers, which, according the Adams, the air force "did not need."

The Eisenhower administration's attempt to limit the production of guided missiles and military jet aircraft in 1956 produced a firestorm of criticism. LeMay supported Gen. NATHAN TWINING'S contention that a "bomber gap" existed between the United States and the USSR. Symington and Sen. HENRY JACKSON (D-Wash.) repeatedly charged that the United States was seriously behind the Soviet Union in the production and development of missiles. Symington's subcommittee held hearings on American military air strength in April 1956. In testimony during those hearings, LeMay maintained that the USSR would surpass the United States in striking power of long-range bombers between 1958 and 1960.

LeMay became vice chief of staff of the air force in April 1957. He also retained command of SAC. After the Soviet Union launched its satellite, *Sputnik*, in the fall of 1957, the military pressed the administration to increase defense spending. Once again, LeMay was in the forefront. In testimony before the Senate Preparedness Subcommittee in December 1957, he repeated his demand for rapid expansion of the manned bomber fleet. He said that his previous requests for larger appropriations had "fallen on deaf ears" at the White House and that, even when Congress had appropriated such funds, the administration had impounded them. LeMay reiterated his warning that failure to provide planes, bases, and intercontinental ballistic missiles would result in the United States falling behind the Soviet Union in striking power. On this occasion, he set mid-1959 as the date when the United States would lose its lead in air power. That, he predicted, would "invite a cataclysmic preemptive strike by the superior communist intercontinental ballistic missile force at some future date." In response to earlier testimony by the army's chief of staff, Gen. MAXWELL D. TAYLOR, LeMay forcefully opposed the idea that funds be diverted from the air force to increase conventional forces and derided the army's preoccupation with conventional war. Air power, he argued, provided a wide variety of military capabilities. To those who questioned the effectiveness of bombers in a guerrilla war, he responded, "I do not understand why a force that will deter a big war will not deter a small war too, if we want it to and say it will."

In 1961, President JOHN F. KENNEDY promoted LeMay to air force chief of staff. LeMay continued to champion the production of manned bombers in opposition to Secretary of Defense Robert S. McNamara's belief that, in an age of missiles, the manned bomber was becoming obsolete. High officials in the administrations of both Kennedy and LYNDON B. JOHNSON feared that LeMay might become a formidable political threat upon his retirement and therefore repeatedly extended his tour of duty at the Pentagon. After LeMay did retire in 1965, he joined the board of Network Electronics Corporation and became an outspoken critic of the Johnson administration's restrictions on bombing raids in both North and South Vietnam. LeMay advocated massive air strikes against North Vietnam's ports, depots, and supply lines. In 1968, George C. Wallace chose LeMay to be his vice presidential running mate on the American Independent Party ticket. During the campaign, LeMay denounced Johnson's decision to halt the bombing of North Vietnam and promised that, if elected, he and Wallace would resume the air war and, if necessary, use nuclear weapons to defeat the North. The ticket won 13.4 percent of the popular vote. LeMay died of a heart attack at March Air Force Base in California on October 1, 1990.

—MSM

Lewis, John L(lewellyn)

(1880–1969) president, United Mine Workers of America

The son of a coal miner and policeman, John L. Lewis was born in Lucas Co., Iowa, on February 12, 1880. In his early teens, he moved with his family to Des Moines, and returned with them to Lucas Co. in the late 1890s. He left school to go to work in the mines and in 1901 became a charter member of a local of the United Mine Workers of America (UMW). After working at mining sites in the West, he returned to Lucas in 1905. Two years later, he ran unsuccessfully for mayor and entered business as a feed and grain distributor. The business failed, and soon after, in 1909, the entire Lewis family moved to the coal mining town of Panama, Ill. In 1910, Lewis won election as president of Local 1475 of the UMW. He launched a successful campaign for state workers' compensation laws and state laws regulating safety in the mines. A dynamic orator and a skillful organizer, he rose quickly in the labor movement. His activities drew the attention of Samuel Gompers, the head of the American Federation of Labor (AFL), and Lewis became a field representative for the AFL in 1911. The job enabled him to travel widely through mining areas and to build a strong personal following within the miners' union. Lewis became vice president of the UMW in 1917 and took over many of the duties of the ailing president, Frank Hayes. At the beginning of 1920, Hayes resigned, and Lewis became acting president. Later that year, Lewis won election as president of what was then the largest union in the AFL. He held that position for the next 40 years.

An active Republican, Lewis backed Warren Harding, Calvin Coolidge, and Herbert Hoover during the 1920s. That decade, however, saw a rapid decline of the UMW. Despite Lewis's insistence that labor and capital shared common interests, the UMW encountered fierce opposition from coal mining companies. Bituminous coal companies drove the UMW from mines in the Appalachian region. Operators in Illinois, Indiana, Ohio, and Pennsylvania insisted that competition from southern mines required reductions in wages and tonnage. Things were little better in the anthracite mines of northeastern Pennsylvania. Faced with difficult conditions and declining membership, Lewis became convinced that the union could not afford internal divisions and consolidated his control. He used armed force and election fraud to crush left-wing opposition in the union.

The coming of the Great Depression exacerbated Lewis's problems and those of the UMW. Membership continued to decline, and the union's financial condition grew worse. Lewis responded by ruthlessly suppressing his opponents in the union. On the other hand, the coming of the New Deal presented opportunities. Taking advantage of provisions of the National Industrial Recovery Act, Lewis launched a massive and successful organizing campaign in the coalfields. Through National Recovery Administration codes and collective bargaining, the UMW gained better wages and union security provisions. These successes enabled the union to compile an enormous treasury and thrust Lewis into a prominent role in the larger union movement.

Lewis believed that mass-production industries should be organized on an industry-wide, rather than a craft, basis. In 1935, Lewis joined with other AFL leaders interested in industry-wide organizing to form the Committee for Industrial Organizations (CIO). The CIO succeeded in establishing unions in the automobile, rubber, steel, and electrical appliance industries. The recession of 1937 to 1939 made further gains difficult, and jurisdictional conflicts with the craft unions of the AFL further impeded the success of the CIO. Moreover, Lewis's critics charged that he had allowed communists to gain influence in the CIO. The AFL expelled the CIO in 1938, and the CIO reconstituted itself as the Congress of Industrial Organizations. As president of the CIO, Lewis quickly found himself in conflict with other leaders of the organization who hoped to quickly repair the rift with the AFL.

Lewis was also at odds with other leaders of the CIO over national politics. Lewis aggressively supported Roosevelt in 1936; indeed, he created

Labor's Non-Partisan League, which poured more than $500,000 into Roosevelt's campaign that year. During the late 1930s, however, Lewis came into increasing conflict with the administration, particularly over matters of foreign policy. When World War II broke out in Europe, Lewis opposed American intervention and charged that Roosevelt's support for Great Britain and his program of increased defense production threatened to involve the United States in a war to save the British Empire. While other leaders of the CIO remained fervently loyal to Roosevelt, Lewis endorsed Wendell Wilkie for the presidency in 1940. On October 25, Lewis gave a radio address in which he vowed to step down as president of the CIO if Roosevelt were elected. After the election, Lewis kept that promise.

Lewis made an unsuccessful bid to regain control of the CIO, and then pulled the UMW out of the organization in 1942. After the American entry into the war, Lewis and the UMW supported the war effort and endorsed the No Strike Pledge made by the AFL and CIO in December 1941. Lewis, however, came to regard Roosevelt and the War Labor Board as duplicitous in dealing with what Lewis regarded as legitimate demands for increased wages to make up for wartime inflation. In 1943, Lewis repudiated the no-strike pledge and led a series of strikes that brought a torrent of public criticism. Lewis also earned the resentment of other labor leaders who adhered to the pledge in the face of dissatisfaction from their rank-and-file membership.

After the war, Lewis continued his confrontational approach toward mine operators and the federal government. In 1946, he demanded a royalty on each ton of coal mined, which would be used to finance union health and welfare benefits. After a series of strikes that led the government to seize control of the mines, Lewis reached a settlement with federal administrators that became the basis for a permanent royalty agreement with the coal industry that funded health care and pension benefits for miners. On the other hand, his defiance of a federal court injunction cost him and his union enormous fines.

The UMW briefly rejoined the AFL in 1946 and 1947, but the UMW remained isolated from the rest of the labor movement during the 1940s

and 1950s. Lewis nonetheless hoped to reunite the AFL and CIO under his leadership. Alternatively, he sought to bring together union heads dissatisfied with the leadership of the two major federations. None of these schemes came to fruition, and Lewis focused his attention almost exclusively on the affairs of his own union. The coal miners, however, no longer commanded the public attention they once did, and Lewis faded from national prominence.

Further, he and the UMW faced new challenges in the 1950s. Faced with competition from oil, natural gas, and hydroelectricity, the demand for bituminous coal diminished, and coal operators sought to cut labor costs. Large operators did this by increasing productivity through mechanization. In addition, the emergence of the Tennessee Valley Authority as a major consumer of coal fostered hundreds of small, nonunion mines in Kentucky and Tennessee that remained competitive by not having to pay royalty payments to the UMW's welfare and retirement fund. These developments weakened Lewis's union by reducing both the size of the workforce under its jurisdiction and its employed membership.

In response to these developments, Lewis took a more collaborative approach to relations with the owners. He sanctioned deals with employers in financial difficulties that undercut standard UMW contracts. Since the UMW's pension and health care programs depended on the royalty for each ton of coal produced, the union cooperated in mechanization programs that resulted in the elimination of jobs. In order to insure the prevention of work stoppages, he tightened his control of the UMW.

In addition, Lewis acted as an industry spokesman in Washington, where he argued for government promotion of coal exports and stricter mine-safety laws. This position had the covert aim of forcing small companies out of business by imposing on them the same expensive safety standards required of larger producers. The big coal companies also urged Lewis to organize the growing number of nonunion mines, since the larger mechanized enterprises could benefit from lower labor costs only if other producers could not achieve the same advantage by simply operating on a nonunion basis. With Lewis's tacit approval, his aide

W. A. "Tony" Boyle, initiated virtual guerrilla war in the unorganized areas. Bands of UMW agents converged on nonunion operations. They marched the miners out of the pits at gunpoint and in many cases coerced them into joining the union.

In return for Lewis's assistance, the industry accorded major concessions on wages and benefits to the UMW. Although the number of working miners fell by three-fifths between 1947 and 1960, creating extensive and chronic unemployment in the coal-producing regions, those UMW members who remained employed earned the highest hourly wage in American industry by 1959. During the same period, moreover, the union's income actually grew despite declining membership, since it was based on a per ton royalty rather than a payroll tax. As a result, the UMW became a wealthy institution. Its assets in 1960 totaled some $110 million—almost as much as the Teamsters, auto, steel, and machinists unions combined. With an industrialist from Cleveland, CYRUS EATON, serving as his informal adviser, Lewis used the health and welfare fund to build a partially concealed financial empire for the union. Eventually the union acquired major stock holdings in several coal companies and a controlling interest in the National Bank of Washington, the capital's second largest bank. In 1960, Lewis resigned as UMW president and became president emeritus. He died in Washington, D.C., on June 11, 1969.

—MSM

Liebman, Marvin

(1923–1997) *secretary, Committee for One Million against the Admission of Communist China to the United Nations*

Born in Brooklyn, New York, on July 21, 1923, Liebman attended New York University. A member of the Young Communist League and the American Communist Party during the 1930s and 1940s, Liebman resigned in protest against the purging of Earl Browder. Drafted into the army during World War II, Liebman served until 1944, when he was dismissed after his homosexuality was discovered. He worked for various Zionist groups and then became involved in the right-wing Israeli terrorist organization, the Irgun Zvai Leumi. While work-

ing for the International Rescue Committee, which aided refugees from the Iron Curtain, Liebman came to view the USSR as a threat to world peace. In 1952, he helped start Aid to Refugee Chinese Intellectuals. During the 1950s, Liebman became a public relations specialist, working first for Harold L. Oram, Inc. In 1957, he founded his own firm, Marvin Liebman Associates Inc., which represented conservative organizations. Richard Dudman, a journalist, called him "the best single-action group organizer on the Far Right."

Liebman was one of the principal organizers of the Committee for One Million against the Admission of Communist China to the United Nations, created in 1953. On October 22, 1953, Liebman and other supporters of Nationalist China presented President Eisenhower with a petition signed by 210 prominent Americans calling for the United States to oppose the admission of Communist China to the UN. The event was the first step in a massive drive to get 1 million American signatures on the document and thus throw the weight of public opinion against the possibility that the administration might support the admission of Communist China. Liebman handled the publicity and fund-raising for the committee. The 1-millionth American signed the petition on July 6, 1954. The committee planned the conclusion of the campaign to coincide with the Geneva Conference on Indochina as an indication of public displeasure with the possibility of the United States negotiating with the Communists at the conference.

Liebman then set out to turn the committee into a permanent lobbying organization designed to be a watchdog over the administration's China policy. In 1955, the Committee for One Million became the Committee of One Million, with Marvin Liebman as its secretary. Although the group contained individuals from both political parties, most members were conservative Republicans. The committee had three goals: creation of a bipartisan foreign policy; opposition to "appeasement" of communists by the West, especially the United States; and resistance to "indirect" communist aggression in Southeast Asia. Liebman kept the committee members informed of the progress of Americans and neutralist nations who lobbied for China's entry into the UN. In addition, he publicly opposed any trade with mainland China and lobbied extensively against the relaxation of the American economic boycott of the communist regime. Both administration officials and Democratic leaders reiterated their support for the organization's positions.

During the Kennedy and Johnson administrations, the Committee of One Million continued to function as an effective lobby influencing American policy toward China. Liebman worked for the presidential campaign of BARRY GOLDWATER in 1964. In 1968, he closed Marvin Liebman Associates. Between 1969 and 1975, he was managing director of Sedgemoor Productions in London. During his time there, he produced or coproduced nine West End theater productions as well as touring and out-of-town productions, two television films, and three feature films. Liebman returned to the United States in 1975 and organized Marvin Liebman, Inc., a firm that performed the same functions as the earlier Marvin Liebman Associates. His client list included Friends of Free China, Friends of Jim Buckley, the Committee of Single Taxpayers, the American-Chilean Council, Firing Line, and Covenant House.

Liebman worked on the presidential campaign of Ronald Reagan in 1980. After Reagan's victory, Liebman became consultant to the Office of Policy and Planning for Action (June through October 1981), consultant to the Office of Public Affairs for the U.S. Department of Education (October 1981 to February 1982), and director of the Office of Public Affairs and director of Special Projects for the National Endowment of the Arts (February 1982 to July 1987).

In 1990, while serving as director of special projects at the Federal Trade Commission, Liebman published an open letter to his long-time friend, WILLIAM F. BUCKLEY, in Buckley's *National Review*. The letter announced Liebman's homosexuality and condemned what he believed to be rampant homophobia in conservative Republican circles. From then on, he devoted himself to gay activism. He became founding chairman of the Log Cabin Republicans and in 1992 published his memoirs, *Coming Out Conservative*. In an article published that same year, he wrote: "To be gay, conservative and Republican is not a contradiction. I'm proud to be all three." In addition to his activities on behalf

of single-issue groups, Liebman was a founding member of three of the most significant institutions of modern conservatism: *The National Review*, Young Americans for Freedom, and the Conservative Union. He died of heart failure in Washington, D.C., on March 31, 1997.

—MSM

Lindsay, John V(liet)
(1921–2000) *executive assistant to the attorney general, U.S. congressman, mayor of New York*

The son of an investment banker, Lindsay was born in Manhattan, N.Y., on November 24, 1921. He grew up in homes on Riverside Drive and Park Avenue, summered on Long Island, and attended the Buckley School for Boys in New York and Saint Paul's preparatory school in Concord, N.H. Upon his graduation from Yale University in 1943, he enlisted in the U.S. Naval Reserve. Rising from ensign to lieutenant while serving as a gunnery officer, he participated in the invasion of Sicily and served aboard destroyers in the South Pacific. After receiving his discharge in 1946, Lindsay returned to Yale, where he earned his law degree in 1948. While in law school, Lindsay met HERBERT BROWNELL JR., a prominent lawyer and political operative, who became Lindsay's mentor. Brownell helped Lindsay get a job with the firm of Webster, Sheffield & Chrystie. Brownell also guided Lindsay's entry into liberal Republican politics. Lindsay became head of the New York Young Republican Club and, in 1952, founded the Youth for Eisenhower organization. Lindsay's work at the Republican convention that year further impressed Brownell, who, after Eisenhower's inauguration, became attorney general. In 1955, Lindsay became Brownell's executive assistant and served as liaison to the White House, the cabinet, and Congress. While working for Brownell, Lindsay played a significant role in shaping and working for passage of legislation affecting civil rights and immigration.

In 1958, Lindsay ran for Congress from New York's 17th District, which included Harlem, Greenwich Village, the East Side, and the affluent neighborhoods along Fifth and Park avenues where Lindsay had been raised. Lindsay won the election and served the Silk Stocking District for four terms.

In Congress, he was an outspoken supporter of civil rights and voted for the Civil Rights Act of 1964. He also involved himself with issues relating to immigration and refugees. On a number of issues, such as housing, school construction, and foreign aid, he voted more frequently with the Democrats than with his own party. In addition, he was one of the first members of Congress to oppose the war in Vietnam.

Lindsay's independent Republicanism played well in his district, but it had the effect of isolating him in Congress. He turned to local politics and in 1965 ran for mayor of New York as a fusion candidate (nominated by both the Republican and Liberal parties). When he won the election, he became the first Republican to hold that office since 1941; he was also one of the youngest mayors in the city's history.

Lindsay's tenure would be marked by strife and controversy. Historians disagree over whether Lindsay contributed significantly to the collapse of New York City or merely presided over it. Only hours after his inauguration, the city's transportation workers went out on a strike that lasted 13 days. The strike cost the city some $1.5 billion, and Lindsay capitulated, granting the union twice the benefits it initially demanded. The generous settlement set a precedent for New York's other municipal unions. Throughout his administration, Lindsay and New York faced as series of strikes by public service workers, including nationally publicized strikes by teachers and sanitation workers.

A strong advocate of civil rights for African Americans, Lindsay initiated a number of programs designed to aid African-American communities. After the assassination of MARTIN LUTHER KING, JR., he walked through the streets of Harlem, with his jacket off and his tie loosened, talking to people in an effort to calm an angry community. Compared to cities such as Detroit, Newark, and Los Angeles, New York experienced relatively little violence and property damage.

Even as Lindsay won a national reputation as a groundbreaking innovator in urban civil rights programs, however, in his own city, Lindsay's efforts on behalf of poor blacks and Hispanics encountered opposition from politicians and middle-class constituents. One reform that Lindsay initiated in education had disastrous results. He gave control of some schools, including those in the Ocean Hill–Brownsville district of Brooklyn, to black community activists. When the administrator of the Ocean Hill–Brownsville district dismissed a group of largely Jewish teachers, the United Federation of Teachers called a strike that closed 85 percent of the city's schools for 55 days. The bitter, racially divisive strike tainted relations between African Americans and Jews for years to come. Similarly, a proposal to build low-income housing in the middle-class, largely Jewish, area of Forest Hills, Queens, ignited a firestorm of racial and class animosities.

During Lindsay's tenure, New York quadrupled welfare benefits, doubled its welfare roles, and initiated a variety of costly social programs. To pay for these, he created new taxes, raised existing ones, borrowed money, and engaged in "creative bookkeeping." Higher taxes accelerated the exodus of businesses and the middle class from the city and further alienated the white working and middle classes. These resentments came to a head in 1969, when a huge snowstorm hit the city. While major arteries were quickly cleared, the streets of Queens remained unplowed. For many, the incident came to symbolize the Lindsay administration, which they saw as favoring minority groups and the affluent in Manhattan, while ignoring the needs of the white working and middle classes.

Running for reelection in 1969, Lindsay lost the Republican nomination but won the general election as a Liberal-Fusion candidate, in spite of garnering only 42 percent of the vote. His second term was marred by disclosures of police corruption, prison riots, racial animosities, and the deteriorating financial condition of the city. Under Lindsay, the city's debt grew from $2.5 billion to $9 billion. The year after Lindsay left office, the city nearly went into bankruptcy.

In the mid and late 1960s, Lindsay and NELSON ROCKEFELLER jockeyed for the leadership of the liberal wing of the Republican party. Their rivalry degenerated into a bitter personal feud. Moreover, Lindsay's relationship with the administration of RICHARD M. NIXON grew increasingly confrontational. Lindsay announced his switch to the Democratic party in August 1971. Spurred on by his aides, Lindsay made a bid for the Democratic presidential nomination in 1972. His short-lived presidential campaign was a disaster. With many of his programs in shambles and without a base of support in any party, Lindsay chose not to run for reelection in 1973 and returned to his old law firm. He also served as an occasional host on ABC's television program, *AM America*, a predecessor of *Good Morning America*, and published two volumes of memoirs as well as a novel. In his one attempted political comeback, he failed to gain the Democratic nomination for the U.S. Senate in 1980.

Poor health and financial difficulties plagued his later years. He failed to qualify for a New York City pension by several years. When Webster, Sheffield folded in 1991, Lindsay joined Mudge Rose Guthrie Alexander & Ferdon. When that firm, too, went out of business in 1995, he was left without health insurance or retirement benefits. Lindsay, who suffered from Parkinson's disease, faced financial ruin. Friends came to his rescue and in 1997 secured for him a position as consul to the New York City Commission for the United Nations, which gave him a salary and health benefits. After a period of time, it also made him eligible for a city pension. Nevertheless, his health continued to deteriorate. After suffering two heart attacks and two strokes, as well as collapsing in public on two occasions, he retired to a senior community on Hilton Head Island in South Carolina in 1999. He died there of complications from pneumonia and Parkinson's disease on December 19, 2000.

—MSM

Lippmann, Walter
(1889–1974) *journalist*

The son of a well-to-do Jewish family, Lippmann was born in New York City on September 23, 1889. He attended private schools and Harvard University, which he left in May 1910, just weeks before receiving his master's degree in philosophy, to become a reporter for a socialist newspaper, the *Boston Common*. Lippmann then worked briefly for Lincoln Steffens's *Everybody's Magazine* before becoming secretary to the socialist mayor of Schenectady, N.Y., in 1912. That experience imbued him with a distrust for reformers and political machinery. In 1913, he published his first book, *A Preface to*

Politics. In it, he criticized American progressives for concentrating on abstract goals, for their moralism, and for their confidence in reason. He urged progressives to draw on the ideas of Sigmund Freud, whose psychoanalytic theories had just begun to draw attention in America. The book brought him to the attention of Theodore Roosevelt, and also Herbert Croly, who was about to launch a magazine to promote Roosevelt's New Nationalism. Croly brought Lippmann on board as an editor. Before the first issue of that journal, *The New Republic*, came out in November 1914, Lippmann published his second book, *Drift and Mastery*. By this time, Lippmann rejected socialism and modified the ideas he had espoused in *A Preface to Politics*. He advocated a scientifically managed society run by a public-minded elite. By 1916, Lippmann had become convinced that the United States could not permit the defeat of Great Britain in the world war, and wrote a series of editorials intended to bring the United States into the war on the side of Great Britain and France. After the United States entered the war in 1917, Lippmann took a job with the government and played a role in the drafting of President Woodrow Wilson's Fourteen Points.

After the war, Lippmann wrote a series of articles on the role of the press, which he then published as a book, *Liberty and the News* (1920). He expanded his ideas in *Public Opinion* (1922), in which he questioned the foundation of democracy. The average person's perceptions, he argued, were the product of propaganda, prejudice, and a failure to engage the issues. Such a person seemed incapable of making informed, rational decisions; yet the theory of democracy depended on the ability of the average person to make intelligent decisions. Lippmann offered an answer to this problem by proposing that trained, unbiased experts be given the task of sorting out the news and presenting it to the public. Lippmann went still further in *The Phantom Public* (1925), in which he suggested that the public be removed from the substance of decision making. Experts, he maintained, should left to make the decisions, and the public's role would be to ratify or reject the decisions by removing experts whose decisions with which it disagreed.

Lippmann left *The New Republic* in 1922 to take a job as head of the editorial page at the *New York*

World, a liberal newspaper. When the *World* closed its doors in 1931, Lippmann went to work for the *New York Herald Tribune*, a conservative newspaper, as a syndicated columnist. His column, Today and Tomorrow, brought him a national audience. He became known for his ability to analyze current controversies and both relate them to larger issues and place them in a historical context.

By the 1930s, the one-time socialist and Wilsonian interventionist had become an advocate of maintaining a degree of distance from the affairs of Europe and Asia and a critic of the New Deal. While he supported the recovery programs of the early New Deal, he became increasingly hostile to what he regarded as Franklin Roosevelt's drift toward socialism. In 1937, he published *The Good Society*, an attempt to find a middle ground between laissez-faire capitalism and tyrannical collectivism. Lippmann early on recognized the threat posed by the fascist powers in Europe and advocated a policy of armed neutrality for the United States. After the Munich Conference in 1938, however, he worried that France and Great Britain could not contain Nazi Germany. With the German invasion of Poland in 1939, Lippmann shifted his position and urged lifting the arms embargo to Great Britain and France. He supported Roosevelt's destroyers-for-bases deal and lend-lease. Hitler's aggression destroyed Lippmann's faith in neutrality and international organizations. The erstwhile Wilsonian idealist emerged as a convinced realist. In *U.S. Foreign Policy: Shield of the Republic* (1943), Lippmann argued that isolation was impossible for the United States and that idealistic schemes could not substitute for military power and alliances. Therefore, the maintenance of peace in the postwar world demanded the continued alliance of the United States, Great Britain, and the Soviet Union.

By the end of World War II, Lippmann had emerged as one of America's most respected and influential political critics. His opinions on foreign affairs, in particular, carried great weight. He believed strongly in the necessity of continuing cooperation among the allied powers, which led him to view the emergence of the cold war with alarm. Lippmann blamed the United States and Great Britain as well as the Soviet Union for the collapse of great power comity and urged keeping the lines of communication with the Soviets open. In 1947 he wrote a series of articles which he later published as a book, *The Cold War* (1947). In it, he sought a middle ground between GEORGE F. KENNAN's policy of containment and Henry Wallace's dream of a unified and cooperative world based on the United Nations. Lippmann believed that America should base its policy on the "realities of the balance of power." While he recognized the need to counter Soviet expansion, he thought that Kennan's approach would commit the United States to unlimited intervention. He rejected the idea that the Soviets sought expansion for ideological reasons and stressed that Soviet interest in eastern Europe had its origins in history rather than communist doctrine. For Lippmann, the primary focus of the cold war was Europe, and particularly Germany. He recommended the neutralization of Germany and the withdrawal of both Soviet and American troops from the continent.

As the cold war took shape, Lippmann supported the Truman Doctrine and the Marshall Plan. At the same time, he objected to their presentation in terms of an ideological crusade. Even as he joined the broad consensus in support of the cold war, he remained a perceptive analyst of it.

Lippmann supported DWIGHT D. EISENHOWER for the presidency in 1952, in part because he believed that a Republican president was needed to check the excesses of Sen. JOSEPH R. McCARTHY (R-Wis.). After Eisenhower's victory, however, Lippmann became a frequent critic of the new president. In 1953, he accused Eisenhower of abdicating the power of the presidency and held Eisenhower responsible for allowing McCarthy to continue his rampage.

In 1955, Lippmann published *Essays in the Public Philosophy*, which continued his uncomfortable engagement with democracy. He viewed with alarm and disdain politicians who allowed themselves to be led by public opinion. While skeptical of mass democracy, he remained unwilling to turn to undemocratic methods. He asserted that democracy should be based on natural law and that natural law should confine the currents of public opinion.

An obdurate critic of Secretary of State JOHN FOSTER DULLES, Lippmann denounced Dulles's failure to define clearly the administration's "New

Look" (the reliance on air power, technology, and nuclear weapons as the primary deterrent against Soviet expansion or an attack by the Soviet Union) or to elaborate on the consequences of "massive retaliation."

When the Communist Chinese began shelling the offshore islands of Quemoy and Matsu in the fall of 1954, Lippmann opposed an American intervention. He contended that the islands had no strategic importance for Taiwan (Formosa) and advocated that the Nationalist Chinese withdraw from them. Moreover, Lippmann regarded the alliance with Chiang Kai-shek (Jiang Jieshi) as a liability that could draw the United States into an unnecessary war.

With respect to Germany, Lippmann continued to support a gradual movement toward a unified, demilitarized, and neutral Germany. When it became apparent that this was unrealistic, he advocated a mutual reduction of foreign troops in Germany and efforts to normalize relations between the East and West German governments.

After a trip to the USSR, Lippmann published an analysis of relations between the United States and the Soviet Union. *The Communist World and Ours*, published in 1957, criticized American reliance on military pacts to contain Soviet expansion. The only way to prevent communism's expansion, he wrote, was for the United States to demonstrate to developing countries that the American system could match communist achievements and do so in a more humane way. Lippmann also contended that without Soviet troops in Eastern Europe, communist regimes would find it difficult to survive. Therefore, he argued that the United States should support an end to the military occupation of Europe.

Disillusioned with Eisenhower, Lippmann enthusiastically supported JOHN F. KENNEDY for the presidency in 1960. He regarded Kennedy as the first presidential candidate since Roosevelt who could stir and unite the American people. Once Kennedy assumed the presidency, however, Lippmann became increasingly critical of the president's foreign and domestic policies. After Kennedy was assassinated, Lippmann initially threw his fervent support to LYNDON JOHNSON, whom he called "a man for this season," but broke with the Johnson administration over the war in Vietnam. Between 1960 and 1965, the CBS network did seven one-hour interviews with Lippmann, an indication of his status as an observer of the American political scene. Beginning in 1965, Lippmann began to criticize the administration's policy in Vietnam. The columnist turned not only against Johnson's policy in Vietnam but against Johnson himself. In 1967, Lippmann stopped writing his newspaper column, although he continued to write a column for *Newsweek* (which he began in 1963) for another year. He returned to New York, where he lived until his death there on December 14, 1974.

—MSM

Lipset, Seymour Martin
(1922–2006) *sociologist*

The son of a Russian-Jewish immigrant who worked as a printer, Lipset was born in New York City on March 18, 1922. Through his father, he was introduced to the politics of the printer's union, which would later become the subject of one of his major studies. He became involved in the Young People's Socialist League during his high school years. The degeneration of socialism in the Soviet Union into a totalitarian form of government profoundly influenced Lipset. By the time he graduated from the City College of New York in 1943, he was a Social Democrat. After completing his B.A., Lipset enrolled in the Ph.D. program in sociology at Columbia University, where he studied under Robert K. Merton. He taught at the University of Toronto from 1946 to 1948 and was an assistant professor at the University of California at Berkeley from 1948 to 1950.

Lipset's first book, *Agrarian Socialism* (1950), was a revised version of his doctoral dissertation on the Cooperative Commonwealth Federation, a mass socialist party that had arisen in Canada during World War II. The study intended to force a revision of conventional explanations for the weakness of socialist movements in North America.

Lipset left Berkeley in 1950 to take a position at Columbia, where he taught until 1956. In 1955, he published an important article on the origins of what he called "the radical right." According to Lipset, this group deserved the term radical because "it desire[d] to make far-reaching changes in American institutions." The radical right rejected the New Deal, or, as Lipset put it, "refuse[d] to accept the recent past," and viewed "our entire foreign policy" since the recognition of the Soviet Union as "appeasement, treason, and treachery." Lipset argued that the origins of the radical right lay in "status politics," which he described as "political movements whose appeal is to the not uncommon resentments of individuals or groups who desire to maintain or improve their social status." Like Theodor Adorno's *The Authoritarian Personality* (1950), on which Lipset drew heavily, Lipset regarded the Right as a form of political deviancy.

In 1956, in collaboration with other members of the Bureau of Applied Social Research, Lipset published *Union Democracy*. The book won him a reputation as one of the nation's leading sociologists. In it, he and his associates countered the widespread notion in sociology that organizations necessarily developed an elite governing body. The scholars did this by describing the democratic practices maintained within the International Typographical Union (ITU), one of America's oldest and most powerful labor organizations. They showed how a healthy level of disagreement was generated most easily among people who regard themselves as social equals. Equality and conflict then combined to provide the framework for two-party democracy. The book conceded the uniqueness of the ITU and that most labor unions were in fact dominated by only a very small minority. Lipset nonetheless implied that under conditions of equality and conflict, democracy would work.

In 1960, Lipset published *Political Man*, which won wide recognition as a classic of contemporary sociology. In it Lipset identified himself as "a man of the left" who made common cause with those who sought to "extend democracy" and reduce social stratification. Further, he associated those values with Americanism; despite its status as the world's "wealthiest capitalist nation," he argued, the United States was also committed to the broad extension of economic and cultural opportunities. Moreover, this contributed to the stability of American society. Labor unions had abandoned attempts to nationalize private property and concentrated on higher wages, benefits, and political reforms, which

did not "require or precipitate" the sort of "extremism" on the part of labor leaders or corporate executives that typified the conflicts of the 1930s. The book also presented the concept of "working-class authoritarianism." By that, Lipset meant that "the less sophisticated and more economically insecure a group" was, the more likely its members were to accept a simplistic ideology or political program. Thus, he maintained, authoritarian movements of the left and right often found a social base in such groups. Making a distinction between "economic" and "noneconomic liberalism," Lipset argued that support for economic liberalism correlated inversely with higher social and economic standing, but support for noneconomic liberalism was associated with higher educational attainment and a greater level of sophistication. He concluded, therefore, that movements propounding both antielitism (economic liberalism) and intolerance of groups or ideas identified as different ("noneconomic illiberalism") would appeal to the less privileged. He located a powerful base of support for Sen. JOSEPH R. McCARTHY (R-Wis.) among just such groups. The "lower a person is in socio-economic status or educational attainment," wrote Lipset, "the more likely he is to support McCarthy, favor restrictions on civil liberties, and back a 'get tough' policy with the communist states."

Lipset returned to Berkeley in 1956. From 1962 to 1966, he also headed the Institute of International Studies at the University of California. In *The First New Nation* (1963), Lipset returned to several of the themes he first discussed in his essay on the radical right in 1955. He maintained that the emphasis on competition and success among nonelite Americans led to pressure to violate the "rules of the game" in politics or other areas of life. After the disturbances at Berkeley in 1964, he turned his attention to an analysis of student unrest. Lipset accepted a position as George D. Markham professor of government and sociology at Harvard University in 1966. His views had moved to the right, and, the following year, he published *Student Politics*. Lipset returned to his examination of the radical right in *The Politics of Unreason* (1970), a book he coauthored with Earl Rabb that "traced the connections and similarities (as well as the major differences) among right-wing extremist tendencies in American history." As had Lipset in much of his earlier work, *The Politics of Unreason* once again characterized the extreme right as a social aberration. Although he and his work were attacked by the New Left, Lipset remained an influential voice within the academic community. He moved to Stanford University as Caroline S. G. Munro professor of political science and sociology in 1975 and remained there until he accepted a position as the Hazel professor of public policy at George Mason University in 1990. He also held a position as a senior fellow at the Hoover Institution. His recent works included *Continental Divide: The Values and Institutions of the United States and Canada* (1990), *American Exceptionalism: A Double-Edged Sword* (1996), and, with Earl Rabb, *Jews and the New American Scene* (1996). Lipset died in Arlington, Va., on December 31, 2006.

Lodge, Henry Cabot

(1902–1985) *ambassador to the United Nations*

The product of a distinguished New England family that traced its ancestry in America back to the colonial period, Henry Cabot Lodge was born in Nahant, Mass., on July 5, 1902. After the death of his father in 1909, Lodge was raised by his grandfather and namesake, Sen. Henry Cabot Lodge, Sr. (R-Mass.). The younger Lodge was educated in Paris and at Harvard, from which he graduated cum laude in 1924. Upon graduating from Harvard, he went to work as a journalist, first with the *Boston Transcript* (1924 to 1927) and then with the *New York Herald-Tribune* (1927 to 1933). He also became an officer in the army reserve.

In 1933, Lodge won election as a Republican to the Massachusetts House of Representatives. Three years later, he defeated James M. Curley, a veteran Democratic politician, for a seat in the U.S. Senate. Lodge entered politics as a conservative Republican, but the international crisis of the late 1930s and the political success of the New Deal convinced him that, to remain viable, the Republican party needed to embrace internationalism and abandon its hostility to the basic structures of the New Deal. With the American entry into World War II, he took temporary leave from the Senate and served with an American tank unit in Libya. After win-

ning reelection to the Senate in 1942, he resigned from the Senate in 1944 to serve with the army in Europe. He rose from captain to lieutenant colonel and won a Bronze Star.

Lodge returned to the Senate in 1947 after defeating the Democratic incumbent, David I. Walsh, for his seat in 1946. In the Senate, Lodge supported the United Nations and aid for European reconstruction. In domestic matters, while critical of the New Deal's massive bureaucracies and what he regarded as its excessive interference with the private sector, Lodge supported a variety of social programs. These positions brought him into conflict with the conservative wing of his party and its leader, ROBERT A. TAFT (R-Ohio). Republican losses in the election of 1948 persuaded Lodge that, unless the party moved toward the center, it faced extinction. Nevertheless, the party's conservative wing dominated the Republican membership in Congress, and Lodge voted against the majority of his party in the Senate over 40 percent of the time between 1949 and 1952.

By the early 1950s, Lodge came to the conclusion that, if it were to survive, the Republican party needed to find a presidential candidate who could defeat Taft for the nomination and win the general election. He became convinced that DWIGHT D. EISENHOWER was such a candidate. Lodge first met with Eisenhower in June 1950 and failed to persuade the general to commit himself to a campaign. Eisenhower did agree, however, that if he thought that his candidacy was necessary to save the two-party system, he would answer the call of "public duty."

Lodge visited Eisenhower in Paris in July 1951 and thought that he had made some progress in persuading Eisenhower to run. At another meeting, on September 4, 1951, Lodge warned Eisenhower that gaining the nomination would be more difficult than winning the general election and insisted that Eisenhower permit the use of his name in Republican primaries. He also urged that political professionals be allowed to take over the Citizens for Eisenhower organization. Unless Eisenhower acted quickly, warned Lodge, Taft would lock up the nomination. In November, a group of political leaders, including THOMAS E. DEWEY and some of his key advisers from his presidential bid in 1948, met and named Lodge as Eisenhower's campaign manager. Among other things, Lodge had the advantage of not being identified with Dewey, who was anathema to the right wing of the party.

Lodge spent the last days of 1951 and the early days of 1952 attempting to persuade a reluctant Eisenhower to become a candidate. On December 8, 1951, Lodge told Eisenhower that if he did not return to the United States and make a positive announcement, the nomination would go to Taft. A parade of liberal or Eastern Republicans came to Paris urging Eisenhower to run. The attempt to enlist Eisenhower ran into difficulties when doubts arose regarding the general's party affiliation. In early January 1952, Lodge sent a letter to SHERMAN ADAMS indicating that the general's "voting record was that of a Republican." In fact, Eisenhower had dictated the content of the letter.

On January 6, 1952, Lodge called a press conference to announce that he would enter Eisenhower's name on the Republican ballot in the New Hampshire primary. At the conference, he read the letter he had sent to Adams maintaining that Eisenhower was a Republican. When reporters asked for verification, Lodge suggested that they ask the general himself. Although irritated at Lodge's presumption, Eisenhower released a statement indicating that "Lodge's announcement . . .

Henry Cabot Lodge at a press conference at the White House, July 23, 1953 *(Dwight D. Eisenhower Library and Museum)*

gives an accurate account of the general tenor of my political convictions and of my Republican voting record."

On February 10, Lodge staged a rally at Madison Square Garden, attended by 33,000 wildly enthusiastic, cheering partisans, in support of the general's candidacy. The demonstration of his popularity helped convince Eisenhower to run, but he did not yet become an active candidate. Despite his absence, Eisenhower won the New Hampshire primary. Encouraged by the showing, Lodge visited the general yet again in April and solicited his promise to return to the United States in June to campaign. During the ensuing months, Lodge stumped the country making speeches for Eisenhower.

By late spring and early summer, the Eisenhower campaign seemed likely to be derailed by Taft's popularity with party regulars, particularly in the Midwest and South. By late June, the contest appeared very close. In selecting the delegation from Texas, Taft's supporters in that state had arbitrarily ignored substantial support for Eisenhower expressed at precinct-level meetings held by the party. Lodge and the Eisenhower organization turned the dispute into a moral issue. Taft's lieutenants responded ineffectively. At the Republican convention, delegates voted to seat a pro-Eisenhower delegation from Texas in place of Taft's slate. Delegates also voted to seat pro-Eisenhower delegates from Georgia and Louisiana, although the issues in those states appeared less clear-cut than in Texas. The successful challenges to Taft delegations from these states provided Eisenhower with the votes necessary for a victory on the first ballot.

His preoccupation with Eisenhower's campaign led Lodge to neglect his own race for reelection against Rep. JOHN F. KENNEDY (D-Mass.). Backed by his family's wealth and influence, Kennedy ran an innovative and lavishly funded campaign. Moreover, Lodge encountered fierce opposition from Taft Republicans in Massachusetts, many of whom voted for Kennedy. In the end, Lodge lost by 70,000 votes out of 2.3 million votes cast.

After winning the election, Eisenhower made Lodge his liaison to the Truman administration to effect a smooth transition of power. Eisenhower also appointed Lodge to be ambassador to the United Nations and elevated the position to cabinet rank.

In addition, Eisenhower made the new ambassador a member of the National Security Council.

Lodge viewed himself not as the head of an embassy who was obliged to take direction from the State Department but rather as one of Eisenhower's senior policy advisers. Lodge had authority to speak at UN debates without prior clearance from Washington. The president often remarked that his ambassador had articulated the position he would have taken had he been consulted.

At the UN, Lodge presented a hard line with respect with the Soviet Union and responded to its positions in debates swiftly and aggressively. At the same time, he sought to keep lines of communication with them open and maintained cordial relations with Soviet diplomats in private. Lodge's patrician manner, his facility with languages, and his sense of humor made him an effective representative at the UN. He needed all the skills he could muster as he dealt with a series of difficult matters, including the coup in Guatemala in 1954, the Suez Crisis and the Hungarian uprising in 1956, and the American intervention in Lebanon in 1958. He also had to manage relations with the newly independent states in Asia and Africa and the neutralist bloc led by India. Lodge responded to the challenge of newly independent and developing countries by becoming the leading advocate of international development initiatives within the administration. Lodge functioned as Eisenhower's official representative and accompanied the Soviet premier, Nikita Khrushchev, on his 12-day tour through the United States in 1959. Lodge also was present at the talks between Khrushchev and Eisenhower at Camp David.

In 1960, Lodge resigned his post to accept the Republican party's vice presidential nomination on a ticket headed by Vice President RICHARD M. NIXON. A highly visible and popular figure as ambassador to the UN and an important link to the liberal wing of the party, Lodge brought a lot to the ticket. Nevertheless, Nixon and Lodge lost to the Democratic ticket of Kennedy and LYNDON B. JOHNSON that November.

Kennedy appointed Lodge ambassador to Vietnam in 1963. Lodge resigned as the post in 1964 because of his wife's ill health. At the request of President Lyndon Johnson, Lodge made a tour of countries belonging to the North Atlantic Treaty

Organization in August and September 1964 in order to brief their leaders regarding American policy in Vietnam. In February 1965, he became a presidential "consultant" on Vietnam and took part in the deliberations that led to the decision to launch an air war. In July 1965, Johnson asked Lodge to return to Vietnam as ambassador. Back in Vietnam, Lodge continued to advocate social reforms to raise the living standards of the rural population. He remained steadfast in his belief that the United States should not permit the communists to take over South Vietnam. In November 1966, he opened secret negotiations with North Vietnam designed to explore the North's reaction to a possible halt of the bombing. Encouraged by what he regarded as a favorable response from Hanoi, Lodge attempted to persuade policy makers in Washington to halt the bombing temporarily. He ultimately proved unsuccessful, and the talks collapsed. Lodge resigned his post in April 1967. In March 1968, Johnson asked Lodge to become a member of the Senior Advisory Group on Vietnam. Lodge served as ambassador to Germany from April 1968 to January 1969. When Richard Nixon became president in January 1969, he appointed Lodge chief U.S. negotiator at the Paris peace talks with North Vietnam. The talks proved unsuccessful, and Lodge resigned in December 1969. Between 1970 and 1977, Lodge served as envoy to the Vatican for Presidents Nixon and GERALD R. FORD, after which he retired to Beverly, Mass. He died there on February 27, 1985. Lodge wrote two volumes of memoirs, *The Storm Has Many Eyes: A Personal Narrative* (1973) and *As It Was: An Inside View of Politics and Power in the '50s and '60s* (1976).

Long, Earl K(emp)

(1895–1960) *governor of Louisiana*

Long was born in Winnfield, La., on August 26, 1895. He grew up in the shadow of his older brother, Huey, and would remain in that shadow even after Huey's death. Unlike his brother, Earl Long was an indifferent student. Following Huey's example, he dropped out of school after finishing the 11th grade and began a successful career as a traveling salesman. Earl attended Loyola University and was admitted to the Louisiana bar in 1926. Earl

played a crucial role in helping Huey win election to the Louisiana Railroad Commission in 1918; Earl gave him money and drove all over the district campaigning for Huey. Earl also proved effective in persuading local political leaders to support Huey. Earl provided similar assistance when Huey ran unsuccessfully for governor in 1923. Four years later, Earl helped Huey win the governorship; once again, he provided financial support and stumped the state for Huey. Huey named Earl attorney for the inheritance tax collector, one of the most lucrative state jobs, although not an influential one. Earl served as Huey's legislative liaison and organized Long machines in parishes. Although Huey was brighter and quicker than Earl, Earl was better with people. When the lower house of the state legislature impeached Huey in 1929, Earl played a key role in helping to avoid a trial in the state senate.

In the election of 1931, Earl wanted to run for lieutenant governor on Huey's ticket, but Huey, who had already been elected to the U.S. Senate, would not allow it. Earl defiantly ran as an independent but finished a distant third. The episode resulted in a split between the brothers that lasted for three years, during which time Earl publicly campaigned for Huey's opponents and testified against his brother at a Senate hearing investigating voting fraud in Louisiana. The brothers reconciled in 1934, the year before Huey was assassinated.

Earl Long ran for lieutenant governor on the Long machine's ticket in 1936. The gubernatorial candidate was Richard W. Leche. Leche and Long won, and Earl once again functioned as the administration's legislative liaison. Long also helped mend relations with the administration of President Franklin D. Roosevelt; these relations had ruptured under the stress of Huey's aspirations for the presidency and his demagogic attacks on Roosevelt. Although Earl engaged in bribery and took graft, he managed to keep a distance from the wholesale corruption of Leche's administration. Revelations about the corruption of the administration led to the governor's resignation in June 1939, and Long served as governor for the remaining 11 months of Leche's term. Long ran for the governor's office in his own right in 1940, but the scandals associated with the Long machine led to his defeat by Sam H. Jones, an anti-Long reformer. Four years later, Earl ran for lieutenant governor and lost, a defeat that seemed to end his political career.

In 1948, however, Long again squared off against Jones for the governorship. He pledged to "share the wealth" without raising taxes, to increase welfare benefits, to provide hot lunches for school-children, and to raise teachers' salaries. He won the support of organized labor and defeated Jones in a runoff primary. As governor, he raised taxes for rich and poor alike. He used the revenue to pay for large increases in state spending for old-age pensions, schools, hospitals, roads, bridges, mental asylums, and other benefits. He also equalized pay for black and white schoolteachers and, under the threat of lawsuits by the National Association for the Advancement of Colored People (NAACP), expanded black voter registration. Although his programs were popular, Long's reversion to the machine-style politics of his brother cost him public support. He abolished the state civil service and fired hundreds of state employees. He attempted to gain control over the state universities and to reduce the municipal independence of the city of New Orleans. Under Long, mobsters like Frank Costello and Carlos Marcello expanded their illegal enterprises, including gambling and vice, all over southern Louisiana. Unable constitutionally to succeed himself as governor, Long supported a district judge, Carlos Spaht, for governor in 1952. Public revulsion at the excesses of the Long administration, however, led to the election of an anti-Long reform candidate, Robert F. Kennon.

Long had always taken a moderate position (at least for a southern governor) on racial issues. After the Supreme Court declared segregated public schools unconstitutional in May 1954, however, Long publicly proclaimed himself "1,000 percent" for segregation. Nevertheless, he ran for the governor's office in 1956 as a racial moderate. His campaign emphasized economic issues, and he denounced politicians who used race to avoid or confuse other matters. After winning the first primary outright against four opponents and then the general election, he once again assumed the governor's office.

Long accomplished less in his second administration than he had in his first. He did force a tax increase through the legislature in 1958, and the legislature repealed the state's right-to-work-law for nonagricultural workers. Race, however, dominated Long's second term as governor.

Long attempted to avoid taking a firm stand on desegregation. He recommended no legislation to enforce white supremacy and warned against passing "a lot of segregation bills—even though I would favor them" on the ground that the Supreme Court would strike them down. On the other hand, he signed the anti-integration bills sent to him by the legislature. Like Gov. James E. Folsom of Alabama, Long refused to join other southern governors in denouncing the Supreme Court's ruling. Unlike Folsom, however, Long did not oppose massive resistance.

A little-known state senator named William E. Rainach emerged as the leader of massive resistance in Louisiana. The president of the segregationist Citizens' Councils, Rainach became chair of the Joint Legislative Committee to Maintain Segregation. The Citizens' Councils made use of a provision in Louisiana's constitution that permitted citizens to challenge "illegally" registered voters and purged 31,000 black voters from the voting rolls. Long had not opposed Rainach, the Committee to Maintain Segregation, or the Citizens' Councils so long as they confined their activities to passing segregation laws. Long drew the line, however, at disfranchising voters who normally cast their ballots for the Longs. "If those colored people helped build this country, if they could fight in its army, then I'm for giving them the vote," stated Long. Further, he asserted that "a candidate should go after every vote he can get." In September 1958, Rainach attempted to purge black voters from the registration rolls in Long's home parish, an action the governor denounced as partisan. When the legislature met in 1959, Rainach and the Committee to Maintain Segregation supported legislation to further restrict voting rolls; Long countered with a bill to protect registered voters.

At the height of this confrontation, in May 1959, Long suffered a breakdown. Long and his wife of 26 years separated in late 1958, and Long went on a series of sprees during the first five months of 1959. He drank excessively and conducted highly publicized affairs with Blaze Starr and other strippers. In May 1959, Long put forward a scheme that would have allowed him to retain power, despite the prohibition against a governor serving two consecutive terms. He proposed to resign in favor of the lieutenant governor while he ran for reelection. This came at the same time the state senate rejected his measure to protect registered voters from purges. In a televised address to a joint legislative session, he lost control. He denounced the legislature in the most abusive language; he cursed and shouted. Long entered the John Sealy Clinic in Galveston, Tex., and then Southeast Louisiana Hospital in Mandeville, where he was treated for paranoid schizophrenia. More likely, he suffered from manic depression. After his release from the hospital, he took off on a wild vacation that took him to several western states and to Mexico.

By 1960, the race issue cut into Long's base of support in northern Louisiana. He ran for lieutenant governor on a ticket headed by James A. Noe, a former governor. Noe and Long lost the primary in December 1959. At the same time, however, Long finished ahead of the incumbent, Harold McSween, in a primary race for a seat in the U.S. House of Representatives. In spite of his continuing erratic behavior (in April 1960, for example, he walked out of a luncheon given for the president of France, Charles de Gaulle, in New Orleans), Long defeated McSween in a runoff primary in August 1960. On the day of his victory, Long suffered a massive heart attack. He died in Alexandria, La., on September 5, 1960.

—MSM

Long, Russell B(illiu)
(1918–2003) *U.S. senator*

The eldest son of Huey Long, the governor of Louisiana and U.S. senator whose political machine dominated Louisiana from the late 1920s to the mid-1930s, Russell Long was born in Shreveport, La., on November 3, 1918. He received a B.A. from Louisiana State University in 1941 and an LL.B. from its law school in 1942. The same year he graduated from law school, he was admitted to the bar. He served in the U.S. naval reserve from June 1942 until his discharge as a lieutenant in December 1945. Upon his discharge from the service, he began to practice law in Baton Rouge. In

1948, Long helped his uncle, EARL LONG win the Democratic gubernatorial nomination. Later that year, he ran for a seat in the U.S. Senate left vacant by the death of John H. Overton and narrowly defeated an anti-Long candidate, ROBERT F. KENNON, in the Democratic primary. In November, he won the general election to fill the last two years of Overton's unexpired term. Long won election to a full term in 1950. He would go on to win reelection in 1956, 1962, 1968, 1974, and 1980.

A moderate southern senator, Long exercised his greatest influence as a member of the Senate Finance Committee, on which he began serving in 1953. He consistently sought to expand Social Security. In 1954, he unsuccessfully proposed, against the wishes of the Eisenhower administration, an amendment that would have increased Old Age and Survivors Insurance benefits without cutting the public assistance checks of beneficiaries. Two years later, Long criticized the Finance Committee for eliminating disability payments to workers who became disabled after age 50. In 1958, Long made an unsuccessful attempt to increase public assistance payments to the aged, blind, and disabled.

In 1954, Long unsuccessfully opposed Eisenhower's proposed cut in dividend income taxes. Instead, he supported an amendment by Sen. WALTER F. GEORGE (D-Ga.) that would have replaced it with an increased personal exemption. The next year, Long supported a Democratic effort to grant a $20 tax credit to all persons. That, too, failed to pass.

While greatly admiring his father, Long acknowledged some differences in their approach to politics. "He wanted to tax it away from those who had it," Long once said of his father, but the younger Long maintained that "I wouldn't keep anybody rich from getting richer." Long generally supported tax cuts for business, and he staunchly supported the natural gas, oil, sulfur, and sugar interests that loomed so large in Louisiana's economy. In 1955, he unsuccessfully attempted to persuade the Senate to give domestic sugar producers a larger share of the expanding American market at the expense of Cuban producers. He obtained passage of a similar measure the following year.

In 1956, Long supported a controversial measure to exempt independent producers of natural gas from federal rate controls. Although Eisenhower was favorably inclined toward the bill, he vetoed the measure after the revelation of improper lobbying activities by representatives of the natural gas industry. Two years later, Long cosponsored a compromise proposal that would have exempted only smaller independent producers from federal regulation, but it did not reach the Senate floor.

In 1957, Long opposed an attempt to reduce the 27.5 percent oil depletion allowance for large oil companies while retaining the rate for smaller operators. He argued that the measure would give advantages to small, but personally wealthy, independent producers while harming the small, low-income investor in the larger companies.

A critic of foreign aid, Long annually attempted to cut funds for foreign-assistance programs. In 1955, he asked, "Why do we insist on treating foreigners better than we treat Americans?" He believed that any treaty entered into by the United States should exact equal obligations from the other countries. On that basis, Long voted against the Korean Mutual Defense Treaty of 1954 and the renegotiated Japanese Mutual Defense Treaty of 1960.

When HUBERT H. HUMPHREY became vice president in January 1965, Long was chosen majority whip. The following year, he assumed the chair of the Finance Committee, which he held until Republicans took control of the Senate in 1981. Long mastered the rules of the Senate and, in spite of a halting manner of speech, was an effective debater. However, his heavy drinking in the 1950s and 1960s made him less than dependable, and he annoyed many of his colleagues with his willingness to delay the business of the Senate. In the 1960s, he opposed what he called "forced integration" and voted against the Civil Rights Act of 1964. He later claimed that he voted with the southern bloc only because it would have cost him his seat not to do so. In 1969, he lost his post as whip to Sen. Edward Kennedy (D-Mass.).

Long tended to adopt an aggressive approach to foreign policy. When Brazil seized a subsidiary of International Telephone and Telegraph in 1962, Long sponsored legislation halting aid to any country that seized American property. He opposed the Nuclear Test Ban Treaty and strongly supported the landing of American troops in Santo Domingo, Dominican Republic, in 1965 and the American involvement in Vietnam.

Long did not seek reelection in 1986 and took up the practice of law in Washington, D.C., and Baton Rouge. He resided primarily in Washington, where he died of an apparent heart attack on May 9, 2003.

—MSM

Lovestone, Jay

(1898–1990) *director, Free Trade Union Committee*
Born to Jewish parents in Lithuania on December 24, 1898, Jacob Liebstein immigrated to the United States with his parents in 1907. The family settled in New York, and Liebstein changed his name to Jay Lovestone. He attended City College, from which he graduated in 1918. While there, he became active in the Socialist Party. After graduating from college, he was a delegate to the founding convention of the American Communist Party, which split from the Socialist Party in 1919, and quickly emerged as a major figure in the new party. He edited the party's theoretical journal, *The Communist*, in 1921 and worked in the party's underground apparatus during the early 1920s. Upon the death of the party's general secretary, Charles Ruthenberg, in 1927, Lovestone succeeded him. During the struggle for succession in the Soviet Union after Lenin's death, factions emerged within the Communist Party USA (CPUSA) loyal to competing Soviet leaders. Lovestone led a faction that supported Nikolay Bukharin and, on orders from Moscow, led a purge of the American followers of Leon Trotsky. At that time, Lovestone also argued for a revision of Marxist-Leninist theory regarding the United States. He predicted that capitalism in the United States was securely ensconced and would continue to expand for a long period. Because of this special circumstance, he maintained, the struggle against capitalism could not successfully follow traditional Marxist-Leninist strategies. Rather, he concluded, communists in the United States should advocate nonrevolutionary policies. This doctrine would later become known as "American exceptionalism."

After Bukharin fell from power, a delegation from the Comintern asked Lovestone to step down as party secretary in favor of William Z. Foster, a supporter of Joseph Stalin. Lovestone declined to surrender his leadership and went to Moscow to argue his case. After a confrontational meeting with Stalin, he returned to the United States, only to be expelled from the party. Lovestone and a small group of followers established a new party that they somewhat optimistically named Communist Party (Majority). Given that the party never numbered more than a few hundred members, it soon changed its name to Communist Party (Opposition). Later, the CP(O) became the Independent Communist Labor League and, in 1938, the Independent Labor League of America. The party published a journal, *Revolutionary Age*, which later became *Workers' Age*. The group was popularly known as the Lovestoneites.

After his expulsion, Lovestone formed an alliance with DAVID DUBINSKY, the anticommunist president of the International Ladies' Garment Workers' Union (ILGWU). Following an unsuccessful attempt to take over the United Auto Workers in 1938, Lovestone's politics began to change. Outraged at the execution of Bukharin, he moved away from communism and worked more closely with Dubinsky in the American Federation of Labor (AFL). Lovestone disbanded the Independent Labor League in 1940. When World War II broke out in Europe, he supported American intervention and became head of the Committee to Defend America, which sought to mobilize support for Great Britain and its allies. He also worked for an effort by the ILGWU's international affairs program to help labor leaders escape from countries occupied by the Axis powers.

Dubinsky appointed Lovestone director of the ILGWU's International Affairs Department in 1943. The following year, Lovestone became director of the AFL's Free Trade Union Committee (FTUC), which attempted to rebuild labor movements in Europe and Japan. The FTUC worked with noncommunist labor unions in other countries to prevent communists from gaining influence in labor movements. His activities brought him into contact with James Jesus Angleton, the counterintelligence chief of the CIA.

After the war, Lovestone used money from American trade unions and the CIA to build anticommunist labor organizations throughout the world. He worked behind the scenes to help create the International Confederation of Free Trade Unions (ICFTU), which was established to coun-

ter the influence of the World Federation of Trade Unions (WFTU), in which both communist and noncommunist unions, including the Congress of Industrial Organizations (CIO), cooperated. Lovestone served as director of the ICFTU from its inception in 1949 until 1963.

During the 1950s, Lovestone shifted his attention from Western Europe to Latin America. With continued assistance from the CIA, the FTUC worked through the Inter-American Regional Organization of Workers (ORIT) to train pro-U.S. labor leaders in Central and South America. Lovestone later admitted that many of these engaged in intelligence work for Washington. Unionists trained by ORIT took part in the "liberation army" of Col. Carlos Castillo Armas, which overthrew Guatemala's president, Jacobo Arbenz Guzmán, in June 1954. After the overthrow of Arbenz, Serafino Romualdi, head of the AFL's Latin America committee, went to Guatemala to help reorganize the country's labor movement and eliminate communist influence from it.

Lovestone's policy toward Cuba was more ambivalent. He protested Fulgencio Batista's coup d'état in 1952 but refrained from criticizing the regime too harshly so long as Batista allowed the Cuban Confederation of Labor (CTC) to function legally. When the collapse of Batista's government seemed inevitable, however, the AFL's FTUC approached Fidel Castro, offering support in exchange for a guarantee that the CTC would be permitted to operate in the event Castro took power. Castro rejected the offer, and, after he seized power, the AFL-CIO denounced him for turning Cuba into an outpost of Soviet communism.

Lovestone's intransigent anticommunism and his ties with the government aroused increasing controversy within the American labor movement. Although the FTUC supported North African unionists fighting French colonialism and denounced apartheid in South Africa, Lovestone generally subordinated questions of democracy and national independence to what he regarded as the overriding need to oppose communist expansion. A member of the Committee of One Million against the Admission of Communist China to the UN and of the Council against Communist Aggression (both of which supported Chiang Kai-shek [Jiang

Jieshi]), Lovestone opposed any steps towards an accord with the communist world. As a result, AFL representatives in the ICFTU found themselves increasingly at odds during the 1950s with Western European socialist labor leaders, who favored a relaxation of cold war tensions. WALTER REUTHER and other leaders of the CIO grew increasingly critical of Lovestone. At their insistence, the FTUC was officially disaffiliated from the merged AFL-CIO in 1955. With GEORGE MEANY's support, however, Lovestone maintained control of foreign labor operations, and Lovestone continued as Meany's chief adviser on foreign affairs.

Lovestone played a leading role in the creation of the American Institute for Free Labor Development (AIFLD) in 1961. The organization was designed to counter communist influence in Latin America, particularly in the aftermath of the Cuban revolution. It sponsored various programs to train Latin American labor leaders and to plan union housing projects, banks, and other projects.

In 1963, Lovestone became director of the AFL-CIO's International Affairs Department, through which millions of dollars from the CIA were channeled to anticommunist activities internationally, particularly in Latin America. Lovestone used his position to build regional anticommunist labor federations. He attempted to rally support within the AFL-CIO for the war in Vietnam and against President RICHARD NIXON's policy of détente in the 1970s. In addition, he brought the leadership of the AFL-CIO together with military, corporate, and political figures to form the Committee on the Present Danger in the mid-1970s to advocate increased military spending. Lovestone continued as director of the International Affairs Department until his retirement in 1974, after which he continued to work as a consultant to the AFL-CIO and to the garment workers. He died in New York City on March 8, 1990.

—MSM

Luce, Clare Boothe
(1903–1987) *ambassador to Italy*

The daughter of a pit-orchestra violinist (and sometime businessman) and a dancer, Ann Clare Boothe was born in New York City on April 10, 1903. Her parents separated when she was eight,

and she lived with her mother in genteel poverty. Raised in Chicago and Memphis, she attended several private schools, including Miss Mason's School in Tarrytown, N.Y., from which she graduated in 1919. Boothe then became a student at Clare Tree Major's School of the Theatre in Manhattan. In 1923, she married George T. Brokaw, a millionaire son of a clothing manufacturer. The marriage ended in divorce six years later, and Boothe resumed her maiden name. Boothe joined the staff of *Vogue* as an editorial assistant in 1930. A year later, she became an associate editor of the magazine. In addition to her editorial duties, she contributed satirical sketches, which were collected and published as *Stuffed Shirts* in 1931. She was promoted to managing editor of *Vanity Fair* in 1933. The following year she resigned from the magazine to write a newspaper column and to work on her first play.

Her debut as a playwright, *Abide with Me*, opened on Broadway in November 1935 to overwhelmingly negative reviews. That same month, she married HENRY R. LUCE, an editor and publisher who had founded *Time* and *Fortune*. He would go on to create *Life* (which was rumored to be his wife's suggestion) and *Sports Illustrated*. The Broadway production of Clare Luce's second play, *The Women*, opened in December 1936. Although critics panned this effort, too, audiences loved it. The play ran for 657 performances, went on tour, and was made into a motion picture. This satire about wealthy, idle wives and divorcées, which the *New York Times* would later describe as "the apotheosis of feminine bitchiness," involved a devoted wife whose husband had been lured away by a saleswoman. Luce's next play, *Kiss the Boys Goodbye* (1938), which she characterized as a political allegory about American fascism, was a satire on the widely publicized search for an actress to play Scarlett O'Hara in the film version of *Gone with the Wind*. Her next play, *Margin for Error* (1939), concerned the murder of a Nazi agent and was a combination of comedy and melodrama.

With the outbreak of World War II in Europe, Luce turned her attention to public affairs. In the spring of 1940, she traveled around Europe as a correspondent for *Life*; her observations were published as a book, *Europe in the Spring* (1940). In the summer of 1940, she became active in Republican

Dwight D. Eisenhower talks with Clare Boothe Luce. *(Library of Congress)*

politics and supported Wendell Wilkie for the presidency. Campaigning for Wilkie in the general election, she criticized President Franklin D. Roosevelt for failing to prepare the country for war. In 1941 she toured China with her husband and reported for *Life* on that country's war with Japan. After the United States entered the war, Luce toured Africa, India, China, and Burma for *Life* in early 1942.

Luce ran for a seat in the House of Representatives from Connecticut's fourth district in 1942. Campaigning on the claim that Roosevelt led the nation into war unprepared, she defeated six opponents in the Republican primary and the Democratic candidate in the general election. Her initial speech in the House attacked Vice President Henry Wallace's proposal for postwar freedom of the air, which Luce described as "globaloney." The speech was warmly received by conservatives and isolationists, and she received an appointment to

the Military Affairs Committee. Throughout her two terms, Luce was a consistent and forceful advocate for American servicemen and raised important issues regarding their eventual return to civilian life. Although she frequently attacked the Roosevelt administration's foreign policy, she generally voted to support it. In 1944, she gave the keynote address at the Republican National Convention and won a second term in Congress. After visiting American troops in Italy over Christmas 1944, she returned to Congress urging aid for Italian war victims. Despite her own flirtation with communism in the 1930s, she warned early on against what she perceived to be a communist threat. In 1945, she began speaking about the danger of communism, particularly the threat it posed to China, and what she regarded as the weak position Roosevelt and HARRY S. TRUMAN had taken with respect to that threat. She warned that the failure of the United States to be "firm, precise, and clear in our foreign policy . . . will result in an increasing drift towards world catastrophe." After the death of her 19-year-old daughter in an automobile accident in 1944, Luce found solace in discussions with the Rev. FULTON SHEEN, which led to her conversion to Catholicism in 1946. Not long after her widely publicized conversion, she announced that she would not seek reelection.

In 1947, Luce wrote a series of articles on her conversion for *McCall's* magazine. Her screenplay for *Come to the Stable* was nominated for an Academy Award in 1949, and two years later, she wrote another play, *Child of the Morning*. She also edited a collection of essays about saints, titled *Saints for Now* published in 1952.

In the spring of 1952, Luce declared her support of the candidacy of DWIGHT D. EISENHOWER. She also made an unsuccessful bid for the Republican nomination for a seat in the U.S. Senate from Connecticut. Luce campaigned hard for Eisenhower in the general election; she made almost 50 speeches on radio and television.

In February 1953, Eisenhower named her ambassador to Italy. After confirmation by the Senate in March, she moved to Rome. Luce arrived in Italy during a period of strained relations between the two countries.

In the postwar years, the United States had exerted economic and political pressure to prevent Italy's communist party from gaining control of the government. In 1953, the U.S.-backed government of Premier Alcide de Gaspari faced an election in which it appeared that his Christian Democratic Party would lose its majority. Believing that the only way to save Italy from a communist takeover was to maintain de Gaspari, Luce did everything in her power to ensure his victory. Just before the election, she saw to it that de Gaspari appeared on *Time's* cover. The accompanying article extolled him as a bulwark of Italian religion and morality and denounced Italian communists as wolves slashing at "the shaky legged colt of Italian democracy." Luce also made a speech suggesting that, if de Gaspari lost, it would have grave consequences for Italian-American relations. Despite her efforts, which some Italian politicians denounced as open meddling, de Gaspari's government fell two months after the election.

Luce's concern over communist influence in the Italian labor movement prompted her in 1954 to protest the American decision to purchase material for the North Atlantic Treaty Organization's defense needs from foreign suppliers. The policy was designed to help restore the industrial capacity of America's allies, but Luce warned that it had the effect of aiding communist unions. She threatened to resign unless the United States canceled such contracts with plants at which communist unions were in control. Eisenhower and Secretary of State JOHN FOSTER DULLES gave her substantial latitude in dealing with the matter. Luce threatened to cut off U.S. government contracts with Fiat, Italy's largest manufacturer, and, as a result, the communists lost control of the company's union in the spring of 1955.

One of her most significant contributions as ambassador was the role she played in resolving the dispute, dating back to the end of World War II, between Italy and Yugoslavia over control of Trieste. Luce pressed for a resolution of the dispute, arguing that it provided the strongest issue for the Italian communist party, and supported the idea that a conference between Italy and Yugoslavia be held in a neutral country. Negotiations took place in London in 1953 and recommenced in the spring of 1954. By August, however, they had bogged down; Yugoslavia's Marshal Josip Tito insisted on more than the Italians, backed by the British and American representatives, were prepared to grant. The Eisenhower administration became convinced that Tito's hard line was motivated, at least in part, by a desire to draw domestic attention away from his country's poor harvest. Thus, the United States offered Yugoslavia wheat, but not directly as a quid pro quo in exchange for concessions at the negotiating table. The strategy contributed to a settlement, and the dispute over Trieste was formally settled in October 1954. Italy got the city of Trieste and the surrounding territory, in exchange for which Yugoslavia received territorial concessions.

Luce resigned her post in 1956, citing ill health. She had been afflicted with a mysterious illness that turned out to be arsenic poisoning caused by flakes of paint falling from the ceiling of her residence.

Eisenhower nominated Luce to be ambassador to Brazil in February 1959, but the nomination ran into fierce opposition from Sen. WAYNE MORSE (D-Oreg.), who objected to her views on Roosevelt's policies during World War II and to what he regarded as her meddling in Italian domestic politics. Luce nonetheless won the approval of the Senate Foreign Relations Committee and overwhelming confirmation by the full Senate, but Morse continued his attacks. Luce retaliated with the observation that her difficulties with Morse went "back some years," to when the senator "was kicked in the head by a horse." In fact, Morse had been kicked by a horse, but not in the head. Her comments created a furor, during which Eisenhower defended her but her husband publicly urged her to resign because the conflict had made it impossible for her to function effectively. Heeding her husband's wishes, she resigned three days after her confirmation.

Luce then resumed her career as a writer and continued to play an active role in Republican politics. In the early 1960s, she moved more towards the conservative wing of the party. She supported Sen. BARRY GOLDWATER of Arizona for the top spot on the Republican ticket in 1964 and seconded his nomination at the Republican National Convention. Later that summer, she declared her own candidacy for a seat in the U.S. Senate from New York on the Conservative Party ticket. On the eve of the Conservative Party's convention, at the urging of both liberal Republicans and Goldwater, she withdrew from the contest. Her husband retired that same year, and they withdrew to a home they owned in Phoenix, where she devoted herself largely to social life. After her husband's death in 1967, she moved to Honolulu, where she lived until 1983. There, she continued to write articles and went back to writing plays. However, her return to the theater, *Slam the Door Softly* (1970), attracted little attention. She served as a member of the President's Foreign Intelligence Advisory Board from 1973 to 1977 and again from 1982 to 1987. She moved to Washington, taking an apartment at the Watergate complex, in 1983. She lived there until she died at home on October 9, 1987.

—MSM

Luce, Henry R(obinson)
(1898–1967) *journalist*

The son of a Presbyterian missionary, Luce was born in Tengchow (Dengzhou), China, on April 3, 1898. Raised in China, where he learned to speak Chinese before he spoke English, he was educated in Chefoo (a British public school), the Hotchkiss School, and Yale University. At Yale, he helped to edit the *Daily News* and was an enthusiastic supporter of U.S. entry into World War I. He served in the Reserve Officers Training Corps at Yale, went to boot camp near Columbia, S.C., and received his commission as a second lieutenant in the army late in 1918. The armistice was signed before he could get to Europe, so he returned to Yale, where he graduated in 1920. He studied briefly at Oxford and, upon his return to the United States, took a job as a reporter for the *Chicago Daily News*. In 1923, with Briton Hadden, a friend from Hotchkiss, Yale, and the army, Luce launched a weekly news magazine they called *Time*. As the enterprise got underway, Luce ran the business affairs and Hadden handled editorial matters. After a somewhat rocky start, the magazine attracted a growing readership. Part of the new magazine's success was that it offered straightforward (some said simplistic) explanations of events in a fast-paced, complicated, and increasingly interconnected world. The magazine was irreverent, clever, and, above all, readable. Moreover, *Time* shared the values of its largely educated, middle-class readership.

When Hadden died in 1929, Luce took over the editorial duties as well. In 1930, Luce launched a new magazine, *Fortune*, aimed at businesspeople. It, too, was a success. Luce and his first wife got a divorce in 1935, and, that same year, he married CLARE BOOTHE, an editor and playwright. Time Inc., as Luce named his expanding business ventures, began producing newsreels called "The March of Time" in 1935. Innovative and well-produced, the series was an instant success. In late 1936, Luce bought out the first issue of a new picture magazine, *Life*, which was also an immediate success.

Luce rejected journalistic objectivity, and his magazines intended to persuade, as well as to inform, their readers. During the 1930s, Luce's publications attacked the New Deal for its spending and its restrictions on free enterprise. Luce threw himself and his magazines behind China's attempts to resist the Japanese invasion. In addition to using his media empire to publicize Japanese atrocities, Luce organized United China Relief (1941–46), which raised millions of dollars for the government of Chiang Kai-shek (Jiang Jieshi). Although China held a special interest for him, Luce, as the 1930s went on, became increasingly concerned about the rise of Hitler's Germany. As much as he disliked and distrusted Roosevelt, Luce supported the president's moves to aid the Allies and to rearm the United States. In domestic matters, Luce played a central role in promoting the presidential candidacy of Wendell L. Wilkie, who became the Republican nominee in 1940.

In February 1941, Luce published an editorial in *Life* titled "The American Century," in which he argued that the United States should assume its rightful place as the dominant power in the world. The country already exercised enormous economic and cultural influence; it should face up to the reality of its place in world politics. With that power, he argued, came the responsibility to "exert upon the world the full impact of our influence, for such purposes as we see fit and by such means as we see fit." Luce urged that the United States enter the war and, upon an Allied victory, use its power to build a free, peaceful, and orderly world.

The threat of communism and the need to meet that threat aggressively, particularly in Asia, emerged as a central concern for Luce. As World War II progressed, Luce became an increasingly strident advocate of Chiang; the publisher also evinced growing concerns about the America's wartime ally, the Soviet Union. During the postwar years, Luce and his publications continued to promote Chiang and to urge the containment of communism in both Europe and Asia. He refused to blame the failures of the Nationalist Chinese on Chiang and instead charged that liberals and communist sympathizers had given bad advice to the American government. Luce and *Time* were early critics of Sen. JOSEPH R. McCARTHY (R-Wis.), but both the publisher and his publications made charges similar to those put forward by the junior senator from Wisconsin against many of McCarthy's targets in the Truman administration.

Luce backed DWIGHT D. EISENHOWER for the Republican presidential nomination in 1952 and used his magazines to advance the general's candidacy, first for the nomination and then for the presidency. When Eisenhower defeated Sen. ROBERT A. TAFT (R-Ohio) for the nomination, some of Taft's supporters blamed Luce and his publications. In its coverage of the general election, *Time* presented Eisenhower as a smiling, earnest candidate and portrayed his opponent, ADLAI STEVENSON, in a much less favorable light. Similarly, Stevenson's running mate, JOHN SPARKMAN, received hostile treatment, while the Republican vice presidential nominee, RICHARD M. NIXON, got favorable coverage, even after the revelation of his private political fund.

After Eisenhower won the election, Luce had high hopes in particular for the new secretary of state, JOHN FOSTER DULLES, whom he had promoted through his media empire since the mid-1940s. The publisher expected Dulles to initiate a policy of rolling back communism in eastern Europe and Asia. Instead, Luce was disappointed when the new administration continued the policy of containment. He nevertheless muted his public criticism of Eisenhower and Dulles.

Luce worried about the expansion of communism everywhere, but his greatest concern lay in Asia. Thus, he urged that the United States take a strong stand in Indochina, where communist insurgents threatened French colonial rule. During the siege of the French garrison at Dien Bien Phu, Luce advocated direct American intervention. After the administration did not intervene, Luce supported the decision to prevent Vietnamese elections, which would likely have brought the communists into power, and an expanded American role in the region.

Luce also supported the administration's "New Look" defense policy, which relied on air power, technology, and the nuclear deterrent to contain the Soviet Union. On the other hand, he remained suspicious of Eisenhower's attempts to reach some sort of accord with the Soviets. The publisher opposed any thaw in the cold war. When the Soviet premier, Nikita Khrushchev, visited the United States in 1959, Luce's publications took every opportunity to remind the public of Khrushchev's phrase, "We will bury you."

In 1959, rioting broke out in Bolivia after an incendiary article in *Time* quoted an official at the U.S. embassy in that country to the effect that the United States had spent $129 million without notable results. Further, according to the story, the official stated that the only way to solve Bolivia's problems was to abolish the country and divide it and its problems among its neighbors.

Luce's publishing empire flourished in the 1950s. He had a remarkable eye for editorial talent and paid well enough to attract it. By the end of the decade, *Life* sold 6 million copies a week and *Time* sold 2 million copies. In addition, Luce launched a new publication, *Sports Illustrated*, in 1954, and the weekly sports magazine was an immediate success. He exercised enormous influence. Foreign leaders sought him out and, in his many travels abroad, Luce received treatment usually accorded only to a visiting statesman.

Despite his earlier support for Richard Nixon, Luce and his publications initially declined to back either candidate during the election of 1960, at least in part because of Luce's friendship with Joseph P. Kennedy, the father of the Democratic candidate, JOHN F. KENNEDY. Luce announced that he would carefully examine each candidate's stand against communism as a primary factor in considering an endorsement. In October, *Life* came out for Nixon, but the publications of Time Inc. covered the elections in an uncharacteristically balanced manner.

In the 1960s, Luce continued to campaign against communism. He praised Kennedy's handling of the Cuban missile crisis and advocated American support for South Vietnam and the regime of Ngo Dinh Diem. Luce retired as editor in chief at *Time* in April 1964, but continued to exercise editorial control over his magazines as editorial chairman. Luce supported LYNDON B. JOHNSON for the presidency in 1964 and remained firm in his support for the American effort in Vietnam, even after it became apparent that Johnson's escalation of the conflict was not winning the war. Television and its nightly news reports weakened the appeal of *Life*; visual images of news events and far away places became more common. Nevertheless, Luce's publishing empire remained highly profitable. He died in Phoenix, Ariz., on February 28, 1967.

—MSM

Lucy, Autherine J(uanita)

(1929–) *school desegregation figure*

The youngest of nine children, Lucy was born on October 5, 1929, on her parents' farm near Shiloh, Ala. She attended public schools in Shiloh and graduated from Linden Academy in 1947. She attended Selma University in Selma, Ala., and Miles College, a church-supported black school in Fairfield, Ala., from which she graduated with a B.A. in English in 1952. She then decided to go to graduate school at the University of Alabama to get a degree in library science. After initially accepting her, the university denied her admission and urged her to seek admission to Alabama State College (for Negroes) in Montgomery. She turned to the National Association for the Advancement of Colored People (NAACP) for help. The NAACP legal team, led by THURGOOD MARSHALL, filed suit in July 1953. On June 29, 1955, a federal district court ruled in Lucy's favor. The judge, H. Hobart Grooms, found that Lucy had been "denied admission to the University of Alabama solely on account of [her] race and color." The court issued an injunction against officials at the university from denying her the right to enroll based on her color.

Officials of the University of Alabama appealed Grooms's decision, not so much because they believed that they would win, but to demonstrate that they were doing everything possible to keep the university segregated. On October 10, 1955, the Fifth Circuit Court of Appeals upheld Grooms's decision, calling it "well considered."

Although it admitted her as a student beginning with the second semester, the university prohibited Lucy from staying in the dormitories or using any of the dining facilities. On February 2, 1956, the night before classes began, students held protest rallies, and a cross was burned on the front lawn of the dean of students. The following day, Lucy attended her first classes, where she sat in a row occupied by no other students. On February 6, a mob of perhaps 1,000 people, composed of students, townspeople, and even people from outside the state, pelted Lucy with eggs and tried to block her way. Two deans escorted her, but by noon the crowd was out of control. University officials arranged for a highway patrol car to remove her from the campus and asked

Gov. James E. Folsom to send the National Guard. Folsom declined and observed that "it is normal for all races not to be overly fond of each other." "We are not," he reassured the public, "excited." That evening, the university suspended Lucy, ostensibly for her own safety. Leonard Wilson, a leader of the mob, was expelled. The university took no other action against the rioters.

On February 9, lawyers for the NAACP filed a contempt of court action against the university, in which they accused administrators of failing to prevent the mob and conspiring with the mob to defy the court's injunction. The president of the university denounced the charge as "untrue, unwarranted, and outrageous." At a court hearing later in the month, Marshall withdrew the conspiracy charge, stating that a careful investigation had failed to substantiate it. On February 29, Judge Grooms dismissed the contempt action but ruled that the university had to reinstate Lucy. That evening, the board of trustees expelled Lucy on disciplinary grounds for having made "false and baseless" accusations against officials of the university.

Throughout the crisis, Lucy stayed with relatives in Birmingham, where she received numerous threatening phone calls. On March 1, she flew to New York City for rest and medical attention. Eight days later, her attorneys went to court to challenge the university's expulsion order. On January 18, 1957, Judge Grooms refused to overturn the trustees' action in expelling Lucy. That decision, he held, was based on disciplinary grounds and not on her race. In the meantime, Lucy had married a college sweetheart, the Reverend Hugh Foster, and moved to Texas. She ended her fight to gain admission to the University of Alabama.

The crisis at the University of Alabama attracted national publicity, and the outcome was generally perceived as a victory for pro-segregation forces. Neither state nor local officials made a serious effort to disperse or control the rioters. At a press conference on February 8, President Dwight D. Eisenhower resisted the idea the that federal government should intervene. While publicly deploring the "defiance of law," he reminded reporters that local authorities and university officials had "not yet had an opportunity . . . to settle this thing." He said that he hoped to avoid federal action "as long as that State, from its governor on down, will do its best to straighten it out."

The Fosters lived in Texas for 17 years, where they had five children and Autherine Lucy Foster worked as a teacher. In 1974, the family moved back to Alabama, and Autherine Lucy Foster worked as a substitute teacher. Two professors at the University of Alabama invited her to speak to a class in 1988, after which several faculty members worked to get her expulsion overturned. The university's trustees officially reversed her expulsion in April 1988, and the next year she enrolled in the University of Alabama as a master's student in elementary education. She received her degree in the spring of 1992, at the same commencement ceremony in which her daughter received an undergraduate degree in corporate finance.

—MSM

M

MacArthur, Douglas, II

(1909–1997) *counselor of the State Department; ambassador to Japan, Belgium, Austria, and Iran*

The nephew of General Douglas MacArthur, Douglas MacArthur was born in Bryn Mawr, Pennsylvania, on July 5, 1909. His father was a captain in the navy; his maternal grandfather was a rear admiral; and his paternal grandfather, General Arthur MacArthur, retired as the army's senior officer. Douglas MacArthur attended Milton Academy and graduated from Yale University, where he majored in history and economics, in 1932. After spending a few months in the merchant marine and more than two years as a first lieutenant in the Officers' Reserve Corps, he joined the foreign service in 1935. His first overseas assignment was vice-consul in Vancouver, British Columbia, Canada. Later in the 1930s, he held posts in Italy and France. At the outbreak of World War II, he was serving as a diplomatic secretary in Vichy, France. After France surrendered in 1940, the Germans occupied most of the country. The remnant came under control of a puppet government, headed by Marshal Philippe Pétain, that ruled from Vichy. MacArthur became third secretary to the U.S. embassy in Vichy. When the Germans occupied Vichy France in 1942, they interned MacArthur and the rest of the embassy staff until they were exchanged in 1944. MacArthur returned to the United States in March 1944 and later that year became assistant political adviser to General Dwight D. Eisenhower, the Supreme Commander of the Allied forces in Europe. After the liberation of Paris, MacArthur became head of the political section of the U.S. embassy in Paris, a post he held until 1948. After serving as first secretary in Brussels for a year, he returned to Washington in 1949 as chief of the State Department's Division of Western European Affairs. He then became deputy director of the Office of Regional Affairs. From 1951 to 1953, he was a political adviser to Eisenhower, who had become supreme commander of NATO forces.

When Eisenhower became president in January 1953, he appointed MacArthur counselor of the State Department. MacArthur attended the conference that led to the signing, in September 1954, of the Southeast Asia Collective Defense Treaty, which created the Southeast Asia Treaty Organization (SEATO). The signatories (the United States, Great Britain, France, Australia, New Zealand, Pakistan, the Philippines, and Thailand) agreed to develop military capabilities adequate for their own defense and for collective security; they further agreed to consult in the event of common danger and to expand trade and technical programs. The Geneva Accords prevented the formal participation of Laos, Cambodia, and South Vietnam in SEATO, but a separate protocol stated that the allies would consider any threat to those countries as a danger to their own "peace and security." MacArthur also worked on the peace treaty with Austria.

MacArthur became ambassador to Japan in 1957. A major issue he had to deal with involved the security pact signed by Japan and the United States in 1952, which had subsequently proved unsatisfactory to both parties. To many Japanese, the pact's provision for the maintenance of American troops in Japan amounted to a virtual occupation. To some Americans, including JOHN FOSTER DULLES, the treaty, which obligated the United States to participate in the defense of Japan, seemed to downplay the need for the rearmament of Japan. Particularly in the aftermath of the Korean War, Dulles thought it urgent to rearm Japan against the threat of Communist expansion in Asia. MacArthur negotiated a new security pact, signed in January 1960. It committed both the United States and Japan to resist "the armed attack against either party in territories under the administration of Japan." It also removed specific limitations on Japanese sovereignty in the earlier treaty and provided that the United States would consult the Japanese government before making major changes in the use of American troops or bases in Japan.

Even though it redressed some Japanese grievances, the new treaty ran into opposition in Japan. Socialists and Communists vigorously opposed the treaty. Leftist-led demonstrations against the treaty in May and June 1960 led to the cancellation of a visit by President Eisenhower scheduled for the day the treaty would take effect. Initially, Prime Minister Kishi Nobusuke refused to ask Eisenhower to cancel the trip, and MacArthur urged the president to make the trip as scheduled unless Kishi asked him not to come. On June 10, TOM STEPHENS and JAMES HAGERTY, acting as an advance party for Eisenhower's trip, arrived at the airport in Tokyo, where they were met by MacArthur. On the way to the embassy, their car was surrounded by demonstrators and held for 15 minutes. The American officials had to be rescued by helicopter. Amid continuing rioting, Kishi "postponed" the invitation to Eisenhower, and, one week later, resigned as prime minister. Nevertheless, the Diet approved the treaty, and Kishi's party was returned to power in the next elections, in which the far left lost seats.

As ambassador to Belgium from 1961 to 1965, MacArthur helped to coordinate efforts to rescue foreign hostages held in the former Belgian Congo. He served as assistant secretary of state for congressional relations from 1965 to 1967 and, in 1966, was named career ambassador, the highest rank in the foreign service. MacArthur was ambassador to Austria from 1967 to 1969 and to Iran from 1969 to 1972. During his service in the latter post, Iranian extremists attempted to kidnap him.

After retiring from the State Department in 1972, MacArthur became a business consultant in the United States and Europe. He died on November 15, 1997, in Washington, D.C.

—MSM

Macdonald, Dwight
(1906–1982) *writer, editor*

The son of an attorney, Dwight Macdonald was born in New York City on March 24, 1906. After graduating from Phillips Exeter Academy in 1924 and Yale University in 1928, his first job was in the executive training program at Macy's. He soon got a job at *Time* magazine, where he wrote stories about business and finance. This led, in 1929, to a job as an associate editor of Henry Luce's new business magazine, *Fortune*. Macdonald would later claim that his experience on the magazine increased his revulsion with capitalism and moved his politics farther to the left. He resigned from *Fortune* in 1936 after editors toned down his savage attack on U.S. Steel in an article about the company. The following year, he became an editor of the *Partisan Review*, which Philip Rahv and William Phillips had recently moved out of the Stalinist camp. In its new incarnation, the magazine was committed to modernism in the arts and radical, but anti-Stalinist, politics. Although it had a small circulation, the magazine exercised considerable influence among intellectuals. Macdonald emerged as perhaps the most politicized of the magazine's editors. The Moscow Trials moved his politics to staunch anti-Stalinism. He became a Trotskyist and joined the Socialist Workers Party in 1938. With the Nazi-Soviet Pact and the Soviet Union's invasion of Finland, Macdonald joined a group, led by Max Schactman, that split from the Socialist Workers Party and formed the Workers Party, which condemned the invasion of Finland. He remained with the Workers Party until 1941.

Macdonald's Marxist perspective and his growing commitment to pacifism led him to oppose World War II. This ultimately caused him, in

1943, to break with the *Partisan Review*, which maintained what it described as "critical support" of the Allied cause. In 1944, Macdonald founded *Politics*, a monthly magazine, as an outlet for his anti-Stalinist, antifascist, and anti–New Deal views. Macdonald was its owner, publisher, editor, proofreader, and most frequent contributor. Over the years he put out *Politics*, Macdonald's own politics moved toward anarchism and pacifism. He became critical of Marxist thought and rejected knee-jerk allegiance to the working class (which he found not just conservative but "rabidly nationalistic") and to trade unions (which, he maintained, had "quite lost touch with the humane and democratic ideals" in which they had once believed). Macdonald turned his attention increasingly to questions of depersonalization in modern society and the resulting apathy of its citizenry. At the same time, he began to turn away from literary criticism and to focus his attention on popular culture. Contributions from Albert Camus, Simone Weil, Bruno Bettelheim, Marianne Moore, Mary McCarthy, C. WRIGHT MILLS, and Paul Goodman (not to mention Macdonald's own wry and stylish pieces) made *Politics*, which became a quarterly in 1947, one of the best journals on the left. Money troubles, the desire to devote more time to his own writing, and the cold war (which made it difficult even for so bumptious a radical as Macdonald to withhold his allegiance from the West) all contributed to Macdonald's decision to close down *Politics* in 1949.

Macdonald threw in with the West only reluctantly. He pointed out similarities between the United States and the Soviet Union: both pursued imperialist foreign policies in the name of which they suppressed indigenous revolutionary movements, and both created societies "where the few have too much and the many too little." For Macdonald, however, there were distinctions. The United States may have used its economic might to dominate western Europe, but the Soviets took the Baltic states by brute force. If Americans failed to appreciate their civil liberties, Soviet citizens had none. Macdonald, therefore, gave his "critical" support to the "imperfect" West as the "lesser evil." Despite his reservations about the West, at some point in the 1950s, he moved from anti-Stalinism to anticommunism.

By the early 1950s, Macdonald had abandoned sectarian politics and turned to cultural criticism. His main objection to totalitarianism was its "censorship . . . [and use of] exile and imprisonment to punish dissident thought." The result, he concluded, was a culture more tasteless and sterile than the worst of Hollywood, television, or pulp fiction. Yet he warned that the pressures of the cold war had transformed the United States and other Western countries into more rigidly managed and hierarchical societies. Alarmed by the dominance of "vast superstates" that managed their societies through elaborate bureaucracies, Macdonald found an antidote in individuals and the idea that individuals must, at least at times, deny the state their cooperation. Therefore, his writing turned to what he described as the "small" questions: "What is a good life? How do people really live and feel and think in their everyday lives? What are the most important human needs? How can they be satisfied best here and now? Who am I? How can I live lovingly, truthfully, pleasurably?" The true calling of a radical intellectual should therefore, according to Macdonald, involve an analysis of matters relating to work, family, sex, and art.

For Macdonald, the decline of a traditional elite that dominated not just politics but culture and the arts and the parallel rise of an urban bourgeoisie with its own conception of cultural entertainment, while "desirable politically," brought "unfortunate results culturally." This combined with technological developments that made possible the inexpensive production and distribution of cultural products (books, magazines, reproductions of images, phonographs, movies, radio, television) to create mass culture. A consequence was the emergence of "middlebrow" culture, which Macdonald campaigned against unceasingly. Culture, he argued, had become another form of ostentatious consumption and display. He railed against pretensions of coffee table books, the Book-of-the-Month Club, Thornton Wilder's play *Our Town*, magazines such as *Harper's* and the *Saturday Review of Literature*, the Revised Standard Version of the Bible (which replaced the "poetic intensity" of the King James Version with "tepid expository prose"), and the "folk fakery" of the popular musical *Oklahoma!*. For Macdonald, the "simple vulgarity" of the tabloid press or pulp fiction was preferable to the insufferable good intentions and pretensions of middlebrow culture.

Macdonald unleashed a stream of invective against kitsch, a term he used for superficial, commercialized art. He described kitsch as a "homogenization process that distributes the globules of cream evenly throughout the milk instead of allowing them to float separately on the top. It thus destroys all values, since value judgements imply discrimination." For Macdonald, the real threat to high culture was not honest trash. Rather it was the poetry and fiction of the *Atlantic Monthly* or the social message films of Stanley Kramer. These self-conscious, devitalized versions of the fine arts brought art down to the level of mass appeal and presented themselves as high culture. In doing so, they placed a cap on culture.

From 1951 to 1971, Macdonald wrote on cultural and literary topics for the *New Yorker*. He was special editor for *Encounter* from 1956 to 1957. For all his commitments to Marxism, Trotskyism, anarchism, and pacifism, Macdonald was essentially a skeptic. Moreover, he was first and foremost a critic. He was at his best when subjecting other people's ideas, ideologies, and language to his incisive scrutiny and pointing out their flaws with his own witty and scathing prose. Take, for example, his comparison of reading the Revised Standard Version to "walking through an old city that has just been given, if not a saturation bombing, a thorough going-over."

He was film critic for *Esquire* from 1960 through 1966. The American involvement in Vietnam rekindled his interest in politics. In 1967, he changed his column in *Esquire* from film criticism to politics and used it to express his unqualified opposition to the war between 1967 and 1969. Macdonald also lent his support to Students for a Democratic Society and the student revolt at Columbia University in 1968. Between 1956 and 1977, he was a visiting professor at several American universities, including Northwestern, the University of Texas, Yale, and the University of California at San Diego.

Although a highly influential intellectual, Macdonald never wrote a scholarly book or even one devoted to a sustained argument. He was, in the tradition of H. L. Mencken, a learned journalist devoted to serious issues. His best form was the essay, and his books all appeared originally as magazine articles. *Henry Wallace: The Man and the Myth* (1948) appeared first in *Politics*, as did *The Root Is Man* (1953). *Memoirs of a Revolutionist* (1957), which recounted his political journey, was a collection of reprinted pieces. Perhaps his most influential works, *Against the American Grain* (1962) and *Discriminations* (1974), were collections of essays that elaborated his critique of American culture and politics. The lengthy lead essay in *Against the American Grain*, "Masscult and Midcult," gave the greatest exposition to his assertion that mass entertainment was "an instrument of domination" and that the middlebrow "instead of being transitional—'the price of progress'"—would "become a debased, permanent standard." To make his point, he cited the popularity of Herman Wouk and Pearl Buck.

For all his intelligence and insight, Macdonald was capable of monumentally foolish statements: "Europe has its Hitlers, but we have our Rotarians." Further, as Delmore Schwartz once observed about Macdonald, "none of his political predictions come true." No less a figure than Leon Trotsky once remarked that "Every man has a natural right to be stupid; but Dwight Macdonald abuses the privilege."

Macdonald spent his final years in New York City, where he died on December 19, 1982.

—MSM

Mack, Richard A(lfred)

(1909–1963) *commissioner, Federal Communications Commission*

Born in Miami, Florida, on October 2, 1909, Richard Mack graduated from the University of Florida in 1932 and for the next nine years worked as an insurance salesman, credit manager, and executive in a farm supply company. He served as an infantry officer during World War II, rising to the rank of colonel. In 1947, he returned to Florida and was appointed to the state Railroad and Public Utilities Commission. In that capacity, he assumed a leading role in requiring utilities to undergo a detailed financial examination when requesting rate increases. For two years, he chaired the commission. Many observers in Florida predicted that he would eventually become the state's governor or U.S. senator. In May 1955, President Dwight D. Eisenhower appointed Mack to a seven-year term on the Federal Communications Commission (FCC).

During the early months of 1958, the House Special Subcommittee on Legislative Oversight conducted an investigation of six regulatory agencies, including the FCC. As a result of the probe, the subcommittee's chief counsel, BERNARD SCHWARTZ, charged Mack with plotting to fix the granting of a license to Miami's television channel 10. In February 1957, Mack had joined three other members of the FCC in voting to allocate the lucrative Miami channel to Public Service, Inc., a subsidiary of National Airlines. In doing so, they overruled the opinion of an FCC examiner, Herbert Scharfman, who had recommended that the license be awarded to A. Frank Katzentine, the owner-operator of WKAT, an AM radio station in Miami. Scharfman regarded National Airlines as the "least qualified" of the four applicants.

Well-publicized hearings held by the subcommittee during February 1958 revealed that National Airlines had contacted Thurman Whiteside, an attorney from Miami with a reputation as a political "fixer" and a close friend of Mack. Moreover, Whiteside had lent the commissioner $7,830, interest free, since 1950. Of this, Mack had received $2,650 after joining the FCC. Further, Mack had "no specific recollection" of having repaid the money and thought that some portion of it had been "forgiven." In addition, Whiteside had secured Mack an interest in two companies. Mack acknowledged both his friendship with Whiteside and having borrowed money from the lawyer but denied that he committed his vote to "anybody." The loans, Mack argued, were "small amounts." He further pointed out that he had known Whiteside since grammar school and that his had not been a deciding vote. For his part, Whiteside, who apparently accepted no money from National Airlines, freely admitted to having approached Mack on behalf of the airline "several" times. Whiteside also testified that he had forgiven none of the loans and that the balance due was only $250. Both National Airlines and WKAT had made efforts to exert political influence on the process. However, the extensive, complicated, and confusing financial transactions between Mack and Whiteside did not withstand scrutiny.

Although Mack and Whiteside maintained that they did nothing wrong, it became apparent to everyone else that, at the very least, Mack had been hopelessly compromised. The chair of the subcommittee, OREN HARRIS (D-Ark.), told Mack that, while it was possible that he had been used as a "tool" in the affair, the best service the commissioner could render at that point would be to submit his resignation. Clearly shaken, Mack said that he would "seriously consider [the chairman's] remarks." *Newsweek* reported that his appearance before the subcommittee "had reduced Mack from an urbane, self-confident, 'bright young man' of Florida Democratic politics to a broken and weary man." Although the administration maintained an official silence with respect to the affair, reporters believed that Eisenhower's chief of staff, SHERMAN ADAMS, and the White House counsel, GERALD MORGAN, told Mack to resign or face immediate dismissal. Mack submitted his letter of resignation on March 3, 1958. In it, he declared that "I feel in my heart that I have done no wrong and my conscience is clear." He complained that his "character and good name had been sacrificed to political expediency" but acknowledged that his usefulness as a commissioner "had been brought into question." The president accepted Mack's resignation within an hour. "Without attempting to pass judgment upon the question you have raised in your letter," replied Eisenhower, "I, nevertheless, agree with you that your usefulness as a member of the commission is so seriously impaired that you are wise to tender your resignation."

A grand jury indicted both Mack and Whiteside for conspiracy in September 1958. The subsequent trial lasted 14 weeks and resulted in a hung jury in July 1959. A second trial, scheduled for early 1960, was postponed several times because of the defendants' poor health. Mack descended into alcoholism and on several occasions spent time in psychiatric institutions. His wife divorced him for desertion. Whiteside stood trial alone and was acquitted in October 1960. In 1961, after Mack was held "temporarily incompetent," the prosecution dropped plans for a second trial. On November 26, 1963, the Miami police found Mack dead, apparently of natural causes, in a rooming house. He had been dead for four or five days.

—MSM

Magnuson, Warren G(rant)
(1905–1989) *U.S. senator*

Born in Moorhead, Minnesota, on April 12, 1905, Magnuson was orphaned at three weeks and adopted by a family of Swedish immigrants, whose name he took. He moved with his new family to North Dakota, where he attended public schools, the University of North Dakota at Grand Forks, and North Dakota State College. At the age of 19, he rode the freight trains west to Seattle, where he worked at several jobs while completing his education. Magnuson graduated from the University of Washington in 1926 and earned his law degree there in 1929. He practiced law in Seattle until he won election as a Democrat to the state legislature in 1932. In the legislature, Magnuson helped secure passage of legislation providing unemployment compensation and old age pensions. He worked in the office of the prosecuting attorney of King County, Washington (which encompassed Seattle), and became an assistant U.S. district attorney in 1933. After serving as the prosecuting attorney of King County from 1934 to 1936, he won election in 1936 to a seat in the U.S. House of Representatives that had been vacated by the suicide of Representative Marion Zioncheck (D-Wash.). A staunch supporter of the New Deal, Magnuson aggressively backed public works projects to provide employment and revive his state's economy, which had been hit particularly hard by the depression. An officer in the naval reserve, he spent eight months on active duty during World War II.

Magnuson won election to the U.S. Senate in 1944. He resigned his House seat in early December 1944, when he received a gubernatorial appointment to fill the last few weeks of the unexpired term of the senator he was elected to succeed, Homer T. Bone (D-Wash.), who had resigned to accept an appointment as a federal judge. In the postwar years, Magnuson succeeded in channeling large amounts of federal aid to Washington for dams, the timber industry, fisheries, and the maritime industry. He also voted for federal aid to

state unemployment compensation funds in 1945 and for the retention of price controls in 1946. A strong supporter of organized labor, Magnuson fought against the Taft-Hartley Act in 1947 and introduced a bill in 1950 that restored the maritime union hiring hall. He cosponsored the bill that created the National Institutes of Health in 1948. In foreign policy, Magnuson supported the Truman administration's policy of containment. Magnuson won reelection in 1950 and subsequently in 1956, 1962, 1968, and 1974.

During the Eisenhower administration, Magnuson's seniority on key committees enhanced his ability to deliver federal defense contracts and resource development projects to his state. In 1952, he became chair of the powerful Interstate and Foreign Commerce Committee (later renamed the Commerce Committee). He also served on the Appropriations Committee and the Aeronautics and Space Sciences Committee. Washington's economic boom in the 1950s, which was based on large federal expenditures on aircraft, atomic installations, and naval yards located in the state, owed much to Magnuson's efforts. As a result, despite his liberal, pro-labor voting record in the Senate, Magnuson gained the support of business interests in the state.

Magnuson opposed the Republican "partnership" policy, which encouraged private business, rather than the federal government, to develop natural resources. He denounced it as a "giveaway" to "favored corporations." In 1954, when the administration endorsed a bill to permit a local public utility to build and operate a $360 million hydroelectric dam on the Columbia River at Priest Rapids, Washington, he condemned the measure as a first step in ceding public water sites to private interests. Magnuson eventually dropped his opposition, however, and declared that even a nonfederal project was better than no project at all.

Beginning in the late 1950s, Magnuson became a leading advocate of government-sponsored research in oceanography as an aid to national defense. Citing the nuclear submarine program's need for information about ocean tides, currents, and weather, he urged the creation of a federal office funded long-range (rather than an annual budgetary basis) to coordinate the oceano-graphic activities of different government agencies. In 1960, Magnuson sponsored legislation to establish a new division of marine sciences in the National Science Foundation, but the bill failed to pass the House.

During the Kennedy administration, Magnuson's activity on the Commerce Committee began to shift from the advocacy of local interests to issues of broader national significance. He figured prominently in the passage of the controversial public accommodations section of the Civil Rights Act of 1964. During the Johnson and Nixon years, Magnuson played a leading role in consumer and environmental legislation. He contributed to the passage of laws dealing with automobile safety, flammable fabrics, truth in packaging, and warning labels on cigarette packages. Magnuson's seniority and his seats on key committees enabled him to look after the economic interests of his home state and Seattle. He chaired the Commerce Committee from 1955 to 1979 and the Appropriations Committee from 1977 to 1981. During the Ninety-sixth Congress (1979–81), he served as president pro tempore of the Senate. After losing his bid for reelection in 1980 to the Republican nominee, Slade Gorton, Magnuson returned to the practice of law. He died in Seattle on May 20, 1989.

—MSM

Mahon, George H(erman)

(1900–1985) *U.S. congressman; chairman, Department of Defense Subcommittee of the Appropriations Committee*

George Mahon was born on a cotton farm in the village of Mahon, near Haynesville, Louisiana, on September 22, 1900. He migrated with his family to rural west Texas in 1908. The family settled on a farm in Mitchell County, where Mahon attended public schools, graduating in 1918. He earned a B.A. from Simmons University (now Hardin-Simmons) in Abilene, Texas, in 1924 and an LL.B. from the University of Texas in 1925. After gaining admission to the bar in 1925, he practiced law in Colorado (now Colorado City), Texas. Before long, he entered politics, winning election as county attorney for Mitchell County in 1926. He served as

district attorney for the 32nd judicial district from 1927 to 1933 and won election as a Democrat to a seat in the U.S. House of Representatives from the newly created 19th congressional district in 1934. Subsequently, he was reelected to that seat 21 consecutive times.

Mahon effectively promoted the economic interests of his district. As he gained seniority, he brought cotton subsidies and federal facilities to the 19th district. During the 1930s, he supported the agricultural programs of the New Deal and began to acquire the seniority that would make him a power in the House. He gained a seat on the powerful House Appropriations Committee in 1939 and also served on its War Department Subcommittee, which later became the Defense Department Subcommittee. In foreign affairs, he strongly supported the policies of the Roosevelt and Truman administrations.

Mahon consistently opposed civil rights legislation and generally opposed the interests of organized labor. He supported the Taft-Hartley Act in 1947. When the Democrats regained control of the House in 1949, he became chair of the Defense Department Subcommittee.

Although a fiscal conservative, Mahon generally opposed the Eisenhower administration's efforts to cut the military budget. As the ranking Democrat on the Defense Department Subcommittee in 1953, he led the panel's minority members in opposing a proposed $5 billion cut in appropriations for the air force. Mahon insisted that the air force would need 143 wings by 1955, rather than the 120 wings requested by the president. As it turned out, the Republican-controlled Congress reduced funding for the air force even more than the administration had requested.

The Democrats regained control of Congress in the elections of 1954, and Mahon once again became chair of the Defense Department Subcommittee. He warned that the Soviet Union was gaining on the United States in nuclear capability, and he therefore urged steady yearly increases in the rate of military spending in order to maintain American superiority. Confronted with the administration's proposed increase of $3 billion in 1957, however, Mahon called for economy, and his committee cut the president's requests by almost $2.6

billion. The Senate subsequently restored $972 million of the funds cut by the House. In July, as conferees sought to find an acceptable compromise between the House and Senate versions of the bill, Eisenhower announced that he was reducing the armed forces by 100,000 men. This weakened the argument for the Senate version, and the conference report in July added $199 million to the House bill. Following the Soviet Union's launch of *Sputnik*, the first artificial satellite, in October 1957, Mahon abruptly ended his efforts to cut military budgets. He and his panel began urging larger defense appropriations than the administration thought wise.

With the death of Representative Clarence Cannon (D-Mo.) in 1964, Mahon assumed the chair of the full Appropriations Committee and thus became one of the most influential members of the House. Long a friend and ally of LYNDON B. JOHNSON, Mahon supported President Johnson's policy in Vietnam but joined his southern Democratic colleagues in opposing the president's proposals for civil rights, Medicare, regional development, and the war on poverty. In the second half of the 1960s, Mahon became increasingly concerned about high levels of government spending and the growing deficit. Despite his concerns about spending, Mahon supported increased defense expenditures during the 1960s and, in the later part of the decade, backed the development of a "China-oriented" antiballistic missile defense system. Although he differed with Johnson over domestic policy, he and Johnson remained on good terms.

His seniority and important committee chairmanships made Mahon a powerful figure during the administrations of RICHARD M. NIXON and GERALD FORD. By the time Mahon retired, he had set a record for the longest tenure as chair of the House Appropriations Committee. Despite his enormous influence, he was largely unknown outside of Washington. By his own admission, Mahon was not a "headline man"; he made few speeches and earned a reputation as a hardworking and effective legislator. He did not stand for reelection in 1978 and retired to Colorado City, where he lived until his death in San Angelo, Texas, on November 19, 1985.

—MSM

Mann, Thomas (Clifton)

(1912–1999) *ambassador to El Salvador, assistant secretary of state for economic affairs, ambassador to Mexico, assistant secretary of state for inter-American affairs*

Thomas Clifton Mann was born on November 11, 1912, in Laredo, Texas, a town on the Mexican border. In high school, he excelled both in the classroom and at athletics. After earning a B.A. and an LL.B. from Baylor University in 1934, he practiced law with his father and brothers in his hometown until World War II. Unable to join the armed forces because of his poor eyesight, Mann joined the State Department in 1942, where, because of his fluency in Spanish, he specialized in Latin American affairs and international economics. During the war, he worked for the Office of Economic Warfare and was posted in Uruguay. He became a Foreign Service officer in 1947 at the request of the assistant secretary of state for American republic affairs, SPRUILLE BRADEN. After working as Braden's special assistant for a few months, Mann left for Caracas, Venezuela, in August 1947 to take charge of the embassy's political and petroleum affairs. He directed the State Department's Office of Middle American Affairs from January 1950 to the end of the year, when he was named deputy assistant secretary in the Bureau of Inter-American Affairs. In August 1953, Mann became embassy counselor in Athens and assumed similar duties in Guatemala City in September 1954. From October 1955 to September 1957, he was ambassador to El Salvador.

In September 1957, Mann was appointed assistant secretary of state for economic affairs. As a function of this position, he represented the United States at many international trade conferences. In his dealings with foreign nations, he preferred to concentrate on immediate problems and to avoid long-term economic planning. In December 1958, for example, he criticized Brazil's president, Juscelino Kubitschek de Oliveira's call for "Operation Pan America," a massive and ambitious long-range development program. Kubitschek argued that economic development would raise living standards, encourage democracy, and undercut support for left-wing revolutionaries. At the same time, Kubitschek maintained that, given the poor infrastructure and political unrest in the region, economic development would require government action to encourage private economic development. He called on the United States to shoulder a large part of the cost. Mann argued that the United States was already doing its share to help Latin America and suggested that Latin American countries should focus on realistic short-term plans.

The hostile reception to Vice President RICHARD NIXON's visit to Latin America in the spring of 1958 and a fact-finding trip by the president's brother, MILTON EISENHOWER, prompted the administration to review its policy toward Latin America. The administration sought to encourage democratic governments, revised import restrictions on commodities from Latin America, and gave a more sympathetic hearing to Kubitschek's ideas.

Mann was particularly concerned about stabilizing prices of raw materials and increasing markets for Latin American goods. In 1958, he induced Latin American coffee-producing nations, perennially plagued by large surpluses and low prices, to institute controls on production to stabilize prices. A year later, he brought coffee-producing African nations into the agreement. In December 1958, Mann pledged U.S. cooperation with the Organization of American States's plan to develop common market areas in Latin America.

Mann was one of the first to argue that, in view of the communist threat, economic policy had to be designed with attention to its political ramifications. Despite his reservations, in 1959 Mann supported the administration's plan to create an Inter-American Development Bank, with an initial capitalization of $1 billion, of which the United States would subscribe $450 million. When Castro called for the United States to undertake a $30 billion aid program in Latin America, Mann, although he never directly responded to Castro's challenge in public, argued that the United States was already supporting all feasible projects, mainly through international bank loans.

After his appointment as assistant secretary of state of inter-American affairs in July 1960, Mann and C. DOUGLAS DILLON, undersecretary of state of economic affairs, attended the meeting of the Inter-American Economic Conference in Bogotá that September. With the notable exception of Cuba, the United States and all other Latin American nations agreed to the Act of Bogotá, a common policy for a "new and vigorous" attack on the sources of political unrest and economic underdevelopment. Emphasizing action on housing, agrarian reform, health, and education, the measure was an expanded version of President Eisenhower's social development plan, which pledged an initial fund of $550 million. In view of the increasingly leftist stance of the Castro regime, some in the United States criticized the program as an ill-timed attempt to ensure Latin American support for U.S. policies. Nonetheless, the Act of Bogotá, along with the Inter-American Development Bank and other policies, formed the basis for President JOHN F. KENNEDY's Alliance for Progress.

From March 1961 to December 1963, Mann served as ambassador to Mexico. On December 14, 1963, just three weeks after the assassination of John F. Kennedy, President LYNDON B. JOHNSON, named Mann assistant secretary of state for inter-American affairs. Johnson also named Mann to head the Alliance for Progress and appointed him to be the president's special assistant to coordinate the Latin American policy of all departments. Observers credited Mann with the formulation of the Johnson administration's policy for Latin America. Critics regarded that policy as a shift away from the idealism of the Kennedy years and toward a policy that focused on the interests of American businesses. A self-styled pragmatist, Mann stressed economic development and protection of American investments over social and political reform. Further, Mann gave priority to supporting anticommunist governments, rather than opposing military regimes. In February 1965, Mann was named undersecretary of state for economic affairs, although he continued to advise Johnson on Latin American affairs. That same year, he played a minor role in Johnson's decision to send marines to the Dominican Republic to put down what Johnson and Mann regarded as a communist threat, a decision denounced by Senator J. WILLIAM FULBRIGHT (D-Ark.). Mann left government for private life in April 1966 and served as president of the Automobile Manufacturers Association from 1967 to 1971. He died at his home in Austin, Texas, on January 23, 1999.

—MSM

Mansfield, Mike (Michael) (Joseph)

(1903–2001) *U.S. senator, majority leader*

The son of Irish immigrants, Mansfield was born in New York City's Greenwich Village on March 16, 1903. After his mother died in 1906, he was sent to live with relatives in Great Falls, Montana. Mansfield left school in the eighth grade and, after lying about his age, joined the navy not long before the United States entered World War I. He served as a seaman during World War I, as a private in the army from 1919 to 1920, and as a private first class in the marine corps from 1920 to 1922. His service in the marine corps took him to the Philippines, Japan, and China, an experience that would have a substantial role in shaping his later career. He worked as a "mucker" (the job entailed using a shovel to clear away rocks and debris) in the copper mines of Butte, Montana, for the next eight years. While working in the mines, he enrolled as a special student at Montana School of Mines, where he took college courses and high school correspondence courses at the same time. In 1930, he entered Montana State University (now the University of Montana) in Missoula, where he earned a B.A. in 1933 and an M.A. in 1934. He began teaching there in 1933 as a professor of Latin American and Far Eastern history.

Mansfield made an inauspicious debut in public life when he ran last in a three-way race for the Democratic nomination for a seat in the U.S. House of Representatives in 1940. Two years later, however, he won election to that same seat. He was reelected to the House four times. Because he had taught Asian and Latin American history and was interested in foreign policy, he was given a place on the Foreign Affairs Committee. His military service in Asia and his experience teaching about the region helped him establish himself as something of an expert in the region within the House. In 1944, President Franklin D. Roosevelt sent him to China on a fact-finding tour. Four years later, Mansfield was a delegate to the ninth Inter-American Conference in Colombia. In 1951 and 1952, he sat on the American delegation to the UN General Assembly.

While generally liberal, his voting record on domestic matters was uneven, particularly with respect to civil liberties. During the Truman administration, he supported the extension of price controls, an increase in the minimum wage, and a bill to abolish the poll tax. He opposed the creation of the House Un-American Activities Committee and the Taft-Hartley Act. On the other hand, Mansfield voted for the McCarran Internal Security Act and the Mundt-Nixon bill. In foreign policy, he backed the Marshall Plan but was less enthusiastic about aid to Greece and Turkey.

In 1952, Mansfield won the Democratic nomination to challenge Senator Zales N. Ecton (R-Mont.), who was up for reelection. Although the Republicans won the White House and control of both houses of Congress that year, Mansfield defeated the incumbent. He went on to win reelection in 1958, 1964, and 1970. His interest and experience in foreign affairs gained him an assignment on the Foreign Relations Committee. Mansfield quickly became a leading critic of the Eisenhower administration's foreign aid program, contending that it was too extensive and indiscriminate. He also thought it poorly administered. In June 1953, he attacked the president's mutual security bill, because, he alleged, it prepared for "never-ending foreign aid on a large scale." In July 1954, he called for an end to foreign economic aid except for technical assistance and a few other programs. Five years later, he unsuccessfully proposed that the administration be required to reduce all nonmilitary grant aid (as opposed to technical assistance and loans) to zero within three years. He also suggested, as efficiency measures, transferring the functions of the semiautonomous International Cooperation Administration to the State Department and shifting responsibility for military aid from the State Department to the Defense Department. The Senate rejected the former proposal, but the latter was incorporated into the Mutual Security Act of 1959.

Mansfield emerged as an important figure in formulating the Democratic congressional response to the Eisenhower administration's foreign policy. At joint hearings of the Foreign Affairs and Armed Services Committees in February 1957, Mansfield and Senator Hubert H. Humphrey (D-Minn.) amended the administration's version of the Eisenhower Doctrine, which would have permitted the president to use American armed forces at his discretion to block communist expansion in the Middle East. The Humphrey-Mansfield amendment, which was incorporated into the final version, stated that the United States was prepared, if the president believed it necessary, to provide such assistance when requested by the nation attacked. Reflecting the bipartisanship of foreign policy during the cold war era, Eisenhower appointed Mansfield as a delegate to the Southeast Asia Conference of 1954 that drafted the SEATO pact (to which Mansfield was a signatory) and as a member of the U.S. delegation to the UN General Assembly in 1958.

In 1957, Majority Leader LYNDON B. JOHNSON (D-Tex.) selected Mansfield to replace Senator Earle Clements (D-Ky.) as majority whip. Many observers believed that Johnson chose Mansfield because he believed the Montanan unassertive and unlikely to challenge the majority leader's authority. As whip, Mansfield's tasks included helping persuade Senate Democrats to vote as the leadership wished and making sure that his Democratic colleagues were on the floor for roll calls. He preferred a low-key, conciliatory approach to arm-twisting.

Throughout the Eisenhower administration, Mansfield generally voted as a liberal on domestic legislation. In August 1959, he voted to override a presidential veto of a housing bill, and the following May he backed an attempt to override a veto of a bill providing for area redevelopment. Mansfield supported the Civil Rights Acts of 1957 and 1960. As majority whip, however, he opposed amendments proposed by liberals that would have strengthened what became the Civil Rights Act of 1960.

Mansfield succeeded Johnson as majority leader in 1961. In contrast to Johnson, whose arm-twisting and deal-making made him the most powerful majority leader in the history of the Senate, Mansfield opted for a more low-key, collegial approach. Some of his Democratic colleagues criticized him for failing to exert leadership. Liberals, in particular, faulted him for working too closely with the minority leader, Senator EVERETT M. DIRKSEN (R-Ill.). An early supporter of Ngo Dinh Diem, Mansfield had a change of heart after a visit to Vietnam in 1962 and advised President JOHN F. KENNEDY that the United States should avoid further involvement in Vietnam. During the presidency of Lyndon Johnson, Mansfield was mildly critical of the administration's policy in Vietnam in public; in private, he attempted to persuade Johnson that military victory

was impossible. After RICHARD M. NIXON became president, however, Mansfield emerged as a frequent and public critic of the war in Vietnam.

During Nixon's tenure, Mansfield sought to increase the Senate's influence over the conduct of foreign policy. In addition to supporting the Cooper-Church and McGovern-Hatfield amendments, he introduced his own amendment calling for the withdrawal of all U.S. military forces from Vietnam within nine months. Mansfield's measure passed the Senate but failed in the House. Further, he was a principal architect of the War Powers Act, which limited the president's ability to commit American troops abroad without the consent of Congress. Mansfield also repeatedly, and without success, proposed reducing American forces in Europe by half.

The controversial Mansfield amendment of 1973 expressly limited grants for defense research given by the Advanced Research Projects Agency (ARPA) to projects with direct military applications. Critics maintained that the amendment had a devastating impact on American science, since ARPA was a major funding source for basic research. In March 1976, Mansfield announced that he would not seek reelection. At that point, he had served as majority leader longer than anyone else. Mansfield served as ambassador to Japan from 1977 to 1988. From 1989 until his death from congestive heart failure on October 5, 2001, he lived in Washington, D.C., and served as senior adviser to Goldman Sachs. President George H. W. Bush awarded him the Presidential Medal of Freedom in January 1989.

—MSM

Mansure, Edmund F(orsman)
(1901–1992) *administrator, General Services Administration*
Born in Chicago, Illinois, on March 14, 1901, Mansure graduated from Dartmouth College in 1924 and Kent College of Law. He went to work for the E. L. Mansure Company, which manufactured textiles, and was promoted to vice president in 1925. Mansure gained admission to the Illinois bar in 1927. He became president of E. L. Mansure in 1935 and chairman of the board in 1952. During this time, he also served on numerous state

commissions. When the Republicans captured the White House in 1952, William J. Balmer, an insurance broker from Chicago and vice chairman of the Cook County Executive Committee of the Republican Party, pushed for Mansure to receive an appointment to a position in the new administration. President DWIGHT D. EISENHOWER chose Mansure to head the General Services Administration (GSA) in April 1953.

David Frier, a political scientist, maintained that Mansure was an inept administrator, immersed in trivia, incapable of overseeing his subordinates, and unable to withstand pressure from top officials to use the GSA to reward the party faithful. One of Mansure's neighbors described him as a man who "could easily get over his head in very shallow water."

In October 1955, Mansure became implicated in a scandal involving U.S. Commissioner of the Public Building Service PETER STROBEL, who was charged with using his post to further his private interests. Mansure acknowledged that he had allowed Strobel to retain a 90 percent interest in the engineering firm of Strobel and Salzman, although he told the commissioner that he had to give up "active management" of the firm. Mansure did not check the legality of this action with the attorney general or question Strobel when the latter took a year and a half to sign the government's code of ethics and was dilatory in providing the GSA with a list of his firm's clients. Although it was fairly clear that Strobel did not set out to use his office to enrich himself, several of Strobel's dealings did violate or skirt the edges of regulations relating to ethics and conflicts of interest. The Justice Department investigated and did not initiate criminal proceedings, but, at the very least, Strobel's activities gave the appearance of impropriety. Strobel resigned his post in November 1955.

In August 1955, Herbert Solow published an article in *Fortune*, in which he alleged that the GSA was "Washington's most durable mess" and was guilty of "favoritism, factionalism, sloppiness, and waste." According to Solow, Mansure, who had been appointed to clean up the mess, had only contributed to it. Solow further implied that outside political interests, Balmer in particular, exercised undue influence over Mansure. The article paid particular attention to the awarding of contracts for the expansion of a government-owned nickel refinery in Nicaro, Cuba.

The Frederick Snare Corporation had constructed the plant during World War II. After the war, the plant had been shut down, but the Korean War created sufficient demand that the plant was reactivated in 1952. The government authorized an expansion of the plant the following year. The contract went to a 50-50 partnership between Snare Corp. and Merritt-Chapman and Scott, a large construction company with little experience in Cuba. Snare accepted the partnership reluctantly. The GSA chose National Lead Company, which owned the majority of Nickel Processing Corporation (the company that had operated the nickel refinery in Nicaro for the U.S. government), as the supervisory contractor for the expansion. National Lead supported Merritt-Chapman and Scott, apparently at least in part because it had dealings with a subsidiary of Merritt.

As a result of the article, the House Special Government Activities Subcommittee began an inquiry into the expansion of the plant at Nicaro in January 1956. Its probe, although unable to determine for certain the reasons for granting the contract to National Lead, established that Mansure's decision to select National Lead came after his staff had advised him that having National Lead supervise the expansion would cost considerably more than having the Public Buildings Service supervise it. Moreover, the chair of the GSA's Nickel-Graphite Committee wrote a memorandum in which he urged that the contract be let to Snare, since it was the only American company that had demonstrated the ability to do major construction work in Cuba.

If unable to state positively what factors accounted for the arrangements for the expansion, the congressional subcommittee drew a strong inference that Mansure had been under heavy pressure from members of Congress, executive departments, and the Republican Party to reward the party faithful. At the subcommittee's hearings, Randall Cremer, executive vice president of Snare, testified that he had awarded two-thirds of the insurance brokerage contract to the firm of Balmer and Moore because Mansure had told him to do so. Following Cremer's testimony, Mansure held a news conference at which he denied that he had instructed Cremer to give the contract to a "specific firm" but acknowledged that he wanted to place the contract with a midwestern "firm friendly to the [Republican] Party." Mansure said that he was "sick and tired" of the brokerage business going to Democratic firms from the East.

Testimony before the subcommittee established that the GSA had long been considered a "political" agency and that Mansure had been under heavy pressure from members of Congress and the Republican National Committee to place loyal Republicans in his agency and to award contracts accordingly. Mansure told an editor for *Fortune* that "half the Cabinet made recommendations for the [Nicaro] job." LEONARD HALL, the chairman of the Republican National Committee, had opposed giving the contract to a firm that "had been at the Democratic trough for twenty years." Apparently, some regarded Snare as a "New Deal" company, because it had repeatedly received contracts from Democratic administrations. Cremer attempted to persuade Hall that no Democrats held top positions at Snare. Moreover, although no proof emerged that Hall or any other Republican solicited support from companies seeking the contract for the expansion at Nicaro, the top seven officials at Snare substantially increased their contributions to Republicans in the elections of 1954. However embarrassing these revelations may have been, neither the Justice Department nor the subcommittee took action against Mansure.

Under heavy pressure from the administration, Mansure resigned in February 1956, citing "personal obligations," and returned to head E. L. Mansure Company. He died in Menlo Park on January 25, 1992.

Marshall, Thurgood

(1908–1993) *director-counsel, NAACP Legal Defense and Educational Fund; Supreme Court justice*

Marshall was born on July 2, 1908, in Baltimore, Maryland, and raised in that city. His father was head steward at the Gibson Island Club (a favorite of Washington's power brokers) and his mother a teacher. After graduating from Lincoln University in 1930 and from Howard University School of

Law, where he finished first in his class, in 1933, Marshall began to practice law in Baltimore. He became active in the National Association for the Advancement of Colored People (NAACP) and lobbied members of Maryland's congressional delegation in support of a federal antilynching bill. He also handled legal matters for the local branch of the NAACP. Marshall worked with Charles Hamilton Houston, chief legal counsel for the NAACP, to gain the admission of a black student into the University of Maryland' law school in *Murray v. Pearson* (1936). In May 1936, Marshall became assistant special counsel to the NAACP. Two years later, he succeeded Houston as special counsel for the NAACP. When the NAACP Legal Defense and Educational Fund was established as a separate entity in 1939, he was appointed its director-counsel. As head of the NAACP's legal program, Marshall led the organization's legal assault on segregation. Gregarious and seemingly tireless, Marshall traveled throughout the South to represent black litigants in court as well as to promote and encourage local NAACP chapters.

In 1939, Marshall won a decision in federal district court striking down racial pay differentials for teachers in Anne Arundel County, Maryland. The following year, after suffering a defeat in district court, Marshall won a decision from the Fourth Circuit Court of Appeals striking down racial pay differentials for teachers in Norfolk, Virginia. He also won a remarkable string of victories in the U.S. Supreme Court. In *Smith v. Allwright* (1944), his second appearance before the Supreme Court, Marshall persuaded the justices to strike down Texas's all-white primary. Another victory came in 1948, when, in *Shelley v. Kraemer*, the Court ruled that restrictive covenants were legally unenforceable.

Education was a primary focus of the NAACP's attack on segregation. In *Missouri ex rel. Gaines v. Canada* (1938), which Houston had argued, the Supreme Court had struck down Missouri's policy of providing for black applicants to its law school by paying for tuition at law schools in neighboring states that accepted African Americans. Marshall built on that decision in *Sipuel v. Oklahoma State Board of Regents* (1948), in which the Court ruled that Oklahoma could not require a black applicant to wait until there were enough black students to make a separate black law school practicable. Under the Fourteenth Amendment, the Court declared, Oklahoma had to provide a qualified black applicant with a legal education "as soon as it [did] for applicants of any other group." Marshall won two landmark victories in 1950. In *Sweatt v. Painter,* the Court held that Texas's attempt to meet its obligation under the Fourteenth Amendment by creating a separate law school for black students fell short. Whether one looked at the faculty, student body, or library, the Court could not find "substantial equality." Further, the Court found that "the University of Texas Law School possesses to a far greater degree those qualities which are incapable of objective measurement but which make for greatness in a law school," including the reputation of the faculty, the position and influence of the alumni, and the school's prestige. In *McLaurin v. Oklahoma,* the justices ruled that, having admitted George McLaurin to its doctoral program in education (since it offered no such program for African Americans in the state), the state could not segregate him in the classroom, dining hall, or library. Once the state had met its constitutional requirement by admitting McLaurin to the University of Oklahoma, held the Court, he was entitled to "the same treatment at the hands of the state as students of other races."

After *Sweatt* and *McLaurin,* Marshall turned his attention to segregated public schools. In addition to shifting from graduate and professional schools to primary and secondary schools, Marshall and his aides also turned their attack directly on segregation Marshall supervised the preparation of five cases challenging the validity of racial segregation in public schools. He personally represented the plaintiffs from Clarendon County, South Carolina, in one of the suits. On May 17, 1954, the Supreme Court ruled unanimously, in *Brown v. Board of Education,* that segregated public schools were "inherently unequal" and therefore violated the equal protection of the Fourteenth Amendment. The Court did not, however, order an immediate remedy. Conceding that the cases presented problems of "considerable complexity," the justices ordered further argument on the question of implementation the following term. In the second round of arguments, Marshall urged the Court to order desegregation of

public schools no later than the fall term of 1956. In May 1955, however, the Court remanded the cases to lower courts with instructions that the courts require that the local school districts make a "prompt and reasonable start toward full compliance" and enter orders to admit the plaintiffs to public schools "on a racially nondiscriminatory basis with all deliberate speed." Over the next several years, Marshall and the NAACP undertook a massive program of litigation to enforce the *Brown* decision.

Along with several other lawyers from the NAACP, Marshall represented AUTHERINE LUCY in her suit to gain admission to the University of Alabama and won a Supreme Court ruling on her behalf in October 1955. Lucy enrolled on February 1 under the protection of campus police. Unruly crowds constantly harassed her, and, on February 6, 1956, Marshall was with her when an angry mob grew violent, which led university authorities to have her removed from campus in a highway patrol car. After the trustees suspended Lucy on the next day, ostensibly for her own safety, Marshall sought a contempt order against the university's officials for failing to control the mob. He also overplayed his hand by alleging that the university's administrators conspired with the mob, an allegation that he later withdrew. A federal district judge found that the officials of the university had not violated his earlier order but ordered that Lucy be reinstated. The trustees, however, expelled Lucy for making unfounded charges against the administration. When Marshall challenged that, the district judge ruled that Lucy had been expelled for disciplinary reasons, not on the basis of her race. At that point, Lucy was physically and emotionally exhausted, and she chose not to appeal the decision.

Marshall was also counsel for the black students who desegregated Central High School in Little Rock, Arkansas, in the fall of 1957. When Governor ORVAL FAUBUS used the National Guard to block the implementation of a court order mandating the admission of the students in September 1957, Marshall got an injunction barring the governor from further interference with the school's desegregation plan. Later in the school year, the local school board sought to postpone its desegregation program for two-and-a-half years. In a special term of the Supreme Court, held in September 1958, Marshall argued against the delay and won a unanimous decision ordering continuation of the plan to desegregate.

Marshall also handled cases extending the principle established in *Brown* to areas such as public recreation and public transit. In 1955, he won decisions in the Supreme Court striking down racial segregation on beaches and in bathhouses maintained by the state of Maryland and the city of Baltimore (*Dawson v. Mayor and City Council of Baltimore* [1955]) and in a municipal golf course in Atlanta (*Holmes v. Atlanta*, 1955). He participated in the suit, growing out of the bus boycott in Montgomery, Alabama, that resulted in the Court's decision, in November 1956, upholding a ruling by the Fifth Circuit Court of Appeals that segregation in local transportation violated the Fourteenth Amendment.

During the late 1950s, Marshall continued the NAACP's attack on legal segregation and defended the organization from attempts by southern states to close down its operations within their borders. A number of southern states enacted legislation effectively outlawing the NAACP, and Marshall won a series of decisions in the Supreme Court overturning such laws. In his last oral argument before the Supreme Court as an advocate for the NAACP, Marshall successfully contended that segregation in restaurants and other facilities at bus terminals involved in interstate travel violated federal law (*Boynton v. Virginia* [1960]).

During his final years with the NAACP, Marshall coordinated the legal defense of hundreds of students arrested during the sit-ins, the Freedom Rides, and similar nonviolent protests. He headed the team that wrote the brief for the case in which the Court reversed the convictions of blacks arrested for peaceful lunch counter sit-ins.

In September 1961, President JOHN F. KENNEDY appointed Marshall to a seat on the Second Circuit Court of Appeals. Opposition from southern senators held up his confirmation for a year. When President LYNDON B. JOHNSON appointed him solicitor general in July 1965, Marshall became the first African American to hold that office. Johnson nominated him to the Supreme Court on June 13, 1967. The Senate confirmed the nomination that

August, making Marshall the first African American to sit on the nation's highest court. On the Court, he was a liberal activist who voted most frequently with Chief Justice EARL WARREN and Justice WILLIAM BRENNAN. Never as great a jurist as he was an advocate, Marshall played a subordinate role in his early years on the Court; he wrote few majority opinions or dissents. As the Court moved to the right in the 1970s, he became more assertive and dissented in an increasing number of cases. Although he wrote opinions in a wide variety of fields, his most significant contributions came in constitutional law. He wrote for the majority in *Stanley v. Georgia* (1969), which held that individuals had a right to possess obscene materials in their own homes, and *Police Department of Chicago v. Mosley* (1972), which ruled that government may not constitutionally favor some types of speech over others. In two dissents, *Dandridge v. Williams* (1970) and *San Antonio Independent School District v. Rodriguez* (1973), Marshall criticized the two-tiered equal protection analysis that regarded classification based on race and other suspect categories as subject to strict scrutiny while all other classifications had only to meet the test of rationality. Marshall proposed a more flexible "sliding scale." The Court never adopted his theory, but his consistent advocacy of this position did appear to move the Court in the direction of greater flexibility. Marshall supported affirmative action on the ground that the Constitution had not been color-blind in the past and remedial action was therefore necessary. He entered a vigorous dissent in *City of Richmond v. Croson* (1989), in which the majority struck down a municipal ordinance that set aside 30 percent of the money appropriated for public contracting for companies owned by African Americans or other minorities. Marshall supported abortion rights and strongly opposed the death penalty. In 1972, the Court struck down the death penalty as it was then practiced. After the Court upheld revised statutes providing for the death penalty in *Gregg v. Georgia* (1976), Marshall dissented in every death penalty case.

Unlike most other justices, Marshall's greatest contributions came before his elevation to the Court. His groundbreaking work for the NAACP made him a symbol of the black struggle for legal equality. He was one of the most successful advocates before the Supreme Court in American history. On the Court, however, he was neither an outstanding justice nor an especially creative one. In his last years as a justice, Marshall became increasingly alienated and embittered, prone to injudicious outbursts both on and off the bench. He retired from the Court in 1991 and died in Bethesda, Maryland, on January 24, 1993.

—MSM

Martin, Joseph W(illiam), Jr.
(1884–1968) *U.S. congressman, Speaker of the House, minority leader*

The son of a blacksmith, Martin was born in North Attleboro, Massachusetts, on November 3, 1884. Following the death of his father, Martin went to work at the age of six delivering newspapers to help support his family. After graduating from North Attleboro High School in 1902, he turned down a scholarship to Dartmouth College and became a reporter for the *North Attleboro Leader* and then for the *North Attleboro Sun*. In 1908, he and several associates purchased the local Republican paper, the *Evening Chronicle*. With Martin as editor and publisher, the paper quadrupled its circulation. He eventually bought out his partners, purchased an insurance agency in 1918, and, in 1944, added a weekly, the *Franklin* (Massachusetts) *Sentinel*, to his holdings. Martin retained ownership of both newspapers and the insurance agency until his death. His work as a journalist drew him toward politics, and in 1911 he ran successfully for a seat in the Massachusetts House of Representatives. After serving three one-year terms as a Republican in the state house (1912–14), he won election to the state senate, where he served three consecutive one-year terms (1915–17). Martin did not stand for reelection in 1917 but returned to politics in 1922 as executive secretary of the state Republican committee in an effort to help heal a split in the state party. In 1924, he won election to the U.S. House of Representatives.

In the House, he voted as an economic conservative. In many regards, he was typical of a small-town businessman who represented a district of small towns and modest-sized cities with many self-owned businesses. Martin rose quickly in the Republican ranks and in 1929 received an assignment to the powerful Rules Committee. Following the elections of 1930, in which Republicans lost control of the House, Martin served as assistant whip from 1931 to 1933.

After the election of Franklin D. Roosevelt in 1932, Martin established a cordial relationship with the new president, who rewarded him with federal projects and services for his home district. In the House, Martin was appointed to the unofficial position of assistant minority leader in 1933. He opposed most New Deal measures, but he was not an ideologue. He supported New Deal programs that brought benefits to New England and opposed those that had little to offer his constituents. In foreign policy, he was a moderate isolationist. He opposed Lend-Lease and the repeal of the Neutrality Acts. Martin's rise in his party derived less from ideology than from his reputation as a skillful legislative technician. In 1939, his colleagues elected him minority leader. Martin reached out to disaffected southern Democrats to build an effective anti–New Deal coalition.

After the Republicans won control of Congress in the elections of 1946, he became Speaker of the house. As Speaker, he preferred to lead through persuasion rather than coercion. At the same time, he used traditional methods to exert his authority when necessary. In his memoirs, Martin recalled that "no Republican went on an important committee without my approval." He helped pass President HARRY S. TRUMAN's proposal for aid to Greece and Turkey as well as the Marshall Plan. Domestically, however, he opposed most of the administration's Fair Deal and, as Speaker, successfully blocked many of Truman's proposals, including national health insurance and public housing. Under his leadership, the House passed the Taft-Hartley Act over Truman's veto and passed the Twenty-second Amendment, which limited presidents to two terms in office. After the Democratic victory in the elections of 1948, Martin once again became minority leader.

In April 1951, Martin became involved in the dispute between Truman and General Douglas MacArthur over the conduct of the Korean War. On April 5, Martin, a supporter of MacArthur, made public the contents of a letter he had received from the general criticizing the administration's conduct of the war and its decision not to use Nationalist Chinese troops in the conflict. The letter contributed to Truman's decision to recall MacArthur on April 11.

After Republicans won the presidency and both houses in the elections of 1952, Martin again became Speaker. He was disappointed in President Dwight D. Eisenhower's legislative agenda because he thought it too similar to those of Roosevelt and Truman. Martin also believed that Eisenhower's approach failed to reflect the views of most Republicans in the House. As the leader of his party in the lower chamber, however, he felt duty bound to support the president. For example, Martin personally favored Representative DANIEL REED's (R-N.Y.) tax cut bill in 1953 but bottled the measure up in the Rules Committee at the request of the administration. Eisenhower's proposed reciprocal trade bill of 1953 was similar to measures that Martin had opposed since the 1930s, but on this, too, the speaker backed the president.

One of the few issue on which Martin broke with the president was the bill for the St. Lawrence Seaway in 1954. There was widespread opposition to the measure in Martin's home district, where many worried that the seaway would divert traffic from the port of Boston. Despite pressure from the president, Martin persisted in opposing the bill. Ultimately, the bill passed without Martin's support.

In the elections of 1954, Democrats regained control of both houses of Congress, and Martin once again became minority leader. He blamed the party's electoral reverses in part on Eisenhower, whom he thought insufficiently partisan and unwilling to help build up local and state Republican organizations. Martin criticized Eisenhower in particular for failing to consult either members of Congress or party officials on matters of patronage. The Republican leader in the House contended that it was impossible to strengthen the party without rewarding the party faithful with jobs. He further faulted Eisenhower for failing to appoint "assistants who could solve political problems with professional skill." Martin also thought that Eisenhower made a big mistake by dealing with Congress primarily through subordinates and not having enough personal contact with members of the legislative branch.

Conservative by temperament rather than ideology, Martin had worked his way up through party ranks by pragmatically adjusting to the exigencies of politics rather than attempting to effect fundamental change in the political system. His approach made Martin acutely aware of the pressures his colleagues faced from constituents, and he generally did not press Republican representatives to vote for bills proposed by the administration that were unpopular in their home districts.

Martin's friendship with the Democratic leader in the House, SAM RAYBURN (D-Tex.), which dated back to the 1930s, also mitigated the Republican leader's partisanship. On occasion, he helped Rayburn pass bills as a personal favor. During the 85th Congress (1957–58), for example, he used his influence with Republicans on the Rules Committee to aid Rayburn in bringing to the floor several bills favored by the liberal Democratic Study Group.

Ironically, just as Martin criticized Eisenhower for insufficient partisanship, Martin encountered similar criticism from Republicans both in and out of Congress. Many Republicans believed that he did not sufficiently stress the need for party discipline and unity. Others thought he made too much of an effort to accommodate Rayburn.

After Republicans lost the congressional elections in 1954 and again in 1956, Martin's deputy, Representative CHARLES HALLECK (R-Ind.), explored the possibility of challenging Martin for the party's leadership. On both occasions, Eisenhower, seeking to avoid internecine warfare, urged him not to, and Halleck decided not to run. After the Democratic landslide in the off-year elections of 1958, however, Halleck once again demonstrated an interest in challenging for the minority leadership. Many in the Republican caucus believed that they needed younger, more vigorous leadership and regarded Martin as too willing to cooperate with Rayburn. This time, moreover, Eisenhower, who attributed the electoral reverses in part to Martin's ineffective leadership, let it be known that he would not discourage Halleck. Many interpreted this as an indication of support for Halleck. Further, some of the president's aides reportedly actively supported Halleck. On January 6, 1959, Halleck defeated Martin in the Republican caucus by a vote of 74 to 70. In *My First Fifty Years in Politics* (1960), Martin bitterly blamed Eisenhower and Vice President Richard M. Nixon for his defeat. "I knew," he wrote, "that if either of them merely spoke a word for me any revolt would be quelled. This was little enough to expect in view of what I had done for them, sometimes to my own distinct political disadvantage."

Following his defeat, Martin's influence in Congress and the Republican party declined rapidly. In 1966, he was defeated in his district's Republican congressional primary. Martin died of peritonitis while vacationing in Hollywood, Florida, on March 6, 1968.

—MSM

Martin, William McChesney
(1906–1998) *chairman, Board of Governors of the Federal Reserve System*

The son of a prominent banker who helped draft the Federal Reserve Act of 1913 and served as president of the Federal Reserve Bank of St. Louis, William McChesney Martin, Jr., was born in St. Louis, Missouri, on December 17, 1906. He graduated from Yale University, where he majored in English and Latin, in 1928. His first job was as a bank examiner in the Federal Reserve Bank of St. Louis. Martin then became head of the statistical department of A. G. Edwards & Sons, a brokerage firm based in St. Louis. He became the youngest partner in the firm's history and in 1931 acquired a seat on the New York Stock Exchange (NYSE).

He joined a group that pressed for reform of the structure of the New York Stock Exchange in the aftermath of the stock market crash of 1929. His activities on behalf of reform led to his election to the NYSE's board of governors in 1935 and to president of the exchange in 1938. At the age of 31, he was the youngest person ever to hold the position. Inducted into the army as a private in 1941, he was commissioned as an officer the following year. He served with the Munitions Allocation Board as well as the army liaison to Congress and eventually supervised the Lend-Lease program to the Soviet Union. At the end of the war, he was discharged as a colonel.

In February 1946, President Harry S. Truman appointed him president and chairman of the board of the Export-Import Bank, formed to grant loans to foreign countries. Three years later, Martin became assistant secretary of the Treasury for monetary affairs. While serving in that post, he engineered the famous Accord between Treasury and the Federal Reserve Board. During World War II, the Federal Reserve supported the price of government securities, which enabled the government to borrow at low interest rates. After the war, the Federal Reserve became increasingly uneasy with this arrangement, because it made it impossible for the Federal Reserve to control the supply of money. Both Mariner Eccles and Thomas McCabe as chairmen of the Federal Reserve Board pushed to free the Federal Reserve Board from "pegging" bond prices. The secretary of the Treasury, John Snyder, wanted to keep the government's cost of borrowing low and opposed the move. Martin sided with the Federal Reserve; he considered a free capital market essential for the economy. The conflict became heated in August 1950, when the Federal Reserve raised short-term interest rates. This led to a series of conflicts between the Federal Reserve on one side and Snyder and Truman on the other. In February 1951, Martin negotiated an agreement, known as the Accord, that called for the restructuring of part of the federal government's long-term debt and freeing the Federal Reserve from "pegging" the bond market. McCabe, who had opposed the president, resigned soon after the Accord was reached, and Truman named Martin to chair the Board of Governors of the Federal Reserve System.

Although Martin had functioned mainly as a conciliator in the resolution of the conflict between the Treasury and the Federal Reserve, the Accord reflected his belief in the independence of the Federal Reserve and a free market in the buying and selling of domestic securities. Martin sternly defended these principles in his two decades as chair of the Federal Reserve. He also watched diligently for signs of inflation and used the power of the Federal Reserve to fight it.

During the presidency of Dwight D. Eisenhower, Martin's conservative attitude toward credit aroused controversy. As chief steward of the country's money supply, he was the most influential exponent of a policy of "tight money" (restricting credit to banks in order to moderate the pace of economic expansion and curtail inflation). He accomplished this chiefly by raising reserve requirements of banks belonging to the Federal Reserve System and by increasing the rediscount rate (the rate of interest charged by the Federal Reserve on loans to member banks).

In the spring of 1953, Martin tightened credit to reinforce the Eisenhower administration's effort to fight inflation. At about the same time, Martin made major speeches in which he asserted that the Federal Reserve's action must be held to a minimum. His statement that "use of the discount window is a privilege not a right" led many dealers in government securities to conclude that the Federal Reserve would be cutting off credit to member banks. According to *Fortune*, "the 'bond panic' of May 1953 followed. The Federal Reserve had to jump in with heavy open market purchases before apprehension subsided."

Over the decade, Martin steadily enforced a policy of tighter money. The rediscount rate rose from 1.5 percent in early 1954 to 3 percent by 1960. Democratic politicians and many economists denounced Martin's policy, charging that tight money was a major cause of the recessions of the 1950s. Martin persistently defended his actions. In December 1956, he argued that a proposed drop in interest rates would only increase the money supply and accelerate inflation. He insisted, moreover, that the credit crunch was due more to high demand for credit than to any action by the Federal Reserve. "Creating more money will not create more goods," he maintained. "It will only intensify demands for the current supply of labor and materials. That is outright inflation."

In addition to the direct impact he exerted on financial policy, Martin often added his prestigious counsel to public debates on other economic issues. Throughout the 1950s, he argued against Democratic proposals to stimulate the economy by cutting taxes. Opposing a congressional plan to lower personal income taxes, he said in February 1954: "If you increase the money consumers have . . . there is no guarantee that the consumer will spend the money. . . . Emphasis needs to be on the production side at this juncture." In June 1957, Martin argued that a proposed tax cut would make the Federal Reserve's effort to curb inflation "well-nigh

impossible." During the recession of 1958, he again opposed a tax cut to stimulate the economy.

In 1955, during the Senate Banking and Currency Committee's probe into fluctuations in the stock market, Martin defended his free market principles. Criticizing proposals to ban buying stocks on credit, he said: "The stock market should not be denied access to credit unless you want to promote a lower standard of living." He insisted that higher margin requirements were not "cure-alls for all stock market excesses" and defended risk-taking and speculation as the "proper function" of a securities market.

In 1956, Eisenhower appointed Martin to a full 14-year term on the Federal Reserve's Board of Governors. In the late 1950s, in spite of criticism, Martin maintained restrictions on credit. During the campaign of 1960, his policies became a topic of debate. Senator JOHN F. KENNEDY (D-Mass.) attacked tight money, and his Republican opponent, Vice President RICHARD M. NIXON, promised to uphold the "independence" of the Federal Reserve. After his defeat, however, Nixon blamed his loss in part on the Federal Reserve's slow response to the recession in 1960.

During the 1960s, Martin remained to many conservatives the symbol of a sound dollar. To populists like Representative WRIGHT PATMAN (D-Tex.), however, he represented policies that enriched big banks and Wall Street while choking small business. Martin got along well with Presidents Kennedy and Johnson and eased monetary policy for a time to accommodate their stimulative fiscal policies. During the Vietnam War, interest rates rose to their highest levels since the 1920s, and Martin once again became the focus of controversy. In December 1968, President-elect Nixon, who wanted to name ARTHUR BURNS to chair the Federal Reserve Board, offered Martin the position of secretary of the Treasury. Martin declined the offer and indicated that he intended to serve the remainder of his term on the Federal Reserve Board, which ran until January 1970. Several months before the expiration of Martin's term, Nixon announced that Burns would replace Martin when the latter's term ended. When Martin's term expired at the end of January 1970, he returned to private life. He held a variety of directorships of firms and nonprofit organizations. He died at his home in Washington, D.C., on July 27, 1998.

—MSM

Matthews, J(oseph) B(rown)

(1894–1966) *staff director, Permanent Subcommittee on Investigations of the Senate Government Operations Committee*

Born in Hopkinsville, Kentucky, on June 28, 1894, J. B. Matthews attended Asbury College in Wilmore, Kentucky. In 1915, he went to Java in the Dutch East Indies (now Indonesia) as a Methodist missionary. He worked as treasurer for the mission and wrote a hymnal in the Malay language. Returning to the United States in 1921, he earned a D.B. and a M.A. from Drew University and then a S.T.M. from Union Theological Seminary in New York. At that time, he embraced the ideas of the Social Gospel movement. After preaching in Bound Brook, New Jersey, he got a job in 1924 at Scarritt College, a Methodist institution in Nashville, Tennessee, where he taught Hebrew and religious history. His activities on behalf of Robert LaFollette's 1924 presidential campaign, his pacifism, and his sermons opposing segregation and child labor led to his forced resignation in 1928. He then taught Hebrew at Fisk and Howard University, two black colleges. In 1929, Matthews became executive secretary of the pacifist Fellowship of Reconciliation. That same year, he joined the Socialist Party. The Fellowship of Reconciliation, an organization devoted to racial and religious toleration, fired him in 1933, after Matthews, speaking to a crowd of 15,000 at Madison Square Garden, advocated a dictatorship of the proletariat to stop Hitler. He became involved with a number of pro-Soviet organizations, as a result of which the Socialist Party suspended him in 1935.

In 1933, he went to work for Consumers' Research (CR), where he assisted with product testing, wrote articles, and gave lectures. He quickly rose to become vice president. With Ruth Shallcross, he coauthored *Partners in Plunder* (1935), which assailed the "business dictatorship in the U.S." Matthews later called it a "stinking, nasty book" and said "God forgive me for writing that." During the mid-1930s, Matthews turned sharply

to the right. He was one of three managers who led the opposition to a strike against CR in 1935. His son, who was a replacement worker at CR during the strike, was dragged off a bus and beaten by strikers. The strike ended in a victory for management but resulted in Matthews's banishment from leftist circles.

In 1938, Matthews published an autobiography, *Odyssey of a Fellow Traveler.* That same year, he appeared as a star witness before the Special House Committee on Un-American Activities (HUAC) and named 94 "Communist front groups" with which he had been associated. The chair of the committee, Martin Dies (D-Tex.), subsequently hired him as chief investigator. In that capacity, Matthews supervised the collection and indexing of a massive body of information on communist-inspired activity. He left HUAC in 1945, taking with him his voluminous files based on the committee's investigations, which included a private list of 22,000 alleged "fellow travelers" (a term he claimed to have introduced into the American language). Upon leaving HUAC, Matthews went to work for John A. Clements Associates and worked as a consultant to Hearst publications. He continued to maintain a network of connections with disillusioned former communists.

Matthews came to the aid of Senator JOSEPH R. McCARTHY (R-Wis.) in 1950, after the senator's allegations that the State Department harbored communists led to a congressional investigation. Matthews provided much of the documentation for McCarthy's charges against the State Department and used his contacts with the powerful conservative publisher, William Randolph Hearst, Jr., to persuade the Hearst papers to support McCarthy. In 1953, McCarthy named Matthews staff director for the Senate Government Operations Committee's Permanent Subcommittee on Investigations, which McCarthy chaired. Shortly after his appointment, an article by Matthews titled "Reds in Our Churches" appeared in the *American Mercury.* Its allegation that "the largest single group supporting the Communist apparatus in the United States is composed of Protestant clergymen" provoked a storm of protest. Democratic members of the subcommittee demanded that Matthews be fired. McCarthy at first refused but gave in after the

White House released a statement condemning the article. The Republican majority on the subcommittee, however, responded with a face-saving motion giving the chair exclusive power to hire and fire staff. This led the Democratic minority to boycott the subcommittee.

After being fired from the Permanent Subcommittee on Investigations, Matthews wrote for several right-wing periodicals and gave lectures. In the 1960s, his name appeared on the masthead of *American Opinion*, the periodical of the extreme right-wing John Birch Society. Matthews died in New York City on July 16, 1966.

—MSM

McCarran, Patrick A(nthony)
(1876–1954) *U.S. senator*

The son of Irish Catholic immigrants, McCarran was born in Reno, Nevada, on August 8, 1876. He attended public schools and the University of Nevada at Reno. When his father suffered an injury, McCarran withdrew from college and went home to run the family's sheep ranch. He became involved in local politics and won election to the state legislature as a free silver Democrat in 1902. In addition to ranching and politics, he studied law, and, after losing a bid for the state senate in 1904, he passed the bar exam and was admitted to the bar in 1905. He moved to Tonopah, a mining boom town, and began to practice law. In 1906, he won election as district attorney for Nye County. A political maverick, McCarran soon made enemies within the state's Democratic Party. A failed attempt to unseat an incumbent member of the U.S. House of Representatives in the Democratic primary in 1908 further alienated him from the state's Democratic establishment. Nevertheless, he won election to the Nevada Supreme Court in 1912 and served from 1913 to 1918. In 1916, he made an unsuccessful bid to unseat an incumbent for the Democratic nomination to the U.S. Senate. That decision would come back to haunt him. Two years later, the opposition of powerful Democrats cost him his bid for reelection to the supreme court. After running unsuccessfully for a seat in the U.S. Senate again in 1926, he finally won election to that body in 1932.

Although he came into office with the Roosevelt landslide, he quickly emerged as an opponent of the New Deal. His outspoken and determined resistance to Franklin D. Roosevelt's court packing plan in 1937 earned him both national attention and Roosevelt's enmity. Because of his opposition to the New Deal, McCarran had to fight for the Democratic nomination in 1938 and again in 1944; he captured the nomination both times and went on to win the general election. During the Truman administration, McCarran played an important role in the resurgence of congressional conservatism. As chair of the Senate Judiciary Committee, he also became a leading figure in the anticommunist crusade of the late 1940s and early 1950s. McCarran's attacks often focused on liberals, who, he charged, naively advanced the cause of communism. In 1950, he sponsored the Internal Security Act, known as the McCarran Act, which required that all "communist-action" and "communist front" organizations register with the Subversive Activities Control Board and disclose the names of their officers and members. Under provisions of the act, communists were denied passports and barred from working for the government or in the defense industry. The measure also provided that the Justice Department could deport subversive aliens or bar them from entering the United States. In addition, the act contained a provision, originally introduced by liberal Democrats, authorizing the president to declare an "internal security emergency," during which the attorney general had authority to detain anyone whom he had "reason to believe" might engage in subversive activities. Truman vetoed the measure, but Congress promptly overrode the veto.

McCarran was one of the few Democrats who endorsed Senator JOSEPH R. MCCARTHY's (R-Wis.) charges that communists had infiltrated the Roosevelt and Truman administrations. Like McCarthy, McCarran maintained that communist subversion had corrupted the State Department and American foreign policy. After appointing himself chair of the Judiciary Committee's newly established Internal Security Subcommittee in 1951, McCarran set up connections between his subcommittee and the FBI. He investigated communist influence in labor unions, the entertainment industry, and higher education. From mid-1951 to mid-1952, he conducted an investigation of the Institute of Pacific Relations (IPR), a left-leaning think tank devoted to the study of Asian affairs. McCarran blamed government officials associated with the IPR for the "loss" of China. The senator focused his attention on Owen Lattimore, a professor at Johns Hopkins and an expert on the Far East, who was editor of the IPR's journal, *Public Affairs*. In 12 days of testimony, Lattimore belligerently responded to questions and allegations. Some of the professor's responses to detailed, specific questions, however, were contradicted by documents seized in an earlier raid by agents of the McCarran committee. McCarran repeatedly pressed the Truman administration to indict Lattimore for perjury. Although the Justice Department got a grand jury to indict Lattimore, an appellate court threw out four of the seven counts and found the others doubtful.

McCarran's concern about domestic subversion led him to sponsor legislation reforming immigration laws. In 1948, he helped draw up the Displaced Persons Act, which permitted the admission of roughly 200,000 refugees. Despite criticism that the measure discriminated against Jews and Catholics from Eastern Europe, the senator refused to budge. Congress passed new legislation in 1950 that permitted freer immigration. In 1952, McCarran and Representative Francis E. Walter (D-Pa.) introduced a complete overhaul of the immigration and naturalization laws. The McCarran-Walter Act repealed the nearly total ban on immigration from Asia. Although McCarran himself did not approve of immigration from non-European countries, he recognized the propaganda value of eliminating the racial bar. Reflecting McCarran's views, the law set an annual quota of 100 people from each nation of Asia and the Pacific. Moreover, the measure retained the principle of national origins and the quota system established in the 1920s. In doing so, it favored immigration from Western Europe and continued to exclude most Eastern Europeans. Finally, the bill broadened the grounds for excluding and deporting aliens. Congress passed the bill over Truman's veto in 1952.

After that, however, McCarran's power began to slip. Both presidential candidates in 1952 disassociated themselves from the McCarran-Walter Act. Eisenhower repudiated the measure as a "blasphemy against democracy." McCarran further alienated the Democratic Party establishment by disavowing the party's nominee, ADLAI STEVENSON, who, sneered McCarran, "wouldn't know a Democrat if he saw one." Even in Nevada, the rapid growth of Las Vegas undermined the senator's power. Further, his close connections with the state's gambling interests became public. To make matters worse, the Republicans won control of both houses of Congress, which cost McCarran his committee chairmanships. Despite all this and his isolation from his party, he still remained influential in the Senate.

In his first State of the Union message, Eisenhower asked Congress to pass a new immigration bill. In April 1953, Eisenhower requested emergency legislation to admit 240,000 non-quota immigrants, most of them refugees from Eastern Europe. McCarran opposed the measure. The president met privately with the senator from Nevada but later admitted to Republican congressional leaders that "I made about as much impression on him as beating on a steel lid with a sponge." McCarran successfully prevailed on the Senate to reduce substantially the number of immigrants eligible for admission and to provide screening procedures to ensure against "communist infiltration."

McCarran supported efforts by conservatives to bring foreign policy under the control of Congress. In 1953, he joined several conservative Republican senators, led by McCarthy, in an effort to block the nomination of CHARLES E. BOHLEN as ambassador to the Soviet Union. Even though Bohlen had the firm support of Secretary of State JOHN FOSTER DULLES, McCarran and other opponents of the nomination linked the career diplomat to what they termed Truman's policy of appeasement toward the Soviet Union. Despite the opposition, the administration stood behind the nomination, and Bohlen was eventually confirmed. Throughout 1953 and into 1954, McCarran supported the Bricker Amendment, a series of proposed amendments to the U.S. Constitution that would have limited the president's power to enter treaties. Eisenhower opposed the measure, and in February 1954 it narrowly failed to win the necessary two-thirds majority in the Senate.

Even though, as chair of the Internal Security Subcommittee, McCarran had come to resent

McCarthy's encroachment on the subcommittee's mandate to investigate subversion, McCarran managed to impede efforts to censure McCarthy throughout the summer of 1954. On September 27, 1954, after the Watkins Committee recommended censure, McCarran gave a speech on the Senate floor attacking the committee and its recommendation. The next day, after addressing a political rally in Hawthorne, Nevada, McCarran collapsed and died of a heart attack.

—MSM

McCarthy, Eugene J(oseph)
(1916–2005) *U.S. congressman and senator*

Born in Watkins, Minnesota, on March 29, 1916, McCarthy attended public schools in Watkins and graduated from St. John's University in Minnesota in 1935. After college, he spent nine months as a novitiate in a Benedictine monastery. He then taught in public high schools until 1940. After receiving a master's degree in sociology and economics from the University of Minnesota in 1939, he taught at St. John's from 1940 to 1943. McCarthy worked as a civilian for the War Department's Military Intelligence Division during 1944. From 1946 to 1949, he was an instructor of sociology and economics at St. Thomas College in Minnesota. He served as acting head of the sociology department.

He entered politics in 1947 as a supporter of HUBERT HUMPHREY, who had been the principal figure in uniting the Minnesota Democratic-Farmer-Labor Party and was then struggling for control of the party with the communist-led left wing. McCarthy won election to the U.S. House of Representatives as a Democrat in 1948 and won reelection four times. In the House, McCarthy compiled a liberal, pro-labor voting record and generally supported the Eisenhower administration on foreign policy. In 1952, McCarthy engaged in a nationally televised debate (on NBC's *American Forum of the Air*) with the publicity-seeking anticommunist, Senator JOSEPH R. MCCARTHY (R-Wis.), when no senator was willing to confront the demagogue from Wisconsin. Eugene McCarthy began to express concern about the unsupervised activities of the Central Intelligence Agency in 1955 and introduced legislation to create a congressional watchdog com-

mittee. McCarthy organized an informal caucus of liberal House Democrats in 1956. Although the group achieved little in the way of legislation, it was formally reconstituted as the Democratic Study Group in 1959, and it played an important role in the battle to reform the House Rules Committee in 1961. This, in turn, helped pave the way for the enactment of liberal legislation in the 1960s.

He won election to the Senate in 1958 by defeating a two-term incumbent, EDWARD THYE (R-Minn.). Thye was hurt by his association with the farm policies of the Eisenhower administration, which were unpopular in Minnesota. Assigned to the Public Works Committee and the Finance Committee, McCarthy compiled a consistently liberal voting record, yet he managed to avoid alienating powerful conservatives in his party such as Senator HARRY BYRD (D-Va.) and Senator ROBERT KERR (D-Okla.). In 1959, McCarthy became one of the first senators to oppose Eisenhower's nominee for secretary of commerce, LEWIS STRAUSS. McCarthy charged that, as chairman of the Atomic Energy Commission, Strauss had gone "beyond reasonable limits" in refusing to cooperate with Congress.

Majority Leader LYNDON JOHNSON (D-Tex.) named McCarthy to chair the newly created Special Senate Subcommittee on Unemployment Problems in 1959. Over the next six months, the committee held hearings in 12 states and heard 538 witnesses. Its report, published in March 1960, warned that the postwar baby boom would swell a workforce already afflicted with growing unemployment. In response to that situation, the report proposed a 12-point plan, including aid to distressed areas, stimulative economic policies, job retraining programs, higher unemployment benefits, longer eligibility for unemployment benefits, and expanded public works.

McCarthy drew national attention for his speech nominating ADLAI STEVENSON at the Democratic Convention in 1960. He pleaded with the convention, "Do not reject this man. Do not reject this man who made us all proud to be Democrats." His highly emotional speech had little impact on the outcome of the convention; Senator JOHN F. KENNEDY (D-Mass.) had more than enough delegates to secure the nomination. McCarthy won reelection to the Senate in 1964 by the largest popular majority of any Democratic candidate in the history of

Minnesota. With his dry wit and aloof demeanor, McCarthy stood apart from his Senate colleagues. He often seemed bored by the Senate and was frequently absent. Not surprisingly, he failed to attain substantial influence within that body.

McCarthy's greatest impact on American politics came in 1968, when, based on his opposition to the war in Vietnam, he challenged President Lyndon Johnson for the Democratic nomination. McCarthy's strong showing in the New Hampshire primary that March revealed a strong undercurrent of antiwar sentiment and contributed to Johnson's decision later that month not to seek reelection. McCarthy and Senator ROBERT F. KENNEDY (D-N.Y.) bitterly contested the primaries until Kennedy was assassinated in June. Although McCarthy had won victories in Wisconsin and Oregon, the Democratic Convention nominated Vice President Hubert Humphrey. After the convention, McCarthy went to the French Riviera and then covered the World Series for *Life* magazine (McCarthy had played semiprofessional baseball as a young man). He did not endorse Humphrey until the last week of the campaign—and then managed only a pallid endorsement. The Republican candidate, RICHARD M. NIXON, narrowly defeated Humphrey in the November election.

After the election, McCarthy continued to behave in a manner many regarded as erratic. He gave up his seat on the Foreign Relations Committee, knowing full well that his replacement would be Gale McGee (D-Wyo.), a hawk on the war in Vietnam. McCarthy did not stand for reelection to the Senate in 1970. He ran marginal campaigns for the presidency in 1972, 1976, 1988, and 1992. In 1980, he endorsed Ronald Reagan, the Republican nominee, for the presidency. McCarthy made a bid for a Senate seat from Minnesota in 1982, but failed to gain his party's nomination. He was a prolific author, whose books included *Frontiers in American Democracy* (1960), *A Liberal Answer to the Conservative Challenge* (1964), *The Limits of Power* (1967), *The Year of the People* (1969), and *Up 'Til Now* (1987), a political memoir. He also published a volume of poetry, *Other Things and the Aardvark* (1970). His last book, published in January 2005, was a collection of essays and poems, titled *Parting Shots from My Brittle Bow: Reflections on American Politics and*

Life. After retiring from the Senate, he moved to Rappahannock County, Virginia, where he lived alone for nearly 20 years in the foothills of the Blue Ridge Mountains. McCarthy died of Parkinson's disease on December 10, 2005, in an assisted living facility in Georgetown.

McCarthy, Joseph R(aymond)

(1908–1957) *U.S. senator; chairman, Government Operations Committee; chairman, Permanent Subcommittee on Investigations of the Government Operations Committee*

The fifth of seven children, McCarthy was born on his father's farm near Grand Chute, Wisconsin, on November 14, 1908. Upon completing eighth grade, McCarthy left school and raised chickens on land rented from his father. After a bout with influenza contributed to the failure of his poultry business, McCarthy took a job as a clerk in a Cash-Way store. The hardworking and popular young man soon became a manager. Shortly after that, he was transferred to manage a new store at Manawa, Wisconsin. He returned to high school in 1929 and completed four years of work in one year, while holding a job as an usher in a movie theater.

McCarthy entered the school of engineering at Marquette University in Milwaukee but shifted to law after two years. At Marquette, McCarthy was known as an intensely competitive and talkative young man. He received his LL.B. in 1935 and was admitted to the Wisconsin bar the same year. He opened a private legal practice in Manawa but attracted little business. McCarthy occupied his time by joining a number of civic and fraternal organizations, including the Young Democratic Club. He attracted the attention of Mike G. Eberlein, an established lawyer from the nearby town of Shawano, who offered him a job. In 1936, he ran unsuccessfully as the Democratic candidate for district attorney of Shawano County, Wisconsin. Three years later, he ran for judge of the tenth circuit court (a nonpartisan office) and, conducting a tireless campaign, upset an incumbent who had held the position for 24 years. On the bench, McCarthy disposed of a huge backlog of cases within a matter of months.

Waiving his judicial deferment, McCarthy volunteered for service in the Marine Corps in 1942 and was assigned to the South Pacific as an intelligence officer, whose job was to debrief combat pilots returning from their missions. Although in subsequent political campaigns he called himself "Tail-Gunner Joe," he did not fly in combat. McCarthy had not resigned his judgeship, and Wisconsin law barred judges from running for any other public office during the term for which they were elected. In addition, military regulations forbade servicemen from speaking on political issues. Despite these prohibitions, he entered the Wisconsin Republican senatorial primary in 1944 against the incumbent, Senator ALEXANDER WILEY (R-Wis.). McCarthy obtained a leave to go home and campaign. He skirted the ban on servicemen speaking on political issues with subterfuges such as "if I weren't in uniform, I would say . . ." McCarthy ran a vigorous campaign but ultimately lost to Wiley. McCarthy asked to be relieved from active duty in February 1945 and resigned his commission the following month. He won reelection to his judgeship in 1945.

In 1946, McCarthy entered the Republican primary for the state's other seat in the Senate, held by Robert M. La Follette, Jr., the leader of Wisconsin's Progressive Party. That year, however, La Follette disbanded the Progressive Party and entered the Republican primary. McCarthy benefited from the state Republican leadership's dislike for La Follette and from the senator's record of pursuing national issues to the neglect of state interests. In addition, many trade unionists refused to follow La Follette into the Republican Party and cast their votes in the Democratic primary. McCarthy campaigned indefatigably and defeated the incumbent by 5,000 votes. He went on to defeat his Democratic opponent, Howard McMurray, in the general election by a landslide, garnering 620,000 votes to his opponent's 279,000.

During his first three years in the Senate, McCarthy compiled an undistinguished record. While his voting record on domestic matters was generally conservative, he did not vote consistently against New Deal types of programs. On foreign policy, he leaned toward moderate internationalism. McCarthy became known as the "Pepsi-Cola Kid"

for his efforts on behalf of that company to decontrol sugar (it should be noted that beet producers in Wisconsin also wanted decontrol). In 1947 and 1948, he played a role in blocking public housing legislation sponsored by Senator ROBERT TAFT (R-Ohio). His opposition to public housing derived, at least in part, from favors he received from the Lustron Corporation, a manufacturer of prefabricated housing. In 1949, McCarthy, whose district had a large German population, questioned whether 73 Nazi SS troopers, 43 of whom received the death penalty, had been fairly convicted by an American war crimes tribunal. The charges against the German defendants grew out of their involvement in the Malmédy Massacre, in which the SS mowed down American prisoners of war with machine guns during the Battle of the Bulge. The convictions had undergone scrutiny by the War Crimes Review Board and the office of the Judge Advocate, which found some procedural irregularities but concluded that the trials were "essentially fair."

During the late 1940s, internal subversion became a major national issue. Many Republicans charged that communist supporters had infiltrated the administrations of Presidents Franklin D. Roosevelt and HARRY S. TRUMAN. While rejecting the accusation, Truman established a Loyalty Program

Senator Joseph McCarthy testifying before the Senate Foreign Relations committee, March 14, 1950 *(Dwight D. Eisenhower Library and Museum)*

in 1947, which provided for the review of all government employees and applicants for government
employment. The program denied those under
review basic procedural safeguards, and, under it,
thousands of government workers lost their jobs.
Moreover, Truman and other Democrats accused
conservative Republicans, who did not support
large defense budgets, multilateral defense pacts,
universal military training, and conscription, of
being dupes of communists.

Competing charges of disloyalty and insufficient vigilance against communism increased in
intensity in 1949, with the communist victory in
China, the detonation of a Soviet atomic device,
and the conviction under the Smith Act of American leaders of the Communist Party for conspiring to advocate the violent overthrow of the U.S.
government. The conviction of Alger Hiss for perjury in 1950 further agitated the public. While a
member of the State Department, Hiss had passed
documents to WHITTAKER CHAMBERS in the 1930s
and subsequently lied about it before the House
Committee on Un-American Activities. The same
month as Hiss's conviction, Klaus Fuchs, a British
scientist who worked on the Manhattan Project,
confessed to passing atomic secrets to the Soviets.

McCarthy initially paid little attention to the
issue of internal communist subversion. Early
in 1950, however, he was looking for an issue to
elevate his profile in preparation for his bid for
reelection in 1952. At a Lincoln Day speech to
a Republican women's group in Wheeling, West
Virginia, on February 9, 1950, McCarthy charged
that there were 205 or 57 Communists in the
State Department. He did not speak from a prepared text, and accounts of his charges differed.
Later, on the Senate floor, he claimed to have 108
documented cases. The charges were not original;
much of the speech was a verbatim repetition of
charges made over several years by conservatives in
both parties. Moreover, several other Republicans
speaking on Lincoln Day made similar remarks.
McCarthy's spectacular and exaggerated claims,
however, attracted headlines.

The Senate established a special subcommittee of the Senate Foreign Relations Committee
in late February to investigate McCarthy's claims.
The leadership chose Senator Millard Tydings, a

conservative Democrat from Maryland, to head the
subcommittee. In July the Democratic majority on
the panel issued a report denouncing McCarthy's
charges as false and condemning him for unethical tactics. The Republican minority on the committee defended McCarthy and called the report a
whitewash of the State Department. The hearings
attracted considerable publicity and did nothing to
diminish the attention McCarthy got.

In June 1950, Senator MARGARET CHASE SMITH
(R-Maine) and six other liberal Republican senators
issued a "Declaration of Conscience" criticizing
McCarthy for making irresponsible charges. Many
Republicans who believed McCarthy's accusations
reckless did not criticize the junior senator from
Wisconsin because the issue of internal subversion
had proved to be an effective political weapon, and
they did not want to vitiate the issue or to risk a
reaction that would discredit the entire party.

Many Democrats feared that, if they attacked
McCarthy, it would appear to confirm that they
were soft on communism. Moreover, in the campaign of 1950, McCarthy campaigned against
a number of leading Democrats who lost their
seats in the November elections, including Scott
Lucas (D-Ill.), the majority leader, and, most notably, Millard Tydings. In fact, all of the candidates
against whom McCarthy campaigned ran ahead
of their state party tickets. Tydings, in particular,
lost for a variety of reasons unrelated to McCarthy or concerns about communists in government.
The results, however, seemed to demonstrate
not only McCarthy's popularity but his ability to
defeat political enemies. Members of both parties
refrained from criticizing McCarthy for fear that he
would turn his attacks on them and cost them their
seats. Moreover, anticommunism was a bipartisan
doctrine. Conservative Democrats, such as Senator
PAT MCCARRAN of Nevada, Representative John E.
Rankin of Mississippi, and Representative Martin
Dies, Jr., of Texas, had warned of communists in
government (often conflating liberals with communists) and conducted investigations long before
McCarthy had taken up the issue. The strident
anticommunist rhetoric of the Truman administration and of cold war liberals as well as the Truman
administration's response to McCarthy's charges
gave credence to the allegations.

McCarthy was not the first of the vocal anti-communists; neither was he the most effective. He was, however, the loudest and most reckless. His success depended only in part on postwar concerns about communism abroad and at home. McCarthy's attacks were calculated to take advantage of resentments caused by social strains in American society. He focused much of his vituperation against an educated, eastern elite that would later be called the Establishment. McCarthy heaped scorn on "dilettante diplomats" and those who were "born with silver spoons in their mouths." The Ivy League and Anglophile affectations of DEAN ACHESON, Truman's secretary of state, made irresistible targets for McCarthy's invective. McCarthy's own skills as a demagogue also contributed to his rapid rise. Unlike most demagogues, McCarthy did not give stem-winding, highly emotional speeches. Rather, he spoke in a monotone, even as he made his most outrageous charges. The delivery lent credence to his accusations, in that they seemed to be unemotional and therefore "factual." When criticized, he charged his accuser with being pro-communist or soft on communism. McCarthy also employed a technique that one commentator called the "multiple untruth"; he threw out a series of charges, and, before they could be checked or disproved, he had moved on to other charges. The disclaimers never caught up to the allegations. Finally, McCarthy made effective use of the press. He issued sensational accusations just before deadlines. What were reporters to do? If a reporter held the story until the facts could be checked, other papers would beat his paper to the story. Further, if the accusations turned out to be true, the reporter who did not go with the story would likely be out of a job. Moreover, reporters could console themselves with the thought that it was news that a U.S. senator had made such allegations.

McCarthy's charges became more sensational and increasingly outlandish. Speaking on the floor of the Senate, he denounced Secretary of Defense George C. Marshall as a traitor. Marshall had served as army chief of staff during World War II and later as secretary of state. He was one of the most respected figures in America, but it was an indication of McCarthy's power of intimidation that no one in the Senate objected when McCarthy charged

Marshall with participating in a "great conspiracy" that accounted for the series of setbacks America had suffered at the hands of the communists since the end of World War II. McCarthy taunted the secretary of state, Dean Acheson, calling him the "Red Dean of Fashion."

In August 1951, Senator WILLIAM BENTON (D-Conn.) introduced a resolution calling on the Rules Committee to examine McCarthy's conduct to determine if he should be expelled from the Senate. The resolution was referred to the committee's Subcommittee on Privileges and Elections, which had only recently issued a report critical of McCarthy's unethical actions in the Maryland senatorial election of 1950. After an investigation that dragged on for over a year, the subcommittee issued a report, written largely by Senator THOMAS HENNINGS (D-Mo.), that raised questions about McCarthy's finances but did not call for action against him.

McCarthy's notoriety made him made him both a prominent figure and an issue in the elections of 1952. Curiously, though, the senator played no role in the campaign for the Republican presidential nomination in 1952. The Republican nominee, DWIGHT D. EISENHOWER, detested McCarthy. Moreover, Eisenhower was a personal friend of Marshall, to whom he owed his rapid advancement during World War II. JOSEPH ALSOP and STEWART ALSOP published a report that Eisenhower would not campaign in Wisconsin on behalf of McCarthy or in Indiana on behalf of Senator WILLIAM JENNER (R-Ind.), another critic of Marshall. In fact, Eisenhower had told his staff not to make plans to visit Wisconsin. At a press conference in August, an irate Eisenhower declared that he had "no patience with anyone who can find in his [Marshall's] record of service for this country anything to criticize." Eisenhower went on to call his former superior a patriot and to proclaim that there was "nothing of disloyalty in General Marshall's soul." When aides pressed on the candidate the need to campaign in Wisconsin, Eisenhower reluctantly agreed. He asked a speechwriter, EMMET JOHN HUGHES, to include a tribute to Marshall in the speech scheduled for October 3 in McCarthy's home state. At an appearance in Indiana, Eisenhower endorsed the Republican ticket in the state but pointedly did not mention Jenner's name, even though the senator had introduced him and remained on the platform. As Eisenhower's campaign headed into Wisconsin, the state's Republican governor, WALTER KOHLER, begged the candidate not to attack McCarthy in Wisconsin, because it would split the Republican Party in the state. The Republican nominee also met with McCarthy and told the senator in no uncertain terms what he thought of him. Eisenhower defended Marshall and, over McCarthy's objections, indicated his intent to make a laudatory reference to Marshall. Ultimately, however, Kohler's repeated entreaties, supported by several of Eisenhower's senior aides, persuaded the candidate to cut the statement regarding Marshall from the speech. The press had an advance copy of the speech and interpreted the deletion as a surrender to McCarthy.

McCarthy campaigned for conservative Republicans in several states and famously referred to the Democratic presidential nominee, ADLAI STEVENSON, as "Alger . . . I mean Adlai." At first glance, the outcome of the elections seemed to confirm McCarthy's power. Three of the four Democratic senatorial incumbents he campaigned against lost, including William Benton of Connecticut and the majority leader, Ernest W. McFarland of Arizona. McCarthy himself won reelection by a comfortable margin, although he ran well behind Eisenhower. McCarthy ran even farther behind Fred Zimmerman, the anti-McCarthy Republican candidate for secretary of state. Indeed, McCarthy ran behind all other Republican candidates for statewide office. Further, all of the defeated Democrats against whom McCarthy campaigned ran ahead of the national ticket in their states. McCarthy's power was more apparent than real, but the appearance counted.

Republicans won control of both houses of Congress in 1952, and McCarthy became chair of the Senate Committee on Government Operations and its subcommittee on investigations. For the committee's chief counsel, he chose ROY MARCUS COHN, an ambitious and caustic attorney from Manhattan, who had served as prosecutor in the trial of JULIUS AND ETHEL ROSENBERG for passing secrets to the Soviets. Although it was not the brief of his committee, McCarthy launched a series of investigations into "communist influence" in the federal government.

Immediately after the elections of 1952, McCarthy announced his intention to cooperate with the new Republican administration. Beginning in January 1953, however, he joined Republican conservatives who objected to Eisenhower's nominations of General WALTER BEDELL SMITH as undersecretary of state and JAMES B. CONANT as U.S. high commissioner to Germany. In March, McCarthy joined the far more serious conservative opposition, led by Senator STYLES BRIDGES (R-N.H.) and Senator PAT MCCARRAN (D-Nev.), to Eisenhower's nominee for ambassador to the Soviet Union, CHARLES E. BOHLEN. McCarthy questioned the loyalty of Bohlen, who had served in the State Department under Roosevelt and Truman. When Secretary of State JOHN FOSTER DULLES said that there was "no substantial evidence" for doubting Bohlen's patriotism, McCarthy called Dulles a liar. Bohlen was ultimately confirmed, but not without a protracted and nasty dispute.

Several of Eisenhower's advisers wanted him to denounce McCarthy publicly. Others hoped to avoid confrontation with the junior senator from Wisconsin, fearing that an open break would cause a rift in the Republican Party that would threaten the president's legislative program. Eisenhower repeatedly expressed in private both his disgust for McCarthy and his unwillingness to "get down in the gutter with that guy."

McCarthy announced in late March 1953 that he had negotiated an agreement with a group of Greek shipowners, in which they had promised to cease trade with Communist China and North Korea. The State Department dismissed McCarthy's claims as "phony," and HAROLD STASSEN, the director of the U.S. Foreign Operations Administration, denounced McCarthy for "undermining" the administration's conduct of foreign affairs. Subsequently, Dulles issued a conciliatory statement, and, at a press conference, Eisenhower suggested that Stassen might have meant "infringed on" rather than "undermined." Stassen dutifully accepted Eisenhower's interpretation.

Meanwhile, McCarthy launched a series of investigations that attracted headlines but failed to expose any communists. In February 1953, he began an investigation of the Voice of America. He insinuated that the cancellation of some broadcasts and the improper location of transmitters had been done to further the communist cause. McCarthy also investigated the Government Printing Office. In April, the Permanent Subcommittee on Investigations looked into the overseas libraries operated by the State Department. McCarthy sent Cohn and the panel's chief consultant, G. DAVID SCHINE, on a tour of the libraries in Europe. At home, McCarthy called before his subcommittee allegedly leftist writers whose works appeared in those libraries. Alarmed by McCarthy's attacks, officials in the State Department ordered the libraries to remove material written by "Communists, fellow travelers, et cetera." Some books were burned. This proved too much for Eisenhower, who, speaking without notes at the commencement exercises of Dartmouth College in June, admonished students, "Don't join the book burners. Don't think you are going to conceal faults by concealing evidence that they ever existed. Don't be afraid to go in your library and read every book." When asked at a press conference to link those comments to McCarthy, Eisenhower refused, citing his policy "never [to] talk personalities."

McCarthy suffered an embarrassment after he hired J. B. MATTHEWS as executive director of the staff for the Permanent Subcommittee on Investigations in June 1953. A conservative Methodist minister in the 1920s and early 1930s, Matthews became a Marxist and an atheist in 1935. Three years later, he again reversed course and became a right-wing anticommunist. Just before he joined the subcommittee's staff, an article by Matthews appeared in the July issue of *American Mercury* charging that "the largest single group supporting the Communist apparatus in the United States today is composed of Protestant clergymen." The subcommittee's ranking minority member, Senator JOHN MCCLELLAN (D-Ark.), and the other Democratic members of the panel demanded that Matthews be dismissed. McCarthy refused, but the article generated a storm of protest. McCarthy understood that Matthews would have to go. While Vice President Richard Nixon stalled McCarthy, the administration arranged for the National Conference of Christians and Jews to send a telegram

protesting Matthews's article and for Eisenhower to issue a sympathetic response that stated, "Generalized and irresponsible attacks that sweepingly condemn the whole of any group of citizens are alien to America." Matthews resigned and McCarthy accepted the resignation "very reluctantly." The sequence of events made it seem that McCarthy had decided to let Matthews go only under pressure from the administration.

Democrats on the subcommittee challenged McCarthy's right to hire staff unilaterally. In a straight party line vote, however, the subcommittee confirmed McCarthy's authority to hire and fire staff. The Democrats on the subcommittee walked out.

McCarthy rebounded from the Matthews fiasco by announcing, the day after Matthews's resignation, that he intended to investigate the Central Intelligence Agency. While he never carried through on that investigation, the announcement alone diverted attention from his problems with Matthews. The senator's next investigation brought him into a head-on collision with the administration.

McCarthy began an investigation of the army and the Defense Department in September 1953. He investigated civilian personnel and army intelligence before turning his attention, in October, to civilian scientists working at the Army Signal Corps Engineering Laboratories at Fort Monmouth, New Jersey. In November, McCarthy briefly pursued allegations of subversion and espionage in defense plants, but in December he returned to Fort Monmouth.

Another issue in late 1953 brought McCarthy's dissatisfaction with the administration into public view. In November, Attorney General HERBERT BROWNELL made public documents indicating that former president Truman had proceeded with the nomination of Harry Dexter White to be executive director of the International Monetary Fund after information revealing that White had engaged in espionage for the Soviet Union had been passed to top officials in the Truman administration. Truman initially denied having seen the reports on White and charged Brownell with *McCarthyism* (a term first used by the *Washington Post*'s cartoonist, Herbert L. Block). Truman later changed his story when documents revealed that the reports had, indeed, come to his attention. In any case, McCarthy, furious with Truman's use of his name, demanded equal time on television to respond. In his reply to Truman, however, McCarthy focused his attack on the Eisenhower administration, which he criticized for allowing American allies to continue to trade with Communist China and for failing to dismiss JOHN PATON DAVIES, a foreign service officer and one of McCarthy's favorite targets. The junior senator from Wisconsin also took issue with the president's recently expressed hope that the problem of internal subversion would have been dealt with so efficiently that it would play no role in the congressional elections of 1954.

In December 1953, McCarthy discovered the case of IRVING PERESS, an army dentist stationed at Camp Kilmer, New Jersey, whom the army had commissioned as a captain in October 1952. At the time he began active duty in January 1953, Peress, a member of the left-wing American Labor Party, had responded to a form concerning membership in subversive organizations by writing "federal constitutional privilege." Military intelligence investigated Peress and found "sufficient evidence" to "warrant his removal." In August, Peress responded to an interrogatory by filling in his name, address, date of birth, and the names of his parents. In answer to the remaining questions, he again wrote "federal constitutional privilege." Through a series of bureaucratic slipups, Peress was not dismissed, despite repeated recommendations to that effect, and was promoted to the rank of major in November 1953 under the provisions of the Doctor's Draft. The army did not get around to removing Peress until mid-January 1954, when it relieved the dentist from active duty and allowed him to choose a date for his discharge within 90 days. Peress chose March 31. In the meantime, McCarthy called Peress to testify before the Permanent Subcommittee on Investigations. The dentist appeared at an executive session on January 30, 1954, and claimed immunity under the Fifth Amendment in response to questions about the Communist Party. On February 1, Peress asked for immediate release from the army; that same day, McCarthy wrote a letter to ROBERT STEVENS, secretary of the army, demanding that Peress be court-martialed. Stevens acknowledged that the system had broken down in the Peress case

but maintained that the army did not have sufficient evidence to court-martial Peress.

McCarthy called the commanding officer of Camp Kilmer, General RALPH ZWICKER, a West Point graduate who had served with distinction under Eisenhower's command in World War II, to testify before the subcommittee on February 18. As Zwicker testified, McCarthy became increasingly frustrated and abusive. The senator questioned whether Zwicker had "the brains of a five-year-old child" and told the general that "any man . . . who protects communists is not fit to wear that uniform." Stevens announced that he would not permit Zwicker to appear before the subcommittee again. "I cannot," he explained, "permit loyal officers of our Armed Forces to be subjected to such unwarranted treatment." McCarthy ordered Stevens to appear before the subcommittee.

In an effort to make peace, Stevens met with McCarthy and other Republicans on the subcommittee over lunch on February 24. Stevens agreed to permit further testimony and release the names of those responsible for the promotion and honorable discharge of Peress; perhaps he received some assurances that the committee would accord decent treatment to witnesses. When the supposedly secret lunch ended, a group of reporters and photographers was waiting. Senator KARL MUNDT (R–S. Dak.) read a "memorandum of understanding," indicating that the secretary of the army had agreed to release the "names of everyone involved in the promotion and honorable discharge of Peress" and make them available to testify before the subcommittee. The statement did not include a word about the treatment of witnesses. A startled Stevens refused to comment and left, after which McCarthy bragged that the secretary had abjectly surrendered.

Eisenhower was infuriated by McCarthy's treatment of Zwicker, by the role that EVERETT DIRKSEN (R–Ill.) and Mundt played in the lunch meeting, and by Stevens's seeming ineptitude. Still, the president had no intention of engaging McCarthy publicly. He thought that if a president attacked a senator, the Senate would rally around one of its own. Further, he believed that McCarthy wanted publicity above all and that a frontal assault by the president would provide him with the publicity he craved. Instead,

Eisenhower worked behind the scenes to isolate and embarrass the senator. He had his staff draft a revised memorandum of understanding that guaranteed respectful treatment for army officers called before the subcommittee. The president summoned Dirksen to the White House and told him that he wanted the new agreement released that day in the name of Stevens and the Republicans on the committee. That effort failed when McCarthy, angry at the implication that officers had been mistreated in the past, refused to sign off on the new agreement. The president attempted to make the best of the situation by having Stevens issue a statement to reporters from the office of JAMES HAGERTY, the White House press secretary. The statement reiterated Stevens's position that Zwicker had been mistreated and claimed that he had received promises at the lunch meeting that, in the future, witnesses would not be browbeaten or humiliated.

Eisenhower followed up with a series of statements supporting the secretary of the army. In his first press conference after Zwicker's appearance before McCarthy's committee, Eisenhower acknowledged that the army had made "serious errors" in its handling of the Peress case, but he went on to praise Zwicker for his patriotism and noted that the general had been "decorated for gallantry in the field." The president also said that he expected that members of the executive branch be accorded "respect and courtesy" when they appeared before congressional panels and made it clear that the "primary responsibility" in that regard lay with the Republican members of Congress. In an indirect comment on McCarthy, he observed, "I regard it as unfortunate when we are diverted from grave problems—one of which is vigilance against any kind of internal subversion—through disregard of the standards of fair play recognized by the American people." McCarthy responded with an intemperate and, given the restrained nature of Eisenhower's remarks, disproportionate attack on Eisenhower.

By early March, opposition to McCarthy became apparent within Republican ranks. Republican congressional leaders considered various "fair play" guidelines for investigating committees. In a radio broadcast on March 9, Senator RALPH FLANDERS (R-Vt.) ridiculed the disparity between McCarthy's exaggerated claims and his modest achievements: "He dons his war paint. He goes into his war dance. He emits war whoops. He goes forth into battle and proudly returns with the scalp of a pink dentist." Later that day, Eisenhower wrote Flanders a letter praising his remarks. That evening, EDWARD R. MURROW devoted his entire television program, *See It Now*, to a denunciation of McCarthy and his methods. On March 12, Nixon gave the administration's formal response to a nationally broadcast speech by Adlai Stevenson, in which the Democratic presidential aspirant attacked the Republican administration and focused on its inability to deal with McCarthy. Nixon called for "fair and proper" procedures in the hunt for communists in government. "Men who have in the past done effective work exposing Communists in this country," said the vice president, "have, by reckless talk and questionable methods, made themselves the issue, rather than the cause they believe in so deeply."

McCarthy suffered a major blow on March 11, when Annie Lee Moss testified before his subcommittee. In February, McCarthy, most likely acting on a tip from someone in the FBI, had alleged that Moss, a civilian employee of the Army Signal Corps, had been a communist. Moss had worked at the Pentagon since World War II, starting out as a cafeteria worker and rising to the position of communications clerk. By the time she appeared before the subcommittee, she had been suspended from her job and was unemployed. She certainly did not look like a major security risk. An African-American woman in her 40s, Mrs. Moss arrived bundled in an overcoat and wearing frayed white gloves. Inarticulate, poorly educated, and seemingly baffled by the charges she was facing, she evoked considerable sympathy. The Democrats on the subcommittee made the most of what seemed to be a cruel assault on an innocent and helpless victim. The fact that three A. L. Mosses were listed in the Washington phone book added to the appearance of charges levied with careless disregard for the facts. However disastrous the Moss case proved for McCarthy, another event later that day overshadowed it.

On the afternoon of March 11, the army alleged that McCarthy and Cohn had sought preferential treatment for Schine, who had been drafted the previous year. McCarthy responded the following day by accusing the army of holding the former aide hostage in an effort to blackmail him into ending his investigation of the armed forces. Amid a flurry of charges and countercharges, an investigation was clearly in order. Over the objection of its Democratic members, McCarthy's own subcommittee voted to look into the matter. After considerable haggling, in which the administration played a role behind the scenes, McCarthy temporarily gave up his seat on the panel for the investigation. Mundt assumed the chair for the hearings, and Senator HENRY DWORSHAK (R-Idaho) filled McCarthy's seat. McCarthy won the right to cross-examine witnesses, a right also accorded to the army. Since the charges also involved Cohn, Ray Jenkins would serve as counsel to the subcommittee. The army chose JOSEPH WELCH, a distinguished trial lawyer from Boston, as its attorney.

Guided by the minority leader, LYNDON B. JOHNSON (D-Tex.), Democrats in the Senate demanded that the hearings be televised. At Eisenhower's insistence, Republican leaders agreed. The president believed that, given a chance to see McCarthy in action, the public would be repulsed. The hearings commenced on April 22 and lasted 36 days. ABC and the Dumont network carried the entire proceedings live, and they attracted an audience of millions.

From the opening of the Army-McCarthy hearings, the junior senator from Wisconsin dominated the proceedings. He made extensive use of his right to cross-examine and constantly interrupted the proceedings with points of order. McCarthy bullied witnesses, behaved rudely, at one point or another attacked every member of the committee, and made personally abusive comments to one of the Democrats on the subcommittee, Senator STUART SYMINGTON (D-Mo.). Moreover, McCarthy and his staff lost considerable credibility when Jenkins introduced a doctored photograph of Schine and Stevens. The photo was apparently intended to suggest that Stevens had befriended Schine in an effort to head off McCarthy's investigation of the army. Welch demonstrated that the photo had been cropped, and he traced the alteration of the photo to McCarthy's staff.

The highlight of the hearings came on June 9, when Welch badgered Cohn to give him the name of a single communist in government. McCarthy interrupted to charge that Welch had tried to introduce one into the hearings. The senator observed that Frederick Fisher, a member of Welch's law firm originally slated to participate in the hearings, had been a member of the National Lawyers Guild, which McCarthy described as "an organization which was named, oh, years and years ago, as the legal bulwark of the Communist Party." Addressing McCarthy directly, Welch said, "Until this moment, I think I never really gauged your cruelty or your recklessness." Welch, who appeared close to tears, explained that Fisher had left the Lawyers Guild years before. As Welch told it, when he brought his team to Washington, he asked if there were anything in their backgrounds that "would hurt anybody." When Fisher disclosed his past membership in the Lawyers Guild, Welch said that he decided to send him back to Boston. (In fact, Welch had met with members of the administration, who urged him not to use Fisher.) "Little did I dream," Welch continued, "you could be so reckless and so cruel as to do an injury to that lad." When McCarthy persisted, Welch asked, "Have you no sense of decency, sir, at long last? Have you left no sense of decency?"

The hearings produced no clear-cut winners, but, by the time they ground to a close on June 17, McCarthy's methods had turned many against him. An increasing number of newspapers came out against the senator. Under intense pressure from Republicans, Roy Cohn resigned as counsel to the subcommittee on July 19. Several other aides to McCarthy resigned under fire. Efforts to craft a bipartisan report failed, and, on September 1, the subcommittee released a majority report, mildly critical of McCarthy, a more harshly critical minority report, and supplementary statements by Dirksen and CHARLES POTTER (R-Mich.). All of them agreed that McCarthy bore responsibility for permitting Cohn to attempt improperly to influence the army on behalf of Schine, that Stevens and JOHN ADAMS (the army's general counsel) had to some degree attempted to influence McCarthy's investigation of Fort Monmouth, and that neither Stevens nor Adams was soft on communism.

By this time, however, the political ground had begun to shift. Back on June 11, Flanders handed McCarthy a message indicting his intention to take the floor and make a speech critical of McCarthy. He then introduced a resolution calling for McCarthy's removal from the chair of the Permanent Subcommittee on Investigations and its parent committee until the senator from Wisconsin answered questions raised about his finances in the Hennings report of January 1953. By threatening to take the unprecedented step of stripping McCarthy of his committee chairs, Flanders aroused the opposition of traditionalists in the Senate and, most especially, that of southerners who saw it as a threat to the seniority system. In July, he withdrew his resolution and in its place offered one that called for censure of McCarthy. Soon after that, Flanders, Senator J. WILLIAM FULBRIGHT (D-Ark.), and Senator WAYNE MORSE (I-Oreg.) introduced amendments that listed specific charges. On August 2, the resolution was referred to a six-member committee to be selected by the vice president. Working closely with Johnson and the Republican leader, WILLIAM KNOWLAND (R-Calif.), Nixon named six moderate conservatives from the South or West who had not taken a strong stand either for or against McCarthy. The committee had no liberals, no presidential contenders, and no media hounds. The chair was Senator ARTHUR WATKINS (R-Utah), who was determined to run dignified, orderly proceedings.

The committee adopted a set of rules designed to minimize McCarthy's potential for disruption. They allowed either McCarthy or his lawyer, but not both, to conduct cross-examinations. This put pressure on McCarthy, who was not the most skilled lawyer, to allow his attorney to handle the cross-examinations and therefore muzzle himself. The committee also barred television cameras from the hearing room. From the beginning of the hearings on August 31, 1954, Watkins exercised firm control over the proceedings. When McCarthy attempted to interject himself in defiance of the panel's rules of procedure, Watkins gaveled him to order.

The rules of the Senate did not define censure or prescribe a specific punishment for it. Moreover, the Senate had resorted to the step only infrequently. The committee therefore needed to define what McCarthy had done that warranted censure without weakening the legitimate senatorial power and prerogatives that McCarthy had abused. On September 27, the committee released a unanimous report recommending censure on two counts. One involved McCarthy's refusal to appear before the Subcommittee on Privileges and Elections in 1952 and his abuse of Hennings. The other related to his treatment of General Zwicker, which the committee described as "reprehensible."

Although the subcommittee's report made some sort of condemnation of McCarthy virtually inevitable, neither party wanted to deal with the matter until after the elections. In the meantime, the political landscape was shifting. Unlike in 1950 or 1952, McCarthy played almost no role in the elections of 1954. The senator's office issued a statement explaining that he had turned down hundreds of invitations to speak in order to devote himself to his committee work, but virtually no one wanted his support. He had become an embarrassment and a liability to his party. The election brought bad news for McCarthy. Democrats regained control of both houses, and liberal Democratic incumbents did well, while a number of right-wing Republican incumbents went down to defeat. The results added to the impression that the senator's power had waned.

The Watkins Committee filed its report with the Senate on November 8. Two days later, McCarthy responded to the charges read by Watkins with a speech in which he asserted that the Communist Party had "made a Committee of the Senate its unwitting handmaiden." The attack on the Watkins Committee served only to convince the uncommitted to vote for censure. Several attempts to broker a compromise that involved an apology by McCarthy failed. Johnson carefully kept his Democrats in check to avoid any appearance of partisanship. Just before the vote, Johnson told Watkins that at least a dozen Democrats intended to vote against the charge relating to McCarthy's abuse of Zwicker. Watkins and the other members of his committee quickly agreed to drop the charge involving Zwicker and substitute one that condemned McCarthy for his abuse of the Watkins Committee. The resolution for censure carried by a vote of 67 to 22. Johnson kept the Democrats in line, which accounted for 44 votes. The Republicans divided evenly, 22 to 22. The Eastern, or liberal, Republicans voted for the resolution; the Midwestern conservatives voted against it. Wayne Morse of Oregon, the Senate's lone independent, also voted yea. Two senators were absent and unrecorded, Alexander Wiley and, in a profile of something other than courage, JOHN F. KENNEDY (D-Mass.). McCarthy voted "present."

Eisenhower invited Watkins to the White House on December 3 and congratulated him for a job well done. On December 7, an infuriated McCarthy lashed out at the president. He said that he had been "mistaken" to believe that Eisenhower would vigorously seek to remove communists from government and apologized for having supported the general in 1952. The attack on Eisenhower appalled even McCarthy's staunchest supporters. He became a political pariah.

McCarthy spent his remaining two-and-a-half years in the Senate in obscurity. The Democratic victory in 1954 stripped him of his committee chairs, which deprived him of control of the committee's staff and budget. Further, he could no longer control what matters the committee would investigate. McCarthy occasionally attempted to attract attention with sensational charges of internal subversion. In March 1955, for instance, he charged that Dulles had hired 150 men to censor the records of the Yalta Conference. In 1955 and 1956, he attacked the Supreme Court for decisions limiting the investigating power of Congress. By this time, however, no one was listening. His friends deserted him, and he suffered another public humiliation when the Eisenhowers announced that McCarthy and his wife were not on the guest list for events at the White House. In 1956, McCarthy urged Republicans to repudiate Eisenhower and nominate the director of the FBI, J. Edgar Hoover, for the presidency.

Always a heavy drinker, McCarthy's drinking got out of hand during the Army-McCarthy hearings. After several stays in Bethesda Naval Hospital to dry out, he began drinking heavily again when the Senate took up the resolution to censure him. If not in the year before, certainly after the vote to condemn him, he became a full-fledged alcoholic. He lost interest in his duties as a senator and fretted obsessively about those who had "betrayed" him. As he proceeded to drink himself into oblivion, his

health deteriorated, and his visits to Bethesda Naval Hospital became more frequent. The ailments for which he was treated included cirrhosis, hepatitis, and delirium tremens. Among the few friends who continued to visit him was ROBERT F. KENNEDY. McCarthy entered Bethesda Naval Hospital for the last time on April 28, 1957. He died there on May 2, 1957.

The concern with internal subversion did not end with McCarthy's disgrace or with his death. The Senate condemned McCarthy for exceeding the bounds of decency and for violating the Senate's code of ethics. It did not repudiate his crusade against communism. With the easing of cold war tensions in the second half of the 1950s, however, the political climate began to change. By the 1960s, McCarthy had few defenders, and the term *McCarthyism* had become common usage for the levying of reckless and unfounded allegations.

—MSM

McClellan, John L(ittle)

(1896–1977) *U.S. senator; chairman, Government Operations Committee; chairman, Select Committee on Improper Activities in the Labor or Management Field*

The son of a country lawyer and teacher, John McClellan was born in Sheridan, Arkansas, on February 25, 1896. Although he never attended college, McClellan studied law in his father's office and was admitted to the bar in 1913 at the age of 17. He commenced the practice of law in Sheridan. During World War I, he enlisted in the army and served as a first lieutenant in the aviation section of the Army Signal Corps from 1917 to 1919. Upon leaving the service, he moved to Malvern, Arkansas, where he served as city attorney from 1920 to 1926 and as prosecuting attorney for the state's seventh judicial district from 1927 to 1930. McClellan won election to the U.S. House of Representatives in 1934 and reelection in 1936. As a member of Congress, he supported most of the New Deal, although he opposed Roosevelt's plan to pack the Supreme Court and a federal antilynching bill. After running unsuccessfully in the Democratic senatorial primary in 1938, he returned to the practice of law in Camden, Arkansas, until he won election to the Senate in 1942. He held that seat in the Senate until his death.

During his first decade or so in the Senate, his voting record was typical for a southern Democrat. He voted consistently against civil rights and against most Fair Deal programs, although he did back some conservation and social welfare measures. In 1947, he supported the Taft-Hartley Act, which placed restrictions on organized labor. With respect to foreign policy, he balanced his belief in fiscal restraint with his commitment to anticommunism, internationalism, and a strong military. McClellan supported both aid to Greece and Turkey and the Marshall Plan. He was appointed to the powerful Appropriations Committee in 1949 and assumed the chair of the Executive Departments Committee, which became the Government Operations Committee in 1952.

After the Republicans won control of the Senate in the elections of 1952, Senator JOSEPH R. McCARTHY (R-Wis.) became chair of the Government Operations Committee. As the ranking minority member of the Permanent Subcommittee on Investigations, also chaired by McCarthy, McClellan did not oppose the panel's investigations of alleged communist infiltration of government agencies, but he did occasionally take exception, sometimes vigorously, to what he regarded as McCarthy's undemocratic methods.

In July 1953, a controversy erupted over a magazine article, written by the subcommittee's newly appointed staff director, J. B. MATTHEWS, that alleged "the largest single group supporting the Communist apparatus in the United States today is composed of Protestant clergymen." McClellan demanded that Matthews be dismissed. McCarthy initially refused but eventually had to accept Matthews's resignation. After the committee adopted a motion to give the chair sole power to hire and fire staff on a straight party-line vote, McClellan led the panel's Democrats in an unprecedented walkout. He also threatened to oppose renewal of the subcommittee's funding for the following year. In January 1954, after McCarthy agreed to relinquish exclusive authority over staff appointments and to allow the minority to hire its own counsel, the Democrats returned to the panel. In March, McClellan urged that the Army-McCarthy hearings

be televised, but did not play a major part in the hearings themselves. Still his sober, lawyerly questions and, as the *Saturday Evening Post* put it, his "dour visage" and "funereal aspect" brought him to national attention.

When the Democrats won control of the Senate in the elections of 1954, McClellan regained the chair of the Government Operations Committee and named ROBERT F. KENNEDY chief counsel of the Permanent Subcommittee on Investigations. Under McClellan's direction, the panel launched a series of probes into charges of graft and corruption in the handling of government contracts for military supplies. Hearings held in July 1955 on the business connections of Air Force Secretary HAROLD E. TALBOTT and other officials in the Defense Department revealed that Talbott, after taking his post at the Pentagon, had continued to hold 50 percent of the stock in an industrial engineering firm that did business with the military. As a result of the investigation, Talbott resigned in August.

McClellan was appointed to chair the Special Committee to Investigate Political Activities, Lobbying, and Campaign Contributions in March 1956. The Senate established the panel after Senator Francis Case (R-S. Dak.) disclosed that he had rejected a $2,500 campaign contribution from a lobbyist interested in the natural gas bill. After hearings in May, in which lobbyists for various businesses and labor unions testified about their efforts to influence senators, the committee recommended legislation to regulate lobbying and campaign financing. It required that all political committees report expenditures and limit individual campaign contributions to $15,000 a year. McClellan sponsored a bill that incorporated those proposals, but strong opposition from the U.S. Chamber of Commerce, the National Association of Manufacturers, and other business groups prevented the measure from reaching the floor of the Senate.

The subcommittee's continuing investigation of procurement policies in the Defense Department led in 1956 to the exposure of the involvement of leading East Coast gangsters in the manufacturing and trucking of military uniforms. The panel released its findings in January 1957, and the report prompted demands for a major investigation of corruption in labor-management relations. Two

Senate committees, the Permanent Subcommittee on Investigations and the Labor Subcommittee of the Labor and Public Welfare Committee, claimed jurisdiction. Management groups did not want the Labor Subcommittee, which liberals dominated, to conduct the inquiry. Unions objected to McClellan's panel undertaking it. On January 30, the Senate established a Select Committee on Improper Activities in the Labor or Management Field, made up of four members from each party and from both subcommittees. McClellan chaired the select panel and chose Robert F. Kennedy as its chief counsel.

The McClellan Committee held hearings in several cities over two-and-a-half years. It exposed abuses of power by labor leaders, including theft, embezzlement, and misuse of union funds; rigging of union elections; "sweetheart" contracts unfavorable to workers, for which management rewarded union officials; ties with organized crime; and the use of violence and threats against both employers and their own rank and file. Although the committee initially took elaborate steps to avoid the appearance of taking sides between unions and management, its investigation focused on corruption in unions, especially the Teamsters.

Hearings in early 1957 featured DAVE BECK, president of the Teamsters, who repeatedly took the Fifth Amendment in response to charges that he had taken union funds to pay for personal investments and real estate. Indicted for tax fraud and other crimes and suspended from the AFL-CIO Executive Council, Beck resigned his post with the Teamsters. That October JAMES HOFFA succeeded Beck, and he, too, was called before the McClellan Committee to answer allegations regarding his involvement with organized crime. As the committee's chief counsel, Robert F. Kennedy supervised the investigation and led the questioning of witnesses. The hearings documented Hoffa's extensive ties with organized crime figures. On numerous occasions, Kennedy listed names of racketeers on Hoffa's payroll and asked if Hoffa were aware of their past and if he intended to remove them from their positions. Hoffa promised to dismiss those tied to organized crime, but he never did. The panel also uncovered evidence of how Teamsters officials enriched themselves by extorting money from companies with which the Teamsters had con-

tracts in exchange for labor peace. Employers paid off the Teamsters officials by putting them on the payroll for doing nonexistent jobs. The committee further found that Hoffa personally profited from his connections with the Teamsters. Evidence of Hoffa's wrongdoing contributed greatly to convincing Congress of the need for legislation to prevent corruption in organized labor.

Although the hearings focused on the Teamsters, the McClellan Committee also probed the United Textile Workers, Bakery and Confectionery Workers, and some smaller unions. As a result of the panel's findings, the AFL-CIO expelled the Teamsters, the Bakery and Confectionery Workers, and the laundry workers union in December. At the insistence of the Republicans on the committee, the investigation included WALTER REUTHER and his United Auto Workers. Unlike Hoffa, however, Reuther's personal activities easily withstood congressional scrutiny.

While continuing its hearings, the committee issued an interim report on March 24, 1958. Describing Hoffa as a national menace running a "hoodlum empire," the panel recommended legislation that would regulate health and welfare funds and pension funds, ensure democratic procedures in unions, and curb the activities of middlemen in labor-management disputes. As a result, in April the Labor Subcommittee, chaired by Senator JOHN F. KENNEDY (D-Mass.), reported favorably on a bill, introduced in the previous session by Senator PAUL DOUGLAS (D-Ill.), that provided for public disclosure of information about pension and welfare funds. The Senate passed the measure without a dissenting vote in August.

Responding to pressure from Republicans, who demanded more comprehensive labor reform, McClellan, in June 1958, endorsed a second, broader labor reform measure, known as the Kennedy-Ives bill. The measure included: restrictions on the authority of national and international unions to place locals under trusteeship, conditions and standards for the election of union officers, a code of ethical practices, and amendments to the Taft-Hartley Act favored by building trades unions. The bill won the endorsement of the AFL-CIO, and the Senate passed it in June. The House, however, rejected it.

Early in 1959, Senators Kennedy and SAM ERVIN (D-N.C.), with the backing of the Democratic leadership, introduced a new measure containing the same relatively modest reform proposals as the Kennedy-Ives bill. Republicans wanted more thoroughgoing reform, but they lacked the numbers in the Senate to gain passage of a bill of their own. Therefore, they recommended amending the Kennedy-Ervin bill so as to address the abuses revealed by the McClellan Committee's investigation.

McClellan's influence with a large block of southern Democrats and his standing in the Senate as a whole made him the key figure in shaping the legislation that ultimately passed. When the debate over the Kennedy-Ervin bill began in April, McClellan demanded the elimination of the changes to the Taft-Hartley Act desired by the AFL-CIO. Kennedy refused, which prompted Ervin to withdraw his sponsorship and released a number of southern senators from their obligation to support the measure. McClellan made an impassioned speech on April 22, in which he introduced an amendment containing a "bill of rights" for union members that attempted to guarantee their rights to vote, speak, and resort to law. Kennedy and most liberals in the Senate opposed the measure as too great an interference in the internal affairs of the labor movement. Nevertheless, McClellan's amendment narrowly passed.

The addition of McClellan's amendment rendered the bill unacceptable to Kennedy. The AFL-CIO also withdrew its support of the legislation. Subsequently, and with McClellan's approval, the measure was modified to qualify the language in the equal rights section and to eliminate a provision granting the secretary of labor authority to seek injunctions in federal court against union officials. Southerners worried that those provisions might serve as precedent for future civil rights legislation. The Senate passed the final version on April 25 and sent it to the House.

On the other side of Capitol Hill, the House passed a measure sponsored by Representatives PHILIP LANDRUM (D-Ga.) and ROBERT GRIFFIN (R-Mich.) on August 15. The Landrum-Griffin bill contained several recommendations made by McClellan that the Senate had earlier rejected, including prohibitions against secondary boycotts

by unions and curbs on picketing. The measure also included provisions that prevented individuals with criminal records from holding positions of leadership in unions and increased fines and prison sentences for union officials convicted of misusing union funds. In September 1959, Congress passed the Landrum-Griffin Act, and President Eisenhower signed it into law.

McClellan consistently opposed civil rights legislation. In 1956, he signed the Southern Manifesto, which called on states to resist the Supreme Court's decision striking down segregation in public schools. He opposed civil rights legislation sponsored by the Eisenhower administration and passed by Congress in 1957 and 1960. During the confrontation over the desegregation of Central High School in Little Rock, Arkansas, McClellan attempted unsuccessfully to mediate between the state's governor, ORVAL FAUBUS, and President Eisenhower. When Eisenhower sent federal troops to enforce the order of a federal court, McClellan vehemently denounced the president's action.

During the 1960s, McClellan continued his opposition to civil rights legislation, voting against the Civil Rights Act of 1964 and the Voting Rights Act of 1965. He consistently supported tougher criminal penalties and broader powers for police; McClellan argued that decisions by the Supreme Court expanding the rights of those accused of crimes hampered law enforcement. While opposed to most of LYNDON JOHNSON's Great Society, McClellan supported the Elementary and Secondary Education Act (1965) and usually supported aid for the rural South. Although a fiscal conservative on most domestic issues, McClellan and Senator ROBERT KERR (D-Okla.) worked for more than two decades to obtain over $1 billion in federal funds for the Arkansas River Navigation Project. Throughout the 1960s, McClellan supported the war in Vietnam. He backed President RICHARD M. NIXON's policy of Vietnamization but opposed expanding the conflict into Laos and Cambodia. Throughout it all, he continued to conduct investigations. In 1963, he headed probes of organized crime (that included spectacular testimony by Joseph Valachi on the activities of La Cosa Nostra), the relationship between the Agriculture Department and Billie Sol Estes, a well-connected financier from

Texas, and the Defense Department's awarding of a contract for the production of the TFX aircraft. McClellan also presided over inquiries relating to missile procurement, race riots, and campus unrest. Upon the death of Senator ALLEN J. ELLENDER (D-La.), the chair of the Appropriations Committee, in 1972, McClellan gave up his seat on the Government Operations Committee to become chair of the Appropriations Committee. He held that position until he died in Little Rock on November 27, 1977.

—TLH

McCloy, John J(ay)

(1895–1989)   *chairman of the board, Chase National Bank; presidential adviser*

The son of a claims officer for the Penn Mutual Life Insurance Company, John McCloy was born in Philadelphia, Pennsylvania, on March 31, 1895. Just before McCloy's sixth birthday, his father died, after which the child was raised by his mother, who devoted herself to the advancement of her sole surviving child. Her hairdressing business put her in touch with wealthy and influential people, and she made sure her son benefited from those contacts. McCloy attended Peddie School in Hightstown, New Jersey, and graduated from Amherst College in 1916. In the summers of 1915 and 1916, he attended the reserve officers' training camp in Plattsburg, New York, and earned a commission as a second lieutenant in the army reserve. He entered Harvard Law School in the fall of 1916 but left after his first year to enlist in the U.S. Army. After seeing limited action in France during World War I as a provisional second lieutenant in a field artillery brigade, he returned to Harvard in 1919 and received his law degree in 1921. Upon graduating from law school, he went to New York to take a position with the prestigious firm of Cadwalader, Wickersham, and Taft. In 1924, McCloy moved to Cravath, Henderson & de Gersdorff. His work took him to Europe, where he worked on several postwar reconstruction projects. After returning to the United States, he represented Schechter Poultry in *Schechter Poultry Corporation v. United States* (1935), in which the Supreme Court declared the National Industrial Recovery Act unconstitutional.

Throughout the 1930s, McCloy was involved in an effort to gain compensation for Bethlehem Steel for an explosion that took place in 1916 at a munitions depot on Black Tom Island in New York Harbor. By demonstrating that the explosion was the work of saboteurs operating on orders from the German government, he won a $50 million award for his clients in 1939.

His experience with the Black Tom case, his concern about Nazi expansionism, and his friendship with Secretary of War Henry Stimson led to McCloy's appointment as a consultant to Army Intelligence in 1940. He became assistant secretary of war in 1941. In that capacity, he was involved in some of the major policy decisions made both during the lead-up to America's entry into the war and during the war itself. He was a primary lobbyist for lend-lease legislation. Within the councils of the administration, McCloy supported the internment of Japanese Americans and coordinated the development of the program. Although he regarded the decision to intern Japanese Americans as inevitable and necessary, he did make efforts to moderate the conditions of the internees. Another important decision in which McCloy was involved was the decision not to bomb Auschwitz or the railheads servicing the concentration camp; he advised against it. He participated in the creation of the Office of Strategic Services, the forerunner of the Central Intelligence Agency, and was also involved in the construction of the Pentagon, the establishment of the United Nations, and the planning for the Dumbarton Oaks Conference. In the later stages of the war, one of his assignments was the administration of occupied areas. McCloy and Stimson successfully opposed the plan, advanced by Secretary of the Treasury Henry Morgenthau, to strip Germany of its industrial capacity. In the debate over whether to use the atomic bomb on Japan, McCloy argued for issuing a warning before the bomb was used.

In January 1946, McCloy joined the law firm of Milbank, Tweed, Hope & Hadley, as a name partner. Nevertheless, he continued to heed the call to public service. He became president of the International Bank for Reconstruction and Development (later the World Bank) in February 1947. McCloy energetically lobbied Congress to approve the Marshall Plan. In June 1949, he replaced General LUCIUS CLAY as military governor of Germany. Two months later, when the three Western zones of occupation were combined to form the Federal Republic of Germany, McCloy became U.S. high commissioner for Germany. He worked to restore the German economy and supervised the transition of West Germany from an occupied zone to a sovereign state. Under McCloy, the role of the United States changed from occupier to partner. Indeed, McCloy advocated transferring authority to the German government at a more rapid rate than either his superiors in Washington or the British, French, or Soviet governments approved. The ever pragmatic McCloy preferred the restoration of Germany to its punishment. His administration employed the services of notorious former Nazi officials, including Klaus Barbie and Franz Six. Limited though it was, denazification was more extensive in the American zone than it was in those of the British or French. Even that modest commitment yielded to other considerations as the cold war emerged and the West worried about Soviet expansion and espionage. Given those concerns, the high commissioner cared less about excluding Nazis than he did about making Germany strong enough to resist the Soviets. McCloy stirred up controversy when he reduced the sentences of dozens of ex-Nazis convicted at the Nuremberg War Crime Trials, including Alfred Krupp, who had been convicted for using slave labor in his family's armament factories. McCloy also pushed for European integration. After serving as high commissioner for three years, he left Germany in 1952.

Eisenhower considered McCloy for secretary of state, a position that went to JOHN FOSTER DULLES. In January 1953, McCloy became chairman of Chase National Bank and arranged the merger with the Bank of Manhattan that created Chase Manhattan Bank. If Chase were to take over the Bank of Manhattan, it would have required the approval of every stockholder in the Bank of Manhattan. McCloy avoided this difficulty by having the smaller Bank of Manhattan absorb Chase. The merger took place in March 1955, and McCloy became chairman of what was the second largest commercial bank in the United States. He aggressively moved the bank into foreign markets.

Beyond his work at Chase Manhattan, McCloy influenced policy through membership in a host of elite institutions. He served on the board of directors of several corporations, including the United Fruit Company, the American Telephone and Telegraph Company, the Dreyfus Corporation, Westinghouse Electric Corporation, and Allied Chemical Corporation. In addition, he cofounded the American Council on Germany and chaired both the Council on Foreign Relations and the Ford Foundation (1953–70). As chair of the Council on Foreign Relations, McCloy picked a professor of government at Harvard named HENRY KISSINGER to head a study of the impact of nuclear weapons on foreign policy. Such behind-the-scenes influence led the journalist RICHARD ROVERE to call McCloy the "chairman of the establishment." In 1956 and 1957, McCloy went to Egypt as special financial adviser on the Suez Crisis to Dag Hammarskjöld, the secretary-general of the United Nations. McCloy also served as a special adviser on disarmament to President Eisenhower.

McCloy retired from Chase Manhattan in December 1960 and returned to Millbank, Tweed. He represented the major oil companies and had better access to some Middle Eastern governments than did the State Department. Throughout the decade of the 1960s, he accepted high-level diplomatic assignments for the Kennedy and Johnson administrations. An adviser to Kennedy on disarmament, he helped draft the legislation creating the U.S. Arms Control and Disarmament Agency in 1961. During the Cuban Missile Crisis in 1962, Kennedy named McCloy to head a team that worked out the details for the withdrawal of Soviet missiles from Cuba. LYNDON JOHNSON called on McCloy to serve on the Warren Commission, appointed to investigate the assassination of JOHN F. KENNEDY. McCloy also served as President Johnson's special envoy to the mutual defense talks between the United States, Great Britain, and West Germany in 1966.

Although he had reservations about American policy in Vietnam, McCloy, when asked, supported Johnson's policy. In 1968, McCloy became a member of the Senior Advisory Group on Vietnam, convened by Johnson to consider the military's request for more than 200,000 additional troops in Vietnam.

Despite his dissatisfaction with the conduct of the war, he did not press for a dramatic change. Ultimately, though, the group, dubbed "the Wise Men" by the press, reported to Johnson that the war could not be won without unacceptable risks and unacceptable costs; the time had come to disengage.

In the 1970s, President James E. Carter sought McCloy's advice on various matters relating to foreign policy, but, in general, the elder statesman had little influence on Carter or his administration. On at least one occasion, however, he did prevail. When the United States refused to give the exiled shah of Iran permission to enter the United States, McCloy vigorously and successfully lobbied the Carter administration to admit the fatally ill former ruler. The decision prompted angry radicals in Iran to take over the U.S. embassy. McCloy received more respectful treatment from Carter's successor, Ronald W. Reagan. In his last years, McCloy maintained an office in New York and resided in Stamford, Connecticut, where he died on March 11, 1989.

—MSM

McCone, John A(lex)

(1902–1991) *director, Atomic Energy Commission*
Born into a prosperous family in San Francisco, California, on January 4, 1902, McCone attended public schools and graduated from the University of California at Berkeley in 1922. After graduating from college, he went to work as a riveter and boilermaker for the Llewellyn Iron Works, where he rose to become construction manager in the late 1920s. Llewellyn merged with the Consolidated Steel Corporation in 1929, and McCone became executive vice president and director of Consolidated in 1933. McCone left Consolidated in 1937 and joined with a college classmate, Stephen Bechtel, to form their own engineering firm, Bechtel-McCone. The successful business made McCone a millionaire within a decade. During World War II, Bechtel-McCone made military aircraft; the company also became involved in shipbuilding. As head of the California Shipbuilding Corporation during World War II, McCone directed construction of almost 500 ships. After the war, McCone left the partnership and became

president and sole proprietor of the Joshua Hendy Iron Works (later the Joshua Hendy Corporation), a shipping firm in Los Angeles.

In 1947, Truman appointed McCone to the Air Policy Commission, formed to consider the role of air power in American defense policy. The commission recommended the creation of an independent air force. McCone served as a special deputy to Secretary of Defense James V. Forrestal in 1948, after which he returned to private business. In June 1950, McCone became undersecretary of the air force. He fought for a larger share of the defense budget for the air force and was assigned responsibility for accelerating the production of war planes. McCone strenuously advocated the development of guided missiles and urged President HARRY TRUMAN to embark on a program, under a single director, to develop these weapons. Truman rejected the proposal. McCone again returned to private business in 1951.

In June 1958, President Eisenhower nominated McCone to succeed LEWIS STRAUSS as head of the Atomic Energy Commission (AEC). Confirmed the following month, McCone implemented the "Atoms for Peace" program, which promoted civilian uses of nuclear power. McCone initially opposed a nuclear test ban; he believed that the United States needed more time for research. By 1959, however, he supported the president's one-year moratorium on testing. That year, McCone attended talks with the Soviets in Geneva on controlling nuclear energy. The talks stalled over the issue of on-site inspections and conditions for underground testing.

McCone supported the administration's efforts to expand international research on the peaceful uses of atomic energy. These included a plan to disseminate information on nuclear reactors to members of the North Atlantic Treaty Organization. In 1958 he signed a treaty between the United States and West Germany, France, Italy, Belgium, Luxembourg, and the Netherlands in which the United States provided a loan of $135 million and a 20-year supply of uranium to fuel allied reactors. The agreement also called for a joint commitment of $100 million for a combined American-European research effort. In 1959, McCone helped formulate a pact with the Soviet

Union establishing a joint U.S.–USSR program of nuclear research that included the exchange of scientists and research data.

During the last half of the decade, the AEC came under criticism for suppressing information on radioactive fallout. With an eye on the presidential contest in 1960, Senator HUBERT H. HUMPHREY (D-Minn.), in March 1959, charged that the agency had been "playing down the dangers of radioactive fallout as it pursued its weapons program." He asserted that data had been withheld because it cast doubt on government statements about the danger of atomic weapons tests. The senator charged that "the [AEC], . . . with its important and primary interest in the field of atomic weapons and power, [was] not the best agency to conduct research on fallout and its effects on human health and heredity." McCone denied that the AEC had suppressed information; he did, however, call on the National Academy of Sciences to arrange a governmentwide review of the issue. In October 1960, the AEC reduced the maximum permissible radioactive dosage for workers in nuclear plants.

A lifelong Republican, McCone resigned his post with the AEC in January 1961. In the aftermath of the Bay of Pigs, however, President JOHN F. KENNEDY appointed McCone to head the Central Intelligence Agency (CIA). As director, McCone helped restore morale and placed greater emphasis on intelligence-gathering functions. He served on the Executive Committee, a group of top advisers assembled to advise the president during the Cuban Missile Crisis, and opposed the American-backed coup against Ngo Dinh Diem in 1963. McCone clashed with President LYNDON B. JOHNSON over American policy in Vietnam. His disagreements with Johnson over policy and Johnson's failure to support McCone's efforts to centralize intelligence operations led McCone to resign in April 1965.

McCone went back to managing the Joshua Hendy Corporation, which he sold in 1969. He also served as a director of International Telephone and Telegraph Corporation. After the race riot in Watts in 1965, Governor EDMUND G. BROWN, SR., named McCone to chair a commission appointed to study the causes of the riots. McCone died at his home in Pebble Beach, California, on February 14, 1991.

—MSM

McCormack, John W(illiam)
(1891–1980) *U.S. congressman, House majority leader, House minority whip*

The son of a stonemason, McCormack was born in Boston, Massachusetts, on December 21, 1891. He grew up in South Boston and attended public schools until the age of 13, when he left to support his family after the death of his father. After working as a newsboy and an errand boy for a brokerage house, he took a job as an office boy in a law firm. While working for the law firm, he studied law and passed the bar examination in 1913. McCormack began to practice law in South Boston and showed a talent for the profession. Politics, however, soon attracted him. In 1917, he won election as a delegate to the Massachusetts Constitutional Convention, which convened that year. He resigned to enlist as a private in the army and served stateside. He won election to the Massachusetts House of Representatives as a Democrat in 1919, serving three consecutive one-year terms beginning in 1920. He won election to the state senate in 1923 and served as leader of the Democratic minority in 1925 and 1926. In the latter year, he tried to win a seat in the U.S. House of Representatives and mounted an unsuccessful campaign for the Democratic nomination against a veteran incumbent, Rep. James A. Gallivan (D-Mass.). When Gallivan died in 1928, McCormack won a special election to fill the seat, which he held until his retirement in 1971.

In the House, McCormack quickly attracted the attention of the minority leader, John Nance Garner (D-Tex.), with his diligence and unswerving obedience. When Garner became speaker in 1931, he appointed the relatively junior McCormack to the Ways and Means Committee as a reward for his loyalty. McCormack's reputation for protecting the interests of his party led to his appointment as chair of the Special Committee on Un-American Activities in 1934. Although the committee was formed primarily to look into Nazi and anti-Semitic organizations, McCormack focused the committee's attention on the Communist Party. In 1937, McCormack provided crucial support for SAM RAYBURN's (D-Tex.) successful bid to become majority leader. Three years later, Rayburn became speaker of the House, and McCormack succeeded Rayburn as majority leader.

For the next 22 years, McCormack served as Rayburn's lieutenant. Known for his highly partisan and flamboyant debating style, McCormack often antagonized colleagues with his sarcasm. Dealing with his fellow members on an individual basis, however, he was less abrasive. Within the Democratic caucus, he developed a reputation as a compromiser who could mediate between liberal northerners and conservative southerners.

Throughout the 1930s and 1940s, McCormack consistently supported the domestic legislative agenda of the Roosevelt and Truman administrations. He played a role in drafting the Social Security Act of 1935 and supported Franklin D. Roosevelt's plan to pack the Supreme Court. In foreign policy, he was an isolationist until the outbreak of World War II in Europe, at which point he shifted to internationalism and supported Roosevelt's cautious moves toward American intervention. After Truman became president, McCormack lined up votes for the Employment Act of 1946 and unsuccessfully attempted to block the congressional override of Truman's veto of the Taft-Hartley Act. Always an aggressive opponent of communism, McCormack strongly supported resistance to communist expansion after the war. He backed aid to Greece and Turkey in 1947, the Marshall Plan, and the decision to send American forces to Korea. When the Republicans won both houses in the elections of 1946, McCormack became minority whip. With the return of the Democrats to power in 1949, he again became majority leader.

As chair of the Democratic platform committee in 1952, McCormack preached the importance of party unity and helped reach a compromise between southern and northern delegates on the civil rights plank. Similarly, after Eisenhower won election to the presidency, McCormack supported Rayburn's policy of moderate opposition to the policies of the Eisenhower administration during the 1950s. At the same time, McCormack provided a hectoring, partisan voice for the Democratic opposition. Despite his intense partisanship and his scolding rhetoric, McCormack consistently demonstrated a willingness to compromise. Democratic representatives of either a more intellectual or a more ideologically liberal bent regarded McCormack as a machine politician with little concern for principles. McCor-

mack, in turn, regarded such colleagues as idealists or ideologues, who, relying on their formal educations, took positions based on ideas or theories but had no grasp of political reality.

From 1953 to 1955, when Republicans controlled the House, McCormack once again assumed the role of minority whip. In 1953, he opposed reduction in new public housing units passed by the Republican-controlled Congress. With the return of the Democrats to majority status after the elections of 1954, McCormack became majority leader for the third time. In 1955, he backed an unsuccessful Democratic effort to provide individual taxpayers with an income tax credit of $20. In 1959, McCormack and Rayburn successfully introduced a bill to extend the period of eligibility for unemployment compensation by three months. The following year, McCormack used a parliamentary maneuver to bring to the floor a bill providing for area redevelopment. Although Congress passed the measure, Eisenhower vetoed it.

As a devout Catholic with close ties to the church hierarchy, McCormack was fiercely anticommunist. He backed the repressive Communist Control Act of 1954, which denied legal standing to the Communist Party. That same year, he questioned the adequacy of the administration's defense budget. McCormack was a consistent critic of the "New Look," which cut military budgets and relied on air power, technology, and the nuclear deterrent. He did not always oppose Eisenhower on defense issues. In 1955, he urged an "overwhelming" vote in favor of the Formosa Resolution, requested by President Eisenhower, that authorized the president to use armed force "if in his judgment it became necessary" to defend Formosa, the Pescadores, and "closely related localities." In that situation, McCormack thought it important to display unity. Some Democrats, however, objected that the resolution gave the president excessively broad authority. McCormack argued that the "calculated risks" entailed in passing the resolution were less than those that resulted from inaction. In the late 1950s, he repeatedly called for an increase in spending on defense.

Although both were Irish Catholics from the Bay State, McCormack and Senator JOHN F. KENNEDY (D-Mass.) did not enjoy a cordial relationship. Separated by almost a generation, as well as by disparities of wealth and education, McCormack repeatedly clashed with his younger colleague. The two fought a number of battles over control of the Democratic Party in Massachusetts. McCormack kept his distance from Kennedy's unsuccessful attempt to capture the vice presidential nomination in 1956. Nevertheless, McCormack chaired the pro-Kennedy Massachusetts delegation to the Democratic convention in 1960. At the convention, he helped overcome opposition to Kennedy's choice of Lyndon Johnson (D-Tex.), the majority leader in the Senate, as his running mate. McCormack campaigned for Kennedy in the general election.

After Kennedy became president, McCormack almost always supported his legislative programs. Still relations between the two remained frosty. In 1961, McCormack successfully opposed Kennedy's proposal for federal aid to education because it did not provide support to parochial schools. The following year, McCormack's nephew, Edward J. McCormack, Jr., and Edward Kennedy, the president's youngest brother, waged a bitter contest in the Democratic primary for a seat in the U.S. Senate from Massachusetts. Kennedy won the primary and the general election. After Rayburn's death in January 1962, McCormack became Speaker. Although he dutifully attempted to line up support for Kennedy's domestic agenda, he had little success getting southern Democrats to back the president's proposals. After Kennedy was assassinated and Johnson assumed the presidency, McCormack became first in line to succeed to the presidency under the Presidential Succession Act of 1947. McCormack remained first in line until the swearing-in of Hubert Humphrey on January 20, 1965. That caused many in Congress to reconsider the issue of succession. Some in Congress believed that he should have resigned the speakership because of his advanced age. In 1965, Congress passed a constitutional amendment providing for the appointment of a vice president in the event of a vacancy. The states ratified the Twenty-fifth Amendment in 1967.

After Johnson became president, McCormack forged a good working relationship with him and supported Johnson's Great Society. During the 1960s, McCormack found his leadership under increasing attack. Younger liberal Democrats criticized him for his defense of the seniority system and his deference to senior southern Democrats; as the decade wore on, they objected to his support of the war in Vietnam. At the start of the new Congress in 1969, Morris Udall (D-Ariz.) challenged him for the speakership. McCormack comfortably defeated Udall, but his support of President Richard M. Nixon's policies in Vietnam and his continuing resistance to institutional change in the House further alienated younger and liberal Democrats. Further, in 1969, *Life* magazine reported that McCormack's administrative assistant, Martin Sweig, and one of McCormack's friends, Nathan Voloshen, had engaged in influence peddling. In May 1970, a federal grand jury indicted them and cleared McCormack of any wrongdoing, after which the Speaker, who earlier that year had survived a no-confidence vote in the Democratic caucus, announced that he would not seek reelection. Not long after his departure from the House, McCormack returned to Boston, where he lived in quiet retirement until his death in Dedham, Massachusetts, on November 22, 1980.

—MSM

McDonald, David J(ohn)

(1902–1979) *president, United Steelworkers of America*

The son of a skilled Irish Catholic steelworker, McDonald was born in Pittsburgh, Pennsylvania, on November 22, 1902. At the age of 16, he began working for U.S. Steel, but he went to high school in the evenings and graduated in 1919, after which he went to work as a typist for Wheeling Steel. In 1923, he became the personal secretary to Philip Murray, a vice president of the United Mine Workers. For most of the next three decades, McDonald's career followed Murray's. McDonald worked as Murray's aide during the bitter strikes in the Appalachian coalfields in the 1920s, in the successful organizing drives of the early New Deal era, and in the formation of the Congress of Industrial Organizations (CIO). In 1936, the president of the CIO, John L. Lewis, named Murray to head an organizing drive in the steel industry, and Murray appointed McDonald secretary-treasurer of the

Steel Workers Organizing Committee (SWOC). When Murray became president of the CIO in 1940, McDonald assumed more of the day-to-day duties of running the SWOC, which became the United Steelworkers of America (USWA) in 1942. Murray was the new organization's president and McDonald its secretary-treasurer. After World War II, McDonald advocated purging leftists from the USWA and the CIO. Many had come to regard McDonald as Murray's heir apparent, but, by the early 1950s, McDonald's relations with his mentor had become strained. Murray criticized McDonald's expensive tastes and flamboyant lifestyle; he may also have feared that his onetime protégé was plotting to oust him. At the USWA convention in 1952, Murray managed to get the organization to strip the position of secretary-treasurer of much of its power. When Murray died in late 1952, however, McDonald swiftly consolidated his position, and the executive board named him interim president of the USWA, which by then had 1 million members. The following year, McDonald ran unopposed for the presidency.

McDonald preferred a conciliatory approach to labor-management relations and advocated what he called a "mutual trusteeship" for the steel industry. In 1953, almost immediately after winning the election for the presidency, he conducted a two-week tour of steel plants with BENJAMIN FAIRLESS, chief executive officer of the U.S. Steel Corporation. In 1953 and 1954, the USWA won wage increases and a noncontributory pension plan. Employers in the steel industry, however, increasingly resisted wage demands by the USWA, and that led to two major strikes in the 1950s. Secretary of the Treasury GEORGE HUMPHREY stepped in to settle a work stoppage in 1956. Humphrey convinced the industry to give the steelworkers a generous economic package, which it immediately passed on to buyers in the form of higher prices. When negotiations for a new contract opened in 1959, McDonald insisted that high profits and productivity in the steel industry justified a substantial increase in wages without price increases. At that time, however, the most important issue was the loss of jobs to automation. The USWA sought to maintain control over work rules in the plants in order to safeguard jobs (employment in steel had dropped from 540,000 to 461,000 during the preceding decade). On the other side, the steel industry wanted the freedom to introduce new methods of production. The impasse resulted in a strike, which began in July and shut down 85 percent of the country's steel production capacity. After 116 days, the president invoked the emergency provisions of the Taft-Hartley Act and ordered the Justice Department to seek an 80-day injunction to end the strike. Industry leaders expected this "cooling-off" period to induce the workers to approve management's last offer. When polls indicated that they would reject it and resume the strike, Vice President RICHARD NIXON personally intervened to obtain a settlement favoring the union's position.

With the merger of the AFL and CIO in 1955, McDonald became a vice president of the combined organization and a member of its executive board. Even as he rose through the ranks of labor, he faced internal opposition within the USWA. In 1955, a coalition of district directors unsuccessfully opposed his candidate for vice president of the union. The next year, McDonald pushed through a two-dollar-a-month increase in dues that inspired a Dues Protest Movement among the rank and file. The leader of that protest, Donald Rarick, a little-known grievance committeeman, ran against McDonald in 1957 and won 35 percent of the vote in the first contested election in the USWA's history. Rarick's strong showing, despite McDonald's control of the union's treasury and its 1,000-strong staff (both of which he used to his advantage in the election), indicated the existence of considerable dissatisfaction with McDonald.

As Democrats jockeyed for the presidential nomination in 1960, McDonald became an early and enthusiastic backer of Senator JOHN F. KENNEDY (D-Mass.), even though the senator from Massachusetts refused to back a USWA proposal for a 32-hour workweek that was intended to preserve jobs in the industry. Unlike others in the AFL-CIO leadership, McDonald supported Senator LYNDON B. JOHNSON (D-Tex.) for the vice presidential nomination. At the Democratic National Convention, after Kennedy announced that he had selected Johnson as his running mate, McDonald worked to overcome labor's opposition to Johnson.

Early in Kennedy's presidency, McDonald cooperated with the administration to coordinate the USWA's bargaining strategy with the government's economic policy. Fearing inflation, the administration urged that all collective bargaining settlements be limited to the annual increase in productivity. Kennedy specifically urged the USWA and the steel industry to reach an accord within the administration's guidelines. Ignoring opposition from within his wage policy committee, McDonald reached an agreement with the industry in March 1962. The contract called for an increase of 10 cents an hour in fringe benefits but no across-the-board wage increase. The agreement fell well within the administration's guidelines but was the first USWA contract since 1942 that did not contain an increase in wages. The steel companies raised prices anyway, which resulted in a confrontation between Kennedy and U.S. Steel that ultimately led the companies to roll back the price increase. In June 1963, McDonald negotiated another contract with no across-the-board wage increase. The modest gains proved unpopular with many workers, especially in light of McDonald's lavish lifestyle. Moreover, some within the union's leadership resented the fact that McDonald negotiated the settlement in secret through a labor-management "Human Relations Committee." In 1965, the secretary-treasurer of the USWA, I. W. Abel, defeated McDonald for the union presidency in a close race.

After losing the presidency of the USWA, McDonald retired to Palm Springs, California, and published an autobiography, *Union Man*, in 1969. He died of cancer in Palms Springs on August 8, 1979.

—MSM

McElroy, Neil H(olsler)

(1904–1972) *secretary of defense*

Neil McElroy was born in Berea, Ohio, on October 30, 1904. After graduating from Harvard University in 1925, he began a long career with Procter & Gamble, a soap-manufacturing concern based in Cincinnati. Starting as a door-to-door salesman, he became director of the promotions department in 1929, vice president and general manager in 1946, and president in 1948. By that time, Procter & Gamble had the largest advertising budget of any company in the world. Under McElroy's director-

ship, company profits expanded from $28.6 million in 1949 to $59.3 million in 1956.

McElroy chaired the White House Conference on Education in 1955 and 1956. When, in 1957, CHARLES E. WILSON informed President DWIGHT D. EISENHOWER of his intention to resign as secretary of defense, Eisenhower chose McElroy to replace Wilson. McElroy agreed to accept the post on the condition that he would take a leave of absence rather than resign from Procter & Gamble. In order to avoid any conflict of interest, Procter & Gamble would drop the small number of defense contracts it held. McElroy also stipulated that he would serve only two years. The president agreed to both conditions, and McElroy was sworn in on October 9.

McElroy entered the Pentagon in the midst of controversy. In August 1957, the Soviet Union had launched the world's first intercontinental ballistic missile (ICBM). Two months later, it placed into orbit *Sputnik*, the world's first artificial satellite. These events shook public confidence in America's defenses and initiated a debate on military organization and weapons development programs. A number of powerful senators, among them STUART SYMINGTON (D-Mo.), HENRY JACKSON (D-Wash.), and LYNDON B. JOHNSON (D-Tex.), called for more rapid production of missiles. In response, McElroy defended Eisenhower's plan for doing everything possible to increase production within the guidelines of the existing defense budget.

Shortly after the launch of *Sputnik*, Eisenhower authorized McElroy to seek a supplemental appropriation of $1.26 billion for the remainder of fiscal year 1958. The additional money was to accelerate existing programs to develop intermediate range ballistic missiles (IRBM) and ICBMs, protect the strategic bomber force, improve detection devices, and speed up development of an antimissile missile. Eisenhower and McElroy privately acknowledged that two-thirds of the supplementary funding served "more to stabilize public opinion than to meet the real need for acceleration." McElroy consolidated control of all military missile programs in a new agency that reported directly to him. He emphasized the development of IRBMs, which the United States had in advanced stages of testing, and argued that with proper deployment overseas they would be as effective as Soviet ICBMs. Waiving final tests, he ordered the air force's Thor and army's Jupiter IRBMs into production, with projected deployment in the United Kingdom by the end of 1958 and in Europe soon after. McElroy also ordered accelerated development of the navy's Polaris IRBM and the Minuteman ICBM, the latter of which was scheduled to become operational in the early 1960s.

Although he consistently attempted to control defense spending, Eisenhower remained conscious of the danger of placing economy above preparedness. In the aftermath of *Sputnik*, Eisenhower and McElroy resisted pressure from Democratic critics to spend more money on defense and the development of missiles. They adjusted some priorities and added modest sums to defense expenditures, but they resisted massive increases in spending on defense. In November 1957, McElroy testified before the Senate Preparedness Subcommittee. He admitted that the USSR was "obviously" ahead of the United States in missiles that could put a satellite into orbit, but he refused to agree that the Soviets led in long-range missiles. Several months later, McElroy argued against a crash program for missile development. He maintained that "a rather frantic . . . program would be of dubious effectiveness" and stated that there was "little we can do to make a significant change in the date by which we can achieve the first operational intercontinental ballistic missile."

McElroy also rebutted Symington's allegation that the Soviet Union had surpassed the United States in total military strength and argued that the United States did not need a total reorganization of its defense plans. At an American Legion Convention in September, he said "the spending of more tax dollars would, at this time, be an unwarranted risk of your money." "There is a point," he declared, "beyond which granting huge sums on untried weapons would be foolhardy—would, in fact, endanger [U.S.] economic and even . . . military security."

When Eisenhower proposed a plan for the reorganization of the Defense Department in 1958, McElroy played a major role in defending the plan to Congress and the public. Submitted in the spring, the legislation proposed to consolidate operational units of the U.S. armed forces under unified commands reporting directly to the secretary of defense. Further, under its provisions, most defense funding would be appropriated to the Defense Department, rather than the individual services. The measure would also have created a central authority to oversee all research and development in the Pentagon. The bill that emerged from Congress gave Eisenhower most of what he wanted. However, Congress added a provision that gave the service secretaries and chiefs of staff the right to go, on their own initiative, to Congress with "any recommendations relating to the Department of Defense they might deem proper." Eisenhower called it "legalized insubordination" but in the end accepted it as a necessary compromise and signed the Defense Reorganization Act into law on August 6. The president gave McElroy considerable credit for its passage.

McElroy strongly supported military assistance and sought to mobilize congressional and public support for the program. "Military assistance," he said, "is to the defense of our Country as fire prevention is to fire fighting. You can have the best, most modern sprinkling system in our factory, but it will be useless if you don't take steps to prevents fires from getting out of control before they reach your plant." Despite his efforts, congressional opposition limited expenditures for military aid.

As he intended, McElroy remained at the Defense Department only two years. He left in December 1959 and returned to Procter & Gamble as chairman of the board. During the next decade, McElroy also served as director of the General Electric Company, the Chrysler Corporation, and the Equitable Life Insurance Company. He stepped down as chairman of the board at Procter & Gamble in October 1971 and became chairman of the company's executive committee. McElroy died of cancer in Cincinnati, Ohio, on November 30, 1972.

—MSM

McKay, Douglas
(1893–1959) *secretary of the interior*

The son of a carpenter, Douglas McKay was born in Portland, Oregon, on June 24, 1893. While in high school, he delivered papers and worked as a meat-cutter. He left high school without receiving a diploma and worked as an office boy for two years before entering Oregon State College, from which he graduated in 1917. He enlisted as an officer in the army during World War I and served in Europe, where he was wounded. After his return to the United States, he began working as an insurance salesman in 1923 and then sold cars until 1927, when he opened his own auto agency. McKay entered politics as a Republican and won election as mayor of Salem in 1932. He was elected to the Oregon state senate in 1934 and held that office until 1948 except for a brief period from 1942 to 1943, during which he served in the army.

McKay won a three-way race for governor in 1948. As governor, he was a fiscal conservative who opposed the expansion of federal authority and advocated state and local responsibility. In general, he favored private over public development of natural resources, but he supported city-owned water projects. He won reelection in 1950.

Although identified with the conservative wing of the Republican Party, McKay doubted that the leader of that wing, Senator ROBERT A. TAFT (R-Ohio), could win the presidency in 1952. McKay therefore became an early supporter of General DWIGHT D. EISENHOWER for the nomination. The governor of Oregon first came to Eisenhower's attention during the Republican National Convention of 1952, when he sent a telegram to the National Committee urging the seating of a pro-Eisenhower delegation from Texas. In January 1953, Eisenhower appointed him secretary of the interior. The president wanted a westerner for the job because of the importance of conservation and the development of water power to that area. At the same time, the president wanted someone who was not from a state involved in a dispute over water rights to the Colorado River or another disputed river that flowed across state lines. Eisenhower also wanted an individual who shared his desires to balance the budget and to limit the federal government's role in the development of natural resources. McKay fit those criteria.

As secretary of the interior, McKay generally favored reversing the trend toward the nationalization of hydroelectric power but did not support dismantling the Tennessee Valley Authority. His approach mirrored Eisenhower's vision, in which the federal government would cooperate with state governments, local public groups, and private enterprise in building facilities. In July 1953, McKay presented a draft statement of the new administration's power policy. The paper reversed the Truman administration's emphasis on federal development of power and placed responsibility on local communities for supplying power needs. The Interior Department would build plants only if "economically justified and feasible" and if the project was too large to be financed privately or by local government. Even before presenting this proposal, McKay announced that the Interior Department would withdraw the Truman administration's objection to the Federal Power Commission's granting a license to the Idaho Power Company to build the Oxbow Dam. This effectively blocked plans for a large, federally built dam at Hell's Canyon in Idaho. After two years of hearings, the Federal Power Commission granted the Idaho Power Company the license in August 1955.

His positions and his combative personality made McKay one of the most controversial figures in Eisenhower's cabinet. McKay supported the Submerged Lands Act of 1953, which redeemed Eisenhower's campaign pledge to give control of oil-rich tidelands to the states. Critics called the secretary "give-away McKay."

His critics also alleged that McKay favored business interests and Republicans over Democrats. In April 1953, McKay announced that Albert M. Day, director of the Wildlife Service since 1946, would be replaced by John L. Farley, former head of the California Fish and Game Commission, who then worked for a paper-manufacturing firm. The secretary's critics accused McKay of preferring Farley because of his ties to Alaska salmon packers and commercial hunters. That same month, McKay announced the resignation of a career civil servant, Marion Clawson, as director of the Bureau of Land Management. McKay said he would appoint Clawson's successor and reinstate the former director in a lower-paying job. Clawson denied he had resigned and asked McKay to explain his dismissal. The secretary then charged him with insubordination and denied him the other position. Soon afterward, McKay nominated Tom Lyon to replace John J. Forbes as director of the Bureau of Mines. United Mine Workers President JOHN L. LEWIS protested the nomination on the grounds that Lyon advocated that the states rather than the federal government administer the Mine Safety Act. Subsequent hearings revealed that Lyon held a pension from the Anaconda Copper Co. that could be revoked at their displeasure. The nomination was withdrawn in June 1953. By the summer, Eisenhower insisted that all high-ranking appointments in the Interior Department be given his personal scrutiny.

McKay's most important achievement was the series of improvements he made to the national park system. Early in 1954, Eisenhower sent a memo to the secretary voicing his concern about the deterioration of the parks. McKay thereafter developed a program of improvements known as "Mission 66," a 10-year plan designed to preserve and improve parks as well as to prepare them to accommodate an expected 80 million visitors in 1966. The secretary also succeeded in protecting park lands, notably blocking a possible transfer of lands in the Wichita Wildlife Refuge for use by the army. Further, the department instituted exacting guidelines for oil and gas leasing in wildlife areas and added nine new wildlife reserves. McKay supervised the addition of 400,000 acres to the parks from 1953 to 1956.

McKay also implemented plans that attempted to further the integration of Native Americans into American society. The so-called termination policy, developed during the Truman administration, proposed to end federal relations with the tribes at the earliest possible time and attempted to promote assimilation. While McKay was secretary, the Department of Interior terminated federal supervision over six Indian groups. The policy encountered resistance from Indian tribes. In addition to the termination policy, the federal government attempted to encourage voluntary relocation from reservations to cities. This intended to ease economic pressures on reservations and to promote integration. Opposition to these policies led the Eisenhower administration to reverse itself in 1958.

In March 1956, McKay resigned to challenge Senator WAYNE MORSE's (D-Oreg.) bid for reelection. Although he waged a vigorous campaign,

McKay suffered the first defeat of his political career. Subsequently, in 1957, McKay became chair of the International Joint Commission, which dealt with boundary water problems between the United States and Canada. He died in Salem, Oregon, on July 22, 1959.

—MSM

McKeldin, Theodore Roosevelt
(1900–1974) *governor of Maryland, mayor of Baltimore*

The son of a Scotch-Irish immigrant stonemason who later became a policeman, McKeldin was born in Baltimore, Maryland, on November 20, 1900. In a working class family of 11 children, money was scarce, and McKeldin left school at the age of 14 to help support the family. While working as an office boy for Alexander Brown & Sons and then for a bank, he attended night school. After earning the equivalent of a high school diploma, he attended night classes at the University of Maryland Law School and earned his LL.B. in 1925. McKeldin practiced law and began his political career in 1927, when he worked for the mayoral campaign of William F. Broening, a prominent Republican. When Broening won the election, he appointed McKeldin to be his executive secretary. McKeldin returned to his private law practice in 1931 but remained active in Republican politics. He ran unsuccessfully for mayor of Baltimore in 1939. Three years later, he was the Republican nominee for governor of Maryland, but lost to the Democratic incumbent, Herbert R. O'Connor. In 1943, after a vigorous door-to-door campaign, McKeldin won an upset victory over the incumbent mayor of Baltimore, Howard Jackson. Running in an overwhelmingly Democratic city, McKeldin won by more than 20,000 votes. A powerful, often florid, orator, McKeldin became the most prominent Republican in his state for the next 25 years.

As mayor, he revised the city charter and initiated plans for a civic center, an international airport, an expressway system, and urban renewal. A long-time opponent of racial segregation, he appointed the first African-American members of the school board and hired black members for his personal staff and to work in the city solicitor's office. While serving as mayor, McKeldin ran again for the governorship in 1946 but lost. When his term as mayor expired in 1947, he returned to the practice of law and studied economics at Johns Hopkins University. McKeldin ran for governor a third time in 1950 and won a landslide victory over the incumbent, William Preston Lane, Jr., who had pushed through an unpopular sales tax.

As governor, McKeldin faced a legislature controlled by Democrats. He launched an extensive program of reform and reconstruction. He appointed a commission, headed by his lifelong friend and adviser, SIMON E. SOBELOFF, to study state government. The Commission on State Government and Bureaucratic Administration (also known as the Little Hoover Commission or the Sobeloff Commission) did an exhaustive study of every aspect of state government, including taxation, budgeting, and the structure of the executive branch. McKeldin also put in place a 12-year program for the construction of highways. One of the major achievements of his administration was the completion in 1952 of the Chesapeake Bay Bridge, a project begun under his predecessor, which linked Maryland's Eastern Shore with the western part of the state. His administration reformed unemployment and workers' compensation laws. McKeldin also continued his support for civil rights. He worked to integrate the state's beaches, parks, and buses. McKeldin supported the basic structure of the New Deal and endorsed many aspects of HARRY S. TRUMAN's Fair Deal, although he criticized the corruption of the Truman administration. An early and outspoken opponent of Senator JOSEPH R. MCCARTHY (R-Wis.), McKeldin denounced what he described as the senator's "smear technique," "big lie," and "sly innuendo."

Through his activities in the Southern Governors' Conference and other bodies, McKeldin emerged as a leading eastern, or liberal, Republican. In an effort to deny the Maryland delegation to Senator ROBERT TAFT (R-Ohio), the favorite of the conservative wing of the party, McKeldin announced his candidacy as a favorite son for the party's presidential nomination in the spring of 1952. Subsequently, McKeldin joined the parade of liberal and moderate Republicans who went to Paris to persuade General DWIGHT D. EISENHOWER to seek the Republican nomination. At the Republican National Convention, McKeldin was chosen to give the speech nominating Eisenhower. His nationally televised speech won widespread praise.

McKeldin won reelection as governor in 1954 by defeating Harry C. ("Curley") Byrd, a popular former president of the University of Maryland. During his second term, McKeldin became involved in the crisis over the desegregation of Central High School in Little Rock, Arkansas. In September 1954, Governor ORVAL FAUBUS of Arkansas obstructed a federal court order requiring the desegregation of Central High School. Eisenhower responded by nationalizing the Arkansas National Guard and sending elements of the 101st Airborne to enforce the order. Predictably, the action received a hostile reception among southern officeholders. The Southern Governors' Conference established a committee, composed of moderates and chaired by Governor LUTHER HODGES of North Carolina, to meet with the president and seek the withdrawal of the troops. McKeldin was one of four members of that committee. Eisenhower informed the governors that, if they could persuade Faubus to assume responsibility for maintaining order, he would withdraw the federal troops and return the Arkansas National Guard to state control. After difficult negotiations with Faubus, in which he repeatedly proved untrustworthy, the committee of southern governors acknowledged defeat. McKeldin issued a blast at Faubus, in which he accused the governor of Arkansas of "double-crossing" the committee.

Barred by the state constitution from running for a third term, McKeldin decided to enter the race for mayor of Baltimore in 1959. This time, he was defeated. After leaving the governor's mansion in 1959, McKeldin remained active in politics and won election to a second term as mayor of Baltimore in 1963. Back in the mayor's office, he continued his support of racial equality. Before Congress passed the Civil Rights Act of 1964, he undertook several pioneering initiatives to bring about social equality in the city. His reputation as a strong supporter of civil rights enabled him to defuse racial tensions in the city. Although Baltimore experienced race riots, it did not suffer the extensive damage some cities did. In one instance, McKeldin avoided a confrontation between a group of African Americans and the National Guard by approaching the crowd and saying: "My brothers, my sisters, what is the problem?" The erstwhile rioters extended a warm welcome to the mayor, chatted with him for a while, and then dispersed. When the Congress of Racial Equality (CORE) made Baltimore one of its "target cities," McKeldin worked with the organization and called for an end to discrimination in employment. He embarked on a massive program of urban renewal, which included the redevelopment of the city's inner harbor, construction of a new municipal building, and urban renewal. In 1964, McKeldin backed New York's governor, Nelson A. Rockefeller, for the Republican presidential nomination. When the conservative Senator BARRY GOLDWATER (R-Ariz.) won the Republican presidential nomination, McKeldin bolted the party and supported LYNDON B. JOHNSON for the presidency. That decision strained his relations with the Republican Party. On the other hand, McKeldin enjoyed good relations with the Johnson administration, which enabled him to obtain a large loan from the federal government for the development of Baltimore's Inner Harbor.

After his second term as mayor expired in 1967, McKeldin remained active in public affairs and continued his activities with various community and charitable organizations. An early opponent of the U.S. involvement in the war in Vietnam, he was appointed by Johnson to a panel of American observers chosen to supervise the elections in South Vietnam in September 1967. Johnson also appointed McKeldin to the U.S. Indian Claims Commission. Under pressure from Goldwater, Nixon did not reappoint McKeldin to the Indian Claims Commission when the latter's term ended in 1969. In the later part of his political career, McKeldin became committed to the abolition of capital punishment. He testified against the death penalty before Congress in 1968. A forceful and outspoken supporter of the state of Israel, he was a founder and president of the America-Israel Society. His successor as mayor appointed McKeldin to the board of municipal zoning appeals in 1971. McKeldin died at his home in Baltimore on August 10, 1974.

—MSM

McLeod, R(obert) W(alter) Scott

(1914–1961) *administrator, Bureau of Security, Consular Affairs and Inspection; ambassador to Ireland*

Scott McLeod was born in Davenport, Iowa, on June 17, 1914. After graduating from Grinnell College in 1937, he sold advertising for the *Des Moines Register and Tribune*. In 1938, he took a job as police reporter for the *Cedar Rapids Gazette*. After working as an FBI agent from 1942 to 1949, he served as administrative assistant to Senator STYLES BRIDGES (R-N.H.) from 1949 to 1953. While working for Bridges, a powerful voice of the Republican right, McLeod helped to write the Republican report protesting President HARRY S. TRUMAN's dismissal of General Douglas MacArthur. McLeod's work as Bridges's administrative assistant also brought him to the attention of Senator JOSEPH R. McCARTHY (R-Wis.).

During Truman's second term, the State Department was shaken by allegations that some of its employees were guilty of disloyalty. When the administration of DWIGHT D. EISENHOWER took office in 1953, the new secretary of state, JOHN FOSTER DULLES, was determined to avoid the kind of problems Truman and his secretary of state, DEAN ACHESON, had with Congress. At the administration's request, Congress created a new position, undersecretary of state for administration and operations. Dulles chose Donald B. Lourie, the president of the Quaker Oats Company, to be undersecretary for administration and operations. Lourie chose McLeod as the State Department's chief security officer. The appointment of McLeod, an ally of McCarthy, was widely regarded as an attempt to appease the right wing of the Republican Party. As administrator of security, consular affairs, and inspection, McLeod served as the State Department's security liaison with the FBI, the Central Intelligence Agency, and Congress. In addition, it fell to him to implement Eisenhower's Executive Order 10450, which replaced Truman's Loyalty Program with a new program designed to ensure that the employment of any government worker was "clearly consistent" with national security. The order also shifted responsibility for administering the program to heads of departments and agencies, who were to establish security programs within their departments. McLeod insisted that, in order to carry out his duties, the office of personnel be placed under his authority. He considered every job at the State Department as a sensitive position and ordered the FBI to conduct a full field investigation on all employees. McLeod hired two dozen ex-FBI agents and within three weeks had fired 21 employees for alleged homosexuality. He and his team looked at what was on top of desks, inside drawers, and in file cabinets. They even examined what employees read. McLeod's activities had a detrimental effect on the morale of employees at the State Department.

McLeod proved a constant thorn in the side of the administration. He kept on his desk an autographed photo of McCarthy. His methods soon upset Dulles, and McLeod's agreement to give McCarthy limited access to the State Department's classified personnel files particularly rankled the secretary of state. Even more infuriating were McLeod's efforts to interfere with the confirmation of CHARLES E. BOHLEN as ambassador to the Soviet Union in March 1953. A career diplomat and an expert on Soviet affairs, Bohlen had served as an interpreter and adviser at Yalta. His association with Yalta made him a target for conservatives, including Bridges, who had demanded that the new administration repudiate the Yalta accords. In reviewing the FBI's report on Bohlen, McLeod found that the FBI's investigation of the nominee had turned up some derogatory information, which it acknowledged was speculative and unreliable. Nevertheless, McLeod attempted to use the material to block Bohlen's confirmation. He not only informed Dulles of the derogatory information, but he passed it on to leading opponents of the nomination, including Bridges, Senator PAT MCCARRAN (D-Nev.), and McCarthy. Dulles personally examined the FBI report and testified before the Foreign Relations Committee that "there [was] not a whisper of a suggestion" that Bohlen was a security risk. The Foreign Relations Committee unanimously recommended approval of the nomination, but this did not quell the opposition of furious conservatives. Eisenhower publicly supported the nomination, and Dulles announced that he had informed the president of all derogatory information in Bohlen's file. Dulles also reiterated his support for the nomi-

nation and declared that he and McLeod agreed on the final evaluation of Bohlen. McLeod met with General WILTON ("JERRY") PERSONS, Eisenhower's congressional liaison, to complain that he and Dulles did not agree on Bohlen. Frustrated over the response he received at the White House, McLeod threatened to resign, but SHERMAN ADAMS, Eisenhower's chief of staff, bluntly told him not to do so. McLeod then related his experience at the White House to McCarthy. In the face of bitter opposition in the Senate led by McCarran, Bridges, and McCarthy, the majority leader, ROBERT TAFT (R-Ohio), proposed that one senator from each party review the FBI report on Bohlen. Taft and JOHN SPARKMAN (D-Ala.), the Democratic vice presidential nominee in 1952, examined the report and secured a statement from McLeod that he had seen only the report (as opposed to the "raw files"). During the debate on the floor of the Senate, Taft and Sparkman informed their colleagues that they found nothing in the report to prevent Bohlen's confirmation. Indeed, Taft declared that Bohlen was "a completely good security risk in every respect." The Senate overwhelmingly confirmed Bohlen.

McLeod's activities during the confirmation battle displeased his superiors. Eisenhower told Dulles that he would have the president's support if he fired McLeod. Dulles, however, worried about the trouble firing McLeod would stir up with McCarthy and his allies. In the end, McLeod wrote a letter of apology, and Dulles decided not to fire him. When Bohlen met with the president just before departing for Moscow, Eisenhower told him that McLeod's appointment was "an error on our part" but that "it would be a worse error to dismiss him."

McLeod further irritated Eisenhower by supporting McCarthy's investigation into the Voice of America and its parent, the International Information Agency. On several occasions, McLeod's partisanship, heavy-handed tactics, and seeming ineptitude embarrassed the administration. In testimony before a subcommittee of the House Appropriations Committee in early 1954, McLeod admitted that he had purged only 11 people from the State Department for "loyalty reasons"; in seven of the cases, the process had begun under the Truman administration. McLeod came under criticism for making a series of highly partisan speeches on Lincoln Day 1954. In February 1954, JOSEPH ALSOP and STEWART ALSOP published a scathing attack on McLeod in their influential column. On March 1, 1954, the administration stripped McLeod of authority over State Department personnel, although he remained in charge of departmental security matters. In August 1954, five former diplomats published a letter in the *New York Times* attacking McLeod and his methods.

As supervisor of the passport and visa divisions and the office of special consular services, McLeod had responsibility for enforcing the Refugee Act of 1953, a measure designed to allow more than 200,000 refugees from communist countries to enter the United States over and above the existing quotas. McLeod insisted on such a careful screening of each immigrant that only nine refugees gained admission under the act in 1953–54. This angered EDWARD CORSI, a special adviser for immigration affairs. After leaving the State Department, Corsi testified before a subcommittee of the Senate Judiciary Committee that the administration of the Refugee Act was a national scandal.

Partly to remove McLeod from a position in which he had attracted so much criticism, Eisenhower nominated McLeod as ambassador to Ireland in 1957. Democratic senators opposed the nomination. During the debate over McLeod's confirmation, Senator JOSEPH CLARK (D-Pa.) attacked him as a "symbol of the witch hunter." Despite the opposition, the Senate voted overwhelmingly to confirm McLeod. At the end of the Eisenhower administration, McLeod resigned his position as ambassador. In 1961, he received an appointment as general counsel to Republican members of the Senate Appropriations Committee. He died of a heart attack in Concord, New Hampshire, on November 7, 1961.

—MSM

McNamara, Patrick V(incent)

(1894–1966) *U.S. senator*

The son of Irish immigrants, McNamara was born in North Weymouth, Massachusetts, on October 4, 1894. He attended public schools in Weymouth and the Bethlehem Steel Company's Fore River Appren-

tice School in Quincy, Massachusetts, from 1912 to 1916. While working as a pipe fitter at the Fore River Shipyard, he played semiprofessional football. He moved to Detroit, Michigan, in 1921 to head a construction gang for the Grinell Company. Subsequently, he worked for two mechanical contracting firms. He was job superintendent for R. L. Spitzley Company from 1922 to 1926 and worked as general superintendent of H. Kelly Company from 1926 to 1930. After the depression curtailed construction, McNamara went to work as a maintenance foreman for the Chrysler Corporation in 1931. He returned to mechanical contracting with the Donald Miller Company in 1934. Even though he had moved into management, McNamara held a succession of unpaid offices in the Pipe Fitters Local 636 of the American Federation of Labor before becoming president of that union in 1937. He held that office without pay until he entered the Senate in 1955. McNamara also served as vice president of the Detroit Federation of Labor from 1939 to 1945, for which he also declined payment. In 1945, McNamara joined the Stanley-Carter Company, a mechanical contracting firm, first as superintendent of construction and customer contact man, then as head of labor relations, and, from 1950 to 1954, as vice president in charge of sales.

McNamara first held public office during World War II, when he served as rent director of the Detroit area for the Office of Price Administration from 1942 to 1945. After the war, he served on the Detroit Common Council from 1946 to 1948 and the Detroit Board of Education from 1949 to 1955. He sought the Democratic nomination for a seat in the U.S. Senate in 1954. Few gave him much of a chance against his opponent in the primary, Blair Moody, a former senator who had the backing of Governor G. MENNEN WILLIAMS and the party organization. When Moody died a month before the primary, however, the Democratic organization shifted its support to McNamara. In the general election, he faced the Republican incumbent, HOMER FERGUSON, who was seeking a third term. McNamara campaigned against the Eisenhower administration's economic, labor, and farm policies. He called for a repeal of the Taft-Hartley Act, advocated federal aid to education, and denounced the Eisenhower administration's foreign policy. In November, he defeated Ferguson by 40,000 votes.

McNamara established a liberal voting record in the Senate. In 1956, he opposed a bill that would have exempted independent natural gas producers from the Federal Power Commission's rate regulations. He supported a federally funded dam and power facility at Hell's Canyon in 1957 and backed measures providing for federal support for public housing, public works, and education. In addition, he supported the Truman administration's rigid price supports for agriculture. The liberal Americans for Democratic Action gave him a 100 percent rating in 1957.

McNamara was a strong supporter of civil rights. In November 1956, he was one of six liberal senators who issued a 16-point "Democratic Declaration of 1957." It called not only for equal voting and educational rights for African Americans, but also for a "reasonable" substitute for Senate rule 22, which required a two-thirds vote to cut off debate. Making it easier to invoke cloture would have denied southern Democrats their most effective tool in thwarting civil rights legislation, the filibuster. In 1957, McNamara supported the Eisenhower administration's civil rights bill, including the controversial Title III, which authorized the Justice Department to seek injunctions in civil rights cases. McNamara opposed an amendment that would have required jury trials for those who violated federal court injunctions relating to voting rights. As passed, the Civil Rights Act of 1957 did not include Title III and did include the jury trial amendment. Three years later, McNamara supported what became the Civil Rights Act of 1960, a measure designed to protect black voting rights.

McNamara was also a strong supporter of organized labor. He consistently backed efforts to increase the minimum wage. In February 1959, he introduced a bill to establish a minimum wage for farmworkers of 75 cents per hour. As a member of the Select Committee on Improper Activities in the Labor or Management Field, established in 1957 to investigate corruption in unions and industry, McNamara opposed the investigation of the United Auto Workers (UAW) proposed by KARL MUNDT (R-S. Dak.) and BARRY GOLDWATER (R-Ariz.). McNamara also opposed the committee's report,

issued on March 24, 1958, which found extensive corruption in labor unions and collusion between labor leaders and management. He charged that, despite an effort to "give a semblance of balance," the overall effect of the report was "to frame a blanket indictment against the labor movement." McNamara resigned from the committee on March 31. The AFL-CIO Committee on Political Education gave him a 100 percent rating in 1958.

McNamara won reelection in 1960 by 120,000 votes. In 1961, he sponsored and served as floor manager for a bill that raised the minimum wage to $1.25 an hour and extended coverage to an additional 3.6 million workers. As ranking member of the Senate Committee on Labor and Public Welfare and chair of its subcommittee on labor, McNamara had a hand in enacting much of President LYNDON B. JOHNSON's Great Society legislation. In 1965, he played a significant role in gaining passage of Medicare and federal aid to education. McNamara chaired the Special Committee on Aging during the 87th Congress and the Public Works Committee during the 88th and 89th Congresses. Ill much of the time after going under major surgery in 1960, McNamara announced in early 1966 that he would not seek reelection. He died in Bethesda, Maryland, on April 30, 1966, less than a year before his second term expired.

—MSM

Meany, George
(1894–1980) *union leader*

The son of an Irish Catholic plumber and union official, Meany was born in New York City on August 16, 1894. He grew up in the Bronx and left school at the age of 14 to work as a messenger for an advertising agency. In 1910, he became a plumber's helper. Upon becoming a journeyman in 1917, he joined Local 463 of the Plumber's Union. He won a seat on the executive board in 1919. Meany was elected to his first full-time union office (business agent of Local 463) in 1922; he never worked as a plumber again. In 1932, he became the building trades' delegate to the New York central labor council and was elected to the executive board of the New York State Federation of Labor. Two years later, he won election as president of the New York Federation of Labor, a post that made him the chief labor spokesperson in Albany and put him in close contact with the Roosevelt administration and the national leadership of the American Federation of Labor (AFL). Meany proved a skillful lobbyist, and in 1940 the president of the AFL, William Green, chose him to be secretary-treasurer of the AFL.

During World War II, Meany served on the National Defense Mediation Board and the War Labor Board. Through his activities in government and within the AFL, he became the architect of an activist role for the AFL in international affairs. In the postwar years, as Green's health failed, Meany assumed increasing responsibility for running the AFL's day-to-day activities. Meany helped lead the AFL's fight against passage of the Taft-Hartley Act in 1947, but he supported the noncommunist affidavits required of union officials under the law. He also worked closely with the American government in building anticommunist trade unions abroad and was instrumental in the formation of the pro-Western International Confederation of Free Trade Unions in 1949.

When Green died in November 1952, the AFL's executive council named Meany president. Although a firm business unionist who remained loyal to the craft traditions of the AFL, Meany was less hostile to the rival Congress of Industrial Organizations (CIO) than others in the AFL's hierarchy. One of his first acts as president was to revive merger negotiations (which had been suspended in 1950) with the CIO. The CIO's president, WALTER REUTHER, also favored unity but insisted on several preconditions, including the establishment of machinery to resolve jurisdictional disputes between industrial and craft unions and the elimination of organized crime from AFL affiliates.

In 1953, Meany moved against the East Coast's International Longshoremen's Association (ILA), which had long been dominated by gangsters (a situation brought to public attention by the New York State Crime Commission in 1952 and 1953). After the ILA's president, Joseph Ryan, refused to reform the union's hiring system and fire officers with criminal records, the AFL, at Meany's initiative, voted to expel the longshoremen. The AFL chartered a new union, the International Brother-

hood of Longshoremen, but New York's dockworkers rejected the AFL's alternative.

In June 1953, Meany reached an agreement with Reuther on a no-raiding pact, which essentially froze the existing jurisdictions of AFL and CIO unions. Although several large AFL affiliates, including the Carpenters and Teamsters, disliked the pact, it was an important step toward an eventual merger, which took place in February 1955. Since the AFL was nearly twice as large as the CIO, Meany assumed the presidency of the new AFL-CIO in December 1955. Reuther became a vice president and head of the Industrial Union Department. CIO leaders agreed to retain the loose structure of the AFL, which gave wide autonomy to member unions.

Among the politically more aggressive labor leaders of the postwar period, Meany in 1947 helped found Labor's League for Political Education, the political arm of the AFL, which worked closely with the Democratic Party. He also persuaded the AFL to break officially with its nonpartisan tradition for the first time by endorsing the Democratic presidential nominee, ADLAI STEVENSON, in 1952. The AFL's primary political objective from 1947 on, however, was to secure the repeal of the Taft-Hartley Act. Although disappointed that DWIGHT D. EISENHOWER defeated Stevenson in 1952, leaders of the AFL applauded the new president's pledge to back certain revisions of the Taft-Hartley law, including provisions for striking workers to vote in representation elections and a requirement that employers as well as union officers sign noncommunist affidavits. The appointment of MARTIN DURKIN, head of Meany's own plumbers' union, as secretary of labor encouraged labor leaders and raised their hopes for amending the Taft-Hartley Act. In early 1953, Eisenhower established a committee to make recommendations regarding the revision of the Taft-Hartley Act. Meany worked with the committee, primarily through Durkin. The committee proposed 19 amendments to the Taft-Hartley law, including a repeal of section 14b, which permitted states to pass laws barring the union shop. Senator ROBERT TAFT (R-Ohio), the majority leader, died the day that Eisenhower intended to send the proposals to Congress. Concluding that it would have been tactless to ask for amendments to Taft's bill on the day of his death, the administration delayed submitting the proposals. Taft's death had other consequences, as well. It would have taken someone with Taft's standing to shepherd the amendments through Congress, and Taft did not support all of them. The new Republican leader in the Senate, WILLIAM KNOWLAND of California, was less able and less sympathetic to revising the act. Moreover, opponents within the administration, led by Secretary of Commerce SINCLAIR WEEKS and pressure from business groups, persuaded the president to withdraw his support. Believing that he had been betrayed, Durkin resigned in August 1953. After that, labor lobbyists spent the rest of the decade devoting their efforts to fending off conservative proposals to strengthen Taft-Hartley.

Meany believed in social unionism (the idea that organized labor should advance the larger cause of social justice). Even after the merger, however, the combined AFL-CIO found it difficult to realize its legislative goals. In 1957, for example, Meany threw the organization's resources behind an effort to win health insurance for the aged. Organized labor's lobbyists succeeded in blocking a bill, sponsored by the administration, that would have provided for underwriting health insurance through private companies, rather than the social security system; but they could not secure passage of the measure backed by the AFL-CIO.

Meany blamed the conservative coalition in Congress as much as the administration for labor's legislative defeats. He grew increasingly skeptical of electoral activity, particularly because many southern Democrats were beyond the political reach of unions. In 1956, Meany unsuccessfully sought to withhold the AFL-CIO's endorsement from Stevenson. Meany reasoned that, even if the Democrats won the presidency, the same antilabor forces would continue to control congressional committees.

While Meany differed with Eisenhower on many domestic issues, he supported the president's defense and foreign policies. Under Meany's leadership, the AFL cooperated with the Foreign Operations Administration, the State Department, the Defense Department, and other government agencies in carrying out labor programs overseas as well as realizing broader policy objectives of the administration. In 1953 and 1954, Meany and his staff worked with the Central Intelligence Agency to topple the government of Guatemala's president, Jacobo Arbenz Guzmán. In an effort to weaken the communist-dominated Guatemalan labor federation, the AFL created a rival union, the leaders of which joined the "liberation army" led by General Carlos Castillo Armas. After the overthrow of Arbenz in June 1954, however, Armas and the new government proceeded to suppress all trade unions in Guatemala.

In his staunch commitment to combating communist influence in the international labor movement and to defending what he perceived to be the national interests of the United States, Meany was strongly influenced by JAY LOVESTONE, the head of the AFL foreign affairs department and a former leader of the Communist Party. Under Meany's aegis, Lovestone set up a network, most of whom had been associates of his in the Communist Party, stationed in various parts of the world. These operatives had large, often untraceable, funds at their disposal. In the 1960s, a series of articles in American newspapers and magazines revealed that much of that money came from government sources, including the CIA. After the merger of the AFL and the CIO, Lovestone's operations became a source of conflict between Meany and Reuther, who wanted to work through the International Confederation of Free Trade Unions (ICFTU). Meany and Lovestone regarded the ICFTU as insufficiently anticommunist and preferred to channel financial aid and political direction independently to trade unions abroad.

Public exposures of union corruption in 1957 forced Meany to take action. The Senate Select Committee on Improper Activities in the Labor or Management Field, headed by Senator JOHN L. McCLELLAN (D-Ark.), began an investigation of the International Brotherhood of Teamsters in January. Meany instructed AFL-CIO officials to cooperate with the investigation. The McClellan Committee quickly compiled a mountain of evidence against the president of the Teamsters, DAVE BECK. Investigators alleged that Beck had taken more than $30,000 in union funds to pay for personal gifts and real estate. After Beck refused to answer more than 90 questions before the committee in March, Meany had him suspended from his seat on the AFL-CIO executive council. The McClellan Committee then turned its attention to Beck's successor, JAMES HOFFA.

In October 1957, Meany recommended that the Teamsters be suspended from the AFL-CIO pending the removal of Beck, Hoffa, and other officials. The leaders of the Teamsters refused to initiate internal reforms, and in December the AFL-CIO voted to expel the union. At the same time, Meany moved against several smaller unions that had been subjects of the McClellan Committee's investigations. The AFL-CIO expelled two unions, the Bakers and Confectioners and the Laundry Workers, and placed a third, the United Textile Workers, on probation. Even as he took action against racketeers in the AFL-CIO, Meany denounced the McClellan Committee as "little more than a vehicle of reactionary elements seeking to discredit the American labor movement" and complained that the Senate investigations ignored corrupt practices by business.

The revelations of the McClellan Committee led to growing demands in Congress for government regulation of the finances, internal governance, and strike activities of unions. In 1958, partly to forestall more stringent legislation, the AFL-CIO endorsed a bill sponsored by Senators JOHN F. KENNEDY (D-Mass.) and IRVING IVES (R-N.Y.). The bill included restrictions on the authority of national and international unions to place locals under trusteeships, conditions and standards for the election of union officers, and a code of ethical practices. It also included several amendments to the Taft-Hartley Act favored by building trades unions. Business groups and congressional conservatives worked to eliminate the amendments sought by the building trades unions. The Kennedy-Ives bill passed the Senate in June but died in the House.

Reacting aggressively to what it perceived as the threat of antilabor legislation, the AFL-CIO threw its resources into the congressional elections of 1958. It sought to defeat right-to-work proposals that had been placed on several state ballots and to elect its "friends" to office. In the elections that November, 70 percent of the candidates backed by the AFL-CIO's Committee on Political Education won. Meany hailed the results as a vindication of organized labor, despite the unfavorable publicity generated by the McClellan Committee's investigations.

After the off-year elections of 1958, the Senate was almost two-thirds Democratic, and Republicans warned of a "labor-bossed Congress." It came as a surprise to Meany, therefore, when the AFL-CIO's efforts to block reform proposals collapsed in the new Congress. In April 1959, the Senate Subcommittee on Labor, dominated by liberals, reported out a bill, drawn in close cooperation with representatives of the AFL-CIO. At the insistence of McClellan, however, the bill was amended to include a "bill of rights" aimed at guaranteeing democratic procedures in union governance. The bill of rights included the rights to vote, speak, and resort to law. Meany and other labor leaders strongly opposed the amendment. The Senate modified the bill of rights to meet some of organized labor's objections and passed the measure. In the House, however, a coalition of southern Democrats and Republicans, supported by the administration, introduced a substitute measure, known as the Landrum-Griffin bill. The Landrum-Griffin bill contained McClellan's proposals as well as additional amendments strengthening prohibitions against secondary boycotts and curbing picketing rights. Despite strong opposition from the AFL-CIO, the bill passed in August, and President Eisenhower signed it into law on September 14.

During the late 1950s, Meany came under increasing criticism from Reuther and other former CIO leaders for what they regarded as his insufficiently dynamic leadership and his hard-line position on the cold war. Reuther urged Meany to throw the AFL-CIO's resources into organizing the estimated 26 million nonunion workers in the United States. Meany, however, remained unwilling to ask individual unions to abandon their jurisdictional claims in joint organizing drives. In his public remarks on foreign policy, Meany consistently opposed détente with the Soviet Union and denounced neutral nations, such as India, for being, "in effect," allies of communism. When Soviet leaders Anastas Mikoyan and Nikita Khrushchev visited the United States in 1959, Meany refused them permission to tour the AFL-CIO headquarters in Washington, D.C., or to address the AFL-CIO convention in San Francisco. Meany also criticized Reuther for meeting with them.

Like corruption, racism proved a difficult issue for Meany and the AFL-CIO in the 1950s. Meany himself supported civil rights, but he was reluctant to confront racial injustice within the labor movement. Although the AFL-CIO pledged itself in 1955 to the rapid elimination of racial discrimination within its ranks, Meany came under fire from black unionists and civil rights leaders, particularly when, in 1956, the AFL-CIO admitted two railroad unions that barred nonwhites from membership. In 1958, the NAACP filed complaints with the AFL-CIO civil rights department against the locals of 12 unions for discriminatory seniority provisions, systematic exclusion of African Americans from leadership positions, and other forms of bias. In the following year, A. PHILIP RANDOLPH, head of the black Brotherhood of Sleeping Car Porters, brought these and other complaints to the floor of the AFL-CIO convention. After an angry exchange, during which Meany demanded of Randolph, "Who in the hell appointed you guardian of the Negro members in America?," the AFL-CIO refused to expel the accused locals.

Meany strongly backed John F. Kennedy at the Democratic National Convention in July 1960. He favored Senator HENRY JACKSON (D-Wash.) for the second spot on the ticket and was shocked when Kennedy chose Senator LYNDON B. JOHNSON (D-Tex.) as his running mate. Meany held Johnson, the Senate majority leader, responsible for allowing the Landrum-Griffin Act to pass. Only Reuther's strenuous efforts on Kennedy's behalf prevented the AFL-CIO caucus at the convention from publicly condemning the selection of Johnson. Not until August did the AFL-CIO's executive council, with Meany's consent, finally endorse the ticket.

Meany applauded the social welfare legislation proposed by the Kennedy administration but criticized the president for failing to reduce unemployment. At the same time, he threw the AFL-CIO's support behind Kennedy's anticommunist initiatives in foreign policy. Meany helped to create the largely government-funded American Institute for Free Labor Development, which trained Latin American union leaders to oppose anti–U.S. regimes.

Racial issues continued to plague the AFL-CIO and its leader. In June 1961, Randolph submitted a stinging report accusing the AFL-CIO of "tokenism in civil rights" and calling for the expulsion of those unions that continued to practice discrimi-

nation. Meany responded by attempting to undercut Randolph's standing within the AFL-CIO. He appointed a committee to investigate Randolph's charges. In October, the committee brought forward a resolution "censuring" the black leader for "causing the gap that has developed between organized labor and the Negro community." Despite the harsh rhetoric and sometimes bruising tactics, Meany and Randolph reached an accord; the AFL-CIO dropped its censure resolution and, at its convention in December 1961, adopted a resolution calling for "appropriate action" against unions that persisted in discriminatory practices.

After Kennedy was assassinated, Meany enthusiastically supported the Johnson administration's Great Society programs. Meany's earlier hostility to Johnson developed into a close friendship. Believing that labor did not have the capacity to eliminate discriminatory practices within its own ranks, Meany supported legislation prohibiting discrimination in employment. He was one of the architects of the provision prohibiting job discrimination in the Civil Rights Act of 1964. Meany also supported Johnson's foreign policy, in particular the war in Vietnam.

Meany mobilized AFL-CIO efforts on behalf of Senator HUBERT HUMPHREY's (D-Minn.) presidential candidacy in 1968. After RICHARD M. NIXON defeated Humphrey for the presidency, Meany supported Nixon's foreign policy, particularly with respect to the war in Vietnam, but opposed many of Nixon's domestic initiatives. In 1972, Meany regarded the antiwar position of the Democratic presidential nominee, Senator GEORGE MCGOVERN (D-S. Dak.), as absurd. In addition, the countercultural lifestyle of many of McGovern's supporters appalled the culturally conservative Meany. He withheld the AFL-CIO's endorsement and its resources from McGovern. As the Watergate scandal developed, however, the AFL-CIO became the first major organization to call for Nixon to resign.

In his last years, Meany typified what many criticized in the labor movement. He was remote from the rank and file; he was ambivalent toward the claims of minorities and women; he clung to older ways of doing things in an age of rapid economic, social, and cultural change. He finally left office in November 1979 and died in Bethesda, Maryland, on January 10, 1980.

—MSM

Merchant, Livingston T(allmadge)

(1903–1976) *assistant secretary of state for European affairs, ambassador to Canada, deputy undersecretary of state for political affairs, undersecretary of state for political affairs*

A descendant of Oliver Wolcott, Jr., secretary of the Treasury under George Washington and John Adams, and General William Floyd, a signer of the Declaration of Independence, Livingston Merchant was born in New York City on November 23, 1903. He graduated from Hotchkiss School in 1922 and from Princeton University in 1926, after which he joined the Boston branch of Scudder, Stevens & Clark and embarked on a successful career as an investment counselor. He became a partner in 1930. After the Japanese attack on Pearl Harbor, Merchant joined the State Department as assistant chief of its division of defense materials. He held a number of positions in the economic division, including economic counselor at the United States embassy in Paris. In 1947, he joined the Foreign Service and was posted as counselor in Nanking, China, where he served until the defeat of the Nationalist Chinese. He went to Taiwan briefly before being called to Washington in 1949 to become assistant secretary of state for Far Eastern affairs.

In March 1953, Secretary of State JOHN FOS-TER DULLES named Merchant assistant secretary of state for European affairs. During his three years in that position, he accompanied President DWIGHT D. EISENHOWER to Berlin in 1954 and to London, Geneva, and Paris the following year. He was a principal planner of the summit conference held at Geneva in July 1955 to discuss the unification of Germany and the status of Berlin. At the conference, he served as a top adviser to Eisenhower. He subsequently participated in a series of conferences in preparation for a meeting of foreign ministers in October 1955 that focused on Germany and the relaxation of East-West tensions.

Eisenhower nominated Merchant as ambassador to Canada in April 1956. Merchant assumed his post at a time of increasing tension between the two countries. The Canadian Conservative Party was accusing the Liberal government of "selling out to foreign capital" (i.e., the United States) through its policy of encouraging foreign investment. By appointing a high-ranking diplomat as ambassador, Eisenhower hoped to demonstrate that the United States recognized the importance of Canada and took cognizance of its problems. Nevertheless, relations between the two countries remained cool throughout Merchant's tour.

In 1959, Secretary of State CHRISTIAN HERTER sent Merchant to Panama in an attempt to ease tensions following anti-American riots over control of the Canal Zone. Despite his assurances that Panama maintained titular sovereignty over the area under the treaty of 1903 and his suggestions that the United States would increase economic aid, Merchant failed to stop the violence. He returned to Washington as deputy undersecretary of state for political affairs in August 1959 and became undersecretary of state for political affairs in January 1960. Merchant played a significant role in planning for the 1959 meeting of foreign ministers in Geneva to discuss the matter of Berlin. He also participated in that meeting.

President JOHN F. KENNEDY appointed Merchant ambassador to Canada in 1961, where he served until his retirement from the Foreign Service in 1962. Merchant served as the president's special representative for Multilateral Force Negotiations in 1963. From 1965 to 1968, he was executive director of the International Bank for Reconstruction and Development. Merchant died in Washington, D.C., on May 15, 1976.

—MSM

Metcalf, Lee

(1911–1978) *U.S. congressman and senator*

The son of a bank cashier, Metcalf was born in Stevensville, Montana, on January 28, 1911. He grew up on his family's 300-acre farm outside Stevensville. After attending Montana State University (later the University of Montana) for a year, he transferred to Stanford University, from which he graduated, and earned an LL.B. degree from Montana State University in 1936. That same year, he was elected as a Democrat to the Montana House of Representatives. In 1937, he was appointed an assistant state attorney general, a post he held until 1941, when he resigned to embark on the private practice of law. Metcalf enlisted in the army in December 1942, attended officers' training school, was commissioned, and participated in the Normandy invasion and the Battle of the Bulge. With the defeat of Germany, his duties focused on the care and repatriation of displaced persons. He also helped to draft ordinances for local elections in Germany. After his discharge from the army as a first lieutenant in April 1946, Metcalf was elected later that year to a six-year term as an associate justice of the Montana Supreme Court. In 1952, he ran successfully for the U.S. House of Representatives from Montana's first district, which comprised the western third of the state.

From his first term in Congress, Metcalf established a reputation as a liberal on domestic issues. An outspoken supporter of conservation, he played a role in defeating a grazing lands bill in 1953 that conservationists and wildlife groups opposed because, they argued, it would have made grazing permits on federal lands tantamount to ownership. The following year, Metcalf led the successful floor opposition to a timberlands exchange bill that would have required the federal government to give private interests timber rights on federal lands in payment for land requisitioned by the government. Metcalf first added several amendments to the measure, including one specifying that timber rights, but not title, would be transferred to private interests. He then moved successfully to recommit the bill to the Interior Committee. On other issues, Metcalf was a critic of private utility companies and their rate structures. He also advocated federal aid to education and consumer protection.

In 1957, Metcalf was one of the founders of a caucus of young liberal Democratic representatives known as the Democratic Study Group. He joined 27 representatives in issuing the caucus's policy statement, which included recommendations for federal aid for school construction, medical education, and housing; repeal of the Taft-Hartley Act; extension of the coverage of the Fair Labor Standards Act; protection of civil rights; and revision of immigration and naturalization laws to eliminate the national origins rule.

Later in 1957, Metcalf was one of the members of the Education and Labor Committee who voted unsuccessfully to deny the panel's chair, Representative GRAHAM A. BARDEN (D-N.C.), the right to appoint subcommittee chairs and staff members. In 1958, Metcalf and Senator James E. Murray (D-Mont.), a member of the Labor and Public Welfare Committee, cosponsored a bill to provide federal aid for the construction of schools and for scholarships. Congress instead passed a somewhat more modest bill backed by the administration. The senators from Montana reintroduced their bill again the following year, but the Murray-Metcalf bill stalled in the Rules Committee.

Metcalf won election to the U.S. Senate in 1960. He was subsequently reelected in 1966 and 1972. In the Senate, he continued to focus his attention on education, the regulation of private utility companies, and conservation. He introduced a bill in 1962 to protect national recreation areas, fish, and wildlife from destruction by federal highway construction programs. The bill never passed. In 1963, Metcalf also fought unsuccessfully for the construction in southern Montana of a federal dam able to produce commercial power. He published a book, *Overcharge* (1967), in which he maintained that states could not effectively regulate private utility companies because they did not have the resources to discipline the industry. Metcalf continued his support for federal aid to education and was a major supporter of the Elementary and Secondary Education Act of 1965. In the late 1960s and into the 1970s, Metcalf continued to support conservation, congressional reform, and legislation to protect consumers. Suffering from ill health, he announced in 1977 that he would not stand for reelection in 1978. He died in Helena, Montana, on January 12, 1978.

—MSM

Meyner, Robert B(aumle)

(1908–1990) *governor of New Jersey*

The son of a silk-loom fixer, Robert B. Meyner was born in Easton, Pennsylvania, on July 3, 1908. He moved with his family to Phillipsburg, New Jersey, where he attended public schools. Meyner earned his undergraduate degree from Lafayette

College and an LL.B. from Columbia University Law School. After receiving his law degree in 1933, he opened a private law practice in Phillipsburg. He ran unsuccessfully for the state senate in 1941. Following service in the navy during World War II, during which he rose to the rank of lieutenant commander, Meyner made an unsuccessful bid for a seat in the U.S. House of Representatives in 1946. He won election to the state senate in 1947 as a Democrat. Meyner became minority leader in 1950 and chair of the state party convention in 1951. Despite his rise in the party, he lost his bid for reelection in 1951.

In 1953, Meyner won the Democratic gubernatorial primary against the candidate of the powerful Hudson County machine. In the general election, he ran on a platform that stressed the need to combat organized crime, revise taxes, and increase aid to public schools. He also accused his Republican opponent, a wealthy building contractor, of seeking clemency for a labor racketeer. Meyner went on to win the general election by 153,000 votes.

In office, Meyner governed as a fiscal conservative and a centrist. He often promoted legislation with bipartisan appeal. During his first term, he aggressively supported state funding for education and a plan to restructure the state government. In 1956, he presided over the opening of the state's first medical college at Seton Hall. He also undertook several large public works projects. In 1954, he began the 164-mile-long Garden State Parkway, and, the following year, he established the Delaware Basin Authority.

Many of Meyner's proposals were not enacted into law, in part because he lacked a strong political base. The Democratic Hudson County machine was in decline, and Republican Bergen County was growing. Further, Meyner's decision in March 1954 to remove former governor Harold G. Hoffman as employment security director on charges of corruption did little to endear him to John V. Kenny, the boss of Hudson County. When Hoffman died a few months later, Meyner made public a confession left by the disgraced official that admitted to having embezzled some $300,000 in state funds.

Meyner became a prominent figure at the Governors' Conference in 1954, and many regarded him as a possible vice presidential candidate in 1956. However, he announced that he would not seek national office and would run for another term as governor. His slate of uncommitted delegates easily won the New Jersey presidential primary in May 1956, defeating a slate pledged to Senator ESTES KEFAUVER (D-Tenn.). At the Democratic National Convention in August, Meyner threw his support to ADLAI STEVENSON.

In November 1957, Meyner won reelection by a large margin, becoming the first governor of New Jersey to serve two four-year terms. His second term saw passage of the Water Supply Act of 1958, which provided $40 million to build reservoirs along the Raritan River and develop New Jersey's groundwater resources. He also got approval for a "green acres" bond issue in 1961 that provided $60 million to buy land for public use. This made New Jersey one of the first states to approve large-scale recreational land purchases.

Meyner spent much of his second term traveling abroad and visiting national Democratic leaders in an attempt to position himself as a contender for the Democratic presidential nomination in 1960. He failed to garner much support, however. In addition, throughout the spring of 1960, Joseph P. Kennedy busily gathered support for his son, Senator JOHN F. KENNEDY (D-Mass.), among politicians in northern New Jersey. Angered by what he regarded as the elder Kennedy's presumption, the governor bound New Jersey's delegation to his candidacy through the first ballot at the convention. His decision was motivated by more than pique; he hoped to prevent Kennedy from winning the nomination and to wind up with the second spot on a ticket headed by Stevenson. At the Democratic National Convention in July 1960, Meyner did not release his delegates in time to put Kennedy over the top, and, consequently, after Kennedy won the election, he did not offer Meyner a position in the new administration.

After leaving public office, Meyner returned to the practice of law. He attempted a political comeback in 1969 and won the Democratic primary for governor. In the general election, he lost badly to the Republican candidate, William T. Cahill. Meyner died in Captiva, Florida, on May 27, 1990.

—MSM

Miller, Arthur

(1915–2005) playwright

The son of a Jewish immigrant father from Radomizl, Poland, and an American-born mother whose family came from the same town, Arthur Miller was born in New York City on October 17, 1915. His father ran a successful coat-manufacturing business that collapsed during the Great Depression. Although the family was not particularly observant, Miller's Jewish upbringing played a central role in shaping his character and worldview. After graduating from Abraham Lincoln High School in 1932, Miller held several jobs before settling down as a shipping clerk in a warehouse for auto parts. He enrolled at the University of Michigan in 1934, where he won two Avery Hopwood awards for playwriting and received his B.A. in 1938. Upon graduating, he returned to New York and took a series of jobs that included writing for the Federal Theater Project and working as a steamfitter at the Brooklyn Navy Yard. Rejected from military service because of an old football injury to his knee, Miller spent World War II writing radio dramas and working part-time as a steamfitter and truck driver. He toured army camps to collect material for a movie, *The Story of GI Joe*, based on a book by Ernie Pyle. In 1944, he published a journal of the tour titled *Situation Normal*. That same year, the Broadway production of his play *The Man Who Had All the Luck* opened and closed after four performances. The play focused on a man whose puritan instincts made him unable to accept his extraordinary good fortune and who therefore behaved in a self-destructive manner to prove that he had control of his life. Despite its lack of commercial success, the play won a Theater Guild Award. In 1945, Miller published a novel *Focus*, which examined American anti-Semitism.

His first critical and commercial success was *All My Sons*, presented in 1947, for which he won the New York Drama Critic's Circle Award. Dealing with themes that would drive his most significant works, the play tells the story of Joe Kellner, the owner of a small factory who, during World War II, allows cracked cylinder heads to be shipped to the air force in order to save his contract with the government. As a result, 21 pilots die in crashes.

Arthur Miller *(Library of Congress)*

Kellner lets his partner take the blame, but eventually his own son exposes him.

In 1949, Miller wrote *Death of a Salesman*, which also won the Circle Award as well as a Pulitzer Prize and a Tony. The work portrays the disintegration of Willy Loman, a traveling salesman forced to confront his failures at work and in his personal life. Willy has imbued his sons with his own grandiose dreams and the shallow values that guide his career as a salesman. He has built a career on "a smile and a shoeshine." "Be liked and you will never want," he preaches. Willy has always regarded his son, Biff, as the embodiment of his hopes and dreams for the future. Biff, however, is heading nowhere; he wanders through a series of low-paid menial jobs and a life of petty crime. Once the star of his high school football team, Biff was about to start college on a football scholarship when he discovered his father's infidelity, after which he dropped out of school and embarked on the path that led to his present state. Willy's other son works in a department store. Willy himself is no longer the hotshot salesman he once was but cannot bring himself to come to terms with the failure of his dreams, which, in a larger sense, is the failure of the American dream. When his young boss fires him, Willy pleads for his job, declaring that "a man is not a piece of fruit." The loss of Willy's job adds one more worry to the life of his careworn wife. Acknowledging that Willy is not "a great man" or "the finest character that ever lived," Willy's wife cries, "but he's a human being, and a terrible thing is happening to him. So attention must be paid." The loss of his job brings Willy partial awareness, but he clings to the fantasy of his dreams for himself and for Biff. The salesman commits suicide by crashing his car, fortified by the thought that Biff will receive the insurance.

With Willy's plea for his job and his wife's famous assertion that "attention must be paid," Miller denounced the cruelties of American capitalism. The playwright regarded as even more inhumane, however, the tantalizing dream that hid the true nature of the system. Intellectual journals dismissed the play as an exercise in sentimentality, melodrama, or Marxist propaganda. *Death of a Salesman*, however, had a profound effect on audiences.

During the 1940s, Miller associated with a number of communist writers and signed numerous appeals and protests by groups the U.S. government classified as communist front organizations. He was appalled by the anticommunist excesses of the early cold war and, in 1950, wrote an adaptation of Henrik Ibsen's drama, *An Enemy of the People*, in which the hero resisted pressure to conform to prevailing ideology. Miller's third Broadway play, *The Crucible*, produced in 1953, brought him to the forefront of the controversy over domestic subversion and Senator JOSEPH R. MCCARTHY's (R-Wis.) charges that communists had infiltrated the national government. The play dealt with the struggle of individuals to hold on to both their integrity and their lives when confronted by the witch-hunters of 17th-century Salem, Massachusetts. In Miller's version, John Proctor, when faced with a choice between death and compromising his conscience, declined to save himself at the expense of his honor. Playgoers readily drew the obvious parallel between congressional investigators and the Puritans who conducted the witch trials. Some connected the play to the trial of JULIUS and ETHEL ROSENBERG. Although the play won a

Tony, it did not do especially well at the box office. Five months after it opened, Miller restaged the play himself. Although better received, the revised version was not especially successful, either. Some critics remained unconvinced by the analogy of the witch hunts in Salem to the hearings conducted by the House Un-American Activities Committee (HUAC) and Senator McCarthy. Several pointed to a manifest failure in the comparison; there had never been witches, but there were communists.

In 1954, Miller published an ironic attack on congressional investigators titled "Every American Should Go to Jail: A Modest Proposal for the Pacification of the Public Temper." Predictably, Miller drew the attention of the HUAC, which called him to testify during its hearings in 1956 on the unauthorized use of U.S. passports. By the time HUAC subpoenaed Miller, its hearings had largely run out of steam. Even though Miller had made himself a likely target by signing countless leftist petitions in the past, the committee did not subpoena him until after the announcement of his engagement to Marilyn Monroe, the actress and sex symbol. The issue, at least ostensibly, was Miller's eligibility to travel abroad, given his communist leanings. Because Miller was an internationally respected figure, HUAC conducted its investigation in a rather restrained manner. The historian Walter Goodman described Miller's testimony as "responsive, collected and only moderately sententious." Facing accusations of having signed numerous statements connected with allegedly pro-communist organizations and of having made a formal application to join the Communist Party, Miller conceded his activities with the communists in the 1940s but denied that he applied to or joined the Communist Party. In addition, he stated that "I would not now support a cause or movement dominated by Communists." Members of the committee mildly praised him for his example of "repentance," but he angered the panel by refusing to offer the names of communists with whom he had associated. "My conscience," he declared, "will not permit me to use the name of another person and bring trouble to him." Miller was cited for contempt of Congress and received a $500 fine and a 30-day suspended jail sentence. He appealed and in 1958 won a reversal of the contempt citation.

Throughout the 1950s and 1960s, Miller continued to write plays in a style sometimes described as "social realism." These included *A Memory of Two Mondays* (1955), a reminiscence of Miller's time working in the auto parts warehouse, and *A View from the Bridge* (1955), the story of an Italian-American longshoreman whose jealousy over his niece leads him to turn in two of his wife's relatives as illegal immigrants. Neither of these social dramas had the power of *Death of a Salesman*.

Miller adapted one of his short stories into a screenplay for *The Misfits* (1961). The movie starred Monroe, whom Miller had married in 1956, and Clark Gable. Miller's next play, *After the Fall* (1964), was his most overtly autobiographical work. It examined his married life with Monroe as well as his relationships with artists who named names during the anticommunist investigations. Some critics regarded the play, written shortly after Miller's divorce from Monroe, as a cruel, even indecent, way of getting even. *Incident at Vichy* (1965), a long one-act play based on an actual incident, dramatized 90 minutes in the lives of a group of men waiting to be interviewed by the Gestapo in 1942. As Miller presented it, those content to avoid complicity in Nazi crimes shared the guilt of the persecutors. With his next play, *The Price* (1968), Miller returned to domestic drama. The play involved the intense confrontation between two estranged brothers, one a surgeon and the other a police officer who gave up the chance for a more promising career to support their father, brought together by their father's death. *The Price*, which did reasonably well financially and received some critical praise, turned out to be Miller's last success on Broadway.

Miller continued to be politically active in the 1960s. He was elected president of P.E.N., the International Association of Writers, in 1965. He spoke against the war in Vietnam at the first teach-ins at the University of Michigan in 1965 and rejected an invitation to the White House in protest against the war. In 1968, he served as a delegate for Senator EUGENE MCCARTHY (D-Minn.) at the Democratic National Convention.

Miller continued to write plays into the first decade of the 21st century, but they found neither the commercial nor critical success of his earlier works. Critics attacked his later work as moralistic and turgid. This, in turn, led Miller to make some corrosive statements about the American theater. Miller also wrote short stories, a novella, travel books, and an autobiography, *Timebends: A Life* (1987). Miller died at his home in Roxbury, Connecticut, on February 10, 2005.

The Great Depression, which Miller regarded as the most significant event of American history with the possible exception of the Civil War, hovered over Miller's works. His best plays explored the emptiness of the American dream. World War II and the Holocaust provided another rich vein for Miller. His works exploring those events included *All My Sons, Incident at Vichy, Broken Glass*, and, in 1980, *Playing for Time* (a dramatization for television of a book about a Jewish woman who survived Auschwitz by playing the violin for Nazi officers). Some critics found his didacticism and the ostentatious display of his liberal conscience difficult to swallow. Even when commenting on Miller's earlier work, Robert Brustein wrote that when Miller "evokes our sympathy for the common man, we are confronted less with works of art than with political acts or social gestures." Critics also complained that his dialogue represented more the attempt of a playwright determined to convey his message to an audience than the voice of authentic human beings. For all that, Miller's best plays continue to resonate with audiences. Miller staged *Death of a Salesman* in China in the 1980s, and *The Crucible* became a Hollywood movie in the 1990s.

—MSM

Millikin, Eugene D(onald)

(1891–1958) *U.S. senator; chairman, Senate Finance Committee*

The son of a dentist, Eugene Millikin was born in Hamilton, Ohio, on February 12, 1891. He enrolled in the University of Colorado Law School in 1910. Upon graduating in 1913, he began to practice law in Salt Lake City, Utah. He embarked on a career in politics as executive secretary to the governor of Colorado, George Carlson, from 1915 to 1917. During World War I, Millikin enlisted as a private in the Colorado National Guard. He saw action in France and was mustered out a lieutenant colonel. After the war, he formed a law partnership in Denver, Colorado, with Karl Schuyler. When Schuyler was elected to the U.S. Senate in 1932, Millikin accompanied him to Washington as his secretary but returned to Colorado the next year after Schuyler died in an automobile accident. Millikin resumed his corporate law practice and served as president of the Kinney-Coastal Oil Company.

In 1941, Millikin, a Republican, was appointed to the Senate to fill a vacancy created by the death of Senator Alva Adams (D-Colo.). He was elected to serve the remainder of Adams's term in 1942 and won election to full terms in 1944 and 1950. A close ally of Senator ROBERT TAFT (R-Ohio), Millikin shared Taft's fiscal conservatism but was rather more inclined to support internationalism in foreign policy. Millikin provided important support for the ratification of the United Nations Charter, the Marshall Plan, and the North Atlantic Treaty. In domestic matters, he became an expert in the intricacies of trade and taxation. After the Republicans won control of both houses of Congress in the elections of 1946, he chaired the Finance Committee during the 80th Congress. When the Democrats regained control of Congress in the elections of 1948, Millikin became the ranking Republican on the Finance Committee. On domestic issues, he was consistently friendly to business and often devoted his technical expertise and formidable skill in debate to the creation of corporate tax breaks. He believed that the accumulation of wealth served the national interest. Someone with an income of $500,000 a year, he once argued, "has the big estate . . . to maintain. . . . He has three Cadillacs. . . . They must be garaged, oiled, greased, and driven." Millikin also opposed most Democratic social programs. During the administration of HARRY S. TRUMAN, Millikin opposed the Full Employment Act of 1946, public housing, and federal aid to education. An effective and increasingly powerful senator, Millikin shunned the limelight, preferring to work behind the scenes.

Millikin supported Taft for the Republican nomination in 1952, but when DWIGHT D. EISENHOWER defeated Taft, the senator from Colorado played a useful role in bringing the party together for the general election. Eisenhower won the White House, and Republicans captured majorities in both houses of Congress. When Republicans organized the Senate in 1953, Millikin resumed the chair of the Finance Committee. In addition, he became chair of the Senate Republican Conference, sat on the Joint Committee on Atomic Energy, and was the second ranking Republican on the Interior and Insular Affairs Committee. Millikin was one of a handful of congressional Republicans who met once a week to discuss policy with the president. In January 1954, *Business Week* characterized him as "probably the most influential Republican in the Senate."

For the most part, Millikin exercised his influence on behalf of the Eisenhower administration's programs. According to *Congressional Quarterly*, his voting record placed him among the five most frequent supporters of the administration in the Senate. Even more important from the administration's point of view was his reliability as chair of the Finance Committee, particularly since his counterpart in the House, Representative DANIEL REED (R-N.Y.), the chair of the Ways and Means Committee, proved difficult to deal with and often defied the administration.

For example, the administration requested a six-month extension of the excess profits tax, which passed the House in July 1953 only after experiencing great difficulty in Reed's committee. In the Senate, however, Millikin rushed the measure through the Finance Committee without holding hearings; it passed the Senate by a voice vote. In another instance, Millikin opposed an amendment by Senator JOHN WILLIAMS (R-Del.) to raise the business tax credit from $25,000 to $100,000, which would have required approval of the revised bill by the House (something Millikin likened to "passing a kidney stone"). The administration objected to the amendment, and Millikin pleaded successfully against it.

In 1954, Millikin fought for an amendment exempting from taxation a portion of income derived from stock dividends. The Senate passed the amendment but then reversed itself. The conference committee partly restored the provision exempting dividends. Millikin also successfully led Republican opposition to an attempt by Democrats to amend the same bill to raise the personal tax exemption from $600 to $700. Democrats accused the bill and Millikin of favoring the affluent over those with lower incomes.

Millikin did not always support the administration. Initially inclined to support the Bricker amendment, Millikin sought a compromise with the president, who adamantly opposed it. In the end, Millikin went against the president's wishes and voted for the George amendment, a compromise that the administration rejected. Millikin also voted against the censure of Senator JOSEPH R. McCARTHY (R-Wis.).

With respect to trade policy, Millikin steered a moderate course between his own protectionist leanings and the administration's desire to renew reciprocal trade agreements. In June 1954, he guided through the Senate passage of a one-year extension of the agreements. In April 1955, he tried to limit extension to two years instead of three, but he lost in the Finance Committee by a vote of eight to seven. He did win passage of an "escape clause" amendment to limit certain imports if they "contributed materially" to a "threat of serious injury" to a domestic industry. Advocates of free trade charged that Millikin's amendment "watered down" the bill, but the Senate passed it in that form.

From his senior position on the Interior Committee, Millikin was an influential supporter of the Colorado River Storage Project, a billion-dollar program to construct water storage facilities along the Upper Colorado River Basin. Many regarded Millikin's vote for the St. Lawrence Seaway in 1954 as a trade-off for the administration's support of the Colorado River project. The Senate approved the Colorado River project in 1955; the House passed it a year later.

Throughout his tenure in the Senate, Millikin generally favored lower taxes and reducing the size of the federal government. His strongest commitment, however, was to a balanced budget. Despite his influence and ability, Millikin never demonstrated any ambitions for the presidency and spurned opportunities to be Republican leader in the Senate. Ailing from arthritis, he did not seek reelection in 1956. Millikin died of pneumonia in Denver, Colorado, on July 26, 1958.

—MSM

Mills, C(harles) W(right)
(1916–1962) sociologist

The product of a middle-class family of Irish and English descent, C. Wright Mills was born in Waco, Texas, on August 28, 1916. His father was an insurance agent, and Mills grew up in Sherman, Fort Worth, and Dallas, where he attended Catholic schools and public high schools. After a year at Texas A&M, Mills enrolled at the University of Texas, from which he received a B.A. in 1938 and an M.A. in philosophy and sociology in 1939. He then enrolled in the doctoral program in sociology at the University of Wisconsin, where he wrote his dissertation under Hans Gerth and received his degree in 1942. His dissertation, later published as *Sociology and Pragmatism* (1964), dealt with professionalization in higher education and the role of pragmatism in that process. After teaching sociology at the University of Maryland from 1942 to 1946, he moved to Columbia University, where he remained for the rest of his career and emerged as one of the most widely read and controversial critics of postwar American society.

Using the methodologies of Karl Marx, Max Weber, and Karl Mannheim, Mills sought to identify the changing relationships of social and political power in the United States and to offer prescriptions for radical change. Fundamentally opposed to liberal social scientists' ideas of objective scholarship, Mills also increasingly diverged from traditional Marxist approaches. His *New Men of Power* (1948) offered a sociological portrait of labor leaders and a study of their political attitudes. Mills concluded that support for a labor party, which he thought necessary to represent the interests of American workers, had declined among labor leaders since the 1930s. Leaders of large unions were attracted to oligarchy, liberalism, and the retention of their own power. Rather than a money elite, they formed a power elite that contested with other elites. Mills, however, contended that the power labor union leaders had achieved since World War II provided them with a basis to form a radical coalition with intellectuals and white collar workers capable of "stopping the main drift towards war and slump."

In *White Collar: The American Middle Classes* (1951), Mills described the emergence of a new American middle class, made up not of the independent entrepreneurs that typified the "old middle class" but of "the small creature who is acted upon but who does not act, who works alone unnoticed in somebody's office or store, never talking loud, never talking back, never taking a stand." Mills argued that the white collar workers of the mid-20th century were analogous to the industrial workers of the late 19th century. They did not have ownership, did routinized, repetitive tasks, and had little or no control over their work, the final product, or the workplace. In one important respect, however, they were worse off than their 19th-century counterparts. Early industrial workers had to sell only their time and energy; in the bureaucratic environment of the mid-20th century, the white collar workers had to sell their personalities as well.

Mills published *The Power Elite* in 1956. In it, he asserted that the American political system was not truly democratic. For Mills, contrary to Marxists and Weberians, power lay neither in the process of production nor in the market. The growth of large-scale bureaucracies, the development of new techniques for the manipulation of people, and the emergence of a vast military establishment armed with weapons of mass destruction, Mills maintained, gave rise to an interconnected elite of military, governmental, and industrial leaders that wielded unprecedented power. He attacked the theory, propounded by JOHN KENNETH GALBRAITH, that "countervailing powers" checked the power of corporations. Real power, Mills maintained, was exercised by an "overlapping" alliance composed of major corporate leaders, top military brass, and a handful of politicians. These leaders made decisions in private and rarely even engaged in "public or . . . Congressional debate." Mills also attacked the ideas of SEYMOUR MARTIN LIPSET and DANIEL BELL, two sociologists who celebrated the "pluralistic" character of American politics and the "end of ideology." Mills argued that "mass society" was easily manipulated and that therefore the policies of the power elite could not be effectively opposed. Neither education, religion, television, nor movies possessed any truly independent organization or ideology to counter the pervasive influence of the power elite. Therefore, Mills concluded, workers had come to accept the values sponsored by the power elite, and

they yearned for nothing more than white collar jobs and suburban homes. The study came in for severe criticism from some sociologists, including Bell, who argued that the theory of a "power elite" implied a "unity of purpose and community of interest" among the elite, which Mills had asserted rather than proved.

Mills expanded his focus on the elite in *The Causes of World War Three* (1958). The book suggested an international power elite, one that, to be sure, did not share an ideology but that "in structural trend and in official action" became "increasingly alike." Mills regarded a new and devastating war as almost unavoidable, because the existing power structure left the fate of the world in the hands of an isolated few whom he regarded as both unscrupulous and incompetent. He further argued that the "balance of blame" was shifting from the Soviet bloc to the West. Mills's professional colleagues essentially ignored the book; it embarrassed even members of the intelligentsia, whom Mills had courted for years.

In *The Sociological Imagination* (1959), Mills claimed that only an exertion of leadership by a new generation of intellectuals could prevent the catastrophe he described in *The Causes of World War Three*. Before they could assert such leadership, however, Mills maintained that intellectuals would have to direct their research away from abstract issues and toward "urgent public issues and instant human trouble." Thus, *The Sociological Imagination* took on what Mills saw as the two dominant tendencies of sociology in his day, the hyperbolic pretension of what he termed "Grand Theory" and the irrelevant, narrow, microscopic focus of "Abstracted Empiricism." Mills called for a sociological imagination that "enables us to grasp history and biography and the relations between the two within society. . . . No social study that does not come back to the problems of biography, of history and of their intersections within a society has completed its intellectual journey."

In his "Letter to the New Left" (1960), Mills called attention to a new kind of radicalism. A cultural elite (a "young intelligentsia") comprising radical students and professors was creating an intellectually fresh "New Left." This movement manifested itself in the protests against the House

Un-American Activities Committee and in its participation in the Civil Rights movement.

Mills was staunchly anticommunist and anti-Soviet until the late 1950s, but visits to Poland in 1956 and the USSR in 1960 left him ambivalent about communist societies. *Listen Yankee! The Revolution in Cuba* (1960), published after a trip to Cuba in the summer of 1960, vigorously defended the Cuban Revolution (with which Mills identified himself through the use of the word "we") and did much to generate enthusiasm for the Castro government among the American student Left. Irving Louis Horowitz, a political scientist and Mills's biographer, wrote that "Mills embraced the Cuban Revolution because it seemed to confirm his long-held pet theories about the decline of liberalism in the West and the growing embrace of democratic values by Marxist states." While Mills demonstrated some apprehension about the lack of democracy in Cuba, he argued that the new regime was building the preconditions for a good society and warned that the United States would attempt to destroy the revolution by force. This unbridled polemic led many of his professional colleagues to write him off as a sociologist.

Mills died of a heart attack in West Nyack, New York, on March 20, 1962. His work greatly influenced the development of the New Left during the 1960s. Both Mills's ideas and his style influenced "The Port Huron Statement," the manifesto that brought the Students for a Democratic Society to public attention in 1962. Readings of Mills gave rise to New Left concepts such as "participatory democracy." Although most widely known as the precursor or patron saint of the New Left of the 1960s, Mills's own work was deeply grounded in the concerns of the late 1940s and 1950s. His most creative work elaborated on the link between culture and politics, as well as the relationship between the larger society and the private discontent of an individual pointed out by writers such as DAVID RIESMAN and WILLIAM WHYTE. Moreover, Mills's work reflected the concerns of the postwar American affluent society; it focused less on the material plight of disadvantaged groups or on programs to help them than on the psychological and moral strains afflicting the middle class. In addition, Mills always exaggerated his own status as an outsider (young New Leftists embraced his image as a motorcycle-riding, cabin-building Texan). There was, to be sure, an element of truth in that image. Unconstrained by the direction of his discipline, by its commitment to objective scholarship, or by academic collegiality, Mills scathingly attacked his fellow sociologists for focusing on narrow and irrelevant topics. None of this endeared him to academic social scientists, many of whom dismissed his work as journalistic or polemical. Nevertheless, Mills addressed large topics (what he called "the big questions") and, particularly in *White Collar*, demonstrated an impressive ability to analyze powerful and significant trends shaping his society.

—MSM

Mills, Wilbur D(aigh)

(1909–1992) *U.S. congressman; chairman, Ways and Means Committee*

The son of a prosperous (at least by local standards) owner of a general store, Wilbur Mills was born on May 24, 1909, in Kensett, Arkansas. He attended public schools and graduated from Searcy (Arkansas) High School in 1926 and four years later from Hendrix College in Conway, Arkansas. A champion debater in college and salutatorian of his class, Mills entered Harvard Law School in 1930. He returned to Arkansas without receiving a degree in 1933 and took a job as a cashier in a bank his father had acquired. Mills was elected county and probate judge for White County, an office he held from 1934 to 1938, when he won a seat as a Democrat in the U.S. House of Representatives. At the time, Mills was the youngest person ever elected to Congress. He subsequently won reelection 18 consecutive times with little or no opposition.

His experience in law and banking led to his assignment to the House Banking and Currency Committee in 1939. A protégé of SAM RAYBURN (D-Tex.), Mills rose in the House after Rayburn became Speaker in 1940. Rayburn's sponsorship gained Mills an appointment to the Ways and Means Committee in 1943, an uncommonly swift ascension to the powerful committee responsible for writing tax legislation. Mills industriously applied himself to the details of government finance and trade legislation; by the 1950s, he became the House's foremost expert on taxes. Although he supported much of the Fair Deal, Mills voted for the Taft-Hartley Act and to override President HARRY S. TRUMAN's veto of the measure. Throughout the late 1940s and early 1950s, Mills voted for anticommunist laws. He also supported an excess profits tax to help pay for the Korean War. In foreign policy, Mills regularly supported the Truman administration; he voted for aid to Greece and Turkey, the Marshall Plan, and the North Atlantic Treaty.

During the administration of DWIGHT D. EISENHOWER, Mills generally voted as a moderate; from 1953 to 1960, he voted for positions favored by the liberal Americans for Democratic Action an average of 45 percent of the time on major issues. He voted against statehood for Alaska and Hawaii and against the Saint Lawrence Seaway project; he voted for public housing, the federal highway program, and federal aid for the prevention of water pollution. Worried that it might become a lever to enforce school desegregation, Mills opposed federal aid for school construction. Although not an especially outspoken segregationist, he consistently opposed civil rights legislation and in 1956 signed the Southern Manifesto, which denounced the Supreme Court's ruling in *Brown v. Board of Education* (1954) that segregated public schools were unconstitutional.

In 1953, Mills supported the extension to the end of the year of the excess profits tax levied during the Korean War. The next year, he voted in favor of an unsuccessful amendment to substitute general tax relief for a bill, sponsored by the Eisenhower administration, providing for preferential treatment of income from dividends. Early in 1955, Mills introduced a Democratic plan to give a tax credit of $20 to every taxpayer and his dependents. The measure passed the House by a vote of 234 to 201, but the Senate rejected it. A proponent of reciprocal trade treaties and lowered tariffs, Mills worked on the Ways and Means Committee to block protectionist amendments to trade bills.

With the death of Representative JERE COOPER (D-Tenn.) in December 1957, Mills assumed the chair of the Ways and Means Committee, one of the most powerful positions in the House. Besides deliberating on legislative matters such as taxes, trade, and Social Security, the committee

functioned as the House Democratic Committee on Committees, which gave out committee assignments to Democratic representatives. Mills's mastery of the complexities of the tax code won him general respect that augmented his power. He became an unusually powerful chair of an unusually powerful committee.

Mills suffered a defeat in his first major test as the chair. In response to the economic recession and the growing number of workers whose unemployment benefits were exhausted, the Ways and Means Committee, under Mills's leadership, passed a controversial bill providing 16 additional weeks of federally financed unemployment payments to roughly 3 million people whose benefits had run out and making additional workers eligible for benefits. The Eisenhower administration opposed the bill, as did a coalition of conservative Republicans and southern Democrats. On May 1, 1958, Mills introduced the measure in the House, which rejected it by a vote of 223 to 165. This rebuff had a far-reaching effect on Mills. It accentuated his native caution and sharpened his sensitivity to the climate of opinion in the House as a whole. After that, he held bills in his committee until he had formed a broad consensus behind them and was certain of approval by the House. Some have argued that this led to his famous role in the delay and obstruction of controversial social and economic legislation during the 1960s.

Mills enjoyed greater success in his management of the administration's trade program in 1958. With the support of most of his Democratic colleagues on the committee, he won approval of a five-year extension of the Reciprocal Trade Agreements Act together with a provision granting the president the authority to cut tariffs by 25 percent at a top rate of 5 percent a year. Mills's first hurdle on the House floor was a protectionist substitute offered by Representative Richard Simpson (R-Pa.), which Mills called "far worse than no extension at all." The House rejected Simpson's substitute by a vote of 234 to 147 and passed the committee's bill by 317 to 98. The Senate reduced the extension to three years and the president's power to cut tariffs to 15 percent. The compromise version that emerged from the conference committee set the figures at four years and 20 percent.

Beginning in 1960, Mills played a crucial role in the struggle over providing medical care for the aged. He blocked a liberal proposal, known as Medicare, that would have provided free medical care for the aged financed through the Social Security system. The American Medical Association vehemently opposed the plan, and Mills feared alienating the officials of his state's medical society, which exerted a powerful influence in Arkansas politics. Moreover, as a fiscal conservative, he questioned the feasibility of financing an ambitious program out of the Social Security system. In response to pressure from the Democratic leadership, Mills agreed to consider the plan. In the end, he remained opposed to it, and, on June 3, 1960, the bill failed in the Ways and Means Committee by a vote of 17 to 8.

Mills then arranged passage of his own bill, which permitted the federal government to make matching grants to the states to provide medical care for the elderly poor. Unlike Medicare, Mills's plan applied only to the elderly indigent and only in those states that chose to extend medical aid. In addition, the plan was financed out of general revenues, not the Social Security system. It passed the House by a vote of 380 to 83. With some modifications inspired by Senator ROBERT KERR (D-Okla.), the Senate enacted the measure, known as the Kerr-Mills Act, in August. Subsequently, Mills bottled up legislation providing for Medicare in the Ways and Means Committee until 1965, when it became apparent that a majority of the House favored the program. He then supported the measure and became the chief architect in the House of the bill that passed Congress that year.

Mills played a similar role in the tax battles of the 1960s. Both when President JOHN F. KENNEDY proposed a sweeping tax cut in 1963 and when President LYNDON B. JOHNSON requested a 10 percent surcharge on income taxes in 1967, Mills initially opposed the measures, out of both fiscal conservatism and doubt about the receptivity of the House. After he had extracted sufficient concessions involving spending limits or budget cuts and shaped each plan to his satisfaction, he steered the bills to passage in his committee and on the floor of the House. During the presidency of RICHARD M. NIXON, Mills made common cause with the Republican administration in opposing busing to achieve

racial integration, supporting the war in Vietnam, and backing Nixon's unsuccessful attempt to reform the welfare system. Fearing that it meant the loss of congressional power, he steadfastly opposed Nixon's plans for revenue sharing.

Despite his often-repeated aim of making a thorough revision of the complicated and inequitable tax code, Mills never attempted major tax reform during his tenure as chair of the Ways and Means Committee. In fact, he generally smothered reform proposals within the committee. In October 1974, Mills became embroiled in a scandal involving his relationship with an Argentine stripper named Annabel Battistella, who performed under the name Fanne Foxe, and public displays of drunkenness. Despite the unfavorable headlines and jokes on late-night television, he won reelection that November. However, Mills stepped down as chair of the Ways and Means Committee in December 1974. He confessed to being an alcoholic and entered a hospital for treatment. Mills retired from Congress in January 1977 and went to work as a tax consultant, lobbyist, and lawyer for the Washington office of Shea, Gould, Climenko & Casey, a law firm based in New York. In the early 1980s, he returned to Kensett, where he resided until he collapsed at his home and died in a hospital in Searcy, Arkansas, on May 2, 1992.

—MSM

Minton, Sherman
(1890–1965) *associate justice, U.S. Supreme Court*

Born in Georgetown, Indiana, on October 20, 1890, Minton attended public schools and earned an LL.B. in 1915 from Indiana University, where he graduated at the head of his class in the law college. He received an LL.M. from Yale the following year and commenced the practice of law in New Albany, Indiana. Minton served as a captain in the Motor Transport Corps from 1917 to 1919 and spent a year overseas. After his military service, he returned to New Albany to practice law. He moved to Miami, Florida, in 1925 and practiced law there until 1928, when he returned to New Albany. In 1933, Minton became counselor of the Indiana Public Service Commission. He won election as a Democrat to the U.S. Senate from Indiana in 1934. An enthusiastic and outspoken supporter of the New Deal, Minton aggressively criticized the Supreme Court's decisions striking down New Deal legislation during 1935 and 1936. In 1937 he backed Franklin D. Roosevelt's plan to pack the Supreme Court. Defeated for reelection in 1940, Minton briefly served as an administrative assistant in the Executive Office of the President in 1941. In May of that year, Roosevelt named him to the U.S. Court of Appeals for the Seventh Circuit. HARRY S. TRUMAN, who had known Minton since their days together in the Senate, appointed him to the Supreme Court in September 1949. Minton took the oath of office on October 12.

Based on his record in the Senate, most observers believed that Minton would be a liberal on the Court. Indeed, some conservative senators attempted to call him before the Senate Judiciary Committee so that they could question him on his support for the Court packing plan and other matters. Minton declined to appear. Contrary to expectations, his accession to the bench helped to create a conservative bloc that held sway for the next four years. In the summer of 1949, two of the Court's more liberal justices, Frank Murphy and Wiley B. Rutledge, died. Truman appointed TOM C. CLARK to replace Murphy and Minton to replace Rutledge. The two new justices, along with Truman's two other appointments to the Court, HAROLD H. BURTON and Chief Justice FRED M. VINSON, moved the Court to the right, especially on issues relating to civil liberties.

The basis of Minton's conservatism lay in his commitment to judicial restraint. The controversies of the 1930s convinced him that the judiciary should allow the executive and legislative branches, as well as the states, the greatest latitude to make policy. The Court, believed Minton, should not interfere with any constitutionally permissible actions by the other branches, however unwise the justices might think them. As a result, Minton voted to uphold the government's position in most cases involving civil liberties and the rights of those accused of a crime.

During the early years of the cold war, Minton supported virtually all of the government's antisubversive programs and actions. In *Dennis v. U.S.* (1951), he voted with the majority to uphold the convictions of leaders of the American Communist Party for violating the Smith Act by conspiring to overthrow the government of the United States. He dissented when, in *Joint Antifascist Refugee Committee v. McGrath* (1951), the Court struck down procedures established by Truman's federal loyalty program that allowed the attorney general to place groups on a list of subversive organizations without a hearing. Minton wrote the majority opinion in *Adler v. Board of Education of New York* (1952), upholding a law passed by New York State that provided for the dismissal of public school teachers on grounds of disloyalty and accepted membership in certain organizations as evidence of disloyalty.

Similarly, Minton consistently supported the government's power to intervene in the economy. He joined Vinson in dissent when the Court declared unconstitutional Truman's seizure of the steel mills during the Korean War (*Youngstown Sheet & Tube Co. v. Sawyer* [1952]).

Under Chief Justice EARL WARREN, Minton continued to vote in a similar fashion, but he found himself more frequently in the minority. He dissented in April 1956, when the Court, in *Pennsylvania v. Nelson*, overturned a state sedition law on the ground that federal action had preempted the field. In another case the same month, Minton objected to a majority ruling that a local government could not discharge a professor solely because he invoked the Fifth Amendment during a federal investigation (*Slochower v. Board*). He dissented again in June 1956, when the Court held, in *Cole v. Young*, that federal employees could not be summarily suspended as security risks if they held nonsensitive jobs. Minton joined the majority, however, in *Peters v. Hobby* (1955), which held that the Civil Service Commission's Loyalty Review Board had exceeded its authority when it reviewed of its own initiative and found unfit a consultant to the Public Health Service who had already been cleared twice by the Health Service's departmental loyalty board.

In criminal cases, Minton was extremely reluctant to upset a conviction when the defendant made no claim of innocence but charged that the government had made procedural errors in the course of arrest and prosecution. In *Lutwak v. United States* (1953), he wrote that "a defendant is entitled to a fair trial but not a perfect one." Minton also disliked interfering with the criminal justice systems of the states. For that reason, he dissented in April 1956 when the Court ruled, in *Griffin v. Illinois*, that the states must furnish a trial transcript to an indigent defendant if the transcript was necessary to appeal a conviction.

In civil rights cases, Minton generally voted to outlaw racial and religious discrimination. He believed that the government had no constitutional power to discriminate and that the Court could legitimately intervene to protect minority rights against infringement by the government. Minton joined with the majority in *Shelley v. Kraemer* (1948) to hold restrictive covenants that barred sales to minorities judicially unenforceable. He also voted with the majority to require the admission of a black student to the University of Texas Law School in *Sweatt v. Painter* (1950) and to force the University of Oklahoma to end discriminatory practices against a graduate student in *McLaurin v. Oklahoma* (1950). Speaking for the Court in *Barrows v. Jackson* (1953), Minton held that state courts could not force a property owner to pay damages to his neighbors for violating a restrictive covenant by selling his property to African Americans. Minton also joined a unanimous court in *Brown v. Board of Education* (1954), which ruled that racial segregation in public schools was unconstitutional. Minton, however, was the lone dissenter in May 1953, when the Court decided that the pre-primary elections of the Jaybird Democratic Association in one Texas county were in effect state actions and therefore could not exclude African Americans. Minton asserted that the association was purely private and that, however undesirable its policy of barring African Americans, the Constitution did not prohibit such discrimination by private organizations. "I am not concerned in the least," he wrote, "as to what happens to the Jaybirds or their unworthy scheme. I am concerned about what this court says is state action."

Declining health led Minton to retire from the Court on October 15, 1956. A warm, gregarious, and unpretentious man who often used earthy language, "Shay" Minton was well liked by all his colleagues throughout his years on the bench. He was not, however, a leading figure on the Court, and he wrote few significant opinions. He did not have an outstanding intellect, and analysts of the Court have overwhelmingly ranked him as an undistin-

guished justice. Following his retirement, Minton was active in the Indiana Bar Association. He died in New Albany on April 9, 1965.

—MSM

Mitchell, Clarence, M., Jr.
(1911–1984)   *director, Washington Bureau, NAACP*
Born in Baltimore, Maryland, on March 8, 1911, Clarence Mitchell attended public schools and graduated from Lincoln University in 1932. He worked as a reporter for the *Baltimore Afro American* from 1933 to 1936, when he left to do a year of graduate study at the Atlanta School of Social Work on a National Urban League fellowship. After completing the program in 1937, he worked briefly as director of the Maryland office of the Division of Negro Affairs of the National Youth Administration. In November 1937, he became executive secretary of the Urban League office in St. Paul, Minnesota. He took a job in 1941 with the Negro Employment and Training Branch in the labor division of the Office of Production Management. Initially, he worked as field employment assistant but was quickly promoted to assistant director of the department. In January 1943, Mitchell was appointed associate director of the division of field operations for the Fair Employment Practices Committee (FEPC); he became director of field operations in 1945. After the war, Congress discontinued the agency, and Walter White, executive secretary of the NAACP, hired Mitchell in 1946 as labor secretary in the organization's Washington bureau. Four years later, Mitchell became director of the Washington bureau. In that capacity, Mitchell served as a lobbyist, presented the NAACP's point of view in the *Crisis* (the NAACP's magazine), and worked with the executive branch to promote enforcement of civil rights.

An important force in shaping and articulating the NAACP's ideas and goals during the 1950s, Mitchell believed that change would be brought about through legislation, action by sympathetic whites, and public relations, rather than by direct-action protests by African Americans. In the early 1950s, the NAACP worked for peaceful desegregation through legal challenges to segregation as well as efforts to persuade the executive and legislative branches to take action. The military became one of the prime targets for executive action, because an executive order could force immediate desegregation of the armed services. In 1953, Mitchell publicly charged that desegregation of military bases was proceeding too slowly. The Eisenhower administration moved expeditiously against segregation on military bases. Mitchell also charged that local opposition was blocking desegregation in locally run schools on military posts and in local schools receiving aid to accommodate the presence of military dependants. In these areas, complexities of the situations made it difficult for the administration to respond as effectively.

Mitchell opposed the congressional seniority system because it often placed southern Democrats at the head of important committees, where they could block civil rights bills. He singled out Senator JAMES O. EASTLAND (D-Miss.), chair of the Judiciary Committee, for particular criticism and threatened that blacks would vote Republican if Democrats did not support civil rights demands.

Mitchell advocated withholding federal funds from segregated areas as a means of advancing desegregation. In 1955, he supported amendments, offered by Representative ADAM CLAYTON POWELL, JR. (D-N.Y.), to bills sponsored by the Eisenhower administration providing federal aid for the construction of schools and for training national reserve units. The so-called Powell amendments banned aid to school districts or reserve units that practiced segregation. The Powell amendment became part of the National Reserve Training Act. Eisenhower opposed the Powell amendment to the school construction bill as "extraneous"; besides, he argued, the Supreme Court had declared segregated public schools unconstitutional. Bills providing for federal aid for school construction both with and without the Powell amendment failed to pass Congress. Mitchell also demanded in 1955 that the government refuse to pay the expenses of South Carolina's delegation to the first White House Conference on Education because the state resisted desegregation of its schools.

Mitchell focused his attention on the extension of voting rights, because he believed that increased black suffrage would result in gains in other fields. In 1956, he urged the NAACP to

give top priority to a bill that would "protect the right to vote and . . . protect individuals against violence." That year, the administration proposed a civil rights bill that would have elevated the civil rights section of the Justice Department to the status of a division, provided for a civil rights commission, granted the attorney general authority to enter civil suits to desegregate, and provided protection for black voting rights. The majority leader, LYNDON B. JOHNSON (D-Tex.), consigned the bill to the deep freeze of Eastland's Judiciary Committee. The administration called for passage of the measure again the following year. By the time the bill passed Congress in 1957, the provision granting the attorney general authority to file civil suits had been deleted, and the protection of voting rights had been substantially weakened. In its final form, the Civil Rights Act of 1957 disappointed Mitchell, and he lobbied for the Civil Rights Act of 1960, which attempted to shore up protections of voting rights. That, too, proved inadequate to protect black voting rights.

Mitchell continued to press for civil rights legislation during the 1960s and 1970s. In addition to his position at the NAACP, he served as legislative chairman of the Leadership Conference on Civil Rights. He was disturbed by what he considered President JOHN F. KENNEDY's foot-dragging on black civil rights. In contrast, he praised President Lyndon B. Johnson's strong stand on behalf of civil rights and lobbied extensively for the Civil Rights Act of 1964 and the Voting Rights Act of 1965. Alone among black leaders who met with Johnson in March 1968, Mitchell supported the president's decision to seek passage of a fair housing law in Congress. The others favored an executive order. Events bore out Mitchell's judgment when, in April, Congress passed the Fair Housing Act of 1968. Mitchell lobbied for passage of extensions of the Voting Rights Act in 1970 and 1975. He attacked the Nixon administration as "anti-Negro" and marshaled support to defeat two of Nixon's nominees to the Supreme Court, CLEMENT F. HAYNSWORTH and G. Harold Carswell.

Mitchell attended night classes at the University of Maryland School of Law and graduated in 1962. He gained admission to the bar in 1965. After Nixon left office, Mitchell continued as director of the NAACP's Washington bureau and the organization's chief lobbyist through the administration of GERALD FORD and into that of Jimmy Carter. He retired from the NAACP in 1978 but served as a consultant to the organization and practiced law in Baltimore; he also was a delegate to the United Nations. Mitchell received numerous awards, including the NAACP's Spingarn Medal in 1969. Carter presented him with the Medal of Freedom in 1980. Mitchell died in Baltimore, Maryland, on March 18, 1984.

—MSM

Mitchell, James P(aul)

(1900–1964) *assistant secretary of the army, secretary of labor*

Mitchell was born in Elizabeth, New Jersey, on November 12, 1900. His father, who edited a trade journal, died in 1912, which left the family in straitened financial circumstances. Although he had to contribute to the family's support, Mitchell graduated from high school in 1917. He worked for several years in a grocery store before opening a small "butter and egg" dairy store in 1919 and opened a second store in 1921. When they failed in 1923, Mitchell worked as a truck driver and then as a salesman. In 1929, he became an expediter for the Western Electric Company. The following year, he was transferred to the personnel department. Laid off in 1932, he served for four years as director of the Union County Emergency Relief Association. He returned to Western Electric in 1936, but the company lent his services to the Works Projects Administration, where he was put in charge of labor relations in New York City.

Beginning in 1940, Mitchell served as director of industrial personnel for the War Department, where he had responsibility for the administration of nearly 1 million employees. Returning to private business in 1945, he directed personnel and industrial relations for R. H. Macy & Company until 1947, when he became vice president in charge of labor relations at Bloomingdale Brothers. Even while working in the private sector, Mitchell conducted studies of employment for the U.S. Army in Germany and served on the personnel advisory board of the first Hoover Commission.

Mitchell supported DWIGHT D. EISENHOWER for president in 1952. In April 1953, the new president appointed him assistant secretary of the army in charge of manpower and reserve affairs. He remained there until October, when MARTIN DURKIN resigned as secretary of labor because he thought that Eisenhower had gone back on a commitment to support his attempts to amend the Taft-Hartley Act. Eisenhower quickly named Mitchell to replace Durkin.

Eisenhower regarded Mitchell as one of the most capable members of his cabinet and respected Mitchell for what the president regarded as the secretary's moderation and realistic approach to labor problems. Mitchell did not wish to be considered the voice of organized labor in government. Rather, he regarded the secretary of labor as a servant of the public. At the same time, he resisted the influence of the more conservative members of the administration, particularly SINCLAIR WEEKS, the secretary of commerce, with whom he frequently

James P. Mitchell, Secretary of Labor *(Dwight D. Eisenhower Library and Museum)*

clashed. As secretary of labor, he opposed right-to-work laws, sought to improve conditions for vulnerable workers such as migrant farmworkers, elderly workers, and handicapped workers. Mitchell strove consistently to promote better relations between labor and management. Further, he demonstrated an early awareness of the nation's growing need for an adequate supply of trained workers. Finally, he improved the efficiency of his department and encouraged the upgrading of civil servants rather than bringing in political appointees.

In general, Mitchell did not believe that the government should intervene frequently in labor disputes. In accord with Mitchell's advice, Eisenhower declined to intervene in strikes against the Louisville and Nashville Railroad in 1954 (in spite of pressure from several governors and members of Congress) and Southern Bell Telephone the same year. Nevertheless, Mitchell's reputation with union leaders as "very able and fair" and a "shrewd bargainer" made him an effective mediator. In 1956, Mitchell announced that he would not act to prevent a steel strike, although he did quietly meet with leaders of the industry and persuaded them to make an offer that prevented a strike. Moreover, he played a major role in the settlement of the steel strike in 1959. That strike began on July 15 and continued for 116 days before it was halted by an 80-day injunction invoked under the Taft-Hartley Act. During the last weeks of 1959, Mitchell and Vice President RICHARD M. NIXON worked behind the scenes to reach an agreement. Finally, a settlement was announced on January 4, 1960. The unions and major steel companies agreed to wages and benefits costing 41 cents over two-and-one-half years; management abandoned its demands for increased efficiency. Although Mitchell played a central role in the negotiations, he yielded the public spotlight to Nixon.

Shortly after assuming office, Mitchell backed an increase in the minimum wage of 75 cents an hour. He wished, however, to hold off the increase until the economy improved. When the issue came before Congress in 1955, labor pushed for $1.25, while the Eisenhower administration submitted an increase of 90 cents. Congress passed a bill raising the figure to $1, a figure that the administration had agreed in advance was acceptable, and Eisenhower

signed the measure. Mitchell opposed a further increase in 1957 on the ground that it would be inflationary.

The secretary also sought to increase the number of workers covered under the federal minimum wage. He extended coverage to industries dealing with office machinery, electric lamps, structural steel, pulp, and water. He liberally interpreted the Walsh-Healey Act, determining the prevailing minimum wages in various industries. Consequently, workers on government contracts in the soft coal as well as the woollen and worsted industries received raises.

In response to the corruption in unions uncovered by the Senate Committee on Improper Relations in the Labor or Management Field, Mitchell, in January 1958, drew up proposed legislation for the administration designed to end labor racketeering and to "provide greater protection for the rights of individual workers, the public, and management and unions." The legislation required unions to file annual financial reports, certify they operated under democratic procedures, and obliged employers and unions to report financial dealings with each other. It prohibited collusion between labor and management and set criminal penalties for bribes, embezzlement, and misappropriation of union funds. In addition, it called for efforts to tighten laws against secondary boycotts and certain types of organizational picketing.

Congress took only limited action on the proposals during 1958. In August, Eisenhower signed a law designed to safeguard pension and welfare funds by requiring disclosure of financial operations. A second measure, sponsored by Senators JOHN F. KENNEDY (D-Mass.) and IRVING IVES (R-N.Y.), dealt with labor corruption. The Kennedy-Ives bill contained some of the anticorruption measures favored by the administration. It also included several changes in the Taft-Hartley Act strongly supported by organized labor. Mitchell opposed the measure. He thought that the "imperfections, omissions or loopholes" made it "almost impossible to administer" and would give union members only "illusory protection." He also objected to the fact that the bill did not tighten the ban on secondary boycotts or bar organizational picketing. The bill passed the Senate but failed in the House.

Eisenhower resubmitted Mitchell's program the following year. The administration wanted particularly to strengthen procedures dealing with secondary boycotts and "blackmail picketing." After vigorous struggles in both the House and the Senate, these provisions eventually made their way into the Landrum-Griffin Act, which Eisenhower signed into law in September 1959. The law included a "bill of rights" for union members that included the rights to secret and fair elections of union officials. The measure also required unions to file reports on union funds with the Department of Labor.

Mitchell strongly supported civil rights for African Americans. In one of his first acts as secretary, he told the National Council of Negro Women that, beginning on November 16, 1953, all contracts with the government of the District of Columbia would contain a clause banning discrimination. During the administration's internal debate over civil rights legislation in 1956 and 1957, Mitchell was one of the strongest voices in the administration for a measure that would effectively protect the rights of African Americans. Congress substantially weakened the legislation proposed by the administration before passing it. As passed by Congress, the Civil Rights Act of 1957 disappointed Mitchell, who called it "weak, watered-down and, in my opinion, ineffectual."

Mitchell greatly improved the efficiency of his office. He established the new career position of undersecretary of labor and three positions of deputy assistant secretary of labor. He added the office of research and development to his department. Mitchell established the practice of meeting regularly with heads of independent agencies, such as the National Labor Relations Board, the Federal Mediation and Reconciliations Service, and the National Retirement Board. Under his leadership, the budget of the Department of Labor rose from $28 million in fiscal 1954 to $53 million by fiscal 1960.

Mitchell left government at the end of the Eisenhower administration and ran unsuccessfully as the Republican nominee for governor of New Jersey in 1961. That same year, he joined the Crown Zellerbach Corporation as a consultant and a director. In 1962, he became senior vice president of industrial relations for the West Coast Pulp and Paper Company. Mitchell resided in Hillsborough,

California, until his death from a heart attack in New York City on October 19, 1964.

—MSM

Mitchell, Stephen A(rnold)
(1903–1974) *chairman, Democratic National Committee*

Born in Rock Valley, Iowa, on March 3, 1903, Mitchell graduated from Creighton University preparatory school in 1921. He then ran the family farm before working as an assistant credit manager in a dry goods company and as credit and sales manager for General Motors Acceptance Corporation. After completing a business course at Creighton University in 1926, he moved to Washington, D.C., and attended Georgetown University Law School at night. Mitchell received his LL.B. in 1928. He worked as an executive for General Motors in New York until 1932, when he joined the Chicago law firm of Taylor, Miller, Busch & Boyden. The firm made him a partner in 1936. Mitchell served as head of the French division of the Lend-Lease Administration from 1942 to 1944 and then worked for the State Department as adviser on French economic affairs. In 1945, he returned to the private practice of law.

Mitchell became one of the postwar generation of Democratic politicians known as "Stevenson Democrats." Upper middle class in origin, these reformers had not set foot in a political clubhouse before 1945. Between 1945 and 1947, Mitchell advocated reform in the Democratic Party of Illinois. In 1947, he sought an appointment as U.S. district attorney. He unsuccessfully attempted to gain the support of the Cook County machine, and the appointment went to Otto Kerner. That same year, ADLAI E. STEVENSON asked for Mitchell's help in securing the senatorial nomination. The Cook County machine, worried that the maverick Democrat, PAUL DOUGLAS, might become governor, preferred to see Douglas run for the Senate and offered Stevenson the gubernatorial nomination. Mitchell played an active role in Stevenson's successful campaign for governor.

In March 1952, Mitchell was appointed chief counsel to a subcommittee of the House Judiciary Committee charged with investigating corruption in the Justice Department. In April, the attorney general, J. Howard McGrath, fired a special counsel appointed to investigate the matter, and Truman announced McGrath's resignation. The subcommittee's report, released in October, criticized McGrath's "deplorable lack of knowledge" of his department and his lack of "enthusiasm" for moving against corruption. Mitchell worked with the new attorney general, James P. McGranery, in reorganizing the department.

Mitchell helped begin the draft Stevenson movement that helped Stevenson win the Democratic nomination for the presidency in 1952. Hoping to counter Republican charges of Democratic corruption, Stevenson appointed Mitchell as chair of the Democratic National Committee. The Democratic candidate chose Mitchell because the latter was personally loyal to him, was not associated with the Truman administration, and had been involved in the investigation of corruption in the Justice Department. The decision infuriated Truman. During the campaign, Mitchell scheduled television time, raised funds, and administered the party's treasury.

Mitchell's most difficult task was maintaining unity within the Democratic Party while distancing Stevenson from the unpopular Truman administration. He announced that Stevenson would hold a series of meetings with Democratic politicians and candidates. Mitchell also assured party regulars that the nominee believed that the fruits of victory should go to those "laboring in the vineyards." In September, after the *New York Post* revealed that the Republican vice presidential nominee, RICHARD M. NIXON, had a "secret" political fund, Mitchell attempted to use the issue of corruption against the Republicans. He immediately demanded that Eisenhower ask for Nixon's resignation. It turned out, however, that the fund was no secret; Nixon had answered questions about it from reporters. Moreover, Nixon successfully confronted the charges in a televised speech, and it came out that Stevenson had a similar fund. The issue probably did more to harm Stevenson than the Republican ticket. In the end, Mitchell's efforts to separate Stevenson from Truman and the corruption of Truman's administration failed. The American electorate gave DWIGHT D. EISENHOWER a large margin of victory in November, and the Republicans carried both houses of Congress.

After the election, Mitchell retained the chair of the Democratic National Committee. He raised money to pay off Stevenson's campaign debt of $830,000. Perhaps his most difficult task was to maintain unity within a party riven by competing interests. Northern liberals, big city bosses, and powerful southern officeholders struggled for influence in the party. In addition, Mitchell attempted to counter charges that the party was drifting to the left and to mount an effective opposition to Eisenhower and his administration. Reacting to criticism from conservatives that the party was too closely linked to the liberal organization, Americans for Democratic Action (ADA), Mitchell attempted to minimize the significance of the ADA. He mentioned that he had never seen a "live" member and maintained that Democratic candidates could "get along without" endorsement by the ADA. In an interview with the *Chicago Sun Times*, Mitchell charged that the organization was injuring the Democratic Party because it competed for the same money from wealthy liberals.

Mitchell continually confronted the problem of promoting opposition to an administration led by a popular president widely perceived as a father figure. While most prominent Democrats were content to attack Eisenhower's programs, Mitchell attacked Eisenhower personally. In March 1954, he announced that the president should be held responsible for the actions of all Republicans and charged that Eisenhower backed McCarthyism as the Republicans' best formula for success. Five months later, Mitchell charged Eisenhower with cronyism for supporting the Dixon-Yates contract, which provided for a private utility to replace the Tennessee Valley Authority as the Atomic Energy Commission's chief supplier of power in that region. Mitchell charged that Bobby Jones (the professional golfer, a friend of the president, and director of one of the companies involved in the proposal) had influenced Eisenhower's decision. Both Eisenhower and Jones denied the charge. The attack backfired against Mitchell and the Democrats, who were never able to substantiate the allegations of improper relations between Eisenhower and Jones. The *New*

York Times accused Mitchell of making unfair and unsubstantiated allegations.

Mitchell's greatest success as the chair of his party was the campaign of 1954, in which Democrats won back both houses of Congress. In December 1954, Mitchell publicly announced that he wished to return to his law practice. Before stepping down, he saw to it that his successor would be a liberal able to hold the center of the party. Mitchell's personal choice, PAUL BUTLER, became his successor.

Mitchell remained active in Democratic politics throughout the decade. While chairman and after stepping down, he worked to strengthen Stevenson's connection with southern leaders. In particular, he cultivated Representative SAM RAYBURN (D-Tex.) and Senator RICHARD RUSSELL (D-Ga.). In early 1956, Mitchell helped organize a committee to promote Stevenson's candidacy for the presidency. That year, Mitchell also made an unsuccessful attempt to gain the nomination for governor. Although his own bid failed, Mitchell helped Stevenson win the Democratic presidential nomination in August. One of his major contributions was to help stave off efforts by segregationists to splinter the party. At the Democratic convention, he contributed to the prevention of a dispute over a loyalty oath like the one that disrupted the convention four years earlier. Mitchell set up a special advisory committee on rules that came up with a resolution acceptable to most party members. The compromise stated that it was understood that state Democratic parties would put the names of the convention's nominees on the ballot. Mitchell also negotiated a weak civil rights plank in the Democratic platform of 1956 that helped prevent a walkout by southerners. He again served with Stevenson's campaign in the general election. After Eisenhower defeated Stevenson by an even greater margin than four years earlier, Mitchell returned to his law practice.

In April 1960, Mitchell ran unsuccessfully for the Democratic gubernatorial nomination in Illinois. From 1964 to 1966, he was director of communication on administrative affairs for the American Council on Education. He subsequently served as a vice president for education with the Raytheon Corporation, vice president for research and public service at the University of Oklahoma, and vice president for development at Nova University in Fort Lauderdale, Florida. In 1968, Mitchell worked for the unsuccessful presidential candidacy of Senator EUGENE MCCARTHY (D-Minn.). Mitchell died in New Taos, Mexico, on April 23, 1974.

—MSM

Monroney, A(lmer) S(tillwell) Mike
(1902–1980) *U.S. senator*

The son of a pioneer family, Monroney was born in Oklahoma City, Oklahoma, on March 2, 1902. He attended public schools in Oklahoma City and received a B.A. from the University of Oklahoma in 1924. After graduating, he went to work as a reporter and political writer for the *Oklahoma News*. His career as a journalist was cut short in 1928, when his father became seriously ill and Monroney had to take over the family's furniture business. Over the next 10 years, he ran the business and became active in civic affairs, serving as president of the Oklahoma City Rotary Club and the Oklahoma City Retailer's Association. He was elected as a Democrat to the U.S. House of Representatives in 1938 and won reelection in five successive races. In Congress, he supported most of the New Deal and Fair Deal. During the 1940s, Monroney gained public attention as a champion of congressional reform. He sponsored legislation to reduce the number of committees, modify seniority rules, and limit the power of the Rules Committee. In foreign policy, he supported the expansion of the U.S. Navy and Lend-Lease before the United States entered World War II. Subsequently, he backed most of the foreign policies of the Roosevelt and Truman administrations.

In 1950, Monroney narrowly defeated an incumbent senator in the Democratic primary and then easily defeated the Republican candidate in the general election. In the Senate, Monroney was one of the few senators who challenged Senator JOSEPH R. MCCARTHY (R-Wis.) during the last years of the administration of HARRY S. TRUMAN. After DWIGHT D. EISENHOWER became president, Monroney continued to speak out against the demagogue from Wisconsin. In July 1953, Monroney charged McCarthy with making a "shambles" of the State Department's Foreign Service and endangering the Central Intelligence Agency. He also ridiculed a tour of Europe made by two of McCarthy's aides, ROY COHN and G. DAVID SCHINE. Monroney dismissed their search for subversive literature in American overseas libraries as a "keystone cops" chase. As a member of the Interstate and Foreign Commerce Committee, Monroney unsuccessfully opposed the nomination of Robert E. Lee, an associate of McCarthy, to the Federal Communications Commission. Monroney was one of the few senators who supported a resolution by Senator RALPH FLANDERS (R-Vt.) calling for McCarthy's removal from his committee chairmanships and later voted for the resolution to censure McCarthy.

Despite his reputation as a reformer in the House, Monroney did not always support proposals aimed at reforming the rules of the Senate. He opposed attempts by liberals in 1953 and 1957 to ease the requirements for cloture in an effort to pass civil rights legislation. Nevertheless, Monroney voted for the Civil Rights Acts of 1957 and 1960. A strong supporter of foreign aid programs, he sponsored a resolution in 1958 that led to the eventual establishment of the International Development Association to provide long-term, low-interest loans to foreign countries. In 1955, Monroney became chair of the Aviation Subcommittee of the Interstate and Foreign Commerce Committee. He supported legislation in 1956 and 1958 that led to the establishment of the Federal Aviation Administration. Aviation emerged as his primary area of expertise and interest. He strongly supported efforts to aid the aviation industry and sponsored legislation providing grants to airports. At the same time, he never forgot the folks back home; throughout his years in the Senate, Monroney obtained millions of dollars for aviation and aeronautics projects in Oklahoma. He also favored the oil depletion allowance, agricultural price supports, soil conservation programs, rural electrification projects, and efforts to manage resources. In addition, Monroney continued his support for federal aid to education. In 1960, he joined with Senator JOSEPH S. CLARK (D-Pa.) to propose an amendment to the school aid bill that would have authorized federal funds in the amount of $20 per school-age child for the construction of classrooms and to increase the salaries of teachers. The Senate passed the bill, but it died in the House Rules Committee.

During the 1960s, Monroney supported most of the programs of the Kennedy and Johnson administrations and backed the war in Vietnam. He also continued to support aid to the aviation industry and renewed his interest in congressional reform. In his one effort to join the Democratic leadership, he ran for majority whip in 1965 but lost to Senator RUSSELL LONG (D-La.). Although Monroney easily won reelection in 1956 and 1962, he lost his bid for a fourth term by a decisive margin. Upon leaving the Senate, he worked as a consultant to several aviation companies before retiring in 1974. He died in Rockville, Maryland, on February 13, 1980.

—MSM

Morgan, Gerald D(emuth)

(1908–1976) *special presidential assistant for congressional liaison, White House administrative assistant, special counsel to the president, deputy assistant to the president*

The son of a lawyer, Morgan was born in New York City on December 19, 1908. He graduated from Hotchkiss School in 1926, Princeton University in 1930, and Harvard Law School in 1933. After working in the office of the solicitor for U.S. Steel Corporation for a year, he moved to Washington, D.C., to become assistant legislative counsel for the House of Representatives. He entered private law practice in Louisville, Kentucky, in 1938 but returned to his former position with the House a year later. In 1945, he became a partner in the law firm of Morgan and Calhoun in Washington. During the postwar period, he also undertook numerous assignments for House panels, including the Foreign Affairs and Un-American Activities Committees. Most notably, Morgan served as counsel to the Republican majority of the House Labor Committee between 1947 and 1949 and played a major role in drafting the Taft-Hartley Act.

Morgan took no part in the presidential campaign in 1952 and had never met DWIGHT D. EISENHOWER before the latter became president. Nevertheless, in February 1953, Eisenhower appointed him a special presidential assistant. Morgan worked under General WILTON B. PERSONS in the congressional liaison office.

Morgan's appointment rested mainly on the strength of his work on the Taft-Hartley Act, and his early duties dealt primarily with issues relating to labor. During the opening months of the administration, he was involved in the attempt to formulate a labor policy that would attract support from labor while retaining the loyalty of the conservative wing of the Republican Party and groups that traditionally supported the Republican Party, such as the National Association of Manufacturers. When Eisenhower named BERNARD SHANLEY to head a committee to study a revision of the Taft-Hartley Act, Morgan was assigned to assist Shanley. Morgan helped draft a series of 19 amendments to the Taft-Hartley Act, many of which had the support of organized labor. Taft died the day that Eisenhower planned to submit the proposals to Congress, and the administration agreed that it would have been impolitic to send the amendments to Congress on the day that the sponsor of the original act died. Taft's death greatly dimmed any prospect for passage of the proposed amendments. Without Taft's prestige and influence, particularly with the Republican right, the amendments had little chance of passing. Moreover, the election of WILLIAM KNOWLAND (R-Calif.) as majority leader made passage even more unlikely. Further, Secretary of Commerce SINCLAIR WEEKS mobilized an effective campaign against the proposals, which were never sent to Capitol Hill.

Morgan became embroiled in the controversy over how to deal with Senator JOSEPH R. MCCARTHY (R-Wis.), particularly after the demagogue from Wisconsin turned his vitriolic attacks on the administration. One group in the White House urged the president publicly to repudiate McCarthy; the other, including Morgan, favored "getting along" with the senator. By early 1954, however, Eisenhower concluded that McCarthy's attacks had become too blatant to ignore, and Morgan helped devise a moderate retaliatory policy that called for exposing McCarthy's more irresponsible charges to public scrutiny and attempting to limit the interrogation of White House personnel by congressional committees.

In February 1955, Morgan was promoted to the post of special counsel to the president. In that capacity, he helped develop Eisenhower's legislative program. Morgan handled all bills the administration planned to introduce to Congress and advised the president on legislation not initiated by the administration. Morgan helped formulate the administration's response to the so-called Powell amendment. That amendment, offered by Representative ADAM CLAYTON POWELL, JR., (D-N.Y.) to a bill sponsored by the administration that called for federal aid for the construction of schools, would have withheld funds from school districts that practiced racial segregation. Predictably, southerners resolutely attempted to defeat the amendment. In addition, many northern members of Congress also opposed the amendment on the ground that it would jeopardize the passage of the entire bill. For a variety of reasons, including Powell's frequent support of the administration, Eisenhower considered backing the amendment, but the president's primary concern in this instance was the national shortage of classrooms. Morgan cautioned against wholehearted support of the amendment because it would leave Eisenhower open to charges that he was less than sincere about passing the aid for school construction. Eisenhower adopted a position similar to the one Morgan suggested. Ultimately, the Powell amendment failed, as did the larger bill. Morgan also lobbied for the administration's civil rights bill in 1956, which became the Civil Rights Act of 1957, and took part in the meeting between Eisenhower and Governor ORVILLE FAUBUS of Arkansas in which they attempted to resolve the crisis set off by a court order to desegregate Little Rock's Central High School.

As special counsel, Morgan also advised and often accompanied members of the administration called to testify before congressional committees. When, in 1955 and 1956, SHERMAN ADAMS refused to testify before the House Government Operations Committee about charges of conflict of interest, Morgan counseled him to plead executive privilege. In 1958, Adams was called before the House Committee on Legislative Oversight to answer questions concerning favors he allegedly did for BERNARD GOLDFINE, a financier from Boston, and gifts he had received from Goldfine. When Adams testified, Morgan accompanied him. Morgan was involved in the discussions that led to Adams's resignation in September 1958.

Following Adams's departure, Persons replaced Adams as chief of staff, and Morgan became Persons's deputy. Persons, who came from Alabama, felt emotionally incapable of remaining objective on issues relating to civil rights, and he asked Morgan to handle such matters.

When Eisenhower left office, Morgan returned to private law practice. He returned to public service in 1971 as vice president for public and governmental affairs for the National Railroad Passenger Corporation (Amtrak). In 1973, he joined the Washington law firm of Hamel, Park, McCabe and Saunders. Morgan died on June 15, 1976, while vacationing on St. Vincent Island in the West Indies.

—MSM

Morrison, deLesseps S(tory)
(1912–1964) *mayor of New Orleans*

The son of a parish district attorney, deLesseps Morrison was born in New Roads, Louisiana, on January 18, 1912. His maternal lineage included Ferdinand deLesseps, the builder of the Suez Canal, and Sidney Story, an alderman in New Orleans who established the city's regulated, legalized red-light district that came to bear his name. Ill with cancer, Morrison's father committed suicide in 1929. His modest estate was ruined by the stock market crash later that year, leaving the family in greatly reduced circumstances. DeLesseps Morrison worked his way through Louisiana State University, graduating in 1932 with a B.A. and a commission as a second lieutenant in the U.S. Army Reserve. Two years later, he earned a law degree from LSU. Upon finishing law school, he took a job as a lawyer with the National Recovery Administration (NRA). After the Supreme Court declared the NRA unconstitutional in 1935, Morrison formed a law firm with his half brother and a family friend, HALE BOGGS. Morrison became involved with reform politics in New Orleans in 1936. Three years later, he helped form the People's League of Independent Voters, which opposed the Long machine that dominated the Democratic Party and therefore politics in Louisiana. Morrison won a seat in the state legislature in 1940. He went on active duty with the army shortly after Pearl Harbor and rose to the rank of colonel.

While still serving in the army, he was reelected in 1944.

In 1946, Morrison ran as the reform candidate for mayor of New Orleans against the incumbent, Robert S. Maestri, who had the backing of the Long machine. With the support of veterans organizations, African Americans, and reform groups, Morrison defeated Maestri in the Democratic primary. In a heavily Democratic city in a state dominated by Democrats, winning the Democratic primary was tantamount to winning election. After going through the formality of sweeping the general election, Morrison took office in May 1946. He held the office for the next 15 years.

As mayor, Morrison gained a national reputation as a reformer and as an executive concerned with public relations. He used his charisma and urbane persona to create a new image for New Orleans. Morrison's administration stressed efficiency and economy in government. He reformed the city government, revamped the municipal purchasing system, and reorganized the police department. During the late 1940s, he defeated Earl Long's attempts to end the city's home rule. In a successful effort to increase trade and industry, the mayor established the first municipal international relations office in the United States. He also toured the Caribbean and South America as a goodwill ambassador for the city. Morrison undertook an extensive construction program to rebuild the decaying downtown area, provide housing for veterans, and expand recreational facilities. He built a new civic center and a new bridge across the Mississippi River. Conscious of the growing black electorate, Morrison gave symbolic recognition to the African-American community in New Orleans and improved municipal services and facilities in black areas. The mayor nonetheless maintained his commitment to segregation.

Despite Morrison's reputation as a reformer, critics often charged that his efforts produced more illusion than substance. Described by a reporter as "the consummate political animal," the mayor developed his own political machine and placed many of his supporters in key posts. When revelations of police corruption rocked the city in the early 1950s, Morrison used a variety of means to hamper the investigation. Throughout his administration, rumors persisted that Morrison had contacts with the city's underworld. Even his popular construction program imposed a financial burden on the city at a time it, like many other urban centers, was losing its tax base as the middle class fled to the suburbs. Further, investigations revealed that the city had used poor materials and shoddy construction methods in many of those projects. With respect to African Americans, Morrison's policies proved, in many cases, to be tokenism. Few blacks had positions of responsibility in the local party or municipal government.

During the 1950s, Morrison faced growing demands by African Americans for desegregation. Because he needed to maintain support from both blacks and whites, the mayor attempted to maintain a moderate position. He courted the black vote and expended political favors to the black community; nevertheless, he never publicly or privately challenged segregation. In the second half of the decade, federal court orders to desegregate encountered massive resistance, and Morrison's style of racial moderation became increasingly difficult to sustain. While resisting pressure from die-hard segregationists, Morrison urged civil rights groups to accept gradual integration and to refrain from direct action protests. The mayor's attempt at moderation pleased neither side.

Morrison faced his most difficult test when Judge J. SKELLEY WRIGHT, who had originally ordered the Orleans Parish School Board to "make arrangements for admission of children . . . on a racially non-discriminatory basis with all deliberate speed" in 1956, ordered the desegregation of the city's public schools in 1960. During the period after Wright's decision in 1956, Morrison sought to equalize black schools in New Orleans in an effort, as he put it, "to remove the causes that would create agitation among the races." His dual objectives, as he explained in a letter written in June 1959, were to "[keep] down mixing and . . . not [have] any trouble." Wright's decision in 1960 made Morrison's position untenable. After a survey indicated that white parents preferred desegregation to closing the schools, the mayor opposed Governor JIMMIE H. DAVIS's attempts to take over the system and shut it down. Nevertheless, he refused to come out in favor of desegregation. The desegregation of schools in New Orleans that November was accompanied by sometimes violent demonstrations. The city's police protected the students from physical injury but initially did not arrest any demonstrators. Only as the violence escalated did the police make arrests, and most of those arrested were African American. Morrison made a televised address asking for an end to the civil disturbances, which some critics claimed could have been avoided had the mayor taken a more assertive stand in the crisis. He also asked parents to keep their children in school and made it clear that the New Orleans police department was not "enforcing the federal court orders relative to school integration"; rather, they were "only maintaining law and order."

While serving as mayor, Morrison made unsuccessful bids for the governorship in 1956 and 1960. His urbane cosmopolitanism and Roman Catholicism proved a liability in rural, Protestant areas of Louisiana. He also faced opposition from the Long machine and from segregationists, who resented his moderate position on desegregation. In 1961, Morrison mounted an unsuccessful attempt to amend the city's charter so that he could run for a fifth term.

In June 1961, Morrison accepted the post of ambassador to the Organization of American States, where his primary assignment was to promote the Alliance for Progress in Latin American countries. He resigned the position in 1963 to make another bid for the governorship of Louisiana the following year. Morrison lost a runoff election for the Democratic nomination. As it had in 1960, Morrison's moderate position on desegregation cost him many votes and probably the election. After the election, Morrison accepted a job with a bank in New Orleans. Governor John McKeithen appointed him to head a committee charged with bringing new business into the state. Morrison died in a plane crash near Ciudad Victoria, Mexico, on May 22, 1964.

—MSM

Morrow, E. Frederic

(1909–1994) *White House administrative assistant, administrative officer for special projects*

The son of a minister, Morrow was born in Hackensack, New Jersey, on April 20, 1909. Upon graduating from Bowdoin College in 1930, he took a job with the Works Progress Administration in Englewood, New Jersey, after which he worked as a bank messenger. He then worked for *Opportunity* magazine, the official organ of the National Urban League (NUL). After two years with the NUL, he went to work in 1937 as coordinator of branches for the National Association for the Advancement of Colored People (NAACP). Called up by his draft board, Morrow volunteered for military service in 1942. He served throughout the war in the United States and rose to the rank of major. Immediately after being mustered out in October 1946, he entered Rutgers University School of Law on the GI Bill. Upon completing his law degree in September 1948, he clerked for a lawyer in Englewood before becoming a writer for the public affairs division of CBS television. He remained with CBS until 1952, when he took a leave of absence to work as a consultant for DWIGHT D. EISENHOWER's presidential campaign.

After the election, Eisenhower's chief of staff, SHERMAN ADAMS, informed Morrow that the president-elect had asked him to offer Morrow a position on the White House staff. Adams advised Morrow to resign his position at CBS. Six months passed, while Morrow lived on his savings. Finally, BERNARD SHANLEY, special counsel to the president, informed Morrow that there would not be a place for him in the White House. Through the efforts of Charles Willis, Jr., an assistant to Adams, Morrow received an offer of a position as adviser on business affairs in the Department of Commerce.

In July 1955, Morrow joined the White House as administrative officer for special projects. During his tenure at the White House, Morrow frequently encountered frustration and embarrassment. He believed that he served as a "whipping boy" for the black press and their dissatisfaction with the policies of the Eisenhower administration. Further, he found the behavior of some of his colleagues on the White House staff correct but cold. In addition, he found his duties too vaguely defined. Although Morrow hoped to avoid becoming a specialist on racial issues, he was sometimes called upon to represent the president before black organizations or to attend state functions.

The failure of Eisenhower and his administration to take a stronger public position on civil rights

frustrated Morrow. In his journal, he stated that the White House handled civil rights issues "like a bad dream." As early as the summer of 1955, Morrow, troubled by the racial violence in the South after the *Brown* decisions, urged Sherman Adams and Maxwell Rabb to convince the president to speak out against it. Though sympathetic, Adams and Rabb fretted about the lack of black support for Eisenhower and warned that the president could not afford to alienate white southern voters. Moreover, advisers such as WILTON B. PERSONS and GERALD MORGAN argued for a cautious policy on civil rights. In the wake of the murder of EMMETT TILL, Morrow suggested that either Adams or Vice President RICHARD M. NIXON meet with a group of black leaders. This earned the ire of Rabb, who told Morrow that the president had called for a commission to study the problem of civil rights and make recommendations. Moreover, Rabb fulminated about the lack of appreciation among black leaders for the steps the administration had taken.

The arrest of black leaders in Montgomery in February 1956 prompted Morrow once again to write to Adams. This time, he asked for permission to meet with black leaders to explain the actions the administration was taking in the field of civil rights. Adams thought the situation too politically fraught and expressed concern for Morrow's safety in such a situation.

Morrow participated in the Republican National Convention in San Francisco in 1956, but the uncertainty of his role made him uncomfortable. In addition, the president's acceptance speech disappointed Morrow. It addressed civil rights issues only in passing.

After the election, Morrow served as a marshal in the inaugural parade, after which, at Eisenhower's invitation, he took a seat in the president's box. Still, Morrow rankled at what he perceived to be cold treatment from some colleagues on the White House staff, and he remained impatient with the administration's cautious approach to civil rights matters.

Morrow found Vice President Richard M. Nixon among the most sympathetic members of the administration. He accompanied the vice president on an official trip to Africa in 1957, a principal purpose of which was to participate in the celebration of the birth of Ghana as an independent nation.

In Ghana, Nixon met MARTIN LUTHER KING, JR., and invited the rising black leader to visit him in Washington.

In June 1957, Morrow wrote a memorandum to Adams urging that the president meet with a group of black leaders. Adams thought the meeting a good idea but thought it should not take place until after the congressional battle over the administration's civil rights bill had resolved itself. Congress passed the Civil Rights Act of 1957, a substantially weakened version of the administration's bill, in August. Morrow regarded it as "a pitiful, watered down version of the original bill emasculated by amendments added by southern senators," and expressed his hope that the president would veto it. Eisenhower had no wish to veto a civil rights measure, much less one originally introduced by his own administration and the first civil rights bill to pass Congress since Reconstruction. The president signed the measure into law in early September. Whatever Morrow's reservations about the act, its passage cleared the way for the president to meet with black leaders, but the desegregation crisis at Little Rock's Central High School further delayed the meeting.

By fall 1957, Morrow became increasingly frustrated by his position. He felt awkward "standing on platforms all over the country, trying to defend the administration's record on civil rights" when he was frustrated by its unwillingness to act more forcefully. Further, in October, Morrow was transferred to work for ARTHUR LARSON, who had recently been chosen as Eisenhower's principal speechwriter. Although reluctant to make the change, Morrow agreed. As it turned out, he never established a satisfactory working relationship with Larson and repeatedly requested to be reassigned.

In April 1958, Morrow returned to his former position in the president's executive office. He played a role in organizing Eisenhower's meeting with a group of black leaders, which finally took place in June 1958. When Max Rabb, who had handled minority affairs, left the White House staff in the spring of 1958, Morrow was given the assignment of dealing with matters relating to civil rights and African Americans. Not only did Morrow find himself in a position he had earlier hoped to avoid, but the departure of Sherman Adams deprived him of someone who had been a source of personal support as well as access to the president. Adams's replacement was Persons, a southerner who was uncomfortable dealing with civil rights issues. Persons urged Morrow to take such matters to Morgan or "anyone else," including the president, rather than to him.

Morrow became increasingly frustrated with his situation, and, in April 1959, he gave speeches to the Wayne County Republican Club in Detroit and the Republican Woman's Convention in Washington in which he criticized the Republican Party for failing to reach out to black voters. The speeches drew considerable public attention. The address to the Republican Women's Club in particular prompted a flood of complaints to the White House; although it prompted numerous expressions of support as well. In 1960, with the presidential campaign in the offing, Morrow repeatedly sent memos to LEONARD HALL, the Republican national chairman, and Senator THRUSTON MORTON (R-Ky.), former national chairman, urging them to make efforts to mobilize and attract black voters. Morrow's recommendations were brushed aside. Nevertheless, Morrow, who had enjoyed a warm relationship with Nixon, took a two-month leave of absence from the White House to work for Nixon's presidential campaign. Once he joined the campaign, however, Morrow found himself shunted to the side. When Martin Luther King, Jr., was jailed in Atlanta on a minor charge, Morrow beseeched Nixon's staff to have the candidate take some action. Morrow's pleas fell on deaf ears. Morrow believed that the decision by the Democratic nominee, JOHN F. KENNEDY, to intercede in the situation won him the election.

As the Eisenhower administration wound down, Morrow could not find a job in private business commensurate with his abilities and experience. He rejected jobs that focused on a company's relations with African Americans. Upon leaving the White House in 1961, Morrow became a vice president of public affairs of the African-American Institute in New York. Morrow became an assistant vice president at the Bank of New York in 1964. Three years later, he became a vice president and was promoted to a division head in 1969. He retired in 1975, after which he worked as an executive associate at the Educational Testing Service. Morrow published a version of the journal he kept in the White House,

Black Man in the White House, in 1963 and an autobiography, *Forty Years a Guinea Pig*, in 1980. He died in New York City on July 19, 1994.

—MSM

Morse, Wayne (Lyman)
(1900–1974) *U.S. senator*

Born on his parents' farm near Madison, Wisconsin, on October 20, 1900, Wayne Morse received a B.A. from the University of Wisconsin in 1923 and an M.A. from the same institution the following year. In 1924, he enrolled at the University of Minnesota for a graduate degree in speech but switched to law and earned a law degree in 1928. He became an assistant professor of law at the University of Oregon in 1929, rising to associate professor in 1930 and full professor in 1931. While serving as dean of the University of Oregon Law School from 1931 to 1944, he earned a doctorate of jurisprudence at Columbia University in 1932. Morse specialized in labor law, and, in 1938, Frances Perkins, the secretary of labor, named him labor arbitrator for the Pacific Coast. He won recognition as a leading arbitrator, and that reputation led President Franklin D. Roosevelt to appoint him to the War Labor Board in 1942. Morse resigned two years later to protest what he considered excessive concessions to John L. Lewis's United Mine Workers.

Running as a Republican, Morse won election in 1944 to the U.S. Senate from Oregon. He quickly established a reputation as a liberal maverick willing to break from his party on key issues. In addition to generally supporting President Harry S. Truman's domestic and foreign policies, he not only voted against but filibustered to prevent passage of the Taft-Hartley Act. Further, Morse joined Senator Margaret Chase Smith (R-Me.) in attacking the anticommunist antics of Senator Joseph R. McCarthy (R-Wis.). Morse's consistent refusal to compromise and his self-righteous attitude alienated many members of the Senate, and not just those in his own party. Fortunately for Morse, his independence and outspokenness proved popular with his constituents.

After winning reelection in 1950, Morse continued to feud with his own party. The Republican leader, Robert A. Taft (R-Ohio), denied Morse a seat on the Foreign Relations Committee. Morse began to attack Republican leaders, including the party's presidential nominee in 1952, Dwight D. Eisenhower, for failing to repudiate McCarthy. After the Republican National Convention, Morse left the Republican Party and campaigned for the Democratic nominee, Adlai Stevenson. Morse cited the choice of Richard M. Nixon as the vice presidential candidate and what he described as the conservative platform as his reasons for bolting.

When the Senate convened in January 1953, Morse ostentatiously brought a folding chair into the chamber and placed it in the aisle that divided the Republicans from the Democrats. Nevertheless, in the vote to organize the chamber, he cast his ballot for the Republicans, giving them narrow control of the Senate (had Morse voted with the Democrats, it would have produced a tie that would have left the deciding vote with the vice president and the Republicans in control). The Republican leadership, however, denied him key committee assignments, including a place on the Labor Committee.

A strong supporter of federal power and resource development, Morse opposed the submerged lands bill, which granted ownership of offshore oil deposits to the states. In a speech that lasted 22 hours and 26 minutes, Morse attacked the bill as a "raid on the public domain." That speech broke the Senate record for a filibuster. (The record lasted only a few years, until Strom Thurmond (D-S.C.) broke it filibustering against a civil rights bill in 1957.) Despite Morse's efforts, the submerged lands bill passed the Senate, and Eisenhower signed it into law in May 1953. From 1951 to 1955, Morse annually introduced a bill that would have provided for public construction of a dam and power plant at Hell's Canyon on the Snake River in Idaho. The measure failed each time.

Although an early critic of McCarthy, Morse was a cautious one. He joined other liberals in debating specific charges McCarthy had made but at the same argued for the need to investigate subversives. After McCarthy assumed the chair of the Senate Government Operations Committee, Morse muted his attacks on the junior senator from Wisconsin. Morse's biographer, A. Robert Smith, maintained that this was because McCarthy was investigating a lobbyist from Oregon who was close to Morse.

When the movement to censure McCarthy gained force during 1954, Morse once again took out after the senator from Wisconsin more aggressively.

After the elections of 1954, the Democrats controlled one more seat in the Senate than the Republicans, with Morse as an Independent. Had Morse voted with the Republicans, the result would have been a tie, and the vice president would have cast the deciding vote for the Republicans. Instead, Morse voted for Democratic control of the chamber. In February 1955, he officially switched to the Democratic Party, induced, in part, by the promise of a seat on the Foreign Relations Committee. Morse became a strident critic of the administration. In addition, he became a leading opponent of the admission of evidence gained from wiretaps in federal courts and annually introduced a bill requiring members of Congress to disclose their outside sources of income. Morse ran for reelection in 1956 as a Democrat and won a third term.

A staunch supporter of civil rights, Morse voted against the Civil Rights Act of 1957 because he believed it too weak. As a member of the District of Columbia Committee, he was the leading proponent in the Senate of home rule for the nation's capital, the population of which was approximately half African American. Morse vigorously opposed the administration's policy of promoting private ownership on the public domain and its foreign policy, most notably concerning the offshore islands of Taiwan.

Morse earned a well-deserved reputation for vicious personal attacks on those who differed with him. During a debate on the construction of federal power facilities, he charged that President Eisenhower was as corrupt as DAVE BECK, the president of the Teamsters who was then under investigation for using his position for personal gain. In 1958, Morse campaigned for Oregon's governor, Robert D. Holmes, and repeatedly reminded voters that the Republican challenger, Mark Hatfield, had been involved in an auto accident in which a young girl had been killed. Some observers believed that Morse's conduct contributed to the defeat of Holmes. That same year, Morse broke with his protégé, Senator RICHARD NEUBERGER (D-Oreg.), because the younger man had supported some of the administration's proposals, including the Civil Rights Act of 1957.

Characterizing Senators JOHN F. KENNEDY (D-Mass.) and HUBERT H. HUMPHREY (D-Minn.) as "phony liberals," Morse entered the race for the Democratic presidential nomination in 1960. Defeats in the District of Columbia, Maryland, and Oregon primaries, however, ended his campaign. After his disastrous showing in the presidential primaries, Morse continued his career in the Senate. In 1961, he became chair of the subcommittee on education, from which position he gave important support to federal aid to education. Morse supported most of the domestic legislation proposed by the administrations of Kennedy and LYNDON B. JOHNSON. He enjoyed a particularly good working relationship with Johnson, who appointed him to two emergency labor relations boards. Ironically, in both instances he angered the unions involved, and they worked against his reelection in 1968. An early opponent of the war in Vietnam, Morse was one of only two senators to vote against the Gulf of Tonkin Resolution in 1964. ERNEST GRUENING (D-Alaska) was the other. Throughout the rest of his career in the Senate, Morse vigorously opposed the war in Vietnam. In 1966, he introduced an amendment to repeal the Gulf of Tonkin Resolution, which went down to defeat by a vote of 95 to 5.

Morse lost his bid for reelection in 1968 to the Republican nominee, Robert Packwood. After leaving the Senate, he worked as a lecturer and labor arbitrator. He was a distinguished visiting scholar at the State University of New York from 1969 to 1970. Morse ran against Hatfield for Oregon's other seat in the Senate in 1972 but lost that election, too. He won the Democratic senatorial primary for his old seat in 1974 but died of kidney failure while campaigning in Portland, Oregon, on July 22, 1974.

—MSM

Morton, Thruston B(allard)

(1907–1982) *assistant secretary of state for congressional relations, U.S. senator, Republican national chairman*

Thruston Morton was born in Louisville, Kentucky, on August 19, 1907. The product of an old and wealthy Kentucky family, he attended Woodberry Forest School in Virginia and Yale University.

Upon graduating from Yale in 1929, Morton went to work for Ballard and Ballard, the family's grain and milling firm. He enlisted in the navy before the United States entered World War II and served in the Pacific during the war. In 1946, he returned to Kentucky, where he became president of Ballard and Ballard. That November he was elected as a Republican to the U.S. House of Representatives, where he aligned himself with the liberal and internationalist wing of his party. Reelected in 1948 and 1950, Morton supported the Tennessee Valley Authority, was an early advocate of federal aid to education, and backed President HARRY S. TRUMAN's major initiatives in foreign policy (including aid to Greece and Turkey, the Marshall Plan, and the North Atlantic Treaty Organization). In addition to defending the basic structure of the New Deal, he emerged as an outspoken critic of Senator JOSEPH R. MCCARTHY (R-Wis.). Morton announced that he would not seek reelection in 1952. He managed JOHN SHERMAN COOPER's successful campaign for the U.S. Senate in 1952 and that same year was the lone supporter of DWIGHT D. EISENHOWER among Kentucky's 20 delegates to the Republican National Convention.

Following Eisenhower's inauguration in January 1953, he named Morton assistant secretary of state for congressional relations. In that post, Morton played an important role in defeating a constitutional amendment, proposed by Senator JOHN W. BRICKER (R-Ohio), designed to limit the president's power to make treaties. Morton's efforts earned him the enmity of conservative groups, in particular the John Birch Society. Morton also fought to save the reciprocal trade bill from defeat by a Republican Congress. As he had in Congress, Morton took exception to McCarthy's approach to fighting communism. While acknowledging the severity of the threat posed by communism, Morton declared that it did not warrant the destruction of American liberties. "You cannot," he maintained, "chip away part of the structure of liberty without beginning to destroy the entire structure."

In 1956, Morton resigned his post to run for the Senate. He defeated the incumbent, Earle Clements, by a narrow margin, aided by the president's presence at the top of the Republican ticket and a split between Kentucky's governor, A. B. "HAPPY"

CHANDLER and Clements. Chandler withheld his support from Clements. In the Senate, Morton loyally backed the administration's programs. In 1957 and 1958, he was Eisenhower's most consistent supporter in the upper house. A longtime opponent of racial segregation, he backed the administration's civil rights bill in 1957. Morton joined liberals in the Senate in attempting to prevent the addition of an amendment to the bill, sponsored by southern Democrats, requiring a jury trial for those accused of violating injunctions protecting black voting rights. Nevertheless, the amendment passed and substantially weakened the law. In 1957, Morton supported the Eisenhower Doctrine, which provided for military and economic aid to the Middle East and granted the president authority to send American troops to any nation in the region that faced "overt armed aggression by any country controlled by international communism" and requested assistance. Morton cosponsored a bill with Cooper that called for $1.6 billion in federal aid to education over four years.

When MEADE ALCORN retired as Republican national chairman in 1959, Morton replaced him and held the position for two years. He defended the administration against criticism after the Soviets downed a U-2 spy plane. At the Republican National Convention in 1960, Morton had substantial backing for the vice presidential nomination, but RICHARD M. NIXON chose HENRY CABOT LODGE instead. Morton easily won reelection in 1962. Although disappointed that the conservative BARRY GOLDWATER captured the Republican nomination in 1964, Morton loyally supported the party's ticket. He favored civil rights and programs to alleviate poverty in Appalachia but opposed many of President LYNDON B. JOHNSON's other domestic programs. An initial supporter of American military involvement in Vietnam, he became disillusioned by 1967 and called for a withdrawal of American forces. In February 1968, he announced that he would not seek a third term in the Senate. He urged Governor NELSON A. ROCKEFELLER to run for the Republican presidential nomination in 1968 and became cochair of Rockefeller's campaign. When Rockefeller lost to Nixon, Morton joined Nixon's campaign; his brother, Rogers C. B. Morton, was Nixon's floor manager at the convention. Morton returned to Louisville, where he was vice chairman of the Liberty National Bank and Trust Company. He also served on the board of directors for a number of companies and pursued his lifelong interest in thoroughbred horses, serving as president of the American Horse Council and chairman of the board of Churchill Downs. Morton died in Louisville on August 14, 1982.

—MSM

Mundt, Karl E(arl)

(1900–1974) U.S. senator

The son of a small businessman, Karl Mundt was born in Humboldt, South Dakota, on June 3, 1900. He attended public schools in Humboldt, Pierre, and Madison, South Dakota. After receiving his B.A. at Carleton College in Minnesota in 1923, he returned to South Dakota and taught high school speech and social science in Bryant. From 1924 to 1927, he served as the town's superintendent of schools. He earned an M.A. in education at Columbia University in 1927, after which he taught speech at Beadle State Teachers College in Madison, South Dakota, from 1927 to 1936. While at Beadle State, he also worked with his father in the Mundt Loan and Investment Company. He attained prominence as a civic leader, and his interest in conservation issues brought him into politics. In 1927, he was elected state president of the Izaak Walton League, a group interested in conservation. He also served on the South Dakota State Game and Fish commission from 1931 to 1937. Following an unsuccessful run for Congress in 1936, he won a seat in 1938. As a Republican candidate in South Dakota's largely German and conservative corn belt, his platform was anti-British and isolationist. Following that path once he entered Congress, Mundt opposed the Selective Service Act of 1940 and Lend-Lease in 1941. After the Japanese attack on Pearl Harbor, however, he threw himself behind the American war effort.

Mundt received an appointment to the Special House Committee on Un-American Activities, known as the Dies Committee, in 1943. As World War II drew to a close, Mundt became one of the most outspoken advocates of anticommunism in both foreign and domestic policy. After the war, he was appointed to the successor to the Dies Committee, the House Un-American Activities Committee (HUAC). Mundt led the Republican attack on the Truman administration's loyalty program in the late 1940s. Presiding over HUAC's investigations of alleged communist infiltration of government departments in 1948, Mundt took an active role in the investigation of the charge by WHITTAKER CHAMBERS that Alger Hiss, a former government official, had been a communist. Information developed during that investigation led a grand jury to indict Alger Hiss for perjury the following year. In 1948, Mundt and Representative RICHARD M. NIXON (R-Calif.) cosponsored a bill that required the American Communist Party to register its membership with the Department of Justice, denied communists passports, and barred communists from federal employment.

Mundt won election to the Senate in 1948 and promptly introduced a similar measure in that body. Truman strongly opposed the Mundt bills, but in 1950 Congress overrode Truman's veto to pass the omnibus Internal Security Act, known as the McCarran Act, which incorporated the provisions Mundt sponsored. Despite his vigorous (some would have said extreme) anticommunism, Mundt defied stereotypes. Unlike most midwestern conservative Republicans, he supported the creation of the United Nations Educational, Scientific and Cultural Organization.

When the Senate convened in January 1953, Mundt was assigned to the Government Operations Committee and to its Permanent Subcommittee on Investigations, both of which were chaired by Senator JOSEPH R. MCCARTHY (R-Wis.). Mundt had strongly supported McCarthy's anticommunist crusade ever since the senator from Wisconsin rose to prominence in 1950, and he worked closely with McCarthy on the subcommittee's wide-ranging probes of alleged communist subversion. In January and February 1954, however, after McCarthy began an investigation of the army, Mundt joined other Republicans on the panel in an effort to forestall a public rupture between the subcommittee and the army or between the subcommittee and the administration. Acting as a mediator at a luncheon on February 24, Mundt drew up a "memorandum of understanding" in which the Secretary of the Army ROBERT STEVENS conceded the right of the chair of the subcommittee to question army officers. Prompted by news reports that described the agreement as a "capitulation" by Stevens, the army proceeded with its plans to expose the activities of McCarthy and the subcommittee's counsel, Roy Cohn, on behalf of G. David Schine, a sometime staff member of the subcommittee (and friend of Cohn) who had been drafted. In March, the subcommittee voted to investigate the dispute. McCarthy temporarily resigned from the panel in order to testify, and Mundt reluctantly accepted the job of acting chairman for the duration of the Army-McCarthy hearings. After unsuccessfully attempting to bar the press from the committee room, he took almost no active part in the nationally televised proceedings. Moreover, he proved unable to control either the junior senator from Wisconsin or Joseph N. Welch, the counsel for the army and McCarthy's principal adversary. Despite the decline in McCarthy's popularity after the hearings, Mundt remained one of his strongest partisans and worked to prevent the Senate from condemning McCarthy's conduct. Although he voted against it, Mundt proved unable to prevent the Senate from passing a resolution censuring McCarthy in December 1954.

As the issue of communism in government began to wane after 1954, Mundt's name faded from public prominence. He remained a powerful force for conservatism in the Senate, however, and regularly opposed social welfare programs and domestic spending. He also advocated government regulation of labor unions. Although he voted with the conservative coalition of southern Democrats and conservative Republicans on most issues, Mundt consistently supported civil rights and measures to protect the environment. He sponsored legislation establishing the National Endangered Species List.

As a member of the Permanent Subcommittee on Investigations, Mundt was appointed in January 1957 to the Select Committee on Improper Activities in the Labor or Management Field, chaired by Senator John McClellan (D-Ark.). Following investigations of corruption in the International Brotherhood of Teamsters and other unions, the panel conducted hearings in February and March 1958 on a violent strike by the United Auto Work-

ers (UAW) against the Kohler Company of Kohler, Wisconsin. Mundt and other Republicans on the McClellan Committee initiated the probe partly to embarrass the committee's counsel, Robert F. Kennedy, and the panel's liberal Democrats, who had close political ties with the UAW's president, Walter Reuther. Amid angry charges of partisanship and "whitewashing" that nearly resulted in the breakup of the panel, the investigation of the UAW produced little evidence to support allegations of corruption by officials of the UAW. The committee's Republicans, Mundt, Barry Goldwater (R-Ariz.), and Carl Curtis (R-Neb.), pressed for a separate inquiry into the UAW's political activities, but the Democrats blocked it.

During the Kennedy administration, Mundt once again became involved in several high-profile investigations, including a probe by the Investigations Subcommittee in 1962 of the relationship between the Agriculture Department and Billie Sol Estes, a financier from Texas, and hearings in 1963 on the Defense Department's conduct in awarding contracts for the TFX fighter bomber. Mundt won a fourth term in 1966 but in 1969 suffered a debilitating stroke that prevented him from carrying on his duties in the Senate. In 1972, the Republican leadership in the Senate relieved him of his posts as ranking Republican on the Government Operations Committee and second-ranking minority member on the Foreign Relations and Appropriations Committees. Mundt did not stand for reelection in 1972 and died in Washington, D.C., on August 16, 1974.

—MSM

Muñoz Marín, Luis

(1898–1980) *governor, Puerto Rico*

The son of Luis Muñoz Rivera, the "George Washington of Puerto Rico," Muñoz was born in San Juan, Puerto Rico, on February 18, 1898. Raised in New York and Washington, D.C., he attended Georgetown Preparatory School from 1911 to 1915 and studied law for a year at Georgetown University. Upon the death of his father in 1916, Muñoz left law school to become secretary to the resident commissioner from Puerto Rico. He also edited his father's papers for publication, wrote articles for the *Baltimore Sun* and several magazines (including the *Nation*), and published two books of his own essays. Muñoz moved to New York in 1918, where he worked as a freelance writer and founded a magazine dedicated to Latin American culture. He moved to San Juan in 1931, where he was editor of a newspaper and a founder, in 1932, of the Liberal Party, which supported political independence for Puerto Rico. Although his party lost the elections in 1932, Muñoz won a seat in the Puerto Rican senate. He used his cultural and political contacts in the United States to help bring money from the Roosevelt administration to Puerto Rico. During this period, Muñoz came to the conclusion that independence did not serve the interests of Puerto Rico, which led to a split with the Liberal Party in 1937. The following year, Muñoz founded the Popular Democratic Party (PPD), which mobilized support of the rural masses with promises of land reform, electricity, education, and access to medical services. After the PPD won an unexpected victory in the elections of 1940, Muñoz became president of the senate. Legislation passed in 1941 gave the government the power to acquire land and divide it among the landless. With the cooperation of the appointed governor, Rexford Tugwell, the PPD majority also enacted legislation providing electricity, water, schools, and medical clinics. Subsequently, the PPD won the elections of 1944 in a landslide and went on to win the next five elections.

After World War II, Muñoz concluded that Puerto Rico could not support a growing population on a solely agricultural base. He helped create "Operation Bootstrap," an economic development program designed to attract industry to the island. He also sought to increase the island's autonomy from the United States. Puerto Rico gained the right to elect its own governor in 1947, and the following year Muñoz became the island's first elected governor. In 1950, President HARRY S. TRUMAN signed Public Law 600, which allowed Puerto Ricans to draft their own constitution. In a referendum the following year, Puerto Rican voters approved the American legislation. Convinced that independence was not the best course for Puerto Rico, Muñoz proposed autonomy as an alternative to independence or statehood. In July 1952, the people of Puerto Rico ratified a constitution

that established the island as a commonwealth in free association with the United States. Under this arrangement, the residents of Puerto Rico paid no federal income taxes and did not vote in presidential elections. Further, they did not have voting representation in Congress but had a resident commissioner. Finally, the United States represented Puerto Rico in foreign affairs and provided it with military protection. In the same year they ratified the constitution, the people of Puerto Rico elected Muñoz to a second term as governor.

Throughout the 1950s, Muñoz maintained that commonwealth status ensured the island's fiscal and cultural autonomy while providing the benefits of U.S. citizenship. However, he faced growing opposition from pro-independence and pro-statehood movements. The Nationalist Party regarded Muñoz as a traitor, and in 1950 five Nationalists were killed in an attempt to assassinate the governor. That same year, two Nationalists attacked Blair House, where President Harry S. Truman was staying while the White House underwent renovation. In 1954, several members of the Nationalist Party sprayed bullets in the chamber of the U.S. House of Representatives and wounded five members of Congress. Muñoz immediately flew to Washington to condemn the shootings and assure the American public that the majority of Puerto Ricans wanted to continue the island's ties to the United States. Communist countries made use of the calls for Puerto Rican independence in their propaganda and asserted that Puerto Rico's commonwealth status was a cover for U.S. colonial domination.

For Muñoz, however, the greater immediate threat came from the pro-statehood Republican Party of Puerto Rico. In the gubernatorial election of 1956, Muñoz won a third term, but the Republicans received 25 percent of the vote, twice as much as they received four years earlier. Recruited mainly from the island's growing middle class, Republicans held that commonwealth status could be no more than a transitional solution. After all, they argued, the U.S. Congress could rescind the law that provided for the commonwealth at any time. In contrast, statehood offered a permanent solution that guaranteed Puerto Ricans U.S. citizenship. Republicans acknowledged the drawback of having to pay federal taxes, but they contended that the dignity and equality conferred by statehood made it a good bargain. Further, they maintained that statehood would provide the stability necessary for further economic development. Muñoz did not respond to the challenge posed by the Republicans until 1959, when the Legislative Assembly controlled by the PPD called on the U.S. Congress to clarify aspects of the relationship between the United States and Puerto Rico established in the Federal Relations Act. The Fernos-Murray bill, which would have slightly augmented Puerto Rican autonomy, addressed some of these concerns, but it was never reported out of committee.

During the 1950s, Operation Bootstrap registered impressive economic gains. Industrial production and per capita income increased. Industry became the dominant economic activity on the island. The improved economic performance owed partly to a large migration to the mainland. Nevertheless, it enhanced Muñoz's image at home and abroad. In 1955, Muñoz proposed "Operation Serenity," a vaguely defined cultural program, which became an effort to upgrade education and to preserve the island's Hispanic traditions and rural values.

Muñoz also sought to play a larger role in U.S.-Latin American relations. In 1958, he asserted that Puerto Rico, because of its Hispanic heritage, its relationship with the United States government, and its prosperity, could best translate U.S. political and economic ideals to Latin Americans. Similarly, Puerto Rico was in a position to explain Latin American aspirations to North America. In March 1958, he told a Senate committee that Latin America had not received its fair share of U.S. foreign aid and urged the United States to undertake more extensive efforts to develop the economies of the Western Hemisphere and to support democratic movements. After Fidel Castro took power in Cuba, Muñoz defended the new regime and, throughout 1959, explained its political violence as a consequence of the brutality of the Batista regime. In time, however, Muñoz became a severe critic of Castro and his regime.

Muñoz won a fourth term as governor in 1960, but the controversy over the island's commonwealth status continued. Faced with growing support for pro-independence and pro-statehood movements,

Muñoz suggested to President JOHN F. KENNEDY in 1962 that a plebiscite of the people of Puerto Rico would be the best way finally to decide the issue. Once Kennedy agreed, Muñoz declined his party's nomination for a fifth term in 1964 and returned to the island's senate. He put forward his friend and secretary of state, Roberto Sánchez Vilella, for governor. Muñoz campaigned vigorously for commonwealth status, and 60 percent of voters chose it over either independence or statehood when the plebiscite was held in 1967. The next year, however, the PPD lost the governorship to the pro-statehood New Progressive Party. The question of the island's status was only one issue with which Muñoz and the PPD had to contend. Operation Bootstrap, which had seemed so successful in the 1950s, looked less impressive by the 1960s, when Puerto Rico was plagued by high unemployment. Despite his party's defeat, Muñoz won reelection to the senate in 1968. In May 1970, however, he resigned and traveled in Europe, where he wrote his memoirs. He returned to Puerto Rico in 1972 and campaigned extensively for the PPD in the elections of that year. His efforts contributed to the PPD's victory in the gubernatorial election. Muñoz retired from active politics in 1975 and died in San Juan on April 30, 1980.

—MSM

Murphy, Robert D(aniel)

(1894–1978) *ambassador to Japan, assistant secretary of state for United Nations affairs, deputy undersecretary of state for political affairs, undersecretary of state*

The son of a steamfitter and railroad worker, Robert Murphy was born in Milwaukee, Wisconsin, on October 28, 1894. He attended Marquette Academy and Marquette University before earning an LL.B. from George Washington University in 1920. Upon receiving his degree, he joined the foreign service in 1921 and was posted as vice-consul to Zurich. During the 1920s, Murphy served in a variety of positions in Washington and Europe. He was vice-consul in Munich from 1921 to 1923 and consul there from 1923 to 1925. After serving briefly as counsel in Seville in 1925, he returned to Washington and worked in the State Department from 1926 to 1930. While in Washington, he earned an LL.M. from George Washington University in 1928.

Murphy was assigned in 1930 as consul to the American embassy in Paris, where he remained until 1941. From 1936 to 1939, he also served as first secretary, and he became counselor of the embassy in 1939. He was the ranking American diplomat when the Germans entered the French capital. In May 1940, he was assigned as chargé d'affaires to Vichy, the capital of the collaborationist government headed by Marshal Philippe Pétain. Murphy headed the embassy until the arrival of Ambassador William Leahy in January 1941. In early 1941, President Franklin D. Roosevelt named Murphy as his personal representative to French North Africa. After the United States entered World War II, Murphy became chief civilian affairs officer on General DWIGHT D. EISENHOWER's staff. In that capacity, Murphy negotiated a deal with Admiral François Darlan, the Vichy commander in chief, under the terms of which Darlan would not oppose Allied landings in North Africa. After the French surrendered, Murphy and General MARK CLARK negotiated the Clark-Darlan Agreement, which left Vichy administrators in office. Murphy drew considerable criticism from the press in the United States and Great Britain for dealing with Darlan, a famously Anglophobic and anti-Semitic fascist.

Murphy became chief civilian affairs officer at the Allied headquarters on November 8, 1942. The next month, he was named political adviser to the supreme allied commander. After attending the Casablanca Conference in 1943, Murphy was assigned as the principal civilian representative of the president and State Department with the Allied command in Italy. One of his duties was to help negotiate the surrender of Italy. In September 1944, Murphy became Eisenhower's chief adviser on German affairs. He attended the Potsdam Conference in July 1945 as a member of the occupation government of Germany.

After the war, Murphy served in a variety of posts. From 1945 to 1949, he remained in Germany with the rank of ambassador and served as political adviser to General LUCIUS CLAY. He returned to Washington in February 1949 to become director of the State Department's Office of German and Austrian Affairs. In September 1949, he was appointed ambassador to Belgium. He became the United States's first postwar ambassador to Japan in 1952. When Eisenhower entered the White House in 1953, he named a new ambassador to Japan, and Murphy served as an adviser to General Mark Clark, then engaged in negotiations for a cease-fire in the Korean War.

After the Korean armistice was signed in July 1953, Secretary of State JOHN FOSTER DULLES appointed Murphy assistant secretary of state for United Nations affairs. Although Murphy was theoretically in charge of the U.S. mission, HENRY CABOT LODGE, the ambassador to the UN, demanded autonomy from the State Department. Lodge, who had the backing of Eisenhower and Dulles, got his way.

In November 1953, Eisenhower appointed Murphy deputy undersecretary for political affairs. During the Eisenhower administration, Murphy acted as the State Department's chief troubleshooter. In 1954, Eisenhower sent Murphy to Belgrade to advance stalled negotiations between Italy and Yugoslavia over Trieste. The following year, Murphy returned to Belgrade to negotiate better military and economic cooperation between Yugoslavia and the United States.

As recognition for his service, Murphy received the rank of career ambassador in 1956. That same year, Murphy headed a mission to dissuade the British prime minister, Anthony Eden, from military action against Egypt after Gamal Abdel Nasser nationalized the Suez Canal. The mission proved unsuccessful, and, in November 1956, a joint French and British expedition seized the canal.

Murphy continued to handle some of the most sensitive diplomatic assignments. In 1958, he helped mediate a dispute between France and Tunisia triggered by the French bombing of a Tunisian village that harbored Algerian rebels. Murphy crafted an agreement under which France withdrew all of its troops in Tunisia to a base at Bizerte. Tunisia granted France the right to occupy the base indefinitely in exchange for recognition of Tunisian sovereignty over it.

Eisenhower sent Murphy to Lebanon in July 1958 following the landing of American troops there at the request of Lebanon's president, Camille Chamoun. The show of force was intended to prevent a possible coup by pro-Nasser elements agitated by Chamoun's maneuvering to retain office beyond the stipulated term. Murphy facilitated an agreement that paved the way for Chamoun's departure and the election of General Fuad Chehab, a candidate acceptable to both sides.

In 1959, Murphy helped work out an agreement providing for an exchange of visits between Eisenhower and the Soviet premier, Nikita Khrushchev. While Khrushchev did tour the United States, the U-2 incident resulted in the cancellation of Eisenhower's visit to the Soviet Union.

After retiring from the Foreign Service in 1959, Murphy joined the board of directors of Corning Glass Works. He became chairman of the board in 1964 and honorary chairman of Corning International in 1971. Throughout the 1960s and 1970s, Murphy served on a number of presidential commissions on foreign intelligence activities. He published his memoirs, *Diplomat Among Warriors*, in 1964. Murphy died in New York City on January 9, 1978.

—MSM

Murrow, Edward R(oscoe)

(1908–1965) *television journalist*

Born Egbert Roscoe Murrow on April 25, 1908, near Greensboro, North Carolina, Murrow moved, at the age of five, with his family to rural northwest Washington State. He attended public schools and worked his way through Washington State College (later Washington State University) in Pullman, where he graduated Phi Beta Kappa in 1930. While in college, he majored in speech, was active in student politics, and changed his first name to Edward. He was elected president of the National Student Federation in 1929. After graduating, Murrow led the National Student Federation for two years. He then worked as assistant director of the Institute of International Education from 1932 until 1935, when he began a long career with the Columbia Broadcasting System (CBS). Murrow went to London as director of CBS's European operations in 1937. He hired a newspaper man, William L. Shirer, to cover the continent for CBS. The two men reported on the Anschluss and the crisis in the Sudetenland, which Hitler claimed for Germany.

When World War II broke out, Murrow was based in London. During the Battle of Britain in 1940, he achieved national recognition for radio broadcasts bringing to America firsthand accounts of the blitz. His signature opening, "This . . . is London," and his dramatic live reporting gripped audiences. The drama of his reporting came not through hyperbole, but rather through calm, terse, intense description. Murrow hired a group of reporters who went on to shape modern broadcasting, including Eric Sevareid, Charles Collingwood, Howard K. Smith, Richard C. Hottelet, Larry LeSueur, and Winston Burdett. Murrow preferred to hire print journalists, because, as he put it, "I'm hiring reporters, not announcers." Later in the war, Murrow broadcast from North Africa and the European continent. He was the first Allied correspondent to enter the Nazi concentration camp at Buchenwald.

Murrow returned to America after World War II as a vice president of news operations, but he returned to the air in 1947 with an evening report on radio called *Edward R. Murrow with the News*. He and Fred W. Friendly, a producer, teamed to create a series of historical record albums called *I Can Hear It Now*. This led to a weekly program on CBS radio called *Hear It Now*.

Murrow entered the new field of television in the early 1950s doing editorial tailpieces on the *CBS Evening News* and covering special events. Beginning in 1951, together with Friendly, he produced *See It Now*, a 30-minute weekly adaptation of *Hear It Now*. Anchored by Murrow, the program usually dealt with a provocative topic. *Person-to-Person*, a weekly informal interview program hosted by Murrow, premiered in October 1953. Although the show did interviews with serious individuals, such as the Cuban revolutionary Fidel Castro and Secretary of State JOHN FOSTER DULLES, it was basically devoted to celebrity interviews. Guests included Gypsy Rose Lee, the renowned stripper, and Marilyn Monroe, the movie star and sex symbol. The level of conversation rarely rose above what the *New York Times* described as "urbane small talk."

See It Now was, in general, the more serious of the two shows. Murrow had been cautious about dealing with the issues relating to the Red Scare and Senator JOSEPH R. McCARTHY, JR. (R-Wis.), and had done very little with those matters on television until October 1953. Friendly later recalled that "Murrow felt we had to be careful that we weren't too far ahead of public opinion." By October 1953, however, there were signs of impatience with McCarthy both in the Senate and in the White House. On October 20, Murrow presented the case of Lieutenant Milo Radulovich on *See It Now*. The air force planned to muster out Radulovich as a security risk because of anonymous reports about the left-wing sympathies of his father and sister. Investigators sent by Murrow and Friendly found no evidence to support the allegations, and the broadcast argued for the exoneration of Radulovich. The program generated a public outcry, and the air force reinstated the young lieutenant.

On March 9, 1954, Murrow devoted a program to the noisiest and most irresponsible of the anticommunists. Friendly and the staff of *See It Now* put together film clips of McCarthy's career, and Murrow wrote a denunciation of the senator's methods. Making no attempt at balance, Murrow's team chose clips that showed McCarthy at his worst, picking his nose, belching, giggling at his own jokes, browbeating witnesses, and contradicting himself. At the end of the program, Murrow told viewers that "we must not confuse dissent with disloyalty." "This is," he declared, "no time for men who oppose Senator McCarthy's methods to be silent."

At the outset of his program, Murrow offered McCarthy equal time. The junior senator from Wisconsin took up the offer and presented his defense in early April. He accused Murrow of past involvement with subversive groups and of being "the symbol, the leader and the cleverest of the jackal pack" who would attack "anyone who dares to expose individual Communists." The senator's inept rebuttal only reinforced the image presented in the original broadcast. William S. Paley, chairman of CBS, thought that McCarthy's reply did more damage to the senator than Murrow's original program.

Contrary to conventional wisdom, Murrow and the *See It Now* program did not bring down McCarthy. McCarthy had already begun to slip in the polls and opposition to the senator from Wisconsin had begun to find its voice in the Senate by the time Murrow took to the air. By the time of the broadcast, even conservative Republican

Edward R. Murrow broadcasting the 1956 election returns *(Library of Congress)*

newspapers had begun to turn against McCarthy. Similarly, Eisenhower's vigorous defense of his secretary of defense, ROBERT STEVENS, after McCarthy launched his attack on the army came before Murrow's broadcast and played a role in altering public opinion. An editorial in the *New York Post*, then a liberal paper and one of the first to attack McCarthy, chided Murrow: "'This is no time for men who oppose Sen. McCarthy's methods to keep silent,' said Ed as he leaped gracefully aboard the crowded band-wagon."

The programs on Radulovich and McCarthy generated largely favorable responses. Some programs, however, created problems for the management of CBS. A broadcast in January 1954 focused on an amendment, sponsored by Senator JOHN W. BRICKER (R-Ohio), to restrict the president's power to enter treaties. Bricker accused Murrow of slanting the program to discredit the proposal. Frank

Stanton, the president of CBS, regretted the broadcast on Bricker.

Despite occasional high ratings when it covered a particularly controversial subject, *See It Now* generally did not attract large audiences. After the programs devoted to McCarthy, *See It Now* ran as a weekly program for one more season. During that season (1954–55), Murrow, chain-smoking all the while, narrated a two-part series on the relationship between smoking and cancer. In January 1955, he interviewed J. ROBERT OPPENHEIMER, the renowned physicist who had been denied a federal security clearance. Although it ended as a weekly broadcast, the show continued as a series of special reports for CBS News. The show's final broadcast, "Watch on the Ruhr," which dealt with postwar Germany, aired in July 1958. The following season, the show became *CBS Reports*, and Murrow's role and authority were reduced.

Beginning in 1958, Murrow hosted a talk show, *Small World*, which brought together political figures by remote telecasting for one-on-one debates. He also continued to host *Person-to-Person*, but Murrow grew increasingly disenchanted with CBS. When CBS removed *See It Now* from its regular schedule after 1955, Murrow's relations with Stanton, which had never been especially cordial, deteriorated. At a convention of radio and TV news directors in 1958, Murrow shocked his audience with an angry address in which he attacked the television networks for their emphasis on profit and called on them to donate one or two regularly scheduled shows for public affairs programs. In October 1959, the president of CBS publicly criticized *Person-to-Person*, and Murrow bitterly denounced Stanton. Murrow took a sabbatical starting in the summer of 1959, during which he contributed to *CBS Reports* and *Small World*. His last major telecast was "Harvest of Shame," an installment of *CBS Reports* that aired in November 1960 and reported on the plight of migrant farmworkers.

Because of his popularity, Murrow was sought out as a candidate for political office. In 1958, a coalition of liberal Democrats in New York, led by ELEANOR ROOSEVELT, attempted to persuade Murrow to run for the U.S. Senate from their state. After conferring with former president HARRY S. TRUMAN and others, Murrow decided not to run.

The press frequently mentioned him as a senatorial candidate again in 1962.

Murrow left CBS in 1961 to serve as director of the United States Information Agency in the Kennedy administration. After being diagnosed with cancer in October 1963, Murrow had an operation to remove his left lung. Three months later, he resigned as head of the United States Information Agency. After that, he was in and out of hospitals until his death from cancer in Pawling, New York, on April 27, 1965.

—MSM

Muste, A(braham) J(ohannes)
(1885–1967) *clergyman, peace activist*

Born in Zierikzee, the Netherlands, on January 8, 1885, A. J. Muste moved with his family to Michigan in 1891. His upbringing and early education in schools sponsored by the Dutch Reformed Church of America were both politically and religiously conservative. He attended Hope Preparatory School and Hope College, from which he graduated in 1905. After teaching Greek and Latin for a year at Northwestern Classical Academy in Iowa, he entered the theological seminary of the Dutch Reformed Church in New Brunswick, New Jersey. Upon his graduation in 1909, he was ordained as a Dutch Reformed minister and took a position as minister at the Fort Washington Collegiate Church in Washington Heights. From 1909 to 1913, he attended Union Theological Seminary, where he earned a bachelor of divinity degree and was exposed to liberal Christian theology. Muste resigned his ministry at Fort Washington Collegiate Church in 1914 because he no longer accepted Calvinist doctrine and had ceased to believe in a literal interpretation of the Bible. He moved to Newton, Massachusetts, where he became minister of the Central Congregational Church.

As the preparedness controversy raged in 1915, Muste read the works of Christian mystics and moved toward pacifism. His pacifism put him in opposition to his congregation, and he resigned in 1917. He became a mediator for the Fellowship of Reconciliation (FOR), a nondenominational, pacifist organization, in 1918. One purpose of the FOR was to promote the nonviolent conciliation of labor disputes, and in 1919 Muste was a leader of a strike of textile workers in Lawrence, Massachusetts. This led to his election as general secretary of the Amalgamated Textile Workers of America. In 1921, he became chairman of the faculty of Brookwood Labor College in Katonah, New York. Although the American Federation of Labor (AFL) provided funds for the school, the leaders of the AFL distrusted the college because its faculty advocated industrial unions and the formation of an independent labor party, positions antithetical to the AFL. In spite of his nonorthodox views, Muste won election as vice president of the American Federation of Teachers in 1923. In the late 1920s, he became a Trotskyist, which put him at odds with the AFL. He founded and became chair of the Conference for Progressive Labor Action (CPLA) in 1929. The depression brought financial difficulties and factionalism to Brookwood Labor College, and Muste left the institution in 1933.

During the early years of the depression, Muste and the CPLA played an important role in the creation of unemployment leagues to promote the cause of the jobless, but his campaign never became a national mass movement. Muste and his followers moved gradually to an independent Marxist position and formed the American Workers Party (AWP) in 1933. A year later, the AWP merged with the orthodox Trotskyist Communist League of America to form the Workers Party. In 1935, however, the Trotskyists ousted him as party leader. Wounded by the loss of his chairmanship, Muste left for a tour of Europe. While visiting the Église Saint-Sulpice in Paris, he experienced what he described as a "reconversion" to pacifism. Although he remained a socialist and continued to believe that the achievement of a just society required a significant disruption of the social order, he believed this should be achieved through nonviolent means.

Upon returning to the United States in 1936, he also returned to the FOR as industrial secretary. From 1937 to 1940, he was director of the Presbyterian Labor Temple in New York City. Muste's efforts, however, shifted increasingly from the labor movement to pacifism. As executive secretary of FOR from 1940 to 1953, Muste made opposition to racial discrimination part of FOR's agenda. Following up on that initiative, several staff members

of FOR formed the Congress of Racial Equality (CORE) in 1942. Muste served on CORE's national advisory board until his death. He and his followers, including James Farmer, BAYARD RUSTIN, and George Hauser, exercised considerable influence on the developing Civil Rights movement. Muste was also active in the antinuclear movement from its earliest days after World War II. He organized protests against the buildup of nuclear weapons, nuclear testing, and civil defense. In the larger cause of pacifism, he worked on behalf of conscientious objectors confined by the U.S. government during World War II, organized protests against conscription, and opposed the cold war. In 1948, he joined 300 ministers in calling on all young men to refuse to register for conscription or serve in the armed forces.

His retirement from FOR in 1953 did not slow his activities on behalf of the causes to which he was committed. In 1954, he promoted the Third Way International Movement, which sought to unify all groups opposed to the policies of the U.S. and Soviet blocs. As chair of the American Third Camp Committee, he helped found *Liberation* magazine in 1956. The following year, Muste joined several peace groups in forming the Committee for Nonviolent Action to stage direct action protests. He also served as its national chairman. An organizer of the first protests at nuclear testing sites, Muste was arrested for trespassing on the grounds of the Mercury Project in Nevada in 1957 and at the missile base in Mead, Nebraska, two years later. He was also active in organizing the Polaris Action Project in New London, Connecticut, in 1960 and participated in the annual protests against civil defense drills held at New York's City Hall Park from 1955 to 1961. Muste's followers helped organize the National Committee for a Sane Nuclear Policy (SANE).

Although a committed anticommunist, Muste carried on an open dialogue with communists and defended their civil liberties. In 1955, he, ELEANOR ROOSEVELT, and NORMAN THOMAS appeared before the Senate Internal Security Subcommittee. Although he offered to discuss his views with J. EDGAR HOOVER personally, Muste refused to comply with any governmental agency or official engaged in an investigation of religious or political opinions. During the same year, he organized the

American Forum for Socialist Education, an educational group sponsoring debates in which communists were invited to participate.

Until his death in 1967, Muste traveled widely for the cause of peace. In 1963, he helped establish the International Confederation for Disarmament and Peace as a rival to the communist-sponsored World Peace Council, which he criticized for endorsing the Chinese communist position in the war in Vietnam. A prominent opponent of U.S. involvement in Southeast Asia, Muste took an active part in organizing rallies, vigils, and marches to protest the war in Vietnam. In January 1967, he was one of three clergymen who met with Ho Chi Minh in North Vietnam for what they described as a "very frank, very cordial" meeting. Muste died in New York City on February 11, 1967.

—MSM

Nathan, Robert (Roy)

(1908–2001) *economist, national chairman, Americans for Democratic Action*

Born and raised in Dayton, Ohio, on December 25, 1908, Nathan worked his way through the University of Pennsylvania, where he earned a bachelor's degree in economics (1931) and an M.S. in economics (1933) from the Wharton School. He immediately went to work for the Commerce Department but resigned in June 1934 to work for the Pennsylvania Emergency Relief Board. While there, he served as a part-time consultant to and with the President's Commission on Economic Security, which played a central role in developing the Social Security system. Nathan returned to the Commerce Department in December 1934 as chief of the National Income Section (later the National Income Division), where he remained until 1940. While at Commerce, he earned a law degree from Georgetown University in 1938. During the 1930s, Nathan criticized what he described as the nation's lackadaisical approach to increasing production. From 1940 to 1942, he was associate director of research and statistics of the National Defense Advisory Commission. Shortly after Pearl Harbor, he was appointed chairman of the planning committee of the War Production Board. In 1945, he became director of the Office of War Mobilization and Reconversion (OWMR). Considered one of the most talented of the New Deal economists, he published *National Income in the U.S.* in 1939 and *Mobilizing for Abundance* five years later. In 1946, Nathan resigned from the OWMR in protest against the policies of its director, John Snyder, a conservative banker from Missouri, who was moving quickly to remove all wartime controls on the economy. Nathan founded his own consulting firm, Robert R. Nathan Associates, to advise labor unions, businesses, and foreign governments. An early member of the Americans for Democratic Action (ADA), Nathan served as the organization's leading spokesman on economic policy during the Truman and Eisenhower years. In 1949, he joined other liberal economists in advocating a massive federal spending program to pull the economy out of a recession that began earlier that year.

Nathan was a frequent and vocal critic of the Eisenhower administration. He called for greater stimulation to the economy during recessions and more extensive tax relief for lower incomes. Six months after Eisenhower's inauguration, Nathan presented the first of many ADA critiques of the administration's economic policies. He criticized Eisenhower's failure to pursue economic planning and charged that the incomes of farmers were shrinking, security prices were dropping, and business was jittery. Speaking for the ADA, he called for a pledge of full employment, aid to farmers, a tax cut, expansion of public housing, and an increase in the minimum wage from $0.75 to $1.25 an hour. During testimony before the Joint Committee on the Economic Report in 1956, Nathan advocated tax relief for lower income groups and repeal of loopholes favoring wealthy taxpayers and corporations.

Nathan proposed a similar economic plan to counter the recession in 1958. Testifying before the House Ways and Means Committee in January of that year, he called for a tax cut and an increase in spending for education, mental health, and housing. Even if this unbalanced the federal budget, he maintained, it would "arrest the recession." On April 6, Nathan expanded the scope of his proposals by suggesting federal grants to the needy, a federal food stamp program, extended and enlarged unemployment benefits, and a "vigorous program" to rebuild depressed areas.

In foreign policy, Nathan stressed the importance of economic instead of military aid. In his opinion, the administration's "emphasis on military might and de-emphasis on economic and social considerations [was] playing havoc with America's role in world affairs." Nathan predicted that "hundreds of millions for economic development can save billions for defense and war." He was particularly impressed with the economic progress of South Vietnam and in 1959 predicted it would outproduce the communist North. The people of South Vietnam, he said, "are hard working and capable and have demonstrated their determination to suffer and fight for high ideals and for freedom and independence."

Nathan served as an adviser to the presidential campaign of Senator HUBERT HUMPHREY (D-Minn.) in 1960. After Senator JOHN F. KENNEDY (D-Mass.) captured the Democratic nomination and went on to defeat RICHARD M. NIXON in November, Nathan served on the economic transition team. In office, Kennedy often consulted Nathan on economic matters. When Humphrey ran for the presidency in 1968, Nathan once again served as an adviser to the campaign. He stepped down as president of Robert R. Nathan Associates in 1978 but remained chairman of the board until shortly before his death in Bethesda, Maryland, on September 4, 2001.

—MSM

Neuberger, Richard (Lewis)

(1912–1960) *U.S. senator*

Born in Portland, Oregon, on December 26, 1912, Neuberger attended public schools there and graduated from the University of Oregon in 1935, where he studied journalism and was editor of the campus newspaper. Although initially a political conservative, he moved to the left by 1933. While at the University of Oregon, he studied law from 1933 to 1934. After graduating, he wrote for national magazines. He also wrote or coauthored three books, including a highly critical examination of the Townsend Plan for old age pensions, a biography of Senator George William Norris, and a history of the Pacific Northwest. In 1939, he became the Pacific Northwest correspondent for the *New York Times*. The following year, he won election as a Democrat to the Oregon house of representatives. He resigned his seat to join the army in 1942. Commissioned a lieutenant, his service included time on the staff of the general assigned to construct the Alaska Highway and an assignment as military adviser to the U.S. delegation at the San Francisco Conference in 1945. After the war, Neuberger returned to journalism, but he almost immediately reentered politics. In 1946, he ran unsuccessfully for the state senate. Two years later, he won the seat. When his wife, Maurine, was elected to the state house of representatives in 1950, the Neubergers became the first married couple to serve in a state legislature at the same time.

In 1954, Neuberger ran for the U.S. Senate against the incumbent, Guy Cordon, (R-Oreg.); an advocate of the transfer of offshore oil reserves to the states. Neuberger attacked Cordon as an opponent of conservation and, with the aid of ADLAI STEVENSON and WAYNE MORSE (I-Oreg.), Neuberger won a narrow victory. Neuberger's stunning upset helped the Democrats regain control of the Senate.

In the Senate, Neuberger backed housing legislation, conservation measures, government financing of federal election campaigns, rigid price supports for farmers, and statehood for Alaska. With respect to local and regional interests, he strongly advocated preservation of the Klamath Basin and the Oregon Dunes. He also supported the Hell's Canyon Dam. In 1957, the liberal Americans for Democratic Action gave him a 100 percent rating, as did the AFL-CIO's Committee on Political Education the following year. Neuberger joined Morse in criticizing Eisenhower's economic policies. Unlike Morse, however, he got along with the

Democratic leadership in the Senate. As Neuberger received increasingly favorable attention from the press, his relations with Morse deteriorated and eventually became a noted political feud.

A strong supporter of civil rights for African Americans, Neuberger was one of six Democratic senators who announced in 1956 that they would attempt to abolish Senate Rule 22, which required a two-thirds vote of the membership to cut off debate, in order to facilitate the passage of civil rights legislation. Contained in the six-point "Democratic Declaration of 1957," this proposal also called on Congress to guarantee black voting and educational rights. The majority leader in the Senate, LYNDON B. JOHNSON (D-Tex.), opposed the motion to amend Rule 22, and it was tabled in January 1957. Neuberger supported another unsuccessful attempt to change the rule in 1959.

Neuberger aggressively backed the Civil Rights Act of 1957 and resisted attempts to weaken the proposal. In July, he unsuccessfully opposed a motion to delete Title III, which granted the federal government authority to enter civil suits to further desegregation. The following month, he again unsuccessfully fought a southern attempt to weaken the bill by guaranteeing a jury trial to people charged with criminal contempt. Neuberger chided Eisenhower for what the senator alleged was the president's lukewarm support of the proposal. He declared that the president was responsible for its fate, and charged that his apathy had "made infinitely more difficult the task of those" who favored "meaningful and effective civil rights legislation." The senator from Oregon remained silent about the role of Johnson, who crafted the agreement to eliminate Title III and add the jury trial amendment to Title IV.

Neuberger vigorously supported increased public housing and voted in August 1959 for a bill that would have promoted urban renewal and provided 37,000 new units of housing as well as loans and grants to aid homeowners, the elderly, colleges, and hospitals. That September he joined an unsuccessful attempt to overturn Eisenhower's veto of the proposal. Neuberger also voted to override the president's veto of a billion-dollar public works bill that month. In that case, the Senate successfully overrode the veto.

Diagnosed with cancer in 1958, Neuberger underwent radiation therapy, which seemed to be proceeding successfully, and he was planning to run for a second term in 1960 when he died unexpectedly of a cerebral hemorrhage in Portland on March 9, 1960. The governor of Oregon appointed H. S. Lusk, a justice of the state supreme court, to complete Neuberger's term. In November 1960, however, Neuberger's widow, Maurine Brown Neuberger, won election to her husband's seat in the Senate.

—MSM

Newsom, Herschel D(avis)

(1905–1970) *master, the National Grange*

Born in Bartholomew County, Indiana, on May 1, 1905, Herschel Newsom grew up on his family's farm. He graduated from Indiana University in 1926 with a B.A. in chemistry and then, like his Quaker forebears, became a farmer. A member of the Grange, an agrarian social and self-help organization, since his days as a schoolboy, Newsom became especially active in the organization in the 1930s. He was chosen master of the Columbus Subordinate Grange of Bartholomew County in 1933 and was elected master of the Indiana State Grange in 1937, an office which his father had once held and which Newsom retained for 13 years. He joined the National Grange's executive committee in 1946 and became its chairman in 1949. In November of the following year, he was elected master of the National Grange.

The election of Newsom reflected increasingly conservative trends in the national farm organization. Newsom claimed that he was elected because he opposed "excessive governmental control of farm production in our daily lives." The Grange, which claimed to be the oldest farm organization in the world (founded in 1867), was politically on the middle ground between the two other large U.S. farm groups, the conservative American Farm Bureau Foundation (AFBF) and the liberal National Farmers Union (NFU). Especially strong in New England, Ohio, and the Northwest, the Grange, or "Patrons of Husbandry," had over 850,000 dues-paying members, which made it larger than the NFU, but smaller than the AFBF.

Under Newsom's leadership, the Grange tended to take a conservative position on farm issues during the early years of the Eisenhower administration. Newsom applauded Secretary of Agriculture EZRA TAFT BENSON's farm program, including his plans to return American agriculture to the free market system and solve the problems of overproduction and declining farm income by reducing acreage controls, price supports, and direct subsidies. Newsom, however, believed that immediate abolition of process supports would be ruinous for American farmers, who had, under the administration of HARRY S. TRUMAN, enjoyed 90 percent of parity price supports for basic crops. Speaking before the Senate Agriculture and Forestry Committee in March 1954, he recommended gradual cuts. Newsom also backed Benson's efforts to expand sales of U.S. farm products abroad, suggesting that they be integrated with a two-price system for wheat and cotton. Under a two-price system, higher prices would be maintained for farm products in the United States, while prices would be lowered on the international market, so that American farmers could successfully compete with foreign producers. In February 1955, as farm income continued the steady decline begun at the end of the Korean War, Newsom spoke out strongly against a measure to restore 90 percent of parity price supports.

Gradually, however, Newsom and the Grange, representing many small farmers, became dissatisfied with the administration, which, they argued, favored the interests of large growers. By 1956, Newsom's disenchantment seemed complete. In November, he rejected the choice between 100 percent of parity price supports advocated by the NFU and most Democrats and the flexible support price program of Secretary Benson. Rather, Newsom wanted an individual commodity-by-commodity approach to price supports and dual parity that guaranteed farmers high prices on food for domestic consumption but unsupported market prices on exports. In addition, Newsom and the Grange called for the creation of a bipartisan commission to study and recommend equitable revisions in the federal tax structure. Newsom opposed tax cuts that would require deficit financing. If tax cuts were possible, however, he argued that they should be given to the lower income brackets. He also advocated the repeal of excise taxes on farm equipment not used on highways and suggested that the government use farm surpluses, not dollars, in foreign economic aid programs. In opposition to the administration, Newsom supported congressional efforts in 1958 to prevent the reduction in price support levels for a number of commodities. In June 1959, Newsom said that Congress had the responsibility to develop a workable farm program, whether or not the president would sign it. Referring to a compromise farm bill, he attacked Eisenhower, saying that "we may eventually have a President who will sign it."

Finally, in a speech before the annual national meeting of the Grange in November 1959, Newsom reversed his position on price supports by asserting that to attempt to remove the government from agriculture or any other area of the economy "is worst than sheer folly . . . it is tantamount to economic disaster." He went on to say that "the nation can afford neither a continuation of the present system of price supports and subsidies nor a return to full free competition for agriculture." He opposed price fixing but argued that government measures should ensure a certain level of farm income, just as they helped determine industrial prices and the wages of labor.

During the Kennedy and Johnson years, Newsom worked closely with Secretary of Agriculture ORVILLE FREEMAN to win adoption of the two-price wheat support plan the Grange had advocated for many years. In 1968, Newsom left the Grange to become U.S. tariff commissioner. He died in Washington, D.C., on July 2, 1970, after suffering a heart attack.

—MSM

Niebuhr, Reinhold
(1892–1971) *theologian*

The son of a German immigrant minister, Niebuhr was born in Wright City, Missouri, on June 21, 1892. He grew up in Missouri and Illinois and was educated at Elmhurst College near St. Louis and Eden Theological Seminary in Missouri, from which he received a bachelor of divinity in 1913. That same year, he was ordained a minister. When his father died in the spring of 1913, Niebuhr served as interim pastor for his father's congregation before departing that fall to attend Yale Divinity School, where he received a second bachelor of divinity in 1914 and an M.A. in 1915. Upon completing his M.A., Niebuhr became a minister of the Bethel Evangelical Church in Detroit, where he was active in labor, pacifist, and socialist movements. When America entered World War I, Niebuhr sought to Americanize his largely German congregation. After the war, Niebuhr became a well-known voice for liberal Protestantism. He could command a pulpit like few of his day. His sermons awed listeners with their energy and erudition. A supporter of the Social Gospel, Niebuhr constantly drew on the book of Amos and urged that justice "run down as waters and righteousness as a mighty stream." Beginning in 1922, Niebuhr was a regular contributor to the *Christian Century*, a leading organ of liberal Protestantism. He advocated the creation of a labor party and urged liberal Protestants to side with labor in its struggle with capital. In the mid-1920s, Niebuhr moved toward socialism.

In 1929, he became an associate professor of ethics at Union Theological Seminary in New York and an editor of the socialist publication, *World Tomorrow*. Niebuhr ran as a socialist candidate for the state senate from Manhattan's Upper West Side in 1930 but made a very poor showing. He ran for Congress from the same district in 1932 and received less than 5 percent of the vote. Although Niebuhr remained a socialist for the rest of the decade, he concluded that voters had rejected socialism, and he withdrew from active participation in party affairs.

Throughout the 1930s, Niebuhr engaged in an extensive reexamination of his ethical and political beliefs. This ultimately led him to reject socialism on religious grounds. He concluded that it was a form of idolatry to believe that human beings could conceive and bring about God's kingdom on earth. Niebuhr first broke with many of his liberal and socialist colleagues in 1932 with the publication of *Moral Man and Immoral Society*. In it, he rejected the liberal Protestant goal of bringing about a community of "perpetual peace and brotherhood" on Earth. Niebuhr conceded that individuals might sometimes behave in a moral and altruistic manner, but he nonetheless insisted that social groups, especially those as large as nations, operated only

according to their particular interests. This "realistic" perspective led him to abandon pacifism as irrelevant to contemporary problems.

One result of his philosophical reassessment was that, during the 1930s, Niebuhr turned his energies to religious, rather than secular, organizations. He also devoted himself more to the study of theology. Critics, including his own brother, H. Richard Niebuhr, a professor of ethics at Yale Divinity School and an important neoorthodox theologian, faulted *Moral Man and Immoral Society* for its vision of unending social conflict and its lack of any message of hope. In his theological explorations, Reinhold Niebuhr was influenced by Paul Tillich, a German theologian who joined Union Seminary in 1933. Tillich focused on the idea of myth and used it to argue that, contrary to liberal Christianity, Christianity was more than an ethical imperative. Niebuhr's *An Interpretation of Christian Ethics* (1935) revealed the influence of Tillich in its analysis of two important Christian "myths," the Creation and the Fall. Christianity's ethical force, Niebuhr wrote, derived from belief in a Creator who loved people but judged them and from the belief that humans were responsible for their own sins. The same year he published *An Interpretation of Christian Ethics*, he became William E. Dodge, Jr., Professor of Applied Christianity, a chair he held until 1955.

As the 1930s drew to a close, Niebuhr's theology was also influenced by the threat of European fascism. He was among the first radical American Christians to argue that class struggle had to yield to a "united front" against fascism. At the Oxford Conference on Church, Community, and State in 1937, he argued that the international crisis resulted not only from economic conditions but from human nature. Liberals and communists, he maintained, were equally deluded. Communists thought that changing the economic system would bring social harmony; liberals thought that human beings were essentially good and needed only the proper education to construct a good society. Christians, said Niebuhr, knew better; the doctrine of original sin, which humanists rejected, taught the imperfect nature of human beings and the imperfectability of any society they would produce. Moreover, he argued, experience demonstrated that truth on a daily basis. That same year, Niebuhr published *Beyond Tragedy*.

In 1939, with Europe at war, Niebuhr delivered the Gifford Lectures at the University of Edinburgh. The publication of those lectures in two volumes as *The Nature and Destiny of Man* (1941, 1943) established him as a major theologian and an important force in American culture. Niebuhr's most significant theological contribution was to revive the doctrine of original sin. Humans, he taught, had the freedom and creativity to do good works, but this led them to overestimate themselves. They came to think of themselves as creators of their own destinies, saw in themselves limitless potential, and strove to create perfection.

Niebuhr broke with the Socialist Party in 1940 because of its noninterventionism. Niebuhr favored American aid to the Allies because he regarded the Nazis as a threat to Western civilization. He played a leading role in founding the Union for Democratic Action (UDA) in 1941 and served as its chair. Noncommunist, pro-labor, and aggressively antifascist, UDA included in its membership a substantial number of former socialists who rejected the party's isolationism. Also in 1941, Niebuhr founded *Christianity and Crisis*, a biweekly paper dedicated to the proposition that "the halting of totalitarian aggression is a prerequisite to world peace and order" and designed to combat the influence of *Christian Century*, a pacifist organ. After the United States entered the war, Niebuhr vigorously supported the war effort. The Office of War Information sent him to England to give talks to American troops and to the British public. Niebuhr was also one of the few American intellectuals to call attention to the plight of Europe's Jews.

Niebuhr applied the theological insights of the *Nature and Destiny of Man* to political theory in *The Children of Light and the Children of Darkness* (1944). In it, he argued that the Children of Darkness (fascists), driven by the will to power, led to totalitarianism. Similarly, however, the foolish Children of Light (communists), driven by a utopian zeal, led to totalitarianism, as well. Indeed, the two extremes were guilty of the same sin, the original sin of intellectual pride. They ignored the imperfect nature of human beings and were willing to destroy freedom and anyone who got in their way in order to create their vision of a perfect society. Hope lay in the Children of Light who recognized the inherently imperfect nature of humans and applied that insight to political theory. Embracing democracy, a system he once believed needed to be replaced through class struggle, Niebuhr wrote: "Man's capacity for justice makes democracy possible, but man's inclination to injustice makes democracy necessary." Hope rested in what ARTHUR SCHLESINGER, JR., later called the "vital center."

Neoorthodoxy, with its emphasis on original sin, struck a chord with the American public in the years after World War II. Liberal Christianity offered no explanation for Hitler, the concentration camps, or Stalin. Neoorthodoxy did. The *Children of Light and the Children of Darkness* provided an ideological, not to mention theological, basis for emerging cold war liberalism, which supported a strong anticommunist foreign policy and New Deal liberalism at home. Niebuhr became involved in the founding of the Liberal Party of New York and served as its vice chairman. He was also a founder of the Americans for Democratic Action (ADA) and served on its board. The ADA became the leading organization of cold war liberals.

During the 1950s, Niebuhr emerged as one of the major intellectual spokesmen for anticommunist liberalism. Such prominent liberals as Schlesinger and Senator HUBERT HUMPHREY (D-Minn.) regarded Niebuhr as the father of "realistic liberalism." GEORGE F. KENNAN, the architect of the policy of containment, called him "the father of us all."

In *The Irony of American History* (1952), Niebuhr once again wrote in defense of pragmatic democracy. He pointed out ironic similarities between the United States and its adversary in the cold war, the Soviet Union. Both nations had origins in the confidence of humans to master their own destiny and to create an ideal society. Approaching the American experience as ironic, he maintained that American dreams had repeatedly been forced to yield in the face of "recalcitrant forces" that "have a power and persistence beyond our reckoning"; nevertheless, Americans were responsible for their own fate. Therefore, Niebuhr contended that people should commit themselves to political action, despite the virtual inevitability that it would fall short of complete success. In the process, he cautioned, people should guard against inflated and unrealistic hopes.

Throughout the 1950s, Niebuhr remained a powerful force in debates over domestic affairs. A stroke in 1952 left one arm partly paralyzed and made it difficult for him to speak. He traveled less but continued to write extensively on politics and religion. Niebuhr attacked Senator JOSEPH R. MCCARTHY (R-Wis.) for undermining anticommunism with his reckless and irresponsible accusations. Throughout the Eisenhower administration, Niebuhr continued to campaign for social welfare programs. He was an outspoken supporter of the Supreme Court's decision in *Brown v. Board of Education* (1954), but, consistent with his pessimistic view of human nature, he expressed little hope for an easy resolution of racial problems in the United States. For his part, Niebuhr directed his personal attention almost exclusively to combating segregation within the church.

The rise of evangelicalism caused Niebuhr considerable concern. In an article that appeared in *Life* magazine in July 1957, he attacked BILLY GRAHAM and the wave of revivalism then sweeping the country. Niebuhr believed that Graham's emphasis on personal conversion and spiritual rebirth evaded the problem of social injustice. Indeed, Graham's "wholly individualistic" conception of sin was "almost completely irrelevant" to the collective problems faced by American society, such as racial prejudice and economic injustice.

In foreign policy, Niebuhr's realism resulted in an emphasis on America's need to live up to its responsibilities as leader of the free world. He held that nations were fundamentally immoral entities that could not be expected to cooperate with one another but, instead, were constantly involved in conflict. Niebuhr, therefore, insisted that foreign policy be based on maintaining a balance of power and that the United States had to serve as the primary counterweight to the totalitarian communist nations. International organizations such as the United Nations played little role in his thought, because they were not based on the realities of power politics. Thus, when the United States turned to the United Nations for a resolution of the Suez Crisis in 1956, he complained that President DWIGHT D. EISENHOWER was guilty of both collaborating with the USSR against the interest of American allies and of compounding the error by pretending that the United Nations constituted a legitimate international authority. Niebuhr consistently advocated a strong American position in foreign affairs, particularly in Europe, which he considered the most important arena of international conflict. He warned consistently against committing American military forces in Asia, primarily because he worried that it might prompt Soviet aggression in Europe.

In 1955, Niebuhr became Charles A. Briggs Graduate Professor of Ethics and Theology. He also served as vice president of Union Theological Seminary after 1955.

By 1959, when he published *The Structure of Nations and Empires*, Niebuhr had somewhat softened his position on the cold war. He conceded that the Soviet Union had moved away from the absolute despotism of the Stalin era, and he hoped that change would ultimately serve to ease international tensions. He even discerned a ray of hope in the "ultimate irony" of the contemporary situation: security could be established "under the umbrella of an atomic stalemate."

Niebuhr retired in 1960 but continued his role as social, religious, and political commentator until his health declined in the mid-1960s. Although he had supported LYNDON B. JOHNSON for the presidency in 1964, Niebuhr became an outspoken critic of the war in Vietnam after the escalation of American involvement in 1965. He died in Stockbridge, Massachusetts, on June 1, 1971.

—MSM

Nixon, Richard M(ilhous)
(1913–1994) *37th president of the United States*

Born in Yorba Linda, California, on January 9, 1913, to a Quaker family of modest means, Richard Nixon was the second of five sons. His father, Frank Nixon, owned a lemon grove in Yorba Linda. When the grove failed in 1922, he moved his family to nearby Whittier, California, where he opened a gasoline station and general store. Beginning at the age of 10 or 11, Richard Nixon worked in his father's store and as a part-time farm laborer.

An extremely diligent and studious young man, Nixon was student body president and an outstanding debater at both Whittier High School and Whittier College. In 1934, he received his B.A., graduating second in his college class. Nixon received a scholarship to attend Duke University Law School, where he earned his LL.B. in 1937 and ranked third in his class. He explored getting a job with a prestigious law firm in New York City, but only one showed any interest in him. After an unsuccessful attempt to get a job with the FBI, Nixon returned to Whittier to practice law with the firm of Wingert & Bewley.

A month after the Japanese attacked Pearl Harbor, Nixon went to Washington and began working for the tire-rationing section of the Office of Price Administration (OPA). He later stated that, although he had been a liberal in law school, his experience with the inefficient bureaucracy at the OPA made him more conservative. In August 1942, Nixon resigned from the OPA and enlisted in the navy. He was assigned to the Combat Air Transport Command in the South Pacific as a lieutenant, junior grade. Nixon returned to the United States in August 1944 for a series of postings. At the end of the war, he was assigned to Baltimore, where he negotiated the termination of defense contracts.

Before Nixon was mustered out of the service in January 1946, a group of prominent Republicans in Whittier and its vicinity asked him to run for Congress against the liberal Democratic incumbent, Rep. Jerry Voorhis. Elected with the Roosevelt landslide of 1936, Voorhis had enthusiastically embraced the New Deal's social legislation and, indeed, wished to extend it further. With the end of the depression, the electorate had moved more toward the center,

President Eisenhower and Vice President Richard Nixon, August 21, 1954 *(Dwight D. Eisenhower Library and Museum)*

and Voorhis, who had entered politics with Upton Sinclair's End Poverty in California campaign, remained at the left of the spectrum of American politics. Nixon won the Republican primary and then waged an energetic and aggressive campaign against Voorhis. He linked the incumbent to the Congress of Industrial Organizations's (CIO) political action committee (PAC). He charged that it was communist-dominated and that Voorhis had voted for almost all measures supported by the CIO-PAC. Voorhis responded clumsily and attempted to hide the fact that he had received endorsements from several local CIO-PACs. Nixon was particularly effective in a series of five debates with his opponent. Dissatisfaction with the process of economic reconversion after the war made 1946 a Republican year; the party won control of both houses of Congress. Nixon defeated Voorhis, garnering roughly 66,000 votes to his opponent's 50,000.

In Congress, Nixon was assigned to the House Un-American Activities Committee (HUAC) and the Education and Labor Committee. On the former panel, he played a key role in pressing the investigation of Alger Hiss, whom WHITTAKER CHAMBERS accused of having been a Soviet spy while serving in the State Department during the 1930s. As head of a special subcommittee, Nixon doggedly pursued Chambers's allegations. He arranged for a meeting between Hiss and Chambers before HUAC in August 1948. That confrontation, at which Hiss denied having known Chambers or having passed documents to him, led to Hiss's conviction for perjury in 1950. The Hiss case brought Nixon to national attention, but it also made him, as he wrote in his memoirs, "one of the most controversial figures in Washington." In 1948, Nixon also cosponsored the Nixon-Mundt bill to require the registration of communist political organizations and their members and communist-front groups and their officers. The measure did not pass, but portions of it were incorporated into the Internal Security Act of 1950.

Although conservative on many domestic issues, Nixon advocated raising the amount of money a retiree could earn and still receive benefits from Social Security. He also voted for federal support for housing and federal aid to education. In foreign affairs, he was an internationalist. In 1947,

he supported President HARRY S. TRUMAN's program of aid to Greece and Turkey. During the same year, he served on a 19-member select panel, popularly known as the Herter Committee, that went on a fact-finding mission to Europe. He joined his colleagues on the panel in strongly endorsing the Marshall Plan.

Under California's cross-filing system, Nixon won both the Republican and Democratic congressional primaries in 1948. Two years later, he ran for a seat in the Senate vacated by Sheridan Downey (D-Calif.), who chose to retire when confronted with serious opposition in the Democratic primary. Unopposed in the Republican primary, Nixon faced in the general election Rep. Helen Gahagan Douglas (D-Calif.), who had emerged as the winner in a bitter Democratic primary race, during which her opponent, Ralph M. Boddy, accused her of left-wing sympathies and branded her the "pink lady." The contest between Nixon and Douglas was a vicious one. Repeating the strategy he had employed in 1946 and echoing Boddy's charges, Nixon alleged that "my opponent is a member of a small clique which joins the notorious Communist party-liner [Representative] Vito Marcantonio in voting time after time against measures that are for the security of this country." Nixon's campaign organization distributed a pink-colored flyer that linked the voting records of Douglas and Marcantonio. Douglas responded by calling Nixon "Tricky Dick" and describing her opponent and his supporters as "a backwash of young men in dark shirts," clearly implying that they were fascists. Nixon won the election with almost 2.2 million votes to Douglas's 1.5 million.

His election to the Senate marked Nixon's emergence as a significant, if highly divisive, political figure. His success in linking the Democratic Party and the Truman administration with subversive influences enraged liberal Democrats and many intellectuals. They regarded him as a notorious smear artist and opportunist who would employ any means to win elections. Republicans, on the other hand, regarded Nixon as a rising star who had played a key role in pushing one of the party's major issues. As a freshman senator, Nixon quickly became one of the most sought-after Republican speakers in the country. In the Senate, he attacked

Truman's handling of the Korean War, criticized the corruption of the Truman administration, and demanded the removal of communists and communist sympathizers from government.

Even before DWIGHT D. EISENHOWER got the Republican presidential nomination in 1952, two of his top political advisers, THOMAS E. DEWEY, the governor of New York, and HERBERT BROWNELL, began seriously to consider Nixon as a running mate for the general. As a California delegate to the Chicago National Republican Convention in July, Nixon was committed to his state's favorite son, Governor EARL WARREN. Between the two leading contenders for the nomination, however, Nixon favored Eisenhower over Senator ROBERT A. TAFT (R-Ohio), largely because he believed Eisenhower had a better chance to win. Warren's supporters charged that Nixon was surreptitiously aiding Eisenhower's candidacy to assure himself the second spot on the ticket. Nixon publicly restated his commitment to Warren and declared him to be the strongest of the dark horse candidates. Moreover, as a member of California's delegation, he was bound by law to vote for Warren on the first ballot. A few hours after Eisenhower won the nomination, Brownell informed Nixon that he would be the vice presidential nominee. Eisenhower's advisers thought that the selection of Nixon would help mollify conservative supporters of Taft. They also believed that Nixon's youth and his identification with the issue of subversive influence in Washington would aid the ticket. Finally, Nixon provided geographical balance.

On September 18, just after Nixon had begun his ambitious national campaign, the *New York Post*, a Democratic and sensationalist tabloid, ran a screaming headline over a story asserting that a group of wealthy businessmen had established a "secret fund" of somewhat over $18,000 for the candidate's personal use. The article referred to a fund created by some of Nixon's supporters in California after Nixon's election to the Senate in 1950. Nixon responded that the money was used only to help pay the expenses involved in his extensive speaking tours. He dismissed the charges as "another typical smear by the same left wing elements which have fought me ever since I took part in the investigation of . . . Alger Hiss." When STEPHEN A. MITCH-

ELL, chair of the Democratic National Committee, demanded Nixon's resignation, Nixon snapped that Mitchell should ask for the resignation of the Democrats' vice-presidential nominee, Senator JOHN SPARKMAN (D-Ala.), whose wife was on his Senate payroll. However, Eisenhower was running a campaign against corruption in Washington, and a number of Republican newspapers immediately called for Nixon's withdrawal from the ticket. The majority of Eisenhower's top advisers believed that Nixon should resign. Eisenhower responded more calmly and cautiously. He issued a public statement in which he declared that he believed "Dick Nixon to be an honest man" and expressed his confidence that Nixon would "place all the facts before the American people." On September 20, however, Eisenhower told reporters in an informal press conference that Nixon would have to prove himself "clean as a hound's tooth."

Eisenhower's chief of staff, SHERMAN ADAMS, arranged for a thorough examination of the fund by a leading law firm in Los Angeles, Gibson, Dunn and Crutcher, and the accounting house of Price Waterhouse. The report revealed that the fund was not a secret, that it had been used exclusively for political purposes, and that it had violated no law. Moreover, the day Price Waterhouse delivered its report, the story broke that the Democratic nominee, ADLAI STEVENSON, had a similar fund.

To clear his name and retain his place on the ticket, Nixon made a half-hour televised speech on September 23. He denied that he used the fund for personal expenses and that any of the contributors had received special favors from him. After giving what he called a "complete" account of his financial holdings, Nixon observed: "It isn't very much, but Pat and I have the satisfaction that every dime we've got is honestly ours." He said that his wife, Pat, to whom the camera cut when references were made to her, did not own a mink coat but only a "respectable Republican cloth coat." (This was a reference to a mink coat that had been given by an attorney for a firm that received a loan from the Reconstruction Finance Corporation [RFC] to an examiner for the RFC whose wife was a stenographer in the White House. The mink coat became a symbol of corruption of the Truman administration.) Having made full financial disclosure, Nixon called on Stevenson and Sparkman to do the same. Nixon did admit to having received a gift from a supporter in Texas; it was a cocker spaniel, and his daughters loved it. The older of his two daughters, Tricia, had named it Checkers, and, he continued, "regardless of what they say about it, we're going to keep it." The address subsequently came to be known as the Checkers speech. At the end of the speech, Nixon urged viewers to let the Republican National Committee know whether they thought he should stay on the ticket.

Although a highly combative politician, Nixon sometimes gave way to despair following an intense effort to overcome adversity. Immediately after the broadcast, he believed that the speech had been a failure because he had gone over his allotted half-hour and had been cut off the air. Moreover, he had urged the audience to contact the Republican National Committee but had forgotten to tell them where to "wire and write." When Eisenhower indicated that he needed more time to make up his mind concerning his running mate's status, Nixon dictated a telegram of resignation to ARTHUR SUMMERFIELD, chairman of the Republican National Committee. MURRAY CHOTINER, Nixon's campaign manager, destroyed the message. As it turned out, public reaction to the speech was overwhelmingly favorable. On the evening of September 24, Eisenhower met Nixon at the airport in Wheeling, West Virginia, and told him, "You're my boy."

Resuming his campaign, Nixon charged that the Democrats had been soft on communism and had permitted subversive influences to penetrate the national government. To demonstrate his own experience in dealing with subversives, Nixon, in a nationally televised campaign address on October 13, described his role in the Hiss affair. In the same speech, he created a political stir by criticizing Stevenson for having attested to Hiss's good character at the latter's trial.

Eisenhower and Nixon won in a landslide that November, and Nixon became an unusually active and visible vice president. He traveled extensively, visiting the Far East in 1953, Central America in 1955, Africa and Rome in 1957, South America in 1958, and the Soviet Union in 1959. He also served on the National Security Council. Eisenhower established a precedent by assigning Nixon to preside over meetings of the cabinet and National Security Council in the president's absence.

Nixon's most important role in the administration, particularly in the early years of the Eisenhower presidency, was as a congressional liaison and political adviser. He also served as a liaison to the Republican right and, in particular, to Senator JOSEPH R. MCCARTHY (R-Wis.). Nixon urged Eisenhower to avoid directly attacking McCarthy. The vice president argued that a break between the president and the senator from Wisconsin could split the Republican Party and open the administration to charges of being soft on communism. In March 1953, after McCarthy had made personal efforts to stop Greek ship operators from trading with communist China, HAROLD STASSEN, chief of the Mutual Security Administration, denounced the senator for "undermining" President Eisenhower's foreign policy. Nixon, who believed that the public approved of McCarthy's efforts, arranged a conference between the senator and Stassen's superior, Secretary of State JOHN FOSTER DULLES. Dulles issued a statement praising McCarthy for acting in the national interest, and McCarthy promised to coordinate his actions with the State Department. In May 1953, McCarthy wrote a letter to the president asking why the administration was not attempting to end Western trade with communist countries. Nixon persuaded him to recall the letter. However, when McCarthy's attacks on the army made reconciliation impossible, Nixon abandoned his role as mediator. Speaking on behalf of the administration in a televised broadcast on March 13, 1954, he asserted that "men who have in the past done effective work exposing Communism in this country have, by reckless talk and questionable methods, made themselves the issue, rather that the cause they believe in so deeply."

In the congressional elections of 1954, Nixon campaigned extensively on behalf of Republican candidates. He charged that "the candidates running on the Democratic ticket in the key states are almost without exception members of the Democratic Party's left-wing clique which has been so blind to the Communist conspiracy and has tolerated it in the United States." Nixon warned that if the Democrats regained control of Congress, President Eisenhower's firm stand against communism would be jeopardized. To demonstrate Eisenhower's effectiveness in dealing with subversives, he claimed that thousands of security risks had been dismissed or had resigned from the federal government under the president's loyalty-security program. Nixon's attacks on Democrats were so heated that in June Eisenhower called him in and told him to tone it down. That fall, Nixon campaigned tirelessly, repeatedly attacking Democratic candidates, but the Democrats captured both houses of Congress.

Nixon's Checkers speech, his position on McCarthy, and his activities in the campaigns of 1952 and 1954 convinced his opponents more strongly than ever that he was an unscrupulous politician. Beginning in 1955, however, his image began to soften, even in the eyes of some of his staunchest foes, and there was talk of a new Nixon. The process began with President Eisenhower's heart attack on September 24, 1955. During the subsequent weeks of Eisenhower's hospitalization, Nixon maintained a low profile, played down the significance of his role, and avoided any appearance of attempting to use the circumstances for political gain. He presided over meetings of the cabinet and National Security Council from his own chair rather than the president's. In the White House, he used a conference room rather than the president's office. Nixon's restraint enhanced his prestige both within the administration and in the country at large.

Even as his standing with the public rose, Nixon considered leaving politics. In 1954, he had carried an extraordinarily heavy burden during the campaign and was a frequent target for Democratic attacks. The combination wore on him, and Nixon decided not to run again in 1956. In reality, leaving politics was never really an option for Nixon, and Eisenhower's heart attack in 1955 placed the vice presidency in a new light. Moreover, any shift to a different political office, such as running for the Senate or entering the cabinet, looked like a step down, so Nixon decided that he would run for reelection in 1956. Eisenhower, however, suggested to Nixon that it might be better for him to take a cabinet post. After a period of indecision, which proved agonizing to Nixon, the president announced in April that he wanted his vice president to remain on the ticket. Eisenhower's reluctance derived from his complicated relationship with Nixon and some

concerns that Nixon might cost the ticket votes. His advisers, however, convinced the president that Nixon was important in maintaining support from the right wing of the Republican Party.

Nixon's campaign for reelection in 1956 contributed to his new image. During that campaign, Nixon largely abandoned his customary electoral strategy of attack and concentrated on defending the record of the Eisenhower administration. He told the public that the president had extricated the country from the Korean War without abandoning principle. Nixon also pointed to the healthy state of the economy and gainsaid the arguments that Republican policies led to economic depression and that the Democrats were the party of the working and poor people. Eisenhower still used him to answer Stevenson, who was again the Democratic nominee and who resorted to some shrill and personal attacks, but this time Nixon did so deftly and without going after Stevenson personally or challenging his patriotism. Eisenhower and Nixon won in a landslide.

During Eisenhower's second term, Nixon's foreign travels added significantly to his political standing. Even before the second term officially began, Eisenhower sent him to Austria in December 1956 to draw public attention to the Soviet Union's brutal repression of Hungary and the plight of Hungarian refugees. The leftist violence that plagued Nixon's tour of South America in May 1958 served to enhance Nixon's stature. In Lima, Peru, Nixon faced down a stone-throwing crowd at San Marcos University. In Caracas, Venezuela, a raging mob smashed the windows of his automobile, and troops arrived just in time to prevent him from being dragged from the car and killed. His courage and calmness in the face of great physical danger earned him considerable respect.

In July 1959, Nixon went to Moscow to open the American National Exhibition at Sokolniki Park. He was the highest-ranking American official to visit the Soviet Union since Premier Nikita S. Khrushchev's rise to power. On the day after his arrival, Nixon and Khrushchev engaged in a heated exchange, which continued as they visited the American Exhibition, where they debated the respective merits of capitalism and communism. Part of the discussion took place in the model kitchen of the exhibition, and the argument became known as the kitchen debate. Nixon's refusal to back down from the blustering Soviet premier and his spirited, effective defense of the United States burnished his reputation at home.

From the earliest days of Eisenhower's presidency, Nixon had been one of the strongest advocates of civil rights within the administration. As chairman of the President's Committee on Government Contracts, Nixon assumed an important role in the administration's efforts to eliminate discrimination practiced by contractors with the federal government and with Washington, D.C. He also figured prominently in the attempt to eliminate segregation from the nation's capital.

During Eisenhower's second term, Nixon made an effort to disassociate himself from the Republican Right and establish himself as a moderate. His support for civil rights constituted an important part of that undertaking. When the administration's civil rights bill was before Congress in 1957, he opposed southern attempts to eliminate Title III, a provision granting the attorney general the power to enforce desegregation through federal court action. He also argued against an amendment, sponsored by southern senators, granting jury trials in criminal contempt cases arising from the measure. The bill nevertheless emerged from Congress without Title III and with the jury-trial amendment. Two years later, Eisenhower considered sending Congress a measure that would merely have extended the life of the Civil Rights Commission. Nixon, Attorney General WILLIAM ROGERS, Health, Education and Welfare Secretary ARTHUR S. FLEMMING, and Labor Secretary JAMES MITCHELL argued forcefully and successfully for a more comprehensive civil rights bill. In a related matter, Nixon lent his support to senators wishing to modify the filibuster rule. In 1957 and again in 1959, he aided their cause by making favorable procedural decisions as president of the Senate.

On a trip to Africa in 1957, Nixon met MARTIN LUTHER KING, JR., the civil rights activist, and invited him to visit the vice president's office when they returned to the United States. King took him up on the offer, and he and his aide RALPH ABERNATHY had a cordial meeting with Nixon. The vice president also supported federal aid to educa-

tion, even though southern members of Congress worried that the federal government would use that aid to advance desegregation by denying it to school districts that continued to segregate. In addition, Nixon supported the decision to invite a group of African-American leaders to meet with the president.

In 1958, Nixon led those within the cabinet who favored more assistance for the unemployed and for depressed areas to fight the recession. Early the following year, he fought successfully in the cabinet to keep federal aid to education on the administration's legislative agenda. In December 1959 and January 1960, Nixon also established a reputation as a conciliator by helping to settle a steel strike that lasted 116 days.

In the second half of the 1950s, Nixon emerged as one of the strongest advocates within the administration of foreign economic aid, including to neutralist nations. He argued that economic aid was even more important than military assistance. In 1957, Eisenhower assigned him to help draw up mutual assistance, technical, and direct aid programs.

Nixon's support for foreign economic aid was a component of his approach to containment. Throughout Eisenhower's presidency, Nixon advocated a hard-line policy toward communist expansion. In 1954, he suggested, off the record, the possibility of sending troops to Indochina if the French pulled out. Four years later, he stated that, regardless of American public opinion, the administration should stand by its commitment to defend the tiny islands of Quemoy and Matsu, which were occupied by the Chinese Nationalists, against attack from Chinese Communists. Nixon's hard line, however, was not without nuance. In 1959, he met Cuban premier Fidel Castro and reported to the president that "he is either incredibly naïve about Communism or under Communist discipline." Nixon's "guess" was "the former." At the same time, the vice president acknowledged the Cuban dictator's "great gift of leadership" and suggested that it might be possible to "orient him in the right direction." Apparently, Nixon soon abandoned that idea. In his book, *Six Crises*, however, Nixon claimed that, after his meeting with Castro, he urged the arming and training of Cuban exiles in the United States and Latin American countries.

While suspicion of Nixon among Democrats and intellectuals became somewhat muted during the late 1950s, it did not disappear. Their long-held distrust surfaced when Eisenhower suffered a stroke in November 1957 that substantially incapacitated him for two weeks. In January 1958, Eisenhower drafted a letter to Nixon indicating that if the president became incapacitated and was aware of it, he would inform Nixon, and the vice president would assume the duties of the presidency. If, however, the president were so disabled as to be unaware of his incapacity, Nixon would "decide upon the devolution" of presidential powers and serve as acting president until the incapacity had ended. Questions over the constitutionality of this arrangement in part reflected anxiety over the possibility of Nixon's becoming chief executive. The vice president's characterization of Democrats as "radicals" in the 1958 congressional elections revived the suspicion among his traditional opponents that the new Nixon image was nothing more than a façade.

Immediately after the elections of 1958, Nixon gave his political backers permission to begin organizing a campaign for the Republican presidential nomination in 1960. The only significant obstacle was NELSON ROCKEFELLER, who had been elected governor of New York that year and emerged as the leader of the eastern, or liberal, wing of the party. However, Nixon, having assiduously campaigned for Republican candidates across the country since the early 1950s, was the solid favorite of state and local party leaders. Moreover, Nixon was a logical compromise for a divided party. He began his career identified with the conservative wing of the party but had served for eight years as vice president in an administration identified with the eastern wing. After testing the waters, Rockefeller announced in December 1959 that he would not seek the nomination.

To win the general election, Nixon needed the full support of Rockefeller and the party's liberal wing. In July 1960, Rockefeller and Nixon met at the former's Fifth Avenue apartment in New York City. The governor used his influence to secure changes in the Republican platform that stressed stronger efforts in the areas of military preparedness and economic growth. Although the "Treaty of Fifth Avenue" upset many conservative Republicans

and was denounced by Senator BARRY GOLDWATER (R-Ariz.) as a "Munich," Nixon won the nomination almost unanimously on July 27. He chose HENRY CABOT LODGE as his running mate. As ambassador to the United Nations, Lodge had gained national popularity through televised debates in the UN.

Since Nixon was the candidate of the minority party, he had to win the support of considerable numbers of voters who did not identify themselves as Republicans. To gain the support of independents and Democrats, he tried to establish clear differences between himself and his opponent, Senator JOHN F. KENNEDY (D-Mass.). Nixon stressed his belief in the free enterprise system and criticized Kennedy for allegedly promising to solve all problems through federal intervention. Since, however, Nixon wanted to present himself as a middle-of-the-road figure, he did not take a clear-cut position against popular social welfare programs. In fact, he and Kennedy had few differences on domestic issues.

In the field of foreign policy, Nixon criticized Kennedy for stating that Quemoy and Matsu were strategically worthless and indefensible, but this issue aroused little interest. Meanwhile, Kennedy took the offensive on the issue of policy toward Cuba. Although the Democratic candidate knew that the Eisenhower administration was training Cuban exiles for an invasion of Cuba, he denounced the president for not supporting the exiles and advocated an intervention similar to the one being planned. Nixon, who knew and strongly approved of the invasion plans but could not acknowledge them, denounced Kennedy for urging the violation of another country's sovereignty. Although Kennedy took a somewhat more belligerent position on the cold war than Nixon and urged a substantial increase in defense spending and, in particular, in spending on conventional forces, Nixon also wanted an increase in the defense budget and more conventional forces. With respect to foreign and defense policies, little separated the two candidates.

One of Nixon's advantages in the election was the continuing popularity of President Eisenhower and the aging hero's endorsement of Nixon, but the usefulness of this backing was somewhat vitiated at a presidential press conference on August 24. When asked to give an example of an important idea of

Nixon's that he had adopted, Eisenhower replied, "If you give me a week, I might think of one." Despite the subsequent explanation that Eisenhower merely wanted to end the press conference and indicate that he would answer the following week, the remark raised questions about the enthusiasm of Eisenhower's support. The president's electoral inactivity during September and October further eroded the significance of Eisenhower's endorsement.

Nixon was better known to the public than Kennedy and, unlike his opponent, could claim executive experience. Both of these advantages, however, were minimized by the four nationally televised debates between Nixon and Kennedy in September and October. Nixon agreed to the debates in part because of his success in the debate against Voorhis in 1946, the effectiveness of his 1952 Checkers speech, and the favorable reaction to his debate with Khrushchev in 1959. However, the mere presence of Kennedy on the same stage presented them as equals; it enormously diminished Nixon's advantage as the sitting vice president. Further, the debates exposed Kennedy to audiences of perhaps as many as 70 million people and materially cut into Nixon's advantage in name recognition. Furthermore, Kennedy's ability more or less to hold his own in the debates weakened the argument that he was too inexperienced to be president.

The first debate, held on September 26, particularly hurt Nixon. He had lost weight during a recent period of hospitalization. As a result, the candidate appeared gaunt, and his clothes seemed oversized. Moreover, Nixon wore a gray suit, white shirt, and blue tie. The gray suit showed up on black-and-white television as gray, the white shirt reflected light and showed up as gray, and the blue tie appeared gray. Nixon blended into the backdrop. Kennedy, whose aides were more savvy about television, wore a navy suit, which showed up black, a blue shirt, which appeared white, and a red tie, which appeared black. Kennedy appeared crisper and more defined. The networks offered both candidates professional makeup artists, but both refused. Kennedy, however, knew that a suntan looked good on television and had made sure that he was tanned before the debates. Just before the first debate, his aides made him up with Max Factor's Cream Puff.

Nixon's aides tried to cover his five o'clock shadow with Shavestick, which Nixon, who sweated profusely under television lights, promptly sweated off. One reporter described Nixon as looking "like a picture on a post office bulletin board." Significantly, a majority of those who watched the debate on television gave Kennedy the edge in the debate, while a majority of those who listened to the debate on radio believed that Nixon had won. The debate became a classic example for those who argued that the visual media projected image more prominently than substance. Unfortunately for Nixon, many more people watched the debate on television than listened on the radio. Although many people believed that Nixon won the final three debates, he did not enjoy a decisive advantage, and, in any event, those debates drew smaller audiences and made substantially less impact than the first one.

Kennedy won the election with an electoral vote margin of 303 to 219. His advantage in the popular vote, though, was only 113,000 votes out of 69 million, the smallest winning percentage in history to that time. Further, there was considerable evidence of fraudulent returns in Illinois and Texas, where Kennedy won by narrow margins. Reversals of the results in those states would have given the election to Nixon, but recounts would have been time-consuming and probably would not have changed the outcome. Kennedy's running mate, LYNDON B. JOHNSON, controlled the process in Texas to the point that no challenge was likely to succeed in that state. Thus, despite considerable pressure from some Republicans to demand a recount, Nixon refused to do so.

In mid-November 1960, President-elect Kennedy offered Nixon a temporary foreign assignment, but the vice president declined. Instead, he retired to private life and joined a law firm in Los Angeles. In March 1962, he published *Six Crises*, an account of six difficult episodes in his life. Persuaded by friends, Nixon entered the race for governor of California in 1962. He ran a spiritless race and lost the general election by a decisive margin to the incumbent, EDMUND "PAT" BROWN. The loss was a devastating blow to a politician who had been a national political figure for well over a decade. Nixon compounded matters at a press conference on the morning after the election. He charged that reporters had been biased against him throughout his career and ranted: "You won't have Nixon to kick around anymore because, gentlemen, this is my last press conference." Many believed that the intemperate display had ended Nixon's political career. The following year, Nixon joined the New York City law firm of Mudge, Stern, Baldwin & Todd, which became Nixon, Mudge, Rose, Guthrie, Anderson & Mitchell.

Before long, however, Nixon returned to the political wars. He campaigned dutifully for the GOP's presidential candidate, Senator Barry Goldwater (R-Ariz.), in 1964. After Goldwater lost in a landslide to Johnson and Republicans suffered disastrous reverses in Congress, Nixon continued to work hard for the party. He campaigned vigorously for many Republican candidates during the congressional elections of 1966, in which the Republicans gained 47 seats in the House and three in the Senate. This helped Nixon win the Republican presidential nomination in 1968, and he went on to defeat narrowly Vice President HUBERT HUMPHREY and George Wallace, the governor of Alabama, who ran on a third-party ticket and made an impressive showing, in the general election.

During his first term, Nixon gradually withdrew American ground forces from South Vietnam while resuming the bombing of North Vietnam and ordering an incursion into Cambodia. At the same time, Nixon charted a new course for the policy of containment by establishing détente with the Soviet Union and an opening to mainland China. Although his was not the first administration to recognize the Sino-Soviet split, his was the first to make it a focal point of foreign policy. In February 1972, he visited China. Practicing triangular relations, he effectively played the two communist superpowers off against each other. Moreover, allowing the Soviet Union and China to contain each other enabled him to end the draft, which undermined the antiwar movement. In one of his most significant achievements, Nixon negotiated a Strategic Arms Limitation Treaty with the Soviets, which, among other things, limited the deployment of antiballistic missiles and thereby halted a new round of the arms race.

With respect to domestic policy, he proposed a massive overhaul of the welfare system with his Family Assistance Plan. His administration banned tobacco advertising on television and made substantial gains in the protection of the environment. Nixon also supported health and safety protection for workers, built more units of public housing than all previous administrations combined, and undertook a massive expansion of the food stamp program. In an effort to control inflation, Nixon resorted first to Keynesian tactics and then to wage and price controls. One of Nixon's innovations was the New Federalism, whereby the federal government distributed several billion dollars of tax receipts each year directly to the states to be spent as they wished. Partly in an effort to appeal to southern Democrats, Nixon opposed court-ordered busing as a means to achieve desegregation.

Nixon won a landslide reelection victory over Senator George McGovern (D-S. Dak.) in 1972. In early 1973, Nixon reached an agreement to end American involvement in the Vietnam War. During his second term, however, suspicion mounted that he was covering up high-level complicity in a break-in at the Democratic National Headquarters in the Watergate complex by employees of his reelection committee in June 1972. The trial of the burglars and televised hearings before the Senate select committee established to investigate the matter uncovered Nixon's participation in the cover-up that began immediately after the unsuccessful break-in. After extensive hearings, the House Judiciary Committee voted articles of impeachment in July 1974. Nixon resigned in August 1974, after a court order forced him to release tape recordings of White House conversations that conclusively proved his involvement in the cover-up from its earliest stages. His successor, GERALD R. FORD, granted him a full pardon in September 1974.

After his resignation, Nixon worked hard to rehabilitate his reputation and to establish himself as a senior statesman. He enjoyed surprising success in that regard, but the cloud of Watergate always hung over him. Following a brief exile in California, he returned to the East Coast, where he lived first in New York and then in New Jersey. He traveled extensively (visiting China five times, where he was treated like a visiting head of state). In addition to publishing a two-volume memoir in 1978, Nixon offered advice to his successors as president and wrote extensively on foreign policy.

His books on foreign policy included *The Real War* (1980), *Leaders* (1982), *Real Peace*, (1983), *No More Vietnams* (1985), and *1999* (1988). Nixon died in Park Ridge, New Jersey, on April 22, 1994. Even at his death, Nixon remained a controversial figure, so much so that the *New York Times*, in an obituary that ran in its Sunday late edition of April 24, 1994, blatantly misrepresented what the notorious "pink sheet" from the 1950 senatorial election actually said.

—MSM

Norstad, Lauris
(1907–1988) *supreme commander, Allied forces, Europe*

The son of a Lutheran minister who had emigrated from Norway, Norstad was born in Minneapolis, Minnesota, on March 24, 1907. He graduated from the U.S. Military Academy at West Point in 1930 and was commissioned a second lieutenant in the cavalry. In 1931, he transferred to the army air corps. During the early 1930s, he served as commander of the 18th Pursuit Group at Schofield Barracks in Hawaii. He served with the 9th Bomb Group and graduated from the Air Corps Tactical School. When the Japanese attacked Pearl Harbor, he was the assistant chief of staff for intelligence of the air force. After the United States entered the war, General Harold H. "Hap" Arnold, commanding general of the army air forces, named Norstad to his advisory council. Assigned to the Twelfth Air Force as assistant chief of staff for operations, Norstad helped plan and direct the air campaign for the invasion of North Africa in 1942. His activities brought him to the attention of General DWIGHT D. EISENHOWER, the Allied commander. In early 1943, Norstad was promoted to brigadier general, and, in December of that year, he became director of operations of the Mediterranean Allied Air Forces. In that capacity, he helped plan the air campaign for the invasions of Sicily and Italy in 1943. His next assignment took him to Washington, D.C., in 1944 as chief of staff of the Twentieth Air Force. There, he took part in planning B-29 raids on Japan. Norstad became assistant chief of air staff for planning in 1945 and the following year was on the War Department's general staff.

In 1946, Eisenhower secured Norstad's appointment as director of the Plans and Operations Division of the War Department General Staff. He was involved in the negotiations that led to the unification of the armed forces under the Defense Department in 1947. In that context, he was instrumental in establishing the air force as an independent branch of the armed services. In October 1947, he was promoted to lieutenant general and made air force vice chief of staff for air operations in charge of planning for air defense. Norstad assumed command of the U.S. Air Force in Europe in 1950 and the following year became commander of Allied air forces in central Europe. Norstad was made a full general in 1952, the youngest American to date to achieve that rank. In 1953, he was named air deputy to the Supreme Allied Commander, Europe (NATO), where he helped formulate atomic strategy and modernize the military communications system.

Norstad became Supreme Commander of Allied Forces, Europe, in November 1956. Sensitive to the growing European belief that the alliance was too dependent on U.S. military power, he advocated the strengthening of NATO forces to respond to both conventional and nuclear warfare. He warned against British troop reductions in 1957 and the following year chided NATO foreign ministers for dilatoriness in meeting troop commitments. In April 1958, he asked for a buildup of active battalions in Europe over a five-year period.

While defending the maintenance of conventional troops in Europe as a first deterrent against Russian attack, Norstad believed that land-based ballistic missiles were a necessary component of defense and an important symbol of power. In November 1958, he announced a plan to increase the number of NATO battalions equipped with short-range missiles from 30 to 100 over a five-year period. Norstad opposed a total reliance on strategic nuclear arms and advocated arming NATO forces with tactical atomic weapons. He initially defended U.S. control of the arms but by 1959 proposed that the alliance build its own nuclear force.

The general believed that a militarily strong Germany was vital for the security of western Europe. In 1958, he rejected a Polish plan to make central Europe a demilitarized zone free of nuclear weapons. He believed that such weapons were "absolutely indispensable" to NATO's effectiveness. As a result of his efforts, the Western European Union Council granted West Germany permission to build surface-to-air and air-to-air missiles in 1959. During the Berlin crisis of 1958–59, West Germany was equipped with rockets capable of carrying atomic warheads. They were placed under Norstad's control.

In the 1960s, Norstad often came into conflict with the administration of President JOHN F. KENNEDY. Norstad, who worked assiduously to develop closer working ties between governments in the NATO alliance, envisioned himself as a servant of the international alliance, a position that did not always sit well with the Kennedy administration. Norstad's continued calls for a NATO nuclear force often ran counter to American policy. Moreover, he thought that Kennedy placed too much emphasis on conventional forces in a nuclear age and continued his advocacy of the importance of tactical nuclear weapons. Although Norstad was scheduled to relinquish his NATO command on November 1, 1962, the Cuban missile crisis led NATO to ask him to continue in his post. Norstad retired from NATO and from the U.S. Air Force on January 2, 1963. After leaving the air force, he became president of the international division of Owens-Corning Fiberglass. He later became chairman and chief executive officer of Owens-Corning. He also served as a member of the company's board of directors. President RICHARD M. NIXON named Norstad to the President's Commission on an All-Volunteer Force and to the General Advisory Committee on Arms Control and Disarmament. Norstad retired from Owens-Corning in 1972 and died in Tucson, Arizona, on September 12, 1988.

—MSM

O'Mahoney, Joseph C(hristopher)

(1884–1962) *U.S. senator*

One of 11 children of Irish immigrant parents, O'Mahoney was born on November 5, 1884, in Chelsea, Massachusetts. He attended Columbia University from 1905 to 1907 and worked as a newspaper reporter for the *Boulder* (Colorado) *Herald* from 1908 until 1916, when he became city editor for the *Cheyenne* (Wyoming) *State Leader.* Originally a Progressive Republican, O'Mahoney switched to the Democratic Party the year he joined the *State Leader,* which was owned by the Democratic governor of Wyoming. When the newspaper's owner, John B. Kendrick, became a U.S. senator in 1917, O'Mahoney went to Washington as his executive secretary. While in Washington, O'Mahoney earned an LL.B. from Georgetown University in 1920. He opened law offices in Washington and Cheyenne and served as city attorney of Cheyenne from 1929 to 1931. From 1924 to 1930, he served as vice chairman of the Democratic Party's state committee. During that time, he ran unsuccessfully for the U.S. Senate in 1924 and 1928. O'Mahoney had a substantial hand in writing the Democratic Party platform in 1932 and served as the vice chairman of the national campaign later that year. When Franklin D. Roosevelt won the election, O'Mahoney was rewarded with an appointment as first assistant postmaster general in 1933. Later that year, Kendrick died, and O'Mahoney was appointed to serve the remainder of his old patron's term. In Novem-ber 1934, O'Mahoney won an election to a full term. He was reelected in 1940 and 1946.

In the Senate, O'Mahoney served on several important committees, including Appropriations, Judiciary, and Interior. An implacable opponent of big business, O'Mahoney supported most of the New Deal. Along with other western progressives, however, there were limits on the extent to which he was willing to tolerate the expansion of the federal government's authority. He also balked at backing Roosevelt's court-packing plan. O'Mahoney opposed legislation abolishing the poll tax, largely because he believed that changes in suffrage regulations required a constitutional amendment. Whatever his other views, he consistently supported legislation that favored the interests of constituents in Wyoming, particularly with respect to oil, livestock, and the use of land and water.

O'Mahoney was best known for his support for the regulation of big business. In one of his first actions in the Senate, he introduced a bill that would have required all corporations to obtain a federal license. In 1938, he introduced legislation to create the Temporary National Economic Committee. During its existence from 1938 to 1941, O'Mahoney chaired the committee, which was composed of six members of Congress and six members of the executive branch. From his positions on key committees, he pushed for the dismantling of monopolies, measures encouraging small business, and the regulation of insurance companies. O'Mahoney also advocated a greater role for the federal government in the management of the economy. From 1949 to 1952, O'Mahoney chaired the Interior Committee.

O'Mahoney lost his bid for reelection in 1952 and returned to the private practice of law. When Wyoming's other Senate seat became vacant with the death of the Democratic incumbent, Lester C. Hunt, in 1954, O'Mahoney won election both to serve out the remainder of Hunt's term and to a full term.

In 1955, O'Mahoney emerged as one of the strongest opponents of the Dixon-Yates contract, which provided for a private company to build a plant to provide power to the Tennessee Valley Authority (TVA) to replace the power that the TVA sold to the Atomic Energy Commission. The decision infuriated advocates of public power and created a minor scandal when it came out that a consultant to the Bureau of the Budget had been simultaneously advising the Dixon-Yates company. When the city of Memphis decided to build its own municipal power plant, which freed up power from the TVA for use by the AEC, President DWIGHT D. EISENHOWER took the opportunity to cancel the Dixon-Yates contract. Later, O'Mahoney opposed the confirmation of LEWIS STRAUSS as secretary of commerce in 1959, largely because he objected to Strauss's support, as head of the AEC, in favor of private power in the Dixon-Yates matter.

In 1956, O'Mahoney chaired a subcommittee of the Judiciary Committee that reviewed the nomination of SIMON E. SOBELOFF, the solicitor general, to the Court of Appeals for the Fourth Circuit. Southerners bitterly opposed the nomination because of Sobeloff's support for desegregation and blocked the nomination when it was originally sent to the Senate in 1955. O'Mahoney conducted the hearings fairly and cut off unfounded attempts at character assassination. Ultimately, the nomination cleared the subcommittee and the Judiciary Committee as a whole; the Senate confirmed the nominee in July 1956.

O'Mahoney was a central figure in striking a deal in the Senate that amended the administration's civil rights bill in 1957 to provide for jury trials for those charged with criminal contempt for violating black voting rights. The majority leader, LYNDON B. JOHNSON (D-Tex.), arranged for western senators to vote to amend the civil rights measure in exchange for the support of southern Democrats for the Hell's Canyon Dam. The amendment substantially weakened the Civil Rights Act of 1957.

On other issues, O'Mahoney was a leading supporter of statehood for Alaska and Hawaii. He first offered bills providing for statehood for the two territories in 1952. Continuing his opposition to economic concentration, O'Mahoney sponsored a bill that would have required "concentrated industries" to give notification or offer public justification for price increases. He also offered legislation to ban automakers from operating finance firms.

After suffering a stroke in 1959, O'Mahoney decided not to run for reelection in 1960. He died in Bethesda, Maryland, on December 1, 1962.

—MSM

Oppenheimer, J. Robert
(1904–1967) *physicist, Atomic Energy Commission consultant*

The son of a wealthy German-born textile importer, J. Robert Oppenheimer was born in New York City on April 22, 1904. Raised in the luxury of his family's lavish apartment in Manhattan and summer home on Long Island, he graduated from the Ethical Culture School in Manhattan and from Harvard University, summa cum laude, in 1925. He went to Cambridge University for graduate study in experimental physics but found that he was no good at it. Drawn to theoretical physics, Oppenheimer left Cambridge for the University of Göttingen, where he received his doctorate in 1927. After a year as a National Research Council Fellow (1927–28), he began teaching concurrently at the California Institute of Technology and the University of California at Berkeley in 1929. His comprehensive command of theoretical physics won him a prominent place among American physicists, and he attracted a large, devoted group of students. During the early 1930s, Oppenheimer explored aspects of the newly discovered positron and developed a new theory of cosmic ray showers. Prior to the outbreak of World War II, he helped develop the theory of gravitational collapse, later used to explain quasars. His work demonstrated both brilliance and a certain carelessness. He often failed to follow up on his most profound insights.

Oppenheimer demonstrated little interest in politics before 1936. However, his exposure to the left-wing ideology shared by many intellectuals of the period and his awareness of the harsh treatment of Jews in Nazi Germany rapidly aroused strong political commitments. Perhaps above all, his engagement to Jean Tatlock, who joined the Communist Party, drew him into leftist circles, even as his father's death in 1937 made Oppenheimer a wealthy man. Although he probably never formally belonged to the Communist Party, he joined and contributed money to many left-wing and fellow-traveling organizations. In 1940, he married Katherine "Kitty" Puening, a former communist whose first husband died fighting for the Republican government during the Spanish civil war. According to his own account, Oppenheimer began to disengage himself from political activity in 1940 and apparently completed this withdrawal within two years. However, his left-wing involvement led some government officials to consider him a security risk when he joined the Manhattan Project, formed to develop the atomic bomb. These doubts continued, even as he undertook the direction of the Manhattan Project's facility at Los Alamos, New Mexico, in 1943. Oppenheimer recruited an impressive group of scientists to Los Alamos. In addition, his broad knowledge of physics and his charismatic personality enabled him to mediate between the military bureaucracy and the individualistic scientists, to ease clashes between people with enormous egos working under incredible pressure, and to help solve both theoretical and practical problems.

For all his achievements as a scientist and administrator, his past left-wing affiliations and his personal life raised continuing questions about whether Oppenheimer was a security risk. He added to those questions when he spent an evening at the home of his former fiancée, Jean Tatlock, in June 1943. Counterintelligence officers had followed him to Tatlock's home, and their superiors recommended that he be dismissed. General Leslie A. Groves, who was in charge of the entire Manhattan Project, overruled their recommendation on the ground that Oppenheimer was "absolutely essential to the Project." Tatlock committed suicide in January 1944.

In August 1943, Oppenheimer reported to security officers that a friend of his had approached scientists on the project about passing information to the Soviets. The incident, the details of which remain somewhat murky, involved Haakon Chevalier, a member of the French Department at Berkeley and a close friend of Oppenheimer. In late 1942, George Eltenton, a British engineer with communist sympathies, approached Chevalier and asked him to tell Oppenheimer that "he had means . . . of getting technical information to Soviet scientists." Chevalier passed Eltenton's message to Oppenheimer sometime in the winter of 1942–43. When Oppenheimer told security officials about the incident in 1943 (after learning that one of his former students, a leftist, had been dismissed from the Manhattan Project), Oppenheimer refused to divulge Chevalier's name until specifically ordered to do so by Groves. The intelligence report on the matter concluded that Oppenheimer posed no real threat to security. According to the report, the scientist was "deeply concerned with gaining a worldwide reputation" and, toward that end, wanted very much to keep his job. In short, his ambition would guarantee his loyalty. Still, Oppenheimer's failure to report the incident immediately and his conflicting accounts of it concerned intelligence officials, who monitored his activities closely throughout the war.

The first atomic device was detonated on July 16, 1945, at Alamogordo, New Mexico. The atomic bombs dropped on Hiroshima and Nagasaki in August 1945 and the subsequent Japanese surrender won Oppenheimer international acclaim as "the father of the atomic bomb." During the war, Oppenheimer assumed that the bomb would be used. Indeed, he advised against a technical demonstration and argued for use of the weapon against Japan. Soon after the use of the weapon, however, he began to question the scientists' social responsibility for its development. Despite his reservations, he played a leading role in molding atomic policy after the war. He was the main author of the Acheson-Lilienthal report, which called for international control of nuclear energy, and of the Baruch Plan for UN supervision of atomic power. The Soviet

Union rejected both of these proposals in 1946. Oppenheimer was named chairman of the General Advisory Committee (GAC) of the Atomic Energy Commission (AEC) in 1946. The following year, he became director of Princeton University's Institute for Advanced Study.

During the Truman administration, Oppenheimer became embroiled in the controversy over the development of the hydrogen (fusion) bomb. The possibility of creating such a device had been explored during the war, but the project had been halted by seemingly insuperable technical obstacles. EDWARD TELLER and others working on the fusion weapon nevertheless advocated continuing the project. When the Soviet Union exploded its first atomic device in August 1949, Teller and Ernest O. Lawrence lobbied aggressively to develop a hydrogen bomb. Oppenheimer and the majority of GAC members recommended only further theoretical study of the hydrogen bomb. They questioned the weapon's military usefulness and the morality of escalating the nuclear arms race. Oppenheimer himself thought it better to equip conventional forces in Europe with tactical nuclear weapons. The Joint Chiefs of Staff disagreed, and in 1950 President Truman authorized a crash program to develop the hydrogen bomb. During the Korean War, Oppenheimer participated in Project Vista, which proposed the development of small tactical nuclear weapons for conventional ground warfare as alternatives to the massive strategic bombing favored by the air force.

If Oppenheimer had enemies on the Right, he also alienated former friends on the Left when he named a former student as having once been a communist in testimony before the House Un-American Activities Committee. Perhaps, as Kai Bird and Martin Sherwin argued in their comprehensive biography of Oppenheimer, he was truly afraid of any association with his onetime radical friends and colleagues because "their company represented a link to his political past and therefore a threat to his political future."

In 1952, Truman named Oppenheimer chairman of a special State Department Advisory Committee on Disarmament. The committee's report, published in July 1953, urged the administration to speak more openly about the realities of nuclear warfare. It recommended a larger role in defense policymaking for the western European nations and called for the accelerated development of continental air defense. Oppenheimer also reiterated his warning against total reliance on strategic nuclear weapons and again urged the development of tactical ones. The Eisenhower administration, however, rejected Oppenheimer's proposals in favor of the New Look in military policy, which reduced overall military spending and focused defense policy on the delivery of nuclear weapons to strategic targets by air.

When LEWIS STRAUSS, who considered Oppenheimer a security risk, became chair of the AEC in 1953, he quickly moved to revoke the scientist's security clearance. In November 1953, William L. Borden, former executive director of the Joint Committee on Atomic Energy, sent FBI Director J. EDGAR HOOVER a letter in which he accused Oppenheimer of disloyalty. The letter outlined Oppenheimer's earlier ties to the Left, charged that he had brought communists to work on the Manhattan Project, and maintained that he had retarded the development of the hydrogen bomb. Borden stated that "more probably than not he has since been functioning as an espionage agent."

As a result of Borden's letter, President DWIGHT D. EISENHOWER ordered Oppenheimer's security clearance suspended pending a review. In December 1953, Strauss presented a list of charges. Strauss offered Oppenheimer the option of either resigning as a consultant with the AEC or requesting a hearing. Oppenheimer demanded a hearing. As was the case with many such hearings during that period, it fell far short of due process. Strauss had the FBI tap Oppenheimer's phones and those of his lawyer. Moreover, Strauss denied security clearance to Lloyd K. Garrison, Oppenheimer's principal lawyer, thus denying him access to classified materials used against Oppenheimer.

Oppenheimer's hearing before a special three-member board began on April 12, 1954. His eligibility for reinstatement was to be determined in accordance with the AEC's personnel security clearance criteria. Concrete actions, such as sabotage or espionage, were considered grounds for denial of clearance, as were political attitudes and associations. The board was also bound by Eisenhower's

Executive Order 10450 (1953), which required that employment be "clearly consistent with the interests of national security." In its review, the board considered the FBI's file on Oppenheimer, although the scientist and his lawyers lacked the clearance necessary for access to the material.

Numerous scientists, including HANS BETHE, LINUS PAULING, and ALBERT EINSTEIN expressed shock at the charges against Oppenheimer and affirmed their confidence in him. At the hearing, most of the witnesses testified in favor of Oppenheimer; however, several, most notably Teller, spoke against reinstating him. The only leading scientist to testify against reinstatement, Teller acknowledged Oppenheimer's loyalty but testified to doubts about his judgment, particularly with respect to his opposition to the development of the H-bomb.

Oppenheimer denied that he had opposed the development of the bomb after Truman had ordered it and asserted that he had worked for the project's success. He acknowledged his past involvement with left-wing groups but stated that he had "never accepted Communist dogma or theory" and that he had become completely disillusioned with the communist movement. He dismissed Chevalier's approach to him as inconsequential. When, however, lawyers for the AEC confronted him with the more damning description of the encounter he had given during the war, Oppenheimer acknowledged that his original story was a "lie," a "cock-and-bull story" for which he had no explanation other than he had behaved like an "idiot." Referring to the charge that he had hired communists to work on the Manhattan Project, Oppenheimer said that "past associations did not necessarily disqualify a man from employment, if we had confidence in his integrity and dependability."

On May 27, the security board unanimously declared Oppenheimer a "loyal citizen" who "seems to have had a high degree of discretion reflecting an unusual ability to keep to himself vital secrets." It is also found that, despite moral, political, strategic, and technical opposition to the hydrogen bomb, Oppenheimer had done nothing to frustrate its production after Truman's decision in 1950. However, two of the three board members, Gordon Gray, former secretary of the army, and Thomas Morgan of the Sperry Rand Corporation, voted

that Oppenheimer's clearance should remain suspended on the ground that his "continuing conduct and associations . . . reflected a serious disregard for the requirements of the security system." Ward V. Evans, a chemist, dissented.

Oppenheimer filed an appeal with the AEC in June, but on June 29 the commission announced its four-to-one decision against reinstatement. The majority, including Strauss, said that its decision was based on "proof of fundamental defects in his character" and the finding that "his association with persons known to him to be Communists has extended far beyond the tolerable limits of prudence and self-restraint." They cited examples of what they termed "falsehoods, evasions and misrepresentations" in his dealings with the FBI, the Counter Intelligence Corps, and the AEC, especially in his account of the Eltenton incident.

Although his defenders saw Oppenheimer as a victim of the virulent anticommunism of the postwar period, they also considered him the target of personal vendettas carried on by Strauss and a group of scientists around Teller. They believed that Oppenheimer, already vulnerable because of his unpopular associations and views, had magnified these tensions with what JOSEPH ALSOP and STEWART ALSOP called his "regrettable tendency to be contemptuous of government flatfeet" and his unwillingness "willingly [to] suffer people whom he considered wrong." Without doubt, Oppenheimer exacerbated differences over policy by treating opponents rudely and contemptuously.

After the AEC's decision, Oppenheimer remained at Princeton, and, in October 1954, he was unanimously reelected director of the Institute for Advanced Study by the university's trustees. Nevertheless, according to Garrison, "the blow [of the AEC's ruling] was a lasting one which he took with him to his grave." The great physicist Isidor I. Rabi agreed that the hearing "achieved what [Oppenheimer's] opponents wanted to achieve; it destroyed him." In 1957, when the launching of the Soviet satellite *Sputnik* generated fresh interest in government-sponsored scientific projects, the possibility was raised of a new hearing that might clear Oppenheimer. However, Strauss announced in January 1958 that the case would not be reopened unless Oppenheimer could present "substantial new evidence." When JOHN McCONE succeeded Strauss as chairman of the AEC later that year, he ordered a legal review of the case. Lawyers for the AEC found "a messy record" and "a primitive abuse of the judicial system," but took no further action.

The Federation of American Scientists petitioned the AEC to reopen the case after JOHN F. KENNEDY became president. The commission again declined to do so. Kennedy did, however, invite Oppenheimer to a White House dinner for Nobel Prize winners at which GLENN SEABORG, the AEC's new chairman, offered him a new hearing. Oppenheimer declined. In 1962, Kennedy decided to vindicate Oppenheimer by presenting him with the AEC's Enrico Fermi Award but postponed the controversial award until after the 1962 elections. He was assassinated before Oppenheimer received the honor. President LYNDON B. JOHNSON made the award in December 1963. Oppenheimer stepped down from his position at the Institute for Advanced Study in 1966 and died of throat cancer in Princeton, New Jersey, on February 18, 1967.

—MSM

Pace, Frank, Jr.

(1912–1988) *chief executive officer, General Dynamics Corporation*

Born in Little Rock, Arkansas, on July 5, 1912, Pace was educated at the Hill School in Pottstown, Pennsylvania, and earned a bachelors degree from Princeton in 1933. After receiving his law degree from Harvard in 1936, he joined the Arkansas district attorney's office. He served as the assistant district attorney for the 12th judicial district until 1938, when he became general counsel to the Arkansas Revenue Department, a post he held until 1940. Pace worked as his father's legal partner in 1941 but left the following year to join the Air Transport Command, where he served as a personnel and administrative officer and rose to the rank of major.

In 1946, Pace went to work for the federal government as the attorney general's special assistant on tax matters; after only a few months he left to become executive assistant to the postmaster general. Pace remained there from 1946 until 1948, when President HARRY S. TRUMAN appointed him assistant director of the Bureau of the Budget. In January 1949, he succeeded James Webb as budget director. The following year, Truman named Pace to succeed Gordon Gray as secretary of the army. At the end of the Truman administration, Pace resigned his post and returned to private business. Nevertheless, he remained active in the Democratic Party and in 1954 turned down the post of chairman of the Democratic National Committee.

In May 1953, Pace was called before the Senate Armed Services Committee's Preparedness Subcommittee, which was investigating ammunition shortages in Korea. He testified that until January 1953 fighting in Korea was done solely with World War II surplus, leaving reserves severely depleted. The subcommittee's final report determined that these shortages had resulted in the "needless loss of American lives," but that "revised procedures had replenished stocks."

In 1953, Pace became executive vice president and a director of the General Dynamics Corporation (GD). He became vice chairman and senior vice president of operations and fiscal affairs in 1955. Two years later, he moved up to chief executive officer. During his tenure, GD became one of the nation's prime defense contractors. In the period from 1950 to 1956, the company held contracts worth $4.07 billion. From 1956 to 1957, it was second only to North American Aviation, with defense contracts totaling $1.33 billion. GD's electric boat division built the first atomic-powered submarine, the *Nautilus*, as well as two subsequent models. The company also received contracts to build the Atlas intercontinental ballistic missile and an experimental atomic-powered aircraft. Pace joined a group of American businessmen who, at a meeting with Soviet leader Nikita Khrushchev in 1959, expressed their hopes for disarmament. The industrialists said that, under capitalism, "production for consumption" would be more profitable than production for the military.

During the Eisenhower administration, Pace served on several government committees, including the President's Commission on National Goals, formed in 1959 to set general domestic and foreign policy goals for the 1960s. The panel's report, issued in November 1960, called for "extraordinary personal responsibility, sustained effort and sacrifice" to achieve "high and difficult goals" in the period of "grave danger" ahead. It assumed that the cold war would continue and that bigger military outlays would be necessary. It stressed the need to increase domestic economic growth and aid the economic development of underdeveloped nations, which would be the focus of East-West struggle during the 1960s. In addition to an expanding economy, the major domestic goals included improved secondary and college-level education open to all, aid to the arts, and reform of the federal bureaucracy. The report declared that "vestiges of religious prejudice, handicaps to women, and, most important, discrimination on the basis of race must be recognized as morally wrong, [and] economically wasteful." The panel emphasized the importance of the right to vote and urged that, if necessary, the federal government take steps to insure every citizen the right to vote.

Pace resigned as chief executive officer of GD in 1962. He founded the International Executive Service Corporation, a nonprofit service organization, in 1964 and headed the organization until 1982. President LYNDON B. JOHNSON appointed Pace to be the first chairman of the Public Broadcasting Corporation in 1968. Pace founded the National Executive Service Corps, which helped other nonprofit organizations fill management positions, in 1977 and served as its chair until his death in Greenwich, Connecticut, on January 8, 1988.

—MSM

Packard, Vance (Oakley)
(1914–1996) *author and social critic*

Born in Granville Summit, Pennsylvania, on May 22, 1914, Vance Packard moved with his family in 1924 to State College, Pennsylvania, where his father worked for Pennsylvania State College (later Pennsylvania State University), first as a farmhand, then as foreman, and eventually as superintendent of the college farm. An English major, Packard received his B.A. from Pennsylvania State College in 1936. He received an M.A. from Columbia University's Graduate School of Journalism the following year. After working as a reporter for the *Boston Daily Record*, he worked as a reporter and editor for the Associated Press from 1938 until 1942, when he became a writer and editor for *American Magazine*. In the postwar era, *American Magazine*, a mass-circulation monthly, offered its readers an anticommunist foreign policy, centrist domestic politics, and a celebration of American consumer culture. After that magazine folded in 1956, Packard wrote briefly for *Collier's*, until it, too, went out of business at the end of 1956. With the failure of *Collier's*, Packard devoted himself to writing books. In 1950, he had published *Animal I.Q.*, which dealt with animal intelligence and instinct. Research for that project led him to investigate work being done by the Institute for Motivational Research in New York, a private corporation used by advertising agencies.

Packard published *The Hidden Persuaders* in 1957. The book discussed the manipulative methods used by the advertising industry to sell products. Many of the newer techniques were developed through "motivational research," which used basic psychological testing and in-depth interviewing of sample consumers to determine human desires and motivations that could be met with advertising campaigns. Packard showed how Madison Avenue sought to stimulate "impulse buying" by indirectly appealing to deep human fears, urges, and desires. "Many of us," he warned, "are being influenced and manipulated, far more than we realize, in the patterns of our everyday lives." Packard reserved his harshest criticism for "subliminal projection," a new technique in which words or images were flashed on television or a movie screen too rapidly to be recognized by the conscious mind. The unconscious picked up the advertising message, however, and directed the consumer to satisfy the subliminal suggestion. Packard maintained that before the 1950s advertising had been largely a matter of proclaiming the virtues of one product over another through appeals to the conscious mind; he advocated a return to this method and urged the industry to adopt a code of ethics. At a time when the nation was concerned with propaganda, brainwashing, and the effects of television, *The Hidden Persuaders* remained on the *New York Times* Best Seller List for a year. Representatives of the advertising industry attacked the book and denied that subliminal projection had ever been used in the marketplace.

Packard followed up with two more spectacular best sellers, *The Status Seekers* (1959) and *The Waste Makers* (1960), although neither sold as well as *The Hidden Persuaders*. In *The Status Seekers*, Packard argued that the "gloss of prosperity" led many to maintain that class lines were being eliminated in the United States. To the contrary, he argued that, while class lines were being redefined, they were becoming increasingly rigid, as Americans tried desperately "to find new ways to draw lines that will separate the elect from the non-elect." Facing impersonal, routine work with large corporations and deriving less satisfaction and prestige from their jobs, Americans turned to material consumption for comfort and status. In this, they received encouragement from advertisers and market researchers.

The Waste Makers maintained that once an economy had achieved prosperity and the wide diffusion of consumer goods, business tended to try to maintain that prosperity by convincing consumers to buy replacements or more advanced models. Manufacturers and advertisers therefore sought to develop a "throwaway spirit" in consumers. They achieved this in part through planned obsolescence. A product became outmoded through the introduction of a newer product that performed the same function better, when it broke or wore out, or when a still sound product became less desirable because of a change in styling or fashion. Although he saw some potential for abuse, Packard granted that planned "obsolescence of function" led to better products. He focused more on "obsolescence of quality," criticizing shoddy production of products designed to wear out in a specified period of time, and "obsolescence of desirability," rebuking advertisers for encouraging consumers to discard perfectly serviceable products. The result, he maintained, was massive waste of natural and human resources.

The three books written at the end of the 1950s established Packard's reputation. Over the next four decades, he continued to publish books at a frenetic pace. *The Pyramid Climbers* (1962) explored the nature of competition for advancement in modern corporations and its impact on managers and executives. Packard examined corporate demands for structured lives and conformity and concluded that those who gained success in the corporate structure were loyal, adaptable, and deferential. Their main attribute was the ability not to antagonize anyone. *The Naked Society* (1964) warned that new technologies, such as computerized filing and surveillance techniques, combined with new attitudes to allow increasing invasion of the privacy of the average American. *The Sexual Wilderness* (1968) chronicled the sexual confusion that accompanied the decline of traditional values. *A Nation of Strangers* (1972) argued that corporate transfers had created a nation of rootless and lonely people. *The People Shapers* (1977) analyzed the use of psychological and biological testing to manipulate human behavior. *Our Endangered Children* (1983) posited that the preoccupation with money, status, sex, and power ignored the needs of children. *Ultra Rich: How Much Is Too Much* (1989) explored the lives of 30 Americans whose average net worth was $330 million. Professional sociologists criticized his work for its lack of statistical rigor, his reliance on anecdotes, and its derivative nature. Nevertheless, he brought significant issues and the work of others to a large public. His earlier works in particular added phrases such as "hidden persuaders" and "status seekers" to the language. He died at his summer home on Martha's Vineyard, Massachusetts, on December 12, 1996.

—MSM

Parks, Rosa (McCauley)
(1913–2005) *civil rights activist*

Born in Tuskegee, Alabama, on February 4, 1913, Rosa McCauley went to a private school run by women from the North and attended Alabama State College in Montgomery. In 1932, she married Raymond Parks, a barber who was active in civil rights causes. To help support the household, she took in sewing, worked as a housekeeper and at a hospital, and was briefly a life insurance agent. During World War II, she worked at an army air force base. Rosa Parks was also active in black community affairs and worked for her church, for the Montgomery Voters League, and for the NAACP.

From 1943 to 1957, she served as secretary of the local branch of the NAACP.

On December 1, 1955, Parks boarded a city bus in downtown Montgomery to return home from her job as a seamstress at the Montgomery Fair department store. Shortly after she sat down, the driver ordered Parks to give up her seat on the racially segregated bus to a white man. Montgomery's segregation ordinance required that the first 10 rows of buses be reserved for whites only and the rear 10 for blacks. In the middle rows, white riders sat from front to back and black riders sat from back to front, but black and white riders could not share a row. If the bus became crowded, black passengers sitting farthest to the front were required to surrender their seats to whites. When the driver ordered her to surrender her seat, Parks quietly refused to move, and the driver called the police, who arrested and jailed her. Her dignified bearing assured that the police charged her with violating the segregation ordinance, rather than disorderly conduct. E. D. Nixon, the president of the Montgomery branch of the NAACP, accompanied by Clifford and Virginia Durr, two white civil rights activists, secured Parks's release on bail, and her trial was set for the following Monday, December 5. Although her husband opposed the idea, she became a test case to challenge the segregation ordinance.

By the time of this incident, Montgomery's bus system had become a particularly sore spot within the black community. The bus drivers, all of whom were white, often behaved abusively toward black passengers. African Americans had to pay their fare at the front door but then get off the bus and board through the rear door. Drivers would sometimes drive off after a black passenger had paid but before he had reached the rear entry. In the year before Parks's arrest, three other black women had refused to give up their seats and had been arrested, and there had been talk of a protest. Following one of these incidents, the black community did organize a citizens' committee to negotiate with the bus company management for improved treatment, but no results came from their meeting.

The arrest of Rosa Parks, a gentle and dignified woman who was highly respected in the black community, proved to be a catalyst for protest.

The night Parks was arrested, the Women's Political Council, a group of black women activists, drafted a letter calling for a boycott of the city's buses. In addition to Nixon, local Baptist ministers, including RALPH ABERNATHY and MARTIN LUTHER KING, JR., became involved. The boycott began on December 5, the day of Parks's trial, in which she was found guilty of violating the segregation law and fined $10. That day, virtually no African Americans rode the buses. A group of black leaders met that afternoon to discuss strategy and make plans for the mass meeting scheduled for that evening. They formed an organization to coordinate the protest, the Montgomery Improvement Association (MIA), and chose Martin Luther King, Jr., as its leader. The boycott continued for 381 days and resulted in a Supreme Court decision striking down Montgomery's segregation ordinance. The Montgomery boycott catapulted King to national prominence and inaugurated an era of nonviolent protest against racial segregation and discrimination.

According to Parks, her refusal to give up her bus seat in December 1955 was wholly unprompted and unplanned. She had no idea, she later declared, that it would cause the reaction it did. The story that she refused to move because she was tired after a long day of work became part of the myth of the Montgomery bus boycott. In fact, she was an activist who had long believed segregation unjust and knew exactly what she was doing. She had previously defied Montgomery's segregation laws on buses and had attended an interracial workshop at the Highlander Folk School. Moreover, her comportment forced police to charge her with disobeying the segregation ordinance, thereby bringing it into court. In her autobiography, *Rosa Parks: My Story* (1992), she wrote: "People always say that I didn't give up my seat because I was tired, but that wasn't true. I was not tired physically, or no more tired than I usually was at the end of a working day. I was not old . . . No, the only tired I was, was tired of giving in."

During the boycott, Parks served on the program committee and the executive board of the Montgomery Improvement Association (MIA), the organization set up to organize the protest. She occasionally traveled to other parts of the country to help raise funds for the MIA. In January 1956, she was fired from her job at the Montgomery Fair and had to take in sewing at home. She also received many threatening and harassing phone calls, and her husband encountered pressure at work.

Represented by the NAACP, the MIA filed suit in federal court challenging the constitutionality of the segregation ordinance on February 1, 1956. On June 5, a three-judge panel voted in favor of the plaintiffs. The Supreme Court upheld that ruling on November 13.

In August 1957, Rosa and Raymond Parks along with her mother moved to Detroit, Michigan, where Rosa's brother lived. She worked as a dressmaker for several years and, beginning in 1965, as a receptionist and staff assistant in the office of Detroit representative John Conyers, Jr. (D-Mich.). Although she did not have a major role in the Civil Rights movement of the 1960s, Parks joined King's Southern Christian Leadership Conference, remained a member of the NAACP, and participated in several protests, including the March on Washington in 1963 and the march from Selma to Montgomery in 1964. For the part she played in touching off the Montgomery bus boycott, Parks has been called "the mother of the civil rights movement." In later years, she was frequently honored by civil rights organizations. The federal government added to her honors; she received the Presidential Medal of Freedom in 1996 and the Congressional Gold Medal in 1999. Parks died in Detroit on October 25, 2005.

—MSM

Parsons, J(ames) Graham

(1907–1991) *ambassador to Laos, deputy assistant secretary of state for Far Eastern affairs, assistant secretary of state for Far Eastern affairs*

Born in New York, New York, on October 28, 1907, Parsons graduated from the Groton School, received his B.A. from Yale in 1929, and did graduate work at New York University. He then embarked on a diplomatic career. Parsons was private secretary to the American ambassador to Japan from 1932 to 1936 and served as vice-consul in Havana, Ottawa, and Mukden (Manchuria) from 1936 to 1943. He then became the State Department's representative on the Permanent Joint Board of Defense of the United States and Canada. From 1945 to 1947, he was assistant chief of the division of British Commonwealth Affairs. After service as the assistant to the president's representative to the pope from 1947 to 1948 and at the New Delhi and Nepal consulates from 1948 to 1950, Parsons returned to the State Department as deputy director of the Office of European Regional Affairs from 1951 to 1953. He then served as deputy chief of mission and minister at the American embassy in Tokyo. Parsons became ambassador to Laos in 1956 and remained there until 1957, when he became deputy assistant secretary of state for Far Eastern affairs. He was promoted to assistant secretary of state for the Far East in 1959.

Shortly thereafter, the House Government Operations Committee charged that, during his tenure in Laos, Parsons had "abetted" bribery and inefficiency in the disbursement of American aid. The panel maintained that he had removed a government auditor who was investigating charges of bribery in the program. The State Department, however, defended Parsons, praising his "superb job" in overseeing the distribution of aid.

In 1960, Parsons became involved in a dispute within the administration over the U.S. policy toward Laos. That August, a Laotian air force captain, Kong Le, overthrew the American-backed government of Phoumi Nosavan and turned administrative power over to neutralist Prince Souvanna Phouma. Souvanna then attempted to form a coalition government composed of Phoumi's supporters, neutralists, and members of the communist Pathet Lao. Phoumi refused to accept Souvanna's offer of a position in the new government. Instead he decided to use his control of the Royal Laotian Army to regain control of the country through a military campaign.

Parsons supported a neutralist government, as did Ambassador WINTHROP BROWN. Both men believed it would be impossible to form a pro-Western government in Laos, because of the corruption of the Phoumi regime and the growing nationalist feelings among the Laotians. At the same time, Parsons distrusted Souvanna, because he regarded the prince as naïve about communism. Higher officials in the State Department, fearing that Souvanna would be another Fidel Castro, demanded his replacement. During August, Parsons worked in Washington to keep U.S. policy options open, while giving Brown a chance to persuade Souvanna to form a coalition government acceptable to the United States.

In the beginning of October, the United States cut off military aid to Laos. On October 12, Parsons led a mission to that country to explain the conditions under which the United States would support Souvanna. He demanded that the prince end discussions with the communists about entry into a coalition government, resume talks with Phoumi and agree to give him a major role in the cabinet, and move his government away from Vientiane to Luang Prabang, where pro-Western influences were strongest. Finally, Parsons urged the prince to restrain Kong Le, who had been distributing U.S. military aid to the communists. Souvanna refused.

Fearing that Souvanna would turn to the Soviet Union for military aid, Parsons and Brown worked for the resumption of assistance. They could not, however, get Souvanna to agree to acceptable terms. Souvanna, facing an insurgency led by Phoumi, turned to the USSR for help. After that, Parsons joined his superiors in working for Souvanna's ouster. In December, a series of coups and countercoups drove Souvanna into exile, and the country moved toward civil war. As the Eisenhower administration came to a close, policy makers in Washington considered the possibility of an American intervention in Laos.

With respect to neighboring Vietnam, Parsons advocated a policy of supporting the government of Ngo Dinh Diem but also of pressing him to reform his government. Parsons met with Diem in Saigon on October 18, 1960, to present that position. By the end of 1960, Parsons had become increasingly pessimistic about the prospects of South Vietnam under Diem.

Parsons was appointed ambassador to Sweden in February 1961. He resigned that post in 1967 to become senior foreign service inspector. In 1969, Parsons was appointed deputy chairman of the U.S. delegation to the Strategic Arms Limitation Talks. He retired in 1972 and died in Lyme, Connecticut, on October 20, 1991.

—MSM

Parsons, Talcott
(1902–1979) *sociologist*

The son of a Congregationalist minister, Parsons was born in Colorado Springs, Colorado, on December 13, 1902. He was raised in Colorado and attended public schools until his family moved to New York City in 1918. Parsons graduated from the Horace Mann School in 1920 and received his B.A. in biology from Amherst College in 1924. At Amherst, he chaired the college's chapter of the Student League for Industrial Democracy and, as he later wrote, was an enthusiast "for the Russian Revolution and for the rise of the British Labour Party." Although he began college with the intention of going to medical school, he was attracted to the social sciences. He did graduate work from 1924 to 1925 at the London School of Economics, where he studied under the anthropologist Bronislaw Malinowski. The following year, Parsons attended Heidelberg University and was introduced to the sociological writings of Max Weber, about whom little was known in the United States. After spending a year as an instructor of economics and sociology at Amherst from 1926 to 1927, he went to Harvard as an instructor in the economics department. Parsons received his doctorate from Heidelberg in 1927. Three years later, he published his translation of Weber's *The Protestant Ethic and the Spirit of Capitalism*, which argued that Protestantism, particularly Calvinism, played a significant role in the development of capitalism in Europe.

From 1927 to 1931, Parsons taught sociology at Harvard in the departments of economics and social ethics. When the university established a separate department of sociology in 1931, Parsons joined it. Parsons's first major work, *The Structure of Social Action*, was published in 1937. In it he posited a common theme of "voluntaristic" theory (the idea that humans functioned as conscious actors in social situations) in the writings of Alfred Marshall, Vilfredo Pareto, Emile Durkheim, and Max Weber. Parsons used this theme to construct a system situated between the individualism of classic liberal theory and the organicism of theories such as Marxism. He criticized orthodox economics for its emphasis on rational efficiency as a motivation for human behavior. That alone, he maintained, could not explain the phenomenon of social order. He argued that common values drew people into an organized social system, a process he dubbed "common value integration." Society grew out of the actions of individuals as they were constrained and motivated by a complex set of norms and values.

During the next 20 years, Parsons developed and refined his theory. He wrote several essays during the 1930s in which he argued that the noneconomic forces in social organization argued against governmental and economic policy derived from strict laissez-faire economics. Maintaining that mechanisms of the market could be controlled without leading to economic disaster, Parsons supported the regulatory and social welfare measures of the New Deal.

Among the motives other than rational economic self-interest he identified as contributing to social cohesion, Parsons included the service orientation of modern professions. He predicted that values of professionalism, such as expertise, universalism, and loyalty to professional organizations, would play an increasingly important role in shaping modern society. Parsons planned to demonstrate that with an empirical study of the American medical profession, but the political crisis in Europe drew his attention in the later 1930s.

As Europe moved toward war, Parsons wrote articles for both professional and public consumption on Nazism and Japanese militarism and became an active interventionist. During the war, he worked for the Foreign Economic Administration and Harvard's School for Overseas Administration, established to train military officers for administrative posts in occupied territories. Parsons also collaborated with members of Harvard's anthropology and psychology departments to study the ways in which social structure, culture, and personality combined to create the national character of the belligerent nations. In 1943, this group proposed a new interdisciplinary program in the social sciences. Soon after the war, this program became the Department of Social Relations, which Parsons headed. This collaboration had a significant impact on Parsons's work; he became more deeply interested in psychoanalysis, and Freud's work became an important element of his social theory.

Parsons's career in the years after World War II reflected major trends in American academic and political life. Based on the experience of the war years, the federal government supported various sorts of scholarship in the early cold war era. Parsons worked with the Social Science Research Council to gain funding for research in the social sciences. As the cold war evolved, Parsons supported the Truman administration's policy toward the Soviet Union but also expressed his support for the British Labour government and the social democracy of Sweden. Although strongly anticommunist, Parsons stood against some of the excesses of anticommunism in the late 1940s and early 1950s. When the state university system of California imposed a loyalty oath on faculty members, Parsons supported professors in the system who objected to the oath. He believed that the fear of communism had reached exaggerated proportions and, in "Social Strains in America" (Parsons's contribution to Daniel Bell's anthology, *The New American Right* [1955]), argued that the red scare could be "understood as a relatively acute symptom of the strains which accompany a major change in the situation and structure of American society." Among those strains, he identified the changing role of the United States in world affairs, the expanded role of government in American life, and the social insecurity of ethnics, who had "risen rapidly in the economic and social scale" but remained "sensitive about their full acceptance."

The years after World War II also saw Parsons emerge as a leader of his discipline. He served as president of the American Sociological Society in 1949. In 1951, he published *The Social System*. In it, Parsons attempted a comprehensive theory of social behavior, which he called a "structural-functional" theory of society. He envisioned society as a system tending toward equilibrium, in which various "control mechanisms" established roles and directed action to conform with accepted norms. The book presented what became known as Parsonian theory.

While Parsons insisted that empirical studies could proceed only after the system was conceptualized in its entirety, *The Social System* contained a case study of the Soviet Union. Writing about two years before Stalin's death, Parsons argued that Stalinism distinguished itself from Nazism by proving more adaptive to outside conditions. The process of adaptation, however, would ultimately mean that the USSR would have to give up any serious hope of realizing the communist society its founders had envisioned. As an industrial nation, it would find itself moving closer and closer to the kinds of values espoused in the United States. In sharp contrast to such theorists as HANNAH ARENDT, who saw the whole world as moving toward totalitarianism, Parsons maintained that the totalitarian nations, once industrialized, would become increasingly democratic or face collapse. The book's extreme formalism and almost total lack of reference to empirical data prompted considerable criticism, as did its clotted, nearly impenetrable prose, but the work nonetheless had a significant impact on both American and European sociology.

In 1955, Parsons published *Family, Socialization and Interaction Process.* This attempt to integrate psychoanalysis and social theory demonstrated his continuing effort to construct a comprehensive social theory. *Economy and Society: A Study in the Integration of Economic and Social Theory* (1956), cowritten with Neil Smelser, was an attempt to establish the beginnings of a synthesis of economics and sociology. Parsons thought that the artificial separation of these disciplines in the university reflected existing institutional arrangements rather than a lack of common interests and concerns. His belief that the various academic disciplines dealt with aspects of social life and could be integrated for a comprehensive analysis of the social world reflected his overriding goal, a comprehensive explanatory model of social behavior. In addition to the social system, Parsons posited three other systems: a personality system, a cultural system, and the behavioral-organic system (the physical environment in which society functioned). He argued that, in order to survive, each system had to meet one of four functional prerequisites: adaptation, goal attainment, integration, and latency. The functional prerequisite for the behavioral-organic system was adaptation to the physical environment. The functional prerequisite for the personality system was "goal attainment" (a means of mobilizing resources to achieve objectives). Integration (coordinating social roles and establishing normative restraints) was the functional prerequisite for the social system, and "latency," or "pattern maintenance" (a means of instilling basic values),

was the functional prerequisite for the cultural system. This "four-function paradigm" formed the basis for Parsons's subsequent work.

In *Structure and Process in Modern Societies* (1960), Parsons attempted to discover the defining principles of formal organizations, but once again he offered a case study. He returned to McCarthyism as an example of "a relatively acute symptom of the strains which accompany a major change in the situation and structure of American society." His analysis closely followed the one he offered in "Social Strains in America" and differed little from the explanations offered by social scientists such as SEYMOUR MARTIN LIPSET and DANIEL BELL, except that Parsons was more confident that right-wing movements posed no real threat to American society.

In the 1960s, Parsons became involved in the struggle for black civil rights. He took a leading role in protesting segregation at a hotel chosen for the convention of the American Sociological Society in 1961. His commitment also manifested itself in *The American Negro* (1965), a volume of essays he coedited.

Parsons's later contributions never departed from his central organizing principles and his concern with integrating the various academic disciplines. He published *Societies: Evolutionary and Comparative Perspectives* (1966), *Politics and the Social Structure* (1969), and *The System of Modern Societies* (1971), an attempt to answer his critics and offer historical grounding for his theoretical conception of societal evolution. Although he continued to write primarily on a theoretical level, he also contributed more substantive studies such as *The American University* (1973). Reflecting his prominence in American intellectual life, he served as president of the American Academy of Arts and Sciences from 1967 to 1971. After more than 40 years at Harvard, Parsons retired in 1973. He died in Munich, Germany, on May 8, 1979.

The emergence of the academic left in the 1960s challenged Parsons's ideas and his dominant place in sociology. As early as 1956, Lewis Coser, in *The Functions of Social Conflict*, charged that Parsons's focus on the phenomenon of order in social life downplayed the role of social conflict. C. WRIGHT MILLS, in *The Sociological Imagination* (1959), also attacked Parsons for his ponderous style and for what Mills regarded as his abandonment of a critical perspective on the problems of modern society. In the late 1960s and early 1970s, leftist graduate students in sociology regarded Parsons as the embodiment of the establishment and hidebound anticommunism. They found him too uncritical of American society and uninterested in or hostile to disruptive popular movements. More fundamentally, they argued that Parsons's approach failed to account for social change. While not entirely unfounded, these criticisms ignored Parsons's support for the Civil Rights movement and for the antiwar campaigns of EUGENE MCCARTHY in 1968 and GEORGE MCGOVERN in 1972. Feminists also criticized his work on family structure. Critics of all stripes found an easy target in Parsons's dense and sometimes undecipherable prose. The 1980s, however, saw a revival of interest in Parsons's work.

—MSM

Passman, Otto E(rnest)

(1900–1988) *U.S. congressman; chairman, Foreign Operations Subcommittee of the House Appropriations Committee*

Born on a farm near Franklinton, in Washington Parish, Louisiana, on June 27, 1900, Passman was the son of poor sharecroppers. After leaving school at 13, he worked at various jobs and attended night classes. He graduated from Baton Rouge High School and Soule Business College in Bogalousa, Louisiana. In 1929, Passman moved to Monroe, Louisiana, where he established a successful business manufacturing commercial refrigerators and distributing wholesale restaurant equipment. He joined the navy as a lieutenant in 1942 and served as a procurement officer. Discharged a lieutenant commander in 1944, he returned to his business. In 1946, he won election to Congress from Louisiana's largely rural fifth district and was subsequently reelected 14 times, usually without opposition.

During the Eisenhower years, Passman usually voted with southern Democrats. He opposed civil rights measures and advocated high price supports for farmers as well as curbs on labor unions. Assigned to the House Appropriations Committee in 1949, Passman developed an expertise in budgetary matters, and he soon emerged as the lower chamber's leading opponent of foreign aid. In 1955, Representative Clarence Cannon (D-Mo.), the conservative chairman of the Appropriations Committee, appointed Passman to head that panel's foreign operations subcommittee, which initiated congressional consideration of foreign aid appropriation bills. With Cannon's support, Passman led an annual and usually successful effort to cut the administration's requests for foreign assistance funds substantially. The subcommittee's recommendations were always quickly ratified by the full 50-member committee and, with this powerful backing, easily passed the House.

Immediately upon assuming the chairmanship, Passman slashed $627 million from the mutual security appropriations bill in 1955, most of which the Senate subsequently restored. The following year, the subcommittee approved a $4 billion ceiling on foreign aid, in spite of Passman's warning that "the best way to destroy friends [overseas] . . . is to start supporting them with gifts and favors." The appropriations bill, as enacted in July 1956, assigned $3.7 billion for operations abroad, some $1 billion less than the sum requested by the administration.

The Eisenhower administration could bring little effective pressure to bear on Passman to modify his stand. For one thing, his district contained no military bases or defense plants that the administration could threaten to remove or close. In 1957, Eisenhower invited Passman to a private conference at the White House with the president, Secretary of State JOHN FOSTER DULLES, and the joint chiefs of staff. Passman proved so recalcitrant, however, that the angry president afterward asked an aide to remind him "never to invite that fellow down here again." Later that year, Passman cut the administration's foreign aid request by 25 percent, despite a threat by the president to call a special session of Congress to force the House to vote the full amount.

Although the Senate usually restored some of the House-initiated foreign aid cuts, Passman was such an intransigent negotiator at House-Senate conferences that the final appropriations bill always fell far below the administration's original request. In 1958, Eisenhower prevailed on Speaker SAM RAYBURN (D-Tex.) for help in dealing with

Passman. Rayburn, who promised to "do his best," personally pleaded with Passman to add more than the $220 million he had offered as a compromise to Senate conferees. The adamant chairman replied: "If they get $220 million, they'll be damn lucky. They can have [the money] in a half hour, or they can get it in 10 days." The Senate finally yielded to Passman's terms.

During the Kennedy and Johnson years, Passman continued to be the most powerful foe of foreign assistance programs on Capitol Hill. When Cannon died in 1964, however, the new chair of the Appropriations Committee, GEORGE H. MAHON (D-Tex.), who did not share Passman's views on foreign aid, curtailed the subcommittee chairman's power both on his own panel and in the House as a whole. Facing accusations that he cheated on his congressional expense accounts and used his influence to persuade foreign governments to ship rice in ships owned by the St. John Maritime Company, Passman failed to win the Democratic primary election for his seat in 1976. After leaving Congress on January 3, 1977, he resided in Monroe, Louisiana. In 1979, Passman stood trial for taking $273,000 from Tongsun Park, a Korean rice trader, in exchange for using his influence on Park's behalf. Passman died in Monroe on August 13, 1988.

—MSM

Pastore, John O(rlando)

(1907–2000) *U.S. senator*

The son of an Italian immigrant tailor, John Pastore was born on March 17, 1907. His father's death in 1916 left the family in straitened circumstances. Pastore went to public schools and attended night classes offered by Northeastern University Law School at a Y.M.C.A. in Providence, Rhode Island, while working as a claims adjuster for Narragansett Electric Company. After graduating in 1931 and gaining admission to the bar the following year, he opened a private legal practice in Providence. His law practice attracted few clients, however, and Pastore decided to enter politics. In 1933, he asked the local political boss, Tommy Testa, to back him for the Democratic nomination for a seat in the General Assembly. With Testa's support, Pastore won the election in a strongly Republican district in 1934

and was reelected two years later. He served as assistant state attorney general from 1937 to 1938 and again from 1940 to 1944. After winning election as lieutenant governor in 1944, he succeeded to the governorship in 1945, when the governor, J. Howard McGrath, accepted an appointment as solicitor general in the Truman administration. Pastore was elected governor in 1946 and reelected in 1948.

In 1950, Pastore won election to a seat in the U.S. Senate vacated by McCrath, who had resigned to become Truman's attorney general. Pastore became the first U.S. senator of Italian descent. He won reelection in 1952, 1958, 1964, and 1970. During his first years in the Senate, Pastore established a liberal record on domestic affairs, supporting federal funds for public housing, hospitals, medical care, and medical research. He also favored raising corporate and personal income taxes in the higher brackets. In foreign policy, the senator supported HARRY S. TRUMAN's requests for foreign aid and opposed efforts to limit the number of troops the president might send to Europe. In 1952, Pastore actively campaigned against the McCarran immigration bill, which Congress passed over Truman's veto. The same year, he directed ADLAI STEVENSON's presidential campaign among Italian Americans.

Pastore continued to back federal housing, school construction, and public works bills throughout the Eisenhower administration. In 1954, he led the Senate opponents of a measure exempting independent natural gas producers from rate regulation by the Federal Power Commission. He supported Eisenhower's foreign aid requests and backed efforts to end the national origins quota system in immigration statutes.

Pastore supported the Civil Rights Act of 1957; however, he voted twice to eviscerate the measure in Congress. He voted to delete part III of the administration's proposal, which would have given the attorney general wide powers to seek injunctions in any type of civil rights case with or without the consent of the alleged victim. Pastore held that it would give the attorney general excessively broad and insufficiently defined powers and further argued that, by antagonizing southerners, it would jeopardize the entire bill. Pastore also voted for an amendment to the measure that guaranteed jury trials not only in criminal contempt cases arising from the voting rights provisions of the law but also in cases stemming from more than 40 other laws.

As a member of the Joint Committee on Atomic Energy, Pastore focused much of his attention on the questions of nuclear power development. In late 1954, he spearheaded Democratic efforts to delay the signing of the Dixon-Yates contract until the incoming 84th Congress, which Democrats controlled, had an opportunity to study it. The contract would have permitted a private utility to construct generating facilities near West Memphis, Arkansas, to supply the Atomic Energy Commission (AEC) with power. The Dixon-Yates Company would have replaced the Tennessee Valley Authority as the power producer for the agency. The administration approved the agreement but cancelled it in July 1955, after revelations of a possible conflict of interest in awarding the contract.

During the 1950s, Pastore supported efforts to stimulate private research and development of the peaceful uses of atomic energy. In 1954, he backed measures designed to limit the patent rights on inventions used in producing fissionable materials in order to encourage private initiative. Two years later, he urged the production of demonstration reactors to spread nuclear technology. Pastore stated in 1957 that he backed government research in the use of atomic energy for peaceful purposes, but "the minute it becomes competitive . . . [and] no longer research, the government ought to get out of the operation, because that would be socialism."

Pastore supported the administration's desire to share atomic energy information with friendly nations. In 1954, he offered an amendment to the atomic energy bill of that year giving the president the right to deal with groups of nations as well as with individual countries in sharing atomic energy for peaceful uses. The amendment failed. Four years later, Pastore chaired the Joint Atomic Energy Subcommittee on Agreements for Cooperation, which formulated a measure to permit free exchange of atomic information and materials between the United States and its allies. He guided the bill through Congress; the president signed it on July 2.

Pastore strongly supported the domestic programs of the Kennedy and Johnson administrations. In 1963, he provided important backing for the Kennedy administration's treaty with the Soviet Union banning atmospheric nuclear testing. He also played an important role in obtaining passage of the Civil Rights Act of 1964. Although generally liberal on economic issues, Pastore tended to take more conservative positions on social and cultural issues. Initially a strong supporter of the war in Vietnam, Pastore moved away from that position during the presidency of RICHARD M. NIXON. Pastore retired from the Senate at the beginning of 1977 and resided in Cranston, Rhode Island, and North Kingstown, Rhode Island, until his death in Cranston on July 15, 2000.

—MSM

Patman, (John) (William) Wright
(1893–1976) *U.S. congressman; chairman, Select Small Business Committee*

The son of a tenant cotton farmer, Patman was born in Patman's Switch, Texas, on August 6, 1893. After graduating from high school in 1912, he studied law on his own and raised cotton as a sharecropper so that he could complete his legal studies at Cumberland University in Tennessee. He received his LL.B. degree there in 1916, was admitted to the bar the same year, and served as assistant county attorney of Cass County, Texas, in 1916 and 1917. During World War I, Patman served stateside in the army from 1917 to 1919. After the war, Patman won election to the Texas house of representatives in 1920 and was reelected in 1922. Two years later, he moved to Texarkana, where he was elected district attorney, serving from 1924 to 1929. In 1928, Patman won a seat in the U.S. House of Representatives; he won election to the next 23 congresses.

Patman represented the poor northeastern corner of Texas and quickly gained a reputation as a controversial populist enemy of concentrated wealth. After the Great Depression began, he emerged as a harsh critic of the policies of President HERBERT HOOVER and Secretary of the Treasury Andrew Mellon. In 1932, he called for the impeachment of Mellon. Patman also supported legislation that would have mandated the immediate payment of bonuses promised to veterans of World War I but not scheduled for payment until 1940. He maintained that the measure would stimulate the economy by increasing consumer demand. The bill did not pass until 1936, when Congress overrode a veto by President Franklin D. Roosevelt to enact it. Patman blamed its failure to stem the depression on what he believed was the nullifying effect of a Federal Reserve Board decision to double reserve requirements for banks.

In 1936, Patman coauthored the Robinson-Patman Act, also known as the Anti-Chain Store Act. It sought to protect small retailers by prohibiting wholesalers from giving price breaks to large-volume dealers and by banning chain stores from cutting prices only in areas served by small competitors. Patman also unsuccessfully sought legislation that would have imposed punitive taxes on chain stores. After receiving an appointment to the House Committee on Banking and Currency in 1937, he used that position to wage war against holding companies and interlocking directorates.

During World War II, he helped small businesses win an enlarged share of defense contracts. The Murray-Patman Act established a Smaller War Plants Corporation to finance the conversion of small plants to production for the war effort. After the war, Patman played a key role in the enactment of the Employment Act of 1946, which created the Council of Economic Advisers and the Congressional Joint Economic Committee. The act also established as a national policy the objective of promoting "maximum employment, production and purchasing power."

The creation of the Small Business Administration (SBA) in 1953 was in large measure due to the efforts of Patman, who since 1940 had worked for the establishment of regional credit banks for small businesses. In 1953, Patman unsuccessfully attempted to amend the bill creating the SBA to increase the revolving fund from $250 million to $500 million and strike the limit of $100,000 in loans for any single firm. When the Select Small Business Committee was created in 1955, Patman became its chair. Two years later, he failed in an effort to boost the maximum loan for individual firms, by then set at $250,000, to $1 million.

In 1958, Patman introduced a bill to replace the SBA with a federal system of small business capital banks, to be located in each of the 12 Federal Reserve districts. Under pressure from the administration, the proposal was modified to create the Small Business Investment Division (SBID) within the SBA. As enacted into law, the SBID was authorized to lend money to state and federally chartered small business investment companies that provided credit to small businesses.

Patman believed that the concentrated power large commercial banks wielded through the Federal Reserve System threatened the welfare of the small businessmen, farmers, and individuals of little or modest means. He charged that the Federal Reserve's tight money policy and high interest rates benefited commercial banks but restricted economic growth and caused unemployment. Rejecting the contention that low interest rates would cause inflation, he asserted that the Federal Reserve could check inflation by increasing its member banks' reserve requirements. Beginning in the 1930s, Patman continually introduced legislation to restructure the Federal Reserve to end its independence of the federal government and thereby reduce the influence of the financial community upon it. These efforts had always failed, and they continued to fail during the 1950s.

Patman also charged that commercial banks dominated the Federal Reserve's Open Market Committee, which controlled the nation's money supply by buying and selling government securities. In 1955, he stated that the Open Market Committee "has the greatest financial power of any single group in all history" and introduced a resolution authorizing the Banking and Currency Committee, of which he was a member, to investigate it. The resolution failed to gain passage.

In addition to his attempts to regulate banking, Patman persistently tried to check the power of large corporations. He vainly opposed the sale of federal rubber plants in 1953, arguing that only "the big rubber companies" would have the resources to bid for them. In 1955, he failed in an effort to strengthen the penalties faced by corporations and their responsible executives for violations of the Sherman Antitrust Act. Patman favored fines up to 5 percent of a corporation's total assets and jail sentences from 30 days to one year. The following year, he sponsored a bill requiring corporations worth more than $1 million to notify the

Justice Department and the Federal Trade Commission about merger intentions and giving the government more power to prohibit mergers. The House passed a bill incorporating Patman's proposals, but the Senate did not act on it. In 1959, Patman vigorously opposed a measure prohibiting states from taxing certain types of income earned by interstate businesses. He contended that the bill would give "a great advantage to interstate chains" in their competition with small retailers. Despite his efforts, the bill was signed into law in September.

Although Patman generally favored liberal domestic legislation, he opposed measures against racial discrimination. In 1956, he signed the Southern Manifesto protesting the Supreme Court's decision in the school desegregation cases two years earlier. He also voted against the Civil Rights Acts of 1957 and 1960.

In 1961, Patman, through the Select Small Business Committee, began a probe of private tax-exempt foundations. The following year, the panel, in the first of a series of reports, charged that many of these foundations were means of tax evasion. In 1963, Patman became chairman of the Banking and Currency Committee. That same year, the committee issued a report charging that there was an extensive network of interlocking connections between banks. An expanded report in 1966 alleged connections between banks and between banks and other financial institutions. In 1970, he successfully opposed the plan of the Nixon administration to provide $200 million in loan guarantees to save the Penn Central Railroad.

Patman used his chairmanship of the Banking and Currency Committee as a forum to present his views on Federal Reserve reform and to interrogate banking and Federal Reserve officials. His years in the chair were marked by controversy. Patman maintained that he attracted criticism because he investigated and attacked powerful monied interests. Members of his committee, however, charged that he was arbitrary and dictatorial. In 1975, the House Democratic caucus ousted Patman as chair of the Banking and Currency Committee. He died of pneumonia at the Bethesda Naval Medical Center in Maryland on March 7, 1976.

—MSM

Patterson, John (Malcolm)

(1921–) *attorney general of Alabama, governor of Alabama*

Patterson was born in Goldville, Alabama, on September 27, 1921. He joined the army in 1939 and served during World War II in Sicily, Italy, southern France, and Germany. After his discharge from the army as a major at the end of World War II, Patterson studied law at the University of Alabama and received his LL.B. in 1949. He then commenced the practice of law with his father, Albert Patterson, in Phenix City, Alabama. John Patterson's legal career was interrupted when he was recalled into the army during the Korean War. After serving from 1951 to 1953, he returned to his law practice. Albert Patterson led the opposition to the racketeers who controlled Phenix, and in 1954 he ran for state attorney general with a pledge to rid the city of gangsters. The elder Patterson won the election but was assassinated before he could take office. John Patterson ran in a special election to take his father's place and was elected attorney general in 1955.

During Patterson's four-year term, he devoted considerable effort to combating organized crime. He was also a strenuous opponent of integration and achieved prominence for his efforts to stop the operations of the NAACP in Alabama. In 1956, he brought suit against the NAACP for failing to register under state law as a foreign corporation and for supporting the Montgomery bus boycott, which he deemed illegal. As a result, a state circuit judge issued a restraining order prohibiting the group from operating in the state. At the end of the decade, litigation was still being carried on over the issue, and the NAACP was unable to conduct business in Alabama until 1964.

Patterson ran for governor of Alabama in 1958. During the campaign, he solicited the backing of individuals associated with the Ku Klux Klan, and several officers of the Klan campaigned for him. After finishing first among candidates in the Democratic primary in May, he defeated George C. Wallace in a runoff the following month by 315,000 votes to 250,000 and went on easily to defeat his Republican opponent in November.

In his inaugural address, Patterson reiterated his adamant opposition to integration. He

warned that if pressure for desegregation continued, Alabama's schools might be closed and "not be
reopened in your lifetime or mine." In September
1959, during one of his weekly radio addresses to
the state, Patterson pledged to "scrap the whole
public school system of this state before I would
submit to any integration of our schools." The following month, Patterson urged state officials to
refuse cooperation with the Federal Civil Rights
Commission, which was investigating black voter
registration complaints. In December, he signed
legislation permitting voter registration boards to
limit registration activities to predominantly white
precincts.

Despite his opposition to integration, Patter-
son opposed a break with the national Democratic
Party. In June 1959, Patterson became one of the
first public figures to endorse Senator JOHN F. KEN-
NEDY (D-Mass.) for president. At the Southern
Governors Conference in October 1959, he joined
Governors LEROY COLLINS of Florida and LUTHER
HODGES of North Carolina in opposing a southern
bolt from the party in 1960 over civil rights.

In March 1960, as chairman of the state's Board
of Education, Patterson ordered the president of
the state-supported black Alabama State College to
expel a group of students who had taken part in sit-
in protests in Montgomery. Patterson and the state
board of education also instigated a purge of the
faculty. Later in the month, the *New York Times* published a fund-raising advertisement, which charged
that Patterson had locked the school's dining room
"to starve" the students. The governor charged
that the *Times* had published "false and defamatory
matter," and the newspaper responded by retract-
ing two paragraphs of the advertisement. Patterson,
however, asserted that this did not represent a "full
and fair retraction," and on May 30, 1960, he filed
a $1 million libel suit against the *Times*.

In 1961, after civil rights activists engaged in
a Freedom Ride from Washington, D.C., to New
Orleans encountered violence in Birmingham,
Alabama, Attorney General ROBERT F. KENNEDY
reached an agreement with Patterson to provide
police protection for the freedom riders' journey
from Birmingham to the city limits of Montgomery,
at which point Montgomery's police commissioner
had assured the governor that the city police would

assume responsibility to protect the bus. When the
bus pulled into the terminal in Montgomery on
May 20, 1961, there was no police protection. After
a mob savagely beat the freedom riders, Patterson
denounced those who would "take the law into their
own hands." On the following day, after a violent
white mob surrounded a civil rights rally held in
the First Baptist Church in Montgomery, Patterson declared martial law in the city and sent the
National Guard to maintain order. He remained,
however, an unyielding foe of integration and, when
the governor of Mississippi, ROSS BARNETT, defied
federal authority by attempting to block the desegregation of the University of Mississippi in September 1962, Patterson backed him.

Patterson's suit against the *Times* was pending in state court when the Supreme Court handed
down a decision in a related suit, *New York Times
v. Sullivan* (1964). In that case, the Court held that
public officials could not recover damages for criticism of their official performance unless they could
prove deliberate malice. Following that decision,
Patterson dropped his suit.

After retiring from the governorship in January
1963 under the provision of the state constitution
barring consecutive terms, Patterson practiced law
in Montgomery. He entered the Democratic gubernatorial primary in 1966 but polled only about 4
percent of the vote. He ran unsuccessfully for chief
justice of the Alabama Supreme Court in 1972
but was appointed to the State Court of Criminal
Appeals in 1984 and held that position until he
retired in 1997.

—MSM

Patton, James G(eorge)

(1902–1985) *president, National Farmers Union*

Born in Bazar, Kansas, on November 8, 1902, Patton grew up in an experimental community in Colorado called Nucla (New Utopia Cooperative Land
Association). His father, a populist and a socialist,
took the young Patton to political meetings. After
the death of his father in 1920, Patton attended
Western State College in Gunnison, Colorado,
and worked as a physical education instructor. He
returned to Western State as business manager from
1927 to 1929 but left to take a job selling insurance.

He joined the Colorado Farmers Union (CFU) in 1932 and established the Farmers Union Mutual Life Association, a cooperative insurance program. He then became executive secretary of the CFU in 1934 and its president in 1938. In 1940, he was elected president of the National Farmers Union (NFU). Based mainly in the Great Plains and Rocky Mountain states, the NFU represented the interests of small family farms. Patton revitalized the NFU, expanded its membership, and brought it into a close alliance with the Roosevelt administration and organized labor. The NFU became the most liberal of the nation's three major farm organizations.

Deeply suspicious of corporations, Patton believed that family farmers were essential to the political and social health of the country. He rejected the doctrine of scarcity (limiting agricultural and industrial output), which he maintained reflected the interests of large corporations. Patton believed that small farmers had to form a powerful national union and accept the fact that "we live in a legislated economy, . . . in which . . . almost every citizen now looks to Washington and Government for something."

Patton emerged as a major figure in American liberalism with interests that extended far beyond the area of farm policy. During World War II, fear of overproduction and declining prices gave way to concerns over shortages and inflation. Patton's answer was an expansion of production in agriculture and industry along with price controls. Patton also sought to insure the prosperity of farmers through subsidies. This brought Patton and the NFU closer to the Roosevelt administration.

In the years after World War II, Patton advocated federal aid to education and a national health plan. Although he initially had some substantial disagreements with the direction of President HARRY S. TRUMAN's agricultural policies, the administration moved closer to his positions and those of the NFU. Indeed, Patton came to exert considerable influence on the Truman administration. He contributed to the creation of the United Nations Food and Agriculture Organization in 1945 and served on the public advisory board that helped administer the Marshall Plan. Patton recognized that industry, not agriculture, dominated the American economy and concluded that consumption, rather than pro-

duction, determined the fortunes of small farmers. His proposals for maintaining full employment and full production in the postwar economy constituted the basis for the Employment Act of 1946. Patton was close to Secretary of Agriculture Charles F. Brannan, and the Brannan Plan, which proposed maintaining subsidy payments while ending restrictions on production, reflected Patton's approach.

Under President Eisenhower, Patton was appointed to the public advisory board of the Foreign Operations Administration in 1953. The following year, he served as chairman of the Commission on School Support in Rural Areas, which presented a report to the White House Conference on Education in December 1955. Patton's influence in agriculture was generally diminished during the Eisenhower years, and his approach to agricultural policy frequently clashed with that of Secretary of Agriculture EZRA TAFT BENSON. Nevertheless, as the leader of an organization representing 250,000 farm families, Patton still wielded considerable lobbying power. In 1954, Congress passed an NFU-sponsored law, inspired by Patton, that made possible the shipment of surplus food to needy countries. The following year, Patton proposed a "soil bank," a plan designed to alleviate the nation's chronic overproduction of basic crops by paying farmers to take portions of their land out of cultivation. Secretary Benson adopted the idea, and in 1956 the administration sponsored and Congress passed legislation enacting a soil bank.

Patton spent much of the Eisenhower years fighting Benson's farm policies. Benson sought to cut the overproduction of basic crops by reducing the price at which the government would take the surplus of a given crop off the market. Thus, Benson reasoned, prices for farm products would decline, encouraging greater efficiency and discouraging overproduction. Eventually, American agriculture would operate under the classical supply and demand market, and the government could conclude its role as the buyer of crops. Patton believed that a reduction of the level of price support payments, as advocated by Benson, would mean the collapse of farm prices, the economic ruin of thousands of farmers, the destruction of the family farm, and vast social dislocation nationally. Patton favored continued federal management of

energy. In the environment of the developing cold war, Pauling's ideas carried little weight.

Pauling's efforts on behalf of world peace took a variety of forms. He helped to organize a Congress for Peace, held in Mexico City, in 1949. The State Department denounced the group for "providing an apologia for the Moscow point of view." The following year, he helped to found a "peace crusade."

Pauling's activities led Senator JOSEPH R. MCCARTHY (R-Wis.) to accuse him of being a communist. Pauling denied the charges, replying, "I am not even a theoretical Marxist." Nevertheless, his name appeared in 1955 on a list, put together by the Senate Internal Security Subcommittee, of "most active and typical sponsors of Communist fronts in the past." The State Department denied him a passport in 1952. Later that year, he was issued a "limited passport" for travel to Great Britain and France. After his work on the chemical bond won the Nobel Prize in chemistry in 1954, however, the State Department issued him an unrestricted passport so that he could travel to Stockholm to receive the award.

Ironically, Pauling's theory of resonance offended Stalin, who found it incompatible with communist ideology. In 1951, the Soviet Union denounced the theory as "pseudo-scientific" and "hostile to the Marxist view," because it was hostile to dialectical materialism. Pauling responded with an attack on Stalinist science.

During the 1950s, Pauling explored the biochemical aspects of schizophrenia, the structure of hemoglobin, and the nature of nucleic acids. In the early years of the decade, James D. Watson and Francis Crick regarded Pauling as an inspiration and a rival. As it turned out, Pauling's work on proteins laid the groundwork for what many regarded as the most important scientific discovery of the 20th century, but his own theories in that area, which proposed a triple helix structure, proved a failure. In 1953, Watson and Crick demonstrated that the genetic strands of DNA formed a double helix, for which they were later awarded a Nobel Prize.

Pauling's ideas about peace and the threat of nuclear weapons became increasingly influential after 1955. By that time, fears that the cold war might turn hot had begun to moderate, and the red scare had abated. Moreover, both the United States and the USSR had developed massive nuclear arsenals capable of destroying their enemies. Even more important, scientists were beginning to discover the genetic and pathological effects of radioactive fallout from atomic blasts. In response to these dangers, a number of scientists, particularly those in the biological sciences, joined Pauling in demanding an end to nuclear testing. In 1955, Pauling was a leading participant at the first Pugwash Conference, composed of scientists who supported disarmament. Two years later, he presented the UN with a petition, signed by over 9,000 scientists, urging immediate cessation of nuclear tests. Pauling's petition won increased support when Albert Schweitzer broadcast an appeal for a test ban.

Pauling continued his plea for disarmament in a book titled *No More War*, published in 1958. In that work, he warned that the United States and the USSR already had enough nuclear weapons to destroy each other completely and that atomic tests produced radioactive strontium 90 and carbon 14, which could cause cancer, leukemia, and birth defects. Pauling maintained that the arms race was due to misunderstanding and ignorance. Once people were informed of all the dangers of fallout, nuclear war would be impossible for rational people. "I believe that the development of these terrible weapons forces us to move into a new period of peace and reason, when world problems are not solved by war or by force," wrote Pauling, "but are solved by the application of man's power of reason, in a way that does justice to all nations and that benefits all people."

In February 1958, Pauling debated the effects of radioactive fallout with EDWARD TELLER, the developer of the H-bomb and a major scientific proponent of continued testing. That year he also participated in an unsuccessful suit against the Defense Department and the Atomic Energy Commission, in an effort to prevent them from conducting further atomic weapons tests.

In 1960, the Senate Internal Security Subcommittee subpoenaed Pauling to testify "on Communist participation in, or support of, a propaganda campaign against nuclear testing." Pauling denied knowledge of any communist involvement and refused to give the names of scientists who had helped to circulate the petitions against testing. He stressed that his own opposition to nuclear testing derived from his concern for the biological effects of radiation. Never given to moderation in his views, Pauling warned that if people's dentists recommended annual or semiannual full mouth X-rays for children, they should "change dentists."

Pauling continued his efforts on behalf of nuclear disarmament through the 1960s. On October 10, 1963, the same day that a partial nuclear test ban treaty went into effect, it was announced that he had won the Nobel Peace Prize for 1962. This made him the only winner of two unshared Nobel Prizes. During the 1960s, Pauling participated in the movement against American military involvement in Vietnam and continued his scientific research. He left Caltech in 1963 and moved to the Center for the Study of Democratic Institutions. In 1967, he went to the University of California at San Diego as a professor of chemistry and left there for Stanford University in 1969, where he remained until 1974. When confronted with mandatory retirement, he established the Linus Pauling Institute of Science and Medicine. Pauling touched off a controversy with the publication of his book, *Vitamin C and the Common Cold*, in 1970. In it, he argued that large doses of vitamin C would build up the immune systems in humans and protect them against infectious diseases, including the common cold. Subsequently, a number of controlled experiments failed to find any connection between vitamin C and the prevention of the common cold. Unchastened, Pauling expanded his claims and suggested that large doses of vitamin C might also help in the treatment of cancer. In 1979, a study of patients with advanced cancer conducted by the Mayo Clinic and published in *The New England Journal of Medicine* reported that vitamin C provided no such benefits. Pauling continued to dose himself with large quantities of vitamin C. He died of cancer at his ranch at Big Sur, California, on August 19, 1994.

—MSM

Peale, Norman Vincent
(1898–1993) *clergyman*

The son of a Methodist pastor, Peale was born in Bowersville, Ohio, on May 31, 1898. Following the Methodist itinerant tradition, the family moved frequently. As a boy, Peale earned money by delivering newspapers, working in a grocery, and selling pots and pans door to door. He graduated from Ohio Wesleyan University in 1920 with a B.A. in liberal arts. Upon graduating, he worked as a reporter for newspapers in Ohio and Michigan, but, within a year, he enrolled at Boston University School of Theology. After his ordination as a minister in the Methodist Episcopal Church in 1922, Peale took a pastorship in Rhode Island. He continued his studies at Boston University and received an M.A. and a Bachelor of Sacred Theology in 1924. Soon after completing his work at Boston University, he moved to Brooklyn, New York, where he became assistant pastor at St. Mark's Methodist Church. He then took over a failing congregation in another section of Brooklyn, where he increased membership from 40 to 900 and built a new church. In 1927, he moved to the University Methodist Church in Syracuse, New York. There he increased attendance at Sunday services and began a successful outreach program for college students. He also became one of the first clergymen to broadcast his own radio program.

Peale began his long affiliation with New York City's Marble Collegiate Church in 1932. In order to accept the pastorship there, he had to change his religious affiliation to the Reformed Church in America. Overwhelmed by the emotional problems of his congregants, he turned to psychiatry for help. In 1937, he began a collaboration with Dr. Smiley Blanton, a psychiatrist who had trained in Vienna with Freud. The two men established a clinic affiliated with the Marble Collegiate Church. The clinic expanded into the Blanton-Peale Institute of Religion and Health, which also trained pastoral counselors. In 1951, the clinic became the American Foundation of Religion and Psychiatry; Peale served as its president. Peale enlisted the aid of rabbis, priests, psychologists, and social workers in his clinic with the aim of helping patients sort out their mental problems and lead happier, Christian lives.

From his post in New York City, Peale built a national following. He offered a brand of Christianity that exhorted believers to have full faith in their own ability to achieve inner peace and the love of God. Peale preached to a packed church weekly, but he reached a much larger audience over radio. Beginning in 1935, he preached weekly on a radio program called *The Art of Living*, which ran on the NBC network. Physically, he seemed an unlikely candidate for a charismatic preacher. He was short and plump, and one observer likened his visage to that of a "benign owl."

Peale published his first book, also called *The Art of Living*, in 1937. In it, he taught that "applied Christianity helps people to tap reservoirs of power within themselves." Over the next 15 years, he wrote five more books, including *You Can Win* (1938) and *A Guide to Confident Living* (1948), as well as countless inspirational articles. In 1945, Peale founded the magazine *Guideposts*, which he hoped would become "an organ for a great, positive Christian movement." A compact, monthly publication modeled after *The Reader's Digest*, the magazine contained inspirational stories.

Peale's books sold modestly well until the religious revival after World War II, which he helped to create. He achieved a new level of success in 1952 with the publication of *The Power of Positive Thinking*. Many of the ideas presented in the book appeared in Peale's earlier works, but *The Power of Positive Thinking* struck a responsive chord. It remained on the best-seller list of the *New York Times* for 186 consecutive weeks and became one of the best-selling inspirational books of all time.

Written in a simple style with familiar references, *The Power of Positive Thinking* taught that positive thoughts and sentiments would cause positive things to happen, or, as Peale put it, "affirmative attitudes help make their own affirmations come true." His biblical source, according to Peale, was Jesus' statement, "Be of good cheer. I have overcome the world." Basically, the book was a collection of anecdotes, stories about people (for the most part men) who had lost the sense of themselves under the pressures of work, family, and society. Moreover, their health had begun to suffer as a result. Key to the stories were the psychological and spiritual remedies Peale had prescribed. For Peale, the key to recovery was the Mind, which, for him, was a positive vision of the subconscious. To release the power of the subconscious, the conscious mind had to surrender to the Divine Presence or Mind. The technique for doing so was positive thinking.

Peale reduced his technique to a series of simple steps; he urged his readers to picturize, prayerize, actualize. In other words, Peale advised his subjects to envision a desired goal, engage in affirmative prayer in order to learn God's will about the goal, and, if God's will supported the goal, to take practical steps to realize it. Each chapter contained "confidence-concepts," "faith attitudes," "energy-producing thoughts," or "spirit-lifters."

The book drew on the New Thought tradition, which traced its origins to a 19th-century faith healer from Maine named Phineas Quimby. Quimby treated patients by encouraging them to rely on mental (meaning spiritual) ability to tap into the restorative power of divine energy. One of his followers, Mary Baker Eddy, became the founder of Christian Science.

Critics argued that Peale's book lacked any theological or philosophical analysis. Instead it gave advice on how to break "the worry habit," maintain constant energy, be liked by people, and release each individual's "creative mind." Peale himself never intended the book to be a theological treatise. He later recalled that "many ministers said my book was oversimplified and wasn't couched in the correct ecclesiastical language. That was true. It was written in simple language because I was trying to reach people who were not in church."

Peale employed a wide variety of media to transmit his message. In addition to his books, radio program, and *Guideposts*, he began distributing his sermons widely in the early 1940s. With the arrival of television, Peale moved into the new medium. In 1952, he began a weekly television program called *What's Your Trouble?* that achieved high ratings and ran until 1968. He also wrote a newspaper column, "Confident Living," which was syndicated nationally and carried by more than 200 newspapers. Finally, he wrote a regular advice column for *Look* magazine.

Peale's enormous popularity came at the peak of a strong religious revival in America. Peale, along with fellow television personality Bishop FULTON J. SHEEN and the evangelism of BILLY GRAHAM, set the tone of the postwar religious revival. During the Eisenhower administration, polls showed that fully 97 percent of Americans said they believed in God. Many of the most admired preachers of the time, like Peale, promised a path to a happier earthly existence through Christian faith. As Peale put it, "God and the doctor, that's what I give them. Anxiety is the great American disease."

Although Peale won millions of converts, he also attracted many critics, particularly among more scholarly religious thinkers. Critics regarded him as the embodiment of many of the worst elements of American religion. According to them, Peale preached a utilitarian and shallow faith that avoided issues of sin and guilt. Neoorthodox Christian theologians like REINHOLD NIEBUHR who stressed original sin and the paltry ability of humankind to redeem itself through its own works, regarded Peale's religion as an insipid, secularized faith. From a different perspective, political liberals and advocates of the social gospel chastised Peale for his emphasis on individual solutions and his complacency about social problems.

Peale also encountered criticism for his public political pronouncements. In the elections of 1952 and 1956, he openly urged the election of DWIGHT D. EISENHOWER. During the election of 1960, he headed a group of Protestant religious leaders who questioned whether the separation of church and state could be maintained if Senator JOHN F. KENNEDY (D-Mass.), a Catholic, were elected. Charged with propagating anti-Catholic sentiments, Peale submitted his resignation to Marble Collegiate Church officials, but his congregation refused to accept it. Although Peale withdrew from the position that the election of a Catholic threatened the separation of church and state, he continued to support Kennedy's opponent, Vice President RICHARD M. NIXON. After that controversy, he made no further formal partisan pronouncements.

The ever-active Peale continued throughout the late 1950s and 1960s to publish books, articles, and columns, speak on television and radio, and travel extensively to preach before devoted audiences. In 1963, his life story was portrayed in the film, *One Man's Way*. Maintaining that the clergy ought to stay out of politics, Peale criticized religious leaders who took a public position against the war in Vietnam; nevertheless, he tended to favor Republican politicians and expressed his own conservative views on political and social issues. President RICHARD M. NIXON often requested that Peale

preach at White House services, and, at Nixon's request, he made a tour of war-torn South Vietnam in 1969. That same year, he was elected president of the Reformed Church in America. In the 1970s, he retained his pastorship at Marble Collegiate Church, contributed to *Guideposts* publications, and headed the Foundation for Christian Living, an organization that distributed pamphlets, books, and recordings of his sermons. Toward the end of his active ministry, he placed greater emphasis on the Christian view of repentance. "I am," he declared, "a very traditional Christian, and a sense of guilt is important." However, he still regarded "too much guilt" as "unhealthy." Peale retired as senior minister of the Marble Collegiate Church in 1984. That same year, President Ronald Reagan awarded him the Presidential Medal of Freedom. Peale died at his estate in Pawling, New York, on December 24, 1993.

—MSM

Pearson, Drew (Andrew) (Russell)
(1897–1969) *syndicated columnist*

The son of a college professor, Pearson was born in Evanston, Illinois, on December 13, 1897. He moved with his family to Pennsylvania in 1902, when his father became a professor of speech at Swarthmore College. After attending a local prep school and Exeter Academy, he graduated from Swarthmore in 1919. Pearson then went to the Balkans as a relief worker for the British Red Cross. After briefly returning to the United States in 1921, during which time he taught geography at the University of Pennsylvania, he then traveled throughout the Far East, earning money as a foreign correspondent. After a brief stint teaching at Columbia University, Pearson returned to journalism. In 1926, he became foreign editor of *United States Daily* (later to become *U.S. News and World Report*). Pearson joined the *Baltimore Sun* in 1929. He became head of the paper's Washington bureau, where he met journalist Robert S. Allen, with whom he published *Washington Merry-Go-Round* in 1931. An anecdotal account of political life behind the scenes in Washington, it melded partisan reporting and gossip into an attack on the Hoover administration. A sequel, *More Merry-Go-Round*, came out in

1932. Although both books were published anonymously, the identities of the authors became known after the second book, and Pearson and Allen lost their jobs. The two journalists then started a syndicated column, "Washington Merry-Go-Round," in December 1932. Syndicated by United Features, it began with a dozen newspapers and increased that number to 350 by 1941 and to about 600 in 1969. Pearson and Allen collaborated on two more books during the 1930s, both of which attacked the conservative Supreme Court. In addition, Pearson and Allen articulated their particular brand of liberal reformism on a popular radio program that ran on the ABC network beginning in 1938. During World War II, Allen severed the partnership to join the army; Pearson carried on alone. He hired David Karr as his chief assistant in 1943 and added Jack Anderson to his staff in 1945. In the late 1950s, Pearson began to share his writing chores and byline with Jack Anderson. He carried on the radio program until 1955.

In the postwar era, Pearson became one of the most influential political columnists in the country. He offered a combination of news, rumor, sensationalism, and a sense of taking his readers on a private guided tour through the corridors of power. The column exuded a smug sense of certainty, even when his information was tenuous. At the same time, no one could deny that Pearson had excellent sources within the government, and he broke some big stories.

Pearson used his column first and foremost to expose the incompetence or corruption of public officials. It also reflected his liberalism, and, although he went after Democratic as well as Republican wrongdoers, he took particular aim at conservative and right-wing figures. In 1948, Pearson began an investigation of Congressman John Parnell Thomas, the chair of the House Un-American Activities Committee. Based on information sent to him by Thomas's secretary, Pearson charged that Thomas had put friends on his congressional payroll. They did no work and kicked back part of their salaries to Thomas. The revelations forced Thomas to resign, and he was later convicted on criminal charges and sent to prison.

Pearson attacked Senator JOSEPH R. MCCARTHY's (R-Wis.) anticommunist campaign and, in turn, became a target of McCarthy. Pearson often supported groups under investigation by the House Un-American Activities Committee and used alleged communists, including Alger Hiss, Owen Lattimore, and Harry Dexter White, as sources for his column. Furthermore, Pearson vigorously denounced McCarthy personally and exposed the senator's exaggerated war record, his income tax evasion, his connections with the housing lobby, and his lack of evidence to substantiate his allegations. In December 1950, McCarthy physically attacked Pearson at Washington's swank Sulgrave Club. McCarthy sought to destroy Pearson's radio program by organizing a sponsors' boycott that almost succeeded in removing the liberal journalist from the airwaves.

Corruption remained Pearson's main focus. His "Washington Merry-Go-Round" column of September 1, 1955, revealed that PETER STROBEL, commissioner of public buildings and the second-ranking official at the Government Services Administration (GSA), had retained his ties with the consulting engineering firm of Strobel and Salzman after accepting his position with the government. Pearson also accused Strobel of refusing to provide his superior with a list of the firm's clients, an omission that prevented the government from determining whether it was doing business with any customers of Strobel and Salzman. A second column disclosed that Strobel had pressed his firm's claim against the Army Corps of Engineers for work done after the corps had expanded the scope of work beyond the initial contract and that the commissioner had refused to sign a conflict-of-interest form until his superior at the GSA "practically ordered" him to do so. Subsequently, Pearson granted Strobel two opportunities to reply to the varied charges, but Strobel ignored Pearson's offers.

Pearson's charges against Strobel prompted an investigation of the GSA by the House Antitrust Subcommittee. While the subcommittee turned up numerous irregularities, it divided evenly on the question of whether Strobel's conduct constituted either a conflict of interest or a violation of the GSA's code of ethics. Strobel resigned in November 1955, reportedly under pressure from the White House, although the administration denied it.

In January 1958, Pearson, after receiving information leaked from the House Special Subcommittee on Legislative Oversight, revealed in his column that the panel had voted to hamstring its inquiry into the Federal Communications Commission (FCC) because, in Pearson's words, "the facts were too hot to handle." Pearson accused Republicans on the subcommittee in particular of trying to bury the investigation and noted that the Republicans' view of corruption in government had changed substantially since the Truman administration.

That column also broke the story of suspicious circumstances surrounding the FCC's decision to award a television license in Miami, Florida, to National Airlines. Pearson asserted that one of the FCC commissioners, RICHARD MACK, had promised a lawyer from Miami who was "close" to National Airlines that he would support National's application.

A few days later, the columnist charged that the chairman of the FCC, JOHN DOERFER, had been reimbursed for a western junket in 1954 by both the television industry and the government. Prompted by his crusading zeal, the subcommittee's chief counsel, BERNARD SCHWARTZ, pressed the case, although not always in the most ethical manner. Several major newspapers compared his tactics to those of McCarthy. In the end, the subcommittee fired Schwartz for the manner in which he conducted the investigation, but the probe eventually resulted in the resignations of both Doerfer and Mack.

Toward the end of the decade, Pearson began to attack Eisenhower. In June 1958, at a time when the House Special Committee on Legislative Oversight was investigating the relationship between top presidential adviser SHERMAN ADAMS and Boston financier BERNARD GOLDFINE, Pearson accused the president of accepting several yards of vicuna material from Goldfine. Though admitting that Goldfine had offered the present, the White House hotly denied that the president had accepted the gift. It insisted that the gift had gone to a friend of the president's, whose name he could not recall. About a month later, Pearson's associate, Jack Anderson, was caught bugging Goldfine's hotel room. In response, Pearson, mimicking Eisenhower's defense of Adams, said that he would not dismiss Anderson

and that his assistant was "imprudent, but I need him." In May 1960, Pearson alleged that various business tycoons had given Eisenhower gifts that the president used to buy machinery, livestock, and agricultural tools for his Gettysburg farm.

During the 1960s, Pearson broke the story that Senator THOMAS J. DODD (D-Conn.) had diverted over $100,000 from campaign contributions to his own use. In 1967, the Senate censured Dodd for conduct "contrary to accepted morals" that tended to bring the Senate into disrepute. Pearson also reported on the financial dealings of Representative ADAM CLAYTON POWELL (D-N.Y.) that led to his removal from the House. In one of his more spectacular revelations, Pearson reported that, as attorney general, ROBERT F. KENNEDY had authorized electronic surveillance of MARTIN LUTHER KING, JR. Pearson coauthored two books with Jack Anderson: *U.S.A.: Second-Class Power* (1958) and *The Case Against Congress* (1968). His first novel, *The Senator* (1968), was ghostwritten by Gerald Green and met with unfavorable reviews. Nevertheless, Pearson's reputation was at its height and his column at a peak of popularity when he died of a heart attack in Washington, D.C., on September 1, 1969.

—MSM

Percy, Charles H(arting)

(1919–   ) *president, Bell and Howell Corporation; chairman, Republican Platform Committee*

Born in Pensacola, Florida, on September 27, 1919, Percy grew up in Chicago, Illinois, where his father worked as a bank manager and then an office manager for Bell & Howell, a small camera company. As a child, Charles Percy sold magazines. Later, while attending high school, he held a series of jobs. With the help of his Sunday school teacher, Joseph H. McNabb, who was president of Bell & Howell, Percy joined a student training program at the company in 1936. Percy received a scholarship to attend the University of Chicago the following year. After working part-time in dormitory cafeterias and the college library, he took over a cooperative agency that sold food, linen, coal, and appliances to dormitories and fraternity houses. Percy turned the operation into a moneymaking enterprise and, in the process, earned a substantial amount of money.

In 1941, when Percy graduated with a B.A. in economics, his campus cooperative agency was grossing $150,000 a year. His cut of the profits was $10,000. While in college, Percy worked for Bell & Howell over the summers. Upon graduating, he immediately joined Bell & Howell on a full-time basis and became manager of the newly formed war contracts department. In 1942, he became assistant corporate secretary and was named to the board of directors. Percy enlisted in the navy as an apprentice seaman in 1943; by the time of his discharge in 1945 he had risen to the rank of lieutenant. Returning to Bell & Howell, Percy became corporate secretary for industrial relations and foreign manufacturing programs in 1946. When McNabb died in January 1949, Percy was elected president of the company, making him the youngest man until then to head a major U.S. corporation.

Under Percy's leadership, Bell & Howell grew rapidly during the 1950s and 1960s. The company became the largest manufacturer of camera equipment in the country. Percy also oversaw the company's diversification, and Bell & Howell doubled its sales to $22 million within the first two years of his presidency. He instituted a number of policies designed to benefit employees, including a profit-sharing plan and a retirement program. He maintained close relations with employees, delegated responsibility to managers, and established joint employee-executive boards concerned with research, merchandising, and plant safety. Percy also earmarked a large percentage of working capital for product research. By 1961, sales of products introduced under his presidency accounted for 82 percent of Bell & Howell's $100 million annual gross. At a time when most camera manufacturers feared imports and favored high tariffs, Percy favored low reciprocal tariffs and aggressively sought to penetrate foreign markets. His interest in overseas markets led him to make trips abroad, which, along with his concern for tariff policy, sparked his interest in politics.

Percy began his political career as a precinct captain for the Republican Party in 1946. In the mid-1950s, he became a protégé of President DWIGHT EISENHOWER. In April 1954, Percy served as spokesman for a delegation of more than 30 business leaders who met with the president at the White House to discuss foreign and economic policy. In an arranged exchange of letters released to the press, Percy supported Eisenhower's trade policies, and Eisenhower, who had called for a three-year extension of reciprocal trade agreements with authority for moderate tariff reductions, indicated his willingness to settle for a one-year extension. Percy became finance chairman of the Illinois Republican Party in August 1955. The following year, Eisenhower chose Percy as his special ambassador to attend presidential inauguration ceremonies in Peru and Bolivia. After the Republicans suffered a resounding defeat in the congressional elections of 1958, Eisenhower invited Percy to meet with him and others to discuss the party's future.

Speaking with Vice President RICHARD NIXON and MEADE ALCORN, the chair of the Republican National Committee, Percy proposed a committee to enunciate Republican programs and goals. Subsequently, the Republican National Committee created a Committee on Program and Progress in February 1959 and selected Percy to chair it. He released the group's four-part report, titled *Decisions for a Better America*, in October 1959. Intended as a vision of long-range goals for the Republican Party, the report, by inference, backed most policies of the Eisenhower administration.

Eisenhower and Nixon chose Percy to head the Republican platform committee in 1960. Percy supported Nixon for president and tailored a platform that accorded with the recommendations in *Decisions for a Better America* and the vice president's wishes. Governor NELSON ROCKEFELLER of New York, however, wanted a stronger civil rights plank and a commitment to more spending on national defense. Determined to head off a floor fight, Nixon met with Rockefeller four days before the party's national convention in July and agreed to a statement of understanding. Eisenhower objected to the wording on defense, and Nixon worked out language acceptable to the president. Eventually, the platform committee worked out a series of compromises. After the convention, Nixon declined most of Percy's offers of assistance and lost Illinois by 8,800 voters.

Percy stepped down as chief executive officer of Bell & Howell in 1963 (although he retained his position as chairman of the board) in order to run for governor of Illinois in 1964. Although he won the Republican nomination, he lost to the Democratic incumbent Otto G. Kerner. Two years later, however, he defeated the Democratic incumbent PAUL DOUGLAS for a seat in the U.S. Senate. Percy won reelection in 1972 and 1978. In the Senate, he established a reputation as one of the most liberal Republicans in the body. An outspoken critic of the war in Vietnam, he cosponsored with Senator JACOB JAVITS (R-N.Y.) the War Powers Act. In domestic affairs, he supported mass transit, housing programs, federal aid to education, consumer protection, and the food stamp program. His votes against the confirmation of Supreme Court nominees CLEMENT F. HAYNSWORTH and G. Harold Carswell, along with other votes, earned him a place on President Nixon's enemies list. A member of the Senate's Special Committee on Aging, Percy became a leading advocate for the needs of the elderly and presented a series of proposals in *Growing Old in the Country of the Young* (1974). He explored running for the presidency in 1968 and 1976 but dropped out early in both races. Percy lost his bid for reelection in 1984. He resides in Washington, D.C.

—MSM

Peress, Irving

(1917–) *U.S. Army officer*

The son of a tailor, Peress was born in the Bronx on July 31, 1917. Raised in Manhattan, he graduated from George Washington High School and City College, where he enrolled in the Reserve Officers' Training Corps. Although City College was a hotbed of leftist political activism, Peress remained largely apolitical through college and dental school at New York University, from which he received his degree in 1940. He became involved in left-wing politics through his wife, who, as Peress later recalled, "came from a more politically advanced family." After graduating from dental school, he applied for a commission as a dentist in the army but was rejected for health reasons. He established a private practice in Queens, New York. After World War II, Peress emerged as a leader of the American Labor Party. By the time the military was drafting older doctors and dentists for the Korean War,

Peress had an active private practice. Upon receiving his notice, Peress deliberately gained weight to increase his hypertension in an effort to fail his physical exam. The subterfuge failed, and he was inducted.

His brief career as an army draftee became a major issue in the confrontation between Senator JOSEPH R. McCARTHY (R-Wis.) and high officials in the military and administration in 1954. Peress was commissioned as a captain in the Army Reserve in October 1952 under the doctors' draft law. He began active duty in the Dental Corps in January 1953 and was assigned to Fort Lewis, Washington, from which he was to go to Yokohama, Japan. He received emergency compassionate leave because his wife and daughter were under psychiatric care and then was assigned to Camp Kilmer, New Jersey.

When commissioned in 1952, he signed a form swearing that he had never belonged to an organization that sought to alter the government by unconstitutional means. Decades later, Peress explained that he did not consider "the American Labor Party or the Communist Party subversive organizations." On subsequent forms, however, he wrote "federal constitutional privilege" in response to questions about membership in organizations declared subversive by the attorney general. In February 1953, shortly after Peress went on active duty, Army Intelligence was notified that he had written "federal constitutional privilege" on a loyalty form. In August 1953, he received an interrogatory citing the evidence against him and giving him a chance to reply. Once again he wrote "federal constitutional privilege" across the papers. The investigation concluded that sufficient evidence of communist tendencies existed to warrant the dentist's discharge as a security risk. In September 1953, while the investigation was in progress, Peress requested a promotion to the rank of major, for which he automatically qualified by his age and previous experience in the Army Reserve. His request was approved, but at the same time the commanding officer at Camp Kilmer, General RALPH W. ZWICKER, wrote a letter to his superiors recommending Peress's discharge. In November, the Pentagon ordered him released at the earliest possible date.

In December 1954, McCarthy, who had been investigating alleged communists in the army, subpoenaed Peress to appear before the Senate Government Operations Committee's Permanent Investigations Subcommittee. At a hearing on January 30, the dentist declined to answer all questions about his political activities. McCarthy, in turn, demanded his court-martial. In the meantime, the army, in mid-January 1954, had ordered Peress's honorable discharge and had given him the usual 90 days to select a termination date. He chose March 31. After his appearance before McCarthy's committee, however, Peress met with Zwicker on February 1 and asked for his immediate separation from the army. The army announced his honorable discharge on February 2.

On February 18, McCarthy's subcommittee heard testimony from a New York policewoman who had joined the Communist Party as an undercover agent. She testified that Peress and his wife had attended meetings and that he had attended a leadership class run by the party. She further stated that she believed Peress had been a member. When Peress appeared, he refused to answer any questions relating to communist affiliations; he did, however, say that he would oppose any group that advocated the violent overthrow of the government. He also said that anyone who equated invoking the Fifth Amendment with guilt was guilty of subversion and quoted the Book of Psalms: "His mischief shall return upon his own head and his violence shall come down upon his own pate." McCarthy launched a diatribe against the army for granting the dentist an honorable discharge. Later that day, General Zwicker testified. Stiff and at times unresponsive, Zwicker refused to disclose the names of those who had promoted and then honorably discharged Peress. Thereupon, McCarthy questioned whether Zwicker had "the brains of a five-year-old child" and whether the highly decorated veteran of World War II was "fit to wear that uniform." McCarthy's attack on Zwicker brought the simmering hostility between the army and the senator to a boiling point and set off the chain of events that led to the Army-McCarthy hearings in the spring of 1954 and ultimately to the Senate's condemnation of McCarthy in the winter of that year.

In March 1955, after the Republicans had lost control of the Senate, the Permanent Investigations Subcommittee, with Senator JOHN MCCLELLAN (D-

Ark.) replacing McCarthy as the chair, reopened hearings on the Peress case. Four months later, the subcommittee filed a report criticizing the army's handling of the matter and recommending changes in military security procedures. The report, however, found no evidence of subversion.

After the hearings, Peress returned to his dental practice in Queens. He sold his practice in 1980 and retired in 2003. He lives in New York City. In 2005, an interviewer asked him if he had changed his views about communism. He responded that he was "a true believer until the not-too-distant past." Asked if he had any regrets, Peress replied: "No. None at all. True believers don't have regrets."

—MSM

Persons, Wilton B(urton)

(1896–1977) *special assistant to the president, deputy assistant to the president, White House chief of staff*

Born in Montgomery, Alabama, on January 19, 1896, Persons attended Starke University School and graduated from Alabama Polytechnic Institute (later Auburn University) with a degree in electrical engineering in 1916, after which he went to work for the Western Electric Company. In August 1917, he was commissioned as a second lieutenant in the Coast Artillery Reserve, and, in October of that year, became a first lieutenant in the Coast Artillery Corps of the Regular Army. Persons served in France during World War I. After the war, he remained in the army and served at a number of posts. In 1923, he transferred to the signal corps and was promoted to captain. He spent the second half of the 1920s as a professor of military science and tactics at the University of Minnesota. In order to prepare himself for an administrative career, he entered Harvard Business School in 1929 and graduated, magna cum laude, two years later with an M.B.A. degree. His next assignment was with the office of the chief signal officer in Washington, D.C. In 1933, the army transferred him to the office of the assistant secretary of war, where he served as liaison with the Military Affairs Committee of the House of Representatives. Promoted to major in 1935, Persons entered Command and General Staff School in 1937, from which he graduated the following year. After graduating from the Air Corps Tactical School in 1939, he joined the office of the chief of staff, where he directed liaison with Congress. He received a promotion to lieutenant colonel in August 1940 and became chief of the liaison branch of the office of the deputy chief of staff of the army in December 1941. During World War II, Persons continued at his post. When General DWIGHT D. EISENHOWER assumed command of the Allied forces in Europe, he asked that Persons, an old friend, be assigned to his staff. The army chief of staff, General George C. Marshall, considered Persons so valuable that he turned down Eisenhower's request.

During the postwar period, Persons rose to the rank of major general and became director of legislative liaison for the army and later for the Department of Defense. Forced to retire from the army in 1949 because of poor health, Persons became superintendent of the Stanton Military Academy. When Eisenhower became supreme commander of the North Atlantic Treaty Organization (NATO) forces in 1951, Persons returned to active duty as a member of Eisenhower's staff. Persons again retired from the army in August 1952. After returning to the United States, he joined the Republican National Committee. During the presidential campaign of 1952, Persons served as liaison between Eisenhower and congressional Republicans.

A few weeks after winning the election, Eisenhower placed Persons in charge of congressional liaison. In that position, Persons used his extensive experience on Capitol Hill and his warm personality to gain passage of the administration's legislative agenda. Persons became extremely popular with members of Congress, due at least in part to his ability to arrange a White House audience for them as well as his great respect for congressional prerogatives and sensibilities.

Persons was one of President Eisenhower's more conservative advisers, in part, because of his belief that the administration needed the support of the Republican Right to pass its legislative agenda. He opposed any move by Eisenhower to denounce Senator JOSEPH R. MCCARTHY's (R-Wis.) vitriolic attacks on communists in government, even after McCarthy began to turn his fire on the administration. Persons believed that such an approach would

accomplish little other than dividing the Republican Party. When McCarthy attempted to prevent the appointment of CHARLES BOHLEN as ambassador to the Soviet Union and denounced him as a traitor, Persons counseled Eisenhower to act with caution. After McCarthy excoriated the army for lax loyalty procedures, Persons again pleaded for presidential restraint. Persons's recommendations had great weight with Eisenhower, who never publicly attacked McCarthy.

The issue of civil rights deeply troubled Persons. As a white southerner, he was uncomfortable about pushing for desegregation. Furthermore, his political instincts told him that a strong position in favor of desegregation would lose Eisenhower support in the south. Members of the White House staff who favored a stronger stand in defense of civil rights regarded Persons as a roadblock. FREDERIC MORROW, a black presidential assistant, remembered that White House staff meetings on civil rights proved "hard going" and especially pointed to Persons, who "while a 'liberal Southerner' [was] obviously deeply affected by and emotional about" the "changes in southern customs decreed by the Supreme Court." Persons was so close to the president that his deep disquietude over civil rights policy noticeably affected Eisenhower's civil rights policy, which for the most part reflected a cautious approach to the issue.

Eisenhower admired Persons both personally and professionally; the president later remembered coming "to respect his ability, particularly as a coordinator among individuals holding vigorous and differing views." In September 1958, Persons was promoted to White House chief of staff to replace the departing SHERMAN ADAMS. Despite his utter devotion to Eisenhower, Persons's effectiveness in that post was a matter of dispute. Some saw him as a liberator of information flowing to the president and appreciated his more relaxed style, while others believed that he created "an atmosphere of indecision and fear" that paralyzed the inner workings of the White House. Members of Congress in both parties preferred dealing with the affable Persons over the curt Adams.

As chief of staff, Persons found civil rights a particularly difficult issue. While assuring Morrow that the door to the chief of staff's office would always be open to him, Persons asked that Morrow take matters relating to civil rights to GERALD MORGAN. Persons explained that his brother was a former governor of Alabama and that the issues of civil rights and desegregation had almost caused a rift in his family.

After the election of 1960, Persons served as Eisenhower's liaison to the transition team of JOHN F. KENNEDY. Upon leaving the White House, Persons became headmaster of Graham-Dex Preparatory School in Palm Beach, Florida. He also accepted a position as a director of Univis Corporation. Persons died in Ft. Lauderdale, Florida, on September 5, 1977.

—MSM

Potter, Charles E(dward)

(1916–1979)   *U.S. senator*

Born in Lapeer, Michigan, on October 30, 1916, Potter grew up in rural Michigan. He attended public schools and did social work while studying at Michigan State Normal College (later Eastern Michigan University). After earning his B.A. in 1938, he became administrator of the Bureau of Social Aid in Cheboygan County, Michigan, and held that position until he enlisted as a private in the U.S. Army in 1942. During World War II, Potter served with distinction as an infantry officer in France. He was seriously wounded in 1945 and, as a result, lost both legs. After his discharge from the service in 1946 as a major, he worked for the Retraining and Reemployment Administration. In 1947, Potter ran as a Republican in a special election to fill a seat in the House of Representatives left vacant by the death of an incumbent and won. He won reelection in 1948 and 1950. A member of the House Un-American Activities Committee, he used that as a credential during his successful bid in 1952 to fill the Senate seat left vacant by the death of Arthur Vandenberg (R-Mich.). That same year, he won election to a full term. Potter made anticommunism the major focus of his campaign against his Democratic opponent, Blair Moody. His strategy, however, mattered less than the presidential candidacy of DWIGHT D. EISENHOWER. Potter rode Eisenhower's coattails and defeated Moody by 45,000 votes.

During the 83rd Congress (1953–54), Potter served on the Permanent Investigations Subcommittee, chaired by Senator JOSEPH R. MCCARTHY (R-Wis.). Like other Republican members of the panel, Potter tried to prevent an open break between McCarthy and the Republican administration. Potter nevertheless had his limits. When the head of the subcommittee's staff, J. B. MATTHEWS, published an article alleging that the Protestant clergy was "the largest single group supporting the Communist apparatus in the United States today," Potter joined the Democrats on the subcommittee in demanding that Matthews resign.

In 1954, when McCarthy intensified his investigation of subversion in the army (apparently in retaliation for complaints by the army that he had sought special treatment for his former aide, G. DAVID SCHINE), Potter joined Senators EVERETT DIRKSEN (R-Ill.) and KARL E. MUNDT (R-S. Dak.) in attempting to forestall the probe. McCarthy nevertheless proceeded with his investigation, and Potter was horrified at the senator from Wisconsin's abuse of General RALPH ZWICKER. Potter was also shocked after the army released its "chronology" of the efforts of ROY COHN, chief counsel of Permanent Subcommittee on Investigations, on behalf of Schine. In the resulting Army-McCarthy hearings, Potter, encouraged by the administration and by the president himself, sought to bring the proceedings to an early close. On June 17, the last day of the investigation, Potter issued a dramatic statement saying he was convinced "that the principal accusation of each side in this controversy was born out by testimony." He further asserted that the testimony heard by the subcommittee was "saturated with statements which were not truthful and which might constitute perjury in the legal sense." The statement also called for the dismissal of employees "who have played top roles on both sides" and an overhaul of the subcommittee's staff. In the end, however, Potter signed the subcommittee's majority report of September 1954, which criticized McCarthy only mildly. At the same time, he filed his own "supplementary views" that essentially restated the position he had taken on June 17. In December 1954, Potter voted for the resolution censuring McCarthy.

Although he claimed, at times, to be an Eisenhower Republican, Potter often voted against the administration. In 1954, he supported the Bricker amendment, which would have limited the president's treaty-making powers and which the administration strongly opposed. During the 1956 congressional session, Potter opposed the administration on the natural gas bill, the farm bill, and the sale of air force jets to Yugoslavia.

Potter actively supported strong civil rights legislation in 1957. With other proponents of civil rights, he opposed an amendment granting jury trials to those who violated court orders protecting black voting rights. "The jury trial question is a strawman," he declared in July and bluntly noted that the justification for the "denial of jury trials is obvious: in many instances Southern juries do not convict white men of offenses against Negroes." Although the jury trial amendment passed, Potter voted for the final version of the civil rights bill in August.

Even though he owed his election to the Senate to Eisenhower, Potter sought to separate himself from the administration when he ran for reelection in 1958. During the recession in 1957–58, he joined a group of Republican senators who unsuccessfully proposed a tax cut as an economic stimulant. To critics who thought the move inflationary, Potter responded, in March 1958, that "it is rather hard to get [his constituents] concerned about inflation when 350,000 people [in Michigan] are unemployed." In June 1958, Potter became one of the first Republican senators to call for the dismissal of the president's chief aide, SHERMAN ADAMS, who was accused of influence peddling.

Potter's political maneuvers failed. In a heavily Democratic year, he lost his Senate seat to Lieutenant Governor PHILIP A. HART by a margin of 170,000 votes. Potter quit active politics and remained in Washington. He worked as an industrial consultant and an international securities executive. In 1965, he published an account of the Army-McCarthy hearings, *Days of Shame*. As the Watergate scandal unfolded, he became, in March 1974, one of three trustees charged with overseeing disbursements of the $3.57 million surplus from President RICHARD M. NIXON's reelection campaign in 1972. Potter resided in Queenstown, Maryland, until his death in Washington, D.C., on November 23, 1979.

—MSM

Potter, David M(orris)
(1910–1971) *historian*

Born in Augusta, Georgia, on December 6, 1910, Potter graduated from Emory University in 1932. He then went to graduate school at Yale University, where he studied with the great southern historian, Ulrich Bonnell Phillips. Potter received a M.A. in 1933 and his Ph.D. in 1940; his dissertation was later published as *Lincoln and His Party in the Secession Crisis* (1942). Based on extensive research and written in graceful and lucid prose, the book became a classic. While working on his doctorate, Potter taught at the University of Mississippi from 1936 to 1938 and then took a job at Rice Institute in Houston, Texas, where he taught until 1942, when he accepted an appointment at Yale. He remained at Yale for 19 years.

In 1950, Potter delivered the Walgreen Lectures at the University of Chicago. Published in a revised form in 1954 as *People of Plenty: Economic Abundance and the American Character*, those lectures became what was quite likely his most significant book. *People of Plenty* reflected both Potter's interest in social science methodology and his involvement in the consensus school of American history. Progressive historians such as Charles A. Beard, Vernon Parrington, and Matthew Josephson emphasized the theme of conflict in American history. In contrast, Potter stressed the shared values of Americans and argued that consensus, rather than conflict, was the dominant theme of the American experience.

In contrast to Frederick Jackson Turner, who had argued that the frontier shaped the American character, Potter maintained that material abundance played the central role in forming the American character. Very much a product of its time, *People of Plenty* reflected both the growing influence of the social and behavioral sciences in the postwar era and the emergence of the American studies movement, an interdisciplinary search for the unique characteristics of America and the nature of an American character. In his search for what made America unique and what defined the American character, Potter found the key to that character in "economic abundance—not the abundance of locked-up natural resources to which man lacks the technological key but the abundance of usable goods produced from these resources—which the people of the United States have possessed in far greater degree than any other national population." As a consequence of that abundance, he concluded, "American life is geared to success rather than to status." Abundance also accounted for the competitive nature of the American character. "Increased abundance," he wrote, "means increased rewards in the competitive struggle. Increased rewards mean an increased premium upon efficiency in competition." Further, Potter argued, these conditions produced "a condition of mobility far more widespread and pervasive than any previous society or previous era of history." This, in turn, gave rise to the American commitment to equality. "Abundance," Potter wrote, "has influenced American life in many ways, but there is perhaps no respect in which this influence has been more profound than in the forming and strengthening of the American ideal and practice of equality, with all that the ideal has implied for the individual in the way of opportunity to make his own place in society and of emancipation from a system of status." Potter was not uncritical of the American experience and recognized that the ideal and practice of equality were not always realized and that opportunity was not equally shared. For instance, minorities did not share fully in the opportunities of American life. Potter nevertheless argued that, despite differences in wealth, status, and racial or ethnic background, Americans shared a consensus based on the drive for economic success and social mobility.

Potter readily conceded that abundance and social mobility exacted costs. The very mobility of American society denied its people the comfort of having a place in an organic social order. According to Potter, however, the benefits conferred by abundance outweighed the costs. Foremost among them, he maintained, was American democracy.

In 1961, he moved to Stanford University, where he was head of the history department from 1965 to 1968, and served for six years as director of the American studies program. In 1968, his book *The South and the Sectional Conflict* received the Jules F. Landry Award from Louisiana State University Press and was nominated for a National Book Award. In reviewing that work, Martin Duber-man, a historian at Princeton University, wrote that "David Potter may be the greatest living historian in the United States." That same year, Potter delivered the Walter Lynwood Fleming Lectures at Louisiana State University. His Fleming Lectures were published in 1972 as *The South and the Concurrent Majority*. Widely recognized as one of the preeminent historians of his generation, he was elected president of the Organization of American Historians in April 1970 and elected president of the American Historical Association in December of the same year. In addition to producing impressive scholarship, he was a dedicated teacher who drew hundreds of undergraduates to his classes and a revered mentor of graduate students.

Potter died in Palo Alto, California, on February 18, 1971. At the time of his death, he was working on several projects. At his request, Don Fehrenbacher finished compiling a collection of Potter's previously published essays, *History and American Society: Essays of David M. Potter* (1973), and completed Potter's magisterial work on the coming of the Civil War, *The Impending Crisis, 1848–1861* (1976).

—MSM

Poulson, Norris
(1895–1982) *mayor of Los Angeles*

The son of Danish immigrants, Poulson was born on a ranch near Haines in Baker County, Oregon, on July 23, 1895. At an early age, he moved with his family to nearby Baker City. He graduated from Baker High School and attended Oregon Agricultural College (later Oregon State University) from 1913 to 1914. In the fall of 1914, he attended business college in Baker City, Oregon, and went to work as an accountant in February 1915. The following year, he became a farmer. Poulson moved to Los Angeles, California, in 1923, where he worked as a bookkeeper for two years until beginning an accounting practice of his own. He took correspondence courses and night classes at Southwestern University to prepare him to become a certified public accountant, which he did in 1933 and then worked at that occupation before entering politics as a Republican. After serving in the California Assembly from 1938 to 1942, he won election to the

U.S. House of Representatives in 1942. He lost his bid for reelection in 1944 but returned to Congress in 1946 and served until his resignation in 1953. In Congress, he was one of the leaders in California's dispute with Arizona over rights to water from the Colorado River.

In 1953, Poulson ran for mayor of Los Angeles against the incumbent Fletcher Bowron, who had held the office for 15 years. Poulson campaigned on the issue of air pollution, a problem he charged the incumbent had ignored. He aroused interest with his proposal that Congress grant tax rebates to industrial firms that installed antipollution equipment. In addition, he promised to ask the Public Health Service, the Department of Agriculture, and the Bureau of Mines for assistance in clearing up Los Angeles's smog. Poulson also attacked Bowron's support for a large public housing project in Chavez Ravine known as Elysian Park Heights. Poulson won the election in May and was reelected in 1957.

As mayor, Poulson was instrumental in the construction of the Los Angeles International Airport and in expanding the Los Angeles Harbor. He also played an important role in integrating the city's fire department and police department. His administration began a controversial garbage recycling program. Perhaps most notably, Poulson took the lead in persuading baseball's Brooklyn Dodgers to move to Los Angeles.

Poulson's activities as mayor involved him in national issues. He took an interest in the development of a civil defense program. Speaking on the NBC television program *American Forum of the Air* in February 1956, he insisted that the federal government had a duty to lay down guidelines for civil defense and arouse the public from its lethargy on the matter. Concerns about the effects of nuclear testing also commanded Poulson's attention. When the city health department reported that radioactive fallout in Los Angeles had increased 20 percent above the acceptable level following a test in Nevada in October 1958, he called President DWIGHT D. EISENHOWER to demand that the testing be discontinued immediately.

In the late 1950s, Poulson was active in the U.S. Conference of Mayors. As vice president of the Conference of Mayors in 1958, Poulson, a vigorous supporter of federal aid for urban redevelopment, joined New York City mayor ROBERT WAGNER, JR., in urging Eisenhower to release $450 million already granted by Congress for that purpose and to allocate $350 million annually over the next 10 years for redevelopment. On another issue, he supported the administration's position. In a statement at the Conference of Mayors, he opposed an increase of defense spending in light of the recent Soviet missile and satellite launchings. He said, "I fail to see what we could gain if we concentrate on a defense program that would make it necessary to neglect important local programs that mean so much for morale, loyalty and the prosperity necessary to support the federal government, especially in times of crisis." Chosen president of the Conference of Mayors in September 1958, Poulson pleaded with the Eisenhower administration to reconsider threats to cut off aid to housing development and recommended that the proposed federal contribution to slum clearance projects be raised from two-thirds to 80 percent of costs.

In September 1959, Poulson caused a minor diplomatic incident when Soviet premier Nikita Khrushchev visited his city. Throughout the day, Khrushchev constantly touted the superiority of the Soviet Union. At a civic dinner, the mayor argued with the Soviet leader about the merits of capitalism and infuriated Khrushchev by chiding him for his comment that "we will bury you." Poulson said, "We tell you in the friendliest of terms possible we are planning no funerals, yours or ours." Khrushchev at first threatened to return home, but, four days later, he extended Poulson an invitation to visit Russia and gave him a gift of bottles of vodka and caviar. Khrushchev later devoted two-and-a-half pages of his memoirs to "that little Mayor of Los Angeles."

Poulson lost his bid for reelection in 1961 to Samuel Yorty. Some observers attributed Poulson's narrow defeat (he lost by only 15,000 votes) to the disaffection of African Americans and Mexican Americans, who believed that he had ignored their problems. Poulson served as California's water commissioner from 1963 to 1969. He resided in Tustin, California, until his death in Orange, California, on September 25, 1982.

—MSM

Powell, Adam Clayton, Jr.

(1908–1972) *U.S. congressman*

The son of a pastor of the Abyssinian Baptist Church, Powell was born in New Haven, Connecticut, on November 29, 1908. He moved with his family to New York City in 1909, when his father became minister of the Abyssinian Baptist Church there. Raised in comfort, Powell graduated from Colgate University in 1930 and earned an M.A. from Columbia University in 1932. In his last year at Colgate, Powell decided to become a minister. During the 1930s, he directed a soup kitchen at his father's church, and in 1930 he became business manager of the church and director of its community center. In 1936, he began publishing a column in the *Amsterdam News*, a black weekly newspaper. At the age of 29, he succeeded his ailing father as pastor of the Abyssinian Baptist Church. Powell used his pulpit to plead for civil rights and social progress for African Americans. He organized boycotts of unions and companies that discriminated against African Americans. In 1941, Powell became the first African American to be elected to the New York City Council. When a new congressional district was created for Harlem in 1944, Powell ran for the seat and won. In Congress, he advocated a permanent Fair Employment Practices Commission, elimination of the poll tax in federal elections, and an end to racial segregation in the armed forces.

During the 1950s, Powell emerged as a leading spokesman for civil rights in the House. In the early months of the Eisenhower administration, he accused several officials of the administration of "virtually countermanding" the president's orders to desegregate military facilities. After Eisenhower and Powell exchanged conciliatory letters, the bases were quietly desegregated.

Powell attempted to further integration by attaching amendments to various appropriations bills stipulating that federal funds could not be spent on projects that practiced segregation. The most controversial of the so-called Powell amendments came in 1956, when he attempted to attach the rider to a bill providing federal aid for the construction of schools. Eisenhower, whose administration proposed the bill, opposed the amendment as "extraneous." Although a coalition of northern Democrats and Republicans in the House passed the amendment, even many who voted for it criticized the proposal. Liberals such as Eleanor Roosevelt and Adlai Stevenson thought that Powell's action would defeat or delay desperately needed funding for schools to respond to demands created by the baby boom. When the House voted on the bill, which included the Powell amendment, conservative Republicans and southern Democrats combined to kill the measure.

During the early years of the Eisenhower administration, Powell publicly praised the president for his contributions to the cause of desegregation. Thanks to Powell's generally friendly relations with the Eisenhower administration, he was able in 1954 to arrange for the emperor of Ethiopia, Haile Selassie, to visit the Abyssinian Baptist Church. Early in 1956, Powell declared his support for Eisenhower and asserted that the president had made "the greatest contribution to civil rights in the history of the United States." Two weeks later, however, Powell accused Eisenhower of "dodging the issue." Nevertheless, in the same statement, he denounced Adlai Stevenson, the leading Democratic candidate, for "middle-of-the-road shilly-shallying, pussyfooting, doubletalking." After meeting with Eisenhower on October 11, Powell again reversed himself and endorsed Eisenhower for reelection. The congressman explained that Eisenhower had a laudable record on civil rights and a good image abroad. In addition, he accused Stevenson, by then the Democratic nominee, of having snubbed him.

Powell's endorsement of Eisenhower angered the Democratic boss of New York City, Carmine DeSapio, who, along with district leaders in Harlem, decided to challenge Powell in the Democratic primary of 1958. Powell campaigned hard and, in one speech, warned DeSapio and Hulan Jack, the black borough president of Manhattan, to avoid walking the streets of Harlem. The NAACP and other leading civil rights groups deplored the statement. Powell retracted it, won the primary, made his peace with DeSapio, and went on to win reelection.

Powell's flamboyant personality, his poor attendance record in the House, and his questionable financial and personal activities compromised his effectiveness as a civil rights leader. During the

1950s, he and several members of his staff were targets of a number of investigations. Several people in his office, as well as leading officials of the Abyssinian Baptist Church, were convicted of income tax evasion and embezzlement. Beginning in 1951, Powell himself had to defend a charge of preparing fraudulent income tax returns for his wife. He was finally acquitted in 1960. That same year, a woman from Harlem, whom he had accused of being a "bag-woman" (graft collector) for the New York City police, sued Powell for defamation and won. Powell refused to pay or to respond to subpoenas to appear in court to explain his failure to comply with the ruling.

As a consequence of the seniority system, Powell became chair of the House Education and Labor Committee in 1961. Legislation such as the Minimum Wage Bill of 1961, the Vocational Education Act, the Manpower Development and Training Act, and the Elementary and Secondary Education Act came out of his committee, as did the renewal of the National Defense Education Act. In addition, Title VI of the Civil Rights Act of 1964 authorized federal agencies to withhold aid from institutions that practiced racial segregation or discrimination; effectively, it enacted a version of the Powell amendment. Although Powell worked closely with Presidents JOHN F. KENNEDY and LYNDON B. JOHNSON to pass their domestic programs, his reputation was tarnished by his conduct. He spent tax dollars on lavish pleasure trips and often missed votes in Congress. His defiance of the court in his defamation case led to a citation first for civil contempt and then for criminal contempt of court in 1966. Powell avoided arrest by staying away from New York and taking up residence in Bimini. In 1967, a select committee of the House began an investigation into his alleged misuse of committee funds and his continuing contempt of New York State courts. Its report recommended that Powell be censured and stripped of his seniority. The full House went beyond the recommendations of the select committee and voted to expel him in March 1967, but, without making an appearance in Harlem, Powell won the special election to fill his vacant seat in a landslide. He also raised enough money to pay off the judgment against him. For two years, his seat remained vacant. After Powell won

election again in 1968, the House voted to seat him in January 1969, but it stripped him of his seniority and fined him for improper use of payroll and travel funds. In 1969, the Supreme Court ruled that the House had improperly excluded Powell in 1967.

Although Powell returned to the House, his power had faded. The loss of his seniority cost him his committee chair. Adding to his difficulties, in 1969 he was hospitalized with cancer. In 1970, State Assemblyman Charles B. Rangel ran against Powell in the Democratic primary and narrowly defeated him. Powell died of cancer in Miami, Florida, on April 4, 1972.

—MSM

Powers, Francis Gary
(1929–1977) *U-2 pilot*

The son of a coal miner, Powers was born in Burdine, Kentucky, on August 17, 1929. After graduating from Milligan College in Johnson, Tennessee, he enlisted in the U.S. Air Force in 1950. He underwent basic training and went on to advanced training and gunnery school. He hoped to serve in the Korean War but came down with appendicitis; by the time he recovered, the war was over. In July 1953, he was stationed at Turner Air Force Base, near Albany, Georgia. In January 1956, the Central Intelligence Agency (CIA) recruited Powers to serve as a pilot in the new U-2 program. Planned and supervised by RICHARD M. BISSELL, JR., a special assistant to the director of intelligence, ALLEN W. DULLES, the program had been conceived in 1955 after the Soviet Union had rejected President DWIGHT D. EISENHOWER's "Open Skies" proposal for mutual aerial surveillance. The U-2, designed and built by Lockheed Aircraft, could fly for extended periods at very high altitudes and was capable of taking detailed photographs of Earth from that altitude.

Following a training period in the United States, Powers was assigned to a U-2 squadron stationed at Incirclick Air Force Base in Turkey. In late 1956, the squadron, publicly identified as a weather observation group, began flights over the Soviet Union and the Middle East. Powers flew over the Mediterranean Sea to monitor naval movements during the Suez Crisis. He also flew a number of missions over the Soviet Union and Eastern Europe. The U-2 overflights proved extremely successful in supplying the United States with intelligence data. The Soviet military soon became aware of the flights but could not stop them, because its fighter planes could not reach the altitude at which the U-2s flew. By 1958, the Soviet Union had begun firing missiles at the planes but failed to hit any. Unwilling to admit publicly that they were unable to prevent such overflights, the Soviets never revealed their existence.

On May 1, 1960, Powers embarked on a flight from Peshawar, Pakistan, to Bodø, Norway. A near miss by a Soviet surface-to-air missile badly damaged the fragile plane, which crashed near the city of Sverdlovsk. Powers bailed out of the plane and was captured. Although the plane had been equipped with self-destruction devices and Powers supplied with a pin soaked in shellfish toxin to commit suicide, he used neither.

The CIA became nervous after losing contact with Powers. On May 2, officials announced, through the National Aeronautics and Space Administration (NASA), that a weather observation plane had been lost over Turkey. Three days later, however, the Soviet premier, Nikita S. Khrushchev, disclosed that the Soviets had shot down an American reconnaissance plane. He charged that the flight was "an aggressive provocation" aimed at wrecking the forthcoming summit conference scheduled to take place in Paris later that month. Khrushchev asked if the flight had been authorized by Eisenhower or was an independent act of "Pentagon militarists."

Convinced that if the plane had been shot down there was no chance that the pilot could survive, American officials denied the Soviet charges and continued to claim that the craft was a weather plane that had gone off course. On May 7, Khrushchev announced that Powers was alive and had confessed to having been on an intelligence mission sponsored by the CIA. Khrushchev also displayed five photos (actually counterfeits) that he claimed had been developed from film found in the wreckage.

Following the Soviet disclosures, the State Department admitted that Powers had been on a spy mission. Secretary of State CHRISTIAN HERTER and Vice President RICHARD M. NIXON defended the flights as necessary to prevent a surprise attack by the Soviet Union and implied that the flights would continue. Despite pressure to fire Allen Dulles, Eisenhower, who did not like scapegoats, took personal responsibility for the U-2 flights at a press conference on May 11.

Upon arriving in Paris on the eve of the scheduled summit, Khrushchev demanded that Eisenhower apologize for the flights or he would cancel the conference. Eisenhower announced that he had ended the flights but accused Khrushchev of using the issue to torpedo the summit. He refused to discuss the subject further. When the summit conference convened on May 16, Khrushchev blustered and the Soviets walked out; the summit broke up before it got under way. Shortly thereafter, the Soviet Union withdrew its invitation to Eisenhower to visit the country. The U-2 incident and the collapse of the Paris summit marked the end of a period of improved relations between the United States and the USSR that had followed Khrushchev's visit to the United States in 1959.

Charged with espionage against the Soviet Union, Powers pleaded guilty at his public trial in Moscow on August 17. He testified to details of the U-2 program and said that he was "deeply repentant" and "profoundly sorry" for his role in the overflights. Although the charge carried a death sentence, he received a sentence of three years' imprisonment and seven years of hard labor. As a result of his behavior at the trial and his failure to activate the aircraft's self-destruct equipment, Powers came under some criticism in the United States. Some also criticized him for not using the suicide pin.

On February 10, 1962, the Soviets exchanged Powers and an American student, Frederic Pryor, for a Soviet spy, Rudolf Abel (KGB Colonel Vilyam Fisher). Upon his release, Powers again faced criticism for his actions after his plane was hit. After extensive debriefing by the CIA, Lockheed, and the air force, Powers appeared on March 6, 1962, before a select committee of the Senate Armed Services Committee, chaired by Senator RICHARD RUSSELL (D-Ga.). The committee determined that Powers had followed orders, divulged no critical information, and conducted himself "as a fine young man under dangerous circumstances."

Powers left the CIA in October 1962 and joined Lockheed as a test pilot. He worked there until 1970, when he coauthored a book about the incident, *Operation Overflight: A Memoir of the U-2 Incident*. During the 1970s, he piloted a helicopter and reported on traffic for the radio station KGIL in Los Angeles. In late 1976, he joined KNBC, a television station, where he piloted a helicopter to report on fires, police chases, and other news. He died when his helicopter crashed while he was covering a brush fire in Los Angeles on August 1, 1977.

—MSM

Prettyman, E(lijah) Barrett

(1891–1971) *U.S. Court of Appeals judge*

Born in Lexington, Virginia, on August 23, 1891, Prettyman graduated from Randolph-Macon College in 1910 and received an M.A. from the same institution a year later. Following his graduation from Georgetown University Law School in 1915, he was admitted to the bar in Virginia and practiced law in Hopewell from 1915 to 1917. He served in the army during World War I and, after his discharge as a captain, became a special attorney for the Internal Revenue Department from 1919 to 1920, when he returned to private law practice in Washington, D.C. For the next 25 years, he alternated between private practice and government service as general counsel of the Bureau of Internal Revenue (1933–34) and as corporation counsel of the District of Columbia (1934–36). During this period, he also taught taxation at Georgetown University Law School.

In 1945, Prettyman was appointed judge of the U.S. Court of Appeals for the District of Columbia. Sitting on that court, through which much litigation involving the government passed, Prettyman wrote several important decisions involving internal security and constitutional rights. In 1952, he wrote the majority opinion in a decision upholding the Subversive Activities Control Act of 1950, known as the McCarran Act, which required the Communist Party to register as a subversive organization dominated by the Soviet Union.

During the Eisenhower administration, Prettyman wrote several important opinions involving

the conduct of congressional investigations of communist subversion and the rights of the Communist Party. In July 1954, speaking for the majority, he dismissed the key count in the perjury indictment of Professor Owen Lattimore, an adviser to the State Department whose leftist views had brought him under the scrutiny of Senator JOSEPH R. MCCARTHY (R-Wis.). When Lattimore appeared before Senator PAT MCCARRAN's Internal Security Subcommittee in 1952, he told the subcommittee that he had never been a "sympathizer or any other kind of promoter of Communism or Communist interests." McCarran pressed the Justice Department to bring charges of perjury based on that statement and several other, more specific statements. Judge Luther Youngdahl of the U.S. District Court for the District of Columbia dismissed four of the seven counts. Writing for the court of appeals, Prettyman restored two of the four counts dismissed by Youngdahl. On the key count, that Lattimore had denied having been a communist sympathizer, Prettyman held that the charge was "void for vagueness," because neither the indictment nor the statute defined "sympathizer."

In December 1954, Prettyman wrote the majority opinion in *Communist Party v. Subversive Activities Control Board*, which upheld the Internal Security Act of 1950. The ruling affirmed an order by the Subversive Activities Control Board (SACB) that the Communist Party register with the Justice Department as a communist-action organization. The decision upheld the provision of the act requiring registration of the Communist Party. Describing the American Communist Party as part of a world communist movement whose purpose was the "destruction of all presently existing national governments" and "the establishment of a world dictatorship under Communist auspices," Prettyman ruled that the act constituted a reasonable exercise by Congress of its power to protect the nation against a worldwide communist conspiracy. In addition, the decision held valid the administrative procedures set forth in the Internal Security Act. The court further ruled that the act did not violate the First or Fifth Amendment. According to the decision, the law did not unconstitutionally impinge on freedom of speech because "the right to unimpeded expression of views does not apply to unimpeded conduct," and "a purpose to establish a totalitarian dictatorship is a program of action rather than of mere discussion. It can be met with action by the government." The statute did not violate the right against self-incrimination, declared Prettyman, since revealed membership in the Communist Party was not, in itself, a violation of any criminal statute. The Supreme Court overturned the Court of Appeals for the District of Columbia in 1956 on the ground that it had erred in not granting the Communist Party's motion to reopen the case for reconsideration of the reliability of evidence offered by tainted witnesses.

After rehearing the matter, the SACB issued a revised report in December 1956 that once again ordered the Communist Party to register. The board denied a petition by the Communist Party to examine reports made to the FBI by four of the attorney general's witnesses. The court of appeals reversed and remanded the case to the board with an order to make the reports available to the Communist Party.

Prettyman became chief judge in 1958. Not long after that, the Communist Party's litigation against the Internal Security Act returned to the court of appeals. After further administrative proceedings, the SACB once again ordered the Communist Party to register. In July 1959, with Prettyman in the majority, the court once again affirmed the ruling of the Subversive Activities Control Board.

Prettyman retired as chief judge in December 1960 but continued to sit on the court. During the Kennedy administration, he served on several presidential panels, including the President's Advisory Commission on Narcotics and Drug Abuse and the Administrative Conference formed to recommend improvement in the administration of federal agencies. Prettyman also headed the board of inquiry that investigated the conduct of FRANCIS GARY POWERS, the pilot of a U-2 plane shot down over the Soviet Union, while he was held prisoner by the Soviets. In *Communist Party v. United States* (1967), Prettyman wrote a separate concurring opinion when the Court of Appeals reversed the conviction of the Communist Party for failing to register under the provisions of the Internal Security Act. The majority opinion found the provisions

of the statute "hopelessly at odds" with the Fifth Amendment, because it singled out the Communist Party for subjection to the "combined sanction of compelled disclosure and criminal punishment." Prettyman died in Washington, D.C., on August 4, 1971.

—MSM

Proxmire, (Edward) William
(1915–2005) *U.S. senator*

The son of a prominent surgeon in Chicago, Proxmire was born in Lake Forest, Illinois, on November 11, 1915. He attended the Hill School in Pottstown, Pennsylvania, and received his B.A. from Yale in 1938. After earning a masters degree in business administration from Harvard in 1940, he took an entry-level job with J. P. Morgan in New York. After the Japanese attack on Pearl Harbor, he enlisted in the army and served in the army Counterintelligence Corps. Discharged as a lieutenant in 1946, he resumed graduate study and received a second master's degree, in public administration, from Harvard in 1948. The following year, Proxmire moved to Wisconsin. He worked as a reporter and political analyst for the *Capital Times* in Madison from 1949 to 1950, when he was fired. He worked briefly for a union newspaper and had a weekly radio show sponsored by the American Federation of Labor. In 1950, he defeated a six-term incumbent in the Democratic primary and the Republican nominee in the general election for a seat in the state assembly. As assemblyman, Proxmire distinguished himself by criticizing the tactics used by Senator JOSEPH R. MCCARTHY (R-Wis.) in his investigations of domestic subversion. During the 1950s, Proxmire ran unsuccessfully for governor three times; he lost to WALTER KOHLER in 1952 and 1954 and to Vernon Thompson in 1956.

When McCarthy died in May 1957, Proxmire won the Democratic nomination and defeated Kohler in the special election that August. Most observers had predicted that Kohler would win easily, but Proxmire conducted an intense, energetic campaign. His platform called for closing corporate tax loopholes and raising personal exemptions. He also promised to increase farm incomes by raising price supports and advocated lower lending rates.

Proxmire attacked President DWIGHT D. EISEN-HOWER rather than Kohler and won an upset victory that made him the first Democratic senator from Wisconsin in 25 years. He won reelection in 1958, 1964, 1970, 1976, and 1982.

In the Senate, Proxmire established a reputation as a maverick. A loner, he was frequently at odds with members of his own party. Early in his first term, he clashed with the majority leader, LYN-DON B. JOHNSON (D-Tex.) over civil rights legislation. Proxmire thought Johnson had compromised too much on the Civil Rights Act of 1957. He also attacked Johnson's support of tax breaks for the oil industry. When Proxmire was passed over for a seat on the Banking and Currency Committee in February 1958, he denounced Johnson for his "unwholesome and arbitrary power" and demanded more frequent caucuses of the Democratic Party.

In many respects, Proxmire was a liberal. He supported civil rights legislation and voted for the Civil Rights Act of 1957. The following year, he joined an unsuccessful bipartisan effort to enact a measure granting the government greater powers to end school segregation. On other matters, he backed increased agricultural price supports, medical care for the elderly financed through Social Security, and reforms designed to tax corporate interest and dividends at their source. During his first year in Congress, Proxmire received a 100 percent rating from the AFL-CIO's Committee on Political Action. During the last years of Eisenhower's presidency, he voted against measures supported by the administration more frequently than any other Democrat in the Senate save one.

Proxmire favored housing and urban renewal measures. In March 1958, he and three other Democrats proposed lending $2 billion in construction funds to states and cities in order to combat the recession. He opposed Eisenhower's call for a partial federal withdrawal from urban renewal in early 1959. When the Banking and Currency Committee authorized $1 billion for more housing than Eisenhower had requested, Proxmire insisted on an even larger appropriation.

At the same time, he departed from his liberal colleagues on important issues. For example, Proxmire became known as a vocal opponent of government waste and favored a balanced budget.

Throughout the 1960s, Proxmire continued to irritate friend and foe alike. He opposed some of President JOHN F. KENNEDY's nominations because he detected a conflict of interest. He even filibustered against one for 19 hours. A fierce opponent of the war in Vietnam, he criticized the administrations of both Lyndon Johnson and RICHARD M. NIXON. During the 1970s, Proxmire carried on a widely publicized campaign against waste in federal government. In 1975, he began issuing press releases that announced a monthly Golden Fleece Award to bring attention to wasteful spending by the government. Proxmire's critics pointed out that some of his awards went to projects in basic science that led to important breakthroughs. Most basic research, they noted, could be made to look foolish. In spite of his opposition to government spending, he was a powerful advocate of the expensive system of dairy price supports, which benefited Wisconsin's large dairy industry. He also conducted a one-man campaign, beginning in 1967, to persuade the Senate to ratify the United Nations Genocide Convention, passed in 1948. He made daily speeches, over 3,000 of them, until the Senate ratified the treaty in 1986.

Proxmire chaired the Senate Banking Committee from 1975 to 1981 and again from 1987 until his retirement. He used the position to push for laws requiring lenders to disclose true rates of loans and advocated legislation giving consumers access to their credit ratings. In addition, he consistently pushed for more competition in the financial services industry.

Although generally a liberal, he earned the ire of feminists for his position on abortion (he was booed at a convention of feminists in 1982) and of fellow Democrats for his vote to confirm President Ronald W. Reagan's nomination of William H. Rehnquist to be chief justice of the Supreme Court. Proxmire remained best known for his ascetic approach to politics. Not only did he oppose wasteful and frivolous government spending, but he applied the same approach to his own activities. For a span of more than 20 years, from 1966 to 1988, he did not miss a roll call vote. In his last two campaigns, he accepted no contributions. During each of those campaigns, he spent less than $200, which he paid for out of his own pocket. He also paid for his own plane fares.

Many of his colleagues regarded him as a self-centered grandstander. Certainly, Proxmire stood out as something of an eccentric in the Senate. A physical culturist, he engaged in vigorous daily exercise and limited himself to a spartan diet. He reprimanded aides for eating junk food and published a book about fitness in 1973 titled *You Can Do It: Senator Proxmire's Exercise, Diet and Relaxation Plan.* Unusually concerned with his personal appearance, he had a well-publicized hair transplant and a facelift. At the same time, his frugality extended to his wardrobe, and he was known for wearing inexpensive suits. Declaring that he was "just too old," Proxmire did not stand for reelection in 1988. He resided in Washington, D.C., until Alzheimer's disease forced him to move to a nursing home in Sykesville, Maryland, where he died on December 15, 2005.

MSM

Pusey, Nathan M(arsh)

(1907–2001) president, Harvard University

Pusey was born in Council Bluffs, Iowa, on April 4, 1907. After attending public schools, he earned a scholarship to Harvard, where he graduated magna cum laude in 1928 with a B.A. in English. After touring France and Italy, he taught at Riverdale Country Day School in New York before entering graduate school at Harvard in 1931. He earned a master's degree in ancient history the following year and took up a fellowship at the American School of Classical Study in Athens, Greece. Pusey began teaching at Lawrence College, in Appleton, Wisconsin, in 1935. After completing his Ph.D. at Harvard in 1937, he taught Greek and ancient history at Scripps College and Wesleyan University before becoming president of Lawrence College in 1944. Although a Republican and normally apolitical, Pusey cosponsored a campaign tract opposing the reelection of Senator JOSEPH R. MCCARTHY (R-Wis.) in 1952. In June 1953, Pusey was named president of Harvard to succeed JAMES B. CONANT. The university announced that Pusey would reemphasize undergraduate education and the humanities.

McCarthy responded to Pusey's appointment by telling a reporter that "Harvard's loss is Wisconsin's gain" and that Pusey was "a rabid anti-anti-Communist," who hid "a combination of bigotry and intolerance behind a cloak of phony, hypocritical liberalism." Soon after Pusey assumed office, McCarthy attacked both Harvard and Pusey. In the spring of 1953, the House Un-American Activities Committee (HUAC) had conducted an investigation of Harvard. One witness, Wendell H. Furry, an associate professor of physics, had earlier appeared before HUAC and denied that he was a communist as of March 1, 1951, but invoked the Fifth Amendment regarding his activities before that date. Harvard retained Furry. In November 1953, McCarthy charged that a "smelly mess" existed at Harvard and alleged that "Communist professors" at the university exposed students to Marxist "indoctrination." In a telegram to Pusey, McCarthy asked what action the president intended to take in Furry's case. In January 1954, Furry appeared before McCarthy's subcommittee. The physics professor testified about his own activities but refused to discuss other people. McCarthy fumed, "To me it is inconceivable that a university which has the reputation of being a great university would keep this type of a creature on teaching our children." McCarthy described Harvard as "a privileged sanctuary for Fifth Amendment Communists" and called for the dismissal of four faculty members. His accusations played into stereotypes of Harvard and other elite colleges. John Fox, the publisher of the *Boston Post* and a Harvard graduate, referred to his alma mater as "Kremlin on the Charles."

Pusey responded by saying that he was "not aware" of any communists on the faculty and stated his opposition to employing communists. Both he and the dean of the faculty, McGeorge Bundy, refused to hire former members of the Communist Party for faculty or administrative positions. At the same time, Pusey stated that he did not regard pleading the Fifth Amendment "as confession of guilt."

Pusey served as Harvard's president for 18 years. A devout Episcopalian, he raised money for the divinity school and criticized the "almost idolatrous preoccupation with the secular order." There was, he said, an "almost desperate urgency" for religious education at Harvard. That view found little support among Harvard's faculty. Pusey oversaw a dramatic expansion of the university's physical plant; he built more than 30 new buildings that almost doubled the floor space of the university. During his presidency, Harvard's endowment grew from $304 million to over $1 billion. Moreover, Harvard, like other major universities, received more and more direct support for pure and applied research. Money from the federal government accounted for one-fourth of Harvard's operating income in 1960. Pusey also oversaw the implementation of need-blind admissions.

Despite these achievements, his last years as president were troubled ones. The student protest movement of the late 1960s confounded him. Angry students protesting the war in Vietnam twice forced Pusey to shut down the campus before the spring semester's scheduled conclusion. Pusey complained that "learning has almost ceased" in many universities because of the violent actions of "a small group of overeager young . . . who feel they have a special calling to redeem society." In 1969, students occupied University Hall, which housed most of the university's administrative offices, to protest the presence of ROTC on campus. Pusey summoned the Cambridge police, who evicted the protesters; in the process, 45 people were injured and 197 arrested. Pusey maintained that he had called in the police to protect "freedom within the university." "People cannot," he said, "use force or violence to interfere with the normal workings" of the university. In his mind, he fought "for the same principles" when he called in the police to prevent coercive attempts to disrupt the university as when he opposed McCarthy. Most faculty and students disagreed; the action destroyed Pusey's already tenuous support within the university. He retired as president in 1971.

After leaving Harvard, Pusey became president of the Andrew W. Mellon Foundation, a position he held from 1971 to 1975. He also served on the boards of several charitable organizations and, from 1979 to 1980, as president of the United States Board for Christian Higher Education in Asia. Pusey wrote two books, *The Age of the Scholar* (1963) and *American Higher Education, 1945–1970: A Personal Report* (1978). He died in New York City on November 14, 2001.

—MSM

Quarles, Donald A(ubrey)

(1894–1959) *assistant secretary of defense for research and development, secretary of the air force, deputy secretary of defense*

The son of a dentist, Quarles was born in Van Buren, Arkansas, on July 30, 1894. He graduated from high school at the age of 15. Already known for his enormous appetite for work, he taught school in his hometown while taking summer courses at the University of Missouri before entering Yale University at the age of 18. After receiving a B.A. in math and physics in 1917, he entered the army and saw action in France and Germany during World War I. After his discharge as a captain, he joined the division of Western Electric Company that later became Bell Telephone Laboratories and by 1940 was director of the Transmission Development Department, which included the company's radar program. During World War II, he directed the radar installation at Bell Laboratories and had responsibility for developments in telephone equipment for both military and commercial purposes. Quarles was appointed in 1946 to the Joint Research and Development Board's newly created Committee on Electronics; he became chair of the Committee on Electronics in 1949. In March 1952, he became vice president of Western Electric and president of Sandia Corporation, a subsidiary operating atomic research laboratories at White Sands, New Mexico.

Quarles was appointed assistant secretary of defense for research and development in 1953, an assignment that gave him responsibility for billions of dollars worth of missile and satellite programs. He oversaw programs to develop an intercontinental ballistic missile (ICBM), an intermediate range ballistic missile (IRBM), and an Earth-orbiting satellite.

Eisenhower chose Quarles as secretary of the air force in August 1955. Because Congress was in recess, Quarles received an interim appointment until Congress confirmed the nomination in February 1956. Known as an exceptionally hard worker, Quarles's major problem was to maintain American military superiority and proceed with new programs

President Einsenhower and Donald Quarles, December 23, 1958 *(Dwight D. Eisenhower Library and Museum)*

despite reductions in defense spending. Quarles had to press the development of new missiles without sacrificing American superiority in traditional weaponry, such as B-52 bombers. During an appearance before the House Appropriations Subcommittee in 1956, he testified that manned planes, rather than missiles, would be the air force's essential weapon for at least five more years. Heatedly defending the need for more bombers, he denied that the ICBM was some sort of ultimate weapon that ended the arms race and precluded the need for development of better conventional weapons. At the same time, the administration gave highest priority to development of both the ICBM and IRBM.

Quarles gained a reputation as a "hard-liner" who supported the administration's New Look defense policy. He insisted that mutual deterrence would not preclude American use of nuclear weapons and warned that no aggressor should presume that the United States would fight a war with conventional weaponry, at it had in Korea.

Although Quarles sought more money for the air force than the president requested, he defended the administration's pared-down military appropriations requests and assured members of Congress that American retaliatory capability was more secure than ever. He continued to emphasize, as he had through his tenure as secretary of the air force, that the American advantage in quality more than made up for any Soviet numerical superiority in planes or missiles. Nevertheless, Quarles and NATHAN F. TWINING, chief of staff of the air force, justified the air force's expenditure of nearly $1 bil-

lion that Congress had appended to the previous year's allocation for the air force. They maintained that, although Soviet production of bombers was proceeding at a slower rate than previously predicted, the Soviets were catching up and that the additional funds were needed.

In April 1957, Quarles was confirmed as deputy secretary of defense, the second-ranking civilian position in the Pentagon. At that post, he continued to assert that the United States retained superiority in ICBMs over the Soviet Union. He argued for a calm, rational response to the Soviet Union's successful launch of a satellite in the fall of 1957. At a series of meetings in the White House during late October 1957, Quarles defended the policy of not mixing the science and defense establishments, as the Soviet Union had done. While not minimizing the Soviet achievement, he saw nothing to indicate that the Soviets had a technological or military advantage over the United States and pointed out that the army thought that it could have launched a satellite a year earlier. Further, he stressed that the United States should not panic and accelerate its satellite program. Quarles took the same positions in public during a two-day investigation of the American missile and space program by a subcommittee of the House Appropriations Committee in November 1957. His pleas fell on deaf ears. In reaction to *Sputnik*, Congress increased funds for defense and space exploration.

Quarles died in his sleep of an apparent heart attack in Washington, D.C., on May 8, 1959.

—MSM

Radford, Arthur W(illiam)

(1896–1973) *chairman, Joint Chiefs of Staff*

The son of an electrical engineer, Radford was born in Chicago, Illinois, on February 27, 1896. As a child, he moved with his family first to Riverside, Illinois, and then to Grinnell, Iowa. After failing to gain an appointment at West Point, he entered the U.S. Naval Academy at Annapolis at the age of 16. Upon graduating in 1916, he saw action as an ensign on the battleship *South Carolina* during World War I. Following the war, Radford trained as a naval aviator and served in a variety of assignments. He was attached to the Bureau of Aeronautics from 1921 to 1923 and was stationed with aviation units aboard the USS *Aroostook*, the USS *Colorado*, and the USS *Pennsylvania* from 1923 to 1927. Radford served as a fighter squadron commander on the carrier *Saratoga* from 1929 to 1931. After several more assignments, he commanded the naval air station in Seattle, Washington, from 1937 to 1940 and served as executive officer of the carrier USS *Yorktown* from 1940 to 1941. Then, he served briefly with the Office of the Chief of Naval Operations, after which he established a naval air station at Trinidad, British West Indies. He became director of aviation training in the Bureau of Aeronautics in December 1941. Promoted to captain in January 1942, he remained director of aviation training until April 1943. In July 1943, Radford was promoted to rear admiral and given command of Carrier Division Eleven. From December 1943 to March 1944, he served as chief of staff for Admiral John Towers, commander of the Pacific Fleet's air forces. He was assigned to Washington, D.C., as assistant to the deputy chief of naval operations for air from December 1943 to March 1944. Radford became commander of Carrier Division Six in November 1944, a position he held to the end of the war. After a brief stint as air commander of the Pacific Fleet, he was promoted to vice admiral in January 1946. He was given command of the Second Task Fleet, Atlantic, in February 1947 and appointed vice chief of naval operations in January 1948. Radford opposed the unification of the armed forces in 1947 and, in the fall of 1949, was a leading figure in the revolt of the admirals against the Truman administration's emphasis on strategic air power. In April 1949, he was promoted to full admiral and took command of the Pacific Fleet.

During the Korean War, Radford had responsibility for all naval operations. A vigorous anticommunist who declared that the United States would not be secure as long as communists controlled mainland China, the admiral gained the support of powerful congressional Republicans such as Senator ROBERT TAFT of Ohio. When, after winning the presidential election in 1952, DWIGHT D. EISENHOWER made a trip to Korea, he met with Radford, who impressed him. Partly to placate the right wing of his party, Eisenhower selected Radford to be chairman of the Joint Chiefs of Staff in May 1953.

Radford was one of the chief architects of the Eisenhower administration's so-called New Look in defense policy. The Korean War convinced Radford

Admiral Arthur Radford, Chairman of the Joint Chiefs of Staff *(Dwight D. Eisenhower Library and Museum)*

against guerrilla warfare. Finally, they contended that the New Look did not provide a credible defense, because the United States would not be the first nation to use nuclear weapons in the event of hostilities.

Radford took a hard-line position toward Asian communism that was often at odds with Eisenhower's own policies. In March 1954, the French chief of staff, General Paul Henry Ely, requested immediate American aid to lift the communist siege of Dien Bien Phu in northern Vietnam. Eisenhower placed a series of conditions on American military assistance, including freedom for the associated states of French Indochina, British participation, and the involvement of at least some Southeast Asian nations. The French general went to Radford, who was more receptive, and they approved joint U.S.-French plans for an air strike against positions held by the Vietminh around Dien Bien Phu. Radford thought that Eisenhower might not be able to resist pressure to intervene as a French defeat became imminent.

On April 3, 1954, Dulles called a meeting at the State Department at which Radford outlined his plans for intervention to eight senior senators. The admiral had to admit that they did not have the unanimous support of the other chiefs and that the bombings could bring China into the war. The army chief of staff, General MATTHEW B. RIDGWAY, strongly dissented and maintained that the bombings would be inconclusive and might lead to the introduction of American troops. The senators shared Ridgway's skepticism toward the proposed operation. The following day, Radford met with Eisenhower, who rejected the admiral's proposal. Until the fall of Dien Bien Phu on May 7, Radford persisted in calling for the United States to intervene.

Radford took a similarly hard line when Chinese communist shore batteries began shelling the Nationalist-held islands of Quemoy and Matsu on September 3, 1954. Three days later, the joint chiefs, headed by Radford, voted three to one (with Ridgway dissenting) to recommend that Eisenhower authorize Chiang Kai-shek to bomb the mainland. If the Communists retaliated, the group suggested that U.S. forces be placed in the islands and that the United States

of the futility of engaging in conventional ground warfare. He also questioned the need to have American troops in western Europe when the United States had nuclear superiority over the Soviet Union. Based on these considerations, Radford, his fellow chiefs of staff, and Secretary of State JOHN FOSTER DULLES formulated a policy that stressed a reliance on air power, technology, and strategic nuclear weapons. Radford believed that the New Look had many advantages. First, American troops would not be called upon to fight unpopular wars, such as that in Korea. Second, having supersonic bombers armed with nuclear weapons ready to attack at any moment would deter Soviet and Chinese aggression. Third, the New Look enabled the administration to reduce defense budgets, since the weapons systems cost less than maintaining large numbers of conventional forces around the world.

Critics of the policy argued that it meant a return to unilateralism. They also maintained that the threat of nuclear attack would prove ineffective join the bombing raids. Radford believed that war between the United States and Communist China was inevitable and that it would be better to fight China when it was weak than wait until it had grown in strength. Eisenhower, however, thought that the islands had little strategic value and wanted to avoid a general war with China. By late October, when the Chinese appeared ready to launch an invasion, the chiefs still operated on the assumption that the United States would strike the mainland when the assault occurred. Eisenhower instructed them to abandon that assumption. If the Chinese invaded Taiwan, he wanted the Seventh Fleet to take defensive action while he called an emergency session of Congress. The president wanted no strike against the Chinese mainland without first consulting Congress.

In January 1955, when the Chinese shelled the Tachen Islands (200 miles to the north of Taiwan), Radford once again urged the United States to bomb the mainland. Eisenhower rejected Radford's recommendation. In the spring of 1955, Eisenhower tried to defuse the crisis by suggesting that Chiang reduce the number of his troops on Quemoy and Matsu, a gesture that he hoped the mainland Chinese might reciprocate. Eisenhower sent Radford and Assistant Secretary of State Walter Robertson to present the plan to the Nationalist leader, who rejected it. In the end, however, the Communists reduced their shelling of the islands and, by the middle of May 1955, ended it.

Radford also took a hard line toward the Soviet Union and publicly opposed any attempt at a disarmament agreement with the Soviets. In May 1957, shortly before he retired, Radford dismissed the possibility with the comment, "we cannot trust the Russians on . . . anything." At a press conference, Eisenhower made a point of saying that "it seems to me that the more any intelligent man thinks about the possibilities of war today, the more he would understand you have got to work on this business of disarmament."

A man with a tough, no-nonsense manner, Radford remained a controversial figure throughout his career. Although acknowledged as a brilliant naval officer, his tendency to dominate those around him drew criticism, as did his tendency to portray his own views as those of the chiefs of staff.

Following his retirement in 1957, Radford served on government committees to study military aid and the merchant marine. He also served on the boards of directors of several corporations. Radford served as Vice President RICHARD M. NIXON's military adviser during the presidential campaign of 1960. Four years later, Radford again was an adviser to the Republican presidential candidate, Senator BARRY GOLDWATER (R-Ariz.). Radford died in Bethesda, Maryland, on August 17, 1973.

—MSM

Rand, Ayn
(1905–1982) *writer*

Born Alisa Zinovévna Rozenbaum in Saint Petersburg, Russia, on February 2, 1905, Rand lived through the Russian Revolution during her school years. She supported the February Revolution in 1917 but denounced the Bolshevik Revolution from the outset. Victory for the Bolsheviks brought the confiscation of her father's pharmacy and her family's financial and social ruin. In 1921, she entered the University of Petrograd where she read history and from which she graduated in 1924. That same year, she entered the State Institute for Cinema Arts to study screenwriting. She went to the United States in 1926 on a temporary visa to visit relatives in Chicago and never returned to Russia. Before long, she moved to Hollywood, where she found work as an extra, a filing clerk, office head of the wardrobe department, and a scriptwriter. She became a naturalized citizen in 1931.

Between 1932 and 1942, she produced two novels, three plays, and numerous movie scripts. She sold her first screenplay, *Red Pawn*, to Universal Studios in 1932. Her first stage play, staged in Hollywood as *Woman on Trial*, was later performed in New York as *The Night of January 16th*. She moved to New York in 1935, when her play began its run, and worked as a secretary for an architectural firm. Rand completed her first novel, *We the Living*, in 1933. It depicted the brutality of life under communist rule in the Soviet Union. Numerous publishers rejected it before the Macmillan Company published it in 1936. American reviewers and intellectuals responded coolly to the play's anticommunist message. She published a second novel, *Anthem*, in 1938.

Published by Bobbs-Merrill in 1943 after being rejected by 12 other publishers, her third novel, *The Fountainhead*, received generally unfavorable reviews but became a best seller. Set in an architectural firm, the book dramatized her own philosophy, which came to be known as objectivism. Rand held that all virtue stemmed from individual creativity and that the egotistical pursuit of rationally defined self-interest accounted for all great achievements. She maintained, however, that in the 20th century mass democracy, egalitarianism, and the altruistic ideals of Christianity all militated against individual genius. Rand identified the theme of *The Fountainhead* as "individualism versus collectivism, not in politics, but in man's soul," and its purpose as "a defense of egoism in its real meaning."

The novel's hero, Howard Roark, has so much talent and is such an individualist that his work, though brilliant, receives little recognition. He refuses to compromise his designs to satisfy clients and is eventually forced to take a job at a granite quarry. Upon his return to architecture, he is again thwarted by small-minded orthodoxy. When one of his designs is adulterated by mediocre minds, he dynamites the building. At his trial, Roark delivers an impassioned defense of the value of selfishness, the importance of creators, and the need to remain true to oneself. The jury acquits him.

Rand returned to Hollywood in 1943 to help write the screenplay for the film version of *The Fountainhead*. The movie, starring Gary Cooper and Patricia Neal, did not come out until 1949. When released, the film fared well at the box office, and Rand stayed in Hollywood to write screenplays for the Hal Wallis Studio.

A fervent anticommunist, Rand appeared before the House Un-American Activities Committee (HUAC) in 1947 to testify about the discrepancy between her own experiences and the way the film *Song of Russia* (1943) portrayed life in the Soviet Union. She also produced a pamphlet, called *Screen Guide for Americans*, designed for distribution to writers in Hollywood. It advised them not to smear industrialists or denigrate the free enterprise system in their scripts.

Rand moved to New York in 1951, where she devoted herself to her next novel, on which she had been working since 1943. Published in 1957, *Atlas Shrugged* tells the story of Dagny Taggart, a female railroad executive who, along with other creators, is hampered by government regulation and attempts to socialize major industries. A group of industrialists and other creators and innovators withdraw from a society dominated by social "parasites" and retire to a remote valley. The leader of this "strike of the mind," John Galt, goes on the airwaves to explain the strike. As the economy crumbles, the government offers to make Galt the economic dictator, but he refuses, even after being tortured. In an armed confrontation, Taggart and other strikers rescue Galt and retreat to the valley. Eventually, facing a state of collapse, the country is forced to call them back to positions of responsibility and respect.

Rand asserted "that man exists for his own sake" and "that the pursuit of his own happiness is his highest moral purpose." She advocated laissez-faire capitalism, which would guarantee free trade and, implicitly, the economic dominance of the creative elite. Philosophically, she placed total faith in reason. She held that "objective reality exists independently of any perceiver or of the perceiver's emotions, feelings, wishes, hopes, or fears." Further, the human mind was capable of grasping this reality and applying it to life. She rejected all religions because she thought that they limited individual capacities and impulses. "My philosophy," she wrote in the appendix to *Atlas Shrugged*, "in essence, is the concept of man as a heroic being, with his own happiness as the moral purpose of his life, with productive achievement as his noblest activity and reason as his only absolute."

Rand won a devout following for her ideas, and her novels continued to sell well. Her wide popularity gave her a platform to espouse her own ideology and to comment on political issues. After *Atlas Shrugged*, she turned to nonfiction to communicate her ideas. Usually identified as a conservative, she often differed from other theorists of the Right. Indeed, Rand and her followers often clashed with other conservatives, particularly those associated with WILLIAM F. BUCKLEY, JR., and his magazine, the *National Review*, which she called the "worst and most dangerous magazine in America." Reviewing *Atlas Shrugged* in the *National Review*, WHITTAKER CHAMBERS called the book "sophomoric" and "remarkably silly." Further, he asserted that it could be "called a novel only by devaluing the term." Most disturbing to Chambers, however, was what he described as the book's "antireligious gospel of philosophic materialism," which he contended argued for the same godless system as the Soviet Union. Garry Wills, the scholar and journalist, claimed that Rand was not a conservative at all; her characters worked from "the first principle of historical Liberalism . . . the immediate perfectibility of man." Because of intellectual differences and personal animosities, objectivism was not absorbed into the emerging conservative mainstream.

After 1960, Rand continued to write and expound on her philosophy in a number of books: *For the New Intellectual* (1961), *The Virtue of Selfishness* (1964), *Capitalism: The Unknown Ideal* (1966), *Introduction to Objectivist Epistemology* (1967), *The Romantic Manifesto* (1971), *The New Left: The Anti-Industrial Revolution* (1971), and *Philosophy, Who Needs It?* (1982). She held visiting lectureships at prestigious universities, including Yale, Princeton, and Columbia. Rand edited the *Objectivist Newsletter* from 1962 to 1965 and an expanded periodical, *The Objectivist*, from 1966 to 1971. She also edited the *Ayn Rand Letter* from 1971 to 1976. Through these publications, she expressed her own eclectic tastes (she loved both Rachmaninoff and Mickey Spillane). Her books and periodical writing elaborated on the ideas in her fiction; they also defended her fiction against critics. Throughout it all, Rand advocated individualism and capitalism while condemning religion.

She supported BARRY GOLDWATER's campaign for the presidency in 1964. During the 1970s, she attracted followers among college students and became something of a cult figure among libertarians. Rand, however, spurned libertarians as a "random collection of emotional hippies-of-the-right who seek to play at politics without a philosophy." She supported GERALD R. FORD for president in 1976 but opposed Ronald W. Reagan, whom she regarded as lacking a program or an "ideology of life." Further, she wrote, since Reagan "denies the right to abortion, he cannot be the defender of any rights."

However popular her novels, Rand probably would not have inspired a movement had it not

been for Nathaniel Branden, whom she met in 1950 when he was a student at UCLA and wrote her a fan letter. In the mid-1950s, they became lovers, even though both were married. Later Branden became the spokesperson for Rand's movement and her manager. In 1968, Rand learned that he had another lover and severed relations with him; she ordered her followers to do the same. The affair did not seem to disrupt Rand's marriage to Frank O'Connor. The couple, who wed in 1929, remained married until his death in 1979.

Rand had major surgery for cancer in 1975 and died in New York City on March 6, 1982.

—MSM

Randall, Clarence B(elden)

(1891–1967) *chairman, Commission on Foreign Economic Policy; special consultant to the president on foreign economic policy; special assistant to the president on foreign economic policy*

The son of a shopkeeper, Randall was born in Newark Valley, New York, on March 5, 1891. He studied at the Methodist-affiliated Wyoming Seminary in Kingston, Pennsylvania, from 1906 to 1908 and then attended Harvard University, from which he graduated Phi Beta Kappa in 1912. After earning an LL.B. at Harvard in 1915, his high ranking in his class earned him an offer from the prestigious New York law firm, Cadwalader, Wickersham & Taft. He turned down the offer and began practicing law with a cousin in Ishpeming, Michigan. His career was interrupted by service in the army during World War I. After enlisting, he served as a lieutenant and aide to a general in France. Randall returned to his practice after the war and in 1925 joined Inland Steel Company. After a visit to a coal mining camp in Wheelwright, Kentucky, where he found appalling conditions, Randall ordered that the camp be rebuilt to provide a higher standard of living. He became vice president of Inland Steel in 1930, president in 1949, and chairman of the board in 1953. Under his leadership, the company became, by 1952, the seventh-largest steelmaker in the United States.

During the postwar period, Randall served as a consultant on steel and coal to the Economic Cooperation Administration, created to implement the Marshall Plan. He also emerged as a leading spokesperson for the steel industry. While he frequently spoke against policies of the Roosevelt and Truman administrations that he regarded as "socialist" or "collectivist," he also insisted that industry respond to human needs. Early in his own career, Randall helped to draft Michigan's worker's compensation law. When President HARRY S. TRUMAN seized the steel mills in 1952, the leaders of the steel industry chose Randall as spokesperson for the nation's 92 steel companies. He became a national figure when he gave a speech carried on all television and radio networks in which he denounced Truman's action. The Supreme Court later declared Truman's seizure of the mills unconstitutional.

Randall became an important figure in the Eisenhower administration's attempts to encourage freer trade. In August 1953, President DWIGHT D. EISENHOWER appointed Randall to chair the 17-member Commission on Foreign Economic Policy, known as the Randall Commission. The commission's report, issued in January 1954, recommended that Eisenhower extend the reciprocal trade program for three years. It also advised a reduction of tariffs "on products which are not being imported or which are being imported in negligible volume" to 50 percent of the rates in effect on January 1, 1945, even without reciprocal concessions. Finally, it called for a reduction to 50 percent ad valorem any tariff rate in excess of that figure.

The Randall Commission also proposed a revision of foreign economic policy. It suggested giving grants to countries unable to maintain their own security while making loans to nations in need of economic aid. Although supporting the ban on exports to Communist China and North Korea as well as efforts to block trade in military materials with eastern Europe, the panel recommended increased trade with eastern Europe to "serve to penetrate the Iron Curtain and advance the day when normal relationships with . . . Eastern Europe may be resumed." Further, the commission's report argued, such trade would benefit the economies of western Europe.

Both foreign and domestic officials greeted the report with favor. Impressed with Randall's work, Eisenhower appointed him as a special consultant to the White House to help formulate trade legislation. Not all reaction was favorable, though. In March 1954, 17 economic experts at a conference on U.S. foreign economic policy held at Princeton University attacked the panel's recommendations. They charged that the report failed to consider long-term questions in American foreign economic policy, such as European integration, and they faulted it for ignoring the domestic recession and particular problems involved in American trade with underdeveloped nations.

Congress, too, proved reluctant to accept the commission's recommendations. Eisenhower proposed a three-year extension of the Reciprocal Trade Act, instead of the usual one-year extension, and asked for authority to cut tariffs more deeply. Congress blocked the program in 1954. After a bitter struggle, Eisenhower signed legislation in 1955 that provided for the extension of reciprocal trade agreements and implementation of tariff cuts over a three-year period.

Randall retired as chair of the board of directors of Inland Steel in April 1956, but he continued to serve as a consultant to the government. In July, he was appointed special assistant on foreign economic policy, and he later became chair of the President's Council on Foreign Economic Policy. In that position, he criticized American business leaders for failing to act more aggressively to prevent Soviet economic penetration of underdeveloped nations. In May 1958, Randall proposed a liberalization of travel restrictions between communist and Western nations to ease tensions. Eisenhower applauded the recommendation as a "powerful influence on behalf of peace."

Randall continued to serve as a consultant to government during the administration of JOHN F. KENNEDY. From 1961 to 1963, he headed a presidential panel reviewing federal pay schedules and in 1963 became chairman of the State Department's advisory committee on international business problems. President LYNDON B. JOHNSON awarded him the Presidential Medal of Freedom in 1963. Randall expressed his views in a number of books, including *A Creed for Free Enterprise* (1952), *A Foreign Economic Policy for the United States* (1954), *Over My Shoulder* (1956), *The Communist Challenge to American Business* (1959), *The Folklore of Management* (1961), and

The Executive in Transition (1967). After suffering a heart attack, Randall died in Ishpeming, Michigan, on August 4, 1967.

—MSM

Randolph, A(sa) Philip
(1889–1979) *president, Brotherhood of Sleeping Car Porters*

The son of a minister in the African Methodist Episcopal Church, A. Philip Randolph was born in Crescent City, Florida, on April 15, 1889. He graduated from the Cookman Institute (later Bethune-Cookman College) in Jacksonville, Florida, in 1911 and, frustrated by the economic limitations he faced in the south, joined the prewar migration of southern African Americans to New York City. He worked at various jobs while taking night courses in political science, economics, and philosophy at City College of New York. Randolph joined the Socialist Party soon after his arrival in New York and in 1917 cofounded *The Messenger*, which was, according to its slogan, the "only magazine of scientific radicalism in the world published by Negroes." The magazine reflected the pacifism of its founders and opposed American participation in World War I. It also urged African Americans to demand better wages and working conditions in wartime industries. In addition, the publishers concluded that African Americans could achieve full citizenship rights only through force, either economic or physical. At this time, Randolph also began his lifelong association with the trade union movement. During World War I, he attempted to unionize black shipyard workers in Virginia and organized a small local for elevator operators in New York City.

During the 1920s, *The Messenger* began publishing the work of young black writers and poets and became an important voice of the Harlem Renaissance. In 1925, Randolph began a campaign to unionize the employees on Pullman sleeping cars. *The Messenger* became the official organ of the Brotherhood of Sleeping Car Porters. After a 12-year struggle, the Brotherhood of Sleeping Car Porters gained recognition from the Pullman Company in 1937. By that time, Randolph had emerged as one of the nation's most prominent black lead-

ers. He served as president of the National Negro Congress in 1935.

After World War II broke out in Europe and the United States prepared for the possibility of war, many Americans found work in defense industries. Discrimination, however, often barred African Americans from such jobs. In 1941, Randolph's threat to organize a march on Washington by over 50,000 African Americans persuaded a reluctant President Franklin D. Roosevelt to issue an executive order banning racial discrimination in defense plants and government employment. The order also created a temporary Fair Employment Practices Committee (FEPC).

After World War II, the emerging cold war led President HARRY S. TRUMAN to ask Congress for a peacetime draft. Randolph turned his attention on desegregation of the armed services. His campaign, along with the defection of southern delegates from the Democratic convention in 1948, pressed Truman to issue an executive order ending segregation in the military.

When Randolph brought the Brotherhood of Sleeping Car Porters into the American Federation of Labor (AFL) in 1935, many unions in the AFL excluded African Americans. Beginning that year, Randolph annually introduced a resolution at the AFL convention calling on the group both to devote more energy to organizing black workers and to expel member locals that continued to discriminate. Randolph's eloquent words and resonant baritone voice failed to sway the delegates. Indeed, many delegates chose to leave the convention hall during Randolph's yearly appearance at the podium. William Green and GEORGE MEANY, who succeeded Green as president in 1952, defended the AFL's policy, established by Samuel Gompers, that left racial policies exclusively to the locals.

When JOHN L. LEWIS, president of the United Mine Workers and one of the few white leaders of organized labor to oppose racial discrimination, walked out of the AFL and formed the Congress of Industrial Organizations (CIO), Randolph went with him. The AFL merged with the CIO in 1955, and the constitution of the new AFL-CIO contained a strong antidiscrimination provision. A vice president of the merged union, Randolph demanded immediate enforcement of the antidiscrimination policy. At the executive council meeting in 1956, he moved that the AFL bar the Brotherhood of Locomotive Firemen and Engineers, known for its discrimination against African Americans, until the union ended its racist policies. Meany, who preferred to work behind the scenes to end discrimination, opposed the motion. The executive council supported Meany's position.

Randolph's advocacy of racial equality repeatedly led him into conflict with the merged union's leadership. At the national convention in 1959, Randolph introduced a resolution to deny entry to the International Longshoremen's Association. Meany indignantly asked Randolph why he had not first discussed the proposal with the executive council. The president then reprimanded Randolph for not "playing on the team" and advised Randolph to sit "a little closer to the trade union movement and pay a little less attention to outside organizations." A few moments later, Randolph introduced another resolution calling for the expulsion of two railroad brotherhoods if they did not cease discriminating within six months. Meany, who supported gradual desegregation, opposed the time limit. He warned Randolph that integration might not be achieved in their lifetime. Randolph then introduced a third resolution calling for the expulsion of member unions charged with racism. Meany then exploded, "Who the hell appointed you the guardian of all the Negroes in America?" Randolph responded, "Brother President, let's not get emotional."

Meany's outburst publicized the problem of racism in labor unions. Although Randolph and Meany sought to downplay the incident, their rift persisted. In 1960, Randolph and other black unionists formed the Negro American Labor Council (NALC) to fight for change within the AFL, and Randolph became its first president. In October 1961, the AFL-CIO censured him for once again urging the union to take disciplinary action against segregated unions. Meany told the press, "We can only get moving on civil rights if he comes to our side and stops throwing bricks at us."

During the four years he held the presidency of the NALC, Randolph sought persistently to combat racism in the labor movement from within the AFL-CIO. This placed him in an increasingly sensitive position. The AFL-CIO's leadership took offense at Randolph's efforts to eliminate racist policies by member unions; younger militants in the black labor organization wanted to adopt a more confrontational posture toward the AFL-CIO and challenged Randolph's leadership. At its convention in 1961, the AFL-CIO effectively rescinded the censure of Randolph and passed a resolution in support of civil rights. In November 1962, Randolph opposed a campaign, sponsored by the NAACP, to decertify trade union locals that discriminated against minority workers. Randolph's position was that "we must carry out our fight within the house of labor."

Randolph worked closely with other civil rights leaders during the 1950s and 1960s. He was an organizer of the Prayer Pilgrimage in support of civil rights legislation in 1957. He sponsored a Youth March for Integrated Schools in both 1958 and 1959. In 1963, he was an organizer of the March On Washington, at which MARTIN LUTHER KING, JR., delivered his famous speech proclaiming his dream of racial equality.

Nevertheless, Randolph took a different approach from most black leaders of that era. While King and ROY WILKINS agitated for civil rights, Randolph fought for the elimination of economic barriers faced by African Americans. A socialist and a dedicated trade unionist, he focused on economic solutions to America's racial problems.

Randolph enthusiastically supported LYNDON B. JOHNSON's equalize war on poverty and opposed American intervention in Vietnam because it diverted funds from programs designed to reduce or eliminate poverty. At the Democratic National Convention in 1964, Randolph supported a compromise, sponsored by Johnson, that would have allowed the Mississippi Freedom Democratic Party (MFDP) two seats. The MFDP, which challenged the all-white delegation from Mississippi, rejected the compromise. By the end of the 1960s, younger, more militant members of the Civil Rights movement eclipsed Randolph, and some dismissed him as an Uncle Tom. In September 1968, an aged and ailing Randolph retired as president of the Brotherhood of Sleeping Car Porters. He died in New York City on May 16, 1979.

—MSM

Rankin, J(ames) Lee

(1907–1996) *solicitor general*

Born in Hartington, Nebraska, on July 8, 1907, Rankin attended public schools and earned his B.A. from the University of Nebraska in 1928. He received his LL.B. from the same institution in 1930. Upon graduating from law school, he joined a law firm in Lincoln, Nebraska, and became a partner in 1935. In the late 1930s, he developed an interest in Republican politics. In 1948, Rankin served as Nebraska manager for the presidential campaign of Thomas E. Dewey. Four years later, he chaired Dwight D. Eisenhower's election committee in Nebraska. After winning the presidency, Eisenhower appointed Rankin assistant attorney general in charge of the office of legal counsel, where Rankin worked under his friend and fellow Nebraskan, Attorney General Herbert Brownell.

Rankin served as chief adviser to Brownell in the formation of legal policy from 1953 to 1956. Since the Eisenhower administration had not yet appointed a solicitor general, Rankin appeared before the Supreme Court, in December 1953, as an amicus curiae in *Brown v. Board of Education*. Representing the U.S. government's position, he supported the position of the black plaintiffs that segregated public schools violated the equal protection clause of the Fourteenth Amendment. The Supreme Court struck down segregated public schools in May 1954. In other matters, Rankin helped draft legal opinions on the questions of U.S. agricultural trade with the Soviet Union and on presidential succession. He also played an instrumental role in resolving conflicting claims by western states to the Colorado River.

Eisenhower announced Rankin's appointment as solicitor general in August 1956. Because of his role in *Brown* and his close identification with civil rights, many observers thought that southern senators might block his confirmation, but the Senate approved Rankin's nomination in May 1957. As solicitor general, Rankin had responsibility for all government briefs and arguments in cases before the Supreme Court. He also decided which cases the government would appeal; only the attorney general could overrule his decisions. During the Supreme Court term in 1956–57, Rankin argued for the government in several cases arising from

congressional investigations of alleged communist activities. He argued unsuccessfully that the Court should sustain the conviction of John T. Watkins, an organizer for the United Automobile Workers, for contempt of Congress arising from his refusal to divulge the names of persons linked with communist activities. Later that year, he argued, again unsuccessfully, to uphold the conviction of Julius Shields under the Smith Act.

During 1957 and 1958, Rankin became embroiled in the dispute over whether the states or the federal government owned tidelands oil. In December 1957, Eisenhower reaffirmed his support for the Submerged Lands Act of 1953, which gave states jurisdiction offshore up to the three-mile limit. Eisenhower further stated that he hoped the Court would rule in favor of Texas's claims of ownership beyond that point. Rankin supported the opposing view, maintaining that the federal government was entitled to oil revenues from drilling beyond the three-mile limit. Two days after Eisenhower's statement, Attorney General William P. Rogers overruled Rankin and gave assurances that the Justice Department's final brief would not conflict with the president's position.

Rankin pressed for implementation of a court order desegregating Central High School in Little Rock, Arkansas. In August 1957, he argued that delaying desegregation on the basis of segregationist sentiment within the community would breed disrespect for the law and lead to violence. The Supreme Court upheld this view and ordered the immediate desegregation of Central High School. The following year, Rankin joined Thurgood Marshall, the lead attorney for the NAACP's Legal Defense Fund, in urging immediate desegregation of Little Rock's remaining high schools. The Supreme Court again upheld the solicitor general's position. In March 1960, Rankin brought a challenge to a law passed by Alabama's state legislature that had redrawn the boundaries of Tuskegee, Alabama, effectively to exclude black voters. The Supreme Court struck down the law in 1961.

With the end of the Eisenhower administration, Rankin entered private practice in New York City. He represented the American Civil Liberties Union when it acted as a friend of the court in *Gideon v. Wainwright* (1962), in which the Supreme

Court held that an indigent person accused of a crime had a right to be provided legal counsel at public expense. In 1963 and 1964, he served as general counsel to the President's Commission to Investigate the Assassination of President Kennedy (generally known as the Warren Commission). In December 1965, JOHN V. LINDSAY, the mayor-elect, named Rankin corporation counsel for New York City, a position he held from 1966 to 1972, when he resigned to enter practice with his son. Rankin also taught constitutional law at New York University Law School. He retired in 1978 and moved to Weston, Connecticut. In 1993, he moved to Los Gatos, California, where, beginning in 1995, he suffered a series of strokes. He died in Santa Cruz, California, on June 26, 1996.

—MSM

Rankin, Karl L(ott)

(1898–1991) *ambassador to Taiwan, ambassador to Yugoslavia*

The son of a clergyman, Rankin was born in Manitowoc, Wisconsin, on September 4, 1898. He grew up in Topeka, Kansas, and graduated from Mercersburg Academy in Pennsylvania in 1916. After serving in the navy during World War I, he attended the California Institute of Technology. He studied engineering at Zurich's Federal Polytechnic Institute in 1920 and 1921 and received a B.S. in civil engineering from Princeton University in 1922. After graduating, he served as a field engineer in Turkey and supervised construction for the Near East Relief in the USSR (Caucasus region) from 1922 to 1925. He managed a real estate development company from 1925 to 1927.

In 1927, Rankin began a career in the foreign service as assistant trade commissioner in Prague. During the 1930s and 1940s, he served as commercial attaché and counselor for economic affairs in various European capitals. He was in Brussels when the Nazis overran Belgium in 1940. That same year, he achieved the rank of consul. In 1941, he was in Belgrade when the Luftwaffe bombed the city. When the Japanese attacked Pearl Harbor and invaded the Philippines in December 1941, Rankin was in Manila and was interned by the Japanese. After 21 months in detention, he was repatriated in an exchange of prisoners. He then served in Cairo and Athens (1944–45, 1947–49), Belgrade (1945–46), and Vienna (1946–47). In 1948, he became a career minister, the highest rank for nonpolitical appointees in the State Department. Rankin was transferred to the Far East in 1949, where he held the post of consul general in Canton, Hong Kong, and Macao. From 1950 to 1953, he was minister and chargé d'affaires at Taipei. In February 1953, President DWIGHT D. EISENHOWER named Rankin ambassador to Nationalist China (Taiwan).

As ambassador, Rankin supported the American commitment to defend Taiwan against an invasion by the Chinese Communists, but he opposed American aid to the Nationalist effort to maintain possession of the offshore islands of Quemoy and Matsu. As early as October 1953, he encouraged Chiang's government to formulate a mutual security pact with the United States, and in July 1954 he conducted negotiations for such an agreement. After Communist China began shelling Quemoy and Matsu in September 1954, Rankin attempted to minimize the islands' importance. When the Joint Chiefs of Staff recommended military action against Communist China over the incident, Eisenhower declined to take such action and pressed for the conclusion of a mutual defense pact with the Nationalists. Rankin supported the president's position. He reported to Washington that the Nationalist strategy was to "exaggerate the military danger" of a Communist conquest of Quemoy and Matsu as a means of gaining more American aid and warned the Nationalist foreign minister, George Yeh, against precipitating war with the mainland over the islands. The mutual security pact was finally signed in December 1954.

When Secretary of State JOHN FOSTER DULLES made a trip to Taipei in February 1955, Nationalist leaders told him how vital the islands were to Taiwan's defense. Rankin cabled the State Department that Yeh "may have exaggerated their importance." Rankin maintained that the loss of the islands would be "very serious but not necessarily disastrous." Significantly, Dulles, who advocated action against the mainland, failed to consult Rankin during his visit.

Rankin was not successful in cultivating the goodwill of the population of Taiwan. On May 24,

1957, he was mobbed during anti-American riots at the American embassy following the murder of a peeping tom by an American solider. Thirty-three thousand Nationalist troops restored order the following day.

Rankin became ambassador to Yugoslavia in January 1958. He served at that post until 1961, when he resigned from the diplomatic corps. In 1964, he published his autobiography, *China Assignment*. He died in Kennebunk, Maine, on January 15, 1991.

—MSM

Rauh, Joseph L(ouis)

(1911–1992) *lawyer, national chairman, Americans for Democratic Action*

The son of a German immigrant who had established a business manufacturing shirts, Rauh was born in Cincinnati, Ohio, on January 3, 1911. He graduated from Harvard College magna cum laude in 1932 and Harvard Law School, where he finished first in his class, in 1935. Rauh then served as law clerk at the Supreme Court, first to Justice Benjamin Cardozo and then to Justice FELIX FRANKFURTER. He also worked for several New Deal agencies. Commissioned a lieutenant in 1942, Rauh served on the staff of the army's Pacific Command and rose to the rank of lieutenant colonel. From 1946 to 1947, he was deputy to Wilson Wyatt, head of the Veterans Emergency Housing Program. In 1947, Rauh joined Wyatt and other liberals in leaving the Truman administration to protest what they regarded as its conservative direction.

Rauh was one of a group of liberals who, in 1947, formed Americans for Democratic Action (ADA) to advocate the expansion of New Deal welfare programs, federal regulation of the economy, and protection of civil liberties. At the same time, the ADA explicitly rejected "any association with communism or sympathizers with communism in the United States" and espoused an internationalist, anticommunist foreign policy. Rauh was selected chair of the ADA's executive committee that year, a position he held until he served as national vice chairman from 1952 to 1955. He was chairman from 1955 to 1957, after which he resumed the post of vice chairman.

During the Truman and Eisenhower administrations, Rauh supported liberal causes in his private law practice as well as in his activities with the ADA. His clients included WALTER REUTHER's United Auto Workers and A. PHILIP RANDOLPH's Brotherhood of Sleeping Car Porters. Rauh represented Lillian Hellman, ARTHUR MILLER, John T. Watkins, and William Remington when they testified before the House Un-American Activities Committee. When Miller was indicted on charges of contempt of Congress in 1956 for refusing to identify former associates who had attended meetings of the Communist Party, Rauh represented him. Although Miller was convicted in trial court, a federal appeals court overturned his conviction. After Remington, an economist with the Commerce Department, was convicted of perjury for denying that he had been a member of the Communist Party, Rauh represented him on appeal. Rauh carried the case of Watkins, who had been convicted of contempt for refusing to disclose the names of persons who had been communists but were no longer members of the party, to the Supreme Court and in 1957 won a decision denying the right of the House Un-American Activities Committee to use its investigative powers simply for the purpose of exposure. Despite his aggressive defense of those accused of communism, Rauh refused to defend avowed communists.

As chief spokesman for the ADA during the Eisenhower administration, Rauh repeatedly attacked the administration for failing to pursue liberal goals. Never given to understatement, Rauh stated in 1954 that "Eisenhower has produced the saddest excuse for a legislative program since McKinley." The following year, he held the president personally responsible for heading "the most corrupt administration since Harding."

Although most of Rauh's rhetorical fire was directed at Republicans, Democrats were not exempt. In 1956, he accused Senator LYNDON B. JOHNSON (D-Tex.) of bringing the Democratic Party "to the lowest point in 25 years" by imitating, rather than opposing, Eisenhower. Rauh also questioned ADLAI STEVENSON's credibility as the leader of the liberal wing of the Democratic Party. Stevenson's statement in 1956 that moderation "is the spirit of our times," which many regarded as a call for caution on civil rights, particularly distressed

Rauh, who wrote Stevenson and urged him to make a strong statement supporting school desegregation and condemning discrimination in voting. Stevenson responded by claiming that his position on civil rights was clear. Rauh replied, "Ike has the squatter's rights on the middle road. Let him have it."

At the Democratic convention in 1956, Rauh and the ADA lobbied for a plank in the platform calling for support of the Supreme Court's decision in *Brown v. Board of Education* (1954), which struck down segregated public schools. One month before the convention, Senator HUBERT H. HUMPHREY (D-Minn.) promised to back Rauh, but the senator withdrew his pledge when his name emerged as a possible vice presidential candidate. Stevenson and the ADA's honorary chair, ELEANOR ROOSEVELT, also opposed Rauh's proposed plank, and it was not reported to the floor.

In 1960, the ADA's national board warned the Democratic Party that, to win the election, it had to nominate a liberal who would offer "a clear alternative to the reactionary Republican candidate." To accomplish this, Rauh's strategy was to stop Johnson. Rauh calculated that the candidacies of Humphrey and Senator JOHN F. KENNEDY (D-Mass.) had divided liberals in the party. Rauh supported Humphrey, the more liberal of the two candidates, and he worried that, if Stevenson entered the race, a three-way split among liberals would deadlock the convention and throw the nomination to Johnson. Rauh therefore publicly called on liberals to end their sentimental loyalty to Stevenson. When Humphrey withdrew from the race, Rauh endorsed Kennedy.

As he had in 1956, Rauh demanded a strong civil rights plank in the Democratic platform. In July 1960, he appeared before the platform committee to present the ADA's call for strong federal action to end all forms of racial discrimination. To his surprise, the delegates approved a plank far closer to his wishes than the one in the 1956 platform.

Kennedy's selection of Johnson as his running mate personally embarrassed Rauh, who had promised many supporters of Stevenson that their candidate would get the second spot on the ticket. Rauh denounced the choice of Johnson as a "double cross" of liberals and predicted that the Texan would be a disaster for the ticket. He joined a group of liberals

in an abortive stop Johnson movement. When it failed, however, Rauh enthusiastically campaigned for the ticket.

During the 1960s, Rauh continued to serve as spokesperson for the ADA. Relations between the ADA and the Kennedy administration were not close. Rauh repeated his demands for civil rights measures and criticized the Kennedy administration for failing to prohibit the use of federal funds for the construction of racially segregated housing. He also opposed the Kennedy administration's bill to legalize wiretapping in certain instances. Beginning in 1964, Rauh served as the general counsel of the Leadership Conference on Civil Rights, a coalition of national civil rights groups. At the Democratic convention in 1964, he represented the Mississippi Freedom Democratic Party in its efforts to supplant the segregationist delegation from Mississippi. Rauh lobbied vigorously for the Civil Rights Act of 1964, the Voting Rights Act of 1965, and the Fair Housing Act of 1968. He opposed the war in Vietnam and supported Senator EUGENE MCCARTHY'S (D-Minn.) antiwar candidacy in 1968. During the administration of RICHARD M. NIXON, Rauh opposed the nominations of CLEMENT F. HAYNSWORTH and G. Harold Carswell to the Supreme Court. During the 1970s, he mobilized amicus curiae briefs supporting affirmative action in *Regents of the University of California v. Bakke* (1978). Rauh died in Washington, D.C., on September 3, 1992.

—MSM

Rayburn, Samuel T(aliaferro)
(1882–1961) U.S. congressman, Speaker of the House, minority leader

The son of a Confederate veteran and poor farmer, Rayburn was born in Roane County, Tennessee, on January 6, 1882. When he was five, the family moved to Fannin County in northeastern Texas, where his father bought a 40-acre cotton farm. Rayburn attended rural schools and left home to attend East Texas Normal College (later East Texas State Teachers College), where he earned his tuition by doing various chores at the college. After graduating in 1903, Rayburn taught at local schools. In 1906, he won election as a Democrat to the state house of representatives and held that seat from

1907 to 1913. In between legislative sessions, he studied law at the University of Texas. Rayburn was admitted to the bar in 1908, after which he began to practice law in Bonham, Texas. After being elected speaker of the Texas house in 1912, he became the youngest speaker in the history of Texas.

As a candidate for the U.S. House of Representatives in 1912, Rayburn advocated income and inheritance taxes, low tariffs, direct election of U.S. senators, and the right of recall at the state and local level. After winning the Democratic primary by a narrow margin, he easily carried the general election. He won reelection 24 consecutive times, during which time he never even had a Republican opponent. In Congress, Rayburn backed most of President Woodrow Wilson's domestic programs but offended organized labor, which had little influence in his predominantly rural district, by voting against child labor bills and opposing the nationalization of railroads. He became an ally of John Nance Garner, a fellow Texan and power in the House of Representatives. Rayburn served as Garner's campaign manager when the latter unsuccessfully sought the Democratic presidential nomination in 1932. After Franklin D. Roosevelt won the nomination, Rayburn served as Garner's representative in the negotiations that led Roosevelt to select Garner as his running mate.

Roosevelt easily won the election in November, and Rayburn subsequently supported most New Deal programs and played a major role in the passage of regulatory legislation. As chair of the House Interstate and Foreign Commerce Committee from 1931 to 1937, Rayburn sponsored the Federal Securities Act of 1933, the Securities Exchange Act of 1934, the Public Utility Holding Company Act of 1935, and the Rural Electrification Act of 1936. After becoming majority leader in 1937, he worked closely with Roosevelt to map out legislative strategy. In 1939, Rayburn began an unsuccessful effort to win a place on the national Democratic ticket in 1940. However, when the Speaker of the House, William B. Bankhead (D-Ala.), died in September 1940, Rayburn was unanimously elected to succeed him. Rayburn firmly supported all of Roosevelt's war measures, except gasoline rationing, which powerful oil interests in Texas opposed.

Rayburn was President HARRY S. TRUMAN's chief supporter in Congress and one of his closest advisers. With the notable exception of civil rights measures, Rayburn backed most of Truman's domestic program, including proposals for national health insurance, housing, education, and an increase in the minimum wage. As minority leader from 1947 to 1949, Rayburn opposed the Taft-Hartley Act, tried to limit Republican cuts in Truman's programs, and attempted to block tax reductions favoring higher incomes. In foreign policy, Rayburn supported the Truman Doctrine and the Marshall Plan. Although he supported much of the New Deal and Fair Deal, colleagues regarded him as more of a centrist than a liberal. In 1947, Rayburn declined Truman's offer of the vice presidential nomination.

Rayburn became Speaker again after the elections of 1948. In January 1949, he succeeded in securing the adoption of the 21-day rule, a measure that reduced the power of the Rules Committee, which was dominated by conservative southern Democrats. A coalition of southern Democrats and conservative Republicans had been able to block the flow of legislation to the floor of the House. Two years later, however, the next Congress refused to adopt the 21-day rule. Rayburn often tried to forge compromises between the Truman administration and southern Democrats in Congress. In 1951, for example, he proposed a compromise solution to the controversy over whether the federal or state governments should control offshore oil. In doing so, he offended the oil interests, which favored state jurisdiction. Although inclined to search all possible avenues of cooperation with the Soviet Union, Rayburn reluctantly came to support Truman's policy of containment. In January 1951, he broke the record of Henry Clay for length of service as Speaker.

When President Truman announced in March 1952 that he would not seek reelection, Senator A. S. "MIKE" MONRONEY (D-Okla.) attempted to mount a campaign for Rayburn's nomination as a presidential nominee acceptable to both the north and the south. That strategy ran quickly into trouble. ALLAN SHIVERS, the Democratic governor of Texas and a political enemy of Rayburn, dominated the state Democratic convention and chose its delegation to the Democratic National Convention.

Without support from his own state, Rayburn had virtually no chance to win the party's nomination.

As the permanent chair of the national convention in Chicago, Rayburn used his power to gain the presidential nomination for Truman's candidate, ADLAI STEVENSON. Senator ESTES KEFAUVER (D-Tenn.) had won some impressive victories in the primaries and led on the first two ballots at the convention. Kefauver's forces, sensing imminent victory, wanted a third roll call immediately. Rayburn, however, called a recess to enable Truman, who was en route to Chicago, to meet with key figures at the convention. Stevenson won the nomination on the third ballot.

During the 1950s, Rayburn worked with the Eisenhower administration to enact its foreign policy. As minority leader in the 83rd Congress, Rayburn backed the extension of the Reciprocal Trade Agreements Act and opposed efforts by conservative Republicans to cut $2 billion from the administration's foreign aid package in 1953. The following year, he opposed the Bricker amendment, which would have limited the president's power to make treaties.

On domestic matters, Rayburn and Eisenhower were both centrists and agreed on most basic issues. Although the Speaker generally supported Eisenhower's domestic initiatives, he sometimes opposed the administration. In 1953, he worked against a measure, backed by the administration, that would have stripped the Southwest Power Administration of authority to transmit electricity to Rural Electrification Administration cooperatives. The next year, he opposed a bill to free the stock issues of middle-size companies from the jurisdiction of the Securities and Exchange Commission and a tax cut that Democrats charged would primarily benefit corporations.

In the elections of 1954, Democrats regained control of Congress, and Rayburn once again became Speaker. During his previous tenure in that post, Rayburn had gained a reputation as one of the strongest Speakers in U.S. history. Speakers in the 19th century had maintained their power through the right to make committee assignments and sit on the Rules Committee, which controlled the flow of legislation from the committees of original jurisdiction to the floor. In the Progressive uprising against

Speaker Joe Cannon, sometimes called the Revolution of 1910, the Speaker lost those powers. Rayburn, however, was able to dominate the chamber through persuasion and informal influence, based in large measure on respect for his legendary integrity (he accepted no money from lobbyists, refused travel expenses for speaking tours, and went on only one congressional junket during his 48 years in Congress, for which he paid his own way), his lack of pretension, and his effectiveness as a conciliator of factional disputes. He exercised indirect control of the legislative process and committee assignments through his relationships with chairs of committees and subcommittees. Rayburn enforced party discipline through similar methods; only rarely did he use his power to influence committee assignments or in other ways advance or impede the careers of his colleagues. Although he claimed that he never asked a member to vote against his principles, the Speaker generally expected Democratic representatives to vote for legislation supported by their leaders. He famously advised freshmen representatives: "If you want to get along—go along."

With the Democrats in the majority after the elections of 1954, Rayburn and Eisenhower worked more closely than before. In 1955 and 1956, the Speaker again supported reciprocal trade and foreign aid bills supported by the administration. Although up to that point he had consistently opposed civil rights measures, Rayburn quietly lent his support to the administration's civil rights bill in 1956. Even though the great majority of southern Democrats in the House opposed it, the measure passed the lower chamber. Southern Democrats, however, blocked it in the Senate.

Rayburn came into conflict with some Democratic liberals in 1955 when he backed the Formosa Resolution, which gave the president authority to use U.S. troops in defense of Taiwan and the Pescadores in case of attack by the Chinese Communists. A number of representatives believed that congressional authorization was superfluous and that the resolution represented an effort by the administration to procure blanket approval for any actions it might take. The Speaker, however, contended that presenting a united front to the world should be the foremost consideration of Congress. The resolution passed the House by a vote of 410 to 3.

Rayburn again served as permanent chair for the Democratic National Convention in 1956. He actively promoted his protégé, Senate Majority Leader LYNDON B. JOHNSON (D-Tex.) for the vice presidential nomination. Toward that end, he helped Johnson wrest control of the party organization in Texas from Shivers. Despite Rayburn's strenuous objections, however, Stevenson, who once again captured the presidential nomination, left the choice of a running mate to the convention. The leading contenders included Kefauver and Senator JOHN F. KENNEDY (D-Mass.). On the second ballot, Kennedy was only 40 votes short of a majority when the Kentucky delegation asked for recognition to transfer its 30 votes from Senator ALBERT GORE (D-Tenn.) to Kennedy. Rayburn, however, recognized the Tennessee delegation, which switched its votes from Gore to Kefauver. This reversed the trend to Kennedy and enabled Kefauver eventually to win the nomination. Although Rayburn did not have a high opinion of Kennedy at the time, it was not entirely clear whether the Speaker's action was calculated to deny Kennedy the nomination.

After the elections of 1956, Rayburn and Johnson came under increasing fire from Democratic liberals for being too conciliatory toward Eisenhower and for not promoting comprehensive welfare legislation. In November 1956, PAUL BUTLER, the chair of the national party, formed the Democratic Advisory Council (DAC). Butler intended it as a vehicle to enable liberals to circumvent the Democratic leadership in the House and Senate in formulating the party's legislative programs. Rayburn and Johnson refused to join the group, and, without their participation, the panel had little influence.

In 1957, Rayburn cooperated with the administration to obtain passage of the first civil rights law since Reconstruction. The House passed the administration's proposals largely intact, but the Senate substantially weakened the measure. Rayburn accepted the Senate's watered-down version of the administration's civil rights bill and got it through conference committee and the full House. Rayburn again cooperated in passing the Civil Rights Act of 1960, aimed at protecting black voting rights.

In response to the obstructionism of the Rules Committee, liberals in the House formed the Dem-

ocratic Study Group (DSG) in an effort to increase their influence. With the assistance of the minority leader, JOSEPH MARTIN (R-Mass.), Rayburn was able to pry some bills backed by the DSG from the Rules committee, which was chaired by the conservative HOWARD W. SMITH (D-Va.). Major legislation, however, such as a multibillion dollar housing bill, languished in the Rules Committee, and members of the DSG became increasingly impatient with the party's leadership.

Shortly after the Democratic sweep in the congressional elections of 1958, Representative CHET HOLIFIELD (D-Calif.), speaking for the DSG, demanded Rayburn's assistance in reestablishing the 21-day rule. The Speaker refused on the grounds that the inevitably bitter struggle over the rule would polarize the Democratic Party going into the presidential election of 1960. He promised, however, to induce the Rules Committee to report out all major bills sent to it during the 1959–60 congressional term. Rayburn did secure release of the housing bill in 1959 (which Eisenhower vetoed) but failed to keep his promise on a number of other bills, including area redevelopment and aid to schools.

Some liberal publications began to refer to Rayburn as an "Eisenhowercrat" in 1959. Rayburn's inability to force passage of liberal legislation resulted at least in part from the selection of Representative CHARLES HALLECK (R-Ind.) to replace Martin as minority leader in January 1959. Rayburn and Martin had maintained a cooperative relationship, but Halleck was more partisan and combative than his predecessor. He replaced two Republican moderates on the Rules Committee with more conservative members and was not inclined to use his influence on Rayburn's behalf.

Rayburn also assumed a more partisan stance. In the presidential year of 1960, the Speaker gave his support to a five-part package of social legislation, which the Eisenhower administration strongly opposed. Democrats intended, by introducing the legislative proposals, to focus on differences between the parties and provide the Democratic ticket with issues on which to run. It also appeased liberals in Congress, who had long agitated for more liberal and partisan leadership in Congress. Congress rejected bills providing for an increase in the minimum wage and more extensive coverage, health care for the aged under Social Security, federal aid for school construction, and housing programs. Eisenhower vetoed the one measure to pass Congress, federal loans and grants for redevelopment of economically depressed areas.

Beginning in 1959, Rayburn backed Johnson's bid for the presidency. He urged Johnson to enter the primaries, but Johnson believed that leaders in the House and Senate would provide him with the votes he needed from their states' delegations. Rayburn declined to serve once again as chair of the Democratic National Convention in order to serve as Johnson's floor manager and nominated Johnson at the convention. When Kennedy offered Johnson the vice presidential nomination, Rayburn at first urged his fellow Texan to reject it. Rayburn initially thought the office would be a political dead end but changed his mind after speaking with Kennedy. Rayburn campaigned heavily for the Democratic ticket in Texas, which Kennedy carried by a narrow margin of 46,000 votes.

In January 1961, Rayburn, with Kennedy's support, sought to gain control of the Rules Committee. On January 31, the House voted 217–212 to enlarge the panel from 12 to 15 members. The new members of the committee consisted of two Democratic supporters of the administration and one Republican. This gave liberals a majority on the committee and paved the way for the social legislation passed in the 1960s. Rayburn's modified version of Kennedy's minimum wage bill, tailored to meet objections of Republicans and southern Democrats, became the basis of legislation adopted in May 1961. Suffering from cancer, Rayburn flew home to Bonham, Texas, in August 1961 and died there on November 16, 1961. His 17 years as Speaker was the longest tenure in history.

—MSM

Reed, Daniel A(lden)

(1875–1959) *U.S. congressman; chairman, Ways and Means Committee*

Born in Sheridan, New York, on September 15, 1875, Reed attended public schools and received an LL.B. from Cornell University in 1898. After being admitted to the bar in 1900, he practiced law in Chautauqua County. He served as an attorney for the excise department of the state of New York from 1903 to 1909. Reed then became the football coach at Cornell University from 1909 to 1918. He served as a member of the Special Food Conservation Mission to France and Britain in 1917 and 1918. Upon his return to the United States, New York's 43rd district elected him to the U.S. House of Representatives as a Republican in 1918. He won reelection 20 successive times, serving in the House from March 4, 1919, until his death in 1959.

During his first decade in Congress, his major concerns were education and serving the interests of New York State. In 1932, he obtained a seat on the powerful Ways and Means Committee, where he emerged as a supporter of sound money and strict limits on federal spending. An advocate of reduced taxes, he authored a bill in 1950 to raise exemptions to $700 and reduce most excise levies by 10 percent to 20 percent.

When the Republicans won control of Congress in the elections of 1952, Reed became chair of the Ways and Means Committee. In the first year of the Eisenhower administration, he opposed the president on two tax bills. On January 3, he introduced a bill to advance the scheduled elimination of an 11 percent increase in personal income taxes, passed to help fund the Korean War, from January 1, 1954, to July 1, 1953. Eisenhower refused to countenance a tax cut until he had a balanced budget. Reed also attempted to block a bill backed by the administration to extend the excess profits tax on corporations, also passed during the Korean War, from June 30, 1953, to December 31, 1953. Eisenhower later recalled using "every possible reason, argument, and device" in an effort to persuade Reed. When that failed, the president exerted pressure on Republican members of Congress. On February 16, Ways and Means favorably reported Reed's bill to move up the elimination of the increase in income taxes, but, with the help of Speaker JOE MARTIN (R-Mass.), the administration succeeded in bottling up Reed's measure in the Rules Committee. The Ways and Means Committee began hearings on the measure to extend the excess profits tax in June. Reed remained adamantly opposed to the extension and rejected Eisenhower's personal appeals to allow a vote by the committee. The president and congressional leaders decided to circumvent Reed if necessary, and on June 25, the Rules Committee, at the behest of Martin, took the extraordinary step of reporting the bill to the House without a report from Ways and Means. Reed hinted at resigning from Congress in protest. The Republican leadership in the House avoided a showdown by postponing a vote by the House on the decision by the Rules Committee scheduled for June 29. On July 8, the Ways and Means Committee overrode Reed's objections and voted to report the bill providing for an extension of the excess profits tax. Reed then offered two compromise versions of the measure, both of which the Ways and Means Committee also rejected. Congress passed the administration's proposal, and Eisenhower signed it into law in July.

Reed also opposed the administration's reciprocal trade policy. In January 1954, Eisenhower asked for a three-year extension of the Reciprocal Trade Agreements Act. Old Guard Republicans, including Reed, opposed the measure, and the president settled for a bill providing for a one-year extension. Although Reed voted for the compromise measure, he condemned the principle of reciprocal trade. He cautioned against the danger of allowing cheap Japanese goods into the United States. Further, he warned, "the insatiable desire to promote exports at any cost has made it possible for our enemies to obtain from our own shores the war materials which they needed in order to wage aggressive war." In 1955 and 1958, when reciprocal trade bills included longer extensions and presidential power to cut tariffs, Reed voted against the measures.

When Democrats regained control of Congress in the elections of 1954, Reed adopted a more partisan role as a defender of the administration. In 1955, he attacked a proposal, supported by Democrats, to cut income taxes; he asserted that defense and other urgent spending made a reduction unwise. The following year, Congress voted a temporary increase in the statutory limit on the public debt for fiscal 1957. Noting that the limit was less than those for 1955 and 1956, Reed praised "the magnificent accomplishments of this Administration in putting the fiscal affairs of the nation in order." In 1958, he introduced a bill incorporating Eisenhower's suggestion that the states assume responsibility for federally financed programs in the areas of vocational education, waste-treatment facilities, planning for slum clearance, and repair of public facilities damaged in natural disasters.

Reed's record on civil rights was somewhat mixed. Although he was one of the few Republicans who opposed federal legislation to ban the poll tax, he did support antilynching legislation. During the Eisenhower administration, Reed voted for the Civil Rights Act of 1957.

He died in Washington, D.C., on February 19, 1959.

—MSM

Reed, Stanley F(orman)
(1884–1980) *associate justice, U.S. Supreme Court*

The son of a physician, Reed was born in Minerva, Kentucky, on December 31, 1884. After attending local private schools, he earned a B.A. from Kentucky Wesleyan College in 1902 and a second B.A. from Yale University in 1906. He studied law at the University of Virginia, Columbia University, and the Sorbonne but never earned a law degree. Upon gaining admission to the Kentucky bar in 1910, he established a successful law practice in Maysville and Ashland. He spent nine years as a single practitioner and then became a partner in Worthington, Browning and Reed. During that time, he became active in Democratic politics. In 1912, he won election to the first of two consecutive terms in the Kentucky general assembly. After serving in the army during World War I, he returned to Maysville and his legal practice until 1929, when President HERBERT HOOVER appointed him general counsel to the Federal Farm Board. Hoover appointed him general counsel to the Reconstruction Finance Corporation (RFC) in 1932. Reed remained at the RFC under the new administration of Franklin D. Roosevelt. In March 1935, Roosevelt named him solicitor general. As solicitor general, he defended major New Deal legislation before the Supreme Court. Although he won 11 of the 13 cases he argued before the nation's highest court, he suffered major defeats when the justices struck down the National Industrial Recovery Act in *Schechter Poultry Corporation v. United States* (1935) and the Agricultural Adjustment Act in *United States v. Butler* (1936).

Roosevelt appointed him to succeed George Sutherland on the Supreme Court in 1938. Widely regarded as a liberal at the time of his elevation to the Court, Reed's career as a justice did not bear out that estimation. An advocate of judicial restraint, he believed that the judiciary should defer to the legislature and the executive unless their actions were clearly unconstitutional. In his early years on the bench, he voted to sustain federal economic regulations and social welfare laws. During the administration of HARRY S. TRUMAN, however, his commitment to judicial restraint and his own inclination to favor the power of the executive and the legislature led him to vote consistently to sustain the exercise of governmental authority, particularly in the area of internal security, at the expense of individual liberties. When the Court rejected the argument that Truman had constitutional authority to issue an executive order seizing privately owned steel mills in *Youngstown Sheet & Tube Co. v. Sawyer* (1952), Reed joined Chief Justice FRED M. VINSON's dissent. In *American Communication Association v. Douds* (1950), Reed voted with the majority to sustain the noncommunist oath provision of the Taft-Hartley Act. He also voted with the majority to sustain the conviction of communist leaders under the Smith Act in *Dennis v. United States* (1951). Reed wrote for the majority in *Carlson v. Landon* (1952), which sustained the right of the government to jail alien communists and hold them without bail until the attorney general's office determined whether they could be deported.

During the Eisenhower administration, Reed continued to support the government's antisubversive efforts. When the majority ruled, in *Peters v. Hobby* (1955), that the Civil Service Commission's Loyalty Review Board had exceeded its authority by auditing on its own initiative a favorable judgment by a departmental loyalty board and ordering the dismissal of a consultant with the Public Health Service, Reed dissented. A year later, Reed wrote for the minority when the Court struck down Pennsylvania's antisubversive law on the ground that Congress had preempted the field (*Pennsylvania v. Nelson* [1956]) and dissented when the majority held that government employees could be dismissed as security risks only if they held sensitive positions (*Cole v. Young* [1956]).

In supporting judicial restraint, Reed generally sided with Justices FELIX FRANKFURTER and ROBERT JACKSON against the judicial activists and civil libertarians on the Court led by HUGO BLACK and WILLIAM O. DOUGLAS. He interpreted the Bill of Rights narrowly. In *United Public Workers v. Mitchell* (1947), Reed wrote for the majority in a decision that rejected the argument of federal employees that the Hatch Act denied them rights guaranteed by the First Amendment. According to Reed, "It is accepted constitutional doctrine that fundamental human rights are not absolute. This court must balance the extent of the guarantees of freedom against Congressional enactment to protect a democratic society against the supposed evil of political partisanship by employees of the government." Writing for the majority in *Adamson v. California* (1947), Reed explicitly rejected Black's theory that the Fourteenth Amendment incorporated the Bill of Rights and therefore applied it to the states. Perhaps Reed's fullest expression of his views came in *Breard v. City of Alexandria, Louisiana* (1951), in which he wrote that the First and Fourteenth Amendments "have never been treated as absolute. Freedom of speech or press does not mean that one can talk or distribute where, when and how he chooses." Similarly, in *Poulos v. State of New Hampshire* (1953), Reed upheld the conviction of Poulos for failing to obtain a license to conduct a religious service in a park. The Court, declared Reed, had never held that rights guaranteed by the First Amendment could not be regulated. Rather, it "had indicated approval of reasonable nondiscriminatory regulations by governmental authority that preserve peace, order and tranquility."

In criminal cases, Reed was reluctant to upset a conviction on the grounds that a confession had been coerced. He voted to do so only when presented with strong evidence of coercion. His opinion in *Adamson v. California* rejected the application of the Fifth Amendment's guarantee against self-incrimination to the states.

Reed's record with respect to civil rights was mixed. His Kentucky background notwithstanding, he voted to support black claims for equality of treatment in *Missouri ex rel. Gaines v. Canada* (1938), *Sipuel v. Oklahoma State Board of Regents* (1948), *Sewatt v. Painter* (1950), and *McLaurin v.*

Oklahoma State Board of Regents (1950). Reed also wrote the opinion for the majority in *Smith v. Allwright* (1944), which struck down Texas's white primary. In *District of Columbia v. John R. Thompson Co., Inc.* (1953), Reed, despite some personal reservations, joined a unanimous Court in upholding a Reconstruction-era municipal statute banning discrimination in places of public accommodation in Washington, D.C. He balked, however, when it came to holding racial segregation itself unconstitutional. The first of what would be five companion cases consolidated under the heading *Brown v. Board of Education* reached the Court in the fall of 1952. These cases presented the Court with the issue of the constitutionality of segregation. Reed believed that segregation did not violate the Fourteenth Amendment so long as blacks received equal treatment. When the justices first discussed the cases in conference, Reed alone held that view. After a series of legal maneuverings and re-arguments, the justices met in early 1954 to vote on the cases. Reed apparently prepared to write a dissent. In the end, Chief Justice EARL WARREN persuaded Reed to make the Court's decision striking down segregated public schools unanimous by asking him whether a lone dissent by a southerner would be the best thing for the country.

Reed retired from the Court in February 1957. Assessing Reed's tenure on the bench, C. Herman Pritchett, a political scientist and analyst of the Supreme Court, described the justice as "a 'center judge,' occupying generally a middle position between the Court's conservative and liberal wings" but one who tilted to the right on cases involving civil liberties.

Following his retirement, Reed divided his time between Washington and his farm near Maysville. In November 1957, President DWIGHT D. EISENHOWER named him to chair the United States Civil Rights Commission crated by the Civil Rights Act of 1957. Reed withdrew from the job in December, because he feared that his service in an investigatory and advisory post might lower public respect for the impartiality of the judiciary, of which he was still a member. Subsequently, he accepted numerous assignments to hear cases in the U.S. Court of Claims and the U.S. Court of Appeals for the District of Columbia. With his health failing, he withdrew from all public activities in 1967 and retired to Huntington, New York, where he died on April 2, 1980.

—MSM

Reston, James
(1909–1995) *journalist*

Born in Clydebank, Scotland, on November 3, 1909, Reston emigrated with his parents to Dayton, Ohio, at the age of 11. When his parents became naturalized citizens, he automatically gained the same status. After graduating in 1932 from the University of Illinois, where he captained the Big Ten championship golf team, Reston returned to Ohio to begin his newspaper career as sports editor of the *Springfield Daily News*. After a brief stint as publicity director for the Cincinnati Reds, he joined the Associated Press in 1934 as a sportswriter based in New York. In 1937, the Associated Press sent Reston to London, where he covered sports and the British Foreign Office. Reston joined the London bureau of the *New York Times* on September 1, 1939, the day Adolf Hitler's armies marched into Poland. His coverage of the Nazi bombing of London and his account of the blitz in *Prelude to Victory* (1942) established him as one of the most promising reporters on the *Times*. He was assigned to the Washington bureau in December 1940. In late 1942, Reston took a leave of absence from the paper to work for the Office of War Information. He returned to the *Times* in 1944 to become the administrative assistant to Arthur Hayes Sulzberger, the paper's publisher. Reston went back to Washington as national correspondent in 1945; he became diplomatic correspondent in 1948.

In 1953, Reston succeeded ARTHUR KROCK as head of the Washington bureau. An astute judge of journalistic talent, Reston revitalized the bureau by hiring promising young reporters and nurturing them. He introduced a sense of informality in the bureau that was decidedly absent under his predecessor. His liberalism also contrasted with Krock's conservatism. In addition to his managerial responsibilities, Reston published his own column three times a week. Reston's observations on foreign affairs gained him national recognition. His articles combined realism with a strong sense of morality that derived from his strict Presbyterian upbringing.

By the time President DWIGHT D. EISENHOWER and Secretary of State JOHN FOSTER DULLES came to power, Reston had moderated his earlier hard-line anti-Soviet views. Reston enjoyed a cordial personal relationship with Dulles and, by the journalist's own account, "spent more time with him than with any other secretary of state from the forties to the nineties." Dulles served as a source for Reston, but this did not prevent the columnist from frequently criticizing the secretary of state and the foreign policy of the Eisenhower administration. Reston was especially harsh after Dulles, in an interview with *Life* magazine in January 1956, explained that on three occasions he had taken the United States to the "brink" of war to face down communist aggression.

Although strongly drawn to Eisenhower's opponent in 1952, ADLAI STEVENSON, whose virtues Reston extolled in his column, the journalist, troubled by Stevenson's lack of decisiveness, voted for Eisenhower in that election. During Eisenhower's first term, Reston criticized the president for being "a symbol of the atmosphere of the time: optimistic, prosperous, escapist, pragmatic, friendly, attentive at moments of crisis and comparatively inattentive the rest of the time."

Reston detested Senator JOSEPH R. MCCAR-THY (R-Wis.) and his anticommunist antics. By his own later calculation, however, Reston and the *Times* were cautious in taking on the senator, particularly in the early days of his crusade against communists in government. By the spring of 1954, however, Reston openly attacked the junior senator from Wisconsin. In March 1954, Reston condemned the administration for "playing a waiting game" with McCarthy in the expectation that the American people would get bored with the senator or that he would discredit himself. Reston acknowledged the likelihood of the latter in particular. However, the columnist warned, McCarthyism would not likely disappear, irrespective of what happened to McCarthy. So long as the nation lived in fear of atomic war and remained "unadjusted to the terrible responsibilities of world leadership," new McCarthys would emerge to exploit the "fears and frustrations of the people." The senator from Wisconsin, asserted Reston, "did not create this situa-

tion; he merely exploited it." Moreover, McCarthy had already won "a considerable victory" in that he "has demonstrated, in the atmosphere of fear, that violence and deceit can be made to pay in American political life." The journalist claimed that McCarthy had already silenced many honorable men in Congress and elsewhere and seized control of a large part of the Republican Party. Worse still, Reston suggested, the junior senator from Wisconsin had become a model for rising young politicians on Capitol Hill. Reston concluded that, for a variety of reasons, Congress was unlikely to put a stop to McCarthy's nonsense; the responsibility therefore fell to the president.

When Eisenhower left office in 1961, Reston delivered an assessment of the president's eight years. "He was a good man in a wicked time; a consolidator in a world crying for innovation; a conservative in a radical age; a tired man in a period of turbulence and energetic action." In Eisenhower's own terms, however, Reston acknowledged that "he has had a successful administration;" the president had successfully avoided what he feared most—war and depression. Further, Eisenhower had broken the isolationist tradition of his party and presided over an era of prosperity. "Swift action" on his part blocked "Communist thrusts in Guatemala and in Lebanon." The United States helped end the Suez Crisis and avoided intervention in Hungary. The administration accepted truces in Indochina, Korea, the Formosa Straits, and Berlin. In those instances, Reston wrote, "nothing has been settled but nothing vital to the free world has been lost." In domestic affairs, Reston praised Eisenhower for consolidating the policies of the New Deal and the Fair Deal. In conclusion, wrote Reston, "President Eisenhower at least maintained enough power to deter the big war and the big depression, that was his . . . objective from the start."

Reston continued writing his column into the 1960s and 1970s. He stepped down as bureau chief in 1964 to concentrate on his column. In 1968, he became executive editor of the *New York Times*. After 13 months, he relinquished the position of editor in favor of spending more time on his column. His nationally syndicated column appeared regularly until 1987, at which point he became a senior columnist. He retired from the *Times* in 1989.

During his 50-year association with the *Times*, he won two Pulitzer Prizes (for reporting in 1944 and 1956) and was awarded the Presidential Medal of Freedom in 1986. Reston published a collection of his columns, titled *Sketches in the Sand*, in 1967, and *Deadline*, a volume of memoirs, in 1991. He died of cancer in New York on December 6, 1995.

David Halberstam, whom Reston recruited to the *Times*, described Reston as "the dominant Washington journalist of the fifties." No one had more high-level sources than Reston, and some critics charged that he treated them too kindly in print. Reston retorted that "hatchet men" could not get their calls returned, which left them only with their opinions. "I wouldn't like that," he concluded, "because my own opinions aren't that good." Reston's column was at its best when breaking a story or working closely from his own reporting.

—MSM

Reuther, Walter P.

(1907–1970) *president, United Automobile Workers*

The son of an immigrant German brewery worker and union leader, Walter Reuther was born in Wheeling, West Virginia, on September 1, 1907. Raised in a tightly knit socialist family, he attended high school in Wheeling but left at 16 to go to work. After working as a handyman, he became an apprentice as a tool and die maker. Reuther moved to Detroit in 1927, where he became a skilled tool and die worker at the Ford Motor Company. He went to work on the night shift and earned a high school diploma from Fordson High School. He then enrolled in Detroit City College (later Wayne State University). The Great Depression politicized Reuther and his brothers, Victor and Roy. Reuther campaigned vigorously for Norman Thomas's presidential candidacy in 1932. After that, he and Victor set out on a world tour, which included a 16-month sojourn as skilled workers in a Soviet auto factory. Returning to Detroit in 1935, Reuther plunged into labor organizing and socialist politics. In 1936, he became a full-time organizer for the United Automobile Workers (UAW). Although technically ineligible for membership in the UAW because he did not work in the auto industry, he was elected to its executive board when the union declared its independence from the American Federation of Labor (AFL) in 1936. Reuther played a significant role in the sitdown strikes that began in 1936 and in the establishment of UAW Local 174, of which he became president. Local 174 quickly came to represent 30,000 workers. Subsequently, the UAW became the largest union in the nation, and Reuther emerged as its most influential leader.

Like many other radical unionists, Reuther resigned from the Socialist Party in the late 1930s and endorsed the alliance between the Congress of Industrial Organizations (CIO) and Franklin D. Roosevelt's Democratic Party. In 1940, the Reuther brothers formed a caucus that fought for control of the UAW against a leadership coalition that included a small but influential communist group. With World War II underway and the United States contemplating the possibility of entering the war, Reuther proposed an aircraft production board, made up of representatives from government, industry, and labor, that would have exerted considerable control over production. Business leaders strongly opposed the plan. After the United States entered the war, Reuther initially backed the labor movement's no-strike pledge but lent his support to wildcat strikes by UAW members. Immediately after the war ended, he led a dramatic 113-day strike against General Motors (GM). Reuther's unprecedented demands for a wage increase without price increases and for union access to company books in order to prove that GM could afford such a concession earned him the allegiance of most noncommunist militants in the auto industry. It also earned him a wide following among left-liberals outside union ranks and led to his election as the president of the UAW in March 1946. Emerging as a leading spokesman for aggressive, politically oriented unionism, Reuther denounced the Truman administration and called for the formation of a labor party.

During the late 1940s, however, Reuther consolidated his control of the UAW and shifted away from radicalism and toward an acceptance of the existing structure of American politics and industrial relations. He became a power within the national Democratic Party and sought incremental social and economic advances for UAW members through collective bargaining. The contracts he signed with the auto industry in 1948 included a cost-of-living adjustment, determined by the general price index, and an annual "improvement factor," tied to increases in productivity.

In 1952, Reuther won election as president of the CIO. Early the following year, he reached agreement with GEORGE MEANY, president of the American Federation of Labor (AFL), to revive the dormant Joint AFL-CIO Unity Committee, a first step toward a merger of the two labor federations. As a precondition of unification, Reuther demanded a no-raiding agreement and serious action against racketeering in AFL unions. The AFL partially fulfilled these conditions by expelling the gangster-dominated International Longshoremen's Association in 1953 and agreeing to curb competition for bargaining rights where CIO unions had already won contracts. The willingness of many CIO leaders to unify on the AFL's terms, however, undermined Reuther's ability to win further concessions on these issues.

In February 1955, Reuther attended a meeting of the AFL Executive Council in Miami Beach, where he reached an agreement for a merger between the two large labor federations. A plan, drawn up by the CIO's counsel, ARTHUR GOLDBERG, won acceptance by both sides. Under Goldberg's proposal, the AFL retained both the presidency and the secretary-treasurership of the new organization. Reuther became one of 27 vice presidents and head of the Industrial Union Department. The merger became final in December 1955 at the founding convention of the AFL-CIO.

When the UAW and the Big Three automakers (GM, Ford, and Chrysler) entered contract talks in 1955, production was at record-breaking levels. Workers, however, endured annual layoffs during model changeovers. Reuther proposed a guaranteed annual wage for autoworkers and selected Ford as the target company for the union's campaign. Rather than risk a strike while its major competitor, GM, continued to operate, Ford offered a "supplemental unemployment benefit" plan (SUB), which called for the company to put five cents an hour into a fund that would be used to provide payments to laid-off workers. In combination with federal unemployment compensation, this guaranteed UAW members between 60 and 65 percent of their normal take-home play for up to 26 weeks of a layoff. GM and Chrysler also accepted the SUB plan. Many at the time regarded the industry's adoption of the SUB as a stunning success for the UAW. However, Reuther's willingness to forgo a substantial wage increase antagonized skilled tool, die, and maintenance workers, who complained that their wage rates were falling behind the scales of AFL craft unions. Dissidents formed a rival organization, the Society of Skilled Trades, and petitioned the National Labor Relations Board for recognition in several plants. The UAW and the auto industry combined to block its efforts to win bargaining rights.

In 1957, Reuther proposed a shorter workweek without a reduction in pay. The timing was not propitious; a recession that year hit the auto industry hard, which reduced the UAW from 1.5 to 1.1 million members. Reuther concluded that the companies, which had nearly 1 million new cars in inventory, could afford to postpone production for an extended period, so he decided to avoid a strike. He therefore backed down on the demand for a shorter workweek and called instead for a profit-sharing plan. When the Big Three rejected that proposal, too, Reuther further reduced demands to improvements in the SUB, increases in pensions, and other fringe benefits. After four months of negotiations, during which union members continued to work without a contract, the UAW settled for what amounted to little more than a three-year renewal of the old contracts. The contracts signed in 1958 were the first in the UAW's history that did not include any major gains.

Under Reuther's leadership, the UAW became a dominant influence in Michigan's Democratic Party in the late 1940s. The influence of the UAW transformed a weak, relatively conservative state party into one of the most liberal and politically effective Democratic organizations in the country. The union mobilized Detroit's large population of autoworkers to help elect Governor G. MENNEN WILLIAMS for seven consecutive terms between 1948 and 1960 and to defeat two conservative Republican senators. During the 1950s, Reuther emerged as a leading voice for the labor-liberal coalition within the national Democratic Party.

In alliance with the NAACP and the Americans for Democratic Action (ADA), Reuther led an effort on behalf of a strong civil rights plank at the Democratic Convention of 1956. Despite his warning that the Democrats could not maintain the support of both southern segregationists and labor, Reuther pulled back from a floor fight over the platform. A strong supporter of ADLAI STEVENSON, he used his influence to prevent the Michigan delegation from backing AVERELL HARRIMAN at the convention and to win the AFL-CIO's endorsement for Stevenson in the general election.

An early and outspoken critic of corruption in the labor movement and an advocate of greater democracy within unions, Reuther parted company with most union leaders when he welcomed the investigation of racketeering in organized labor by the Senate Select Committee on Improper Activities in the Labor or Management Field, known as the McClellan Committee after its chair, Senator JOHN MCCLELLAN (D-Ark.). After the McClellan Committee's initial investigation of the International Brotherhood of Teamsters, Reuther called for the expulsion of that union from the AFL-CIO and played a major role in the formulation of codes of ethical practices for the AFL-CIO. In 1957, the UAW established a Public Review Board, consisting of seven prominent clergymen, lawyers, and professors, with authority to hear and make binding decisions on the appeals of union members against the UAW executive board.

Senators BARRY GOLDWATER (R-Ariz.), KARL MUNDT (R-S. Dak.), and CARL CURTIS (R-Neb.) urged the McClellan Committee to investigate the UAW. Over the objections of its chief counsel, ROBERT F. KENNEDY, the committee held hearings on the UAW between February 1958 and September 1959. The investigation focused on a prolonged strike by the UAW against the Kohler Company, a manufacturer of bathroom fixtures. Republican members of the committee tried to link the union to criminal activity and large-scale violence. They failed, however, to uncover corruption on a scale significant enough to equate the UAW with the Teamsters and other corrupt unions targeted by the committee.

Almost immediately after the merger of the AFL and CIO, differences in style and policies led to friction between Reuther and Meany. During the late 1950s, Reuther criticized Meany for what Reuther regarded as the AFL-CIO's complacency at home and its rigid anticommunism abroad. Reuther particularly took aim at Meany's unwillingness to curb jurisdictional raids by craft unions on industrial unions and his refusal to throw substantial resources into large-scale organizing drives. He further attacked Meany for holding meetings of the executive council at luxury hotels in Florida rather than meeting in the industrial cities of the North. With respect to foreign policy, Reuther objected to the government-supported, often clandestine overseas operations of Meany's aide, JAY LOVESTONE, who was head of the Free Trade Union Committee. These disagreements surfaced when top Soviet leaders visited the United States in 1959. Meany pointedly boycotted two union delegations led by Reuther that met with Soviet deputy premier Anastas Mikoyan and premier Nikita Khrushchev.

Generally regarded as the most influential labor leader at the Democratic National Convention in 1960, Reuther helped to deliver the nomination to Senator JOHN F. KENNEDY (D-Mass.). Although Kennedy's selection of Senator LYNDON B. JOHNSON (D-Tex.) as his running mate shocked Reuther at first, he quickly fell into line behind the ticket and dissuaded the Michigan delegation from staging a floor fight over the nomination. Reuther also succeeded in preventing the AFL-CIO executive council from condemning Johnson.

During the 1960s, as local UAW leaders and rank-and-file members became more concerned with noneconomic grievances involving production standards and working conditions, Reuther encountered significant internal opposition to his policies. Recurrent wildcat strikes followed the negotiation of each companywide contract. At the same time, his disagreements with George Meany grew more intense. In 1968, Reuther formally withdrew the UAW from the AFL-CIO. The 60s were frustrating years for Reuther. Demands for civil rights, black power, and women's liberation joined the antiwar movement to replace Reuther and the labor movement at the cutting edge of social activism. Indeed, many of these movements regarded Reuther and his generation of labor leaders as obstacles or enemies. On May 9, 1970, Reuther and his wife were killed near Pellston, Michigan, when their chartered jet crashed on landing.

—MSM

Ribicoff, Abraham A(lexander)

(1910–1998) *U.S. congressman, governor of Connecticut*

The son of a Jewish immigrant from Poland who worked as a peddler and factory worker, Ribicoff was born in New Britain, Connecticut, on April 9, 1910. He grew up in a poor section of New Britain, where he attended public schools and worked delivering groceries and selling newspapers. Afer graduating from high school, he worked for a year at a factory that made zippers and buckles in New Britain to earn money to attend New York University. After a year, the company sent him to manage sales in its office in Chicago. He began taking night classes at the University of Chicago and, even though he had not completed a college degree, gained admission to the University of Chicago Law School, where he was editor of the law review. After graduating from law school in 1933, he returned to Connecticut, was admitted to the bar, and established a private practice in Hartford. In 1938, Ribicoff won election as a Democrat to the state's general assembly, where he served two terms and won acclaim from journalists as that state's "most able representative." From 1941 to 1943 and again from 1945 to 1947, Ribicoff served as a police court judge in Hartford.

Ribicoff won election to the U.S. House of Representatives in 1948 and was reelected in 1950. Assigned to the House Foreign Affairs Committee, he helped to formulate the Australia-New Zealand-U.S. defense pact and the Philippine Security Treaty. Though generally known as a moderate and a supporter of the Truman administration, Ribicoff backed the Internal Security (McCarran) Act of 1950. Near the end of his second term in the House, he ran in an election to fill the unexpired Senate term of Brien McMahon (D-Conn.), who had died in July 1952. Ribicoff lost a close election to his Republican opponent, PRESCOTT BUSH, and, at the end of his term in the House, returned to private practice with his brother's law firm in Hartford.

In 1954, Ribicoff ran for governor against the Republican incumbent, John Davis Lodge. After a campaign in which he stressed the need to reform state government and increase state revenues, Ribicoff emerged the winner by 3,115 votes. His narrow victory and the fact that Republicans controlled the state legislature led Ribicoff to adopt a cautious, nonpartisan approach as governor. Avoiding new programs and reforms, he stressed administrative efficiency by eliminating or consolidating 20 state agencies. He held daily press conferences and kept state officials alert by calling department heads for information on questions he could not answer.

Ribicoff gained national attention in early 1956 with a campaign for highway safety that punished convicted speeders with automatic suspensions of their licenses for 30 days or more. As a result of the campaign and increased state spending for highway safety measures, traffic fatalities in Connecticut fell 11 percent from their level the year before. When Republicans complained that the penalties were too severe, Ribicoff derisively dubbed them the "pro-speeding" party.

Ribicoff's administration was so popular that it temporarily upset the normally close balance between Republicans and Democrats in Connecticut. Ribicoff won reelection by nearly 247,000 votes in 1958, and Democrats riding his coattails took control of the state legislature for the first time since 1876. The Democratic victory, however, brought little change in the customary caution of the governor, who often spoke of "the integrity of compromise." He did submit a bill to the legislature to eliminate Connecticut's outmoded system of county government, which had responsibility only for placing foster children and managing county jails. Passed by the legislature in May 1959, the bill transferred county functions to the state and abolished the county tax on cities and towns.

His record as governor brought him to prominence in the national Democratic Party, and Ribicoff increased his influence through his early support of the presidential aspirations of Senator JOHN F. KENNEDY (D-Mass.), with whom he became friends when they served together in the House. Ribicoff backed Kennedy's unsuccessful bid for the vice presidential nomination in 1956 and nominated Kennedy for the vice presidency at the convention. Along with John Bailey, the Democratic chairman of Connecticut, Ribicoff planned Kennedy's strategy in New England for the presidential race in 1960. Ribicoff served as Kennedy's chief spokesperson at the annual Governors' Conference in June 1960 and later that year was one of Kennedy's floor managers at the Democratic National Convention in Los Angeles.

In return for his services during the campaign, Kennedy offered Ribicoff his choice of cabinet posts in the new administration. According to Kennedy's aides and biographers, ARTHUR SCHLESINGER, JR., and Theodore Sorensen, Ribicoff would have liked to serve as attorney general but thought it unwise for a Jewish official to preside over the prosecution of controversial civil rights cases in the South. He chose instead the position of secretary of health, education, and welfare (HEW) and resigned as governor at the end of 1960 to take up the post. Ribicoff spent much of his time as head of HEW advocating the administration's legislative programs for health care for the elderly and federal aid to education. Congress passed neither. Frustrated by a hostile Congress and a federal bureaucracy he considered cumbersome and unresponsive, he resigned his post in the cabinet in July 1962 and returned to politics in Connecticut. Ribicoff won election to the Senate in 1962 and was reelected by wide margins in 1968 and 1974. As chair of the Government Operations Subcommittee on Executive Reorganization, he gained wide attention for supporting motor vehicle safety standards, Medicare, federal aid to education, and environmental regulation. One of the most memorable moments of his career came in 1968, when he nominated Senator George McGovern (D-S. Dak.) for the presidency at the Democratic National Convention in Chicago. At a convention held amid protests against the war in Vietnam, Ribicoff accused Chicago's mayor, Richard Daley, of employing "Gestapo tactics" to suppress the protests. Daley shouted an epithet at Ribicoff from the floor, and turmoil broke out at the convention. In 1972, Ribicoff again nominated McGovern, who won the nomination but lost in a landslide to RICHARD M. NIXON. Ribicoff announced that he would not seek reelection in 1980.

After leaving the Senate, he joined the law firm of Kaye, Scholer, Fierman, Hays & Handler in New York City and resided in Cornwall Bridge, Connecticut. He died in New York City on February 22, 1998.

—MSM

Rickover, Hyman G(eorge)

(1900–1986) *director of naval research, Atomic Energy Commission, director of nuclear propulsion, Navy Bureau of Ships*

Rickover was born in Makow, in Russian Poland, on January 29, 1900. Fleeing poverty and anti-Semitism, his father emigrated to the United States and brought his family over in 1906. Rickover grew up in a Jewish area of Chicago, attended public schools there, and graduated from the naval academy in 1922. He served on the USS *La Vallette* and the USS *Nevada* before returning to Annapolis for a year at the naval postgraduate school, where he studied electrical engineering. He earned a M.Sc. in engineering from Columbia University in 1929. After attending submarine school in 1930, Rickover served on *S-48*, first as an engineer and then as executive officer. He served on the battleship *New Mexico* from 1935 to 1937, when he assumed command of the minesweeper *Finch*. Later in 1937, he became an engineering duty officer and served at the Cavite navy yard in the Philippines. In August 1939, he was assigned to the electrical section of the Bureau of Ships and became chief of the section in December 1940, a position he held throughout World War II and for which he received a Legion of Merit. Rickover left the electrical section in March 1945 to assume command of a planned naval repair base at Okinawa, but Japan surrendered before the base was completed.

After the war, the navy sent him to receive training in nuclear power at Oak Ridge, Tennessee, and to explore the possibility of using nuclear power for ship propulsion. The law that created the Atomic Energy Commission (AEC) gave it a monopoly on the development of atomic energy. In February 1949, Rickover became head of a joint navy-AEC program to develop nuclear propulsion. Under Rickover's guidance, construction of the nuclear-powered submarine *Nautilus* began in June 1952 and was completed in January 1954. Between 1954 and 1959, the navy constructed three nuclear surface warships: the destroyer *Bainbridge*, the cruiser *Long Beach*, and the aircraft carrier *Enterprise*.

Despite his obvious ability, Rickover generated intense animosity. Although nuclear-powered ships offered many advantages over conventional ships, many naval officers opposed the construction of a nuclear navy, because the cost of constructing such ships was considerably higher than that of conventional ships. In the face of stiff opposition, Rickover fought hard for his nuclear ships. In addition, he assembled a crack staff for his nuclear projects during the 1950s and offended some in the service by prizing ability over rank. His incessant demands for high-quality work at low cost did not endear him to private industry, either. Further, his autocratic personal style won him no friends. His outspoken views and abrasive manner made him unpopular with his superiors, and Rickover was twice overlooked for promotion until an act of Congress promoted him from captain to rear admiral in 1953. He was promoted to vice admiral in 1958.

Rickover's experiences with personnel as well as his dissatisfaction with substandard workmanship by civilian contractors led him frequently to attack American education. In a series of public statements, he declared that U.S. students were ill prepared to meet the demands of an increasingly technological society. In February 1958, Rickover stated that, if necessary, he favored transferring money from the Defense Department to raise teachers' pay and improve education. He asserted that education was more important than defense expenditures and urged federal standards for teachers. He placed the blame for America's inadequate educational system principally on "professional educators" and warned Congress not to "make the mistake of strengthening the position of state boards of education." In 1959, he published *Education and Freedom*, which argued for higher standards, especially in math and science. The book also called for the establishment of national standards and warned that other nations provided their children with a better education. Particularly in the context of the cold war, Rickover asserted that America's inferior public schools placed the nation at risk. He wrote that "Education is the most important problem facing the United States today" and warned that "only the massive upgrading of the scholastic standards of our schools will guarantee the future prosperity and freedom of the Republic."

During the Kennedy administration, Rickover clashed with Secretary of Defense Robert S. McNamara over construction of a second nuclear-powered aircraft carrier, which Rickover strongly

and unsuccessfully advocated. In the early 1960s, he also continued his public criticism of the American educational system. He published *Swiss Schools and Ours: Why Theirs Are Better* (1962) and *American Education: A National Failure* (1963). President LYNDON B. JOHNSON waived mandatory retirement for Rickover in 1964, which allowed the admiral to continue in the service. During the Johnson years, Rickover deplored the navy's acceptance of inferior materials, which he contended stemmed from the close connection between business and the military. Promoted to admiral in 1973, he remained on active duty until 1981 and retired on January 19, 1982. His interest in naval technology ranged widely. In 1976, he published a technical inquiry into the destruction of the battleship *Maine*, which led to the Spanish-American War. Rickover died in Arlington, Virginia, on July 8, 1986.

—MSM

Ridgway, Matthew B(unker)
(1895–1993)   *army chief of staff*

The son of an army colonel, Matthew B. Ridgway was born in Fort Monroe, Virginia, on March 3, 1895, and raised on various army posts. Following his graduation from West Point in 1917, he spent World War I in the United States as a company commander and adjutant with the Third Infantry Regiment. From 1918 to 1924, he taught romance languages at West Point and became manager of the athletics program, during which time he was promoted to captain. He spent the interwar years serving in assignments in Central America, the Far East, and the United States. Promoted to major in 1932, he attended Command and General Staff School from 1933 to 1935, after which he served as assistant chief of staff for operations with the VI Corps. He attended the U.S. Army War College from 1936 to 1937 and was chief operations officer for the Fourth Army from 1937 to 1939. From 1939 to 1942, Ridgway was assigned to the war plans division of the War Department's general staff. While serving there, he was promoted to colonel. During World War II, Ridgway played an important role in the creation of army airborne units and, as commanding general of the 82nd Airborne Division, participated in the invasion of Sicily, the Italian campaign, and the invasion of Normandy. Ridgway became commander of XVIII Corps, which comprised three airborne divisions. His men were engaged in some of the heaviest fighting of the European campaign.

Ridgway received a promotion to lieutenant general in 1945 and, by the end of the war, was one of the army's most respected combat commanders. From 1945 to 1948, he briefly commanded U.S. forces in the Mediterranean theater and had extended assignments with the Military Staff Committee of the United Nations and the Inter-American Defense Board. In 1948, he was appointed head of the Caribbean command and the following year became deputy chief of staff for administration and training. After a brief stint as army deputy chief of staff, Ridgway commanded the Eighth Army during the Korean War. When President HARRY S. TRUMAN relieved General Douglas A. MacArthur, commander of the UN forces, in 1951, Ridgway replaced him. In 1952, he succeeded General DWIGHT D. EISENHOWER as supreme commander of the North Atlantic Treaty Organization (NATO) forces.

After assuming the presidency, Eisenhower appointed Ridgway army chief of staff in August 1953. Ridgway soon clashed with the administration over its "New Look" defense policy, which relied on technology, air power, and the nuclear deterrent. The administration's approach stemmed partly from a desire to reduce spending on defense and partly from a reaction to the Korean War. Cuts under this policy hit the army hardest. In 1954, Ridgway joined General JAMES M. GAVIN in protesting the New Look's cutbacks in the defense budget and reductions in army personnel. Instead, Ridgway called for a policy that provided for carefully measured responses to aggression with conventional forces in instances that did not warrant the use of nuclear weapons. Eisenhower regarded Ridgway's opposition to cuts in the army as "parochial," and relations between the two became strained.

In debates over military policy, Ridgway often served as a voice of moderation, countering the more belligerent policies of Admiral ARTHUR RADFORD, chairman of the Joint Chiefs of Staff. When the administration was considering a request from the French for U.S. military intervention in French Indochina during the spring of 1954, Ridgway opposed Radford's plan for air strikes. Ridgway doubted that the air power alone could achieve the objective and feared that, if bombing failed, there would be a strong temptation to send American ground troops. Ridgway ordered a team of experts to evaluate the situation in Indochina. Their subsequent report concluded that the United States was not ready to fight a guerrilla war of the type being carried on in the area. Eisenhower eventually decided against using military force to aid the French.

Ridgway also opposed Radford's recommendations after Communist China began shelling the Nationalist-held islands of Quemoy and Matsu in the fall of 1954. Radford and the majority of the Joint Chiefs argued that, although the islands had no strategic value to Taiwan, their loss would bring a collapse of Nationalist morale, which, in turn, would have implications for the defense of Asia. They therefore recommended that Eisenhower permit Chiang Kai-shek to bomb the mainland. If Quemoy were attacked, they urged that the United States intervene militarily. The only dissenter among the Joint Chiefs, Ridgway argued that it was not the military's responsibility to judge the psychological value of the island and urged restraint. Once again, Eisenhower decided against military intervention.

Frustrated by his constant disagreements with the president and other members of the Joint Chiefs and nearing the end of his term as army chief of staff, Ridgway retired from the army in June 1955 and became head of the Mellon Institute, an industrial research center. He held that position for five years. "Throughout my two years as Chief of Staff," he later recalled, "I felt I was being called upon to tear down, rather than build up, the ultimately decisive element in a properly proportioned fighting force." He published a volume of memoirs, *Soldier*, in 1956. A few days before his retirement, he expressed his views on the need for a "viable strategy for Cold War situations" to meet aggression in the "mountains of Greece and Korea or the jungles of Indochina."

After leaving the military, Ridgway continued to oppose the administration's emphasis on air power and the nuclear deterrent. He criticized what he regarded as the elevation of politics above the national interest. As a member of the Association of the U.S. Army, he worked for acceptance of his views on limited wars, which gained increasing support among congressional leaders and academic strategists. In a report of the association in 1960, Ridgway outlined a proposal for the reorganization of the army into a "mobile ready force" capable of fighting small wars. The plan eventually won acceptance as part of the Kennedy administration's "flexible response."

As the United States escalated its involvement in Vietnam during the 1960s, Ridgway was one of the military leaders, along with Gavin, who attempted to persuade the Johnson administration to limit American participation. In 1966, he argued that the government should maintain a middle course between unilateral withdrawal and all-out war. A member of the Senior Advisory Group on Vietnam, which met with President LYNDON B. JOHNSON during March 1968, Ridgway continued to stress nonmilitary options in the conflict. By 1970, he supported a planned withdrawal. In the 1970s, Ridgway opposed the volunteer army and the admission of women into the service academies. The Pentagon's decision in 1979 to order paratroopers to stop wearing the red beret infuriated him. President Ronald Reagan awarded Ridgway the Presidential Medal of Freedom in 1986. Ridgway received the Congressional Gold Medal in 1991. He died in Fox Chapel, Pennsylvania, on July 26, 1993.

—MSM

Riesman, David

(1909–2002) *sociologist*

The son of a German-born professor of medicine at the University of Pennsylvania, David Riesman was born in Philadelphia, Pennsylvania, on September 22, 1909. He attended William Penn Charter School and Harvard University, from which he graduated Phi Beta Kappa in 1931. He went to Harvard Law School, where he was an editor of the Harvard Law Review and received his LL.B. in 1934. Upon completing a law degree, Riesman received a fellowship that enabled him to spend an additional year studying with FELIX FRANKFURTER at Harvard Law

School. Admitted to the bars of Massachusetts and the District of Columbia in 1935, he became a clerk to Supreme Court Justice Louis D. Brandeis. Riesman then practiced law in Boston and, from 1937 to 1941, was professor of law at the University of Buffalo. He took up a visiting research fellowship at Columbia Law School in 1941. During his career in academic law, he published several books and articles on human rights and employment law. From 1942 to 1943, he served as deputy assistant district attorney in New York County, after which he spent three years as an executive at the Sperry Gyroscope Company on Long Island. He joined the faculty of social sciences at the University of Chicago as a visiting associate professor in 1946. Three years later, he became a full professor.

In 1950, he published *The Lonely Crowd*. Riesman's thesis was that Americans had once been "inner-directed" people, who lived by internalized values. Postwar Americans, however, were becoming "other directed" people, who took their cues from peers and the mass media. Whereas radicals of the 1930s railed against selfishness and competition, Riesman was far more concerned about society's encroachments on the individual. As Riesman put it, the "problem for people" in postwar America was less the "material environment" than "other people."

The book argued that in societies with a stable population, an essentially static social order, and little technological change (such as medieval Europe), the dominant character type was "tradition-directed." Such people lived their lives by a set of rules "dedicated to a very large degree by power relations among the various age and sex groups, the clans, castes, professions—relations which have endured for centuries and are modified but slightly." Patterns of life were dictated by rituals, custom, and religious practices. In periods of technological advance, economic expansion, and social mobility, people developed a capacity to set goals for themselves, influenced by values implanted in childhood that stressed a belief in personal choice, initiative, individual responsibility, and achievement. These values guided individuals throughout their lives. Riesman characterized the people produced by such societies as "inner-directed." During periods when consumption overtook production, when scarcity gave way to abundance, the dominant character type became "other directed." Such people desired to be part of a larger community to the extent that they constantly adjusted their values and morality to fit in with the group. "While all people want and need to be liked by some of the people some of the time," wrote Riesman, "it is only the modern other-directed types who make this their chief source of direction."

Riesman identified inner-direction as "the typical character of the 'old' middle class—the banker, the tradesman, the small entrepreneur, the technically oriented engineer." Other-direction, he maintained, was "becoming the typical character of the 'new' middle class—the bureaucrat, the salaried employee . . . etc." Perhaps, Riesman suggested, postwar affluence had produced a class whose economic progress had come so quickly that the social and psychological adjustments that would normally accompany such a development lacked the time to evolve.

Yale University Press printed 3,000 copies of *The Lonely Crowd* and had to order 13 additional printings before an abridged version, published as one of Anchor Books's "quality paperbacks" series, appeared in 1953. According to a study conducted by Herbert Gans in 1997, *The Lonely Crowd* went on to sell more copies than any work of sociology before or since.

A boldly speculative work, *The Lonely Crowd*, written with Riesman's assistants, Nathan Glazer and Reuel Denny, represented a marked departure from the statistically driven works that dominated sociology at that time and, as such, encountered skepticism from sociologists. On the other hand, it won praise from virtually all other quarters. The literary critic Lionel Trilling called it "one of the most interesting books I have read." Irving Howe, the writer and literary critic, thought the book "often strikingly brilliant" and praised especially its description of the effects of other-directed values on Americans and American culture. Riesman appeared on the cover of *Time* magazine in September 1954. *The Lonely Crowd* became the first of a succession of books examining the American character, most of which focused attention on the power of the mass over the individual. Among those were C. WRIGHT MILLS's *White Collar* (1951), DAVID POTTER's *People of Plenty* (1954), WILLIAM WHYTE's *The Organization Man* (1956), John

Keats's *The Crack in the Picture Window* (1956), and VANCE PACKARD's *The Status Seekers* (1959).

Riesman left the University of Chicago in 1958 to join Harvard University's Department of Social Relations. When it broke up, he joined Harvard's new department of sociology, where he taught until his retirement. His other books include *Faces in the Crowd: Individual Studies in Character and Politics* (1952, based on a collection of interviews dealing with issues raised in *The Lonely Crowd*), *Thorstein Veblen: A Critical Interpretation* (1953), *Individualism Reconsidered and Other Essays* (1954), *Constraint and Variety in American Higher Education* (1956), *Abundance for What* (1964), *The Academic Revolution* (1968), *The Perpetual Dream* (1978), and *On Higher Education* (1980), which dealt with the rise of student power on college campuses.

In the 1950s and early 1960s, Riesman supported a number of liberal causes, most notably the antinuclear movement. He served as faculty adviser to Tocsin, a peace group at Harvard and Radcliffe, and was editor of *The Correspondent*, the journal of the Committee (later Council) of Correspondence, an association of antinuclear academics. Beginning with the student protests at the University of California at Berkeley in 1964, however, he opposed the student radicals of the 1960s. Riesman maintained that the establishment they hoped to destroy, however flawed, was a social web critical to a free society. In the late 1960s, he criticized the discipline of sociology for "becoming so politicized" that it was "hard to bring sober people into it."

Never one to follow the crowd, lonely or otherwise, Riesman held a number of opinions that many regarded as heretical or merely eccentric. He maintained, for example, that no student should go to college less than 500 miles from home "without good reason." He did not favor coeducation, because he thought it tended to produce students whose behavior conformed to accepted gender patterns. As Riesman saw it, young women influenced their male associates to choose careers compatible with domesticity.

Upon his retirement from Harvard in 1980, Riesman became professor emeritus and continued to reside in Cambridge. He died in Binghamton, New York, on May 10, 2002.

—MSM

Rivers, L(ucius) Mendel

(1905–1970) *U.S. congressman*

The son of a small farmer who also owned a turpentine still, Rivers was born in Gumville, South Carolina, in Berkeley County, on September 28, 1905. Rivers's father died in 1914, and the boy moved with his mother to northern Charleston County. Rivers took odd jobs to help support his family. He attended public schools, where he excelled as an athlete and, after graduating in 1926, played semiprofessional baseball. Rivers attended the College of Charleston from 1926 to 1929 and the University of South Carolina from 1929 to 1931. He graduated from neither institution but was admitted to the bar in 1932. After practicing law for a brief time, he ran unsuccessfully for the state legislature in 1932 but won a special election to fill a vacancy in the state legislature the following year. He served until 1936, when he took a position as a special attorney with the Justice Department.

In 1940, Rivers resigned from the Justice Department and ran against Alfred Von Kolnitz in the Democratic primary for a congressional seat that represented Charleston and vicinity. Rivers ran behind his opponent in Charleston but, thanks to his strong showing in rural areas, won the primary. In an overwhelmingly Democratic state, the general election was little more than a formality. For the next three decades, he served in Congress, usually facing only token opposition in his bids for reelection. Upon entering the House, Rivers received an assignment to the Naval Affairs Committee, which in 1947 was merged into the new Armed Services Committee. During his first years in Washington, he tended to support the Roosevelt administration, but he soon shifted to more conservative politics. He supported the Taft-Hartley Act and other restrictions on organized labor. An ardent segregationist, he opposed civil rights and antilynching legislation. In 1948, Rivers backed the presidential candidacy of Governor STROM THURMOND of South Carolina, who ran on the States Rights (Dixiecrat) ticket. As a member of the Armed Services Committee, he consistently backed large defense expenditures and a hard line in the cold war. In 1950, Rivers publicly urged President HARRY S. TRUMAN to threaten North Korea with the atomic bomb. He consistently supported antisubversive legislation.

Rivers backed DWIGHT D. EISENHOWER for the presidency in 1952. Nevertheless, he opposed the Eisenhower administration's cuts to defense spending. Rivers believed that military strength provided the only real guarantee of American security. Not only did he oppose reductions in defense spending, but he advocated substantially increased spending on the military throughout the 1950s. In 1955, he unsuccessfully offered an amendment to a supplemental appropriations bill that would have nearly doubled funds for navy public works. The following year, he backed a bill providing for a pay raise for the military. In 1960, Rivers headed a special subcommittee of the Armed Services Committee on military airlifts, which recommended an extensive program for modernizing the Military Air Transport Service (MATS). As a result, the military purchased more powerful airplanes to expand and update the MATS fleet.

From the beginning of his career in Congress, Rivers used his position on the Armed Services Committee to secure a vast array of military installations for his district. In 1955, he served as vice chair of a special subcommittee examining military land transfers. Shortly after that, he headed a special subcommittee investigating the Pentagon's property acquisitions. Between 1955 and 1960, the navy established a marine corps air station at Beaufort; the air force built a recreation center at Berkeley and an unmanned radar site at Parris Island. The army located a national guard office in Hampton and an army reserve installation in Charleston. Rivers's tireless efforts to locate military installations in his district once led CARL VINSON (D-Ga.), the chair of the Armed Services Committee and a close ally of Rivers, to remark, "You put anything else down there in your district, Mendel, it's gonna sink."

Throughout the Eisenhower administration, Rivers passionately defended segregation. He was highly critical of the Supreme Court's ruling in 1954 that declared segregated public schools unconstitutional. He signed the Southern Manifesto, which condemned the decision and urged all legal means to resist it. In addition, Rivers joined the White Citizens' Council, an organization formed to preserve segregation; he was the only member of South Carolina's congressional delegation to do so. In Congress, Rivers opposed every civil rights measure that came before the House in the 1950s and 1960s.

On occasion, however, Rivers supported social welfare measures opposed by the Eisenhower administration. In 1958, he voted for an increase in Social Security benefits that the president thought too costly. The following year, he backed two housing bills that Eisenhower vetoed because of their cost.

In 1960, Rivers supported a bill to cut the Cuban sugar quota in retaliation for the policies of Cuba's premier, Fidel Castro. During the floor debate on the bill, he urged further action. He urged his colleagues to "revise our sugar quota and take the next step tomorrow, and probably the ultimate step will be to occupy that island to save those people. Let us take that step. Our stature is dwindling. Let us build it up while time remains."

Rivers succeeded Vinson as chair of the Armed Services Committee in 1965. During that year, he clashed with President LYNDON B. JOHNSON and Secretary of Defense Robert S. McNamara over the closing of military bases and a pay raise for the military. Rivers failed in an attempt to secure congressional veto power over base closings but did succeed in doubling the military pay raise requested by the administration.

One of the strongest congressional supporters of the war in Vietnam, he called for the use of nuclear weapons in that conflict. Rivers's enthusiasm for weapons systems exceeded that of the most ambitious military officials in the Pentagon. He also regarded himself as the champion of the common soldier, which led him to take positions that sometimes brought him into conflict with military leaders. Unswerving in his support for the war in Vietnam, Rivers criticized the antiwar movement in the most vitriolic of terms. He continued to obtain military installations for his district, and, by the late 1960s, defense-related facilities accounted, according to reports, for more than one-third of the total payroll in the Charleston area. Never as consistent in his conservatism on domestic issues as he was in his support for the military and an aggressive foreign policy, Rivers supported a number of Great Society programs in the second half of the 1960s. He voted for housing subsidies, the

food stamp program, antipoverty legislation, and mass transit. He continued, however, to oppose civil rights legislation.

An alcoholic, Rivers was a binge drinker. He remained sober most of the time but periodically embarked on unrestrained bouts of drinking. The columnist DREW PEARSON wrote that Rivers was a "security risk" and included an indictment of Rivers in his book, *The Case Against Congress* (1968). Rivers stopped drinking and remained sober the last two years of his life. He underwent open-heart surgery in Birmingham, Alabama, on December 11, 1970, and died of heart failure there on December 28, 1970.

—MSM

Roberts, C(harles) Wesley
(1902–1976) *chairman, Republican National Committee*

Born in Oskaloosa, Kansas, on December 14, 1902, Roberts attended public schools and Kansas State College before becoming part-owner and coeditor of three small-town newspapers in Kansas. After serving as campaign manager for the Republican gubernatorial nominee in 1936, he became the assistant chairman of the Kansas Republican State Committee in 1938. The following year, he became secretary to Governor Payne Ratner. After service as a major in the marines during World War II, he became chairman of the Kansas Republican Party in 1947. He resigned three years later to manage the successful senatorial campaign of FRANK CARLSON. Although he did not hold any office in the Republican Party of Kansas after 1950, he remained a powerful figure in Kansas's majority party. Together with Carlson and Governor Edward Arn, Roberts led the conservative, or "palace guard," wing of the state Republican Party, which engaged in bitter intraparty conflict with the more progressive "young Turks" faction, led by Lieutenant Governor Fred Hall and the aging Alf Landon.

Carlson was an early supporter of DWIGHT D. EISENHOWER's presidential candidacy, and, in 1952, he managed Eisenhower's preconvention headquarters in Washington. After the convention, Roberts became director of organization of the Republican National Committee. In January 1953, the outgoing chairman of the Republican National Committee, ARTHUR SUMMERFIELD, designated Roberts as his successor. The national committee immediately ratified the selection, and President Eisenhower expressed his "hearty approval."

Less than one month after he assumed office, the *Kansas City Star* reported that Roberts had received a commission of $11,000 for helping a fraternal order sell a hospital building to the state in 1951. Even though he held no official position in the state's Republican Party at that time, Roberts had used his connections as a state party leader to influence an appropriation by the state legislature. To add to the scandal, there was some question as to whether the state already owned the facility. Moreover, Roberts had failed to register as a lobbyist and failed to inform any state officials and legislators with whom he dealt that he represented private parties. Roberts responded that he had not acted as a lobbyist but as a "public relations counsel." Republican rivals in Kansas pressed the attack on Roberts. A special committee of the state legislature, on which the Arn faction had a majority, charged Roberts with having "deliberately and intentionally" violated the "spirit" if not the "letter" of the state's law requiring the registration of lobbyists.

Upon release of the committee's report, Roberts resigned as chairman of the Republican National Committee after what was described as a "heart to heart" talk with Eisenhower at the White House. He had filled the post for nine weeks. Eisenhower, who had campaigned vigorously against corruption in the Truman administration, issued a statement describing Roberts's move as "a wise one" and quickly named LEONARD HALL as Roberts's successor. Roberts returned to his newspapers and his insurance agency. In August 1953, the attorney general of Kansas announced that, although it left him with "a feeling of real frustration," he would not press criminal charges against Roberts because the latter's action "did not violate our statute as it now is written."

Roberts became a public relations consultant with Lehman Brothers in New York and then with Goodbody and Company. Later, he opened his own public relations company in Washington, D.C. Roberts died in Alexandria, Virginia, on April 9, 1976.

—MSM

Robertson, A(bsalom) Willis
(1887–1971) *U.S. senator; chairman, Senate Banking and Currency Committee*

Born in Martinsburg, West Virginia, on May 27, 1887, Robertson moved with his parents to Lynchburg, Virginia, in 1891. He attended public schools, after which he graduated from the University of Richmond in 1907 and from its law department in 1908. Admitted to the bar in 1908, he began to practice law in Rockbridge County, Virginia. Robertson served as a Democratic member of the Virginia senate from 1916 to 1922. During World War I, he served in the U.S. Army as assistant camp adjutant at Camp Lee, Virginia, and in the adjutant general's office in Washington, rising to the rank of major. Robertson served as the commonwealth's attorney for Rockbridge County from 1922 to 1928. He was commissioner of the state Commission of Game and Inland Fisheries from 1926 until 1932, when he won election to the U.S. House of Representatives. He was reelected six consecutive times.

In the House, Robertson established himself as a conservative who, according to the historian J. Harvie Wilkinson, "personified Spartan discipline, pioneer individualism, Puritan and Calvinist morality." Robertson voted against most New Deal measures and with the Roosevelt administration on foreign policy. Like HARRY BYRD, whose Democratic machine dominated politics in Virginia from the late 1920s to the middle of the 1960s, Robertson opposed racial integration, social welfare programs, and the growth of the federal government. Although part of the Byrd machine, Robertson was not personally close to Byrd himself. Indeed, he was not Byrd's first choice to fill the vacancy in the Senate created by the death of Carter Glass in 1946. Robertson, however, seemed less likely than Byrd's first choice to arouse the ire of the machine's opponents. Subsequently, Robertson won the election, entered the Senate on November 6, 1946, and was reelected to full terms in 1948, 1954, and 1960.

In the Senate, Robertson supported the Taft-Hartley Act in 1947 and voted against public housing. He did support President HARRY S. TRUMAN's seizure of the steel industry. In addition, he voted for aid to Greece and Turkey in 1947 and the Marshall Plan in 1948. He also strongly supported the North Atlantic Treaty Organization.

In 1948, Robertson became convinced that General DWIGHT D. EISENHOWER was the only potential candidate for the presidency who could unite the nation and deal with the Soviet Union. Accordingly, Robertson urged his southern colleagues to join him in persuading Truman to step aside and in drafting Eisenhower. His arguments failed to persuade other southern members of Congress. When it became evident that Eisenhower would not run as a Democrat in 1948, Robertson became the first significant officeholder in Virginia to announce his support for Truman. In 1951, however, Robertson advanced Eisenhower for the presidency. When it became clear that Eisenhower was a Republican, Robertson contacted Bernard Baruch, the influential financier, and asked him to work to make Eisenhower the Republican candidate in 1952.

During the Eisenhower administration, Robertson focused his attention on preventing the expansion of the federal government. He also supported conservative fiscal policies, particularly those designed to balance the budget. Those concerns led him to oppose the continuation of rent controls and the creation of a permanent Small Business Administration in 1953. While he favored the bill that established the St. Lawrence Seaway Development Corporation in 1954, Robertson wanted to use the toll money collected on the waterway to reduce the national debt. In 1957, Robertson successfully opposed federal construction of a hydroelectric dam at Hell's Canyon, Idaho; the project, he believed, should be left to private developers. In 1958, he opposed accelerating the administration's interstate highway program as inflationary. Despite his fiscal conservatism, Robertson consistently supported high defense spending. In 1956, he was one of 13 members of the Senate Appropriations Committee who supported a $1.6 billion increase in the amount the House voted for the air force.

In 1956, Robertson headed a subcommittee that attempted to develop a legislative program for revising the U.S. banking code. At the request of the panel, the agencies involved in regulating banking submitted more than 175 proposed amendments. In December, a 27-member advisory committee filed a report that urged increased federal authority over interstate bank mergers and embodied more

than 200 legislative recommendations. Finally, in 1960, Congress passed the Bank Merger Act, which prohibited mergers or consolidations of federally insured banks "without the prior written consent" of the appropriate supervisory agency.

Robertson became chairman of the Banking and Currency Committee in 1958. In that post, he emerged as the leading spokesman on fiscal matters for the conservative coalition of southern Democrats and Republicans. He cautioned that if the government's deficit of $12.9 billion continued to rise, foreign and domestic capital would flee the dollar. Robertson also warned against inflation but discouraged wage and price controls, which he believed ineffective. In 1959, he was the only member of his committee to support the administration and vote against an additional $1 billion in housing appropriations. Eisenhower vetoed this bill as too costly, and Robertson led the committee in rewriting it to meet the president's objections.

A committed segregationist, Robertson opposed the Supreme Court's decision in *Brown v. Board of Education* (1954) that struck down segregated public schools. In 1956, he signed the Southern Manifesto, which denounced the decision as a "clear abuse of judicial power" and urged the use of all legal means to oppose it. When President Eisenhower nominated Solicitor General SIMON E. SOBELOFF to a seat on the Fourth Circuit Court of Appeals in 1956, Robertson opposed Sobeloff's confirmation. He accused the solicitor general of "prejudice" against the South on the issue of segregation. Despite the efforts of Robertson and other segregationists, the Senate overwhelmingly confirmed Sobeloff.

Robertson worried about the ability of southern members of Congress to maintain the influence they had exerted throughout the first half of the 20th century. He and Senator J. STROM THURMOND (D-S.C.) led an unsuccessful fight to keep Alaska out of the Union, because they feared its admission would dilute southern congressional strength.

Unlike Byrd, who maintained a resounding silence, Robertson at least nominally supported the Democratic national ticket in 1960. During the Kennedy and Johnson administrations, Robertson continued to oppose civil rights and social welfare legislation. Running for reelection in 1966, he was narrowly defeated by William B. Spong in the Virginia Democratic primary. Having lost the election, Robertson resigned early in order to give Spong seniority. After Robertson left the Senate, he was a consultant to the National Bank for Reconstruction and Development from 1966 to 1968, when he retired. He resided in Lexington, Virginia, until his death there on November 1, 1971.

—MSM

Robeson, Paul B(ustill)

(1898–1976) *entertainer, political activist*

The son of a Protestant minister who had been a slave until he ran away to join the Union Army at the age of 15, Paul Robeson was born in Princeton, New Jersey, on April 9, 1898. His mother, a schoolteacher of African, Indian, and English heritage, died when he was a child. In 1910, Robeson moved with his father to Somerville, New Jersey, where he attended public schools. He won a competitive scholarship to attend Rutgers College (later Rutgers University), where he was the lone African American in his class and only the third to attend the college. An outstanding student, he was on the varsity debate team, won class prizes in oratory each of his four years, won election to Phi Beta Kappa as a junior, and was valedictorian of his class. Robeson's athletic achievements equaled his academic performance. He earned a total of 12 varsity letters in baseball, basketball, football, and track. An outstanding end on both offense and defense, Robeson was twice named to the All-American team in football. After receiving his B.A. in 1919, he entered Columbia University Law School, where he supported himself by playing professional football. While in law school, Robeson became involved in the theater, largely through the influence of his wife, Eslanda. He made his professional debut on Broadway in 1922. Upon earning his LL.B. in 1923, he joined a law firm in New York City. Discrimination within the firm and in the legal profession generally led him to quit after a few months to pursue a career in acting. In 1924, he appeared in the lead role of two plays by Eugene O'Neill, *The Emperor Jones* and *All God's Chillun Got Wings*. In 1930, Robeson played Othello in London to great acclaim. In addition to his acting, he embarked on a career as a singer in 1925. Eschewing classical music in favor of African-American spirituals and folk songs, he went on concert tours, performed on radio, and made over 300 recordings. His bass baritone as well as his acting talent made him a star of several musicals, the best known of which was *Show Boat*. Robeson also appeared in 11 motion pictures, including *The Emperor Jones* (1933) and *Show Boat* (1936).

Introduced to socialism by George Bernard Shaw in 1928, Robeson became a prominent spokesperson for black aspirations and various left-wing causes. Dismayed by racism in America, he lived in Europe for most of the 1930s and returned to the United States only for concerts or roles in films. Robeson toured the Soviet Union in 1934 and was impressed by the warm reception he received as well as what he perceived to be an absence of discrimination based on class or race. After that, he returned to Moscow for extended stays and learned Russian. As the 1930s progressed, he actively opposed fascism, racism, and imperialism. In Britain, he gave benefit performances for refugees from fascist countries and for left-wing British groups. He went to Spain in 1938 to perform for Republican troops.

With the outbreak of World War II, Robeson returned to the United States, where he was outspoken in his criticism of American racism and his praise for the Soviet Union. The causes he supported included organized labor, the desegregation of professional baseball, and Pan-Africanism. Although Robeson's political activities attracted some criticism, it did not hurt his career, in large part because the Soviet Union and the United States were allies during the war. In 1943, he became the first African American to play Othello with a white supporting cast on Broadway. His performance received rave reviews. The following year, he received the Spingarn Medal, the highest award offered by the National Association for the Advancement of Colored People.

After the war, however, he continued to praise the Soviet Union and to compare the United States unfavorably to the communist state. As American relations with the Soviet Union deteriorated, his position became increasingly unpopular. In 1946, he appeared before a committee of the state legislature of California and denied that he had ever been a member of the Communist Party. Subsequently, he refused to answer any questions about his political affiliations before investigating committees as a matter of conscience and constitutional right. Meanwhile, he continued to attack American racism and to defend the Soviet experiment. A founder of the Progressive Party, he campaigned for its nominee, Henry Wallace, in the presidential election of 1948. The following year, he pronounced it "unthinkable" that African Americans would "go to war on behalf of those who have oppressed us for generations against a country [the Soviet Union] which in one generation has raised our people to the full dignity of mankind." That remark drew criticism from the press, including the black press, and most civil rights organizations. The House Un-American Activities Committee (HUAC) called black witnesses to refute Robeson's contention and labeled him a "communist sympathizer." A scheduled performance by Robeson at a music festival in Peekskill, New York, sponsored by the radical Civil Rights Congress, touched off rioting. In 1950, the State Department revoked Robeson's passport because he had refused to sign a noncommunist oath, as then required. Robeson fought the decision in the courts for eight years; in the meantime, he could not leave the country. While his case was still pending, in 1958 the Supreme Court ruled in a similar case that the State Department could not withhold passports because of an applicant's "beliefs and association," and the State Department issued him a passport.

Throughout the 1950s, Robeson continued his strident attacks on American policy. He denounced the American involvement in Korea and what he described as the "genocide" of African Americans. The Soviet Union awarded him the Stalin Peace Prize in 1952, which provided further ammunition for his critics. The political controversies brought an end to his career. Robeson was blacklisted, and his income fell from more than $100,000 in 1947 to roughly $6,000 in 1952.

In 1956, HUAC called him to appear at hearings on the revocation of U.S. passports. He refused to answer most questions on constitutional grounds and used the platform to denounce racism and express his love for the Soviet people. Although HUAC threatened him with contempt, it took no action against him.

By the late 1950s, the emerging Civil Rights movement and the passing of the red scare opened the door for the rehabilitation of Robeson's reputation. In 1958, he published *Here I Stand*, in which he once again declared his admiration for the Soviet Union and his belief in "the principles of scientific Socialism" but denied having ever "been involved in any international conspiracy." The book urged a "Negro people's movement," which, he insisted, "must be led by Negroes." Rejecting gradualism, he called for "mass action" of the "aroused and militant" black masses. In addition to the book, he gave a series of concerts, including sold-out performances at Carnegie Hall, and recorded an album. After the Supreme Court's decision paved the way for the restoration of his passport, Robeson left for Europe to restart his career.

Although he returned to the Soviet Union to a rousing welcome, his time there was an unhappy one. Years of political attacks, the disruption of his career, and harassment by the government had taken its toll on his health and his state of mind. A circulatory ailment and emotional instability led to frequent hospitalizations. He attempted suicide, and excessive treatment with drugs as well as electroshock therapy probably caused brain damage. He returned to the United States in 1963, where he lived in seclusion until his death in Philadelphia on January 23, 1976.

—MSM

Rockefeller, Nelson A(ldrich)
(1908–1979) undersecretary of health, education and welfare; special assistant to the president; governor of New York

The son of John Davison Rockefeller, Jr., a businessman and philanthropist, Nelson Rockefeller was born in Bar Harbor, Maine, on July 8, 1908. His grandfather, John D. Rockefeller, was the founder of the Standard Oil Company and one of the richest men in the world. After graduating from Dartmouth College in 1930, Nelson Rockefeller worked in the family's Chase National Bank. From 1935 to 1940, he served as a director of Creole Petroleum Company, an affiliate of Standard Oil that had substantial holdings in Venezuela. During that time, he developed an interest in Latin American affairs and became convinced of the need for massive economic assistance to that region for both humanitarian and commercial reasons. He became president of Rockefeller Center in 1938.

In 1940, President Franklin D. Roosevelt appointed Rockefeller coordinator of the Office of Inter-American Affairs, where he oversaw an economic and cultural program for Latin America. From 1944 to 1945, Rockefeller served as assistant secretary of state for Latin American affairs. After World War II, he founded the American International Association for Economic and Social Development, a private, nonprofit organization created to channel private capital from the United States to improve social and economic conditions in underdeveloped nations, particularly in Latin America. He also founded the International Basic Economy Corporation to promote economic development in Latin America. From 1950 to 1951, he advised President HARRY S. TRUMAN on the implementation of the Point Four program.

A liberal Republican, Rockefeller backed General DWIGHT D. EISENHOWER in the presidential election of 1952. Three weeks after Eisenhower's victory, the president-elect appointed Rockefeller to chair the President's Advisory Committee on Government Organization. Following one of the committee's recommendations, Eisenhower in 1953 sought legislation to create a cabinet-rank Department of Health, Education and Welfare (HEW) to replace the Federal Security Agency. When the department was created the following year, Rockefeller became its undersecretary. In that post, Rockefeller originated the Eisenhower administration's proposal for a federal health reinsurance plan to encourage private insurance companies to extend coverage to more people.

Rockefeller left HEW in 1954 to become special assistant to the president for cold war planning. He criticized what he regarded as a piecemeal approach and attempted to promote expanded long-range economic and military aid programs. His major initiative, known as "Open Skies," proposed that the United States and the Soviet Union each allow the other to make aerial inspections of nuclear installations, thus precluding the possibility of a surprise attack. Eisenhower presented the plan at the Geneva summit in 1955. Rockefeller's

grand schemes encountered strong opposition from fiscal conservatives, such as Secretary of the Treasury GEORGE M. HUMPHREY and Undersecretary of State HERBERT HOOVER, JR. Humphrey blocked Rockefeller's path to the cabinet, and, at the end of 1955, a frustrated Rockefeller left Washington and returned to New York.

To promote the kind of comprehensive programs he favored, Rockefeller initiated the Special Studies Project of the Rockefeller Brothers Fund in 1956. The project brought together some of the best minds in the country to make policy recommendations in the areas of defense, education, and economics. HENRY A. KISSINGER, director of Harvard's Center for International Affairs, oversaw the study that produced the best known of these reports. Published in 1958 as "International Security: The Military Aspect," the report warned that the Soviet Union was advancing more rapidly than the United States in many crucial areas of military technology and that "if not reversed, this trend . . . will place the free world in dire jeopardy." The report criticized the Eisenhower administration's reliance on the nuclear deterrent, air power, and technology and argued for a more flexible defense policy. Toward that end, it urged a major increase in the defense budget as well as an ability and willingness to engage in conventional warfare. The report received considerable publicity in 1958, and Rockefeller used its recommendations and those of other reports done by the Special Studies Project to develop policy proposals in his subsequent political campaigns.

After his experiences in appointive federal positions, Rockefeller concluded that he had to win elective office to implement his ideas. In 1956, he began preparations to run for governor of New York. That year he became chair of the Committee on the Preparation of the State Constitutional Convention and, through that position, made contact with state and local party leaders. He won the Republican gubernatorial nomination with ease in 1958, but some prominent Republicans worried that Rockefeller's name and wealth might damage his prospects. However, the fact that W. AVERELL HARRIMAN, the incumbent governor and his opponent, was also the scion of a fabulously wealthy family minimized that problem. Few substantive issues separated the candidates. Rockefeller repeatedly charged that Harriman dealt with problems on a piecemeal basis and did not develop long-term goals. An enthusiastic and exuberant campaigner, Rockefeller also made extensive use of expert political technicians. In addition, he outspent Harriman by $1.8 to $1.1 million. In the end, Rockefeller won by more than half a million votes. He went on to win reelection three times.

During the first two years of his administration, Rockefeller laid the foundation for extensive social welfare programs. Early in 1959, he successfully procured from the legislature an increase in the state income tax to finance the programs on a pay-as-you-go basis, as mandated by the state's constitution. Later in the year, he appointed a three-member committee on higher education. In 1960, it recommended the establishment of a new state university with two new graduate schools and the transformation of the 11 state teachers' colleges into liberal arts schools. During Rockefeller's tenure as governor, the state university system expanded from 38,000 students on 28 campuses to 246,000 students on 71 campuses. In 1960, Rockefeller succeeded in establishing a State Housing Finance Authority, with a borrowing capacity of $2 billion, to encourage investment of private capital in housing for middle-income families. Rockefeller signed New York State's first minimum wage bill in 1960. It set the minimum wage at $1 an hour. That same year, he announced plans to build a $4 million fallout shelter in Albany to accommodate 2,200 employees. Rockefeller failed, however, to win passage of his plan for mandatory shelters in public and private buildings.

Rockefeller saw the governorship of New York as a stepping-stone to the presidency. Immediately after his election as governor, he set up a large campaign organization to seek his party's nomination. He endorsed liberal domestic programs, such as civil rights, expanded aid to education, and advocated federal reinsurance of private health insurance. In defense and foreign policy, he took a hard line, urging resumption of underground nuclear tests and calling for caution in the expansion of trade with the communist bloc.

To promote his presidential candidacy, Rockefeller went on a nationwide tour in the fall of 1959. Although he received a warm reception from the public and favorable treatment in the press, Republican leaders clearly favored Vice President RICHARD M. NIXON. After concluding that he could not wrest the nomination from Nixon, Rockefeller withdrew from the race in December 1959. Hoping to influence the Republican platform, he declined to endorse Nixon unqualifiedly and continued to express his views, particularly with respect to defense. Reflecting the conclusions of the report by the Rockefeller Brothers Fund's Special Studies Project, he stated that America's military position relative to the Soviet Union had been declining for 15 years and insisted upon the need for greater defense spending. In early July, Rockefeller met with CHARLES H. PERCY, the chair of the Republican Platform Committee, to discuss the preliminary draft of the platform and to press his views. Rockefeller wanted a dramatic increase in military spending, a stronger civil rights plank, federal aid to education, and programs to promote unity in the Western Hemisphere and among North Atlantic nations. Percy, who had laboriously crafted a skillful compromise that bridged the gaps in a deeply divided party, had no inclination to rewrite the platform at Rockefeller's insistence. On July 25, 1960, shortly before the Republican Platform Committee adopted its final draft, Rockefeller met with Nixon at the governor's apartment on Fifth Avenue in New York City. In what became known as the Treaty of Fifth Avenue, Nixon agreed to incorporate a number of Rockefeller's demands into the platform. The agreement outraged conservatives in the party, who decried the influence of the eastern, or liberal, wing of the party. Senator BARRY M. GOLDWATER (R-Ariz.) called it "the Munich of the Republican Party."

During the early and middle 1960s, Rockefeller established or expanded a large number of social welfare programs. He increased the state's minimum wage to $1.15 an hour, expanded state aid to education, and established programs to deter juvenile delinquency. In addition, he gained passage of civil rights legislation to ban discrimination in housing, lending, and places of public accommodation. A zealous advocate of fallout shelters, he signed a bill in April 1961 that granted up to $100 in real estate tax exemptions to homeowners who built shelters. In November of that year, he signed a bill that provided $100 million in state matching funds for schools and colleges that constructed fallout shelters.

The vast array of social welfare programs enormously expanded the state's budget. Rockefeller employed additional tax increases and voter-approved bond issues to provide funds for these programs. When the electorate began rejecting the bond issues, he created a system of over 40 quasi autonomous state authorities empowered to issue bonds and pay for them by imposing fees for the use of services provided by the state authorities.

Rockefeller easily won reelection in 1962. During the campaign, he promised no tax increases, but to meet the cost of his programs, he had to ask for a substantial tax increase in 1963. The request generated considerable resentment among voters.

After Nixon's defeat in 1960, Rockefeller emerged as the early front-runner for the nomination in 1964. His personal life became an issue after his divorce and remarriage. Nevertheless, he ran for the Republican presidential nomination in 1964 but lost to the far more conservative Goldwater, whom Rockefeller described as "an extremist." Rockefeller's refusal to endorse Goldwater in the general election infuriated the conservative wing of his party.

Rockefeller won reelection as governor in 1966 by a discouragingly narrow margin. He remained, however, the acknowledged leader of his party's liberal wing and made another try for the presidential nomination in 1968, only to lose to Nixon for a second time.

Faced with increasing criticism over his enormous expenditures in New York and the continuing hostility of Republican conservatives throughout the country, Rockefeller began moving to the right in the late 1960s. He supported the Nixon administration and served as Nixon's emissary to Latin America in 1969. When inmates at the state prison in Attica rioted and took hostages in 1971, Rockefeller refused to negotiate and ultimately ordered an assault on the prison. In 1973, he resigned as governor and established a study group called the Commission for Critical Choices for Americans. Some political observers believed that he intended to use the commission as a springboard for another

presidential bid. At this point, his career took an unexpected turn. After Nixon was forced to resign the presidency in 1974 and Vice President GERALD R. FORD succeeded him, Ford nominated Rockefeller to fill the vacant office of the vice president. Congress confirmed him in December 1974. Rockefeller served only a little over a year in the office. As it became clear that Ronald Reagan intended to mount a campaign for the Republican nomination in 1976, the challenge from the right wing of the party made Rockefeller something of a liability for Ford. In November 1975, Rockefeller announced that he did not want to be renominated for the vice presidency. Upon leaving the vice presidency in January 1977, Rockefeller retired from politics. He devoted time to his business affairs and his art collection. Rockefeller died in New York on January 26, 1979.

—MSM

Rogers, William P(ierce)

(1913–2001) *deputy attorney general, attorney general*

The only son of a former bank director who was reduced to working at a management position at a paper mill after the bank failures of the Great Depression, Rogers was born in Norfolk, New York, on June 23, 1913. Raised by maternal grandparents after the death of his mother, Rogers spent his teen years in Canton, New York. After graduating as the class valedictorian at Canton High School, Rogers won a scholarship to attend Colgate University, where he earned his B.A. in 1934. He then went to Cornell Law School, where he edited the *Cornell Law Review*, was a member of the Order of the Coif, and graduated fifth in his class in 1937. He passed the bar later that year. After working briefly with the prestigious Wall Street firm of Cadwalader, Wickersham and Taft, he took a job as assistant district attorney under THOMAS E. DEWEY in 1938. As part of a 60-person team Dewey formed to prosecute organized crime in New York, Rogers worked on roughly 1,000 cases, largely involving bookmaking and racketeering. He left the district attorney's office in 1942 to join the U.S. Navy and served as a lieutenant junior grade aboard the USS *Intrepid*.

At the end of the war, Rogers returned to the district attorney's office, where he was chief of the bureau of special sessions under District Attorney FRANK HOGAN. The Republicans won control of Congress in the elections of 1946, and in April 1947 Rogers, a Republican, became counsel to the Senate Special Committee to Investigate the National Defense Program. In July, he became chief counsel. When that committee was succeeded by the Senate Investigations Subcommittee of the Executive Expenditures Committee in 1948, Rogers continued as counsel to the subcommittee. After the Democrats regained control of Congress in the elections of 1948, Senator CLYDE R. HOEY (D-N.C.), who had been impressed by Rogers's nonpartisanship, asked Rogers to remain.

While serving as committee counsel, Rogers became friendly with a freshman member of the House, RICHARD M. NIXON (R-Calif.), who, as a member of the House Un-American Activities Committee, was investigating charges that Alger Hiss had passed documents to the Soviets in the 1930s. Nixon told Rogers what he knew and asked Rogers to examine the files. After evaluating the evidence, Rogers advised Nixon to proceed. Rogers and Nixon became close friends, a relationship that continued after Rogers returned to New York in 1950 to practice law with Dwight, Royall, Harris, Koegel and Caskey.

Rogers followed Dewey in supporting DWIGHT D. EISENHOWER's bid for the presidency in 1952. At the Republican National Convention, Rogers played an important role in the effort to persuade the Credentials Committee to seat delegates loyal to Eisenhower from Louisiana, Texas, Georgia, and Florida rather than those committed to Senator ROBERT TAFT (R-Ohio). After Eisenhower secured the nomination, he chose Nixon as his running mate, and Rogers served as an adviser to Nixon during the campaign. When the *New York Post*, a Democratic newspaper, alleged that Nixon had a "secret" slush fund, Rogers helped ward off demands from Republicans that Nixon resign from the ticket. He also advised Nixon to present his case to the public and helped to arrange and prepare what became known as Nixon's Checkers speech, the favorable response to which kept Nixon on the ticket.

When Eisenhower assumed the presidency, Rogers became deputy attorney general. In that capacity, he served as chief liaison between the Justice Department and Congress. His responsibilities included drafting legislative proposals and lobbying for the administration's legislative proposals relating to the administration of justice. He was instrumental, for example, in obtaining passage of the Civil Rights Act of 1957. In addition, he had primary responsibility for developing lists of potential judicial nominees.

Rogers remained close to Nixon throughout the Eisenhower administration. In late 1953, he went with the vice president to a meeting with Senator JOSEPH R. MCCARTHY (R-Wis.) in an effort to persuade the senator to pull back from his attacks on communists in government and thus prevent a split between the senator and the president. After Nixon heard of Eisenhower's heart attack in September 1955, he escaped the press and spent the night at Rogers's house, where the two discussed the problems of temporarily assuming presidential powers as well as the possibility of permanent succession should Eisenhower not survive. Rogers advised Nixon to "act scrupulously like a Vice-President— not like an Acting President." When Eisenhower suffered a small stroke in 1957, Rogers performed a similar role. After the Hungarian revolt in 1956, Rogers accompanied Nixon on a trip to Europe to visit refugees. Writing in the early 1960s, Nixon described Rogers as a "cool man under pressure" on whose "excellent judgment" he could rely.

When Attorney General HERBERT BROWNELL resigned in October 1957, Eisenhower appointed Rogers to replace him. As attorney general, Rogers made enforcement of civil rights measures a major concern. Rogers maintained that his views on the matter did not differ in the slightest from Brownell's. Nevertheless, the more personable Rogers enjoyed better relations with southern members of Congress than did his predecessor. As provided for in the Civil Rights Act of 1957, Rogers set up the civil rights division of the Justice Department. He oversaw prosecution of cases involving the denial of black voting rights. In 1958, after defiance of a federal court order to desegregate Little Rock's Central High School had led to federal intervention in 1957, Rogers established a committee in the

Justice Department to deal with the federal aspects of desegregation. In 1960, Rogers recommended stronger measures to guarantee black voting rights, which formed the basis for the Voting Rights Act of 1960.

Eisenhower's health problems brought the issue of presidential infirmity to the fore. In 1958, Rogers advocated a constitutional amendment that would have allowed the president to issue a written statement initiating and terminating the vice president's assumption of presidential powers. Rogers led the administration's attempt to persuade Congress to approve the measure and send it to the states, but Congress did not act on it.

An excellent administrator, Rogers initiated a number of reforms at Justice. He established a program to recruit top students from leading law schools for positions in the department. In 1958, Rogers instituted a special unit to combat racketeering. That organization was eventually integrated into the prosecutory arm of the Justice Department.

Rogers also convinced a reluctant Eisenhower of the necessity of instituting antitrust suits against General Electric and Westinghouse. During the spring of 1960, Rogers represented the administration on a goodwill trip to West Africa.

In 1960, Rogers acted as a policy adviser to Nixon's presidential campaign. After Nixon's loss to JOHN F. KENNEDY, Rogers rejoined his old law firm, which became Royall, Koegel, Rogers, and Wells, as a senior partner. His law practice thrived (his clients included the Washington Post Company and the Dreyfus Fund), but he interrupted it for occasional public service. In 1965, he became a member of the U.S. delegation to the UN General Assembly, and in 1967 he served as a delegate to the United Nations Committee on Southwest Africa. Although Rogers did not play an important role in Nixon's campaign for the White House in 1968, when Nixon won the election he appointed Rogers secretary of state. That fact that Rogers had only limited experience in foreign affairs led many to conclude that Nixon intended to call the shots in foreign policy. Rogers established good relations with Congress and proved to be a skillful negotiator. However National Security Advisor HENRY KISSINGER, was a more aggressive bureaucratic politician and claimed far more publicity

than the secretary of state, who seemed very much in the background. Nixon excluded Rogers from negotiations with the Soviet Union that led to the Strategic Arms Limitation Talks (SALT) and with the Chinese that led to the establishment of diplomatic relations. Rogers played a larger role in the Middle East. In 1969, he proposed a plan that called for Israel to withdraw from territories occupied since the 1967 war in exchange for a commitment to peace by Arab nations. Neither side accepted the plan. Rogers did succeed in obtaining a cease-fire agreement between Egypt, Jordan, and Israel. Analysts debated the extent to which Rogers influenced foreign policy. In part, this was because, as Rogers put it, he and the president thought "a lot alike." He did disagree, however, with the decision to invade Cambodia in 1970 without apparent effect.

After repeated clashes with Kissinger, Rogers resigned in 1973 and returned to Rogers and Wells (later Clifford, Chance, Rogers and Wells). In his later years, Nixon told an aide, Monica Crowley, that "the way I treated Rogers was terrible. . . . I regret that because Rogers was smart and a good man." Rogers returned once again to public service in 1986, when President Ronald W. Reagan asked him to head the investigation into the explosion of the space shuttle *Challenger*. Rogers continued to practice law until shortly before his death in Bethesda, Maryland, on January 2, 2001.

—MSM

Romney, George W(ilcken)

(1907–1995) *chairman of the board and president, American Motors Corporation*

Romney was born in a Mormon colony in Chihuahua, Mexico, on July 8, 1907. Although American citizens and monogamists, his parents had moved to Mexico with a group of Mormons when Congress outlawed polygamy in the 1880s. After Pancho Villa expelled American nationals, Romney returned with his family to the United States and lived briefly in Texas and Idaho before settling in Utah. He attended Latter-Day Saints University but left without completing a degree to serve for two years as a missionary in England and Scotland. Upon his return, Romney briefly attended the University of

Utah before moving to Washington, D.C., where he attended George Washington University. He never did earn a college degree. In Washington, he worked as an aide to Senator David I. Walsh (D-Mass.) in 1929 and 1930. After working for the Aluminum Corporation of America from 1930 to 1931, he became a lobbyist for the aluminum industry from 1932 to 1938. In 1939, he began working as a lobbyist for the Automobile Manufacturers Association (AMA). During his years with the AMA, Romney became close friends with George Mason, an officer and later president of Nash-Kelvinator, Inc., manufacturers of automobiles and home appliances. Under pressure to groom a successor, Mason hired Romney as his assistant in April 1948 and made him vice president two years later. In 1950, Romney oversaw initial production of a small, low-priced car, the Rambler, which could go 35 miles on a gallon of gasoline. Sales proved sluggish through the first half of the decade, and the Nash division operated at a deficit. In January 1954, Nash-Kelvinator joined with Hudson Motor Car Company to form the American Motors Corporation (AMC). Mason headed the new corporation.

Upon Mason's death in late 1954, Romney became chairman, president, and general manager. When continued losses pushed AMC to the brink of financial ruin in 1956, Romney successfully negotiated a revolving bank credit of $45 million. In 1956–57, he headed off an attempted takeover of AMC by Louis Wolfson, a stock manipulator.

As head of AMC, Romney risked the company's future on the production of small cars. He limited and finally ended production of AMC's full-sized Hudson and Nash models while continuing to promote the Rambler. In contrast the "Big Three"—General Motors, Ford, and Chrysler—marketed large models, which Romney derided as the "dinosaur in our driveway" and "gas guzzlers."

An economic recession in 1957–58 transformed Romney into an honored prophet. As aggregate automobile sales declined, AMC's production rose from 100,000 in 1956 to 500,000 in 1958 and a similar figure in 1959. For the next three years, the Big Three had to follow Romney's lead. Chrysler presented its own compact models in 1960 and abandoned its full-sized DeSoto. Ford lost millions on its Edsel.

A frequent critic of the auto industry, Romney appeared in 1958 before the Senate Judiciary Subcommittee on Antitrust and Monopoly, where he attacked "excess concentration of power in any form." The size of the Big Three and its accompanying advantages, he said, made the "barriers to entry" for prospective producers nearly prohibitive. As a consequence, he pointed out, it had "been 34 years since a new United States manufacturer has successfully entered the automotive industry." In addition, he claimed that smaller producers like AMC and Studebaker had "contributed relatively more basic product pioneering than their bigger competitors." Nevertheless, he charged, the Big Three had been slow to adapt their innovations. He offered the Rambler as an example. To remedy the situation, Romney recommended the dismemberment of General Motors into several fully autonomous companies.

In his testimony, Romney attacked the United Automobile Workers (UAW) and its president, Walter Reuther, with equal fervor. "Big labor," he told the antitrust panel, "represented just as great a threat to freedom in America as did the business monopoly." He denounced industrywide bargaining as unfair to smaller manufacturers and berated the UAW for wage increases that outpaced increases in productivity.

As a relatively inexperienced but independent-minded executive, Romney never had cordial relations with the UAW. Fearing a loss of managerial authority, he fought constantly with local leaders over productivity and once threatened to close a plant over the issue. Although AMC avoided costly, prolonged strikes in the 1950s, it also paid higher wages than the Big Three.

Beginning in 1959, Romney became involved in state politics. In June of that year, he led the formation of a nonpartisan committee, "Citizens for Michigan," which sought to revise the state constitution. In November 1960, voters approved the group's proposal for a constitutional convention, and Romney served as a delegate and vice president of the convention in 1961–62. He ran for governor in 1962 as a Republican and defeated the Democratic incumbent, John B. Swainson. Despite the opposition of the UAW, voters in 1963 approved the constitution drafted by the convention. The approval of the new constitution made Romney a national figure. Some Republican leaders looked at him as an alternative to NELSON ROCKEFELLER, the liberal governor of New York, and BARRY GOLDWATER, the conservative senator from Arizona, for the party's presidential nomination in 1964. After demonstrating some initial interest, Romney took himself out of the presidential race in May 1963. A moderate, he criticized the right-wing John Birch Society and forced the resignation of a Republican district leader who belonged to it. He also called on the Republican Party to support civil rights legislation and joined a march favoring open housing in June 1963. Romney won reelection in 1964 and election to a four-year term under the state's new constitution in 1966. By the end of 1966, Romney had emerged as the front-runner for the Republican presidential nomination in 1968. He proved, however, spectacularly inept in dealing with the national press. An early supporter of the war in Vietnam who had moved away from that position, he explained his change in thinking by stating that during a tour of Vietnam in 1965 he had been "brainwashed" by American officials. The remark proved disastrous and led many in the press to speculate that perhaps Romney did not have all that much grey matter to wash. He withdrew from the race two weeks before the first primary. The Republican nominee RICHARD M. NIXON, won the election and chose Romney to serve as secretary of housing and urban development. In that position, Romney found himself frequently at odds with Nixon. Romney pleaded unsuccessfully for an expansion of housing programs, federal programs to aid cities, and other domestic initiatives. In his frustration, he publicly criticized the administration's approach to housing and to inflation. Shortly after Nixon won reelection in 1972, Romney resigned his position in the cabinet. Romney became chairman and chief executive officer of the National Center for Voluntary Action, a nonprofit organization he had helped form in 1970 to encourage greater voluntary participation by citizens in solving national problems. After leaving the cabinet, he retired from politics but did campaign for his son, Mitt Romney, who ran unsuccessfully in 1994 for the Senate seat held by Senator Edward M. Kennedy (D-Mass.). George Romney died at his home in Bloomfield Hills, Michigan, on July 26, 1995.

—MSM

Rooney, John J(ames)
(1903–1975) *U.S. congressman*

The son of Irish immigrants, Rooney was born in New York City on November 29, 1903. He attended St. Francis Preparatory School and College. After earning an LL.B. from Fordham University in 1925, he practiced law in Brooklyn, until he was appointed assistant district attorney of Kings County, New York, by District Attorney William O'Dwyer in 1940. Rooney's relentless and effective prosecutions of illegal gamblers attracted the attention of the Democratic machine in Brooklyn, which chose him to run in a special election in June 1944 to fill a seat in the U.S. House of Representatives vacated by the death of the incumbent. Rooney won the election and entered the House as the representative of a constituency consisting of mixed ethnic and economic backgrounds. He won reelection without a serious challenge for almost 30 years.

Rooney built a reputation in the House as a liberal Democrat who usually voted with his party's majority on foreign and domestic policy legislation. While he remained largely unknown to the general public, behind the scenes he became one of the most powerful politicians in the United States. In 1946, he received an appointment to the House Appropriations Committee and to its Subcommittee on the State and Justice Departments, the Judiciary and Related Federal Agencies. From 1949 until his retirement in 1975, he served as chair of that subcommittee (except for two years, from 1953 to 1955, when Republicans controlled the House). The parsimonious Rooney rigorously scrutinized those departments whose budgets were subject to his committee's approval. His close examination of the most minute budgetary details struck fear in the heart of bureaucrats. The *Saturday Evening Post* described him as a master at "making an appropriations-hunting civil servant appear like a confidence man." Not only did he terrorize witnesses and dominate his own subcommittee, but the full Appropriations Committee and the House leadership rarely questioned his recommendations.

Although Rooney unquestionably saved taxpayers money by his budget slashing—in 1959 he claimed to have eliminated $1 billion in spending during the previous decade—he was frequently criticized for failing to perceive expenditures in terms of a larger, cohesive policy. In 1958, columnist JAMES RESTON described Rooney as a "powerful" but "negative" force in Congress. Reston referred specifically to a meeting with President Eisenhower during 1958, in which an advisory group of the Foreign Service Institute (FSI) revealed that 50 percent of the Foreign Service officer corps did not have a speaking knowledge of any foreign language. Indeed, many U.S. ambassadors could not speak the languages of the countries they served. The advisory group informed a startled Eisenhower that Rooney's meager budget appropriations made adequate language training impossible. Rooney defended himself by citing examples of extravagance and waste by the FSI, and a group of State Department officials publicly supported him as a valuable inspiration for examining their own spending policies.

The State Department was often subject to Rooney's most vigorous interrogations. The plain-speaking Brooklynite could be disdainful of the elite, "striped-pants" officials of the State Department who "don't know what they're talking about." In 1955, he refused a request by the State Department for extra funds for ambassadors, calling the money "booze allowances for cookie pushers." Officials claimed Rooney's decisions kept people of moderate means out of ambassadorial service. After returning from an overseas tour in 1955, Rooney aimed his criticism at the United States Information Agency. He called the organization "futile" and charged it with being "more interested in propagandizing the American public than in combating Communism overseas." In 1957, Rooney sponsored a bill to pare down appropriations for the United States Information Agency, claiming that its efforts during the Hungarian uprising had been "almost a complete failure."

Unlike other agencies subject to Rooney's budgetary control, the FBI did not suffer from verbal harassment and cuts in appropriations. The agency's director, J. EDGAR HOOVER, and Rooney shared a mutual admiration and political philosophy. Hoover's appearances before the subcommittee usually brought forth from the chairman praise for the FBI's fiscal efficiency and open-ended questions intended to provide Hoover the opportunity to expound on his positions. Historian Sanford Unger claimed that Rooney was informed of some of the FBI's more controversial counterintelligence activities. The FBI viewed his tacit approval of them as tantamount to congressional approval. Conversely, the FBI regarded a directive from Rooney as a congressional mandate. Critics charged Rooney with inadequate oversight of FBI operations and lax control over the money allocated to the agency.

Rooney's voting record in the House reflected the varied constituency he served, which included substantial numbers of Jews, Irish Americans, African Americans, Hispanics, and immigrants from the Near East. Rooney voted in 1953 for increased immigration quotas, particularly for countries subject to communist oppression. A staunch defender of Israel, he supported the Eisenhower Doctrine, which permitted the president to use armed forces to aid Middle Eastern nations threatened by communism. He voted for the Civil Rights Acts of 1957 and 1960 as well as for the expanded public works bill of 1959.

Rooney supported the domestic policy programs of Presidents JOHN F. KENNEDY and LYNDON B. JOHNSON. He voted for Medicare, urban renewal, and child care measures. In foreign policy, he supported the war in Vietnam. Rooney survived challenges in the Democratic primaries in 1968, 1970, and 1972 by candidates who opposed his position on the war and his ties to the Brooklyn Democratic machine. In 1970 and 1972, Rooney's campaign accepted illegal contributions from unions and shipping interests in his district. This led the courts to order a rerun of the Democratic primary in 1972. Pressure from the Democratic machine in Brooklyn helped persuade Rooney not to stand for reelection in 1974. Upon his retirement, he lived in Washington, D.C., until his death there on October 26, 1975.

—MSM

Roosevelt, (Anna) Eleanor
(1884–1962) *political figure*

A daughter of the younger brother of Theodore Roosevelt, Eleanor Roosevelt was born in New York City on October 11, 1884. She was eight when her mother died, after which she was raised by her maternal grandmother. Her father died two years later. After receiving tutoring in her home, she went to finishing school in London. Returning to the United States at the age of 18, she made her debut in New York society. She also joined the National Consumers League and worked at the Rivington Street Settlement House. In 1905, she married her fifth cousin Franklin D. Roosevelt. They had a daughter and four sons. During the early years of her marriage, she encouraged her husband's political career. He won election to the state legislature in 1910 and became assistant secretary of the navy in 1913. When the United States entered World War I, Eleanor worked for navy relief, visited the wounded, and helped run a Red Cross canteen.

In 1918, Eleanor discovered that her husband was having an affair with her friend and social secretary, Lucy Mercer. She offered him a divorce, which he declined and agreed not to see Lucy Mercer again. Eleanor's discovery of the affair marked the end of marital intimacy; their relationship evolved into one of, as she put it, "just respect and affection." As she and her husband led increasingly separate lives, she threw herself into a series of social and political causes.

Franklin Roosevelt resigned as assistant secretary of the navy to run as the Democratic vice presidential nominee in 1920. Even the optimistic Franklin did not expect the Democratic ticket to win, and it did not. After polio paralyzed Franklin in 1921, Eleanor devoted herself to nursing her husband. While Franklin undertook the long and grueling process of therapy, Eleanor became involved in the Democratic Party and frequently stood in for her husband at party functions. His paralysis provided a public rationale for her activism. Eleanor developed her own interests in world disarmament, the creation of an international organization to keep peace, and the rights of women and minorities. She took leadership roles in the League of Women Voters, the Women's Trade Union League, and the Women's City Club. From 1924 to 1928, she served as finance chairman of the Women's Division of New York's Democratic State Committee. By 1928, she was head of the Women's Division of the Democratic National Committee. In that capacity, she campaigned for the Democratic nominee, Al Smith, who lost decisively to HERBERT HOOVER. Eleanor also took an active role in her husband's successful gubernatorial campaigns in 1928 and 1930.

After Franklin Roosevelt became president in 1933, Eleanor continued to champion social reform. She traveled thousands of miles to win support for New Deal legislation and was the New Deal's most forceful advocate of civil rights for African Americans. In 1935, she began a syndicated newspaper column "My Day," which she used first to discuss women's issues and, after 1939, to advance her views on public affairs. At the Democratic convention in 1940, her speech from the podium helped her friend Henry Wallace win the vice presidential nomination. After the United States entered World War II in December 1941, she served as assistant director of the Office of Civilian Defense, created by an executive order that gave the agency responsibility for providing for protection of civilians, organizing volunteer efforts, and maintaining morale. Critics lambasted several of her appointments (including a couple of close friends at substantial salaries) and some of her ideas, such as defense-related programs in drama and dance. She resigned in February 1942. Throughout the war, she traveled extensively, touring Britain and visiting American troops in the Pacific and Caribbean.

Shortly after her husband's death in 1945, Roosevelt returned to public life. She accepted an appointment as a U.S. delegate to the United Nations. In 1946, she served as chairman of the Commission on Human Rights and played a central role in drafting the Universal Declaration of Human Rights, which the UN adopted in 1948. She left her post at the UN in 1953.

During the 1950s, Roosevelt traveled extensively to promote the UN and other causes. Under the auspices of the American Association for the United Nations, she delivered countless speeches defending the international organization and urging the United States to adopt the Universal Declaration of Human Rights. She also visited numerous countries, including India, Yugoslavia, and Poland. On these trips, she promoted increased cultural contacts to break down barriers between East and West.

In 1957, Roosevelt traveled to the Soviet Union. The most prominent American to visit that country since the early cold war, she received an invitation from Premier Nikita S. Khrushchev to meet with him in Yalta. At the meeting, the two candidly exchanged their views of the cold war, and Roosevelt raised the question of human rights, pointing particularly to the Soviet Union's refusal to permit its Jews to emigrate to Israel. She returned to the Soviet Union the following year and hosted Khrushchev in Hyde Park in 1959.

Roosevelt frequently criticized the Eisenhower administration's foreign policy. She objected to what she considered the administration's too heavy reliance on military aid to prevent the expansion of communism and advocated a greater emphasis on economic aid. In addition, she criticized what she regarded as Secretary of State JOHN FOSTER DULLES's unilateralism and often questioned his failure to use the UN in international crises.

Although sympathetic to the plight of European Jews during and after World War II, in private she expressed some anti-Semitic attitudes typical of her time and class. A strong supporter of Israel, she questioned the Eisenhower administration's decision to send arms to conservative Arab states, which she regarded as a threat to Israel's security. In 1956, she denounced Dulles's decision not to grant Egyptian president Gamal Abdel Nasser a loan to build the Aswan Dam. The former first lady maintained that had the money not been withheld, Nasser would not have been forced to turn to the Soviet Union.

Roosevelt also objected to what she regarded as the administration's tacit position that equated neutralism with pro-communism. She argued that for a nation such as India to remain nonaligned and a democracy served the interests of the United States. As she saw it, India's first priority was social and economic development, not choosing sides in the cold war. The former first lady deplored congressional efforts to cut back on foreign aid to India in retaliation for its friendly relations with the Soviet Union.

Late in the decade, she maintained that the administration did not do enough to seek a nuclear test ban treaty. She suggested that the United States reduce its testing as a gesture to encourage the Soviet Union to agree to end testing.

In domestic policy, Roosevelt served as a leading voice for liberal Democrats and advocated extend-

ing the programs of the New Deal and Fair Deal. She supported the expansion of public housing and slum clearance, increased aid to the rural poor, and job training programs for the unemployed. Roosevelt remained a particularly vigorous proponent of civil rights and desegregation.

Roosevelt supported ADLAI STEVENSON for president in 1952 and 1956, and he frequently consulted her on important matters. She enthusiastically worked for Stevenson in the primaries in 1956 and defended him against liberals, including ROY WILKINS of the NAACP, who accused him of ambivalence on civil rights. She also worked tirelessly for him in the general election.

Following Stevenson's defeat, Roosevelt turned her attention to Democratic politics in New York. In conjunction with HERBERT LEHMAN and THOMAS FINLETTER, she helped organize a Democratic reform movement to unseat CARMINE DeSAPIO, the boss of the Tammany machine, as Democratic leader in New York County. In 1961, they succeeded in breaking his power.

Roosevelt favored Stevenson for the presidency in 1960 and made the speech seconding his nomination at the convention. She was initially cool toward the candidacy of Senator JOHN F. KENNEDY (D-Mass.). In a magazine article in 1958, she had criticized him for having been "evasive" with respect to Senator JOSEPH R. McCARTHY (R-Wis.). She also thought that Kennedy's father exercised too much influence over him. Once Kennedy claimed the nomination, however, Roosevelt supported him. After his election, Kennedy appointed her to advisory commissions on the status of women and on the Peace Corps. He also reappointed her as a delegate to the UN. She continued to write her columns and travel until her death at her home in New York City on November 7, 1962.

—MSM

Roosevelt, Kermit, Jr.

(1916–2000) *Central Intelligence Agency official*
The son of a banker and shipping line official and the grandson of Theodore Roosevelt, Kermit ("Kim") Roosevelt was born in Buenos Aires, Argentina, on February 16, 1916. He grew up in Oyster Bay, New York, graduated from Harvard in

1938, and then taught history at Harvard and the California Institute of Technology. During World War II, he served in the Office of Strategic Services and, after the war, joined its successor, the Central Intelligence Agency (CIA), where he became an expert on Middle Eastern affairs.

Roosevelt played an important role in the coup that overthrew Iranian premier Mohammed Mossadeq in 1953. In 1951, Mossadeq accepted the support of the country's Communist Party and nationalized the giant Anglo-Iranian Oil Company. The British withdrew their technical people, shutting down the world's largest oil refinery at Abadan, and took the position that any oil purchased from Iran was stolen, in effect imposing a de facto embargo on Iranian oil. The boycott devastated the Iranian economy but hardened Mossadeq's resolve. The young shah, Mohammed Reza Pahlavi, who had opposed nationalizing the Anglo-Iranian Oil Company, attempted to dismiss Mossadeq in mid-1952, but rioting led by nationalists and Tudeh (Iran's Communist Party) forced the shah to reverse himself. In October 1952, Mossadeq broke diplomatic relations with the British.

Lacking the resources to drive Mossadeq from power, the British turned to the United States for help. The British made their approach through the CIA. In cooperation with the British Foreign Office, the American State Department and CIA decided to topple Mossadeq and reinstall a pro-Western government. The plan, known as Operation Ajax, involved using money from the CIA to buy the loyalty of Iranian army officers and a street mob. Roosevelt was chosen to direct the operation.

In July 1953, Mossadeq dissolved parliament and called for a plebiscite. In the meantime, he ruled by decree. Tudeh staged riots in Teheran. Mossadeq won 99.4 percent of the votes in the plebiscite on August 5. Three days later, the Soviet Union announced that it had entered negotiations to provide financial aid to Iran.

Roosevelt had arrived in Iran on July 19 with a large bankroll provided by the CIA. He met with officers of the Iranian army and the shah. After the plebiscite and the announcement of negotiations with the Soviets, Roosevelt organized demonstrations against Mossadeq. Amid antiroyalist rioting, led by Tudeh, the shah panicked and fled the country on August 16. During the next few days, Roosevelt organized demonstrations in favor of the shah and coordinated activities with the armed forces. On August 19, after several days of fighting in the streets, Mossadeq surrendered. The shah returned to the country and to power on August 22. A month later, President DWIGHT D. EISENHOWER awarded Roosevelt the National Security Medal in a closed-door ceremony.

Roosevelt was also involved in the unsuccessful attempt to persuade Egypt's president Gamal Abdel Nasser not to accept military aid from the Soviets. In mid-August 1955, Roosevelt was sent to Egypt. At the same time, Secretary of State JOHN FOSTER DULLES sent Undersecretary of State GEORGE ALLEN to Egypt with a stern letter warning that the arms deal could hand Egypt over to the communists. Although Roosevelt's role remained unclear, it prompted some critics to charge that the CIA had undercut official U.S. policy.

Roosevelt resigned from the CIA in 1958 and became government relations director for the Gulf Oil Corporation. Gulf named him a vice president in 1960. Four years later, he formed his own corporation, Roosevelt and Associates, which specialized in assisting American firms with business interests in the Middle East. In 1975, a Senate Foreign Relations subcommittee reported that Roosevelt had used his CIA contacts in Saudi Arabia and Iran in an effort to win government contracts for Northrop Corporation, a large aircraft manufacturer. Roosevelt retired in the late 1970s. In 1979, he published *Countercoup: The Struggle for the Control of Iran*, an account of his role in the overthrow of Mossadeq. Roosevelt died in Cockeysville, Maryland, on June 8, 2000.

—MSM

Rose, Alex

(1898–1976) *president, United Hatters, Cap and Millinery Workers International Union; vice chairman, Liberal Party*

The son of a prosperous tanner, Rose was born in Olesh Royz, Russian Poland, on October 15, 1898. Since Jews were largely excluded from universities, Rose left Poland at the age of 15, intending to study medicine in the United States. World War

I, however, cut him off from his parents' support, and he became a sewing machine operator in a millinery shop. In 1918, Rose, who had been active in the Labor Zionist Organization, joined the Jewish Legion of the British army, and served for two years in the Middle East. After his return to the United States, he defeated a communist-backed candidate for secretary-treasurer of his local in the Cloth, Hat, Cap and Millinery Workers Union (CHCMW). He became a vice president of the union in 1927 and retained that post when the CHCMW merged with the United Hatters of North America to form the United Hatters, Cap and Millinery Workers International Union (UHCMW) in 1934.

When Max Zaritsky, president of the UHCMW, died in 1950, the executive board appointed Rose president; later that year, he won election to the position. As president, he led a successful 45-week strike in 1953–54 against the Hat Corporation of America in Norwalk, Connecticut. Usually, however, Rose strove to work with manufacturers to bolster the industry's declining fortunes, particularly in the Northeast, where the union had its base. The settlement of an eight-day strike in the cap industry during July 1958 included an agreement by manufacturers and the union to join in promoting sales and in campaigning against less expensive imported and nonunion caps.

Rose believed that the job security of his union members depended on the health of their respective industries; in 1949, he wrote that "the class struggle is a thing of the past in my union." Under Rose, the UHCMW lent $250,000 to the Kartiganer Hat Corporation in 1954. The following year, a smaller loan to a hat firm in Baltimore enabled it to resume production. In 1958, the union began to invest in real estate in New York City's garment district to prevent millinery companies from being dispossessed or from sustaining large rent increases. The following year, the Merrimac Hat Corporation of Massachusetts faced liquidation, and the UHCMW purchased it to save the jobs of the company's workers. The company remained in business for a decade with Rose as its chairman of the board. It closed when it could not compete with inexpensive imports from Czechoslovakia.

Rose entered politics in 1936, when, joined by DAVID DUBINSKY, president of the Interna-

tional Ladies Garment Workers Union, and others, he helped to found the American Labor Party (ALP). The unionists established the party because they feared that the rivalry between the American Federation of Labor (AFL) and the Congress of Industrial Organizations (CIO) would impede mobilization of the labor vote to support President Franklin D. Roosevelt's bid for a second term. Over time, however, Rose and Dubinsky became increasingly concerned at the communist influence in the party, and they withdrew from it in 1944. That same year, along with REINHOLD NIEBUHR, a leading theologian who had also left the ALP, they formed the Liberal Party as an anticommunist alternative. Rose became a vice chairman and key leader of the group. The ALP supported Henry A. Wallace, the Progressive Party's candidate in 1948, a decision that proved fatal to that party. The Liberals supported the successful candidacy of President HARRY S. TRUMAN.

The Liberal Party occasionally ran congressional candidates, but the major goal of the organization was to influence the policies of the New York Democratic Party by endorsing those of its nominees who met the Liberals' political standards. In 1954, for example, the support of Rose and the Liberal Party proved decisive in gaining the Democratic gubernatorial nomination for W. AVERILL HARRIMAN. Rose occasionally supported independent or Republican candidates, in part to maintain his leverage with the Democrats.

During the 1950s, the Liberal Party's program included reform of labor legislation in New York State, repeal of the Taft-Hartley Act, a higher minimum wage, tax reform at both the state and national levels, antidiscrimination legislation, more federal aid for housing programs, and increased consumer protection through new and existing state and federal agencies. The party endorsed the basic objectives of American foreign policy in the cold war and offered strong support for the United Nations, which the party's state chairman, A. A. Berle, called "the only agency capable of restoring [international] stability."

In spite of the small size of his union, Rose also played an important role in national labor affairs. With other garment union leaders, he frequently petitioned the Eisenhower administration to raise the federal minimum wage. In 1957, he chaired a special committee of the AFL-CIO created to review a recommendation of the federation's Ethical Practices Committee to expel the Teamsters for corruption in its leadership. Behind the scenes, Rose sought unsuccessfully to reach an accord that would have allowed the Teamsters to remain in the AFL-CIO. In the end, he recommended to the AFL-CIO's convention that the Teamsters be expelled, and the convention endorsed that recommendation. When JAMES HOFFA mysteriously disappeared in 1975, Rose said, "If Hoffa had done what we told him to, the teamsters would still be in the federation, and he would still be alive." Rose advocated the establishment of a "labor FBI" by the federation to combat the kind of corruption found in the Teamsters.

Rose eschewed the AFL-CIO's official position of neutrality during the campaign for the Democratic presidential nomination in 1960 and endorsed Senator JOHN F. KENNEDY (D-Mass.) not long after the senator won the Wisconsin primary in April. He and ARTHUR GOLDBERG, special counsel to the AFL-CIO, were the first important labor leaders to back Kennedy. Rose called the Kennedy campaign "a public referendum" on Jimmy Hoffa, a reference to the roles that ROBERT KENNEDY and John Kennedy played in the investigation of the Teamsters's leader. Another Kennedy supporter, WALTER REUTHER, president of the United Auto Workers, joined Goldberg and Rose as AFL-CIO liaison representatives at the Los Angeles Democratic Convention in July. The group objected vehemently to Kennedy's choice of Senator LYNDON B. JOHNSON (D-Tex.) as his running mate but later helped rally other liberals to the national ticket.

Rose continued to play a dominant role in the Liberal Party through the 1960s and well into the 1970s. The party's chief accomplishment during this period was to help elect JOHN V. LINDSAY mayor of New York. By the 1970s, however, some within the party came to regard Rose as autocratic and out of touch with recent developments in politics, particularly the emergence of the women's movement. Whatever success the Liberal Party enjoyed, the UHCMW suffered, as increasing numbers of Americans went hatless and foreign competition ate into the remaining market. Rose's union shrank

from almost 100,000 to 16,000. In the mid-1960s, the union proposed raising his salary from $20,000 to $30,000; Rose rejected the raise and cut his pay to $17,500, the lowest salary for the president of any international union in the country. He continued to draw that salary through the inflationary late 1960s and 1970s until his death in New York City on December 28, 1976.

—MSM

Rosenberg, Ethel G(reenglass)
(1915–1953) *convicted espionage agent*

Ethel Greenglass was born in New York City on September 28, 1915, and raised in poverty on Manhattan's East Side. While in school, she studied piano and sang in Hugh Ross's Schola Cantorum, in the Yiddish theater, and at small neighborhood gatherings. Upon graduating from Seward Park High School at 15, she went to work as a clerk for a shipping company. Four years later, she was fired after she organized a strike of 150 women workers. Subsequently, she found another job as a stenographer and became involved in union activities and various radical causes. She joined the Young Communist League and became a member of the American Communist Party. Ethel first met JULIUS ROSENBERG, the man who would become her husband, in 1936. They married in 1939, after which the couple initially lived with Julius's mother. In 1940, Julius took a position as a junior engineer with the Army Signal Corps. The Rosenbergs moved into an apartment in Knickerbocker Village in New York in 1942, and Ethel stayed at home with the couple's two sons.

Julius, who had been a member of the Communist Party, began spying for the Soviets in 1942. The following year, David Greenglass, Ethel's brother, was drafted into the army and assigned to the Manhattan Project at Los Alamos, New Mexico, as a machinist. Julius informed the Soviets of this development and, along with Ethel, approached David's wife, Ruth Greenglass, a devoted communist, about obtaining technical information through David. Ruth Greenglass, in turn, recruited her husband, who was also a loyal Communist.

In February 1945, the Army Signal Corps fired Julius on the ground that he had been a member of the Communist Party, a charge he denied. He then started a machine shop with David Greenglass, Ethel's brother. The business never did well, and the partners bickered.

In 1950, Klaus Fuchs, a German-born British physicist, was arrested in Great Britain and confessed to passing information about the atomic bomb to the Soviets. Harry Gold, the courier for Fuchs, was also arrested and confessed. Two members of Rosenberg's ring, Joel Barr and Alfred Sarant, fled to Europe and eventually to the Soviet Union, where they became leading computer scientists. In June 1950, Greenglass was arrested for spying for the Soviet Union. He confessed, implicating his wife and Julius Rosenberg. In July, the FBI arrested Julius Rosenberg on charges that he had been a central figure in a Soviet spy ring during World War II that had passed information on the atomic bomb to the Soviet Union. On August 11, Ethel was arrested for helping to transmit information about the atomic bomb to the Soviet Union during 1944 and 1945.

Gold and Greenglass pleaded guilty to charges of espionage, while the Rosenbergs and MORTON SOBELL maintained their innocence. Julius and Ethel Rosenberg went on trial for conspiracy to commit espionage rather than treason, because the USSR had been an ally of the United States at the time of the alleged acts. At the trial, which began on March 6, 1951, the U.S. government alleged that both Rosenbergs were operatives in an espionage ring that included Fuchs, a Russian diplomat, and two Americans, Harry Gold and Morton Sobell. Greenglass testified that he made drawings of precision molds for the bomb's high-explosive lenses and passed them to Gold, who then transmitted the information to the Soviets. Gold's testimony corroborated these allegations, and Greenglass's wife, Ruth Greenglass, testified that Ethel had typed the notes provided by David Greenglass. Ruth Greenglass had made the allegation for the first time only 10 days before the Rosenbergs' trial, and David had changed his testimony to support that of his wife. The Rosenbergs' lawyer, Emanuel Bloch, an attorney of no particular distinction who had little experience in criminal law, did not cross-examine Greenglass effectively and did not cross-examine Gold at

all. After an unexpectedly short three-week trial, the jury returned guilty verdicts. Judge Irving Kaufman sentenced the Rosenbergs to the electric chair and Sobell to 30 years in prison. Greenglass and Gold received lesser prison terms.

The trial and its aftermath provoked impassioned responses. Many at the time believed that the evidence against the Rosenbergs proved their guilt beyond a shadow of a doubt; others held firmly to the belief that Julius and Ethel were victims of a political trial in a country swept by anticommunist hysteria. All over the world, people of various political backgrounds formed committees either to protest the Rosenbergs' death sentences or insist on their innocence. A primary vehicle for pro-Rosenberg sentiment in the United States was the Committee to Secure Justice in the Rosenberg Case. Many of the organizations supporting the Rosenbergs turned out to have been sponsored by communists and part of an orchestrated campaign of propaganda. These groups gained momentum for their cause when the Court of Appeals for the Second Circuit rejected the Rosenbergs' first appeal in February 1952. Over the next few months, the Rosenberg Committee collected over $1 million, while international protests grew with each newly decreed date of execution.

By early 1953, a number of distinguished scientists were pleading for the Rosenbergs. Dr. Harold Urey, a nuclear chemist who had been involved in the development of the atomic bomb, derided Greenglass's testimony, declaring a man of Greenglass's abilities was "wholly incapable" of transmitting the complex mechanics of atomic weapons. Subsequent evidence proved Urey badly mistaken. ALBERT EINSTEIN joined Urey in a plea for clemency.

In late December 1952, Judge Kaufman rejected a motion for a reduction in the Rosenbergs' sentence, but he did grant a stay of execution to allow for a formal appeal for clemency to President HARRY S. TRUMAN, who declined to act on it. When President DWIGHT D. EISENHOWER took office, he inherited the Rosenbergs' formal plea for clemency, which he rejected in February 1953. Eisenhower described his decision as a difficult one, but he believed that the evidence pointed clearly to their guilt. Their crime, he said in his formal rejection, "involved the deliberate betrayal of the entire nation and could very well result in the death of many, many thousands of innocent citizens."

After Eisenhower refused clemency, the Rosenbergs' lawyers, led by Bloch, worked feverishly in appellate courts and the U.S. Supreme Court to win reviews of the conviction and stays of execution. Public appeals reached a crescendo in June 1953 as the Rosenbergs' third scheduled date of execution approached. The government of Poland offered the couple asylum. The president of France, Vincent Auriol, made a quiet plea for clemency to Eisenhower, as did Nobel Prize winners François Mauriac and Léon Jouhaux. In Italy, leftists were joined in the protests by the right-wing press and Pope Pius XII. Forty members of the British Parliament urged Eisenhower to stop the executions, and crowds in Israel accused the U.S. government of anti-Semitism (perhaps ignoring the fact that the judge and two lead prosecutors were also Jewish). In communist countries, pleas for the Rosenbergs were incorporated into vitriolic anti-American propaganda.

On June 15, the Supreme Court once again refused, by a five-to-four vote, to review the case; and marshals set June 18 as the date for the couple's execution. On June 16, two lawyers who had had no previous connection with the defense appeared before Supreme Court Justice WILLIAM O. DOUGLAS and argued that the Atomic Energy Act of 1946 had superseded the Espionage Act of 1917 and that the district court had improperly imposed the death penalty without the recommendation of a jury. Douglas held that the claim presented a substantial question of law and granted a stay of execution on June 17. Attorney General HERBERT BROWNELL petitioned the Court to vacate the stay, and, on June 18, Chief Justice FRED M. VINSON took the highly unusual step of calling together the recessed Court to consider Douglas's action. On June 19, after almost three hours of intense and emotional argument, the Court ruled that the Atomic Energy Act did not displace the penalties established by the Espionage Act. Moreover, since the actions that formed the basis for the conviction had taken place before passage of the Atomic Energy Act, any alleged inconsistencies with the penalties of the Espionage Act were irrelevant. President Eisenhower refused a second plea for clemency by the

Rosenbergs, and on the evening of June 19, Julius and Ethel Rosenberg went to the electric chair at the prison in Ossining, New York, aware of an offer from the Justice Department to spare their lives if they confessed and cooperated in tracking down other spies. The Rosenbergs maintained their innocence to the end.

Their deaths touched off scattered emotional demonstrations—some of grief, some of satisfaction—around the world. Eight protest strikes were reported in Italy, while 400 demonstrators were arrested in Paris. In New York City, 5,000 people gathered to denounce the action and pray.

Public interest in the Rosenberg case continued during the ensuing decades. Numerous writers and researchers reopened the case. During the 1960s, amid growing distrust of the government and doubts about the cold war, several works weighed in on behalf of the Rosenbergs. In 1969, *The United States v. Julius and Ethel Rosenberg*, a play by Donald Freed, portrayed the couple as victims of blind injustice. Walter and Miriam Schneir raised evidentiary questions about the government's case in their book, *Invitation to an Inquest* (1965). With the passage of the amended Freedom of Information Act in 1974, defenders of the Rosenbergs obtained the release of many, albeit heavily censored, documents from FBI files. While these documents raised questions about the fairness and legality of the trial, the information released in the mid-1970s did not support Julius's innocence. The documents did suggest, however, that the government brought Ethel into the case in an attempt to force a confession from her husband. In 1983, Ronald Radosh, a historian formerly associated with the New Left, and Joyce Milton, a freelance writer, published *The Rosenberg File*, which strongly challenged the Schneirs' evidence. Radosh and Milton concluded that the Rosenbergs had been guilty.

After the fall of the Soviet Union, the Russian government released documents that indicated that Julius Rosenberg had provided information to the NKVD. His main contact, Alexander Feklisov, met Julius on more than 50 occasions over a three-year period, beginning in 1942. Feklisov himself said that Julius had passed military secrets to him but never had important information about the atomic bomb.

In 1995, the National Security Agency released intercepted Soviet consular communiqués from the years 1942 to 1945, which had been decoded as part of the Venona project. The intercepted cable traffic provided conclusive evidence that Julius Rosenberg had been a Soviet agent, code named "Liberal," and that he had actively engaged in espionage. More than that, he had supervised other agents. After the release of the Venona decrypts, even the Schneirs publicly conceded that Julius Rosenberg had been a Soviet spy. The Venona documents, however, contained no evidence that Ethel had directly engaged in espionage. Indeed, the fact that Soviet documents referred to her as "Ethel," rather than a code name, would seem to indicate that the Soviets at least did not consider her a valuable asset. On the other hand, a cable from the Soviet consulate in New York in November 1944 described Ethel as "well developed politically" (which meant that she believed unquestioningly in the party line) and indicated that she "knows about her husband's work." Moreover, she played an active role in recruiting Ruth Greenglass.

In 2001, David Greenglass claimed that he had committed perjury and falsely implicated his sister to protect his wife and children. At this point, it seems safe to say that Julius Rosenberg was a Soviet spy and part of a ring that passed documents relating to the atomic bomb to the Soviet Union. Ethel Rosenberg's direct involvement in espionage remains unproved, although she knew of and supported the activities of her husband and brother.

The execution of the Rosenbergs continues to be a contentious matter. The government did not want to execute them, the prosecutor did not recommend the death penalty, and no less an anticommunist than J. EDGAR HOOVER, director of the FBI, opposed the execution. The government used the threat of execution to press for a confession. Although the government knew the identity of the other members of Julius Rosenberg's ring through the Venona intercepts, it did not want to reveal the existence of the Venona project. This accounts for the decision to bring in Ethel, who was clearly an accessory, and for sticking with the threat of execution. The option to cooperate with U.S. intelligence and save themselves remained open to the Rosenbergs until they were put to death.

The Rosenbergs, however, remained true believers. The letters they wrote to each other while awaiting execution read less like letters from people facing imminent death than activists or propagandists pleading someone else's cause. The letters are replete with sloganeering references to "our social duty to our fellow man" and pledges to "take our stand with the people fighting for peace and right." They make no reference to communism or the Communist Party; the Rosenbergs maintained the fiction to the end. In her plea to Eisenhower for clemency, Ethel even accused the United States of anti-Semitism for prosecuting the Rosenbergs. "The great democratic United States," she wrote, "is proposing the savage destruction of a small unoffending Jewish family." Ironically, at that very time, the USSR, the country for which the Rosenbergs chose to die, was engaged in a pogrom, as Stalin's government rounded up Jews falsely accused of taking part in the "Doctors' Plot." Perhaps Sam Roberts, a reporter for the *New York Times* and author of *The Brother: The Untold Story of Atomic Spy David Greenglass and How He Sent His Sister, Ethel Rosenberg, to the Electric Chair* (2002), got it right when he wrote: "By martyring themselves," the Rosenbergs "contributed more to the cause of world communism than they ever had as spies."

—MSM

Rosenberg, Julius

(1918–1953) *convicted espionage agent*

The son of a garment worker, Rosenberg was born in New York City on May 12, 1918, and brought up on the Lower East Side. The product of a poor, Orthodox Jewish family, he received religious instruction at Downtown Talmud Torah and Hebrew High School in New York. He attended public schools and graduated from Seward Park High School. With the encouragement of Ethel Greenglass, whom he first met in 1936, he completed his B.S. degree in electrical engineering at the City College of New York in 1939. While there, he devoted himself to left-wing politics and organized the Steinmetz Society, an affiliate of the Young Communist League. Soon after graduating from City College, Julius married Ethel Greenglass. In 1940, he took a position as a junior engineer with the Army Signal Corps. His job involved inspecting electrical equipment manufactured by defense contractors in New York and New Jersey.

In 1942, he began working for the Soviet Union. According to Alexander Feklisov, Rosenberg's main Soviet handler, "Julius never accept[ed] any kind of compensation." Further, Rosenberg "was not just a valuable source himself," but "also the linchpin of a network" of growing importance. While acting as the on-site inspector for the army at Emerson Radio and Phonograph, Rosenberg stole a proximity fuse and passed it to the Soviets. (Rosenberg's theft of the proximity fuse was more valuable to the Soviets than the information about the atomic bomb that he later provided to them.) When Ethel's brother, David Greenglass, was drafted in 1943 and assigned to the technical support staff at the Manhattan Project, Rosenberg recruited his brother-in-law to collect information for the Soviets. The Army Signal Corps fired Rosenberg in March 1945, when a security check turned up information that he had been a member of the Communist Party, a charge he denied. At that point, the Soviets deactivated Rosenberg; although he continued to carry out occasional specific missions.

After losing his job with the Signal Corps, Rosenberg started a machine shop with David Greenglass and another brother of Ethel's, Bernie. The business achieved little success, and the partners bickered. Rosenberg and his wife were arrested in 1950 on charges of arranging to pass documents relating to the atomic bomb to the Soviet Union during World War II. He was executed in the prison at Ossining, New York, on June 19, 1953. *See* ETHEL ROSENBERG.

—MSM

Ross, Robert Tripp

(1903–1981) *deputy assistant secretary of defense for legislative affairs, assistant secretary of defense for legislative and public affairs*

Born in Washington, North Carolina, on June 4, 1903, Ross attended public schools and spent much of his early life working in drug stores. He got married after graduating from high school and left his job as a drug store clerk to try to sell real estate in Florida. A series of other sales jobs followed until finally Ross moved to New York City in 1929 and found work as a clerk in a pharmacy of a large hotel. Once described as a "pleasant, gregarious, outgoing man," by 1940 he was managing a large pharmacy in Jackson Heights.

In 1946, Ross ran successfully as a Republican for a seat in the U.S. House of Representatives. He lost his bid for reelection in 1948, after which he became an officer in a company, owned by his second wife's family, that manufactured clothing and athletic equipment. Ross ran to regain his seat in 1950 but was again defeated. Upon the resignation of Representative T. VINCENT QUINN (D-N.Y.), however, Ross won a special election in February 1952 to fill the unexpired term. His campaign emphasized the issues of "crime, corruption and Communism" in the Truman administration. Ross lost his bid for reelection to a full term in November 1952 and in 1953 accepted the post of the New York State Republican Committee's representative in Washington, D.C.

Ross received an appointment as deputy assistant secretary of defense for legislative affairs in March 1954. Nearly one year later, he was promoted to assistant secretary of defense for legislative and public affairs. Controversy marked his tenure in that position. In late March 1955, Secretary of Defense CHARLES E. WILSON issued a memorandum directing that information released by the Defense Department make a "constructive contribution to the primary mission of the Department of Defense." Ross's rigid interpretation of Wilson's order elicited charges of censorship not only from congressional committees and reporters, but also from the secretaries of the armed services and even from members of the Joint Chiefs of Staff. The military officials protested that Ross censored their speeches to stifle all difference of opinion with the administration's defense policy.

In November 1955, Representative John E. Moss (D-Calif.), the chairman of the House Government Operations Subcommittee on Information, canceled a scheduled hearing on government information policies, largely because of Ross's refusal to cooperate. During the summer of 1956, the subcommittee issued a report charging that the Defense Department's policies were the "most restrictive" of any government agency. For his part,

Ross consistently maintained that "security" was the only basis on which he withheld information.

Ross again clashed with Congress in October 1956, when he accused three powerful senators of bilking the public for free air transportation from Europe to the United States. On October 20, he announced that the air force was sending two 66-passenger planes to Europe at a round-trip cost of $20,000 merely to bring home Senators JOHN L. MCCLELLAN (D-Ark.), JOHN STENNIS (D-Miss.), and DENNIS CHAVEZ (D-N. Mex.). All three heatedly denied Ross's charges. They claimed they had arranged to return on scheduled military flights and that the administration charged them with seeking special treatment for no other reason than to embarrass the Democratic Party. When McClellan and Stennis subsequently arrived together from Madrid on a regularly scheduled military flight and demanded a retraction of the charges, Ross apologized and conceded that they had never requested special treatment.

Ross's most serious difficulties began in January 1957, when both the Senate Permanent Investigations Subcommittee, led by McClellan, and the House Government Operations Subcommittee, led by Representative CHET HOLIFIELD (D-Calif.), began investigations of conflict-of-interest charges leveled against him. The accusations stemmed from a contract for wind-resistant trousers, in the amount of $834,150, that the army had awarded to Wynn Enterprises of Knoxville, Tennessee, of which Ross's second wife was president. (Ross had been vice president, sales manager, and public relations director for the Knoxville branch, although he claimed to have resigned before running for Congress in February 1952.) The controversy gained momentum when the Amalgamated Clothing Workers Union charged that the Southern Athletic Company, controlled by Herman D. ("Breezy") Wynn, Ross's brother-in-law, had received more than $4 million in government contracts over a two-year period despite repeated violations of federal labor law.

Appearing before the Senate Permanent Investigations Subcommittee, Ross denied any conflict of interest or violation of legal or ethical codes but admitted that he had arranged a conference between his brother-in-law, Herman Wynn, and a marine general. Ross maintained that this meeting only concerned the quality of some baseball uniforms produced for the marines by one of the Wynn companies. His appearance before McClellan's subcommittee seemed to have shaken Ross, and Holifield's subcommittee in the House was gearing up for hearings of its own.

Faced with the growing pressure of two congressional investigations, Ross resigned on February 14, 1957. Subsequently, McClellan conceded that Ross had probably done nothing illegal, but, as the senator put it, "whether he did anything improper is a matter of opinion." Subsequent hearings by the House Government Operations Subcommittee revealed that Ross had not severed all ties with companies owned by the Wynn family. Southern Athletic listed Ross as a vice president from 1952 to 1956. In fairness to Ross, he was apparently unaware that he had ever been an officer of the firm. Breezy Wynn attributed the annual reports listing Ross as a vice president to an "auditor's error."

Ross quickly secured an appointment as assistant commissioner of borough works in Queens, a position he held from March 1957 to January 1958. He served as vice president of the Merchandising Apparel Company from 1959 to 1968. Ross resided in Jackson Heights until his death there on October 1, 1981.

—MSM

Rossiter, Clinton L(awrence), III

(1917–1970) *professor of government, Cornell University*

Born in Philadelphia, Pennsylvania, on September 18, 1917, Clinton Rossiter grew up in Bronxville, New York. He attended Westminster School in Simsbury, Connecticut, and Cornell University, from which he graduated in 1939. He then went on to earn an M.A. in politics from Princeton University in 1941 and a Ph.D. in constitutional law, also from Princeton, in 1942. During World War II, Rossiter served in the navy and saw action in the Pacific. Discharged with the rank of lieutenant, he received an appointment as instructor in political science at the University of Michigan in the fall of 1946. In 1947, he returned to Cornell as assistant professor of government and remained there for the rest of his career. He was promoted to associate professor in 1949 and became a full professor in 1954.

Rossiter quickly established himself as one of the leading interpreters of the American experience. His scholarly work concentrated on conservative thought, and Rossiter associated himself with moderate conservatism of the sort espoused by Edmund Burke, the 18th-century British political thinker. Rossiter's own writing was distinguished by an elegant, highly literary style. His early books included *Constitutional Dictatorship: Crisis Government in the Modern Democracies* (1948), which argued that, in times of crisis, democracies often turned to dictatorship, and *The Supreme Court and the Commander in Chief* (1951). *Seedtime of the Republic: The Origin of the American Tradition of Political Liberty*, published in 1953, described the American Revolution as an effort to conserve British liberties, motivated by a philosophy of ethical, ordered liberty. The book offered a laudatory analysis of American political institutions and traditions of freedom. *Seedtime of the Republic* received widespread acclaim; it won the Bancroft Prize and the Woodrow Wilson Award.

Conservatism in America (1955) traced the history of conservative thought in England and America. As Rossiter described it, "conservatism is full of harsh doubts about the goodness and equality of men, the wisdom and possibilities of reform and the sagacity of the majority. . . . In the final reckoning, however, it defends the desire for human liberty hardly less staunchly than it does the need for social order." The book acknowledged the limits conservatism faced in America, because the United States was "a progressive country with a Liberal tradition" and "a liberal [political] mind." Indeed, Rossiter contended that pure Burkean conservatism was "irrelevant" to America. Arguing that the *Federalist Papers*, rather than Burke's work, should serve as the principal source for modern conservatives, Rossiter criticized conservatives who rejected New Deal programs for engaging in a hopeless effort to return to the past. His stated goal was "to sober and strengthen the American liberal tradition, not to destroy it." Predictably, the work infuriated RUS-SELL KIRK and other conservatives.

Rossiter's own conservatism consisted of a desire for gradual, contained progress; a distrust of majoritarianism, of which he regarded McCarthy-

ism as a deplorable example; and a commitment to leadership by an aristocracy of talent. During the 1950s, Rossiter backed civil rights, world peace, and the United Nations. Many conservatives, particularly those associated with *National Review* magazine, denounced Rossiter's views as virtually indistinguishable from those of liberals.

In *The American Presidency* (1956), Rossiter described the American presidency as "one of the few truly successful institutions created by men in their endless quest for the blessings of free government." The office, he argued, had served the American republic well. His *Parties and Politics* (1960) praised the two-party system's effectiveness in providing for peaceful change and articulating the majority will. In *Marxism: The View from America* (1960), Rossiter advocated peaceful coexistence with the Soviet Union, asserting that "we must not slide hopelessly into an apocalyptic view of the struggle between their system and ours, lest we slam the door forever on all hopes of an evolution in Communism that would make it possible for East and West to live together in a reasonably peaceful world."

Rossiter served as chair of his department from 1956 to 1959 and in 1959 was named John L. Senior Professor of American Institutions. He also held various positions outside his own university. From 1953 to 1960, he served as a consultant to the Ford Foundation's Fund for the Republic, in which capacity he headed a team of 10 scholars that produced a series of books on communist influence in the United States. In addition, Rossiter was a consultant to the Rockefeller Foundation from 1956 to 1958 and a contributor to the report of the President's Commission on National Goals, published in 1960.

In the early 1960s, Rossiter toured extensively throughout the world as a visiting lecturer for the State Department. He published *Conservatism in America: The Thankless Persuasion* in 1962. His *Alexander Hamilton and the Constitution* (1964) praised Hamilton for his role in creating an industrial society with an effective national government. In 1966, his *1787: The Grand Convention* took issue with the idea that the Constitution represented a conservative step back from the democratic ideals of the Declaration of Independence. Rossiter asserted that the Constitution emerged logically from the aspirations expressed in 1776 and that it saved the infant republic from chaos. In 1966, Rossiter received an invitation to lecture at the Academy of Sciences of the Soviet Union. Cornell experienced widespread student unrest in 1969 and 1970. Rossiter initially joined a number of senior faculty in calling for a return to order. When the university's president, a close friend of Rossiter's, reached an accommodation with black students, however, Rossiter broke with his colleagues and supported the agreement. Rossiter died in at his home in Ithaca, New York, an apparent suicide, on July 11, 1970. His *The American Quest, 1790–1860* (1971) appeared posthumously.

—MSM

Rovere, Richard H(alworthy)
(1915–1979) *journalist*

The son of an electrical engineer, Richard Rovere was born in Jersey City, New Jersey, on May 5, 1915. After attending public schools in New York City and Stony Brook School on Long Island, he earned his B.A. at Bard College in upstate New York, where he was editor of the school newspaper and became first a socialist and then a communist. After graduation in 1937, Rovere joined the staff of *New Masses*, a communist weekly, which, he said later, "consistently, indeed slavishly followed the Communist line." "Like many others at the time," he reflected, "I looked at brutal authoritarianism and saw discipline." The signing of the Nazi-Soviet Pact in August 1939 deeply disillusioned Rovere, who quit *New Masses* and turned away from the Communist Party, which he had never officially joined. Over the next five years, he wrote as an anticommunist liberal for *The Nation* and, beginning in 1943, for *Common Sense*, the organ of the League for Independent Political Action. He clashed with other members of the staff and left *Common Sense* after less than a year. In 1944, he began writing for *Harper's* and the *New Yorker*.

Early in his association with the *New Yorker*, Rovere wrote mostly on nonpolitical topics. He contributed profiles of colorful individuals, some political and many not. His subjects ranged from New York politicians, such as Newbold Morris and Edward Flynn, to John Gunther (a journalist), Bruno

Furst (a memory expert), and Henry Blackman Sell (an author and literary critic turned meatpacker). Based on the strength of a series of stories Rovere wrote about the campaign of 1948, in particular a widely read article he had written in *Harper's* on New York's governor, THOMAS E. DEWEY, the editors of the *New Yorker* hired Rovere as a regular political columnist. In the more than 30 years he wrote Letter from Washington (later Affairs of State), Rovere became one of the most respected and influential political journalists in America. Rovere covered Washington from New York; rather than breaking stories based on his own investigations, he wrote detached, analytical accounts of controversial topics. For the most part, his columns displayed little evidence of his younger polemical attitude. Rovere's reputation rested on the wit, distinctive style, and quality of his analyses.

Rovere's most vivid journalism dealt with personalities, and his language came closest to passionate when he wrote about the anticommunist crusader Sen. JOSEPH R. McCARTHY (R-Wis.). His pieces on McCarthy for the *New Yorker* mingled amusement, revulsion, and incredulity. Rovere described his first encounter with McCarthy, during which the senator offered a formidable stack of documents intended to prove a contention he had made. Rovere gradually realized that the papers were all either irrelevant, contradictory to the senator's own case, or useless.

In 1959, Rovere published a popular, controversial character study of McCarthy, *Senator Joe McCarthy*. Characterizing the senator as "in many ways the most gifted demagogue ever bred on these shores," Rovere called McCarthy a "master of flimflammery" and a "champion liar." As Rovere saw it, McCarthy was not "totalitarian in any significant sense, or even reactionary. . . . If he was anything at all in the realm of ideas, principles, doctrines, he was a species of nihilist; he was an essentially destructive force, a revolutionist without any revolutionary vision, a rebel without a cause." For all his talents as a demagogue, Rovere wrote, McCarthy "lacked the most necessary and awesome of demagogic gifts—a belief in the sacredness of his own mission."

In *Senator Joe McCarthy*, Rovere described McCarthy's technique as the "multiple untruth." According to Rovere, the multiple untruth "need not be a particularly large untruth but can instead be a long series of loosely related untruths, or a single untruth with many facets. In either case, the whole is composed of so many parts that anyone wishing to set the record straight will discover that it is utterly impossible to keep all the elements of the falsehood in mind at the same time." By boldly scattering falsehoods and distortions, McCarthy was able to stay ahead of the slow-moving process of factual refutation, while enjoying a full measure of publicity from his accusations.

The book's analysis of McCarthy was devastating. In McCarthy, Rovere found a rare case, "a true cynic and a true hypocrite." "Beyond mischief," wrote Rovere, "he never accomplished anything." Much as he characterized McCarthy as a mountebank, Rovere dismissed the man's cause as "a headlong flight from reality. It elevated the ridiculous and ridiculed the important." Rovere concluded his work: "McCarthy offered a powerful challenge to freedom, and he showed us to be more vulnerable than many of us had guessed to a seditious demagogy—as well as less vulnerable than some of us feared."

Rovere wrote noteworthy assessments of the other major political figures of the time. He praised President HARRY S. TRUMAN for acting vigorously in the face of staggering crises, in which he showed "moral courage under pressure, even a kind of moral grace." Rovere supported Truman's intervention in Korea: "Aggression had at that moment to be resisted . . . had we failed to respond, the slave world would have been greatly emboldened, the free world greatly dispirited." In July 1953, Rovere cited the American intervention in Korea as "the turning point of the world struggle against Communism."

Rovere eulogized Senator ROBERT TAFT (R-Ohio) as a "man of character." In a less flattering portrait of Vice President RICHARD NIXON, Rovere wrote in 1955 that, although Nixon had taken many stands, "there is no discernible pattern to his commitments." Rovere was struck by "the flexibility that suggests an almost total indifference to policy. Nixon appears to be a politician with an advertising man's approach to his work. Policies are products to be sold to the public—this one today, that one tomorrow, depending on the discounts and the state of the market."

Rovere's collection of essays, *Affairs of State: The Eisenhower Years*, published in 1956, offered an appraisal of DWIGHT D. EISENHOWER's performance as president. In it, Rovere coupled praise for the president's foreign policy with criticism of his conduct of domestic affairs. Recognizing that "such challenges as he chose to meet he met well," he lauded Eisenhower for fulfilling the urgent tasks of holding together the Western alliance and saving Western civilization "in a spirit of decency and maturity." However, Rovere criticized the president's attitude toward the rest of the government as "neglectful." "Once Eisenhower has found a first-class automobile dealer, cotton broker, or razor manufacturer to head a department, he has acted as if the public interest has been satisfied and his own responsibility discharged." For Rovere, Eisenhower's program was nothing more than "a pastiche of pieties." Rovere concluded that Eisenhower's presidency had "left the country almost exactly as he found it."

In 1962, Rovere wrote a retrospective assessment of Eisenhower that took his second term into account. He found the second four years disappointing but reiterated his essential judgment. Eisenhower's "command decisions" in foreign affairs were "generally wise," while his responses to domestic problems were complacent and inadequate. Beginning in the late 1960s, some of Eisenhower's harshest critics, including left-leaning journalists Murray Kempton and I. F. STONE, reassessed Eisenhower and found much to praise in his conduct of the presidency. In 1971, Rovere published a rebuttal to their work, titled "Eisenhower Revisited—A Political Genius? A Brilliant Man?," in the *New York Times Magazine*. Acknowledging that "after the various agonies of the Johnson and Nixon years, Ike's record and behavior look increasingly attractive," Rovere nonetheless contended that, "with hindsight, we can see that practically all of the problems that bedeviled us in the sixties had been worsening in the fifties." Rovere contended that the increasingly popular characterization of Eisenhower as a "political genius" arose from the simple fact that the United States did not go to war while he was president, a circumstance Rovere attributed as much to luck as good management.

By the late 1950s, Rovere had established himself as a leading political commentator and expanded his activities well beyond his column for the *New Yorker.* He was a correspondent for *Spectator* (a British review of politics, literature, and the arts) from 1954 to 1962 and served on the board of editors of the *American Scholar* from 1958 to 1967. He taught at Columbia University from 1957 to 1959 and lectured at Yale University in 1972 and 1973.

In 1962, Rovere published *The American Establishment and Other Reports, Opinions and Speculations.* The title essay, which originally appeared that same year in *Esquire,* contained a satiric listing of those elite institutions and individuals most influential in American life. The public took the piece at face value, and it contributed a phrase to the language. During the 1960s, he also published *The Goldwater Caper* (1965) and *Waist Deep in the Big Muddy: Personal Reflections on United States Policy* (1968). The latter reflected his growing disgust with the Vietnam War, an enterprise that he thought threatened "all mankind," could "liberate no one," and became "daily more unconscionable." Rovere published a volume of memoirs, *Arrivals and Departures: A Journalist's Memoirs,* in 1976 and wrote his last regular political column for the *New Yorker* in August 1979. He died in Poughkeepsie, New York, on November 23, 1979. A posthumous book, *Final Reports: Personal Reflections on Politics and History in Our Time,* came out in 1984.

—MSM

Rowe, James H(enry), Jr.
(1909–1984) *attorney*

Born in Butte, Montana, on June 1, 1909, Rowe earned his B.A. from Harvard University and graduated from Harvard Law School in 1934. The following year, he clerked for Justice Oliver Wendell Holmes. From 1935 to 1938, he worked for various New Deal agencies. Through the influence of Thomas Corcoran, one of President Franklin D. Roosevelt's aides and a top political fixer, Rowe landed a low-level job in the White House, as an assistant to Roosevelt's son, James. In 1939, Rowe became an administrative assistant to the president. Rowe went to the Justice Department in 1941 as an assistant attorney general. He served as a lieutenant

in the navy in the Pacific from 1943 to 1945. After the war, he was a technical adviser to the International Military Tribunal that tried Nazi leaders at Nuremberg, Germany. He left government in 1946 to form a law firm in Washington with Corcoran. During the Truman administration, Rowe advised the president on how to deal with the Republican-dominated 80th Congress and helped plan strategy for the presidential campaign of 1948.

During the Eisenhower administration, Rowe advised such Democratic leaders as Senator LYNDON B. JOHNSON (D-Tex.), ADLAI STEVENSON, and Senator HUBERT HUMPHREY (D Minn.). Rowe was particularly close to Johnson, whom he urged to speak out in opposition to the administration's programs. The senator, however, preferred to cooperate with Eisenhower. Rowe served as an intermediary between Stevenson and Johnson. Beginning in 1954, he advised Stevenson to court Johnson; Rowe argued that Stevenson would need Johnson's help to win the Democratic presidential nomination in 1956. Rowe's advice paid off; after initial wavering, Johnson endorsed Stevenson.

Rowe initially supported Johnson for the presidential nomination in 1960. However, after Johnson assured him in 1959 that he would not be a candidate, Rowe supported Humphrey. The senator from Minnesota valued Rowe's advice, despite warnings from supporters that Rowe backed him only to divide liberals in the party. Humphrey's aides believed that Rowe intended to create a three-way deadlock between Stevenson, Senator JOHN F. KENNEDY (D-Mass.), and Humphrey, so that the convention would draft Johnson.

In late 1959, Rowe developed a strategy for Humphrey's upcoming campaign. Because Humphrey was relatively unknown outside the Midwest and had only limited funds, Rowe urged him to devote all his time to campaigning in selected primaries. With enough victories in the primaries, Rowe figured, Humphrey could obtain the votes of a minimum of 150 to 200 delegates and thus enter the convention as a strong candidate in a floor fight. Rowe's plan failed when Humphrey lost primaries in Wisconsin and West Virginia. Following the defeat in West Virginia, Rowe urged Humphrey to continue campaigning, but Humphrey withdrew from the race. Rowe then encouraged Johnson to seek the nomination. At the convention, Rowe served as Johnson's leading floor manager.

Rowe remained Johnson's confidant throughout the 1960s. In 1964, he was part of the inner circle that directed Johnson's presidential campaign. He was instrumental in convincing Johnson not to offer the vice presidential nomination to ROBERT F. KENNEDY and to chose Humphrey as a running mate. In late 1967, Rowe began planning Johnson's presidential campaign for 1968. Following the Tet offensive in February 1968, Rowe was a member of the Senior Advisory Group on Vietnam that urged Johnson not to escalate the war further. Johnson followed Rowe's advice and, at the end of March, announced that he was limiting the bombing of North Vietnam. The president surprised many people, including his close friend Rowe, by also announcing his withdrawal from the presidential race. Rowe managed Humphrey's unsuccessful campaign for the presidency in 1968. During the 1970s, Rowe continued to be active in Democratic politics. From 1965 to 1971, he was a member of Harvard's Board of Overseers. Rowe died in New York City on June 17, 1984.

—MSM

Rusk, Dean

(1909–1994) *president, Rockefeller Foundation; secretary of state*

The son of a country schoolteacher, small farmer, and Presbyterian minister, Dean Rusk was born in Cherokee County, Georgia, on February 9, 1909. At the age of three, he moved with his family to Atlanta, Georgia, where his father worked as a mail carrier. He started school in second grade, having taught himself to read from his brother's textbooks, and graduated from Boys' High School in Atlanta in 1925. He worked for two years in a law office and entered Davidson College in North Carolina in 1927. After graduating magna cum laude in 1931, he attended St. John's College at Oxford University as a Rhodes Scholar. There, he earned a master's degree in politics, economics, and philosophy in 1934. Later that year, Rusk became a professor of government at Mills College in California and in 1936 dean of the faculty. While continuing to hold his position at Mills College, he studied law at the

University of California at Berkeley. A captain in the army reserve, Rusk was called to active duty in 1940. Not long before Pearl Harbor, he received a transfer to military intelligence and was assigned to the War Department. In 1943, he was promoted to major and assigned to the staff of General Joseph Stilwell. Rusk participated in the first and third Burma campaigns; he was appointed deputy chief of staff and promoted to colonel. Recalled to Washington in June 1945, he served as assistant chief of the Operations Division of General Staff of the War Department.

After his discharge in February 1946, Rusk joined the State Department as assistant chief of the Division of International Security Affairs. That summer, Rusk became special assistant to the secretary of war. He returned to the State Department in March 1947 as director of the Office of Special Political Affairs, where he was directly involved in policy concerning the establishment of the state of Israel. By 1950, Rusk had risen to deputy undersecretary. Rusk requested and received an appointment as assistant secretary of state for Far Eastern affairs in March 1950. Although a demotion, it was the job he wanted. A dedicated anticommunist, Rusk supported American military intervention in Korea, although he opposed any invasion of China. Rusk left the State Department to become president of the Rockefeller Foundation in 1952.

As president of the Rockefeller Foundation during the 1950s, Rusk directed the distribution of about $250 million to developing nations in Asia, Africa, and Latin America to help them improve their methods of agriculture and promote health and social welfare. Under Rusk's leadership, scientists working for the Rockefeller Foundation promoted the green revolution by improving the yields of rice and producing new varieties of rust-resistant wheat. The foundation also funded research by the National Academy of Sciences in 1955 and 1956 on the health hazards of nuclear fallout. It later supported research by Cornell University, the University of Chicago, and the Social Science Research Council to ensure the safety of the peaceful use of atomic energy. In 1956, Rusk traveled to Hungary and Austria, where he directed the distribution of aid to Hungarian scholars and scientists afer the failed Hungarian revolt.

As head of the Rockefeller Foundation, Rusk also played a role in protecting academic freedom. In 1954, the Republican majority on the House Special Committee to Investigate Tax-Exempt Foundations charged that the Rockefeller, Carnegie, Ford, and other foundations "directly supported 'subversion' by supporting attacks upon our social and governmental system and financing the promotion of socialism and collectivist ideas." The three-member majority—Representatives B. Carroll Reece (R-Tenn.), Jesse P. Wolcott (R-Mich.), and Angier L. Goodwin (R-Mass.)—believed the foundations had "propagandized blindly for the United Nations," had supported assignment of articles by the Encyclopedia of the Social Sciences to communist and other leftist writers, and had promoted excessive moral relativism in research. To the committee's majority, a striking example of this was the Rockefeller Foundation's support of ALFRED KINSEY's studies on sex. Responding to these charges, Rusk denied the Rockefeller Foundation was infiltrated by communists. He emphasized that the foundation would never try to control the type of research it funded and would fight any attempt by the government to use taxation to infringe on freedom of thought.

As secretary of state during the administration of President JOHN F. KENNEDY, Rusk generally played an advisory role. Kennedy chose Rusk over more prominent candidates because the president intended to shape his own foreign policy. Rusk later claimed to have had reservations about the invasion of Cuba and acknowledged that he had been excluded from the decision-making process and had been too deferential to the president. Initially, Rusk favored keeping the United States out of Vietnam, but after 1963 he came to support U.S. involvement. During the administration of LYNDON B. JOHNSON, Rusk played a leading role in formulating and defending American policy in Vietnam as the war escalated. After the Tet offensive in February 1968, Johnson announced that he would not seek another term, de-escalated the American military commitment, and entered into negotiations with North Vietnam. Rusk, who apparently disapproved of the talks, took little part in them. After leaving the government in January 1969, Rusk found that many elite universities would not even consider him for a faculty appointment. In

1970, he became Sibley Professor of International Law at the University of Georgia. After retiring from teaching in 1984, he published a volume of memoirs, *As I Saw It*, in 1990. Rusk died in Athens, Georgia, on December 20, 1994.

—MSM

Russell, Richard B(revard), Jr.
(1897–1971) *U.S. senator; chairman, Armed Services Committee*

The son of a lawyer and judge, Russell was born in Winder, Georgia, on November 2, 1897. He graduated from the Seventh District Agricultural and Mechanical School in Powder Springs, Georgia, in 1914, and from Gordon Military Institute in 1915 before earning a law degree from the University of Georgia in 1918. After serving in the navy for 79 days during World War I, during which time he never left Atlanta, Russell returned to Winder to practice law with his father. In 1920, he won election as a Democrat to the Georgia General Assembly; he served in that body from 1921 to 1931 and as its speaker from 1927 until 1931. In November 1930, Russell was elected governor. The following January, his father, the chief justice of Georgia, administered the oath of office. Having promised economy in government during his campaign, he reduced his salary, consolidated executive departments, bureaus, and commissions, and established a state purchasing department. He built highways and made efforts to improve education.

In November 1932, Russell won a special election to fill a vacancy in the U.S. Senate created by the death of William J. Harris (D-Ga.). Russell subsequently won election to a full term in 1936 and was reelected in 1942, 1948, 1954, 1960, and 1966. Early in his career, he supported most New Deal legislation and demonstrated particular enthusiasm for agricultural price supports, rural electrification, and farm loans. By the mid-1930s, Russell began to depart from the New Deal on labor legislation. He refused to support President Franklin D. Roosevelt's plan to pack the Supreme Court. Throughout his career in the Senate, Russell opposed measures aimed at altering race relations in the South. He led filibusters against antilynching bills in 1935 and 1937. Whatever differences he may have had with Roosevelt over domestic policy, in the years preceding American entry into World War II, Russell backed the president's foreign policy. In the mid-1930s, Russell had opposed the World Court and voted for the Neutrality Act. By the end of the decade, he voted several times for funds to strengthen America's defenses. He supported an end to the mandatory arms embargo and the establishment of Selective Service in 1940 and voted for lend-lease legislation in 1941.

Russell quickly rose to prominence in the Senate based on his friendly manner, his ability to mediate differences, his honesty, his oratorical ability, and his parliamentary skills. Upon his arrival in the Senate, he managed to get appointed to the Appropriations Committee, perhaps the most powerful committee in the upper chamber. He also received appointments to other key committees, including Immigration, Manufactures, and Naval Affairs (from which he moved in 1947 to the newly created Armed Services Committee). In addition to serving on two of the Senate's most powerful committees, Appropriations and Armed Services, Russell was a member of the Democratic Policy Committee and the Democratic Steering Committee. In the 79th Congress, he chaired the Committee on Manufactures. By the second half of the 1940s, he had emerged as the leader of the southern caucus. Although a skilled debater, he gave few speeches on the Senate floor, preferring to work behind the scenes, but no one exercised more influence on his colleagues.

Like many southerners on Capitol Hill, Russell became an opponent of social welfare programs after the war. He did, however, serve as chief sponsor of the National School Lunch Act of 1946, which not only provided nutrition for schoolchildren but subsidized agriculture as well. In foreign policy, Russell rejected the idea that the United States should police the world. He nevertheless believed that the United States should receive special rights to bases that it had helped to build during World War II. As relations with the Soviets deteriorated, Russell supported the Truman Doctrine and the Marshall Plan, the latter without much enthusiasm.

Russell resented the report of the President's Committee on Civil Rights, which recommended, among other things, the establishment of a perma-

nent Fair Employment Practices Commission and the abolition of segregation in the armed forces. He thought that the committee had gathered information intended to confirm the preconceived notions of its members. Truman's message calling for passage of some of the committee's recommendations alarmed Russell and other southerners in Congress. In March 1948, a group of 21 southern senators met and agreed to rally behind Russell's leadership to block any civil rights legislation.

Disillusioned with Truman, Russell was among the many Democrats of various political views who favored General DWIGHT D. EISENHOWER for the Democratic nomination that year. When Eisenhower disavowed any interest in the presidency, Russell, as leader of the southern bloc in the Senate, permitted his name to be entered in nomination at the Democratic National Convention. A regional candidate, he received only 263 votes to Truman's 947½.

Russell led southern opposition to the inclusion of a strong civil rights plank in the Democratic platform in 1948. When the convention rejected the modest plank backed by Truman and proposed by the platform committee in favor of a stronger endorsement of civil rights, southern delegates walked out of the convention, bolted from the Democratic Party, and nominated South Carolina's governor, STROM THURMOND (D-S.C.), for the presidency on the States Rights Party (Dixiecrat) ticket. Russell did not join the Dixiecrats and, shortly before the election, gave Truman a pro forma endorsement. He took no part in the national campaign.

In 1951, Russell became chair of the Armed Services Committee, a position he held until 1953, when the Republicans gained control of the Senate. After the elections of 1954, the Democrats regained control of the upper house, and Russell resumed the chairmanship of the Armed Services Committee, which he held until 1969. Although strongly anticommunist, Russell did not believe that the United States could do much to prevent China from falling to the communists. He thought it unwise to base American foreign policy on undependable allies and opposed the use of American force abroad when the national interest did not clearly dictate it. For Russell, a strong military capability provided the best way to provide for America's defense. In 1951, he headed a joint investigation by the Armed Services Committee and the Foreign Relations Committee into Truman's dismissal of General Douglas MacArthur. Russell's impartial, restrained, and expeditious handling of the proceedings helped to defuse an explosive issue.

In 1952, Russell actively sought the Democratic presidential nomination. He presented himself as a conservative and declared that "I do not think this dangerous period is the time to strike out on new adventures that could lead this country down the road to socialism." In an attempt to broaden the base of his appeal, Russell advocated reform of the Taft-Hartley Act (even though he had voted to pass the law over Truman's veto). He remained, however, a sectional candidate and ran third on all three ballots at the national convention. His highest tally came on the second ballot, when he received 294 votes. Russell endorsed the party's nominee, ADLAI E. STEVENSON, in October but took little part in the campaign.

An intelligent, unpretentious, and courteous man, Russell devoted his life entirely to the Senate. He never married, worked long hours, and avoided the outward trappings of power. Russell was one of the most respected members of the Senate, and his colleagues regarded him as the embodiment of the best traditions of the upper chamber. Many observers believed that he would have become president had he not been a southerner at a time when the South's position on race diverged strongly from that of the rest of the country. Russell's unsuccessful presidential bid in 1952, which clearly demonstrated the limits faced by southern conservatives, somewhat embittered him. He subsequently decided to forgo any ambition for a national office role and devote his abilities, including his formidable parliamentary skill, to leading the powerful bloc of southerners who chaired committees and subcommittees in the Senate. In 1953, he passed over an opportunity to become minority leader and instead secured the position for his friend and protégé, Senator LYNDON B. JOHNSON (D-Tex.).

Throughout the 1950s, many informed political observers considered Russell the most influential member of the Senate. Russell used that influence to maintain high levels of price support for basic commodities. The antics of Senator JOSEPH R. McCARTHY (R-Wis.) embarrassed Russell. McCarthy's coarse language, his reckless charges, and his abuse of witnesses who appeared before his committee appalled the dignified Georgian. Russell would not, however, support cutting off funds for McCarthy's committee, because he refused to interfere with the operations of a legitimately constituted committee of the Senate.

During the Eisenhower administration, Russell led the southern bloc in its fight against racial integration and measures designed to protect the civil rights of African Americans. Throughout his career, Russell refused to engage in race-baiting and opposed lynching and other forms of racist violence. He was nevertheless a dedicated white supremacist and fought vigorously against all federal efforts to intrude upon southern society. By the mid-1950s, however, Russell proved willing to make strategic compromises rather than engage in hopeless, die-hard obstruction.

When the Supreme Court struck down segregation in public schools (*Brown v. Board of Education* [1954]), Russell issued a statement calling the decision "a flagrant abuse of judicial power" that violated rights "plainly guaranteed" to the states by the Constitution. In 1956, Strom Thurmond drafted a Declaration of Constitutional Principles, more popularly known as the Southern Manifesto, attacking the Supreme Court's decision. When a number of moderate southern members of Congress refused to sign the manifesto, a committee headed by Russell produced a new draft that excluded some of the most inflammatory language. The final draft, largely written by Russell, declared that *Brown* had overstepped the Court's authority and called on southern states to use "any lawful means" to resist it. Nineteen senators and 77 members of the House signed the document.

That same year, the House passed legislation proposed by the Eisenhower administration. Parliamentary maneuvering killed the bill in the Senate. In 1957, the administration once again sent the measure to Congress, and it once again passed the House. Designed primarily to protect black voting rights, it also established a presidential civil rights commission and elevated the civil rights section of the Justice Department to the status of a division.

The most controversial provision granted the attorney general authority to file civil suits to further desegregation. Before the Senate considered the bill, Russell warned that it would be "vigorously resisted by a resolute group of senators." Johnson went to Russell and warned his mentor that a filibuster would damage the Democratic Party and might result in the loss of Congress. It would also most likely result in a change to the Senate's Rule 22, which provided for unlimited debate and required a two-thirds vote for cloture. Without control of the committee chairs and without even the threat of a filibuster, Johnson admonished, southerners would lose any ability to influence civil rights legislation, much less the ability to block it. In exchange for a promise not to filibuster, Russell and his allies extracted a promise to eliminate provisions giving the president power to use troops to enforce existing civil rights laws and permitting the attorney general to initiate civil action for injunctive relief in civil rights cases. They also added a provision guaranteeing a jury trial in contempt cases arising from interference with the exercise of the right to vote.

On August 24, Russell declared that southern leaders remained "unalterably opposed" to the bill. However, reflecting a recognition that the compromise was the best the southerners could hope to obtain, he added that "there was no collective agreement that we would undertake to talk the proposition to death." On August 28, Thurmond conducted a solo filibuster against the bill for a record 24 hours and 18 minutes before he physically collapsed. With Thurmond's theatrics out of the way, the Senate passed the bill (Russell voted against it), and Eisenhower signed the Civil Rights Act of 1957 into law. Russell contended that Thurmond's stunt could have created an "unparalleled disaster" by prompting an attempt by supporters of civil rights to revoke the concessions the southerners had obtained. Russell denounced Thurmond, asserting that "if I had undertaken a filibuster for personal political aggrandizement, I would have forever reproached myself for being guilty of a form of treason against the people of the South."

In 1960, Russell and 17 other members of the southern bloc managed, with the aid of a filibuster, to weaken legislation proposed by the administration designed primarily to strengthen the voting rights provisions of the Civil Rights Act of 1957. Southerners succeeded in amending a plan for court-appointed referees to help African Americans register and vote so as to reduce the power of the referees. They also killed a provision enabling the federal government to pay half the costs incurred by local schools for desegregation and an amendment strengthening provisions prohibiting companies with federal contracts from engaging in discriminatory employment practices. As in 1957, Russell denounced the final version of the civil rights bill but did not attempt to block its passage.

As chairman of the Armed Services panel, Russell opposed attempts by the Eisenhower administration to cut the military budget; he also opposed the New Look, which was intended to save money and avoid another limited war by stressing nuclear deterrence over conventional forces. During Senate debate over a defense appropriations bill in 1955, Russell stated that General MATTHEW B. RIDGWAY had asserted that the cuts in the army's manpower proposed by the administration would "endanger national security." In spite of Russell's plea and his position as chair of the Armed Services Committee, he could not prevent reductions in defense spending.

Early in 1956, following indications that the Soviet Union had made significant advances in developing long-range bombers, Russell appointed Senator STUART SYMINGTON (D-Mo.) to chair a special five-member panel to investigate the state of American air power. The Democratic majority criticized defense cuts proposed by the administration and warned that the USSR might soon have superiority in the air. Later in the year, Russell joined a 13–12 majority on the Appropriations Committee in a vote to increase funding for the air force by $800 million more than the administration's request. After Secretary of Defense CHARLES WILSON described the increase as "phony," Russell, always jealous of congressional prerogatives, denounced the secretary for having "treated the Congress with disdain . . . at times almost with contempt." He charged that Wilson "has sought to intimidate the officers of the Armed Services from fully expressing their opinions to, and advising with, the Congress." The final bill signed by the president contained most of the increase in air force funding.

Russell often criticized what he regarded as excessive expenditures on foreign aid. While he did not oppose all foreign aid, he maintained that it should be temporary in nature and distributed sparingly. In fact, Russell never voted for a foreign aid bill after 1952. Throughout the Eisenhower administration, he objected to what he called throwing money around the world and insisted on careful scrutiny of the administration's requests for foreign aid. In 1957, Russell posed the major obstacle in the Senate to passage of the Eisenhower Doctrine and an appropriation for $200 million in economic aid to countries in the Middle East. He proposed that the economic assistance should be postponed until Congress made its annual study of the entire foreign aid program. His amendment, however, went down to defeat on the floor by a vote of 28 to 58.

In 1956, Russell, who had a close political and personal relationship with Johnson, backed Johnson's bid for the Democratic presidential nomination. Four years later, however, a rift developed between them over Johnson's efforts as majority leader to pass the civil rights bill in 1960. The rift widened when Johnson accepted the Democratic vice presidential nomination after the party's national convention had adopted a stronger civil rights platform than Russell could countenance. The friendship between Johnson and Russell, however, withstood the strains of politics; although Russell initially declined to back the national ticket, he gave his endorsement after Johnson made a personal appeal.

Russell remained a formidable figure during the 1960s, but a declining one. The election of 16 new Democratic senators, mostly liberals, in 1958 served to reduce Russell's power. He served on the Warren Commission, which investigated the assassination of President JOHN F. KENNEDY. Russell's adamant opposition to President Johnson's civil rights bills resulted in stinging defeats. A southern filibuster failed when the Senate invoked cloture to pass the Civil Rights Act of 1964. The next year, Russell proved unable to prevent passage of the Voting Rights Act. He opposed most of Johnson's Great Society but remained close to Johnson, who trusted the advice of the Georgian. Although Russell had misgivings about American involvement in Vietnam, he maintained that, since a commitment

had been made, the United States should use all necessary military force to win the war. In 1969, Russell gave up his chairmanship of the Armed Services panel to become head of the Appropriations Committee. On January 21, 1971, during his seventh term in the Senate, Russell died of respiratory insufficiency in Washington, D.C.

—MSM

Rustin, Bayard
(1910–1987) *civil rights leader*

An illegitimate child raised by his Quaker maternal grandparents, Rustin was born in West Chester, Pennsylvania, on March 17, 1910. He attended public schools and studied at Wilberforce College, Cheney State Teachers College, and the College of the City of New York, but he never earned a degree. In 1936, he joined the Young Communist League because he believed that communists "seemed to be the only people who had civil rights at heart." He broke with the communists in 1941 when, after the Nazi invasion of the Soviet Union, the Communist Party abandoned its opposition to World War II and subordinated social protest to the cause of defeating Germany. From then on, Rustin devoted himself to civil rights and pacifism.

Soon after breaking with the communists, Rustin joined the Fellowship of Reconciliation (FOR), a nondenominational, pacifist religious group that opposed the war and racial injustice. His work brought him into contact with A. PHILIP RANDOLPH, the president of the Brotherhood of Sleeping Car Porters and a leading activist for black civil rights. In 1941, Rustin helped organize Randolph's March on Washington Movement, which demanded fair employment practices in the nation's burgeoning defense industries. Randolph postponed the planned march on Washington when President Franklin D. Roosevelt issued an executive order banning racial discrimination by defense contractors. Rustin opposed the decision to cancel the march and accused Randolph of compromising his principles.

In 1941, Rustin helped found the Congress of Racial Equality (CORE) and went to work for the organization as a field secretary. He went to prison from 1943 to 1945 for refusing military service in

World War II. Upon his release, he became chairman of the Free India Committee and three years later went to India to study Gandhi's nonviolent protest. In 1947, Rustin participated in CORE's Journey of Reconciliation, the first Freedom Ride into the South. During that protest, he was convicted of violating segregation laws and spent weeks on a road gang in North Carolina. At about the same time, he became director of the Committee Against Discrimination in the Armed Forces. Pressure from that group contributed to President HARRY S. TRUMAN's decision to issue an executive order barring discrimination in the services in 1948.

Rustin resigned his post with CORE in 1953 to become executive director of the pacifist War Resisters League. His commitment to pacifism took him to many places around the world. He traveled to Britain in 1959 to help the Campaign for Nuclear Disarmament organize its first march to "ban the bomb." In 1960, Rustin was arrested in France for protesting atomic tests in the Sahara.

From 1955 to 1964, Rustin served as chief tactician of the Civil Rights movement. In 1955, he helped MARTIN LUTHER KING, JR., organize the bus boycott in Montgomery, Alabama, and Rustin played a significant role in the formation of King's philosophy of nonviolence. Rustin stressed the tactical as well as the moral advantages of nonviolent direct action. In October 1956, he wrote that "insofar as the Negro retains the nonviolent approach, he will be able to win white sympathy and frustrate the aims of the White Citizens Council [white supremacists]. . . ." If, however, white racists succeeded in provoking blacks to violence, Rustin contended, "Negroes will lose their moral initiative, liberals will become even more frightened and inactive and a deeper wedge will be driven between white and black workers." He also asserted that ongoing nonviolent direct action would exert immediate economic and social pressure on the South and was more important than "a one-shot performance at the polls in November."

In 1957, at King's request, Rustin drew up plans for the organization of the Southern Christian Leadership Conference, which advocated racial equality through nonviolent means. That year he also wrote a series of statements used by King and the Rev. RALPH ABERNATHY at a meeting with Vice President RICHARD M. NIXON. The statements included the assertions that federal action was necessary to end racial discrimination and that neither political party had been sufficiently active in promoting civil rights. They also demanded that President Eisenhower make an appeal to the nation on behalf of racial equality and that Nixon make a trip to the South and "speak out in moral terms" for civil rights in general and voting rights in particular.

Although committed to nonviolent direct action and civil disobedience, Rustin believed in the need to create alliances with white reformers, particularly sympathetic elements in the labor movement. Rustin emphasized the need for an interracial coalition of poor people, because he believed that gaining civil rights alone would not remedy the issue of poverty in the black community.

In June 1960, Rustin drafted a letter that King sent to both national parties proposing action on civil rights. It called on them to repudiate the segregationists within their ranks; to reduce, in accordance with the Fourteenth Amendment, the congressional representation of areas denying blacks the right to vote; to endorse explicitly the Supreme Court's 1954 school desegregation decision as both morally correct and the law of the land; and to oppose colonialism in Africa. The letter also urged Congress to include in the civil rights bill then under consideration a section empowering the federal government to bring suits on behalf of African Americans who had been denied civil rights and to frame the bill so as to place responsibility for the protection of black voting rights in the hands of the president rather than the southern courts. That same year, Rustin organized demonstrations at both the Republican and Democratic National Conventions.

Rustin served as chief planner of the March on Washington for Jobs and Freedom that took place in August 1963. More than 250,000 people attended the rally to support civil rights legislation and to listen to speeches that included King's "I Have a Dream" speech. In 1964, Rustin organized a one-day boycott of public schools in New York City to demonstrate support for more rapid integration of New York's school system. With the Civil Rights Act of 1964 and the Voting Rights Act of 1965, the Civil Rights movement achieved its greatest success. At the same time, some younger activists turned to Black Power and rejected nonviolence. Rustin opposed black nationalism and calls for violence in the mid-1960s, calling instead for an alliance of organized labor, African Americans, and liberals under the umbrella of the Democratic Party. Black militants derided him as an Uncle Tom, and Rustin, in response, moved closer to his white allies. During a strike of teachers in New York City in 1968, Rustin supported the United Federation of Teachers against the demands of African-American militants who demanded community control of the schools. In 1964, Rustin became executive director of the newly created A. Philip Randolph Institute. In that post, he attempted to strengthen ties between African Americans and the trade union movement. Rustin also maintained strong ties with the American-Jewish community. His advocacy of harmony between the black and Jewish communities became a major emphasis of his later years, and he condemned growing anti-Semitism among African Americans. That and his strong support of the state of Israel were controversial among African Americans. Some African Americans accused him of greater devotion to white liberal, labor, and Jewish causes than to black causes. Months before he died, he acknowledged in an interview with the *Village Voice* that he was a homosexual. He had previously downplayed his sexual orientation because public knowledge of the fact would have limited his effectiveness on behalf of civil rights, pacifism, and other causes. Rustin died in New York City on August 24, 1987.

—MSM

S

Salisbury, Harrison E(vans)
(1908–1993) *journalist*

Born in Minneapolis, Minnesota, on November 14, 1908, Harrison Salisbury attended the University of Minnesota, where he began his career in journalism as editor of the student newspaper and a part-time reporter for the *Minneapolis Journal*. He graduated in 1930 and began his 18-year association with the United Press (UP, later United Press International). Beginning in St. Paul, Salisbury was successively assigned to the Chicago bureau in 1931, the Washington bureau in 1934, and foreign desk of the New York office in 1940. He went to Britain in 1943 as manager of UP's London bureau. From January to September 1944, he covered the Soviet Union and the war on the Eastern front. In late 1944, Salisbury returned to the United States to become UP's foreign news editor. In 1946, Salisbury published his first book, *Russia on the Way*, which compared the United States to a Soviet Union exhausted by the war.

Salisbury joined the *New York Times* as its Moscow bureau chief in 1949. For the next five years, he wrote about internal changes in the Soviet Union caused by Stalin's policies and the pressures of the cold war. Soviet authorities censored his dispatches, a fact that remained unknown in the United States at the time and led some to conclude that he was excessively sympathetic to the Soviet Union. Salisbury later criticized the *Times* for not printing a notice that the reports were subject to Soviet censorship. In September 1954, he requested a transfer from Moscow. After returning to the United States, Salisbury published 14 articles in a series titled "Russia Re-viewed," which detailed life in the Soviet Union and Stalin's terror. Salisbury won the 1955 Pulitzer Prize for his candid appraisal of life in the Soviet Union, including, as he later described it, "the drunkenness, the bureaucracy and the famine of goods, services and ideas after nearly 40 years of Bolshevism." The articles were published as a book, *American in Russia*, in 1954. The book included a large amount of narrative material on aspects of Soviet life that few Americans saw. He described the customs and attitudes of the diverse nationalities that made up the Soviet Union and made it clear that ethnic nationalism had not died with the Russian Revolution.

Salisbury took what he termed a "realistic position" on relations with the Soviet Union after Stalin's death. He believed in the possibility of coexistence with the Soviet Union. In his view, patience, common sense, and the application of a little "honey as well as vinegar to the critical joints" of the Communist regime might enable the two superpowers to survive in peace. He cautioned, however, that the United States had to remain militarily strong "for to be second best in a nuclear war was unthinkable folly." He saw a possible danger to improved relations when young Soviet army officers, with little contact with the West, came to power. Moreover, Salisbury believed the leadership of the Soviet Union displayed a new flexibility that the United States did not match.

Following his return to the United States, Salisbury worked as New York City correspondent for the *Times*. He remained one of the leading American experts on foreign affairs and lectured extensively on the topic. In 1957, he visited Bulgaria and Albania, nations virtually closed to most Americans. The following year, he became the second American reporter to travel through Mongolia since World War II. He returned to the Soviet Union in 1959 and again in 1961–62. The first of these trips produced *To Moscow—and Beyond: A Reporter's Narrative* (1960), which reported that life in the Soviet Union had improved under Nikita Khrushchev.

In the wake of the sit-in protests in 1960, the *Times* sent Salisbury to report on the racial situation in the South. He filed a story that the paper ran on its front page in which he described the fear and anxiety he found in Birmingham, Alabama. In it, he wrote that "every inch of middle ground has been fragmented by the emotional dynamite of racism, enforced by the whip, the razor, the gun, the bomb, the torch, the club, the knife, the mob, the police and many branches of the state's apparatus." City officials, including T. Eugene ("Bull") Connor, sued Salisbury and the *Times* for libel. After dismissing the other cases, a lower court awarded damages to Connor in 1964, but the United States Court for the Fifth Circuit overturned that decision.

Salisbury served as director of national coverage for the *Times* from 1962 to 1964 and assistant managing editor from 1964 to 1972. A trip to China and countries sharing a border with it resulted in a series of articles and a book, *Orbit of China* (1967). Salisbury traveled to North Vietnam to inspect the consequences of American bombing campaigns there during 1966. He reported that what the administration of President LYNDON B. JOHNSON described as surgical bombing inflicted heavy casualties among civilians. Salisbury rewrote the articles into a book, *Behind the Lines*, published in 1967.

In 1970, Salisbury became the first editor of the Op-Ed page of the *Times*, which ran columns and articles by outside contributors to present a variety of views beyond those of the *Times*'s own columnists. He became associate editor in 1972, a year before he reached the age of mandatory retirement. After retiring from the *Times*, Salisbury continued to write, producing 11 more books, including *Black*

Night, White Snow: Russia's Revolutions, 1905–1917 (1978), and *The Long March: The Untold Story* (1985). Salisbury happened to be in Beijing's Tiananmen Square in June 1989 when the pro-democracy demonstrations broke out, and, although he left Beijing before the Chinese army attacked the protesting students, Salisbury reported on the experience in *Tiananmen Diary: Thirteen Days in June* (1989). He suffered a heart attack and died while riding in an automobile outside of Providence, Rhode Island, on July 5, 1993.

—MSM

Salk, Jonas E(dward)
(1914–1995) *professor of epidemiology and preventive medicine, University of Pittsburgh*

The son of Orthodox Jewish immigrants from Poland, Salk was born in New York City on October 28, 1914. After graduating from Townsend Harris High School, Salk received his B.S. from the City College of New York in 1934 and his M.D. from New York University in 1939. He began, in 1940, a two-year internship at Mount Sinai Hospital in New York City. In 1942, he won a research fellowship in epidemiology at the University of Michigan, where he worked with the celebrated microbiologist, Dr. Thomas Francis, Jr., and helped develop antiinfluenza vaccines using a killed virus to stimulate the production of antibodies. During and after World War II, Salk served as a consultant on epidemic diseases, first to the War Department and then to the secretary of the army. He was appointed professor at the University of Pittsburgh School of Medicine and director of its virus research laboratory in 1947.

At the request of the National Foundation for Infantile Paralysis (later the March of Dimes), Salk began research on a vaccine against poliomyelitis. Although other researchers, including Dr. Albert Sabin, had been working on a weakened ("attenuated") live-virus vaccine, the National Foundation provided support for Salk's efforts to develop a killed-virus vaccine. After developing techniques to confirm the theory that there were three varieties of the virus, Salk and his team set about developing a vaccine that could provide protection against all of them. Salk killed ("inactivated") the polio viruses

Dr. Jonas Salk receives a citation at a White House ceremony, April 22, 1955 *(Dwight D. Eisenhower Library and Museum)*

by exposing them to formaldehyde long enough so that the viruses could not cause paralytic polio but not so long that the viruses would be insufficiently potent to generate sufficient antibodies to provide immunity. Salk injected himself, his family, and members of his lab with the killed-virus vaccine. In 1952, Salk vaccinated residents of two institutions in Pennsylvania, the Polk State School and the D. T. Watson Home for Crippled Children. The subjects developed sufficient antibodies to protect against the disease, and none became ill. Salk formally announced the results of his trial in the *Journal of the American Medical Association (JAMA)* in March 1953. Two days before the publication of his results in *JAMA*, however, Salk made public his results on a nationwide broadcast on CBS radio, which violated scientific decorum and earned him a reputation among many in the scientific community as a publicity seeker.

Sabin, Salk's leading rival, denounced the Salk vaccine as "insufficiently tested for mass trial" and "potentially unsafe." The National Foundation did a field test of Salk's vaccine in 1954. The massive trial involved over 1 million children in 44 states. More than 400,000 children received the vaccine; roughly the same number received placebos, and a third group was observed but not injected. Overall, more than 300,000 doctors, nurses, public health officials, teachers, principals, and volunteers participated in the trial.

Salk became a national hero in April 1955, when a team at the University of Michigan, headed by Francis, reported that the massive test of the vaccine had been a success. "The vaccine," declared Francis, "works. It is safe, effective, and potent." Released on the 10th anniversary of the death of Franklin Roosevelt (who had been crippled by polio as a young man), the report generated a national wave of excitement and relief. On April 23, President DWIGHT D. EISENHOWER awarded Salk a citation "for his extraordinary achievement."

Later that month, six pharmaceutical companies received federal licenses to manufacture and distribute the vaccine. Batches from Cutter Laboratories of Berkeley, California, however, had failed to eliminate the live polio virus, and 204 people were infected with the disease; most became paralyzed, and 11 died. Salk maintained that the laboratory had not precisely followed his instructions for killing the virus. The surgeon general of the United States temporarily halted the injections. After tightening safety standards for manufacturing the vaccine, the inoculations resumed.

The nationwide vaccination program also became the focus of political controversy. In May, the Eisenhower administration proposed that Congress appropriate $28 million in grants to states to vaccinate needy children. A rival proposal, introduced in June by LISTER HILL (D-Ala.), the chair of the Senate Labor and Public Welfare Committee, called for $135 million to provide free vaccines for all children. The American Medical Association (AMA) supported the administration's bill, while an official of the National Foundation for Infantile Paralysis gave implied approval to Hill's proposal. Congress passed Hill's measure, and Eisenhower signed the bill in August.

The program was overwhelmingly successful. In June 1956, Salk told an AMA meeting that 100 percent prevention of polio was possible through the administration of vaccine booster shots. Between 1955 and 1967, paralytic polio cases averaged 2,000 a year, compared with 20,000 to 30,000 cases a year before the vaccine's widespread use.

Salk became a hero to the public, a symbol of the possibilities of modern science. Some in the scientific community, however, dismissed Salk as a capable but unoriginal researcher and a publicity hound. He did not win the Nobel Prize or election to the National Academy of Sciences.

During the late 1950s and early 1960s, Salk worked on a single vaccine to stimulate immunity to several viral diseases simultaneously. At the same time, Sabin continued to develop a live-virus vaccine that could be administered orally. In June 1961, the AMA adopted a resolution recommending the massive use of Sabin's oral live-virus polio vaccine, which offered "longer protection" than Salk's dead-virus vaccine. Salk challenged the recommendation, describing it as "questionable," but by the mid-1960s, the Sabin vaccine had replaced the Salk vaccine in the United States. However, other countries, including Canada, continued to use the Salk vaccine.

Salk founded and became director of the Salk Institute for Biological Studies in La Jolla, California, in 1963. The city donated land for the institute, and the March of Dimes provided funds to build it. Salk turned his attention to the role of the immune system in cancer and multiple sclerosis. In the late 1980s, he attempted to develop a vaccine against AIDS. He died in San Diego, California, on June 23, 1995.

—MSM

Saltonstall, Leverett
(1892–1979) *U.S. senator*

The scion of one of Massachusetts's oldest, wealthiest, and most politically prominent families, Leverett Saltonstall was born in Chestnut Hill, Massachusetts, on September 1, 1892. Educated at private schools, he received a B.A. from Harvard College in 1914. After graduation from Harvard Law School in 1917 and service as a lieutenant in the field artillery during World War I (including six months in France), he returned to Boston, was admitted to the Massachusetts bar, and joined his uncle in the law firm of Gaston, Snow, Saltonstall, and Hunt. A Republican, Saltonstall first entered local politics in 1920 as an alderman in Newton, Massachusetts. In 1922, he won election to the lower house of the general court (the state legislature), in which he served for the next 14 years, the last eight as speaker. He ran unsuccessfully for lieutenant governor in 1936. Two years later, however, he defeated James Michael Curley, the former mayor of Boston, for the governorship. Although elected in a stunning upset, Saltonstall proved a popular governor. His administration reduced the state deficit by 90 percent, and he won reelection easily in 1940 and 1942. In 1944, Saltonstall won an election to fill the unexpired Senate term of HENRY CABOT LODGE, JR., who had resigned to return to army service. He was elected to a full term in 1948 and reelected in 1954 and 1960.

In the Senate, Saltonstall was an effective legislator, whose strength lay in drafting legislation and negotiating in conference committee. Although he voted against much of President HARRY S. TRUMAN's Fair Deal legislation, Saltonstall's support for aid to Greece and Turkey, the Marshall Plan, and the North Atlantic Treaty earned him a reputation as a liberal. He also assiduously served the interests of his constituents. A strong supporter of civil liberties, he emerged as an early opponent of what he believed were the excesses of Senator JOSEPH McCARTHY's (R-Wis.) anticommunist campaign and vigorously opposed McCarthy's attacks on Secretary of State DEAN ACHESON and Secretary of Defense George C. Marshall.

Saltonstall rose rapidly to a position of party leadership. He served on the powerful Appropriations and Armed Services Committees throughout his career in the Senate and as Republican whip from 1949 to 1957. An internationalist in foreign policy, Saltonstall was not consistently liberal or conservative on domestic issues. Personally respected and a moderate within the Republican Party, he rose to leadership because he was acceptable to both wings of a bitterly divided party. Particularly on foreign policy, Saltonstall aligned himself with the internationalist, or liberal, wing of the Republican Party. This led him to urge General DWIGHT D. EISENHOWER to run for the presidency in 1952 and to play an active role in promoting the general's candidacy for the Republican nomination.

During the early years of Eisenhower's presidency, Saltonstall held the post of Republican whip. Considered the most liberal member of the party's leadership in the upper house, Saltonstall was more sympathetic to the administration's program during the Republican-controlled 83rd Congress (1953–55) than either Majority Leader WILLIAM KNOWLAND (R-Calif.) or HOMER FERGUSON (R-Mich.), chair of the Republican Policy Committee. Saltonstall strongly opposed the Bricker amendment, designed to limit the president's treaty-making powers. As chair of the Armed Services Committee in 1953 and 1954 and after that as ranking Republican on the committee, Saltonstall backed the administration's requests for foreign aid.

Saltonstall continued to oppose McCarthy during the 1950s but adopted a cautious approach toward motions to censure the Wisconsin Republican. Facing reelection in 1954, Saltonstall backed efforts to delay consideration of the Watkins Committee report, which recommended McCarthy's censure, until after the campaign. When the censure vote was taken in December 1954, however, he was the only member of the Republican leadership to vote for the motion.

Saltonstall became chair of the Republican Senate Conference in 1957, a position he held until he left the Senate 10 years later.

During the administrations of JOHN F. KENNEDY and LYNDON B. JOHNSON, Saltonstall maintained a moderately liberal voting record and a relatively low public profile. Pressure from the Massachusetts Republican Party, which supported the political aspirations of the state's African-American attorney general, Edward Brooke, led Saltonstall to retire from the Senate in 1967 in order to allow Brooke to seek his seat. Saltonstall retired to Dover, Massachusetts, where he lived until his death there on June 17, 1979.

—MSM

Sarnoff, David

(1891–1971)　*chairman of the board, Radio Corporation of America*

Born to a poor Jewish family in Uzlian, a small village near Minsk in what is now Belarus, on February 27, 1891, David Sarnoff came to the United States with his family at the age of nine. The family settled on New York's Lower East Side. To help support his family, Sarnoff sold newspapers, made deliveries for a butcher, and sang in a synagogue. He attended public schools and took night classes at the Educational Alliance, a settlement house on the Lower East Side. Following his father's death in 1906, he quit high school to work as a messenger boy for the Commercial Cable Company.

During the next three decades, Sarnoff rose from messenger boy to chairman of the board of one of America's largest corporations. He took a job with the American Marconi Company as an office boy and rose to become a wireless telegraph operator. In his spare time, he studied all aspects of radio electronics. After several assignments as a wireless operator, he became manager of the Marconi wireless station located on the roof of the John Wanamaker department store. On April 14, 1912, Sarnoff picked up faint signals indicating that the *Titanic* had struck an iceberg and was sinking. Sarnoff alerted other ships and the press. He remained at his equipment for 72 hours, until he had the names of all the survivors. Rising rapidly through the ranks of American Marconi, Sarnoff received promotions to radio inspector, assistant chief engineer, and contract manager. He became the company's commercial manager in 1917. Two years later, British Marconi sold American Marconi to General Electric, which formed the Radio Corporation of America (RCA); soon after, Westinghouse joined the RCA alliance. Sarnoff became commercial manager of RCA.

Sarnoff became general manager of RCA in 1921. Early on, he recognized the potential of radio. In 1920, he wrote a memo in which he proposed bringing music into the home by wireless, thereby making radio a "household utility." The memo claimed that he had urged American Marconi to manufacture "radio music boxes" back in 1915. To provide programming and thereby increase the market for RCA radio receivers, he persuaded RCA to organize what proved to be the country's first successful commercial radio network, the National Broadcasting Company (NBC), in 1926. Sarnoff also engineered the purchase of the Victor Talking Machine Company, the nation's largest manufacturer of records and phonographs. He used the Victor facilities to manufacture units that combined a radio and a phonograph in the same set. Elected to RCA's board in 1927, Sarnoff became the company's executive vice president in 1928. He served as acting president in 1928, when the company's president, James G. Harbord, took a leave of absence to campaign for HERBERT HOOVER. RCA profited greatly from Sarnoff's vision, both through the manufacture of radio sets and through the sale of advertising time for NBC radio programs.

As the motion picture business retooled for sound, RCA entered the field with a recording process developed by General Electric. To secure a market, the company entered an agreement with the Keith-Albee-Orpheum chain of theaters in 1928 to form Radio-Keith-Orpheum (R.K.O.). Once again, Sarnoff's ability to envision the commercial potential of new communications technology served RCA well.

Sarnoff became president of RCA in 1930. That same year, the Justice Department filed suit against RCA for monopoly and restraint of trade. Sarnoff led the company's fight against the government's suit, and, in the end, agreed to a consent decree in 1932 that called for GE and Westinghouse to divest their stock in RCA and NBC. NBC became a wholly owned subsidiary of RCA. RCA agreed to license its patents to competitors. Through Sarnoff's skilled negotiations, RCA emerged as an independent company that owned two networks (NBC-red and NBC-blue), broadcast stations, facilities to provide ship-to-shore communications, manufacturing facilities, and experimental laboratories. It also owned Radio City, a new complex of buildings in midtown Manhattan. Sarnoff was president of the newly independent company.

Sarnoff became chairman of the board of RCA in 1947. That year RCA's income reached about $300 million. (RCA had earned $2 million in 1920, Sarnoff's first full year with the company.) *Forbes* magazine listed Sarnoff as one of America's "Fifty Foremost Business Leaders" in 1947.

As he had with radio, Sarnoff emerged early on as a leading promoter of commercial television, and RCA proved the ultimate beneficiary. In 1923, he predicted the advent of television and, seven years later, of color TV. When an engineer, Vladimir Zworykin, met with Sarnoff to explain his concept of an electronic camera, Sarnoff underwrote Zworykin's efforts to develop television. Beginning in the 1930s, long before TV became commercially feasible, RCA began investing heavily in television. It inaugurated regular telecasts at the 1939 World's Fair. However, technical problems and World War II interrupted the development of commercial TV until the late 1940s.

Sarnoff served with the Signal Corps during World War II. He had requested a commission with the U.S. Navy during World War I and been denied (he believed anti-Semitism was the reason). Commissioned a lieutenant colonel in 1924, Sarnoff became a full colonel in 1931. He was called to active duty in World War II, during which he worked for General DWIGHT D. EISENHOWER and coordinated communications on D-day. He emerged from the war a brigadier general and from then on preferred to be called General Sarnoff. During the war, RCA lost a suit to block an FCC ruling that required RCA to divest itself of one of its radio networks. The company sold NBC-blue, which became ABC.

In the early years of television, RCA-NBC led the trade in profits and station access. The company got its black-and-white sets on the market in 1946. Sarnoff's unquestioned faith in television's eventual significance reflected his lifelong belief in research and development. By 1955, the corporation reported netting $1 billion from the sales, royalties, and services of television. RCA led the communications field in the number of patents granted. Between 1950 and 1961, Sarnoff committed an estimated $130 million to develop color TV. He also won a battle with CBS to establish the standards for color TV. In 1950, the Federal Communications Commission (FCC) had approved a system developed by CBS that was not compatible with black-and-white televisions. Sarnoff, whose scientists at RCA were working on a color system compatible with black-and-white sets, objected. Sarnoff pressed the FCC to reverse itself, which it did in 1953.

Sarnoff did not limit his interest to radio and television. In the early 1950s, he engaged in a feud with Edwin Howard Armstrong over the development of FM radio and related patents. In 1958, RCA introduced the first stereo records. That same year, it entered electronic data processing, a field then effectively dominated by International Business Machines Corporation. In four years, RCA spent $100 million on the project. The investment illustrated Sarnoff's recognition of the technological links between communications research and fields unrelated to entertainment. It also marked the beginning of RCA's transformation into a conglomerate.

When Eisenhower became president, Sarnoff advised him on cold war strategy. As chairman of the Citizens Advisory Committee on Utilization of Manpower in the Armed Services, he recommended in February 1953 an "at least 10 percent" cut in the defense budget. The panel's report anticipated the administration's New Look defense policy. Sarnoff wrote long memoranda to government leaders on the use of technology for the military. He proposed the use of electronics to detect and even to intercept incoming missiles. Television, he argued, could become the "eyes of the top command" and enable commanders to coordinate military action on land, sea, and air. In 1955, Sarnoff recommended the creation of a cabinet-level propaganda chief, delegated to use mass communications to help the United States win the cold war. In that spirit, RCA's Sarnoff Research Center created special Radio Free Europe receivers, unbreakable and incapable of being jammed.

Sarnoff retired as RCA's chief executive officer in 1966 in favor of his son Robert, whom he had made president of NBC in 1955. Sarnoff remained as chairman of the board, but his involvement in management declined. After a prolonged illness, he died in New York City on December 12, 1971.

—MSM

Saulnier, Raymond J(oseph)

(1908–2009) *chairman, Council of Economic Advisers*
Born in Hamilton, Massachusetts, on September 20, 1908, Raymond Saulnier received a B.S. in economics from Middlebury College in Vermont in 1929 and an M.A. from Tufts University in 1931. He earned his Ph.D. at Columbia University in 1938, where he wrote his thesis on monetary theory. Saulnier joined Columbia's economics faculty in 1934 and served as an instructor at Columbia College until 1938, when he moved over to Bar-

nard College as an assistant professor; he became a full professor in 1949. An authority on banking and mortgage finance, he published *Industrial Banking Companies and Their Credit Practices* (1940), *Contemporary Monetary Theory* (1941), *Business Finance and Banking* (1947), and *Urban Mortgage Lending by Life Insurance Companies* (1956). In 2000, reflecting on *Contemporary Monetary Theory*, Saulnier said: "At the time, the conventional wisdom was Keynesian, but I was persuaded that the great man overrated the antirecessionary effect . . . of the government spending and tax cuts he favored, and underestimated the capacity of an enterprise system to heal itself."

In 1946, Saulnier became director of the financial research division of the National Bureau of Economic Research, where his colleague at Columbia, Dr. ARTHUR BURNS, was director of research. When Burns went to Washington as chairman of the Council of Economic Advisers (CEA) in 1953, he named Saulnier a special consultant to the CEA. President DWIGHT D. EISENHOWER appointed Saulnier to the council in April 1955 and named him to succeed Burns as chairman in November 1956.

According to *Fortune* magazine, Saulnier was "a trifle more conservative than Burns" and did not enjoy the "intimate kind of rapport" his predecessor had enjoyed with the president. Particularly at the outset of his tenure as chair of the CEA, Saulnier's influence in the economic policymaking councils of the Eisenhower administration did not equal that of Secretary of the Treasury GEORGE HUMPHREY or Eisenhower's personal economic adviser, GABRIEL HAUGE. *Newsweek* reported in March 1958 that politicians on Capitol Hill considered Saulnier to be less forceful than either Burns or the last chairman of the CEA under a Democratic administration, LEON KEYSERLING.

Nevertheless, Eisenhower depended on Saulnier for advice of a technical and predictive nature, and gradually the economist's counsel acquired greater weight in the White House. Most concerned with the stability of the business cycle, Saulnier was less inclined to regard inflation as the paramount economic problem than were Hauge, Secretaries of the Treasury George Humphrey and ROBERT ANDERSON, and the chairman of the Federal Reserve Board, WILLIAM MCCHESNEY MARTIN. For most of 1957, he argued unsuccessfully against the Federal Reserve's "tight money" policy. In Saulnier's view, the economic indicators called for a stimulus, but the Federal Reserve raised the rediscount rate in August from 3 percent to 3.5 percent. In November, however, faced with a deepening economic recession, the Federal Reserve lowered the rediscount rate. In the next few months, it also lowered bank reserve requirements in an effort to shore up the sagging economy by making money for lending more available.

Within the administration, Saulnier argued for a more stimulative fiscal policy against pressures from the Treasury and the Bureau of the Budget to reduce the budget. Eisenhower met with his top economic advisers in October 1957 and heard unanimous concern that the economy seemed to be sinking into a recession. Saulnier warned that federal revenues might fall short of predictions. "We must," he urged, "take every measure to prevent a sharp decline in the economy." As the 1957–58 recession worsened, Saulnier's case against a budget surplus for fiscal 1959 appeared more persuasive. The Soviet Union's launching of *Sputnik* in October 1957 spurred an increase in military spending, while Saulnier also succeeded in gaining more funds for the construction of schools and highways. He also favored lengthening the duration of unemployment insurance and stimulating private investment in housing through the provision of more liberal mortgage insurance by the government. In May, Saulnier reported at a cabinet meeting that the downward trend of the economy had abated but not yet flattened. Worried about the inflationary effect of a tax cut, Eisenhower, supported by Anderson, resisted reducing taxes. In April and May, unemployment began to drop, and, by June and July, industrial production, personal income, nonagricultural employment, and new home construction all increased.

In an interview with *U.S. News and World Report* in April 1959, Saulnier declared that the "cornerstone" of the Eisenhower economic program was a balanced budget for fiscal 1961. He maintained that tax reduction was desirable but not possible without a balanced budget. At the same time, he proposed a number of tax revisions: liberalized depreciation allowances for businesses, lower tax rates on high incomes, elimination of various excise taxes, and the institution of a manufacturer's sales tax. In addition, Saulnier emphasized that, if the United States

were to achieve a higher rate of economic growth, it needed to keep the money supply in check, hold down wage increases so as not to cause inflation, and push ahead with automation.

Despite the continuing threat of inflation, Saulnier rejected wage and price controls. "It is in the absence of controls," he said, "that we have the freedom that gives our economy its dynamic quality. We don't want to lose that quality in the process of trying to avoid cost and price inflation." In August 1959, Saulnier stated that general price stability could be achieved only if, in industries "where productivity gains are especially rapid," management cut prices and labor accepted raises less than the full productivity gain. The reference was generally understood to refer to the steel industry in particular. Saulnier, however, continued to reject any system of mandatory wage and price restraint.

Saulnier remained in his post until January 1961. Later that year, he resumed teaching at Barnard, where he remained until he retired from teaching in 1973 and became professor emeritus. In 1991, he published *Constructive Years*, an account of the economic policies of the Eisenhower administration. Saulnier remained active in politics and worked for Ellen R. Sauerbrey's unsuccessful campaign for governor of Maryland in 1998. In early 2009, he cited the government's contribution to the credit boom through its encouragement of lending, particularly through Fannie Mae, as a major cause of the recession. He died in Chestertown, Maryland, on April 30, 2009.

—MSM

Schine, G(erard) David

(1927–1996) *chief consultant, Permanent Subcommittee on Investigations of the Senate Government Operations Committee*

The son of a wealthy hotel magnate, Schine was born in Gloversville, New York, on September 11, 1927. He attended Andover Academy and entered Harvard University in 1945. Shortly after Schine graduated in 1949, his father made him president of Schine Hotels, Inc., although his father retained operational control. The easygoing, handsome Schine was interested in a show business career and tried writing popular songs. He went to nightclubs, dated starlets, and indulged his tastes for expensive cars and cigars.

Schine also wrote a six-page pamphlet called "Definitions of Communism" that was printed privately and placed in every room in the Schine chain of hotels. In 1952, he met ROY COHN, an assistant U.S. attorney specializing in cases involving subversion. The young men became close friends and traveled the Manhattan social circuit together.

When Cohn became chief counsel for Senator JOSEPH R. MCCARTHY's (R-Wis.) Permanent Subcommittee on Investigations in January 1953, he brought Schine along as the panel's unpaid chief consultant. Although Schine's qualifications for conducting investigative work were unclear, he worked closely with Cohn in directing McCarthy's probes of alleged subversives in the International Information Administration, the Voice of America, and the State Department early in 1953.

In April 1953, Schine and Cohn went on an 18-day, seven-country tour of Europe on behalf of the subcommittee to determine if the State Department's overseas libraries contained pro-communist literature. Trailed by hostile European reporters, they blazed from city to city, called on diplomats, held press conferences, and collected documents. They received extensive coverage by the press, both in America and in Europe, almost all of it negative and some of it mocking. Critics of the two men charged them with immature and farcical behavior that damaged America's prestige abroad. Some of their actions undoubtedly made them seem callow. They referred to *Commonweal* as a "Communist Catholic magazine." One German newspaper reported that Schine chased Cohn, swatting him with a rolled-up magazine, through a hotel lobby in Munich. Journalists also claimed to have overheard them making snide remarks in public about alleged homosexuality among State Department employees. Their visits demoralized American embassies and consulates.

As a result of their activities and pressure exerted by McCarthy at home, the State Department ordered its libraries to remove works by "Communist, fellow-travelers, et cetera." That decision drew criticism from President DWIGHT D. EISENHOWER. In a commencement address at Dartmouth College in June 1953, Eisenhower urged the undergraduates not to "join the book-burners."

In July 1953, Schine received notice of his impending induction into the army. At that time,

McCarthy was involved in an acrimonious investigation of alleged communist infiltration of the Army Communications Center at Fort Monmouth, New Jersey. McCarthy and Cohn interceded to prevent any interruption in Schine's duties as a member of the subcommittee's staff and made several unsuccessful attempts to get him an officer's commission or a job at the U.S. Military Academy. After Schine was inducted as a private in November, Cohn continued to exert pressure on his behalf, making numerous telephone calls to Schine's commanding officers and to army counsel JOHN G. ADAMS.

In January 1954, Eisenhower's chief of staff, SHERMAN ADAMS, urged the army to draft a chronology of the attempts by McCarthy and Cohn to secure preferential treatment for Schine. In March, after McCarthy had stepped up his attacks against the army, the chronology was released. The document revealed that Schine had received such privileges as exemptions from KP and barracks cleaning duties as well as regular weekend passes. On March 16, the subcommittee voted to investigate the army's accusations as well as a set of countercharges by McCarthy and Cohn. McCarthy alleged that the army was holding Schine "hostage" and that ROBERT STEVENS, the secretary of the army, had attempted to "blackmail" the committee into dropping the investigation of Fort Monmouth.

The subcommittee's hearings, known as the Army-McCarthy hearings, began in April. Late that month, the panel was presented with a photo of Schine and Stevens. It was apparently intended to suggest that Stevens made an effort to be friendly toward Schine in the hope that the subcommittee would drop its investigation of the army. The army's counsel, JOSEPH WELCH, produced an enlargement of the photo indicating that the image presented to the subcommittee had been cropped to exclude other individuals. Welch traced the cropping to a member of McCarthy's staff.

During the investigation, McCarthy admitted under cross-examination that Schine had no investigative experience to qualify him for a position with the subcommittee but said that Schine had worked on a plan for psychological warfare against communism. Senator HENRY JACKSON (D-Wash.) later ridiculed the plan, mocking its proposals for the use of pinups, billboards, and bumper stickers. Despite the fact that his case was a central theme in the hearings, Schine testified only briefly concerning the authenticity of the photograph that purported to show him alone with Stevens.

The hearings proved inconclusive as to whether McCarthy had used undue influence on behalf of Schine. McCarthy's conduct during the nationally televised hearings, however, led the Senate to censure him on December 2, 1954.

Before his discharge in 1955, Schine served with a military police unit in Anchorage and rose to the rank of corporal. Upon leaving the army, he served as president of the Ambassador Hotel in Los Angeles, which was part of the chain owned by his father (who also owned theaters, radio stations, and real estate holdings). During the next two decades, he established a show-business management firm, a movie production company (he produced the Oscar-winning film, *The French Connection*), and a music publishing concern. He lived in Los Angeles, California, and died when a single-engine plane piloted by his son crashed shortly after takeoff from Burbank, California, on June 19, 1996.

—MSM

Schlesinger, Arthur M(eier), Jr.
(1917–2007) *historian*

The son of the distinguished American historian, Arthur Schlesinger, Sr., Arthur Bancroft Schlesinger was born in Columbus, Ohio, on October 15, 1917. Out of respect for his father, the younger Schlesinger, when in his middle teens, changed his name to Arthur Meier Schlesinger, Jr. Arthur Schlesinger, Sr., moved first to the University of Iowa and then, in 1924, to Harvard University. The younger Schlesinger attended Phillips Exeter Academy and Harvard College, from which he graduated summa cum laude in 1938. As a senior, he wrote an honors thesis on the 19th-century American thinker, Orestes Brownson. During a year at Peterhouse College of Cambridge University, he turned the thesis into a book, *Orestes Brownson: A Pilgrim's Progress*, which was published in 1939 to favorable reviews. After the year at Cambridge, Schlesinger returned to Harvard as a member of the prestigious Society of Fellows and began work on a book about the era of Andrew Jackson. During World War II, he worked in

Washington for the Office of War Information and the Office of Strategic Services. Immediately after the war, he remained in Washington and worked as a freelance journalist. In 1945, he published *The Age of Jackson*, for which he won the Pulitzer Prize for history in 1946. The book challenged the then traditional interpretation, pioneered by Frederick Jackson Turner, which associated democracy with the frontier, and argued that the popular democracy of the Jacksonian era had its origins in the cities and workers of the Northeast. Schlesinger essentially cast the age of Jackson as an earlier version of the New Deal in which the people struggled to wrest control from the propertied interests, an interpretation that subsequent historians largely demolished.

In 1947, Schlesinger joined his father on the Harvard faculty. That same year, he helped organize the Americans for Democratic Action (ADA), an organization of anticommunist liberals who advocated a hard line in the cold war. During the postwar period, he wrote articles for numerous magazines and published *The Vital Center* (1949), a manifesto for cold war liberals. In it, Schlesinger called for a strong and realistic liberalism that rejected the notion that human nature was benign and society perfectible. "The Soviet experience," he wrote, "on top of the rise of fascism, reminded my generation rather forcibly that man was, indeed, imperfect." Accordingly, liberals should abandon the utopian solutions of the communist left. Following the ideas of political scientist De Witt C. Poole, Schlesinger suggested that the traditional linear political graph should be bent into a circle. The extremes of left and right, he maintained, shared many more characteristics than those that set them apart: "The totalitarian left and the totalitarian right meet at last on the murky grounds of tyranny and terror." In times of crisis, he argued, the right would turn to fascism and the left would turn to communism. Freedom rested in the "vital center." The political center he admired possessed a tough-minded realism, a commitment to freedom, and an "unconditional rejection of totalitarianism." Liberals, he reminded his readers, "have values in common with most members of the business community—in particular, a belief in free society—which they do not have in common with the totalitarians."

In 1952, Schlesinger took a leave of absence from Harvard to join ADLAI STEVENSON's campaign staff as a speechwriter. Although some on Stevenson's staff regarded Schlesinger as too liberal, Stevenson stood by him, and the two men developed a close friendship. After the campaign, Schlesinger returned to Harvard, where he became a full professor in 1954.

Schlesinger headed the research and writing group in Stevenson's campaign in 1956. He advocated emphasizing the idea that the Republican Party was the party of big business and special interests, while the Democratic Party represented the people. Since Eisenhower had established a reputation as a president of peace, Schlesinger recommended that Stevenson emphasize domestic over foreign policy issues.

Through his history and his journalism, Schlesinger repeatedly expressed liberal thinking on important issues in the postwar era. Like many liberals, his record on civil liberties during the early days of the cold war and the red scare was uneven. Although convinced that some sort of loyalty program was necessary, he found the procedures set forth in President HARRY S. TRUMAN's executive order "inexcusably defective." Schlesinger opposed Senator JOSEPH R. MCCARTHY's (R-Wisc.) anticommunist crusade and in 1954 wrote a defense of J. ROBERT OPPENHEIMER, the former director of the wartime Manhattan Project, who had been denied security clearance by the Eisenhower administration.

Schlesinger was often pessimistic in his assessment of the social changes of the decade. He believed that the economic advances since World War II had been bought at the price of communal disintegration and the loss of cultural diversity. He wrote often of the oppressive standardization of life in the new suburbs and of the emptiness of white-collar existence. Even though the so-called New Conservatives, led by RUSSELL KIRK, addressed the same issues, Schlesinger attacked their work. He insisted that in America conservatism meant a defense of business interests before all else. Partisan to the point of arrogance, he asserted that the idea of a conservative intellectual was a contradiction in terms. Schlesinger worked hard to create the image of the Democratic Party as a party of "creative liberalism," guided by intellectuals.

Throughout the 1950s, Schlesinger continued to pursue his work as a historian. From 1957 to 1960, he published three volumes of *The Age of Roosevelt*. The fruit of nearly 15 years of research, the unabashedly admiring work portrayed Roosevelt as a strong and innovative reformer as well as the enduring model of progressive leadership. The tensions he identified in American society of the 1930s bore a striking similarity to those he found in the age of Jackson. As had *The Age of Jackson*, the trilogy about Roosevelt associated American liberalism with a strong president who used his power in a pragmatic fashion. The book won praise for the power of its sweeping narrative.

Not satisfied to write history and polemics, Schlesinger remained active in the political arena. Schlesinger, who had backed JOHN F. KENNEDY's unsuccessful bid for the Democratic vice presidential nomination in 1956, shifted his support from Stevenson to Kennedy in 1960 and was a key figure in winning the support of the ADA and the liberal intellectual community for Kennedy. Although many ADA members accused him of being a traitor, Schlesinger himself did not regard his shift as a dramatic one. He wrote in 1960 that "in his eight years as titular leader Stevenson renewed the Democratic Party. . . . Kennedy today is the heir and the executor of the Stevenson revolution."

During the campaign for the general election, Schlesinger joined Kennedy's campaign staff and published *Kennedy or Nixon: Does It Make Any Difference?*, a short book that favorably contrasted Kennedy with his Republican opponent, Vice President RICHARD M. NIXON. Much of the book compared the two candidates' personalities. Schlesinger alleged, improbably, that if Nixon were elected, the country would "sink into mediocrity and cant and payola and boredom." He argued, more plausibly, that Nixon "lacks taste." After the election, Kennedy appointed Schlesinger special adviser to the president. In that capacity, Schlesinger concentrated on Latin American affairs. After a trip to South America with George McGovern, director of the Food for Peace Program, Schlesinger returned and, at Kennedy's request, prepared a white paper on Cuba that endorsed the Cuban revolution against Fulgencio Batista but condemned the direction in which Fidel Castro had taken it. Although he was close to the source of power at the Kennedy White House, the degree of his influence was debatable. After the assassination of Kennedy, Schlesinger served briefly in the administration of LYNDON B. JOHNSON but felt shunted aside; he left in January 1964.

In 1965, Schlesinger published, *A Thousand Days: John F. Kennedy in the White House*, a work that earned him the Pulitzer Prize for biography. The work celebrated Kennedy's youth, vigor, and what Schlesinger regarded as his unsentimental, pragmatic liberalism. The admiring portrait presented Kennedy as an agent of progressive change at home and abroad. It also glorified what Schlesinger considered to be the sophistication of the policy makers in the administration. Schlesinger became Albert Schweitzer Professor of the Humanities at the City University of New York in 1966. He at first defended, though not uncritically, the Johnson administration's conduct of the war in Vietnam. By 1966, however, he moved to a measured opposition. In *The Bitter Heritage: Vietnam and American Democracy*, published late that year, he argued for an end to the war because of its "ugly side-effects" at home. He favored an immediate halt to the bombing of North Vietnam and a gradual de-escalation. Although he moved closer to the burgeoning opposition to the war, he opposed the New Left, which attacked the entire direction of American foreign policy since World War II. In October 1967, he published an article in *Foreign Affairs* attacking the New Left, or revisionist, historians of the early cold war. Not satisfied with intellectual engagement, he remained involved with ROBERT F. KENNEDY, whom he initially advised not to challenge President LYNDON JOHNSON in the 1968 primaries. Once Kennedy entered the race for the nomination, however, Schlesinger strongly supported him. After Kennedy's assassination, Schlesinger threw his support to McGovern.

During the early 1970s, Schlesinger was a leading academic critic of the Nixon administration. In 1973, he published *The Imperial Presidency*, which attacked the growing centralization of power in the executive branch. Schlesinger was less impressed with strong presidency when it was held by someone with whom he disagreed. He traced the expansion of presidential power to distortions created by the cold war and nuclear weapons.

Robert F. Kennedy and His Times, published in 1978, presented Robert Kennedy as his brother's heir and someone who, like his brother, had developed the potential for greatness as a leader but was killed before he could realize that potential. In his unstinting efforts to celebrate Robert Kennedy, he even found some nice things to say about the McCarthy committee, for which Kennedy had been minority counsel. Schlesinger did, however, acknowledge that Kennedy had played a larger role in attempting to overthrow Castro than that which had been portrayed in *A Thousand Days*.

A prolific writer who claimed never to have been troubled by writer's block, Schlesinger continued to publish regularly over the next two decades. *The Cycles of American History* (1986) argued that the country alternated between periods of liberalism, in which it turned toward government and social causes, and periods of conservatism, in which it turned against government and toward private gratification. In 1991, he published *The Disuniting of America*, an attack on multiculturalism. In it, he condemned the rise of political correctness and rejected identity politics that he believed threatened to divide the country. He advocated the traditional American melting pot as a preferable model. Several black scholars in particular attacked the book and its author in highly personal terms. Schlesinger retired from teaching in 1994. His last book, *War and the American Presidency* (2005), was an unbridled attack on the war in Iraq. Schlesinger published *A Life in the Twentieth Century* (2000), the first volume of a planned two-volume memoir. He never completed the second volume, but an edited volume of his diaries from 1952 to 2000 was published in 2007.

Schlesinger died in New York City on February 28, 2007. One might dismiss Schlesinger as a partisan whose presentist concerns marred his historical judgment. On the other hand, one could argue that he did what historians have always done; he explained to the American people their past in a way that made sense to them.

—MSM

Schwartz, Bernard

(1923–1997) *chief counsel, Subcommittee on Legislative Oversight of the House Commerce Committee*

Born in New York City on August 25, 1923, Bernard Schwartz completed seven years of study in four by simultaneously attending the City College of New York, where he earned a B.S. in 1944, and New York University, from which he received an LL.B. in the same year. He went on to earn an LL.M. at Harvard in 1945 and a doctorate from Cambridge University in 1947. Schwartz joined the faculty of New York University Law School in 1947 and, over the next few years, wrote numerous articles and books on the Supreme Court and administrative law. During the early years of the Eisenhower administration, he served as counsel to the Second Hoover Commission on Executive Branch Reorganization and the House Government Information Subcommittee. In March 1957, Schwartz, at age 33, became chief counsel to a subcommittee of the House Interstate and Foreign Commerce Committee, known as the Special Committee on Legislative Oversight.

Created in February 1957 at the urging of House Speaker SAM RAYBURN (D-Tex.), this Subcommittee on Legislative Oversight was charged with investigating improper influence by regulated industries on federal regulatory agencies and political pressure on those agencies. To chair the subcommittee, OREN HARRIS (D-Ark.), chair of the Commerce Committee, appointed Representative Morgan M. Moulder (D-Mo.). Under Schwartz's direction, the subcommittee's staff concentrated on six of 20 government agencies: the Civil Aeronautics Board (CAB), the Federal Power Commission (FPC), the Federal Trade Commission (FTC), the Interstate Commerce Commission (ICC), the Securities and Exchange Commission (SEC), and the Federal Communications Commission (FCC).

Schwartz encountered obstruction from various agencies and from within Congress. For a monthlong period ending on October 17, 1957, the chair of the CAB, James R. Durfee, denied Schwartz's staff access to pertinent records. Schwartz also came under congressional criticism for sending the 38 commissioners a detailed questionnaire inquiring about personal gifts, loans, and other favors presented by companies subject to the regulators' authority. "Never before," Representative Joseph O'Hara (R-Minn.) complained, "has any congressional investigating group started out by assuming everyone was crooked."

In January 1958, Schwartz submitted a memorandum urging a sweeping investigation of the FCC. The subcommittee declined to undertake the sort of

investigation Schwartz recommended, and someone leaked the memo to DREW PEARSON, the newspaper columnist. Schwartz later admitted to leaking the memo to the *New York Times*, but claimed that he did so only after the story had appeared in Pearson's column. The memo accused several members of the FCC, including its chair, JOHN DOERFER, of official misconduct and improper fraternization with the industry. Specifically, Schwartz charged them with billing the government for expenses paid for by broadcasting figures, accepting gifts and loans, and discussing matters pending before the agency with the parties involved. As a result of these relationships, the memo alleged, the agency exhibited "a most disturbing inconsistency" in its awards of station licenses. In testimony before the subcommittee on February 3, Doerfer denounced what he considered Schwartz's irresponsible tactics in investigating the commission and leaking the memo. At the hearing, it came out that Doerfer had accepted reimbursement from a television station and the National Association of Radio and Television Broadcasters for a trip and then submitted travel vouchers to the government for the trip. Doerfer attributed the double reimbursement to a mistake. It also turned out that he had received travel expenses and honoraria for speeches to broadcasting groups at several resorts. Further, he received partial reimbursement for one of the trips from the government. Nevertheless, the hearings established neither illegality nor impropriety on Doerfer's part.

Schwartz's investigative tactics and his treatment of witnesses before the subcommittee came under heavy fire. Southern Democratic and Republican members resented Schwartz's method of cross-examining Doerfer and disapproved of his leak to the *Times*. On February 10, the panel voted seven-to-four to dismiss Schwartz. Chairman Moulder, two other Democratic members, and one Republican voted against his removal. Moulder resigned as chairman in protest, and Harris assumed the post. Schwartz immediately accused Harris, most subcommittee members, and later Speaker Rayburn of seeking "a bipartisan whitewash." Schwartz repaid the loyalty of Moulder with the comment that "he [Moulder] turned out to be a weak man."

The day following his ouster, Schwartz made a series of sensational charges against leading officials in the administration. He declared that FCC

Commissioner Richard A. Mack was guilty of conflict of interest in granting a license to a TV station in Miami. He also added the names of New York's former governor, Thomas E. Dewey, and the president's chief aide, Sherman Adams, to his list of influence peddlers.

Not content with that, Schwartz took documents he had been working on, which he eventually gave to Senator Wayne Morse (D-Oreg.). The subcommittee subpoenaed Schwartz to detail his accusations. It also demanded and received the "working papers" Schwartz had given to Morse. Before the subcommittee in mid-February, Schwartz presented additional materials strongly suggesting unlawful action by Mack and improper ones by Adams in his dealings with regulatory agencies.

Schwartz also revealed that he had secretly wiretapped an interview with Mack in 1957. The wiretapping, together with Schwartz's headline-catching list of influence peddlers, caused some liberal journals and politicians—and a great many Republican ones—to criticize Schwartz's investigative methods, which several compared to those of Senator Joseph R. McCarthy (R-Wis.). The liberal *New Republic* described Schwartz as "unprincipled"; Senator Morse called for an end to all government wiretaps.

Schwartz's appearance before the subcommittee received extensive coverage by the national news media and forced further investigations. Once hopeful of restricting the subcommittee's activities, Harris pursued Schwartz's allegations. After Schwartz's testimony, Attorney General William Rogers ordered the FBI to investigate Mack; and, after appearing before the subcommittee, Mack resigned. By September, the once-powerful Sherman Adams had quit his job at the White House. The cumulative effects of the subcommittee's hearings, which lasted well into 1958, seriously damaged the Republican Party's already bleak prospects for the congressional elections in November. New legislation enacted in 1960 revised commission procedure.

Schwartz returned to New York University in 1963 as Edwin D. Webb Professor of Law, a position he held for nearly 30 years. Schwartz was best known as a legal scholar, whose work ranged from the Napoleonic Code to federal regulatory agencies. His most important writings, however, dealt with the Supreme Court and the justices who served on it. He wrote *The Supreme Court: Constitutional Revolution in Retrospect* (1957), a five-volume *Commentary on the Constitution of the United States* (1963–68), *Swann's Way: The School Busing Case and the Supreme Court* (1986), and *Behind Bakke: The Supreme Court and Affirmative Action* (1988). He compiled *The Unpublished Opinions of the Warren Court* (1985), *The Unpublished Opinions of the Burger Court* (1988), and *The Unpublished Opinions of the Rehnquist Court* (1996). Published in 1996, *Decision: How the Supreme Court Decides Cases* sold more copies than any of his other titles. In addition to his books on the Court and its decisions, Schwartz published *Super Chief*, a comprehensive biography of Chief Justice Earl Warren, in 1983. Schwartz retired from New York University in 1992. He then accepted an appointment as Chapman Distinguished Professor of Law at the University of Tulsa, where he remained until his death in Tulsa, Oklahoma, on December 23, 1997.

—MSM

Scott, Hugh D(oggett)
(1900–1994) *U.S. congressman and senator*

Born in Fredericksburg, Virginia, on November 11, 1900, Scott graduated from Randolph-Macon College in 1919 and received a law degree from the University of Virginia in 1922. That same year, he was admitted to the bar and began to practice law in Philadelphia. From 1926 to 1941, he served as assistant district attorney in that city. Scott won election as a Republican to the U.S. House of Representatives in 1940 and again in 1942. He resigned from the House to serve in the navy from 1944 to 1946, rising to the rank of captain in the naval reserves. Scott returned to the House in 1947 and served for 12 more years. A consistent internationalist, he supported the Lend-Lease Act in 1941, aid to Greece and Turkey in 1947, and the Marshall Plan. In 1948, Thomas E. Dewey, the Republican presidential nominee, chose Scott to chair the Republican National Committee, a post Scott held until 1949.

A moderate Republican, Scott supported public housing, rent control, and abolition of the poll tax. On other issues, he adopted more traditional Republican positions. He supported lower taxes and the Taft-Hartley Act (1947), which labor unions regarded as antilabor. As a member of the more liberal, internationalist wing of the party, Scott opposed the selection of Senator ROBERT A. TAFT (R-Ohio) as the party's presidential nominee in 1952 and was an early participant in the draft Eisenhower movement. In February 1952, Scott was among 19 representatives who wrote to Eisenhower urging him to seek the GOP nomination. During the presidential campaign, Scott chaired Eisenhower's headquarters committee.

In the mid-1950s, Scott and Representatives KENNETH KEATING (R-N.Y.) and JACOB JAVITS (R-N.Y.), all moderate to liberal members of the House from the Northeast with urban constituencies, favored civil rights legislation. Their urging contributed to the administration's decision to submit civil rights legislation to Congress in January 1956. The next month, Scott and Representative ADAM CLAYTON POWELL, JR. (D-N.Y.), announced that a group of House members was determined to bring legislation protecting the right to vote before the House. In May 1957, Scott joined a majority on the Rules Committee that favored reporting a civil rights bill. On the floor, he opposed a southern attempt to weaken the bill by guaranteeing a jury trial to persons violating court orders protecting voting rights.

Over the opposition of the Republican machine in Pennsylvania, Scott won the Republican nomination for a seat in the Senate in 1958 and defeated Governor GEORGE LEADER in the general election. As a senator, Scott continued to stand toward the left of his party, voting to override the president's veto of a housing bill in 1959 and the veto of an area redevelopment bill in 1960. In March 1960, he was among 16 senators who signed a cloture petition in an unsuccessful effort to end a southern filibuster of what became the Civil Rights Act of 1960.

Although Scott's voting record was significantly more liberal than those of most Republicans on Capitol Hill, he frequently served as a partisan spokesman in Congress. In 1955, Democrats criticized the tax cuts of the previous year as tailored to the interests of big business and called for a $20 personal income tax credit. Scott denounced the proposal as a "gimmick . . . [to] buy the votes of the American people at 20 bucks a head." Five years

later, he attacked Democratic senatorial opposition to the nomination of LEWIS STRAUSS as secretary of commerce, describing it as "a well-planned attempt at legislative lynching."

In 1962, Scott attempted to make the Republican Party in Pennsylvania more attractive to liberal voters by successfully promoting Representative William Scranton for governor. Two years later, Scott led an effort to block BARRY M. GOLDWATER, a conservative senator from Arizona, from gaining the Republican nomination for the presidency. Toward that end, Scott urged Scranton to enter the race against Goldwater. Nevertheless, when Goldwater won the nomination, Scott supported the national ticket. Scott continued to support civil rights for African Americans; he voted for civil rights acts in 1964, 1965, and 1968. He backed New York's liberal governor, NELSON A. ROCKEFELLER for the Republican nomination in 1968. When RICHARD M. NIXON won the nomination, however, Scott campaigned for him.

In September 1969, Scott became minority leader in the Senate. During the Nixon administration, his voting record became more conservative; he nevertheless coauthored the Voting Rights Act of 1970. Scott split with the administration and opposed the nomination of CLEMENT F. HAYNSWORTH to the Supreme Court (a decision Scott later regretted). The following year, he supported the president's nomination of G. Harrold Carswell (another decision Scott came to regret). Moreover, although he had supported the war under the administrations of JOHN F. KENNEDY and LYNDON B. JOHNSON, Scott became decidedly more dovish during the Nixon administration. During the Watergate scandal of 1973–74, Scott initially supported the president. The minority leader urged Nixon to release tape recordings of conversations in the Oval Office in the belief that they would exonerate the president. Nixon resisted, but after the courts ordered the release of the tapes and they revealed Nixon's participation in a cover-up, Scott informed the president that he could not survive impeachment proceedings. Compromised by his defense of President Nixon and by charges that he had received illicit contributions from the Gulf Oil Corporation (something for which the Senate Ethics Committee cleared him of any wrongdoing), Scott did not seek reelection in 1976. Scott practiced law in Washington, D.C., from 1977 to 1987. He died in Falls Church, Virginia, on July 21, 1994.

—MSM

Seaborg, Glenn T(heodore)

(1912–1999) *associate director, Lawrence Radiation Laboratory; chancellor, University of California, Berkeley; member, President's Science Advisory Committee*

Seaborg was born in Ishpeming, Michigan, on April 19, 1912. At the age of 10, he moved with his family to a suburb of Los Angeles. After receiving his B.A. from the University of California at Los Angeles in 1934, he went on to earn his doctorate in chemistry from the University of California at Berkeley in 1937. Seaborg became a research associate at Berkeley in 1937. He was appointed an instructor of chemistry in 1939 and promoted to assistant professor in 1941. His studies of atomic structure led to the discovery of numerous new isotopes of common elements by 1940. Seaborg's major achievement, however, was the extraction of plutonium, a new element with fissionable properties, from uranium. In 1941 Seaborg's team transmuted an isotope of uranium into a new element, plutonium 239, by bombarding it with neutrons. The achievement contributed to the development of the atomic bomb. During World War II, Seaborg worked on the Manhattan Project as section chief of the metallurgical laboratory at the University of Chicago. His unit separated enough plutonium to be used in experiments at the laboratories at Los Alamos, New Mexico. Eventually, Seaborg's team produced enough to be used to build two atomic bombs, including the one dropped on Nagasaki, Japan. Seaborg was among seven scientists working on the bomb who, in June 1945, sent a report to the secretary of war calling for a demonstration of the atomic bomb in an uninhabited place before its use in warfare. Known as the Franck Report, this statement forecast a dangerous atomic arms race and urged international control of nuclear weapons in the postwar period.

After the war, Seaborg returned to Berkeley in 1946 as a full professor. He was head of the nuclear chemistry research section at the Lawrence Radia-

tion Laboratory from 1954 to 1958 and associate director from 1954 to 1961. His research proved the existence of several transuranium elements, and in 1951 he won the Nobel Prize in chemistry. Seaborg was also a member of the Atomic Energy Commission's (AEC) General Advisory Committee (GAC) from 1946 to 1950. He was out of the country and did not attend a meeting of the GAC, held in October 1949, where members of the committee, including its chair, J. ROBERT OPPENHEIMER, declared their opposition to a crash program to develop the hydrogen bomb. Seaborg had indicated his support for the project in a letter sent to Oppenheimer earlier that month. "Although I deplore the prospect of our country's putting tremendous effort into the H-bomb," wrote Seaborg, "I must confess that I have been unable to come to the conclusion that we should not." In 1950, President Truman ordered the AEC to develop the weapon.

Seaborg's letter became a point of contention in the Oppenheimer security hearings in 1954. Responding to charges that the scientist had been disloyal, President Eisenhower ordered Oppenheimer's security clearance suspended in late 1953, pending a hearing. The charges were based on Oppenheimer's prewar associations with pro-communist groups and his postwar ambivalence toward the development of the hydrogen bomb. At the AEC's security hearing in April, all the scientists who had served on the GAC with Oppenheimer in 1949 testified on Oppenheimer's behalf except Seaborg. The hearing revealed conflicting evidence concerning whether or not Oppenheimer had informed other members about Seaborg's letter supporting the project. Citing Oppenheimer's conduct, the testimony regarding Seaborg's letter, as well as other incidents, the board ruled, two to one, to maintain the suspension.

Seaborg became chancellor of the Berkeley campus in 1958. The following year, Eisenhower appointed him to the President's Science Advisory Committee.

President JOHN F. KENNEDY appointed Seaborg head of the AEC in 1961. The following year, Seaborg offered Oppenheimer a new hearing, which the latter declined. As chair of the AEC, Seaborg advocated resumption of U.S. nuclear tests after the Soviet Union resumed testing in 1961. Nevertheless, he supported the nuclear test ban treaty in 1963, which banned aboveground testing. Indeed, the treaty was a disappointment to Seaborg, who had hoped for a comprehensive ban. While the AEC's role expanded greatly in the late 1960s, it drew frequent criticism from those who considered its safeguards against atomic accidents inadequate. In 1971, Seaborg resigned as its chair and returned to the University of California. In 1983, President Ronald Reagan appointed Seaborg to serve on the National Commission on Excellence in Education. The final draft of the report did not satisfy Seaborg, because he thought it did not adequately portray the urgency of the situation. He stated that deficiencies in education made the United States a "nation at risk." His comments led to the drafting of a new introduction and gave the report its famous title. Demonstrating his concern with the quality of science education, he became a professor in Berkeley's graduate school of education in 1983. The recipient of many awards and honors, Seaborg received the Enrico Fermi Award of the AEC, the Priestly Medal of the American Chemical Society, and (in 1991) the National Medal of Science. He died in Lafayette, California, on February 25, 1999.

—MSM

Seaton, Frederick A(ndrew)

(1909–1974) *assistant secretary of defense for legislative affairs, administrative assistant for congressional liaison, deputy assistant to the president, secretary of the interior*

Born in Washington, D.C., on December 11, 1909, Seaton was raised in Manhattan, Kansas, where his father, a former secretary to Senator Joseph L. Bristow (R-Kan.), owned and published two newspapers. Seaton attended public schools and Kansas State Agricultural College (later Kansas State University) from 1927 to 1931. Upon graduation from college, he became associate editor and business manager of Seaton Publications of Manhattan. While continuing his career in journalism, Seaton became active in the Young Republicans Club beginning in 1932 and served as vice chair of the Kansas Republican State Committee from 1934 to 1937. During the presidential campaign of 1936, he

served as secretary to Alfred M. Landon, the Republican nominee. In 1937, Seaton moved to Nebraska and became publisher and general manager of the *Hastings Daily Tribune*. He bought KHAS Radio in Hastings and acquired radio stations in Manhattan and Coffeyville, Kansas. Perhaps his most powerful outlet was *Western Farm Life Magazine*, which eventually grew to 160,000 subscribers in 10 states. Seaton served in Nebraska's state legislature from 1945 to 1949. He was Nebraska state chairman for HAROLD STASSEN's unsuccessful bid for the Republican presidential nomination in 1948. Upon the death of Senator Kenneth S. Wherry (R-Neb.), Governor Val Peterson appointed Seaton to fill the vacant seat in December 1951. Seaton did not stand for election to the vacancy and served until November 4, 1952.

During the presidential campaign of 1952, Seaton served on DWIGHT D. EISENHOWER's campaign staff as a deputy to SHERMAN ADAMS. He was involved in formulating the campaign's strategy in the wake of RICHARD NIXON's Checkers speech. After the campaign, Seaton returned to Kansas to run his growing media business, which by this time included a television station.

In September 1953, Eisenhower appointed Seaton an assistant secretary of defense. At that post, he persuaded Secretary of Defense CHARLES E. WILSON to hold weekly press conferences and improve relations between the Defense Department and Congress. In February 1955, Seaton joined the White House staff as the president's administrative assistant for congressional liaison. He was promoted to deputy assistant to the president in charge of patronage and liaison in June.

After DOUGLAS MCKAY resigned as secretary of the interior, Eisenhower was anxious to mollify tensions within the department generated by McKay's controversial personnel policies and abrasive personality. Therefore, he offered the position to the even-tempered Seaton in May 1956. The appointment drew widespread approval, and Seaton's friendly, open-door policies soon established him as a popular figure within the department.

Seaton vigorously pursued McKay's policies in the area of developing national parks. Attendance at parks reached record highs during his tenure. Spending on the park system increased substantially, more than half a million acres were added to the system, and a 29th national park was established on the island of St. John in the Virgin Islands.

Seaton also followed McKay's initiatives with respect to Native Americans. Termination, a policy designed to end federal relations with the tribes, encountered opposition from many tribes. The product of a variety of motives, termination initially amounted to a program of forced assimilation. The federal government also placed greater emphasis on relocating Native Americans to the cities. In an effort to ease economic pressures on reservations and to accelerate assimilation, Indians who relocated were provided with housing and jobs. Seaton also launched educational programs, providing courses on the reservations as well as vocational training for those from 18 to 35 years old. In addition, he fostered the development of job opportunities near the reservations. By 1958, problems associated with termination and protests from various tribes led the administration to halt the policy of termination without the consent of the affected tribe.

While McKay had supported the use of private enterprise to develop resources whenever possible, Seaton promoted joint federal/private cooperation. He endorsed teamwork projects in the Trinity River division and San Luis unit of the Central Valley Project in California, and he promoted the Fryingpan Arkansas Project in Colorado, construction of which began in fall 1956. Seaton continued the hydro-generating program in the Pacific Northwest. In 1959, facilities for 5.8 million kilowatts were either under construction or scheduled for completion by 1969. For fiscal 1960, the Bureau of Reclamation planned a $9 million program of construction involving 59 projects.

Seaton made protection of wildlife a major goal of the department. In 1958, he sponsored the duck stamp amendment, raising from $2 to $3 the fee for duck stamps (used as hunting licenses). The proceeds went to the acquisition of additional national refuges for waterfowl. He also prohibited the leasing of oil and gas reserves on refuges except for the purposes of drainage. That same year, Seaton promoted amendments to the Coordination Act of 1946 designed to further wildlife conservation. Under the original act, agencies and groups constructing water projects were required to include

features to prevent harm to wildlife. The amendments went further and ordered agencies to consider ways of enhancing and developing new fish and wildlife resources. The measure was one of the most important conservation bills of the postwar era.

Development of resources remained another major priority. In 1958, Seaton detailed for a Senate internal affairs subcommittee a plan for federal subsidization of domestic protection of copper, lead, zinc, and other minerals. He furthered the construction of a $12 million helium extraction plant, completed in November 1959. The secretary also administered the mandatory import controls on crude oil, which Congress passed in 1959 and were designed to nourish domestic production and development.

Seaton led the drive in the White House and Congress that resulted in statehood for Alaska in 1958 and Hawaii in 1959. Some Republicans singled out the secretary as a possible vice presidential candidate in 1960.

Seaton left government in January 1961 and returned to the Seaton Publishing Company. In 1962, he ran for governor of Kansas, unsuccessfully challenging the Democratic incumbent, Frank B. Morrison. Seaton then returned to his business, which included eight newspapers, radio stations, and television stations in Nebraska and Kansas. He lived in Hastings until his death in Minneapolis, Minnesota, on January 17, 1974.

—MSM

Service, John S(tewart)
(1909–1999) *Foreign Service officer*

The son of American missionaries, Service was born in Chengdu, China, on August 3, 1909. After spending his early years in China, where he attended a boarding school in Shanghai, he returned with his family to the United States in 1924 and graduated from high school in Berkeley, California. He graduated from Oberlin College in 1931 and spent a year doing graduate work in art history. In 1933, he passed the Foreign Service examination but did not receive an official appointment until 1935. After serving as a Foreign Service clerk at the U.S. consulate in Kunming, China, he was named language attaché at the embassy in Beijing in 1936. He was posted to Shanghai in 1938. As the Japanese army advanced, Service relocated in 1941 to the wartime Nationalist capital at Chungking, where he served as political officer. After meeting with Mao Zedong in 1944, Service wrote a memo praising the Communist leader and describing the Nationalist government as corrupt and ineffective. His views got back to the Nationalist government and angered the China lobby in the United States. Service was called back from China in 1944 and returned to Washington. He went back to China as an adviser to the army. Once again, however, his views got him in trouble. A letter urging the United States to support the Communists in order to reduce casualties in an expected allied invasion, however, outraged Roosevelt's personal envoy, General Patrick J. Hurley, who sent Service back to Washington.

In 1945, Service was arrested and charged with passing confidential material to Phillip Jaffe, editor of *Amerasia*, a leftist scholarly magazine dealing with Asia. The FBI had recorded (without a warrant) a meeting in which Service briefed Jaffe about U.S. policy toward China and gave him reports that Service had written criticizing the government of Chiang Kai-shek. Service himself had classified some of the reports he gave to Jaffe as secret. Acknowledging that he had committed an "indiscretion," Service defended himself, claiming such practices were normal. Rather than engaging in espionage for the Soviets, it seems that Service improperly leaked government information in the hope that it would influence American policy. He believed that a civil war was inevitable in China and that the corruption and incompetence of the Nationalist government doomed it to failure. Therefore, he maintained, the United States should establish friendly relations with the Communists. A grand jury declined to indict him, although it handed down indictments in two related cases, and Service was reinstated in the State Department that same year.

During the next six years, Service faced a series of investigations by the State Department and its loyalty board, some prompted by Senator JOSEPH R. McCARTHY's (R-Wis.) charges that the department was harboring disloyal Americans. In each case, the loyalty board cleared Service. The undersecretary of state also reviewed the loyalty board's findings and approved them. In addition, a Senate committee found that Service had simply written the "facts as he saw them." On December 13, 1951, however, the loyalty review board of the Civil Service Commission audited the departmental proceedings. The loyalty review board found "reasonable doubt as to his loyalty" and recommended dismissal. Secretary of State DEAN ACHESON did so the following day, basing his action on the McCarran rider to the State Department appropriation bill of 1947 that gave the secretary of state absolute discretion to remove from office any employee when he deemed it in the national interest.

Service decided to challenge the constitutionality of Acheson's action. In 1956, a federal district court ruled that the loyalty review board had no authority to audit favorable decisions by departments and ordered that doubts of Service's loyalty be stricken from his record. The court also held that, under the McCarran rider, Acheson had a right to discharge Service and therefore refused to order his reinstatement.

On January 17, 1957, by a vote of eight to zero, the Supreme Court affirmed the lower court's ruling that the loyalty review board had no authority to review decisions favorable to the accused. The Court further held that, under State Department regulations, Acheson had no right to overrule the final decision of the undersecretary of state and, in doing so, had violated Service's rights. The Court then returned the case to the lower court, which reinstated Service to the State Department with all back pay. The decision, along with others handed down on "Red Monday," marked a significant shift from the Court's willingness to grant the government wide latitude in the interests of national security to a concern for the rights of individuals.

Service returned to work in September 1957 and was assigned to make a survey of how the department could save money in shipping the household goods of Foreign Service officers sent to new posts. In 1959, he was transferred to Liverpool, England, as consul. Service retired three years later and earned a master's degree from the University of California at Berkeley. He become library curator at the Center for Chinese Studies at the University of California at Berkeley. In 1971, he visited Communist China. He died in Oakland, California, on February 3, 1999.

—MSM

Shanley, Bernard M(ichael)

(1903–1992) *special counsel to the president, presidential appointments secretary*

Born in Newark, New Jersey, on August 3, 1903, Shanley studied briefly at Columbia University in 1925 and then attended law school at Fordham University, from which he graduated in 1928. From 1929 to 1952, he practiced law in Newark, New Jersey. During World War II, he served in the army, rising to the rank of captain. After the war, he returned to his law practice and held directorships in several insurance companies. From early in his career, he was actively involved with the Republican Party in New Jersey and served as chairman of the New Jersey Republican Committee for an Effective Assembly and of the executive committee of the Republican National Committee.

A longtime supporter of HAROLD STASSEN, Shanley became national chairman of the Stassen for President Volunteer Committee in late 1951. However, by the Republican National Convention of June 1952, Shanley had switched his support to DWIGHT D. EISENHOWER, and he worked for the Eisenhower campaign during the general election campaign.

On the recommendation of SHERMAN ADAMS, who had worked closely with him during the campaign, Shanley was appointed White House special counsel in January 1953. The following month, he became involved in the administration's debate over possible revision of the Taft-Hartley Act. Secretary of Labor MARTIN DURKIN wanted substantial changes to Taft-Hartley. Reflecting the views of organized labor, he wanted, among other things, to eliminate the right-to-work provision and to permit secondary boycotts. SINCLAIR WEEKS, the secretary of commerce, opposed such changes. Along with GERALD D. MORGAN, assistant congressional liaison, Shanley produced a position paper attempting to reconcile differences between Durkin and Weeks. It detailed what the administration needed to attract labor votes without losing sup-

port from the National Association of Manufacturers, a powerful, traditionally Republican business organization. The Shanley-Morgan draft included many of Durkin's proposals and called for substantial revisions of the Taft-Hartley Act, especially of its more antilabor sections. However, Senator ROBERT A. TAFT (R-Ohio) died the day that Eisenhower planned to submit the proposals to Congress, and the administration agreed that it would be impolitic to send the amendments to Congress on the day that the sponsor of the original act died. In addition, Taft's death greatly dimmed any prospect for passage of the proposed amendments. Without Taft's prestige and his influence, particularly with the Republican Right, the amendments had little chance of passing. Moreover, the election of Senator WILLIAM KNOWLAND (R-Calif.) to replace Taft as majority leader made passage even more unlikely. In addition, Weeks mobilized an effective campaign against the proposals within the administration, and they were never sent to Capitol Hill. When Durkin resigned in September 1953, he accused Shanley and Morgan of sabotaging their own reform proposals as well as his own efforts to revise the statute.

Shanley later performed public relations assignments for the Eisenhower administration. In November 1953, Eisenhower handed Shanley the task of dealing with protests from the press about the administration's policies and public utterances. Shortly thereafter, Shanley embroiled himself in controversy when he implied that 1,456 government employees who lost their jobs had been dismissed as "subversives." In February 1954, Shanley admitted that his statement had been an "unfortunate mistake" and apologized. Nevertheless, ADLAI STEVENSON took the opportunity to denounce the Republican Party and the Eisenhower administration for using McCarthyite tactics in the "deception." Although Shanley and others had declared them to be traitors and subversives, Stevenson said, the only concrete fact was that the government reluctantly admitted it found "only one alleged active Communist" in all its security investigations.

In January 1955, Shanley assumed the post of appointments secretary following the resignation of THOMAS E. STEPHENS. Shanley resigned that fall to resume his law practice but returned to the White

House in January 1956. In November 1957, Shanley again resigned to seek the Republican senatorial nomination from New Jersey. The following April, he lost to Winthrop Kean in the primary.

Shanley returned to his law practice and remained politically active in the 1960s. He was appointed to the Republican National Committee in 1960, serving until 1964. He won the New Jersey Republican senatorial nomination in 1964 but lost the general election to Democrat HARRISON WILLIAMS. In 1968, he became vice chairman of the Republican National Committee for the northeastern region and remained on it until the year he died. His law firm, Shanley and Fisher, grew into one of the largest in New Jersey; at the time of Shanley's death, it had 140 lawyers. He resigned as Republican national committeeman in 1992. Shanley died in Bernardsville, New Jersey, on February 25, 1992.

—MSM

Sheen, Fulton J(ohn)

(1895–1979) *clergyman*

Born in El Paso, Illinois, on May 8, 1895, Peter John Sheen early on adopted his mother's maiden name and used it throughout his life. After completing high school at Spalding Institute in Peoria, Illinois, in 1913, he began lengthy and distinguished university training at St. Viator College of Illinois, receiving his B.A. in 1917 and M.A. in 1919. He studied at St. Paul's Seminary in Minnesota in 1919 and was ordained as a priest the same year. Sheen earned a Bachelor of Sacred Theology degree and a Bachelor of Canon Law degree from Catholic University in 1920, and a Ph.D. at the University of Louvain in 1923. After studying at the Sorbonne, he earned an S.T.D. from the Collegio Angelico in Rome in 1924. Sheen briefly taught theology at St. Edmunds College in Ware, England, and published his doctoral dissertation as *God and Intelligence in Modern Philosophy* (1925). It won considerable acclaim and established its author as a leading Catholic philosopher. The University of Louvain awarded Sheen the Agrégé en Philosophie, making him the first American to receive the prestigious degree. He served briefly in 1925 and 1926 as curate of St. Patrick's Church in a poor parish in Peoria, Illinois. In 1926, Sheen accepted appointment to the philosophy department of Catholic University, a position he held until 1950.

Early in his career, Sheen became one of the most popular spokesmen for Catholicism in America. He lectured at Catholic universities and accepted invitations to speak at churches nationwide. He also wrote many books and articles during the 1930s and 1940s, and a few of the books sold well. His effectiveness as an orator led Catholic officials to choose him in 1930 to appear as the featured speaker on the weekly radio program "Catholic Hour," carried by NBC and sponsored by the National Council of Catholic Men. The program was intended to make the doctrines of the church more familiar to Americans. Sheen became extremely popular; he drew an estimated audience of 4 million listeners.

Made a papal chamberlain in 1934 and elevated to monsignor the following year, Sheen became known during the 1930s and 1940s not only as an articulate preacher who brought many converts to the Catholic church—including prominent ex-communists Elizabeth Bentley and Louis Budenz—but also as a firm anticommunist who supported Generalissimo Francisco Franco in the Spanish civil war. During World War II, Sheen's sermons combined piety with patriotism. Along with his message of anticommunism (he denounced America's wartime alliance with the Soviet Union), he taught that social reform derived from spiritual regeneration and advocated the church's program of Catholic Action as a middle ground between capitalism and communism. After the war, he opposed any concessions to the USSR or relaxation of the cold war. In *Communism and the Conscience of the West* (1948), he held the "Western world" responsible for communism and urged it to repent and return to Christianity.

During the postwar religious revival, Catholicism worked its way into the American religious mainstream, and Sheen played a major role in that development. In 1950, he was named the national director of the Society for the Propagation of the Faith, an international Catholic organization that distributed funds for missionary activities. Consecrated auxiliary bishop of New York in 1951, Sheen continued to spread his message through a variety of media. A prolific writer, he published a number of books, including *Peace of Soul* and *Life of Christ*, as well as two newspaper columns ("Bishop Sheen Writes" and "God Love You").

Many Catholics expected him to rise to greater prominence in the church hierarchy, but while bringing converts to the church he made enemies among its officials. Described by a biographer, Rev. D. P. Noonan, as a "consummate egocentric," Sheen could, according to Noonan, "captivate, inspire, persuade and stimulate" on the one hand and "belittle, antagonize, and alienate" on the other.

Launched in 1951, Sheen's television program, "Life Is Worth Living," won consistently high ratings on the DuMont and ABC networks. Airing at 8:00 on Tuesday evenings opposite the comedian Milton Berle's popular entertainment show on NBC, Sheen was the only competitor ever to challenge Berle, at times drawing a larger audience than the man known as Mr. Television. At its peak, Sheen's program drew 10 million viewers, including large numbers of Protestants and Jews. After DuMont folded in 1955, Sheen moved his program to ABC. Speaking before a live audience, Sheen appeared in full liturgical regalia, and his almost hypnotic gaze, his reassuring smile, and his calm, though theatrical, delivery captivated his viewers. Noonan described Sheen's program as "not a dogmatic one, but a mixture of common sense, logic and Christian ethics" that did not attempt to proselytize for Catholicism. Presented through anecdotes and moral lessons, Sheen's subjects ranged from war, motherhood, psychiatry, teenagers, death, and democracy to the divine sense of humor. A recurring theme was communism and the danger it posed to the United States. He based discussions on Franz Kafka's *The Trial*, Fyodor Dostoyevsky's *The Brothers Karamazov*, St. Augustine's *Confessions*, and St. Thomas Aquinas's *Summa Theologica*. All were presented in a comforting, nonintimidating manner, and Sheen frequently supplemented his unscripted discussions with jokes solicited from friends or derived from books of humor. Sheen received an Emmy Award in 1952, and the program was honored with the Freedom Foundation Award the next year. Describing him as "America's best known Roman Catholic priest," *Time* magazine put Sheen on its cover in 1952. Sheen's pro-

gram went off the air in 1957 but resumed in 1959 and continued until 1965. Printed transcripts of the programs were compiled in five volumes, titled *Life Is Worth Living* and published between 1953 and 1957. The individual volumes repeatedly appeared on the best-seller lists. Bishop Sheen returned all revenues connected with the program to the Society for the Propagation of the Faith.

Like many other Catholics in the United States during the 1950s, Bishop Sheen believed that communism posed the most ominous threat to freedom and that Christianity and the church constituted the most powerful force opposing it. Never timid about pointing to what he believed was communist subversion, he, in 1952, accused American communists of having attempted to infiltrate the Catholic priesthood in 1936. At the same time, he professed not to sympathize with the methods of Senator JOSEPH R. MCCARTHY (R–Wis.).

Sheen continued to write books and syndicated columns in the late 1950s and 1960s. He also participated in the Second Vatican Council. His expected promotion in the church did not materialize, because, at least many believed, he had incurred the disfavor of the archbishop of New York FRANCIS SPELLMAN. After refusing Spellman's offer of a bishopric in New York City, he received an appointment from Pope Paul VI as bishop of Rochester, New York, in 1966. Sheen had little previous experience as a parish leader, and he shocked his conservative congregation by determinedly introducing the reforms of Vatican II, his ecumenical overtures to the community, and his advocacy of a variety of liberal political causes. Not only did he focus attention on the poor of the inner cities, but in 1967 he became the first major Catholic figure to urge a total and immediate withdrawal of American troops from Vietnam. He later modified his position and supported President RICHARD M. NIXON's policy of Vietnamization. In 1969, Sheen resigned his bishopric in Rochester and became titular archbishop of Newport, Wales. Thereafter, he made occasional appearances on television and radio programs and contributed to national and religious magazines. He died in New York City on December 9, 1979.

—MSM

Shivers, Allan

(1907–1985) *governor of Texas*

The son of a prominent judge, Allan Shivers was born in Lufkin, Texas, on October 5, 1907. He grew up near Woodville, Texas, and moved with his family to Port Arthur, Texas, where he graduated from high school in 1924. Shivers entered the University of Texas but dropped out after a year to work at an oil refinery. He returned to the University of Texas in 1928 and received his B.A. in 1931. Soon after graduating, he passed the state bar exam, although he did not complete his LL.B. at the University of Texas until 1933. After receiving his law degree, he returned to Port Arthur and opened a law office. In 1934, Shivers won election as a Democrat to the state senate, where he focused his attention on defending his state's ownership of tidelands oil and gas properties claimed by the federal government. He held his seat in the state senate until 1947. From 1943 to 1945, he served in the army and was assigned to the Allied military government in North Africa, Italy, France, and Germany. Discharged from the army as a major, Shivers returned to Texas and managed his father-in-law's business enterprises, including a substantial citrus farm. In 1946, Shivers won election as lieutenant governor. Reelected with the incumbent governor, Beauford H. Jester, in 1948, Shivers became governor in July 1949, when Jester died of a heart attack. Shivers easily won election in November 1950. As governor, he reorganized state government to make it more efficient and expanded state services, funding them by pushing tax increases through the state legislature. His administration increased appropriations for retirement benefits for state employees, aid for the elderly, teachers' salaries, roads, and bridges. It also provided funding for private charity organizations. A strong believer in states' rights, the governor continued to assert Texas's claim to tidelands oil, which put him at odds with the administration of HARRY S. TRUMAN. When Truman vetoed a bill that would have vested ownership of tidelands in the states, Shivers broke with the national Democratic Party.

During the presidential campaign of 1952, DWIGHT D. EISENHOWER stated that he favored state control of offshore oil deposits, and Shivers endorsed him for president. Conservative Democrats, or "Shivercrats" as they came to be called, helped Eisenhower win 53 percent of the vote in Texas that November. Shivers won reelection at the same time, running on both Republican and Democratic tickets.

Shivers made public comments harshly critical of the Supreme Court's decision in *Brown v. Board of Education* (1954), which struck down segregation in public schools. His actions, however, were more moderate. In August 1955, he appointed an advisory committee on segregation to recommend ways of preventing integration. Yet Texas passed no legislation impeding voluntary compliance with the Court's decision, and the state offered assistance in implementing locally developed desegregation plans. By the end of 1955, 84 districts in Texas had desegregated, more than the rest of the southern states combined.

During the mid-1950s, however, Shivers found himself losing his political base. In 1954, the governor faced a challenge for renomination from the liberal RALPH YARBOROUGH and was forced into a bitter runoff. Charges of corruption and malpractice in his administration further embarrassed the governor (a scandal in the Veterans Land Board was particularly harmful), even though he was never implicated in any of the scandals.

Faced with declining popularity, Shivers seized the idea of interposition to unite his followers. Conceived to obstruct the *Brown* decision, the theory of interposition maintained that each state had a right to interpose itself between the federal government and the state's citizens if a federal law or court decision was contrary to the Constitution. By extension, opponents of *Brown* argued for consolidating public school authority under state government instead of local school boards, thus placing the "sovereignty of the state" between local school officials and federal courts. In February 1956, Shivers called on the state Democratic Party to conduct a referendum on interposition and, if the voters endorsed it, to place the doctrine in the party platform. The following month, the governor promoted an interposition plank for the Democratic national platform. This led to a conflict over control of the state delegation to the Democratic National Convention in 1956. In May, a moderate coalition led by Representative SAM RAYBURN (D-Tex.) and Senator LYNDON JOHNSON

(D-Tex.) ousted Shivers as party leader and wrote a statement denouncing interposition but supporting states rights. The state convention named Johnson its favorite son candidate for president.

Although Johnson and Rayburn wrested control of the state delegation from Shivers, the issue of interposition did not go away. In July, the white supremacist Citizens' Councils, with Shivers's support, forced a statewide referendum on three propositions to maintain segregation, one of which called for interposition. All three received heavy approval. The large vote for segregation reinforced Shivers's stand. In the fall of 1956, under the guise of maintaining order, Shivers used Texas Rangers to block federal court orders to admit African-American students to schools in Mansfield and Texarkana. President Eisenhower took no action on the matter. According to Eisenhower's attorney general, HERBERT BROWNELL, "there was no Court-ordered plan to desegregate and obviously no violation of a Court order and no rioting that got beyond the capability of local authorities." Therefore, Brownell "advised President Eisenhower that we did not have requisite Federal jurisdiction to enter the Mansfield case."

Shivers endorsed Eisenhower for president in 1956, and the president carried Texas in November. Shivers had announced in March that he would not run for a fourth term. The governor threw his support to a moderately conservative Democrat, PRICE DANIEL, who defeated Yarborough for the Democratic nomination and went on to win election as governor. In late 1956, the advisory committee Shivers had appointed returned 21 proposals to maintain segregation. They came too late for his signature and awaited action by the new administration.

After completing an unprecedented seven-and-a-half years as governor, Shivers retired from politics in January 1957. He returned to private life and managed his business interests. He served as chairman of Western Pipe Line, Inc., a large construction concern, Austin National Bank (later InterFirst Bank Austin), and Texas Commerce Bank. In addition, he remained active in public affairs. Shivers was president of the United States Chamber of Commerce and served as chair of the advisory board of the Export-Import Bank of the United States.

In 1973, he was appointed to a six-year term as a member of the board of regents of the University of Texas, which he chaired for four years. Shivers died of a massive heart attack in Austin, Texas, on January 14, 1985.

—MSM

Short, Dewey

(1898–1979) *U.S. congressman; chairman, Armed Services Committee; assistant secretary of the army for civil-military affairs*

Born in Galena, Missouri, on April 7, 1898, Short attended public schools and Marrionville College in Missouri. He began campaigning for Republican candidates at age 18. He served in the infantry during World War I, after which he received a B.A. from Baker University in 1919 and a Bachelor of Sacred Theology from Boston University in 1922. He studied theology and philosophy at Heidelberg University, the University of Berlin, and Oxford University and took law courses at Harvard. Short became a professor of ethics, psychology, and political philosophy at Southwestern College in Winfield, Kansas, in 1923, and pastor of the Grace Methodist Episcopal Church in Springfield, Missouri, in 1927. He won election as a Republican to the U.S. House of Representatives from Missouri in 1928. Although he lost his bid for reelection in 1930 and ran unsuccessfully for the Republican nomination for a Senate seat in 1932, redistricting enabled him to return to the House in 1934.

Short strongly objected to the New Deal's concentration of power in the federal government. In 1935, he unleashed a verbal tirade against the New Deal that attracted national attention. *Time* magazine ran a story about the speech.

In 1939, Short became the second-ranking Republican on the Military Affairs Committee. After a trip to Europe, he became a leading isolationist and was proposed as a vice presidential candidate at the 1940 Republican National Convention. Short maintained his distrust of foreign entanglements and opposed lend-lease in March 1941. Following World War II, he urged the United States to build Pacific bases to counter Soviet aggression and predicted that Korea would be a "hot spot." Short became ranking Republican on the Armed Services

Committee in 1949 and supported creation of the Department of Defense during the 80th Congress (1947–48). In September 1952, he urged that UN forces in Korea go "all the way" to the Yalu River and end the division of that country.

After Republicans gained control of Congress in the elections of 1952, Short became chair of the Armed Services Committee. The Korean War occupied most of the first six months of his term. In January, Short dismissed charges brought by Representative CLARE E. HOFFMAN (R-Mich.) that the army had staged a useless Korean raid to impress visitors. While President Eisenhower tried to set the stage for peace talks in April, Short urged that negotiations be delayed until the communists permitted international inspection of prison camps. When a truce was signed in July, Short stated that military victory would have been possible if the army had not been restricted.

In May 1953, Eisenhower conferred with Short over his proposed budget for 1953. The president stressed the fact that it gave the air force $20 billion, "more than 40 percent of all defense funds," as part of an effort to build 120 combat wings by July 1955. After the conference, Short announced that the administration did not deserve "full credit" for the buildup. He and other members of Congress had originally proposed increasing the number of combat wings to 143 by July 1955. Nevertheless, Short supported Eisenhower's budget.

Short became involved in the debate over the defense reorganization bill drafted by the administration and sent to Congress in April. The plan was intended to streamline and improve the Department of Defense by making the chairman of the Joint Chiefs of Staff responsible for the staff's work and giving him tenure power over personnel. Short initially opposed the plan as possibly leading to a "military dictatorship," but BRYCE HARLOW, of the White House congressional liaison staff, persuaded him to support it. With the backing of Short and the ranking Democrat on the committee, Representative CARL VINSON (D-Ga.), the reorganization plan was approved by the House and went into effect in June 1953.

Short attempted to calm American fears of nuclear attack in April 1954 by announcing that U.S. A-bomb defenses were "in pretty good shape" and saying it was "silly" to talk of evacuating large cit-

ies. He counseled moderation in July when Senate Majority Leader WILLIAM F. KNOWLAND (R-Calif.) stated that the United States should quit the UN if Communist China were admitted. The Democratic leadership supported Knowland, but other senators and Short announced that they opposed withdrawal.

The Democrats regained control of Congress in the elections of 1954, and Short lost his chairmanship. In June 1956, he opposed an $800 million supplemental increase in air force funds proposed by a House-Senate conference committee and opposed by the administration. Short objected to the increase on the grounds that the air force lacked facilities and manpower to make efficient use of the extra money and that it would lead to an unbalanced budget. The additional funding was nevertheless approved.

Short lost his seat in the House to Democrat Charles H. Brown in November 1956. The following February, Eisenhower nominated him to be assistant secretary of the army for civil-military affairs. The Senate confirmed his selection in March. In August 1957, he declared that decreased purchases of weapons by the armed services due to inflation would not seriously impair American defenses. In 1959, Short told a subcommittee of the House Armed Services Committee that charges of enlisted men being used to perform menial chores for officers were exaggerated. He retained his post until the end of the Eisenhower administration.

After leaving government, he lived in Washington, D.C., where he died on November 19, 1979.

—MSM

Shuman, Charles B(aker)

(1907–   ) *president, American Farm Bureau Federation*

Born in Sullivan, Illinois, on April 27, 1907, Shuman grew up on a family farm, attended public schools, and earned a B.S. from the University of Illinois College of Agriculture in 1928. The following year, he earned a master's degree in agronomy from the University of Illinois. He joined the American Farm Bureau Federation in 1929 and became increasingly active in farm organizations during the 1930s. He said that in those years he "learned about bureaucracy." Although a Democrat, he opposed many of

Franklin D. Roosevelt's agricultural policies. Shuman became a member of the board of directors of the Illinois Agricultural Association in 1941 and its president in 1945. In the latter year, Shuman also became a director of the American Farm Bureau Federation (AFBF).

Albert B. Kline, president of the AFBF, retired in 1954, and Shuman was unanimously elected to succeed him. The largest general farm organization in the United States, the AFBF had a membership of over 1.6 million farm families, concentrated mainly in the midwest. Originally, the AFBF supported the New Deal's agricultural policies. By the late 1930s, however, it became increasingly hostile to the New Deal. With the start of World War II, the AFBF broke with the agricultural policies of the Roosevelt administration. The election of Kline as president in 1947 reflected the organization's break from the New Deal. Under Shuman, the AFBF continued to oppose New Deal farm policies. By the 1950s, critics charged that the AFBF represented large commercial farmers. In response to such charges, Shuman said that "we represent either big or little farmers. We're a cross section of the entire farm population." However, observers noted that the AFBF membership included many farmers whose substantial holdings inclined them to oppose government controls. In contrast, members of the next two largest farm organizations, the National Farmers Union and the National Grange, tended to own small and medium-sized farms.

As an advocate of the free enterprise system, Shuman generally favored the policies of the Eisenhower administration's secretary of agriculture, EZRA TAFT BENSON. In Shuman's first year as president of the AFBF, he strongly backed Benson's proposal for flexible price supports for basic farm products. For Shuman, it represented a feasible, gradual method of returning American agriculture to the free market. When, in 1955, Democrats and some farm organizations called for a return to rigid price supports at 90 percent of parity, Shuman characterized the plan as a "backward step" that would "wreck this economy" and further depress declining agricultural income.

Shuman applied his philosophy of free enterprise and his opposition to government interference even more consistently than Benson. In September 1955, he rejected Benson's plan for the government to purchase pork to support its price. Instead, Shuman proposed a program calling for promotion to increase the use of pork and lard and to develop export markets (including in the Soviet bloc). Shuman and the AFBF consistently viewed the expansion of foreign markets as a superior strategy to government price supports as a means of increasing farm income.

For the most part, however, Shuman found the policies of the Eisenhower administration congenial. He overcame his aversion to government interference in agriculture in January 1956, when he told the Senate Agriculture and Forestry Committee that Benson's plan for a soil bank, which intended to reduce overproduction by having the government pay farmers to remove acreage from cultivation and use it to plant soil-building crops, was a "step in the right direction." Congress eventually passed a bill that included some, but not all, of the AFBF's recommendations. In both 1956 and 1958, Shuman supported Eisenhower's vetoes of farm bills that sought to restore high price supports. Eisenhower signed legislation supported by the AFBF that allowed farmers to file for refunds of federal tax on gasoline used on farms, added more funding for school milk programs, and provided more funding for the eradication of brucellosis.

Throughout the 1960s, Shuman was highly critical of the agricultural policies of the Kennedy and Johnson administrations. He especially opposed Democratic efforts to impose strict marketing controls. The owner of a farm that produced corn, cattle, and soybeans, Shuman left the AFBF in 1974 but remained active on the boards of a number of agencies and companies, including the Export-Import Bank, the Economic Development Administration, the Illinois Power Company, and the Chicago Mercantile Exchange.

—MSM

Shuttlesworth, Fred L(ee)

(1922–   ) *president, Alabama Christian Movement for Human Rights; secretary, Southern Christian Leadership Conference*

Born in Mount Meigs, Alabama, a small agricultural community, on March 18, 1922, Shuttlesworth grew up near Birmingham, Alabama, where he attended public schools and was the valedictorian of Rosedale High School. After high school, he worked as a handyman and moved to Mobile, Alabama, and worked at the Brookley Field Air Force Base. Although raised a Methodist, he joined a Baptist congregation and became a minister. After attending Cedar Grove Seminary, Shuttlesworth received a B.A. from Selma College in 1951 and a B.S. from Alabama State College in 1952. While attending Selma College, he began preaching in 1948 at two rural churches near Selma. Later that year, he moved to the First Baptist Church of Selma. The strong-willed, some would say arrogant, Shuttlesworth clashed with the deacons and resigned in December 1952. He spent four months as a guest preacher until, in March 1953, he became pastor of Birmingham's Bethel Baptist Church. There Shuttlesworth began to involve himself in civil rights causes. He led an unsuccessful attempt in 1955 to get African Americans placed on the local police force. He joined the NAACP, and when the organization was outlawed in Alabama in 1956, he helped establish the Alabama Christian Movement for Human Rights (ACMHR) to continue the fight for black equality in Birmingham. Shuttlesworth was elected its first president.

Called the Johannesburg of America by some African Americans, Birmingham was governed in the late 1950s by officials who firmly opposed any attempts at desegregation. As leader of the movement to desegregate the city, Shuttlesworth headed many attempts to end segregation in local public facilities. In early December 1956, Shuttlesworth attended the Institute on Nonviolence and Social Change, sponsored by the Montgomery Improvement Association, the group, led by MARTIN LUTHER KING, JR., that conducted the boycott of Montgomery's city buses. He returned to Birmingham and set about applying the lessons he had learned at the institute. On December 20, 1956, shortly after the Supreme Court had declared segregation on local transportation unconstitutional in a case arising from the Montgomery bus boycott, Shuttlesworth called on the city commissioners to end segregated seating on Birmingham's buses. A bomb made from six sticks of dynamite destroyed his home on Christmas night, injuring the church's deacon and

two of Shuttlesworth's children. Shuttlesworth was uninjured and the next day led roughly 250 African Americans onto local buses, where they sat in the seats reserved for whites. Following the arrest of 21 African Americans, Shuttlesworth called off the demonstrations until the segregation law could be tested in the courts. The 21 African Americans were convicted in January 1957, and the ACMHR appealed. In October 1958, just before a scheduled federal court hearing on the law, the city commission repealed the statute and passed a new one authorizing the bus company to establish its own segregation rules. Shuttlesworth then helped organize a test of this new ordinance. Thirteen African Americans were arrested on October 20 for sitting in seats reserved for whites, and Shuttlesworth himself was arrested the next day for having incited the protest. The ACMHR initiated a legal challenge to the new law the next month, and a federal district court ruled the new ordinance unconstitutional in December 1959.

Shuttlesworth also tried to desegregate the waiting rooms at Birmingham's railroad terminal in March 1957. That September he tried to enroll four black children, two of them his own, at a white high school. A mob savagely beat him outside the building, and the children were refused admission. Shuttlesworth filed a suit challenging Alabama's pupil placement law, passed in 1955 with the intent to forestall school desegregation. In November 1958, the U.S. Supreme Court ruled that the statute was not unconstitutional on its face. An attempt to dynamite Shuttlesworth's church in June 1958 failed only because a volunteer guarding the church found the bomb and moved it into the street before it exploded. The church sustained broken windows and cracked plaster. In late 1959, the ACMHR filed suit to desegregate Birmingham's parks. During the spring of 1960, Shuttlesworth aided student sit-ins in Birmingham and was arrested for his participation. In 1961, he served as the main contact in Alabama for the Freedom Rides and coordinated activities that saved the freedom riders after a mob attacked them in Anniston.

Along with Martin Luther King, Jr., Shuttlesworth helped organize the Southern Christian Leadership Conference (SCLC) in 1957. He was elected its secretary and became one of King's top aides in the SCLC. He spoke at the prayer pilgrimage in Washington, D.C., in May 1957. The city commissioners of Montgomery, Alabama, sued Shuttlesworth, three other black ministers, and the *New York Times* for libel in April 1960 because of an ad placed in the *Times* criticizing municipal officials. At trial, the jury returned a verdict for L. B. Sullivan, one of the commissioners, in the amount of $500,000. In a landmark decision, the Supreme Court overturned the $500,000 judgment against the defendants in March 1964 (*New York Times v. Sullivan*).

Combative, stubborn, and blunt, Shuttlesworth antagonized colleagues in the Civil Rights movement as well as his opponents. He became pastor of the Revelation Baptist Church in Cincinnati, Ohio, in 1961, but remained president of the ACMHR and a leader of Birmingham's movement for integration. Shuttlesworth suggested and then took a leadership role in a major antisegregation campaign in Birmingham in the spring of 1963. He invited King to come to Birmingham to participate in the campaign to desegregate the city. During those demonstrations, Shuttlesworth was hospitalized after water from a fire hose slammed him into a wall. He participated in other desegregation campaigns sponsored by the SCLC and remained a key aide to King during the 1960s.

Shuttlesworth became pastor of the Greater New Light Baptist Church in Cincinnati, Ohio, in 1966 and in 1988 became director of the Shuttlesworth Housing Foundation, created to assist low-income families in obtaining housing. In 2004, he became president of the SCLC but resigned in November 2004, less than a year later, alleging that the vice chairman was guilty of financial neglect and personal improprieties. Shuttlesworth complained that "deceit, mistrust and a lack of spiritual discipline and truth have eaten at the core of this once-hallowed organization."

—MSM

Smathers, George A(rmistead)
(1913–2007) *U.S. senator*

The son of a judge and Democratic leader in New Jersey who moved to Florida for his health, George Smathers was born in Atlantic City, New Jersey, on November 14, 1913, and moved to Miami with his family at the age of six. He attended public schools and received his B.A. in 1936 and LL.B. in 1938 from the University of Florida. After gaining admission to the bar in 1938, he began to practice law in Miami. A protégé of Senator Claude Pepper (D-Fla.), a strong supporter of the New Deal, Smathers became assistant U.S. district attorney in 1940. He joined the marine corps in 1942, served for 39 months in the Pacific, and was discharged a major in 1945. After the war, he briefly prosecuted war frauds for the government as a special assistant to the U.S. attorney general. With the aid of Pepper, Smathers won a seat in the House of Representatives in 1946 and reelection in 1948.

Although regarded as a "Pepper man" in the House, Smathers turned sharply to the right when he challenged his mentor for the senatorial nomination in 1950. The Florida primary attracted national attention in what was viewed as the first major test of the communist issue in the elections of 1950. Smathers attacked his opponent, who had long advocated friendlier relations with the USSR and had spoken before organizations later characterized as communist front groups, as a communist sympathizer bent on entangling the state in "the spiraling spider web of the Red network." The most important issue in the campaign, however, was the New Deal-Fair Deal tradition itself, with which Pepper was closely identified. Backed by a coalition of powerful business interests that opposed Pepper's liberal stands on taxes and labor legislation, Smathers appealed to upper-income voters, including many Republicans, with a program of economic conservatism and opposition to what he called "creeping socialism" in Washington. Smathers defeated Pepper by 60,000 votes and went on to win the general election in November. He won reelection in 1956 and 1962.

As a senator during the 1950s, Smathers was a conservative on social and economic issues, an outspoken defender of racial segregation in the South, and a foe of civil rights legislation. He became a close aide to Senate Majority Leader LYNDON B. JOHNSON (D-Tex.) and a powerful member of the small group of senators, known as the Senate establishment, who made committee appointments and could often decide the fate of legislation. Johnson placed him in charge of the Senate Democratic Elections Committee in 1956, where he used his position to disburse campaign money to conservatives and build important political connections among influential southern senators. Smathers's power was enhanced still further when he served as acting majority leader in Johnson's absence.

During the Eisenhower administration, Smathers used his influence on Capitol Hill to promote bills that advanced the interests of oil companies and railroads, some of which were clients of his law firm. He was one of the leading backers of the successful drive in 1953 to vest control of the oil-rich tidelands with the state governments and not the federal government. As chairman of the Commerce Committee's Surface Transportation Subcommittee, Smathers introduced the Transportation Act of 1958. The measure aided financially pressed railroads by granting them loan guarantees for the purchase of new equipment and making it easier for them to discontinue unprofitable passenger services.

When he served in the House, Smathers met and befriended Representative JOHN F. KENNEDY (D-Mass.). In 1959, Smathers became the head of the committee directing Kennedy's presidential campaign in the South. However, Smathers frequently failed to give his support to measures supported by the administration after Kennedy was elected, despite their friendship. Some suggested that, rather than ideology, his voting patterns reflected a desire to aid his law firm's clients and his campaign contributors. After Johnson became president, Smathers remained a powerful force in the Senate and frequently advised the president. He opposed the nomination of THURGOOD MARSHALL to the Supreme Court and the Civil Rights Act of 1964. After the enfranchisement of some 300,000 African Americans in Florida in 1964, however, Smathers became more liberal on many domestic issues. Although he voted against adding Medicare to the amendments to Social Security in 1964, when the entire bill, including Medicare, came to the floor, Smathers voted for it. He also supported the Voting Rights Act of 1965. His attempts to satisfy his constituents and his continuing efforts to aid the associations and businesses that supported his campaigns resulted in a sometimes contradictory voting pattern during the Johnson administration. Smathers remained a powerful force in the Senate during the 1960s, but toward the latter part of the decade, as many of his business dealings became known, he became the target of frequent charges of influence peddling. Claiming poor health, he did not seek reelection in 1968. After leaving the Senate, Smathers stayed in Washington, where he practiced law and established a lucrative lobbying practice that represented a powerful alliance of rail, trucking, and water transportation interests. He served on the board of directors of Winn-Dixie Stores, Inc., and Aerodex, a defense contractor. Smathers died on a private island near Miami, Florida, on January 20, 2007.

—MSM

Smith, Earl E. T.
(1903–1991) *ambassador to Cuba*

The son of a prominent New York family, Smith was born in Newport, Rhode Island, on July 8, 1903. After attending Yale University from 1926 to 1928, he became a founding member of Paige, Smith & Remick, an investment brokerage firm, in 1920. He remained with the firm until the late 1930s. President Franklin D. Roosevelt appointed Smith to the Office of Production Management, later the War Production Board, in 1941. Smith served in the U.S. Air Army during World War II and was discharged as a lieutenant colonel. During the 1950s, he actively entered Republican politics, serving from 1954 to 1955 as chairman of the Florida State Finance Committee and from 1954 to 1956 as a member of the Republican National Finance Committee.

In June 1957, Eisenhower appointed Smith ambassador to Cuba. Smith had no diplomatic experience and did not speak Spanish, but he did have personal ties to Cuban political and business leaders developed over frequent trips to Cuba in the previous 30 years. Justifying his appointment, Smith said he "knew Cuba well and . . . felt I could judge the thoughts and moods of the Cuban people."

Smith's appointment marked an official change in the attitude of the State Department toward the government of General Fulgencio Batista. During the early years of the decade, the United States had supported the Cuban dictator, but by 1957 the State Department, aware of growing opposition to the repressive regime among broad segments of the Cuban population and within the United States, abandoned this policy. The outgoing ambassador, Arthur Gardner, had supported Batista uncritically; Smith was instructed to adopt a position of neutrality in the conflict between the government and the leftist rebels led by Fidel Castro.

Smith's initial activities as ambassador reflected the change in policy. Arriving in Cuba in mid-July, he quickly created an image that differed markedly from that of his predecessor. In a press conference on July 24, he said, "We have nothing substantial to make us believe [that Castro's movement] is red-inspired." After witnessing the Cuban police attack a group of Cuban mothers demonstrating against Batista's regime, Smith issued a statement deploring the "excessive police action." The statement concerned Eisenhower, who thought it unwise for an "ambassador to make statements about local conditions." Secretary of State JOHN FOSTER DULLES told the president that Smith's reaction was "technically incorrect"; nevertheless, Dulles thought that Smith's indiscretion was "a human thing to do."

As the revolt in Cuba progressed, the State Department remained divided over which side to support. Smith, however, became increasingly anti-Castro. He believed that Castro's movement was infiltrated by communists, that Castro would fail to honor international obligations or foreign investments, and that communists would benefit from the overthrow of Batista. Smith advised Washington to support Batista, who had promised to hold fair elections, at least until an alternative to Castro could be found. In early 1958, the Batista government used U.S. military equipment to quell disturbances in Cienfuegos in violation of a military assistance agreement with the United States signed in 1951. Moreover, in bombing rebel positions, Batista's air force inflicted heavy civilian casualties. In reaction, the anti-Batista faction in the State Department convinced the administration to end arms shipments to the dictator in March 1958. Smith vigorously opposed the action, which he maintained only weakened the chances of eventual constitutional order in Cuba. Smith's diplomacy came apart in November 1958, when Batista rigged the election

to ensure a victory for his chosen candidate, Dr. Andrés Rivero Aguero. Although disappointed by the fraudulent elections, Smith considered Rivero Aguero preferable to Castro and unsuccessfully urged the Eisenhower administration to recognize him. In December 1958, Smith, under instructions from Washington, reluctantly informed Batista that "the United States will no longer support the present government of Cuba."

Although the Eisenhower administration opposed Castro's movement, it remained unconvinced that Castro was a communist or that he posed a threat to the United States. On December 31, 1958, Batista fled Cuba, and Castro took power. Whatever its misgivings about the new regime, the Eisenhower administration was prepared to try to establish a working relationship with it. The State Department quickly extended recognition to the new government. At the urging of Undersecretary of State CHRISTIAN HERTER, Eisenhower reluctantly replaced Smith with Philip W. Bonsal, the ambassador to Bolivia and a career diplomat who had long advocated social and economic reform in Latin America. Eisenhower accepted Smith's resignation on January 20, 1959.

During hearings before the Subcommittee to Investigate the Administration of the Internal Security Act and Other Internal Security Laws in 1960, Smith charged that the Central Intelligence Agency, officials in the State Department, officials connected with the U.S. embassy in Cuba, and "segments of the press" had contributed to Batista's downfall. Acknowledging that the Batista government "was overthrown because of corruption, disintegration from within," he maintained that "we helped overthrow the Batista dictatorship which was pro-American only to install the Castro dictatorship which is pro-Russian." Smith published an account of the Cuban Revolution in his book, *The Fourth Floor* (1962), in which he argued that Castro's victory was a disaster for both Cuba and the United States and one that could have been avoided.

After his resignation from government service, Smith returned to his business interests. He became director of the Bank of Palm Beach and Trust Corporation and the U.S. Sugar Corporation. President JOHN F. KENNEDY offered him a position as ambassador to Switzerland, which Smith declined because Switzerland managed American interests in Cuba. He remained active in Republican politics and was a member of the Republican platform committee in 1960 and 1980. Smith served as mayor of Palm Beach from 1971 to 1977. President Ronald W. Reagan appointed him to the Presidential Commission on Broadcasting to Cuba in 1982. Smith died at his home in Palm Beach, Florida, on February 15, 1991.

—MSM

Smith, Gerald L(yman) K(enneth)
(1898–1976) *national director, Christian Nationalist Crusade*

The son of a poor farmer and evangelical preacher, Gerald L. K. Smith was born in Pardeeville, Wisconsin, on February 27, 1898. Raised in small towns in Wisconsin, he graduated from Viroqua High School, where he was a champion debater, and in 1918 from Valparaiso University in Indiana. At the age of 19, Smith heard a spiritual call and became a minister in the Disciples of Christ Church, the same denomination for which his father and grandfather preached. In 1929, he moved to Louisiana for his wife's health and took a position as minister of the Kings Highway Christian Church in Shreveport. Smith's popularity as a preacher helped double the church's membership. He proved an adept fundraiser and began a series of local radio broadcasts.

Smith was also active as a social reformer and union organizer. From his arrival in Louisiana, Smith had admired Huey P. Long. Smith developed a personal relationship with Long when the preacher urged the governor to support legislation to protect homeowners from foreclosures on their mortgages. After Long won election to the U.S. Senate, Smith periodically visited him in Washington. When Long returned to Louisiana, Smith was a constant companion. Smith's political activities brought him into conflict with his congregation and, facing the prospect of dismissal, he resigned. After briefly associating himself with William Dudley Pelley, a fascist who openly based his organization on Adolf Hitler's Nazi Party, Smith joined Long's staff. When, in 1934, Long launched the "Share Our Wealth" crusade, a populist movement to redistribute income and build public projects, Smith became an orga-

nizer for the Share Our Wealth Society. Smith's oratorical skills won the admiration of no less an authority than H. L. Mencken, who called him "the greatest rabble-rouser since Peter the Hermit" and "the champion boob-bumper of all epochs." Smith's intense devotion to Long eventually made even "the Kingfish" uncomfortable.

Following Long's assassination in September 1935, Smith appointed himself Long's successor and scrambled to maintain control of the Share Our Wealth movement, but he encountered opposition from other members of the Long machine, most of whom despised him. Immediately after Long's assassination, Smith made sensational charges of conspiracies, and several days after the funeral, his opponents had him arrested for incitement to riot and deported from Louisiana. Unlike Long, who had avoided race baiting, Smith moved the Share Our Wealth movement in the direction of white supremacy. In fact, however, he was leading a movement that no longer existed. He had no funds or base of support. Indeed, he lacked access to the organization's mailing lists or even an office.

Looking for a new movement, Smith then affiliated himself with Dr. Francis E. Townsend, a doctor from California who proposed generous pensions for old people, providing they retired and spent the pensions. This, Townsend argued, would both take care of the elderly and, by increasing purchasing power, end the depression. An ardent opponent of President Franklin Roosevelt, whom he characterized as "Franklin Delano Jewsvelt," Smith joined with Townsend and Father Charles Coughlin, a priest who had a huge radio following for his anti-Semitic ravings, to found the Union Party in 1936. The party nominated William Lemke, a member of Congress from North Dakota, for president. Lemke received fewer than a million votes. After the failure of the Union Party, Smith moved to Detroit and founded the Committee of One Million, a racist, anti-Semitic, and isolationist organization. Following the Japanese attack on Pearl Harbor, Smith, in 1942, founded a racist, pro-fascist paper *The Cross and the Flag*, which soon found its way onto the Attorney General's list of seditious publications. He also founded the America First party and ran for the U.S. Senate in 1942; he finished a distant third. Smith formed the Christian Nationalist party and ran for president as its candidate in 1944, 1948, and 1956. A fringe candidate, he failed to get on the ballot in most states. Smith founded the Christian Nationalist Crusade in 1947 to realize his dream of "a white, Christian America." Its platform called for "deportation of Zionists," the breakup of "Jewish Gestapo organizations," the deportation of blacks to Africa, and the dissolution of the United Nations.

After the war, Smith toured the nation giving anti-Semitic harangues, for which he drew large crowds. He supported Senator JOSEPH R. McCAR-THY's (R-Wis.) crusade against communists in government. In 1952, Smith denounced Republican presidential candidate DWIGHT EISENHOWER as "a Swedish Jew" and hence unfit for office. That year, he supported General Douglas MacArthur for president. Vice President RICHARD NIXON's humble Protestant beginnings and anticommunism appealed to Smith. Running for reelection in 1956, Nixon received Smith's unsolicited support, which he immediately disavowed.

Smith denounced the Supreme Court's decisions banning segregation in public schools and asserting constitutional protection for works he deemed pornographic. On many occasions, he demanded that "the pro-criminal, pro-Communist, pro-pornographic Supreme Court must be impeached." He castigated Congress as "impotent, insipid and cowardly" when it passed civil rights legislation in 1957 and that same year called Senator McCarthy's death "murder." Smith characterized himself as "the persecuted victim of a gang of international character assassins" that had destroyed McCarthy, dismissed MacArthur during the Korean conflict, and campaigned to "destroy" the House Un-American Activities Committee.

As the 1950s progressed, Smith devoted himself increasingly to writing. He continued to publish *The Cross and the Flag* and began a newsletter for his followers. Moving his home base to Los Angeles in 1953, he fulminated against the welfare state, desegregation of the races, and fluoridation of water. Continually appealing for funds from his followers, Smith amassed a fortune by the end of the decade. Some observers speculated that Smith was motivated purely by financial gain. "Religion and patriotism, keep going on that, it's the only way you can really get them het up," he said, "and then a

fellow like myself . . . will have the people with him hook, line and sinker. I'll teach them how to hate."

Smith's views became even more extreme and his popularity declined in the late 1950s. In 1964, he moved to Eureka Springs, Arkansas, where he erected a seven-story statue of Jesus, the Christ of the Ozarks. He added a Bible museum and a Christian art gallery. In 1968, he began staging an anti-Semitic passion play that aroused considerable controversy. Smith's entrepreneurship and aggressive fund-raising enabled him to maintain lavish homes in Los Angeles, Tulsa, and Eureka Springs. He died in Los Angeles, California, on April 15, 1976.

—MSM

Smith, H. Alexander
(1880–1966) *U.S. senator*

The son of a physician, Smith was born in New York City on January 30, 1880. He attended Cutler School in New York City, graduated from Princeton University in 1901, and earned his law degree from Columbia University in 1904. After gaining admission to the New York bar, he suffered an attack of tuberculosis and in 1905 moved to Colorado to regain his health. He opened a law practice there and also pursued interests in mining, public utilities, railroads, and real estate. Deeply influenced by his Princeton professor Woodrow Wilson's idea of an international organization to prevent wars, Smith joined the League to Enforce Peace. When the United States entered World War I, Smith worked for the Federal Food Administration as HERBERT HOOVER's assistant. After the war, he participated in Hoover's European relief program. Smith then returned to Princeton in 1919 as the university's executive secretary, where he supervised the modernization of the curriculum. He held that post until 1927, when he became a lecturer in the Department of Politics. In 1932, Smith resumed the practice of law with a prestigious New York law firm.

A lifelong Republican, Smith worked for the election of Hoover as president in 1928 and 1932. In 1934, he became the treasurer of the Republican Party of New Jersey and seven years later was elected state party chairman. He was a member of the Republican National Committee from 1942 to 1943. Campaigning on a platform that stressed acceptance of the country's increasing role in world affairs, Smith won election to fill a vacant seat in the U.S. Senate from New Jersey in 1944. He was reelected in 1946 and 1952.

In the Senate, Smith continued to support U.S. involvement in world affairs. He backed American entry into the United Nations and supported the Truman administration on most issues relating to foreign policy, including aid to Greece and Turkey and the Marshall Plan. On the question of policy toward China, however, he broke with the president. Smith joined such supporters of the Nationalist government as Senator WILLIAM KNOWLAND (R-Calif.) in advocating all-out aid to the Nationalists in the civil war against the Communists. When the Nationalist government fell in 1949, Smith joined the so-called China bloc in the Senate that pressed the government to refuse to recognize the Communist regime and to oppose its entry into the UN.

Smith maintained his militant stand on China throughout the Eisenhower administration. He was a member of the steering panel of the Committee of One Million, founded in 1953 to prevent the admission of Communist China to the UN. The following year, he traveled to Taiwan and returned to the United States reporting that Chiang Kai-shek urged the United States to give him the "green light" for an invasion of the mainland. In January 1955, Smith said he would favor a UN blockade of the mainland as a last-ditch action to free U.S. prisoners of war held by the Communists. During the Quemoy and Matsu crisis of 1958, when Communist China renewed shelling the Nationalist-held offshore islands, the senator said the United States should definitely fight to prevent Communist seizure of the islands.

Smith was troubled by the way Senator JOSEPH R. MCCARTHY (R-Wis.) conducted his anticommunist crusade. While he never publicly attacked McCarthy, he did express support for Senator MARGARET CHASE SMITH's (R-Me.) Declaration of Conscience and did take to the floor of the Senate to defend Ambassador Philip C. Jessup, one of McCarthy's targets. Known as a conciliator in the Senate, Smith sought to moderate calls to censure McCarthy in 1954. On June 15, Senator RALPH FLANDERS (R-Vt.) announced that within two weeks he would introduce a resolution to censure the Wis-

consin Republican. The measure would state that McCarthy's conduct was "unbecoming a member of the United States Senate . . . contrary to senatorial tradition, and tended to bring the Senate into disrepute, and such conduct is thereby condemned." One week later, on July 31, Smith proposed that the Senate discard the Flanders resolution in favor of one providing for a special committee of three Republicans and three Democrats, with Vice President RICHARD M. NIXON as ex-officio chairman, to study "problems created by the fact that there had been infiltration of Communists and others security risks into sensitive positions and the method and procedures employed in exposing and eliminating such security risks." Smith's plan never got off the ground. The following week, Smith, in a television interview, said that the move to censure "had embarrassed" his efforts to get McCarthy to go to Eisenhower with an "offer to work with the government and not against it." Smith, however, voted for the condemnation of the senator in December 1954.

In general, Smith supported the foreign policy of the Eisenhower administration. He differed more frequently with Eisenhower on domestic matters. Smith believed in voluntary desegregation of schools ("You'll never do it with paratroopers," he said.), the right of states to pass right to work laws, and that an expanding national government posed a threat to individual freedom. Quiet, thoughtful, and deeply religious, Smith believed that reform had to come from a spiritual awakening, rather than a coercive central government.

Smith decided not to seek reelection to the Senate in 1958. He then served as special consultant to the secretary of state from 1959 to 1960. In 1959, he attended the Colombo Conference at which he proposed an ambitious American foreign aid program for Asia. Smith then retired from public life. He died in Princeton, New Jersey, on October 27, 1966.

—MSM

Smith, Howard W(orth)

(1883–1976) *U.S. congressman; chairman, House Rules Committee*

Born in Broad Run, Virginia, on February 2, 1883, Smith attended the Bethel Military Academy and received his Bachelor of Laws degree from the

University of Virginia in 1903. After graduating, he practiced law in Alexandria and invested in real estate. He was assistant general counsel to the Alien Property Custodian in 1917 and 1918 and commonwealth attorney of Alexandria from 1918 to 1922. He served as judge of the Alexandria Corporation Court from 1922 to 1928 and judge of the 16th Circuit Court of Virginia from 1928 to 1930. Elected as a Democrat to the House of Representatives in 1930, he won reelection 17 consecutive times before failing to gain the Democratic nomination in 1966.

Judge Smith, as he preferred to be called, established a conservative record in the House. He consistently opposed civil rights legislation and what he regarded as excessive federal spending. By the late 1930s, he became a member of the conservative coalition of southern Democrats and conservative Republicans who resisted the programs of President Franklin D. Roosevelt and the New Deal. The president and labor unions unsuccessfully attempted to defeat Smith in the Democratic primary in 1938. During the 1940s, he became known principally as the author of the Smith Act (1939), which gave the government the right to prosecute anyone advocating the violent overthrow of the U.S. government, and of the Smith-Connally Wartime Labor Disputes Act (1943), which was passed during World War II and limited the right to strike during national emergencies.

In 1955, Smith became chair of the Rules Committee. Often called the "third house" of Congress, this panel determined the length and manner of floor debate on a bill and whether the House should enter into conference with the Senate if the two bodies passed different, but similar, bills. Polls taken by legislators and journalists consistently ranked Smith as one of the most powerful men on Capitol Hill—second only to House Speaker SAM RAYBURN (D-Tex.). Smith was often called "the traffic cop of the House" (a term he resented), because he controlled what bills his committee should vote on and whether they should proceed to the floor. He used the Rules Committee's power, its universal reach, and its byzantine procedures to obstruct measures that would have increased Social Security coverage, public housing, and the minimum wage.

Smith used all his legislative skill to block civil rights legislation. He bragged that he had defeated every civil rights measure introduced since the early 1930s. In March 1956, he joined 100 other southern members of Congress in signing the Southern Manifesto. This declaration denounced the Supreme Court's 1954 public school desegregation decision and pledged to fight it through every lawful means. Smith introduced it into the House, where he presented a fiery defense of states rights against federal usurpation of local power. He said that he had "a sacred obligation" to warn his fellow Americans that the decision contravened the Constitution.

In 1956 and 1957, Smith attempted to prevent passage of a civil rights bill backed by the Eisenhower administration. A bill passed the House in 1956, only to die in the Senate. Supporters reintroduced the measure the following year. In August 1957, the House leadership called a meeting with Smith to clear the way for the full chamber to consider the measure. Smith, however, could not be found in Washington. His office finally informed the public that he had needed to return to one of his dairy farms because a barn had burned down. Rayburn humorously stated he knew that Smith would have done anything to prevent a vote on the bill, "but I never suspected he would resort to arson." Smith delayed committee consideration of a civil rights bill for over a month and was finally forced, as a result of a petition from his own committee, to hold hearings. He then arranged for a large number of opponents to testify before his panel in a further attempt to stall the bill. However, because the administration and leaders in the House favored the measure, Smith finally was forced to report it favorably to the House floor. The House passed the bill in June, and it became the Civil Rights Act of 1957.

In 1960, Smith almost succeeded in killing the central portion of another civil rights bill, which provided for voting referees to enroll black voters. He and his fellow southern Democrats supported an amendment supported by liberals in the hope that Republicans would then join them in voting down the whole section. The amended segment of the bill was voted down. However, the Republicans offered a new plan that was similar to the original version. Ultimately, Smith could not prevent passage of the Voting Rights Act of 1960.

A fiscal conservative who opposed the expansion of federal government spending, Smith was more successful in blocking or slowing down legislation related to housing and education. During the last days of the 85th Congress (1957–58), Smith avoided holding hearings on a dozen major bills, including relief to depressed areas and mineral subsidies, by simply disappearing. He returned after a week, saying "he had had some hay on his farm that needed tending."

In April 1956, the Supreme Court ruled that states had no power to punish persons for advocating the forcible overthrow of the federal government. Smith disagreed with the decision and introduced legislation giving the states the right to pass their own acts. The measure failed.

Smith's power began to decline in the 1960s. During the Kennedy administration, Speaker Sam Rayburn engineered reforms that enlarged the Rules Committee and changed its procedures, effectively reducing Smith's power. This paved the way for civil rights and liberal legislation that the aged congressman opposed. After LYNDON B. JOHNSON became president, Smith attempted to kill what became the Civil Rights Act of 1964 by adding an amendment barring sex discrimination. The measure passed with Smith's amendment. As a result of reapportionment, he lost the primary election in 1966. Smith then resumed his practice of law and tended to his dairy farms. He died in Alexandria, Virginia, on October 3, 1976.

—MSM

Smith, Margaret Chase

(1897–1995) *U.S. senator*

The daughter of a barber, Margaret Chase was born in Skowhegan, Maine, on December 14, 1897. After graduating from Skowhegan High School in 1916, she taught in a local primary school. In 1917, she began working as a switchboard operator and later as an executive of the local telephone company. Beginning in 1919, she worked in the circulation, advertising, and editorial departments of the *Skowhegan Independent Reporter,* a weekly newspaper. She left the paper after eight years to become

office manager of a local textile mill. In May 1930, Chase married Clyde Harold Smith, a wealthy and prominent Republican 23 years her senior who served in the U.S. House of Representatives from 1936 to 1940. When Representative Smith died in 1940, Margaret Chase Smith won a special election in June 1940 to fill his seat. She was reelected in November 1940, 1942, 1944, and 1946.

In the House, Smith supported military preparedness and an internationalist foreign policy. She voted for the Selective Service Act in 1940 and Lend-Lease in 1941. Later, she voted with the six other congresswomen to defeat the House proposal withdrawing half of the funds for day-care facilities for wartime factory workers. After the war, she continued to support a strong military. Appointed to the new Armed Services Committee in 1947, she fought for the Woman's Armed Services Integration Act of 1948, which improved the status of women in the military. On purely domestic matters, Smith demonstrated a strong independent streak. Although strongly supported by Maine's organized labor movement, she voted with other Republicans to override President Truman's veto of the Taft-Hartley bill in 1947. She had backed the Dies Committee's investigation of un-American activities in 1945 but did not support the establishment of a permanent House Un-American Activities Committee in 1950.

Smith decided to run for an open seat in the U.S. Senate in 1948 and became the first woman to hold a seat in that body without first having been appointed to it. She won reelection in 1954, 1960, and 1966. In the Senate, Smith became one of the first senators to condemn Senator JOSEPH R. McCARTHY's (R-Wis.) anticommunist crusade. She had served with McCarthy on the Executive Expenditures Committee, and they had become good friends. She came to realize, however, that the documents McCarthy often distributed did not support his charges. On June 1, 1950, she made a speech introducing a Declaration of Conscience, a statement attacking McCarthy that she and six other senators had signed. In that speech, she declared that "the greatest deliberative body in the world . . . has . . . been debased to the level of a forum of hate and character assassination sheltered by the shield of congressional immunity." She concluded that she did not "want to see the Republican Party ride to victory on the four horsemen of calumny—fear, ignorance, bigotry, and smear." McCarthy responded by sneeringly referring to the signers of the Declaration of Conscience as "Snow White and the Six Dwarfs." Subsequently, McCarthy supported her opponent in Maine's Republican primary of 1954, but Smith won by a margin of five to one. That December, Smith voted in favor of censuring the Wisconsin Republican. Perhaps because of these efforts, Lee Mortimer and Jack Lait implied in their book, *U.S.A. Confidential,* that Smith was pro-communist, an allegation that led Smith to bring a successful suit for libel in 1956. She was awarded $1 million.

An independent senator, Smith joined Republicans in supporting the reduction of funds for the Tennessee Valley Authority and voting for state ownership of offshore oil in 1953. She also backed civil rights legislation supported by the Eisenhower administration in 1957 and 1960. However, Smith voted for the Democratic depressed areas bill in 1959, despite Eisenhower's opposition. She also voted against LEWIS L. STRAUSS, Eisenhower's nominee for secretary of commerce, in 1959. Another demonstration of her independence came when she proposed a constitutional amendment in December 1960 providing for the direct nomination and election of the president and the vice president and the elimination of the electoral college.

As an active member of the Senate Armed Services Committee, Smith chaired a five-member subcommittee in 1953 to investigate a shortage of ammunition in Korea. Maintaining her support for a strong military, she voted with the Democrats, over Republican objections, for an additional half million dollars for the air force beyond Eisenhower's request in 1956.

During the administrations of JOHN F. KENNEDY and LYNDON B. JOHNSON, Smith was one of only a few Republicans who generally supported the domestic policies of those administrations. On the other hand, she accused the Kennedy administration of lacking the will to use nuclear weapons when necessary and opposed the nuclear test ban treaty in 1963. The ranking Republican on the Armed Services Committee after 1967, Smith consistently voted for expenditures for the Vietnam War. She answered 2,941 consecutive roll calls in the Senate until a hip operation in 1968 forced her to miss a vote. During the Nixon administration, she opposed the Safeguard antiballistic missile system and the supersonic transport. In 1970, she stated that those on the radical Left who advocated violence and shouted down their opponents posed at least as great a threat as McCarthy and the radical Right had in the early 1950s. Smith was defeated for reelection in November 1972. She died at her home in Skowhegan on May 29, 1995.

—MSM

Smith, Walter Bedell
(1895–1961) *undersecretary of state*

A descendent of 18th-century settlers, Smith was born in Indianapolis, Indiana, on October 5, 1895. From early childhood, he wanted to be an army officer. A talented but indifferent student, he lacked the record or influence to gain an appointment to West Point. He became a private in the Indiana National Guard in 1911, while attending St. Peter and Paul's School. Within a year, he became company sergeant and in 1916 went with his unit to participate in the expedition to Mexico. When the United States entered World War I, he went to officer training school and was deployed to France as a second lieutenant. After being wounded in action along the Marne, he was assigned to the Bureau of Military Intelligence in the War Department, the first of a series of staff positions in which he demonstrated exceptional skills as a manager. Promoted to first lieutenant during the war, he received a regular army commission after the passage of the National Defense Act of 1920. During the 1920s, Smith was assigned to the Bureau of the Budget and in 1929 went to the Philippines, where he received his promotion to captain. Advancement came gradually during the interwar years, but at the infantry school Smith impressed Major Omar N. Bradley and General George C. Marshall. He also attended command and general staff school and the Army War College. When George C. Marshall became chief of staff, he named Major Smith to be assistant to the secretary of the general staff. Smith's loyalty, competence, and willingness to accept responsibility greatly impressed Marshall. Promoted to lieutenant colonel and then to colonel, Smith became secretary to the general staff in September 1941. He was a brigadier general in 1942, when he became General DWIGHT D. EISENHOWER's chief of staff. Promoted to major general, Smith oversaw Eisenhower's headquarters and managed the staff. Brusque and irascible, Smith's personality differed markedly from that of the genial and generally conciliatory Eisenhower. The two men developed a close relationship and made a formidable team. Smith served as Eisenhower's sounding board, trusted confidante, and troubleshooter. He helped to plan and coordinate the invasions of North Africa and Italy, and in 1943 he negotiated the surrender of Italy. Promoted to lieutenant general in early 1944, Smith helped plan the invasion of France later that year. Eisenhower assigned him responsibility for negotiating the surrender of Nazi Germany. Immediately following World War II, Smith served as the chief of staff of the American occupation forces in Germany. He returned to Washington in January 1946 as chief of the Operations and Planning Division of the Joint Chiefs of Staff.

In February 1946, President HARRY S. TRUMAN appointed Smith ambassador to the Soviet Union, an experience he later described in his book *My Three Years in Moscow* (1950). His time in the Soviet Union turned Smith into a hard-line cold warrior. He returned home in 1949 to resume his military career as commander of the first army. In September 1950, Truman appointed him head of the Central Intelligence Agency (CIA).

Smith resigned from the CIA in 1953 to become undersecretary of state. Because JOHN FOSTER DULLES focused on formulating policy and traveling abroad, Smith held the major responsibility for administering the State Department. He expected to function as a close adviser to Eisenhower and to have substantial influence on the administration's foreign policy, but Dulles's centralization of decision making in his own hands frustrated Smith's expectations.

In spring 1954, Smith headed the National Security Council's Special Committee on the United States and Indochina, formed to study the American response to the deteriorating situation in French Indochina. By that time, the French had concluded that without massive American aid the

beleaguered fortress of Dien Bien Phu would fall to the Viet Minh. The committee issued a report advocating equipping and training an effective force drawn from the people of the associated states and recommending the creation of a mutual Asian defense treaty, underwritten by the major Western powers, to protect Southeast Asia from further communist aggression. The report contributed to the decision to create the Southeast Asia Treaty Organization later that year.

Desperate to maintain the post at Dien Bien Phu, the French chief of staff, General Paul Henry Ely, asked Eisenhower for direct American military intervention in March. In early April, Eisenhower held a meeting with five of his most trusted advisers to discuss Indochina. Smith, joined by Dulles and Admiral ARTHUR W. RADFORD, argued for American military intervention, if the conditions Eisenhower had set were met. Those conditions involved the use of a multinational force, including Asian forces from the Philippines and Thailand, and French guarantees of independence for the associated states.

In an interview with CBS television on April 11, Smith explained the importance of Indochina for American strategy and economic interests in Asia. If this area fell to the communists, he predicted, the other free states would fall like dominoes to the enemy. Many observers considered Smith to be one of the leading hawks in the administration.

With the opening of the Geneva Conference on Korea and Indochina on April 26, and the fall of Dien Bien Phu on May 7, 1954, Smith privately conceded that Vietnam would be partitioned into a communist-controlled northern zone and a Western-dominated southern area. Smith succeeded Dulles as head of the U.S. delegation to the Geneva Conference. He was instructed to play a passive role and not approve any settlement that would turn territory over to the communists. He announced that the United States "took note" of the Geneva settlement on July 24 that temporarily partitioned Vietnam until free elections could be held.

Smith resigned from the State Department in October 1954 and became vice president of the American Machine and Foundry Company. He continued to serve as an unofficial adviser to Eisenhower and Dulles on disarmament matters, was appointed to a committee to study mutual security, and served on a number of corporate boards. He also wrote a second book, *Eisenhower's Six Great Decisions: Europe 1944–1945*, published in 1956. Smith died in Washington, D.C., on August 9, 1961.

—MSM

Smylie, Robert E.

(1914–2004) *governor of Idaho*

Born in Marcus, Idaho, on October 31, 1914, Robert E. Smylie graduated from the College of Idaho in 1938 and earned a law degree at George Washington University in 1942. Following service in the coast guard during World War II, he practiced law and became active in Republican politics in Idaho. He became deputy attorney general in 1947. Later that year, the attorney general, Robert Ailshie, died, and the governor of Idaho appointed Smylie to complete Ailshie's term. A year later, Smylie won election to the office and served until 1954. In office, he became deeply involved in the controversy over private versus federal development of a hydroelectric dam in Hell's Canyon on the Snake River.

During the early years of the Eisenhower administration, Smylie emerged as a prominent critic of federal development of hydroelectric power. He opposed the federal plan for a high dam, because he feared that the loss of state control of water rights would result in the diversion of water to neighboring states and because the giant dam would despoil the scenic Hell's Canyon area. Smylie favored the private development of three smaller dams spread along the Snake River. He faced opposition from other governors in the Northwest, powerful members of Congress from Idaho, and Oregon's senator WAYNE MORSE (Ind.-Oreg.), who argued that the dam was necessary for a cheap hydroelectric power system throughout the Northwest. In 1954, Smylie ran for governor of Idaho on a plank opposing the dam. In a state more concerned with water rights than cheap electrical power, Smylie won the election by 50,000 votes.

As governor, Smylie continued to oppose the dam. In hearings before the Senate Interior Committee in April 1955, he testified that federal development would be "tragic" and called for its "swift rejection," declaring that "75 percent of the people of Idaho" agreed with his position. A year later, in July 1956, the Senate killed the bill that would have authorized a federal hydroelectric plant at Hell's Canyon.

Smylie went on to serve two more terms as governor. During his last term, he obtained passage of a sales tax to support local schools, extended the state's parks and recreation program, and established a water resources board. He opposed gambling in Idaho, but the state legislature passed a measure providing for pari-mutuel betting over his veto. Smylie opposed Senator BARRY GOLDWATER'S (R-Ariz.) bid for the Republican presidential nomination in 1964. After Goldwater won the nomination, Smylie supported him only reluctantly. After Goldwater's devastating defeat, Smylie attempted to oust Dean Burch, a supporter of Goldwater, as head of the Republican National Committee. Burch subsequently resigned. Smylie's more activist agenda and his opposition to Goldwater earned him the ire of conservative Republicans in Idaho, and he lost the 1966 Republican nomination to Don Samuelson, a relative unknown. After his term expired, Smylie retired to his legal practice in Boise. He served as trustee, chair of trustees, and acting president of the University of Idaho. Smylie died in Boise on July 17, 2004.

—MSM

Sobell, Morton

(1917–) *convicted espionage agent*

Born in New York City on April 11, 1917, Sobell attended City College of New York, where he was friendly with JULIUS ROSENBERG, Joel Barr, Alfred Sarant, and Max Elitcher. After graduating in 1938, he moved to Washington, D.C., to work for the navy Bureau of Ordinance. He earned an M.A. in electrical engineering from the University of Michigan in 1942, returned briefly to the navy, and then moved to Schenectady, N.Y., to work for the General Electric Company. Later, he and his family returned to New York City, where he did research for the Reeves Instrument Company, which held government contracts for classified work.

In 1950, following the arrests and confessions of Klaus Fuchs, a British physicist who had worked on the Manhattan Project, and his courier,

Harry Gold, the Soviets alerted key members of Rosenberg's espionage ring. Two of them, Barr and Sarant, fled to Europe and later to the Soviet Union. Sobell fled with his family to Mexico, where he was arrested in August 1950 and turned over to American authorities, who charged him with conspiracy to commit espionage. Although not accused of activities related to espionage at Los Alamos, he was tried with Julius and ETHEL ROSENBERG. At the trial, evidence against him fell into two areas: testimony that he was involved in an espionage apparatus with the Rosenbergs and charges that he and his family took flight to Mexico in order to avoid his own arrest. The case against Sobell depended heavily on the testimony of Elitcher, another alleged conspirator, a former communist, and a former friend of Sobell, whom Rosenberg had recruited in 1944. Elitcher had been a high school friend of Sobell and a college classmate of Sobell and Julius Rosenberg. Sobell had invited Elitcher to join the Young Communist League (the branch was organized by Julius Rosenberg). Elitcher testified that he had accompanied Sobell on a trip to deliver material to Julius Rosenberg. He also testified that Sobell and Rosenberg had attempted to recruit him to the Communist Party and to espionage and that Sobell had asked him for classified pamphlets relating to an antisubmarine device the navy Bureau of Ordinance was developing. Lawyers for the defense did not effectively discredit Elitcher's testimony. Letters Sobell wrote from Mexico and reports of his activities there also proved damaging to him. He used a variety of aliases and, after the arrest of the Rosenbergs became public on July 18, he cashed in his family's return airplane tickets and attempted to book passage to Europe on a ship. Later, he maintained that he had been kidnaped in Mexico and delivered illegally to FBI agents at the border. Sobell was found guilty, along with the Rosenbergs, and given a maximum 30-year sentence.

From the moment of his arrest, Sobell steadfastly asserted his innocence. Many who believed the Rosenbergs had been unjustly convicted also believed that Sobell had suffered abuse at the hands of the law. In fact, many people who thought the Rosenbergs guilty still claimed that he had not received a fair trial. After the execution of the Rosenbergs, money and legal efforts that had been devoted to their defense was used to aid the Committee to Free Morton Sobell (an organization led by his wife, Helen).

On the advice of his lawyers, Sobell never testified on his own behalf during the original trial. In 1953, he regretted that action. He submitted to the Court of Appeals (which had previously upheld his conviction by a 2-1 vote) an affidavit detailing his activities before he left the United States and after he arrived in Mexico. Again he denied any involvement in espionage and challenged the government to verify his own account of events. The court rejected his appeal. Sobell learned of the rejection from a cell in Alcatraz Federal Penitentiary, where he had been transferred in late 1952. His supporters charged that the government placed him in one of the nation's most notorious prisons in order to induce him to confess to nonexistent crimes.

In 1957, the Supreme Court refused for the eighth time to review Sobell's case. The following year, he was transferred from Alcatraz to the Atlanta Penitentiary, a medium security facility. In 1963, he moved to a prison in Springfield, Missouri, for medical treatment, and in 1965 he was transferred to the federal facility in Lewisburg, Pennsylvania.

President JOHN F. KENNEDY received an appeal for clemency on behalf of Sobell that included the names and statements of MARTIN LUTHER KING, JR., Senator LEE METCALF (D-Mont.), REINHOLD NIEBUHR, scientist Harold Urey, and historian Maxwell Geismar. Kennedy declined to grant clemency.

In 1962, Sobell became eligible for parole; but it was refused. After serving 17 years and 9 months in prison, he was released in 1969 with time off for good behavior. He again faced court proceedings in 1971, when his parole board denied him permission to attend anti–Vietnam War demonstrations or speak before a communist-sponsored group. Sobell filed suit, charging violation of his constitutional rights. Terming the parole board's reasons for denial "silly," a federal judge decided for Sobell. In 1974, Sobell wrote *On Doing Time*, a book describing the background of his case and his experiences in federal prisons. He returned to school to update his education and training and then worked as an engineer in medical electronics. In their book, *The Rosenberg File* (1983), Ronald Radosh and Joyce Milton concluded that "though by no means the complete innocent he has always publicly claimed to be, Morton Sobell was a peripheral figure in Rosenberg's espionage ring." Sobell continued to maintain his innocence, even after release of the Venona intercepts in 1995, which appeared conclusively to identify him as a Soviet spy. In *Engineering Communism: How Two Americans Spied for Stalin and Founded the Soviet Silicon Valley* (2005), Steven T. Usdin, a writer on science policy, argued convincingly that Barr, Salant, and Sobell passed to the Soviets technology that proved "extremely valuable to the USSR, especially during the early years of the cold war." In September 2008, Sobell admitted to an interviewer that he had been a spy.

Sobeloff, Simon E(rnest)

(1894–1973) *U.S. solicitor general, court of appeals judge*

The son of Russian Jewish immigrants, Sobeloff was born in Baltimore, Maryland, on December 3, 1894. At the age of 12, he went to work in the law office of William F. Broening. After serving as a page in the U.S. House of Representatives, he attended Loyola College in Baltimore from 1911 to 1912 and graduated from the University of Maryland School of Law in 1915. While still in law school, Sobeloff clerked for the chief judge of the supreme bench of Baltimore and was admitted to the bar in 1914. After graduating, he began to practice law. Over the next 25 years, Sobeloff established a successful private legal practice, which was frequently interrupted by his appointment to public positions. He served as assistant city solicitor in Baltimore (1919–23), as deputy city solicitor (1927–31), and as U.S. attorney for Maryland (1931–34). Although he returned to private practice in 1934, he continued public service in a number of capacities. He remained on the unemployment commission and served as labor arbitrator for the garment industry in Baltimore. An outspoken opponent of racial discrimination, Sobeloff testified before Congress in support of a federal antilynching bill in 1934. The following year, Judge Eugene O'Dunne appointed him to investigate the failure of the Baltimore Trust Company.

Sobeloff was a close friend and adviser of THEODORE ROOSEVELT McKELDIN, a rising liberal Republican politician, and when McKeldin became mayor of Baltimore in 1943, he chose Sobeloff as city solicitor. After the Democrats won the city elections in 1947, the new mayor prevailed on Sobeloff to remain as city solicitor. Later in the year, Sobeloff returned to private practice, but he continued to serve as counsel to the Baltimore Housing Authority and as a legal consultant to the mayor. Sobeloff took an active role in McKeldin's campaign for governor of Maryland in 1950. After McKeldin won the election, Sobeloff served as "first minister" in the governor's "kitchen cabinet," and McKeldin appointed Sobeloff to head a special commission on the reorganization of state government. In April 1952, McKeldin and Sobeloff went to Paris to urge General DWIGHT D. EISENHOWER to seek the Republican nomination that year. That summer, Sobeloff wrote the speech with which McKeldin nominated Eisenhower at the Republican National Convention. Eisenhower won the Republican nomination and went on to defeat ADLAI E. STEVENSON in the general election. In December 1952, McKeldin appointed Sobeloff chief judge of the Maryland court of appeals, the state's highest court.

Eisenhower nominated Sobeloff to be solicitor general of the United States in January 1954, and the Senate confirmed the nomination on February 25. As solicitor general, Sobeloff represented the federal government before the Supreme Court and decided which cases to appeal from lower to higher federal courts. In 1955, Sobeloff presented the government's case regarding the implementation of *Brown v. Board of Education* (1954), which held segregated public schools unconstitutional. In that decision, the Court had called for further argument on how to implement its ruling. The solicitor general proposed a plan that gave local school boards primary responsibility for developing desegregation plans, which would then be reviewed by the district courts. The government's plan further recommended that the Supreme Court should instruct district judges to approve programs for gradual integration as long as they made a prompt and reasonable start toward desegregation. At the same time, Sobeloff contended, district courts should be instructed not to let local officials frustrate the process of school desegregation. In its decision of May 31, 1955, known as *Brown II*, the Supreme Court

Swearing-in of Simon E. Sobeloff as solicitor general of the United States, February 25, 1954 *(Dwight D. Eisenhower Library and Museum)*

unanimously adopted a position very similar to that put forward by Sobeloff, but it did not include the government's suggestion of a 90-day deadline for school districts to propose an acceptable plan to desegregate.

Sobeloff split with the administration over the issue of internal security. He overruled attorneys who wanted to appeal a district judge's dismissal of the indictment of Owen Lattimore, a professor at Johns Hopkins and expert on Asia who had been indicted for perjury after his testimony before a congressional committee. Sobeloff came into direct conflict with the administration over the case of John P. Peters, a professor of medicine at Yale University who had been a consultant to

the U.S. Public Health Service until dismissed as a security risk under the Truman administration's loyalty program. After Peters was cleared by the agency's loyalty board, the Civil Service Commission Loyalty Review Board reviewed the matter and recommended Peters's dismissal. The board refused to reveal the source or nature of the information it had against Peters, and the doctor challenged the board's procedures in court. Skeptical about the evidence against Peters and dissatisfied with the procedures, Sobeloff proposed that the government confess error. When the administration decided to press the case, Sobeloff refused to argue the government's position. Although Sobeloff defended the government's position in other loyalty and security cases, he refused to do so in this instance because he considered the board's methods a violation of due process. Assistant Attorney General WARREN E. BURGER argued for the government. The Supreme Court decided the case in Peters's favor in June 1955 but did so on narrow, technical grounds.

On July 14, 1955, Eisenhower nominated Soboloff to a judgeship on the Fourth Circuit Court of Appeals, which included Maryland, Virginia, West Virginia, North Carolina, and South Carolina. Southern Democratic senators, led by Olin D. Johnston (D-S.C.), opposed the appointment because of Soboloff's opposition to segregation and his participation in the *Brown* case. They managed to prevent action on the nomination until Congress adjourned. Eisenhower resubmitted the nomination in 1956. After a long and bitter confirmation battle, the Senate finally approved Soboloff's nomination on July 16, 1956, by a vote of 64-19. The only opposition came from southern Democrats and four right-wing Republicans (JOSEPH R. McCARTHY [R-Wis.], WILLIAM JENNER [R-Ind.], HERMAN WELKER [R-Idaho], and JOHN J. WILLIAMS [R-Del.]) who resented his role in the *Peters* case. Soboloff was sworn in as a circuit court judge on July 19 and became chief judge of the Fourth Circuit in March 1958.

During his 17-year tenure on the Fourth Circuit, his opinions broke new ground in criminal justice reform, legislative reapportionment, and civil rights. In the many school desegregation cases heard by the Fourth Circuit in the late 1950s, Soboloff voted regularly to sustain district court orders mandating the admission of black pupils to previously all-white schools. In September 1958, he refused to stay three such desegregation orders for Warren County, Charlottesville, and Norfolk, Virginia. Governor J. LINDSAY ALMOND, JR., closed the schools in those districts, in accordance with the state's "massive resistance" laws. Soboloff sat on the three-judge federal court that held the Virginia school closing laws unconstitutional on January 19, 1959. Token school desegregation followed shortly thereafter in several Virginia communities.

In other types of cases, Soboloff consistently demonstrated a concern for protecting individual rights, and he gained recognition as a forceful advocate of civil libertarian principles. He was highly regarded by fellow jurists and lawyers, who respected his legal learning, his clear and vigorous legal prose, and his judicious approach to cases.

Soboloff led the Fourth Circuit away from the position that the Supreme Court had mandated desegregation, not integration. During the 1960s, he became frustrated with the slow pace of school desegregation and demonstrated increasing willingness to overturn evasive local laws as well as to insist on full and immediate, rather than partial and gradual, compliance with *Brown*. He resigned as chief judge in December 1964 when he reached the mandatory retirement age of 70, but he remained a fully active member of the court. His last opinion in a civil rights case was a dissent in *Swann v. Charlotte-Mecklenburg Board of Education* (1970), in which he voted to uphold the first use of court-ordered busing to achieve integration. The Supreme Court adopted his position the following year. Soboloff became a senior circuit judge in 1971 and died in Baltimore on July 11, 1973.

—MSM

Sparkman, John J(ackson)

(1899–1985) *U.S. senator; chairman, Senate Select Small Business Committee; chairman, Housing Subcommittee of the Senate Banking and Currency Committee*

The son of a sharecropper, Sparkman was born in Morgan County, Alabama, on December 20, 1899. He worked his way through college and law school. After enrolling at the University of Alabama in 1916, he enlisted in the U.S. Army in 1918 and later joined the Reserve Officers' Training Corps. He returned to the University of Alabama and earned a B.A. in 1921, an LL.B. in 1923, and an M.A. in history and political science in 1924. Admitted to the bar in 1925, he established a law practice in Huntsville, Alabama. In 1936, he won election to the House of Representatives, where he supported most New Deal programs. He was particularly interested in the creation of the Tennessee Valley Authority, which played a major role in the development of northern Alabama, the region he represented.

In 1946, Sparkman won a special election to fill a Senate vacancy created by the death of Senator John H. Bankhead (D-Ala.). He was reelected in 1948, 1954, 1960, 1966, and 1972. Unlike most southern Democrats, Sparkman supported President HARRY S. TRUMAN's Fair Deal. As a member of the Joint Committee on Housing and as chairman of the Banking and Currency Committee's Housing Subcommittee, he played a key role in the passage of almost all housing legislation during the late 1940s, the 1950s, and the early 1960s. He voted against overriding Truman's veto of the Taft-Hartley Act in 1947 and consistently supported the Small Business Administration. In foreign policy, he backed aid to Greece and Turkey, the Marshall Plan, and the North Atlantic Treaty.

A strong segregationist, Sparkman refused to support Truman's civil rights program. He opposed the inclusion of the controversial civil rights plan in the 1948 Democratic platform and supported STROM THURMOND's candidacy on the States Rights Party (Dixiecrat) ticket. Following the election, he helped bring the southern insurgents back into the Democratic Party.

At the Democratic National Convention in 1952, Sparkman played an important role in crafting a civil rights plank that appeased both supporters of civil rights and segregationists. Sparkman declared that the plank "represents as near a meeting of the minds as we can work out." Impressed by Sparkman's work on the platform, ADLAI STEVENSON, the presidential nominee, chose Sparkman to be the Democratic Party's vice presidential candidate in 1952. In choosing Sparkman, Stevenson hoped to retain the loyalty of the South and to satisfy liberals, many of whom accepted Sparkman because of his support for New Deal and Fair Deal legislation. During the campaign, Sparkman made 400 speeches and traveled 36,000 miles. He defended the party's ambiguous civil rights plank, which called on the federal government to "exercise the powers vested in it by the Constitution" to end discrimination in employment and protect African Americans from intimidation. Nevertheless, he refused to commit himself to aid efforts to curb Senate filibusters or back a fair employment practices commission.

Sparkman spent a large portion of his campaign defending the Truman administration against charges of corruption and of tolerating subversives in government. Attempting to counter accusations that Truman had been soft on communism,

Sparkman quoted a 1945 statement by Republican candidate DWIGHT D. EISENHOWER that "nothing guides Russian policy so much as the desire for friendship with the U.S." Sparkman added that "there are more Communist infiltrators from Eisenhower's own Columbia University than from any other school in the U.S." He criticized the Republican candidate for associating with Senators WILLIAM JENNER (R-Ind.) and JOSEPH R. McCARTHY (R-Wis.), the two major critics of Eisenhower's former commander General George C. Marshall. Sparkman expressed confidence that America would not "stomach a crusade" that included such men. When the Republican candidate for the vice presidency, RICHARD NIXON, faced charges that he had a secret political fund, Nixon noted that Sparkman employed his wife on his Senate staff. The Alabama senator angrily replied that his wife earned "every dollar she got."

Following the defeat of the Democratic ticket, Sparkman returned to the Senate as one of the most respected leaders of the Democratic Party. He played a leading role in the controversy over Eisenhower's nomination of CHARLES BOHLEN as ambassador to the Soviet Union in 1953. The Republican right, led by McCarthy and Jenner, contended that the diplomat had been involved in the alleged "sell-out of Eastern Europe" during the Yalta Conference and implied that the State Department was covering up evidence of disloyalty found in his security record. Sparkman and Senator ROBERT TAFT (R-Ohio) were chosen to review the record. After examining the files, the two men informed the Senate that Bohlen had no subversive ties. The nomination was then confirmed.

As one of the senior members of the Foreign Relations Committee, Sparkman frequently criticized the administration's diplomacy. In spring 1954, he charged that the Geneva Conference on Indochina, which partitioned Vietnam, was a surrender of Southeast Asia to the communists. During the Quemoy-Matsu crisis in the fall of the same year, Sparkman warned that a possible blockade of the mainland, contemplated by some members of the administration, would invite war. He labeled Eisenhower's handling of the Suez Crisis in 1956 the worst diplomatic disaster in memory. In 1957, he did support the Eisenhower Doctrine, which gave the president the right to use troops to aid Middle Eastern nations threatened by communists. At the same time, however, Sparkman argued that economic help was more important in ensuring political stability in the area.

As chair of the Senate Small Business Committee and the Housing Subcommittee of the Senate Banking and Currency Committee, Sparkman supported federal aid for small businesses and increased government spending on housing. He lobbied for corporate income tax relief and the establishment of a federally insured loan program to help small businesses. During the recession of 1958 and 1959, Sparkman advocated an ambitious housing program to stimulate the economy and improve the housing of the poor. He charged that the administration had abandoned the plan, set up during the Truman years, to provide decent housing for all. In March 1958, he introduced an emergency housing bill designed to stimulate residential construction. The legislation gave the Federal National Mortgage Association $1 billion to buy Federal Housing Association and Veterans Administration insured mortgages and extend Veterans Administration mortgages and loan programs. The president signed the bill, with some reluctance, in April. The following year, Sparkman submitted an ambitious omnibus housing bill that focused on urban renewal and the stimulation of construction of rental as well as private housing units. However, the majority leader, Senator LYNDON B. JOHNSON (D-Tex.) oversaw the introduction of major cuts on the Senate floor in an effort to avoid a presidential veto. Despite the cuts, Eisenhower vetoed the bill as too costly.

During the Eisenhower administration, Sparkman continued to oppose civil rights for African Americans. He joined 100 other southern members of Congress in signing the Southern Manifesto, which denounced the Supreme Court's decision striking down segregated public schools and pledged to reverse it by "all lawful means." Sparkman opposed civil rights legislation in 1957 and 1960. In 1957, he supported successful attempts to weaken the administration's civil rights bill by deleting authority for the attorney general to file civil suits to further desegregation and by including a proposal to provide a jury trial for those charged with contempt for violating court orders protect-

ing black voting rights. In 1959, he voted against modifying Rule 22, which dealt with the procedures for filibusters.

Sparkman remained active in national Democratic politics during the 1950s. In early 1956, he endorsed Stevenson's presidential candidacy. In March, the Democratic National Committee requested that the senator respond to Eisenhower's announcement that he would seek a second term in spite of his recent illness. Sparkman raised the possibility that Eisenhower would be a part-time president and that much power would be delegated to appointed officials. This, he said, would demote the office of president and play havoc with the separation of powers under the Constitution. He urged his audience to "think carefully" before "allowing such a fundamental change."

In the 1960s, Sparkman opposed Medicare and Medicaid as too costly. He supported the war in Vietnam and attacked antiwar protestors for treasonously obstructing the American military effort. During the late 1960s and early 1970s, Sparkman became one of the most powerful Democratic senators. He assumed the chair of the Banking Committee in 1967, and in 1975 he succeeded Senator J. WILLIAM FULBRIGHT (D-Ark.) as head of the Senate Foreign Relations Committee. Sparkman did not stand for reelection in 1978. He died in Huntsville, Alabama, on November 16, 1985.

—MSM

Spellman, Francis Cardinal
(1889–1967) *Roman Catholic archbishop of New York*

The son of a grocery store proprietor, Spellman was born in Whitman, Massachusetts, on May 4, 1889. After attending public schools and graduating from Fordham College in New York in 1911, he entered the seminary and was sent to the North American College in Rome. Awarded a doctorate in theology and ordained a Roman Catholic priest in 1916, he returned to Boston, first as a pastor (from 1916 to 1918) and then as a member of the staff of the diocesan newspaper, *The Pilot*. Spellman became a member of the chancery staff in 1922 and archivist of the archdiocese in 1924. He went to Rome in 1925, where he was named director of the Knights of Columbus playgrounds in Rome and appointed an official of the congregation for the Extraordinary Affairs of the Church. Named auxiliary bishop of Boston in 1932, Spellman clashed repeatedly with the archbishop. His close relationship with the new pope, Pius XII, led to Spellman's appointment as the archbishop of New York in 1939. With the outbreak of World War II, Spellman played a central role in establishing a diplomatic relationship between the United States and the Holy See in Rome. In late 1939, he was named vicar for U.S. armed forces. After the United States entered the war, Spellman took on the role of mobilizing Catholic support for the war effort. Pius XII named him a cardinal in 1946.

After the war, Spellman, a theological conservative, became a determined and outspoken enemy of communism. He also emerged as one of the most powerful clergymen in America. During the postwar period, as Catholics moved rapidly into the middle class and took a more prominent role in national politics, his influence increased. A successful fund-raiser, he built churches and schools in New York and helped finance Catholic missionary work abroad. The cardinal also distributed money for relief of refugees from communist-controlled areas. As vicar-general of the U.S. armed forces, he visited American troops around the world and was often identified with the interests of the American military.

Spellman opposed communist expansion in Eastern Europe and Asia. During the Eisenhower administration, he was particularly concerned about preventing a communist takeover of Indochina. In a speech given before the American Legion National Convention in August 1954, Spellman condemned the Geneva Accords of July 1954, which partitioned Vietnam. He labeled the truce "taps for the buried hopes of freedom in Southeast Asia," and he warned that it was a further step toward the communist goal of total world domination. On a visit to South Vietnam in January 1955, he brought with him a check for $100,000 to help the refugees who had fled from the North. In that same year, with the assistance of Joseph Kennedy, Spellman helped influence the Eisenhower administration to support South Vietnam's premier, Ngo Dinh Diem.

The cardinal also supported the pro-American government of Syngman Rhee in South Korea.

Beginning in 1951, Spellman flew to Korea each Christmas to offer encouragement to American soldiers stationed there. In January 1956, he described Korea as "the most difficult theater of defense against atheistic forces."

Opposed to any attempts toward peaceful coexistence with the Soviet Union, Spellman feared that any lack of vigilance on the part of the United States would lead to a communist takeover. In September 1959, one week before the Soviet premier Nikita Khrushchev arrived on a visit to the United States, the cardinal summoned the archdiocese to participate in an hour of prayer for America. Moscow did not take Spellman's attacks in silence; he was often a target for Soviet invective.

Spellman's anticommunism led him to embrace Senator JOSEPH R. McCARTHY's (R-Wis.) anticommunist crusade and to defend him against his critics. In an address in Brussels, delivered in October 1953, the cardinal rebuked European critics of McCarthyism and said that Americans would not be dissuaded from their determination to root out communist subversives. In April 1954, during a communion breakfast at which McCarthy was present, Spellman complimented the senator for his exposure of communists. The cardinal continued his support of the senator even after the Senate voted to condemn him in December 1954.

A vigorous opponent of what he considered to be pornography, Spellman called on Catholics to boycott several motion pictures. In December 1956, the cardinal, in one of his rare addresses from the pulpit of St. Patrick's Cathedral, denounced a film called *Baby Doll* and exhorted Catholics to refrain from viewing it.

During the 1960s, Spellman participated in the Second Vatican Council and was elected one of its 10 presidents. The most active American prelate at the proceedings, he played an instrumental role in securing an official declaration on religious liberty. At home, the cardinal became involved in the battles surrounding federal aid to education and the Supreme Court's decision banning organized prayer in the public schools. His strong support of the Vietnam War brought him into conflict both with Pope Paul VI and with Catholic antiwar activists in the United States Despite their disagreement, Pope Paul refused Spellman's offer in October 1966 to resign as archbishop because of his age. The cardinal died in New York City of a stroke on December 2, 1967.

—MSM

Stanley, Thomas B(ahnson)
(1890–1970) *governor of Virginia*

Born on July 16, 1890, near Spencer, Virginia, and raised on a small tobacco farm, Thomas Stanley received a degree in accounting from Eastern Business College in Poughkeepsie, N.Y. He established a furniture manufacturing firm in conservative southern Virginia in 1924. The town that grew up around it bears his name. Stanley won election to the Virginia House of Delegates in 1930 and became its speaker in 1942. A member of the conservative Byrd organization that dominated Virginia politics, he won a seat in the U.S. House of Representatives in 1946. Reelected twice, he opposed a large part of President HARRY S. TRUMAN's Fair Deal legislation.

At the request of Senator HARRY BYRD (D-Va.), Stanley resigned from Congress to run for governor in 1953. Campaigning on a platform that pledged the continuation of the poll tax, a pay-as-you-go balanced budget, and an adherence to the Byrd machine's conservative principles, he beat back the Republicans' strongest challenge of the century.

As governor, Stanley became embroiled in the controversy that followed the Supreme Court's decision striking down segregated public schools. In response to the decision, Stanley initially counseled moderation and announced he would work toward a plan acceptable to Virginians while obeying the Court's edict. At the same time, he set about subverting the Court's decision. He summoned black leaders to Richmond and asked them to reject integration. They refused. Segregationists mobilized, and members of the state legislature demanded that the governor take a more forceful position in opposition to the Court's decision. Even more important, Byrd pressed the governor to take a stronger stand against desegregation. In June 1954, Stanley announced he would "use every legal means at my command to proclaim resistance to the court order" and promoted repeal of the state's constitutional provision requiring that the state maintain a public school system.

With segregationist sentiment hardening, in August he appointed a Commission on Public Education to study the problem. The panel, weighted with political regulars and conservatives, was headed by state senator Garland Gray, a leading member of the Byrd organization and a militant segregationist. In January 1955, the Gray Commission, as the panel became known, issued a preliminary report. It declared that the majority of Virginians opposed racial integration of public schools and advised the governor that the commission would develop a program to prevent it. In November 1955, the Gray Commission recommended legislation that vested authority for pupil placement with local school boards. It also proposed legislation exempting children assigned to integrated schools from compulsory attendance laws. Finally, the commission recommended that parents who objected to their children attending integrated schools be eligible for tuition grants to help their children attend private schools. Stanley praised the plan and convened the state legislature to approve the tuition grants. This required amending the state's constitution, and a referendum was scheduled for January 1956. Voters overwhelmingly approved the amendment, and Byrd interpreted the results as total endorsement of segregation.

During the early months of 1956, segregationist forces gained momentum within the state. Powerful leaders in the Byrd organization, including Stanley, demanded a showdown with the Supreme Court and a rejection of what they termed its illegal demand for desegregation. Along with other leaders of the Byrd organization, Stanley adopted interposition, a doctrine that called on states to interpose their authority between their citizens and unconstitutional decisions of the Supreme Court. Stanley called a conference of southern governors at Richmond, Virginia, in January 1956, at which he endorsed a resolution calling on states to interpose their sovereignty between the federal government and local school boards to prevent desegregation. Virginia's general assembly adopted an interposition resolution in February 1956.

In July, Stanley reversed himself, rejecting the local-option features of the Gray Commission's report as conducive to integration. Rent with internal dissension, the commission also rejected its own report. Stanley convened a special session of the legislature in August 1956. He recommended 13 anti-integration bills, including a controversial proposal empowering the governor to close integrated schools. The state would provide funding for the private education of students and for the salaries of teachers and principals displaced by the closing of their schools. The legislation permitted city councils of closed schools to petition the governor to reopen the schools but denied state funding to integrated schools. The state legislature enacted the governor's anti-integration program. The program led to the actual closing of some schools in the state and was eventually struck down by the Fourth Circuit Court of Appeals.

After his term as governor expired in January 1958, Stanley returned to his furniture manufacturing business. He was director of First National Bank of Bassett, Virginia, and chaired a commission to study state and local taxes. Stanley died in Martinsville, Virginia, on July 11, 1970.

—MSM

Stanton, Frank

(1908–2006) *president, Columbia Broadcasting System*

The son of an industrial arts teacher, Stanton was born in Muskegon, Michigan, on March 20, 1908. He grew up in Dayton, Ohio, and received his B.A. from Ohio Wesleyan in 1930. He earned a M.A. (1932) and Ph.D. (1935) in psychology from Ohio State University. While in graduate school, Stanton invented a device that could be installed inside a radio receiver to keep track of what programs it played. This so impressed an executive at the Columbia Broadcasting System (CBS) that he offered Stanton a job in the research department. As director of research at CBS between 1938 and 1945, he worked closely with and helped support the work of sociologist Paul Lazarsfeld, a pioneer in public opinion calculation and social statistics. Stanton became vice president and general manager of CBS in 1945 and president in 1946. Although the chairman of CBS and its founder, William F. Paley, remained the ultimate arbiter of power, Stanton administered the network at a time of its expansion into television. Stanton saw the potential of

television earlier than Paley did; although, for his own part, Stanton cared little for show business and discounted RCA's huge investments in color TV. Under pressure from advertisers and pressure groups, Stanton approved requiring employees of CBS to take an oath of loyalty to the U.S. government. He also created a security office to investigate the political leanings of employees.

Unlike Paley, Stanton maintained a high visibility. In May 1954, during the Senate hearings on UHF-VHF stations, Stanton defended VHF (Channels 2–13) against charges made by the struggling UHF station operators. (CBS owned five VHF stations in five of the largest markets.) He attacked PAY-TV saying television could not long survive "half fee, half free." An articulate and forceful speaker, he repeatedly defended the national networks whenever Congress proposed regulating them. To critics of TV program content, both in the Congress and elsewhere, Stanton countered that "a program in which a large portion of the audience is interested is by that very fact . . . in the public interest."

Like its competition, CBS had standardized its TV programming by the late 1950s. Predominantly live shows gave way to film. *I Love Lucy*, a CBS program, set an industry pattern for situation comedy, as did *The Honeymooners*, which CBS won away from the doomed DuMont network.

In the 1950s, CBS News, once the industry leader, lost ground to the National Broadcasting Company (NBC). *See It Now*, coproduced by EDWARD R. MURROW, began to lose sponsors and lost its regular time spot after the 1954–55 season. Unlike DuMont and the American Broadcasting Company, CBS did not cover the Army-McCarthy hearings. Stanton later tried, unsuccessfully, to secure broadcast rights to the Senate hearings on McCarthy's censure.

In 1959, following revelations that producers had rigged the popular quiz show, *The $64,000 Question*, Stanton forced the executive in charge of the program to resign and canceled other quiz shows on the network. The quiz show scandals greatly embarrassed the national networks, whose chief executives actually had exerted less control over the programs than had the shows' individual producers and advertisers. Interestingly, opinion surveys showed a general indifference to the affair, but Stanton and his fellow broadcasters feared that the episode might result in greater government regulation. In May 1959, he announced that, henceforth, CBS would exercise far greater authority in program operation. He also pledged to revise the news division by presenting regular prime-time one-hour documentaries. "We are determined," he said, "to press the [television] medium to its fullest development as an informational force." In October he canceled all quiz programs and programming "conceits," such as canned applause and laughter.

Stanton played a leading role in bringing about the presidential debates of 1960. Long opposed to the equal time section of the Federal Communications Act of 1934, he continually argued that its literal interpretation compelled networks to offer equal access to candidates of every minor party. Congress suspended the equal time rule in August 1960, and Stanton personally devoted great attention to producing the debates between Senator JOHN F. KENNEDY (D-Mass.) and Vice President RICHARD M. NIXON. After the debates in September, Republicans criticized CBS for placing too much light on the pale face of their candidate. Stanton's arrangements, however, greatly pleased Kennedy.

In December 1960, President-elect Kennedy offered Stanton the directorship of the United States Information Agency. When Stanton declined the post, Kennedy appointed Murrow. In 1971, CBS broadcast an investigative report, titled "The Selling of the Pentagon," that covered a $30 million campaign by the Defense Department to improve its image. The House Interstate and Foreign Commerce Committee demanded that CBS turn over material cut from the program. Stanton refused to comply, and the committee cited him for contempt. The full House, however, voted down the citation. Stanton remained president of CBS until 1971 and stayed on as vice president until his retirement in 1973. After leaving CBS, Stanton became chairman and chief operating officer of the American Red Cross. He also served on the boards of the Rockefeller Foundation, the Carnegie Institution, and the Harvard board. He died in Boston on December 24, 2006.

—MSM

Stassen, Harold E(dward)

(1907–2001) director, Mutual Security Administration; director, Foreign Operations Administration; special assistant to the president for disarmament

The son of a farmer, Stassen was born in West St. Paul, Minnesota, on April 13, 1907. Hard-driving and persistent, he graduated from high school by the age of 15 and entered the University of Minnesota in 1922. He worked at a variety of jobs, including stints as a grocery clerk and a Pullman car conductor, to help finance his education. After receiving his B.A. in 1927, he entered the University of Minnesota Law School, where he received his law degree in 1929. Stassen also found time to organize and become the first chairman of the Minnesota Young Republican League.

Upon graduating from law school, Stassen and a classmate opened a law office and established a thriving private practice. Stassen also entered politics, campaigning successfully in 1929 for county attorney of Dakota County, Minnesota, an office he occupied from 1930 to 1938. In 1938, with the support of the Young Republicans, Stassen overcame strong opposition from the incumbent, Elmer A. Benson, and the old guard of the state's Republican Party to win election as governor of Minnesota. Chosen to give the keynote address at the Republican National Convention in 1940, he was reelected governor in 1940 and again in 1942. In 1943, Stassen resigned his office to go on active duty in the U.S. Naval Reserve. Entering the navy as a lieutenant commander, he served on the staff of Admiral William F. Halsey in the Pacific. He left the navy as a captain.

In 1945, Stassen was a delegate to the San Francisco conference that led to the formation of the United Nations. After that, he directed his efforts toward an eventual presidential bid. He was the first to enter the race for the Republican nomination in 1948. In his yearlong campaign, Stassen ran on a platform espousing progressive Republicanism in domestic affairs and international cooperation in foreign policy. Stassen wanted a system of modern capitalism whose strength and stability would rule out any serious economic depression and which would also be responsive to human needs. He opposed the isolationist wing of the Republican Party and believed that the United States should be willing to face war if necessary to overcome totalitarianism. After some early primary wins, Stassen lost the nomination in 1948 to THOMAS E. DEWEY.

Four years later, Stassen again ran for the Republican presidential nomination. General DWIGHT D. EISENHOWER's campaign staff, of which Stassen himself was a central figure, believed that Stassen's candidacy would be a useful tool to draw delegates from Senator ROBERT TAFT (R-Ohio), Eisenhower's major opponent. They also assumed that Stassen would switch his delegates to Eisenhower during the convention.

When the Republican National Convention convened, however, Stassen remained hopeful of his own nomination. He resisted all pressures within his Minnesota delegation to declare for Eisenhower. At the conclusion of the first ballot, when he received the votes of only 19 delegates, Stassen withdrew his name for the nomination and advised his delegates to support Eisenhower. Minnesota's shift provided Eisenhower with a narrow majority. Stassen opposed the selection of RICHARD M. NIXON as Eisenhower's running mate. After allegations surfaced that Nixon had maintained a "secret" political fund, Stassen wrote a letter to Eisenhower suggesting that he drop out of the race and that EARL WARREN replace him.

After Eisenhower won the election, he appointed Stassen director of the Mutual Security Program, a post he held from 1953 to 1955. In that capacity, he headed the foreign aid program and pushed the administration for increased emphasis on economic aid. In January 1955, Stassen supported agricultural expert WOLF LADEJINSKY, dismissed from his job at the Agriculture Department by Secretary of Agriculture EZRA TAFT BENSON as a security risk. At the behest of Eisenhower, Stassen gave Ladejinsky a position in the Foreign Operations Administration comparable to the one he had lost and released a detailed statement explaining why he had cleared Ladijinsky on the security charges.

In March 1955, Eisenhower, disturbed by the prospect of an arms race with the Soviet Union, created the position of special assistant to the presi-

dent for disarmament, with cabinet rank, and named Stassen to fill the post. The former governor was to develop and negotiate a plan for disarmament with the Soviet Union. In response to a Soviet offer, Eisenhower suggested a plan called Open Skies at the Geneva summit conference in July. He offered to swap military blueprints with the Soviets and suggested that the United States was willing, if the Soviets were, to allow complete aerial surveillance and photography to prevent a surprise attack.

Over the next two years, Stassen worked to develop this general statement into a specific proposal and attempted to get powerful forces within the administration to accept disarmament. Secretary of State JOHN FOSTER DULLES, in particular, opposed any accommodation with the Soviet Union on the issue. He feared that, because the New Look focused on strategic nuclear weapons as America's primary deterrent, any arms limitation agreement would jeopardize U.S. security. Stassen, on the other hand, believed that as the two superpowers reached nuclear parity, the United States must begin serious arms control discussions with the Soviets. Stassen was particularly anxious to stop nuclear testing while the United States had the numerical and technological advantage.

During the 1950s, Stassen remained active in Republican politics. In 1956, the liberal Stassen mounted a campaign to replace Nixon as the vice presidential nominee. On July 23, he suggested that the governor of Massachusetts, CHRISTIAN A. HERTER, would make a stronger candidate. Stassen said "the negative side" of the Eisenhower-Nixon ticket was most apparent in polls of "the best informed and the younger voters." He maintained that Nixon would only decrease support for the party. He pointed to the findings of private polls that showed an Eisenhower-Herter ticket would run 6 percent stronger than an Eisenhower-Nixon ticket. In these public pronouncements, Stassen insisted that he was acting "as an individual and not as a representative of the President." Stassen also asked his supporters not to advance his own name for the vice presidential nomination.

Almost every major figure in the Republican Party rallied to Nixon's side. The former governor of New York, THOMAS E. DEWEY, regarded Nixon's renomination as "all settled." Senator BARRY GOLD-

WATER (R-Ariz.) suggested that the GOP give Stassen a "transfer" to the Democratic Party for "trying to create dissent in an otherwise harmonious" party. On August 22, Stassen had a private meeting with Eisenhower. Immediately thereafter, Stassen made a public statement of his decision to give Vice President Nixon his "full support" and called upon the GOP to "close ranks" for the campaign.

In 1957, the United States and the Soviet Union outlined tentative proposals at meetings held in London under the direction of a subcommittee of the UN Disarmament Commission. The United States proposed an end to nuclear testing with an elaborate system of on-site inspections to ensure compliance. The Soviet Union, on the other hand, opposed inspection, believing secrecy would help it compensate for U.S. superiority in nuclear weapons. In addition, it called for a halt to the use of hydrogen bombs long before a cutoff in fissionable material production, a step that would inhibit use of the superior U.S. Air Force. The USSR also asked for aerial inspection of Europe outside the Soviet Union.

The tacit intention to include West Germany under the provision for aerial inspection immediately provoked the German chancellor Konrad Adenauer, a friend of Dulles, who demanded reassurance that his nation's interests would not be endangered. Dulles gave that reassurance and effectively blocked Stassen's further efforts to form a mutually acceptable accord with the Soviets.

During the London Conference, Stassen made a diplomatic blunder that led to his fall from grace in the eyes of the administration. After Eisenhower met with his advisers on disarmament, he authorized Stassen to return to London with a "talking paper" that proposed to offer the Soviets a moratorium on testing in exchange for future limitations on the production of nuclear weapons. Other elements of the paper included an aerial inspection scheme, a plan to prohibit the use of nuclear weapons except in defense or retaliation in case of nuclear attack, and a clause calling for the devotion of future production of fissionable material to peaceful purposes. Eisenhower stressed the tentative nature of the talking paper and told Stassen to show it to the British and French and get their approval before presenting it to the Soviets. Without any prior consulta-

tion with America's allies, Stassen gave the paper to the Soviets, who announced that the United States and the Soviet Union were near an agreement. The British prime minister Harold Macmillan opposed any test ban; the British had just exploded their first hydrogen bomb and wanted to conduct more tests. A furious Macmillan complained directly to Eisenhower.

The president reprimanded Stassen for the "acute embarrassment" his action had caused. Stating publicly that the unanimous assent of the allies would be necessary for any agreement, Dulles himself went to the conference to present the Western position. His usefulness at an end, Stassen resigned his post in February 1958.

After leaving the government, Stassen practiced law in Philadelphia and remained active in politics. In 1958 and 1966, he lost races for the Republican gubernatorial nomination in Pennsylvania. In 1960, he opposed Richard Nixon's nomination for the presidency at the Republican National Convention. Eight years later, Stassen ran for the presidency on a peace platform calling for the de-escalation of the war in Vietnam. His repeated campaigns for the Republican presidential nomination made him a standing joke and provided fodder for late night talk shows on television. He died in Bloomington, Minnesota, on March 4, 2001.

—MSM

Stennis, John C(ornelius)
(1901–1995) *U.S. senator*

The son of a prosperous farmer, Stennis was born in Kemper County, Mississippi, on August 3, 1901. Raised in rural Mississippi, he received his B.A. from Mississippi Agricultural and Mechanical College (later Mississippi State University) in 1923 and his LL.B. from the University of Virginia in 1927. He maintained a law practice while serving in the Mississippi House of Representatives from 1928 to 1932 and then won election to the position of district prosecuting attorney, which he held from 1932 to 1937. Appointed to a circuit court judgeship in 1937, he sat on the bench for a decade. Stennis won a special election in 1947 to fill the seat in the U.S. Senate left vacant by the death of Theodore Bilbo (D-Miss.), the noted segregationist demagogue. In a race to replace Bilbo, Stennis, a calm, genteel, and dignified southerner, downplayed the race issue but made clear his support for a "reasonable and proper segregation." He won reelection in 1952, 1958, 1964, 1970, 1976, and 1982.

Once in the Senate, he aligned himself with fellow conservative southern Democrats in opposing civil rights and much social welfare legislation. In 1948, he opened a filibuster of an anti–poll tax bill. He voted for the Internal Security Act of 1950 and the McCarran-Walter Immigration Act of 1952. In foreign policy, Stennis supported most of President Truman's policies to contain the Soviet Union, including the Marshall Plan in 1947 and the North Atlantic Treaty in 1949. A protégé of Senator RICHARD B. RUSSELL (D-Ga.), Stennis received appointments to the Armed Services Committee and the Appropriations Committee.

Stennis often opposed the Eisenhower administration's foreign policy, voting to limit foreign aid and opposing American troop commitments abroad. Although he had originally supported the Marshall Plan, he voted to lower its budget, and in 1953 he backed reduced foreign aid to western Europe. In 1956 he again voted for cuts in President Eisenhower's proposals for foreign aid and military assistance. Stennis opposed the U.S. Mutual Defense Treaty with Korea in 1954, arguing that the United States was "stretching-out" its commitments so thinly that it might not be able "to deliver." Instead of a formal treaty, he proposed a "firm declaration of assurances" that the United States would "stand by Korea under present conditions."

Stennis advocated a cautious policy toward American military involvement in Vietnam. In 1954, he warned against sending American technicians to Indochina because he thought it might provoke renewed fighting in Korea. When French forces were besieged by the communists at Dien Bien Phu that spring and the French government pleaded for U.S. military assistance, Stennis worried that the Western allies would again be content to have the United States assume the burden of the fighting. He stated that he could not think of any circumstances in which "our land troops should go into Indochina and be committed in this war area." When Senator JOHN F. KENNEDY (D-Mass.) warned that a French or U.S. military victory there was

impossible, Stennis called it "the finest statement I have heard on this subject."

Respected by his fellow senators for his personal integrity, Stennis was selected in 1954 to sit on the Senate Select Committee to Study Censure Charges, chaired by Senator ARTHUR WATKINS (R-Utah). The six members of the committee assembled in fall 1954 to study a resolution censuring Senator JOSEPH R. McCARTHY (R-Wis.) for his conduct in carrying out his investigations of Communists in government. Although strongly anticommunist, Stennis believed that McCarthy had violated traditional Senate standards of prudence and fairness. For him the issue was "one purely of political morality in senatorial conduct," not partisan or ideological conflict. In joining the committee's unanimous vote to recommend censure, Stennis rejected what he described as McCarthy's "slush and slime as a proper standard of senatorial conduct." He warned his colleagues that "something big and fine will have gone from this chamber" if it condoned the behavior of the senator from Wisconsin. The Senate censured McCarthy in December, by a vote of 67–22.

During the 1950s, Stennis was one of the Senate's most prominent opponents of civil rights legislation. An acknowledged authority on Senate procedures, he often used this knowledge to dilute or delay legislation through filibuster and manipulation of other parliamentary measures. In 1956, he joined 100 other southern members of Congress in signing the Southern Manifesto, which assailed the U.S. Supreme Court's decision striking down segregated public schools. While basing its attack on legal grounds, the group made it clear that its members would oppose any federal attempts to desegregate schools. Stennis voted against the Civil Rights Acts of 1957 and 1960. In 1959, he supported a proposed constitutional amendment to grant states and localities the right to decide questions of school desegregation. Some observers believed Stennis to be trapped by a constituency that favored segregation. Others, like Aaron Henry, a civil rights activist, saw Stennis as "shrewd and sophisticated in promulgating segregation" and perhaps more dishonest for doing so.

Stennis opposed most social welfare legislation. He supported only limited federal aid to education, despite the fact that Mississippi schools remained among the poorest in the nation. In 1960, he opposed raising the national minimum wage from $1 to $1.25 and the same year voted against a plan to provide medical benefits to the elderly through Social Security funds.

As a member of the Armed Services Committee, Stennis generally supported the military's budget requests and opposed the Eisenhower administration's New Look, which increased reliance on air power and the nuclear deterrent while reducing military spending. In the late 1950s, Stennis joined other Democratic senators who accused the Eisenhower administration of allowing a missile gap to develop. Claiming the United States was behind the USSR in numbers of missiles, he urged more intense research and production in the missile program. During partisan wrangling over a supposed "deterrent gap" in 1960, Stennis championed the B-70 bomber as "essential" to U.S. security.

Despite his earlier reservations about intervening in Indochina, Stennis provided important support for Presidents John F. Kennedy and LYNDON B. JOHNSON as they escalated the American involvement. Although he had earlier opposed a unilateral American effort, he believed that, once engaged, the United States had to uphold its commitment with a full military effort. After the Tet offensive, Stennis began to have doubts about American policy. In 1969, Stennis became chairman of the Armed Forces Committee.

Stennis's reputation for personal integrity drew him into some of the messiest political situations of his era. In 1967, Stennis chaired an investigation of Senator THOMAS DODD (D-Conn.) that resulted in Dodd's censure for misuse of congressional funds. During the Watergate scandal, President RICHARD M. NIXON came under pressure in 1973 to release the tape recordings of conversations in the Oval Office. He released transcripts of the recordings, but demands for the tapes continued. As a compromise, Nixon offered to let Stennis, as the representative of Congress, listen to the tapes and verify the White House transcripts of them. Opposed by the special prosecutor and members of Congress, the compromise collapsed. Although he refrained from race baiting, Stennis opposed civil rights measures throughout his tenure in the Senate. Toward

the end of his career, he moderated that position somewhat. He used his position on the Appropriations Committee to direct large amounts of federal funding to his state. In September 1987, Stennis announced that he would not run for reelection in 1988. Upon his retirement, he moved to Starkville, Mississippi, where he was involved with the John C. Stennis Institute of Government and the John C. Stennis Center for Public Service at Mississippi State University. He died in Jackson, Mississippi, on April 23, 1995.

—MSM

Stephens, Thomas E(dwin)
(1903–1988) *presidential appointments secretary*

Born in Ireland on October 18, 1903, Stephens graduated from St. Lawrence University in 1932 and received a law degree from Brooklyn Law School. He then served as assistant corporate counsel for the city of New York, beginning in 1938 representing the city at the state legislature in Albany. In 1936, Stephens began private practice with the firm of Lord, Day and Lord. He left in 1938 to become administrative assistant to the president of the New York City Council. During World War II, he served in Europe as a major in the army air corps. After the war, he became active in national Republican politics as director of the campaign division of the Republican National Committee in 1945 and 1946. He worked as a tactician for THOMAS E. DEWEY's successful campaign for the Republican presidential nomination in 1948; during the general election, he served as assistant to the Republican national campaign manager. After working as administrative assistant to Senator JOHN FOSTER DULLES (R-N.Y.) in 1949, he served as secretary of the New York State Republican Committee from 1950 to 1952. He joined DWIGHT D. EISENHOWER's presidential campaign during the primaries and became an aide to Eisenhower during the general election.

On the advice of SHERMAN ADAMS, President Eisenhower appointed Stephens appointments secretary with the title of special counsel in January 1953. Stephens's new position involved little formal counseling. Instead, he dealt with many small but significant details of the White House routine, choosing speaking invitations for the president and coordinating security arrangements with the Secret Service. He also arranged and logged Eisenhower's appointments. More informally, Stephens was the staff's chief comedian and practical joker. Eisenhower relied on his "genius for breaking up a tense discussion with exactly the right comment."

Stephens also contributed to the Eisenhower administration as a political adviser. He possessed shrewd political instincts and was a thoroughly perceptive judge of people. Eisenhower believed Stephens to be one of his most "politically astute" aides, and the president's reliance upon his appointments secretary as a "rock of good sense and sound judgment" gave Stephens more influence than most people in Washington realized.

Although ill health and the need to resume private law practice forced Stephens to resign as appointments secretary in January 1955, he continued to advise Eisenhower and on occasion to perform some duties for the White House. He worked on Eisenhower's reelection campaign in 1956 and served as an advance man at the Republican National Convention. With the resignation of Stephens's replacement, BERNARD SHANLEY, Stephens resumed his old post as appointments secretary in March 1958. When Eisenhower left office in January 1961, Stephens announced his intention to enter business. Two years later, however, he returned to politics, helping coordinate operations for the manager of NELSON A. ROCKEFELLER's campaign for reelection as governor of New York. In 1964, Stephens participated in Rockefeller's unsuccessful presidential bid and KENNETH B. KEATING's losing battle to retain his U.S. Senate seat. Four years later, Stephens again aided Rockefeller's unsuccessful presidential campaign and Senator JACOB K. JAVITS's (R-N.Y.) victorious bid for reelection. Stephens died in Clearwater, Florida, on May 15, 1988.

—MSM

Stevens, Robert T(en Broeck)

(1899–1983) *secretary of the army*

Born in Fanwood, New Jersey, on July 31, 1899, Stevens graduated from Phillips Academy in Andover, Massachusetts, in 1917. He served as a second lieutenant in the field artillery during World War

I. After the war, he earned a B.A. at Yale in 1921. He then entered the family textile business (J. P. Stevens and Co., founded in 1813 by Nathaniel Stevens). Stevens worked in manufacturing and merchandising before becoming president in 1929. In 1933, he was an administrative representative in the industry section of the National Recovery Administration. From 1934 to 1953, he was the director of the Federal Reserve Bank of New York. In 1940, he was appointed to head the National Defense Advisory Commission. During World War II, he served as a colonel in the office of the quartermaster general and handled the procurement of textiles for the army. After the war, he returned to J. P. Stevens as chairman of the board.

President-elect Eisenhower appointed him secretary of the army in December 1952. When the nomination was sent to the Senate Armed Services Committee, the majority of the committee asked Stevens to dispose of his stock in companies that did business with the Defense Department. Stevens promised that he would sell all holdings except his stock in the J. P. Stevens Co., frankly citing sentimental reasons for the exception. The committee refused to permit the exception, and Stevens agreed to sell the stock totaling $1.4 million.

While in office, Stevens was called upon to answer charges that budget cutbacks were impairing the army's effectiveness. In response to a special Senate inquiry into alleged shortages of ammunition in Korea, Stevens, in March 1953, assured the senators that production and supply were increasing rapidly. In July of that year, he told a subcommittee of the Senate Appropriations Committee that the proposed cut of about $1 million from the estimates presented by HARRY S. TRUMAN would not adversely affect the army's current combat effectiveness.

In the summer of 1953, Stevens began a tense, yearlong ordeal when Senator JOSEPH R. McCARTHY (R-Wis.), chairman of the Permanent Subcommittee on Investigations, launched a probe into possible communist infiltration of the army. McCarthy's attack focused on the army signal corps laboratories at Fort Monmouth, New Jersey. On November 16, he promised "evidence of actual stealing of classified materials" at Monmouth, a claim that contradicted the findings of an inquiry by the army, which maintained that there was no evidence of "current" spying. The subcommittee met with opposition from army officers, who refused to reveal the names of officials who had given security clearances to people suspected of communist connections. In his first encounter with McCarthy, Stevens, whom the senator termed "a fine, naive, not-too-brilliant" Republican businessman, appeared conciliatory. He promised to review the problem and indicated a desire to cooperate with the subcommittee. The matter was eventually dropped.

In January 1954, a new investigation brought Stevens and McCarthy to loggerheads. Dr. IRVING PERESS, a dentist and a member of the left-wing American Labor Party, had been inducted into the army in October 1952. A month later, in accordance with the automatic provisions of the Doctor Draft Act, Peress was promoted to the rank of major. When given a loyalty questionnaire, he refused to answer any questions regarding his political beliefs. In December, the army bureaucracy had discovered Peress's refusal, and the adjutant general ordered Peress discharged within 90 days. The army then gave him an honorable discharge. Infuriated, McCarthy insisted that Peress should have been court-martialed. On February 2, Peress asked that his discharge become effective immediately, and the army followed the path of least resistance. McCarthy demanded to know the identity of Pentagon officials who had promoted Peress and then ordered his discharge. In testimony before the subcommittee on February 18, General RALPH W. ZWICKER refused to reveal the names of those involved. Thereupon, McCarthy asserted that Zwicker, a highly decorated officer who had served with distinction in World War II, was "not fit to wear that uniform." Stevens directed Zwicker to refuse to appear for further questioning and denounced McCarthy's behavior as unwarranted. The secretary of the army announced that he would personally testify.

Stevens's order brought the senator and the administration into open conflict over what constituted the proper relation between the executive and legislative branches of government. In an effort to head off a major dispute, Vice President RICHARD M. NIXON and WILTON ("JERRY") PERSONS, Eisenhower's congressional liaison, arranged for a lunch meeting between the Republicans on the subcommittee and Stevens. At the meeting on February 24, Stevens agreed to cooperate with McCarthy if the senator accorded proper respect to the army's personnel. After the lunch, Senator KARL MUNDT (R-S. Dak.) read a "memorandum of understanding" between the army and the subcommittee, in which Stevens agreed to permit officers to appear before the subcommittee and to give it the names of those involved in the promotion and discharge of Peress. It seemed as though Stevens had capitulated completely; the press reported the meeting as an abject surrender to McCarthy. Nixon, Stevens, Deputy Attorney General WILLIAM ROGERS, Eisenhower's press secretary, JAMES HAGERTY, and several others worked out a statement, revised and approved by the president, claiming the secretary had in no way departed from his principle that army personnel were not to be "brow-beaten or humiliated." It further declared that Stevens had received assurances from members of the subcommittee along those lines. After Senator EVERETT N. DIRKSEN (R-Ill.) failed to get the Republicans on the subcommittee publicly to assure respectful treatment of officers, Stevenson read the statement at a press conference.

The army then took the offensive against McCarthy. On March 11, 1954, Stevens released a report stating that McCarthy and ROY M. COHN, the subcommittee's counsel, had intervened and even made direct threats to army officials in an effort to assure favored treatment for G. DAVID SCHINE, a former consultant to McCarthy's subcommittee who had been drafted into the army in November of the previous year. Stevens issued the report to each Republican member of the panel and to the press. Embarrassed and caught off guard, McCarthy labeled the report "blackmail" and, in addition, accused Stevens of trying to divert his attention to an investigation of the air force and navy. Cohn charged that it was a subterfuge to halt the probe of alleged subversives at the Monmouth laboratories.

McCarthy's Senate Permanent Investigations Subcommittee voted to hold hearings on the charges and countercharges. The nationally televised probe began on April 22, 1954, and continued until June 17. Most of the examination was devoted to petty haggling interrupted by McCarthy's calling, "point of order, Mr. Chairman!" In the words of historian Charles Alexander, "Even the closest followers could make little sense of the confused proceedings." Stevens himself had only a minor role in the hearings. The public's attention focused on the dramatic clashes between McCarthy and the army's chief counsel, JOSEPH WELCH. The hearings revealed McCarthy at his most boorish and ruthless and contributed to his downfall in December 1954. Assessing Stevens's role in the senator's political demise, the *New York Times* wrote that "[Stevens's] courage and persistence . . . was the beginning of McCarthy's own downfall as a power in the Senate."

Stevens resigned from his post on July 20, 1955, for what he termed "compelling personal consideration" and returned to the presidency of J. P. Stevens and Company. From 1963 to 1964, he was president of the American Textile Manufacturers. Stevens died in Edison, New Jersey, on January 31, 1983.

—MSM

Stevenson, Adlai E(wing)

(1900–1965) *Democratic presidential candidate*

Born in Los Angeles, California, on February 5, 1900, Stevenson was the grandson of Adlai Stevenson, vice president in Grover Cleveland's second term, and the son of Lewis Stevenson, a businessman who was active in Illinois Democratic politics. The younger Adlai Stevenson attended the Choate School in Wallingford, Connecticut, and graduated from Princeton University in 1922. At the insistence of his father, Stevenson went to Harvard Law School, but he flunked out after his second year. He worked for his family's newspaper in Bloomington, Illinois, and studied law at Northwestern University, receiving a J.D. degree in 1926. The following year, Stevenson joined Cutting, Moore & Sidley, an old and established law firm in Chicago.

Stevenson became special counsel to the Agricultural Adjustment Administration in 1933 and the following year transferred to the Federal Alcohol Control Administration as assistant general counsel. More a loyal Democrat than an ideologically devoted New Dealer, he returned to his law practice in Chicago in 1935. Six years later, Stevenson

went back to Washington as special assistant to Secretary of the Navy Frank Knox. In 1945, Stevenson became special assistant to Secretary of State Edward Stettinius. Later in the year, he was appointed U.S. minister and representative to the Preparedness Commission for the United Nations. He was senior adviser to the American delegation to the first session of the UN General Assembly, which opened in London in January 1946. Stevenson served as an alternate delegate at subsequent sessions in 1946 and 1947.

Needing a respectable candidate to improve the party's image, Chicago's political boss, Jacob Avery, urged Stevenson to run for governor of Illinois in 1948. Stevenson then ran as a reform candidate against what he charged was the scandal-ridden administration of the Republican incumbent, Governor Dwight H. Green. Stevenson defeated Green by 572,000 votes, the largest plurality in Illinois history.

Stevenson's accomplishments as governor included a reform of the state police force that substituted a merit system for political appointments, a doubling of state aid to schools, an increase in unemployment compensation and pensions for the aged and blind, and a 10-year road building program. The Illinois legislature declined to approve his proposals for establishing a fair employment practices commission, imposing greater restrictions on gambling, reforming the criminal justice system, and revising the state's constitution. Stevenson vetoed a bill requiring a loyalty oath, claiming that it infringed upon the right of free speech and the presumption of innocence.

From the time of his election as governor, Stevenson was mentioned as a possible Democratic presidential candidate for 1952. After Senator ESTES KEFAUVER (D-Tenn.) won the New Hampshire primary, President HARRY S. TRUMAN decided not to run and offered Stevenson his endorsement. Stevenson persistently said that he did not want to be a presidential candidate and would run for another term as governor. Some observers believed that he really did not want the nomination. Others claimed that he did not want to be associated with the unpopular Truman administration and thought he could win the election only if nominated by a popular draft. The success of Kefauver, whose committee in the Senate held widely publicized investigations into organized crime, in the early primaries alarmed Democratic city bosses, and they found an alternative in Stevenson.

Despite Stevenson's refusal to encourage a national movement on his behalf and his assertions that he would not even accept a draft, a Stevenson-for-President movement began to form in February 1952. In order to get the nomination, he had to defeat not only Kefauver but Mutual Security Director W. AVERELL HARRIMAN and Senator RICHARD B. RUSSELL (D-Ga.), who had also announced their candidacies for the nomination. In July, at the Democratic National Convention in Chicago, Stevenson ran second (with 273 votes) to Kefauver (with 340 votes) on the first ballot. But no candidate came close to the 615 1/2 votes needed for nomination. After Kefauver made only minor gains on the second ballot, Stevenson was selected on the fourth. He chose Senator JOHN SPARKMAN (D-Ala.), a segregationist who had supported much of the New Deal, as his running mate.

In his acceptance speech, Stevenson appealed for an issue-oriented campaign based on thought rather than emotion. His comment, "Let's talk sense to the American people," became for many the trademark of his campaign. Liberal intellectuals in particular came to admire what they perceived to be the thoughtful, analytical, and urbanely witty character of his speeches and his minimization of traditional campaign ballyhoo. In fact, Stevenson's speeches contained more rhetoric than substance.

If some liberal intellectuals swooned, to many others Stevenson's style smacked of uncertainty, indecisiveness, and a lack of fighting spirit. President Truman, for one, complained that Stevenson's campaign was not aggressive. Stevenson was overheard early in the Democratic National Convention saying to the Illinois delegation, "I do not dream myself fit for the job [of President]," a comment that reinforced the impression of uncertainty. Moreover, Stevenson was a moderately conservative Democrat, who remained uncomfortable with organized labor and minorities.

Furthermore, Stevenson's campaign was haunted by the record of the beleaguered Truman administration. He supported the president's major domestic and foreign policies, including

Adlai Stevenson arriving at the White House, February 17, 1953 *(Dwight D. Eisenhower Library and Museum)*

Truman's conduct of the stalemated war in Korea. The Democratic nominee stated that the fight against communism was a long and difficult one and that only persistence, not miracles, could end the conflict on favorable terms. On October 24, his Republican opponent promised to go to Korea. Stevenson contended that this promise was a grandstand play without meaningful content, but many observers believed that it clinched the election for Eisenhower.

On the domestic front, Republicans had a field day reminding voters of the scandals that marred the Truman administration. They also attempted to link Stevenson to their charge that the Truman administration was soft on communism and had allowed subversive elements to penetrate the national government. On October 10, Senator RICHARD M. NIXON (R-Calif.), the Republican vice-presidential nominee, denounced Stevenson for having testified favorably regarding the character of Alger Hiss at the latter's trial for perjury in 1949 and called Stevenson a "graduate of DEAN ACHE-SON's spineless school of diplomacy." On October 27, Senator JOSEPH R. MCCARTHY (R-Wis.), who had repeatedly impugned Stevenson's patriotism, said that if he could board Stevenson's campaign train with a club, he might be able to make a "good American out of him."

Stevenson also had the misfortune to run against a popular war hero, General DWIGHT D. EISENHOWER. Nothing Stevenson did could combat Eisenhower's overwhelming, nonpartisan popularity. Contrary to Stevenson's stated hope, the campaign did not center around a clear-cut debate over issues. Stevenson opposed McCarthyism, calling for "free enterprise for the mind," and took a cautious position in favor of civil rights for African Americans. However, Stevenson's supporters and many independent observers contended that Eisenhower won support across the political spectrum by presenting himself as a trustworthy father figure who stood above not only parties but issues. Eisenhower won a substantial victory in the popular vote (33.9 million to 27.3 million) and swept the electoral college by 442 to 89. Eisenhower even made inroads into the Solid South, capturing the southern states of Virginia, Florida, and Texas as well as the border states of Oklahoma and Tennessee.

In March 1953, Stevenson began a six-month tour of the Far East, Middle East, and Europe. Upon his return, he wrote a series of articles for *Look* magazine. He stated that, in the cold war, "anti-Communist preaching wins few hearts." The United States, he said, had to promote economic development in backward countries and live up to its ideals by rejecting McCarthyism and opposing Western colonialism.

As its most recent presidential candidate, Stevenson was the unofficial national voice of the Democratic Party, and in that capacity he remained in the public eye. At the Democratic National Committee's Southern Conference in March 1954, he denounced McCarthyism, stating that "it is wicked and it is subversive for public officials to try deliberately to replace reason with passion; to substitute hatred for honest difference." He also attacked the New Look defense policy recently announced by Secretary of State JOHN FOSTER DULLES, which relied on the use of strategic nuclear weapons as the primary defense against Soviet attack and expansion. Stevenson warned that the Soviet Union also had massive retaliatory power and that implementation of the plan "would certainly mean World War III and atomic counter-retaliation." In 1955, he opposed the Formosa resolution sponsored by the administration on the grounds that it committed the Senate to support almost any action the president might choose to protect Nationalist China against Communist Chinese attack, including defense of what he believed were the strategically worthless islands of Quemoy and Matsu. In a radio address on April 11, Stevenson warned that the United States might lose allies if it went to war over those islands.

During the period between the elections of 1952 and 1956, Stevenson criticized the Eisenhower administration and the state of American society. According to Stevenson, while the American standard of living was high, the people had little sense of purpose beyond the acquisition of material goods. Warning against complacency and conformity in a speech at Smith College, he attacked the theory of education whose main purpose was the production of citizens "who can fit painlessly into the social pattern." Stevenson's admirers regarded such comments as an extension and deepening of his political criticism of President Eisenhower, whose alleged blandness and lack of creative ideas or strong commitments they blamed for the emphasis on conformity.

By the summer of 1955, Stevenson believed that he was the best available candidate for the Democratic presidential nomination in 1956. On November 15, 1955, he formally announced his candidacy. Stevenson emphasized what he believed to be the excessive influence of business interests on the Eisenhower administration. On the issue of race, he hoped to reconcile the northern and southern wings of the party by taking a moderate stand on civil rights. Thus, he advocated gradualism in the enforcement of the Supreme Court's decision in *Brown v. Board of Education* (1954), which declared segregated public schools unconstitutional, and expressed the hope that southern moderates would be able to implement the ruling without the use of federal force. His major opponents, Kefauver and Harriman, who was by then governor of New York, took a more liberal position on civil rights.

After Stevenson received a surprisingly low write-in vote in the New Hampshire primary in March 1956 and suffered a stunning defeat at Kefauver's hands later in the month in the Minnesota primary, he altered his customary campaign style. Kenneth S. Davis, Stevenson's biographer, wrote: "Gone from his prepared talks were the witticisms that had sparkled from his speeches of '52; gone was the evident reluctance to campaign for the presidency as though it were a popularity prize. The new Stevenson was bussed by pretty girls in California, donned cowboy boots in Arizona, carried a stuffed alligator and thumped a bass fiddle in Florida and everywhere shook hands by the hundreds, the thousands." He went on to win successive primaries in Illinois, New Jersey, Pennsylvania, Alaska, Alabama, the District of Columbia, Oregon, Florida, and California. Stevenson won the nomination on the first ballot at the Democratic National Convention in August. He then surprised the convention by allowing it to choose his running mate; the delegates selected Kefauver.

In the general election rematch with Eisenhower, Stevenson continued to deviate from his 1952 campaign style. He followed a brutally crowded schedule, concentrating on key states, counties, and wards. Some of his speeches reflected the haste with which they were written. At his worst, Stevenson suggested that Eisenhower, who had suffered a heart attack, might not live through a second term, which would make Nixon the president. The Democratic nominee also engaged in a personal attack on the president's brother, Milton Eisenhower. Although disturbed by Stevenson's more traditional style of campaigning, his supporters comforted themselves with the thought that the candidate raised provocative ideas. Addressing the American Legion convention on September 5, Stevenson stated that the draft could be ended in the "foreseeable future," because the modern armed forces needed technically skilled specialized personnel serving for long periods rather than partly trained men enlisted for brief terms. Eisenhower denounced the suggestion as "incredible folly" that led "down the road of surrender." Republicans ridiculed Stevenson for claiming to know more about

military matters than the president, who had spent a career in the military and commanded the European theater during World War II.

On October 15, during a nationwide television appearance, Stevenson suggested that the United States unilaterally halt further testing of H-bombs in the hope that the Soviet Union would reciprocate. (He had made a similar proposal the preceding April.) Stevenson argued that such a cessation could be a first step toward nuclear disarmament or at least toward a halt to the poisoning of the atmosphere with radioactive fallout. He contended that any subsequent Soviet H-bomb explosions could be detected and that the United States could then resume its tests. The administration believed that testing could not be monitored adequately without on-site inspection in the countries participating in a moratorium, and it therefore opposed any unilateral halt. Stevenson's suggestion became a political debacle when Soviet premier Nikolai A. Bulganin, in a letter to President Eisenhower on October 21, backed the Democratic candidate's proposal and called for a test suspension without inspection.

Eisenhower had not lost his nonpartisan appeal since 1952, and he now spoke with the authority of an incumbent. Furthermore, Stevenson's controversial proposals probably cost him votes. He was defeated even more soundly in 1956 than in his first presidential bid, receiving only 73 electoral votes to Eisenhower's 457. Eisenhower extended his inroads into the South, capturing Oklahoma, Kentucky, Tennessee, Texas, Louisiana, Florida, and Virginia. The incumbent received 35.6 million votes to Stevenson's 26.0 million.

In late November 1956, Stevenson joined with National Democratic Chairman PAUL BUTLER in establishing the Democratic Advisory Council. It was created to serve as a national voice for the party. Stevenson played the leading role in drawing up the council's statements and papers. In addition, he continued to speak throughout the country after his second defeat, and his speeches gained national attention. In fall 1957, the administration decided to invite Stevenson to help draw up an American program for the North Atlantic Treaty Organization (NATO) and participate in the forthcoming NATO conference in Paris. Stevenson decided not to attend the conference but agreed to work on the program. He stressed the importance of programs to improve living conditions in backward countries and stated in one of his memoranda that "if the Atlantic Community had multilateral economic and trade development plans it would mean a lot more to many people than its purely military anti-Communism does now." However, his views had little influence on the American position at the conference, which stressed military might in deterring the spread of communism.

During the summer of 1958, Stevenson visited the Soviet Union and met with Soviet premier Nikita S. Khrushchev. Stevenson concluded that the current leadership of the USSR was more sensitive to public opinion than Stalin and was more pragmatic than ideological. Therefore, he believed, the Kremlin would seriously weigh the desire of the people in the Soviet Union and throughout the world for peace.

Stevenson repeatedly declined to seek a third presidential nomination in 1960. Early in that year, however, liberals in the Democratic Party, led by George Ball, THOMAS FINLETTER, and Senator MIKE MONRONEY (D-Okla.), formally organized a draft Stevenson movement. Stevenson made no effort to stop it. The strategy of the movement was to try to prevent any of the active candidates from winning on the first ballot and then, according to Kenneth Davis, "stampede the Convention in much the same way as the Wilkie amateurs had stampeded the Republican Convention of 1940."

That strategy came apart when Senator JOHN F. KENNEDY (D-Mass.) defeated Senator HUBERT H. HUMPHREY (D-Minn.) in the West Virginia primary and severely damaged hopes for a deadlocked convention. Despite demonstrations by thousands of enthusiastic Stevenson supporters outside the convention hall and a tumultuous 20-minute demonstration inside, Kennedy won the nomination on the first ballot at the July gathering. Stevenson received the votes of only 79 1/2 delegates and finished fourth.

Although many people regarded Kennedy as an idealistic young man who represented a continuation of the Stevensonian tradition in the Democratic Party, Stevenson and a number of other Democratic liberals regarded the party's nominee as a cold, ambitious politician without a strong commitment to principles. Kennedy, like many others, regarded Stevenson as indecisive and prissy. Whatever his misgivings about the Democratic nominee, Stevenson disliked Vice President Nixon, the Republican nominee, far more. Stevenson's support of Kennedy induced many Democratic liberals such as ELEANOR ROOSEVELT to give their wholehearted support to the senator from Massachusetts.

During the primary campaign, Kennedy had indicated that he would give Stevenson a high post in his administration. Stevenson expected to be appointed secretary of state, but instead Kennedy offered him the post of ambassador to the United Nations. A disappointed Stevenson accepted it. In April 1961, Stevenson was not informed about the American role in the Bay of Pigs invasion, and he denied American involvement before the Security Council. Upon learning the truth, he was enraged. Stevenson's advocacy of concessions and negotiations during the Cuban missile crisis of 1962 earned him a reputation as a dove in an administration of hawks. Subsequently, his influence in the administration, which had never been great, declined, and he was forced to defend policies that he had no role in formulating. Stevenson retained his post under President LYNDON B. JOHNSON, hoping to have a larger role in the formulation of policy; he was to be disappointed again. Stevenson died of a heart attack in London on July 14, 1965.

—MSM

Stewart, Potter

(1915–1985) *associate justice, U.S. Supreme Court*
Stewart was born in Jackson, Michigan, where his family was vacationing, on January 23, 1915. He came from an affluent and prominent family in Cincinnati; his father served as mayor of the city and chief justice of the Ohio Supreme Court. Potter Stewart grew up in Cincinnati and attended the Hotchkiss School in Lakeville, Connecticut. Stewart graduated from Yale in 1937, and, after a year studying international law at Cambridge University in England, he entered Yale Law School, from which he graduated in 1941. Stewart went to work with a firm on Wall Street, but, after the Japanese attack on Pearl Harbor, he joined the navy as an officer and saw action in the Atlantic and Mediter-

ranean. After the war, he worked with a Wall Street law firm and then returned to Cincinnati in 1947. There, he joined a leading law firm and entered politics. Stewart served as a city council member from 1950 to 1953. President DWIGHT D. EISENHOWER appointed him to the Sixth Circuit Court of Appeals in April 1954. Stewart soon emerged as a leading federal circuit judge, admired for his closely reasoned and well-written opinions.

Mentioned as a possible Supreme Court nominee as early as 1957, Stewart was appointed to the high court when HAROLD BURTON retired in October 1958. Stewart began serving on the Court under a recess appointment that month. The Senate confirmed his nomination in May 1959, by a vote of 70–17, with the opposition coming from southern Democrats who disliked Stewart's position on civil rights.

Throughout his career on the nation's highest bench, he adopted a moderate, pragmatic approach. He tended to favor First Amendment rights, particularly free speech and religion, as well as the equal protection of African Americans and other minorities. He also strongly favored guarantees of the right to counsel. At the same time, he tended to support state criminal laws. Stewart often functioned as a swing justice, who moved between the Court's liberal and conservative wings. During his first term, for example, he joined the majority in two cases in which a closely divided Court upheld the contempt convictions of witnesses who had refused to answer questions or produce information for congressional and state anticommunist investigations. Later the same month (June 1959), however, Stewart voted to overturn a federal industrial security program because Congress had never authorized certain of the procedures used.

Stewart tended toward a policy of judicial restraint, but he was willing to intervene if government violated procedural rights or encroached too greatly on individual liberties. In general, however, he preferred to overturn government action on the narrowest possible grounds. In *Bates v. Little Rock* (1960), Stewart spoke for the majority to void the convictions of two officials of the Arkansas NAACP who had refused to give their membership lists to local authorities. The Court held that the forced disclosure would cause an unwarranted intrusion into

the right of free association. Stewart's opinion for the Court in *Shelton v. Tucker* (1960) ruled unconstitutional an Arkansas law requiring public school teachers to list all organizations to which they had belonged in the past five years. Such a requirement, Stewart held, was too extreme an infringement on free association. Stewart demonstrated his concern for First Amendment rights in *Kingsley Picture Corporation v. Regents* (1959). Writing for the majority, he overturned a ban imposed by the regents of the University of the State of New York on the showing of the film *Lady Chatterley's Lover.*

Justice Stewart had a special concern for the right to counsel and wrote two opinions for the Court in February and June of 1959 overturning convictions in which the defendant had been denied counsel. On other criminal rights issues, however, he was a moderate. In March 1959, for example, he voted to hold that persons tried for the same offense in federal and state courts had not been subjected to double jeopardy.

Stewart found himself in dissent more often once a clear liberal majority emerged on the Court in the early 1960s. He voted with the liberals in many cases involving the right to counsel, civil rights, and obscenity, but he opposed them on most criminal rights issues (including *Miranda v. Arizona* [1966], in which the Court held that an accused had to be informed of his rights), on legislative reapportionment, and in many loyalty-security cases.

Whichever side he came down on, his opinions won praise for their concise, lucid, and literate style. Stewart was one of the Court's great phrasemakers. In *Braunfeld v. Brown* (1961), Stewart dissented from a decision upholding the constitutionality of a Sunday closing statute. "Pennsylvania," wrote the justice, "has passed a law which compels an Orthodox Jew to choose between his religious faith and economic survival. . . . It is a choice which I think no State can constitutionally demand." An obscenity case, *Jacobellis v. Ohio* (1964), led Stewart to craft his most memorable phrase. The Court overturned the conviction of a theater manager for showing the French film, *Les Amants.* In a concurring opinion, Stewart wrote: "I shall not today attempt further to define the kinds of material I understand to be embraced within [the term hard-core pornography]; and perhaps I could never succeed in intelligibly doing so. But I know it when I see it, and the motion picture involved in this case is not that." At that point, Stewart believed that states could ban hard-core pornography but not other sexually explicit material. A few years later, he came to the conclusion that judges should stay out of obscenity cases except when the obscenity was advertised salaciously or pandered to children (*Redrup v. New York* [1967]).

In 1969, amid speculation in the press that he might be elevated to the chief justiceship to succeed EARL WARREN, Stewart paid a call on President RICHARD M. NIXON. He told Nixon that history indicated that it was unwise to promote an associate justice.

Stewart voted to strike down state death penalty statutes in *Furman v. Georgia* (1972), because they were unevenly applied. In another of his most frequently quoted turns of phrase, Stewart wrote: "These death sentences are cruel and unusual in the same way that being struck by lightning is cruel and unusual." Ultimately, however, he supported the constitutionality of the death penalty.

One of his most significant opinions came in *Jones v. Mayer Co.* (1968). That decision revived long-dormant legislative protections for African Americans against discrimination in housing. He also voted to uphold stronger enforcement of fair employment statutes but argued for color-blind applications when he saw affirmative action programs leading to racial quotas.

Stewart retired in 1981. After that, he continued to sit for several years as a judge on federal courts of appeals. He died in Hanover, New Hampshire, on December 7, 1985.

—MSM

Stone, I(sidor) F(einstein)

(1907–1989) *journalist, editor, publisher*

The son of Jewish immigrants from Russia, Isidor Feinstein (he legally changed his name to I. F. Stone at the age of 30) was born in Philadelphia, Pennsylvania, on December 24, 1907. His family moved in 1914 to Haddonfield, New Jersey, where his parents owned a dry goods store. During his high school years, he worked for the *Haddonfield Press* and the *Camden* (New Jersey) *Evening Courier.* He

attended the University of Pennsylvania, where he studied philosophy but left in 1927 before the end of his junior year. While in college, he wrote for the *Philadelphia Inquirer* and the *Philadelphia Record.* Upon leaving college, Stone became an editorial writer for the *Camden Evening Courier.* A member of the Socialist Party's New Jersey State Committee, Stone did publicity work for NORMAN THOMAS's presidential campaign in 1928. Soon afterward, he divorced himself from partisan political activity to pursue a career in journalism.

In 1931, Stone became an editorial writer for the *Philadelphia Record.* He argued that conventional liberal solutions were inadequate to rescue the nation from the depression. Though an advocate of centralized authority and planning, he criticized what he considered to be President Franklin D. Roosevelt's "fascist" tendencies. In 1933, Stone became the chief editorial writer for the staunchly pro-Roosevelt *New York Post.* In 1937, he changed his legal name to I. F. Stone and published his first book, *The Court Disposes,* in which he supported Roosevelt's plan to enlarge the Supreme Court. Stone became associate editor of *The Nation* in 1938; two years later, he moved to Washington to become the magazine's capitol editor. He continued to work at *The Nation* but in 1942 began writing as well for the liberal newspaper *PM.*

He published *Underground to Palestine* (1946), based on his experiences with a group of slightly over 1,000 Jewish survivors of Hitler's death camps as they ran the British naval blockade to immigrate to Palestine. "If those ships were illegal," he wrote, "so was the Boston Tea Party." Two years later, he published another pro-Zionist book, *This Is Israel.* When *PM* folded in 1949, Stone joined the *New York Daily Compass.*

Stone criticized the Truman administration's anticommunist foreign policy from a leftist perspective. In November 1947, he denied that the Soviet Union maintained its rule in eastern Europe only by brutal terror and asserted that the planned economies of that region brought benefits to industrial and agricultural workers. The following year, he supported the Progressive Party's presidential candidate, Henry A. Wallace, who urged accommodation with the USSR. Stone refused to accept the American government's explanation of the causes of the Korean War, and in his *Hidden History of the Korean War* (1952), argued that the United States and South Korea had provoked the North Korean invasion of South Korea. Stone's critics contended that he cast U.S. policy in the worst possible light and Soviet policy in the best possible light.

After the *Daily Compass* folded in 1952, Stone began publishing *I. F. Stone's Weekly*, an independent radical newsletter, in January 1953. Stone maintained the autonomy of the publication by rejecting advertising. He did all the research, reporting, and editing, while his wife managed the newsletter's business affairs. A staunch opponent of Senator JOSEPH R. MCCARTHY (R-Wis.), Stone wrote in April 1953 that "no one is doing so much to damage the country's prestige abroad and its power to act effectively at home." However, he did not spare McCarthy's foes, stating in March 1954 that they accepted his underlying premise that communism was an evil conspiracy against the peace and stability of the world. "To acquiesce in the delusions which create a panic," Stone wrote, "is no way to stem it."

After visiting the Soviet Union in 1956, Stone alienated many of his leftist subscribers and friends with his scathing assessment of that country and its society. Workers there, he asserted, were "more exploited than in Western welfare states." The Soviet Union, he wrote, "is not a good society, and it is not led by honest men." For all his criticism of the United States, he acknowledged that "there are very few countries in which you can spit in the eye of the Government and get away with it. It's not possible in Moscow."

Stone regarded Eisenhower as a lackadaisical chief executive who was indifferent to the responsibilities of his office. In March 1959, he described the president as "a cardiac case whose chief interest is in getting away from his job as often as possible for golf and bridge." Stone was one of the few prominent journalists who attacked the administration's foreign and domestic policies from a radical point of view. In January 1958, he charged that Secretary of State JOHN FOSTER DULLES sought to promote the arms race to force the USSR to increase its arms budget and thus maintain poverty and increase domestic tension within the Soviet bloc. During March 1959, Stone wrote that the Berlin crisis

demonstrated that leaders in the United States and the USSR believed in "their sacred right to consign millions to death if they so choose."

Stone praised the Supreme Court's decision in *Brown v. Board of Education* (1954), which struck down segregated public schools. On a number of occasions, he attacked the Eisenhower administration for not vigorously investigating the lynching of blacks in the South, and in May 1958 he chided the president for urging black leaders to be patient in the face of the slow pace of integration. In August 1958, Stone warned that if African Americans were not assimilated into American society, they might become embittered and turn from integration to racist nationalism.

In addition to his dissident views, Stone was known for turning up facts that would otherwise have gone unnoticed. He pored over official documents for information. A critic of the U.S. insistence upon on-site inspection as a condition for the cessation of nuclear tests, Stone discovered in 1958 that the Atomic Energy Commission's first underground test had been detected 2,600 miles away.

In 1961, Stone regarded President JOHN F. KENNEDY as a promising liberal, but, in December 1963, he wrote that Kennedy "was no more than an enlightened conservative, cautious as an old man for all his youth, with a basic distrust of the people." He defended the Warren Commission report on Kennedy's assassination, which concluded Lee Harvey Oswald had acted alone. Stone was an early and relentless critic of President LYNDON B. JOHNSON's policies in Vietnam, and, as a result, during the mid- and late 1960s, his newsletter became increasingly popular. In 1964, his account of the Gulf of Tonkin incident, based on a close reading of official documents, undermined the government account of events.

Fiercely independent, Stone infuriated virtually all of his readers at some point. He deplored the turn to violence by the New Left and black militants in the late 1960s. For all his commitment to free speech, he refused to defend pornography. After the Arab-Israeli war of 1967, he called on Israel to compensate Arab refugees and to turn over the occupied territories to create a Palestinian state.

As Stone's health failed, he changed his newsletter to a biweekly in 1968. He ceased publication of the newsletter in December 1971 but continued to write for *The Nation* and the *New York Review of Books*. Stone taught himself classical Greek and published *The Trial of Socrates* in 1988. It was his best-selling book and his last one. He died in Boston, Massachusetts, on June 18, 1989.

—MSM

Strauss, Leo
(1899–1973) *philosopher*

Born in Kirchhain, Germany, on September 20, 1899, Strauss was raised in a Jewish household that observed the ceremonial laws but was little concerned with Jewish knowledge. His father and uncle operated a farm supply and livestock business they inherited from their father. He attended the Kirchhain *Volksschule* and the *Rektoratsschule*, a private, Protestant institution, before enrolling at the Gymnasium Philippinum in 1912. After graduating in 1917, Strauss began the summer session at the University of Marburg but was conscripted into the German army during World War I, serving from July 1917 to December 1918. German universities allowed students to switch freely from one to the other, and Strauss attended Marburg, Frankfurt am Main, and Berlin before receiving his doctorate in 1921 at the University of Hamburg. After a postdoctoral year at the University of Freiburg-im-Breisgau that began in 1922, Strauss took a position at the Academy of Jewish Research in Berlin. His first book, *Spinoza's Critique of Religion as the Foundation of His Science of the Bible*, was published in 1930. Strauss received a Rockefeller fellowship in 1932 and went to Paris, where he studied medieval Jewish and Islamic philosophy. After extending his Rockefeller fellowship for a second year, he decided not to return to Germany, where the Nazis had come to power. He moved to Britain in 1934 and found temporary employment at the University of Cambridge. While in Britain, he published *Philosophy and Law: Contributions to the Understanding of Maimonides and His Predecessors* (1935) and *The Political Philosophy of Thomas Hobbes* (1936).

Unable to find permanent employment in Britain, he moved to the United States in 1937. After briefly holding a position as a research fellow at Columbia University, Strauss held a tenuous position at the New School for Social Research from 1938 to 1948. He became a U.S. citizen in 1944. Despite financial difficulties, he managed to remain productive, publishing *On Tyranny* in 1948. Strauss became a professor of political science at the University of Chicago in 1949. For the first time in his life, he held a secure position and earned a salary that sustained a comfortable standard of living.

Strauss combined a commitment to historical tradition with a suspicion of innovation. After leaving Germany, Strauss, who was trained in Jewish and Greek philosophy, did expand his interests to include the 17th-century philosopher Thomas Hobbes. His later writing demonstrated a concern with natural law and natural rights. He elaborated on those concerns in *Natural Right and History* (1953). Strauss believed that the highest American principles, expressed in the Declaration of Independence, had been eroded, by a variety of forces, including the positivist tendency of political science.

Strauss believed that the true message of a text could be discerned through close reading and the application of principles and reason. While the average reader would understand a text in one way ("exoteric"), the careful and properly educated reader would grasp its true ("esoteric") meaning. As Strauss put it: "The real opinion of an author is not necessarily identical with that which he expressed in the largest number of passages." Strauss demonstrated this idea with his own innovative reading of classical texts. In *Persecution and the Art of Writing* (1952), he put forward the possibility that philosophers wrote esoterically to avoid persecution by the state or religious authorities.

Moreover, he posited a correlation between reading well and leading the good life. His application of classical philosophy to politics offered an alternative to the "value free" social science of his day. Through argument and practice, he made a case for the history of political thought, which had fallen out of favor in political science, a discipline enamored with the scientific methodologies of behaviorism. Strauss traced the turning point in political philosophy to Machiavelli. By denying the certainty of a God who punished wrongdoing, Machiavelli rejected Christian virtue, which was upheld by the belief in such a God. Since virtue was unattainable, Machiavelli taught that political order had to be based on humans as they existed and therefore had to take into account their mediocrity and their vices. Against this, Strauss proposed to restore ancient philosophy as a legitimate political critique. He argued for the need to understand the ancient philosophers from their own perspective and then to apply that understanding to modern political affairs.

Strauss remained deeply suspicious of liberalism, which he believed intrinsically led to relativism and ultimately to nihilism. Its commitment to toleration meant that liberalism was unable to distinguish "timeless wisdom" from "mere opinion." Further, he regarded mass rule as conducive to mediocrity. Strauss's early writings demonstrated the extent to which his intellectual development was shaped by his experience as a Jew living in Germany's Weimar Republic. During those years, he observed a liberal state so tolerant that it tolerated communists and Nazis who eventually destroyed it.

Strauss was interested in the investigation of ultimate truths, which he referred to as "first things." In a lecture delivered in 1967, "Jerusalem and Athens," Strauss considered at length whether reason or revelation represented to road to truth. As he saw it, until the modern era, the central question of the Western tradition was whether the Bible or "first philosophy" provided the key to the highest life.

For many years, the standard interpretation of Strauss was that, although drawn to Jerusalem (revelation), he ultimately chose Athens (reason). His most significant work consisted of studies of classical political thought, including *The City and Man* (1964) and *Studies in Platonic Political Philosophy* (1983), and Strauss won a deserved reputation as a creative and sophisticated interpreter of Plato and his school.

In the 1990s, however, a German edition of Strauss's collected works made available his early writings, which contained substantial consideration of Jewish issues, and the State University of New York Press published the first volumes of a planned multivolume translation of Strauss's writing on Judaism. Once again, his experience as a German Jew who lived through the early 20th century and the Weimar period proved formative. Strauss concluded that assimilation, the 19th-century liberal

answer to the Jewish question, had failed. Liberalism, or assimilation, he maintained, demanded effectively renouncing Jewishness as the price of equal citizenship. That price, he argued, was too high. In addition, since the 1890s, central Europe had experienced a rise of virulent anti-Semitism, and liberal societies had proved unable and unwilling to protect their Jews against persecution. Strauss considered carefully other Jewish responses to modernity. During his late teens, Strauss embraced Zionism as a pragmatic response to the situation. Ultimately, however, he concluded that Zionism was consistent with the ethos of modern liberalism. A secular movement, it avoided the question of Jewish authenticity. As was the case with so many of his generation, World War I shattered Strauss's confidence in reason and the prospects for a peaceable resolution of the Jewish question. He rejected the notion, advanced by the German philosopher Hermann Cohen (1842–1918) and widely discussed during Strauss's days as a student, that Judaism was a religion of reason and as such was the basis of modern rationalism. Strauss concluded that such an approach stripped Judaism of all intrinsically religious content. If, therefore, reason did not provide the answer, perhaps revelation did.

Strauss held the Robert Maynard Hutchins Distinguished Service Professorship at Chicago until 1969, when he moved to Claremont Men's College (later Claremont McKenna College) in California. In 1970, he moved to St. John's College in Annapolis, Maryland, where he was the Scott Buchanan Distinguished Scholar in residence until his death in Annapolis on October 18, 1973.

—MSM

Strauss, Lewis L(ichtenstein)

(1896–1974) *chairman, Atomic Energy Commission*
The son of a an executive who worked for a wholesale shoe manufacturer, Strauss was born in Charleston, West Virginia, on January 31, 1896. Raised in Richmond, Virginia, he attended public schools. Strauss wanted to become a physicist but his father suffered financial reverses and could not afford to send his son to college. Instead, Strauss went to work in his father's business. When the United States entered World War I, Strauss served as HERBERT HOOVER's

personal secretary in the U.S. Food Administration. After the war, Hoover went to Paris to run the American Relief Administration, and Strauss went with him. Strauss then joined the leading Wall Street banking house of Kuhn, Loeb and Company in 1919 and became a partner in 1929. He worked for Hoover's presidential campaign in 1928 and also became active in philanthropic and cultural affairs, especially within the American Jewish community. A member of the U.S. Naval Reserve since 1925, Strauss was ordered to active duty early in 1941 and assigned to the Bureau of Ordnance. During World War II, he coordinated production and procurement of ordnance. In 1944, he went to work for Secretary of the Navy James Forrestal, where he focused on economic reconversion. At the end of the war in 1945, President HARRY S. TRUMAN made him a rear admiral, an honor only rarely extended to reservists.

In 1946, Truman appointed Strauss to a three-year term on the newly created Atomic Energy Commission (AEC), a civilian agency formed to oversee nuclear development. During the late

Lewis L. Strauss, chairman of the Atomic Energy Commission and acting secretary of commerce *(Dwight D. Eisenhower Library and Museum)*

1940s, Strauss joined EDWARD TELLER in advocating the immediate development of the hydrogen bomb as a means of maintaining American military supremacy over the Soviet Union. Other members of the commission, including its head, David Lillenthal, and its general advisory committee, headed by J. ROBERT OPPENHEIMER, opposed development of the hydrogen bomb. They argued that work on the weapon should be restricted to the theoretical level for technical, strategic, and moral reasons. Truman sided with Strauss and ordered the AEC to proceed with development of the hydrogen bomb in 1950. Strauss left the AEC later that year.

In March 1953, President DWIGHT D. EISENHOWER named Strauss chairman of the AEC. The following year, he became involved in the Oppenheimer security hearings. In late 1953, Oppenheimer, then an AEC consultant, had his security clearance suspended following charges relating to his prewar association with left-wing groups and his ambivalence about developing the H-bomb. A special AEC security board found Oppenheimer "loyal" but voted two to one to deny him clearance in April, based on the fact that he had associated with communists and lied about it. Oppenheimer then appealed his case to the full AEC. The commission ruled four to one in May to withhold clearance. Strauss was among the majority, which stated that the decision was based on "proof of fundamental defects in [Oppenheimer's] character." Ironically, Strauss had made every effort to persuade Senator JOSEPH R. MCCARTHY (R-Wis.) not to attack Oppenheimer, because he thought that it would generate support for Oppenheimer in the scientific community, but some people compared him to McCarthy.

Strauss also became embroiled in the Dixon-Yates contract, which exploded into a major political controversy in 1954–55. The Tennessee Valley Authority (TVA) proposed building a new steam plant at Fulton, Tennessee, to supply power to the city of Memphis. The consumption of TVA power by the AEC's installations at Paduca meant that the city of Memphis would face a shortage of electricity within four years. Eisenhower, who preferred the private development of power, could not see the justification for the federal government to pay for a plant to supply power to a particular city. He ordered JOSEPH DODGE, the director of the Bureau of the Budget, and Strauss to explore the possibilities of having private industry build the plant. A private combine headed by EDGAR DIXON, president of Middle South Utilities, and EUGENE YATES, chairman of the board of the Southern Company, organized the Mississippi Valley Generating Company to build a plant that would supply power to the TVA to replace the power the TVA sold to the AEC. Strauss enthusiastically endorsed this plan, describing it as "fair" and "a splendid example" of private enterprise serving public interests. After the Dixon-Yates proposal received approval from the AEC, TVA, and Bureau of the Budget, Eisenhower approved it. The contract was signed in October. Congressional Democrats, however, denounced it as an attempt to curb the TVA. Four months later, a Senate investigation revealed that Adolphe Wenzell, the consultant to the Bureau of the Budget who had recommended the plan, was a member of the bank that was to finance the Dixon-Yates plant. As a result of this disclosure and the decision of the city of Memphis to build its own municipal power plant (which freed up power from the TVA for use by the AEC), Eisenhower ordered the AEC to cancel the contract in July 1955.

During the 1950s, Strauss continued to oppose a nuclear test ban despite the heated debate over the effects of radioactive fallout. In 1954, fallout from an H-bomb test caused radiation sickness among Japanese fishermen on a trawler hundreds of miles from the test site. Reports also circulated that radioactive fish had reached Japan. At a press conference following the incident, Strauss argued that radiation levels would decrease rapidly. Japanese scientific studies failed to substantiate the claim and convinced many scientists that Strauss was trying to cover up the effects of atomic testing. The official AEC report on the incident, issued 11 months later, minimized the effects and claimed no long-term problems, but it did little to allay the public's fears.

As the controversy over the effects of testing continued, the administration, following Strauss's advice, emphasized the importance of U.S. nuclear supremacy while stressing the peaceful uses of nuclear energy. As part of this policy, Eisenhower announced the Atoms for Peace program in 1955. Under the plan, the International Atomic Energy Agency was established to increase the supply of fissionable materials available to other nations for nonmilitary purposes.

The rancor and bitterness generated by the debate over the danger of radioactive fallout continued through the end of the decade, and Strauss continued to defend the increasingly unpopular tests. In 1956, Strauss announced that within four years the United States would develop methods for localizing fallout from atomic blasts. Two years later, however, he was forced to withdraw the claim.

Strauss further enraged proponents of a test ban in March 1958, when the AEC announced that the maximum distance for detection of an underground atomic blast was 250 miles. Critics charged that the announcement was designed to sabotage attempts to achieve an atmospheric nuclear test ban treaty, which was dependent on U.S. ability to detect Soviet underground explosions. Challenges to Strauss's statement forced the AEC to admit one week later that a blast could be detected 2,300 miles away.

Strauss's steadfast opposition to a test ban conflicted with the Eisenhower administration's growing commitment to reach agreement on such a treaty in the late 1950s. In 1958, Strauss declined Eisenhower's offer of reappointment to another five-year term as AEC chairman, saying that "circumstances beyond the control of either of us make a change in the chairmanship . . . advisable." The administration announced in June that Strauss would become Eisenhower's special assistant for Atoms for Peace.

In October 1958, Eisenhower appointed Strauss to replace SINCLAIR WEEKS as secretary of commerce. However, his role in the Dixon-Yates affair and the Oppenheimer hearings, as well as his hostility to a test ban, generated strong opposition to his confirmation. Moreover, by the time hearings on his nomination began, the Democrats had won a decisive victory in the congressional elections of 1958 and enjoyed a majority of 30 seats in the Senate. Although Eisenhower defended Strauss as "a valuable public servant . . . of the utmost integrity and competence" and refused to withdraw the appointment, the Senate rejected the nomination 49 to 46 on June 19, 1959. He became the first cabinet appointee to be denied confirmation since 1925, and he resigned June 30. After leaving the government, Strauss published his memoirs,

Men and Decisions (1962), and remained active in philanthropy during the 1960s. He worked for the presidential campaigns of BARRY GOLDWATER in 1964 and RICHARD M. NIXON in 1958. He died at his estate in Culpepper, Virginia, on January 21, 1974.

—MSM

Streibert, Theodore C(uyler)
(1899–1987) *director, United States Information Agency*

Born in Albany, New York, on August 29, 1899, Streibert graduated from Wesleyan University in 1921 and received an M.B.A. from Harvard two years later. He remained at Harvard Business School, first as a research staff member for three years and then moved to New York as an executive in the film industry. He returned to Harvard Business School in 1929 as assistant dean and held that position until 1933. He simultaneously began a career in radio in 1933. Over the next 18 years, he was vice president, general manager, and, in 1945, president of radio station WOR. He also served as treasurer, vice president, and, from 1949 to 1951, chairman of the board of the Mutual Broadcasting System. During the opening months of the Eisenhower administration, Streibert served as an adviser to the International Information Administration and to the U.S. high commissioner in Germany.

Eisenhower appointed Streibert to be the first director of the proposed U.S. Information Agency (USIA) in July 1953. The Senate confirmed the appointment on August 3, two days after Congress passed the law creating the agency. Streibert's task was to reorganize the department and restore morale in the wake of Senator JOSEPH R. McCARTHY's (R-Wis.) attacks and severe budget cuts. The director created the office of policy and programs to centralize administration and appointed assistant directors for the four geographical divisions compromising the USIA to coordinate policy. These assistants determined content as well as policy. Because of budget cuts, the director was forced to close 26 overseas libraries, reduce Voice of America (VOA) broadcasts by 25 percent, and reduce staff by more than one-third. However, he was able to increase allocations for the office of pri-

vate cooperation, which was designed to get American business and labor involved in sponsorship of USIA activities. Although regarded as somewhat high-handed, Streibert was able to improve staff morale, increase efficiency, and upgrade the quality of his personnel.

Streibert was continually forced to defend his agency against McCarthy's charges that it was infiltrated by communists. At the end of 1953, his office of security conducted an investigation in which he reported that "there were no Communists discovered" in the USIA. Streibert told the Senate Foreign Relations Committee in January 1954 that he had combed his agency and that only about 20 out of 7,800 employees had been dismissed as security risks. After Eisenhower's advisory committee on information suggested in February that McCarthy discontinue his probe of the Voice of America because he was hurting the agency's reputation, McCarthy threatened to call Streibert to testify before his Senate Permanent Investigations Subcommittee. Streibert responded with an address to Congress in which he defended the VOA. He told Congress that the agency tried to stress the facts and avoid "strident and propagandist material," and he proudly claimed that a poll of east European refugees rated the VOA as their favorite show. He assured Congress that he had dismissed security risks and banned works by communist authors in USIA libraries.

Despite Streibert's announcement that the USIA would "concentrate on objective factual news reporting and appropriate commentaries," the agency reflected the cold war thinking of the time. The USIA praised the United States–sponsored overthrow of the leftist Arbenz regime in Guatemala, calling it a victory of free men over "red colonialism." It also tried to convince India and Egypt to renounce their neutralist policies, but it failed.

Streibert was particularly concerned to depict the dark side of Soviet totalitarianism. He focused a large portion of the agency's resources on publicizing Russian repression of the Hungarian revolt in 1956. The director also launched a "worldwide offensive to explore this spurious intellectual and ideological appeal of Communism." He ordered 54 selected books for USIA libraries, including such titles as *Forced Labor in Soviet Russia* and *Death of Science in Russia.*

In February 1955, Eisenhower appointed Streibert a member of the National Security Council's operations coordinating board. Beginning in 1956, he was invited to attend cabinet meetings. However, his influence on policymaking was slight. Streibert continued to advocate a hard line in the cold war and questioned the easing of tension between the United States and the USSR that followed the summit conference in 1955.

Streibert resigned his post in November 1956 and joined the business staff of Nelson and Lawrence Rockefeller. In 1960, he became a vice president of the Time-Life Broadcasting Corporation and served as president of the Radio Free Europe Fund from 1962 to 1965. He died at his home in Laurel Hollow, Long Island, on January 18, 1987.

—MSM

Strobel, Peter A(ndres)

(1901–1980) *commissioner, Public Buildings Service, General Services Administration*

Born in Denmark on May 22, 1901, Strobel graduated from Copenhagen's Technical University with a degree in civil engineering at the age of 24. He immediately emigrated to the United States, accompanied by his wife and daughter. After a long apprenticeship in the building trades, Strobel worked as chief structural engineer at the New York World's Fair of 1939. During World War II, he designed prefabricated army barracks and portable airplane hangers. After the war, his new firm, Strobel and Salzman, built shopping centers, railroad stations, and the cosmotron building at Brookhaven National Laboratory.

Upon the recommendation of the Republican National Committee, Strobel was appointed commissioner of the Public Buildings Service (PBS) of the General Services Administration (GSA) in 1954. As commissioner, Strobel operated 6,000 government buildings, supervised the construction of over 100 others, and directed the 45 factories of the National Industrial Reserve. In accepting the position as commissioner, he willingly accepted a cut in his income from the $100,000 he earned annually in the private sector to $14,800. "Perhaps," he said at the time of his appointment, "I can partly pay back this country for what it has done for me."

In September 1955, columnist DREW PEARSON charged that Strobel had not dissolved his connection with Strobel and Salzman after becoming commissioner. Strobel demanded an opportunity to refute the charges but refused to do so in Pearson's column.

When the House Judiciary Committee's Antitrust Subcommittee opened hearings on the matter in October, Strobel cooperated fully. He admitted maintaining a 90 percent interest in his engineering firm, but he insisted that he never "used or sought to use my official position to further the firm's interests." Strobel acknowledged that, while commissioner, he pressed his firm's claim for $7,500 against the Corps of Engineers, unaware that he was violating a law forbidding federal employees from acting as agents in claims against the government. He also negotiated a $71,050 contract with the corps after being appointed commissioner but before taking office. The commissioner's testimony revealed that he had recommended several of Strobel and Salzman's clients for PBS contracts, including one for work on the new $46 million Central Intelligence Agency headquarters. However, he maintained that his firm received no profits from the jobs. The subcommittee also learned that Strobel had not signed the required standard of conduct statement, stipulating that employees get written approval before engaging in outside business activity, and had not submitted a list of his firm's clients to the agency until August 1955.

In evaluating Strobel's testimony, the chairman of the subcommittee, EMANUEL CELLER (D-N.Y.), said that, although some of the commissioner's actions might have been in violation of the criminal code, Strobel was not an intentionally dishonest man. Celler set November 22 as the deadline to hear what action the GSA contemplated against him. Strobel resigned on November 8 and returned to his firm amid rumors that members of the White House staff pressed him to resign. In April 1956, The Antitrust Subcommittee voted 4-3 to clear Strobel of unethical conduct. The Justice Department decided not to initiate criminal charges against him. He died in Palm Beach, Florida in March, 1980.

—MSM

Sulzberger, C(yrus) L(eo)

(1912–1993) *journalist*

Born in New York City on October 27, 1912, Sulzberger was a nephew of Arthur Hays Sulzberger, publisher of the *New York Times* from 1935 to 1961. His cousin, Arthur Ochs Sulzberger, published the paper from 1963 to 1992. Following his graduation (magna cum laude) from Harvard in 1934, Sulzberger began a career in journalism. Because of his family connections to the *Times*, he decided to try to make his name elsewhere. He went to work for the *Pittsburgh Press*. After a year, he moved to the United Press, where he covered labor, the Treasury Department, and the Federal Reserve system. He later wrote for the *London Evening Standard*. In 1939, he joined the *New York Times* as the Balkan bureau manager. During his first three years with the paper he traveled more than 100,000 miles through 30 countries reporting on World War II.

In 1944, Sulzberger became the chief foreign correspondent for the *New York Times* and headed its foreign desk. The paper gave him his own column in 1954. His column, "Foreign Affairs," appeared three times a week on the editorial page until 1970, when it moved to the Op-Ed page. He argued that powerful leaders, such as HARRY S. TRUMAN, Joseph Stalin, Charles de Gaulle, and Winston Churchill, rather than ideas shaped history. Reflecting his belief that great men shaped events, his column focused on interviews with and profiles of foreign leaders. Through Sulzberger's writing, these individuals emerged as personalities. Sulzberger began by holding interviews with Secretary of State JOHN FOSTER DULLES and former secretary of state DEAN ACHESON. From these discussions, the journalist was able to outline the differences in attitudes between the two cold warriors. Dulles emerged as a moralist anxious to carry on a crusade against communism, while Acheson appeared as a realist maintaining that morality produced useless slogans. Churchill and de Gaulle were Sulzberger's favorite subjects. He thought of both as symbols of the most positive and negative expressions of their cultures. Sulzberger called them "the last of the giants of the past age."

Sulzberger wrote two books on foreign policy during the Eisenhower administration, both of which synthesized views he had expressed in his columns. The first book, *The Big Thaw: A Personal Exploration of the "New" Russia and the Orbit Countries* (1956), discussed what he saw as the relaxation of Stalin's oppressive internal policies following the dictator's death. Sulzberger argued that the Soviets were extending this "thaw," in varying degrees, to its satellite nations. He believed the West would benefit from this because it could lead to a breakup of monolithic communism. In response to these developments, he advised the United States to encourage more "Titoist heresies" in eastern Europe. The publication of Sulzberger's book coincided with the Soviet suppression of the Hungarian revolt. At least one reviewer suggested that Sulzberger might want to revise his thesis in light of events in Hungary.

In 1959, Sulzberger published *What's Wrong with U.S. Foreign Policy*. Reiterating a theme that first emerged in his writing during the 1940s, he criticized the United States for failing to demonstrate a strong enough sense of realism and direction in its policies. Sulzberger urged the United States to stop using abstract ideology as a means of interpreting the intentions of its rivals. Russian imperialism, he argued, rather than Marxism, motivated Soviet leaders. Reflecting the importance he placed on the individuals who molded policy, Sulzberger recommended that greater care should be used in the selection of diplomats.

Sulzberger's contacts with the famous and powerful gained him many exclusive stories, and he won praise for his ability to uncover news and place it in context. At the same time, reviewers and academic critics often criticized his books for being pompous, repetitious, and overwhelmed by trivial detail. Many objected that the author injected himself too much into his columns and books.

Throughout the 1960s and 1970s, Sulzberger continued to be one of the nation's leading observers of foreign policy. Through his travels to distant lands, his meetings with foreign leaders, and his contacts with foreign policy experts at home and abroad, Sulzberger continued to document and interpret the changes in American diplomacy. He published a volume of memoirs, *A Long Row of Candles*, in 1969. *The Fall of Eagles* (1977) dealt with the collapse of the Hapsburg, Hohenzollern, and Romanov dynasties. Another volume of memoirs, *Seven Continents and Forty Years*, which contained numerous brief, sharply drawn portraits of world leaders, was published in 1977. Sulzberger gave up his column on the Op-Ed page of the *Times* in 1978 but continued to write. He died in Paris on September 20, 1993.

—MSM

Summerfield, Arthur E(llsworth)
(1899–1972) *postmaster general*

The son of a rural mail carrier, Arthur Summerfield was born in Pinconning, Michigan, on March 17, 1899. He left school at the age of 13 and worked for the Weston-Mott Company and then for the Buick Motor Company. During World War I, he worked for the ammunition department of the Chevrolet plant in Flint, Michigan. He entered the real estate business in 1919 and became a distributor in Flint for the Pure Oil Company in 1924. He developed the latter business into one of the largest individual oil distributorships in the state. In 1929, he also launched the Summerfield Chevrolet Company, which eventually became one of the largest dealerships in the nation, with branches throughout his home state of Michigan. In 1937, he gave up his Pure Oil business and the following year became president of Bryant Properties Corporation, a profitable real estate business.

Summerfield entered politics during Wendell Willkie's campaign for the presidency in 1940. Seeing the failure of the local Republicans to mobilize support for Willkie, Summerfield organized his own county committee. Willkie carried the county, a factor crucial for the Republican's upset victory in Michigan. The automobile magnate thus earned a reputation as an effective political organizer.

Summerfield unsuccessfully sought the Republican nomination for Michigan secretary of state in 1942. The following year, he became finance director for the state's Republican Central Committee. He expanded the party's drives, which had concentrated on the wealthy, to include Republicans of all means. The method proved so successful that several other states adopted it. During World War II, he assisted in mobilizing manpower for the war effort and directed Flint's war chest campaign. Summerfield was elected to the Republican National Committee in 1944. Two years later, he made an unsuccessful bid for the Republican nomination for a seat in the U.S. Sen-

ate. In 1946, Summerfield was named to the party's national finance committee. There his fame as a money raiser approached the "legendary," according to one newspaper.

During the postwar period, Summerfield attempted to promote Senator Arthur S. Vandenberg (R-Mich.) for president, but the senator declined to run. In 1948, the Republican presidential candidate THOMAS E. DEWEY, contemplated appointing Summerfield national chairman. However, Summerfield removed his name from consideration. The following year, he accepted the chairmanship of the Republican national strategy committee. In that capacity, he designed the strategy for the congressional elections of 1950. After coming into conflict with the party's chairman, Guy C. Gabrielson, Summerfield resigned.

Summerfield headed the Michigan delegation to the Republican National Convention in 1952. Although he had initially backed Senator ROBERT A. TAFT of Ohio for the nomination, prior to the convention he shrewdly announced his neutrality in the race between General DWIGHT D. EISENHOWER and Taft. The morning of the nomination meeting, he threw his support behind Eisenhower, which helped create momentum for Eisenhower's candidacy. Thirty-five of Michigan's 45 delegates voted for Eisenhower on the first ballot. Pennsylvania, the other large uncommitted state, then joined Michigan in coming out for Eisenhower. Following the convention, Summerfield became chairman of the Republican National Committee. During the summer, he successfully unified the party, which had been split by the bitter primary fight between Taft and Eisenhower.

After Eisenhower's victory in November, he announced that Summerfield would become postmaster general, a position traditionally held by one of the top functionaries of the victorious party. Summerfield surprised many by resigning as Republican national chairman and refusing to use the postal service for patronage.

In taking over the postal department, Summerfield sought to introduce business techniques to improve service and reduce the department's operating deficit. He appointed new managers to top administrative positions, made financial statements available at the end of each month, and streamlined administration. In addition, he reorganized the Postal Service's transportation patterns, standardized equipment throughout the nation to keep costs down, and closed uneconomical post offices and ended uneconomical routes. Summerfield devoted substantial resources to invest in new machinery. He persuaded Eisenhower to veto pay increases for postal workers on four different occasions, which alienated employees of the Postal Service. In 1956, Summerfield claimed that he had sharply reduced the deficit. His critics charged that the reduction resulted more from a rise in the postage rates and clever bookkeeping tricks. They also questioned the success of his reforms, charging that improvements in the department tended to be cosmetic—newly painted mailboxes, new uniforms for mailmen, and the availability of chained pens on desks in front of postal windows.

During his tenure as postmaster general, Summerfield experimented with several ways to speed the mails. In 1959, a guided missile carried 3,000 letters from a submarine in the Atlantic to a field near Jacksonville, Florida. He heralded the flight as the first known "official use of missiles by any Post Office Department in any nation." The following year, he demonstrated an electronic facsimile system to deliver mail across the nation in seconds. Letters were put on a postal form and transmitted over television microwaves. This system, however, proved too costly to operate.

Summerfield's attempts to modernize the department were often hindered by Congress, which controlled the postal budget. The legislature refused rate increases Summerfield believed necessary for modernization or to fund purchases of new equipment. The postmaster general also wanted to increase salaries of management personnel to attract better administrators, but Congress focused its attention on average postal workers, raising their pay by 8 percent in 1955. That decision appealed to the political instincts of members of Congress, but it added to Summerfield's operating costs without corresponding rate increases. The postmaster general also discovered that politics made it difficult to close uneconomic local post offices. Many members of Congress pressed him to reopen them, and he was forced to do so to maintain their support for his budget.

Summerfield waged an energetic campaign against obscene material sent through the mail. He believed that the courts had upheld his authority to bar pornography. In 1959, he reported that 315 arrests had been made that year on such charges. Intending to demonstrate the dangerous and offensive nature of the matter he sought to ban from the mails, Summerfield arranged an exhibition of seized pornographic material in Washington, D.C. Rather than persuading the public that it needed to be protected from such matter, the exhibit provoked tittering and sneers. That same year, Summerfield attempted to ban from the mails a new, unexpurgated edition of D. H. Lawrence's novel, *Lady Chatterley's Lover*. He stated, "Any literary merit the book may have is far outweighed by the pornographic and smutty passages and words, so that the book taken as a whole, is an obscene and filthy work." A federal district court ruled against Summerfield's action, and, on March 25, 1960, a federal court of appeals unanimously upheld the lower court's ruling. The Justice Department decided not to appeal the decision to the Supreme Court.

Following his retirement from public service, Summerfield returned to his business ventures and raised funds for BARRY GOLDWATER's presidential campaign in 1964. Summerfield died in West Palm Beach, Florida, on April 26, 1972.

—MSM

Symington, (William) Stuart
(1901–1988) *U.S. senator*

Symington was born on June 26, 1901, into a wealthy family in Amherst, Massachusetts, where his father taught Romance languages at Amherst College. He was raised in Baltimore, Maryland. After service as a second lieutenant in the army during World War I (he never left the United States), he attended Yale University but left in 1923 without taking a degree. He worked briefly as a newspaper reporter in Baltimore and as an iron molder in his uncles' company in Rochester, New York. In 1925, he became president of Eastern Clay Products. During the next 12 years, he served as chief operating officer of three other companies, moving first to Buffalo and then to Baltimore. He took over foundering enterprises and made them into financial successes.

Symington's greatest business achievement came as president of the Emerson Electric Manufacturing Company from 1938 to 1945. When he joined the firm, it was suffering from serious labor and financial problems. Symington successfully negotiated with the unit of the United Electrical, Radio and Machine Workers that represented Emerson and started a profit-sharing program. As a result, the employees rallied to the support of the company, profits rose, and Emerson was the only large war plant in St. Louis not to have labor problems during World War II.

After the war, President HARRY S. TRUMAN appointed Symington head of the Surplus Property Board, where he directed the disposal of $90 billion in surplus war property. As director, Symington helped alleviate the housing shortage for veterans by ordering federal agencies to turn over to states without charge surplus materials, equipment, and land for emergency housing. In 1946, Truman appointed Symington assistant secretary of war for air. After passage of the Armed Forces Unification Bill in 1947, Symington became the first secretary of the air force. Believing that the United States had to act from a position of military superiority against the expansionist policies of the Soviet Union, Symington became a leading proponent of increased defense spending. He particularly advocated the development of a large nuclear-equipped air force as the cornerstone of a modern defense system. In 1950, shortly before the Korean War, Symington resigned to protest a series of cuts in military spending. Truman appointed him to chair the National Security Resources Board. A year later, at Truman's request, Symington took over the scandal-ridden Reconstruction Finance Corporation.

Symington ran for the Democratic nomination for a seat in the U.S. Senate from Missouri in 1952. Although Truman had already committed to support his opponent, Symington won the primary. He easily won the general election in November and won reelection in 1958, 1964, and 1970. From the time he arrived in the Senate, he served on the Armed Services Committee, and other members deferred to him as an expert on defense. While a liberal on domestic issues, he was known primarily for his devotion to protecting the interests of the Defense Department and particularly the air

force. Shortly after taking his seat, he criticized the United States for lagging behind the Soviet Union in the development of missiles and bombers. Symington alleged that the cuts in defense spending proposed by the Eisenhower administration would leave the country vulnerable to a strategic bombing campaign, an allegation that, in private, Eisenhower referred to as "pure rot."

Several years later, Symington joined such military men as General NATHAN TWINING in suggesting that a "bomber gap" existed between the United States and the USSR. In April 1956, Symington headed a special subcommittee of the Senate Armed Forces Committee that held hearings on the state of American airpower. In a Senate speech in May, he stated, "It is now clear that the U.S. . . . may have lost control of the air" and called for an accounting of U.S. air strength. During three months of hearings, the panel heard testimony from a number of military leaders, including Air Force general CURTIS LEMAY, who predicted that the United States would be behind the Soviets in airpower within the decade unless spending was increased. Representatives of the administration, however, defended the president's limited budget and maintained that U.S. defenses would continue to be superior to those of the USSR. Following testimony by Secretary of Defense CHARLES WILSON, Symington charged that the Defense Department was considering going against the wishes of Congress by refusing to increase production. He also maintained that someone in the department was misleading the American people in describing comparative U.S. and USSR defense strengths. At a meeting with Republican congressional leaders, Eisenhower dismissed the agitation as "purely political."

The subcommittee's majority report, issued in January 1957, concluded that U.S. vulnerability to sudden attack had "increased greatly" and that the Soviet Union exceeded America in combat aircraft and would soon close the "quality gap." The report alleged that "the United States has never been more vulnerable to Soviet attack than now" and charged that the Eisenhower administration had placed financial considerations ahead of defense requirements. At a press conference, Eisenhower dismissed the alarmist findings of the report. He acknowledged that "the vulnerability of any nation is probably greater today than it ever was, because one bomb today can do the damage of probably all that we dropped on Germany in World War II." On the other hand, he maintained that "we are in as good a position as we have ever been in time of peace. And I don't believe that the position by any manner of means is deteriorating at the rate that some people would have you think."

After the Soviet Union launched *Sputnik*, Symington stepped up his attack. In 1959, Symington charged that a "missile gap" existed between the United States and the USSR. He predicted that the Soviet Union would soon have a three-to-one lead over the United States in operational intercontinental ballistic missiles. That, he maintained, would enable the Russians to "wipe out our entire manned and unmanned retaliatory force" with a single blow. Eisenhower invited Symington to a private meeting in which, according to a memorandum of the conference, Eisenhower pointed out that "it would be out of character for him to be indifferent to valid assessments of Soviet strength." Symington remained undeterred.

During the early 1950s, Symington was an outspoken and fierce opponent of Senator JOSEPH R. MCCARTHY (R-Wis.). In February 1953, as a member of McCarthy's Permanent Investigations Subcommittee, Symington defended Annie Lee Moss, a clerk in the Pentagon whom McCarthy had charged with having seen decoded messages while being a member of the Communist Party. Symington believed that the Annie Lee Moss under investigation was actually the wrong Annie Lee Moss, since three appeared in the Washington, D.C., telephone directory. He offered to help her find another job if she was fired as a result of McCarthy's inquiry.

Symington also played a principal role in the Army-McCarthy hearings the following year, during which, according to the historian Robert Griffith, Symington was "McCarthy's most intransigent foe."

When Republicans on the subcommittee tried to get the hearings adjourned, Symington, with the cooperation of the White House, pressed for their continuation. Accused by McCarthy of using the investigation to destroy the Republican Party and Eisenhower, Symington assured the nationwide television audience watching the hearings that he was "not afraid of anything about [McCarthy] or anything [McCarthy had] to say, at any time, any place, anywhere."

In 1959, Symington entered the campaign for the Democratic presidential nomination. His central issue was an attack on Eisenhower's defense policies. Although he had the backing of former president Harry S. Truman, Symington's candidacy failed. Avoiding what proved to be the decisive primary campaigns, he had based his hopes on a deadlocked convention. After Senator JOHN F. KENNEDY (D-Mass.) won the nomination, Symington was mentioned as a possible running mate, but that went to Senator LYNDON B. JOHNSON (D-Tex.).

During the 1960s, Symington continued his advocacy of increased military spending. Beginning in 1961, he chaired the Foreign Relations Committee. Although an early supporter of the war in Vietnam, the senator became an opponent of the war by late 1967. Reversing his early belief that the United States had to take a dominant role in defense of the world, Symington called on President RICHARD M. NIXON in 1973 to bring home many of the U.S. servicemen throughout the world because of the detrimental effect large-scale defense commitments had on the American economy. Symington also fought for the reassertion of congressional authority in foreign policy. He did not run for reelection in 1976. After leaving the Senate, he became vice chairman of First American Bankshares. He lived in New Canaan, Connecticut, until his death there on December 14, 1988.

—MSM

T

Taber, John

(1880–1965) *U.S. congressman; chairman,*
Appropriations Committee

The son of an attorney, Taber was born on May 5, 1880, in Auburn, New York, where he attended public schools. After receiving a B.A. degree from Yale University in 1902, he attended the New York Law School for one year. Following his admission to the New York bar in 1904, he joined his father's practice in Auburn. In 1918, he established his own practice. Early in his career, Taber became involved in Republican Party politics. He sat as a special judge of the county court from 1910 to 1918. In 1922, he won election to the U.S. House of Representatives from New York's Finger Lakes region. His district reelected Taber 19 consecutive times.

During his first term, he was named to the Appropriations Committee and served on it for the rest of his career in the House. Throughout the 1920s, Taber established a reputation as a fiscal conservative, but he exercised little influence. After the Democratic landslide in 1932 wiped out the senior Republicans on the Appropriations Committee, Taber became the ranking minority member. Throughout the New Deal, he consistently voted against social welfare programs. He also opposed federal intervention on behalf of African Americans; he voted against bills outlawing the poll tax and making lynching a federal offense as well as the Fair Employment Practices Commission. In foreign policy, Taber was an isolationist until 1941, when he declared his support for Lend-Lease aid. After the

United States entered the war, Taber enthusiastically supported appropriations for the war effort. He remained, however, staunchly opposed to President Franklin D. Roosevelt's domestic programs.

After HARRY S. TRUMAN became president, Taber once again attempted to cut government spending and continued to oppose social welfare measures. He attempted to block federal grants for school lunches and supported the Taft-Hartley Act while opposing wage and price controls and public housing. Although he often took internationalist positions in foreign affairs, he was a critic of foreign economic aid programs. When the Republicans gained control of Congress after the elections of 1946, Taber became chairman of the Appropriations Committee. He declared his intention to cut Truman's proposal for a $37.5 billion budget by $6 billion and to reduce the federal payroll by half. Although Taber did force reductions in domestic programs, the savings were more than offset by increased spending on the cold war. He also failed in his efforts to eliminate half of federal employees. Taber played a key role in cutting foreign relief funds in 1947 but fought unsuccessfully for substantial reductions in Marshall Plan appropriations the following year. The Democrats regained control of Congress after the elections of 1948, and Taber reverted to ranking minority member.

The election of 1952 brought DWIGHT D. EISENHOWER to the White House and returned the Republicans to control in Congress. Taber once again assumed the chair of the Appropriations

Committee in 1953. In July 1953, Taber's panel cut $700 million from Eisenhower's $5.1 billion foreign aid request, despite a personal appeal by the president at a breakfast meeting with the representative from New York. Most of the cuts were in the area of economic assistance. In order to secure the expeditious enactment of a foreign military aid package, however, Taber was willing to accept a somewhat higher level of economic aid at the House-Senate conference two weeks later. He urged the House to approve the bill as it came out of conference on the ground that "the world is facing a very difficult situation" and "we have got . . . to develop military strength sufficient to combat the Communist threat." The following year, after the French defeat at Dien Bien Phu in northern Vietnam, Taber defended that year's foreign aid bill. He believed that recent international developments required the United States to "do whatever we can to build up support for the defense of the Far East, Southeast Asia and the Western Pacific."

During his second term as chairman, he repeatedly took to the floor to defend cuts made by his committee. In 1953, the Appropriations Committee eliminated provisions providing for aid to schools in areas that had increased enrollment as a result of the Korean War. The entire House restored that provision, and Taber took the floor in a futile effort to reinstate the cut. That same year, he successfully fought off House efforts to increase the $60 million appropriation for the State Department's International Information Administration (IIA) approved by his committee. In opposing any increase above the level recommended by his committee, Taber charged that there were "thousands and thousands of incompetents" on the IIA payroll. Followers of Senator JOSEPH R. MCCARTHY (R-Wis.) voted with Taber because they believed that the IIA harbored left-wingers. The following year, Taber successfully opposed an effort in the whole House to restore funding for the Census Bureau to do a business census. He argued that such censuses were of no help to business and "have just historic value." Finally, in 1953, he voted against an increase in Social Security payments and the inclusion of 750,000 new workers.

After the Democrats regained control of Congress in the 1954 elections, Taber reverted to the status of ranking Republican on the Appropriations Committee. For the remainder of the decade, he was particularly vehement in opposing public works projects. In 1956, Taber asserted that "we cannot go along continuing to pile up projects that are . . . to cost a tremendous amount of money and yet have the nation land right side up." A critic of the Tennessee Valley Authority (TVA), he attacked an appropriation for additional TVA power facilities in 1956 and the following year unsuccessfully attempted on the House floor to cut funding for the TVA from $13.3 million to $3.5 million. Continuing his budget-minded approach to foreign economic aid, Taber unsuccessfully attempted in 1960 to eliminate appropriations for U.S. participation in the International Development Association (IDA), which he denounced as a "giveaway."

During the administration of JOHN F. KENNEDY, Taber opposed most New Frontier legislation. In 1962, he announced that he would not seek reelection. He returned to Auburn, New York, where he died on November 22, 1965.

—MSM

Taft, Robert A(lphonso)

(1889–1953) *U.S. senator; Senate majority leader*

The grandson of Ulysses Grant's attorney general and son of the 27th president and 10th chief justice of the United States, Robert A. Taft was born on September 8, 1889, in Cincinnati, Ohio. After graduating first in his class at both Yale in 1910 and Harvard Law School in 1913, he returned to Cincinnati to practice law. During World War I, he was an assistant counsel to U.S. Food Administrator HERBERT HOOVER. Taft won election as a Republican to the Ohio house of representatives in 1920. During his six years in that body, he opposed prohibition and the Ku Klux Klan. His colleagues elected him Republican floor leader in 1925 and speaker in 1926. Taft retired from the legislature in 1926 and resumed his career with Taft, Stettinius and Hollister. He served a term in the state senate from 1931 to 1932. A firm opponent of President Franklin D. Roosevelt's New Deal, Taft ran for the U.S. Senate in 1938 and won. He was reelected in 1944 and 1950. His intelligence, mastery of detail, and expertise on parliamentary procedure made

Taft a leader of the Republican minority from the time he entered the Senate.

Taft quickly emerged as the most articulate champion of the Republican Party's midwestern, conservative, isolationist wing. He repeatedly denounced most New and Fair Deal social programs as both wasteful and hazardous to individual liberties. He denounced expanding government bureaucracies as "creeping socialism." His stature was such that, after only a year in the Senate, he emerged as a serious candidate for the Republican presidential nomination. At the Republican National Convention in 1940, Taft and THOMAS E. DEWEY, the leader of the eastern, liberal, internationalist wing of the party, battled to a standstill, and the nomination went to Wendell Willkie on the sixth ballot.

Throughout the 1930s, Taft had opposed American military intervention in Europe. Although appalled by Nazism, he believed that the United States should go to war against Hitler only if attacked. Thus, he opposed the Lend-Lease bill in 1941 and other measures he thought likely to bring the United States into World War II. At the same time, Taft supported military preparedness and aid to Britain "consistent with the policy of staying out of the war." Among other things, Taft feared that a war would contribute to the growth of government and expansion of presidential power. World War II bore out Taft's concerns. In the Senate, Taft alone raised constitutional objections to legislation providing for the forced removal of Japanese and Japanese Americans, although he swallowed his objections when the bill passed by a voice vote without dissent.

In 1944, Taft put aside his ambition for the presidency and backed JOHN BRICKER, the governor of Ohio, for the Republican nomination. Bricker, however, lost the nomination to Dewey. In the general election, Roosevelt defeated Dewey. When Roosevelt died not quite three months into his fourth term, HARRY S. TRUMAN became president.

Taft doggedly led the congressional opposition to Truman's administration. Taft's reputation as a grim reactionary, however, derived more from his stern demeanor than from ideological rigidity. On occasion, he veered sharply from conservative orthodoxy. Beginning in 1945 and 1946, for example, Taft sponsored decidedly liberal measures

providing for federally funded public housing and aid to education.

His signature legislative achievement, however, infuriated organized labor. A rash of strikes in the postwar period led to demands to curb organized labor. Truman himself called for legislation that banned secondary boycotts and strikes arising from jurisdictional disputes between unions. As chair of the Senate Labor Committee, Taft became a key player in crafting reform of the National Labor Relations Act. The Labor-Management Relations Act of 1947 (known as the Taft-Hartley Act), which became law after Congress overrode Truman's veto, outlawed secondary boycotts, banned the closed shop, authorized the president to order an 80-day "cooling off" period to forestall strikes that threatened national health or safety, required union officials seeking certification by the National Labor Relations Board to sign noncommunist oaths, and required unions to file financial reports with the Department of Labor. Union leaders decried the measure as a "slave labor act" and warned that it would destroy organized labor. It did no such thing.

With respect to foreign policy, Taft rejected calls by some Republican leaders after the war for bipartisanship in foreign policy. Skeptical of postwar Europe's military and economic weakness, Taft took exception to Truman's primary focus on western Europe in the struggle against communist expansion. Like many midwestern conservative Republicans, Taft believed that America's primary interests lay across the Pacific. He nevertheless supported aid to Greece and Turkey and, after some reluctance, the Marshall Plan.

Taft again sought the presidential nomination in 1948. He had the loyalty of party regulars in the Midwest, but his results in the primary elections were disappointing. At the convention, Dewey's forces were better organized, and Taft lost the nomination to Dewey, whom Truman defeated in a stunning upset that November.

During Truman's second term, Taft clashed repeatedly with the administration on foreign policy. He voted against the North Atlantic Treaty, which created the North Atlantic Treaty Organization (NATO). Although Taft later accepted American membership in NATO, he sought reductions in America's military commitment to the alliance.

The senator excoriated the Truman administration for "losing" China to the Communists. After North Korea invaded South Korea in June 1950, Taft denounced the "outrageous act of aggression," which he thought "in all probability was instigated by Soviet Russia." Had Truman gone to Congress for a joint resolution approving the dispatch of American air and naval forces, declared Taft, he would have voted for it. Nevertheless, he criticized Secretary of State DEAN ACHESON for publicly excluding Korea from the defense perimeter of the United States and thereby encouraging the North Koreans. He also attacked Truman for failing to get congressional approval for the military action.

Senator JOSEPH R. MCCARTHY (R-Wis.) presented Taft with a dilemma. McCarthy's charges that communists had infiltrated the State Department and the Truman administration placed Taft, the unquestioned leader of the midwestern Republicans in the Senate, in a difficult situation. Taft believed that there was some truth to the charges. Moreover, he recognized the political value of such attacks on the Truman administration. On the other hand, Taft had a solid record in support of civil liberties, and, in private, Taft complained that McCarthy did not "check his statements very carefully," "overstated a good case," and "made allegations which are impossible to prove which may be embarrassing before we get through." When it became clear that McCarthy's particular allegations were unfounded, Taft distanced himself from the junior senator from Wisconsin.

Dewey's defeats at the hands of Roosevelt and Truman discredited him in the eyes of conservative Republicans, who detested him anyway. Conversely, Taft's unilateralist approach to foreign policy alarmed the internationalist wing of the party, as did his dour personality and the thought that he could not win a general election. Given Taft's popularity with party loyalists, the eastern wing of the party, led by Dewey, sought a candidate whose personal popularity could derail Taft's seemingly certain nomination. They found such a candidate in DWIGHT D. EISENHOWER.

The battle for the Republican nomination in 1952 was tightly contested. At the convention in Chicago, the outcome turned on a challenge mounted by the Eisenhower forces to the credentials of the Taft delegates from Texas, Louisiana, and Georgia. The superior organization and strategy of Eisenhower's supporters led to victory in the struggle over the contested southern delegations and ultimately to Eisenhower's nomination.

Taft's last and narrowest defeat for the nomination proved his greatest personal disappointment, and his defeat embittered many loyal party workers. Recognizing the need to unify the party, Eisenhower met with Taft at the nominee's headquarters on Morningside Heights in September. After a long breakfast meeting, Taft emerged to endorse his former rival. Taft released a statement to reporters that sketched out an agreement that he and Eisenhower had reached. Taft acknowledged that he and the nominee held differing views on foreign policy, but the statement declared that the two men agreed on what Taft described as the most important issue in the campaign: the struggle for "liberty" against "creeping socialism in every domestic field." In addition, the statement committed the candidate to reduce the budget and taxes as well as to support the basic elements of the Taft-Hartley Act. Critics, including liberal Republicans, denounced the agreement as the "surrender at Morningside Heights."

In the weeks after his election, Eisenhower displayed only the most formal regard for Taft's sensibilities. Several of the president's choices for his cabinet annoyed the senator, who thought that the selections included too many leaders of big business. None perturbed him more, however, than the nomination of MARTIN DURKIN, a Democrat, labor leader, and avowed foe of the Taft-Hartley Act, as secretary of labor. Taft called Durkin's selection "incredible."

Eisenhower's lopsided victory in November helped Republicans gain control of both houses of Congress, and, in December 1952, Republican senators unanimously elected Taft majority leader. Ever the party loyalist, Taft tried to put aside the frustrations of the previous year. Although his party held only a narrow, 48–47 majority, Taft constructed a working majority in support of most of Eisenhower's domestic program. He proved to be a loyal and effective majority leader.

Senator McCarthy posed Taft's first major problem as majority leader. Supporting some of McCarthy's broader goals, Taft had early on defended the controversial anticommunist investigator despite private misgivings over his methods and doubts over the extent of a domestic communist menace. Taft also worried that McCarthy might embarrass the new Republican administration. He therefore charged Senator WILLIAM JENNER (R-Ind.), chairman of the Internal Security Committee, with the responsibility for investigating domestic subversion and relegated McCarthy to the chairmanship of the previously insignificant Government Operations Committee. There, Taft reasoned, "We've got McCarthy where he can't do any harm." Events proved him incorrect.

Eisenhower's nomination of CHARLES BOHLEN to be ambassador to the Soviet Union provided Taft with the greatest single challenge during his majority leadership. Largely because of Bohlen's participation in the controversial Yalta Conference of 1945, McCarthy and other militantly anticommunist Republican senators quickly denounced him as a security risk. Sensing a potentially disastrous rift within his own ranks and an early humiliation for the new president, Taft personally examined Bohlen's FBI file. He found nothing to validate charges made by the nominee's detractors. Taft refused to allow McCarthy to examine the confidential file. With the full weight of his own impeccable anticommunist credentials, Taft ardently defended Bohlen, thus assuring his confirmation in March, by a vote of 74 to 13. The votes against the nomination came from McCarthy and a handful of Republican right-wingers.

Defense policy continued to divide Eisenhower and Taft after the election. In February 1953, Taft gave a speech that anticipated the president's own farewell address by declaring, "We could destroy our liberty by a military and foreign expenditure in time of peace so great that a free economic system cannot survive." Excessive military spending, he warned, might make America a "garrison state." He failed, however, to convert Eisenhower during an April budget meeting; Eisenhower refused to reduce Defense Department requests for fiscal 1954. The president did acquiesce to Taft's suggestion that, as part of an overall effort to distinguish his image from that of his predecessor, he should replace all members of the Joint Chiefs of Staff, including his old army comrade Omar Bradley.

Though essentially loyal to Eisenhower, Taft publicly differed with the president on certain aspects of foreign policy. He criticized NATO's dependence on American military power and called upon European members to play a larger role. He remained more anxious over communist expansion in Asia than in Europe. In a widely reported speech on Korea during May 1953, Taft faulted the United Nations for impeding the war there. If truce negotiations failed, Taft suggested that the United States must "reserve to ourselves a completely free hand" and expand operations against China. America, he insisted, should insist on a free, united Korea. The White House quickly released a statement making it clear that the administration did not share Taft's opinions.

Taft became seriously ill with cancer in the late spring and died in New York City on July 31, 1953. In June, he had selected WILLIAM F. KNOWLAND (R-Calif.) as his successor. Robert Taft possessed rare intelligence, courage, and integrity. Years later his various positions found support among a wide range of people. Democrats quoted his speeches in favor of public housing, and New Left scholars praised his skepticism toward a cold war leviathan state. Many conservative Republican partisans continued to seek revenge for Taft's defeat in 1952 well into the 1960s. They realized their goal with the nomination of BARRY GOLDWATER in 1964 and Ronald Reagan in 1980. The conservative wing ultimately seized control of the Republican Party. In 1959, the Senate designated Taft as one of the five greatest senators in history.

—MSM

Talbott, Harold E(lstner)

(1888–1957) *secretary of the air force*

Born in Dayton, Ohio, on March 31, 1888, Talbott attended the Hill School, in Pottstown, Pennsylvania, spent two years at Yale University, and joined his father's construction company in 1911. Along with a group of investors, he and his father founded the Dayton-Wright Airplane Company (a successor to the Orville Wright Company) in 1916. Talbott served as its president from 1916 to 1923. When the United States entered World War I, Dayton-Wright became the leading supplier of aircraft to the American military. In September 1918, Talbott was commissioned a major in the air service of the signal corps and assigned to France. The signing of the armistice resulted in the cancellation of his assignment. An investigation led by Charles Evans Hughes revealed that Dayton-Wright's cost-plus contracts with government resulted in profits of approximately $3.5 million. Talbott and his partners received salaries of $100,000, which were charged to the government as part of the cost of production. The government attempted to prosecute the firm in 1922, but the case was dismissed. The sale of Dayton-Wright to General Motors in 1920 made Talbott wealthy. Talbott moved to New York City in 1924. He was one of the original investors in the Chrysler Corporation and served as chairman of North American Aviation in the early 1930s.

After serving as aircraft production director of the War Production Board during 1942–43, Talbott joined the board of directors of Chrysler Corporation in 1944 and also served as a member of the finance committee of the Electric Auto-Lite Company. Beginning in the 1930s, he became a fundraiser for the Republican Party. He raised money for the presidential campaigns of Wendell L. Willkie in 1940 and Thomas E. Dewey in 1944 and 1948. Talbott served as chairman of the Republican National Finance Committee in 1948–49. An early supporter of Dwight D. Eisenhower for the presidency in 1952, Talbott raised money for Eisenhower's campaign that year.

President-elect Eisenhower nominated Talbott air force secretary in December 1952. Because of regulations requiring government personnel to divest themselves of stock held with firms that had government contracts, Talbott was forced to sell his stock in Chrysler and Electric Auto-Lite. However, he was allowed to continue his partnership with Paul Mulligan & Company, a general management engineering firm. The Senate confirmed Talbott by a vote of 76 to 6 in February 1953.

As secretary of the air force, Talbott improved the pay and living conditions of those serving in the air force. He also founded the Air Force Academy and oversaw the expansion of the air force from 98 to 122 wings.

In July 1955, however, the Senate Permanent Investigations Subcommittee, chaired by John L. McClellan (D-Ark.), brought charges of conflict of interest against Talbott. At hearings held by the Permanent Investigations Subcommittee, McClellan asked Talbott if he had used his influence to obtain business for Mulligan and Company. Talbott denied that he had; the people he had approached had been personal friends for many years. The probe, however, revealed that Talbott had solicited clients for the Mulligan Company using air force stationery. Although Talbott claimed that the prospective clients were not defense contractors, he had successfully negotiated new contracts with Olin Industries, Owens-Illinois Glass Company, and Avco Company, all of which held contracts with the Defense Department. Moreover, profits for the Mulligan Company had risen substantially since Talbott's appointment, and the secretary's personal income from the firm had averaged over $50,000 per year after his appointment.

The most damaging testimony was the revelation that the Radio Corporation of America (RCA) had declined to renew a contract with the Mulligan Company after failing to secure an advisory opinion from the Justice Department clearing it of impropriety under the conflict-of-interest laws. Talbott reportedly told an attorney for RCA that his position was "foolish" and that RCA should "come off [its] high horse and stop acting so high and mighty." Claiming that his memory was hazy, he still maintained that he had never made the alleged statement about RCA. John Johnson, general counsel to the air force, testified that Talbott had asked him to investigate whether a contract between RCA and Mulligan would constitute a conflict of interest. Johnson concluded that such a contract would neither violate existing laws nor be improper. He met with Attorney General Herbert Brownell to get official approval, but Brownell declined to approve it.

As a result of the hearings and newspaper coverage, Talbott was forced to resign in August 1955. His letter of resignation asserted that his conduct had been "within the bounds of ethics" and blamed his predicament on "distorted publicity." In a letter accepting Talbott's resignation, Eisenhower praised Talbott's "unexcelled" diligence in the administration of his department and his "fine accomplishments as Secretary" but stated that "under the circumstances, your decision was the right one." In private, Eisenhower, who considered Talbott "a warm personal friend" and "a splendid public servant," believed that the secretary had been "guilty of indiscretions" and had "made a mistake in trying to do his own work."

Talbott received a spectacular farewell at Bolling Air Force Base and received the Medal of Freedom, the Defense Department's highest civilian award, from Secretary of Defense CHARLES WILSON. Talbott returned to the business world "to make a little dough" and died of a stroke while vacationing in Palm Beach, Florida, on March 2, 1957.

—MSM

Talmadge, Herman E(ugene)
(1913–2002) *governor of Georgia, U.S. senator*

The son of Eugene Talmadge, the fiery white supremacist and anti–New Deal governor of Georgia during the 1930s, Herman Talmadge was born in McRae, Georgia, on August 9, 1913. After earning his law degree from the University of Georgia in 1936, Talmadge joined his father's law firm in Atlanta. He managed his father's unsuccessful bid for a seat in the U.S. Senate in 1938. Two years later, Talmadge managed his father's successful campaign for reelection as governor. He entered the navy in 1941 as an ensign and saw action in the Pacific theater during World War II. Discharged in November 1945 with the rank of lieutenant commander, Talmadge returned to his law practice. When Eugene Talmadge entered the Democratic primary for governor in 1946, Herman once again managed the campaign. After winning the nomination, which was tantamount to winning election in Georgia, Eugene Talmadge became seriously ill. Concerned that the nominee would not survive, his followers mounted a write-in campaign in the general election for Herman Talmadge, who won enough votes to finish second to his father. In December 1946, shortly before the inauguration, the governor-elect died.

The constitution of Georgia did not clearly provide for such an eventuality, and a fierce controversy broke out between the Talmadge and anti-Talmadge factions of the Democratic Party. In January

1947, the state legislature chose Herman Talmadge to succeed his father. The outgoing governor, Ellis G. Arnall, however, refused to surrender his office. Talmadge responded by deploying units of the state police and the National Guard to seize control of the state capitol and the governor's mansion. Arnall then abdicated his claim to the governorship in favor of the incoming lieutenant governor, Melvin E. Thompson, who took the oaths for both lieutenant governor and governor. Talmadge continued to occupy the executive departments, but, after 67 days, the state's supreme court ruled that the legislature had acted improperly in electing Talmadge and awarded the office to Thompson.

The ultimate resolution came in a special primary election between Talmadge and Thompson in 1948. Adopting his father's campaign trademarks (red suspenders and chewing tobacco), Talmadge projected a properly rustic image. He also adopted his father's campaign tactics and exploited the racial fears of rural whites. Talmadge won the election.

While in office, Talmadge increased expenditures for health, education, and welfare, particularly for vocational schools, roads, and mental hospitals. He paid for these by pushing a sales tax through the legislature. At the same time, he made every effort to prevent African Americans from participating in politics. During his election campaign, Talmadge had promised to establish a new voter registration system, based on educational requirements, that would have barred 80 percent of the state's potential black voters. The law was enacted but never enforced; Talmadge's supporters realized that it would disqualify an equally large number of poor white voters. In another effort to exclude African Americans from voting, Talmadge unsuccessfully attempted to revive the poll tax, which had been repealed in 1945, as a means of restricting black voting.

By 1950, the Talmadge administration faced serious financial problems, and Talmadge faced a strong challenge from Thompson in the gubernatorial primary. Talmadge stressed the threat posed to white supremacy by the Truman administration's Fair Employment Practices Commission. Emphasizing his own unambiguous commitment to segregation, he portrayed Thompson, who had ties to the national administration, as an ally of integrationists. Placed on the defensive, Thompson spent most of the campaign denying Talmadge's accusations. Talmadge won renomination and, inevitably, reelection.

As the urbanization of Georgia threatened Talmadge's rural base (he bragged that he had never carried a county with a streetcar line), he responded by sponsoring a amendment to the state constitution in 1952 that would have extended and formalized the county unit system, thereby increasing the already disproportionate electoral weight of the least populous counties. When presented as a referendum, the measure went down to defeat by 29,000 votes. At the same time, however, Talmadge made overtures to urban voters by encouraging new industries and expanding state services. Ultimately, he won a substantial urban following while retaining the allegiance of rural dwellers.

Talmadge's reaction to the Supreme Court's decision striking down segregated public schools (*Brown v. Board of Education* [1954]) enhanced Talmadge's prestige in Georgia. He declared that "there aren't enough troops in the whole United States to make the white people of this state send their children to school with colored children" and predicted that "blood will run in Atlanta's streets." Soon after the Court's ruling, the governor put forward a constitutional amendment that permitted the substitution of private schools for the state's public school system. Voters in Georgia overwhelmingly endorsed this device to avoid desegregation. As a result of his aggressive opposition to desegregation, Talmadge achieved virtually complete domination of the state's Democratic organization by the mid-1950s. In 1956, he defeated the longtime incumbent, WALTER F. GEORGE (D-Ga.), in the Democratic primary and went on to win election to the U.S. Senate. During the campaign, he declared that "God advocates segregation." He won reelection in 1962, 1968, and 1974.

Despite his reputation for political demagoguery, Talmadge quickly established a reputation among his fellow senators as an intelligent and well-informed legislator. During the Kennedy and Johnson administrations, he unfailingly opposed civil rights legislation (including the Civil Rights Act of 1964 and the Voting Rights Act of 1965) and supported measures favorable to business interests.

During the late 1960s, however, as the number of black voters in the state increased, Talmadge became less vehement in his opposition to civil rights measures, even though he continued to vote against them. Although a strong supporter of the war in Vietnam during the Kennedy and Johnson administrations, he became an opponent of the war during the administration of President RICHARD M. NIXON. By 1969, Talmadge questioned the wisdom of fighting a war that, in his opinion, the government was not attempting to win. Subsequently, he called on Nixon to withdraw American troops from Indochina in 1971. Talmadge served on the Senate Select Committee to Investigate Presidential Campaign Activities, known as the Watergate Committee, in 1973. In the late 1960s and early 1970s, as urban and African-American voters made up an increasingly large proportion of the electorate in Georgia, Talmadge became more inclined to vote for social welfare programs. For example, he helped develop the food stamp program and sponsored a school lunch program passed in 1970. In the mid-1970s, personal problems, including a messy divorce and alcohol abuse, derailed his career. The Senate Ethics Committee looked into irregularities in his campaign and office expenses. Denounced by the Senate for "reprehensible" financial misconduct in October 1979, Talmadge survived a tough primary challenge but lost the general election in 1980 to Mack Mattingly, who became the first Republican senator from Georgia since Reconstruction. Talmadge returned to Hampton, Georgia, where he resumed the practice of law. He died in Hampton on March 21, 2002.

—MSM

Taylor, Maxwell D(avenport)
(1901–1987) *army chief of staff*

The son of an attorney, Taylor was born in Keytesville, Missouri, on August 26, 1901. Stirred by his maternal grandfather's tales of the Confederate army, Taylor decided on a military career. After graduating from Northeast High School in Kansas City, he won appointment to West Point and graduated fourth in a class of 102 in 1922. Commissioned a second lieutenant, he joined the corps of engineers, attended engineers school, and was assigned to duty in Maryland, Hawaii, and Washington. Taylor transferred to the artillery in 1926. His demonstrated talent for languages won him an assignment to Paris in order to polish his French. He returned to West Point to teach French and Spanish from 1927 to 1932. After attending field artillery school and the command and general staff school (from which he graduated in 1935), Taylor received a posting to the U.S. embassy in Tokyo, where he served from 1935 to 1939. During the interwar years, advancement came slowly, and Taylor did not receive his promotion to captain until 1935. In 1939 he served as assistant military attaché in Beijing. Promoted to major in 1940, he served in the war plans division. He attended the army war college in 1940 and then served as commander of the 12th Field Artillery Battalion from 1940 to 1941. When the Japanese attacked Pearl Harbor, Taylor was chief of staff to General MATTHEW B. RIDGWAY, commander of the 82nd Infantry Division. He received promotions to lieutenant colonel in December 1941 and to colonel in February 1942. Promoted to brigadier general in December 1942, Taylor served as artillery commander of the 82nd Airborne Division and participated in the invasions of Sicily and Italy. After one especially risky mission in Italy, for which Taylor won a Silver Star, General DWIGHT D. EISENHOWER praised him for discharging his "weighty responsibilities . . . with unerring judgment." Promoted to major general, Taylor assumed command of the 101st Airborne Division in May 1944 and became the first American general to land in France on D-day. Taylor was injured during Operation Market Garden in September 1944 and missed the Battle of the Bulge. As the 101st held out desperately against the German offensive at Bastogne, Belgium, Taylor returned to join the drive to relieve his unit.

After the war, Taylor became superintendent of West Point in September 1945. He expanded the curriculum to include a greater emphasis on the liberal arts. In 1949, he became chief of staff of the U.S. Army's European command and later that year became commander of the American forces in Berlin. Taylor returned to the Pentagon in 1951 as deputy chief of staff of operations and administration, a position he held until assuming command of the Eighth Army in February 1953, during the final stages of the Korean War. In April 1955, he began a brief assignment as U.S. and UN commander in the Far East. That June, President Eisenhower selected Taylor to replace General Ridgway as army chief of staff. Ridgway had opposed Eisenhower's cuts in the defense budget and particularly his cuts in the army.

Prompted by a desire to hold down defense spending and a reluctance to commit American fighting men to unpopular wars, the administration's New Look defense policy focused on airpower and the nuclear deterrent. The administration announced that the United States would avoid debilitating ground wars such as the Korean conflict and would instead respond "swiftly and selectively" with nuclear power to stop communist aggression.

In his initial years as army chief of staff, Taylor avoided public criticism of Eisenhower's defense policy, although he almost immediately came into conflict with the chairman of the Joint Chiefs of Staff, Admiral ARTHUR W. RADFORD, who supported the New Look. Taylor advocated a policy of "flexible response," which required a larger conventional military and larger defense budgets. "Air power," he argued, "is our initial line of defense, but no one has proved to my satisfaction that we will have only world wars to be settled only by big bangs. . . . infantrymen at one time or another become indispensable. . . . The atom bomb is no weapon to counter a coup d'etat." When he testified in 1957 at the House Appropriations Committee's hearings on the proposed defense budget for fiscal 1958, he strongly endorsed the Defense Department's military funding request and outlined ways in which the army was spending funds more efficiently.

Months later, before the Senate Appropriations Committee, Taylor reiterated his strong support for Eisenhower's budget. He casually admitted that he had originally urged greater funding for long-range modernization of conventional forces, but he did not complain about being turned down. He did, however, warn that as the United States and USSR reached nuclear parity, the Soviet Union would grow increasingly reluctant to risk nuclear war. Consequently, the threat of subversion and limited wars would increase greatly. To meet such a danger, he maintained, the United States needed a well-equipped, highly prepared army, ready to "intervene quickly with substantial forces." At that time, no one on the committee regarded Taylor's comments as especially important, nor did the general himself consider them anything other than a plea for the restoration of cuts the House had made in the administration's defense budget.

The Soviet Union's launch of *Sputnik* in the fall of 1957 opened a debate within the various branches of the military on defense strategy. Taylor, with the backing of top navy personnel, spoke for a group that advocated the capacity to fight "limited wars." He contended that *Sputnik* portended the end of American nuclear superiority and that conventional forces (especially army units) would therefore become vitally important in the era of stalemate to follow. He opposed a primary reliance on missiles and nuclear weapons on the ground that they limited options. In contrast, a faction headed by the air force proposed that the United States increase funding for strategic aircraft and missiles in order to maintain its traditional nuclear superiority.

Taylor's demands for increased defense spending brought him into conflict with Eisenhower. The president angrily criticized Taylor's failure to appreciate the broader considerations, particularly economic factors, involved in constructing defense policy. As a result of his stand, Taylor was eased out of his position as army chief of staff. When his term ended in June 1959, he retired from the army but continued to express his views, both in print and on television.

In 1960 he published *The Uncertain Trumpet*, a biting attack on the administration's New Look. Instead of a policy that he argued would lead either to general war or to compromise and defeat, Taylor advocated a "flexible response" that would enable the United States to respond to "anything from general war to infiltration, aggression," or subversion. Taylor focused particularly on the ability to fight small, local wars, where the use of nuclear weapons was inappropriate. He believed that such a policy could be achieved only by building up both conventional and nuclear forces.

Taylor's book impressed JOHN F. KENNEDY, who used the arguments to attack the Eisenhower administration's defense policy during his presiden-

tial campaign in 1960. Taylor's ideas about limited war in particular influenced Kennedy. Early in his presidency, Kennedy named Taylor to conduct an investigation of the failed invasion at the Bay of Pigs. Kennedy created a new post of military representative of the president and convinced Taylor to return to active duty to assume that position in July 1961. Taylor became chairman of the Joint Chiefs of Staff in October 1962. His theories shaped America's early military response to the war in Vietnam. Kennedy had sent him on a mission to South Vietnam in October 1961, after which he reported that the situation was deteriorating and urged the president to increase economic and military aid to the government in Saigon. Following Taylor's advice, Kennedy increased American involvement. Taylor was also instrumental in gaining the support of the Joint Chiefs of Staff for the Nuclear Test Ban Treaty in 1963. After Kennedy's assassination, Taylor continued as chairman of the Joint Chiefs under President LYNDON B. JOHNSON. In July 1964, Johnson appointed Taylor ambassador to Vietnam. In that capacity, Taylor controlled the American forces then in Vietnam and played an important role as the United States escalated its involvement. Taylor remained at that post until July 1965, when he returned to the United States as a special consultant to the president. He continued in that position until the end of the Johnson administration. In retirement, Taylor published *Precarious Security* in 1976. He lived in Washington, D.C., where he died on April 19, 1987.

—MSM

Teller, Edward
(1908–2003) *associate director, Lawrence Livermore Laboratory, Atomic Energy Commission*

The son of a well-to-do Jewish lawyer, Teller was born in Budapest, Hungary, on January 15, 1908. At the age of 18, he left the increasingly anti-Semitic atmosphere of Hungary for Germany and the Institute of Technology at Karlsruhe. Intrigued by physics, especially the new theory of quantum mechanics, Teller transferred to the University of Munich in 1928. He completed his doctorate at the University of Leipzig in 1930 and then joined the faculty of the University of Göttingen. After the

Nazis came to power in 1933, Teller fled Germany. In 1934, he went to Denmark, where he worked at the Institute for Theoretical Physics under the renowned Danish physicist, Niels Bohr. From there, Teller emigrated first to England, where he held a job at the University of London, and then, in 1935, to the United States, where he took up a position at George Washington University. He became an American citizen in 1941.

In 1941, Teller joined the Manhattan Project, the top secret project that developed the atomic bomb. He worked at the University of Chicago with Enrico Fermi and at the University of California at Berkeley with J. ROBERT OPPENHEIMER. In 1942, he participated in a planning seminar, convened by Oppenheimer, to discuss the development of atomic weapons. At that meeting, Teller raised the possibility of creating a bomb that worked through the thermonuclear fusion of isotopes of hydrogen and deuterium (heavy hydrogen). In 1943, Teller went to Los Alamos, New Mexico, where a laboratory had been established for research on the atomic bomb. His ambition to create a fusion bomb led to friction with Oppenheimer, the laboratory's director, who insisted that the laboratory concentrate on the development of a fission weapon (a less complicated device that worked by splitting the atom). Moreover, the development of a hydrogen bomb encountered major scientific and technological obstacles. Despite his focus on a fusion weapon and his sometimes egocentric behavior, Teller made valuable contributions to the development of the atomic bomb. Following the first successful test of an atomic bomb in 1945, the sense of urgency surrounding the development of the H-bomb diminished.

After the war, Teller turned down an offer to remain at Los Alamos as director of the theoretical division and returned to the University of Chicago in 1946. During the postwar period, Teller played an important part in the debate among nuclear scientists over the role of atomic weapons. He supported the Baruch Plan that called for the creation of an atomic development authority under the auspices of the United Nations. The Soviet rejection of the Baruch Plan convinced Teller that hopes for an accommodation with the Soviet Union were chimerical and that an arms race was inevitable. He believed that, in order to maintain American military superiority over the Soviet Union, the United States should work on developing a hydrogen bomb. The explosion of the Soviet Union's first atomic device in 1949 induced Teller to push for a crash program to develop the H-bomb. Ernest O. Lawrence, a physicist from the University of California at Berkeley, joined Teller in advocating development of the hydrogen bomb. Military leaders supported their position. The majority of the Atomic Energy Commission's (AEC) General Advisory Committee (GAC), including its chairman, Robert Oppenheimer, however, opposed the plan on moral and technical grounds. They questioned the project's military value, believed that it would escalate the arms race, and thought it too costly as well as fraught with technical problems. These scientists recommended gradual development of the "Super," as the H-bomb was called. President HARRY S. TRUMAN supported Teller's position and ordered a crash program in 1950.

Teller returned to Los Alamos to work on developing the weapon. In 1952, Teller, who had lobbied for the creation of a second center for thermonuclear research, left Los Alamos for the newly created laboratory at Livermore, California, a branch of the Berkeley Radiation Laboratory. A thermonuclear device was successfully tested in November 1952, and the first hydrogen bomb was detonated in May 1954. Teller became known as "the father of the hydrogen bomb," a title he detested.

Teller played a central role in the Oppenheimer security hearings of 1954. Oppenheimer's security clearance had been suspended in 1953 on the grounds that his prewar leftist associations and his reluctance to develop the H-bomb raised significant doubts about his loyalty. Of the six scientists involved in the H-bomb controversy who testified at the AEC hearing, only Teller supported denying Oppenheimer's security clearance. Teller told the security board that he considered Oppenheimer a loyal American and that Oppenheimer's direction of Los Alamos, both as a scientist and as an administrator, constituted "a very outstanding achievement." Nevertheless, Teller stated his belief that Oppenheimer had hindered work on the development of a thermonuclear weapon, which Teller argued might have been produced "about four years earlier" if "at the end of the war people like Oppenheimer had lent . . . moral support" to the project. "If it is a question of wisdom and judgment, as demonstrated by actions since 1945," concluded Teller, "then I would say one would be wiser not to grant clearance." The board agreed with Teller.

Teller served as director of the Lawrence Livermore National Laboratory (which he, along with Ernest Lawrence, had helped found) from 1958 to 1960. After that, he continued as an associate director and held a professorship of physics at the University of California at Berkeley. He also chaired the committee that founded the Space Sciences Laboratory at Berkeley.

As the dangers of radioactive fallout became publicized in the late 1950s, demands for a nuclear test ban grew. Teller continued to support tests because he thought them necessary not only to maintain American military superiority but also to improve nuclear weapons and solve the problem of fallout. In meetings with the president and congressional committees in 1957 and 1958, Teller assured government leaders that the United States would produce a "clean bomb," free of fallout, within four or five years. Although he conceded that "thousands of genetic mutations might result from test radioactivity," he warned that the United States "may be sacrificing millions of lives in a 'dirty' nuclear war later" if it agreed to a test ban.

After the Soviet Union launched *Sputnik* in 1957, Teller advocated space research for both its scientific and its military value. He also recommended that the government develop plans for quick industrial recovery from a nuclear missile attack and that it institute a massive fallout shelter program. Teller participated in a panel sponsored by the Rockefeller Brothers Fund that, in its report released in January 1958, urged "substantially increased defense expenditures."

In the 1960s, Teller continued to oppose a nuclear test ban; indeed, he stepped down as director of Lawrence Livermore in order to lobby against the test ban. During the administration of JOHN F. KENNEDY, Teller continued to press for nuclear tests. In 1963, at Senate hearings on the nuclear test ban treaty, Teller was the most influential scientist to testify against ratification. In subsequent years, he persisted in his advocacy of a strong national defense. He made headlines in the 1970s

by promoting the development of nuclear fusion as an alternative source of energy. Teller became a senior research fellow at the Hoover Institute for the Study of War, Revolution and Peace at Stanford University in 1975. In the 1980s, he defended the development of a strategic missile defense system. President George W. Bush presented Teller with the Presidential Medal of Freedom in 2003. Teller died in Palo Alto, California, on September 9, 2003.

—MSM

Thomas, Charles S(arks)

(1897–1983) *undersecretary of the navy, assistant secretary of defense for supply and logistics, secretary of the navy*

Born in Independence, Missouri, on September 28, 1897, Thomas moved with his parents to Los Angeles, California, in 1911. He attended the University of California at Berkeley during 1915–16 before transferring to Cornell University. Thomas left school during his junior year to serve as a naval aviator during World War I. In 1919, he joined the Los Angeles investment house of George H. Burr Company, subsequently becoming a partner and vice president. Named vice president and general manager of Foreman and Clark, Incorporated, a retail clothing manufacturer, in 1932, he saved the company from bankruptcy during the depression and advanced to become president and director by 1937.

During World War II, Thomas became special assistant first to Artemus L. Gates, assistant secretary of the navy for air, and later to Secretary of the Navy James L. Forrestal. After the war, Thomas returned to Foreman and Clark. He also served as airport commissioner of Los Angeles from 1945 to 1950 and assumed several corporate directorships, including one with Lockheed Aircraft Corporation.

In February 1953, President DWIGHT D. EISENHOWER appointed Thomas undersecretary of the navy and five months later promoted him to assistant secretary of defense for supply and logistics. Thomas's duties were similar in both capacities. His major project was to formulate a single catalogue of equipment used by the three armed services, thus preventing duplication and saving money.

In March 1954, Eisenhower nominated Thomas to be secretary of the navy. As secretary, Thomas faced several vexing matters relating to loyalty and security. In October, acting on the recommendation of Vice President RICHARD M. NIXON, Thomas suspended the security clearance of Edward U. Condon, an authority on quantum mechanics who had worked as Oppenheimer's deputy at Los Alamos and then as director of the National Bureau of Standards from 1945 to 1951. In the late 1940s, as president of the American Physical Society, Condon called for closer working relations with the Soviet Union. This raised the ire of J. Parnell Thomas (R-N.J.), the chair of HUAC. The scientist insisted that the secretary of commerce have his loyalty investigated. Soon after the Commerce Department's loyalty board cleared Condon. However, in 1948, HUAC issued a report calling him "one of the weakest links in our atomic security." Condon left the government in 1951 and went to work for Corning Glass Works. Since Corning held classified contracts, Condon required security clearance, which he had received. At Nixon's urging, Thomas suspended Condon's security clearance on the ground that the scientist had knowingly or unknowingly associated with alleged Soviet espionage agents. After initially announcing his readiness to be cleared "a fifth time," Condon resigned from Corning.

In August 1955, Thomas announced that he would personally review the case of Eugene W. Landy, a graduate of the U.S. Merchant Marine Academy who had been denied a commission in the naval reserve because his mother had been a member of the Communist Party from 1937 to 1947 and still subscribed to the party's organ, the *Daily Worker.* Landy's mother protested that she had left the party at her son's urging. Thomas appointed a special review board, which, in late September, recommended against issuing Landy's commission. Thomas, however, overruled the board and made Landy an ensign in the naval reserve.

Thomas spent much of his time as secretary of the navy attempting to defend the administration's policy of reducing the military budget. In January 1958, he testified before the House Armed Services Committee that the navy and the marine corps could maintain and even increase their striking power

Newly sworn in Secretary of the Navy Charles S. Thomas shakes hands with President Eisenhower, May 3, 1954 *(Dwight D. Eisenhower Library and Museum)*

despite the administration's budget cuts, which resulted in reductions of both manpower and vessels. Two years later, the secretary returned to Capitol Hill to defend the administration's program, which eschewed large increases in the military budget and instead emphasized more efficient use of equipment on hand over the building of costly new weapons systems. "In essence," said the navy secretary, "the United States could not endure if it either permitted its military arsenal to rust," or if "in response to some transient danger," it undertook a "prolonged and full mobilization during peace time."

In March 1957, shortly after his testimony before the House, Thomas resigned as secretary of the navy. That June, he became chairman of the Republican National Finance Committee. From 1958 to 1960, he was president and chief executive officer for Trans World Airlines. He became president of the Irvine Company of Tostin, California, in 1960, a post he held until his retirement in 1966. In 1971, President Richard Nixon appointed Thomas chairman of the National Tourism Review Commission, a group composed of business leaders and government officials organized to encourage foreign travel in the United States. Thomas died in Corona del Mar, California, on October 17, 1983.

—MSM

Thomas, Norman M(attoon)

(1884–1968) *peace and reform advocate*

Descended from three generations of ministers, Thomas was born in Marion, Ohio, on November 20, 1884. After graduating from Marion High School in 1901, he spent a year at Bucknell University before transferring to Princeton University as a pre-divinity student. Thomas graduated as valedictorian of his class at Princeton in 1905. He then engaged in social work at the Spring Street Presbyterian Church's settlement house in a working-class section of New York City. He became a minister's assistant at New York's Christ Church and then associate pastor of the Brick Presbyterian Church. He received a B.D. from Union Theological Seminary, a leading center for the Social Gospel, in 1911 and became pastor of the East Harlem Presbyterian Church in New York City. He also directed the American House, a settlement house in an immigrant neighborhood.

Thomas opposed American participation in World War I. In 1917, he joined the Fellowship of Reconciliation, a religious pacifist group and edited its official organ, the *New World* (which soon became the *World Tomorrow*), from 1918 to 1921. That same year, he helped to found the National Civil Liberties Bureau (later the American Civil Liberties Union [ACLU]).

Thomas supported the socialist candidate, Morris Hillquit, for mayor of New York in 1917. The next year, Thomas joined the Socialist Party and resigned from the ministry. He advocated a gradual, democratic transition to socialism. His views blended traditional Marxism with tenets of the Social Gospel. Although sympathetic to the Bolsheviks, he criticized their rejection of democracy. He departed from the overwhelming majority of his party and argued that racism constituted a social problem independent of economics.

In 1921, Thomas left the *World Tomorrow* and became associate editor of the *Nation*, a liberal magazine. A year later, he became coordinator of the League for Industrial Democracy. He briefly edited the socialist daily paper, the *New York Leader*, but in 1922 his wife inherited a trust fund that provided the couple with a comfortable income. Freed from the need to earn an income, Thomas devoted himself to various causes. He was the Socialist candidate for governor of New York in 1924 and mayor of New York City the following year. During the 1920s, he emerged as a leading figure in the Socialist Party, and, on the death of Eugene Debs in 1926, Thomas became the party's national leader. Thomas headed its national ticket in every presidential election from 1928 through 1948. He advocated unemployment insurance, child labor laws, legislated minimum wages and maximum hours, collective bargaining, programs to retrain workers in declining or obsolete industries, and government planning of the economy. His most successful electoral effort came in 1932, when he polled about 3 percent of the total vote. Thomas supported some elements of the New Deal, but, for the most part, he remained critical of President Franklin D. Roosevelt and his programs. Thomas regarded the New Deal as an effort to prop up a doomed system and attacked its limitations.

For all of Thomas's rhetorical skills, he was a poor organizer and administrator. During the depression, his party disintegrated into warring factions and lost ground to the communists.

Unlike many on the left, Thomas was not taken by the illusion of the Soviet Union. After touring the Soviet Union and Spain in 1937, he castigated the USSR as an oppressive society and denounced Stalin's purges and show trials.

The Spanish civil war caused Thomas to question his commitment to pacifism. Nevertheless, he opposed American intervention in the burgeoning European crisis. In 1938, he founded the Keep America Out of War Committee. He was associated with the America First Committee, the most powerful anti-interventionist group, but broke off that association after Charles Lindbergh, one of the organization's founders, made an anti-Semitic speech. Based on the experience of World War I, Thomas viewed war as a threat to American democracy. When World War II broke out in Europe, Thomas opposed American entry. After the Japanese attack on Pearl Harbor, however, he offered "critical support" to the war effort. Thomas's reluctant endorsement of the war cost the Socialist Party support, as did his outspoken opposition to the internment of Japanese Americans.

During the late 1940s, Thomas was a forceful critic of Soviet despotism and expansionism.

He denounced Henry A. Wallace, the Progressive Party presidential candidate in 1948, as an apologist for Soviet aggression and an advocate of peace by appeasement of Stalin. Nevertheless, Thomas favored international agreements to reduce arms and in 1950 called on President HARRY S. TRUMAN to propose disarmament at the United Nations. During the same year, Thomas urged the Socialist Party to abandon its increasingly ineffectual electoral efforts, but its national convention rejected this proposal.

The red scare presented Thomas with a difficult balancing act. He had helped purge communists from the ACLU's leadership in 1940. In the late 1940s, he denounced Senator JOSEPH R. MCCARTHY's (R-Wis.) campaign against communists in government as a threat to civil liberties and defended the right of communists to engage in legal political activity. There were limits, however, to Thomas's defense of communists. He drew a distinction between dissenters and conspirators and regarded communists as conspirators. Thus, he did not believe that communists had a right to hold positions as teachers or sensitive government jobs.

Widely admired even by those who strongly disagreed with his views, Thomas refrained from expressions of personal animosity and tempered his often impassioned rhetoric with wit. Even opponents acknowledged his integrity and genuine compassion for the weak. Furthermore, he explicitly rejected Leninism and advocated instead the peaceful establishment of a democratic form of socialism.

During the 1950s, Thomas's prestige rose still further, because he became increasingly identified as an individual advocate of reform rather than as a partisan leader of the Socialist Party. Thomas continued to act as a spokesman for the group, but, over the course of the decade, he gave up his posts in the dwindling organization. In 1952, he supported the Socialist ticket and campaigned for it, but he developed an admiration for ADLAI E. STEVENSON, the Democratic presidential nominee and a fellow Princetonian. In private, Thomas made it clear that he hoped Stevenson would win in 1952 and again in 1956.

After DWIGHT D. EISENHOWER became president, Thomas continued to balance his opposition to communism with concern for civil liberties. He continued to excoriate McCarthy and urged clemency for JULIUS AND ETHEL ROSENBERG, even though he believed them guilty. Thomas met with Eisenhower in October 1953 to protest the exclusion of Socialists from policy-making positions and the broad definition government officials had given to such posts. Thomas was always sensitive to the notion that Socialists were disloyal. In addition, the State Department and Mutual Security Agency were dismissing Socialists who did not hold policy-making positions. Eisenhower agreed that Socialists should not be barred from jobs that did not involve making policy. Thomas emerged from the meeting impressed with the president, whom he found "an extremely decent man" who "showed a much better understanding of what Socialism really was than I expected."

While Thomas condemned communist tyranny, he supported peaceful coexistence with the Soviet Union because he thought it necessary in order to avoid a nuclear holocaust. He persistently advocated disarmament and placed part of the blame for failures to achieve arms reductions upon the United States. In 1955, Thomas criticized the Eisenhower administration for rejecting a British and French proposal, accepted by the Soviet Union, to reduce conventional forces. Two years later, he condemned the United States for turning down a Soviet plan for a monitored moratorium on nuclear tests.

In 1957, Thomas and NORMAN COUSINS were key figures in organizing the Committee for a Sane Nuclear Policy (SANE). In 1960, the group held a rally in New York City, attended by more than 17,000 people, to urge an end to nuclear testing and a concerted effort to end poverty. That same year, Senator THOMAS DODD (D-Conn.), vice chairman of the Internal Security Subcommittee, charged that SANE was heavily infiltrated by communists and fellow travelers. The organization's national board issued a policy statement, endorsed by Thomas, barring communists from membership in the organization. Shortly afterward, 37 members of SANE's New York City chapter, which openly opposed this policy, were subpoenaed by Senate investigators. The national board, at Thomas's insistence, refused to come to their defense. Subsequently, the board revoked the local chapter's charter.

Thomas favored Stevenson for the Democratic presidential nomination in 1960. When Senator JOHN F. KENNEDY (D-Mass.) captured the nomination, Thomas reluctantly backed him in the general election. Thomas testified before a Senate committee in July 1963 as a supporter of the administration's civil rights bill, which he regarded as a worthwhile but timid step toward ending racial injustice. During the administration of President LYNDON B. JOHNSON, Thomas stridently criticized America's military involvement in Vietnam. A stroke forced him to withdraw from public life in 1967. Thomas died in Huntington, New York, on December 19, 1968.

—MSM

Thompson, Frank, Jr.

(1918–1989) *U.S. congressman*

The son of a newspaperman and the nephew of a Democratic leader in New Jersey, Thompson was born in Trenton, New Jersey, on July 16, 1918. He attended public and parochial schools, Wake Forest College in Winston-Salem, North Carolina, and Wake Forest Law School. He served in the navy from 1941 to 1948 and saw action in the Pacific, where he won the Bronze Star. After gaining admission to the bar in 1948, he practiced law in Trenton. In 1949, he won election as a Democrat to the New Jersey state assembly. He served in the assembly until he won election to Congress in 1954 as a self-styled "New Deal-Fair Deal Democrat of the Adlai Stevenson School." During his campaign, he called for a bipartisan foreign policy and drastic revision of the Taft-Hartley Act.

In the House, Thompson voted in agreement with the AFL-CIO Committee on Political Education's (COPE) recommendations on most issues. As a member of the Education and Labor Committee, he quickly emerged as a leading advocate of federal aid to education. In January 1959, Thompson sponsored a bill, drafted by the National Education Association, to provide $1.3 billion in federal grants to local school districts for the construction of schools and teachers' salaries. He claimed that the bill would finance 25,000 new classrooms and, through provisions for federal-state matching funds, would encourage the states to build 15,000 to 16,000

more. In January 1960, the Senate passed a version of the proposal, but strong conservative opposition threatened its passage in the House. Responding to pressure from the administration to water down the bill, Thompson removed the provisions for aid to teachers' salaries and amended it to require equal matching of federal with state funds during every year of the proposed four-year program.

Passage of the bill was further threatened by an anti-segregation rider attached by Representative ADAM CLAYTON POWELL, JR. (D-N.Y.). Recalling that a similar rider had led to the defeat of a bill to provide funds for school construction in 1956, Thompson accused conservatives in the House of supporting the Powell amendment solely to prevent the bill's final passage. He declared that individual school districts defying court orders to desegregate could be denied funds under the bill "without the addition of any amendment," because the Constitution was "self-enacting." The bill passed with the rider attached in May 1960. However, the House Rules Committee killed the measure by refusing to authorize a House-Senate conference, which might have resolved the differences between the House and Senate versions.

Despite his opposition to the Powell amendment, Thompson generally supported civil rights throughout his congressional career. In 1959, he helped bring a number of younger liberal members of Congress together in the Democratic Study Group, and he led an unsuccessful fight the same year to curb the power of the conservative-dominated Rules Committee to keep legislation from the floor. Limiting the power of the Rules Committee would have prevented its ability to block civil rights legislation.

Thompson actively supported JOHN F. KENNEDY in the presidential campaign of 1960, and, after Kennedy won the election, Thompson introduced the new administration's proposal for federal aid to schools in 1961. A key sponsor of legislation that created the National Endowment for the Arts and the National Endowment of he Humanities, Thompson also authored the bill that established the John F. Kennedy Center for the Performing Arts in Washington, D.C. Thomas lost his bid for reelection in 1980 after being caught up in the Abscam scandal. Posing as a rich Arab sheik and his aides, federal agents offered to bribe several American public officials. The investigation led to the conviction of Thompson and six other members of Congress for bribery and conspiracy. Thompson served two years of a three-year prison sentence. After unsuccessful appeals of his conviction, he went to prison from 1983 to 1985. Upon leaving Congress, he resided in Alexandria, Virginia, until his death in Bethesda, Maryland, on July 22, 1989.

—MSM

Thompson, Llewellyn E., Jr.

(1904–1972) *high commissioner for and ambassador to Austria, ambassador to the Soviet Union*

The son of a rancher, Thompson was born in Las Animas, Colorado, on August 24, 1904. He graduated from the University of Colorado in 1928 and then entered the School of Foreign Service at Georgetown University. The following year, he joined the Foreign Service and was sent to Ceylon (later Sri Lanka) as vice consul. In 1933, Thompson moved to Geneva, Switzerland, where, over the next seven years, he served as vice-consul and then as consul. During the latter half of the decade, he also worked as adviser to the conferences of the International Labour Organization. Thompson returned to the United States in 1940 and attended the army war college. In November 1940, Thompson was appointed second secretary and consul at the American embassy in Moscow. In 1941, the German army reached the gates of Moscow. Most of the Soviet government, including the foreign ministry, as well as the foreign diplomatic corps moved to Kuibyshev. Thompson remained in Moscow through the siege and won the admiration of the Soviets for his willingness to share their risks and hardship. President Franklin D. Roosevelt awarded Thompson the Medal of Freedom for his service.

During the last year of the war and in the decade after its end, Thompson's career progressed through a series of increasingly important assignments. From 1944 to 1946, he was stationed at the United States embassy in London. Following the war, Thompson returned to Washington, where he held a number of administrative positions in the State Department: chief of the division of Eastern European affairs from 1946 to 1947, deputy director

for European affairs from 1947 to 1949, and deputy assistant secretary of state for European affairs from 1949 to 1950. In June 1950, he became counselor of the embassy in Rome. President HARRY S. TRUMAN appointed Thompson high commissioner to Austria in July 1952.

As commissioner, Thompson spent a good deal of his time negotiating the Trieste settlement of 1954 and the Austrian State Treaty of 1955. Both Italy and Yugoslavia claimed the key port of Trieste, which had been placed under the jurisdiction of the United Nations following World War II. In 1954, after eight months of patient negotiations with both sides, Thompson worked out an agreement. Italy and Yugoslavia signed an agreement in October, under which Italy took possession of the northern half of the disputed territory, including the city of Trieste, and Yugoslavia occupied the southern area, including the Slovene town of Crevatini. Thompson later recalled that the agreement "was one of the few things we have done that even the Russians approved."

Simultaneously, Thompson worked on the Austrian State Treaty, signed in May 1955. After World War II, Austria had been placed under the joint occupation of France, Great Britain, the USSR, and the United States. Over the next 10 years, the United States made repeated attempts to negotiate a treaty ending the occupation, but the Soviet Union, fearing a revitalized, pro-Western Austria bordering on Eastern Europe, refused to normalize relations. In 1955, however, the USSR dramatically announced its willingness to negotiate the issue. In 11 days of arduous bargaining, Thompson worked out the final terms of an agreement. Under the treaty, Austria regained its independence in return for its military neutrality.

In 1957, Eisenhower appointed Thompson ambassador to the Soviet Union. Since Secretary of State JOHN FOSTER DULLES dominated policy making, Thompson had little role in molding American policy toward the Soviet Union. He served primarily as a reporter of events and a negotiator who arranged many of the top-level conferences of the period. At Thompson's urging, Eisenhower invited Soviet premier Nikita Khrushchev to visit the United States in 1959. The ambassador arranged the trip, accompanied the Soviet leader, and also took part in the meetings between Khrushchev and Eisenhower at Camp David, Maryland. The "spirit of Camp David" marked a notable relaxation of tensions in the cold war. Following the visit, Thompson was instrumental in laying the groundwork for the ill-fated Paris summit conference of 1960, which was cancelled after the downing of a U-2 intelligence plane over the Soviet Union. Despite the incident, Thompson maintained good relations with Khrushchev and the Soviet foreign minister, Andrei Gromyko. In 1960, Thompson achieved the rank of career ambassador.

Thompson remained in Moscow for the first two years of the administration of President JOHN F. KENNEDY. During this period, he helped to arrange the Vienna summit conference in 1961. In fall 1962, Thompson returned to Washington as ambassador at large and special adviser to the State Department on Soviet affairs. He aided in the negotiations leading to the nuclear test ban treaty in 1963. After LYNDON B. JOHNSON became president, Thompson served as acting deputy undersecretary of state from 1964 to 1966. Johnson appointed him ambassador to Moscow in 1967, a post he held until 1969. Adam Ulam, a specialist on Soviet affairs at Harvard, called Thompson, "the most effective of our Moscow envoys" in the post–World War II period. Thompson retired from the Foreign Service in January 1969, but President RICHARD M. NIXON called him back to serve on the American delegation to the strategic arms limitation talks. Thompson retired for a second time in 1971 and died in Bethesda, Maryland, on February 2, 1972.

—MSM

Thurmond, Strom

(1902–2003) *U.S. senator*

The son of a lawyer and politician, Thurmond was born in Edgefield, South Carolina, on December 5, 1902. He received a B.S. from Clemson College in 1923 and worked as a high school teacher until, after winning election as county school superintendent in 1928, he took office in July 1929. While working as school superintendent, Thurmond studied law with his father. Thurmond was admitted to the South Carolina bar in 1930 and almost immediately elected as attorney for Edgefield. In 1933,

Thurmond won election to the state senate from Edgefield. In the legislature, he supported a number of social welfare programs, including the state's first bill providing aid to the aged, the blind, and needy children. In 1938, the state legislature elected Thurmond to fill a vacancy as a circuit judge; two years later, the legislature elected him to a full term. A member of the U.S. Army Reserves, Thurmond enlisted in the army as a captain immediately after the Japanese attacked Pearl Harbor. By 1944, he was a lieutenant colonel in a civil affairs unit with the 82nd Airborne, and he landed in France by glider on D-day. Among other decorations, he won the Bronze Star and French Croix de Guerre. Thurmond resumed his judgeship after being discharged from the service in January 1946, but he stepped down from the post the following May to run for governor. His opponents in the Democratic primary charged him with being a New Dealer and hinted that he was receiving money from the Congress of Industrial Organizations. Nevertheless, he won his party's nomination, which was tantamount to election in South Carolina. As the state's chief executive, Thurmond increased appropriations for education and health care facilities, led a successful drive to repeal the poll tax, and backed a bill establishing a minimum wage and maximum hours. After a mob in Greenville lynched an African American accused of robbing and killing a white taxi driver, Thurmond appointed a tough prosecutor who obtained indictments against 28 alleged members of the mob. A jury, however, acquitted all of the defendants. Thurmond won praise for his strong stand against lynching. He also pressed to improve black schools and appointed an African American to the state Hospital Advisory Council.

Thurmond entered the national political scene, however, as a staunch conservative. In 1948, when liberals, led by HUBERT H. HUMPHREY, forced a stronger civil rights plank into the Democratic platform at the National Democratic Convention, some of the southern delegates walked out of the convention. They then organized a third party, the States' Rights Democrats (popularly known as the Dixiecrats), and nominated Thurmond for president. Opposing what he regarded as federal encroachment upon the constitutional powers of the states, Thurmond denounced Truman's civil rights and social welfare programs as well as the president's call for federal control of tidelands oil. Above all, Thurmond opposed racial integration. "All the laws of Washington and all the bayonets of the Army," he declared, "cannot force the Negro into our homes, into our schools, our churches and our places of recreation and amusement." Thurmond received nearly 1.2 million popular votes, almost all from the south, and captured 38 electoral votes (he carried Alabama, Louisiana, Mississippi, and South Carolina). In subsequent national campaigns, Thurmond did not endorse the Democratic national ticket.

In 1950, Thurmond challenged the incumbent, Senator Olin D. Johnston (D-S.C.), in the Democratic senatorial primary. Though at least as committed a segregationist and white supremacist as Thurmond, Johnston had remained loyal to the Democratic Party in 1948. Johnston defeated Thurmond, who moved to Aiken and returned to the private practice of law. In 1952, Thurmond once again bolted from the national Democratic Party and backed DWIGHT D. EISENHOWER for the presidency.

Thurmond reentered politics in 1954, when incumbent senator Burnet R. Maybank (D-S.C.) died after winning renomination in the Democratic primary. The South Carolina Democratic Executive Committee, dominated by loyalist Democrats, chose State Senator Edgar A. Brown to replace Maybank as the party's nominee. The Dixiecrat faction of the party and Governor JAMES F. BYRNES opposed the selection. With the support of the governor and the Dixiecrats, Thurmond mounted a write-in campaign in the general election. He defeated Brown by 59,000 votes, becoming the first person to win a seat in the U.S. Senate through a write-in campaign. In the meantime, Byrnes had appointed Charles E. Daniel to serve the remaining four months of Maybank's term. Daniel resigned on December 24, 1954, in order to allow Thurmond to have seniority over other first-term senators. Byrnes appointed Thurmond to fill the remaining days of Daniel's term.

In the Senate, Thurmond joined the Democratic caucus. During the campaign, he had promised that, if elected, he would resign in 1956 and run in the Democratic primary. True to his word, he resigned his seat in April 1956 and won the Demo-

cratic primary (with no opposition) as well as the general election to fill the remainder of his term. He served in the Senate until 2003.

Thurmond was one of Congress's most aggressive opponents of integration and civil rights legislation. In 1956, he initiated a movement among southern members of Congress to issue a Declaration of Constitutional Principles as a challenge to the Supreme Court's decision in *Brown v. Board of Education* (1954), which struck down segregated public schools. Thurmond wrote the initial draft, which contained sections endorsing the doctrine of interposition and declaring the Court's decision to be unconstitutional and illegal. He and Senator HARRY F. BYRD (D-Va.) circulated the draft among southern members, but moderates refused to sign it unless the clauses endorsing interposition and declaring the Court's decision unconstitutional were removed. As modified by Senator RICHARD B. RUSSELL (D-Ga.) and others, the declaration, popularly known as the Southern Manifesto, was presented to Congress on March 12, 1956, with the signatures of 19 southern senators and 81 southern members of the House. It described the *Brown* decision as "a clear abuse of judicial power" and urged the states "to resist forced integration by any lawful means."

In 1957, Thurmond conducted a record-breaking filibuster against a civil rights bill aimed primarily at protecting black voting rights. Before the measure, originally proposed by the administration, came to a vote in the Senate, opponents substantially weakened it by deleting provisions authorizing the president to use troops to enforce existing civil rights laws and permitting the attorney general to institute civil action for preventive relief in civil rights cases. It was further diluted by the addition of an amendment permitting jury trials in criminal contempt cases brought against those who obstructed black voting rights. Most southern members of Congress believed that the final version of the bill did not pose a serious threat to their region's racial practices and that it was the most favorable measure they could obtain. On August 28, Senator SAM ERVIN (D-N.C.), speaking on behalf of senior southern senators, said there would be no filibuster against it. Later in the day, however, Thurmond began a one-man filibuster that lasted 24 hours and

18 minutes, the longest in Senate history to that time. Many of his fellow southerners believed that Thurmond's action could have created a backlash leading to a strengthening of the bill. Agreeing with Senator HERMAN TALMADGE's (D-Ga.) description of the filibuster as a "grandstand" performance, they branded Thurmond an opportunist who would seek to advance his political career even at the risk of the southern cause.

Thurmond opposed the expansion of the public sector of the economy and national social welfare programs. In 1956, he joined three colleagues on the Public Works Committee in issuing a minority report opposing public power development at Niagara Falls. They stated that private enterprise had pioneered the project and that public development would be "tantamount to saying that all public resources must be publicly developed." The Senate passed the bill, but it died in the House Rules Committee. In 1960, Thurmond successfully amended a minimum wage bill to reduce the number of workers covered by overtime pay provisions. That bill died in conference.

Thurmond advocated an anticommunist foreign policy and was skeptical of efforts to reduce East-West tensions. In 1955, he backed a bill authorizing the president to use U.S. forces in defense of Taiwan and the Pescadores Islands, warning that "war might come as the result of any display of weakness, of disunity or of hesitation." Five years later, Thurmond joined Senators Russell, CLAIR ENGLE (D-Calif.), and THOMAS DODD (D-Conn.) in leading the unsuccessful opposition to the Antarctic Treaty, signed by 12 nations including the United States and the USSR. The senators contended that the pact did not fully ensure against secret Soviet military operations in Antarctica and that it gave the Soviet Union equal rights with the United States in an area in which the United States had previously predominated.

Throughout his career in the Senate, Thurmond paid careful attention to issues that had an impact on his constituents. In March 1955, Thurmond expressed reservations about a reciprocal trade bill sponsored by the administration, because he worried about the effects tariff reductions would have on South Carolina's textile industry. The measure would have permitted the president to reduce

tariffs up to 15 percent for three successive years beginning July 1, 1955. Since it seemed likely that a treaty with Japan lowering textile tariffs would be concluded before July 1, Thurmond feared that his state's textile enterprises might be severely injured. In April, however, Senator WALTER GEORGE (D-Ga.) successfully proposed an amendment moving up the effective date of the president's new power to reduce tariffs to January 1, 1955. This eliminated the possibility of a double reduction of the tariff on textiles in 1955. Once the George amendment was adopted, Thurmond supported the bill.

During the early 1960s, Thurmond continued to vote as a conservative on most matters. He became increasingly alienated from the national Democratic Party, especially after President LYNDON B. JOHNSON chose Humphrey as his running mate. Moreover, Thurmond found the Republican nominee for the presidency, Senator BARRY M. GOLDWATER (R-Ariz.), ideologically compatible and liked him personally. In September 1964, in order to demonstrate his support for Goldwater, Thurmond became a Republican. As he left the Democratic Party, Thurmond blasted it for "leading the evolution of our country to a socialist dictatorship," for having "forsaken the people to become the party of minority groups, power-hungry union leaders, political bosses and big businessmen looking for government contracts and favors," for encroaching on "the private lives of the people," and for supporting "judicial tyranny." Thurmond uniformly opposed President Johnson's Great Society programs while criticizing the administration for using insufficient military force in Southeast Asia. In 1968, his forceful advocacy of RICHARD M. NIXON's bid for the Republican presidential nomination kept most southern delegates to the Republican National Convention out of the camp of California's governor, Ronald W. Reagan. In order to attract support in the South, Thurmond advised Nixon not to press too hard on school desegregation and not to choose a northern liberal as a running mate. In the 1970s, as the number of black voters in South Carolina increased, Thurmond moved away from his earlier segregationist positions without ever renouncing them. He became one of the first southern senators to hire a black aide, supported the extension of the Voting Rights Act in 1982, voted for strengthening the Fair Housing Act in 1988, and supported making Martin Luther King, Jr., Day a federal holiday. When Republicans took control of the Senate in 1981, they elected Thurmond president pro tempore. He served until the Democrats regained control of the upper house after the elections of 1986. When the Republicans returned to power in 1995, Thurmond again became president pro tempore.

A fitness buff, Thurmond exercised vigorously and abstained from alcohol, tobacco, coffee, tea, and Coca-Cola. During his last years in the Senate, he became hard of hearing but refused to use a hearing aid. After collapsing on the floor of the Senate in October 2001, he moved into Walter Reed Army Medical Center. From then on, he had to be helped on and off the Senate floor by aides. He did not stand for reelection in 2002 and retired from the Senate in January 2003. After leaving the Senate, he returned to Edgefield, where he lived until his death there on June 26, 2003.

—MSM

Thye, Edward J(ohn)
(1896–1969) *U.S. senator*

Thye was born in Frederick, South Dakota, on April 26, 1896. In early childhood, he moved with his parents to Minnesota, where the family settled on a farm near Northfield. Thye attended public schools, the Minneapolis Tractor and Internal Combustion School, and the American Business College. After the United States entered World War I in 1917, he enlisted as a private in the U.S. Army Air Corps and served overseas. Following his discharge as a second lieutenant, he worked as a tractor expert for a local manufacturing concern. Thye resigned in 1922 and became a successful dairy farmer. His political career began in 1925 with his election to the local school board. In 1929, he became president of the Dakota County Farm Bureau, a position he held for a decade. In the early 1930s, Thye met HAROLD STASSEN. When Stassen decided to run for governor in 1938, Thye campaigned actively on his behalf. Stassen appointed Thye state dairy and food commissioner and deputy commissioner of agriculture in 1939. When Stassen ran for reelection in 1942, Thye joined him on the ticket as the Republican candidate for lieutenant governor. Stassen and

Thye carried the election that fall. When Governor Stassen resigned to go on active duty with the navy in 1943, Thye became governor. He subsequently won election to the office in 1944. As governor, Thye approved a low-cost, pre-paid medical care plan, launched extensive highway construction, and set up a state postwar planning commission. He also earned a reputation for his ability to settle labor disputes.

Thye ran for the U.S. Senate in 1946. In the primary campaign, Thye attacked the incumbent, Senator Henrik Shipstead (R-Minn.), for his isolationist record, and defeated him by a wide plurality. Thye then went on to win the general election. In the Senate, he became a prominent proponent of a bipartisan foreign policy during the Truman administration. Thye sided with the president on aid to Greece and Turkey, the North Atlantic Security Pact, and the foreign mutual aid bill. He won reelection in 1952.

A liberal Republican, Thye championed aid to education and civil rights legislation during the 1950s. He also supported the Eisenhower administration's foreign policy. The senator backed the Refugee Relief Act of 1953, the creation of the St. Lawrence Seaway Development Corporation in 1954, the Formosa Resolution of 1955, and the Eisenhower Doctrine of 1957.

Thye was particularly concerned about the problems of the small farmer. He consistently opposed Secretary of Agriculture EZRA TAFT BENSON's plans to phase out price supports for farm commodities. In 1954, the senator opposed the secretary's farm program, which established a flexible scale of price supports, from 75 percent to 90 percent of parity, for basic farm commodities. A member of the Senate Agriculture and Forestry Committee, Thye supported extension of the existing rigid price system at 90 percent of parity. He thought that lower prices, an inevitability with growing postwar surpluses, would result in greater production as farmers tried to maintain their existing income levels. Thye recommended that surpluses be reduced through production controls "before we start tampering with the price supports." In late April 1954, he introduced an amendment to the Agricultural Act of 1949 limiting the downward adjustment of price supports on dairy products.

It was defeated, and parity on dairy products was reduced to 75 percent.

In 1956, Thye supported a bill providing for price supports at 90 percent of parity and a "soil bank." The Eisenhower administration had proposed the soil bank, under which farmers could receive payments from the federal government for removing a specified amount of land from production and putting it back into ungrazed grass, forest, or water storage. The administration had also recommended flexible price supports. Democrats in Congress amended the administration's proposal and reintroduced high, rigid price supports. President Eisenhower vetoed it, citing the provision calling for a return to 90 percent of parity as "unacceptable." Two years later, Thye again failed to prevent a reduction of price supports on dairy products.

Thye lost his Senate seat to EUGENE J. MCCARTHY in 1958. Upon leaving the Senate, Thye resumed his agricultural interests and remained active in Republican politics and civic affairs. In 1960, Thye represented Minnesota as a delegate at large at the Republican National Convention. He died at his farm in Northfield, Minnesota, on August 28, 1969.

Till, Emmett L(ouis)

(1941–1955) *lynching victim*

Emmett Till was born near Chicago, Illinois, on July 25, 1941. His parents divorced two years later, and Till was raised by his mother. In the summer of 1955, Till's mother sent him to visit his great-uncle Moses Wright, a sharecropper who lived in LeFlore County, Mississippi, near the town of Money. On the evening of August 24, Till and a group of black teenagers went into Money. They entered a store owned by Roy Bryant and his wife, Carolyn. Roy Bryant was out of town, and his wife was behind the counter. Witnesses disagreed about precisely what happened, but, apparently on a dare by some of the other teenagers, Till asked Carolyn Bryant for a date. One of Till's cousins pulled him from the store; as they departed, Till whistled at Mrs. Bryant. Although Carolyn Bryant decided not to tell her husband about the incident, Roy Bryant later learned about it from a black customer. On August 28, Bryant, accompanied by his half-brother, J. W.

Milam, went to the cabin in which Wright and his wife, Elizabeth, lived. Bryant and Milam abducted Till, pistol-whipped him, and murdered him. Till's savagely mutilated body was pulled from the Tallahatchie River on August 31. It was tied to a cotton gin fan to weigh it down. Till's mother demanded that the body be returned to Chicago and insisted on an open casket, so that "the world" could "see what they did to my boy."

Till arrived in Mississippi when racial tension was high. The White Citizens Council had publicly defended segregation and had called for resistance to the Supreme Court's decision in *Brown v. Board of Education* (1954), which declared segregated public schools unconstitutional. Several African Americans had been murdered throughout the South in reprisal for attempts to register black voters. In LeFlore County, threats and intimidation had stopped African Americans from voting in the primary of August 1955.

Authorities arrested Bryant and Milam on August 29. They admitted abducting the boy to question him about having whistled at and insulted Mrs. Bryant but denied killing him. A grand jury indicted the two men for murder. At the subsequent trial, Wright dramatically identified Bryant and Milam as the men who had kidnapped Till. Nevertheless, an all-white jury acquitted Bryant and Milam after deliberating little more than an hour. A grand jury later refused to indict Bryant and Milam for kidnapping. In an article that appeared in *Look* magazine in 1956, the two men admitted that they had killed Till.

The Eisenhower administration responded carefully to the Till case. Civil rights experts in the Justice Department carefully studied the case but concluded that neither the murder of Till nor the acquittal of his killers violated existing federal law. The attorney general, HERBERT BROWNELL, believed that the case dramatized the lack of federal authority to enforce a constitutional promise. Moreover, as he pointed out, the "horrible nature of the facts involved" generated considerable pressure on the Justice Department to act. Further, many people mistakenly assumed that, since Till was a citizen of Illinois and was murdered in Mississippi, there were sufficient grounds to invoke federal jurisdiction.

The verdict aroused a storm of protest throughout the world and increased efforts to win strong government support for civil rights. The NAACP, the Jewish Labor Committee, the Brotherhood of Sleeping Car Porters, and other organizations held protest demonstrations in the North to demand that President Eisenhower call a special session of Congress to enact an antilynching law. When he announced his candidacy for the Democratic presidential nomination in October 1955, Senator ESTES KEFAUVER (D-Tenn.) made the Till case a cornerstone of his position on civil rights. He said that, if elected, he would ask Congress for antilynching legislation.

In a cabinet meeting held in December 1955, Brownell mentioned the mounting pressure on the Justice Department to investigate racial violence in the South, particularly the Till case. Vice President RICHARD M. NIXON suggested that the administration call for a congressional investigation. Southern Democrats, he argued, would block any legislation that emerged from the investigation, and that would shift the onus onto the Democrats.

In public, the administration adopted a cautious tone. On ABC's "College Press Conference," WILLIAM P. ROGERS, the deputy attorney general, called the fact that the killers had not been brought to justice a "real black mark" on the American system of justice. In an address to the National Urban League a few weeks later, Rogers called the verdict a "serious black mark."

With the exception of Kefauver, leading Democrats matched the administration's caution. ADLAI STEVENSON, preparing to mount another run for the presidency, failed to speak out on the Till case. Indeed, when Till's mother attempted to take her case to the public, Stevenson condemned her appearances as "a spectacle parading around the country." In private, he expressed exasperation that the matter constantly came up, and, when a reporter raised the Till case at a press conference, Stevenson cut off the questioner.

The murder of Emmet Till and the subsequent acquittal of his killers provided an impetus for the Eisenhower administration to ask Congress for civil rights legislation in 1956. Wanting no part of a bill that would create internecine conflict in the Democratic Party in an election year, the majority leader,

LYNDON B. JOHNSON (D-Tex.), consigned the bill to Senator JAMES O. EASTLAND's (D-Miss.) Judiciary Committee, from which it never emerged. The following year, after substantially weakening the measure, Congress passed the Civil Rights Act of 1957. Till's murder also spurred support for the burgeoning Civil Rights movement. Although a number of African Americans were murdered in the South, and particularly in Mississippi, the youth of the victim, the savagery of the crime, and the determination of Till's mother not to let the matter pass quietly made the Till case a focal point for the indictment of the southern social system.

—MSM

Timmerman, George B(ell)
(1881–1966) *U.S. district judge*

Timmerman was born in Edgefield County, South Carolina, on March 28, 1881. After receiving his law degree from South Carolina College in 1902, Timmerman entered private practice and became involved in local Democratic politics. After winning election as solicitor for South Carolina's Fifth Judicial Circuit in 1904, he served in that office from 1905 to 1920. In the following years, he established a successful legal practice and held office as a member of the state house of representatives in 1923–24 and as state highway commissioner from 1931 to 1939. A Democratic state committeeman from 1938 to 1942, Timmerman was named a federal district court judge for South Carolina by President Franklin D. Roosevelt in 1942.

As a member of a federal three-judge panel in May 1951, Timmerman heard a case challenging public school segregation in Clarendon County, South Carolina. The suit was the first in a series of cases brought by the NAACP to mount a frontal assault on racial segregation in public primary and secondary schools. In June 1951, Timmerman joined the opinion of Judge John J. Parker, chief judge of the Fourth Circuit Court of Appeals, which ruled that segregated public schools did not violate the Constitution, that the schools for African Americans in Clarendon County were not equal to those for whites, and that the black schools had to be made equal to those for whites. Judge J. Waties Waring dissented. The three-judge panel held a rehearing in early March 1952. Ten days later, the panel handed down its ruling. The court found that, while the schools had not yet been equalized, South Carolina had undertaken a good-faith effort toward equalization and that the black schools would achieve substantial equality by the beginning of the school year in fall 1952. The court therefore saw no purpose in disrupting the schools so near to the end of the academic year. The NAACP appealed the case to the Supreme Court, where it was joined by four other cases (from Kansas, Delaware, Virginia, and Washington, D.C.). On May 17, 1954, the Supreme Court ruled that segregated public schools were inherently unequal and therefore unconstitutional (*Brown v. Board of Education*). In compliance with this decision, Timmerman and his colleagues in July 1955 enjoined officials in Clarendon County from enforcing racial segregation in local public schools.

Judge Timmerman soon made it clear, however, that he remained a confirmed segregationist, that he strongly disapproved of the Supreme Court's decision, and that he would issue an order to desegregate only when he had no alternative. While his son, South Carolina's governor, GEORGE B. TIMMERMAN, JR., led South Carolina's efforts to oppose desegregation in the late 1950s, the judge attempted to limit the scope of the Court's decree in *Brown*. In April 1955, he dismissed a case challenging South Carolina's laws requiring segregation on buses. *Brown*, he held, applied only to public education. The Fourth Circuit Court of Appeals reversed Timmerman in July, ruling that *Brown* had invalidated legally enforced segregation in other public facilities, including transportation, and remanded the case for trial. Timmerman dismissed the suit a second time for more technical reasons in June 1956, but the appellate court again reversed his decision that November.

In March 1956, South Carolina adopted a law forbidding the employment of NAACP members as teachers in the state, and Timmerman sat on the three-judge federal panel that heard a challenge to the statute. The court voted two-to-one to dismiss the case in January 1957. In a concurring opinion, Timmerman wrote that the law was "designed to protect young minds from the poisonous effects of NAACP propaganda," and he believed it fully con-

stitutional. The case was appealed to the Supreme Court, but the state legislature, recognizing the likelihood of an adverse ruling, repealed the law before the Court could act.

In August 1959, Judge Timmerman dismissed a suit challenging segregated facilities at the municipal airport terminal in Greenville, South Carolina. In his opinion, Timmerman declared that whites "still have the right to choose their own companions and associates and to preserve the integrity of the race with which God Almighty has endowed them." The Fourth Circuit reversed Timmerman's action in April 1960. At the trial in October, Timmerman again ruled against the black plaintiff. In December, the court of appeals ordered him to issue an injunction against enforcing laws requiring the segregation of the airport. In February 1961, Timmerman issued the order prohibiting segregated facilities at the air terminal but made it clear that he did so only because a higher court had commanded it.

In July 1957, Timmerman criticized the Supreme Court in a speech to a Rotary Club in Thomson, Georgia. In addition to the school desegregation decision, Timmerman objected to the Court's judgments in cases involving loyalty-security measures and criminal rights. He attacked the Court as a "hierarchy of despotic judges that is bent on destroying the finest system of government ever designed."

Timmerman retired from the federal bench at the age of 81 in October 1962. He then lived with his son in Batesburg, South Carolina, until his death in Columbia, South Carolina, on April 22, 1966.

—MSM

Timmerman, George Bell, Jr.
(1912–1994) *governor of South Carolina*

The son of a conservative and white supremacist federal judge from South Carolina, George Bell Timmerman, Jr., was born in Anderson, South Carolina, on August 11, 1912. After attending the Citadel and the University of South Carolina, from which he graduated in 1934, Timmerman received his LL.B. from the University of South Carolina in 1937. He was admitted to the bar that year and practiced law with his father, GEORGE BELL TIMMERMAN. After serving in the U.S. Naval Reserve from 1942 to 1946, Timmerman returned home and won election as lieutenant governor. He took office in 1947 and won reelection to the office in 1950. During his second term in office, he served under Governor JAMES F. BYRNES, one of the South's most prominent advocates of states' rights and opponents of desegregation.

Running on a platform supporting states' rights and opposing the Supreme Court's decision in *Brown v. Board of Education* (1954), which outlawed school segregation, Timmerman won election as governor in 1954. In his inaugural address, he asserted that the Court had usurped powers that the Constitution had never intended it to have. The Court's exercise of such powers, he argued, "endanger[ed] the future freedom of all citizens."

As governor, Timmerman focused primarily on opposing desegregation. He urged Congress to limit the authority of the Supreme Court. With three other southern governors, he issued a statement endorsing the doctrine of interposition in 1956. This doctrine held that the sovereign states had the power and right to intercede if the federal government overstepped its legitimate authority. In such a situation, states had the right to interpose their authority between the federal government and the states' citizenry. Even Timmerman had reservations about interposition, however. "We do not believe that nullification will help us in South Carolina," he said. Moreover, while he believed that the people of his state would support closing parks and other public amenities, he did not think that they were "prepared to bring a crisis in our schools." The press called the South Carolina General Assembly's session in 1956 the "Segregation Session," because it passed a series of laws designed to block integration. Timmerman supported a measure, passed in 1956, making members of the NAACP ineligible for state employment; he declared that the group exerted "constant pressure on its members contrary to the principles upon which the economic and social life of our state rests." Timmerman condemned the enactment of civil rights legislation sponsored by the Eisenhower administration as "dastardly." After Eisenhower sent federal troops to enforce a court order to desegregate Little Rock's Central High School, Timmerman accused the president of "trying to set himself up as a dictator" and resigned his commission in the naval reserves.

Timmerman also tried to suppress dissent in the state's black colleges. When a Hungarian refugee enrolled in previously all-black Allen University in September 1957, talk of communist influence at the school spread. The governor informally advised the school's board of trustees to dismiss faculty members who favored desegregation. When the board refused, the governor cancelled the school's accreditation. The following January, Timmerman devoted a large part of his annual address to alleged communist influence in black colleges. In that speech, he charged that three members of the faculty at another black college, Benedict University, were subversive. Political pressure mounted against the black schools throughout the spring. They finally surrendered and dismissed the accused professors. Their accreditation was then restored.

During 1956, Timmerman devoted considerable energy to building a new Dixiecrat coalition, which would promote a united southern front at the Democratic National Convention. He presented his plan at two conferences held in Atlanta during July and August but received little support. Advocates of conciliation, led by Mississippi's governor, JAMES COLEMAN, dominated the discussion, and southern delegates went to the national convention in August intent on working for change within the party. Democrats from South Carolina, led by Timmerman and Senator STROM THURMOND (D-S.C.), continued to criticize the national party. Eventually, however, Timmerman and the state's Democratic Party endorsed the presidential ticket. In November, ADLAI STEVENSON carried the state.

Limited by law to one term, Timmerman returned to his law practice in 1959. He served as a Democratic elector in the presidential election of 1964. In 1967, Timmerman received an appointment as a circuit judge, a position he held until his retirement in 1984. He continued to hear cases part time until 1988. Timmerman died in Columbia, South Carolina, on November 29, 1994.

—MSM

Truman, Harry S.
(1884–1972) *president of the United States*
The son of a farmer, Truman was born in Lamar, Missouri, on May 8, 1884. He moved with his family

to Independence, Missouri, in 1890. Afflicted with poor eyesight from birth, he did not participate in sports and related awkwardly with other boys. He was equally awkward with girls. He learned to play the piano and worked hard in school. Despite his efforts, he was not an outstanding student. After graduating from high school in 1901, he worked as a timekeeper for a construction company and then as a bank clerk. In 1906, along with his parents and siblings, Truman began managing a farm owned by his maternal grandmother and uncle. He joined the Masonic order as well as other fraternal organizations and belonged to a national guard artillery battery from 1905 to 1911. As the United States moved toward war in 1917, Truman rejoined the national guard. Elected lieutenant by the newly formed 129th Artillery Regiment, he attended advanced artillery school in France. Promoted to captain, he was given command of Battery D, which saw combat in France. Truman returned home in 1919 and formed a partnership with an army comrade, Eddie Jacobson, in a haberdashery shop in downtown Kansas City. Ever the joiner, Truman took an active role in the Reserve Officers Association, the American Legion, and a downtown improvement group. During the postwar economic downturn, Truman's business failed in 1922. Debts from that failure would plague him for years.

With the support of Tom Pendergast, boss of the powerful Democratic machine in Kansas City, Truman won election as judge of the Eastern District of Jackson County. Despite the title, the position was not a legal one; it was analogous to that of a county commissioner. In office, he dutifully dispensed patronage to members of the machine and overlooked various ethical and legal violations of his associates. A split in the Democratic Party contributed to Truman's defeat in his bid for reelection two years later. He became membership director of the local automobile club and took a couple of night classes at Kansas City School of Law. In 1926, with the Pendergast machine firmly in control of the local Democratic Party, Truman won election as presiding judge of Jackson County (elected from the entire county) and occupied that position for eight years. He built a county road system and a new courthouse while continuing to distribute patronage to the Pendergast machine.

Despite his loyal performance as a member of the Pendergast organization, Truman earned a reputation as something of a reformer. Further, while his personal conduct in office fell short of spotless, he was regarded as "honest" by the standards of the Pendergast machine.

Truman became the Pendergast machine's candidate for the U.S. Senate in 1934. Through his own tireless campaigning and the efforts of the Pendergast machine, Truman won the Democratic nomination and easily carried the general election. In the Senate, he consistently supported President Franklin D. Roosevelt's domestic and foreign policies. A party loyalist, he backed even Roosevelt's court packing plan. Throughout his first term, Truman dutifully obtained patronage for the Pendergast machine and remained an obscure backbencher. Some in the Washington press corps referred to him as "the gentleman from Pendergast." His personal finances remained shaky, and, at one point, he obtained a favorable mortgage from the Jackson County school fund. As chair of subcommittees of the Interstate and Foreign Commerce Committee, he did play a role in passing the Civil Aeronautics Act of 1938 and the Railroad Transportation Act of 1940.

Tom Pendergast went to jail for income tax evasion in 1939. Unlike many of the boss's political associates, Truman never abandoned his patron. Pendergast's troubles, however, came at a bad time for Truman, who had to run for reelection in 1940. His chances were considered so slim that Roosevelt sent word that he would appoint Truman to a seat on the Interstate Commerce Commission if the senator would step aside in favor of another Democrat. Truman defied Roosevelt and ran for a second term. To the surprise of almost everyone, Truman narrowly defeated Governor Lloyd Stark for the Democratic nomination and went on to win a hard-fought victory in the general election.

Truman first gained national prominence in 1941, when he chaired the Special Committee to Investigate Contracts under the National Defense Program (known as the Truman Committee). His panel uncovered waste, extravagance, and misconduct in military procurement and the nation's defense industries. The committee also exposed abuses by contractors and labor unions.

In 1944, the left wing of the Democratic Party favored the renomination of Henry A. Wallace for vice president, but southerners and conservatives objected strenuously. Conservatives in the party backed presidential assistant JAMES F. BYRNES for the vice presidency, but liberals, labor, and African Americans resolutely opposed him. Roosevelt was in a strong position as he sought a fourth term; the party needed a candidate who would not divide the party or harm the ticket. Truman emerged as a logical compromise candidate. Southerners liked him; he came from a border state and had supported Senator Pat Harrison (D-Miss.) for majority leader over the administration's choice, Senator Alban Barkley (D-Ky.). On the other hand, Truman had consistently voted for New Deal measures, which made him acceptable to liberals and labor. The press dubbed the choice of Truman "the Missouri Compromise."

Roosevelt and Truman won the election in November, and Truman took office in January 1945. He had served as vice president for only 83 days when Roosevelt died on April 12, 1945. Truman, who had not been closely briefed by Roosevelt on the progress of the war, was thrust into the position of guiding the American war effort during the last months of the conflict and formulating foreign policy during the postwar period. In July, Truman met with the leaders of the Soviet Union and Great Britain at Potsdam, Germany. At the meeting, the United States and Britain issued an ultimatum to Japan demanding unconditional surrender. The Japanese government dismissed the ultimatum. In August, Truman approved the use of the recently developed atomic bomb. After the destruction of Hiroshima on August 6 and Nagasaki on August 9, the Japanese surrendered on August 14.

Relations with the Soviet Union and the United States deteriorated rapidly after the war ended. A strong stand by the United States resulted in the Soviet Union's withdrawal from Iran. While he still harbored hope, at least occasionally, that he could deal with Stalin, Truman grew increasingly convinced that the Soviets were hopelessly intransigent. Truman came to accept the view of GEORGE F. KENNAN that the Soviet Union was an expansionist power, driven by internal dynamics, and that the United States should respond by containing it. When Henry

Wallace, the secretary of agriculture, publicly criticized the administration's policy toward the Soviet Union in September 1946, Truman dismissed him. The administration implemented the containment policy through the Truman Doctrine and the Marshall Plan. In 1947, Truman called for American aid to Greece and Turkey in order to prevent communist insurgents from taking over those countries. In asking for that aid, Truman articulated what became known as the Truman Doctrine: "I believe that it must be the policy of the United States to support free peoples who are resisting attempted subjugation by armed minorities or by outside pressures." Later that year, Secretary of State George C. Marshall announced a program of massive economic aid for the reconstruction of Europe, which became known as the Marshall Plan. When the Soviets blockaded West Berlin in June 1948, Truman used an airlift to resupply the city. In 1949, Truman secured ratification of the North Atlantic Treaty, which created the North Atlantic Treaty Organization (NATO), a mutual defense pact.

Although Truman secured a general consensus on these measures, he proved less successful in domestic policy. The first problem he confronted was reconversion of the economy. Truman and his advisers focused primarily on preventing a recession. In fact, that did not turn out to be a problem. The pent-up consumer demand created by the war made inflation the primary issue. Truman's policies, intended to stimulate the economy, further fueled inflationary pressures. In September 1945, he presented a 21-point program, which included an increase in unemployment compensation, a rise in the minimum wage, housing legislation, increased public works, and tax reductions. Runaway inflation led to a series of strikes. Truman's threat to draft striking railway workers alienated organized labor.

Truman's less-than-sure handling of reconversion led to a sweeping Republican victory in the congressional elections of 1946. The Republican campaign slogan ("Had Enough?") proved devastatingly effective, and Republicans emerged from the election with a substantial majority in the House and a slim majority in the Senate. After the election, however, the worst of the disruptions caused by reconversion eased. The shortages disappeared, and the number of strikes declined. Moreover, freed from a Democratic Congress that received his initiatives coolly, Truman found his political footing as an adversary of a Republican Congress. He portrayed himself as a bold, visionary leader hampered by a reactionary Congress. Truman put forward a program of social legislation designed to preserve and expand the New Deal that would also solidify Truman's standing with liberals in the party and establish the foundation for his campaign for reelection in 1948. He proposed increased aid to farmers, an increase in the minimum wage, a program to increase the stock of new housing, and slum clearance. In response to an outbreak of racial violence in the South, Truman appointed a President's Committee on Civil Rights in December 1947. The panel's report, "To Secure These Rights," issued in October 1947, frankly addressed racial discrimination in American society. In February 1948, Truman called for enactment of some of the commission's recommendations, including a federal antilynching bill, the elimination of the poll tax, and creation of a Fair Employment Practices Commission. Congress rejected most of Truman's proposals; although it did enact the housing program. Truman also vetoed 62 bills during the 80th Congress, including the Taft-Hartley Act, which Congress passed over his veto. That veto solidified Truman's standing with organized labor.

Going into 1948, Truman had created a broad base of support for his foreign policy and made significant strides toward rebuilding the Democratic presidential coalition. Nevertheless, his chances for reelection seemed slim. Wallace ran for president on the Progressive Party ticket and attracted voters from the left wing of the Democratic Party. Truman also lost the right wing of his party when liberals at the Democratic convention pushed through a strong civil rights plank over the objections of Truman and his managers. As a result, southern delegates walked out and subsequently formed a third party (the States' Rights Democrats, or Dixiecrats). They nominated Governor STROM THURMOND of South Carolina for the presidency. Confronted with the defection of the southerners and needing to mend fences with liberals, Truman issued an executive order banning discrimination in the armed forces (although he subsequently did little to enforce it).

The Republicans nominated THOMAS E. DEWEY, the leader of the eastern, or liberal, wing of their party. While Dewey ran a restrained campaign, Truman vehemently attacked the Republican Congress and charged that, if left to their own devices, they would undo the New Deal. In November, Truman fell just short of a majority of the popular vote (his opponents divided the remainder), but he won a comfortable victory in the electoral college. Democrats regained control of both houses of Congress.

After winning election in his own right, Truman presented to Congress a domestic program he called the Fair Deal, which proposed several extensions of the New Deal. It included a housing bill, federal aid to education, national health insurance, a repeal of the Taft-Hartley Act, civil rights legislation, and the Brannan Plan (named for the secretary of agriculture, Charles Brannan, the plan proposed to pay subsidies to farmers while allowing prices of agricultural goods to drop to market levels). Congress passed a housing bill, an increase of Social Security benefits, an increase in the minimum wage, and a few other modest extensions of the New Deal. Most of Truman's program, however, went down to defeat. Under LEON KEYSERLING, the chair of the Council of Economic Advisers, the Truman administration emphasized economic growth, rather than redistribution, as the goal of liberalism.

Despite the containment of communism in Europe, the United States suffered a series of reverses in the cold war. Mainland China fell to Mao Zedong's Communists in 1949, and that same year the Soviet Union exploded its first atomic device. In January 1950, Truman approved development of a thermonuclear bomb. In June 1950, North Korea, controlled by a communist government, invaded South Korea. Truman's conduct of the Korean War aroused controversy. He concluded that the North Korean aggression had to be resisted. At the same time, the president favored a restoration of the status quo that had existed before the North Korean invasion of the South. Moreover, he decided not to ask Congress for a declaration of war. Thanks to a temporary boycott by the Soviet Union, the Truman administration got the United Nations Security Council to condemn the invasion. After American forces managed to hold a defense perimeter around the port of Pusan, General Douglas MacArthur staged a successful amphibious landing at Inchon and inflicted a devastating defeat on the North Korean invaders. Hoping for a much-needed victory in the cold war, Truman approved an advance into North Korea with the intent of unifying Korea under a noncommunist government. As they advanced deep into North Korea, American forces encountered Chinese troops. By late November 1950, the United Nations forces were once again in full-scale retreat. Truman rejected MacArthur's proposal to expand the conflict by bombing mainland China. The president worried about the possibility of a Soviet move against western Europe and the possibility of a third world war. MacArthur took his case to Republican congressional leaders, and Truman relieved MacArthur of his command in April 1951. Initially the general rallied considerable support, particularly among those who were already critical of the Truman administration for having allegedly lost China to the communists. The furor over the dismissal subsided after a few weeks, but the conflict settled into a bloody stalemate that lasted until the end of Truman's presidency.

The cold war and the war in Korea fed fears of communist subversion. In 1945, an FBI raid on the offices of *Amerasia*, a left-leaning journal devoted to foreign policy, discovered classified State Department documents. The following year, a Canadian Royal Commission uncovered evidence of Soviet spying in Canada and the United States. Truman initiated a loyalty program for federal employees in 1947. In January 1950, a jury convicted Alger Hiss, a former assistant secretary of state, of perjury for denying in testimony before Congress that he had passed documents to the Soviets. That same year, Dr. Klaus Fuchs, a German-born scientist who held British citizenship and had worked on the Manhattan Project, was arrested in England and confessed to spying for the Soviets. The arrest of Fuchs led to the arrest of JULIUS AND ETHEL ROSENBERG, as well as others belonging to the ring led by Julius Rosenberg. Amid these disturbing events, an obscure Republican senator from Wisconsin, JOSEPH R. MCCARTHY, gained national attention in February 1950 with charges that the State Department harbored communists. McCarthy made a series of spectacular allegations but could prove none of

them. Nevertheless, the charges made by McCarthy and others plagued the Truman administration.

Under attack for failing to end the Korean stalemate and for failing to root out communists in government, Truman became increasingly unpopular. In addition, his administration was plagued by corruption, ranging from the small-time influence peddling of the president's military aide, Harry Vaughan, to more serious breaches. During the Truman administration, the Reconstruction Finance Corporation became, in the words of Truman's favorably inclined biographer, Alonzo Hamby, "a hotbed of political favoritism." The most serious incidents involved wrongdoing in the Bureau of Internal Revenue and the Tax Division of the Justice Department. Fifty-seven functionaries of the Bureau of Internal Revenue had to be dismissed or were forced to resign by the end of 1951. Charles Oliphant, chief counsel of Internal Revenue, resigned under pressure after accepting gifts in exchange for favors. Assistant Attorney General T. Lamar Caudle was dismissed in 1951 and later convicted of conspiracy. Attorney General J. Howard McGrath failed to moved against corruption in his department, and Truman had to force his resignation.

On March 29, 1952, Truman announced that he would not seek reelection. He publicly professed to oppose a third term as a matter of principle, but he realized that he had virtually no chance of winning another term. His approval rating fell to 23 percent after he fired MacArthur, and it never got higher than 32 percent for the rest of his term in office. Moreover, Truman's announcement came after Senator ESTES KEFAUVER (D-Tenn.) soundly trounced the sitting president in New Hampshire's presidential preference primary. Truman offered to support Chief Justice FRED VINSON and General DWIGHT D. EISENHOWER, both of whom declined to seek the Democratic nomination. Eisenhower ultimately decided to run for the Republican nomination. Truman then turned to ADLAI E. STEVENSON, the governor of Illinois. Stevenson, however, believed that he could not win if he were too closely associated with an unpopular administration. Anticipating a draft, he insisted upon his noncandidacy. After winning the nomination, Stevenson carefully maintained some distance from the administration. Stevenson's strategy offended the president; in addition to which, Truman disliked the candidate's low-keyed style. Despite the personal friction between the president and the candidate, Truman campaigned aggressively for Stevenson. Given Truman's unpopularity, that may have been a liability for Stevenson. In subsequent years, Truman asserted that Stevenson's defeat was the candidate's own fault. In any event, Eisenhower overwhelmingly defeated Stevenson in November.

In his final State of the Union message, on January 7, 1953, Truman warned Soviet premier Joseph V. Stalin that war would mean ruin for the USSR. He also stressed the necessity for the West to resist communist expansion without plunging the world into atomic conflict. With respect to domestic policy, Truman cautioned against legislation aimed at domestic communism that would promote an "enforced conformity." He further asserted that the economy had "grown tremendously" under his administration, and, while acknowledging increases in prices, he said that income had increased more.

Later that year, Truman became embroiled in a controversy that raised a fundamental issue involving the relationship between the executive and legislative branches of the federal government. On November 6, Attorney General HERBERT BROWNELL charged that Truman knew that the late Harry Dexter White was a Russian spy when he promoted White from assistant secretary of the Treasury to U.S. executive director of the International Monetary Fund in 1946. Governor JAMES F. BYRNES of South Carolina, who had been Truman's secretary of state at the time, backed the charge, but Truman heatedly denied it. On November 10, the House Un-American Activities Committee (HUAC) subpoenaed Truman, Byrnes, and Supreme Court Justice TOM C. CLARK, Truman's former attorney general. Such a summons to an ex-president was unprecedented. Two days later, Truman rejected it. He offered to testify regarding any acts unrelated to his presidential role but said that the constitutional position of the presidency would be jeopardized if he accepted the congressional subpoena to testify about his conduct as president. The chair of the HUAC, Representative Harold H. Velde (R-Ill.), decided that he would not attempt to compel Truman to appear before the panel.

After leaving the White House, Truman retired to Independence, Missouri, where he wrote his memoirs. He remained a public figure during the 1950s, periodically criticizing the Eisenhower administration for its domestic policies and particularly for its cuts in defense spending. Truman, who thought of himself as an active and decisive chief executive, denounced Eisenhower as a "do-nothing" president in April 1956. Truman also remained active in Democratic politics. In August 1956, he announced his support for New York's governor, AVERELL HARRIMAN, for the Democratic presidential nomination. Truman said that the governor's "long experience in top government positions" made him the best candidate. Three days later, the ex-president stated at a news conference that he did not think Stevenson could win the election. Nonetheless, after Stevenson captured the nomination, Truman campaigned vigorously for him in the general election. Eisenhower trounced Stevenson even more decisively than he had in 1952.

After the election of 1956, Truman became a member of the newly created Democratic Advisory Council (DAC). Formed at the urging of Democratic national chairman PAUL BUTLER, the DAC was designed to provide a means of developing Democratic legislative programs in a forum independent of the Speaker of the house, SAM RAYBURN (D-Tex.), and the majority leader of the Senate, LYNDON B. JOHNSON (D-Tex.), whom liberals in the party regarded as too conservative. Other members of the DAC included Stevenson, ELEANOR ROOSEVELT, and Senator Estes Kefauver. In 1958, Truman joined other DAC members in proposing stronger civil rights legislation, curbs on Senate filibusters, a higher minimum wage, and other measures.

In 1957, the Harry S. Truman Library Institute for National and International Affairs, built by private subscription and given to the government, opened its doors in Independence. It housed the ex-president's papers, the papers of members of his administration, a large collection of books, and many exhibits. Truman subsequently spent much of his time working in an office there.

Truman declined to attend the Democratic National Convention in 1960 on the ground that it had been rigged in advance to assure the nomina-

<col>
</col>

---

tion for Senator JOHN F. KENNEDY (D-Mass.). However much he disliked the Kennedy family, party loyalty and his loathing for Kennedy's opponent, Vice President RICHARD M. NIXON, led Truman to campaign actively for Kennedy in 1960, as he had for Stevenson four years earlier.

During the 1960s, Truman gave his public support to Kennedy's policies and even more enthusiastic support to President Lyndon B. Johnson's Great Society. Although he endorsed the civil rights legislation passed during Johnson's presidency, Truman criticized civil rights demonstrators at the New York World's Fair in 1964 and the following year called the civil rights march in Selma, Alabama, a "silly" effort to attract attention. In April 1965, he described MARTIN LUTHER KING, JR., as a "troublemaker." Truman consistently supported Johnson's policy in Vietnam. He died in Kansas City, Missouri, on December 26, 1972.

By the late 1950s, many Americans had come to regard Truman as a beneficent elder statesman endowed with an earthy common sense that made his judgments superior to those of intellectuals. During 1961 and 1962, Truman gave extensive recorded interviews to Merle Miller. After Truman's death, Miller published selections of the transcripts as *Plain Speaking: An Oral Biography of Harry S. Truman* (1973). The book served to rekindle interest in Truman and to reinforce the public image of Truman as a plain-speaking figure possessed of an uncommon amount of common sense. *Plain Speaking* revealed many of Truman's resentments and contained highly negative comments about many people, including the entire Kennedy family, which he regarded as power hungry, Stevenson, whom he considered a "sissy," and Tom Clark, whose elevation to the Supreme Court he regarded as his worst mistake as president and whom he described as a "dumb son of a bitch."

Historians have drawn a more reserved image of Truman. At his best, concluded Hamby, Truman was decisive; at his worst, he was impetuous. Truman was not good at giving formal speeches, and his poor eyesight made it difficult for him to read transcripts. Truman's sometimes awkward efforts made a marked contrast with Roosevelt's magnificent speeches. Hamby also contended that Truman "carried a lot of latent, unfocused anger" as a result of his failures in business and the criticism he received for his association with the corrupt Pendergast machine. In addition, noted Hamby, Truman worked exceedingly hard and experienced a great deal of stress, which "reinforced a tendency toward ill-tempered and unpresidential outbursts." Truman tended to appoint friends and cronies to high places. Constitutional historians generally regard his four appointments to the Supreme Court as the least distinguished set of appointments to the Court in American history. In spite of his support for civil rights legislation, Truman retained prejudices of his small-town Missouri upbringing. Eben Ayers's diary reveals that Truman regularly used the word "nigger," and the president was prone to occasional anti-Semitic outbursts, some of which he recorded in his own diary ("The Jews, I find, are very, very selfish."). Another sympathetic biographer, Robert Donovan wrote: "Still, he had come from a world of two-bit politicians, and its aura was one that he never was able to shed entirely. And he did retain certain characteristics of machine-bred politicians: intense partisanship, partisan loyalty, a certain insensitivity about the transgressions of political associates, and a disinclination for the companionship of intellectuals and artists. Mostly, his personal friends were plain, obscure, even mediocre men who shared his love of politics and poker." Yet Truman guided the United States through the early days of the cold war, and, through his administration's emphasis on Keynesian demand management as a means to achieve growth and avoid questions of redistribution, he helped recast liberalism for the postwar era.

—MSM

Tuttle, Elbert Parr

(1897–1996) *general counsel to the Treasury Department, federal appellate judge*

Born in Pasadena, California, on July 17, 1897, Tuttle moved with his family first to Washington, D.C., and then in 1906 to Hawaii. He attended Punahou Academy in Honolulu and graduated from Cornell University in 1918. Upon graduating, he enlisted in the U.S. Army as a "flying cadet" in the artillery's observation corps. He was still in training when World War I ended, and Second Lieutenant Tuttle joined the U.S. Army Reserve. In 1919, Tuttle went to work as a reporter and editorial writer for the *New York Evening World*. He returned to Cornell for law school and worked as a reporter to support himself. Tuttle compiled an excellent record in law school and became editor-in-chief of the law review. Upon receiving his LL.B. in 1923, he and William Sutherland, his brother-in-law, decided to practice law together and founded a law firm in Atlanta, Georgia. Their practice thrived, and Sutherland, Tuttle & Brennan (later Sutherland Asbill & Brennan) became a leading law firm. Sutherland specialized in corporate tax law, and Tuttle devoted himself to general practice. Tuttle also did a good deal of pro bono work and took cases for the American Civil Liberties Union (ACLU). In 1931, as a major in the national guard, Tuttle commanded a unit that prevented a mob from lynching an African-American man accused of raping a white woman. Subsequently, the accused man was convicted and sentenced to death. Tuttle filed a petition with a federal district judge in which he argued that the presence of the mob effectively denied the defendant due process. The judge denied the petition, and Tuttle appealed to the Fifth Circuit Court of Appeals, which granted a new trial. Tuttle and Sutherland also challenged the constitutionality of a state statute prohibiting incitement to insurrection. After losing in the state courts, Tuttle appealed the case to the U.S. Supreme Court, which struck down the statute by a five to four vote. The ACLU asked Tuttle to take a case of a convicted counterfeiter who had been unable to afford legal representation at his trial. After losing in the lower courts, Tuttle took an appeal to the Supreme Court and won a decision establishing the right to counsel for every defendant charged with a crime in federal courts (*Johnson v. Zerbst*, 1938). Tuttle also served on the board of trustees of two black colleges, Spelman College and Morehouse College.

When the United States entered World War II, Tuttle, who had remained in the reserves, turned down a desk job and the rank of full colonel. Instead, he chose to go on active combat duty as a lieutenant colonel commanding the 304th Field Artillery Battalion of the 77th Infantry Division. He served in the Pacific theater and won the Legion of Merit, a Bronze Star, and a Purple Heart. After the war, he remained in the reserves as commanding general of the 108th Airborne Division until he retired in 1950.

When the war ended, Tuttle returned to his law practice and became active in Republican politics. He gravitated toward the Republican Party because he opposed the segregationist Democratic Party in Georgia. Tuttle once described the Democratic Party of Georgia as "paternalistic at best, and autocratic at worst." He saw "nothing 'democratic' about it at all except the name." In early 1952, Tuttle became vice chairman of the Southern Conference for Eisenhower, part of the movement to draft General DWIGHT D. EISENHOWER to run as the Republican presidential nominee. At the Republican National Convention, Tuttle led the pro-Eisenhower delegation from Georgia that challenged the traditional Republican leadership in his state, which supported Senator ROBERT A. TAFT of Ohio. Tuttle also played an active role in Eisenhower's general election campaign. After Eisenhower won the election, he appointed Tuttle general counsel of the Treasury Department in 1953. The following year, Eisenhower appointed Tuttle to a newly created seat on the Fifth Circuit Court of Appeals. At that time, the Fifth Circuit comprised Louisiana, Mississippi, Texas, Alabama, Georgia, and Florida.

Tuttle became a federal appellate judge a few months after the Supreme Court ruled segregated public schools unconstitutional in *Brown v. Board of Education* (1954). Much of his career on the federal bench would deal with the implementation of that ruling. A week after the *Brown* decision, a friend asked Tuttle if he had seen what the Court had done. "Oh, yes," replied Tuttle, "but they'll fall in line." Experience proved him wrong. Along with three other judges on the Fifth Circuit (JOHN MINOR WISDOM, John R. Brown, and Richard Rives), Tuttle played a central role in desegregating the Deep South. Beginning in the late 1950s, the Fifth Circuit handed down a series of rulings desegregating public schools and striking down discrimination in voting, jury selection, and employment. Tuttle wrote the opinion for the majority upholding Federal District Judge J. SKELLY WRIGHT's order to desegregate public schools in New Orleans. In 1961, Tuttle ordered the admission of two black students to the University of Georgia. The following year, Tuttle joined in the majority opinion ordering the admission of an African American, James H. Meredith, to the University of Mississippi. After massive civil rights demonstrations in Birmingham in 1963, the Birmingham school board suspended black students who had taken part in the demonstrations. Tuttle issued an order commanding the school board to permit the students to return to school.

Tuttle became chief judge of the Fifth Circuit in 1961. He stepped down as chief judge in 1967 and took senior judge status in 1968. When the Fifth Circuit was divided into the Fifth and new 11th Circuits in 1981, Tuttle became a senior judge of the 11th Circuit. President James Earl Carter presented him with the Presidential Medal of Freedom in 1981. Tuttle continued to sit until his death in Atlanta on June 23, 1996.

—MSM

Twining, Nathan F(arragut)

(1897–1982) *air force chief of staff; chairman, Joint Chiefs of Staff*

The son of a banker, Twining was born in Monroe, Wisconsin, on October 11, 1897. He was a direct descendant of settlers who landed at Plymouth and of military men who fought in the Revolutionary War. As a youth, he moved with his family to Portland, Oregon, where he attended public schools and joined the Oregon National Guard. Called to active duty in 1916, Twining served under General John J. Pershing along the Mexican border. He then attended the United States Military Academy at West Point, where he completed an abbreviated wartime course in 1918 and became a second lieutenant. Twining served briefly with the Allied occupation forces in Germany. After being promoted to first lieutenant in 1920 and completing infantry school, he received flight training in Texas during 1923 and 1924. He transferred to the air service in November 1926 and spent the next three years as a flight instructor. Between 1930 and 1936, he was stationed in Hawaii, Texas, and Louisiana. Promoted to captain in 1935, he attended the tactical school at Maxwell Field in Alabama and the command and general staff school in 1936 and 1937. After serving in Texas, where he was promoted to major, Twining was assigned to Washington,

D.C., as a member of the staff of the chief of the air corps in August 1940. He became a lieutenant colonel in July 1941. Not long after the United States entered World War II, he became assistant executive to the chief of staff of the army air force and received a promotion to full colonel. In July 1942, he was promoted to brigadier general and assigned to the South Pacific as chief of staff of army forces. In January 1943, Twining became commanding general of the 13th Air Force and saw action in the Solomon Islands. He returned to Washington in November 1943 but soon received orders to assume command of the 15th Air Force and saw action in the Mediterranean theater. After VE Day, he returned to the Pacific and, as commander of the 20th Air Force, oversaw firebombing raids on Japan and the missions that dropped atomic bombs on Hiroshima and Nagasaki. At the end of the war, Twining held the temporary rank of lieutenant general. After the war, he held a series of posts in the United States. He received his promotion to major general in 1948 and became vice chief of staff in 1950.

President DWIGHT D. EISENHOWER appointed him air force chief of staff in May 1953. Twining's selection reflected Eisenhower's desire to reduce American reliance on conventional forces and his emphasis on airpower, technology, and the nuclear deterrent. The general supported Eisenhower's belief that the primary American deterrent should be a mobile nuclear strike force capable of meeting any threat. However, Twining objected to the cuts in conventional forces and defense spending that accompanied the administration's New Look. In testimony before the Senate Armed Services Committee in 1953, he stated that proposed cuts in the air force would delay creation of the 143 wings he deemed necessary for American security. He also warned that the United States could not maintain its superiority over the Soviet Union without enough trained men and that the air force could not attract or keep such men because of low pay.

In 1956, Twining joined a number of air force generals and members of Congress in warning of an impending "bomber gap" with the USSR. Appearing before the Senate Appropriations Committee's Subcommittee on Defense in May, Twining said that "the people above" him had cut $272 million

Swearing-in of General Nathan F. Twining as chairman of the Joint Chiefs of Staff, August 15, 1957 *(Dwight D. Eisenhower Library and Museum)*

from his funds for air force bases. He further stated that he would have to request more money if all installations and early warning systems were to be completed by the targeted date of 1958. He informed the subcommittee that he had asked for six additional wings of B-52 type bombers to increase the Strategic Air Command by 300 planes but that Eisenhower was still considering his request. Twining assured the congressmen that the United States could deter a Soviet attack "this year" but questioned how long the advantage would continue. After a trip to the Soviet Union in July, he again reported that the Russians were outproducing the United States in modern planes and catching up in the quality of the aircraft they produced. Congress added nearly $1 billion dollars to the administration's request for the air force in fiscal 1957.

Despite his disagreements with some of the administration's policies, Twining retained Eisenhower's trust, and in 1957 the president appointed him to succeed Admiral Arthur Radford as chairman of the Joint Chiefs of Staff. Twining defended Eisenhower's plan for cutting back production of B-52s and for the development of the XB-70 bomber. An advocate of the Jupiter and Atlas missiles as well as the navy's submarine-launched Polaris missile, Twining nevertheless defended the administration's reluctance to commit unlimited sums of money to the development of missiles. Questioned by Senator Dennis Chavez (D-N. Mex.), chair of the Senate Subcommittee on Defense, Twining explained that less money would be needed in fiscal 1958 than in fiscal 1957, because intelligence reported a slower rate of Soviet bomber production than anticipated.

Further, he assured the subcommittee, "I know of nothing that could be done to give us operationally effective ballistic missiles appreciably sooner."

Twining advocated American intervention in the Middle East and Asia to contain communism. In spring 1954, he proposed that the United States use tactical atomic weapons to relieve the besieged French garrison at Dien Bien Phu in northern Vietnam. When the Communist Chinese began shelling Quemoy and Matsu in September of that same year, Twining joined Radford, then chairman of the Joint Chiefs of Staff, in recommending that the Nationalist Chinese be permitted to bomb the mainland and suggesting that American aircraft enter the battle if the Communists retaliated. In 1958, when Lebanon's president, Camille Chamoun, requested American forces to help quell a pro-Nasser insur-gency, Twining successfully argued for the landing of U.S. Marines in Lebanon.

Following an operation for lung cancer in 1959, Twining retired in September 1960. He became chairman of the board of the publishing firm Holt, Rinehart and Winston, Inc. He remained a strong anticommunist. He went before Congress to testify against the limited nuclear test ban treaty of 1963 and supported the American involvement in Vietnam. In 1964, Twining served as an adviser to the Republican presidential nominee, Senator BARRY GOLDWATER (R-Ariz.). Two years later, Twining ran unsuccessfully as the Republican candidate for the U.S. Senate from New Hampshire. He retired from Holt, Rinehart and Winston in 1967 and died at Lackland Air Force Base in San Antonio, Texas, on March 29, 1982.

—MSM

Vandenberg, Hoyt S(anford)

(1899–1954) *air force chief of staff*

A descendent of early Dutch settlers and the nephew of an influential Republican senator, Arthur Vandenberg (R-Mich.), Hoyt Vandenberg was born in Milwaukee, Wisconsin, on January 24, 1899. Following his graduation from West Point in 1923, he began a career in army aviation. After filling a number of routine assignments, Vandenberg attended the air corps tactical school from 1934 to 1935, command and general staff school from 1935 to 1936, and the army war college from 1938 to 1939. After completing his studies at the army war college, he received a promotion to major and an assignment to the plans division in the office of the chief of the air corps. After becoming a full colonel in January 1942, he went to Britain with General Henry Arnold, the chief of the army air forces, in June 1942. Vandenberg helped plan the air operations for the Allied invasion of North Africa and later participated in the operation. He became chief of staff to General James Doolittle, commander of the 12th Air Force. Vandenberg flew 26 combat missions and became known as the "flying general." He won the Silver Star and the Distinguished Flying Cross. Promoted to brigadier general in December 1942, he continued to serve as Doolittle's chief of staff when Doolittle assumed command of the Northwest African Strategic Air Force. In August 1943, he became one of four deputy chiefs of staff on Arnold's staff. Promoted to major general, Vandenberg joined General DWIGHT D. EISENHOWER's staff in March 1944. He helped plan air support for the D-day invasion. In August 1944, Vandenberg assumed command of the Ninth Air Force. After receiving a promotion to lieutenant general, he returned to army air forces headquarters in May 1945. In January 1946, Eisenhower appointed Vandenberg director of intelligence on the War Department's general staff. In July of that year, President HARRY S. TRUMAN named him director of the Central Intelligence Group, a predecessor of the Central Intelligence Agency. Vandenberg returned to the army air corps in May 1947 and in September became the first vice chief of staff of the newly independent air force. Upon his promotion to full general a month later, he became, at the age of 49, the youngest member of the military to hold that rank. Truman appointed him air force chief of staff in April 1948.

During the postwar period, Vandenberg lobbied for a strong air force, which he considered essential in light of Soviet advances in the production of jet fighters and bombers. He also was a leading figure in the drive for a unified armed services and a strong proponent of the development of the hydrogen bomb. In 1951, Vandenberg joined other members of the Joint Chiefs of Staff in defending President Harry S. Truman's dismissal of General Douglas MacArthur from his Korean command. Vandenberg was scheduled to retire as air force chief of staff in 1952, but his term was extended 14 months so that he could retire with 30 years of service and at the highest rank he had attained in the air force.

During the last months of his tenure, Vandenberg was an outspoken critic of the Eisenhower administration's proposed cuts in the defense budget.

In May 1953, Secretary of Defense CHARLES WILSON announced a $5 billion reduction in appropriations for the air force. The cut precluded the service's anticipated expansion to 143 wings. Vandenberg testified against the cuts before the Senate Appropriations Committee in June. He warned that 143 wings was the absolute minimum needed for U.S. air defense and that anything short of that goal "would increase the risk to national security beyond the dictates of national prudence." He claimed that the air force was being crippled by limitations on personnel, base construction, appropriations, force levels, and expenditures and research. Vandenberg claimed that he had heard no sound military reason for the cut "at a time when we face an enemy who has more modern jet fighters than we have and enough long range bombers to attack this country in a sudden all-out atomic effort." He charged that Wilson's plan would leave the United States with a "second-best air force" inadequate to meet growing Soviet strength. It would be a "one-shot" service, which would not have any reserve strength if the Soviets launched an all-out atomic war against the United States.

Secretary of Defense Wilson and Secretary of the Air Force HAROLD E. TALBOTT challenged Vandenberg's assertions, claiming the cuts would not impair American airpower. Eisenhower met with Republican congressional leaders and explained that the air force was ordering and acquiring new planes before it had the personnel to fly them or bases from which they might operate. Vandenberg retired on June 30, 1953. The cuts went into effect immediately after Vandenberg's retirement.

Vandenberg underwent surgery for prostate cancer in May 1952 but soon returned to work. Not long after he retired, however, he suffered a relapse and entered Walter Reed Army Hospital in Washington, D.C., where he remained until his death from the cancer on April 2, 1954.

—MSM

Van Doren, Charles L(incoln)

(1926–   ) *college instructor, television quiz show contestant, writer*

The product of a distinguished intellectual family, Charles Van Doren was born in New York City on February 12, 1926. His father, Mark Van Doren, was a poet and critic who taught at Columbia University and won a Pulitzer Prize for poetry; his mother, Dorothy, a novelist, had been an editor of the *Nation*. An uncle, Carl Van Doren, was a historian who held a Pulitzer Prize for biography. Charles Van Doren earned his B.A. from St. John's College in Maryland in 1947. After receiving an M.A. in mathematics at Columbia University, Van Doren switched to English literature. He began doctoral studies in English and worked as an instructor at Columbia. Upon completion of his dissertation on William Cowper, an 18th-century British poet, the newly minted Ph.D. received an assistant professorship at Columbia in 1959.

While a graduate student and instructor at Columbia, Van Doren gained national attention as a quiz show contestant during the 1956–57 television season. Beginning in late 1955, evening game programs, awarding large cash prizes, emerged as the most popular programs on TV. Van Doren appeared on *Twenty-One*, a (Jack) Barry and (Dan) Enright production. Possessing good looks and an appealing, boyish charm, Van Doren proved an immediate hit as a contestant. After a series of ties, he defeated the reigning champion, Herbert Stempel, in December 1956 and went on to win $129,000. During Van Doren's 14 appearances, *Twenty-One* climbed to the top of the television ratings. Van Doren became a national celebrity, and he appeared on the cover of *Time* magazine on February 11, 1957. Vivian Nearing, a lawyer whose husband had earlier lost to Van Doren, defeated Van Doren, after three dramatic ties, in March 1957. The National Broadcasting Company, which aired *Twenty-One*, capitalized on Van Doren's continuing popularity by signing him to a contract and making him a host for the network's popular morning program, the *Today Show*.

While Van Doren cohosted *Today* in August 1958, the *New York World-Telegram* carried a story in which Stempel charged that his appearances on *Twenty-One*, along with those of other contestants, had been staged by Barry and Enright. Van Doren denied Stempel's allegations on *Today* and persisted in defending the programs well into 1959. In August 1958, however, a guest on another quiz show, *Dotto*, found materials left behind by another contestant that contained the answers to the questions on that day's program. The information made its way to Manhattan's district attorney, FRANK S. HOGAN, who assigned an assistant district attorney, Joseph Stone, to began an investigation of all TV quiz programs. Stone convened a grand jury and took testimony from over 100 contestants, most of whom, including Van Doren, swore that they knew nothing about rigging the shows. By October, Stone procured an indictment of Albert Freedman, the producer of *Dotto* and *Twenty-One*. Ratings for the programs plummeted, and NBC canceled *Twenty-One* in October 1958. After the grand jury completed its work in June 1959, a Manhattan judge took the unusual step of keeping its report confidential. Prior to its release, the chairman of the House Commerce Committee, OREN HARRIS (D-Ark.) launched an inquiry and subpoenaed Van Doren and others in October.

On November 2, Van Doren made a dramatic appearance before a Subcommittee on Legislative Oversight (a subcommittee of the House Commerce Committee), chaired by Harris. Van Doren admitted that he had been given the answers to questions beforehand, that he had been coached on how to deliver his responses, and that he had agreed to lose to Nearing "in a dramatic manner." Van Doren said "I was deeply involved, deeply involved in a deception . . . I have deceived my friends—and I had millions of them." In Van Doren's account, the producers of *Twenty-One* had persuaded him that his cooperation would create goodwill for "the intellectual life." Van Doren also admitted to lying before the grand jury. He resigned from Columbia's faculty that day; the next day, NBC fired him.

Van Doren's confession shocked the nation and altered the networks' programing. The intellectual from Columbia had been a much-admired figure, and his fall disillusioned many TV viewers. Yet surveys indicated that a majority of Americans did not hold Van Doren and other participants either legally or morally culpable for their actions. Most of the condemnation of quiz show producers and panelists came from opinion leaders—editors, ministers, and the like—not the public at large. On November 8, President DWIGHT D. EISENHOWER expressed "dismay" that anyone would "conspire to confuse and deceive the American people." He blamed the advertisers ("the grey-flanneled hucksters from Madison

Avenue") and compared the event to the "fix" of the 1919 World Series. Because of the vague wording of communications law, however, the federal government took no action against the programs' producers or the networks. For their part, the networks, led by FRANK STANTON at CBS, canceled the quiz shows and scheduled more "public service" programming, including news and cultural programs.

Van Doren moved to Chicago, where he avoided the limelight. Hogan's office obtained perjury indictments against Van Doren and 13 other contestants in October 1960; most pleaded guilty, and all received suspended sentences in January 1962. Van Doren remained out of the public eye but began a successful career as a writer and editor. He became an editor at Praeger Books and wrote several books under a pseudonym. In 1973, he became editorial vice president of the *Encyclopædia Britannica*. Eventually, in the mid-1980s, he began publishing under his own name. His works include *The Idea of Progress* (1967), *The Joy of Reading* (1985), and *A History of Knowledge* (1991). In 2008, Van Doren published an account of his experiences on the quiz shows and his life since that episode in the *New Yorker*. He lives in Cornwall, Connecticut.

—MSM

Velde, Harold H(immel)
(1910–1985) *U.S. congressman; chairman, Un-American Activities Committee*

The son of parents of East Frisian and German ancestry, Harold Velde was born on a farm near Parkland, Illinois, on April 1, 1910. He grew up in rural Illinois. Velde attended Bradley University from 1927 to 1929 and graduated from Northwestern University in 1931. After teaching high school from 1931 to 1935, he enrolled in law school at the University of Illinois, from which he graduated in 1937. He practiced law in his home state until he entered the army signal corps in 1942. After a year of military service, Velde became an agent in the FBI's sabotage and counterespionage division. In 1946 he won election as a county judge in Illinois.

Velde won a seat in the U.S. House of Representatives in 1948 after campaigning on the slogan, "Get the Reds out of Washington and Washington out of the Red." He gained a reputation in Congress as an ardent anticommunist, alarmed by what he saw as widespread subversion within the U.S. government. His background in the FBI landed him a post on the House Un-American Activities Committee (HUAC). After Republicans won control of Congress in the elections of 1952, Velde became chair of the panel.

During 1953–54, HUAC held a record 178 days of hearings. Velde led HUAC investigations of the motion picture industry, education, and labor—areas the committee had investigated in previous years. However, he broke new ground in March 1954 by announcing that a probe of the nation's clergy was "entirely possible." His charges that the clergy spent more time in questionable politics than in the ministry ignited protests from church groups, citizens, and fellow members of Congress. One member of HUAC, Representative Franklin D. Roosevelt, Jr. (D N.Y.), introduced a resolution calling for the removal of Velde as chair. The American Council of Christian Churches supported Velde's charges, and a Gallup poll showed 36 percent of the public in favor of a probe. General public disapproval, however, prevented him from vigorously pursuing the investigation, though several clergymen did testify before the panel. At one point, Velde charged those church leaders who had criticized his allegations with the "sin" of subversion.

During Velde's term as chairman, HUAC continued investigations of the entertainment industry, long a favorite target. In March 1953, Velde took HUAC to Los Angeles to hear testimony from various writers, performers, and technicians who had been accused of having communist ties. In May, HUAC investigators in New York interrogated such celebrities as Artie Shaw, Carin K. Burrows, Robert Rossen, and Lionel Stander. These and other investigations stirred intense public debate over constitutional rights of due process and protection against self-incrimination versus the alleged need to uncover American communists. In March 1953, a group of 23 actors and motion picture workers sued Velde and other congressmen who had served on HUAC in 1951 because they had been blacklisted in the industry after they refused to testify before the committee. State courts in California later dismissed the case.

HUAC's probe of communist infiltration in education got off to a bad start when Velde inaccu-

rately accused Mrs. Eugene Meyer, wife of the chairman of the board of the *Washington Post*, of having praised the USSR in a letter to a Soviet publication. In fact, the letter had been sent by a "Mrs. G. S. Mayer." When that came out, Velde promptly fired the HUAC investigator on the case. He defended himself by saying that it was "better to wrongly accuse one person of being a Communist" than to allow the true party members to roam freely. In February 1953, Velde elicited from Dr. Robert Davis the names of 21 people whom he claimed were fellow communists while he taught at Harvard University from 1937 to 1939. The list of names included Daniel Boorstin and Granville Hicks, both of whom had since become anticommunists. The investigations moved to Philadelphia in November 1953, where the Communist Party had gained more support among teachers in the 1930s than in any other major city on the East Coast except New York. Philadelphia's board of education suspended 26 Philadelphia teachers who had appeared before Velde's committee. In 1954, HUAC cited for contempt of Congress nine witnesses who had refused to testify in the committee's investigations of alleged communist educators in Philadelphia and New York City.

Velde captured the attention of the nation in November 1953 when he issued, without prior approval of HUAC, subpoenas to former president Harry S. Truman, former secretary of state JAMES BYRNES, and former attorney general TOM CLARK. Velde did so after Attorney General HERBERT BROWNELL charged that Truman had appointed an accused communist, Harry Dexter White, to the International Monetary Fund (IMF) after receiving an FBI report that indicated White had spied for the USSR. The account Byrnes gave to reporters supported Brownell's version on several key points. Although Truman, Byrnes, and Clark expressed a willingness to cooperate with HUAC, each rejected the subpoena after it was served. Truman declined to respond on grounds of executive privilege; Byrnes, then governor of South Carolina, cited states' rights; and Clark, then a justice of the Supreme Court, cited judicial privilege. President Eisenhower declared he would not have subpoenaed Truman or Clark. Truman made a nationally televised address devoted primarily to denouncing Brownell. The former president claimed that he deliberately allowed White's nomination to go through, because the appointment to the IMF was "much less sensitive—if it was sensitive at all—than the position" White held as assistant secretary of the Treasury. Further, asserted Truman, the FBI did not want to tip its hand until the investigation had been completed and White had been separated from government service "promptly" when the investigation was concluded. Both assertions were false. In testimony before the Senate Internal Security Committee, the director of the FBI, J. EDGAR HOOVER, contradicted Truman's version of the story. Nevertheless, Velde's decision to subpoena Truman offended many Americans, and HUAC took no further action on the subpoenas.

Velde continued his HUAC investigations throughout the 1953–54 session, opening hearings on alleged subversives in the navy and expanding probes of supposed communist infiltration of labor unions. Although raised voices and accusations continually flew through HUAC's hearing rooms, Velde himself never won the notoriety that his more-famous colleague, Senator JOSEPH R. McCARTHY (R-Wis.), achieved.

Velde did not stand for reelection in 1956 and retired from office in 1957. He practiced law in Urbana, Illinois, and Washington, D.C., until 1969, when he became regional counsel for the General Services Administration. He retired and took up residence in Sun City, Arizona, in 1974, where he lived until his death there on September 1, 1985.

—MSM

Viereck, Peter (Robert) (Edwin)

(1916–2006) *historian, poet, political commentator*
The son of a German immigrant and reporter, Viereck was born in New York City on August 5, 1916. He studied in Germany and in Switzerland in his early youth and attended Phillips Exeter Academy. After receiving his undergraduate degree, summa cum laude, from Harvard University in 1937, he remained at Harvard to earn an M.A. in European history in 1939 and a Ph.D. in European history in 1942. During his academic career at Harvard, he received numerous awards, including Phi Beta Kappa and a fellowship to Oxford University.

In early 1940, the *Atlantic Monthly* invited Viereck to write an essay about "the meaning of young liberalism for the present age." Viereck produced an essay titled "But—I'm a Conservative!" Published in the April issue, the essay asked: "Why should any young man want to be a conservative, on a globe where so much needs changing?" In response, Viereck observed that "I have watched the convention of revolt harden into dogmatic ritual." He called for a "new conservatism" to counter the "storm of totalitarianism" abroad and the moral relativism and soulless materialism that dominated domestic life. Nazism and communism, Viereck argued, shared a fundamental utopianism that sanctioned the murder of anyone or any group perceived as an obstacle to creating the perfect society. Moreover, since liberalism represented a milder version of the same view (a belief in the innate goodness of humanity and the perfectibility of human society), it offered no adequate defense against totalitarianism. Viereck identified a conservative faith, rooted in the understanding that within the inherent "nature of man" lay "the ultimate source of evil," as the only hope to save Western civilization from attempts to subvert it, subjugate it, or perfect it.

Viereck published his first book, *Metapolitics from the Romantics to Hitler,* in 1941. The son of George Sylvester Viereck, a famous Nazi supporter who was convicted of conspiring with the Nazis in 1941 and spent four years in prison, Peter Viereck published the book while his father was on trial. In addition to presenting a searing critique of Nazi ideology, which he saw as "irreconcilable" with the American way of life, Viereck rejected the then-orthodox idea that Nazism grew out of the authoritarian Prussian tradition and argued instead that Nazism developed from romantic German nationalist movements of the 19th century. The book received praise from scholars and critics.

After the United States entered World War II, Viereck served in the army's psychological warfare branch, where he analyzed Nazi propaganda and rose to the rank of sergeant. After the war, he took a job teaching literature at Harvard. He taught at Smith College from 1946 to 1947 and began a long career at Mount Holyoke College in 1948.

In 1949, he published *Conservatism Revisited: The Revolt Against Revolt,* which immediately established him as a forceful expositor of conservatism in America. Expanding on the ideas he had presented in the *Atlantic Monthly*, Viereck criticized the collectivism of both fascism and Stalinism for robbing the individual of dignity. Calling for cooperation between the moderate Right and the moderate Left, he advocated a reformist conservatism, based on the "necessity and supremacy of Law and of absolute standards of conduct." Continuing his assault on what he regarded as the naive belief in the essential goodness of humans, he ridiculed the idea of the "common, natural man." "We don't need a 'century of the common man,'" wrote Viereck; "we have had it already, and it has only produced the commonest man, the impersonal and irresponsible and uprooted mass-man." In terms reminiscent of REINHOLD NIEBUHR, Viereck rejected the "cult" of Rousseau and the "natural man," instead emphasizing the inherently sinful and imperfect nature of humans. "In his natural instincts," wrote Viereck, "every modern baby is still born a cave-man baby. What prevents today's baby from remaining a cave man is the conservative force of law and tradition." He defined conservatism as "the political secularization of the doctrine of original sin." Viereck's conservatism did not advocate laissez-faire capitalism but was "incompatible with fascist or Stalinist collectivism." Above all, he based his conservatism firmly in "the four ancestries of western man": the Judaic, Hellenic, Roman, and medieval intellectual traditions. The book gave a name to a new intellectual movement.

Throughout the 1950s, Viereck continued his call for a "new conservatism." He intended the term to distinguish what he called "ethical" conservatism from what he derisively called "Old Guard," "McKinley-style" Republicanism. As the 1950s progressed, however, it became clear that Viereck's vision differed from that espoused by other philosophers of the Right. In the words of historian John P. Diggins, Viereck sought a synthesis of "philosophical conservatism and political liberalism." Indeed, many conservatives criticized Viereck's rejection of 19th century laissez-faire capitalism, his support for many of the reforms of the New Deal, and his endorsement of ADLAI STEVENSON as the foremost political exponent of his own brand of conservatism. Moreover, while Viereck disdained

ideologies of the far Left, he had considerably less enthusiasm for attacking liberals than did other conservatives. Indeed, he retained hope that liberals and conservatives would unite against all forms of totalitarianism. Although strongly anticommunist, he formulated a conservatism grounded primarily in philosophical and moral principles. He believed that economic theories were hollow unless set in an ethical context.

Unlike some other conservatives, Viereck vehemently repudiated Senator JOSEPH R. MCCARTHY (R-Wis.) and the popular movement the senator helped create. Along with a group of pluralist social scientists (including RICHARD HOFSTADTER, DAVID RIESMAN, Nathan Glazer, and TALCOTT PARSONS), Viereck contributed an essay ("The Revolt Against the Elite") to *The New American Right* (1955), edited by DANIEL BELL. In contrast to those who saw McCarthyism as an outgrowth of conservatism, Viereck viewed McCarthyism as radically anti-conservative, as a kind of populist phenomenon ("the same old isolationist, Anglophobe, Germanophile revolt of radical populist lunatic-fringers against the eastern, educated Anglicized elite"). According to Viereck, McCarthyism was a form of pseudo-conservatism, "a leftist instinct behind a *self-deceptive* [emphasis in the original] rightist veneer." After all, McCarthy attacked the most conservative and organic institutions as well as the American elite. Further, the anticommunism of the postwar era was "populism gone sour." For Viereck, McCarthyism represented "the revenge of the noses that for twenty years of fancy parties were pressed against the outside window pane." He expounded his thesis more fully in *The Unadjusted Man* (1956). Viereck's position further alienated him from many anticommunist conservatives.

Viereck, however, also rebuked those of McCarthy's critics who in his view deliberately minimized the communist threat. In addition, he denounced the foreign policy of containment of communism, which he regarded as "heartless" for consigning eastern European peoples to communism without offering them hope of liberation in the future.

Viereck's views prevented him from becoming part of the ideological conservative group that coalesced in the mid-1950s around the *National Review*, edited by WILLIAM F. BUCKLEY, JR. In

1956, Frank Meyer, the culture editor of *National Review*, published an article in that journal denouncing Viereck for passing off "unexceptionably liberal sentiments" as "conservative philosophy." Meyer dismissed Viereck as a "counterfeit conservative." That same year, Willmoore Kendall, a conservative political philosopher, published an article in the *National Review* attacking Viereck for lecturing others on "how to be a conservative and yet agree with the Liberals about Everything."

Although noted primarily for his philosophical and political views and writings, Viereck considered literature his first love and wrote numerous books of poetry. He won a Pulitzer Prize in 1949 for his collection of poetry, *Terror and Decorum* (1948), and served as a distinguished visiting professor of poetry at several universities in the United States and abroad. In the mid-1960s, Viereck stopped writing about politics and devoted his efforts to poetry and Russian history, which he taught at Mount Holyoke College until his retirement in 1987. He published a long poem, "Archer in the Marrow: The Applewood Cycles," in 1987. Even after retiring from Mount Holyoke, he continued to teach a survey course in Russian history until 1997. In his final lecture at Mount Holyoke, he warned the undergraduates "If you kill out of love or for a perfect utopia, you never stop killing because human nature is always imperfect." Viereck died at his home in South Hadley, Massachusetts, on May 13, 2006.

—MSM

Vincent, John Carter
(1900–1972) *Foreign Service officer*

The son of a real estate and insurance salesman, Vincent was born in Seneca, Kansas, on August 19, 1900. He moved with his family to Macon, Georgia, in 1906. After graduating from Mercer University in 1923, he passed the exams to qualify for an appointment in a U.S. consulate. He received his first posting, to Changsha, China, in 1924. He went from Changsha to Hankou. In 1928, he began a two-year program in Chinese language at Beijing. He became fluent in Chinese and, over the next decade, served as a diplomatic officer in a number of major Chinese cities. He was assigned to Jinan from 1930 to 1931. Between 1931 and 1936, he

was stationed in Shen-yang (Mukden) and then in Darien. He witnessed firsthand the Japanese conquest of Manchuria. In 1936, he returned to Washington to serve on the China desk of the State Department's division of Far Eastern affairs. After a brief assignment in Europe (1939–40), he returned to China, serving first in Shanghai. In 1941, Vincent rose to first secretary of the U.S. embassy in Chongqing (Chunking), China's wartime capital. He became counselor of the embassy in 1942. During his years in China, Vincent developed close personal relationships with Zhou Enlai (Chou Enlai), one of the Communist leaders, and Chiang Kai-shek (Jiang Jieshi), the Nationalist leader whom Vincent thought could unify the nation following the war. However, Vincent became increasingly critical of Chiang, whose government seemed incapable of resisting the Japanese, opposing the communist insurgency, or maintaining the loyalty of the people. Further, the pervasive corruption of Chiang's government along with his dictatorial methods disillusioned Vincent. Vincent became convinced that his government needed to institute substantial internal reforms, and he urged the American government to require Chiang to implement such reforms before it granted more aid. In 1944, Vincent was recalled to Washington to head the China division of the Office of Far Eastern Affairs. Throughout the war, President Franklin D. Roosevelt ignored Vincent's advice. In the postwar era, however, Vincent emerged as perhaps the most influential China specialist in the State Department.

Recognized as the Foreign Service's leading expert on China, Vincent received a promotion to director of the State Department's Office of Far Eastern Affairs in 1945. As the conflict between Chiang and the Communist forces led by Mao Zedong (Mao Tse-tung) escalated, Vincent was one of the architects of General George C. Marshall's mission to China in 1945–47. Vincent advised the secretary of state, JAMES F. BYRNES, that the United States should limit military and economic assistance to Chiang until his Nationalist government implemented reforms. The delegation headed by Marshall was instructed to urge Chiang to make necessary reforms and to attempt some sort of reconciliation with the Communists. Vincent hoped that a political settlement with the Communists would buy time for the reforms to get underway. The failure of the mission convinced Vincent that Chiang would lose the civil war with the Communists, regardless of the amount of American support. Vincent, therefore, recommended that the United States reduce military and economic aid. After Marshall became secretary of state in 1947, he adopted Vincent's recommendations.

In January 1947, Vincent was named to the rank of career minister. His appointment, however, ran into opposition from conservative Republicans and members of the China lobby, who accused him of adopting positions similar to those of the Communist Party line. Vincent won confirmation in July, but Republicans had exacted a promise that he would not be sent to an important post in the far east. Vincent was assigned to Switzerland.

Following the defeat of the Nationalists by the Communists in 1949, Vincent came under fire by officials in the State Department who had disagreed with his approach (particularly the Japan specialists), members of the China lobby, and conservative Republicans. Some accused him to attempting to engineer a Communist victory. Senator JOSEPH R. McCARTHY (R-Wis.) charged Vincent with sabotaging the Marshall mission by placing impossible demands on Chiang and urged that Vincent be fired. In 1950, the Tydings Committee investigated McCarthy's allegations and found nothing to support his charges against Vincent. Indeed, the Democratic majority on the committee accused McCarthy of perpetrating "a fraud and a hoax" upon the American people.

Vincent received a posting to Tangier, Morocco, in 1951. The assignment carried less prestige and a cut in salary. Also in 1951, the Senate Internal Security Subcommittee, under the leadership of Senator PATRICK McCARRAN (D-Nev.), accused Vincent of having used his influence to shift American policy in favor of the Communists. McCarthy then renewed his demand that Vincent be removed from the State Department. A State Department loyalty board cleared Vincent, but the Civil Service Loyalty Review Board reviewed the decision and concluded that there was reasonable doubt about Vincent's loyalty. President HARRY S. TRUMAN and Secretary of State DEAN ACHESON formed a new panel, headed by Learned B. Hand, a highly respected federal appellate judge, to review the case.

The panel had not completed its work when the Eisenhower administration took office. In March 1953, Secretary of State JOHN FOSTER DULLES decided not to rely on the panel and resolved the matter himself. He reversed the loyalty review board and ruled that there was no reasonable doubt about Vincent's loyalty. Nevertheless, Vincent's "reporting of the facts, evaluation of the facts, and policy advice during the period under review show a failure to meet the standard which is demanded of a Foreign Service officer." Offered the choice of resigning or being dismissed, Vincent chose to preserve his pension and quit. During their last meeting, Dulles asked Vincent to discuss China. "After all," explained Dulles, Vincent knew "the situation there better than just about anybody."

Critics charged that Vincent's departure, one of several in the State Department during the period, weakened the Foreign Service. Many Foreign Service officers took it as a sign that Dulles would not protect them from right-wing attacks, and some analysts have suggested that prompted many officers to make policy recommendations on the basis of accepted ideology rather than on expert opinion. In fact, some officers took heart from the fact that Dulles had vindicated Vincent on the charge of disloyalty. Virtually all, however, were dismayed by the dismissal for poor reporting.

Vincent told reporters that the Eisenhower administration should abandon the idea that the United States had "lost China," which he called a "phony idea" peddled by the China lobby. Only by acknowledging this could the administration free Foreign Service officers from "a fear that loyalty to Chiang Kai-shek is a test of loyalty to the U.S.A." and thus make possible the development of "an objective and, we hope, effective policy regarding China."

At the age of 52, Vincent retired to Cambridge, Massachusetts. He wrote and lectured on foreign affairs and maintained an informal association with the East Asian Research Center at Harvard and the Radcliffe Seminars. The Foreign Policy Association's speakers bureau advertised him as a lecturer on Asia and China, but he had few offers. In subsequent years, Vincent opposed the American intervention in Vietnam and criticized America's unwillingness to establish relations with the People's Republic of China. Chou En-lai invited him to visit China in 1972, but Vincent could not accept the invitation because he was suffering from terminal cancer. He died in Cambridge, Massachusetts, on December 3, 1972.

—MSM

Vinson, Carl
(1883–1981) *U.S. congressman; chairman, Armed Services Committee*

Vinson was born on November 18, 1883, in Baldwin County, Georgia, near the town of Milledgeville. After graduating from the Georgia Military College, Vinson entered Mercer University in Macon, Georgia, where he received his LL.B. degree in 1902. After gaining admission to the Georgia bar, he practiced law in Milledgeville with the firm of Hines and Vinson. He won election to two terms as the prosecuting attorney for Baldwin County and served from 1906 to 1909. Vinson served in the Georgia House of Representatives from 1909 to 1912. Upon narrowly losing his bid for reelection in 1912, he received an appointment as judge of Baldwin County Court, a position he held from 1912 to 1914, when he was elected judge of the Baldwin County Court. In 1914, Vinson won election to the U.S. House of Representatives as a Democrat. He served without interruption until January 3, 1965.

In the House, Vinson was assigned to the House Naval Affairs Committee in 1917 and emerged as a forceful advocate of military preparedness. He became chair of the Naval Affairs Committee in 1932. For the remainder of the decade, he pressed for a major enlargement of the navy. Vinson not only resisted a proposal by President Franklin D. Roosevelt to cut funding for the navy but pushed naval expansion bills through the House in 1938, 1939, and 1940. As relations with Japan worsened and Europe moved toward war, Vinson advocated a two-ocean navy. During World War II, he supported legislation to curb strikes in defense industries and other legislation restricting labor unions. This made him unpopular with union leaders.

At the end of World War II, Vinson unsuccessfully opposed President HARRY S. TRUMAN's call for merging the separate military service depart-

ments into a unified Defense Department. When the Defense Department was created in 1947, the military committees in the House were combined to form the Armed Services Committee. Two years later, when the Democrats regained control of Congress, Vinson became chair of the Armed Services Committee. The following year, he attacked reductions in military expenditures proposed by Defense Secretary Louis Johnson.

Although not widely known outside of Congress, Vinson played a crucial role in the formulation and passage of bills related to the military. He dominated his committee by dividing the panel into subcommittees without specific jurisdictions (except for the Subcommittee on Special Investigations) and deciding himself which subcommittee would receive each bill. Vinson thereby determined who would introduce bills on the House floor. On the floor itself, he was, according to Speaker SAM RAYBURN (D-Tex.), the "best legislative technician in the House." The lower chamber passed almost all legislation approved by his committee.

A leading advocate of a strong military establishment, Vinson supported the army officers, led by Chief of Staff MAXWELL TAYLOR, who criticized the Eisenhower administration's New Look defense policy. They believed that the strategy placed too much emphasis upon nuclear weapons and did not prepare the country to fight limited wars. In particular, Vinson opposed attempts to reduce conventional forces. In January 1955, he attacked a proposal by the administration to reduce the strength of the army from 1.1 to 1 million men. The following month, Vinson ended his opposition, reportedly because the administration promised that troop strength would not be reduced below 900,000 men. Three years later, the Appropriations Committee approved a request by the administration to cut the army's strength to 870,000 men. On the floor of the House, however, some members of the Armed Services panel, backed by Vinson, led a successful drive to restore the troop level to 900,000.

Vinson jealously guarded what he considered to be the prerogatives of his committee and of Congress with respect to military matters. In 1956, the administration proposed a reorganization of the Defense Department that would have established an office of assistant secretary for research and development for each of the services. Vinson declared that he had no objection to the plan, but complained that he had not been informed of the proposal until it was sent to Capitol Hill. He therefore opposed the measure, and his committee voted unanimously to recommend disapproval.

Vinson opposed attempts to secure civil rights for African Americans. In 1956, he joined 100 other members of Congress who signed the Southern Manifesto, which denounced the Supreme Court's decision in *Brown v. Board of Education* (1954) and urged resistance to it by all lawful means. He opposed civil rights legislation, including the Civil Rights Acts of 1957 and 1960.

In 1958, Vinson opposed a plan by the administration to strengthen the authority of the secretary of defense. The congressman particularly objected to a proviso that appropriated all funds to the secretary rather than to the separate service departments and allowed the secretary flexibility in shifting funds between the departments to meet new military developments. Vinson denounced this proposal as an invitation to Congress to "surrender its constitutional responsibilities." Vinson also objected to provisions of the plan that removed restrictions on the secretary's power to reassign combat functions and personnel among the three service departments. Further, he opposed a proviso repealing the law, passed in 1947, that stipulated the departments were to be separately administered by their respective secretaries. The Armed Service Committee's version of the reorganization plan reflected Vinson's views. The bill passed by Congress and signed by the president did not appropriate funds to the secretary of defense. It did, however, grant him increased authority to reassign combat functions and strengthen his administrative authority over the three departments (while maintaining the separate organization of the departments).

In 1960, Representative F. EDWARD HÉBERT (D-La.), chair of the Special Investigations Subcommittee, proposed a bill to limit the hiring of retired military officers by the defense industry on the ground that they exerted influence upon their former colleagues still in the military. The bill would have barred retired officers for two years after their retirement from helping a private company secure a defense contract. It would have imposed a $10,000

fine, two years' imprisonment, and denial of retirement pay during the period of violation. In the full Armed Services Committee, however, Vinson successfully eliminated the penalties providing for fine and imprisonment. The House approved the committee's version of the measure, but the Senate took no action on the measure.

During the early and mid-1960s, Vinson opposed efforts by the administrations of JOHN F. KENNEDY and LYNDON B. JOHNSON to phase out manned bombers in favor of missiles. He attacked Secretary of Defense Robert S. McNamara's efforts to transfer powers from the services to the Defense Department.

During the Kennedy administration, Vinson broke with southern members of Congress and supported a proposal by Speaker Sam Rayburn to enlarge the House Rules Committee. Rayburn's objective was to reduce the power of Representative HOWARD W. SMITH (D-Va.) to block legislation. The measure narrowly passed the House in 1961. In 1964, Vinson announced that he would not seek reelection. By that time, he had become the first person to serve in the House for 50 years. Upon leaving Congress, he retired to Milledgeville, where he lived until his death there on June 1, 1981.

—MSM

Vinson, Fred(erick) M(oore)

(1890–1953) *chief justice of the U.S. Supreme Court*

The son of the local jailer, Vinson was born in Louisa, Kentucky, on January 22, 1890. He graduated from Kentucky Normal College in 1908 and earned a B.A. at Centre College in Kentucky the following year. While attending law school at Centre College, he taught mathematics and played semiprofessional baseball. After receiving his law degree in 1911 and gaining admission to the Kentucky bar the same year, Vinson practiced law in Louisa. He became the city attorney of Louisa in 1913. Vinson entered the army in 1918 and was attending officer training camp in Arkansas when the war ended. Discharged from the military, he returned to Louisa and won election as commonwealth attorney for the 32nd Judicial District. In January 1924, he won a special election to fill a vacant seat representing Kentucky's Ninth Congressional District. Reelected in the fall of 1924 and again in 1926, he joined the Democratic minority in the House of Representatives. During his two terms, he had little impact. In 1928, he served as Al Smith's campaign manager in Kentucky. Herbert Hoover resoundingly defeated Smith, and Vinson lost his own seat in the Republican landslide of that year. Vinson returned to private practice in Ashland, Kentucky, but, riding a Democratic tide, won election to the House in 1930. Assigned to the Ways and Means Committee, he quickly established himself as an expert on taxation. With the election of Franklin D. Roosevelt in 1932, Vinson became an important member of the House, because virtually all New Deal measures contained some tax provision. A loyal supporter of Roosevelt, Vinson helped develop New Deal tax programs and coauthored the Guffy Coal Act of 1935. Vinson even backed Roosevelt's plan to pack the Supreme Court in 1937.

Roosevelt nominated Vinson to the U.S. Circuit Court of Appeals for the District of Columbia in December 1937. After receiving confirmation from the Senate, Vinson took his seat on the bench in May 1938. A competent but pedestrian judge, Vinson demonstrated some traits that would mark his later judicial career. He tended to favor governmental authority in general and in particular against claims that government had infringed on individual liberties.

At Roosevelt's request, Vinson resigned from the court in May 1943 to serve as director of economic stabilization. Roosevelt named him federal loan administrator in March 1945. One month later, the president called on Vinson to replace JAMES F. BYRNES as director of the Office of War Mobilization and Reconversion. Vinson was a key adviser to President HARRY S. TRUMAN, who appointed him secretary of the Treasury in July 1945. Upon the death of Chief Justice Harlan Fiske Stone, Truman nominated Vinson to be chief justice of the Supreme Court on June 6, 1946. Truman admired Vinson's record of government service and his political philosophy. He also hoped that the genial, patient Kentuckian, who had a reputation as a skilled negotiator and compromiser, would be able to bring unity to a bitterly divided Supreme Court. Ideological and personal differences led to friction between a liberal faction, led by Justices HUGO L. BLACK and WIL-

LIAM O. DOUGLAS, and a faction devoted to judicial restraint, led by Justices ROBERT H. JACKSON and FELIX FRANKFURTER.

Vinson failed to bring the warring justices together. Debates over the extent to which the Court should defer to the elected branches of government and whether the Fourteenth Amendment applied the Bill of Rights to the states continued to divide the Court during Vinson's tenure. While he did help reduce some of the personal friction between the justices, Vinson's own philosophy placed him with the Frankfurter/Jackson wing of the Court and against the judicial activists led by Black and Douglas. Beginning in 1949, however, when Truman named two more justices to the Court, Vinson was able to bring together a bloc of five justices that dominated the Court until 1953.

The group led by Vinson generally upheld government interests against claims of individual rights. Vinson himself wrote the Court's opinion in two significant cases. In May 1950, the Court upheld the provision of the Taft-Hartley Act that required union leaders to sign affidavits swearing that they were not and had never been members of the Communist Party (*American Communications Association v. Douds*). In June 1951, it upheld the provision of the Smith Act that made it a crime to teach or advocate violent overthrow of the government (*Dennis v. U.S.*). Vinson believed that the government needed broad powers to deal with the threat of communism at home and abroad in particular, but he believed that the government needed leeway to deal with other national and international problems as well. The chief justice favored a restrained, limited role for the Supreme Court and was willing to give wide latitude to the executive and legislative branches, especially in matters relating to internal security. Thus, Vinson repeatedly favored government policy on internal security over claims of individual rights. According to C. Herman Pritchett, a leading legal scholar, Vinson's record made him, "very nearly the most negative member of the Court on libertarian claims."

Vinson's deference to government action manifested itself in other ways as well. He wrote the opinion for the majority when the Court upheld Truman's seizure of coal mines following a nationwide strike (*U.S. v. United Mine Workers and John L.*

Lewis [1947]). The chief justice dissented when the Court held that Truman had exceeded his statutory and constitutional authority by seizing the nation's steel mills (*Youngstown Sheet & Tube Company v. Sawyer* [1952]). In addition, Vinson took a conservative position on most issues involving the rights of those accused of crimes, particularly on matters relating to search and seizure.

With respect to civil rights, however, the Vinson Court established a relatively liberal and unified record. The chief justice himself wrote some of his most important opinions in this area. In May 1948, he spoke for a unanimous Court that held restrictive covenants barring the sale of residential property to African Americans and other minorities legally unenforceable (*Shelley v. Kraemer*). Two decisions in June 1950 undermined the separate but equal doctrine that derived from *Plessy v. Ferguson* (1896). Speaking for a unanimous Court in *Sweatt v. Painter*, Vinson held that a separate law school for African Americans established by Texas as an alternative to the University of Texas did not meet the test of equality and therefore the exclusion of Heman Sweatt from the University of Texas Law School on the basis of his race constituted a denial of the equal protection guaranteed by the Fourteenth Amendment. By any quantitative measure, held the chief justice, the black law school did not measure up. Even more important, wrote Vinson, "the University of Texas Law School possesses to a far greater degree those qualities which are incapable of objective measurement but which make for greatness in a law school." *McLaurin v. Oklahoma* presented a related, but different, issue. Since Oklahoma did not provide a comparable graduate education for African Americans, it admitted a black graduate student to the doctoral program in education at the University of Oklahoma. The state admitted the student, however, "on a segregated basis." George McLaurin had to sit in an alcove adjacent to the classroom, to eat at a specified table in the dining hall and at a different time, and to study at a specified desk on the mezzanine floor of the library. While the case was on appeal, the state mitigated the restrictions. McLaurin was allowed to sit in the classroom but had to sit in a separate row designated "Colored." He could eat at the regular time, but at a separate table, and use a speci-

fied desk on the main floor of the library. Writing again for a unanimous Court, Vinson held that such restrictions impaired McLaurin's ability to learn. Having admitted McLaurin to graduate study, the university had to treat him as it did other students. Neither decision overturned *Plessy*, but the holding in *Sweatt* made it difficult for a state to maintain a segregated law school.

Nevertheless, the chief justice was among the more cautious members of the Court on the race question. His opinions expanded the rights of minorities, but only as far as was needed to decide the issue at hand. He resisted calls from other justices to strike down legally enforced segregation. Moreover, Vinson occasionally dissented from decisions favorable to the rights of African Americans. In his final term on the Court, for example, Vinson alone dissented when, in June 1953, the majority extended the rule of *Shelley v. Kraemer* and held that neighbors could not sue a white homeowner for damages when he violated a restrictive covenant by selling to African Americans.

In 1952, the Court granted review in five cases that challenged the constitutionality of segregation per se in public schools. In June 1953, the Court ordered the litigants to reargue the case in the fall and to answer specific questions about the intent of the Congress that adopted the Fourteenth Amendment and the power of Congress or the courts to abolish segregation under that amendment. Vinson did not live to hear the reargument. Under Vinson's successor, EARL WARREN, the Court struck down segregated public schools in these cases, known collectively as *Brown v. Board of Education* (1954).

In June 1953, Vinson and the Court became involved in the case of JULIUS AND ETHEL ROSENBERG, who had been sentenced to death for passing atomic secrets to the Soviet Union. The Supreme Court three times refused to review the Rosenbergs' conviction and, on June 15, 1953, denied what seemed to be all final motions in their case. Two days later, however, Justice William O. Douglas granted a stay of execution because a new legal argument had been raised on behalf of the convicted couple. A lawyer new to the case argued that the Atomic Energy Act of 1956 had superseded the Espionage Act of 1917 and that the district court therefore had no authority to impose the death penalty without the recommendation of a jury. Vinson immediately called a special session of the Court. On June 18, the justices heard oral arguments on whether to uphold Douglas's stay. The following day, Vinson read the decision of a six-to-three majority, which held that the Atomic Energy Act did not displace the penalties of the Espionage Act. Moreover, since the activities for which the Rosenbergs had been convicted took place before passage of the Atomic Energy Act, any alleged consistency was irrelevant. Therefore, the Court vacated the stay of execution. The Rosenbergs were executed later that day.

Vinson died of a heart attack at his home in Washington, D.C., on September 8, 1953. Neither a philosopher nor a legal theorist, he never developed an overarching theory of the Constitution. Vinson adopted a pragmatic approach guided by his belief in democratically elected leaders and in a strong national government. During his tenure as chief justice, the Court generally exercised restraint and permitted other branches of government the freedom he thought they should have. In the years after his death, many legal scholars regarded him as an unsuccessful chief justice. He was certainly not the Court's intellectual leader, and he proved unable to unify a bitterly divided Court. To be sure, he inherited a Court divided by judicial philosophy and personal conflicts. While he managed to calm the personal conflicts to a limited degree, the ideological disputes continued unabated. Although the Vinson Court did take steps to advance the legal status of African Americans, John P. Frank, the noted legal scholar, observed that Vinson presided over the reversal of a trend that began in the 1930s toward judicial protection of civil liberties. To some extent, assessments of Vinson have depended largely on whether the observer believed that the needs of the time justified the judicial restraint the Vinson Court normally displayed, especially in civil liberties cases.

—MSM

Vorys, John M(artin)

(1896–1968) *U.S. congressman*

The son of a lawyer and active Republican, Vorys was born in Lancaster, Ohio, on June 16, 1896. After attending public schools in Lancaster and Columbus, he received his B.A. in 1918 from Yale University, where he lettered in football and belonged to the Skull and Bones Society. During World War I, he served overseas as a pilot in the U.S. Naval Air Service and retired to inactive service in 1919 with the rank of lieutenant. Vorys taught for a year in Changsha, China. During 1921 and 1922, he served as an assistant secretary of the American delegation to the conference on the Limitation of Arms and Pacific and Far East Affairs (the Washington Naval Conference). Vorys earned a law degree at Ohio State University in 1923. A Republican, Vorys served in the Ohio General Assembly from 1923 to 1924 and sat in the Ohio State Senate from 1925 to 1926. In 1938, he won election to the U.S. House of Representatives on a platform opposing the New Deal. He was reelected nine consecutive times.

Appointed to the House Foreign Affairs Committee, Vorys initially supported isolationist policies. Throughout the 1920s and 1930s, he had opposed Wilsonian internationalism. Moreover, as Europe moved closer to war, he worried that the United States would be drawn into the war and President Franklin D. Roosevelt would exploit the opportunity to expand presidential power. When in 1939 Roosevelt sought to repeal a law that provided for an embargo of the sale of arms to any nation at war, Vorys offered an amendment that helped sink the measure. Later that year, after Germany invaded Poland, Congress repealed the embargo. Vorys opposed Lend-Lease aid to Great Britain and a peacetime draft. Following the Japanese attack on Pearl Harbor, Vorys, like many others who had been identified as "isolationist," modified his views. He concluded that the United States would need to take a more active role in international affairs and in 1943 supported the Fulbright Resolution, which put the House on record in favor of American entry into a postwar international organization. Vorys remained opposed, however, to the idea of a single world state and determined that the United States should abandon only enough sovereignty to make an international organization workable.

After the war, Vorys, along with Senator Arthur Vandenberg (R-Mich.), led the Republican Party to bipartisan support for internationalism. Vorys alienated some members of his own party by supporting aid for Greece and Turkey as well as the Marshall Plan. Despite his vital support for Truman's policy of containment, he was infuriated by what he perceived to be the administration's indifference to the "loss" of China.

Vorys became an important figure in the debates over foreign aid. During the Truman administration, he opposed foreign aid grants and recommended that assistance take the form of long-term loans. In 1951, he was the author of the Vorys Compromise, which won approval by the House of a plan to send massive shipments of wheat to India and to allow India to pay for the wheat over several decades at a low rate of interest in return for a long-term repayment plan. The following year, his amendments to the Truman administration's aid budget accounted for a substantial part of the $1.7 billion eliminated from the request. Vorys was a strong supporter of Senator Robert A. Taft (R-Ohio) for the Republican presidential nomination in 1952.

After Dwight D. Eisenhower defeated Taft and won the general election, Vorys often acted as spokesman for the Eisenhower administration and defender of presidential authority. During the first year of the Eisenhower administration, Vorys defended the president's requests for foreign aid. On February 23, 1953, he introduced legislation containing a draft of the president's call for a resolution criticizing the Soviet Union for violating the "clear intent" of the Yalta Accords and "subjugating" whole nations. Five days later, the Foreign Affairs Committee unanimously approved the measure. The resolution did not satisfy the Old Guard of the Republican Party. Stalin's death, however, provided an excuse to shelve the resolution and thereby avoid a fight within the Republican Party. Also in the first year of Eisenhower's presidency, Vorys opposed Taft's proposal for a congressional investigation of the Korean War. "I doubt if you can investigate the past conduct of a war that is going on without having the committee influence the current war," he said, "and I don't think a congressional committee can conduct a war." In 1955, he pushed for approval of the Formosa Resolution, which authorized the president to use the armed forces to defend Taiwan and the neighboring Pescadores against a possible invasion by the Chinese Communists.

In 1956, Vorys opposed the Hardy amendment to the Mutual Security Act, which would have required the executive branch to refer relevant documents to Congress before spending foreign aid funds. Vorys said, "An executive cannot be independent if somebody else has the right to look not only at his mail but at every scrap of information." The amendment was defeated. In 1957, Vorys opposed the Senate version of the Eisenhower Doctrine, giving the president power to aid Middle Eastern nations threatened by communism, because it deleted the House's authorization for the president to use troops "as he deemed necessary."

Vorys was a key defender of the administration's foreign aid program in the 1950s. According to the *New York Times*, the congressman was a "trimmer" rather than a "slasher" of White House foreign aid budgets. Debating the Mutual Security Act in 1953, he urged approval of what he called the "smallest foreign aid bill in five years." Vorys attempted to keep congressional cuts to $500 million, but Congress shaved off $1 billion from the administration's military and economic aid requests. The following year, under his management, the president's request passed with a substantially smaller cut.

Vorys was appointed to the Commission on Foreign Economic Policy in 1953. In January 1954, the panel released its final report suggesting methods for improving the nation's international trade situation. These included a three-year extension of the Tariffs Agreement Act and other proposals to encourage international trade. It recommended reducing tariffs, reorienting U.S. foreign aid toward making loans instead of grants, and increasing trade with Soviet satellites. Eisenhower submitted a program to Congress based on the commission's recommendations, but most of the proposals remained stalled on Capitol Hill throughout 1954. After a bitter struggle in 1955, Vorys succeeded in getting approval of the extension of reciprocal trade agreements and implementation of tariff cuts over a three-year period.

Vorys did not seek reelection in 1958. After retiring from the House in January 1959, he resumed the practice of law. In 1961, President John F. Kennedy appointed him to a commission studying the cost of political campaigns. Vorys died of a respiratory ailment in Columbus, Ohio, on August 25, 1968.

—MSM

Wadsworth, James J(eremiah)

(1905–1984) *representative to the United Nations*

The product of a wealthy Hudson Valley family that traced its ancestry back to the colonial period, Wadsworth was born in Groveland, New York, on June 12, 1905. His relatives included John Hay, Lincoln's private secretary who later served as secretary of state, and his father was a U.S. senator. He attended Fay School and St. Mark's School. Following his graduation from Yale University in 1927, Wadsworth returned to his family estate to manage his own dairy farm. Wadsworth won election as a Republican to the New York Assembly in 1930 and served until 1941 (he did not run for reelection in 1940). Upon leaving the legislature, he went to work for the Curtis-Wright Corporation in Buffalo, New York, where he rose to the position of assistant manager of industrial relations and earned a reputation as a skillful labor negotiator. In 1945, he was appointed director of the public service division of the War Assets Administration. Between 1946 and 1948, he headed the governmental affairs department of the Air Transport Association.

In 1948, Wadsworth became a special assistant to PAUL G. HOFFMAN, head of the Economic Cooperation Administration. In that capacity, he helped line up congressional support for the Marshall Plan. In June 1950, he became administrator of the civil defense office of the National Security Resources Board. The following year, he received an appointment as deputy administrator of the Civil Defense Administration.

At the urging of HENRY CABOT LODGE, the incoming administration's designated ambassador to the United Nations and a Yale classmate of Wadsworth's, President DWIGHT D. EISENHOWER appointed Wadsworth deputy representative to the UN in 1953. He sat on the Economic and Social Council and was an alternate representative to the Technical Assistance Conference. As a representative, Wadsworth had no policy-making role but served as spokesman for the administration on many sensitive issues. He opposed the blanket admission of new members, which could lead to the entrance of Communist China to the international organization, and barred any negotiations on Korean unification until North Korea recognized the "authority of the United Nations in repelling the Communist invasion of South Korea." Wadsworth also urged the Security Council in 1955 to censure Israel for attacking the Gaza Strip. He advised the Arab nations to recognize the right of Israel to exist and recommended that they resettle Palestinian refugees from Israel permanently and regard them "not as temporary residents but as fellow citizens and co-sharers of the Near East's future."

Wadsworth's primary responsibilities involved disarmament and atomic energy. As deputy representative to the UN Disarmament Commission, Wadsworth took part in negotiations for arms reduction. Speaking before the General Assembly in October 1954, he voiced the Eisenhower administration's policy that disarmament must be accompanied by an effective inspection system. "We cannot stop an arms race unless all the racers stop running," he said, "and we cannot know whether all the racers have stopped running if one of them insists on running on a concealed track. For the free world to stop arming while the Soviet Union keeps on increasing its strength would be an invitation to the very war we seek to avoid."

As U.S. representative to the Disarmament Commission's Subcommittee on Atomic Control, Wadsworth reiterated the administration's demand for an end to secrecy in nuclear development and ready access to atomic installations for inspection purposes. In May 1955, he cautioned that Soviet proposals for a self-inspection system "still appear to fall short of the minimum safety requirements." He responded unequivocally to Soviet foreign minister Andrei Y. Vishinsky's demand in October 1954 that the UN Security Council be given veto powers in any disarmament formula. Wadsworth believed that Vishinsky's proposal would make the Soviets the supreme arbiter in deciding which disarmament violations were to be punished.

Wadsworth gradually achieved a reputation as the administration's "chief troubleshooter." His abilities as a negotiator earned him the praise of many of his colleagues in the UN. During 1956, he handled the extremely delicate negotiations leading to the formulation of the Statute of the International Atomic Agency, establishing a 70-nation organization to further peaceful use of atomic energy. In October 1956, Dr. João Carlos Muniz of Brazil, chairman of the council that elaborated the fine points of the statute, called it a "monument to Wadsworth."

In February 1958, Secretary of State JOHN FOSTER DULLES appointed Wadsworth to replace HAROLD STASSEN as chief U.S. disarmament negotiator. Wadsworth represented the United States at the disarmament conference in Geneva, Switzerland. Although the United States and the Soviet Union continued to disagree on the issue of inspections (the United States pressed for on-site inspections, while the Soviets would agree only to "seismic" inspections from outside national borders), they reached agreement on 17 of 21 articles that became part of the treaty signed in 1963.

Wadsworth later replaced Henry Cabot Lodge in September 1960 as permanent U.S. representative to the UN. He proved to be a popular diplomat,

known for his informal manner and ready laugh as well as his diplomatic expertise. The Russians who worked with him found him "serious, not a cold warrior." Wadsworth left his UN post in 1961. He served as a government consultant during the 1960s, and President LYNDON B. JOHNSON appointed him to he Federal Communications Commission, on which he sat from 1965 to 1970. Wadsworth retired to his family farm in the Genesee Valley of upstate New York. He died in Rochester, New York, on March 13, 1984.

—MSM

Wagner, Robert F(erdinand), Jr.
(1910–1991) *mayor of New York City*

The son of the popular senator Robert F. Wagner, Sr. (D-N.Y.), Wagner was born in New York City on April 20, 1910. Raised in the Yorkville section of Manhattan, he attended Taft School and in 1933 graduated from Yale University. After receiving his law degree from Yale in 1937, he ran successfully for a seat in the New York State Assembly. Reelected in 1938 and 1940, he resigned in 1941 to join the army air corps. He served as an intelligence officer in Europe and rose to the rank of lieutenant colonel. After World War II, Wagner returned to New York and resumed his political career. With the support of Tammany Hall, New York City's Democratic machine, he advanced rapidly. Mayor William O'Dwyer appointed Wagner city tax commissioner in 1946, commissioner of housing and buildings in 1946, and chairman of the city planning commission in 1947. In 1949, Wagner won election as Manhattan borough president. While serving in that office, he made an unsuccessful bid for the Democratic senatorial nomination in 1952.

In 1953, CARMINE DESAPIO, the powerful Democratic Party leader in Manhattan, became disillusioned with Mayor Vincent Impellitteri and, anxious to improve Tammany's image, chose Wagner as his candidate for the Democratic mayoral nomination. Although not a charismatic leader, Wagner's excellent staff, his capacity for hard work, and his ability to make well-thought-out decisions earned him praise from the press and informed observers. His forceful advocacy of improved schools gained him the support of the powerful Parent-Teachers Association, and his father's popularity further enhanced his standing. Moreover, he had managed to avoid the kind of scandals that had rocked the previous Democratic administrations. All of this made him a strong candidate. In the primary, Wagner condemned the incumbent for increases in rent, taxes, and transit fares. He particularly stressed the problem of overcrowded classrooms. With the support of unions and reformers anxious to rid the party of the scandals of the Impellitteri years, Wagner won the primary by over 160,000 votes. He easily defeated the Republican candidate, Harold Riegelman, in the general election.

As mayor, Wagner became known for the steady, methodical, and cautious way in which he attacked the city's problems. He used his administrative abilities and formidable political skills to bring about important improvements in the city. Wagner carefully avoided offending New York's many interest groups, and he often delayed decisions until assured of broad political support.

During Wagner's first two terms, he built 123,000 units of middle-income housing, increased school construction, improved welfare services, opened new parks, modernized the city's building code, successfully pressed the city council to pass a fair housing law, recognized the right of municipal employees to unionize, and undertook a substantial program of highway construction. He appointed greater numbers of African Americans and Puerto Ricans to political and governmental positions than did his predecessors. Wagner also supported the performance of Shakespeare's plays in Central Park. In an extremely popular move, he hired 3,000 additional policemen and transferred others from desk jobs to street assignments; incidents of major crime in the city declined by 21 percent. When a blue-ribbon panel suggested closing 30 firehouses to save $1 million a year, Wagner yielded to popular pressure and refused to shut them down.

The mayor also took important steps to improve city government. He created the office of city administrator to coordinate the activities of various departments and hired expert administrators for top-level posts. Although obligated to DeSapio and Tammany Hall for his election, he refused to put political hacks in policy-making positions. The

press praised him for increasing the professionalism of the city's contracting process and for the quality of his appointments to high-level offices, particularly commissioners. Acutely aware of his need for Tammany's support, however, he rarely took low-level jobs away from political appointees and did not interfere with established political practices and customs.

During the late 1950s, Wagner pressed unsuccessfully for revision of the city charter to concentrate executive and administrative power in the hands of the mayor and legislative power in the city council. His reforms were intended to simplify the government's structure, limit political rivalries, and unify the city administration. In 1958, Wagner asked the state legislature to authorize a commission to revise the charter, but the measure did not pass. The following year, he proposed a city law establishing the commission, and the state responded by forming its own panel. The state commission's first report was essentially a political document that criticized the administration of the city. In February 1960, Wagner countered by creating a city panel of high-ranking municipal officials to recommend revision of the charter. Facing the prospect of two commissions preparing conflicting reports, the state legislature enlarged the committee and authorized the mayor to appoint two of its 11 members. Wagner then dissolved his task force. In 1961, voters approved the new charter. It gave the mayor greater power in preparing the capital budget and administering the expense budget, where the Board of Estimate had previously exercised total control. At the same time, it reduced the power of the borough presidents, effectively limiting their patronage.

Yet, despite these accomplishments, Wagner's city could not escape the problems that beset major urban areas during the 1950s. In 1957, New York experienced a seven-day subway strike. The following year, Wagner recognized the right of municipal workers to unionize. With newfound power and the threat of a strike, the city's unions began to extract substantial increases in wages and benefits, which, according to some observers, laid the basis for the city's fiscal problems during the 1970s. Although Manhattan experienced a boom in the construction of office buildings and luxury housing, a good many of the city's residential areas decayed. Thousands of poor African Americans and Hispanics moved into the city, while the white middle class fled to the suburbs. The increasing population of poor people was accompanied by a rising crime rate, de facto school segregation, and growing unemployment. The loss of the city's tax base to the suburbs made it more difficult for the city government to respond to these issues.

In 1957, New York lost the Giants to San Francisco and the Dodgers to Los Angeles. Wagner appointed a commission to investigate the possibility of bringing the National League back to New York. That commission and the mayor proved instrumental in bringing a new franchise, the Mets, to a new stadium in Queens.

During his first two terms, Wagner sought both to remain friendly with DeSapio and to establish independence from the Democratic boss. The Tammany leader was Wagner's chief political adviser and regularly counseled him on patronage matters. Attempting to follow his father into the U.S. Senate, Wagner, with DeSapio's support, won the Democratic nomination in 1956 but lost in the general election to the Republican candidate, JACOB JAVITS. In his bid for reelection as mayor in 1957, Wagner gained the support of all five of the city's Democratic leaders and the backing of the Liberal Party as well. He won an overwhelming 72 percent of the vote. This gave him the opportunity to divorce himself from DeSapio, and the two became rivals during Wagner's second term.

In 1961, Wagner broke with Tammany Hall and, with the support of Democratic reformers such as HERBERT LEHMAN and ELEANOR ROOSEVELT, sought his third term by running against bossism in the Democratic primary. Although he lost the support of all five of New York's Democratic Party leaders, Wagner defeated DeSapio's candidate, Arthur Levitt, and went on to win reelection, defeating Louis J. Lefkowitz.

During Wagner's third term, the Lincoln Center for the Performing Arts opened, the city fluoridated its water, and the city hosted the World's Fair in 1964. Nevertheless, he faced a series of problems, including racial violence and shortfalls of municipal revenues. He committed the city to borrowing at unprecedented levels to meet current expenses, thereby establishing a precedent that contributed

to the city's fiscal crisis in the following decade. Wagner declined to run for a fourth term in 1965 and was succeeded by a liberal Republican, JOHN V. LINDSAY. After leaving the mayor's office, Wagner practiced law with the firm of Wagner, Quillinan & Tenant. President LYNDON B. JOHNSON appointed him ambassador to Spain in 1968. Wagner resigned at the end of the Johnson administration and ran for mayor in 1969 but lost the Democratic primary to Mario Procaccino. In 1976, his law firm merged into Finley, Kumble, Wagner, Heine, Underberg, Manley, Myerson & Casey. President James Carter appointed him unofficial representative to the Vatican in 1978, a position he held until 1981. Wagner left Finley, Kumble in 1987 and joined Fischbein, Badillo & Wagner. He died in New York City on February 12, 1991.

—MSM

Walter, Francis E(ugene)
(1894–1963) *U.S. congressman; chairman, Subcommittee on Immigration Affairs of the Judiciary Committee; chairman, Un-American Activities Committee*

Born in Easton, Pennsylvania, on May 26, 1894, Walter graduated from the Princeton (New Jersey) Preparatory School in 1912. He attended Lehigh University and George Washington University, where he earned his B.A. After serving in the air service of the U.S. Navy during World War I, he earned an LL.B. from Georgetown University in 1919. He returned to Easton, was admitted to the bar in 1919, and began to practice law. In addition to practicing law, Walter served as a director of the Broad Street Trust Company in Philadelphia and of the Easton National Bank. In 1928, he was appointed solicitor of Norhampton County, Pennsylvania. He won election as a Democrat to the House of Representatives in 1933 and served in the House continuously until his death. During his early years in the House, he supported the New Deal, especially those programs that brought benefits to his district. During Roosevelt's second term, however, he became increasingly worried about the growth and increasing power of the federal bureaucracy. Walter served in the naval air service for six months during World War II.

During the postwar era, Walter emerged as a conservative on many issues. In 1946, he and Senator PAT MCCARRAN (D-Nev.) sponsored the Administrative Procedure Act, which required the publication of regulations promulgated by federal agencies in the Federal Register. Walter supported efforts to limit the power of organized labor and congressional efforts to combat communist influence at home and abroad. He became the second-ranking member of the House Un-American Activities Committee (HUAC) in 1949. That year, he introduced an unsuccessful bill to deprive members of the Communist Party of American citizenship. In 1950, as chair of a subcommittee of HUAC, he led an investigation of communist activities in Hawaii. The following year, he served as acting chair of the committee in a second round of hearings on communist influence in the film industry.

Walter also became an influential figure in formulating immigration policy. In 1950, he sponsored legislation to allow more displaced persons to come to the United States and to remove racial barriers to naturalization. As a delegate to the International Committee for European Migration in 1951, he worked to place immigrants in countries other than the United States. In 1952, he cosponsored the McCarran-Walter Act, which passed despite opposition from liberals in Congress. Passed over President HARRY S. TRUMAN's veto, the act continued immigration quotas established in 1924, which were based on ratios of foreign born to the nation's population reported in the 1920 census. The measure had the practical effect of severely limiting the number of eastern and southern European and Asian immigrants. It also extended the grounds for excluding or deporting immigrants. Critics attributed Walter's harsh legislation to his fear of communist infiltration through foreign immigration.

During the next eight years, six of them as chairman of the Judiciary Committee's Subcommittee on Immigration Affairs, Walter consistently opposed President DWIGHT D. EISENHOWER's efforts to reform the McCarran-Walter Act. Eisenhower proposed using the census of 1950 as a basis for quotas and pooling the unused quotas. Walter blocked such changes and warned that they would increase the danger of communist subversion. In 1953, the president managed to secure passage of the Refugee Relief Act, designed to admit 215,000 non-quota immigrants over the next three years. In 1956, the State Department hired EDWARD CORSI, a respected former immigration official, to administer the law. Walter forced the removal of Corsi from his post, in part because Corsi had criticized the McCarran-Walter Act. Walter also charged that Corsi had once been affiliated with communist front organizations, an allegation that he never substantiated. Eisenhower continued his struggle against Walter in 1956 by recommending major revisions in immigration laws, including the removal of national origins quotas and liberalization of policies affecting refugees from communist countries. Once again Walter was able to block major changes. Later in 1956, however, he departed from his hard-line position and proposed the admission of 5,000 refugees from the Hungarian revolt. One month later, however, Walter was "thoroughly convinced" that many of the new refugees had been communists in Hungary, and he urged that they be admitted as "parolees." In Eisenhower's final year, Walter again thwarted the president's efforts to increase immigration and change admission procedures.

When HUAC was chaired by HAROLD VELDE (R-Ill.) from 1953 to 1955, Walter earned a reputation as one of the more fair and temperate investigators on that panel. Upon assuming the chair of HUAC in 1955, however, his own words and actions took on a new stridency that intensified over the next nine years. In 1955, HUAC investigated one of its familiar targets, the entertainment industry. The hearings turned up little new information. In the spring of 1956, the committee began an investigation of alleged unauthorized use of U.S. passports. In particular, Walter expressed concern about the dissemination of anti-American views. As a result of the hearings, HUAC issued eight contempt citations, none of which were upheld in the courts. The U.S. Supreme Court ruled in 1958 that the State Department had not been authorized by Congress to withhold passports on the basis of "beliefs and associations." Walter immediately pressed for tighter legislative controls on passports.

In July 1958, HUAC probed the Fund for the Republic, set up by the Ford Foundation. Commentator Walter Goodman wrote that Walter suspected the group of campaigning against his immigration law. Furthermore, the liberal foundation was committed to support the "elimination of restrictions on freedom of thought." At the center of the confrontation was the financing by the fund of a critical report on blacklisting in the entertainment industry. During the hearings, it became clear that while Walter would not admit to the existence of a blacklist, he backed the exclusion of communists. Walter attacked the fund as a tax-exempt organization supporting dubious, anti-American activities. In HUAC's annual report of 1956, he declared that 200,000 people in the United States, "the equivalent of 20 combat divisions of enemy troops," were aiding the subversion of U.S. political affairs. HUAC recommended tighter postal and passport controls and more severe punishment for individuals who "obstructed" congressional hearings.

In subsequent years, HUAC chose targets that had been heavily investigated in previous congressional sessions, including the labor movement, the churches, and the entertainment industry. HUAC went to California in 1957 to investigate suspected communists in the education system. In an unusual action, HUAC released names to local school boards and delegated to them the authority to hear testimony that would be duly recorded for HUAC's later study. Numerous teachers lost their jobs at the hands of local school board officials. Walter incurred the wrath of Protestant ministers in 1960, when he endorsed charges that communists had infiltrated the churches.

HUAC held hearings in San Francisco in 1959, which provoked demonstrations opposing HUAC's activities. In 1960, HUAC produced a movie, *Operation Abolition*, that depicted the demonstrations as communist-inspired and directed. The film received considerable criticism as a blatantly deceptive and manipulative journalistic enterprise.

During the administration of President JOHN F. KENNEDY, Walter continued to block efforts to overhaul the McCarran-Walter Act and warned Congress about the danger of importing subversion. While he frequently disagreed with the Kennedy administration on immigration and internal security, he supported much of Kennedy's proposed economic and social legislation. Indeed, Walter acted as a key operative for the president on numerous congressional votes. Walter's HUAC had

a diminishing role in U.S. affairs during the early 1960s. He died in Washington, D.C., of leukemia on May 31, 1963.

—MSM

Warren, Earl
(1891–1974) *chief justice of the U.S. Supreme Court*
The son of Scandinavian immigrants, Warren was born in Los Angeles, California, on March 19, 1891. His mother came from Sweden, and his father, who worked as a railroad mechanic for the Southern Pacific Railroad, came from Norway. Earl Warren grew up in Bakersfield, California, and attended the University of California, where he received an undergraduate degree in 1912 and a law degree in 1914. After working for private firms, which he found unsatisfying, Warren enlisted in the army when the United States entered World War I in 1917. He spent most of the war training recruits and was discharged as a first lieutenant in December 1918. Upon leaving the army, he became a deputy city attorney in Oakland in 1919 and the following year took a position as a deputy district attorney in Alameda County, California. After advancing to chief deputy in 1923, Warren was appointed in 1925 to fill the last year of District Attorney Ezra DeCoto's term when DeCoto accepted an appointment to the state railroad commission. Warren won election to a full term in 1926 and reelection in 1930 and 1934. In the 13 years he served as district attorney, Warren built a reputation as an honest, efficient, and fair-minded prosecutor. He received national attention for his advocacy of the professionalization of law enforcement and the use of science in law enforcement, as well as his support for cooperation between jurisdictions. Although he was an aggressive prosecutor, no higher court ever overturned a conviction obtained by his office.

Although he was a Republican, Warren's appeal transcended partisan affiliation. When he ran for state attorney general in 1938, he won the primaries of the Republican, Democratic, and Progressive Parties. Running with little more than token opposition, he swept to victory in the general election. As California's attorney general, he reorganized his department and focused on prosecuting vice and organized crime. After Pearl Harbor, Warren

President Eisenhower and Earl Warren, governor of California, July 13, 1953 *(Dwight D. Eisenhower Library and Museum)*

enthusiastically supported the internment of Japanese Americans. At the same time, however, he issued an opinion holding that the state personnel board could not deny state employees of Japanese descent their rights as civil servants.

Running as a Republican, Warren won the first of three successive terms as governor in 1942. Although never a charismatic figure, his hearty public persona, plain manner of expression, and progressive but pragmatic approach to issues won him a personal following that extended across party lines. Warren's liberal Republicanism alienated some conservatives but won over substantial numbers of Democrats. Indeed, when he ran for reelection in 1946, he did so as the nominee of both the Republican and Democratic Parties. He won in a landslide. In his bid for a third term, he carried every county in the state.

As governor, Warren made appointments virtually without regard to party affiliation. He increased old age pensions and unemployment benefits, overhauled the state penal system, expanded unemployment coverage, and inaugurated a public works program that built new schools, highways, hospitals, and parks to meet the needs of the state's rapidly expanding population. He supported lower taxes, proposed a statewide compulsory health insurance program, and opposed the dismissal of professors at the University of California who refused to sign a loyalty oath. Warren did, however, support a loyalty pledge for all state employees, and he signed a bill outlawing the Communist Party in California. Over all, he established a socially progressive record and earned a reputation as a governor with an open mind.

A candidate for the Republican presidential nomination in 1948, Warren swung California's delegation to Governor THOMAS E. DEWEY of New York on the final ballot. After Dewey claimed the nomination, he selected Warren as his running mate. Although heavily favored to win the general election, Dewey and Warren lost to President HARRY S. TRUMAN and his running mate, Alben Barkley.

Warren made another bid for his party's presidential nomination in 1952. At the Republican National Convention in July, the California delegation, which Warren led, voted for a resolution to bar contested delegates from voting on the credentials of other contested delegates. The so-called fair play resolution amounted to a vote to seat delegates who supported DWIGHT D. EISENHOWER and helped Eisenhower win the nomination. During the general election campaign, Warren campaigned for Eisenhower in California.

Warren's support for Eisenhower seems not to have been part of any quid pro quo. Following the election, Eisenhower telephoned Warren to inform him that he would not be offered a position in the cabinet. The president-elect had considered Warren for the position of attorney general, but that went to HERBERT BROWNELL, whose legal and political advice Eisenhower greatly valued. Eisenhower then remarked that he intended to offer Warren the first vacancy on the Supreme Court. Eisenhower, at least, did not consider the commitment to be a concrete one; Warren, by all indications, did. In any event, no one expected the first vacancy to be the chief justice. In the meantime, Eisenhower offered Warren the position of solicitor general, which Warren accepted. Before the nomination was made public, however, Chief Justice FRED VINSON died early in September 1953. The president considered other possible appointees before settling on Warren. Eisenhower announced Warren's nomination as chief justice on September 30, saying that he had chosen the Californian for his "integrity, honesty, middle-of-the-road philosophy, experience in Government, [and] experience in the law." Eisenhower gave Warren a recess appointment, and the new chief justice was sworn in on October 5, the day the Court's new term started. The Senate confirmed his nomination by a unanimous voice vote on March 1, 1954.

Warren took the helm of a court bitterly divided between a faction of judicial activists, led by Hugo Black and William O. Douglas, and a faction dedicated to judicial restraint, led by Felix Frankfurter and Robert H. Jackson. Under Vinson's ineffective leadership, the ideological divisions persisted unabated, even though the personal animosities had calmed somewhat.

In December 1953, soon after Warren took his seat, the Court heard arguments in five cases held over from its previous session, which challenged the constitutionality of racial segregation in public schools. The cases came from four states and the District of Columbia. When the justices met to consider the case, Warren suggested that, contrary to their usual practice, they discuss the matter before voting on it. Over the next few months, Warren demonstrated his exceptional skills as a politician and managed to unite the Court behind a decision to overturn segregated public schools. After the justices finally voted in late February or March 1954, Warren undertook to write the opinion himself. On May 17, 1954, he announced the Court's decision in *Brown v. Board of Education*, his first major opinion as chief justice. In a deliberately low-key manner, Warren read the decision of a unanimous Court, which held that racially segregated public schools were inherently unequal and therefore deprived children of equal protection of the laws guaranteed by the Fourteenth Amendment. He left open the question of how this decision should be implemented and called for further argument on that issue. In a second opinion handed down that day, Warren, again speaking for a unanimous Court, ruled that segregated public schools in the District of Columbia violated the due process clause of the Fifth Amendment. A year later, on May 31, 1955, Warren spoke once more for a unanimous Court, this time on the question of implementation. In that decision, the Court ruled that school desegregation

was to begin immediately and proceed "with all deliberate speed."

The most famous and perhaps the most important of Warren's many major decisions, *Brown* did not explicitly overturn *Plessy v. Ferguson* (1896). Therefore, it did not strike down segregation in other public facilities, but the logic of *Brown* was clear. Appellate courts struck down segregated parks, swimming pools, and other facilities. In 1963, the Court ruled, in *Johnson v. Virginia*, that "a State may not constitutionally require segregation of public facilities." *Brown* effectively ended the legality of the South's Jim Crow system and helped set in motion major changes in American race relations.

Warren's particular contribution in *Brown* lay in his ability to gain unanimity among the justices. Although several prior rulings had suggested that the Court might outlaw segregation in *Brown*, the outcome was by no means assured. More important, a unanimous Court, which was invaluable in such a momentous decision, proved difficult to secure. Even some justices who personally found segregation abhorrent questioned whether the Court had the constitutional authority to overturn it. Warren got his unanimous decision by his handling of the issue in conference, his discussion of the cases with individual justices, and the moderate phrasing of the final opinion. Similarly, his decision to put off the matter of implementation helped promote unanimity, even though it did not, as Warren hoped, promote southern acceptance of the decision.

Addressed to the American polity as well as judges and lawyers, Warren's opinion in *Brown* was short and nontechnical. In terms easily accessible to the general public, it eloquently argued that segregation harmed black students and therefore violated their constitutional rights. On the other hand, it lacked, in the words of legal historian Paul Finkelman, "technical precision and rigorous [legal] analysis." Opponents, and even some supporters, of the *Brown* decision, criticized Warren's opinion for its absence of solid legal analysis and argument, as well as its reliance on social science. Many civil rights advocates expressed dissatisfaction with the gradualist formula for implementation the Court adopted in the second decision.

Aside from *Brown*, Warren in his first years on the bench turned out to be the moderate and rather cautious jurist most observers expected him to be when he was appointed. In his first term, for example, he voted to uphold a state gambling conviction based on illegally seized evidence and to sustain medical authorities in the state of New York when they suspended a doctor's license to practice because he had refused to cooperate with a congressional investigation into communism.

By mid-1956, however, Warren aligned himself with the Court's more activist and libertarian members. His shift became evident through a series of controversial cases involving loyalty and security issues in which he consistently voted in favor of individual claimants and against the government, though he did so on a variety of grounds. In April 1956, Warren, speaking for a majority of six justices, overturned the conviction of a well-known communist under Pennsylvania's anti-sedition statute (*Pennsylvania v. Nelson*). The chief justice held that Congress had preempted this field with the Smith Act of 1940. Warren again spoke for the Court in *Watkins v. U.S.* (1957), which reversed the contempt conviction of an officer in a labor union who, while willing to answer questions about himself and others he knew to be members of the Communist Party, had refused to answer questions before a subcommittee of the House Un-American Activities Committee (HUAC) about people who had once been members of the party but no longer were. Warren ruled that the subcommittee had failed to show that the questions asked were pertinent to the subject under investigation, but he added to this narrow holding a lengthy essay which insisted that congressional committees were subject to constitutional limitations and that congressional investigations had to be related to a legitimate legislative purpose. "There is," wrote Warren, "no Congressional power to expose for the sake of exposure."

In a companion case reversing a similar contempt conviction under state law, Warren, writing for a plurality, also limited the investigative power of the states (*Sweezy v. New Hampshire* [1957]). The legislature of New Hampshire had given the state's attorney general authority to investigate subversive persons and activities. Called before the attorney general, Paul M. Sweezy, a left-wing professor, refused to answer questions about the content of the lecture he had given at the state university. The

attorney general petitioned to county court to ask the professor the same questions. When Sweezy refused to answer, the court held him in contempt. The Supreme Court reversed that conviction. Basing his opinion on a narrow question, Warren, writing for himself and three other justices, held that the legislature had not specified that it desired the information about which the attorney general had questioned Sweezy. Two other justices voted to set aside the conviction but did so on the ground that the questions put to Sweezy infringed upon his constitutionally protected academic and political freedom.

The decisions in *Watkins* and *Sweezy* aroused considerable controversy. Some members of Congress openly and harshly criticized the Court. Senator WILLIAM JENNER (R-Ind.) introduced a bill that would have limited the appellate jurisdiction of the Supreme Court in cases involving the functions of congressional committees, security programs administered by the executive branch, and state laws dealing with subversion. Representative HOWARD SMITH (D-Va.) introduced a bill to limit the discretion of the Court in determining that statutes passed by Congress had preempted the field. None of the various anti-Court bills became law.

The congressional reaction overestimated the reach of the *Watkins* and *Sweezy* cases. In June 1959, the Court upheld contempt convictions in two cases very similar to those decided in 1957. Focusing on the limited nature of the Court's decision in *Watkins*, a narrow majority of the Court (five to four) voted, in *Barenblatt v. U.S.*, to uphold the conviction for contempt of Congress of a teacher who had refused to answer questions before a subcommittee of HUAC. The questions posed in this case, held the majority, were "pertinent" to the investigation, which, moreover, fell within the committee's purview. Decided the same day as *Berenblatt*, *Uphaus v. Wyman* upheld the conviction of Willard Uphaus for refusing to divulge the names of the people who attended a "World Fellowship" camp in New Hampshire. The majority distinguished this case from Sweezy in that it involved no question of academic freedom, the legislature clearly wanted the questions answered, and the government's interest in "self-preservation" outweighed "individual rights in an associational privacy which . . . were here tenuous at best." The chief justice dissented in both *Berenblatt* and *Sweezy*.

During the 1960s, when new appointments created a liberal majority, Warren led an increasingly activist Court whose rulings were marked by a concern for protecting individual liberties and promoting equality. Although he exercised considerable influence on the Court, unlike Chief Justice John Marshall, Warren did not assign to himself all of the most important decisions in which he joined the majority. Indeed, many of the decisions that define the Warren Court were written by other justices. For example, Warren did not write for the Court in *Mapp v. Ohio* (1961), which excluded evidence seized without a warrant; *Engel v. Vitale* (1961), which struck down mandated or state-sanctioned prayers in public schools; *Gideon v. Wainwright* (1963), which extended the Sixth Amendment's right to counsel to defendants in state courts; and *Griswold v. Connecticut* (1965), which struck down state prohibitions on the use of contraceptives and established a constitutional right to privacy. Warren did not even assign himself the opinion in a case he considered the most significant of his tenure, *Baker v. Carr* (1962), in which the justices ruled that federal courts could decide legislative apportionment issues. The Court later ordered reapportionment on the basis of "one man, one vote" (*Gray v. Sanders* [1964]).

Warren did, however, write opinions in a number of highly significant cases. In *Miranda v. Arizona* (1966), Warren wrote the decision for a five-to-four majority which held that suspects had to be informed of their right to remain silent and that anything a suspect said could be held against him or her in court. In addition, suspects had to be informed of their right to counsel and their right to have counsel appointed if they could not afford one. These so-called Miranda warnings reshaped the administration of criminal justice in the United States. In *Reynolds v. Sims* (1964), a case dealing with legislative reapportionment, Warren held that legislative districts should be based on population. "Legislators," he memorably wrote, "represent people, not trees or acres."

The Warren Court expanded the rights of those suspected or accused of crime, overturned much of the loyalty-security apparatus of the 1950s, held organized prayer and Bible reading in public schools unconstitutional, and expanded the scope of freedom of speech and of the press. By the time Warren retired in June 1969, the Court had wrought a constitutional revolution in several areas, and its rulings had made a profound impact on American social and political life.

In November 1963, President LYNDON B. JOHNSON appointed Warren to head a presidential commission assigned to investigate the assassination of President JOHN F. KENNEDY. Warren balked at the assignment; he questioned the appropriateness of his service on an extrajudicial investigative panel. Johnson prevailed on the chief justice, who acceded to the president. Johnson hoped that the Warren Commission would squelch burgeoning speculation that Kennedy's assassination was the result of a conspiracy. The Warren Commission found that Lee Harvey Oswald, acting alone, assassinated Kennedy. For a variety of reasons, the commission did not do a good job of investigating the matter, and the shortcomings of its report subsequently fueled conspiracy theories. Ironically, in spite of all of the report's inadequacies, the weight of scholarly opinion supports the Warren Commission's conclusion that Lee Harvey Oswald assassinated Kennedy.

Johnson announced that he would not seek reelection on April 1, 1968. Convinced that RICHARD M. NIXON, a longtime political enemy and the frontrunner for the Republican presidential nomination, would win the election, Warren decided to resign. That decision seems to have been based on Warren's fear that Nixon would appoint his successor. Johnson nominated Associate Justice Abe Fortas to replace Warren and Homer Thornberry, a judge from Texas, to replace Fortas. Ironically, a scandal involving Fortas's financial dealings forced him to withdraw his nomination. Warren agreed to remain on the Court, but the scandal forced Fortas to resign from the Court. Warren remained in office until Nixon appointed WARREN E. BURGER to the chief justiceship. Nixon appointed Harry Blackmun to the vacancy created by Fortas's resignation.

After leaving the Court, Warren wrote his memoirs and gave public lectures. He died in Washington, D.C., on July 9, 1974.

Aside from those who objected to the outcome of particular cases, the Warren Court encountered criticism for reaching out to decide controversial issues and for being too result-oriented in its rulings. Even some supporters of the Court's decisions conceded that the justices acted more like legislators than judges in the way they made new policy. Warren answered these criticisms by asserting that the Court had an obligation to decide all cases properly placed before it, however controversial the issues. For Warren, the Court's special function lay in guaranteeing the constitutional protections afforded to individuals, especially those least likely to receive them.

Neither a great legal scholar nor judicial philosopher, Warren was not even an especially skilled legal craftsman. Most analysts, however, regard him as one of the most important and influential chief justices, perhaps second only to John Marshall. Warren believed in fairness and common sense and regarded them as more appropriate bases for decisions than the fine points of judicial philosophy.

—MSM

Washington, Val(ores) (James)

(1903–1995) *Republican national committeeman, director of minorities*

Born in Columbus, Indiana, on September 18, 1903, Washington graduated from Indiana University in 1924. He worked as an editor and publisher of the *Gary* (Indiana) *Sun* from 1924 to 1926. For the next eight years, he was a freelance writer, specializing in political articles and features. In 1934, he joined the *Chicago Defender,* Chicago's African-American Newspaper, where he worked as the paper's business, advertising, and general manager. He remained with the *Defender* until 1941, when he became a member of the Illinois Commerce Commission, a position he held until 1948.

An active Republican, he became executive assistant to the campaign director of the Republican National Committee (RNC) in 1946. At the same time, he received an appointment to the headquarters staff of the RNC as director of minorities. In that capacity, he had responsibility for planning and executing strategies to win black voters back to the Republican Party. Two years later, he served as assistant campaign manager to

HERBERT BROWNELL, who ran THOMAS E. DEWEY's presidential campaign.

During the presidential campaign of 1952, Washington served as the RNC's official spokesman for the campaign of DWIGHT D. EISENHOWER on African-American issues. In support of Eisenhower's campaign in 1952, Washington wrote in *The Crisis:* "Historically, 3,000,000 Negro slaves found emancipation through the Republican party eighty-nine years ago. In 1952, this same party offers the surest and best chance, the most practical, realistic and honest program through which this minority . . . can achieve their present political ambition of full citizenship." Washington defended Eisenhower against charges that he had supported segregation in the military. Just before the election, he persuaded the National Council of Negro Democrats to endorse Eisenhower.

During the Eisenhower administration, Washington served as an adviser to the president and as an administrative liaison to Congress on minority affairs. During the campaign, Eisenhower had promised to include qualified African Americans for positions in his administration. Eisenhower assigned responsibility for seeking out black candidates to SHERMAN ADAMS. Washington was responsible for gathering the names of likely candidates. He played a role in obtaining an appointment for E. FREDERIC MORROW as adviser on business affairs in the Department of Commerce and then in getting Morrow a position as administrator for special projects in the White House. In the latter post, Morrow became the first African American to hold an executive post in the White House. Washington also played a role in the appointment of J. Ernest Wilkins as assistant secretary of labor. Other appointments for which Washington could claim some responsibility included Frank Snowden as cultural attaché in Rome, Clifton Wharton as minister to Romania, John B. Eubanks as head of the Rural Improvements Staff of the U.S. Operations Mission of the International Cooperation Administration, and Robert Lee Brokenburr, Charles H. Mahoney, and Archibald J. Carey as members of the American delegation to the United Nations. In addition, Washington constantly urged Republican officials at all levels of government to appoint African Americans to their staffs.

Washington offered advice, which was not always welcome, to the Eisenhower administration on racial matters. He urged Eisenhower to demonstrate "warmth, sympathy, and solid helpfulness" to school districts that complied with the Supreme Court's ruling, in *Brown v. Board of Education*, that segregated public schools were unconstitutional. He also suggested that federal aid for school construction be extended to districts that desegregated. Washington also argued for a public statement from the administration condemning the murder of EMMETT TILL. Going into the election of 1956, Washington pressed for an increase in the RNC's budget to attract black voters. During the campaign, Washington aggressively defended the administration's record. In 1957, Washington strongly supported the administration's civil rights bill and strenuously objected when key sections were cut and weakened.

At the end of the Eisenhower administration, Washington left the Republican National Committee and founded an import/export firm based in Washington, D.C. When Ronald Reagan won the presidential election in 1980, Washington told *Ebony* magazine that Reagan would open doors for African Americans.

Washington died of a heart attack at his home in Upper Marlboro, Maryland, on April 23, 1995.

—MSM

Watkins, Arthur V(ivian)
(1886–1973) *U.S. senator*

A Mormon whose grandparents were among the early pioneers of Utah, Arthur Watkins was born in Midway, Utah, on December 18, 1886. He moved with his family to Vernal, Utah, in the mid-1890s. He studied at Brigham Young Academy (later Brigham Young University) from 1903 to 1906. After teaching grade school for a year, he left for New York City to serve two years as a missionary. He remained to study law at New York University and Columbia University, from which earned a law degree in 1912. Watkins returned to Vernal in 1913, where he gained admission to the bar, entered the practice of law with a family friend, and edited a weekly newspaper. After losing a race for county attorney in Uintah County, in which he ran on the

Progressive ticket, he received an appointment as assistant county attorney of Salt Lake County in 1914. When the Republicans were turned out of office the following year, Watkins lost his position and practiced law in Centerville, Utah. Health problems interfered with his work as a lawyer, and, beginning in 1919, he managed a ranch owned by his cousins, which he turned into Utah's first commercial turkey farm. During the early 1920s, he resumed the practice of law in American Fork and relocated to Orem in 1925, where he also leased a commercial fruit farm. He served as judge for the fourth judicial district in Utah from 1928 to 1933. After an unsuccessful attempt to gain a seat in the House of Representatives in 1936, he won election as a Republican to the U.S. Senate in 1946. He was reelected in 1952.

A conservative on domestic issues and a unilateralist in foreign policy, Watkins associated himself with the midwestern, conservative wing of the Republican Party led by Senator ROBERT A. TAFT (R-Ohio). Anxious to assert congressional control over foreign policy, he introduced a reservation to the North Atlantic Treaty of 1949 that would have required congressional approval before committing American forces to combat. The Senate rejected his reservation. Later he criticized President HARRY S. TRUMAN's decision to send troops to Korea without seeking congressional approval. Watkins also favored more aid to Nationalist China and less to Europe.

A strong advocate of western water development, Watkins worked to gain support for the Upper Colorado River Storage Project, which Congress passed in 1956. As head of the Indian Affairs Subcommittee, he took the lead in efforts to end federal trust relationships with numerous tribes.

Although a strong anticommunist, Watkins remained noncommittal on Senator JOSEPH R. McCARTHY's (R-Wis.) anticommunist crusade during the early 1950s. Nevertheless, Watkins played a key role in the events leading to the Senate's condemnation of McCarthy in late 1954. In July, Senator RALPH FLANDERS (R-Vt.) introduced a resolution to censure McCarthy for conduct "unbecoming a member of the U.S. Senate . . . contrary to senatorial traditions, and tending to bring the Senate into disrepute." Senators WILLIAM FULBRIGHT (D-Ark.)

and WAYNE MORSE (Ind.-Oreg.) later added 33 specific complaints against McCarthy. The leaders of the Senate created a special select committee to investigate the charges and chose six "neutral" senators to serve on it. The members of the committee, highly respected by their colleagues, all came from the moderately conservative group that held the balance of power in both parties. None had taken a strong stand on McCarthy. Watkins's reputation as a stern moralist, devoted to order, propriety, and the traditions of the Senate, made him a logical choice for chair. In addition, Watkins was a member of the Internal Security Subcommittee and had impeccable anticommunist credentials.

When the committee's hearings began on August 31, Watkins clearly intended to exercise full control and not to allow McCarthy to turn the hearings into a circus or a showcase for himself. The committee forbade smoking and television cameras in the hearing room. Further, the rules established by the committee permitted either McCarthy or his lawyer (but not both) to cross-examine a given witness. By eliminating the senators who had introduced the censure motion as witnesses, the committee deprived McCarthy of anyone to attack. Moreover, Watkins forced McCarthy to obey the rules and adhere to standards of relevance. With grim determination and effectiveness, Watkins used the gavel to cut off McCarthy's outbursts.

The Watkins Committee decided to consider 13 charges divided into five general categories, including contempt of the Senate, receipt of classified information, encouragement of federal employees to violate the law, abuse of fellow senators, and abuse of General RALPH W. ZWICKER, who had appeared before McCarthy's Government Operations Committee during its investigation of the army. Over many tedious hours and days, the panel and an admittedly bored McCarthy heard a mass of evidence documenting the behavior of the junior senator from Wisconsin. The unanimous committee's report, issued on September 27, recommended censure on two counts: contempt of the Senate for failing to appear before the Subcommittee on Privileges and Elections in 1952 and for abusing General Zwicker. The report described McCarthy's conduct as "contumacious, denunciatory, unworthy, inexcusable and reprehensible." Neither party espe-

cially wanted to bring the matter to a vote before the elections in November. The Senate leadership postponed a vote by the full Senate on the censure resolution until after the November elections. During the interim, Senator McCarthy denounced Watkins as "cowardly and stupid."

On the first day of debate, November 10, 1954, Watkins presented his committee's charges before the Senate. Afflicted with a painful spastic abdominal muscle, Watkins did not waver under attacks by McCarthy and his allies. In a speech inserted into the *Congressional Record* on November 15, McCarthy accused the Watkins Committee of becoming a "unwitting handmaiden" of the communists. Watkins then told the Senate that McCarthy should be censured for his attacks on the panel. This charge replaced the one dealing with the abuse of Zwicker. Later in the proceedings, an angry Watkins elicited tears from some of his colleagues and applause from others as he described McCarthy's attack on the Select Committee as a blow against the Senate itself. He challenged that body, "What are you going to do about it?"

On December 2, the censure resolution passed by a margin of 67–22. Afer the vote, STYLES BRIDGES (R-N.H.), one of McCarthy's supporters, demanded of Vice President RICHARD M. NIXON, then presiding, whether the word "censure" appeared in the resolution. Nixon acknowledged that it did not and, exercising his prerogative as presiding officer to change the title of a resolution to conform to its text, eliminated the word censure from the title. No one, however, could misinterpret the Senate's forceful condemnation. McCarthy himself observed that "it wasn't exactly a vote of confidence." Soon afterward, President Eisenhower personally congratulated Watkins for his excellent work, a fact that provoked charges of "lynching" from McCarthy's remaining supporters.

After the McCarthy investigation, Watkins receded from the public eye. He lost his bid for reelection in 1958, when the former governor of Utah, J. BRACKEN LEE, who personally disliked Watkins, ran as an independent in the general election and split the Republican vote. As a result, the Democratic candidate, Frank Moss, was elected senator. After leaving the Senate, Watkins served briefly as a consultant to the secretary of the interior. Appointed to the Indian Claims Commission in 1959, he became chair of the commission in 1960. After retiring from the commission in 1967, he returned to Salt Lake City. In 1973, he moved to Orem, where he died on September 1, 1973.

—MSM

Watson, Thomas J(ohn), Jr.
(1914–1993) *president, International Business Machines Corporation*

The son of the head of International Business Machines Corporation (IBM), Watson was born in Dayton, Ohio, on January 8, 1914. He attended the Hun School in Princeton, New Jersey, and graduated from Brown University in 1937. That same year, he joined IBM as a salesman. When the United States entered World War II, Watson joined the New York National Guard and later received a commission as a second lieutenant in the army air corps. By the time he was discharged in 1945, he held the rank of lieutenant colonel. After the war, Watson returned to IBM, where he demonstrated managerial ability and a flair for salesmanship in the rapidly growing corporation, which made punch card tabulating machinery (adding machines). Young Watson rose rapidly through the company. His father placed him as assistant to the executive vice president. Watson became a vice president of IBM in 1946 and later that year was elected to the board of directors. In 1949, he became executive vice president.

Watson became president of IBM in 1952. His father was chairman of the board and chief executive officer. Watson assumed the position of chief executive officer in 1956, and, when the elder Watson died a few months later, his son became the major force behind the company. Watson oversaw changes in the company's benefits and pension policies that included offering medical insurance for employees and stock options for managers. He also decentralized the company's corporate structure.

During the mid-1950s, Watson led the company into the computer industry. IBM had funded efforts to develop an electronic computer during World War II but had not demonstrated any interest in developing computers for commercial use. The elder Watson believed them too expensive and too unreliable. Nevertheless, electronic computers could make calculations many times faster than the conventional business equipment produced by IBM that operated with electric motors, levers, and punch cards. After the Census Bureau purchased a UNIVAC computer, built by another company, to process census information, the younger Watson moved to get IBM into the business. During the Korean War, Watson persuaded his father that the company should develop computers to sell to the military. The result was the 701 Data Processing Machine. IBM developed a version for commercial use (the IBM 702) in 1954. In these computers, transistors replaced vacuum tubes; and the machines could store data on magnetic tape. Under Watson's direction, the sales and profits of IBM skyrocketed. Watson vastly increased IBM's spending on research and development, and the company's research division turned out increasingly advanced models to meet the increasing demand for sophisticated equipment. In the late 1950s, IBM developed a computer network to link a string of radar stations for the air force. That technology became the basis for the first commercial online computer network, which IBM built for American Airlines and began operating in 1964.

IBM's dominant position in the sale of office equipment brought unwelcome attention from the federal government, which filed an antitrust lawsuit against the company in 1952. Watson persuaded his father to sign a consent agreement to settle the matter in 1956. IBM agreed to sell, as well as lease, its office equipment, share some of its patents, and separate its service operations from the rest of the company. Watson calculated that the agreement would primarily effect the firm's older equipment and that settling the matter would free the company to expand its business in computers. By 1960, IBM had become one of the nation's leading corporations and the dominant producer of computers. That year its profits reached over $168 million.

Unlike many of the important business executives of the period, Watson was a liberal Democrat who opposed neither high levels of government spending nor the high tax rates necessitated by such spending. In a speech before the National Association of Manufacturers (NAM) in 1959, he maintained that a liberal welfare state was necessary to achieve U.S. goals at home and abroad. He argued that the Soviet Union's success in raising its standard of living impressed underdeveloped nations, which were tempted to follow its example. Watson, however, maintained that the American economic system provided an even more appealing model and asked businessmen to realize that the nation must do everything in its power to help other countries adopt it. Watson told his audience that business leaders should not complain about high taxes. The American people desired a stronger nation, a balanced budget, and the same or even lower taxes. "These three goals," Watson said, "are incompatible. One of our first sacrifices must be a willingness to accept higher taxes if necessary." Watson's speech received polite but restrained applause.

The following year, Watson testified before a Senate subcommittee examining the economic and military threat posed by the Soviet Union. He said that, although he disliked government controls of business, he accepted them as necessary in the cold war. He remarked, "I would rather have greater control by our government under the present system than to discover one day that business-as-usual has not been sufficient to win the battle." As he had in his speech to the NAM, Watson stressed that only liberalism could prevent the spread of communism.

Watson stepped down as president in 1961, but he continued as chairman of the board and chief executive officer. During the 1960s and 1970s, IBM grew to be one of the largest multinational corporations in the world. Under Watson's direction, the company spent $5 billion on the development of a new generation of computers. Introduced in 1964, the System/360 used hard drives instead of magnetic tape and integrated circuits instead of transistors. The new line of computers proved so successful that IBM expanded its already large share of the market. Several competitors, including Honeywell, RCA, and General Electric, dropped out of the market.

A close friend of President John F. Kennedy, Watson served on a number of important advisory committees, including the Committee on Labor Management Policy, the National Advisory Council for the Peace Corps, and the Citizens Committee for International Development. In 1969, the government brought an antitrust suit to break up the company. In response, Watson "unbundled" the pricing of computer hardware from that of maintenance and software. That prompted the development of a new industry of independent software makers.

Watson suffered a heart attack in 1970, after which he stepped down as chairman and chief executive officer in 1971. He continued on the board of directors and headed its executive committee until 1979. In 1977, President Jimmy Carter named Watson to chair the General Advisory Committee on Arms Control and Disarmament. Two years later, Carter appointed him ambassador to the Soviet Union. Watson's hopes for substantial gains in arms reduction evaporated when the Soviet Union invaded Afghanistan, but he continued as ambassador until the end of the Carter administration. He returned to IBM's board of directors in 1981 and served until 1984. After that, Watson devoted himself to philanthropic activities. In the 1980s, the microchip and the growth of personal computers did what the government had never been able to achieve; it broke IBM's hold on the computer market. Watson died in Greenwich, Connecticut, on December 31, 1993.

—MSM

Weeks, Sinclair

(1893–1972) *secretary of commerce*

Sinclair Weeks was born in West Newton, Massachusetts, on June 15, 1893. His father founded the brokerage house of Hornblower & Weeks and served as a Republican mayor of Newton, a member of Congress, a U.S. senator, and Calvin Coolidge's secretary of war. Weeks graduated from Harvard in 1914 and went to work for First National Bank of Boston. A member of the Massachusetts National Guard, he served on the Mexican border in 1916. When the United States entered World War I, Weeks enlisted in the army. Rising from second lieutenant to captain, he saw action in France as commander of battery B of the 101st Artillery of the 26th Division. Upon his discharge from the army in 1919, Weeks returned to First National Bank. In 1923, his father-in-law, whose health was failing, prevailed on Weeks to help manage Reed & Barton, a silver manufacturing firm, and United States Fastener Company, which made fasteners for clothing. Weeks negotiated a merger with United States Fastener's main competitor, creating United-Carr Fastener Corporation in 1929. Under Weeks's careful leadership both United-Carr and Reed & Barton weathered the Great Depression in good shape.

Weeks also began a career in politics. After losing a race for alderman in Newton in 1921, he won the seat the following year. Reelected three times, he served from 1923 to 1930 and, during the later part of his tenure, became president of the board of aldermen. Weeks won election as mayor of Newton in 1929. He performed his duties as mayor during mornings and evenings and devoted the afternoons to running his businesses. While initiating public works projects, he kept the city's debt under control. He won reelection in 1931 and 1933. Driven by his opposition to what he regarded as President Franklin D. Roosevelt's reckless spending, Weeks sought the Republican nomination for the U.S. Senate in 1936. He narrowly lost the nomination to HENRY CABOT LODGE, JR., but he soon assumed the chair of the Republican state committee. From 1941 to 1953, he was a member of the Republican National Committee, and he served as treasurer of that body from 1940 to 1944. He chaired the Republican Finance Committee from 1949 to 1952. A director of the National Association of Manufacturers as well as a number of major corporations, he exercised considerable influence in the business community and served as an important link between business leaders and the Republican Party. Weeks took an active role in the presidential campaign of Wendell L. Willkie in 1940.

When Lodge resigned from the Senate in 1944 to enlist in the army, Governor LEVERETT SALTONSTALL appointed Weeks to fill the vacant seat. Weeks did not run for the seat that September. During nearly a year in the Senate, Weeks was an outspoken opponent of Roosevelt's domestic programs. He then returned to his role as a party functionary. He supported Senator Arthur H. Vandenberg's unsuccessful bid for the Republican presidential nomination in 1948 and engineered a draft of Representative CHRISTIAN A. HERTER for the Massachusetts gubernatorial nomination in 1952. Herter subsequently defeated his Democratic opponent.

Weeks became the first member of the Republican National Committee to declare his support for the candidacy of General DWIGHT D. EISENHOWER. Senator ROBERT TAFT (R-Ohio) had the support of most party regulars, but Weeks helped to organize Eisenhower's primary drive and then helped swing delegates to Eisenhower's candidacy during the Republican National Convention. In a much publicized statement, Weeks urged Taft to withdraw from the race, calling on the senator to "perform a supreme act of self-denial" that would "electrify the country, instantly unite the Party[,] . . . guarantee victory and save the country." Taft, predictably, rejected the suggestion. After Eisenhower defeated Taft for the nomination, Weeks became chair of the Republican National Finance Committee and raised a record amount of money for the fall campaign.

After the election, President-elect Eisenhower approached Weeks about assuming the chairmanship of the Republican National Party, which became vacant when ARTHUR SUMMERFIELD resigned to become postmaster general. Weeks, however, expressed a preference for becoming secretary of commerce, a position he though would enable him to use his skills as a manager and to promote the interests of American businesses.

As secretary of commerce, Weeks quickly emerged as the most aggressively pro-business member of Eisenhower's cabinet. During the

President Eisenhower and Secretary of Commerce C. Sinclair Weeks, October 19, 1954 *(Dwight D. Eisenhower Library and Museum)*

closing months of 1952, Eisenhower asked Weeks to head a panel formed to study the question of ending the wage and price controls imposed by the Truman administration. The commission recommended an end to price controls and a return to a free market. Based on historical experience, the panel maintained, controls had coped only with the symptoms of inflation rather than its basic causes. The panel therefore recommended they be reserved only for extreme emergencies and then used only for short periods of time. Weeks argued that controls would "distort and impede our production effort." He conceded that removing controls might result in rising prices but maintained that the long-range effect would be salutary. Eisenhower followed Weeks's advice and in February 1953 ordered the removal of all wage and some price controls at once.

During the first year of the administration, Weeks became involved in a debate within the administration over modifying the Taft-Hartley Act of 1947, which labor opposed because of its restrictions on unions. The principal proponent of revision, Secretary of Labor MARTIN DURKIN, wanted to drop the act's provision requiring union leaders to sign noncommunist affidavits, abolish "right-to-work" laws, give unions more control over membership, and permit secondary boycotts. In addition, he hoped to minimize the jurisdiction of state courts in labor disputes. Eisenhower rejected extreme revisions and supported amending the legislation to eliminate only those provisions that could be used to "smash unions." Weeks, on the other hand, saw the attempt at revision as an opportunity to strengthen the act. He was particularly anxious to clarify the authority of states in labor disputes to prevent "erroneous" interpretations of the statutes.

Weeks and Durkin clashed bitterly over the revision of Taft-Hartley. In an effort to resolve the dispute, presidential assistants BERNARD SHANLEY and GERALD MORGAN drew up a 19-point memorandum suggesting a position for the administration. Most of the points reflected Durkin's position. The memorandum eventually became the basis for a draft of a message to be forwarded to Congress on July 31. Taft, however, died that day, and, because he had coauthored the original legislation, the White House delayed action. It seemed impolitic to submit revisions of the act the day its original sponsor died. Further, Taft's death greatly diminished any prospect for passage of amendments. Without Taft's prestige and influence, particularly with the Republican Right, the amendments had little chance of gaining congressional approval. In the meantime, Weeks, joined by Vice President RICHARD NIXON, maneuvered behind the scenes to kill the message. They convinced the president that alienating business and supporters of states' rights would be politically disastrous. During the early part of September, Eisenhower informed Durkin that the 19 points would not be forwarded to Congress. Durkin resigned from the cabinet.

Weeks became involved in another well-publicized clash in 1953—this time within his own department. Dr. Allen V. Austin, head of the National Bureau of Standards (NBS), announced that a product advertised as giving longer life to storage batteries proved ineffective in a scientific test. On March 31, Weeks attempted to force Austin's resignation on the ground that he had made a subjective judgment. However, public opposition to what appeared to be political interference with the scientific process and sentiment within the NBS (400 employees threatened to resign) forced Weeks to establish a panel of scientists to rule on the product. The committee not only backed Austin's conclusions but insisted that he remain on the job. Recognizing his own mistake, Weeks retreated. Weeks and Austin eventually became friends and worked closely together.

Weeks consistently advocated turning over government operations to private industry whenever possible. In 1954, he oversaw the sale of the Inland Waterways Corporation's barge lines to a syndicate from the Midwest. Weeks also faced criticism for his department's use of business leaders as unpaid management consultants; by 1957, he curtailed his department's use of such consultants.

Weeks often came across as an unyielding conservative. Even President-elect Eisenhower noted in his diary that he found Weeks "so completely conservative in his views that he seems to be illogical. I hope . . . that he will soon become a little bit more aware of the world as it is today." During his years as secretary of commerce, however, Weeks frequently supported the president's "modern Republicanism."

He backed Eisenhower's commitment to more open trade and led the fight for Eisenhower's reciprocal trade program, even though many manufacturers opposed it. Although known as a hard-liner on communism, he nevertheless issued regulations in August 1957 permitting an increase in the export of "peaceful" goods to Poland. The move incurred the wrath of members of the Republican Right. Weeks served as liaison between the cabinet and various subcommittees during the planning stages of the St. Lawrence Seaway, a project for which he was a vigorous advocate. He fought for U.S. membership in the antiprotectionist Organization of Trade Cooperation, broadened Weather Bureau services, modernized the air navigation system, furthered legislation to assist railroads, administered the nation's largest peacetime shipbuilding program for merchant ships, expanded the fair trade program, and expanded his department's activities in research and the gathering of statistics. In addition, Weeks furthered the passage of the Federal Highway Act of 1956. In his memoirs, Eisenhower wrote that "the great highway system would stand as a memorial to the man in my cabinet who headed the department responsible for it."

Weeks retired from the cabinet in November 1958 for personal and financial reasons. In 1959, he was elected director of the First National Bank of Boston, a post he had resigned to join the cabinet. Five years later, he joined Hornblower & Weeks, Hemphill, Noyes, as a limited partner. Despite his business activities, Weeks spent much of his time on his farm in Lancaster, New Hampshire. He died in Concord, Massachusetts, on January 7, 1972.

—MSM

Welch, Joseph N(ye)

(1890–1960) *special counsel, U.S. Army*

The son of poor English-born parents, Welch was born in Primghar, Iowa, on October 22, 1890. He clerked in a real estate office for two years to save enough money to attend college. After graduating Phi Beta Kappa from Grinnell College in 1914, he went to Harvard Law School on a scholarship. After receiving his LL.B. in 1917, he enrolled in the army's officer candidate school, which he was attending when World War I ended. After serving

with the legal division of the U.S. Shipping Board, he joined the Boston firm of Hale and Dorr in 1919. A highly successful trial lawyer, he became a partner in 1923 and senior partner in 1936.

In April 1954, Welch agreed to serve as special counsel for the army in its dispute with Senator JOSEPH R. McCARTHY (R-Wis.), a position for which Welch took no pay. Welch immediately filed 29 charges with the Senate Government Operations Committee's Permanent Investigations Subcommittee, chief among them that McCarthy and his aide ROY M. COHN "had improperly pressed the Army to promote Private G. DAVID SCHINE," a former member of McCarthy's staff.

The hearings, which opened before the subcommittee on April 22, attempted to sort out a confusing myriad of charges and countercharges. The accuracy of specific allegations or facts proved less influential than impressions and images. McCarthy's menacing appearance, his angry outbursts, his rudeness, his personal attacks, and his abuse of procedure had more impact on the public than the substantive matters before the panel. Moreover, McCarthy's crude behavior stood in marked contrast to Welch's civility, dry wit, legal skill, and self-composure. The experienced trial attorney refused to let McCarthy's antics distract him, and Welch continually needled McCarthy. Welch also surgically dissected McCarthy's "evidence." He exposed a doctored photograph of Secretary of the Army Robert T. Stevens and Schine, which purportedly showed that the two had been friendly at a time when Stevens claimed to be angry over improper pressure on Schine's behalf. When McCarthy claimed to have a copy of a letter from J. EDGAR HOOVER, director of the FBI, that warned army officials of security problems, Welch dismissed the document as "a carbon copy of precisely nothing."

McCarthy increasingly lost control of his temper and became more and more reckless. Toward the end of the 36-day hearings, the mounting personal animosity between Welch and McCarthy exploded in a celebrated exchange. During Welch's heated cross-examination of Cohn, the army's attorney badgered Cohn about the exact number and the names of communists or subversives in defense plants. "I don't want the sun to go down while they're still in there," intoned Welch. McCarthy interrupted and said that "in view of Mr. Welch's request that, uh, the information be given if we know of anyone who might be performing any work for the Communist Party, I think we should tell him that he has in his law firm a young man named [Frederick G.] Fisher whom he recommended incidentally to do the work on this Committee, who has been, for a number of years, a member of an organization [the National Lawyers Guild] which is named, oh years and years ago, as the legal bulwark for the Communist Party." Charging Welch with trying to "burlesque" the hearings, McCarthy added that he doubted the lawyer had "any conception of the danger of the Communist Party." Visibly shaken, Welch responded that "Until this moment, Senator, I think I never really gauged your cruelty or your recklessness." Welch went on to explain that Fisher had been a member of the guild only briefly, while in law school and for a few months after, and that he had since become a promising lawyer and a Republican. When he decided to represent the army, Welch explained, he had asked James St. Clair to be his assistant and told St. Clair to choose another lawyer in the firm to assist him. St. Clair chose Fisher. When Welch asked if either of the younger lawyers had anything in their pasts that might prove embarrassing, Fisher said that he had belonged to the National Lawyers Guild, and Welch sent Fisher back to Boston in order to avoid any possible controversy. Welch's account was something less that the truth. Welch sent Fisher back to Boston only after consulting with members of the White House staff. Moreover, Welch did not say that both sides in the Army-McCarthy hearings had agreed not to raise the matter. Turning to McCarthy, he said, "Little did I dream you could be so reckless and so cruel as to do an injury to that lad. . . . If it were in my power to forgive you for your reckless cruelty, I would do so. I like to think I'm a gentle man, but your forgiveness will have to come from some one other than me." When McCarthy persisted, Welch cut him short, pleading with the senator not to "assassinate this lad further." Welch then demanded: "Have you no sense of decency, sir, at long last? Have you left no sense of decency?" He then left the room to the applause of the spectators.

According to many observers, McCarthy's attack on Welch's associate was his single most damaging

blunder during the hearings. Although McCarthy's popularity had already begun to slide, the hearings, McCarthy's attack on Fisher, and Welch's memorable response contributed to a growing sense of national outrage at the senator's actions. More important, McCarthy's rash disregard for the Senate's procedures and decorum alienated a substantial bipartisan bloc in the upper house and led to his eventual condemnation by the Senate in December 1954.

Welch returned to his law practice. As a result of the hearings, however, he became a nationally popular figure. He appeared on a number of television shows and in 1959 played a judge in the film *Anatomy of a Murder.* He died on October 6, 1960, in Hyannis, Massachusetts.

—MSM

Welker, Herman
(1906–1957) *U.S. senator*
Born on December 11, 1906, in Cambridge, Idaho, Welker grew up in rural Idaho, attended public schools, and worked his way through the University of Idaho and its law school, where he received his LL.B. in 1929. While still a student, he was appointed the prosecuting attorney of Washington County, Idaho, in 1928. He held that position until 1936, when he left his home state for Los Angeles, where he set up private law practice. After serving in the army air corps in 1943 and 1944, he established a law practice in Payette, Idaho, and then won election as a Republican to the state senate in 1948. Two years later, he won a seat in the U.S. Senate by the largest margin in a senatorial election in Idaho since 1936. He credited his victory to the support of his ally, Senator JOSEPH R. McCARTHY (R-Wis.).

A vehement anticommunist, Welker joined the small group of ultraconservative Republicans in the Senate. Like McCarthy, he attributed most of the nation's problems to Democratic appeasement and misrule. In 1951, he supported a complete ban on Western trade with the Soviet bloc. He also favored drastic cuts in foreign aid to Europe, which he regarded as the home of numerous left-wing groups. In domestic affairs, Welker supported a measure giving states title to tidelands oil. He was one of McCarthy's strongest supporters in the upper house. As a member of the Senate Subcommittee on Privileges and Elections, he attempted to delay the panel's investigation of McCarthy in 1952 and resigned from the subcommittee that September, protesting that the subcommittee was being used as a "political vehicle by the Democratic Party."

Welker remained on the extreme right of the Republican Party after DWIGHT D. EISENHOWER became president and frequently came into conflict with the new president and his administration. On domestic issues, Welker supported limiting government intervention in the private sector. He voted to cut appropriations for the Tennessee Valley Authority and opposed wage and price controls as well as tax increases. An extreme cold warrior, in 1953, Welker opposed Eisenhower's nomination of CHARLES BOHLEN as ambassador to the Soviet Union because of the career diplomat's role in what Welker termed the "Truman-Acheson policy of appeasement" toward the Soviet Union. Also in 1953, Welker argued against an emergency immigration bill, designed to admit increased numbers of refugees from eastern Europe. The following year, he vigorously opposed U.S. recognition of Communist China. In 1954, Welker accused ARTHUR H. DEAN, the U.S. negotiator of the Korean armistice, of supporting appeasement and of collaborating with Communist China. He assailed Dean as an "ex-official spokesmen" of the Institute of Pacific Relations, which many on the Right believed had links to communists. Also in 1954, he supported the Bricker amendment, which was designed to limit the president's treaty-making power.

The senator from Idaho was known for his vitriolic style in debate. Reporter RICHARD ROVERE observed that Welker was "capable of more hatred than McCarthy, as well as more ideology." During the debate over a resolution to censure McCarthy in November 1954, Welker served as floor manager for the junior senator from Wisconsin. Welker vigorously defended McCarthy, whom he called "one of the greatest living champions of human liberty, and one of the greatest living foes of Communist slavery," and attacked the Watkins Committee's recommendation to censure McCarthy. If passed, Welker charged, such a resolution would indirectly promote the aims of communist conspirators.

On November 16, Welker told the Senate that the Constitution provided for punishing senators for "disorderly behavior but did not for the specification in the censure resolution—conduct unbecoming a senator or . . . contrary to senatorial traditions." The following day, Welker said that there was no precedent for censuring McCarthy, that many senators had assailed colleagues with violent language without being censured. He predicted that he himself would be censured for defending McCarthy. Welker protested repeatedly that senators showed "disrespect" for McCarthy by their sparse attendance during Welker's presentation of the defense case. Even some of McCarthy's supporters questioned Welker's vitriolic rhetoric. On December 2, the Senate condemned McCarthy by a vote of 67–22.

In 1955, Senator McCarthy named Welker and FBI director J. EDGAR HOOVER as "good candidates to replace Eisenhower as President." In 1956, Welker lost his bid for reelection to FRANK CHURCH. After leaving the Senate, he practiced law in Boise, Idaho, and owned a farm. In early 1957, Welker participated in a meeting of right-wing Republicans, during which he joined a series of speakers who denounced the direction of the Eisenhower administration and "modern Republicanism." Welker died of a brain tumor in Bethesda, Maryland, on October 30, 1957.

—MSM

Whittaker, Charles E(vans)
(1901–1973) *associate justice, Supreme Court*

The son of a farmer, Whittaker was born near Troy, Kansas, on February 22, 1901. He dropped out of school after the ninth grade. After working as a farmer for two years, he went to Kansas City to study law. He worked as an office boy in a law office while earning the equivalent of a high school diploma. Whittaker completed his high school work in 1922 and enrolled in the University of Kansas City's law school. Working his way through law school, he passed the state bar exam in 1923, a year before his graduation. Upon graduating, he joined the prestigious Kansas City law firm of Watson, Gage & Ess, where he specialized in litigation and business planning for a largely corporate clientele. He became a partner in 1940, and his name was added to the firm's name in 1942. He remained with that firm until he took a seat on the federal bench.

In July 1954, President DWIGHT D. EISEN-
HOWER named Whittaker to a federal district court
judgeship in Kansas City. Although not politically
active, Whittaker was a Republican, well regarded
by political leaders in Kansas, and a close friend of
the president's brother, Arthur Eisenhower. Moreover, since Democrats held both Senate seats from
Missouri, the White House took a more active role
in seeking out nominees for a vacancy on the federal
district court in that state. As a judge, Whittaker
demonstrated great industry and efficiency. Eisenhower promoted him to a seat on the U.S. Court of
Appeals for the Eighth Circuit in July 1956. Upon
the retirement of Justice STANLEY REED, Eisenhower nominated Whittaker to the Supreme Court
in March 1957. The American Bar Association
warmly endorsed his nomination, and the Senate
quickly confirmed him.

On the bench, Whittaker aligned himself with
the Court's more conservative members. On occasion, however, he joined an opinion upholding a
particularized individual right against encroachment by the government. For example, he joined
with the other members of the Court in taking a
firm stand against segregation. Nevertheless, on
most issues, Whittaker voted against individual
claims of civil liberties and in favor of the needs of
government and social order. He wrote the majority opinion in *Mulcahey v. Catalanotte* (1957), which
upheld the deportation of an alien for trafficking
in narcotics, even though that crime had not been
grounds for deportation when he committed it. The
decision upheld a section of the Immigration and
Nationality Act of 1952. A year later, Whittaker
joined a five-justice majority in *Beilan v. Board of
Education* (1958), which sustained the dismissal
for incompetence of a public school teacher who
refused to answer questions by the school superintendent about the teacher's communist affiliations. Whittaker dissented in *Kent v. Dulles* (1958),
when the Court ruled that the State Department
lacked an adequate statutory basis to deny a citizen a passport because of his political beliefs. In
two cases decided in June 1959, the justice voted
to uphold the contempt convictions of witnesses
who had refused to answer questions or produce
records for congressional and state investigations
of communism. In *Barenblatt v. U.S.*, Whittaker

voted with the majority to uphold the conviction
for contempt of Congress of a teacher who had
refused to answer questions before a subcommittee
of the House Un-American Activities Committee.
Whittaker also voted with the majority in *Uphaus
v. Wyman*, which upheld a conviction for contempt
in a state court for refusing to divulge the names of
people who attended a World Fellowship camp in
New Hampshire

Whittaker did occasionally vote with the
Court's liberals in cases involving the First Amendment and issues relating to loyalty and security. In
January 1958, his opinion for the Court in *Staub
v. City of Baxley* declared unconstitutional a local
ordinance that required union organizers to obtain
permits before they could solicit workers to join
a union. Whittaker held that the ordinance gave
too wide discretion to city officials. Whittaker also
voted with the majority in *Trop v. Dulles* (1958)
to overturn a federal statute that punished desertion from the armed forces in a time of war with
a loss of citizenship. On a case decided the same
day, however, he voted with the majority in *Perez v.
Brownell* (1958), which held that a deserter from the
armed forces who had left the country for Mexico
and voted in a Mexican election had relinquished
his citizenship.

In criminal rights cases, Whittaker also tended
to favor the claims of government. In *Bartkus v.
Illinois* (1959), he joined the majority in a decision
holding that an individual acquitted in a federal
court could then be tried for the same offense in a
state court without violating the safeguard against
double jeopardy. Whittaker dissented in *Mapp
v. Ohio* (1961), in which the Court extended the
exclusionary rule to state criminal proceedings. In
some criminal cases, such as those involving allegedly coerced confessions, Whittaker was accused of
inconsistency because he would vote opposite ways
in largely similar cases without clearly explaining
his reasons for doing so.

Although a modest, sincere man who worked
extremely hard while on the Court, Whittaker was
not a distinguished justice. Neither an outstanding
judicial theorist nor a legal craftsman, he wrote very
few opinions of any significance. He articulated no
judicial philosophy and agonized over decisions.
Leon Friedman wrote that Whittaker "was not

fitted intellectually or physically for the job" of a Supreme Court justice. On the advice of his physician, Whittaker retired from the Court in March 1962 and returned to corporate practice. He died in Kansas City, Missouri, on November 26, 1973.

—MSM

Whyte, William H(ollingsworth), Jr.
(1917–1999) *journalist and sociologist*

The son of a railroad executive, Whyte was born in West Chester, Pennsylvania, on October 1, 1917. Known as Holly, he attended St. Andrew's School in Middletown, Delaware, and Princeton University, from which he graduated with a degree in English in 1939. He then attended the Vick School of Applied Merchandising to prepare for a position as a junior executive with the Vick Chemical Company. He enlisted in the Marine Corps in 1941 and served in the Pacific. He was discharged with the rank of captain in 1945. After leaving the service, he took a job with *Fortune* magazine in 1946. He rose to the position of assistant managing editor of *Fortune* by the time he published *The Organization Man* in 1956.

The *Organization Man* joined DAVID RIESMAN's *The Lonely Crowd* (1950) and C. WRIGHT MILLS's *White Collar* (1956) in offering a powerful and literate critique of the forces promoting conformity in mid-20th century American society. Whyte described the decline of entrepreneurship and risk-taking that accompanied the bureaucratization of corporate business and argued that bold visions of entrepreneurial individualists were giving way to "the modest aspirations of organization men who lower their sights to achieve a good job with adequate pay and proper pension and a nice house in a pleasant community populated with people as nearly like themselves as possible." "In our attention to making the organization work," he warned, "we have come close to deifying it." Even worse, he maintained, "we . . . [are] denying that there is—or should be—a conflict between the individual and the organization. This denial is bad for the organization. It is worse for the individual." "Fight the organization," Whyte advised his readers, "but not self-destructively." Writing from "the optimistic premise that individualism is as possible in our

times as in others," Whyte urged people to seek "individualism within organizational life."

Perhaps even more important, White warned that the "organizational ethos," based on a desire for security and characterized by conformity, had spread to academic and scientific institutions and, indeed, to suburbia. He contended that American society was changing from one shaped by a Protestant ethic, characterized by work, sacrifice, responsibility, to a "social ethic," defined by the organization. As Whyte explained it, the "social ethic" was belief that "of himself, [man] is isolated, meaningless; only as he collaborates with others does he become worthwhile, for by sublimating himself in the group, he helps to produce a whole that is greater than the sum of its parts." Therefore, according to the social ethic, there should be no conflict between the individual and society.

Although often lumped together with social critics rooted in a radical or left liberal tradition, such as Riesman and Mills, Whyte came from a different perspective. A Princeton graduate, a former junior executive with Vicks (makers of Vaporub), and a journalist for a popular business magazine, Whyte was not interested in bringing down the organization; he was interested in creating space for individuals within it.

Whyte left *Fortune* in 1958 to devote himself to other pursuits. While working at the magazine, he had encountered and impressed Laurence S. Rockefeller, the philanthropist, who shared Whyte's interest in conservation and urban development. Rockefeller subsequently subsidized a number of Whyte's projects involving rural land use, beautification, reclamation, city planning, suburban growth, and civic design. Whyte's study, *Conservation Easements*, published by the Urban Land Institute in 1959, helped to win passage of open-space legislation in California, New York, Connecticut, and Massachusetts.

For the next 10 years, Whyte devoted himself to issues relating to conservation and urban sprawl. He wrote reports for the Outdoor Recreation Resources Review Commission and the American Conservation Commission. A member of President LYNDON B. JOHNSON's Task Force on Natural Beauty, Whyte wrote the initial draft of its final report. His proposal for urban beautification led to passage of a $50 million program to plant trees in urban areas. Whyte argued for the preservation of rural lands and open areas in *Cluster Development* (1964) and *The Last Landscape* (1968).

In 1969, Whyte took part in the New York City Planning Commission's development of a comprehensive plan for the city. His work with the planning commission led him to wonder how people actually used the spaces provided for by the plan. In particular, he was curious about the effectiveness of incentive zoning. A grant to study street life in New York and other cities, provided by the National Geographic Society, enabled Whyte to establish the Street Life Project, a pioneering study of urban dynamics and pedestrian behavior. He and his team observed and filmed the use of corporate plazas, urban streets, parks, and other open spaces in New York City; they charted the movement of pedestrians. Whyte opposed what he described as "the fortressing of America," typified by windowless walls, concrete courtyards, and features that discouraged people from sitting ("The human backside," he once commented, "is a dimension architects seem to have forgotten."). He was interested in "schmoozing patterns, the rituals of street encounters," and he explored why "people flocked to some plazas and left others empty." "It is difficult to design a space that will not attract people," he observed; "what is remarkable is how often this has been accomplished." Whyte championed the creation of space that encouraged social interaction and civic engagement. Above all, he advocated designing public spaces based on studies of how people used such spaces. The years of observation and time-lapse photography compiled for the Street Life Project became the basis of "The Social Life of Small Urban Places," a documentary that ran on the Public Broadcasting System. He expanded that documentary into a book, *The Social Life of Small Urban Spaces* (1980), in which he wrote: "I end then in praise of small spaces. . . . It is not just the number of people using them, but the larger number who pass by and enjoy them vicariously . . . For a city, such places are priceless, whatever the cost." In 1988, he published *City: Rediscovering the Center.*

Whyte died in New York City on January 12, 1999.

—MSM

Wiley, Alexander
(1884–1967) *U.S. senator*

The son of Norwegian immigrants, Wiley was born in Chippewa Falls, Wisconsin, on May 26, 1884. He grew up on his father's farm and, as a young man, worked as a lumberjack. Wiley studied to become a Lutheran minister at Augsburg College in Minneapolis from 1902 to 1904. Abandoning his plans to become a minister, he entered the University of Michigan Law School in 1904 and then transferred to the University of Wisconsin's law school, from which he graduated in 1907. Admitted to the bar that same year, Wiley returned to Chippewa Falls, where he set up a law practice. Over the next 32 years, his practice thrived. He served three terms as district attorney (1909–15), and, building on his success as a lawyer, he purchased a dairy farm, was a bank director, served on the school board, and joined a number of civic and fraternal organizations. Wiley also traveled the state delivering inspirational talks. In 1933, he won election as president of the Kiwanis International for the Wisconsin and Upper Michigan district. His statewide contacts provided him with the base to win the Republican nomination for governor in 1936. He lost the general election to the popular incumbent, Philip LaFollette. Two years later, however, Wiley won a seat in the U.S. Senate. He won reelection in 1944, 1950, and 1956.

A conservative Republican, Wiley opposed Franklin D. Roosevelt's New Deal legislation and American entry into World War II. After Pearl Harbor, however, he renounced his isolationist views and joined the internationalist wing of the Republican Party led by Senator Arthur Vandenberg (R-Mich.). In 1945, Wiley became the second-ranking Republican member of the Foreign Relations Committee, which Vandenberg chaired. Wiley supported American entry into the UN and worked closely with the administration of HARRY S. TRUMAN to obtain passage of legislation implementing the Marshall Plan and the North Atlantic Treaty, the two cornerstones of the president's containment policy toward the Soviet Union. Wiley, however, broke with the administration over its China policy. A member of the so-called China bloc in the Senate, he called for all-out aid to Chiang Kai-shek in the civil war against the Communists. Wiley supported Truman's decision to commit American forces to

Korea but criticized the president's decision to fire General Douglas MacArthur as the commander of Allied forces in Korea. In domestic matters, Wiley assumed an important role when, after the Republicans won control of both houses of Congress in the elections of 1946, he became chair of the Judiciary Committee in 1947. He cooperated with the Truman administration to establish the practice of consulting local bar associations on the qualifications of judicial nominees. In addition, he supported the Taft-Hartley Act and served on the Kefauver Committee, appointed to investigate organized crime.

Wiley opposed Senator JOSEPH R. McCARTHY (R-Wis.), both on moral grounds and because of internal state politics, but he approached the matter with caution. In a letter to his son written in 1950, Wiley described McCarthy's techniques as "rather vicious." Nevertheless, after Truman launched into a tirade against McCarthy and other conservative Republicans at a press conference, Wiley issued a press release the same month in which he called on Truman to stop trying to "smear McCarthy." Running for reelection in 1950, Wiley set aside his personal distaste for McCarthy and his methods and praised his junior colleague for sounding the alarm about "the danger of Communist penetration." In the spring of 1952, Wiley delivered a speech during which he made a favorable reference to DEAN ACHESON, a favorite target of the Republican Right. In reaction to Wiley's speech, the *Chicago Tribune*, a conservative paper, condemned the senator as a "Truman Republican and an Acheson stooge." The paper also charged that he was an "expert on betrayal," as sinister as Alger Hiss. McCarthy's supporters in the Senate also attacked Wiley, implying that Acheson had seduced an "illiterate country bumpkin inflated to the point of bombast." Despite the denunciations, Wiley refused to retract his statement. During the debate over a resolution to censure McCarthy, Wiley arranged to be in Brazil.

Upon the death of Vandenberg in 1951, Wiley became the ranking minority member of the Senate Foreign Relations Committee. As chair of the Foreign Relations Committee from 1953 to 1954 and as its ranking minority member from 1955 to 1960, Wiley was a major supporter of the Eisenhower administration's foreign policy and often defended it against challenges from the Republican Right. In

1953, he supported the appointment of CHARLES BOHLEN as ambassador to the Soviet Union. The right wing of the Republican Party regarded Bohlen as too closely associated with the "Truman-Acheson policies of appeasement."

Wiley consistently supported the North Atlantic Treaty Organization, and he favored a strong, rearmed West Germany as its leading European power. Although he believed that the United States should not recognize Communist China and should oppose its admission to the UN, he refused to join Republican conservatives in criticizing the British and French governments for recognizing and trading with the Beijing regime. He thought that attacking America's allies would play into Moscow's hands by splitting the Atlantic alliance. Although deeply concerned about communist electoral victories in western Europe, he concluded that they reflected a discontent with existing governments rather than acceptance of communist ideology.

Wiley led the opposition in the Senate to the Bricker amendment, which would have curbed the president's treaty-making powers. As a result, the Wisconsin Republican State Convention, dominated by McCarthy and his supporters, censured him in June 1953. On May 26, 1956, Wiley's 72nd birthday, the Republican State Convention denied him its endorsement. It chose instead Representative Glen R. Davis, who had supported the Bricker amendment and advocated a reduction in foreign aid. After leaving the hall, Wiley, sobbing, vowed to run anyway. In September, he won the primary by 9,700 votes out of more than 424,000 cast. Wiley then went on to win the general election.

In 1962, Governor Gaylord Nelson defeated Wiley in his bid for reelection. Although he had his differences with the Eisenhower administration, Wiley regarded himself as a "modern Republican." He supported a modest welfare state and an internationalist foreign policy. During the administration of JOHN F. KENNEDY, Wiley generally voted as a conservative on domestic legislation, except for civil rights, which he strongly supported. While generally backing the president's diplomacy, Wiley called for more aggressive action against Cuba.

A back-slapping, joke-telling politician, Wiley published a small book, *Laughing with Congress* (1947), in which he recounted humorous incidents relating to Congress. Critics regarded him as something of a buffoon for his cliché-ridden speeches and his corny political stunts, but Wiley's image led some to overlook his hard work and his usually sound political instincts. Afer leaving the Senate, he resided in Washington, D.C., until a few days before his death from a stroke in Germantown, Pennsylvania, on October 26, 1967.

—MSM

Wilkins, Roy
(1901–1981) executive director, NAACP

The son of a minister who was forced to find work tending a brick kiln, Wilkins was born in St. Louis, Missouri, on August 30, 1901. His mother died when Wilkins was only four, after which he was raised by an aunt and uncle in St. Paul, Minnesota. Wilkins grew up in an integrated, working-class neighborhood and went on to attend the University of Minnesota, where he majored in sociology and wrote for the campus newspaper. In 1922, he became editor of a failing black weekly, the *Appeal*. During his senior year, he joined the St. Paul, Minneapolis, chapter of the NAACP and became its secretary. After graduating in 1923, he went to work as a reporter for the *Kansas City Call*, a weekly black newspaper, and eventually became its managing editor. In Kansas City, he encountered Jim Crow for the first time. While working for the *Call*, he became active in a number of causes involving the city's black community. In 1930, Wilkins worked against Senate confirmation of Judge John J. Parker, an allegedly racist nominee to the U.S. Supreme Court. That same year, he also worked to defeat Senator Henry J. Allen (R-Kan.), a segregationist. His activities brought him to the attention of Walter White.

When White replaced James Weldon Johnson as executive secretary of the National Association for the Advancement of Colored People (NAACP) in 1931, he offered his former position as assistant secretary to Wilkins. The NAACP was dedicated to the elimination of racial discrimination, primarily through lawsuits and legislative lobbying. In his new position, Wilkins had a number of responsibilities. He investigated conditions of black workers on the Mississippi levees in December 1931. White assigned Wilkins to serve as the NAACP's

point man on the Scottsboro Case, which involved nine young black men accused of raping two white women while traveling on a freight train. Wilkins also edited the NAACP's organ, the *Crisis*, from 1934 to 1949 and ran the national office during White's frequent absences. His many activities included participation in the planning of A. PHILIP RANDOLPH's proposed March on Washington in 1941, efforts to end rioting in Harlem in 1943, and service as a consultant to the U.S. delegation to the conference in San Francisco that established the charter for the United Nations.

When White took a leave of absence from the NAACP in 1949, Wilkins became acting executive secretary. In 1950, he organized an Emergency Civil Rights Mobilization in Washington, D.C., to lobby on behalf of civil rights legislation. Upon White's return in May 1950, the board of directors relieved him of some of his duties. They selected Wilkins to handle the daily administrative duties. When White retired in 1955, Wilkins replaced him as executive secretary (a title later changed to executive director) of the 240,000-member organization.

Wilkins oversaw the NAACP's legal and legislative efforts, ran the national office, made speeches throughout the country, wrote pamphlets, and raised funds. One of his first activities after becoming executive secretary was to help raise money to support the Montgomery bus boycott led by MARTIN LUTHER KING, JR. Wilkins, however, focused his primary attention on attempts to integrate southern schools. In June 1955, the national office urged southern chapters of the NAACP to petition local school boards to implement the Supreme Court's decision in *Brown v. Board of Education* (1954), which struck down segregation in public schools.

In 1956, Wilkins attacked both major political parties for taking weak positions on civil rights. He criticized Democratic presidential aspirant ADLAI E. STEVENSON in February for favoring a go-slow approach to granting African Americans their rights as citizens. In August, Wilkins unsuccessfully urged the Republican platform committee to promise to amend the rules of the Senate to make it easier to end filibusters. Subsequently, he criticized both national party platforms as inadequate. Since the NAACP was a nonpartisan organization, Wilkins expressed no preference in the presidential race.

In February 1957, Wilkins testified before a subcommittee of the House Judiciary Committee in support of the administration's civil rights bill, which he described as "minimum legislation." Before its enactment by Congress, the Senate eliminated the crucial Title III, which would have permitted the attorney general to file civil suits in cases of civil rights violations. Nevertheless, Wilkins decided to support the bill, which established a civil rights commission, elevated the Civil Rights Section of the Justice Department to the status of a division, and provided some protection for black voting rights. It was, he concluded, the best that could be obtained at the moment. He also thought that it represented an historic breakthrough that would open the way for more far-reaching legislation in the future. Wilkins convinced the Leadership Conference on Civil Rights, a coalition of groups opposing racial discrimination, to support the measure.

On June 23, 1958, Wilkins, King, A. Philip Randolph, and Lester B. Granger met with President Eisenhower to present a nine-point program to further civil rights. The plan included the organization of a White House conference on school desegregation, the granting of funds to officials and community groups seeking to promote the desegregation of schools, the denial of federal funds for segregated institutions, the assurance of federal protection against terrorist bombings in the South, and the enactment of what had been Title III of the original civil rights bill presented to Congress in 1957. The black leaders received a polite audience from the president. Wilkins denounced the Civil Rights Act of 1960, which extended the voting rights protection of the legislation passed in 1957. Under the act, he declared, "the Negro has to pass more check points and more officials than he would if he were trying to get the United States gold reserves in Fort Knox. It's a fraud." In that year, he again denounced the civil rights planks of both parties as inadequate and participated in picketing the Democratic National Convention. He and other civil rights leaders believed that, among other things, the major parties should repudiate the segregationists within their ranks and, in accordance with the Fourteenth Amendment, back a reduction of congressional

representation in areas where African Americans were denied the right to vote.

The decade after 1955 brought new challenges to the NAACP and its leader. Direct action protest commanded the attention of the nation and the black community. The Montgomery bus boycott, the lunch counter sit-ins of 1960, and the Freedom Rides brought new leaders to the fore and led to the creation of new organizations. At the NAACP's convention in 1960, Wilkins praised direct action as a means of promoting desegregation in the South. He announced in the spring that the NAACP would support student sit-ins at lunch counters and that the organization itself would stage wade-ins in the summer to integrate swimming facilities. Wilkins nevertheless held firm in his belief that legal and political action offered the best chance for advancing black civil rights. The effectiveness of direct action, he believed, was limited, as was its applicability to a national scale.

Wilkins and Clarence Mitchell, the NAACP's top lobbyist, played a major role in obtaining major civil rights legislation in the 1960s. Pressure from the NAACP under Wilkins helped to convince President JOHN F. KENNEDY to issue an executive order in 1962 that banned discrimination in federally financed housing. Wilkins and Mitchell cooperated with President LYNDON B. JOHNSON and lobbied Congress to obtain passage of the Civil Rights Act of 1964 and the Voting Rights Act of 1965. Wilkins participated in the March on Washington in 1963, the march from Selma to Montgomery in 1965, and the continuation of James Meredith's March Against Fear in 1966.

By the mid-1960s, however, the direction of the black struggle for equality was changing. Wilkins resisted growing demands for black nationalism and black separatism. He regarded Stokely Carmichael as a huckster and opposed his call for black power in 1966. In his memoirs, Wilkins wrote that "black power was just a slogan, loaded words, not a real program." His attack on black power in his keynote address at the NAACP's convention in 1966 drew the ire of many younger and more militant African Americans. Wilkins denounced the growing number of nationalist and separatist groups. While he understood the frustrations that led to such violence, he condemned the black riots in many northern cities. Unlike many civil rights activists who spoke out against the war in Vietnam, Wilkins believed that the issues of civil rights and peace should be kept separate.

By the late 1960s, Wilkins's moderate stands made him a target for criticism by black militants. Within the NAACP, a group of younger, more militant members called for him to step down. Police broke up a plot by the Revolutionary Action Movement to assassinate Wilkins. In the late 1960s and early 1970s, Wilkins opposed separate dormitories and dining halls for black college students. "I had been against black apartheid all my life," he explained in his memoirs. Wilkins retired as executive director in 1977. He died in New York City on September 8, 1981.

—MSM

Williams, G(erhard) Mennen
(1911–1988) *governor of Michigan*

A product of a wealthy and prominent family, Williams was born in Detroit, Michigan, on February 23, 1911. His grandfather founded the Mennen Company, which made soaps and toiletries, his father was the head of a company that made pickles. G. Mennen Williams, or Soapy as he was known, grew up in a privileged Episcopalian and Republican home. After attending the exclusive Salisbury School in Connecticut, Williams earned his B.A. from Princeton University, where he graduated Phi Beta Kappa in 1933. As president of the Young Republican Club at Princeton, he campaigned for HERBERT HOOVER in 1932. Williams then surprised his family by becoming an enthusiastic supporter of the New Deal and joining the Democratic Party.

He earned a law degree from the University of Michigan in 1936 and that same year went to Washington to serve as an attorney for the Social Security Board. The following year, Michigan's governor, Frank Murphy, appointed Williams assistant attorney general. When Murphy became U.S. attorney general in 1939, Williams joined his staff as an administrative assistant. President Franklin D. Roosevelt appointed Murphy to the Supreme Court in 1940, after which Williams remained briefly at the Justice Department before moving to the Office of Price Administration (OPA). In 1942, Williams

enlisted in the navy and served in the Pacific as an air combat intelligence officer on aircraft carriers. Upon leaving the navy in 1946 with the rank of lieutenant commander, he took a position as deputy director of the Michigan office of the OPA. In 1947, he became a partner in the law firm of Griffiths, Williams, and Griffiths in Detroit. Williams engaged in Democratic Party politics and in 1947 received an appointment to the state liquor control commission.

Supported by the Michigan Democratic Club (a liberal organization founded by Williams and his law partners designed to wrest control of the state party from JAMES HOFFA, the president of the Teamsters), the Congress of Industrial Organizations, and many liberals, Williams ran for governor in 1948. Williams defeated Hoffa's candidate in the primary and ran in the general election on a platform that called for improved housing, roads, and education as well as increases in farm supports, unemployment compensation, and veterans' benefits. It also strongly supported civil rights for African Americans and promised to repeal Michigan's "little Taft-Hartley" act, which restricted some activities of organized labor. With the support of African Americans, ethnic voters, and the United Automobile Workers, Williams won the general election. Given his patrician background, his folksy style of campaigning brought derision from his critics. It was nevertheless effective; he went on to win five more terms in a state where Democrats had previously enjoyed little success.

During the 1950s, Williams earned a reputation as one of the most liberal governors in the nation. He modernized Michigan's courts, built more schools, and reformed state prisons. To win public support for his programs, he formed bipartisan commissions of experts to study proposals and make recommendations. The panels recommended legislation to aid the handicapped, improve the juvenile justice system, and reform election procedures. A committed supporter of civil rights, Williams proposed a fair employment practices law in 1948, which the Republican-dominated legislature passed in 1955. The governor also got the legislature to ban discrimination in the sale of real estate. Williams appointed many African Americans to state offices, including positions in his cabinet and on the state courts.

Williams had less success in implementing his ambitious social agenda. Soon after taking office, the governor requested state corporate and personal income taxes to finance his proposals for programs to improve education, hospitals, prisons, unemployment benefits, and health care. The Republican-controlled legislature repeatedly turned down his requests, preferring an increase in sales and user taxes. Increases in general revenue, however, enabled Williams to take modest steps toward implementing his proposals. The stalemate between the governor and the legislature led the state to the brink of bankruptcy by the late 1950s. The difficult battle over taxes and the state's precarious financial position contributed to Williams's decision not to seek reelection in 1960.

As the governor of one of the nation's largest states, Williams's name frequently came up as a possible presidential or vice presidential candidate. He never denied interest in either office. At the Democratic National Convention in 1952, the governor was Michigan's favorite-son candidate. Williams supported Senator ESTES KEFAUVER (D-Tenn.) with the expectation that, if the senator won the presidential nomination, he might select Williams as the vice presidential nominee. The nomination, however, went to ADLAI STEVENSON. Political commentators once again mentioned Williams as a presidential contender in 1956, but his forceful advocacy of civil rights, his belief that segregation had to end throughout the nation, and his pro-union record made him unacceptable to the southern Democrats. One incident in particular irritated southerners. Invited to speak at a Democratic fund-raising event in Birmingham, Alabama, in 1955, Williams initially accepted the invitation, but, after finding out that African Americans would be banned from the affair, he publicly refused to attend.

The animosity of southerners in the party did not diminish Williams's enthusiasm for civil rights. In 1957, Williams published an article in the *Nation*, in which he appealed to the Democratic Party to take a more forceful position in support of civil rights for black Americans. The United States, he warned, could not afford to face the world as a nation that did not adhere to its founding principles.

Although he considered it, Williams did not mount a serious candidacy for the Democratic

nomination in 1960. He expressed some interest in Senator JOHN F. KENNEDY's (D-Mass.) candidacy but initially remained skeptical of Kennedy's commitment to liberalism. After a meeting with Kennedy, however, Williams endorsed him on the spot. At the Democratic National Convention, the governor urged delegates from uncommitted states to support Kennedy, who won the Democratic nomination and defeated Vice President RICHARD M. NIXON in the general election that November.

Williams hoped for a position in the cabinet, but Kennedy did not offer him one. In 1961, Kennedy appointed Williams assistant secretary of state for African affairs. After the assassination of Kennedy, Williams had less influence. LYNDON B. JOHNSON, whom Williams had opposed for the vice presidency, became president. Williams remained at the State Department until 1966, when he made an unsuccessful bid for the Senate. Johnson appointed Williams ambassador to the Philippines in 1968, a position he held until 1969. Williams won election to the Michigan Supreme Court in 1970 and served as chief justice from 1982 until his retirement in 1986. He lived in Grosse Pointe Farms until his death in Detroit on February 2, 1988.

—MSM

Williams, Harrison A(rlington), Jr.
(1919–2001) *U.S. congressman and senator*
Born in Plainfield, New Jersey, on December 10, 1919, Williams attended public schools in Plainfield and received a B.A. degree from Oberlin College in 1941. He studied briefly at Georgetown University's School of Foreign Service and worked as a copy boy for the *Washington Post*. After service as a flight instructor in the navy during World War II, he worked as a steelworker in Lorain, Ohio. Williams enrolled in Columbia University Law School and received an LL.B. in 1948. He practiced law in New Hampshire for a year and then returned to Plainfield, where he worked as "a combination clerk and babysitter" for a conservative Republican lawyer. Williams gained admission to the state bar in 1951. That same year, Williams ran unsuccessfully for the state assembly; the following year, he failed in an effort to win a seat on the Plainfield City Council.

In August 1953, Representative CLIFFORD P. CASE, a liberal Republican, resigned his seat from New Jersey's sixth district to run for the Senate. In November 1953, Williams ran as the Democratic candidate in the special election for the seat. The sixth district, which encompassed Union County, had been controlled by Republicans since its creation in 1932. Because the Democratic Party regarded the race as hopeless, Williams had to finance the campaign with his own money. He promised to follow in Case's political footsteps, and he benefited from the successful campaign of the Democratic candidate for governor, ROBERT MEYNER. In the end, Williams defeated his opponent by a narrow margin. He won reelection by a more substantial margin in 1954.

In Congress, Williams supported an anticommunist foreign policy and liberal social programs at home. During 1954, he backed government-supported urban renewal and an extension of unemployment benefits. In 1955, he favored the elimination of the national origins quota system for immigration and the following year supported the Powell amendment, stipulating that no federal aid would go to segregated schools. A fervent cold warrior, he introduced a resolution in 1955 that condemned Soviet violations of agreements that nation had signed with the United States and urged that measures be taken to inform the American people of such infractions. The next year, Williams successfully offered an amendment to the Mutual Security Act terminating all aid to Yugoslavia unless the president declared such aid in the national interest.

In 1956, Williams lost his seat in Congress. His largely Republican district went overwhelmingly for President DWIGHT D. EISENHOWER, and, even though Williams ran well ahead of the national Democratic ticket, it was not enough. He returned to the private practice of law and continued to be involved in Democratic politics. In 1957, he played a major role in Governor Meyner's campaign for reelection. He served as chairman of the Meyner for Governor Clubs, and Meyner's substantial victory revived Williams's political fortunes. The following year, the governor helped him win the state organization's endorsement for the Senate. As a result of Meyner's backing and the economic reces-

sion of 1958, Williams carried the general election by 85,000 votes. He thereby became the first Democrat to win election as senator from New Jersey since 1936.

Williams immediately aligned himself with the Democratic liberals in the Senate. During his first month as a senator, Williams joined the chamber's liberals in backing a proposal by Senator PAUL DOUGLAS (D-Ill.) to change the rules of the Senate to enable a majority vote to end a filibuster. The measure went down to defeat by a vote of 67–28. In March 1960, he joined in an unsuccessful effort to end a southern filibuster against a civil rights bill sponsored by the Eisenhower administration. That same year, he successfully offered an amendment to increase funding for housing for the elderly from $5 million to $50 million (the final bill provided $20 million). He also backed Senator PATRICK V. McNAMARA's (D-Mich.) abortive attempt to provide health care to the elderly through the Social Security system. Williams chaired the Labor and Public Welfare Committee's Special Migratory Labor Subcommittee from its inception in 1959. In June 1961, the subcommittee recommended legislation providing for the extension of the minimum wage to agricultural workers, the application of the child labor provisions of the Fair Labor Standards Act to agriculture, federal registration of farm labor contractors, the inclusion of agricultural employment under the National Labor Relations Act, and the establishment of matching federal grants to the states for education and health programs designed to help migrant workers. Congress passed most of these measures during the administrations of JOHN F. KENNEDY and LYNDON B. JOHNSON. However, the bills providing for a federal minimum wage for agricultural workers and the inclusion of agricultural workers under the collective bargaining and other labor laws did not pass.

A party loyalist, Williams consistently ranked among those senators who voted most frequently with his party. During the Kennedy and Johnson administrations, he regularly backed social welfare programs. He also initially supported the war in Vietnam. In 1966, however, he joined 14 other senators in signing a letter to President Johnson calling for continued suspension of air strikes against North Vietnam. Williams nevertheless voted for appropriations for the war in 1967 and 1968. Not until 1969, when a Republican occupied the White House, did Williams's voting record reflect his doubts about the war in Vietnam and the cold war. In that year, he voted to bar American ground troops from Laos and Thailand; he also voted against the antiballistic missile program. In 1970, Williams voted for the Cooper-Church amendment, which cut off funds for American forces in Indochina after the end of the year.

Personal and ethical problems plagued Williams's last years in the Senate. According to journalist Franklin Pierce, Williams "undercut his own effectiveness for years by heavy drinking . . . until he finally went on the wagon around the end of 1968." In spite of his problems, Williams won reelection in 1970 by a comfortable margin and assumed the chair of the Senate Labor and Public Welfare Committee in January 1971. During the 1970s, he became interested in mine safety and actively maintained his concern for the welfare of the elderly. He sought ways to mitigate the impact of inflation on the elderly and in 1972 introduced a bill designed to prevent abuses of private pension plans (that bill became a law in 1974). Williams also supported the Occupational Safety and Health Act of 1970, the Philadelphia Plan (which required contractors with the federal government in the construction industry to hire quotas of minority workers), and banking reform. He easily won reelection in 1976. One of the congressional targets in an FBI sting operation known as ABSCAM, Williams was convicted on charges of bribery and conspiracy in May 1981. He was fined $50,000 and sentenced to three years in prison. Facing near-certain expulsion from the Senate, he resigned his seat on March 11, 1982. After his release from prison, Williams resided in Bedminster, New Jersey, until his death in Denville, New Jersey, on November 18, 2001.

—MSM

Williams, John J(ames)
(1904–1988) *U.S. senator*

The ninth of 11 children, John Williams was born in Frankford, Delaware, on May 17, 1904. He grew up on a farm in southern Delaware. After graduating from Frankford's high school, he moved to nearby Millsboro and set up a feed business with his brother. The business prospered, and the brothers expanded their ventures to include a hatchery for chickens and turkeys, farms, and timberland. An active Rotarian, a Mason, and a Sunday school teacher, Williams won election to the town council in 1940; he served 14 years in that office.

Despite his obscurity, Williams entered the race for the U.S. Senate in 1946. He disapproved of the way President HARRY S. TRUMAN's administration handled the postwar economic reconversion. In particular, he opposed the continuation of wartime economic regulations. Running for the seat of a popular Democratic incumbent, he had little opposition for the Republican nomination. Few gave him any chance to win the general election, but he campaigned vigorously against government controls and big budgets and was swept into office on the Republican tide of that year. He won reelection in 1952, 1958, and 1964.

In the Senate, he voted, for the most part, as a conservative. He opposed agricultural price support programs, opposed the continuation of the Office of Price Administration, supported tax cuts, and called for a reduction in the number of federal employees. He also worked to promote the poultry industry of Delaware. In foreign policy, he voted against aid to Greece and Turkey in 1947 and the implementation of the Marshall Plan in 1948. He did, however, support the North Atlantic Treaty.

Williams devoted a considerable amount of his time and effort to investigating fraud and abuse in the government. Assigned to the Committee to Investigate the National Defense, Williams participated in the investigation of the companies owned by HOWARD HUGHES. In 1949, he exposed massive discrepancies in the bookkeeping of the Commodities Credit Corporation. The most noteworthy accomplishment of Williams's first term in this regard was his investigation of corruption within the Bureau of Internal Revenue (BIR). From his seat on the Committee on Interstate and Foreign Commerce, he led an investigation that uncovered extensive corruption and favoritism in the BIR. His report, issued in 1951, led to action by Congress and the Justice Department; by November 1953, Williams reported that 380 IRS employees had been fired and over 200 indicted for crimes including bribery, extortion, and embezzlement. The so-called Truman tax scandals led to a reorganization of the system and the establishment of the Internal Revenue Service. Under the new system, tax collectors ceased to be political appointments and were brought under the civil service.

Throughout the 1950s and 1960s, Williams continued to conduct his independent investigations of fraud, waste, and mismanagement within the federal government. Operating without a staff and eschewing the fanfare of committee hearings, he relied on agency informants, the General Accounting Office (GAO), and his own dogged thoroughness. In the mid-1950s, for example, he criticized the government for paying over $2 million for radar equipment to a British manufacturer, then declaring the equipment surplus and selling it back for $114,000. In 1960, he criticized the air force for buying 272,710 screws for $1 each from a contractor who paid the manufacturer 5.5 cents each.

In addition to such waste, Williams sought to expose and eliminate some of the perquisites enjoyed by government employees. His favorite targets were overseas trips taken by members and employees of Congress at public expense. In February 1957, he demanded that public accounting be made of "counterpart funds" (foreign currency supplied by nations receiving aid from the United States) spent by congressional employees on foreign travel. In May 1960, the Senate adopted, by a vote of 68–0, an amendment proposed by Williams that required members of Congress and congressional staff members to submit itemized public accountings of money spent on foreign travel. A House-Senate conference committee cut the amendment. An amendment Williams offered to prohibit government employees from traveling at a reduced rate on any American ship suffered a similar fate in June 1958, but it finally passed in June 1960.

In 1957, Williams tried to return the unused portion of the stationery allowance for his office to the Treasury, which declined to accept the money. This led Williams to a decade-long effort to remedy this situation. Finally, in 1968, Congress passed legislation providing for the return of unexpended congressional stationery allowances to the Treasury. Williams's campaigns against waste and favor-

itism won him the sobriquet "the conscience of the Senate."

During the Eisenhower years, Williams served on the Finance Committee and the Agriculture and Forestry Committee. In 1960, he left the latter for the Foreign Relations Committee. On the Finance Committee, his general opposition to high taxation and big government found expression in actions such as his proposed amendment to the 1953 extension of the excess profits tax. The amendment would have raised the amount of corporate income exempt from the tax from $25,000 to $100,000, but it was defeated, 52–34.

On the other hand, Williams strove to eliminate various tax loopholes favored by others on the Finance Committee. Throughout the 1950s, he tried and failed to lower the 27.5 percent oil depletion allowance. Williams also voted against various tax reductions. For example, in June 1958 he voted not to repeal the 3 percent excise tax on freight shipments and the 10 percent levy on passenger travel. Among 15 Republican senators seeking reelection that year, he was the only one to vote against the popular tax cuts.

Consistent in his support of free markets, Williams supported the Eisenhower administration's farm program, which proposed to make price supports more flexible. In June 1956, Williams said that rigid price supports continued "to stimulate wasteful production." In the same month, Williams opposed additional airline subsidies. "Let us not fool ourselves," he said; "this is a little extra gravy for a special group that has already been riding the gravy train." He also sought to reduce subsidies to the maritime industry.

One of the most conservative members of the Senate on domestic issues, Williams consistently voted against social welfare legislation. In 1959 and 1960, he voted against a foreign aid authorization, federal aid to education, federal aid to depressed areas, an increase in the minimum wage, larger appropriations for housing and public works, and a Democratic plan to provide medical care for the elderly through the Social Security system.

A moderate on civil rights issues, Williams believed that the Supreme Court's decision striking down segregated public schools (*Brown v. Board of Education* [1954]) encroached on the right of states to establish their own policies with respect to education. Nevertheless, he opposed extralegal opposition to the decision. When an agitator from a group that called itself the National Association for the Advancement of White People came to Delaware in the aftermath of the *Brown* decision, Williams publicly called for order. He stated that, while citizens might disagree with the Supreme Court's decision (as he acknowledged that he did), they had a civic duty to observe the law as declared by the Court. He voted for the Civil Rights Acts of 1957, but not until the measure was amended to provide a jury trial for those charged with criminal contempt for interfering with black voting rights. He also voted for the Civil Rights Act of 1960.

Beginning in 1958, a subcommittee of the House Interstate and Foreign Commerce Committee investigated charges that Eisenhower's chief of staff, SHERMAN ADAMS, had accepted a vicuna coat and other gifts from BERNARD GOLDFINE, an industrialist, and had allowed Goldfine to pay some of Adams's hotel bills. Moreover, the committee looked into charges that Adams had used his influence on behalf of Goldfine, who had tax problems as well as regulatory problems with the Securities and Exchange Commission. In 1959, Williams called for the resignation of Adams.

During the 1960s, Williams continued to pursue his one-man investigations and to champion more stringent ethical requirements for Congress. He opposed several of President JOHN F. KENNEDY's ambassadorial appointments because of their involvement in questionable business dealings. In 1962, he requested an investigation of Billie Sol Estes, a Texan who had fraudulently manipulated the Department of Agriculture's programs of crop control allotments and grain storage. In 1963, an independent inquiry by Williams turned up important information on the unethical practices (including tax fraud and influence peddling) of Robert G. ("Bobby") Baker, secretary to the Senate majority and a protégé of LYNDON B. JOHNSON. Williams's investigation uncovered much of the information used in the subsequent hearings of the Senate Rules Committee. Although he was not on the Rules Committee, he was invited to sit in on its sessions. His insistence on a thorough investigation of the matter brought him into conflict with

the committee. Williams clashed with the committee when it voted to limit the investigation to staff members, thereby excluding senators. His activities also earned him the enmity of Johnson, who made a serious, but ultimately unsuccessful, effort to defeat Williams in his bid for reelection in 1964.

Williams initially criticized the Johnson administration for what he regarded as a half-hearted commitment to Vietnam, but by 1967 he concluded that victory was improbable and that negotiations would have to end the conflict. Williams did not support the incursion into Cambodia ordered by President RICHARD M. NIXON in 1970. At the same time, he opposed the Cooper-Church amendment, which would have cut off funding for the war. Moreover, Williams was appalled by actions of antiwar demonstrators. Much as he had done with respect to opposition to the *Brown* decision in 1954, he called on people to observe the law and to maintain order.

When President Johnson sought a tax increase in 1969, Williams, recognizing that an increase was inevitable, began to lobby for simultaneous and mandatory cuts in federal spending. Williams opposed the Nixon administration's Family Assistance Plan, a proposal to reform the welfare system. He also voted against the nomination of CLEMENT F. HAYNSWORTH to the Supreme Court. Williams chose not to run for a fifth term in 1970. He resigned from the Senate on December 31, 1970, in order to give his successor and protégé, William V. Roth, Jr., seniority over other members elected in 1970. After leaving the Senate, he retired to his home in Millsboro, Delaware, and devoted his efforts to real estate and farming. He died in Lewes, Delaware, on January 11, 1988.

—MSM

Wilson, Charles E(rwin)
(1890–1961) *secretary of defense*

The son of a high school principal, Charles Wilson was born in Minerva, Ohio, on July 18, 1890. He moved with his family to Mineral City, Ohio, in 1894; 10 years later, the family moved to Pittsburgh, Pennsylvania. Wilson earned a degree in electrical engineering from the Carnegie Institute of Technology in 1909. He then went to work at

Charles E. Wilson, Secretary of Defense *(Dwight D. Eisenhower Library and Museum)*

Westinghouse Electric as an apprentice engineer. There he designed the company's first motor for automobile starters and by 1916 was in charge of all of Westinghouse's production of electrical equipment for automobiles. During World War I, he designed dynamotors and radio generators for the military. He also designed a primitive crystal set for use by the infantry. In 1919, Wilson joined the Remy Electric Company, a subsidiary of General Motors (GM), as chief engineer and sales manager of the company's automobile division; he became general manager of the company in 1925. When Remy merged with Delco in 1926, Wilson became president and general manager of the combined company. In 1928, Wilson moved to the parent company as a vice president and special assistant to Alfred P. Sloan, the head of GM. Wilson joined GM's board of directors and became executive vice president in 1934. When GM's president, William S. Knudsen, went to Washington in 1940 to become director of defense production, Wilson became acting president. Upon Knudsen's resignation in 1941, Wilson became president of GM.

Wilson led the company through World War II and the postwar era. Under his leadership, the company geared up for military production, although it continued to produce automobiles for civilian use until early 1942. Between 1942 and 1945, the company sold $13.4 billion worth of goods; production for the military accounted for over 90 percent of that total. GM made tanks, armored trucks, aircraft, arms, and ammunition. GM accounted for the production of approximately one-quarter of all tanks, armored cars, and airplane engines built in the United States during the war. It made almost half the machine guns and carbines as well as two-thirds of heavy trucks. Soon after the war, Wilson replaced Sloan as GM's chief executive officer and continued as president of the company. He oversaw the company's reconversion to civilian production. By the end of the 1940s, GM made more than 6 million cars and trucks annually and accounted for 43 percent of new car sales.

Wilson also became a prominent figure in postwar labor relations. He helped create a social contract under which big business gave recognition to organized labor and paid good wages and benefits in exchange for stability, predictability, and control over the process of production. From the mid-1930s until he left the company to go to Washington, Wilson led GM in its bargaining with the United Auto Workers (UAW). Immediately after World War II, WALTER REUTHER, the head of the UAW, led a 113-day strike against GM, demanding a wage increase without price increases. Wilson refused to yield to those demands. Over the years, however, Wilson developed a mutually respectful relationship with Reuther. In 1948, Wilson introduced the cost-of-living adjustment, which tied wages to government price indexes. He also agreed to regular pay increases tied to increases in productivity. The plan drew praise from labor leaders and won rapid acceptance. The contract GM negotiated with the UAW in 1950, known as the Treaty of Detroit, established a pension plan for GM's workers. At the same time, Wilson and GM steadfastly refused to surrender control over personnel or the details of production.

After winning the presidential election in 1952, DWIGHT D. EISENHOWER named Wilson secretary of defense. Eisenhower had first become impressed with Wilson when, as army chief of staff, he consulted the executive on problems relating to production and supply. The president-elect thought it a good idea for the secretary of defense to have expertise in management as well as procurement, storage, transportation, and distribution. As head of GM, Wilson had such qualifications, and Eisenhower offered him the position in late 1952.

Wilson almost immediately became a center of controversy. During hearings on his nomination, members of the Senate Armed Services Committee expressed concern that his holdings of stock in General Motors, the nation's largest defense contractor, could constitute a conflict of interest. Members of the panel, therefore demanded that he sell his nearly 40,000 shares worth approximately $2.5 million. Wilson objected in what at least some of the senators regarded as an arrogant manner. For Wilson, the whole matter was infuriating; he was leaving a job that paid some $600,000 a year for one that paid $22,500. Asked if he would be able to make a decision in the national interest even if it had "extremely adverse" consequences for General Motors, Wilson answered, "Yes, sir, I could. I cannot conceive of one because for years, I thought what was good for the country was good for General Motors and vice versa." Subsequently he was frequently misquoted as having said "What's good for General Motors is good for the country." After Eisenhower told him that he would have to sell his stock, Wilson announced on January 22 that he would do so; the following day, the Senate overwhelmingly approved his nomination.

Wilson saw his role as mainly administrative and operational rather than as one involving the formulation of policy. Eisenhower would make military policy and Secretary of State JOHN FOSTER DULLES would give instructions on foreign affairs. During his first year at Defense, Wilson undertook a major reorganization of the department. The secretary cut nearly 40,000 civilian employees from the Defense Department staff, canceled or held up many military building programs, and instituted the "narrow base" approach to procurement, which directed production to large, and presumably more

efficient, suppliers. His reorganization gave the service secretaries more responsibility. It strengthened civilian control, facilitated implementation of the secretary's decisions, improved communications, and provided better means for strategic planning. By the end of his first year, Wilson pared his staff from 3,100 to 2,400.

Throughout his tenure as secretary of defense, Wilson never established good relations with the press. Known as a generally good-natured fellow and an excellent man to work under, he nevertheless had an unfortunate habit of putting his foot in his mouth. When asked his opinion about assistance for unemployed workers, he stated that he preferred "hunting dogs to kennel-fed dogs because the hunting dogs or bird dogs would get out and hunt for what they wanted; whereas the kennel-fed dog would set back his haunches and yelp." The fact that this occurred during the congressional elections in 1954 made the matter all the worse. On another occasion, Wilson stated that he wanted to cut back the National Guard and added that the guard was not much of a fighting force. He then said that those who enlisted in the guard during the Korean War did so to evade regular military service. That brought a public rebuke from the president, who called it "a very . . . unwise statement." The secretary's propensity for unfortunate public statements led JAMES RESTON, a columnist for the *New York Times*, to quip that Wilson invented the automatic transmission so that he would be free to drive with one foot in his mouth.

Regardless of his lack of verbal discretion, Wilson lined up behind Eisenhower's New Look defense policy, which called for a reduction in the defense budget and reliance on airpower, technology, and the nuclear deterrent rather than costly conventional forces. In his usual blunt manner, Wilson said that the shift in policy would give the United States "a bigger bang for a buck." From the outset, the policy encountered fierce resistance from Democrats and some Republicans. Between December 1953 and June 1955, the army's budget was cut from nearly $13 billion to $7 billion; its manpower was reduced from 1.5 million to 1 million men. During the same period, the navy and marines contracted from 1 million to 870,000 men. On the other hand, the number of air force personnel rose from 950,000 in 1953 to 970,000 in 1955, and its budget increased from $16.4 billion in 1955 to $18 billion in fiscal 1957.

By 1955, many prominent military officials publicly opposed the administration's New Look. Wilson issued a gag directive to stop their writing. However, the retiring chief of staff, General MATTHEW B. RIDGWAY, leaked proof of the army's discontent and published a series of articles in *Life* magazine. Wilson's order became a source of criticism of him and the administration.

Opposition to the New Look along with fierce interservice rivalries frustrated Wilson. By the mid-1950s, critics accused the New Look for weakening the nation's military and limiting its flexibility. Moreover, Eisenhower lost patience with Wilson's verbal gaffes and became frustrated with Wilson's unwillingness to make decisions. Even in the quotidian running of the department, an area where one would have expected Wilson to excel, Wilson disappointed Eisenhower, who thought that Wilson wanted to pass on too many decisions to the president. "Look here, Charlie," a frustrated president told his defense secretary, "I want *you* to run Defense. We *both* can't run it, and I *won't* run it. I was elected to worry about a lot of things other than the day-to-day operations of a department."

Weary of the disputes and the pace, Wilson submitted his resignation in August 1957 and left the Defense Department in October. He returned to his business activities, which included a dairy farm in Michigan, a cattle ranch in Florida, and a plantation in Louisiana. Wilson also served as a member of the board of directors of General Motors, a director of the National Bank of Detroit, and chairman of the Michigan advisory committee to the U.S. Commission on Civil Rights. He died at his plantation in Norwood, Louisiana, on September 26, 1961. His obituary in the *New York Times* misquoted him as having said: "What's good for General Motors is good for the country."

—MSM

Wilson, Sloan
(1920–2003) *author*

The son of a university professor, Wilson was born in Norwalk, Connecticut, on May 8, 1920. After attending Phillips Exeter Academy, he entered Harvard College in 1938, where he majored in psychology and philosophy. Wilson interrupted his education in 1942 to join the coast guard. Commissioned a reserve ensign, he served in the North Atlantic and South Pacific before his discharge as a lieutenant in 1945. The following year, he returned to Harvard and received his B.A. He wrote articles for the *New Yorker* and other magazines about how former servicemen were adjusting, or failing to adjust, to civilian life. In 1947, Wilson published *Voyage to Somewhere*, his first novel, which was based on his wartime experience in the South Pacific. Following a brief stint as a reporter for the *Providence Journal*, he joined *Time* magazine as a reporter and then became an assistant to Roy Larsen, the president of Time-Life. From 1949 to 1952, he worked for the National Citizens Commission for Public Schools. In 1952, Wilson became information director and an assistant professor of English at the University of Buffalo. He left the University of Buffalo in 1955. That same year, he was appointed as assistant director of the White House Conference on Education. He worked at *Parents* magazine and the *New York Herald-Tribune* before becoming a freelance writer in 1958.

Wilson published *The Man in the Gray Flannel Suit* in July 1955. It quickly became a best seller. Distinguished in neither style nor composition, the novel nevertheless attracted the interest of middle-class America. Wilson wrote about a new type of American who staffed the growing service sector of the economy, in particular those who worked in the media and advertising industries. These white-collar workers and their world had already drawn the attention of DAVID RIESMAN in *The Lonely Crowd* (1950) and C. WRIGHT MILLS in *White Collar* (1950). They were also the subject of WILLIAM WHYTE's *The Organization Man* (1956). The organization men described by Riesman, Whyte, Mills, and Wilson worked in unsatisfying circumstances to produce an intangible product. Fleeing cities for the good life in suburbia, these commuters found fulfillment illusory there, too. Despite a reasonable income that provided a comfortable middle-class life, the pressures on the men in gray flannel proved endless: a bigger house, a better car, private schools for the children. Moreover, these men found themselves cut off from traditional values like heroism, found no purpose in work or suburban life, and saw no way to deal with their problems. Wilson's novel dealt with the malaise of these conformist, status-hungry, executive commuters.

The central figure of Wilson's novel, Tom Rath, is a veteran of World War II who works for a charitable foundation and likes the work. He and Betsy, his wife of 12 years, have three small children and live in an unprepossessing house in Westport, Connecticut. Tom's income will not support their social aspirations, and their lives are blighted by "a thousand petty shabbinesses"; the house needs repair, as does their car and washing machine. Driven by the desire to make more money, Tom gives up his job at the foundation and takes a job at the Union Broadcasting Corporation. In order to succeed, he must become Whyte's organization man. In the end, he quits the rat race but gets rich anyway. The happy ending blunts the social criticism of the book; as the novel closes, he is about to develop the land left to him by his grandmother. Whatever its artistic shortcomings, the novel struck a chord, and its title entered the language.

The book received mixed reviews. The reviewer for the *New York Times* called it "a good novel—neat, smooth and reportorially exact in its account of the pressures, problems and tribal customs of the men in grey flannel suits, the ambitious commuters who are too young to be either successes or failures but whose time is running out." Perhaps because the egocentric head of the fictional Union Broadcasting Corporation in the novel resembled Roy Larsen, the president of *Time* magazine, the review in *Time* dismissed *The Man in the Gray Flannel Suit* as "upper-middle-class soap opera."

In 1956, the novel was made into a movie directed by Nunally Johnson and starring Gregory Peck and Jennifer Jones. The movie received widespread critical acclaim that the book did not. It was also a hit at the box office.

Wilson followed his first success with *A Summer Place*, published in 1958. The story revolves around Ken and Sylvia, teen lovers divided by wealth and social status. Ken, the son of a Swedish immigrant, is working as a lifeguard at a resort in Pine Island, Maine, where Sylvia's family arrives as guests. In spite of her love for Ken, Sylvia's parents push her into marriage with a young man,

Bart, from a wealthy family. An alcoholic boor, Bart loses the fortune he inherited from his father and has to turn the family house on Pine Island into an inn. Ken, who becomes rich through his work as a research chemist, marries Helen, a woman obsessed with status and appearances. The plot gets under way when Ken and Helen book rooms at the inn owned by Bart and Sylvia. Ken's daughter, Molly, and Sylvia's son, Johnny, are attracted to each other. Ken and Sylvia have an affair that results in divorce for both of them. Eventually Ken and Sylvia marry and, when Molly becomes pregnant by Johnny, the reunited couple guides their children to marry.

The book's frank depiction of adultery, divorce, and teenage sex attracted considerable attention when it was published. Wilson also satirized racial and religious bigotry. Taken together, *A Summer Place* and *The Man in the Gray Flannel Suit* challenged the American dream of personal happiness through economic success. Driven by a high-powered advertising campaign, sales of *A Summer Place* earned Wilson over a million dollars. Many serious writers and critics were repelled by what they regarded as the crass campaign to sell the book (and perhaps by jealousy); they spurned Wilson as greedy and commercial. *A Summer Place* became a film in 1959 starring Troy Donahue and Sandra Dee.

Wilson's greatest success as a novelist came in the 1950s. Over a dozen subsequent novels received an indifferent response from critics and enjoyed nothing like the sales of *The Man in the Gray Flannel Suit* or *A Summer Place*. Wilson published *A Sense of Values* in 1960 and the following year took a job teaching English at New York University. He began drinking heavily and sank into depression and alcoholism. His career turned downward, but he continued to write, publishing *Georgie Winthrop* in 1963, *Janus Island* in 1967, and *All the Best People* in 1970. He found help for his psychological problems in the form of drug therapy and overcame his alcoholism with the assistance of family. In 1976, he published *What Shall We Wear to This Party?*, which described his life before and after the mid-1950s and received a warmer critical reception than the fiction he wrote after the 1950s.

He based *Ice Brothers* (1979) on his experience as commander of a trawler in the North Atlantic and another novel, *Pacific Interlude* (1982), on his experiences in the South Pacific. *Small Town* (1978) and *The Greatest Crime* (1980) failed to attract critical acclaim or to sell well. A sequel to *The Man in the Gray Flannel Suit, The Man in the Gray Flannel Suit II* (1984) took Tom Rath, amicably divorced from Betsy, to Washington to work for the Kennedy administration. The sequel was a critical and commercial flop.

Wilson lived in Florida for many years and, for a time in the 1980s, was a distinguished writer in residence at Rollins College in Florida. He moved in 1999 to Colonial Beach, Virginia, where he died on May 25, 2003.

—MSM

Wisdom, John Minor

(1905–1999) *federal appellate judge*

Wisdom was born into a prominent family in New Orleans, Louisiana, on May 17, 1905. His father, a cotton broker, businessman, and a member of the old Democratic establishment of New Orleans, had belonged to the White League, which opposed the integrated city government of New Orleans during Reconstruction. John Minor Wisdom earned his B.A. from Washington and Lee University in 1925. After spending a year as a graduate student in English literature at Harvard, he returned to New Orleans to study law and received his LL.B. from Tulane University in 1929. Upon graduating first in his law school class, he remained in New Orleans, where he established a successful practice, specializing in estates and trusts. Wisdom also taught part time at Tulane Law School. During World War II, he rose to the rank of lieutenant colonel in the legal service of the U.S. Army. While still in law school, Wisdom became concerned that Huey Long threatened democracy in Louisiana, so he joined the Republican Party. After the war, he became convinced that one-party rule had led to political stagnation in the South. In the late 1940s and early 1950s, Wisdom devoted considerable time and effort trying to build a Republican Party in Louisiana. His efforts brought him into contact with ELBERT PARR TUTTLE, who was trying to establish a Republican Party in Georgia; their efforts attracted the attention of national Republican leaders.

Wisdom was active in promoting the candidacy of DWIGHT D. EISENHOWER for the presidency in 1952. Tuttle and Wisdom helped launch the Eisenhower movement in the South, and, in February 1952, a group of 15 Eisenhower supporters from the South chose Wisdom to chair the Southern Conference for Eisenhower; Tuttle served as vice chair. Wisdom traveled Louisiana, helping to organize local conventions to choose members for the Louisiana delegation to the Republican National Convention. A pro-Eisenhower slate, which included Wisdom, contested the party regulars, who supported Senator ROBERT A. TAFT (R-Ohio). Similar challenges came from Georgia and Texas. After a brilliant and lawyerly presentation by Wisdom, the Credentials Committee seated the pro-Eisenhower delegation from Louisiana; Tuttle's delegation from Georgia lost in the Credentials Committee but defeated the pro-Taft regulars in a vote on the convention floor. The defeat of the party regulars from the South led to Eisenhower's victory in the battle for the nomination.

During the general election, Wisdom campaigned for Eisenhower in Louisiana. After the election, he continued his involvement in politics and won election as Republican National Committeeman from Louisiana, a position he held from 1952 until he went on the bench. President Eisenhower appointed him to the president's Committee on Government Contracts, chaired by Vice President RICHARD M. NIXON and created to insure that contractors with the federal government did not discriminate for reasons of race, religion, creed, or national origin.

Possessed of a scholarly bent, Wisdom published articles in the areas of admiralty as well as estates and trusts. In addition, he engaged in a wide variety of civic activities, including service as president of the New Orleans Council of Social Agencies and as a board member of the National Urban League. A courtly and courteous individual, Wisdom, in spite of his outspoken opposition to segregation, managed to retain the friendship of conservatives with whom he had been raised. A member of the social elite, Wisdom continued his affiliations with exclusive private clubs and Mardi Gras crewes that excluded African Americans and Jews. Wisdom defended his decision not to resign from such organizations by pointing out that the members knew how he stood "on these matters" and that his resignation would not have changed their views.

In 1957, President Eisenhower appointed Wisdom to the U.S. Court of Appeals for the Fifth Circuit. There he joined Tuttle, whom Eisenhower had named to the Fifth Circuit in 1954. At that time, the Fifth Circuit comprised Louisiana, Florida, Alabama, Mississippi, Texas, and Georgia. Tuttle emerged as the leader of the court. Particularly after he became chief judge in 1961, Tuttle performed a role similar to that of EARL WARREN on the Supreme Court.

Widely read in history, literature, and political philosophy, as well as law, Wisdom quickly emerged as the intellectual leader of the Fifth Circuit. His elegantly crafted opinions defined the philosophical and legal matters facing the court. He aligned himself with the court's liberal, antisegregationist bloc, which included Tuttle, Richard T. Rives, and John R. Brown. These four judges led the Fifth Circuit in desegregating the Deep South as they implemented the Supreme Court's decision in *Brown v. Board of Education* (1954). Wisdom played a large role in leading the court to interpret *Brown* as demanding not just an end to segregated public schools but an end to discrimination in voting, employment, and jury selection. Similarly, the Fifth Circuit held that *Brown* required the desegregation of public parks, playgrounds, community centers, and cultural facilities. Careful legal craftsmanship, a broad knowledge of history, and graceful prose characterized Wisdom's many decisions for the court.

Wisdom came to the court with the belief that segregation, as he said in an interview in 1983, "was just plain wrong." His courageous stand against segregation made him the target of political vituperation by segregationist politicians as well as more direct and personal assaults. He received threatening phone calls, rattlesnakes were thrown into the courtyard garden of his home, and two of his pet dogs were poisoned. Wisdom nevertheless refused to get an unlisted phone number and claimed never to have lost a friend.

Wisdom wrote many of the decisions that broke down legal segregation in the Deep South. In 1961 he struck down Louisiana's school closing law after St. Helena Parish voted to close its public schools rather than to desegregate (*St. Helena Parish School Board v. Hall*).

He also wrote the decision in 1962 that found that the University of Mississippi had denied admission to James Meredith solely on the basis of his race (*Meredith v. Fair*). Wisdom castigated the university officials for engaging "in a carefully calculated campaign of delay, harassment and masterly inactivity" and ordered the admission of Meredith to the university. The decision led to three days of rioting in which three people were killed. Writing for the court, in *United States v. Louisiana* (1963), Wisdom struck down a Louisiana statute that required black voters to interpret passages of the United States Constitution or that of the state of Louisiana to pass the literacy test. "We hold," wrote Wisdom, "that this wall, built to bar Negroes from access to the franchise, must come down." The decision included a masterly history of direct and indirect means of excluding black political participation in Louisiana.

Wisdom wrote the opinion in *U.S. v. Jefferson County* (1968), which held that the Constitution did not merely forbid legally enforced segregation but required integration. "The law," wrote Wisdom, "imposes an absolute duty to . . . disestablish segregation" as well as "an absolute duty to integrate." He advocated "the planned organized undoing of the effects of past segregation" and, in doing so laid the philosophical groundwork for affirmative action. "The only school desegregation plan that meets constitutional standards," he wrote, "is one that works."

Wisdom took senior judge status in 1977 but continued to hear cases into his 90s. In 1993, President William Jefferson Clinton awarded Wisdom the Presidential Medal of Freedom. Wisdom died in New Orleans on May 15, 1999.

—MSM

Wolfson, Louis E(lwood)

(1912–2007) *industrialist*

The son of Russian Jewish immigrants, Wolfson was born in St. Louis, Missouri, on January 28, 1912. He grew up in Jacksonville, Florida, where he excelled in athletics. A football star in high school, he also boxed professionally under the name "Kid Wolf" as a youth. He attended the University of Georgia, but he left after two years to work in his father's scrap yard. Wolfson raised $10,000 to start Florida Pipe and Supply Company, which dealt in building materials. Before long, he had created a substantial business. During World War II, Florida Pipe and Supply held over $4.5 million in government contracts. After the war, he extended his interests into real estate and shipbuilding. At the end of the war, he bought a surplus shipyard in Jacksonville from the government. He bought Merritt-Chapman & Scott Corporation, a conglomerate that began as a construction firm but expanded into ship building, chemicals, and money lending.

In 1949, he became majority shareholder and board chairman of Capital Transit Company, which provided streetcar and bus service for Washington, D.C. In that capacity, he became a favorite villain of the capital city. That image became firmly ensconced when he admitted to *Time* magazine that he had milked the company of its surplus by paying large dividends to shareholders, many of whom were his associates. In the meantime, fare prices went up, the company's profits lagged, and a strike shut down operations for 51 days in the summer of 1955. On August 1, 1955, Congress voted to revoke Wolfson's franchise. After O. Roy Chalk took over the system, customers continued to complain about fare hikes and poor service.

Wolfson regarded himself as a savior of moribund businesses who turned out stagnant leadership and revived failing enterprises. Typically, he bought up companies whose book values exceeded the value of their common stock and then moved in with his own management. In fact, he did successfully revive a number of failing firms. His aggressive management style, though, contributed to his reputation as a corporate raider concerned only with making money for himself and his associates. By the mid-1950s, he had built an empire worth roughly $200 million.

Between 1954 and 1958, Wolfson attempted to win control of two major corporations: Montgomery Ward & Company, the nation's second largest retailer, and American Motors Corporation (AMC), the fourth largest domestic auto producer. Wolfson's campaign to control Montgomery Ward commenced in August 1954, when the financier and his associates began to purchase large blocks of the company's common stock. Management problems at Montgomery Ward aided Wolfson's cause. The company's chairman of the board, SEWELL AVERY, though past his 80th birthday, still single-handedly ran the company and had allowed it to stagnate. Despite a protracted eight-month struggle and a court fight, Wolfson failed to acquire Ward; he secured just under 1 percent of the company's stock. Through his initiative, however, he won for himself and two allies places on the board of directors and forced Avery's retirement. Wolfson declared Avery's resignation to be a victory for his side, which had "succeeded in infusing new blood into the Ward management." Curiously, Wolfson quit the board in January 1956.

A year later, Wolfson attempted to gain control of AMC, which had been created when several auto concerns had merged in January 1954. Wolfson had owned a large number of shares in one of those companies, Hudson, and used this block as the base for his acquisitions. In October 1956, Wolfson threatened AMC president GEORGE ROMNEY with a stock takeover unless he partially liquidated some of AMC's assets. Unable to compete with the industry's three leaders and in desperate need of new financing, AMC management appeared vulnerable. Romney, however, persuaded Wolfson, by then the largest individual stockholder, to delay acting against management and not to demand a place on the board of directors. Wolfson issued a statement in support of Romney and dropped his campaign. Wolfson profited from his cooperation. By 1958, AMC had markedly improved its sales and earnings. As his the value of his stock rose, Wolfson sold his holdings for a profit of $2 million.

During the mid-1960s, Wolfson became the target of an investigation by the Securities and Exchange Commission (SEC) into his manipulation of the stock of Continental Enterprises, a company in which Wolfson held a controlling interest. Ultimately, he was convicted in 1967 and again in 1968 on federal charges stemming from stock sales. The first conviction involved Wolfson's sale of unregistered shares in Continental Enterprises. He did not deny the specifics of the allegations but argued that the law was misapplied. In September 1967, he was convicted on 19 counts of conspiracy and illegal stock sales. His lawyers appealed all the way to the Supreme Court, which refused to hear the appeal. Wolfson served nine months in federal prison and paid a substantial fine. The second conviction, for perjury, obstruction of justice, and filing misleading annual reports, involved an investigation by the SEC into Merritt-Chapman & Scott. The U.S. Court of Appeals for the Second Circuit reversed this conviction in 1970. Two subsequent trials resulted in hung juries. Wolfson agreed to a plea bargain in which he pleaded no contest to the charges and avoided additional time in prison.

Wolfson's ties to Supreme Court justice Abe Fortas contributed to the withdrawal of Fortas's nomination to replace EARL WARREN as chief justice and led to Fortas's resignation from the Court in May 1969. In January 1966, not long after taking his seat as an associate justice, Fortas agreed to serve as a consultant to Wolfson's charitable foundation, in exchange for which the foundation paid Fortas an annual fee of $20,000 for the rest of his life. At that time, Wolfson was already under investigation for suspected securities violations. After Wolfson was indicted, Fortas returned the money in December 1966 and recused himself from the case. Nevertheless, when *Life* magazine published an article about Fortas's arrangement in May 1969, the public outcry forced the justice's resignation from the Court.

In the late 1960s, Wolfson lived in Miami Beach, Florida. He established Harbor View Farm, a thoroughbred horse farm near Ocala, Florida. He bred, raised, and raced Affirmed, a horse that won the Triple Crown in 1978. Wolfson died at his home in Bal Harbour, Florida, on December 30, 2007.

—MSM

Wright, J(ames) Skelly

(1911–1988) *U.S. district court judge*

The son of a city building superintendent and plumbing inspector, Wright was born in New Orleans, Louisiana, on January 14, 1911. He grew up in a working-class neighborhood and attended the city's public schools. Wright went to Loyola University on a scholarship and graduated from that institution in 1931. That year he began teaching mathematics and English at Fortier High

School. While working as a high school teacher, he attended Loyola University Law School, from which he received a degree in 1934. He continued teaching at Fortier until 1935 and held an appointment as a lecturer in English history at Loyola from 1936 to 1937. Through the political connections of an uncle, Wright became an assistant U.S. attorney for New Orleans in 1937; he remained in that position until he entered the coast guard in 1942. During World War II, he served as commander of a submarine chaser in the North Atlantic and then as an attaché at the American embassy in London. After leaving the coast guard in 1945, he returned to the U.S. attorney's office in New Orleans as senior assistant to U.S. attorney Herbert Christenberry. In spring 1946, Wright opened a law office in Washington, D.C. The next year, he entered a partnership with two other attorneys. Wright's practice primarily dealt with maritime and shipping matters. In 1948, he returned to New Orleans as U.S. attorney for the eastern district of Louisiana. The following year, President HARRY S. TRUMAN appointed Wright to a U.S. district court judgeship for the eastern district of Louisiana.

As a district judge during the 1950s, Wright presided over many cases involving desegregation and civil rights. Even before the Supreme Court declared segregated public schools unconstitutional in *Brown v. Board of Education* (1954), Wright ordered the admission of black students to the law school at Louisiana State University on the ground that the law school for African Americans at Southern University was not equal to the white institution. In 1957, he held that laws designed to keep Louisiana State University and other state universities segregated were unconstitutional. The following year, he ordered the desegregation of transportation facilities in New Orleans. In 1959, Wright ruled unconstitutional a law banning sports events in which both whites and blacks participated, and in 1960 he ordered registrars in Washington parish registrars to restore African Americans to the voting rolls.

However controversial those decisions may have been, Wright's decisions desegregating the public schools of New Orleans made him the most hated man in the state. In 1952, the NAACP filed a suit against the Orleans Parish School Board to desegregate the public schools (*Bush v. Orleans Parish School Board*). Both the NAACP and the school board assented to Wright's decision to postpone a ruling until the Supreme Court had decided *Brown*. In the aftermath of *Brown*, Louisiana joined other southern states in employing a number of devices to thwart desegregation. One such device was the enactment of pupil placement laws. In February 1956, Wright sat on a three-judge panel that struck down Louisiana's pupil placement laws. Then, sitting alone, Wright ordered the school board to make arrangements to desegregate "with all deliberate speed" but explained that his order did not require it be done "overnight" or "even in a year or more." The Fifth Circuit Court of Appeals upheld Wright's order.

A series of appeals delayed action on the case, but in 1959 the NAACP got Wright to order the school board to submit a desegregation plan by March 1960. When it refused, Wright ordered integration to begin in September 1960 on a grade-per-year basis. In response, the governor of Louisiana, JIMMIE DAVIS, took control of the schools under a recently enacted statute in an attempt to close them and thus maintain segregation. Wright then issued restraining orders prohibiting the school closings. On November 14, four black first graders entered two previously all-white schools amid the protests of taunting white mobs. In 1962, Wright issued his final order in the matter of public schools in New Orleans. Frustrated with the lack of progress toward desegregation, he ordered the public schools of New Orleans to desegregate beginning with the fall term. Wright ruled that pupils in first through sixth grades could choose to attend the school nearest his or her home rather than the school to which the school board had assigned the pupil. Wright's successor, Frank Ellis, modified the ruling in May to require only the first grade be integrated by September 1962. On appeal, the Fifth Circuit modified Ellis's order. The appellate court ruled that students in grades one through three should be given the option to attend the school nearest their residence and that the option be extended to the first five grades by 1964.

In the course of the litigation over public schools in New Orleans, Wright became a pariah. Crosses were burned on his lawn; he received threatening telephone calls; state politicians denounced him in the most immoderate language and even urged citizens to defy his orders. Federal marshals guarded his home and escorted him to and from his chambers. Old friends refused to recognize him.

If it were possible, Wright further alienated the people of New Orleans and Louisiana when he held in 1962 that Tulane University was a "public institution" because it received a "very substantial state subsidy." Therefore, he reasoned, the university was subject to the Fourteenth Amendment's ban on state-sanctioned discrimination. Accordingly, he ordered the university to admit two black students.

President JOHN F. KENNEDY considered appointing Wright to the Fifth Circuit Court of Appeals but ultimately decided not to, because he thought opposition from southern senators would make confirmation unlikely. Instead, Kennedy appointed Wright to the U.S. Court of Appeals for the District of Columbia in 1962. As an appellate judge during the 1960s, Wright continued to hand down important civil rights decisions. In a special circumstance, Wright sat as a district judge in 1967 and heard a controversial case involving segregation in the public schools of Washington, D.C. Wright ruled unconstitutional a tracking system that resulted in the de facto segregation of black students in the District of Columbia's public schools (*Hobson v. Hanson*). During the 1970s, Wright handed down significant decisions dealing with the Alaska pipeline, military justice, and nuclear reactors. In 1973, Wright was a member of the circuit court that ordered President RICHARD M. NIXON to release the Watergate tapes. Wright served as chief judge of the Court of Appeals for Washington, D.C., from 1978 to 1981. He took senior judge status in 1987. Wright died at his home in Westmoreland Hills, Maryland, on August 6, 1988.

—MSM

Y

Yarborough, Ralph W(ebster)

(1903–1996) *U.S. senator*

Born on a farm in Chandler, Texas, on June 8, 1903, Yarborough went to local schools before attending the U.S. military academy in 1919 and 1920. He then taught school in Henderson County while attending Sam Houston State Teacher's College. He also worked in agriculture and building oil tanks. He paid his way to Europe by working on a freighter and lived in Germany, where he was assistant secretary for the American Chamber of Commerce in Berlin. After returning to the United States, Yarborough received an LL.B. from the University of Texas at Austin in 1927 and was admitted to the Texas bar in the same year. He joined a law firm in El Paso. He served as an assistant attorney general of Texas from 1931 to 1935. From 1936 to 1941, he served as a judge of the 53rd judicial district. In 1938, Yarborough ran unsuccessfully for state attorney general. A member of the Texas national guard in the 1930s, he joined the army in 1943. During World War II, he served as an infantry officer in Europe and in the occupation government of Japan. He won a bronze star. After his discharge as a lieutenant colonel in 1946, he practiced law in Austin.

During the 1950s, Yarborough emerged as the leader of the small group of liberal Democrats in Texas. In 1952, he entered his party's Democratic primary against the incumbent governor, ALLAN SHIVERS. A conservative, Shivers dominated the Democratic Party in Texas. Yarborough ran as a neopopulist; he supported social reform and opposed the powerful Texas business establishment. Shiv-

ers soundly defeated him, receiving 833,000 votes to Yarborough's 488,000 votes. In the presidential election that year, Shivers led the state organization in its decision to back the Republican presidential candidate, DWIGHT D. EISENHOWER.

Two years later, Yarborough, denouncing Shivers for his endorsement of Eisenhower, ran against the governor again, this time losing by 90,000 votes. In a nasty campaign, Yarborough accused Shivers of corruption in a scandal involving the Veteran's Land Board. Shivers accused Yarborough of supporting integration and being a tool of labor unions and communists. In fact, both men campaigned on platforms that directly or indirectly supported segregation. Shivers appealed openly to racial prejudice. Yarborough, on the other hand, professed his opposition to "forced" desegregation. Yarborough's stronger showing was aided by the growing cohesiveness of Texas's liberals, comprised of intellectuals, populist East Texas farmers, trade unionists, African Americans, and Mexican Americans. The previous year, liberals had formed the Democratic Organizing Committee with the support of House Minority Leader SAM RAYBURN (D-Tex.), who wanted to reestablish the loyalty of the state organization to the national party.

In 1956, Yarborough entered his third successive gubernatorial primary. In a runoff election, he faced U.S. senator PRICE DANIEL (D-Tex.) and lost by fewer than 4,000 votes. When Daniel resigned from the Senate to assume the governorship, Yarborough ran in a special election to fill Daniel's vacant seat. In April 1957, Yarborough won a plurality in the special election against a Democrat and a Republican who split the conservative vote. Seeking a full term in 1958, Yarborough defeated conservative William A. Blakley in the Democratic primary and easily won the general election.

During his early years in the Senate, Yarborough compiled a generally liberal record. He voted for Democratic bills in 1959 providing funding for housing and area redevelopment. He also supported unsuccessful efforts to override President Eisenhower's vetoes of those measures. He supported the National Defense Education Act of 1958, which provided loans and grants to universities and their students. He backed the Civil Rights Acts of 1957 and 1960. He was one of only five southern senators to vote for the Civil Rights Act of 1957. In the 86th Congress (1959–61), according to *Congressional Quarterly*, Yarborough voted with the southern Democratic-Republican conservative coalition on only 23 percent of key roll call votes and against it 67 percent of the time.

Yarborough, however, joined the predominantly conservative Texas congressional delegation in defending the state's powerful oil interests. In March 1958, during a debate over a reciprocal trade bill, he stated that voluntary import quotas on foreign oil were not working and that "enforceable import quotas are critically needed." In June of the following year, he voted against an amendment to a tax bill offered by Senator Paul H. Douglas (D-Ill.) that would have reduced the depletion allowance on oil and gas wells.

In the early 1960s, Yarborough engaged in a biter quarrel with Governor John Connally, the leader of the state's moderate and conservative Democrats, for control of the state party. When President John F. Kennedy was assassinated in Dallas on November 22, 1963, Yarborough rode in an open vehicle two cars behind the presidential limousine in the motorcade. Yarborough crassly criticized the Secret Service agents for not responding quickly enough. In an example of political grandstanding, Yarborough sponsored federal legislation to provide assistance to the family of J. D. Tippitt, the police officer killed by Lee Harvey Oswald, Kennedy's assassin. Yarborough won reelection in 1964. Yarborough defeated George H. W. Bush, a future president of the United States, to win a third

term in 1964. During the mid and late 1960s, Yarborough voted for President Lyndon B. Johnson's Great Society measures. He urged legislation in the areas of civil rights, education, public health, and the environment. He either sponsored or cosponsored the Elementary and Secondary Education Act of 1965, the Higher Education Act of 1965, and revisions of the G.I. Bill in 1966. He also cowrote the Endangered Species Act of 1973.

While he generally supported Johnson's domestic policies, he split with the president on the war in Vietnam. In 1968, he endorsed antiwar candidate Senator Eugene McCarthy (D-Minn.) for the presidency. Two years later, Lloyd Bentsen, Jr., a heavily financed conservative, defeated Yarborough in the Democratic senatorial primary. Bentsen's campaign stressed the breakdown of law and order, urban riots, and Yarborough's opposition to the war in Vietnam. Afer leaving the Senate, Yarborough returned to the practice of law in Austin. He made a bid to return to the Senate in 1972 but lost in the primary. He maintained an active law practice, concentrating on the oil and gas business, almost up to his death in Austin, Texas, on January 27, 1996.

—MSM

Yates, Eugene A(dams)

(1880–1957) *chairman of the board, Southern Company, Inc.*

Born on November 7, 1880, in Elizabeth, New Jersey, Yates graduated from Rutgers University in 1902 with a B.S. in civil engineering. After graduating, he worked in the construction industry in New York City until he moved to Alabama in 1912 to become chief engineer of the Alabama Power Company. He rose to be general manager of Alabama Power, and, recognizing the advantages of an integrated network, he played a central role in the creation of Southeastern Power and Light in 1924. Southeastern Power and Light was a holding company that created an interconnected system out of the assets of Alabama Power, Georgia Power, Gulf Power, and Mississippi Power. With the formation of Southeastern Power and Light, Yates became vice president and general manager of the company. In 1930, Southeastern Power and Light merged into the Commonwealth and Southern

Corporation, which included five northern companies and six southern companies, and Yates became vice president of Commonwealth and Southern. In the mid-1940s, the federal government forced the dissolution of Commonwealth and Southern under the Public Utility Holding Company Act. Four of the southern companies (Alabama Power, Georgia Power, Gulf Power, and Mississippi Power) were deemed to be an integrated system and were thus allowed to remain under common ownership. A new holding company, the Southern Company, was formed for that purpose. Yates became president of Southern Company in 1947 and chairman of its board in 1950.

In 1954, Yates joined EDGAR H. DIXON, president of Middle South Utilities, in forming the Mississippi Valley Generating Company. They proposed to build a $107 million electric generating plant at West Memphis, Arkansas, to sell power to the Atomic Energy Commission (AEC). The consumption of power by the AEC's installation at Paducah, Kentucky, taxed the capacity of the Tennessee Valley Authority (TVA) to meet the demands of the city of Memphis, which faced the prospect of a shortage of electricity in four years. The TVA proposed building a new steam plant at Fulton, Tennessee, to supply power to the city of Memphis. President DWIGHT D. EISENHOWER, who preferred private development of power, could not see a justification for the federal government to pay for a plant to supply power to a particular city. He ordered JOSEPH DODGE, the director of the Bureau of the Budget, and LEWIS L. STRAUSS, the chair of the AEC, to explore the possibility of having private industry build the plant. In response, Dixon and Yates organized the Mississippi Valley Generating Company to build a plant to supply power to the TVA to replace the power that the TVA sold to the AEC. The Dixon-Yates proposal won acceptance by the AEC, TVA, and Bureau of the Budget. Upon the recommendation of the Bureau of the Budget, Eisenhower approved the proposal. The decision infuriated advocates of public power and created something of a scandal when it came out that a consultant to the Bureau of the Budget, Adolphe Wenzell, had been simultaneously advising the Dixon-Yates company. Ultimately, the city of Memphis decided to build its own power plant,

which freed up power from the TVA for use by the AEC. Eisenhower took the opportunity to cancel the Dixon-Yates contract and thus avoid a continuing controversy.

Yates died of a heart attack in New York City on October 5, 1957.

—MSM

York, Herbert F(rank)

(1921–2009) *chief scientist, Advanced Research Projects Agency, Department of Defense; director of defense research and engineering, Department of Defense*

Born in Rochester, New York, on November 24, 1921, York graduated with honors in physics from the University of Rochester in 1942 and earned an M.A. there the following year. Upon completing his M.A., he joined the Manhattan Project as a physicist at Ernest Lawrence's Radiation Laboratory at Berkeley and at Oak Ridge, Tennessee, where he worked on the electromagnetic separation of uranium 235. At the end of World War II, he went to the University of California at Berkeley to study for a doctorate. Awarded his Ph.D. in 1949, York then worked as a consultant at the laboratory at Los Alamos, New Mexico. In 1950, he became an assistant professor at the University of California and led a team engaged in the development of nuclear and thermonuclear weapons at the California Radiation Laboratory. He oversaw the expansion of the laboratory and in 1952 became the first director of Lawrence Livermore Radiation Laboratory.

When, in 1957, the Soviet Union launched *Sputnik*, the first human-made satellite, it caused a national alarm in the United States. President DWIGHT D. EISENHOWER created the President's Scientific Advisory Commission (PSAC) in 1957 and appointed York to it. York served from 1957 to 1961. In March 1958, he took a leave of absence from the Lawrence Livermore Radiation Laboratory in order to become chief scientist of the Defense Department's Advanced Research Projects Agency (ARPA). The ARPA supervised the development of rockets, satellites, and other space-related projects by the armed services. It also had responsibility for planning and implementing future American ventures into space.

While Eisenhower believed that military applications formed the primary basis of America's interest in space ("because they bear on our immediate safety"), the scientists at the PSAC made a case for the purely scientific possibilities of the space program. They, and some within the administration, argued that it would be better for nonmilitary research in space to be conducted by a civilian agency. Although Eisenhower worried about the cost of duplication, he agreed to proceed with a dual effort. ARPA would oversee military applications and the scientists at ARPA would design a civilian agency that would be responsible for developing nonmilitary applications. JAMES KILLIAN, head of the PSAC, appointed York to a panel to determine how the space program would be organized and what its objectives should be. Among the scientists on that panel, York was more inclined to rely primarily on the ARPA; others placed greater emphasis on a civilian agency devoted to scientific exploration. In the end, the panel recommended expanding the National Advisory Committee for Aeronautics into the National Aeronautics and Space Administration to oversee the civilian space program. With respect to the overall objectives of the space program, York argued strenuously for the importance of military projects in space. After PSAC presented its final report, Eisenhower asked the committee to prepare a version for the public. "Introduction to Outer Space," written primarily by York and Nobel laureate Edward Purcell, emphasized the scientific benefits of space exploration. The projects it mentioned included satellites to help forecast weather and instrumented probes to the moon. The report also warned against exploiting "space science at the cost of weakening our efforts in other scientific endeavours."

In discussions within the PSAC, York supported a proposal by the ARPA that called for four more *Explorer* satellites and three lunar probes. York stressed the need to reach the moon ahead of the Soviets and warned of "the *Sputnik*-like reaction" that would follow a successful Soviet lunar probe. After gaining the approval of the president, the Pentagon released a statement briefly explaining the ARPA's program and downplaying any hint of a race with the Soviets to hit the moon. In April 1958, before the House Select Committee on Astronau-

tics and Space Exploration, York comprehensively outlined the ARPA space itinerary, which included the lunar probes and especially the development of more powerful rocket engines to place larger satellites into orbit around Earth.

Interservice rivalries led to expensive and wasteful duplication in the development of missiles. In guiding a reorganization of the Joint Chiefs of Staff through Congress, Eisenhower included the creation of a new position, director of defense research and engineering. Effectively, the director of defense research and engineering would serve as a "missile czar"; it would fall to the director to clamp down on interservice rivalries and facilitate the orderly and coherent development of new weapons. In December 1958, Eisenhower appointed York to the newly created position.

While at that post, York played a central role in the military aspects of the space program and was often called on to defend its more controversial elements. In March 1959, for example, a White House report prepared by the PSAC made public details of Project Argus, which conducted nuclear tests in space during 1958. York denied that the project's three ionospheric bursts posed any danger of radioactive fallout, despite the fact that the tests had generated intense radioactivity, which was trapped in the earth's magnetic field.

After leaving the Pentagon in 1961, York became the first chancellor of the University of California at San Diego. He served in that capacity until 1964 and again from 1970 to 1972. President JOHN F. KENNEDY appointed him to the general advisory committee of the U.S. Arms Control and Disarmament Agency in 1962. During the administration of President LYNDON B. JOHNSON, York served again on the PSAC from 1964 to 1968. Throughout the 1960s and 1970s, York consistently expressed his opposition to the arms race between the Soviet Union and the United States. In 1970, he published *Race to Oblivion: A Participant's View of the Arms Race*, which detailed his view of the weakness of the antiballistic missile. In 1972, York joined Senator George McGovern's (D-S. Dak.) presidential campaign as cochairman of its national security panel and supported the senator's announced intention of reducing "wasteful and dangerous elements" in the defense budget. During the presidency of Jimmy Carter, York served as U.S. ambassador to the Comprehensive Test Ban negotiations in Geneva, Switzerland, from 1979 to 1981. In 1982, York founded and directed the Institute of Global Conflict and Cooperation at UC San Diego. He is director emeritus of the Institute on Global Conflict and Cooperation at UC San Diego and serves as chair of the university's scientific and academic advisory committee. In addition to *Race to Oblivion*, York has written *Arms Control* (1973), *The Advisors: Oppenheimer, Teller and the Superbomb* (1976), *Making Weapons, Talking Peace: A Physicist's Journey from Hiroshima to Geneva* (1987), *A Shield in Space? Technology, Politics and the Strategic Defense Initiative*, with Sanford Lakoff (1988), and *Arms and the Physicist* (1995). In 2000, President William Jefferson Clinton awarded York the Enrico Fermi Award for his contributions to nuclear deterrence and arms control. York died in San Diego, California, on May 19, 2009.

—MSM

Young, Milton R(uben)
(1897–1983) *U.S. senator*

The son of a grain farmer and real estate dealer, Young was born on his father's farm in Berlin, North Dakota, on December 6, 1897. After graduating from high school in 1915, he attended North Dakota Agricultural College and Graceland College in Iowa before becoming a grain farmer and real estate dealer. In his first race for public office, Young won election to the school board in 1924 and, running as a Republican, won a seat in the lower house of the state legislature in 1932. Two years later, he won election to the state senate. He served in the upper house until March 1945, when Governor Fred Aandahl appointed him to fill a vacancy in the U.S. Senate created by the death of Senator John Moses (D-N. Dak.). Young then won a special election in June 1946 to complete the term, and in 1950 won election to a full term by a margin of more than two to one. He won reelection in 1956, 1962, 1968, and 1974.

Generally conservative in his voting, Young opposed most of the legislation sent to Congress by the administration of President HARRY S. TRUMAN. Young supported the Taft-Hartley Act of 1947, the Internal Security Act of 1950, and the Immigration

Act of 1952. As a senator from one of the nation's leading wheat-producing states, however, he was one of the foremost advocates of high price supports for agricultural products. By his own reckoning, Young was "a farmer first and a Republican second." Although he tended to vote with the midwestern, conservative wing of the Republican Party in foreign policy, he did vote for aid to Greece and Turkey in 1947 and the Marshall Plan in 1948. Thereafter, however, he consistently voted to cut economic aid to western Europe, and he was one of 13 senators to vote against the North Atlantic Treaty in 1949.

During the administration of DWIGHT D. EISENHOWER, Young vigorously criticized the system of flexible price supports advocated by the secretary of agriculture, EZRA TAFT BENSON. In February 1953, Benson set off a storm of controversy when he declared that price supports "encourage uneconomic production" and should be used only as "disaster insurance." By October, Young called for Benson's resignation. During the debate over the administration's omnibus farm bill in 1954, Young asserted that "the lowering of price supports . . . will result in drastically reduced prices received by farmers." Moreover, he warned that it would "hurt the Republicans in farm states." Young voted for a version of the bill, passed by the House, that set the minimum level of support at 80 percent. When the House-Senate conference produced a bill setting the minimum at 75 percent, Young opposed it. In 1956, Young successfully amended a farm bill to establish 90 percent support for millable varieties of wheat for that year. Three years later, during debate over price supports for wheat, he warned that the administration's plan for reducing supports would ruin all but large farmers. Young voted for a bill offering farmers the option of 90 percent support and a 25 percent acreage reduction or 50 percent support and no restriction on acreage. The president, however, vetoed the measure.

On issues other than agriculture, Young usually voted with the conservative wing of his party. In February 1954, he voted for the Bricker amendment, which would have imposed limits on the treaty-making powers of the president. Young opposed the censure of Senator JOSEPH R. McCARTHY (R-Wis.) in December 1954. On the other hand, he generally voted for civil rights measures.

In February 1956, Young voted for a bill to exempt independent gas producers from federal price regulation. President Eisenhower vetoed the measure after it came out that gas lobbyists had exerted improper influence on Congress. A newspaper in North Dakota declared that Young had "sold out" by supporting the bill. Young, who faced an election later that year, demanded an investigation. The editor of the newspaper appeared in late May before a special Senate panel investigating corrupt practices and declared that the charge had not been meant literally. The probe was dropped, and Young won reelection in November by a margin of 108,000 to 63,000 votes.

For all his seniority, Young remained virtually unknown outside of North Dakota. He received national attention briefly, however, in 1961, when he denounced the John Birch Society and warned that it was gaining influence within Republican circles in North Dakota. In 1962, he was the only Republican who voted for a bill, recommended by the administration of President JOHN F. KENNEDY, that provided for strict control of wheat and feed grain production. During the administration of President LYNDON B. JOHNSON, Young opposed Medicare and the war on poverty. He advocated cuts in spending for health, education, and welfare programs. Some programs of the Great Society gained his favor. He supported manpower training programs and provided important backing for the Model Cities program in 1966. Continuing his record of support for civil rights, Young voted for the Civil Rights Act of 1964, but he opposed the Voting Rights Act of 1965 and voted against the use of federal funds to achieve integration through busing. In the second half of the 1960s, Young became concerned over his state's loss of population and its low per capita income; in response, he played a central role in obtaining large military contracts for his state. Young opposed American intervention in Indochina as early as 1954 and continued to oppose the war in Vietnam throughout the 1960s on the ground that the area was "militarily untenable." He nevertheless consistently voted to provide funding for the war.

In 1974, he decided to seek reelection at the age of 76. He narrowly defeated a popular former governor, William Guy. A recount in December gave him a victory by 186 votes. Over his long career in the Senate, he used his position on the Senate Appropriations Committee to obtain seven major water projects, air force bases at Minot and Grand Forks, and several research laboratories for his state. Late in his career, he told a reporter that he was more proud of the federal largesse he brought to his state than any other accomplishment in the Senate. Young did not stand for reelection in 1980 and retired to Sun City, Arizona, where he lived until his death there on May 31, 1983.

—MSM

Z

Zwicker, Ralph W(ise)

(1903–1991) *army officer*

Born in Stoughton, Wisconsin, on April 17, 1903, Zwicker grew up in Madison and spent a year at the University of Wisconsin before attending the U.S. Military Academy at West Point. After graduating from West Point in 1923, he was commissioned a second lieutenant in the infantry. Assigned to the Third Infantry Regiment, he reported for duty at Fort Snelling, Minnesota. In 1930, he was assigned to Schofield Barracks, Hawaii. He graduated from the company officer's course at the infantry school in 1933, after which he returned to the Third Infantry Regiment. Upon receiving a promotion to first lieutenant in July 1933, he commanded one of the original companies of the Civilian Conservation Corps. He became an instructor at West Point in 1934 and in 1939 was assigned to the 38th Infantry. Zwicker returned to the Infantry School in 1941 as an instructor. He then completed command and general staff school at Fort Leavenworth. During World War II, he served in Normandy (where he participated in the assault landings on Omaha Beach on D-day), northern France, the Ardennes, the Rhineland, and Central Europe. Serving first as a regimental commander of the Second Infantry Division and then as then as its chief of staff, he won a Silver Star, the Legion of Merit, a Bronze Star, and decorations from Britain and France. After the war, he attended the Naval War College in 1945 and the National War College from 1945 to 1946. He served with the operation and training division of the Army General Staff from 1947 to 1949 and was transferred to the European Command Headquarters in 1949. For two years, he commanded the 18th Infantry Regiment of the First Infantry Division. Zwicker returned to the United States as an instructor at the National War College in 1952 and in 1953 served briefly as assistant division commander of the Fifth Infantry Division. Promoted to brigadier general in March 1953, he became the commanding officer at Camp Kilmer, New Jersey, in July 1953.

In that capacity, Zwicker became a key figure in the confrontation between Senator JOSEPH R. MCCARTHY (R-Wis.) and the army in 1954. Beginning in the fall of 1953, the Senate Government Operations Committee's Permanent Investigations Subcommittee, chaired by McCarthy, intensified its investigations of alleged subversive activity in the army. It demanded access to the army's loyalty and security files and summoned officers for questioning. On January 30, 1954, the panel questioned Major IRVING PERESS, an army dentist at Camp Kilmer. Peress had refused to answer questions on a form asking about membership in subversive organizations. In addition, he refused to respond to a subsequent interrogatory from army intelligence. After an investigation, army intelligence concluded that sufficient evidence existed to warrant the dentist's discharge as a security risk. Through a series of bureaucratic blunders, the army did not act immediately on the recommendation to discharge Peress. In September 1953, while the army's investigation was in progress, Peress requested a promotion to the rank of major, for which he automatically qualified by his age and previous experience in the army reserve. His request was approved. When Zwicker became aware of the matter in October, he wrote a letter to his superiors urging that Peress be relieved from duty immediately as a security risk. In November, the Pentagon decided to release the dentist at the earliest possible date. Outraged at Peress's promotion to major, Zwicker approached McCarthy and in December provided the senator's staff with information about the matter.

McCarthy, who had been investigating alleged communists in the army, subpoenaed Peress to appear before the Permanent Investigations Subcommittee. At a hearing on January 30, 1954, at which McCarthy was the only senator present, the dentist declined to answer all questions about his political activities. McCarthy, in turn, demanded the dentist's court-martial. In the meantime, in mid-January 1954, the army had ordered Peress's honorable discharge and had given him the usual 90 days within which to select a termination date. He chose March 31. After his appearance before McCarthy's committee, however, Peress met with Zwicker on February 1 and asked for his immediate separation from the army. The army announced his honorable discharge on February 2.

On February 18, McCarthy's subcommittee heard further testimony on the Peress matter. After several witnesses had testified in the morning, Zwicker appeared before the subcommittee that afternoon in a closed hearing. Stiff and at times unresponsive, the general infuriated McCarthy. McCarthy accused Zwicker of "double-talk," to which the general replied that he did not like "to have anyone impugn my honesty, which you just about did." McCarthy responded: "either your honesty or your intelligence; I can't help impugning one or the other." When McCarthy pressed Zwicker regarding Peress's discharge, the general found himself defending the very bureaucratic bungling that had infuriated him and that he had tried to correct. McCarthy questioned whether Zwicker had "the brains of a five-year-old child" and whether the highly decorated veteran of World War II was "fit to wear that uniform." McCarthy ordered the general to appear again before the committee the following Tuesday, February 26.

McCarthy's treatment of Zwicker brought the simmering hostility between the army and McCarthy to a boiling point and set off the chain of events that led to the Army-McCarthy hearings in the spring of 1954 and ultimately to the Senate's condemnation of McCarthy at the end of that year. Fuming at his treatment by McCarthy, Zwicker returned to Camp Kilmer, wrote a report of his encounter with the senator, and sent it to the Pentagon. The chief of staff, MATTHEW B. RIDGWAY, took the matter to the secretary of the army, ROBERT T. STEVENS. On Saturday, February 20, Stevens issued an order forbidding army officers to appear before McCarthy's subcommittee. He telephoned McCarthy to inform the senator of his intention, in response to which, McCarthy told Stevens to appear before the committee on Thursday. The next day, Stevens released a statement to the press indicating that he had ordered Zwicker not to appear for the second interrogation before the subcommittee because he was "unwilling to have so fine an officer . . . run the risk of further abuse."

In response to demands by both Republicans and Democrats, the unedited transcript of Zwicker's testimony was made public. The *New York Times* printed the entire transcript. When reporters contacted Zwicker, the general said that he supported McCarthy's efforts to rid the government of communists "100 percent" but that "there's a way to do it."

Under pressure from Vice President RICHARD M. NIXON and WILTON PERSONS who headed Eisenhower's congressional liaison office, Republicans on McCarthy's subcommittee (EVERETT DIRKSEN of Illinois, KARL MUNDT of South Dakota, and CHARLES POTTER of Michigan) attempted to avoid a head-on collision between McCarthy and the administration. They set up a lunch attended by Stevens, McCarthy, Mundt, and Dirksen on Wednesday, February 24. At the end of the lunch, perhaps 50 reporters and photographers, who had obviously been tipped off, awaited the group. Mundt read a "memorandum of understanding," which made it seem that Stevens had given in to virtually all of McCarthy's demands. Mundt's memorandum declared that Stevens had agreed to permit officers to appear before the subcommittee, to give the committee the names of all military personnel involved in Peress's promotion, and to make those involved in the decision available to the subcommittee. Zwicker's second appearance was postponed, and Stevens's appearance, scheduled for the following day, was canceled. During the meeting, Stevens had received a promise from the senators that army officers called to testify would be treated fairly. Mundt's memorandum, however, did not include that commitment. Faced with news reports that characterized the agreement as a "capitulation" to McCarthy and under pressure from the White House staff, Stevens attempted to work out a compromise with the Republicans on the subcommittee. When that failed, Stevens went to the White House to release a statement, prepared in consultation with Eisenhower's aides, in which he declared that he would not permit officers to be "browbeaten or humiliated" by a congressional committee and that he had received assurances from members of the subcommittee that they would not allow this to happen. When Stevens finished, Eisenhower's press secretary, JAMES HAGERTY, told reporters that the president had seen Stevens's statement and endorsed it "100 percent."

The incident involving Zwicker led to the final break between McCarthy and the administration. In a press conference on March 3, Eisenhower praised Zwicker and demanded that members of the executive branch be treated with respect and courtesy when they appeared before Congress. On March 11, the army released its "chronology," which accused McCarthy and his top aide, ROY COHN, of attempting to seek preferential treatment for G. DAVID SCHINE, a friend of Cohn's and a consultant to McCarthy's committee. This led to the Army-McCarthy hearings. In July, Senator RALPH FLANDERS (R-Vt.) introduced a motion to censure McCarthy. The speech with which Flanders introduced the motion referred to three particulars, one of which charged that McCarthy had exhibited "habitual contempt for people" and offered his questioning of Zwicker as an example. The leadership of the Senate referred the resolution to a select bipartisan committee, which in September recommended that McCarthy be censured on two counts—contempt of the

Senate and his "inexcusable" and "reprehensible" treatment of Zwicker. During the Senate debate on the censure resolution, however, the charge that McCarthy had abused Zwicker was dropped without a vote on December 2 and replaced by a charge that McCarthy had abused the select committee. Some feared that censuring McCarthy for his conduct as a committee chair would set an unfortunate precedent and limit the ability of committee chairs in examining witnesses. Others thought that Zwicker had provoked McCarthy. The Senate passed the resolution to censure McCarthy later the same day.

Soon after his confrontation with McCarthy, Zwicker was transferred to Japan, where he became commanding general of the Southwestern Command, Armed Forces Far East. After the Democrats won control of Congress in the elections of 1954, the Permanent Subcommittee on Investigations reopened its investigation into the Peress matter. Called to testify once again, Zwicker's testimony generated new controversy. Both the subcommittee's chair, Senator JOHN McCLELLAN (D-Ark.) and its minority counsel, ROBERT F. KENNEDY, believed that Zwicker had lied on the stand. In April 1955, McClellan referred the matter to Attorney General HERBERT BROWNELL and asked whether the Justice Department should bring action for perjury. The Justice Department sat on the matter for more than a year and decided to bring no action.

In 1957, during hearings conducted by the Senate Armed Services Committee on his nomination to the rank of major general, Zwicker discussed his testimony in 1954. He admitted that he may have been uncooperative in order to avoid accidentally revealing classified information. The committee ignored McCarthy's demand that Zwicker be indicted for perjury, and the Senate approved the nomination on April 1, 1957, with only McCarthy and Senator George W. Malone (R-Nev.) dissenting. Zwicker was assigned to command the 24th Infantry Division in Korea. In May 1958, he assumed command of the XX Army Corps (Reserve).

Zwicker retired from the army in 1960 and worked as a military analyst with the Research Analysis Corporation in McLean, Virginia. He lived in Falls Church, Virginia, and then McLean.

In an interview with *Newsweek* magazine in 1969, Zwicker maintained that McCarthy's accusations had deleterious effects on his life, health, and career in the army. He claimed that his promotion to major general, which had been originally recommended in 1954, was delayed while the FBI investigated McCarthy's charges. Ironically, the general revealed that, before appearing before McCarthy's subcommittee, "I was not unsympathetic with the Senator." Zwicker died at Fort Belvoir, Virginia, in August 1991.

—MSM

APPENDIXES

CHRONOLOGY

1951

October 16—Sen. Robert A. Taft announces his candidacy for the Republican presidential nomination.

1952

January 6—Sen. Henry Cabot Lodge enters Gen. Dwight D. Eisenhower's name in the New Hampshire Republican presidential primary.

January 23—Sen. Estes Kefauver announces his candidacy for the Democratic presidential nomination.

March 11—Eisenhower wins the New Hampshire Republican presidential primary with 50.4 percent of the vote. Taft garners 38.9 percent. In the Democratic primary, Kefauver defeats Pres. Harry S. Truman. Kefauver gets 55.4 percent of the vote to Truman's 44.5 percent.

March 18—In the Minnesota primary, Eisenhower polls 108,692 write-in votes to 129,076 for favorite-son candidate Harold Stassen. The result convinces Eisenhower to seek the Republican presidential nomination.

March 29—President Truman announces he will not seek reelection.

April 8—Truman seizes steel mills to avoid a strike.

April 22—In the Pennsylvania primary, Eisenhower receives over 847,420 votes, a figure larger than the combined totals of his Democratic and Republican opponents.

May 27—The Texas State GOP Convention selects rival Taft and Eisenhower delegations to the Republican National Convention despite wide majorities won by Eisenhower delegates in local party conventions.

June 2—Eisenhower retires from the army to campaign for the Republican presidential nomination. In *Youngstown Sheet and Tube Co. v. Sawyer*, the Supreme Court declares Truman's seizure of the steel mills unconstitutional

June 27—Congress passes the Immigration and Nationality (McCarran-Walter) Act over Truman's veto.

July 2—At the Republican Governors Convention in Houston, Tex., 23 governors, including three Taft supporters, sign a manifesto urging that contested delegates be kept from voting on the seating of others at the national convention. The move favors Eisenhower forces.

July 7—The Republican National Convention opens in Chicago. It is the first presidential nominating convention to be televised nationally.

July 9—In a key test of disputed delegates, the Republican National Convention votes to seat a Georgia delegation favoring Eisenhower. Eisenhower delegates from six other states, Texas, Florida, Mississippi, Kansas and Missouri are subsequently seated.

July 11—Eisenhower defeats Taft for the Republican presidential nomination on the first ballot. Sen. Richard M. Nixon is chosen as the vice presidential candidate.

July 19—The Democratic National Committee approves a loyalty oath requiring each delegation to "exert every honorable means" to get the party's nominees on its state ballot.

July 21—The Democratic National Convention opens in Chicago.

July 24–25—The Louisiana, South Carolina, and Virginia delegations to the Democratic National Convention win full voting rights despite their refusal to take the loyalty pledge.

July 25—Puerto Rico becomes a U.S. commonwealth.

July 26—Gov. Adlai E. Stevenson wins the Democratic presidential nomination on the third ballot. He selects Sen. John J. Sparkman as the vice presidential candidate.

August 22—At a news conference in Denver, Eisenhower makes an indirect reference to Sen. Joseph R. McCarthy when he says that he would not "give a blanket endorsement to any man who does anything that I believe to be un-American in its methods and procedures" but that he would back Republican candidates for Congress.

August 25—Eisenhower tells the American Legion Convention in New York that the United States should help the people of communist countries "liberate" themselves. Eisenhower also defends Gen. George C. Marshall and says he had "no patience" with anyone who criticized Marshall.

September 23—In a nationally televised address, later known as the "Checkers Speech," Nixon defends himself against charges that he had misused money from a secret political fund.

October 3—Eisenhower delivers a campaign address in Milwaukee. Under pressure from local Republican leaders, he deletes a portion praising Gen. George C. Marshall, an old friend under attack by McCarthy.

October 24—Eisenhower announces that, if elected, he will go to Korea.

November 1—The United States explodes the world's first hydrogen (fusion) bomb.

November 4—Eisenhower defeats Stevenson in the presidential election by over 6 million votes and receives 442 of 531 electoral votes. The Republicans gain control of both houses of Congress by very narrow margins: 221 to 211 in the House and 48 to 47 in the Senate. There is one independent in each house.

December 2–5—Fulfilling his campaign pledge, Eisenhower visits Korea.

1953

January 20—Eisenhower is inaugurated 34th president of the United States.

February 2—In his State of the Union address, Eisenhower announces that there is no "sense or logic" in the United States assuming "defensive responsibilities on behalf of Chinese Communists." He will therefore, withdraw the Seventh Fleet from the Formosa Strait between Taiwan and mainland China. He also announces that he will let wage and price controls end by April 30.

February 4—McCarthy begins a loyalty-security probe of the State Department.

February 5—Eisenhower names Charles E. Bohlen as ambassador to the USSR, touching off a battle with the right wing of the Republican Party. Conservatives accused Bohlen of being part of the "Truman-Acheson policy of appeasement" toward the USSR.

February 11—Eisenhower declines to grant executive clemency to Ethel and Julius Rosenberg, under death sentences for transmitting atomic secrets to the USSR.

February 20—Dulles submits the Captive Peoples Resolution to Congress. It rejects "any interpretations or applications" of secret World War II agreements "which have been perverted to bring about the subjugation of free peoples" and deplores Soviet "totalitarian imperialism" in Eastern Europe. The resolution disappoints the Republican Right, because it fails to repudiate the Yalta Accords.

February 28—The Senate Permanent Investigations Subcommittee, chaired by McCarthy, opens televised hearings on subversion in the Voice of America.

March 4—Dulles announces his acceptance of the resignation of State Department China expert John Carter Vincent, under attack by McCarthy.

March 5—Marshal Joseph Stalin dies.

March 9—Rep. Harold Velde suggests investigation of subversive influences among the clergy.

March 10—Congress shelves the Captive Peoples Resolution following the announcement of Stalin's death.

March 27—Despite strong opposition, the Senate confirms Charles Bohlen as ambassador to the Soviet Union.

March 30—Congress authorizes a new, cabinet-level Department of Health, Education, and Welfare.

April 2—Japan and the United States sign a 10-year treaty of friendship, commerce, and navigation.

April 4–21—McCarthy aides Roy Cohn and G. David Schine tour Europe in search of subversive literature in U.S. Information Agency libraries.

April 16—Eisenhower addresses the American Society of Newspaper Editors. His speech, "A Chance for Peace" warn of the dangers of the arms race.

April 20—The Subversive Activities Control Board determines that the U.S. Communist Party is a subversive political organization controlled by the Soviet Union and orders it to register as such with the attorney general.

April 27—Eisenhower issues Executive Order 10450, instituting a loyalty-security program for the executive branch. It replaces the loyalty program instituted by Truman.

May 19—In a nationwide address, Eisenhower calls for a six-month extension of the excess profits tax beyond June 30, 1953.

May 22—Eisenhower signs the Tidelands Oil bill, giving coastal states title to offshore oil within three miles of shore (10.5 miles for Texas and Florida).

June 14—In a speech at Dartmouth College, Eisenhower urges the undergraduates not to "join the book burners," a reference to the Cohn and Schine European trip.

June 17—Workers in East Germany riot to protest factory speedups and food shortages. Russian tanks are brought in to quell the uprising.

June 19—The Rosenbergs are executed for giving atomic secrets to the USSR.

July 2—The Senate Foreign Relations Committee approves a resolution praising the East Germans' "patriotic defiance of Communist tyranny" and calling for German unification on the basis of free elections.

July 9—Eisenhower denounces an article by McCarthy aide J. B. Matthews charging Protestant clergymen with forming "the largest single group supporting the communist apparatus."

July 10—The Senate Permanent Investigations Subcommittee's three Democratic members, Sens. Henry Jackson, John McClellan, and Stuart Symington, resign in protest after the panel votes to give McCarthy sole power to hire and fire staff members.

July 27—The United States and North Korea sign an armistice at Panmunjom. The treaty calls for a demilitarized zone along the 38th parallel and the voluntary repatriation of prisoners of war.

July 31—Taft dies of cancer.

August 7—Eisenhower signs the refugee relief bill, which permits 214,000 over-quota refugees to enter the United States during the next three years.

August 12—The USSR explode its first hydrogen bomb.

August 19—The House Un-American Activities Committee releases its report on organized communism in the United States. The report recommends that membership in the Communist Party be considered as prima facie evidence of violation of the Smith Act and urges legislation to prohibit misuse of the Bill of Rights to withhold information from congressional committees.

August 19–22—A coup, engineered by the Central Intelligence Agency (CIA), overthrows the leftist government of Premier Mohammad Mossadegh in Iran and installs a pro-Western regime loyal to Shah Pahlevi.

August 31—McCarthy begins an investigation of possible communist infiltration in the armed forces.

September 10—Secretary of Labor Martin P. Durkin resigns because of the administration's failure to revise the Taft-Hartley Act.

September 22—The American Federation of Labor expels the International Longshoremen's Association for failing to rid itself of corruption.

October 5—Earl Warren is sworn in as chief justice of the United States.

October 23—The White House announces that in the first four months of its new security program, 1,456 persons have been dropped from the federal payroll. (863 were dismissed, and 593

resigned when notified of "unfavorable" reports about them.)

November 6—Attorney General Herbert Brownell, Jr., charges that Truman promoted Harry Dexter White to U.S. executive director of the International Monetary Fund (IMF) in 1946, despite warnings from the FBI that White was a "Russian spy."

November 16—In a nationwide radio-TV broadcast Truman defends his actions and charges that the Eisenhower administration is "embracing McCarthyism for political advantage."

December 3—Eisenhower orders Dr. J. Robert Oppenheimer's security clearance suspended, pending a review.

December 4–7—President Eisenhower, British prime minister Winston Churchill, and French premier Joseph Laniel confer in Bermuda on the exchange of atomic information.

December 8—Eisenhower delivers his "Atoms for Peace" speech at the UN, proposing the creation of an international atomic energy agency to pool resources for the peaceful development of nuclear energy.

1954

January 11—Eisenhower sends Congress a farm program recommending flexible price supports.

January 12—Secretary of State John Foster Dulles makes a speech in which he announces that the United States will in the future meet aggression with "a great capacity to retaliate instantly by means and places of our own choosing."

January 21—The navy launches the first nuclear powered submarine the *S.S. Nautilus*.

January 26—Sens. Jackson, McClellan, and Symington resume membership in the Senate Permanent Investigations Subcommittee after McCarthy capitulates to their demands for a greater role in subcommittee investigations.

January 26—The Senate approves the U.S.-South Korean Mutual Defense Treaty.

February 1—McCarthy demands the court-martial of army dentist Irving Peress for his early affiliation with left-wing organizations.

February 8—In *Irvine v. California*, the Supreme Court affirms a state court conviction that was based on evidence from illegal electronic surveillance.

February 10—Eisenhower tells newsmen that he can conceive of no greater tragedy than for the United States to become involved in all-out war in Indochina.

February 18—The Berlin Conference of foreign ministers fails to reach an agreement on the reunification of Germany.

February 18—During an investigation of alleged subversion in the army, McCarthy accuses the army of "coddling Communists" and disparages Gen. Ralph W. Zwicker as "not fit to wear that uniform" and lacking "the brains of a five-year-old child."

February 26—By a vote of 50-42, the Senate defeats the Bricker amendment, which would have limited the president's treaty-making powers.

March 1—Firing from the House visitors' gallery, three Puerto Rican nationalists wound five members of Congress.

March 1—The United States sets off its second hydrogen bomb at Bikini Atoll in the Pacific Ocean. The force of the explosion inadvertently exposes 379 persons to radiation, including 23 Japanese fishermen seriously burned on a ship 70–90 miles from the blast center.

March 8—The United States and Japan sign a mutual defense treaty, providing for the gradual rearmament of Japan.

March 9—On *See It Now*, Edward R. Murrow accuses McCarthy of habitually using half-truths

and of repeatedly stepping over the "line between investigating and persecuting."

March 11—The army releases a report listing the dates on which the status of Private G. David Schine was discussed by army officials and McCarthy or members of his subcommittee staff. The next day, McCarthy accuses the army of "blackmail" and "trying to use Schine as a hostage to pressure us to stop our hearings on the Army."

March 13—The Organization of American States adopts a U.S.-sponsored resolution calling for joint action against any Latin American state falling under communist control.

March 20—French chief of staff Gen. Paul Henry Ely flies to Washington seeking direct U.S. military aid for the beleaguered French garrison at Dien Bien Phu in northern Vietnam.

March 29—Dulles calls for united action in Indochina.

March 31—Eisenhower signs a bill providing for an estimated $999 million annual reduction in federal excise taxes.

April 14—The army files formal charges with the Senate Permanent Investigations Subcommittee, accusing McCarthy and Cohn of trying to obtain preferential treatment for Schine "by improper means."

April 20—McCarthy denounces army charges against him and charges Assistant Secretary of Defense Struve Hensel with malfeasance and attempting to try to interfere with his subcommittee's investigation of the army.

April 22–June 17—The Senate Permanent Investigations Subcommittee holds public hearings into conflicting charges made by the army and McCarthy.

April 26—The Geneva Conference on Korea and Indochina opens with foreign ministers of 19 nations, including Communist China, present.

May 4—Dulles withdraws from the Geneva Conference after his plan for a South Asian defense alliance fails.

May 7—The French garrison at Dien Bien Phu surrenders after a 55-day siege.

May 13—Eisenhower signs a bill authorizing the joint U.S.-Canadian construction of the St. Lawrence Seaway.

May 17—In *Brown v. Board of Education*, the Supreme Court unanimously rules that segregated public schools are "inherently unequal" and therefore unconstitutional.

May 24—In *Galvan v. Press*, the Supreme Court upholds a provision of the Internal Security Act of 1950 making past membership in the Communist Party grounds for deportation of an alien.

June 9—Army counsel Joseph Welch reproaches McCarthy for "cruelty and recklessness" in trying to "assassinate" the reputation of Frederick Fisher, a member of Welch's Boston law firm.

June 11—Sen. Ralph Flanders introduces a resolution to remove McCarthy from his committee chairmanships until he answers charges stemming from his action in the 1952 election.

June 14—Eisenhower signs legislation to add the words "under God" to the Pledge of Allegiance to the Flag.

June 18–25—A CIA-supported coup takes place in Guatemala, ousting the leftist government of Jacobo Arbenz.

June 29—In a controversial 4-1 decision, the Atomic Energy Commission refuses to reinstate Dr. J. Robert Oppenheimer's security clearance for access to classified information on nuclear technology. The verdict is based on "proof of fundamental defects in his character" and his associations with communists.

July 10—Eisenhower signs Public Law 480, which provides for foreign disposal of surplus farm commodities.

July 21—The Geneva Conference on Indochina ends with the signing of the Geneva Accords, partitioning Vietnam at the 17th parallel and providing for unified elections within two years.

July 22—Eisenhower signs the Chemical Amendments of 1954 (Miller Act), designed to protect consumers from chemical residues left in food products by setting "poison residue tolerances."

July 30—Flanders introduces a resolution charging McCarthy with "personal contempt" of the Senate for refusing to answer questions about finances and for the "frivolous and irresponsible" conduct of his aides.

August 2—Eisenhower signs the Housing Act of 1954, which provides funds for 35,000 houses to serve families displaced by various urban redevelopment programs.

August 2—The Senate votes to refer the Flanders resolution to a select bipartisan committee of "neutral" senators headed by Sen. Arthur V. Watkins.

August 4—Eisenhower signs the Watershed Protection and Flood Prevention Act of 1954, authorizing federal aid in construction of small watershed projects to prevent floods and conserve soil.

August 5—Eisenhower signs the Reed Act, which establishes a $200 million loan fund from which states with high unemployment could draw to pay unemployment insurance.

August 10—Eisenhower signs the Securities Information bill, which permits greater distribution of information on new investment security issues.

August 16—Eisenhower signs the Internal Revenue Code of 1954, which cuts personal taxes by up to $1.36 billion and moves the deadline for personal income tax returns from March 15 to April 15.

August 20—Eisenhower signs the Immunity Act of 1954, which allows congressional committees to grant immunity from prosecution to witnesses giving self-incriminatory testimony in security cases.

Critics charge the measure forces witnesses to testify or go to jail.

August 23—Eisenhower vetoes a bill providing a 5 percent increase in the salaries of federal employees.

August 24—Eisenhower signs the communist control bill of 1954. Sponsored by liberal Democrats, the measure outlaws the Communist Party and makes its members subject to the provisions and penalties of the Internal Security Act of 1950.

August 28—Eisenhower signs the 1954 agricultural bill, which institutes a flexible scale of farm support prices to stem overproduction of surplus crops.

August 30—Eisenhower signs the 1954 atomic energy bill, which permits private industry to use nuclear fuels and build and operate nuclear power plants.

August 31–September 13—The Watkins Committee holds hearings on the censure of McCarthy.

September 1—The Social Security Act is amended to increase benefits and add new category of beneficiaries.

September 3—Communist China begins heavy shelling of the Pescadores claimed by Nationalist China.

September 3—Eisenhower signs the espionage and sabotage bill of 1954, which authorizes the death penalty for peacetime espionage and sabotage.

September 8—Australia, Great Britain, France, New Zealand, Pakistan, the Philippines, Thailand, and the United States form the Southeast Asian Treaty Organization (SEATO), pledging joint action in defense of member nations. Nationalist China is excluded from the alliance.

September 27—The Watkins Committee unanimously recommends the censure of McCarthy for his conduct toward the Senate Subcommittee on Privileges and Elections during the 82nd Congress

and for his treatment of Gen. Zwicker during the Army-McCarthy hearings.

November 2—In mid-term elections, the Democrats gain control of Congress by 29 votes in the House and one in the Senate. They also oust Republicans from eight state governorships.

November 5—Dulles announces the dismissal of career diplomat John Paton Davies, Jr., who had been attacked by McCarthy.

November 11—The Atomic Energy Commission (AEC) signs the Dixon-Yates contract permitting a private utility combine to build a generating plant in the Tennessee Valley to feed power into the Tennessee Valley Authority system and supply the Atomic Energy Commission's installations in the area.

November 23—The Dow Jones Industrial average regains its 1929 peak of 381.

December 2—The United States and Nationalist China sign a mutual defense treaty, pledging American retaliation if Communist China attacks Taiwan.

December 2—The Senate votes, 67-22, to condemn McCarthy for obstructing the elections subcommittee in 1952, abusing Sen. Watkins and the Select Committee to Study Censure, and insulting the Senate during the censure proceedings.

December 11—Eisenhower creates a Council of Foreign Economic Policy, headed by Joseph M. Dodge, to coordinate foreign aid activities and develop foreign economic policies.

December 28—Dulles indicates at a press conference that aggression in western Europe would be met with tactical atomic weapons.

1955

January 1—U.S. Foreign Operations Administration begins to supply direct financial aid to South Vietnam, Cambodia, and Laos.

January 10—Eisenhower asks Congress for new powers to reduce foreign trade barriers, including a three year extension of the Reciprocal Trade Agreements Act.

January 13—Eisenhower asks Congress to inaugurate a military reserve plan, to extend the Selective Service System, and to raise military pay, allowances, and benefits.

January 28—Congress passes the Formosa Resolution, giving Eisenhower discretionary powers to use U.S. forces in the defense of Taiwan and the Pescadores. It is the first time Congress has granted a president such war-making powers in peacetime.

February 8—Eisenhower proposes a three-year $7 billion federal-state-local school construction program to Congress.

February 18—Sen. Lister Hill accuses Adolphe Wenzell, a Bureau of the Budget consultant, of conflict of interest in connection with the Dixon-Yates contract. Hill also denounces Budget director Rowland Hughes for concealing Wenzell's actions.

February 23—Eisenhower states that the United States would stop testing atomic weapons only under a workable disarmament agreement with effective international inspection.

March 23—By voice vote, the House adopts a minimum standard of conduct for House Committee investigations. It bars "one-man hearings" and assures witnesses the right to counsel and the opportunity to rebut testimony tending to "defame, degrade or incriminate" them.

March 31—Eisenhower signs a bill providing for an increase of $745 million annually in military pay and allowances.

April 1—The Senate ratifies the treaty ending the occupation of West Germany.

April 12—Scientists announce that the Salk vaccine is "safe, effective and potent" in preventing polio.

April 20—During testimony before a Senate Judiciary subcommittee, dismissed State Department special adviser on refugees Edward J. Corsi charges that the management of the Refugee Relief Act of 1953 is "a national scandal" and that the emphasis on security investigation of refugees had made their admission incidental.

April 21—The United States ends its occupation of Germany.

May 9—West Germany is admitted to full membership in the North Atlantic Treaty Organization (NATO).

May 15—The United States, Great Britain, France, and the USSR sign a peace treaty with Austria, granting it full independence in return for political neutrality.

May 26—The Senate Banking and Currency Committee issues its report on the rise of stock market prices in 1954. The panel describes an "increase in unhealthy speculative developments," and it recommends tightening existing federal regulations and undertaking further study of abuses.

May 31—In *Brown v. Board of Education*, the Supreme Court hands down a ruling implementing its earlier school desegregation decision. It places the burden on local authorities to begin desegregation immediately and proceed with "all deliberate speed."

June 21—The reciprocal trade program is extended for three years.

June 30—In his second speech to the UN, Eisenhower calls for a "new kind of peace," in which the atom will be used for productive purposes.

June 30—A 12-hour steel strike of 600,000 workers is settled with an hourly wage increase averaging 15¢. Steel prices increase an average of $7.50 a ton.

June 30—The Second Hoover Commission submits its final report, recommending that government not compete with the private sector.

June 30—Eisenhower signs a bill authorizing an increase of $6 billion in the public debt.

July 1—Eisenhower signs a bill requiring the inscription "In God We Trust" on all currency.

July 11—Following an announcement that the city of Memphis has voted to build its own electrical generating plant, Eisenhower cancels the Dixon-Yates contract.

July 18–23—President Dwight D. Eisenhower, Premier Nikolai Bulganin, Prime Minister Winston Churchill, and Premier Edgar Faure hold a summit conference at Geneva. The major topic is German unification.

July 21—Eisenhower submits his "Open Skies" proposal at the Geneva summit conference. He suggests that the USSR and the United States exchange military blueprints and allow mutual air reconnaissance over their military installations.

August 1—Air Force secretary Harold E. Talbott resigns following a Senate Permanent Investigations Subcommittee probe of his activities in promoting Defense Department contracts with the Paul Mulligan Co., of which he is part owner.

August 4—Rejecting proposals for federal construction of a single high dam at Hell's Canyon on the Snake River, the Federal Power Commission grants the private Idaho Power Co. a 50-year license to build and operate three low hydroelectric dams in the same area.

August 8—The first conference on the peaceful uses of atomic energy opens in Geneva. Seventy-three nations are represented.

August 9—Eisenhower signs a bill creating a 12-member bipartisan commission to review the government's loyalty-security program.

August 12—Eisenhower signs the poliomyelitis vaccination bill, which provides free vaccines for children under 20 and pregnant women, regardless of ability to pay.

August 28—Emmett Till, a 15-year-old African American, is kidnapped after allegedly propositioning a white woman. Three days later, his body is recovered from the Tallahatchie River. An all-white jury later acquits the two white men accused of the murder.

September 24—Eisenhower suffers a "moderately severe" heart attack.

September 30—Film actor James Dean, symbol of alienated youth, dies in a car crash.

October 27—The foreign ministers of the United States, Great Britain, France, and the USSR meet in Geneva to discuss disarmament, German unification and East-West relations.

November 15—Adlai Stevenson announces his candidacy for the Democratic nomination for president in 1956.

November 25—The Interstate Commerce Commission bans racial segregation on interstate trains and buses.

December 1—Rosa Parks is arrested for refusing to give up her bus seat to a white man in Montgomery, Alabama.

December 5—Under the leadership of Martin Luther King, Jr., African Americans in Montgomery, Alabama, begin a 54-week boycott of city buses.

December 5—The American Federation of Labor and the Congress of Industrial Organizations merge. George Meany becomes president of the new organization.

December 16—Kefauver announces his candidacy for the Democratic presidential nomination.

1956

January 5—In his State of the Union address, Eisenhower recommends the creation of a bipartisan commission to investigate denial of voting rights.

January 13—Eisenhower names a panel of eight prominent citizens, headed by James Killian, to monitor the activities of the CIA.

January 16—In an interview with *Life* magazine, Dulles defends his "brinkmanship" policies, saying that the United States has gone "to the verge of war" to maintain peace. He states that "the ability to get to the verge without getting into the war is the necessary art." "We walked to the brink, and we looked it in the face."

January 24—At a conference in Richmond, Virginia, four southern governors endorse the doctrine of interposition. They pledge the use of state power to prevent desegregation by interposing the "sovereignty of the state between local school board officials and federal courts."

February 3—Autherine Lucy attempts to integrate formerly all-white University of Alabama. She is suspended four days later because her presence "threatens public order."

February 6—General Services Administrator Edward Mansure resigns in the midst of a congressional probe of political influence in granting government contracts.

February 17—Eisenhower vetoes a bill to free natural gas producers from direct federal rate control after Sen. Francis Case reveals that he received a $2,500 campaign contribution from persons favoring the measure.

February 25—Eisenhower declares he will seek reelection.

March 1—The national minimum wage is increased from 75¢ to $1 per hour.

March 12—One hundred and one southern senators and representatives issue a Declaration of Constitutional Principles, known as the Southern Manifesto, denouncing the Supreme Court's desegregation decision and pledging to use all "lawful means" to resist it.

March 13—Eisenhower and Kefauver win the New Hampshire presidential primaries. Nixon gets a heavy vote of confidence with over 22,000 write-in votes for his renomination.

March 20—Kefauver scores an upset victory over Adlai E. Stevenson in the Minnesota presidential primary, winning by over 50,000 votes.

March 26—The Supreme Court, in *Ullman v. U.S.*, upholds the Immunity Act.

April 2—In *Pennsylvania v. Nelson*, the Supreme Court rules that the Smith Act of 1940, the Internal Security Act of 1950, and the Communist Control Act of 1954 preempt state sedition laws.

April 9—In *Slochower v. Board of Education*, the Supreme Court rules that a state cannot discharge an employee for invoking the Fifth Amendment before a congressional committee.

April 11—The Senate rejects, 27-59, a proposal to establish a joint congressional committee to review the activities of the CIA and other intelligence operations.

April 11—Eisenhower signs a bill authorizing the Upper Colorado River Project, one of the largest water projects undertaken by the federal government.

April 18—The State Department announces agreement among 12 nations, including the USSR, to charter the International Atomic Energy Agency.

April 26—Nixon announces that Eisenhower is "delighted" to have him on the ticket as the vice presidential candidate.

May 10—The Senate cites several newsmen for contempt of Congress because of their refusal to answer questions on communism during an Internal Security Subcommittee probe into Communist penetration of the press.

May 28—Eisenhower signs the Agricultural Act of 1956. It establishes the "Soil Bank" program to compensate farmers for land left fallow in attempts to reduce surpluses. Alternatively, farmers are permitted to contract with the Agriculture Department to convert productive land to specified conservation projects.

May 29—Stevenson narrowly defeats Kefauver in Florida's Democratic presidential primary.

June 9—Eisenhower suffers an attack of ileitis and has emergency surgery.

June 9—New York's governor, Averell Harriman, announces his candidacy for the Democratic presidential nomination.

June 11—In *Cole v. Young*, the Supreme Court rules that government employees in "non-sensitive" positions cannot be dismissed as security risks under the Internal Security Act of 1950.

June 19—The House Special Government Activities Subcommittee files a report on its probe of the $43 million expansion of a government-owned nickel project at Nicaro, Cuba. The Democratic majority finds "political and private influence" in the contract award.

June 29—Eisenhower signs the highway bill of 1956, which provides for the largest road-building program in U.S. history. The measure authorizes $32.4 billion for the construction of over 40,000 miles of controlled access road.

July 5—The House defeats an administration-backed federal aid-to-education bill authorizing $1.6 billion for school construction. The defeat is, in part, attributed to a controversial Powell amendment, which prohibited aid to segregated schools.

July 19—At the close of fiscal year 1956, the U.S. budgetary surplus is $1.75 billion.

July 19—Dulles announces that the United States is withdrawing the offer of a $56 million grant to Egypt for construction of the proposed $1.3 billion Aswan High Dam.

July 23—The House passes a civil rights bill, sponsored by the administration, focusing on the protection of voting rights. Parliamentary maneuvers prevent the bill from reaching the Senate floor.

July 23—Liberals, led by Stassen, recommend nominating the governor of Massachusetts, Christian A. Herter, as the Republican vice presidential candidate instead of Nixon.

July 31—Kefauver withdraws from the race for the Democratic presidential nomination, and throws his support to Adlai Stevenson.

August 16—Stevenson is selected as the Democratic Party's presidential nominee on the first ballot at the Chicago convention. Stevenson unexpectedly throws the choice of a vice presidential running mate to the convention.

August 16—Liberals fail in an attempt to insert a strong civil rights plank in the Democratic platform.

August 17—Kefauver wins the Democratic vice presidential nomination in a dramatic two-ballot contest with Sen. John F. Kennedy.

August 22—The Republican National Convention nominates Eisenhower and Nixon for reelection.

August 23—The Federal Reserve Board raises the discount rate from 2 ¾ percent to 3 percent.

October 9—Commerce and Labor Departments report that factory workers' average weekly wage is at a record $81 for the month of September, with average factory pay exceeding $2 an hour for the first time. Nonfarm employment is at a record 52,100,000; unemployment is down to 1,988,000, the lowest figure since November 1953.

October 23—An armed revolt begins in Budapest, Hungary. As demanded by the rebels, the imprisoned Imre Nagy, a moderate communist, is brought back to head the government.

October 29—Pursuant to an agreement with Britain and France, Israel invades the Gaza Strip and the Sinai Peninsula, driving toward the Suez Canal.

October 30—A joint British-French ultimatum to Israel and Egypt demands immediate cessation of all fighting and withdrawal of military forces to positions at least 10 miles from the Suez Canal.

October 31—As Anglo-French forces attack Egyptian installations around the Suez Canal Zone, Eisenhower declares himself opposed to the use of force to settle international disputes.

November 2—The United States offers $20 million worth of food and medical supplies to Hungary.

November 4—Khrushchev orders Soviet armored units to crush the Hungarian "fascists." Thirty thousand Hungarians and 7,000 Russians die in the ensuing conflict, which ends a year of unrest and dissent in the Soviet satellites.

November 4—In a letter to Bulganin, Eisenhower urges "in the name of humanity and in the cause of peace" that the USSR halt the bloodshed in Hungary.

November 5—The UN votes to organize a police force to restore peace in the Middle East.

November 6—Eisenhower wins reelection in a landslide, defeating Stevenson by over 9 million votes and capturing 457 out of 531 electoral votes.

November 8—Eisenhower announces that he has directed the Refugee Relief Administration to speed the processing of Hungarian refugees.

November 13—In *Gayle v. Browder*, the Supreme Court unanimously decides that the Montgomery, Alabama, city ordinance requiring racial segregation in buses is unconstitutional.

December 6—Eisenhower orders an air and sea lift to bring 21,500 Hungarian refugees to the United States by January 1, 1957 or shortly thereafter.

December 10—The Supreme Court rules, in *Amalgamated Meat Cutters and Butcher Workmen of North*

America v. NLRB, that a union cannot be penalized because an officer files a false non-communist affidavit with the National Labor Relations Board.

December 31—Sociologist C. Wright Mills's book *The Power Elite* is published.

1957

January 10–11—Martin Luther King, Jr., and 60 other black leaders from 10 southern states meet in Atlanta to form the Southern Christian Leadership Conference.

January 21—Eisenhower is inaugurated for his second term. He becomes the first president limited by the Twenty-Second Amendment.

January 30—The Senate adopts a resolution setting up the Select Committee on Improper Activities in the Labor or Management Field, chaired by John McClellan.

February 25—The Supreme Court, in *Butler v. Michigan*, overturns a Michigan law intended to protect children from obscenity. Justice Felix Frankfurter writes that, by banning all such material, the law denies adults access to material that is unsuitable only for children.

March 7—Congress approves the Eisenhower Doctrine, giving the president the authority to use military force in the Middle East to preserve "the independence and integrity" of Middle Eastern nations and prevent "overt armed aggression from . . . international Communism."

March 24—Eisenhower and British prime minister Harold Macmillan issue a joint communiqué, after four-day conference at Bermuda, stating that the United States has agreed to supply guided missiles to Great Britain.

March 26–27—Teamster Union president Dave Beck testifies before the McClellan Committee on links between the Teamsters and organized crime.

April 11—The House of Representatives votes to authorize $250,000 for a Special Subcommittee on

Legislative Oversight to probe federal regulatory agencies.

April 13—Postmaster General Arthur E. Summerfield halts Saturday post office operations because of Congress's failure to vote supplemental funds for the balance of the fiscal year.

April 16—Normal post office service resumes after Eisenhower signs a $41 million supplemental appropriations bill.

April 29—The army's first nuclear power reactor is dedicated at Fort Belvoir, Virginia.

May 2—Sen. Joseph McCarthy dies of acute liver failure.

May 4—In testimony before the House Ways and Means Committee, Health, Education and Welfare secretary Arthur S. Flemming proposes that the states set up federally subsidized Medicare systems to provide health insurance for persons over 65.

May 14—The United States resumes military aid to Yugoslavia, which had been halted because of Tito's reconciliation with the USSR.

June 3—In *U.S. v. duPont*, the Supreme Court holds that duPont's acquisition of 23 percent of General Motors Co. stock violates the Clayton Antitrust Act.

June 3—In *Jencks v. U.S.*, the Supreme Court rules that the government must permit defendants access to reports made to the FBI by witnesses who testified against the defendant.

June 3–6—The United States formally joins the Military Committee of the Baghdad Pact at a meeting of the Council of Ministers in Karachi, Pakistan.

June 17—In *Yates v. U.S.*, the Supreme Court rules that advocating an "abstract doctrine" of overthrowing the government is not punishable under the Smith Act.

June 17—In *Watkins v. U.S.*, the Supreme Court overturns John Thomas Watkins's conviction for contempt of Congress. In his opinion for the majority, Warren holds that congressional investigations must be related to a legitimate legislative purpose.

June 17—In *Sweezy v. New Hampshire*, the Supreme Court reverses the contempt conviction of a professor who had refused to answer questions concerning the content of his lectures and his earlier activities in the Progressive Party.

June 24—The Supreme Court, in *Roth v. U.S.*, rules that obscenity is not protected by the First Amendment and that state and federal obscenity laws are therefore constitutionally permissible.

July 11—Twenty of 22 leading nuclear scientists attending a conference at Pugwash, Nova Scotia, warn that misuse of nuclear energy could lead to the annihilation of humanity.

July 16—Secretary of Defense Charles Wilson orders the armed forces reduced by 100,000 men by the end of 1957.

July 20—The Southern Regional Council reports that in 11 southern states only 25 percent of the eligible black voters are registered, compared with 60 percent of the white voters.

August 12—Eisenhower signs a bill authorizing New York State to construct a $600 million power plant at Niagara Falls.

August 13—The Senate Finance Committee approves a proposal, sponsored by Sen. Robert S. Kerr, under which the federal and state governments would share in paying medical expenses for needy aged persons.

August 21—Eisenhower announces a U.S. offer to suspend nuclear weapons tests for two years in return for a Soviet agreement to halt production of fissionable material for weapons and to establish an inspection system.

August 25—The Special Radiation Subcommittee of the Joint Atomic Energy Committee reports that the effect of radioactive fallout is negligible but might increase if atomic tests increase.

August 28—Sen. Strom Thurmond stages a 24-hour 27-minute filibuster in an effort to prevent Senate passage of a civil rights bill.

August 29—The Senate passes a civil rights bill focusing on voting rights.

September 1—Rev. Dr. Billy Graham's New York City crusade ends with a rally in Times Square. An estimated 2 million people attended his nightly meetings and 56,767 persons responded with "decisions for Christ."

September 4—The governor of Arkansas, Orval E. Faubus, orders national guardsmen to bar nine black students from entering Little Rock's Central High School.

September 9—Eisenhower signs the Civil Rights Act of 1957, establishing a 6-person bipartisan commission with power to study all aspects of the matter of "equal protections of the laws under the Constitution." It also elevates the Civil Rights Section of the Justice Department to the status of a division and protects black voting rights. It is the first civil rights act in 82 years.

September 14—Faubus and Eisenhower confer at Newport, Rhode Island, on the question of the desegregation of Little Rock's Central High School.

September 20—Faubus removes national guardsmen from Little Rock's Central High School in compliance with a federal court injunction.

September 23—Federal officers secretly escort the nine black students into the Little Rock high school building. With an enraged white mob outside and harassment of the students inside the school, the students are removed after three hours.

September 24—Eisenhower federalizes the Arkansas national guard and sends federal troops to Little Rock to enforce a court order desegregating Central High.

October 4—The Soviet Union launches the first artificial earth satellite, *Sputnik*, into orbit.

October 19—The Atomic Energy Commission reports that, according to current estimates, harm to Americans from H-bomb testing appears to be within "tolerable limits."

November 3—The USSR launches *Sputnik II.*

November 7—In response to the Soviet space launchings, Eisenhower appoints James Killian, president of the Massachusetts Institute of Technology, to manage a program of scientific improvement in the U.S. defense program.

November 7—The Gaither Report, leaked to the press, finds that because of increased Soviet spending, the USSR will achieve missile superiority over the United States by 1959. The group recommends increased military spending and the development of a fallout shelter program to meet the challenge.

November 13—In a nationwide address, Eisenhower proposes a considerable increase in defense appropriations to meet the threat of scientific advances by the USSR. The increase is less than Democrats are demanding.

November 25—Sen. Lyndon Johnson's Preparedness Subcommittee of the Senate Armed Services Committee begins an inquiry into the history, status, and future of the nation's missile and satellite programs.

November 25—Eisenhower suffers a mild stroke.

December 6—America's first attempt to launch a space satellite ends in failure as the Vanguard rocket explodes on its launchpad before a national TV audience.

December 6—AFL-CIO votes overwhelmingly to expel the Teamsters Union for failing to purge itself of corrupt leadership.

December 15—Eisenhower rejects an appeal by Indian prime minister Jawaharlal Nehru for a halt in nuclear weapons tests.

December 16–19—At the Paris NATO meeting, the United States convinces Great Britain, Italy, and Turkey to station U.S. intermediate range missiles on their territory.

December 17—The United States successfully fires the Atlas, its first intercontinental ballistic missile.

December 18—The first commercial nuclear electric generating plant goes into operation at Shippingport, Pennsylvania.

1958

January 5—The Rockefeller Brothers Fund releases a report, prepared by Henry Kissinger, warning of massive Soviet success in improving technology and approaching military weapons parity with the United States. It advocates larger defense expenditures and a buildup of conventional forces.

January 7—Eisenhower requests that Congress appropriate an additional $1.4 billion to speed up and expand missile and air defenses.

January 9—Eisenhower's State of the Union message stresses the need for an accelerated defense effort and the reorganization of the Defense Department to curb interservice rivalry.

January 12—In a letter to Bulganin, Eisenhower urges that "outer space should be used only for peaceful purposes."

January 13—Eisenhower sends his fiscal 1959 budget to Congress. It provides for moderate increases in military spending and cutbacks in other areas.

January 13—Linus Pauling releases a petition signed by 9,235 scientists, including 36 Nobel Prize laureates, calling for an international nuclear test ban.

January 27—Eisenhower urges enactment of an "emergency" four-year program to improve education, especially in mathematics and the sciences.

January 30—Eisenhower requests that Congress extend the reciprocal trade program for five years.

January 31—An army rocket team, led by Dr. Wernher von Braun, sends the first U.S. satellite, *Explorer I*, into orbit.

February 10—Bernard Schwartz is dismissed as chief counsel of the Special House Committee on Legislative Oversight after he accuses committee members of trying to whitewash the investigation of federal regulatory agencies.

February 22—In a televised address, former president Harry S. Truman charges the Eisenhower administration with bringing on the recession.

February 27—Eisenhower signs a bill temporarily raising the national debt limit from $275 to $285 billion.

March 5—Eisenhower vetoes a bill granting funds for the development of a nuclear-powered airplane.

March 31—The USSR announces a unilateral suspension of nuclear tests.

April 1—Eisenhower signs the emergency housing bill to stimulate housing construction by calling for federal purchase of new home mortgages and providing additional money for federal loans on veterans' housing.

May 1—The coast guard arrests four pacifists attempting to sail their ship into the U.S. atomic testing site in the South Pacific. Protests against nuclear testing increase.

May 3—The United States proposes a treaty providing for demilitarization of the Antarctic.

May 8—Eisenhower orders the removal of federalized national guardsmen from Little Rock's Central High School.

May 15—Nixon returns from a stormy 18-day tour of eight South American republics. During the tour, he was often assailed by anti-American mobs protesting alleged U.S. support of dictators.

May 20—Eisenhower delivers a nationwide radio-TV address stating that an economic upturn is in the making and promising an early decision on proposed tax reductions.

May 26—Eisenhower asks Congress to extend excise and corporation income taxes for one year.

June 4—Eisenhower signs a bill extending unemployment benefits to counter the recession. Under the measure, the federal government grants financial aid to states to enable them to extend coverage for an average of eight weeks.

June 5—The House Special Subcommittee on Legislative Oversight begins hearings on conflict-of-interest charges involving Sherman Adams.

June 16—In *Kent v. Dulles*, the Supreme Court rules that the State Department lacked statutory authority to withhold passports to applicants because of their alleged communist beliefs or associations.

June 17—Adams denies before the House Special Subcommittee on Legislative Oversight that he had interceded with federal agencies on behalf of Bernard Goldfine. Adams acknowledges, however, that he might have "acted more prudently" in inquiring about matters involving Goldfine.

June 30—In *NAACP v. Alabama*, the Supreme Court holds that the NAACP has the right, by freedom of association, not to divulge its membership list.

July 1—Nuclear scientists representing the Western and Soviet blocs meet in Geneva to convene a "conference of experts to study the possibility of detecting violations of possible agreement on suspension of nuclear weapons tests."

July 15—Eisenhower orders U.S. Marines to Lebanon in response to a request from President Camille Chamoun for assistance.

July 29—Eisenhower signs a bill creating the National Aeronautics and Space Administration (NASA) to direct U.S. nonmilitary space activities.

August 1—New postal rates go into effect: Regular mail rises from 3¢ to 4¢ an ounce, domestic airmail from 6¢ to 7¢.

August 6—Eisenhower signs a bill reorganizing the Defense Department. The measure strengthens the powers of the secretary of defense and creates a directorate of defense research and engineering.

August 12—U.S. Marines begin withdrawing from Lebanon.

August 22—Eisenhower offers to halt U.S. nuclear tests for one year. He also proposes that the nuclear powers meet in Geneva to seek an agreement on suspending nuclear tests and setting up an inspection system.

August 23—Eisenhower signs a bill creating the Federal Aviation Agency to supervise air transportation safety.

August 23—Communist China resumes shelling Quemoy and Matsu.

September 2—Eisenhower signs the National Defense Education Act, providing loans for college students and funds to encourage young people to enter teaching careers, particularly in higher education and the sciences.

September 2—Eisenhower signs the excise tax technical changes bill. The measure is the first important revision of the general excise tax provisions of the Internal Revenue Code since 1932.

September 9—Eisenhower orders federal agencies to cut their employment levels by 2 percent in fiscal 1959 to absorb a pay raise voted by Congress.

September 11—On national TV, Eisenhower reiterates the United States's commitment to defend Quemoy and Matsu.

September 22—Accused of conflict of interest, Sherman Adams resigns as Eisenhower's chief aide.

September 25—A federal grand jury indicts former Federal Communications Commission member Richard A. Mack and Miami attorney Thurman Whiteside on charges of conspiracy to defraud the United States.

September 27—In a statewide referendum, Arkansas voters reject school desegregation.

September 28—In *Cooper v. Aaron*, the Supreme Court denies a request from the Little Rock, Arkansas, school board for additional time to implement its desegregation plan.

October 6—Beijing announces a one week suspension of its bombardment of Quemoy.

October 7—NASA initiates Project Mercury, its first program for manned space flight.

November 4—In midterm elections, the Democrats increase their majorities in both houses of Congress. They control the Senate by 30 seats and the House by 128. Democrats also win 26 gubernatorial races, leaving only 14 Republican governors in office.

November 10—Khrushchev calls on the United States, Great Britain, and France to "give up the remnants of the occupation regime in Berlin" and announces his intention to sign a peace treaty with East Germany. This, he implies, would terminate Allied rights in West Berlin.

November 11–December 18—The United States and USSR hold an inconclusive conference on the Prevention of Surprise Attack in Geneva.

November 22—The United States reaffirms its intention to "maintain the integrity" of West Berlin.

November 27—Khrushchev announced a six-month deadline for a settlement on Berlin.

December—The John Birch Society is founded.

December 14—The United States, Britain, and France formally reject Soviet demands for their withdrawal from West Berlin.

December 20—John Kenneth Galbraith publishes *The Affluent Society*.

1959

January 1—Fidel Castro's guerrilla forces overthrow the Batista regime in Cuba.

January 2—The USSR achieves the world's first moon shot as *Lunik I* passes within a few thousand miles of the moon.

January 3—Eisenhower proclaims Alaska the 49th state.

January 5—The White House releases a statement by its science advisory committee questioning the reliability of techniques for detecting underground nuclear tests.

February 2—Eisenhower outlines to Congress a 10-year space program to launch a satellite or space probe vehicle each month starting in mid-1959.

February 5—In a special message to Congress, Eisenhower submits a seven-point civil rights program that includes support for school integration.

March 23—The peacetime draft is extended until July 1, 1963.

March 30—In *Abbate v. U.S.* and *Bartkus v. Illinois*, the Supreme Court rules that a person may be tried for the same offense in federal and state courts without infringing on the freedom from double jeopardy.

April 4—In an address at Gettysburg College, Eisenhower makes his first commitment to maintain South Vietnam as a separate national state.

April 9—NASA selects seven astronauts for Project Mercury.

April 13—Eisenhower proposes a ban on atmospheric nuclear testing.

April 15—Suffering from terminal cancer, Dulles resigns as secretary of state.

April 15–28—Castro visits the United States.

April 18—Christian Herter is named secretary of state.

April 25—The St. Lawrence Seaway opens.

May 11—The foreign ministers of the United States, Great Britain, France, and the USSR meet in Geneva to begin talks on the problems of Berlin, German reunification, an all-German peace treaty, and European security.

May 24—Dulles dies of cancer.

May 27—Soviet ultimatum on Berlin expires without incident.

June 8—In *Barenblatt v. U.S.*, the Supreme Court upholds the conviction for contempt of Congress of a witness who had refused to testify before HUAC about his beliefs or his membership in a communist organizations.

June 8—Eisenhower asks Congress to abolish the interest ceiling on U.S. savings and treasury bonds and to raise the public debt limit to $295 billion.

June 11—Postmaster General Arthur Summerfield bans a new unexpurgated edition of D. H. Lawrence's *Lady Chatterley's Lover* from the mails.

June 19—The Senate refuses to confirm Lewis Strauss as secretary of commerce.

June 27—The United States denounces Cuba before the Organization of American States for contributing to Caribbean tensions and for its slanderous attacks upon the United States.

June 29—In *Kingsley International Pictures v. Regents*, the Supreme Court unanimously strikes down a ban by the Regents of the University of the State of New York on showing the film version of D. H. Lawrence's *Lady Chatterley's Lover*. The Court leaves the general question of obscenity unclear.

June 30—The public debt limit is raised temporarily to $295 billion. The permanent cap is raised to $285 billion.

July 7–September 10—The House Armed Services Committee holds hearings on the employment of retired military officers by industry.

July 15—Despite Eisenhower's call for further negotiations, 500,000 steelworkers go on strike against the 28 companies that normally produce 85 percent to 90 percent of America's steel.

July 24—Nixon and Khrushchev engage in a political debate at a preview of the U.S. exhibition in Moscow. The discussion, held in the kitchen of a so-called typical American home, becomes known as the "kitchen debate."

August 1—In a radio-TV address from Moscow, Nixon tells the Soviet people that they will continue to live in an era of fear, suspicion, and tension if Khrushchev tries to promote the communization of countries outside the USSR.

August 12—Four Little Rock public high schools, closed since 1958 to avoid integration, reopen.

August 21—Hawaii is officially proclaimed the 50th state.

August 26—Eisenhower vetoes an omnibus public works bill.

August 31—The Joint Atomic Energy Committee's Special Subcommittee on Radiation issues a report concluding that further nuclear tests could be hazardous and urging the establishment of a national civil defense system.

September 8—The Civil Rights Commission issues its first report on voting rights. It finds that only 25 percent of eligible black voters are registered in 10 southern states and outlines a dozen specific legislative measures to assure African Americans their full voting rights.

September 10—Congress overrides Eisenhower's veto of the omnibus public works bill.

September 14—Eisenhower signs a bill exempting TV and radio news from having to provide equal time to all competing political candidates in cases where one has appeared in a newscast or interview.

September 14—Eisenhower signs the Labor Management Reporting and Disclosure Act (Landrum-Griffin Act) designed to crack down on corruption in unions. It also includes provisions protecting members from unfair actions by their unions and revises the ban on secondary boycotts.

September 15—Soviet premier Khrushchev arrives in the United States on a goodwill visit.

September 15–27—Agreements made during congenial talks between Khrushchev and Eisenhower at Camp David, Maryland, prepare the way for a summit meeting the following year.

October 1—Federal taxes on gasoline are increased by 1¢ per gallon to finance the national highway program.

October 12—The United States places an embargo on all exports to Cuba, except medical supplies and food.

October 19—The U.S. Development Loan Fund releases a major policy statement announcing that future loans to underdeveloped countries must be spent on U.S. goods.

October 21—District Judge Herbert Sorg signs an 80-day Taft-Hartley injunction ordering the United Steelworkers to halt their 99-day strike.

October 26—Eisenhower announces his firm intention to defend the U.S. naval base at Guantánamo, Cuba.

October 31—Eisenhower's announced moratorium on nuclear testing expires, but Eisenhower asks for no new tests.

November 3—Panamanian nationalists riot over U.S. domination of the Panama Canal Zone.

November 6—The Senate Subcommittee on Legislative Oversight concludes hearings on rigged TV quiz shows. No indictments are handed down, although several contestants, including Charles Van Doren, testified that they were coached on answers and told when to lose.

November 7—The Supreme Court upholds the 80-day injunction, issued under the Taft-Hartley Act, halting the 116-day steel strike.

December 1—The United States, USSR, and 10 other nations sign the Antarctic Treaty, establishing a nuclear-free zone around the Antarctic ice mass and setting up inspection and enforcement procedures.

December 3—Eisenhower embarks on an 11-nation goodwill tour of Europe, Asia, and North Africa.

December 30—The navy commissions the *S.S. George Washington*, the first nuclear-powered submarine designed to fire Polaris missiles.

December 30—Sen. Hubert Humphrey begins his campaign for the Democratic presidential nomination in 1960.

1960

January 2—Kennedy announces his candidacy for the Democratic presidential nomination.

January 4—Negotiators for the United Steelworkers and 11 major steel producers reach an agreement on a new contract.

January 9—Nixon announces his candidacy for the Republican presidential nomination.

January 19—The United States and Japan sign the Mutual Security Treaty, under which both countries pledge to maintain and develop their capacities to resist armed attacks.

January 26—Formally restating U.S. policy, Eisenhower reaffirms that there will be no reprisals against Cuba or intervention in its internal affairs.

February 1—Black students peacefully sit in at segregated lunch counters in Greensboro, North Carolina.

February 22–March 7—Eisenhower undertakes a four-nation goodwill tour of Latin America.

March 8—Kennedy wins the New Hampshire Democratic primary with a record 42,969 votes.

March 10—Federal Communications Commission chairman John Charles Doerfer resigns effective March 14, as a result of conflict-of-interest charges raised by the Special House Subcommittee on Legislative Oversight.

March 15—The 10-Nation Disarmament Conference begins in Geneva.

March 15—Eisenhower meets with West German chancellor Konrad Adenauer at the White House, assuring him of U.S. support in maintaining the freedom of West Berlin.

March 16—Eisenhower endorses Nixon as his successor.

March 17—Eisenhower formally approves a CIA plan to train Cuban emigrés for an invasion of the island.

March 31—The House Ways and Means Committee kills the Forand plan to provide hospital and nursing home care for the elderly, financed through Social Security.

April 1—The United States launches *Tiros I*, the first weather satellite, which will provide televised pictures of cloud cover over the earth's surface.

April 3—Daniel Bell's *The End of Ideology: On the Exhaustion of Political Ideas in the Fifties* is published.

April 8—The Senate, by a vote of 71-18, passes a civil rights bill that gives increased authority to the federal courts and Civil Rights Commission to prevent the disenfranchisement of black voters in the South.

April 22—In a television speech, Castro charges that the United States is plotting to overthrow his government.

April 26—Kennedy wins the Pennsylvania Democratic presidential primary.

May 1—Francis Gary Powers, on a U-2 reconnaissance flight for the CIA, is shot down over the USSR by a surface-to-air missile.

May 2—Caryl Chessman is executed for first-degree rape at San Quentin prison in California, despite worldwide protests.

May 3—A spokesman for NASA announces that a U-2 "research airplane," gathering weather data for NASA and the Air Force Weather Service, has apparently crashed in Turkey.

May 5—Khrushchev reveals that an American aircraft has been shot down over Soviet air space and angrily declares it an act of "aggressive provocation." Two days later, he produces Powers and the remnants of the U-2 plane.

May 6—Eisenhower signs the Civil Rights Act of 1960.

May 7—Eisenhower announces that the United States will resume underground nuclear testing as part of research on detecting such blasts.

May 7—The State Department admits that the U-2 plane was "probably" endeavouring to obtain intelligence information.

May 9—Secretary of State Christian Herter strongly defends the need for the aerial intelligence program to counter the USSR's ability to prepare secretly for a surprise attack.

May 9—The Federal Drug Administration approves Enovid, an oral contraceptive for women, for public sale.

May 10—Kennedy defeats Humphrey in the West Virginia Democratic primary by 77,305 votes. Humphrey withdraws from the presidential race.

May 11—In his first public comment on the U-2 incident, Eisenhower accepts personal responsibility for the U-2 flights.

May 16—After three hours, the Paris summit meeting collapses when Khrushchev vehemently demands that Eisenhower apologize for the U-2 flights, punish the culprits responsible, and ban future flights. He also revokes his invitation to Eisenhower to visit the USSR later in the spring.

May 27—Eisenhower announces the termination of U.S. economic aid to Cuba.

May 31—In *U.S. v. States of La., Tex., Miss., Ala., and Fla.*, the Supreme Court upholds the Submerged Lands Act of 1953 by which the United States granted oil rights in submerged lands to coastal states up to three miles offshore.

June 2—The Federal Reserve Board authorizes a reduction in the discount rate from 4 percent to 3 ½ percent.

June 7—A surgeon general's report on the mission of the Public Health Service underscores the growing danger of environmental health factors.

June 8—Eisenhower signs legislation directing the surgeon general to make a study of the effects of motor vehicle exhaust fumes on the public health.

June 12—Eisenhower leaves on a two-week goodwill tour of 12 Far Eastern countries.

June 16—Thousands of Japanese riot against the U.S.-Japanese security treaty. Eisenhower cancels his visit to Japan.

June 20—In *Hannah v. Larche*, the Supreme Court upholds the right of the Civil Rights Commission to hold hearings in which the identity of those submitting complaints remains confidential.

June 27—In *Elkins v. U.S.*, the Supreme Court rules that evidence obtained by state officers during an illegal search is inadmissible in federal courts.

June 27—The 10-Nation Disarmament Conference ends with no movement on either side.

July 1—Congress overrides Eisenhower's veto of a bill providing pay increases for federal employees.

July 6—In retaliation for the seizure of millions of dollars worth of American property, the United States cuts Cuba's sugar import quota by 700,000 tons.

July 9—Eisenhower asserts that the United States will never permit the establishment of a communist regime in the Western Hemisphere.

July 13—Kennedy wins the Democratic presidential nomination on the first ballot at the Los Angeles convention. Johnson is chosen vice presidential candidate at the following session.

July 22—Eisenhower orders a 3 percent reduction in the number of federal employees.

July 22–23—In a meeting with New York's governor, Nelson Rockefeller, Nixon agrees to a stronger platform on civil rights, defense, and foreign policy in exchange for Rockefeller's support for the presidential nomination. The press dubs the meeting the "Treaty of Fifth Avenue."

July 25—Nixon easily wins the Republican presidential nomination on the first ballot in Chicago.

August 7—Castro announces "forcible expropriation" of all U.S.-owned companies.

August 19—A Soviet military tribunal sentences Powers to 10 years in prison for espionage.

August 20—The United States joins other members of the Organization of American States in voting to sever diplomatic relations with the Dominican Republic as well as to impose economic sanctions and a complete arms embargo on it for its "acts of aggression" in participating in a plot to overthrow the Venezuelan government.

August 24—In response to a reporter's query for an example of a major idea Nixon has contributed to the administration, Eisenhower replies, "If you give me a week, I might think of one. I don't remember."

September 11—The Inter-American Economic Conference adopts the "Act of Bogota," an extensive social and economic aid program for Latin America.

September 13—Eisenhower signs a bill making the fixing of TV quiz shows a federal crime and giving the Federal Communications Commission power to tighten restrictions on deceptive broadcasting practices.

September 13—Eisenhower signs amendments to Social Security that provide federal aid to states to establish programs providing medical care for poor and low-income elderly.

September 22—Eisenhower addresses the UN General Assembly, proposing national self-determination for African colonies and a five-point program of economic and educational assistance to be administered through the UN.

September 26—Kennedy and Nixon hold the first of four televised debates between the presidential candidates.

October 17—National variety store chains: Woolworth, Kresge, W.T. Grant, and McCrory-McLellan announce that lunch counters in their stores have been integrated in more than 100 southern cities.

October 19—The United States prohibits export to Cuba of all goods except food and medical supplies.

October 24—U.S. church membership for 1959 is reported to have risen to a record 112,226,905 at year's end.

October 28—The United States requests the Organization of American States to investigate reports that Cuba is receiving large shipments of arms from the Soviet bloc.

November 1—Eisenhower announces that the United States would take "whatever steps" necessary to maintain the U.S. naval base at Guantánamo, Cuba.

November 8—Kennedy defeats Nixon in the presidential election by 113,057 votes and receives 303 of the 537 electoral votes. The Democrats retain control of both the House and the Senate.

November 14—Rioting accompanies the desegregation of two elementary schools in New Orleans.

November 17—The CIA briefs Kennedy on its involvement in training Cuban exiles in Guatemala to overthrow Castro.

November 18—Eisenhower orders U.S. naval units to patrol Central American waters to prevent communist-led invasions of either Guatemala or Nicaragua.

November 19—Eisenhower's science advisory committee urges the federal government and all other elements of the national community to assume a greater role in supporting, strengthening, and expanding basic scientific research and graduate education in science.

November 27—Eisenhower's Commission on National Goals issues a report calling for "extraordinary personal responsibility" and sustained "effort and sacrifice" from "every American" in the 1960s to help the United States achieve "high and difficult goals" in the period of "grave danger" ahead.

December 5—In *Boynten v. Virginia*, the Supreme Court rules that racial discrimination in bus terminal facilities serving interstate passengers violates the Interstate Commerce Act.

December 7—Kefauver's Senate Antitrust and Monopoly Subcommittee begins an investigation of pricing in the prescription drug industry.

December 7—The Office of Education announces that a record 3.6 million students are pursuing college degrees.

December 14—Western European nations, the United States, and Canada sign an agreement in Paris creating an Organization for Economic Cooperation and Development.

1961

January 3—Eisenhower breaks diplomatic relations with Cuba.

January 17—Eisenhower delivers an eloquent farewell address to the nation, in which he warns that America "must guard against the acquisition of unwarranted influence, whether sought or unsought, by the military-industrial complex."

PRINCIPAL U.S. GOVERNMENT OFFICIALS OF THE EISENHOWER YEARS

SUPREME COURT

Fred M. Vinson, Chief Justice 1946–53
Earl Warren, Chief Justice 1953–69
Hugo L. Black 1937–71
William J. Brennan, Jr. 1956–90
Harold H. Burton 1945–58
Tom C. Clark 1949–67
William O. Douglas 1939–75

Felix Frankfurter 1939–62
John Marshall Harlan 1955–71
Robert H. Jackson 1941–54
Sherman Minton 1949–56
Stanley F. Reed 1938–57
Potter Stewart 1958–81
Charles E. Whittaker 1957–62

EXECUTIVE DEPARTMENTS

Department of Agriculture
Secretary of Agriculture
   Ezra Taft Benson, 1953–61

Undersecretary
   True D. Morse, 1953–61

Assistant Secretaries
   J. Earl Coke, 1953–54
   John H. Davis, 1953–54
   Ross Rizley, 1953–54
   Ervin L. Peterson, 1954–60
   Earl L. Butz, 1954–57
   James A. McConnell, 1955
   Marvin L. McLain, 1956–60
   Don Paarlberg, 1957–58
   Clarence L. Miller, 1958–61

Administrative Assistant Secretary
   Ralph S. Roberts, 1953–61

Department of Commerce
Secretary of Commerce
   Sinclair Weeks, 1953–58
   Lewis L. Strauss, (acting) 1958–59
   Frederick H. Mueller, 1959–61

Undersecretary
   Walter Williams, 1953–58
   Frederick H. Mueller, 1958–59
   Philip A. Ray, 1959–61

Undersecretary for Transportation
   Robert B. Murray, Jr. 1953–55
   Louis S. Rothschild, 1955–58
   John J. Allen, Jr., 1959–61

Assistant Secretary for Administration
James C. Worthy, 1954–55
George T. Moore, 1955–61

Assistant Secretary for International Affairs
Samuel W. Anderson, 1953–55
Harold C. McClellan, 1955–57
Henry Kearns, 1957–60
Bradley Fisk, 1960–61

Assistant Secretary for Domestic Affairs
Craig R. Sheaffer, 1953
Lothair Teetor, 1953–55
Frederick H. Mueller, 1955–58
Carl F. Oechsle, 1958–61

Department of Defense
Secretary of Defense
Charles E. Wilson, 1953–57
Neil H. McElroy, 1957–59
Thomas S. Gates, Jr., 1959–61

Deputy Secretary of Defense
Roger M. Kyes, 1953–54
Robert B. Anderson, 1954–55
Reuben B. Robertson, Jr., 1955–57
Donald A. Quarles, 1957–59
Thomas S. Gates, Jr., 1959
James H. Douglas, Jr., 1959–61

Secretary of the Air Force
Harold Talbott, 1953–55
Donald A. Quarles, 1955–57
James H. Douglas, Jr., 1957–59
Dudley C. Sharp, 1959–61

Secretary of the Army
Robert T. Stevens, 1953–55
Wilbur M. Brucker, 1955–61

Secretary of the Navy
Robert B. Anderson, 1953–54
Charles S. Thomas, 1954–57
Thomas S. Gates, Jr., 1957–59
William B. Franke, 1959–61

Assistant Secretary of Defense (Comptroller)
Wilfred J. McNeil, 1949–59
Franklin B. Lincoln, 1959–61

Assistant Secretary of Defense (Engineering)
Frank D. Newbury, 1953–57

* Reorganized under Assistant Secretary (Research and Engineering), 1957

Assistant Secretary of Defense (Health and Medical)
Dr. Melvin A. Casberg, 1953–54
Dr. Frank B. Berry, 1954–61

* Reorganized under Assistant Secretary (Manpower) 1961

Assistant Secretary of Defense (International Security Affairs)
Frank C. Nash, 1953–54
H. Struve Hensel, 1954–55
Gordon Gray, 1955–57
Mansfield D. Sprague, 1957–58
John N. Irwin, II, 1958–61

Assistant Secretary of Defense (Legislative and Public Affairs)
Frederick A. Seaton, 1953–55
Robert Tripp Ross, 1955–57

* Reorganized under Assistant Secretary (Public Affairs), 1957

Assistant Secretary of Defense (Manpower)
John A. Hannah, 1953–54
Carter L. Burgess, 1954–57
William H. Francis, Jr., 1957–58
Charles C. Finucane, 1958–61

Assistant Secretary of Defense (Public Affairs)
Murray Snyder, 1957–61

Assistant Secretary of Defense (Properties and Installations)
Franklin G. Floete, 1953–56
Floyd S. Bryant, 1956–61

* Reorganized under Assistant Secretary (Installations and Logistics), 1961

Assistant Secretary of Defense (Research and Development)
Donald A. Quarles, 1953–55
Dr. Clifford C. Furnas, 1955–57

* Reorganized under Assistant Secretary (Research and Engineering), 1957

Assistant Secretary of Defense (Research and Engineering)
Frank D. Newbury, 1957
Paul D. Foote, 1957–58

* Reorganized under Directorate of Defense Research and Engineering, 1958

Assistant Secretary of Defense (Supply and Logistics)
Charles S. Thomas, 1953–54
Thomas P. Pike, 1954–56
E. Perkins McGuire, 1956–61

* Reorganized under Assistant Secretary (Installations and Logistics), 1961

*Director of Defense Research and Engineering**
Herbert F. York, 1958–61

* Created from the Assistant Secretariat of Defense (Research and Engineering), 1958

Joint Chiefs of Staff
Chairman
Gen. of the Army Omar N. Bradley, U.S. Army, 1949–53
Adm. Arthur W. Radford, U.S. Navy, 1953–57
Gen. Nathan F. Twining, U.S. Air Force, 1957–60
Gen. Lyman L. Lemnitzer, U.S. Army, 1960–62

Chief of Staff, U.S. Army
Gen. J. Lawton Collins, 1949–53
Gen. Matthew B. Ridgeway, 1953–55
Gen. Maxwell D. Taylor, 1955–59
Gen. Lyman L. Lemnitzer, 1959–60
Gen. George H. Decker, 1960–62

Chief of Naval Operations
Adm. William M. Fechteler, 1951–53
Adm. Robert B. Carney, 1953–55
Adm. Arleigh A. Burke, 1955–61

Chief of Staff, U.S. Air Force
Gen. Hoyt S. Vandenberg, 1948–53
Gen. Nathan F. Twining, 1953–57
Gen. Thomas D. White, 1957–61

Commandant of the Marine Corps
Gen. Lemuel C. Shepherd, 1952–55
Gen. Randolph McC. Pate, 1956–59
Gen. David M. Shoup, 1960–63

Department of Health, Education and Welfare
Secretary
Oveta Gulp Hobby, 1953–55

Marion B. Folsom, 1955–58
Arthur S. Flemming, 1958–61

Undersecretary
Nelson A. Rockefeller, 1953–54
Harold C. Hunt, 1955–57
John A. Perkins, 1957–58
Bertha S. Adkins, 1958–61

Assistant Secretary
Russell R. Larmon, 1953–55
Bradshaw Mintener, 1955–57
Edward Foss Wilson, 1957–60

Assistant Secretary for Program Analysis
Roswell B. Perkins, 1954–57

Assistant Secretary for Legislation
Elliot L. Richardson, 1957–59
Robert A. Forsythe, 1960–61

Department of the Interior
Secretary of the Interior
Douglas McKay, 1953–56
Frederick A. Seaton, 1956–61

Undersecretary
Ralph A. Tudor, 1953–54
Clarence A. Davis, 1954–57
Olin H. Chilson, 1957–58
Elmer F. Bennett, 1958–61

Assistant Secretary—Fish and Wildlife
Ross L. Leffler, 1957–61

Assistant Secretary—Mineral Resources
Felix E. Wormser, 1953–57
Royce A. Hardy, 1957–61

Assistant Secretary—Public Land Management
Orme Lewis, 1953–55
Wesley A. D'Ewart, 1955–56
Olin H. Chilson, 1956–57
Roger C. Ernst, 1957–60
George W. Abbott, 1960–61

Assistant Secretary—Water and Power Development
Fred G. Aandahl, 1953–61

Administrative Assistant Secretary
D. Otis Beasley, 1952–65

Department of Justice

Attorney General
Herbert Brownell, Jr., 1953–57
William P. Rogers, 1957–61

Deputy Attorney General
William P. Rogers, 1953–57
Lawrence E. Walsh, 1957–60

Solicitor General
Simon E. Sobeloff, 1954–55
J. Lee Rankin, 1956–61

Assistant Attorney General/Administration
S. A. Andretta, 1950–65

Assistant Attorney General/Antitrust Division
Stanley N. Barnes, 1953–56
Victor R. Hansen, 1956–59
Robert A. Bicks, (acting) 1960–61

Assistant Attorney General/Civil Division
Warren E. Burger, 1953–56
George Cochran Doub, 1956–60

Assistant Attorney General/Civil Rights Division
W. Wilson White, 1957–59
Joseph M. F. Ryan, Jr., (acting) 1959–60
Harold R. Tyler, Jr., 1960–61

Assistant Attorney General/Criminal Division
Warren Olney, III, 1953–57
Malcolm Anderson, 1958–59
Malcolm R. Wilkey, 1959–61

Assistant Attorney General/Internal Security Division
William F. Tompkins, 1954–58
J. Walter Yeahley, 1959–70

Assistant Attorney General/Lands Division
Perry W. Morton, 1953–61

Assistant Attorney General/Office of Alien Property
Dallas S. Townsend, 1953–60

Assistant Attorney General/Office of Legal Counsel
J. Lee Rankin, 1953–56
Malcolm R. Wilkey, 1958–59
Robert Kramer, 1959–61

Assistant Attorney General/Tax Division
H. Brian Holland, 1953–56
Charles K. Rice, 1956–61

Department of Labor

Secretary of Labor
Maurice J. Tobin, 1948–53
Martin P. Durkin, 1953
Lloyd A. Mashburn, (acting) 1953
James P. Mitchell, 1953–61

Undersecretary
Michael J. Galvin, 1949–53
Lloyd A. Mashburn, 1953
Arthur Larson, 1954–56
James T. O'Connell, 1957–61

Deputy Undersecretary
Millard Cass, 1955–71

Assistant Secretary for Labor-Management Relations
John J. Gilhooley, 1957–61

Assistant Secretary for Employment and Manpower
Rocco C. Siciliano, 1953–57
Newell Brown, 1957–60
Walter C. Wallace, 1960–61
Jerry R. Holleman, 1961–62

Assistant Secretary for International Labor Affairs
Philip M. Kaiser, 1949–53
Spencer Miller, Jr., 1953–54
J. Ernest Wilkins, 1954–58
George C. Lodge, 1958–61
George L. P. Weaver, 1961–69

Assistant Secretary for Standards and Statistics
Harrison C. Hobart, 1953–54

Post Office Department

Postmaster General
Arthur E. Summerfield, 1947–61

Deputy Postmaster General
Charles R. Hook, Jr., 1953–55
Maurice H. Stans, 1955–57
Edson O. Sessions, 1957–59
John M. McKibbin, 1959–61

Assistant Postmaster General/Bureau of Operations
Norman R. Abrams, 1953–57
John M. McKibbin, 1957–59
Bert B. Barnes, 1959–61

Assistant Postmaster General/Bureau of Transportation
John C. Allen, 1953–54
E. George Siedle, 1954–59
George M. Moore, 1959–61

Assistant Postmaster General/Bureau of Finance
Albert J. Robertson, 1953–56
Hyde Gillette, 1957–61

Assistant Postmaster General/Bureau of Facilities
Ormonde A. Kieb, 1953–59
Rollin D. Barnard, 1959–61

Assistant Postmaster General/Bureau of Personnel
Eugene J. Lyons, 1953–59
Frank E. Barr, 1960–61

State Department

Secretary of State
John Foster Dulles, 1953–59
Christian A. Herter, 1959–61

Undersecretary
Walter B. Smith, 1953–54
Herbert Hoover, Jr., 1954–57
Christian A. Herter, 1957–59
C. Douglas Dillon, 1959–61

Undersecretary for Administration
Donold B. Lourie, 1953–54
Charles E. Saltzman, 1954

Undersecretary for Economic Affairs
C. Douglas Dillon, 1958–59

Undersecretary for Political Affairs
Robert D. Murphy, 1959
Livingston T. Merchant, 1959–61

Deputy Undersecretary
H. Freeman Matthews, 1950–53

Deputy Undersecretary for Administration
Carlisle H. Humelsine, 1950–53
Loy W. Henderson, 1955–61

Deputy Undersecretary for Economic Affairs
Samuel C. Waugh, 1955
Herbert V. Prochnow, 1955–56
C. Douglas Dillon, 1957–58

Deputy Undersecretary for Political Affairs
Robert D. Murphy, 1953–59
Livingston T. Merchant, 1959
Raymond A. Hare, 1960–61

Assistant Secretary for Administration
Edward T. Wailes, 1953–54
Isaac W. Carpenter, Jr., 1954–55, 1957
Walter K. Scott, 1958–59
Lane Dwinell, 1959–61

Assistant Secretary for African Affairs
Joseph C. Satterthwaite, 1958–61

Assistant Secretary for Congressional Relations
Thruston B. Morton, 1953–56
Robert C. Hill, 1956–57
William B. Macomber, Jr., 1957–61

Assistant Secretary for Controller
Isaac W. Carpenter, Jr., 1955–57

Assistant Secretary for Economic Affairs
Harold F. Linder, 1952–53
Samuel C. Waugh, 1953–55
Thorsten V. Kalijarvi, 1957
Thomas C. Mann, 1957–60
Edwin M. Martin, 1960–62

Assistant Secretary for European Affairs
Livingston T. Merchant, 1953–56, 1958–59
C. Burke Elbrick, 1957–58
Foy D. Kohler, 1959–62

Assistant Secretary for Far Eastern Affairs
John M. Allison, 1952–53
Walter S. Robertson, 1953–59
J. Graham Parsons, 1959–61

Assistant Secretary for Inter-American Affairs
John M. Cabot, 1953–54
Henry F. Holland, 1954–56
Roy R. Rubottom, Jr., 1957–60
Thomas C. Mann, 1960–61

Assistant Secretary for International Organization Affairs
David McK. Key, 1954–55
Francis O. Wilcox, 1955–61

Assistant Secretary for Near Eastern, South Asian & African Affairs
Henry A. Byroade, 1952–55

George V. Allen, 1955–56
William M. Rountree, 1956–59

* Reorganized as Near Eastern and South Asian Affairs, 1958 G. Lewis Jones, 1959–61

Assistant Secretary for Policy Planning
Robert R. Bowie, 1955–57
Gerard C. Smith, 1957–61

Assistant Secretary for Public Affairs
Carl W. McCardle, 1953–57
Andrew H. Berding, 1957–61

Assistant Secretary for United Nations Affairs
John D. Hickerson, 1949–53
Robert D. Murphy, 1953
David McK. Key, 1953–54

* Reorganized as International Organization Affairs, 1954

Department of the Treasury

Secretary of the Treasury
George M. Humphrey, 1953–57
Robert B. Anderson, 1957–61

Undersecretary
Marion B. Folsom, 1953–55
W. Randolph Burgess, 1955–57
Fred C. Scribner, Jr., 1957–61

Undersecretary for Monetary Affairs
W. Randolph Burgess, 1954–55
H. Chapman Rose, 1955–56
Julian B. Baird, 1957–61

Assistant Secretaries
H. Chapman Rose, 1953–55
Andrew N. Overby, 1952–57
Laurence B. Robbins, 1954–61
David W. Kendall, 1955–57
A. Gilmore Flues, 1958–61
Tom B. Coughran, 1957–58
T. Graydon Upton, 1958–60

Assistant Secretary for Fiscal Affairs
Edward F. Bartelt, 1945–55
William T. Heffelfinger, 1955–62

Administrative Assistant Secretary
William W. Parsons, 1950–59
A. E. Weatherbee, 1959–70

REGULATORY COMMISSIONS AND INDEPENDENT AGENCIES

Atomic Energy Commission

Joseph Campbell, 1953–54
Gordon E. Dean, 1949–53; Chairman, 1950–53
John F. Floberg, 1957–60
John S. Graham, 1957–62
W. F. Libby, 1954–59
John A. McCone, 1958–61; Chairman, 1958–61
Thomas E. Murray, 1950–57
Loren K. Olson, 1960–62
Henry D. Smyth, 1949–54
Lewis L. Strauss, 1946–50; Chairman, 1953–58
Harold S. Vance, 1955–59
John Von Neumann, 1955–57
John H. Williams, 1959–60
Robert E. Wilson, 1960–64
Eugene M. Zuckert, 1952–54

Civil Aeronautics Board

Joseph P. Adams, 1951–56
Alan S. Boyd, 1959–65; Chairman, 1961–65
Harmar D. Denny, 1953–59
James R. Durfee, Chairman, 1956–60
Whitney Gillilland, 1959–76
Chan Gurney, 1951–65; Chairman, 1954
Louis J. Hector, 1957–59
Josh Lee, 1945–55
G. Joseph Minetti, 1956–74
Ross Rizley, 1955–56; Chairman, 1955–56
Oswald Ryan, 1945–54; Chairman, 1953

Federal Communications Commission

Robert T. Bartley, 1952–72
T. A. M. Craven, 1956–63

John S. Cross, 1958–62
John C. Doerfer, 1953–60; Chairman, 1957–60
Frederick W. Ford, 1957–65; Chairman, 1960–61
Frieda B. Hennock, 1948–55
Rosel H. Hyde, 1946–69; Chairman, 1953–54, 1966–69
Robert E. Lee, 1953
Richard A. Mack, 1955–58
George C. McConnaughey, 1954–57; Chairman, 1954–57
Eugene H. Merrill, 1952–53
George E. Sterling, 1948–54
Paul A. Walker, 1945–53; Chairman, 1952–53
Edward M. Webster, 1947–56

Federal Power Commission
Thomas C. Buchanan, 1948–53; Chairman, 1952–53
William R. Connole, 1955–60
Seaborn L. Digby, 1953–58
Dale E. Doty, 1952–54
Claude L. Draper, 1945–56
John B. Hussey, 1958–60
Arthur Kline, 1956–61
Jerome K. Kuykendall, 1953–61; Chairman, 1953–61
Nelson Lee Smith, 1945–55; Chairman, 1947–50
Frederick Stueck, 1954–61
Paul A. Sweeny, 1960–61
Harrington Wimberly, 1945–53

Federal Reserve Board
C. Canby Balderston, 1954–66
Rudolph M. Evans, 1945–54
G. H. King, Jr., 1959–63
William McC. Martin, Jr., 1951–70; Chairman, 1951–70
Paul E. Miller, 1954

A. L. Mills, Jr., 1952–65
J. L. Robertson, 1952–73
Charles N. Shepardson, 1955–67
M. S. Szymczak, 1945–61
James K. Vardaman, Jr., 1946–58

Federal Trade Commission
Sigurd Anderson, 1955–64
Albert A. Carretta, 1952–54
John Carson, 1949–53
John W. Gwynne, 1953–59; Chairman, 1955–59
Edward F. Howrey, 1953–55; Chairman, 1953–55
William C. Kern, 1955–62
Earl W. Kintner, 1959–61; Chairman, 1959–61
Lowell B. Mason, 1945–56; Chairman, 1949–50
James M. Mead, 1949–55; Chairman, 1950–53
Edward K. Mills, Jr., 1960–61
Robert T. Secrest, 1954–61
Stephen J. Spingarn, 1950–53
Edward T. Tait, 1956–60

Securities and Exchange Commission
Clarence H. Adams, 1952–56
J. Sinclair Armstrong, 1953–57; Chairman, 1955–57
Donald C. Cook, 1949–53; Chairman, 1952–53
Ralph H. Demmler, 1953–55; Chairman, 1953–55
Edward N. Gadsby, 1957–61; Chairman, 1957–61
A. Jackson Goodwin, Jr., 1953–55
Earl Freeman Hastings, 1956–61
Richard B. McEntire, 1946–53
Andrew Downey Orrick, 1955–60
Harold C. Patterson, 1955–60
Paul R. Rowen, 1948–55
James C. Sargent, 1956–60
Byron D. Woodside, 1960–67

HOUSE OF REPRESENTATIVES

Alabama
George W. Andrews (D) 1944–71
Laurie C. Battle (D) 1947–55

Frank W. Boykin (D) 1935–63
Carl Elliott (D) 1949–65
George M. Grant (D) 1938–65

George Huddleston, Jr. (D) 1955–65
Robert E. Jones (D) 1947–77
Albert Rains (D) 1945–65
Kenneth A. Roberts (D) 1951–65
Armistead I. Selden, Jr. (D) 1953–69

Alaska
Ralph J. Rivers (D) 1959–67

Arizona
Harold A. Patten (D) 1949–55
Stewart L. Udall (D) 1955–61
John J. Rhodes (R) 1953–83

Arkansas
Dale Alford (D) 1959–63
E. C. Gathings (D) 1939–69
Oren Harris (D) 1941–66
Brooks Hays (D) 1943–59
Wilbur D. Mills (D) 1939–77
W. F. Norrell (D) 1939–61
James W. Trimble (D) 1945–67

California
Jeffery Cohelan (D) 1959–71
Robert L. Condon (D) 1953–55
Clyde Doyle (D) 1945–47; 1949–63
Clair Engle (D) 1943–59
Harlan D. Hagen (D) 1953–67
Chet Holifield (D) 1943–75
Harold T. Johnson (D) 1959–81
George A. Kasem (D) 1959–61
Cecil R. King (D) 1942–69
John J. McFall (D) 1957–78
Clem Miller (D) 1959–62
George P. Miller (D) 1945–73
John E. Moss (D) 1953–78
James Roosevelt (D) 1955–65
D. S. Saund (D) 1957–63
John F. Shelley (D) 1949–64
Harry R. Sheppard (D) 1937–65
B. F. Sisk (D) 1955–79
Samuel W. Yorty (D) 1951–55
John J. Allen, Jr. (R) 1947–59
John F. Baldwin (R) 1955–66
Ernest K. Bramblett (R) 1947–55
Charles S. Gubser (R) 1953–75
Edgar W. Hiestand (R) 1953–63

Patrick J. Hillings (R) 1951–59
Carl Hinshaw (R) 1939–56
Joseph F. Holt, III (R) 1953–61
Craig Hosmer (R) 1953–75
Allan O. Hunter (R) 1951–55
Donald L. Jackson (R) 1947–61
J. Leroy Johnson (R) 1943–57
Glenard P. Lipscomb (R) 1953–70
Gordon L. McDonough (R) 1945–63
William S. Mailliard (R) 1953–74
John Phillips (R) 1943–57
Norris Poulson (R) 1943–45; 1947–53
Hubert B. Scudder (R) 1949–59
H. Allen Smith (R) 1957–73
Charles M. Teague (R) 1955–74
James B. Utt (R) 1953–70
Bob Wilson (R) 1953–81
J. Arthur Younger (R) 1953–67

Colorado
Wayne N. Aspinall (D) 1949–73
Byron L. Johnson (D) 1959–61
Byron G. Rogers (D) 1951–71
J. Edgar Chenoweth (R) 1941–49; 1951–65
William S. Hill (R) 1941–59

Connecticut
Chester Bowles (D) 1959–61
Emilio Q. Daddario (D) 1959–71
Thomas J. Dodd (D) 1953–57
Robert N. Giaimo (D) 1959–81
Donald J. Irwin (D) 1959–61; 1965–69
Frank Kowalski (D) 1959–63
John S. Monagan (D) 1959–73
Albert W. Cretella (R) 1953–59
Edwin H. May, Jr. (R) 1957–59
Albert P. Morano (R) 1951–59
James T. Patterson (R) 1947–59
Antoni N. Sadlak (R) 1947–59
Horace Seely-Brown, Jr. (R) 1947–49; 1951–59;
    1961–63

Delaware
Harris B. McDowell, Jr. (D) 1955–57; 1959–67
Harry Haskell, Jr. (R) 1957–59
Herbert B. Warburton (R) 1953–55

Florida
Charles E. Bennett (D) 1949–93

Courtney W. Campbell (D) 1953–55
Dante B. Fascell (D) 1955–93
James A. Haley (D) 1953–77
A. Sydney Herlong, Jr. (D) 1949–69
William C. Lantaff (D) 1951–55
Chester B. McMullen (D) 1951–53
D. R. (Billy) Matthews (D) 1953–67
Dwight L. Rogers (D) 1945–54
Paul G. Rogers (D) 1955–79
Robert L. F. Sikes (D) 1941–44; 1945–79
William C. Cramer (R) 1955–71

Georgia
Iris F. Blitch (D) 1955–63
Paul Brown (D) 1933–61
A. Sidney Camp (D) 1939–54
James C. Davis (D) 1947–63
John J. Flynt, Jr. (D) 1954–79
E. L. Forrester (D) 1951–65
Phil M. Landrum (D) 1953–77
Henderson Lanham (D) 1947–57
Erwin Mitchell (D) 1958–61
J. L. Pilcher (D) 1953–65
Prince H. Preston, Jr. (D) 1947–61
Carl Vinson (D) 1914–65
W. M. Wheeler (D) 1947–55

Hawaii
Daniel K. Inouye (D) 1959–63

Idaho
Gracie Pfost (D) 1953–63
Hamer H. Budge (R) 1951–61

Illinois
James B. Bowler (D) 1953–57
Charles A. Boyle (D) 1955–59
William L. Dawson (D) 1943–70
Thomas S. Gordon (D) 1943–59
Kenneth J. Gray (D) 1955–75
John C. Kluczynski (D) 1951–75
Roland V. Libonati (D) 1957–65
Peter F. Mack, Jr. (D) 1949–63
William T. Murphy (D) 1959–71
James C. Murray (D) 1955–57
Thomas J. O'Brien (D) 1933–39; 1943–64
Barratt O'Hara (D) 1949–51; 1953–69

Melvin Price (D) 1945–88
Roman C. Pucinski (D) 1959–73
Dan Rostenkowski (D) 1959–95
George E. Shipley (D) 1959–79
Sidney R. Yates (D) 1949–63; 1965–99
Leo E. Allen (R) 1933–61
Leslie C. Arends (R) 1935–75
C. W. (Runt) Bishop (R) 1941–55
Fred E. Busbey (R) 1943–45; 1947–49; 1951–55
Emmet F. Byrne (R) 1957–59
Robert B. Chiperfield (R) 1939–63
Marguerite Stitt Church (R) 1951–63
Harold R. Collier (R) 1957–75
Edward J. Derwinski (R) 1959–83
Elmer J. Hoffman (R) 1959–65
Richard W. Hoffman (R) 1949–57
Edgar A. Jonas (R) 1949–55
Russell W. Keeney (R) 1957–58
William E. McVey (R) 1951–58
Noah M. Mason (R) 1937–63
Robert H. Michel (R) 1957–95
Chauncey W. Reed (R) 1935–56
Timothy P. Sheehan (R) 1951–59
Edna Oakes Simpson (R) 1959–61
Sid Simpson (R) 1943–58
William L. Springer (R) 1951–73
Harold H. Velde (R) 1949–57
Charles W. Vursell (R) 1943–59

Indiana
Joseph W. Barr (D) 1959–61
John Brademas (D) 1959–81
Winfield K. Denton (D) 1949–53; 1955–67
Randall S. Harmon (D) 1959–61
Earl Hogan (D) 1959–61
Ray J. Madden (D) 1943–77
J. Edward Roush (D) 1959–69; 1971–77
Fred Wampler (D) 1959–61
E. Ross Adair (R) 1951–71
John V. Beamer (R) 1951–59
William G. Bray (R) 1951–75
Charles R. Brownson (R) 1951–59
Shepard J. Crumpacker, Jr. (R) 1951–57
Charles A. Halleck (R) 1935–69
Cecil M. Harden (R) 1949–59
Ralph Harvey (R) 1947–59; 1961–66
D. Bailey Merrill (R) 1953–55

F. Jay Nimtz (R) 1957–59
Earl Wilson (R) 1941–59; 1961–65

Iowa

Steven V. Carter (D) 1959
Merwin Coad (D) 1957–63
Neal Smith (D) 1959–95
Leonard G. Wolf (D) 1959–61
Paul Cunningham (R) 1941–59
James I. Dolliver (R) 1945–57
H. R. Gross (R) 1949–75
Charles B. Hoeven (R) 1943–65
Ben F. Jensen (R) 1939–65
John H. Kyl (R) 1959–65; 1967–73
Karl M. LeCompte (R) 1939–59
Thomas E. Martin (R) 1939–55
Fred Schwengel (R) 1955–65; 1967–73
Henry O. Talle (R) 1939–59

Kansas

J. Floyd Breeding (D) 1957–63
Newell A. George (D) 1959–61
Denver D. Hargis (D) 1959–61
Howard S. Miller (D) 1953–55
William H. Avery (R) 1955–65
Myron V. George (R) 1950–59
Clifford R. Hope (R) 1927–57
Edward H. Rees (R) 1937–61
Errett P. Scrivner (R) 1943–59
Wint Smith (R) 1947–61

Kentucky

Frank W. Bruke (D) 1959–63
Frank Chelf (D) 1945–67
Noble J. Gregory (D) 1937–59
William H. Natcher (D) 1953–94
Carl D. Perkins (D) 1949–84
Brent Spence (D) 1931–63
Frank A. Stubblefield (D) 1959–75
John C. Watts (D) 1951–71
Garrett L. Withers (D) 1952–53
James S. Golden (R) 1949–55
John M. Robsion, Jr. (R) 1953–59
Eugene Siler (R) 1955–65

Louisiana

Hale Boggs (D) 1941–43; 1947–72

Overton Brooks (D) 1937–61
F. Edward Hebert (D) 1941–77
George S. Long (D) 1953–58
Harold B. McSween (D) 1959–63
James H. Morrison (D) 1943–67
Otto E. Passman (D) 1947–77
T. Ashton Thompson (D) 1953–65
Edwin E. Willis (D) 1949–69

Maine

Frank M. Coffin (D) 1957–61
James C. Oliver (D) 1937–43; 1959–61
Robert Hale (R) 1943–59
Clifford G. McIntire (R) 1952–65
Charles P. Nelson (R) 1949–57

Maryland

Daniel B. Brewster (D) 1959–62
George H. Fallon (D) 1945–71
John R. Foley (D) 1959–61
Samuel N. Friedel (D) 1953–71
Edward A. Garmatz (D) 1947–73
Thomas F. Johnson (D) 1959–63
Richard E. Lankford (D) 1955–65
James P. S. Devereux (R) 1951–59
DeWitt S. Hyde (R) 1953–59
Edward T. Miller (R) 1947–59
Frank Small, Jr. (R) 1953–55

Massachusetts

Edward P. Boland (D) 1953–89
James A. Burke (D) 1959–79
Harold D. Donohue (D) 1947–75
Thomas J. Lane (D) 1941–63
John W. McCormack (D) 1928–71
Torbert H. Macdonald (D) 1955–76
Thomas P. (Tip) O'Neill, Jr. (D) 1953–87
Philip J. Philbin (D) 1943–71
William H. Bates (R) 1950–69
Silvio O. Conte (R) 1959–91
Laurence Curtis (R) 1953–63
Angier L. Goodwin (R) 1943–55
John W. Heselton (R) 1945–59
Hastings Keith (R) 1959–73
Joseph W. Martin, Jr. (R) 1925–67
Donald W. Nicholson (R) 1947–59
Edith Nourse Rogers (R) 1925–60
Richard B. Wigglesworth (R) 1928–59

Michigan
Charles C. Diggs, Jr. (D) 1955–80
John D. Dingell (D) 1933–55
John D. Dingell, Jr. (D) 1955–
Martha W. Griffiths (D) 1955–74
Donald Hayworth (D) 1955–57
John Lesinski, Jr. (D) 1951–65
Thaddeus M. Machrowicz (D) 1951–61
George D. O'Brien (D) 1937–39; 1941–47; 1949–55
James G. O'Hara (D) 1959–77
Louis C. Rabaut (D) 1935–47; 1949–61
John B. Bennett (R) 1943–45; 1947–64
Alvin M. Bentley (R) 1953–61
William S. Broomfield (R) 1957–93
Elford A. Cederberg (R) 1953–78
Charles E. Chamberlain (R) 1957–74
Kit Francis Clardy (R) 1953–55
George A. Dondero (R) 1933–57
Gerald R. Ford (R) 1949–73
Robert P. Griffin (R) 1957–66
Clare E. Hoffman (R) 1935–63
August E. Johansen (R) 1955–65
Victor A. Knox (R) 1953–65
Robert J. McIntosh (R) 1957–59
George Meader (R) 1951–65
Charles G. Oakman (R) 1953–55
Paul W. Shafer (R) 1937–54
Ruth Thompson (R) 1951–57
Jesse P. Wolcott (R) 1931–57

Minnesota
John A. Blatnik (D) 1947–74
Joseph E. Karth (D) 1959–77
Coya Knutson (D) 1955–59
Eugene J. McCarthy (D) 1949–59
Fred Marshall (D) 1949–63
Roy W. Wier (D) 1949–61
H. Carl Andersen (R) 1939–63
August H. Andresen (R) 1925–33; 1935–58
Harold C. Hagen (FL) 1943–45; (R) 1945–55
Walter H. Judd (R) 1943–63
Odin Langen (R) 1959–71
Ancher Nelsen (R) 1959–75
Joseph P. O'Hara (R) 1941–59
Albert H. Quie (R) 1958–79

Mississippi
Thomas G. Abernethy (D) 1943–73
William M. Colmer (D) 1933–73

Frank E. Smith (D) 1951–62
Jamie L. Whitten (D) 1941–95
John Bell Williams (D) 1947–68
W. Arthur Winstead (D) 1943–65

Missouri
Richard Bollin (D) 1949–83
Charles H. Brown (D) 1957–61
Clarence Cannon (D) 1923–64
A. S. J. Carnahan (D) 1945–47; 1949–61
George H. Christopher (D) 1949–51; 1955–59
W. R. Hull, Jr. (D) 1955–73
Paul C. Jones (D) 1948–69
Frank M. Karsten (D) 1947–69
Morgan M. Moulder (D) 1949–63
William J. Randall (D) 1959–77
Leonor K. Sullivan (D) 1953–77
William C. Cole (R) 1943–49; 1953–55
Thomas B. Curtis (R) 1951–69
Jeffrey P. Hillelson (R) 1953–55
Dewey Short (R) 1929–31; 1935–57

Montana
LeRoy H. Anderson (D) 1957–61
Lee Metcalf (D) 1953–61
Wesley A. D'Ewart (R) 1945–55
Orvin B. Fjare (R) 1955–57

Nebraska
Lawrence Brock (D) 1959–61
Donald F. McGinley (D) 1959–61
Jackson B. Chase (R) 1955–57
Glenn Cunningham (R) 1957–71
Carl T. Curtis (R) 1939–54
Robert D. Harrison (R) 1951–59
Roman L. Hruska (R) 1953–54
A. L. Miller (R) 1943–59
Phil Weaver (R) 1955–63

Nevada
Walter S. Baring (D) 1949–53; 1957–73
C. Clifton Young (R) 1953–57

New Hampshire
Perkins Bass (R) 1955–63
Norris Cotton (R) 1947–54
Chester E. Merrow (R) 1943–63

New Jersey

Hugh J. Addonizio (D) 1949–62
Dominick V. Daniels (D) 1959–77
Cornelius E. Gallagher (D) 1959–73
Edward J. Hart (D) 1935–55
Charles R. Howell (D) 1949–55
Peter W. Rodino, Jr. (D) 1949–89
Alfred D. Sieminski (D) 1951–59
Frank Thompson, Jr. (D) 1955–80
T. James Tumulty (D) 1955–57
Harrison A. Williams (D) 1953–57
James C. Auchincloss (R) 1943–65
William T. Cahill (R) 1959–70
Gordon Canfield (R) 1941–61
Clifford P. Case (R) 1945–53
Vincent J. Dellay (R) 1957–58; (D) 1958–59
Florence P. Dwyer (R) 1957–73
Peter H. B. Frelinghuysen, Jr. (R) 1953–75
Milton W. Glenn (R) 1957–65
T. Millet Hand (R) 1945–56
Robert W. Kean (R) 1939–59
Frank C. Osmers, Jr. (R) 1939–43; 1951–65
George M. Wallhauser (R) 1959–65
William B. Widnall (R) 1950–74
Charles A. Wolverton (R) 1927–59

New Mexico

John J. Dempsey (D) 1935–41; 1951–58
Antonio M. Fernandez (D) 1943–56
Joseph M. Montoya (D) 1957–64
Thomas G. Morris (D) 1959–69

New York

Victor L. Anfuso (D) 1951–53; 1955–63
Charles A. Buckley (D) 1935–65
Emanuel Celler (D) 1923–73
Irwin D. Davidson (D) 1955–56
James J. Delaney (D) 1945–47; 1949–78
Isidore Dollinger (D) 1949–60
James G. Donovan (D) 1951–57
Thaddeus J. Dulski (D) 1959–75
Leonard Farbstein (D) 1957–71
Sidney A. Fine (D) 1951–56
Jacob H. Gilbert (D) 1960–71
James C. Healey (D) 1956–65
Louis B. Heller (D) 1949–54
Lester Holtzman (D) 1953–61
Edna F. Kelly (D) 1949–69
Eugene J. Keogh (D) 1937–67

Arthur G. Klein (D) 1941–45; 1946–56
Abraham J. Multer (D) 1947–67
Leo W. O'Brien (D) 1952–67
Adam C. Powell, Jr. (D) 1945–67; 1969–71
John J. Rooney (D) 1944–74
Franklin D. Roosevelt, Jr. (L) 1949–51; (D) 1951–55
Alfred E. Santangelo (D) 1957–63
Samuel S. Stratton (D) 1959–89
Ludwig Teller (D) 1957–61
Herbert Zelenko (D) 1955–63
Robert R. Barry (R) 1959–65
Frank J. Becker (R) 1953–65
Albert H. Bosch (R) 1953–60
W. Sterling Cole (R) 1935–57
Frederic R. Coudert, Jr. (R) 1947–59
Steven B. Derounian (R) 1953–65
Edwin B. Dooley (R) 1957–63
Francis E. Dorn (R) 1953–61
Paul A. Fino (R) 1953–68
Ralph A. Gamble (R) 1937–57
Charles E. Goodell (R) 1959–68
Ralph W. Gwinn (R) 1945–59
Seymour Halpern (R) 1959–73
Jacob K. Javits (R) 1947–54
Bernard W. (Pat) Kearney (R) 1943–59
Kenneth B. Keating (R) 1947–59
Clarence Kilburn (R) 1940–65
Henry J. Latham (R) 1945–58
John V. Lindsay (R) 1959–65
William E. Miller (R) 1951–65
Harold C. Ostertag (R) 1951–65
John R. Pillion (R) 1953–65
Alexander Pirnie (R) 1959–73
Edmund P. Radwan (R) 1951–59
John H. Ray (R) 1953–63
Daniel A. Reed (R) 1919–59
R. Walter Riehlman (R) 1947–65
Howard W. Robison (R) 1958–75
Katharine St. George (R) 1947–65
John Taber (R) 1923–63
Dean P. Taylor (R) 1943–61
Stuyvesant Wainwright (R) 1953–61
Jessica McC. Weis (R) 1959–63
J. Ernest Wharton (R) 1951–65
William R. Williams (R) 1951–59

North Carolina

Hugh Alexander (D) 1953–63
Graham A. Barden (D) 1935–61

Herbert C. Bonner (D) 1940–65
Frank E. Carlyle (D) 1949–57
Richard Thurmond Chatham (D) 1949–57
Harold D. Cooley (D) 1934–67
Charles B. Deane (D) 1947–57
Carl T. Durham (D) 1939–61
L. H. Fountain (D) 1953–83
David M. Hall (D) 1959–60
Woodrow W. Jones (D) 1950–57
A. Paul Kitchin (D) 1957–63
Alton Lennon (D) 1957–73
Ralph J. Scott (D) 1957–67
George A. Shuford (D) 1953–59
Roy A. Taylor (D) 1960–77
Basil L. Whitener (D) 1957–69
Charles R. Jonas (R) 1953–73

North Dakota
Quentin N. Burdick (D) 1959–60
Usher L. Burdick (R) 1935–45; 1949–59
Otto Krueger (H) 1953–59
Don L. Short (R) 1959–65

Ohio
Thomas L. Ashley (D) 1955–81
Robert E. Cook (D) 1959–63
Robert Crosser (D) 1913–19; 1923–55
Michael A. Feighan (D) 1943–71
Wayne L. Hays (D) 1949–76
Michael J. Kirwan (D) 1937–70
Robert W. Levering (D) 1959–61
Walter H. Moeller (D) 1959–63; 1965–67
James G. Polk (D) 1931–41; 1949–59
Robert T. Secrest (D) 1933–42; 1949–54; 1963–66
Charles A. Vanik (D) 1955–81
William H. Ayres (R) 1951–71
A. D. Baumhart, Jr. (R) 1941–42; 1955–61
George H. Bender (R) 1939–49; 1951–54
Jackson E. Betts (R) 1951–73
Frances P. Bolton (R) 1940–69
Oliver P. Bolton (R) 1953–57; 1963–65
Frank T. Bow (R) 1951–72
Clarence J. Brown (R) 1939–65
Cliff Clevenger (R) 1939–59
David Dennison (R) 1957–59
Samuel L. Devine (R) 1959–81
John E. Henderson (R) 1955–61

William E. Hess (R) 1929–37; 1939–49; 1951–61
Thomas A. Jenkins (R) 1925–59
Delbert L. Latta (R) 1959–89
William M. McCulloch (R) 1947–73
J. Harry McGregor (R) 1940–58
Ward M. Miller (R) 1960–61
William E. Minshall (R) 1955–75
Paul F. Schenck (R) 1951–65
Gordon H. Scherer (R) 1953–63
John M. Vorys (R) 1939–59
Alvin F. Weichel (R) 1943–55
H. Frazier Reams (Ind.) 1951–55

Oklahoma
Carl Albert (D) 1947–77
Ed Edmondson (D) 1953–73
John Jarman (D) 1951–75; (R) 1975–77
Toby Morris (D) 1947–53; 1957–61
Tom Steed (D) 1949–81
Victor Wickersham (D) 1941–47; 1949–57; 1961–65
Page Belcher (R) 1951–73

Oregon
Edith Green (D) 1955–74
Charles O. Porter (D) 1957–61
Al Ullman (D) 1957–81
Homer D. Angell (R) 1939–55
Sam Coon (R) 1953–57
M. Harris Ellsworth (R) 1943–57
A. Walter Norblad (R) 1946–64

Pennsylvania
William A. Barrett (D) 1945–47; 1949–76
Vera D. Buchanan (D) 1951–55
James A. Byrne (D) 1953–73
Earl Chudoff (D) 1949–58
Frank M. Clark (D) 1955–74
John H. Dent (D) 1958–79
Herman P. Eberharter (D) 1937–58
Daniel J. Flood (D) 1945–47; 1949–53; 1955–80
Kathryn E. Granahan (D) 1956–63
William T. Granahan (D) 1945–47; 1949–56
William J. Green, Jr. (D) 1945–47; 1949–63
Elmer J. Holland (D) 1942–43; 1956–68
Augustine B. Kelley (D) 1941–57
William S. Moorhead (D) 1959–81
Thomas E. Morgan (D) 1945–77

Robert N. C. Nix (D) 1958–79
Stanley A. Prokop (D) 1959–61
James M. Quigley (D) 1955–57; 1959–61
George M. Rhodes (D) 1949–69
Herman Toll (D) 1959–67
Francis E. Walter (D) 1933–63
Edward J. Bonin (R) 1953–55
Alvin R. Bush (R) 1951–59
Joseph L. Carrigg (R) 1951–59
Robert J. Corbett (R) 1939–41; 1945–71
Willard S. Curtin (R) 1957–67
Paul B. Dague (R) 1947–67
Douglas H. Elliott (R) 1960
Ivor D. Fenton (R) 1939–63
James G. Fulton (R) 1945–71
Leon H. Gavin (R) 1943–63
Louis E. Graham (R) 1939–55
Benjamin F. James (R) 1949–59
Carroll D. Kearns (R) 1947–63
Karl C. King (R) 1951–57
John A. Lafore, Jr. (R) 1957–61
Samuel K. McConnell, Jr. (R) 1944–57
William H. Milliken, Jr. (R) 1959–65
Walter M. Mumma (R) 1951–61
John P. Saylor (R) 1949–73
Herman T. Schneebeli (R) 1960–77
Hugh Scott (R) 1941–45; 1947–59
Richard M. Simpson (R) 1937–60
S. Walter Stauffer (R) 1953–55; 1957–59
James E. Van Zandt (R) 1939–43; 1947–63
J. Irving Whalley (R) 1960–73

Rhode Island
John E. Fogarty (D) 1941–44; 1945–67
Aime J. Forand (D) 1937–39; 1941–61

South Carolina
Robert T. Ashmore (D) 1953–69
Joseph R. Bryson (D) 1939–53
W. J. Bryan Dorn (D) 1947–49; 1951–75
Robert W. Hemphill (D) 1957–64
John L. McMillan (D) 1939–73
James P. Richards (D) 1933–57
John J. Riley (D) 1945–49; 1951–62
L. Mendel Rivers (D) 1941–70

South Dakota
George S. McGovern (D) 1957–61

E. Y. Berry (R) 1951–71
Harold O. Lovre (R) 1949–57

Tennessee
Ross Bass (D) 1955–64
Jere Cooper (D) 1929–57
Clifford Davis (D) 1940–65
Robert A. Everett (D) 1958–69
Joe L. Evins (D) 1947–77
James B. Frazier, Jr. (D) 1949–63
J. Carlton Loser (D) 1957–63
Tom Murray (D) 1943–67
J. Percy Priest (D) 1941–56
Pat Sutton (D) 1949–55
Howard H. Baker (R) 1951–64
B. Carroll Reece (R) 1921–31; 1933–47; 1951–61

Texas
Lindley Beckworth (D) 1939–53; 1957–67
John J. Bell (D) 1955–57
Lloyd M. Bentsen, Jr. (D) 1948–55
Jack Brooks (D) 1953–95
Omar Burleson (D) 1947–78
Bob Casey (D) 1959–76
Martin Dies, Jr. (D) 1931–45; 1953–59
John Dowdy (D) 1952–73
O. C. Fisher (D) 1943–75
Brady Gentry (D) 1953–57
Frank Ikard (D) 1951–61
Paul J. Kilday (D) 1939–61
Joe M. Kilgore (D) 1955–65
Wingate H. Lucas (D) 1947–55
John E. Lyle (D) 1945–55
George H. Mahon (D) 1935–79
Wright Patman (D) 1929–76
W. R. Poage (D) 1937–78
Sam Rayburn (D) 1913–61
Kenneth Began (D) 1947–55
Walter Rogers (D) 1951–67
J. T. Rutherford (D) 1955–63
Olin E. Teague (D) 1946–78
Albert Thomas (D) 1937–66
Clark W. Thompson (D) 1933–35; 1947–66
W. Homer Thornberry (D) 1949–63
J. Franklin Wilson (D) 1947–55
James C. Wright (D) 1955–89
John Young (D) 1957–79
Bruce Alger (R) 1955–65

Utah
David S. King (D) 1959–63; 1965–67
William A. Dawson (R) 1947–49; 1953–59
Henry Aldous Dixon (R) 1955–61
Douglas R. Stringfellow (R) 1953–55

Vermont
William H. Meyer (D) 1959–61
Winston L. Prouty (R) 1951–59

Virginia
Watkins M. Abbitt (D) 1948–73
Thomas N. Downing (D) 1959–77
J. Vaughan Gary (D) 1945–65
Porter J. Hardy (D) 1947–69
Burr P. Harrison (D) 1946–63
W. Pat Jennings (D) 1955–67
Edward J. Robeson, Jr. (D) 1950–59
Howard W. Smith (D) 1931–67
Thomas B. Stanley (D) 1946–53
William M. Tuck (D) 1953–69
Joel T. Broyhill (R) 1953–74
Richard H. Poff (R) 1953–72
William C. Wampler (R) 1953–55; 1967–83

Washington
Julia B. Hansen (D) 1960–74
Don Magnuson (D) 1953–63
Hal Holmes (R) 1943–59
Walt Horan (R) 1943–65
Russell V. Mack (R) 1947–60
Catherine May (R) 1959–71
Thomas M. Pelly (R) 1953–73
Thor C. Tollefson (R) 1947–65
Jack Westland (R) 1953–65

West Virginia
Cleveland M. Bailey (D) 1945–47; 1949–63
M. G. Burnside (D) 1949–53; 1955–57
Robert C. Byrd (D) 1953–59
Ken Hechler (D) 1959–77
M. Elizabeth Kee (D) 1951–65
Robert H. Mollohan (D) 1953–57; 1969–83
John M. Slack, Jr. (D) 1959–80
Harley O. Staggers (D) 1949–81
Arch A. Moore, Jr. (R) 1957–69
Will E. Neal (R) 1953–55; 1957–59

Wisconsin
Gerald T. Flynn (D) 1959–61
Lester R. Johnson (D) 1953–65
Robert W. Kastenmeier (D) 1959–91
Henry S. Reuss (D) 1955–83
Clement J. Zablocki (D) 1949–83
John W. Byrnes (R) 1945–73
Glenn R. Davis (R) 1947–57; 1965–74
Merlin Hull (R) 1929–31; (Prog.) 1935–47; (R)
    1947–53
Charles J. Kersten (R) 1947–49; 1951–55
Melvin R. Laird (R) 1953–69
Alvin E. O'Konski (R) 1943–73
Lawrence H. Smith (R) 1941–58
Donald E. Tewes (R) 1957–59
William K. Van Pelt (R) 1951–65
Gardner R. Withrow (R) 1931–35; (Prog.) 1935–
    39; (R) 1949–61

Wyoming
William H. Harrison (R) 1951–55; 1961–65;
    1967–69
E. Keith Thomson (R) 1955–60

SENATE

Alabama
Lister Hill (D) 1938–69
John J. Sparkman (D) 1946–79

Alaska
E. L. Bartlett (D) 1959–69
Ernest Gruening (D) 1959–69

Arizona
Carl Hayden (D) 1927–69
Barry M. Goldwater (R) 1953–65; 1969–87

Arkansas
J. William Fulbright (D) 1945–75
John L. McClellan (D) 1943–77

California
Clair Engle (D) 1959–64
William F. Knowland (R) 1945–59
Thomas H. Kuchel (R) 1953–69

Colorado
John A. Carroll (D) 1957–63
Edwin C. Johnson (D) 1937–55
Gordon Allott (R) 1955–73
Eugene D. Millikin (R) 1941–57

Connecticut
Thomas J. Dodd (D) 1959–71
Prescott Bush (R) 1953–63
William A. Purtell (R) 1952–59

Delaware
J. Allen Frear, Jr. (D) 1949–61
John J. Williams (R) 1947–71

Florida
Spessard L. Holland (D) 1946–71
George P. Smathers (D) 1951–69

Georgia
Walter F. George (D) 1923–57
Richard B. Russell (D) 1933–71
Herman E. Talmadge (D) 1957–81

Hawaii
Oren E. Long (D) 1959–63
Hiram Fong (R) 1959–77

Idaho
Frank Church (D) 1957–81
Henry C. Dworshak (R) 1947–49; 1949–62
Herman Welker (R) 1951–57

Illinois
Paul H. Douglas (D) 1949–67
Everett M. Dirksen (R) 1951–69

Indiana
Vance Hartke (D) 1959–77
Homer E. Capehart (R) 1945–63
William E. Jenner (R) 1944–45; 1947–59

Iowa
Guy M. Gillette (D) 1936–45; 1949–55
Bourke B. Hickenlooper (R) 1945–69
Thomas E. Martin (R) 1955–61

Kansas
Frank Carlson (R) 1951–69
Andrew F. Schoeppel (R) 1949–62

Kentucky
Alben W. Barkley (D) 1927–49; 1955–56
Earle C. Clements (D) 1950–57
Robert Humphreys 1956–57
John Sherman Cooper (R) 1946–49; 1952–55;
   1956–73
Thruston B. Morton (R) 1957–69

Louisiana
Allen J. Ellender (D) 1937–72
Russell B. Long (D) 1948–87

Maine
Edmund S. Muskie (D) 1959–80
Frederick G. Payne (R) 1953–59
Margeret Chase Smith (R) 1949–73

Maryland
J. Glenn Beall (R) 1953–65
John Marshall Butler (R) 1951–63

Massachusetts
John F. Kennedy (D) 1953–60
Leverett Saltonstall (R) 1945–67

Michigan
Philip A. Hart (D) 1959–76
Pat V. McNamara (D) 1955–66
Homer Ferguson (R) 1943–55
Charles E. Potter (R) 1953–59

Minnesota
Hubert H. Humphrey (D) 1949–64; 1971–78
Eugene J. McCarthy (D) 1959–71
Edward J. Thye (R) 1947–59

Mississippi
James O. Eastland (D) 1941; 1943–78
John C. Stennis (D) 1947–89

Missouri
Thomas C. Hennings, Jr. (D) 1951–60
Stuart Symington (D) 1953–77

Montana
Mike Mansfield (D) 1953–77
James E. Murray (D) 1934–61

Nebraska
Hazel H. Abel (R) 1954
Eva K. Bowring (R) 1954
Hugh A. Butler (R) 1941–54
Carl T. Curtis (R) 1935–79
Dwight P. Griswold (R) 1952–54
Roman L. Hruska (R) 1954–77
Sam W. Reynolds (R) 1954

Nevada
Alan Bible (D) 1954–75
Howard W. Cannon (D) 1959–83
Pat McCarran (D) 1933–54
Ernest S. Brown (R) 1954
George W. Malone (R) 1947–59

New Hampshire
H. Styles Bridges (R) 1937–61
Norris Cotton (R) 1954–75
Charles W. Tobey (R) 1939–53
Robert W. Upton (R) 1953–54

New Jersey
Harrison A. Williams, Jr. (D) 1959–82
Clifford P. Case (R) 1955–79
Robert C. Hendrickson (R) 1949–55
H. Alexander Smith (R) 1944–59

New Mexico
Clinton P. Anderson (D) 1949–73
Dennis Chavez (D) 1935–62

New York
Herbert H. Lehman (D) 1949–57
Irving M. Ives (R) 1947–59

Jacob K. Javits (R) 1957–81
Kenneth B. Keating (R) 1959–65

North Carolina
Sam J. Ervin, Jr. (D) 1954–75
Clyde R. Hoey (D) 1945–54
B. Everett Jordan (D) 1958–73
Alton Lennon (D) 1953–54
W. Kerr Scott (D) 1954–58
Willis Smith (D) 1950–53

North Dakota
Quentin N. Burdick (D) 1960–92
C. Norman Brunsdale (R) 1960
William Langer (R) 1941–59
Milton R. Young (R) 1945–81

Ohio
Thomas A. Burke (D) 1954
Frank J. Lausche (D) 1957–69
Stephen M. Young (D) 1959–71
George H. Bender (R) 1954–57
John W. Bricker (R) 1947–59
Robert A. Taft (R) 1939–53

Oklahoma
Robert S. Kerr (D) 1949–63
A. S. Mike Monroney (D) 1951–69

Oregon
Richard L. Neuberger (D) 1955–60
Guy Cordon (R) 1944–55
Wayne Morse (R) 1945–52; (Ind.) 1952–55; (D)
    1955–69

Pennsylvania
Joseph S. Clark (D) 1957–69
James H. Duff (R) 1951–57
Edward Martin (R) 1947–59
Hugh Scott (R) 1959–77

Rhode Island
Theodore Francis Green (D) 1937–61
John O. Pastore (D) 1950–77

South Carolina
Charles E. Daniel (D) 1954
Olin D. Johnston (D) 1945–65

Burnet R. Maybank (D) 1941–54
Strom Thurmond (D) 1954–56, 1956–64; (R)
    1964–
Thomas A. Wofford (D) 1956

South Dakota
Francis Case (R) 1951–62
Karl E. Mundt (R) 1948–73

Tennessee
Albert Gore (D) 1953–71
Estes Kefauver (D) 1949–63

Texas
William A. Blakley (D) 1957
Price Daniel (D) 1953–57
Lyndon B. Johnson (D) 1949–61
Ralph W. Yarborough (D) 1957–71

Utah
Frank E. Moss (D) 1959–77
Wallace F. Bennett (R) 1951–75
Arthur V. Watkins (R) 1947–59

Vermont
George D. Aiken (R) 1941–75
Ralph E. Flanders (R) 1946–59
Winston L. Prouty (R) 1959–71

Virginia
Harry Flood Byrd (D) 1933–65
A. Willis Robertson (D) 1946–66

Washington
Henry M. Jackson (D) 1953–83
Warren G. Magnuson (D) 1944–81

West Virginia
Robert C. Byrd (D) 1959–
Harley M. Kilgore (D) 1941–56
William R. Laird, III (D) 1956
Matthew M. Neely (D) 1923–29; 1931–41; 1949–
    58
Jennings, Randolph (D) 1958–85
John D. Hoblitzell, Jr. (R) 1958
Chapman Revercomb (R) 1943–49; 1956–59

Wisconsin
William Proxmire (D) 1957–89
Joseph R. McCarthy (R) 1947–57
Alexander Wiley (R) 1939–63

Wyoming
Lester C. Hunt (D) 1949–54
Gale W. McGee (D) 1959–77
Joseph C. O'Mahoney (D) 1934–53; 1954–61
Edward D. Crippa (R) 1954
Frank A. Barrett (R) 1953–59

GOVERNORS

Alabama
James E. Folsom (D) 1947–51; 1955–59
Gordon Persons (D) 1951–55
John Patterson (D) 1959–63

Alaska
William A. Egan (D) 1959–67

Arizona
Howard Pyle (R) 1951–55
Ernest W. McFarland (D) 1955–59
Paul Fannin (R) 1959–65

Arkansas
Francis Cherry (D) 1953–55
Orval E. Faubus (D) 1955–67

California
Earl Warren (R) 1943–53
Goodwin J. Knight (R) 1953–59
Edmund G. Brown (D) 1959–67

Colorado
Dan Thornton (R) 1951–55
Ed. C. Johnson (D) 1955–57
Stephen L. McNichols (D) 1957–63

Connecticut
John Davis Lodge (R) 1951–55
Abraham A. Ribicoff (D) 1955–61

Delaware
J. Cabel Boggs (R) 1953–60

Florida
Dan McCarty (D) 1953
Charley E. Johns (D) (acting) 1953–55
LeRoy Collins (D) 1955–61

Georgia
Herman Talmadge (D) 1948–55
Marvin Griffin (D) 1955–59
Ernest Vandiver (D) 1959–63

Hawaii
William F. Quinn (R) 1959–63

Idaho
Len B. Jordan (R) 1951–55
Robert E. Smylie (D) 1955–67

Illinois
William G. Stratton (R) 1953–61

Indiana
George N. Craig (R) 1953–57
Harold W. Handley (R) 1957–61

Iowa
William S. Beardsley (R) 1949–54
Leo A. Hoegh (R) 1954–57
Herschel C. Loveless (D) 1957–61

Kansas
Edward F. Arn (R) 1951–55
Fred Hall (R) 1955–57
George Docking (D) 1957–61

Kentucky
Lawrence W. Wetherby (D) 1950–56
Albert B. Chandler (D) 1956–59
Bert T. Combs (D) 1959–63

Louisiana
Robert F. Kennon (D) 1952–56
Earl K. Long (D) 1956–60
Jimmie H. Davis (D) 1960–64

Maine
Burton M. Cross (R) 1953–55
Edmund S. Muskie (D) 1955–59
Clinton A. Clauson (D) 1959
John H. Reed (R) 1960–67

Maryland
Theodore R. McKeldin, Jr. (R) 1951–59
J. Millard Tawes (D) 1959–67

Massachusetts
Christian A. Herter (R) 1953–57
Foster Furcolo (D) 1957–61

Michigan
G. Mennen Williams (D) 1949–61

Minnesota
C. Elmer Anderson (R) 1951–55
Orville L. Freeman (D) (FL) 1955–61

Mississippi
Hugh White (D) 1952–56
James P. Coleman (D) 1956–60
Ross R. Barnett (D) 1960–64

Missouri
Phil M. Donnelly (D) 1953–57
James T. Blair, Jr. (D) 1957–61

Montana
J. Hugo Aronson (R) 1953–61

Nebraska
Robert B. Crosby (R) 1953–55
Victor E. Anderson (R) 1955–59
Ralph G. Brooks (D) 1959–60

Nevada
Charles H. Russell (R) 1951–59
Grant Sawyer (D) 1959–67

New Hampshire

Hugh Gregg (R) 1953–55
Lane Dwinell (R) 1955–59
Wesley Powell (R) 1959–63

New Jersey

Alfred E. Driscoll (R) 1947–54
Robert B. Meyner (D) 1954–62

New Mexico

Edwin L. Mechem (R) 1951–55; 1957–59; 1961–
  62
John F. Simms, Jr. (D) 1955–57
John Burroughs (D) 1959–61

New York

Thomas E. Dewey (R) 1943–55
Averell Harriman (D) 1955–59

North Carolina

William B. Umstead (D) 1953–54
Luther H. Hodges (D) 1955–61

North Dakota

C. Norman Brunsdale (R) 1951–57
John E. Davis (R) 1957–61

Ohio

Frank J. Lausche (D) 1945–47; 1949–57
C. William O'Neill (R) 1957–59
Michael V. DiSalle (D) 1959–63

Oklahoma

Johnston Murray (D) 1951–55
Raymond Gary (D) 1955–59
J. Howard Edmondson (D) 1959–63

Oregon

Paul L. Patterson (R) 1952–56
Robert D. Holmes (D) 1957–59
Mark O. Hatfield (R) 1959–67

Pennsylvania

John S. Fine (R) 1951–55
George M. Leader (D) 1955–59
David L. Lawrence (D) 1959–63

Rhode Island

Dennis J. Roberts (D) 1951–59
Christopher Del Sesto (R) 1959–61

South Carolina

James F. Byrnes (D) 1951–55
George B. Timmerman, Jr. (D) 1955–59
Ernest F. Hollings (D) 1959–63

South Dakota

Sigurd Anderson (R) 1951–55
Joe J. Foss (R) 1955–59
Ralph Herseth (D) 1959–61

Tennessee

Frank G. Clement (D) 1953–59
Buford Ellington (D) 1959–63

Texas

Allan Shivers (D) (R) 1949–57
Price Daniel (D) 1957–63

Utah

J. Bracken Lee (R) 1949–57
George D. Clyde (R) 1957–65

Vermont

Lee E. Emerson (R) 1951–55
Joseph B. Johnson (R) 1955–59
Robert T. Stafford (R) 1959–61

Virginia

John S. Battle (D) 1950–54
Thomas B. Stanley (D) 1954–58
J. Lindsay Almond, Jr. (D) 1958–62

Washington

Arthur B. Langlie (R) 1949–57
Albert Rossellini (D) 1957–65

West Virginia

William C. Marland (D) 1953–57
Cecil H. Underwood (R) 1957–61

Wisconsin
Walter J. Kohler (R) 1951–57
Vernon W. Thomson (R) 1957–59
Gaylord A. Nelson (D) 1959–63

Wyoming
Frank A. Barrett (R) 1951–53
C. J. Rogers (R) 1953–55
Milward L. Simpson (R) 1955–59
J. J. Hickey (D) 1959–61

SELECTED PRIMARY DOCUMENTS

All documents were taken from the Public Papers of the Presidents of the United States: Dwight D. Eisenhower 1953–1961. The Presidency Project. Available online. URL: http://www.presidency.ucsb.edu/ws/.

1. First Inaugural Address, January 20, 1953

My friends, before I begin the expression of those thoughts that I deem appropriate to this moment, would you permit me the privilege of uttering a little private prayer of my own.

And I ask that you bow your heads.

Almighty God, as we stand here at this moment my future associates in the executive branch of government join me in beseeching that Thou will make full and complete our dedication to the service of the people in this throng, and their fellow citizens everywhere.

Give us, we pray, the power to discern clearly right from wrong, and allow all our words and actions to be governed thereby, and by the laws of this land. Especially we pray that our concern shall be for all the people regardless of station, race, or calling.

May cooperation be permitted and be the mutual aim of those who, under the concepts of our Constitution, hold to differing political faiths; so that all may work for the good of our beloved country and Thy glory. Amen.

My fellow citizens:

The world and we have passed the midway point of a century of continuing challenge. We sense with all our faculties that forces of good and evil are massed and armed and opposed as rarely before in history.

This fact defines the meaning of this day. We are summoned by this honored and historic ceremony to witness more than the act of one citizen swearing his oath of service, in the presence of God. We are called as a people to give testimony in the sight of the world to our faith that the future shall belong to the free.

Since this century's beginning, a time of tempest has seemed to come upon the continents of the earth. Masses of Asia have awakened to strike off shackles of the past. Great nations of Europe have fought their bloodiest wars. Thrones have toppled and their vast empires have disappeared. New nations have been born.

For our own country, it has been a time of recurring trial. We have grown in power and in responsibility. We have passed through the anxieties of depression and of war to a summit unmatched in man's history. Seeking to secure peace in the world, we have had to fight through the forests of the Argonne, to the shores of Iwo Jima, and to the cold mountains of Korea.

In the swift rush of great events, we find ourselves groping to know the full sense and meaning of these times in which we live. In our quest of understanding, we beseech God's guidance. We summon all our knowledge of the past and we scan all signs of the future. We bring all our wit and all our will to meet the question:

How far have we come in man's long pilgrimage from darkness toward light? Are we nearing the light—a day of freedom and of peace for all mankind? Or are the shadows of another night closing in upon us?

Great as are the preoccupations absorbing us at home, concerned as we are with matters that deeply affect our livelihood today and our vision of the future, each of these domestic problems is dwarfed by, and often even created by, this question that involves all human kind.

This trial comes at a moment when man's power to achieve good or to inflict evil surpasses the brightest hopes and the sharpest fears of all ages. We can turn rivers in their courses, level mountains to the plains. Oceans and land and sky are avenues for our colossal commerce. Disease diminishes and life lengthens.

Yet the promise of this life is imperiled by the very genius that has made it possible. Nations amass wealth. Labor sweats to create—and turns out devices to level not only mountains but also cities. Science seems ready to confer upon us, as its final gift, the power to erase human life from this planet.

At such a time in history, we who are free must proclaim anew our faith.

This faith is the abiding creed of our fathers. It is our faith in the deathless dignity of man, governed by eternal moral and natural laws.

This faith defines our full view of life. It establishes, beyond debate, those gifts of the Creator that are man's inalienable rights, and that make all men equal in His sight.

In the light of this equality, we know that the virtues most cherished by free people—love of truth, pride of work, devotion to country—all are treasures equally precious in the lives of the most humble and of the most exalted. The men who mine coal and fire furnaces and balance ledgers and turn lathes and pick cotton and heal the sick and plant corn—all serve as proudly, and as profitably, for America as the statesmen who draft treaties and the legislators who enact laws.

This faith rules our whole way of life. It decrees that we, the people, elect leaders not to rule but to serve. It asserts that we have the right to choice of our own work and to the reward of our own toil. It inspires the initiative that makes our productivity the wonder of the world. And it warns that any man who seeks to deny equality among all his brothers betrays the spirit of the free and invites the mockery of the tyrant.

It is because we, all of us, hold to these principles that the political changes accomplished this day do not imply turbulence, upheaval or disorder. Rather this change expresses a purpose of strengthening our dedication and devotion to the precepts of our founding documents, a conscious renewal of faith in our country and in the watchfulness of a Divine Providence.

The enemies of this faith know no god but force, no devotion but its use. They tutor men in treason. They feed upon the hunger of others. Whatever defies them, they torture, especially the truth.

Here, then, is joined no argument between slightly differing philosophies. This conflict strikes directly at the faith of our fathers and the lives of our sons. No principle or treasure that we hold, from the spiritual knowledge of our free schools and churches to the creative magic of free labor and capital, nothing lies safely beyond the reach of this struggle.

Freedom is pitted against slavery; lightness against the dark.

The faith we hold belongs not to us alone but to the free of all the world. This common bond binds the grower of rice in Burma and the planter of wheat in Iowa, the shepherd in southern Italy and the mountaineer in the Andes. It confers a common dignity upon the French soldier who dies in Indo-China, the British soldier killed in Malaya, the American life given in Korea.

We know, beyond this, that we are linked to all free peoples not merely by a noble idea but by a simple need. No free people can for long cling to any privilege or enjoy any safety in economic solitude. For all our own material might, even we need markets in the world for the surpluses of our farms and our factories. Equally, we need for these same farms and factories vital materials and products of distant lands. This basic law of interdependence, so manifest in the commerce of peace, applies with thousand-fold intensity in the event of war.

So we are persuaded by necessity and by belief that the strength of all free peoples lies in unity; their danger, in discord.

To produce this unity, to meet the challenge of our time, destiny has laid upon our country the responsibility of the free world's leadership.

So it is proper that we assure our friends once again that, in the discharge of this responsibility, we Americans know and we observe the difference between world leadership and imperialism; between firmness and truculence; between a thoughtfully calculated goal and spasmodic reaction to the stimulus of emergencies.

We wish our friends the world over to know this above all: we face the threat—not with dread and confusion—but with confidence and conviction.

We feel this moral strength because we know that we are not helpless prisoners of history. We are free men. We shall remain free, never to be proven guilty of the one capital offense against freedom, a lack of stanch faith.

In pleading our just cause before the bar of history and in pressing our labor for world peace, we shall be guided by certain fixed principles.

These principles are:

(1) Abhorring war as a chosen way to balk the purposes of those who threaten us, we hold it to be the first task of statesmanship to develop the strength that will deter the forces of aggression and promote the conditions of peace. For, as it must be the supreme purpose of all free men, so it must be the dedication of their leaders, to save humanity from preying upon itself.

In the light of this principle, we stand ready to engage with any and all others in joint effort to remove the causes of mutual fear and distrust among nations, so as to make possible drastic reduction of armaments. The sole requisites for undertaking such effort are that—in their purpose—they be aimed logically and honestly toward secure peace for all; and that—in their result—they provide methods by which every participating nation will prove good faith in carrying out its pledge.

(2) Realizing that common sense and common decency alike dictate the futility of appeasement, we shall never try to placate an aggressor by the false and wicked bargain of trading honor for security. Americans, indeed all free men, remember that in the final choice a soldier's pack is not so heavy a burden as a prisoner's chains.

(3) Knowing that only a United States that is strong and immensely productive can help defend freedom in our world, we view our Nation's strength and security as a trust upon which rests the hope of free men everywhere. It is the firm duty of each of our free citizens and of every free citizen everywhere to place the cause of his country before the comfort, the convenience of himself.

(4) Honoring the identity and the special heritage of each nation in the world, we shall never use our strength to try to impress upon another people our own cherished political and economic institutions.

(5) Assessing realistically the needs and capacities of proven friends of freedom, we shall strive to help them to achieve their own security and well-being. Likewise, we shall count upon them to assume, within the limits of their resources, their full and just burdens in the common defense of freedom.

(6) Recognizing economic health as an indispensable basis of military strength and the free world's peace, we shall strive to foster everywhere, and to practice ourselves, policies that encourage productivity and profitable trade. For the impoverishment of any single people in the world means danger to the well-being of all other peoples.

(7) Appreciating that economic need, military security and political wisdom combine to suggest regional groupings of free peoples, we hope, within the framework of the United Nations, to help strengthen such special bonds the world over. The nature of these ties must vary with the different problems of different areas.

In the Western Hemisphere, we enthusiastically join with all our neighbors in the work of perfecting a community of fraternal trust and common purpose.

In Europe, we ask that enlightened and inspired leaders of the Western nations strive with renewed vigor to make the unity of their peoples a reality. Only as free Europe unitedly marshals its strength can it effectively safeguard, even with our help, its spiritual and cultural heritage.

(8) Conceiving the defense of freedom, like freedom itself, to be one and indivisible, we hold all continents and peoples in equal regard and honor. We reject any insinuation that one race or another, one people or another, is in any sense inferior or expendable.

(9) Respecting the United Nations as the living sign of all people's hope for peace, we shall strive to make it not merely an eloquent symbol but an effective force. And in our quest for an honorable peace, we shall neither compromise, nor tire, nor ever cease.

By these rules of conduct, we hope to be known to all peoples.

By their observance, an earth of peace may become not a vision but a fact.

This hope—this supreme aspiration—must rule the way we live.

We must be ready to dare all for our country. For history does not long entrust the care of freedom to the weak or the timid. We must acquire proficiency in defense and display stamina in purpose.

We must be willing, individually and as a Nation, to accept whatever sacrifices may be required of us. A people that values its privileges above its principles soon loses both.

These basic precepts are not lofty abstractions, far removed from matters of daily living. They are laws of spiritual strength that generate and define our material strength.

Patriotism means equipped forces and a prepared citizenry. Moral stamina means more energy and more productivity, on the farm and in the factory. Love of liberty means the guarding of every resource that makes freedom possible—from the sanctity of our families and the wealth of our soil to the genius of our scientists.

And so each citizen plays an indispensable role. The productivity of our heads, our hands, and our hearts is the source of all the strength we can command, for both the enrichment of our lives and the winning of the peace.

No person, no home, no community can be beyond the reach of this call. We are summoned to act in wisdom and in conscience, to work with industry, to teach with persuasion, to preach with conviction, to weigh our every deed with care and with compassion. For this truth must be clear before us: whatever America hopes to bring to pass in the world must first come to pass in the heart of America.

The peace we seek, then, is nothing less than the practice and fulfillment of our whole faith among ourselves and in our dealings with others. This signifies more than the stilling of guns, easing the sorrow of war. More than escape from death, it is a way of life. More than a haven for the weary, it is a hope for the brave.

This is the hope that beckons us onward in this century of trial. This is the work that awaits us all, to be done with bravery, with charity, and with prayer to Almighty God.

2. "Open Skies" Address, July 21, 1955

Mr. Chairman, Gentlemen:

Disarmament is one of the most important subjects on our agenda. It is also extremely difficult. In recent years the scientists have discovered methods of making weapons many, many times more destructive of opposing armed forces—but also of homes, and industries and lives—than ever known or even imagined before. These same scientific discoveries have made much more complex the problems of limitation and control and reduction of armament.

After our victory as Allies in World War II, my country rapidly disarmed. Within a few years our armament was at a very low level. Then events occurred beyond our borders which caused us to realize that we had disarmed too much. For our own security and to safeguard peace we needed greater strength. Therefore we proceeded to rearm and to associate with others in a partnership for peace and for mutual security.

The American people are determined to maintain and if necessary increase this armed strength for as long a period as is necessary to safeguard peace and to maintain our security.

But we know that a mutually dependable system for less armament on the part of all nations would be a better way to safeguard peace and to maintain our security.

It would ease the fears of war in the anxious hearts of people everywhere. It would lighten the burdens upon the backs of the people. It would make it possible for every nation, great and small, developed and less developed, to advance the standards of living of its people, to attain better food, and clothing, and shelter, more of education and larger enjoyment of life.

Therefore the United States government is prepared to enter into a sound and reliable agreement making possible the reduction of armament. I have directed that an intensive and thorough study of this subject be made within our own government. From these studies, which are continuing, a very important principle is emerging to which I referred in my opening statement on Monday.

No sound and reliable agreement can be made unless it is completely covered by an inspection and reporting system adequate to support every portion of the agreement.

The lessons of history teach us that disarmament agreements without adequate reciprocal inspection increase the dangers of war and do not brighten the prospects of peace.

Thus it is my view that the priority attention of our combined study of disarmament should be upon the subject of inspection and reporting.

Questions suggest themselves.

How effective an inspection system can be designed which would be mutually and reciprocally acceptable within our countries and the other nations of the world? How would such a system operate? What could it accomplish?

Is certainty against surprise aggression attainable by inspection? Could violations be discovered promptly and effectively counteracted?

We have not as yet been able to discover any scientific or other inspection method which would make certain of the elimination of nuclear weapons. So far as we are aware no other nation has made such a discovery. Our study of this problem is continuing. We have not as yet been able to discover any accounting or other inspection method of being certain of the true budgetary facts of total expenditures for armament. Our study of this problem is continuing. We by no means exclude the possibility of finding useful checks in these fields.

As you can see from these statements, it is our impression that many past proposals of disarmament are more sweeping than can be insured by effective inspection.

Gentlemen, since I have been working on this memorandum to present to this Conference, I have been searching my heart and mind for something that I could say here that could convince everyone of the great sincerity of the United States in approaching this problem of disarmament.

I should address myself for a moment principally to the Delegates from the Soviet Union, because our two great countries admittedly possess new and terrible weapons in quantities which do give rise in other parts of the world, or reciprocally, to the fears and dangers of surprise attack.

I propose, therefore, that we take a practical step, that we begin an arrangement, very quickly, as between ourselves—immediately. These steps would include:

To give to each other a complete blueprint of our military establishments, from beginning to end, from one end of our countries to the other; lay out the establishments and provide the blueprints to each other.

Next, to provide within our countries facilities for aerial photography to the other country—we to provide you the facilities within our country, ample facilities for aerial reconnaissance, where you can make all the pictures you choose and take them to your own country to study, you to provide exactly the same facilities for us and we to make these examinations, and by this step to convince the world that we are providing as between ourselves against the possibility of great surprise attack, thus lessening danger and relaxing tension. Likewise we will make more easily attainable a comprehensive and effective system of inspection and disarmament, because what I propose, I assure you, would be but a beginning.

Now from my statements I believe you will anticipate my suggestion. It is that we instruct our representatives in the Subcommittee on Disarmament in discharge of their mandate from the United Nations to give priority effort to the study of inspection and reporting. Such a study could well include a step by step testing of inspection and reporting methods.

The United States is ready to proceed in the study and testing of a reliable system of inspections and reporting, and when that system is proved, then to reduce armaments with all others to the extent that the system will provide assured results.

The successful working out of such a system would do much to develop the mutual confidence which will open wide the avenues of progress for all our peoples.

The quest for peace is the statesman's most exacting duty. Security of the nation entrusted to his care is his greatest responsibility. Practical progress to lasting peace is his fondest hope. Yet in pursuit of his hope he must not betray the trust placed in him as guardian of the people's security. A sound place—with security, justice, well-being, and freedom for the people of the world—*can* be achieved, but only by patiently and thoughtfully following a hard and sure and tested road.

3. Eisenhower Doctrine, January 5, 1957

To the Congress of the United States:

First may I express to you my deep appreciation of your courtesy in giving me, at some inconvenience to yourselves, this early opportunity of addressing you on a matter I deem to be of grave importance to our country.

In my forthcoming State of the Union Message, I shall review the international situation generally. There are worldwide hopes which we can reasonably entertain, and there are worldwide responsibilities which we must carry to make certain that freedom—including our own—may be secure.

There is, however, a special situation in the Middle East which I feel I should, even now, lay before you.

Before doing so it is well to remind ourselves that our basic national objective in international affairs remains peace—a world peace based on justice. Such a peace must include all areas, all peoples of the world if it is to be enduring. There is no nation, great or small, with which we would refuse to negotiate, in mutual good faith, with patience and in the determination to secure a better understanding between us. Out of such understandings must, and eventually will, grow confidence and trust, indispensable ingredients to a program of peace and to plans for lifting from us all the burdens of expensive armaments. To promote these objectives, our government works tirelessly, day by day, month by month, year by year. But until a degree of success crowns our efforts that will assure to all nations peaceful existence, we must, in the interests of peace itself, remain vigilant, alert and strong.

I.

The Middle East has abruptly reached a new and critical stage in its long and important history. In past decades many of the countries in that area were not fully self-governing. Other nations exercised considerable authority in the area and the security of the region was largely built around their power. But since the First World War there has been a steady evolution toward self-government and independence. This development the United States has welcomed and has encouraged. Our country supports without reservation the full sovereignty and independence of each and every nation of the Middle East.

The evolution to independence has in the main been a peaceful process. But the area has been often troubled. Persistent cross-currents of distrust and fear with raids back and forth across national boundaries have brought about a high degree of instability in much of the Mid East. Just recently there have been hostilities involving Western European nations that once exercised much influence in the area. Also the relatively large attack by Israel in October has intensified the basic differences between that nation and its Arab neighbors. All this instability has been heightened and, at times, manipulated by International Communism.

II.

Russia's rulers have long sought to dominate the Middle East. That was true of the Czars and it is true of the Bolsheviks. The reasons are not hard to find. They do not affect Russia's security, for no one plans to use the Middle East as a base for aggression against Russia. Never for a moment has the United States entertained such a thought.

The Soviet Union has nothing whatsoever to fear from the United States in the Middle East, or anywhere else in the world, so long as its rulers do not themselves first resort to aggression.

That statement I make solemnly and emphatically.

Neither does Russia's desire to dominate the Middle East spring from its own economic interest in the area. Russia does not appreciably use or depend upon the Suez Canal. In 1955 Soviet traffic through the Canal represented only about three fourths of 1% of the total. The Soviets have no need for, and could provide no market for, the petroleum resources which constitute the principal natural wealth of the area. Indeed, the Soviet Union is a substantial exporter of petroleum products.

The reason for Russia's interest in the Middle East is solely that of power politics. Considering her announced purpose of Communizing the world, it is easy to understand her hope of dominating the Middle East.

This region has always been the crossroads of the continents of the Eastern Hemisphere. The Suez Canal enables the nations of Asia and Europe to carry on the commerce that is essential if these countries are to maintain well-rounded and prosperous economies. The Middle East provides a gateway between Eurasia and Africa.

It contains about two thirds of the presently known oil deposits of the world and it normally supplies the petroleum needs of many nations of Europe, Asia and Africa. The nations of Europe are peculiarly dependent upon this supply, and this dependency relates to transportation as well as to production! This has been vividly demonstrated since the closing of the Suez Canal and some of the pipelines. Alternate ways of transportation and, indeed, alternate sources of power can, if necessary, be developed. But these cannot be considered as early prospects.

These things stress the immense importance of the Middle East. If the nations of that area should lose their independence, if they were dominated by alien forces hostile to freedom, that would be both a tragedy for the area and for many other free nations whose economic life would be subject to near strangulation. Western Europe would be endangered just as though there had been no Marshall Plan, no North Atlantic Treaty Organization. The free nations of Asia and Africa, too, would be placed in serious jeopardy. And the countries of the Middle East would lose the markets upon which their economies depend. All this would have the most adverse, if not disastrous, effect upon our own nation's economic life and political prospects.

Then there are other factors which transcend the material. The Middle East is the birthplace of three great religions—Moslem, Christian and Hebrew. Mecca and Jerusalem are more than places on the map. They symbolize religions which teach that the spirit has supremacy over matter and that the individual has a dignity and rights of which no despotic government can rightfully deprive him. It would be intolerable if the holy places of the Middle East should be subjected to a rule that glorifies atheistic materialism.

International Communism, of course, seeks to mask its purposes of domination by expressions of good will and by superficially attractive offers of political, economic and military aid. But any free nation, which is the subject of Soviet enticement, ought, in elementary wisdom, to look behind the mask.

Remember Estonia, Latvia and Lithuania! In 1939 the Soviet Union entered into mutual assistance pacts with these then independent countries; and the Soviet Foreign Minister, addressing the Extraordinary Fifth Session of the Supreme Soviet in October 1939, solemnly and publicly declared that "we stand for the scrupulous and punctilious observance of the pacts on the basis of complete reciprocity, and we declare that all the nonsensical talk about the Sovietization of the Baltic countries is only to the interest of our common enemies and of all anti-Soviet provocateurs." Yet in *1940*, Estonia, Latvia and Lithuania were forcibly incorporated into the Soviet Union.

Soviet control of the satellite nations of Eastern Europe has been forcibly maintained in spite of solemn promises of a contrary intent, made during World War II.

Stalin's death brought hope that this pattern would change. And we read the pledge of the Warsaw Treaty of 1955 that the Soviet Union would follow in satellite countries "the principles of mutual respect for their independence and sovereignty and non-interference in domestic affairs." But we have just seen the subjugation of Hungary by naked armed force. In the aftermath of this Hungarian tragedy, world respect for and belief in Soviet promises have sunk to a new low. International Communism needs and seeks a recognizable success.

Thus, we have these simple and indisputable facts:

1. The Middle East, which has always been coveted by Russia, would today be prized more than ever by International Communism.
2. The Soviet rulers continue to show that they do not scruple to use any means to gain their ends.
3. The free nations of the Mid East need, and for the most part want, added strength to assure their continued independence.

III.

Our thoughts naturally turn to the United Nations as a protector of small nations. Its charter gives it primary responsibility for the maintenance of international peace and security. Our country has given the United Nations its full support in relation to the hostilities in Hungary and in Egypt. The United Nations was able to bring about a cease-fire and withdrawal of hostile forces from Egypt because it was dealing with governments and peoples who had a decent respect for the opinions of mankind as reflected in the United Nations General Assembly. But in the case of Hungary, the situation was different. The Soviet Union vetoed action by the Security Council to require the withdrawal of Soviet armed forces from Hungary. And it has shown callous indifference to the recommendations, even the censure, of the General Assembly. The United Nations can always be helpful, but it cannot be a wholly dependable protector of freedom when the ambitions of the Soviet Union are involved.

IV.

Under all the circumstances I have laid before you, a greater responsibility now devolves upon the United States. We have shown, so that none can doubt, our dedication to the principle that force shall not be used internationally for any aggressive purpose and that the integrity and independence of the nations of the Middle East should be inviolate. Seldom in history has a nation's dedication to principle been tested as severely as ours during recent weeks.

There is general recognition in the Middle East, as elsewhere, that the United States does not seek either political or economic domination over any other people. Our desire is a world environment of freedom, not servitude. On the other hand many, if not all, of the nations of the Middle East are aware of the danger that stems from International Communism and welcome closer cooperation with the United States to realize for themselves the United Nations goals of independence, economic well-being and spiritual growth.

If the Middle East is to continue its geographic role of uniting rather than separating East and West; if its vast economic resources are to serve the well-being of the peoples there, as well as that of others; and if its cultures and religions and their shrines are to be preserved for the uplifting of the spirits of the peoples, then the United States must make more evident its willingness to support the independence of the freedom-loving nations of the area.

V.

Under these circumstances I deem it necessary to seek the cooperation of the Congress. Only with that cooperation can we give the reassurance needed to deter aggression, to give courage and confidence to those who are dedicated to freedom and thus prevent a chain of events which would gravely endanger all of the free world.

There have been several Executive declarations made by the United States in relation to the Middle East. There is the Tripartite Declaration of May 25, 1950, followed by the Presidential assurance of October 31, 1950, to the King of Saudi Arabia. There is the Presidential declaration of April 9, 1956, that the United States will within constitutional means oppose any aggression in the area. There is our Declaration of November 29, 1956, that a threat to the territorial integrity or political independence of Iran, Iraq, Pakistan, or Turkey would be viewed by the United States with the utmost gravity.

Nevertheless, weaknesses in the present situation and the increased danger from International Communism, convince me that basic United States policy should now find expression in joint action by the Congress and the Executive. Furthermore, our joint resolve should be so couched as to make it apparent that if need be our words will be backed by action.

VI.

It is nothing new for the President and the Congress to join to recognize that the national integrity of other free nations is directly related to our own security.

We have joined to create and support the security system of the United Nations. We have reinforced the collective security system of the United Nations by a series of collective defense arrangements. Today we have security treaties with 42 other nations which recognize that our peace and security are intertwined. We have joined to take decisive action in relation to Greece and Turkey and in relation to Taiwan.

Thus, the United States through the joint action of the President and the Congress, or, in the case of treaties, the Senate, has manifested in many endangered areas its purpose to support free and independent governments—and peace—against external menace, notably the menace of International Communism. Thereby we have helped to maintain peace and security during a period of great danger. It is now essential that the United States should manifest through joint action of the President and the Congress our determination to assist those nations of the Mid East area, which desire that assistance.

The action which I propose would have the following features.

It would, first of all, authorize the United States to cooperate with and assist any nation or group of nations in the general area of the Middle East in the development of economic strength dedicated to the maintenance of national independence.

It would, in the second place, authorize the Executive to undertake in the same region programs of military assistance and cooperation with any nation or group of nations which desires such aid.

It would, in the third place, authorize such assistance and cooperation to include the employment of the armed forces of the United States to secure and protect the territorial integrity and political independence of such nations, requesting such aid, against overt armed aggression from any nation controlled by International Communism.

These measures would have to be consonant with the treaty obligations of the United States, including the Charter of the United Nations and with any action or recommendations of the United Nations. They would also, if armed attack occurs, be subject to the overriding authority of the United Nations Security Council in accordance with the Charter.

The present proposal would, in the fourth place, authorize the President to employ, for economic and defensive military purposes, sums available under the Mutual Security Act of 1954, as amended, without regard to existing limitations.

The legislation now requested should not include the authorization or appropriation of funds because I believe that, under the conditions I suggest, presently appropriated funds will be adequate for the balance of the present fiscal year ending June 30. I shall, however, seek in subsequent legislation the authorization of $200,000,000 to be available during each of the fiscal years 1958 and 1959 for discretionary use in the area, in addition to the other mutual security programs for the area hereafter provided for by the Congress.

VII.

This program will not solve all the problems of the Middle East. Neither does it represent the totality of our policies for the area. There are the problems of Palestine and relations between Israel and the Arab States, and the future of the Arab refugees. There is the problem of the future status of the Suez Canal. These difficulties are aggravated by International Communism, but they would exist quite apart from that threat. It is not the purpose of the legislation I propose to deal directly with these problems. The United Nations is actively concerning itself with all these matters, and we are supporting the United Nations. The United States has made clear, notably by Secretary Dulles' address of August 26, 1955,

that we are willing to do much to assist the United Nations in solving the basic problems of Palestine.

The proposed legislation is primarily designed to deal with the possibility of Communist aggression, direct and indirect. There is imperative need that any lack of power in the area should be made good, not by external or alien force, but by the increased vigor and security of the independent nations of the area.

Experience shows that indirect aggression rarely if ever succeeds where there is reasonable security against direct aggression; where the government disposes of loyal security forces, and where economic conditions are such as not to make Communism seem an attractive alternative. The program I suggest deals with all three aspects of this matter and thus with the problem of indirect aggression.

It is my hope and belief that if our purpose be proclaimed, as proposed by the requested legislation, that very fact will serve to halt any contemplated aggression. We shall have heartened the patriots who are dedicated to the independence of their nations. They will not feel that they stand alone, under the menace of great power. And I should add that patriotism is, throughout this area, a powerful sentiment. It is true that fear sometimes perverts true patriotism into fanaticism and to the acceptance of dangerous enticements from without. But if that fear can be allayed, then the climate will be more favorable to the attainment of worthy national ambitions.

And as I have indicated, it will also be necessary for us to contribute economically to strengthen those countries, or groups of countries, which have governments manifestly dedicated to the preservation of independence and resistance to subversion. Such measures will provide the greatest insurance against Communist inroads. Words alone are not enough.

VIII.

Let me refer again to the requested authority to employ the armed forces of the United States to assist to defend the territorial integrity and the political independence of any nation in the area against Communist armed aggression. Such authority would not be exercised except at the desire of the nation attacked. Beyond this it is my profound hope that this authority would never have to be exercised at all.

Nothing is more necessary to assure this than that our policy with respect to the defense of the area be promptly and clearly determined and declared. Thus the United Nations and all friendly governments, and indeed governments which are not friendly, will know where we stand.

If, contrary to my hope and expectation, a situation arose which called for the military application of the policy which I ask the Congress to join me in proclaiming, I would of course maintain hour-by-hour contact with the Congress if it were in session. And if the Congress were not in session, and if the situation had grave implications, I would, of course, at once call the Congress into special session.

In the situation now existing, the greatest risk, as is often the case, is that ambitious despots may miscalculate. If power-hungry Communists should either falsely or correctly estimate that the Middle East is inadequately defended, they might be tempted to use open measures of armed attack. If so, that would start a chain of circumstances which would almost surely involve the United States in military action. I am convinced that the best insurance against this dangerous contingency is to make clear now our readiness to cooperate fully and freely with our friends of the Middle East in ways consonant with the purposes and principles of the United Nations. I intend promptly to send a special mission to the Middle East to explain the cooperation we are prepared to give.

IX.

The policy which I outline involves certain burdens and indeed risks for the United States. Those who covet the area will not like what is proposed. Already, they are grossly distorting our purpose. However, before this Americans have seen our nation's vital interests and human freedom in jeopardy, and their fortitude and resolution have been equal to the crisis, regardless of hostile distortion of our words, motives and actions.

Indeed, the sacrifices of the American people in the cause of freedom have, even since the close of World War II, been measured in many billions of dollars and in thousands of the precious lives of our youth. These sacrifices, by which great areas of the

world have been preserved to freedom, must not be thrown away.

In those momentous periods of the past, the President and the Congress have united, without partisanship, to serve the vital interests of the United States and of the free world.

The occasion has come for us to manifest again our national unity in support of freedom and to show our deep respect for the rights and independence of every nation—however great, however small. We seek not violence, but peace. To this purpose we must now devote our energies, our determination, ourselves.

4. Speech Concerning Little Rock, September 24, 1957

Good Evening, My Fellow Citizens:

For a few minutes this evening I want to speak to you about the serious situation that has arisen in Little Rock. To make this talk I have come to the President's office in the White House. I could have spoken from Rhode Island, where I have been staying recently, but I felt that, in speaking from the house of Lincoln, of Jackson and of Wilson, my words would better convey both the sadness I feel in the action I was compelled today to take and the firmness with which I intend to pursue this course until the orders of the Federal Court at Little Rock can be executed without unlawful interference.

In that city, under the leadership of demagogic extremists, disorderly mobs have deliberately prevented the carrying out of proper orders from a Federal Court. Local authorities have not eliminated that violent opposition and, under the law, I yesterday issued a Proclamation calling upon the mob to disperse.

This morning the mob again gathered in front of the Central High School of Little Rock, obviously for the purpose of again preventing the carrying out of the Court's order relating to the admission of Negro children to that school.

Whenever normal agencies prove inadequate to the task and it becomes necessary for the Executive Branch of the Federal Government to use its powers and authority to uphold Federal Courts, the President's responsibility is inescapable.

In accordance with that responsibility, I have today issued an Executive Order directing the use of troops under Federal authority to aid in the execution of Federal law at Little Rock, Arkansas. This became necessary when my Proclamation of yesterday was not observed, and the obstruction of justice still continues.

It is important that the reasons for my action be understood by all our citizens.

As you know, the Supreme Court of the United States has decided that separate public educational facilities for the races are inherently unequal and therefore compulsory school segregation laws are unconstitutional.

Our personal opinions about the decision have no bearing on the matter of enforcement; the responsibility and authority of the Supreme Court to interpret the Constitution are very clear. Local Federal Courts were instructed by the Supreme Court to issue such orders and decrees as might be necessary to achieve admission to public schools without regard to race—and with all deliberate speed.

During the past several years, many communities in our Southern States have instituted public school plans for gradual progress in the enrollment and attendance of school children of all races in order to bring themselves into compliance with the law of the land.

They thus demonstrated to the world that we are a nation in which laws, not men, are supreme.

I regret to say that this truth—the cornerstone of our liberties—was not observed in this instance.

It was my hope that this localized situation would be brought under control by city and State authorities. If the use of local police powers had been sufficient, our traditional method of leaving the problems in those hands would have been pursued. But when large gatherings of obstructionists made it impossible for the decrees of the Court to be carried out, both the law and the national interest demanded that the President take action.

Here is the sequence of events in the development of the Little Rock school case.

In May of 1955, the Little Rock School Board approved a moderate plan for the gradual desegregation of the public schools in that city. It provided that a start toward integration would be made at the present term in the high school, and that the plan would be in full operation by 1963. Here I might say that in a number of communities in Arkansas integration in the schools has already started and without violence of any kind. Now this Little Rock plan was challenged in the courts by some who believed that the period of time as proposed in the plan was too long.

The United States Court at Little Rock, which has supervisory responsibility under the law for the plan of desegregation in the public schools, dismissed the challenge, thus approving a gradual rather than an abrupt change from the existing system. The court found that the school board had acted in good faith in planning for a public school system free from racial discrimination.

Since that time, the court has on three separate occasions issued orders directing that the plan be carried out. All persons were instructed to refrain from interfering with the efforts of the school board to comply with the law.

Proper and sensible observance of the law then demanded the respectful obedience which the nation has a right to expect from all its people. This, unfortunately, has not been the case a Little Rock. Certain misguided persons, many of them imported into Little Rock by agitators, have insisted upon defying the law and have sought to bring it into disrepute. The orders of the court have thus been frustrated.

The very basis of our individual rights and freedoms rests upon the certainty that the President and the Executive Branch of Government will support and insure the carrying out of the decisions of the Federal Courts, even, when necessary with all the means at the President's command.

Unless the President did so, anarchy would result.

There would be no security for any except that which each one of us could provide for himself.

The interest of the nation in the proper fulfillment of the law's requirements cannot yield to opposition and demonstrations by some few persons.

Mob rule cannot be allowed to override the decisions of our courts.

Now, let me make it very clear that Federal troops are not being used to relieve local and state authorities of their primary duty to preserve the peace and order of the community. Nor are the troops there for the purpose of taking over the responsibility of the School Board and the other responsible local officials in running Central High School. The running of our school system and the maintenance of peace and order in each of our States are strictly local affairs and the Federal Government does not interfere except in a very few special cases and when requested by one of the several States. In the present case the troops are there, pursuant to law, solely for the purpose of preventing interference with the orders of the Court.

The proper use of the powers of the Executive Branch to enforce the orders of a Federal Court is limited to extraordinary and compelling circumstances. Manifestly, such an extreme situation has been created in Little Rock. This challenge must be met and with such measures as will preserve to the people as a whole their lawfully-protected rights in a climate permitting their free and fair exercise.

The overwhelming majority of our people in every section of the country are united in their respect for observance of the law—even in those cases where they may disagree with that law.

They deplore the call of extremists to violence.

The decision of the Supreme Court concerning school integration, of course, affects the South more seriously than it does other sections of the country. In that region I have many warm friends, some of them in the city of Little Rock. I have deemed it a great personal privilege to spend in our Southland tours of duty while in the military service and enjoyable recreational periods since that time.

So from intimate personal knowledge, I know that the overwhelming majority of the people in the South—including those of Arkansas and of Little Rock—are of good will, united in their efforts to preserve and respect the law even when they disagree with it.

They do not sympathize with mob rule. They, like the rest of our nation, have proved in two great wars their readiness to sacrifice for America.

A foundation of our American way of life is our national respect for law.

In the South, as elsewhere, citizens are keenly aware of the tremendous disservice that has been done to the people of Arkansas in the eyes of the

nation, and that has been done to the nation in the eyes of the world.

At a time when we face grave situations abroad because of the hatred that Communism bears toward a system of government based on human rights, it would be difficult to exaggerate the harm that is being done to the prestige and influence, and indeed to the safety, of our nation and the world.

Our enemies are gloating over this incident and using it everywhere to misrepresent our whole nation. We are portrayed as a violator of those standards of conduct which the peoples of the world united to proclaim in the Charter of the United Nations. There they affirmed "faith in fundamental human rights" and "in the dignity and worth of the human person" and they did so "without distinction as to race, sex, language or religion."

And so, with deep confidence, I call upon the citizens of the State of Arkansas to assist in bringing to an immediate end all interference with the law and its processes. If resistance to the Federal Court orders ceases at once, the further presence of Federal troops will be unnecessary and the City of Little Rock will return to its normal habits of peace and order and a blot upon the fair name and high honor of our nation in the world will be removed.

Thus will be restored the image of America and of all its parts as one nation, indivisible, with liberty and justice for all.

Good night, and thank you very much.

5. Address to the American People on Science in National Security, November 7, 1957

My subject tonight is Science in National Security.

Originally this talk was to be part of one I intend to make in Oklahoma City next week. However, I found that I could not possibly deal with this subject in just one address. So tonight I shall concentrate on the most immediate aspects of this question of the relationship of science to the defense of our country.

Let me tell you plainly what I am going to do in this talk and those to follow.

I am going to lay the facts before you—the rough with the smooth. Some of these security facts are reassuring; others are not—they are sternly demanding. Some require that we resolutely continue lines of action now well begun. Others require new action, and still others new dimensions of effort. After putting these facts and requirements before you, I shall propose a program of action—a program that will demand the energetic support of not just the government but every American, if we are to make it successful.

I

First: some facts about our present security posture. It is one of great strength—but by no means should this assurance satisfy any of us. Our defenses must be adequate not just today, but tomorrow and in all the years to come, until under the safety of these defenses, we shall have secured a durable and just peace for all the world.

As of now, the United States is strong. Our nation has today, and has had for some years, enough power in its strategic retaliatory forces to bring near annihilation to the war-making capabilities of any other country.

This position of present strength did not come about by accident. The Korean War had the effect of greatly expanding our peacetime defense forces. As we began the partial demobilization of these forces we undertook also an accelerated program of modernization.

As a first step, scientific surveys were instituted soon after the Korean Armistice. The result was a decision to give a "New Look" to the defense establishment, depending for increased efficiency more upon modern science and less upon mere numbers of men.

In succeeding years there has been an across-the-board program to bring all units of our defense into line with the possibilities of modern technology. There has been, also, a high level of expenditure on research and development for defense—now running in the aggregate at something over $5 billion a year.

Later, scientific surveys focused attention and emphasis on long range ballistic missiles. Development on this item got into high gear more than two years ago. We have since been spending a billion dollars a year on this item alone.

Before discussing some of the things we urgently need to do, I would like to give you a few samples of the things that have been done in recent years by our military forces, scientists and engineers to put current scientific discovery at the service of your defense.

In our diversified family of missiles, we have weapons adapted to every kind of distance, launching and use. There are now thirty-eight different types either in operation or under development.

All combat vessels of the Navy built since 1955 have guided missiles in place of, or to supplement, guns. The Navy has in both oceans, submarines which can rise to the surface and launch, in a matter of minutes, a missile carrying a nuclear warhead, and submerge immediately—while the missile is guided to a target hundreds of miles away.

The Navy possesses an atomic depth bomb.

Since Korea, both the Army's and Navy's anti-aircraft guns have been largely replaced by surface-to-air missiles. All of our new interceptor aircraft are armed with air-to-air missiles.

Many of the traditional functions of the Army's artillery and support aircraft have been taken over by guided missiles. For example, we have already produced, in various distance ranges, hundreds of Matador, Honest John and Corporal missiles. To give you some idea of what this means in terms of explosive power: Four battalions of Corporal missiles alone are equivalent in fire power to all the artillery used in World War II.

Some of these missiles have their own built-in mechanisms for seeking out and destroying a target many miles away. Thus, the other day, a Bomarc missile, by itself, sought out a fast-moving, unmanned airplane 45 miles at sea and actually met it head-on.

Except for a dwindling number of B-36s, there is hardly an airplane in the combat units of the Air Force that was in them even as late as the Korean conflict. The B-52 jet bomber, supported by its jet tankers, is standard in our Strategic Air Command. Again, to show you what this means in terms of power: One B-52 can carry as much destructive capacity as was delivered by all the bombers in all the years of World War II combined. But the B-52 will, in turn, be succeeded by the B-58, a supersonic bomber.

Atomic submarines have been developed. One ran almost sixteen days without surfacing; another cruised under the polar ice cap for over five days.

A number of huge naval carriers are in operation, supplied with the most powerful nuclear weapons and bombers of great range to deliver them. Construction has started which will produce a carrier to be driven by atomic power.

Since 1956 we have developed nuclear explosives with radioactive fall-out of less than 4 percent of the fall-out of previous large weapons. This has obvious importance in developing nuclear defenses for use over our own territory.

In numbers, our stock of nuclear weapons is so large and so rapidly growing that we are able safely to disperse it to positions assuring its instant availability against attack, and still keep strong reserves. Our scientists assure me that we are well ahead of the Soviets in the nuclear field, both in quantity and in quality. We intend to stay ahead.

We have already shown that we can, with the precision to make it a useful military weapon, fire a large ballistic missile well over a thousand miles. Our ballistic test missiles have had successful flights to as much as 3,500 miles. An intercontinental missile is required, and we have some of them in an advanced state of development. But, because of our many forward positions, for us an intermediate range missile is for some purposes as good as an intercontinental one.

A different kind of missile, the air-breathing Snark, recently travelled over a guided course for 5,000 miles and was accurately placed on target.

We have fired three rockets to heights between 2,000 and 4,000 miles, and have received back much valuable information about outer space.

One difficult obstacle on the way to producing a useful long-range weapon is that of bringing a missile back from outer space without its burning up like a meteor, because of friction with the earth's atmosphere.

Our scientists and engineers have solved that problem. This object here in my office is an experimental missile—a nose cone. It has been hundreds of miles to outer space and back. Here it is, completely intact.

These illustrations—which are of course only a small sample of our scientists' accomplishments—I give you merely to show that our strength is not static but is constantly moving forward with technological improvement.

Long-range ballistic missiles, as they exist today, do not cancel the destructive and deterrent power of our Strategic Air Force.

The Soviet launching of earth satellites is an achievement of the first importance, and the scientists who brought it about deserve full credit and recognition. Already, useful new facts on outer space have been produced, and more are on the way, as new satellites with added instruments are launched.

Earth satellites, in themselves, have no direct present effect upon the nation's security. However, there is real military significance to these launchings, which I have previously mentioned publicly. Their current military significance lies in the advanced techniques and the competence in military technology they imply, evidenced, for example, by the powerful propulsion equipment necessarily used.

But in the main, the Soviets continue to concentrate on the development of war-making weapons and supporting industries. This, as well as their political attitude in all international affairs, serves to warn us that Soviet expansionist aims have not changed. The world has not forgotten the Soviet military invasions of such countries as Finland and Poland, their support of the war in Korea, or their use of force in their ruthless suppression of Hungarian freedom.

Eternal vigilance and increased free world military power, backed by our combined economic and spiritual strength, provide the only answer to this threat until the Soviet leaders themselves cease to consume their resources in warlike and expansionist purposes and turn them to the well-being of their own peoples.

We frankly recognize that the Soviets are building up types of power that could, if we were attacked, damage us seriously. This is because no defensive system today can possibly be air-tight in preventing all break-throughs of planes and weapons.

To aid in protecting against this, we, in partnership with Canada, have long been constructing a continental defense system reaching from far out in the Pacific around the northern edge of this continent and across the Atlantic approaches. This is a complex system of early warning radars, communication lines, electronic computers, supersonic aircraft, and ground-to-air missiles, some with atomic warheads. This organization and equipment is under constant improvement; emphasis on this improvement must be increased.

In addition to retaliatory and continental defense forces, we and our allies maintain strong ground and naval units in strategic areas of the world. In the strength and readiness of all these varied kinds of power—retaliatory, defensive and local—properly distributed and supported, lies the real deterrent to the outbreak of war. This fact brings home to all of us the tremendous importance to this country of our Allies. Not only do they maintain large military forces as part of our combined security, but they provide vital bases and areas that permit the effective deployment of all our forces for defense.

It is my conviction, supported by trusted scientific and military advisers, that, although the Soviets are quite likely ahead in some missile and special areas, and are obviously ahead of us in satellite development, as of today the over-all military strength of the free world is distinctly greater than that of the communist countries.

We must see to it that whatever advantages they have, are temporary only.

II

The next question is: How about the future?

I must say to you, in all gravity, that in spite of both the present over-all strength and the forward momentum of our defense, it is entirely possible that in the years ahead we could fall behind. I repeat: we could fall behind—unless we now face up to certain pressing requirements and set out to meet them at once.

I address myself to this problem knowing that for every American it surmounts any division among us of whatever kind. It reminds us once again that we are not partisans of any kind, we are Americans! We will close ranks as Americans, and get on with the job to be done.

According to my scientific friends, one of our greatest, and most glaring, deficiencies is the failure of us in this country to give high enough priority to scientific education and to the place of science in our national life.

Of course, these scientists properly assume that we shall continue to acquire the most mod-

ern weapons in adequate numbers as fast as they are produced; but their conviction does expose one great future danger that no amount of money or resources currently devoted to it can meet. Education requires time, incentive and skilled teachers.

They believe that a second critical need is that of giving higher priority, both public and private, to basic research.

As to these long range requirements, I shall have something to say next week.

Tonight I shall discuss two other factors, on which prompt action is possible.

The first is the tragic failure to secure the great benefits that would flow from mutual sharing of appropriate scientific information and effort among friendly countries.

Most great scientific advances of the world have been the product of free international exchange of ideas. There is hardly a nation that has not made some significant contribution to modern science.

There instantly comes to mind the contribution of Britain to jet propulsion, radar, and infra-red rays; Germany to rocketry, x-rays, and sulfa drugs; Italy to wireless telegraphy; France to radio activity; and Japan to magnetics.

In the free world, we all have a lot to give and a lot to gain in security through the pooling of scientific effort. Why should we deny to our friends information that we are sure the Soviets already have?—information our friends could use toward our mutual security.

Why, for want of the fullest practicable sharing, should we waste American research funds and talent struggling with technological problems already mastered by our friends?

Here is a way in which, at no cost, we can dramatically and quickly magnify the scientific resources at the disposal of the free world.

The second immediate requirement is that of greater concentration of effort and improved arrangements within the government in the fields of science, technology and missiles—including the continuing requirement for the closest kind of Executive-Legislative cooperation.

III

As to action: I report the following items to you tonight.

The first thing I have done is to make sure that the very best thought and advice that the scientific community can supply, heretofore provided to me on an informal basis, is now fully organized and formalized so that no gap can occur. The purpose is to make it possible for me, personally, whenever there appears to be any unnecessary delay in our development system, to act promptly and decisively.

To that end, I have created the office of Special Assistant to the President for Science and Technology. This man, who will be aided by a staff of scientists and a strong Advisory Group of outstanding experts reporting to him and to me, will have the active responsibility of helping me follow through on the program that I am partially outlining tonight and next week.

I am glad to be able to tell you that this position has been accepted by Dr. James R. Killfan, President of the Massachusetts Institute of Technology. He is a man who enjoys my confidence, and the confidence of his colleagues in the scientific and engineering world, and in the government.

Through him, I intend to be assured that the entire program is carried forward in closely-integrated fashion, and that such things as alleged inter-service competition or insufficient use of overtime shall not be allowed to create even the suspicion of harm to our scientific and development program. Moreover, Dr. Killfan will see to it that those projects which experts judge have the highest potential shall advance with the utmost possible speed. He will make sure that our best talent and the full necessary resources are applied on certain high-priority top-secret items that, for security reasons, I know you will not expect me to enumerate.

In looking to Dr. Killfan to discharge these responsibilities, I expect him to draw upon the full abilities of the scientists and engineers of our country.

Second: In the Defense Department is an official, directly responsible to the Secretary, in charge of missile development. I have directed that the Secretary make certain that the Guided Missile Director is clothed with all the authority that the Secretary himself possesses in this field, so that no administrative or inter-service block can occur. Dr. Killfan will, of course, work intimately with this official.

Third: The Secretary of Defense and I have agreed that any new missile or related program hereafter originated will, whenever practicable, be put under a single manager and administered without regard to the separate services.

Fourth: There will be laid before the Congress proposed legislation to remove legal barriers to the exchange of appropriate technological information with friendly countries.

Fifth: If the necessary authority is granted, I shall support, along the lines of the agreement reached with Prime Minister Macmillan, a Scientific Committee organized within NATO to carry out an enlarged Atlantic effort in research. Similar action in SEATO and comparable organizations will be studied. And, to help carry out these measures of mutual effort, the Secretary of State will appoint a Science Adviser to himself and Science Attaches in appropriate places abroad.

At any point in any of these actions where additional legal authority proves necessary, that authority will be asked of Congress at the outset of its next session. These matters will be discussed in my forthcoming bipartisan meeting with the leaders of Congress. They will be requested to consider every feasible step to hasten needed legislative action.

These, my friends, are the most immediate steps that are under way in scientific areas as they bear upon security.

Even in two talks I cannot, by any means, cover the entire subject of defense, but only selected questions of pressing and current importance. Accordingly, I am not at this time even alluding to a number of key items bearing strongly on defense, such as mutual aid, and Civil Defense. Likewise I have not dwelt upon the urgent need for greater dispersal in the Strategic Air Command, or for providing all the means that will enable airplanes to take off in the shortest possible time after receipt of warning.

In this whole effort it is important to see that nothing is wasted on non-essentials. Defense today is expensive, and growing more so. We cannot afford waste.

It misses the whole point to say that we must now increase our expenditures of all kinds on military hardware and defense—as, for example, to heed demands recently made that we restore all personnel cuts made in the armed forces.

Certainly, we need to feel a high sense of urgency. But this does not mean that we should mount our charger and try to ride off in all directions at once.

We must clearly identify the exact and critical needs that have to be met. We must then apply our resources at that point as fully as the need demands. This means selectivity in national expenditures of all kinds. We cannot, on an unlimited scale, have both what we must have and what we would like to have.

We can have both a sound defense, and the sound economy on which it rests—if we set our priorities and stick to them and if each of us is ready to carry his own share of the burden.

In conclusion: Although for tonight's purposes I stress the influence of science on defense, I am not forgetting that there is much more to science than its function in strengthening our defense, and much more to our defense than the part played by science. The peaceful contributions of science—to healing, to enriching life, to freeing the spirit—these are the most important products of the conquest of nature's secrets. And the spiritual powers of a nation—its underlying religious faith, its self-reliance, its capacity for intelligent sacrifice—these are the most important stones in any defense structure.

Above all, let me say for all to hear that, so far as we are concerned, the amassing of military might never has been—and never will be—devoted to any other end than defense and the preservation of a just peace.

What the world needs today even more than a giant leap into outer space, is a giant step toward peace. Time and again we have demonstrated our eagerness to take such a step. As a start in this direction, I urge the Soviets now to align themselves with the practical and workable disarmament proposals, approved yesterday by a large majority in the United Nations.

Never shall we cease to hope and work for the coming of the day when enduring peace will take these military burdens from the back of mankind, and when the scientist can give his full attention, not to human destruction, but to human happiness and fulfillment.

Thank you—and good night.

6. "Military-Industrial Complex" Address, January 17, 1961

My fellow Americans:

Three days from now, after half a century in the service of our country, I shall lay down the responsibilities of office as, in traditional and solemn ceremony, the authority of the Presidency is vested in my successor.

This evening I come to you with a message of leave-taking and farewell, and to share a few final thoughts with you, my countrymen.

Like every other citizen, I wish the new President, and all who will labor with him, Godspeed. I pray that the coming years will be blessed with peace and prosperity for all.

Our people expect their President and the Congress to find essential agreement on issues of great moment, the wise resolution of which will better shape the future of the Nation.

My own relations with the Congress, which began on a remote and tenuous basis when, long ago, a member of the Senate appointed me to West Point, have since ranged to the intimate during the war and immediate post-war period, and, finally, to the mutually interdependent during these past eight years.

In this final relationship, the Congress and the Administration have, on most vital issues, cooperated well, to serve the national good rather than mere partisanship, and so have assured that the business of the Nation should go forward. So, my official relationship with the Congress ends in a feeling, on my part, of gratitude that we have been able to do so much together.

II.

We now stand ten years past the midpoint of a century that has witnessed four major wars among great nations. Three of these involved our own country. Despite these holocausts America is today the strongest, the most influential and most productive nation in the world. Understandably proud of this pre-eminence, we yet realize that America's leadership and prestige depend, not merely upon our unmatched material progress, riches and military strength, but on how we use our power in the interests of world peace and human betterment.

III.

Throughout America's adventure in free government, our basic purposes have been to keep the peace; to foster progress in human achievement, and to enhance liberty, dignity and integrity among people and among nations. To strive for less would be unworthy of a free and religious people. Any failure traceable to arrogance, or our lack of comprehension or readiness to sacrifice would inflict upon us grievous hurt both at home and abroad.

Progress toward these noble goals is persistently threatened by the conflict now engulfing the world. It commands our whole attention, absorbs our very beings. We face a hostile ideology—global in scope, atheistic in character, ruthless in purpose, and insidious in method. Unhappily the danger is poses promises to be of indefinite duration. To meet it successfully, there is called for, not so much the emotional and transitory sacrifices of crisis, but rather those which enable us to carry forward steadily, surely, and without complaint the burdens of a prolonged and complex struggle—with liberty the stake. Only thus shall we remain, despite every provocation, on our charted course toward permanent peace and human betterment.

Crises there will continue to be. In meeting them, whether foreign or domestic, great or small, there is a recurring temptation to feel that some spectacular and costly action could become the miraculous solution to all current difficulties. A huge increase in newer elements of our defense; development of unrealistic programs to cure every ill in agriculture; a dramatic expansion in basic and applied research—these and many other possibilities, each possibly promising in itself, may be suggested as the only way to the road we wish to travel.

But each proposal must be weighed in the light of a broader consideration: the need to maintain balance in and among national programs—balance between the private and the public economy, balance between cost and hoped for advantage—balance between the clearly necessary and the comfortably desirable; balance between our essential requirements as a nation and the duties imposed by the nation upon the individual; balance between actions of the moment and the national welfare of the future. Good judgment seeks balance and progress; lack of it eventually finds imbalance and frustration.

The record of many decades stands as proof that our people and their government have, in the main, understood these truths and have responded to them well, in the face of stress and threat. But threats, new in kind or degree, constantly arise. I mention two only.

IV.

A vital element in keeping the peace is our military establishment. Our arms must be mighty, ready for instant action, so that no potential aggressor may be tempted to risk his own destruction.

Our military organization today bears little relation to that known by any of my predecessors in peacetime, or indeed by the fighting men of World War II or Korea.

Until the latest of our world conflicts, the United States had no armaments industry. American makers of plowshares could, with time and as required, make swords as well. But now we can no longer risk emergency improvisation of national defense; we have been compelled to create a permanent armaments industry of vast proportions. Added to this, three and a half million men and women are directly engaged in the defense establishment. We annually spend on military security more than the net income of all United States corporations.

This conjunction of an immense military establishment and a large arms industry is new in the American experience. The total influence—economic, political, even spiritual—is felt in every city, every State house, every office of the Federal government. We recognize the imperative need for this development. Yet we must not fail to comprehend its grave implications. Our toil, resources and livelihood are all involved; so is the very structure of our society.

In the councils of government, we must guard against the acquisition of unwarranted influence, whether sought or unsought, by the military-industrial complex. The potential for the disastrous rise of misplaced power exists and will persist.

We must never let the weight of this combination endanger our liberties or democratic processes. We should take nothing for granted. Only an alert and knowledgeable citizenry can compel the proper meshing of the huge industrial and military machinery of defense with our peaceful methods and goals, so that security and liberty may prosper together.

Akin to, and largely responsible for the sweeping changes in our industrial-military posture, has been the technological revolution during recent decades.

In this revolution, research has become central; it also becomes more formalized, complex, and costly. A steadily increasing share is conducted for, by, or at the direction of, the Federal government.

Today, the solitary inventor, tinkering in his shop, has been over-shadowed by task forces of scientists in laboratories and testing fields. In the same fashion, the free university, historically the fountainhead of free ideas and scientific discovery, has experienced a revolution in the conduct of research. Partly because of the huge costs involved, a government contract becomes virtually a substitute for intellectual curiosity. For every old blackboard there are now hundreds of new electronic computers.

The prospect of domination of the nation's scholars by Federal employment, project allocations, and the power of money is ever present—and is gravely to be regarded.

Yet, in holding scientific research and discovery in respect, as we should, we must also be alert to the equal and opposite danger that public policy could itself become the captive of a scientific-technological elite.

It is the task of statesmanship to mold, to balance, and to integrate these and other forces, new and old, within the principles of our democratic system—ever aiming toward the supreme goals of our free society.

V.

Another factor in maintaining balance involves the element of time. As we peer into society's future, we—you and I, and our government—must avoid the impulse to live only for today, plundering, for our own ease and convenience, the precious resources of tomorrow. We cannot mortgage the material assets of our grandchildren without risking the loss also of their political and spiritual heritage. We want democracy to survive for all generations to come, not to become the insolvent phantom of tomorrow.

VI.

Down the long lane of the history yet to be written America knows that this world of ours, ever growing smaller, must avoid becoming a community of dreadful fear and hate, and be instead, a proud confederation of mutual trust and respect.

Such a confederation must be one of equals. The weakest must come to the conference table with the same confidence as do we, protected as we are by our moral, economic, and military strength. That table, though scarred by many past frustrations, cannot be abandoned for the certain agony of the battlefield.

Disarmament, with mutual honor and confidence, is a continuing imperative. Together we must learn how to compose differences, not with arms, but with intellect and decent purpose. Because this need is so sharp and apparent I confess that I lay down my official responsibilities in this field with a definite sense of disappointment. As one who has witnessed the horror and the lingering sadness of war—as one who knows that another war could utterly destroy this civilization which has been so slowly and painfully built over thousands of years—I wish I could say tonight that a lasting peace is in sight.

Happily, I can say that war has been avoided. Steady progress toward our ultimate goal has been made. But, so much remains to be done. As a private citizen, I shall never cease to do what little I can to help the world advance along that road.

VII.

So—in this my last good night to you as your President—I thank you for the many opportunities you have given me for public service in war and peace. I trust that in that service you find some things worthy; as for the rest of it, I know you will find ways to improve performance in the future.

You and I—my fellow citizens—need to be strong in our faith that all nations, under God, will reach the goal of peace with justice. May we be ever unswerving in devotion to principle, confident but humble with power, diligent in pursuit of the Nation's great goals.

To all the peoples of the world, I once more give expression to America's prayerful and continuing aspiration:

We pray that peoples of all faiths, all races, all nations, may have their great human needs satisfied; that those now denied opportunity shall come to enjoy it to the full; that all who yearn for freedom may experience its spiritual blessings; that those who have freedom will understand, also, its heavy responsibilities; that all who are insensitive to the needs of others will learn charity; that the scourges of poverty, disease and ignorance will be made to disappear from the earth, and that, in the goodness of time, all peoples will come to live together in a peace guaranteed by the binding force of mutual respect and love.

SELECTED BIBLIOGRAPHY

General Studies of the 1950s

Diggins, John Patrick. *The Proud Decades: America in War and Peace, 1941–1960.* New York: Norton & Co., 1988.

Donaldson, Gary. *Abundance and Anxiety: America, 1945–1960.* Westport, Conn.: Praeger Books, 1997.

Goldman, Eric. *The Crucial Decade.* New York: Vintage Books, 1961.

Halberstam, David. *The Fifties.* New York: Villard Books, 1993.

Jezer, Mark. *The Dark Ages: Life in the United States, 1946–1960.* Boston: South End Press, 1982.

Kallen, Stuart. *The 1950s.* Chapel Hill: University of North Carolina Press, 2000.

Mayer, Michael S. (ed.). *The Eisenhower Presidency and the 1950s.* Boston: Houghton Mifflin Company, 1998.

Oakley, J. Ronald. *God's Country: America in the Fifties.* New York: Dembner Books, 1986.

O'Neill, William. *American High: The Years of Confidence 1945–1960.* New York: Free Press, 1986.

Reichard, Gary. *Politics as Usual: The Age of Truman and Eisenhower.* Arlington Heights, Ill.: Harlan Davidson, 1988.

Young, William and Nancy. *The 1950s.* Westport, Conn.: Greenwood Press, 2004.

Dwight D. Eisenhower and the Eisenhower Administration

Adams, Sherman. *First Hand Report: The Story of the Eisenhower Administration.* New York: Harper, 1961.

Alexander, Charles C. *Holding the Line: The Eisenhower Era, 1952–1961.* Bloomington: Indiana University Press, 1975.

Ambrose, Stephen. *Eisenhower: Soldier and President.* New York: Simon & Schuster, 1983.

———. *Eisenhower: The President.* New York: Simon & Schuster, 1984.

Bischoff, Gunter, and Stephen Ambrose (eds.). *Eisenhower: A Centenary Assessment.* Baton Rouge: Louisiana State University Press, 1995.

Burk, Robert. *Dwight D. Eisenhower: Hero and Politician.* Boston: Twayne Publishers, 1986.

Cook, Blanche. *The Declassified Eisenhower.* Garden City, N.Y.: Doubleday Books, 1981.

Damms, Richard V. *The Eisenhower Presidency, 1955–1961.* London: Longman, 2002.

Eisenhower, Dwight D. *Mandate For Change.* Garden City, N.Y.: Doubleday Books, 1963.

———. *Waging Peace.* Garden City, N.Y.: Doubleday Books, 1965.

Ewald, William Bragg, Jr. *Eisenhower the President: Crucial Days: 1951–1960.* Englewood Cliffs, N.J.: Prentice Hall, 1981.

Ferrell, Robert H. (ed.). *The Eisenhower Diaries.* New York: W. W. Norton & Co., 1981.

Greenstein, Fred I. *The Hidden-Hand Presidency: Eisenhower as Leader.* New York: Basic Books, 1982.

Griffith, Robert W. (ed.). *Ike's Letters to a Friend, 1941–1958.* Lawrence: University of Kansas Press, 1984.

Kinnard, Douglas. *Eisenhower: Soldier-Statesman of the American Century.* Washington, D.C.: Potomac Books, 2002.

Krieg, Joann. *Dwight D. Eisenhower: Soldier, President, Statesman.* New York: Greenwood Press, 1987.

Larson, Arthur. *Eisenhower: The President That Nobody Knows.* New York: Charles Scribner's Sons, 1968.

Lee, R. Alton. *Dwight D. Eisenhower: Soldier and Statesman.* Chicago: Burnham Publishing, 1981.

Mayer, Michael S. (ed.). *The Eisenhower Presidency and the 1950s.* Boston: Houghton Mifflin, 1998.

Murray, Charles. *Losing Ground: American Social Policy, 1950–1980.* New York: Basic Books, 1984.

Neal, Steve. *The Eisenhowers.* Lawrence: University of Kansas Press, 1984.

Pach, Chester, and Elmo Richardson. *The Presidency of Dwight D. Eisenhower.* Lawrence: University of Kansas Press, 1991.

Parmet, Herbert. *Eisenhower and the American Crusades.* New York: Macmillan, 1972.

Pickett, William B. *Dwight David Eisenhower and American Power.* Wheeling, Ill.: Harlan Davidson, 1995.

Warshaw, Shirley Anne. *Reexamining the Eisenhower Presidency.* Westport, Conn.: Greenwood Press, 1993.

Politics

Bartley, E. R. *The Tidelands Oil Controversy.* Austin: University of Texas Press, 1953.

Bean, Louis H. *Influences in the 1954 Mid-Term Elections.* Washington, D.C.: Public Affairs Institute, 1954.

Dallek, Robert. *Lone Star Rising: Lyndon Johnson and His Times, 1908–1960.* New York: Oxford University Press, 1991.

Eulau, Heinz. *Class and Party in the Eisenhower Years: Class Roles in Perspective in the 1952 and 1956 Elections.* New York: Free Press of Glencoe, 1962.

Harris, Louis. *Is There a Republican Majority?* New York: Harper, 1954.

Johnson, Walter (ed.). *The Papers of Adlai E. Stevenson.* Boston: Little, Brown, 1972.

———. *How We Drafted Stevenson.* New York: Knopf, 1955.

Lodge, Henry Cabot. *As It Was: An Inside View of Politics and Power in the '50s and '60s.* New York: Norton, 1976.

Lubell, Samuel. *Revolt of the Moderates.* New York: Harper, 1956.

Martin, Joe. *My First Fifty Years in Politics.* New York: McGraw-Hill, 1960.

Matthews, Donald R. *U.S. Senators and Their World.* Chapel Hill: University of North Carolina Press, 1960.

Morgan, Iwan W. *Eisenhower versus "The Spenders": The Eisenhower Administration, the Democrats, and the Budget, 1953–60.* New York: St. Martin's Press, 1990.

Redding, Jack. *Inside the Democratic Party.* Indianapolis: Bobbs-Merrill, 1958.

Reichard, Gary. *The Reaffirmation of Republicanism: Eisenhower and the 83rd Congress.* Knoxville: University of Tennessee Press, 1985.

Richardson, Elmo. *Dams, Parks, and Politics: Resource Development and Preservation in the Truman-Eisenhower Era.* Lexington: University Press of Kentucky, 1973.

Rovere, Richard. *The American Establishment and Other Reports, Opinions, and Speculations.* New York: Harcourt, Brace & World, 1962.

Soth, Lauren. *Farm Trouble.* Princeton: Princeton University Press, 1957.

Stone, I. F. *The Haunted Fifties.* New York: Random House, 1963.

Theoharis, Athan. *The Yalta Myths: An Issue in U.S. Politics, 1945–1955.* Columbia: University of Missouri Press, 1970.

Thomson, C. A. H., and F. N. Shattuck. *The 1956 Presidential Campaign.* Washington, D.C.: Brookings Institute, 1960.

Tillet, Paul (ed.). *Inside Politics: The National Conventions, 1960.* Dobbs Ferry, N.Y.: Oceana Publications, 1962.

Weinstein, Allen, and Alexander Vassilev. *The Haunted Wood: Soviet Espionage in America—The Stalin Era.* New York: Random House, 1999.

Wildavsky, Aaron. *Dixon-Yates: A Study in Power Politics.* New Haven: Yale University Press, 1962.

Willoughby, William B. *The St. Lawrence Waterway: A Study in Politics and Diplomacy.* Madison: University of Wisconsin Press, 1961.

Wills, Garry. *Nixon Agonistes: The Crisis of the Self-Made Man.* Boston: Houghton Mifflin, 1970.

Congress

Bass, Jack, and Marilyn W. Thompson. *Strom: The Complicated Personal and Political Life of Strom Thurmond*. New York: Public Affairs, 2005.

Bolling, Richard. *House Out of Order*. New York: Dutton, 1965.

Bowles, Chester. *Promises to Keep*. New York: Harper & Row, 1971.

Clark, Joseph S. *The Senate Establishment*. New York: Hill & Wang, 1963.

Douglas, Paul H. *In the Fullness of Time*. New York: Harcourt Brace Jovanovich, 1972.

Evans, Rowland, and Robert Novak. *Lyndon B. Johnson: The Exercise of Power*. New York: New American Library, 1966.

Flanders, Ralph E. *Senator from Vermont*. Boston: Little, Brown, 1961.

Fontenay, Charles L. *Estes Kefauver*. Knoxville: University of Tennessee Press, 1980.

Gorman, Joseph B. *Kefauver: A Political Biography*. New York: Oxford University Press, 1971.

Gruening, Ernest H. *Many Battles*. New York: Liveright, 1973.

Huitt, Ralph K., and Robert L. Peabody (eds.). *Congress: Two Decades of Analysis*. New York: Harper & Row, 1969.

Humphrey, Hubert H. *The Education of a Public Man: My Life and Politics*. Garden City, N.Y.: Doubleday, 1976.

Johnson, Haynes, and Bernard M. Gwertzman. *Fulbright: The Dissenter*. Garden City, N.Y.: Doubleday Books, 1968.

Manley, John F. *The Politics of Finance: The House Ways and Means Committee*. Boston: Little, Brown, 1970.

Martin, Joseph. *My First Fifty Years in Politics*. New York: McGraw-Hill, 1973.

McAdams, Alan K. *Power and Politics in Labor Legislation*. New York: Columbia University Press, 1964.

McNeil, Neil. *Dirksen: Portrait of a Public Man*. New York: World Publishing Co., 1970.

Montgomery, Gayle B., and James W. Johnson. *One Step from the White House: The Rise and Fall of Senator William F. Knowland*. Berkeley: University of California Press, 1998.

Nevins, Allan. *Herbert Lehman and His Era*. New York: Scribner, 1963.

Ognibene, Peter I. *Scoop: The Life and Politics of Henry M. Jackson*. New York: Stein & Day, 1975.

Patterson, James. *Mr. Republican: A Biography of Robert A. Taft*. Boston: Houghton Mifflin, 1972.

Pearson, Drew, and Jack Anderson. *The Case against Congress*. New York: Simon & Schuster, 1967.

Potter, Charles. *Days of Shame*. New York: Coward-McCann, 1965.

Powell, Adam Clayton. *Adam by Adam*. New York: Dial Press, 1971.

Robertson, David. *Sly and Able: A Political Biography of James F. Byrnes*. New York: Norton, 1994.

Schapsmeier, Edward L., and Frederick H. Schapsmeier. *Dirksen of Illinois*. Urbana: University of Illinois Press, 1985.

Sheele, Henry Z. *Charlie Halleck*. New York: Exposition Press, 1966.

Smith, A. Robert. *The Tiger in the Senate: The Biography of Wayne Morse*. Garden City, N.Y.: Doubleday Books, 1962.

Smith, Margaret Chase. *Declaration of Conscience*. New York: Doubleday, 1972.

Steinberg, Alfred. *Sam Rayburn*. New York: Hawthorn Books, 1975.

Sykes, Jay G. *Proxmire*. Washington, D.C.: R. B. Luce, 1972.

Wellman, Paul I. *Stuart Symington: Portrait of a Man with a Mission*. Garden City, N.Y.: Doubleday Books, 1960.

White, William S. *Citadel: The Story of the United States Senate*. New York: Harper, 1957.

———. *The Taft Story*. New York: Harper, 1954.

Red Scare

Adams, John G. *Without Precedent: The Story of the Death of McCarthyism*. New York: Norton, 1983.

Anderson, Jack, and Ronald May. *McCarthy: The Man, the Senator and the "ism."* Boston: Beacon Press, 1952.

Bayley, Edwin R. *Joe McCarthy and the Press*. Madison: University of Wisconsin Press, 1981.

Brown, Ralph S., Jr. *Loyalty and Security: Employment Tests in the U.S.* New Haven: Yale University Press, 1958.

Buckley, William F., Jr., and L. Brent Bozell. *McCarthy and His Enemies: The Record and Meaning*. Chicago: University of Chicago Press, 1954.

Caute, David. *The Great Fear: The Anti-Communist Purge under Truman and Eisenhower.* New York: Simon & Schuster, 1978.

Chambers, Whittaker. *Odyssey of a Friend: Whittaker Chambers' Letters to William F. Buckley Jr. 1954–61.* New York: National Review, 1969.

Cohn, Roy. *McCarthy.* New York: New American Library, 1968.

Cook, Fred J. *The Nightmare Decade: The Life and Times of Sen. Joseph McCarthy.* New York: Random House, 1971.

Eden, Anthony. *The Suez Crisis of 1956.* Boston: Beacon Press, 1966.

Ewald, William Bragg. *McCarthyism and Consensus.* Lanham, Md.: University Press of America, 1986.

———. *Who Killed Joe McCarthy?* New York: Simon & Schuster, 1984.

Freeland, Richard. *The Truman Doctrine and the Origins of McCarthyism.* New York: Knopf, 1972.

Fried, Albert. *McCarthyism: The Great American Red Scare: A Documentary History.* New York: Oxford Press, 1997.

Fried, Richard M. *Men against McCarthy.* New York: Columbia University Press, 1976.

———. *Nightmare in Red: The McCarthy Era in Perspective.* New York: Oxford University Press, 1990.

Goodman, Walter. *The Committee.* New York: Farrar, Straus and Giroux, 1968.

Griffith, Robert. *The Politics of Fear: Joseph McCarthy and the Senate.* Lexington: University of Kentucky Press, 1970.

Griffith, Robert, and Athan Theoharis (eds.). *The Specter: Original Essays on the Cold War and McCarthyism.* New York: New Viewpoints, 1974.

Haynes, John. *Red Scare or Red Menace.* Chicago: Ivan R. Dee, 1996.

Klehr, Harvey, and John Earl Haynes. *The American Communist Movement: Storming Heaven Itself.* New York: Twayne Publishing, 1992.

Klehr, Harvey, John Earl Haynes, and Fredrikh Igorevich Firsov. *The Secret World of American Communism.* New Haven: Yale University Press, 1995.

Latham, Earl. *The Communist Controversy in Washington.* Cambridge: Harvard University Press, 1966.

Matusow, Harvey. *False Witness.* New York: Cameron & Kahn, 1955.

Morgan, Ted. *Reds: McCarthyism in Twentieth-Century America.* New York: Random House, 2003.

O'Brien, Michael. *McCarthy and McCarthyism in Wisconsin.* Columbia: University of Missouri Press, 1980.

O'Reilly, Kenneth. *Hoover and the Un-Americans: The FBI, HUAC, and the Red Menace.* Philadelphia: Temple University Press, 1983.

Oshinsky, David. *A Conspiracy So Immense: The World of Joe McCarthy.* New York: Free Press, 1983.

Powers, Richard Gidd. *Secrecy and Power: The Life of J. Edgar Hoover.* New York: Free Press, 1987.

Reeves, Thomas. *The Life and Times of Joe McCarthy.* New York: Stein & Day, 1982.

Rogin, Michael Paul. *The Intellectuals and McCarthy.* Cambridge: Harvard University Press, 1967.

Rovere, Richard. *Senator Joe McCarthy.* New York: Harcourt, Brace, 1959.

Schrecker, Ellen. *The Age of McCarthyism: A Brief History With Documents.* Boston: Bedford Books of St. Martin's Press, 1994.

———. *Many Are the Crimes: McCarthyism in America.* Boston: Little, Brown, 1998.

———. *No Ivory Tower: McCarthyism and the Universities.* New York: Oxford University Press, 1986.

Theoharis, Athan. *Seeds of Repression.* Chicago: Quadrangle Books, 1971.

Watkins, Arthur. *Enough Rope.* Englewood Cliffs, N.J.: Prentice Hall, 1969.

Weinstein, Allen. *Perjury: The Hiss-Chambers Case.* New York: Random House, 1978.

Weinstein, Allen, and Alexander Vassiliev. *The Haunted Wood.* New York: Random House, 1999.

Ybarra, Michael J. *Washington Gone Crazy: Senator Pat McCarran and the Great American Communist Hunt.* Hanover, N.H.: Steerforth Press, 2004.

Foreign Policy

Alteras, Isaac. *Eisenhower and Israel: U.S.-Israeli Relations, 1953–1960.* Gainesville: University Press of Florida, 1993.

Ambrose, Stephen. *Rise to Globalism: American Foreign Policy since 1938.* New York: Penguin Books, 1988.

Anderson, David. *Trapped by Success: The Eisenhower Administration and Vietnam, 1953–1961.* New York: Columbia University Press, 1991.

Arnold, James R. *The First Domino: Eisenhower, the Military, and America's Intervention in Vietnam.* New York: W. Morrow, 1991.

Baldwin, David. *Economic Development and American Foreign Policy, 1943–1962.* Chicago: University of Chicago Press, 1966.

Bandle, Robert E. *Geneva: 1954.* Princeton: Princeton University Press, 1969.

Berding, Andrew H. *Dulles on Diplomacy.* Princeton: Van Nostrand, 1965.

Beschloss, Michael. *Mayday: Eisenhower, Khrushchev, and the U-2 Affair.* New York: Harper & Row, 1986.

Bill, James A. *The Eagle and the Lion: The Tragedy of American-Iranian Relations.* New Haven: Yale University Press, 1983.

Bill, James A., and William Roger Louis. *Musaddiq: Iranian Nationalism and Oil.* Austin: University of Texas Press, 1988.

Billings-Yun, Melanie. *Decision against War: Eisenhower and Dien Bien Phu, 1954.* New York: Columbia University Press, 1988.

Bonsal, Phillip W. *Cuba, Castro, and the United States.* Pittsburgh: University of Pittsburgh Press, 1971.

Bowie, Robert R., and Richard W. Immermann. *Waging Peace: How Eisenhower Shaped an Enduring Cold War Strategy.* New York: Oxford University Press, 1998.

Bowles, Chester. *Africa's Challenge to the Americans.* Berkeley: University of California Press, 1957.

Boyle, Peter (ed.). *The Churchill-Eisenhower Correspondence.* Chapel Hill: University of North Carolina Press, 1990.

Campbell, John C. *Defense of the Middle East.* New York: Published for the Council on Foreign Relations by Harper, 1960.

Clayton, Lawrence. *Peru and the United States: The Condor and the Eagle.* Athens: University of Georgia Press, 1999.

Cook, Blauche Wiesen. *The Declassified Eisenhower.* New York: Penguin, 1984.

Deshpande, Javashri. *Indonesia: The Impossible Dream: The United States and the 1958 Rebellion.* New Delhi: Prachi Prakashan, 1981.

Devillers, Phillip, and Jean Lacoutre. *End of a War: Indo-China, 1954.* New York: Praeger, 1969.

Divine, Robert. *Eisenhower and the Cold War.* New York: Oxford University Press, 1981.

Dockrill, Saki. *Eisenhower's New-Look National Security Policy, 1953–61.* New York: St. Martin's Press, 1996.

Draper, Theodore. *Castro's Revolution.* New York: Praeger, 1962.

Drummond, Roscoe, and Gaston Coblentz. *Duel at the Brink: John Foster Dulles' Command of American Power.* Garden City, N.Y.: Doubleday Books, 1960.

Dulles, Eleanor Lansing. *John Foster Dulles: The Last Year.* New York: Harcourt, Brace & World, 1963.

Dulles, Foster Rhea. *American Policy toward Communist China, 1949–1969.* New York: Crowell, 1972.

Dunn, Frederick S. *Peacemaking and the Settlement with Japan.* Princeton: Princeton University Press, 1963.

Eisenhower, Milton. *The Wine Is Bitter.* Garden City, N.Y.: Doubleday Books, 1963.

Elliot, William Y., et al. *The Political Economy of American Foreign Policy.* New York: Holt, 1955.

Fall, Bernard B. *The Two Viet-Nams: A Political and Military Analysis.* New York: Praeger, 1963.

Fernea, Robert, et al. *The Iraqi Revolution of 1958: The Old Social Classes Revisited.* New York: I. B. Tauris, 1991.

Finer, Herman. *Dulles over Suez.* Chicago: Quadrangle Books, 1964.

Finletter, Thomas K. *Foreign Policy: The Next Phase.* New York: Published for the Council on Foreign Relations by Harper, 1958.

———. *Power and Policy: U.S. Foreign Policy and Military Power in the Hydrogen Age.* New York: Harcourt, Brace, 1954.

Foot, Rosemary. *A Substitute for Victory: The Politics of Peacemaking at the Korean Armistice Talks.* Ithaca, N.Y.: Cornell University Press, 1990.

Gardner, Lloyd. *Approaching Vietnam: From World War II through Dienbienphu, 1941–1954.* New York: W. W. Norton & Co., 1988.

Garthoff, Raymond. *Assessing the Adversary: Estimates by the Eisenhower Administration of Soviet*

Intentions and Capabilities. Washington, D.C.: Brookings Institute, 1991.

Gasiorowski, Mark J., and Malcolm Byrne (eds.). *Mohammad Mosaddeq and the 1953 Coup in Iran.* Syracuse, N.Y.: Syracuse University Press, 2004.

Gelber, Lionel. *America in Britain's Place: The Leadership of the West and Anglo-American Unity.* New York: Praeger, 1961.

Gembone, Michael D. *Eisenhower, Somoza, and the Cold War in Nicaragua, 1953–1961.* Westport, Conn.: Praeger, 1999.

Gleijeses, Piero. *Shattered Hopes: The Guatemala Revolution and the United States, 1944–1955.* Princeton: Princeton University Press, 1991.

Gray, William Glenn. *Germany's Cold War: The Global Campaign to Isolate East Germany, 1949–1969.* Chapel Hill: University of North Carolina Press, 2003.

Gukin, Michael. *John Foster Dulles: A Statesman and His Times.* New York: Columbia University Press, 1972.

Gurtov, Melvin. *The First Vietnam Crisis: Chinese Communist Strategy and United States Involvement, 1953–1954.* New York: Columbia University Press, 1967.

Hahn, Peter. *Caught in the Middle East: U.S. Policy toward the Arab-Israeli Conflict, 1945–1961.* Chapel Hill: University of North Carolina Press, 2006.

———. *The United States, Great Britain, and Egypt, 1945–1956: Strategy and Diplomacy in the Early Cold War.* Chapel Hill: University of North Carolina Press, 1991.

Halberstam, David. *The Best and the Brightest.* New York: Random House, 1972.

———. *The Making of a Quagmire.* New York: Random House, 1965.

Heiss, Mary Ann. *Empire and Nationhood: The United States, Great Britain, and Iranian Oil, 1950–1954.* New York: Columbia University Press, 1997.

Henderson, John W. *The United States Information Agency.* New York: Praeger, 1969.

Higgins, Trumball. *The Perfect Failure: Kennedy, Eisenhower, and the C. I. A. at the Bay of Pigs.* New York: Norton, 1987.

Hoopes, Townsend. *The Devil and John Foster Dulles.* Boston: Little, Brown, 1973.

Hughes, Emmett J. *America the Vincible.* Garden City, N.Y.: Doubleday Books, 1959.

Immerman, Richard (ed.). *The C. I. A. and Guatemala: The Foreign Policy of Intervention.* Austin: University of Texas Press, 1982.

———. *John Foster Dulles and the Diplomacy of the Cold War.* Princeton: Princeton University Press, 1990.

———. *John Foster Dulles: Piety, Pragmatism and Power in U.S. Foreign Policy.* Wilmington, Del.: Scholarly Resources, 1999.

Iriye, Akira, and Warren Cohen. *The Great Powers in East Asia, 1953–1960.* New York: Columbia University Press, 1990.

Jones, Howard P. *Indonesia: The Possible Dream.* New York: Harcourt Brace Jovanovich, 1971.

Kahin, George, and John W. Lewis. *The United States in Vietnam.* New York: Dial Press, 1969.

Kalicki, J. H. *The Pattern of Sino-American Crises: Political-Military Interactions in the 1950s.* New York: Cambridge University Press, 1975.

Kaufman, Burton. *Trade and Aid: Eisenhower's Economic Foreign Policy, 1953–1961.* Baltimore: Johns Hopkins University Press, 1982.

Kennan, George F. *Realities of American Foreign Policy.* Princeton: Princeton University Press, 1954.

Kingseed, Cole C. *Eisenhower and the Suez Crisis of 1956.* Baton Rouge: Louisiana State University Press, 1995.

Kissinger, Henry A. *Nuclear Weapons and Foreign Policy.* New York: Published for the Council on Foreign Relations by Harper, 1957.

Knorr, Klaus (ed.). *NATO and American Security.* Princeton: Princeton University Press, 1959.

Krebs, Ronald R. *Dueling Visions: U.S. Strategy towards Eastern Europe under Eisenhower.* College Station, Tex.: A&M University Press, 2001.

Krenn, Michael. *The Chains of Interdependence: U.S. Policy toward Central America, 1945–1954.* Armonk, N.Y.: M. E. Sharpe, 1996.

Kunz, Diane B. *The Economic Diplomacy of the Suez Crisis.* Chapel Hill: University of North Carolina Press, 1991.

Lansdale, Edward G. *In the Midst of Wars: An American's Mission to Southeast Asia.* New York: Harper & Row, 1972.

Lesch, David. *Syria and the United States: Eisenhower's Cold War in the Middle East.* Boulder, Colo.: Westview Press, 1997.

Lewis, Gordon K. *Puerto Rico: Freedom and Power in the Caribbean.* New York: Monthly Review Press, 1963.

Lieberman, Robert. *The Strangest Dream: Communism, Anticommunism, and the U.S. Peace Movement, 1945–1963.* New York: Syracuse University Press, 2000.

McAllister, James. *No Exit: America and the German Problem, 1943–1954.* Ithaca, N.Y.: Cornell University Press, 2002.

McClellan, Grant S. (ed.). *U.S. Policy in Latin America.* New York: H. W. Wilson Co., 1963.

Melanson, Richard, and David Mayers. *Reevaluating Eisenhower: American Foreign Policy in the 1950s.* Urbana: University of Illinois Press, 1987.

Mezerik, A. G. *Cuba and the United States.* New York: International Review, 1960.

Nash, Philip. *The Other Missiles of October: Eisenhower, Kennedy and the Jupiters, 1957–1963.* Chapel Hill: University of North Carolina Press, 1994.

Neff, Donald. *Warriors at Suez: Eisenhower Takes America into the Middle East.* New York: Linden Press/Simon & Schuster, 1981.

Osgood, Kenneth. *Total Cold War: Eisenhower's Secret Propaganda Battle at Home and Abroad.* Lawrence: University of Kansas Press, 2002.

Osgood, Robert E. *NATO: The Entangling Alliance.* Chicago: University of Chicago Press, 1962.

Planek, Charles R. *The Changing Status of German Reunification in Western Diplomacy, 1955–1966.* Baltimore: Johns Hopkins University Press, 1967.

Rabe, Stephen. *Eisenhower and Latin America: The Foreign Policy of Anticommunism.* Chapel Hill: University of North Carolina Press, 1988.

Ridgway, Matthew B. *The Korean War: How We Met the Challenge: How All-out Asian War Was Averted: Why MacArthur Was Dismissed: Why Today's War Objectives Must Be Limited.* Garden City, N.Y.: Doubleday, 1967.

Roosevelt, Kermit. *Countercoup: The Struggle for Control in Iran.* New York: McGraw-Hill, 1979.

Rosenberg, Victor. *Soviet-American Relations, 1953–1960: Diplomacy and Cultural Exchange during the Eisenhower Presidency.* Jefferson, N.C.: McFarland & Co., 2005.

Ross, Robert, and Jiang Changbin. *Reexamining the Cold War: U.S.-China Diplomacy, 1954–1973.* Cambridge: Harvard University Press, 2001.

Ruane, Kevin. *The Rise and Fall of the European Defense Community.* New York: St. Martin's Press, 2000.

Rubin, Barry. *Paved with Good Intentions: The American Experience and Iran.* New York: Oxford University Press, 1980.

Schick, Jack M. *The Berlin Crisis, 1958–1962.* Philadelphia: University of Pennsylvania Press, 1971.

Schlesinger, Stephen, and Stephen Kinzer. *Bitter Fruit: The Untold Story of the American Coup in Guatemala.* Garden City, N.Y.: Doubleday Books, 1982.

Smith, Jean E. *The Defense of Berlin.* Baltimore: Johns Hopkins University Press, 1963.

Smith, Merriman. *A President's Odyssey.* New York: Harper, 1961.

Stevenson, Charles A. *The End of Nowhere, American Policy toward Laos since 1954.* Boston: Beacon Press, 1972.

Tananbaum, Duane. *The Bricker Amendment: A Test of Eisenhower's Vertical Leadership.* Ithaca, N.Y.: Cornell University Press, 1988.

Theoharis, Athan G. *The Yalta Myths.* Columbia: University of Missouri Press, 1970.

Vigneras, Marcel. *Rearming the French.* Washington, D.C.: Office of the Chief of Military History, Dept. of the Army, 1957.

Weissman, Stephen R. *American Foreign Policy in the Congo: 1960–1964.* Ithaca, N.Y.: Cornell University Press, 1974.

Welch, Jr., Richard E. *Response to Revolution: The United States and the Cuban Revolution, 1959–1961.* Chapel Hill: University of North Carolina Press, 1985.

Westad, Odd Arne. *Brothers in Arms: The Rise and Fall of the Sino-Soviet Alliance, 1945–1963.* Stanford: Stanford University Press, 1998.

Williams, William Appleman. *The U.S., Cuba, and Castro: An Essay on Revolution and the Dissolution of Empire.* New York: Monthly Review Press, 1962.

Winand, Pascaline. *Eisenhower, Kennedy, and the United States of Europe.* New York: St. Martin's Press, 1993.

Wittner, Lawrence S. *Rebels against War: The American Peace Movement 1941–1960*. New York: Columbia University Press, 1969.

Yagulo, Selim. *Containing Arab Nationalism: The Eisenhower Doctrine and the Middle East*. Chapel Hill: University of North Carolina Press, 2004.

Yergin, Daniel. *The Prize: The Epic Quest for Oil, Money, and Power*. New York: Simon & Schuster, 1991.

Disarmament

Dean, Arthur H. *Test Ban and Disarmament: The Path of Negotiation*. New York: Published for the Council on Foreign Relations by Harper & Row, 1966.

Levine, Robert A. *The Arms Debate*. Cambridge: Harvard University Press, 1963.

National Lawyer's Guild. *A Summary of Disarmament Documents, 1945–1962*. San Francisco: National Lawyers Guild, International Law Committee, Subcommittee on Disarmament, 1963.

Roberts, Chalmers M. *The Nuclear Years: The Arms Race and Arms Control, 1945–1970*. New York: Praeger, 1970.

Schelling, Thomas C., and Morton H. Halperin. *Strategy and Arms Control*. New Haven: Yale University Press, 1961.

Spanier, John W., and Joseph L. Nogee. *The Politics of Disarmament: A Study in Soviet-American Gamesmanship*. New York: F. A. Praeger, 1962.

Intelligence and Espionage

Agee, Philip. *Inside the Company: CIA Diary*. New York: Stonehill, 1975.

Ambrose, Stephen, and Richard H. Immerman. *Ike's Spies: Eisenhower and the Espionage Establishment*. Garden City, N.Y.: Doubleday Books, 1981.

Dulles, Allen W. *The Craft of Intelligence*. New York: Harper & Row, 1963.

Garber, Marjorie, and Rebecca Walkowitz. *Secret Agents: The Rosenberg Case, McCarthyism, and Fifties America*. New York: Routledge, 1995.

Grose, Peter. *Gentleman Spy: The Life of Allen Dulles*. Boston: Houghton Mifflin, 1994.

May, Gary. *Un-American Activities: The Trials of William Remington*. New York: Oxford University Press, 1994.

Powers, Francis Gary, and Curt Gentry. *Operation Overflight*. New York: Rinehart & Winston, 1970.

Sanders, Frances Stonar. *The Cultural Cold War: The CIA and the World of Arts and Letters*. New York: W. W. Norton & Co., 1999.

Srodes, James. *Allen Dulles: Master of Spies*. Washington, D.C.: Regnery, 1999.

Taubman, Philip. *Secret Empire: Eisenhower, the CIA, and the Hidden Story of America's Space Espionage*. New York: Simon & Schuster, 2003.

Theoharis, Athan. *Beyond the Hiss Case: The FBI, Congress, and the Cold War*. Philadelphia: Temple University Press, 1982.

———. *Chasing Spies: How the FBI Failed in Counterintelligence, but Promoted the Politics of McCarthyism in the Cold War Years*. Chicago: Ivan R. Dee, 2002.

U.S. Commission on CIA Activities within the United States. *Report to the President by the Commission on CIA Activities within the United States*. Washington, D.C.: U.S. Government Printing Office, 1975.

U.S. Senate, Select Committee on Intelligence Activities. *Alleged Assassination Plots Involving Foreign Leaders*. Washington, D.C.: U.S. Government Printing Office, 1975.

U.S. Senate, Select Committee on Intelligence Activities. *Intelligence Activities and the Rights of Americans*. Washington, D.C.: U.S. Government Printing Office, 1976.

Weinstein, Allan, and Alexander Vassiliev. *The Haunted Wood: Soviet Espionage in America—the Stalin Era*. New York: Random House, 1999.

Defense Policy

Alian, Richard. *American Defense Policy from Eisenhower to Kennedy, 1957–1961*. Athens: Ohio University Press, 1975.

Aron, Raymond. *The Great Debate: Theories of Nuclear Strategy*. Garden City, N.Y.: Doubleday Books, 1965.

Baldwin, Hanson W. *The Great Arms Race: A Comparison in U.S. and Soviet Power Today*. New York: Praeger, 1958.

Beard, Edmund. *Developing the ICBM: A Study in Bureaucratic Politics*. New York: Columbia University Press, 1976.

Bechhoefer, G. *Postwar Negotiations for Arms Control.* Washington, D.C.: Brookings Institute, 1961.

Bottome, Edgar M. *The Missile Gap: A Study of the Formation of Political and Military Policy.* Rutherford, N.J.: Fairleigh Dickinson University Press, 1971.

Brodie, Bernard. *Strategy in the Missile Age.* Princeton: Princeton University Press, 1959.

Caralay, Demetrios. *The Politics of Military Unification.* New York: Columbia University Press, 1966.

Craig, C. *Destroy the Village: Eisenhower and Thermonuclear War.* New York: Columbia University Press, 1998.

Dietchman, Seymour. *Limited War and American Defense Policy.* Cambridge: Harvard University Press, 1964.

Divine, Robert A. *Blowing on the Wind: The Nuclear Test Ban Debate.* New York: Oxford University Press, 1978.

Dornberger, Walter. *V-2.* New York: Viking Press, 1954.

Gavin, James. *War and Peace in the Space Age.* New York: Harper, 1958.

Geelhoed, E. Bruce. *Charles E. Wilson and the Controversy at the Pentagon, 1953–1957.* Detroit: Wayne State University Press, 1979.

Gilpin, Robert. *American Scientists and Nuclear Weapons Policy.* Princeton: Princeton University Press, 1962.

Halperin, Morton H. *Limited War in the Nuclear Age.* New York: Wiley, 1963.

Huntington, Samuel P. *Changing Patterns of Military Politics.* New York: Free Press of Glencoe, 1962.

———. *The Common Defense: Strategic Programs in National Politics.* New York: Columbia University Press, 1961.

Kahn, Herman. *On Thermonuclear War.* Princeton: Princeton University Press, 1960.

Kaufmann, William W. *The Requirements of Deterrence, Memorandum No. 7.* Princeton: Princeton University Press, 1954.

Kissinger, Henry H. *Nuclear Weapons and Foreign Policy.* Washington, D.C.: Harper, 1957.

Kolodziej, Edward A. *The Common Defense and Congress, 1945–1963.* Columbus: Ohio State University Press, 1966.

Lider, Julian. *Towards a Nuclear Doctrine: The 1950s.* Stockholm: Swedish Institute of International Affairs, 1981.

Miksche, F. O. *The Failure of Atomic Strategy and a New Proposal for the Defense of the West.* New York: Praeger, 1958.

Morgenstern, Oskar. *The Question of National Defense.* New York: Random House, 1959.

Murray, Joseph P. *From Yalta to Disarmament: Cold War Debate.* New York: Monthly Review Press, 1961.

Osgood, Robert E. *Limited War: The Challenge to American Security.* Chicago: University of Chicago Press, 1957.

Schilling, Warner, et al. *Strategy, Politics, and Defense Budget.* New York: Columbia University Press, 1962.

Schwiebert, Ernest G. *A History of Air Force Ballistic Missiles.* New York: F. A. Praeger, 1965.

Smith, Bruce L. R. *The Rand Corporation: Case Study of a Nonprofit Advisory Agency.* Cambridge: Harvard University Press, 1966.

Snead, David L. *The Gaither Committee, Eisenhower, and the Cold War.* Columbus: Ohio State University Press, 1998.

Snyder, Glenn H. *Deterrence and Defense: Toward a Strategy of National Security.* Princeton: Princeton University Press, 1961.

Taylor, Maxwell. *Swords and Plowshares.* New York: W. W. Norton, 1972.

Theoharis, Athan, and John Stuart Cox. *The Boss: J. Edgar Hoover and the Great American Inquisition.* Philadelphia: Temple University Press, 1988.

Turner, Gordon G., and Richard D. Challener. (eds.). *National Security in the Nuclear Age: Basic Facts and Theories.* New York: Praeger, 1960.

Wang, Jessica. *American Science in an Age of Anxiety: Scientists, Anticommunism, and the Cold War.* Chapel Hill: University of North Carolina Press, 1999.

Waskow, Arthur I. (ed.). *The Debate over Thermonuclear Strategy.* Boston: Heath, 1965.

Space

Bates, David R. (ed.). *Space Research and Exploration.* New York: W. Sloane Associates, 1958.

Bergaust, Erik. *Reaching for the Stars.* Garden City, N.Y.: Doubleday Books, 1960.

Boyd, Robert Lewis. *Space Research by Rocket and Satellite.* New York: Harper, 1960.

Cox, Donald. *The Space Race: From Sputnik to Apollo.* Philadelphia: Chilton Books, 1962.

Dickson, Paul. *Sputnik: The Shock of the Century.* New York: Walker Publishing, 2001.

Divine, Robert. *The Sputnik Challenge: Eisenhower's Response to the Soviet Satellite.* New York: Oxford University Press, 1993.

Green, Constance McLaughlin, and Milton Lomask. *Vanguard: A History.* Washington, D.C.: Smithsonian Institution Press, 1971.

McDougall, Walter A. *The Heavens and Earth: A Political History of the Space Age.* New York: Basic Books, 1985.

Rosholt, Robert L. *An Administrative History of NASA, 1958–1963.* Washington, D.C.: Scientific and Technical Information Division, National Aeronautics and Space Administration, 1963.

Schwiebert, Ernest G., et al. *A History of the US Air Force Ballistic Missiles.* New York: F. A. Praeger, 1965.

Shelton, William. *American Space Exploration: The First Decade.* Boston: Little, Brown, 1967.

Sobel, Lester A. *Space: From Sputnik to Gemini.* New York: Facts On File, 1965.

Swenson, Lloyd S., Jr., et al. *The New Ocean: A History of Project Mercury.* Washington, D.C.: Scientific and Technical Division, Office of Technology Utilization, National Aeronautics and Space Administration, 1966.

Witkin, Richard (ed.). *The Challenge of Sputnik.* Garden City, N.Y.: Doubleday Books, 1958.

Wolfe, Tom. *The Right Stuff.* New York: Farrar, Straus, Giroux, 1979.

Civil Rights and Minorities

Bartley, Numan. *The Rise of Massive Resistance: Race and Politics in the South during the 1950s.* Baton Rouge: Louisiana State University Press, 1969.

Bates, Daisy. *The Long Shadow of Little Rock.* New York: David McKay Co., 1962.

Branch, Taylor. *Parting the Waters: America in the King Years, 1954–1963.* New York: Simon & Schuster, 1988.

Burk, Robert. *The Eisenhower Administration and Black Civil Rights.* Knoxville: University of Tennessee Press, 1984.

Ely, James W. *The Crisis of Conservative Virginia.* Knoxville: University of Tennessee Press, 1976.

Fairclough, Adam. *To Redeem the Soul of America: The Southern Christian Leadership Conference and Martin Luther King, Jr.* Athens: University of Georgia Press, 1987.

Freyer, Tony. *The Little Rock Crisis: A Constitutional Interpretation.* Westport, Conn.: Greenwood Press, 1984.

Friedman, Leon (ed.). *Argument: The Oral Argument before the Supreme Court in* Brown v. Board of Education of Topeka, *1952–1955.* New York: Chelsea House Publishers, 1969.

Garcia, Mario. *Mexican Americans: Leadership, Ideology, and Identity, 1930–1960.* New Haven: Yale University Press, 1989.

Garrow, David. *Bearing the Cross: Martin Luther King, Jr., and the Southern Christian Leadership Conference.* New York: W. Morrow, 1986.

Gates, Robbins L. *The Making of Massive Resistance.* Chapel Hill: University of North Carolina Press, 1962.

Hays, Brooks. *A Southern Moderate Speaks.* Chapel Hill: University of North Carolina Press, 1959.

Hickey, Neil, and Edwin Hickey (eds.). *Adam Clayton Powell and the Politics of Race.* New York: Fleet Publishing Corp., 1966.

Howard-Pitney, David. *Martin Luther King, Malcolm X, and the Civil Rights Struggle of the 1950s and 1960s.* New York: Bedford/St. Martin's, 2004.

Jackson, Walter. *Gunnar Myrdal and America's Conscience: Social Engineering and Racial Liberalism, 1938–1987.* Chapel Hill: University of North Carolina Press, 1990.

King, Martin Luther, Jr. *Stride toward Freedom: The Montgomery Boycott.* New York: Harper, 1958.

Lawson, Steven. *Black Ballots: Voting Rights in the South, 1944–1969.* New York: Columbia University Press, 1976.

Lewis, Anthony. *Portrait of a Decade.* New York: Random House, 1964.

Lewis, David L. *King: A Critical Biography.* New York: Praeger, 1970.

Lincoln, C. Eric (ed.). *Martin Luther King, Jr.: A Profile.* New York: Hill & Wang, 1970.

Malcolm X. *Autobiography of Malcolm X.* New York: Grove Press, 1965.

McMillen, Neil. *The Citizens' Council: Organized Resistance to the Second Reconstruction, 1954–1964.* Urbana: University of Illinois Press, 1964.

Meier, August, and Elliot Rudwick. *CORE: A Study in the Civil Rights Movement, 1942–1968.* New York: Oxford University Press, 1973.

Morris, Aldon. *The Origins of the Civil Rights Movement: Black Communities Organizing for Change.* New York: Free Press, 1984.

Muse, Benjamin. *Ten Years of Prelude: The Story of Integration since the Supreme Court's 1954 Decision.* New York: Viking Press, 1961.

———. *Virginia's Massive Resistance.* Bloomington: Indiana University Press, 1961.

Newby, I. A. *Challenge to the Court: Social Scientists and the Defense of Segregation, 1954–1966.* Baton Rouge: Louisiana State University Press, 1969.

Nichols, David A. *A Matter of Justice: Eisenhower and the Beginning of the Civil Rights Revolution.* New York: Simon & Schuster, 2007.

Oates, Stephen B. *Let The Trumpet Sound: The Life of Martin Luther King, Jr.* New York: Harper & Row, 1982.

Powell, Adam Clayton, Jr. *Adam by Adam.* New York: Dial Press, 1971.

Robinson, Jo Ann. *The Montgomery Bus Boycott and the Women Who Started It.* Knoxville: University of Tennessee Press, 1987.

Sarrat, Reed. *The Ordeal of Desegregation: The First Decade.* New York: Harper & Row, 1966.

Silverman, Corinne. *The Little Rock Story.* University, Ala.: Published for the IPC by Bobbs-Merrill, 1959.

Smith, Bob. *They Closed Their Schools: Prince Edward County, Virginia, 1951–1964.* Chapel Hill: University of North Carolina Press, 1965.

Smith, J. Douglas. *Managing White Supremacy: Race, Politics, and Citizenship in Jim Crow Virginia.* Chapel Hill: University of North Carolina Press, 2002.

Webb, Clive (ed.). *Massive Resistance.* New York: Oxford University Press, 2005.

Wilhoit, Francis M. *The Politics of Massive Resistance.* New York: G. Braziller, 1973.

Wolters, Raymond. *The Burden of Brown.* Knoxville: University of Tennessee Press, 1984.

Woodward, C. Vann. *The Strange Career of Jim Crow.* New York: Oxford University Press, 1974.

Workman, William D., Jr. *The Case for the South.* New York: Devin-Adair Co., 1960.

Social

Barmash, Isadore. *More Than They Bargained for: The Rise and Fall of Korvettes.* New York: Lebhar-Friedman/Chain Store Publishing Co., 1981.

Bernard, Richard M., and Bradley R. Rice. *Sunbelt Cities: Politics and Growth since World War II.* Austin: University of Texas Press, 1983.

Bremner, Robert H., and Gary W. Reichard. *Reshaping American Society and Institutions, 1945–1960.* Columbus: Ohio State University Press, 1982.

Clark, Alison J. *Tupperware: The Promise of Plastic in 1950's America.* Washington, D.C.: Smithsonian Institute Press, 1999.

Conant, James B. *The American High School Today.* New York: McGraw-Hill, 1959.

Gans, Herbert J. *The Levittowners: Ways of Life and Politics in a New Suburban Community.* New York: Pantheon Books, 1967.

Gelfand, Mark. *A Nation of Cities: The Federal Government and Urban America, 1933–1965.* New York: Oxford University Press, 1975.

Gilbert, James. *A Cycle of Outrage: America's Reaction to the Juvenile Delinquent in the 1950's.* New York: Oxford University Press, 1986.

Hayden, Dolores. *Building Suburbia: Green Fields and Urban Growth, 1820–2000.* New York: Pantheon Books, 2003.

Hirsch, Arnold. *Making the Second Ghetto: Race and Housing in Chicago, 1940–1960.* New York: Cambridge University Press, 1983.

Jackson, Kenneth T. *Crabgrass Frontier: The Suburbanization of the United States.* New York: Oxford University Press, 1985.

Jacobs, Jane. *The Death and Life of Great American Cities.* New York: Random House, 1961.

Jones, James H. *Alfred C. Kinsey: A Public/Private Life.* New York: W. W. Norton, 1997.

Jones, Landon. *Great Expectations: America and the Baby Boom Generation.* New York: Coward, McCann & Geoghegan, 1980.

Keats, John. *Crack the Picture Window.* Boston: Houghton Mifflin, 1957.

Love, John. *McDonalds: Behind the Arches.* New York: Bantam Books, 1986.

Miller, Zane. *Suburb: Neighborhood and Community in Forest Park, Ohio, 1935–1976.* Knoxville: University of Tennessee Press, 1981.

Muller, Peter. *Contemporary Sub/Urban America.* Englewood Cliffs, N.J.: Prentice Hall, 1981.

Packard, Vance Oakley. *The Status Seekers.* New York: D. McKay Co., 1959.

Palladino, Grace. *Teenagers: An American History.* New York: Basic Books, 1996.

Reed, James. *The Birth Control Movement and American Society: From Private Vice to Public Virtue.* Princeton: Princeton University Press, 1978.

Schulman, Bruce. *From Cotton Belt to Sunbelt: Federal Policy, Economic Development, and the Transformation of the South, 1938–1980.* New York: Oxford University Press, 1991.

Szatmary, David P. *Rockin in Time: A Social History of Rock-and-Roll.* Englewood Cliffs, N.J.: Prentice Hall, 1991.

Teaford, John. *The Twentieth-Century American City: Problem, Promise, and Reality.* Baltimore: Johns Hopkins University Press, 1986.

Culture

Appy, Christian G. *Cold War Constructions: The Political Culture of United States Imperialism, 1945–1966.* Amherst: University of Massachusetts Press, 2000.

Bestor, Arthur. *Educational Wastelands.* Urbana: University of Illinois Press, 1953.

Biskind, Peter. *Seeing Is Believing: How Hollywood Taught Us to Stop Worrying and Love the Fifties.* New York: Pantheon Books, 1983.

Booker, M. Keith. *The Post-Utopian Imagination: American Culture in the Long 1950s.* Westport, Conn.: Greenwood Press, 2002.

Boyer, Paul. *By the Bomb's Early Light: American Thought and Culture at the Dawn of the Atomic Age.* New York: Pantheon, 1985.

Carter, Paul *Another Part of the Fifties.* New York: Columbia University Press, 1983.

Cook, Bruce. *The Beat Generation.* New York: Scribner, 1971.

Foreman, Joel (ed.). *The Other Fifties.* Urbana: University of Illinois Press, 1997.

Fox, Stephen. *The Mirror Makers.* New York: Morrow, 1984.

Gilbert, James. *A Cycle of Outrage: America's Reaction to the Juvenile Delinquents of the 1950s.* New York: Oxford University Press, 1986.

———. *Men in the Middle: Searching for Masculinity in the 1950s.* Chicago: University of Chicago Press, 2005.

Gillette, Charles. *The Sound of the City: The Rise of Rock and Roll.* New York: Pantheon Books, 1984.

Guralnick, Peter. *Last Train to Memphis: The Rise of Elvis Presley.* Boston: Little, Brown, 1994.

Henriksen, Margot A. *Dr. Strangelove's America: Society and Culture in the Atomic Age.* Berkeley: University of California Press, 1997.

Hine, Thomas. *Populuxe.* New York: Knopf, 1986.

Kuznick, Peter J., and James Gilbert. *Rethinking Cold War Culture.* Washington, D.C.: Smithsonian Institute Press, 2001.

Lhamon, W. T. *Deliberate Speed: The Origins of a Cultural Style in the American 1950s.* Washington D.C.: Smithsonian Institute Press, 1990.

Lipsitz, George. *Class and Culture in Cold War America: A Rainbow at Midnight.* New York: Praeger, 1981.

May, Larry (ed.). *Recasting America: Culture and Politics in the Age of the Cold War.* Chicago: University of Chicago Press, 1989.

McNally, Dennis. *Desolate Angel: Jack Kerouac, the Beat Generation, and America.* New York: Random House, 1979.

Miles, Barry. *Ginsburg: A Biography.* New York: Simon & Schuster, 1989.

Nicosia, Gerald. *Memory Babe: A Critical Biography of Jack Kerouac.* New York: Grove Press, 1983.

Potter, David. *People of Plenty: Economic Abundance and the American Character.* Chicago: University of Chicago Press, 1954.

Schudson, Michael. *Advertising, the Uneasy Persuasion.* New York: Basic Books, 1984.

Szatmary, David. *Rockin' in Time: A Social History of Rock-and-Roll.* Englewood Cliffs, N.J.: Prentice Hall, 1991.

Wakefield, Dan. *New York in the Fifties.* Boston: Houghton Mifflin/Seymour Lawrence, 1992.

Walker, Jeff. *The Ayn Rand Cult.* Chicago: Open Court, 1999.

Ward, Ed, et al. *Rock of Ages: The Rolling Stone History of Rock and Roll.* New York: Rolling Stone Press: Summit Books: Distributed by Simon & Schuster, 1986.

Werner, Craig A. *Change Is Gonna Come: Music, Race and the Soul of America*. New York: Plume, 1998.

Whitfield, Stephen. *The Culture of the Cold War*. Baltimore: Johns Hopkins University Press, 1996.

Whyte, William. *The Organization Man*. New York: Simon & Schuster, 1956.

Wright, Bradford W. *Comic Book Nation: The Transformation of Youth Culture in America*. Baltimore: Johns Hopkins University Press, 2001.

Intellectual

Arendt, Hannah. *The Origins of Totalitarianism*. New York: Harcourt, Brace, 1951.

Bell, Daniel. *The End of Ideology: On the Exhaustion of Political Ideas in the 1950s*. Glencoe, Ill.: Free Press, 1960.

Bloom, Alexander. *Prodigal Sons: The New York Intellectuals and Their World*. New York: Oxford University Press, 1986.

Brewer, John D. *C. Wright Mills and the Ending of Violence*. New York: Palgrave Macmillan, 2003.

Buckley, William F., Jr. *God and Man at Yale*. Chicago: Regnery, 1951.

Charters, Ann. *Kerouac*. New York: St. Martin's Press, 1994.

Diggins, John P. *Up from Communism: Conservative Odysseys in American Intellectual History*. New York: Harper & Row, 1975.

East, John P. *The American Conservative Movement: The Philosophical Founders*. Chicago: Regnery Books, 1986.

Fielder, Leslie. *An End to Innocence*. Boston: Beacon Press, 1955.

Fox, Richard. *Reinhold Niebuhr*. New York: Pantheon Books, 1985.

Gormon, Paul R. *Left Intellectuals and Popular Culture in Twentieth-Century America*. Chapel Hill: University of North Carolina Press, 1996.

Gotfried, Paul. *The Conservative Movement*. New York: Twayne Publishers, 1993.

Halliwell, Martin. *The Constant Dialogue: Reinhold Niebuhr and American Intellectual Culture*. Lanham, Md.: Rowman & Littlefield Publishers, 2005.

Horowitz, Irving Louis. *C. Wright Mills: An American Utopian*. New York: Free Press, 1983.

Kateb, George. *Hannah Arendt: Politics, Conscience, Evil*. Totowa, N.J.: Rowman & Allanheld, 1984.

King, Richard H. *Race, Culture, and the Intellectuals, 1940–1970*. Baltimore: Johns Hopkins University Press, 2004.

Macdonald, Dwight. *Discriminations*. New York: Grossman Publishers, 1974.

———. *Politics Past: Essays in Political Criticism*. New York: Viking Press, 1957.

Mattson, Kevin. *Intellectuals in Action: The Origins of the New Left and Radical Liberalism, 1945–1970*. University Park: University of Pennsylvania Press, 2002.

McAllister, Ted V. *Revolt against Modernity: Leo Strauss, Eric Voegelin, and the Search for a Postliberal Order*. Lawrence: Kansas University Press, 1996.

McDonald, W. Wesley. *Russell Kirk and the Age of Ideology*. Columbia: University of Missouri Press, 2004.

Mills, C. Wright. *The Power Elite*. New York: Oxford University Press, 1956.

———. *White Collar*. New York: Oxford University Press, 1951.

Nash, George H. *The Conservative Intellectual Movement in America since 1945*. New York: Basic Books, 1976.

Pells, Richard. *The Liberal Mind in a Conservative Age: American Intellectuals in the 1940s and 1950s*. New York: Harper & Row, 1985.

Potter, David M. *People of Plenty*. Chicago: University of Chicago Press, 1954.

Tar, Zoltan. *The Frankfurt School: The Critical Theories of Max Horkheimer and Theodor W. Adorno*. New York: Wiley, 1977.

Tilman, Rick. *C. Wright Mills: A Native Radical and His American Intellectual Roots*. University Park: University of Pennsylvania Press, 1984.

Whitfield, Stephen. *A Critical American: The Politics of Dwight Macdonald*. Hamden, Conn.: Archon Books, 1984.

Whyte, William H., Jr. *The Organization Man*. New York: Simon & Schuster, 1956.

Young-Bruehl, Elizabeth. *Hannah Arendt: For the Love of the World*. New Haven: Yale University Press, 2004.

Religion

Anker, Roy. *Self-help and Popular Religion in Modern American Culture.* Westport, Conn.: Greenwood Press, 1999.

Boyer, Paul. *When Time Shall Be No More: Prophecy and Belief in Modern American Culture.* Cambridge: Harvard University Press, 1992.

Fox, Richard. *Reinhold Niebuhr.* New York: Pantheon Books, 1985.

George, Carol. *God's Salesman: Norman Vincent Peale and the Power of Positive Thinking.* New York: Oxford University Press, 1993.

Gilbert, James. *Redeeming Culture: American Religion in an Age of Science.* Chicago: University of Chicago Press, 1997.

Hart, D. G. *Deconstructing Evangelicalism: Conservative Protestantism in the Age of Billy Graham.* Grand Rapids, Mich.: Baker Academic, 2004.

Herberg, Will. *Protestant, Catholic, Jew: An Essay in American Religious Sociology.* Garden City, N.Y.: Doubleday, 1955.

Hunter, James Davidson. *Culture Wars: The Struggle to Define America.* New York: Basic Books, 1991.

Martin, William. *A Prophet with Honor: The Billy Graham Story.* New York: Quill, 1991.

May, Henry. *Ideas, Faiths, and Feelings: Essays on American Intellectual and Religious History, 1952–1982.* New York: Oxford University Press, 1983.

McLoughlin, William. *Billy Graham: Revivalist in a Secular Age.* New York: Ronald Press, 1960.

Ribuffo, Leo. *The Old Christian Right: The Protestant Far Right from the Depression to the Cold War.* Philadelphia: Temple University Press, 1983.

Wuthnow, Robert. *The Restructuring of American Religion: Society and Faith since World War II.* Princeton: Princeton University Press, 1988.

Education

Cremin, Lawrence. *American Education: The Metropolitan Experience, 1876–1980.* New York: Harper & Row, 1988.

Hampel, Robert. *The Last Little Citadel: American High Schools since 1940.* Boston: Houghton Mifflin, 1986.

Ravitch, Diane. *The Troubled Crusade: American Education, 1945–1980.* New York: Basic Books, 1983.

Silberman, Charles. *Crisis in the Classroom: The Remaking of American Education.* New York: Random House, 1970.

Media

Abell, Tyler (ed.). *Drew Pearson Diaries, 1949–1959.* New York: Holt, Rinehart and Winston, 1974.

Allen, Craig. *Eisenhower and the Mass Media: Peace, Prosperity, & Prime-Time TV.* Chapel Hill: University of North Carolina Press, 1993.

Alsop, Joseph, and Stewart Alsop. *The Reporter's Trade.* New York: Reynal, 1958.

Anderson, Kent. *The History and Implications of the Quiz Show Scandals.* Westport, Conn.: Greenwood Press, 1978.

Aronson, James. *The Press and the Cold War.* Indianapolis: Bobbs-Merrill, 1970.

Barnouw, Erik. *Tube of Plenty: The Evolution of American Television.* New York: Oxford University Press, 1975.

Baughman, James. *The Republic of Mass Culture: Journalism, Filmmaking, and Broadcasting in America since 1941.* Baltimore: Johns Hopkins University Press, 1992.

Bliss, Edward (ed.). *In Search of Light: The Broadcasts of Edward R. Murrow, 1938–1961.* New York: Knopf, 1967.

Booker, M. Keith. *Monsters, Mushroom Clouds, and the Cold War: American Science Fiction and the Roots of Postmodernism, 1946–1964.* Westport, Conn.: Greenwood Press, 2001.

Cloud, Stanley, and Lynne Olson. *The Murrow Boys.* Boston: Houghton Mifflin, 1996.

Davies, Richard. *America's Obsession: Sports and Society since 1945.* Ft. Worth, Tex.: Harcourt Brace College Publishers, 1994.

Diamond, Edwin, and Stephen Bates. *The Spot: The Rise of Political Advertising on Television.* Cambridge: Harvard University Press, 1993.

Dougherty, Thomas Patrick. *Cold War, Cool Medium: Television, McCarthyism, and American Culture.* New York: Columbia University Press, 2003.

Krock, Arthur. *In The Nation 1932–1966.* New York: McGraw-Hill, 1966.

————. *Memoirs: Sixty Years on the Firing Line.* New York: Funk & Wagnalls, 1968.

Marling, Karal Ann. *As Seen on TV: The Visual Culture of Everyday Life in the 1950s.* Cambridge: Harvard University Press, 1994.

Metz, Robert. *CBS: Reflections in a Bloodshot Eye.* Chicago: Playboy Press, 1975.

Michie, Allan A. *Voices through the Iron Curtain: The Radio Free Europe Story.* New York: Dodd, Mead, 1963.

Reston, James. *Sketches in the Sand.* New York: Knopf, 1967.

Rojecki, Andrew. *Silencing the Opposition: Antinuclear Movements and the Media in the Cold War.* Urbana: University of Illinois Press, 1999.

Sayre, Nora. *Running Time: Films of the Cold War.* New York: Dial Press, 1982.

Sulzberger, C. L. *A Long Row of Candles: Memoirs and Diaries, 1934–1954.* New York: Macmillan, 1969.

Swanberg, W. A. *Luce and His Empire.* New York: Scribner, 1972.

Thomson, Charles A. *Television and Presidential "Politics": The Experience in 1952 and the Problems Ahead.* Washington: Brookings Institute, 1956.

Watson, Mary Ann. *Defining Visions: Television and the American Experience since 1945.* Fort Worth, Tex.: Harcourt Brace College Publishers, 1998.

Women

Breines, Wini. *Young, White, and Miserable: Growing Up Female in the Fifties.* Boston: Beacon Press, 1992.

D'Emilio, John. *Sexual Politics, Sexual Communities: The Making of a Homosexual Minority in the United States, 1940–1970.* Chicago: University of Chicago Press, 1983.

Harrison, Cynthia. *On Account of Sex: The Politics of Women's Issues, 1945–1968.* Berkeley: University of California Press, 1988.

Kaledin, Eugenia. *Mothers and More: American Women in the 1950s.* Boston: Twayne Publishers, 1984.

Lynn, Susan. *Progressive Women in Conservative Times: Racial Justice, Peace, and Feminism, 1945 to the 1960s.* New Brunswick, N.J.: Rutgers University Press, 1987.

May, Elaine Tyler. *Homeward Bound: American Families in the Cold War Era.* New York: Basic Books, 1988.

Meyerowitz, Joanne J. *Not June Cleaver: Women and Gender in Postwar America, 1945–1960.* Philadelphia: Temple University Press, 1994.

Rupp, Leila J., and Verta Taylor. *Survival in the Doldrums: The American Women's Rights Movement, 1945 to the 1960s.* New York: Oxford University Press, 1987.

Solinger, Ricky. *Wake Up, Little Susie: Single Pregnancy and Race before* Roe v. Wade. New York: Routledge, 1992.

Courts

Barrow, Deborah J., and Thomas G. Walker. *A Court Divided: The Fifth Circuit Court of Appeals and the Politics of Judicial Reform.* New Haven: Yale University Press, 1988.

Bickel, Alexander. *Politics and the Warren Court.* New York: Harper & Row, 1965.

Cox, Archibald. *The Warren Court: Constitutional Decisions as an Instrument of Reform.* Cambridge: Harvard University Press, 1968.

Dunne, Gerald. *Hugo Black and the Judicial Revolution.* New York: Simon & Schuster, 1977.

Freyer, Tony (ed.). *Justice Hugo Black and Modern America.* Tuscaloosa: University of Alabama Press, 1990.

de Grazia, Edward. *Girls Lean Back Everywhere: The Law of Obscenity and the Assault on Genius.* New York: Random House, 1992.

Horwitz, Morton J. *The Warren Court and the Pursuit of Justice.* New York: Hill & Wang, 1998.

Kluger, Richard. *Simple Justice: The History of* Brown v. Board of Education *and Black America's Struggle for Equality.* New York: Knopf, 1976.

Lytle, Clifford M. *The Warren Court and Its Critics.* Tucson: University of Arizona Press, 1968.

Murphy, Paul. *The Constitution in Crisis Times, 1918–1969.* New York: Harper & Row, 1972.

Murphy, Terrence J. *Censorship: Government and Obscenity.* Baltimore: Helicon, 1963.

Paul, James C. N., and Murray L. Schwartz. *Federal Censorship: Obscenity in the Mail.* Westport, Conn.: Greenwood Press, 1961.

Peltason, J. W. *Fifty-Eight Lonely Men: Southern Federal Judges and School Desegregation.* New York: Harcourt, Brace & World, 1961.

Pritchett, C. Herman. *Civil Liberties and the Vinson Court.* Chicago: University of Chicago Press, 1954.

———. *Congress versus the Supreme Court, 1957 to 1960.* New York: Da Capo Press, 1961.

———. *The Political Offender and the Warren Court.* Boston: Boston University Press, 1958.

Read, Frank T., and Lucy S. McGough. *Let Them Be Judged: The Judicial Integration of the Deep South.* Metuchen, N.J.: Scarecrow Press, 1978.

Rembar, Charles. *The End of Obscenity.* New York: Random House, 1968.

Sabin, Arthur J. *In Calmer Times: The Supreme Court and Red Monday.* Philadelphia: University of Pennsylvania Press, 1999.

Sayler, Richard H., et al. (eds.). *The Warren Court: A Critical Analysis.* New York: Chelsea House, 1969.

Schwartz, Bernard, and Stephen Lesher. *Inside the Warren Court, 1953–1969.* Garden City, N.Y.: Doubleday, 1983.

Schwartz, Bernard. *Super Chief: Earl Warren and His Supreme Court—A Judicial Biography.* New York: New York University Press, 1983.

Silverstein, Mark. *Constitutional Faiths: Felix Frankfurter, Hugo Black, and the Process of Judicial Decision Making.* Ithaca, N.Y.: Cornell University Press, 1984.

Simon, James F. *The Antagonists: Hugo Black, Felix Frankfurter, and Civil Liberties in Modern America.* New York: Simon & Schuster, 1989.

Tushnet, Mark (ed.). *The Warren Court in Historical and Political Perspective.* Charlottesville: University Press of Virginia, 1993.

Vestal, Theodore M. *The Eisenhower Court and Civil Liberties.* Westport, Conn.: Praeger, 2002.

Weaver, James D. *Warren: The Man, the Court, the Era.* Boston: Little, Brown, 1967.

Wilkinson, J. Harvie. *From Brown to Bakke: The Supreme Court and School Integration, 1954–1978.* New York: Oxford University Press, 1979.

Business, Labor, and the Economy

Baldwin, Daniel A. *Economic Development and American Foreign Policy, 1943–1962.* Chicago: University of Chicago Press, 1966.

Berle, Adolf A. *The American Economic Republic.* New York: Harcourt, Brace & World, 1963.

Blough, Roger. *The Washington Embrace of Business.* New York: Columbia University Press, 1976.

Bremner, Robert. *Chairman of the Fed: William McChesney Martin, Jr., and the Creation of the American Financial System.* New Haven: Yale University Press, 2004.

Brody, David. *Workers in Industrial America.* New York: Oxford University Press, 1993.

Chinoy, Eli. *Automobile Workers and the American Dream.* Garden City, N.Y.: Doubleday, 1955.

Cray, Ed. *Chrome Colossus: General Motors and Its Times.* New York: McGraw-Hill, 1980.

Duffy, Gavan. *Demons and Democrats: 1950s Labor at the Crossroads.* North Melbourne, Vic., Australia: Freedom Publishing Co., 2002.

Dulles, Foster Rhea, and Melvyn Dubofsky. *Labor in America, a History.* New York: Crowell, 1960.

Fones-Wolf, Elizabeth A. *Selling Free Enterprise: The Business Assault on Labor and Liberalism, 1945–1960.* Urbana: University of Illinois Press, 1994.

Galbraith, John Kenneth. *The Affluent Society.* Boston: Houghton Mifflin, 1958.

———. *American Capitalism: The Concept of Countervailing Power.* Boston: Houghton Mifflin, 1952.

Gerstle, Gary. *Working-Class Americanism: The Politics of Labor in an Industrial City, 1914–1960.* New York: Cambridge University Press, 1989.

Goulden, Joseph C. *Meany: The Unchallenged Strongman of American Labor.* New York: Atheneum, 1972.

Hession, Charles H. *John Kenneth Galbraith and His Critics.* New York: New American Library, 1972.

Himmelberg, Robert. *Antitrust and Business Regulation in the Postwar Era, 1946–1954.* New York: Garland Publishing, 1994.

Holmans, A. E. *United States Fiscal Policy, 1945–1959.* New York: Oxford University Press, 1961.

James, Ralph C., and Estelle James. *James Hoffa and the Teamsters: A Study of Union Power.* Princeton: Princeton University Press, 1965.

Kaplan, A. D. H. *Big Enterprise in a Competitive System.* Washington, D.C.: Brookings Institute, 1964.

Kendrick, John. *Productivity Trends in the United States.* New York: Arno Press, 1961.

Kovaleff, Phillip. *Business and Government during the Eisenhower Administration: A Study of the Antitrust Policy of the Antitrust Division of the Justice Department.* Athens: Ohio University Press, 1980.

Larrowe, Charles P. *Harry Bridges: The Rise and Fall of Radical Labor in the United States.* New York: L. Hill, 1972.

Lee, R. Alton. *Eisenhower and Landrum-Griffin: A Study in Labor Management Politics.* Lexington: University Press of Kentucky, 1990.

Lewis, Wilfred, Jr. *Federal Fiscal Policy in the Postwar Recessions.* Washington, D.C.: Brookings Institute, 1962.

Lilienthal, David E. *Big Business: A New Era.* New York: Harper, 1953.

Mighell, Ronald L. *American Agriculture: Its Structure and Place in the Economy.* New York: Wiley, 1955.

Minchin, Timothy. *Fighting against the Odds: A History of Southern Labor since World War II.* Gainesville: University Press of Florida, 2005.

Morgan, Iwan. *Eisenhower versus "The Spenders": The Eisenhower Administration, the Democrats, and the Budget, 1953–1960.* New York: St. Martin's Press, 1990.

Radosh, Ronald. *American Labor and the United States Foreign Policy.* New York: Random House, 1969.

Reagan, Michael. *The Managed Economy.* New York: Oxford University Press, 1963.

Reuther, Victor G. *The Brothers Reuther.* Boston: Houghton Mifflin, 1976.

Russell, Thaddeus. *Out of the Jungle: Jimmy Hoffa and the Remaking of the American Working Class.* Philadelphia: Temple University Press, 2003.

Saulnier, Raymond. *Constructive Years: The U.S. Economy under Eisenhower.* Lanham, Md.: University Press of America, 1991.

Sloan, John. *Eisenhower and the Management of Prosperity.* Lawrence: University of Kansas Press, 1991.

Sobel, Robert. *The Age of Giant Corporations: A Microeconomic History of American Business, 1914–1970.* Westport: Greenwood Press, 1972.

Triflin, Robert. *Gold and the Dollar Crisis.* New Haven: Yale University Press, 1961.

Vatter, Harold G. *The U.S. Economy in the 1950s.* New York: Norton, 1963.

Warner, W. Lloyd, and James Abegglen. *Big Business Leaders in America.* New York: Harper, 1955.

White, Lawrence J. *The Automobile Industry since 1945.* Cambridge: Harvard University Press, 1971.

Ziegler, Robert. *American Workers, American Unions, 1920–1985.* Baltimore: Johns Hopkins University Press, 1986.

Biographies

Abernathy, Ralph. *And the Walls Came Tumbling Down: An Autobiography.* New York: Harper & Row, 1989.

Abramson, Rudy. *Spanning the Century: The Life of William Averell Harriman, 1891–1986.* New York: W. Morrow, 1992.

Acheson, Dean. *Morning and Noon.* Boston: Houghton Mifflin, 1965.

———. *Present at the Creation: My Years in the State Department.* New York: Norton, 1969.

Aczel, Amir D. *God's Equation: Einstein, Relativity, and the Expanding Universe.* New York: Four Walls Eight Windows, 1999.

Adams, John Gibbon. *Without Precedent: The Story of the Death of McCarthyism.* New York: W. W. Norton, 1983.

Adams, Sherman. *Firsthand Report: The Story of the Eisenhower Administration.* New York: Harper, 1961.

Aiken, George D., and Samuel B. Hand. *The Essential Aiken: A Life in Public Service.* Burlington: University of Vermont Press, 2004.

Albert, Carl Bert, and Danney Goble. *Little Giant: The Life and Times of Speaker Carl Albert.* Norman: University of Oklahoma Press, 1990.

Allison, John M. *Ambassador from the Prairie: Or, Allison Wonderland.* Boston: Houghton Mifflin, 1973.

Almquist, Leann Grabavoy. *Joseph Alsop and American Foreign Policy: The Journalist as Advocate.* Lanham, Md.: University Press of America, 1993.

Alsop, Joseph W. *I've Seen the Best of It: Memoirs.* New York: Norton, 1992.

Alsop, Stewart O. *Stay of Execution: A Sort of Memoir.* Philadelphia: Lippincott, 1973.

Ambrose, Stephen E. *Eisenhower: Soldier, General of the Army, President-elect, 1890–1952.* New York: Simon & Schuster, 1983.

———. *Eisenhower: The President.* New York: Simon & Schuster, 1984.

———. *Milton S. Eisenhower, Educational Statesman.* Baltimore: Johns Hopkins University Press, 1983.

———. *Nixon: Ruin and Recovery, 1973–1990.* New York: Simon & Schuster, 1991.

———. *Nixon: The Education of a Politician, 1913–1967.* New York: Simon & Schuster, 1987.

———. *Nixon: The Triumph of a Politician, 1962–1972.* New York: Simon & Schuster, 1989.

Anderson, Jervis. *A. Philip Randolph: A Biographical Portrait.* New York: Harcourt Brace Jovanovich, 1973.

———. *Bayard Rustin: Troubles I've Seen: A Biography.* New York: HarperCollins Publishers, 1997.

Anderson, John F. *The Kefauver Story.* New York: Dial Press, 1956.

Ashby, LeRoy. *Fighting the Odds: The Life of Senator Frank Church.* Seattle: Washington State University Press, 1994.

Ashmore, Harry S. *Unseasonable Truths: The Life of Robert Maynard Hutchins.* Boston: Little, Brown, 1989.

August, Jack L. *Vision in the Desert: Carl Hayden and Hydropolitics in the American Southwest.* Fort Worth: Texas Christian University Press, 1999.

Ausmus, Harry J. *Will Herberg: From Right to Right.* Westport, Conn.: Greenwood Press, 1987.

Baker, James T. *Eleanor Roosevelt.* Fort Worth, Tex.: Harcourt Brace, 1999.

———. *Eric Hoffer.* Boston: Twayne, 1982.

———. *Brooks Hays.* Macon, Ga.: Mercer University Press, 1989.

Baker, Liva. *Felix Frankfurter.* New York: Coward-McCann, 1969.

Baker, Richard A. *Conservation Politics: The Senate Career of Clinton P. Anderson.* Albuquerque: University of New Mexico Press, 1985.

Ball, Howard. *A Defiant Life: Thurgood Marshall and the Persistence of Racism in America.* New York: Crown Publishers, 1998.

———. *Hugo L. Black: Cold Steel Warrior.* New York: Oxford University Press, 1996.

———. *Of Power and Right: Hugo Black, William O. Douglas and America's Constitutional Revolution.* New York: Oxford University Press, 1992.

Barnard, John. *Walter Reuther and the Rise of the Auto Workers.* Boston: Little, Brown, 1983.

Barnouw, Dagmar. *Visible Spaces: Hannah Arendt and the German-Jewish Experience.* Baltimore: Johns Hopkins University Press, 1990.

Bartlett, Donald. *Empire: The Life, Legend and Madness of Howard Hughes.* New York: Norton, 1979.

Bartlett, Paul D. *James Bryant Conant, 1893–1978: A Biographical Memoir.* Washington, D.C.: National Academy Press, 1983.

Bass, Jack, and Marilyn W. Thompson. *Strom: The Complicated Personal and Political Life of Strom Thurmond.* New York: Public Affairs, 2005.

Bass, Jack. *Ol' Strom: An Unauthorized Biography of Strom Thurmond.* Atlanta: Longstreet, 1998.

———. *Taming the Storm: The Life and Times of Judge Frank M. Johnson and the South's Fight over Civil Rights.* New York: Doubleday, 1993.

Bates, Daisy. *The Long Shadow of Little Rock: A Memoir.* New York: David McKay Co., 1962.

Beal, John Robinson. *John Foster Dulles: A Biography.* New York: Harper, 1957.

Beatty, Jack. *The World According to Peter Drucker: The Life and Work of the World's Greatest Management Thinker.* New York: Free Press, 1998.

Becker, William. *The Governor's Office under Edmund G. Brown, Sr.* Berkeley: University of California Press, 1981.

Bennett, Lerone. *What Manner of Man: A Biography of Martin Luther King, Jr.* Chicago: Johnson Publishing Co., 1968.

Bergen, Bernard J. *The Banality of Evil: Hannah Arendt and "The Final Solution."* Lanham, Md.: Rowman & Littlefield Publishers, 1998.

Bernstein, Jeremy. *Hans Bethe: Prophet of Energy.* New York: Basic Books, 1980.

———. *Oppenheimer: Portrait of an Enigma.* Chicago: Ivan R. Dee, 2005.

Berthelot, Helen W. *Win Some, Lose Some: G. Mennen Williams and the New Democrats.* Detroit: Wayne State University Press, 1995.

Biggs, Bradley. *Gavin.* Hamden, Conn.: Archon Books, 1980.

Bilby, Kenneth W. *The General: David Sarnoff and the Rise of the Communications Industry.* New York: Harper & Row, 1986.

Biles, Roger. *Crusading Liberal: Paul H. Douglas of Illinois.* DeKalb: Northern Illinois University Press, 2002.

———. *Richard J. Daley: Politics, Race, and the Governing of Chicago.* DeKalb: Northern Illinois University Press, 1995.

Bingham, June. *Courage to Change: An Introduction to the Life and Thought of Reinhold Niebuhr.* New York: Scribner, 1961.

Bird, Kai, and Martin J. Sherwin. *American Prometheus: The Triumph and Tragedy of J. Robert Oppenheimer.* New York: Knopf, 2005.

Bird, Kai. *The Chairman: John J. McCoy, The Making of the American Establishment.* New York: Simon & Schuster, 1992.

Bissell, Richard M., and Jonathan Lewis. *Reflections of a Cold Warrior: From Yalta to the Bay of Pigs.* New Haven: Yale University Press, 1996.

Bitner, William C. *Frank J. Lausche: A Political Biography.* New York: Studia Slovenica, 1976.

Bixby, Roland. *Standing Tall: The Life of Senator Norris Cotton.* Crawfordsville, Ind.: Lakeside Press, 1988.

Black, Hugo. *A Constitutional Faith.* New York: Knopf, 1968.

Blackburn, Julia. *Daisy Bates in the Desert.* New York: Pantheon Books, 1994.

Blossom, Virgil T. *It Has Happened Here.* New York: Harper, 1959.

Blumberg, Stanley A. *Edward Teller: Giant of the Golden Age of Physics: A Biography.* New York: Scribner's, 1990.

———. *Energy and Conflict: The Life and Times of Edward Teller.* New York: Putnam, 1976.

Blumenson, Martin. *Mark Clark.* New York: Congdon & Weed/St. Martin's Press, 1984.

Bohlen, Charles. *Witness to History, 1929–1969.* New York: Norton, 1973.

Booth, T. Michael. *Paratrooper: The Life of General James M. Gavin.* New York: Simon & Schuster, 1994.

Bortz, Arn. *John J. Rooney: Democratic Representative from New York.* Washington, D.C.: Grossman, 1972.

Boulard, Garry. *The Big Lie: Hale Boggs, Lucille May Grace, and Leander Perez in 1951.* Gretna, La.: Pelican Publishing Co., 2001.

Bowles, Chester. *Promises to Keep: My Years in Public Life, 1941–1969.* New York: Harper & Row, 1971.

Boyle, Peter G. *Eisenhower.* Harlow, England: Longman/Pearson, 2005.

Brackenridge, R. Douglas. *Eugene Carson Blake, Prophet with Portfolio.* New York: Seabury Press, 1978.

Braden, Spruille. *Diplomats and Demagogues: The Memoirs of Spruille Braden.* New Rochelle, N.Y.: Arlington House, 1971.

Branch, Taylor. *Parting the Waters: America in The King Years, 1954–1963.* New York: Simon & Schuster, 1988.

Branden, Barbara. *The Passion of Ayn Rand.* Garden City, N.Y.: Doubleday, 1986.

Brazelton, W. Robert. *Designing US Economic Policy: An Analytical Biography of Leon Keyserling.* New York: Palgrave, 2001.

Bremner, Robert. *Chairman of the Fed: William McChesney Martin, Jr., and the Creation of the Modern American Financial System.* New Haven: Yale University Press, 2004.

Bridge, William. *John J. Sparkman: Democratic Senator from Alabama.* Washington, D.C.: Grossman, 1972.

Brinkley, Douglas. *Rosa Parks.* New York: Viking, 2000.

Broadwater, Jeff. *Adlai Stevenson and American Politics.* New York: Twayne, 1994.

Brown, David. *Richard Hofstadter: An Intellectual Biography.* Chicago: University of Chicago Press, 2006.

Brown, Stuart Gerry. *Conscience in Politics: Adlai E. Stevenson in the 1950s.* Syracuse, N.Y.: Syracuse University Press, 1961.

Brown, Winthrop G. *Postmark Asia: Letters of an American Diplomat to His Family from India, Laos, and Korea, 1957–1966.* New York: Brown, 1990.

Brownell, Herbert, and John P. Burke. *Advising Ike: The Memoirs of Attorney General Herbert Brownell.* Lawrence: University Press of Kansas, 1993.

Buckley, Thomas C. *Lauris Norstad: From Red Wing to Paris*. Red Wing, Minn.: Goodhue County Historical Society, 1990.

Burke, Bob. *Bryce Harlow: Mr. Integrity*. Oklahoma City: Oklahoma Heritage Association, 2000.

Burke, Robert F. *Dwight D. Eisenhower: Hero and Politician*. Boston: Twayne, 1986.

Burner, David. *Herbert Hoover: A Public Life*. New York: Knopf, 1979.

———. *John F. Kennedy and a New Generation*. New York: Pearson/Longman, 2005.

Bush, Vannevar. *Pieces of the Action*. New York: Morrow, 1970.

Byer, Barry K. *Thomas E. Dewey: A Study in Political Leadership*. New York: Taylor & Francis, 1979.

Byrd, Harry Flood. *Defying the Odds: An Independent Senator's Historic Campaign*. Harrisonburg, Va.: R. R. Donnelley & Sons Co., 1998.

Byrd, Robert C. *Robert C. Byrd: Child of the Appalachian Coalfields*. Morgantown: West Virginia University Press, 2005.

Caldwell, Bruce. *Hayek's Challenge: An Intellectual Biography of F. A. Hayek*. Chicago: University of Chicago Press, 2003.

Cannon, Elaine. *Boy of the Land, Man of the Lord*. Salt Lake City: Bookcraft, 1989.

Cannon, James M. *Time and Chance: Gerald Ford's Appointment with History*. New York: HarperCollins, 1994.

Cantor, Milton. *Max Eastman*. New York: Twayne Publishers, 1970.

Caro, Robert A. *The Years of Lyndon Johnson: Means of Ascent*. New York: Knopf, 1990.

———. *The Years of Lyndon Johnson: The Path to Power*. New York: Knopf, 1982.

Carter, Barbara. *The Road to City Hall: How John V. Lindsay Became Mayor*. Englewood Cliffs, N.J.: PrenticeHall, 1967.

Celler, Emanuel. *You Never Leave Brooklyn: The Autobiography of Emanuel Celler*. New York: J. Day Co., 1953.

Chambers, Whittaker, and William F. Buckley, Jr. *Odyssey of a Friend: Whittaker Chambers' Letters to William F. Buckley, Jr., 1954–1961*. New York: Putnam, 1970.

Chambers, Whittaker. *Witness*. Chicago: Regnery Gateway, 1984.

Chandler, Happy. *Heroes, Plain Folks, and Skunks*. Chicago: Bonus Books, 1989.

Charters, Ann. *Kerouac*. New York: St. Martin's Press, 1974.

Chase, James. *Acheson: The Secretary of State Who Created the American World*. New York: Simon & Schuster, 1998.

Chessman, Caryl. *Cell 2455: Death Row*. Englewood Cliffs, N.J.: Prentice Hall, 1954.

———. *The Face of Justice*. Englewood Cliffs, N.J.: Prentice Hall, 1958.

Childs, Marquis, and James Reston, eds. *Walter Lippman and His Times*. New York: Harcourt, Brace, 1959.

Christenson, Cornelia V. *Kinsey: A Biography*. Bloomington: Indiana University Press, 1971.

Church, F. Forrester. *Father and Son: A Personal Biography of Senator Frank Church of Idaho*. New York: Harper & Row, 1985.

Clancy, Paul R. *Just a Country Lawyer: A Biography of Senator Sam Ervin*. Bloomington: Indiana University Press, 1974.

Clark, Hunter R. *Justice Brennan: The Great Conciliator*. Secaucus, N.J.: Carol Publishing Group, 1995.

Clark, Mark W. *From the Danube to the Yalu*. London: George G. Harrap & Co., 1954.

Clark, Ronald William. *Einstein: The Life and Times*. New York: World Publishing Co., 1971.

Cleveland, Martha. *Charles Percy: Strong New Voice from Illinois: A Biography*. Jacksonville, Ill.: Harris-Wolfe, 1968.

Cochran, Bert. *Adlai Stevenson: Patrician among Politicians*. New York: Funk & Wagnalls, 1969.

Coffey, Thomas M. *Iron Eagle: The Turbulent Life of General Curtis LeMay*. New York: Crown Publishers, 1986.

Coffin, Tristram. *Senator Fulbright: Portrait of a Public Philosopher*. New York: Dutton, 1966.

Cohen, Adam, and Elizabeth Taylor. *American Pharaoh: Mayor Richard J. Daley: His Battle for Chicago and the Nation*. Boston: Little, Brown, 2000.

Cohn, Roy, and Sidney Zion. *The Autobiography of Roy Cohn*. Secaucus, N.J.: Lyle Stuart, 1988.

Cohodas, Nadine. *Strom Thurmond and the Politics of Southern Change*. New York: Simon & Schuster, 1993.

Colburn, Don. *Chet Holifield: Democratic Representative from California.* Washington, D.C.: Grossman, 1972.

Collier, Peter. *The Fords: An American Epic.* New York: Summit Books, 1987.

Collins, J. Lawton. *Lightning Joe: An Autobiography.* Baton Rouge: Louisiana State University Press, 1979.

Conkin, Paul Keith. *Big Daddy from the Pedernales: Lyndon Baines Johnson.* Boston: Twayne, 1986.

Conrad, Glenn R. *Creed of a Congressman: F. Edward Hebert of Louisiana.* Lafayette, La.: USL History Series, University of Southwestern Louisiana, 1971.

Cook, Gay. *F. Edward Hébert, Democratic Representative from Louisiana.* Washington, D.C.: Grossman, 1972.

————. *John C. Stennis, Democratic Senator from Mississippi.* Washington, D.C.: Grossman, 1972.

Cook, James F. *Carl Vinson: Patriarch of the Armed Forces.* Macon, Ga.: Mercer University Press, 2004.

Cooney, John. *The American Pope: The Life and Times of Francis Cardinal Spellman.* New York: Times Books, 1984.

Cooper, Richard J. *Politics of Progress: How Governor George M. Leader Modernized Pennsylvania State Government.* Harrisburg: Pennsylvania Valley Publishers, 1982.

Cormier, Frank, and William J. Eaton. *Reuther.* Englewood Cliffs, N.J.: Prentice Hall, 1970.

Cotton, Norris. *In the Senate: Amidst the Conflict and the Turmoil.* New York: Dodd, Mead, 1978.

Cottrell, Robert C. *Izzy: A Biography of I. F. Stone.* New Brunswick, N.J.: Rutgers University Press, 1992.

Cousins, Norman. *Human Options.* New York: Norton, 1983.

Cox, Patrick. *Ralph W. Yarborough: The People's Senator.* Austin: University of Texas Press, 2001.

Cremin, Lawrence Arthur. *Richard Hofstadter (1916–1970): A Biographical Memoir.* Syracuse, N.Y.: National Academy of Education, 1972.

Crispell, Brian Lewis. *Testing the Limits: George Armistead Smathers and Cold War America.* Athens: University of Georgia Press, 1999.

Crosswell, D. K. *The Chief of Staff: The Military Career of General Walter Bedell Smith.* New York: Greenwood Press, 1991.

Cunningham, Barry. *Mr. District Attorney: The Story of Frank S. Hogan and the Manhattan D.A.'s Office.* New York: Mason/Charter, 1977.

Currey, Cecil B. *Edward Lansdale: The Unquiet American.* Boston: Houghton Mifflin, 1988.

Dallek, Robert. *An Unfinished Life: John F. Kennedy, 1917–1963.* Boston: Little, Brown, 2003.

————. *Flawed Giant: Lyndon Johnson and His Times, 1961–1973.* New York: Oxford University Press, 1995.

————. *Lone Star Rising: Lyndon Johnson and His Times, 1908–1960.* New York: Oxford University Press, 1991.

Danish, Max D. *The World of David Dubinsky.* Cleveland: World Publishing Co., 1957.

Dauer, Richard P. *A North-South Mind in an East-West World: Chester Bowles and the Making of the Cold War.* Westport, Conn.: Praeger, 2005.

Davies, Richard O. *Defender of the Old Guard: John Bricker and American Politics.* Columbus: Ohio State University Press, 1993.

Davis, Daniel S. *Mr. Black Labor: The Story of A. Philip Randolph, Father of the Civil Rights Movement.* New York: E. P. Dutton, 1972.

D'Emilio, John. *Lost Prophet: The Life and Times of Bayard Rustin.* New York: Free Press, 2003.

Depoe, Stephen P. *Arthur M. Schlesinger, Jr., and the Ideological History of American Liberalism.* Tuscaloosa: University of Alabama Press, 1994.

Desmond, James. *Nelson Rockefeller: A Political Biography.* New York: Macmillan, 1964.

Dew, Sheri L. *Ezra Taft Benson: A Biography.* Salt Lake City: Deseret Book Co., 1987.

Diggins, John P. *The Liberal Persuasion: Arthur Schlesinger, Jr., and the Challenge of the American Past.* Princeton: Princeton University Press, 1997.

Dirksen, Everett McKinley. *The Education of a Senator.* Urbana: University of Illinois Press, 1998.

DiSalle, Michael V. *Second Choice.* New York: Hawthorne Books, 1966.

Dobbs, Ricky F. *Yellow Dogs and Republicans: Allan Shivers and Texas Two-Party Politics.* Dallas: Texas A&M University Press, 2005.

Donovan, Robert J. *Conflict and Crisis: The Presidency of Harry S. Truman, 1945–1948.* New York: Norton, 1977.

———. *Eisenhower: The Inside Story.* New York: Harper, 1956.

———. *Tumultuous Years: The Presidency of Harry S. Truman, 1949–1953.* New York: Norton, 1982.

Dorough, C. Dwight. *Mr. Sam.* New York: Random House, 1962.

Douglas, Paul H. *In the Fullness of Time.* New York: Harcourt Brace Jovanovich, 1971.

Douglas, William O. *The Court Years, 1939–1975: The Autobiography of William O. Douglas.* New York: Random House, 1980.

Draper, Hal. *The Mind of Clark Kerr: His View of the University Factory & the "New Slavery."* Boston: New England Free Press, 1964.

Dreher, Carl. *Sarnoff: An American Success.* New York: Quadrangle Books, 1977.

Drosnin, Michael. *Citizen Hughes.* New York: Holt, Rinehart & Winston, 1985.

Drucker, Peter F. *Adventures of a Bystander.* New York: Harper & Row, 1979.

Drukman, Mason. *Wayne Morse: A Political Biography.* Portland: Oregon Historical Society Press, 1997.

Dryden, Hugh L. *Hugh L. Dryden's Career in Aviation and Space.* Washington, D.C.: NASA, 1996.

Duberman, Martin B. *Paul Robeson.* New York: Knopf, 1998.

Dubinsky, David. *David Dubinsky: A Life with Labor.* New York: Simon & Schuster, 1977.

Dubovsky, Melvyn, and Warren Van Tine. *John L. Lewis: A Biography.* New York: Quadrangle Books, 1977.

Dulles, Allen. *The Craft of Intelligence.* New York: Harper & Row, 1963.

Duncan, Anne Shipley. *The Making of an Anti-Communist Crusader: A Political Biography of Walter H. Judd.* South Hadley, Mass.: Mount Holyoke College, 1982.

Duncan, Francis. *Rickover and the Nuclear Navy: The Discipline of Technology.* Annapolis: Naval Institute Press, 1990.

Dunne, Gerald T. *Hugo Black and the Judicial Revolution.* New York: Simon & Schuster, 1977.

Durden-Smith, Jo. *100 Most Infamous Criminals.* New York: MetroBooks, 2004.

Dyckman, Martin A. *Floridian of His Century: The Courage of Governor LeRoy Collins.* Gainesville: University Press of Florida, 2006.

Dyke, Richard Wayne. *Chet Holifield: Master Legislator and Nuclear Statesman.* Lanham, Md.: University Press of America, 1996.

Dzuback, May Ann. *Robert M. Hutchins: Portrait of an Educator.* Chicago: University of Chicago Press, 1991.

Edwards, Bob. *Edward R. Murrow and the Birth of Broadcast Journalism.* Hoboken, N.J.: Wiley, 2004.

Edwards, Lee. *Goldwater: The Man Who Made a Revolution.* Washington, D.C.: Regnery Publishing Co., 1995.

———. *Missionary for Freedom: The Life and Times of Walter Judd.* New York: Paragon House, 1990.

Eggler, Bruce. *The Life and Career of Hale Boggs.* New Orleans: New Orleans States-Item, 1973.

Eisenhower, Dwight D. *At Ease: Stories I Tell to Friends.* Garden City, N.Y.: Doubleday, 1967.

———. *The White House Years.* 2 vols. Garden City, N.Y.: Doubleday, 1963–65.

Eisenhower, Milton S. *The President Is Calling.* Garden City, N.Y.: Doubleday, 1974.

Eisler, Kim Isaac. *A Justice for All: William J. Brennan, Jr., and the Decisions That Transformed America.* New York: Simon & Schuster, 1993.

Elliot, Gary. *Senator Alan Bible and the Politics of the New West.* Reno: University of Nevada Press, 1994.

Emmet, John Hughes. *The Ordeal of Power: A Political Memoir of the Eisenhower Years.* New York: Atheneum, 1963.

Ervin, Sam J. *Preserving the Constitution: The Autobiography of Senator Sam J. Ervin, Jr.* Charlottesville, Va.: Michie Co., 1984.

Ettinger, Elzbieta. *Hannah Arendt/Martin Heidegger.* New Haven: Yale University Press, 1995.

Evans, Rowland, and Robert Novak. *Lyndon B. Johnson: The Exercise of Power.* New York: Signet, 1966.

Fallows, James M. *Warren G. Magnuson, Democratic Senator from Washington.* Washington, D.C.: Grossman, 1972.

Fassett, John D. *New Deal Justice: The Life of Stanley Reed of Kentucky.* New York: Vantage Press, 1994.

Fast, Howard. *Being Red.* Boston: Houghton Mifflin, 1990.

Ferrell, Robert (ed.). *The Eisenhower Diaries.* New York: Norton, 1981.

Ferrell, Robert H. *Harry S. Truman and the Modern American Presidency.* Boston: Little, Brown, 1983.

Fleischman, Harry. *Norman Thomas—A Biography: 1884–1968.* New York: Norton, 1969.

Flemming, Bernice. *Arthur Flemming: Crusader at Large.* Washington, D.C.: Caring Publishing, 1991.

Folsing, Albrecht. *Einstein: A Life in Science.* New York: Oxford University Press, 1994.

Fontenay, Charles L. *Estes Kefauver: A Biography.* Knoxville: University of Tennessee Press, 1980.

Ford, Gerald R. *A Time to Heal: The Autobiography of Gerald Ford.* New York: Harper & Row, 1979.

Fox, Richard Wightman. *Reinhold Niebuhr: A Biography.* New York: Pantheon Books, 1985.

Frady, Marshall. *Billy Graham: A Parable of American Righteousness.* Boston: Little, Brown, 1979.

Frank, John P. *Clement Haynsworth, the Senate, and the Supreme Court.* Charlottesville: University of Virginia Press, 1991.

Frankfurter, Felix. *Felix Frankfurter Reminisces.* New York: Reynal, 1960.

Frasca, Dom. *Vito Genovese: King of Crime.* New York: Avon Books, 1963.

Freyer, Tony. *Hugo L. Black and the Dilemma of American Liberalism.* Glenview, Ill.: Little, Brown, 1990.

Fried, Richard M. *Men against McCarthy.* New York: Columbia University Press, 1976.

Galbraith, John Kenneth. *A Life in Our Time: Memoirs.* Boston: Houghton Mifflin, 1981.

Gamble, Andrew. *Hayek: The Iron Cage of Liberty.* Boulder, Colo.: Westview Press, 1996.

Gannon, Robert I. *The Cardinal Spellman Story.* Garden City, N.Y.: Doubleday, 1962.

Garber, Marjorie B. *Secret Agents: The Rosenberg Case, McCarthyism, and Fifties America.* New York: Routledge, 1995.

Gardner, Trevor. *My First Eighty Years.* Edinburgh: Pentland Press, 1998.

Garraty, John Arthur. *Henry Cabot Lodge: A Biography.* New York: Knopf, 1953.

Garrow, David J. *Bearing the Cross: Martin Luther King, Jr. and the Southern Christian Leadership Conference.* New York: W. Morrow, 1986.

Geelan, Agnes. *The Dakota Maverick: The Political Life of William Langer, Also Known as "Wild Bill" Langer.* Fargo, N.D.: Geelan, 1975.

Gelman, Irwin F. *The Contender: Richard Nixon, The Congress Years, 1946–1952.* New York: Free Press, 1999.

Gentry, Curt. *J. Edgar Hoover: The Man and His Secrets.* New York: Norton, 1991.

George, Carol. *God's Salesman: Norman Vincent Peale & the Power of Positive Thinking.* New York: Oxford University Press, 1993.

Gerhardt, Uta. *Talcott Parsons: An Intellectual Biography.* Cambridge: Cambridge University Press, 2002.

Gerhart, Eugene C. *America's Advocate: Robert H. Jackson.* Indianapolis: Bobbs-Merrill, 1958.

Gibbons, Francis M. *Ezra Taft Benson: Statesman, Patriot, Prophet of God.* Salt Lake City: Deseret Book Co., 1996.

Gibson, M. Allen. *Beautiful upon the Mountains: A Portrait of Cyrus Eaton.* Hantsport, N.S.: Lancelot Press, 1977.

Gill, Kenny. *Jimmy Davis: More Than Sunshine.* Many, La.: Sweet Dreams Publishing Co., 2000.

Gilliam, Dorothy Butler. *Paul Robeson: All-American.* Washington, D.C.: New Republic Book Co., 1976.

Ginsberg, Allen. *Journals: Early Fifties, Early Sixties.* New York: Random House, 1977.

———. *Journals: Mid-Fifties, 1954–1958.* New York: HarperCollins, 1995.

Gleisser, Marcus. *The World of Cyrus Eaton.* New York: A. S. Barnes, 1965.

Goertzel, Ted. *Linus Pauling: A Life in Science and Politics.* New York: Basic Books, 1995.

Gold, Ben. *Memoirs.* New York: W. Howard, 1984.

Goldberg, Robert Alan. *Barry Goldwater.* New Haven: Yale University Press, 1995.

Goldman, Roger, and David Gallen. *Justice William J. Brennan, Jr.: Freedom First.* New York: Caroll & Graf, 1994.

Goldwater, Barry M. *Goldwater.* New York: Doubleday, 1988.

Goodchild, Peter. *J. Robert Oppenheimer: Shatterer of Worlds.* Boston: Houghton Mifflin, 1981.

Goodwin, Doris Kearns. *Lyndon Johnson and the American Dream.* New York: Harper & Row, 1976.

Goold-Adams, Richard. *The Time of Power: A Reappraisal of John Foster Dulles.* London: Weidenfeld &Nicolson, 1962.

Gordon, Arthur. *One Man's Way: The Story and Message of Norman Vincent Peale.* Englewood Cliffs, N.J.: PrenticeHall, 1972.

Gore, Albert. *Let the Glory Out: My South and Its Politics.* New York: Viking Press, 1972.

Gorman, Joseph Bruce. *Kefauver: A Political Biography.* New York: Oxford University Press, 1971.

Gottfried, Martin. *Arthur Miller: His Life and Work.* Cambridge: Harvard University Press, 2003.

Goulden, Joseph C. *Meany.* New York: Atheneum, 1972.

Grafton, Carl. *Big Mules and Branchheads: James E. Folsom and Political Power in Alabama.* Athens: University of Georgia Press, 1985.

Graham, Billy. *Just as I Am: The Autobiography of Billy Graham.* San Francisco: Harper, 1997.

Graubard, Stephen R. *Kissinger: Portrait of a Mind.* New York: Norton, 1973.

Green, George N. *The Establishment in Texas Politics: The Primitive Years, 1938–1945.* Norman: University of Oklahoma Press, 1984.

Greene, Lee Seifert. *Lead Me On: Frank Goad Clement and Tennessee Politics.* Knoxville: University of Tennessee Press, 1982.

Griffin, Winthrop. *Humphrey: A Candid Biography.* New York: Morrow, 1965.

Griffith, Robert. *The Politics of Fear: Joseph R. McCarthy and the Senate.* Lexington: University Press of Kentucky, 1970.

Grose, Peter. *Gentleman Spy: The Life of Allen Dulles.* Boston: Houghton Mifflin, 1994.

Gruening, Ernest. *Many Battles: The Autobiography of Ernest Gruening.* New York: Liveright, 1973.

Gugin, Linda and James E. St. Clair. *Sherman Minton: New Deal Senator, Cold War Justice.* Indianapolis: Indiana Historical Society, 1997.

Guhin, Michael A. *John Foster Dulles: A Statesman and His Times.* New York: Columbia University Press, 1972.

Haas, Edward F. *DeLesseps S. Morrison and the Image of Reform: New Orleans Politics, 1946–1961.* Baton Rouge: Louisiana State University Press, 1974.

———. *The Age of the Longs: Louisiana, 1928–1960.* Lafayette: University of Louisiana at Lafayette, 2001.

Haberman, Aaron L. *Andrew J. Goodpaster Papers, 1930–1997.* New York: Marshall George Research, 2000.

Hack, Richard. *Hughes: The Private Diaries, Memos and Letters: The Definitive Biography of the First American Billionaire.* Beverly Hills: New Millennium Press, 2001.

Hager, Thomas. *Force of Nature: The Life of Linus Pauling.* New York: Simon & Schuster, 1995.

Hall, Bill. *Frank Church: D.C. & Me.* Pullman: Washington State University Press, 1995.

Hamilton, Charles. *Adam Clayton Powell, Jr.: The Political Biography of an American Dilemma.* New York: Atheneum, 1991.

Hamilton, Nigel. *JFK: Reckless Youth.* New York: Random House, 1992.

Hamilton, Virginia. *Lister Hill: Statesman from the South.* Chapel Hill: University of North Carolina Press, 1987.

Hannah, John A. *A Memoir.* East Lansing: Michigan State University Press, 1980.

Harbaugh, William Henry. *Lawyer's Lawyer: The Life of John W. Davis.* New York: Oxford University Press, 1973.

Hardeman, D. B., and Donald C. Bacon. *Rayburn: A Biography.* Austin: University of Texas Press, 1987.

Harris, T. George *Romney's Way: A Man and an Idea.* Englewood Cliffs, N.J.: Prentice Hall, 1967.

Hartley, Robert E. *Charles H. Percy: A Political Perspective.* Chicago: Rand McNally, 1975.

Hass, Eric. *Dave Beck Labor Merchant: The Case History of a Labor Leader.* New York: New York Labor News, 1955.

Hatch, Alden. *Ambassador Extraordinary: Clare Boothe Luce.* New York: Holt, 1956.

Haygood, Will. *King of the Cats: The Life and Times of Adam Clayton Powell, Jr.* Boston: Houghton Mifflin, 1993.

Heidepriem, Scott. *A Fair Chance for a Free People: Biography of Karl E. Mundt, United States Senator.* Madison, S.D.: Leader Print Co., 1988.

Heinemann, Ronald L. *Harry Byrd of Virginia.* Charlottesville: University Press of Virginia, 1996.

Henault, Marie. *Peter Viereck.* New York: Twayne, 1969.

Henry, Charles P. *Ralph Bunche: Model Negro or American Other?* New York: New York University Press, 1999.

Hentoff, Nat. *Peace Agitator: The Story of A. J. Muste.* New York: Macmillan, 1982.

———. *A Political Life: The Education of John V. Lindsay.* New York: Knopf, 1969.

Herken, Gregg. *Brotherhood of the Bomb: The Tangled Lives and Loyalties of Robert Oppenheimer.* New York: Henry Holt and Co., 2002.

Hershberg, James G. *James B. Conant: Harvard to Hiroshima and the Making of the Nuclear Age.* New York: Knopf, 1993.

Herskowitz, Mickey. *Duty, Honor, Country: The Life and Legacy of Prescott Bush.* Nashville: Rutledge Hill Press, 2003.

Hession, Charles H. *John Kenneth Galbraith and His Critics.* New York: New American Library, 1972.

Heymann, C. David. *RFK: A Candid Biography.* New York: Dutton, 1998.

Hickey, Neil. *Adam Clayton Powell and the Politics of Race.* New York: Fleet Publishing Corp., 1965.

Hirsch, H. N. *The Enigma of Felix Frankfurter.* New York: Basic Books, 1981.

Hodges, Luther H. *Businessman in the Statehouse: Six Years as Governor of North Carolina.* Chapel Hill: University of North Carolina Press, 1962.

Hoff, Joan. *Herbert Hoover: Forgotten Progressive.* Boston: Little, Brown, 1975.

———. *Without Precedent: The Life and Career of Eleanor Roosevelt.* Bloomington: Indiana University Press, 1984.

Hoffa, James R. *Hoffa: The Real Story.* New York: Stein & Day, 1975.

Hoffecker, Carol E. *Honest John Williams: U.S. Senator from Delaware.* Newark: University of Delaware Press, 2000.

Hoffman, Banesh, and Helen Dukas. *Albert Einstein, Creator and Rebel.* New York: New American Library, 1972.

Holmes, Sven Erik. *Gordon Allot: Republican Senator from Colorado.* Washington: Grossman Publishers, 1972.

Holmwood, John. *Talcott Parsons.* Aldershot, England: Ashgate, 2006.

Hook, Sidney. *Out of Step: An Unquiet Life in the 20th Century.* New York: Harper & Row, 1987.

Hoopes, Townsend. *The Devil and John Foster Dulles.* Boston: Little, Brown, 1973.

Hoover, Herbert. *Memoirs.* New York: Macmillan, 1952.

Hope, Cliff. *Quiet Courage: Kansas Congressman Clifford R. Hope.* Manhattan, Kans.: Sunflower University Press, 1997.

Horowitz, Daniel. *Vance Packard & American Social Criticism.* Chapel Hill: University of North Carolina Press, 1994.

Horowitz, Irving Louis. *C. Wright Mills: An American Utopian.* New York: Free Press, 1983.

Hughes, Emmet John. *The Ordeal of Power.* New York: Atheneum, 1963.

Hulsey, Byron C. *Everett Dirksen and His Presidents: How a Senate Giant Shaped American Politics.* Lawrence: University Press of Kansas, 2000.

Humphrey, Hubert H. *The Education of a Public Man: My Life and Politics.* Garden City, N.Y.: Doubleday, 1976.

Huthmacher, J. Joseph. *Senator Robert F. Wagner and the Rise of Urban Liberalism.* New York: Atheneum, 1968.

Hyman, Sidney. *The Lives of William Benton.* Chicago: University of Chicago Press, 1969.

Ingalls, Robert P. *Herbert H. Lehman and New York's Little New Deal.* New York: New York University Press, 1975.

Isaacson, Walter. *Kissinger: A Biography.* New York: Simon & Schuster, 1992.

Iverson, Peter. *Barry Goldwater: Native Arizonan.* Norman: University of Oklahoma Press, 1997.

Ivey, Pete. *Luther H. Hodges, Practical Idealist.* Minneapolis: Denison, 1968.

James, Ralph C. *Hoffa and Teamsters: A Study in Union Power.* Princeton: Princeton University Press, 1965.

Javits, Jacob K. *Javits: The Autobiography of a Public Man.* Boston: Houghton Mifflin, 1981.

Jeansonne, Glen. *Gerald L. K. Smith, Minister of Hate.* New Haven: Yale University Press, 1988.

Johnpoll, Bernard. *Pacifist's Progress: Norman Thomas and the Decline of American Socialism.* Chicago: Quadrangle Books, 1970.

Johnson, Haynes Bonner. *Fulbright: The Dissenter.* Garden City, N.Y.: Doubleday, 1968.

Johnson, Lyndon Baines. *The Vantage Point.* New York: Holt, Rinehart & Winston, 1971.

Jones, James H. *Alfred C. Kinsey: A Public/ Private Life.* New York: W. W. Norton, 1997.

Jones, Ken, and Hubert Kelly. *Admiral Arleigh (31-Knot) Burke: The Story of a Fighting Sailor.* Annapolis, Md.: Naval Institute Press, 2001.

Jordan, Robert S. *Norstad: Cold War NATO Supreme Commander: Airman, Strategist, Diplomat.* New York: St. Martin's Press, 2000.

Judis, John. *William F. Buckley, Jr.: Patron Saint of the Conservatives.* New York: Simon & Schuster, 1988.

Kahn, E. J. *The China Hands: America's Foreign Service Officers and What Befell Them.* New York: Viking Press, 1975.

Kalb, Marvin. *Kissinger.* Boston: Little, Brown, 1974.

Kaplan, Gisela T., and Clive S. Kessler. *Hannah Arendt: Thinking, Judging, Freedom.* Sydney: Allen & Unwin, 1989.

Katcher, Leo. *Earl Warren: A Political Biography.* New York: McGraw-Hill, 1967.

Kateb, George. *Hannah Arendt: Politics, Conscience, Evil.* Totowa, N.J.: Rowman & Allanheld, 1984.

Katz, Leonard. *Uncle Frank: The Biography of Frank Costello.* New York: Drake Publishers, 1973.

Kaufman, Robert Gordon. *Henry M. Jackson: A Life in Politics.* Seattle: University of Washington Press, 2000.

Keeley, Joseph Charles. *The China Lobby Man: The Story of Alfred Kohlberg.* New Rochelle, N.Y.: Arlington House, 1969.

Kelly, Daniel. *James Burnham and the Struggle for the World.* Wilmington, Del.: ISI Books, 2002.

Kelly, George Edward. *Man of Steel: The Story of David J. McDonald.* New York: North American Book Co., 1954.

Kemper, Donald J. *Decade of Fear: Senator Hennings and Civil Liberties.* Columbia: University of Missouri Press, 1965.

Kendrick, Alexander. *Prime Time: The Life of Edward R. Murrow.* Boston: Little, Brown, 1969.

Kennan, George Frost. *Memoirs, 1950–1963, George F. Kennan.* London: Hutchinson, 1973.

Kennedy, Eugene C. *Himself: The Life and Times of Mayor Richard J. Daley.* New York: Viking Press, 1978.

Kennedy, Robert Francis, Jr. *Judge Frank M. Johnson, Jr.: A Biography.* New York: Putnam, 1978.

Kerouac, Jack. *Windblown World: The Journals of Jack Kerouac, 1947–1954.* New York: Viking Press, 2004.

Kerr, Clark. *The Gold and the Blue: A Personal Memoir of the University of California, 1949–1967.* Berkeley: University of California Press, 2001.

Khedouri, F. N. *Carl T. Curtis: Republican Senator from Nebraska.* Washington, D.C.: Grossman, 1972.

Kiepper, James J. *Styles Bridges: Yankee Senator.* Sugar Hill, N.H.: Phoenix Publishing, 2001.

Killian, James Rhyne. *Sputnik, Scientists, and Eisenhower: A Memoir of the First Special Assistant to the President for Science and Technology.* Cambridge: Harvard University Press, 1977.

Kinch, Sam. *Allan Shivers: The Pied Piper of Texas Politics.* Austin: University of Texas Press, 1974.

King, Martin Luther, Jr. *Stride toward Freedom: The Montgomery Story.* New York: Harper, 1958.

———. *The Autobiography of Martin Luther King, Jr.* New York: Warner Books, 1998.

Kinkead, Gwen. *J. Caleb Boggs: Republican Senator from Delaware.* Washington, D.C.: Grossman Publishers, 1972.

Kirk, Russell. *The Sword of Imagination: Memoirs of a Half-Century of Literary Conflict.* Grand Rapids, Mich.: William B. Eerdmans Publishing, 1995.

Kistiakowsky, George B. *A Scientist at the White House.* Cambridge: Harvard University Press, 1976.

Klitzman, Stephen. *Sam J. Ervin, Jr.: Democratic Senator from North Carolina.* Washington, D.C.: Grossman, 1972.

Kluger, Jeffrey. *Splendid Solution: Jonas Salk and the Conquest of Polio.* New York: G.P. Putnam's Sons, 2004.

Klurfeld, Herman. *Behind the Lines: The World of Drew Pearson.* Englewood Cliffs, N.J.: Prentice Hall, 1968.

Koerner, James D. *Hoffer's America.* La Salle, Ill.: Library Press, 1973.

Kohl, Robert, and Cynthia Stokes Brown. *She Would Not Be Moved: How We Tell the Story of Rosa Parks and the Montgomery Bus Boycott.* New York: W. W. Norton, 2005.

Kramer, Joe. *Allen Ginsberg in America*. New York: Random House, 1969.

Krock, Arthur. *In the Nation*. New York: McGraw-Hill, 1966.

Kurtz, Michael L. *Earl K. Long: The Saga of Uncle Earl and Louisiana Politics*. Baton Rouge: Louisiana State University Press, 1990.

Lachicotte, Alberta Morel. *Rebel Senator: Strom Thurmond of South Carolina*. New York: Devin-Adair Co., 1966.

Lankford, Nelson D. *The Last American Aristocrat: The Biography of David K. E. Bruce, 1898–1977*. Boston: Little, Brown, 1996.

Lansdale, Edward G. *In the Midst of Wars: An American's Mission to Southeast Asia*. New York: Harper & Row, 1972.

Larrowe, Charles P. *Harry Bridges: The Rise and Fall of Radical Labor in the United States*. New York: L. Hill, 1972.

Larson, Arthur. *Eisenhower: The President Nobody Knew*. New York: Scribner, 1968.

———. *A Twentieth-Century Life: The Memoirs of Arthur Larson*. Sioux Falls, S.D.: Center for Western Studies, 1997.

Lash, Joseph P. *Eleanor: The Years Alone*. New York: Norton, 1972.

Lasky, Victor. *Arthur J. Goldberg: The Old and the New*. New Rochelle, N.Y.: Arlington House, 1970.

———. *Never Complain, Never Explain: The Story of Henry Ford II*. New York: R. Marek Publishers, 1981.

LeMay, Curtis, with McKinley Kantor. *Mission with LeMay: My Story*. New York: Doubleday, 1965.

Leonard, Rodney E. *Freeman: The Governor Years, 1955–1960*. Minneapolis: Hubert H. Humphrey Institute of Public Affairs, 2003.

Levine, Daniel. *Bayard Rustin and the Civil Rights Movement*. New Brunswick, N.J.: Rutgers University Press, 2000.

Levine, Erwin L. *Theodore Francis Green: The Washington Years, 1937–1960*. Providence, R.I.: Brown University Press, 1971.

Lewis, David L. *King: A Critical Biography*. New York: Praeger, 1970.

Lewis, Tom. *Empire of the Air: The Men Who Made Radio*. New York: E. Burlingame Books, 1991.

Lichtenstein, Nelson. *The Most Dangerous Man in Detroit: Walter Reuther and the Fate of American Labor*. New York: Basic Books, 1995.

Liebling, A. J. *The Earl of Louisiana*. New York: Simon & Schuster, 1961.

Liebman, Marvin. *Coming Out Conservative: An Autobiography*. San Francisco: Chronicle Books, 1992.

Lindsay, John V. *Journey into Politics*. New York: H. W. Wilson Co., 1967.

Livingston, Jeffery C. *Swallowed by Globalism: John M. Vorys and American Foreign Policy*. Lanham, Md.: University Press of America, 2001.

Lodge, Henry Cabot. *As It Was: An Inside View of Politics and Power in the '50s and '60s*. New York: Norton, 1976.

———. *The Storm Has Many Eyes*. New York: Norton, 1973.

Longley, Kyle. *Senator Albert Gore, Sr.: Tennessee Maverick*. Baton Rouge: Louisiana State University Press, 2004.

Loth, David Goldsmith. *A Long Way Forward: The Biography of a Congresswoman Frances P. Bolton*. New York: Longmans, Green, 1957.

Ludwick, Jim. *Mansfield: The Senator from Montana*. Missoula, Mont.: The Missoulian, 1988.

Lule, Jack. *Radical Rules: I. F. Stone's Ethical Perspective*. New York: HarperBusiness, 1992.

Lyon, Peter. *Eisenhower: Portrait of the Hero*. Boston: Little, Brown, 1974.

Lyons, Eugene. *David Sarnoff: A Biography*. New York: Harper & Row, 1966.

———. *Herbert Hoover: A Biography*. Garden City, N.Y.: Doubleday, 1964.

Lythgoe, Dennis L. *Let 'em Holler: A Political Biography of J. Bracken Lee*. Salt Lake City: Utah State Historical Society, 1982.

MacArthur, Douglas. *Reminiscences*. New York: McGraw-Hill, 1964.

MacKown, Craig. *Jacob K. Javits: Republican Senator from New York*. Washington, D.C.: Grossman Publishers, 1972.

MacNeil, Neil. *Dirksen: Portrait of a Public Man*. New York: World Publishing Co., 1970.

MacPherson, Myra. *All Governments Lie: The Life and Times of Rebel Journalist I. F. Stone*. New York: Scribner, 2006.

Mahoney, Tom. *The Story of George Romney: Builder, Statesman, Crusader.* New York: Harper, 1960.

Manchester, William Raymond. *American Caesar: Douglas MacArthur, 1880–1964.* Boston: Little, Brown, 1978.

Maney, Kevin. *The Maverick and His Machine: Thomas Watson and the Making of IBM.* New York: J. Wiley & Sons, 2003.

Manis, Andrew Michael. *A Fire You Can't Put Out: The Civil Rights Life of Birmingham's Reverend Fred Shuttlesworth.* Tuscaloosa: University of Alabama Press, 1999.

Mann, Peggy. *Ralph Bunche: UN Peacemaker.* New York: Coward, McCann & Geoghegan, 1975.

Mann, Robert. *Legacy to Power: Senator Russell Long of Louisiana.* New York: Paragon House, 1992.

Markmann, Charles L. *The Buckleys: A Family Examined.* New York: W. Morrow, 1973.

Martin, John Bartlow. *Adlai Stevenson and the World.* Garden City, N.Y.: Doubleday, 1977.

———. *Adlai Stevenson of Illinois: The Life of Adlai E. Stevenson.* Garden City, N.Y.: Doubleday, 1976.

Martin, Joseph W. *My First Fifty Years in Politics.* New York: McGraw-Hill, 1960.

Mason, Lowell B. *Senator Saltonstall Hits a Home Run.* New York: Rand McNally, 1956.

Matteson, Robert Eliot. *Harold Stassen: His Career, The Man, and the 1957 London Arms Control Negotiations.* Minneapolis: Desk Top Ink, 1993.

Matthews, Christopher. *Kennedy & Nixon: The Rivalry That Shaped Postwar America.* New York: Simon & Schuster, 1996.

Matthews, Thomas G. *Luis Munoz Marin.* New York: American R.D.M. Corp., 1967.

May, Gary. *China Scapegoat: The Diplomatic Ordeal of John Carter Vincent.* Washington, D.C.: New Republic Books, 1979.

Mayer, Milton Sanford. *Robert Maynard Hutchins: A Memoir.* Berkeley: University of California Press, 1993.

Mayers, David Allan. *George Kennan and the Dilemmas of US Foreign Policy.* New York: Oxford University Press, 1988.

Mazo, Earl. *Richard Nixon: A Political and Personal Biography.* New York: Harper, 1959.

McAdams, Alan K. *Power and Politics in Labor Legislation.* New York: Columbia University Press, 1964.

McCallum, John Dennis. *Dave Beck.* Mercer Island, Wash.: Writing Works, 1978.

McCarthy, Eugene J. *Parting Shots from My Brittle Bow: Reflections on American Politics and Life.* Golden, Colo.: Fulcrum Publishing, 2004.

McCullough, David G. *Truman.* New York: Simon & Schuster, 1992.

McDonald, David J. *Union Man.* New York: Dutton, 1969.

McFarland, Linda. *Cold War Strategist: Stuart Symington and the Search for National Security.* Westport, Conn.: Greenwood Press, 2001.

McKeever, Porter. *Adlai Stevenson: His Life and Legacy.* New York: Morrow, 1989.

McLellan, David S. *Dean Acheson: The State Department Years.* New York: Dodd, Mead & Co., 1976.

McMillan, Priscilla. *The Ruin of J. Robert Oppenheimer and the Birth of the Modern Arms Race.* New York: Viking, 2005.

McNally, Dennis. *Desolate Angel: Jack Kerouac, the Beat Generation, and America.* New York: Random House, 1979.

McNaughton, Frank. *Mennen Williams of Michigan, Fighter for Progress.* New York: Oceana Publications, 1960.

Meilinger, Phillip. S. *Hoyt S. Vandenberg: The Life of a General.* Bloomington: Indiana University Press, 1989.

Mendelson, Wallace (ed.). *Felix Frankfurter: The Judge.* New York: Reynal, 1964.

Merkley, Paul. *Reinhold Niebuhr: A Political Account.* Montreal: McGill-Queen's University Press, 1975.

Merry, Robert. *Taking on the World: Joseph and Stewart Alsop—Guardians of the American Century.* New York: Viking, 1996.

Metress, Christopher. *The Lynching of Emmett Till: A Documentary Narrative.* Charlottesville: University of Virginia Press, 2002.

Michelman, Frank I. *Brennan and Democracy.* Princeton: Princeton University Press, 1999.

Miles, Barry. *Ginsberg: A Biography.* New York: Simon & Schuster, 1989.

Miller, Arthur Selwyn. *A Capacity for Outrage: The Judicial Odyssey of J. Skelly Wright.* Westport, Conn.: Greenwood Press, 1984.

Miller, Arthur. *Timebends: A Life.* New York: Grove Press, 1987.

Miller, Richard Lawrence. *Whittaker: Struggles of a Supreme Court Justice.* Westport, Conn.: Greenwood Press, 2002.

Miller, William J. *Henry Cabot Lodge: A Biography.* New York: Heineman, 1967.

Millet, Anna L., and John A. Millet. *Blatnik: Democratic Representative from Minnesota.* Washington, D.C.: Grossman Publishers, 1972.

Mitchell, William C. *Sociological Analysis and Politics: The Theories of Talcott Parsons.* Englewood Cliffs, N.J.: Prentice Hall, 1967.

Mollenhoff, Clark R. *George Romney, Mormon in Politics.* New York: Meredith Press, 1968.

Montgomery, Gayle B., and James Johnson. *One Step from the White House: The Rise and Fall of Senator William F. Knowland.* Berkeley: University of California Press, 1998.

Morgan, Anne Hodges. *Robert S. Kerr: The Senate Years.* Oklahoma City: University of Oklahoma Press, 1977.

Morgan, Ted. *A Covert Life: Jay Lovestone, Communist, Anticommunist, and Spymaster.* New York: Random House, 1999.

Morganthau, Ruth S. *Pride without Prejudice: The Life of John Pastore.* Providence, R.I.: Rhode Island Historical Society, 1989.

Morris, Joe Alex. *The Richardson Dilworth Story.* Philadelphia: Mercury Books, 1962.

Morris, Roger. *Richard Milhous Nixon: The Rise of an American Politician.* New York: Holt, 1990.

Morris, Sylvia Jukes. *Rage for Fame: The Ascent of Clare Boothe Luce.* New York: Random House, 1997.

Morrow, E. Frederic. *Black Man in the White House.* New York: Coward-McCann, 1963.

———. *Forty Years a Guinea Pig.* New York: Pilgrim Press, 1980.

Moscow, Warren. *The Last of the Big-Time Bosses: The Life and Times of Carmine DeSapio and the Rise and Fall of Tammany Hall.* New York: Stein & Day, 1971.

Moss, Leonard. *Arthur Miller.* New York: Twayne Publishers, 1967.

Murph, Dan. *Texas Giant: The Life of Price Daniel.* Austin: University of Texas Press, 2001.

Murphy, Bruce Allen. *Wild Bill: The Legend and Life of William O. Douglas.* New York: Random House, 2003.

Murphy, Robert D. *Diplomat among Warriors.* Garden City, N.Y.: Doubleday, 1964.

Nashel, Jonathan. *Edward Lansdale's Cold War.* Amherst: University of Massachusetts Press, 2005.

Naske, Claus M. *Ernest Gruening: Alaska's Greatest Governor.* Fairbanks: University of Alaska Press, 2004.

Nevins, Allan. *Herbert H. Lehman and His Era.* New York: Scribner, 1963.

Newman, Roger K. *Hugo Black: A Biography.* New York: Fordham University Press, 1997.

Niehoff, Richard O. *John A. Hannah: Versatile Administrator and Distinguished Public Servant.* Lanham, Md.: University Press of America, 1989.

Nixon, Richard M. *Six Crises.* New York: Doubleday, 1962.

———. *RN: The Memoirs of Richard Nixon.* New York: Grosset & Dunlap, 1978.

Noer, Thomas J. *Soapy: A Biography of G. Mennen Williams.* Ann Arbor: University of Michigan Press, 2005.

Noonan, D. P. *The Passion of Fulton Sheen.* New York: Dodd, Mead, 1972.

Oates, Stephen. *Let the Trumpet Sound: The Life of Martin Luther King, Jr.* New York: Harper & Row, 1982.

Oberdorfer, Don. *Senator Mansfield: The Extraordinary Life of a Great Statesman and Diplomat.* Washington, D.C.: Smithsonian Books, 2003.

O'Brien, F. William. *Justice Reed and the First Amendment.* Washington: Georgetown University Press, 1958.

O'Brien, Michael. *Philip Hart: The Conscience of the Senate.* East Lansing: Michigan State University Press, 1995.

O'Connor, Len. *Clout: Mayor Daly and His City.* Chicago: H. Regnery Co., 1975.

Odenkirk, James E. *Frank J. Lausche: Ohio's Great Political Maverick.* Wilmington, Ohio: Orange Frazer Press, 2005.

Ognibene, Peter J. *Scoop: The Life and Politics of Henry M. Jackson.* New York: Stein & Day, 1975.

Ohnson, Robert David. *Ernest Gruening and the American Dissenting Tradition.* Cambridge: Harvard University Press, 1998.

Olson, James. *Stuart Symington: A Life.* Columbia: University of Missouri Press, 2003.

O'Neill, William J. *The Last Romantic: A Life of Max Eastman.* New York: Oxford University Press, 1970.

Oshinsky, David M. *A Conspiracy So Immense: The World of Joe McCarthy.* New York: Free Press, 1983.

Parker, Joseph B. *The Morrison Era: Reform Politics in New Orleans.* Gretna, La.: Pelican Publishing Co., 1974.

Parker, Richard. *John Kenneth Galbraith: His Life, His Politics, His Economics.* New York: Farrar, Straus, & Giroux, 2005.

Parks, Rosa. *My Story.* New York: Dial Books, 1992.

Parmet, Herbert S. *Eisenhower and the American Crusade.* New York: Macmillan, 1972.

———. *Jack: The Struggles of John F. Kennedy.* New York: Dial Press, 1980.

———. *JFK: The Presidency of John F. Kennedy.* New York: Dial Press, 1983.

———. *Richard Nixon and His America.* Boston: Little, Brown, 1990.

Parmet, Robert D. *The Master of Seventh Avenue: David Dubinsky and the American Labor Movement.* New York: New York University Press, 2005.

Parrish, Michael E. *Felix Frankfurter and His Times.* New York: Free Press, 1982.

Parthenakis, Thomas. *George M. Humphrey: Secretary of the Treasury, 1953–1957: A Political Biography.* Kent, Ohio: Kent State University Press, 1986.

Patner, Andrew. *I. F. Stone: A Portrait.* New York: Pantheon Books, 1988.

Patterson, James T. *Mr. Republican: A Biography of Robert A. Taft.* Boston: Houghton Mifflin, 1972.

Patterson, Lillie. *A. Philip Randolph: Messenger for the Masses.* New York: Facts On File, 1996.

Peale, Norman Vincent. *The True Joy of Positive Living: An Autobiography.* New York: Morrow, 1984.

Pearson, Drew. *Diaries, 1949–1959.* New York: Holt, Rinehart and Winston, 1974.

Perlstein, Rick. *Before the Storm: Barry Goldwater and the Unmaking of the American Consensus.* New York: Hill & Wang, 2001.

Perret, Geoffrey. *Eisenhower.* New York: Random House, 1999.

———. *Jack.* New York: Random House, 2002.

———. *Old Soldiers Never Die: The Life of Douglas MacArthur.* New York: Random House, 1996.

Persico, Joseph E. *The Imperial Rockefeller: A Biography of Nelson A. Rockefeller.* New York: Simon & Schuster, 1982.

Petkas, Peter J. *Lee Metcalf Democratic Senator from Montana.* Washington, D.C.: Grossman Publishers, 1972.

Pfau, Richard. *No Sacrifice Too Great: The Life of Lewis L. Strauss.* Charlottesville: University Press of Virginia, 1984.

Pfeffer, Paula F. *A. Philip Randolph: Pioneer of the Civil Rights Movement.* Baton Rouge: Louisiana State University Press, 1990.

Phillips, William. *Yarborough of Texas.* Washington, D.C.: Acropolis Books, 1969.

Pickett, William B. *Dwight David Eisenhower and American Power.* Wheeling, Ill.: Harlan Davidson, 1995.

———. *Homer E. Capehart: A Senator's Life, 1897–1979.* Indianapolis: Indiana Historical Society, 1990.

Pilat, Oliver. *Drew Pearson: An Unauthorized Biography.* New York: Harper's Magazine Press, 1973.

Piszkiewicz, Dennis. *Wernher von Braun: The Man Who Sold the Moon.* Westport, Conn.: Praeger, 1998.

Pollock, John Charles. *Billy Graham, Evangelist to the World: An Authorized Biography of the Decisive Years.* San Francisco: Harper & Row, 1979.

Polmar, Norman. *Rickover.* New York: Simon & Schuster, 1982.

Pomeroy, Wardell Baxter. *Dr. Kinsey and the Institute for Sex Research.* New York: Harper & Row, 1972.

Potter, Charles E. *Days of Shame.* New York: Coward-McCann, 1965.

Potter, E. B. *Admiral Arleigh Burke.* New York: Random House, 1990.

Powell, Adam Clayton, Jr. *Adam by Adam: The Autobiography of Adam Clayton Powell, Jr.* New York: Dial Press, 1971.

Powers, Francis Gary, with Curt Gentry. *Operation Overflight: The U-2 Spy Pilot Tells His Story for the First Time.* New York: Rinehart & Winston, 1970.

Powers, Richard Gid. *Secrecy and Power: The Life of J. Edgar Hoover.* New York: Collier Macmillan, 1987.

Press, Howard. *C. Wright Mills.* Boston: Twayne Publishers, 1978.

Prochnau, William W. *A Certain Democrat: Senator Henry M. Jackson: A Political Biography.* Englewood Cliffs, N.J.: Prentice Hall, 1972.

Pruessen, Ronald W. *John Foster Dulles: The Road to Power.* New York: Free Press, 1982.

Pullen, Dale. *George H. Mahon: Democratic Representative from Texas.* Washington, D.C.: Grossman, 1972.

Puryear, Elmer L. *Graham A. Barden: Conservative Carolina Congressman.* Buie's Creek, N.C.: Campbell University Press, 1979.

Quiring, Virginia M. *The Milton S. Eisenhower Years at Kansas State University.* Manhattan: Kansas State University Press, 1986.

Radcliff, William Franklin. *Sherman Minton: Indiana's Supreme Court Justice.* Indianapolis: Guild Press of Indiana, 1996.

Radford, Arthur William. *From Pearl Harbor to Vietnam: The Memoirs of Admiral Arthur W. Radford.* Stanford: Hoover Institution Press, 1980.

Radosh, Ronald, and Joyce Milton. *The Rosenberg File.* London: Weidenfeld & Nicolson, 1983.

Rakove, Milton L. *Don't Make No Waves—Don't Back No Losers: An Insider's Analysis of the Daley Machine.* Bloomington: Indiana University Press, 1975.

Rankin, Karl. *China Assignment.* Seattle: University of Washington Press, 1964.

Ranville, Michael. *To Strike a King: The Turning Point in the McCarthy Witch Hunts.* Troy, Mich.: Momentum Books, 1997.

Raucher, Alan. *Paul G. Hoffman: Architect of Foreign Aid.* Lexington: University Press of Kentucky, 1985.

Reed, Roy. *Faubus: The Life and Times of an American Prodigal.* Fayetteville: University of Arkansas Press, 1997.

Reeves, Andre E. *Congressional Committee Chairmen: Three Who Made an Evolution.* Lexington: University Press of Kentucky, 1993.

Reeves, Thomas. *America's Bishop: The Life and Times of Fulton J. Sheen.* San Francisco: Encounter Books, 2001.

———. *The Life and Times of Joe McCarthy: A Biography.* New York: Stein & Day, 1982.

Reich, Cary. *The Life of Nelson A Rockefeller: Worlds to Conquer, 1908–1958.* New York: Doubleday, 1996.

Reis, Ronald A. *Jonas Salk: Microbiologist.* New York: Ferguson, 2006.

Reston, James. *Deadline: A Memoir.* New York: Random House, 1991.

Reuther, Victor G. *The Brothers Reuther and the Story of the UAW: A Memoir.* Boston: Houghton Mifflin, 1976.

Rice, Ross R. *Carl Hayden: Builder of the American West.* Lanham, Md.: University Press of America, 1994.

Richards, Robert D. *Uninhibited, Robust, and Wide Open: Mr. Justice Brennan's Legacy to the First Amendment.* Boone, N.C.: Parkway Publishers, 1994.

Rivers, Margaret Middleton. *Mendel: Slices of Life with an American Statesman.* Charleston: Quin Press, 2000.

Rivlin, Benjamin. *Ralph Bunche: The Man and His Times.* New York: Holmes & Meier, 1990.

Roberts, George C. *Paul M. Butler: Hoosier Politician and National Political Leader.* Lanham, Md.: University Press of America, 1987.

Robertson, David. *Sly and Able: A Political Biography of James F. Byrnes.* New York: Norton, 1994.

Robinson, Archie. *George Meany and His Times: A Biography.* New York: Simon & Schuster, 1981.

Robinson, Jo Ann. *Abraham Went Out: A Biography of A. J. Muste.* Philadelphia: Temple University Press, 1981.

Robinson, Paul A. *The Modernization of Sex.* New York: Harper & Row, 1976.

Rockwell, Theodore. *The Rickover Effect: How One Man Made a Difference.* Annapolis: Naval Institute Press, 1992.

Rodgers, William. *Think: A Biography of the Watsons and IBM.* New York: Stein & Day, 1969.

Roosevelt, Kermit. *Countercoup: The Struggle for the Control of Iran*. New York: McGraw-Hill, 1979.

Rosenkranz, E. Joshua, and Bernard Schwartz. *Reason and Passion: Justice Brennan's Enduring Influence*. New York: Oxford University Press, 1994.

Rovere, Richard H. *Arrivals and Departures: A Journalist's Memoirs*. New York: Macmillan, 1976.

———. *Final Reports: Personal Reflections on Politics and History in Our Time*. Garden City, N.Y.: Doubleday, 1984.

———. *Senator Joe McCarthy*. New York: Harcourt, Brace, 1959.

Rowan, Carl Thomas. *Dream Makers, Dream Breakers: The World of Justice Thurgood Marshall*. Boston: Little, Brown, 1993.

Rowe, James N. *Five Years to Freedom*. Boston: Little, Brown, 1971.

Royko, Mike. *Boss: Richard J. Daley of Chicago*. New York: Dutton, 1971.

Ruddy, Michael T. *The Cautious Diplomat: Charles E. Bohlen and the Soviet Union, 1929–1969*. Kent, Ohio: Kent State University Press, 1986.

Rusk, Dean. *As I Saw It*. New York: Norton, 1990.

Russell, George B. *J. Bracken Lee: The Taxpayer's Champion*. New York: R. Speller, 1961.

Russell, Thaddeus. *Out of the Jungle: Jimmy Hoffa and the Remaking of the Working Class*. New York: Knopf, 2001.

Rustin, Bayard. *Down the Line*. Chicago: Quadrangle Books, 1971.

Salisbury, Harrison E. *A Journey for Our Times: A Memoir*. New York: Harper & Row, 1983.

Salter, Elizabeth. *Daisy Bates*. New York: McCann & Geoghegan, 1972.

Saltonstall, Leverett. *Salty: Recollections of a Yankee in Politics*. Boston: Boston Globe, 1976.

Sandbrook, Dominic. *Eugene McCarthy: The Rise and Fall of Postwar American Liberalism*. New York: Alfred A. Knopf, 2004.

Scates, Shelby. *Warren G. Magnuson and the Shaping of Twentieth-Century America*. Seattle: University of Washington Press, 1997.

Schaffer, Howard B. *Chester Bowles: New Dealer in the Cold War*. Cambridge: Harvard University Press, 1993.

Schapsmeier, Edward L., and Frederick H. Schapsmeier. *Ezra Taft Benson and the Politics of Agriculture: The Eisenhower Years, 1953–1961*. Danville, Ill.: Interstate Printers & Publishers, 1975.

———. *Dirksen of Illinois: Senatorial Statesman*. Urbana: University of Illinois Press, 1998.

Schecter, Barbara R. *Clarence J. Brown: Republican Representative from Ohio*. Washington, D.C.: Grossman Publishers, 1972.

Scheele, Henry Z. *Charlie Halleck: A Political Biography*. New York: Exposition Press, 1966.

Schlesinger, Arthur M. *A Life in the Twentieth Century*. Boston: Houghton Mifflin, 2000.

———. *Robert Kennedy and His Times*. Boston: Houghton Mifflin, 1978.

Schneir, Walter, and Miriam Schneir. *Invitation to an Inquest: A New Look at the Rosenberg-Sobell Case*. New York: Dell Publishing Co., 1968.

Schoenbaum, Thomas J. *Waging Peace and War: Dean Rusk in the Truman, Kennedy, and Johnson Years*. New York: Simon & Schuster, 1988.

Schriftgiesser, Karl. *The Gentleman from Massachusetts: Henry Cabot Lodge*. Boston: Little, Brown, 1944.

Schumacher, Michael. *Dharma Lion: A Critical Biography of Allen Ginsberg*. New York: St. Martin's Press, 1992.

Schwartz, Bernard. *Super Chief: Earl Warren and His Supreme Court: A Judicial Biography*. New York: New York University Press, 1983.

———. *The Professor and the Commissions*. New York: Knopf, 1959.

Schweber, S. S. *In the Shadow of the Bomb: Bethe, Oppenheimer, and the Moral Responsibility of the Scientist*. Princeton: Princeton University Press, 2000.

Scimecca, Joseph A. *The Sociological Theory of C. Wright Mills*. Port Washington, N.Y.: Kennikat Press, 1977.

Scott, Nathan. *Reinhold Niebuhr*. Minneapolis: University of Minnesota Press, 1963.

Seaborg, Glenn. *A Chemist in the White House: From the Manhattan Project to the End of the Cold War*. Washington, D.C.: American Chemical Society, 1998.

———. *Adventures in the Atomic Age: From Watts to Washington*. New York: Farrar, Straus and Giroux, 2001.

Serafini, Anthony. *Linus Pauling: A Man and His Science*. New York: Paragon House, 1989.

Service, John S. *State Department Duty in China: The McCarthy Era and After, 1933–1977.* Berkeley: University of California Press, 1981.

Shadegg, Stephen. *Clare Boothe Luce: A Biography.* New York: Simon & Schuster, 1970.

Sheed, Wilfrid. *Clare Boothe Luce.* New York: Dutton, 1982.

Sheen, Fulton J. *Treasure in Clay: The Autobiography of Fulton J. Sheen.* Garden City, N.Y.: Doubleday, 1980.

Sheridan, Walter. *The Rise and Fall of Jimmy Hoffa.* New York: Saturday Review Press, 1972.

Sherman, Janann. *No Place for a Woman: A Life of Senator Margaret Chase Smith.* New Brunswick, N.J.: Rutgers University Press, 2000.

Sherman, Michael. *The Political Legacy of George D. Aiken: Wise Old Owl of the Senate.* Montpelier: Vermont Historical Society, Countryman Press, 1995.

Shire, Al. *Oveta Culp Hobby.* Houston: Western Lithograph, 1997.

Shuman, Charles B. *Reminisces.* Sullivan, Ill.: C. B. Shuman, 1998.

Sikora, Frank. *The Judge: The Life and Opinions of Alabama's Frank M. Johnson, Jr.* Montgomery: Black Belt Press, 1992.

Silverstein, Mark. *Constitutional Faiths: Felix Frankfurter, Hugo Black, and the Process of Judicial Decision Making.* Ithaca, N.Y.: Cornell University Press, 1984.

Simon, James F. *Independent Journey: The Life of William O. Douglas.* New York: Harper & Row, 1980.

———. *The Antagonists: Hugo Black, Felix Frankfurter and Civil Liberties in Modern America.* New York: Simon & Schuster, 1989.

Sims, George. *The Little Man's Big Friend: James E. Folsom in Alabama Politics, 1946–1958.* University: University of Alabama, 1985.

Sloane, Arthur. *Hoffa.* Cambridge: Harvard University Press, 1991.

Smant, Kevin J. *How Great the Triumph: James Burnham, Anticommunism, and the Conservative Movement.* Lanham, Md.: University Press of America, 1992.

Smiley, Sara Judith. *The Political Career of Thruston B. Morton: The Senate Years, 1956–1968.* Lexington: University Press of Kentucky, 1975.

Smith, Arthur Robert. *The Tiger in the Senate: The Biography of Wayne Morse.* Garden City, N.Y.: Doubleday, 1962.

Smith, Craig Alan. *Failing Justice: Charles Evans Whittaker on the Supreme Court.* Jefferson, N.C.: McFarland & Co., 2005.

Smith, Glenn H. *Langer of North Dakota: A Study in Isolationism, 1940–1959.* New York: Garland Publishing, 1979.

Smith, Jean Edward. *Lucius D. Clay: An American Life.* New York: Holt, 1990.

Smith, Margaret Chase. *Declaration of Conscience.* New York: Doubleday, 1972.

Smith, Richard Norton. *Thomas E. Dewey and His Times.* New York: Simon & Schuster, 1982.

Smith, Steven B. *Reading Leo Strauss: Politics, Philosophy, Judaism.* Chicago: University of Chicago Press, 2006.

Smylie, Robert E. *Governor Smylie Remembers.* Moscow: University of Idaho Press, 1998.

Sobell, Morton. *Doing Time.* New York: Scribner, 1974.

Solberg, Carl. *Hubert Humphrey: A Biography.* New York: Norton, 1984.

Sorensen, Theodore C. *Kennedy.* New York: Harper & Row, 1965.

Sperber, A. M. *Murrow: His Life and Times.* New York: Freundlich Books, 1986.

Srodes, James. *Allen Dulles: Master of Spies.* Washington, D.C.: Regnery, 1999.

Stacks, John F. *Scotty: James B. Reston and the Rise and Fall of American Journalism.* Boston: Little, Brown, 2003.

St. Clair, James E. *Chief Justice Fred M. Vinson of Kentucky: A Political Biography.* Lexington: University Press of Kentucky, 2002.

Stebenne, David L. *Arthur J. Goldberg: New Deal Liberal.* New York: Oxford University Press, 1996.

———. *Modern Republican: Arthur Larson and the Eisenhower Years.* Bloomington: Indiana University Press, 2006.

Steel, Ronald. *Walter Lippman and the American Century.* New Brunswick, N.J.: Rutgers University Press, 1980.

Steibel, Warren. *Cardinal Spellman: The Man.* New York: Appleton-Century, 1966.

Steinberg, Alfred. *Sam Rayburn: A Biography.* New York: Hawthorn Books, 1975.

Stern, Phillip M. *The Oppenheimer Case: Security on Trial.* New York: Harper & Row, 1969.

Stockley, Grif. *Daisy Bates: Civil Rights Crusader from Arkansas.* Jackson: University of Mississippi Press, 2005.

Stone, Ronald H. *Reinhold Niebuhr: Prophet to Politicians.* Nashville: Abingdon Press, 1972.

Stuhlinger, Ernst. *Wernher von Braun, Crusader for Space: A Biographical Memoir.* Malabar, Fla.: Krieger Publishing, 1994.

Sulzberger, C. L. *A Long Row of Candles: Memoirs and Diaries, 1934–1954.* New York: Macmillan, 1969.

————. *Seven Continents and Forty Years: A Concentration of Memoirs.* New York: Quadrangle/New York Times Book Co., 1977.

Sussman, Robert. *Wright Patman, Democratic Representative from Texas.* Washington, D.C.: Grossman, 1972.

Swan, Patrick. *Alger Hiss, Whittaker Chambers, and the Schism in the American Soul.* Wilmington, Del.: ISI Books, 2003.

Swanberg, W. A. *Luce and His Empire.* New York: Scribner, 1972.

————. *Norman Thomas, the Last Idealist.* New York: Scribner, 1976.

Sykes, Jay G. *Proxmire.* Washington, D.C.: R. B. Luce, 1972.

Talbot, Allen R. *The Mayor's Game: Richard Lee of New Haven and the Politics of Change.* New York: Harper & Row, 1967.

Tamadge, Herman E. *Talmadge: A Political Legacy, a Politician's Life.* Atlanta: Peachtree Publishers, 1987.

Tanenhaus, Sam. *Whittaker Chambers: A Biography.* New York: Random House, 1997.

Tanguay, Daniel. *Leo Strauss: An Intellectual Biography.* New Haven: Yale University Press, 2006.

Tarrant, John J. *Drucker: The Man Who Invented the Corporate Society.* Boston: Cahners Books, 1976.

Taylor, Henry D. *Arthur V. Watkins: My Stake President.* Salt Lake City: Henry D. Taylor, 1985.

Taylor, John M. *General Maxwell Taylor: The Sword and the Pen.* New York: Doubleday, 1989.

Taylor, Maxwell D. *Swords and Plowshares.* New York: Norton, 1972.

Teiser, Ruth. *Remembering William F. Knowland.* Berkeley: University of California Press, 1981.

Teller, Edward. *Memoirs: A Twentieth-Century Journey in Science and Politics.* Cambridge: Harvard University Press, 2001.

Ter Horst, Jerald F. *Gerald Ford and the Future of the Presidency.* New York: Third Press, 1974.

Theoharis, Athan G. *The Boss: J. Edgar Hoover and the Great American Inquisition.* Philadelphia: Temple University Press, 1988.

Thomas, Evan. *Robert Kennedy and His Times.* Boston: Houghton Mifflin, 1978.

Thomas, Helen Shirley. *Felix Frankfurter, Scholar on the Bench.* Baltimore: Johns Hopkins University Press, 1960.

Tower, Elizabeth A. *Alaska's Homegrown Governor: A Biography of William A. Egan.* Anchorage: Publication Consultants, 2003.

Traister, Daniel. *Being Read: The Career of Howard Fast.* Philadelphia: University of Pennsylvania Libraries, 1994.

Tushnet, Mark. *Making Civil Rights Law: Thurgood Marshall and the Supreme Court, 1931–1961.* New York: Oxford University Press, 1994.

Tytell, John. *Naked Angels: The Lives and Literature of the Beat Generation.* New York: McGraw-Hill, 1976.

Ungar, Sanford J. *The FBI.* Boston: Little, Brown, 1975.

Urquhart, Brian. *Ralph Bunche: An American Life.* New York: W. W. Norton, 1993.

Vigil, Maurilio E. *Parallels in the Careers of Two Hispanic US Senators.* El Paso: Chicano Studies, University of Texas, 1985.

Von Hoffman, Nicholas. *Citizen Cohn.* New York: Doubleday, 1988.

Wagy, Tom. *Governor LeRoy Collins of Florida: Spokesman of the New South.* University: University of Alabama Press, 1985.

Walker, Jeff. *The Ayn Rand Cult.* Chicago: Open Court, 1998.

Wallace, Patricia Ward. *Politics of Conscience: A Biography of Margaret Chase Smith.* Westport, Conn.: Praeger, 1995.

Walsh, George. *Public Enemies: The Mayor, the Mob, and the Crime That Was.* New York: Norton, 1980.

Walters, Helen B. *Wernher von Braun, Rocket Engineer.* New York: Macmillan, 1964.

Wanock, Alvin Timothy. *Associate Justice Tom C. Clark: Advocate of Judicial Reform.* Ann Arbor: University of Michigan Press, 1973.

Warren, Earl. *The Memoirs of Earl Warren.* Garden City, N.Y.: Doubleday, 1977.

Watson, Denton. *Lion in the Lobby: Clarence Mitchell, Jr.'s Struggle for the Passage of Civil Rights Laws.* New York: Morrow, 1990.

Watson, Thomas J. *Father, Son & Co.: My Life at IBM and Beyond.* New York: Bantam Books, 1990.

Weaver, John D. *Warren: The Man, the Court, the Era.* Boston: Little, Brown, 1967.

Weeks, Stuart B. *The Lord of Cat Bow.* Brookline, N.H.: Hobblebush Books, 2003.

Weill, Gus. *You Are My Sunshine: The Jimmie Davis Story: An Affectionate Biography.* Waco, Tex.: Word Books, 1977.

Weintraub, Stanley. *MacArthur's War: Korea and the Undoing of an American Hero.* New York: Free Press, 2000.

Wellman, Paul Iselin. *Stuart Symington: Portrait of a Man with a Mission.* Garden City, N.Y.: Doubleday, 1960.

White, Edward G. *Earl Warren: A Public Life.* New York: Oxford University Press, 1982.

White, Marjorie Longenecker. *Birmingham Revolutionaries: The Reverend Fred Shuttlesworth and the Alabama Christian Movement for Human Rights.* Macon, Ga.: Mercer University Press, 2000.

White, William Smith. *The Taft Story.* New York: Harper, 1954.

Whitfield, Stephen J. *The Critical American: The Politics of Dwight Macdonald.* Hamden, Conn.: Archon Books, 1984.

Wicker, Tom. *One of Us: Richard Nixon and the American Dream.* New York: Random House, 1991.

Wickman, Patricia R. *The Uncommon Man: George Smathers of Florida.* New York: Wickman, 1993.

Wides, Louise DeCosta. *Edith Green: Democratic Representative from Oregon.* Washington, D.C.: Grossman Publishers, 1972.

Wilder, Phillip. *Meade Alcorn and the 1958 Election.* New York: Holt, 1959.

Wilkins, Roy. *Reminiscences.* New York: Columbia University Press, 1972.

———. *Standing Fast: The Autobiography of Roy Wilkins.* New York: Viking Press, 1982.

Wilkinson, J. Harvey III. *Harry Bird and the Changing Face of Virginia Politics, 1945–1966.* Charlottesville: University of Virginia Press, 1968.

Williams, Juan. *Thurgood Marshall: American Revolutionary.* New York: Times Books, 1998.

Wilson, Augusta E. *Liberal Leader in the House: Frank Thompson, Jr.* Washington, D.C.: Acropolis Books, 1968.

Wilson, Sloan. *What Shall We Wear to This Party?: The Man in the Gray Flannel Suit Twenty Years Before and After.* New York: Arbor House, 1976.

Winchell, Mark Royden. *Too Good to Be True: The Life and Work of Leslie Fiedler.* Columbia: University of Missouri Press, 2002.

Winters, Susan Cramer. *Enlightened Citizen: Frances Payne Bolton and the Nursing Profession.* New York: University of Virginia, 1997.

Wisoff, Marilyn. *H. R. Gross: Republican Representative from Iowa.* Washington, D.C.: Grossman Publishers, 1972.

Witfield, Stephen J. *A Death in the Delta: The Story of Emmett Till.* New York: Free Press, 1988.

Wolf, George, and Joseph DiMona. *Frank Costello: Prime Minister of the Underworld.* New York: Morrow, 1974.

Woods, Randall Bennett. *Fulbright: A Biography.* New York: Cambridge University Press, 1995.

Wreszin, Michael. *A Rebel in Defense of Tradition.* New York: Basic Books, 1994.

Yarbrough, Tinsley. *John Marshall Harlan: Great Dissenter of the Warren Court.* New York: Oxford University Press, 1992.

———. *Judge Frank Johnson and Human Rights in Alabama.* University: University of Alabama Press, 1981.

Yoder, Edwin. *Joe Alsop's Cold War: A Study of Journalistic Influence and Intrigue.* Chapel Hill: University of North Carolina Press, 1995.

York, Herbert F. *Arms and the Physicist.* Woodbury, N.Y.: American Institute of Physics, 1995.

Young, Nancy Beck. *Wright Patman: Populism, Liberalism, & the American Dream.* Dallas: Southern Methodist University Press, 2000.

Young-Bruehl, Elisabeth. *Hannah Arendt: For The Love of the World.* New Haven: Yale University Press, 1982.

Youngs, J. William T. *Eleanor Roosevelt: A Personal and Public Life.* New York: Pearson/Longman, 2006.

Zachary, G. Pascal. *Endless Frontier: Vannevar Bush, Engineer of the American Century.* New York: Free Press, 1997.

Zeiler, Thomas W. *Dean Rusk: Defending the American Mission Abroad.* Wilmington, Del.: Scholarly Resources, 2000.

Zieger, Robert H. *John L. Lewis: Labor Leader.* Boston: Twayne Publishers, 1988.

Zimmerman, Carroll L. *Insider at SAC: Operations Analysis under General LeMay.* Manhattan, Kans.: Sunflower University Press, 1988.

Zimmerman, Richard G. *Call Me Mike: A Political Biography of Michael V. DiSalle.* Kent, Ohio: Kent State University Press, 2003.

INDEX

Boldface page numbers indicate main headings; *italic* page numbers indicate illustrations.